August 13-17, 2017
Halifax, NS, Canada

Association for
Computing Machinery

Advancing Computing as a Science & Profession

KDD2017

KDD'17

Proceedings of the 23rd ACM SIGKDD International Conference on

Knowledge Discovery and Data Mining

Sponsored by:

ACM SIGKDD & ACM SIGMOD

Supported by:

DiDi, Amazon, Microsoft, Alibaba Group, Facebook, SAS, CapitalOne, Criteo Research, Google, E-AI, Siemens, LinkedIn, Huawei, Booking.com, Honeywell, American Express, Oracle, Western Digital, Open Innovation KNIME, Institut Tutte, Uber, Two Sigma, Cambridge University Press, MIT Press, Springer, & Syngenta

Association for Computing Machinery

Advancing Computing as a Science & Profession

The Association for Computing Machinery
2 Penn Plaza, Suite 701
New York, New York 10121-0701

Notice to Past Authors of ACM-Published Articles
ACM intends to create a complete electronic archive of all articles and/or other material previously published by ACM. If you have written a work that has been previously published by ACM in any journal or conference proceedings prior to 1978, or any SIG Newsletter at any time, and you do NOT want this work to appear in the ACM Digital Library, please inform permissions@acm.org, stating the title of the work, the author(s), and where and when published.

ISBN: 978-1-4503-4887-4 (Digital)

ISBN: 978-1-4503-5669-5 (Print)

Additional copies may be ordered prepaid from:

ACM Order Department
PO Box 30777
New York, NY 10087-0777, USA

Phone: 1-800-342-6626 (USA and Canada)
+1-212-626-0500 (Global)
Fax: +1-212-944-1318
E-mail: acmhelp@acm.org
Hours of Operation: 8:30 am – 4:30 pm ET

Printed in the USA

KDD 2017 Chairs' Welcome Message

It is our great pleasure to welcome you to the 2017 ACM Conference on Knowledge Discovery and Data Mining – KDD 2017. We hope that the content and the professional networking opportunities at KDD 2017 will help you to succeed professionally by enabling you to: identify new technology trends; learn from contributed papers, presentations, and posters; discover new tools, processes and practices; identify new job opportunities; and hire new team members.

The terms "Data Science", "Data Mining" and "Big Data" have, in the last few years, grown out of research labs and gained presence in the media and in everyday conversations. We also hear these terms on social media and from decision makers at various level of governments and corporations. The impact of these technologies is felt in almost every walk of life. Importantly, the current rapid progress in data science is facilitated by the timely sharing of newly discovered and developed representations and algorithms between those working in research and those interested in industrial deployment. It is the hallmark of KDD conferences in the past that they have been the bridge between theory and practise, the great facilitator and catalyst for this exchange. Researchers and practitioners meet in person and interact in a meaningful way over several days. The conference program, with its three parallel tracks - the Research Track, the Applied Data Science Track and the Applied Invited Speakers Track - brings the two groups together. Participants are welcome to freely attend any track, and the events common for all tracks.

The conference this year continues with its tradition of a strong tutorial and workshop program on leading edge issues of data mining during the first two days of the program. The last three days are devoted to contributed technical papers, describing both novel, important research contributions, and deployed, innovative solutions. Three keynote talks, by Cynthia Dwork, Bin Yu, and Renée J. Miller touch on some of the hard, emerging issues before the field of data mining. With a growing industry around AI assistants, our KDD Panel brings together industry experts in this field to spawn discussions and an exchanges of ideas. We have an outstanding lineup of industry speakers sharing their experiences and expertise in deploying industrial data mining solutions. We continue a strong hands-on tutorial program, in which participants will learn how to use practical data science tools. In order to broaden the impact of KDD and to increase the participation of attendees who would greatly benefit from the conference but would have otherwise found it financially challenging to attend, we reserved a substantial budget for travel grants. KDD 2017 awarded a record USD 145k for student travel and also set aside USD 25k to enable smaller startups to attend. With the new "Meet the Experts" sessions, KDD 2017 also gives researchers and practitioners a unique opportunity to form professional networks and to share their perspectives with others interested in the various aspects of data science. We hope that the KDD 2017 conference will serve as a meeting ground for researchers, practitioners, funding agencies and investors to help create new algorithms and commercial products.

The table below summarizes numerically different elements of the conference program and provides acceptance rates, whenever applicable.

Venue or Track	Reviewed	Accepted	Acceptance Rate
Research Track Papers	748	64*, 66+	8.6*, 8.8+
Applied Data Science Track Papers	390	36*, 50+	9.2*,12.8+
Workshops	36	22	61.1
Tutorials	35	22	62.8
Hands-on Tutorials	8	8	NA
Applied Data Science Talks	Invited	11	NA
Regular Keynotes	Invited	3	NA
Panels	Invited	2	NA

Papers: *oral, +poster

Putting together KDD 2017 has been a wonderful team effort by the members of the organizing committee. We thank the authors and the speakers for providing the content of the program. We are grateful to the program committee and the senior program committee, who worked very hard in reviewing papers and providing feedback for authors. Finally, we thank the numerous sponsors and ACM SIGKDD for their support in hosting the conference.

We hope that you will find this program interesting and thought-provoking, and that the conference will provide you with a valuable opportunity to share ideas with other researchers and practitioners from institutions around the world. We also hope that the conference facilities, and the host city of Halifax, Nova Scotia, Canada, will provide a friendly environment and many opportunities for such fruitful discussions and exchanges.

Stan Matwin *(General Chair)*
Shipeng Yu *(General Chair)*
Faisal Farooq *(Associate General Chair)*
KDD'17 Chairs

Table of Contents

KDD 2017 Research Papers (Oral Papers)

KDD 2017 Research Papers (Poster Papers)

KDD 2017 Applied Data Science Papers (Oral Papers)

KDD 2017 Applied Data Science Papers (Poster Papers)

KDD 2017 Conference Organization

KDD 2017 Organizing Committee

General Chairs
- Stan Matwin (Dalhousie University)
- Shipeng Yu (LinkedIn)

Associate General Chair
- Faisal Farooq (IBM)

Research Track Program Chairs
- Ravi Kumar (Google)
- Tina Eliassi-Rad (Northeastern University)

Applied Data Science Track Program Chairs
- Roberto J. Bayardo (Google)
- Charles Elkan (Amazon & UCSD)

Applied Data Science Invited Talks Chairs
- Usama Fayyad (Barclays)
- Evangelos Simoudis (Synapse Partners)
- Ashok Srivastava (Verizon)

Workshop Chairs
- Leman Akoglu (CMU)
- Tijl De Bie (Ghent University & University of Bristol)

Tutorial Chairs
- Yan Liu (University of Southern California)
- Jianyong Wang (Tsinghua University)

Hands-on Tutorial Chairs
- HangHang Tong (Arizona State University)
- Ritwik Kumar (Apple)

Publications Chair
- Rómer Rosales (LinkedIn)

Poster Chairs
- Jing Gao (University at Buffalo)
- Xiaoguang Wang (Alibaba)

Local Arrangements Chair
- Evangelos Milios (Dalhousie University)

KDD Cup Chairs
- Lei Li (Toutiao Lab and Byte Dance)
- Danai Koutra (University of Michigan)

Panel Chairs
- Andrew Tomkins (Google)
- Muthu Muthukrishnan (Rutgers)

Media and Publicity Chairs
- Tiger Zhang (LinkedIn)
- Aijun An (York University)

Sponsorship Chair
- Claudia Perlich (Dstillery)
- Diana Inkpen (University of Ottawa)

Best Paper Chairs
- Deepak Agarwal (LinkedIn)
- Jennifer Neville (Purdue University)

Doctoral Dissertation Award Chair
- Tanya Berger-Wolf (UIC)

Web Chair
- Derek Young (Amazon)

Innovation and Service Award Chair
- Wei Wang (UCLA)

Test-of-Time Paper Award Chair
- Qiang Yang (HKUST)

Social Network Chairs
- Jingrui He (Arizona State University)
- Xia "Ben" Hu (Texas A&M University)

Student Travel Awards Chair
- Qiaozhu Mei (University of Michigan)

Treasurer
- Ying Li (DataSpark)

Video and Streaming Chair
- Marko Grobelnik (IJS)

Job Matching Chair
- Jiliang Tang (Michigan State University)

Social Impact Chairs
- Mohak Shah (Bosch Research)
- Rayid Ghani (University of Chicago)

Research Track Senior Program Committee

Naoki Abe (IBM Research)
Arindam Banerjee (University of Minnesota)
Paul Bennett (Microsoft Research)
Tanya Berger-Wolf (University of Illinois at Chicago)
Wray Buntine (Monash University)
James Caverlee (Texas A&M University)
Hong Cheng (The Chinese University of Hong Kong)
Flavio Chierichetti (Sapienza University)
Diane Cook (Washington State University)
Cristian Danescu-Niculescu-Mizil (Cornell University)
Anirban Dasgupta (IIT Gandhinagar)
Ian Davidson (U.C. Davis)
Martin Ester (SFU)
Peter Flach (University of Bristol)
Benjamin C. M. Fung (McGill University)
Johannes Fürnkranz (TU Darmstadt)
Thomas Gaertner (University of Nottingham)
Aristides Gionis (Aalto University)
David Gleich (Purdue University)
Dimitrios Gunopulos (University of Athens)
Stratis Ioannidis (Northeastern University)
Panos Ipeirotis (New York University)
George Karypis (University of Minnesota)
Eamonn Keogh (UC Riverside)
Tamara Kolda (Sandia National Laboratories)
Jure Leskovec (Stanford)
Edo Liberty (Yahoo Labs)
Chih-Jen Lin (National Taiwan University)
Tie-Yan Liu (Microsoft Research Asia)
Qiaozhu Mei (University of Michigan)
Katharina Morik (TU Dortmund)
Benjamin Moseley (Washington University in St. Louis)
Siegfried Nijssen (Katholieke Universiteit Leuven)
Srinivasan Parthasarathy (Ohio State University)
B. Aditya Prakash (Virginia Tech)
Matteo Riondato (Two Sigma Investments, LP)
Arno Siebes (Universiteit Utrecht)
Ambuj Singh (University of California, Santa Barbara)
Yizhou Sun (UCLA)
Jie Tang (Tsinghua University)
Dacheng Tao (The Hong Kong Polytechnic University)
Evimaria Terzi (Boston University)
Charalampos Tsourakakis (Harvard University)
Sergei Vassilvitskii (Google)
Tim Weninger (University of Notre Dame)
David P. Woodruff (IBM Almaden)
Elad Yom-Tov (Microsoft Research)
Jeffery Xu Yu (Chinese Univ. of Hong Kong)
Yisong Yue (California Institute of Technology)
Mohammed Zaki (RPI)

Applied Data Science Track Senior Program Committee

Kamal Ali (Apple Inc.)
Shlomo Berkovsky (CSIRO)
Chiranjib Bhattacharyya (Indian Institute of Science)
Albert Bifet (Telecom ParisTech)
Kofi Boakye (Yahoo)
Alexey Borisov (University of Amsterdam & Yandex)
Tilmann Bruckhaus (Intuit)
Edith Cohen (Google Research)
Brain d'Alessandro (Zocdoc)
Jesse Davis (KU Leuven)
Dmitriy Fradkin (Siemens)
Glenn Fung (American Family Insurance)
Ariel Fuxman (Google)
Byron Galbraith (Talla)
Rayid Ghani (University of Chicago)
Moises Goldszmidt (Apple)
Jingrui He (Arizona State University)
Diane Hu (Etsy)
Vanja Josifovski (Pinterest)
Pallika Kanani (Oracle Labs)
Nick Koudas (University of Toronto)
Hang Li (Huawei Technologies)
Tie-Yan Liu (Microsoft Research Asia)
Yoelle Maarek (Yahoo Research)
Jérémie Mary (Univ. Lille / Inria Lille Nord Europe)
Julian Mcauley (UC San Diego)
Gabor Melli (Sony Interactive Entertainment)
Nina Mishra (Amazon)
S Muthukrishnan (Rutgers University)
Vijay Narayanan (Microsoft)
Jennifer Neville (Purdue University)
Nikunj Oza (NASA)
Alessandro Panconesi (Sapienza University of Rome)
Hanchuan Peng (Allen Inst)
Florian Pinel (IBM)
Naren Ramakrishnan (Virginia Tech)
Nikhil Rao (Technicolor Research)
D. Sculley (Google)
Srinivasan Sengamedu (Amazon)
Pavel Serdyukov (Yandex)
Dou Shen (Microsoft Adcenter Labs)
Gautam Shroff (Tata Consultancy Services)
Le Song (Georgia Tech)
Isabelle Stanton (Google)
V.S. Subrahmanian (University of Maryland)
Jimeng Sun (Georgia Tech)
Vincent S. Tseng (National Chiao Tung University)
Peter van der Putten (LIACS Leiden University & Pegasystems)
Fei Wang (Cornell University)
Graham Williams (Microsoft)
Josh Wills (Rui Yan)
Rui Yan (Peking University)
Martin Zinkevich (Google)

Research Track Program Committee

Bruno Abrahao (Stanford University)
Tim Althoff (Stanford University)
Aris Anagnostopoulos (Sapienza University of Rome)
Ira Assent (Aarhus University)
Renato Assuncao (Universidade Federal de Minas Gerais)
Stephen Bach (Stanford University)
Mohammad Taha Bahadori (Georgia Institute of Technology)
Eric Balkanski (Harvard University)
Richard Baraniuk (Rice University)
Nicola Barbieri (Tumblr)
Senjuti Basu Roy (New Jersey Institute of Technology)
Gustavo Batista (University of São Paulo)
Andras A. Benczur (Institute for Computer Science and Control, Hungarian Academy of Sciences)
Austin Benson (Stanford University)
Klaus Berberich (Max Planck Institute for Informatics)
Michael Berthold (University of Konstanz)
Alex Beutel (Google)
Sahely Bhadra (Network Science Institute, Northeastern University)
Smriti Bhagat (Facebook)
Aditya Bhaskara (University of Utah)
Siddhartha Bhattacharyya (Information and Decision Sciences, College of Business, University of Illinois, Chicago)
Jinbo Bi (University of Connecticut)
Jiang Bian (Microsoft Research)
Albert Bifet (Telecom ParisTech)
Mustafa Bilgic (Illinois Institute of Technology)
Christian Böhm (Ludwig-Maximilians-Universität München)
Klemens Böhm (Karlsruhe Institute of Technology (KIT))
Francesco Bonchi (The ISI Foundation, Turin, Italy)
Rajesh Bordawekar (IBM research)
Alessandro Bozzon (Delft University of Technology)
Ulf Brefeld (Leuphana Universität Lüneburg)
David Buttler (Lawrence Livermore National Laboratory)
Jose Cadena (Virginia Tech)
Deng Cai (Zhejiang University)
B. Barla Cambazoglu (NTENT Inc.)
Jian Cao (Shanghai Jiao Tong University)
Longbing Cao (University of Technology Sydney)
Michele Catasta (Ecole Polytechnique Fédérale de Lausanne)
Jeffrey Chan (University of Melbourne)
Vineet Chaoji (Amazon)
Duen Horng Chau (Georgia Tech)
Sanjay Chawla (Qatar Computing Research Institute (QCRI), HBKU, Doha, Qatar)
Bee-Chung Chen (LinkedIn)
Enhong Chen (University of Science & Technology of China)
Ming-Syan Chen (National Taiwan University)
Ping Chen (UMB)
Rui Chen (Samsung Research America)
Shu-Ching Chen (Florida International University)
Shuo Chen (Blizzard Entertainment)
Songqing Chen (George Mason University)
Wei Chen (Microsoft Research Asia)
Yixin Chen (Washington University)
James Cheng (Chinese University of Hong Kong)
Ingemar Cox (University College London & University of Copenhagen)
Mark Crovella (Boston University)
Philippe Cudre-Mauroux (University of Fribourg)
Bin Cui (Peking University)
Abhimanyu Das (Google)
Mahashweta Das (Visa Research)
Gianluca Demartini (University of Sheffield)
Ayhan Demiriz (Gebze Technical University)
Alex Deng (Microsoft)
Amit Dhurandhar (IBM TJ Watson)
Djellel Eddine Difallah (University of Fribourg)
Bolin Ding (Microsoft Research)
Nemanja Djuric (Uber ATG)
Guozhu Dong (Wright State University)
Yuxiao Dong (University of Notre Dame)
Petros Drineas (Purdue)
Nan Du (Google)
Saso Dzeroski (Jozef Stefan Institute)
Alina Ene (Boston University)
Alessandro Epasto (Google Research)
Alex Fabrikant (Google Research)
Boi Faltings (Ecole Polytechnique Federale de Lausanne)
Liyue Fan (State University of New York Albany)

Research Track Program Committee (continued)

Ad Feelders (Universiteit Utrecht)
Yun Fu (Northeastern University)
Pavid Fuhry (The Ohio State University)
Aram Galstyan (USC/ISI)
Joao Gama (University Porto)
Bin Gao (Microsoft Research)
Byron Gao (Texas State University)
Jing Gao (University at Buffalo)
David Garcia (ETH Zurich)
Wolfgang Gatterbauer (Carnegie Mellon University)
Yong Ge (The University of North Carolina at Charlotte)
Rumi Ghosh (University of Southern California)
Amol Ghoting (LinkedIn Corporation)
Fosca Giannotti (Istituo di Scienza e Tecnologie dell'Informazione, National Research Council of Italy)
Derek Greene (University College Dublin)
Quanquan Gu (University of Virginia)
Francesco Gullo (UniCredit)
Krishna Gummadi (MPI-SWS)
Stephan Günnemann (Technical University of Munich)
Abhishek Gupta (LinkedIn)
Wook-Shin Han (POSTECH)
Mohammad Hasan (Indiana University Purdue University, Indianapolis)
Xiaofeng He (East China Normal University)
Andreas Hotho (University of Wuerzburg)
Cho-Jui Hsieh (UC Davis)
Hsun-Ping Hsieh (National Taiwan University)
Chun-Nan Hsu (UC San Diego)
Xia Ben Hu (Texas A&M University)
Jun Huan (University of Kansas)
Sheng-Jun Huang (Nanjing University of Aeronautics and Astronautics)
Yen E. H. Ian (Carnegie Mellon University)
Tomoharu Iwata (NTT)
Szymon Jaroszewicz (Institute of Computer Science, Polish Academy of Sciences)
David Jensen (University of Massachusetts Amherst)
Shuiwang Ji (WSU)
Yexi Jiang (Florida International University)
Wen Jin (Independent Researcher)
Panos Kalnis (King Abdullah University of Science and Technology)
U Kang (Seoul University University)
Murat Kantarcioglu (University of Texas at Dallas)
Ben Kao (The University of Hong Kong)
Komal Kapoor (University of Minnesota Twin Cities)
Amin Karbasi (Yale University)
Panagiotis Karras (Aalborg University)
Hisashi Kashima (Kyoto University)
Latifur Khan (UTD)
Emre Kiciman (Microsoft Research)
Deguang Kong (Yahoo Research)
Xiangnan Kong (Worcester Polytechnic Institute)
Nicolas Kourtellis (Telefonica Research)
Ioannis Koutis (University of Puerto Rico-Rio Piedras)
Tim Kraska (Brown University)
Srijan Kumar (University of Maryland, College Park)
Himabindu Lakkaraju (Stanford University)
Laks Lakshmanan (University of British Columbia)
Theodoros Lappas (Stevens Institute of Technology)
Longin Jan Latecki (Temple University)
Neal Lathia (Skyscanner)
Silvio Lattanzi (Google)
Kyumin Lee (Utah State University)
Kristen Lefevre (Google)
Kristina Lerman (University of Southern California)
Cheng Li (University of Michigan)
Cheng-Te Li (National Cheng Kung University)
Chengkai Li (University of Texas at Arlington)
Jiuyong Li (University of South Australia)
Kai Li (University of Central Florida)
Shuai Li (University of Cambridge)
Yanen Li (University of Illinois at Urbana-Champaign)
Zhenhui Li (Penn State University)
Hsuan-Tien Lin (National Taiwan University)
Xuemin Lin (The University of New South Wales)
Chuanren Liu (Rutgers Business School)
Guimei Liu (Institute for Infocomm Research)
Huan Liu (Arizona State University)
Jun Liu (SAS Institute Inc.)
Xuanzhe Liu (Peking University)
David Lo (Singapore Management University)
Peter Lofgren (Stanford)
Felipe Llinares Lopez (Swiss Federal Institute of Technology, Zürich)
Bo Long (Yahoo! Labs)
Yin Lou (Airbnb)
Chang-Tien Lu (Virginia Tech)
Patrick Lucey (STATS)
Jiebo Luo (University of Rochester)

Research Track Program Committee (continued)

Ping Luo (Institute of Computing Technology, CAS)
Hao Ma (Microsoft Research)
Shuai Ma (Beihang University)
Richard Maclin (University of Minnesota Duluth)
Malik Magdon-Ismail (Rensselaer Polytechnic Institute)
Anirban Majumder (Amazon)
Hiroshi Mamitsuka (Kyoto University)
Nikos Mamoulis (University of Hong Kong)
Amin Mantrach (Yahoo!)
Michael Mathioudakis (Aalto University)
Julian Mcauley (UC San Diego)
Wagner Meira Jr. (Universidade Federal de Minas Gerais)
Weiyi Meng (Binghamton University)
Pauli Miettinen (Max Planck Institute for Informatics)
Baharan Mirzasoleiman (Swiss Federal Institute of Technology, Zürich)
Dunja Mladenic (Jozef Stefan Institute)
Joshua Moore (Cornell)
Sebastian Moreno (Universidad Adolfo Ibañez)
Abdullah Mueen (University of New Mexico)
Kamesh Munagala (Duke University)
Emmanuel Müller (Hasso-Plattner-Institute)
Mirco Nanni (KDD-Lab ISTI-CNR Pisa)
Olfa Nasraoui (University of Louisville)
Wilfred Ng (The Hong Kong University of Science and Technology)
Feiping Nie (Northwestern Polytechnical University, China)
Zaiqing Nie (Microsoft Research Asia)
Eirini Ntoutsi (Gottfried Wilhelm Leibniz Universität Hannover)
Tim Oates (University of Maryland Baltimore County)
Zoran Obradovic (Temple University)
Rasmus Pagh (IT University of Copenhagen)
Themis Palpanas (Paris Descartes University)
Rong Pan (Sun Yat-sen University)
Rina Panigrahy (Microsoft Research)
Evangelos Papalexakis (University of California Riverside)
Jian Pei (Simon Fraser University)
Bryan Perozzi (Google Research)
Francois Petitjean (Monash University)
Bernhard Pfahringer (University of Waikato)
Dinh Phung (Deakin University)
Claudia Plant (University of Vienna)
Tao Qin (Microsoft Research Asia)
Vladan Radosavljevic (Uber Advanced Technology Group)
Chedy Raïssi (INRIA)
Karthik Raman (Google)
Jan Ramon (INRIA)
Huzefa Rangwala (George Mason University)
Sayan Ranu (IIT Delhi)
Chotirat Ratanamahatana (Chulalongkorn University)
Xiang Ren (University of Illinois at Urbana-Champaign)
Steffen Rendle (Google)
Matthias Renz (Ludwig-Maximilians University)
Bruno Ribeiro (Purdue University)
Manuel Gomez Rodriguez (MPI for Software Systems)
Oleg Rokhlenko (Amazon)
Salvatore Ruggieri (Dipartimento di Informatica, Università di Pisa)
Joerg Sander (University of Alberta)
Raul Santos-Rodriguez (University of Bristol)
Nishanth Sastry (King's College London)
Assaf Schuster (Technion)
C. Seshadhri (University of California, Santa Cruz)
Aneesh Sharma (Twitter Inc)
Pannaga Shivaswamy (Netflix Inc.)
Milad Shokouhi (Microsoft)
Vikas Sindhwani (IBM Research)
Yaron Singer (Harvard University)
Kaushik Sinha (Wichita State University)
Kevin Small (Amazon)
Yangqiu Song (The Hong Kong University of Science and Technology)
Anna Squicciarini (The Pennsylvania State University)
Mudhakar Srivatsa (IBM T.J. Watson Research Center)
Michael Steinbach (University of Minnesota)
Torsten Suel (New York University)
Mahito Sugiyama (Osaka University)
Masashi Sugiyama (RIKEN/The University of Tokyo)
Huan Sun (The Ohio State University)
Jimeng Sun (Georgia Tech)
Einoshin Suzuki (Kyushu University)
Adith Swaminathan (Cornell University)
Ichiro Takeuchi (Nagoya Institute of Technology)
Partha Talukdar (Indian Institute of Science)
Chenhao Tan (Cornell University)
Jian Tang (University of Michigan)
Yufei Tao (The University of Queensland)

Research Track Program Committee (continued)

Nikolaj Tatti (Aalto University)
Kai-Ming Ting (Federation University Australia)
Volker Tresp (Siemens AG)
Panayiotis Tsaparas (University of Ioannina)
Vincent S. Tseng (National Chiao Tung University)
Antti Ukkonen (Finnish Institute of Occupational Health)
Jaideep Vaidya (Rutgers University)
Kush Varshney (IBM Thomas J. Watson Research Center)
Michail Vlachos (IBM Research)
Jilles Vreeken (Max-Planck Institute for Informatics and Saarland University)
Slobodan Vucetic (Temple University)
Anil Kumar Vullikanti (Virginia Tech)
Can Wang (Zhejiang University)
Dashun Wang (Kellogg School of Management, Northwestern University)
Dong Wang (University of Notre Dame)
Guan Wang (Nio Automotive)
Hongning Wang (University of Virginia)
Jian Wang (LinkedIn Corporation)
Ke Wang (Simon Fraser University)
Ting Wang (Lehigh University)
Wei Wang (UCLA)
Xiang Wang (IBM Research)
Takashi Washio (ISIR, Osaka Univ.)
Ingmar Weber (Qatar Computing Research Institute)
Robert West (École Polytechnique Fédérale de Lausanne)
Anthony Wirth (The University of Melbourne)
Ran Wolff (Yahoo Labs)
Raymond Chi-Wing Wong (The Hong Kong University of Science and Technology)
Weng-Keen Wong (Oregon State University)
Jungie Wu (Beihang University)
Xindong Wu (University of Louisiana of Lafayette)
Xintao Wu (University of Arkansas)
Keli Xiao (Stony Brook University)
Xiaokui Xiao (Nanyang Technological University)
Hui Xiong (Rutgers University)
Chang Xu (University of Technology Sydney)
Jiajing Xu (Pinterest)
Xiaowei Xu (University of Arkansas at Little Rock)
Takeshi Yamada (NTT Communication Science Laboratories)
Xifeng Yan (University of California at Santa Barbara)
Zhijun Yin (Twitter)
Hsiang-Fu Yu (Amazon)
Kui Yu (Hefei University of Technology)
Lei Yu (Binghamton University)
Xiao Yu (Google)
Yang Yu (Nanjing University)
Chunqiu Zeng (Florida International University)
Duo Zhang (Kunlun Inc.)
Kun Zhang (Carnegie Mellon University)
Min-Ling Zhang (School of Computer Science and Engineering, Southeast University)
Peng Zhang (Fictitious Economics & Data Technology Research Centre)
Ping Zhang (IBM Thomas J. Watson Research Center)
Rui Zhang (IBM Research - Almaden)
Shichao Zhang (Guangxi Normal University)
Weinan Zhang (Shanghai Jiao Tong University)
Wenlu Zhang (Old Dominion University)
Xiang Zhang (The Pennsylvania State University)
Ya Zhang (Shanghai Jiao Tong University)
Yu Zhang (HKUST)
Zhenjie Zhang (Advanced Digital Sciences Center)
Bo Zhao (Pinterest)
Peixiang Zhao (Florida State University)
Yuchen Zhao (AppDynamics)
Vincent W. Zheng (Advanced Digital Sciences Center)
Yu Zheng (Microsoft Research)
Jiayu Zhou (Michigan State University)
Mianwei Zhou (Yahoo Lab)
Wenjun Zhou (University of Tennessee)
Feida Zhu (Singapore Management University)
Xingquan Zhu (Florida Atlantic University)

Applied Data Science Track Program Committee

Talel Abdessalem (Télécom ParisTech, Université Paris-Saclay)
Puneet Agarwal (Tata Consultancy Services)
John-Mark Agosta (Microsoft)
Amr Ahmed (Google Research)
Nesreen Ahmed (Intel Labs)
Jae-Wook Ahn (University of Pittsburgh)
Ioannis Akrotirianakis (Siemens)
Bo An (Nanyang Technological University)
Azin Ashkan (Google)
Kun Bai (MIG Tencent Company)
Gagan Bansal (Microsoft)
Rohan Baxter (ATO)
Michael Bendersky (Google)
Charlie Berger (Oracle)
Debarun Bhattacharjya (IBM T.J. Watson Research Center)
Sourangshu Bhattacharya (IIT KGP)
Jiang Bian (Microsoft Research)
Joseph Bockhorst (American Family Insurance)
Alessandro Bria (University of Cassino)
Donna Byron (IBM)
Diane Chang (Intuit)
Abon Chaudhuri (Walmart Labs)
Daizhuo Chen (Dstillery & Columbia Business School)
Feng Chen (SUNY Albany)
Jie Chen (University of South Australia)
Kuan-Ta Chen (Academia Sinica)
Zhengzhang Chen (NEC Laboratories America, Inc.)
Zhitang Chen (Huawei Technologies)
Juan Colmenares (Samsung Research America)
Prakash Mandayam Comar (Amazon)
James Cook (Google)
Peng Cui (Tsinghua University)
Bo Dai (Georgia Tech)
Hanjun Dai (Georgia Institute of Technology)
Kamalika Das (NASA Ames Research Center)
Danielle Dean (Microsoft)
Cheng Deng (Xidian University)
Lipika Dey (TCS Innovation Lab Delhi)
Sauptik Dhar (Robert Bosch)
Weicong Ding (Amazon)
Yuxiao Dong (University of Notre Dame)
Zhenhua Dong (Huawei Technologies)
Pinar Donmez (Microsoft)
Alexey Drutsa (Yandex & Lomonosov Moscow State University)
Nan Du (Google Research)
Hoda Eldardiry (PARC)
Thomas Emerson (Freddie Mac)
Theodoros Evgeniou (INSEAD)
Mehrdad Farajtabar (Georgia Institute of Technology)
Luca Foschini (Evidation Health)
Sorelle Friedler (Haverford College)
Ravi Ganti (Walmart Labs, San Bruno)
Pierre Garrigues (Yahoo)
Mina Ghashami (University of Utah)
Shalini Ghosh (SRI)
Balaji Gopalan (Google)
Mihajlo Grbovic (Airbnb)
Tamara Greasby (Oracle Data Cloud)
Elena Grewal (Airbnb)
Sudipto Guha (University Of Pennsylvania)
Gleb Gusev (Yandex)
Eui-Hong (Sam) Han (The Washington Post)
Tj Hazen (Microsoft)
Arjen Hommersom (Open University of the Netherlands)
Mahmud Shahriar Hossain (University of Texas at El Paso)
Joshua Huang (Shenzhen University)
Samuel Huston (Google)
Hsun-Ping Hsieh (National Cheng Kung University)
Monica Hsu (Intuit)
Alex Jaimes (Columbia University)
Vijay Manikandan Janakiraman (USRA/NASA AMES Research Center)
Warren Jin (CSIRO)
Xiaoming Jin (Tsinghua University)
Purushottam Kar (Indian Institute of Technology Kanpur)
Alexandros Karatzoglou (Telefonica Research)
Tom Kenter (University of Amsterdam)
Krishnaram Kenthapadi (LinkedIn)
Brendan Kitts (AOL)
Noam Koenigstein (Microsoft)
Yun Sing Koh (University of Auckland)
Alek Kolcz (Pushd)
Konstantinos Kollias (Google Research)

Applied Data Science Track Program Committee (continued)

James Kunz (Google)
Henry Leung (University of Calgary)
Cheng-Te Li (National Cheng Kung University)
Shuai Li (University of Cambridge)
Yun Li (Nanjing University of Posts and Telecommunications)
Xiaoli Li (Institute for Infocomm Research)
Shou-De Lin (National Taiwan University)
Lin Liu (University of South Australia)
Yiqun Liu (Tsinghua University)
Yuchen Liu (UCLA)
Sean Lorenz (Senter)
Kun Lui (LinkedIn)
Qiang Ma (Yahoo! Inc.)
Amogh Mahapatra (Apple)
Anirban Majumder (Amazon)
Gideon Mann (Bloomberg LP)
Manish Marwah (Hewlett Packard Labs)
Charalampos Mavroforakis (Boston University)
Wannes Meert (KU Leuven)
Sam Michalka (Olin College)
Boriana Milenova (Oracle)
Avishkar Misra (Oracle)
Gianmarco De Francisci Morales (Qatar Computing Research Institute)
Robert Moskovitch (Deutsche Telekom Laboratories at Ben-Gurion University)
Abdullah Mueen (University of New Mexico)
Saikat Mukherjee (Intuit)
Shubha Nabar (Salesforce)
Nagarajan Natarajan (University of Texas Austin)
Richi Nayak (Queensland University of Technology - Brisbane, Australia)
See-Kiong Ng (National University of Singapore)
Karl Ni (In-Q-Tel)
Scott Nicholson (Consultant)
Alexandros Ntoulas (LinkedIn)
John O'Donovan (University of California Santa Barbara)
Neil O'Hare (Yahoo! Research)
Kok-Leong Ong (La Trobe University)
Girish Palshikar (Tata Consultancy Services Limited)
Debprakash Patnaik (Amazon.com)
Wen-Chih Peng (National Chiao Tung University)
Luisa Polania (AMFAM)
Foster Provost (NYU)
Vladan Radosavljevic (Uber Advanced Technology Group)
Balaraman Ravindran (Indian Institute of Technology Madras)
Bruno Ribeiro (Purdue University)
Marco Tulio Ribeiro (University of Washington)
Alex Sadovsky (Oracle Data Cloud)
Nima Sarshar (Apple)
Ed Seabolt (IBM)
Bin Shao (Microsoft Research Asia)
Li Shen (Indiana University School of Medicine)
Conglei Shi (IBM T.J. Watson Research Center)
Larisa Shwartz (IBM T.J. Watson Research Center)
Mauro Sozio (Télécom ParisTech)
Francesca Spezzano (Boise State University)
Jacob Spoelstra (Microsoft)
Ori Stitelman (dstillery)
Yifan Sun (Technicolor Research)
Can Ozan Tan (Harvard Medical School)
Wei Tan (IBM)
Liang Tang (Google)
Dan Tecuci (Ernst & Young (EY))
Marko Tkalcic (Free University of Bozen-Bolzano)
Yongxin Tong (Beihang University)
Tanguy Urvoy (France Telecom R&D)
Hamed Valizadegan (NASA Ames Research Center)
Christophe Van Gysel (University of Amsterdam)
Jan Van Haaren (KU Leuven)
Lav Varshney (University of Illinois at Urbana-Champaign)
Lovekesh Vig (TCS Research, New Delhi)
Chenguang Wang (IBM Research)
Dingding Wang (Florida Atlantic University)
John Wang (Facebook)
Pengyuan (Penelope) Wang (University of Georgia)
Quan Wang (Chinese Academy of Sciences)
Taifeng Wang (Microsoft Research Asia)
Renato Werneck (Amazon)
Melinda Han Williams (Dstillery)
Yinglong Xia (Huawei Research America)
Cao Xiao (IBM T.J. Watson Research Center)
Bo Xie (Georgia Tech)
Jun Xu (Chinese Academy of Sciences)
De-Nian Yang (Academia Sinica)
Hongxia Yang (Alibaba Group)

Applied Data Science Track Program Committee (continued)

Pei Yang (South China University of Technology)
Yuan Yao (Nanjing University)
Yanfang Ye (West Virginia University)
Shi Yu (American Family Insurance)
Mingxuan Yuan (Huawei Noah Arklab)
Morteza Zadimoghaddam (Google Research)
Chunqiu Zeng (FIU)
Yiye Zhang (Weill Cornell Medical College)
Yuyu Zhang (Georgia Institute of Technology)
Xi Zhang (Weill Cornell Medical College)
Yu Zheng (Microsoft Research)
Zhi Zhou (Allen Institute for Brain Science)
Yada Zhu (IBM T.J. Watson Research Center)
Albrecht Zimmermann (Université Caen Normandie)

KDD 2017 Sponsors & Supporters

Sponsor: ACM SIGKDD

Supporters: Diamond

Supporters: Platinum

Supporters: Gold

sas

Capital One

Supporters: Silver

criteo research

Google

EAI

SIEMENS
Ingenuity for life

LinkedIn

Supporters: Bronze

HUAWEI

Booking.com

Honeywell

THE POWER OF CONNECTED

AMERICAN EXPRESS

ORACLE

Supporters: Lanyard Sponsor

Open for Innovation

KNIME

Supporters: KDD CUP Sponsor

Supporters: Research Track Best Paper Award

Supporters: Industry/Government Track Best Paper Award

Supporters: Dissertation Award

Supporters: Student Travel Awards

Exhibitors:

WiFi Sponsor:

What's Fair?

Cynthia Dwork
Microsoft Research / Harvard University
cdwork@gmail.com

ABSTRACT

Data, algorithms, and systems have biases embedded within them reflecting designers' explicit and implicit choices, historical biases, and societal priorities. They form, literally and inexorably, a codification of values. "Unfairness" of algorithms – for tasks ranging from advertising to recidivism prediction – has attracted considerable attention in the popular press. The talk will discuss the nascent mathematically rigorous study of fairness in classification and scoring.

Author Keywords

Algorithmic bias; data bias; system bias; fairness; classification fairness; scoring fairness; data mining.

KDD'17, August 13-17, 2017, Halifax, NS, Canada.

ACM ISBN 978-1-4503-4887-4/17/08.
DOI: http://dx.doi.org/10.1145/3097983.3105807

BIOGRAPHY

Cynthia Dwork, Distinguished Scientist at Microsoft Research, is renowned for placing privacy-preserving data analysis on a mathematically rigorous foundation. A cornerstone of this work is differential privacy, a strong privacy guarantee frequently permitting highly accurate data analysis. Dwork has also made seminal contributions in cryptography and distributed computing. She is a member of the US National Academy of Sciences and the US National Academy of Engineering, and is a Fellow of the American Academy of Arts and Sciences and the American Philosophical Society. Beginning January, 2017, Dwork will be the Gordon McKay Professor of Computer Science at the Harvard Paulson School of Engineering, the Radcliffe Alumnae Professor at the Radcliffe Institute for Advanced Study, and Professor by Affiliation at Harvard Law School.

The Future of Data Integration

Renée J. Miller
University of Toronto
miller@cs.toronto.edu

ABSTRACT

The value of data explodes when it is integrated. In this talk, I present some important innovations in data integration over the last two decades. These include data exchange [1], which provides a foundation for reasoning about the correctness of transformed data, and the use of declarative mappings in integration [2]. I discuss how data mining has been used to facilitate data integration, including constraint discovery [3], mapping discovery [4], and in schema discovery to combat database decay and facilitate integration [5,6]. I present some important new data integration challenges that arise in data science. These include the use of mining for query and visualization recommendation over massive data lakes [7] and data set search, finding datasets of interest at interactive speeds [8].

CCS Concepts/ACM Classifiers

• Data integration; data exchange; information integration; data mining; data cleaning

Author Keywords

Data science

BIOGRAPHY

Renée J. Miller is a fellow of the Royal Society of Canada and a Professor of Computer Science. She has been named a fellow of the ACM and Bell Canada Chair of Information Systems. She received the US Presidential Early Career Award for Scientists and Engineers (PECASE), the highest honor bestowed by the United States government on outstanding scientists and engineers beginning their careers. She received an NSF CAREER Award, the Premier's Research Excellence Award, and an IBM Faculty Award. She and her co-authors received the ICDT Test-of-Time Award for their influential 2003 paper establishing the foundations of data exchange. She has served on the Board of Trustees of the VLDB Endowment and as President of the Endowment. Her research is funded by NSERC, NSF, IBM, SAP, and Bell Canada among others. She received her PhD in Computer Science from the University of Wisconsin, Madison and Bachelor's degrees in Mathematics and in Cognitive Science from MIT.

KDD'17, August 13-17, 2017, Halifax, NS, Canada.

ACM ISBN 978-1-4503-4887-4/17/08.
DOI: http://dx.doi.org/10.1145/3097983.3105809

REFERENCES

[1] R. Fagin, Ph. G. Kolaitis, R. J. Miller, L. Popa. Data Exchange: Semantics and Query Answering. Theoretical Computer Science, 336(1):89-124, May 2005.

[2] R. Fagin, L. M. Haas, M. A. Hernandez, R. J. Miller, L. Popa, Y. Velegrakis. Clio: Schema Mapping Creation and Data Exchange. Conceptual Modelling: Foundations & Applications, 198-236, 2009.

[3] F. Chiang and R. J. Miller, Discovering Data Quality Rules. PVLDB 1(1):1166-1177, 2008.

[4] A. Kimmig, A. Memory, R. J. Miller, L. Getoor. A Collective Probabilistic Approach to Schema Mapping Discovery. IEEE ICDE, 921-932, 2017.

[5] R. J. Miller and P. Andritsos. Schema Discovery. IEEE Data Engineering Bulletin, 26(3):40-45, 2003.

[6] P. Andritsos, R. J. Miller, P. Tsaparas. Information-Theoretic Tools for Mining Database Structure from Large Data Sets. ACM SIGMOD, 33(2):731-742, 2004.

[7] E. Kandogan, M. Roth, P. M. Schwarz, J. Hui, I. G. Terrizzano, C. Christodoulakis, R. J. Milller. LabBook: Metadata-Driven Social Collaborative Data Analysis. IEEE Big Data, 431-440, 2015.

[8] E. Zhu, F. Nargesian, K. Q. Pu, R. J. Miller. LSH Ensemble: Internet-Scale Domain Search. PVLDB, 9(12):1185-1196 2016.

Three Principles of Data Science: Predictability, Stability, and Computability

Bin Yu
Departments of Statistics and EECS
University of California, Berkeley
binyu@berkeley.edu

ABSTRACT

In this talk, I'd like to discuss the intertwining importance and connections of three principles of data science in the title in data-driven decisions.

Making prediction as its central task and embracing computation as its core, machine learning has enabled wide-ranging data-driven successes. Prediction is a useful way to check with reality. Good prediction implicitly assumes stability between past and future. Stability (relative to data and model perturbations) is also a minimum requirement for interpretability and reproducibility of data driven results (cf. Yu, 2013). It is closely related to uncertainty assessment. Obviously, both prediction and stability principles cannot be employed without feasible computational algorithms, hence the importance of computability.

The three principles will be demonstrated in the context of two neuroscience projects and through analytical connections. In particular, the first project adds stability to predictive modeling used for reconstruction of movies from fMRI brain signlas for interpretable models. The second project use predictive transfer learning that combines AlexNet, GoogleNet and VGG with single V4 neuron data for state-of-the-art prediction performance. Our results lend support, to a certain extent, to the resemblance of these CNNs to brain and at the same time provide stable pattern interpretations of neurons in the difficult primate visual cortex V4.

B. Yu (2013). Stability. Bernoulli, 19 (4), 1484-1500. (Invited paper for the Special Issue commemorating the 300th anniversary of the publication of Jakob Bernoullis Ars Conjectandi in 1712).

KDD'17, August 13-17, 2017, Halifax, NS, Canada.

ACM ISBN 978-1-4503-4887-4/17/08.
DOI: http://dx.doi.org/10.1145/3097983.3105808

Applied Data Science Invited Talks Track at KDD-2017

The Applied Data Science (ADS) Invited Talks Track at KDD-2017 is a continuation of what has now become a "7-year tradition" at KDD conferences. This is the second year the track operates under the ADS name, an evolution from its origins at KDD-2011 as the "Industry Practice Expo".

The KDD Conference on Knowledge Discovery and Data Mining (KDD) is the world's first, largest and best conference on Data Science, Data Mining, and Knowledge Discovery. It brings together a healthy mix of academic researchers, industry and government researchers, and practitioners from a wide range of institutions and fields. The primary focus on KDD is on peer-reviewed research contributions and the academic advancement of the field. This is an important goal and in fact the KDD conference is now recognized as the most competitive and prestigious forum for presenting high quality research results. KDD, being fundamentally an applied field, needs the strong representation of applied work of big impact. Over the years of running the conference we observed that our initial speaker-selection approach needed to be re-thought because of the important contributions made to the field outside traditional academic, industrial and government research laboratories.

The result of this re-thinking was to create a forum that exposes important contributions to Data Science through Big Data Applications that address strategic problems. We wanted to effectively capture the rising importance of Data Science and Machine Learning especially in the Big Data environment where structured and unstructured data create special challenges, and of course present new opportunities. The goal of the Invited Talks Track is to curate contributions from leaders in our field who have made important contributions through the development of a system, the creation of a new and important business, or the development and market introduction of a product,. Some of these important contributions may never see an academic paper or detailed peer-reviewed paper written about them, yet they are of critical importance to our very applied field.

To give you an idea of how rapidly growing this area is, and how this sector of our industry and promises to be highly disruptive across many industries, we cite a couple of articles out of a plethora of such coverage: According to IDC, the global revenues from Big Data and business will grow from $130.1 billion in 2016 to more than $203 billion in 2020, at a compound annual growth rate (CAGR) of 11.7% [1]. Furthermore, to quote from a Forbes article: ""Data monetization" will become a major source of revenues, as the world will create 180 zettabytes of data (or 180 trillion gigabytes) in 2025, up from less than 10 zettabytes in 2015." [2]

Over the past nine months we have worked hard to create a strong program of invited speakers. The focus is first and foremost on applications: deployed, real-world applications addressing strategic problems in industry, in private or public sectors, with quantifiable value delivered. This year we particularly focused on two areas that, in our opinion, are not getting sufficient attention in the Data Science, and Machine Learning communities: the establishment of actual repeatable benchmarks for the field and the creation of tools to track, manage, and bring order and repeatability to the (often messy) work environment of Data Scientists.

The Invited Talks are clustered around the following themes:

Data Science in Sensor Data: David Potere, CEO of Tellus Labs will speak on how common the analysis of spaceborne data has become in his talk: "Spaceborne data enters the mainstream." A related topic is analysis of climate data and will be covered by Professor Vipin Kumar of the

University of Minnesota. Professor Jonathan How of MIT will cover the issues of uncertainty in learning and planning when it comes to dealing with this type of data.

Benchmarks & Process Management in Data Science: Eduardo Ariño de la Rubia, Chief Data Scientist of Domino Data Lab will speak on experiences with large enterprises in deploying process management tools for data scientists. Szilard Pafka, Chief Scientist of Epoch will share experiences and learnings from attempting to uild large scale benchmark metrics and data sets in the field.

Understanding Behavior with Data Science: Professor Andy Berglund, of the University of Florida will speak on "Mining Big Data in NeuroGenetics to Understand Muscular Dystrophy." Mainak Mazumdar, EVP and Chief Research Officer of Nielsen will speak on challenges in media measurement with BigData and Paritosh Desai, SVP Enterprise Data and Analytics of Target addresses the real considerations of successfully delivering results at a large retailer with his talk: "It Takes More than Math and Science to Hit the Bullseye with Data."

Applied Machine Learning: Joshua Bloom, VP of Data and Analytics of GE speaks on machine learning is practical industrial/manufacturing settings.

Rajesh Parekh, Director of Analytics at of Facebook delivers a talk on "Designing AI at Scale to Power Everyday Life." Professor Longbing Cao of UTS speaks on the dramatic results achieved with applying data science for tax enforcement in working with the Australian Taxation Office.

These talks present a rare opportunity to hear from the very best in the field about the most exciting topics when it comes to building highly scalable platforms for Data Science and deploying practical, real-world applications. Our invited speakers will share key insights from their experiences and present valuable lessons learned.

Invited Panel Session: The ADS Invited talks track concludes with a Invited Panel Session titled: **"Benchmarks and Process Management in Data Science: Will We Ever Get Over this Mess?"** which addresses the issues of benchmarks and management of the work environments of Data Scientists to achieve consistency, objectivity, and repeatability.This panel will be moderated by Usama Fayyad of Open Insights. The panelists are: Arno Candel, CTO of H20.ai; Eduardo Ariño de la Rubia, Chief Data Scientist of Domino Data Lab; Szliard Pafka, Chief Scientist of Epoch, Anthony Chong, Founder and CEO of IKASI; and Jeong Yoon Lee, Technical Evangelist at Microsoft.

REFERENCES

[1] See IDC report: *Worldwide Semiannual Big Data and Analytics Spending Guide* - https://www.idc.com/getdoc.jsp?containerId=prUS41826116 - October 2016.

[2] See Forbes Magazine article: "6 Predictions For The $203 Billion Big Data Analytics Market" - https://www.forbes.com/sites/gilpress/2017/01/20/6-predictions-for-the-203-billion-big-data-analytics-market/#61f37fe82083 - January 2017.

Usama M. Fayyad *(Open Insights)*
Evangelos Simoudis *(Synapse Partners)*
Ashok Srivastava *(Verizon)*

More than the Sum of its Parts: Building Domino Data Lab

Eduardo Ariño de la Rubia
Domino Data Lab
eduardo@dominodatalab.com

ABSTRACT

Industry has always leveraged cutting edge quantitative research techniques. From finance and insurance, to marketing and manufacturing, efficiencies and advantages have been seized through measurement, prediction, and the generation of insights– but never at this scale. Organizations which previously may have employed one or two data scientists are now scaling the work to dozens if not hundreds of practitioners. Where previously only a handful of organizations could boast that they were leveraging machine learning and statistical models, now it's a rarity to find an untouched industry or player. Organizations are now faced with the challenges of empowering, scaling, and measuring this workforce to sustain the transformation to the prediction economy. In this talk, I will discuss how and why we built the Domino Data Lab platform. I will talk about the challenges we faced technologically, organizationally and culturally when bringing a system of record to data science.

Author Keywords

Domino Data Lab; industrial machine learning; data science; data science scalability; data science organization.

BIOGRAPHY

Eduardo Arino de la Rubia is chief data scientist at Domino Data Lab. Eduardo is a lifelong technologist with a passion for data science who thrives on effectively communicating data-driven insights throughout an organization. He is a graduate of the MTSU Computer Science department, completed graduate studies in negotiation, conflict resolution, and peace-building from CSUDH, the General Assembly's Data Science program, and the Johns Hopkins Coursera Data Science specialization. You can follow him on Twitter as @earino.

KDD'17, August 13-17, 2017, Halifax, NS, Canada.

ACM ISBN 978-1-4503-4887-4/17/08.
http://dx.doi.org/10.1145/3097983.3106682

Mining Big Data in NeuroGenetics to Understand Muscular Dystrophy

Andy Berglund
University of Florida
USA
aberglund@ufl.edu

ABSTRACT

The recent advances in genome sequencing and analyses of the billions of base pairs in genomic data have been a boon for moving forward our understanding of human disease. In this talk I will describe how genome sequencing has dramatically improved our understanding of the most common adult form of muscular dystrophy, which is myotonic dystrophy. Two different genetic mutations cause thousands of changes in the cells and tissues of myotonic dystrophy patients. Genome sequencing has allowed us to precisely determine the degree of changes across patients, correlate these changes to disease symptoms and allow us to determine quickly in cell and animal models the effectiveness of therapeutic strategies for myotonic dystrophy.

Author Keywords

Genome sequencing; genomic data; muscular dystrophy; myotonic dystrophy; data mining.

BIOGRAPHY

Andy Berglund is a Preeminence Professor of Biochemistry and Molecular Biology in the College of Medicine at the University of Florida. He is the Director of Informatics and Sequencing in the Center for NeuroGenetics. Before joining the faculty at Florida, Andy was a Professor of Chemistry and Biochemistry at the University of Oregon, Associate Dean of Graduate Education and Co-Director of the Bioinformatics Graduate Internship Program. Andy holds a BA in Biochemistry from the University of Colorado and a PhD in Biochemistry from Brandeis University.

KDD'17, August 13-17, 2017, Halifax, NS, Canada.

ACM ISBN 978-1-4503-4887-4/17/08.
http://dx.doi.org/10.1145/3097983.3105813

Industrial Machine Learning

Josh Bloom
GE
josh.bloom@ge.com

ABSTRACT
The ongoing digitization of the industrial-scale machines that power and enable human activity is itself a major global transformation. But the real revolution—in efficiencies, in improved and saved lives—will happen as machine learning automation and insights are properly coupled to the complex systems of industrial data. Leveraging a systems view of real-world use cases from aviation to transportation, I contrast the needs and approaches of consumer versus industrial machine learning. Particularly, I focus on three key areas: combining physics-based models to data-driven models, differential privacy and secure ML (including edge-to-cloud strategies), and interpretability of model predictions.

Author Keywords
Industrial machine learning; physics-based models; data-driven models; differential privacy; secure machine learning; interpretability; data mining.

BIOGRAPHY
Dr. Joshua Bloom is VP of Data & Analytics at GE Digital where he serves as the technology and research lead bringing machine learning applications to market within the GE ecosystem. He was co-founder and CTO of Wise.io, which was acquired by GE Digital in 2016 and has been an astronomy professor at the University of California, Berkeley since 2005. Josh has been awarded the Moore Foundation Data-Driven Investigator Prize and the Pierce Prize from the American Astronomical Society; he is also a former Sloan Fellow, Junior Fellow at the Harvard Society, and Hertz Foundation Fellow; he holds a PhD from Caltech and degrees from Harvard and Cambridge University.

KDD'17, August 13-17, 2017, Halifax, NS, Canada.

ACM ISBN 978-1-4503-4887-4/17/08.
DOI: http://dx.doi.org/10.1145/3097983.3105817

Behavior Informatics to Discover Behavior Insight for Active and Tailored Client Management

Longbing Cao
Advanced Analytics Institute, University of Technology Sydney, Australia
Longbing.Cao@gmail.com

ABSTRACT

Behavior is ubiquitous, and behavior intelligence and insight play an important role in data understanding and business problem-solving. *Behavior Informatics* [1, 2] emerges as an important tool for discovering behavior intelligence and behavior insight. As a computational concept, behavior captures the aspects of the demographics of behavioral subjects and objects; social relationships or norms governing the interactions between behaviors of an individual or a group; behavior sequences or networks and their dynamics; and the impact or effect generated by the behaviors undertaken by subjects on objects. Accordingly, a behavior model [2] captures the subject and the object of a behavior or behavior sequence, the activities conducted by its subject on objects, and the relationships between activities; behavior subject, object, activities and relationships are characterized by their respective attributes. As a result, a behavior is represented as a behavior attributes-based vector; and a subject's behaviors at a time period form a vector-based sequence, namely, represented as a behavior attribute vector-based matrix [3]. With such behavior modeling and from the informatics perspective, behavior informatics takes a top-down approach to systematically and deeply represent, model, reason about, and aggregate behaviors [4]; and a bottom-up approach to analyze and learn behavior occurrences, non-occurrences, dynamics, impact, and utility [2].

Accordingly, for a real-life problem, first, its data is converted to *behavioral data* according to the above behavior model, characterized by the relevant activities that form behavior sequences, and the properties of subjects, objects, activities, and relationships. Second, analytical tasks, such as behavior pattern analysis, abnormal behavior detection, coupled analysis of group behaviors, modeling of behavior impact and utility, discovery of high impact and high utility behaviors, analysis of non-occurring behaviors, and analysis of behavior evolution and dynamics, can be undertaken on such behavioral data. In this way, complex behaviors are quantifiable, computable [5], and manageable.

This talk introduces some of real-life applications of behavior informatics in core business, capital markets and government services. It involves complex individual and group behaviors in relevant business, the interactions between clients and service providers, and relevant behavior sequences and attributes. The examples demonstrate the personalized and early prediction, the prevention and intervention of abnormal behaviors, and the active and tailored management of suspicious clients. Examples include the detection of pool manipulation through analyzing coupled sequences [3] of trading behaviors from multiple associated accounts in stock markets, the intervention of high-impact [6] behaviors in social security for preventing overpayments, the quantification and identification of high-utility [7] behaviors, the identification of and tailored intervention on self-finalizing versus non-self-finalizing taxpaying behaviors [8, 9], and even the impact of non-occurring behaviors [10] in debt recovery and prevention. The real-life case studies show the value and potential of behavior informatics for handling complex and challenging risk management, fraud and non-compliance, and for active and tailored client management in business problems. The examples are associated with highly significant economic benefits and social impact as a result of applying the resultant behavior insight and behavior intelligence[1].

KDD'17, August 13-17, 2017, Halifax, NS, Canada.

ACM ISBN 978-1-4503-4887-4/17/08.
DOI: http://dx.doi.org/10.1145/3097983.3105818

CCS CONCEPTS

• **Information systems applications** → Data Mining; • **Modeling and simulation** → Simulation types and techniques

KEYWORDS

Behavior informatics, behavior computing, behavior intelligence, behavior insight, behavior modeling, user modeling, coupled behavior analysis, non-occurring behavior

REFERENCES

[1] Longbing Cao, et al. Behavior Informatics: A New Perspective. IEEE Intelligent Systems, 29(4): 62-80, 2014.

[2] Longbing Cao, In-depth Behavior Understanding and Use: the Behavior Informatics Approach, Information Science, 180(17); 3067-3085, 2010.

[3] Longbing Cao, Yuming Ou, Philip S Yu. Coupled Behavior Analysis with Applications, IEEE Trans. on Knowledge and Data Engineering, 24(8): 1378-1392, 2012.

[4] Can Wang, Longbing Cao, Chi-Hung Chi. Formalization and Verification of Group Behavior Interactions. IEEE T. Systems, Man, and Cybernetics: Systems 45(8): 1109-1124, 2015.

[5] Longbing Cao, Philip S Yu (Eds). Behavior Computing: Modeling, Analysis, Mining and Decision, Springer, 2012.

[6] Longbing Cao. Zhao Y., Zhang, C. Mining Impact-Targeted Activity Patterns in Imbalanced Data, IEEE Trans. on Knowledge and Data Engineering, 20(8): 1053-1066, 2008.

[7] Junfu Yin, Zhigang Zheng, Longbing Cao. USpan: An Efficient Algorithm for Mining High Utility Sequential Patterns, KDD 2012, 660-668.

[8] Zhigang Zheng, Wei Wei, Chunming Liu, Wei Cao, Longbing Cao, Maninder Bhatia. An effective contrast sequential pattern mining approach to taxpayer behavior analysis, World Wide Web 19(4): 633-651, 2016.

[9] Australian Taxation Office. Commissioner of Taxation Annual Report 2012-2013.

[10] Longbing Cao, Philip S. Yu, Vipin Kumar. Nonoccurring Behavior Analytics: A New Area. IEEE Intelligent Systems 30(6): 4-11, 2015.

[11] Yanchang Zhao, Huaifeng Zhang, Longbing Cao, Chengqi Zhang and Hans Bohlscheid. Mining Both Positive and Negative Impact-Oriented Sequential Rules From Transactional Data, PAKDD2009, pp.656-663.

It Takes More than Math and Engineering to Hit the Bullseye with Data

Paritosh Desai
Target
paritosh.desai@target.com

ABSTRACT

Adopting algorithmic decision-making in a large and complex enterprise such as a Fortune 50 retailer like Target takes much more than clean, reliable data and great data mining capabilities. Yet data practitioners too often start with advanced math and fancy algorithms, rather than working hand-in-hand with business partners to identify and understand the biggest business problems. (Then teams should move onto how algorithms can be applied to those problems.) Another key step for data scientists at large organizations: ensuring that their business partners – the merchants, marketers and supply chain experts – have a baseline understanding of advanced models as well as the proper analytical support tools. Obtaining widespread buy-in and enthusiasm also requires providing a user-friendly interface for business partners with optionality and flexibility that allows the intelligence to be applied to the many varied issues facing a modern retailer, from personalization to supply chain transformation to decisions on assortment and pricing. This talk will explore effective practices and processes — the do's and don'ts — for data scientists to succeed in large, complex organizations like a retailer with 1,800+ stores, major marketing campaigns across multiple channels and a fast growing online business.

Author Keywords

Data science; decision-making; practices and processes; online business; data mining.

BIOGRAPHY

Paritosh Desai is the Chief Data and Analytics Officer at Target. He oversees the work of the Enterprise Data, Analytics & Business Intelligence (EDABI) team, while owning responsibility for enterprise data management and governance. Paritosh and his team are focused on creating value from Target's data assets across all enterprise functions. Under Paritosh's direction, Target has brought in a world-class team of data scientists, engineers and analysts who have created tools and data products that drive decision making across the company. The team's work includes technology that powers personalization capabilities – from product recommendations to ads – as well as IoT applications, fraud detection, supply chain optimization and demand forecasting. The team is also instrumental in creating test-and-measure opportunities for Target experiences, both in stores and online. Paritosh joined Target in 2013, with a background in designing and delivering data science based decision support systems using various advanced data science algorithms and web-scale technologies, primarily for the retail industry. He previously served as Senior Director of Data Science at Gap Inc., where his focus was on applying predictive models for analyzing and affecting customer behavior, inventory planning decisions, and personalization. Before this, he held senior roles at IBM-owned retail analytics firm, DemandTec. Paritosh holds a Ph.D. in Operations Research from Stanford University.

KDD'17, August 13-17, 2017, Halifax, NS, Canada.

ACM ISBN 978-1-4503-4887-4/17/08.
DOI: http://dx.doi.org/10.1145/3097983.3105816

Planning and Learning under Uncertainty: Theory and Practice

Jonathan P. How
MIT

ABSTRACT

This talk will describe recent progress on modeling, planning, learning, and control of autonomous systems operating in dynamic environments, with an emphasis on addressing the challenges faced on various timescales. For example, autonomous robotic agents need to plan/execute safe paths and avoid imminent collisions given noisy sensory information (short timescale), learn how to interact with other agents (possibly humans) with intents that are not known (medium timescale), and perform complex cooperative tasks given imperfect models and knowledge of the environment and teammate actions (long timescale). These tasks are often constrained to be done using onboard computation and perception, which can add significant complexity to the system. The talk will highlight several recently developed solutions to these challenges that have been implemented to demonstrate high-speed agile flight of a quadrotor in unknown, cluttered environments, autonomous navigation of a ground vehicle in complex indoor environments alongside pedestrians, and real-time cooperative multiagent planning with an onboard deep learning-based perception system.?

KDD'17, August 13-17, 2017, Halifax, NS, Canada

ACM 978-1-4503-4887-4/17/08...$15.00.
DOI: http://dx.doi.org/10.1145/3097983.3105812

Big Data in Climate: Opportunities and Challenges for Machine Learning

Anuj Karpatne
Department of Computer Science and Engineering,
University of Minnesota
karpa009@umn.edu

Vipin Kumar
Department of Computer Science and Engineering,
University of Minnesota
kumar001@umn.edu

ABSTRACT

The climate and Earth sciences have recently undergone a rapid transformation from a data-poor to a data-rich environment. In particular, massive amount of data about Earth and its environment is now continuously being generated by a large number of Earth observing satellites as well as physics-based earth system models running on large-scale computational platforms. These massive and information-rich datasets offer huge potential for understanding how the Earth's climate and ecosystem have been changing and how they are being impacted by humans actions. We discuss the challenges involved in analyzing these massive data sets as well as opportunities they present for both advancing machine learning as well as the science of climate change.

KEYWORDS

Climate Science, Earth Observation Data, Machine Learning

1 OPPORTUNITIES FOR BIG DATA

Climate science has experienced a rapid transformation from a data-poor to a data-rich phase in the last few decades, with data from Earth-observing satellites launched by organizations such as NASA, SpaceX, and European Space Agency (ESA), and massive volumes of data from model simulations that are being generated by multiple groups of climate scientists across the world. The growing size and richness of climate data provide numerous opportunities for data science to improve our understanding of the Earths climate. They also provide answers to some of the pressing questions related to climate change mitigation and adaptation [18, 19].

First, data science methods can play a major role in discovering key climatic processes such as teleconnections, which represent pairs of distant regions in the world that show coupled climate activity. A well-known example of such phenomena is the El-Nino Southern Oscillation in the West Pacific Ocean. Automated discovery of teleconnections using data science methods (e.g., recent network-based algorithms [12]) can help us discover previously unknown phenomena

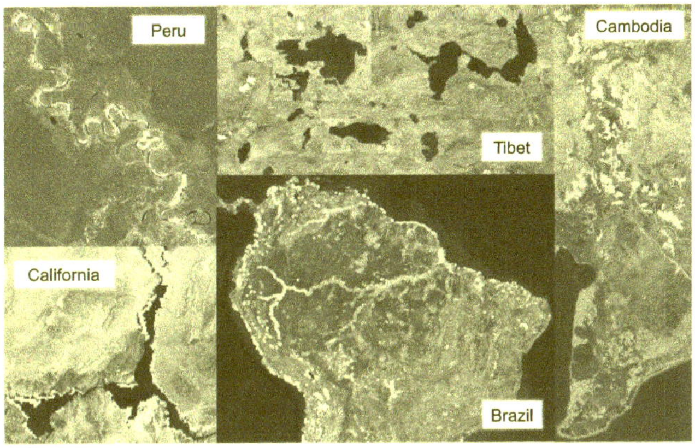

Figure 1: Examples of changes identified by our global surface water monitoring system (green indicates loss of water and red indicates gain in water in the last 15 years). This includes river migrations in floodplains of Peru (possibly aided by increased soil erosion due to deforestation in the Amazonian tropical forests), expanding glacial lakes in Tibet due to melting glaciers, declining water supplies in drought-stricken lakes of California and Cambodia, and increasing constructions of dams and reservoirs in Brazil and around the world that have a variety of ecological impacts. (Image backgrounds are courtesy of Bing Aerial Imagery.)

in climate[15, 16]. We can also use data science methods to identify relationships in climate science that exist beyond pairs of regions such as tripoles [3, 14]. Insights gained from such analyses can also help in evaluating and refining climate models based on their ability to reproduce vital climatic processes.

Second, the vast amount of remote sensing data being collected by Earth-observing satellites can help us monitor critical environmental resources and their interactions with the changing climate. Some examples include monitoring the dynamics of surface water bodies [2, 13] that are impacted by changing climate and human actions (Figure ??), mapping tropical forest fires [1, 17] that are one of the major contributors of greenhouse gas emissions worldwide, monitoring conversions of tropical forests to oil palm plantations [8–10] and understanding how extreme rainfall patterns are impacted by climate change [6].

KDD '17, August 13-17, 2017, Halifax, NS, Canada

ACM ISBN 978-1-4503-4887-4/17/08.
https://doi.org/10.1145/3097983.3105810

2 CHALLENGES AND RESEARCH NEEDS

Although big data in climate offers numerous research opportunities and the data science community is increasingly becoming eager to explore applications in climate domains [7], there are a number of challenges in utilizing the full potential in climate data for accelerating scientific discovery, relative to the level of success achieved by data science in the commercial arena.

One challenge is that, while traditional data science algorithms are designed for handling well-defined objects, such as items bought in market-basket transactions or lists of friends in social networks, objects of interest in climate science often appear as loosely defined patterns in continuous space-time fields that evolve over space and time. For example, ocean eddies (swirling bodies of water and nutrients in the ocean) appear as changes in sea surface height data with loose boundaries around their edges.

Another challenge is that climate science problems often involve the complex nature of relationships among physical variables that are difficult to extract from the limited number of climate records. For example, high-quality sensor measurements of climate variables on a global scale are only available for the recent past (40 to 100 years). This limits the usefulness of several state-of-the-art data science algorithms such as deep learning, whose success in speech and image recognition problems have been greatly enabled by the internet-scale availability of data in these domains. In fact, black-box data science methods, that are oblivious to the rich understanding of the physical processes driving climatic phenomena, have met with limited success in climate science [4].

To fully capitalize the power of big data for accelerating scientific discovery in the domain of climate, there is an increasing interest in developing a systematic way of integrating climate science knowledge in state-of-the-art data science algorithms. This theory-guided data science paradigm [5, 11] is expected to be a key enabler in advancing our knowledge of the Earths climate system and informing adaptation and mitigation policies related to combating climate change.

3 ACKNOWLEDGMENTS

This work was supported by NSF grant IIS-1029771 and NASA awards 14-CMAC14-0010 and NNX12AP37G.

REFERENCES

[1] 2017. Global Burned Area Mapping using Satellite Data. https://z.umn.edu/fireviewer. (2017). [Online; accessed 14-July-2017].
[2] 2017. Global Surface Water Monitoring System. http://z.umn.edu/monitoringwater. (2017). [Online; accessed 14-July-2017].
[3] Saurabh Agrawal, Gowtham Atluri, Anuj Karpatne, William Haltom, Stefan Liess, Snigdhansu Chatterjee, and Vipin Kumar. 2017. Tripoles: A New Class of Relationships in Time Series Data. In *Knowledge Discovery and Data Mining*. ACM.
[4] Peter M Caldwell, Christopher S Bretherton, Mark D Zelinka, Stephen A Klein, Benjamin D Santer, and Benjamin M Sanderson. 2014. Statistical significance of climate sensitivity predictors obtained by data mining. *Geophysical Research Letters* 41, 5 (2014), 1803–1808.
[5] James H Faghmous and Vipin Kumar. 2014. A big data guide to understanding climate change: The case for theory-guided data science. *Big data* 2, 3 (2014), 155–163.
[6] Subimal Ghosh, Debasish Das, Shih-Chieh Kao, and Auroop R Ganguly. 2012. Lack of uniform trends but increasing spatial variability in observed Indian rainfall extremes. *Nature Climate Change* 2, 2 (2012), 86–91.
[7] Climate Informatics. 2017. International Conference on Climate Informatics. http://climateinformatics.org. (2017). [Online; accessed 14-June-2017].
[8] Xiaowei Jia, Ankush Khandelwal, James Gerber, Kimberly Carlson, Paul West, and Vipin Kumar. 2016. Learning large-scale plantation mapping from imperfect annotators. In *Big Data (Big Data), 2016 IEEE International Conference on*. IEEE, 1192–1201.
[9] Xiaowei Jia, Ankush Khandelwal, N Guru, James Gerber, Kimberly Carlson, Paul West, and Vipin Kumar. 2017. Predict land covers with transition modeling and incremental learning. In *SIAM International Conference on Data Mining*. SIAM.
[10] Xiaowei Jia, Ankush Khandelwal, Guruprasad Nayak, James Gerber, Kimberly Carlson, Paul West, and Vipin Kumar. 2017. Incremental Dual-memory LSTM in Land Cover Prediction. In *Knowledge Discovery and Data Mining*. ACM.
[11] Anuj Karpatne, Gowtham Atluri, James Faghmous, Michael Steinbach, Arindam Banerjee, Auroop Ganguly, Shashi Shekhar, Nagiza Samatova, and Vipin Kumar. 2017. Theory-guided data science: A new paradigm for scientific discovery. In *IEEE Transactions on Knowledge and Data Engineering, arXiv: 1612.08544*.
[12] Jaya Kawale, Stefan Liess, Arjun Kumar, Michael Steinbach, Peter Snyder, Vipin Kumar, Auroop R Ganguly, Nagiza F Samatova, and Fredrick Semazzi. 2013. A graph-based approach to find teleconnections in climate data. *Statistical Analysis and Data Mining: The ASA Data Science Journal* 6, 3 (2013), 158–179.
[13] Ankush Khandelwal, Anuj Karpatne, Miriam Marlier, Julia Kim, Dennis Lettenmaier, and Vipin Kumar. 2017. An Approach for Global Monitoring of Surface Water Extent Variations Using MODIS Data. In *Remote Sensing of Environment*.
[14] Stefan Liess, Saurabh Agrawal, Snigdhansu Chatterjee, and Vipin Kumar. 2017. A Teleconnection between the West Siberian Plain and the ENSO Region. *Journal of Climate* 30, 1 (2017), 301–315.
[15] Stefan Liess, Arjun Kumar, Peter K Snyder, Jaya Kawale, Karsten Steinhaeuser, Frederick HM Semazzi, Auroop R Ganguly, Nagiza F Samatova, and Vipin Kumar. 2014. Different modes of variability over the Tasman Sea: Implications for regional climate. *Journal of Climate* 27, 22 (2014), 8466–8486.
[16] Mengqian Lu, Upmanu Lall, Jaya Kawale, Stefan Liess, and Vipin Kumar. 2016. Exploring the Predictability of 30-Day Extreme Precipitation Occurrence Using a Global SST–SLP Correlation Network. *Journal of Climate* 29, 3 (2016), 1013–1029.
[17] Varun Mithal, Guruprasad Nayak, Vipin Kumar, Ankush Khandelwal, Nikunj C. Oza, and Rama Nemani. 2017. RAPT: Rare Class Prediction in Absence of True Labels. In *Transactions on Knowledge and Data Engineering*.
[18] University of Minnesota. 2017. Understanding Climate Change: A Data Driven Approach. http://climatechange.cs.umn.edu/. (2017). [Online; accessed 14-June-2017].
[19] National Science Foundation Report. 2016. Using data to better understand climate change. https://nsf.gov/discoveries/disc_summ.jsp?cntn_id=189519. (2016). [Online; accessed 14-July-2017].

Addressing challenges with Big Data for Media Measurement

Mainak Mazumdar
Nielsen
mainak.mazumdar@nielsen.com

ABSTRACT

The digital media and TV - which is increasingly digitized, have amassed and generating enormous amount of data. While extremely useful, the big data generated by these platforms poses unique challenges for Data Scientists working on developing measurement framework and metrics. Most practitioners optimize speed and scale at the expense of accuracy, which is critical for any measurement. And, the trade-off between bias and variance is not in consideration. In this paper, we will demonstrate how Nielsen is combining proprietary ground truth data and methodologies with Big Data to address the accuracy and bias/variance challenges. We argue that high quality ground truth or training set is pre-requisite to deploying Big Data for high quality media measurement. To illustrate the point, we will share how Nielsen is combining its proprietary high quality panels with Set Top Box for TV measurement in the U.S.

Author Keywords
Digital media; TV; media measurement; data mining; big data; proprietary data

KDD'17, August 13-17, 2017, Halifax, NS, Canada.

ACM ISBN 978-1-4503-4887-4/17/08.
http://dx.doi.org/10.1145/3097983.3105814

BIOGRAPHY

Mainak Mazumdar leads the Data Science organization for the Nielsen Company. This includes supporting new initiatives for the such as deploying RPD into US Local TV, launching Total Audience and globalize Digital Ad Ratings, ecommerce and AI. In addition, Mainak launched new competencies in Big Data, Machine Learning/ AI and Data Integration to deploy newer forms of methods in our business. Prior to Nielsen he has held executive positions at Simulmedia, GfK, and Google.

Machine Learning Software in Practice: Quo Vadis?

Szilárd Pafka
Epoch
2644 30th St 2nd Fl
Santa Monica, CA 90401
szilard.pafka@epoch.com

ABSTRACT

Due to the hype in our industry in the last couple of years, there is a growing mismatch between software tools machine learning practitioners wish for, what they would truly need for their work, what's available (either commercially or open source) and what tool developers and researchers focus on. In this talk we will give a couple of examples of this mismatch. Several surveys and anecdotal evidence show that most practitioners work most of the time (at least in the modeling phase) with datasets that fit in the RAM of a single server, therefore distributed computing tools are very often overkill. Our benchmarks (available on github [1]) of the most widely used open source tools for binary classification (various implementations of algorithms such as linear methods, random forests, gradient boosted trees and neural networks) on such data show over 10x speed and over 10x RAM usage difference between various tools, with "big data" tools being the most inefficient. Significant performance gains have been obtained by those tools that incorporate various low-level (close to CPU and memory architecture) optimizations. Nevertheless, we will show that even the best tools show degrading performance on the multi-socket servers featuring a high number of cores, systems that have become widely accessible more recently. Finally, while most of this talk is about performance, we will also argue that machine learning tools that feature high-level easy-to-use APIs provide increasing productivity for practitioners and therefore are preferable.

CCS CONCEPTS

• **Computing methodologies → Supervised learning by classification**;

KEYWORDS

binary classification; software implementations; training speed; memory footprint; accuracy

REFERENCES

[1] Szilárd Pafka. 2016. A Benchmark for the Scalability, Speed and Accuracy of Machine Learning Libraries for Binary Classification. https://github.com/szilard/benchm-ml. (2016).

KDD '17, August 13-17, 2017, Halifax, NS, Canada

ACM ISBN 978-1-4503-4887-4/17/08.
https://doi.org/10.1145/3097983.3106683

Designing AI at Scale to Power Everyday Life

Rajesh Parekh
Facebook
rgparekh@fb.com

ABSTRACT

The majority of the experiences and interactions people have on Facebook today are made possible with AI. Well over 1 billion people enjoy unique, personalized experiences on Facebook that are powered by a wealth of AI and machine learning algorithms. AI is an incredibly fast-moving field: engineers and researchers across the company are turning the latest research breakthroughs into tools, platforms, and infrastructure that make it possible for anyone at Facebook to use AI in the experiences and products they build. This talk will look at how Facebook is conducting and applying industry-leading research to help drive advancements in AI disciplines like computer vision, language understanding, speech and video. We will also talk about building an infrastructure that anyone at Facebook can use to easily reuse algorithms in different products, scale to run thousands of simultaneous custom experiments, and give concrete examples of how employees across the company are able to leverage these platforms to build new AI products and services.

Author Keywords
Artificial Intelligence; Facebook; computer vision; language understanding; speech; video; machine learning infrastructure

KDD'17, August 13-17, 2017, Halifax, NS, Canada.

ACM ISBN 978-1-4503-4887-4/17/08.
DOI: http://dx.doi.org/10.1145/3097983.3105815

BIOGRAPHY

Dr. Rajesh Parekh is Director of Analytics at Facebook. Applying big data analytics to solve challenging business problems and building empathy for the people who use Facebook's products is his passion, and he has 20 years' experience building and leading global data teams. Dr. Parekh leads analytics for Facebook's Applied Machine Learning efforts, which involves using advanced data analytics to build state-of-the-art AI technologies that power a large variety of products across Facebook.

Prior to Facebook, Dr. Parekh was the Vice President of Data Science at Groupon where he built products for large-scale personalization, sales-automation, and marketing optimization. He also worked at Yahoo Labs building display advertising targeting products, at Blue Martini Software developing data mining products for e-commerce, and at Allstate solving insurance problems like cross-sell, retention, and fraud.

Dr. Parekh earned his Ph.D. in Computer Science specializing in Artificial Intelligence from Iowa State University. He is the founding the co-chair of the Applied Data Science Invited Talks track at the KDD conference and is currently serving as co-chair for the Applications track at the IEEE DSAA'2017 conference.

Spaceborne Data Enters the Mainstream

David Potere
Tellus Laboratories
USA
david@telluslabs.com

ABSTRACT

Thanks to a diverse constellation of Earth observing satellites, humanity is effectively looking everywhere, at everything, all the time. And we've been quietly doing so for a long time. The challenge is that for many years these massive data archives have been stranded from operational, cloud-based, modern data science. That is changing fast. In this session we'll do a rapid primer on satellite imagery as a source of novel data about our Earth and discuss how machine learning is a key force for translating all of this Earth data into real insights. We'll use the global agriculture system as a case in point, highlighting some of potential that a spaceborne perspective brings to this vital sector of the economy. Along the way, we will explore some of the beautiful imagery of our home planet that fuels this new class of insights.

Author Keywords

Satellite imagery; spaceborne data; data mining; machine learning; agriculture system.

BIOGRAPHY

David is the co-founder and CEO of TellusLabs, a Boston-based startup that combines decades of satellite imagery with a machine learning platform to answer critical, time-sensitive economic and environmental questions. David co-founded Boston Consulting Group's global data science practice. At TellusLabs, David is combining his love of satellite remote sensing with nearly a decade of practical experience addressing the geospatial and data-driven questions of the Fortune 500. Prior to BCG, David served as a Surface Warfare Officer in the US Navy. He received an AB from Harvard College, an MA in satellite remote sensing from Boston University, and a PhD in geo-demography from Princeton.

KDD'17, August 13-17, 2017, Halifax, NS, Canada.

ACM ISBN 978-1-4503-4887-4/17/08.
http://dx.doi.org/10.1145/3097983.3105811

Benchmarks and Process Management in Data Science: Will We Ever Get Over the Mess?

Usama M. Fayyad
Open Insights
San Francisco, CA
usama@open-insights.com

Arno Candel
H2O.ai, Inc.
Mountain View, CA
arno@h2o.ai

Eduardo Ariño de la Rubia
Domino Data Lab
San Francisco, CA
eduardo@dominodatalab.com

Szilárd Pafka
Epoch
Santa Monica, CA
szilard.pafka@epoch.com

Anthony Chong
IKASI
Palo Alto, CA
anthony.chong@ikasi.ai

Jeong-Yoon Lee
Microsoft
Los Angeles, CA
jeongyoon.lee@microsoft.com

ABSTRACT

This panel aims to address areas that are widely acknowledged to be of critical importance to the success of Data Science projects and to the healthy growth of KDD/Data Science as a field of scientific research. However, despite this acknowledgement of their criticality, these areas receive insufficient attention in the major conferences in the field. Furthermore, there is a lack of actual actions and tools to address these areas in actual practice. These areas are summarized as follows:

1. Ask any data scientist or machine learning practitioner what they spend the majority of their time working on, and you will most likely get an answer that indicates that 80% to 90% of their time is spent on "Data Chasing", "Data Sourcing", "Data Wrangling", "Data Cleaning" and generally what researchers would refer to—often dismissively—as "Data Preparation". The process of producing statistical or data mining models from data is typically "messy" and certainly lacks management tools to help manage, replicate, reconstruct, and capture all the knowledge that goes in 90% of activities of a Data Scientists. The intensive Data Engineering work that goes into exploring and determining the representation of problem and the significant amount of "data cleaning" that ensues creates a plethora of extracts, files, and many artifacts that are only meaningful to the data scientist.
2. The severe lack of Benchmarks in the field, especially ones at big data scale is an impediment to true, objective, measurable progress on performance. The results of each paper are highly dependent on the large degree of freedom an author has on configuring competitive models and on determining which data sets to use (often Data that is not available to others to replicate results on)
3. Monitoring the health of models in production, and deploying models into production environments efficiently and effectively is a black art and often an ignored area. Many models are effectively "orphans" with no means of getting appropriate health monitoring. The task of deploying a built model to production is frequently beyond the capabilities of a Data Scientists and the understanding of the IT team.

For a typical company, a Machine Learning or Data Science expert is a major investment; yet these people are in such hot demand, that likelihood of churn is high. Typically, when a data scientist is replaced, the process pretty much starts over with a tabula rasa... In fact, I would argue most data scientists coming back to tasks they built themselves 1-2 years before are unable to reconstruct what they did.

For this panel, we have selected a unique set of experts who have different experiences and perspectives on these important problems and how they should be dealt with in real environments. It is our hope that the panel discussion will not only produce recommendations on what to do about these painful impediments to successful project deployments, but also serve as an eye opener for the research community to the importance of paying close attention to issues of Data and Model Management in KDD, as well the need to think carefully about the lifecycle of models and how they can be managed, maintained, and deployed systematically.

Without addressing these critical deployment and practice issues, our field will be challenged to grow in a healthy and sustainable way. The expert panelists for this panel along with the panel moderator: Usama Fayyad are listed below along with their biographical sketches.

KDD '17, August 13-17, 2017, Halifax, NS, Canada

ACM ISBN 978-1-4503-4887-4/17/08
https://doi.org/10.1145/3097983.3120998

CCS CONCEPTS

• Information systems→Information systems applications→Data mining
• Computing methodologies→Supervised learning by classication;
• Computing methodologies→Data and Model Management
• Social and professional topics→Professional topics→Management of computing and information systems→File systems management
• Information systems→Data management systems→Information integration

KEYWORDS

Performance benchmarks; software implementations; training speed; memory footprint; accuracy, model management, model deployment and monitoring, Data benchmarks

Panelist: Arno Candel

Dr. Arno Candel is the Chief Technology Officer at H2O.ai, the makers of the distributed and scalable open-source machine-learning platform H2O. Arno is also the main author of H2O's Deep Learning and a key contributor to H2O's GBM and DRF algorithms, and recently has been working on GPU algorithms and Driverless AI. Arno spent the last 5+ years designing and implementing high-performance machine-learning algorithms. Previously, he spent a decade in high-performance computing and ran his code on the world's largest supercomputers as a staff scientist at SLAC National Accelerator Laboratory, where he participated in US DOE scientific computing initiatives and collaborated with CERN on next-generation particle accelerators.

Arno holds a PhD and Masters summa cum laude in Physics from ETH Zurich, Switzerland. He has authored dozens of scientific papers and is a sought-after conference speaker. Arno was named "2014 Big Data All-Star" by Fortune Magazine and featured by ETH GLOBE in 2015. Follow him on Twitter: @ArnoCandel.

Panelist: Eduardo Ariño de la Rubia

Eduardo Arino de la Rubia is chief data scientist at Domino Data Lab. Eduardo is a lifelong technologist with a passion for data science who thrives on effectively communicating data-driven insights throughout an organization. He is a graduate of the MTSU Computer Science department, completed graduate studies in negotiation, conflict resolution, and peacebuilding from CSUDH, the General Assembly's Data Science program, and the Johns Hopkins Coursera Data Science specialization. You can follow him on Twitter as @earino.

Panelist: Szilárd Pafka

Szilard studied Physics in the 90s and has obtained a PhD by using statistical methods to analyze the risk of financial portfolios. Next, he has worked in a bank quantifying and managing market risk. About a decade ago he moved to California to become the Chief Scientist of a credit card processing company doing everything data (analysis, modeling, data visualization, machine learning, data infrastructure etc). He is also the founder/organizer of several meetups in Los Angeles (R, data science etc) and the data science community website datascience.la. He is teaching data science and machine learning in graduate programs at CEU (Europe) and UCLA (California).

Panelist: Anthony Chong

Anthony is the founder/CEO of IKASI. Prior to founding IKASI he helped start the social media advertising company Adaptly, where he was the first employee. Anthony was the Head of Optimization (Data Science), where he was responsible for building their Data Science team, tackling problems ranging from automated ad content and bidding optimization to sentiment analysis. He helped grow the company from three people in an apartment to over 80 employees. Anthony received his BS from the California Institute of Technology, in Computer Science. Anthony serves on the Board of Directors of the Caltech Alumni Association.

Panelist: Jeong-Yoon Lee

Jeong is Technical Evangelist at Microsoft, where he promotes and helps adoption of new Machine Learning technologies among enterprises and communities. He is also Science Advisor at Conversion Logic, where he served as Chief Data Scientist and developed marketing analytics platforms with cutting edge ML models for enterprise clients. Prior to Conversion Logic, Jeong was Lead Applied Science Engineer at Demand Media, where he deployed Machine Learning pipelines for titling, pricing and deduplication algorithms for eHow.com and eNom.com. Jeong was also Co-Founder of Neofect, a smart rehabilitation solution company, and Micro ML, a Machine Learning solution provider for embedded IoT devices.

As an avid competitor, Jeong has participated in over 70 Data Science competitions, won 6 times including KDD Cup 2012 and 2015, finished Top 10 8 times including the Deloitte, AARP, Criteo competitions, and was ranked Top 10 at Kaggle in 2015.

Jeong earned his Ph.D. in Computer Science and M.S. in Electrical Engineering from University of Southern California. He earned his B.S. in Electrical Engineering from Seoul National University.

MODERATOR: Usama Fayyad

Usama is CEO of Open Insights in Silicon Valley which he reactivated after leaving his position as Chief Data Officer and Group Managing Director at Barclays in London (2013-2016). He is served as Interim CTO for Stella.AI a Mountain View, CA and is acting Chief Operations & Technology Officer for MTN's new division: MTN2.0 aiming to extend Africa's largest telco into new revenue streams beyond Voice & Data.

In 2010 Usama was appointed as founding Executive Chairman of OASIS-500 by King Abdullah II of Jordan to build a tech startup investment fund and accelerator in Jordan and MENA Region. He was also Chairman, Co-Founder and CTO of Blue Kangaroo, a mobile search engine service for offers based in Silicon Valley 2011-2013. In 2008, Usama founded Open Insights, a US-based data strategy, technology and consulting firm that helps enterprises deploy data-driven solutions that effectively and dramatically grow revenue and competitive advantage.

Usama became the world's first Chief Data Officer at Yahoo!'s when he served as CDO & EVP (2004-2008) after Yahoo! acquired his second startup: DMX Group, a data mining and data strategy consulting and technology company specializing in Big Data Analytics and Data Science for Fortune 500 clients. In 2000 Usama left his leadership position at Microsoft to co-found and serve as Chairman and CEO digiMine (Audience Science). At Microsoft, he spent 5 years leading the data mining and exploration group at Microsoft Research and headed the data mining products group for Microsoft's server division.

Usama held a leadership role at NASA's Jet Propulsion Laboratory (1989-1996) where his work garnered him the Lew Allen Award for Excellence in Research from Caltech, as well as a U.S. Government medal from NASA.

Usama has published over 100 technical articles on data mining, Artificial Intelligence, machine learning, and databases. He holds over 30 patents, is a Fellow of the Association for Advancement of Artificial Intelligence and a Fellow of the ACM. He has edited two influential books on data mining and served as editor-in-chief on two key industry journals. Usama earned his Ph.D. in engineering in AI/Machine Learning from the University of Michigan, Ann Arbor. He holds two BSE's in Engineering, MSE Computer Engineering and M.Sc. in Mathematics. He is active in the academic community with several adjunct professor posts and is the only person to receive both the ACM's SIGKDD Innovation Award (2007) and Service Award (2003). He serves on several private/public boards

The Future of Artificially Intelligent Assistants

Muthu Muthukrishnan
Rutgers University
New Brunswick, NJ
muthu@cs.rutgers.edu

Andrew Tomkins
Google
Mountain View, CA
tomkins@google.com

Larry Heck
Google
Mountain View, CA
larryheck@google.com

Deepak Agarwal
LinkedIn
Sunnyvale, CA
dagarwal@linkedin.com

Alborz Geramifard
Amazon
Boston, MA
alborzg@amazon.com

ABSTRACT

Artificial Intelligence has been present in literature at least since the ancient Greeks. Depictions present a wide range of perspectives of AI ranging from malefic overlords to depressive androids. Perhaps the most common recurring theme is the AI Assistant: C3PO from Star Wars; the Jetson's Rosie the Robot; the benign hyper-efficient Minds of Iain M. Banks's Culture novels; the eerie HAL 9000 of Arthur C. Clarke's 2001: A Space Odyssey. Today, artificially intelligent assistants are actual products in the marketplace, based on startling recent progress in technologies like speaker-independent speech recognition. These products are in their infancy, but are improving rapidly. In this panel, we will address the product and technology landscape, and will ask a series of experts in the field plus the members of the audience to take a stance on what the future of artificially intelligent assistants will look like.

KEYWORDS

Artificial Intelligence; intelligent assistants; conversational bots; speech recognition.

Panelist: Larry Heck

Larry Heck is a Research Director at Google leading an advanced R&D effort behind the Google Assistant. From 2009--2014, he was the Chief Scientist of the Microsoft Speech products team and later a Distinguished Engineer in Microsoft Research. In 2009, he co--founded the initiative that led to Microsoft's Cortana personal assistant. From 2005 to 2009, he was Vice President of Search & Advertising Sciences at Yahoo!, responsible for the creation, development, and deployment of the algorithms powering Yahoo! Search, Yahoo! Sponsored Search, Yahoo! Content Match, and Yahoo! display advertising. From 1998 to 2005, he was with Nuance Communications and served as Vice President of R&D, responsible for natural language processing, speech recognition, voice authentication, and text-to-speech synthesis technology. He began his career as a researcher at the Stanford Research Institute (1992-1998), initially in the field of acoustics and later in speech research with the Speech Technology and Research (STAR) Laboratory. Dr. Heck received the PhD in Electrical Engineering from the Georgia Institute of Technology in 1991. He is a Fellow of the IEEE and holds over 50 United States patents.

Panelist: Alborz Geramifard

Alborz Geramifard is currently a machine learning manager at Amazon, leading the conversational AI team in Alexa Boston. He has led more than a dozen NLU Models for Alexa. Before joining Amazon, he was a postdoctoral associate at MIT's Laboratory for Information and Decision Systems. Alborz received his PhD from MIT working on representation learning and safe exploration in large-scale sensitive sequential decision-making problems in 2012. He completed his MSc at University of Alberta in 2008, where he worked on data efficient online reinforcement learning techniques. His research interests lie in machine learning with the focus on reinforcement learning, natural language understanding, planning, and brain and cognitive sciences. Alborz was the recipient of the NSERC postgraduate scholarships 2010-2012 program.

Panelist: Deepak Agarwal

Deepak Agarwal is currently leading AI and ML efforts across LinkedIn. He is most well known for his work on personalization and recommender systems and has published a book on the topic. He has also published extensively in top-tier computer science conferences and has coauthored several patents. He is a Fellow of the American Statistical Association and has served on the Executive Committee of Knowledge

KDD '17, August 13-17, 2017, Halifax, NS, Canada

ACM ISBN 978-1-4503-4887-4/17/08
https://doi.org/10.1145/3097983.3120999

Discovery and Data Mining (KDD). Deepak regularly serves on program committees of various conferences in the field of AI and computer science. He is also an associate editor of two flagship statistics journals.

MODERATOR: Muthu Muthukrishnan

Muthu Muthukrishnan is a Distinguished Professor of Computer Science at Rutgers Univ. He has previously worked at Microsoft, Google, AT&T and Bell Labs. His research interest is in design and analysis of algorithms with applications to streaming, online auctions, IP networking, scheduling, string analysis and so on. He heads the Massive Data Analysis Lab (MassDAL) at Rutgers University.

MODERATOR: Andrew Tomkins

Andrew joined Google Research in 2009, where he serves as an engineering director, currently working on machine learning and understanding of geo data. Prior to these projects, he worked on measurement, modeling, and analysis of content, communities, and users on the World Wide Web. Before joining Google, he spent four years at Yahoo! serving as chief scientist of search, and eight years at IBM's Almaden Research Center, where he served as chief scientist on the WebFountain project. Andrew has authored over 100 technical papers and 90 issued patents. He received Bachelors degrees in Mathematics and Computer Science from MIT, and a PhD in CS from Carnegie Mellon University.

Learning Certifiably Optimal Rule Lists

Elaine Angelino
EECS, UC Berkeley
Berkeley, CA 94720
elaine@eecs.berkeley.edu

Nicholas Larus-Stone
Daniel Alabi, Margo Seltzer
SEAS, Harvard University
Cambridge, MA 02138
nlarusstone@college.harvard.edu
{alabid@g, margo@eecs}.harvard.edu

Cynthia Rudin
Duke University
Durham, NC 27708
cynthia@cs.duke.edu

ABSTRACT

We present the design and implementation of a custom discrete optimization technique for building rule lists over a categorical feature space. Our algorithm provides the optimal solution, with a certificate of optimality. By leveraging algorithmic bounds, efficient data structures, and computational reuse, we achieve several orders of magnitude speedup in time and a massive reduction of memory consumption. We demonstrate that our approach produces optimal rule lists on practical problems in seconds. This framework is a novel alternative to CART and other decision tree methods.

CCS CONCEPTS

• Computing methodologies → Discrete space search; Classification and regression trees;

KEYWORDS

Rule lists; Decision trees; Optimization; Interpretable models

1 INTRODUCTION

As machine learning continues to gain prominence in socially-important decision-making, the interpretability of predictive models remains a crucial problem. Our goal is to build models that are both highly predictive and easily understood by humans. We use rule lists, also known as decision lists, to achieve this goal. Rule lists are lists composed of if-then statements, which are easily interpreted; the rules give a reason for each prediction (Figure 1).

Constructing rule lists, or more generally, decision trees, has been a challenge for more than 30 years; most approaches use greedy splitting techniques [4, 32, 34]. Recent approaches use Bayesian analysis, either to find a locally optimal solution [6] or to explore the search space [25, 45]. These approaches achieve high accuracy while also managing to run reasonably quickly. However, despite the apparent accuracy of the rule lists generated by these algorithms, there is no way to determine either if the generated rule list is optimal or how close it is to optimal, where optimality is defined with respect to minimization of a regularized loss function.

KDD '17, August 13-17, 2017, Halifax, NS, Canada

ACM ISBN 978-1-4503-4887-4/17/08...$15.00
https://doi.org/10.1145/3097983.3098047

Optimality is important, because there are societal implications for a lack of optimality. Consider the recent ProPublica article on the COMPAS recidivism prediction tool [23]. It highlights a case where a black-box, proprietary predictive model is being used for recidivism prediction. The authors show that the COMPAS scores are racially biased, but since the model is not transparent, no one (outside of the creators of COMPAS) can determine the reason or extent of the bias [23], nor can anyone determine the reason for any particular prediction. By using COMPAS, users implicitly assumed that a transparent model would not be sufficiently accurate for recidivism prediction, *i.e.*, they assumed that a black box model would provide better accuracy. We wondered whether there was indeed no transparent and sufficiently accurate model. Answering this question requires solving a computationally hard problem. Namely, we would like to both find a transparent model that is optimal within a particular pre-determined class of models and produce a certificate of its optimality, with respect to the regularized empirical risk. This would enable one to say, for this problem and model class, with certainty and before resorting to black box methods, whether there exists a transparent model. While there may be differences between training and test performance, finding the simplest model with optimal training performance is prescribed by statistical learning theory.

To that end, we consider the class of rule lists assembled from pre-mined frequent itemsets and search for an optimal rule list that minimizes a regularized risk function, R. This is a hard discrete optimization problem. Brute force solutions that minimize R are computationally prohibitive due to the exponential number of possible rule lists. However, this is a worst case bound that is not realized in practical settings. For realistic cases, it is possible to solve fairly large cases of this problem to optimality, with the careful use of algorithms, data structures, and implementation techniques.

We develop specialized tools from the fields of discrete optimization and artificial intelligence. Specifically, we introduce a special branch-and-bound algorithm, called Certifiably Optimal RulE ListS (CORELS), that provides (1) the optimal solution, (2) a certificate of optimality, and (3) optionally, a collection of near-optimal solutions and the distance between each such solution and the optimal one. The certificate of optimality means that we can investigate how

if ($age = 23-25$) **and** ($priors = 2-3$) **then predict** *yes*
else if ($age = 18-20$) **then predict** *yes*
else if ($sex = male$) **and** ($age = 21-22$) **then predict** *yes*
else if ($priors > 3$) **then predict** *yes*
else predict *no*

Figure 1: An example rule list that predicts two-year recidivism for the ProPublica dataset, found by CORELS.

close other models (*e.g.*, models provided by greedy algorithms) are to optimal. In particular, we can investigate if the rule lists from probabilistic approaches are nearly optimal or whether those approaches sacrifice too much accuracy in the interest of speed.

The efficacy of CORELS depends on how much of the search space our bounds allow us to prune; we seek a tight lower bound on R. The bound we maintain throughout execution is a maximum of several bounds that come in three categories. The first category of bounds are those intrinsic to the rules themselves. This category includes bounds stating that each rule must capture sufficient data; if not, the rule list is provably non-optimal. The second type of bound compares a lower bound on the value of R to that of the current best solution. This allows us to exclude parts of the search space that could never be better than our current solution. Finally, our last type of bound is based on comparing incomplete rule lists that capture the same data and allows us to pursue only the most accurate option. This last class of bounds is especially important – without our use of a novel *symmetry-aware map*, we are unable to solve most problems of reasonable scale. This symmetry-aware map keeps track of the best accuracy over all observed permutations of a given incomplete rule list.

We keep track of these bounds using a modified *prefix tree*, a data structure also known as a trie. Each node in the prefix tree represents an individual rule; thus, each path in the tree represents a rule list such that the final node in the path contains metrics about that rule list. This tree structure, together with a search policy and sometimes a queue, enables a variety of strategies, including breadth-first, best-first, and stochastic search. In particular, we can design different best-first strategies by customizing how we order elements in a priority queue. In addition, we are able to limit the number of nodes in the tree and thereby enable tuning of space-time tradeoffs in a robust manner. This tree structure is a useful way of organizing the generation and evaluation of rule lists.

CORELS targets large (not massive) problems, where interpretability and certifiable optimality are important. We illustrate the efficacy of our approach using (1) the ProPublica COMPAS dataset [23], for the problem of two-year recidivism prediction, and (2) the New York Civil Liberties Union (NYCLU) 2014 stop-and-frisk dataset [30], to predict whether a weapon will be found on a stopped individual who is frisked or searched. We produce certifiably optimal, interpretable rule lists that achieve the same accuracy as approaches such as random forests. This calls into question the need for use of a proprietary, black box algorithm for recidivism prediction.

Our work overlaps with the thesis presented by Larus-Stone [24]. We have also written a long version of this report that includes proofs to all bounds in §3, additional bounds and empirical results, and further implementation and data processing details [1].

Our code is at **https://github.com/nlarusstone/corels**.

2 RELATED WORK

Since every rule list is a decision tree and every decision tree can be expressed as an equivalent rule list, the problem we are solving is a version of the "optimal decision tree" problem, though regularization changes the nature of the problem (as shown through our bounds). The optimal decision tree problem is computationally hard, though since the late 1990's, there has been research on building optimal decision trees using optimization techniques [2, 13, 14]. A particularly interesting paper along these lines is that of Nijssen and Fromont [31], who created a "bottom-up" way to form optimal decision trees. Their method performs an expensive search step, mining all possible leaves (rather than all possible rules), and uses those leaves to form trees. Their method can lead to memory problems, but it is possible that these memory issues can be mitigated using the theorems in this paper.[1] None of these methods used the tight bounds and data structures of CORELS.

Because the optimal decision tree problem is hard, there are a huge number of algorithms such as CART [4] and C4.5 [32] that do not perform exploration of the search space beyond greedy splitting. Similarly, there are decision list and associative classification methods that construct rule lists iteratively in a greedy way [26–28, 34, 37, 40, 41, 46]. Some exploration of the search space is done by Bayesian decision tree methods [7, 8, 12] and Bayesian rule-based methods [25, 45]. The space of trees of a given depth is much larger than the space of rule lists of that same depth, and the trees within the Bayesian tree algorithms are grown in a top-down greedy way. Because of this, authors of Bayesian tree algorithms have noted that their MCMC chains tend to reach only locally optimal solutions. The RIPPER algorithm [10] is similar to the Bayesian tree methods in that it grows, prunes, and then locally optimizes. The space of rule lists is smaller than that of trees, and has simpler structure. Consequently, Bayesian rule list algorithms tend to be more successful at escaping local minima and can introduce methods of exploring the search space that exploit this structure—these properties motivate our focus on lists. That said, the tightest bounds for the Bayesian lists (namely those of Yang et al. [45], upon whose work we build), are not nearly as tight as those of CORELS.

Tight bounds, on the other hand, have been developed for the (immense) literature on building disjunctive normal form (DNF) models, a good example of this is the work of Rijnbeek and Kors [33]. For models of a given size, since the class of DNF's is a proper subset of decision lists, our framework can be restricted to learn optimal DNF's. The field of DNF learning includes work from the fields of rule learning/induction (e.g., early algorithms [9, 15, 29]) and associative classification [41]. Most papers in these fields aim to carefully guide the search through the space of models. If we were to place a restriction on our code to learn DNF's, which would require restricting predictions within the list to the positive class only, we could potentially use methods from rule learning and associative classification to help order CORELS' queue, which would in turn help us eliminate parts of the search space more quickly.

Some of our bounds, including the minimum support bound (§3.7, Theorem 3.8), come from Rudin and Ertekin [36], who provide flexible mixed-integer programming (MIP) formulations using the same objective as we use here; MIP solvers in general cannot compete with the speed of CORELS.

CORELS depends on pre-mined rules, which we obtain here via enumeration. The literature on association rule mining is huge, and any method for rule mining could be reasonably substituted.

CORELS' main use is for producing interpretable predictive models. There is a growing interest in interpretable (transparent,

[1] There is no public version of their code for distribution as of this writing.

comprehensible) models because of their societal importance (see [3, 11, 16, 18, 20, 21, 38, 39, 42]). There are now regulations on algorithmic decision-making in the European Union on the "right to an explanation" [19] that would legally require interpretability of predictions. There is work in both the DNF literature [35] and decision tree literature [17] on building interpretable models. Interpretable models must be so sparse that they need to be heavily optimized; heuristics tend to produce either inaccurate or non-sparse models.

Interpretability has many meanings, and it is possible to extend the ideas in this work to other definitions of interpretability; these rule lists may have exotic constraints that help with ease-of-use. For example, Falling Rule Lists [44] are constrained to have decreasing probabilities down the list, and thus could be easier to use. We are currently working on bounds for Falling Rule Lists [5] similar to those presented here, but even CORELS' basic support bounds do not hold for the falling case.

The models produced by CORELS are predictive only; they cannot be used for policy-making. It is possible to adapt CORELS' framework for causal inference [43], dynamic treatment regimes [47], or cost-sensitive dynamic treatment regimes [22] to help with policy design. Both Wang and Rudin [44] and Lakkaraju and Rudin [22] use Monte Carlo searches to explore the space of rule lists. CORELS could potentially be adapted to handle these kinds of interesting problems.

3 LEARNING OPTIMAL RULE LISTS

3.1 Notation

We restrict our setting to binary classification. Let $\{(x_n, y_n)\}_{n=1}^N$ denote training data, where $x_n \in \{0,1\}^J$ are binary features and $y_n \in \{0,1\}$ are labels. Let $\mathbf{x} = \{x_n\}_{n=1}^N$ and $\mathbf{y} = \{y_n\}_{n=1}^N$, and let $x_{n,j}$ denote the j-th feature of x_n.

A rule list $d = (r_1, r_2, \dots, r_K, r_0)$ of length $K \geq 0$ is a $(K+1)$-tuple consisting of K distinct association rules, $r_k = p_k \rightarrow q_k$, for $k = 1, \dots, K$, followed by a default rule r_0. Figure 1 illustrates a 4-rule list, $d = (r_1, r_2, r_3, r_4, r_0)$. An association rule $r = p \rightarrow q$ is an implication corresponding to the conditional statement, "if p, then q." In our setting, an antecedent p is a Boolean assertion that evaluates to either true or false for each datum x_n, and a consequent q is a label prediction. For example, $(x_{n,1} = 0) \wedge (x_{n,3} = 1) \rightarrow (y_n = 1)$ is an association rule. The final default rule r_0 in a rule list can be thought of as a association rule $p_0 \rightarrow q_0$ whose antecedent p_0 simply asserts true.

Let $d = (r_1, r_2, \dots, r_K, r_0)$ be a rule list, where $r_k = p_k \rightarrow q_k$ for each $k = 0, \dots, K$. We introduce a useful alternate rule list representation: $d = (d_p, \delta_p, q_0, K)$, where we define $d_p = (p_1, \dots, p_K)$ to be d's prefix, $\delta_p = (q_1, \dots, q_K) \in \{0,1\}^K$ gives the label predictions associated with d_p, and $q_0 \in \{0,1\}$ is the default label prediction. For the rule list in Figure 1, we would write $d = (d_p, \delta_p, q_0, K)$, where $d_p = (p_1, p_2, p_3, p_4)$, $\delta_p = (1,1,1,1)$, $q_0 = 0$, and $K = 4$.

Let $d_p = (p_1, \dots, p_k, \dots, p_K)$ be an antecedent list, then for any $k \leq K$, we define $d_p^k = (p_1, \dots, p_k)$ to be the k-prefix of d_p. For any such k-prefix d_p^k, we say that d_p starts with d_p^k. For any given space of rule lists, we define $\sigma(d_p)$ to be the set of all rule lists whose prefixes start with d_p:

$$\sigma(d_p) = \{(d'_p, \delta'_p, q'_0, K') : d'_p \text{ starts with } d_p\}. \tag{1}$$

If $d_p = (p_1, \dots, p_K)$ and $d'_p = (p_1, \dots, p_K, p_{K+1})$ are two prefixes such that d'_p starts with d_p and extends it by a single antecedent, we say that d_p is the parent of d'_p and that d'_p is a child of d_p.

A rule list d classifies datum x_n by providing the label prediction q_k of the first rule r_k whose antecedent p_k is true for x_n. We say that an antecedent p_k of antecedent list d_p captures x_n in the context of d_p if p_k is the first antecedent in d_p that evaluates to true for x_n. A prefix captures those data captured by its antecedents; for a rule list $d = (d_p, \delta_p, q_0, K)$, data not captured by the prefix d_p are classified according to the default label prediction q_0.

Let β be a set of antecedents. We define $\text{cap}(x_n, \beta) = 1$ if an antecedent in β captures datum x_n, and 0 otherwise. For example, let d_p and d'_p be prefixes such that d'_p starts with d_p, then d'_p captures all the data that d_p captures: $\{x_n : \text{cap}(x_n, d_p)\} \subseteq \{x_n : \text{cap}(x_n, d'_p)\}$.

Now let d_p be an ordered list of antecedents, and let β be a subset of antecedents in d_p. Let us define $\text{cap}(x_n, \beta \mid d_p) = 1$ if β captures datum x_n in the context of d_p, *i.e.*, if the first antecedent in d_p that evaluates to true for x_n is an antecedent in β, and 0 otherwise. Thus, $\text{cap}(x_n, \beta \mid d_p) = 1$ only if $\text{cap}(x_n, \beta) = 1$; $\text{cap}(x_n, \beta \mid d_p) = 0$ either if $\text{cap}(x_n, \beta) = 0$, or if $\text{cap}(x_n, \beta) = 1$ but there is an antecedent α in d_p, preceding all antecedents in β, such that $\text{cap}(x_n, \alpha) = 1$. For example, if $d_p = (p_1, \dots, p_k, \dots, p_K)$ is a prefix, then

$$\text{cap}(x_n, p_k \mid d_p) = \left(\bigwedge_{k'=1}^{k-1} \neg\, \text{cap}(x_n, p_{k'}) \right) \wedge \text{cap}(x_n, p_k)$$

indicates whether antecedent p_k captures datum x_n in the context of d_p. Now, define $\text{supp}(\beta, \mathbf{x})$ to be the normalized support of β,

$$\text{supp}(\beta, \mathbf{x}) = \frac{1}{N} \sum_{n=1}^{N} \text{cap}(x_n, \beta), \tag{2}$$

and similarly define $\text{supp}(\beta, \mathbf{x} \mid d_p)$ to be the normalized support of β in the context of d_p,

$$\text{supp}(\beta, \mathbf{x} \mid d_p) = \frac{1}{N} \sum_{n=1}^{N} \text{cap}(x_n, \beta \mid d_p), \tag{3}$$

Next, we address how empirical data constrains rule lists. Given training data $(\mathbf{x}, \mathbf{y})$, an antecedent list $d_p = (p_1, \dots, p_K)$ implies a rule list $d = (d_p, \delta_p, q_0, K)$ with prefix d_p, where the label predictions $\delta_p = (q_1, \dots, q_K)$ and q_0 are empirically set to minimize the number of misclassification errors made by the rule list on the training data. Thus for $1 \leq k \leq K$, label prediction q_k corresponds to the majority label of data captured by antecedent p_k in the context of d_p, and the default q_0 corresponds to the majority label of data not captured by d_p. In the remainder of our presentation, whenever we refer to a rule list with a particular prefix, we implicitly assume these empirically determined label predictions.

Our method is technically an associative classification method since it leverages pre-mined rules.

3.2 Objective function

Define a simple objective function for a rule list $d = (d_p, \delta_p, q_0, K)$:

$$R(d, \mathbf{x}, \mathbf{y}) = \ell(d, \mathbf{x}, \mathbf{y}) + \lambda K. \tag{4}$$

This objective function is a regularized empirical risk; it consists of a loss $\ell(d, \mathbf{x}, \mathbf{y})$, measuring misclassification error, and a regularization term that penalizes longer rule lists. $\ell(d, \mathbf{x}, \mathbf{y})$ is the fraction of training data whose labels are incorrectly predicted by d. In our setting, the regularization parameter $\lambda \geq 0$ is a small constant; *e.g.*, $\lambda = 0.01$ can be thought of as adding a penalty equivalent to misclassifying 1% of data when increasing a rule list's length by one.

3.3 Optimization framework

Our objective has structure amenable to global optimization via a branch-and-bound framework. In particular, we make a series of important observations, each of which translates into a useful bound, and that together interact to eliminate large parts of the search space. We discuss these in depth in what follows:

- Lower bounds on a prefix also hold for every extension of that prefix. (§3.4, Theorem 3.1)
- If a rule list is not accurate enough with respect to its length, we can prune all extensions of it. (§3.4, Lemma 3.2)
- We can calculate *a priori* an upper bound on the maximum length of an optimal rule list. (§3.5, Theorem 3.5)
- Each rule in an optimal rule list must have support that is sufficiently large. This allows us to construct rule lists from frequent itemsets, while preserving the guarantee that we can find a globally optimal rule list from pre-mined rules. (§3.7, Theorem 3.8)
- Each rule in an optimal rule list must predict accurately. In particular, the number of observations predicted correctly by each rule in an optimal rule list must be above a threshold. (§3.7, Theorem 3.9)
- We need only consider the optimal permutation of antecedents in a prefix; we can omit all other permutations. (§3.8, Theorem 3.10 and Corollary 3.11)
- If multiple observations have identical features and opposite labels, we know that any model will make mistakes. In particular, the number of mistakes on these observations will be at least the number of observations with the minority label. (§3.10, Theorem 3.14)

We present additional theorems and all proofs in [1].

3.4 Hierarchical objective lower bound

We can decompose the misclassification error into two contributions corresponding to the prefix and the default rule:

$$\ell(d, \mathbf{x}, \mathbf{y}) \equiv \ell_p(d_p, \delta_p, \mathbf{x}, \mathbf{y}) + \ell_0(d_p, q_0, \mathbf{x}, \mathbf{y}),$$

where $d_p = (p_1, \ldots, p_K)$ and $\delta_p = (q_1, \ldots, q_K)$;

$$\ell_p(d_p, \delta_p, \mathbf{x}, \mathbf{y}) = \frac{1}{N} \sum_{n=1}^{N} \sum_{k=1}^{K} \text{cap}(x_n, p_k \mid d_p) \wedge \mathbb{1}[q_k \neq y_n]$$

is the fraction of data captured and misclassified by the prefix, and

$$\ell_0(d_p, q_0, \mathbf{x}, \mathbf{y}) = \frac{1}{N} \sum_{n=1}^{N} \neg\, \text{cap}(x_n, d_p) \wedge \mathbb{1}[q_0 \neq y_n]$$

is the fraction of data not captured by the prefix and misclassified by the default rule. Eliminating the latter error term gives a lower bound $b(d_p, \mathbf{x}, \mathbf{y})$ on the objective,

$$b(d_p, \mathbf{x}, \mathbf{y}) \equiv \ell_p(d_p, \delta_p, \mathbf{x}, \mathbf{y}) + \lambda K \leq R(d, \mathbf{x}, \mathbf{y}), \quad (5)$$

where we have suppressed the lower bound's dependence on label predictions δ_p because they are fully determined, given $(d_p, \mathbf{x}, \mathbf{y})$.

Algorithm 1 Branch-and-bound for learning rule lists.

Input: Objective function $R(d, \mathbf{x}, \mathbf{y})$, objective lower bound $b(d_p, \mathbf{x}, \mathbf{y})$, set of antecedents $S = \{s_m\}_{m=1}^M$, training data $(\mathbf{x}, \mathbf{y}) = \{(x_n, y_n)\}_{n=1}^N$, initial best known rule list d^0 with objective $R^0 = R(d^0, \mathbf{x}, \mathbf{y})$
Output: Provably optimal rule list d^* with minimum objective R^*

```
(d^c, R^c) ← (d^0, R^0)                ▷ Initialize best rule list and objective
Q ← queue( [ ( ) ] )                    ▷ Initialize queue with empty prefix
while Q not empty do                     ▷ Stop when queue is empty
    d_p ← Q.pop( )                       ▷ Remove prefix d_p from the queue
    if b(d_p, x, y) < R^c then           ▷ Bound: Apply Theorem 3.1
        R ← R(d, x, y)                   ▷ Compute objective of d_p's rule list d
        if R < R^c then                  ▷ Update best rule list and objective
            (d^c, R^c) ← (d, R)
        end if
        for s in S do                    ▷ Branch: Enqueue d_p's children
            if s not in d_p then
                Q.push( (d_p, s) )
            end if
        end for
    end if
end while
(d^*, R^*) ← (d^c, R^c)                  ▷ Identify provably optimal solution
```

Furthermore, $b(d_p, \mathbf{x}, \mathbf{y})$ gives a lower bound on the objective of *any* rule list whose prefix starts with d_p.

Theorem 3.1 (Hierarchical objective lower bound). *Define $b(d_p, \mathbf{x}, \mathbf{y}) = \ell_p(d_p, \delta_p, \mathbf{x}, \mathbf{y}) + \lambda K$, as in (5). Also, define $\sigma(d_p)$ to be the set of all rule lists whose prefixes starts with d_p, as in (1). Let $d = (d_p, \delta_p, q_0, K)$ be a rule list with prefix d_p, and let $d' = (d'_p, \delta'_p, q'_0, K') \in \sigma(d_p)$ be any rule list such that its prefix d'_p starts with d_p and $K' \geq K$, then $b(d_p, \mathbf{x}, \mathbf{y}) \leq R(d', \mathbf{x}, \mathbf{y})$.*

To generalize, consider a sequence of prefixes such that each prefix starts with all previous prefixes in the sequence. It follows that the corresponding sequence of objective lower bounds increases monotonically. This is precisely the structure required and exploited by branch-and-bound, illustrated in Algorithm 1.

Specifically, the objective lower bound in Theorem 3.1 enables us to prune the state space hierarchically. While executing branch-and-bound, we keep track of the current best (smallest) objective R^c, thus it is a dynamic, monotonically decreasing quantity. If we encounter a prefix d_p with lower bound $b(d_p, \mathbf{x}, \mathbf{y}) \geq R^c$, then by Theorem 3.1, we do not need to consider *any* rule list $d' \in \sigma(d_p)$ whose prefix d'_p starts with d_p. For the objective of such a rule list, the current best objective provides a lower bound, *i.e.*, $R(d', \mathbf{x}, \mathbf{y}) \geq b(d'_p, \mathbf{x}, \mathbf{y}) \geq b(d_p, \mathbf{x}, \mathbf{y}) \geq R^c$, and thus d' cannot be optimal.

Next, we state an immediate consequence of Theorem 3.1.

Lemma 3.2 (Objective lower bound with one-step lookahead). *Let d_p be a K-prefix and let R^c be the current best objective. If $b(d_p, \mathbf{x}, \mathbf{y}) + \lambda \geq R^c$, then for any K'-rule list $d' \in \sigma(d_p)$ whose prefix d'_p starts with d_p and $K' > K$, it follows that $R(d', \mathbf{x}, \mathbf{y}) \geq R^c$.*

Therefore, even if we encounter a prefix d_p with lower bound $b(d_p, \mathbf{x}, \mathbf{y}) \leq R^c$, if $b(d_p, \mathbf{x}, \mathbf{y}) + \lambda \geq R^c$, then we can prune all prefixes d'_p that start with and are longer than d_p.

3.5 Upper bounds on prefix length

At any point during branch-and-bound execution, the current best objective R^c implies an upper bound on the maximum prefix length we might still have to consider.

Theorem 3.3 (Upper bound on prefix length). *Consider a state space of all rule lists formed from a set of M antecedents. Let L(d) be the length of rule list d and let R^c be the current best objective. For all optimal rule lists $d^* \in \operatorname{argmin}_d R(d, \mathbf{x}, \mathbf{y})$*

$$L(d^*) \leq \min\left(\lfloor R^c/\lambda \rfloor, M\right), \tag{6}$$

where λ is the regularization parameter.

Corollary 3.4 (Simple upper bound on prefix length). *For all optimal rule lists $d^* \in \operatorname{argmin}_d R(d, \mathbf{x}, \mathbf{y})$,*

$$L(d^*) \leq \min\left(\lfloor 1/2\lambda \rfloor, M\right). \tag{7}$$

For any particular prefix d_p, we can obtain potentially tighter upper bounds on prefix length for all prefixes that start with d_p.

Theorem 3.5 (Prefix-specific upper bound on prefix length). *Let $d = (d_p, \delta_p, q_0, K)$ be a rule list, let $d' = (d'_p, \delta'_p, q'_0, K') \in \sigma(d_p)$ be any rule list such that d'_p starts with d_p, and let R^c be the current best objective. If d'_p has lower bound $b(d'_p, \mathbf{x}, \mathbf{y}) < R^c$, then*

$$K' < \min\left(K + \left\lfloor \frac{R^c - b(d_p, \mathbf{x}, \mathbf{y})}{\lambda} \right\rfloor, M\right). \tag{8}$$

We can view Theorem 3.5 as a generalization of our one-step lookahead bound (Lemma 3.2), as (8) is equivalently a bound on $K' - K$, an upper bound on the number of remaining 'steps' corresponding to an iterative sequence of single-rule extensions of a prefix d_p.

3.6 Upper bounds on prefix evaluations

In this section, we use Theorem 3.5's upper bound on prefix length to derive a corresponding upper bound on the number of prefix evaluations made by Algorithm 1. We present Theorem 3.6, in which we use information about the state of Algorithm 1's execution to calculate, for any given execution state, upper bounds on the number of additional prefix evaluations that might be required for the execution to complete. The relevant execution state depends on the current best objective R^c and information about prefixes we are planning to evaluate, *i.e.*, prefixes in the queue Q of Algorithm 1. We define the number of *remaining prefix evaluations* as the number of prefixes that are currently in or will be inserted into the queue.

Theorem 3.6 (Upper bound on the number of remaining prefix evaluations). *Consider the state space of all rule lists formed from a set of M antecedents, and consider Algorithm 1 at a particular instant during execution. Let R^c be the current best objective, let Q be the queue, and let $L(d_p)$ be the length of prefix d_p. Define $\Gamma(R^c, Q)$ to be the number of remaining prefix evaluations, then*

$$\Gamma(R^c, Q) \leq \sum_{d_p \in Q} \sum_{k=0}^{f(d_p)} \frac{(M - L(d_p))!}{(M - L(d_p) - k)!}, \tag{9}$$

$$\textit{where} \quad f(d_p) = \min\left(\left\lfloor \frac{R^c - b(d_p, \mathbf{x}, \mathbf{y})}{\lambda} \right\rfloor, M - L(d_p)\right). \tag{10}$$

Proof. The number of remaining prefix evaluations is equal to the number of prefixes that are currently in or will be inserted into queue Q. For any such prefix d_p, Theorem 3.5 gives an upper bound on the length of any prefix d'_p that starts with d_p:

$$L(d'_p) \leq \min\left(L(d_p) + \left\lfloor \frac{R^c - b(d_p, \mathbf{x}, \mathbf{y})}{\lambda} \right\rfloor, M\right) \equiv U(d_p). \tag{11}$$

This gives an upper bound on the number of remaining prefix evaluations: $\Gamma(R^c, Q) \leq \sum_{d_p \in Q} \sum_{k=0}^{U(d_p)-L(d_p)} P(M - L(d_p), k)$. □

The proposition below is a naïve upper bound on the total number of prefix evaluations over the course of Algorithm 1's execution. It only depends on the number of rules and the regularization parameter λ; *i.e.*, unlike Theorem 3.6, it does not use algorithm execution state to bound the size of the search space.

Proposition 3.7 (Upper bound on the total number of prefix evaluations). *Define $\Gamma_{tot}(S)$ to be the total number of prefixes evaluated by Algorithm 1, given the state space of all rule lists formed from a set S of M rules. For any set S of M rules,*

$$\Gamma_{tot}(S) \leq \sum_{k=0}^{K} \frac{M!}{(M-k)!}, \quad \textit{where} \quad K = \min(\lfloor 1/2\lambda \rfloor, M). \tag{12}$$

Proof. By Corollary 3.4, $K \equiv \min(\lfloor 1/2\lambda \rfloor, M)$ gives an upper bound on the length of any optimal rule list. We obtain (12) by viewing our problem as finding the optimal selection and permutation of k out of M rules, over all $k \leq K$. □

3.7 Lower bounds on antecedent support

In this section, we give two lower bounds on the normalized support of each antecedent in any optimal rule list; both are related to the regularization parameter λ.

Theorem 3.8 (Lower bound on antecedent support). *Let $d^* = (d_p, \delta_p, q_0, K) \in \operatorname{argmin}_d R(d, \mathbf{x}, \mathbf{y})$ be any optimal rule list, with objective R^*. For each antecedent p_k in prefix $d_p = (p_1, \ldots, p_K)$, the regularization parameter provides a lower bound, $\lambda \leq \operatorname{supp}(p_k, \mathbf{x} \mid d_p)$, on the normalized support of p_k.*

Thus, we can prune a prefix d_p if any of its antecedents captures less than a fraction λ of data, even if $b(d_p, \mathbf{x}, \mathbf{y}) < R^*$. The bound in Theorem 3.8 depends on the antecedents, but not the label predictions, and thus does not account for misclassification error. Theorem 3.9 gives a tighter bound by leveraging this information.

Theorem 3.9 (Lower bound on accurate antecedent support). *Let $d^* \in \operatorname{argmin}_d R(d, \mathbf{x}, \mathbf{y})$ be any optimal rule list, with objective R^*; let $d^* = (d_p, \delta_p, q_0, K)$, with prefix $d_p = (p_1, \ldots, p_K)$ and labels $\delta_p = (q_1, \ldots, q_K)$. For each rule $p_k \rightarrow q_k$ in d^*, define a_k to be the fraction of data that are captured by p_k and correctly classified:*

$$a_k \equiv \frac{1}{N} \sum_{n=1}^{N} \operatorname{cap}(x_n, p_k \mid d_p) \wedge \mathbb{1}[q_k = y_n]. \tag{13}$$

The regularization parameter provides a lower bound, $\lambda \leq a_k$.

Thus, we can prune a prefix if any of its rules correctly classifies less than a fraction λ of data. While the lower bound in Theorem 3.8

is a sub-condition of the lower bound in Theorem 3.9, we can still leverage both – since the sub-condition is easier to check, checking it first can accelerate pruning. In addition to applying Theorem 3.8 in the context of constructing rule lists, we can furthermore apply it in the context of rule mining (§3.1). Specifically, it implies that we should only mine rules with normalized support of at least λ; we need not mine rules with a smaller fraction of observations.[2] In contrast, we can only apply Theorem 3.9 in the context of constructing rule lists; it depends on the misclassification error associated with each rule in a rule list, thus it provides a lower bound on the number of observations that each such rule must correctly classify.

3.8 Equivalent support bound

If two prefixes capture the same data, and one is more accurate than the other, then there is no benefit to considering prefixes that start with the less accurate one. Let d_p be a prefix, and consider the best possible rule list whose prefix starts with d_p. If we take its antecedents in d_p and replace them with another prefix with the same support (that could include different antecedents), then its objective can only become worse or remain the same.

Formally, let D_p be a prefix, and let $\xi(D_p)$ be the set of all prefixes that capture exactly the same data as D_p. Now, let d be a rule list with prefix d_p in $\xi(D_p)$, such that d has the minimum objective over all rule lists with prefixes in $\xi(D_p)$. Finally, let d' be a rule list whose prefix d'_p starts with d_p, such that d' has the minimum objective over all rule lists whose prefixes start with d_p. Theorem 3.10 below implies that d' also has the minimum objective over all rule lists whose prefixes start with *any* prefix in $\xi(D_p)$.

Theorem 3.10 (Equivalent support bound). *Define $\sigma(d_p)$ to be the set of all rule lists whose prefixes start with d_p, as in (1). Let $d = (d_p, \delta_p, q_0, K)$ be a rule list with prefix $d_p = (p_1, \dots, p_K)$, and let $D = (D_p, \Delta_p, Q_0, \kappa)$ be a rule list with prefix $D_p = (P_1, \dots, P_\kappa)$, such that d_p and D_p capture the same data, i.e.,*

$$\{x_n : \text{cap}(x_n, d_p)\} = \{x_n : \text{cap}(x_n, D_p)\}. \quad (14)$$

If the objective lower bounds of d and D obey $b(d_p, \mathbf{x}, \mathbf{y}) \le b(D_p, \mathbf{x}, \mathbf{y})$, then the objective of the optimal rule list in $\sigma(d_p)$ gives a lower bound on the objective of the optimal rule list in $\sigma(D_p)$:

$$\min_{d' \in \sigma(d_p)} R(d', \mathbf{x}, \mathbf{y}) \le \min_{D' \in \sigma(D_p)} R(D', \mathbf{x}, \mathbf{y}). \quad (15)$$

Thus, if prefixes d_p and D_p capture the same data, and their objective lower bounds obey $b(d_p, \mathbf{x}, \mathbf{y}) \le b(D_p, \mathbf{x}, \mathbf{y})$, Theorem 3.10 implies that we can prune D_p. Next, in Sections 3.9 and 3.9.1, we highlight and analyze the special case of prefixes that capture the same data because they contain the same antecedents.

3.9 Permutation bound

If two prefixes are composed of the same antecedents, *i.e.*, they contain the same antecedents up to a permutation, then they capture the same data, and thus Theorem 3.10 applies. Therefore, if one is more accurate than the other, then there is no benefit to considering prefixes that start with the less accurate one. Let d_p be a prefix, and consider the best possible rule list whose prefix starts with d_p. If we permute its antecedents in d_p, then its objective can only become worse or remain the same.

[2] We describe our application of this idea in the appendix of our long report [1].

Formally, let $P = \{p_k\}_{k=1}^K$ be a set of K antecedents, and let Π be the set of all K-prefixes corresponding to permutations of antecedents in P. Let prefix d_p in Π have the minimum prefix misclassification error over all prefixes in Π. Also, let d' be a rule list whose prefix d'_p starts with d_p, such that d' has the minimum objective over all rule lists whose prefixes start with d_p. Corollary 3.11 below, which can be viewed as special case of Theorem 3.10, implies that d' also has the minimum objective over all rule lists whose prefixes start with *any* prefix in Π.

Corollary 3.11 (Permutation bound). *Let π be any permutation of $\{1, \dots, K\}$, and define $\sigma(d_p)$ to be the set of all rule lists whose prefix starts with d_p, as in (1). Let $d = (d_p, \delta_p, q_0, K)$ and $D = (D_p, \Delta_p, Q_0, K)$ denote rule lists with prefixes $d_p = (p_1, \dots, p_K)$ and $D_p = (p_{\pi(1)}, \dots, p_{\pi(K)})$, respectively, i.e., the antecedents in D_p correspond to a permutation of the antecedents in d_p. If the objective lower bounds of d and D obey $b(d_p, \mathbf{x}, \mathbf{y}) \le b(D_p, \mathbf{x}, \mathbf{y})$, then the objective of the optimal rule list in $\sigma(d_p)$ gives a lower bound on the objective of the optimal rule list in $\sigma(D_p)$:*

$$\min_{d' \in \sigma(d_p)} R(d', \mathbf{x}, \mathbf{y}) \le \min_{D' \in \sigma(D_p)} R(D', \mathbf{x}, \mathbf{y}). \quad (16)$$

Thus if prefixes d_p and D_p have the same antecedents, up to a permutation, and their objective lower bounds obey $b(d_p, \mathbf{x}, \mathbf{y}) \le b(D_p, \mathbf{x}, \mathbf{y})$, Corollary 3.11 implies that we can prune D_p. We call this symmetry-aware pruning, and we illustrate the subsequent computational savings next in §3.9.1.

3.9.1 Upper bound on prefix evaluations with symmetry-aware pruning. Here, we present an upper bound on the total number of prefix evaluations that accounts for the effect of symmetry-aware pruning (§3.9). Since every subset of K antecedents generates an equivalence class of $K!$ prefixes equivalent up to permutation, symmetry-aware pruning dramatically reduces the search space.

Algorithm 1 describes a breadth-first exploration of the state space of rule lists. Now suppose we integrate symmetry-aware pruning into our execution of branch-and-bound, so that after evaluating prefixes of length K, we only keep a single best prefix from each set of prefixes equivalent up to a permutation.

Theorem 3.12 (Upper bound on prefix evaluations with symmetry-aware pruning). *Consider a state space of all rule lists formed from a set S of M antecedents, and consider the branch-and-bound algorithm with symmetry-aware pruning. Define $\Gamma_{tot}(S)$ to be the total number of prefixes evaluated. For any set S of M rules,*

$$\Gamma_{tot}(S) \le 1 + \sum_{k=1}^{K} \frac{1}{(k-1)!} \cdot \frac{M!}{(M-k)!}, \quad (17)$$

where $K = \min(\lfloor 1/2\lambda \rfloor, M)$.

Proof. By Corollary 3.4, $K \equiv \min(\lfloor 1/2\lambda \rfloor, M)$ gives an upper bound on the length of any optimal rule list. The algorithm begins by evaluating the empty prefix, followed by M prefixes of length $k = 1$, then $P(M, 2)$ prefixes of length $k = 2$, where $P(M, 2)$ is the number of size-2 subsets of $\{1, \dots, M\}$. Before proceeding to length $k = 3$, we keep only $C(M, 2)$ prefixes of length $k = 2$, where $C(M, k)$ denotes the number of k-combinations of M. Now, the number of length $k = 3$ prefixes we evaluate is $C(M, 2)(M - 2)$. Propagating this forward gives $\Gamma_{tot}(S) \le 1 + \sum_{k=1}^{K} C(M, k-1)(M - k + 1)$. □

Pruning based on permutation symmetries thus yields significant computational savings. Let us compare, for example, to the naïve number of prefix evaluations given by the upper bound in Proposition 3.7. If $M = 100$ and $K = 5$, then the naïve number is about 9.1×10^9, while the reduced number due to symmetry-aware pruning is about 3.9×10^8, which is smaller by a factor of about 23. If $M = 1000$ and $K = 10$, the number of evaluations falls from about 9.6×10^{29} to about 2.7×10^{24}, which is smaller by a factor of about 360,000. While 10^{24} seems infeasibly enormous, it does not represent the number of rule lists we evaluate. As we show in §5, our permutation bound in Corollary 3.11 and our other bounds together conspire to reduce the search space to a size manageable on a single computer. The choice of $M = 1000$ and $K = 10$ in our example above corresponds to the state space size our efforts target. $K = 10$ rules represents a (heuristic) upper limit on the size of an interpretable rule list, and $M = 1000$ represents the approximate number of rules with sufficiently high support (Theorem 3.8) we expect to obtain via rule mining (§3.1).

3.10 Equivalent points bound

The bounds in this section quantify the following: If multiple observations that are not captured by a prefix d_p have identical features and opposite labels, then no rule list that starts with d_p can correctly classify all these observations. For each set of such observations, the number of mistakes is at least the number of observations with the minority label within the set.

Consider a dataset $\{(x_n, y_n)\}_{n=1}^N$ and also a set of antecedents $\{s_m\}_{m=1}^M$. Define distinct observations to be equivalent if they are captured by exactly the same antecedents, *i.e.*, $x_i \neq x_j$ are equivalent if

$$\frac{1}{M} \sum_{m=1}^{M} \mathbb{1}[\text{cap}(x_i, s_m) = \text{cap}(x_j, s_m)] = 1. \quad (18)$$

Notice that we can partition a dataset into sets of equivalent points; let $\{e_u\}_{u=1}^U$ enumerate these sets. Let e_u be the equivalent points set that contains observation x_i. Now define $\theta(e_u)$ to be the normalized support of the minority class label with respect to set e_u, *e.g.*, let $e_u = \{x_n : \forall m \in [M], \mathbb{1}[\text{cap}(x_n, s_m) = \text{cap}(x_i, s_m)]\}$, and let q_u be the minority class label among points in e_u, then

$$\theta(e_u) = \frac{1}{N} \sum_{n=1}^{N} \mathbb{1}[x_n \in e_u] \, \mathbb{1}[y_n = q_u]. \quad (19)$$

The existence of equivalent points sets with non-singleton support yields a tighter objective lower bound that we can combine with our other bounds; as our experiments demonstrate (§5), the practical consequences can be dramatic. First, for intuition, we present a general bound in Proposition 3.13; next, we explicitly integrate this bound into our framework in Theorem 3.14.

Proposition 3.13 (General equivalent points bound). *Let $d = (d_p, \delta_p, q_0, K)$ be a rule list, then $R(d, \mathbf{x}, \mathbf{y}) \geq \sum_{u=1}^{U} \theta(e_u) + \lambda K$.*

Now, recall that to obtain our lower bound $b(d_p, \mathbf{x}, \mathbf{y})$ in (5), we simply deleted the default rule misclassification error $\ell_0(d_p, q_0, \mathbf{x}, \mathbf{y})$ from the objective $R(d, \mathbf{x}, \mathbf{y})$. Theorem 3.14 obtains a tighter objective lower bound via a tighter lower bound on the default rule misclassification error, $0 \leq b_0(d_p, \mathbf{x}, \mathbf{y}) \leq \ell_0(d_p, q_0, \mathbf{x}, \mathbf{y})$.

Theorem 3.14 (Equivalent points bound). *Let d be a rule list with prefix d_p and lower bound $b(d_p, \mathbf{x}, \mathbf{y})$, then for any rule list $d' \in \sigma(d)$ whose prefix d'_p starts with d_p,*

$$R(d', \mathbf{x}, \mathbf{y}) \geq b(d_p, \mathbf{x}, \mathbf{y}) + b_0(d_p, \mathbf{x}, \mathbf{y}), \quad \text{where} \quad (20)$$

$$b_0(d_p, \mathbf{x}, \mathbf{y}) = \frac{1}{N} \sum_{u=1}^{U} \sum_{n=1}^{N} \neg\, \text{cap}(x_n, d_p) \wedge \mathbb{1}[x_n \in e_u] \, \mathbb{1}[y_n = q_u].$$

4 IMPLEMENTATION

For every prefix d_p evaluated during Algorithm 1's execution, we compute the objective lower bound $b(d_p, \mathbf{x}, \mathbf{y})$ and sometimes the objective $R(d, \mathbf{x}, \mathbf{y})$ of the corresponding rule list d. These calculations are the dominant computations and motivate our use of a highly optimized library, designed by Yang et al. [45], for representing rule lists and performing operations encountered in evaluating functions of rule lists. Furthermore, we exploit the hierarchical nature of the objective function and its lower bound to compute these quantities incrementally throughout branch-and-bound execution.

We implement our algorithm using a collection of optimized data structures: a trie (prefix tree), a symmetry-aware map, and a queue. The trie acts like a cache, keeping track of prefixes that we have already evaluated and are also still of interest. Each node in the trie contains metadata associated with that corresponding rule list; the metadata consists of bookkeeping information such as what child rule lists are feasible and the lower bound and accuracy for that rule list. We also track the best observed minimum objective and its associated rule list.

The symmetry-aware map supports symmetry-aware pruning. We implement this using the C++ STL unordered_map, to map all permutations of a set of antecedents to a key, whose value contains the best ordering of those antecedents (*i.e.*, the prefix with the smallest lower bound). Every antecedent is associated with an index, and we call the numerically sorted order of a set of antecedents its canonical order. Thus by querying a set of antecedents by its canonical order, all permutations map to the same key. This map dominates memory usage for problems that explore longer prefixes. Before inserting permutation P_i into the symmetry-aware map, we check if there exists a permutation P_j of P_i already in the map. If no such permutation exists, then we insert P_i in the map. Otherwise, if a permutation P_j exists and the lower bound of P_i is better than that of P_j, we update the map and remove P_j and its subtree from the trie. Else, if P_j exists and has a better lower bound than P_i, we do nothing (*i.e.*, we do not insert P_i into the symmetry-aware map or the trie).

We use a queue to store all of the leaves of the trie that still need to be explored. We order entries in the queue to implement several different policies, including breadth-first search (BFS) and best-first search. For best-first we use a priority queue, ordered by either the lower bound, the objective, or a custom priority metric. In preliminary work (not shown), we also experimented with stochastic exploration processes that do not require a queue; instead, these follow random paths from the root to leaves. Developing such methods could be an interesting direction for future work. We find that ordering by the lower bound and other priority metrics often leads to a shorter runtime than using BFS.

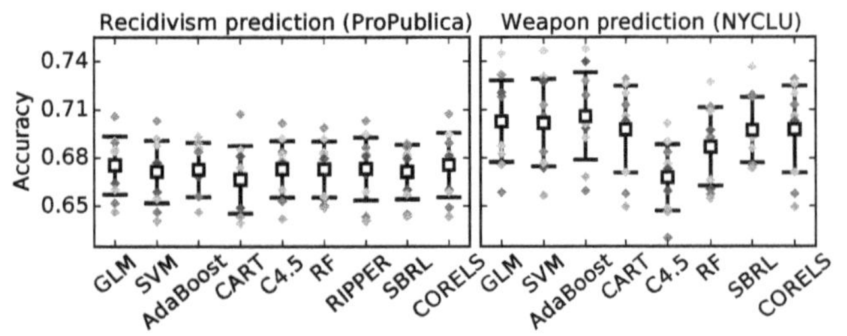

Figure 2: Test accuracy means (white squares), standard deviations (error bars), and values (colors correspond to folds). For CORELS, $\lambda = 0.005$ (left) and $\lambda = 0.01$ (right).

Mapping our algorithm to our data structures produces the following execution strategy. While the trie contains unexplored leaves, a scheduling policy selects the next prefix to extend. Then, for every antecedent that is not already in this prefix, we calculate the lower bound, objective, and other metrics for the rule list formed by appending the antecedent to the prefix. If the lower bound of the new rule list is less than the current minimum objective, we insert that rule list into the symmetry-aware map, trie, and queue, and, if relevant, update the current minimum objective. If the lower bound is greater than the minimum objective, then no extension of this rule list could possibly be optimal, thus we do not insert the new rule list into the tree or queue. We also leverage our other bounds from §3 to aggressively prune the search space.

During execution, we garbage collect the trie. Each time we update the minimum objective, we traverse the trie in a depth-first manner, deleting all subtrees of any node with lower bound larger than the current minimum objective. At other times, when we encounter a node with no children, we prune upwards, deleting that node and recursively traversing the tree towards the root, deleting any childless nodes. This garbage collection allows us to constrain the trie's memory consumption, though in our experiments we observe the minimum objective to decrease only a few times.

5 EXPERIMENTS

Our experimental analysis addresses four questions: (1) How does CORELS' accuracy and model size compare to that of other algorithms? (2) How rapidly do the objective value and its lower bound converge, for different values of λ? (3) How much does each of the implementation optimizations contribute to CORELS' performance? (4) How rapidly does CORELS prune the search space? We present additional empirical results and further implementation and data processing details in a long version of this report [1].

All timed results ran on a server with two Intel Xeon E5-2699 v4 (55 MB cache, 2.20 GHz) processors and 756 GB RAM. Except where we mention a memory constraint, all experiments can run comfortably on smaller machines, *e.g.*, a laptop with 16GB RAM.

We focus on two problems: (1) Predicting which individuals in the ProPublica COMPAS dataset [23] recidivate within two years ($N = 7,215$). Our rule mining procedure yields $M = 156$ single- and two-clause antecedents. (2) Using the NYCLU 2014 stop-and-frisk dataset [30] to predict whether a weapon will be found on a stopped individual who is frisked or searched. We identify a subset of 29,595 records for stopped individuals who were frisked and/or searched. Of these, criminal possession of a weapon was identified in about 5% of instances, thus we resampled due to class imbalance. In the first

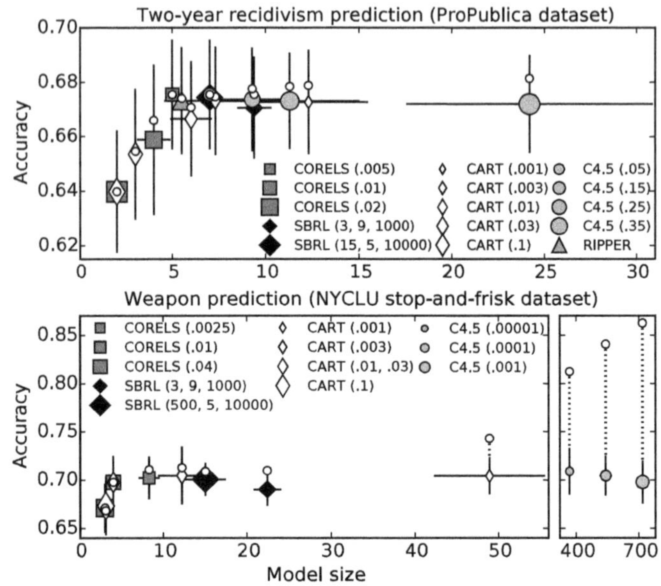

Figure 3: Training and test accuracy as a function of model size. In the legend, numbers in parentheses are algorithm parameters that we vary for CORELS (λ), CART (cp), C4.5 (C), and SBRL (η, λ, i), where i is the number of iterations. Legend markers and error bars indicate means and standard deviations, respectively, of test accuracy across cross-validation folds. Small circles mark training accuracy means. Top: ProPublica dataset. No models exhibit significant overfitting. Bottom: NYCLU dataset. CART with $cp = 0.001$ overfits; C4.5 finds large models and dramatically overfits. Note the broken horizontal axis and change in scale.

two subsections below, we use $M = 28$ single-clause antecedents; in the latter two, we add negations of some, yielding $M = 46$.

Accuracy and model size: We first ran a 10-fold cross validation experiment using CORELS and eight other algorithms:[3] logistic regression, support vector machines, AdaBoost, CART, C4.5, random forests, RIPPER,[4] and scalable Bayesian rule lists (SBRL).[5] Figure 1 shows an optimal rule list that CORELS learns for the ProPublica dataset. Figure 2 shows that there were no statistically significant differences in algorithm accuracies – the difference between folds was far larger than the difference between algorithms. We conclude that CORELS produces models whose accuracy is comparable to those found via other algorithms. Figure 3 summarizes differences in accuracy and model size for CORELS and other tree (CART, C4.5) and rule list (RIPPER, SBRL) learning algorithms. For both problems, CORELS can learn short rule lists without sacrificing accuracy.

Convergence and regularization: We illustrate several views of CORELS execution traces, for the NYCLU stop-and-frisk dataset with $M = 28$ antecedents, for the same three regularization parameters ($\lambda = 0.04, 0.01, 0.025$) as in Figure 3 (bottom). The panels in Figure 4 plot example execution traces, from a single cross-validation fold, of both the current best objective value R^c and the lower

[3]We use standard R packages, with default parameter settings, for the first seven. By default, CART and C4.5 use complexity parameters $cp = 0.01$ and $C = 0.25$, respectively.
[4]We were unable to execute RIPPER for the NYCLU problem.
[5]Code for SBRL can be found at https://github.com/Hongyuy/sbrlmod. By default, SBRL sets $\eta = 3$, $\lambda = 9$, the number of chains to 11 and iterations to 1,000.

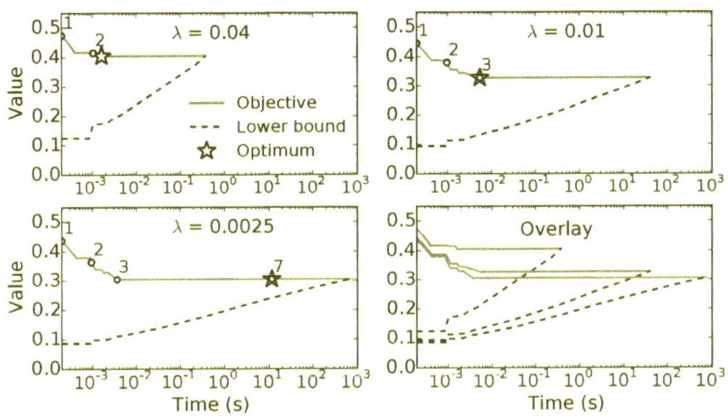

Figure 4: Example CORELS execution traces (NYCLU). Objective value (lines) and lower bound (dashes) for CORELS. Numbered points along the trace of the objective value indicate when the length of the best known rule list changes and are labeled by the new length. For each value of λ, a star marks the optimum and the time at which it was achieved. Bottom right: Overlay of the three traces.

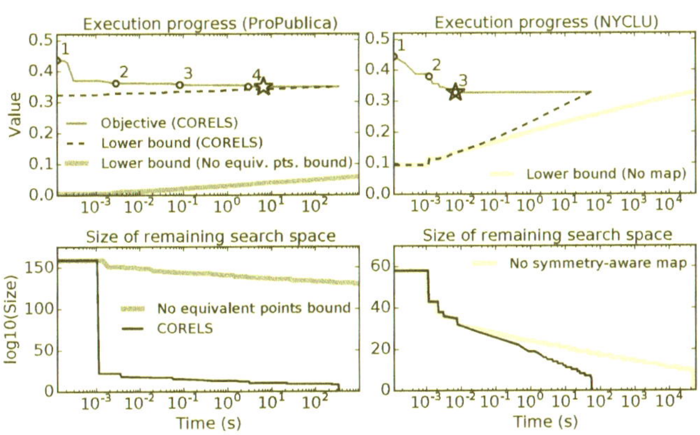

Figure 5: Significant algorithm optimizations for ProPublica (left) and NYCLU (right). Top: Objective value (thin lines) and lower bound (dashes) for CORELS, as in Figure 4, and lower bound (thick lines) for separate executions of variants without equivalent points (left) and permutation (right) bounds. Bottom: Upper bound on remaining search space size, for CORELS (thin lines) and variants (thick lines).

bound $b(d_p, \mathbf{x}, \mathbf{y})$ of the prefix d_p being evaluated. These plots illustrate that CORELS certifies optimality when the lower bound matches the objective value. In these examples, CORELS achieves the optimum in a small fraction of the total execution time.

As λ decreases, these times increase because the search problems become more difficult. In particular, CORELS must evaluate longer prefixes: across 10 cross-validation folds, the maximum evaluated prefix lengths are 6, 11, and 16-17, for $\lambda = 0.04$, 0.01, and 0.025, respectively. Consequently, our data structures grow in size: *e.g.*, across folds, the mean number of queue elements are 1,900 (100), 170,000 (1,300), and 2,400,000 (170,000), with standard deviations shown in parentheses, for $\lambda = 0.04$, 0.01, and 0.025, respectively.

Algorithm optimizations: We determine the efficacy of each of our bounds and data structure optimizations. In the remainder, we show results using the ProPublica dataset. Table 1 provides summary

Algorithm variant	t_{total} (min)	t_{opt} (s)	i_{total} ($\times 10^6$)	Q_{max} ($\times 10^6$)	K_{max}
CORELS	5.4 (1.6)	8 (2)	1.7 (0.4)	1.3 (0.4)	5-6
BFS priority queue	6.4 (2.0)	34 (21)	3.5 (1.4)	2.6 (1.2)	5-6
No support bounds	10.0 (3.3)	12 (4)	2.7 (0.8)	2.2 (0.7)	5-6
No symmetry-aware map	56.8 (22.3)	21 (6)	16.0 (5.9)	14.5 (5.7)	5-6
No lookahead bound	70.0 (22.0)	8 (2)	18.5 (5.9)	17.1 (5.5)	6-7
No equivalent pts bound	>87	>3744	>1004	>987	≥10

Table 1: Per-component performance improvement (ProPublica). Columns report total execution time, time to optimum, number of queue insertions, maximum queue size, and maximum evaluated prefix length. The first row shows CORELS; subsequent rows show variants that each remove one implementation optimization or bound. We terminated each experiment in the last row once the size of the trie reached 10^9 nodes (each execution consumed ~350GB RAM). In all but the final row and column, we report means (and standard deviations) over 10 cross-validation folds; in the final row, we report the minimum values across folds.

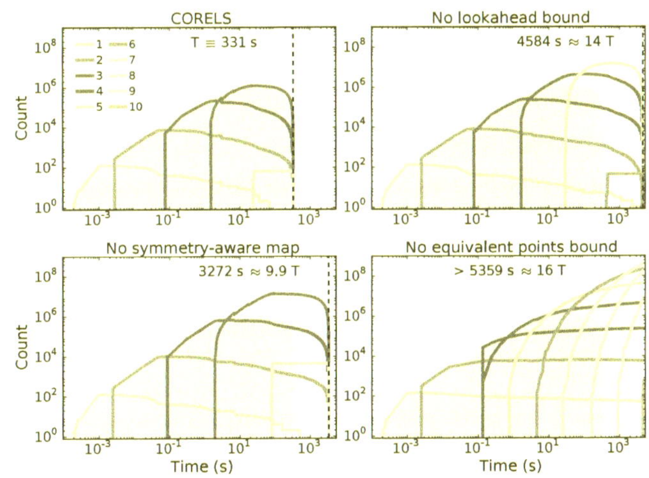

Figure 6: Queue composition (ProPublica). Numbers of prefixes in the queue (log scale), labeled and colored by length, for CORELS (top left) and without three specific implementation optimizations or bounds. Gray shades the area beneath the total number of queue elements for CORELS, *i.e.*, the sum over all lengths in the top left figure. For comparison, we replicate the same gray region in all subfigures.

statistics for experiments using the full CORELS implementation and variants that each remove a specific optimization. Figure 6 presents a view of the same experiments, focusing on three of our optimizations. These plots depict the number of prefixes of a given length in the queue during the algorithm's execution.

State space pruning: Figure 5 highlights the most significant algorithm optimizations for our two problems: the equivalent points bound for the ProPublica dataset (left) and the symmetry-aware map for the NYCLU dataset (right). On the left, for CORELS (thin lines), the objective drops quickly, achieving the optimal value within 10 seconds. CORELS certifies optimality in less than 6 minutes: the objective lower bound steadily converges to the optimal objective (top) as the search space shrinks (bottom). We dynamically and incrementally calculate $\lfloor \log_{10} \Gamma(R^c, Q) \rfloor$, where $\Gamma(R^c, Q)$

is the upper bound on remaining search space size (Theorem 3.6); this adds some computational overhead. In the same plots, we also show a separate execution of CORELS without the equivalent points bound (Theorem 3.14). This execution is far from complete: the lower bound is far from the optimum objective value (top) and much of the search space remains unexplored (bottom). On the right, CORELS achieves the optimum objective in well under a second and certifies optimality in less than a minute. Removing the permutation bound (Corollary 3.11), and thus the symmetry-aware map, increases the execution time by orders of magnitude.

6 CONCLUSION

CORELS is an efficient and accurate algorithm for constructing provably optimal rule lists. Optimality is particularly important in domains where model interpretability has social consequences, *e.g.*, recidivism prediction. While achieving optimality on such discrete optimization problems is computationally hard in general, we aggressively prune our problem's search space via a suite of bounds. This makes realistically sized problems tractable. CORELS is amenable to parallelization, which should allow it to scale to even larger problems.

ACKNOWLEDGEMENTS

E.A. is supported by the Miller Institute for Basic Research in Science, University of California, Berkeley, and is hosted by Prof. M.I. Jordan at RISELab. C.D.R. is supported in part by MIT-Lincoln Labs.

REFERENCES

[1] E. Angelino, N. Larus-Stone, D. Alabi, M. Seltzer, and C. Rudin. 2017. Learning certifiably optimal rule lists for categorical data. *Preprint at arXiv:1704.01701* (April 2017).

[2] K. P. Bennett and J. A. Blue. 1996. *Optimal Decision Trees.* Technical Report. R.P.I. Math Report No. 214, Rensselaer Polytechnic Institute.

[3] I. Bratko. 1997. Machine learning: Between accuracy and interpretability. In *Learning, Networks and Statistics.* International Centre for Mechanical Sciences, Vol. 382. Springer Vienna, 163–177.

[4] L. Breiman, J. H. Friedman, R. A. Olshen, and C. J. Stone. 1984. *Classification and Regression Trees.* Wadsworth.

[5] C. Chen and C. Rudin. 2017. Optimized Falling Rule Lists and Softly Falling Rule Lists. (2017). Work in progress.

[6] H. A. Chipman, E. I. George, and R. E. McCulloch. 1998. Bayesian CART model search. *J. Amer. Statist. Assoc.* 93, 443 (1998), 935–948.

[7] H. A. Chipman, E. I. George, and R. E. McCulloch. 2002. Bayesian treed models. *Machine Learning* 48, 1 (2002), 299–320.

[8] H. A. Chipman, E. I. George, and R. E. McCulloch. 2010. BART: Bayesian additive regression trees. *The Annals of Applied Statistics* 4, 1 (2010), 266–298.

[9] P. Clark and T. Niblett. 1989. The CN2 induction algorithm. *Machine Learning* 3 (1989), 261–283. Issue 4.

[10] W. W. Cohen. 1995. Fast Effective Rule Induction. In *Twelfth International Conference on Machine Learning (ICML).* 115–123.

[11] R. M. Dawes. 1979. The robust beauty of improper linear models in decision making. *American Psychologist* 34, 7 (1979), 571–582.

[12] D. Dension, B. Mallick, and A.F.M. Smith. 1998. A Bayesian CART algorithm. *Biometrika* 85, 2 (1998), 363–377.

[13] D. Dobkin, T. Fulton, D. Gunopulos, S. Kasif, and S. Salzberg. 1996. Induction of shallow decision trees. (1996).

[14] A. Farhangfar, R. Greiner, and M. Zinkevich. 2008. A Fast Way to Produce Optimal Fixed-Depth Decision Trees. In *International Symposium on Artificial Intelligence and Mathematics (ISAIM 2008).*

[15] Eibe Frank and Ian H. Witten. 1998. Generating Accurate Rule Sets Without Global Optimization. In *Proceedings of the Fifteenth International Conference on Machine Learning (ICML '98).* 144–151.

[16] A. A. Freitas. 2014. Comprehensible classification models: a position paper. *ACM SIGKDD Explorations Newsletter* 15, 1 (2014), 1–10.

[17] M. Garofalakis, D. Hyun, R. Rastogi, and K. Shim. 2000. Efficient Algorithms for Constructing Decision Trees with Constraints. In *Proceedings of the Sixth ACM SIGKDD International Conference on Knowledge Discovery and Data Mining (KDD'98).* 335–339.

[18] C. Giraud-Carrier. 1998. Beyond predictive accuracy: What?. In *Proceedings of the ECML-98 Workshop on Upgrading Learning to Meta-Level: Model Selection and Data Transformation.* 78–85.

[19] B. Goodman and S. Flaxman. 2016. European Union regulations on algorithmic decision-making and a "right to explanation". In *ICML Workshop on Human Interpretability in Machine Learning (WHI).*

[20] R. C. Holte. 1993. Very simple classification rules perform well on most commonly used datasets. *Machine Learning* 11, 1 (1993), 63–91.

[21] J. Huysmans, K. Dejaeger, C. Mues, J. Vanthienen, and B. Baesens. 2011. An empirical evaluation of the comprehensibility of decision table, tree and rule based predictive models. *Decision Support Systems* 51, 1 (2011), 141–154.

[22] H. Lakkaraju and C. Rudin. 2017. Cost-sensitive and Interpretable Dynamic Treatment Regimes Based on Rule Lists. In *Proceedings of the Artificial Intelligence and Statistics (AISTATS).*

[23] J. Larson, S. Mattu, L. Kirchner, and J. Angwin. 2016. How We Analyzed the COMPAS Recidivism Algorithm. *ProPublica* (2016).

[24] N. L. Larus-Stone. 2017. *Learning Certifiably Optimal Rule Lists: A Case For Discrete Optimization in the 21st Century.* (2017). Undergraduate thesis, Harvard College.

[25] B. Letham, C. Rudin, T. H. McCormick, and D. Madigan. 2015. Interpretable classifiers using rules and Bayesian analysis: Building a better stroke prediction model. *Annals of Applied Statistics* 9, 3 (2015), 1350–1371.

[26] W. Li, J. Han, and J. Pei. 2001. CMAR: Accurate and efficient classification based on multiple class-association rules. *IEEE International Conference on Data Mining* (2001), 369–376.

[27] B. Liu, W. Hsu, and Y. Ma. 1998. Integrating classification and association rule mining. In *Proceedings of the 4th International Conference on Knowledge Discovery and Data Mining (KDD '98).* 80–96.

[28] M. Marchand and M. Sokolova. 2005. Learning with decision lists of data-dependent features. *Journal of Machine Learning Research* 6 (2005), 427–451.

[29] R.S. Michalski. 1969. On the quasi-minimal solution of the general covering problem. In *Proceedings of the Fifth International Symposium on Information Processing.* 125–128.

[30] New York Civil Liberties Union. 2014. Stop-and-Frisk Data. (2014). http://www.nyclu.org/content/stop-and-frisk-data.

[31] S. Nijssen and E. Fromont. 2010. Optimal constraint-based decision tree induction from itemset lattices. *Data Mining and Knowledge Discovery* 21, 1 (2010), 9–51.

[32] J. R. Quinlan. 1993. *C4.5: Programs for Machine Learning.* Morgan Kaufmann.

[33] P. R. Rijnbeek and J. A. Kors. 2010. Finding a Short and Accurate Decision Rule in Disjunctive Normal Form by Exhaustive Search. *Machine Learning* 80, 1 (July 2010), 33–62.

[34] R. L. Rivest. 1987. Learning Decision Lists. *Machine Learning* 2, 3 (Nov. 1987), 229–246.

[35] U. Rückert and L. De Raedt. 2008. An experimental evaluation of simplicity in rule learning. *Artificial Intelligence* 172 (2008), 19–28.

[36] C. Rudin and S. Ertekin. 2015. Learning Optimized Lists of Rules with Mathematical Programming. (2015). Unpublished.

[37] C. Rudin, B. Letham, and D. Madigan. 2013. Learning Theory Analysis for Association Rules and Sequential Event Prediction. *Journal of Machine Learning Research* 14 (2013), 3384–3436.

[38] S. Rüping. 2006. *Learning interpretable models.* Ph.D. Dissertation. Universität Dortmund.

[39] G. Shmueli. 2010. To explain or to predict? *Statist. Sci.* 25, 3 (Aug. 2010), 289–310.

[40] M. Sokolova, M. Marchand, N. Japkowicz, and J. Shawe-Taylor. 2003. The Decision List Machine. In *Advances in Neural Information Processing Systems (NIPS '03)*, Vol. 15. 921–928.

[41] K. Vanhoof and B. Depaire. 2010. Structure of association rule classifiers: A review. In *Proceedings of the International Conference on Intelligent Systems and Knowledge Engineering (ISKE '10).* 9–12.

[42] A. Vellido, J. D. Martín-Guerrero, and P. J.G. Lisboa. 2012. Making machine learning models interpretable. In *Proceedings of the European Symposium on Artificial Neural Networks, Computational Intelligence and Machine Learning.*

[43] F. Wang and C. Rudin. 2015. Causal Falling Rule Lists. *Preprint at arXiv:1510.05189* (Oct. 2015).

[44] F. Wang and C. Rudin. 2015. Falling Rule Lists. In *Proceedings of Artificial Intelligence and Statistics (AISTATS).*

[45] H. Yang, C. Rudin, and M. Seltzer. 2017. Scalable Bayesian Rule Lists. In *Proceedings of the 34th International Conference on Machine Learning (ICML '17).*

[46] X. Yin and J. Han. 2003. CPAR: Classification based on predictive association rules. In *Proceedings of the 2003 SIAM International Conference on Data Mining (ICDM '03).* 331–335.

[47] Y. Zhang, E. B. Laber, A. Tsiatis, and M. Davidian. 2015. Using decision lists to construct interpretable and parsimonious treatment regimes. *Biometrics* 71, 4 (2015), 895–904.

Improved Degree Bounds and Full Spectrum Power Laws in Preferential Attachment Networks

Chen Avin
Ben Gurion University of the Negev
Be'er-Sheva, Israel
avin@cse.bgu.ac.il

Zvi Lotker
Ben Gurion University of the Negev
Be'er-Sheva, Israel
zvilo@cse.bgu.ac.il

Yinon Nahum
Weizmann Institute of Science
Rehovot, Israel
yinon.nahum@weizmann.ac.il

David Peleg
Weizmann Institute of Science
Rehovot, Israel
david.peleg@weizmann.ac.il

ABSTRACT

Consider a random preferential attachment model $G(p)$ for network evolution that allows both node and edge arrivals. Starting with an arbitrary nonempty graph G_0, at each time step, there are two possible events: with probability $p > 0$ a new node arrives and a new edge is added between the new node and an existing node, and with probability $1 - p$ a new edge is added between two existing nodes. In both cases, the involved existing nodes are chosen at random according to preferential attachment, i.e., with probability proportional to their degree. $G(p)$ is known to generate *power law networks*, i.e., the fraction of nodes with degree k is proportional to $k^{-\beta}$. Here $\beta = (4-p)/(2-p)$ is in the range $(2, 3]$.

Denoting the number of nodes of degree k at time t by $m_{k,t}$, we significantly improve some long-standing results. In particular, we show that $m_{k,t}$ is concentrated around its mean with a deviation of $O(\sqrt{t})$, which is independent of k. We also tightly bound the expectation $\mathbb{E}\left[m_{k,t}\right]$ with an additive error of $O(1/k)$, which is independent of t. These new bounds allow us to tightly estimate $m_{k,t}$ for a considerably larger k values than before. This, in turn, enables us to estimate other important quantities, e.g., the size of the k-rich club, namely, the set of all nodes with a degree at least k.

Finally, we introduce a new generalized model, $G(p_t, r_t, q_t)$, which extends $G(p)$ by allowing also *time-varying* probabilities for node and edge arrivals, as well as the formation of new components. We show that the extended model can produce power law networks with any exponent β in the range $(1, \infty)$. Furthermore, the concentration bounds established for $m_{k,t}$ in $G(p)$ also apply in $G(p_t, r_t, q_t)$.

KEYWORDS

preferential attachment; degree bounds; power law

KDD '17, August 13-17, 2017, Halifax, NS, Canada
© 2017 ACM. 978-1-4503-4887-4/17/08...$15.00
DOI: 10.1145/3097983.3098012

1 INTRODUCTION

1.1 Background

Preferential attachment is one of the prevalent mechanisms for network evolution, in the context of both social networks and other complex systems, and considerable efforts have been invested in studying its properties and behavior. The basic idea in preferential attachment is that "the rich get richer", which translates in a network evolution context to the concept that nodes with high degrees have a better chance to gain new edges, i.e., the probability that a node gains a new edge is proportional to its degree.

A key feature of preferential attachment models is that they are known to generate networks with a power law degree distribution [18], i.e., a distribution where the fraction of nodes with degree k is proportional to $k^{-\beta}$ for some fixed β. The power law degree distribution has been observed in many real life networks (and complex systems), as well as non-network scenarios, and is thought to be a universal property. For example, the preferential attachment model itself was proposed by Price [19] to explain observed power law degree distributions in citation networks and later by Barabasi et al. [4] in order to explain the observed heavy-tailed degree distributions in various other networks.

Specifically, consider the following model $G(p)$ defined in [6]. Starting at time 0 with a graph consisting of a single node with a single self-loop, at time t, with probability $p > 0$ a new node arrives and a new edge is added between the new node and an existing node, and with probability $1 - p$ a new edge is added between two existing nodes. In both cases, existing nodes are chosen at random according to preferential attachment, i.e., with probability proportional to their degree. Letting $m_{k,t}$ denote the number of nodes with degree k at time t, and setting

$$\beta = \frac{4-p}{2-p} \in (2,3] \qquad \text{and} \qquad M_k = \frac{2}{4-p}\prod_{j=1}^{k-1}\frac{j}{j+\beta},$$

the following is shown in [6].

Lemma 1.1. *[6] In the $G(p)$ model the following hold:*

(i) M_k is proportional to $k^{-\beta}$.
(ii) For every **fixed** *k we have*

$$\lim_{t\to\infty}\frac{\mathbb{E}\left[m_{k,t}\right]}{p\cdot t} = M_k .$$

(iii) For every integers k, t and real $c \geq 0$ we have

$$\mathbb{P}\left[|m_{k,t} - p \cdot M_k \cdot (t+1)| \geq 2k\sqrt{t} \cdot \sqrt{c + \ln 2 + (k-1)\ln(t+1)}\right] \leq e^{-c} .$$

Note that while (ii) suggests that the fraction of nodes with degree k obeys a power law with exponent β, it only holds for fixed k and only in the limit ($t \to \infty$). Therefore, it is insufficient in order to estimate $\mathbb{E}\left[m_{k,t}\right]$ for large k, e.g., $k = \sqrt{t}$. Also note that (iii) implies a deviation of $O(\sqrt{k^3 \cdot t \cdot \ln t})$ for $m_{k,t}$ from $p \cdot M_k \cdot (t+1)$. This deviation bound is somewhat dissatisfactory since it increases with k, contrary to the intuition that $m_{k,t}$ should become more concentrated as k increases.

1.2 Paper Contributions

The contribution of our paper is threefold. First, we improve Lemma 1.1(ii) by providing bounds on $\mathbb{E}\left[m_{k,t}\right]$ for every k and t, rather than only for fixed k's and only in the limit $t \to \infty$. This, in turn, allows us to estimate various quantities in $G(p)$, for example, the number of nodes with degree $k = \sqrt{t}$, which was not known before. Our second contribution lies in significantly improving the best previously known concentration bounds for $m_{k,t}$ given by Lemma 1.1(iii), established over a decade ago. Specifically, we bound the deviation by $O(\sqrt{t})$, independent of k, Our third contribution is introducing an extended preferential attachment model that can produce a power law network with any exponent in the range $(1, \infty)$.

Let us now describe our results in more detail. Letting $e_t = e_0 + t$ denote the number of edges at time t, we first prove the following theorem.

THEOREM 1.2. *In the $G(p)$ model, for every integers $t \geq 0$ and $1 \leq k \leq 2e_t$ we have*

$$\mathbb{E}\left[m_{k,t}\right] \leq p \cdot M_k \cdot e_t - \frac{p^2(1-p)}{2(2-p)} \cdot M_k + \frac{c^*}{k} , \quad (1)$$

$$\mathbb{E}\left[m_{k,t}\right] \geq p \cdot M_k \cdot e_t + p(1-p)M_k - \frac{2p(e_0+1-p)}{k(4-p)} , \quad (2)$$

where $c^* = \max\left\{2e_0 \,,\, 2e_1(1-p) \,,\, 2e_1^2 p \,,\, -\frac{8}{\ln(1-p)}\right\}$.

Clearly, Thm. 1.2 implies Lemma 1.1(ii). Note, however, that it also implies a considerably tighter estimate for $\mathbb{E}\left[m_{k,t}\right]$, namely, $|\mathbb{E}\left[m_{k,t}\right] - p \cdot M_k \cdot e_t| \leq O(1/k)$, and thus can be applied to estimate $\mathbb{E}\left[m_{k,t}\right]$ for any $k = o(t^{1-p/2})$.

Also note that Thm. 1.2 may be used to bound the expected size of the "rich club". Formally, defining the *k-rich club* of the network at time t to be the set of all nodes with degree at least k, and denoting its size by

$$RC_{k,t} = \sum_{j \geq k} m_{j,t} ,$$

we prove the following corollary.

COROLLARY 1.3. *In the $G(p)$ model, for every integers $t \geq 0$ and $1 \leq k \leq 2e_t$ we have*

$$\mathbb{E}\left[RC_{k,t}\right] \leq p \cdot e_t \cdot (\varphi_k - \varphi_{2e_t+1}) + c^* \cdot \ln\left(\frac{2e_t}{k-1}\right), \quad (3)$$

$$\mathbb{E}\left[RC_{k,t}\right] \geq p \cdot e_t \cdot (\varphi_k - \varphi_{2e_t+1}) - \frac{2e_0}{3} \cdot \ln\left(\frac{2e_t+1}{k}\right), \quad (4)$$

where $\varphi_z = (1 + (1-p/2)z)M_z = \Theta(z^{1-\beta})$.

Note that Cor. 1.3 implies $|\mathbb{E}\left[m_{k,t}\right] - pe_t(\varphi_k - \varphi_{2e_t+1})| = O(\ln(t/k))$, and thus can be applied to estimate $RC_{k,t}$ for any $k = o((t/\ln t)^{1-p/2})$.

For our second contribution, we prove the following rather general theorem, which extends Lemma 1.1(iii) by bounding any weighted combination of $m_{k,t}$ values. For integer $t \geq 0$ and reals $\boldsymbol{\varepsilon} = (\varepsilon_1, \ldots, \varepsilon_{2e_t}) \in \mathbb{R}^{2e_t}$, let $\Delta_{\boldsymbol{\varepsilon}} = \max_{i,j} |\varepsilon_i - \varepsilon_j|$ be the maximum distance between any two coordinates of $\boldsymbol{\varepsilon}$, and $\|\boldsymbol{\varepsilon}\|_\infty = \max_i |\varepsilon_i|$ be the maximum distance between a coordinate and 0. Also let $S_t(\boldsymbol{\varepsilon}) = \sum_{k=1}^{2e_t} \varepsilon_k \cdot m_{k,t}$.

THEOREM 1.4. *In the $G(p)$ model, for every integer $t \geq 0$, real $c \geq 0$, and reals $\boldsymbol{\varepsilon} = (\varepsilon_1, \varepsilon_2, \ldots, \varepsilon_{2e_t}) \in \mathbb{R}^{2e_t}$, we have*

$$\mathbb{P}\left[S_t(\boldsymbol{\varepsilon}) - \mathbb{E}\left[S_t(\boldsymbol{\varepsilon})\right] \geq \sqrt{2ct} \cdot (2\Delta_{\boldsymbol{\varepsilon}} + 2\max(\Delta_{\boldsymbol{\varepsilon}}, \|\boldsymbol{\varepsilon}\|_\infty))\right] \leq e^{-c} ,$$

$$\mathbb{P}\left[S_t(\boldsymbol{\varepsilon}) - \mathbb{E}\left[S_t(\boldsymbol{\varepsilon})\right] \leq -\sqrt{2ct} \cdot (2\Delta_{\boldsymbol{\varepsilon}} + 2\max(\Delta_{\boldsymbol{\varepsilon}}, \|\boldsymbol{\varepsilon}\|_\infty))\right] \leq e^{-c} .$$

Note that Thm. 1.4 suggests that $m_{k,t}$ is concentrated around its mean with a deviation of $O(\sqrt{t})$. This is given by the following direct corollary.

COROLLARY 1.5. *In the $G(p)$ model, for every integers $k \geq 0, t \geq 0$ and real $c \geq 0$, we have*

$$\mathbb{P}\left[m_{k,t} - \mathbb{E}\left[m_{k,t}\right] \geq \sqrt{32ct}\right] \leq e^{-c},$$

$$\mathbb{P}\left[m_{k,t} - \mathbb{E}\left[m_{k,t}\right] \leq -\sqrt{32ct}\right] \leq e^{-c}.$$

Note that Thm. 1.4 also suggests that $RC_{k,t}$ is concentrated around its mean with a deviation of $O(\sqrt{t})$. This is given by the following direct corollary.

COROLLARY 1.6. *In the model $G(p)$, for every integers $k \geq 0, t \geq 0$ and real $c \geq 0$, we have*

$$\mathbb{P}\left[RC_{k,t} - \mathbb{E}\left[RC_{k,t}\right] \geq \sqrt{32ct}\right] \leq e^{-c},$$

$$\mathbb{P}\left[RC_{k,t} - \mathbb{E}\left[RC_{k,t}\right] \leq -\sqrt{32ct}\right] \leq e^{-c},$$

For our third contribution, we consider a rather general preferential attachment model $G(p_t, r_t, q_t)$ for network evolution that allows three types of events. Starting with an arbitrary nonempty graph G_0, at time t, the following three types of events may occur. i) **Node arrival event:** with probability p_t a new node arrives and a new edge is added between the new node and an existing node. ii) **Edge arrival event:** with probability r_t a new edge is added between two existing nodes, and iii) **Component arrival event:** with probability $q_t = 1 - p_t - r_t$ two new nodes arrive and a new edge is added between them. In the first two cases, existing nodes that participate in the event are chosen at random according to preferential attachment.

The model $G(p_t, r_t, q_t)$ was previously studied with null q_t and constant p_t, i.e., $q_t = 0$ and $p_t = p > 0$ for all t. It is known

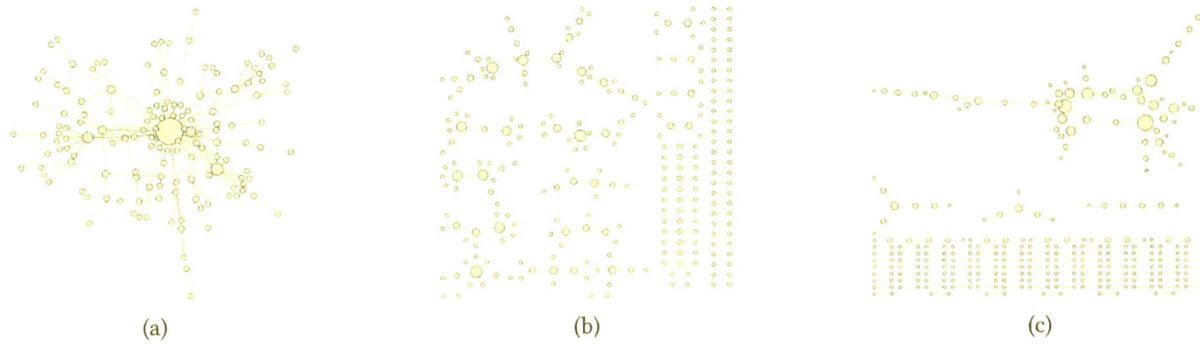

Figure 1: Three networks generated by the model $G(p_t, r_t, q_t)$. Each with 200 edges. Node sizes are proportional to their degrees. (a) No component events: $p_t = 0.75, r_t = 0.25, q_t = 0$. This is the standard model with one connected component. Here $\beta = 2.6$. (b) No edge events: $p_t = 0.75, r_t = 0, q_t = 0.25$. We obtain many connected components. Here $\beta = 3\frac{2}{3}$. (c) No node events: $p_t = 0, r_t = 0.25, q_t = 0.75$. One giant component emerges. Here $\beta = 5$.

that for the special case where q_t is null and p_t is constant, the resulting graph consists of a single connected component and obeys a power law with exponent $\beta = (4-p)/(2-p) \in (2,3]$. In this paper, we extend the model by allowing p_t to vary over time, and even diminish as t tends to infinity. The rationale for this is that it allows us to model situations where the nodes already existing in the network continue to create new connections among themselves, hence as their number grows, the fraction of new edge events grows as well. This also allows the model both to account for changes in the growth rate of large networks, and to explain phenomena which were observed empirically in many networks, but could not be captured by the original model. Such examples are *densification* [17] (i.e., unbounded average degree as the network grows), power law distribution with exponent smaller than 2 or larger than 3 [7], multiple connected components, etc. We show that in this model it is possible to obtain networks obeying a power law with any exponent in the range $(1,\infty)$. In particular, letting $y_t = p_t + 2q_t$, we show that whenever $\lim_{t\to\infty} y_t = y < 2$, $\sum_{i=1}^{\infty} y_i = \infty$ and $\lim_{t\to\infty} t \cdot y_{t+1} / \sum_{j=1}^{t} y_j = \Gamma > 0$, the resulting network obeys a power law with exponent $\beta = 1 + \frac{2\Gamma}{2-y}$. Thus selecting the parameters so as to satisfy $y_t = t^{\alpha-2}$ $(1 < \alpha < 2)$ yields networks obeying a power law with exponent $\beta = \alpha$. Likewise, setting the parameters to satisfy $y_t = 1/\ln(t+2)$ yields networks obeying a power law with exponent $\beta = 2$, and aiming for $y_t = 2 - 2/(\alpha - 1)$ $(\alpha > 2)$ yields networks obeying a power law with exponent $\beta = \alpha$. In addition, we show that Thm. 1.4 applies also in the extended model $G(p_t, r_t, q_t)$, see Thm. 3.1. Figure 1 presents networks generated by the model $G(p_t, r_t, q_t)$ for selected parameters p_t, r_t and q_t.

1.3 Related Work

The first to consider a *preferential attachment* based network evolution process was Price [19] who studied citation networks. Motivated by early work of Simon [20] who showed power laws in non networked settings like wealth, city sizes and word distributions, Price was interested in a network model that will generate a power law degree distribution. He proposed a directed graph model where a new paper cites an existing paper i with probability $\frac{q_i+a}{\sum_i q_i+a} = \frac{q_i+a}{n(c+a)}$, where q_i is the number of papers that already cite i (i.e., the in-degree of i), a is a positive constant and c is the average (in- and out-)degree. So a new paper generates on average c citations. This model leads to a power law distribution of the in-degrees with exponent $\beta = 2 + \frac{a}{c} > 2$.

Barabási and Albert [4] independently proposed their model for growing undirected networks and coined the term "preferential attachment". In their model each new node adds exactly c new edges, each of which connects to (existing) node i with probability $d(i)/(\sum_v d(v))$, where $d(v)$ is the degree of node v. It can be shown directly, or by a careful reduction from Price's model (setting $a = c$), that this leads to a power law degree distribution with $\beta = 3$.

The model proposed here is a generalization of the one introduced in [1, 8] and we follow the formulation of Chung and Lu [6]. They analyzed an undirected network evolution with two types of preferential attachment events: a node event with probability p and an *edge event* with probability $1-p$. As discussed later on, this leads to a power law with $\beta = \frac{4-p}{2-p} \in (2,3]$.

A different type of models are the *copying* based models [15, 16]. In the simple copy model, every new node that joins the network adds a single directed edge. It selects an existing node u uniformly at random and then connects to u with probability $1-p$ or to the single node that u points to with probability p. It can then be shown that the in-degree distribution follows a power law with exponent $\beta = 1 + \frac{1}{p} \in (2,\infty)$.

While models with time varying probabilities were considered before [9, 11–14], they have not captured the full range $(1,\infty)$.

The exponent β of the power law has a significant impact on the networks structure. In [2] we studied the core size in preferential attachment models. It can be shown that for $\beta = 2$, the core size becomes *sublinear* in the network size, which may have implications on the size of elites in social networks [3].

Additional study of large scale social networks has revealed several other universal properties, for example the "small-world" phenomena, short average path lengths, navigability and high clustering coefficients.

The rest of the paper is organized as follows. Section 2 presents the model formally. Section 3 establishes improved concentration bounds for $m_{k,t}$, Section 4 establishes bounds for $\mathbb{E}\left[m_{k,t}\right]$, and section 5 deals with power laws for degree distributions, proves their existence, and analyzes their exponent.

2 THE GENERALIZED $G(p_t, r_t, q_t)$ MODEL

In this section we describe a generalization of the preferential attachment model $G(p)$ defined in Ch. 3.1 of [6]. $G(p)$ has one parameter, p, assumed therein to be constant with t. Here we allow p to vary with t. Let us now introduce the model $G(p_t, r_t, q_t)$ formally.

Consider a sequence $(G_t)_{t=1}^{\infty}$ of graphs, $G_t = (V_t, E_t)$, where V_t (respectively, E_t) denotes the set of nodes (resp. edges) in G_t and $n_t = |V_t|$ (resp. $e_t = |E_t|$). Let $d_t(w)$ denote the degree of node w in G_t. Starting from an arbitrary initial nonempty graph G_0, for $t \geq 1$ the graph G_t is constructed from G_{t-1} at time t by performing either a *node event* with probability $p_t \in [0,1]$, an *edge event* with probability r_t, or a *component event* with probability $q_t = 1 - p_t - r_t$.

In a node event, a new vertex v is added to the graph, along with a new edge selected using *preferential attachment.* Formally, the new edge is (v,u), where $u \in V_{t-1}$ is chosen with probability proportional to its degree, i.e., $\gamma_t(u) = d_{t-1}(u)/(\sum_{w \in V_{t-1}} d_{t-1}(w))$. In an edge event, a new edge (u,w) is added, where both $u, w \in V_{t-1}$ are chosen by preferential attachment, independently of each other, i.e., (u,w) is chosen with probability $\gamma_t(u) \cdot \gamma_t(w)$. Finally, in a component event, two new nodes v and u are added, along with a new edge (v,u). Note that exactly one edge is added at each time step, so the number of edges in the graph G_t is $e_t = e_0 + t$ and the sum of degrees is $2e_t = 2(e_0 + t)$.[1] We also have

$$\mathbb{E}[n_t] = n_0 + \sum_{j=1}^{t}(p_j + 2q_j).$$

3 CONCENTRATION BOUNDS FOR $m_{k,t}$

We now establish Thm. 1.4. To do that, we prove the following more general theorem.

For integer $t \geq 0$ and reals $\boldsymbol{\varepsilon} = (\varepsilon_1, \ldots, \varepsilon_{2e_t}) \in \mathbb{R}^{2e_t}$, let $\Delta_{\boldsymbol{\varepsilon}} = \max_{i,j} |\varepsilon_i - \varepsilon_j|$ be the maximum distance between any two coordinates of $\boldsymbol{\varepsilon}$, and $\|\boldsymbol{\varepsilon}\|_\infty = \max_i |\varepsilon_i|$ be the maximum distance between a coordinate and 0. Also let $S_t(\boldsymbol{\varepsilon}) = \sum_{k=1}^{2e_t} \varepsilon_k \cdot m_{k,t}$.

Theorem 3.1. *In the $G(p_t, r_t, q_t)$ preferential attachment model, for every integer $t \geq 0$, real $c \geq 0$, and reals $\boldsymbol{\varepsilon} = (\varepsilon_1, \varepsilon_2, \ldots, \varepsilon_{2e_t}) \in \mathbb{R}^{2e_t}$, we have*

$$\mathbb{P}\left[S_t(\boldsymbol{\varepsilon}) - \mathbb{E}[S_t(\boldsymbol{\varepsilon})] \geq \sqrt{2ct} \cdot (2\Delta_{\boldsymbol{\varepsilon}} + 2\max(\Delta_{\boldsymbol{\varepsilon}}, \|\boldsymbol{\varepsilon}\|_\infty))\right] \leq e^{-c},$$
$$\mathbb{P}\left[S_t(\boldsymbol{\varepsilon}) - \mathbb{E}[S_t(\boldsymbol{\varepsilon})] \leq -\sqrt{2ct} \cdot (2\Delta_{\boldsymbol{\varepsilon}} + 2\max(\Delta_{\boldsymbol{\varepsilon}}, \|\boldsymbol{\varepsilon}\|_\infty))\right] \leq e^{-c}.$$

Note that Thm. 3.1 suggests a deviation of $O(\sqrt{t})$ from the mean. This can be obtained by setting all the coordinates in $\boldsymbol{\varepsilon}$ to zero except for a single ε_k which is set to 1, yielding the following.

Corollary 3.2. *In the model $G(p_t, r_t, q_t)$, for every integers $k \geq 0, t \geq 0$ and real $c \geq 0$, we have*

$$\mathbb{P}\left[m_{k,t} - \mathbb{E}\left[m_{k,t}\right] \geq \sqrt{32ct}\right] \leq e^{-c},$$
$$\mathbb{P}\left[m_{k,t} - \mathbb{E}\left[m_{k,t}\right] \leq -\sqrt{32ct}\right] \leq e^{-c},$$

Note that for $k > 2e_t$, we have $m_{k,t} = 0$ and Cor. 3.2 follows trivially. Thm. 3.1 also implies concentration bounds for $RC_{k,t}$. This can be obtained by using a vector $\boldsymbol{\varepsilon}$ in which $\varepsilon_i = 0$ for $i < k$ and $\varepsilon_i = 1$ for $i \geq k$, yielding the following.

Corollary 3.3. *In the model $G(p_t, r_t, q_t)$, for every integers $k \geq 0, t \geq 0$ and real $c \geq 0$, we have*

$$\mathbb{P}\left[RC_{k,t} - \mathbb{E}\left[RC_{k,t}\right] \geq \sqrt{32ct}\right] \leq e^{-c},$$
$$\mathbb{P}\left[RC_{k,t} - \mathbb{E}\left[RC_{k,t}\right] \leq -\sqrt{32ct}\right] \leq e^{-c},$$

Finally, note that Thm. 3.1 implies Thm. 1.4, Cor. 3.2 implies Cor. 1.5, and Cor. 3.3 implies Cor. 1.6 as a special case since the model $G(p)$ can be obtained from the model $G(p_t, r_t, q_t)$ by setting $p_t = p$ and $q_t = 0$.

The rest of this section is dedicated to proving Thm. 3.1.

3.1 Recursive Relation for $m_{k,t}$

As a first step, we find a recursive representation for $m_{k,t+1}$ in terms of $m_{k',t}$ for smaller $k' \leq k$. Note that $m_{0,t} = m_{0,0}$ for every t. Also note that the number of edges at time t is $e_t = e_0 + t$. Hence, since the sum of the degrees at time t equals $2e_t$, we have $m_{k,t} = 0$ for $k > 2e_t$. Therefore, we focus on $m_{k,t}$ for $1 \leq k \leq 2e_t$.
Let $\mathcal{F}_t$ denote the σ-algebra generated by the graphs $G_0, \ldots, G_t$. Intuitively, $\mathcal{F}_t$ encodes all the history until time t. Fix $k \geq 2$. Since $0 \leq d_{t+1}(v) - d_t(v) \leq 2$ for every node v and time t, we have

$$\mathbb{E}\left[m_{k,t+1} \mid \mathcal{F}_t\right] = \sum_{\{v \,:\, k-2 \leq d_t(v) \leq k\}} \mathbb{P}[d_{t+1}(v) = k]. \quad (5)$$

Recalling that $\gamma_t(v) = d_{t-1}(v)/\sum_{w \in V_{t-1}} d_{t-1}(w)$, for every node v such that $d_{t+1}(v) = k$, there are at most three possible values for $d_t(v)$:

(i) $d_t(v) = k - 2$ and at time $t + 1$ there was an edge event where the edge (v,v) was added (this happens with probability $r_{t+1} \cdot (\gamma_{t+1}(v))^2$).
(ii) $d_t(v) = k - 1$ and at time $t + 1$ there was either a node event involving v (this happens with probability $p_{t+1} \cdot \gamma_{t+1}(v)$) or an edge event where the edge (v,w) $w \neq v$ was added (this happens with probability $r_{t+1} \cdot 2\gamma_{t+1}(v) \cdot (1 - \gamma_{t+1}(v))$).
(iii) $d_t(v) = k$ and at time $t+1$ there was either a node event where v was not involved (this happens with probability $p_{t+1} \cdot (1 - \gamma_{t+1}(v))$), an edge event where the edge (u,w) $v \notin \{u,w\}$ was added (this happens with probability $r_{t+1} \cdot (1 - \gamma_{t+1}(v))^2$) or a component event (this happens with probability q_{t+1}).

Letting $\alpha_{k,t} = k/(2e_t)$, for every v such that $d_t(v) = i$ we have $\gamma_{t+1}(v) = \alpha_{i,t}$. Denoting

$$A_{k,t} = p_{t+1}(1 - \alpha_{k,t}) + r_{t+1} \cdot (1 - \alpha_{k,t})^2 + q_{t+1},$$
$$B_{k,t} = p_{t+1} \cdot \alpha_{k,t} + 2 \cdot r_{t+1} \cdot \alpha_{k,t} \cdot (1 - \alpha_{k,t}),$$
$$C_{k,t} = r_{t+1} \cdot \alpha_{k,t}^2,$$

we have

$$A_{k,t} + B_{k,t} + C_{k,t} = 1 \quad (6)$$

and $A_{k,t}, B_{k,t}, C_{k,t} \geq 0$ for every $0 \leq k \leq 2e_t$. Furthermore, by Eq. (5), for every $k \geq 2$ we have

$$\mathbb{E}\left[m_{k,t+1} \mid \mathcal{F}_t\right] = m_{k,t} \cdot A_{k,t} + m_{k-1,t} \cdot B_{k-1,t} + C_{k-2,t} \cdot m_{k-2,t}. \quad (7)$$

[1] Here a self loop increments the degree of a node by two.

Similarly, for $k = 1$ we have

$$\mathbb{E}\left[m_{1,t+1} \mid \mathcal{F}_t\right] = A_{1,t} \cdot m_{1,t} + p_{t+1} + 2q_{t+1} . \quad (8)$$

Letting

$$X_{k,t} = \begin{cases} m_{k-1,t} \cdot B_{k-1,t} + m_{k-2,t} \cdot C_{k-2,t} & k \geq 2 , \\ p_{t+1} + 2q_{t+1} & k = 1 , \end{cases}$$

Eq. (7) and (8) can be rewritten as

$$\mathbb{E}\left[m_{k,t+1} \mid \mathcal{F}_t\right] = m_{k,t} \cdot A_{k,t} + X_{k,t} . \quad (9)$$

Taking expectation on both sides, we get

$$\mathbb{E}\left[m_{k,t+1}\right] = \mathbb{E}\left[m_{k,t}\right] \cdot A_{k,t} + \mathbb{E}\left[X_{k,t}\right] . \quad (10)$$

3.2 Analysis of the Martingale $\mathbb{E}\left[m_{k,t} \mid \mathcal{F}_\ell\right]$

For integers $0 \leq \ell \leq t$ and $0 \leq k \leq 2e_t$, denote $Y_\ell^{k,t} = \mathbb{E}\left[m_{k,t} \mid \mathcal{F}_\ell\right]$, where the expectation is taken over all that occurred from time $\ell + 1$ till time t. By the law of total expectation, we have

$$\begin{aligned} \mathbb{E}\left[Y_\ell^{k,t} \mid \mathcal{F}_{\ell-1}\right] &= \mathbb{E}\left[\mathbb{E}\left[m_{k,t} \mid \mathcal{F}_\ell\right] \mid \mathcal{F}_{\ell-1}\right] \\ &= \mathbb{E}\left[\mathbb{E}\left[m_{k,t} \mid \mathcal{F}_\ell, \mathcal{F}_{\ell-1}\right] \mid \mathcal{F}_{\ell-1}\right] \\ &= \mathbb{E}\left[m_{k,t} \mid \mathcal{F}_{\ell-1}\right] = Y_{\ell-1}^{k,t} . \end{aligned}$$

Therefore, $Y_0^{k,t}, Y_1^{k,t}, \ldots, Y_t^{k,t}$ is a martingale (with respect to the filtration $\mathcal{F}_0 \subseteq \cdots \subseteq \mathcal{F}_t$). This general construction is commonly referred to as a Doob Martingale [10]. Therefore, for a vector $\boldsymbol{\varepsilon} = (\varepsilon_1, \ldots, \varepsilon_{2e_t}) \in \mathbb{R}^{2e_t}$, letting

$$Y_\ell^t(\boldsymbol{\varepsilon}) = \sum_{k=1}^{2e_t} \varepsilon_k \cdot Y_\ell^{k,t} = \sum_{k=1}^{2e_t} \varepsilon_k \cdot \mathbb{E}\left[m_{k,t} \mid \mathcal{F}_\ell\right],$$

we have that $Y_0^t(\boldsymbol{\varepsilon}), Y_1^t(\boldsymbol{\varepsilon}) \ldots, Y_t^t(\boldsymbol{\varepsilon})$ is also a Doob martingale (with respect to the same filtration $\mathcal{F}_0 \subseteq \cdots \subseteq \mathcal{F}_t$). We next bound the difference between consecutive elements in the sequence. For $1 \leq \ell \leq t$ and reals $\boldsymbol{\varepsilon} = (\varepsilon_1, \ldots, \varepsilon_{2e_t}) \in \mathbb{R}^{2e_t}$, let

$$\Delta_\ell^t(\boldsymbol{\varepsilon}) = |Y_\ell^t(\boldsymbol{\varepsilon}) - Y_{\ell-1}^t(\boldsymbol{\varepsilon})|.$$

LEMMA 3.4. *For every $1 \leq \ell \leq t$ and $\boldsymbol{\varepsilon} = (\varepsilon_1, \ldots, \varepsilon_{2e_t})$, we have*

$$\Delta_\ell^t(\boldsymbol{\varepsilon}) \leq 2\Delta_{\boldsymbol{\varepsilon}} + 2\max(\Delta_{\boldsymbol{\varepsilon}}, \|\boldsymbol{\varepsilon}\|_\infty).$$

PROOF. Fixing ℓ, the proof is by induction on t. For $t = \ell$, letting

$$\Psi_1 = \sum_{k=1}^{2e_\ell} \varepsilon_k \cdot (m_{k,\ell} - m_{k,\ell-1}) ,$$

$$\Psi_2 = \varepsilon_1 \cdot (p_\ell + 2q_\ell) + \sum_{k=1}^{2e_\ell} \varepsilon_k \cdot ((1 - A_{k,\ell-1})m_{k,\ell-1} - X_{k,\ell-1}) ,$$

by Eq. (9) we have

$$\begin{aligned} \Delta_\ell^\ell(\boldsymbol{\varepsilon}) &= \left|\sum_{k=1}^{2e_\ell} \varepsilon_k \cdot \left(\mathbb{E}\left[m_{k,\ell} \mid \mathcal{F}_\ell\right] - \mathbb{E}\left[m_{k,\ell} \mid \mathcal{F}_{\ell-1}\right]\right)\right| \\ &= \left|\sum_{k=1}^{2e_\ell} \varepsilon_k \cdot (m_{k,\ell} - A_{k,\ell-1} \cdot m_{k,\ell-1} - X_{k,\ell-1})\right| \\ &= | - \varepsilon_1 \cdot (p_\ell + 2q_\ell) + \Psi_1 + \Psi_2| . \end{aligned} \quad (11)$$

Note that

$$\Psi_1 = \begin{cases} 2\varepsilon_1, & \text{At time } \ell \text{ a compenent event occurred,} \\ \varepsilon_1 + \varepsilon_{i+1} - \varepsilon_i, & \text{At time } \ell \text{ a new node was connected to an existing node of degree } i, \\ \varepsilon_{i+2} - \varepsilon_i, & \text{At time } \ell \text{ a self loop was added to a node of degree } i, \\ \varepsilon_{i+1} - \varepsilon_i + \varepsilon_{j+1} - \varepsilon_j, & \text{At time } \ell \text{ a new edge was added between two distinct existing nodes with degrees } i \text{ and } j. \end{cases}$$

Therefore, we have

$$\begin{aligned} |\Psi_1 - \varepsilon_1 \cdot (p_\ell + 2q_\ell)| &\leq \max(2|\varepsilon_1|, |\varepsilon_1| + \Delta_{\boldsymbol{\varepsilon}}, (p_\ell + 2q_\ell)|\varepsilon_1| + 2\Delta_{\boldsymbol{\varepsilon}}) \\ &\leq (p_\ell + 2q_\ell)\Delta_{\boldsymbol{\varepsilon}} + 2\max(|\varepsilon_1|, \Delta_{\boldsymbol{\varepsilon}}) . \end{aligned}$$

For Ψ_2, recalling that $m_{k,\ell-1} = 0$ for every $k > 2e_{\ell-1}$, and by Eq. (6) we obtain

$$\begin{aligned} |\Psi_2| &= \left|\sum_{k=1}^{2e_\ell} m_{k,\ell-1} \left((1 - A_{k,\ell-1})\varepsilon_k - B_{k,\ell-1}\varepsilon_{k+1} - C_{k,\ell-1}\varepsilon_{k+2}\right)\right| \\ &= \left|\sum_{k=1}^{2e_\ell} m_{k,\ell-1} \left(B_{k,\ell-1}(\varepsilon_k - \varepsilon_{k+1}) + C_{k,\ell-1}(\varepsilon_k - \varepsilon_{k+2})\right)\right| \\ &\leq \sum_{k=1}^{2e_\ell} m_{k,\ell-1} \left(B_{k,\ell-1} \cdot \Delta_{\boldsymbol{\varepsilon}} + C_{k,\ell-1} \cdot 2\Delta_{\boldsymbol{\varepsilon}}\right) \\ &= (p_\ell + 2r_\ell)\Delta_{\boldsymbol{\varepsilon}} \sum_{k=1}^{2e_\ell} \alpha_{k,\ell-1} m_{k,\ell-1} = (p_\ell + 2r_\ell)\Delta_{\boldsymbol{\varepsilon}} . \end{aligned}$$

Plugging this into Eq. (11), we obtain

$$\begin{aligned} \Delta_\ell^\ell(\boldsymbol{\varepsilon}) &\leq |\Psi_1 - \varepsilon_1 \cdot (p_\ell + 2q_\ell)| + |\Psi_2| \\ &\leq (2p_\ell + 2r_\ell + 2q_\ell)\Delta_{\boldsymbol{\varepsilon}} + 2\max\{|\varepsilon_1|, \Delta_{\boldsymbol{\varepsilon}}\} \\ &= 2\Delta_{\boldsymbol{\varepsilon}} + 2\max\{|\varepsilon_1|, \Delta_{\boldsymbol{\varepsilon}}\} \leq 2\Delta_{\boldsymbol{\varepsilon}} + 2\max\{\|\boldsymbol{\varepsilon}\|_\infty, \Delta_{\boldsymbol{\varepsilon}}\} . \end{aligned}$$

Hence the induction basis holds. Next, assuming the claim for t, we prove it for $t + 1$. By the law of total expectation and Eq. (9),

$$\begin{aligned} Y_\ell^{t+1}(\boldsymbol{\varepsilon}) &= \sum_{k=1}^{2e_{t+1}} \varepsilon_k \cdot \mathbb{E}\left[m_{k,t+1} \mid \mathcal{F}_\ell\right] \\ &= \sum_{k=1}^{2e_{t+1}} \varepsilon_k \cdot \mathbb{E}\left[\mathbb{E}\left[m_{k,t+1} \mid \mathcal{F}_t\right] \mid \mathcal{F}_\ell\right] \\ &= \sum_{k=1}^{2e_{t+1}} \varepsilon_k \cdot \mathbb{E}\left[A_{k,t} \cdot m_{k,t} + X_{k,t} \mid \mathcal{F}_\ell\right] \\ &= \varepsilon_1 \cdot (p_t + 2q_t) + \sum_{k=1}^{2e_t} \tilde{\varepsilon}_k \cdot \mathbb{E}\left[m_{k,t} \mid \mathcal{F}_\ell\right] \\ &= \varepsilon_1 \cdot (p_t + 2q_t) + Y_\ell^t(\tilde{\boldsymbol{\varepsilon}}) , \end{aligned}$$

where $\tilde{\varepsilon}_k = \varepsilon_k \cdot A_{k,t} + \varepsilon_{k+1} \cdot B_{k,t} + \varepsilon_{k+2} \cdot C_{k,t}$ and $\tilde{\boldsymbol{\varepsilon}} = (\tilde{\varepsilon}_1, \ldots, \tilde{\varepsilon}_{2e_t})$.[2] Therefore, by the induction hypothesis we have

$$\begin{aligned} \Delta_\ell^{t+1}(\boldsymbol{\varepsilon}) &= \left|Y_\ell^{t+1}(\boldsymbol{\varepsilon}) - Y_{\ell-1}^{t+1}(\boldsymbol{\varepsilon})\right| = \left|Y_\ell^t(\tilde{\boldsymbol{\varepsilon}}) - Y_{\ell-1}^t(\tilde{\boldsymbol{\varepsilon}})\right| \\ &= \Delta_\ell^t(\tilde{\boldsymbol{\varepsilon}}) \le 2\Delta_{\tilde{\boldsymbol{\varepsilon}}} + 2\max(\|\tilde{\varepsilon}\|_\infty, \Delta_{\tilde{\boldsymbol{\varepsilon}}}) \\ &\le 2\Delta_{\boldsymbol{\varepsilon}} + 2\max(\|\boldsymbol{\varepsilon}\|_\infty, \Delta_{\boldsymbol{\varepsilon}}) , \end{aligned}$$

noting that every coordinate of $\tilde{\boldsymbol{\varepsilon}}$ is a convex combination of three coordinates of $\boldsymbol{\varepsilon}$, so $\|\tilde{\boldsymbol{\varepsilon}}\|_\infty \le \|\boldsymbol{\varepsilon}\|_\infty$ and $\Delta_{\tilde{\boldsymbol{\varepsilon}}} \le \Delta_{\boldsymbol{\varepsilon}}$. The lemma follows. □

Proof of Thm. 3.1: By Lemma 3.4, we may apply Azuma's inequality to the martingale $Y_0^t(\boldsymbol{\varepsilon}), Y_1^t(\boldsymbol{\varepsilon}), \ldots, Y_t^t(\boldsymbol{\varepsilon})$, and obtain for every $\lambda \ge 0$

$$\mathbb{P}[Y_t^t(\boldsymbol{\varepsilon}) - Y_0^t(\boldsymbol{\varepsilon}) \ge \lambda] \le \exp\left(-\frac{\lambda^2}{2t \cdot (2\Delta_{\boldsymbol{\varepsilon}} + 2\max(\Delta_{\boldsymbol{\varepsilon}}, \|\boldsymbol{\varepsilon}\|_\infty))^2}\right),$$

$$\mathbb{P}[Y_t^t(\boldsymbol{\varepsilon}) - Y_0^t(\boldsymbol{\varepsilon}) \le -\lambda] \le \exp\left(-\frac{\lambda^2}{2t \cdot (2\Delta_{\boldsymbol{\varepsilon}} + 2\max(\Delta_{\boldsymbol{\varepsilon}}, \|\boldsymbol{\varepsilon}\|_\infty))^2}\right).$$

Noting that $Y_t^t(\boldsymbol{\varepsilon}) = \sum_{k=1}^{2e_t} \varepsilon_k \cdot m_{k,t}$ and $Y_0^t = \sum_{k=1}^{2e_t} \varepsilon_k \cdot \mathbb{E}\left[m_{k,t}\right]$ and letting $\lambda = \sqrt{2ct} \cdot (2\Delta_{\boldsymbol{\varepsilon}} + 2\max(\Delta_{\boldsymbol{\varepsilon}}, \|\boldsymbol{\varepsilon}\|_\infty))$, Thm. 3.1 follows. □

4 IMPROVED BOUNDS FOR $\mathbb{E}\left[m_{k,t}\right]$

We now prove Thm. 1.2 for $G(p)$. Consider the model $G(p)$, which can be derived from the model $G(p_t, r_t, q_t)$ by setting $p_t = p$ and $q_t = 0$ for every t. Thus we obtain the simplified expressions

$$\begin{aligned} A_{k,t} &= 1 - \frac{(2-p)k}{2e_t} + (1-p) \cdot \frac{k^2}{4e_t^2} , \\ B_{k,t} &= \frac{(2-p)k}{2e_t} - 2(1-p) \cdot \frac{k^2}{4e_t^2} , \\ C_{k,t} &= (1-p) \cdot \frac{k^2}{4e_t^2} . \end{aligned}$$

Recall that $\beta = \frac{4-p}{2-p}$ and $M_k = \frac{2}{4-p} \prod_{j=1}^{k-1} \frac{j}{j+\beta}$.

Proof of Thm. 1.2 : To prove Ineq. (1), letting

$$\ell_{k,t} = \mathbb{E}\left[m_{k,t}\right] - \left(pe_t - \frac{p^2(1-p)}{2(2-p)^2}\right) \cdot M_k - \frac{c^*}{k} ,$$

it suffices to show that $\ell_{k,t} \le 0$ for every t and $1 \le k \le 2e_t$. We show this by induction on t. For $t = 0$, since $e_t \ge 1$, we have

$$k \cdot \ell_{k,0} \le k \cdot \mathbb{E}\left[m_{k,0}\right] - c^* \le k \cdot \mathbb{E}\left[m_{k,0}\right] - 2e_0 \le 0 ,$$

where the last inequality follows since $\sum_{k=1}^{2e_0} k \cdot m_{k,0} = 2e_0$, hence the basis of the induction holds. Assuming the claim for t, we prove it for $t+1$. For $k = 1$, by Eq. (10), it can be shown that

$$\begin{aligned} \ell_{1,t+1} &= A_{1,t} \cdot \ell_{1,t} + \frac{p(1-p)M_1}{4e_t} \\ &\quad - \left(c^* - \frac{p^2(1-p)M_1}{2(2-p)^2}\right)(1 - A_{1,t}) \\ &\le 0 + \frac{p(1-p)M_1}{4e_t} - \left(c^* - \frac{p(1-p)M_1}{2}\right) \cdot \frac{1}{2e_t} \\ &= \frac{p(1-p)M_1 - c^*}{2e_t} \le \frac{1-2e_0}{2e_t} \le 0 . \end{aligned}$$

For $2 \le k \le 2e_t$, by Eq. (10), it can be shown that

$$\begin{aligned} \ell_{k,t+1} &= A_{k,t} \cdot \ell_{k,t} + B_{k-1,t} \cdot \ell_{k-1,t} + C_{k-2,t} \cdot \ell_{k-2,t} \\ &\quad - \frac{p(1-p)M_k}{2(2-p)^2 e_t}\left(\frac{p^2(1-p)}{2(2-p)^2 e_t} + \frac{4-p}{k-1}\left(1 - \frac{p(1-p)}{2(2-p)^2 e_t}\right)\right) \\ &\le A_{k,t} \cdot \ell_{k,t} + B_{k-1,t} \cdot \ell_{k-1,t} + C_{k-2,t} \cdot \ell_{k-2,t} \le 0 . \end{aligned}$$

For $2e_{t+1} - 1 \le k \le 2e_{t+1}$, we have

$$k \cdot \ell_{k,t+1} \le k \cdot \mathbb{E}\left[m_{k,t+1}\right] - c^* .$$

Note that for $k = 2e_{t+1}$ and $m_{k,t+1} = 1$, necessarily the initial graph G_0 is composed of a single node (of degree $2e_0$) and only edge events occur until time $t+1$, thus

$$\begin{aligned} k \cdot \ell_{k,t+1} &\le 2e_{t+1} \cdot (1-p)^{t+1} - c^* \\ &\le \max\left\{2e_1(1-p) , \frac{2}{-\ln(1-p)}\right\} - c^* \le 0 , \end{aligned}$$

where the second inequality follows by maximizing over the range $t \ge 0$. Finally, for $k = 2e_{t+1} - 1$ and $m_{k,t+1} > 0$, we analyze the two possible cases. In the first case, the initial graph G_0 is composed of two nodes, one of degree 1 and the other of degree $2e_0 - 1$. Therefore, necessarily only edge events occur until time $t+1$, thus

$$k \cdot \ell_{k,t+1} \le (2e_{t+1} - 1) \cdot (1-p)^{t+1} - c^* \le 0 ,$$

as before. In the second case, the initial graph G_0 is composed of a single node v_0 (of degree $2e_0$). Therefore, exactly t edge events (involving the edge (v_0, v_0)) and one node event occur until time $t+1$. Therefore,

$$\begin{aligned} k \cdot \ell_{k,t+1} &\le (2e_{t+1} - 1) \cdot (1-p)^t \cdot p \cdot t - c^* \\ &\le 2e_{t+1}^2 \cdot (1-p)^t \cdot p - c^* \\ &\le \max\left\{2e_1^2 \cdot p , \frac{8p}{(\ln(1-p))^2}\right\} - c^* \le 0 , \end{aligned}$$

where the third inequality follows by maximizing over the range $t \ge 0$, thus concluding the proof of Ineq. (1). To prove Ineq. (2), letting

$$Z_{k,t} = p(e_t + 1 - p)M_k - \frac{p(e_0 + 1 - p)M_1}{k} - \mathbb{E}\left[m_{k,t}\right] ,$$

it suffices to show that $Z_{k,t} \le 0$ for every $t \ge 0$ and $1 \le k \le 2e_t$. We show this by induction on t. For $t = 0$, since $\beta > 1$, we have

$$\frac{Z_{k,0}}{p(e_0 + 1 - p)} \le M_k - \frac{M_1}{k} \le -\frac{M_1}{k} + M_1 \prod_{j=1}^{k-1} \frac{j}{j+1} = 0 .$$

[2] Note that $\boldsymbol{\varepsilon} \in \mathbb{R}^{2e_{t+1}}$ and $\tilde{\boldsymbol{\varepsilon}} \in \mathbb{R}^{2e_t}$, thus $Y_\ell^{t+1}(\boldsymbol{\varepsilon})$ and $Y_\ell^t(\tilde{\boldsymbol{\varepsilon}})$ are well defined.

Assuming the claim for t, we prove for $t+1$. For $k=1$, by Eq. (10), it can be shown that

$$\begin{aligned} Z_{1,t+1} &= A_{1,t}\cdot Z_{1,t} - \frac{p(1-p)}{2e_t(4-p)} - p\cdot e_0\cdot M_1\,(1-A_{1,t}) \\ &\le A_{1,t}\cdot Z_{1,t} - 0 - 0 \le 0\,. \end{aligned}$$

For $2 \le k \le 2e_t$, by Eq. (10), it can be shown that

$$\begin{aligned} Z_{k,t+1} &= A_{k,t}\cdot Z_{k,t} + B_{k-1,t}\cdot Z_{k-1,t} + C_{k-2,t}\cdot Z_{k-2,t} \\ &+ \frac{p(1-p)M_k}{e_t}\left(-1+\frac{1+(1-p)/e_t}{2(2-p)^2}\left(\frac{4-p}{k-1}-p\right)\right) \\ &\le 0+0+0+\frac{p(1-p)M_k}{e_t}\left(-1+\frac{1+(1-p)/e_t}{2-p}\right) \\ &\le \frac{p(1-p)M_k}{e_t}\left(-1+\frac{1+(1-p)}{2-p}\right) = 0\,, \end{aligned}$$

and for $2e_{t+1}-1 \le k \le 2e_{t+1}$, since $\beta \ge 2$, we have

$$\begin{aligned} Z_{k,t+1} &\le p(e_{t+1}+1-p)M_k - \frac{p(e_0+1-p)M_1}{k} \\ &\le p(e_{t+1}+1-p)M_1\prod_{j=1}^{k-1}\frac{j}{j+2} - \frac{p(e_0+1-p)M_1}{k} \\ &= \frac{pM_1}{k}\left(\frac{2e_{t+1}}{k+1} - e_0 + (1-p)\left(\frac{2}{k+1}-1\right)\right) \\ &\le \frac{pM_1}{k}\,(1-1+(1-p)\,(1-1)) = 0\,, \end{aligned}$$

thus concluding the proof of Ineq. (2). Theorem 1.2 follows. □

We now prove Cor. 1.3 using Thm. 1.2.

Proof of Cor. 1.3 : By Ineq. (1),

$$\begin{aligned} \mathbb{E}\left[RC_{k,t}\right] &= \sum_{j=k}^{2e_t}\mathbb{E}\left[m_{j,t}\right] \le p\cdot e_t\sum_{j=k}^{2e_t}M_j + c^*\sum_{j=k}^{2e_t}1/j \\ &\le c^*\cdot\ln\left(\frac{2e_t}{k-1}\right) + p\cdot e_t\sum_{j=k}^{2e_t}M_j\,. \end{aligned}$$

Noting that $M_j = \varphi_j - \varphi_{j+1}$, Ineq. (3) follows. The proof of Ineq. (4) is similar. □

5 POWER LAW IN $G(p_t, r_t, q_t)$

In this section, we show that the in the $G(p_t, r_t, q_t)$ model, it is possible to obtain networks obeying a power law degree distribution with any exponent in the range $(1,\infty)$, thus expanding the range of $(2,3]$ obtainable in the standard $G(p)$ model (see Lemma 1.1).

5.1 Existence of Power Law

The following lemma can be found in [6].

LEMMA 5.1. *[6] Suppose that a sequence $\{a_t\}$ satisfies the recurrence relation*

$$a_{t+1} = \left(1-\frac{b_t}{t+t_1}\right)a_t + c_t \;\; for\; t \ge t_0\,.$$

Furthermore, suppose $\lim_{t\to\infty} b_t = b > 0$ and $\lim_{t\to\infty} c_t = c$. Then $\lim_{t\to\infty} a_t/t$ exists and $\lim_{t\to\infty} a_t/t = c/(1+b)$.

We use Lemma 5.1 to prove the following generalized lemma.

LEMMA 5.2. *Suppose that a sequence $\{a_t\}$ satisfies the recurrence relation*

$$a_{t+1} = \left(1-\frac{b_t}{t+t_1}\right)a_t + c_t \;\; for\; t \ge t_0\,. \tag{12}$$

Furthermore, letting $\{s_t\}$ be a sequence of reals satisfying $\lim_{t\to\infty} s_t/s_{t+1} = 1$, and $d_t = t(1-s_t/s_{t+1})$, suppose that $\lim_{t\to\infty} b_t = b$, $\lim_{t\to\infty} c_t\cdot t/s_t = c$, $\lim_{t\to\infty} d_t = d$ and $b+d>1$. Then $\lim_{t\to\infty} a_t/s_t$ exists and $\lim_{t\to\infty} a_t/s_t = c/(b+d)$.

Note that Lemma 5.1 is a special case of Lemma 5.2 obtained by setting $s_t = t$.

PROOF. Denote

$$\begin{aligned} a_t^* &= \frac{a_t\cdot t}{s_t}\,, \\ b_t^* &= \frac{t+t_1}{t}\cdot\left(d_t - \frac{s_t}{s_{t+1}}\right) + \frac{t+1}{t}\cdot\frac{s_t}{s_{t+1}}\cdot b_t\,, \\ c_t^* &= c_t\cdot\frac{t+1}{s_{t+1}}\,. \end{aligned}$$

By Eq. (12),

$$\begin{aligned} a_{t+1}^* &= \frac{a_{t+1}\cdot(t+1)}{s_{t+1}} = \left(1-\frac{b_t}{t+t_1}\right)a_t\cdot\frac{t+1}{s_{t+1}} + c_t\cdot\frac{t+1}{s_{t+1}} \\ &= \left(1-\frac{b_t^*}{t+t_1}\right)a_t^* + c_t^*\,. \end{aligned}$$

Since $\lim_{t\to\infty} b_t^* = b+d-1 > 0$, and $\lim_{t\to\infty} c_t^* = c$, we may apply Lemma 5.1, and obtain $\lim_{t\to\infty}\frac{a_t}{s_t} = \lim_{t\to\infty}\frac{a_t^*}{t} = \frac{c}{b+d}$. □

The following theorem and corollary complete the proof of a power law in $G(p_t, r_t, q_t)$.

THEOREM 5.3. *Consider $G(p_t, r_t, q_t)$ and let $y_t = p_t + 2q_t$. Assume that $\lim_{t\to\infty} y_t = y < 2$, $\sum_{t=1}^{\infty} y_t = \infty$ and $\lim_{t\to\infty} t\cdot y_{t+1}/\sum_{j=1}^{t} y_j = \Gamma > 0$. Then letting $\beta = 1+\frac{2\Gamma}{2-y}$, the limit $M_k = \lim_{t\to\infty}\frac{\mathbb{E}[m_{k,t}]}{\mathbb{E}[n_t]}$ exists for every $k \ge 1$ and*

$$M_k = \frac{\Gamma}{\Gamma+1-y/2}\cdot\prod_{j=1}^{k-1}\frac{j}{j+\beta}\,. \tag{13}$$

PROOF. By induction on k. For $k=1$, consider Eq. (10). By applying Lemma 5.2 with $(t_1, s_t, a_t, b_t, c_t)$ set to $(e_0, \mathbb{E}[n_t], \mathbb{E}[m_{1,t}], e_t(1-A_{1,t}), y_{t+1})$, yielding the limits $b = 1-y/2$, and $c = d = \Gamma$, Eq. (13) follows. Assuming the claim for $k-1$, we prove it for k. Consider Eq. (10). Applying Lemma 5.2 with $(t_1, s_t, a_t, b_t, c_t)$ set to $(e_0, \mathbb{E}[n_t], \mathbb{E}\left[m_{k,t}\right], e_t(1-A_{k,t}), B_{k-1,t}\cdot\mathbb{E}\left[m_{k-1,t}\right] + C_{k-2,t}\cdot\mathbb{E}\left[m_{k-2,t}\right])$, we obtain the limits $d = \Gamma$, $b = k\cdot(1-y/2)$ and by the induction hypothesis,

$$c = \lim_{t\to\infty}\frac{c_t\cdot t}{s_t} = (k-1)\left(1-\frac{y}{2}\right)M_{k-1}\,.$$

Therefore, M_k exists and

$$M_k = \frac{(k-1)\,(1-y/2)\,M_{k-1}}{k\cdot(1-y/2)+\Gamma} = \frac{k-1}{k-1+\beta}\cdot M_{k-1}\,.$$

□

Corollary 5.4. *Under the assumptions stated in Thm. 5.3, M_k is proportional to $k^{-\beta}$.*

Proof. Consider Eq. (13). By the First Order Condition [5], a differentiable function f is convex if and only if $f(x_2) \geq f(x_1) + f'(x_1)(x_2 - x_1)$ for every x_1 and x_2. Applying this with $(f(z), x_1, x_2)$ set to $(z^\beta, 1, 1 + 1/j)$, we obtain

$$\prod_{j=1}^{k-1} \frac{j}{j+\beta} = \prod_{j=1}^{k-1}\left(1+\frac{\beta}{j}\right)^{-1} \geq \prod_{j=1}^{k-1}\left(1+\frac{1}{j}\right)^{-\beta} = k^{-\beta}.$$

Applying the First Order Condition with $(f(z), x_1, x_2)$ set to $(z^\beta, 1, 1 - 1/(j+\beta))$, we obtain

$$\prod_{j=1}^{k-1} \frac{j}{j+\beta} = \prod_{j=1}^{k-1}\left(1-\frac{\beta}{j+\beta}\right) \leq \prod_{j=1}^{k-1}\left(1-\frac{1}{j+\beta}\right)^{\beta} = \left(\frac{\beta}{k-1+\beta}\right)^{\beta} \leq \beta^\beta \cdot k^{-\beta}.$$

Therefore, $c_1 \cdot k^{-\beta} \leq M_k \leq c_2 \cdot k^{-\beta}$ for some positive constants c_1, c_2 and every $k \geq 1$. □

Note that $\lim_{t\to\infty} \mathbb{E}[n_t] = \infty$. Thus n_t is concentrated around $\mathbb{E}[n_t]$, yielding an expected power law with exponent β. Furthermore, for $y_t = \omega(1/\sqrt{t})$, we have $\mathbb{E}[n_t] = \omega(\sqrt{t})$. By Thm. 5.3, $\mathbb{E}\left[m_{k,t}\right] = \Omega(\mathbb{E}[n_t]) = \omega(\sqrt{t})$ for fixed k. Therefore, by Thm. 3.1, $m_{k,t}$ is concentrated around $\mathbb{E}\left[m_{k,t}\right]$, thus the power law is obtained almost surely.

5.2 Power Law Exponent Characterization

In Sect. 5.1 we showed that letting $y_t = p_t + 2q_t$, and whenever $\lim_{t\to\infty} y_t = y < 2$, $\sum_{t=1}^{\infty} y_t = \infty$ and $\lim_{t\to\infty} t \cdot y_{t+1} / \sum_{j=1}^{t} y_j = \Gamma > 0$, the resulting network obeys a power law with exponent $\beta = 1 + \frac{2\Gamma}{2-y}$. Under these assumptions, we have $\beta > 1$. The following lemma shows that any value of β in the range $(1, \infty)$ is attainable for some possible choice of the probabilities p_t, r_t and q_t.

Lemma 5.5. *For any $x \in (1, \infty)$, there exists a choice of p_t, r_t, q_t such that in $G(p_t, r_t, q_t)$ the resulting network follows a power law degree distribution with exponent $\beta = x$.*

Proof. Consider the following three cases.

(i) For $x \in (2, \infty)$, setting $y_t = 2 - 2/(x-1) \in (0, 2)$ for every t and applying Cor. 5.4, we obtain a power law with exponent $\beta = 1 + \frac{2}{2-(2-2/(x-1))} = x$.

(ii) For $x \in (1, 2)$, setting $y_t = t^{x-2}$ for every t, we have

$$\frac{t^{x-1}}{\int_{j=0}^{t} j^{x-2} dj} = \frac{(x-1)\cdot t^{x-1}}{[j^{x-1}]_{j=0}^{t}} = x - 1.$$

Therefore,

$$\Gamma = \lim_{t\to\infty} \frac{y_{t+1}\cdot t}{\sum_{j=1}^{t} y_j} = \lim_{t\to\infty}\frac{(t+1)^{x-2}\cdot t}{\sum_{j=1}^{t} j^{x-2}} = \lim_{t\to\infty} \frac{t^{x-1}}{\int_{j=0}^{t} j^{x-2} dj} = x - 1.$$

By Cor. 5.4, $G(p_t, r_t, q_t)$ follows a power law degree distribution with exponent $\beta = 1 + 2\Gamma/(2-y) = 1 + 2(x-1)/(2-0) = x$.

(iii) For $x = 2$, setting $y_t = 1/\ln(t+2)$ for every t, we have

$$\Gamma = \lim_{t\to\infty} \frac{y_{t+1}\cdot t}{\sum_{j=1}^{t} y_j} = \lim_{t\to\infty} \frac{t/\ln(t+3)}{\sum_{j=1}^{t} 1/\ln(j+2)} = \lim_{t\to\infty} \frac{t/\ln(t+3)}{t/\ln t} = 1.$$

By Cor. 5.4, $G(p_t, r_t, q_t)$ follows a power law degree distribution with exponent $\beta = 1 + 2\Gamma/(2-y) = 1 + 2/(2-0) = 2$.

□

We now show that component events are needed in $G(p_t, r_t, q_t)$ in order to obtain a power law with exponent larger than 3, namely, in a model with no component events, the exponent β is restricted to the range $(1, 3]$.

Lemma 5.6. *Assume $\lim_{t\to\infty} y_t = y$ and $\lim_{t\to\infty} y_{t+1} \cdot t / \sum_{j=1}^{t} y_j = \Gamma$. Then:*

(i) For $y > 0$, we have $\Gamma = 1$.
(ii) For $y = 0$ we have $\Gamma \leq 1$. Here $0/0$ is interpreted as 0.

Proof. Let $\bar{y}_t = \frac{1}{t}\sum_{j=1}^{t} y_j$. For $y > 0$, we have also $\lim_{t\to\infty} \bar{y}_t = y$, so $\lim_{t\to\infty} y_{t+1} \cdot t / \sum_{j=1}^{t} y_j = y/y = 1$. Part (i) follows. Turning to (ii), for $y = 0$, if $y_t = 0$ for infinitely many t's, then clearly $\Gamma = 0$. Otherwise, there exists t_0 such that $y_t > 0$ for every $t \geq t_0$. Consider the following positive descending subsequence. For every $i \geq 1$ we let t_i be the minimum integer such that $t_i > t_{i-1}$ and $y_{t_i} \leq y_{t_{i-1}}$. The minimum exists since $y_{t_{i-1}}$ is positive and $\lim_{t\to\infty} y_t = 0$. By construction, $y_{t_i} \leq y_t$ for every $t \in [t_{i-1}, t_i]$. Since $(y_{t_i})_{i=0}^{\infty}$ is descending, we have $y_{t_i} \leq y_t$ for every $t \in [t_0, t_i]$, thus letting

$$Q(i) = \frac{y_{t_i+1}\cdot t_i}{\sum_{j=1}^{t_i} y_j} \leq \frac{y_{t_i+1}\cdot t_i}{\sum_{j=t_0}^{t_i} y_j} \leq \frac{y_{t_i+1}\cdot t_i}{(t_i - t_0 + 1)\cdot y_{t_i+1}} = \frac{t_i}{t_i - t_0 + 1},$$

it follows that $\Gamma = \lim_{i\to\infty} Q(i) \leq \lim_{i\to\infty} t_i/(t_i - t_0 + 1) = 1$. □

Corollary 5.7. *Consider $G(p_t, r_t, q_t)$. Assume $\lim_{t\to\infty} q_t = 0$, $\lim_{t\to\infty} y_t = y$, $\sum_{j=1}^{t} y_j = \infty$, and $\lim_{t\to\infty} y_{t+1} \cdot t / \sum_{j=1}^{t} y_j = \Gamma > 0$. Then the resulting graph follows a power law degree distribution with exponent $\beta \in (1, 3]$.*

Proof. By Cor. 5.4, $G(p_t, r_t, q_t)$ follows a power law degree distribution with exponent $\beta = 1 + 2\Gamma/(2-y) > 1$. By Lemma 5.6, for $0 < y \leq 1$ we have $\beta = 1 + \frac{2}{2-y} \in (2, 3]$ and for $y = 0$ we have $\beta = 1 + \Gamma \in (1, 2]$. □

6 CONCLUSIONS AND DISCUSSION

Consider the preferential attachment model $G(p)$ described in [6]. The contribution of this paper is threefold. First, we improve the concentration bounds on the number of nodes of degree k at time t, denoted $m_{k,t}$. Specifically, we show that $m_{k,t}$ is concentrated around its mean with a deviation of $O(\sqrt{t})$, an improvement of the previously known deviation of $O(\sqrt{k^3 t \ln t})$. These bounds also allow us to bound the concentration of the k-rich club, namely the number of nodes with degree at least k.

Second, we bound the expectation of $m_{k,t}$, showing that $\mathbb{E}\left[m_{k,t}\right] = pM_k e_t \pm O(1/k)$, where $\beta = 1 + \frac{2}{2-p}$ and $M_k =$

(a) (b)

Figure 2: An example of two different networks with the same power law exponent $\beta = 5$. Each with 200 edges. (a) No edge events: $p_t = 0.5, r_t = 0, q_t = 0.5$. Many connected components. (b) No node events: $p_t = 0, r_t = 0.25, q_t = 0.75$. A giant connected component.

$\frac{2}{4-p}\prod_{j=1}^{k-1}\frac{j}{j+\beta}$ is proportional to $k^{-\beta}$, and $e_t = e_0 + t$ is the number of edges at time t. This allows us to estimate $\mathbb{E}\left[m_{k,t}\right]$ for any $k = o(t^{1-p/2})$, and the k-rich club, namely $\mathbb{E}\left[RC_{k,t}\right] = \sum_{j\geq k}\mathbb{E}\left[m_{j,t}\right]$, for any $k = o((t/\ln t)^{1-p/2})$.

Third, we extend the $G(p)$ model in a natural way to a model $G(p_t, r_t, q_t)$, by allowing the creation of new connected components, and time varying p. This results in a model for networks obeying a power law degree distribution with any exponent β in the full spectrum $1 < \beta < \infty$.

The new model allows us to point out some delicate issues that come up in the analysis of social networks. Let us mention two such examples. The first deals with the difference between the degree distribution in the network as a whole and that of the largest component in the same network. Consider the case where $p_t = q_t = 1/2$ for every t, thus there are no edge events. An illustration of the generated network appears in Figure 2(a). By Thm. 5.3, we obtain $y = 1.5$, $\Gamma = 1$ and so the whole network follows a power law degree distribution with exponent $\beta = 5$. However, any single component of this network is created using node events only, and hence can be described within the classical preferential attachment model of Barabási and Albert [4], or in our model $G(p_t, r_t, q_t)$ with $p_t = 1$. By Thm. 5.3, the degree distribution in this component follows a power law with exponent $\hat{\beta} = 3$, which is considerably different from $\beta = 5$, the exponent of the entire network. The surprising implication is that, focusing on studying the largest component alone might be insufficient for determining the correct power law exponent of the network as a whole.

The second example highlights yet another important feature of our model, namely, that it can generate many networks with the same power law distribution, but strikingly different structure. To illustrate this, consider the case where $r_t = 0.25$ and $q_t = 0.75$ for every t, thus there are no node events. An illustration of the generated network appears in Figure 2(b). By Thm. 5.3, the generated network follows a power law with exponent $\beta = 5$. While the above two networks display the same power law distribution, they also differ in some of their properties. For example, it can be shown that only the latter will have a single giant component, which follows a power law degree distribution with exponent $\beta = 5$. These examples emphasize some of the advantages of our extended preferential attachment model. We leave the formal proof of the above claims to the complete version of the paper.

REFERENCES

[1] William Aiello, Fan Chung, and Linyuan Lu. Random evolution in massive graphs. In *Handbook of massive data sets*, pages 97–122. Springer, 2002.

[2] Chen Avin, Zvi Lotker, Yinon Nahum, and David Peleg. Core size and densification in preferential attachment networks. In *Automata, Languages, and Programming*, pages 492–503. Springer, 2015.

[3] Chen Avin, Zvi Lotker, David Peleg, Yvonne Anne Pignolet, and Itzik Turkel. Core-periphery in networks: an axiomatic approach. *arXiv preprint arXiv:1411.2242*, 2014.

[4] A-L. Barabási and R. Albert. Emergence of scaling in random networks. *Science*, 286:509–512, 1999.

[5] S. Boyd and L. Vandenberghe. *Convex optimization*. Cambridge Univ. Press, 2004.

[6] F.R.K. Chung and L. Lu. *Complex graphs and networks*. AMS, 2006.

[7] Aaron Clauset, Cosma Rohilla Shalizi, and Mark EJ Newman. Power-law distributions in empirical data. *SIAM review*, 51(4):661–703, 2009.

[8] Colin Cooper and Alan M Frieze. A general model of undirected web graphs. In *Algorithms—ESA 2001*, pages 500–511. Springer, 2001.

[9] Colin Cooper and Pawe l Pra lat. Scale-free graphs of increasing degree. *Random Structures & Algorithms*, 38(4):396–421, 2011.

[10] Joseph L Doob. Regularity properties of certain families of chance variables. *Transactions of the American Mathematical Society*, 47(3):455–486, 1940.

[11] S. N. Dorogovtsev and J. F. F. Mendes. Effect of the accelerating growth of communications networks on their structure. *Phys. Rev. E*, 63:025101, Jan 2001.

[12] Sergey N Dorogovtsev and JFF Mendes. Accelerated growth of networks. *arXiv preprint cond-mat/0204102*, 2002.

[13] Sergey N Dorogovtsev and Jose FF Mendes. Evolution of networks. *Advances in physics*, 51(4):1079–1187, 2002.

[14] M. J. Gagen and J. S. Mattick. Accelerating, hyperaccelerating, and decelerating networks. *Phys. Rev. E*, 72:016123, Jul 2005.

[15] Jon M Kleinberg, Ravi Kumar, Prabhakar Raghavan, Sridhar Rajagopalan, and Andrew S Tomkins. The web as a graph: measurements, models, and methods. In *Computing and combinatorics*, pages 1–17. Springer, 1999.

[16] Ravi Kumar, Prabhakar Raghavan, Sridhar Rajagopalan, Dandapani Sivakumar, Andrew Tompkins, and Eli Upfal. The web as a graph. In *Proceedings of the nineteenth ACM SIGMOD-SIGACT-SIGART symposium on Principles of database systems*, pages 1–10. ACM, 2000.

[17] J. Leskovec, J. Kleinberg, and C. Faloutsos. Graph evolution: Densification and shrinking diameters. *Trans. Knowledge Discovery from Data*, 1:2, 2007.

[18] M. Newman. *Networks: An Introduction*. Oxford Univ. Press, 2010.

[19] D. de Solla Price. A general theory of bibliometric and other cumulative advantage processes. *J. Amer. Soc. Inform. Sci.*, 27(5):292–306, 1976.

[20] H.A. Simon. On a class of skew distribution functions. *Biometrika*, pages 425–440, 1955.

Unsupervised Network Discovery for Brain Imaging Data

Zilong Bai
University of California, Davis
Computer Science
zlbai@ucdavis.edu

LCDR Peter Walker
Naval Medical Research Center
peter.b.walker.mil@mail.mil

Anna Tschiffely
Naval Medical Research Center
anna.e.tschiffely.ctr@mail.mil

Fei Wang
Cornell University
Healthcare Policy and Research
feiwang03@gmail.com

Ian Davidson
University of California, Davis
Computer Science
davidson@cs.ucdavis.edu

ABSTRACT

A common problem with spatiotemporal data is how to simplify the data to discover an underlying network that consists of cohesive spatial regions (nodes) and relationships between those regions (edges). This network discovery problem naturally exists in a multitude of domains including climate data (dipoles), astronomical data (gravitational lensing) and the focus of this paper, fMRI scans of human subjects. Whereas previous work requires strong supervision, we propose an unsupervised matrix tri-factorization formulation with complex constraints and spatial regularization. We show that this formulation works well in controlled experiments with synthetic networks and is able to recover the underlying ground-truth network. We then show that for real fMRI data our approach can reproduce well known results in neurology regarding the default mode network in resting-state healthy and Alzheimer affected individuals.

CCS CONCEPTS

• **Information systems** → *Clustering*;

KEYWORDS

network discovery; spatial regularization; spatiotemporal data; fMRI; brain

1 INTRODUCTION

Network discovery is crucial in analyzing complex spatiotemporal data in a multitude of applications, such as ocean temperature monitoring[14], climate modeling[8], astronomical data[12], and the subject of this paper, fMRI scans of human subjects[4]. Simplifying such spatiotemporal data into a network of cohesive spatial regions (nodes) and relationships between those regions (edges) offers great insight. Consider the focus of this paper, discovering cognitive networks in fMRI data. It is well known that the 70,000 voxels in a typical fMRI scan can be grouped into 116 anatomical regions[16]; what is unknown is how those regions are coactive to form a functional network for different tasks. Our earlier work[4] addresses this problem by adding strong supervision in the form of the anatomical regions' boundaries.

In this paper we remove this requirement that the regions are given and instead require our method to discover their boundaries and the connectivity between them *without supervision*. Figure 1 shows a simplified example involving a single slice of brain activity. This problem is particularly difficult given that these studies rarely involve more than 100 patients, rendering methods such as deep learning inapplicable.

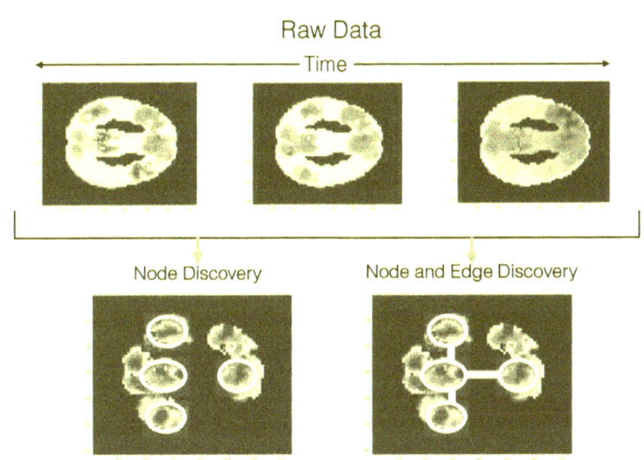

Figure 1: Our aim is to take spatiotemporal data and simultaneously discover nodes and edges to uncover the underlying network the person possesses without any supervision.

Though unsupervised matrix factorization methods such as the Orthogonal Nonnegative Matrix tri-Factorization (ONMtF) algorithms in [6] and [9] can be applied, they are not directly applicable to spatiotemporal problems. As shown in Figure 2a, when we set the rank of factorization to *six*, ONMtF cannot correctly discover *six* spatially continuous nodes; it can only discover *six* clusters of voxels with relatively high intra-cluster correlations. Even if we recursively apply this method by dividing the brain into two regions (using a factor 2, i.e. rank-2, ONMtF) and then divide each of those

KDD '17, August 13-17, 2017, Halifax, NS, Canada

ACM ISBN 978-1-4503-4887-4/17/08...$15.00
https://doi.org/10.1145/3097983.3098023

into two regions and so forth, the results are that recursive ONMtF cannot separate non-adjacent nodes even in the third recursion as shown in Figure 2b. To be interpreted as a cognitive network, the spatial regions must be continuous as these allow explanations in terms of the anatomical atlas as we have done in the captions of Figures 10, 11 and 12.

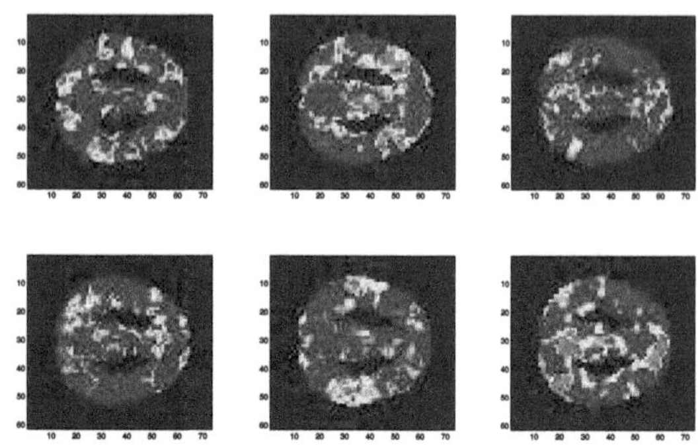

(a) A typical orthogonal non-negative symmetric matrix rank-6 tri-factorization by using ONMtF [6] .

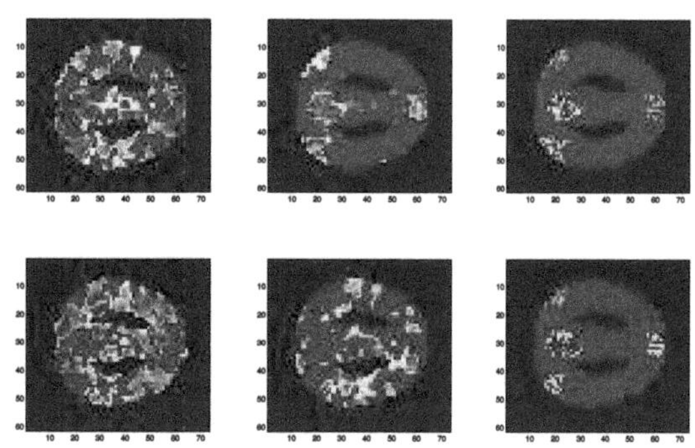

(b) Recursive foreground/background separation with ONMtF [6] for the typical scan sequence. Each column represents a 2 way factorization, one of which is then further refined.

Figure 2: The limitations of prior work (ONMtF [6]) for spatiotemporal data. Compare with Figure 10.

In this work, we extend the previous formulation of matrix tri-factorization (see Equation (1)) by adding a spatial regularizer (see Equation (2)). This is a non-trivial extension and produces a new type of solver involving new multiplicative update rules and a non-negative least squares solver. Our main contributions are as follows:

- We formulate a novel tri-factorization with spatial continuity regularization (ONMtF-SCR). This produces a novel non-negative least squares solver (Equation (17)) and multiplicative update rules (Equation (10)).
- The tri-factorization allows a natural representation where one matrix represents the nodes and another the associations between the nodes, thus simultaneously discovering nodes and edges in one framework.
- Our tri-factorization allows the discovery of networks without strong supervision. This produces results where each factor/node can be interpreted as an activated anatomical region and most importantly can generate new insights.
- We verify that our method discovers interpretable nodes that reproduce well known results in neurology regarding the default mode network in resting-state healthy and Alzheimer affected individuals for fMRI scans of human subjects.

We begin this paper by discussing related works about both the problem and the model. In the next section, we introduce and define the unsupervised network discovery problem. In the third section, we present our formulation of orthogonal non-negative matrix tri-factorization with continuity regularization; our solver is presented in the subsequent section. Extensive experiments were conducted to evaluate our approach first on synthetic networks where the ground truth is known and then on fMRI data. Finally, we conclude our work.

2 RELATED WORK

This work is related to two areas: the application domain of network discovery and underlying formulation of matrix tri-factorization.

2.1 Network Discovery

Most work on network discovery focuses on either node identification or edge identification but to our knowledge not simultaneously discovering both as we propose. Furthermore, finding a network with heterogeneous edges to our knowledge has not been addressed. A variety of current data mining tools have been used to determine, in an unsupervised setting, clusterings of voxels (what we refer to as nodes/regions) that appear to exhibit relatively high connectivity or covary with each other in systematic ways [2, 17]. Another stream of research focuses on just identifying connectivity between given brain regions using dynamic belief networks [3], and our own work using sparse inverse covariance estimation [15]. Some supervised learning work could be used to predict the existence of a network. Such work performs dimension reduction, followed by classification or regression, on the 4D array provided by the Blood Oxygenation Level Dependence (BOLD) fMRI [5]. However, probing functional connectivity goes far beyond a yes or no question of whether two regions are functionally connected; activity in one region can lag, excite another region, or coordinate only in certain circumstances [11].

Early work [1] used projection methods to uncover the subset of voxels that are co-active. For example principal component analysis can be used to determine which subset of the voxels have similar co-activation patterns. Here the data to project consists of a matrix $Cohort \times Voxel$. The projection vector's sign can be interpreted as an indicator vector for those voxels that are coactive. This work only provides a coarse measurement of the network as it divides the voxels into "in network" and "out of network". Later work is more refined in that it discovers the individual parts of the network. This work can naturally be modeled as a tensor decomposition problem into k factors using PARAFAC where each factor corresponds to an anatomical region. Consider a slice of activity modeled as an order 3 tensor: $x \times y \times time$. Then the decomposition produces factor matrices $A \times B \times T$ where A is $x \times k$, B is $y \times k$ and T is $t \times k$. The outer-product of each column of the matrices (i.e. A_i and B_i) produces a spatial pattern which can be interpreted as a combination of voxels that are co-active according to the vector T_i. However, such a formulation does not discover spatial patterns that correspond to anatomical regions. To overcome this, strong supervision must used as we did in our earlier work [4]. However, use of such strong supervision means making a strong prior assumption that this anatomical region information is known and accurate which is often not the case if the study involves complex understudied settings where neuroplasticity (brain reconfiguration) occurs such as TBI (traumatic brain injury), PTSD (post traumatic stress disorder) and Alzheimer affected individuals.

Finally, finding consensus networks in populations is primarily done by visual inspection of ICA components of rasterized data; little work focuses on finding similarities and differences between two cohorts (sub-populations).

2.2 Matrix tri-Factorization

Matrix tri-factorization with non-negative constraints has been applied to simplify traffic data [10]. As we focus on discovering interpretable cognitive networks, the discovered nodes should be non-overlapped clusters of voxels. Among various models for matrix tri-factorization, the model most related to our work is [6], in which multiplicative algorithms are proposed for solving matrix tri-factorization with orthogonality constraints on clustering indicator matrices to ensure non-overlapped clusters. An Orthogonal Non-negative Matrix tri-Factorization (ONMtF) model for symmetric matrix is formulated in Equation (1). However, the orthogonality constraints are *incapable* of discovering nodes with spatial continuity as shown in empirical experiments on fMRI scans (See Figure 2).

$$\underset{\mathbf{F}\geq 0, \mathbf{M}\geq 0}{Minimize} \|\mathbf{X} - \mathbf{FMF}^T\|_F^2 \quad s.t. \quad \mathbf{F}^T\mathbf{F} = \mathbf{I} \tag{1}$$

To our knowledge, the use of *non-negative matrix tri-factorization with spatial continuity regularization* to discover cognitive networks is novel and is particularly challenging when *orthogonality* is incorporated on top of these requirements. More specifically, our work differs from [6] in our novelty of incorporating spatial continuity into the multiplicative update rule for **F** and using nonnegative least squares solver to solve for symmetric **M**.

3 PROBLEM OVERVIEW AND DEFINITION

We now discuss our proposed contributions at the functional level and go into more details with respect to formulations and solvers in the next sections. fMRI is a predominant method for capturing brain activity as it processes information [7, 18] with a natural question being to simplify the activity into the underlying cognitive network. The example in Figure 1 shows that there are multiple groups of voxels which coactivate together even though they are spatially far apart.

Problem 1 ***Unsupervised Network Discovery Problem***
Input: $\mathcal{D} \in \mathbb{R}^{Spatial \times Temporal}$, *k the number of nodes to discover.*
Output: A collection of k non-overlapping continuous nodes $\mathbf{F}_1 \ldots \mathbf{F}_k$ *where* $\mathbf{F}_i \in [0,1]^{Spatial}, \forall i \neq j, \mathbf{F}_i^T\mathbf{F}_j = 0$,
$\mathbf{M} \in \mathbb{R}^{k \times k}$ *a measure of association between the nodes.*

In this paper we take $\mathcal{D}$ and convert it to an affinity/similarity matrix **X** between the voxels.

3.1 Problem Formulation: ONMtF-SCR

In this section we formulate the network discovery problem as a non-negative symmetric matrix tri-factorization model with orthogonality constraint and spatial continuity regularization (ONMtF-SCR) as shown in Equation (2).[1]

$$\begin{aligned} &\underset{\mathbf{F}\geq 0, \mathbf{M}\geq 0}{Minimize} \|\mathbf{X} - \mathbf{FMF}^T\|_F^2 + \beta tr(\mathbf{F}^T\Theta\mathbf{F}) \\ &s.t. \quad \mathbf{F}^T\mathbf{F} = \mathbf{I} \end{aligned} \tag{2}$$

The Modeling Assumptions Made. We first discuss how Equation (2) simplifies the underlying behavior in the fMRI data. The tri-factorization effectively rewrites the fMRI image as a linear combination of subnetworks in the form $\sum_{i,j} (\mathbf{M})_{ij}\mathbf{F}_{*i}\mathbf{F}_{*j}^T$ as diagrammatically shown in Figure 3. Here the *weighted* **outer** product of $\mathbf{F}_{*i}$ and $\mathbf{F}_{*j}$ represents a subgraph consisting of node i and j, and the weight $\mathbf{M}_{ij}$ thus indicates the amount of inter-node (or intra-node if $i = j$) associations between node i and j. In this way the network is modeled as a series of node pairs with a strength of association of each pair.

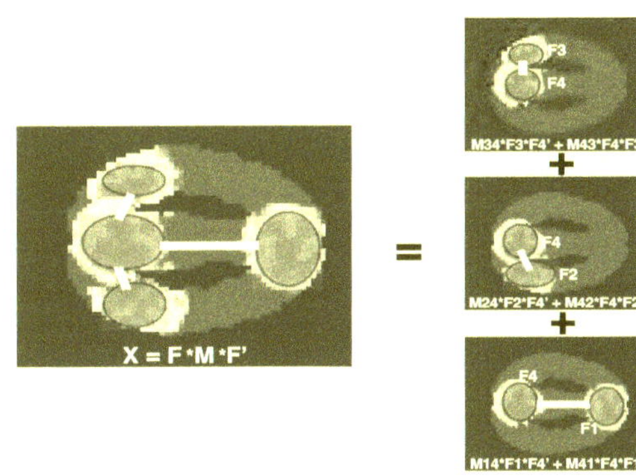

Figure 3: How our formulation models a complex network as a linear combination of simpler parts. The example 4-node underlying network is decomposed into a linear combination of three subnetworks.

Interpretation of ONMtF-SCR for Medical Imaging. Here **X** can be the correlations between each pair of voxels over time according to the BOLD values taken from the fMRI scans.

F is the node indicator matrix. Each column of **F** is a nonnegative ($\mathbf{F}_{i,j} \geq 0, \forall i,j$) and normalized ($\|\mathbf{F}_{*j}\|_2 = 1, \forall j$) indicator vector where $\mathbf{F}_{i,j}$ denotes the membership weight of voxel i in node j. The columns of **F** are orthogonal to each other ($\mathbf{F}_{*i}^T\mathbf{F}_{*j} = 0, \forall i \neq j$) to guarantee that the discovered nodes are **non-overlapping**.

M is a symmetric non-negative matrix that describes the associations/interactions between the nodes indicated by **F**. The entries of **M** can be used to construct the edges between the nodes of the functional network shown in Figure 1.

[1] In this paper superscript " T " denotes matrix transpose, and "tr()" represents matrix trace calculation.

The Spatial Regularizer. Spatial continuity within each discovered node is enforced by the regulation term $\beta tr(\mathbf{F}^T\Theta\mathbf{F})$ where Θ is a penalty matrix that discourages voxels located far apart spatially from being clustered into the same node. Note our regularizer is very general and does not simply state the adjacent columns (or rows) in the matrix $\mathbf{X}$ should be together. Any forms of spatial properties can be used. Specifically, Θ is a reciprocal Gaussian Kernel matrix for each pair of voxels within brain area as shown in Equation (3). Vectors $\mathbf{v}_i$ and $\mathbf{v}_j$ indicate the spatial $x-y$ locations of voxels i and j on the slice of the brain image this paper evaluates. The diagonal entries of Θ *enforce L-2 norm sparsity regularization* on the region indicator vectors.

$$(\Theta)_{ij} = e^{\frac{\|\mathbf{v}_i-\mathbf{v}_j\|_2^2}{2\sigma^2}} \tag{3}$$

The spatial continuity regularization in Equation (2) is incorporated to improve the interpretability of discovered networks since the orthogonality constraint *does not* guarantee each discovered node to be spatially continuous.

Solving Equation (2) **Directly is Challenging.** One common approach to solve constrained optimization problems is the Lagrangian multiplier method and accordingly the Lagrangian function of Equation (2) is derived below.

$$\begin{aligned} L(\mathbf{F},\mathbf{M},\lambda) &= tr(\mathbf{XX}) - 2tr(\mathbf{XFMF}^T) + \beta tr(\mathbf{F}^T\Theta\mathbf{F}) \\ &+ tr(\mathbf{FMF}^T\mathbf{FMF}^T) + tr(\lambda(\mathbf{F}^T\mathbf{F})) - tr(\lambda) \end{aligned} \tag{4}$$

The presence of the 4th-order term $tr(\mathbf{FMF}^T\mathbf{FMF}^T)$ in Equation (4) makes directly solving it extremely challenging and it *cannot* be reduced to $tr(\mathbf{FM}^2\mathbf{F}^T)$ unless $\mathbf{F}^T\mathbf{F} \equiv \mathbf{I}$ is guaranteed through each iteration of the solver.

4 ALGORITHM FOR SOLVING ONMTF-SCR

In this section we present the solver for ONMtF-SCR in Algorithm 1. Given the difficulty of directly solving Equation (2) there are two possible directions: *1)* Simplify the formulation or *2)* Approximately solve the complex formulation. The formulation cannot be simplified, as each part of it is essential to formulate the problem of unsupervised network discovery, and it is our desire to address the problem directly. Thus, the latter option is taken: instead of directly solving Equation (2), the problem is reformulated into two subproblems, which are then solved within one framework. Particularly, multiplicative update rules are developed for solving the node discovery subproblem, and a non-negative least squares subproblem is solved for edge discovery. Our experiments suggest the solutions found are effective on both synthetic and real-world data.

4.1 Unsupervised Node Discovery Subproblem

To solve the node discovery subproblem, Equation (2) is simplified to Equation (5) by substituting the term $\mathbf{FM}^T$ with a single optimization matrix variable $\mathbf{G}$ while keeping both the orthogonality constraints and spatial regularization on $\mathbf{F}$.

$$\begin{aligned} &\underset{\mathbf{F}\geq 0,\mathbf{G}\geq 0}{Minimize}\|\mathbf{X}-\mathbf{FG}^T\|_F^2 + \beta tr(\mathbf{F}^T\Theta\mathbf{F}) \\ &s.t. \quad \mathbf{F}^T\mathbf{F} = \mathbf{I} \end{aligned} \tag{5}$$

This simplification makes it plausible to derive multiplicative update rules that can be efficiently applied to obtain an effective solution for $\mathbf{F}$ and $\mathbf{G}$. The Lagrangian of Equation (5) is given by Equation (6) with the $r \times r$ symmetric matrix λ as Lagrangian multipliers.

Algorithm 1 Algorithm for Network Discovery.

Require: i. Θ: Spatial continuity penalty matrix (constructed with spatial bandwidth σ)
ii. β: Weight of spatial continuity regularization
iii. r: Rank of factorization
Output: $\mathbf{F}$, $\mathbf{M}$

```
Initialization: Randomly initialize F_{s×r} and G_{s×r};
Solve Equation (5) and set F for node discovery:
while Termination condition not satisfied do
    Update F with Equation (10), λ calculated with Equation (14);
    Update G with Equation (11);
end while
Solve Equation (17) and set M for edge discovery;
Rescale M with Equation (18);
Rescale F with Equation (19);
return: F, M
```

$$L(\mathbf{F},\mathbf{G},\lambda) = \|\mathbf{X}-\mathbf{FG}^T\|_F^2 + \beta tr(\mathbf{F}^T\Theta\mathbf{F}) + tr(\lambda(\mathbf{F}^T\mathbf{F}-\mathbf{I})) \tag{6}$$

Since $\|\mathbf{X}-\mathbf{FG}^T\|_F^2 = tr((\mathbf{X}-\mathbf{FG}^T)(\mathbf{X}-\mathbf{FG}^T)^T)$, partial differentiation over $\mathbf{F}$ on $L(\mathbf{F},\mathbf{G},\lambda)$ is given by Equation (7)

$$\frac{\partial L(\mathbf{F},\mathbf{G},\lambda)}{\partial \mathbf{F}} = -2\mathbf{XG} + 2\mathbf{FG}^T\mathbf{G} + 2\beta\Theta\mathbf{F} + 2\mathbf{F}\lambda \tag{7}$$

A local optima is obtained when Equation (7) is set to 0 and by using *KKT* (*Karush-Kuhn-Tucker*) complementary condition [6] yields:

$$(-2\mathbf{XG} + 2\mathbf{FG}^T\mathbf{G} + 2\beta\Theta\mathbf{F} + 2\mathbf{F}\lambda)_{ik}\mathbf{F}_{ik} = 0 \tag{8}$$

This is equivalent to Equation (9) if either $\mathbf{F}_{ik} = 0$ or the left factor is equal to 0.

$$(-2\mathbf{XG} + 2\mathbf{FG}^T\mathbf{G} + 2\beta\Theta\mathbf{F} + 2\mathbf{F}\lambda)_{ik}\mathbf{F}_{ik}^2 = 0 \tag{9}$$

Hence,

Multiplicative Update Rule for F

$$\mathbf{F}_{i,k} \leftarrow \mathbf{F}_{i,k}\sqrt{\frac{(\mathbf{XG})_{i,k}}{(\mathbf{FG}^T\mathbf{G} + \beta\Theta\mathbf{F} + \mathbf{F}\lambda)_{i,k}}} \tag{10}$$

By partial differentiation over $\mathbf{G}$ on $L(\mathbf{F},\mathbf{G},\lambda)$,

Multiplicative Update Rule for G

$$\mathbf{G}_{i,k} \leftarrow \mathbf{G}_{i,k}\frac{(\mathbf{X}^T\mathbf{F})_{i,k}}{(\mathbf{G}(\mathbf{F}^T\mathbf{F}))_{i,k}} \tag{11}$$

An approximate compact expression for λ can be derived by summing over i in Equation (8) (a technique also used by [6]):

$$\begin{aligned} &(-\mathbf{F}^T\mathbf{XG} + (\mathbf{F}^T\mathbf{F})(\mathbf{G}^T\mathbf{G}) + (\mathbf{F}^T\mathbf{F})\lambda + \beta\mathbf{F}^T\Theta\mathbf{F})_{k,k} = 0 \\ &(-\mathbf{F}^T\mathbf{XG} + (\mathbf{G}^T\mathbf{G}) + \lambda + \beta\mathbf{F}^T\Theta\mathbf{F})_{k,k} = 0 \end{aligned} \tag{12}$$

Hence,

$$\lambda_{k,k} = (\mathbf{F}^T\mathbf{XG} - \mathbf{G}^T\mathbf{G} - \beta\mathbf{F}^T\Theta\mathbf{F})_{k,k} \tag{13}$$

By ignoring the non-negativity of $\mathbf{F}$, approximate off-diagonal entries of $\lambda_{i,j}, i \neq j$ can be obtained, which lead to compact expression for λ:

$$\lambda = (\mathbf{F}^T\mathbf{XG} - \mathbf{G}^T\mathbf{G} - \beta\mathbf{F}^T\Theta\mathbf{F}) \tag{14}$$

In contrast to the ONMF with only orthogonality constraints in [6], the update rule of F in our model is novel in incorporating spatial continuity regularization with Θ and β.

4.2 Edge Discovery Subproblem

In the second stage we aim to recover the association matrix **M**. As suggested by the simplification in the first stage, a straightforward way looks for the solution of the nonnegative least squares problem in Equation (15).

$$\underset{\mathbf{M}\geq 0}{Minimize}\|\mathbf{G}-\mathbf{F}\mathbf{M}^T\|_F^2 \tag{15}$$

However, it is crucial to note that the solution **M** to subproblem 15 need *not* be symmetric (as **G** is not definitely within the space spanned by the column vectors of **F** due to the *non-negativity* constraint) which is a requirement for the simpler networks we explore with the original formulation 2. Hence we use Equation (16) to solve for the symmetric edge discovery subproblem. Note Equation (16) can be equivalently rewritten as Equation (17) in the form of standard nonnegative least squares problem, which can be efficiently solved by various existing solvers. We make use of the result that the structure of the Kronecker product of two identical **F** matrices in Equation (17) guarantees the solution **M** reshaped from $vec(\mathbf{M})$ to be symmetric. Note our nonnegative least squares solver for the core matrix **M** is different from the multiplicative update rule used in [6] for tri-factorizations.

Symmetric Edge Discovery Solver

$$\underset{\mathbf{M}\geq 0}{Minimize}\|\mathbf{X}-\mathbf{F}\mathbf{M}\mathbf{F}^T\|_F^2 \equiv \tag{16}$$

$$\underset{\mathbf{M}\geq 0}{Minimize}\|(\mathbf{F}\otimes\mathbf{F})vec(\mathbf{M})-vec(\mathbf{X})\|_2^2 \tag{17}$$

where $\otimes$ is the Kronecker product and $vec(\cdot)$ is the vectorization of a matrix (i.e. stack columns altogether).

4.3 Rescaling for Reproducibility of M and F.

Since the columns of **F** solved from Equation (5) are normalized, **M** solved from Equation (17) is affected by the sizes of the clusters. **M** is rescaled with Equation (18) such that **M** only reflects weighted correlations within/between nodes. Correspondingly, **F** needs to be rescaled with Equation (19) after rescaling **M** to make the maximum entry of each column in **F** equal to 1.

$$\mathbf{M}_{i,j} \leftarrow \mathbf{M}_{i,j} * (max(\mathbf{F}_{*i}) * max(\mathbf{F}_{*j})), \forall i,j \tag{18}$$

$$\mathbf{F}_{i,j} \leftarrow \frac{\mathbf{F}_{i,j}}{\underset{i}{max}(\mathbf{F}_{i,j})}, \forall i,j \tag{19}$$

In the experimental results for showing the relative strength of the correlations between and within the discovered nodes, **M** is further rescaled with Equation (20).

$$\mathbf{M}_{i,j} \leftarrow \frac{\mathbf{M}_{i,j}}{\underset{i,j}{max}(\mathbf{M}_{i,j})} \tag{20}$$

5 EXPERIMENTS

Previously we showed the limitations of existing ONMtF formulation (see Equation (1)) [6] for functional network discovery (Figure 2). Here we evaluate the performance of our network discovery method with experiments on both synthetic networks and networks generated from real fMRI spatiotemporal data. For the synthetic network experiments we use anatomical region structures from an anatomical atlas to define the functional nodes and background regions (Figure 4) but create artificial ground truth interactions (Figure 5). For real world data we compare results of finding networks in young, elderly and demented individuals and present typical results.

Setting Parameters. The matrix Θ (see Equation (3)) determines the penalty for placing two non-adjacent voxels in the same cluster. To use our regularizer we need to set two parameters: σ (the bandwidth of the kernel) and β (the regularizer weight). The parameter σ effectively specifies the diameter of continuous regions that our method discovers. The parameter β controls the tradeoff between the continuity regularization on the discovered nodes and how well our decomposition model reconstructs the original graph.

Using cross-validation we set $\sigma = 7$, $\beta = 40$. This parameter setting achieves the following: *1)* one continuous node with strong intra-cluster correlation will not be partitioned into two nodes, while two spatially separated nodes with strong inter-cluster correlation will not be clustered into one node; *2)* our method guarantees the continuity within each discovered node while achieving a reasonable reconstruction of the original graph with the decomposition model.

All MATLAB code to reproduce the experimental results in this paper will be available on `github` [2].

5.1 Synthetic Network Experiments With The Brain Atlas

Here we conduct experiments on different synthetic networks. The underlying regions we use are from the *Automated Anatomical Labeling (AAL) Atlas* (see Figure 4) and we create artificial associations between the nodes/regions to answer the following questions regarding the potentials of our method:

(1) How our method performs on a *simple network*, where the functional nodes of underlying network are both strongly self-correlated and strongly inter-correlated (see Figure 5a).

(2) How our method performs on a *degrading network*, where there is strong correlation within each individual node, but the inter-cluster correlation gradually decreases. This network is common in demented individuals (see Figure 5b).

(3) How our method performs on a degraded network with *local noise* in the form of weak correlations within each background (remaining) region (see Figure 5c). This is a setting that mirrors patients with the PTSD pathology.

(4) How our method performs when there are networks with *global noise*. Here there are not only strong inter-correlations between the set of functional nodes but also weak correlations between functional nodes and the background regions (see Figure 5d).

The synthetic networks $\mathbf{X}_{syn}$ are constructed from $\mathbf{F}_{syn}\mathbf{M}_{syn}\mathbf{F}_{syn}^T$ where $\mathbf{F}_{syn}$ is the indicator matrix for the segments of the synthetic brain activation network and $\mathbf{M}_{syn}$ describes the average intra/inter-cluster correlations of the segments. We now describe how we create the synthetic regions and their interactions.

[2] https://github.com/ZilongBai/KDD2017.git

Label	Correlation Definition
C_f	Within the same functional node
C_{ff}	Between different functional nodes
C_b	Within the same background region
C_{fb}	Between functional node and background region
C_{bb}	Between different background regions

Table 1: Definitions of different types of correlations for synthetic networks.

	C_f	C_{ff}	C_b	C_{fb}	C_{bb}
1.	1.0	1.0	0.0	0.0	0.0
2.	1.0	[0.1, 0.9]	0.0	0.0	0.0
3.	1.0	0.6	[0.1, 0.8]	0.0	0.0
4.	1.0	0.8	0.5	[0.1, 0.9]	0.0

Table 2: Specification of M_{syn}, the synthetic correlation matrix, for different settings. *1. Simple Network, 2. Degrading Network, 3. Local Noise, 4. Global Noise.*

Creating Realistic But Synthetic Regions. The spatial region of the entire synthetic brain network is partitioned into eight major segments (based on the anatomical atlas) to synthesize the real brain activation as shown in Figure 4. Each segment is comprised of multiple spatially adjacent anatomical regions. The four segments on the first row of Figure 4 are spatially separated nodes that comprise the underlying functional network; the four segments on the second row of Figure 4 are remaining parts that serve to synthesize background regions.

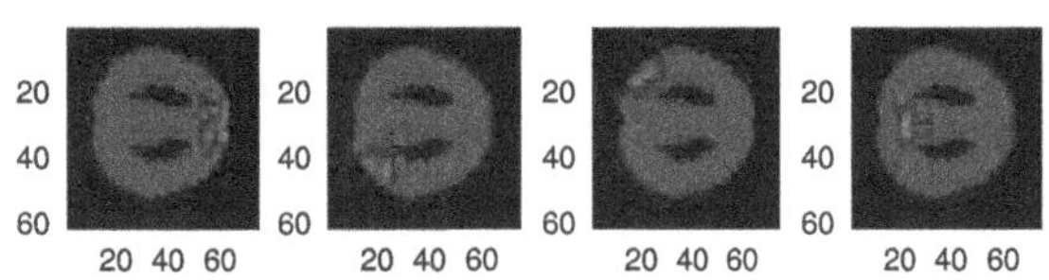

(a) Functional Nodes

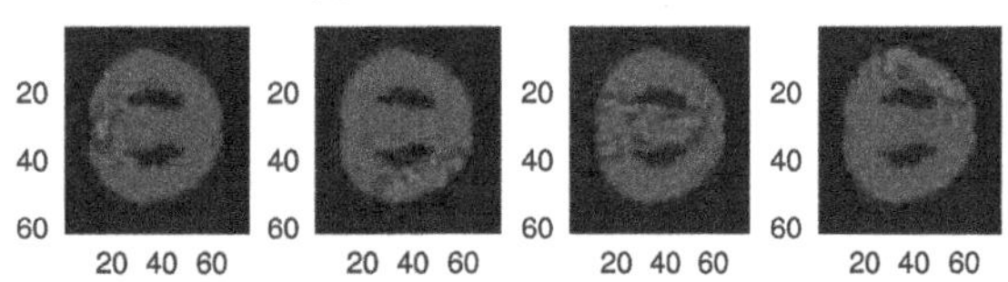

(b) Background Regions

Figure 4: Synthetic nodes/regions used in our experiments.

Creating Synthetic Activations. Figure 5 visually shows examples of synthetic node interaction matrices. Here we include precise details for reproduciblity of experiments, which are important as we show how we increase the challenge of the network discovery problem. To construct $\mathbf{M}_{syn}$ we define 5 major types of correlations which we label as C_f, C_{ff}, C_b, C_{fb}, C_{bb}. Here the suffix f means functional node and b means background region as shown in Figure 4. Details of their definitions are in Table 1. Specifically for the entires of $\mathbf{M}_{syn}$:

- $\mathbf{M}_{syn}(i, i) = C_f, 1 \le i \le 4$,
- $\mathbf{M}_{syn}(i, i) = C_b, 5 \le i \le 8$,
- $\mathbf{M}_{syn}(i, j) = C_{ff}, 1 \le i, j \le 4, i \ne j$,
- $\mathbf{M}_{syn}(i, j) = C_{bb}, 5 \le i, j \le 8, i \ne j$,
- $\mathbf{M}_{syn}(i, j) = C_{fb}, 1 \le i \le 4, 5 \le j \le 8$,
- $\mathbf{M}_{syn}(i, j) = C_{fb}, 5 \le i \le 8, 1 \le j \le 4$

A network is then defined by a combination of these different types of correlations and allows us to meaningfully test in a variety of situations. In our work we construct four synthetic settings defined formally in Table 2 and visually in Figure 5.

Results for Synthetic Networks With Our Method. Figure 6 and Figure 7 respectively show the discovered functional nodes $\mathbf{F}_{dis}$ and associations of nodes $\mathbf{M}_{dis}$ for each example ground truth network. $\mathbf{F}_{dis}$ should be compared with the ground truth functional nodes in Figure 4. Similarly, $\mathbf{M}_{dis}$ should be compared to the ground truth correlations between functional nodes in Figure 5.

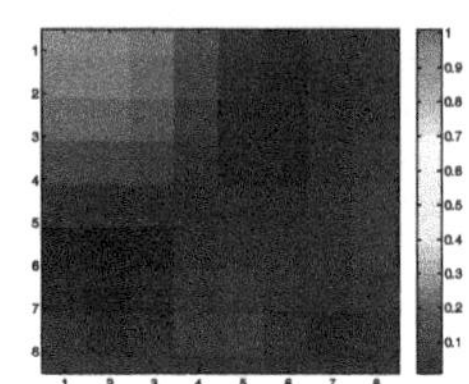

(a) Simple Network

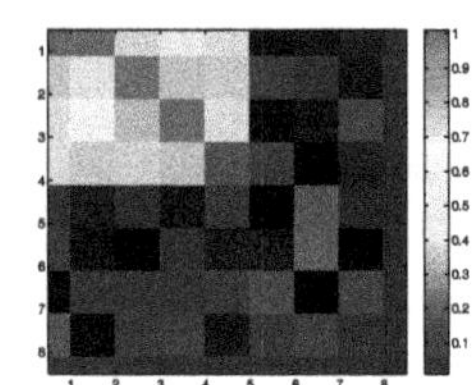

(b) Degrading Network

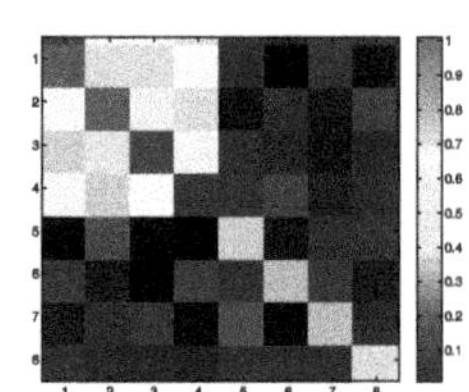

(c) Local Noise

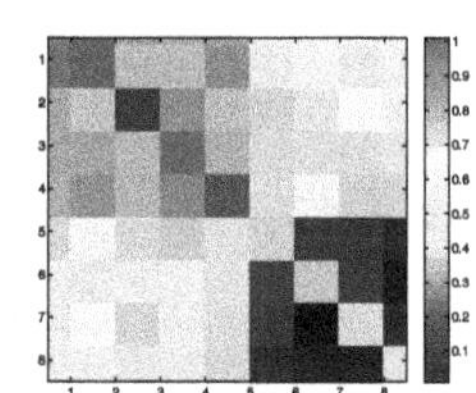

(d) Global Noise

Figure 5: Example synthetic correlation matrices M_{syn} of synthetic settings *1,2,3,4*. Each graph shows the edges of eight component networks (four functional nodes and four background regions from Figure 4). The *top left* 4×4 *patch of each graph shows the ground truth correlations of synthetic functional nodes our method attempts to recover.* The colors indicate the strength of each correlation.

5.2 Quantifying Node Discovery

Whilst in the previous section one can visually compare the ground truth (top row of Figure 4) with the recovered nodes in our four settings (Figure 6), here we quantify how good our method is at recovering the underlying nodes in various challenging situations.

To evaluate the performance of the proposed algorithm, we define a performance metric as follows:

Definition (Node Discovery Accuracy) Node Discovery Accuracy (NDA) of functional node i is defined as the maximum cosine similarity between all discovered nodes and the ground-truth functional

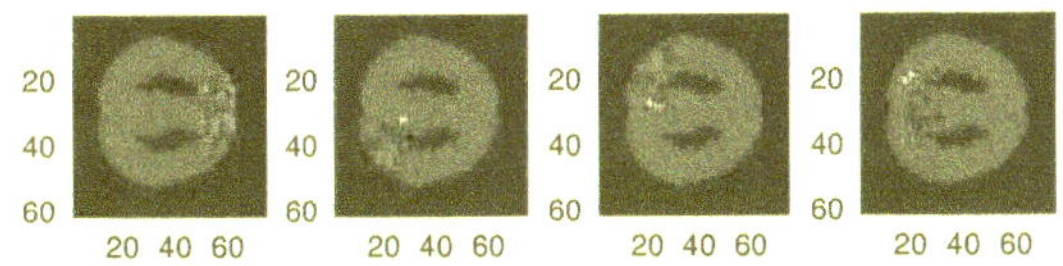

(a) Simple Network

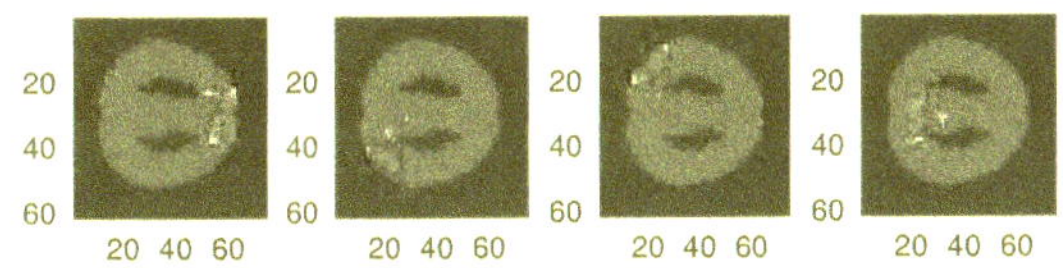

(b) Degrading Network

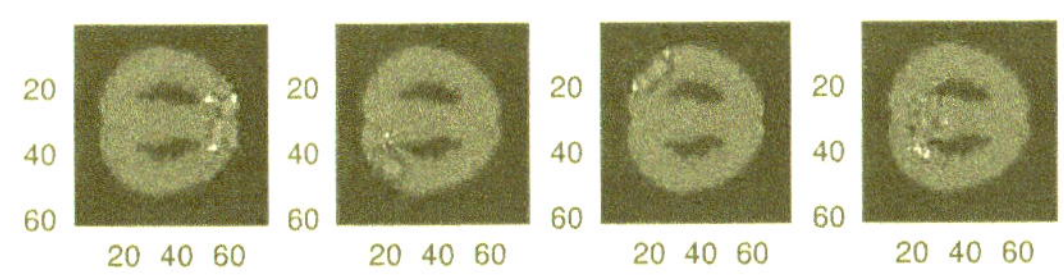

(c) Local Noise

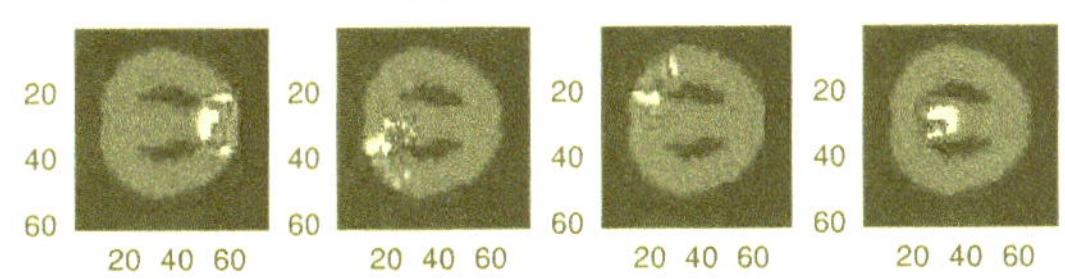

(d) Global Noise

Figure 6: Recovered functional nodes F_{dis} from the example synthetic networks in synthetic settings *1,2,3,4*. Compare with the top row of Figure 4, which is the ground truth. Our method recovers functional nodes with various complex shapes in the presence of different noises. The spatial properties of the ground-truth nodes are preserved accurately in the recovered nodes.

node i (see Equation (21)).

$$accuracy(node_i) = \max_{1 \leq j \leq r} \frac{\mathbf{F}^T_{dis(*,j)} \mathbf{F}_{syn(*,i)}}{\|\mathbf{F}_{dis(*,j)}\|_2 \|\mathbf{F}_{syn(*,i)}\|_2} \tag{21}$$

where F_{dis} denotes the discovered nodes of rank-r factorization; F_{syn} denotes the indicator matrix of ground-truth synthetic functional nodes/background regions as shown in Figure 4, with $F_{syn(*,i)}$, $1 \leq i \leq r$ for functional nodes. Cosine similarity enables NDA to provide fair comparison between different nodes without being affected by their sizes.

Figure 8 shows the NDA results of the four underlying functional nodes in *Degrading Network*, *Local Noise* and *Global Noise*. As one progresses along the x-axis in each graph the situations become more and more challenging. In *Degrading Network* (Figure 8a), the x-axis of this graph shows C_{ff} changing from 0.1 to 0.9. Whilst discovery of node 1,2, and 3 remain unaffected by the increasing strength of correlations between synthetic functional nodes, it becomes more challenging for our method to recover node 4 as its NDA drops significantly when C_{ff} increases to greater than 0.6. In the settings with *Local Noise* (Figure 8b), the x-axis represents C_b increasing from 0.1 to 0.8. It shows that our method is robust against the increasing correlation within each background region

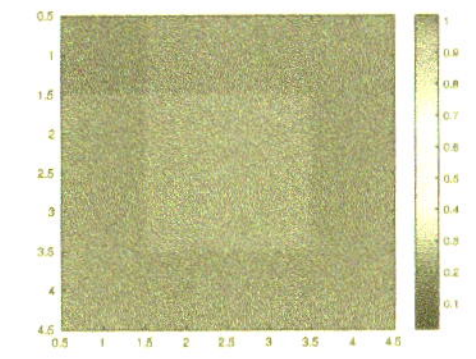

(a) Simple Network

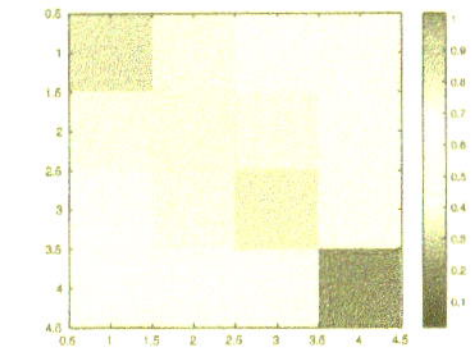

(b) Degrading Network

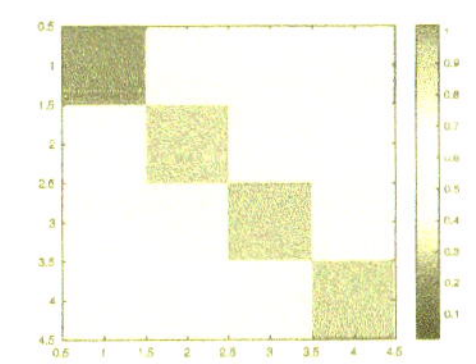

(c) Local Noise

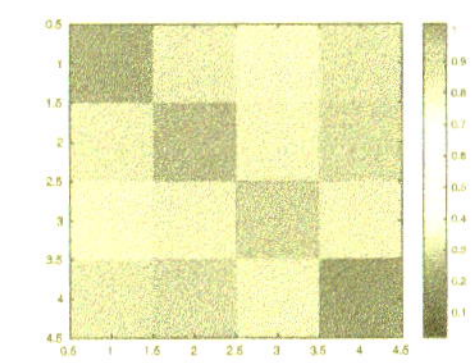

(d) Global Noise

Figure 7: Discovered interactions M_{dis} between functional nodes from the example synthetic networks of the four synthetic settings with our rank-4 factorization. *Compare with the top left* 4×4 *patches of the graphs from Figure 5 which are the ground truth edges between synthetic functional nodes. Our method performs well in recovering interactions between functional nodes in the face of different noises.*

until $C_b \geq 0.8$ (note $C_{ff} = 0.6$ as specified in Table 2-3). It becomes notably challenging to accurately discover nodes in the presence of *Global Noise* (Figure 8c). The x-axis tells C_{fb} increasing from 0.1 to 0.9. Unlike Figures 8a and 8b, the NDA of node 3 drops to lower than 0.8 when $C_{fb} > 0.7$; the NDA of node 4 decreases to lower than 0.6 when $C_{fb} \geq 0.6$. Note node 4 completely fails to be discovered when $C_{fb} = 0.3$.

In summary, our approach is robust against various types of noise to certain extents. Comparing to other nodes, node 4 tends to be more susceptible to various noises and is particularly vulnerable to the *Global Noise*. This can be explained by the spatial properties of node 4: it has the most irregular shape amongst all synthetic functional nodes and is *surrounded* by background regions. The exceptional drop at $C_{fb} = 0.3$ in the presence of *Global Noise* (Figure 8c) can be explained by the difficulty of capturing the most appropriate solutions with 20 randomly initialized experiments for its particular shape, location, and size. We also witness that node 3 tends to suffer along with node 4 in the face of significant *Global Noise*. This can be explained by: *i)* the two synthetic functional nodes are closely located in spatial domain; *ii)* the space between them is filled up with some synthetic background regions.

5.3 Experiment with Real Brain Imaging Data

In these experiments we work on trying to discover the underlying networks in real fMRI data from ADNI [3]. The matrix **X** in Equation (5) is constructed by calculating the absolute Pearson correlation between each pair of voxels based on their temporal activations and hence represents a correlation/similarity matrix. In this paper for ease of visualization, we focus on the activation network on

[3] http://adni.loni.usc.edu/study-design/collaborative-studies/dod-adni/

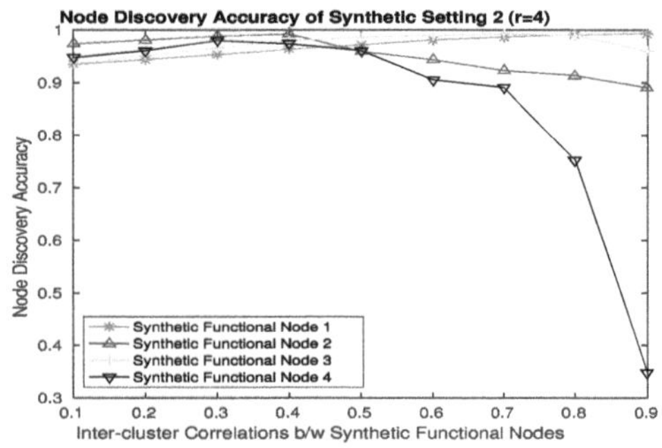

(a) Degrading Network

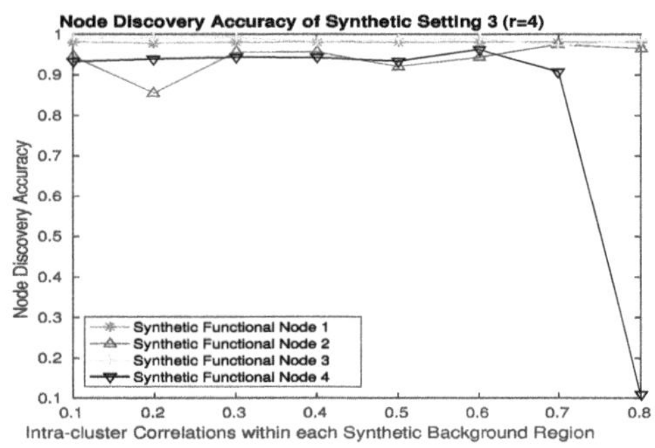

(b) Local Noise

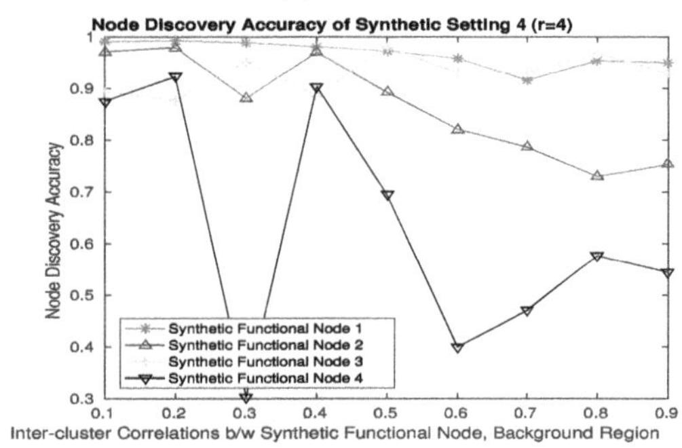

(c) Global Noise

Figure 8: Node discovery accuracy measured by Equation (21) for different synthetic networks. The higher the NDA, the better the node discovery performance. In each graph the network discovery difficulty increases along the x-axis from left to right. The interactions (correlations) of functional nodes and background regions of each graph are specified in Table 2. Each synthetic setting is tested with 20 randomly initialized experiments and the tri-factorization solution with the lowest relative reconstruction error is chosen.

the 36*th* slice of each 3-dimensional scan image. The data contains three cohorts of individuals: **y** young normal subjects, **o** old normal subjects and **d** old demented (Alzheimer affected) subjects at resting state. At resting state it is well known that even the most diseased individual will exhibit the well known default mode network (DMN) (Figure 9). We expect the strength of the DMN to diminish from **y** to **o** to **d** and for parts of the DMN to become missing for demented individuals. Figures 10, 11 and 12 illustrate the network

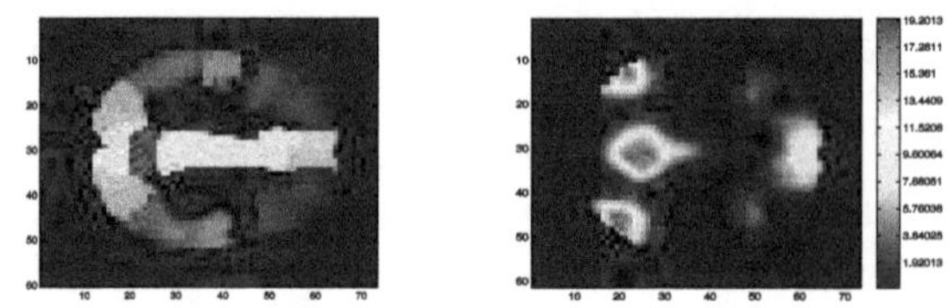

Figure 9: Left: Anatomical structures/nodes in the brain at slice 36. Different colors represent different nodes. Right: The subset of structures that form the default mode network (DMN). This network activates while a person is in resting state.

discovered by our method using a rank-6 factorization. For each of the cohorts we present the results of one typical subject and the average network discovery result. Similar to our synthetic experiments, we conduct multiple experiments with random initialization on the same subject and select the tri-factorization solution with the lowest relative reconstruction error. The results from experiments on real fMRI data demonstrate the capability of our method to reproduce the well known results in neurology [7] regarding the default mode network in resting-state subjects. Figure 10 shows a strong and completely intact DMN for a young healthy person as expected whilst Figure 11 shows for a healthy elderly subject a mostly intact but weakened network. Most importantly, Figure 12 shows that a demented individual's network is not intact in that the front cingular is missing from the network. This behavior has been observed previously [13]. The percentage amounts listed in part (c) of Figures 10, 11 and 12 are significant. What they indicate is that our method was able to simplify the network into regions

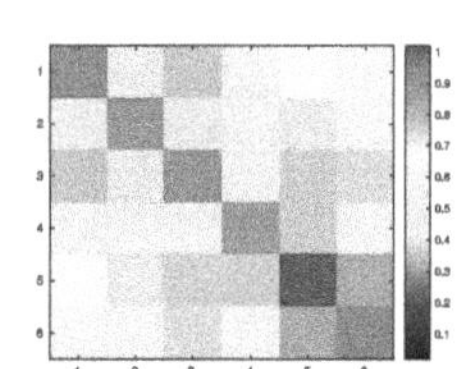

(a) Discovered edges

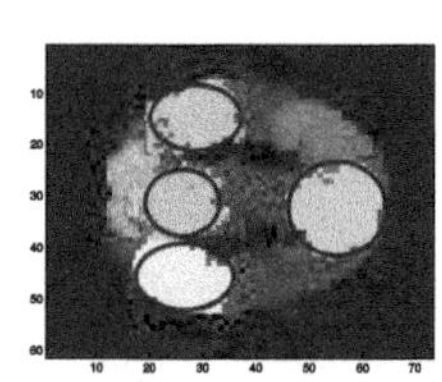

(b) Discovered Network

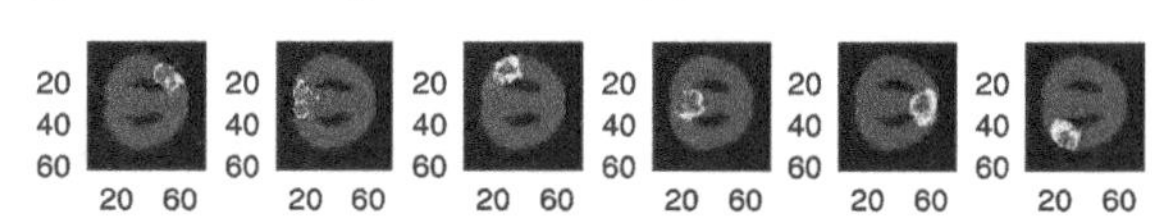

(c) Discovered nodes and corresponding largest covered anatomical regions (cosine similarity) from left to right: Frontal Inf. Oper. R. (59.12%), Cuneus L. (59.15%), Precentral L. (66.61%), Precuneus R. (48.45%), SupraMarginal L. (61.10%), Frontal Sup. Medial. L. (50.56%).

Figure 10: Network discovered from a typical young normal subject. Normal activities are discovered from the *Parietal and Occipital Lobes* (ice blue and lemon regions in (b)), the *Cingulum Region Posterior* (sea foam region in (b)), the *Frontal Cortex* (lime region in (b)).

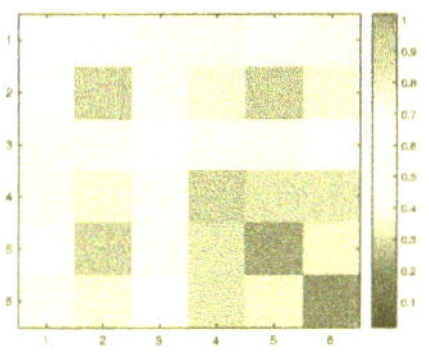

(a) Discovered edges

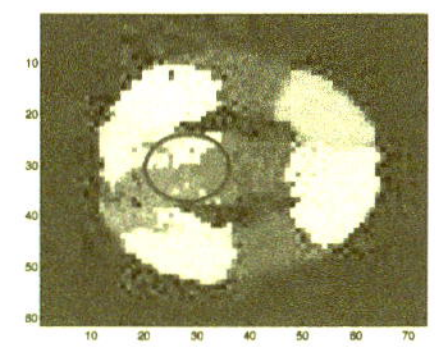

(b) Discovered Network

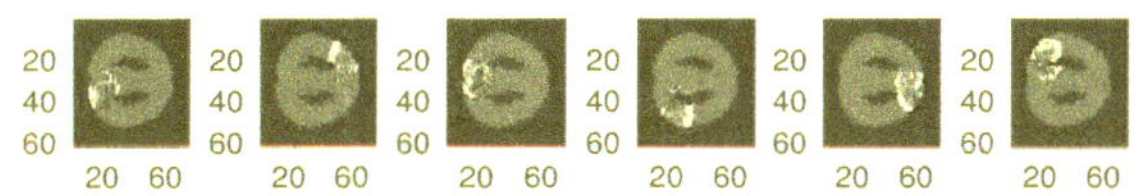

(c) Discovered nodes and corresponding largest covered anatomical regions (cosine similarity) from left to right: Precuneus R. (28.49%), Occipital Mid. R. (61.59%), Angular L. (56.42%), SupraMarginal R. (59.52%), Frontal Sup. Medial. L. (44.60%), Occipital Mid. L. (51.63%).

Figure 11: Network discovered from a typical elderly normal subject. The *Parietal and Occipital Lobes* and *Frontal Cortex* regions are discovered as seen in the typical young normal scan. The region within black oval in (b) shows some activity on the edge of *Cingulum Region Posterior* but not as much as in Alzheimer affected patient, which likely indicates normal slowed activity that comes with normal aging.

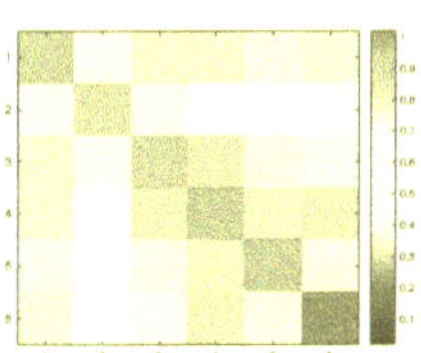

(a) Discovered edges

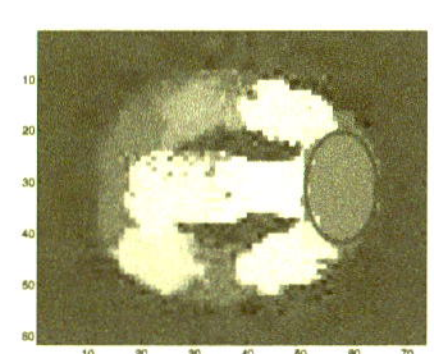

(b) Discovered Network

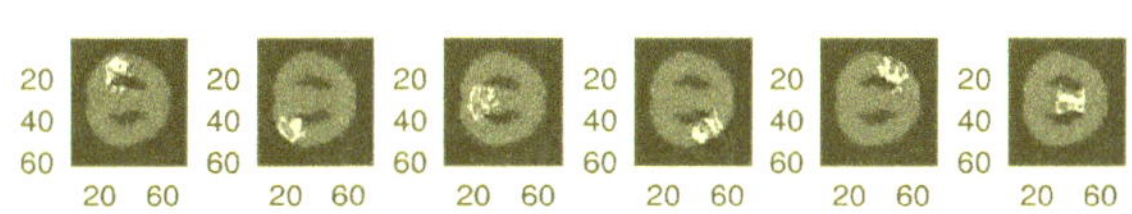

(c) Discovered nodes and corresponding largest covered anatomical regions (cosine similarity) left to right: SupraMarginal R. (23.28%), Angular L. (63.27%), Precuneus L. (51.63%), Frontal Inf. Oper. L. (48.40%), Frontal Inf. Oper. R. (54.92%), Cingulum Mid. L. (40.46%).

Figure 12: Network discovered from a typical elderly demented subject (Alzheimer affected individual). The *Occipital and Angular* are discovered with retarded activity levels likely due to Alzheimer's disease. The region within black oval in (b) shows that *Frontal Cortex* is not discovered as a functional node; hypo-activity of this region shows possible lack of decision making or executive function likely due to Alzheimer's disease. The *Cingulum Region Anterior* in lemon is discovered as a functional node, showing the relative overactivity of cingulum that may manifest as depression. Depression is common in Alzheimer's disease affected patients.

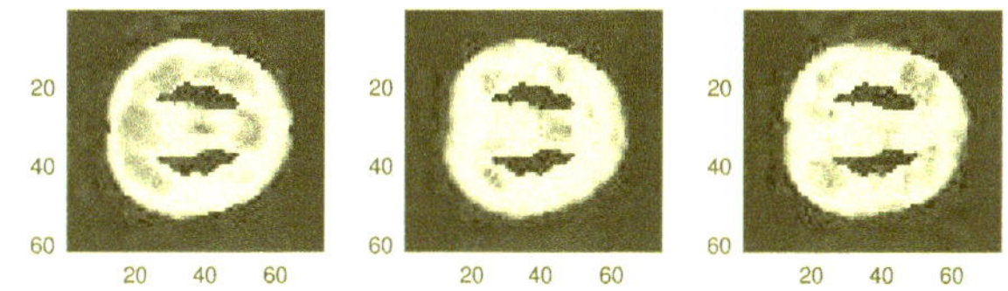

Figure 13: Average network discovery result of each cohort. Left: young normal, 40 fMRI scans. Middle: elderly normal, 19 fMRI scans. Right: elderly demented (Alzheimer affected), 21 fMRI scans.

that matched known anatomical regions **despite not** being given those regions, that is without any supervision.

6 CONCLUSION

In this paper, we pose the problem of unsupervised network discovery involving the discovery of regions with cohesive behavior (the nodes) and the relationship between those regions (the edges) from spatiotemporal data. Though previous work has solved the problem of *either* node discovery *or* edge discovery, to our knowledge no method has been proposed to simultaneously solve both without supervision. We formulate the unsupervised network discovery problem as a nonnegative matrix tri-factorization with orthogonality constraints and a novel spatial continuity regularizer to ensure easily interpretable and useful results. We develop effective solvers for the formulation with *i)* novel update rules for node discovery, *ii)* nonnegative least squares solver for edge discovery. We explored the strength of our methods with extensive experiments on a variety of synthetic but realistic networks and on real world datasets. On synthetic data our method demonstrates robustness in the presence of different kinds of background noise. For real world data, we are not able to present all individuals' results due to space, but we show an average result and the result of a typical subject for each cohort. These results are consistent with known earlier work [2] and demonstrate the significance of our method: it has the potential to effectively explore new networks in scenarios where specific domain knowledge is unavailable or insufficient. This model can be applied to spatiotemporal data from other domains if their node discovery requires geometrical continuity within each node.

ACKNOWLEDGMENTS

This research is supported by NSF Grant IIS-1422218 'Functional Network Discovery for Brain Connectivity' and The Henry M. Jackson Foundation Grant 'Small World and Other Graph Properties in Brains'. Peter B. Walker is a military service member. This work was prepared as part of his official duties. Title 17 U.S.C. 101 defines U.S. Government work as a work prepared by a military service member or employee of the U.S. Government as part of that person's official duties. The opinions of the authors do not necessarily reflect those of the United States.

REFERENCES

[1] Dan A Alcantara, Owen Carmichael, Will Harcourt-Smith, Kirstin Sterner, Stephen R Frost, Rebecca Dutton, Paul Thompson, Eric Delson, and Nina Amenta. 2009. Exploration of shape variation using localized components analysis. *IEEE transactions on pattern analysis and machine intelligence* 31, 8 (2009), 1510–1516.

[2] Jessica R Andrews-Hanna, Jay S Reidler, Jorge Sepulcre, Renee Poulin, and Randy L Buckner. 2010. Functional-anatomic fractionation of the brain's default network. *Neuron* 65, 4 (2010), 550–562.

[3] John Burge, Terran Lane, Hamilton Link, Shibin Qiu, and Vincent P Clark. 2009. Discrete dynamic Bayesian network analysis of fMRI data. *Human brain mapping* 30, 1 (2009), 122–137.

[4] Ian Davidson, Sean Gilpin, Owen Carmichael, and Peter Walker. 2013. Network Discovery via Constrained Tensor Analysis of fMRI Data *(KDD '13)*. ACM, New York, NY, USA, 194–202.

[5] Federico De Martino, Francesco Gentile, Fabrizio Esposito, Marco Balsi, Francesco Di Salle, Rainer Goebel, and Elia Formisano. 2007. Classification of fMRI independent components using IC-fingerprints and support vector machine classifiers. *Neuroimage* 34, 1 (2007), 177–194.

[6] Chris Ding, Tao Li, Wei Peng, and Haesun Park. 2006. Orthogonal nonnegative matrix t-factorizations for clustering *(KDD '06)*. ACM, 126–135.

[7] Christopher R Genovese, Nicole A Lazar, and Thomas Nichols. 2002. Thresholding of statistical maps in functional neuroimaging using the false discovery rate. *Neuroimage* 15, 4 (2002), 870–878.

[8] Forrest M Hoffman, William W Hargrove Jr, David J Erickson III, and Robert J Oglesby. 2005. Using clustered climate regimes to analyze and compare predictions from fully coupled general circulation models. *Earth Interactions* 9, 10 (2005), 1–27.

[9] Keigo Kimura, Yuzuru Tanaka, and Mineichi Kudo. 2014. A Fast Hierarchical Alternating Least Squares Algorithm for Orthogonal Nonnegative Matrix Factorization.. In *ACML*.

[10] Chia-Tung Kuo, James Bailey, and Ian Davidson. *A Framework for Simplifying Trip Data into Networks via Coupled Matrix Factorization.* Chapter 83, 739–747.

[11] Pierre-Jean Lahaye, Jean-Baptiste Poline, Guillaume Flandin, Silke Dodel, and Line Garnero. 2003. Functional connectivity: studying nonlinear, delayed interactions between BOLD signals. *Neuroimage* 20, 2 (2003), 962–974.

[12] Marc Postman and P Murdin. 2001. Distribution of Galaxies, Clusters, and Superclusters. *Encyclopedia of Astronomy and Astrophysics* (2001).

[13] Marcus E Raichle and Abraham Z Snyder. 2007. A default mode of brain function: a brief history of an evolving idea. *Neuroimage* 37, 4 (2007), 1083–1090.

[14] Marian Scott, Claire Miller, Francesco Finazzi, and Ruth Haggarty. 2013. Coherency in space of lake and river temperature and water quality records. (2013).

[15] Liang Sun, Rinkal Patel, Jun Liu, Kewei Chen, Teresa Wu, Jing Li, Eric Reiman, and Jieping Ye. 2009. Mining brain region connectivity for alzheimer's disease study via sparse inverse covariance estimation *(KDD '09)*. ACM, 1335–1344.

[16] Nathalie Tzourio-Mazoyer, Brigitte Landeau, Dimitri Papathanassiou, Fabrice Crivello, Olivier Etard, Nicolas Delcroix, Bernard Mazoyer, and Marc Joliot. 2002. Automated anatomical labeling of activations in SPM using a macroscopic anatomical parcellation of the MNI MRI single-subject brain. *Neuroimage* 15, 1 (2002), 273–289.

[17] Vincent G van de Ven, Elia Formisano, David Prvulovic, Christian H Roeder, and David EJ Linden. 2004. Functional connectivity as revealed by spatial independent component analysis of fMRI measurements during rest. *Human brain mapping* 22, 3 (2004), 165–178.

[18] Peter B Walker and Ian N Davidson. 2011. Exploring new methodologies for the analysis of functional magnetic resonance imaging (fMRI) following closed-head injuries. In *Foundations of Augmented Cognition. Directing the Future of Adaptive Systems.* Springer, 120–128.

Patient Subtyping via Time-Aware LSTM Networks

Inci M. Baytas
Computer Science and Engineering
Michigan State University
428 S Shaw Ln.
East Lansing, MI 48824
baytasin@msu.edu

Cao Xiao
Center for Computational Health
IBM T. J. Watson Research Center
1101 Kitchawan Rd
Yorktown Heights, NY 10598
cxiao@us.ibm.com

Xi Zhang
Healthcare Policy and Research
Weill Cornell Medical School
Cornell University
New York, NY 10065
sheryl.zhangxi@gmail.com

Fei Wang
Healthcare Policy and Research
Weill Cornell Medical School
Cornell University
New York, NY 10065
few2001@med.cornell.edu

Anil K. Jain
Computer Science and Engineering
Michigan State University
428 S Shaw Ln.
East Lansing, MI 48824
jain@cse.msu.edu

Jiayu Zhou
Computer Science and Engineering
Michigan State University
428 S Shaw Ln.
East Lansing, MI 48824
jiayuz@msu.edu

ABSTRACT

In the study of various diseases, heterogeneity among patients usually leads to different progression patterns and may require different types of therapeutic intervention. Therefore, it is important to study patient subtyping, which is grouping of patients into disease characterizing subtypes. Subtyping from complex patient data is challenging because of the information heterogeneity and temporal dynamics. Long-Short Term Memory (LSTM) has been successfully used in many domains for processing sequential data, and recently applied for analyzing longitudinal patient records. The LSTM units are designed to handle data with constant elapsed times between consecutive elements of a sequence. Given that time lapse between successive elements in patient records can vary from days to months, the design of traditional LSTM may lead to suboptimal performance. In this paper, we propose a novel LSTM unit called Time-Aware LSTM (T-LSTM) to handle irregular time intervals in longitudinal patient records. We learn a subspace decomposition of the cell memory which enables time decay to discount the memory content according to the elapsed time. We propose a patient subtyping model that leverages the proposed T-LSTM in an auto-encoder to learn a powerful single representation for sequential records of patients, which are then used to cluster patients into clinical subtypes. Experiments on synthetic and real world datasets show that the proposed T-LSTM architecture captures the underlying structures in the sequences with time irregularities.

CCS CONCEPTS

•**Applied computing** →**Health informatics;** •**Mathematics of computing** →*Time series analysis;* •**Computing methodologies** →*Cluster analysis;*

KDD'17, August 13–17, 2017, Halifax, NS, Canada.
© 2017 ACM. 978-1-4503-4887-4/17/08...$15.00
DOI: http://dx.doi.org/10.1145/3097983.3097997

KEYWORDS

Patient subtyping, Recurrent Neural Network, Long-Short Term Memory

1 INTRODUCTION

Clinical decision making often relies on medical history of patients. Physicians typically use available information from past patient visits such as lab tests, procedures, medications, and diagnoses to determine the right treatment. Furthermore, researchers use medical history and patient demographics to discover interesting patterns in patient cohorts, to study prognosis of different types of diseases, and to understand effects of drugs. In a nut shell, large-scale, systematic and longitudinal patient datasets play a key role in the healthcare domain. Examples such as Electronic Health Records (EHRs), whose adoption rate increased by 5% between 2014 and 2015 [1] in the healthcare systems in the United States, facilitate a systematic collection of temporal digital health information from variety of sources.

With the rapid development of computing technologies in health-care, longitudinal patient data are now beginning to be readily available. However, it is challenging to analyze large-scale heterogeneous patient records to infer high level information embedded in patient cohorts. This challenge motivates the development of computational methods for biomedical informatics research [5, 16, 23, 27, 30]. These methods are required to answer different questions related to disease progression modeling and risk prediction [8, 9, 13, 21, 29, 31].

Patient Subtyping, which seeks patient groups with similar disease progression pathways, is crucial to address the heterogeneity in the patients which ultimately leads to precision medicine where patients are provided with treatments tailored to their unique health status. Patient subtyping facilitates the investigation of a particular type of complicated disease condition [5]. From the data mining perspective, patient subtyping is posed as an unsupervised learning task of grouping patients according to their historical records. Since these records are longitudinal, it is important to capture the relationships and the dependencies between the elements of the

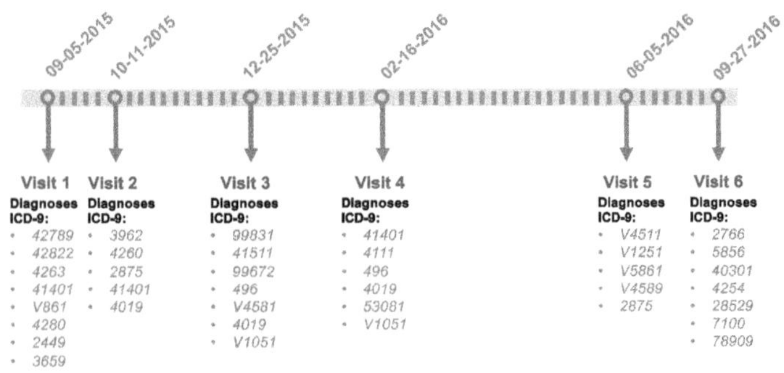

Figure 1: An example segment of longitudinal patient records. The patient had 6 office visits between Sept 5, 2015 and Sept 27, 2016. In each visit, diagnosis of the patient was given by a set of ICD-9 codes. Time spans between two successive visits can vary, and may be months apart. Such time irregularity results in a significant challenge in patient subtyping.

record sequence in order to learn more effective and robust representations, which can then be used in the clustering stage to obtain the patient groups.

One powerful approach which can capture underlying structure in sequential data is Recurrent Neural Networks (RNNs), which have been applied to many areas such as speech recognition [15], text classification [20], video processing [12, 25], and natural language processing [26]. In principle, time dependencies between the elements can be successfully captured by RNNs, however traditional RNNs suffer from vanishing and exploding gradient problems. To handle these limitations, different variants of RNN have been proposed. Long-Short Term Memory (LSTM) [17] is one such popular variant which can handle long term event dependencies by utilizing a gated architecture. LSTM has recently been applied in health informatics [4, 6] with promising results.

One limitation of the standard LSTM networks is that it cannot deal with irregular time intervals. But, the time irregularity is common in many healthcare applications. To illustrate this, one can consider patient records, where the time interval between consecutive visits or admissions varies, from days to months and sometimes a year. We illustrate this in Figure 1 using a sample medical record segment for one patient. Notice that the time difference between records varies from one month to a few months. Such varying time gaps could be indicative of certain impending disease conditions. For instance, frequent admissions might indicate a severe health problem and the records of those visits provide a source to study progression of the condition. On the other hand, if there are months between the two successive records, dependency on the previous memory should not play an active role to predict the current outcome.

To address the aforementioned challenges in patient subtyping, we propose an integrated approach to identify patient subtypes using a novel Time-Aware LSTM (T-LSTM), which is a modified LSTM architecture that takes the elapsed time into consideration between the consecutive elements of a sequence to adjust the memory content of the unit. T-LSTM is designed to incorporate the time irregularities in the memory unit to improve the performance of the standard LSTM. The main contributions of this paper are summarized bellow:

- A novel LSTM architecture (T-LSTM) is proposed to handle time irregularities in sequences. T-LSTM has *forget, input, output* gates of the standard LSTM, but the memory cell is adjusted in a way that longer the elapsed time, smaller the effect of the previous memory to the current output. For this purpose, elapsed time is transformed into a weight using a time decay function. The proposed T-LSTM learns a neural network that performs a decomposition of the cell memory into short and long-term memories. The short-term memory is discounted by the decaying weight before combining it with the long-term counterpart. This subspace decomposition approach does not change the effect of the current input to the current output, but alters the effect of the previous memory on the current output.
- An unsupervised patient subtyping approach is proposed based on clustering the patient population by utilizing the proposed T-LSTM unit. T-LSTM is used to learn a single representation from the temporal patient data in an auto-encoder setting. The proposed T-LSTM auto-encoder maps sequential records of patients to a powerful representation capturing the dependencies between the elements in the presence of time irregularities. The representations learned by the T-LSTM auto-encoder are used to cluster the patients by using the k-means algorithm.

Supervised and unsupervised experiments on both synthetic and real world datasets show that the proposed T-LSTM architecture performs better than standard LSTM unit to learn discriminative representations from sequences with irregular elapsed times.

The rest of the paper is organized as follows: related literature survey is summarized in Section 2, technical details of the proposed approach are explained in Section 3, experimental results are presented in Section 4, and the study is concluded in Section 5.

2 RELATED WORK

Computational Subtyping with Deep Networks. A similar idea as presented in this study was proposed in [24], but for supervised problem settings. Pham *et al.* introduced an end-to-end deep network to read EHRs, saves patient history, infers the current state and predicts the future. Their proposed approach, called "DeepCare", used LSTM for multiple admissions of a patient, and also addressed the time irregularities between the consecutive admissions. A single vector representation was learned for each admission and was used as the input to the LSTM network. Forget gate of standard LSTM unit was modified to account for the time irregularity of the admissions. In our T-LSTM approach, however the memory cell is adjusted by the elapsed time. The main aim of [24] was answering the question "What happens next?". Therefore, the authors of [24] were dealing with a supervised problem setting whereas we deal with an unsupervised problem setting.

There are several studies in the literature using RNNs for supervised tasks. For instance, in [13], authors focused on patients suffering from kidney failure. The goal of their approach was to predict whether a patient will die, the transplant will be rejected, or transplant will be lost. For each visit of a patient, the authors tried to answer the following question: which one of the three conditions will occur both within 6 months and 12 months after the visit? RNN was used to predict these aforementioned endpoints. In [21], LSTM was used to recognize patterns in multivariate time series of clinical measurements. Subtyping clinical time series was posed as a multi-label classification problem. Authors stated that diagnostic labels without timestamps were used, but timestamped diagnoses were obtained. LSTM with a fully connected output layer was used for the multi-label classification problem.

In [9] authors aimed to make predictions in a similar way as doctors do. RNN was used for this purpose and it was fed by the patient's past visits in a reverse time order. The way RNN was utilized in [9] is different than its general usage. There were two RNNs, one for visit-level and the other for variable-level attention mechanisms. Thus, the method proposed in [9] could predict the diagnosis by first looking at the more recent visits of the patient, and then determining which visit and which event it should pay attention.

Another computational subtyping study [8] learned a vector representation for patient status at each time stamp and predicted the diagnosis and the time duration until the next visit by using this representation. Authors proposed a different approach to incorporate the elapsed time in their work. A softmax layer was used to predict the diagnosis and a ReLU unit was placed at the top of the GRU to predict the time duration until the next visit. Therefore, the elapsed time was not used to modify the GRU network architecture but it was concatenated to the input to be able to predict the next visit time. On the other hand, authors in [4] aimed to learn patient similarities directly from temporal EHR data for personalized predictions of Parkinson's disease. GRU unit was used to encode the similarities between the sequences of two patients and dynamic time warping was used to measure the similarities between temporal sequences.

A different approach to computational subtyping was introduced in [10]. Their method, called Med2Vec, was proposed to learn a representation for both medical codes and patient visits from large scale EHRs. Their learned representations were interpretable, therefore Med2Vec did not only learn representations to improve the performance of algorithms using EHRs but also to provide interpretability for physicians. While the authors did not use RNN, they used a multi-layer perceptron to generate a visit representation for each visit vector.

Auto-Encoder Networks. The purpose of our study is patient subtyping which is an instance of unsupervised learning or clustering, therefore we need to learn powerful representations of the patient sequences that can capture the dependencies and the structures within the sequence. One of the ways to learn representations by deep networks is to use auto-encoders. Encoder network learns a single representation of the input sequence and then the decoder network reconstructs the input sequence from the representation learned by the encoder at the end of the input sequence. In each iteration, reconstruction loss is minimized so that the learned representation is effective to summarize the input sequence. In [25] LSTM auto-encoders were used to learn representations for video sequences. Authors tested the performance of the learned representation on supervised problems and showed that the learned representation is able to increase the classification accuracy.

Auto-encoders are also used to generate a different sequence by using the representation learned in the encoder part. For instance, in [7], one RNN encodes a sequence of symbols into a vector representation, and then the decoder RNN map the single representation into another sequence. Authors of [7] showed that their proposed approach can interpret the input sequence semantically and can learn its meaningful representation syntactically.

3 METHODOLOGY

3.1 Time-Aware Long Short Term Memory

3.1.1 Long Short-Term Memory (LSTM). Recurrent neural network (RNN) is a deep network architecture where the connections between hidden units form a directed cycle. This feedback loop enables the network to keep the previous information of hidden states as an internal memory. Therefore, RNNs are preferred for problems where the system needs to store and update the context information [3]. Approaches such as Hidden Markov Models (HMM) have also been used for similar purposes, however there are distinctive properties of RNNs that differentiates them from conventional methods such as HMM. For example, RNNs do not make the assumption of Markov property and they can process variable length sequences. Furthermore, in principle, information of past inputs can be kept in the memory without any limitation on the time in the past. However, optimization for long-term dependencies is not always possible in practice because of vanishing and exploding gradient problems where the value of gradient becomes too small and too large, respectively. To be able to incorporate the long-term dependencies without violating the optimization process, variants of RNNs have been proposed. One of the popular variants is Long Short-Term Memory (LSTM) which is capable of handling long-term dependencies with a gated structure [17].

A standard LSTM unit comprises of forget, input, output gates, and a memory cell, but the architecture has the implicit assumption of uniformly distributed elapsed time between the elements of a sequence. Therefore, the time irregularity, which can be present in a longitudinal data, is not integrated into the LSTM architecture. For instance, the distribution of the events in a temporal patient record is highly non-uniform such that the time gap between records can vary from days to years. Given that the time passed between two consecutive hospital visits is one of the sources of decision making in the healthcare domain, an LSTM architecture which takes irregular elapsed times into account is required for temporal data. For this purpose, we propose a novel LSTM architecture, called Time-Aware LSTM (T-LSTM), where the time lapse between successive records is included in the network architecture. Details of T-LSTM are presented in the next section.

3.1.2 Time-Aware LSTM (T-LSTM). Regularity of the duration between consecutive elements of a sequence is a property that does not always hold. One reason of the variable elapsed time is the nature of the EHR datasets, where the frequency and the number of patient records are quite unstructured. Another reason is missing information in the longitudinal data. In case of the missing data, elapsed time irregularity impacts predicting the trajectory of the temporal changes. Therefore, an architecture that can overcome this irregularity is necessary to increase the prediction performance. For EHR data, varying elapsed times can be treated as a part of the information contained in the medical history of a patient, hence it should be utilized while processing the records.

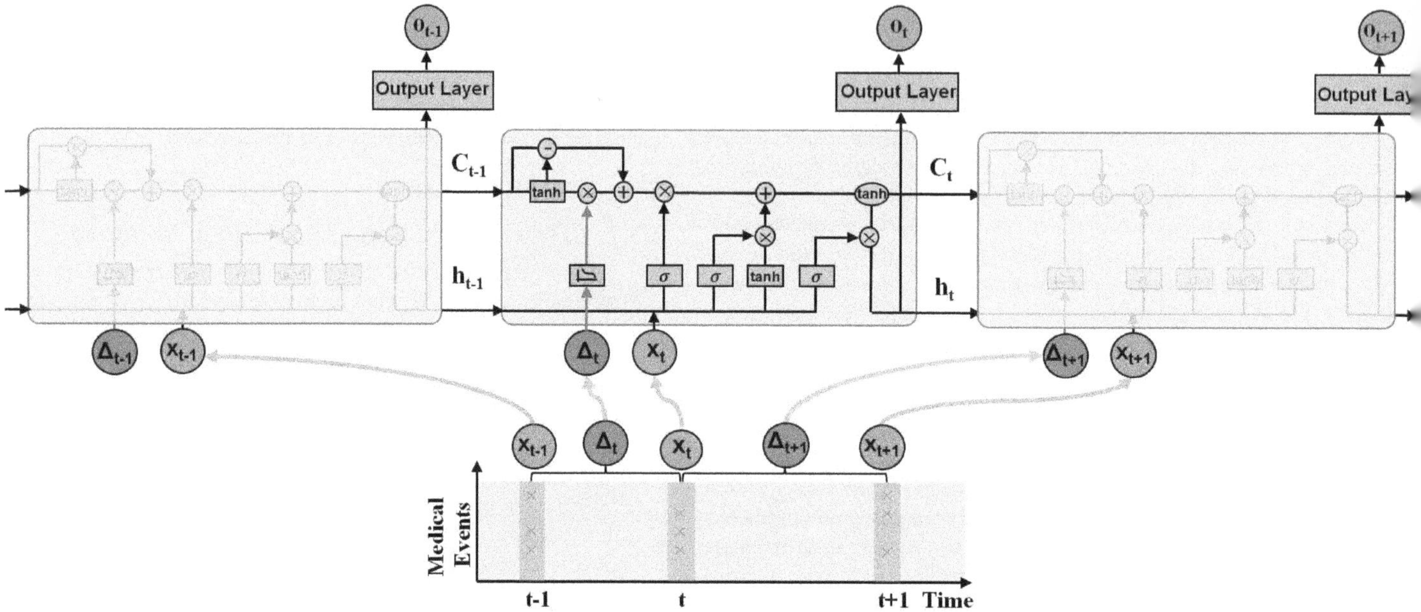

Figure 2: Illustration of the proposed time-aware long-short term memory (T-LSTM) unit, and its application on analyzing healthcare records. Green boxes indicate networks and yellow circles denote point-wise operators. T-LSTM takes two inputs, input record and the elapsed time at the current time step. The time lapse between the records at time $t-1$, t and $t+1$ can vary from days to years in healthcare domain. T-LSTM decomposes the previous memory into long and short term components and utilizes the elapsed time (Δ_t) to discount the short term effects.

T-LSTM is proposed to incorporate the elapsed time information into the standard LSTM architecture to be able to capture the temporal dynamics of sequential data with time irregularities. The proposed T-LSTM architecture is given in Figure 2 where the input sequence is represented by the temporal patient data. Elapsed time between two immediate records of a patient can be quite irregular. For instance, time between two consecutive admissions/hospital visits can be weeks, months and years. If there are years between two successive records, then the dependency on the previous record is not significant enough to affect the current output, therefore the contribution of the previous memory to the current state should be discounted. The major component of the T-LSTM architecture is the subspace decomposition applied on the memory of the previous time step. While the amount of information contained in the memory of the previous time step is being adjusted, we do not want to lose the global profile of the patient. In other words, long-term effects should not be discarded entirely, but the short-term memory should be adjusted proportional to the amount of time span between the records at time step t and $t-1$. If the gap between time t and $t-1$ is huge, it means there is no new information recorded for the patient for a long time. Therefore, the dependence on the short-term memory should not play a significant role in the prediction of the current output.

T-LSTM applies the memory discount by employing the elapsed time between successive elements to weight the short-term memory content. To achieve this, we propose to use a non-increasing function of the elapsed time which transforms the time lapse into an appropriate weight. Mathematical expressions of the subspace decomposition procedure are provided in Equation Current hidden state. First, short-term memory component (C^S_{t-1}) is obtained by a network. Note that this decomposition is data-driven and the parameters of the decomposition network are learned simultaneously with the rest of network parameters by back-propagation. There is no specific requirement for the activation function type of the decomposition network. We tried several functions but did not observe a drastic difference in the prediction performance of the T-LSTM unit, however tanh activation function performed slightly better. After the short-term memory is obtained, it is adjusted by the elapsed time weight to obtain the discounted short-term memory ($\hat{C}^S_{t-1}$). Finally, to compose the adjusted previous memory back (C^*_{t-1}), the complement subspace of the long-term memory ($C^T_{t-1} = C_{t-1} - C^S_{t-1}$) is combined with the discounted short-term memory. Subspace decomposition stage of the T-LSTM is followed by the standard gated architecture of the LSTM. Detailed mathematical expressions of the proposed T-LSTM architecture are given below:

$$C^S_{t-1} = \tanh\left(W_d C_{t-1} + b_d\right) \quad \text{(Short-term memory)}$$

$$\hat{C}^S_{t-1} = C^S_{t-1} * g\left(\Delta_t\right) \quad \text{(Discounted short-term memory)}$$

$$C^T_{t-1} = C_{t-1} - C^S_{t-1} \quad \text{(Long-term memory)}$$

$$C^*_{t-1} = C^T_{t-1} + \hat{C}^S_{t-1} \quad \text{(Adjusted previous memory)}$$

$$f_t = \sigma\left(W_f x_t + U_f h_{t-1} + b_f\right) \quad \text{(Forget gate)}$$

$$i_t = \sigma\left(W_i x_t + U_i h_{t-1} + b_i\right) \quad \text{(Input gate)}$$

$$o_t = \sigma\left(W_o x_t + U_o h_{t-1} + b_o\right) \quad \text{(Output gate)}$$

$$\tilde{C} = \tanh\left(W_c x_t + U_c h_{t-1} + b_c\right) \quad \text{(Canditate memory)}$$
$$C_t = f_t * C_{t-1}^* + i_t * \tilde{C} \quad \text{(Current memory)}$$
$$h_t = o * \tanh\left(C_t\right), \quad \text{(Current hidden state)}$$

where x_t represents the current input, h_{t-1} and h_t are previous and current hidden states, and C_{t-1} and C_t are previous and current cell memories. $\left\{W_f, U_f, b_f\right\}$, $\{W_i, U_i, b_i\}$, $\{W_o, U_o, b_o\}$, and $\{W_c, U_c, b_c\}$ are the network parameters of the forget, input, output gates and the candidate memory, respectively. $\{W_d, b_d\}$ are the network parameters of the subspace decomposition. Dimensionalities of the parameters are determined by the input, output and the chosen hidden state dimensionalities. Δ_t is the elapsed time between x_{t-1} and x_t and $g(\cdot)$ is a heuristic decaying function such that the larger the value of Δ_t, less the effect of the short-term memory. Different types of monotonically non-increasing functions can be chosen for $g(\cdot)$ according to the measurement type of the time durations for a specific application domain. If we are dealing with time series data such as videos, the elapsed time is generally measured in seconds. On the other hand, if the elapsed time varies from days to years as in the healthcare domain, we need to convert the time lapse of successive elements to one type, such as days. In this case, the elapsed time might have large numerical values when there are years between two consecutive records. As a guideline, $g(\Delta_t) = 1/\Delta_t$ can be chosen for datasets with small amount of elapsed time and $g(\Delta_t) = 1/\log(e + \Delta_t)$ [24] is preferred for datasets with large elapsed times.

In the literature, studies proposing different ways to incorporate the elapsed time into the learning process can be encountered. For instance, elapsed time was used to modify the forget gate in [24]. In T-LSTM, one of the reasons behind adjusting the memory cell instead of the forget gate is to avoid any alteration of the current input's effect to the current output. The current input runs through the forget gate and the information coming from the input plays a role to decide how much memory we should keep from the previous cell. As can be seen in the expressions of *Current memory* and *Current hidden state* in Equation Current hidden state, modifying the forget gate directly might eliminate the effect of the input to the current hidden state. Another important point is that, the subspace decomposition enables us to selectively modify the short-term effects without losing the relevant information in the long-term memory. Section 4 shows that the performance of T-LSTM is improved by modifying the forget gate, which is named as Modified Forget Gate LSTM (MF-LSTM) in this paper. Two approaches are adopted from [24] for comparison. First approach, denoted by MF1-LSTM, multiplies the output of the forget gate by $g(\Delta_t)$ such as $f_t = g(\Delta_t) * f_t$. whereas MF2-LSTM utilizes a parametric time weight such as $f_t = \sigma\left(W_f x_t + U_f h_{t-1} + Q_f q_{\Delta_t} + b_f\right)$ where $q_{\Delta_t} = \left(\frac{\Delta_t}{60}, \left(\frac{\Delta_t}{180}\right)^2, \left(\frac{\Delta_t}{360}\right)^3\right)$ when Δ_t is measured in days similar to [24].

Another idea to handle the time irregularity could be imputing the data by sampling new records between two consecutive time steps to have regular time gaps and then applying LSTM on the augmented data. However, when the elapsed time is measured in days, so many new records have to be sampled for the time steps which have years in between. Secondly, the imputation approach might have a serious impact on the performance. A patient record contains detailed information and it is hard to guarantee that the imputed records reflect the reality. Therefore, a change in the architecture of the regular LSTM to handle time irregularities is suggested.

3.2 Patient Subtyping with T-LSTM Auto-Encoder

In this paper, patient subtyping is posed as an unsupervised clustering problem since we do not have any prior information about the groups inside the patient cohort. An efficient representation summarizing the structure of the temporal records of patients is required to be able to cluster temporal and complex EHR data. Auto-encoders provide an unsupervised way to directly learn a mapping from the original data [2]. LSTM auto-encoders have been used to encode sequences such as sentences [32] in the literature. Therefore, we propose to use T-LSTM auto-encoder to learn an effective single representation of the sequential records of a patient. T-LSTM auto-encoder has T-LSTM encoder and T-LSTM decoder units with different parameters which are jointly learned to minimize the reconstruction error. The proposed auto-encoder can capture the long and the short term dependencies by incorporating the elapsed time into the system and learn a single representation which can be used to reconstruct the input sequence. Therefore, the mapping learned by the T-LSTM auto-encoder maintains the temporal dynamics of the original sequence with variable time lapse.

In Figure 3, a single layer T-LSTM auto-encoder mechanism is given for a small sequence with three elements $[X_1, X_2, X_3]$. The hidden state and the cell memory of the T-LSTM encoder at the end of the input sequence are used as the initial hidden state and the memory content of the T-LSTM decoder. First input element and the elapsed time of the decoder are set to zero and its first output is the reconstruction ($\hat{X_3}$) of the last element of the original sequence (X_3). When the reconstruction error E_r given in Equation 1 is minimized, T-LSTM encoder is applied to the original sequence to obtain the learned representation, which is the hidden state of the encoder at the end of the sequence.

$$E_r = \sum_{i=1}^{L} \left\|X_i - \hat{X}_i\right\|_2^2, \tag{1}$$

where L is the length of the sequence, X_i is the ith element of the input sequence and $\hat{X}_i$ is the ith element of the reconstructed sequence. The hidden state at the end of the sequence carries concise information about the input such that the original sequence can be reconstructed from it. In other words, representation learned by the encoder is a summary of the input sequence [7]. The number of layers of the auto-encoder can be increased when the input dimension is high. A single layer auto-encoder requires more number of iterations to minimize the reconstruction error when the learned representation has a lower dimensionality compared to the original input. Furthermore, learning a mapping to low dimensional space requires more complexity in order to capture more details of the high dimensional input sequence. In our experiments, a two layer T-LSTM auto-encoder, where the output of the first layer is the input of the second layer, is used because of the aforementioned reasons.

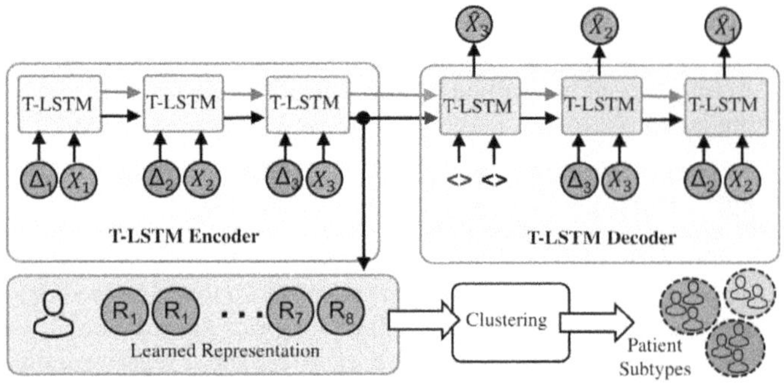

Figure 3: Clustering patients with a single-layer T-LSTM Auto-Encoder. Blue arrows denote the cell memory and the black arrows denote the hidden states. After the representations (R_i, $i = 1, 2, \cdots, 8$) are learned for the population, we can cluster the patients and obtain subtypes for each group as the prominent common medical features of the group. Number of layers should be increased in case of dimensionality reduction to be able to capture more complex structure with fewer iterations compared to single layer.

Given a single representation of each patient, patients are grouped by the k-means clustering algorithm. Since we do not make any assumption about the structure of the clusters, the simplest clustering algorithm, k-means, is preferred. In Figure 3, a small illustration of clustering the patient cohort for 8 patients is shown. In this figure, learned representations are denoted by R. If R has the capability to represent the distinctive structure of patient sequence, then clustering algorithm can group patients with similar features (diagnoses, lab results, medications, conditions, and so on) together. Thus, each patient group has a subtype, which is a collection of common medical features present in the cluster. Given a new patient, learned T-LSTM encoder is used to find the representation of the patient and the subtype of the cluster which gives the minimum distance between the cluster centroid and the new patient's representation is assigned to the new patient. As a result, T-LSTM auto-encoder learns powerful single representation of temporal patient data that can be easily used to obtain the subtypes in the patient population.

4 EXPERIMENTS

In this section, experimental results on synthetic and real world datasets are reported. For synthetic data, two sets of experiments were conducted such as a classification task on a publicly available synthetic EHR dataset and a clustering task with auto-encoder setting on a randomly generated synthetic data. Comparisons between T-LSTM, MF1-LSTM, MF2-LSTM [24], LSTM, and logistic regression are made. The application of T-LSTM auto-encoder on patient subtyping is presented on a real world dataset (PPMI) and subtyping results are discussed. T-LSTM [1] was implemented in Tensorflow and mini-batch stochastic Adam optimizer was used during experiments. All the weights were learned simultaneously and in data-driven manner. Same network settings and parameters were used for all the deep methods for comparison. Therefore, fixed number of epochs were chosen during the experiments instead of using a stopping criteria. Since there are variable size sequences in longitudinal patient data, batches with same sequence sizes were generated instead of padding the original sequences with zero to make every sequence same length. In this study, we did not use the publicly available large scale ICU dataset, MIMIC [18]. MIMIC is an ICU data, therefore sequence length for the majority of patients is very small such as one or two admissions. Even though MIMIC is an important public source for healthcare research, it is not suitable for our purpose such that very short sequences do not enable us to analyze long and short term dependencies and the effect of the elapsed time irregularities.

[1] Available at https://github.com/illidanlab/T-LSTM

Table 1: Supervised synthetic EHR experimental results, average AUC of testing on 10 different splits. Training and testing ratio was chosen as 70% and 30%, respectively.

Methods	Avg. Test AUC	Stdev.
T-LSTM	**0.91**	0.01
MF1-LSTM	0.87	0.02
MF2-LSTM	0.82	0.09
LSTM	0.85	0.02
LR	0.56	0.01

4.1 Synthetic Dataset

4.1.1 Supervised Experiment. In this section, we report experimental results for a supervised task on an artificially generated EHR data which can be found in [2]. The aforementioned data has electronic records of up to 100,000 patients with lab results, diagnoses, and start and end dates of the admissions. Each patient has a unique patient ID similar to real world EHR data. We refer to the reference study [19] for further details of the data generation process. Although the dataset is artificially generated, it contains similar characteristics as a real EHR data. In this experiment, target diagnoses was Diabetes Mellitus and the task was a binary classification problem. Input of the network was the sequence of admissions and the output was the predicted label as one-hot vector. Therefore, regular recurrent network setting was utilized for this task instead of auto-encoder. Feature of one admission was a multi-hot vector containing the diagnoses given in the corresponding admission and the vocabulary size was 529. For this purpose, 6,730 patients were sampled with an average of 4 admissions. For this task, a single layer T-LSTM, MF1-LSTM and MF2-LSTM networks were tested to compare the performance based on area under ROC curve (AUC) metric for 50 epochs. In this experiment, number of hidden and softmax layer neurons were chosen as 1028 and 512, respectively. In addition, performance of the traditional logistic regression (LR) classifier was also analyzed. In logistic regression experiments, admissions were aggregated for each patient without incorporating the elapsed time. We also tried to incorporate the elapsed time as a weight by using the same non-increasing function used in T-LSTM during the aggregation of admissions. However, this approach did not improve the performance in our case. The results are summarized in Table 1.

As it can be seen from the Table 1, T-LSTM has a better performance than the baseline approaches. The way to represent the sequential data could be improved further for logistic regression, but aggregation of the admissions for each patient did not perform

[2] http://www.emrbots.org/

Table 2: Average Rand index of k-means over 10 runs. T-LSTM auto-encoder outperforms LSTM and MF1-LSTM auto-encoders. This result indicates that the time irregularities should be considered to capture the temporal dynamics of a sequence.

Method	Mean RI	Std
T-LSTM	0.96	0.05
MF1-LSTM	0.85	0.13
LSTM	0.90	0.09

well for this task. Supervised experiments show that LSTM networks can enable us to leverage the time aspect of the EHR data better. In addition, modifying the cell memory yields a better classification performance. According to our observation, MF1-LSTM and MF2-LSTM have better and sometimes similar results as the traditional LSTM for the tasks in our experiments.

4.1.2 Unsupervised Experiment. In this experiment, we investigate the expressive power of the representation learned from the T-LSTM auto-encoder. For this purpose, a synthetic data was randomly generated and the clustering results were evaluated. Since we know the ground truth of the synthetic data, we computed the Rand index (RI), given in Equation 2 [22], of the clustering to observe the discriminative power of the learned representations. A large value of Rand index indicates that the learned representations are clustered close to the ground truth.

$$\mathrm{RI} = (\mathrm{TP} + \mathrm{TN})/(\mathrm{TP} + \mathrm{FP} + \mathrm{FN} + \mathrm{TN}), \tag{2}$$

where TP, TN, FP, FN are true positive, true negative, false positive and false negative, respectively. Note that $0 \leq \mathrm{RI} \leq 1$.

The results on a synthetic dataset containing 4 clusters generated from a mixture of normal distributions with four different means and the same covariance are reported. A data point in the synthetic dataset is a sequence of vectors and the values of the sequences are increasing with time. Some of the elements in the sequences are discarded randomly to introduce unstructured elapsed time and obtain variable sequence lengths of sizes 4, 6, 18, 22, and 30. Dimensionality of the vectors was 5 and the dimension was reduced to 2 by the T-LSTM auto-encoder to be able to plot the representations in a 2-D space. Thus, the input and the output of the T-LSTM auto-encoder were 5 dimensional input and the reconstructed sequences, respectively. The hidden state dimension of the second layer T-LSTM encoder was chosen as 2, therefore the learned representations were 2-dimensional single vectors. The learned representations were clustered by k-means, where k was set to 4. Representation learning was repeated 10 times with different initializations of k-means and the average Rand index of clustering is reported for T-LSTM, LSTM and MF1-LSTM auto-encoders in Table 2. The non-increasing heuristic function was chosen as $g(\Delta_t) = 1/\log(e + \Delta_t)$. For this experiment, we compared the performances of T-LSTM, MF1-LSTM and LSTM excluding MF2-LSTM. Since the time gap of the data used in this experiment does not relate to an actual time measurement such as days, MF2-LSTM was excluded.

Table 2 shows that the T-LSTM outperforms the baselines and T-LSTM auto-encoder can learn the underlying structure of the input sequence with varying elapsed times such that the representations obtained by T-LSTM encoder could be clustered. In this example, performance of MF1-LSTM was obtained better than LSTM on average. A visual example of one of the trials is also shown in Figure 4 where the 2-dimensional representations obtained by the three approaches were plotted.

In Figure 4 different colors denote ground truth assignments of different clusters. Representations learned by T-LSTM yields more compact groups in the 2-D space leading to a more accurate clustering result compared to the standard LSTM and MF1-LSTM. As it can be observed from the Figures 4c and 4b, directly multiplying the forget gate with the time coefficient does not always enables a modification which leverages the time irregularity in our experiments. Even though MF1-LSTM produced a higher Rand index, there are examples, such as Figure 4, where LSTM actually learns a better representation than MF1-LSTM. The change in the objective values of T-LSTM, MF1-LSTM and LSTM with respect to the number of epochs are also compared in Figure 5 for the trial illustrated in Figure 4. It is observed that the modifications related to the time irregularity does not affect the convergence of the original LSTM network in a negative way.

4.2 Parkinson's Progression Markers Initiative (PPMI) Data

In this section, we present experimental results for a real world dataset. Parkinson's Progression Markers Initiative (PPMI) is an observational clinical and longitudinal study comprising of evaluations of people with Parkinson's disease (PD), those people with high risk, and those who are healthy [11]. PPMI aims to identify biomarkers of the progression of Parkinson's disease. PPMI data is a publicly available dataset which contains clinical and behavioral assessments, imaging data, and biospecimens, therefore PPMI is a unique archive of PD [11]. As with many EHRs, PPMI is a longitudinal dataset with unstructured elapsed time. Therefore, T-LSTM is a suitable approach for prediction and clustering of PPMI dataset.

In our experiments, we used the pre-processed PPMI data of 654 patients given in [4]. Che *et al.* [4] collected patients with Idiopathic PD or non PD, imputed missing values, used one-hot feature form for categorical values, and encoded data abnormalities as 1 and 0. As a result, dataset we used has $15,636$ records of 654 patients with an average of 25 sequences (minimum sequence length is 3). Authors of [4] also categorized data as features and targets, where the features are related to patient characteristics and the targets correspond to the progression of PD. A total of 319 features consist of motor symptoms/complications, cognitive functioning, autonomic symptoms, psychotic symptoms, sleep problems, depressive symptoms, and hospital anxiety and depression scale. A total of 82 targets are related to motor sign, motor symptom, cognition, and other non-motor factors [4]. Summary of the PPMI data used in this paper can be found in Table 3.

As it can be seen in Table 3, the elapsed time is measured as months. From 1 month to nearly 2 years gap between successive records of patients is encountered in the dataset. Several experiments were conducted on PPMI data to show the performance of the proposed subtyping approach.

4.2.1 Target Sequence Prediction. In this experiment, T-LSTM is used to predict the target sequence of each patient. For this purpose, we divided the data into different train (70%)-test (30%) splits and

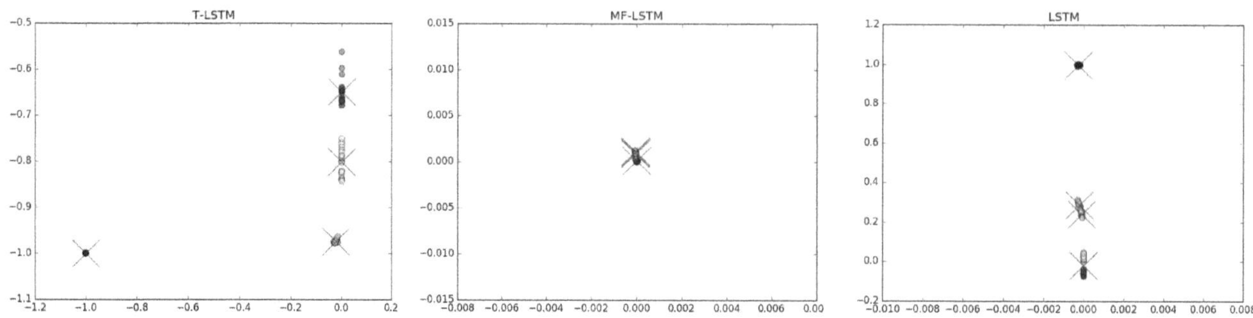

(a) T-LSTM Auto-Encoder (b) MF1-LSTM Auto-Encoder (c) LSTM Auto-Encoder

Figure 4: Illustration of the clustering results. Different colors denote ground truth assignments of different clusters. T-LSTM auto-encoder learns a mapping for the sequences such that 4 separate groups of points can be represented in the 2-D space.

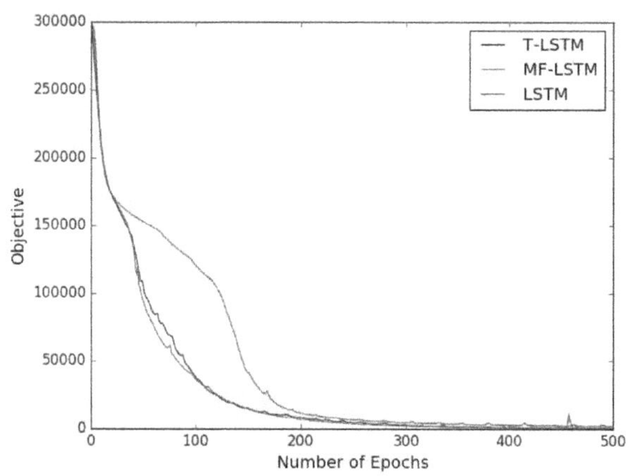

Figure 5: Change in the objective values of T-LSTM, MF1-LSTM and LSTM with respect to 500 epochs. It is observed that the modifications related to the time irregularity does not deteriorate the convergence of the original LSTM network.

Table 3: Details of PPMI data used in this study. Elapsed time encountered in the data is measured in months and it varies between 1 month to nearly 2 years. Here, the elapsed time interval is not the time interval of PPMI data recording, but elapsed times seen in records of individual patients.

Number of Patients	654
Elapsed Time Interval	[1, 26]
Average Sequence Length	25
Feature Dimensionality	319
Target Dimensionality	82

report the mean square error (MSE) between the original target sequence and the predicted target sequence. Average MSEs of 10 different train-test splits for T-LSTM, LSTM, MF1-LSTM and MF2-LSTM are given in Table 4. Same step size and the number of epochs were used for all the three methods. The non-increasing heuristic function of the elapsed time was chosen as $g(\Delta_t) = 1/\log(e + \Delta_t)$ for PPMI data.

Table 4: Average mean square error (MSE) for 10 different train-test splits for T-LSTM, LSTM, MF1-LSTM, and MF2-LSTM. T-LSTM yielded a better result than the standard LSTM in the presence of the unstructured time gaps. Elapsed time was multiplied by 30 while applying MF2-LSTM since the time lapse is measured in months.

MSE	T-LSTM	MF1-LSTM	MF2-LSTM	LSTM
Mean	0.50	0.53	0.51	0.51
Std	0.018	0.017	0.012	0.017

We also investigated target features on which T-LSTM performed the best. The commonly encountered target features where the T-LSTM provided lower MSE than LSTM, MF1-LSTM and MF2-LSTM are reported in Table 5. The main observation about the target features in Table 5 is that they are related to the effects of Parkinson's disease on the muscle control such as finger tapping, rigidity, and hand movements. In addition, T-LSTM predicted the target value of Bradykinesia, which encompasses several of the problems related to movement, and MoCA (Montreal Cognitive Assessment) Total Score, which assesses different types of cognitive abilities with lower error than other methods. This result shows that the reported target features are sensitive to elapsed time irregularities and discounting the short-term effects by the subspace decomposition of memory cell helps to alleviate this sensitivity.

4.2.2 Patient Subtyping of PPMI Data. In this experiment, T-LSTM auto-encoder was used to obtain subtypes of the patients in the PPMI dataset. The T-LSTM encoder was used to learn a representation from the input feature sequence of each patient and the T-LSTM decoder generated the target sequence. Parameters of the auto-encoder were learned to minimize the squared error between the original target sequence and the predicted target sequence. The learned representations were used to cluster the patients by the k-means algorithm as discussed before.

Since we do not know the ground truth for the clustering, we conducted a statistical analysis to assess the subtyping performance. For this purpose, clustering results were statistically analyzed at the time of 6 years follow-up in the PPMI study. Features including

Table 5: Some common target features from PPMI dataset on which T-LSTM performed better than LSTM and MF1-LSTM during 10 trials. These target features are mainly related to the effects of Parkinson's disease on muscle control.

Code	Name
NP3BRADY	Global spontaneity of movement
NP3RIGRU	Rigidity - RUE(Right Upper Extremity)
NP3FTAPR	Finger Tapping Right Hand
NP3TTAPR	Toe tapping - Right foot
NP3PRSPR	Pronation-Supination - Right Hand
NP3HMOVR	Hand movements - Right Hand
NP3RIGN	Rigidity - Neck
NP2DRES	Dressing
PN3RIGRL	Rigidity - RLE (Right Lower Extremity)
DFBRADYP	Bradykinesia present and typical for PD
NP3RTARU	Rest tremor amplitude - RUE
NP3PTRMR	Postural tremor - Right Hand
MCATOT	MoCA Total Score

demographics, motor severity measures such as Unified Parkinson's Disease Rating Scale (MDSUPDRS), Hoehn and Yahr staging (H&Y), non-motor manifestations such as depression, anxiety, cognitive status, sleep disorders, imaging assessment such as DaTScan, as well as cerebrospinal fluid (CSF) biomarkers were taken into account. In order to interpret the clustering results in terms of subtyping, we compared the clusters using Chi-square test for the categorical features, F-test for the normal continuous features, Kruskal-Wallis test for the non-normal continuous features, and Fisherfis exact test for the high sparsity features. According to the previous Parkinson's disease studies, if the p-values of the aforementioned features are less than 0.05, a significant group effect is considered for the associated features [14]. Thus, if a method can obtain higher number of features with small p-values, it means that method provides a more sensible patient subtyping result.

Since we do not know the ground truth groups of the patient population, we tried several k values for the k-means algorithm. We often observed that there were two main clusters, therefore we reported the clustering results for $k = 2$. We conducted several tests with different parameters. According to our observation, LSTM yielded very few features with p-values less than 0.05 and most of the patients were generally grouped into one cluster. In Table 6, features of small p-values and cluster means of the features are presented for T-LSTM, MF1-LSTM and MF2-LSTM. As it can be seen from the table, T-LSTM has more discriminative features than MF1-LSTM and MF2-LSTM.

In Table 6, high cluster mean indicates that the symptoms of the corresponding feature are more severe for that cluster and the PD patients have lower cluster mean for DaTScan feature. Note that one of the observed features of T-LSTM in Table 6 is MoCA which was predicted better by T-LSTM in the target sequence prediction experiment. Finally, we illustrate the patient subtyping results of T-LSTM with heat map illustration in Figure 6. In this figure, shade of red color represents the cluster mean which is higher than the total mean of the patients and the shades of blue color show lower mean values for the corresponding feature with the p-value< 0.05. Subtypes and features which are significant for each subtype can be observed from the heat map. For instance, DaTSCAN features were found to be significant for subtype I, whereas subtype II was defined by BJLO (Benton Judgement Line Orientation) and MoCA features. Note that the dataset contains healthy subjects as well. It is known that PD patients have lower DaTScan SBR values than healthy subjects [28]. Hence, we can conclude from Figure 6 that subtype II can be considered as PD patients. We can also observe from Figure 6 that cluster means of BJLO and MoCA are very low (darker shades of blue) for subtype I compared to subtype II.

Table 6: Results of the statistical analysis for T-LSTM, MF1-LSTM and MF2-LSTM. DaTScan1 corresponds to DaTScan SBR-CAUDATE RIGHT, DaTScan2 is DaTScan SBR-CAUDATE LEFT, and DaTScan4 is DaTScan SBR-PUTAMEN LEFT.

Feature	P-Value	Cluster1 Mean	Cluster2 Mean
T-LSTM			
BJLO	9.51×10^{-8}	16.5	24.7
MoCA	0.001	40.0	41.2
DaTScan1	0.042	2.29	2.07
DaTScan2	0.027	2.31	2.08
DaTScan4	0.001	1.4	1.1
MF1-LSTM			
CSF-Total tau	0.007	87.9	46.72
MoCA	2.16×10^{-17}	47.5	41.05
SDM	0.005	58.5	41.5
MF2-LSTM			
HVLT-Retention	0.03	0.84	0.83
SDM	0.007	36.61	41.68

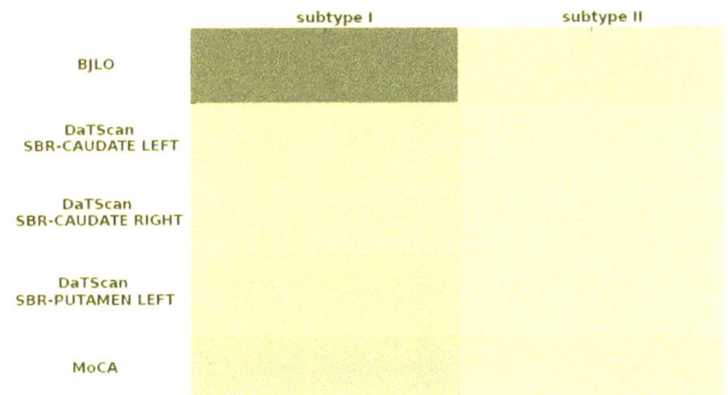

Figure 6: Heat map illustration of the patient subtyping results of T-LSTM for two clusters. Shade of red represents the cluster mean which is higher than the total mean of the patients and the shades of blue show lower mean values for the corresponding feature with p-value< 0.05.

5 CONCLUSION

In this paper, we propose a novel LSTM unit, called time-aware LSTM (T-LSTM) which can deal with irregular elapsed times between the successive elements of sequential data. Examples include medical records which are complex temporal data with varying sequence lengths and elapsed times, and video sequence with missing frames. T-LSTM does not have any assumption about the elapsed time measure such that the time gap does not have to be measured in days or years and thus it can be adopted by other domains dealing with different types of sequences. T-LSTM adjusts the previous memory content of an LSTM unit by a decaying function of the elapsed time in a way that longer the time lapse, less the influence of the previous memory content on the current output. The proposed T-LSTM was tested for supervised and unsupervised tasks on synthetic data and real world datasets. Patient subtyping, which can be defined as clustering sequential patient records, was analyzed on a publicly available real world dataset called Parkinson's Progression Markers Initiative (PPMI). For the subtyping purpose, T-LSTM auto-encoder was used to learn powerful representations for the temporal patient data, and the learned representations were used to cluster the patient population. In future work, we plan to apply the proposed approach to several other real datasets to observe the behaviour of our method for patient populations with different characteristics.

ACKNOWLEDGMENTS

Data used in the preparation of this article were obtained from the Parkinson's Progression Markers Initiative (PPMI) database (http://www.ppmi-info.org/data). For up-to-date information on the study, visit http://www.ppmi-info.org. PPMI a public-private partnership is funded by the Michael J. Fox Foundation for Parkinson's Research and funding partners, including abbvie, Avid, Biogen, Bristol-Mayers Squibb, Covance, GE, Genentech, GlaxoSmithKline, Lilly, Lundbeck, Merk, Meso Scale Discovery, Pfizer, Piramal, Roche, Sanofi, Servier, TEVA, UCB and Golub Capital. This research is supported in part by the Office of Naval Research (ONR) under grants number N00014-17-1-2265 (to JZ and AKJ), N00014-14-1-0631 (to JZ and AKJ) and National Science Foundation under grants IIS-1565596 (to JZ), IIS-1615597 (to JZ) and IIS-1650723 (to FW).

REFERENCES

[1] 2017. Health IT Dashboard. Retrieved at https://dashboard.healthit.gov/quickstats/quickstats.php. (2017).

[2] Yoshua Bengio, Aaron Courville, and Pascal Vincent. 2014. Representation Learning: A Review and New Perspectives. *arXiv:1206.5538v3[cs.LG]* (2014). https://arxiv.org/abs/1206.5538

[3] Yoshua Bengio, Patrice Simard, and Paolo Frasconi. 1994. Learning Long-Term Dependencies with Gradient Descent is Difficult. *IEEE Transactions on Neural Networks* 5, 2 (March 1994), 157–166.

[4] Chao Che, Cao Xiao, Jian Liang, Bo Jin, Jiayu Zhou, and Fei Wang. 2017. An RNN Architecture with Dynamic Temporal Matching for Personalized Predictions of Parkinson's Disease. In *Proceedings of the 2017 SIAM International Conference on Data Mining*.

[5] Zhengping Che, David Kale, Wenzhe Li, Mohammad Taha Bahadori, and Yan Liu. 2015. Deep Computational Phenotyping. In *Proceedings of the 21th ACM SIGKDD International Conference on Knowledge Discovery and Data Mining*. ACM, 507–516.

[6] Zhengping Che, Sanjay Purushotham, Kyunghyun Cho, David Sontag, and Yan Liu. 2016. Recurrent Neural Networks for Multivariate Time Series with Missing Values. *arXiv preprint arXiv:1606.01865* (2016).

[7] Kyunghyun Cho, Bart van Merrienboer, Caglar Gulcehre, and Dzmitry Bahdanau et al. 2014. Learning Phrase Representations using RNN Encoder-Decoder for Statistical Machine Translation. *arXiv:1406.1078v3[cs.CL]* (2014). https://arxiv.org/pdf/1406.1078v3

[8] Edward Choi, Mohammad Taha Bahadori, Andy Schuetzy, Walter F. Stewarty, and Jimeng Sun. 2016. Doctor AI: Predicting Clinical Events via Recurrent Neural Networks. *arXiv:1511.05942v11 [cs.LG]* (2016). https://arxiv.org/pdf/1511.05942v11.pdf

[9] Edward Choi, Mohammad Taha Bahadori, Andy Schuetzy, Walter F. Stewarty, and Jimeng Sun. 2016. RETAIN: Interpretable Predictive Model in Healthcare using Reverse Time Attention Mechanism. *arXiv:1608.05745v3 [cs.LG]* (2016). https://arxiv.org/pdf/1608.05745v3.pdf

[10] Edward Choi, Mohammad Taha Bahadori, Elizabeth Searles, Catherine Coffey, Michael Thompson, James Bost, Javier Tejedor-Sojo, and Jimeng Sun. 2016. Multi-layer Representation Learning for Medical Concepts. In *Proceedings of the 22nd ACM SIGKDD International Conference on Knowledge Discovery and Data Mining KDD16*. Association for Computing Machinery (ACM). http://dx.doi.org/10.1145/2939672.2939823

[11] Ivo D. Dinov, Ben Heavner, Ming Tang, Gustavo Glusman, Kyle Chard, and Mike Darcy et al. 2016. Predictive Big Data Analytics: A Study of Parkinson's Disease Using Large, Complex, Heterogeneous, Incongruent, Multi-Source and Incomplete Observations. *PLoS ONE* 11, (8):e0157077 (August 2016).

[12] Jeff Donahue, Lisa Anne Hendricks, Marcus Rohrbach, Subhashini Venugopalan, Sergio Guadarrama, Kate Saenko, and Trevor Darrell. 2016. Long-term Recurrent Convolutional Networks for Visual Recognition and Description. *arXiv:1411.4389v4[cs.CV]* (2016). https://arxiv.org/pdf/1411.4389.pdf

[13] Cristobal Esteban, Oliver Staeck, Yinchong Yang, and Volker Tresp. 2016. Predicting Clinical Events by Combining Static and Dynamic Information Using Recurrent Neural Networks. *arXiv:1602.02685v1 [cs.LG]* (2016). https://arxiv.org/pdf/1602.02685v1.pdf

[14] Seyed-Mohammad Fereshtehnejad, Silvia Ros-Romenets, Julius B. M. Anang, and Ronald B. Postuma. 2015. New Clinical Subtypes of Parkinson Disease and Their Longitudinal Progression: A Prospective Cohort Comparison With Other Phenotypes. *JAMA Neurol* 72, 8 (2015), 863–873.

[15] Alex Graves, Abdel rahman Mohamed, and Geoffrey Hinton. 2013. Speech Recognition with Deep Recurrent Neural Networks. *arXiv:1303.5778[cs.NE]* (2013). https://arxiv.org/abs/1303.5778

[16] Joyce C Ho, Joydeep Ghosh, and Jimeng Sun. 2014. Marble: High-Throughput Phenotyping from Electronic Health Records via Sparse Nonnegative Tensor Factorization. In *Proceedings of the 20th ACM SIGKDD International Conference on Knowledge Discovery and Data Mining*. ACM, 115–124.

[17] Sepp Hochreiter and Jürgen Schmidhuber. 1997. Long Short-Term Memory. *Neural computation* 9, 8 (1997), 1735–1780.

[18] Alistair EW Johnson, Tom J Pollard, Lu Shen, Li-wei H Lehman, Mengling Feng, Mohammad Ghassemi, Benjamin Moody, Peter Szolovits, Leo Anthony Celi, and Roger G Mark. 2016. MIMIC-III, A Freely Accessible Critical Care Database. *Scientific Data* 3 (2016).

[19] Uri Kartoun. 2016. A Methodology to Generate Virtual Patient Repositories. *arXiv:1608.00570 [cs.CY]* (2016). https://arxiv.org/ftp/arxiv/papers/1608/1608.00570.pdf

[20] Siwei Lai, Liheng Xu, Kang Liu, and Jun Zhao. 2015. Recurrent Convolutional Neural Networks for Text Classification. In *Proceedings of the Twenty-Ninth AAAI Conference on Artificial Intelligence*.

[21] Zachary C. Lipton, David C. Kale, Charles Elkan, and Randall" Wetzell. 2016. Learning to Diagnose with LSTM Recurrent Neural Networks. *arXiv:1511.03677v6 [cs.LG]* (2016). https://arxiv.org/pdf/1511.03677v6.pdf

[22] Christopher D. Manning, Prabhakar Raghavan, and Hinrich Schutze. 2008. *Introduction to Information Retrieval*. Cambridge University Press.

[23] Benjamin M. Marlin, David C. Kale, Robinder G. Khemani, and Randall C. Wetzel. 2012. Unsupervised Pattern Discovery in Electronic Health Care Data using Probabilistic Clustering Models. In *Proceedings of the 2nd ACM SIGHIT International Health Informatics Symposium*. ACM, 389–398.

[24] Trang Pham, Truyen Tran, Dinh Phung, and Svetha Vankatesh. 2016. DeepCare: A Deep Dynamic Memory Model for Predictive Medicine. *arxiv:1602.00357v1 [stat.ML]* (February 2016). https://arxiv.org/pdf/1602.00357v1.pdf

[25] Nitish Srivastava, Elman Mansimov, and Ruslan Salakhutdinov. 2016. Unsupervised Learning of Video Representations using LSTM. *arXiv:1502.04681v3[cs.LG]* (2016). https://arxiv.org/abs/1502.04681

[26] Tsung-Hsien Wen, Milica Gasic, Nikola Mrksic, Pei-Hao Su, David Vandyke, and Steve Young. 2015. Semantically Conditioned LSTM-based Natural Language Generation for Spoken Dialogue Systems. In *Proceedings of the 2015 Conference on Empirical Methods in Natural Language Processing*. 1711–1721.

[27] Ting Xiang, Debajyoti Ray, Terry Lohrenz, Peter Dayan, and P Read Montague. 2012. Computational Phenotyping of Two-person Interactions Reveals Differential Neural Response to Depth-of-thought. *PLoS Comput Biol* 8, 12 (2012), e1002841.

[28] Yu Zhang, I-Wei Wu, Duygu Tosun, Eric Foster, and Norbert Schuff. 2016. Progression of Regional Microstructural Degeneration in Parkinsonfis Disease: A Multicenter Diffusion Tensor Imaging Study. *PLOS ONE* (2016).

[29] Jiayu Zhou, Zhaosong Lu, Jimeng Sun, Lei Yuan, Fei Wang, and Jieping Ye. 2013. Feafiner: Biomarker Identification from Medical Data Through Feature Generalization and Selection. In *Proceedings of the 19th ACM SIGKDD International Conference on Knowledge Discovery and Data Mining*. 1034–1042.

[30] Jiayu Zhou, Fei Wang, Jianying Hu, and Jieping Ye. 2014. From Micro to Macro: Data Driven Phenotyping by Densification of Longitudinal Electronic Medical Records. In *Proceedings of the 20th ACM SIGKDD International Conference on Knowledge Discovery and Data Mining*. ACM, 135–144.

[31] Jiayu Zhou, Lei Yuan, Jun Liu, and Jieping Ye. 2017. A Multi-Task Learning Formulation for Predicting Disease Progression. In *Proceedings of the 17th ACM SIGKDD International Conference on Knowledge Discovery and Data Mining*. 814–822.

[32] Xiaoqiang Zhou, Baotian Hu, Qingcai Chen, and Xiaolong Wang. 2015. An Auto-Encoder for Learning Conversation Representation Using LSTM. In *Proceedings of the 22nd International Conference on Neural Information Processing, ICONIP 2015*. 310–317. http://dx.doi.org/10.1007/978-3-319-26532-2_34

Robust Top-k Multiclass SVM for Visual Category Recognition

Xiaojun Chang
Language Technologies Institute
Carnegie Mellon University
cxj273@gmail.com

Yao-Liang Yu
School of Computer Science
University of Waterloo
yaoliang.yu@uwaterloo.ca

Yi Yang*
Centre for Artificial Intelligence
University of Technology Sydney
yi.yang@uts.edu.au

ABSTRACT

Classification problems with a large number of classes inevitably involve *overlapping* or *similar* classes. In such cases it seems reasonable to allow the learning algorithm to make mistakes on similar classes, as long as the true class is still among the top-k (say) predictions. Likewise, in applications such as search engine or ad display, we are allowed to present k predictions at a time and the customer would be satisfied as long as her interested prediction is included. Inspired by the recent work of [15], we propose a very generic, robust multiclass SVM formulation that directly aims at minimizing a *weighted* and *truncated* combination of the *ordered* prediction scores. Our method includes many previous works as special cases. Computationally, using the Jordan decomposition Lemma we show how to rewrite our objective as the difference of two convex functions, based on which we develop an efficient algorithm that allows incorporating many popular regularizers (such as the ℓ_2 and ℓ_1 norms). We conduct extensive experiments on four real large-scale visual category recognition datasets, and obtain very promising performances.

KEYWORDS

Top-k Multiclass SVM, Visual Category Recognition

Figure 1: Video examples from the FCVID dataset [11]. The objects in Figure (a) and Figure (b) have some overlapping, and the objects in Figure (c) and Figure (d) are similar.

1 INTRODUCTION

The multiclass classification problem is a fundamental task in the filed of machine learning and computer vision [3, 8, 10, 20, 32]. It plays a central role in many vision applications, *e.g.*, object recognition, image segmentation, and scene classification [21], which can all be reduced to the task of discriminating multiple categories. Multiclass classification is difficult because the classifier needs to distinguish an object from a large number of categories, potentially overlapping and similar to each other [5, 17]. Indeed, even conservative estimates suggest that there are tens of thousands of object classes in the visual world [2]. The multiclass classification problem can be solved by naturally extending the binary classification technique with the 1-vs-all or 1-vs-1 strategy [22]. These include neural networks [25], decision trees [1], and Support Vector Machines [4].

When the number of visual categories becomes large, the visual recognition problem becomes extremely challenging in the presence of *overlapping* or *similar* classes [9]. We illustrate this phenomenon in Figure 1, where Fig. (a) and Fig. (b) have some overlapping classes while Fig. (c) and Fig. (d) have similar classes. One might ask, is it possible, or even expected, for a human to predict correctly on a first attempt?

Perhaps not. Therefore, for such challenging circumstances, it makes sense to allow the learning algorithm to present k predictions altogether to the user, as long as the true category is among the top-k predictions. This assumption also aligns with many real applications, such as ad display or search engine [12, 13, 18]. Generally, the customer will still be happy as long as her item of interest is included in the top-k candidates [14].

Recently, [15] proposed the top-k multiclass SVM as a direct method to optimize for top-k performance. It strictly generalizes the multiclass SVM based on a tight convex upper bound of the top-k error. The traditional multiclass formulation of [4] aims at separating the correct class with the top-1 confusing class, which can be too stringent for applications with severe class overlapping. In contrast, the top-k extension in [15] gives the algorithm some slack by ignoring the $k-1$ most confusing labels.

The major limitation of the existing top-k extension is its sensitivity to abnormal observations, *i.e.*, outliers, after all its loss is still convex [31]. To overcome this limitation, we propose a very generic, robust multiclass SVM formulation. Its goal is to directly minimize a *weighted* and *truncated* combination of the ordered prediction scores. Particularly, the proposed algorithm allows to "give up" focusing on any training pair that incurs an excessively

KDD'17, , August 13–17, 2017, Halifax, NS, Canada

ACM ISBN 978-1-4503-4887-4/17/08.
https://doi.org/10.1145/3097983.3097991

large loss, namely, outliers. We also show that the algorithm includes many previous multiclass SVMs as special cases. Based on the Jordan decomposition Lemma, we propose an efficient algorithm that allows incorporating many popular regularizers. Lastly, we conduct extensive experiments on several real large-scale visual category recognition datasets. The experiment results confirm the effectiveness of our algorithm.

Paper organization: We first review some related works on multiclass SVM and its recent top-k extension in Section 2. Then we introduce the proposed Robust Top-k Multiclass SVM in Section 3, followed by the detailed computational algorithm in Section 4. Experiments are conducted in Section 5. Finally, Section 6 concludes this paper.

2 PRELIMINARY

In this section we first recall the multiclass SVM of [4] and the recent top-k extension due to [15].

Given a training sample $(\mathbf{x}_i, y_i), i = 1, \ldots, n$, where $\mathbf{x}_i \in \mathcal{X} \subseteq \mathbb{R}^d$ and $y_i \in \mathcal{Y} := \{1, \ldots, c\}$, the multiclass SVM [4] aims at minimizing the following regularized empirical risk:

$$\min_{W=[\mathbf{w}_1,\ldots,\mathbf{w}_c]^\top \in \mathbb{R}^{c\times d}} \sum_{i=1}^n \bar{\ell}_i(W) + \lambda \|W\|_\mathsf{F}^2, \tag{1}$$

where the loss $\bar{\ell}_i$ on the i-th training example is given as

$$\bar{\ell}_i = \bar{\ell}_i(W) := \max_{j\in\mathcal{Y}} \{\mathbb{1}_{j\neq y_i} + \langle \mathbf{w}_j, \mathbf{x}_i\rangle - \langle \mathbf{w}_{y_i}, \mathbf{x}_i\rangle\}, \tag{2}$$

$\|W\|_\mathsf{F}$ is the Frobenius norm, and $\lambda \geq 0$ controls the tradeoff between the model fitting on the training data and the model complexity. Here we use the notation $\mathbb{1}_A$ for the indicator which is 1 iff A is true, and 0 otherwise. The inner product $\langle \mathbf{w}_j, \mathbf{x}_i\rangle$ is the score of the i-th example w.r.t. the j-th class.

To predict the label of a test point $\mathbf{x}$, we use the max-rule[1]:

$$\hat{y} = \operatorname*{argmax}_{j\in\mathcal{Y}} \langle \mathbf{w}_j, \mathbf{x}\rangle. \tag{3}$$

From this prediction rule it is clear that the prediction is correct, *i.e.*, $\hat{y} = y(\mathbf{x}) =: y$, iff the scores satisfy

$$\langle \mathbf{w}_y, \mathbf{x}\rangle > \langle \mathbf{w}_j, \mathbf{x}\rangle, \ \forall j \neq y. \tag{4}$$

Accordingly, the multiclass loss $\bar{\ell}_i$ in Equation (2) is designed to enjoy the following property:

$$\bar{\ell}_i(W) = 0 \iff \langle \mathbf{w}_{y_i}, \mathbf{x}_i\rangle \geq \langle \mathbf{w}_j, \mathbf{x}_i\rangle + \mathbb{1}_{j\neq y_i}, \tag{5}$$

which is clearly a sufficient condition to guarantee Equation (4). Due to homogeneity of the objective function (1), changing the margin parameter 1 here to any positive number $\gamma > 0$ amounts to scaling down W and scaling up λ by γ. For simplicity, we do not consider adding a bias term here.

The multiclass SVM formulation above has been successfully applied to many real applications, however, it is less appropriate when we are allowed to predict *a set of labels* $\hat{Y}$ for a test point $\mathbf{x}$ and the prediction is deemed "correct" iff $y = y(\mathbf{x}) \in \hat{Y}$. Recently, [15] considered the following set prediction rule:

$$\hat{Y} = \operatorname*{argmax}_{Y\subseteq\mathcal{Y}, |Y|=k} \sum_{j\in Y} \langle \mathbf{w}_j, \mathbf{x}\rangle, \tag{6}$$

where the cardinality of $\hat{Y}$ is constrained to be k. Namely, we present the k labels whose scores are among the top-k, and the prediction is considered "correct" iff the scores satisfy[2]:

$$\langle \mathbf{w}_y, \mathbf{x}\rangle > (W_{\backslash y}\mathbf{x})_{[k]}, \tag{7}$$

where we use $a_{[k]}$ to denote the k-th largest entry of the vector $\mathbf{a}$, and the matrix $W_{\backslash y} \in \mathbb{R}^{(c-1)\times d}$ removes the y-th row of W. Accordingly, [15] modified the multiclass SVM loss Equation (2) as follows:

$$\tilde{\ell}_i(W) := \max\{0, (W_{\backslash y_i}\mathbf{x}_i)_{[k]} + 1 - \langle \mathbf{w}_{y_i}, \mathbf{x}_i\rangle\} \tag{8}$$

$$= \max\left\{0, \left((W - \mathbf{1}\mathbf{w}_{y_i}^\top)\mathbf{x}_i + \mathbf{1} - \mathbf{e}_{y_i}\right)_{[k]}\right\}, \tag{9}$$

where $\mathbf{e}_j$ is the j-th canonical basis vector, and $\mathbf{1}$ is the all ones vector. Indeed,

$$\tilde{\ell}_i(W) = 0 \iff \langle \mathbf{w}_{y_i}, \mathbf{x}_i\rangle \geq (W_{\backslash y_i}\mathbf{x}_i)_{[k]} + 1, \tag{10}$$

which is a sufficient condition to guarantee Equation (7). Again, the margin parameter 1 here can be replaced with any positive number.

The above top-k extension due to [15] is indeed useful for the following reasons:

- It strictly generalizes the multiclass SVM: Setting $k = 1$ we recover the original multiclass SVM of [4], which is clear by comparing Equation (2) with Equation (8), Equation (3) with Equation (6), Equation (4) with Equation (7), and Equation (5) with Equation (10).
- In retrieval tasks such as search engine or ad display, we may be allowed to present k predictions altogether to the user, who will remain happy as long as she can easily identify the desired outcome from the k candidates.
- The multiclass formulation of [4] aims at separating the correct class with the top-1 confusing class, which is wasteful in applications (*e.g.* image classification with extremely many labels) where the labels inevitably overlap a lot. In contrast, the top-k extension gives the algorithm some slack by ignoring the $k - 1$ most confusing labels (which could well resemble the correct class).

The top-k loss in Equation (8) is unfortunately nonconvex. Instead, [15] proposed the following convex upper bound (up to a rescaling of factor k):

$$\tilde{\ell}_i(W) = \max\left\{0, \sum_{j=1}^k \left((W - \mathbf{1}\mathbf{w}_{y_i}^\top)\mathbf{x}_i + \mathbf{1} - \mathbf{e}_{y_i}\right)_{[j]}\right\}. \tag{11}$$

However, this convex loss may still be dominated by the top-1 confusing class. Moreover, it grows unboundedly as $\|W\|_\mathsf{F} \to \infty$ in the nonseparable case — an indication of non-robustness w.r.t. outliers [31].

3 ROBUST TOP-K MULTICLASS SVM

In this section we further extend the top-k multiclass SVM in two aspects: We introduce weights on the ordered scores, and we truncate the loss to induce robustness. Due to its generality, our formulation includes the aforementioned multiclass SVM works as special cases.

[1] Ties can be broken in any consistent way.

[2] Note that for the set prediction rule Equation (6), we can assume w.l.o.g. that $k \leq c-1$, for otherwise the problem is trivial.

The major limitation of the convex surrogate Equation (11) and also the original nonconvex top-k loss Equation (8), is their sensitivity to abnormal observations, *i.e.* outliers. This is mostly due to the unboundedness of the corresponding losses (as $\|W\|_F \to \infty$). To overcome this limitation, we propose the following truncated loss that extends the multicategory ψ-loss in [19]:

$$\ell_i(W) := \min\left\{ \max\left\{0, \sum_{j=1}^{c} \alpha_j s^i_{[j]}\right\}, \tau\right\}, \tag{12}$$

where we use the following abbreviation for the scores

$$\mathbf{s}^i = (W - \mathbf{1}\mathbf{w}_{y_i}^\top)\mathbf{x}_i + \mathbf{1} - \mathbf{e}_{y_i}, \tag{13}$$

and $\boldsymbol{\alpha} \in \mathbb{R}^k$ is an arbitrary weight that we choose to combine the *ordered* scores. Here $\tau > 0$ is a hyperparameter that we use to *cap* the loss for any training pair. In particular, it allows the algorithm to "give up" focusing on any training pair that incurs an excessively large loss, namely, outliers. In real large application where the training data are inevitably noisy, it is beneficial to use a small τ to exclude outliers.

It is clear that our formulation includes many previous multiclass SVMs as special cases:

- If $\tau = \infty, \alpha_1 = 1, \alpha_2 = \cdots = \alpha_c = 0$, then we recover the multiclass SVM of [4].
- If $\tau = \infty, \alpha_k = 1, \alpha_1 = \cdots = \alpha_{k-1} = \alpha_{k+1} = \cdots = \alpha_c = 0$, then we recover the nonconvex top-k multiclass SVM of [15].
- If $\tau = \infty, \alpha_1 = \cdots = \alpha_k = 1, \alpha_{k+1} = \cdots = \alpha_c = 0$, then we recover the convex surrogate of [15].
- If $\tau = 2, \alpha_1 = 1, \alpha_2 = \cdots = \alpha_c = 0$, then we recover a similar formulation as [19].

We can combine the robust multiclass loss Equation (12) with a regularization function to promote structure, resulting in the composite minimization problem:

$$\min_W \sum_{i=1}^{n} \ell_i(W) + \lambda f(W), \tag{14}$$

where we can choose for instance the l_2^2-norm $f(W) = \|W\|_F^2$ for generalization or the l_1-norm $f(W) = \|W\|_1$ for sparsity. In general, our rosbut loss $\ell_i(W)$ in Equation (12) is not convex, due to the truncation by τ and the arbitrariness of the weight α. However, if $\tau = \infty$ and $\alpha_1 \geq \alpha_2 \geq \cdots \geq \alpha_c$ is monotonically decreasing, such as the multiclass SVM of [4] and the convex surrogate of [15], then the formulation Equation (14) becomes a convex minimization problem. In the next section we develop an efficient algorithm for the general nonconvex setting.

4 COMPUTATIONAL ALGORITHM

The main challenge to numerically solve our formulation Equation (14) is that the robust loss $\ell_i(W)$ defined in Equation (12) is both nonconvex and nonsmooth — a setting where not many algorithms are applicable. Here we propose an efficient implementation based on the difference of convex algorithm (DCA) [28]. The main idea is to decompose a nonconvex function, say ℓ, as the difference of two convex functions, *i.e.* $\ell = g - h$, where both g and h are convex. Note that *not* all nonconvex functions can be written this way, but it is the case for our robust loss (as we shall demonstrate soon). The decomposition is not unique either and we will simply pick a convenient one. The next step is to linearize h at the current iterate, say W_t, so that we have the upper bound

$$\ell(W) \leq g(W) - \langle W - W_t, \nabla h(W_t)\rangle - h(W_t), \tag{15}$$

where $\nabla h(W_t)$ is any subgradient of h at W_t and the inequality follows from the convexity of h. Since the upper bound is now a convex function of W, we can apply our favorite convex optimization algorithm to find its minimizer, which will be W_{t+1}, our next iterate. It is easy to prove that the objective value will decrease monotonically, and with more efforts it can be shown that the algorithm converges to a critical point, see [28]. We note that another possibility is to approximate the robust loss ℓ_i with some (nonconvex) differentiable function, and then apply the ordinary gradient descent.

To implement the above DCA procedure, let us first decompose $\ell_i(W)$ into the difference of two convex functions. For this we need the following well-known (Jordan) decomposition:

Lemma 4.1. *For any vector $\alpha \in \mathbb{R}^c$, we have*

$$\boldsymbol{\alpha} = \boldsymbol{\alpha}^+ + \boldsymbol{\alpha}^-, \ \text{where } \forall j = 1, \ldots, c, \tag{16}$$

$$\alpha_j^+ = \sum_{p=1}^{j} \max\{0, \alpha_p - \alpha_{p-1}\}, \tag{17}$$

$$\alpha_j^- = \sum_{p=1}^{j} \min\{0, \alpha_p - \alpha_{p-1}\}, \tag{18}$$

and by convention $\alpha_0 := 0$.

Clearly, $\boldsymbol{\alpha}^-$ is monotonically decreasing and $\boldsymbol{\alpha}^+$ is monotonically increasing. For instance, for the top-k loss:

$$\boldsymbol{\alpha} = [0, \ldots, 0, \underbrace{1}_{k^{\text{th}}}, 0, \ldots, 0] \tag{19}$$

$$\boldsymbol{\alpha}^+ = [0, \ldots, 0, \underbrace{1}_{k^{\text{th}}}, 1, \ldots, 1] \tag{20}$$

$$\boldsymbol{\alpha}^- = [0, \ldots, 0, \underbrace{-1}_{(k+1)^{\text{th}}}, -1, \ldots, -1], \tag{21}$$

while for the convex upper bound of [15], *i.e.* Equation (11), we have

$$\boldsymbol{\alpha} = [1, \ldots, 1, \underbrace{1}_{k^{\text{th}}}, 0, \ldots, 0] \tag{22}$$

$$\boldsymbol{\alpha}^+ = [1, \ldots, 1, \underbrace{1}_{k^{\text{th}}}, 1, \ldots, 1] \tag{23}$$

$$\boldsymbol{\alpha}^- = [0, \ldots, 0, \underbrace{-1}_{(k+1)^{\text{th}}}, -1, \ldots, -1]. \tag{24}$$

Of course, the decomposition is not unique. For instance, we could also choose $\boldsymbol{\alpha}^- = \boldsymbol{\alpha}, \boldsymbol{\alpha}^+ = 0$ for the latter case above.

Now we can proceed to the robust top-k loss in Equation (12). Since

$$\begin{aligned}\min\{\max\{a, 0\}, \tau\} &= \max\{a, 0\} - \max\{a - \tau, 0\} \\ &= \max\{a^+ + a^-, 0\} - \max\{a^+ + a^- - \tau, 0\} \\ &= \max\{a^-, -a^+\} - \max\{a^- - \tau, -a^+\},\end{aligned}$$

where in the last equality we subtract a^+ from both terms. Therefore, we have the following decomposition for the i-th robust loss:

$$\ell_i(W) = \max\left\{\sum_{j=1}^{c} \alpha_j^- s_{[j]}^i, \sum_{j=1}^{c}(-\alpha_j^+)s_{[j]}^i\right\} \qquad (25)$$

$$- \max\left\{\sum_{j=1}^{c} \alpha_j^- s_{[j]}^i - \tau, \sum_{j=1}^{c}(-\alpha_j^+)s_{[j]}^i\right\}$$

Since both $\boldsymbol{\alpha}^-$ and $-\boldsymbol{\alpha}^+$ are monotonically decreasing, all four sums in Equation (25) are convex functions of W. Since convexity is preserved under taking the maximum, we have successfully decomposed the robust loss $\ell_i(W)$ into the difference of two convex functions.

The next step is to linearize the subtrahend convex function, for which we will need a formula for the subgradient of the convex function $W \mapsto \sum_{j=1}^{c} \beta_j s_{[j]}$, where recall from Equation (13) that s is a linear function of W and $\boldsymbol{\beta}$ is any monotonically decreasing vector. For this purpose we need the following reformulation:

$$\sum_{j=1}^{c} \beta_j s_{[j]} = \max_P \boldsymbol{\beta}^\top P[(W - \mathbf{1}\mathbf{w}_y^\top)\mathbf{x} + \mathbf{1} - \mathbf{e}_y], \qquad (26)$$

where the maximization is over all permutation matrices P. Given W_t, we can find a maximizer P_t easily in (almost) linear time (essentially sorting s), then we can choose the subgradient to be

$$P_t^\top \boldsymbol{\beta}\mathbf{x}^\top - (\boldsymbol{\beta}^\top \mathbf{1})\mathbf{e}_y\mathbf{x}^\top. \qquad (27)$$

Note that the second term does not depend on W_t hence can be precomputed once in the beginning. Lastly, let us recall the well-known subdifferential rule for the max-function $\max\{g, h\}$: the subgradient can be simply chosen as the subgradient of g (resp. h) if g (resp. h) is bigger at the evaluated point. To summarize, a subgradient of the subtrahend in Equation (25) at the current iterate W_t is given in Equation (27) where $\boldsymbol{\beta} = \boldsymbol{\alpha}^-$ if the first term inside the max operator is bigger and $\boldsymbol{\beta} = -\boldsymbol{\alpha}^+$ otherwise.

Denote the subgradient above in Equation (27) as H_t. The next step is to minimize the convex upper bound:

$$\min_W \sum_{i=1}^{n} \ell_i(W; W_t) + \lambda f(W), \quad \text{where} \qquad (28)$$

$$\ell_i(W; W_t) = \max\left\{\sum_{j=1}^{c} \alpha_j^- s_{[j]}^i, \sum_{j=1}^{c}(-\alpha_j^+)s_{[j]}^i\right\} - \langle H_t^i, W\rangle$$

Conveniently, we can evaluate the subgradient of the convex upper bound $\ell_i(W; W_t)$ similarly as before. Note that H_t^i is fixed here. To solve the convex upper bound Equation (28), we use the stochastic forward-backward splitting algorithm of [6]. The algorithm is again iterative, and consists mostly of two steps:

$$W \leftarrow W - \eta \nabla \ell_I(W; W_t) \qquad (29)$$

$$W \leftarrow \mathsf{P}_f^{\eta\lambda}(W) := \operatorname*{argmin}_Z \tfrac{1}{2\eta}\|W - Z\|_{\mathsf{F}}^2 + \lambda f(Z), \qquad (30)$$

where $\nabla \ell_I(W; W_t)$ is the subgradient evaluated at a (uniformly) randomly chosen sample index I, $\eta > 0$ is a small step size, and $\mathsf{P}_f^{\eta\lambda}(W)$ is the proximity operator of the regularizer f. For the

Algorithm 1: DCA for robust top-k multiclass SVM

Initialize $W, \eta, \boldsymbol{\alpha}$.
for $j = 1, \ldots, c$ **do**
  $\alpha_j^+ = \alpha_{j-1}^+ + \max\{0, \alpha_j - \alpha_{j-1}\}$
  $\alpha_j^- = \alpha_{j-1}^- + \min\{0, \alpha_j - \alpha_{j-1}\}$
for $t = 1, 2, \ldots$ **do**
  $H \leftarrow 0$
  for $i = 1, \ldots, n$ **do**
    $\mathbf{s} \leftarrow (W - \mathbf{1}\mathbf{w}_{y_i}^\top)\mathbf{x}_i + \mathbf{1} - \mathbf{e}_{y_i}$
    $[\mathbf{s}, P] \leftarrow \mathsf{sort}(\mathbf{s})$
    if $\mathbf{s}^\top\boldsymbol{\alpha}^- - \tau > \mathbf{s}^\top(-\boldsymbol{\alpha}^+)$ **then**
      $\boldsymbol{\beta} \leftarrow \boldsymbol{\alpha}^-$
    else
      $\boldsymbol{\beta} \leftarrow -\boldsymbol{\alpha}^+$
    $H \leftarrow H + P^\top\boldsymbol{\beta}\mathbf{x}_i^\top - (\boldsymbol{\beta}^\top\mathbf{1})\mathbf{e}_{y_i}\mathbf{x}_i^\top$
  for $m = 1, 2, \ldots$ **do**
    randomly draw I from $\{1, \ldots, n\}$
    $\mathbf{s} \leftarrow (W - \mathbf{1}\mathbf{w}_{y_I}^\top)\mathbf{x}_I + \mathbf{1} - \mathbf{e}_{y_I}$
    $[\mathbf{s}, P] \leftarrow \mathsf{sort}(\mathbf{s})$
    if $\mathbf{s}^\top\boldsymbol{\alpha}^- > \mathbf{s}^\top(-\boldsymbol{\alpha}^+)$ **then**
      $\boldsymbol{\beta} \leftarrow \boldsymbol{\alpha}^-$
    else
      $\boldsymbol{\beta} \leftarrow -\boldsymbol{\alpha}^+$
    $G \leftarrow P^\top\boldsymbol{\beta}\mathbf{x}_I^\top - (\boldsymbol{\beta}^\top\mathbf{1})\mathbf{e}_{y_I}\mathbf{x}_I^\top$
    $W \leftarrow W - \eta(G - H)$
    $W \leftarrow \mathsf{P}_f^{\eta\lambda}(W)$

l_2^2-norm regularizer we have

$$\mathsf{P}_{\|\cdot\|_{\mathsf{F}}^2}^{\eta\lambda}(W) = \tfrac{1}{1+2\eta\lambda}W \qquad (31)$$

while for the l_1-norm regularizer we have

$$\mathsf{P}_{\|\cdot\|_1}^{\eta\lambda}(W) = \operatorname{sign}(W) * \max\{|W| - \eta\lambda, 0\}, \qquad (32)$$

where the algebraic operations are component-wise. For the step size η we can either choose a small value by try-and-error, or use the diminishing rule $\eta_m = O(1/\sqrt{m})$. As shown by [6], this iteration will converge to the minimum objective value in expectation (and in high probability).

We summarize the entire procedure in Algorithm 1, where we make one final modification: Instead of computing the entire subgradient of $\ell_I(W; W_t)$, we rearrange the terms as follows:

$$\min_W \sum_i \max\left\{\sum_{j=1}^{c} \alpha_j^- s_{[j]}^i, \sum_{j=1}^{c}(-\alpha_j^+)s_{[j]}^i\right\} \qquad (33)$$

$$-\langle \sum_i H_t^i, W\rangle + \lambda f(W), \qquad (34)$$

where we treat the terms in Equation (34) as the "regularizer". Therefore, in each iteration we need only sample and compute the subgradient of the first max-term in Equation (33), followed by the proximity operator of the sum in Equation (34), for which we can apply Theorem 3 of [30]. This amounts to subtracting the term $\sum_i H_t^i$ instead of the sampled one H_t^I, hence potentially making more progress in each iteration. It is clear that in each iteration the time and space complexity is (almost) linear in terms of the problem size.

We note that [15] adopted an entirely different algorithm (SDCA of [23]) for their convex upper bound loss Equation (11). However, SDCA optimizes the dual problem and relies on a strongly convex regularizer (such as the ℓ_2^2-norm). Instead, our algorithm here, building on the work of [28] and [6], works for a variety of robust losses (by choosing different weight vector $\boldsymbol{\alpha}$) and any regularizer (as long as its proximity operator is available cheaply, such as the ℓ_1-norm).

5 EXPERIMENTS

In this section, we carry out extensive experiments to validate the performance of the proposed robust top-k multiclass SVM, abbreviated as **rtop-k SVM**.

5.1 Experimental Setup

Datasets: We test on four real visual category recognition datasets.

- Caltech 101 Silhouettes [27]: This dataset was created based on the CalTech 101 image annotations. Each image in the CalTech 101 data set includes a high-quality polygon outline of the primary object in the scene. To create the CalTech 101 Silhouettes data set, each outline is centered and scaled, and then rendered on a *DtimesD* pixel image-plane. It contains 101 classes, each of which has at most 100 training instances. We use features provided by [27].
- MIT Indoor 67 [21]: This is a dataset of 15,620 images over 67 indoor scenes assembled by [21]. The indoor scenes range from specific categories (*e.g.*, dental office) to generic concepts (*e.g.*, mall). We follow their experimental setting in [21] by using 80 images from each class for training and 20 for testing. We extract CNN features of a pre-trained CNN (fc7 layer after ReLU) [24], resulting in 4096-dimensional feature representation.
- UCF 101 [26]: This dataset consists of 13,320 videos with an average length of 6.2 seconds belonging to 101 different action categories. The dataset has 3 standard train/test splits with the training set containing around 9,500 vidoes in each split (the rest are used as testing data). Following the hybrid deep learning framework proposed in [29], we first extract spatial and motion features with two CNNs trained static frames and stacked optical flows respectively. The two types of features are used separately as inputs of the LSTM network for long-term temporal modeling. We apply a regularized fusion network to combine the two features on video level.
- FCVID 239 [11]: The FCVID239 dataset contains 91,223 web videos annotated into 239 categories, covering a wide range of topics like social events (*e.g.*, tailgate part), procedural events (*e.g.*, making cak), objects (*e.g.*, panda), scenes (*e.g.*, beach), *etc.* The "data" category has the largest number of positive videos while "making egg tarts" is the most infrequent category containing only 108 samples. The total duration of FCVID is 4,232 hours with an average video duration of 167 seconds. We use the 4096-dimensional CNN features provided by [11].

Compared Algorithms: To evaluate the performance of the proposed algorithm, we compare with the following alternatives.

- Probabilistic Model for Top-k Classification [27]: The proabilistic model explicitly includes a prior distribution over the number of variables that take on each label. The authors illustrate the utility of the model by exploring applications to top-K classification.
- SVM^{OVA}: The most common technique for multiclass SVMs has been to build the classifier in a one-versus-rest fashion, and to choose the class which classifiers the test datum with greatest margin.
- TopPush [16]: TopPush aims to optimize accuracy at the top that has computational complexity linear in the number of training instances.
- Top-k SVM [15]: The top-k multiclass SVM is a direct method to optimize for top-k performance. The generalization of the well-known multiclass SVM is based on a tight convex upper bound of the top-k error.

5.2 Visual Recognition Experiment

For all the compared algorithms, we cross-validate the regularization parameter λ in the range of 10^{-5} to 10^{3}, extending it when the optimal value is at the boundary. The oficial splits are used for all the compared algorithms. For the proposed algorithm, we also cross-validate the hyperparameter τ in the range of 10^{-1} to 10^{3}. The multiclass SVM of [4] is compared as a baseline. We use LibLinear [7] for SVM^{OVA} and the code provided by [16] for TopPush. For the latter, we use its one-vs-all version for scalability. Two versions of top-k multiclass SVM [15], namely top-k SVM$_\alpha$ and top-k SVM$_\beta$, are also compared. Performance is measured in terms of the top-k accuracy, *i.e.*, the percentage of labels with at least one matching item retrieved within the top-k predictions.

To begin with, we compare all the algorithms with ℓ_2^2-norm regularization. The experimental results on all the used datasets are illustrated in Table 1 and Table 2, from which we make the following observations: First, all alternatives of top-k SVM generally outperform the multiclass SVM of [4], hence demonstrating the benefit of allowing k simultaneous predictions. Second, it is interesting to notice that the alternatives of top-k SVM achieve a decreased top-1 accuracy on MIT Indoor 67 dataset, while achieving a significant improvement in the top-1 accuracy on the other datasets, like UCF 101 and FCVID 239 datasets. This phenomenon is consistent with the intuition that optimizing the top-k accuracy is more appropriate for datasets with a large number of categories, especially when overlapping or similar categories commonly exist. Third, the proposed robust top-k SVM performs better than the other alternatives of top-k SVM. For example, in top-5 accuracy with the proposed rtop-10 SVM, compared with top-10 SVM$_\alpha$: +2.06% on Caltech 101, +1.91% on MIT Indoor 67, +2.39% on UCF 101 and +2.39% on FCVID 239 dataset. This confirms that enhanced robustness does lead to improved performance. Overall, we get systematic increase in top-k accuracy over all the dataset that we used.

To step further, we also compare the performance of top-k SVM$_\alpha$, top-k SVM$_\beta$ and the proposed algorithm, when ℓ_1-norm regularization is used for all the compared alternatives. For space limitation, we only use the Caltech 101 Sihouettes and MIT Indoor 67 datasets in this experiment. The experimental results are reported in Table 3, from which we observe that it is clear the proposed algorithm rtop-k SVM performs the best on both datasets. We attribute this

Table 1: Performance comparison between different multi-class classification algorithms on Caltech 101 Sihouettes and MIT Indoor 67 datasets. Top-k accuracy is used as an evaluation metric. A larger value indicates a better performance.

	Caltech 101 Sihouettes						MIT Indoor 67					
	Top-1 Acc	Top-2 Acc	Top-3 Acc	Top-4 Acc	Top-5 Acc	Top-10 Acc	Top-1 Acc	Top-2 Acc	Top-3 Acc	Top-4 Acc	Top-5 Acc	Top-10 Acc
Top-1 [27]	62.13	73.68	79.59	80.05	83.08	88.65	69.76	78.64	81.64	83.17	84.62	90.83
Top-2 [27]	61.42	72.11	79.23	79.94	83.42	88.93	68.84	77.33	80.87	82.69	83.96	90.14
Top-5 [27]	60.24	70.65	78.71	79.16	83.42	88.93	69.43	78.52	81.29	82.95	84.25	90.47
SVM^{OVA}	61.81	73.13	76.25	77.76	78.89	83.57	71.72	81.49	84.93	86.49	87.39	90.45
TopPush	63.11	75.16	78.46	80.19	81.97	86.95	70.52	83.13	86.94	90.00	91.64	95.90
top-1 SVM_α	62.81	74.60	77.76	80.02	81.97	86.91	73.96	85.22	89.25	91.94	93.43	96.94
top-2 SVM_α	63.11	76.16	79.02	81.01	82.75	87.65	73.06	85.67	90.37	92.24	94.48	97.31
top-3 SVM_α	63.37	76.72	79.67	81.49	83.57	88.25	71.57	86.27	91.12	93.21	94.70	97.24
top-4 SVM_α	63.20	76.64	79.76	82.36	84.05	88.64	71.42	85.67	90.75	93.28	94.78	97.84
top-5 SVM_α	63.29	76.81	80.02	82.75	84.31	88.69	70.67	85.75	90.37	93.21	94.70	97.91
top-10 SVM_α	62.98	77.33	80.49	82.66	84.57	89.55	70.00	85.45	90.00	93.13	94.63	97.76
top-20 SVM_α	59.21	75.64	80.88	83.49	85.39	90.33	65.90	84.10	89.93	92.69	94.25	97.54
top-1 SVM_β	62.81	74.60	77.76	80.02	81.97	86.91	73.96	85.22	89.25	91.94	93.43	96.94
top-2 SVM_β	63.55	76.25	79.28	81.14	82.62	87.91	74.03	85.90	89.78	92.24	94.10	97.31
top-3 SVM_β	63.94	76.64	79.71	81.36	83.44	87.99	72.99	86.34	90.60	92.76	94.40	97.24
top-4 SVM_β	63.94	76.85	80.15	82.01	83.53	88.73	73.06	86.19	90.82	92.69	94.48	97.69
top-5 SVM_β	63.59	77.03	80.36	82.57	84.18	89.03	72.61	85.60	90.75	92.99	94.48	97.61
top-10 SVM_β	64.02	77.11	80.49	83.01	84.87	89.42	71.87	85.30	90.45	93.36	94.40	97.76
top-20 SVM_β	63.37	77.24	81.06	83.31	85.18	90.03	71.94	85.30	90.07	92.46	94.33	97.39
rtop-1 SVM	64.89	77.03	81.18	83.17	84.49	88.49	74.02	85.13	89.96	92.36	94.03	97.69
rtop-2 SVM	64.97	77.65	82.53	83.42	84.73	89.03	73.75	85.58	90.11	92.49	94.06	97.46
rtop-3 SVM	65.23	77.84	82.64	83.29	84.98	89.44	74.12	85.03	89.59	92.28	93.85	96.58
rtop-4 SVM	65.49	78.35	83.12	83.57	84.77	89.97	74.69	85.98	90.03	92.79	94.13	97.39
rtop-5 SVM	65.83	78.89	83.04	83.29	84.53	90.48	73.84	85.86	91.05	92.86	95.16	97.84
rtop-10 SVM	66.21	78.64	83.28	84.02	85.38	91.73	73.28	86.87	91.68	94.74	96.42	98.22
rtop-20 SVM	66.46	77.63	83.21	84.14	84.35	90.21	72.69	85.68	90.28	94.12	94.89	97.85

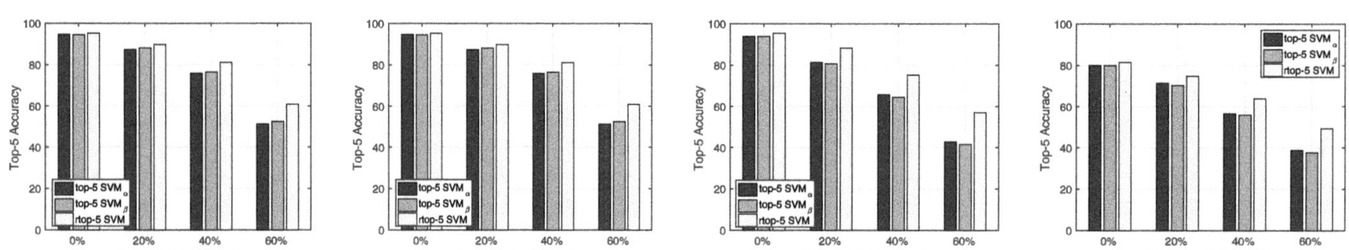

(a) Caltech 101 Sihouettes (b) MIT Indoor 67 (c) UCF101 (d) FCVID

Figure 2: Robust evaluation of the proposed algorithm on Caltech 101 Sihouettes, MIT Indoor, UCF 101 and FCVID datasets.

superiority of the proposed algorithm to the novel truncated loss function in Equation (12).

5.3 Robustness Evaluation

To conduct additional experiments to illustrate robustness of the proposed algorithm, we corrupt a varying percentage (0%, 20%, 40%, 60%) of training samples with outliers and compare the performance of top-k SVM and robust top-k SVM (rtop-k SVM). In this section, we use Top-5 accuracy as an evaluation metric and choose $k = 5$ as an example. We report the experimental results in Figure 2. From the experimental results we have the following observations: (1) With the increase of outlier percentages, the performance of all the

Table 2: Performance comparison between different multi-class classification algorithms on UCF 101 and FCVID datasets. Top-k accuracy is used as an evaluation metric. A larger value indicates a better performance.

	UCF101						FCVID					
	Top-1 Acc	Top-2 Acc	Top-3 Acc	Top-4 Acc	Top-5 Acc	Top-10 Acc	Top-1 Acc	Top-2 Acc	Top-3 Acc	Top-4 Acc	Top-5 Acc	Top-10 Acc
Top-1 [27]	70.85	81.57	86.46	87.28	88.35	90.28	56.85	67.57	72.46	73.29	74.35	76.28
Top-2 [27]	70.24	80.83	86.18	86.93	87.85	89.88	56.24	66.84	72.18	72.94	73.85	75.88
Top-5 [27]	70.66	81.16	86.33	87.15	88.04	90.16	56.67	67.17	72.33	73.15	74.05	76.16
SVM^{OVA}	70.94	83.39	87.29	88.42	89.17	91.68	56.95	69.39	73.30	74.43	75.17	77.68
TopPush	72.49	85.16	88.14	88.98	89.85	92.56	58.50	71.16	74.14	74.98	75.86	78.56
top-1 SVM_α	78.83	88.21	91.20	92.89	93.97	96.80	64.84	74.21	77.21	78.89	79.98	82.80
top-2 SVM_α	78.56	88.18	91.28	93.10	93.87	96.78	64.56	74.19	77.28	79.10	79.88	82.78
top-3 SVM_α	77.98	87.87	91.22	93.13	93.95	96.80	63.99	73.88	77.23	79.13	79.95	82.81
top-4 SVM_α	77.58	87.81	91.12	93.02	93.87	96.75	63.59	73.82	77.12	79.03	79.87	82.76
top-5 SVM_α	77.06	87.68	91.09	92.86	93.95	96.85	63.07	73.68	77.09	78.86	79.95	82.85
top-10 SVM_α	75.61	87.18	90.80	92.84	93.58	96.78	61.62	73.19	76.80	78.85	79.59	82.78
top-20 SVM_α	73.83	85.78	89.92	92.33	93.37	96.71	59.84	71.79	75.93	78.33	79.37	82.71
top-1 SVM_β	78.83	88.21	91.20	92.89	93.97	96.80	64.83	74.21	77.20	78.90	79.98	82.81
top-2 SVM_β	79.14	88.78	91.63	93.02	94.18	97.32	65.15	74.78	77.63	79.02	80.18	83.32
top-3 SVM_β	79.37	88.95	91.84	92.96	93.96	97.11	65.37	74.95	77.85	78.97	79.96	83.11
top-4 SVM_β	79.05	88.36	91.38	92.23	93.96	96.86	65.06	74.37	77.39	78.24	79.96	82.87
top-5 SVM_β	77.85	87.95	91.54	92.51	93.89	95.92	63.85	73.95	77.55	78.52	79.89	81.92
top-10 SVM_β	76.53	87.36	91.33	92.87	93.84	95.87	62.53	73.37	77.34	78.87	79.85	81.87
top-20 SVM_β	74.17	86.04	91.28	92.69	93.12	95.46	60.17	72.04	77.28	78.69	79.13	81.46
rtop-1 SVM	78.97	89.59	92.12	94.03	95.16	97.88	65.01	75.58	78.21	80.04	81.12	83.89
rtop-2 SVM	79.23	90.18	92.58	94.16	95.64	98.02	65.21	76.05	78.51	80.12	81.58	84.04
rtop-3 SVM	79.85	90.35	92.29	94.11	95.23	97.61	65.85	76.19	78.27	80.13	81.06	83.52
rtop-4 SVM	79.28	89.59	91.95	93.64	95.02	97.76	65.38	75.69	77.95	79.64	81.02	83.75
rtop-5 SVM	80.17	90.37	92.58	94.25	95.25	97.62	66.21	76.42	78.68	80.29	81.30	83.62
rtop-10 SVM	81.27	91.54	92.87	94.56	95.76	98.32	67.01	77.39	78.89	80.45	81.65	84.42
rtop-20 SVM	80.15	90.27	92.49	94.01	95.51	98.03	65.97	76.12	78.25	89.86	81.25	84.02

compared algorithms dropped. For example, the performance of the propsoed algorithm decreased from 95.28% to 61.02% when the outlier percentage increases from 0% to 60% on FCVID. (2) As the outlier percentage increases, we can see the performance gain of the proposed robust algorithm becomes more significant, which confirms the robustness of the proposed algorithm.

5.4 Sensitivity Analysis

We conduct some sensitivity ayalysis in this section, to draw further insights of the proposed learning algorithm.

Effect of τ and λ: We conduct experiments to assess the sensitivity of the proposed algorithm w.r.t. the hyperparameter τ. To be more specific, we fix $\lambda = 1$ and record the top-k accuracy by varying τ. We use Top-5 accuracy as an evaluation metric and choose $k = 5$ as an example. The experimental results are reported in Figure 3, from which we observe that the performance is relatively robust against the paremter τ. Generally speaking, the best performance is obtained when τ is in the range of $\{10^0, 10^1\}$. Then we fix τ at 1 and test the sensitivity against the regularization parameter λ. The top-5 accuracy with varying λ is shown in Figure 4, from which we see that the performance degrades when λ is overly large. The best performance is obtained when λ is in the range of $\{10^{-3}, 10^{-2}, 10^{-1}\}$.

Effect of Initialization: The general setting of Equation (14) is nonconvex, hence in theory it could have multiple local optima. In practisce we observed that the computational algorithm always converged to a reasonable solution. To test this point, we repeatedly run Algorithm 1 20 times, each with a different initialization. The results in terms of top-5 accuracy on the four datasets are reported in Figure 5, which confirmed that the proposed algorithm can always get a promising result on all the datasets.

6 CONCLUSION

We have presented a generic, robust multiclass SVM formulation that directly aims at minimizing a weighted and truncated combination of the ordered prediction scores. Computationally, we have proposed an efficient implementation based on the difference of convex algorithm (DCA). Extensive experiments are conducted on four

Table 3: Performance comparison between top-k SVM$_\alpha$, top-k SVM$_\beta$ and the proposed rtop-k SVM while ℓ_1 regularizer is used. Caltech 101 Sihouettes and MIT Indoor 67 datasets are utilized. Top-k accuracy is used as an evaluation metric. A larger value indicates a better performance.

	Caltech 101 Sihouettes						MIT Indoor 67					
	Top-1 Acc	Top-2 Acc	Top-3 Acc	Top-4 Acc	Top-5 Acc	Top-10 Acc	Top-1 Acc	Top-2 Acc	Top-3 Acc	Top-4 Acc	Top-5 Acc	Top-10 Acc
top-1 SVM$_\alpha$	64.21	76.16	78.85	81.47	83.16	88.22	74.03	85.13	89.42	92.29	93.85	97.27
top-2 SVM$_\alpha$	64.98	77.58	79.89	82.32	83.95	89.14	73.15	85.72	90.08	92.55	94.02	97.17
top-3 SVM$_\alpha$	65.23	78.95	80.33	83.19	84.62	89.83	72.18	85.47	89.96	92.89	94.25	97.13
top-4 SVM$_\alpha$	64.98	77.28	80.79	83.58	85.29	90.32	72.23	85.98	91.05	93.19	94.26	97.17
top-5 SVM$_\alpha$	65.03	78.01	81.57	84.19	86.74	91.59	72.26	85.68	90.84	93.08	94.95	97.66
top-10 SVM$_\alpha$	65.32	78.57	81.92	85.23	87.98	91.23	71.93	86.17	91.14	93.98	95.26	98.05
top-20 SVM$_\alpha$	62.48	76.92	82.59	85.31	86.84	92.42	69.87	84.85	90.19	93.22	94.59	97.67
top-1 SVM$_\beta$	64.28	76.29	79.14	82.57	83.17	88.19	74.08	85.18	89.54	92.17	93.94	97.19
top-2 SVM$_\beta$	64.97	78.15	80.48	84.12	84.09	89.98	73.23	85.81	90.04	92.42	94.01	97.25
top-3 SVM$_\beta$	65.38	78.19	81.59	83.27	85.29	89.48	72.14	86.42	89.95	92.75	94.18	97.08
top-4 SVM$_\beta$	65.84	78.47	82.48	84.22	85.29	90.58	72.09	85.83	90.87	93.11	94.18	97.05
top-5 SVM$_\beta$	65.28	79.42	81.98	84.27	86.28	91.24	72.16	85.59	90.81	93.02	94.86	97.34
top-10 SVM$_\beta$	66.42	79.48	82.86	85.21	86.48	91.16	71.83	85.98	90.79	93.58	94.97	97.65
top-20 SVM$_\beta$	65.84	79.11	82.98	85.19	87.04	91.98	71.89	85.19	90.12	92.25	94.19	97.48
rtop-1 SVM	66.52	78.56	82.64	84.67	85.95	89.97	74.13	85.27	90.01	92.88	94.17	97.76
rtop-2 SVM	66.74	79.14	84.15	84.93	86.27	90.52	73.86	85.74	90.26	92.94	94.17	97.58
rtop-3 SVM	66.81	79.37	84.16	84.76	86.18	90.95	74.28	85.19	89.75	92.53	93.99	96.72
rtop-4 SVM	67.03	79.86	84.63	85.02	86.27	91.48	74.84	86.12	90.19	93.04	94.32	97.61
rtop-5 SVM	67.58	80.14	84.59	84.78	86.08	91.92	74.01	85.97	91.14	93.19	95.28	98.04
rtop-10 SVM	67.96	80.39	84.88	85.49	86.63	93.26	73.47	86.98	91.79	95.01	96.54	98.43
rtop-20 SVM	67.28	79.15	84.62	85.36	86.11	91.84	72.85	85.75	90.43	94.26	95.08	97.92

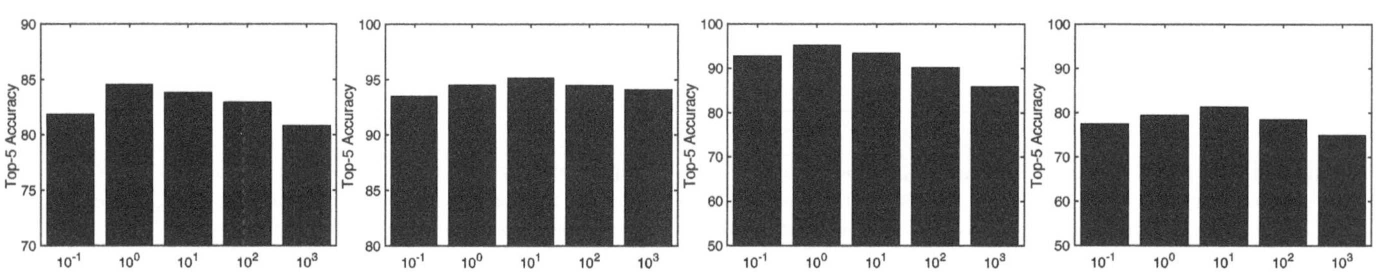

(a) Caltech 101 Sihouettes (b) MIT Indoor 67 (c) UCF101 (d) FCVID

Figure 3: Sensitivity analysis on τ on Caltech 101 Sihouettes, MIT Indoor, UCF 101 and FCVID datasets.

real visual recognition datasets. The experimental results confirm the superiority of the proposed algorithm. In the future, we plan to deploy the proposed robust rtop-k SVM to other applications, *i.e.*, person re-identification problems.

ACKNOWLEDGMENTS

We thank the reviewers for their valuable comments. This work was partially supported by the Data to Decisions Cooperative Research Centre (www.d2dcrc.com.au) and partially supported by NSERC. Disclaimer: The views and conclusions contained herein are those of the authors and should not be interpreted as necessarily representing the official policies or endorsements, either expressed or implied, of the Data to Decisions Cooperative Research Centre (www.d2dcrc.com.au) and NSERC.

REFERENCES

[1] Samy Bengio, Jason Weston, and David Grangier. 2010. Label Embedding Trees for Large Multi-Class Tasks. In *NIPS*.
[2] Irving Biederman. 1987. Recognition-by-components: a theory of human image understanding. *Psychol Rev* (1987).
[3] Antoine Bordes, Léon Bottou, Patrick Gallinari, and Jason Weston. 2007. Solving multiclass support vector machines with LaRank. In *ICML*.

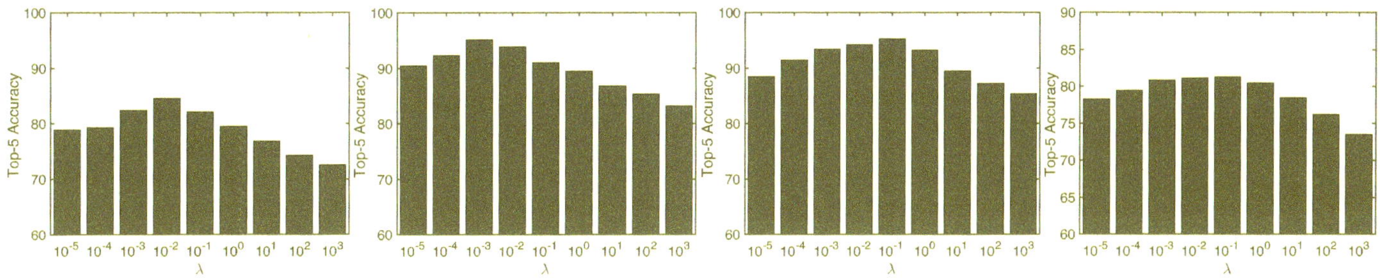

(a) Caltech 101 Sihouettes (b) MIT Indoor 67 (c) UCF101 (d) FCVID

Figure 4: Sensitivity analysis on λ on Caltech 101 Sihouettes, MIT Indoor, UCF 101 and FCVID datasets.

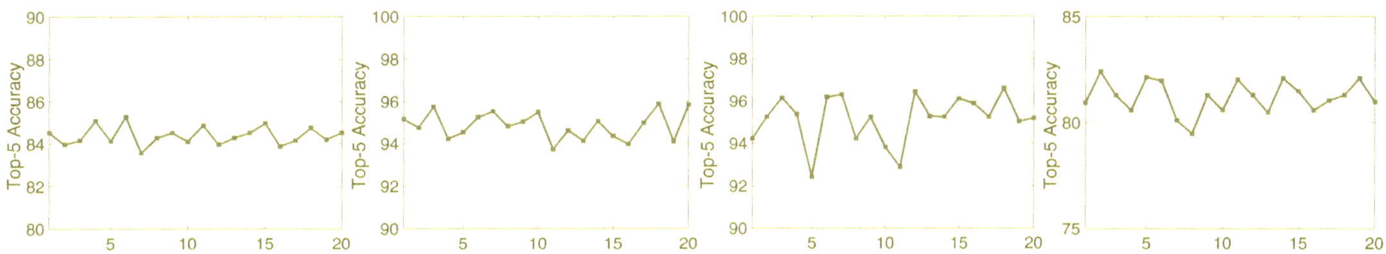

(a) Caltech 101 Sihouettes (b) MIT Indoor 67 (c) UCF101 (d) FCVID

Figure 5: Sensitivity analysis w.r.t. different initializations on Caltech 101 Sihouettes, MIT Indoor, UCF 101 and FCVID datasets.

[4] Koby Crammer and Yoram Singer. 2001. On the algorithmic implementation of multiclass kernel-based vector machines. *Journal of Machine Learning Research* 2 (2001), 265–292.

[5] Jia Deng, Jonathan Krause, Alexander C. Berg, and Fei-Fei Li. 2012. Hedging your bets: Optimizing accuracy-specificity trade-offs in large scale visual recognition. In *CVPR*.

[6] John C. Duchi and Yoram Singer. 2009. Efficient Online and Batch Learning Using Forward Backward Splitting. *Journal of Machine Learning Research* 10 (2009), 2899–2934.

[7] Rong-En Fan, Kai-Wei Chang, Cho-Jui Hsieh, Xiang-Rui Wang, and Chih-Jen Lin. 2008. LIBLINEAR: A Library for Large Linear Classification. *Journal of Machine Learning Research* 9 (2008), 1871–1874.

[8] Tianshi Gao and Daphne Koller. 2011. Discriminative learning of relaxed hierarchy for large-scale visual recognition. In *ICCV*.

[9] Maya R. Gupta, Samy Bengio, and Jason Weston. 2014. Training highly multiclass classifiers. *Journal of Machine Learning Research* 15, 1 (2014), 1461–1492.

[10] Chih-Wei Hsu and Chih-Jen Lin. 2002. A comparison of methods for multiclass support vector machines. *IEEE Transactions on Neural Networks* 13, 2 (2002), 415–425.

[11] Yu-Gang Jiang, Zuxuan Wu, Jun Wang, Xiangyang Xue, and Shih-Fu Chang. 2015. Exploiting Feature and Class Relationships in Video Categorization with Regularized Deep Neural Networks. (2015). arXiv:1502.07209.

[12] Thorsten Joachims. 2002. Optimizing search engines using clickthrough data. In *ACM SIGKDD*.

[13] M. Hadi Kiapour, Xufeng Han, Svetlana Lazebnik, Alexander C. Berg, and Tamara L. Berg. 2015. In *ICCV*.

[14] Maksim Lapin, Matthias Hein, and Bernt Schiele. 2015. Loss Functions for Top-k Error: Analysis and Insights. *CoRR* abs/1512.00486 (2015).

[15] Maksim Lapin, Bernt Schiele, and Matthias Hein. 2015. Top-*k* Multiclass SVM. In *NIPS*.

[16] Nan Li, Rong Jin, and Zhi-Hua Zhou. 2014. Top Rank Optimization in Linear Time. In *NIPS*.

[17] Baoyuan Liu, Fereshteh Sadeghi, Marshall F. Tappen, Ohad Shamir, and Ce Liu. 2013. Probabilistic Label Trees for Efficient Large Scale Image Classification. In *CVPR*.

[18] Li-Ping Liu, Thomas G. Dietterich, Nan Li, and Zhi-Hua Zhou. 2015. Transductive Optimization of Top k Precision. *CoRR* abs/1510.05976 (2015).

[19] Yufeng Liu and Xiaotong Shen. 2006. Multicategory ψ-Learning. *J. Amer. Statist. Assoc.* 101, 474 (2006), 500–509.

[20] John C. Platt, Nello Cristianini, and John Shawe-Taylor. 1999. Large Margin DAGs for Multiclass Classification. In *NIPS*.

[21] Ariadna Quattoni and Antonio Torralba. 2009. Recognizing indoor scenes. In *CVPR*.

[22] Ryan M. Rifkin and Aldebaro Klautau. 2004. In Defense of One-Vs-All Classification. *Journal of Machine Learning Research* 5 (2004), 101–141.

[23] Shai Shalev-Shwartz and Tong Zhang. 2016. Accelerated Proximal Stochastic Dual Coordinate Ascent for Regularized Loss Minimization. *Mathematical Programming* 155, 1 (2016), 105–145.

[24] Karen Simonyan and Andrew Zisserman. 2015. Very Deep Convolutional Networks for Large-Scale Image Recognition. In *ICLR*.

[25] Hyun Oh Song, Stefan Zickler, Tim Althoff, Ross B. Girshick, Mario Fritz, Christopher Geyer, Pedro F. Felzenszwalb, and Trevor Darrell. 2012. Sparselet Models for Efficient Multiclass Object Detection. In *ECCV*.

[26] Khurram Soomro, Amir Roshan Zamir, and Mubarak Shah. 2012. UCF101: A Dataset of 101 Human Actions Classes From Videos in The Wild. *CoRR* abs/1212.0402 (2012).

[27] Kevin Swersky, Daniel Tarlow, Ryan P. Adams, Richard S. Zemel, and Brendan J. Frey. 2012. Probabilistic n-Choose-k Models for Classification and Ranking. In *NIPS*.

[28] Pham Dinh Tao and Le Thi Hoai An. 1998. A D.C. Optimization Algorithm for Solving the Trust-Region Subproblem. *SIAM Journal on Optimization* 8, 2 (1998), 476–505.

[29] Zuxuan Wu, Xi Wang, Yu-Gang Jiang, Hao Ye, and Xiangyang Xue. 2015. Modeling Spatial-Temporal Clues in a Hybrid Deep Learning Framework for Video Classification. In *ACM MM*.

[30] Yaoliang Yu. 2013. On Decomposing the Proximal Map. In *NIPS*.

[31] Yaoliang Yu, Özlem Aslan, and Dale Schuurmans. 2012. A Polynomial-time Form of Robust Regression. In *NIPS*.

[32] Tong Zhang. 2004. Statistical Analysis of Some Multi-Category Large Margin Classification Methods. *Journal of Machine Learning Research* 5 (2004), 1225–1251.

KATE: K-Competitive Autoencoder for Text

Yu Chen
Rensselaer Polytechnic Institute
Troy, NY, USA 12180
cheny39@rpi.edu

Mohammed J. Zaki
Rensselaer Polytechnic Institute
Troy, NY, USA 12180
zaki@cs.rpi.edu

ABSTRACT

Autoencoders have been successful in learning meaningful representations from image datasets. However, their performance on text datasets has not been widely studied. Traditional autoencoders tend to learn possibly trivial representations of text documents due to their confounding properties such as high-dimensionality, sparsity and power-law word distributions. In this paper, we propose a novel k-competitive autoencoder, called KATE, for text documents. Due to the competition between the neurons in the hidden layer, each neuron becomes specialized in recognizing specific data patterns, and overall the model can learn meaningful representations of textual data. A comprehensive set of experiments show that KATE can learn better representations than traditional autoencoders including denoising, contractive, variational, and k-sparse autoencoders. Our model also outperforms deep generative models, probabilistic topic models, and even word representation models (e.g., Word2Vec) in terms of several downstream tasks such as document classification, regression, and retrieval.

CCS CONCEPTS

• **Information systems** → **Data mining**; **Document representation**; *Retrieval tasks and goals*; • **Computing methodologies** → **Neural networks**; *Information extraction*;

KEYWORDS

Representation Learning, Autoencoders, Competitive Learning, Text Analytics

ACM Reference format:
Yu Chen and Mohammed J. Zaki. 2017. KATE: K-Competitive Autoencoder for Text. In *Proceedings of KDD '17, Halifax, NS, Canada, August 13-17, 2017,* 10 pages.
https://doi.org/10.1145/3097983.3098017

1 INTRODUCTION

An autoencoder is a neural network which can automatically learn data representations by trying to reconstruct its input at the output layer. Many variants of autoencoders have been proposed recently [14, 24–26, 35, 39]. While autoencoders have been successfully applied to learn meaningful representations on image datasets (e.g., MNIST [20], CIFAR-10 [15]), their performance on text datasets has not been widely studied. Traditional autoencoders are susceptible to learning trivial representations for text documents. As noted by Zhai and Zhang [42], the reasons include that fact that textual data is extremely high dimensional and sparse. The vocabulary size can be hundreds of thousands while the average fraction of zero entries in the document vectors can be very high (e.g., 98%). Further, textual data typically follows power-law word distributions. That is, low-frequency words account for most of the word occurrences. Traditional autoencoders always try to reconstruct each dimension of the input vector on an equal footing, which is not quite appropriate for textual data.

Document representation is an interesting and challenging task which is concerned with representing textual documents in a vector space, and it has various applications in text processing, retrieval and mining. There are two major approaches to represent documents: 1) **Distributional Representation** is based on the hypothesis that linguistic terms with similar distributions have similar meanings. These methods usually take advantage of the co-occurrence and context information of words and documents, and each dimension of the document vector usually represents a specific semantic meaning (e.g., a topic). Typical models in this category include Latent Semantic Analysis (LSA) [7], probabilistic LSA (pLSA) [12] and Latent Dirichlet Allocation (LDA) [2]. 2) **Distributed Representations** encode a document as a compact, dense and lower dimensional vector with the semantic meaning of the document distributed along the dimensions of the vector. Many neural network-based distributed representation models [5, 18, 22, 27, 36] have been proposed and shown to be able to learn better representations of documents than distributional representation models.

In this paper, we try to overcome the weaknesses of traditional autoencoders when applied to textual data. We propose a novel autoencoder called KATE (for **K**-competitive **A**utoencoder for **TE**xt), which relies on competitive learning among the autoencoding neurons. In the feedforward phase, only the most competitive k neurons in the layer fire and those k "winners" further incorporate the aggregate activation potential of the remaining inactive neurons. As a result, each hidden neuron becomes better at recognizing specific data patterns and the overall model can learn meaningful representations of the input data. After training the model, each hidden neuron is distinct from the others and no competition is needed in the testing/encoding phase. We conduct comprehensive experiments qualitatively and quantitatively to evaluate KATE and to demonstrate the effectiveness of our model. We compare KATE with traditional autoencoders including basic autoencoder, denoising autoencoder [39], contractive autoencoder [35], variational autoencoder [14], and k-sparse autoencoder [24]. We also compare with deep generative models [22], neural autoregressive [18] and variational inference [27] models, probabilistic topic models such as

ACM ISBN 978-1-4503-4887-4/17/08...$15.00
https://doi.org/10.1145/3097983.3098017

LDA [2], and word representation models such as Word2Vec [28] and Doc2Vec [19]. KATE achieves state-of-the-art performance across various datasets on several downstream tasks like document classification, regression and retrieval.

2 RELATED WORK

Autoencoders. The basic autoencoder is a shallow neural network which tries to reconstruct its input at the output layer. An autoencoder consists of an encoder which maps the input $\boldsymbol{x}$ to the hidden layer: $\boldsymbol{z} = g(\boldsymbol{W}\boldsymbol{x} + \boldsymbol{b})$ and a decoder which reconstructs the input as: $\hat{\boldsymbol{x}} = o(\boldsymbol{W}'\boldsymbol{z} + \boldsymbol{c})$; here $\boldsymbol{b}$ and $\boldsymbol{c}$ are bias terms, $\boldsymbol{W}$ and $\boldsymbol{W}'$ are input-to-hidden and hidden-to-output layer weight matrices, and g and o are activation functions. Weight tying (i.e., setting $\boldsymbol{W}' = \boldsymbol{W}^T$) is often used as a regularization method to avoid overfitting. While plain autoencoders, even with perfect reconstructions, usually only extract trivial representations of the data, more meaningful representations can be obtained by adding appropriate regularization to the models. Following this line of reasoning, many variants of autoencoders have been proposed recently [14, 24–26, 35, 39]. The denoising autoencoder (DAE) [39] inputs a corrupted version of the data while the output is still compared with the original uncorrupted data, allowing the model to learn patterns useful for denoising. The contractive autoencoder (CAE) [35] introduces the Frobenius norm of the Jacobian matrix of the encoder activations into the regularization term. When the Frobenius norm is 0, the model is extremely invariant to perturbations of input data, which is thought as good. The variational autoencoder (VAE) [14] is a generative model inspired by variational inference whose encoder $q_\phi(\boldsymbol{z}|\boldsymbol{x})$ approximates the intractable true posterior $p_\theta(\boldsymbol{z}|\boldsymbol{x})$, and the decoder $p_\theta(\boldsymbol{x}|\boldsymbol{z})$ is a data generator. The k-sparse autoencoder (KSAE) [24] explicitly enforces sparsity by only keeping the k highest activities in the feedforward phase.

We notice that most of the successful applications of autoencoders are on image data, while only a few have attempted to apply autoencoders on textual data. Zhai and Zhang [42] have argued that traditional autoencoders, which perform well on image data, are less appropriate for modeling textual data due to the problems of high-dimensionality, sparsity and power-law word distributions. They proposed a semi-supervised autoencoder which applies a weighted loss function where the weights are learned by a linear classifier to overcome some of these problems. Kumar and D'Haro [16] found that all the topics extracted from the autoencoder were dominated by the most frequent words due to the sparsity of the input document vectors. Further, they found that adding sparsity and selectivity penalty terms helped alleviate this issue to some extent.

Deep generative models. Deep Belief Networks (DBNs) are probabilistic graphical models which learn to extract a deep hierarchical representation of the data. The top 2 layers of DBNs form a Restricted Boltzmann Machine (RBM) and other layers form a sigmoid belief network. A relatively fast greedy layer-wise pretraining algorithm [9, 10] is applied to train the model. Maaloe et al. [22] showed that DBNs can be competitive as a topic model. DocNADE [18] is a neural autoregressive topic model that estimates the probability of observing a new word in a given document given the previously observed words. It can be used for extracting meaningful representations of documents. It has been shown to outperform the Replicated Softmax model [11] which is a variant of RBMs for document modeling. Srivastava et al. [36] introduced a type of Deep Boltzmann Machine (DBM) that is suitable for extracting distributed semantic representations from a corpus of documents; an Over-Replicated Softmax model was proposed to overcome the apparent difficulty of training a DBM. NVDM [27] is a neural variational inference model for document modeling inspired by the variational autoencoder.

Probabilistic topic models. Probabilistic topic models, such as probabilistic Latent Semantic Analysis (pLSA) and Latent Dirichlet Allocation (LDA) have been extensively studied [2, 12]. Especially for LDA, many variants have been proposed for non-parametric learning [1, 37], sparsity [8, 40, 43] and efficient inference [4, 38]. Those models typically build a generative probabilistic model using the bag-of-words representation of the documents.

Word representation models. Distributed representations of words in a vector space can capture semantic meanings of words and help achieve better results in various downstream text analysis tasks. Word2Vec [28] and Glove [33] are state-of-the-art word representation models. Pre-training word embeddings on a large corpus of documents and applying learned word embeddings in downstream tasks has been shown to work well in practice [6, 13, 29]. Doc2Vec [19] was inspired by Word2Vec and can directly learn vector representations of paragraphs and documents. NTM [5], which also uses pre-trained word embeddings, is a neural topic model where the representations of words and documents are combined into a uniform framework.

With this brief overview of existing work, we now turn to our competitive autoencoder approach for text documents.

3 K-COMPETITIVE AUTOENCODER

Although the objective of an autoencoder is to minimize the reconstruction error, our goal is to extract meaningful features from data. Compared with image data, textual data is more challenging for autoencoders since it is typically high-dimensional, sparse and has power-law word distributions. When examining the features extracted by an autoencoder, we observed that they were not distinct from one another. That is, many neurons in the hidden layer shared similar groups of input neurons (which typically correspond to the most frequent words) with whom they had the strongest connections. We hypothesized that the autoencoder greedily learned relatively trivial features in order to reconstruct the input.

To overcome this drawback, our approach guides the autoencoder to focus on important patterns in the data by adding constraints in the training phase via mutual competition. In competitive learning, neurons compete for the right to respond to a subset of the input data and as a result, the specialization of each neuron in the network is increased. Note that the specialization of neurons is exactly what we want for an autoencoder, especially when applied on textual data. By introducing competition into an autoencoder, we expect each neuron in the hidden layer to take responsibility for recognizing different patterns within the input data. Following this line of reasoning, we propose the k-competitive autoencoder, KATE, as described below.

3.1 Training and Testing/Encoding

Algorithm 1 KATE: K-competitive Autoencoder

procedure TRAINING
    Feedforward step: $z = tanh(Wx + b)$
    Apply k-competition: $\hat{z}$ = k-competitive_layer(z)
    Compute output: $\hat{x} = sigmoid(W^T \hat{z} + c)$
    Backpropagate error (cross-entropy) and iterate

procedure ENCODING
    Encode input data: $z = tanh(Wx + b)$

The pseudo-code for our k-competitive autoencoder KATE is shown in Algorithm 1. KATE is a shallow autoencoder with a (single) competitive hidden layer, with each neuron competing for the right to respond to a given set of input patterns. Let $x \in \mathbb{R}^d$ be a d-dimensional input vector, which is also the desired output vector, and let $h_1, h_2, ..., h_m$ be the m hidden neurons. Let $W \in \mathbb{R}^{d \times m}$ be the weight matrix linking the input layer to the hidden layer neurons, and let $b \in \mathbb{R}^m$ and $c \in \mathbb{R}^d$ be the bias terms for the hidden and output neurons, respectively. Let g be an activation function; two typical functions are $tanh(x) = \frac{e^{2x}-1}{e^{2x}+1}$ and $sigmoid(x) = \frac{1}{1+e^{-x}}$. In each feed-forward step, the activation potential at the hidden neurons is then given as $z = g(Wx + b)$, whereas the activation potential at the output neurons is given as $\hat{x} = g(W^T z + c)$. Thus, the hidden-to-output weight matrix is simply W^T, being an instance of *weight tying*.

In KATE, we represent each input text document as a log-normalized word count vector $x \in \mathbb{R}^d$ where each dimension is represented as

$$x_i = \frac{log(1 + n_i)}{\max_{i \in V} log(1 + n_i)}, \text{ for } i \in V$$

where V is the vocabulary and n_i is the count of word i in that document. Let $\hat{x}$ be the output of KATE on a given input x. We use the binary cross-entropy as the loss function, which is defined as

$$l(x, \hat{x}) = -\sum_{i \in V} x_i log(\hat{x}_i) + (1 - x_i) log(1 - \hat{x}_i)$$

where $\hat{x}_i$ is the reconstructed value for x_i.

Let H be some subset of hidden neurons; define the **energy** of H as the total activation potential for H, given as: $E(H) = \sum_{h_i \in H} |z_i|$, i.e., sum of the absolute values of the activations for neurons in H. In KATE, in the feedforward phase, after computing the activations z for a given input x, we select the most competitive k neurons as the "winners" while the remaining "losers" are suppressed (i.e., made inactive). However, in order to compensate for the loss of energy from the loser neurons, and to make the competition among neurons more pronounced, we amplify and reallocate that energy among the winner neurons.

KATE uses *tanh* activation function for the k-competitive hidden layer. We divide these neurons into positive and negative neurons based on their activations. The most competitive k neurons are those that have the largest absolute activation values. However, we select the $\lceil k/2 \rceil$ largest positive activations as the positive winners, and reallocate the energy of the remaining positive loser neurons among the winners using an α amplification connection, where

Algorithm 2 K-competitive Layer

function K-COMPETITIVE-LAYER(z)
    sort positive neurons in ascending order $z_1^+ ... z_P^+$
    sort negative neurons in descending order $z_1^- ... z_N^-$
    if $P - \lceil k/2 \rceil > 0$ **then**
        $E_{pos} = \sum_{i=1}^{P - \lceil k/2 \rceil} z_i^+$
        for $i = P - \lceil k/2 \rceil + 1, ..., P$ **do**
            $z_i^+ := z_i^+ + \alpha \cdot E_{pos}$
        for $i = 1, ..., P - \lceil k/2 \rceil$ **do**
            $z_i^+ := 0$
    if $N - \lfloor k/2 \rfloor > 0$ **then**
        $E_{neg} = \sum_{i=1}^{N - \lfloor k/2 \rfloor} z_i^-$
        for $i = N - \lfloor k/2 \rfloor + 1, ..., N$ **do**
            $z_i^- := z_i^- + \alpha \cdot E_{neg}$
        for $i = 1, ..., N - \lfloor k/2 \rfloor$ **do**
            $z_i^- := 0$
    return updated $z_1^+ ... z_P^+, z_1^- ... z_N^-$

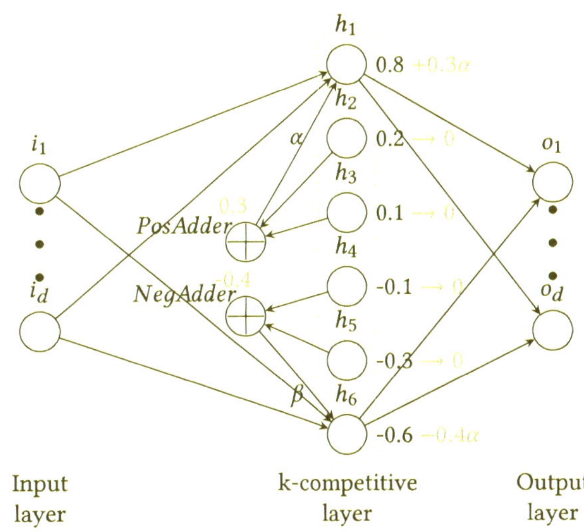

Figure 1: Competitions among neurons. Input and hidden neurons, and hidden and output neurons are fully connnected, but we omit these to avoid clutter.

α is a hyperparameter. Finally, we set the activations of all losers to zero. Similarly, the $\lfloor k/2 \rfloor$ lowest negative activations are the negative winners, and they incorporate the amplified energy from the negative loser neurons, as detailed in Algorithm 2. We argue that the α amplification connections are a critical component in the k-competitive layer. When $\alpha = 0$, no gradients will flow through loser neurons, resulting in a regular k-sparse autoencoder (regardless of the activation functions and k-selection scheme). When $\alpha > 2/k$, we actually boost the gradient signal flowing through the loser neurons. We empirically show that amplification helps improve the autoencoder model (see Sec. 4.4.1 and 4.5). As an example, consider Figure 1, which shows an example feedforward step for $k = 2$. Here, h_1 and h_6 are the positive and negative winners, respectively, since the absolute activation potential for h_1 is $|z_1| = 0.8$, and for h_6 it is $|z_6| = 0.6$. The positive winner h_1 takes away the energy from the positive losers h_2 and h_3, which is $E(\{h_2, h_3\}) = 0.2 + 0.1 = 0.3$.

Likewise, the negative winner h_6 takes away the energy from the negative losers h_4 and h_5, which is $-E(\{h_4, h_5\}) = -(|-0.1| + |-0.3|) = -0.4$. The hyperparameter α governs how the energy from the loser neurons is incorporated into the winner neurons, for both positive and negative cases. That is h_1's net activation becomes $z_1 = 0.8 + 0.3\alpha$, and h_6's net activation is $z_6 = -0.6 - 0.4\alpha$. The rest of the neurons are set to zero activation.

Finally, as noted in Algorithm 1 we use weight tying for the hidden to output layer weights, i.e., we use $\boldsymbol{W}^T$ as the weight matrix, with different biases $\boldsymbol{c}$. Also, since the inputs $\boldsymbol{x}$ are non-negative for document representations (e.g., word counts), we use the *sigmoid* activation function at the output layer to maintain the non-negativity. Note that in the back-propagation procedure, the gradients will first flow through the winner neurons in the hidden layer and then the loser neurons via the α amplification connections. No gradients will flow directly from the output neurons to the loser neurons since they are made inactive in the feedforward step.

Testing/Encoding. Once the k-competitive network has been trained, we simply encode each test input as shown in Algorithm 1. That is, given a test input $\boldsymbol{x}$, we map it to the feature space to obtain $z = tanh(\boldsymbol{W}\boldsymbol{x}+\boldsymbol{b})$. No competition is required for the encoding step since the hidden neurons are well trained to be distinctive from others. We argue that this is one of the superior features of KATE.

3.2 Relationship to Other Models

KATE vs. K-Sparse Autoencoder. The k-sparse autoencoder [24] is closely related to our model, but there are several differences. The k-sparse autoencoder explicitly enforces sparsity by only keeping the k highest activities at training time. Then, at testing time, in order to enforce sparsity, only the αk highest activities are kept where α is a hyperparameter. Since its hidden layer uses a linear activation function, the only non-linearity in the encoder comes from the selection of the k highest activities. Instead of focusing on sparsity, our model focuses on competition to drive each hidden neuron to be distinct from the others. Thus, at testing time, no competition is needed. The non-linearity in KATE's encoding comes from the *tanh* activation function, and the winner-take-all operation via the top k (+ve/−ve) selection and energy reallocation/amplification.

It is important to note that for the k-sparse autoencoder, too much sparsity (i.e., low k) can cause the so-called "dead" hidden neurons problem, which can prevent gradient back-propagation from adjusting the weights of these "dead" hidden neurons. As mentioned in the original paper, the model is prone to behaving in a manner similar to k-means clustering. That is, in the first few epochs, it will greedily assign individual hidden neurons to groups of training cases and these hidden neurons will be re-enforced but other hidden neurons will not be adjusted in subsequent epochs. In order to address this problem, scheduling the sparsity level over epochs was suggested. However, by design our approach does not suffer from this problem since the gradients will still flow through the loser neurons via the α amplification connections in the k-competitive layer.

KATE vs. K-Max Pooling. Our proposed k-competitive operation is also reminiscent of the k-max pooling operation [3] applied in convolutional neural networks. We can intuitively regard k-max pooling as a global feature sampler which selects a subset of k maximum neurons in the previous convolutional layer and uses only the selected subset of neurons in the following layer. Unlike our k-competitive approach, the objective of k-max pooling is to reduce dimensionality and introduce feature invariance via this downsampling operation.

KATE as a Regularized Autoencoder. We can also regard our model as a special case of a fully competitive autoencoder where all the neurons in the hidden layer are fully connected with each other and the weights on the connections between them are fully trainable. The difference is that we restrict the architecture of this competitive layer by using a positive adder and a negative adder to constrain the energy, which serves as a regularization method.

4 EXPERIMENTS

In this section, we evaluate our k-competitive autoencoder model on various datasets and downstream text analytics tasks to gauge its effectiveness in learning meaningful representations in different situations. All experiments were performed on a machine with a 1.7GHz AMD Opteron 6272 Processor, with 264G RAM. Our model, KATE, was implemented in Keras (github.com/fchollet/keras) which is a high-level neural networks library, written in Python. The source code for KATE is available at **github.com/hugochan/KATE**.

dataset	20 news	reuters	wiki10+	mrd
train.size	11,314	554,414	13,972	3,337
test.size	7,532	250,000	6,000	1,669
valid.size	1,000	10,000	1,000	300
vocab.size	2,000	5,000	2,000	2,000
avg.length	93	112	1,299	124
classes/vals	20	103	25	[0, 1]
task	class & DR	MLC	MLC	regression

Table 1: Datasets: Tasks include classification (class), regression, multi-label classification (MLC), and document retrieval (DR).

4.1 Datasets

For evaluation, we use datasets that have been widely used in previous studies [17, 21, 30–32, 44]. Table 1 provides statistics of the different datasets used in our experiments. It lists the training, testing and validation (a subset of training) set sizes, the size of the vocabulary, average document length, the number of classes (or values for regression), and the various downstream tasks we perform on the datasets.

The 20 Newsgroups [17] (www.qwone.com/~jason/20Newsgroups) data consists of 18846 documents, which are partitioned (nearly) evenly across 20 different newsgroups. Each document belongs to exactly one newsgroup. The corpus is divided by date into training (60%) and testing (40%) sets. We follow the preprocessing steps utilized in previous work [18, 27, 36]. That is, after removing stop-words and stemming, we keep the most frequent 2,000 words in the training set as the vocabulary. We use this dataset to show that our model can learn meaningful representations for classification and document retrieval tasks.

The Reuters RCV1-v2 dataset [21] (www.jmlr.org/papers/volume5/lewis04a) contains 804,414 newswire articles, where each document typically has multiple (hierarchical) topic labels. The total number of topic labels is 103. The dataset already comes preprocessed with stopword removal and stemming. We randomly split the corpus into 554,414 training and 25,000 test cases and keep the most frequent 5,000 words in the training dataset as the vocabulary. We perform multi-label classification on this dataset.

The Wiki10+ dataset [44] (www.zubiaga.org/datasets/wiki10+/) comprises English Wikipedia articles with at least 10 annotations on delicious.com. Following the steps of Cao et al. [5], we only keep the 25 most frequent social tags and those documents containing any of these tags. After removing stopwords and stemming, we randomly split the corpus into 13,972 training and 6,000 test cases and keep the most frequent 2,000 words in the training set as the vocabulary for use in multi-label classification.

The Movie review data (MRD) [30–32] (www.cs.cornell.edu/people/pabo/movie-review-data/) contains a collection of movie-review documents, with a numerical rating score in the interval [0, 1]. After removing stopwords and stemming, we randomly split the corpus into 3,337 training and 1,669 test cases and keep the most frequent 2,000 words in the training set as the vocabulary. We use this dataset for regression, i.e., predicting the movie ratings.

Note that among the above datasets, only the 20 Newsgroups dataset is balanced, whereas both the Reuters and Wiki10+ datasets are highly imbalanced in terms of class labels.

4.2 Comparison with Baseline Methods

We compare our k-competitive autoencoder KATE with a wide range of other models including various types of autoencoders, topic models, belief networks and word representation models, as listed below.

LDA [2]: a directed graphical model which models a document as a mixture of topics and a topic as a mixture of words. Once trained, each document can be represented as a topic proportion vector on the topic simplex. We used the gensim [34] LDA implementation in our experiments.

DocNADE [18]: a neural autoregressive topic model that can be used for extracting meaningful representations of documents. The implementation is available at www.dmi.usherb.ca/~larocheh/code/DocNADE.zip.

DBN [22]: a direct acyclic graph whose top two layers form a restricted Boltzmann machine. We use the implementation available at github.com/larsmaaloee/deep-belief-nets-for-topic-modeling.

NVDM [27]: a neural variational inference model for document modeling. The authors have not released the source code, but we used an open-source implementation at github.com/carpedm20/variational-text-tensor-flow.

Word2Vec [28]: a model in which each document is represented as the average of the word embedding vectors for that document. We use Word2Vec$_{pre}$ to denote the version where we use Google News pre-trained word embeddings which contain 300-dimensional vectors for 3 million words and phrases. Those embeddings were trained by state-of-the-art word2vec skipgram model. On the other hand, we use Word2Vec to denote the version where we train word embeddings separately on each of our datasets, using the gensim [34] implementation.

Doc2Vec [19]: a distributed representation model inspired by Word2Vec which can directly learn vector representations of documents. There are two versions named Doc2Vec-DBOW and Doc2Vec-DM. We use Doc2Vec-DM in our experiments as it was reported to consistently outperform Doc2Vec-DBOW in the original paper. We used the gensim [34] implementation in our experiments.

AE: a plain shallow (i.e., one hidden layer) autoencoder, without any competition, which can automatically learn data representations by trying to reconstruct its input at the output layer.

DAE [39]: a denoising autoencoder that accepts a corrupted version of the input data while the output is still the original uncorrupted data. In our experiments, we found that masking noise consistently outperforms other two types of noise, namely Gaussian noise and salt-and-pepper noise. Thus, we only report the results of using masking noise. Basically, masking noise perturbs the input by setting a fraction v of the elements i in each input vector as 0. To be fair and consistent, we use a shallow denoising autoencoder in our experiments.

CAE [35]: a contractive autoencoder which introduces the Frobenius norm of the Jacobian matrix of the encoder activations into the regularization term.

VAE [14]: a generative autoencoder inspired by variational inference.

KSAE [24]: a competitive autoencoder which explicitly enforces sparsity by only keeping the k highest activities in the feedforward phase.

We implemented the AE, DAE, CAE, VAE and KSAE autoencoders on our own, since their implementations are not publicly available.

Training Details: For all the autoencoder models (including AE, DAE, CAE, VAE, KSAE, and KATE), we represent each input document as a log-normalized word count vector, using binary cross-entropy as the loss function and Adadelta [41] as the optimizer. Weight tying is also applied. For CAE and VAE, additional regularization terms are added to the loss function as mentioned in the original papers. As for VAE, we use *tanh* as the nonlinear activation function while as for AE, DAE and CAE, *sigmoid* is applied. As for KSAE, we found that omitting sparsity in the testing phase gave us better results in all experiments.

When training models, we randomly extract a subset of documents from the training set as a validation set, as noted in Table 1, which is used for tuning hyperparameters and early stopping. Early stopping is a type of regularization used to avoid overfitting when training an iterative algorithm. We stop training after 5 successive epochs with no improvement on the validation set. All baseline models were optimized as recommended in original sources. For KATE, we set α as 6.26, learning rate as 2, batch size as 100 (for the Reuters dataset) or 50 (for other datasets) and k as 6 (for the 20 topics case), 32 (for the 128 topics case) or 102 (for the 512 topics case), as determined from the validation set.

4.3 Qualitative Analysis

In this set of qualitative experiments, we compare the topics generated by KATE to other representative models including AE, KSAE, and LDA. Even though KATE is not explicitly designed for the purpose of word embeddings, we compared word representations learned by KATE with the Word2Vec model to demonstrate that our model can learn semantically meaningful representations from text. We evaluate the above models on the 20 Newsgroups data. Matching the number of classes, the number of topics is set to exactly 20 for all models. For both KSAE and KATE, k (the sparsity level/number of winning neurons) is set as 6.

soc.religion .christian	AE	line subject organ articl peopl post time make write good
	KSAE	peopl origin bottom applic mind subject pad europ role christian
	KATE	god christian jesu moral rutger bibl exist religion apr christ
	LDA	god christian jesu church bibl peopl christ man time life
sci.crypt	KATE	govern articl law key encrypt clipper chip secur case distribut
	LDA	key encrypt chip clipper secur govern system law escrow privaci
comp.os.ms-windows.misc	KATE	ca system univers window problem card file driver drive scsi
	LDA	drive card gun control disk scsi system driver hard bu

Table 2: Topics learned by various models.

4.3.1 Topics Generated by Different Models. Table 2 shows some topics learned by various models. As for autoencoders, each topic is represented by the 10 words (i.e., input neurons) with the strongest connection to that topic (i.e., hidden neuron). As for LDA, each topic is represented by the 10 most probable words in that topic. The basic AE is not very good at learning distinctive topics from textual data. In our experiment, all the topics learned by AE are dominated by frequent common words like *line, subject* and *organ*, which were always the top 3 words in all the 20 topics. KSAE learns some meaningful words but only alleviates this problem to some extent, for example, *line, subject, organ* and *white* still appears as top 4 words in 6 topics. For this reason, the output of AE and KSAE is shown for only one of the newsgroups (*soc.religion.christian*). On the other hand, we find that KATE generates 20 topics that are distinct from each other, and which capture the underlying semantics very well. For example, it associates words such as *god, christian, jesu, moral, bibl, exist, religion, christ* under the topic *soc.religion.christian*. It is worth emphasizing that KATE belongs to the class of distributed representation models, where each topic is "distributed" among a group of hidden neurons (the topics are therefore better interpreted as "virtual" topics). However, we find that KATE can generate competitive topics compared with LDA, which explicitly infers topics as mixture of words.

4.3.2 Word Embeddings Learned by Different Models. In AE, KSAE and KATE, each input neuron (i.e., a word in the vocabulary set) is connected to each hidden neuron (i.e., a virtual topic) with different strengths. Thus, each row i of the input to hidden layer weight matrix $\boldsymbol{W} \in \mathbb{R}^{d \times m}$ is taken as an m-dimensional word embedding for word i. In order to evaluate whether KATE can capture semantically meaningful word representations, we check if similar or related words are close to each other in the vector space. Table 3 shows the five nearest neighbors for some query words in the word representation space learned by AE, KSAE, KATE and Word2Vec. KATE performs much better than AE and KSAE. For example KATE lists words like *arm, crime, gun, firearm, handgun* among the nearest neighbors of query word *weapon* while neither AE nor KSAE is able to find relevant words. One can observe that KATE can learn competitive word representations compared to Word2Vec in terms of this word similarity task.

4.3.3 Visualization of Document Representations. A good document representation method is expected to group related documents, and to separate the different groups. Figure 2 shows the PCA projections of the document representations taken from the six main groups in the 20 Newsgroups data. As we can observe, neither AE nor the KSAE methods can learn good document representations. On the other hand, KATE successfully extracts meaningful representations from the documents; it automatically clusters related documents in the same group, and it can easily distinguish the six different groups. In fact, KATE is very competitive with LDA (arguably even better on this dataset, since LDA confuses some categories), even though the latter explicitly learns documents representations as mixture of topics, which in turn are mixture of words. Figure 3 shows the T-SNE based visualization [23] of the above document representations and we can draw a similar conclusion.

4.4 Quantitative Experiments

We now turn to quantitative experiments to measure the effectiveness of KATE compared to other models on tasks such as classification, multi-label classification (MLC), regression, and document retrieval (DR). For classification, MLC and regression tasks, we train a simple neural network that uses the encoded test inputs as feature vectors, and directly maps them to the output classes or values. A simple softmax classifier with cross-entropy loss was applied for the classification task, and multi-label logistic regression classifier with cross-entropy loss was applied for the MLC task. For the regression task we used a two-layer neural regression model (where the output layer is a sigmoid neuron) with squared error loss. The same architecture is used for all methods to ensure fairness. Note that when comparing various methods, the same number of features were learned for all of them except for Word2Vec$_{pre}$ which uses 300-dimensional pre-trained word embeddings and thus its number of features was fixed as 300 in all experiments.

4.4.1 Mean Squared Cosine Deviation among Topics. We first quantify how distinct are the topics learned via different methods. Let $\boldsymbol{v}_i$ denote the vector representation of topic i, and let there be m topics. The cosine of the angle between $\boldsymbol{v}_i$ and $\boldsymbol{v}_j$, given as $\cos(\boldsymbol{v}_i, \boldsymbol{v}_j) = \frac{\boldsymbol{v}_i^T \boldsymbol{v}_j}{\|\boldsymbol{v}_i\| \cdot \|\boldsymbol{v}_j\|}$, is a measure of how similar/correlated the two topic vectors are; it takes values in the range $[-1, 1]$. The topics are most dissimilar when the vectors are orthogonal to each other, i.e., with the angle between them is $\pi/2$, with the cosine of the angle being zero. Define the pair-wise mean squared cosine deviation among m topics as follows

$$MSCD = \sqrt{\frac{2}{m(m-1)} \sum_{i,j>i} \cos^2(\boldsymbol{v}_i, \boldsymbol{v}_j)}$$

Thus, MSCD $\in [0, 1]$, and smaller values of MSCD (closer to zero) imply more distinctive, i.e., orthogonal topics.

Model	weapon	christian	compani	israel	law	hockey	comput	space
AE	effort	close	hold	cost	made	plane	inform	studi
	muslim	test	simpl	isra	live	tie	run	data
	sort	larg	serv	arab	give	sex	program	answer
	america	result	commit	fear	power	english	base	origin
	escap	answer	societi	occupi	reason	intel	author	unit
KSAE	qualiti	god	commit	occupi	back	int	run	data
	challeng	power	student	enhanc	govern	cco	inform	process
	tire	lie	age	azeri	reason	monash	part	answer
	7u	logic	hold	rpi	call	rsa	case	heard
	learn	simpl	consist	sleep	answer	pasadena	start	version
KATE	arm	belief	market	arab	citizen	playoff	scienc	launch
	crime	god	dealer	isra	constitut	nhl	dept	orbit
	gun	believ	manufactur	palestinian	court	team	cs	mission
	firearm	faith	expens	occupi	feder	wing	math	shuttl
	handgun	bibl	cost	jew	govern	coach	univ	flight
Word2Vec	assault	understand	insur	lebanon	court	sport	engin	launch
	militia	belief	feder	isra	prohibit	nhl	colleg	jpl
	possess	believ	manufactur	lebanes	ban	playoff	umich	nasa
	automat	god	industri	arab	sentenc	winner	subject	moon
	gun	truth	pay	palestinian	legitim	cup	perform	gov

Table 3: Five nearest neighbors in the word representation space on 20 Newsgroups dataset.

(a) AE (b) KSAE (c) LDA (d) KATE

Figure 2: PCA on the 20-dimensional document vectors from 20 Newsgroups dataset.

(a) AE (b) KSAE (c) LDA (d) KATE

Figure 3: T-SNE on the 20-dimensional document vectors from 20 Newsgroups dataset.

We evaluate MSCD for topics generated by AE, KSAE, LDA, and KATE. We also evaluate KATE without amplification. In LDA, a topic is represented as its probabilistic distribution over the vocabulary set, whereas for autoencoders, it is defined as the weights on the connections between the corresponding hidden neuron and all the input neurons. We conduct experiments on the 20 Newsgroups dataset and vary the number of topics from 20 to 128 and 512. Table 4 shows these results. We find that KATE has the lowest MSCD values, which means that it can learn more distinctive (i.e., orthogonal) topics than other methods. Our results are much better than LDA, since the latter does not prevent topics from being similar. On the other hand, the competition in KATE drives topics (i.e., the hidden neurons) to become distinct from each other. Interestingly,

Model	20 News		
	20	128	512
AE	0.976	0.722	0.319
KSAE	0.268	0.198	0.056
LDA	0.249	0.059	0.028
KATE $_{no\_amp.}$	0.154	0.069	0.037
KATE	**0.097**	**0.024**	**0.014**

Table 4: Mean squared cosine deviation among topics; smaller means more distinctive topics.

KATE with amplification (i.e., here we have $\alpha = 6.26$) consistently achieves lower MSCD values than KATE without amplification, which verifies the effectiveness of the α amplification connections in terms of learning distinctive topics.

Model	20 News	
	128	512
LDA	0.657	0.685
DBN	0.677	0.705
DocNADE	0.714	0.735
NVDM	0.052	0.053
Word2Vec$_{pre}$	0.687	0.687
Word2Vec	0.564	0.586
Doc2Vec	0.347	0.399
AE	0.084	0.516
DAE	0.125	0.291
CAE	0.083	0.512
VAE	0.724	0.747
KSAE	0.486	0.675
KATE	**0.744**	**0.761**

Table 5: Classification accuracy on 20 Newsgroups dataset.

4.4.2 Document Classification Task. In this set of experiments, we evaluate the quality of learned document representations from various models for the purpose of document classification. Table 5 shows the classification accuracy results on the 20 Newsgroups dataset (using 128 topics). Traditional autoencoders (including AE, DAE, CAE) do not perform well on this task. We observed that the validation set error was oscillating when training these classifiers (also observed in the regression task below), which indicates that the extracted features are not representative and consistent. KSAE consistently achieves higher accuracies than other autoencoders and does not exhibit the oscillating phenomenon, which means that adding sparsity does help learn better representations. VAE even performs better than KSAE on this dataset, which shows the advantages of VAE over other traditional autoencoders. However, as we will see later, VAE fails to consistently perform well across different datasets and tasks. Word2Vec$_{pre}$ performs on par with DBN and LDA even though it just averages all the word embeddings in a document, which suggests the effectiveness of pre-training word embeddings on a large external corpus to learn general knowledge. Not surprisingly, DocNADE works very well on this task as also reported in previous work [5, 18, 36]. Our KATE model significantly outperforms all other models. For example, KATE obtains 74.4% accuracy which is significantly higher than the 72.4% accuracy achieved by VAE.

Table 6 shows multi-label classification results on Reuters and Wiki10+ datasets. Here we show both the Macro-F1 and Micro-F1 scores (reflecting a balance of precision and recall) for different number of features. Micro-F1 score biases the metric towards the most populated labels, while Macro-F1 biases the metric towards the least populated labels. Both Reuters and Wiki10+ are highly imbalanced. For example in Wiki10+, the documents belonging to 'wikipedia' or 'wiki' account for 90% of the corpus while only around 6% of the documents are relevant to 'religion'. Similarly, in Reuters, the documents belonging to 'CCAT' account for 47% of the corpus while there are only 5 documents relevant to 'GMIL'. DocNADE works the very well on this task, but the sparse and competitive autoencoders also perform well. KATE outperforms KSAE on Reuters and remains competitive on Wiki10+. We don't report the results of DBN on Reuters since the training did not end even after a long time.

4.4.3 Regression Task. In this set of experiments, we evaluate the quality of learned document representations from various models for predicting the movie ratings in the MRD dataset, as shown in Table 7 (using 128 features). The coefficient of determination, denoted r^2, from the regression model was used to evaluate the methods. The best possible r^2 statistic value is 1.0; negative values are also possible, indicating a poor fit of the model to the data. In general, other autoencoder models perform poorly on this task, for example, AE even gets a negative r^2 score. Interestingly, Word2Vec$_{pre}$ performs on par with DocNADE, indicating that word embeddings learned from a large external corpus can capture some semantics of emotive words (e.g., good, bad, wonderful). We observe that KATE significantly outperforms all other models, including Word2Vec$_{pre}$, which means it can learn meaningful representations which are helpful for sentiment analysis.

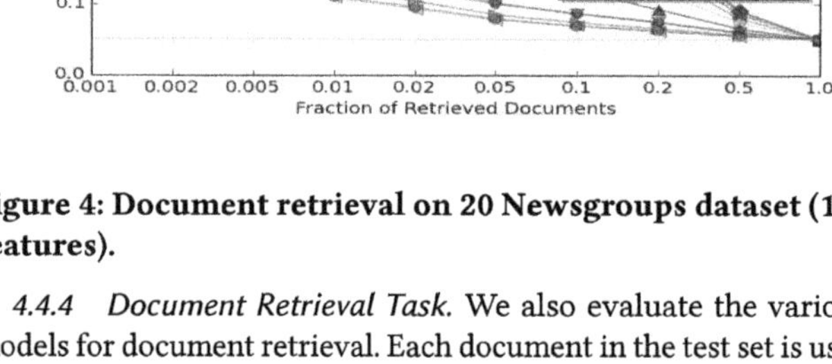

Figure 4: Document retrieval on 20 Newsgroups dataset (128 features).

4.4.4 Document Retrieval Task. We also evaluate the various models for document retrieval. Each document in the test set is used as an individual query and we fetch the relevant documents from the training set based on the cosine similarity between the document representations. The average fraction of retrieved documents which share the same label as the query document, i.e., precision, was used as the evaluation metric. As shown in Figure 4, VAE performs the best on this task followed by DocNADE and KATE. Among the other models, DBN and LDA also have decent performance, but the other autoencoders are not that effective.

Model	Reuters				Wiki10+			
	128		512		128		512	
	Macro-F1	Micro-F1	Macro-F1	Micro-F1	Macro-F1	Micro-F1	Macro-F1	Micro-F1
LDA	0.408	0.703	0.576	0.766	0.442	0.584	0.305	0.441
DBN	-	-	-	-	0.330	0.513	0.339	0.536
DocNADE	**0.564**	**0.768**	**0.667**	**0.831**	**0.451**	0.585	0.423	0.561
NVDM	0.215	0.441	0.195	0.452	0.187	0.461	0.036	0.375
Word2Vec_{pre}	0.549	0.712	0.549	0.712	0.312	0.454	0.312	0.454
Word2Vec	0.458	0.648	0.595	0.761	0.205	0.318	0.234	0.325
Doc2Vec	0.004	0.082	0.000	0.000	0.289	0.486	0.344	0.524
AE	0.025	0.047	0.459	0.651	0.016	0.040	0.382	0.569
DAE	0.275	0.576	0.489	0.685	0.359	0.560	0.375	0.534
CAE	0.024	0.045	0.549	0.726	0.091	0.168	0.404	0.547
VAE	0.325	0.458	0.490	0.594	0.312	0.497	0.373	0.511
KSAE	0.457	0.660	0.605	0.766	0.449	**0.594**	**0.471**	**0.614**
KATE	0.539	0.716	0.615	0.767	0.445	0.580	0.446	0.580

Table 6: Comparison of MLC F1 score on Reuters RCV1-v2 and Wiki10+ datasets.

Model	MRD	
	128	512
LDA	0.287	0.226
DBN	0.277	0.369
DocNADE	0.404	0.424
NVDM	0.199	0.191
Word2Vec_{pre}	0.409	0.409
Word2Vec	0.143	0.136
Doc2Vec	0.052	0.032
AE	-0.001	0.203
DAE	0.067	0.100
CAE	0.018	0.118
VAE	0.111	0.355
KSAE	0.152	0.365
KATE	**0.463**	**0.516**

Table 7: Comparison of regression r^2 score on MRD dataset.

4.4.5 Timing. Finally, we compare the training time of various models. Results are shown in Table 8 for the 20 Newsgroups dataset, with 20 topics. Our model is much faster than deep generative models like DBN and DocNADE. It is typically slower than other autoencoders since it usually takes more epochs to converge. Nevertheless, as demonstrated above, it significantly outperforms other models in various text analytics tasks.

4.5 KATE: Effects of Parameter Tuning

Having demonstrated the effectiveness of KATE compared to other methods, we study the effects of various hyperparameter choices in KATE, such as the number of topics (i.e., hidden neurons), the number of winners k and the energy amplification parameter α. The default values for the number of topics is 128, with $k = 32$ and $\alpha = 6.26$. Note when exploring the effect of the number of topics, we also vary k to find its best match to the given number of topics. Figure 5 shows the classification accuracy on the 20 Newsgroups dataset, as we vary these parameters. We observe that as we increase the number of topics or hidden neurons (in Figure 5a), the accuracy continues to rise, but eventually drops off. We use 128 as the default value since it offers the best trade-off in complexity and performance; only relatively minor gains are achieved in increasing the number of topics beyond 128. Considering the number of winning neurons (see Figure 5b), the main trend is that the performance degrades when we make k larger, which is expected since larger k implies lesser competition. In practice, when tuning k, we find that starting by a value close to around a quarter of the number of topics is a good strategy. Finally, as we mentioned, the α amplification connection is crucial as verified in Figure 5c. When $\alpha = 2/k = 0.0625$, which means there is no amplification for the energy, the classification accuracy is 71.1%. However, we are able to significantly boost the model performance up to 74.6% accuracy by increasing the value of α. We use a default value of $\alpha = 6.26$, which once again reflects a good trade-off across different datasets. It is also important to note that across all the experiments, we found that using the *tanh* activation function (instead of *sigmoid* function) in the k-competitive layer of KATE gave the best performance. For example, on the 20 Newsgroups data, using 128 topics, KATE with *tanh* yields 74.4% accuracy, while with *sigmoid* it was only 56.8%.

5 CONCLUSIONS

We described a novel k-competitive autoencoder, KATE, that explicitly enforces competition among the neurons in the hidden layer by selecting the k highest activation neurons as winners, and reallocates the amplified energy (aggregate activation potential) from the losers. Interestingly, even though we use a shallow model, i.e., with one hidden layer, it outperforms a variety of methods on many different text analytics tasks. More specifically, we perform a comprehensive evaluation of KATE against techniques spanning graphical models (e.g., LDA), belief networks (e.g., DBN), word embedding models (e.g., Word2Vec), and several other autoencoders including the k-sparse autoencoder (KSAE). We find that across tasks such as document classification, multi-label classification, regression and document retrieval, KATE clearly outperforms competing methods or obtains close to the best results. It is very encouraging to note that KATE is also able to learn semantically meaningful representations of words, documents and topics, which we evaluated via both quantitative and qualitative studies. As part of future work, we plan to evaluate KATE on more domain specific datasets, such as bibliographic networks, for example for topic induction and scientific publication retrieval. We also plan to improve the scalability

Model	LDA	DBN	DocNADE	NVDM	Word2Vec	Doc2Vec	AE	DAE	CAE	VAE	KSAE	KATE
Time (s)	399	15,281	4,787	645	977	992	566	361	729	660	489	1,214

Table 8: Training time of various models (in seconds).

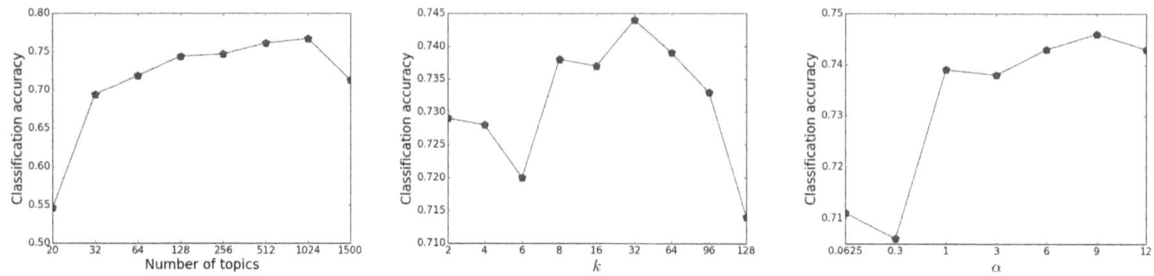

(a) Effect of number of topics **(b) Effect of k** **(c) Effect of α**

Figure 5: Effects of hyper-parameters.

and effectiveness of our approach on much larger text collections by developing parallel and distributed implementations.

ACKNOWLEDGMENTS

This work was supported in part by NSF awards IIS-1302231 and IIS-1738895.

REFERENCES

[1] David M Blei, Thomas L Griffiths, and Michael I Jordan. 2010. The nested chinese restaurant process and bayesian nonparametric inference of topic hierarchies. *Journal of the ACM (JACM)* 57, 2 (2010), 7.
[2] David M Blei, Andrew Y Ng, and Michael I Jordan. 2003. Latent dirichlet allocation. *Journal of Machine Learning Research* 3, Jan (2003), 993–1022.
[3] Phil Blunsom, Edward Grefenstette, and Nal Kalchbrenner. 2014. A convolutional neural network for modelling sentences. In *ACL Meeting*.
[4] Kevin Robert Canini, Lei Shi, and Thomas L Griffiths. 2009. Online Inference of Topics with Latent Dirichlet Allocation.. In *AISTATS*, Vol. 9. 65–72.
[5] Ziqiang Cao, Sujian Li, Yang Liu, Wenjie Li, and Heng Ji. 2015. A Novel Neural Topic Model and Its Supervised Extension.. In *AAAI*. 2210–2216.
[6] Rajarshi Das, Manzil Zaheer, and Chris Dyer. 2015. Gaussian lda for topic models with word embeddings. In *ACL Meeting*. 795–804.
[7] Scott Deerwester, Susan T Dumais, George W Furnas, Thomas K Landauer, and Richard Harshman. 1990. Indexing by latent semantic analysis. *Journal of the American Society for Information Science* 41, 6 (1990), 391.
[8] Jacob Eisenstein, Amr Ahmed, and Eric P Xing. 2011. Sparse additive generative models of text. In *ICML*.
[9] Geoffrey E Hinton, Simon Osindero, and Yee-Whye Teh. 2006. A fast learning algorithm for deep belief nets. *Neural Computation* 18, 7 (2006), 1527–1554.
[10] Geoffrey E Hinton and Ruslan R Salakhutdinov. 2006. Reducing the dimensionality of data with neural networks. *Science* 313, 5786 (2006), 504–507.
[11] Geoffrey E Hinton and Ruslan R Salakhutdinov. 2009. Replicated softmax: an undirected topic model. In *NIPS*. 1607–1614.
[12] Thomas Hofmann. 1999. Probabilistic latent semantic analysis. In *UAI Conf.* 289–296.
[13] Yoon Kim. 2014. Convolutional neural networks for sentence classification. In *EMNLP*.
[14] Diederik P Kingma and Max Welling. 2014. Auto-encoding variational bayes. In *ICLR*.
[15] Alex Krizhevsky. 2009. The CIFAR-10 dataset. www.cs.toronto.edu/~kriz/cifar.html. (2009).
[16] Girish Kumar and Luis F. D'Haro. 2015. Deep Autoencoder Topic Model for Short Texts. In *International Workshop on Embeddings and Semantics*.
[17] Ken Lang. 1995. Newsweeder: Learning to filter netnews. In *ICML*. 331–339.
[18] Hugo Larochelle and Stanislas Lauly. 2012. A neural autoregressive topic model. In *NIPS*. 2708–2716.
[19] Quoc V Le and Tomas Mikolov. 2014. Distributed Representations of Sentences and Documents.. In *ICML*, Vol. 14. 1188–1196.
[20] Yann LeCun, Léon Bottou, Yoshua Bengio, and Patrick Haffner. 1998. Gradient-based learning applied to document recognition. *Proc. IEEE* 86, 11 (1998), 2278–2324.
[21] David D Lewis, Yiming Yang, Tony G Rose, and Fan Li. 2004. Rcv1: A new benchmark collection for text categorization research. *Journal of Machine Learning Research* 5, Apr (2004), 361–397.
[22] Lars Maaloe, Morten Arngren, and Ole Winther. 2014. Deep belief nets for topic modeling. In *Workshop on Knowledge-Powered Deep Learning for Text Mining*.
[23] Laurens van der Maaten and Geoffrey Hinton. 2008. Visualizing data using t-SNE. *Journal of Machine Learning Research* 9, Nov (2008), 2579–2605.
[24] Alireza Makhzani and Brendan Frey. 2014. k-Sparse Autoencoders. In *ICLR*.
[25] Alireza Makhzani and Brendan J Frey. 2015. Winner-take-all autoencoders. In *NIPS*. 2791–2799.
[26] Alireza Makhzani, Jonathon Shlens, Navdeep Jaitly, and Ian Goodfellow. 2016. Adversarial autoencoders. In *ICLR*.
[27] Yishu Miao, Lei Yu, and Phil Blunsom. 2016. Neural Variational Inference for Text Processing. In *ICML*.
[28] Tomas Mikolov, Ilya Sutskever, Kai Chen, Greg S Corrado, and Jeff Dean. 2013. Distributed representations of words and phrases and their compositionality. In *NIPS*. 3111–3119.
[29] Dat Quoc Nguyen, Richard Billingsley, Lan Du, and Mark Johnson. 2015. Improving Topic Models with Latent Feature Word Representations. *Transactions of the Association for Computational Linguistics* 3 (2015), 299–313.
[30] Bo Pang and Lillian Lee. 2004. A sentimental education: Sentiment analysis using subjectivity summarization based on minimum cuts. In *ACL Meeting*. 271.
[31] Bo Pang and Lillian Lee. 2005. Seeing stars: Exploiting class relationships for sentiment categorization with respect to rating scales. In *ACL Meeting*. 115–124.
[32] Bo Pang, Lillian Lee, and Shivakumar Vaithyanathan. 2002. Thumbs up?: sentiment classification using machine learning techniques. In *EMNLP*. 79–86.
[33] Jeffrey Pennington, Richard Socher, and Christopher D Manning. 2014. Glove: Global Vectors for Word Representation.. In *EMNLP*, Vol. 14. 1532–1543.
[34] Radim Řehůřek and Petr Sojka. 2010. Software Framework for Topic Modelling with Large Corpora. In *LREC 2010 Workshop on New Challenges for NLP Frameworks*. 45–50.
[35] Salah Rifai, Pascal Vincent, Xavier Muller, Xavier Glorot, and Yoshua Bengio. 2011. Contractive auto-encoders: Explicit invariance during feature extraction. In *ICML*. 833–840.
[36] Nitish Srivastava, Ruslan R Salakhutdinov, and Geoffrey E Hinton. 2013. Modeling documents with deep boltzmann machines. In *UAI Conf.*
[37] Yee Whye Teh, Michael I Jordan, Matthew J Beal, and David M Blei. 2006. Hierarchical dirichlet processes. *J. Amer. Statist. Assoc.* 101, 476 (2006), 1566–1581.
[38] Yee W Teh, Kenichi Kurihara, and Max Welling. 2007. Collapsed variational inference for HDP. In *NIPS*. 1481–1488.
[39] Pascal Vincent, Hugo Larochelle, Isabelle Lajoie, Yoshua Bengio, and Pierre-Antoine Manzagol. 2010. Stacked denoising autoencoders: Learning useful representations in a deep network with a local denoising criterion. *Journal of Machine Learning Research* 11, Dec (2010), 3371–3408.
[40] Chong Wang and David M Blei. 2009. Decoupling sparsity and smoothness in the discrete hierarchical dirichlet process. In *NIPS*. 1982–1989.
[41] Matthew D Zeiler. 2012. ADADELTA: an adaptive learning rate method. *arXiv* 1212.5701 (2012).
[42] Shuangfei Zhai and Zhongfei Zhang. 2016. Semisupervised Autoencoder for Sentiment Analysis. In *AAAI*.
[43] Jun Zhu and Eric P Xing. 2011. Sparse topical coding. In *UAI Conf.*
[44] Arkaitz Zubiaga. 2009. Enhancing Navigation on Wikipedia with Social Tags. In *5th International Conference of the Wikimedia Community*.

A Minimal Variance Estimator for the Cardinality of Big Data Set Intersection

Reuven Cohen
Department of Computer Science
Technion
Haifa 32000, Israel
rcohen@cs.technion.ac.il

Liran Katzir
Department of Computer Science
Technion
Haifa 32000, Israel

Aviv Yehezkel
Department of Computer Science
Technion
Haifa 32000, Israel
avivy@cs.technion.ac.il

ABSTRACT

In recent years there has been a growing interest in developing "streaming algorithms" for efficient processing and querying of continuous data streams. These algorithms seek to provide accurate results while minimizing the required storage and the processing time, at the price of a small inaccuracy in their output. A fundamental query of interest is the intersection size of two big data streams. This problem arises in many different application areas, such as network monitoring, database systems, data integration and information retrieval. In this paper we develop a new algorithm for this problem, based on the Maximum Likelihood (ML) method. We show that this algorithm outperforms all known schemes in terms of the estimation's quality (lower variance) and that it asymptotically achieves the optimal variance.

CCS CONCEPTS

• **Information systems** →**Data stream mining;**

KEYWORDS

Data mining; Streaming algorithms; Cardinality estimation; Set intersection

ACM Reference format:

Reuven Cohen, Liran Katzir, and Aviv Yehezkel. 2017. A Minimal Variance Estimator for the Cardinality of Big Data Set Intersection. In *Proceedings of KDD'17, August 13–17, 2017, Halifax, NS, Canada.*, , 9 pages.
DOI: http://dx.doi.org/10.1145/3097983.3097999

1 INTRODUCTION

Classical processing algorithms for database management systems usually require several passes over (static) data sets in order to produce an accurate answer to a user query. However, for a wide range of application domains, the data set is very large and is updated on a continuous basis, making this approach impractical. For this reason, there is a growing interest in developing "streaming algorithms" for efficient processing and querying of continuous data streams in data stream management systems (DSMSs). These algorithms seek to provide accurate results while minimizing both the required storage and the processing time per stream element, at the price of a small inaccuracy in their output [2, 7, 11, 20]. Streaming algorithms for DSMSs typically summarize the data stream using a small sketch, and use probabilistic techniques in order to provide approximate answers to user queries. Such big data streams appear in a wide variety of computer science applications. They are common, for example, in computer networks, where detailed usage statistics (such as the source IP addresses of packets) from different parts of the network need to be continuously collected and analyzed for various security and management tasks.

A fundamental query of interest is the intersection size of two big data streams. Consider two streams of elements, $\overline{A}$ and $\overline{B}$, taken from two sets A and B respectively. Suppose that each element may appear more than once in each stream. Let $n = |\overline{A} \cap \overline{B}|$. For example, for $\overline{A} = a, b, c, d, a, b$ and $\overline{B} = a, a, c, c$, we get that $n = 2$ is the cardinality of $A \cap B$. Finding n is a problem that arises in many different application areas such as network monitoring, database systems, data integration and information retrieval [4, 5].

One can find the exact value of n by computing the intersection set C in the following way. For every element $b_i \in B$, compare b_i to every $a_j \in A$ and $c_k \in C$. If $b_i \notin C$ and $b_i \in A$, add b_i to C. After all the elements are treated, return the number of elements in C. This naive approach does not scale if storage is limited or if the sets are very large. In these cases, the following estimation problem should be solved. Given two streams of elements (with repetitions) $\overline{A} = a_1, a_2, \ldots, a_p$, and $\overline{B} = b_1, b_2, \ldots, b_q$, such that A and B are the respective sets of the two streams, and $n = |A \cap B|$, find an estimate $\widehat{n}$ of n using only m storage units, where $m \ll n$.

The cardinality $|A \cap B|$ can be estimated in a straightforward manner using the inclusion-exclusion principle: $\widehat{|A \cap B|} = \widehat{|A|} + \widehat{|B|} - \widehat{|A \cup B|}$, taking advantage of the fact that estimating $|A|$, $|B|$ and $|A \cup B|$ with good accuracy (small variance) is easy. However, we will later show that this scheme produces inaccurate results. In [2], it is proposed to estimate the Jaccard similarity, defined as $\rho(A, B) = \frac{|A \cap B|}{|A \cup B|}$. The idea is to estimate $|A \cup B|$, and then to extract $|A \cap B|$.

KDD'17, August 13–17, 2017, Halifax, NS, Canada.
© 2017 ACM. 978-1-4503-4887-4/17/08...$15.00
DOI: http://dx.doi.org/10.1145/3097983.3097999

A third scheme, proposed in [11], suggests that $|\widehat{A \cap B}| = \frac{\widehat{\rho(A,B)}}{\rho(A,B)+1}(|\widehat{A}| + |\widehat{B}|)$. With respect to the above three estimation schemes, the main contributions of this paper are as follows:

(1) **We present and analyze a new unbiased estimator, based on the Maximum Likelihood (ML) method, which outperforms the above three schemes by having a lower variance.**
(2) **The new estimator has the optimal (minimum) variance of any unbiased set intersection estimator. We present an analysis of this variance.**

There are several previous works on set intersection estimators (e.g., [2, 11, 24]), but none is based on the Maximum Likelihood (ML) estimator, which asymptotically achieves the optimal (lower bound) variance. The most relevant attempt is a very recent work [24], which describes a "pseudo-likelihood based method". This method is claimed by the authors to be asymptotically equivalent to a maximum likelihood estimator. In this paper, we derive, for the first time, the complete maximum likelihood estimator and provide a full proof.

The rest of the paper is organized as follows. Section 2 provides the motivation for this work and discusses a wide variety of applications for which accurate estimation of set intersection cardinality is required. Section 3 discusses previous work and presents the three previously known schemes. Section 4 presents our new Maximum Likelihood (ML) estimator. It also shows that the new scheme achieves optimal variance and that it outperforms the three known schemes. Section 5 presents simulation results confirming that the new ML estimator outperforms the three known schemes. Section 6 presents analysis results of the three previous schemes. Finally, Section 7 concludes the paper.

2 MOTIVATION AND APPLICATIONS

Many real world problems from different disciplines require estimation of the cardinality of set intersection. In this section we describe some of them.

Relational database management systems have achieved great success in the past forty years. One of the main reasons is that each system uses declarative query languages, such as SQL, which allow to describe a query without specifying how it should be executed. This abstraction has greatly benefited users and developers, who no longer need to understand how the data is actually stored and manipulated by these languages. At the same time, declarative query languages allow great flexibility in choosing different plans for a given query. A plan is a tree-like structure that encodes query sub-parts. Each node indicates some operator, such as scan, sort, or join. In order to produce efficient, low-cost, execution plans, every database system contains a query optimizer that can estimate the cost of each plan.

Query optimizers usually define the cost of a query according to its predicted CPU and I/O overhead. To estimate these quantities, an optimizer needs to estimate the input/output cardinalities of each operator in the plan. For example, in join and conjunctive queries, the order in which intersections are processed by the database system significantly affects the performance, and the optimizer needs to know the number of distinct tuples in each intersection in order to choose the best strategy. Thus, the query optimizer needs to accurately estimate set intersection cardinalities. In addition, by estimating the set intersection cardinality between all involved tables, the optimizer can estimate the size of the join/conjunction outcome.

Another discipline where estimating the set intersection cardinality is important is network management and security [14, 15, 20]. For example, web administrators would like to measure the increase in popularity of their sites, e.g., to estimate the number of users who accessed the web server during the last 24 hours, but not during the previous week. This can be translated into the problem of estimating the cardinality of $|V_t \setminus V_w| = |V_t| - |V_t \cap V_w|$, where V_t is the stream of users (e.g., their source IP addresses) who visited the site today, and V_w is the stream of users who visited the site during the previous week.

Estimating the set intersection cardinality also allows real-time detection of network and security anomalies. As an example, consider a network where packets are received from a router. Let R be the set of IP flows that enter the network through the router. We hereby describe two important monitoring applications:

(a) Suppose that all incoming flows must pass through a firewall. To verify this, one needs to verify that the set $R \cap F$ is equal to F, where F is the set of flows that traverse the firewall. This can be translated into the problem of estimating $|R \cap F|$ and verifying that it is "close enough" to $|F|$.
(b) Internet policy enforcement: The Internet is composed of many Autonomous Systems (AS). Two neighboring ASs can have a peering or a customer-provider relationship. The relationship determines which packets can be forwarded from one to the other. For example, an AS is not allowed to forward a packet to a peer AS if the ultimate destination of the packet is a client of the first AS. By estimating set intersection cardinality between the stream of packets received from each neighboring AS, an AS can discover routing violations and anomalies.

Our last application example is finding textually similar documents in a large corpus such as the web or a collection of news articles. In this case, $a_i \in A$ and $b_j \in B$ could be sets of sub-strings found within two text documents. Then, $|A \cap B|$ represents the number of sub-strings shared by both documents, and $\frac{|A \cap B|}{|A \cup B|}$ can be used as a "similarity index". Among many applications, this allows plagiarism detection and pruning of near-duplicate search results in search engines.

3 RELATED WORK AND PREVIOUS SCHEMES

The database research community has extensively explored the problem of data cleaning: detecting and removing errors and inconsistencies from data to improve the quality of databases [22]. Identifying which fields share similar values, identifying join paths, estimating join directions and sizes, and detecting inclusion dependencies are well-studied aspects of this problem [1, 8, 11, 17, 21]. For example, in [11] the authors present several methods for finding related database fields. Their main idea is to hash the values of each field and keep a small sketch that contains the minimal hash values for each. Then, the Jaccard similarity is used to measure similarities between fields. In [1], the authors study the related problem of detecting inclusion dependencies, i.e., pairs of fields A and B such that $A \subseteq B$, and they present an efficient way to test all field pairs in parallel.

3.1 The Cardinality Estimation Problem

Algorithms for estimating the cardinality of set intersection use estimations of $|A|$, $|B|$, and $|A \cup B|$. These estimations can be found using well-known algorithms for the following cardinality estimation problem:

Instance: A stream of elements $x_1, x_2, \ldots, x_s$ with repetitions. Let c be the number of different elements, namely $c = |\{x_1, x_2, \ldots, x_s\}|$.

Objective: Find an estimate $\widehat{c}$ of c using only m storage units, where $m \ll c$.

This problem has received a great deal of attention in the past decade thanks to the growing number of important real-time "big data" applications, such as estimating the propagation rate of viruses, detecting DDoS attacks [14, 15], and measuring general properties of network traffic [20].

Many works address the cardinality estimation problem [7, 9, 12, 16, 19, 20] and propose statistical algorithms for solving it. These algorithms are usually limited to performing only one pass on the received packets and using a fixed small amount of memory. A common approach is to hash every element into a low-dimensional data sketch, which can be viewed as a uniformly distributed random variable. Then, one of the following schemes is often used to estimate the number of distinct elements in the set:

(1) Order-statistics based estimators: In this family of schemes, the identities of the smallest (or largest) k elements are remembered for the considered set. These values are then used for estimating the total number of distinct elements [2, 9, 16, 19]. The family of estimators with $k = 1$ (where the minimal/maximal identity is remembered) is also known as min/max sketches.

(2) Bit-pattern based estimators: In this family of schemes, the highest position of the leftmost 1-bit in the binary representation of the identity of each element is remembered and then used for the estimation [7, 12].

If only one hash function is used, the schemes estimate the value of n with an infinite variance. To bound the variance, both schemes repeat the above procedures for m different hash functions and use their combined statistics for the estimation[1].

A comprehensive overview of different cardinality estimation techniques is given in [7, 20]. State-of-the art cardinality estimators have a standard error of about $1/\sqrt{m}$, where m is the number of storage units [6]. The best known cardinality estimator is the HyperLogLog algorithm [12], which belongs to the family of min/max sketches and has a standard error of $1.04/\sqrt{m}$, [12]. For instance, this algorithm estimates the cardinality of a set with 10^9 elements with a standard error of 2% using $m = 2,048$ storage units.

For the rest of the paper we consider the HyperLogLog algorithm [12] for solving the cardinality estimation problem. The estimator uses $O(1)$ operations per element, and is very efficient because it maintains the m sketches using only two hash functions, h_1 and h_2. The first function is used for hashing each element into a uniformly distributed variable (the element's sketch), and the second for splitting each element into one of m buckets. These m buckets replace the need for m different hash functions. In addition, in order to increase computation speed, the estimator does not keep the value of the maximal sketch for each bucket, but rather only the highest position of the leftmost 1-bit of each sketch i.e., the largest $i \geq 0$ such that the $i - 1$ leftmost bits are all 0.

3.2 Previous Schemes

Cardinality estimation algorithms can be used for estimating the cardinality of set intersection. As mentioned in Section 1, a straightforward technique is to estimate the intersection using the following inclusion-exclusion principle:

$$\widehat{|A \cap B|} = \widehat{|A|} + \widehat{|B|} - \widehat{|A \cup B|}.$$

This method will be referred to as Scheme-1. Other set intersection estimators first estimate the Jaccard similarity $\rho(A, B) = \frac{|A \cap B|}{|A \cup B|}$. The value of ρ ranges between 0, when the two sets are completely different, and 1, when the sets are identical.

An efficient and accurate estimate of ρ can be computed as follows [3]. Each item in A and B is hashed into $(0, 1)$, and the maximal value of each set is considered as a sketch that represents the whole set. To improve accuracy, m hash functions are used, and the sketch of each set is a vector of m maximal values. Given a set $A = \{a_1, a_2, \ldots, a_p\}$ and m different hash functions $h_1, h_2, \ldots, h_m$, the maximal hash value for the jth hash function can be formally expressed as:

$$x_A^j = \max_{i=1}^{p} \{h_j(a_i)\} \quad , \quad 1 \leq j \leq m,$$

and the sketch of A is:

$$X_{(A)} = \left\{x_A^1, x_A^2, \ldots, x_A^m\right\}.$$

[1] Stochastic averaging can be used to reduce the number of hash functions from m to only two [13].

$X_{(B)}$ is computed in the same way. Then, the two sketches are used to estimate the Jaccard similarity of A and B:

$$\widehat{\rho(A,B)} = \frac{\sum_{j=1}^{m} I_{x_A^j == x_B^j}}{m}, \quad (1)$$

where the indicator function $I_{x_A^j == x_B^j}$ is 1 if $x_A^j = x_B^j$, and 0 otherwise. To shorten our notation, for the rest of the paper we use ρ to indicate $\rho(A,B)$.

After estimating the Jaccard similarity, previous works use some algebraic manipulation on it in order to estimate the set intersection cardinality [2, 11]. Specifically, the scheme proposed in [2] estimates both the Jaccard similarity and $|A \cup B|$, and then uses

$$\widehat{|A \cap B|} = \widehat{\rho(A,B)} \cdot \widehat{|A \cup B|}.$$

This scheme will be referred to as Scheme-2. The third scheme discussed in this paper, referred to as Scheme-3, is presented in [11]. It estimates the Jaccard similarity, $|A|$, and $|B|$, and then uses

$$\widehat{|A \cap B|} = \frac{\widehat{\rho(A,B)}}{\rho(A,B)+1}(\widehat{|A|} + \widehat{|B|}).$$

The above equation is obtained by substituting the Jaccard similarity definition into $\frac{\rho(A,B)}{\rho(A,B)+1}$, which yields that

$$\frac{\rho(A,B)}{\rho(A,B)+1} = \frac{|A \cap B|}{|A \cap B| + |A \cup B|} = \frac{|A \cap B|}{|A| + |B|}.$$

In [1, 18], the set intersection estimation problem is solved using smaller sample sets. While these techniques are simple and unbiased, they are inaccurate for small sets. In addition, they are sensitive to the arrival order of the data, and to the repetition pattern.

Recent work [24] provides a "pseudo-likelihood based method" for estimating the set intersection cardinality. The method is claimed by the authors to be asymptotically equivalent to a maximum likelihood estimator, but there is no proof for this claim. In this paper, we derive the complete maximum likelihood estimator and provide a full proof.

4 A NEW MAXIMUM LIKELIHOOD SCHEME WITH OPTIMAL VARIANCE

In this section we present a new unbiased estimator for the set intersection estimation problem. Because this estimator is based on the Maximum Likelihood (ML) method, it achieves optimal variance and outperforms the three known schemes.

Maximum-Likelihood estimation (ML) is a method for estimating the parameters of a statistical model. For example, suppose we are interested in the height distribution of a given population, but are unable to measure the height of every single person. Assuming that the heights are Gaussian distributed with some unknown mean and variance, the mean and variance can be estimated using ML and only a small sample of the overall population. In general, for a given set of data samples and an underlying statistical model, ML finds the values of the model parameters that maximize the likelihood function, namely, the "agreement" of the selected model with the given sample.

In the new scheme, we first find the (probability density) likelihood function of the set intersection estimation problem, $L(x_A = s, x_B = t; \theta)$; namely, given $\theta = (a, b, n)$ as the problem parameters[2], this is the probability density of s to be the maximal hash value for A and t to be the maximal hash value for B. Then, we look for values of the problem parameters that maximize the likelihood function.

Table 1 shows some of the notations we use for the rest of the paper.

notation	value
n	$\lvert A \cap B\rvert$
u	$\lvert A \cup B\rvert$
a	$\lvert A\rvert$
b	$\lvert B\rvert$
α	$\lvert A \setminus B\rvert$
β	$\lvert B \setminus A\rvert$

Table 1: Notations

4.1 The Likelihood Function of the Set Intersection Estimation Problem

We first find the likelihood function for one hash function h_k, namely, $L(x_A = s, x_B = t; \theta)_k$, and then generalize it for all hash functions. Recall that for the kth hash function, $x_A^k = \max_{i=1}^{a}\{h_k(a_i)\}$ and $x_B^k = \max_{j=1}^{b}\{h_k(b_j)\}$. To simplify the notation, we shall omit the superscript k for x_A^k and x_B^k, and use x_A and x_B respectively.

We use $\text{PDF}_U(w)$ to denote the probability density function (PDF) of a uniformly distributed random variable U(0, 1) at w. Denote the elements in $A \cap B$ as $\{z_1, z_2, \ldots, z_n\}$. Thus, the elements in A and the elements in B can be written as $\{x_1, x_2, \ldots, x_\alpha, z_1, z_2, \ldots, z_n\}$ and $\{y_1, y_2, \ldots, y_\beta, z_1, z_2, \ldots, z_n\}$ respectively (see Table 1).

We now divide the likelihood function according to the three possible relations between x_A and x_B: $x_A = x_B$, $x_A > x_B$ and $x_A < x_B$.

Case 1: $x_A = x_B$

When $x_A = x_B = s$ holds, the element with the maximal hash value must belong to $A \cap B$. The likelihood function of θ given this outcome is

$$L(x_A = x_B = s; \theta) = \sum_{i=1}^{n} \text{PDF}_U(s) \cdot \Pr\left(x_{(A \cup B)\setminus\{z_i\}} < s\right) = \sum_{i=1}^{n} s^{u-1} = n \cdot s^{u-1}. \quad (2)$$

[2]The set intersection estimation problem has six identifying parameters $(n, u, a, b, \alpha, \beta)$, only three of which are needed to derive the others.

This equality holds because there are n possible elements in $A \cap B$ whose hash value can be the maximum in $A \cup B$, and because $\text{PDF}_U(s) = 1$.

Case 2: $x_A < x_B$

In order to have $x_A < x_B$, where $x_A = s$ and $x_B = t$, the maximal hash value in B must also be in $B \setminus A$, and its value must be t. The likelihood function of θ in this case is

$$L(x_{B\setminus A} = t; \theta) = \sum_{j=1}^{\beta} \text{PDF}_U(t) \cdot \Pr\left(x_{(B\setminus A)\setminus\{y_j\}} < t\right) = \beta \cdot t^{\beta-1}.$$

In addition, the maximal hash value in A must be s. The probability density for this is

$$L(x_A = s; \theta) = \sum_{e \in A} \text{PDF}_U(s) \cdot \Pr\left(x_{A\setminus\{e\}} < s\right) = as^{a-1}.$$

Thus,

$$L(x_A < x_B, x_A = s, x_B = t; \theta) = as^{a-1} \cdot \beta t^{\beta-1}. \quad (3)$$

Case 3: $x_A > x_B$

This case is symmetrical to the previous case. Thus, the likelihood function of θ in this case is

$$L(x_A > x_B, x_A = s, x_B = t; \theta) = \alpha s^{\alpha-1} b t^{b-1}.$$

Thus, the likelihood function for set intersection is

$$L(x_A = s, x_B = t; \theta)_k = \begin{cases} ns^{u-1} & x_A = x_B \\ \beta t^{\beta-1} a s^{a-1} & x_A < x_B \\ \alpha s^{\alpha-1} b t^{b-1} & x_A > x_B \end{cases}.$$

We now use the following indicator variables:

(1) $I_1 = 1$ if $x_A = x_B$, and $I_1 = 0$ otherwise,
(2) $I_2 = 1$ if $x_A < x_B$, and $I_2 = 0$ otherwise,
(3) $I_3 = 1$ if $x_A > x_B$, and $I_3 = 0$ otherwise,

to obtain that

$$L(x_A = s, x_B = t; \theta)_k = (ns^{u-1})^{I_1} \cdot (\beta t^{\beta-1} a s^{a-1})^{I_2} \cdot (\alpha s^{\alpha-1} b t^{b-1})^{I_3}. \quad (4)$$

Eq. (4) states the likelihood function for one hash function. To generalize this equation to all m hash functions, denote $S = (s_1, s_2, \ldots, s_m)$ and $T = (t_1, t_2, \ldots, t_m)$ as the m-dimensional vectors of s and t for each hash function.

COROLLARY 4.1.
The likelihood function for the set intersection estimation problem, for all m hash functions, satisfies:

$$L(x_A = S, x_B = T; \theta) = \prod_{k=1}^{m} \Big((n(s_k)^{u-1})^{I_{1,k}} \cdot (\beta(t_k)^{\beta-1} a(s_k)^{a-1})^{I_{2,k}} \cdot (\alpha(s_k)^{\alpha-1} b(t_k)^{b-1})^{I_{3,k}} \Big),$$

where $I_{1,k}$ is the value of I_1 for hash function k, and the same holds for $I_{2,k}$ and $I_{3,k}$. ■

It is usually easier to deal with the log of a likelihood function than with the likelihood function itself. Because the logarithm is a monotonically increasing function, its maximum value is obtained at the same point as the maximum of the function itself. In our case,

$$\begin{aligned}\log L(x_A = S, x_B = T; \theta) &= \log \prod_{k=1}^{m} L(x_A^k = s_k, x_B^k = t_k; \theta)_k \\ &= \sum_{k=1}^{m} \log L(x_A^k = s_k, x_B^k = t_k; \theta)_k \\ &= \sum_{k=1}^{m} I_{1,k} \cdot \log\left(n \cdot (s_k)^{u-1}\right) \\ &+ \sum_{k=1}^{m} I_{2,k} \cdot \log\left(\beta \cdot (t_k)^{\beta-1} \cdot a \cdot (s_k)^{a-1}\right) \\ &+ \sum_{k=1}^{m} I_{3,k} \cdot \log\left(\alpha \cdot (s_k)^{\alpha-1} \cdot b \cdot (t_k)^{b-1}\right). \end{aligned} \quad (5)$$

4.2 The New Scheme

We use Corollary 4.1 in order to find $\theta = (a, b, n)$ that maximizes Eq. (5). Note that there must be a single global optimum to Eq. (5) because this function is concave (sum of linear and logarithmic functions). Let $g(a, b, n)$ and $\mathbb{H}(a, b, n)$ be the gradient and the Hessian matrix of the log-likelihood function. Namely, g is the vector whose components are the partial derivatives of the log-likelihood function for the problem parameters $\theta = (a, b, n)$:

$$g(a, b, n) = \left(\frac{\partial \log L}{\partial a}, \frac{\partial \log L}{\partial b}, \frac{\partial \log L}{\partial n}\right), \quad (6)$$

and $\mathbb{H}$ is the matrix of the second-order partial derivatives of the log-likelihood function

$$\mathbb{H}_{i,j} = \frac{\partial^2}{\partial \theta_i \partial \theta_j} \log L \quad , 1 \le i, j \le 3, \quad (7)$$

where $\theta_1 = a$, $\theta_2 = b$ and $\theta_3 = n$.

The new scheme finds the maximum of the log-likelihood function, i.e., the root of its gradient $g(a, b, n)$. Practically, this is done using iterations of the Newton-Raphson method on the gradient and Hessian matrix g and H. Starting from an initial estimation $\widehat{\theta_0} = (\widehat{a_0}, \widehat{b_0}, \widehat{n_0})$, the Newton-Raphson method implies that a better estimation is $\widehat{\theta_1} = \widehat{\theta_0} - H^{-1}(\widehat{\theta_0}) \cdot g(\widehat{\theta_0})$. The process is repeated, namely,

$$\widehat{\theta_{l+1}} = \widehat{\theta_l} - H^{-1}(\widehat{\theta_l}) \cdot g(\widehat{\theta_l}), \quad (8)$$

until a sufficiently accurate estimation is reached. This idea is summarized in the following algorithm.

ALGORITHM 1.
(A Maximum Likelihood scheme for the set intersection estimation problem)
The scheme gets as an input the sketches of the sets $\{x_A^k\}_{k=1}^m$ and $\{x_B^k\}_{k=1}^m$, where x_A^k and x_B^k are the maximal hash values of A and B respectively for the kth hash function, and returns an estimate of their set intersection cardinality.

1) *Estimate* $a_0 = \widehat{a}$, $b_0 = \widehat{b}$ *and* $\widehat{u}$ *using any cardinality estimation algorithm, such as [12].*
2) *Estimate the Jaccard similarity* $\widehat{\rho}$ *from the given sketches of* A *and* B.
3) *Find the maximum of the likelihood function* L *(Eq. (5)) as explained above; use* $n_0 = \widehat{\rho} \cdot \widehat{u}$ *as an initial value of* n *(see Scheme-2 in Section 3), and* a_0, b_0 *as an initial values of* a *and* b *respectively.*
4) *Return* $\widehat{n}$.

When we implemented Algorithm 1, we discovered that 3 Newton-Raphson iterations are enough for the algorithm to converge. Each Newton-Raphson step requires only a simple inversion of a 3x3 matrix and thus incurs only negligible computational effort. However, instead of reaching full convergence, we can use one of the "previous schemes" (namely, Scheme-1, Scheme-2 or Scheme-3 from Section 3) as initial estimation, and then run only a single Newton-Raphson iteration to improve the result. **Therefore, while our new scheme performs significantly better than Scheme-1, Scheme-2, and Scheme-3 (has smaller variance), it does not require a longer running time.**

4.3 The Optimal Variance of the New Estimator

The new estimator proposed above is based on Maximum Likelihood and thus it asymptotically achieves optimal variance [23] with respect to min/max-sketch algorithms[3]. Note that all main previous works, and in particular the three schemes described in Section 3, are based upon min/max-sketches. We now use the Cramer-Rao bound to compute this optimal variance.

The Cramer-Rao bound states that the inverse of the Fisher information matrix is a lower bound on the variance of any unbiased estimator [23]. The Fisher information matrix $\mathbb{F}_{i,j}$ is a way of measuring the amount of information that a random variable X carries about an unknown parameter θ upon which the probability of X depends. It is defined as:

$$\mathbb{F}_{i,j} = -\mathbb{E}\left[\frac{\partial^2}{\partial\theta_i\partial\theta_j}\log L\right]. \qquad (9)$$

We now use the log-likelihood function (Eq. (5)) to derive this matrix for the set intersection estimation problem:

$$\mathbb{F}(a,b,n) = m \cdot \begin{pmatrix} \frac{\beta}{u}\cdot\frac{1}{a^2}+\frac{1}{u\cdot\alpha} & 0 & \frac{-1}{u\cdot\alpha} \\ 0 & \frac{\alpha}{u}\cdot\frac{1}{b^2}+\frac{1}{u\cdot\beta} & \frac{-1}{u\cdot\beta} \\ \frac{-1}{u\cdot\alpha} & \frac{-1}{u\cdot\beta} & \frac{1}{u\cdot n}+\frac{1}{u\cdot\beta}+\frac{1}{u\cdot\alpha} \end{pmatrix},$$

where each term is derived due to algebraic manipulations and derivatives of the log-likelihood function. Note that the expected values of the indicator variables $I_{1,k}, I_{2,k}$ and $I_{3,k}$ are required to derive the matrix. For $I_{1,k}$ we get:

$$\mathbb{E}[I_{1,k}] = \Pr\left(x_A^k = x_B^k\right) = \frac{n}{u} \quad , 1 \le k \le m.$$

[3]The optimality holds also with respect to bottom-k sketches, as they are statistically equivalent to min/max-sketches.

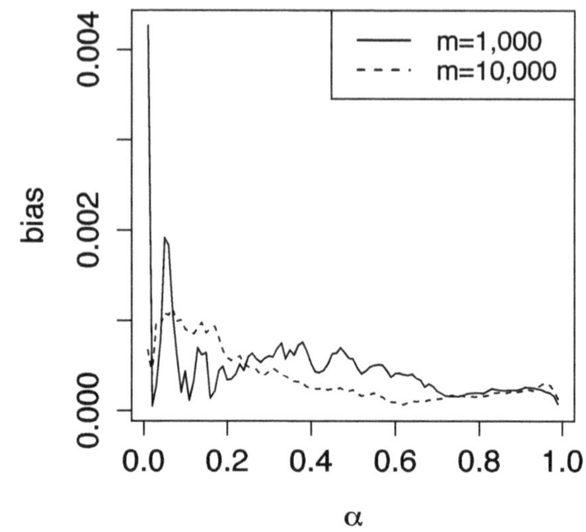

Figure 1: The bias of the new ML scheme for $f = 1$ and for different α values, for $m = 1,000$ and $m =$ 10,000

The first equality is due to the definition of $I_{1,k}$, and the second is due to [3]. The following are obtained in the same way for every $1 \le k \le m$:

(1) $\mathbb{E}[I_{2,k}] = \Pr\left(x_A^k < x_B^k\right) = \frac{\beta}{u}$.
(2) $\mathbb{E}[I_{3,k}] = \Pr\left(x_A^k > x_B^k\right) = \frac{\alpha}{u}$.

Let $\widehat{|A \cap B|}$ be an unbiased estimator for the set intersection estimation problem. Then, according to the Cramer-Rao bound, $\text{Var}\left[\widehat{|A \cap B|}\right] \ge (\mathbb{F}^{-1})_{3,3}$, where $(\mathbb{F}^{-1})_{3,3}$ is the term in place $[3,3]$ in the inverse Fisher information matrix. Finally, from the computation of the term $(\mathbb{F}^{-1})_{3,3}$, we can obtain the following corollary:

COROLLARY 4.2.
$\text{Var}\left[\widehat{|A \cap B|}\right] \ge (\mathbb{F}^{-1})_{3,3}$, *where,*

$$(\mathbb{F}^{-1})_{3,3} = \frac{n\cdot u}{m}\cdot\frac{(b^2+\alpha\beta)(a^2+\alpha\beta)}{\alpha\cdot n(a^2+\alpha\beta)+\beta\cdot n(b^2+\alpha\beta)+(a^2+\alpha\beta)(b^2+\alpha\beta)}.$$

5 SIMULATION STUDY

In this section we examine the performance of our new ML estimator and show that it indeed outperforms the three known schemes when using the same memory. We simulate different data sets and estimate set intersection cardinality using the new scheme as well as the three previous schemes. We then measure the improvement (in percentages) of the new scheme over each previous scheme.

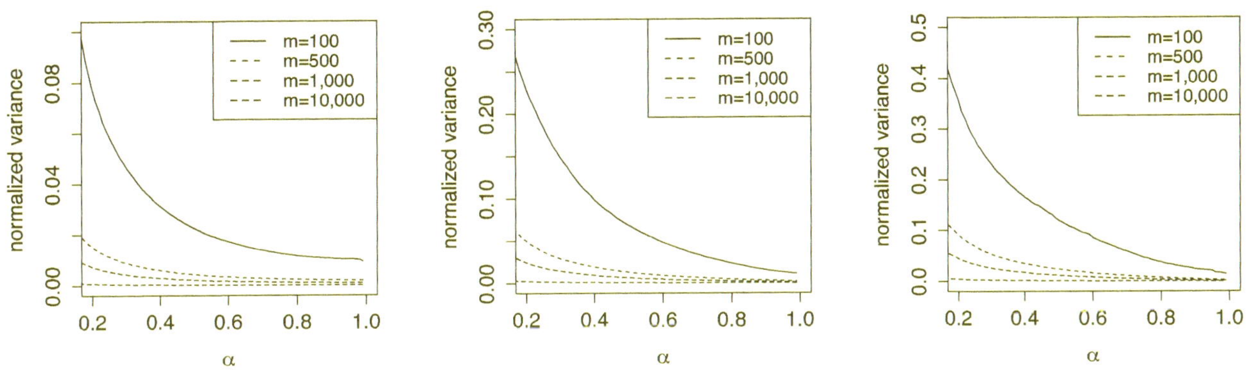

(a) $f = 1$ (b) $f = 5$ (c) $f = 10$

Figure 2: The normalized variance of the new ML scheme for different values of f, α and m

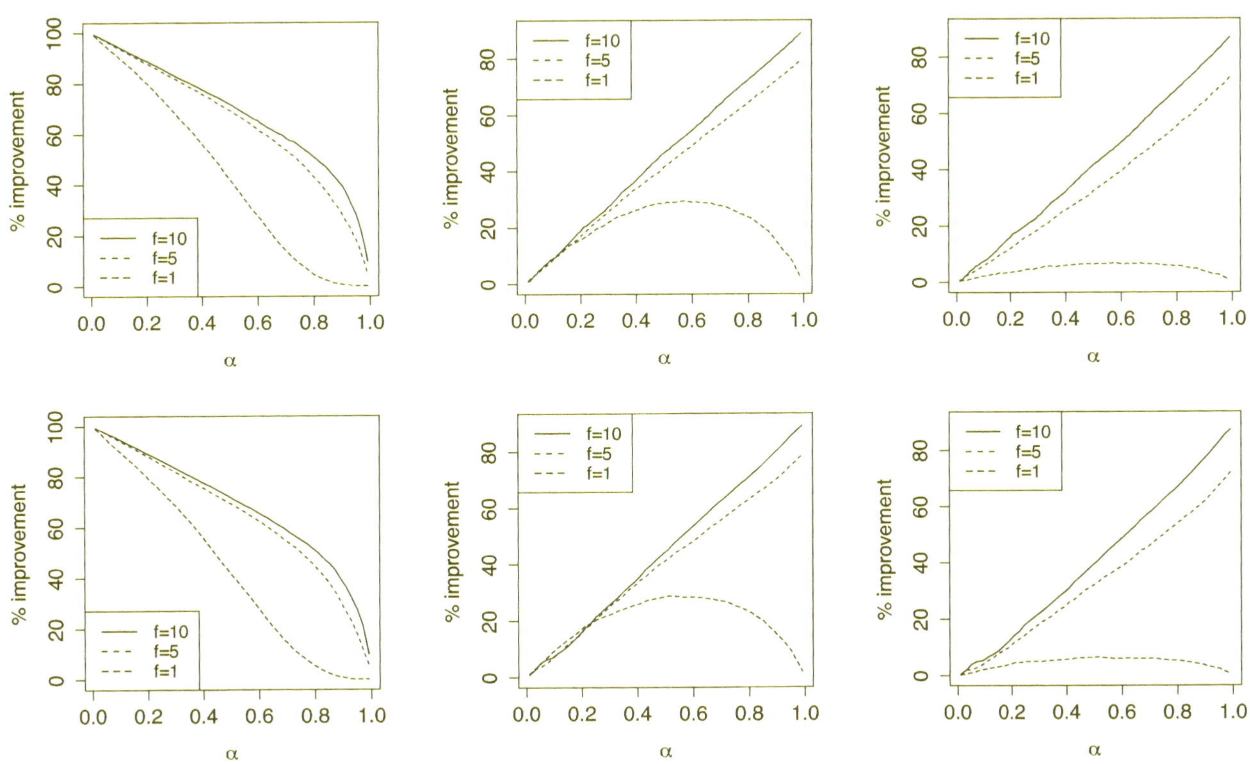

(a) Scheme-1 (b) Scheme-2 (c) Scheme-3

Figure 3: The percentage of variance improvement of the new ML scheme over each of the other schemes for different values of f and α; the upper graphs are for $m = 10,000$ and the lower graphs are for $m = 1,000$

In the simulation, we use the HyperLogLog algorithm [12] to estimate $|A|$, $|B|$ and $|A \cup B|$. We then estimate $\widehat{|A \cap B|}$ for each of the four schemes, for $f \in \{1, 5, 10\}$ and for $\alpha \in \{0, 0.01, 0.02, \ldots, 0.98, 0.99, 1\}$, where

(1) $|A| = a = 10^6$;
(2) $|B| = a \cdot f$, where $f > 0$;
(3) $|A \cap B| = a \cdot \alpha$, where $0 \leq \alpha \leq 1$.

We repeat the test for 10,000 different sets. Thus, for each of the four schemes, and for each f and α values, we get a vector of 10,000 different estimations. Then, for each f and α values, we compute the variance and bias of this vector, and view the result as the variance and bias of the estimator (for the specific f and α values). Each such computation is represented by one point in the graph. Let $v_{f,\alpha} = (\widehat{n_1}, \ldots, \widehat{n_{10^4}})$ be the vector of estimations for a specific scheme and for specific f and α values. Let $\mu = \frac{1}{10^4}\sum_{i=1}^{10^4} \widehat{n_i}$, be the mean of $v_{f,\alpha}$. The bias and variance of $v_{f,\alpha}$ are computed as follows:

$$\text{Bias}(v_{f,\alpha}) = \left|\frac{1}{n}(\mu - n)\right|$$

and

$$\text{Var}\left[v_{f,\alpha}\right] = \frac{1}{10^4}\sum_{i=1}^{10^4}(\widehat{n_i} - \mu)^2.$$

Figure 1 presents the bias of the ML estimator for $f = 1$, different α values, and two values of m: $m = 1,000$ and $m = 10,000$ (recall that m is the number of hash values used for the estimations of $\widehat{|A|}$, $\widehat{|B|}$ and the Jaccard similarity $\widehat{\rho}$). We can see that the bias is very small for all α and m values. We got very similar results for bigger f values as well.

Figure 2 presents the normalized variance ($\text{Var}\left[\frac{\widehat{n}}{n}\right]$) of our ML estimator for different f and α values, and for $m \in \{100, 500, 1000, 10000\}$. As expected, the normalized variance decreases as the number of hash values (m) increases, or as α increases. Overall, the normalized variance is very small for all values of α, f and m, indicating that the new scheme is very precise.

After showing that the new ML scheme indeed yields good results, we now compare its performance to that of Schemes 1-3. When comparing the statistical performance of two algorithms, it is common to look at their MSE (mean squared error) or RMSE, where MSE $= (\text{Bias}(\widehat{\theta}))^2 + \text{Var}\left[\widehat{\theta}\right]$, and RMSE $= \sqrt{(\text{Bias}(\widehat{\theta}))^2 + \text{Var}\left[\widehat{\theta}\right]}$. In our case, because all the estimators are unbiased, we compare only their variance. We define the "relative variance improvement" of the new ML scheme over each scheme as

$$\frac{\text{Var}\left[\widehat{\theta_i}\right] - \text{Var}\left[\widehat{\theta_{ML}}\right]}{\text{Var}\left[\widehat{\theta_i}\right]},$$

where θ_i is the estimator of the ith scheme, and θ_{ML} is the new ML estimator.

Figure 3 presents the simulation results for two values of m: $m = 10,000$ (upper graphs) and $m = 1,000$ (lower graphs). **We can see that the new ML estimator outperforms the three schemes for all values of α and f, and for both values of m.** This improvement varies between 100% to a few percent.

6 ANALYSIS OF THE THREE PREVIOUS SCHEMES

We have conducted a full analysis of the asymptotic statistical performance (bias and variance) of the three previous schemes. Due to space constraints, this analysis is not included in this short version of the paper, and the reader is referred to the full technical report [10]. For the sake of completeness, we give here the final results of the analysis.

Analysis of Scheme-1 (Theorem 8 in the full paper [10])

$\frac{\widehat{n_1}}{n} \to \mathcal{N}(1, V)$, where

$$V = \frac{1}{mn^2}(u^2 - a^2 - b^2) - \frac{2a \cdot b}{m \cdot u \cdot n} + \frac{2u \cdot (a^2(b^2 + \alpha\beta) + b^2(a^2 + \alpha\beta))}{m \cdot Z \cdot n},$$

In addition m is the number of storage units, and Z satisfies:

$$Z = \alpha \cdot n(a^2 + \alpha\beta) + \beta \cdot n(b^2 + \alpha\beta) + (a^2 + \alpha\beta)(b^2 + \alpha\beta).$$

Analysis of Scheme-2 (Theorem 9 in the full paper [10])

$$\frac{\widehat{n_2}}{n} \to \mathcal{N}\left(1, \frac{1}{m\rho}\right),$$

where m is the number of storage units.

Analysis of Scheme-3 (Theorem 11 in the full paper [10])

$$\frac{\widehat{n_3}}{n} \to \mathcal{N}\left(1, \frac{1}{m}(1 + \frac{2ab}{u(a+b)} + (\alpha+\beta)\frac{u^2}{n(a+b)^2})\right),$$

where m is the number of storage units.

To verify that the asymptotic variance of the new scheme is indeed better (lower) than the asymptotic variances of the three previous schemes, we compute the analyzed asymptotic variance of each of the four schemes according to Corollary 4.2 and the theorems above from the full paper [10], for $f \in \{1, 5, 10\}$ and for $\alpha \in \{0, 0.01, 0.02, \ldots, 0.98, 0.99, 1\}$; as in Section 5, $f = \frac{|B|}{|A|}$ and $\alpha = \frac{|A \cap B|}{|A|}$. Figure 4 shows the improvement (in percentages) of the analyzed asymptotic variance of the new scheme over each of the three previous schemes. The results are for $|A| = 10^6$ and $m = 100$, but note that the improvement is affected only by α and f and not by the value of m.

We can see that the analyzed asymptotic variance of the new ML estimator indeed outperforms the analyzed asymptotic variances of the three schemes for all values of α and f.

One can see the similarity between this figure, which presents the **expected** improvement of the new scheme over each of the three schemes according to their analysis, and Figure 3, which presents the **actual** improvement according to the simulations variance. In other words, the improvement of the new scheme over each scheme in the simulations in Section

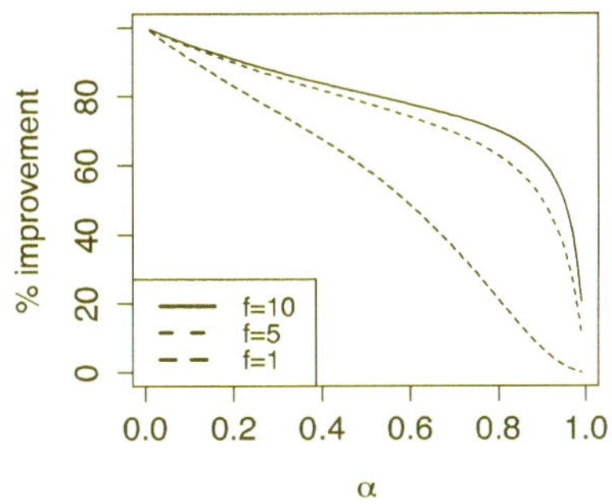

(a) Improvement over Scheme-1

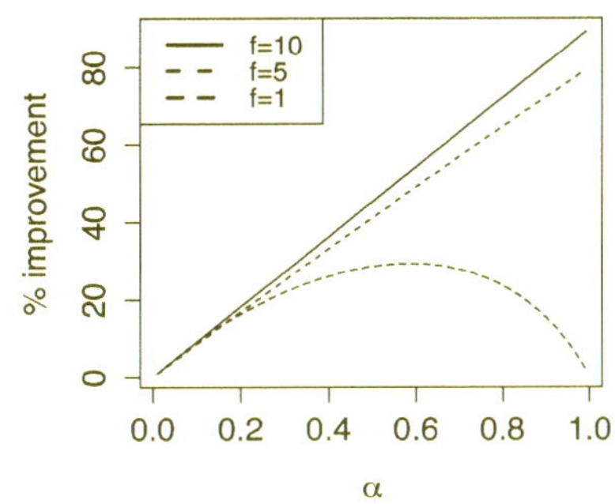

(b) Improvement over Scheme-2

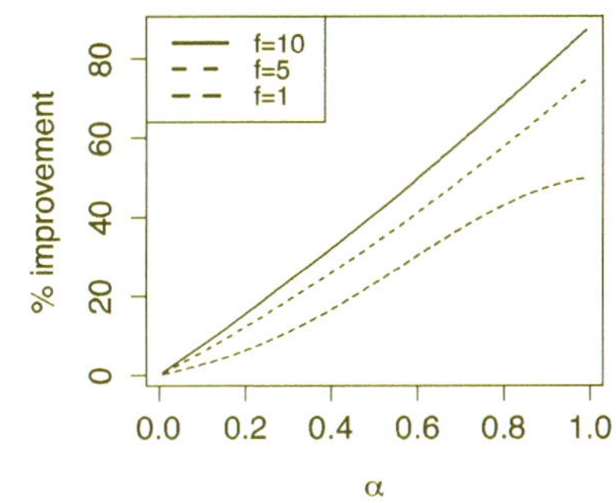

(c) Improvement over Scheme-3

Figure 4: The percentage of variance improvement of the new ML scheme over each of the other schemes for different values of f and α

5 is very close to the improvement expected by our analysis of the four schemes.

7 CONCLUSION

In this paper we studied the problem of estimating the number of distinct elements in the set intersection of two streams. We computed the likelihood function of the problem and used it to present a new estimator, based on the ML method. We also found the optimal variance of any unbiased set intersection estimator, which is asymptotically achieved by our new ML scheme. We can conclude that our new scheme outperforms the three known schemes, significantly improves the variance (precision) of the estimator, and yields better results than the three previously known schemes.

REFERENCES

[1] J. Bauckmann, U. Leser, F. Naumann, and V. Tietz. Efficiently detecting inclusion dependencies. In *ICDE*, pages 1448–1450, 2007.
[2] K. S. Beyer, P. J. Haas, B. Reinwald, Y. Sismanis, and R. Gemulla. On synopses for distinct-value estimation under multiset operations. In *SIGMOD Conference*, pages 199–210, 2007.
[3] A. Z. Broder. On the resemblance and containment of documents. In *IEEE Compression and Complexity of Sequences 1997*, pages 21–29.
[4] A. Z. Broder. Identifying and filtering near-duplicate documents. In *CPM*, pages 1–10, 2000.
[5] A. Z. Broder, S. C. Glassman, M. S. Manasse, and G. Zweig. Syntactic clustering of the web. *Computer Networks*, 29(8-13):1157–1166, 1997.
[6] P. Chassaing and L. Gérin. Efficient estimation of the cardinality of large data sets. In *Proceedings of the 4th Colloquium on Mathematics and Computer Science*, volume AG of *Discrete Mathematics & Theoretical Computer Science Proceedings*, pages 419–422, 2006.
[7] P. Clifford and I. A. Cosma. A statistical analysis of probabilistic counting algorithms. *Scandinavian Journal of Statistics*, 2011.
[8] C. Clifton, E. Housman, and A. Rosenthal. Experience with a combined approach to attribute-matching across heterogeneous databases. In *DS-7*, pages 428–451, 1997.
[9] E. Cohen and H. Kaplan. Tighter estimation using bottom k sketches. *PVLDB*, 1(1):213–224, 2008.
[10] R. Cohen, L. Katzir, and A. Yehezkel. A minimal variance estimator for the cardinality of big data set intersection. *CoRR*, abs/1606.00996, 2016.
[11] T. Dasu, T. Johnson, S. Muthukrishnan, and V. Shkapenyuk. Mining database structure; or, how to build a data quality browser. In *SIGMOD Conference*, pages 240–251, 2002.
[12] P. Flajolet, É. Fusy, O. Gandouet, and F. Meunier. Hyperloglog: the analysis of a near-optimal cardinality estimation algorithm. In *Analysis of Algorithms (AofA) 2007*. DMTCS.
[13] P. Flajolet and G. N. Martin. Probabilistic counting algorithms for data base applications. *J. Comput. Syst. Sci.*, 31:182–209, Sep. 1985.
[14] É. Fusy and F. Giroire. Estimating the number of active flows in a data stream over a sliding window. In D. Panario and R. Sedgewick, editors, *ANALCO*, pages 223–231. SIAM, 2007.
[15] S. Ganguly, M. N. Garofalakis, R. Rastogi, and K. K. Sabnani. Streaming algorithms for robust, real-time detection of ddos attacks. In *ICDCS*, page 4. IEEE Computer Society, 2007.
[16] F. Giroire. Order statistics and estimating cardinalities of massive data sets. *Discrete Applied Mathematics*, 157:406–427, 2009.
[17] M. A. Hernández and S. J. Stolfo. Real-world data is dirty: Data cleansing and the merge/purge problem. *Data Min. Knowl. Discov.*, 2(1):9–37, 1998.
[18] H. Köhler. Estimating set intersection using small samples. In *ACSC*, pages 71–78, 2010.
[19] J. Lumbroso. An optimal cardinality estimation algorithm based on order statistics and its full analysis. In *Analysis of Algorithms (AofA) 2010*. DMTCS.
[20] A. Metwally, D. Agrawal, and A. E. Abbadi. Why go logarithmic if we can go linear?: Towards effective distinct counting of search traffic. In *Proceedings of the 11th International Conference on Extending Database Technology: Advances in Database Technology*, EDBT '08, pages 618–629.
[21] A. E. Monge. Matching algorithms within a duplicate detection system. *IEEE Data Eng. Bull.*, 23(4):14–20, 2000.
[22] E. Rahm and H. H. Do. Data cleaning: Problems and current approaches. *IEEE Data Eng. Bull.*, 23(4):3–13, 2000.
[23] J. Shao. *Mathematical Statistics*. Springer, 2003.
[24] D. Ting. Towards optimal cardinality estimation of unions and intersections with sketches. In *Proceedings of the 22nd ACM SIGKDD International Conference on Knowledge Discovery and Data Mining, 2016*, pages 1195–1204.

HyperLogLog Hyperextended: Sketches for Concave Sublinear Frequency Statistics

Edith Cohen
Google Research, USA
Tel Aviv University, Israel
edith@cohenwang.com

ABSTRACT

One of the most common statistics computed over data elements is the number of distinct keys. A thread of research pioneered by Flajolet and Martin three decades ago culminated in the design of optimal approximate counting sketches, which have size that is double logarithmic in the number of distinct keys and provide estimates with a small relative error. Moreover, the sketches are composable, and thus suitable for streamed, parallel, or distributed computation.

We consider here all statistics of the frequency distribution of keys, where a contribution of a key to the aggregate is concave and grows (sub)linearly with its frequency. These fundamental aggregations are very common in text, graphs, and logs analysis and include logarithms, low frequency moments, and cap statistics.

We design composable sketches of double-logarithmic size for all concave sublinear statistics. Our design combines theoretical optimality and practical simplicity. In a nutshell, we specify tailored mapping functions of data elements to output elements so that our target statistics on the data elements is approximated by the (max-) distinct statistics of the output elements, which can be approximated using off-the-shelf sketches. Our key insight is relating these target statistics to the *complement Laplace* transform of the input frequencies.

1 INTRODUCTION

We consider data presented as elements $e = (e.key, e.value)$ where each element has a *key* and a positive numeric *value* > 0. This data model is very common in streaming or distributed aggregation problems. A well-studied special case is where $e.value \equiv 1$ for all elements.

One of the most fundamental statistics over such data is the number of distinct keys: $\text{Distinct}(E) = |\{e.key \mid e \in E\}|$. Exact computation of the statistics requires maintaining a structure of size that is linear in the number of distinct keys. A pioneering design of Flajolet and Martin [14] showed that an approximate count can be obtained in a streaming model using structures ("sketches") of logarithmic size. Since then, a rich research strand proposed and analysed a diverse set of approximate counting sketches and deployed them for a wide range of applications [17].

KDD'17, August 13-17, 2017, Halifax, NS, Canada.
 978-1-4503-4887-4/17/08.
DOI: http://dx.doi.org/10.1145/3097983.3098020

Distinct counting sketches can be mostly classified as based on sampling (MinHash sketches) or on random projections (linear sketches). Both types of structures are mergeable/composable: This means that when the elements are partitioned, we can compute a sketch for each part separately and then obtain a corresponding sketch for the union from the sketches of each part. This property is critical for making the sketches suitable for parallel or distributed aggregation.

The original design of [14] and the leading ones used in practice use sample-based sketches. In particular, the popular Hyperloglog sketch [13] has double logarithmic size $O(\epsilon^{-2}+\log\log n)$, where n is the number of distinct keys and ϵ is the target normalized root mean squared error (NRMSE). Since this size is necessary to represent the approximate count, Hyperloglog is asymptotically optimal. We note that the Hyperloglog sketch contains ϵ^{-2} registers which store exponents of the estimated count. Thus, explicit representation of the sketch has size $O(\epsilon^{-2}\log\log n)$, but one can theoretically use instead a single exponent and ϵ^{-2} constant-size offsets (e.g. [4, 20]) to bring the sketch size down to $O(\epsilon^{-2}+\log\log n)$, albeit by somewhat increasing updates complexity. Another point is that Hyperloglog uses random hash functions which have logarithmic-size representations. If we considers the hash representation to be part of the sketch [1, 20]), we get a logarithmic lower bound on sketch size. Here we follow [13, 14] and consider the hash representation to be provided by the platform, which is consistent with practice where hash functions are reused and shared by multiple sketches.

We now consider other common statistics over elements. In particular, statistics expressed over a set of (key, weight) pairs, where the weight w_x of a key x, is defined to be the sum of the values of data elements with key x:

$$w_x = \sum_{e \mid e.key=x} e.value\ .$$

Keys that are not active (no elements with this key) are defined to have $w_x = 0$. Note that if all elements have value equal to 1, then w_x is the number of occurrences of key x. For a nonnegative function $f(w) \geq 0$ such that $f(0) \equiv 0$, we define the *f-statistics* of the data as $\sum_x f(w_x)$. We will find it convenient to work with the notation $W(w)$ for the number of keys with $w_x = w$. Equivalently, we can treat W as a distribution over weights w_x that is scaled by the number of distinct keys. We can then express the f-statistics (with a slight notation abuse) as

$$f(W) = \int_0^\infty W(w) f(w) dw\ . \tag{1}$$

The study of sketches that approximate f-statistics over streams of elements was formalized and popularized in a seminal paper by Alon, Matias, and Szegedy [1]. The aim is to the fundamental tradeoff between sketch size and approximating quality for different statistics.

We focus here on functions f that are concave with (sub)linear nonnegative growth-rate. Equivalently, these functions are the nonnegative *span* $\overline{\text{cap}}$ (all nonnegative linear combinations) of *cap* functions

$$\text{cap}_T(w) \equiv \min\{T, w\}\text{ , parameterized by } T > 0\ .$$

Notable members of $\overline{\text{cap}}$ that parametrize a spectrum between distinct count ($f(w) = 1$) and sum ($f(w) = w$) include *frequency moments* $f(w) = w^p$ in the range $p = [0, 1]$ (sum is $p = 1$ and distinct count is $p = 0$), cap functions (sum is realized by cap_∞ and distinct count by cap_1 when element values are integral and by $f(w) = \text{cap}_T(w)/T$ as $T \to 0$ generally), and *softcap* functions

$$\widetilde{\text{cap}}_T(w) = T(1 - \exp(-w/T))\ . \quad (2)$$

Softcap is a smooth approximation of cap: For $w \ll T$ we have $\widetilde{\text{cap}}_T(w) \approx w$, for $w \gg T$ we have $\widetilde{\text{cap}}_T(w) \approx T$, and for all T, w:

$$\forall w,\ (1 - 1/e)\text{cap}_T(w) \le \widetilde{\text{cap}}_T(w) \le \text{cap}_T(w)\ . \quad (3)$$

Other important $\overline{\text{cap}}$ members are $\log(1 + w)$ and capped moments.

Statistics in $\overline{\text{cap}}$ are used in applications to decrease the impact of very frequent keys and increase the impact of rare keys. It is a common practice to weigh frequencies, say degree of nodes in a graph [24] or frequency of a term in a corpus [22, 30], by a sublinear function such as w^p for $p \in (0, 1)$ or $\log(1 + w)$. In many applications, the ability to approximate the statistics over the raw data, without the cost of aggregation, can be very useful. One example is online advertising [16, 26], where data elements are opportunities to show ads to users (keys) that are interacting with various apps on different platforms. An advertisement campaign specifies a maximum number of times T an ad can be displayed to the same user, so the number of qualifying impressions corresponds to cap_T statistics of the data. Statistics are computed over past data in order to estimate the number of qualifying impressions when designing a campaign. Another example is the computation of word embeddings, where each word has a focus and context embedding so that (a function) of the inner product captures the respective co-occurrence frequencies. Glove [27] demonstrated a significant benefit when weighting cooccurrences by $f(w) = \min\{1, w/T\}^\alpha$ for $\alpha < 1$ (instead of $f(w) = w$). Typically, the text corpus is presented as complete text documents, and elements (focus-context pairs) in arbitrary order are extracted in a distributed pass.

There is a very large body of work on the topic of approximating statistics over streamed or distributed data and it is not possible to mention it all here. Most of the prior work uses linear sketches (random linear projections). A sketch for the second moment, inspired by the JL transform [19], was presented by [1]. Indyk [18] followed with a beautiful construction based on stable distributions of sketches of size $O(\epsilon^{-2}\log^2 n)$ for moments in $p \in [0, 2]$. Braverman and Ostrovsky [2] presented an umbrella construction of polylogarithmic-size sketch structures, based on L_2 heavy hitter sketches, for all monotone f-statistics that are sketchable in polylogarithmic size. The construction is illuminating but not practical (high degree of the polylog and constant factors).

Sample-based sketches for $\overline{\text{cap}}$ functions were presented by the author [6]. The sketch is a weighted sample of keys that supports approximate cap-statistics on domain queries (subsets of the keys). The framework generalizes both distinct reservoir sampling [21, 31] and the sample and hold stream sampling [7, 12, 15]. The size and quality tradeoffs of the sample are very close (within a small constant) to those of an optimal sample that can be efficiently computed over aggregated data (set of key and weight pairs). Roughly, a sample of $O(\epsilon^{-2})$ keys suffices to approximate $\text{cap}_T(W)$ unbiasedly with coefficient of variation (CV) ϵ. Moreover, a *multi-objective* (universal) sample (see [5, 10]) of $O(\epsilon^{-2}\log n)$ keys can approximate with CV ϵ *any* f-statistics for $f \in \overline{\text{cap}}$. When this method is applied to sketching statistics of the full data, we can hash key identifiers to size $O(\log n)$ (to obtain uniqueness with very high probability) and obtain sketches of size $O(\epsilon^{-2}\log n)$ and a multi-objective sketches of size $O(\epsilon^{-2}\log^2 n)$. One weakness of the design is that these sketches are not fully composable: They apply on streamed elements (single pass) or take two passes over distributed data elements.

The remaining fundamental challenge was to design composable sketches of size $O(\epsilon^{-2}\log n)$ for each $\overline{\text{cap}}$ statistics and a composable multi-objective sketch of size $O(\epsilon^{-2}\log^2 n)$. Given the practical significance of the problem, we seek simple and highly efficient designs. A further theoretical challenge is to design sketches that meet or approach the double-logarithmic representation-size lower bound of $O(\epsilon^{-2} + \log\log n)$.

Contributions overview and organization

We address these challenges and make the following contributions. We show that *any* statistics in the *softcap span* $\overline{\widetilde{\text{cap}}}$ can be approximated with the essential effectiveness and estimation quality of Hyperloglog. That is, we present composable sketches of size $O(\epsilon^{-2} + \log\log n)$ and estimators with NRMSE ϵ and good concentration. The softcap span $\overline{\widetilde{\text{cap}}} \subset \overline{\text{cap}}$ is the set of functions that can be expressed as

$$f(w) = \int_0^\infty a(t)(1 - e^{-wt})dt\ ,\ \text{where } a(t) \ge 0\ . \quad (4)$$

The span includes all softcap functions, low frequency moments ($f(w) = w^p$ with $p \in (0, 1)$), and $\log(1 + w)$. We also present a composable *multi-objective* sketch for $\overline{\widetilde{\text{cap}}}$. This is a single structure that is larger by a logarithmic factor than a single distinct counter and supports the approximations of *all* $\overline{\widetilde{\text{cap}}}$ statistics. Finally, we consider statistics in $\overline{\text{cap}}$ that are not in $\overline{\widetilde{\text{cap}}}$ and show how to approximate them within small relative errors (12%) using differences of approximate $\overline{\widetilde{\text{cap}}}$ statistics.

Our main component is a framework, illustrated in Figure 1, that reduces the sketching of the target statistics to sketching distinct statistics. We specify randomized functions M that map data elements of the form $e = (e.key, e.value)$ to sets of *output elements*. Each output element $e' \in M(e)$ contains an *output key* (*outkey*) $e'.key$ (which generally is from a different domain than the input keys) and an optional value $e'.value \ge 0$. For a multiset of data elements W, we obtain a corresponding multiset of output elements

$$E = M(W) = \bigcup_{e \in W} M(e)\ .$$

The mapping functions are crafted so that the approximate statistics of the set of data elements W can be obtained from approximations

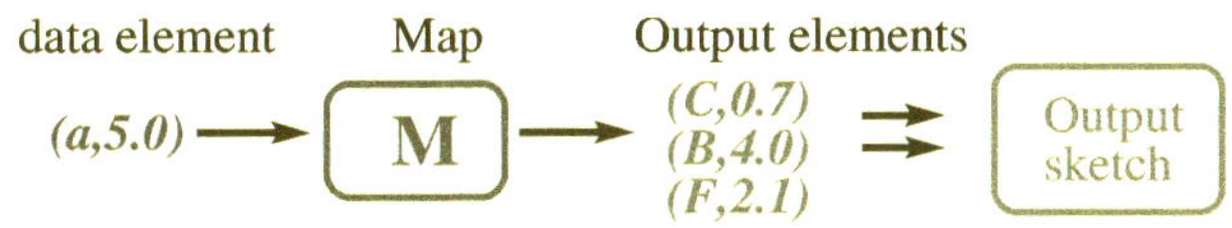

Figure 1: Element processing framework

of other statistics of the output elements E. In particular, if we have a composable sketch for the output statistics, we obtain a composable sketch for the target statistics. Note that our mapping functions are randomized, therefore the set E is a random variable and so is any (exact) statistics on E. We refer to the value of the output statistics on the output elements as a *measurement* of W. When we sketch the output elements, we refer to the resulting estimate as an *approximate measurement* of W.

The output statistics we use are the distinct count $\text{Distinct}(E)$, which allows us to leverage approximate distinct counters as black boxes, and the more general *max-distinct* statistics $\text{MxDistinct}(E)$, defined as the sum over distinct keys of the maximum value of an element with the key:

$$\text{MxDistinct}(E) = \sum_x m_x \,, \qquad (5)$$
$$\text{where } m_x \equiv \max_{e \in E \mid e.key=x} e.value \,,$$

which also can be sketched in double logarithmic size. Note that when all elements have value 1, $\text{MxDistinct}(E) = \text{Distinct}(E)$.

For multi-objective approximations we use *all-threshold* sketches that allows us to recover, for any threshold $t > 0$, an approximation of

$$\text{TDistinct}_t(E) = \text{Distinct}\{e \in E \mid e.value \leq t\}, \qquad (6)$$

which is the number of distinct keys that appear in at least one element $e \in E$ with value $e.value \leq t$. The size of the all-threshold sketch is larger by only a logarithmic factor than the basic distinct count sketch.

The paper is organized as follows. In Section 2 we define the *complement Laplace transform* $\mathcal{L}^c[W](t)$ of the frequency distribution W, which is its distinct count minus its Laplace transform at t. We have the relation

$$T\,\mathcal{L}^c[W](1/T) = \widetilde{\text{cap}}_T(W) \,, \qquad (7)$$

that is, the transform at $1/T$ multiplied by T is the $\widetilde{\text{cap}}_T$ statistics of the data. In Section 3 we define a mapping function for any $t > 0$, so that $\mathcal{L}^c[W](t)$, and hence $\widetilde{\text{cap}}_{1/t}$-statistics, is approximated by the respective Distinct measurement. We refer to this as a measurement of $\mathcal{L}^c[W]$ at point t.

In Section 4 we consider the span $\overline{\widetilde{\text{cap}}}$ of softcap statistics, that is, all f of the form (4). Equivalently, $a(t)$ is the inverse $\mathcal{L}^c$ transform of f. We derive the explicit form of the inverse transform of all frequency moments with $p \in (0, 1)$ and logarithms. The statistics $f(W)$ for $f \in \overline{\widetilde{\text{cap}}}$ can thus be expressed as

$$f(W) = \mathcal{L}^c[W][a] \equiv \int_0^\infty a(t)\,\mathcal{L}^c[W](t)dt \,.$$

This suggests that we can approximate $f(W)$ using multiple approximate point (Distinct) measurements. In section 5 we show that a single MxDistinct measurement suffices: We present element mapping functions (tailored to f) such that the MxDistinct statistics on output elements approximates $f(W) = \mathcal{L}^c[W][a]$. We refer to this statistics as a *combination* measurement of $\mathcal{L}^c[W]$ using a. A MxDistinct sketch of the output element gives us an approximation of combination measurement which approximates $f(W)$. Finally, we will review the design of HyperLoglog-like MxDistinct sketches.

In Section 6 we consider the multi-objective setting, that is, a single sketch from which we can approximate all $\overline{\widetilde{\text{cap}}}$ statistics. We define a mapping function such that for all $t > 0$, $\text{TDistinct}_t(E)$ is equivalent to a point measurement of $\mathcal{L}^c[W]$ at t. The output elements are processed by an *all-threshold distinct count* sketches, which can be interpreted as all-distance sketches [3, 4] and inherit their properties – In particular, the total structure size has logarithmic overhead over a single distinct counter. The all-threshold sketch allows us to obtain approximate point measurements for any t and combination measurement for any a.

In Section 7 we consider statistics in $\overline{\text{cap}}$ that may not be in $\overline{\widetilde{\text{cap}}}$. We characterize $\overline{\text{cap}}$ as the set of all concave sublinear functions and derive expressions for the *cap transform* which transforms $f \in \overline{\text{cap}}$ to the coefficients of the corresponding nonnegative linear combination of cap functions. We then consider sketching these statistics $f(W)$ using approximate *signed* inverse $\mathcal{L}^c$ transform of the function f. We use separate combinations measurements of the positive and negative components for the approximation. We show that cap_1 is the "hardest" function in that class in the sense that any approximate inverse transform for the function $\text{cap}_1(x) = \min\{1, x\}$ can be extended (while retaining sketchability and approximation quality) to any statistics $f \in \overline{\text{cap}}$, using the cap transform of f. We then derive some approximate transforms for $\text{cap}_1(x)$, and hence for any $\overline{\text{cap}}$ statistics that achieve maximum relative error of 12%.

Section 8 reports some experimental results. We conclude in Section 9. Due to page limitations, many details are omitted. A full version can be found in https://arxiv.org/abs/1607.06517.

2 THE LAPLACE^C TRANSFORM

The *complement Laplace (Laplace^c) transform* $\mathcal{L}^c[W](t)$ at a point $t > 0$ is defined as

$$\mathcal{L}^c[W](t) \equiv \int_0^\infty W(w)(1 - \exp(-wt))dw$$
$$= \int_0^\infty W(w)dw - \mathcal{L}[W(w)](t) \,. \qquad (8)$$

See Figure 2 for an illustration of $\mathcal{L}^c[W](t)$ for a toy distribution W. The first term in (8), $\int_0^\infty W(w)dw \equiv \text{Distinct}(W)$, is the "distinct count" and the second term $\mathcal{L}[W(w)]$ is the Laplace transform of our (scaled) frequency distribution W. Hence the name *complement Laplace* transform. Note that $\mathcal{L}^c[W](t)$ is non-decreasing with t. At the limit when t increases, the second term vanishes and

$$\lim_{t\to+\infty} \mathcal{L}^c[W](t) = \int_0^\infty W(w)dw = \text{Distinct}(W) \qquad (9)$$

is the number of distinct keys in W. At the limit as t decreases

$$\lim_{t\to 0^+} \frac{1}{t}\,\mathcal{L}^c[W](t) = \int_0^\infty W(w)wtdw = t\,\text{Sum}(W) \,, \qquad (10)$$

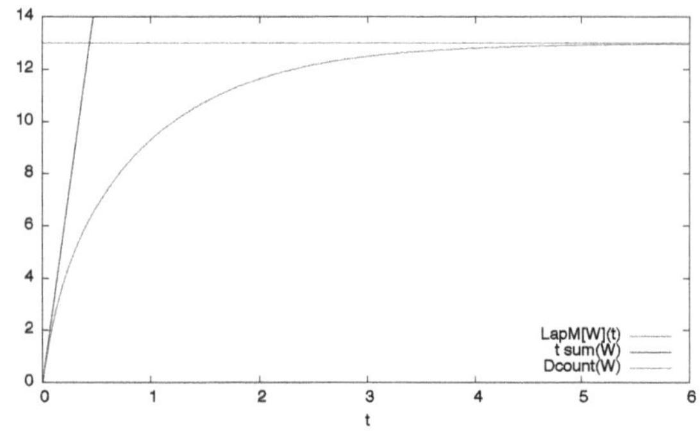

Figure 2: Data W with 10 keys with $w_x = 1$, 2 keys with $w_x = 5$, and one key with $w_x = 10$. The distinct count (number of keys) is Distinct(W) = 13 and the sum is Sum(W) = 30. We have $W(w) = 10\delta(w-1)+2\delta(w-5)+\delta(w-10)$, where δ is Dirac Delta function. The transform (plotted) is $\mathcal{L}^c[W](t) = 10(1-e^{-t})+2(1-e^{-5t})+(1-e^{-10t}) = 13-10e^{-t}-2e^{-5t}-e^{-10t}$. The plot shows the asymptotes $t\,$Sum(W) for small t and Distinct(W) for large t.

where $\mathsf{Sum}(W) = \sum_{e \in W} e.value = \sum_x w_x$ is the sum of the weights of keys. More precisely:

Lemma 2.1. *For $t \leq \frac{\sqrt{\epsilon}}{\max_x w_x}$ and for $t \geq \frac{-\ln \epsilon}{\min_x w_x}$, the transform is approximated within a relative error of at most ϵ by the respective limits* (10) *and* (9).

Proof. For the first claim, note that $wt \leq \sqrt{\epsilon}$. Hence, using the Maclaurin expansion, $|1 - e^{-wt} - wt| \approx (wt)^2/2 \leq \epsilon$. For the second claim, the relative error is $\exp(-wt) \leq \epsilon$. □

The Lemma implies that the fine structure of W is captured by a restricted "relevant" range of t values and is well approximated outside this range by the basic (and composably sketchable) Distinct and Sum statistics. The statistics Distinct(W) is approximated by an off-the-shelf approximate distinct counter applied to data elements. The exact Sum(W) is straightforward to compute composably with a single counter of size $O(\log \mathsf{Sum}(W))$ (assuming integral values). A classic algorithm by Morris [23] (see [4] for a composable version that can handle varying weights) uses sketches of size $O(\epsilon^{-2} + \log\log(\mathsf{Sum}(W))$.

3 LAPLACE^C POINT MEASUREMENTS

We define a mapping function of elements such that the expectation of the (scaled) distinct count of output elements is equal to the Laplace^c transform $\mathcal{L}^c[W](t)$ of W at t. We also establish concentration around the expectation.

The basic element mapping is provided as Algorithm 1. A more efficient variant that performs computation proportional to the number of generated output elements is provided in the full version.

The mapping is parametrized by t and by an integer $r \geq 1$ and uses a set of functions H_i for $i \in [r]$. All we need to assume here is that for all i and keys x, $H_i(x)$ are (nearly) unique. This can be achieved by concatenating x to a string representation of i: $H_i(x) \equiv x \cdot \mathsf{str}(i)$). To obtain output key representation that is logarithmic in r Distinct(W), we can apply a random hash function to the concatenated string. An element e is processed by drawing a set of r independent exponential random variables $y_i \sim \mathsf{Exp}[e.value]$ with parameter $e.value$. For each i such that $y_i < t$, the output key $H_i(e.key)$ is created. Note that the number of output keys returned is between 0 and r.

Algorithm 1: OutKeys$_{t,H}(e)$: Map input element to outkeys

Input: Element $e = (e.key, e.value)$, $t > 0$, integer $r \geq 1$, hash functions H_i $i \in [r]$
Output: A set OutKeys of at most r outkeys
OutKeys ← [] // initialize
foreach $i \in [r]$ **do**
  $y_i \sim \mathsf{Exp}[e.value]$ // independent exponentially distributed with parameter e.value
  if $y_i \leq t$ **then**
    OutKeys.*append*(H_i(*e.key*)) // Append H_i(e.key) to list of output keys
return OutKeys

Our point measurement at t is

$$\widehat{\mathcal{L}^c}[W](t) = \frac{1}{r} \mathsf{Distinct}\left(\bigcup_e \textsc{OutKeys}_{t,H}(e)\right), \quad (11)$$

which is number of distinct output keys generated for all data elements, divided by r. We now show that for any choice of $r \geq 1$, t, and input data W, the expectation of the measurement $\widehat{\mathcal{L}^c}[W](t)$ is equal to the value of the Laplace^c transform of W at t.

Lemma 3.1.

$$\mathsf{E}[\widehat{\mathcal{L}^c}[W](t)] = \mathcal{L}^c[W](t)$$

Proof. The number of distinct outkeys $r\widehat{\mathcal{L}^c}[W](t)$ can be expressed as the sum of r Distinct(W) Poisson events. For each input key x and $i \in [r]$, the event is the appearance (at least once) of the outkey $H_i(x)$. The outkey $H_i(x)$ appears if the minimum $\mathsf{Exp}[e.value]$ draw over elements e with key x is at most t. The minimum of these exponential random variables is exponentially distributed with parameter equal to their sum $w_x = \sum_{e|e.key=x} e.value$. Therefore, the probability of the event is

$$p(w_x, t) = \int_0^t w_x \exp(-w_x y) dy = 1 - \exp(-w_x t) . \quad (12)$$

It follows that the expected contribution of a key x with weight w_x to the sum $r\widehat{\mathcal{L}^c}[W](t)$ is $rp(w_x, t)$. Therefore the expected value of the measurement is

$$\mathsf{E}[\widehat{\mathcal{L}^c}[W](t)] = \frac{1}{r} \int_0^\infty W(w) r p(w,t) dw \equiv \mathcal{L}^c[W](t) .$$

□

We next consider concentration of the measurement. When $t = +\infty$, we have $p(w,t) = 1$, and there is no measurement error. In general, we can bound the relative error by applying the Chernoff bound:

LEMMA 3.2. *For* $\delta < 1$,

$$\Pr[\frac{|\widehat{\mathcal{L}^c}[W](t) - \mathcal{L}^c[W](t)|}{\mathcal{L}^c[W](t)} \geq \delta] \leq 2\exp(-r\delta^2\,\mathcal{L}^c[W](t)/3)\,.$$

The outkeys E are processed by an *approximate* distinct counter which yields an approximate measurement

$$\widehat{\widehat{\mathcal{L}^c}}[W](t) = \frac{1}{r}\widehat{\text{Distinct}}(E) \tag{13}$$

equal to the approximate count of distinct output keys divided by r. Since there are at most r Distinct(W) distinct output keys, the sketch size needed for NRMSE ϵ is $O(\epsilon^{-2}+\log\log(r\,\text{Distinct}(W))) = O(\epsilon^{-2} + \log\log \text{Distinct}(W))$. Note that even a very large r that is polynomial in Distinct(W) will not significantly increase the sketch size. The two sources of error, due to the measurement itself and its approximation, are independent and the bottleneck one is the quality of the approximate distinct counter. When both estimates have NRMSE ϵ with concentration, the error of $\widehat{\widehat{\mathcal{L}^c}}[W](t)$ as an approximation of $\mathcal{L}^c[W](t)$ has NRMSE $\sqrt{2}\epsilon$ with concentration.

While the magnitude of r has negligible effect on sketch size, it does effect element mapping computation. This can be mitigated by using a more efficient algorithm with computation that is linear in the number of generated output keys $O(r(1 - \exp(-te.value))$ (see the full version). Moreover, we can bound the size of r needed to guarantee that our measurement has CV of at most ϵ:

LEMMA 3.3. *When* $t \geq \frac{\sqrt{\epsilon}}{Max(W)}$ *(where* $Max(W) \equiv \max_x w_x$*) and*

$$r \geq \frac{3e}{e-1}\epsilon^{-2.5}\,, \tag{14}$$

the estimator $\widehat{\mathcal{L}^c}[W](t)$ *(defined in* (11)*) has CV at most* ϵ.

PROOF. From Lemma 3.2, it suffices to have

$$r\,\mathcal{L}^c[W](t) \geq 3\epsilon^{-2}\,. \tag{15}$$

From (7) and (3),

$$\mathcal{L}^c[W](t) \geq (1-\frac{1}{e})\sum_x \min\{1, tw_x\} \tag{16}$$

When $t \leq 1/\,\text{Max}(W)$ we have

$$\sum_x \min\{1, tw_x\} = t\,\text{Sum}(W) \geq \sqrt{\epsilon}\frac{\text{Sum}(W)}{\text{Max}(W)} \geq \sqrt{\epsilon}\,.$$

When $t \geq 1/\,\text{Max}(W)$ we have $\sum_x \min\{1, tw_x\} \geq \sum_x \min\{1, \frac{w_x}{\text{Max}(W)}\} \geq 1$. Combining, we get $\mathcal{L}^c[W](t) \geq \frac{e-1}{e}\sqrt{\epsilon}$ and the claim follows using (15). □

Recall from Lemma 2.1 that when $t < \sqrt{\epsilon}/\,\text{Max}(W)$, $\mathcal{L}^c[W](t)$ is well approximated by $t\,\text{Sum}(W)$. Since we do not know Max(W) or Sum(W) in advance, we use the following strategy. Our approximate point measurement algorithm computes both an approximate sum $\widehat{\text{Sum}}(W)$ and approximate count of output elements $\widehat{\text{Distinct}(E)}$ generated by Algorithm 1 with r as in (14). If $\widehat{\text{Distinct}(E)} < 3\epsilon^{-2}$, we return $t\widehat{\text{Sum}}(W)$ and otherwise return (13).

We comment here that using r as in (14) provides seamless worst-case quality guarantees for any t and distribution W. In practice it is often safe to assume that Sum$(W) \gg$ Max(W) and a small value of r suffices. In particular when Sum$(W) \geq \epsilon^{-2.5}$ Max(W) we can use $r = 1$.

4 THE SOFTCAP SPAN

The *softcap span* $\overline{\widetilde{\text{cap}}}$ contains all functions f that can be expressed as nonnegative linear combinations of $\widetilde{\text{cap}}_T$ functions. Equivalently, for some $a(t) \geq 0$,

$$f(w) = \mathcal{L}^c[a](w) = \int_0^\infty a(t)(1-e^{-wt})dt\,. \tag{17}$$

Note that $a(t)$ is the inverse Laplace^c transform of $f(w)$:

$$a(t) = (\mathcal{L}^c)^{-1}[f(w)](t)\,. \tag{18}$$

The following is immediate

LEMMA 4.1. *The relation* (17) *implies that* $a(t) \geq 0$ *satisfies*

$$\int_0^1 a(t)tdt < \infty \text{ and } \int_1^\infty a(t)dt < \infty\,. \tag{19}$$

Table 1 lists explicit expressions for the inverse $\mathcal{L}^c$ transforms of some basic functions in the softcap span (w^p for all $p \in (0, 1)$, and $\ln(1 + w)$). The table also includes other expressions that we will use for sketching the statistics. Our derivations utilized the following Lemma which expresses the inverse $\mathcal{L}^c$ transform of f in terms of the inverse Laplace transform of the derivative of $f(w)$:

LEMMA 4.2.

$$(\mathcal{L}^c)^{-1}[f(w)](t) = \frac{1}{t}\,\mathcal{L}^{-1}[\frac{\partial f(w)}{\partial w}](t)\,,$$

where $\mathcal{L}$ *is the Laplace transform.*

PROOF. We look for a solution $a(t)$ of (17). Differentiating both sides by w we obtain

$$\frac{\partial f(w)}{\partial w} = \int_0^\infty ta(t)e^{-wt}dt = \mathcal{L}[a(t)t](w)\,.$$

□

In preparation for the task of sketching the statistics $f(W)$, we express it in terms of the inverse $\mathcal{L}^c$ transform $a(t)$ of $f(w)$ and the transform $\mathcal{L}^c[W]$ of the frequencies:

$$\begin{aligned} f(W) &= \int_0^\infty f(w)W(w)dw \\ &= \int_0^\infty W(w)\,\mathcal{L}^c[a](w)dw \\ &= \int_0^\infty a(t)\int_0^\infty W(w)(1-e^{-wt})dwdt \\ &= \int_0^\infty a(t)\,\mathcal{L}^c[W](t)dt\,. \end{aligned} \tag{20}$$

When the inverse transform has a discrete form, that is, f is expressed using $\{a_t\}$ for $t \in Y$ as

$$f(w) = \sum_{t\in Y} a_t(1-e^{-wt})\,, \tag{21}$$

(Equivalently, $a(t)$ is a linear combination of Dirac delta functions at $t \in Y$). We can express $f(W)$ in terms of corresponding points of $\mathcal{L}^c[W]$:

$$f(W) = \sum_{t\in Y} a_t\,\mathcal{L}^c[W](t)$$

Table 1: Inverse $\mathcal{L}^c$ transform of basic functions

$f(w)$	$a(t) = (\mathcal{L}^c)^{-1}[f(w)](t)$	$\int_\tau^\infty a(t)dt$	$\int_0^\tau a(t)tdt$
$\widetilde{\text{cap}}_T(w)$	$T\delta_{1/T}(t)$	T, when $y \le 1/T$; 0 otherwise	0 when $\tau < 1/T$
w^p $(p \in (0,1))$	$\frac{p}{\Gamma(1-p)}t^{-(1+p)}$	$\frac{1}{\tau^p\Gamma(1-p)}$	$\frac{p}{(1-p)\Gamma(1-p)}\tau^{1-p}$
$\sqrt{w}$	$\frac{1}{2\sqrt{\pi}}t^{-1.5}$	$\frac{1}{\sqrt{\pi\tau}}$	$\frac{\tau^{0.5}}{\sqrt{\pi}}$
$\log(1+w)$	$\frac{e^{-t}}{t}$	$\int_\tau^\infty \frac{e^{-t}}{t}dt = -\tau\text{Ei}(-\tau)$	$1-e^{-\tau}$

and approximate $f(W)$ using corresponding point measurements of $\mathcal{L}^c[W]$. In the next section we introduce *combination* $\mathcal{L}^c$ measurements which allow us to approximate $\mathcal{L}^c[W][a]$ for any $a(t) \ge 0$ that satisfies (19).

5 COMBINATION $\mathcal{L}^c$ MEASUREMENTS

In this section we show how to sketch $f(W)$ for any $f \in \overline{\widetilde{\text{cap}}}$. We will use the notation

$$\mathcal{L}^c[W][a]_\tau^b \equiv \int_\tau^b a(t)\,\mathcal{L}^c[W](t)dt\ . \quad (22)$$

When the subscript or superscript are omitted, we default to $\tau = 0$ and $b = \infty$. We use the same notation with approximate measurements:

$$\widehat{\widehat{\mathcal{L}^c}}[W][a]_\tau^b = \int_\tau^b a(t)\,\widehat{\widehat{\mathcal{L}^c}}[W](t)dt\ . \quad (23)$$

From Section 4, we can equivalently present a sketch design for $\mathcal{L}^c[W][a]_0^\infty$ where $a(t) \ge 0$ satisfies (19). We define randomized mapping functions of elements, tailored to some $a(t) \ge 0$ and $\tau > 0$, such that the expectation of the (scaled) max-distinct statistics of output elements is equal to $\mathcal{L}^c[W][a]_\tau^\infty$ and establish concentration around the expectation. We estimate the contribution $\mathcal{L}^c[W][a]_0^\tau$ of the low-t regime by a separate Sum(W) sketch.

5.1 Element mapping

Consider $a(t) \ge 0$. Our element processing is a simple modification of the element processing Algorithm 1 for point measurements. The algorithm inputs the function $a()$ (instead of t) and returns output elements (outkey and value pairs) instead of only returning outkeys. Pseudocode is provided as Algorithm 2.

Algorithm 2: OutElements $_{a,\tau,H}(e)$: Map of element e to a set of output elements for a $\mathcal{L}^c[W][a]_\tau^\infty$ measurement

```
Input: Element e = (e.key, e.value), a(t) ≥ 0, integer r ≥ 1,
       hash functions H_i i ∈ [r], τ > 0
Output: OutElements: A set of at most r output elements
OutElements ← []              // initialize
foreach i ∈ [r] do
    y_i ~ Exp[e.value]      // independent exponentially
    distributed with parameter e.value
    v ← ∫_{max{τ,y_i}}^∞ a(t)dt
    if v > 0 then
        OutElements.append((H_i(e.key), v)) // New output
        element
return OutElements
```

Our combination measurement is the max-distinct statistics of the output elements divided by r:

$$\widehat{\mathcal{L}^c[W][a]}_\tau^\infty = \frac{1}{r}\,\text{MxDistinct}\left(\bigcup_{e\in W}\text{OutElements}_a(e)\right)\ . \quad (24)$$

We show that the measurement has expectation equal to $\mathcal{L}^c[W][a]_\tau^\infty$ with good concentration:

LEMMA 5.1.

$$E[\widehat{\mathcal{L}^c[W][a]}_\tau^\infty] = \mathcal{L}^c[W][a]_\tau^\infty$$

$$\forall\delta < 1,\ \Pr[\frac{|\widehat{\mathcal{L}^c[W][a]}_\tau^\infty - \mathcal{L}^c[W][a]_\tau^\infty|}{\mathcal{L}^c[W][a]_\tau^\infty} \ge \delta]$$
$$\le\ 2\exp(-r\delta^2\,\mathcal{L}^c[W][\tau]/3)\ .$$

PROOF. The claim on the expectation follows from linearity of expectation and the claim for point measurements for each t in Lemma 3.1. The concentration follows from Lemma 3.2 which establishes point-wise concentration at each t, combined with the relation

$$\min_{t\in[\tau,\infty)} \mathcal{L}^c[W](t) = \mathcal{L}^c[W](\tau)$$

which follows from monotonicity of $\mathcal{L}^c[W](t)$. □

Note that nonnegativity $a(t) \ge 0$ is necessary for correctness: It ensures monotonicity of $\int_y^\infty a(t)dt$ in y which implies that the maximum indeed corresponds to minimum y.

We now address quality of approximation. From the lemma, quality is bounded by a function of the value of the transform at point τ: $\mathcal{L}^c[W](\tau)$. From our analysis of point measurements, we know that it suffices to ensure that τ and r are large enough so that (15) holds. As with point measurements, we can use $\tau = \sqrt{\epsilon}/\text{Max}(W))$ and r as in (14) to obtain a concentrated measurement of $\mathcal{L}^c[W][a]_\tau^\infty$.

5.2 The low t regime

To obtain an estimate of $\mathcal{L}^c[W][a]_0^\infty$, we need to separately estimate $\mathcal{L}^c[W][a]_0^\tau$. From Lemma 2.1, when $\tau \le \sqrt{\epsilon}/\text{Max}(W)$, we have

$$\mathcal{L}^c[W][a]_0^\tau \approx \int_0^\tau a(t)t\,\text{Sum}(W)dt \approx \widehat{\text{Sum}(W)}\int_0^\tau a(t)tdt\ . \quad (25)$$

The first approximation has relative error at most ϵ. For the second, as discussed earlier, we can use exact Sum(W) or a composable Morris counter sketch that provides an estimate with a well concentrated error of ϵ.

Closed expressions for $\int_0^\tau a(t)tdt$ (used in (25) and for $\int_\tau^\infty a(t)dt$ (used in Algorithm 2) for inverse transforms of basic functions are provided in Table 1. Note that these expressions are bounded and well defined for all a that are inverse $\mathcal{L}^c$ transform of a $\overline{\overline{\text{cap}}}$ function (see Lemma 4.1).

5.3 Putting it together

Our sketch consists of a $\widehat{\text{Sum}}$ sketch applied to data elements W and a $\widehat{\text{MxDistinct}}$ sketch applied to output element E produced by applying the element mapping Algorithm 2 to W. The final estimate we return is

$$\widehat{\widehat{\mathcal{L}^c}}[W][a]_0^\infty = \frac{1}{r}\widehat{\text{MxDistinct}}(E) + \widehat{\text{Sum}}(W)\int_0^\tau a(t)tdt\ . \quad (26)$$

There is one subtlety here that was deferred for the sake of exposition: We do not know Max(W) and therefore can not simply set τ prior to running the algorithm. To obtain the worst-case statistical guarantees we set r as in (14) and set τ adaptively to be the $\ell = 3\epsilon^{-2}$ smallest y value that is generated for a distinct output key. To do so, we extend our sketch to include another component, which we call the *sidelined* set, which is the ℓ distinct output keys with smallest y values processed so far. Note that this sketch component is also composable. The sidelined elements are not immediately processed by the MxDistinct sketch: The processing is delayed until they are taken out of being sidelined, that is, to the point that due to sketch compositions or new arrivals, there are ℓ other distinct output keys with lower y values. Finally, when the sketches are used to extract an estimate of the statistics, we set τ as the largest y in the sidelined set, feed all the sidelined keys to the MxDistinct sketch with value $\int_\tau^\infty a(t)dt$, and apply the estimator (26). We note that explicitly maintaining the sidelined output keys and y value pairs would require $\epsilon^{-2}\log n$ storage. Details on how to obtain the same effect using a double logarithmic size sketch component are provided in the full version.

5.4 Max-distinct sketches

For completeness, we discuss some sketch designs for max-distinct statistics. These sketches generalize MinHash sketches for distinct statistics (see overview in [4]) and are based on composable weighted sampling schemes.

With bottom-k sampling [8, 9, 25, 28, 29] we associate with each element (with a unique key) e an independent random rank value $r_e \sim D[e.value]$ from a distribution D parametrized by $e.value$ (Exponential [28] or uniform $U[0, 1/e.value]$ [25]). The sample includes the k keys with minimum r_e and the corresponding $e.value$. It is easy to see that this can be performed using composable sketches that contain $k = \epsilon^{-2}$ key value pairs. When the keys are not unique, we instead use ranks obtained by applying the respective inverse CDF to $u_{e.key} \sim U[0, 1]$, which is a hash function that maps strings to independent uniform random numbers. What this achieves is that minimum rank of elements with the same key x has distribution $D[m_x]$ and hence the sample distribution is the same as the plain scheme applied to elements (x, m_x) with unique keys. An estimator of the max-distinct statistics $\sum_x m_x$ that is applied to the sample [9, 11] is well-concentrated with CV $1/\sqrt{k-2} \approx \epsilon$. The representation of the sample amounts to storing k key identifiers (or their $O(\log n)$ size hashes) and their respective m_x values resulting in representation size of $O(\epsilon^{-2}\log n)$. The size can be reduced by hashing keys to a domain that is polynomial in k and store approximate consistently-rounded ranks in an offset form.

A different design of max-distinct sketches of size $O(\log\log n + \epsilon^{-2}\log\epsilon^{-1})$ (assuming $1 \leq m_x = O(\text{poly}(n))$) builds on with-replacement weighted sampling [3] and popular distinct counting sketches [13, 14]. Our sketch contain k registers that corresponds to balanced "buckets" of output keys. For balance, we can place all keys in all buckets or apply stochastic averaging and partition the output keys to buckets according to a partition of $[r]$. For an element e with key that falls in bucket i, we compute $-\ln u_{e.key\#i}/e.value$ and if smaller than the current register, replace its value. The distribution of the minimum in the bucket is exponential with parameter equals to the sum of m_x over keys in the bucket (see e.g. [3]). Since the buckets are balanced, each register contains a sample from this distribution and we can estimate the parameter by $k-1$ divided by the sum of the k registers. As in Hyperloglog, we can use consistent (per key/bucket) randomized rounding to an integral power of $(1+\delta)$ and store only the negated exponent y_i for register i. The exponent can be stored in $O(\log\log n)$ bits. For different buckets, we can store one exponent and offsets of expected size $O(1)$ per bucket. To obtain the approximate statistics from the sketch we use the estimator

$$\widehat{\text{MxDistinct}}(E) = (k-1)/\sum_{i=1}^{k} b^{-y_i}\ .$$

6 FULL RANGE $\mathcal{L}^c$ MEASUREMENTS

In this section we present a composable sketch from which we can approximate $\mathcal{L}^c[W](t)$ for all t and $\mathcal{L}^c[w][a]_\tau^\infty$ for all applicable $a() \geq 0$ and τ. Concretely, consider the set of output keys $\text{OutKeys}_t(e)$ generated by Algorithm 1 for input element e when fixing the parameter r, the set of hash functions $\{H_i\}$, and the randomization $\{y_i\}$, but varying t. It is easy to see that the set $\text{OutKeys}_t(e)$ monotonically increases with t until it reaches size r. We can now consider all outkeys generated for input W as a function of t

$$\text{OutKeys}_t(W) \equiv \bigcup_{e\in W}\text{OutKeys}_t(e)\ .$$

The number of distinct outkeys increases with t until it reaches size rn, where n is the number of distinct input keys. Our *full-range* measurement is accordingly defined as the function

$$\widehat{\mathcal{L}^c}[W](t) = \frac{1}{r}\left|\text{OutKeys}_t(W)\right|\ . \quad (27)$$

The full-range element mapping Algorithm 3 returns for each input element e, a set of r output elements $\text{OutElements}_H(e)$ that are outkey and value pairs. The mapping is equivalent to Algorithm 1 except that the point t is not specified and instead the output elements are always generated with value equal to the applicable threshold t.

6.1 Point from full range

We denote the set of output elements generated for all input elements $e \in W$ by OutElements(W). We have that

$$\text{OutKeys}_t(W) = \{e.key \mid e \in \text{OutElements}(W)\text{such that}e.value \leq t\}\ .$$

Therefore, the point measurement for t is

$$\widehat{\mathcal{L}^c}[W](t) = \frac{1}{r}\,\text{Distinct}\{e \in \text{OutElements}(W) \mid e.value \le t\}\,, \tag{28}$$

which is the number of distinct keys in output elements that have value at most t. This measurement is identical to the one we would have obtained using Algorithm 1 with input t.

6.2 Combination from full range

A combination measurement can be computed from a full range measurement using

$$\widehat{\mathcal{L}^c}[W][a]_\tau^\infty = \int_\tau^\infty a(t)\widehat{\mathcal{L}^c}[W](t)dt\,. \tag{29}$$

We show that this formulation is equivalent to a combination measurement (24) obtained by a max-distinct statistics of output elements generated by Algorithm 2:

Lemma 6.1. *Consider $a(t) \ge 0$, $\tau \ge 0$ and element mappings for full-range (Algorithm 3) and combination (Algorithm 2) measurements where the mappings are performed using identical parameter r, hash functions H, and random draws y. Then the corresponding combination measurements (29) and (24) are equal.*

Proof. It is easy to verify that

$$\begin{aligned}\widehat{\mathcal{L}^c[W][a]_\tau^\infty} &= \frac{1}{r}\,\text{MxDistinct}\left(\bigcup_{e\in W}\text{OutElements}_{a,\tau}(e)\right)\\ &= \frac{1}{r}\int_\tau^\infty a(t)|\text{OutKeys}_t(W)|dt\,.\end{aligned}$$

□

6.3 Sketching a full range measurement

The output elements OutElements(W) are processed by a composable *all-threshold* distinct counting sketch. Our all-threshold sketch is a single-point All-Distance Sketch (ADS) [3–5] (universal monotone sample). We refer the reader to [4, 5] for full details and provide here an overview for completeness. The ADS summarizes data elements E that are a set of key value pairs with nonnegative values. From the sketch we can approximate $\text{TDistinct}_t(E)$ (6) for any t and $\int_\tau^\infty a(t)\,\text{TDistinct}_t(E)dt$ for any integrable $a(t) \ge 0$ and τ. Respectively, we obtain from an ADS of the output elements, approximate point $\widehat{\widehat{\mathcal{L}^c}}[W][t]$ and combination $\widehat{\widehat{\mathcal{L}^c}}[W][a]_\tau^\infty$ measurements.

An ADS is a parametric extension of a MinHash sketch: It efficiently represents MinHash sketches for all the sets $\text{OutKeys}_t(W)$ for different t. It retains the sketch structure of the base MinHash sketch and records all the change points t at which the content of a register (of the respective MinHash sketches) changes. At the base we can use almost any MinHash sketch design including HyperLogLog [13] which uses $k = \epsilon^{-2}$ registers that store respective maximum values over processed data elements. As t is increased, the values that the sketch would have stored increase. The ADS records the values and change points t for each register. The total expected number of change points for all k registers is well-concentrated around $k\ln(rn)$. Hence, the overhead factor of all-threshold sketching is $O(\epsilon^{-2}\ln n)$ and the representation of the breakpoints. Since $\mathcal{L}^c[W](t)$ is smooth and Lipschitz, we can limit the precision in which the breakpoints are represented to $\log(1/\epsilon)$ significant bits and use a single exponent and offsets. We can apply the HIP estimator [4, 5] to the ADS (with respect to the swept parameter t) to obtain tighter estimates for all t.

Algorithm 3: $\text{OutElements}_H(e)$: Map of element e to a set of output elements for full range measurement

```
Input: Element e = (e.key, e.value), integer r ≥ 1, hash
       functions {H_i} i ∈ [r]
Output: OutElements: A set of r output elements
OutElements ← []
foreach i ∈ [r] do
    y_i ~ Exp[e.value]      // independent exponentially
    distributed with parameter e.value
    OutElements.append((H_i(e.key), y_i))      // New output
    element
return OutElements
```

7 THE CAP SPAN

In this section we consider sketching statistics for concave sublinear f that may not be in $\overline{\overline{\text{cap}}}$. We show that all concave sublinear f are in the nonnegative span $\overline{\text{cap}}$ of cap functions. We define *cap transform* of f as a function $a(t) \ge 0$ and $A_\infty \ge 0$ such that $\int_0^\infty a(t)dt < \infty$ and

$$f(x) = A_\infty x + \int_0^\infty a(t)\text{cap}_t(x)dt\,.$$

We can express the transform as follows:

Theorem 7.1. *Let $f : [0, \infty]$ be a nonnegative, continuous, concave, and monotone non-decreasing function such that $f(0) = 0$ and $\partial_+ f(0) < \infty$. Then $f \in \overline{\text{cap}}$ with the cap transform:*

$$a(x) = \begin{cases} -\partial^2 f(x) & \textit{when } \partial_-^2 f(x) = \partial_+^2 f(x) \\ (\partial_- f(x) - \partial_+ f(x))\delta_x & \textit{otherwise}\end{cases} \tag{30}$$

$$A_\infty = \partial f(\infty) \tag{31}$$

where δ is the Dirac delta function and $\partial f(\infty) \equiv \lim_{t\to\infty}\partial f(t)$.

7.1 Sketching with signed inverse transforms

We consider sketching statistics for f such that $a(t) = \mathcal{L}^{c^{-1}}[f(w)](t)$ (17) is *signed*. We use the notation $a(t) = a_+(t) - a_-(t)$ where

$$a_+(t) = \max\{a(t), 0\} \text{ and } a_-(t) = \max\{-a(t), 0\}\,. \tag{32}$$

We define $f_+(w) = \mathcal{L}^c[a_+](w)$ and $f_-(w) = \mathcal{L}^c[a_-](w)$. Note that for all w, $f(w) = f_+(w) - f_-(w)$ and in particular $f(W) = f_+(W) - f_-(W)$. Since $a_+, a_- \ge 0$, we can obtain a good approximations $\hat{f}_+(W)$ and $\hat{f}_-(W)$ for each of $f_+(W) = \mathcal{L}^c[W][a_+]$ and $f_-(W) = \mathcal{L}^c[W][a_-]$ using approximate full-range, two combination, or several point measurements when a is discrete and small. We approximate $f(W)$ using the difference $\hat{f}(W) = \hat{f}_+(W) - \hat{f}_-(W)$.

The quality of this estimate depends on a parameter ρ:

$$\rho(a) \equiv \max_w \max \frac{\mathcal{L}^c[a_+](w)}{\mathcal{L}^c[a](w)}, \frac{\mathcal{L}^c[a_-](w)}{\mathcal{L}^c[a](w)} \tag{33}$$

LEMMA 7.2. *For all* W, $f(w) = \mathcal{L}^c[a](w)$,

$$\frac{|f(W) - \hat{f}(W)|}{f(W)} \leq \rho(a)\left(\frac{|\mathcal{L}^c[W][a_+] - \widehat{\mathcal{L}^c}[W][a_+]|}{\mathcal{L}^c[W][a_+]} + \frac{|\mathcal{L}^c[W][a_-] - \widehat{\mathcal{L}^c}[W][a_-]|}{\mathcal{L}^c[W][a_-]}\right)$$

That is, when the components $f_+(W)$ and $f_-(W)$ are estimated within relative error ϵ, then our estimate of $f(W)$ has relative error at most $\epsilon\rho$. In particular, the concentration bound in Lemma 5.1 holds with $\rho\delta$ replacing δ and the sketch size has $\epsilon\rho$ replacing ϵ.

When the exact inverse transform a of f is not defined or has a large $\rho(a)$, we look for an *approximate* inverse transform a such that $\rho(a)$ is small and $f(w) \approx \mathcal{L}^c[a](w)$:

$$\text{relerr}(f, \mathcal{L}^c[a]) = \max_{w>0} \frac{|f(w) - \mathcal{L}^c[a](w)|}{f(w)} \leq \epsilon \quad (34)$$

7.2 From cap_1 to $\overline{\text{cap}}$

We show that from an approximate signed inverse transform of cap_1 we can obtain one with the same quality for any $f \in \overline{\text{cap}}$.

THEOREM 7.3. *Let* $f \in \overline{\text{cap}}$ *and let* $a(t)$ *be the cap transform of* f. *Let* $\alpha(x)$ *be such that* $\mathcal{L}^c[\alpha](w)$ *is an approximation of* cap_1. *Then*

$$c(x) = \int_0^\infty a(T)\alpha(x/T)dT\ , \quad (35)$$

is an approximate inverse transform of f *that satisfies*

$$\rho(c) \leq \rho(\alpha) \quad (36)$$

$$\text{relerr}(f, \mathcal{L}^c[c]) \leq \text{relerr}(\text{cap}_1, \mathcal{L}^c[\alpha]) \quad (37)$$

It follows that to approximate $f(W)$ we do as follows. We compute the cap transform of f and use an approximate inverse transform of cap_1, from which we obtain an approximate inverse transform c of f. We then perform two combination measurements (with respect to the negative and positive components c_+ and c_-). Alternatively, we can use one full-range measurement to estimate both.

7.3 Sketching cap_1

We consider approximate inverse transforms of cap_1. The simplest approximation (see (3)) is to approximate cap_T statistics by $\widetilde{\text{cap}}_T$. The worst-case error of this approximation is $\text{relerr}(\text{cap}_T, \widetilde{\text{cap}}_T) = 1/e \approx 0.37$. Note, however, that the relative error is maximized at $w = T$, but vanishes when $w \ll T$ and $w \gg T$. This means that only distributions that are heavy with keys of weight approximately T would have significant error. Noting that $\widetilde{\text{cap}}_T$ is an underestimate of cap_T, we can decrease the worst-case relative error using the approximation

$$\frac{2e}{2e-1}\widetilde{\text{cap}}_T(w) \quad (38)$$

and obtain $\text{relerr}(\text{cap}_T, \frac{2e}{2e-1}\widetilde{\text{cap}}_T) = \frac{1}{2e-1} \approx 0.23$. This improvement, however, comes at the cost of spreading the error, that otherwise dissipated for very large and very small frequencies w, across all frequencies.

We derive tighter approximations of cap_1 using a signed approximate inverse transform $\alpha()$. We first specify properties of $\alpha()$ so that $\mathcal{L}^c[\alpha]$ has desirable properties as an approximation of cap_1.

To have the error vanish for $w \gg 1$, that is, have $\mathcal{L}^c[\alpha](w) \to 1$ when $w \to +\infty$, we must have

$$\int_0^\infty \alpha(t)dt = 1\ . \quad (39)$$

To have the error vanish for $w \ll 1$, that is, have $\mathcal{L}^c[\alpha](w)/w \to 1$ when $w \to 0$, we must have

$$\int_0^\infty t\alpha(t)dt = 1\ . \quad (40)$$

We show (see full version) that using α of the form

$$\alpha(t) = (A+1)\delta_1(t) - \alpha_1\delta_{\beta_1}(t) - \alpha_2\delta_{\beta_2}(t)\ ,$$

where δ is the Dirac delta function, we obtain the following:

A	β_1	β_2	relerr $\approx$	$\rho(\alpha) <$
10.0	0.9	3.75	0.115	12.4
1.5	0.6	7.97	0.14	2.9

Figure 3 shows $\text{cap}_1(w)$ and various approximations. The single point measurement approximations: $\widetilde{\text{cap}}_1$ and scaled $\widetilde{\text{cap}}_1$ and the two 3-point approximations from the table. One plot shows the functions and the other shows their ratio to cap_1 which corresponds to the relative error as a function of w. The graphs show that the error vanishes for small and large values of w for all but the scaled $\widetilde{\text{cap}}_1$ (38). We can also see the smaller error for the 3-point approximations.

8 EXPERIMENTS

We performed experiments aimed at demonstrating the practicality of our schemes and providing some insights on parameter selection. We implemented the element mapping functions in Python and generated synthetic data elements with values equal to 1 and Zipf distributed keys with parameter $\alpha \in [1, 2]$. Figure 4 shows the measurement error as a function of the parameter r for point measurements and for a combination measurement.

9 CONCLUSION

We presented a novel elegant framework for composable sketching of concave sublinear statistics. We obtain state-of-the-art asymptotic bounds on sketch size together with highly efficient practical solution.

We leave open the intriguing questions of fully understanding the limits of our approach. In particular, whether the scope of sample-based sketching is limited to (sub)linear statistics (we suspect it does) and to precisely quantify the attainable approximation tradeoff for cap_1 (and hence for any $\overline{\text{cap}} \setminus \widetilde{\text{cap}}$ function)

REFERENCES

[1] N. Alon, Y. Matias, and M. Szegedy. The space complexity of approximating the frequency moments. *J. Comput. System Sci.*, 58:137–147, 1999.
[2] V. Braverman and R. Ostrovsky. Zero-one frequency laws. In *STOC*. ACM, 2010.
[3] E. Cohen. Size-estimation framework with applications to transitive closure and reachability. *J. Comput. System Sci.*, 55:441–453, 1997.
[4] E. Cohen. All-distances sketches, revisited: HIP estimators for massive graphs analysis. *TKDE*, 2015.
[5] E. Cohen. Multi-objective weighted sampling. In *HotWeb*. IEEE, 2015. full version: http://arxiv.org/abs/1509.07445.
[6] E. Cohen. Stream sampling for frequency cap statistics. In *KDD*. ACM, 2015. full version: http://arxiv.org/abs/1502.05955.
[7] E. Cohen, N. Duffield, H. Kaplan, C. Lund, and M. Thorup. Algorithms and estimators for accurate summarization of unaggregated data streams. *J. Comput. System Sci.*, 80, 2014.

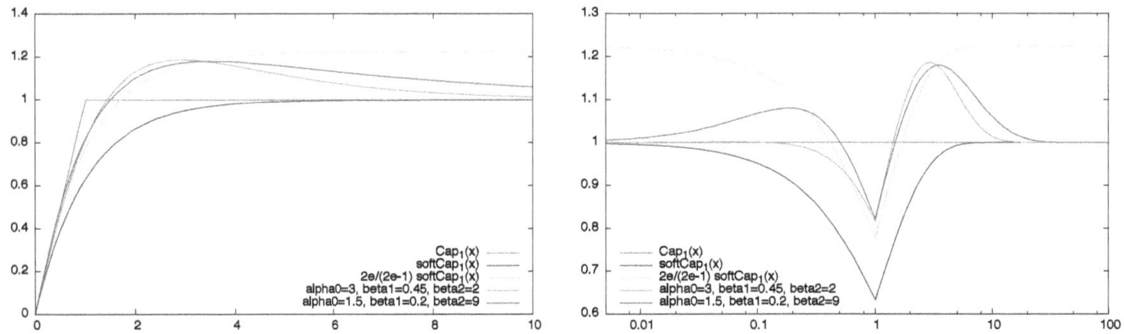

Figure 3: Left: $\text{cap}_1(w)$ function and different approximations: With a single $\mathcal{L}^c$ point measurement we can use the softcap function $\widetilde{\text{cap}}_1(w)$ or scaling it $\frac{2e}{2e-1}\widetilde{\text{cap}}_1(w)$ to minimize the worst-case relative error. We also show two 3 point measurements approximations with different parameters. Right: The corresponding ratio to cap_1 which shows the relative error of the different approximations.

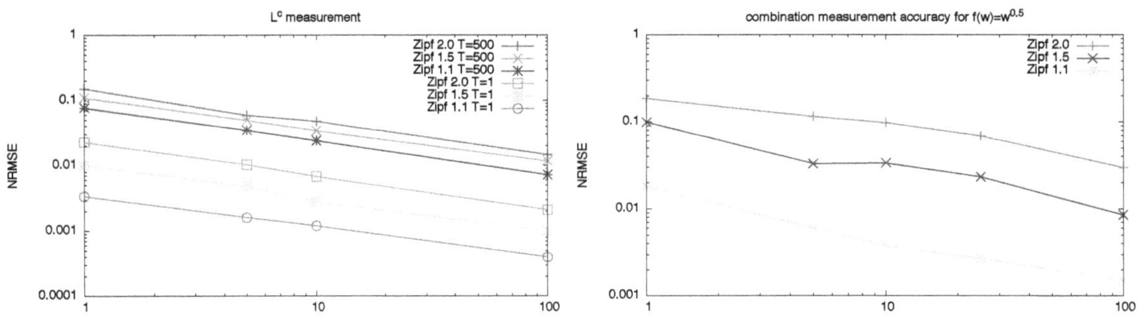

Figure 4: Experiments on 10^5 elements with Zipf-distributed keys (averaged over 200 repetitions), showing measurement error NRMSE as a function of r Left: point measurements $\widehat{\mathcal{L}^c}[W](1/T)$. Right: combination measurement for $f(w) = \sqrt{w}$.

[8] E. Cohen and H. Kaplan. Summarizing data using bottom-k sketches. In *ACM PODC*, 2007.

[9] E. Cohen and H. Kaplan. Tighter estimation using bottom-k sketches. In *Proceedings of the 34th VLDB Conference*, 2008.

[10] E. Cohen, H. Kaplan, and S. Sen. Coordinated weighted sampling for estimating aggregates over multiple weight assignments. *VLDB*, 2(1–2), 2009. full: `http://arxiv.org/abs/0906.4560`.

[11] N. Duffield, M. Thorup, and C. Lund. Priority sampling for estimating arbitrary subset sums. *J. Assoc. Comput. Mach.*, 54(6), 2007.

[12] C. Estan and G. Varghese. New directions in traffic measurement and accounting. In *SIGCOMM*. ACM, 2002.

[13] P. Flajolet, E. Fusy, O. Gandouet, and F. Meunier. Hyperloglog: The analysis of a near-optimal cardinality estimation algorithm. In *Analysis of Algorithms (AofA)*. DMTCS, 2007.

[14] P. Flajolet and G. N. Martin. Probabilistic counting algorithms for data base applications. *J. Comput. System Sci.*, 31:182–209, 1985.

[15] P. Gibbons and Y. Matias. New sampling-based summary statistics for improving approximate query answers. In *SIGMOD*. ACM, 1998.

[16] Google. *Frequency capping: AdWords help*, December 2014. https://support.google.com/adwords/answer/117579.

[17] S. Heule, M. Nunkesser, and A. Hall. HyperLogLog in practice: Algorithmic engineering of a state of the art cardinality estimation algorithm. In *EDBT*, 2013.

[18] P. Indyk. Stable distributions, pseudorandom generators, embeddings and data stream computation. In *Proc. 41st IEEE Annual Symposium on Foundations of Computer Science*, pages 189–197. IEEE, 2001.

[19] W. Johnson and J. Lindenstrauss. Extensions of Lipschitz mappings into a Hilbert space. *Contemporary Math.*, 26, 1984.

[20] D. M. Kane, J. Nelson, and D. P. Woodruff. An optimal algorithm for the distinct elements problem. In *PODS*, 2010.

[21] D. E. Knuth. *The Art of Computer Programming, Vol 2, Seminumerical Algorithms*. Addison-Wesley, 1st edition, 1968.

[22] T. Mikolov, I. Sutskever, K. Chen, G. S. Corrado, and J. Dean. Distributed representations of words and phrases and their compositionality. In *NIPS*, 2013.

[23] R. Morris. Counting large numbers of events in small registers. *Comm. ACM*, 21, 1977.

[24] S. Nandanwar and N. N. Murty. Structural neighborhood based classification of nodes in a network. In *KDD*. ACM, 2016.

[25] E. Ohlsson. Sequential poisson sampling. *J. Official Statistics*, 14(2):149–162, 1998.

[26] M. Osborne. *Facebook Reach and Frequency Buying*, October 2014. http://citizennet.com/blog/2014/10/01/facebook-reach-and-frequency-buying/.

[27] J. Pennington, R. Socher, and C. D. Manning. Glove: Global vectors for word representation. In *EMNLP*, 2014.

[28] B. Rosén. Asymptotic theory for successive sampling with varying probabilities without replacement, I. *The Annals of Mathematical Statistics*, 43(2):373–397, 1972.

[29] B. Rosén. Asymptotic theory for order sampling. *J. Statistical Planning and Inference*, 62(2):135–158, 1997.

[30] G. Salton and C. Buckley. Term-weighting approaches in automatic text retrieval. *Information Processing & Management*, 24(5):513 – 523, 1988.

[31] J.S. Vitter. Random sampling with a reservoir. *ACM Trans. Math. Softw.*, 11(1):37–57, 1985.

Fast Enumeration of Large k-Plexes

Alessio Conte
University of Pisa
conte@di.unipi.it

Donatella Firmani
Roma Tre University
donatella.firmani@uniroma3.it

Caterina Mordente
Be Think Solve Execute
c.mordente@be-tse.it

Maurizio Patrignani
Roma Tre University
patrigna@dia.uniroma3.it

Riccardo Torlone
Roma Tre University
torlone@dia.uniroma3.it

ABSTRACT

k-plexes are a formal yet flexible way of defining communities in networks. They generalize the notion of cliques and are more appropriate in most real cases: while a node of a clique C is connected to all other nodes of C, a node of a k-plex may miss up to k connections. Unfortunately, computing all maximal k-plexes is a gruesome task and state-of-the-art algorithms can only process small-size networks. In this paper we propose a new approach for enumerating large k-plexes in networks that speeds up the search by several orders of magnitude, leveraging on (i) methods for strongly reducing the search space and (ii) efficient techniques for the computation of maximal cliques. Several experiments show that our strategy is effective and is able to increase the size of the networks for which the computation of large k-plexes is feasible from a few hundred to several hundred thousand nodes.

ACM Reference format:
Alessio Conte, Donatella Firmani, Caterina Mordente, Maurizio Patrignani, and Riccardo Torlone. 2017. Fast Enumeration of Large k-Plexes. In *Proceedings of KDD '17, August 13-17, 2017, Halifax, NS, Canada,* 10 pages.
DOI: 10.1145/3097983.3098031

1 INTRODUCTION

In the vast majority of networks representing real-world scenarios the distribution of edges is not uniform and it is often possible to clearly distinguish groups of nodes that are highly connected. The automatic detection of these groups, often called *communities*, helps to discover fundamental properties of large networks in a variety of different domains. For this reason this problem has been largely investigated [14].

A *clique* is a set of nodes in a network with all possible edges among them, and is a formal and strict way of defining a community. So strict, in fact, that cliques are generally thought to be too rigid to be used in practice [17]. A more appropriate notion in many practical cases is the *k-plex*: a set of nodes such that each of them has edges with all the others, with the possible exception of up to k missing neighbors (including itself). So, for example, for $k = 1$, k-plexes are cliques, for $k = 2$, each node may miss one edge, etc. Hence, k-plexes are a simple and intuitive generalization of cliques.

The problem of finding k-plexes arises in social network analysis [4], but it has wider applicability in several important areas employing graph-based data mining [6, 17, 22]. Unfortunately, the detection of all maximal k-plexes in a network is unpractical being hindered by two main problems: (i) maximal k-plexes are even more numerous than maximal cliques, even if most k-plexes are small and not significant; (ii) the most efficient algorithms in the literature for computing maximal k-plexes can only be used on small-size graphs: we show in our experiments that the largest networks we were able to analyze with the algorithm in [6] have a few hundred nodes.

In this paper we propose a solution to the first issue that is also a solution to the second one. Namely, if we restrict the search to *large* k-plexes, which are the most meaningful in practice, we can devise efficient algorithms to detect them.

Indeed, computing all maximal k-plexes does not make sense when the purpose is that of detecting communities. In this respect, it is useful to focus on the relationship between s, the size of a k-plex, and k itself. Starting from $k = 1$, which corresponds to cliques, if we increase the value of k, we obtain progressively sparser communities that are clearly less interesting in practice. In addition, there is a dramatic effect on small k-plexes: it is trivial that if $s \leq k$ a k-plex can be composed of isolated nodes, but it is possible to show that even if $s < 2k$, the k-plex can be disconnected (see Section 5). Hence, small k-plexes do not correspond to communities. In particular, in order to avoid finding the degenerate k-plexes mentioned above, it is natural to impose at least that $s \geq 2k$.

In this framework, our strategy for finding large k-plexes relies on two main observations. First, the complexity of the problem can be reduced in the vast majority of cases on the basis of certain properties of large k-plexes that can be efficiently checked and that allows us to filter out a large portion of the network before starting their search. The second consideration is that, differently to what happens for k-plexes, the state-of-the-art techniques to compute all maximal cliques are able to scale up to millions of nodes by decomposing the network into small blocks [8, 12]. Unfortunately, the decomposition approach cannot be easily adapted to the detection of k-plexes. However, we demonstrate that we can find all k-plexes non-smaller than m by looking in the neighborhood of cliques of a size that depends on k and m. Hence, it turns out that the knowledge of maximal cliques in a network provides a hint for finding all the significant k-plexes.

In sum, our contributions are the following.

KDD '17, August 13-17, 2017, Halifax, NS, Canada

DOI: 10.1145/3097983.3098031

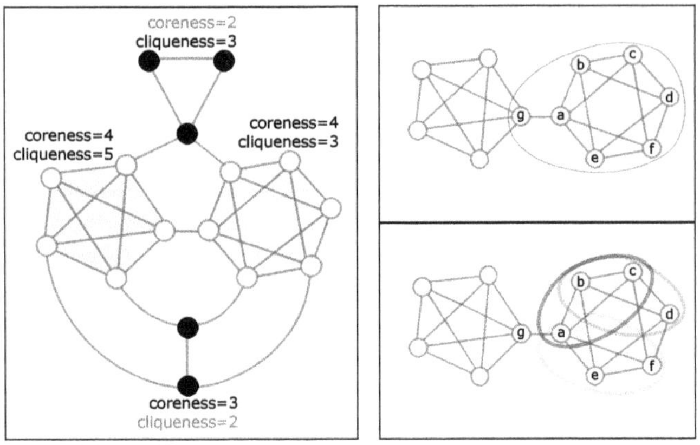

(a) (b)

Figure 1: An example network.

- We present techniques to efficiently compute all *maximum* k-plexes of a network in the hypothesis that they are greater than a fixed threshold, which is adequate to obtain significant results. Our approach is based on the intuition that the efficient computation of all maximal cliques can be exploited to guide the search for k-plexes towards specific portions of the network, filtering out uninteresting parts.
- We propose an algorithm to detect all *maximal* k-plexes whose size is at least a given threshold. The algorithm is based on a decomposition of the network in smaller blocks, which is, to the best of our knowledge, the first decomposition that is proposed for this purpose and, again, is based on the maximal cliques that are detected in the network.
- We illustrate an experimentation showing that these techniques are able to speed up the computation of several orders of magnitude with respect to traditional algorithms, increasing the size of the networks for which computing maximal k-plexes is a feasible task from a few hundred nodes to several hundred thousand nodes.

The rest of this paper is organized as follows. Section 2 contains an overview of our approach and results. Sections 3 and 4 describe in detail our approach to find all largest k-plexes in the network and all the most significant k-plexes, respectively. Section 5 contains the theoretical basis of our algorithms. The efficiency of the algorithms is experimentally measured in Section 6. Finally, Sections 7 and 8 contain related work and our concluding remarks.

2 OVERVIEW

As mentioned in the introduction, our approach is based on two main ideas: (i) before starting the search of k-plexes, we can filter out a relevant portion of the network in which necessary conditions for the presence of large k-plexes do not hold, and (ii) in large networks, cliques can drive the search of k-plexes. While the first point provides an effective way to simplify the problem at hand, the second can lead to an efficient strategy for finding k-plexes.

Let us elaborate on these ideas starting with the problem of finding all k-plexes of *maximum* size. Assume that we have computed all the maximal cliques of a network and let ω be the size of the maximum clique. Then, a maximum k-plex has size at least ω, since cliques are also k-plexes. For example, suppose we are searching for k-plexes in the network in Fig. 1a, which we will use as a running example in this section: we have that $\omega = 5$, since the maximum clique (the blue subgraph on the left hand side) involves five nodes.

At this point, it turns out that two filtering criteria can be applied.

(1) **Coreness** Our first intuition follows from the very definition of k-plex: all the nodes of a k-plex of size m must have degree non-smaller than $m - k$. If we know that the size of a maximum k-plex is at least ω, this means that we can iteratively filter out any node that has degree lower than $\omega - k$. This corresponds to computing the *coreness* of all the nodes of the network (Lemma 5.3), a process that can be executed in linear time [5]. For example, suppose we are searching for 2-plexes in the running example of Fig. 1a for which $\omega = 5$: we can filter out the three black nodes on the top of the picture since they have coreness 2, which is less than $\omega - k = 3$. In larger networks we show that this criterion allows us to cut up to 99% of the nodes.
(2) **Cliqueness** The second intuition is that any node of a k-plex of size m must be included in a clique of a size that depends on m. This is confirmed by Corollary 5.5 stating that any node of a k-plex larger or equal to m is included in a clique of size at least $\lceil m/k \rceil$. Then, if the size of the maximum k-plex is at least ω, we can cut out all nodes that do not belong to any clique of size at least $\lceil \omega/k \rceil$. For example, if we are searching for 2-plexes in the network depicted in Fig. 1a, we can filter out all nodes that do not belong to cliques of size at least $\lceil 5/2 \rceil = 3$, that is, the pair of black nodes in the bottom of the network. We will show in Section 6 that in larger instances this criterion can be tested efficiently and is able to cut up to 98% of the nodes.

Even if some nodes can be filtered out both because their low cliqueness and low coreness, the network in Fig. 1a shows that the two filtering criteria are indeed independent. When both criteria are applied, the size of the network is reduced of magnitude and standard techniques for finding k-plexes may become applicable even to very large networks.

We push ahead this approach to devise a technique that allows us to further increase the tractable cases. In fact, a consequence of Corollary 5.5 is that if the largest k-plex has size p, then the network contains a clique of size at least p/k, which in turn must be less than the size of the maximum clique ω. This implies that the size p of a maximum k-plex in the network cannot exceed $k \cdot \omega$. Hence, the size p of the searched k-plexes is in the interval $[\omega, k \cdot \omega]$. In our running example, this would mean to search in the interval $[5, 10]$. Now we iteratively apply the following algorithm:

(1) We make an educated guess of a value of p in the interval $[\omega, k \cdot \omega]$ that allows us to filter out many nodes based on the cliqueness criterion.
(2) We launch a traditional method to find all k-plexes on such reduced network

(3) If we find some k-plex of size greater or equal than p we are done (our guess was correct and we found all maximum k-plexes).
(4) If we find only k-plexes of size $s \in [\omega, p-1]$, then we know that our guess was too optimistic and we iterate, using $p-1$ as new upper bound and using s as new lower bound (and filtering out nodes based on it).

This technique is effective at least whenever the size p of the largest k-plex is much larger than the size ω of the largest clique, which is a reasonable property for some networks.

Once we have found the largest k-plexes, we may be interested into searching smaller ones. We have noted in the introduction that an exhaustive search does not make much sense, since very small k-plexes are not significant, to the point that they may be even disconnected or composed by a set of isolated nodes. Hence, the second problem we tackle is to find all maximal k-plexes in the network of size bigger than a threshold m.

As mentioned above, our idea is to start from cliques, which are k-plexes but not necessarily maximal, and possibly enlarge them to find maximal k-plexes. Building on the cliqueness criterion, which ensures that each node of a k-plex C of size s is included into a clique of size at least $\lceil s/k \rceil$, we start from each of such cliques K. If we set $m \geq k^2$, we have that $|K| \geq \lceil s/k \rceil > k$, which implies that any other node of C must be adjacent to at least one node of K (in other words, K is a *dominating set* of C). Hence, we can search for C restricting to a block including K and all its adjacent nodes. For example, suppose you are searching for all maximal 2-plexes of size at least 5 in the network in the top of Fig. 1b. Consider any clique of size at least $\lceil s/k \rceil = \lceil 5/2 \rceil = 3$, for example the clique $K = \{a, b, e\}$ (yellow triangle in Fig. 1b). The nodes of any k-plex of size at least 5 containing K are adjacent to K (surrounded nodes of Fig. 1b top).

We further reduce the size of the block by proving that C can be obtained by considering only nodes belonging to K and to other cliques of size at least $\lceil s/k \rceil$ intersecting with K (Lemma 5.7). For example, the 2-plex of size 6 on the right of Fig. 1b is all contained into the clique $\{a, b, e\}$ and three other cliques of size 3 intersecting with K (surrounded nodes of Fig. 1b bottom). This gives rise to an efficient searching algorithm that decomposes the network into blocks each composed of one clique as the core, and all intersecting cliques as the boundary. Each block can be separately processed, possibly in a distributed environment.

3 FINDING MAXIMUM K-PLEXES

In this section, we show our algorithms for enumerating the maximum k-plexes of the input graph G. Intuitively, our approach consists of enumerating all the k-plexes of a targeted sub-graph of G, that we refer to as H, and then selecting the largest ones. Clearly, the smaller is H with respect to G, the faster is solving the problem[1], as long as H contains all the maximum k-plexes of G. Precisely, we aim at extracting a sub-graph H out of G, that is:

(1) small enough to make the enumeration fast;
(2) large enough to capture all maximum k-plexes of G, and allow the computation of a correct solution.

[1] Ideally, H consists exclusively of the nodes of the k-plexes we are looking for.

We design two different sub-graph extraction *criteria*, dubbed CORENESS and CLIQUENESS. Our criteria are of the form "all the k-plexes larger or equal than m consist of nodes with property XYZ", and have the above desiderata for a suitable choice of m. Practically speaking, we make the following observations.

- If m is too small, then the criteria are trivially met by most (or even all) nodes of G (violating the first desiderata);
- If m is too large, then the criteria are met only by few (or even none) nodes of G (violating the second desiderata);

To this end, we show what are the best settings of the threshold m in different scenarios. The theoretical analysis in Section 5 proves that the solution provided by our settings is correct, and the experiments in Section 6 show that the enumeration on the resulting sub-graph is greatly faster than in the input graph.

In the rest of this section, we first describe our criteria and related concepts, then we describe the corresponding algorithms for enumerating maximum k-plexes, based on different choices for the threshold m.

3.1 Criteria

We now describe our CORENESS and CLIQUENESS criteria, and how to use them for extracting the sub-graph H out of G.

Coreness. Our first criterion is the simplest, and it is based on the intuition that all the nodes of a k-plex C, with $|C| \geq m$ have degree non-smaller than $m-k$. Clearly, we do not know a priori what are the nodes of C. However, we can iteratively filter out any node that has degree lower than $m-k$. Formally, this is equivalent to search for the $(m-k)$-*cores* of G. We define this concept in the following.

Definition 3.1. An h-*core* of G is a maximal connected subgraph of G in which all nodes have degree at least h. A node u has *coreness* h if it belongs to a h-core, but not to any $(h+1)$-core.

An h-*core* is one of the connected components of the sub-graph of G formed by repeatedly deleting all nodes of degree less than h. We are now ready to state our coreness criterion, as follows.

CRITERION 1 (CORENESS). *All the k-plexes of G larger or equal than m consist of nodes having coreness larger or equal than $m-k$.*

Cliqueness. Our second criterion is based on the intuition that all the nodes of a k-plex C, with $|C| \geq m$, form smaller cliques with other nodes of C. Informally speaking, if we try to "draw" a k-plex by adding one edge at a time, we soon realize that there are no ways of placing edges without forming progressively larger cliques here and there. Lemma 5.4 in Section 5 proves that every node of C participates in a clique non-smaller than $\frac{m}{k}$. Therefore, we can filter out any node that only participates in smaller cliques. We define this concept in the following.

Definition 3.2. A node u has *cliqueness* h if it belongs to a clique of G of size h, but not to any clique of G of size $h+1$.

We are now ready to state our cliqueness criterion, as follows.

CRITERION 2 (CLIQUENESS). *All the k-plexes of G larger or equal than m consist of nodes having cliqueness larger or equal than $\frac{m}{k}$.*

Computing the sub-graph. Let m be given as input. The procedure prune(G, k, m), shown in Algorithm 1, returns the sub-graph

Algorithm 1 prune(G, k, m) algorithm that computes a sub-graph of G according to Criterion 1 and 2.

1: $G' \leftarrow \{v \in G : G.\texttt{coreness}(v) \geq m - k\}$
2: $H \leftarrow \{v \in G' : G'.\texttt{cliqueness}(v) \geq \frac{m}{k}\}$
3: **return** H

Algorithm 2 max_plexes(G, k) algorithm.

1: $\mathcal{K} \leftarrow$ all_cliques(G)
2: $m \leftarrow \max_{K \in \mathcal{K}} |K|$
3: $H \leftarrow$ prune(G, k, m)
4: $\mathcal{K} \leftarrow$ all_plexes(H, k)
5: P $\leftarrow \text{argmax}_{K \in \mathcal{K}} |K|$
6: **return** P

H resulting from a combination of CORENESS and CLIQUENESS. We first compute the $(m-k)$-cores (line 1), and then we filter out all the nodes with low cliqueness in the cores (line 2). Note that the two criteria can be applied sequentially, in any order. Since computing coreness is easy [5], we chose to apply CORENESS first and compute cliqueness on the smaller graph G' (line 2).

3.2 Algorithms for maximum k-plexes

Let ω be the size of any maximum clique in G. Criterion 2 shows that the size of any maximum k-plex lies in the range $[\omega, k \cdot \omega]$. In principle, for the problem at hand, m can be set anywhere in the interval $[\omega, k \cdot \omega]$. With our desiderata in mind (complete solution and fast enumeration), we identify two alternative strategies that make sense with no prior knowledge on the maximum k-plexes, that we refer to as the *cautious choice* and the *greedy choice.*

- **Cautious choice.** We set $m = \omega$. The pros are that we cannot miss the maximum k-plexes. The cons are that if the size of the maximum k-plex is closer to $k \cdot \omega$ than to ω, H may be much larger than needed.
- **Greedy choice.** We set m in the middle. The pros are that H is very small. The cons are that we may miss the maximum k-plex. To this end, we can iterate in a binary search fashion.

Let us introduce the following useful methods.

- all_cliques(G): The method returns all the maximal cliques of G.
- all_plexes(H, k): The method returns all the maximal k-plexes of the sub-graph H, for a given k, with any appropriate state-of-art method.

Cautious choice. Our first strategy is illustrated in Algorithm 2, that we refer to as max_plexes(). The procedure is very simple. We first enumerate all the maximal cliques of G (line 1), and then extract the sub-graph H using our criteria and the maximum clique size as threshold (line 2–3). Finally, we enumerate all the maximal k-plexes of the sub-graph H, and return the maximum ones (line 4–5). Note that some cliques can be included in the solution. We observed that some instances in our experiments only have one maximum clique C_{max}, that also corresponds to the maximum k-plex. In such extreme cases, the sub-graph H only consists in C_{max}, and we can even do without all_plexes().

Algorithm 3 max_plexes_binary(G, k) algorithm.

1: $\mathcal{K} \leftarrow$ all_cliques(G)
2: $m \leftarrow \max_{K \in \mathcal{K}} |K|$
3: LB $\leftarrow m$
4: UB $\leftarrow k \cdot m$
5: **while** $LB \neq UB$ **do**
6: $\quad x \leftarrow \frac{LB+UB}{2}$ ▷ Pivot
7: $\quad H \leftarrow$ prune(G, k, x)
8: $\quad \mathcal{K} \leftarrow$ all_plexes(H, k)
9: $\quad x' \leftarrow \max_{K \in \mathcal{K}} |K|$
10: $\quad LB \leftarrow \max\{LB, x'\}$
11: $\quad UB \leftarrow \max\{x, x'\}$
12: **end while**
13: P $\leftarrow \text{argmax}_{K \in \mathcal{K}} |K|$
14: **return** P

Greedy choice. Our second strategy is illustrated in Algorithm 3, that we refer to as max_plexes_binary(). We first enumerate all the maximal cliques of G (line 1), as in max_plexes(). After that, rather than using the maximum clique size as threshold, the algorithm attempts to extract a smaller sub-graph by setting m to the middle point of the range $[\omega, k \cdot \omega]$ (line 6–7). Then, we enumerate all the maximal k-plexes of the sub-graph H, and compute the maximum size x' (line 9). If $H = \emptyset$ we set $x' = 0$. The following scenarios are possible.

- If $x' \in [0, x)$, then there are no k-plexes larger than the pivot x and the search continues. The lower-bound does not change (line 10), and the pivot becomes the new upper-bound (line 11).
- If $x' \geq x$, then we found k-plexes non-smaller than the pivot x. The search comes to an end, since the value x' becomes both the new lower-bound (line 10) and the the new upper-bound (line 11).

In particular, if $x' \geq x$, then x' is also the maximum k-plex size of G by our criteria. Equivalently, all the maximum k-plexes of the input graph G must be included in $\mathcal{K}$ (line 8). Therefore, at the end of the search, we return the maximum elements of $\mathcal{K}$ (line 13–14).

Note that if we replace the selection of $x = \frac{LB+UB}{2}$ with $x = \omega$ we obtain the same behavior than max_plexes() algorithm.

4 FINDING LARGE K-PLEXES

Let ω_k be the size of any maximum k-plex of G, as computed for instance with the algorithm max_plexes() in the earlier section. A natural next step is to find all the k-plexes within a range $(1-\epsilon)\omega_k$. One may be tempted to re-use the approach of max_plexes() as a template, and change line 2 of Algorithm 2 by setting $m = (1-\epsilon)\omega_k$. While this is valid in principle, we observed in practice that large k-plexes are more numerous that maximum k-plexes (that in most case only consist of a single max k-plex) even if ϵ is small. On the one hand, this confirms our initial intuition that enumerating all the k-plexes of G is impractical. On the other, this calls for the design of an efficient algorithm specific for the *large k-plexes* problem at hand. To this end, we introduce a third criterion, that we refer to as OVERLAPPINGCLIQUES, which enables the enumeration

Algorithm 4 large_plexes(G, k, m) algorithm.

```
1: H ← prune(G, k, m)
2: 𝒦 ← all_cliques(H)
3: for K ∈ 𝒦 do
4:     B ← boundary(K)
5:     P ← all_plexes(H[B], k)      ▷ H[B] is the subgraph of H induced by B ⊆ V.
6:     for P ∈ P, |P| ≥ m do
7:         yield P                   ▷ duplicates admitted
8:     end for
9: end for
```

Algorithm 5 boundary(K) algorithm.

```
1: B ← ∅
2: for K′ ∈ 𝒦 do
3:     if K′ ∩ K ≠ ∅ then
4:         B ← B ∪ K′
5:     end if
6: end for
7: return B
```

of large k-plexes in networks that are orders of magnitude larger than previously considered.

Overlapping cliques criterion. This is an advanced application of the cliqueness criterion. Let C be a k-plex non-smaller than m. Consider any maximal clique $K \in C$. We know from the cliqueness criterion that $|K| \geq \frac{m}{k}$.

- If $\frac{m}{k} \geq k$, every node of $C \setminus K$ must be adjacent to at least one node $v \in K$, since every node of a k-plex can miss up to $k - 1$ neighbors.
- Every node of $C \setminus K$ must itself participate in a clique K', at least as large as $\frac{m}{k}$.

Intuitively, for large enough k-plexes with $m \geq k^2$, all the nodes of C not in K participate in cliques overlapping with K, that is, sharing at least one node with K. (We provide a proof of this statement in Lemma 5.7.) This allows us to target our search for large k-plexes to the neighborhood of each clique K. More formally, to all the cliques overlapping with K, that we refer to as its *boundary*. We state the overlapping cliques criterion as follows.

Criterion 3 (OverlappingCliques). *All the k-plexes of G with size $m \geq k^2$ consist of nodes either belonging to a clique K s.t. $|K| \geq \frac{m}{k}$, or to overlapping cliques K', s.t. $|K'| \geq \frac{m}{k}$ and $K \cap K' \neq \emptyset$.*

Algorithm for large k-plexes. Our algorithm for large k-plexes is illustrated in Algorithm 4, that we refer to as large_plexes(). The procedure uses the same auxiliary methods than max_plexes() (see Section 3), and the boundary(K) primitive in addition.

- boundary(K): The method returns all the nodes included in a given clique K, or in overlapping cliques.

The large_plexes() algorithm first extracts the sub-graph H using our criteria and the input threshold $m = (1 - \epsilon)\omega_k$ (line 1). Note that prune() selects all the nodes of G, except those that do not participate in any k-plex larger or equal than m. Then, it enumerates all the maximal cliques of the sub-graph H (line 2). The resulting set $\mathcal{K}$ (line 2) only consists of cliques that are larger than $\frac{m}{k}$ (because of the constructive process of H) and thus can be used as "seeds" for growing large k-plexes, according to the OverlappingCliques criterion. Finally, the large_plexes() algorithm iterates over $\mathcal{K}$ (lines 3–9) and for each clique considers its boundary (line 4). Let B the current set returned by boundary(). We first enumerate all the maximal k-plexes of the sub-graph of $H[B]$ of H induced by B (line 5). Then, we return only k-plexes non-smaller than m (lines 6–8), and proceed with the next clique.

In Algorithm 5 we show a simple implementation of the boundary() algorithm. At line 2, the data structure $\mathcal{K}$ is shared with the caller method (i.e., large_plexes()).

Duplicates. Note that the above method can return the same k-plex multiple times (line 7). To this end, we design a clever test, that guarantees that every k-plex is returned at most once. Let C be any k-plex computed by all_plexes($H[B], k$). We define the concept of *parent* clique $P(C)$, and return C only when the current clique is equal to $P(C)$. Specifically, let

- $min(C)$ be the node u in C with smallest id;
- $complete(X, Y)$ be a method that iteratively adds to the clique X the next minimum node in the set Y s.t. X is still a clique;

We define $P(C)$ by construction as in the following equation.

$$P(C) = complete(complete(\{min(C)\}, C), H) \quad (1)$$

Practically speaking, we start from the node u in C with smallest id. Then, the process of construction has two phases. In the first phase, we extend u within C in increasing order of id. Then we keep extending by selecting nodes from the whole H.

We can thus rewrite line 6 as "**if** $P(P) = K$ **then yield** P": this way each k-plex is returned exactly once.

Parallelism. We note that the main operations introduced so far, can be efficiently executed in a distributed setting. Cliques of the input graph and cliqueness values of nodes can be computed in a cluster environment, as shown in [12]. In addition, for large_plexes(), different machines can process different clique boundaries in parallel. We are not aware of parallel techniques for implementing the all_plexes() sub-routine, and we leave this for future work.

5 THEORETICAL BASIS

A *k-plex* $C = (V, E)$ with s nodes, $s \geq 2k$, is a graph such that every node is adjacent at least to all other nodes in C except k. For the sake of simplicity C may refer to both the set of nodes it contains and to the induced graph. We refer to nodes adjacent to a given node u, as *neighbors* of u. A *clique* can be thought of as 1-plex. Any subset of a k-plex is also a k-plex, and a k-plex is also a k + 1-plex. We need to prove the three criteria described in the previous sections, dubbed coreness, cliqueness and OverlappingCliques.

Coreness criterion. Let $\Delta(C)$ denote the *diameter* of C, that is, the largest number of nodes which must be traversed in order to travel from one node to another. While a clique, or a 1-plex, has diameter equals 1, k-plexes with $k > 1$ come in a variety of forms and can have arbitrarily high diameter (which is not a desirable property for a community). However, for $k \leq \frac{s}{2}$ – which means that every node is adjacent more than half nodes in C – the diameter is only at most 2. This is proven in the following.

Lemma 5.1. *If $s \geq 2k$ then $\Delta(C) \leq 2$.*

Proof. If C has diameter larger than 2, there are at least two nodes u and v at distance larger than 2. Since u is missing at most k edges, it has at least $s - k$ neighbors. However, neither u or its neighbors are connected to v and therefore v missing at least $s - k + 2$ edges, which is larger than k if $k \leq \frac{s}{2}$. □

Corollary 5.2. *If $s \geq 2k$ then C is connected.*

We are now ready for proving the coreness criterion.

Lemma 5.3 (Coreness). *Every node in C has coreness at least $s-k$.*

Proof. Let $\delta(u)$ denote the *degree* of a node u, that is, the number of nodes of C adjacent to u. It easy to verify that for every node $c \in C$, $\delta(u) \geq s - k$. A h-core of C is a connected subgraph of C in which all nodes have degree at least h [20]. Since C is connected by Corollary 5.2, C is a $s - k$-core. □

Other criteria. We give the technical lemma below, that we use for deriving the cliqueness and adjacency criteria, and the advanced search principle.

Lemma 5.4. *Every clique $X \subseteq C$, s.t. $|X| < \frac{s}{k}$, is included in a bigger clique X_{big}, s.t. $|X_{big}| \geq \frac{s}{k}$.*

Proof. Let $X \subseteq C$ be any clique of C, s.t. $|X| < \frac{s}{k}$. Let $N \subseteq C$ be the set of nodes which are *not* adjacent to all nodes of X, that is, that are adjacent from 0 to $|X| - 1$ nodes of X. By picking any node $u' \in C \setminus (X \cup N)$, we have that $X' = X \cup \{u'\}$ is a clique of size $|X| + 1$. Since every $u \in X$ can miss at most k neighbors including itself, $|N \cup X| \leq |X|(k-1) + |X| = k|X|$. This means that at most $k|X|$ nodes are excluded for the selection of u'. Let N' be the nodes not adjacent to all nodes of X'. We can repeat the process and grow X', by picking any node $u'' \in C \setminus (X' \cup N')$, until we run out of nodes. Note that the newly-excluded nodes for selecting u'' are u' and its missing neighbors. Such a clique-growing process can be thought of as an iterative process starting from a node and growing a clique – as if X itself were grown after $|X|$ steps of the process – and excluding at most k nodes at a time. Therefore, the process will run at least $\frac{s}{k}$ steps, after which X has been grown to $\frac{s}{k}$ nodes. □

Note that, in case $\frac{s}{k}$ is not integer, the proof yields $|X_{big}| \geq \lceil \frac{s}{k} \rceil$. The cliqueness and the adjacency criteria directly follow.

Corollary 5.5 (cliqueness). *Every node in C has cliqueness at least $\lceil \frac{s}{k} \rceil$.*

Lemma 5.6. *Consider a clique $X \subseteq C$, s.t. $|X| \geq \frac{s}{k}$. If $s \geq k^2$, every node in C either belongs to X or has a neighbors in X.*

Proof. We know that such a clique always exists from Lemma 5.4. Since its size is at least k by assumption, then every $u \in C \setminus X$ has to be adjacent to at least one node in X. □

Our last criterion is a stricter form of the above lemma, which we formalize as follows.

Lemma 5.7 (OverlappingCliques). *Consider a clique $X \subseteq C$, s.t. $|X| \geq \frac{s}{k}$. If $s \geq k^2$, every node in C either belongs to X or to an overlapping clique X', s.t. $|X'| \geq \frac{s}{k}$ and $X \cap X' \neq \emptyset$.*

Graph	n	density	ω	type	File Name
jazz	198	$1.41 \cdot 10^{-1}$	30	collab.	jazz
grQc	5.241	$1.05 \cdot 10^{-3}$	44	collab.	ca-GrQc
geom	6.158	$6.28 \cdot 10^{-4}$	22	collab.	geom
advogato	7.418	$1.75 \cdot 10^{-3}$	19	collab.	advogato
hepPh	12.006	$1.64 \cdot 10^{-3}$	239	collab.	ca-HepPh
astroPh	18.771	$1.12 \cdot 10^{-3}$	57	collab.	ca-AstroPh
newm	22.015	$2.42 \cdot 10^{-4}$	3	collab.	Newman-Cond_mat
mathSci	391.529	$1.14 \cdot 10^{-5}$	25	collab.	MathSciNet
dblp	511.163	$1.43 \cdot 10^{-5}$	115	collab.	dblp20080824_MAX
patents	3.8 M	$2.32 \cdot 10^{-6}$	11	citat.	cit-Patents

Table 1: Real-world networks in our experiments. File name extension is ".nde". Networks are sorted by size n.

Proof. Let u be any node of $C \setminus X$. We know from Lemma 5.6 that exists a node $v \in X$ adjacent to u. Since $\{u, v\}$ is a clique of size 2, we can apply Lemma 5.4 and conclude that both nodes belong to a clique X' larger or equal than $\frac{s}{k}$. Finally, $v \in X \cup X'$. □

6 EXPERIMENTS

In this section, we compare our and previous algorithms over different real-world networks, and show the advantages and limitations of our approach.

Datasets. We considered a mix of real-world networks with various sizes and characteristics. All our networks are publicly available on the LASAGNE meta-repository [1], and come from different human activities. Specifically, we consider:

- small to large collaboration networks, where nodes represent authors of published papers or books, and edges represent co-authorship;
- a large citation network, where nodes represent published papers or books, and edges represent citations;

The networks considered in our experiments, together with their number of nodes (n), density, maximum clique size (ω) and type, are listed in Table 1. In the table, we also list the file name of every network in the repository, for sake of reproducibility.

Implementation details. We implement the auxiliary methods used by our algorithms, with the most recent methods in literature for the corresponding tasks, to the best of our knowledge.

- In `all_cliques`(G), we use the algorithm in [12] for enumerating all the maximal cliques of the input graph G.
- In `all_plexes`(H, k), we use the algorithm in [6] for enumerating all the maximal k-plexes of the sub-graph H.

We implement coreness and cliqueness criteria, respectively, with the method in [5] and the already mentioned algorithm in [12]. Our code is publicly available [2].

Methodology. We compare the execution of our methods for enumerating targeted k-plexes, with the most recent method for enumerating all k-plexes of the input graph [6]. In other words, we compare the algorithms `max_plexes`(G, k), `max_plexes_binary`(G, k), `large_plexes`(G, k, m) with the algorithm `all_plexes`(G, k) over the same input graph, for different values of k and threshold m. To the best of our knowledge, indeed, there are no faster approaches

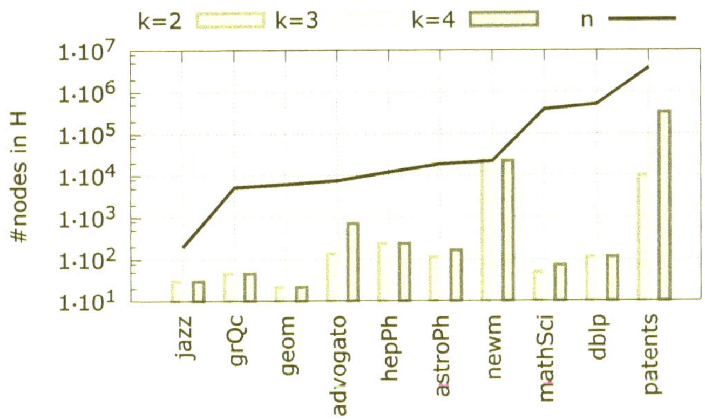

Figure 2: Number of nodes (log scale) in the sub-graph H.

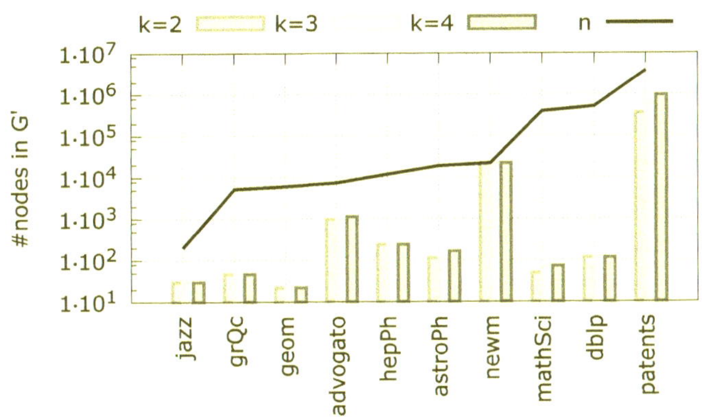

Figure 3: Number of nodes (log scale) surviving the CORENESS criterion.

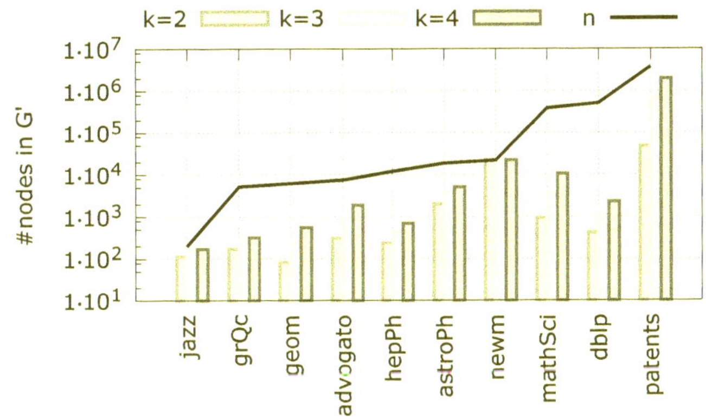

Figure 4: Number of nodes (log scale) surviving the CLIQUENESS criterion.

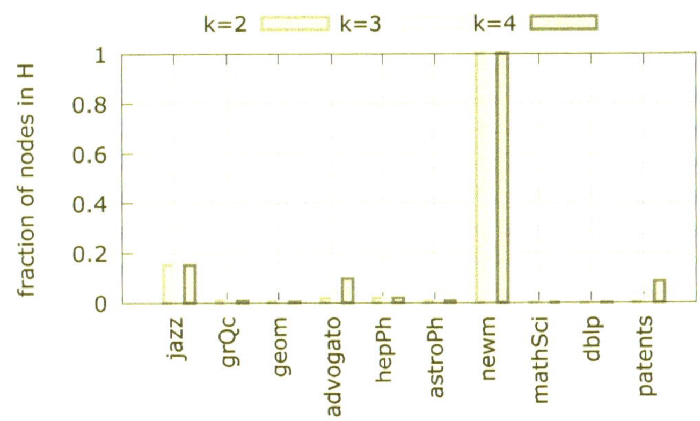

Figure 5: Fraction of nodes surviving CORENESS and CLIQUENESS.

than [6] that are specific for maximum k-plexes and k-plexes non-smaller than a threshold. Targeted enumeration is indeed our contribution.

Test environment. Our experiments were performed on a machine with two CPU Intel Xeon E5-520 units with 4 cores each, running at 2.26GHz, with 8MB of cache and 32GB RAM. The operating system was Linux CentOS 6.7, with kernel version 2.6.32, Java Virtual Machine version 1.8.0_111 (64-Bit) and Python version 2.6.6 (64-Bit). All our executions have a reasonable 6 hours timeout, after which they are interrupted. In the experiments, we show that even the smallest networks with few thousands nodes timeout with traditional methods. Our algorithms, instead, can process networks up to hundreds of thousands of nodes.

6.1 Results

In Figure 2, we show the number of nodes in the sub-graph H computed by the algorithm prune(G, k, m), with different values of k and $m = \omega$, i.e, the maximum clique size. As frame of comparison, we show the number of nodes in G (i.e., n). The figure shows that, except for newm where $\omega = 3$, the sub-graph H is order of magnitudes smaller than G. Notably, for different networks (jazz, geom, hephPh, newm, and dblp), H is left with only the nodes of the maximum k-plex. In such lucky cases we can even skip the execution of the enumeration step all_plexes(H, k). Since the sub-graph produced by a given k is included in the sub-graph produces by $k + 1$, is not surprising that higher values of k yield more nodes in H. (Remember that for $k = n$ we have $G = H$.) However, for most instances, the sub-graph is small with respect to G (thus allowing for faster enumeration of k-plexes) for different values of k. Finally, our criteria have little impact on the newm network, because its maximum clique size is only 3.

Figures 3 and 4 report the number of nodes of G residual after the CORENESS and CLIQUENESS criteria, applied separately. Figure 5 shows the fraction of nodes of G residual after both criteria, applied together as in our prune() algorithm. For the considered networks, most nodes are filtered out by CORENESS. Then, the structures that are too connected to be filtered by CORENESS but too small to play a role in the search for k-plexes non-smaller than ω, are filtered out by CLIQUENESS. Such an additional CLIQUENESS step has bigger impact in advogato and patents. In principle, our CORENESS and CLIQUENESS criteria can be applied repeatedly, in alternation, until there are no more nodes to filter out. In practice, we observed that after three iterations (that is, CORENESS–CLIQUENESS–CORENESS–CLIQUENESS–CORENESS–CLIQUENESS) there were no additional nodes

GRAPH	FULL ENUM	OUR APPROACH		
		CORE	CLIQUE	ENUM
jazz	2 h	0,008 s	0,091 s	no need
grQc	> 6h	0,001 s	0,026 s	1,99 s
geom	> 6h	0,001 s	0,086 s	no need
advogato	> 6h	0,003 s	0,234 s	1 h 45 m
hepPh	> 6h	0,001 s	0,421 s	no need
astroPh	> 6h	0,046 s	0,892 s	2,92 s
newm	> 6h	0,22 s	0,167 s	> 6h
mathSci	> 6h	0,009 s	2,535 s	0,11 s
dblp	> 6h	0,005 s	4,336 s	no need
patents	> 6h	1,148 s	63,258 s	> 6h

Table 2: Running time for finding all the largest 2-plexes.

GRAPH	k	FULL ENUM	OUR APPROACH	
		TIME	TIME	#FOUND
grQc	2	> 6h	4,65 s	3
	4	> 6h	2,7 s	1
astroPh	2	> 6h	5 h 44 m	10
	4	> 6h	> 6h	-
mathSci	2	> 6h	2,75 s	7
	4	> 6h	> 6h	7

Table 3: Running time for finding all k-plexes larger than 80% of the maximum clique.

to filter out of networks in our dataset, and that only few nodes (i.e., less than 10) were removed from second iteration on.

Maximum k-plexes. In Table 2, we show running times for different steps of max_plexes(G, 2), compared to the time required for enumerating all 2-plexes (column "FULL ENUM"), over the same input graph.

- column "CORE" is the time needed for applying CORENESS criterion, and computing an intermediate sub-graph G';
- column "CLIQUE" is the time needed for applying CLIQUENESS criterion over the intermediate sub-graph G', and computing H;
- column "ENUM" is the execution time of large_plexes() over H.

The time for computing our criteria has little impact on the overall running time, which is dominated by the enumeration of 2-plexes of the residual sub-graph when necessary. As a consequence, in all the networks where H is left with only the nodes of the maximum clique, which is in turn also the maximum 2-plex, the computation of max_plexes() ends successfully after fractions of seconds. For such networks, we write "no need" in the "ENUM" column. As frame of comparison, full enumeration of 2-plexes (i.e., as in [6]) requires hours even on our smallest network (jazz), and times out on the other networks.

When H is not as minimal as in the networks with no need for all_plexes(H, k), the running time of max_plexes() still ranges from fractions of seconds (most networks) to 2 h, proportionally to the size of H (see Figure 2 for comparison). In general, we can conclude that the running time of our algorithm mostly depends on the size of the sub-graph computed by prune(). The only two instances that requires more than 6 h are indeed the newm and patents networks, that correspond to the top two largest filtered sub-graphs (see Figure 2).

We observed that the results for higher values of k , namely $k = 3$ and $k = 4$, are similar. This is because the sub-graph H produced with higher valued of k contains only few more nodes than the sub-graph produced with $k = 2$, as shown in Figure 2

Binary search. Our "cautious choice" strategy for the maximum k-plexes is able to process quickly all the networks in Table 2, except newm and patents. For the newm network, we observe that $\omega = 3$ (see Table 1) and the size of the maximum 2-plex is $\omega_2 = 5$, that is, ω_2 is closer to $2 \cdot \omega$ (i.e., the theoretical maximum size for a 2-plex) than to ω. This makes the newm network a good candidate for a "greedy choice" as in the max_plexes_binary() algorithm described in Section 3.2. In practice, the value of ω_2 is not known a priori. However, we can decide for the greedy choice also by observing that ω is small. We observed experimentally for the newm networks that the computation of max_plexes_binary(G,2) terminates after only one iteration in less than our time out. Instead, the network patents is hard to process even with the greedy choice. To improve on this result is a challenging future task.

Large k-plexes. In Table 3, we show the overall running time of large_plexes(G, k, m) on different networks in our dataset, for different values of k. For this experiment, we set $m = 0.8\omega_k$, where ω_k is the maximum k-plex size, as computed by max_plexes(G, k). The time required for enumerating all k-plexes (column "FULL ENUM") of such networks is always larger than our timeout (6 hours). The table also show the number of k-plexes returned (column "FOUND"). All the networks considered contain less than a dozen k-plex non-smaller than $0.8\omega_k$, which are quickly found by our algorithm in most cases. Note that in this experiment we call prune($G, k, 0.8\omega_k$), that is, we compute the sub-graph H using a different threshold than in Figure 2 (possibly $0.8\omega_k \geq \omega$).

The astroPh network requires much more time than other networks. To this end, for this specific network, we plot in Figure 6a the overall running time of large_plexes(G, 2, m) (i.e., for 2-plexes), for m ranging in $[0, \omega_2]$. We computed using max_plexes(G, 2) that $\omega_2 = 57$. On the one side of the spectrum, for $m = 0$, all the 2-plexes ought to be returned (i.e., the same result than all_plexes()). On the other side, for $m = \omega_2$, only a single 2-plex – the maximum 2-plex – is returned. The plot shows that the running time quickly decreases from hours to seconds as m approaches to ω_2. The data-point close to 5 hours corresponds to $m = 0.8\omega_2$, as in Table 3. We compare these results with the cumulative distribution function (CDF) of 2-plexes of astroPh, as reported in Figure 6b. As frame of comparison, we also show CDF of cliques (that are 1-plexes). As expected, most 2-plexes have size smaller than 10^2. For $m > 0.8\omega_2$, which represents the 99th percentile for 2-plexes, the running time of large_plexes() is even smaller than half an hour, confirming the effectiveness of our targeted enumeration system.

[2] The figure may be counter-intuitive to read, as while the portion of 2-plexes larger than 10 is smaller than the one of cliques, the absolute number is still larger.

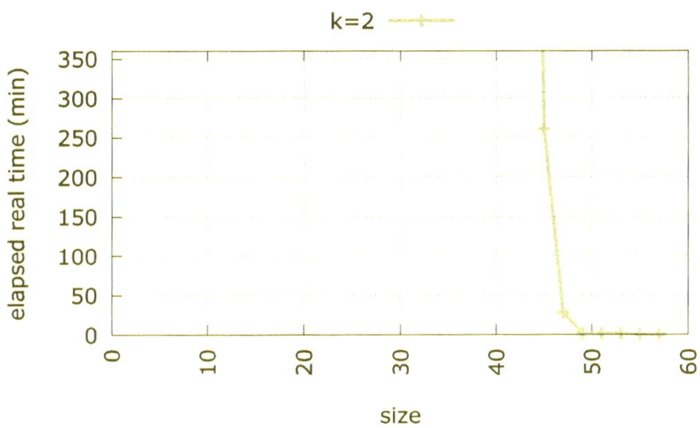

(a) Running time.

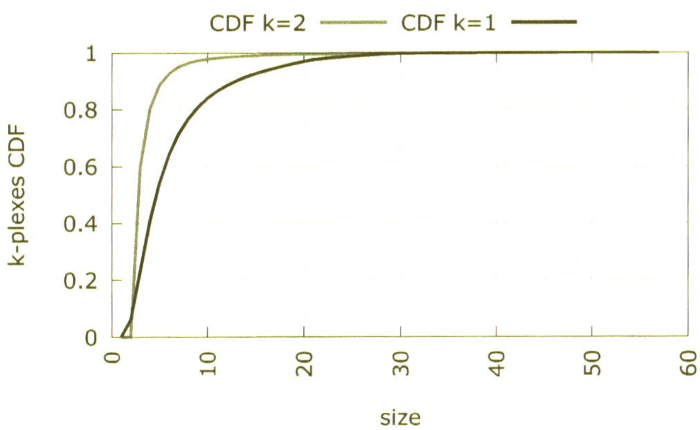

(b) CDF of 2-plexes.

Figure 6: Running time on `large_plexes()` and cumulative distribution function distribution of k-plexes of `astroPh`.

7 RELATED WORKS

In the field of network analysis, dense substructures in graphs (aka dense subgraphs) are associated with communities, or more in general sets of closely related elements [14, 17]. The problem of finding these substructures has been extensively studied for decades, and continues to be the object of cutting edge research. The simplest and most rigorous definition of dense subgraph is the clique, i.e., a subgraph in which all nodes are pairwise connected. Many algorithms for finding all maximal cliques have been developed, most of them being inspired to the Bron-Kerbosh algorithm [7], such as [13, 19] or to the more recent paradigm of *reverse search* [3], such as [10, 11, 15]. The definition of clique may be too strict in some instances, such as in real datasets where data can be noisy and incomplete, so several definitions of pseudo-clique have been produced [17], such as the k-plex [18].

McClosky [16] performs a thorough study to devise exact algorithms for finding the largest k-plex, and heuristics for finding lower upper bounds on its size, exploiting co-k-plexes (i.e., k-plexes on the complement graph) and graph coloring techniques. The usability of the algrorithms for finding the largest k-plex is however limited to small networks, as the running time exceeds the hour for graphs with hundreds of nodes.

Wu et al. [21] propose *Pemp*, a parallel algorithm for enumerating k-plexes, which successfully improves its performance with the usage of multiple cores.

Cohen et al. [9] give a generic framework for enumerating all maximal subgraphs with respect to hereditary and connected hereditary graph properties, i.e., properties that are closed with respect to induced subgraphs and connected induced subgraphs, respectively. Berlowitz et al. [6] apply the framework in [9], together with insights on the k-plex problem, to produce efficient algorithms for the enumeration of maximal k-plexes and maximal connected k-plexes, which are respectively hereditary and connected hereditary. The algorithm for connected k-plexes in [6] outperforms the other state of the art algorithms for enumerating or finding the largest k-plex, and constitutes our baseline for the experimental evaluation.

Other quasi clique models include the one defined by Zhai et al. [22], that is a k-plex with additional connectivity constraint (called *CLB*), and more that can be found in this survey by Pattillo et al. [17].

Real world networks can often be large, with millions of nodes and billions of edges. However, algorithms for finding dense subgraphs tend to have high computational complexity, and the number of solutions can be exponential in the worst case [19]. Thus, a great amount effort was dedicated to find ways to process these difficult networks.

Some [8, 12] have proposed decomposition approaches to limit the memory usage, as this allows in-memory computation on larger instances, and can provide a speedup even when the graph fits in main memory. Others, such as Zhai et al. [22], exploit properties specific to the considered quasi-cliuque model to prune the search space.

8 CONCLUSIONS

We have proposed a novel approach to the enumeration of large k-plexes, a formal and meaningful way to define interesting communities in real-world networks that generalizes the notion of clique. Two main clues have driven our solution:

- a relevant portion of the network can be filtered out well before starting the detection of large k-plexes and
- cliques, which are more restricted but can be computed efficiently, can be used as starting points for the search of k-plexes in the network. The efficiency of the approach over state-of-the-art algorithms has been confirmed by our experiments.

In the future, we intend to further extend the applicability of our approach and tackle the problem of computing large k-plexes on real world networks with millions of nodes. Our future work also includes experimenting with a variety of networks coming from different domains, such as (but not limited to) biological networks, web graphs, and product co-purchasing networks.

ACKNOWLEDGMENTS

We thank the authors of [6] for providing us with their code and for discussions on the subject of this paper.

REFERENCES

[1] http://lasagne-unifi.sourceforge.net. [Online; accessed Feb-2017].
[2] http://patrignani.dia.uniroma3.it/large-k-plexes. [Online; accessed Feb-2017].
[3] David Avis and Komei Fukuda. Reverse search for enumeration. *Discrete Applied Mathematics*, 65(1-3):21 – 46, 1996.
[4] Balabhaskar Balasundaram, Sergiy Butenko, and Illya V. Hicks. Clique relaxations in social network analysis: The maximum k-plex problem. *Oper. Res.*, 59(1):133–142, January 2011.
[5] Vladimir Batagelj and Matjaz Zaversnik. An o(m) algorithm for cores decomposition of networks. *CoRR*, cs.DS/0310049, 2003.
[6] Devora Berlowitz, Sara Cohen, and Benny Kimelfeld. Efficient enumeration of maximal k-plexes. In *Proceedings of the 2015 ACM SIGMOD International Conference on Management of Data*, SIGMOD '15, pages 431–444, New York, NY, USA, 2015. ACM.
[7] Coenraad Bron and Joep Kerbosch. Finding all cliques of an undirected graph (algorithm 457). *Commun. ACM*, 16(9):575–576, 1973.
[8] James Cheng, Linhong Zhu, Yiping Ke, and Shumo Chu. Fast algorithms for maximal clique enumeration with limited memory. In *KDD*, pages 1240–1248, 2012.
[9] Sara Cohen, Benny Kimelfeld, and Yehoshua Sagiv. Generating all maximal induced subgraphs for hereditary and connected-hereditary graph properties. *Journal of Computer and System Sciences*, 74(7):1147 – 1159, 2008.
[10] Carlo Comin and Romeo Rizzi. An improved upper bound on maximal clique listing via rectangular fast matrix multiplication. *CoRR*, abs/1506.01082, 2015.
[11] Alessio Conte, Roberto Grossi, Andrea Marino, and Luca Versari. Sublinear-space bounded-delay enumeration for massive network analytics: Maximal cliques. In *43rd International Colloquium on Automata, Languages, and Programming, ICALP 2016, July 11-15, 2016, Rome, Italy*, pages 148:1–148:15, 2016.
[12] Alessio Conte, Roberto De Virgilio, Antonio Maccioni, Maurizio Patrignani, and Riccardo Torlone. Finding all maximal cliques in very large social networks. In *Proceedings of the 19th International Conference on Extending Database Technology, EDBT 2016, Bordeaux, France, March 15-16, 2016, Bordeaux, France, March 15-16, 2016.*, pages 173–184, 2016.
[13] David Eppstein and Darren Strash. Listing all maximal cliques in large sparse real-world graphs. In *SEA*, pages 364–375, 2011.
[14] Santo Fortunato. Community detection in graphs. *Physics reports*, 486(3):75–174, 2010.
[15] Kazuhisa Makino and Takeaki Uno. New algorithms for enumerating all maximal cliques. In *SWAT*, pages 260–272, 2004.
[16] Benjamin McClosky and Illya V. Hicks. Combinatorial algorithms for the maximum k-plex problem. *J. Comb. Optim.*, 23(1):29–49, 2012.
[17] Jeffrey Pattillo, Nataly Youssef, and Sergiy Butenko. *Clique Relaxation Models in Social Network Analysis*, pages 143–162. Springer New York, New York, NY, 2012.
[18] Stephen B. Seidman and Brian L. Foster. A graph-theoretic generalization of the clique concept. *The Journal of Mathematical Sociology*, 6(1):139–154, 1978.
[19] Etsuji Tomita, Akira Tanaka, and Haruhisa Takahashi. The worst-case time complexity for generating all maximal cliques and computational experiments. *Theor. Comput. Sci.*, 363(1):28–42, 2006.
[20] Douglas Brent West et al. *Introduction to graph theory*, volume 2. Prentice hall Upper Saddle River, 2001.
[21] Bin Wu and Xin Pei. A parallel algorithm for enumerating all the maximal k-plexes. In *Pacific-Asia Conference on Knowledge Discovery and Data Mining*, pages 476–483. Springer, 2007.
[22] Hongjie Zhai, Makoto Haraguchi, Yoshiaki Okubo, and Etsuji Tomita. A fast and complete algorithm for enumerating pseudo-cliques in large graphs. *International Journal of Data Science and Analytics*, 2(3-4):145–158, 2016.

Matrix Profile V: A Generic Technique to Incorporate Domain Knowledge into Motif Discovery

Hoang Anh Dau Eamonn Keogh
University of California, Riverside
USA
{hdau001, eamonn}@ucr.edu

ABSTRACT

Time series motif discovery has emerged as perhaps the most used primitive for time series data mining, and has seen applications to domains as diverse as robotics, medicine and climatology. There has been recent significant progress on the scalability of motif discovery. However, we believe that the current definitions of motif discovery are limited, and can create a mismatch between the user's intent/expectations, and the motif discovery search outcomes. In this work, we explain the reasons behind these issues, and introduce a novel and general framework to address them. Our ideas can be used with current state-of-the-art algorithms with virtually no time or space overhead, and are fast enough to allow real-time interaction and hypotheses testing on massive datasets. We demonstrate the utility of our ideas on domains as diverse as seismology and epileptic seizure monitoring.

KEYWORDS

Time series; matrix profile; motif discovery; interactive data mining

1 INTRODUCTION

The last decade has seen time series motif discovery become a prominent primitive for time series data mining. It has been applied to diverse domains such as climatology, robotics [11], medicine [23] and seismology [24]. Recently there has been significant progress on the scalability of motif discovery, and datasets with lengths in the tens of millions can be routinely searched on conventional hardware [24]. Paradoxically, the ease with which we can now perform motif discovery has revealed some weaknesses in the traditional definition of motifs; there are many situations in which the results of motif search do not align with the user's intent. Below we discuss several examples to help develop the reader's intuitions for this fact. This section is unusually long for a paper's "Introduction", but is warranted by the fact that we are introducing unfamiliar and unintuitive issues.

1.1 Stop-Word Motif Bias

In some datasets, the most interesting repeated patterns may be rare, and "swamped" by more frequent patterns. By analogy with text, we can ask what is the most common "motif" (i.e. word) in Poe's famous poem, *The Raven*? One might imagine that it is the eponymous bird; however, that is only the 13th most common word, with 13 occurrences. The most frequent words with their number of occurrences are "*the*" (56), "*and*" (38), "*I*" (32) ... In retrospect, this finding is not surprising, and we recall that stop-words are removed before any text analytics are performed.

A similar problem occurs in time series. Consider the snippet of ECG data shown in Figure 1. Note that the signal begins with a slightly noisy saw-toothed wave (called the *calibration signal*), which is how the ECG apparatus indicates that it is switched-on, but not detecting a biological signal. Unsurprisingly, the saw-tooth "stop-word" is the best motif in this dataset.

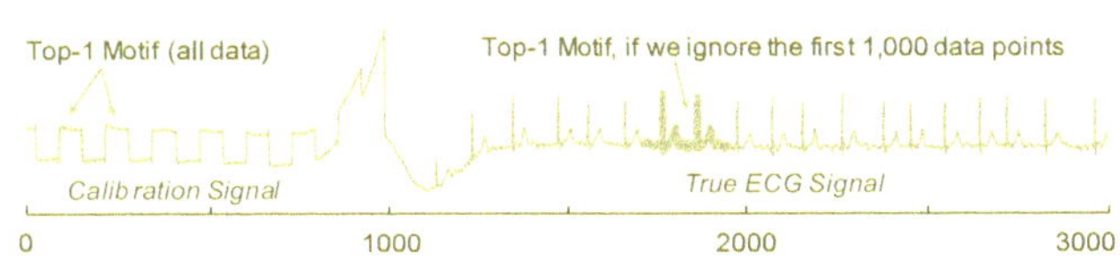

Figure 1: A snippet of ECG data from the LTAF-71 Database [13]. The top motifs come from regions of the calibration signal because they are much more similar than the motifs discovered if we search only data that contains true ECGs.

One might imagine that this issue only affects the *beginning* of signals, and thus could be easily addressed by manual inspection and truncation. Unfortunately, this is not the case. It is very common for sensors to temporarily lose the signal due to poor contact or patient motion, and this issue shows up dozens of times in this 25-hour trace.

It is important to note that the issue of stop-word motifs is not limited to machine artifacts from the recording process. The

KDD '17, August 13-17, 2017, Halifax, NS, Canada

ACM ISBN 978-1-4503-4887-4/17/08...$15.00
http://dx.doi.org/10.1145/3097983.3097993

issue shows up even within "pure" data sources. Again, by analogy, note that a set of text stop-words is context dependent. For example, in a general text search the word "computer" is *not* a stop-word, but for a search within the ACM portal, it *is* a stop-word. The exact same situation occurs with time series. Consider the snippet of ECG data shown in Figure 2. The eye is drawn to the repeated ventricular contractions highlighted in red, but the best motifs by the classic definitions are a pair of normal heartbeats.

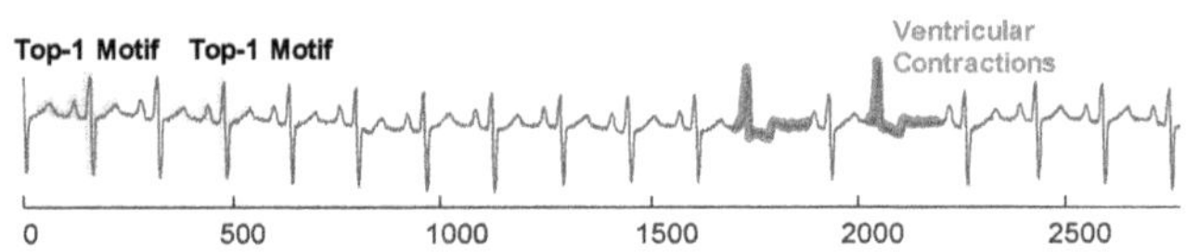

Figure 2: A snippet of ECG data from BIDMC Congestive Heart Failure Database (chf02). The top motif pair are the two highlighted normal heartbeats. However, a cardiologist's eye is drawn here to the two repeated ventricular contractions [13].

Even if the rare motifs are more strongly conserved than the background motifs, we should *still* expect the background motifs to be discovered first. The reason is essentially a real-valued version of the birthday paradox. Consider again the pair of ventricular contractions shown in Figure 2. They are better conserved (under the Euclidean distance) than *most* pairs of normal beats. However, there are fourteen normal beats, therefore there are 91 pairwise combinations that *could* match. With so many possibilities, it is unsurprising that the closest pair will be reported as the best motif.

The toy problem in Figure 2 can be solved by visual inspection, but with time series motif discovery now scaling to datasets of length one-hundred million [24], a more general and automatic solution is required. Finally, we note that this problem is not confined to ECGs or other periodic data. For example, in industrial data the top-K motifs may all correspond to patterns caused by calibration runs or shift changes. These known/uninteresting patterns may obscure a much rarer and unexpected repeated pattern.

1.2 Simplicity Bias in Motif Search

Imagine that we have {C1,C2}, a pair of subsequences that are "complicated" (informally for now, this means having *many peaks and valleys* [1]), and $\{S_1,S_2\}$, a pair subsequences that are "simple". Further imagine that, to your eyes, each pair itself is equally similar. In spite of this imagined subjective equality of similarity, it is almost certain that $D(C_1,C_2)$ is greater than $D(S_1,S_2)$ under Euclidean distance, Dynamic Time Warping or any other effective distance measure [1]. The practical upshot of this is that it will be difficult to find such complicated motifs, as the top-K will be swamped by many simple motifs. To see this, consider the top motif discovered in the EEG snippet shown in Figure 3.

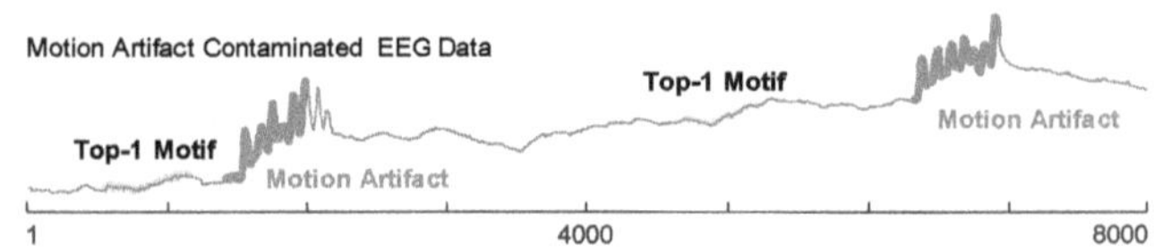

Figure 3: A snippet of an EEG time series in which two motion artifacts were deliberately introduced by the attending physician [16]. Surprisingly, the top-motif does not correspond to the motion artifacts, but to simple regions of "drift".

The result is visually jarring. The two motion artifacts *are* visually similar and *do* have a small Euclidean Distance, yet they are not discovered as the top motif. Instead, two regions of vaguely rising trends are the top motif. The reason for this mismatch between our expectation and the results is understood, but not in this context. In [1], it was demonstrated that the Euclidean distance has a bias toward simple shapes. Quoting [1], "*pairs of complex objects, even those which subjectively may seem very similar to the human eye, tend to be further apart under* (Euclidean) *distance measures than pairs of simple objects.*"

This issue is perhaps the most reported complaint of users of motif discovery tools[1]. Almost all large time series datasets have low complexity regions, which are often uninteresting to the analyst, yet it is virtually certain that all the top-K motifs will come from there.

1.3 Actionability Bias

In many cases a domain expert wants to find not simply the best motif (as defined as the subsequence pair that minimizes their mutual distance), but regularities in the data which are exploitable or actionable in some domain specific ways. Such constraints have been explained to us by various domain experts[1] with statements such as "*I want to find motifs in this web-click data, preferably occurring on or close to the weekend*", or "*I want to find motifs in this oil pressure data, but they would be more useful if they end with a rising trend*", or "*I want to find motifs in this PPG time series data, but it would be better if they happened about five to ten minutes after the accompanying RR time series data was relatively high*".

There is currently no way to support such arbitrary constraints/preferences in motif search. Note that by their very nature, many of these constraints will need to be adjusted in real-time interactive sessions. For example, the user with a preference for a motif that happens near a weekend may be inspired by the quality of the results and wish to sharpen her focus to "*strictly on a weekend*", or she may have been disappointed by the sparse results and reluctantly weaken her constraint to "*preferably not on a Tuesday or Wednesday*". As we

[1] We note that many of the issues we address were reported to us over the last decade by users of motif discovery tools from academia and industry.

will show, we can support this need interactively with almost no overheard of time or space.

1.4 Summary and Outline

We have seen several reasons why classic motif discovery can fail to produce the expected or desired results. The contribution of this work is to produce a single, real-time, intuitive framework that can handle all the above, and many other domain specific constraints that have yet to occur to us. The basic idea behind our approach is to produce a vector that is "parallel" to the original time series and annotates it with the user's constraint(s). As the motif discovery algorithm finds candidate motifs, this annotation vector (AV) is used to re-rank them, allowing the motifs that best balance the fidelity of conservation with the user's constraints to rise to the top.

This only leaves the question of how do we create such annotation vectors? We introduce a generic framework that allows a user to create such vectors, typically with just a few lines of code in a scripting language. For concreteness, we explicitly show the annotation functions that allow us to address all the examples above, and illustrate their utility with detailed case studies. Furthermore, our framework is simple and flexible enough to support domains and constraints that have yet to be explored. Despite the flexibility and expressiveness of our system, we will show that it requires an inconsequential overhead of time and space complexity, relative to the state-of-the-art motif discovery [23][24].

The rest of the paper is organized as follows. In Section 2, we review the related work and introduce necessary notations. In Section 3, we discuss our proposed framework together with several case studies. Section 4 includes a comprehensive quantitative comparison with other motif discovery algorithms in the literature. Finally, we arrive at conclusions and future research in Section 5.

2 RELATED WORK AND NOTATION

We begin with a brief review of related work before introducing the notations needed to understand our proposed framework.

2.1 Related Work

The literature on general time series motif search is large and growing. We refer the reader to [2][7][23] and references therein.

This section is brief. While there are many papers on exploiting motifs, and scaling up motif search, to the best of our knowledge there are no research efforts that even explicitly *note* the issues we tackle, much less *address* them.

Saria and colleagues noted a limitation of the standard motif definition in that it may not readily discover motifs that have significant temporal warping [14]. Similarly, Yankov et al. noted that in some domains we may need to allow uniform scaling to enable meaningful motif discovery [22]. However, both of these issues are largely orthogonal to the issues at hand. In any case, Mueen has argued that these issues are mostly an artifact of searching small datasets, and as we search larger datasets, these issues simply go away (see Section 4.3.2 of [12]).

We do note that in the context of text information retrieval, there is significant work in query-biased (or user-directed) summaries [18]. Such work is in the same spirit as our work, directing the results of a query toward an arbitrary informational need or away from an undesired outcome [10].

2.2 Notation

We begin by defining the data type of interest, *time series*:

Definition 1: A *time series* $T \in \mathbb{R}^n$ is a sequence of real-valued numbers $t_i \in \mathbb{R} : T = [t_1, t_2, \ldots, t_n]$ where n is the length of T.

We are typically not interested in the global properties of a time series, but in the local regions known as *subsequences*:

Definition 2: A *subsequence* $T_{i,m} \in \mathbb{R}^m$ of a time series T is a continuous subset of the values from T of length m starting from position i. Formally, $T_{i,m} = [t_i, t_{i+1}, \ldots, t_{i+m-1}]$.

The particular local property we are interested in in this work is *time series motifs*:

Definition 3: A *time series motif* is the most similar subsequence pair of a time series. Formally, $T_{a,m}$ and $T_{b,m}$ is the motif pair iff $dist(T_{a,m}, T_{b,m}) \leq dist(T_{i,m}, T_{j,m}) \; \forall \, i,j \in [1, 2, \ldots, n-m+1]$ where $a \neq b$ and $i \neq j$, and $dist$ is a function that computes the z-normalized Euclidean distance between the input subsequences [2][5][12][22][23].

We store the distance between a subsequence of a time series with all the other subsequences from the same time series in an ordered array called *distance profile*.

Definition 4: A *distance profile* $D \in \mathbb{R}^{n-m+1}$ of a time series T and a subsequence $T_{i,m}$ is a vector stores $dist(T_{i,m}, T_{j,m}) \; \forall \, j \in [1, 2, \ldots, n-m+1]$, where $i \neq j$.

One of the most efficient ways to locate *exact* time series motifs is to compute the *matrix profile* [23].

Definition 5: A *matrix profile* $P \in \mathbb{R}^{n-m+1}$ of a time series T is a meta time series that stores the z-normalized Euclidean distance between each subsequence and its nearest neighbor where n is the length of T and m is the given subsequence length. The time series motif can be found by simply locating the two lowest values in P (they will have tying values).

Figure 4 illustrates a matrix profile on a small toy dataset.

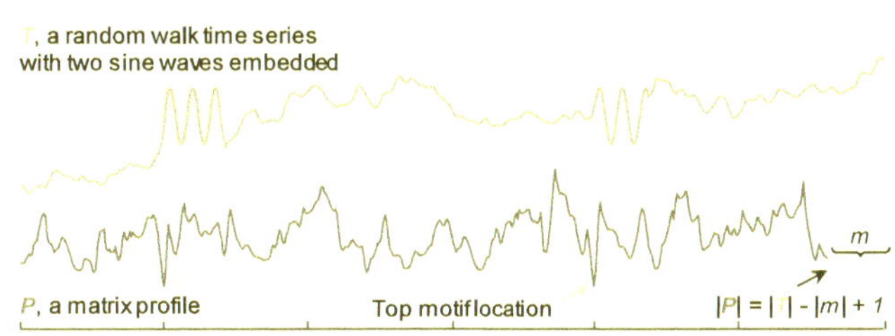

Figure 4: A time series T and its self-join matrix profile P. The ith element of P is the Euclidean distance between the subsequence starting from position i of T and its nearest neighbor.

To avoid trivial matches [12] in which a pattern is matched to itself, or a pattern that largely overlaps with itself, the matrix profile incorporates an "exclusion-zone" concept, which is a region before and after the location of a given query that should be ignored. The exclusion zone is heuristically set to $m/2$.

The time complexity to compute a matrix profile P is $O(n^2)$. This may seem untenable for time series data mining, but several factors mitigate this concern. First, note that the time complexity is independent of m, the length of the subsequences. Secondly, the matrix profile can be computed with an *anytime algorithm*, and in most domains, in just $O(cn\log n)$ steps the algorithm converges to what would be the final solution [23] (c is a small constant). Finally, the matrix profile can be computed with GPUs, cloud computing and other HPC environments that make scaling to at least tens of millions of data points trivial [24]. Even using standard hardware, all the examples in this paper can be computed much faster than real-time. For example, 30 minutes of ECG sampled at 60Hz takes about four minutes to exactly compute the full matrix profile using STOMP [24]. If that was not fast enough, STAMP can produce a very high quality approximation in under five seconds [23].

2.1.1 Summary of this section. Before moving on, we wish to restate the reason for our detailed explanation of the matrix profile. As explained in greater detail in [23], once the matrix profile has been computed, all the top-K motifs are available "for free". For example, the locations of the top-1 motif is simply the (tied) lowest points in the matrix profile. Moreover, all other definitions of motifs (range motifs, top-K motifs etc.) can also be trivially extracted. Thus, we see the computational aspects of motif search largely solved, our contributions are limited to "nudging" the results to be more useful.

3 GUIDED MOTIF SEARCH

The basic idea behind guided motif search is to produce a vector that is "parallel" to the original time series (and to the matrix profile) that encodes the user's domain-dependent *bias(es)*. This vector is then used to modify the matrix profile, changing its shape such that the undesirable solutions are more expensive, and no longer show up in the top-K motifs. We begin by explaining the general domain independent part of our solution in the next section, before showing several examples of how to create domain dependent bias functions.

3.1 The Annotation Vector Framework

The Annotation Vector (AV) plays the role of manipulating the motif search. Recall the notation of matrix profile (MP) elucidated in Section 2.2. The MP is the current state-of-the-art for motif discovery [23][24]. Our main idea is to leverage this MP to discover more meaningful motifs. We achieve this goal by combining the matrix profile with the annotation vector to produce a new matrix profile. We will refer to this as the "Corrected" MP (CMP), as it correctly incorporates the contextual bias for the problem at hand.

The annotation vector AV is a time series consisting of real-valued numbers between [0 - 1]. A low value indicates the subsequence starting at that index is not a desirable motif, and therefore should be biased *against*. Conversely, higher values mean the subsequence at that location should be favored *for* the potential motif pool. Note that the AV has the same length as the matrix profile MP. In Figure 5 we show the annotation vector that encodes the bias: *"I want to find motifs in this traffic data, preferably occurring on or close to the weekend"*.

There may be some scenarios in which the annotation vector AV consists of just 0s and 1s. For example, this would be the case when the desired motifs are strictly limited to within a certain period, such as, *activities between 8am-10am daily*, or at a longer time scale, *activities that happen only during an Olympic year.* For such scenarios, we would assign 0 for AV data points in the untargeted period, and 1 for targeted ones. However, as shown in Figure 5, we allow arbitrary real-number values in the AV, so long as they are in the unit interval.

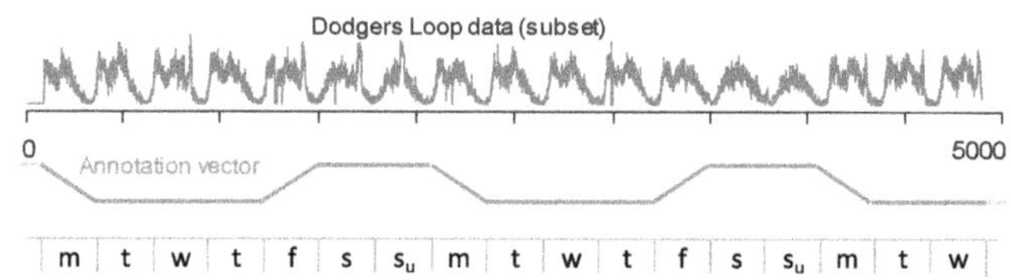

Figure 5: *top*) Seventeen days from the Dodger Loop dataset. *bottom*) The AV that encodes a preference for motifs occurring on or near the weekend.

Having defined the AV, we can now explain how we use it to correct the undesirable results explained above. To do this, we simply produce a Corrected Matrix Profile (CMP) by combining the annotation vector AV and the original matrix profile MP:

$$CMP_i = MP_i + (1 - AV_i) * \max(MP)$$

In the above equation, CMP_i, MP_i and AV_i denote the corrected MP value, the original MP value and the AV value respectively. The $\max(MP)$ term denotes the maximum value of the original MP. The resulting corrected MP can be interpreted as follow: if a region of the time series potentially contains the meaningful motifs, its MP values are left untouched. Otherwise, its MP values are "pushed" higher (increased) to reduce the possibility of any motif in that region appears in the top-K motif list.

In many cases, the annotation vectors can be created by just a few lines of code. Moreover, they can be created in a simple environment such as MS Excel or a scripting language such as Matlab or Python. This is important, since many of the end-users of motif discovery are biologists, medical doctors, seismologists [23] etc., not computer/data scientists.

For example, to produce one week of the AV shown in Figure 5, assuming that the data is sampled once a minute and starts at midnight Sunday, we can use a single line of Matlab:

```
AV = [(1440:-1:1)/1440 zeros(1,1440*3) (1:1440)/1440 ones(1,1440*2)]
```

Which we can interpret as:

AV = [$\text{Mon}_{\text{RampDown}}$ $\text{TueWedThu}_{\text{ConstantLow}}$ $\text{Fri}_{\text{RampUp}}$ $\text{Weekend}_{\text{ConstantHigh}}$]

In the following subsections, we will show how the annotation vector is used in action to guide motif search with several motivating case studies.

3.2 Case Study: Actionability Bias

In this section, we discuss two problems brought to our attention by medical researchers, and we show that they have trivial fixes using our framework.

3.2.1 Suppressing Motion Artifact. We begin with an example brought to our attention by Dr. Gregory Mason of the UCLA Medical Center. Clinicians often want to find motifs in medical telemetry, for example, in data obtained by brain-imaging technique such as fNIRS shown in Figure 6.

This example highlights a problem ubiquitous in this domain [3] [17]. The motif discovered in Figure 6 corresponds to a motion artifact, and has no medical significance. Such motion artifacts plague both clinicians and researchers. For example, an eight-hour sleep study is likely to have dozens or hundreds of such artifacts, as the subject tosses and turns. Note that the example shown in Figure 6 is visually obvious for the reader's benefit; however, more generally, it is not always easy to differentiate between biologically significant patterns and artifacts.

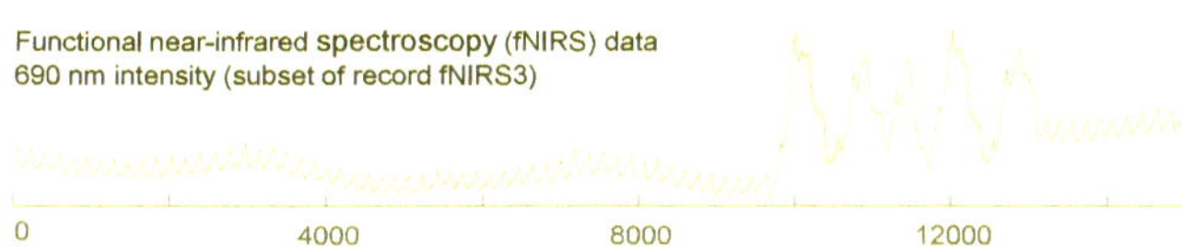

Figure 6: A snippet of fNIRS searched for motifs of length 600. The motifs correspond to an atypical region, which (using external data) we know is due to a sensor artifact.

Nevertheless, we can address this issue for motif discovery in a very simple way, by leveraging the fact that many medical sensors also include an accelerometer. Figure 7 shows the synchronization between the fNIRS data and accompanying accelerator data. Given that the motion of the sensors is *producing* spurious motifs, we can use this motion to produce an annotation vector to suppress *them*.

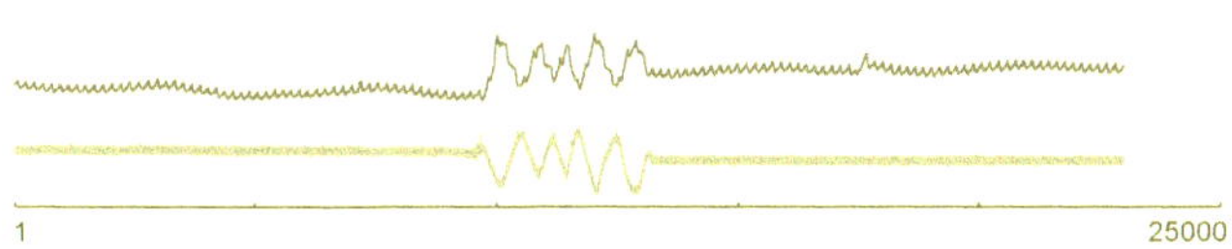

Figure 7: The blue time series is fNIRS data. The red time series is the acceleration of the body-worn sensors. This is a dramatic and visually obvious example of this issue. The problem is typically subtler, but still negatively effects motif discovery.

Concretely, we slide a window of length m across the acceleration time series. We compare the standard deviation of each subsequence with the mean of all the subsequences' standard deviations, and assign the AV value to be either 0 or 1 accordingly (see Figure 8). Our AV data point is 0 if the corresponding subsequence has its standard deviation equal or greater than the mean, indicating regions of unusually large fluctuation.

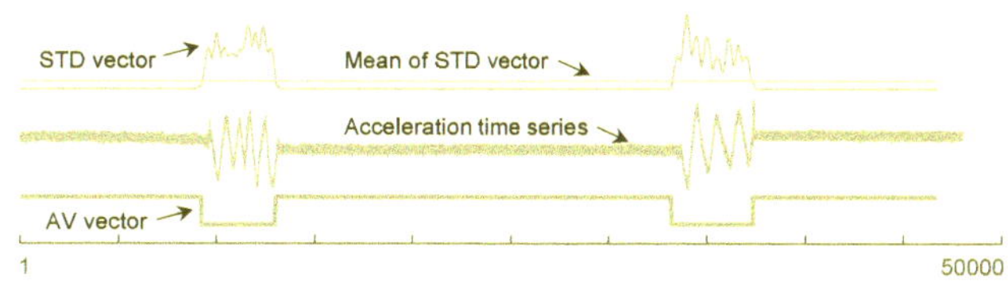

Figure 8: Points above the mean of all subsequences' standard deviation are well aligned with regions of motion artifacts.

To show how little effort this would be for a clinician or researcher, Table 1 contains the full Matlab code used to generate this AV. Naturally, a Matlab guru could write even terser code, but our point is simply that writing an AV is typically only a minute's work.

Table 1: Code to generate the AV for fNIRS example

```
function AV = make_AV(data, subsequenceLength)
for i = 1:length(data) - subsequenceLength + 1
    stdVector(i) = std(data(i:i+subsequenceLength-1));
end
AV(stdVector >= mean(stdVector)) = 0;
AV(stdVector <  mean(stdVector)) = 1;
```

Figure 9.*top* displays the original matrix profile along with the spurious motifs that are discovered with that MP. Figure 9.*bottom* shows the MP corrected with the annotation vector produced by Table 1, enabling medically meaningful motifs from neuronal activity-related signal regions to be discovered.

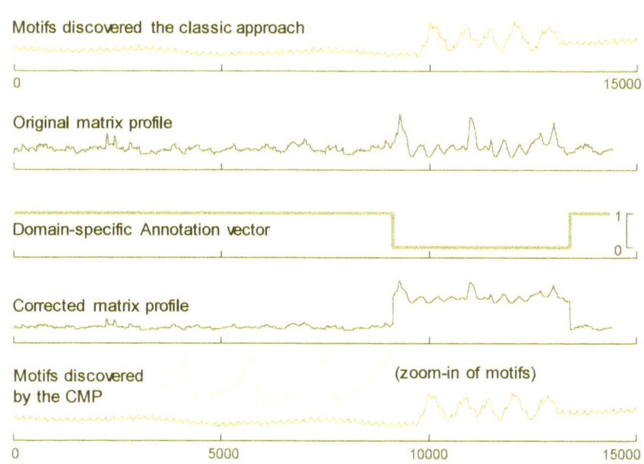

Figure 9: (*top to bottom*) Motifs in fNIRS data discovered using classic motif search tend to be spurious motion artifacts, because the matrix profile is minimized by the highly conserved but specious patterns. If we create an AV using the algorithm in Table 1, and use it to correct the MP, then that CMP allows us to find medically significant motifs.

Note that here we created a *Boolean* AV, which strictly prohibits finding motifs during sensor movement. However, we could also have created a real-valued AV, which simply *bias* the motif search away from regions where movement was noted, in proportion to the magnitude of the motion. As it happens, in this case, the Boolean AV was sufficient to solve the problem. In the next section, we will show an example of an issue that *does* require a real-valued AV.

3.2.2 Suppressing Hard-Limited Artifacts. Here we consider another example of a commonly encountered issue that may prevent us from finding meaningful motifs in medical and industrial datasets. In Figure 10.*bottom* we see that the motif discovered in this Electrooculogram (EOG) has a perfectly flat plateau. This is not reflective of medical reality, but is simply a region where the physical process exceeds the 8-bit precision available to record it [21].

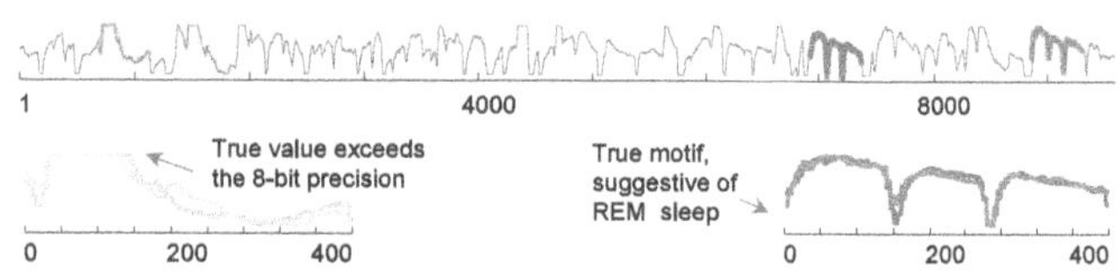

Figure 10: *top*) A snippet of a left-eye EOG sampled at 50 Hz, from an individual with sleep disorder. *bottom*) The top motif may be spurious, as it features a region where the time series indicates only the *maximum* value possible. However, this snippet does have a true motif, with medical significance.

In the many datasets that have this limited precision flaw, we can be guaranteed that most or all of the top motifs will feature some of these constant regions, as the flat regions produce *little cost* in the Euclidean distance calculation[2] that defines motifs. However, as shown in Figure 10.*bottom.right*, the data may be replete with more medically meaningful motifs. It is important to note that we do not wish to completely exclude the possibility of returning motifs with some amount of constant regions. It is just that we want to mitigate the strong bias to finding them exclusively.

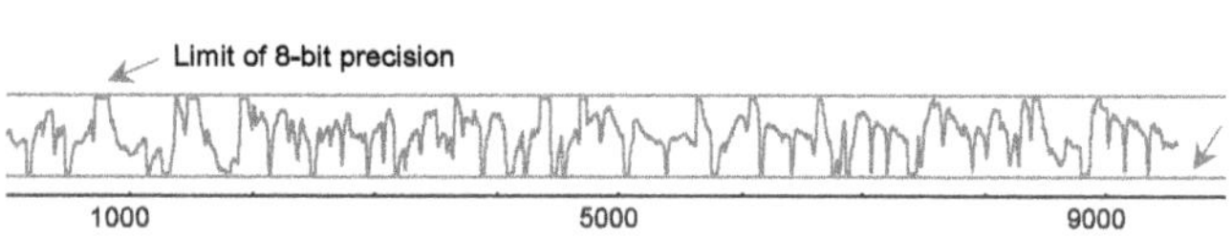

Figure 11: The upper and lower bound of the EOG data indicates the regions where the physical process exceeds the 8-bit precision available to record it.

As the reader will now appreciate after having seen our previous examples, we can easily build an AV to suppress these spurious matches. We begin by recording the maximum and the minimum values of the time series, the constant values touching the red bars shown in Figure 11. We slide a window across the time series to extract subsequences, counting the number of constant values (from being hard-limited above or below) in each sequence. This number over the subsequence length is used as the bias function. A higher value hints that the motifs that include this subsequence may be spurious, as the overflow/underflow regions act like a "don't-care" in the motif distance.

Figure 12 illustrates the results of applying this AV to the problematic example shown in Figure 10. Here again the annotation vector helps to bias away from spurious motifs, by leveraging the original matrix profile with domain specific insights.

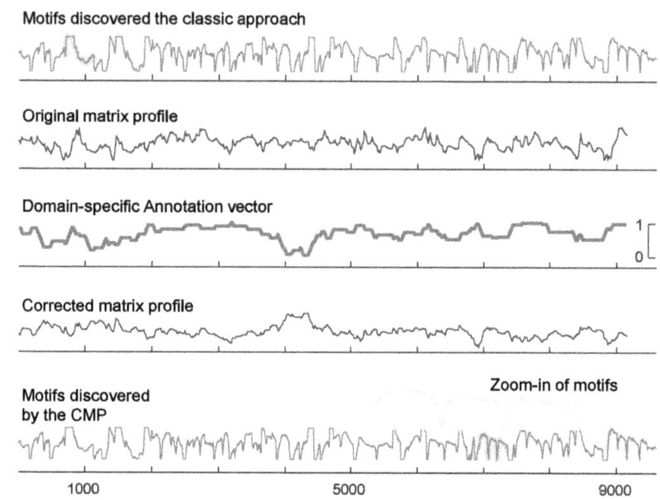

Figure 12: (*top to bottom*) Motifs in the EOG domain that are discovered using classic motif search tend to include hard-limited data, because the matrix profile is minimized by having long constant regions. By creating an AV using the algorithm in Table 2 to correct the MP, we can find true motifs corresponding to ponto-geniculo-occipital waves [6].

Once again, for concreteness, in Table 2 we show the full Matlab code used to make the annotation vector discussed above. As before, this simple fix requires only a minute of coding effort.

Table 2: Code to generate the AV for EOG example

```
function AV = make_AV(data, subsequenceLength)
for i = 1: length(data) - subsequenceLength + 1
  s = data(i:i+subsequenceLength - 1);
  AV(i) = length(s(s == max(data) | s == min(data)));
end
AV = AV - min(AV); % zero one normalization
AV = AV / max(AV); % zero one normalization
AV = 1 - AV;       % AV property conformation
```

3.3 Case Study: Stop-Word Motif Bias

We return to the ECG example presented in Figure 1. Recall that the top motifs of this time series do not come from a true medical signal, but regions of the electrode's calibration signal.

[2] Note, we say *little cost*, not *zero cost*, because when the subsequences are z-normalized, the constant regions may have slightly different heights.

These signals are much more similar than the "genuine" medically significant motifs, and swamp the top-K motif set.

Leveraging similar ideas in text processing, we propose to treat these spurious patterns as a "stop-word" motifs. Our goal is to design an AV that is capable of discounting such motifs. We can make no assumptions about the locations of the stop-word motif, given that they can show up anywhere in the signal.

We assume only that the stop-word motif(s) will be known to the users of our framework, as the stop-words are domain specific. In Figure 13.*top*, we show an example of a stop-word motif that we are targeting. Figure 13.*bottom* displays the annotation vector that can bias the motif discovery away from that stop-word.

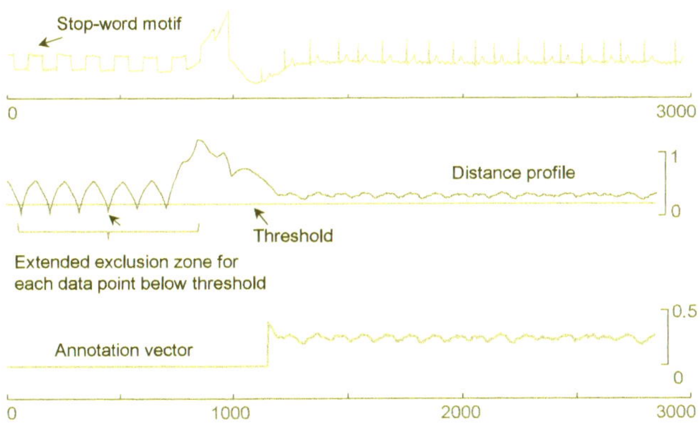

Figure 13: *top*) We annotated a single stop-word from the LTAF-71 Database [13]. *middle*) The stop-words distance profile to the entire dataset was thresholded to create an exclusion zone, which was used to create a AV (*bottom*).

To create the AV here, we measure the similarity between the stop-word subsequence to all subsequences in the time series *T*, by sliding a window of the subsequence length across the time series. This gives a *distance profile* (see Section 2.2 **Definition 4**). We normalize this distance profile to be in range [0 - 1], as shown in Figure 13.*middle*. To convert the normalized distance profile into our final AV vector, we employ a threshold parameter. The threshold chosen indicates how similar the corresponding subsequences are in comparison to the stop-word motif. If we set the threshold to be 0.1, we retrieve the location of subsequences that are 90% stop-word-like.

Having a threshold is generally undesirable, but recall that our framework has completely divorced the computationally trivial AV adjustment from the expensive computation of the matrix profile. Thus, if the threshold is too aggressive or too lax, the user can update it and refresh the results in under a second, even for datasets as large as one million data points.

To generate the final AV vector, we set the stop-word motif location, and all the data up to $3m$ points before and after them to 0, retaining the original values of other data points. This $3m$ "padded" exclusion zone is simply to compensate for the "spikey" valleys of the distance profile.

Figure 14.*top* shows the original MP (left) and the top-1 motif that would have been found using that MP (right, highlighted in green and cyan). Figure 14.*bottom* shows the corrected MP and the corresponding top-1 motif.

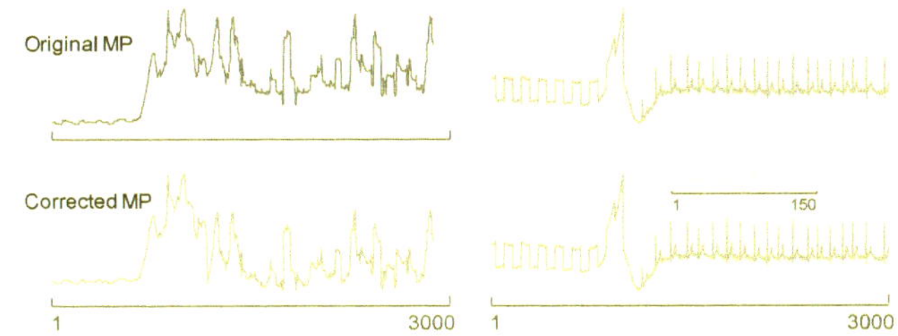

Figure 14: By correcting the MP to bias away from stop-word motifs, we can discover medically meaningful motifs.

3.4 Case Study: Simplicity Bias

The issue of *simplicity bias* has been reported to us by a dozen research groups in the last decade, although not under that name, which we coined for this paper. The problem can be very subtle, but in Figure 15 below we show a strikingly obvious example.

Figure 15: A short snippet of a time series of the flexion of a subject's little finger [9]. Subjectively, most people would expect that two occurrences of consecutive multiple flexions to be the top motif (inset). Instead we find the simple "ramp-up" pattern to be the top motif.

The reason why motif discovery fails to match our expectation here was discussed in Section 1.2, and at length in [1] (in a very different context). Given our guided motif framework, the problem is trivial to solve. We just need to create an AV that penalizes for simplicity.

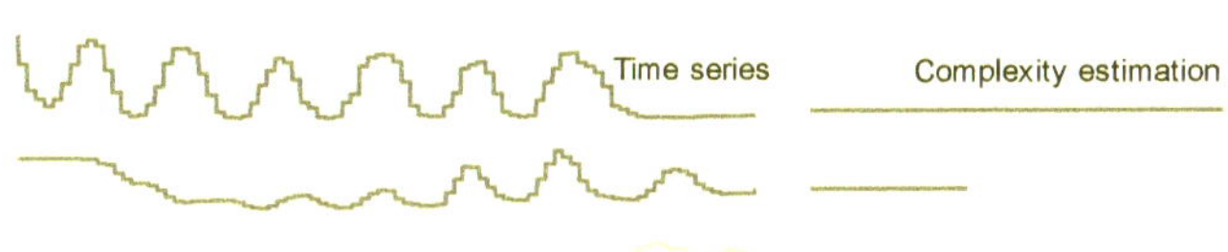

Figure 16: A visual intuition of the complexity estimation of three time series subsequences of different complexity levels according to the algorithm proposed in [1].

To do this, we employ the complexity estimation proposed in [1], which will be referred as CE. The authors of [1] originally embedded CE in a complexity correction factor for the Euclidean distance, making this distance measure complexity-invariant. This complexity estimation is simple (one line of code), parameter-free and has a natural interpretation. Intuitively, time series can be imagined as "chains" or "ropes", and have their complexity measured by "stretching" them and measuring the length of the resulting taut lines, as illustrated in Figure 16. The more complex the time series is, the longer its corresponding line will be.

We slide a window across the time series, measuring the complexity of each subsequence and store them in a complexity vector, as shown by the green (bold) line of Figure 17. We simply normalize this complexity vector to be in range [0 - 1] to obtain the final AV.

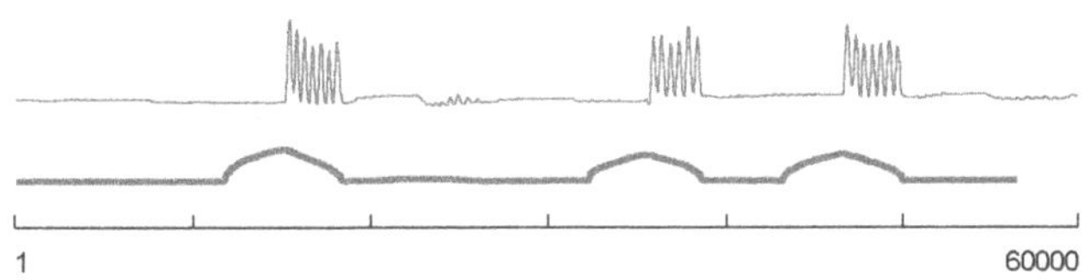

Figure 17: The complexity measure (*bold/bottom*) shown in parallel to the raw data (*fine/top*).

Table 3 contains the Matlab code used to generate the AV.

Table 3: Code to generate AV for ECoG signal

```
function AV = make_AV(data, subsequenceLength)
for i = 1: length(data) - subsequenceLength + 1
   subsequence = data(i:i+subsequenceLength - 1);
   AV(i) = sqrt(sum(diff(subsequence).^2));;
end
AV = AV - min(AV); % zero one normalization
AV = AV / max(AV); % zero one normalization
```

Figure 18 illustrates how the real motifs are uncovered, as opposed to the "ramp-up" patterns that would have dominated if we rely on the classic matrix profile.

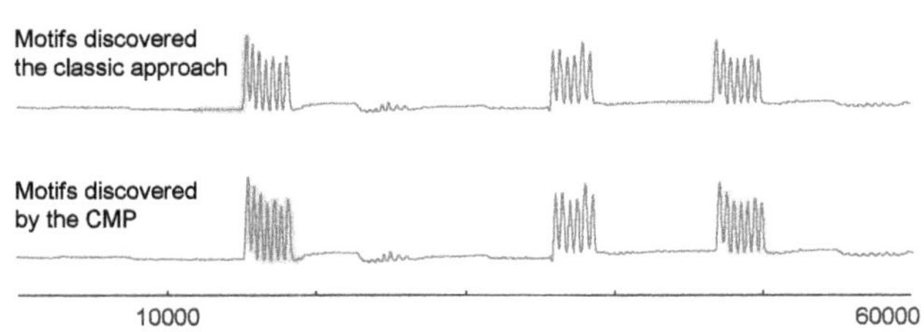

Figure 18: By correcting the matrix profile with an AV using the algorithm in Table 3, we discover the true motifs of finger flexion pattern in the ECoG signal.

To show the ubiquity of this issue, and the generality of our solution, we searched seismology telemetry [24]. Figure 19 illustrates how guided motif search correctly discovers two earthquakes from the same fault, occurring thirteen years apart, in Sonoma Country, CA. The result is impressive given that classic motif search ranks 852 other motifs above this true motif; these higher-ranked motifs are all sensor artifacts [8] that our AV suppresses.

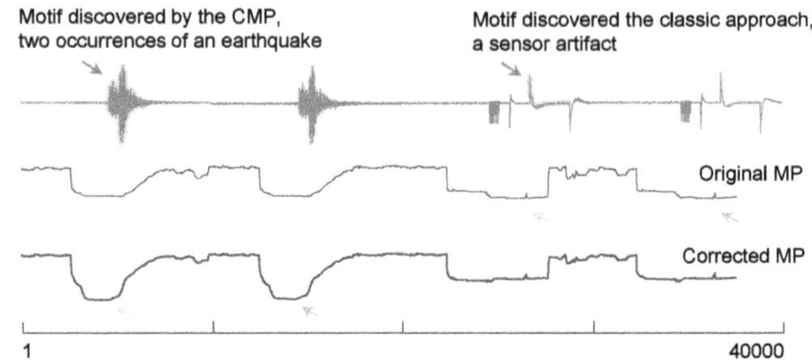

Figure 19: The top motif returned by the classic approach is not an earthquake, but a sensor artifact. Using guided motif search framework, we can avoid such various misleading sensor artifacts, which swamp this 17,279,800 data-points earthquake dataset. The time series shown was edited for visual clarity.

4 EMPIRICAL EVALUATION

To ensure that our experiments are reproducible, we have built a website which contains all data/code/raw spreadsheets for the results, in addition to many experiments that are omitted here for brevity [15]. This commitment to reproducibility extends to all the examples the previous sections. We note that we do not need to compare to rival *algorithms*, but a rival *definition*, the classic motif definition used in several hundred research efforts over the last decade [2][12][23][24].

4.1 Preliminary Tests

We begin with an experiment that is designed to closely model the issue shown in Figure 3, but at a scale that will allow statistically significant results. We produced 1,000 datasets as follows. We created a random walk of length 20,000, then embedded into it two randomly chosen instances from the eight-class MALLAT dataset from the UCR Archive [4]. Figure 20 shows that these synthetic datasets are, at least visually, a good proxy for the real motion artifact contamination data.

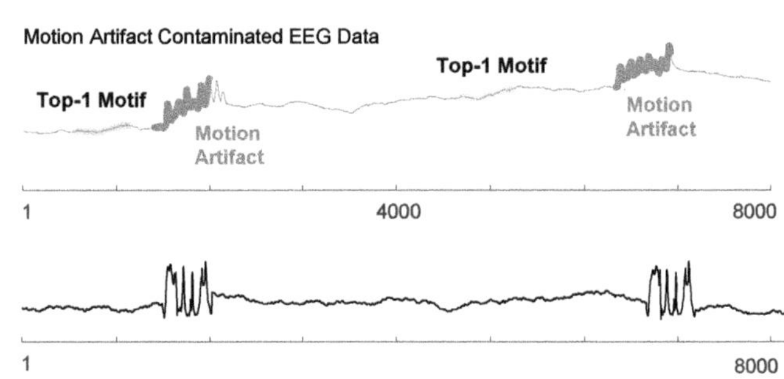

Figure 20: A snippet of real motion artifact contamination data (see also Figure 3) and a snippet of our synthetic proxy for it.

For each dataset, we run motif discovery, and count as a *success*, any answer in which the top-1 returned motifs overlap with *any* part of the embedded motifs.

We test the performance of three alternatives:

- Classic motif search, to reflect what is currently done in the literature (*Classic*) [23].
- Guided Motif Search: In which the AV is created using complexity bias, as discussed in Section 3.4 ($AV_{complexity}$).
- Guided Motif Search: In which the AV is created by counting the number of zeros-crossings ($AV_{ZeroCrossings}$) in the subsequences.

We consider two variants of the AV to test the following informal claim: Once a practitioner understands the issue producing poor motifs, there will almost certainly be many simple fixes possible. Table 4 summarizes the results.

A practitioner that exploited the number of zero-crossings would have seen her hit rate more than double, yet noted there is still room for improvement. Perhaps she would have noticed that random walk data can sometimes have high zero-crossings by chance, and would have turned to a more robust zero-crossings extractor [20]. On the other hand, a more sophisticated practitioner that was aware of complexity bias [1], would have seen essentially perfect results from the first time. In both cases, we see that the simple correction offered by an annotation vector can dramatically improve the utility of motif search. We note in passing these results that they support our claim that the time overhead for guided motif search is inconsequential.

Table 4: Comparison between classic motif search and guided motif search over 1000 datasets of length 20,000. Both two variants of guided motif search outperform classic motif search in terms of accuracy, with extra time overhead of just 0.09 second per run, less than a half of a percent.

Approach	Average success rate	Time per run
Classic	16.3%	22.40 seconds
$AV_{complexity}$	99.9%	22.46 seconds
$AV_{ZeroCrossings}$	38.7%	22.49 seconds

4.2 Guided Motif Search for Event Detection

Sometimes motif discovery is the *endpoint* of data analysis, but more often motif search is a subroutine in a higher-level algorithm. In this section, we show that our framework can also be helpful in such scenarios. We are particularly interested in the problem of building dictionaries from weakly labeled training data. We show that in this case, classic motif search may perform poorly and guided motif search can offer significant improvements.

Figure 21 presents an example of a weakly labeled time series. While the time series snippet represents a 71 seconds long episode of mimicked epileptic seizures [19], the actual seizure is only about 30 seconds long, sandwiched in-between states where the actor was preparing-for/recovering-from her role. This presence of spurious data is what is meant by "weakly labeled". Using classic motif search to find the most conserved pattern in this time series returns top motifs in a non-epileptic region, as shown in Figure 21.*top*. However, using the guided motif search framework (CMP), employing a complexity bias, discovers the top-1 motif in the truly representative seizure region, as shown in Figure 21.*bottom*.

We design the experiment as follows. We first run motif search on the weakly labeled training data for subsequence of length 16 (1 second) to find the top-1 motif pair. We average this motif pair to get the representative pattern for that class. Next, we slide the representative motif across the test (unseen) time series, measuring its distance to all the subsequences. If the difference between a test subsequence and the representative motif is at most three times the distance between the train top-1 motif pair, we mark that subsequence as epilepsy *positive*. Our test set consists of five recordings of mimicking epilepsy seizure and three recordings of walking task concatenated (visualized in Figure 22). We divide the test time series into segments of 36 two-second regions. If we find any hit within each 2 second segment, and the ground truth agrees with that, we denote this as a *true positive*.

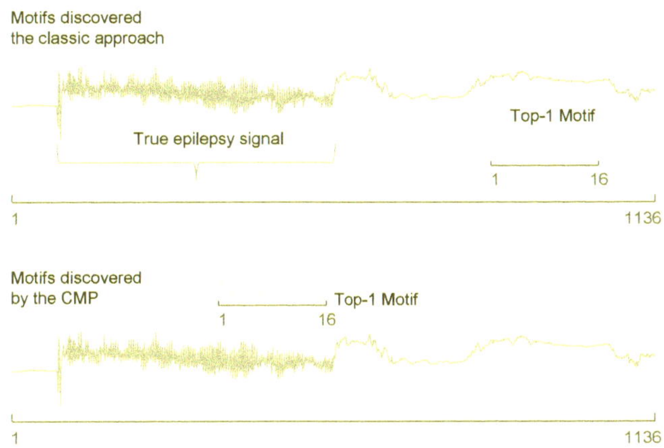

Figure 21: A weakly labeled seizure mimicking captured with accelerometer x-axis reading. *top*) Classic motif search wrongly finds the top motifs in non-representative event regions whilst CMP correctly uncovers the true epileptic patterns (*bottom*). Figure is best viewed in color.

We compare the result of the guided motif search approach using $AV_{complexity}$ with the classic motif search approach. Table 5 shows the full contingency matrix.

Table 5: Contingency matrix. *left*) The classic motif search approach *right*) the guided motif search approach. E denotes Epilepsy. NE denotes Not Epilepsy.

Classic

Prediction	True class: E	True class: NE
E	1	1
NE	66	321

CMP

Prediction	True class: E	True class: NE
E	52	3
NE	15	319

The guided motif search outperforms classic motif search in both metrics, accuracy (95.7% vs. 82.78%) and F-measure (82.78% vs 2.9%). Figure 22 shows a visualization of classification result.

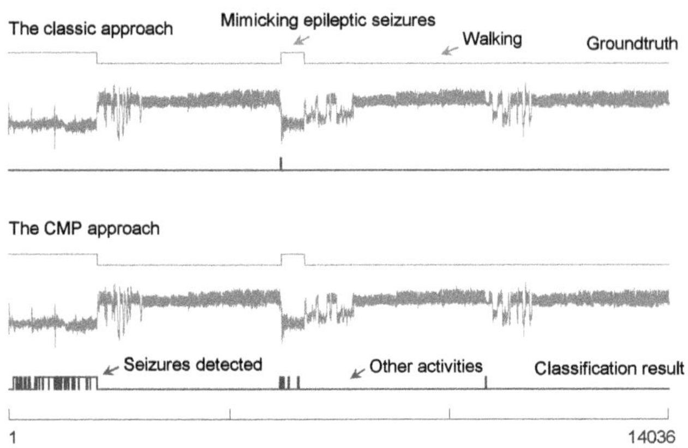

Figure 22: Classification result with the dictionary learned using classic motif search (*top*) and the dictionary built using the guided motif search approach (*bottom*).

This issue of weakly labeled data could be avoided by having an expert manually annotating the dataset, and we acknowledge that the experiment is somewhat contrived. However, we do not always have the luxury of human expert intervention, and in that case, guided motif search with a little insight might take us a long way.

4.3 Time and Space Complexity

The time complexity of our proposed guided motif search is $O(n^2)$, and the space complexity is merely $O(n)$, which is the same as classic motif search using state-of-the-art methods [23][24]. We need $O(n^2)$ for computing the original MP, plus $O(n)$ additional work to compute the AV and produce the corrected MP. To concretely ground these numbers, consider Table 4. It took 22.5 seconds to process 20,000 data points. Given that the data was recorded at 50Hz, this is 400 seconds of wall-clock time, meaning we are about eighteen times faster than real-time.

5 CONCLUSIONS AND FUTURE WORK

We have shown that direct use of classic time motif search can produce unexpected/undesired results in many circumstances, for a variety of domain dependent reasons. We have presented a novel framework for guided motif discovery, which greatly mitigate these issues. In the spirit of reproducible research, we have released all the code and data at [15], to allow others to confirm, extend and exploit our ideas.

We plan to produce a crowdsourced website which catalogues the issues effecting motif discovery, together with the suggested AVs that can fix the issue. We envision that this resource will expand as domain experts provide examples, in the manner of: "*If you are looking for repeating stanzas in Byzantine or Turkish folk songs, we suggest you use this* $AV_{PitchCorrect}$*, otherwise you may find...*"

Finally, all the examples that we have given required the practitioner to understand the issue, and come up with an AV to solve it. In future work, we hope to learn the AV simply by observing the user interact with the raw data.

ACKNOWLEDGMENTS

We thank the many users of motif discovery tools, dating back to 2003 [5], who provided us with both success and failure stories, giving us the insight and motivation to produce this work.

REFERENCES

[1] Batista, Gustavo EAPA, et al. "CID: an efficient complexity-invariant distance for time series." *Data Mining and Knowledge Discovery* 28.3 (2014): 634-669.
[2] Begum, Nurjahan, and Eamonn Keogh. "Rare time series motif discovery from unbounded streams." *Proceedings of the VLDB Endowment* 8.2 (2014): 149-160.
[3] Brigadoi, Sabrina, et al. "Motion artifacts in functional near-infrared spectroscopy: a comparison of motion correction techniques applied to real cognitive data." *Neuroimage* 85 (2014): 181-191.
[4] Chen, Yanping, et al. The UCR Time Series Classification Archive. www.cs.ucr.edu/~eamonn/time_series_data/.
[5] Chiu, Bill, Eamonn J. Keogh, Stefano Lonardi: Probabilistic discovery of time series motifs. KDD 2003: 493-498
[6] Datta, Subimal. "Cellular basis of pontine ponto-geniculo-occipital wave generation and modulation." *Cellular and molecular neurobiology* 17.3 (1997): 341-365.
[7] Hao, Yuan, et al. "Parameter-free audio motif discovery in large data archives." *2013 IEEE 13th International Conference on Data Mining*. IEEE, 2013.
[8] Havskov Jens, and Gerardo Alguacil. Instrumentation in earthquake seismology: modern approaches in geophysics. Vol 22, Springer, Berlin, 2004.
[9] Kubanek, J., et al. "Decoding flexion of individual fingers using electrocorticographic signals in humans." *Journal of neural engineering* 6.6 (2009): 066001.
[10] Liu, Xitong, Hui Fang, and Deng Cai. "Towards Less Biased Web Search." *Proceedings of the 2015 International Conference on The Theory of Information Retrieval*. ACM, 2015.
[11] Mueen, Abdullah, and Eamonn Keogh. "Online discovery and maintenance of time series motifs." *Proceedings of the 16th ACM SIGKDD international conference on Knowledge discovery and data mining*. ACM, 2010.
[12] Mueen, Abdullah, Eamonn J. Keogh, Qiang Zhu, Sydney Cash, M. Brandon Westover. "Exact Discovery of Time Series Motifs." *SDM* 2009: 473-484
[13] Petrutiu, Simona, Alan V. Sahakian, and Steven Swiryn. "Abrupt changes in fibrillatory wave characteristics at the termination of paroxysmal atrial fibrillation in humans." *Europace* 9.7 (2007): 466-470.
[14] Saria, Suchi, Andrew Duchi, and Daphne Koller. "Discovering deformable motifs in continuous time series data." *IJCAI Proceedings-International Joint Conference on Artificial Intelligence*. Vol. 22. No. 1. 2011.
[15] Supporting webpage: http://www.cs.ucr.edu/~hdau001/guided_motif_search/
[16] Sweeney, Kevin T., Seán F. McLoone, and Tomas E. Ward. "The use of ensemble empirical mode decomposition with canonical correlation analysis as a novel artifact removal technique." *IEEE transactions on biomedical engineering* 60.1 (2013): 97-105.
[17] Tak, Sungho, and Jong Chul Ye. "Statistical analysis of fNIRS data: a comprehensive review." *Neuroimage* (2014): 72-91.
[18] Tombros, Anastasios, and Mark Sanderson. "Advantages of query biased summaries in information retrieval." *Proceedings of the 21st annual international ACM SIGIR conference on Research and development in information retrieval*. ACM, 1998.
[19] Villar, Jose R., et al. "Generalized Model for the Classification of Abnormal Movements in Daily Life and its Applicability to Epilepsy Convulsion Recognition." *International Journal of Neural Systems* (2016).
[20] Wall, R. W. "Simple methods for detecting zero crossing." *Proceedings of the 29th Annual Conference of the IEEE Industrial Electronics Society Paper*. Vol. 291. No. 1. 2003.
[21] Whitney, Coralyn W., et al. "Reliability of scoring respiratory disturbance indices and sleep staging." *Sleep* 21.7 (1998): 749-757.
[22] Yankov, Dragomir, et al. "Detecting time series motifs under uniform scaling." *Proceedings of the 13th ACM SIGKDD international conference on Knowledge discovery and data mining*. ACM, 2007.
[23] Yeh, Chin-Chia Michael, et al. "Matrix Profile I: All Pairs Similarity Joins for Time Series: A Unifying View that Includes Motifs, Discords and Shapelets." *IEEE ICDM*. 2016.
[24] Zhu, Yan, et al. "Matrix Profile II: Exploiting a Novel Algorithm and GPUs to Break the One Hundred Million Barrier for Time Series Motifs and Joins." *IEEE ICDM*. 2016.

metapath2vec: Scalable Representation Learning for Heterogeneous Networks

Yuxiao Dong*
Microsoft Research
Redmond, WA 98052
yuxdong@microsoft.com

Nitesh V. Chawla
University of Notre Dame
Notre Dame, IN 46556
nchawla@nd.edu

Ananthram Swami
Army Research Laboratory
Adelphi, MD 20783
ananthram.swami.civ@mail.mil

ABSTRACT

We study the problem of representation learning in heterogeneous networks. Its unique challenges come from the existence of multiple types of nodes and links, which limit the feasibility of the conventional network embedding techniques. We develop two scalable representation learning models, namely *metapath2vec* and *metapath2vec++*. The *metapath2vec* model formalizes meta-path-based random walks to construct the heterogeneous neighborhood of a node and then leverages a heterogeneous skip-gram model to perform node embeddings. The *metapath2vec++* model further enables the simultaneous modeling of structural and semantic correlations in heterogeneous networks. Extensive experiments show that *metapath2vec* and *metapath2vec++* are able to not only outperform state-of-the-art embedding models in various heterogeneous network mining tasks, such as node classification, clustering, and similarity search, but also discern the structural and semantic correlations between diverse network objects.

CCS CONCEPTS

•Information systems →Social networks; •Computing methodologies →Unsupervised learning; Learning latent representations; *Knowledge representation and reasoning;*

KEYWORDS

Network Embedding; Heterogeneous Representation Learning; Latent Representations; Feature Learning; Heterogeneous Information Networks

ACM Reference format:
Yuxiao Dong, Nitesh V. Chawla, and Ananthram Swami. 2017. metapath2vec: Scalable Representation Learning for Heterogeneous Networks. In *Proceedings of KDD '17, August 13-17, 2017, Halifax, NS, Canada, ,* 10 pages.
DOI: http://dx.doi.org/10.1145/3097983.3098036

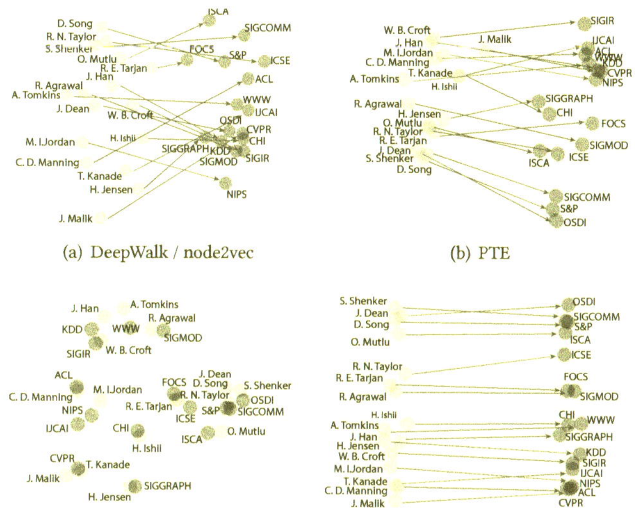

(a) DeepWalk / node2vec (b) PTE (c) *metapath2vec* (d) *metapath2vec++*

Figure 1: 2D PCA projections of the 128D embeddings of 16 top CS conferences and corresponding high-profile authors.

1 INTRODUCTION

Neural network-based learning models can represent latent embeddings that capture the internal relations of rich, complex data across various modalities, such as image, audio, and language [15]. Social and information networks are similarly rich and complex data that encode the dynamics and types of human interactions, and are similarly amenable to representation learning using neural networks. In particular, by mapping the way that people choose friends and maintain connections as a "social language," recent advances in natural language processing (NLP) [3] can be naturally applied to network representation learning, most notably the group of NLP models known as word2vec [17, 18]. A number of recent research publications have proposed word2vec-based network representation learning frameworks, such as DeepWalk [22], LINE [30], and node2vec [8]. Instead of handcrafted network feature design, these representation learning methods enable the automatic discovery of useful and meaningful (latent) features from the "raw networks."

However, these work has thus far focused on representation learning for homogeneous networks—representative of singular type of nodes and relationships. Yet a large number of social and information networks are heterogeneous in nature, involving diversity of node types and/or relationships between nodes [25]. These heterogeneous networks present unique challenges that cannot be handled by representation learning models that are specifically designed for homogeneous networks. Take, for example, a heterogeneous academic network: How do we effectively preserve the concept of "word-context" among multiple types of nodes, e.g., authors, papers, venues, organizations, etc.? Can random walks, such those used in DeepWalk and node2vec, be applied to networks

*This work was done when Yuxiao was a Ph.D. student at University of Notre Dame.

KDD '17, August 13-17, 2017, Halifax, NS, Canada

DOI: http://dx.doi.org/10.1145/3097983.3098036

Table 1: Case study of similarity search in the heterogeneous DBIS data used in [26].

Method	PathSim [26]		DeepWalk / node2vec [8, 22]		LINE (1st+2nd) [30]		PTE [29]		*metapath2vec*		*metapath2vec++*	
Input	meta-paths		heterogeneous random walk paths		heterogeneous edges		heterogeneous edges		probabilistic meta-paths		probabilistic meta-paths	
Query	PKDD	C. Faloutsos	PKDD	C. Faloutsos	PKDD	C. Faloutsos	PKDD	C. Faloutsos	PKDD	C. Faloutsos	PKDD	C. Faloutsos
1	ICDM	J. Han	R. S.	J. Pan	W. K.	C. Aggarwal	KDD	C. Aggarwal	A. S.	C. Aggarwal	KDD	R. Agrawal
2	SDM	R. Agrawal	M. N.	H. Tong	S. A.	P. Yu	ICDM	P. Yu	M. B.	J. Pei	PAKDD	J. Han
3	PAKDD	J. Pei	R. P.	H. Yang	A. B.	D. Gunopulos	SDM	Y. Tao	P. B.	P. Yu	ICDM	J. Pei
4	KDD	C. Aggarwal	G. G.	R. Filho	M. S.	N. Koudas	DMKD	N. Koudas	M. S.	H. Cheng	DMKD	C. Aggarwal
5	DMKD	H. Jagadish	F. J.	R. Chan	S. A.	M. Vlachos	PAKDD	R. Rastogi	M. K.	V. Ganti	SDM	P. Yu

of multiple types of nodes? Can we directly apply homogeneous network-oriented embedding architectures (e.g., skip-gram) to heterogeneous networks?

By solving these challenges, the latent heterogeneous network embeddings can be further applied to various network mining tasks, such as node classification [13], clustering [27, 28], and similarity search [26, 35]. In contrast to conventional meta-path-based methods [25], the advantage of latent-space representation learning lies in its ability to model similarities between nodes without connected meta-paths. For example, if authors have never published papers in the same venue—imagine one publishes 10 papers all in NIPS and the other has 10 publications all in ICML; their "APCPA"-based PathSim similarity [26] would be zero—this will be naturally overcome by network representation learning.

Contributions. We formalize the heterogeneous network representation learning problem, where the objective is to simultaneously learn the low-dimensional and latent embeddings for multiple types of nodes. We present the *metapath2vec* and its extension *metapath2vec++* frameworks. The goal of *metapath2vec* is to maximize the likelihood of preserving both the structures and semantics of a given heterogeneous network. In *metapath2vec*, we first propose meta-path [25] based random walks in heterogeneous networks to generate heterogeneous neighborhoods with network semantics for various types of nodes. Second, we extend the skip-gram model [18] to facilitate the modeling of geographically and semantically close nodes. Finally, we develop a heterogeneous negative sampling-based method, referred to as *metapath2vec++*, that enables the accurate and efficient prediction of a node's heterogeneous neighborhood.

The proposed *metapath2vec* and *metapath2vec++* models are different from conventional network embedding models, which focus on homogeneous networks [8, 22, 30]. Specifically, conventional models suffer from the identical treatment of different types of nodes and relations, leading to the production of indistinguishable representations for heterogeneous nodes—as evident through our evaluation. Further, the *metapath2vec* and *metapath2vec++* models also differ from the Predictive Text Embedding (PTE) model [29] in several ways. First, PTE is a semi-supervised learning model that incorporates label information for text data. Second, the heterogeneity in PTE comes from the text network wherein a link connects two words, a word and its document, and a word and its label. Essentially, the raw input of PTE is words and its output is the embedding of each word, rather than multiple types of objects.

We summarize the differences of these methods in Table 1, which lists their input to learning algorithms, as well as the top-five similarity search results in the DBIS network for the same two queries used in [26] (see Section 4 for details). By modeling the heterogeneous neighborhood and further leveraging the heterogeneous negative sampling technique, *metapath2vec++* is able to achieve the best top-five similar results for both types of queries. Figure 1 shows the visualization of the 2D projections of the learned embeddings for 16 CS conferences and corresponding high-profile researchers in each field. Remarkably, we find that *metapath2vec++* is capable of automatically organizing these two types of nodes and implicitly learning the internal relationships between them, suggested by the similar directions and distances of the arrows connecting each pair. For example, it learns J. Dean → OSDI and C. D. Manning → ACL. *metapath2vec* is also able to group each author-conference pair closely, such as R. E. Tarjan and FOCS. All of these properties are not discoverable from conventional network embedding models.

To summarize, our work makes the following contributions:

(1) Formalizes the problem of heterogeneous network representation learning and identifies its unique challenges resulting from network heterogeneity.
(2) Develops effective and efficient network embedding frameworks, *metapath2vec* & *metapath2vec++*, for preserving both structural and semantic correlations of heterogeneous networks.
(3) Through extensive experiments, demonstrates the efficacy and scalability of the presented methods in various heterogeneous network mining tasks, such as node classification (achieving relative improvements of 35–319% over benchmarks) and node clustering (achieving relative gains of 13–16% over baselines).
(4) Demonstrates the automatic discovery of internal semantic relationships between different types of nodes in heterogeneous networks by *metapath2vec* & *metapath2vec++*, not discoverable by existing work.

2 PROBLEM DEFINITION

We formalize the representation learning problem in heterogeneous networks, which was first briefly introduced in [21]. In specific, we leverage the definition of heterogeneous networks in [25, 27] and present the learning problem with its inputs and outputs.

Definition 2.1. **A Heterogeneous Network** is defined as a graph $G = (V, E, T)$ in which each node v and each link e are associated with their mapping functions $\phi(v) : V \rightarrow T_V$ and $\varphi(e) : E \rightarrow T_E$, respectively. T_V and T_E denote the sets of object and relation types, where $|T_V| + |T_E| > 2$.

For example, one can represent the academic network in Figure 2(a) with authors (A), papers (P), venues (V), organizations (O) as nodes, wherein edges indicate the coauthor (A–A), publish (A–P,

P–V), affiliation (O–A) relationships. By considering a heterogeneous network as input, we formalize the problem of heterogeneous network representation learning as follows.

Problem 1. ***Heterogeneous Network Representation Learning:*** *Given a heterogeneous network G, the task is to learn the d-dimensional latent representations* $\mathbf{X} \in \mathbb{R}^{|V| \times d}$, $d \ll |V|$ *that are able to capture the structural and semantic relations among them.*

The output of the problem is the low-dimensional matrix **X**, with the vth row—a d-dimensional vector X_v—corresponding to the representation of node v. Notice that, although there are different types of nodes in V, their representations are mapped into the same latent space. The learned node representations can benefit various heterogeneous network mining tasks. For example, the embedding vector of each node can be used as the feature input of node classification, clustering, and similarity search tasks.

The main challenge of this problem comes from the network heterogeneity, wherein it is difficult to directly apply homogeneous language and network embedding methods. The premise of network embedding models is to preserve the proximity between a node and its neighborhood (context) [8, 22, 30]. In a heterogeneous environment, how do we define and model this 'node–neighborhood' concept? Furthermore, how do we optimize the embedding models that effectively maintain the structures and semantics of multiple types of nodes and relations?

3 THE *METAPATH2VEC* FRAMEWORK

We present a general framework, *metapath2vec*, which is capable of learning desirable node representations in heterogeneous networks. The objective of *metapath2vec* is to maximize the network probability in consideration of multiple types of nodes and edges.

3.1 Homogeneous Network Embedding

We, first, briefly introduce the word2vec model and its application to homogeneous network embedding tasks. Given a text corpus, Mikolov et al. proposed *word2vec* to learn the distributed representations of words in a corpus [17, 18]. Inspired by it, DeepWalk [22] and node2vec [8] aim to map the word-context concept in a text corpus into a network. Both methods leverage random walks to achieve this and utilize the skip-gram model to learn the representation of a node that facilitates the prediction of its structural context—local neighborhoods—in a homogeneous network. Usually, given a network $G = (V, E)$, the objective is to maximize the network probability in terms of local structures [8, 18, 22], that is:

$$\arg\max_{\theta} \prod_{v \in V} \prod_{c \in N(v)} p(c|v;\theta) \tag{1}$$

where $N(v)$ is the neighborhood of node v in the network G, which can be defined in different ways such as v's one-hop neighbors, and $p(c|v;\theta)$ defines the conditional probability of having a context node c given a node v.

3.2 Heterogeneous Network Embedding: *metapath2vec*

To model the heterogeneous neighborhood of a node, *metapath2vec* introduces the heterogeneous skip-gram model. To incorporate the heterogeneous network structures into skip-gram, we propose meta-path-based random walks in heterogeneous networks.

Heterogeneous Skip-Gram. In *metapath2vec*, we enable skip-gram to learn effective node representations for a heterogeneous network $G = (V, E, T)$ with $|T_V| > 1$ by maximizing the probability of having the heterogeneous context $N_t(v), t \in T_V$ given a node v:

$$\arg\max_{\theta} \sum_{v \in V} \sum_{t \in T_V} \sum_{c_t \in N_t(v)} \log p(c_t|v;\theta) \tag{2}$$

where $N_t(v)$ denotes v's neighborhood with the tth type of nodes and $p(c_t|v;\theta)$ is commonly defined as a softmax function [3, 7, 18, 24], that is: $p(c_t|v;\theta) = \frac{e^{X_{c_t} \cdot X_v}}{\sum_{u \in V} e^{X_u \cdot X_v}}$, where X_v is the vth row of **X**, representing the embedding vector for node v. For illustration, consider the academic network in Figure 2(a), the neighborhood of one author node a_4 can be structurally close to other authors (e.g., a_2, a_3 & a_5), venues (e.g., ACL & KDD), organizations (CMU & MIT), as well as papers (e.g., p_2 & p_3).

To achieve efficient optimization, Mikolov et al. introduced negative sampling [18], in which a relatively small set of words (nodes) are sampled from the corpus (network) for the construction of softmax. We leverage the same technique for *metapath2vec*. Given a negative sample size M, Eq. 2 is updated as follows: $\log \sigma(X_{c_t} \cdot X_v) + \sum_{m=1}^{M} \mathbb{E}_{u^m \sim P(u)}[\log \sigma(-X_{u^m} \cdot X_v)]$, where $\sigma(x) = \frac{1}{1+e^{-x}}$ and $P(u)$ is the pre-defined distribution from which a negative node u^m is drew from for M times. *metapath2vec* builds the the node frequency distribution by viewing different types of nodes homogeneously and draw (negative) nodes regardless of their types.

Meta-Path-Based Random Walks. How to effectively transform the structure of a network into skip-gram? In DeepWalk [22] and node2vec [8], this is achieved by incorporating the node paths traversed by random walkers over a network into the neighborhood function.

Naturally, we can put *random walkers in a heterogeneous network* to generate paths of multiple types of nodes. At step i, the transition probability $p(v^{i+1}|v^i)$ is denoted as the normalized probability distributed over the neighbors of v^i by ignoring their node types. The generated paths can be then used as the input of node2vec and DeepWalk. *However, Sun et al. demonstrated that heterogeneous random walks are biased to highly visible types of nodes—those with a dominant number of paths—and concentrated nodes—those with a governing percentage of paths pointing to a small set of nodes [26].*

In light of these issues, we design meta-path-based random walks to generate paths that are able to capture both the semantic and structural correlations between different types of nodes, facilitating the transformation of heterogeneous network structures into *metapath2vec*'s skip-gram.

Formally, a meta-path scheme $\mathcal{P}$ is defined as a path that is denoted in the form of $V_1 \xrightarrow{R_1} V_2 \xrightarrow{R_2} \cdots V_t \xrightarrow{R_t} V_{t+1} \cdots \xrightarrow{R_{l-1}} V_l$, wherein $R = R_1 \circ R_2 \circ \cdots \circ R_{l-1}$ defines the composite relations between node types V_1 and V_l [25]. Take Figure 2(a) as an example, a meta-path "APA" represents the coauthor relationships on a paper (P) between two authors (A), and "APVPA" represents two authors (A) publish papers (P) in the same venue (V). Previous work has shown that many data mining tasks in heterogeneous information networks can benefit from the modeling of meta-paths [6, 25, 27].

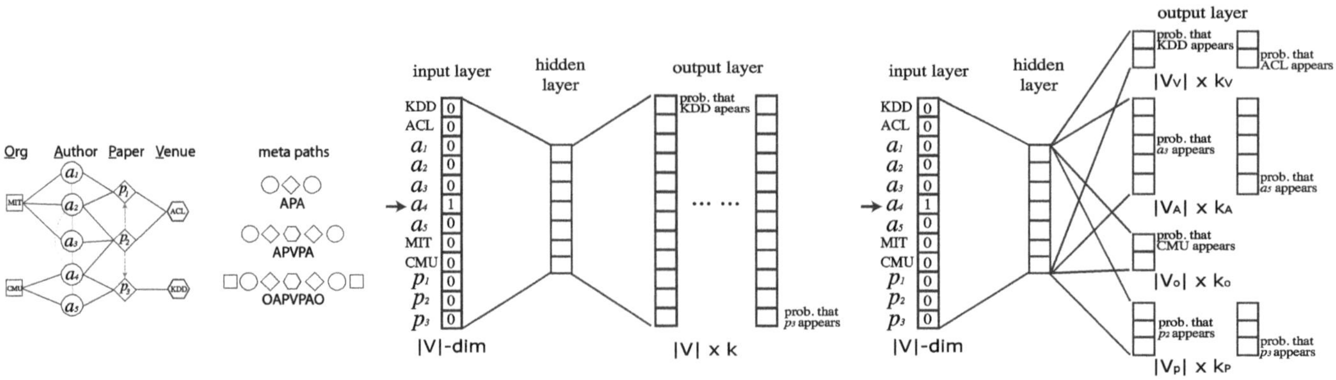

(a) An academic network (b) Skip-gram in *metapath2vec*, node2vec, & DeepWalk (c) Skip-gram in *metapath2vec++*

Figure 2: An illustrative example of a heterogeneous academic network and skip-gram architectures of *metapath2vec* and *metapath2vec++* for embedding this network. (a). Yellow dotted lines denote coauthor relationships and red dotted lines denote citation relationships. (b) The skip-gram architecture used in *metapath2vec* when predicting for a_4, which is the same with the one in node2vec if node types are ignored. $|V|$=12 denotes the number of nodes in the heterogeneous academic network in (a) and a_4's neighborhood is set to include CMU, a_2, a_3, a_5, p_2, p_3, ACL, & KDD, making $k = 8$. (c) The heterogeneous skip-gram used in *metapath2vec++*. Instead of one set of multinomial distributions for all types of neighborhood nodes in the output layer, it specifies one set of multinomial distributions for each type of nodes in a_4's neighborhood. V_t denotes one specific t-type nodes and $V = V_V \cup V_A \cup V_O \cup V_P$. k_t specifies the size of a particular type of one's neighborhood and $k = k_V + k_A + k_O + k_P$.

Here we show how to use meta-paths to guide heterogeneous random walkers. Given a heterogeneous network $G = (V, E, T)$ and a meta-path scheme $\mathcal{P}$: $V_1 \xrightarrow{R_1} V_2 \xrightarrow{R_2} \cdots V_t \xrightarrow{R_t} V_{t+1} \cdots \xrightarrow{R_{l-1}} V_l$, the transition probability at step i is defined as follows:

$$p(v^{i+1}|v_t^i, \mathcal{P}) = \begin{cases} \frac{1}{|N_{t+1}(v_t^i)|} & (v^{i+1}, v_t^i) \in E, \phi(v^{i+1}) = t+1 \\ 0 & (v^{i+1}, v_t^i) \in E, \phi(v^{i+1}) \neq t+1 \\ 0 & (v^{i+1}, v_t^i) \notin E \end{cases} \tag{3}$$

where $v_t^i \in V_t$ and $N_{t+1}(v_t^i)$ denote the V_{t+1} type of neighborhood of node v_t^i. In other words, $v^{i+1} \in V_{t+1}$, that is, the flow of the walker is conditioned on the pre-defined meta-path $\mathcal{P}$. In addition, meta-paths are commonly used in a symmetric way, that is, its first node type V_1 is the same with the last one V_l [25, 26, 28], facilitating its recursive guidance for random walkers, i.e.,

$$p(v^{i+1}|v_t^i) = p(v^{i+1}|v_1^i), \text{ if } t = l \tag{4}$$

The meta-path-based random walk strategy ensures that the semantic relationships between different types of nodes can be properly incorporated into skip-gram. For example, in a traditional random walk procedure, in Figure 2(a), the next step of a walker on node a_4 transitioned from node CMU can be all types of nodes surrounding it—a_2, a_3, a_5, p_2, p_3, and CMU. However, under the meta-path scheme 'OAPVPAO', for example, the walker is biased towards paper nodes (P) given its previous step on an organization node CMU (O), following the semantics of this path.

3.3 *metapath2vec++*

metapath2vec distinguishes the context nodes of node v conditioned on their types when constructing its neighborhood function $N_t(v)$ in Eq. 2. However, it ignores the node type information in softmax. In other words, in order to infer the specific type of context c_t in $N_t(v)$ given a node v, *metapath2vec* actually encourages all types of negative samples, including nodes of the same type t as well as the other types in the heterogeneous network.

Heterogeneous negative sampling. We further propose the *metapath2vec++* framework, in which the softmax function is normalized with respect to the node type of the context c_t. Specifically, $p(c_t|v; \theta)$ is adjusted to the specific node type t, that is,

$$p(c_t|v; \theta) = \frac{e^{X_{c_t} \cdot X_v}}{\sum_{u_t \in V_t} e^{X_{u_t} \cdot X_v}} \tag{5}$$

where V_t is the node set of type t in the network. In doing so, *metapath2vec++* specifies one set of multinomial distributions for each type of neighborhood in the output layer of the skip-gram model. Recall that in *metapath2vec* and node2vec / DeepWalk, the dimension of the output multinomial distributions is equal to the number of nodes in the network. However, in *metapath2vec++*'s skip-gram, the multinomial distribution dimension for type t nodes is determined by the number of t-type nodes. A clear illustration can be seen in Figure 2(c). For example, given the target node a_4 in the input layer, *metapath2vec++* outputs four sets of multinomial distributions, each corresponding to one type of neighbors—venues V, authors A, organizations O, and papers P.

Inspired by PTE [29], the sampling distribution is also specified by the node type of the neighbor c_t that is targeted to predict, i.e., $P_t(\cdot)$. Therefore, we have the following objective:

$$O(\mathbf{X}) = \log \sigma(X_{c_t} \cdot X_v) + \sum_{m=1}^{M} \mathbb{E}_{u_t^m \sim P_t(u_t)}[\log \sigma(-X_{u_t^m} \cdot X_v)] \tag{6}$$

Input: The heterogeneous information network $G = (V, E, T)$, a meta-path scheme $\mathcal{P}$, #walks per node w, walk length l, embedding dimension d, neighborhood size k
Output: The latent node embeddings $\mathbf{X} \in \mathbb{R}^{|V| \times d}$

```
initialize X ;
for i = 1 → w do
    for v ∈ V do
        MP = MetaPathRandomWalk(G, P, v, l) ;
        X = HeterogeneousSkipGram(X, k, MP) ;
    end
end
return X ;

MetaPathRandomWalk(G, P, v, l)
MP[1] = v ;
for i = 1 → l-1 do
    draw u according to Eq. 3 ;
    MP[i+1] = u ;
end
return MP ;

HeterogeneousSkipGram(X, k, MP)
for i = 1 → l do
    v = MP[i] ;
    for j = max(0, i-k) → min(i+k, l) & j ≠ i do
        c_t = MP[j] ;
        X^new = X^old − η · ∂O(X)/∂X (Eq. 7) ;
    end
end
```

ALGORITHM 1: The *metapath2vec++* Algorithm.

whose gradients are derived as follows:

$$\frac{\partial O(\mathbf{X})}{\partial X_{u_t^m}} = (\sigma(X_{u_t^m} \cdot X_v - \mathbb{I}_{c_t}[u_t^m]))X_v \tag{7}$$

$$\frac{\partial O(\mathbf{X})}{\partial X_v} = \sum_{m=0}^{M} (\sigma(X_{u_t^m} \cdot X_v - \mathbb{I}_{c_t}[u_t^m]))X_{u_t^m}$$

where $\mathbb{I}_{c_t}[u_t^m]$ is an indicator function to indicate whether u_t^m is the neighborhood context node c_t and when $m = 0$, $u_t^0 = c_t$. The model is optimized by using stochastic gradient descent algorithm. The pseudo code of *metapath2vec++* is listed in Algorithm 1.

4 EXPERIMENTS

In this section, we demonstrate the efficacy and efficiency of the presented *metapath2vec* and *metapath2vec++* frameworks for heterogeneous network representation learning.

Data. We use two heterogeneous networks, including the AMiner Computer Science (CS) dataset [31] and the Database and Information Systems (DBIS) dataset [26]. Both datasets and code are publicly available[1]. This AMiner CS dataset consists of 9,323,739 computer scientists and 3,194,405 papers from 3,883 computer science venues—both conferences and journals—held until 2016. We construct a heterogeneous collaboration network, in which there are three types of nodes: authors, papers, and venues. The links represent different types of relationships among three sets of nodes—such as collaboration relationships on a paper.

The DBIS dataset was constructed and used by Sun et al. [26]. It covers 464 venues, their top-5000 authors, and corresponding 72,902 publications. We also construct the heterogeneous collaboration networks from DBIS wherein a link may connect two authors, one author and one paper, as well as one paper and one venue.

4.1 Experimental Setup

We compare *metapath2vec* and *metapath2vec++* with several recent network representation learning methods:

(1) DeepWalk [22] / node2vec [8]: With the same random walk path input (p=1 & q=1 in node2vec), we find that the choice between hierarchical softmax (DeepWalk) and negative sampling (node2vec) techniques does not yield significant differences. Therefore we use p=1 and q=1 [8] in node2vec for comparison.
(2) LINE [30]: We use the advanced version of LINE by considering both the 1st- and 2nd-order of node proximity;
(3) PTE [29]: We construct three bipartite heterogeneous networks (author–author, author–venue, venue–venue) and restrain it as an unsupervised embedding method;
(4) Spectral Clustering [33] / Graph Factorization [2]: With the same treatment to these methods in node2vec [8], we exclude them from our comparison, as previous studies have demonstrated that they are outperformed by DeepWalk and LINE.

For all embedding methods, we use the same parameters listed below. In addition, we also vary each of them and fix the others for examining the parameter sensitivity of the proposed methods.

(1) The number of walks per node w: 1000;
(2) The walk length l: 100;
(3) The vector dimension d: 128 (LINE: 128 for each order);
(4) The neighborhood size k: 7;
(5) The size of negative samples: 5.

For *metapath2vec* and *metapath2vec++*, we also need to specify the meta-path scheme to guide random walks. We surveyed most of the meta-path-based work and found that the most commonly and effectively used meta-path schemes in heterogeneous academic networks are "APA" and "APVPA" [12, 25–27]. Notice that "APA" denotes the coauthor semantic, that is, the traditional (homogeneous) collaboration links / relationships. "APVPA" represents the heterogeneous semantic of authors publishing papers at the same venues. Our empirical results also show that this simple meta-path scheme "APVPA" can lead to node embeddings that can be generalized to diverse heterogeneous academic mining tasks, suggesting its applicability to potential applications for academic search services.

We evaluate the quality of the latent representations learned by different methods over three classical heterogeneous network mining tasks, including multi-class node classification [13], node clustering [27], and similarity search [26]. In addition, we also use the embedding projector in TensorFlow [1] to visualize the node embeddings learned from the heterogeneous academic networks.

[1]The network data, learned latent representations, labeled ground truth data, and source code can be found at https://ericdongyx.github.io/metapath2vec/m2v.html

Table 2: Multi-class venue node classification results in AMiner data.

Metric	Method	5%	10%	20%	30%	40%	50%	60%	70%	80%	90%
Macro-F1	DeepWalk/node2vec	0.0723	0.1396	0.1905	0.2795	0.3427	0.3911	0.4424	0.4774	0.4955	0.4457
	LINE (1st+2nd)	0.2245	0.4629	0.7011	0.8473	0.8953	0.9203	0.9308	0.9466	0.9410	0.9466
	PTE	0.1702	0.3388	0.6535	0.8304	0.8936	0.9210	0.9352	0.9505	0.9525	0.9489
	metapath2vec	0.3033	0.5247	0.8033	0.8971	0.9406	0.9532	0.9529	0.9701	0.9683	0.9670
	metapath2vec++	0.3090	0.5444	0.8049	0.8995	0.9468	0.9580	0.9561	0.9675	0.9533	0.9503
Micro-F1	DeepWalk/node2vec	0.1701	0.2142	0.2486	0.3266	0.3788	0.4090	0.4630	0.4975	0.5259	0.5286
	LINE (1st+2nd)	0.3000	0.5167	0.7159	0.8457	0.8950	0.9209	0.9333	0.9500	0.9556	0.9571
	PTE	0.2512	0.4267	0.6879	0.8372	0.8950	0.9239	0.9352	0.9550	0.9667	0.9571
	metapath2vec	0.4173	0.5975	0.8327	0.9011	0.9400	0.9522	0.9537	0.9725	0.9815	0.9857
	metapath2vec++	0.4331	0.6192	0.8336	0.9032	0.9463	0.9582	0.9574	0.9700	0.9741	0.9786

Table 3: Multi-class author node classification results in AMiner data.

Metric	Method	5%	10%	20%	30%	40%	50%	60%	70%	80%	90%
Macro-F1	DeepWalk/node2vec	0.7153	0.7222	0.7256	0.7270	0.7273	0.7274	0.7273	0.7271	0.7275	0.7275
	LINE (1st+2nd)	0.8849	0.8886	0.8911	0.8921	0.8926	0.8929	0.8934	0.8936	0.8938	0.8934
	PTE	0.8898	0.8940	0.897	0.8982	0.8987	0.8990	0.8997	0.8999	0.9002	0.9005
	metapath2vec	0.9216	0.9262	0.9292	0.9303	0.9309	0.9314	0.9315	0.9316	0.9319	0.9320
	metapath2vec++	0.9107	0.9156	0.9186	0.9199	0.9204	0.9207	0.9207	0.9208	0.9211	0.9212
Micro-F1	DeepWalk/node2vec	0.7312	0.7372	0.7402	0.7414	0.7418	0.7420	0.7419	0.7420	0.7425	0.7425
	LINE (1st+2nd)	0.8936	0.8969	0.8993	0.9002	0.9007	0.9010	0.9015	0.9016	0.9018	0.9017
	PTE	0.8986	0.9023	0.9051	0.9061	0.9066	0.9068	0.9075	0.9077	0.9079	0.9082
	metapath2vec	0.9279	0.9319	0.9346	0.9356	0.9361	0.9365	0.9365	0.9365	0.9367	0.9369
	metapath2vec++	0.9173	0.9217	0.9243	0.9254	0.9259	0.9261	0.9261	0.9262	0.9264	0.9266

4.2 Multi-Class Classification

For the classification task, we use third-party labels to determine the class of each node. First, we match the eight categories[2] of venues in Google Scholar[3] with those in AMiner data. Among all of the 160 venues (20 per category × 8 categories), 133 of them are successfully matched and labeled correspondingly (Most of unmatched venues are pre-print venues, such as arXiv). Second, for each author who published in these 133 venues, his / her label is assigned to the category with the majority of his / her publications, and a tie is resolved by random selection among the possible categories; 246,678 authors are labeled with research category.

Note that the node representations are learned from the full dataset. The embeddings of above labeled nodes are then used as the input to a logistic regression classifier. In the classification experiments, we vary the size of the training set from 5% to 90% and the remaining nodes for testing. We repeat each prediction experiment ten times and report the average performance in terms of both Macro-F1 and Micro-F1 scores.

Results. Tables 2 and 3 list the eight-class classification results. Overall, the proposed *metapath2vec* and *metapath2vec++* models consistently and significantly outperform all baselines in terms of both metrics. When predicting for the venue category, the advantage of both *metapath2vec* and *metapath2vec++* are particular strong given a small size of training data. Given 5% of nodes as training data, for example, *metapath2vec* and *metapath2vec++* achieve 0.08–0.23 (relatively 35–319%) improvements in terms of Macro-F1 and 0.13–0.26 (relatively 39–145%) gains in terms of Micro-F1 over DeepWalk / node2vec, LINE, and PTE. When predicting for authors' categories, the performance of each method is relatively stable when varying the train-test split. The constant gain achieved by the proposed methods is around 2-3% over LINE and PTE, and ~20% over DeepWalk / node2vec.

In summary, *metapath2vec* and *metapath2vec++* learn significantly better heterogeneous node embeddings than current state-of-the-art methods, as measured by multi-class classification performance. The advantage of the proposed methods lies in their proper consideration and accommodation of the network heterogeneity challenge—the existence of multiple types of nodes and relations.

Parameter sensitivity. In skip-gram-based representation learning models, there exist several common parameters (see Section 4.1). We conduct a sensitivity analysis of *metapath2vec++* to these parameters. Figure 3 shows the classification results as a function

[2] 1. Computational Linguistics, 2. Computer Graphics, 3. Computer Networks & Wireless Communication, 4. Computer Vision & Pattern Recognition, 5. Computing Systems, 6. Databases & Information Systems, 7. Human Computer Interaction, and 8. Theoretical Computer Science.

[3] https://scholar.google.com/citations?view_op=top_venues&hl=en&vq=eng. Accessed on February, 2017.

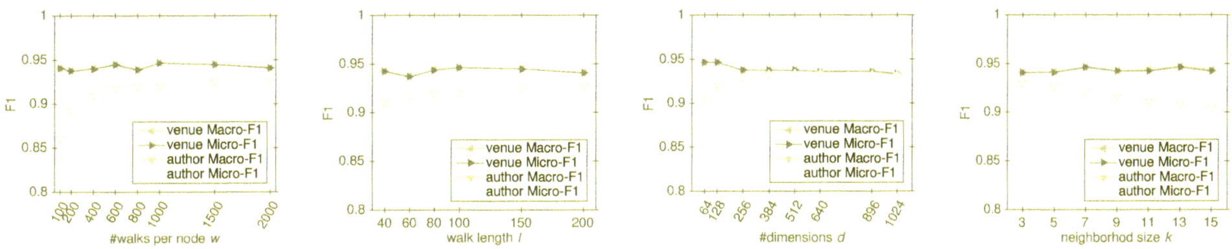

(a) #walks per node w (b) walk length l (c) #dimensions d (d) neighborhood size k

Figure 3: Parameter sensitivity in multi-class node classification. 50% as training data and the remaining as test data.

Table 4: Node clustering results (NMI) in AMiner data.

methods	venue	author
DeepWalk/node2vec	0.1952	0.2941
LINE (1st+2nd)	0.8967	0.6423
PTE	0.9060	0.6483
metapath2vec	0.9274	0.7470
metapath2vec++	0.9261	0.7354

of one chosen parameter when the others are controlled for. In general, we find that in Figures 3(a) and 3(b) the number of walks w rooting from each node and the length l of each walk are positive to the author classification performance, while they are surprisingly inconsequential for inferring venue nodes' categories as measured by Macro-F1 and Micro-F1 scores. The increase of author classification performance converges as w and l reach around 1000 and 100, respectively. Similarly, Figures 3(c) and 3(d) suggest that the number of embedding dimensions d and neighborhood size k are again of relatively little relevance to the predictive task for venues, and k on the other hand is positively crucial to determine the class of a venue. However, the descending lines as the increase of k for author classifications imply that a smaller neighborhood size actually produces the best embeddings for separating authors. This finding differs from those in a homogeneous environment [8], wherein the neighborhood size generally shows a positive effect on node classification.

According to the analysis, *metapath2vec++* is not strictly sensitive to these parameters and is able to reach high performance under a cost-effective parameter choice (the smaller, the more efficient). In addition, our results also indicate that those common parameters show different functions for heterogeneous network embedding with those in homogeneous network cases, demonstrating the request of different ideas and solutions for heterogeneous network representation learning.

4.3 Node Clustering

We illustrate how the latent representations learned by embedding methods can help the node clustering task in heterogeneous networks. We employ the same eight-category author and venue nodes used in the classification task above. The learned embeddings by each method is input to a clustering model. Here we leverage the k-means algorithm to cluster the data and evaluate the clustering results in terms of normalized mutual information (NMI) [26]. In addition, we also report *metapath2vec++*'s sensitivity with respect to different parameter choices. All clustering experiments are conducted 10 times and the average performance is reported.

Results. Table 4 shows the node clustering results as measured by NMI in the AMiner CS data. Overall, the table demonstrates that *metapath2vec* and *metapath2vec++* outperform all the comparative methods. When clustering for venues, the task is trivial as evident from the high NMI scores produced by most of the methods: *metapath2vec*, *metapath2vec++*, LINE, and PTE. Nevertheless, the proposed two methods outperform LINE and PTE by 2–3%. The author clustering task is more challenging than the venue case, and the gain obtained by *metapath2vec* and *metapath2vec++* over the best baselines (LINE and PTE) is more significant—around 13–16%.

In summary, *metapath2vec* and *metapath2vec++* generate more appropriate embeddings for different types of nodes in the network than comparative baselines, suggesting their ability to capture and incorporate the underlying structural and semantic relationships between various types of nodes in heterogeneous networks.

Parameter sensitivity. Following the same experimental procedure in classification, we study the parameter sensitivity of *metapath2vec++* as measured by the clustering performance. Figure 4 shows the clustering performance as a function of each of the four parameters when fixing the other three. From Figures 4(a) and 4(b), we can observe that the balance between computational cost (a small w and l in x-axis) and efficacy (a high NMI in y-axis) can be achieved at around $w = 800{\sim}1000$ and $l = 100$ for the clustering of both authors and venues. Further, different from the positive effect of increasing w and l on author clustering, d and k are negatively correlated with the author clustering performance, as observed from Figures 4(c) and 4(d). Similarly, the venue clustering performance also shows an descending trend with an increasing d, while on the other hand, we observe a first-increasing and then-decreasing NMI line when k is increased. Both figures together imply that $d = 128$ and $k = 7$ are capable of embedding heterogeneous nodes into latent space for promising clustering outcome.

4.4 Case Study: Similarity Search

We conduct two case studies to demonstrate the efficacy of our methods. We select 16 top CS conferences from the corresponding

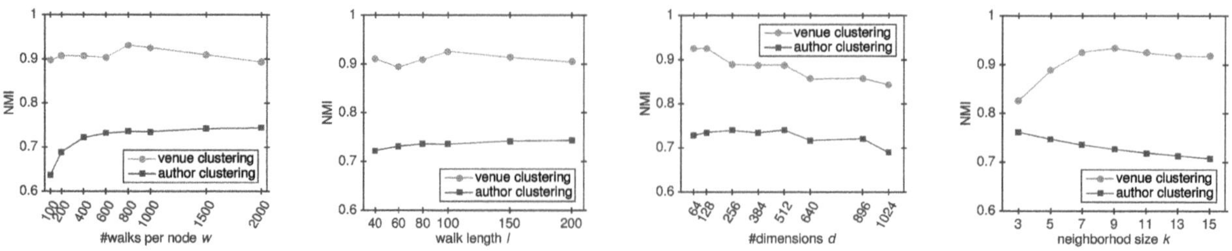

(a) #walks per node w (b) walk length l (c) #dimensions d (d) neighborhood size k

Figure 4: Parameter sensitivity in clustering.

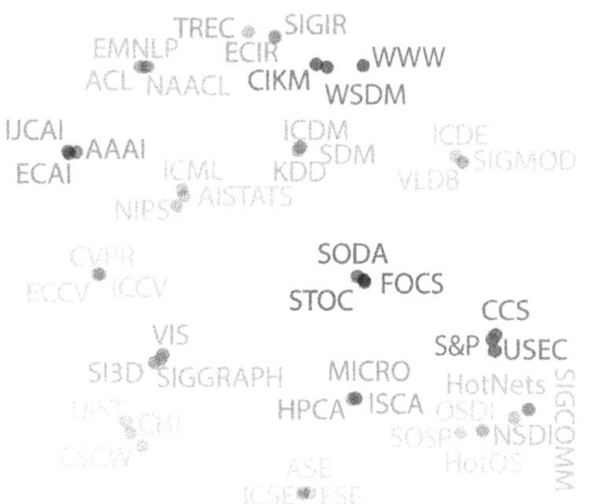

Figure 5: 2D t-SNE projections of the 128D embeddings of 48 CS venues, three each from 16 sub-fields.

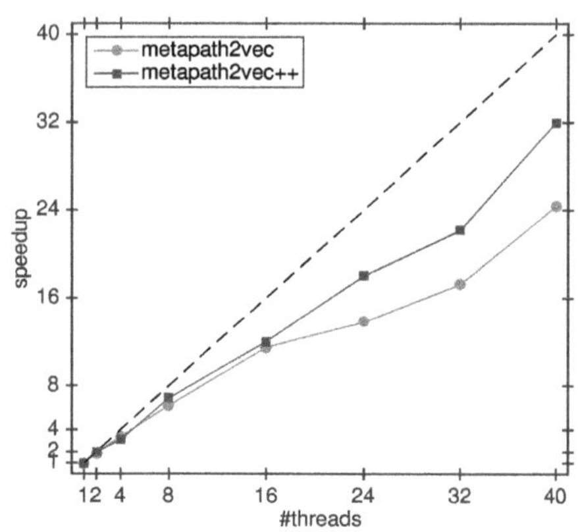

Figure 6: Scalability of *metapath2vec* and *metapath2vec++*.

sub-fields in the AMiner CS data and another 5 from the DBIS data. This results in a total of 21 query nodes. We use cosine similarity to determine the distance (similarity) between the query node and the remaining others.

Table 5 lists the top ten similar results for querying the 16 leading conferences in corresponding computer science sub-fields. One can observe that for the query "ACL", for example, *metapath2vec++* returns venues with the same focus—natural language processing, such as EMNLP (1st), NAACL (2nd), Computational Linguistics (3rd), CoNLL (4th), COLING (5th), and so on. Similar performance can be also achieved when querying the other conferences from various fields. More surprisingly, we find that in most cases, the top three results cover venues with similar prestige to the query one, such as STOC to FOCS in theory, OSDI to SOSP in system, HPCA to ISCA in architecture, CCS to S&P in security, CSCW to CHI in human-computer interaction, EMNLP to ACL in NLP, ICML to NIPS in machine learning, WSDM to WWW in Web, AAAI to IJCAI in artificial intelligence, PVLDB to SIGMOD in database, etc. Similar results can also be observed in Tables 6 and 1, which show the similarity search results for the DBIS network.

4.5 Case Study: Visualization

We employ the TensorFlow embedding projector to further visualize the low-dimensional node representations learned by embedding models. First, we project multiple types of nodes—16 top CS conferences and corresponding top-profile authors—into the same space in Figure 1. From Figure 1(d), we can clearly see that *metapath2vec++* is able to automatically organize these two types of nodes and implicitly learn the internal relationships between them, indicated by the similar directions and distances of the arrows connecting each pair of them, such as J. Dean → OSDI, C. D. Manning → ACL, R. E. Tarjan → FOCS, M. I. Jordan → NIPS, and so on. In addition, these two types of nodes are clearly located in two separate and straight columns. Neither of these two results can be made by the recent network embedding models in Figures 1(a) and 1(b).

As to *metapath2vec*, instead of separating the two types of nodes into two columns, it is capable of grouping each pair of one venue and its corresponding author closely, such as R. E. Tarjan and FOCS, H. Jensen and SIGGRAPH, H. Ishli and CHI, R. Agrawal and SIGMOD, etc. Together, both models arrange nodes from similar fields close to each other and dissimilar ones distant from each other, such as the "Core CS" cluster of systems (OSDI), networking (SIGCOMM), security (S&P), and architecture (ISCA), as well as the "Big AI" cluster of data mining (KDD), information retrieval (SIGIR), artificial intelligence (AI), machine learning (NIPS), NLP (ACL), and vision (CVPR). These groupings are also reflected by their corresponding author nodes.

Second, Figure 5 visualizes the latent vectors—learned by *metapath2vec++*—of 48 venues used in similarity search of Section 4.4,

Table 5: Case study of similarity search in AMiner Data

Rank	ACL	NIPS	IJCAI	CVPR	FOCS	SOSP	ISCA	S&P	ICSE	SIGGRAPH	SIGCOMM	CHI	KDD	SIGMOD	SIGIR	WWW
0	ACL	NIPS	IJCAI	CVPR	FOCS	SOSP	ISCA	S&P	ICSE	SIGGRAPH	SIGCOMM	CHI	KDD	SIGMOD	SIGIR	WWW
1	EMNLP	ICML	AAAI	ECCV	STOC	TOCS	HPCA	CCS	TOSEM	TOG	CCR	CSCW	SDM	PVLDB	ECIR	WSDM
2	NAACL	AISTATS	AI	ICCV	SICOMP	OSDI	MICRO	NDSS	FSE	SI3D	HotNets	TOCHI	TKDD	ICDE	CIKM	CIKM
3	CL	JMLR	JAIR	IJCV	SODA	HotOS	ASPLOS	USENIX S	ASE	RT	NSDI	UIST	ICDM	DE Bull	IR J	TWEB
4	CoNLL	NC	ECAI	ACCV	A-R	SIGOPS E	PACT	ACSAC	ISSTA	CGF	CoNEXT	DIS	DMKD	VLDBJ	TREC	ICWSM
5	COLING	MLJ	KR	CVIU	TALG	ATC	ICS	JCS	E SE	NPAR	IMC	HCI	KDD E	EDBT	SIGIR F	HT
6	IJCNLP	COLT	AI Mag	BMVC	ICALP	NSDI	HiPEAC	ESORICS	MSR	Vis	TON	MobileHCI	WSDM	TODS	ICTIR	SIGIR
7	NLE	UAI	ICAPS	ICPR	ECCC	OSR	PPOPP	TISS	ESEM	JGT	INFOCOM	INTERACT	CIKM	CIDR	WSDM	KDD
8	ANLP	KDD	CI	EMMCVPR	TOC	ASPLOS	ICCD	ASIACCS	A SE	VisComp	PAM	GROUP	PKDD	SIGMOD R	TOIS	TIT
9	LREC	CVPR	AIPS	T on IP	JAIG	EuroSys	CGO	RAID	ICPC	GI	MobiCom	NordiCHI	ICML	WebDB	IPM	WISE
10	EACL	ECML	UAI	WACV	ITCS	SIGCOMM	ISLPED	CSFW	WICSA	CG	IPTPS	UbiComp	PAKDD	PODS	AIRS	WebSci

Table 6: Case study of similarity search in DBIS Data

Rank	KDD	SIGMOD	SIGIR	WWW	WSDM
0	KDD	SIGMOD	SIGIR	WWW	WSDM
1	SDM	PVLDB	TREC	CIKM	WWW
2	ICDM	ICDE	CIKM	SIGIR	SIGIR
3	DMKD	TODS	IPM	KDD	KDD
4	KDD E	VLDBJ	IRJ	ICDE	AIRWeb
5	PKDD	PODS	ECIR	TKDE	CIKM
6	PAKDD	EDBT	TOIS	VLDB	WebDB
7	TKDE	CIDR	WWW	TOTT	ICDM
8	CIKM	TKDE	JASIST	SIGMOD	VLDB
9	ICDE	ICDT	JASIS	WebDB	VLDBJ
10	TKDD	DE Bull	SIGIR F	WISE	SDM

three each from 16 sub-fields. We can see that conferences from the same domain are geographically grouped to each other and each group is well separated from others, further demonstrating the embedding ability of *metapath2vec++*. In addition, similar to the observation in Figure 1, we can also notice that the heterogeneous embeddings are able to unveil the similarities across different domains, including the "Core CS" sub-field cluster at the bottom right and the "Big AI" sub-field cluster at the top right.

Thus, Figures 1 and 5 intuitively demonstrate *metapath2vec++*'s novel capability to discover, model, and capture the underlying structural and semantic relationships between multiple types of nodes in heterogeneous networks.

4.6 Scalability

In the era of big (network) data, it is necessary to demonstrate the scalability of the proposed network embedding models. The *metapath2vec* and *metapath2vec++* methods can be parallelized by using the same mechanism as word2vec and node2vec [8, 18]. All codes are implemented in C and C++ and our experiments are conducted in a computing server with Quad 12 (48) core 2.3 GHz Intel Xeon CPUs E7-4850. We run experiments on the AMiner CS data with the default parameters with different number of threads, i.e., 1, 2, 4, 8, 16, 24, 32, 40, each of them utilizing one CPU core.

Figure 6 shows the speedup of *metapath2vec* & *metapath2vec++* over the single-threaded case. Optimal speedup performance is denoted by the dashed $y = x$ line, which represents perfect distribution and execution of computation across all CPU cores. In general, we find that both methods achieve acceptable sublinear speedups as both lines are close to the optimal line. In specific, they can reach 11–12× speedup with 16 cores and 24–32× speedup with 40 cores used. By using 40 cores, *metapath2vec++*'s learning process costs only 9 minutes for embedding the full AMiner CS network, which is composed of over 9 million authors with 3 million papers published in more than 3800 venues. Overall, the proposed *metapath2vec* and *metapath2vec++* models are efficient and scalable for large-scale heterogeneous networks with millions of nodes.

5 RELATED WORK

Network representation learning can be traced back to the usage of latent factor models for network analysis and graph mining tasks [10, 34], such as the application of factorization models for recommendation systems [14, 16], node classification [32], relational mining [19], and role discovery [9]. This rich line of research focuses on factorizing the matrix/tensor format (e.g., the adjacency matrix) of a network, generating latent-dimension features for nodes or edges in this network. However, the computational cost of decomposing a large-scale matrix/tensor is usually very expensive, and also suffers from its statistical performance drawback [8], making it neither practical nor effective for addressing tasks in big networks.

With the advent of deep learning techniques, significant effort has been devoted to designing neural network-based representation learning models. For example, Mikolov et al. proposed the *word2vec* framework—a two-layer neural network—to learn the distributed representations of words in natural language [17, 18]. Building on word2vec, Perozzi et al. suggested that the "context" of a node can be denoted by their co-occurrence in a random walk path [22]. Formally, they put random walkers over networks to record their walking paths, each of which is composed of a chain of nodes that could be considered as a "sentence" of words in a text corpus. More recently, in order to diversify the neighborhood of a node, Grover & Leskovec presented biased random walkers—a mixture of breadth-first and width-first search procedures—over networks to produce paths of nodes [8]. With node paths generated, both works leveraged the skip-gram architecture in word2vec to model the structural correlations between nodes in a path. In addition, several other methods have been proposed for learning representations in networks [4, 5, 11, 20, 23]. In particular, to learn network embeddings, Tang et al. decomposed a node's context into first-order (friends) and second-order (friends' friends) proximity [30], which was further developed into a semi-supervised model PTE for embedding text data [29].

Our work furthers this direction of investigation by designing the *metapath2vec* and *metapath2vec++* models to capture heterogeneous structural and semantic correlations exhibited from large-scale networks with multiple types of nodes, which can not be handled by previous models, and applying these models to a variety of network mining tasks.

6 CONCLUSION

In this work, we formally define the representation learning problem in heterogeneous networks in which there exist diverse types of nodes and links. To address the network heterogeneity challenge, we propose the *metapath2vec* and *metapath2vec++* methods. We develop the meta-path-guided random walk strategy in a heterogeneous network, which is capable of capturing both the structural and semantic correlations of differently typed nodes and relations. To leverage this method, we formalize the heterogeneous neighborhood function of a node, enabling the skip-gram-based maximization of the network probability in the context of multiple types of nodes. Finally, we achieve effective and efficient optimization by presenting a heterogeneous negative sampling technique. Extensive experiments demonstrate that the latent feature representations learned by *metapath2vec* and *metapath2vec++* are able to improve various heterogeneous network mining tasks, such as similarity search, node classification, and clustering. Our results can be naturally applied to real-world applications in heterogeneous academic networks, such as author, venue, and paper search in academic search services.

Future work includes various optimizations and improvements. For example, 1) the *metapath2vec* and *metapath2vec++* models, as is also the case with DeepWalk and node2vec, face the challenge of large intermediate output data when sampling a network into a huge pile of paths, and thus identifying and optimizing the sampling space is an important direction; 2) as is also the case with all meta-path-based heterogeneous network mining methods, *metapath2vec* and *metapath2vec++* can be further improved by the automatic learning of meaningful meta-paths; 3) extending the models to incorporate the dynamics of evolving heterogeneous networks; and 4) generalizing the models for different genres of heterogeneous networks.

Acknowledgments. We would like to thank Reid Johnson for discussions and suggestions. This work is supported by the Army Research Laboratory under Cooperative Agreement Number W911NF-09-2-0053 and the National Science Foundation (NSF) grants CNS-1629914 and IIS-1447795.

REFERENCES

[1] Martín Abadi, Paul Barham, Jianmin Chen, Zhifeng Chen, Andy Davis, Jeffrey Dean, Matthieu Devin, Sanjay Ghemawat, Geoffrey Irving, and others. 2016. TensorFlow: A system for large-scale machine learning. In *OSDI '16*.
[2] Amr Ahmed, Nino Shervashidze, Shravan Narayanamurthy, Vanja Josifovski, and Alexander J. Smola. 2013. Distributed Large-scale Natural Graph Factorization. In *WWW '13*. ACM, 37–48.
[3] Yoshua Bengio, Aaron Courville, and Pierre Vincent. 2013. Representation learning: A review and new perspectives. *IEEE TPAMI* 35, 8 (2013), 1798–1828.
[4] Shiyu Chang, Wei Han, Jiliang Tang, Guo-Jun Qi, Charu C. Aggarwal, and Thomas S. Huang. 2015. Heterogeneous Network Embedding via Deep Architectures. In *KDD '15*. ACM, 119–128.
[5] Ting Chen and Yizhou Sun. 2017. Task-Guided and Path-Augmented Heterogeneous Network Embedding for Author Identification. In *WSDM '17*. ACM.
[6] Yuxiao Dong, Jing Zhang, Jie Tang, Nitesh V. Chawla, and Bai Wang. 2015. CoupledLP: Link Prediction in Coupled Networks. In *KDD '15*. ACM, 199–208.
[7] Yoav Goldberg and Omer Levy. 2014. word2vec Explained: deriving Mikolov et al.'s negative-sampling word-embedding method. *CoRR* abs/1402.3722 (2014).
[8] Aditya Grover and Jure Leskovec. 2016. Node2Vec: Scalable Feature Learning for Networks. In *KDD '16*. ACM, 855–864.
[9] Keith Henderson, Brian Gallagher, Tina Eliassi-Rad, Hanghang Tong, Sugato Basu, Leman Akoglu, Danai Koutra, Christos Faloutsos, and Lei Li. 2012. Rolx: structural role extraction & mining in large graphs. In *KDD '12*. ACM, 1231–1239.
[10] Peter D Hoff, Adrian E Raftery, and Mark S Handcock. 2002. Latent space approaches to social network analysis. *Journal of the American Statistical association* 97, 460 (2002), 1090–1098.
[11] Xiao Huang, Jundong Li, and Xia Hu. 2017. Label Informed Attributed Network Embedding. In *WSDM '17*. na.
[12] Zhipeng Huang, Yudian Zheng, Reynold Cheng, Yizhou Sun, Nikos Mamoulis, and Xiang Li. 2016. Meta structure: Computing relevance in large heterogeneous information networks. In *KDD '16*. ACM, 1595–1604.
[13] Ming Ji, Jiawei Han, and Marina Danilevsky. 2011. Ranking-based classification of heterogeneous information networks. In *KDD '11*. ACM, 1298–1306.
[14] Yehuda Koren. 2008. Factorization meets the neighborhood: a multifaceted collaborative filtering model. In *KDD '08*. ACM, 426–434.
[15] Yann LeCun, Yoshua Bengio, and Geoffrey Hinton. 2015. Deep learning. *Nature* 521, 7553 (2015), 436–444.
[16] Hao Ma, Dengyong Zhou, Chao Liu, Michael R Lyu, and Irwin King. 2011. Recommender systems with social regularization. In *WSDM '11*. 287–296.
[17] Tomas Mikolov, Kai Chen, Greg Corrado, and Jeffrey Dean. 2013. Efficient Estimation of Word Representations in Vector Space. *CoRR* abs/1301.3781 (2013). http://arxiv.org/abs/1301.3781
[18] Tomas Mikolov, Ilya Sutskever, Kai Chen, Greg S Corrado, and Jeff Dean. 2013. Distributed representations of words and phrases and their compositionality. In *NIPS '13*. 3111–3119.
[19] Jennifer Neville and David Jensen. 2005. Leveraging relational autocorrelation with latent group models. In *Proceedings of the 4th international workshop on Multi-relational mining*. ACM, 49–55.
[20] Mingdong Ou, Peng Cui, Jian Pei, Ziwei Zhang, and Wenwu Zhu. 2016. Asymmetric Transitivity Preserving Graph Embedding. In *KDD '16*. ACM, 1105–1114.
[21] Siddharth Pal, Yuxiao Dong, Bishal Thapa, Nitesh V Chawla, Ananthram Swami, and Ram Ramanathan. 2016. Deep learning for network analysis: Problems, approaches and challenges. In *Military Communications Conference, MILCOM 2016-2016*. IEEE, 588–593.
[22] Bryan Perozzi, Rami Al-Rfou, and Steven Skiena. 2014. DeepWalk: Online Learning of Social Representations. In *KDD '14*. ACM, 701–710.
[23] Xiang Ren, Wenqi He, Meng Qu, Clare R Voss, Heng Ji, and Jiawei Han. 2016. Label noise reduction in entity typing by heterogeneous partial-label embedding. In *KDD '16*. ACM.
[24] Xin Rong. 2014. word2vec Parameter Learning Explained. *CoRR* abs/1411.2738 (2014). http://arxiv.org/abs/1411.2738
[25] Yizhou Sun and Jiawei Han. 2012. *Mining Heterogeneous Information Networks: Principles and Methodologies*. Morgan & Claypool Publishers.
[26] Yizhou Sun, Jiawei Han, Xifeng Yan, Philip S. Yu, and Tianyi Wu. 2011. Pathsim: Meta path-based top-k similarity search in heterogeneous information networks. In *VLDB '11*. 992–1003.
[27] Yizhou Sun, Brandon Norick, Jiawei Han, Xifeng Yan, Philip S. Yu, and Xiao Yu. 2012. Integrating Meta-path Selection with User-guided Object Clustering in Heterogeneous Information Networks. In *KDD '12*. ACM, 1348–1356.
[28] Yizhou Sun, Yintao Yu, and Jiawei Han. 2009. Ranking-based Clustering of Heterogeneous Information Networks with Star Network Schema. In *KDD '09*. ACM, 797–806.
[29] Jian Tang, Meng Qu, and Qiaozhu Mei. 2015. PTE: Predictive Text Embedding Through Large-scale Heterogeneous Text Networks. In *KDD '15*. ACM, 1165–1174.
[30] Jian Tang, Meng Qu, Mingzhe Wang, Ming Zhang, Jun Yan, and Qiaozhu Mei. 2015. LINE: Large-scale Information Network Embedding.. In *WWW '15*. ACM.
[31] Jie Tang, Jing Zhang, Limin Yao, Juanzi Li, Li Zhang, and Zhong Su. 2008. ArnetMiner: Extraction and Mining of Academic Social Networks. In *KDD '08*. 990–998.
[32] Lei Tang and Huan Liu. 2009. Relational learning via latent social dimensions. In *KDD '09*. 817–826.
[33] Lei Tang and Huan Liu. 2011. Leveraging social media networks for classification. *DMKD* 23, 3 (2011), 447–478.
[34] Shuicheng Yan, Dong Xu, Benyu Zhang, Hong-Jiang Zhang, Qiang Yang, and Stephen Lin. 2007. Graph embedding and extensions: A general framework for dimensionality reduction. *IEEE TPAMI* 29, 1 (2007).
[35] Jing Zhang, Jie Tang, Cong Ma, Hanghang Tong, Yu Jing, and Juanzi Li. 2015. Panther: Fast top-k similarity search on large networks. In *KDD '15*. ACM, 1445–1454.

Ego-Splitting Framework: from Non-Overlapping to Overlapping Clusters

Alessandro Epasto
Google Research NY
aepasto@google.com

Silvio Lattanzi
Google Research Zurich
silviol@google.com

Renato Paes Leme
Google Research NY
renatoppl@google.com

ABSTRACT

We propose *ego-splitting*, a new framework for detecting clusters in complex networks which leverage the local structures known as ego-nets (i.e. the subgraph induced by the neighborhood of each node) to de-couple overlapping clusters. Ego-splitting is a highly scalable and flexible framework, with provable theoretical guarantees, that reduces the complex overlapping clustering problem to a simpler and more amenable non-overlapping (partitioning) problem. We can scale community detection to graphs with tens of billions of edges and outperform previous solutions based on ego-nets analysis.

More precisely, our framework works in two steps: a local ego-net analysis phase, and a global graph partitioning phase. In the local step, we first partition the nodes' ego-nets using a partitioning algorithm. We then use the computed clusters to split each node into its *persona* nodes that represent the instantiations of the node in its communities. Finally, in the global step, we partition the newly created graph to obtain an overlapping clustering of the original graph.

KEYWORDS

Overlapping clustering; ego-nets; large-scale graph algorithms.

1 INTRODUCTION

Detecting the clustering structure of real-world networks has emerged as an important primitive in a wide range of data analysis tasks such as community detection [19], event detection [39], spam detection [3], computational biology [22], link prediction [31] and many others. As a result, the study of the topology of real world networks and of their clustering (or community[1]) structure is central in modern network analysis. In particular, in recent years, several models have been introduced to capture the community structure of social networks [25, 27, 28] and numerous empirical studies analyzed the community structures at a macroscopic [21, 28, 29] and microscopic [13, 17] levels. One of the main observations in this line of work is the lack of a clear macroscopic community structure in real world networks. For instance in [29], Leskovec et al. give an empirical evidence that at global level it is rare to observe medium-sized communities (around 100 nodes) with clear clustering properties.

In addition, Abrahao et al. [1] collected empirical evidence showing that real-world communities are rarely detected by commonly used algorithms. In particular, real clusters overlap with each other and haves many edges crossing cluster boundaries. As a result, real world graphs do not exhibit a clear clustering structure at the macroscopic level.

In sharp contrast with these findings, it has been observed that while the community detection problem is hard at a macroscopic level, it becomes simple at a microscopic level [13, 17]. This is especially true when we restrict our attention to local structures know as *ego-nets* (a.k.a. ego-networks) which consist of the subgraph induced over the neighborhood of a single node in the graph. Intuitively, this happens because, even if a node is part of many communities, if we restrict our attention to a node and one of her neighbors, there is only one or a limited number of communities in which the two nodes interact, which present a clearer structure at the level of the neighborhood. In fact, Epasto et al. [17] analyze the ego-nets community structure of several graphs and show that it is possible to detect high quality communities in them using a simple out-of-the-shelf partitioning algorithms.

Inspired by this encouraging observation, we design a novel framework which we call *ego-splitting*. The main idea behind the framework is to use the guidance of local clustering structure to detect overlapping communities. The idea of using local clustering structure to obtain a global clustering is not new, for instance, Coscia et al. [13] recently designed an algorithm based on this approach. In this paper, however, we leverage for the first time this idea to design a highly scalable and flexible framework with provable theoretical guarantees, that reduces the complex overlapping clustering problem to a simpler and more amenable non-overlapping (partitioning) problem. This is particularly interesting because it allows us to use the large literature on non-overlapping clustering to approach the more complex overlapping clustering problem on large-scale graphs.

More formally, our *ego-splitting* framework works in two steps: a local ego-net analysis and a global graph partitioning. In those steps we use two partitioning algorithms $\mathcal{A}^{\ell}$ and $\mathcal{A}^{g}$ as a black box.

The first step of our framework is the ego-nets clustering. In this step for every node u, the framework constructs the ego-nets of u and then uses algorithm $\mathcal{A}^{\ell}$ to partition the neighborhood of u. For each community in the partition *ego-splitting* creates a new replica of u (which we call *persona*) that is associated uniquely with a cluster in the partition. Then we map each edge between nodes in the original graph to an edge between personas. The output of this step is a new graph which we refer to as the *persona* graph where

[1] Note that in the paper we use the terms cluster and community interchangeably.

KDD'17, August 13–17, 2017, Halifax, NS, Canada.
 978-1-4503-4887-4/17/08.
DOI: http://dx.doi.org/10.1145/3097983.3098054

each node u is replaced by a series of copies called the *personas* of u.

Then, in the second step of our framework, the global partition step, *ego-splitting* runs a partitioning algorithm $\mathcal{A}^g$ (potentially the same as $\mathcal{A}^\ell$) on the resulting persona graph and returns the clustering detected by $\mathcal{A}^g$.

To clarify the main intuition behind our framework we now present a visual example in Figure 1 where we show the execution of our method using as clustering algorithms $\mathcal{A}^\ell$ and $\mathcal{A}^g$ the simple connected component algorithm.

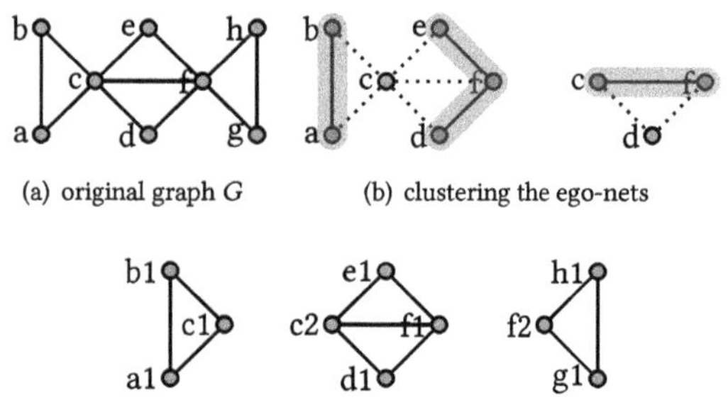

(a) original graph G (b) clustering the ego-nets

(c) splitting the ego we obtain the persona graph

Figure 1: The ego-splitting framework applied to a simple graph to transform an overlapping clustering problem into a partitioning problem.

First, note that in the graph in Figure 1 there are 3 overlapping communities: $\{a,b,c\}, \{c,d,e,f\}, \{f,g,h\}$. In particular nodes c and f are part of two communities. Although, when restricting the attention to the the ego-net of any specific node (which recall, does not includes the node itself), the communities are naturally de-coupled. For instance, consider the ego-net of c in Figure 1(b), when we consider the graph induced on c's neighborhood, the two communities of c are easy to identify–they correspond exactly to the two connected components $\{a,b\}$ and $\{d,e,f\}$. So by using connected components our framework would be able to detect that even if there is one single node c in the graph, c has in reality two *personas* and so it would split c into two different nodes: c_1 and c_2. Note that besides nodes c and f the other nodes participate in a single community. In this case our algorithm keeps these nodes in a unique persona, for instance, d_1 in this case of d.

After the first local step, in the second global step the connected component algorithm can easily detect the overlapping community structure of the graph by partitioning the persona graph in the clusters $\{a_1,b_1,c_1\}$, $\{c_2,d_1,e_1,f_1\}$ and $\{f_2,g_1,h_1\}$ which corresponds to overlapping clusters in the original graph.

Even if this anecdotal example may look artificial at first sight, it captures well the complexity of real world graphs where people or entities are part of a multitude of communities. For example we can imagine node c in Figure 1 as a college student that participates in two clusters representing her college friends and her friends from a sports club. Clearly Figure 1 is an oversimplified scenario but, interestingly we observe empirically that our *ego-splitting* framework works well also in more complex realistic settings. While for the toy example in Figure 1 a simple articulation or bridge detection would work, the ego-splitting framework is able to dis-entangle communities even for highly connected graphs without bridges or articulations as we show in various examples later in the paper.

Notice also that more sophisticated algorithms than simple connected components can be used both at the ego-net clustering and at the persona clustering step. In fact, thanks to its flexibility, our framework can be used to transform any partitioning algorithm in an overlapping clustering algorithm.

Our Contribution. We introduced the new *ego-splitting* framework to reduce the overlapping clustering problem to a non-overlapping partition problem. Our methods scale easily in distributed settings, enabling the analysis of the overlapping community structure in graphs with tens of billions of edges using standard non-overlapping clustering algorithms.

We analyze the performance of the method both experimentally and theoretically. Experimentally we compare the performance of our algorithm against state of the art ego-net based clustering algorithms and measure their performance in terms of standard metrics for clustering detection: F_1-score and Normalized Mutual Information (NMI). We show that ego-splitting outperforms other algorithms in both metrics and both in real-world graphs with labeled communities (amazon, dblp, livejournal, orkut and friendster) and in synthetic benchmark graphs constructed by Lanchinetti et al. [26].

We also analyze ego-splitting theoretically in a random overlapping clusters model, where clusters are chosen to be random subsets of the vertex set and for each cluster we overlay a random Erdös-Renyi graph. We bound the Jaccard similarity between the clusters produced by the algorithm and the original clusters used by the model and show that, for natural ranges of parameters, the algorithm is able to perfectly reconstruct the clusters in the limit.

2 RELATED WORK

The related works span large research areas such ego-net analysis and community detection. In this section we restrict ourselves to reviewing only the most closely related papers in these areas.

The concept of ego-net (or ego-network) was first introduced in the seminal work of Freeman [20]. Then the study of ego-nets established itself at the basis of social network analysis [11, 15, 18, 38]. Recently, a widespread attention has been devoted in the computer science community on mining ego-nets. In their pioneering work, Rees and Gallagher [36] proposed to the use of ego-nets to find a global clustering of the graph. The core idea of their algorithm is to find basic communities by computing the weakly connected components for each ego-net after removing the ego from it. Then to obtain a global clustering they merge communities that overlap significantly. Coscia et al. [13] built on this work employing label propagation algorithms to cluster the ego-nets and analyze different merging strategies. The merging procedures applied are not scalable as they require $O(n^2)$ computation in the worst case. More recently Buzun et al. [12] and Liakos et al. [14] introduced distributed algorithms for the variation of this problem problem. We observe that unfortunately both solutions are more complex and less flexible (they are tailored to the use a specific underlying clustering algorithm) than ours. In addition the authors do not show any theoretical guarantees of their algorithms. The work [14] also assumes to know a set of seeds in each community which the algorithm expands locally. This is a different problem from the one we address of producing an overlapping clustering of the entire graph. To the best of our knowledge we are the first to introduce the concept of *persona graph* and to leverage it for obtaining a scalable and distributed ego-net based overlapping community detection method with provable guarantees.

In a different line of work, McAuley and Leskovec [33] provided a machine learning approach to cluster ego-nets. Subsequently Yang et al. [43] proposed an extension of this model for directed and undirected graphs. Finally, Li et al. [30] extended their learning model to also capture hidden attributes that are not explicitly present in the input.

The literature on community detection is very rich, for a good survey on the topic refer to [19]. Our paper is particularly related to the overlapping community literature. Whang et al. [40] develop an overlapping community detection algorithm based on seed set expansion. The algorithm optimizes for conductances and requires a set of input seeds. Unfortunately, the algorithm does not have any theoretical guarantees. Furthermore, no distributed implementation of the algorithm is presented in the paper. In another paper Amoretti et al. [4] propose a parallel (not distributed) implementation of Demon [13] on mid-size graphs. Other relevant overlapping community algorithms have been presented in [7] and in [23], unfortunately no distributed implementation of those algorithms is known and so they cannot scale to very large graphs. Finally, the overlapping community problem has been analyzed theoretically in several papers [5, 6, 24], although the proposed algorithms are mostly theoretical and have not been evaluated in practice.

Finally, our work is also related to the edge partitioning problem [2, 32]. In the edge partition problem the objective is to find an algorithm to partition the edges in different communities. This problem received significant attention because it allows us to compute an overlapping clustering of the graph by simply computing a partitioning of the edges of the graph. Interestingly, we note here that our framework can be used to obtain scalable algorithms for this problem as well.

3 CLUSTER DETECTION PROBLEM

In the overlapping community detection problem the goal is to design an algorithm $\mathcal{R}$ which consumes an undirected graph $G = (V, E)$ and outputs a collection $\mathcal{S}' = \mathcal{R}(G)$ of (possibly overlapping) subsets of the node set V which we call *clusters*, i.e. each $C \in \mathcal{S}'$ is a subset $C \subseteq V$ and two sets $C, C' \in \mathcal{S}'$ can overlap.

In this paper we try, as much as possible, to be agnostic to a precise definition of what a cluster is. For this reason instead of specific quality function to optimize we use a cluster reconstruction approach to evaluate our method. In a cluster reconstruction formulation we assume that there is a set $\mathcal{S}$ of subsets of the nodes which we call *ground-truth clusters* and the algorithm is tasked with recovering such clusters. Of course, for the detection problem to be meaningful, $\mathcal{S}$ and G must be related in a way that it is possible to extract information about $\mathcal{S}$ from G.

In order for the problem to be more concrete, we define two different scenarios where we want to evaluate our algorithms. The first is that of *labeled datasets*, where graphs come with metadata identifying subsets of nodes that are known to be communities and that we want to retrieve. This is particularly common for social networks (many examples are shown in the experimental section). A second scenario is that of *generative models*, where a random process generates a graph from a set of clusters and the algorithm needs to recover those clusters having only access to the graph. We evaluate our methods in this context in our theoretical analysis.

3.1 Evaluating a detection algorithm

In most cases, exact reconstructions of the communities is unrealistic and we will settle for approximate reconstructions. In the rest of the subsection we define several notions of approximation in comparing two clusterings which are standard in the literature.

Given a ground truth cluster $C \subseteq V$ and reconstructed cluster $C' \subseteq V$ we define the precision $P(C', C) = |C \cap C'|/|C'|$ as the fraction of the reconstruction that is in the ground truth and the recall $R(C', C) = |C \cap C'|/|C|$ as the fraction of the ground truth that is in the reconstruction. The notions of precision and recall are often combined in a single number between 0 and 1 called F_1-score, defined as:

$$F_1(C', C) = 2 \cdot \frac{P(C', C) \cdot R(C', C)}{P(C', C) + R(C', C)}$$

The notion of F_1 has the additional advantage of being symmetric, i.e., $F_1(C', C) = F_1(C, C')$ and of being such that $F_1(C, C') = 1$ iff the sets C and C' are equal.

Now that we can compare two clusters, we define a metric for evaluating the set of clusters detected:

F_1 score. Given a collection of ground truth clusters $\mathcal{S}$ and a collection of detected clusters $\mathcal{S}'$, a widely used [13] measure of accuracy is the F_1 score of the reconstruction with respect to the ground truth as follows:

$$F_1(\mathcal{S}', \mathcal{S}) = \frac{1}{|\mathcal{S}'|} \sum_{C' \in \mathcal{S}'} \max_{C \in \mathcal{S}} F_1(C', C)$$

which corresponds to the average F_1 score of a reconstructed cluster with respect to the best match in the ground truth.

Normalized Mutual Information (NMI). We will also use another standard measure of detection quality based on information theory developed by Lancichinetti and Fortunato [26] and later refined by McDaid et al [34]. The measure was carefully crafted to avoid various pitfalls of previous measures and it is quite involved. We refer to the cited papers for an exact description and a comprehensive discussion of its merits.

4 EGO-SPLITTING FRAMEWORK

The main algorithmic idea in the paper is that each node in the graph is a blend of different *personas*. Instead of seeking to solve the clustering problem directly, we first split each node in different personas. This disentangles the different clusters and makes the graph simpler to cluster.

Before we can describe the procedure in detail we establish notation and define some standard notions in graph theory:

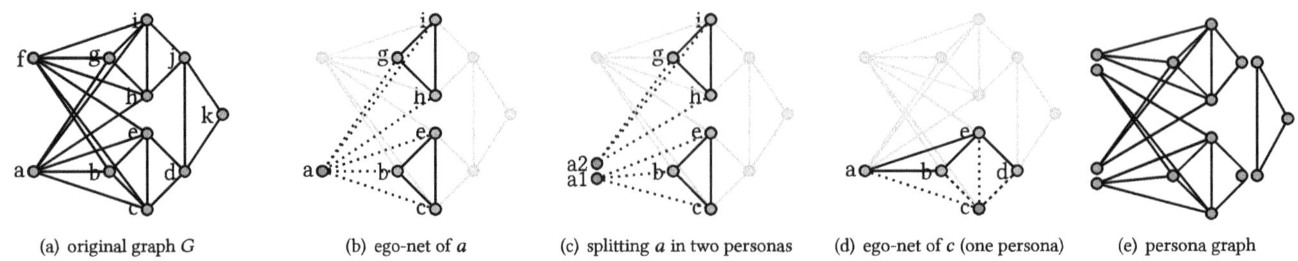

Figure 2: Clustering the ego-nets, splitting the ego and building the persona graph

4.1 Graph Theory Notation

An (undirected, unweighted) graph $G = (V, E)$ consists of a finite set V of nodes and an edge set $E \subset V \times V$ such that $u \neq v$ for each $(u, v) \in E$ and $(u, v) \in E$ iff $(v, u) \in E$.[2]

A *non-overlapping clustering algorithm* $\mathcal{A}$ produces for each graph $G = (V, E)$ a partition $\mathcal{A}(G) = (V_1, \ldots, V_t)$ of variable size. We use the notation $\text{np}_{\mathcal{A}}(G) = t$ to denote the number of sets in the partition. The fact that $\mathcal{A}(G)$ is a partition means that $V_i \cap V_j = \emptyset$ for $i \neq j$ and that $V_1 \cup \ldots V_t = V$. An example of a non-overlapping clustering algorithm is the connected components algorithm, which simply splits the graph into connected components.

Given a graph $G = (V, E)$ and a subset of nodes $U \subset V$, we define the induced graph $G[U] = (U, E \cap U \times U)$. For a node $u \in V$, the neighborhood of u consists of the set of nodes connected to it $N_u = \{v; (u, v) \in E\}$ and the ego-net of u consists of the graph induced on the neighborhood $G[N_u]$. The ego-net represents the local view from node u on the graph connections (notice that the ego-net of u does not include the node u).

4.2 The Framework

The ego-splitting framework provides a general methodology for constructing an overlapping clustering algorithm starting from two (possibly equal) non-overlapping clustering algorithms: the local clustering algorithm $\mathcal{A}^\ell$ and the global clustering algorithm $\mathcal{A}^g$. The ego-splitting algorithm processes a graph G and outputs a set of clusters $\mathcal{S}'$ as follows:

- *Step 1:* For each node u we use the local clustering algorithm to partition the ego-net of u. Let $\mathcal{A}^\ell(G[N_u]) = \{N_u^1, N_u^2, \ldots, N_u^{t_u}\}$ where $t_u = \text{np}(\mathcal{A}^\ell, G[N_u])$.
- *Step 2:* Create a set V' of personas. Each node u in V will correspond to t_u personas in V' denoted by u_i for $i = 1, \ldots, t_u$.
- *Step 3:* Add edges between personas. If $(u, v) \in E$, $v \in N_u^i$ and $u \in N_v^j$ then add an edge (u_i, v_j) to E'.
- *Step 4:* Apply the global clustering algorithm $\mathcal{A}^g$ to $G' = (V', E')$ and obtain a partition $\mathcal{S}''$ of V'.
- *Step 5:* For set $C' \in \mathcal{S}''$ in the partition of V' associate a cluster $C(C') \subseteq V$ formed by the corresponding nodes of V, i.e., $C(C') = \{u \in V | \exists i \text{ s.t. } u_i \in C'\}$. Output $\mathcal{S}' = \{C(C') | C' \in \mathcal{S}''\}$.

In Figure 2 we show an example execution using connected components as clustering method. In Figure 2(b) we depict Step 1 for node a: we look at the ego-net $G[N_a]$ and partition it. In Figure 2(c), we add for each partition of the ego-net a persona of a associated with that partition (Step 2). For example, persona a_1 is associated with nodes b, c, e. In Figure 2(d) we do the same process for node c, but since his ego-net has only one partition, we add single persona of c associated with a, b, e, d. After this is done for all nodes (in parallel), we build the persona graph, depicted in Figure 2(e). In this graph there is an edge for each edge in the original graph, for example, for edge (a, c) in the original graph, we add an edge between the persona of a associated with c (i.e. the persona of a associated with the cluster to which c belongs in the ego-net of a) and the persona of c associated with a (Step 3). Figure 3(a) depicts Step 4 where we apply the global non-overlapping to the persona graph and obtain clusters. Step 5 is finally in Figure 3(b) where we map the clusters defined on personas to overlapping clusters defined on original nodes.

Clustering edges. The transformation from the original graph to the graph of personas can increase the number of nodes in the graph, but keeps the number of edges constant, so in terms of memory, the persona graph consumes the same space as the original one. Also, since there is a one-to-one mapping of the edges in both graphs, the non-overlapping partitions of the persona graph also imply a clustering of the egdes. We are able to say for each edge, which cluster it belongs to. In that sense, our methodology can be also viewed as a edge-disjoint clustering approach.

Ego-splitting at scale. A naïve way to bound all ego-nets could be prohibitively expensive, at the order of $O(nm)$ for $n = |V|$ and $m = |E|$. Epasto et al [17] use a combinatorial bound on the number of triangles to show all ego-nets can be constructed in time $O(m^{3/2})$, which is a considerable gain for sparse graphs. Indeed, the bound in practice can be much better than $O(m^{3/2})$ and depends directly on the number of triangles in the graph. They also show that if T is the time to cluster a graph with m edges, the total work to build all ego-nets and cluster them is $O(\sqrt{m}T + m^{3/2})$. Furthermore they show that this step can be performed in two rounds of MapReduce. One more step is required to build the persona graph and one to associate the clusters of the persona graph to the original nodes. Taking those results together we have:

Theorem 4.1. *If $T_\ell(m)$ and $T_g(m)$ are the total work of the local and global algorithms on a graph of size m (respectively), R_g is the number of rounds of MapReduce required by the global partition*

[2]Notice that our algorithm could be conceivably adapted to directed and weighted graphs but we do not pursue this direction in this paper.

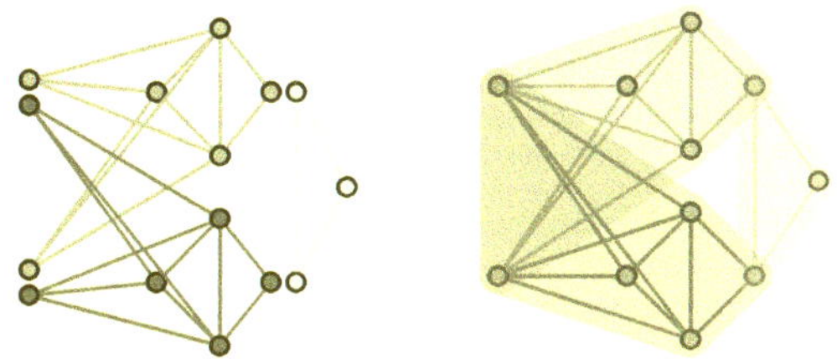

(a) non-overlapping partition of the persona graph (b) overlapping clusters in original graph

Figure 3: Clustering the persona graph

algorithm and if the local partition can be run in memory for each ego-net, the ego-splitting framework can be implemented in $4 + R_g$ *rounds of MapReduce with total work* $O(m^{3/2} + \sqrt{m}T_\ell(m) + T_g(m))$.

Notice for instance that if the both the local and global partitioning algorithms are $O(m)$, and if the global partitioning operates in $O(1)$ rounds we can implement the entire approach using $O(m^{3/2})$ total work and $O(1)$ rounds.

5 PROVABLE RECONSTRUCTION GUARANTEES

We present a generative model with overlapping clusters in which we are able to reconstruct most of the clusters exactly by using the *connected component* algorithm as a non-overlapping partition algorithm both in the ego-net clustering phase and in the persona graph clustering phase. Connected component is arguably the simplest (and most rudimentary) non-overlapping clustering algorithm possible, but its analysis sheds light on the ability of our framework to achieve provable guarantees even using a simple partitioning method as a building block. It is conceivable that using more sophisticated algorithms allows to prove guarantees in other more difficult models.

In our model there are k clusters and each node $u \in V$ is assigned to a cluster $C \in \mathcal{S}$ iid with probability q. Now, between two nodes of each cluster we add an edge with probability p. A different way to describe our model is that we pick k random subsets and overlay an Erdös-Renyi graph on each of those subsets. We are presented with the graph obtained by the union of such random graphs and are asked to reconstruct what are the original subsets chosen.

We will show that for a range of parameters, it is possible to reconstruct most of the random sets with high probability. We don't make any claim that the model corresponds to any real-world network. Our goal here is simply to show that even in highly-connected graphs with heavily overlapping clusters, it is possible to disentangle them by analyzing the local ego-net structures using a simple clustering algorithm in our framework.

Random Overlapping Clusters. We define the generative process $\mathcal{P}(n,k,q,p)$ as the random process that starts with a set of n nodes $V = [n]$ and first sample a collection of k subsets $\mathcal{S}$ as follows: from 1 to k we sample $C \in \mathcal{S}$ by adding each node $u \in V$ to C with probability q, independently.

Now, we sample G as follows: we visit each $C \in \mathcal{S}$ and for each we sample the edge sets E_C as follows: for each $u, v \in C$ with $u \neq v$ we add edge (u,v) to E_C with probability p. In other words, E_C is the edge set of an Erdös-Renyi graph with vertex set C. Now the edge set of the G is simply the union $E = \cup_{C \in \mathcal{S}} E_C$.

We note that the same edge (u,v) can be present in more than one set E_C. In such case we still have only a single edge added to E.

Jaccard similarity of the reconstruction. The ego-splitting algorithm will be given access to G and will process it and produce a set of clusters $\mathcal{S}'$. For sake of the theoretical analysis we will measure the quality of the reconstruction using the simple Jaccard similarity over the set of clusters:

$$J(\mathcal{S},\mathcal{S}') = \frac{|\mathcal{S} \cap \mathcal{S}'|}{|\mathcal{S} \cup \mathcal{S}'|}$$

The Jaccard similarity is such that $0 \leq J(\mathcal{S},\mathcal{S}') \leq 1$ and $J(\mathcal{S},\mathcal{S}') = 1$ iff the reconstruction is exact, i.e., $\mathcal{S} = \mathcal{S}'$. In our experimental evaluation of the algorithm we show results for other more nuanced and widely used quality measures like F_1 score and NMI, notice that Jaccard similarity as defined is a very demanding measure (it consider a cluster with a single error as entirely wrong) and implies also bounds on F_1, since:

$$F_1 = \frac{\sum_{C' \in \mathcal{S}'} \max_{C \in \mathcal{S}} F_1(C',C)}{|\mathcal{S}'|} \geq \frac{|\mathcal{S} \cap \mathcal{S}'|}{|\mathcal{S}'|} \geq \frac{|\mathcal{S} \cap \mathcal{S}'|}{|\mathcal{S} \cup \mathcal{S}'|} = J$$

Our main result is as follows:

Theorem 5.1. *If $\mathcal{S}$ and G are sampled from a $\mathcal{P}(n,k,q,p)$ with $kq \geq 1$ and $p \geq c' \log(npq/2)/(npq/2)$, then:*

$$\mathbb{E}[J(\mathcal{S},\mathcal{S}')] \geq 1 - nk\exp(-\Omega(np^2q)) - O\left(n^3k^2p^2q^6\right)$$

Notice that the assumption $kq \geq 1$ is natural as otherwise nodes have fewer than one cluster in expectation.

To make our model more concrete we first consider the following example:

Example 5.2. In the random overlapping clusters model, for $0 < \epsilon < \frac{1}{6}$ constant, let $k = n$, $q = n^\epsilon/n$ and $p = 1/n^{\epsilon/4}$. Under those parameters each node is on average on $kq = n^\epsilon$ clusters. Each cluster has average size $nq = n^\epsilon$. So a back-of-envelope calculation will get us that the degree of each node is roughly: $n^\epsilon \cdot n^\epsilon \cdot p = n^{1.75\epsilon}$. Since the theorem conditions holds, the Jaccard coefficient is $\mathbb{E}[J(\mathcal{S},\mathcal{S}')] \geq 1 - O(n^{5.5\epsilon}/n)$.

Example 5.3. Set $k = n$, $q = c\log(n)/n$ (for a large enough constant c) and $p = O(1)$. Each node is on average on $O(\log n)$ clusters and each cluster has average size $O(\log n)$. The degree of each node is $O(\log^2 n)$. Since the theorem conditions hold, the Jaccard coefficient is $\mathbb{E}[J(\mathcal{S},\mathcal{S}')] \geq 1 - O((\log^6 n)/n)$.

In either example as $n \to \infty$ the similarity $\mathbb{E}[J(\mathcal{S},\mathcal{S}')] \to 1$ so we achieve perfect reconstruction in the limit.

5.1 Proof of Main Theorem

Our main tools will be Chernoff bounds and the connectivity threshold in the Erdös-Renyi model. We will use the following version of Chernoff bounds: if $X_i \in [0,1]$ are independent random variables and $\mu = \mathbb{E}[\sum_i X_i]$, then:

$$\mathbb{P}\left(|\textstyle\sum_i X_i - \mu| \leq \epsilon\mu\right) \geq 1 - 2\exp(-\epsilon^2\mu/4)$$

The other probability statement we will require is the following. Let $G(n,p)$ be the Erdös-Renyi random graph on n nodes where each edge is added with probability p. The following classical lemma bounds the probability of the graph being connected:

Lemma 5.4. *In the Erdös-Renyi random graph $G(n,p)$ if $p \geq 6\log(n)/n$, then*

$$\mathbb{P}[G(n,p) \text{ is connected}] \geq 1 - \exp(-\Omega(np))$$

The proof of this lemma is standard and thus omitted.

Our first step in proving the theorem will be to analyze the connectivity of the ego-net of u. For each $C \in \mathcal{S}$, let $G_C = (V, E_C)$ and define N_u^C to be the neighborhood of u in graph G_C. Since the final graph G is the union of the edges of the G_C graphs, $N_u = \cup_{C \ni u} N_u^C$.

Ideally we would like to look at the induced graph $G[N_u]$ and from it identify the sets N_u^C and split u into k_u personas, where $k_u = |\{C \in S; u \in C\}|$. If all N_u^C are disjoint and each is a connected component of $G[N_u]$, then we are done.

Our first statement is that for each cluster C and each $u \in C$, the graphs $G_C[C]$ and $G_C[N_u^C]$ are connected with high probability. The proof follows from concentration arguments. For each C we bound the probability that $|C|$ is at least $\frac{1}{2}\mathbb{E}|C|$ using Chernoff bounds and condition on that event, we use Lemma 5.4 to bound the probability that $G_C[C]$ is connected. For $G_C[N_u^C]$ the same argument can be done being more careful regarding which events to condition on. Due to space limitations we omit the proofs of the following two lemmas:

Lemma 5.5. *If $p \geq 6\log(npq/2)/(npq/2)$, then with at least*

$$1 - nk\exp\left(-\Omega(np^2q)\right)$$

probability, the graph $G[C]$ is connected for all $C \in \mathcal{S}$ and $G[N_u^C]$ is connected for all $u \in C \in \mathcal{S}$.

The previous lemma shows that with high probability, node u won't split N_u^C when performing the ego-splitting operation using connected components. However, it is also possible for two clusters to be wrongly merged. The next lemma describes the necessary conditions so that a cluster can be exactly reconstructed:

Lemma 5.6. *Fix a cluster C, if for for all $u \in C$ the following conditions hold:*

1. *the induced graph $G[C]$ is connected.*
2. *the induced graph $G[N_u^C]$ is connected.*
3. *there are no edges between N_u^C and $N_u - N_u^C$.*

then ego-splitting with connected component reconstructs cluster C exactly.

Proof. The three conditions guarantee that for each $u \in C$, when we analyze the graph $G[N_u]$, the set N_u^C will be a connected component, so the local step of ego-splitting will create a persona of u associated with N_u^C. We name this persona u_C.

For each $v \in N_u^C$, the personas u_C and v_C are connected in the personas graph. This component can't contain any other personas than u_C for $u \in C$, otherwise it would imply an edge from N_u^C to $N_u - N_u^C$. □

The following corollary follows directly from the proof of the previous lemma:

Corollary 5.7. *If the induced graph $G[N_u^C]$ and the induced graph $G[C]$ is connected for all C and all $u \in C$, then each connected component of the personas graph corresponds to a cluster $C \in \mathcal{S}$ or to an union of clusters in $\mathcal{S}$. Moreover, under this condition, ego-splitting using connected components outputs at most k clusters.*

Proof. In the conditions of the corollary, each node u will have at most $k_u = |\{C; C \ni u\}|$ personas. We say that a persona of u is compatible with cluster C if the connected component of $G[N_u]$ corresponding to it contains N_u^C. Each persona is compatible with at least one cluster (but can be compatible with more than one). Now, by the same argument as in Lemma 5.6, for each fixed $C \in \mathcal{S}$, all personas compatible with cluster C are connected. Therefore, the personas graph has at most k connected components. □

Lemma 5.6 tells us that if all induced graphs $G[C]$ and $G[N_u^C]$ are connected, there is only one source of errors: edges from N_u^C to $N_u - N_u^C$. We say that an edge (v,w) is bad for u, C if $u, v \in C$, $v \in N_u^C$, $w \in N_u - N_u^C$ and (v,w) is in G.

Lemma 5.8. *Assuming $kq \geq 1$, given $u, v, w \in V$ and C, an edge (v,w) is bad for u, C with probability $O(k^2q^6p^3)$.*

Proof. We need $u, v \in C$, $v \in N_u^C$ and $w \notin C$ which happens with probability $pq^2(1-q)$. Now, to bound the probability that edges (v,w) and (u,w) are in the graph we take the union bound over the following event that there are clusters $C', C'' \neq C$ such that $u, v \in C'$, $v, w \in C''$, (u,w) is added to $G_{C'}$ and (v,w) is added to $G_{C''}$.

- if $C' = C''$ we have that the probability that $u, v, w \in C'$ and edges (u,v) and (v,w) are added is: q^3p^2.
- if $C' \neq C''$ we have that the probability that $u, v \in C'$, $v, w \in C''$ and edges (u,v) and (v,w) are added are: q^4p^2.

So taking the union bound we get that the probability of a bad event is $O(pq^2(1-q)[kq^3p^2 + k^2q^4p^2]) = O(k^2q^6p^3)$. □

Proof of Theorem 5.1. Let D denote the event that $G[C]$ and $G[N_u^C]$ are connected for every $C \in \mathcal{S}$ and $u \in C$. The probability of $\mathbb{P}[D]$ is bounded by Lemma 5.5.

If edge (v,w) is bad for u, C we say that a bad edge event occurred for (v, w, u, C). Lemma 5.8 bounds the probability of each bad edge event. So if B is a random variable measuring the total number of bad edge events, then: $\mathbb{E}[B] = O(n^3k^3q^6p^3)$ by Corollary 5.7, conditioned on D, $|\mathcal{S}'| \leq |\mathcal{S}|$. Also, each bad edge can cause at most two clusters to be merged, therefore: $|\mathcal{S}'| \geq |\mathcal{S}| - 2B$. This implies a bound on the size of the union $|\mathcal{S} \cup \mathcal{S}'| = |\mathcal{S}| + |\mathcal{S}'| - |\mathcal{S} \cap \mathcal{S}'| \leq 2k - (k - 2B) = k + 2B$. Now, we can bound the Jaccard similarity as:

$$J(\mathcal{S}, \mathcal{S}') = \frac{|\mathcal{S} \cap \mathcal{S}'|}{|\mathcal{S} \cup \mathcal{S}'|} \geq \frac{k - 2B}{k + 2B} = 1 - \frac{4B}{k + 2B} \geq 1 - \frac{4B}{k}$$

Computing expectations:

$$\mathbb{E}[J(\mathcal{S}, \mathcal{S}')] \geq \mathbb{E}[J(\mathcal{S}, \mathcal{S}')|D]\mathbb{P}[D] = \left(1 - \frac{4\mathbb{E}[B|D]}{k}\right)\mathbb{P}[D]$$

Using that $\mathbb{E}[B|D]\mathbb{P}[D] \leq \mathbb{E}[B]$ and substituting the bounds for $\mathbb{E}[B]$ and $\mathbb{P}[D]$ we get the desired result. □

Remarks about the model. We can also extend our model to consider edges from two nodes that don't share a cluster. The usual way to incorporate this to the model is to add an edge between any two nodes with some probability r. We defer this discussion to the full version of the paper.

6 EXPERIMENTS

6.1 Experimental setup

We implemented our framework using a large-scale distributed computing infrastructure based on MapReduce.

Clustering algorithms. Our framework can use any non-overlapping clustering algorithm to partition the ego-nets and the persona graph (the two algorithms need not to be the same). For our experimental evaluation we used iterative label propagation clustering algorithms as non-overlapping partitioners in both phases. This choice is motivated by two reasons. First, label propagation algorithms are highly scalable and can be easily implemented in distributed settings. Second, previous ego-net based works have used successfully label propagation algorithms [13, 17].

We use a standard non-overlapping label propagation method based on the Absolute Potts Model technique [37]. This is the same algorithm that was used in [17] to cluster ego-nets so we omit its description here for lack of space. In our experiments in this paper we set the parameter $\alpha = 0.1$ (the penalty for missing a neighbor with a certain label). During the ego-net clustering phase we apply an in-memory version of this algorithm to cluster the ego-net. For the larger datasets, during the persona graph clustering step, the graph may not fit in memory, so we use a distributed variant of the algorithm. In this variant each label update iteration is carried out in parallel and we set $\alpha = 0$.

Pre-processing and post-processing. We use the following two heuristics that improves both the scalability and the accuracy of our methods.

First, we preprocess the graphs to restrict our analysis to at most 2000 neighbors of each node. If a neighbor v of u is not processed in the ego-net of u we discard the edge in the persona graph that corresponds to (u, v). This, besides increasing scalability, also improves the accuracy of the algorithms as high degree nodes are usually hubs connecting multiple communities so using them in the ego-nets can confuse the community structure.

Second, we post-process the overlapping communities produced by the algorithm discarding communities of size at most 4. This is because small communities are less informative. Notice that previous work [13] used a more complex post-processing of the output communities which was $O(n^2)$ while our post-processing is straightforward and fast.

6.2 Comparison with other algorithms

We compare our method with a state of the art ego-net based overlapping clustering algorithm **DEMON** [13]. For this method we use code provided by the authors and we set the parameter $\epsilon = 1$ in the post-processing as suggested (i.e. overlapping clusters are merged if and only if one is subset of the other). Consistently with our method we discard communities of size at most 4.

Table 1: Statistics on the real-world graphs used

Graph	Nodes	Edges	Persona nodes
amazon [42]	334,863	1,851,744	799,080
dblp [42]	317,080	2,099,732	611,068
livejournal [42]	3,997,962	69,362,378	22,970,759
orkut [42]	3,072,441	234,370,166	69,030,8073
friendster [42]	65,608,366	3,612,134,270	1,492,532,217
clueweb12 [9, 10]	955,207,488	67,823,249,559	55,433,497,920

As a baseline, we also used an off-the-shelf distributed overlapping label propagation algorithm (henceforth **OLP**). In this method nodes are allowed to retain up to k most frequent labels. Then a node is assigned to all the at most k clusters defined by the nodes that have retained a label. We fix $k = 3$ in our experiments and keep communities of size at least 5.

6.3 Datasets

Synthetic benchmarks. In the previous section we have shown how our method can provably reconstruct highly overlapping communities in a simple stylized generative model. For our experimental evaluation we employ instead random graphs with planted overlapping clusters produced by the more widely used and sophisticated model of Lanchinetti et al. [26]. We chose this model for consistency with previous ego-net based works [13] and because the model replicates several properties of real-world graphs, such as power law distribution of degrees, varying community sizes and membership of nodes in varying community number.

We refer to [26] for a detailed description of the model. With the code provided online by the authors we generated 3 set of graphs referred as Benchmark-0.01, Benchmark-0.1 and Benchmark-0.3, respectively. Each set of graphs contains 10 random instantiation of the model with the same settings, we report averages over those 10 graphs for all algorithms. The Benchmark-0.01 consist of the same settings of [13] paper which we report here for convenience (`N=1000, k=25, maxk=50, mu=0.01, minc=20, maxc=50, on=500, om=3`) for Benchmark-0.1 and Benchmark-0.3 instead have the following settings (`N=1000, k=10, maxk=50, minc=5, maxc=50, on=100, om=2`) and `mu` set to 0.1 and 0.3, respectively.

Real-world graphs. We analyzed a set of widely used graphs (amazon, dblp, livejournal, orkut, friendster) that have ground truth clusters and are available from the *SNAP* collection. For these graphs, we use the dataset with top quality communities as ground-truth (more details in [42]). The details of the graphs are reported in Table 1. In this table we also report the number of persona nodes identified by our framework using label propagation as clustering algorithm.

We also run our algorithms on the clueweb12 [9, 10] graph which is web graph with tens of billions of edges but for which have no ground truth clusters. All graphs are made undirected ignoring the direction of the edges if present.

6.4 Results on synthetic benchmarks

Example persona graph. To gain an insight on how our framework operates we first provide a visualization of a smaller synthetic graph produced with Lanchinetti et al. model. For sake of visualization we used a graph with only 100 nodes and 9 highly overlapping

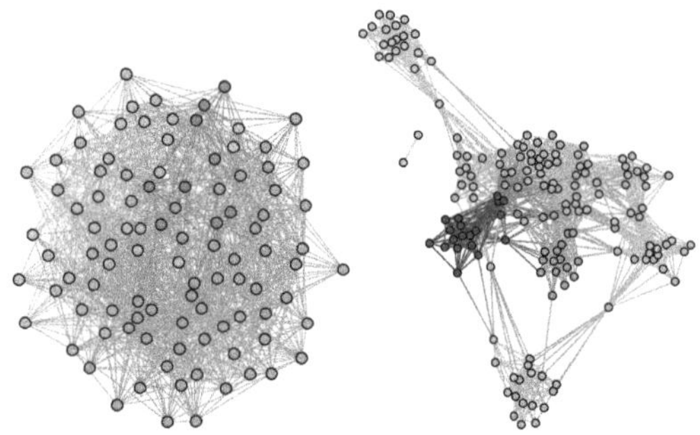

(a) Original Graph (b) Persona Graph

Figure 4: Color visualization of a small synthetic graph and its persona graph.

Table 2: Accuracy in synthetic benchmarks

	Ego-splitting		DEMON		OLP	
Graph	F1	NMI	F1	NMI	F1	NMI
Benchmark-0.01	**0.9368**	**0.9403**	0.4765	0.1670	0.6254	0.3149
Benchmark-0.1	**0.7878**	**0.7100**	0.1200	0.0000	0.7723	0.5571
Benchmark-0.3	**0.6714**	**0.5076**	0.1216	0.0000	0.6151	0.4405

ground-truth communities. Figure 4 shows the both original graph and the persona graph output by our method, as plotted by the standard Gephi [8] tool with the same visualization setting. Both graphs have 1269 edges while the persona graph has 164 nodes (from the 100 nodes in the original graph). The colors represent the communities identified by Gephi on both graphs based the standard non-overlapping modularity-based algorithm of the tool. It is possible to observe that while the community structure in the first graph is not immediately clear, in the second the clusters are visibly more separated. In fact in the first graph Gephi found only 5 communities with a modularity of 0.25 while in the second it found 8 communities with a higher modularity of 0.60. This visually shows how our framework is able to disentangle the communities.

Quantitative analysis. We now provide a more quantitative analysis of the accuracy of our algorithm in reconstruct the ground truth communities in the benchmark graphs. The results are shown in Table 2. The NMI is computed using publicly available implementation of [34], for F_1 we use distributed computing to scale the computation to large community outputs.

It is possible to observe our method using label propagation as clustering algorithm outperforms all other benchmark methods in all the graphs evaluated and in both accuracy measures. Notice how in particular for the benchmark graph Benchmark-0.01 reported in [13] we get close to > 93% F_1 compared to 47% of DEMON [13].

6.5 Results on real graphs

We first report statistics on the communities identified by our algorithm. Figure 5(a) shows the distribution of the size of the overlapping communities identified by our algorithm on the largest social network analyzed Friendster. Notice how the distribution of

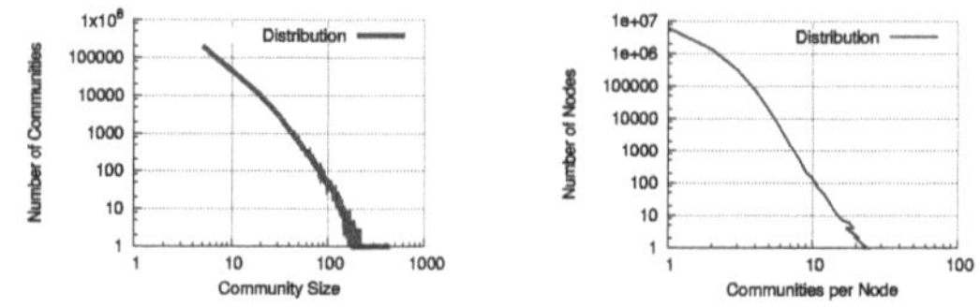

(a) Friendster: Size of the Communities (b) Friendster: Communities per Node

Figure 5: Statistics on the overlapping communities output.

Table 3: Accuracy in real-world graphs

	Ego-splitting		DEMON		OLP	
Graph	F1	NMI	F1	NMI	F1	NMI
amazon	**0.0374**	**0.0809**	0.0337	0.0310	0.0339	0.0450
dblp	**0.1662**	**0.1041**	0.1539	0.0309	0.1448	0.0645
livejournal	**0.0490**	**0.0394**	-	-	0.0115	0.0148
orkut	**0.0332**	0.0060	-	-	0.0267	**0.0129**
friendster	**0.0051**	**0.0008**	-	-	0.0010	0.0006

community sizes follows a clear heavy tailed distribution (the plot is in log scale, the other graphs have similar distributions). This is consistent with previous results in social networks [35]. Consistent with previous studies [28] most communities have < 100 nodes. In total our algorithm outputs the following number of communities in the graphs analyzed: amazon 27,004; dblp 33,626; livejournal 49,954; orkut 131,773; friendster 905,520; clueweb 31,642,414. Figure 5(b) shows for the same graph the distribution of the number of communities to which a node belongs in our output. Notice that a large fraction of nodes belong to more than one community (~ 30% in Friendster) and that again the distribution of participation of nodes in multiple communities is heavy tailed.

Accuracy. Finally, we report the accuracy of our method in real-world graphs with ground-truth communities. The results are in Table 3. Consistently with the results in the random graphs our method outperforms the other two methods in almost all cases. In particular our method has always the highest F_1 score and in all but one case it has the best NMI score. This confirms our theoretical results that shows that splitting the ego's in persona allows the overlapping community structure to be more easily detectable.

Results for DEMON on large graphs are omitted as the algorithm did not finish to run in the allocated time (the method employed a slow post-processing which is not scalable in large graphs).

6.6 Scalability

Finally we evaluate the scalability of our method. In Figure 6 we show the relationship between the total running time our algorithm (total wall-clock time of the distributed execution) and the size of the graph. We report the results as a ratio of the time used to process a graph (resp. number of edges of the graph) and the time used to process our smaller graph amazon (resp. number of edges in amazon). It is possible to observe the high scalability of our method. Even if clueweb has 30000 times more edges the execution

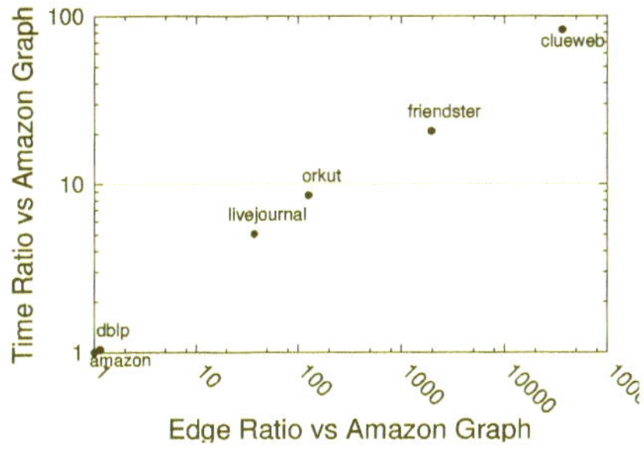

Figure 6: Running time vs size of the graph

time is only 80 times longer that of amazon. This shows that our method can scale to very large graphs with billions of nodes and edges.

7 CONCLUSIONS AND FUTURE WORK

We presented a scalable and flexible framework for finding overlapping clusters. Our empirical and theoretical findings shows that, using the local clustering structure of the ego-nets as guidance, it is possible to disentangle the complex and highly overlapping community structures of real-networks by splitting nodes into their "personas".

For future work, we would like to establish theoretical guarantees in more nuanced models by using more sophisticated partitioning algorithms. Another important direction is to adapt our methods to incremental models of computation, since real world networks are dynamic. Recent work [41] has observed a rich structure in the overlap of communities which could be analyzed to further improve our method. Finally, we believe further analysis of the structural properties of the persona graphs could yield other insights on the social network besides its clustering such as, for instance, the roles of actors in a social network [16].

ACKNOWLEDGMENTS

We thank Sergei Vassilvitskii and Bryan Perozzi for their comments and Bryan for his help with graph visualization. We thank Michele Coscia, Giulio Rossetti, Dino Pedreschi and Fosca Giannotti for making their code available and for their helpful comments.

REFERENCES

[1] B. D. Abrahao, S. Soundarajan, J. E. Hopcroft, and R. D. Kleinberg. A separability framework for analyzing community structure. *TKDD*, 2014.

[2] Y.-Y. Ahn, J. P. Bagrow, and S. Lehmann. Link communities reveal multiscale complexity in networks. *Nature*, 466(7307):761–764, 2010.

[3] L. Akoglu, M. McGlohon, and C. Faloutsos. oddball: Spotting anomalies in weighted graphs. In *PAKDD 2010*, 2010.

[4] M. Amoretti, A. Ferrari, P. Fornacciari, M. Mordonini, F. Rosi, and M. Tomaiuolo. Local-first algorithms for community detection. In *KDWeb 2016*, 2016.

[5] S. Arora, R. Ge, S. Sachdeva, and G. Schoenebeck. Finding overlapping communities in social networks: toward a rigorous approach. In *EC*, 2012.

[6] M. Balcan, C. Borgs, M. Braverman, J. T. Chayes, and S. Teng. Finding endogenously formed communities. In *SODA 2013*.

[7] S. Bandyopadhyay, G. Chowdhary, and D. Sengupta. FOCS: fast overlapped community search. *IEEE Trans. Knowl. Data Eng.*, 27(11):2974–2985, 2015.

[8] M. Bastian, S. Heymann, and M. Jacomy. Gephi: An open source software for exploring and manipulating networks, 2009.

[9] P. Boldi, M. Rosa, M. Santini, and S. Vigna. Layered label propagation: a multiresolution coordinate-free ordering for compressing social networks. In *WWW*, 2011.

[10] P. Boldi and S. Vigna. The WebGraph framework I: Compression techniques. In *WWW 2004*, pages 595–601, Manhattan, USA, 2004. ACM Press.

[11] R. Burt. *Structural Holes: The Social Structure of Competition*. Harvard Press, 1995.

[12] N. Buzun, A. Korshunov, V. Avanesov, I. Filonenko, I. Kozlov, D. Turdakov, and H. Kim. Egolp: Fast and distributed community detection in billion-node social networks. In *2014 IEEE ICDM Workshops*, pages 533–540, 2014.

[13] M. Coscia, G. Rossetti, F. Giannotti, and D. Pedreschi. Uncovering hierarchical and overlapping communities with a local-first approach. *TKDD*, 2014.

[14] A. Delis, A. Ntoulas, and P. Liakos. Scalable link community detection: A local dispersion-aware approach. In *IEEE BigData 2016*, pages 716–725, 2016.

[15] R. I. M. Dunbar and S. G. B. Roberts. Communication in social networks: Effects of kinship, network size and emotional closeness. *Personal Relationships*, 2010.

[16] D. Easley and J. Kleinberg. *Networks, crowds, and markets: Reasoning about a highly connected world*. Cambridge University Press, 2010.

[17] A. Epasto, S. Lattanzi, V. Mirrokni, I. O. Sebe, A. Taei, and S. Verma. Ego-net community mining applied to friend suggestion. *VLDB*, 9(4):324–335, 2015.

[18] M. Everett and S. P. Borgatti. Ego network betweenness. *Social Networks*, 2005.

[19] S. Fortunato. Community detection in graphs. *Physics reports*, 2010.

[20] L. C. T. Freeman. Centered graphs and the structure of ego networks. *Mathematical Social Sciences*, 1982.

[21] M. Girvan and E. J. Newman. Community structure in social and biological networks. *PNAS*, 2002.

[22] L. H. Hartwell, J. J. Hopfield, S. Leibler, and A. W. Murray. From molecular to modular cell biology. *Nature*, 402:C47–C52, 1999.

[23] K. He, Y. Sun, D. Bindel, J. E. Hopcroft, and Y. Li. Detecting overlapping communities from local spectral subspaces. In *IEEE ICDM*, pages 769–774, 2015.

[24] R. Khandekar, G. Kortsarz, and V. S. Mirrokni. On the advantage of overlapping clusters for minimizing conductance. *Algorithmica*, 69(4):844–863, 2014.

[25] R. Kumar, P. Raghavan, S. Rajagopalan, D. Sivakumar, A. Tomkins, and E. Upfal. Random graph models for the web graph. In *FOCS*, 2000.

[26] A. Lancichinetti and S. Fortunato. Benchmarks for testing community detection algorithms on directed and weighted graphs with overlapping communities. *Physical Review E*, 80(1):016118, 2009.

[27] S. Lattanzi and D. Sivakumar. Affiliation networks. In *STOC 2009*.

[28] J. Leskovec, K. J. Lang, A. Dasgupta, and M. W. Mahoney. Community structure in large networks: Natural cluster sizes and the absence of large well-defined clusters. *Internet Mathematics*, 2009.

[29] J. Leskovec, K. J. Lang, and M. W. Mahoney. Empirical comparison of algorithms for network community detection. In *WWW 2010*.

[30] R. Li, C. Wang, and K. C. Chang. User profiling in an ego network: co-profiling attributes and relationships. In *WWW*, 2014.

[31] D. Liben-Nowell and J. Kleinberg. The link-prediction problem for social networks. *journal of the Association for Information Science and Technology*, 58(7):1019–1031, 2007.

[32] W. Liu, X. Jiang, M. Pellegrini, and X. Wang. Discovering communities in complex networks by edge label propagation. *Scientific reports*, 6, 2016.

[33] J. J. McAuley and J. Leskovec. Learning to discover social circles in ego networks. In *NIPS*, 2012.

[34] A. F. McDaid, D. Greene, and N. Hurley. Normalized mutual information to evaluate overlapping community finding algorithms. Oct. 2011.

[35] G. Palla, I. Derényi, I. Farkas, and T. Vicsek. Uncovering the overlapping community structure of complex networks in nature and society. *Nature*, 2005.

[36] B. S. Rees and K. B. Gallagher. Overlapping community detection by collective friendship group inference. In *ASONAM*, 2010.

[37] P. Ronhovde and Z. Nussinov. Local resolution-limit-free potts model for community detection. *Phys. Rev. E*, 2010.

[38] S. Wasserman and K. Faust. *Social network analysis: methods and applications*. Cambridge University Press, 1994.

[39] J. Weng and B.-S. Lee. Event detection in twitter. *ICWSM*, 11:401–408, 2011.

[40] J. J. Whang, D. F. Gleich, and I. S. Dhillon. Overlapping community detection using seed set expansion. In *ACM CIKM'13*, pages 2099–2108, 2013.

[41] J. Yang and J. Leskovec. Overlapping community detection at scale: a nonnegative matrix factorization approach. In *Proceedings of the sixth ACM international conference on Web search and data mining*, pages 587–596. ACM, 2013.

[42] J. Yang and J. Leskovec. Defining and evaluating network communities based on ground-truth. *Knowledge and Information Systems*, 42(1):181–213, 2015.

[43] J. Yang, J. J. McAuley, and J. Leskovec. Detecting cohesive and 2-mode communities indirected and undirected networks. In *WSDM*, 2014.

Contextual Motifs

Increasing the Utility of Motifs using Contextual Data

Ian Fox
Computer Science and Engineering,
University of Michigan
ifox@umich.edu

Lynn Ang
Internal Medicine,
University of Michigan
angly@med.umich.edu

Mamta Jaiswal
Internal Medicine,
University of Michigan
jaiswalm@med.umich.edu

Rodica Pop-Busui
Internal Medicine,
University of Michigan
rpbusui@med.umich.edu

Jenna Wiens
Computer Science and Engineering,
University of Michigan
wiensj@umich.edu

ABSTRACT

Motifs are a powerful tool for analyzing physiological waveform data. Standard motif methods, however, ignore important contextual information (*e.g.*, what the patient was doing at the time the data were collected). We hypothesize that these additional contextual data could increase the utility of motifs. Thus, we propose an extension to motifs, *contextual motifs*, that incorporates context. Recognizing that, oftentimes, context may be unobserved or unavailable, we focus on methods to jointly infer motifs and context. Applied to both simulated and real physiological data, our proposed approach improves upon existing motif methods in terms of the discriminative utility of the discovered motifs. In particular, we discovered contextual motifs in continuous glucose monitor (CGM) data collected from patients with type 1 diabetes. Compared to their contextless counterparts, these contextual motifs led to better predictions of hypo- and hyperglycemic events. Our results suggest that even when inferred, context is useful in both a long- and short-term prediction horizon when processing and interpreting physiological waveform data.

1 INTRODUCTION

In a single day, a continuous glucose monitor can passively collect over 200 times the amount of data one would normally collect using standard blood glucose measurement practices (*e.g.*, manual measurement). Such wearable health monitors have led to the rapid accumulation of large amounts of rich longitudinal health data in the form of time series [25]. Still, in terms of utility, these data have yet to reach their full potential. This is in part do to the fact that we often have an incomplete understanding of the physiological system(s) generating these data. Reasoning about these systems is a central goal of the analysis of physiological time-series data.

KDD '17, August 13-17, 2017, Halifax, NS, Canada

ACM ISBN 978-1-4503-4887-4/17/08...$15.00
https://doi.org/10.1145/3097983.3098068

An increased understanding of these systems could lead to better data-driven predictions and, in turn, better health outcomes. To this end, researchers have sought efficient methods to analyze and represent these time-series data.

Motifs, subsequences that occur in or across signals more often than average, are a popular and useful abstraction for representing and analyzing sequential data [35, 36]. Motifs are short subsequences or patterns that commonly occur within or across signals. For example, we might *discover* a motif representing a rapid heartbeat within an electrocardiogram (ECG) dataset. By representing an ECG signal by whether or not it contains this particular motif, we could learn an association between a rapid heartbeat and a patient's cardiac health (*e.g.*; a rapid heartbeat may be indicative of poor health).

Motifs exhibit several properties that make them an appealing approach for analyzing large physiological datasets, including their broad applicability across a wide range of data types, their resilience to noise, and their inherent interpretability [2, 5, 9, 22, 35].

Despite their useful properties, Van Esbroeck et al. recently showed that, as a feature representation for discriminative algorithms, motifs performed worse than other representation learning schemes [37]. We hypothesize that a key reason for this suboptimal performance is that standard motifs ignore the *context* under which they are generated. Standard motif methods assume that the system which generates the signal, and thus the meaning of the motifs, does not change over the observation period. This assumption is not always reasonable in physiological data.

For example, suppose that the ECG data mentioned earlier were collected under a range of normal living conditions. The ability of the heart rate to vary to accommodate external stressors, called heart rate variability, indicates good cardiac health [14]. Rapid heartbeats would then be an indicator of good health within the context of physical activity, and an indicator of poor health outside that context.

Another, particularly relevant, example can be found in glucose data (*i.e.*, blood sugar levels). In this domain, motifs may represent spikes in blood glucose levels. When interpreting these spikes, it is important to understand the broader context of the signal. Occasional, isolated spikes may be expected as the result of glycemic challenges (such as meals). In contrast, repeated spikes in a temporally localized region could indicate poor glycemic control, a risk factor for long-term health outcomes [12, 23]. Thus, it is not always reasonable to assume that the interpretation of a motif remains constant throughout the signal, especially in physiological data collected under varying conditions.

We address these issues by augmenting motifs with context. Here, we define context as external phenomena affecting the signal, *e.g.*, physical activity in ECG, or meals in glucose data. We present a framework, for understanding physiological time series, that incorporates time-varying context. By adding context, we hypothesize that we can more accurately model the relationship between the signal and outcomes of interest. Importantly, context can be either observed or unobserved. In our blood glucose example, if patients' meals were never recorded, the context would be unobserved. In this common setting, accounting for context is more challenging. In light of these challenges, we:

(1) propose a general motif framework that accounts for context, ***contextual motifs***, and
(2) introduce contextual motif discovery along with techniques to jointly infer context and motifs in a signal when context is unobserved.

One could discover contextual motifs using a two-stage approach in which context and motifs are inferred independently. However, we hypothesize that a joint inference approach will lead to richer motifs, as it allows contextual information to improve motif discovery while simultaneously using motifs to improve context discovery.

Applied to both simulated and real physiological data, our proposed approach improves upon existing motif methods in terms of the discriminative utility of the discovered motifs. We observe a consistent 11-12 percentage point improvement in the area under the ROC curve (AUC) using contextual motifs compared to a contextless baseline, across a range of settings in simulated data. Additionally, applied to a Continuous Glucose Monitoring (CGM) dataset of patients with type 1 diabetes (T1D), our proposed contextual motif discovery techniques led to a 4 and 7.2 point improvement in the AUC when predicting long-term hypo- and hyperglycemic events respectively, compared with a contextless motif discovery method. We demonstrate that our method is capturing a physiologically relevant context for glucose data, demonstrating the potential of joint motif-context inference. These results suggest that, even when context is unobserved, contextual motifs could lead to a better understanding of the physiological system and, therefore, more accurate predictions.

2 BACKGROUND AND PROBLEM STATEMENT

Motifs have been applied across many different fields, including: genetic analysis, activity monitoring, and clinical event prediction [18, 20, 41]. For an in-depth review of motifs and their applications, we refer the reader to the survey paper by Mueen [22]. Here, we limit our discussion to prior work that directly relates to our proposed approach. We introduce vocabulary for discussing different motif discovery approaches. In particular, we differentiate between *data-derived* and *data-generating* motifs. Then, we present our proposed framework, *contextual motifs*, and discuss related work.

2.1 Motifs

2.1.1 History, Definitions, and Notation. The study of motifs originated in the field of genetics [26]. Lin et al. ported the idea of motifs to time-series analysis [15]. While there exist several different definitions of time-series motifs, here, we focus on *support motifs* [22, 35]. Support motifs are the subsequences that are most frequently expressed throughout a dataset [22]. These types of motifs are best suited to capturing inter- and intra-sequence similarity, and are widely used as a result [6, 10, 13, 18, 20, 27].

Before going further, we provide some notation and definitions to make our discussion more precise. We define a *signal* as an ordered observation sequence of the form $\mathbf{x} = (x_1, x_2, \ldots, x_T)$, where T is the signal length. Signals can be any form of ordered data, but here we focus on data ordered by time, also called *time series.* A *subsequence* of a signal is a contiguous subset of observations $\mathbf{x}_{t,k} = [x_t, x_{t+1}, \ldots, x_{t+k-1}]$, here the subsequence has length k. We call the process that generates the signal the *system.* Our goal in time-series analysis is to increase our understanding of the system using the observed signal. Some subsequences help us achieve this goal, whereas others do not. Subsequences that occur more often (*i.e.*, have support) are less likely to be the result of noise, and thus are more likely to reflect structure in the system. This motivates the study of frequently occurring subsequences, or *motifs.*

Previous work has investigated how to increase the discriminative power of motifs. Motifs that are maximally discriminative across classes are known as shapelets [40]. Shapelets extend motifs by using a measure of their predictive power during the discovery step. Other work has sought to discover more discriminative patterns by directly using label information [7, 29]. Our work also extends motif discovery to better predict outcomes. However, we approach this problem in a unsupervised manner. I.e., we focus on learning a richer representation of the signal, leading to the discovery of more informative motifs without using labels. Our approach is complementary to previously proposed supervised methods.

2.1.2 Data-Derived vs. Data-Generating Motifs. Data-derived and data-generating motifs are the two most common frameworks in the motif literature. Data-derived motifs are subsequences that are *derived* from the signal. Data-generating motifs are latent variables that *generate* the signal. See Table 1 for a summary of data-derived versus data-generating motifs.

Data-derived motifs are discovered using a measure of subsequence quality q. A motif $\mathbf{m}_t$ is a subsequence

$$\mathbf{m}_t = \mathbf{x}_{t,k} : q(\mathbf{x}_{t,k}) > n$$

for some quality threshold n. With support motifs, the quality measure q indicates the number of *approximate* occurrences of the subsequence in a dataset. Looking for exactly repeated subsequences is limiting, because noise can perturb even well conserved subsequences. Thus, the vast majority of motif discovery procedures attempt to find approximate motifs.

Data-generating motifs are discovered using a generative model to encode assumptions about how the data were created. These motifs are defined as an ordered sequence of distributions

$$\mathbf{m}_z = [\theta_{z,1}, \theta_{z,2}, \ldots, \theta_{z,k}] : \theta_{z,i} \in \Theta \text{ for } i = 1, \ldots, k$$

Table 1: Summary of Data-Derived vs. Data-Generating Motifs. Both are important types of motifs, and we consider both in developing contextual motifs.

	Discovery	Advantages	Baseline
Data-Derived	search	efficiency	MDLats [18]
Data-Generating	inference	quality	MMM [2]

where elements of Θ parameterize the distribution generating the signal and z is the motif label. Note that under this definition, a motif is not parameterized by the values occurring in the signal, but instead by a sequence of distributions.

The primary difference between these motif types is the method by which they are discovered. Data-derived motif discovery methods focus on search. In contrast, data-generating motif discovery methods emphasize inference. Both approaches are useful to consider. Though data-derived motifs are easier to discover and thus more common in the literature [6, 15, 18, 22, 33], data-generating motifs (also called latent motifs), are typically higher quality [10, 31]. One can naturally extend discovering data-generating motifs to discovering deformable motifs, motifs that have similar structure but vary in duration. This can be particularly relevant in the analysis of physiological data [31].

2.1.3 Discovering Motifs - Baseline Methods. We consider two motif discovery algorithms as baselines. The first is a data-derived motif discovery algorithm, MDLats. Presented by Liu et al. [18], MDLats combines many of the methodological improvements developed in recent literature into an efficient and effective method of discovering support motifs in physiological signals [6, 8, 18]. We will show how MDLats can be applied in a contextual motif framework to further improve discriminative performance.

The second baseline we consider, based on a data-generating motif discovery algorithm proposed by Bailey et al., is a motif mixture model (MMM) [2]. Their method is designed for categorical genomic data, and thus fits a mixture of categorical distributions. As we are working with real-valued physiological time series, we instead use a Gaussian mixture model. We assume each portion of a signal is generated by a set of distributions called a motif. For one signal, $\mathbf{x}$, the generative model is given below:

(1) For $i = 0, \ldots, K$:
   (a) Draw motif label $z_i \sim \text{Cat}(\gamma)$, where γ is the motif mixing parameter
   (b) For $k = 0, \ldots, l_m - 1$:
      (i) Draw observation:

$$x_{i(l_m)+k} \sim \mathcal{N}(\theta_{z_i,\mu_k}, \theta_{z_i,\sigma_k^2})$$

Where K is the signal length divided by the motif length, and θ_{z_i} parameterizes the K component distributions for the motif $\mathbf{m}_{z_i}$

Thus to generate a signal, one draws a categorical motif label z from a categorical distribution parameterized by γ. This motif operates over some period of time called the motif window with length l_m. Observations from the signal are then distributed according to the motif-dependent parameters θ_z.

According to this definition, even noisy, poorly conserved subsequences are technically motifs. Thus, it is common to include a *background* motif, assumed to be poorly conserved, to account for such subsequences. Here, inferring γ and θ_z for each motif $\mathbf{m}_z$ is identical to inference with a Gaussian mixture model. Each mixture component, representing a motif, is an l_m-dimensional Gaussian with a diagonal covariance matrix.

2.2 Contextual Motifs- A Novel Extension

We extend past work on motifs to incorporate context. We represent context as a categorical variable $c_t \in C$ that, at time point t, takes a discrete value $c_t \in \{1, \ldots, n_c\}$, where n_c is the number of distinct contexts. Contextual motifs are then well conserved patterns of contextualized data, representing a motif and the context under which it occurs. Contextual motif discovery is the task of discovering these contextual motifs. Discovery can also be viewed as the process of discovering motifs occurring within similar contexts. This distinction can be important when contexts vary from signal to signal. Without taking context into account, our measure of motif quality q may mistake infrequent contexts with infrequent motifs within a context. For example, a certain quantity of food consumption may always present a distinctive blood glucose pattern in individuals with poor glycemic control. If some glucose signals contained large meals, and others did not, contextless motif discovery could fail to recognize this pattern. When context is observed, as a context signal $\mathbf{x}_C$, discovering contextual motifs is trivial. One can simply apply an existing motif discovery algorithm to each chunk of data occurring under a particular context. Contextual motifs in this simple setting would be tuples $(\mathbf{m}_t, c_i)$.

A more interesting, and perhaps more common, setting is the one in which context is unobserved or unavailable. In the next section, we focus on methods for discovering contextual motifs in this latent setting. We present methods that extend both data-derived and data-generating motifs to contextual motifs. When extending data-derived motifs, we infer context in a two-stage approach. While such an approach could also apply to data-generating motifs, we sought a joint inference approach, in which context and motifs inform one another. Data-generating motifs can be extended using either a two-stage approach or by jointly inferring motifs and context. To perform this joint inference, we propose a generative model based on a subclass of dynamic Bayesian networks [24].

Despite the vast literature studying motifs, and motif discovery methods, there is relatively limited work on considering abstractions based on motifs. Still, we discuss the related work in this area and how it differs from what we propose.

Van Esbroeck et al. considered representing physiological signals using a bag of motifs (a common approach in motif discovery) [38]. But, the authors built upon this representation using a topic modeling approach. In their approach, each topic is associated with a distribution over motifs and each signal is then a distribution over topics. These topics are then used as an abstraction to represent the signal. While the idea of a topic is conceptually similar to context, their method differs from our proposed method in two ways. First, we jointly infer contexts and motifs, whereas they assume that motifs are first discovered and then topics are inferred. Second, the bag-of-motifs approach assumes a static representation of the signal. In contrast, our approach leverages the temporal contiguity of contexts to allow for flexible variation in motif representations both within and across signals.

In other domains, where the order in which motifs occur is important (*e.g.*, genetics) researchers have considered leveraging this temporal ordering to discover better motif representations. In particular, Lin et al. proposed a method based on hierarchical HMMs in which the presence/absence of motifs in one part of a signal affects the presence/absence of motifs in neighboring parts [17]. Again, this is conceptually similar to context, since context can be viewed as a type of inter-motif structure. However, like the method described above, Lin et al.'s method also requires a separate motif discovery step. Our approach combines the discovery steps, enabling joint motif-context discovery.

Finally, others have looked at non-motif based approaches to learning abstractions based on time-series data. For example, Saria et al. examined the joint discovery of generating functions and temporal topics in NICU data [32]. They also used a hierarchical model to represent structure at different temporal levels. However, they assumed the use of base autoregressive generating functions. We instead use motifs as our primitive of choice, for the reasons described above.

3 METHODS

In this section, we propose approaches for discovering contextual motifs when context is unobserved (*i.e.*, latent). In this setting, we begin with a straightforward extension of data-derived motifs to contextual motifs using a two-stage approach. Then, we move on to the more interesting setting, in which we show how to extend data-generating motifs to contextual motifs. In particular, we present a method to jointly discover motifs and context.

3.1 Two-Stage Discovery with Data-Derived Contextual Motifs

By adopting a two-stage approach, we can adapt any existing motif discovery method (data-generating or data-derived) to discover contextual motifs. We can use any context discovery algorithm appropriate to our problem to derive the context signal $\mathbf{x}_C$, followed by the application of a motif discovery algorithm within each context. We note that the motif and context discovery steps in the two-stage approach can be performed in either order.

In our domain of interest, predicting outcomes from blood glucose, two plausible context discovery approaches include:

(1) Expert-Driven Context: Using domain knowledge we can hand-engineer features indicative of certain contexts. For example, large spikes in blood glucose levels typically occur only after meals [1, 21]. Using this knowledge, we created an expert rule,

$$c_t = b\left(\frac{\sum_{i=1}^{k} x_{t-(i-1)} - x_{t-i}}{k}\right)$$

where b is a hand-defined mapping from $\mathbb{R} \longrightarrow C$. Figure 1 illustrates the process of context discovery.

(2) Data-Driven Context: Using an unsupervised method, an HMM, we infer transient structure in the data. The hidden states then are used as context.

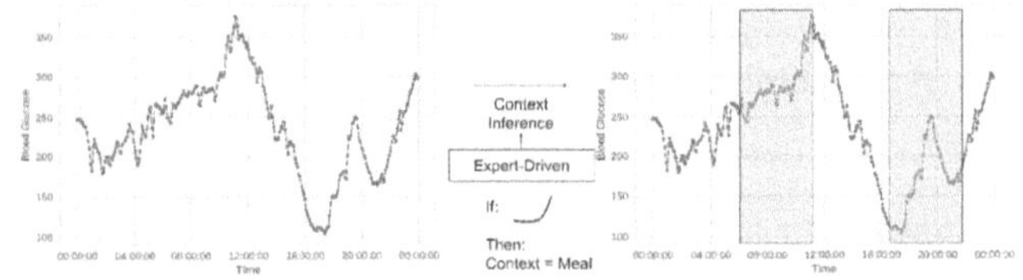

Figure 1: When expert/domain knowledge is available, we can discover context using hand-engineered rules. The rule illustrated here assigns a 'meal' context to a window (highlighted in green) around a sharp increase in blood sugar.

Alternatively, motifs can be used to derive context. If we observe the motif labels $\mathbf{m}$, found via an initial motif discovery step, then we can cluster empirical frequencies within the context windows to derive the contextual motif distribution parameter $\boldsymbol{\gamma}$ and use maximum likelihood estimation to find $\mathbf{c}$. This is similar to the motif topic context introduced by [38], except under this approach context varies over the course of the signal.

While straightforward and flexible, this two-stage approach misses an opportunity to learn richer motifs based on context and vice versa. In the activity monitoring literature it has been noted that motifs are useful for deriving context[20], and as we will demonstrate with our two-stage discovery experiments, context aids motif discovery. This observation inspired our proposed joint inference approach, presented in the next section.

3.2 Joint Discovery with Data-Generating Contextual Motifs

While data-generating motif discovery techniques carry additional computational cost, the increased model flexibility allows for the joint discovery of motifs and context. To achieve this, we modify the data-generating MMM (introduced in Section 2.1.3) to include a context variable. In our proposed *contextual motif mixture model* (CMMM), each context c_i defines a distribution over the set of possible motifs (Figure 2). This definition of context is motivated by previous work done in topic models, where the relative frequencies of primitives (originally, words) gives insight into higher level structure in the data [4]. The CMMM generative model is as follows:

(1) For $i = 0, \ldots, \frac{|\mathbf{x}|}{l_c}$, where l_c is the context window length:
  (a) Pick context $c_i \sim \text{Cat}(\boldsymbol{\alpha})$, where $\boldsymbol{\alpha}$ is the context mixing parameter
  (b) For $j = 0, \ldots, \frac{l_c}{l_m}$:
    (i) Choose motif label $z_j \sim \text{Cat}(\boldsymbol{\gamma}_{c_i})$, where $\boldsymbol{\gamma}_{c_i}$ is the motif mixing parameter for context c_i
    (ii) For $k = 0, \ldots, l_m - 1$:
      (A) Draw observation:

$$x_{l_c i + l_m j + k} \sim \mathcal{N}(\theta_{z_j, \mu_k}, \theta^2_{z_j, \sigma_k})$$

Generating data using this model begins by picking a categorical context c_i that holds for some window in time. If one assumes that context changes slowly relative to the rate of data sampling, context windows may be large. Contexts are selected according to a categorical distribution parameterized by a context mixing parameter $\boldsymbol{\alpha}$.

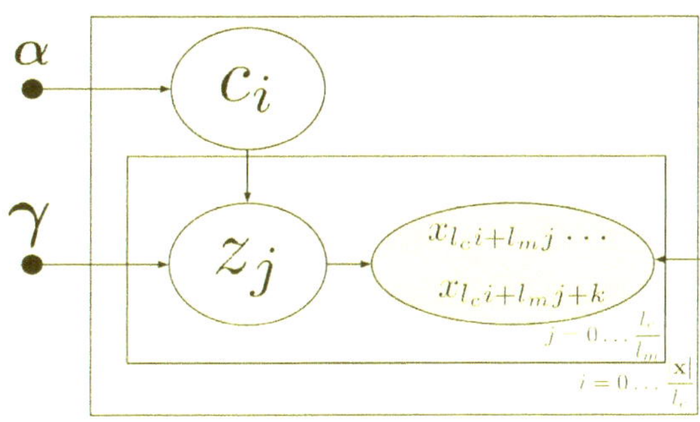

Figure 2: Proposed generative model for the contextual motif generative process. Each context parameterizes a different distribution of motif frequencies.

The selection of a context decides the motif frequency parameter γ_{c_i}, and from this point the model behaves identically to the MMM discussed in Section 2.1.3. This model can be viewed as a hierarchical HMM with a feed-forward context layer. Our notion of context is a temporally contiguous extension of the topics used in the motif topic model of Van Esbroeck et al. [38]. In contrast to their approach, we allow the motif distribution parameter, $\boldsymbol{\gamma}$, to vary over time according to a categorical context variable. We explicitly model motif mixing distributions for each context, but hold the motif parameters constant across all contexts. This allows for the identification of similar contexts across a population.

Using this model, one can infer the specific contexts under which each motif occurs at the same time one infers the motifs, allowing for the *de novo* discovery of contextual motifs.

Discovering the contextual motif representation of a signal requires inferring the motif labels $\mathbf{z} = [z_{j_0}, z_{j_1}, \ldots, z_{j_{|\mathbf{x}|/l_m}}]$ and context labels $\mathbf{c} = [c_{i_0}, c_{i_1}, \ldots, c_{i_{|\mathbf{x}|/l_c}}]$. This is a mixture of mixture models, and thus exact inference on it is intractable. Note that computing the posterior of the latent variables and parameters requires computing:

$$\frac{p(\mathbf{c}, \mathbf{z}, \boldsymbol{\alpha}, \boldsymbol{\gamma}, \boldsymbol{\theta}, \mathbf{x})}{\int_{\boldsymbol{\alpha}} p(\boldsymbol{\alpha}) \sum_{\mathbf{c}} p(\mathbf{c}|\boldsymbol{\alpha}) \int_{\boldsymbol{\gamma}} p(\boldsymbol{\gamma}) \sum_{\mathbf{z}} p(\mathbf{z}|\boldsymbol{\gamma}, \mathbf{c}) \int_{\boldsymbol{\theta}} p(\boldsymbol{\theta}) p(\mathbf{x}|\boldsymbol{\theta}, \mathbf{z})}$$

To perform approximate inference on this model, we use a sampling approach, as is routine with data-generating motif systems [17, 34, 35]. Our sampling method was implemented using the probabilistic programming python module PyMC3 [30]. We sample on the graphical model proposed in Figure 2. We use different sampling methods on the various types of variables in the model to optimize sampling speed and per-sample improvement. We sample the categorical variables **c** and **z** using a Metropolized Gibbs sampler with a uniform proposal distribution [19]. The motif and context mixing parameters, $\boldsymbol{\alpha}$ and $\boldsymbol{\gamma}$, are assumed to have Dirichlet priors to allow for collapsed sampling. They are sampled using Metropolis-Hastings with a Gaussian proposal distribution. Finally, we sample the motif distribution parameter $\boldsymbol{\theta}$ using a No-U-Turn Sampler with dual averaging [11]. This sampler uses gradient information to intelligently guide the sampling steps, and features an adaptive stepsize. These sampling schemes use the default parameters in PyMC3.

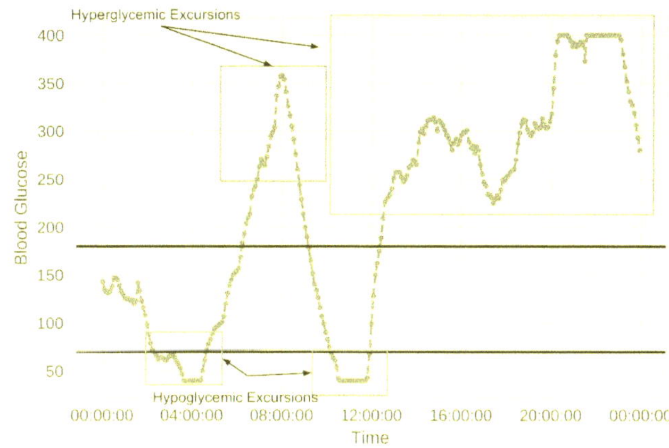

Figure 3: One day of blood glucose in the CGM dataset. Each of the 40 patients has between 21-48 days of data.

To avoid label switching problems when sampling, we use a series of potentials that enforce an ordering on the dimensions of the variable $\boldsymbol{\alpha}$. We also enforce that values of $\boldsymbol{\alpha}$ are above a threshold dependent on n_c, to ensure multiple contexts are used. We draw 2000 samples from the model, where each step iterates over all variables, and derive values using the final 1000.

4 EXPERIMENTS AND RESULTS

To measure the utility of contextual motifs, we compare their discriminative performance to that of contextless motifs across several classification tasks. We also measure the utility of the joint context-motif inference approach compared to a two-stage approach. In the sections that follow, we begin by describing the data used for these experiments and our evaluation procedure. We then present a series of experiments using both data-derived and data-generating motif frameworks on real and simulated physiological data.

4.1 Dataset and Prediction Tasks

4.1.1 CGM Data. Our physiological dataset consists of CGM sessions collected from 40 T1D patients at approximately 3-month intervals over the course of 3 years. The length of each session varies from 3-6 days with glucose measured every 5 minutes. Patients were blinded to their CGM monitor during this time. These monitors, by measuring glucose concentrations in interstitial fluid, accurately infer blood glucose levels between 40-400 mg/dL. The collection and study of these data was approved by a UM Medical School IRB panel.

Due to calibration and sensor errors, the sessions contain periods of missing data. In total, the dataset contains approximately 51.6k hours of glucose data, and is missing around 4.5k hours. To handle these missing data, we use linear interpolation. This is sensible for small chunks of missing data, as glucose data are locally linear. However, we exclude days with contiguous missing periods longer than thirty minutes. After removing days with excessive missing data, 32.4k hours of data occurring across 1,352 days remain. Each of the 40 patients contributes between 21 and 48 days to this total.

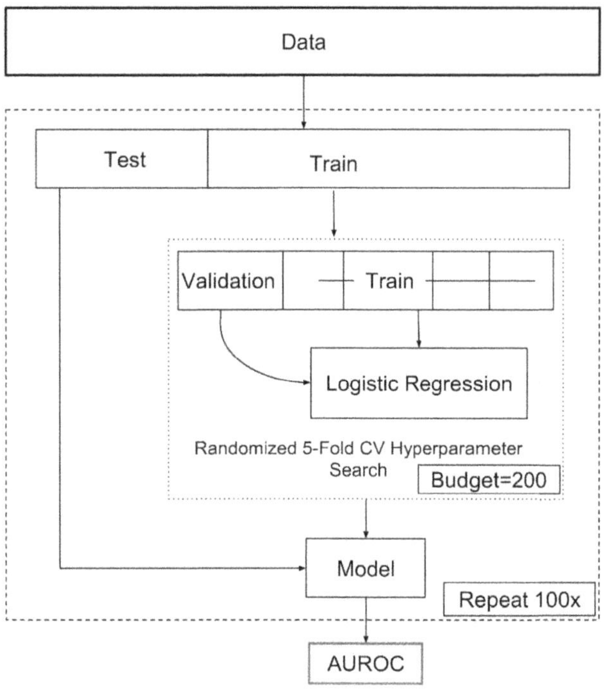

Figure 4: Outline of evaluation process. Data are split, using a patient aware scheme, into train-test splits 100 times. Within each split, the training data are used For model selection. The final classifier is then applied to the test data and the AUC is calculated. We report average AUC across all test sets.

4.1.2 *Evaluation Metric.* To measure the utility of the discovered contextual motifs relative to motifs, we represent each day's worth of data by the number of times each (contextual) motif appears in the signal that day, and use this representation in a supervised learning task. *I.e.*, we transform each signal into a feature vector representing motif counts. Given the fixed length feature representation, any number of machine learning techniques can be used to learn a mapping from the feature vector to the label.

We consider two different supervised learning tasks related to T1D: hypoglycemia (low blood sugar) and hyperglycemia (high blood sugar). Hypoglycemic events are caused by an over administration of insulin, a mismatch in insulin delivery and food absorption, or increased physical activity. They can result in unconsciousness, seizures, irregular heartbeat, and even death [42]. Hyperglycemic events are caused by overconsumption of carbohydrates or an under administration of insulin. In the short term, severe hyperglycemic events can result in coma or can lead to life threatening diabetic ketoacidosis. In the long term, chronic hyperglycemia increases risk for heart disease, nerve damage, kidney damage, and early death [3].

We selected these two tasks for their clinical relevance, but also since they differ substantially in terms of the underlying pathophysiology. Learning a representation that works well across both tasks is more challenging, but ultimately, the goal of this work.

Table 2: Predictive utility of contextual data-derived motifs. Across both short- and long-term prediction horizons we observe an increase in AUC when including expert- and data-driven contextual information, though the data-driven context is more informative. Bold values indicate the best in prediction class.

Prediction Task	Method	AUC (std)	
	Context	Hypo	Hyper
Long-Term	None	0.535 (0.022)	0.527 (0.020)
	Expert-Driven	0.552 (0.023)	0.534 (0.020)
	Data-Driven	**0.607 (0.023)**	**0.567 (0.022)**
Short-Term	None	0.568 (0.017)	0.572 (0.007)
	Expert-Driven	0.586 (0.013)	0.585 (0.009)
	Data-Driven	**0.595 (0.013)**	**0.606 (0.009)**

We investigate performing these tasks over both short- and long-term prediction horizons. For the long-term horizon, we use one day of data to predict whether or not a hypo- or hyperglycemic event will occur in the next day. Due to the large number of hyperglycemic events that occur in our data, we modified the prediction task to predict the occurrence of two or more hyperglycemic events. This task measures our ability to represent a patient's long-term physiological state, giving us a measure of their level of glucose control, and is very challenging to do using only one day of data. For the short-term horizon, we use one day of data to predict if a hypo- or hyperglycemic event will occur in the next 40 minutes. This task was chosen to emphasize the immediate state of the patient, and is clinically motivated by the ability of such short-term prediction to aid closed loop glucose control using an artificial pancreas [39].

We do not focus on the choice of supervised learning algorithm, as our contribution lies in the feature representation method. For consistency, we use a pipeline constructed using sklearn [28] that tunes hyperparameters and fits a regularized logistic regression classifier using patient-aware stratification for cross-validation and train-test splits. An outline of our evaluation process is given in Figure 4. We report results in term of average AUC across test sets.

4.2 Experiments on Real Data

We begin with the results of our experiments on the CGM dataset. We examine the utility of our data-derived contextual motifs, followed by an evaluation of the proposed data-generating contextual motifs.

4.2.1 *Data-Derived Motifs.* Our first set of experiments explores the utility of two-stage inference for data-derived motifs. Using the physiological data described in Section 4.1, we use the baseline data-derived motif discovery method, MDLats, to discover motifs using three different approaches to context:

- None: this represents the baseline motif discovery approach without context, described in Section 2.1.3 (*i.e.*, MDLats). To faithfully reimplement MDLats, we discretized our data using the SAX representation technique [16].
- Expert-Driven: using two-stage inference to add context defined according to the domain rule discussed in Section

Table 3: Predictive utility of contextual data-generating motifs. We note two main trends in these results. First, the short-term task is much easier than the long-term task when using data-generating motifs. Second, CMMM consistently outperforms MMM.

	Method	AUC (std)	
Task	Model	Hypo	Hyper
Long-Term	MMM	0.517 (0.023)	0.588 (0.026)
	CMMM	**0.539 (0.026)**	**0.595 (0.025)**
Short-Term	MMM	0.811 (0.011)	0.841 (0.007)
	CMMM	**0.814 (0.010)**	**0.845 (0.007)**

3.1. This rule is based on the clinically validated measure of glycemic variability, MAGE [1],

- Data-Driven: using two-stage inference to add context defined as the hidden state sequence in an HMM.

We use the learned motif representations to predict both hypo- and hyperglycemic events in the short and long term, using the pipeline discussed in 4.1.2.

The results are presented in Table 2. The results of the baseline approach are poor (*i.e.*, near random). Applied to the long-term task, the contextless baseline achieves an AUC=0.535 and AUC=0.527 for the tasks of predicting hypo- and hyperglycemic events respectively. But this level of predictive performance is not uncommon for such difficult tasks. Encouragingly, if we focus on the differences in performance, incorporating data-driven context leads to a significant increase in performance across *both* tasks (AUC=0.607 and AUC=0.567). These differences are statistically significant at $\alpha = 0.01$, as determined by a two-sided paired t test. For the short-term task performance is still poor. We hypothesize that this is because we do not discover many motifs that occur right before the prediction window. Upon inspection, only 18% of our samples have a motif occurring in the 40 minutes prior to prediction. In a follow-up experiment we tested our data-driven contextual motif model on only those samples with a motif in the last 40 minutes, and achieved AUCs of 0.723 and 0.843 for hypo- and hyperglycemic prediction respectively. This demonstrates that for the short-term task, recent information is critical.

4.2.2 Data-Generating Motifs. In our second set of experiments, we shift to data-generating motifs to test our joint inference approach. This allows us to measure the value of contextual motifs in a different setting (*i.e.*, data-generating vs. data-derived). We compare MMM (presented in Section 2.1.3) against our proposed CMMM on the glucose dataset.

Discovery of data-generating motifs is more computationally intensive than discovering data-derived motifs. As such, we perform motif discovery on a randomly chosen subset of the data (40 days worth). After fitting our models, we apply maximum likelihood estimation to the remainder of the data to find motifs and context across all data, so as to leverage all training data. In a follow up experiment, we used an optimized GMM package [28] and the entire dataset. We did not, however, observe a significant improvement in predictive performance, suggesting that this subsampling has little effect on performance for this particular task.

Table 4: Using motifs and context derived by the CMMM for predicting long- and short-term events. We observe best performance using (motif), though (motif, context) consistently outperforms (motif, noise).

	Method	AUC (std)	
Task	Representation	Hypo	Hyper
Long-Term	(motif)	0.539 (0.026)	0.595 (0.025)
	(motif, context)	0.533 (0.020)	0.591 (0.029)
	(motif, noise)	0.510 (0.025)	0.577 (0.023)
Short-Term	(motif)	0.814 (0.010)	0.845 (0.007)
	(motif, context)	0.810 (0.009)	0.843 (0.008)
	(motif, noise)	0.808 (0.010)	0.843 (0.007)

Based on a grid search over plausible values given our domain, we set the number of different motifs discovered to 20, the length of motifs $l_m = 8$ (representing 40 minutes of glucose data), the length of each context window $l_c = 72$, and the number of contexts to 2. We kept this setting constant across methods, and used the same evaluation metrics, namely AUC, as we did in Section 4.2.1.

The results of our experiments are given in Table 3. Our proposed CMMM approach dominates the MMM approach, outperforming it on all tasks. The results directly compare the discriminative utility of the motifs discovered using MMM and CMMM

In Table 4, we examine the discriminative utility of the inferred context. Compared to motifs alone, motifs plus inferred context appears to do slightly worse. We hypothesize that a reason for the lack of performance improvement when adding context was that our pipeline failed to properly regularize when dimensionality was increased. Thus, we considered a third model in which we added noise to the motifs instead of context. Indeed, we see a decrease in performance when increasing dimensionality using (motifs, noise), even though the actual information present remains constant. In all tasks except short-term hyperglycemic prediction, (motifs, context) outperforms (motifs, noise) ($\alpha = 0.01$), suggesting there is some amount of discriminative information in the context.

It is encouraging that the CMMM is able to discover higher quality motifs in addition to natively discovering contextual motifs. However, the failure of context to consistently improve performance in this task is troubling. We hypothesize this is due to having insufficient data (at the prediction stage, not motif discovery stage) to adequately compensate for the increased dimensionality that context introduces. Thus, to further test the efficacy of contextual motifs, we investigated performance on simulated data.

4.3 Experiments on Simulated Data

To evaluate our proposed contextual motif methods across a range of settings, we turn to experiments using simulated data. Our simulated data are created using the CMMM generative model shown in Figure 2. We create labels for these data following the procedure given below, varying β values to simulate different types of settings:

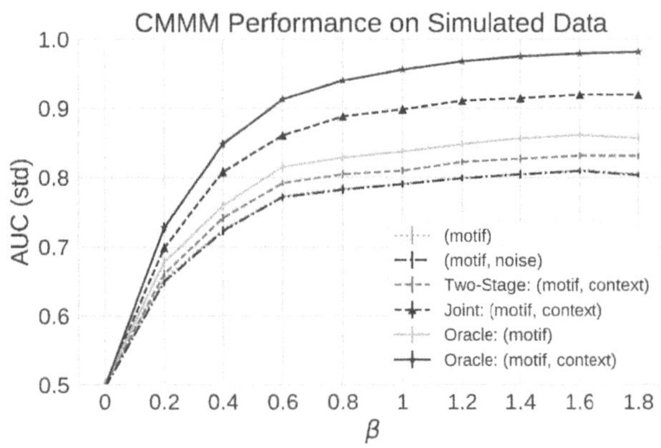

Figure 5: Here we see the efficacy of our proposed CMMM inference method on 10,000 simulated signals as we vary the strength of relationship between contextual motifs and outcome. Using only (motifs) results in suboptimal performance. Two-stage: (motifs, context) improves performance, but not as much as using joint:(motifs, context). Error bars on all lines signify 1 standard deviation.

(1) For contextual motif $(\mathbf{m}, c) \in CM$, the set of all possible contextual motifs that can be generated under a CMMM:
  (a) draw a value for the contextual motif: $v_{(\mathbf{m},c)} \sim \mathbb{U}(-1, 1)$
(2) For each signal in the dataset $\mathbf{x} \in X$:
  (a) Compute a raw score for the signal: $s_{\mathbf{x}} = \sum_{(\mathbf{m},c)\in\mathbf{x}} v_{(\mathbf{m},c)}$
  (b) Transform the score into a Bernoulli parameter:
$$p_{\mathbf{x}} = \frac{\exp(\beta s_{\mathbf{x}})}{1 + \exp(\beta s_{\mathbf{x}})}$$
  (c) Draw the signal's outcome: $y_{\mathbf{x}} \sim \text{Ber}(p_{\mathbf{x}})$

As an upper bound, we compare to two oracles that are based on the ground truth oracle:(motifs) and oracle:(motifs, context). We compare (motifs) inferred by the CMMM, (motifs, noise), two-stage:(motifs, context) (where we use the inferred motifs to derive the motif topic context as described in Section 3.1), and joint:(motifs, context). We vary the importance of the contextual motifs by varying the value of β. This allows us to directly test the efficacy of our proposed methods. We examined predictive performance using 10,000 simulated signals, with identical CMMM hyperparameters to those used in our real data-experiments. We used the same evaluation pipeline as above, with the exception that the number of train-test splits is reduced to 25 since we had more data.

The results are presented in Figure 5. The (motifs) and (motifs, noise) representation perform the worst. The two-stage: (motifs, context) representation provides a minor boost to performance, and joint:(motifs, context) provides a major boost, surpassing the performance of the contextless oracle and approaching the performance of the oracle with context (significant with $\alpha = 0.01$ when $\beta \geq 0.4$).

5 DISCUSSION

Our results confirm both the importance of context in physiological time series and the ability of contextual motifs in capturing this context. Below, we summarize some of the main takeaways of our experiments and present a follow-up analysis in which we take a closer look at what the models actually learned.

Contextual Motifs vs. Motifs. Our first set of experiments demonstrates that contextual motifs are more discriminative than their contextless counterparts, even when context is inferred. In Table 2, we showed that, particularly when using data-driven techniques, contextual motifs are more predictive of both hypo- and hyperglycemic events. These events are, on their face, opposites, as one involves an increase in glucose levels while the other involves a decrease. However, both events are indicative of poor glycemic control. The fact that our inferred context improves the predictive utility for motifs on both tasks suggests that contextual motifs are more informative of the physiological system than motifs alone.

Data-Derived vs. Data-Generating. Our second set of experiments, together with the first set, demonstrate the utility of considering both data-derived and data-generating motif frameworks. The data-derived motif discovery method, MDLats, was able to discover variable length motifs much faster than our data-generating motif discovery methods were able to discover fixed length motifs. However, we observe that the data-generating motif representation was much more useful for the short-term prediction task. In the hypoglycemic task, using the data-generating framework instead of the data-derived framework improved AUC from 0.607 to 0.814. The poor performance of the data-derived motif technique is due in large part to the lack of recent data. In a follow up experiment using the data-derived framework, we achieved an AUC of 0.723 for hypoglycemic prediction on a subset of the test set for which recent data were available. While detrimental for the short-term task, we saw that data-derived motifs can be helpful in other places. For instance, data-derived motifs outperformed data-generating in the long-term hypoglycemia task AUC 0.607 vs. 0.533.

Joint Inference vs. A Two-Stage Approach. Both our second set of experiments in Section 4.2.2 and our experiments on simulated data suggest the utility of a joint inference approach. In our second experiment, the motifs discovered by the CMMM were more discriminative than those discovered by the MMM. Although we did not observe large differences between CMMM motifs with and without context in our real data, some of this appears to have resulted from regularization issues when increasing dimensionality due to insufficient training data. This is evidenced by the decline in performance when a noise context was added. In our large simulated dataset, we did not observe a performance difference between (motifs) and (motifs, noise), suggesting that the regularization issues were a result of the data size and not our pipeline. Additionally, in our simulated experiment we observed a performance increase when we include context (from (motifs) to two-stage: (motifs, context)). Importantly, we observe a much larger performance increase when using the jointly inferred context (from two-stage: (motifs, context) to joint: (motifs, context)). These results suggest that joint inference allows for the discovery of both better motifs and better context.

What are we learning? One of the main advantages of motifs is their interpretability. In Figure 6, we show the motifs we discovered in the CGM data. In this collection, we observe several interesting

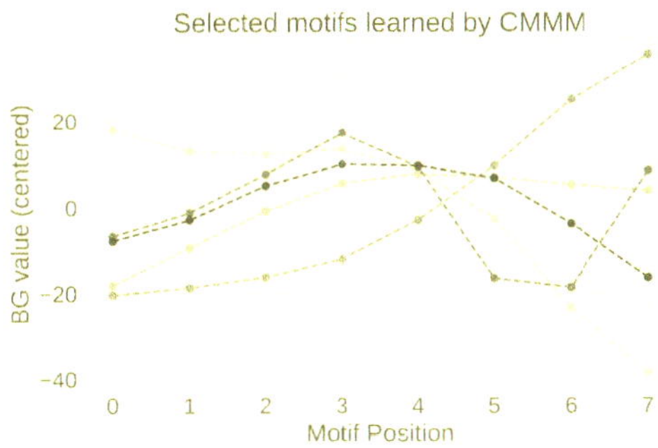

Figure 6: A hand-selected subset of motifs learned from the physiological data, selected to demonstrate the interesting range of motif morphologies present.

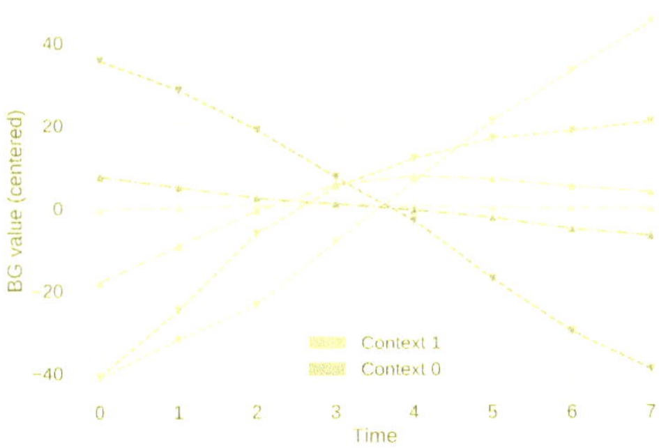

Figure 7: CMMM context comparison. We see that the top motifs under Context 0 have a much wider range of values than those under Context 1. This indicates that our learned context captures period of elevated glucose variability.

patterns, including nonlinear monotonic increases/decreases in glucose levels, demonstrating the nonlinearity of the glucoregulatory system. Additionally we observe 'peak' and 'trough' motifs, which appear indicative of hypo- and hyperglycemic events.

To examine the motifs and contexts we jointly inferred using the CMMM, we examine the difference in motif mixing probabilities under each context ($|\gamma_0 - \gamma_1|$). Here, the context we are learning represents inter-motif structure. The three motifs with the greatest negative and positive difference are shown in Figure 7. These are the motifs which are the most indicative of the context under which they occur. Interestingly, we observe a clinically significant increase in the value range for motifs more likely under context 0 vs. 1. This suggests that context 0 represents periods of elevated glycemic variability, which could indicate the unsupervised, data-driven discovery of post/pre-meal contexts.

Limitations and Extensions. Our current contextual motif approach makes an important assumption: *all contexts are categorical.* This makes sense for binary context sets, such as post/pre-meal. However, it may make sense to consider context along an ordinal scale. E.g., post-large meal, post-small meal, and fasting. One may consider extending the proposed framework to ordinal or even continuous representations.

Our joint inference approach also assumes that the progression of context is memoryless, which may be unreasonable for certain physiological contexts (such as meals). This suggests a possible extension where context labels are generated by a stateful model.

Still, the utility of contextual motifs depends greatly on the context under consideration. Our joint inference method discovers a temporally varying motif topic context, which may or may not be useful depending on the task in question. When the context with the greatest potential utility is unobserved and difficult/impossible to derive from the signal, the utility of contextual motif discovery is limited.

Contextual motifs do not currently take advantage of external labels to discover more discriminative motifs. By combining contextual motifs with existing techniques to improve motif performance, such as shapelets, it may be possible to further improve discriminative ability.

6 SUMMARY AND CONCLUSIONS

In this work, we described how the utility of motifs, as a representation for physiological time-series data, is limited when context is ignored. To address this limitation, we introduced the concept of *contextual motifs* and proposed methods for contextual motif discovery.

We focused on the setting in which context is unobserved, since often one does not have access to contextual information. In this setting, we proposed a technique to jointly infer context and motifs.

We hypothesized that by incorporating context, we can discover more clinically meaningful motifs. To test this hypothesis, we ran a series of experiments on a CGM dataset of subjects with T1D. We considered two tasks: predicting hypo- and hyperglycemic events. Compared to a standard motif representation, our contextual motif discovery algorithms led to an increase in the AUC for both tasks. We conclude that contextual motifs are more discriminative than their contextless counterparts, even in the absence of observed context.

While contextual motifs can be discovered using a two-stage inference approach (Section 3.1), we hypothesized that one could learn higher quality motifs using a joint-inference approach. Our experiments on simulated data confirm this, though the difference is most pronounced when context plays an important role. We conclude that given a large dataset where context is relevant, CMMM is preferred over other approaches.

Contextual motifs present a new, richer, motif framework which augments motif representations to account for the context under which they occur. This new framework can be applied to sequential data in which context plays an important role, such as financial time series, energy-metering data, or physiological signals.

7 ACKNOWLEDGMENTS

This work was supported by the National Science Foundation (NSF award numbers CNS-1330142 and IIS-1553146) and the National Institutes of Health (NIH research grant RO1 NIH/NHLBI-1R01HL102334-01). The views and conclusions in this document are those of the authors and should not be interpreted as necessarily representing the official policies, either expressed or implied, of the NSF or the NIH.

REFERENCES

[1] P. A. Baghurst. Calculating the mean amplitude of glycemic excursion from continuous glucose monitoring data: an automated algorithm. *Diabetes technology & therapeutics*, 13(3):296–302, 2011.

[2] T. L. Bailey and C. Elkan. Fitting a mixture model by expectation maximization to discover motifs in biopolymers. *Proceedings. International Conference on Intelligent Systems for Molecular Biology*, 2:28–36, 1994.

[3] R. M. Bergenstal. Glycemic variability and diabetes complications: Does it matter? simply put, there are better glycemic markers! *Diabetes care*, 38(8):1615–1621, 2015.

[4] D. M. Blei, A. Y. Ng, and M. I. Jordan. Latent Dirichlet allocation. *the Journal of machine Learning research*, 3:993–1022, 2003.

[5] M. Breton and B. Kovatchev. Analysis, modeling, and simulation of the accuracy of continuous glucose sensors. *Journal of Diabetes Science and Technology*, 2(5):853–862, 2008.

[6] J. Buhler and M. Tompa. Finding motifs using random projections. *Journal of computational biology*, 9(2):225–242, 2002.

[7] H. Cheng, X. Yan, J. Han, and C. W. Hsu. Discriminative Frequent Pattern Analysis for Effective Classification. In *2007 IEEE 23rd International Conference on Data Engineering*, pages 716–725, Apr. 2007.

[8] B. Chiu, E. Keogh, and S. Lonardi. Probabilistic discovery of time series motifs. In *Proceedings of the ninth ACM SIGKDD international conference on Knowledge discovery and data mining*, pages 493–498. ACM, 2003.

[9] C. K. Chui. *An introduction to wavelets*, volume 1. Academic press, 2014.

[10] J. Grabocka, N. Schilling, and L. Schmidt-Thieme. Latent time-series motifs. *ACM Transactions on Knowledge Discovery from Data (TKDD)*, 11(1):6, 2016.

[11] M. D. Hoffman and A. Gelman. The no-u-turn sampler: adaptively setting path lengths in hamiltonian monte carlo. *Journal of Machine Learning Research*, 15(1):1593–1623, 2014.

[12] M. Jaiswal, K. McKeon, N. Comment, J. Henderson, S. Swanson, C. Plunkett, P. Nelson, and R. Pop-Busui. Association between impaired cardiovascular autonomic function and hypoglycemia in patients with type 1 diabetes. *Diabetes care*, 37(9):2616–2621, 2014.

[13] K. L. Jensen, M. P. Styczynski, I. Rigoutsos, and G. N. Stephanopoulos. A generic motif discovery algorithm for sequential data. *Bioinformatics*, 22(1):21–28, 2006.

[14] R. E. Kleiger, J. P. Miller, J. T. Bigger, and A. J. Moss. Decreased heart rate variability and its association with increased mortality after acute myocardial infarction. *The American journal of cardiology*, 59(4):256–262, 1987.

[15] J. Lin, E. Keogh, S. Lonardi, and P. Patel. Finding motifs in time series. In *Proc. of the 2nd Workshop on Temporal Data Mining*, pages 53–68, 2002.

[16] J. Lin, E. Keogh, L. Wei, and S. Lonardi. Experiencing sax: a novel symbolic representation of time series. *Data Mining and knowledge discovery*, 15(2):107–144, 2007.

[17] T.-h. Lin, P. Ray, G. K. Sandve, S. Uguroglu, and E. P. Xing. Baycis: a Bayesian hierarchical hmm for cis-regulatory module decoding in metazoan genomes. In *Annual International Conference on Research in Computational Molecular Biology*, pages 66–81. Springer, 2008.

[18] B. Liu, J. Li, C. Chen, W. Tan, Q. Chen, and M. Zhou. Efficient motif discovery for large-scale time series in healthcare. *IEEE Transactions on Industrial Informatics*, 11(3):583–590, 2015.

[19] J. S. Liu. Metropolized gibbs sampler: an improvement. Technical report, Technical report, Dept. Statistics, Stanford Univ, 1996.

[20] D. Minnen, T. Starner, I. Essa, and C. Isbell. Discovering characteristic actions from on-body sensor data. In *2006 10th IEEE international symposium on wearable computers*, pages 11–18. IEEE, 2006.

[21] G. D. Molnar, J. W. Rosevear, E. Ackerman, L. C. Gatewood, W. F. Taylor, et al. Mean amplitude of glycemic excursions, a measure of diabetic instability. *Diabetes*, 19(9):644–655, 1970.

[22] A. Mueen. Time series motif discovery: dimensions and applications. *Wiley Interdisciplinary Reviews: Data Mining and Knowledge Discovery*, 4(2):152–159, 2014.

[23] M. Muggeo, G. Zoppini, E. Bonora, E. Brun, R. C. Bonadonna, P. Moghetti, and G. Verlato. Fasting plasma glucose variability predicts 10-year survival of type 2 diabetic patients: the verona diabetes study. *Diabetes care*, 23(1):45–50, 2000.

[24] K. P. Murphy. Dynamic bayesian networks. *Probabilistic Graphical Models, M. Jordan*, 7, 2002.

[25] T. Nakamura, K. Kiyono, H. Wendt, P. Abry, and Y. Yamamoto. Multiscale analysis of intensive longitudinal biomedical signals and its clinical applications. *Proceedings of the IEEE*, 104(2):242–261, 2016.

[26] S. B. Needleman and C. D. Wunsch. A general method applicable to the search for similarities in the amino acid sequence of two proteins. *Journal of molecular biology*, 48(3):443–453, 1970.

[27] T. Oates. Peruse: An unsupervised algorithm for finding recurring patterns in time series. In *Data Mining, 2002. ICDM 2003. Proceedings. 2002 IEEE International Conference on*, pages 330–337. IEEE, 2002.

[28] F. Pedregosa, G. Varoquaux, A. Gramfort, V. Michel, B. Thirion, O. Grisel, M. Blondel, P. Prettenhofer, R. Weiss, V. Dubourg, et al. Scikit-learn: Machine learning in python. *Journal of Machine Learning Research*, 12(Oct):2825–2830, 2011.

[29] S. Ranu and A. K. Singh. GraphSig: A Scalable Approach to Mining Significant Subgraphs in Large Graph Databases. In *2009 IEEE 25th International Conference on Data Engineering*, pages 844–855, Mar. 2009.

[30] J. Salvatier, T. V. Wiecki, and C. Fonnesbeck. Probabilistic programming in python using pymc3. *PeerJ Computer Science*, 2:e55, 2016.

[31] S. Saria, A. Duchi, and D. Koller. Discovering deformable motifs in continuous time series data. In *IJCAI Proceedings-International Joint Conference on Artificial Intelligence*, volume 22, page 1465, 2011.

[32] S. Saria, D. Koller, and A. Penn. Learning individual and population level traits from clinical temporal data. In *Proc. Neural Information Processing Systems (NIPS), Predictive Models in Personalized Medicine workshop*. Citeseer, 2010.

[33] M. Shokoohi-Yekta, Y. Chen, B. Campana, B. Hu, J. Zakaria, and E. Keogh. Discovery of meaningful rules in time series. In *Proceedings of the 21th ACM SIGKDD International Conference on Knowledge Discovery and Data Mining*, pages 1085–1094. ACM, 2015.

[34] R. Siddharthan, E. D. Siggia, and E. Van Nimwegen. Phylogibbs: a Gibbs sampling motif finder that incorporates phylogeny. *PLoS Comput Biol*, 1(7):e67, 2005.

[35] Z. Syed, C. Stultz, M. Kellis, P. Indyk, and J. Guttag. Motif discovery in physiological datasets: a methodology for inferring predictive elements. *ACM Transactions on Knowledge Discovery from Data (TKDD)*, 4(1):2, 2010.

[36] A. Vahdatpour, N. Amini, and M. Sarrafzadeh. Toward unsupervised activity discovery using multi-dimensional motif detection in time series. In *IJCAI*, volume 9, pages 1261–1266, 2009.

[37] A. Van Esbroeck. *Learning Better Clinical Risk Models*. PhD thesis, The University of Michigan, 2015.

[38] A. Van Esbroeck, C.-C. Chia, and Z. Syed. Heart rate topic models. In *The Twenty-Sixth AAAI Conference on Artificial Intelligence*, volume 1001, page 48109, 2012.

[39] S. A. Weinzimer, G. M. Steil, K. L. Swan, J. Dziura, N. Kurtz, and W. V. Tamborlane. Fully automated closed-loop insulin delivery versus semiautomated hybrid control in pediatric patients with type 1 diabetes using an artificial pancreas. *Diabetes care*, 31(5):934–939, 2008.

[40] L. Ye and E. Keogh. Time series shapelets: a new primitive for data mining. In *Proceedings of the 15th ACM SIGKDD international conference on Knowledge discovery and data mining*, pages 947–956. ACM, 2009.

[41] Q. Zhou and W. H. Wong. Cismodule: de novo discovery of cis-regulatory modules by hierarchical mixture modeling. *Proceedings of the national academy of sciences of the United States of America*, 101(33):12114–12119, 2004.

[42] S. Zoungas, A. Patel, J. Chalmers, B. E. de Galan, Q. Li, L. Billot, M. Woodward, T. Ninomiya, B. Neal, S. MacMahon, et al. Severe hypoglycemia and risks of vascular events and death. *New England Journal of Medicine*, 363(15):1410–1418, 2010.

Unsupervised P2P Rental Recommendations via Integer Programming

Yanjie Fu
Missouri Univ. of Sci. and Tech.
Missouri, USA
fuyan@mst.edu

Guannan Liu*
Beihang University
Beijing, China
liugn@buaa.edu.cn

Mingfei Teng
Rutgers University
NJ, USA
tengmf@gmail.com

Charu Aggarwal
IBM T. J. Watson Research Center
NY, USA
charu@us.ibm.com

ABSTRACT

Due to the sparseness of quality rating data, unsupervised recommender systems are used in many applications in Peer to Peer (P2P) rental marketplaces such as Airbnb, FlipKey, and HomeAway. We present an integer programming based recommender systems, where both accommodation benefits and community risks of lodging places are measured and incorporated into an objective function as utility measurements. More specifically, we first present an unsupervised fused scoring method for quantifying the accommodation benefits and community risks of a lodging with crowd-sourced geo-tagged data. In order to the utility of recommendations, we formulate the unsupervised P2P rental recommendations as a constrained integer programming problem, where the accommodation benefits of recommendations are maximized and the community risks of recommendations are minimized, while maintaining constraints on personalization. Furthermore, we provide an efficient solution for the optimization problem by developing a learning-to-integer-programming method for combining aggregated listwise learning to rank into branching variable selection. We apply the proposed approach to the Airbnb data of New York City and provide lodging recommendations to travelers. In our empirical experiments, we demonstrate both the efficiency and effectiveness of our method in terms of striving a trade-off between the user satisfaction, time on market, and the number of reviews, and achieving a balance between positive and negative sides.

KEYWORDS

Unsupervised Recommendations; Integer Programming; Learning To Optimize;

*Contact author.

KDD'17, August 13–17, 2017, Halifax, NS, Canada.
© 2017 ACM. ISBN 978-1-4503-4887-4/17/08...$15.00
DOI: http://dx.doi.org/10.1145/3097983.3098044

1 INTRODUCTION

The sharing economy has provided travelers more choices beyond traditional hotels with the emergence of Internet-enabled P2P rental markets, e.g., Airbnb (www.airbnb.com), FlipKey (www.flipkey.com), HomeAway (www.homeaway.com), where local residents serve as hosts to provide home stay while travelers search, identify, and compensate their hosts. Although current P2P platforms bring cheaper lodging options for travelers, it is however a very challenging task for the travelers to find satisfactory lodging places in an unfamiliar city due to the following issues: (1) Lodgings are on or off markets dynamically, and thus are lack of quality rating data. For example, some apartments are listed or rented only once. (2) Lodgings are mostly private properties without location planning and hospitality management for travel accommodation purposes. For example, some places may not be convenient for entertainment and sightseeing, or the amenities may not be well equipped. (3) Travelers have little knowledge about the neighborhood environments of the lodgings listed on the markets. For example, some places are located in unsafe neighborhoods with many sexual assaults, gunshots, and thefts.

To facilitate travelers to search lodgings, today's P2P rental platforms provide rankings of posted lodgings, typically using filtering criteria such as price, amenities, review ratings, etc. However, existing approaches are far from adequate due to the following reasons. Since travelers are unfamiliar with destination cities, they may have to probe into as many listings as possible by browsing related review comments from third-party sources, checking the neighborhoods of interested places with Google Map, and communicating with hosts. These may cost tremendous time and efforts, and thus it highly necessitates a smart system to recommend appropriate lodging places, to overcome the lack of quality user ratings, and moreover, to alleviate the information asymmetry between travelers and hosts in the P2P platforms.

There are several challenges in achieving the goal inherent in our system. First, it is difficult to estimate the accommodation benefits and community risks of P2P rentals as they are privately owned and dynamically listed, with limited information publicly available. With the advent of mobile, sensing and Internet technologies, the availability of mobile data including urban geography (e.g., POIs), human mobility (e.g., GPS traces), and public service data (e.g., crimes, noises) are ever increasing. These data can be a source of rich intelligence for scoring accommodation benefits and community risk of lodgings. However, how to score accommodation benefits and community risks of lodgings under unsupervised settings by fusing heterogeneous data is a challenging problem.

Second, a P2P rental recommender system can be viewed in terms of benefit and risk. In other words, the system should have the capability of maximizing accommodation benefits and minimizing community risks. Moreover, users also have personalized constraints. For instance, the cost of a recommended place should be within the user's budget; the availability of a recommended place should be long enough to cover the planed travel days. Therefore, how can we simultaneously achieve multiple objectives? Unlike traditional supervised recommendation algorithms such as collaborative filtering and matrix factorizations, we alternatively formulate this problem as a constrained *I*nteger *P*rogramming (IP), where the utility of recommendations is maximized while constraints are for personalization, in order to navigate these trade-offs in a flexible and meaningful way.

Third, a natural approach for the IP based recommendation problem is the *B*ranch and *B*ound (BB) method. However, traditional BB methods exhaustedly examine every candidate branching variable, in order to find the best branching variable to reduce the gap between the best bound and the current best feasible solution value, and thus are computationally expensive. We adapt the idea of learning by analogy. In reality, it is often possible to collect many other data sets, which have labels or ratings provided by domain experts. Running BB on these labeled datasets can enable us to observe how BB selects branching variables and computes corresponding gains of different branching events. The collected information (i.e., branching variable selection and gains) of BB on labeled datasets can provide a "meta training" collection of the branching behaviors of BB, which can be used to identify the key statistical characteristics of the best branching variables that help BB find the optimal solutions faster.

Along these lines, in this paper, we develop an unsupervised framework for recommending lodging places with awareness of benefit and safety. Specifically, we first extract the features of accommodation benefits for each lodging from urban geography, human mobility, and property amenities data. Besides, we mine the features of community risk for each lodging from the publicly available data of crimes, noises, and complains. In addition, we devise an unsupervised fused scoring method to select, weight, and aggregate the corresponding features into benefit and risk scores for each lodging. Moreover, we construct an optimization objective for recommending lodgings by simultaneously maximizing accommodation benefit and minimizing community risk with respect to personalized constraints. We also develop a learning to IP method by presenting an aggregated listwise branching selector. Finally, we present extensive experiments to demonstrate the enhanced performance of the proposed method using real world P2P rental market data.

2 PRELIMINARIES

In this section, we first introduce the unsupervised recommendations formulation for P2P rental markets, and then detail how to measure accommodation benefits and community risks of a lodging for constructing the utility of a lodging.

2.1 Motivation and Problem Statement

The decision process of finding a lodging place in a P2P rental market is different from that of booking a starred hotel. Travelers not only need to consider personalized constraints (i.e., cost budget, length of stay), but also take into account both the positive and negative factors (i.e., accommodation benefits and community risks), which have been considered in starred hotels but not in P2P rental markets. Formally, considering a set of candidate lodgings, $I = \{1, 2, 3, ..., |I|\}$, let $i \in I$ be the index of a candidate lodging, with $u_i \in U$ being its accommodation benefit, $r_i \in R$ being its community risk, we aim to determine K lodgings as a recommendation set, indicated by a binary decision vector $\mathbf{y}$, by maximizing accommodation benefit, minimizing community risk, while subject to personalized constraints.

We propose to formulate this task as an integer programming as shown in Definition 2.1, where (i) the criteria in terms of benefit and risk is denoted as Discounted Accumulated Gain, DCG(y, U, R), which is in a form of weighted sum of benefits and risks of recommended lodgings. (ii) the criteria in terms of personalized constraints is directly formulated as constraints in the integer programming problem.

Definition 2.1. **Problem Statement.** *Given a set of candidate lodgings, I, each with a benefit measurement and a risk measurement, recommend K lodgings such that the discounted accumulated gain, i.e., DCG(y, U, R), is maximized, while respecting personalized constraints.*

Specifically, each lodging has a normalized benefit score and a normalized risk score, i.e., $DCG(\mathbf{y}, U, R) = \sum_{i \in I} y_i(\lambda u_i - r_i)$. Also, the personalized constraints can be instantiated by two commonly used constraints in lodging search, i.e., cost budget and length of stay. However, in addition to cost and length of stay, the model can be easily extended to more personalized constraints for more sophisticated personalized recommendations. Accordingly, the lodging recommendation problem can be further formulated as follows:

$$\max_{\mathbf{y}} \mathcal{F}(\mathbf{y}) = \sum_{i \in I} y_i(\lambda u_i - r_i) \tag{1}$$

$$s.t. \quad y_i \in \{0, 1\} \tag{2}$$

$$\forall p \in \{i | y_i = 1\} : c_p \leq C \tag{3}$$

$$\forall q \in \{i | y_i = 1\} : t_q \geq T^1 \tag{4}$$

$$\sum_{i \in I} y_i = K \tag{5}$$

where λ is a parameter representing the weight of accommodation benefits compared to community risks. In Constraint (2), $\mathbf{y} = \{0, 1\}^{|I|}$ is a binary vector. $y_i = 1$ indicates that the lodging place i is selected as a recommended lodging place, otherwise $y_i = 0$. Constraint (3) simply states that the maximum cost budget is C. Constraint (4) simply states that the minimum length of stay is T. Constraint (5) states that the number of recommended lodging places is K.

[1] In reality, a user usually input start date and end date for lodging search and reservation. To simplify the formulation of objective function and data processing, we use single input: length of stay. This simplified objective function can be easily adapted for two inputs: start date and end date.

Table 1: Benefit-related features.

Categories	Source	Variable Name	Variable Description
Public Transportation	NYC Taxi Commission	reachability	number of bus stops one can reach by bus in one hour
		transit density	number of bus stops or subway stations in the neighboring circle area of radius one kilometer
		distance to transit	walking distance to the nearest bus stop or subway station
POIs	Foursquare NYC POIs	POI frequency	number of POIs in terms of different POI categories (e.g., shopping, foods, education, entertainment, etc.)
		POI diversity	entropy given POI frequency density over different POI categories
Mobility	Foursquare NYC Checkins	neighborhood popularity	number of smart phone checkins when people visit outdoor places
Space and Amenities	Airbnb NYC	bath rooms	numbers of bath rooms
		bedrooms	numbers of bedrooms
		beds	numbers of beds
		kitchen	binary indicator of kitchen
		Internet	binary indicator of Internet
		TV	binary indicator of TV
		air conditioner	binary indicator of air conditioner
		heat	binary indicator of heat

Table 2: Risk-related features.

Categories	Source	Variable Name	Variable Description
Crime	NYPD	crime frequency	number of criminal events over different offense categories (burglary, felony assault, grand larceny of motor vehicle, murder, rape, robbery)
		crime diversity	entropy given criminal frequency density over different offense categories
Complaints	NYC 311 Service	complaint frequency	complaint frequencies over different complaint types (air, animal, decoration, dirty, electricity, facility, food, human, noise, safety, transport, water)
		complaint diversity	entropy given complaint frequency density over different complaint types

2.2 Unsupervised Scoring of Accommodation Benefits and Community Risks

We first construct benefit-related and risk-related features from heterogeneous lodging related information, and then develop an unsupervised fused scoring method to score the accommodation benefit and community risk of each lodging.

Construction of Benefit-related and Risk-related Features. First, accommodation benefits can be assessed from positive sides based on urban geography, human mobility, and property amenities. Specifically, urban geography data such as public transportations and POIs describe the neighborhood infrastructure near a place; human mobility data such as vehicle GPS traces and check-ins encode the geographic preferences of mobile users and the popularity of a place. Moreover, the information such as space and amenities of a listed lodging is usually specified on the website, which represents the comfortableness and functionality and can be incorporated to estimate the benefit. Table 1 lists the features to depict of accommodation benefits. Second, community risk can be perceived from negative sides of the neighborhoods such as crimes, complains, and noises, which have been publicly available from local government websites. Table 2 lists the features of community risks.

Unsupervised Fused Scoring. We propose a three-step unsupervised method to aggregate the features of benefits (risks) into a single benefit (risk) score. The challenge mainly lies on how to effectively select discriminative features and weigh feature distinctiveness under an unsupervised setting.

Step1: Unsupervised Feature Selection. Features can be selected to be mutually far away from each other such that the information redundancy is minimized. To measure the feature redundancy, we use mutual information for discrete features. Given two features X and Y, the mutual information is computed by $\rho(X,Y) = \sum_{y \in Y} \sum_{x \in X} p(x,y) log(\frac{p(x,y)}{p(x)p(y)})$, where $p(x,y)$ is the joint distribution of X and Y, and $p(x)$ and $p(y)$ are marginal distributions of X and Y, respectively. For continuous features, we use statistical correlation (i.e., Pearson product-moment correlation coefficient) which is given by $\rho(X,Y) = \frac{cov(X,Y)}{\sigma_X \sigma_Y}$, where cov is the covariance and σ_X is the standard deviation of X. Then, we propose a fast algorithm to select non-redundant features. The idea is as follows: we first compute the pair-wise correlation between features, and identify highly-correlated feature pairs, i.e., pairs with absolute values of correlation larger than a threshold α (set to 0.9). From the two features in each identified feature pair, we remove the feature with larger mean absolute correlation (computed as the average of the absolute value of the Pearson correlation of this feature with all other features). By this selection procedure, we are able to obtain a set of features with low redundancy.

Step2: Unsupervised Feature Weighting. The weight of a feature represents the discrimination capability of classifying accommodation benefits or community risks. We propose a Laplacian Score [10] based approach to quantify the weight of each feature. The Laplacian score for a feature is computed based on Laplacian Eigenmaps and Locality Preserving Projection, in order to capture its classification power. Consider a data table $\mathbf{F} \in \mathbb{R}^{P \times Q}$ with P instances and Q features, where the instance $\mathbf{f}_{p,*}$ is the p-th row in $\mathbf{F}$ and the feature $\mathbf{f}_{*,q}$ is the q-th column. To extract the Laplacian Score of the feature q, we first construct an undirected graph with nodes as instances (i.e., rows). Each edge $(p1, p2)$ is associated with a weight representing the Cosine similarity between the row $\mathbf{f}_{p1,*}$ and the row $\mathbf{f}_{p2,*}$. Thereby, we can use a weight matrix $\mathbf{S} \in \mathbb{R}^{P \times P}$ to describe this graph and represent the local structure of the data space F. Finally, the Laplacian Score of the q-th feature is defined by $L_q = \frac{\sum_{p1=1}^{P} \sum_{p2=1}^{P} (f_{p1,q} - f_{p2,q})^2 s_{p1,p2}}{Var(\mathbf{f}_{*,q})}$, where $f_{p1,q}$ is the value at $p1$-th row and q-th column in $\mathbf{F}$, $Var(\mathbf{f}_{*,q})$ is the variance of the q-th column, and $s_{p1,p2} \in \mathbf{S}$.

Step3: Normalization, Aggregation and Scoring. Given features and corresponding weights, we normalize features using a quotient transformation (x/max). Also, we normalize feature weights using another quotient transformation (x/sum). Finally, we combine features and weights into a single score in a form of weighted sum of components. We will apply this method to the benefit feature set and the risk feature set, and extract two corresponding scores for each lodging.

3 LISTWISE LEARNING TO INTEGER PROGRAMMING

We present a learning to integer programming method as an effective solution for the optimization problem, by combining listwise learning to rank and learning by analogy into branch and bound.

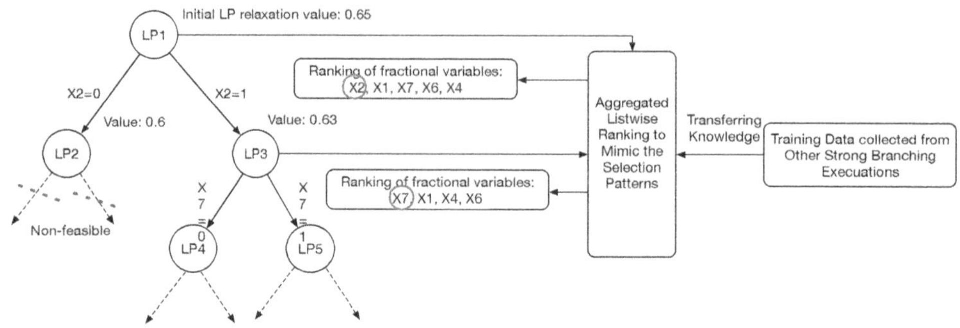

Figure 1: Incorporating Aggregated Listwise Branching Variable Selector into BB to Transfer Knowledge from Strong Branching

3.1 Background of Branch-and-Bound

Compared to probabilistic searching (e.g., genetic algorithm or simulated annealing), BB can solve this objective in a fast, accurate and stable manner. BB begins by finding the optimal solution to the relaxation of the problem without the integer constraints via standard linear programming. If in this solution, the decision variables with integer constraints have integer values, then no further work is required. If one or more integer variables have non-integral solutions, the method chooses one such variable and "branches", creating two new subproblems where the value of that variable is more tightly constrained. These subproblems are solved and the process is repeated, until a solution that satisfies all of the integer constraints is found.

Therefore, it is critical to select proper branching variables effectively and efficiently in BB. One widely-used strategy is strong branching [1]: if a solution E is not integer feasible, let V be the set of candidate branching variables in E with objective value z. For all candidate branching variables $j \in V$, we compute a branching gain g_j as follows: assuming branching E on j downwards and upwards, the two solutions E^+ and E^- of two newly created subproblems have feasible objective values z_j^+ and z_j^-, then the gain g_j for the branching variable j is defined as $g_j = (z_j^+ - z) \times (z_j^- - z)$. Strong branching strategy will identify the best branching variable with maximum gain: $\max_{j \in V} g_j$.

3.2 An Aggregated Listwise Branching Selector

Traditional BB, including strong branching, is a time-consuming process due to its exhaustive strategy. To strive a balance between efficiency and effectiveness, we improve BB by replacing strong branching with a new branching variable selector. We adapt the idea of learning by analogy. It is often possible to collect many other data sets with labels available. Running BB on these labeled datasets can enable us to observe and collect how strong branching computes the branching gains of all candidate variables, selects the best one, and branches upwards and downloads. The branching variables and gains of BB branchings on labeled datasets can be used to identify the key statistical characteristics of the best branching variables that make BB effective and efficient and learn a new branching variable selector.

(i) Data Collection. At every branch in BB, the branching variable selected from multiple candidates can be represented by a binary vector $h = \{0, ..., 0, 1, 0, ..., 0\}$, where 1 indicates "selected" and 0 indicates "not selected". Later, for each candidate branching variable, we extract the features that are related to branching gain as follows:

- Objective function coefficients: Values of objective function coefficients
- Number constraints: Number of constraints that the candidate branching variable participates in.
- Statistics for constraint degree: The degree of a constraint is the number of variables that participate in it. A candidate branching variable may participate in multiple constraints. We use the mean, standard deviation, min, max of the constraint degrees as features.
- Statistics for constraint coefficients: For each candidate branching variable, we can extract a set of coefficients in the constraints the variable participates in. We will use the count, mean, standard deviation, min, max of the set of coefficients as features.
- Statistics for infeasibility: For each candidate branching variable, we count the frequency of selecting the variable that leads to infeasible solutions of subbranches.

Each candidate branching variable, along with its branching gain related features and corresponding binary section label in BB, will be compiled as a training dataset for learning a new branching variable selector. As shown in Figure 1, by incorporating the aggregated listwise branching variable selector into BB, we can mimic the patterns regarding how the strong branching selects the best variables on meta training data by the ranker, and exploit the ranker to enhance our integer programming based recommendations.

(ii) Offline Learning. Next, we construct an aggregated listwise ranking objective to mimic how the Strong Branching strategy selects the best variables for branching. First of all, a BB generates many branches, each of which can be regarded as a ranking task, where the branching variable selector produces a ranking list of candidate branching variables in terms of the features of these candidate variables. Since we can observe many branches, we formulate the modeling of all branches as an aggregated listwise learning to rank problem. From the perspective of generative modeling, we can assume our ranker generates the ranking lists of candidate branching variables in each branch with certain likelihood. Then, learning the branching variable selector is reduced to the problem of maximizing the likelihood of generating the ranking lists in each branch given our branching variable selector. Formally, suppose there are M branches (i.e., ranking tasks). The m-th branch has N_m candidate branching variables. The training data of m-th branch is denoted by $B_m = \{v_{mn}, h_{mn}\}_{n=1}^{N}$, where v_{mn} and h_{mn} respectively represent the branching gain feature vector and the binary selection label of the n-th candidate branching variable in the m-th branch. Given a candidate variable v_{mn}, we linearly combine its branching gain-related features to predict its ranking score to be selected as a branching variable: $w * v_{mn}$, where w is vectorized linear coefficients. Then, we use softmax functions and listwise strategy to model the likelihood of the predicted ranking list in the m-th branch as:

$$\mathcal{L}(B_m|w) = \prod_{n=1}^{N_m} \left(\frac{e^{wv_{mn}}}{\sum_{n'=1}^{N_m} e^{wv_{mn'}}}\right)^{h_{mn}}. \quad (6)$$

The overall likelihood of all the ranking lists of the M branches is

$$\mathcal{L}(B|w) = \prod_{m=1}^{M} \prod_{n=1}^{N_m} \left(\frac{e^{wv_{mn}}}{\sum_{n'=1}^{N_m} e^{wv_{mn'}}}\right)^{h_{mn}} \quad (7)$$

where $B = \{B_m\}_{m=1}^{M}$. With the formulated overall likelihood, the objective is to find the best estimation of w that maximize the overall ranking likelihood. By applying Jensenfis inequality, the logarithm of $\mathcal{L}$ can be approximated by a lower bound $\mathbb{L}$, which is

$$\begin{aligned} log\mathcal{L}(B|w) &= \sum_{m=1}^{M} \sum_{n=1}^{N_m} h_{mn}(wv_{mn} - log \sum_{n'=1}^{N_m} e^{wv_{mn'}}) \\ &\geq \mathbb{L} = \sum_{m=1}^{M} \sum_{n=1}^{N_m} h_{mn}(wv_{mn} - \sum_{n'=1}^{N_m} wv_{mn'}) \end{aligned} \quad (8)$$

After that, we apply a gradient descent method to maximize $\mathbb{L}$ via $w^{\#it+1} = w^{\#it} + \epsilon \frac{\partial(\mathbb{L})}{\partial w}$, where $\#it$ is iteration number.

(iii) Online Selection. After the branching variable selector is learned, the Strong Branching in BB will be replaced by our selector. Given a set of candidate variables for branching, we use the ranker to rank these candidate variables and branch on the top-1 variable upwards and downwards.

3.3 Recommending Lodging Places

Our proposed system accepts the number of recommended lodging places K, maximum price C, and length of stay T as inputs, which are specified based on a user's preference. After solving the objective, we find the optimal binary vector **y** where all the lodging place with indicator 1 will be selected as recommended lodging places. In other words, our proposed system will output a K-sized set of lodging places for the user to explore.

4 EXPERIMENTAL RESULTS

We evaluate the proposed model with real-world data in terms of various tasks.

4.1 Data Description

Table 3 shows the detailed statistics of our real-world data sets for experiments. The data of the lodging places are collected from Airbnb which is a popular website for people to find and rent lodging. It includes the geolocation, neighborhood group (like Manhattan, Brooklyn), room types (private room, entire home), prices, available period and people's ratings and reviews. To estimate the accommodation benefit of the lodging places, we crawled the check-in and POI data from www.foursquare.com. It consists of massive check-in events. Each event is associated with a GPS address, a date, a POI name, a POI category, and comments. For the public transportation, we use the subway data from MTA, which is in the General Transit Feed Specification (GTFS) format, including the information of stops, routes, stop times. To estimate the community risk of the lodging places, we consider 311 complaints data. In New York, 311 is a special telephone number to help local residents to access goverment services and information. The data are composed of a large set of call-in events, each of which are recorded with the complaint type (e.g., Illegal Parking, Noise, Safety), geolocation, location type (e.g., residential, club, restaurant) as well as zip code and created date. The NYPD crime data are also utilized to measure the safety of community. The records in the data are major felony incidents came with timestamp, geolocation and offense type.

Table 3: Statistics of the experiment data.

Data Sources	Properties	Statistics
Airbnb	Number of places	27469
	Size of bounding box (km)	44.28 x 43.175
	Time period of transactions	Jun. 2015 - Sep. 2015
POIs	Number of POIs	12677339
	Number of categories	7
Check-Ins	Number of check-in POIs	12677339
	Number of check-in events	1146283
	Number of POI categories	7
	Time Period	329 days
Crimes	Number of offense types	7
	Number of criminal events	76755
	Number of offense levels	4
	Time Period	36769 days
311 Complaints	Number of location types	137
	Number of complaint types	245
	Number of complaints	9137092
	Time period	4433 days

4.2 Evaluation Metrics

To show the effectiveness of our proposed method, we use Precision, Recall, F-measure, NDCG as evaluation metrics. We evaluate the performance of our proposed method from three aspects: satisfaction ratings, time-on-market (TOM), and review counts. Generally, if a lodging place is good and popular, it is likely that the satisfaction rating of the place is high, the time-on-market of the place is short, and the review count of this place is large.

Precision and Recall. Precision and recall are typically used in a binary rating system. To prepare binary ratings of satisfaction , we collected the original satisfaction scores (ranging from 5 to 1) of each lodging place, and then labeled these lodging places with rating 1 if their satisfaction scores > 4.5, representing the rank of top 10% in population, and rating 0 otherwise. To prepare binary ratings of time-on-market, we collected the number of available days of each lodging place, normalized it by #non-available days / (#available days + #non-available days), and labeled these lodging places with rating 1 if availability ratio > 0.35, representing the rank of top 10% in population, and 0 otherwise. To prepare binary ratings of review counts, we collected the review counts of each lodging place, and then labeled these lodging places with rating 1 if review count > 20, representing the rank of top 10% in population, and 0 otherwise. Thereby, we treat the rating 1 as "relevant" and the rating 0 as "not relevant". Given a set of N recommended lodging places E_N, precision and recall are defined as Precision@N = $\frac{|E_N \bigcap E_{\geq 1}|}{N}$ and Recall@N = $\frac{|E_N \bigcap E_{\geq 1}|}{|E_{\geq 1}|}$, where $E_{\geq 1}$ are the lodging places whose ratings are greater or equal to 3.

F-measure. F-measure combines precision and recall, and is the harmonic mean of precision and recall. Here we use the F_β measure with $\beta = 0.5$, $xF_\beta = (1 + \beta^2) \cdot \frac{\text{Precision} \cdot \text{Recall}}{\beta^2 \text{Precision} + \text{Recall}}$ The F_β measure with $\beta < 1$ indicates more emphasis on precision than recall.

Normalized Discounted Cumulative Gain (NDCG). The discounted cumulative gain (DCG) metric is evaluated over top N lodging places on the ranked accommodation list by assuming that better lodging places should appear earlier in the ranked list. The discounted cumulative gain (DCG@N) is given by

$$DCG[n] = \begin{cases} rel_1 & if\ n = 1 \\ DCG[n-1] + \frac{rel_n}{log_2 n}, & if\ n >= 2 \end{cases} \quad (9)$$

where rel_n is the rating of the lodging place n. Later, given the ideal discounted cumulative gain DCG', NDCG at the n-th position can be computed as NDCG[n]= $\frac{DCG[n]}{DCG'[n]}$. The larger NDCG@N is, the higher top-N ranking accuracy is.

4.3 Baseline Algorithms

Our proposed system accepts the number of recommended lodging places K, maximum price C, and length of stay T, specified by a user, as inputs. Our proposed system will output a K-sized set of lodging places. We thus introduce the following baseline methods for comparison. We name our method as (1) **L-Rec**: we consider both accommodation benefits and community risks, which is exactly our proposed method.

First of all, we compare our method with unsupervised cheaper-first methods. (2) **Price based Ranking (PR)** : we first filter out candidate lodging places based on the constraints of price and length of stay. Then, we rank and select top K cheapest lodging places. In addition, we compare our proposed method with supervised learning-to-rank methods. We then feed a set of lodging places, each of which with extracted features of benefit and risk, as well as corresponding benchmark ratings of satisfaction, time-on-market, and review counts in Airbnb, into the ranking methods for training. After that, we similarly filter out candidate lodging places in terms of price and length of stay, and use the trained models to rank candidate lodging places and select top-K candidates. Specifically, we select three ranking methods: (3) **AdaRank [17]:** AdaRank is a list-wise learning algorithm within the framework of boosting, which can minimize a list-wise loss function. We set tolerance = 0.002 and max consecutive selection count = 5 for AdaRank. (4) **Coordinate Ascent [13]:** it uses domination loss and applies coordinate descent for optimization. We set step base = 0.05, step scale = 2.0, tolerance = 0.001, and slack = 0.001 for Coordinate Ascent . (5) **RankBoost (RB) [8]:** it is a boosted pairwise ranking method, which trains multiple weak rankers and combines their outputs as final rankings. We set the number of iteration = 300, the number of threshold candidates = 10 for RankBoost.

4.4 Parameter Sensitivity of λ

In our objective function, λ controls the weight ratio of accommodation benefits to community risks. We study the sensitivity of

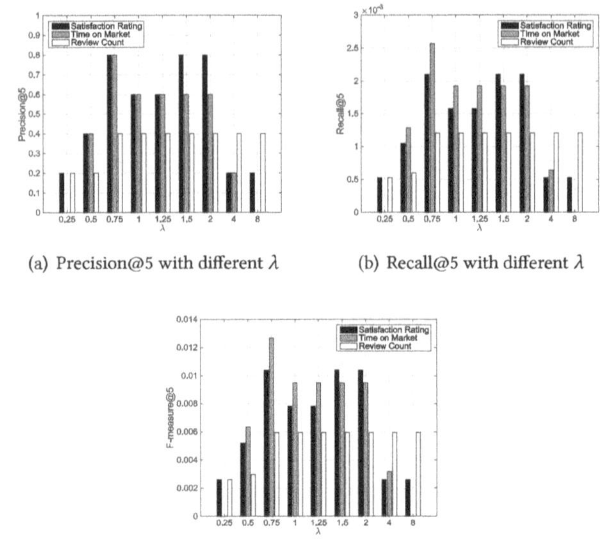

(a) Precision@5 with different λ (b) Recall@5 with different λ

(c) F-measure@5 with different λ

Figure 2: Precision and Recall on satisfaction rating, time on market, and review count with different λ.

λ and identify the best λ. Specifically, we extract the Precision at 5 and Recall at 5 in terms of the benchmark satisfaction ratings, time on market, and review counts, when given different values of λ. Figure 2 shows when λ is set as 0.75, the recommender system achieves the best performances in terms of the three evaluation criteria: satisfaction ratings, time on market, and review counts. A potential interpretation of this finding is that when travelers choose a lodging, they care more about the community risks than the accommodation benefits, since they are traveling to an unfamiliar city and the lodgings on Airbnb are non-standardized hotels. In the next, we will use $\lambda = 0.75$ as a default setting.

4.5 Overall Performances

We compare our method with the baseline methods in terms of Precision and Recall with respect to the three criteria (i.e., satisfaction, time on market, and review counts). Specifically, satisfaction refers to the ratings given by travelers after their stays in the lodging places; time on market refers to the number of days a lodging listing is active on the market, which is an important measurement of popularity and liquidity. The three criteria is used as benchmark ratings (golden standards) for both training and testing in the baseline algorithms. However, the three criteria are only used for testing in our method since our method is unsupervised.

Evaluation on Satisfaction Ratings. We compare our proposed method with the baseline methods in terms of satisfaction ratings. A method is effective if the satisfaction ratings of lodging places recommended by the method are high. In the experiments, we set N as 5, 10, 15, and 20. Figure 3 shows the results of each approach with respect to the three different evaluation metrics. In this figure, we can see that our proposed unsupervised method consistently outperforms not just the price-based ranking method but

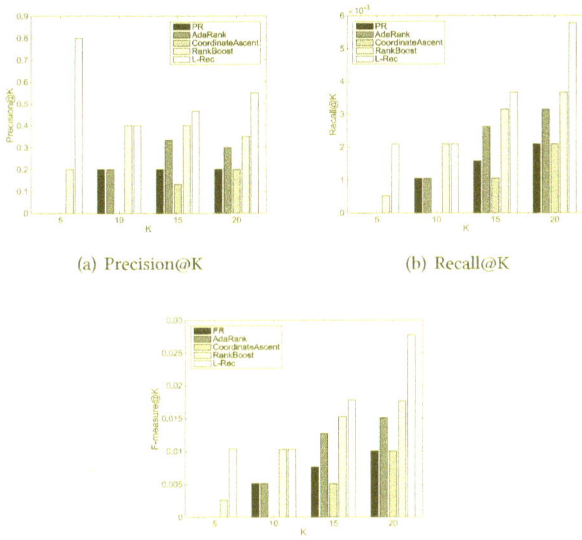

(a) Precision@K (b) Recall@K

(c) F-measure@K

Figure 3: Comparison of different methods in terms of precision and recall on satisfaction rating.

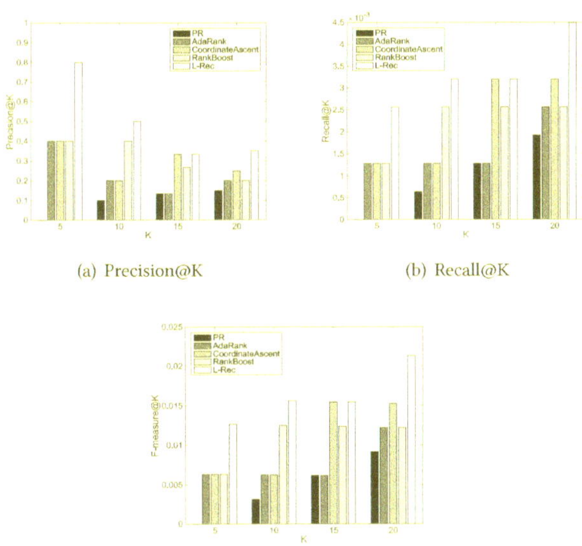

(a) Precision@K (b) Recall@K

(c) F-measure@K

Figure 4: Comparison of different methods in terms of precision and recall on time-on-market.

also the three supervised learning-to-rank methods. The improvement of our unsupervised method is more significant for smaller K, for example, recommending top-5 lodging places.

Evaluation on Time-On-Market. We compare our proposed method with the baseline methods in terms of time on market. A method is effective if the time on market of lodging places recommended by the method are short, which means that the lodgings are quickly rented once they are listed in the rental market. Figure 4 shows that when we look at the performances of predicting time-on-market, our proposed method again consistently outperform the baseline methods, particularly for hitting top-5 and top-20 lodging places. Also, the two supervised methods, AdaRank and RankBoost, are in the second place. The price based ranking again achieves lowest accuracy.

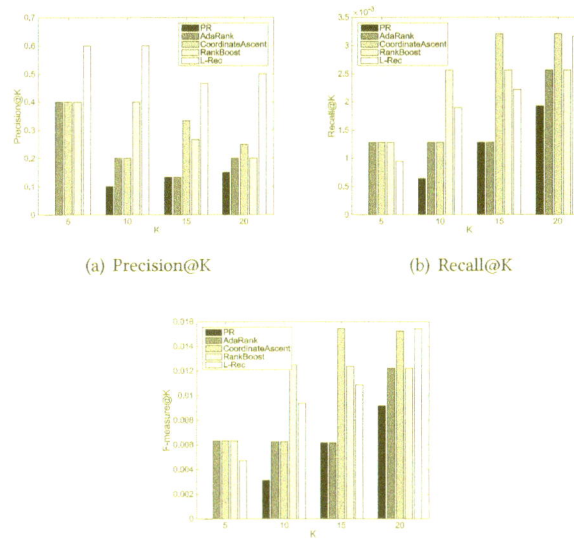

(a) Precision@K (b) Recall@K

(c) F-measure@K

Figure 5: Comparison of different methods in terms of precision and recall on review count.

Evaluation on Review Count. We compare our proposed method with baseline methods in terms of review count. A method is effective if the review numbers of lodging places recommended by the method are large. Figure 5 shows that the performance of our proposed method ranks #1 with respect to precision and ranks #3 in terms of recall. Although Coordinate Ascent and RankBoost methods outperform our method with respect to recall and f-measure, our method still outperforms price based ranking (unsupervised), as well as AdaRank (supervised), which is traditionally expected to outperform our unsupervised method.

Look back to all the three criteria (i.e. satisfaction rating, time-on-market, review count), our method stand out from all the compared methods due to the following aspects: (i) our proposed method strive a balanced performance among the three criteria; (2) our proposed method is unsupervised without expensive quality ratings as supervised information.

4.6 Balance Check between Benefit and Risk

We evaluate our recommendation approach by checking whether it can achieve a balance between accommodation benefits and community risks. Specifically, there are two measures of lodging places, i.e., accommodation benefit scores and community risk scores. If a recommendation system outputs a list of top-K lodging places, we use (i) a benefit emphasis metric, measured by NDCG(benefit) and (ii) a risk emphasis metric, measured by NDCG(risk), to check the balance of a top-K list between benefit emphasis and risk emphasis. To compute the NDCG(benefit) and NDCG(risk) of a top-K

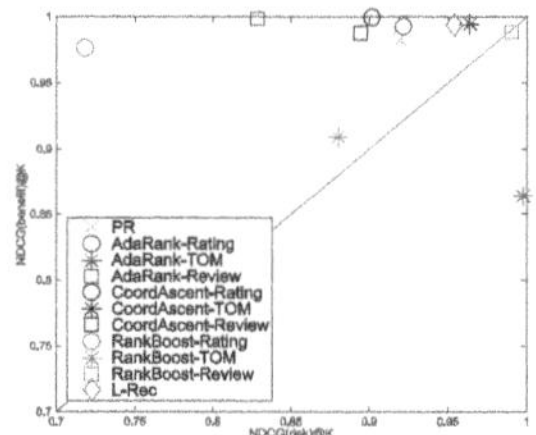

(a) K=5

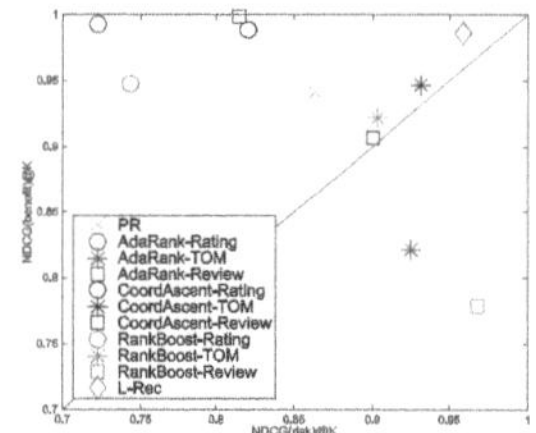

(b) K=10

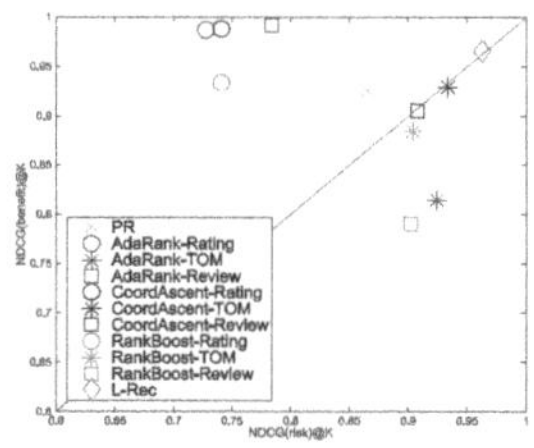

(c) K=15

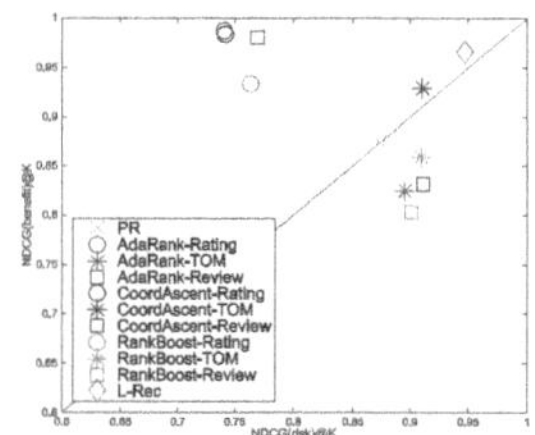

(d) K=20

Figure 6: Balance check on different methods between NDCG(benefit)@K and NDCG(risk)@K. AdaRank-Rating: AdaRank trained on satisfaction ratings; AdaRank-TOM: AdaRank trained on time on market; AdaRank-Review: AdaRank trained on review count. The naming policy is similar for other methods.

list, the relevance scores *rel* in Equation 9 are set to be the benefit score and the risk score, respectively. Intuitively, if a top-K list has higher NDCG(benefit) or NDCG(risk), it means that the list has more emphasis on the positive or negative side. Thereby, we prefer a top-K list with both high NDCG(benefit) and high NDCG(risk). Figure 6 visualizes the balance check of different methods on top-K (K=5, 10, 15, 20) recommendation between benefit emphasis and risk emphasis, where x-axis represents risk emphasis and y-axis represents benefit emphasis. We can observe that our proposed method is located in the upper-right corners of four subfigures. This observation indicates our method has both highest benefit emphasis and highest risk emphasis. Also, with the increase of K, the recommendation results of both our method and the baselines have more emphasis on risks than benefits.

4.7 Efficiency Study

We compare our enhanced learning to integer programming (LIP) with three baseline methods: (i) traditional branch and bound with strong branching (BB) [2] ; (ii) simulated annealing (SA) [3] ; and (iii) genetic algorithm (GA) [4] . While GA and SA are developed for local optimum, BB and our enhanced BB are developed for global optimum. Theoretically, BB and our LIP method can outperform GA and SA with respect to recommendation effectiveness and robustness. Here, we focus on comparing their running time in terms of different percentages of candidate lodging places. Table 4 shows our LIP method can greatly reduce the time cost compared with BB, GA, and SA. The reasons are: GA and SA are probabilistic iterative searching methods and their convergence requires more iterations. Compared with BB, LIP combines both BB and a branching variable selector learned via an aggregated listwise ranking strategy. The selector can mimic and learn how to select the best branching variable. Therefore, LIP method can save time.

[2] https://cran.r-project.org/web/packages/lpSolve/

[3] https://cran.r-project.org/web/packages/GenSA/

[4] https://cran.r-project.org/web/packages/genalg/

Table 4: Running time comparison (in seconds) between our method (LIP) and baseline methods over different percentages of training data.

Percentage	GA	SA	BB	LIP
0.4	663.645	985.657	13.121	**19.134**
0.6	689.848	1064.740	44.873	**30.419**
0.8	759.948	1152.539	152.189	**82.872**
1	867.753	1208.099	235.459	**122.287**

4.8 Discussions

Different from traditional supervised methods (e.g., collaborative filtering, matrix factorization), we focus on an alternative and different perspective by formulating recommendation in P2P environments as an unsupervised problem based on integer programming, where utility of recommendations is maximized by considering positive and negative sides while personalizations are implemented based on constraints. We find that such an unsupervised strategy can be very helpful for simultaneously achieving a balance among multiple criteria (satisfaction, time on market, number of reviews). Also, we adapt the idea of learning by analogy and combine the branch and bound method with a branching variable selector, which is learned by listwise learning to rank. The strategy can improve the efficiency. From the preliminary results, we believe it is promising to exploit more supervised learning methods to learn and mimic the decision making processes of searching optimal solutions in integer programming.

5 RELATED WORK

The related work can be categorized into the following categories: (i) utility-based recommendations; (ii) learning to optimize, (vi) P2P rental markets.

Utility based Recommendations. Our work is relevant to utility based recommendations. Most recommendation approaches utilize users' ratings for items to predict their preferences, and recommend users with items that have highest predicted ratings. Nevertheless, there also exist several work that ignore the ratings due to their low quality and sparsity, and different optimization goals. For instance, users' utility functions are defined to better capture multiple dimensions of recommender systems, since rational users aim to maximize their utility in the decision process [14]. [6] further decomposed the overall product utility as the sum-product of contributions of interest dimensions and the utility in each dimension. [15] incorporated explicit utility into recommendation process, which is revealed by users' actions. A mixed integer programming (MIP) is formulated by introducing the setwise minmax decision rules, and items are recommended by solving the optimization problem. [4] designed a utility function for query search, and recommend queries by optimizing the utility function. [16] defined a marginal net utility function to better match users' purchase decisions in e-commerce websites, and further designed a utility based SVD algorithm to recommend items.

Learning To Optimize. Our work is related to the research of Learning To Optimize that applies machine learning approaches to improve optimization. The idea of learning heuristic functions for combinatorial search algorithms dates back to [5, 12]. Particularly, [5] proposed a learning approach named STAGE to automatically improving search performance on optimization problems. Recently, [2] developed a set of features to describe the states of ongoing optimization procedures and used extremely randomized trees to predict strong branching scores. [3] proposed a machine learning approach to load balancing in parallel branch-and-bound for MIP. [9] presented a method for learning an adaptive node searching order for any class of problem solvable by branch-and-bound. More recently,[11] collected and combined the strong branching scores of all the branching variables during BB into a single global ranking list, and trained a previously-proposed pairwise ranking function for selecting variables. However, in many cases, there is no global metric, i.e., strong branching scores, for compiling a global ranking list of candidate branching variables.

To be generalized, we use binary indicator (selected or not-selected) to represent the local rankings at each branch during BB, and thus there are multiple local ranking lists for the entire BB process. Our proposed aggregated listwise ranking method can aggregate these local ranking lists and collectively learn the patterns about how BB selects the best branching variables. Therefore, our method is more robust and generalized.

P2P Rental Markets. Finally, our work has a connection with P2P rental markets. With regards to the application of P2P rental markets, recent work focused on the market efficiency, searching and ranking problems on the market. [7] studied the efficiency of P2P markets and the effects of ranking algorithms on the search and matching process using internal data from Airbnb. The results show that potential guests engaged in limited search are frequently rejected by hosts, and match at lower rates, while an algorithm with personalized constraints would increase the matching rate by up to 10%. [18] revealed the nuances of user-generated ratings in the context of the sharing economy and find that there only exists weak correlations between the ratings of the listings across different platforms. Our work aims to resolve one of the challenges in P2P rental markets, that is, to address rating sparsity and quality issues, provide effective recommendations, and overcome information imbalance between providers and consumers.

6 CONCLUSION REMARKS

Traditional single rating-based recommender systems (e.g., collaborative filtering) may often encounter challenges when ratings are sparse, dynamic, and expensive. According to Multi-Attribute Utility Theory, choices are made in terms of multiple criteria, which inspire people to seek for information from heterogeneous data sources, and further make choices by navigating the multiple criteria and maximizing utility. Following the decision process, we have presented an unsupervised optimization framework to effectively and efficiently recommend products with the goal of maximizing the utility under multi-criteria concerns. Particularly, we apply the framework to the P2P lodging rental markets.

To accomplish the goal, we firstly propose a fast unsupervised fused scoring method for assessing both the benefits and risks of products from cross-domain data, in order to objectively evaluate the utility of products. Besides, the objective of maximizing the utility is closely related to a knapsack problem, and thus a constrained integer programming problem is formulated to provide flexibility for navigating multiple criteria. In addition, we propose an enhanced branch-and-bound method by incorporating aggregated listwise ranking for enhancing efficiency. The aggregated listwise ranker can mimic and learn the decision policy of strong branching and speed up the selection of branching variables. Finally, the empirical experiments on P2P lodging rental market data has demonstrated the effectiveness in striking a trade-off among user satisfaction, time on market, and number of reviews, while the optimization efficiency is significantly improved.

Acknowledgment. This is research was partially supported University of Missouri Research Board (UMRB) via proposal number: 4991.

REFERENCES

[1] Tobias Achterberg, Thorsten Koch, and Alexander Martin. 2005. Branching rules revisited. *Operations Research Letters* 33, 1 (2005), 42–54.

[2] Alejandro Marcos Alvarez, Quentin Louveaux, and Louis Wehenkel. 2014. A supervised machine learning approach to variable branching in branch-and-bound. In *In ECML*. Citeseer.

[3] Alejandro Marcos Alvarez, Louis Wehenkel, and Quentin Louveaux. 2014. Machine Learning to Balance the Load in Parallel Branch-and-Bound. (2014).

[4] Aris Anagnostopoulos, Luca Becchetti, Carlos Castillo, and Aristides Gionis. 2010. An optimization framework for query recommendation. In *Proceedings of the third ACM international conference on Web search and data mining*. ACM, 161–170.

[5] Justin A Boyan and Andrew W Moore. 1998. Learning evaluation functions for global optimization and boolean satisfiability. In *AAAI/IAAI*. 3–10.

[6] Alexander Felfernig, Bartosz Gula, Gerhard Leitner, Marco Maier, Rudolf Melcher, and Erich Teppan. 2008. Persuasion in knowledge-based recommendation. In *International Conference on Persuasive Technology*. Springer, 71–82.

[7] Andrey Fradkin. 2013. *Search frictions and the design of online marketplaces*. Technical Report. Tech. rep., Working paper, Stanford University.

[8] Yoav Freund, Raj Iyer, Robert E Schapire, and Yoram Singer. 2003. An efficient boosting algorithm for combining preferences. *The Journal of machine learning research* (2003).

[9] He He, Hal Daume III, and Jason M Eisner. 2014. Learning to Search in Branch and Bound Algorithms. In *Advances in Neural Information Processing Systems*. 3293–3301.

[10] Xiaofei He, Deng Cai, and Partha Niyogi. 2005. Laplacian score for feature selection. In *Advances in neural information processing systems*. 507–514.

[11] Elias B Khalil, Pierre Le Bodic, Le Song, George Nemhauser, and Bistra Dilkina. 2016. Learning to Branch in Mixed Integer Programming. In *Thirtieth AAAI Conference on Artificial Intelligence*.

[12] Matthew Lowrie and Benjamin Wah. 1988. Learning heuristic functions for numeric optimization problems. In *Computer Software and Applications Conference, 1988. COMPSAC 88. Proceedings., Twelfth International*. IEEE, 443–450.

[13] Donald Metzler and W Bruce Croft. 2007. Linear feature-based models for information retrieval. *Information Retrieval* (2007).

[14] J von Neumann, Oskar Morgenstern, and others. 1944. *Theory of games and economic behavior*. Vol. 60. Princeton university press Princeton.

[15] Paolo Viappiani and Craig Boutilier. 2009. Regret-based optimal recommendation sets in conversational recommender systems. In *Proceedings of the third ACM conference on Recommender systems*. ACM, 101–108.

[16] Jian Wang and Yi Zhang. 2011. Utilizing marginal net utility for recommendation in e-commerce. In *Proceedings of the 34th international ACM SIGIR conference on Research and development in Information Retrieval*. ACM, 1003–1012.

[17] Jun Xu and Hang Li. 2007. Adarank: a boosting algorithm for information retrieval. In *Proceedings of the 30th annual international ACM SIGIR conference on Research and development in information retrieval*. ACM, 391–398.

[18] Georgios Zervas, Davide Proserpio, and John Byers. 2015. A First Look at Online Reputation on Airbnb, Where Every Stay is Above Average. *Where Every Stay is Above Average (January 23, 2015)* (2015).

The Co-Evolution Model for Social Network Evolving and Opinion Migration

Yupeng Gu
University of California, Los Angeles
Los Angeles, CA
ypgu@cs.ucla.edu

Yizhou Sun
University of California, Los Angeles
Los Angeles, CA
yzsun@cs.ucla.edu

Jianxi Gao
Northeastern University
Boston, MA
j.gao@neu.edu

ABSTRACT

Almost all real-world social networks are dynamic and evolving with time, where new links may form and old links may drop, largely determined by the homophily of social actors (i.e., nodes in the network). Meanwhile, (latent) properties of social actors, such as their opinions, are changing along the time, partially due to social influence received from the network, which will in turn affect the network structure. Social network evolution and node property migration are usually treated as two orthogonal problems, and have been studied separately. In this paper, we propose a co-evolution model that closes the loop by modeling the two phenomena together, which contains two major components: (1) a network generative model when the node property is known; and (2) a property migration model when the social network structure is known. Simulation shows that our model has several nice properties: (1) it can model a broad range of phenomena such as opinion convergence (i.e., herding) and community-based opinion divergence; and (2) it allows to control the evolution via a set of factors such as social influence scope, opinion leader, and noise level. Finally, the usefulness of our model is demonstrated by an application of co-sponsorship prediction for legislative bills in Congress, which outperforms several state-of-the-art baselines.

CCS CONCEPTS

•Information systems →Data mining;

KEYWORDS

Dynamic networks; network generation models; co-evolution

1 INTRODUCTION

Social network analysis has become prevalent as the variety and popularity of information networks increase. In the real world, networks are evolving constantly with links joining and dropping over time. Meantime, properties of social actors in these networks, such as their opinions, are constantly changing as well. One example is the political ideology migration for two parties in U.S. Figure 1 shows the 1-dimensional mean ideology for members in two political parties via ideal point estimation using their historical voting records [12]. A similar discovery can be seen in [2]. We can clearly observe the divergence of ideologies of the two communities (i.e. the Democrats and Republicans), especially the polarization trend since 1960s. A natural question raises, *why such divergence happens and is there any possible intervention we can have to alleviate such polarization?* In this paper, we attempt to interpret this phenomenon and thus propose a unified co-evolution model for link evolution as well as (latent) node property migration in social networks.

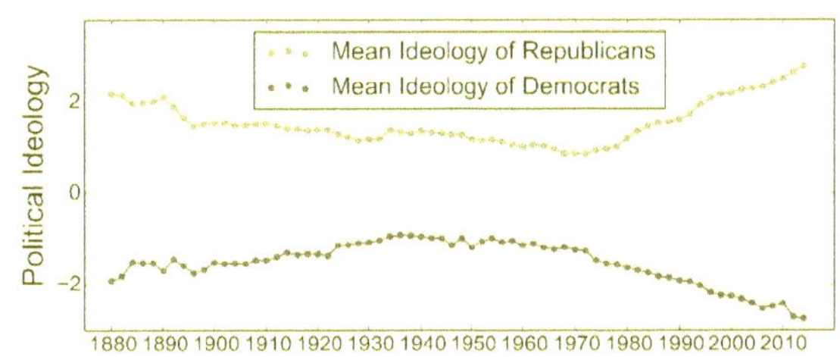

Figure 1: Ideology migration of the two parties in U.S.

On one hand, people in social networks exhibit great diversity and are associated with different properties (e.g., hidden properties such as political ideology). Interactions between individuals are more likely to happen within people that are alike, described as "homophily" in social network analysis [28]. With this principle, network generative models such as blockmodels [18, 44] and latent space models [17] have emerged, where each individual is assigned with a feature vector denoting her latent properties (i.e., a position in a latent space). Individuals that are close in the latent space are likely to have interactions in the network.

On the other hand, like flocks of collectively moving animals, people in social networks comprise a system of interacting, permanently moving units. In fact, the changing of location is ubiquitous among many kinds of creatures in real life: flocks of birds fly and migrate; colonies of ants and drones work and move to seek for foods. This phenomenon is also overwhelming in the realm of social network analysis, where people's latent position (e.g., ideology) are migrating with their crowds (e.g., parties). In other words, individuals are likely to be affected by their friends or who they interact with in the social network. This "social influence" [22, 41] assumption has been widely applied in literature. For example, in an information diffusion model, a person will be activated (i.e. the binary status is switched to "on") if she has enough activated neighbors [14].

Inspired by these observations, in this paper we propose a probabilistic co-evolution model that explains the evolution of networks

KDD'17, August 13–17, 2017, Halifax, NS, Canada.
 ISBN 978-1-4503-4887-4/17/08...$15.00
DOI: http://dx.doi.org/10.1145/3097983.3098002

as well as the migration of node properties, which contains two major components: (1) a network generative model when the node property is known; and (2) a property migration model when the social network structure is known. First, in terms of network evolution, similar to existing work, we assume the network is a reflection of node's latent properties. Our network generative model assumes (1) individuals have a higher chance to interact with people who are alike; and (2) opinion leaders attract more people and thus interact with more people. Second, in terms of property migration, we notice how creatures in biological systems and how particles in molecular systems propagate: they are influenced by their spatial neighbors to a large extent. We generalize the notion of "spatial neighbors" to "friends" in social network, and people's moving direction is influenced by their friends' moving directions.

Simulation shows that our model has several nice properties: (1) it can model a broad range of phenomena such as opinion convergence (i.e., herding) and community-based opinion divergence; and (2) it allows us to control the evolution via a set of factors such as social influence scope, opinion leader, and noise level. By learning system-level parameters via a series of historical snapshots of networks, predictions can be made about the evolution of the whole system in the future. We demonstrate the usefulness of our model by an application of co-sponsorship prediction for legislative bills in Congress, which outperforms several state-of-the-art baselines.

The contributions of our paper are summarized as follows:

- We propose a unified co-evolution model that captures the evolution of network structure as well as the migration of node properties.
- Under different system-level parameter settings, our model is able to exhibit different behaviors of network evolution and property migration.
- Our model is capable of inference via learning from real-world data. Empirical results reveal our advantage over state-of-the-art approaches in terms of a co-sponsorship prediction task.

2 PRELIMINARY OF COLLECTIVE MOTION

In the realm of biological systems, collective motion is one of the most common and spectacular manifestation of coordinated behavior [19, 43]. Flocks of birds fly and migrate uniformly as a group; ants are famous for their large and well-organized hierarchies, and individuals in each hierarchy exhibit highly coherent behaviors; a school of fish swim in a tightly organized way in terms of speed and direction. Collective motion is also observed in phase transition process as in many particle systems, and a well known line of work [42] describes their collective motion model as follows. Each particle moves at a constant rate v, while the direction of motion is determined by the average direction of all others within its neighborhood of radius r, plus some random perturbation. Denoting a particle n's position at time t by $\boldsymbol{x}_n(t)$, it is assumed to be updated according to

$$\frac{d}{dt}\boldsymbol{x}_n(t) = \boldsymbol{v}_n(t) \tag{1}$$

where $\boldsymbol{v}_n(t) = v \cdot (\cos\theta_n(t), \sin\theta_n(t))$ is its moving direction at t. The direction will be consistently adjusted by it spatial neighbors:

$$\theta_n(t+1) = \langle\theta_n(t)\rangle + \Delta\theta \tag{2}$$

where $\langle\theta_n(t)\rangle$ is the direction averaged by n's spatial neighbors within radius r, i.e. $\{m : ||\boldsymbol{x}_n(t) - \boldsymbol{x}_m(t)|| \leq r\}$. v is the absolute value of each particle's velocity and is assumed to remain the same for every particle during the transition process. Noise $\Delta\theta$ is randomly chosen uniformly from interval $[-\eta/2, \eta/2]$, where η controls the noise level.

Spatial neighbors play a crucial role in above systems. Notice that, however, in the setting of social networks, individuals are assumed to receive social influence only from their friends rather than anyone who are close to them. This inspires us to design the co-evolution model as introduced in next section.

3 THE CO-EVOLUTION MODEL

The position migration in biological and molecule systems mentioned in Section 2 are a good analogy to the opinion migration for individuals in social networks. Like flocks of collectively moving animals, people on social networks also comprise a system of interacting, permanently moving units in terms of latent opinions or stances. Different from biological systems, in social networks people form social ties where information propagate through. In other words, every individual is exposed to a group of "friends" and receives influence merely from them. This phenomenon is referred to as "social influence" or "social selection" [7, 22, 41] in literature. In turn, new/old links in social networks may form/drop as a result of individuals' opinion migration, due to "homophily" [28]. Since opinion is an important property of an entity, we use the terms *opinion*, *property* and *feature* interchangeably in this paper, to denote the intrinsic characteristics belonging to an individual on social network.

By putting (1) social influence-based opinion migration and (2) homophily-based network generation together, we then have our co-evolution model, which is introduced in the remaining of this section.

3.1 Social Network Generation

Latent space models [17] assume the snapshot of a static social network is generated based on the positions of individuals in an unobserved social space. This latent space consists of unobserved latent characteristics of people that represent potential tendencies in network relations. In these network generation models, the generation of each link is independent on each other, and is based purely on the positions of two users. We could design any score function $s : \mathcal{R}^K \times \mathcal{R}^K \rightarrow \mathcal{R}$ that assigns a score to a pair of node features $(\boldsymbol{x}_n, \boldsymbol{x}_m)$, which indicates the likelihood of observing the presence of the link in between. The score function is crucial to the network and its properties, and we discuss two possibilities below.

Dot Product-based Score Function. In tons of existing works, dot product of two features vectors is used to capture the similarity between them [3, 21, 30, 31, 40]. However, this generation model contradicts with the following observation.

Obviously, node degree is associated with the choice of score function. The higher chance of a node has to issue links to others, the larger degree it will be. Vector norm plays an important role in inner product; as a result, those actors with a large norm (i.e. $||\boldsymbol{x}_n||$) tend to attract interests from a large group of others, and thus become opinion leaders in the generation process. To demonstrate this, we show the 2-dimensional position of two users A and B as well as their affected regions in Figure 2(a). The affected region of a user is defined as the set of people who can be influenced by her (i.e. their score function exceeds some threshold). User A has a position of $(3, 3)$ and B is located at $(-1, -0.5)$. It is obvious from the plot that user A are far more likely to befriend others (even those with less cosine similarity) than B, simply because A is further away from the origin than B is. In other words, people with extreme stances (i.e. large norms of latent feature vector) will become the opinion leader. However in most cases, the most popular people are either around the center of the entire population, or the center in their community. For example, it is found that radical politicians on the ideology spectrum are hardly party leaders [34]. In addition, each actor has limited resources and energy, which sets a constraint on one's spreadable radius. Preferably, the score function is invariant of the scale, and the affected region should have limited area (i.e. bounded).

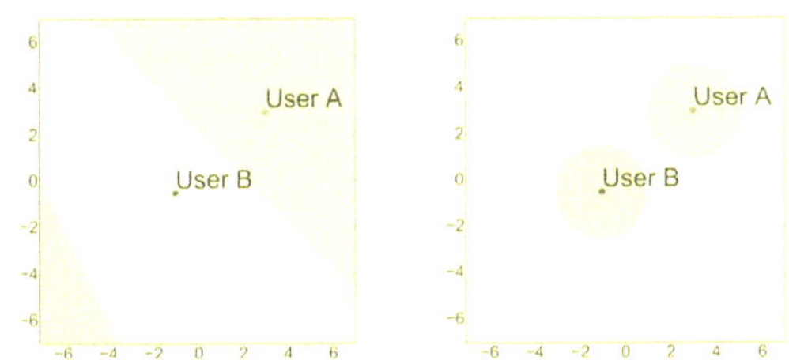

(a) Inner product-based similarity (b) Distance-based similarity

Figure 2: Affected regions (colored area) for two users with different similarity functions. Nodes in the affected region are prone to interact with the corresponding user in the same color (i.e., red region for User A and blue region for User B).

Gravity-based Score Function. We recall that herds of animals have the notion of "spatial neighbors" when they migrate and collaborate. In molecule systems, nearby molecules also account for the majority of the interaction. Inspired by these observations, it is reasonable to set the score function between two users to be based on their Euclidean distance. We adapt the inverse squared gravity formula in our definition of score function. Using the new metric, we show the affected region of two users in Figure 2(b). Although the feature vectors of user A and B have different scales, the spaces of their friend candidates are comparable.

In the graph generation model, when we want to determine the link between two actors, the score function is mapped to a probability using Gaussian function:

$$p_{nm} = \exp(-\frac{1}{\epsilon^2} \cdot \frac{||\boldsymbol{x}_n - \boldsymbol{x}_m||^2}{b_n \cdot b_m}) \tag{3}$$

where ϵ is a model hyper-parameter, and $\{b_n\} \subset \mathbb{R}^+$ is another set of parameters which reflect the popularity of actors. The link will be generated if $p_{nm} > d$, where d is a system parameter which controls sparsity of the network, and a larger d means fewer neighbors an actor can interact with. For geometric interpretation, b_n is proportional to the radius of one's neighborhood, and opinion leaders will be the ones with largest values of b. In other words, opinion leaders are more likely (with higher probability) to interact with other actors. As the formula $\frac{b_n \cdot b_m}{||\boldsymbol{x}_n - \boldsymbol{x}_m||^2}$ resembles the law of gravity, we call this score function as gravity-based.

3.2 Opinion Migration

Similar to the migration of fish and flocks of birds, individuals in social networks also exhibit collective behaviors, which is modeled in this section.

Earlier work [6, 16, 36, 37, 45, 46] on modeling property change is quite straightforward: properties at adjacent timestamps (e.g. $\boldsymbol{x}^{\langle t \rangle}$, $\boldsymbol{x}^{\langle t+1 \rangle}$) are forced to be similar via various kinds of regularization/prior in order to avoid abrupt changes. For example, $\boldsymbol{x}^{\langle t+1 \rangle}$ is assumed to be generated from a Gaussian prior centered on its previous position $\boldsymbol{x}^{\langle t \rangle}$. However, this plausible strategy has two major flaws, which greatly reduce the power of the generation model.

First of all, let us investigate the activity of two actors in Figure 3. Here X-axis denotes the timestamp, and Y-axis denotes the 1-dimensional latent position. According to the migration prior defined above, the behavior of user X and Y are equally possible; however in real life, it is more likely to observe the trajectory of user Y (moving along the same direction) rather than X (oscillating). The same phenomenon is observed in flocks of animals as well: a school of fish tends to move towards some direction instead of wandering around some places.

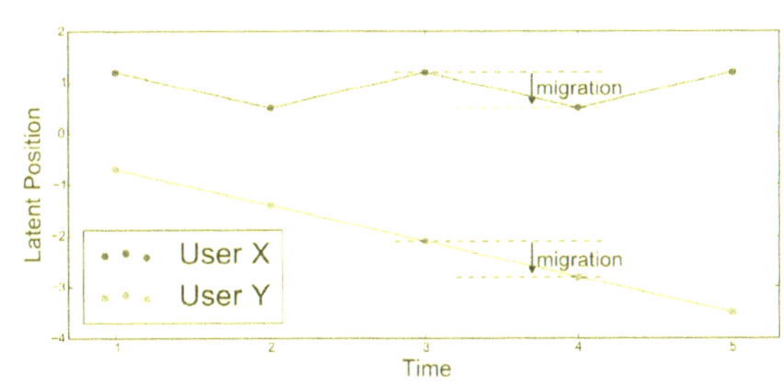

Figure 3: An example of two people's migration.

Secondly, social influence should be involved in the migration process, and the generation model should be able to express different properties of the random network under different system settings. For example, we may observe the polarization of opinions in some networks, i.e. multiple clusters of people heading towards different directions. However, if latent features evolve solely according to their previous positions, it is unlikely that individuals will automatically form several clusters.

In a recent work [16], social influence are included in the generation model. Simply generalizing their binary features into continuous features, we have

$$\boldsymbol{x}_n^{\langle t+1 \rangle} \sim \mathcal{N}\Big((1-\lambda) \cdot \boldsymbol{x}_n^{\langle t \rangle} + \lambda \cdot \langle \boldsymbol{x}_n^{\langle t \rangle} \rangle, \sigma^2\Big) \tag{4}$$

where $\langle \boldsymbol{x}_n^{\langle t \rangle} \rangle$ is the average position of user u_n's neighbors at time t, and $\mathcal{N}(\mu, \sigma^2)$ is the normal distribution with mean μ and variance

σ^2. A toy example of 2-dimensional feature migration under this framework is shown in Figure 4. We see that although two clusters emerge after several steps (nodes in the middle are going upwards and downwards), they are trapped in a local area and refuse to keep moving upwards or downwards since the clusters are formed. In other words, people's opinions will no longer change after communities are developed. The principal reason lies in that propagation model: the moving tendency of nodes is never captured; instead, entities update their positions arbitrarily, and they lack the motivation to move in a stable status.

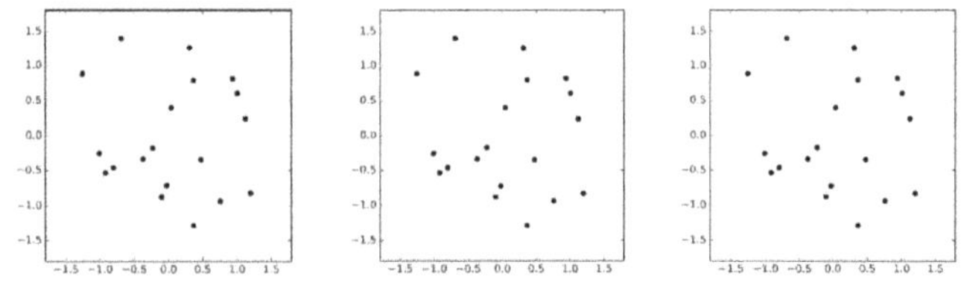

(a) $t = 0$ (initial) (b) $t = 200$ (c) $t = 400$

Figure 4: Position migration of $N = 20$ nodes. 3 nearest neighbors of each node are chosen as friends in the network.

To overcome these problems, a natural approach is to track the historic features, such as setting a global regularization term in addition to features in adjacent steps. However, the lack of Markov property would make the generation process less intuitive and much more complex, and inference would be impossible due to high computational cost. Here we seek for a solution from the propagation in the nature. It is rare to observe a flock of animals turn around frequently; similarly, a person should gradually change her interest in some dimension (e.g. her enthusiasm of a topic may be dropping) instead of keeping switching between two viewpoints. Therefore, we keep track of velocity, i.e., the direction (which can be regarded as the first derivation of displacement), and punish its volatile changes.

Therefore, in terms of opinion migration, we introduce the direction that a user u_n is heading as an angle θ_n, and the latent position of each user will be updated according to the basic displacement formula:

$$\frac{d}{dt}\boldsymbol{x}_n(t) = v \cdot (\cos\theta_n(t),\ \sin\theta_n(t)) \tag{5}$$

where v is a constant factor indicating absolute speed, and the unit vector $(\cos\theta_n(t), \sin\theta_n(t))$ represents u_n's moving direction at time t. In reality, we observe discrete snapshots of social networks. Therefore, we write the above equation in its discrete form as

$$\boldsymbol{x}_n^{\langle t+1\rangle} = \boldsymbol{x}_n^{\langle t\rangle} + v \cdot (\cos\theta_n^{\langle t\rangle},\ \sin\theta_n^{\langle t\rangle}) \tag{6}$$

The remaining question is how $\theta_n^{\langle t\rangle}$ propagates. It is worth noticing how every member in a flock of birds picks its direction. When some flocks of birds head west and others head north, an observer bird is likely to pick either direction instead of south or east. During a migration, people are likely to take similar paths as their families and close friends. This strategy is believed to have advantages such as more efficient explorations for resources and improved decision making in larger groups [43]. In sum, it is very rare that a member chooses to behave oppositely to its friends. When it comes to social networks, people also adopt similar behaviors as their neighbors [22]. We probably have already observed the following facts in our real life. A scholar tends to raise interest in a research topic that is trending among her collaborators. A Democrat is likely to become more liberal, if she feels her acquaintances are going "left" (and vice versa). Social network provides exposure to one's neighbors, and this factor will be reflected in the formation of direction variables. Therefore in our model, a person's moving direction is assumed to be influenced by her neighbors' directions, and is subject to a noise of some magnitude:

$$\theta_n^{\langle t+1\rangle} \sim \mathcal{N}(\langle\theta_n^{\langle t\rangle}\rangle, \sigma^2) \tag{7}$$

where $\langle\theta_n^{\langle t\rangle}\rangle$ is the average direction of u_n's neighbors' (including herself) at time t. In the above case, when a bird observes 10 others heading west and 20 others heading north, the average direction of other birds is about 63° north of west. Therefore in most cases, the observer will fly in a similar direction (follows either the west or north group), as it would incur great penalty if it flies south or east instead. Intrinsically, the parameter σ controls how easily people are influenced by their neighbors (or how strictly a person should follow the trend of their neighbors): larger σ will relax the regularization.

In the discussion above, the dimension of node feature is set to 2 in order to make the propagation process more intuitive. Nevertheless, our method is not subject to this constraint and can be easily generalized to higher dimensional latent spaces using polar/hyperspherical coordinate systems [1]. For example, the direction $(\cos\theta_n(t),\ \sin\theta_n(t))$ in Equation 5 can be replaced by any dimensional unit-length vector with polar coordinates. The average direction determined by Equation 7 simply becomes the (normalized) vector summation. In the remaining of the paper, we will use 2-dimensional representations for visualization purposes.

Note that our regularization on the direction θ already implies the regularization of feature $\boldsymbol{x}$. This is trivial since the change of a variable is reflected in its first derivative. In particular, $||\boldsymbol{x}_n^{\langle t+1\rangle} - \boldsymbol{x}_n^{\langle t\rangle}||$ is fixed for every t, which means abnormal change in the feature space is impossible. Therefore, our model has further contributions while inheriting the advantages of existing propagation approaches.

3.3 Unified Model

Putting them together, the evolution of network and migration of entity opinions happen iteratively after each other in our co-evolution model. At each timestamp t, a network is generated given node latent features (homophily), and node directions are generated according to the network structure (social influence), thus determine the latent feature for the next timestamp $t + 1$ (migration). System-level parameters include sparsity parameter d which controls the sparsity of the graph (i.e. the average number of friends), and noise level σ which implies the deviation of one's direction from the expected value. The generative process of our co-evolution model is summarized in Algorithm 1.

input : number of users N; number of timestamps T; sparsity parameter d; noise level σ.
output : a series of graphs and users' latent positions.
initialization;
for $t = 1$ *to* T **do**
  // graph generation
  for $n, m = 1$ *to* N **do**
    calculate p_{nm};
    determine the link between n and m as $G_{nm}^{\langle t \rangle} = 1$ if $p_{nm} > d$;
  end
  // opinion migration
  if $t == 1$ **then**
    for $n = 1$ *to* N **do**
      sample $\theta_n^{\langle t \rangle} \sim \text{Uniform}[0, 2\pi)$;
      update $\mathbf{x}^{\langle t+1 \rangle} = \mathbf{x}^{\langle t \rangle} + v \cdot (\cos\theta_n^{\langle t \rangle}, \sin\theta_n^{\langle t \rangle})$;
    end
  else
    for $n = 1$ *to* N **do**
      sample $\theta_n^{\langle t \rangle} \sim \mathcal{N}(\langle \theta_n^{\langle t-1 \rangle} \rangle, \sigma^2)$;
      update $\mathbf{x}^{\langle t+1 \rangle} = \mathbf{x}^{\langle t \rangle} + v \cdot (\cos\theta_n^{\langle t \rangle}, \sin\theta_n^{\langle t \rangle})$;
    end
  end
end

Algorithm 1: Generation model for co-evolution

4 SIMULATION

To reveal the properties of our generation model, we run simulations and show the migration of individuals in the network for selected parameters. For initialization, every node is randomly assigned a 2-dimensional initial position in the lattice of $[-L/2, L/2] \times [-L/2, L/2]$ where $L = 5$, as well as a popularity $b \sim \text{Uniform}([1, 2])$. b will be fixed throughout the migration process. Initializations are identical across all parameter settings.

According to [42], we adopt the absolute value of average normalized velocity as a measure for the system status:

$$v_{ave} = \frac{1}{N} \left| \sum_{n=1}^{N} (\cos\theta_n, \sin\theta_n) \right| \quad (8)$$

$v_{ave} \in [0, 1]$ and in general, $v_{ave} = 1$ means completely coherent moving behavior, while $v_{ave} = 0$ means completely randomness, or two groups of equal number of people moving towards opposite directions. In Figure 5 we plot the metric v_{ave} under different parameter settings.

Noise level. Noise level σ controls how uniformly individuals proceed. Intuitively, a large σ will overwrite the direction determined by one's neighbors, thus leads to more random migration behaviors. In Figure 5(a) we can see $v_{ave} \approx 0$ for large σ. People tend to behave collectively in groups with small σ values.

Sparsity parameter. Sparsity parameter d plays a role in the emergence of clusters. A larger value of d leads to a sparser network, therefore people interact with only a few others. In this case, communities are allowed to maintain their own direction, and it is more likely to observe several clusters with different migration directions. On the other hand, when the threshold is small, an individual is easily linked to most others, therefore information is prone to spread through the entire network, making almost all the people to propagate coherently. In Figure 5(b) we can see v_{ave} is larger for smaller d values.

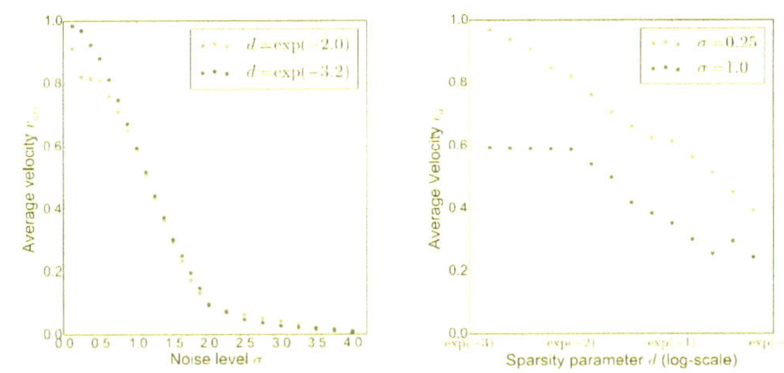

(a) Effect of noise level σ (b) Effect of sparsity parameter d

Figure 5: System-level parameter study

We show people's positions and their moving directions in Figure 6. Each row corresponds to a set of system-level parameters. Absolute value of velocity is set to $v = 0.03$ and moving directions are shown as unit-length arrows starting from one's position. Opinion leaders (top 5% people with largest b) are marked in red.

Observations. We can see in most cases, the opinion leaders are surrounded by others and appear in the center of a community, which agrees with our findings in Section 3.1. In addition, the effect of system-level parameters is also revealed in these examples: networks tend to be very random when noise level σ is large (comparing first and second row). Under a small noise level, sparsity parameter d comes into play: a small d makes the network denser, thus communities have more overlapping entities and are likely to act coherently; while a large d reduces the scope of individuals, and clusters may emerge and head towards different directions (comparing first and third row). In sum, initially, sparsity, small noise and different directions of opinion leaders are necessary in order for opinion convergence within each community, which eventually leads to emergence of clusters.

Intervention. Now back to the question raised in introduction section: how can we alleviate the divergence of communities? From the above observations, one solution is to reduce σ and enlarge d. Under this setting, people are exposed to many others, follow their directions without much perturbation and a uniform global trend is likely to occur. Another alternative is utilizing opinion leaders to advertise and propagate similar directions of migration. Thanks to their high popularity, they are likely to interact with more people in their neighborhood, and thus play a role in deciding others' directions. In Figure 6(a)-6(c), we already observe the emergence of two clusters with different directions. Following Figure 6(c), we flip and fix the directions of the three leaders in the left community as in Figure 7(a); as a result, people in the left cluster will gradually alter their directions following the leaders (Figure 7(a)-7(c)).

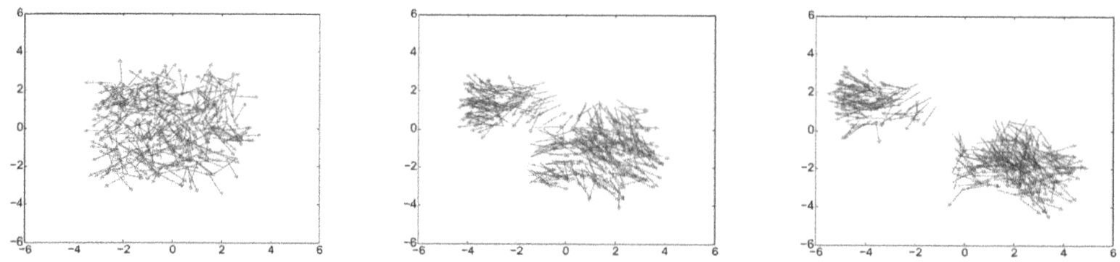

(a) $t = 0$ (init) (b) $t = 40$ (c) $t = 80$

Noise level $\sigma = 0.5$. Sparsity parameter $d = \exp(-0.4)$.

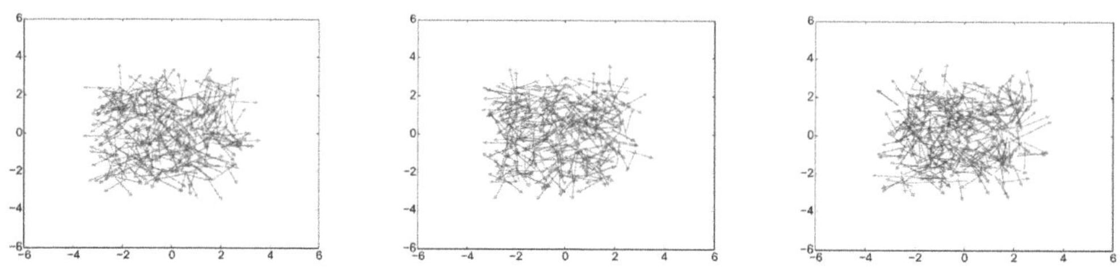

(d) $t = 0$ (init) (e) $t = 40$ (f) $t = 80$

Noise level $\sigma = 2.0$. Sparsity parameter $d = \exp(-0.4)$.

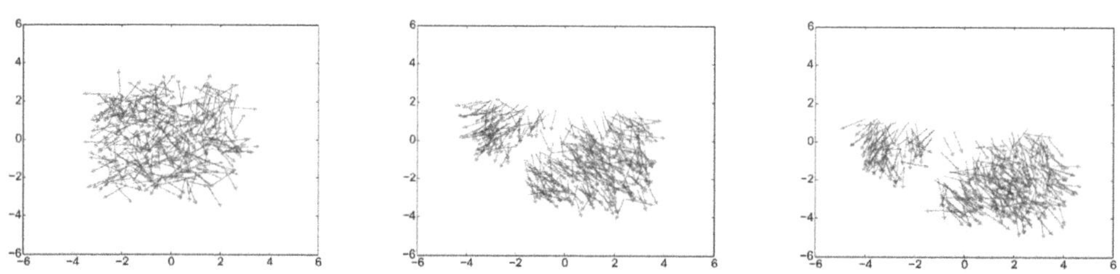

(g) $t = 0$ (init) (h) $t = 40$ (i) $t = 80$

Noise level $\sigma = 0.5$. Sparsity parameter $d = \exp(-2.0)$.

Figure 6: Migration of entities in the network. Each row corresponds to one setting of system parameters.

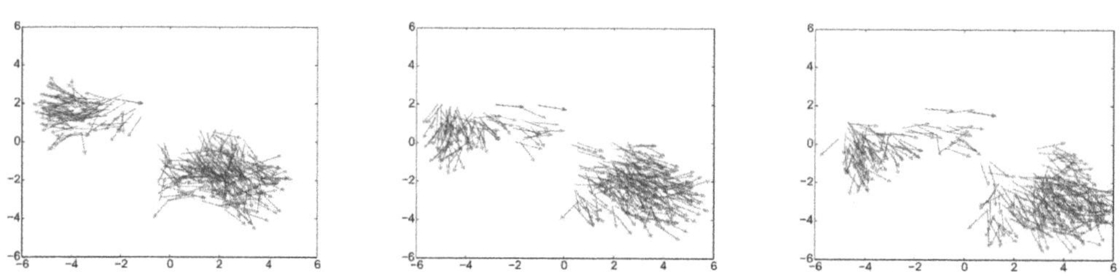

(a) $t = 80$ (b) $t = 120$ (c) $t = 160$

Figure 7: Role of opinion leaders (under the same setting: $\sigma = 0.5$, $d = \exp(-0.4)$).

5 APPLICATION

Apart from the capability of modeling opinion migration and network evolution, a good generation model should be able to explain and predict the behavior of objects given observed data. In general, node properties could be regarded as vector representations or explanatory variables of a node, and are also referred to as node embeddings in some work (e.g. [40]). They usually convey meanings dependent on the network and context, and are flexible enough to be inferred given a variety of real-world networks. In this section we show an application of our co-evolution model, where we predict the cosponsors of bills in the future. Here the node latent properties can be treated as multi-dimensional political ideology as in [5, 32].

5.1 Dataset

Co-sponsorship dataset. A *sponsor* of a bill is a legislator (usually a member from the congress) who introduces a bill or resolution for consideration. A *cosponsor* is another congress member who adds his or her name as a supporter to the sponsor's bill. Cosponsorship contains important information about the social support network between legislators: the closer the relationship between a sponsor and a cosponsor, the more likely it is that the sponsor has directly petitioned the cosponsor for support [11]. We crawled the legislative bills[1] from 1983 ($98th$ congress meeting) till now ($114th$ congress meeting), with a timeframe of 34 years. For bills with a sponsor, we extract all the cosponsors and build links between them. The minimal time unit is set to one month, and we use $H^{\langle t\rangle}$ to denote all the cosponsor links in month t. In order to make the evolution process smoother, a snapshot of network $G^{\langle t\rangle}$ consists of all the people and their cosponsor links within a 12-month period up to month t, and the time window is shifted forwards one month at a time. In other words, $G^{\langle t\rangle} = H^{\langle t-11\rangle} \cup H^{\langle t-10\rangle} \cup \cdots \cup H^{\langle t\rangle}$. Therefore, this series of graphs starts at $t_0 = 12$ and $G^{\langle t_0\rangle}$ contains all the cosponsorship links from Jan. 1, 1983 to Jan. 1, 1984; $G^{\langle t_0+1\rangle}$ contains all the cosponsorship links from Feb. 1, 1983 to Feb. 1, 1984, and so on. This series of evolving networks contain $T = 382$ time slices, $N = 2,180$ legislators, 130,692 bills and 2.1 million cosponsorship links in total.

5.2 Fitting the Data

A graphical model representing our model is shown in Figure 8.

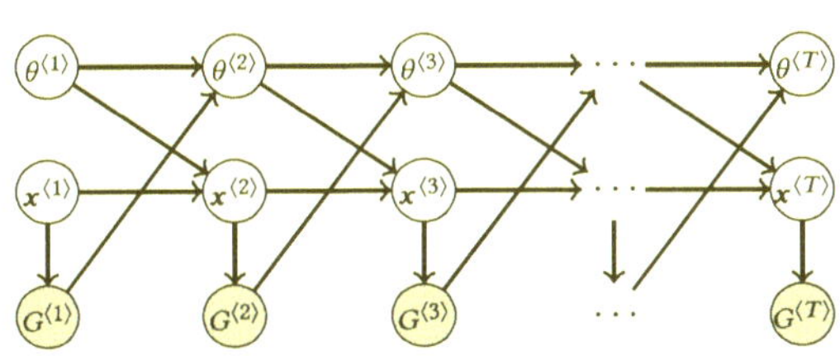

Figure 8: Graphical model representation of our model. Shadowed units represent observed variables.

Our model becomes a probabilistic model during the inference process, therefore each link is no longer deterministically established by a threshold d. The optimal parameters are inferred by maximizing the joint probability of G, $X = \{\boldsymbol{x}^{\langle t\rangle}\}_{t=1}^{T}$, $\Theta = \{\theta^{\langle t\rangle}\}_{t=1}^{T}$ and $\boldsymbol{b} = \{b_n\}_{n=1}^{N}$. From Figure 8 we have

$$X,\Theta,\boldsymbol{b} = \underset{X,\Theta,\boldsymbol{b}}{\operatorname{argmax}} \prod_{t=1}^{T} p(G^{\langle t\rangle}|\boldsymbol{x}^{\langle t\rangle},\boldsymbol{b}) \cdot \prod_{t=2}^{T} p(\theta^{\langle t\rangle}|\theta^{\langle t-1\rangle},G^{\langle t-1\rangle}) \tag{9}$$

s.t.

$$\boldsymbol{x}_n^{\langle t+1\rangle} = \boldsymbol{x}_n^{\langle t\rangle} + v \cdot (\cos\theta_n^{\langle t\rangle},\ \sin\theta_n^{\langle t\rangle}),\ \forall n,t \tag{10}$$

The constraint (Equation 10) makes it much harder to achieve a global estimation of parameters. Therefore, we adopt an approach similar to coordinate ascent algorithm, and update X, Θ and $\boldsymbol{b}$ given each other iteratively.

Update $\boldsymbol{b}$. $\boldsymbol{b}$ can be directly updated using traditional methods (e.g. stochastic gradient ascent) under a unconstrained optimization setting.

Update X and Θ. Initially ($t = t_0$), the optimal positions $\boldsymbol{x}^{\langle t_0\rangle *}$ are estimated by maximizing the likelihood of the first observed graph:

$$\boldsymbol{x}^{\langle t_0\rangle *} = \underset{\boldsymbol{x}^{\langle t_0\rangle}}{\operatorname{argmax}}\, p(G^{\langle t_0\rangle}|\boldsymbol{x}^{\langle t_0\rangle},\boldsymbol{b}) \tag{11}$$

and directions $\theta^{\langle t_0\rangle}$ are initialized uniformly at random in $[0, 2\pi)$. Latent features at the next step $\boldsymbol{x}^{\langle t_0+1\rangle}$ are updated deterministically by our propagation model (Equation 6).

After that, for each timestamp t ($t \geq t_0 + 1$), given the present position $\boldsymbol{x}^{\langle t\rangle}$, previous direction $\theta^{\langle t-1\rangle}$ and the next graph $G^{\langle t+1\rangle}$, we are able to estimate $\theta^{\langle t\rangle *}$ according to:

$$\begin{aligned}
\theta^{\langle t\rangle *} &= \underset{\theta^{\langle t\rangle}}{\operatorname{argmax}}\ \log p(\theta^{\langle t\rangle}|G^{\langle t+1\rangle},\theta^{\langle t-1\rangle},\boldsymbol{x}^{\langle t\rangle},\boldsymbol{b}) \\
&= \underset{\theta^{\langle t\rangle}}{\operatorname{argmax}}\ \left(\log p(G^{\langle t+1\rangle}|\theta^{\langle t\rangle},\boldsymbol{x}^{\langle t\rangle},\boldsymbol{b}) + \log p(\theta^{\langle t\rangle}|\theta^{\langle t-1\rangle},G^{\langle t-1\rangle})\right) \\
&= \underset{\theta^{\langle t\rangle}}{\operatorname{argmax}}\ \left(\log p(G^{\langle t+1\rangle}|\boldsymbol{x}^{\langle t+1\rangle},\boldsymbol{b}) + \log p(\theta^{\langle t\rangle}|\theta^{\langle t-1\rangle},G^{\langle t-1\rangle})\right)
\end{aligned} \tag{12}$$

This concludes an outer-iteration of parameter update. We plot the objective versus the number of outer iterations in Figure 9. Empirically, only a few iterations are needed for convergence, and we let the number to be 3 in all following experiments.

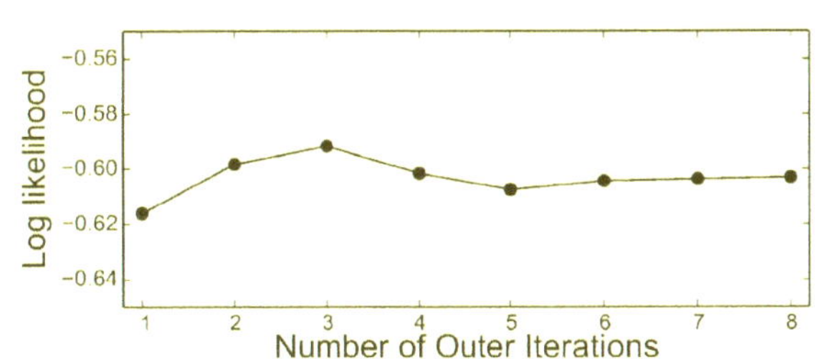

Figure 9: The log likelihood when parameters are updated for multiple rounds.

5.3 Baselines

We compare our co-evolution model of network structure and node opinions (CoNN) with the following baseline methods. For fair comparison, we compare with several models designed for dynamic networks, and dimension of latent features is set to $K = 2$ in all methods. The absolute value of velocity is fixed to be $v = 3 \times 10^{-3}$ in order for the process to be smoother. We let $\sigma = 1$ and $\epsilon = 0.8$ in our method for now. Parameter studies at the end of this section reveal that our method is not sensitive to these parameters.

[1] Data are collected at https://www.govtrack.us

- CoNN_{dot}: The first baseline is a variant of our model where the probability of a link involves a dot product: $p(G_{nm} = 1) = 1/(1+e^{-(x_n \cdot x_m + b_n + b_m)})$. $\{b_n\}$ is a set of variables with meaning similar to our CoNN model.
- Latent feature propagation model (LFP) [16]: The second baseline is the binary latent feature propagation model. Local optimization is adopted in order for their method to scale with our data. The authors kindly share their code.
- Dynamic social network with latent space models (DSNL) [36]: We implement the dynamic social network analysis approach where no social neighbors are considered in propagation. Latent features evolve purely according to their previous positions.
- Phase transition model (PTM) [42]. This approach is proposed to model the behavior of molecules during a phase transition. Directions of molecules are treated as the parameter, and they propagate according to the average of their spatial neighbors. We use our estimated features at the beginning as their initialization, and run simulation for T steps.

We also compare with a state-of-the-art baseline method designed for static networks.

- Large-scale information network embedding (LINE) [40]. This approach embeds information network into low-dimensional vector spaces. We apply LINE on static snapshots of the social graph, and treat the embeddings as node features.

5.4 Co-sponsorship Prediction

In this task, we demonstrate the advantage of our co-evolution model by predicting cosponsors in the future. Specifically, given the observed cosponsor links up to time t_1, a bill in future time t_2 ($t_2 > t_1$) and its sponsor u_n, our goal is to predict the users who will cosponsor it.

Given $G^{\langle t_0:t_1\rangle}$, we are able to learn $\theta^{\langle t_0:t_1-1\rangle}$ and $x^{\langle t_0:t_1\rangle}$. After that, the latent features propagate according to our evolution model, namely

$$\begin{aligned} \theta_n^{\langle s\rangle} &\sim \mathcal{N}(\langle\theta_n^{\langle s-1\rangle}\rangle, \sigma^2) \\ x_n^{\langle s+1\rangle} &= x_n^{\langle s\rangle} + v \cdot (\cos\theta_n^{\langle s\rangle}, \sin\theta_n^{\langle s\rangle}) \end{aligned} \tag{13}$$

for $s = t_1, \cdots, t_2 - 1$ and every user n. Finally, we calculate the pairwise probability of a link from u_n to all other users, rank them and evaluate the AUC score in Figure 11. The X-axis denotes time gap between now and the prediction (in months) ($\Delta t = t_2 - t_1$), and Y-axis denotes the cosponsor prediction AUC for all bills at time t_2, averaged over all pairs of (t_1, t_2) which satisfy $t_2 - t_1 = \Delta t$.

For baseline methods which purely model the propagation of latent features, we have

$$x_n^{\langle s+1\rangle} \sim p_m(x_n^{\langle s\rangle}), \forall n \tag{14}$$

for $s = t_1, \cdots, t_2 - 1$, where $p_m(x_n^{\langle s\rangle})$ is the prior (propagation probability) for the corresponding baseline method m. For baseline methods designed for static networks (i.e. no propagation in terms of latent features), we use the node representation at time t_1 to predict the cosponsors at t_2.

It would also be interesting to study the time delay that a legislator cosponsors a bill. After a bill is initialized, the sponsor may expend considerable efforts recruiting cosponsors with personal contacts so that others will add their names to support the bill later. Only those cosponsors who join within a year are considered. The distribution of the time delay between the initial sponsorship and cosponsor date is shown in Figure 10. When a legislator cosponsors a bill immediately after its initialization, it may indicate that the sponsor and cosponsor are close in some sense. Therefore, we assign a relevant score to cosponsors according to the date of cosponsorship: those who signed their names within the first quartile (most promptly) are assigned with the highest relevance score of 4; those between the first and the second quartile have a relevance score of 3, and so on. Thus, based on the ranking given by the likelihood of a cosponsor, we are able to calculate the normalized discounted cumulative gain (NDCG) of the cosponsorship prediction. The macro-average NDCG_{10} score for each bill is reported in Figure 12. X-axis has the same meaning as the previous task, i.e., the time gap between now and the prediction.

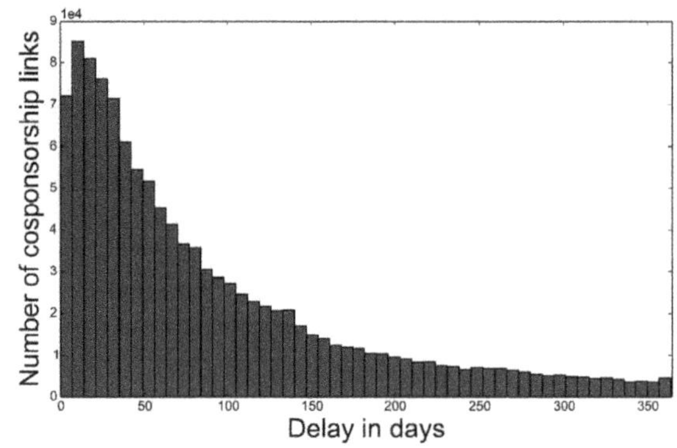

Figure 10: Distribution of time delay. Quartiles: Q_1 = 24, Q_2 = 58, Q_3 = 125.

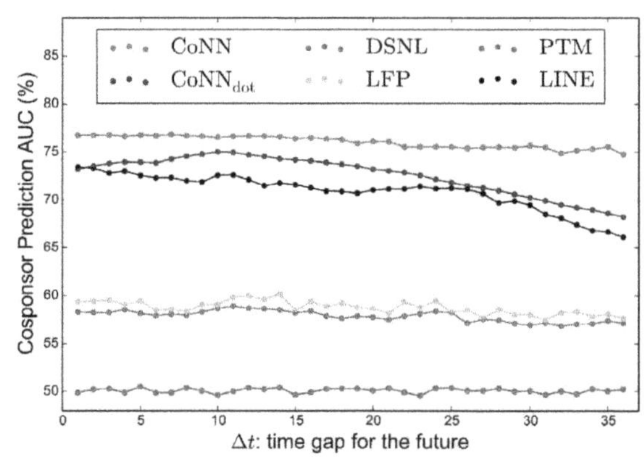

Figure 11: AUC score for cosponsor prediction.

In Table 1 we also show the top 10 people with largest b values in our timeframe (1983-present). They are popular in that many others legislators are likely to cosponsor the bills they drafted. We interpret them as opinion leaders, since cosponsorship implies endorsement and their ideas spread more widely among others. Among the

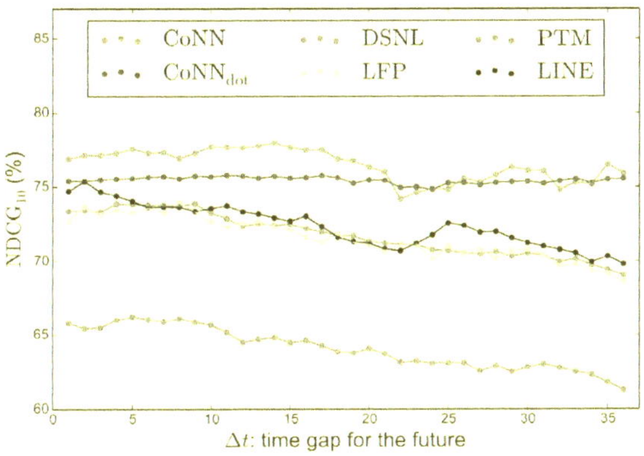

Figure 12: $NDCG_{10}$ for cosponsor prediction.

results, we identify John Kerry (68th U.S. Secretary of State), Albert Gore (45th U.S. Vice President) and Mitch McConnell (the majority leader of the Senate since 2015). Therefore, the opinion leaders and the actual leaders in the legislature have some overlap, and our approach can detect leaders from another perspective.

Rank	Name	Party-State	Time in Congress
1	Paul Simon	Democrat-IL	1975-1997
2	Jay Rockefeller	Republican-WV	1985-2015
3	John Kerry	Democrat-MA	1985-2013
4	Thomas Harkin	Democrat-IA	1975-2015
5	James Terry Sanford	Democrat-NC	1986-1993
6	Albert Gore	Democrat-TN	1983-1993
7	Kent Conrad	Democrat-ND	1987-2013
8	Edward Kennedy	Democrat-MA	1962-2009
9	Mitch McConnell	Republican-KY	1985-present
10	Frank Annunzio	Democrat-IL	1965-1993

Table 1: Popular legislators ranked by b in recent 34 years.

Parameter Study. We plot the performance curve under different choices of hyperparameters (σ, ϵ) in Figure 13. For intuitive comparison, we calculate the average evaluation measure over all possible lengths of time gap (i.e. from $\Delta t = 1$ to 36) as the value on Y-axis. In sum, our inference model is not sensitive to these parameters as long as they lie within a reasonable range.

6 RELATED WORK

Understanding the evolution of link structure and node property has been a promising research topic recently. Traditional interpretations of dynamic networks treat the two problems separately, i.e., the evolution of link structures [4, 9, 24–26, 39, 47] and the evolution of node attributes [13–15, 22].

Under a fixed network structure, various node property propagation models have been proposed, which are better known as the information diffusion model when the node features are binary. The binary feature of each node can be considered as a status,

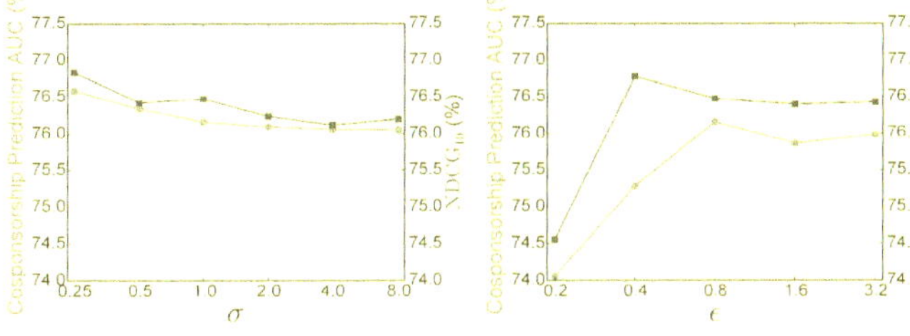

Figure 13: Parameter study on σ and ϵ for CoNN. In the left figure, ϵ is fixed to be 0.8. In the right figure, σ is fixed to be 1.

as whether the node is infested or activated, and it may change according to the network structure. Typically, information diffusion process occurs between nodes that are linked to each other. For example, linear threshold model [14] involves an aggregation of neighbors' weights, and a node is activated if the aggregated weight of its active neighbors exceeds some threshold. Independent cascade model [13] assumes an activating probability for each neighbor of a newly activated node. While binary features reflect the activation status of a node, probabilistic or real-valued features embed every node onto a continuous spectrum, which indicates the relative position between actors. In the DeGroot learning process, every time the opinions of agents are assumed to be updated according to the weighted average of their neighbors [8]. Adjustment in user features after interaction is studied in [7], where similarity of connected users are found to be increasing over time. These methods are limited to the case where network structure does not change over time, and more principled approaches are desired to model user behaviors in dynamic networks.

The evolution of networks is usually modeled as a result of the migration of individuals' features. To model the static snapshots of networks, a variety of methods assume vertices in the network are associated with a latent feature representation, and the observed links are a result of their interaction. Latent class models (blockmodels) assume the probability of a link depends on the communities that the corresponding users engage in [6, 16, 45, 46], and continuous latent feature models embed each node in the network as a position in a lower dimensional Euclidean space, where the features constitute a continuous spectrum that conveys more meaningful messages such as a user's stance (e.g. extreme/moderate) towards a specific topic. These approaches have broad applications in clustering, visualization and so on [17, 29, 33].

Migration of users' latent features is usually modeled as a hidden Markov model (HMM), with network structure being the observed sequence and node features being the latent variables [6, 16, 45, 46]. The distribution of the latent variables depends only on the their previous values, and the value of observed network depends only on the latent variables at the same timestamp. Optimization is usually done using standard forward-backward algorithm [16]. Feature dimension may also be learned automatically from the data, leading to nonparametric methods [10, 20, 23, 35]. The evolution of latent features is modeled as regression of a node's future features to accommodate dynamic networks [27, 36–38]. However, these methods fail to consider the feature migration as part of co-evolution process. In other words, influence from network structure to node feature migration is totally ignored. In addition, as far as we are concerned, all of the existing approaches simply posit the propagation of node features can happen arbitrarily, without considering the direction or tendency when people change their opinions.

7 CONCLUSION

In this paper we present a novel approach for understanding the co-evolution of network structure and opinion migration. Our approach models both the migration of latent features by virtue of network structures, and the evolution of link structures as a result of the change of node features. We analogize the motion of entities in biological and molecular system to propose the latent feature migration model, and social influence is explicitly exhibited in terms of user's moving directions. Various properties of network can be charactered by adjusting the system-level parameters of our generation model, and applications on a real-world dataset reveal our advantage over the state-of-the-art co-evolution approaches.

ACKNOWLEDGEMENT

The authors would like to thank Tina Eliassi-Rad who kindly reviewed an earlier version of this manuscript and provided valuable feedback and suggestions. We would also like to thank the anonymous reviewers for their precious comments. This work is partially supported by NSF CAREER #1741634.

REFERENCES

[1] *N-sphere: Spherical coordinates.* https://en.wikipedia.org/wiki/N-sphere#Spherical_coordinates
[2] *The Polarization of the Congressional Parties.* http://www.voteview.com/political_polarization_2015.htm
[3] Amr Ahmed, Nino Shervashidze, Shravan Narayanamurthy, Vanja Josifovski, and Alexander J Smola. 2013. Distributed large-scale natural graph factorization. In *WWW'13.* 37–48.
[4] Albert-László Barabási and Réka Albert. 1999. Emergence of scaling in random networks. *Science* 286, 5439 (1999), 509–512.
[5] Joshua Clinton, Simon Jackman, and Douglas Rivers. 2004. The statistical analysis of roll call data. *American Political Science Review* 98, 02 (2004), 355–370.
[6] Marco Corneli, Pierre Latouche, and Fabrice Rossi. 2015. Modelling time evolving interactions in networks through a non stationary extension of stochastic block models. In *ASONAM'15.* 1590–1591.
[7] David Crandall, Dan Cosley, Daniel Huttenlocher, Jon Kleinberg, and Siddharth Suri. 2008. Feedback effects between similarity and social influence in online communities. In *KDD'08.* 160–168.
[8] Morris H DeGroot. 1974. Reaching a consensus. *J. Amer. Statist. Assoc.* 69, 345 (1974), 118–121.
[9] Mehrdad Farajtabar, Yichen Wang, Manuel Gomez-Rodriguez, Shuang Li, Hongyuan Zha, and Le Song. 2015. Coevolve: A joint point process model for information diffusion and network co-evolution. In *NIPS'15.* 1954–1962.
[10] James R Foulds, Christopher DuBois, Arthur U Asuncion, Carter T Butts, and Padhraic Smyth. 2011. A dynamic relational infinite feature model for longitudinal social networks. In *Int. Conf. on Artificial Intelligence and Statistics.* 287–295.
[11] James H Fowler. 2006. Connecting the Congress: A study of cosponsorship networks. *Political Analysis* (2006), 456–487.
[12] Sean Gerrish and David M Blei. 2011. Predicting legislative roll calls from text. In *ICML'11.* 489–496.
[13] Jacob Goldenberg, Barak Libai, and Eitan Muller. 2001. Talk of the network: A complex systems look at the underlying process of word-of-mouth. *Marketing letters* 12, 3 (2001), 211–223.
[14] Mark Granovetter. 1978. Threshold models of collective behavior. *Amer. J. Sociology* (1978), 1420–1443.
[15] Daniel Gruhl, Ramanathan Guha, David Liben-Nowell, and Andrew Tomkins. 2004. Information diffusion through blogspace. In *WWW'13.* 491–501.
[16] Creighton Heaukulani and Zoubin Ghahramani. 2013. Dynamic probabilistic models for latent feature propagation in social networks. In *ICML'13.* 275–283.
[17] Peter D Hoff, Adrian E Raftery, and Mark S Handcock. 2002. Latent space approaches to social network analysis. *J. Amer. Statist. Assoc.* 97, 460 (2002), 1090–1098.
[18] Paul W Holland, Kathryn Blackmond Laskey, and Samuel Leinhardt. 1983. Stochastic blockmodels: First steps. *Social networks* 5, 2 (1983), 109–137.
[19] Petter Holme and Mark EJ Newman. 2006. Nonequilibrium phase transition in the coevolution of networks and opinions. *Physical Review E* 74, 5 (2006), 056108.
[20] Katsuhiko Ishiguro, Tomoharu Iwata, Naonori Ueda, and Joshua B Tenenbaum. 2010. Dynamic infinite relational model for time-varying relational data analysis. In *Advances in Neural Information Processing Systems.* 919–927.
[21] Mohsen Jamali and Martin Ester. 2010. A matrix factorization technique with trust propagation for recommendation in social networks. In *RecSys'10.* 135–142.
[22] David Kempe, Jon Kleinberg, and Éva Tardos. 2003. Maximizing the spread of influence through a social network. In *KDD'03.* 137–146.
[23] Myunghwan Kim and Jure Leskovec. 2013. Nonparametric multi-group membership model for dynamic networks. In *Advances in Neural Information Processing Systems.* 1385–1393.
[24] Paul L Krapivsky, Sidney Redner, and Francois Leyvraz. 2000. Connectivity of growing random networks. *Physical review letters* 85, 21 (2000), 4629.
[25] Jure Leskovec, Lars Backstrom, Ravi Kumar, and Andrew Tomkins. 2008. Microscopic evolution of social networks. In *KDD'08.* 462–470.
[26] Jure Leskovec, Deepayan Chakrabarti, Jon Kleinberg, and Christos Faloutsos. 2005. Realistic, mathematically tractable graph generation and evolution, using kronecker multiplication. In *PKDD'05.* 133–145.
[27] Shawn Mankad and George Michailidis. 2013. Structural and functional discovery in dynamic networks with non-negative matrix factorization. *Physical Review E* 88, 4 (2013), 042812.
[28] Miller McPherson, Lynn Smith-Lovin, and James M Cook. 2001. Birds of a feather: Homophily in social networks. *Annual review of sociology* (2001), 415–444.
[29] Aditya Krishna Menon and Charles Elkan. 2011. Link prediction via matrix factorization. In *ECML/PKDD'11.* 437–452.
[30] Tomas Mikolov, Ilya Sutskever, Kai Chen, Greg S Corrado, and Jeff Dean. 2013. Distributed representations of words and phrases and their compositionality. In *NIPS'13.* 3111–3119.
[31] Jeffrey Pennington, Richard Socher, and Christopher D Manning. 2014. Glove: Global Vectors for Word Representation. In *EMNLP'14*, Vol. 14. 1532–1543.
[32] Keith T Poole and Howard Rosenthal. 1985. A spatial model for legislative roll call analysis. *American Journal of Political Science* (1985), 357–384.
[33] Guo-Jun Qi, Charu Aggarwal, Qi Tian, Heng Ji, and Thomas Huang. 2012. Exploring context and content links in social media: A latent space method. *PAMI'12* 34, 5 (2012), 850–862.
[34] Sebastián M Saiegh and others. 2015. Using joint scaling methods to study ideology and representation: Evidence from Latin America. *Political Analysis* 23, 3 (2015), 363–384.
[35] Purnamrita Sarkar, Deepayan Chakrabarti, and Michael Jordan. 2012. Nonparametric link prediction in dynamic networks. *arXiv preprint arXiv:1206.6394* (2012).
[36] Purnamrita Sarkar and Andrew W Moore. 2005. Dynamic social network analysis using latent space models. *ACM SIGKDD Explorations Newsletter* 7, 2 (2005), 31–40.
[37] Purnamrita Sarkar, Sajid M Siddiqi, and Geoffrey J Gordon. 2007. A latent space approach to dynamic embedding of co-occurrence data. In *AISTATS'07.* 420–427.
[38] Daniel K Sewell and Yuguo Chen. 2015. Latent space models for dynamic networks. *J. Amer. Statist. Assoc.* 110, 512 (2015), 1646–1657.
[39] Yizhou Sun, Jie Tang, Jiawei Han, Cheng Chen, and Manish Gupta. 2014. Co-evolution of multi-typed objects in dynamic star networks. *TKDE'14* 26, 12 (2014), 2942–2955.
[40] Jian Tang, Meng Qu, Mingzhe Wang, Ming Zhang, Jun Yan, and Qiaozhu Mei. 2015. Line: Large-scale information network embedding. In *WWW'15.* 1067–1077.
[41] Jie Tang, Jimeng Sun, Chi Wang, and Zi Yang. 2009. Social influence analysis in large-scale networks. In *KDD'09.* 807–816.
[42] Tamás Vicsek, András Czirók, Eshel Ben-Jacob, Inon Cohen, and Ofer Shochet. 1995. Novel type of phase transition in a system of self-driven particles. *Physical review letters* 75, 6 (1995), 1226.
[43] Tamás Vicsek and Anna Zafeiris. 2012. Collective motion. *Physics Reports* 517, 3 (2012), 71–140.
[44] Yuchung J Wang and George Y Wong. 1987. Stochastic blockmodels for directed graphs. *J. Amer. Statist. Assoc.* 82, 397 (1987), 8–19.
[45] Eric P Xing, Wenjie Fu, Le Song, and others. 2010. A state-space mixed membership blockmodel for dynamic network tomography. *The Annals of Applied Statistics* 4, 2 (2010), 535–566.
[46] Kevin S Xu and Alfred O Hero III. 2013. Dynamic stochastic blockmodels: Statistical models for time-evolving networks. In *Social Computing, Behavioral-Cultural Modeling and Prediction.* 201–210.
[47] Elena Zheleva, Hossam Sharara, and Lise Getoor. 2009. Co-evolution of social and affiliation networks. In *KDD'09.* 1007–1016.

Groups-Keeping Solution Path Algorithm for Sparse Regression with Automatic Feature Grouping

Bin Gu
Computer Science and Engineering
University of Texas at Arlington
Texas, 76019, USA
jsgubin@gmail.com

Guodong Liu
Computer Science and Engineering
University of Texas at Arlington
Texas, 76019, USA
mealsd@gmail.com

Heng Huang*
Computer Science and Engineering
University of Texas at Arlington
Texas, 76019, USA
heng@uta.edu

ABSTRACT

Feature selection is one of the most important data mining research topics with many applications. In practical problems, features often have group structure to effect the outcomes. Thus, it is crucial to automatically identify homogenous groups of features for high-dimensional data analysis. Octagonal shrinkage and clustering algorithm for regression (OSCAR) is an important sparse regression approach with automatic feature grouping and selection by ℓ_1 norm and pairwise ℓ_∞ norm. However, due to over-complex representation of the penalty (especially the pairwise ℓ_∞ norm), so far OSCAR has no solution path algorithm which is mostly useful for tuning the model. To address this challenge, in this paper, we propose a groups-keeping solution path algorithm to solve the OSCAR model (OscarGKPath). Given a set of homogenous groups of features and an accuracy bound ε, OscarGKPath can fit the solutions in an interval of regularization parameters while keeping the feature groups. The entire solution path can be obtained by combining multiple such intervals. We prove that all solutions in the solution path produced by OscarGKPath can strictly satisfy the given accuracy bound ε. The experimental results on benchmark datasets not only confirm the effectiveness of our OscarGKPath algorithm, but also show the superiority of our OscarGKPath in cross validation compared with the existing batch algorithm.

CCS CONCEPTS

•Information systems →**Data mining**; **•Computing methodologies** →Machine learning;

KEYWORDS

Solution path, OSCAR, automatic feature grouping, feature selection, sparse regression

*To whom all correspondence should be addressed. This work was partially supported by U.S. NIH R01 AG049371, NSF IIS 1302675, IIS 1344152, DBI 1356628, IIS 1619308 and IIS 1633753.

KDD'17, August 13-17, 2017, Halifax, NS, Canada.
© 2017 ACM. 978-1-4503-4887-4/17/08...$15.00
DOI: http://dx.doi.org/10.1145/3097983.3098010

1 INTRODUCTION

The high-dimensional data are increasingly available in many data mining applications as the data collection technologies evolve. For example, DNA microarray technology can produce a large number of measurements [14, 29]. Medical imaging technologies (*e.g.*, MRI, CT, and Ultrasound) can produce high resolution 3-dimensional and 4-dimensional images [15]. The high resolution images are essentially high-dimensional data defined by the large number of voxels. To efficiently and effectively analyze the high-dimensional data, feature selection techniques have been introduced to identify the significant features associated to response variables [2] and to enhance the prediction tasks. Feature selection methods are particularly important and useful in bioinformatics and computational medicine (also called as biomarker selection).

To conduct the feature selection in high-dimensional data analysis, many sparse learning methods [8, 9, 19, 26, 30, 31] have been proposed. These sparse learning methods use the sparsity-inducing norms (*e.g.* to force the coefficients of non-important features to be zero. As a result, the features which have non-zero coefficients can be easily 'selected'. In the high-dimensional data, the highly correlated features widely exist [13, 15]. However, the sparse learning methods tend to arbitrarily select only one of them as mentioned in [6]. Thus, the estimation can be unstable, and the resulted model is difficult to interpret [33]. Especially, in bioinformatics research, some genes from the same family always work together to show the biological function, thus it is incorrect to only select one of them as biomarker. However, most existing feature selection methods ignore the feature group structure. Although the group LASSO model and its variants have been proposed, these methods require the feature group information to be known in advance [33]. Thus, it is crucial to design new feature selection with automatically identifying homogenous groups of features.

To tackle this challenging problem, several sparse learning methods have been proposed. For example, the elastic net [35] encourages β_i to be close to β_j for highly correlated features i, j by a ℓ_2-norm, where β_i's are the feature coefficients of the regression model. The fused LASSO [27] directly enforces the successive feature coefficients to be similar by the regularizer $|\beta_i - \beta_{i-1}|$, if the features are ordered in some meaningful way. The method proposed by Wu *et al.* [32] uses the ℓ_∞-norm to encourage the equality of coefficients for the features with maximum absolute value. The clustered LASSO [25] constraints all feature coefficients to be similar by the regularizer $\sum_{i<j} |\beta_i - \beta_j|$ (also called pairwise penalty). Different to the above feature grouping which cannot clearly and adaptively reveal the feature group structure, the OSCAR [6] (octagonal shrinkage and clustering algorithm for regression) method

uses the pairwise ℓ_∞-norm to encourage the equality of coefficients for highly correlated features. Among these methods, OSCAR can adaptively capture the feature groups, and clearly reveal the feature group structure by the equality of coefficients. In this paper, we focus on OSCAR model due to the ability of automatic feature grouping. The sparse learning based feature selection models usually have parameters and tuning parameters is time-consuming and could lead to sub-optimal results.

To address the parameter tuning issue and generate stable and optimal results, the solution path algorithm can provide a compact representation of all exact (or approximate) optimal solutions, which is extremely useful for model selection [10]. Several solution path algorithms have been proposed for sparse learning. For example, Rosset and Zhu [23] proposed a solution path algorithm for LASSO. Zhu *et al.* [34] proposed a solution path algorithm for ℓ_1-norm support vector machine. Park and Hastie [21] introduced a solution path algorithm for ℓ_1-norm regularized generalized linear models. Tibshirani and Taylor [28] presented the solution path algorithm for the generalized LASSO, where LASSO and fused LASSO are two special cases of the generalized LASSO. These solution path algorithms were designed for the learning problems with ℓ_1-norm. However, due to the difficulty in treating over-complex representation of the penalty (especially the pairwise ℓ_∞-norm) in OSCAR, there is still no solution path algorithm for OSCAR model. More importantly, we hope that the designed solution path algorithm can efficiently handle the pairwise ℓ_∞-norm. Note that Zhong and Kwok [33] proposed a fast batch algorithm of OSCAR (FastOSCAR) based on the accelerated proximal gradient method, which only gives one solution for one execution, but cannot give a continuous solution path for OSCAR.

In this paper, we propose a novel groups-keeping solution path algorithm for OSCAR (OscarGKPath), which can significantly improve the regularization parameters tuning of OSCAR model. Specifically, given a set of homogenous groups of features produced by a batch algorithm (*e.g.* FastOSCAR) and an accuracy bound ε, our new OscarGKPath algorithm can fit the solutions in an interval of regularization parameters while keeping the feature groups. Theoretically, we prove that any solution in this interval can strictly satisfy the given accuracy bound ε. The entire solution path can be obtained by combining multiple such intervals. We conduct the experiments on seven benchmark datasets. The experimental results confirm the effectiveness and efficiency of our OscarGKPath method.

Notations. β_j denote the j-th element of vector β. Δ denotes the amount of the change of each variable. $\text{sign}(x)$ is a sign function which returns 1 if $x > 0$, otherwise returns -1.

2 REVIEW OF OSCAR MODEL

In this section, we first introduce the formulation of OSCAR, and then provide the optimality conditions of OSCAR correspondingly.

2.1 OSCAR

Given a training set $S = \{(x_i, y_i)\}_{i=1}^{l}$ with $x_i \in \mathbb{R}^d$ and $y_i \in \mathbb{R}$. We assume that y_i is centered, *i.e.*, $\sum_{i=1}^{l} y_i = 0$, and each feature of the training set S is standardized, *i.e.*, $\sum_{i=1}^{l} x_{ij} = 0$ and $\sum_{i=1}^{l} x_{ij}^2 = 1$. Because the response is centered, OSCAR considers a linear regression model without the intercept. Thus, the formulation of OSCAR is considered as follows:

$$\min_{\beta} \quad \frac{1}{2}\sum_{i=1}^{l}\left(y_i - x_i^T\beta\right)^2 \qquad (1)$$
$$s.t. \quad \|\beta\|_1 + c\sum_{j<k}\max\{|\beta_j|, |\beta_k|\} \le t,$$

where the ℓ_1-norm enforces the sparsity, and the pairwise ℓ_1-norm encourages every coefficient pair $|\beta_j|$ and $|\beta_k|$ to be equal which can automatically group highly correlated features. $c \ge 0$ an $t > 0$ are tuning constants. c is controlling the relative weighting of the norms and t is controlling the magnitude. Specially, if $c = 0$, OSCAR degenerates to LASSO. If $c = \infty$, OSCAR clusters all features as a group but without variable selection. Thus, selecting appropriate values of c and t plays an essential role for OSCAR.

The formulation (1) is a constrained optimization problem which can be written in the penalized form (2) according to the subdifferential version of Karush-Kuhn-Tucker (KKT) conditions [24]:

$$F(\beta, \lambda_1, \lambda_2) = \min_{\beta} \quad \frac{1}{2}\sum_{i=1}^{l}\left(y_i - x_i^T\beta\right)^2 \qquad (2)$$
$$+\lambda_1\|\beta\|_1 + \lambda_2\sum_{i<j}\max\{|\beta_i|, |\beta_j|\},$$

where $\lambda_1 \ge 0$ and $\lambda_2 \ge 0$ are two regularization parameters. For a pair of λ_1 and λ_2, there exists a pair of t and c such that (2) and (1) share the same solution, and vice versa. As mentioned above, selecting the values of λ_1 and λ_2 also plays an essential role for OSCAR. This paper will propose a novel group-keeping solution path algorithm for (2) which greatly benefits the regularization parameters tuning in solving OSCAR model.

2.2 Optimality Conditions of OSCAR Model

The formulation (2) has the pair ℓ_∞-norm which make it nontrivial to derive the optimality conditions of OSCAR. In this section, we first derive an equivalent formulation of (2) which is based on the feature groups and orders of the optimal solution, and then present the optimality conditions of OSCAR.

We denote β as an optimal solution of OSCAR. Let $o(j) \in \{1, \cdots, d\}$ denote the order of $|\beta_j|$ among $\{|\beta_1|, |\beta_2|, \cdots, |\beta_d|\}$ such that if $o(j_1) < o(j_2)$, we have: $|\beta_{j_1}| \le |\beta_{j_2}|$. Based on the orders $o(j)$, we can define the feature group $\mathcal{G}_g$ as following:

Definition 2.1. Given the orders $o(j)$ of $|\beta_j|$. The set $\mathcal{G}_g \subseteq \{1, \cdots, d\}$ is called a group of features if the following conditions are satisfied.

(1) $\forall j_1, j_2 \in \mathcal{G}_g$, and $j_1 \ne j_2$, we have $|\beta_{j_1}| = |\beta_{j_2}| \overset{\text{def}}{=} \theta_g$.
(2) If $j \in \{1, 2, \cdots, d\}$ and $j \notin \mathcal{G}_g$, we have that $|\beta_j| \ne \theta_g$.

In Definition 2.1, we denote θ_g as the common value of $|\beta_j|$ for the group $\mathcal{G}_g$. Thus, we have a set of $\mathcal{G}_g$, $g = 1, \cdots, G$, such that $\mathcal{G}_1 \cup \mathcal{G}_2 \cup \cdots \cup \mathcal{G}_G = \{1, 2, \cdots, d\}$, and $0 \le \theta_1 < \theta_2 < \cdots < \theta_G$. Based on the groups $\mathcal{G}_g$, $g = 1, \cdots, G$, the formulation (2) can be rewritten as (3) which is free of the ℓ_1-norm and the pair ℓ_∞-norm:

$$\min_{\theta} \quad \frac{1}{2}\sum_{i=1}^{l}\left(y_i - \tilde{x}_i^T\theta\right)^2 + \sum_{g=1}^{G} w_g\theta_g \qquad (3)$$
$$s.t. \quad 0 \le \theta_1 < \theta_2 < \cdots < \theta_G,$$

where $\widetilde{x}_i = [\widetilde{x}_{i1}\ \widetilde{x}_{i2} \cdots \widetilde{x}_{iG}]$ and $\widetilde{x}_{ig} = \sum_{j \in \mathcal{G}_g} \text{sign}(\beta_j) x_{ij}$. $w_g = \sum_{j \in \mathcal{G}_g} (\lambda_1 + (o(j) - 1)\lambda_2)$.

According to the value of θ_g, we can define an active set: $\mathcal{A} = \{g \in \{1, \cdots, G\} \mid \theta_g > 0\}$. Correspondingly, we define $\overline{\mathcal{A}} = \{1, \cdots, G\} - \mathcal{A}$. Thus, the optimality conditions of (3) can be presented as following:

$$\sum_{i=1}^{l} -\widetilde{x}_{ig} \left(y_i - \widetilde{x}_i^T \theta \right) + w_g = 0, \quad \forall g \in \mathcal{A} \tag{4}$$

$$0 < \theta_{2-|\overline{\mathcal{A}}|} < \cdots < \theta_{G-1} < \theta_G \tag{5}$$

$$\theta_{\overline{\mathcal{A}}} = 0\,. \tag{6}$$

3 OUR NEW SOLUTION PATH ALGORITHM

In this section, we propose a groups-keeping solution path algorithm of OSCAR (*i.e.*, OscarGKPath) with respect to two regularization parameters λ_1 and λ_2. Let $\Delta\lambda = \begin{bmatrix} \Delta\lambda_1 \\ \Delta\lambda_2 \end{bmatrix}$ denote the changes of λ_1 and λ_2, and given a direction $d = \begin{bmatrix} d_1 \\ d_2 \end{bmatrix}$ to $\Delta\lambda$, we have $\Delta\lambda = d\Delta\eta$, where $\Delta\eta$ is a parameter to control the adjustment qualities of λ_1 and λ_2. Thus, OscarGKPath actually tries to produce a solution path of OSCAR with respect to the direction d on λ_1 and λ_2.

Normally, solution path algorithms include two steps, *i.e.*, initializing the solution for a fixed values of λ_1 and λ_2, and computing the solution path based on the initial solution. As mentioned previously, FastOSCAR [33] is a fast batch algorithm of OSCAR based on the accelerated proximal gradient method. As far as we know, so far FastOSCAR is the fastest batch learning algorithm of OSCAR. Thus, we use FastOSCAR to produce the initial solution and the initial groups $\mathcal{G}_g$ to the optimization (3). In the following, we provide the detailed descriptions for computing the solution path based on the initial solution.

Let $\Delta\theta$ represent the changes of the coefficients θ. To compute the solution path, the first issue is which direction of $\Delta\theta$ (denoted by ξ) is with respect to the direction d on λ_1 and λ_2. The key of computing the direction ξ is trying to hold all the solutions satisfying the optimality conditions (4)-(6) during the adjustments (see Fig. 1), given the feature groups. Note that the unchanged feature groups may not be true for new values of λ_1 and λ_2. Thus, the solutions on the direction ξ could be approximate solutions. We use an accuracy bound ε to control the quality of solutions. After computing the direction ξ, the next issue is what maximum adjustment of $\Delta\eta$ (denoted by $\Delta\eta^{max}$) is such that the optimality conditions (4)-(6) will not be satisfied if $\Delta\eta$ exceeds $\Delta\eta^{max}$. After finding the maximum adjustment quantity $\Delta\eta^{max}$, we can update θ, $\lambda_1, \lambda_2, \mathcal{A}, \overline{\mathcal{A}}$ and the orders of θ_g. Repeating this procedure until the duality gap $G(\theta, \lambda_1, \lambda_2) > \varepsilon$ (see Fig. 1). Finally, we should backtrack the last piece of solution path to make sure the end solution to satisfy the accuracy ε, which can be easily implemented by binary search. The above procedure is our OscarGKPath algorithm which is summarized in Algorithm 1.

As mentioned above, three main steps of OscarGKPath are:

(1) computing the directions of $\Delta\theta$;
(2) computing the maximum adjustment of $\Delta\eta$;
(3) and computing the duality gap $G(\theta, \lambda_1, \lambda_2)$.

In the following, we provide the detailed descriptions for these three steps respectively.

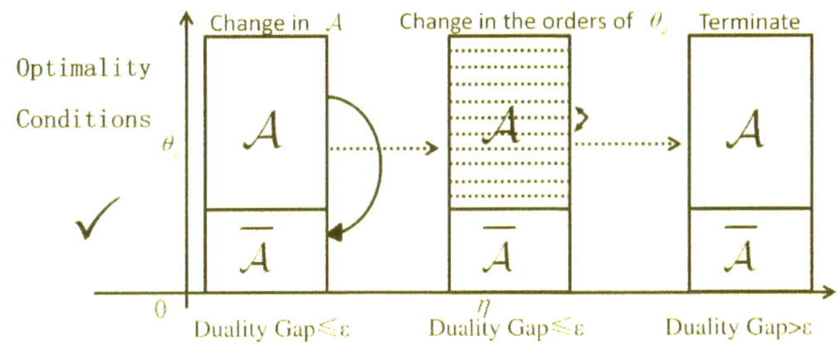

Figure 1: The fundamental principle of OscarGKPath is holding all the solutions satisfying the accuracy bound ε when given a set of feature groups, and adjusting the solutions based on the optimality conditions.

Algorithm 1 OscarGKPath

Input: The direction d, and the accuracy ε, an interval $[\underline{\eta}, \overline{\eta}]$ of η.
Output: Approximate solution path of OSCAR w.r.t. d on λ_1 and λ_2 in an interval of $[\underline{\eta}, \overline{\eta}]$.

1: Compute the solution θ and the groups $\mathcal{G}_g$ for $\eta = \underline{\eta}$ based on FastOSCAR.
2: **repeat**
3: Compute the directions of $\Delta\theta$.
4: Compute the maximum adjustment of $\Delta\eta$.
5: Update η, θ, λ_1, λ_2, $\mathcal{A}$ and the orders of θ_g.
6: Compute the duality gap $G(\theta, \lambda_1, \lambda_2)$ according to Algorithm 1.
7: **until** $\eta > \overline{\eta}$ or $G(\theta, \lambda_1, \lambda_2) > \varepsilon$
8: Backtrack the last piece of solution path to make sure the end solution to satisfy the accuracy ε.

3.1 Compute the Directions of $\Delta\theta$

As mentioned above, the principle during the adjustment of λ_1 and λ_2 is to keep the optimality conditions of OSCAR. According to the optimality condition (4), it is easy to find $\theta_{\overline{\mathcal{A}}}$ is fixed on the bound 0. Only $\theta_{\mathcal{A}}$ have the possibility to be adjusted when changing λ_1 and λ_2. Thus, we have the following linear system:

$$\sum_{i=1}^{l} \widetilde{x}_{ig} \widetilde{x}_{i\mathcal{A}}^T \Delta\theta_{\mathcal{A}} + \widetilde{w}_g \Delta\eta = 0, \quad \forall g \in \mathcal{A}\,, \tag{7}$$

where $\widetilde{w}_g = \sum_{j \in \mathcal{G}_g} (d_1 + (o(j) - 1) d_2)$. Let $\widetilde{W}$ be the $G \times G$ diagonal matrix with $\widetilde{W}_{gg} = \widetilde{w}_g$, and $\widetilde{X}$ be a $l \times G$ matrix whose i-th row is equal to $\widetilde{x}_i^T$. We can represent the above linear system (7) as the following in the matrix form:

$$\underbrace{\widetilde{X}_{*\mathcal{A}}^T \widetilde{X}_{*\mathcal{A}}}_{H_{\mathcal{A}\mathcal{A}}} \Delta\theta_{\mathcal{A}} + \widetilde{W}_{\mathcal{A}\mathcal{A}} \Delta\eta = \mathbf{0}\,. \tag{8}$$

Let $\xi_{\mathcal{A}}$ denote $\frac{\Delta\theta_{\mathcal{A}}}{\Delta\eta}$ (*i.e.*, the direction of $\Delta\theta_{\mathcal{A}}$ *w.r.t.* $\Delta\eta$), the linear system (8) can be rewritten as:

$$H_{\mathcal{A}\mathcal{A}}\xi_{\mathcal{A}} = -\widetilde{W}_{\mathcal{A}\mathcal{A}}. \tag{9}$$

Thus, we can get $\xi_{\mathcal{A}}$ by solving the linear system (9). Traditional way for solving the linear system (9) is by the direct matrix inverse of $H_{\mathcal{A}\mathcal{A}}$. As mentioned in [12, 20], the key matrix $H_{\mathcal{A}\mathcal{A}}$ will encounter singularities. For the robustness of OscarGKPath, we can compute $\xi_{\mathcal{A}}$ based on the QR decomposition with column pivoting [22] without directly computing the inverse of $H_{\mathcal{A}\mathcal{A}}$. Because $\Delta\theta_{\overline{\mathcal{A}}} = \mathbf{0}$, actually we know the direction of $\Delta\theta$.

3.2 Compute the Maximum Adjustment of $\Delta\eta$

After obtaining the linear relationships $\xi_{\mathcal{A}}$, we need to compute the maximum adjustment $\Delta\eta^{max}$ as mentioned previously. As shown in Fig. 1, there are three main types of cases which should be considered for the computation of $\Delta\eta^{max}$.

(1) A certain coefficient θ_g in $\mathcal{A}$ reaches 0. Thus we can compute the maximal possible $\Delta\eta^{\mathcal{A}}$ before a certain θ_g in $\mathcal{A}$ moves to $\overline{\mathcal{A}}$, by the constraints $\theta_g + \xi_g\Delta\eta > 0, \forall g \in \mathcal{A}$ in the optimality conditions of OSCAR.
(2) A pair of feature groups swap their orders of θ_g. As mentioned in (5), the optimality conditions of OSCAR are based on a given orders of θ_g. Thus, we can compute the maximal possible $\Delta\eta^o$ before a pair of adjacent groups $\mathcal{G}_g$ and $\mathcal{G}_{g+1}$ swap their orders, by the constraints $\theta_g + \xi_g\Delta\eta < \theta_{g+1} + \xi_{g+1}\Delta\eta$.
(3) η reaches $\overline{\eta}$, i.e., the termination condition is met. Then the maximal adjustment quantity before the solution path algorithm meets the termination condition is $\overline{\eta} - \eta$.

Thus, the smallest of three values $\{\Delta\eta^{\mathcal{A}}, \Delta\eta^o, \overline{\eta} - \eta\}$ constitutes the maximal adjustment quantity $\Delta\eta^{max}$.

3.3 Check the Duality Gap

The optimization problem $F(\beta)$ is a convex problem. Thus, we can guarantee the solution β is a ε-approximation solution with $F(\beta, \lambda_1, \lambda_2) - F(\beta^*, \lambda_1, \lambda_2) \leq \varepsilon$ by the duality gap $G(\beta, \lambda_1, \lambda_2) = F(\beta, \lambda_1, \lambda_2) - \widetilde{F}(\alpha, \lambda_1, \lambda_2) \leq \varepsilon$, where β^* is an optimal solution of $F(\beta, \lambda_1, \lambda_2)$, α is the dual variable, and $\widetilde{F}(\alpha, \lambda_1, \lambda_2)$ is the dual of $F(\beta, \lambda_1, \lambda_2)$. This conclusion holds because $F(\beta, \lambda_1, \lambda_2) - F(\beta^*, \lambda_1, \lambda_2) \leq G(\beta, \lambda_1, \lambda_2)$ [7].

As discussed in [4, 33], the dual function $\widetilde{F}(\alpha, \lambda_1, \lambda_2)$ can be computed as:

$$\widetilde{F}(\alpha, \lambda_1, \lambda_2) = \max_{\alpha} \quad \frac{-1}{2}\alpha^T\alpha - \alpha^T y \tag{10}$$
$$s.t. \quad \max_{\sum_{j=1}^{d}(\lambda_1 + \lambda_2(o(j)-1))|\beta_j|=1} \alpha^T X\beta \leq 1,$$

where X is an $l \times d$ matrix whose i-th row is equal to x_i^T. Further, [33] proved that the optimal α of $\widetilde{F}(\alpha)$ can be analytically computed as:

$$\alpha = \min\{1, \frac{1}{r^*(X^T\nabla f(\beta))}\}\nabla f(\beta), \tag{11}$$

where $\nabla f(\beta) = X\beta - y$. Assuming the indices of γ are sorted by $|\gamma_1| \leq |\gamma_2| \leq \cdots \leq |\gamma_d|$, we have:

$$r^*(\gamma) = \max_{j\in\{1,2,\cdots,d\}} \frac{\sum_{i=1}^{j}|\gamma_j|}{\sum_{i=1}^{j}\lambda_1 + (i-1)\lambda_2}. \tag{12}$$

The algorithm for computing the duality gap was originally proposed by [33]. In a word, it can be computed according to (10) based on the optimal α of $\widetilde{F}(\alpha, \lambda_1, \lambda_2)$ (11) which is analytically represented. Thus, the duality gap can be computed efficiently. We also present them in Algorithm 2 to be consistent with the formulation of (2).

Algorithm 2 Duality Gap

Input: β or θ, λ_1 and λ_2.
Output: The duality gap $G(\theta, \lambda_1, \lambda_2)$.
1: Compute $\gamma = X^T\nabla f(\beta)$ and sort γ_i in ascend order.
2: Compute $r^*(\gamma)$.
3: Compute the optimal α of $\widetilde{F}(\alpha)$ according to (11).
4: Compute the duality gap $G(\beta, \lambda_1, \lambda_2) = F(\beta, \lambda_1, \lambda_2) - \widetilde{F}(\alpha, \lambda_1, \lambda_2)$ according to (10).

4 ε-APPROXIMATION ANALYSIS OF OSCARGKPATH ALGORITHM

As shown in Algorithm 1, we check the duality gap only for several single points of η. How to guarantee that the whole solution path produced by OscarGKPath is ε-approximation is the focus of this section. In this section, we will prove that any solution in the solution path produced by OscarGKPath can strictly satisfy that $G(\theta, \lambda_1, \lambda_2) \leq \varepsilon$ (Corollary 4.3). In addition, we provide a guideline for choosing $\underline{\eta}$ and $\overline{\eta}$ (Theorem 4.5 and 4.6), which guide the choices for the start and ending points of the interval $[\underline{\eta}, \overline{\eta}]$.

Before answering the question, we first give a definition of piecewise linearity [10] of the solution path as following:

Definition 4.1. Suppose $\theta(\eta)$ is returned by a solution path. The solution $\theta(\eta)$ is called piecewise linear as a function of η, if existing $\underline{\eta} = \eta_0 < \eta_1 < \eta_2 < \cdots < \eta_m = \overline{\eta}$, and the corresponding vectors $\xi^{[1]}, \xi^{[2]}, \cdots, \xi^{[m]}$, such that the solution $\theta(\eta)$ is given exactly or approximately, by $\theta(\eta_k) + \xi^{[k]}(\eta - \eta_k), \forall\eta \in [\eta_k, \eta_{k+1}]$.

Based on Definition 4.1, it is easy to verify that $\theta(\eta)$ produced by OscarGKPath is piecewise linear, where each interval $[\eta_k, \eta_{k+1}]$ corresponds the interval produced by one iteration of OscarGKPath. Based on the piecewise linearity of OscarGKPath, we can prove that all the solutions $\beta(\eta)$, $\forall\eta \in [\eta_k, \eta_{k+1}]$, strictly satisfy that $G(\theta(\eta), \lambda_1, \lambda_2) \leq \varepsilon$ (Theorem 4.5), which means that any solution in the solution path produced by OscarGKPath can strictly satisfy that $G(\theta(\eta), d_1\eta, d_2\eta) \leq \varepsilon$ (Corollary 4.3).

Theorem 4.2. *For the interval $[\eta_k, \eta_{k+1}]$ produced by one iteration of OscarGKPath, we have that all the solutions $\theta(\eta)$, $\forall\eta \in [\eta_k, \eta_{k+1}]$, strictly satisfy that $G(\theta(\eta), d_1\eta, d_2\eta) \leq \varepsilon$.*

Proof. According to (11), we have that $\alpha = \nabla f(\beta)$ if $r^*(X^T\nabla f(\beta)) < 1$, otherwise $\alpha = \frac{1}{r^*(X^T\nabla f(\beta))}\nabla f(\beta)$. We first prove that the solutions $\theta(\eta)$, $\forall\eta \in [\eta_{k-1}, \eta_k]$, strictly satisfy that $G(\theta(\eta), d_1\eta, d_2\eta) \leq \varepsilon$

if $\alpha(\eta) = \nabla f(\beta(\eta))$.

$$\begin{aligned} & F(\theta(\eta), d_1\eta, d_2\eta) \qquad (13) \\ = \ & \frac{1}{2}\|\widetilde{X}\theta(\eta) - y\|^2 + \sum_{g=1}^{G} w_g\theta_g(\eta) \\ = \ & \frac{1}{2}\|\widetilde{X}(\theta(\eta_k) + \xi\Delta\eta) - y\|^2 \\ & + \sum_{g=1}^{G} \widetilde{w}_g(\eta_k + \Delta\eta)(\theta_g(\eta_k) + \xi_g\Delta\eta) \\ = \ & \underbrace{F(\theta(\eta_t))}_{c_1} + \underbrace{\left(\xi^T\xi + \sum_{g=1}^{G}\widetilde{w}_g\xi_g\right)}_{a_1}(\Delta\eta)^2 + \\ & \underbrace{\left(\sum_{g=1}^{G}\widetilde{w}_g(\eta_k\xi_g + \theta_g(\eta_k)) - 2\xi^T(\widetilde{X}\theta(\eta_k) - y)\right)}_{b_1}\Delta\eta \end{aligned}$$

$$\begin{aligned} & -\widetilde{F}(\alpha(\eta), d_1\eta, d_2\eta) \qquad (14) \\ = \ & \frac{1}{2}\alpha(\beta(\eta))^T\alpha(\beta(\eta)) + \alpha(\eta)^T y \\ = \ & \frac{1}{2}\left(X(\beta(\eta_t) + \widetilde{\xi}\Delta\eta) - y\right)^T\left(X(\beta(\eta_t) + \widetilde{\xi}\Delta\eta) - y\right) \\ & + \left(X(\beta(\eta_t) + \widetilde{\xi}\Delta\eta) - y\right)^T y \\ = \ & \underbrace{\widetilde{F}(\alpha(\eta_t))}_{c_2} + \underbrace{\frac{1}{2}\left(X\widetilde{\xi}\right)^T\left(X\widetilde{\xi}\right)}_{a_2}(\Delta\eta)^2 \\ & + \underbrace{\left((X\beta(\eta_t) - y^T)X\widetilde{\xi} + X\widetilde{\xi}^T y\right)}_{b_2}\Delta\eta \end{aligned}$$

where β can be converted from θ, $\widetilde{\xi}$ is the directions of $\Delta\beta$ which also can be converted from ξ. Based on (13)-(14), we can denote $G(\theta(\eta), d_1\eta, d_2\eta)$ as $G(\theta(\eta), d_1\eta, d_2\eta) = a(\Delta\eta)^2 + b\Delta\eta + c$, where

$$a = a_1 + a_2 \qquad (15)$$
$$b = b_1 + b_2 \qquad (16)$$
$$c = c_1 + c_2 \qquad (17)$$
$$\Delta\eta = \eta - \eta_t \qquad (18)$$

Thus, it is easy to verify that $a > 0$ or $a = 0$ and $b \geq 0$. Otherwise, we can get $G(\beta(\eta), d_1\eta, d_2\eta) < 0$ for some $\eta > \eta_t$, which contradicts with the fact $G(\beta(\eta), d_1\eta, d_2\eta) \geq 0$ for all $\eta \geq 0$. Thus, the maximum of $G(\theta(\eta), d_1\eta, d_2\eta)$ for $\eta \in [\eta_k, \eta_{k+1}]$ is either $G(\theta(\eta_t), d_1\eta_t, d_2\eta_t)$ or $G(\theta(\eta_{t+1}), d_1\eta_{t+1}, d_2\eta_{t+1})$. This completes the proof for $\alpha(\eta) = \nabla f(\beta(\eta))$.

If $\alpha = \frac{1}{r^*(X^T\nabla f(\beta))}\nabla f(\beta)$, we have:

$$\begin{aligned} & X^T\nabla f(\beta(\eta)) = X^T(X\beta(\eta) - y) \qquad (19) \\ = \ & X^T X(\beta(\eta_t) + \widetilde{\xi}\Delta\eta) - X^T y \\ = \ & X^T\nabla f(\beta(\eta_t)) + X^T X\widetilde{\xi}\Delta\eta . \end{aligned}$$

Assuming $r^*(\gamma(\eta))$ achieves the maximum at the index j_0, we have:

$$\begin{aligned} r^*(\gamma(\eta)) = \ & \frac{\sum_{i=1}^{j_0}|\gamma_j(\eta)|}{\sum_{i=1}^{j_0}\lambda_1 + (i-1)\lambda_2} \qquad (20) \\ = \ & \frac{\sum_{i=1}^{j_0}|X_{*i}^T\nabla f(\beta(\eta_t)) + X_{*i}^T X\widetilde{\xi}\Delta\eta|}{\sum_{i=1}^{j_0}\lambda_1 + (i-1)\lambda_2} \\ \stackrel{\text{def}}{=} \ & r^*(\gamma(\eta_t)) + \widetilde{a}\Delta\eta . \end{aligned}$$

Thus, we have $\alpha(\eta) = \frac{X(\beta(\eta_t)) - y + \widetilde{\xi}\Delta\eta}{r^*(\gamma(\eta_t)) + \widetilde{a}\Delta\eta}$. Let

$$\begin{aligned} & (X(\beta(\eta_t)) - y + \widetilde{\xi}\Delta\eta)^T y(r^*(\gamma(\eta_t)) + \widetilde{a}\Delta\eta) \\ \stackrel{\text{def}}{=} \ & a_3(\Delta\eta)^2 + b_3\Delta\eta + c_3 , \qquad (21) \end{aligned}$$

we have:

$$\begin{aligned} & -\widetilde{F}(\alpha(\eta), d_1\eta, d_2\eta) \qquad (22) \\ = \ & \frac{(a_2 + a_3)(\Delta\eta)^2 + (b_2 + b_3)\Delta\eta + c_2 + c_3}{(r^*(\gamma(\eta_t)) + \widetilde{a}\Delta\eta)^2} \end{aligned}$$

We can conclude that $\frac{-r^*(\gamma(\eta_t))}{\widetilde{a}} < 0$. Otherwise, it is easy to verify that the duality gap is negative or infinite for some $\Delta\eta > 0$ because the singular point $\Delta\eta = \frac{-r^*(\gamma(\eta_t))}{\widetilde{a}}$. Further, we have that $r^*(\gamma(\eta_t)) > 0$ and $\widetilde{a} > 0$. We have that $a_2 + a_3 > 0$ because $\lim_{\eta\to\infty} -\widetilde{F}(\alpha(\eta), d_1\eta, d_2\eta) = \frac{a_2+a_3}{\widetilde{a}^2}$. Further, $a_2 + a_3$ should be much larger than $-\widetilde{a}^2\widetilde{F}(\alpha(\eta_k), d_1\eta_k, d_2\eta_k)$. Thus, $-\widetilde{F}(\alpha(\eta), d_1\eta, d_2\eta)$ should not be monotonically increasing then decreasing for $\eta > 0$.

Similarly, we can conclude that $a_1 > 0$ or or $a_1 = 0$ and $b_1 \geq 0$. Otherwise, we can get $G(\beta(\eta), d_1\eta, d_2\eta) < 0$ for some $\eta > \eta_t$, which contradicts with the fact $G(\beta(\eta), d_1\eta, d_2\eta) \geq 0$ for all $\eta \geq 0$. Thus, $F(\theta(\eta), d_1\eta, d_2\eta)$ should not be monotonically increasing then decreasing for $\eta > 0$.

Thus, combining the analysis for $-\widetilde{F}(\alpha(\eta), d_1\eta, d_2\eta)$ and $F(\theta(\eta), d_1\eta, d_2\eta)$ as mentioned above, we can conclude that $G(\theta(\eta), d_1\eta, d_2\eta)$ should not be monotonically increasing then decreasing for $\eta > 0$. Thus, the maximum of $G(\theta(\eta), d_1\eta, d_2\eta)$ for $\eta \in [\eta_k, \eta_{k+1}]$ would be at the start point or endpoint of the interval $[\eta_k, \eta_{k+1}]$. This completes the proof. □

Corollary 4.3. *For all solutions $\theta(\eta)$ produced by OscarGKPath, we have that $\theta(\eta)$ satisfies that $G(\theta(\eta), d_1\eta, d_2\eta) \leq \varepsilon$.*

Corollary 4.3 can be easily obtained based on Theorem 4.5. In the following, we give the definition of the maximal of η (denoted by $\eta_{\min}$) such that $\beta(\eta_{\min})$ is a solution of the ordinary least squares. We also give the the definition of the minimum of η (denoted by $\eta_{\max}$) such that $\beta(\eta_{\max}) = \mathbf{0}$. It is intuitive that $[\eta_{\min}, \eta_{\max}]$ is a good choice for the interval $[\underline{\eta}, \overline{\eta}]$ in Algorithm 1.

Definition 4.4. Let $\beta(0) = (\widetilde{X}^T\widetilde{X})^{-1}\widetilde{X}^T y$ is the solution of (2) with $\eta = 0$. $\eta_{\min}$ is the maximal of η in (2) such that $F(\beta(\eta_{\min}), d_1\eta_{\min}, d_2\eta_{\min}) = F(\beta(0), 0, 0)$. Let $\beta(\infty) = \mathbf{0}$ is the solution of (2) with $\eta = \infty$. $\eta_{\max}$ is the minimum of η in (2) such that $F(\beta(\eta_{\max}), d_1\eta_{\max}, d_2\eta_{\max}) = F(\mathbf{0}, \infty, \infty)$.

Theorem 4.5. *We define $t_{\max}$ as*

$$t_{\max} = \min_{v} \quad \|\beta(0) + v\|_1 + \qquad (23)$$

$$\frac{d_2}{d_1}\sum_{j<k}\max\{|\beta(0)_j + v_j|, |\beta(0)_k + v_k|\}$$
$$s.t. \quad X^T v = \mathbf{0}$$

Let $\beta = \beta(0) + v$. We have $\eta_{\min} = \|D^{-1}X^T(X\beta - y)\|_\infty$, where D is a $d \times d$ diagonal matrix with $D_{jj} = d_1 + d_2(o(j) - 1)$.

Proof. According to the subdifferential version of KKT conditions [24], we have that $X^T(X\beta - y) + Dv\eta = \mathbf{0}$, where $v \in \partial\|\beta\|_1$. Thus, we have $\eta = \|D^{-1}X^T(X\beta - y)\|_\infty$ if $\beta \neq \mathbf{0}$. As mentioned in [6], there exists a direct correspondence between t and η. Specifically, the larger t is, and the smaller η. Thus, $\eta_{\min} = \|D^{-1}X^T(X(\beta(0) + v) - y)\|_\infty$. This completes the proof. □

The problem (23) can be solved by the augmented Lagrangian algorithm efficiently with the iteration complexity $O(\log(\epsilon^{-1}))$ [3], where ϵ is the accuracy of the solution.

Theorem 4.6. *Let Ω denote the set of all possible orders for $|\beta = \mathbf{0}|$, and let D^Ω denote the set of all possible D based on a given Ω. We have*

$$\eta_{\max} = \min \quad \|D^{-1}X^T y\|_\infty \qquad (24)$$
$$s.t. \quad D \in D^\Omega$$

Proof. According to the subdifferential version of KKT conditions [24], we have $Dv\eta - X^T y = \mathbf{0}$, where $v \in \partial\|\beta\|_1$. Because $v_j \in [-1, 1]$, we have that $\eta = \|D^{-1}X^T y\|_\infty$. This completes the proof. □

Essentially, (24) is a combinatorial optimization, which can not be solved exactly in polynomial time. In practice, we can set the orders of $|\beta_j|$ as the ones of the $|X^T y|$ in ascending order, which gives a good approximation of $\eta_{\max}$.

5 EXPERIMENTAL RESULTS

In this section, we first describe the experimental setup, and then provide the experimental results and discussions.

5.1 Experimental Setup

5.1.1 Design of Experiments. The experiments include two parts. The first part is to verify the effectiveness of OscarGKPath, and the second part is to show the advantage of OscarGKPath for model selection.

To verify the effectiveness of OscarGKPath, we count the numbers of the iterations (denoted as *#Iterations*) of OscarGKPath and the numbers of calling FastOSCAR (denoted as *#FastOSCAR*) for producing the entire solution path. By counting the *#FastOSCAR*, we want to check how many the calling of FastOSCAR are needed for producing the entire solution path. By counting the *#Iterations*, we empirically show that finite convergence of OscarGKPath. To show the advantage of OscarGKPath for model selection, we compare the running time, cross validation errors and testing errors of our OscarGKPath and the batch algorithm (*i.e.*, FastOSCAR) for 5-fold cross validation.

5.1.2 Implementation Details. We implement our proposed OscarGKPath in MATLAB. As mentioned previously, to the best of our knowledge, the FastOSCAR algorithm [33] is the fastest batch learning algorithm for OSCAR. To compare the run-time at the same platform, we implement the FastOSCAR algorithm in MATLAB to compare the running time of cross validation with our OscarGKPath.

The 5-fold cross validation is done on a two-step grid search strategy [11]. The initial search is done on a 20 coarse grid linearly spaced in the region $\{\log_2 \eta| - 4 \leq \log_2 \eta \leq 15\}$, followed by a fine search on a 20 uniform grid linearly spaced by 0.1 in the $(\log_2 \eta)$ space. To compare the running time of FastOSCAR and OscarGKPath and verify the effectiveness of OscarGKPath, we do the experiments on three representative directions of d, *i.e.*, $\begin{bmatrix} 1 \\ 0.5 \end{bmatrix}$, $\begin{bmatrix} 1 \\ 1 \end{bmatrix}$ and $\begin{bmatrix} 1 \\ 2 \end{bmatrix}$. Thus, we fix $d_1 = 1$, and set $d_2 = 0.5$, 1 and 2 respectively. In the experiments, we set the duality gap $G(\theta(\eta), d_1\eta, d_2\eta) \leq \varepsilon = 0.1 \times F(\beta^*, d_1, d_2)$.

5.1.3 Datasets. Table 1 summarizes the details of seven benchmark datasets used in our experiments, where the first and last two datasets (*i.e.*, YearPredictionMSD, USPS, SensIT Vehicle (combined) and Protein datasets) are from the LIBSVM Data[1], and the IndoorLoc Longitude, IndoorLoc Latitude and Slice Localization datasets are from the UCI benchmark repository [5]. The Left Ventricle and Right Ventricle dataset were collected from 3360 MRI images by hospital and each image has 400 pixels. Both of the datasets are encouraged to find the homogenous groups of features. The Left and right Ventricle datasets are to predict the areas for left ventricle and right ventricle respectively [16, 17]. Note that, the alphabets in the $(\cdot)$ are the abbreviation of the name of the corresponding dataset.

Table 1: The summary of datasets used in our experiments.

Dataset	Sample size	Attributes
YearPredictionMSD(YP)	51,630	90
USPS	7,291	256
Left Ventricle(LV)	3,360	400
Right Ventricle(RV)	3,360	400
IndoorLoc Longitude(InLo)	21,048	529
IndoorLoc Latitude(InLa)	21,048	529
Slice Localization(SL)	53,500	386
SensIT Vehicle Combined	78,823	100
Protein	17,766	357

5.2 Experimental Results and Discussions

Effectiveness of OscarGKPath: Table 2 presents the average numbers of *#Iterations* for OscarGKPath over 10 trials with different values of d_2 on the YearPredictionMSD, USPS, Left Ventricle, Right Ventricle, IndoorLoc Longitude, IndoorLoc Latitude, Slice Localization, SensIT Vehicle Combined and Protein datasets. The results show that OscarGKPath can fit the entire approximate solution path of OSCAR within a finite number of iterations. Table 2 also presents

[1] https://www.csie.ntu.edu.tw/~cjlin/libsvmtools/datasets/

Table 2: Average results of OscarGKPath over 10 trials.

Dataset	Size	*#Iterations*			*#FastOSCAR*		
		$d_2 = 0.5$	$d_2 = 1$	$d_2 = 2$	$d_2 = 0.5$	$d_2 = 1$	$d_2 = 2$
YearPredictionMSD	10,000	2,628	2,742	1,484	8	7	6
	20,000	3,063	2,497	1,694	8	8	7
	30,000	4,012	4,285	2,266	8	8	8
	40,000	3,789	5,128	1,891	8	8	9
USPS	1,500	2,032	2,536	1,874	6	7	7
	3,000	1,865	3,142	2,893	9	9	8
	4,500	3,512	2,892	2,571	10	10	10
	6,000	3,357	4,932	2,974	12	11	11
Left Ventricle	800	7,324	8,731	6,319	10	8	7
	1,600	8,629	10,896	6,232	13	10	9
	2,400	7,149	9,643	6,882	13	12	9
	3,200	9,798	9,921	7,237	14	13	11
Right Ventricle	800	8,163	8,932	6,654	9	8	7
	1,600	8,676	11,324	6,134	11	10	8
	2,400	9,564	9,251	7,234	12	12	10
	3,200	11,941	10,453	8,951	13	12	11
IndoorLoc Longitude	4,200	903	954	502	23	19	12
	8,400	615	891	499	21	18	12
	12,600	469	604	439	24	18	15
	16,800	558	753	695	26	21	11
IndoorLoc Latitude	4,200	7,124	6,212	7,290	6	5	5
	8,400	6,161	7,404	6,260	6	6	5
	12,600	7,908	6,348	4,767	5	5	5
	16,800	5,837	5,210	4,980	5	5	5
Slice Localization	10,000	9,073	8,738	9,346	8	8	7
	20,000	7,330	5,328	7,207	9	8	8
	30,000	4,442	7,620	6,804	8	9	9
	40,000	6,220	9,483	7,896	10	10	9
SensIT Vehicle Combined	5,000	1,844	2,321	2,435	5	6	6
	10,000	1,667	2,073	2,656	5	5	6
	15,000	1,430	2,001	2,092	5	5	5
	20,000	910	1,844	2,012	4	5	5
Protein	3,000	793	937	587	5	4	3
	6,000	765	898	485	6	5	4
	9,000	988	715	689	6	5	4
	12,000	567	815	743	6	6	5

#FastOSCAR for OSCAR over 10 trials with different values of d_2 on different datasets. The results empirically show that only the limited calling of FastOSCAR can produce the entire solution path. Based on the results of *#Iterations* and *#FastOSCAR*, we verify that OscarGKPath is an effective algorithm to fit the entire approximate solution path of OSCAR.

Advantages of OscarGKPath: Fig. 2 plots the running time of OscarGKPath and FastOSCAR in 5-fold cross validation on the YearPredictionMSD, USPS, Left Ventricle, IndoorLoc Longitude, IndoorLoc Latitude, Slice Localization, SensIT Vehicle Combined and Protein datasets with different values of d_2. The results demonstrate that the cross validation based on our OscarGKPath is generally much faster than the one based on FastOSCAR. Because our OscarGKPath only runs five times for the 5-fold cross validation, however, FastOSCAR has to run 400×5 times for the 5-fold cross validation.

Fig. 3 illustrates the cross validation errors and testing errors of OscarGKPath and FastOSCAR for 5-fold cross validation over 10 trials with notched box plot, where the mean squared error (MSE) is used as the performance criterion. From the results, we can find that OscarGKPath performs better than or equally to FastOSCAR on the cross validation errors. This is because that our OscarGKPath fits the entire approximate solution path with a given accuracy bound ε which guarantees that the cross validation error of our OscarGKPath is not worse than the one of FastOSCAR with the same accuracy bound ε. The results of Fig. 3 also confirm the generalization of our OscarGKPath on the testing sets.

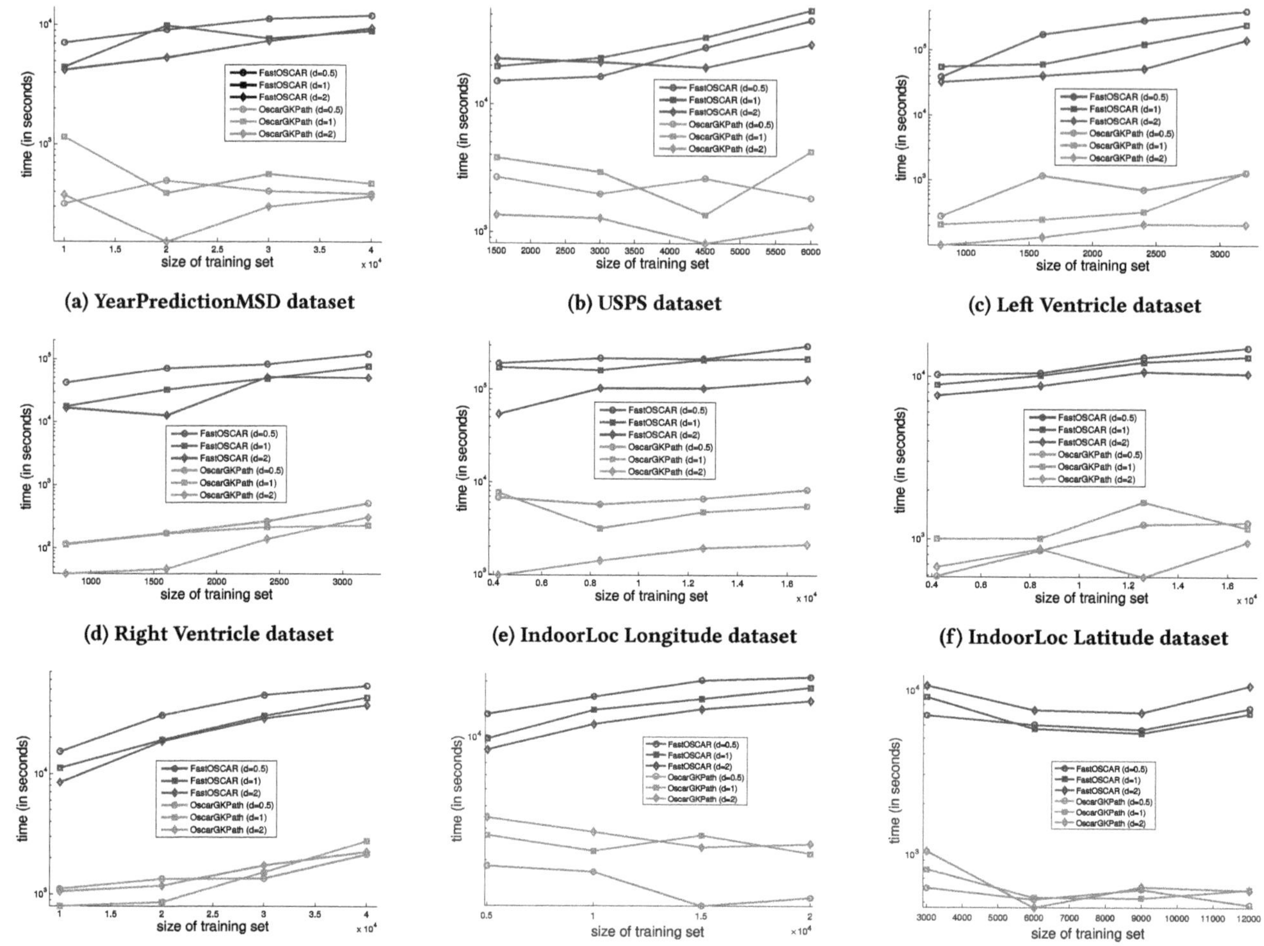

(a) YearPredictionMSD dataset (b) USPS dataset (c) Left Ventricle dataset

(d) Right Ventricle dataset (e) IndoorLoc Longitude dataset (f) IndoorLoc Latitude dataset

(g) Slice Localization dataset (h) SensIT Vehicle Combined dataset (i) Protein dataset

Figure 2: Average running time (in seconds) of OscarGKPath and FastOSCAR with 5-fold cross validation over 10 trials.

In addition to showing the advantage of OscarGKPath for model selection, we also validate the advantage of OSCAR for automatic feature grouping. Facebook Comment Volume dataset from the UCI benchmark repository [5] is originally with 54 features. We select 6 most important features by LASSO and duplicate these features 20 times with noise from $N(0, 0.16)$. Fig. 3 presents the absolute coefficients of OSCAR and LASSO on the revised Facebook Comment Volume dataset. The results show that LASSO arbitrarily selects several (maybe zero) of them from a group. However, OSCAR can group the features automatically, and its solution is closer to the ground truth.

6 CONCLUSION

OSCAR is an effective feature selection approach which can automatically group homogenous features in feature selection process. In this paper, we proposed a novel groups-keeping solution path algorithm of OSCAR (OscarGKPath), which can effectively handle the pairwise ℓ_∞-norm in OSCAR, and produce an approximate solution path. More importantly, we theoretically prove that all solutions from OscarGKPath can strictly satisfy a given accuracy bound ε. OscarGKPath can greatly benefit the regularization parameters tuning of OSCAR and generate stable and optimal results. The experimental results on a variety of datasets not only confirm the effectiveness of our OscarGKPath, but also show the superiority of our OscarGKPath in cross validation compared with the existing batch algorithm. In the further, we plan to extend the OscarGKPath algorithm to the general structured sparse learning method with the ℓ_∞-norm [1, 18].

REFERENCES

[1] Henry Adams, Tegan Emerson, Michael Kirby, Rachel Neville, Chris Peterson, Patrick Shipman, Sofya Chepushtanova, Eric Hanson, Francis Motta, and Lori Ziegelmeier. 2017. Persistence Images: A Stable Vector Representation of Persistent Homology. *Journal of Machine Learning Research* 18, 8 (2017), 1–35.

[2] Charlotte Møller Andersen and Rasmus Bro. 2010. Variable selection in regression a tutorial. *Journal of Chemometrics* 24, 11-12 (2010), 728–737.

[3] Necdet Aybat, Zi Wang, and Garud Iyengar. 2015. An Asynchronous Distributed Proximal Gradient Method for Composite Convex Optimization. In *Proceedings of The 32nd International Conference on Machine Learning*. 2454–2462.

[4] Francis Bach, Rodolphe Jenatton, Julien Mairal, Guillaume Obozinski, and others. 2011. Convex optimization with sparsity-inducing norms. *Optimization for Machine Learning* 5 (2011).

[5] K. Bache and M. Lichman. 2013. UCI Machine Learning Repository. (2013). http://archive.ics.uci.edu/ml

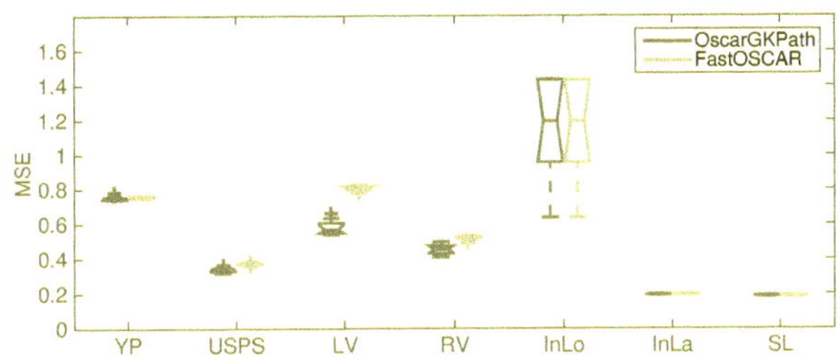

(a) Cross validation errors

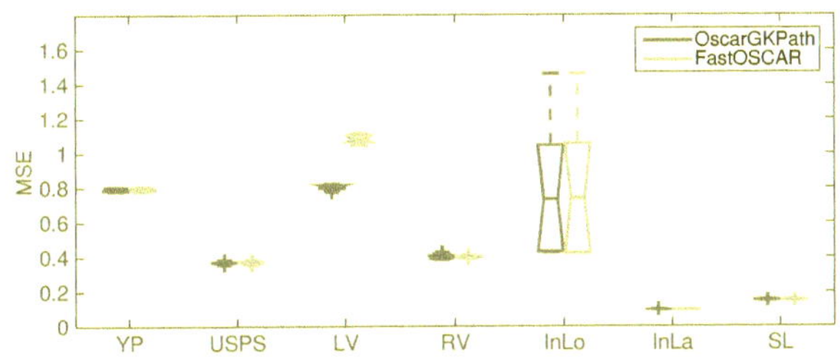

(b) Testing errors

Figure 3: Cross validation errors and testing errors of OscarGKPath and FastOSCAR with 5-fold cross validation over 10 trials.

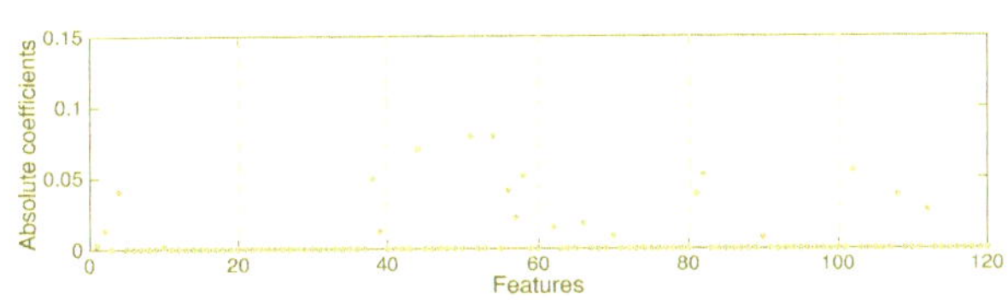

(a) LASSO

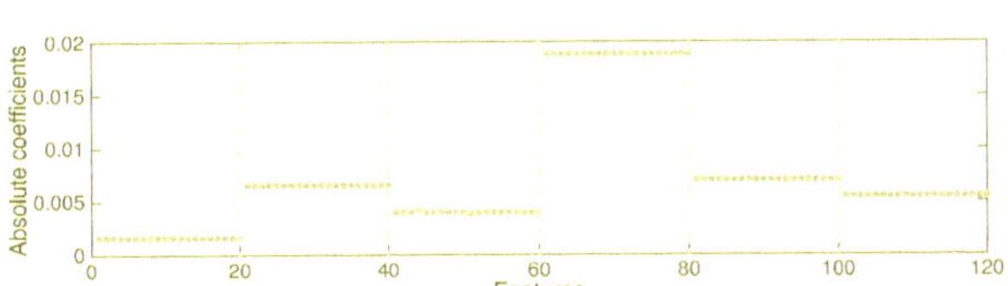

(b) OSCAR

Figure 4: Absolute coefficients of LASSO and OSCAR on the Facebook Comment Volume dataset.

[6] Howard D Bondell and Brian J Reich. 2008. Simultaneous regression shrinkage, variable selection, and supervised clustering of predictors with OSCAR. *Biometrics* 64, 1 (2008), 115–123.

[7] Stephen Boyd and Lieven Vandenberghe. 2004. *Convex optimization.* Cambridge university press.

[8] Xiao Cai, Feiping Nie, and Heng Huang. 2013. Exact Top-k Feature Selection via l2,0-Norm Constraint. *23rd International Joint Conference on Artificial Intelligence (IJCAI)* (2013), 1240–1246.

[9] Xiao Cai, Feiping Nie, Heng Huang, and Chris Ding. 2011. Feature Selection via l2,1-Norm Support Vector Machine. In *IEEE International Conference on Data Mining.* 91–100.

[10] Bin Gu and Charles X Ling. 2015. A New Generalized Error Path Algorithm for Model Selection. In *Proceedings of the 32nd International Conference on Machine Learning (ICML-15).* 2549–2558.

[11] Bin Gu, Victor Sheng, Keng Tay, Walter Romano, and Shuo Li. 2016. Cross Validation Through Two-dimensional Solution Surface for Cost-Sensitive SVM. (2016).

[12] B. Gu and V. S. Sheng. 2016. A Robust Regularization Path Algorithm for ν-Support Vector Classification. *IEEE Transactions on Neural Networks and Learning Systems* PP, 99 (2016), 1–8. https://doi.org/10.1109/TNNLS.2016.2527796

[13] Jiang Gui and Hongzhe Li. 2005. Penalized Cox regression analysis in the high-dimensional and low-sample size settings, with applications to microarray gene expression data. *Bioinformatics* 21, 13 (2005), 3001–3008.

[14] Michael J Heller. 2002. DNA microarray technology: devices, systems, and applications. *Annual review of biomedical engineering* 4, 1 (2002), 129–153.

[15] Gabor T Herman. 1990. A survey of 3D medical imaging technologies. *IEEE engineering in medicine and biology magazine: the quarterly magazine of the Engineering in Medicine & Biology Society* 9, 4 (1990), 15.

[16] Rainer Hoffmann, Giuseppe Barletta, Stephan von Bardeleben, Jean Louis Vanoverschelde, Jaroslaw Kasprzak, Christian Greis, and Harald Becher. 2014. Analysis of left ventricular volumes and function: a multicenter comparison of cardiac magnetic resonance imaging, cine ventriculography, and unenhanced and contrast-enhanced two-dimensional and three-dimensional echocardiography. *Journal of the American Society of Echocardiography* 27, 3 (2014), 292–301.

[17] Roberto M Lang, Luigi P Badano, Victor Mor-Avi, Jonathan Afilalo, Anderson Armstrong, Laura Ernande, Frank A Flachskampf, Elyse Foster, Steven A Goldstein, Tatiana Kuznetsova, and others. 2015. Recommendations for cardiac chamber quantification by echocardiography in adults: an update from the American Society of Echocardiography and the European Association of Cardiovascular Imaging. *Journal of the American Society of Echocardiography* 28, 1 (2015), 1–39.

[18] Julien Mairal, Rodolphe Jenatton, Francis R Bach, and Guillaume R Obozinski. 2010. Network flow algorithms for structured sparsity. In *Advances in Neural Information Processing Systems.* 1558–1566.

[19] Feiping Nie, Heng Huang, Xiao Cai, and Chris Ding. 2010. Efficient and Robust Feature Selection via Joint l2,1-Norms Minimization. *NIPS* (2010).

[20] Chong-Jin Ong, Shiyun Shao, and Jianbo Yang. 2010. An improved algorithm for the solution of the regularization path of support vector machine. *IEEE Transactions on Neural Networks* 21, 3 (2010), 451–462.

[21] Mee Young Park and Trevor Hastie. 2007. L1-regularization path algorithm for generalized linear models. *Journal of the Royal Statistical Society: Series B (Statistical Methodology)* 69, 4 (2007), 659–677.

[22] David Poole. 2014. *Linear algebra: A modern introduction.* Cengage Learning.

[23] Saharon Rosset and Ji Zhu. 2007. Piecewise linear regularized solution paths. *The Annals of Statistics* (2007), 1012–1030.

[24] Andrzej P Ruszczyński. 2006. *Nonlinear Optimization.* Number 13 in Nonlinear optimization. Princeton University Press.

[25] Yiyuan She. 2010. Sparse regression with exact clustering. *Electronic Journal of Statistics* 4 (2010), 1055–1096.

[26] Robert Tibshirani. 1996. Regression shrinkage and selection via the lasso. *Journal of the Royal Statistical Society. Series B (Methodological)* (1996), 267–288.

[27] Robert Tibshirani, Michael Saunders, Saharon Rosset, Ji Zhu, and Keith Knight. 2005. Sparsity and smoothness via the fused lasso. *Journal of the Royal Statistical Society: Series B (Statistical Methodology)* 67, 1 (2005), 91–108.

[28] Ryan Joseph Tibshirani, Jonathan E Taylor, Emmanuel Jean Candes, and Trevor Hastie. 2011. *The solution path of the generalized lasso.* Stanford University.

[29] H. Wang, F. Nie, H. Huang, S. Kim, K. Nho, S. L. Risacher, A. J. Saykin, and L. Shen. 2012. Identifying quantitative trait loci via group-sparse multitask regression and feature selection: an imaging genetics study of the ADNI cohort. *Bioinformatics* 28, 2 (2012), 229–37.

[30] Hua Wang, Feiping Nie, Heng Huang, Shannon Risacher, Chris Ding, Andrew J Saykin, Li Shen, and ADNI. 2011. Sparse Multi-Task Regression and Feature Selection to Identify Brain Imaging Predictors for Memory Performance. In *IEEE Conference on Computer Vision.* 557–562.

[31] Larry Wasserman and Kathryn Roeder. 2009. High dimensional variable selection. *Annals of statistics* 37, 5A (2009), 2178.

[32] Seongho Wu, Xiaotong Shen, and Charles J Geyer. 2009. Adaptive regularization using the entire solution surface. *Biometrika* 96, 3 (2009), 513–527.

[33] Leon Wenliang Zhong and James T Kwok. 2012. Efficient sparse modeling with automatic feature grouping. *IEEE transactions on neural networks and learning systems* 23, 9 (2012), 1436–1447.

[34] Ji Zhu, Saharon Rosset, Trevor Hastie, and Rob Tibshirani. 2004. 1-norm support vector machines. *Advances in neural information processing systems* 16, 1 (2004), 49–56.

[35] Hui Zou and Trevor Hastie. 2005. Regularization and variable selection via the elastic net. *Journal of the Royal Statistical Society: Series B (Statistical Methodology)* 67, 2 (2005), 301–320.

Clustering Individual Transactional Data for Masses of Users

Riccardo Guidotti
ISTI-CNR & University of Pisa, Italy
riccardo.guidotti@isti.cnr.it

Anna Monreale
University of Pisa, Italy
anna.monreale@di.unipi.it

Mirco Nanni
ISTI-CNR, Pisa, Italy
mirco.nanni@isti.cnr.it

Fosca Giannotti
ISTI-CNR, Pisa, Italy
fosca.giannotti@isti.cnr.it

Dino Pedreschi
University of Pisa, Italy
dino.pedreschi@di.unipi.it

ABSTRACT

Mining a large number of datasets recording human activities for making sense of individual data is the key enabler of a new wave of personalized knowledge-based services. In this paper we focus on the problem of clustering individual transactional data for a large mass of users. Transactional data is a very pervasive kind of information that is collected by several services, often involving huge pools of users. We propose *txmeans*, a parameter-free clustering algorithm able to efficiently partitioning transactional data in a completely automatic way. *Txmeans* is designed for the case where clustering must be applied on a massive number of different datasets, for instance when a large set of users need to be analyzed individually and each of them has generated a long history of transactions. A deep experimentation on both real and synthetic datasets shows the practical effectiveness of *txmeans* for the mass clustering of different personal datasets, and suggests that *txmeans* outperforms existing methods in terms of quality and efficiency. Finally, we present a *personal cart assistant* application based on *txmeans*.

1 INTRODUCTION

The most disruptive effect of our always-connected society is *data*, the digital breadcrumbs left behind us as a side effect of our everyday usage of digital technologies. Thanks to these data, human activities are becoming observable, measurable, quantifiable and, predictable. At individual level, each person generates more than 5Gb of data per year. An avalanche of information that, for the most part, consists of *transactions* (or baskets), i.e., a special kind of categorical data in the form of sets of event data, such as the items purchased in a shopping cart, the web pages visited in a browsing session, the songs listened in a time period, the clinical events in a patient's history. Such kind of data may be key enablers of a new wave of knowledge-based services, and of new scientific discoveries.

Several application contexts involve the analysis of a large number of datasets, each one characterized by different properties. For instance, this is the case of individual transactional data – retail sales, web sessions, credit card transactions, etc. – where each user produces historical data that need to be analyzed separately from other users. This requires that a parameter-tuning phase is included in any data mining method we want to apply, driven by the necessity to automatically capture the wide diversity of individual behaviors. Due to the potentially large number of datasets (e.g. users in nowadays massive systems scale up to billion), it is generally unfeasible to determine in an ad-hoc manner the optimal parameter configuration for each of them. Therefore, we need *auto-focus* data mining methods that adjust their parameter setting to the characteristics of the dataset under analysis, to the aim of extracting personalized patterns from transactional data of each user [17].

In this paper we focus on the problem of performing transactional clustering for a large number of different datasets. Given a collection of transactions, transactional clustering consists in discovering groups of homogeneous transactions which share many common items [30]. In the state of the art, all the methods for transactional clustering require either a parameter tuning process that is not automatic, or an extremely heavy automated process that does not scale to large user bases [3, 12, 13, 30, 36]. Hence, repeatedly applying the existing procedures on thousands or millions of different datasets – which is the case when dealing with a large population of users – is simply unfeasible. We refer to this problem, i.e., the separate individual clustering of many individual transactional datasets, as *mass clustering*.

The problem to design parameter-free clustering algorithms has been addressed in the context of non transactional data by solutions like *xmeans* [22], which are perfect for solving many instances of the clustering problems. Unfortunately, they are not directly applicable to transactional data. To the best of our knowledge, the only existing parameter-free transactional clustering algorithms are [5, 7]. Nevertheless, they are based on a scanning schema which is generally not efficient and overestimates the real number of clusters. In addition, they do not provide representative transactions, i.e., the items that characterize the transactions contained in each cluster.

In this paper we propose *txmeans*, a new parameter-free clustering method providing a viable solution to the problem of clustering a massive number of different datasets. Our proposal follows a strategy similar to *xmeans* [22], but is designed and improved for finding clusters in the specific context of transactional data.

Txmeans overcomes the deficiencies of existing methods, indeed, it automatically estimates the number of clusters and, besides extracting the clusters, it provides the *representative transaction* of each cluster, which summarizes the pattern captured by that cluster. *Txmeans* employs a top-down divisive approach which starts from a unique cluster, and then iteratively splits the cluster into two sub-clusters. *Txmeans* calculates the representative baskets as the centroids of the sub-clusters by adopting a procedure described in

KDD '17, August 13-17, 2017, Halifax, NS, Canada

DOI: 10.1145/3097983.3098034

[12]. The representative baskets enable *txmeans* to decide through the *Bayesian Information Criteria* [24] (adapted to transactional data) whether the cluster under analysis needs further partitioning or not. The capability to adapt to specific individual datasets combined with a high efficiency put *txmeans* in the position of outperforming all competitors when transactional clustering must be applied on a very large number of different datasets, both in terms of clusters quality and in terms of running time.

We extensively validate our method using a large array of synthetic and real datasets. *Txmeans*' performance shows stability across diversified situations, including noise and varying clustering structures, and it scales to large datasets. The results suggest that *txmeans* is the best approach for the clustering of a massive number of datasets, but also for the clustering of a single individual dataset *txmeans*'s performance are significantly better than those of the competitors. The proposed approach enables sophisticated processes, based on individual clustering, to offer personalized services such as prediction-based and recommendation-based services.

As final result, we show how to exploit the individual clusters and representative transactions to build a *personal cart assistant* that suggests to the customer the items to put in her shopping list.

The paper is organized as follows. Section 2 discusses the related work. Section 3 defines the problem setting and Section 4 describes our clustering method. Section 5 shows a deep experimentation, while Section 6 illustrates *txmeans* in a recommender system application. Finally, Section 7 concludes the paper.

2 RELATED WORK

In the literature there is a great variety of papers proposing approaches for clustering transactional data. Most existing algorithms require the setting of different parameters which often may be difficult to tune. The first algorithm proposed for transactional clustering is *large item* [30]. It requires a support threshold indicating the minimum number of occurrences for an item to be *large* for a cluster. Through a scan of the transactions, it evaluates a global cost function and decides the cluster for that transaction, or creates a new one. Algorithms like *rock* and *clope* were proposed with the same scanning strategy but different cost functions [13, 35, 36].

The most common parameter is the number of clusters k [12, 15, 32, 37]. *Tkmeans* [12] is an example of this category, and also represents the first attempt to use a clustering strategy – basically the standard *k-means* [27] – different from direct optimization of a cost function. Also our *txmeans* does not minimize a cost function, and it inherits from *tkmeans* the method to extract cluster centroids. Another approach able to extract cluster centroids, but only for categorical dataset, is *k-modes* [6] which employs the mode instead of the mean. A recent approach with a different purpose is proposed in [9]: *purtreeclust* is a method for clustering customers through their purchase trees which are built on the customers transactions. The *txmeans* method can recall *purtreeclust* in the construction of a tree to extract the clusters, however the measure used to perform the split is different, and the predictive clustering trees works only on classical categorical data and not on transactional data.

A further notion widely used in cost functions to measure the similarity of data objects is entropy [2, 3, 8, 19]. In [3] is proposed *coolcat* that iteratively chooses the suitable cluster for each transaction by minimizing the entropy at each step. A similar procedure is followed by the algorithm *limbo* [2]. A dual approach is proposed in [19] where starting from a single cluster a Monte Carlo process is used to select a transaction and to assign it to another cluster to decrease the entropy. The process is repeated until convergence.

Besides parameter tuning, when dealing with transactional data another problem is high dimensionality: it makes algorithms inefficient in terms of execution time and clustering quality. To not suffer from high dimensionality, *subspace* clustering algorithms like [11, 38] have been proposed, with the goal of finding clusters embedded in subspaces of the original data with their own dimensions. Algorithms like [4, 10] use bipartite graph theory to cluster datasets. They generate co-clustering results where columns and rows are simultaneously partitioned. In transactional data this means an unnatural split of the clusters that overlap over a few frequent items. Moreover, they are often memory and time consuming, and inappropriate for clustering large datasets.

Some proposals were made to overcome manual parameter tuning. [8] introduces an entropy-based clustering evaluating the similarity with incremental entropy, and finally, generating a clustering tree containing clusterings with different numbers of clusters. The authors of [34] propose to run their algorithm with different numbers of clusters and choose the result that optimizes a novel index of quality. In terms of execution time this method is clearly inefficient.

Atdc [7] is a parameter-free transactional clustering algorithm which, similarly to our method, adopts a top-down strategy resembling a decision tree algorithm. [5] proposes the *practical* parameter-free method that through scanning automatically identifies clusters even in presence of rare items. Finally, also the *dhcc* algorithm presented in [33] is a parameter-free procedure based on a divisive hierarchical clustering approach. However, *dhcc* is especially designed to work on categorical rather than transactional data.

The main difference between these methods and *txmeans* is the ability to extract centroids, i.e., representative itemsets for each cluster. Moreover, among all the methods in the literature only *txmeans* and *practical* are able to deal with rare and very common items: *rare items* lead algorithms to return singleton clusters, while *very common items* incorrectly causes the merge of different clusters.

3 PROBLEM SETTING

In this section we define the context and the problem we want to solve, i.e., the *mass transactional clustering* problem.

Let $B = \{b_1, \ldots, b_N\}$ be a set of N baskets (or transactions) and $I = \{i_1, \ldots, i_D\}$ a set of D items., a *basket* b_i is defined as a subset of items such that $\emptyset \subset b_i \subseteq I$. Datasets of transactions B are usually denoted as *transactional data*, and represent a special case of high-dimensional categorical data. Indeed, each transactional dataset can be represented as categorical by representing each attribute value as a boolean attribute in I. In the following, we refer to transactional data in the sense of *high-dimensional* categorical datasets which in turns can also be considered as *sparse* categorical datasets.

Definition 3.1 (Transactional Clustering). Given a set of baskets B, we define the *transactional clustering* problem as the partitioning of B into K disjoint sets $\mathbb{C} = \{C_1, \ldots, C_K\}$ such that $\mathbb{C}$ is optimal in terms of homogeneity and simplicity, and for each set C_i a representative transactions r_i is provided.

This means that the baskets in each C_i must exhibit a high degree of overlap in comparison to any transaction in $B \setminus C_i$, while keeping the clustering structure concise. Notice that, in general, the subset $I_i \subseteq I$ of a cluster is not disjoint to the subset $I_j \subseteq I$ of other clusters.

When dealing with applications that involve a large number of logically separated datasets, there is the need of solving many instances of the transactional clustering problem. For instance, each dataset might contain the baskets of a different user and we want to analyze each user separately in order to profile her.

Definition 3.2 (Mass Transactional Clustering). Given a set of users $U = \{u_1, \dots, u_M\}$ each one with her personal set of baskets $\mathcal{B} = \{B_{u_1}, \dots, B_{u_M}\}$, we refer to *mass transactional clustering* as the problem which consists in solving the transactional clustering problem individually on each set B_{u_i} of baskets of each user $u_i \in U$.

Since the number of users $u \in U$ can be very large in real applications, the above problem definition implies some technical requirements on the methods aimed to solve it. First, the clustering of each different user dataset B_{u_i} can yield a different number K_i of clusters, which needs to be automatically determined, since a repeated intervention of an expert manually setting the K_i for each dataset is impractical. Second, since at least M runs of the clustering method are needed, i.e., one for each user dataset B_{u_i}, the algorithm needs to be efficient. Also, each dataset B_{u_i} can be large, depending on the application and the temporal period covered by the data, thus the algorithm needs to be scalable and applicable to big data. Third, in the context of transactional data an important semantic feature is the notion of *cluster representative*, that is a transaction that should represent the characteristics of the transactions belonging to the cluster. Producing such kind of cluster summary is a significant plus, since it provides a simple way to explain the content of the clusters, and can also support various useful personal applications, among which the *personal cart assistant* application described in Section 6 represents a typical example.

While each of the above requirements is satisfied by some existing algorithm, there is no method meeting all of them together. This paper introduces an algorithm able to do it, also being competitive against the state-of-art competitors on each single requirement.

4 PROPOSED METHOD

In this section we describe the components of *txmeans*. Inspired by *xmeans* [22], *txmeans* is a hierarchical divisive clustering method based on iterative bisections with the extraction of a representative transaction for each cluster. Its aim is to reach efficiency without sacrificing the clustering quality and, most important, without parameter tuning. We start by introducing the overall algorithm, and then we present details of the basic functionalities such as stopping criteria, cluster representatives and splitting procedure.

4.1 *Txmeans* Algorithm

In analogy with [7, 22], we address the clustering problem through a top-down, divide-and-conquer strategy: we start from an initial set containing a single cluster, then, iteratively we try to split a cluster in two sub-clusters. *Bisecting* strategies proved to be very effective in several different contexts like when clustering mobility data [14].

Algorithm 1: *txmeans(B)*

```
Input  : B - set of baskets
Output : ℂ - set of clusters, R - set of representative baskets
1  r ← getRepr(B);                                   // extract representatives
2  Q.push(⟨B, r⟩);                                   // initialize queue
3  R ← ∅; ℂ ← ∅;                                      // initialize result
4  while Q ≠ ∅ do
5      ⟨C, r⟩ ← Q.pop();                              // extract from the queue
6      I ← ⋂_{b∈C};                                   // calculate common items
7      C* ← {c \ I | c ∈ C};                          // remove common items from baskets
8      r* ← r \ I;                                    // remove common items from representative
9      C′, C″, r′, r″ ← bisectBaskets(C*);            // split cluster
10     bic_o ← bic({C*}, {r*}, |C*_N|, |C*_D|);       // BIC original
11     bic_s ← bic({C′, C″}, {r′, r″}, |C*_N|, |C*_D|); // BIC splt
12     if bic_s > bic_o then
13         C′ ← {c ∪ I | c ∈ C′}; r′ ← r′ ∪ I;        // restore items
14         C″ ← {c ∪ I | c ∈ C″}; r″ ← r″ ∪ I;        // restore items
15         Q.push(⟨C′, r′⟩); Q.push(⟨C″, r″⟩);        // update queue
16     else
17         ℂ ← ℂ ∪ {C}; R ← R ∪ {r};                  // update result
18     end
19 end
20 return ℂ, R;
```

The general schema of *txmeans*, which implements this approach, is specified in Algorithm 1. The algorithm starts extracting a representative basket r (described in Section 4.3) for the whole dataset B, and puts both B and r into a queue Q that keeps track of the set of baskets still to be considered for splitting (lines 1–2).

At each iteration, a cluster C and its representative r are extracted from Q (line 5). In steps 6–8 the algorithm identifies the items I which are common to all the baskets, and removes them from the transactions of the cluster and from its representative. The results are denoted by $*$. The point of this task is that such items *(i)* provide no useful knowledge for the bisecting step, and *(ii)* a large number of common items tends to *flatten* the similarity values, making it more difficult to appreciate the variability in the other parts of the transactions. Preliminary tests showed that keeping common items affects the splitting step, degrading the overall performance.

Then, the partitioning of C into two disjoint sub-clusters C', C'' is calculated using *bisectBaskets* (described in Section 4.3) over the *clean* transactions (line 9). After that, lines 10–11 calculate the *BIC* (Section 4.2) on the original cluster (bic_o) and on the two sub-clusters (bic_s). Here, $|C_N|$ is the number of baskets in C while $|C_D|$ is the number of different items in C. If the split is useful (line 12) the common items are reinserted, and C', C'' and r', r'' are added to Q (lines 13-15). Otherwise, the original cluster C and its representative basket r are added to the final sets $\mathbb{C}$ and R (line 17).

4.2 *Txmeans* Stopping Criterion

Given a cluster $C \subseteq B$ and two disjoint sub-clusters $C', C'' \subseteq C$, we need a criterion to decide whether the splitting is actually useful, i.e., the split significantly improves the homogeneity of C, in which case it is performed and the procedure reiterates on each sub-cluster.

In the literature, various measures and cost functions are adopted [5, 30]. However, they are all *global* measures which consider the whole partitioning during the clustering process.

A *local* measure to drive this decision is the *Bayesian Information Criterion (BIC)* [24], which selects the model with the highest *BIC* value. *BIC* has been successfully employed in [22] to control the splitting process and to determine the number of clusters. Yet, to the best of our knowledge it was never considered for transactional clustering, since it involves a *variance* computation [16] and thus requires central values for each cluster which are unavailable in most transactional clustering methods. The representative baskets computed in our solution provide exactly this kind of information, thus enabling the use of the *BIC* criteria formalized as follows [22]:

$$bic(N, D, C, r) = \mathcal{L}(N, D, C, r) - \frac{|C|(D+1)}{2} \log |C|$$

$$\mathcal{L} = \sum_{C_i} N_i \log N_i - N_i \log N - \frac{N_i}{2} \log 2\pi - \frac{N_i D}{2} \log \sigma^2 - \frac{N_i - |C|}{2}$$

$$\sigma^2 = \frac{1}{N_i - |C|} \sum_{b_i} dist(b_i, r_{(i)})^2$$

where C and r are the set of clusters and their representatives, $\mathcal{L}$ is the log-likelihood, N=$|C_N|$ and D=$|C_D|$ are the number of baskets and items in C, $|C|$ is the number of clusters (one in bic_o, and two in bic_s, see Algorithm 1), N_i=$|C_i|$ is the number of baskets in cluster C_i, σ^2 is the variance and $r_{(i)}$ is the representative of basket b_i.

According to literature [22], the *BIC* criterion can be adopted with success when the size of the data sample is larger than the data dimensionality, i.e., $N \gg D$. This requirement is typically satisfied by the input dataset B. Moreover, *BIC* is evaluated over each single cluster C, and not the whole dataset (the only exception being the first iteration of the process). Therefore, it is expected that the actual dimensionality, now reduced to $|C_D|$ (i.e., the set of items in cluster C), is such that $|C_D| \ll D$, since clusters group similar transactions. *Txmeans* further strengthens this property by removing the common items in each cluster before splitting. This step influences the computation of *BIC* by changing the similarity values involved in most computations. In particular, *(i)* the effect of items removal is an increase in the values of BIC, since the dimensionality of data decreases, meaning (from a more theoretical perspective) a smaller number of free parameters and therefore a better model; and *(ii)* in practice, we verified experimentally that at each candidate split the effects of item removal on the original cluster (bic_o) and on the new pair of clusters (bic_s) are usually similar enough to keep the split decision unaffected.

4.3 *Txmeans* Bisecting Schema

Center-Based Optimization. At each iteration, the cluster splitting process invoked by *txmeans* tries to divide a cluster C into two compact subgroups $\{C', C''\}$. The criteria we adopt is based on a distance function between the cluster elements and a *representative basket*. More formally, we want to find a partitioning such that:

- C',C'' have corresponding representative baskets r',r'';
- the partitioning minimizes the Sum of Squared Errors

$$SSE = \sum_{b \in C'} dist(b, r')^2 + \sum_{b \in C''} dist(b, r'')^2$$

where $dist(a, b)$ is a distance function based on the measure of overlap of items between sets a and b.

Algorithm 2: $getRepr(B)$

Input : B - set of baskets
Output: r - set of representative baskets

1 $I \leftarrow \bigcup_{b \in B} b \setminus \bigcap_{b \in B} b$; // calculate not common items
2 $\forall i \in I.freq(i) \leftarrow |\{b \in B | i \in b\}|$; // calculate frequencies
3 $i \leftarrow 0$; $r_{(i)} \leftarrow \bigcap_{b \in B} b$; $d_{(i)} \leftarrow \infty$; // initialize variables
4 **while** $I \neq \emptyset$ **do**
5 $\quad m \leftarrow \text{argsmax}_{i \in I} freq(i)$; // set of max-freq items
6 $\quad r_{(i+1)} \leftarrow r_{(i)} \cup m$; // update representative
7 $\quad d_{(i+1)} \leftarrow \sum_{b \in B} dist(b, r_{(i+1)})^2$; // compute SSE
8 $\quad$ **if** $d_{(i)} \leq d_{(i+1)}$ **then** $I \leftarrow \emptyset$; // best representative found
9 $\quad$ **else** $i \leftarrow i + 1; I \leftarrow I \setminus m$; // update variables
10 **end**
11 **return** $r_{(i)}$;

A consequence of our notion of optimality is that each basket belongs to the cluster minimizing the distance with its "centroid", i.e., maximizing the overlap among the items.

Distance Function. While in theory *txmeans* could adopt any distance function $dist(\cdot, \cdot)$ for comparing transactions, in practice, being designed for transactional data, the number of reasonable choices is reduced. According to the literature [30], distances like Euclidean or Manhattan are not suitable in this context. Indeed, the function $dist(a, b)$ should be based on the measure of overlap of items between baskets a and b, which suggests measures such as set intersection, match similarity or Jaccard coefficient. Since the latter is known to be more robust and adequate for sparse vector data (like transactions), *txmeans* adopts Jaccard distance as default. Finally, we want to stress that a strategy like the one proposed by the *k-modes* algorithm for categorical data does not work for sparse transactional data. Indeed, if we binarize a sparse transactional dataset in the corresponding categorical dataset, the zeros usually predominate, and therefore the corresponding modes will be zero for most of the columns, i.e., the centroids will be empty at every iteration. Also, alternative approaches where lower thresholds are adopted (i.e., lower than the 50% involved by the mode) might avoid empty centroids but would introduce a new parameter to set, since each dataset might require a different threshold value.

Representative Baskets. Using Algorithm 2, *txmeans* extracts the *representative baskets* following a parameter-free heuristics defined in [12] that first selects the items contained in every transaction in B (lines 1–3), and then refines such approximation by adding the most frequent items (lines 5–6). This process is iterated as long as each step improves the solution (lines 7–8), thus stopping when a locally optimal representative r is generated. A representative basket is a virtual transaction that (approximately) minimizes the overall distance from all the baskets in the cluster, therefore capturing the items that best characterize it, i.e., the typical combination of items expected to appear in any of its transactions.

Bisecting Schema. *Txmeans* exploits the representative baskets for partitioning a set of baskets B into two disjoint sets C', C'' using the *bisecting* procedure [27] reported in Algorithm 3. First of all, two representatives are selected among the baskets in B (line 2). These initial centroids are selected with *selectInitialCentroids*, which randomly picks several pairs of baskets, and returns the

Algorithm 3: *bisectBaskets*(B)

Input : B - set of baskets
Output: C', C'' - baskets partitioning; r', r'' - repr

1 $i \leftarrow 0$; $SSE_{(i)} \leftarrow \infty$; // init. variables
2 $r'_{(i)}, r''_{(i)} \leftarrow selectInitialCentroids(B)$; // init. variables
3 **while** True **do**
4 $\{C', C''\} \leftarrow assignBaskets(B, \{r'_{(i)}, r''_{(i)}\})$; // assign baskets
5 $r'_{(i+1)} \leftarrow getRepr(C')$; // calculate representative
6 $r''_{(i+1)} \leftarrow getRepr(C'')$; // calculate representative
7 $SSE_{(i+1)} \leftarrow \sum_{b \in C'} dist(b, r'_{(i+1)})^2 + \sum_{b \in C''} dist(b, r''_{(i+1)})^2$; // calc. SSE
8 **if** $SSE_{(i+1)} \geq SSE_{(i)}$ **then**
9 **return** $C', C'', r'_{(i)}, r''_{(i)}$;
10 **end**
11 $i \leftarrow i + 1$; // update variable
12 **end**

pair with the highest distance value. Then *assignBaskets* (line 4) compares each basket $b \in B$ to the two representative baskets r' and r'' and associates it to the closest one. When all baskets have been assigned to a cluster, r' and r'' are re-computed through *getRepr* (lines 5–6). The process is reiterated as long as the SSE decreases (lines 7–9), i.e., the SSE at step i+1 is higher than that of step i.

4.4 Termination and Complexity

We provide a few theoretical properties about *txmeans*, including proofs of termination and computational complexity.

Theorem 4.1 (Termination). *The* txmeans *algorithm terminates for any input dataset.*

Proof. Both Alg. 2 and Alg. 3 terminate for any input data. The stop condition of the loop in Alg. 2 is that I becomes empty, since it decreases strictly monotonically at each iteration (steps 9 or 11–12). Also, Alg. 3 follows the classical *kmeans* structure, and the loop stops when the SSE does not strictly increase. Since the number of possible clusterings, and thus of possible SSE values, is finite, the strictly monotonic sequence of SSE values produced throughout the iterations must eventually reach a (local) minimum in a finite number of steps. Finally, the loop in Alg. 1 iteratively removes a cluster and replaces it with strictly smaller ones. In the worst case all clusters will be broken down to singletons in a finite number of steps. That avoids any possible unbounded loop, leading to termination. □

Theorem 4.2 (Complexity). *The computational complexity of* txmeans *is $O(It \cdot N \cdot K \cdot D)$, where It is the number of iterations required to reach convergence in a run of* bisectBaskets, *N=$|B|$ is the number of transactions in input, K is the number of clusters detected and D is the number of distinct items in the dataset.*

Proof. As mentioned in the proof of Theorem 4.1, the *txmeans* algorithm iteratively splits the initial dataset B into sub-clusters. The number of iterations corresponds to the number K of clusters returned at the end of the computation. All the operations performed at each iteration involve scanning the transactions in the cluster only once, thus the overall cost is $O(N \cdot D)$, notice that the size of the clusters is always $O(N)$ in case all iterations produce extremely unbalanced splits. The only exception is Alg. 3: it follows a *kmeans* structure with k=2, and all the operations performed at each step are linear in the number of transactions and their length. That includes also the calls of Alg. 2, since they involve $O(D)$ iterations each taking only constant-time operations plus the distance computation in step 7. The latter, though apparently requiring $O(N \cdot D)$ time, actually can be computed incrementally along the different iterations (both numerator and denominator of the Jaccard distance monotonically increase at each iteration), thus taking only $O(N)$, and lifting the overall cost of Alg. 2 to $O(N \cdot D)$. There is no clear bound on the number of iterations required by Alg. 3 to converge, which is then kept as a parameter It and leads to a cost equal to $O(It \cdot N \cdot D)$, which dominates the complexity of each iteration of *txmeans*. The overall complexity, thus, results to be $O(It \cdot N \cdot K \cdot D)$. □

The theoretical complexity of *txmeans* is similar or smaller than most competitors in the literature. Where not explicit, we inferred the complexities from the corresponding papers. *Tkmeans* [12], *clope* [36] and *practical* [5] follow a *k-means* structure, i.e., $O(It \cdot N \cdot K \cdot D)$ that is the same as *txmeans*. *Coolcat* [3] has a similar cost, plus a $O(S^2)$ due to the initialization over a sample of size S, that dominates the complexity if $S > \sqrt{N}$. *Atdc* [7] iteratively performs a partitioning having cost $O(It \cdot N)$ followed by a stabilization step $O(It' \cdot N \cdot K)$. The two steps are repeated till convergence, leading to an overall cost of $O(It \cdot It' \cdot It'' \cdot N^2 \cdot K^2)$, where It, It' and It'' are the number of iterations for each component of the algorithm.

4.5 Dealing with Very Large Datasets

We remark that *txmeans* has been designed to solve the mass transactional clustering problem, thus considering that many different datasets must be efficiently clustered without parameter tuning. While this situation usually results in analyzing small- or medium-size datasets, nowadays we might need to move to a "big data" context where each single dataset actually contains a huge set of transactions, therefore calling for a scalable approach.

In this case, *txmeans* can be adapted to integrate a sampling strategy. Thanks to the representative baskets, the clustering can be computed on a subset, then assigning the remaining transactions according to their closest representative basket [3]. The algorithm exploiting the sampling is working as follows. First, it randomly selects a subset $S \subset B$ of S_N transactions from the input dataset B. To do that, it employs the approach proposed in [18] to estimate S_N, i.e., $S_N = ss/(1 + (ss - 1)/N)$, where ss=$Z^2 p(p-1)$. Z and p are fixed and set, respectively, to the z-score of confidence level 99% and to 0.5 (but potentially modifiable for special cases). Then the transactions in S are clustered using Algorithm 1. Finally, the rest of the transactions are associated to the proper cluster using the representatives R through a *k-nearest-neighbour* strategy with k=1.

Empirical results show that, besides efficiency, sampling improves also clustering quality. This is mainly due to noisy and rare items, whose impact appears to be significantly reduced by sampling, since most of them will disappear and thus will not distort the clusters structure. When clear from the context we will refer to *txmeans* using the sampling strategy simply as *txmeans*.

5 EXPERIMENTS

In this section we evaluate the performance of *txmeans* in the context of mass transactional clustering where only parameter-free algorithms or methods using automated techniques for parameters estimation can be employed. Then, we evaluate the scalability of

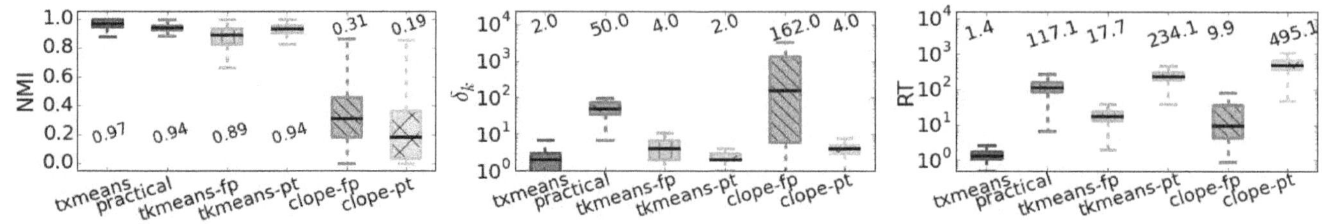

Figure 1: *NMI*, δ_k and *RT* evaluation for comparing algorithms on 10k different dataset with structure *DS*1.

txmeans. We also assess the quality of the clusterings, by studying the *txmeans* performance in various synthetic and real datasets.

5.1 Performance Indicators

To evaluate the clustering quality we compared the clusters returned with the real ones. We quantified the similarity between the two sets of clusters with the *Normalized Mutual Information (NMI)* [29]. *NMI* was preferred over *purity* because *(i)* it is more sensitive to the change in the clustering results, and *(ii)* it takes into account unbalanced distributions and does not necessarily improve when the number of clusters increases (as purity does). Given two sets of clusters $\mathbb{C} = \{c_1 \dots c_k\}$ and $\mathcal{G} = \{g_1 \dots g_{k'}\}$

$$\text{NMI}(\mathbb{C}, \mathcal{G}) = \frac{I(\mathbb{C}, \mathcal{G})}{0.5 * H(\mathbb{C}) + 0.5 * H(\mathcal{G})} \in [0, 1]$$

where $I(\mathbb{C}, \mathcal{G}) = \sum_k \sum_j (|c_k \cap g_j|/N) \log(N|c_k \cap g_j|/|c_k||g_j|)$ is the mutual information [29], and $H(\mathbb{C}) = -\sum_k (|c_k|/N) \log(|c_k|/N)$ is entropy [25]. Good clusterings have a *NMI* $\sim$1, bad clusterings $\sim$0.

Besides *NMI*, we evaluated the *deviation* $\delta_k = |\mathbb{C}| - |\mathcal{G}|$ between the real number of clusters and the number of clusters detected: $\delta_k \sim 0$ when the right number of cluster is detected, $\delta_k > 0$ if more clusters than real ones are detected, $\delta_k < 0$ otherwise.

Finally, we analyzed the running time *RT* (in sec) of the methods. Experiments were run on a Mac OS v10.11.4, 2,6 GHz i5, 8GB DDR3.

5.2 Competitors

We evaluate our method against a set of competitors sharing some features with *txmeans* yet following different algorithmic structures.

Practical [5] and *atdc* [7] are both parameter-free. *Practical* first scans the data and assigns each basket to an existing cluster or to a new one according to a cost function inspired by "tf-idf"; then, it moves the baskets from a cluster to another one. Note how the structure of *practical* and *txmeans* are completely different. *Atdc* adopts a divisive approach similar to *txmeans*, but *atdc* scans the baskets and iterates between a partitioning and a stabilization phase. *Tkmeans* [12] adapts the *k-means* [27] definition of distance to measure transactions dissimilarity, and computes centroids using the same approach of *txmeans*. *Coolcat* [3] works on a random sample of the baskets, as *txmeans*. We also report the performance of *clope* [36] as it represents a reference approach and it was designed for market-basket data, which is analyzed in our case study. *Clope* requires a *repulsion* parameter r that is hard to be interpreted.

We omit the comparison with *rock* [13], *subcad* [11], *limbo* [2], *clicks* [38] and *largeitem* [30], since, according to the literature, are outperformed respectively by *practical*, *atdc* and *clope*. Moreover, we omit the comparison with *k-modes* [6] and *dhcc* [33] because they are designed for categorical data, and with *purtreeclust* [9] because its target is the clustering of users through their transactions.

5.3 Mass Transactional Clustering Evaluation

In this section we evaluate *txmeans* and its competitors with respect to the task of clustering a massive number of different datasets[1]. As already discussed, this is a common situation when the datasets of a large number of users must be clustered in order to accomplish further tasks (as it is discussed and shown in Section 6). As consequence, efficiency in computing every single clustering and freedom from parameters are two mandatory requirements to meet.

Since real datasets containing users' transactions annotated with cluster labels are publicly not available, we used the synthetic data generator employed in [5], that we name *DS*1, to create individual synthetic datasets. *DS*1 was kindly provided by the authors of [7], where the generator is accurately described. *DS*1 allows to specify the following parameters to modify the dataset and the clustering structure: the number of baskets N, the number of items D, the average basket length T, the number of clusters C, the percentage of outliers O (i.e., proportion of items that do not contribute to form any cluster), and the percentage P of overlap among transactions of distinct clusters. Different combinations of O and P allow to simulate various situations, thus enabling an objective experimentation.

By using *DS*1, we generated 100k datasets with characteristics selected randomly in $N \in [1000, 10000]$, $D \in [100, 1000]$, $T \in [10, 30]$, $C \in [4, 16]$, $P \in [0, 50]$, $O \in [0, 30]$. Hence, we test mass transactional clustering using a wide set of different datasets generated with random structures and simulating different users, and we evaluate the performance considering the clusterings of all the datasets.

Moreover, since we are simulating a real application scenario, we are not suggesting the correct setting to the methods requiring parameters. Indeed, for these algorithms we adopt two versions: *fixed parameter (fp)* for which we fix a parameter setting for all the datasets, and *parameter tuning (pt)* for which we simulate the search of the best parameters through an heuristic for each dataset by running each method several times and varying the parameters.

In this experiment we consider the following competitors: *practical* because is the best parameter-free algorithm according to the state of the art, *tkmeans* because uses the same approach as *txmeans* for extracting the centroid, and *clope* because has a completely different approach not requiring to specify as parameter the number of cluster. As shown in the following, *atdc* and *coolcat* have relatively poor performance, even when clustering simple and single datasets. Hence their performance are not reported in this test.

We name the parameter-based competitors with fixed parameters *tkmeans-fp* and *clope-fp*, and those with parameter tuning *tkmeans-pt* and *clope-pt*. For *tkmeans-fp* and *clope-fp* we fix k=6 and r=2 respectively. We used the heuristic technique "knee method" to select the best k and r: we run *tkmeans* for $k \in [4, 16]$ and we store the

[1] The Python code of the algorithms and the data generators is at https://goo.gl/sAJ7WO.

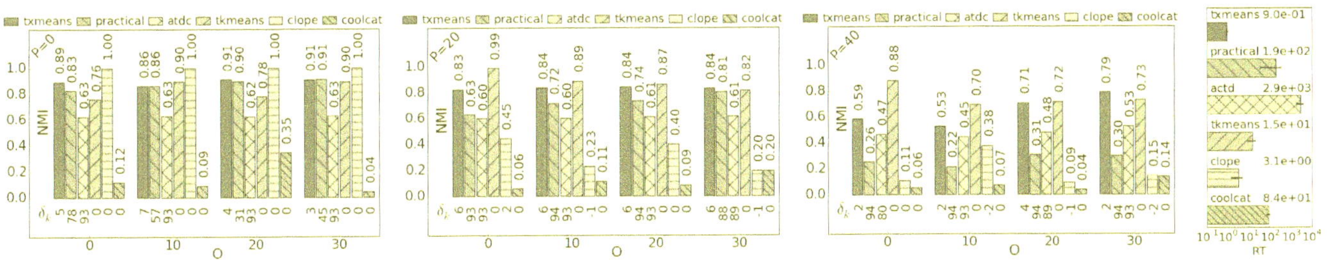

Figure 2: *NMI*, δ_k and *RT* evaluation for comparing algorithms on *DS*1 with *N*=2000, *D*=200, *T*=10 and *C*=6.

SSE for every run. Then we select as best k the one corresponding in the "knee" point in which the SSE curve changes [27]. We adopted a similar technique for *clope* considering the trend change of the *Profit* function [36] with $r \in [0.1, 3.5]$. Note that these parameters cannot be selected by optimizing an evaluation metric like *NMI* because at this stage we do not possess any information about the clustering structure of the dataset we have to analyze.

Figure 1 depicts the boxplots of *NMI*, δ_k, *RT* (from left to right). The numbers represent the median values of each boxplot. *Txmeans* shows remarkably the best performance: it returns for each dataset the purest clusters (a median level of 0.97 *NMI*) in a few seconds without any parameter tuning and it deviates on average of only 2 clusters from the real number. Considering these three aspects at the same time, this level of performance is reached by none of the competitors. *Practical* and *tkmeans-pt* have a *NMI* gap w.r.t. *txmeans* of only 0.03. However, they both have a median *RT* two orders of magnitude greater than *txmeans*. Moreover, while *tkmeans-pt* succeeds in minimizing δ_k, *practical* has an average deviation of ~50 clusters, that is unacceptable because, even if the clusters extracted are pure, they would provided a too dispersed summary of users'patterns for any real application. *Tkmeans-pt* is highly penalized in terms of *RT* by the multiple runs for tuning the number of clusters k, while *tkmeans-fp* has lower running times, but also lower *NMI* and higher δ_k. Note that, *tkmeans-fp* has overall good *NMI* and δ_k because the most frequent number of clusters for the generated datasets is exactly 6. *Clope* is not competitive in none of the versions. In conclusion, *txmeans* is the best algorithm in case of transactional clustering on a massive number of datasets.

5.4 Assessing Clustering Quality

The goal of these experiments is to evaluate the ability of *txmeans* and its competitors to correctly identify clusters under specific circumstances in synthetic datasets and real-world datasets.

Synthetic Datasets. For synthetic datasets, we study the performance when specific datasets among those generated on the previous experiment must be clustered. In particular, we employ *DS*1 to generate different datasets with controlled overlap percentage $P \in \{0, 10, 20, 30, 40, 50\}$ and outliers percentage $O \in \{0, 10, 20, 30\}$ and we fix the other dimensions to N=2000, D=200, T=10, C=6.

In this experiment we offer a significant advantage to parameter-dependent algorithms, by setting their parameters to optimal values: the real number of clusters k for *tkmeans* and *coolcat*, and for *clope* the value of r that minimizes δ_k, with $r \in [1.0, 3.5]$. Finally, the sample S for *coolcat* is selected through the same function adopted by *txmeans*. Figure 2 shows the performance by barplots of *NMI*,

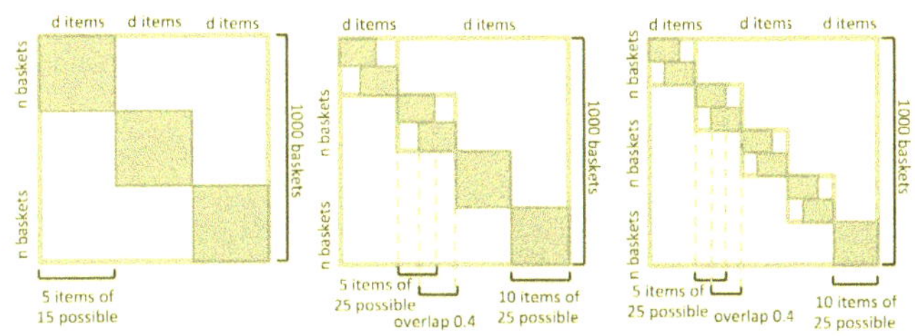

Figure 3: Structure of synthetic data for *DS*2, *DS*3, *DS*4.

Algorithm	DS2			DS3			DS4		
	(N=1000,D=75,C=3)			(N=1000,D=100,C=6)			(N=1000 D=125,C=9)		
	NMI	δ_k	RT	NMI	δ_k	RT	NMI	δ_k	RT
txmeans	0.66	**11.5**	***0.42***	***0.87***	**6.8**	***0.43***	0.83	**10.4**	***0.62***
practical	0.57	51.8	20.96	0.73	***20.7***	6.06	0.68	***36.6***	12.22
atdc	0.53	***49.1***	130.86	0.65	48.4	189.52	0.72	49.5	261.92
tkmeans	***0.67***	-	2.12	0.75	-	3.41	***0.86***	-	4.79
coolcat	0.01	-	14.4	0.22	-	24.97	0.34	-	31.94
clope	**1.00**	-	**0.16**	**0.99**	-	**0.10**	**0.99**	-	**0.10**

Table 1: Clustering performance on *DS*2, *DS*3, *DS*4 datasets. Best performer in bold, second best performer in bold-italic.

with δ_k reported below the bars. When varying the percentage of outliers O for a given level of overlap P, the *NMI* of all the algorithms has small fluctuations. The overall level of *NMI* decreases significantly when P grows. *Txmeans* and *tkmeans* are the two most stable ones, but the latter is given the right number of clusters as input. However, *txmeans* maintains good performance for $P \geq 30$ and O=30 and overcomes also *tkmeans*. *Clope* is the best performer when there is no overlap and no noise, then its performances rapidly decrease for growing P. *Coolcat* is always the worst performer.

Moreover, it is worth to notice that even though the difference of *NMI* between *txmeans* and *practical* can be considered small, *practical* has a significant deviation δ_k, already observed also in Section 5.3, which represents a clear weakness of this approach. Both *practical* and *atdc* largely overestimate the number of clusters, while the overestimation of *txmeans* is very small.

Finally, the average *RT* values are reported on the right of Figure 2. As previously observed, *txmeans* is the most efficient: its *RT* is one order of magnitude smaller than *clope* and two orders of magnitude smaller than *practical*. Furthermore, like *coolcat*, due to the sampling, *txmeans* is also the most constant in *RT*.

We performed additional experiments on other simpler synthetic datasets (*DS2*, *DS3*, *DS4*) generated according to the state of the art [5, 7, 34]. The clustering structure of these dataset is reported in Figure 3. These datasets have a well defined clustering structure, and each basket distinctly belongs to one cluster. *DS2*, has a one-layer clustering with C=3 clusters of the same size and each basket

Algorithm	Mushrooms (N=8124, D=22, C=2)			Zoo (N=101, D=17, C=7)			Congress (N=435 D=16, C=2)		
	NMI	δ_k	RT	NMI	δ_k	RT	NMI	δ_k	RT
txmeans	***0.406***	***3.5***	**1.082**	**0.826**	**-2.2**	0.066	0.358	7.0	0.304
practical	0.001	**-0.5**	***5.775***	0.426	-5.3	***0.029***	***0.470***	**0.3**	***0.124***
atdc	0.216	4.0	33.421	0.736	***-3.0***	0.091	0.297	***1.0***	0.319
tkmeans	0.158	*	302.645	0.773	*	2.161	**0.475**	*	5.448
coolcat	0.005	*	73.184	0.544	*	0.890	0.413	*	13.015
clope	**0.419**	*	7.754	0.796	*	**0.005**	0.382	*	**0.042**

Table 2: Clustering performance on real-world data sets. Best performer in bold, second best performer in bold-italic.

has length T=5 and is characterized by D/C=15 different items. *DS*3 and *DS*4 are built similarly to *DS*1, but they have a two-layer clustering structure: in *DS*3 the top layer has four clusters, two of which have sub-clusters; in *DS*4 the top layer has five clusters, four of which have sub-clusters. In both cases the items overlap in sub-clusters is 0.4 and the average basket length is $T \in \{5, 10\}$.

For each clustering structure *DS*2, *DS*3, *DS*4 we generate ten datasets. Tab. 1 reports the mean value of the evaluation measures. The deviation δ_k is considered only for parameter-free methods. *Clope* is the best performer but we must consider that the best r is provided as input, and that in practice, as previously shown, this requires an extensive tuning. *Txmeans* is the second best performer w.r.t. *NMI* for *DS*3 and the third for *DS*2 and *DS*4 without requiring any tuning. Also *tkmeans* has very good performance. All the parameter-free algorithms overestimate the number of clusters, but the overestimation of *txmeans* is much smaller than that of *practical* and *atdc*. Finally, *txmeans* also has the smallest *RT*. Also these experiments confirm the effectiveness of *txmeans* in extracting in the shortest time the clusters with the highest quality.

Real-World Datasets. Moving to real-world, we analyzed three datasets from the UCI repository[2]: *Mushrooms, Congressional Votes* and *Zoo*. Classes information is used as ground truth for validation.

As showed in Table 2, *txmeans* performs well on all the datasets. Like before, the deviation δ_k is considered only for parameter-free methods. For *Mushrooms* dataset *txmeans* is the second best performer with respect to *NMI* and δ_k and the best performer with respect to *RT*. Good performances are obtained only by *txmeans* and *clope*: *practical* underestimates the number of clusters, while *atdc* overestimates it. The parameter-free algorithms underestimate the real number of species in *Zoo*. Despite this fact, *txmeans* is the best performer and returns a partitioning even better than parameter-based algorithms for which the number of clusters was correctly specified. In *Congressional* dataset *txmeans* is not the best one but the results are comparable to those obtained by the competitors. Overall, the experiments on real datasets suggest that *txmeans* provides consistent and stable results with respect to the competitors confirming the suitability observed on synthetic data.

5.5 Evaluating Scalability

We evaluate the scalability of *txmeans* by observing its performance when varying N, D, C on *DS*1. We fixed $T = 20$, $P = 20\%$, $O = 20\%$.

The *first column* of Figure 4 shows the scalability varying C. For *NMI* we observe that when C is small there are better performances

[2]http://archive.ics.uci.edu/ml/

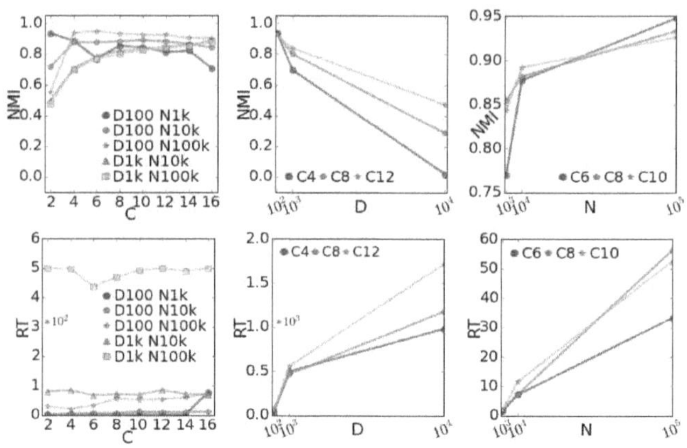

Figure 4: Dataset *DS*1**, scalability w.r.t:** ***(first column)*** **clusters** *C*, ***(second column)*** **items** *D*, ***(third column)*** **baskets** *N*.

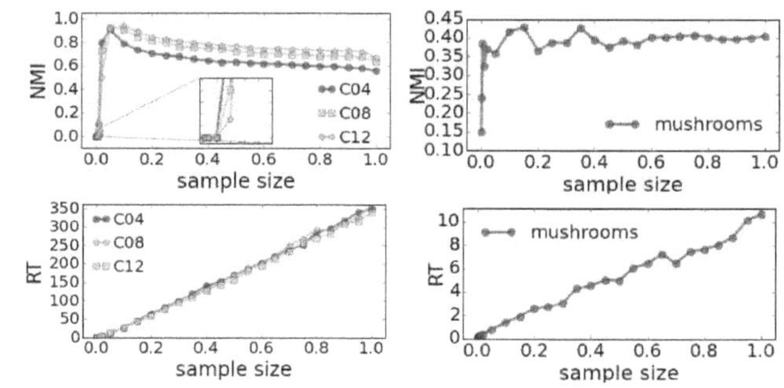

Figure 5: ***NMI*** **and** ***RT*** **varying** *S* **on** *DS*1 (N = *10, 000*, D = *1, 000*, T=20, P=20 **and** O=10) **(left), and on** ***Mushrooms*** **(right).**

with small datasets, while with high C there are better performances for large datasets. The *RT* does not fluctuate when varying C.

The *second column* reports the variation of D with fixed N=100, 000. The *NMI* is influenced by the dataset density, indeed fixing N we observe that increasing D the *NMI* values decrease drastically. However, the *NMI* decreases more slowly for higher number of clusters. The *RT* grows less than linearly in D and it is higher for high C.

Finally, in the *third column* of Figure 4 we observe the scalability varying N (with D=100). The *NMI* grows with N: the more the baskets, the less the noise, and the better are the representatives. The *RT* grows linearly and it is not influenced by C.

5.6 Evaluating Sample Size

In this last experimental section we evaluate the performance of *txmeans* varying the size of the initial sample S both in case of synthetic and real world datasets. Figure 5 *(left)* illustrates the variations of *NMI* and *RT* for *txmeans* on *DS*1 when changing the *sample size* S for a dataset with T=20, D=1, 000, N=10, 000, P=20, O=10, while on the *(right)* we can observe the same indicators for the *Mushrooms* dataset. A clear trend appears for both datasets: a first peak of high values of *NMI* is positioned in a range of sample size between 0.05 and 0.15, then the trend decreases a little before stabilizing. The range [0.05, 0.15] confirms that the function using the z-score [18] that we adopted to select the size S_N of the initial sample S is a good choice. Indeed, it returns samples S with a size which is generally between the 5% and the 20% of the whole dataset. Finally, the *RT* grows linearly with the sample size.

6 REAL CASE STUDY APPLICATION

The efficiency and the freedom from parameters of *txmeans* makes it possible to adopt clustering-based strategies in applications that need to handle mass transactional clustering. We present an application where clustering individual transactional data for masses of users is necessary to build personalized recommendation systems that requires to analyze thousands of shopping sessions datasets. In this context, transactional data are typically treated with simple strategies, while more complex approaches are avoided exactly for the same reasons that motivated the development of *txmeans*. Enabled by the capabilities of *txmeans*, the proposed solution is a first attempt to go in the opposite direction.

The application consists in a *Personal Cart Assistant* suggesting to retail customers potential items to add to their current basket based on their shopping behavior. The suggestions are based on the representative baskets and clusters obtained from their purchasing history. In the following we describe our solution, we present baselines approaches, and we show comparative empirical results.

Personal Cart Assistant. Given the baskets B_u of a customer u, the *personal cart assistant* (*pca*) method cluster B_u using *txmeans* to obtain $\mathbb{C}_u = \{C_1, \ldots, C_k\}$ and $R_u = \{r_1, \ldots, r_k\}$. $P_u = \langle \mathbb{C}_u, R_u \rangle$ is the customer's shopping profile [1] used as basis for a model-based collaborative filtering approach [26, 28]. Then, given the current incomplete basket $L = \{i_1, \ldots, i_n\}$ of user u, *pca* finds the $r_i \in R_u$ which is closer to L in terms of Jaccard distance, and then uses the baskets in C_i to generate suggestions. A weight is associated to each candidate item, computed as the sum of similarities between current basket L and the baskets in C_i that contain the candidate items. Then, only the highest-weight items are suggested. This process is an instance of the general *collaborative filtering* approach, with a set of users (here corresponding to single baskets), user's preferences (the items in L), users selected as similar w.r.t. the user's preferences (the baskets in C_i) based on item bought in the past (r_i). A difference from classical collaborative filtering is that our user's preferences (i.e., the shopping list L) are binary instead of scores [21].

Baselines. We compared the performances of our method against the following baselines. *Last* suggests the items in the last basket purchased. *Rand* suggests random items among those in B_{u_i}. *Most* recommends the most frequent items in B_{u_i}. *Mbcf* is a memory-based collaborative filtering method on transactional data [21]. Although in the literature there are other methods personalized on user behavior, e.g. [23, 31], none of them try to complete the current shopping list, and thus cannot be directly compared.

Real Dataset. We tested our method over real data describing the purchases of the customers of a large Italian supermarket chain. Customers are provided with a loyalty card which allows to link different shopping sessions, and therefore reconstruct their personal shopping history. We analyzed a dataset of 2, 670, 343 shopping sessions occurred in Leghorn province over 2010–2013, corresponding to about $10k$ loyal customers, i.e., customers active in at least ten months every year. For each customer we have $N{\sim}240$ baskets, $D{\sim}100$ different items, and an average basket length T of ~8 items.

Representative Baskets Analytics. The number of clusters per customer ranges from 2 to 22 with a mean of ~5 and a skewed left normal distribution: every customer has her own purchasing behavior made of a different number of patterns. In Table 3 we report the representative baskets of three customers to highlight the differences in terms of number of clusters and baskets composition. Customer A has two very different representatives: the first one contains perishable items while the second one is also related to bathroom products. Customer B always purchases *salad bags, wine* but, the first two representatives are characterized by *apples, tomatoes*, while the second two by *oranges, onions*. The purchases of customer C are characterized by two different patterns: we notice three representatives dominated by *bovine steak, bread, milk*, versus two representatives containing cake ingredients and female personal products. Finally, in general, there is a sort of "matrioska effect" where most of the representatives contain a small kernel of frequent items and larger representatives contain additional frequent item. This delineates two shopping behaviors: *big-purchases* typically performed on a monthly base, containing disparate types of items and not only perishable foods, and *small-purchases* performed more frequently, containing both the favorite and most consumed items together with perishable products.

	Representative Baskets (Support)
A	{bread, breakfast snacks, pasta, yogurt, tomato sauce} (0.55), {basil, body cream, bovine steak, fresh pasta, onions, shampoo, tomatoes, toothpaste} (0.45)
B	{salad bag, wine, apples, tomatoes} (0.17), {salad bag, wine, apples, tomatoes, chocolate, bananas} (0.29), {salad bag, wine, oranges, onions, potatoes} (0.44), {salad bag, wine, oranges, onions, milk, kiwi} (0.12)
C	{bovine steak, bread, milk} (0.11), {bovine steak, bread, milk, fresh cheese, tomato sauce} (0.18), {bovine steak, brad, milk, fresh cheese, tomato sauce, pasta, tomatoes, canned tuna} (0.17), {bread, milk, sugar, absorbent, fresh cheese, eggs} (0.18), {bread, milk, sugar, absorbent, chocolate, flour, fresh cheese, prepared for cakes}(0.36)

Table 3: Examples of representative baskets.

Recommendation Evaluation. The first three years of data is used to extract the representative transactions and the cluster for each customer, while the last year is used for testing. We observe that for each customer ~4 clusters are detected, thus few patterns are needed to represent the shopping behavior of a customer. For each customer we test the methods over each session L, in chronological order, updating the models as follows: *pca* assigns L to a cluster with respect to the representative baskets, *mbcf* considers also L into the model, *most* updates the frequencies of each item in L, *last* becomes L, *rand* also considers the items in L in its choices. Only baskets having length at least $\omega \in [2, 16]$ were considered, and the current basket L in the test set is split in two parts w.r.t. a percentage $\theta \in [0.2, 0.8]$. As quality measure we report the $F_{0.5}$ [20], which puts more emphasis on precision than recall as we focus on providing useful suggestions. The evaluations are aggregated by averaging the scores of all the customers. Figure 6 shows $F_{0.5}$ for the recommenders varying ω and θ. *Pca* performs better than any other approach with a minimum improvement of at least 0.02 (obtained over *mbcf*, the second best method), corresponding to 1 to 3 more items correctly suggested. Figure 6 *(left)*, with varying ω and θ=0.5, shows that the larger is the minimum basket length, the worse are performances. The fact that for short baskets the recommendation is easier reveals that the probability that frequent

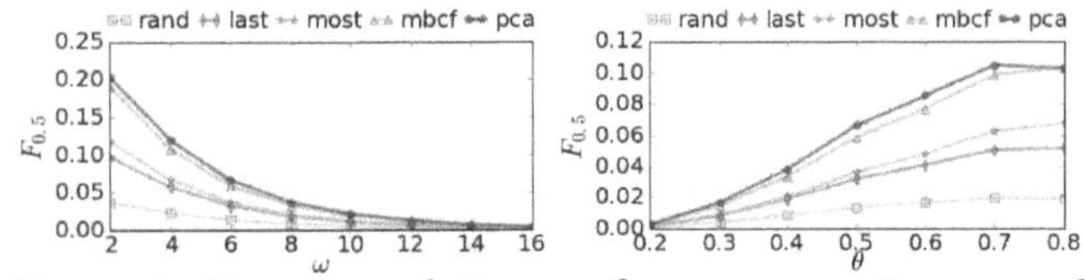

Figure 6: Recommendation performances as $F_{0.5}$ on real dataset varying minimum length ω *(left)*, split θ *(right)*.

items are regularly purchased is high. Figure 6 *(right)* shows that, for $\omega \geq 6$, the larger is the portion θ of L considered, the better are the performances, as expected, and *pca* is the best method.

7 CONCLUSIONS

In this paper we have introduced the mass transactional clustering problem and *txmeans*, a parameter-free transactional clustering algorithm able to partition efficiently a massive number of different datasets and to provide representative transactions for all clusters. Our proposal applies a bisecting strategy to find groups of similar transactions, and gives the possibility to work on a sample of the initial data, making it applicable also in the context of big data. Thanks to these features, *txmeans* is able to outperform existing algorithms both on synthetic and real-world datasets. Finally, we have shown an application scenario on a real retail sale dataset, where we built on top of *txmeans* results a *personal cart assistant*, able to suggest to the customer new items to put in her shopping list.

The main future developments of the work include the improvement of personal recommender systems through the integrated analysis of both individual patterns (already employed in this paper) and collective patterns, obtained by applying *txmeans* on the representative baskets of all customers. Also, we plan to apply *txmeans* to several other contexts. For example, in the analysis of semantically enriched mobility data, *txmeans* might help in the identification of personal point of interests typically visited by people, while in the analysis of individual health indicators it might extract the typical patterns characterizing the health conditions of a person during the daily activities. It would be interesting also applying our algorithm on social media data to infer individual patterns of interests and preferences in terms of music, food, movies, etc. In all these applications the temporal dimension of each transaction might play an important role in the analysis. Unfortunately, the current version of our algorithm does not capture this particular data dimension. Thus, a future research direction would be to extend *txmeans* for considering also the temporal dimension.

ACKNOWLEDGMENTS

This work is partially supported by the European Community H2020 Programnder the funding scheme "INFRAIA-1-2014-2015: Research Infrastructures" grant agreement 654024 (http://www.sobigdata.eu) *"SoBigData"*. We thank UniCoop Tirreno for allowing us to analyze the data and to publish the results.

REFERENCES

[1] Gediminas Adomavicius and Alexander Tuzhilin. 2001. Using data mining methods to build customer profiles. *Computer* 2 (2001), 74–82.
[2] Periklis Andritsos, Panayiotis Tsaparas, and others. 2004. LIMBO: Scalable clustering of categorical data. In *EDBT*. Springer, 123–146.
[3] Daniel Barbará, Yi Li, and Julia Couto. 2002. COOLCAT: an entropy-based algorithm for categorical clustering. In *CIKM*. ACM, 582–589.
[4] Charles-Edmond Bichot. 2010. Co-clustering Documents and Words by Minimizing the Normalized Cut Objective Function. *MMA* 9, 2 (2010), 131–147.
[5] Mohamed Bouguessa. 2011. A practical approach for clustering transaction data. In *MLDM*. Springer, 265–279.
[6] Fuyuan Cao, Jiye Liang, and Liang Bai. 2009. A new initialization method for categorical data clustering. *ESA* 36, 7 (2009), 10223–10228.
[7] Eugenio Cesario, Giuseppe Manco, and Riccardo Ortale. 2007. Top-down parameter-free clustering of high-dimensional categorical data. *TKDE* 19, 12 (2007), 1607–1624.
[8] Keke Chen and Ling Liu. 2005. The" Best K" for entropy-based categorical data clustering. (2005).
[9] Xiaojun Chen and others. 2016. PurTreeClust: A purchase tree clustering algorithm for large-scale customer transaction data. In *ICDE*. IEEE, 661–672.
[10] Inderjit S. Dhillon. 2001. Co-clustering documents and words using bipartite spectral graph partitioning. In *KDD*. 269–274.
[11] Guojun Gan and Jianhong Wu. 2004. Subspace clustering for high dimensional categorical data. *SIGKDD Explorations Newsletter* 6, 2 (2004), 87–94.
[12] Fosca Giannotti, Cristian Gozzi, and Giuseppe Manco. 2002. Clustering transactional data. In *PKDD*. Springer, 175–187.
[13] Saikat Guha, Rajeev Rastogi, and Kyuseok Shim. 1999. ROCK: A robust clustering algorithm for categorical attributes. In *ICDE*. IEEE, 512–521.
[14] Riccardo Guidotti, Roberto Trasarti, and Mirco Nanni. 2015. TOSCA: TwO-Steps Clustering Algorithm for Personal Locations Detection. In *SIGSPATIAL*. ACM, 38:1–38:10.
[15] Zhexue Huang. 1998. Extensions to the k-means algorithm for clustering large data sets with categorical values. *DAMI* 2, 3 (1998), 283–304.
[16] Robert E Kass and Larry Wasserman. 1995. A reference Bayesian test for nested hypotheses and its relationship to the Schwarz criterion. *Journal of the american statistical association* 90, 431 (1995), 928–934.
[17] Eamonn Keogh, Stefano Lonardi, and Chotirat Ann Ratanamahatana. 2004. Towards parameter-free data mining. In *KDD*. 206–215.
[18] JWKJW Kotrlik and CCHCC Higgins. 2001. Organizational research: Determining appropriate sample size in survey research appropriate sample size in survey research. *ITLPJ* 19, 1 (2001), 43.
[19] Tao Li, Sheng Ma, and Mitsunori Ogihara. 2004. Entropy-based criterion in categorical clustering. In *ICML*. 68.
[20] Christopher D Manning, Prabhakar Raghavan, and others. 2008. *Introduction to information retrieval*. Vol. 1. Cambridge university press.
[21] Andreas Mild and Thomas Reutterer. 2003. An improved collaborative filtering approach for predicting cross-category purchases based on binary market basket data. *JRCS* 10, 3 (2003), 123–133.
[22] Dan Pelleg, Andrew W Moore, and others. 2000. X-means: Extending K-means with Efficient Estimation of the Number of Clusters.. In *ICML*, Vol. 1.
[23] Steffen Rendle and others. 2010. Factorizing personalized markov chains for next-basket recommendation. In *WWW*. ACM, 811–820.
[24] Gideon Schwarz and others. 1978. Estimating the dimension of a model. *The annals of statistics* 6, 2 (1978), 461–464.
[25] Claude Elwood Shannon. 2001. A mathematical theory of communication. *SIGMOBILE* 5, 1 (2001), 3–55.
[26] Xiaoyuan Su and Taghi M Khoshgoftaar. 2009. A survey of collaborative filtering techniques. *Advances in AI* 2009 (2009), 4.
[27] Pang-Ning Tan, Michael Steinbach, Vipin Kumar, and others. 2006. *Introduction to data mining*. Vol. 1. Pearson Addison Wesley Boston.
[28] Lyle H Ungar and Dean P Foster. 1998. Clustering methods for collaborative filtering. In *AAAI*, Vol. 1. 114–129.
[29] Nguyen Xuan Vinh, Julien Epps, and James Bailey. 2009. Information theoretic measures for clusterings comparison: is a correction for chance necessary?. In *ICML*. ACM, 1073–1080.
[30] Ke Wang, Chu Xu, and Bing Liu. 1999. Clustering transactions using large items. In *CIKM*. ACM, 483–490.
[31] Pengfei Wang, Jiafeng Guo, and others. 2014. Modeling retail transaction data for personalized shopping recommendation. In *CIKM*. 1979–1982.
[32] Yongqiao Xiao and Margaret H Dunham. 2001. Interactive clustering for transaction data. In *DaWaK*. Springer, 121–130.
[33] Tengke Xiong, Shengrui Wang, André Mayers, and Ernest Monga. 2012. DHCC: Divisive hierarchical clustering of categorical data. *Data Mining and Knowledge Discovery* 24, 1 (2012), 103–135.
[34] Hua Yan, Keke Chen, and Ling Liu. 2006. Efficiently clustering transactional data with weighted coverage density. In *CIKM*. ACM, 367–376.
[35] Yinghui Yang and others. 2005. GHIC: A hierarchical pattern-based clustering algorithm for grouping Web transactions. *TKDE* 17, 9 (2005), 1300–1304.
[36] Yiling Yang, Xudong Guan, and Jinyuan You. 2002. CLOPE: a fast and effective clustering algorithm for transactional data. In *TKDE*. ACM, 682–687.
[37] Ching-Huang Yun, Kun-Ta Chuang, and Ming-Syan Chen. 2006. Adherence clustering: an efficient method for mining market-basket clusters. *Information systems* 31, 3 (2006), 170–186.
[38] Mohammed J Zaki and Markus Peters. 2005. CLICKS: Mining subspace clusters in categorical data via K-partite maximal cliques. In *ICDE*. 355–356.

Network Inference via the Time-Varying Graphical Lasso

David Hallac, Youngsuk Park, Stephen Boyd, Jure Leskovec
Stanford University
{hallac,youngsuk,boyd,jure}@stanford.edu

ABSTRACT

Many important problems can be modeled as a system of interconnected entities, where each entity is recording time-dependent observations or measurements. In order to spot trends, detect anomalies, and interpret the temporal dynamics of such data, it is essential to understand the relationships between the different entities and how these relationships evolve over time. In this paper, we introduce the *time-varying graphical lasso (TVGL)*, a method of inferring time-varying networks from raw time series data. We cast the problem in terms of estimating a sparse time-varying inverse covariance matrix, which reveals a dynamic network of interdependencies between the entities. Since dynamic network inference is a computationally expensive task, we derive a scalable message-passing algorithm based on the Alternating Direction Method of Multipliers (ADMM) to solve this problem in an efficient way. We also discuss several extensions, including a streaming algorithm to update the model and incorporate new observations in real time. Finally, we evaluate our TVGL algorithm on both real and synthetic datasets, obtaining interpretable results and outperforming state-of-the-art baselines in terms of both accuracy and scalability.

1 INTRODUCTION

Applications in many settings, ranging from neurological connectivity patterns [21] to financial markets [23] and social network analysis [1, 22], contain massive sequences of multivariate timestamped observations. Such data can often be modeled as a network of interacting entities, where each entity is a node associated with a time series of data points. In these dependency networks, also known as Markov random fields (MRFs) [16, 26, 33], an edge represents a partial correlation, or a direct effect (holding all other nodes constant) between two entities. An important problem that arises in many applications is using observational data to infer these relationships (*i.e.*, edges) and their evolution over time. In particular, it is necessary to understand how the structure of these complex systems changes over a period of interest (Figure 1). For example, in financial markets, companies can be represented as nodes, and each acts like a "sensor" recording a time series of its stock price. By understanding the relationships within the network and their evolution over time, one can detect anomalies, spot trends, classify events, forecast future behavior, and solve many other problems at the intersection of time series analysis and network science.

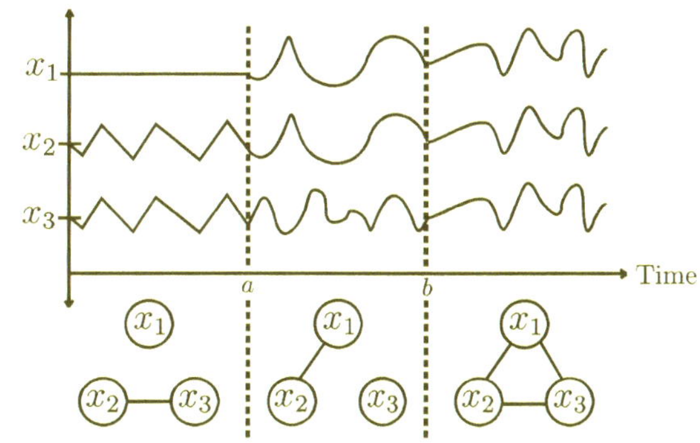

Figure 1: Three sensors with associated time series readings. Based on such data, we infer a time-varying network that reveals 1) the dependencies between the different sensors, and 2) when and how these dependencies change over time.

To learn these dynamic networks, one can model the relationships between the entities through an underlying inverse covariance matrix that changes over time. Doing so allows for inference of a dynamic undirected network, with nodes representing the different entities and edges defining the coupling between them. More precisely, given a multivariate sequence of readings, one can estimate the true inverse covariance matrix $\Sigma^{-1}(t)$ (which changes over time), assuming a Gaussian distribution. The focus is specifically on the inverse covariance because of its increased interpretability: if $\Sigma^{-1}_{ij}(t) = 0$ then, given the values of all the other entities (*i.e.*, nodes), i and j are conditionally independent at time t [17]. Therefore, the inferred network has an edge between i and j at time t if $\Sigma^{-1}_{ij}(t) \neq 0$, denoting a structural dependency between these two entities at that moment in time. In the static case, where Σ^{-1} is constant, this inference is known as the graphical lasso problem [7, 35]. While many efficient algorithms exist for the graphical lasso [2, 14], such methods do not generalize to the time-varying case.

Inferring dynamic networks is challenging mainly because it is difficult to simultaneously estimate both the network itself and the change in its structure over time. This is in part due to the fact that networks can exhibit many different types of changes. The range of possibilities includes a sudden shift of the entire network structure, a single node rewiring all of its connections, or even just one or two edges changing in the whole network. Therefore, any method must be general enough to discover many types of evolutionary patterns, while also being powerful enough to learn this temporal structure over very long time series. As such, solving for time-varying networks is computationally expensive, especially compared to time-invariant inference [6, 19]. There are more parameters, additional coupling, and more complicated dynamics.

KDD '17, August 13-17, 2017, Halifax, NS, Canada

ACM ISBN 978-1-4503-4887-4/17/08...$15.00
https://doi.org/10.1145/3097983.3098037

Standard methods have trouble scaling to large examples, so novel algorithms and techniques are required.

Present Work. In this paper, we formulate time-varying network inference as a convex optimization problem. Thus, our two primary contributions are in formally defining this problem, which we call the *time-varying graphical lasso* (TVGL), and in deriving a scalable optimization method to solve it. Given a sequence of multivariate observations, the TVGL estimates the inverse covariance $\Sigma^{-1}(t)$ of the data to simultaneously achieve three goals: (1) matching the empirical observations, (2) sparsity, and (3) temporal consistency. Matching the empirical observations ensures that our estimated network is well-supported by the data. A sparse inverse covariance prevents overfitting and provides interpretable results via a sparse graphical representation [2, 7]. Temporal consistency is the idea that, most of the time, adjacent timestamps should have very similar (or even identical) estimations of the network. We impose a temporal penalty to limit how the network can evolve, where different penalties induce different dynamics. We suggest five specific penalties that allow us to model different types of temporal variation (or evolutionary patterns) in networks: e.g., smoothly varying networks, rare-but-large-scale shifts, or a single node rewiring its connections. Then, since no scalable methods exist for solving our TVGL problem, we develop a message-passing algorithm using the alternating direction method of multipliers (ADMM) [3]. We derive closed-form solutions for the ADMM subproblems, including one for each of the five unique penalty types, to further speed up the runtime. We also discuss several extensions, including one to convert our approach into a streaming algorithm that can quickly incorporate new data and update our estimate in real time.

We then apply our TVGL method to both real and synthetic datasets. First, we test accuracy and scalability on synthetic examples with known ground truth networks. Our TVGL method leads to accuracy improvements of up to 92% over two state-of-the-art baselines. Furthermore, our ADMM-based implementation is several orders of magnitude faster than other solution methods, able to solve for 5 million unknown variables in under 12 minutes (while other solvers take several hours for even 50 thousand unknowns). Finally, we analyze two real-world case studies, using financial and automobile sensor data, to demonstrate how the TVGL approach can find meaningful insights, understandable structure, and different types of evolutionary patterns in time series data.

Related Work. This work relates to recent advancements in both graphical models and convex optimization. Inferring static networks via the graphical lasso is a well-studied topic [2, 6, 7, 35]. However, previous work on dynamic inference has only focused on a kernel method [36] or an ℓ_1-fused penalty [15, 21, 31]. One of the main contributions of our approach is that it is able to model many different types of network evolutionary patterns, for example a small set of edges rewiring, a single node changing all its edges, or the entire network restructuring at a single time step. This opens up a variety of new applications, several of which we examine in Sections 6 and 7. Whereas previous work allows for only one time-varying pattern [15, 21, 31], we show how the selection of the proper evolutionary penalty is a very important parameter for obtaining accurate results. We also propose several extensions, including a streaming approach, that to the best of our knowledge have not been explored in the literature.

To solve our TVGL problem, we develop an ADMM-based algorithm [3] so that the same framework can incorporate all of the different penalty types that we study. This is necessary because, even though many problem-specific methods exist to solve the standard (static) graphical lasso [7, 14], no ready-to-use methods exist for the time-varying case. To make our algorithm more scalable, we rewrite the ADMM subproblems in terms of proximal operators [6, 21, 27]. This allows us to take advantage of known properties and solution methods to derive closed-form ADMM updates [4, 25], which speed up our solver by several orders of magnitude over a naive ADMM implementation (Section 6.2).

Another common method of time series analysis is the Kalman filter [9], a special type of dynamic factor model [20]. Although used in similar domains, these models are fundamentally different from our network inference approach. They are typically used to predict values of unknown variables, given all previous data. Our algorithm instead learns the underlying dynamic graphical structure of the variables [16, 17]. Thus, our method helps remove the effects of noisy data and adds interpretability to the results. Additionally, we note the difference between our work here and information cascade-based network inference [8, 22], which assumes a viral spreading process over the nodes and aims to infer the links based on the node infection times. We instead aim to uncover the dependency structure (*i.e.*, inverse covariance matrix) based on multivariate time series observations.

2 PROBLEM DEFINITION

Consider a sequence of multivariate observations in $\mathbf{R}^p$ sampled from a distribution $x \sim N(0, \Sigma(t))$. Observations come in at times $0 \leq t_1 \leq \cdots \leq t_T$, where at each time t_i, there are $n_i \geq 1$ different observation vectors over the readings of all the nodes. (For now we assume that the readings are synchronous, where $t_i - t_{i-1}$ is a constant value for all i, but in Section 3.1 we extend this approach to asynchronous observations.) With these samples, we aim to estimate the underlying covariance matrix $\Sigma(t)$, which can change over time. That is, given a changing underlying distribution, we attempt to estimate it based on a sequence of observations. Here, we formulate a convex optimization problem to infer a sequence of sparse inverse covariance matrices, $\Theta_i = \Sigma(t_i)^{-1}$, one for each t_i. These estimates are based on local empirical observation vector(s), as well as coupling constraints with neighboring timestamps' covariance estimates. Recall that a sparse inverse covariance allows us to encode conditional independence between different variables [16].

Inferring Static Networks. We first consider static inference, which is equivalent to the graphical lasso problem [2, 7, 35], and then build on it to extend to dynamic networks. In the static case, $\Sigma(t)$ is constant for all t. Given a series of multivariate readings, this can be written as

$$\text{minimize} - l(\Theta) + \lambda \, \|\Theta\|_{\text{od},1}, \tag{1}$$

where $\|\Theta\|_{\text{od},1}$ is a seminorm of Θ, the off-diagonal ℓ_1-norm, $\sum_{i \neq j} |\Theta_{ij}|$. This lasso penalty enforces element-wise sparsity in our solution for Θ, regulated by the trade-off parameter $\lambda \geq 0$. In Problem (1),

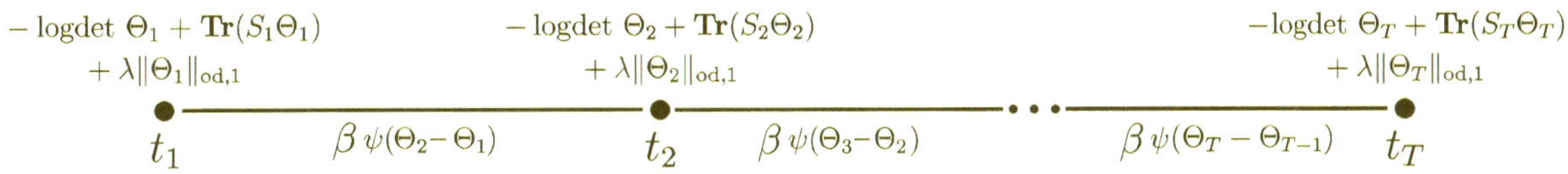

Figure 2: Dynamic network inference can be thought of as an optimization problem on a chain graph, where each node objective solves for a *network slice* at each timestamp, and edge objectives define the penalties that enforce temporal consistency.

$l(\Theta)$ is the log likelihood of Θ (up to a constant and scale) [29, 35],

$$l(\Theta) = n(\log\det\Theta - \mathrm{Tr}(S\Theta)),$$

where Θ must be symmetric positive-definite ($\mathbf{S}_{++}^p$), S is the empirical covariance $\frac{1}{n}\sum_{i=1}^{n} x_i x_i^T$, n is the number of observations, and x_i are the different samples. When S is invertible, $l(\Theta)$ encourages Θ to be close to S^{-1}.

Inferring Dynamic Networks. In order to infer a time-varying sequence of networks, we extend the above approach and allow $\Sigma(t)$ to vary over time. To do so we set up a sequence of graphical lasso problems, each coupled together in a chain to penalize deviations in the estimations, which we call the *time-varying graphical lasso* (TVGL). We solve for $\Theta = (\Theta_1, \ldots, \Theta_T)$, our estimated inverse covariance matrices at times $t_1, \ldots, t_T$,

$$\underset{\Theta\in\mathbf{S}_{++}^p}{\text{minimize}} \quad \sum_{i=1}^{T} -l_i(\Theta_i) + \lambda\,\|\Theta_i\|_{\text{od},1} + \beta\sum_{i=2}^{T}\psi(\Theta_i - \Theta_{i-1}). \tag{2}$$

Here, $l_i(\Theta_i) = n_i(\log\det\Theta_i - \mathrm{Tr}(S_i\Theta_i))$, $\beta \geq 0$, and $\psi(\Theta_i - \Theta_{i-1})$ is a convex penalty function, minimized at $\psi(0)$, which encourages similarity between Θ_{t-1} and Θ_t. We examine in Section 2.1 how different ψ's enforce different behaviors. Note that Problem (2) can be viewed as an optimization problem defined on a chain graph, where each element solves for a different Θ_i, as shown in Figure 2.

Empirical Covariance. The log-likelihood l_i depends on S_i, the empirical covariance at time t_i. In high-dimensional settings, where the number of dimensions p is larger than the number of observations n_i, S_i will be rank deficient and therefore non-invertible. However, our method is well-suited to overcome this problem of an insufficient number of observations. By enforcing structural similarity, each Θ_i borrows strength from the fact that neighboring network estimates should be similar, or even identical, across time. In the extreme case, we are able to estimate a network at a time where there is only one observation. The empirical covariance, $x_i x_i^T$, is rank 1, but between the sparsity and the temporal consistency penalties, our approach can still infer an accurate estimate of the network at that snapshot in time.

Regularization Parameters λ and β. Problem (2) has two parameters, λ and β, which define important values on two trade-off curves. λ determines the sparsity level of the network: small values will better match the empirical data, but will lead to very dense networks, which are less interpretable and often overfit. β determines how strongly correlated neighboring covariance estimations should be. A small β will lead to Θ's which fluctuate from estimate-to-estimate, whereas large β's lead to smoother estimates over time. As $\beta \to \infty$, the temporal deviation penalty gets so large that Problem (2) turns into the original graphical lasso, since a constant Θ will be the solution across the entire time series.

2.1 Encoding Network Evolutionary Patterns

Different types of penalty functions ψ allow us to enforce different behaviors in the evolution of the network structure. In particular, if we have an expectation about how the underlying network may change over time, we are able to encode it into ψ. Here, we define several common temporal patterns and their associated penalty functions. In Sections 6 and 7, we use these to analyze the time-varying dynamics of multiple real and synthetic datasets. For these penalties, note that ψ can sometimes be split into a sum of column-norms. As such, we refer to the j-th column of a matrix X as $[X]_j$.

- **A few edges changing at a time** — Setting $\psi(X) = \sum_{i,j}|X_{i,j}|$, an element-wise ℓ_1 penalty, encourages neighboring graphs to be identical [6, 34]. When the ij-th edge of the network "breaks", or is different at two neighboring times, this penalty still encourages the rest of the graph to remain *exactly* the same. As a result, this penalty is best used in cases where we expect only a handful of edges — at most — to change at a time.
- **Global restructuring** — Setting $\psi(X) = \sum_j \|[X]_j\|_2$, a group lasso ℓ_2 penalty, causes the entire graph to restructure at a select few timestamps, while at all other times, the graph remains piecewise constant [6, 10]. This is useful for event detection and time-series segmentation, as it finds exact times where there is a regime-change, or shift, in the underlying covariance matrix.
- **Smoothly varying over time** — Setting $\psi(X) = \sum_{i,j} X_{i,j}^2$, a Laplacian penalty, causes smooth transitions of the graphical model from timestamp to timestamp. Adjacent graphs will often differ by small amounts, but severe deviations are largely penalized so they rarely occur [30]. This penalty is best used when we want to come up with a smoothly varying estimate over time.
- **Block-wise restructuring** — Setting $\psi(X)$ to an ℓ_∞ penalty, $\psi(X) = \sum_j \left(\max_i |X_{i,j}|\right)$, implies that, when an element in the inverse covariance matrix changes by ϵ at a given time, other elements are free to change by up to that same amount with no additional penalty (except for the original $\ell_{\text{od},1}$ sparsity condition). This is best used when a cluster of nodes suddenly changes its internal edge structure, the rest of the network does not change.
- **Perturbed node** — Setting ψ to the row-column overlap penalty [18], defined as $\psi(X) = \underset{V:V+V^T=X}{\min} \sum_j \|[V]_j\|_2$, yields an interesting behavior. When node i has a reweighting of one edge at time t, this says that the node can rewire all its edges at that same time with a minimal penalty. However the rest of the graph is strongly encouraged to remain the exact same. It is best used in situations where we are looking for single nodes re-locating themselves to a new set of neighbors within the network.

3 EXTENSIONS

Here, we develop three extensions of the basic time-varying graphical lasso. First, we update our approach to allow for asynchronous observations of the data. Then, we derive a method of inferring an estimate at *any* time, even if there is no temporally-local data. Finally, we extend the algorithm so it can be deployed in an application with streaming data and real-time update constraints.

Asynchronous Observations. Problem (2) can be extended to asynchronous settings, where samples are observed at irregularly-spaced intervals. We rewrite the problem as

$$\underset{\Theta \in S_{++}^{p}}{\text{minimize}} \quad \sum_{i=1}^{T} - l_i(\Theta_i) + \lambda \|\Theta_i\|_{\text{od},1} + \beta \sum_{i=2}^{T} h_i \psi\left(\frac{\Theta_i - \Theta_{i-1}}{h_i}\right),$$

where $h_i = t_i - t_{i-1}$, the interval of time between sample $i - 1$ and sample i. This is similar to putting h_i different intermediate Θ's between the two samples (with no loss, since there is no data). Since ψ is convex, we know that the loss is minimized by evenly spreading the change in $\Theta_i - \Theta_{i-1}$ across these h_i steps. We also know from convexity that this penalty gets smaller as h_i gets larger. That is, the temporal consistency penalty is less important when consecutive samples have a large time gap between them. Of course, we can scale this penalty through the regularization parameter β to account for the average frequency of the data.

Inferring Intermediate Networks. With this approach, it is possible to infer the covariance estimation at *any* time, even if there are no observations at that moment in time. This can be very useful if, for example, we want to get a granular estimate of a sharp breakpoint. To infer a network estimate at intermediate time s, we create a dummy node at s and merge it into the chain graph by connecting it to the nearest observation in either direction, $j - 1$ and j. To get an estimate of Θ_s, we solve for

$$\underset{\Theta_s \in S_{++}^{p}}{\text{minimize}} \quad w(s - t_{j-1})\psi(\Theta_s - \Theta_{j-1}) + w(t_j - s)\psi(\Theta_j - \Theta_s).$$

For most common ψ's, this problem has a closed-form solution. With this we can efficiently "upsample" and predict underlying covariances as frequently as our application requires, even if the data has a slower sampling frequency.

Streaming Algorithm. In many applications, it is necessary to deploy a network inference scheme that updates in real time as new observations continue to arrive. Therefore, we require a streaming algorithm to quickly incorporate new data into our model. That is, given that we have solved for a problem with i timestamps, we look for a fast way to update the solution when we receive a new observation at time t_{i+1}.

One approach is to use a warm-start ADMM. With this method, we solve for the $i+1$ covariance matrices using the standard ADMM approach, but the first i Θ's initialize themselves at the value of the solution to the previous problem. However, there are no guarantees as to how many iterations warm-start ADMM may take to converge. In particular, as i gets large, there is a risk that one single additional reading takes a very long time as the new information needs to propagate across the entire time series. Therefore, it may take longer to incorporate the 1000th reading than the 100th. If we want a real-time implementation of this algorithm, we need a way of guaranteeing that it takes the same amount of time to solve, regardless of the current timestamp.

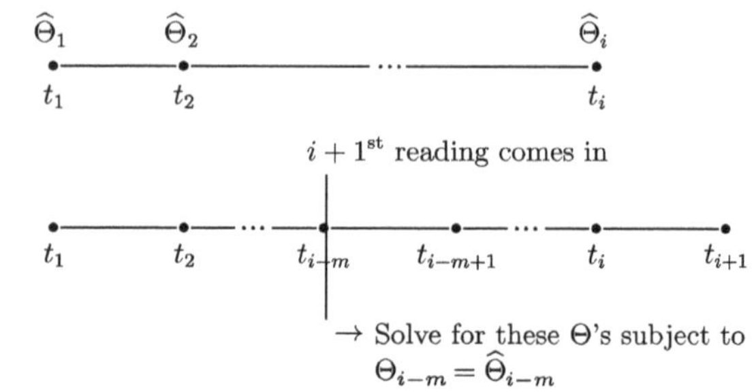

Figure 3: To quickly update our estimates when the observation at t_{i+1} arrives, we re-solve for the most recent m timestamps, while enforcing that Θ_{i-m} must remain the same.

We do so using a small approximation where we fix the result a certain distance in the past, and only solve for the m most recent nodes (Figure 3). Therefore, if the $i + 1$-st reading comes in, we only solve for nodes $i - m$ to $i + 1$, subject to the constraint that $\Theta_{i-m} = \hat{\Theta}_{i-m}$, where $\hat{\Theta}$ is the solution from when there were only i timestamps. We can pick m based on memory limitations, previous breakpoints, or domain expertise.

4 PROPOSED ALGORITHM

When inferring small networks, or those without time-varying dynamics, Problem (2) can be solved using standard interior-point methods. However, our paper focuses on larger examples, where it is infeasible to solve the whole problem at once. Here, we propose the time-varying graphical lasso (TVGL) algorithm, based on the alternating direction method of multipliers (ADMM) [3], a well-established distributed convex optimization approach. With ADMM, we split the problem up into a series of subproblems and use a message-passing algorithm to converge on the globally optimal solution. In this section, we analyze the separable subproblems and develop analytical solutions, which are fast and easy to implement, for every step in the ADMM process. To do so, we rewrite terms in the form of proximal operators [25], which are defined for a matrix $A \in \mathbf{R}^{m \times n}$ and the real-valued function $f(X)$ as

$$\mathbf{prox}_{\eta f}(A) = \underset{X \in \mathbf{R}^{m \times n}}{\text{argmin}} \left(f(X) + 1/(2\eta)\|X - A\|_F^2\right). \tag{3}$$

The proximal operator defines a trade-off for X between minimizing f and being near A. Writing the problems in this form allows us to take advantage of well known properties to find closed-form updates for each of the ADMM subproblems.

4.1 ADMM Solution

To split Problem (2) into a separable form, we introduce a consensus variable $Z = \{Z_0, Z_1, Z_2\} = \{(Z_{1,0}, \ldots, Z_{T,0}), (Z_{1,1}, \ldots, Z_{T-1,1}), (Z_{2,2}, \ldots, Z_{T,2})\}$. With this, we can rewrite Problem (2) as its equivalent problem,

$$\begin{array}{ll} \text{minimize} & \sum_{i=1}^{T} -l_i(\Theta_i) + \lambda \|Z_{i,0}\|_{\text{od},1} + \beta \sum_{i=2}^{T} \psi(Z_{i,2} - Z_{i-1,1}) \\ \text{subject to} & Z_{i,0} = \Theta_i, \ \Theta_i \in S_{++}^{p} \quad \text{for} \quad i = 1, \ldots, T \\ & (Z_{i-1,1}, Z_{i,2}) = (\Theta_{i-1}, \Theta_i) \quad \text{for} \quad i = 2, \ldots, T. \end{array}$$

The corresponding augmented Lagrangian [13] becomes

$$\mathcal{L}_\rho(\Theta, Z, U) = \sum_{i=1}^{T} -l(\Theta_i) + \lambda \|Z_{i,0}\|_{\text{od},1} + \beta \sum_{i=2}^{T} \psi(Z_{i,2} - Z_{i-1,1})$$
$$+ (\rho/2) \sum_{i=1}^{T} \left(\|\Theta_i - Z_{i,0} + U_{i,0}\|_F^2 - \|U_{i,0}\|_F^2 \right)$$
$$+ (\rho/2) \sum_{i=2}^{T} \Big(\|\Theta_{i-1} - Z_{i-1,1} + U_{i-1,1}\|_F^2 - \|U_{i-1,1}\|_F^2$$
$$+ \|\Theta_i - Z_{i,2} + U_{i,2}\|_F^2 - \|U_{i,2}\|_F^2 \Big), \tag{4}$$

where $U = \{U_0, U_1, U_2\} = \{(U_{1,0}, \ldots, U_{T,0}), (U_{1,1}, \ldots, U_{T-1,1}), (U_{2,2}, \ldots, U_{T,2})\}$ is the scaled dual variable and $\rho > 0$ is the ADMM penalty parameter [3, §3.1.1]. ADMM consists of the following updates, where k denotes the iteration number:

$$(a) \quad \Theta^{k+1} := \underset{\Theta \in \mathbf{S}_{++}^p}{\text{argmin}}\ \mathcal{L}_\rho\left(\Theta, Z^k, U^k\right)$$

$$(b) \quad Z^{k+1} = \begin{bmatrix} Z_0^{k+1} \\ Z_1^{k+1} \\ Z_2^{k+1} \end{bmatrix} := \underset{Z_0, Z_1, Z_2}{\text{argmin}}\ \mathcal{L}_\rho\left(\Theta^{k+1}, Z, U^k\right)$$

$$(c) \quad U^{k+1} = \begin{bmatrix} U_0^{k+1} \\ U_1^{k+1} \\ U_2^{k+1} \end{bmatrix} := \begin{bmatrix} U_0^k \\ U_1^k \\ U_2^k \end{bmatrix} + \begin{bmatrix} \Theta^{k+1} - Z_0^{k+1} \\ (\Theta_1^{k+1}, \ldots, \Theta_{T-1}^{k+1}) - Z_1^{k+1} \\ (\Theta_2^{k+1}, \ldots, \Theta_T^{k+1}) - Z_2^{k+1} \end{bmatrix}.$$

Global Convergence. By separating Problem (2) into two blocks of variables, Θ and Z, our ADMM approach is guaranteed to converge to the global optimum. Our iterative algorithm uses a stopping criterion based on the primal and dual residual values being below specified thresholds; see [3].

4.2 Θ-Update

The Θ-step can be split into separate updates for each Θ_i, which can then be solved in parallel:

$$\Theta_i^{k+1} \overset{(a)}{=} \underset{\Theta_i \in \mathbf{S}_{++}^p}{\text{argmin}}\ -\log\det(\Theta_i) + \mathbf{Tr}(S_i\Theta_i) + \frac{1}{2\eta}\|\Theta_i - A\|_F^2$$
$$\overset{(b)}{=} \underset{\Theta_i \in \mathbf{S}_{++}^p}{\text{argmin}}\ -\log\det(\Theta_i) + \mathbf{Tr}(S_i\Theta_i) + \frac{1}{2\eta}\left\|\Theta_i - \frac{A + A^T}{2}\right\|_F^2$$

where (a) holds for $A = \frac{Z_{i,0}^k + Z_{i,1}^k + Z_{i,2}^k - U_{i,0}^k - U_{i,1}^k - U_{i,2}^k}{3}$ and $\eta = \frac{n_i}{3\rho}$, and (b) holds due to the symmetry of Θ_i. This can be rewritten as a proximal operator,

$$\Theta_i^{k+1} = \mathbf{prox}_{\eta(-\log\det(\cdot) + \mathbf{Tr}(S_i \cdot))}\left((A + A^T)/2\right).$$

Since $\frac{A+A^T}{2}$ is symmetric, this has an analytical solution,

$$\Theta_i^{k+1} := \frac{1}{2\eta^{-1}} Q\left(D + \sqrt{D^2 + 4\eta^{-1}I}\right)Q^T, \tag{5}$$

where QDQ^T is the eigendecomposition of $\eta^{-1}\frac{A+A^T}{2} - S_i$ [6, 32]. This is the most computationally expensive task in our algorithm, as decomposing a $p \times p$ matrix has an $O(p^3)$ runtime.

4.3 Z-Update

The Z-update can be split into two parts: Z_0, which refers to the $\|\Theta\|_{\text{od},1}$-penalty that enforces sparsity in the inverse covariance matrices, and (Z_1, Z_2), which denotes the ψ-penalty that minimizes deviations across timestamps. These two updates can be solved simultaneously, and each part can be parallelized even further to speed up computation.

4.3.1 Part 1: Z_0-Update. Each $Z_{i,0}$ can be written as the proximal operator of the $\ell_{\text{od},1}$-norm, which has a known closed-form solution [25]

$$Z_{i,0}^{k+1} = \mathbf{prox}_{\frac{\lambda}{\rho}\|\cdot\|_{\text{od},1}}(\Theta_i^{k+1} + U_{i,0}^k) = S_{\frac{\lambda}{\rho}}(\Theta_i^{k+1} + U_{i,0}^k),$$

where $S_{\frac{\lambda}{\rho}}(\cdot)$ is the element-wise soft-threshold function, for $1 \leq i \neq j \leq p$. The (i,j)-th element of this update is

$$\left(S_{\frac{\lambda}{\rho}}(A)\right)_{ij} = \begin{cases} 0 & |A_{ij}| \leq \frac{\lambda}{\rho} \\ \mathbf{sgn}(A_{ij})(|A_{ij}| - \frac{\lambda}{\rho}) & \text{otherwise.} \end{cases}$$

4.3.2 Part 2: (Z_1, Z_2)-Update. $Z_{i-1,1}$ and $Z_{i,2}$ are coupled together in the augmented Lagrangian, so they must be jointly updated. In order to derive the closed-form solution, we define

$$\tilde{\psi}\left(\begin{bmatrix} Z_1 \\ Z_2 \end{bmatrix}\right) = \psi(Z_2 - Z_1).$$

We now solve a separate update for each (Z_1, Z_2) pair,

$$\begin{bmatrix} Z_{i-1,1}^{k+1} \\ Z_{i,2}^{k+1} \end{bmatrix} = \mathbf{prox}_{\frac{\beta}{\rho}\tilde{\psi}(\cdot)}\left(\begin{bmatrix} \Theta_{i-1}^{k+1} + U_{i-1,1}^k \\ \Theta_i^{k+1} + U_{i,2}^k \end{bmatrix}\right). \tag{6}$$

Part 2-1: (Z_1, Z_2)-Updates for the Sum of Column Norms. For the ℓ_1, ℓ_2, ℓ_2^2, and ℓ_∞ penalties defined in Section 2.1, we solve the proximal operator by utilizing the following two properties [25, 28]:

- If a function f is a composition of another function g with an orthogonal affine transformation, i.e., $f(x) = g(Cx + D)$ and $CC^T = (1/\alpha)I$, then
$$\mathbf{prox}_f(x) = (I - \alpha C^T C)x + \alpha C^T(\mathbf{prox}_{\frac{1}{\alpha}g}(Cx + D) - D).$$
- If f is block-separable, i.e., $f(x) = \sum_j f_j(x_j)$ where $x = (x_1, x_2, \ldots)$, then $\left(\mathbf{prox}_f(v)\right)_j = \mathbf{prox}_{f_j}(v_j)$.

Recall that our goal is to get the analytical solution to (6). To do so, we apply the first property with $f = \tilde{\psi}$, $g = \psi$, $C = \begin{bmatrix} -I & I \end{bmatrix}$, $D = 0$, and $\alpha = \frac{1}{2}$, which converts the (Z_1, Z_2)-update into

$$\begin{bmatrix} Z_{i-1,1}^{k+1} \\ Z_{i,2}^{k+1} \end{bmatrix} \overset{(a)}{=} \frac{1}{2}\begin{bmatrix} \Theta_{i-1}^{k+1} + \Theta_i^{k+1} + U_{i-1,1}^k + U_{i,2}^k \\ \Theta_{i-1}^{k+1} + \Theta_i^{k+1} + U_{i-1,1}^k + U_{i,2}^k \end{bmatrix} + \frac{1}{2}\begin{bmatrix} -E \\ E \end{bmatrix},$$

where (a) holds for

$$E = \mathbf{prox}_{\frac{2\beta}{\rho}\psi}\left(\begin{bmatrix} \Theta_i^{k+1} - \Theta_{i-1}^{k+1} + U_{i,2}^k - U_{i-1,1}^k \end{bmatrix}\right).$$

Now, for each penalty function ψ, we simply need to solve for the corresponding E. We denote $A = \begin{bmatrix} \Theta_{i-1}^{k+1} - \Theta_i^{k+1} + U_{i-1,1}^k - U_{i,2}^k \end{bmatrix}$ and $\eta = \frac{2\beta}{\rho}$. Then, since ψ is just the sum of column-norms and thus block-separable, we simplify E as

$$[E]_j = \left(\mathbf{prox}_{\eta\psi}(A)\right)_j \overset{(b)}{=} \mathbf{prox}_{\eta\phi}([A]_j), \tag{7}$$

where ϕ is the column-norm for ℓ_1, ℓ_2, ℓ_2^2, and ℓ_∞. Note that we have narrowed the $(Z_{i-1,1}, Z_{i,2})$-update in (6) down to just finding E_j in (7), expressed by the proximal operator of ϕ defined on a vector, each of which has a closed form solution as follows:

Element-wise ℓ_1 Penalty. The ℓ_1 proximal operator is

$$[E]_j = \mathbf{prox}_{\eta\|\cdot\|_1}([A]_j) = S_\eta(A_j).$$

This is just the element-wise soft threshold,

$$E_{ij} = S_\eta(A_{ij}) = \begin{cases} 0 & |A_{ij}| \leq \eta \\ \mathbf{sgn}(A_{ij})(|A_{ij}| - \eta) & \text{otherwise.} \end{cases}$$

Group Lasso ℓ_2 Penalty. The proximal operator for the ℓ_2-norm is a block-wise soft thresholding,

$$[E]_j = \mathbf{prox}_{\eta\|\cdot\|_2}([A]_j) = \begin{cases} 0 & \|[A]_j\|_2 \leq \eta \\ (1 - \eta/\|[A]_j\|_2)[A]_j & \text{otherwise.} \end{cases}$$

Laplacian Penalty. The proximal operator for the ℓ_2^2-norm, Laplacian regularization, is given by

$$[E]_j = \mathbf{prox}_{\eta\|\cdot\|_2^2}([A]_j) = (1 + 2\eta)^{-1}([A]_j).$$

This can be rewritten in element-wise form

$$E_{ij} = (1 + 2\eta)^{-1}(A_{ij}).$$

ℓ_∞ Penalty. The proximal operator for the ℓ_∞-norm is

$$[E]_j = \mathbf{prox}_{\eta\|\cdot\|_\infty}([A]_j) = \begin{cases} 0 & \|[A]_j\|_1 \leq \eta \\ [A]_j - \eta S_\sigma([A]_j/\eta) & \text{otherwise,} \end{cases}$$

where σ is the solution to $\sum_{i=1}^{n} \max\{A_{ij}/\eta - \sigma, 0\} = 1$, which has no closed-form solution but can be solved via bisection.

Part 2-2: (Z_1, Z_2)-Update for Perturbed Node Penalty. The perturbed node proximal operator does not have an efficient analytical solution. However, we can solve this new problem by deriving a second ADMM algorithm. Here, in each iteration of our original ADMM solution, we now call this second ADMM solver.

In order to avoid notational conflict, we denote the minimization variables $(Z_{i-1,1}, Z_{i,2})$ as (Y_1, Y_2). We then introduce an additional variable $V = W^T$, and the augmented Lagrangian $\mathcal{L}_\rho$ becomes

$$\mathcal{L}_\rho(V, W, Y_1, Y_2) = \beta\|V\|_2 + \frac{\rho}{2}\left\|\begin{bmatrix} Y_1 \\ Y_2 \end{bmatrix} - \begin{bmatrix} \Theta_{i-1}^{k+1} + U_{i-1,1}^k \\ \Theta_i^{k+1} + U_{i,2}^k \end{bmatrix}\right\|_F^2$$
$$+ \frac{\rho}{2}\left\|V + W - (Y_1 - Y_2) + \tilde{U}_1\right\|_F^2 + \frac{\rho}{2}\left\|V - W^T + \tilde{U}_2\right\|_F^2,$$

where $(\tilde{U}_1, \tilde{U}_2)$ is the scaled dual variable and ρ is the same ADMM penalty parameter as outer ADMM. At the l-th iteration, the three steps in the ADMM update are as follows:

$$(a) \quad V^{l+1} = \mathbf{prox}_{\frac{\beta}{2\rho}\|\cdot\|_2}\left(\frac{Y_1^l - Y_2^l - W^l - \tilde{U}_1^l + ((W^l)^T - \tilde{U}_2^l)^T}{2}\right),$$

which has the following closed form solution for the jth column, with $A = \frac{Y_1^l - Y_2^l - W^l - \tilde{U}_1^l + ((W^l)^T - \tilde{U}_2^l)^T}{2}$,

$$[V^{l+1}]_j = \begin{cases} 0 & \|[A]_j\|_2 \leq \frac{\beta}{2\rho} \\ (1 - 1/(2\rho\|[A]_j\|_2))[A]_j & \text{otherwise.} \end{cases}$$

$$(b) \begin{bmatrix} W^{l+1} \\ Y_1^{l+1} \\ Y_2^{l+1} \end{bmatrix} = (C^T C + 2I)^{-1}\left(2\begin{bmatrix} (V^l + \tilde{U}_2^l)^T \\ \Theta_{i-1}^{k+1} + U_{i-1,1}^k \\ \Theta_i^{k+1} + U_{i,2}^k \end{bmatrix} - C^T D\right),$$

where $C = \begin{bmatrix} I & -I & I \end{bmatrix}$, and $D = (V^l + \tilde{U}_1^l)$.

$$(c) \begin{bmatrix} \tilde{U}_1^{l+1} \\ \tilde{U}_2^{l+1} \end{bmatrix} = \begin{bmatrix} \tilde{U}_1^l \\ \tilde{U}_2^l \end{bmatrix} + \begin{bmatrix} (V^{l+1} + W^{l+1}) - (Y_1^{l+1} - Y_2^{l+1}) \\ V^{l+1} - (W^{l+1})^T \end{bmatrix}.$$

5 IMPLEMENTATION

We have built a custom TVGL Python solver[1] on top of SnapVX [11], an open-source convex optimization package. Our solver takes as inputs the multivariate observations, the regularization parameters, and the type of penalty (ℓ_1, ℓ_2, Laplacian, ℓ_∞, or perturbed node), and it returns the time-varying network. Although TVGL is capable of being distributed across many machines, we instead distribute it across multiple cores of a single large-memory machine.

6 EXPERIMENTS

Here, we run several experiments on synthetic data, where there are clear ground truth networks, to test the accuracy and scalability of our network inference approach. First, we compare our TVGL method to two state-of-the-art baselines to measure accuracy, and we demonstrate the importance of using appropriate penalties for different types of temporal evolutions. Next, we vary the problem size over several orders of magnitude and test our ADMM-based algorithm's scalability compared to three other solution methods.

6.1 Accuracy on Synthetic Data

We first analyze a synthetic problem in which the observations are generated from a changing underlying covariance matrix. This provides a known ground truth network, which we can use to verify the accuracy of our network inference approach.

Experimental Setup. We evaluate two different types of temporal evolutions: a global shift, where the entire structure of the network changes at some time t, and a single node perturbation (which we refer to as a local shift), where one node rewires its connections all at once but the rest of the graph remains the same. We randomly generate the ground truth covariance and subsequent samples using the method outlined by Mohan et al. [19]. For both examples, we generate data in $\mathbf{R}^{10}$ over 100 timestamps, where the shift (either global or local) occurs at time $t = 50$. At each t, we observe 10 independent samples from the true distribution.

From this time series of observations, we then solve for $\Theta_t, t = 1, \ldots, 100$, our estimate of the dynamic network across this time period. Here, we set the regularization parameters λ and β as the values that minimize the Akaike Information Criteria (AIC) [12] (on a separate, independently generated training set).

Baseline Methods. We compare our approach to two different baselines: the static graphical lasso [7] and the kernel method [36]. For the static graphical lasso, we treat each t_i as an independent network. Since our data has 100 time steps, this means we solve 100 independent graphical lasso problems and infer 100 separate networks. For the kernel method, we modify the empirical covariances

[1]Code and solver can be found at http://snap.stanford.edu/tvgl/.

True Shift	Score	Static GL	Kernel	TVGL (ℓ_1)	TVGL (ℓ_2)	TVGL (Perturbed Node)
Local	F_1	0.646	0.768	0.819	0.817	**0.853**
	TD ratio	2.02	2.41	27.9	23.3	**55.5**
Global	F_1	0.496	0.688	0.939	**0.952**	0.943
	TD ratio	1.06	1.80	**47.6**	38.6	36.2

Table 1: F_1 score and Temporal Deviation (TD) ratio for a local and global shift, using the two baselines and three different TVGL evolutionary penalties.

and weight them according to a non-negative kernel function. We set the kernel width to the theoretically guaranteed optimum using the method proposed by Zhou et al. [36].

Performance Measures. We introduce two metrics to measure the accuracy of our estimate:

- **F_1 score:** This measures how closely we capture the true edge structure of the network (*i.e.*, how many of the non-zero elements in the inverse covariance we correctly identify as non-zero). This score is the harmonic mean of the precision and recall.
- **Temporal deviation (TD) ratio:** The temporal deviation, $\|\Theta_i - \Theta_{i-1}\|_F$, shows how much the estimate has changed at each timestamp. This score is the ratio of the temporal deviation at $t = 50$ (where the one "true" shift happened) to the average temporal deviation value across the 100 timestamps.

Experimental Results. We show results for both the local and global shift with several different TVGL penalties in Table 1. In terms of both F_1 score and temporal deviation, our TVGL approach significantly outperforms the two baselines. The TVGL F_1 score is up to 38.4% higher than the kernel method and 91.9% higher than the static graphical lasso. Regardless of penalty type, the TVGL also always has a temporal deviation (TD) ratio at least 9.7 times larger than any of the baseline methods. In fact, for both baselines and both shift types, the largest temporal deviation peak in the time series does *not* occur at $t = 50$. This means that the baselines do not detect that there is a large shift in the network at this time, whereas this sudden change is clearly discovered by TVGL (where the largest peak always occurs at $t = 50$). We later use this idea in Section 7 to detect significant events in real-world time series data.

Selection of Penalty Type. While the TVGL outperformed the two baselines regardless of the penalty type, even greater gains can be achieved by selecting the correct evolutionary penalty. In real world cases, this parameter can be selected by cross-validation or by incorporating domain knowledge, using the descriptions in Section 2.1 to choose the proper penalty based on exactly what type of temporal evolution one is looking for in the data. As shown in Table 1, there are clear benefits from using certain penalties in certain situations. For example, with a local shift, which is well-suited to be analyzed by a perturbed node penalty, choosing this penalty leads to a 5% higher F_1 score and a temporal deviation ratio that is more than twice as large as both the ℓ_1 or ℓ_2 cases. For the Global shift, the ℓ_2 penalty does the best job at reconstructing the time-varying network (largest F_1 score), though the ℓ_1 is better able to identify the sudden shift at $t = 50$ (with its TD ratio 23% larger than either of the other two penalty types). This additional selection parameter, which to the best of our knowledge has not been previously explored in this context, expands the reach of time-varying inference methods by allowing us to model various types of network evolutions with high precision.

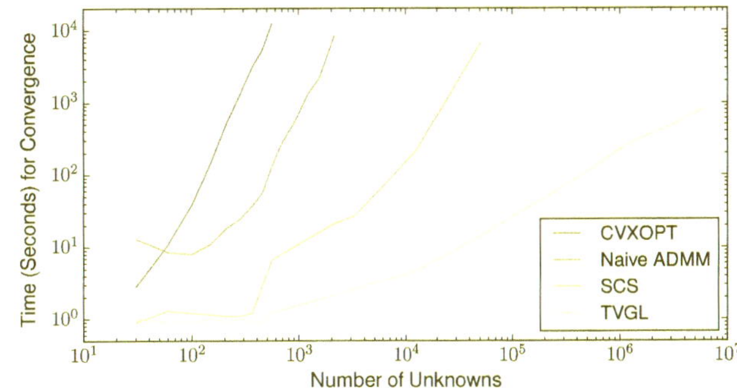

Figure 4: Scalability comparison between our TVGL solver and three other solution methods.

6.2 Scalability of TVGL

Next, we examine the scalability of our TVGL algorithm. We run our TVGL solver on data generated by the method outlined in Section 6.1, and we vary our problem size over several orders of magnitude. Here, we estimate m slices of a n-node network, for a total of $m\frac{n(n+1)}{2}$ unknown variables.

While many algorithms exist to efficiently solve the static graphical lasso problem (*e.g.*, [7, 14]), these cannot be directly applied to our problem because of the time-varying penalties coupling the variables together. Instead, we compare our runtime against three alternative methods that can solve our time-varying problem: two semidefinite programming solvers (CVXOPT [5] and SCS [24]) and a naive ADMM method (without the closed-form updates that we developed in §4). We experiment on a single 40-core CPU where the entire problem fits into memory. We set $m = 10$ and modify n to vary the problem size. Even though our TVGL algorithm can solve for problems with much larger values of m, it is intractable to scale the other methods beyond this point, and we run the experiments in identical conditions to isolate our algorithm's effect on scalability.

We compare the performance of the four solvers in Figure 4. As shown, problems which take hours for the other solvers can be solved in seconds using TVGL. For example, to solve for 50,000 unknowns, TVGL is over 400 times faster than SCS, the second fastest solver (14.3 vs. 6,611 seconds). The main difference in solution time is due to the closed-form ADMM solutions we derived in Section 4.1 for each of the ADMM subproblems. Our problem has a semidefinite programming (SDP) constraint, which is particularly difficult to solve via standard methods. To infer a single n-by-n covariance, the largest per-iteration cost in our algorithm is $O(n^3)$, the cost of an eigendecomposition during the Θ-update. For the same problem, general interior-point methods have a runtime of $O(n^6)$ [19]. These numbers empirically appear to hold true in Figure 4 (recall that the total number of unknowns in the x-axis scales with $O(n^2)$).

7 CASE STUDIES

We next apply the TVGL to two real-world domains to illustrate several basic examples of how our approach can be used to learn meaningful insights from multivariate time series data.

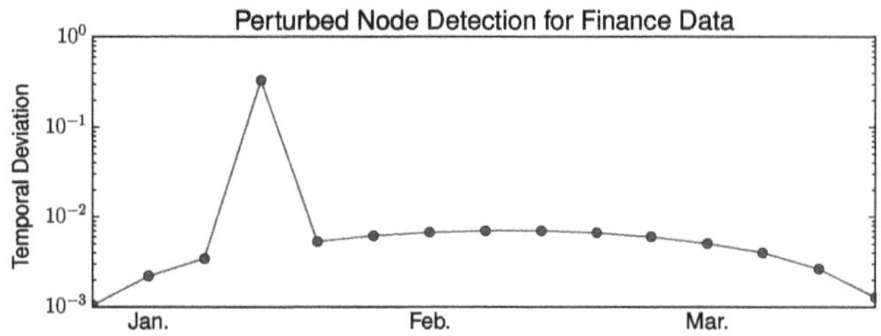

Figure 5: Plot of the temporal deviation of our estimated stock network, which detects a local shift in late January.

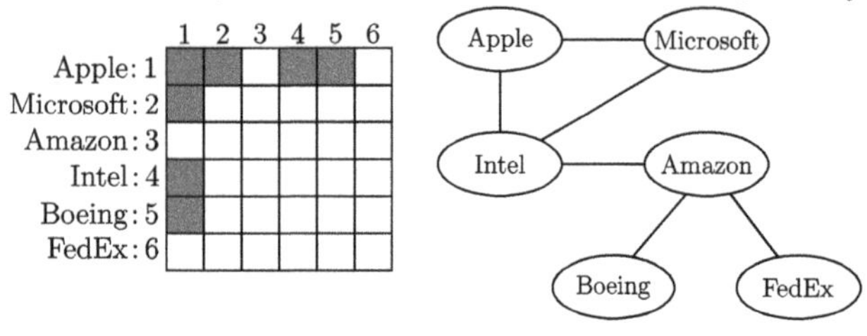

(a) (b)

Figure 6: Sparsity structure of (a) the network change during the local shift, indicating that Apple is the perturbed node, (b) the relationships in the financial network.

7.1 Applications in Financial Data

By examining historical stock prices, we can infer a financial network to model relationships between different companies. Learning the structure of this network is useful because it allows us to devise models of how certain stocks are related, which can be used to predict future prices, understand economic trends, or even diversify a portfolio by avoiding highly correlated stocks. We infer this network by examining the stock prices of several large companies in 2010. We apply our method by treating the closing price of each stock as a daily "sensor" observation. Our inferred graphical representation then shows how the stock prices affect each other.

Identifying Single-Stock Perturbations. We observe daily stock prices for six large American companies: Apple, Google, Amazon, Intel, Boeing, and FedEx. Generally, large companies are well-established in the market, so we would expect their correlation network to change only slightly over time. However, events occasionally occur which cause a sudden shift in the network structure. We look at the dependencies of these companies while using a perturbed node penalty. This enforces a temporal dynamic where single nodes may occasionally reweigh all their connections at once. This typically reflects that something happened to affect just one company, while leaving the rest of the network unchanged. We solve the TVGL optimization problem with a perturbed node penalty and discover that one event stood out as having the *largest single-node effect* on the dynamics between these stocks.

After running our TVGL method, we plot the temporal deviation, $\|\Theta_i - \Theta_{i-1}\|_F$, in Figure 5. We discover that there is a large spike in the temporal deviation score during the last week of January. This represents a significant "shift" in the network at this specific time. We show the network change at this shift in Figure 6(a), where we see that the perturbed stock was Apple. At this timestamp, only Apple's edges were affected, reflecting a local rather than global change in the network. We examined the media to understand what may have caused this shift, and we found that on January 27th, Apple first introduced the original iPad to the public. This corresponds to the exact time that our TVGL method captured a structural change in the network, where it was also able to identify Apple as the cause of this shift.

We also plot the post-announcement network in Figure 6(b). Analyzing the correlation structure yields some insightful relationships. The four technology companies—Apple, Google, Amazon, and Intel—are closely related. The shipping company (FedEx) and the airplane manufacturer (Boeing) are both connected to only one company, Amazon. Amazon heavily depends on both companies to deliver products on time, while both rely on Amazon for a large portion of their business. Interestingly, our model predicts that FedEx and Boeing's stock prices are conditionally independent given Amazon, a trend that holds true across the entire dataset.

Detecting Large-Scale Events. Time-varying inference can also be used to detect significant events that affected the entire network, not just single entities within it. We run a similar experiment to the previous example, except we now include every company in the S&P 500, which covers 500 of the largest US-based public companies. Since we are focusing on macro-level event detection, we look for the maximum temporal deviation with an ℓ_1 penalty. This point in time represents the largest "shock" to the network, the timestamp where our TVGL model detected a large and sudden change. We discover that a shift happens during the week of May 6th, 2010. Surprisingly, we saw that there was in fact a "Flash Crash" that day, where the entire market dropped 9% in a matter of seconds, only to rebound back just minutes later. Our results imply that, even though the market recovered from the crash in terms of stock price values, there were tangible long-term effects on the correlation network between companies in the S&P 500.

7.2 Application to Automobile Sensors

Inferring relationships between interrelated entities is of particular interest to industries with large amounts of sensor data. One such industry is automobiles, where modern cars contain hundreds of sensors measuring everything from the car's velocity to the slope of the road. Inferring a time-varying network of relationships between these sensors is an informative way to understand driving habits, as each driver creates a unique "signature", or dynamic sensor network, while driving. This network can be used to model behavior, compare driver ability, or even detect impaired drivers.

As a second case study, we analyze an automobile sensor dataset, provided by a large car company. We look at a short session where a driver goes down a straight road, makes a right turn, and continues on a new road. We observe eight different sensors every 0.1 seconds: steering wheel angle, steering wheel velocity, vehicle velocity, brake pedal, gas pedal, forward acceleration, lateral acceleration, and engine RPM. Since we do not expect any sudden shifts in this network, we use a Laplacian penalty to enforce a smoothly varying network across time. We run our TVGL algorithm and plot three snapshots of the sensor network in Figure 7: one on the straightaway before the turn, one in the middle of turning, and one after the turn. Note that the "before" and "after" networks look quite similar, since the driver is doing a similar activity (driving straight) on both. The "during" network looks much different, however. The most

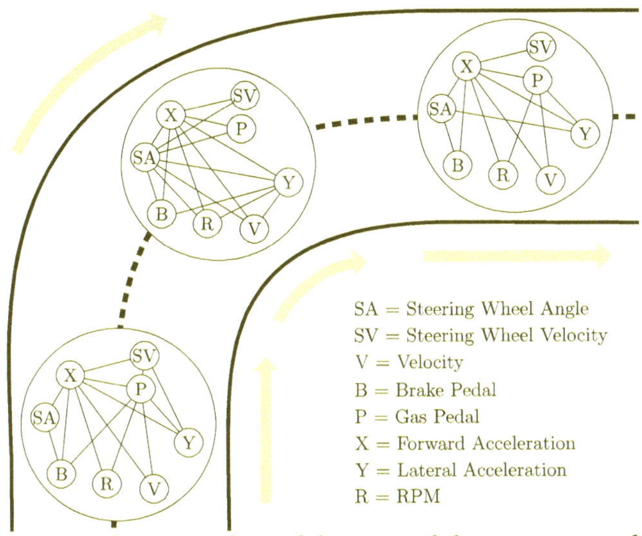

Figure 7: Three snapshots of the automobile sensor network measuring eight sensors, taken (1) before, (2) during, and (3) after a standard right turn.

noticeable difference is that the steering wheel angle sensor (SA) is now centrally located within the network, connected to almost every other node. This means that variations in the other sensors' observations can be largely explained by the steering wheel angle during the turn. For straightaways, on the other hand, the steering angle is on the network periphery, meaning that it is not well suited to explain the other sensor readings.

8 CONCLUSION AND FUTURE WORK

In this paper, we have defined a general method for inferring dynamic networks from timestamped observational data. Our approach, the time-varying graphical lasso, provides a scalable algorithm capable of encoding many different temporal dependencies. This type of modeling allows us to infer structure from large-scale "sensor" deployments. We leave for future work the examination of additional penalty functions to enforce different behaviors in the evolution of the network structure, along with their closed-form proximal operator solutions. There are also new extensions, beyond what was discussed in Section 3, which could be further analyzed. For example, we currently assume that the underlying distribution is zero mean. However, we could model a problem where observations come from a distribution $x \sim N(\mu(t), \Sigma(t))$, and attempt to simultaneously estimate both the mean and covariance as they vary over time. Finally, this work could also be extended to infer correlations across different timestamps. Currently, our algorithm is suited to find simultaneously-related entities, *i.e.*, stocks whose prices move up and down in unison. However, there are other applications where the correlations are not immediate. For example, in brain connectivity networks, neuron A firing at timestamp i could cause neuron B to fire at time $i + 1$. Each of these additions would open up our framework to new potential applications, providing additional benefits to future research in this topic.

Acknowledgements. This work was supported by NSF IIS-1149837, NIH BD2K, DARPA SIMPLEX, DARPA XDATA, Chan Zuckerberg Biohub, SDSI, Boeing, Bosch, and Volkswagen.

REFERENCES

[1] A. Ahmed and E. P. Xing. Recovering time-varying networks of dependencies in social and biological studies. *PNAS*, 2009.
[2] O. Banerjee, L. El Ghaoui, and A. d'Aspremont. Model selection through sparse maximum likelihood estimation for multivariate Gaussian or binary data. *JMLR*, 2008.
[3] S. Boyd, N. Parikh, E. Chu, B. Peleato, and J. Eckstein. Distributed optimization and statistical learning via the alternating direction method of multipliers. *Foundations and Trends in Machine learning*, 2011.
[4] S. Boyd and L. Vandenberghe. *Convex Optimization*. Cambridge University Press, 2004.
[5] J. Dahl and L. Vandenberghe. CVXOPT: A Python package for convex optimization. In *Proc. Eur. Conf. Op. Res*, 2006.
[6] P. Danaher, P. Wang, and D. Witten. The joint graphical lasso for inverse covariance estimation across multiple classes. *JRSS: Series B*, 2014.
[7] J. Friedman, T. Hastie, and R. Tibshirani. Sparse inverse covariance estimation with the graphical lasso. *Biostatistics*, 2008.
[8] M. Gomez Rodriguez, J. Leskovec, and A. Krause. Inferring networks of diffusion and influence. In *KDD*. ACM, 2010.
[9] M. S. Grewal. *Kalman filtering*. Springer, 2011.
[10] D. Hallac, J. Leskovec, and S. Boyd. Network lasso: Clustering and optimization in large graphs. In *KDD*, 2015.
[11] D. Hallac, C. Wong, S. Diamond, R. Sosič, S. Boyd, and J. Leskovec. SnapVX: A network-based convex optimization solver. *JMLR (To Appear)*, 2017.
[12] T. Hastie, R. Tibshirani, and J. Friedman. *The Elements of Statistical Learning*. Springer, 2009.
[13] M. R. Hestenes. Multiplier and gradient methods. *Journal of Optimization Theory and Applications*, 1969.
[14] C.-J. Hsieh, M. A. Sustik, I. S. Dhillon, P. K. Ravikumar, and R. Poldrack. BIG & QUIC: Sparse inverse covariance estimation for a million variables. In *NIPS*, 2013.
[15] M. Kolar, L. Song, A. Ahmed, and E. Xing. Estimating time-varying networks. *The Annals of Applied Statistics*, 2010.
[16] D. Koller and N. Friedman. *Probabilistic Graphical Models: Principles and Techniques*. MIT press, 2009.
[17] S. L. Lauritzen. *Graphical models*. Clarendon Press, 1996.
[18] K. Mohan, M. Chung, S. Han, D. Witten, S.-I. Lee, and M. Fazel. Structured learning of Gaussian graphical models. In *NIPS*, 2012.
[19] K. Mohan, P. London, M. Fazel, D. Witten, and S.-I. Lee. Node-based learning of multiple Gaussian graphical models. *JMLR*, 2014.
[20] P. C. Molenaar. A dynamic factor model for the analysis of multivariate time series. *Psychometrika*, 1985.
[21] R. P. Monti, P. Hellyer, D. Sharp, R. Leech, C. Anagnostopoulos, and G. Montana. Estimating time-varying brain connectivity networks from functional MRI time series. *Neuroimage*, 2014.
[22] S. Myers and J. Leskovec. On the convexity of latent social network inference. In *NIPS*, 2010.
[23] A. Namaki, A. Shirazi, R. Raei, and G. Jafari. Network analysis of a financial market based on genuine correlation and threshold method. *Physica A: Stat. Mech. Apps.*, 2011.
[24] B. O'Donoghue, E. Chu, N. Parikh, and S. Boyd. Conic optimization via operator splitting and homogeneous self-dual embedding. *Journal of Optimization Theory and Applications*, 2016.
[25] N. Parikh and S. Boyd. Proximal algorithms. *Foundations and Trends in Optimization*, 2014.
[26] H. Rue and L. Held. *Gaussian Markov Random Fields: Theory and Applications*. CRC Press, 2005.
[27] K. Scheinberg, S. Ma, and D. Goldfarb. Sparse inverse covariance selection via alternating linearization methods. In *NIPS*, 2010.
[28] L. Vanderberghe. Proximal mapping lecture notes. http://seas.ucla.edu/~vandenbe/236C/lectures/proxop.pdf, 2010.
[29] M. J. Wainwright and M. I. Jordan. Log-determinant relaxation for approximate inference in discrete Markov random fields. *IEEE Tr. on Signal Processing*, 2006.
[30] K. Weinberger, F. Sha, Q. Zhu, and L. Saul. Graph Laplacian regularization for large-scale semidefinite programming. In *NIPS*, 2006.
[31] E. Wit and A. Abbruzzo. Inferring slowly-changing dynamic gene-regulatory networks. *BMC Bioinformatics*, 2015.
[32] D. Witten and R. Tibshirani. Covariance-regularized regression and classification for high dimensional problems. *JRSS: Series B*, 2009.
[33] M. Wytock and J. Z. Kolter. Sparse Gaussian conditional random fields: Algorithms, theory, and application to energy forecasting. *ICML*, 2013.
[34] S. Yang, Z. Lu, X. Shen, P. Wonka, and J. Ye. Fused multiple graphical lasso. *SIAM*, 2015.
[35] M. Yuan and Y. Lin. Model selection and estimation in the Gaussian graphical model. *Biometrika*, 2007.
[36] S. Zhou, J. Lafferty, and L. Wasserman. Time varying undirected graphs. *Machine Learning*, 2010.

Toeplitz Inverse Covariance-Based Clustering of Multivariate Time Series Data

David Hallac, Sagar Vare, Stephen Boyd, Jure Leskovec
Stanford University
{hallac,svare,boyd,jure}@stanford.edu

ABSTRACT

Subsequence clustering of multivariate time series is a useful tool for discovering repeated patterns in temporal data. Once these patterns have been discovered, seemingly complicated datasets can be interpreted as a temporal sequence of only a small number of states, or *clusters*. For example, raw sensor data from a fitness-tracking application can be expressed as a timeline of a select few actions (*i.e.*, walking, sitting, running). However, discovering these patterns is challenging because it requires simultaneous segmentation and clustering of the time series. Furthermore, interpreting the resulting clusters is difficult, especially when the data is high-dimensional. Here we propose a new method of model-based clustering, which we call *Toeplitz Inverse Covariance-based Clustering* (TICC). Each cluster in the TICC method is defined by a correlation network, or Markov random field (MRF), characterizing the interdependencies between different observations in a typical subsequence of that cluster. Based on this graphical representation, TICC simultaneously segments and clusters the time series data. We solve the TICC problem through alternating minimization, using a variation of the expectation maximization (EM) algorithm. We derive closed-form solutions to efficiently solve the two resulting subproblems in a scalable way, through dynamic programming and the alternating direction method of multipliers (ADMM), respectively. We validate our approach by comparing TICC to several state-of-the-art baselines in a series of synthetic experiments, and we then demonstrate on an automobile sensor dataset how TICC can be used to learn interpretable clusters in real-world scenarios.

1 INTRODUCTION

Many applications, ranging from automobiles [32] to financial markets [35] and wearable sensors [34], generate large amounts of time series data. In most cases, this data is multivariate, where each timestamped observation consists of readings from multiple entities, or *sensors*. These long time series can often be broken down into a sequence of states, each defined by a simple "pattern", where the states can reoccur many times. For example, raw sensor data from a fitness-tracking device can be interpreted as a temporal sequence of actions [38] (*i.e.*, walking for 10 minutes, running for 30 minutes, sitting for 1 hour, then running again for 45 minutes). Similarly, using automobile sensor data, a single driving session can be expressed as a sequential timeline of a few key states: turning, speeding up, slowing down, going straight, stopping at a red light, etc. This representation can be used to discover repeated patterns, understand trends, detect anomalies and more generally, better interpret large and high-dimensional datasets.

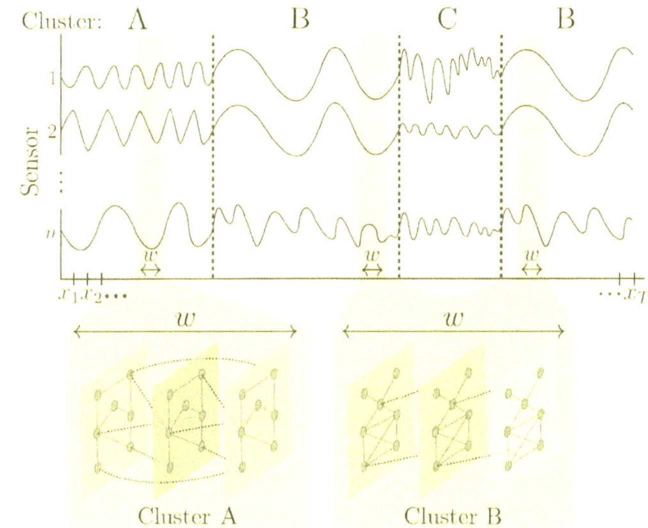

Figure 1: Our TICC method segments a time series into a sequence of states, or "clusters" (*i.e.*, A, B, or C). Each cluster is characterized by a correlation network, or MRF, defined over a short window of size *w*. This MRF governs the (time-invariant) partial correlation structure of *any* window inside a segment belonging to that cluster. Here, TICC learns both the cluster MRFs and the time series segmentation.

To achieve this representation, it is necessary to simultaneously segment and cluster the time series. This problem is more difficult than standard time series segmentation [17, 20], since multiple segments can belong to the same cluster. However, it is also harder than subsequence clustering [3, 43] because each data point cannot be clustered independently (since neighboring points are encouraged to belong to the same cluster). Additionally, even if one is able to simultaneously segment and cluster the data, the question still arises as to how to interpret the different clusters. These clusters are rarely known a priori, and thus are best learned through data. However, without prior knowledge, it is difficult to understand what each of the clusters refers to. Traditional clustering methods are not particularly well-suited to discover interpretable structure in the data. This is because they typically rely on distance-based metrics, such as dynamic time warping [4]. These methods focus

KDD '17, August 13-17, 2017, Halifax, NS, Canada

ACM ISBN 978-1-4503-4887-4/17/08...$15.00
https://doi.org/10.1145/3097983.3098060

on matching the raw values, rather than looking for more nuanced structural similarities in the data, for example how different sensors in a car correlate with each other across time.

In this paper, we propose a new method for multivariate time series clustering, which we call *Toeplitz inverse covariance-based clustering* (TICC). In our method, we define each cluster as a dependency network showing the relationships between the different sensors in a short (time-invariant) subsequence (Figure 1). For example, in a cluster corresponding to a "turn" in an automobile, this network, known as a Markov random field (MRF), might show how the brake pedal at a generic time t might affect the steering wheel angle at time $t + 1$. Here, the MRF of a different cluster, such as "slowing down", will have a very different dependency structure between these two sensors. In these MRFs, an edge represents a partial correlation between two variables [26, 41, 46]. It is important to note that MRFs denote a relationship much stronger than a simple correlation; partial correlations are used to control for the effect of other confounding variables, so the existence of an edge in an MRF implies that there is a *direct* dependency between two variables in the data. Therefore, an MRF provides interpretable insights as to precisely what the key factors and relationships are that characterize each cluster.

In our TICC method, we learn each cluster's MRF by estimating a sparse Gaussian inverse covariance matrix [14, 48]. With an inverse covariance Θ, if $\Theta_{i,j} = 0$, then by definition, elements i and j in Θ are conditionally independent (given the values of all other variables). Therefore, Θ defines the adjacency matrix of the MRF dependency network [1, 45]. This network has multiple layers, with edges both within a layer and across different layers. Here, the number of layers corresponds to the window size of a short subsequence that we define our MRF over. For example, the MRFs corresponding to clusters A and B in Figure 1 both have three layers. This multilayer network represents the time-invariant correlation structure of *any* window of observations inside a segment belonging to that cluster. We learn this structure for each cluster by solving a constrained inverse covariance estimation problem, which we call the *Toeplitz graphical lasso*. The constraint we impose ensures that the resulting multilayer network has a block Toeplitz structure [16] (*i.e.*, any edge between layers l and $l + 1$ also exists between layers $l + 1$ and $l + 2$). This Toeplitz constraint ensures that our cluster definitions are time-invariant, so the clustering assignment does not depend on the exact starting position of the subsequence. Instead, we cluster this short subsequence based solely on the structural state that the time series is currently in.

To solve the TICC problem, we use an expectation maximization (EM)-like approach, based on alternating minimization, where we iteratively cluster the data and then update the cluster parameters. Even though TICC involves solving a highly non-convex maximum likelihood problem, our method is able to find a (locally) optimal solution very efficiently in practice. When assigning the data to clusters, we have an additional goal of *temporal consistency*, the idea that adjacent data in the time series is encouraged to belong to the same cluster. However, this yields a combinatorial optimization problem. We develop a scalable solution using dynamic programming, which allows us to efficiently learn the optimal assignments (it takes just $O(KT)$ time to assign the T points into K clusters). Then, to solve for the cluster parameters, we develop an algorithm to solve the Toeplitz graphical lasso problem. Since learning this graphical structure from data is a computationally expensive semidefinite programming problem [6, 22], we develop a specialized message-passing algorithm based on the alternating direction method of multipliers (ADMM) [5]. In our Toeplitz graphical lasso algorithm, we derive closed-form updates for each of the ADMM subproblems to significantly speed up the solution time.

We then implement our TICC method and apply it to both real and synthetic datasets. We start by evaluating performance on several synthetic examples, where there are known ground truth clusters. We compare TICC with several state-of-the-art time series clustering methods, outperforming them all by at least 41% in terms of cluster assignment accuracy. We also quantify the amount of data needed for accurate cluster recovery for each method, and we see that TICC requires 3x fewer observations than the next best method to achieve similar performance. Additionally, we discover that our approach is able to accurately reconstruct the underlying MRF dependency network, with an F_1 network recovery score between 0.79 and 0.90 in our experiments. We then analyze an automobile sensor dataset to see an example of how TICC can be used to learn interpretable insights from real-world data. Applying our method, we discover that the automobile dataset has five true clusters, each corresponding to a "state" that cars are frequently in. We then validate our results by examining the latitude/longitude locations of the driving session, along with the resulting clustering assignments, to show how TICC can be a useful tool for unsupervised learning from multivariate time series.

Related Work. This work relates to recent advancements in time series clustering and convex optimization. Subsequence clustering of time series data is a well-developed field. Methods include several variations of dynamic time warping [3, 23, 25, 39], symbolic representations [29, 30], and rule-based motif discovery [11, 28]. There has also been work on simultaneous clustering and segmentation of time series data, which is known as time point clustering [15, 49]. However, these methods generally rely on distance-based metrics, which in certain situations have been shown to yield unreliable results [24]. Instead, our TICC method is a model-based clustering approach, similar to clustering based on ARMA [47], Gaussian Mixture [13], or hidden Markov models [43]. To the best of our knowledge, our method is the first to perform time series clustering based on the graphical dependency structure of each subsequence. This provides interpretability to our clusters, prevents overfitting, and, as we show in Sections 6 and 7, allows us to discover types of patterns that other approaches are unable to find. We do so by proposing a structured inverse covariance estimation problem, which we call the Toeplitz graphical lasso. This problem is a variation on the well-known graphical lasso problem [14] where we enforce a block Toeplitz structure on the solution. While many algorithms exist to solve the standard graphical lasso [1, 21, 22], we are not aware of any methods specifically adapted for the block Toeplitz case. We propose an ADMM approach because the overall optimization problem can be split into ADMM-friendly subproblems, where we can derive closed-form proximal operators [5] to quickly solve the optimization problem.

2 PROBLEM SETUP

Consider a time series of T sequential observations,

$$x_{\text{orig}} = \begin{bmatrix} | & | & | & & | \\ x_1 & x_2 & x_3 & \dots & x_T \\ | & | & | & & | \end{bmatrix},$$

where $x_i \in \mathbf{R}^n$ is the i-th multivariate observation. Our goal is to cluster these T observations into K clusters. However, instead of clustering each observation in isolation, we treat each point in the context of its predecessors in the time series. Thus, rather than just looking at x_t, we instead cluster a short subsequence of size $w \ll T$ that ends at t. This consists of observations $x_{t-w+1}, \dots, x_t$, which we concatenate into an nw-dimensional vector that we call X_t. We refer to this new sequence, from X_1 to X_T, as X. Note that there is a bijection, or a bidirectional one-to-one mapping, between each point x_t and its resulting subsequence X_t. (The first w observations of x_{orig} simply map to a shorter subsequence, since the time series does not start until x_1.) These subsequences are a useful tool to provide proper context for each of the T observations. For example, in automobiles, a single observation may show the current state of the car (*i.e.*, driving straight at 15mph), but a short window, even one that lasts just a fraction of a second, allows for a more complete understanding of the data (*i.e.*, whether the car is speeding up or slowing down). As such, rather than clustering the observations directly, our approach instead consists of clustering these subsequences $X_1, \dots, X_T$. We do so in such a way that encourages adjacent subsequences to belong to the same cluster, a goal that we call *temporal consistency*. Thus, our method can be viewed as a form of time point clustering [49], where we simultaneously segment and cluster the time series.

Toeplitz Inverse Covariance-Based Clustering (TICC). We define each cluster by a Gaussian inverse covariance $\Theta_i \in \mathbf{R}^{nw \times nw}$. Recall that inverse covariances show the conditional independency structure between the variables [26], so Θ_i defines a Markov random field encoding the structural representation of cluster i. In addition to providing interpretable results, sparse graphical representations are a useful way to prevent overfitting [27]. As such, our objective is to solve for these K inverse covariances $\Theta = \{\Theta_1, \dots, \Theta_K\}$, one per cluster, and the resulting assignment sets $\mathbf{P} = \{P_1, \dots, P_K\}$, where $P_i \subset \{1, 2, \dots, T\}$. Here, each of the T points are assigned to exactly one cluster. Our overall optimization problem is

$$\underset{\Theta \in \mathcal{T}, \mathbf{P}}{\text{argmin}} \sum_{i=1}^{K} \left[\overbrace{\|\lambda \circ \Theta_i\|_1}^{\text{sparsity}} + \sum_{X_t \in P_i} \left(\overbrace{-\ell\ell(X_t, \Theta_i)}^{\text{log likelihood}} + \overbrace{\beta \mathbb{1}\{X_{t-1} \notin P_i\}}^{\text{temporal consistency}} \right) \right]. \tag{1}$$

We call this the *Toeplitz inverse covariance-based clustering* (TICC) problem. Here, $\mathcal{T}$ is the set of symmetric block Toeplitz $nw \times nw$ matrices and $\|\lambda \circ \Theta_i\|_1$ is an ℓ_1-norm penalty of the Hadamard (element-wise) product to incentivize a sparse inverse covariance (where $\lambda \in \mathbf{R}^{nw \times nw}$ is a regularization parameter). Additionally, $\ell\ell(X_t, \Theta_i)$ is the log likelihood that X_t came from cluster i,

$$\ell\ell(X_t, \Theta_i) = -\frac{1}{2}(X_t - \mu_i)^T \Theta_i (X_t - \mu_i) + \frac{1}{2} \log \det \Theta_i - \frac{n}{2} \log(2\pi), \tag{2}$$

where μ_i is the empirical mean of cluster i. In Problem (1), β is a parameter that enforces temporal consistency, and $\mathbb{1}\{X_{t-1} \notin P_i\}$ is an indicator function checking whether neighboring points are assigned to the same cluster.

Toeplitz Matrices. Note that we constrain the Θ_i's, the inverse covariances, to be block Toeplitz. Thus, each $nw \times nw$ matrix can be expressed in the following form,

$$\Theta_i = \begin{bmatrix} A^{(0)} & (A^{(1)})^T & (A^{(2)})^T & \cdots & \cdots & (A^{(w-1)})^T \\ A^{(1)} & A^{(0)} & (A^{(1)})^T & \ddots & & \vdots \\ A^{(2)} & A^{(1)} & \ddots & \ddots & \ddots & \vdots \\ \vdots & \ddots & \ddots & \ddots & (A^{(1)})^T & (A^{(2)})^T \\ \vdots & & \ddots & A^{(1)} & A^{(0)} & (A^{(1)})^T \\ A^{(w-1)} & \cdots & \cdots & A^{(2)} & A^{(1)} & A^{(0)} \end{bmatrix},$$

where $A^{(0)}, A^{(1)}, \dots, A^{(w-1)} \in \mathbf{R}^{n \times n}$. Here, the $A^{(0)}$ sub-block represents the intra-time partial correlations, so $A^{(0)}_{ij}$ refers to the relationship between concurrent values of sensors i and j. In the MRF corresponding to this cluster, $A^{(0)}$ defines the adjacency matrix of the edges within each layer. On the other hand, the off-diagonal sub-blocks refer to "cross-time" edges. For example, $A^{(1)}_{ij}$ shows how sensor i at some time t is correlated to sensor j at time $t + 1$, and $A^{(2)}$ shows the edge structure between time t and time $t + 2$. The block Toeplitz structure of the inverse covariance means that we are making a time-invariance assumption over this length-w window (we typically expect this window size to be much smaller than the average segment length). As a result, in Figure 1, for example, the edges between layer 1 and layer 2 must also exist between layers 2 and 3. We use this assumption because we are looking for a unique structural pattern to identify each cluster. We consider each cluster to be a certain "state". When the time series is in this state, it retains a certain (time-invariant) structure that persists throughout this segment, regardless of the window's starting point. By enforcing a Toeplitz structure on the inverse covariance, we are able to model this time invariance and incorporate it into our estimate of Θ_i.

Regularization Parameters. Our TICC optimization problem has two regularization parameters: λ, which determines the sparsity level in the MRFs characterizing each cluster, and β, the smoothness penalty that encourages adjacent subsequences to be assigned to the same cluster. Note that even though λ is a $nw \times nw$ matrix, we typically set all its values to a single constant, reducing the search space to just one parameter. In applications where there is prior knowledge as to the proper sparsity or temporal consistency, λ and β can be chosen by hand. More generally, the parameter values can also be selected by a more principled method, such as Bayesian information criterion (BIC) [18] or cross-validation.

Window Size. Recall that instead of clustering each point x_t in isolation, we cluster a short window, or subsequence, going from time $t - w + 1$ to t, which we concatenate into a nw-dimensional vector that we call X_t. The Toeplitz constraint assumes that each cluster has a time-invariant structure, but this window size is still a relevant parameter. In particular, it allows us to learn cross-time correlations (*i.e.*, sensor i at time t affects sensor j at time $t+1$). The larger the window, the farther these cross-time edges can reach. However, we do not want our window to be too large, since it may struggle to properly classify points at the segment boundaries, where our time-invariant assumption may not hold. For this reason, we generally keep the value of w relatively small. However, its exact value should generally be chosen depending on the application, the granularity of the observations, and the average expected segment length. It can also be selected via BIC or cross-validation, though as we discover in Section 6, our TICC algorithm is relatively robust to the selection of this window size parameter.

Selecting the Number of Clusters. As with many clustering algorithms, the number of clusters K is an important parameter in TICC. There are various methods for doing so. If there is some labeled ground truth data, we can use cross-validation on a test set or normalized mutual information [8] to evaluate performance. If we do not have such data, we can use BIC or the silhouette score [40] to select this parameter. However, the exact number of clusters will often depend on the application itself, especially since we are also looking for interpretability in addition to accuracy.

3 ALTERNATING MINIMIZATION

Problem (1) is a mixed combinatorial and continuous optimization problem. There are two sets of variables, the cluster assignments P and inverse covariances Θ, both of which are coupled together to make the problem highly non-convex. As such, there is no tractable way to solve for the globally optimal solution. Instead, we use a variation of the expectation maximization (EM) algorithm to alternate between assigning points to clusters and then updating the cluster parameters. While this approach does not necessarily reach the global optimum, similar types of methods have been shown to perform well on related problems [13]. Here, we define the subproblems that comprise the two steps of our method. Then, in Section 4, we derive fast algorithms to solve both subproblems and formally describe our overall algorithm to solve the TICC problem.

3.1 Assigning Points to Clusters

We assign points to clusters by fixing the value of $\mathbf{\Theta}$ and solving the following combinatorial optimization problem for $\mathbf{P} = \{P_1, \ldots, P_K\}$,

$$\text{minimize} \sum_{i=1}^{K} \sum_{X_t \in P_i} -\ell\ell(X_t, \Theta_i) + \beta \mathbb{1}\{X_{t-1} \notin P_i\}. \qquad (3)$$

This problem assigns each of the T subsequences to one of the K clusters to jointly maximize the log likelihood and the temporal consistency, with the tradeoff between the two objectives regulated by the regularization parameter β. When $\beta = 0$, the subsequences $X_1, \ldots, X_T$ can all be assigned independently, since there is no penalty to encourage neighboring subsequences to belong to the same cluster. This can be solved by simply assigning each point to the cluster that maximizes its likelihood. As β gets larger, neighboring subsequences are more and more likely to be assigned to the same cluster. As $\beta \to \infty$, the switching penalty becomes so large that all the points in the time series are grouped together into just one cluster. Even though Problem (3) is combinatorial, we will see in Section 4.1 that we can use dynamic programming to efficiently find the globally optimal solution for this TICC subproblem.

3.2 Toeplitz Graphical Lasso

Given the point assignments $\mathbf{P}$, our next task is to update the cluster parameters $\Theta_1, \ldots, \Theta_K$ by solving Problem (1) while holding $\mathbf{P}$ constant. We can solve for each Θ_i in parallel. To do so, we notice that we can rewrite the negative log likelihood in Problem (2) in terms of each Θ_i. This likelihood can be expressed as

$$\sum_{X_t \in P_i} -\ell\ell(X_t, \Theta_i) = -|P_i|(\log\det\Theta_i + \mathrm{tr}(S_i\Theta_i)) + C,$$

where $|P_i|$ is the number of points assigned to cluster i, S_i is the empirical covariance of these points, and C is a constant that does not depend on Θ_i. Therefore, the M-step of our EM algorithm is

$$\begin{array}{ll} \text{minimize} & -\log\det\Theta_i + \mathrm{tr}(S_i\Theta_i) + \frac{1}{|P_i|}\|\lambda \circ \Theta_i\|_1 \\ \text{subject to} & \Theta_i \in \mathcal{T}. \end{array} \qquad (4)$$

Problem (4) is a convex optimization problem, which we call the *Toeplitz graphical lasso*. This is a variation on the well-known graphical lasso problem [14] where we add a block Toeplitz constraint on the inverse covariance. The original graphical lasso defines a tradeoff between two objectives, regulated by the parameter λ: minimizing the negative log likelihood, and making sure Θ_i is sparse. When S_i is invertible, the likelihood term encourages Θ_i to be near S_i^{-1}. Our problem adds the additional constraint that Θ_i is block Toeplitz. λ is a $nw \times nw$ matrix, so it can be used to regularize each sub-block of Θ_i differently. Note that $\frac{1}{|P_i|}$ can be incorporated into the regularization by simply scaling λ; as such, we typically write Problem (4) without this term (and scale λ accordingly) for notational simplicity.

4 TICC ALGORITHM

Here, we describe our algorithm to cluster $X_1, \ldots, X_T$ into K clusters. Our method, described in full in Section 4.3, depends on two key subroutines: AssignPointsToClusters, where we use a dynamic programming algorithm to assign each X_t into a cluster, and UpdateClusterParameters, where we update the cluster parameters by solving the Toeplitz graphical lasso problem using an algorithm based on the alternating direction method of multipliers (ADMM). Note that this is similar to expectation maximization (EM), with the two subroutines corresponding to the E and M steps, respectively.

4.1 Cluster Assignment

Given the model parameters (*i.e.*, inverse covariances) for each of the K clusters, solving Problem (3) assigns the T subsequences, $X_1, \ldots, X_T$, to these K clusters in such a way that maximizes the likelihood of the data while also minimizing the number of times that the cluster assignment changes across the time series. Given K potential cluster assignments of the T points, this combinatorial optimization problem has K^T possible assignments of points to clusters, that it can choose from. However, we are able to solve for the globally optimal solution in only $O(KT)$ operations. We do so through a dynamic programming method described in Algorithm (1). This method is equivalent to finding the minimum cost Viterbi path [44] for this length-T sequence, as visualized in Figure 2.

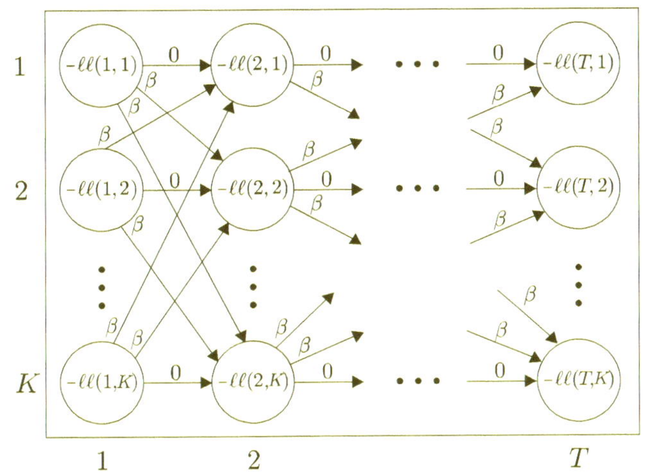

Figure 2: Problem (3) is equivalent to finding the minimum-cost path from timestamp 1 to T, where the node cost is the negative log likelihood of that point being assigned to a given cluster, and the edge cost is β whenever the cluster assignment switches.

Algorithm 1 Assign Points to Clusters

given $\beta > 0$, $-\ell\ell(i, j)$ = negative log likelihood of point i when it is assigned to cluster j.
initialize PrevCost = list of K zeros.
  CurrCost = list of K zeros.
  PrevPath = list of K empty lists.
  CurrPath = list of K empty lists.
for $i = 1, \ldots, T$ **do**
  for $j = 1, \ldots, K$ **do**
    MinIndex = index of minimum value of PrevCost.
    if PrevCost[MinIndex] + β > PrevCost[j] **then**
      CurrCost[j] = PrevCost[j] $-\ell\ell(i, j)$.
      CurrPath[j] = PrevPath[j].append[j].
    else
      CurrCost[j] = PrevCost[minIndex] + $\beta - \ell\ell(i, j)$.
      CurrPath[j] = PrevPath[minIndex].append[j].
  PrevCost = CurrCost.
  PrevPath = CurrPath.
FinalMinIndex = index of minimum value of CurrCost.
FinalPath = CurrPath[FinalMinIndex].
return FinalPath.

4.2 Solving the Toeplitz Graphical Lasso

Once we have the clustering assignments, the M-step of our EM algorithm is to update the inverse covariances, given the points assigned to each cluster. Here, we are solving the Toeplitz graphical lasso, which is defined in Problem (4). For smaller covariances, this semidefinite programming problem can be solved using standard interior point methods [6, 36]. However, to solve the overall TICC problem, we need to solve a separate Toeplitz graphical lasso for each cluster at every iteration of our algorithm. Therefore, since we may need to solve Problem (4) hundreds of times before TICC converges, it is necessary to develop a fast method for solving it efficiently. We do so through the alternating direction method of multipliers (ADMM), a distributed convex optimization approach that has been shown to perform well at large-scale optimization tasks [5, 37]. With ADMM, we split the problem up into two subproblems and use a message passing algorithm to iteratively converge to the globally optimal solution. ADMM is especially scalable when closed-form solutions can be found for the ADMM subproblems, which we are able to derive for the Toeplitz graphical lasso.

To put Problem (4) in ADMM-friendly form, we introduce a consensus variable Z and rewrite Problem (4) as its equivalent problem,

$$\begin{array}{ll} \text{minimize} & -\log\det\Theta + \operatorname{tr}(S\Theta) + \|\lambda \circ Z\|_1 \\ \text{subject to} & \Theta = Z, Z \in \mathcal{T}. \end{array}$$

The augmented Lagrangian [19] can then be expressed as

$$\mathcal{L}_\rho(\Theta, Z, U) := -\log\det(\Theta) + \mathbf{Tr}(S\Theta) + \|\lambda \circ Z\|_1 + \frac{\rho}{2}\|\Theta - Z + U\|_F^2. \quad (5)$$

where $\rho > 0$ is the ADMM penalty parameter, $U \in \mathbf{R}^{nw \times nw}$ is the scaled dual variable [5, §3.1.1], and $Z \in \mathcal{T}$.

ADMM consists of the following three steps repeated until convergence,

$$\begin{aligned} &(a) \quad \Theta^{k+1} := \underset{\Theta}{\operatorname{argmin}}\ \mathcal{L}_\rho\left(\Theta, Z^k, U^k\right) \\ &(b) \quad Z^{k+1} := \underset{Z \in \mathcal{T}}{\operatorname{argmin}}\ \mathcal{L}_\rho\left(\Theta^{k+1}, Z, U^k\right) \\ &(c) \quad U^{k+1} := U^k + (\Theta^{k+1} - Z^{k+1}), \end{aligned}$$

where k is the iteration number. Here, we alternate optimizing Problem (5) over Θ and then over Z, and after each iteration we update the scaled dual variable U. Since the Toeplitz graphical lasso problem is convex, ADMM is guaranteed to converge to the global optimum. We use a stopping criteria based on the primal and dual residual values being close to zero; see [5].

Θ-Update. The Θ-update can be written as

$$\Theta^{k+1} = \underset{\Theta}{\operatorname{argmin}}\ -\log\det(\Theta) + \mathbf{Tr}(S\Theta) + \frac{\rho}{2}\left\|\Theta - Z^k + U^k\right\|_F^2.$$

This optimization problem has a known analytical solution [10],

$$\Theta^{k+1} = \frac{\rho}{2} Q\left(D + \sqrt{D^2 + 4\rho I}\right)Q^T, \quad (6)$$

where QDQ^T is the eigendecomposition of $\frac{Z^k - U^k}{\rho} - S$.

Z-Update. The Z-update can be written as

$$Z^{k+1} = \underset{Z \in \mathcal{T}}{\operatorname{argmin}}\ \|\lambda \circ Z\|_1 + \frac{\rho}{2}\left\|Z - \Theta^{k+1} - U^k\right\|_F^2. \quad (7)$$

This proximal operator can be solved in parallel for each sub-block $A^{(0)}, A^{(1)}, \ldots, A^{(w-1)}$. Furthermore, within each sub-block, each (i, j)-th element in the sub-block can be solved in parallel as well. In $A^{(0)}$, there are $\frac{n(n+1)}{2}$ independent problems (since it is symmetric), whereas for the other $w - 1$ blocks, this number is n^2. Therefore, Problem (7) can be broken down into a total of $(w-1)n^2 + \frac{n(n+1)}{2}$ independent problems. Each of these problems has the same form, and can be solved in the same way.

Algorithm 2 Toeplitz Inverse Covariance-Based Clustering

initialize Cluster parameters Θ; cluster assignments $\mathbf{P}$.
repeat
  E-step: Assign points to clusters $\rightarrow \mathbf{P}$.
  M-step: Update cluster parameters $\rightarrow \Theta$.
until Stationarity.
return $(\Theta, \mathbf{P})$.

We denote the number of times each element appears as R (this equals $2(w-m)$ for sub-block $A^{(m)}$, except for the diagonals of $A^{(0)}$, which occur w times.) We order these R occurrences, and we let $B_{ij,l}^{(m)}$ refer to the index in Z corresponding to the l-th occurrence of the (i,j)-th element of $A^{(m)}$, where $l = 1, \ldots, R$. Thus, $B_{ij,l}^{(m)}$ returns an index (x,y) in the $nw \times nw$ matrix of Z. With this notation, we can solve each of the $(w-1)n^2 + \frac{n(n+1)}{2}$ subproblems of the Z-update proximal operator the same way. To solve for the elements of Z corresponding to $B_{ij}^{(m)}$, we set these elements all equal to

$$\underset{z}{\text{argmin}} \sum_{l=1}^{R} |\lambda_{B_{ij,l}^{(m)}} z| + \frac{\rho}{2}\left(z - (\Theta^{k+1} + U^k)_{B_{ij,l}^{(m)}}\right)^2. \quad (8)$$

We let $Q = \sum_{l=1}^{R} \lambda_{B_{ij,l}^{(m)}}$ and $S_l = (\Theta^{k+1} + U^k)_{B_{ij,l}^{(m)}}$ for notational simplicity. Then, Problem (8) can be rewritten as

$$\underset{z}{\text{argmin}}\ Q|z| + \sum_{l=1}^{R} \frac{\rho}{2}(z - S_l)^2.$$

This is just a soft-threshold proximal operator [37], which has the following closed-form solution,

$$Z_{B_{ij}^{(m)}}^{k+1} = \begin{cases} \frac{\rho \sum_l S_l - Q}{\rho R} & \frac{\rho \sum_l S_l - Q}{\rho R} > 0 \\ \frac{\rho \sum_l S_l + Q}{\rho R} & \frac{\rho \sum_l S_l + Q}{\rho R} < 0 \\ 0 & \text{otherwise.} \end{cases} \quad (9)$$

We fill in the R elements in Z^{k+1} (corresponding to $B_{ij}^{(m)}$) with this value. We do the same for all $(w-1)n^2 + \frac{n(n+1)}{2}$ subproblems, each of which we can solve in parallel, and we are left with our final result for the overall Z-update.

4.3 TICC Clustering Algorithm

To solve the TICC problem, we combine the dynamic programming algorithm from Section 4.1 and the ADMM method in Section 4.2 into one iterative EM algorithm. We start by randomly initializing the clusters. From there, we alternate the E and M-steps until the cluster assignments are stationary (*i.e.*, the problem has converged). The overall TICC method is outlined in Algorithm (2)

5 IMPLEMENTATION

We have built a custom Python solver to run the TICC algorithm[1]. Our solver takes as inputs the original multivariate time series and the problem parameters. It then returns the clustering assignments of each point in the time series, along with the structural MRF representation of each cluster.

[1] Code and solver are available at http://snap.stanford.edu/ticc/.

6 EXPERIMENTS

We test our TICC method on several synthetic examples. We do so because there are known "ground truth" clusters to evaluate the accuracy of our method.

Generating the Datasets. We randomly generate synthetic multivariate data in $\mathbf{R}^5$. Each of the K clusters has a mean of $\vec{0}$ so that the clustering result is based entirely on the structure of the data. For each cluster, we generate a random ground truth Toeplitz inverse covariance as follows [33]:

(1) Set $A^{(0)}, A^{(1)}, \ldots A^{(4)} \in \mathbf{R}^{5\times5}$ equal to the adjacency matrices of 5 independent Erdős-Rényi directed random graphs, where every edge has a 20% chance of being selected.
(2) For every selected edge in $A^{(m)}$ set $A_{jk}^{(m)} = v_{jk,m}$, a random weight centered at 0 (For the $A^{(0)}$ block, we also enforce a symmetry constraint that every $A_{ij}^{(0)} = A_{ji}^{(0)}$).
(3) Construct a $5w \times 5w$ block Toeplitz matrix G, where $w = 5$ is the window size, using the blocks $A^{(0)}, A^{(1)}, \ldots A^{(4)}$.
(4) Let c be the smallest eigenvalue of G, and set $\Theta_i = G + (0.1 + |c|)I$. This diagonal term ensures that Θ_i is invertible.

The overall time series is then generated by constructing a temporal sequence of cluster segments (for example, the sequence "1, 2, 1" with 200 samples in each of the three segments, coming from two inverse covariances Θ_1 and Θ_2). The data is then drawn one sample at a time, conditioned on the values of the previous $w-1$ samples. Note that, when we have just switched to a new cluster, we are drawing a new sample in part based on data that was generated by the previous cluster.

We run our experiments on four different temporal sequences: "1,2,1", "1,2,3,2,1", "1,2,3,4,1,2,3,4", "1,2,2,1,3,3,3,1". Each segment in each of the examples has $100K$ observations in $\mathbf{R}^5$, where K is the number of clusters in that experiment (2, 3, 4, and 3, respectively). These examples were selected to convey various types of temporal sequences over various lengths of time.

Performance Metrics. We evaluate performance by clustering each point in the time series and comparing to the ground truth clusters. Since both TICC and the baseline approaches use very similar methods for selecting the appropriate number of clusters, we fix K to be the "true" number of clusters, for both TICC and for all the baselines. This yields a straightforward multiclass classification problem, which allows us to evaluate clustering accuracy by measuring the macro-F_1 score. For each cluster, the F_1 score is the harmonic mean of the precision and recall of our estimate. Then, the macro-F_1 score is the average of the F_1 scores for all the clusters. We use this score to compare our TICC method with several well-known time series clustering baselines.

Baseline Methods. We use multiple model and distance-based clustering approaches as our baselines. The methods we use are:

- TICC, $\beta = 0$ — This is our TICC method without the temporal consistency constraint. Here, each subsequence is assigned to a cluster independently of its location in the time series.
- GMM — Clustering using a Gaussian Mixture Model [2].
- EEV — Regularized GMM with shape and volume constraints on the Gaussian covariance matrix [13].

	Clustering Method	1,2,1	1,2,3,2,1	1,2,3,4,1,2,3,4	1,2,2,1,3,3,3,1
		Temporal Sequence			
	TICC	**0.92**	**0.90**	**0.98**	**0.98**
Model-Based	TICC, $\beta = 0$	0.88	0.89	0.86	0.89
	GMM	0.68	0.55	0.83	0.62
	EEV	0.59	0.66	0.37	0.88
Distance-Based	DTW, GAK	0.64	0.33	0.26	0.27
	DTW, Euclidean	0.50	0.24	0.17	0.25
	Neural Gas	0.52	0.35	0.27	0.34
	K-means	0.59	0.34	0.24	0.34

Table 1: Macro-F_1 score of clustering accuracy for four different temporal sequences, comparing TICC with several alternative model and distance-based methods.

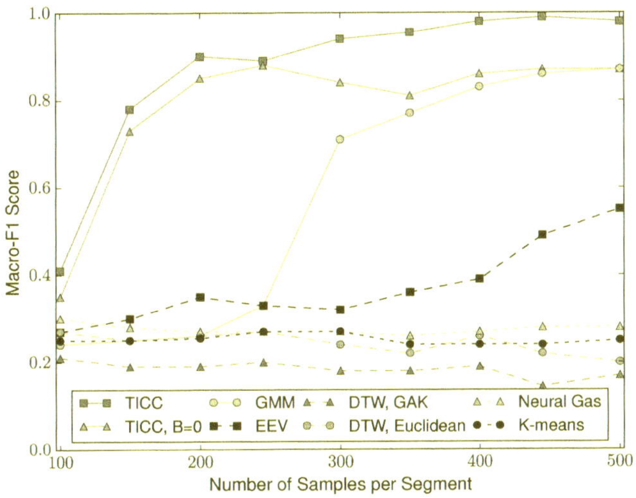

Figure 3: Plot of clustering accuracy macro-F_1 score vs. number of samples for TICC and several baselines. TICC needs significantly fewer samples than the other model-based methods to achieve similar performance, while the distance-based measures are unable to capture the true structure.

- DTW, GAK — Dynamic time warping (DTW)-based clustering using a global alignment kernel [9, 42].
- DTW, Euclidean — DTW using a Euclidean distance metric [42].
- Neural Gas — Artificial neural network clustering method, based on self-organizing maps [12, 31].
- K-means — The standard K-means clustering algorithm using Euclidean distance.

Clustering Accuracy. We measure the macro-F_1 score for the four different temporal sequences in Table 1. Here, all eight methods are using the exact same synthetic data, to isolate each approach's effect on performance. As shown, TICC significantly outperforms the baselines. Our method achieves a macro-F_1 score between 0.90 and 0.98, averaging 0.95 across the four examples. This is 41% higher than the second best method (not counting TICC, $\beta = 0$), which is GMM and has an average macro-F_1 score of only 0.67. We also ran our experiments using micro-F_1 score, which uses a weighted average to weigh clusters with more samples more heavily, and we obtained very similar results (within 1-2% of the macro-F_1 scores). Note that the K clusters in our examples are always zero-mean, and that they are only differentiated by the structure of the data. As a result, the distance-based methods struggle at identifying the clusters, and these approaches have lower scores than the model-based methods for these experiments.

Temporal Sequence	TICC Network Recovery F_1 score
1,2,1	0.83
1,2,3,2,1	0.79
1,2,3,4,1,2,3,4	0.89
1,2,2,1,3,3,3,1	0.90

Table 2: Network edge recovery F_1 score for the four temporal sequences. TICC defines each cluster as an MRF graphical model, which is successfully able to estimate the dependency structure of the underlying data.

Effect of the Total Number of Samples. We next focus on how many samples are required for each method to accurately cluster the time series. We take the "1,2,3,4,1,2,3,4" example from Table 1 and vary the number of samples. We plot the macro-F_1 score vs. number of samples per segment for each of the eight methods in Figure 3. As shown, when there are 100 samples, none of the methods are able to accurately cluster the data. However, as we observe more samples, both TICC and TICC, $\beta = 0$ improve rapidly. By the time there are 200 samples, TICC already has a macro-F_1 score above 0.9. Even when there is a limited amount of data, our TICC method is still able to accurately cluster the data. Additionally, we note that the temporal consistency constraint, defined by β, has only a small effect in this region, since both TICC and TICC, $\beta = 0$ achieve similar results. Therefore, the accurate results are most likely due to the sparse block Toeplitz constraint that we impose in our TICC method. However, as the number of samples increases, these two plots begin to diverge, as TICC goes to 1.0 while TICC, $\beta = 0$ hovers around 0.9. This implies that, once we have enough samples, the final improvement in performance is due to the temporal consistency penalty that encourages neighboring samples to be assigned to the same cluster.

Network Recovery Accuracy. Recall that our TICC method has the added benefit in that the clusters it learns are interpretable. TICC models each cluster as a multilayer Markov random field, a network with edges corresponding to the non-zero entries in the inverse covariance matrix Θ_i. We can compare our estimated network with the "true" MRF network and measure the average macro-F_1 score of our estimate across all the clusters. We look at the same four examples as in Table 2 and plot the results in Table 2. We recover the underlying edge structure of the network with an F_1 score between 0.79 and 0.90. This shows that TICC is able to both accurately cluster the data and recover the network structure of the underlying clusters. Note that our method is the first approach that is able to explicitly reconstruct this network, something that the other baseline methods are unable to do.

Window Size Robustness. We next examine how the selection of window size w affects our results. We run the same "1,2,3,4,1,2,3,4" example, except now we vary the window size w. (Recall that the "true" window size was 5.) Empirically, we discover that any window size between 4 and 15 yields a Macro-F_1 clustering accuracy score of between 0.95 and 0.98. Similarly, our network recovery macro-F_1 score stays between 0.87 and 0.89 for window sizes between 5 and 14. It is only after the window size drops below 4 or above 15 that the results begin to get worse. We observe similar patterns in the

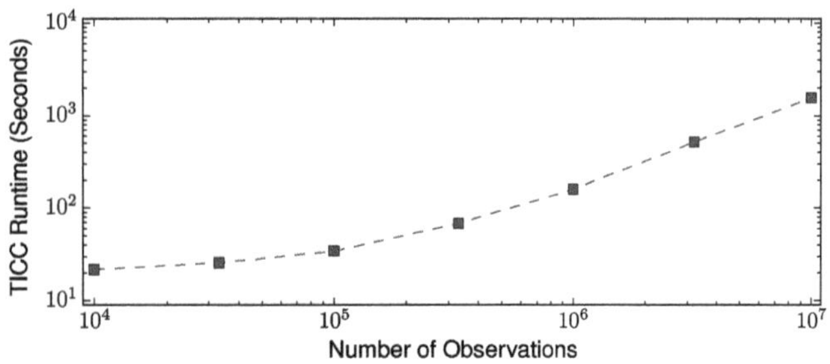

Figure 4: Per-iteration runtime of the TICC algorithm (both the ADMM and dynamic programming steps). Our algorithm scales linearly with the number of samples. In this case, each observation is a vector in $\mathbf{R}^{50}$.

other three examples, so our TICC method appears to be relatively robust to the selection of w.

Scalability of TICC. One iteration of the TICC algorithm consists of running the dynamic programming algorithm and then solving the Toeplitz graphical lasso problem for each cluster. These steps are repeated until convergence. The total number of iterations depends on the data, but typically is no more than a few tens of iterations. Since T is typically much larger than both K and n, we can expect the largest bottleneck to occur during the assignment phase, where T can potentially be in the millions. To evaluate the scalability of our algorithm, we vary T and compute the runtime of the algorithm over one iteration. We observe samples in $\mathbf{R}^{50}$, estimate 5 clusters with a window size of 3, and vary T over several orders of magnitude. We plot the results in log-log scale in Figure 4. Note that our ADMM solver infers each 150×150 inverse covariance (since $nw = 50 \times 3 = 150$) in under 4 seconds, but this runtime is independent of T, so ADMM contributes to the constant offset in the plot. As shown, at large values of T, our algorithm scales linearly with the number of points. Our TICC solver can cluster 10 millions points, each in $\mathbf{R}^{50}$, with a per-iteration runtime of approximately 25 minutes.

7 CASE STUDY

Here, we apply our TICC method to a real-world example to demonstrate how this approach can be used to find meaningful insights from time series data in an unsupervised way.

We analyze a dataset, provided by a large automobile company, containing sensor data from a real driving session. This session lasts for exactly 1 hour and occurs on real roads in the suburbs of a large European city. We observe 7 sensors every 0.1 seconds:

- Brake Pedal Position
- Forward (X-)Acceleration
- Lateral (Y-)Acceleration
- Steering Wheel Angle
- Vehicle Velocity
- Engine RPM
- Gas Pedal Position

Thus, in this one-hour session, we have 36,000 observations of a 7-dimensional time series. We apply TICC with a window size of 1 second (or 10 samples). We pick the number of clusters using BIC, and we discover that this score is optimized at $K = 5$.

We analyze the 5 clusters outputted by TICC to understand and interpret what "driving state" they each refer to. Each cluster has a multilayer MRF network defining its structure. To analyze the result, we use network analytics to determine the relative "importance" of each node in the cluster's network. We plot the betweenness centrality score [7] of each node in Table 3. We see that each of the 5 clusters has a unique "signature", and that different sensors have different betweenness scores in each cluster. For example, the Y-Acceleration sensor has a non-zero score in only two of the five clusters: #2 and #5. As such, we would expect these two clusters to refer to states in which the car is turning, and the other three clusters to refer to intervals where the car is going straight. Similarly, cluster #1 is the only cluster with no importance on the Gas Pedal, and it is also the cluster with the largest Brake Pedal score. Therefore, we expect this state to be the cluster assignment whenever the car is slowing down. We also see that clusters 3 and 4 have the same non-zero sensors, velocity and gas pedal, so we may expect them to refer to states when the car is driving straight and not slowing down, with the most "important" sensor in the two clusters being the velocity in cluster 4. As such, we can use these betweenness scores to interpret these clusters in a meaningful way. For example, from Table 3, a reasonable hypothesis might be that the clusters refer to 1) slowing down, 2) turning, 3) speeding up, 4) cruising on a straight road, 5) driving on a curvy road segment.

	Interpretation	Brake	X-Acc	Y-Acc	SW Angle	Vel	RPM	Gas
#1	Slowing Down	25.64	0	0	0	27.16	0	0
#2	Turning	0	4.24	66.01	17.56	0	5.13	135.1
#3	Speeding Up	0	0	0	0	16.00	0	4.50
#4	Driving Straight	0	0	0	0	32.2	0	26.8
#5	Curvy Road	4.52	0	4.81	0	0	0	94.8

Table 3: Betweenness centrality for each sensor in each of the five clusters. This score can be used as a proxy to show how "important" each sensor is, and more specifically how much it directly affects the other sensor values.

Plotting the Resulting Clusters. To validate our hypotheses, we can plot the latitude/longitude locations of the drive, along with the resulting cluster assignments. Analyzing this data, we empirically discover that each of the five clusters has a clear real-world interpretation that aligns very closely with our estimates based on the betweenness scores in Table 3. Furthermore, we notice that many consistent and repeated patterns emerge in this one hour session. For example, whenever the driver is approaching a turn, he or she follows the same sequence of clusters: going straight, slowing down, turning, speeding up, then going straight again. We plot two typical turns in the dataset, coloring the timestamps according to their cluster assignments, in Figure 5. It is important to note here that the same pattern emerges here for both left and right turns. Whereas distance-based approaches would treat these two scenarios very differently (since several of the sensors have completely opposite values), TICC instead clusters the time series based on structural similarities. As a result, TICC assigns both left and right turns into the same underlying cluster.

8 CONCLUSION AND FUTURE WORK

In this paper, we have defined a method of clustering multivariate time series subsequences. Our method, Toeplitz Inverse Covariance-based Clustering (TICC), is a new type of model-based clustering that is able to find accurate and interpretable structure in the data. Our TICC algorithm simultaneously segments and clusters the data, breaking down high-dimensional time series into a clear sequential timeline. We cluster each subsequence based on its correlation

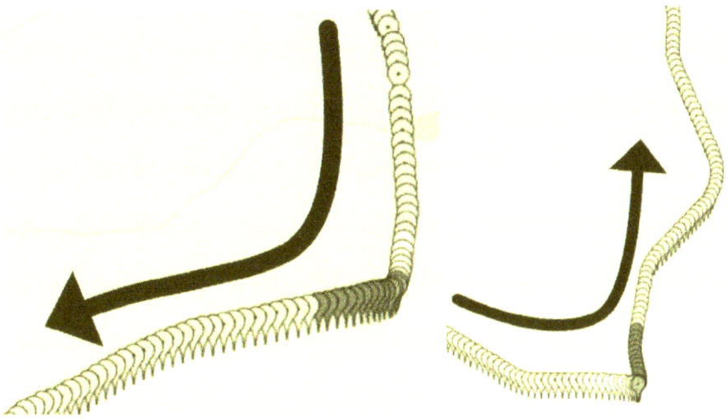

(a) (b)

Figure 5: Two real-world turns in the driving session. The pin color represents cluster assignment from our TICC algorithm (Green = Going Straight, White = Slowing Down, Red = Turning, Blue = Speeding up). Since we cluster based on structure, rather than distance, both a left and a right turn look very similar under the TICC clustering scheme.

structure and define each cluster by a multilayer MRF, making our results highly interpretable. To discover these clusters, TICC alternates between assigning points to clusters in a temporally consistent way, which it accomplishes through dynamic programming, and updating the cluster MRFs, which it does via ADMM. TICC's promising results on both synthetic and real-world data lead to many potential directions for future research. For example, our method could be extended to learn dependency networks parameterized by *any* heterogeneous exponential family MRF. This would allow for a much broader class of datasets (such as boolean or categorical readings) to be incorporated into the existing TICC framework, opening up this work to new potential applications.

Acknowledgements. This work was supported by NSF IIS-1149837, NIH BD2K, DARPA SIMPLEX, DARPA XDATA, Chan Zuckerberg Biohub, SDSI, Boeing, Bosch, and Volkswagen.

REFERENCES

[1] O. Banerjee, L. El Ghaoui, and A. d'Aspremont. Model selection through sparse maximum likelihood estimation for multivariate Gaussian or binary data. *JMLR*, 2008.
[2] J. D. Banfield and A. E. Raftery. Model-based Gaussian and non-Gaussian clustering. *Biometrics*, 1993.
[3] N. Begum, L. Ulanova, J. Wang, and E. Keogh. Accelerating dynamic time warping clustering with a novel admissible pruning strategy. In *KDD*, 2015.
[4] D. J. Berndt and J. Clifford. Using dynamic time warping to find patterns in time series. In *AAAI Workshop on Knowledge Disovery in Databases*, 1994.
[5] S. Boyd, N. Parikh, E. Chu, B. Peleato, and J. Eckstein. Distributed optimization and statistical learning via the alternating direction method of multipliers. *Foundations and Trends in Machine Learning*, 2011.
[6] S. Boyd and L. Vandenberghe. *Convex Optimization*. Cambridge University Press, 2004.
[7] U. Brandes. A faster algorithm for betweenness centrality. *Journal of Mathematical Sociology*, 2001.
[8] T. M. Cover and J. A. Thomas. *Elements of Information Theory*. John Wiley & Sons, 2012.
[9] M. Cuturi. Fast global alignment kernels. In *ICML*, 2011.
[10] P. Danaher, P. Wang, and D. M. Witten. The joint graphical lasso for inverse covariance estimation across multiple classes. *JRSS: Series B*, 2014.
[11] G. Das, K.-I. Lin, H. Mannila, G. Renganathan, and P. Smyth. Rule discovery from time series. In *KDD*, 1998.
[12] E. Dimtriadou. Cclust: Convex clustering methods and clustering indexes. https://CRAN.R-project.org/package=cclust, 2009.
[13] C. Fraley and A. E. Raftery. MCLUST version 3: an R package for normal mixture modeling and model-based clustering. Technical report, DTIC Document, 2006.
[14] J. Friedman, T. Hastie, and R. Tibshirani. Sparse inverse covariance estimation with the graphical lasso. *Biostatistics*, 2008.
[15] A. Gionis and H. Mannila. Finding recurrent sources in sequences. In *RECOMB*, 2003.
[16] R. M. Gray. Toeplitz and circulant matrices: A review. *Foundations and Trends in Communications and Information Theory*, 2006.
[17] D. Hallac, P. Nystrup, and S. Boyd. Greedy Gaussian segmentation of multivariate time series. *arXiv preprint arXiv:1610.07435*, 2016.
[18] T. Hastie, R. Tibshirani, and J. Friedman. *The Elements of Statistical Learning*. Springer, 2009.
[19] M. R. Hestenes. Multiplier and gradient methods. *Journal of Optimization Theory and Applications*, 1969.
[20] J. Himberg, K. Korpiaho, H. Mannila, J. Tikänmaki, and H. T. Toivonen. Time series segmentation for context recognition in mobile devices. In *ICDM*, 2001.
[21] C.-J. Hsieh, M. A. Sustik, I. S. Dhillon, and P. Ravikumar. QUIC: quadratic approximation for sparse inverse covariance estimation. *JMLR*, 2014.
[22] C.-J. Hsieh, M. A. Sustik, I. S. Dhillon, P. K. Ravikumar, and R. Poldrack. BIG & QUIC: Sparse inverse covariance estimation for a million variables. In *NIPS*, 2013.
[23] E. Keogh. Exact indexing of dynamic time warping. In *VLDB*, 2002.
[24] E. Keogh, J. Lin, and W. Truppel. Clustering of time series subsequences is meaningless: Implications for previous and future research. In *ICDM*, 2003.
[25] E. Keogh and M. J. Pazzani. Scaling up dynamic time warping for datamining applications. In *KDD*, 2000.
[26] D. Koller and N. Friedman. *Probabilistic Graphical Models: Principles and Techniques*. MIT press, 2009.
[27] S. L. Lauritzen. *Graphical models*. Clarendon Press, 1996.
[28] Y. Li, J. Lin, and T. Oates. Visualizing variable-length time series motifs. In *SIAM*, 2012.
[29] J. Lin, E. Keogh, S. Lonardi, and B. Chiu. A symbolic representation of time series, with implications for streaming algorithms. In *SIGMOD workshop on Research issues in data mining and knowledge discovery*, 2003.
[30] J. Lin, E. Keogh, L. Wei, and S. Lonardi. Experiencing SAX: a novel symbolic representation of time series. *Data Mining and knowledge discovery*, 2007.
[31] T. M. Martinetz, S. G. Berkovich, and K. J. Schulten. 'Neural-gas' network for vector quantization and its application to time-series prediction. *IEEE Transactions on Neural Networks*, 1993.
[32] C. Miyajima, Y. Nishiwaki, K. Ozawa, T. Wakita, K. Itou, K. Takeda, and F. Itakura. Driver modeling based on driving behavior and its evaluation in driver identification. *Proceedings of the IEEE*, 2007.
[33] K. Mohan, P. London, M. Fazel, D. Witten, and S.-I. Lee. Node-based learning of multiple Gaussian graphical models. *JMLR*, 2014.
[34] F. Mörchen, A. Ultsch, and O. Hoos. Extracting interpretable muscle activation patterns with time series knowledge mining. *International Journal of Knowledge-based and Intelligent Engineering Systems*, 2005.
[35] A. Namaki, A. Shirazi, R. Raei, and G. Jafari. Network analysis of a financial market based on genuine correlation and threshold method. *Physica A: Stat. Mech. Apps.*, 2011.
[36] B. O'Donoghue, E. Chu, N. Parikh, and S. Boyd. Conic optimization via operator splitting and homogeneous self-dual embedding. *Journal of Optimization Theory and Applications*, 2016.
[37] N. Parikh and S. Boyd. Proximal algorithms. *Foundations and Trends in Optimization*, 2014.
[38] J. Pärkkä, M. Ermes, P. Korpipää, J. Mäntyjärvi, J. Peltola, and I. Korhonen. Activity classification using realistic data from wearable sensors. *IEEE Transactions on information technology in biomedicine*, 2006.
[39] T. Rakthanmanon, B. Campana, A. Mueen, G. Batista, B. Westover, Q. Zhu, J. Zakaria, and E. Keogh. Searching and mining trillions of time series subsequences under dynamic time warping. In *KDD*, 2012.
[40] P. J. Rousseeuw. Silhouettes: a graphical aid to the interpretation and validation of cluster analysis. *Journal of computational and applied mathematics*, 1987.
[41] H. Rue and L. Held. *Gaussian Markov Random Fields: Theory and Applications*. CRC Press, 2005.
[42] A. Sarda-Espinosa. Dtwclust. https://cran.r-project.org/web/packages/dtwclust/index.html, 2016.
[43] P. Smyth. Clustering sequences with hidden Markov models. *NIPS*, 1997.
[44] A. Viterbi. Error bounds for convolutional codes and an asymptotically optimum decoding algorithm. *IEEE Transactions on Information Theory*, 1967.
[45] M. J. Wainwright and M. I. Jordan. Log-determinant relaxation for approximate inference in discrete Markov random fields. *IEEE Tr. on Signal Processing*, 2006.
[46] M. Wytock and J. Z. Kolter. Sparse Gaussian conditional random fields: Algorithms, theory, and application to energy forecasting. *ICML*, 2013.
[47] Y. Xiong and D.-Y. Yeung. Time series clustering with ARMA mixtures. *Pattern Recognition*, 2004.
[48] M. Yuan and Y. Lin. Model selection and estimation in regression with grouped variables. *Journal of the Royal Statistical Society: Series B*, 68:49–67, 2006.
[49] S. Zolhavarieh, S. Aghabozorgi, and Y. W. Teh. A review of subsequence time series clustering. *The Scientific World Journal*, 2014.

Efficient Correlated Topic Modeling with Topic Embedding

Junxian He*[1,3], Zhiting Hu*[1,2], Taylor Berg-Kirkpatrick[1], Ying Huang[3], Eric P. Xing[1,2]
Carnegie Mellon University[1] Petuum Inc.[2] Shanghai Jiao Tong University[3]
* Equal contribution {junxianh,zhitingh,tberg,epxing}@cs.cmu.edu , hy941001@sjtu.edu.cn

ABSTRACT

Correlated topic modeling has been limited to small model and problem sizes due to their high computational cost and poor scaling. In this paper, we propose a new model which learns compact topic embeddings and captures topic correlations through the closeness between the topic vectors. Our method enables efficient inference in the low-dimensional embedding space, reducing previous cubic or quadratic time complexity to *linear* w.r.t the topic size. We further speedup variational inference with a fast sampler to exploit sparsity of topic occurrence. Extensive experiments show that our approach is capable of handling model and data scales which are several orders of magnitude larger than existing correlation results, without sacrificing modeling quality by providing competitive or superior performance in document classification and retrieval.

CCS CONCEPTS

•**Computing methodologies → Latent variable models;**

KEYWORDS

Correlated topic models; topic embedding; scalability

1 INTRODUCTION

Large ever-growing document collections provide great opportunities, and pose compelling challenges, to infer rich semantic structures underlying the data for data management and utilization. Topic models, particularly the Latent Dirichlet Allocation (LDA) model [6], have been one of the most popular statistical frameworks to identify latent semantics from text corpora. One drawback of LDA derives from the conjugate Dirichlet prior, as it models topic occurrence (almost) independently and fails to capture rich topical correlations (e.g., a document about virus may be likely to also be about disease while unlikely to also be aboutfi nance). Effective modeling of the pervasive correlation patterns is essential for structural topic navigation, improved document representation, and accurate prediction [5, 9, 37]. Correlated Topic Model (CTM) [5] extends LDA using a logistic-normal prior which explicitly models correlation patterns with a Gaussian covariance matrix.

Despite the enhanced expressiveness and resulting richer representations, practical applications of correlated topic modeling have unfortunately been limited due to high model complexity and poor scaling on large data. For instance, in CTM, direct modeling of pairwise correlations and the non-conjugacy of logistic-normal prior impose inference complexity of $O(K^3)$, where K is the number of latent topics, significantly more demanding compared to LDA which scales only linearly. While there has been recent work on improved modeling and inference [2, 9, 35, 36], the model scale has still limited to less than 1000s of latent topics.Th is stands in stark contrast to recent industrial-scale LDA models which handle millions of topics on billions of documents [8, 42] for capturing long-tail semantics and supporting industrial applications [40], yet, such rich extraction task is expected to be better addressed with more expressive correlation models. It is therefore highly desirable to develop efficient correlated topic models with great representational power and highly scalable inference, for practical deployment.

In this paper, we develop a new model that extracts correlation structures of latent topics, sharing comparable expressiveness with the costly CTM model, while keeping as efficient as the simple LDA. We propose to learn a distributed representation for each latent topic, and characterize correlatedness of two topics through the closeness of respective topic vectors in the embedding space. Compared to previous pairwise correlation modeling, our topic embedding scheme is parsimonious with less parameters to estimate, yetfl exible to enable richer analysis and visualization. Figure 1 illustrates the correlation patterns of 10K topics inferred by our model from two million NYTimes news articles, in which we can see clear dependency structures among the large collection of topics and grasp the semantics of the massive text corpus.

We further derive an efficient variational inference procedure combined with a fast sparsity-aware sampler for stochastic tackling of non-conjugacies. Our embedding based correlation modeling enables inference in the low-dimensional vector space, resulting in *linear* complexity w.r.t topic size as with the lightweight LDA. This allows us to discover 100s of 1000s of latent topics with their correlations on near 10 million articles, which is several orders of magnitude larger than prior work [5, 9].

Our work differs from recent research which combines topic models with word embeddings [3, 10, 22, 29] for capturing word dependencies, as we instead focus on modeling dependencies in the latent topic space which exhibit uncertainty and are inferentially more challenging. To the best of our knowledge, this is thefirst work to incorporate distributed representation learning with topic correlation modeling, offering both intuitive geometric interpretation and theoretical Bayesian modeling advantages.

We demonstrate the efficacy of our method through extensive experiments on various large text corpora. Our approach shows greatly improved efficiency over previous correlated topic models, and scales well as with the much simpler LDA.Th is is achieved without sacrificing the modeling power—the proposed model extracts high-quality topics and correlations, obtaining competitive

KDD'17, August 13-17, 2017, Halifax, NS, Canada.
© 2017 ACM. 978-1-4503-4887-4/17/08...$15.00
DOI: 10.1145/3097983.3098074

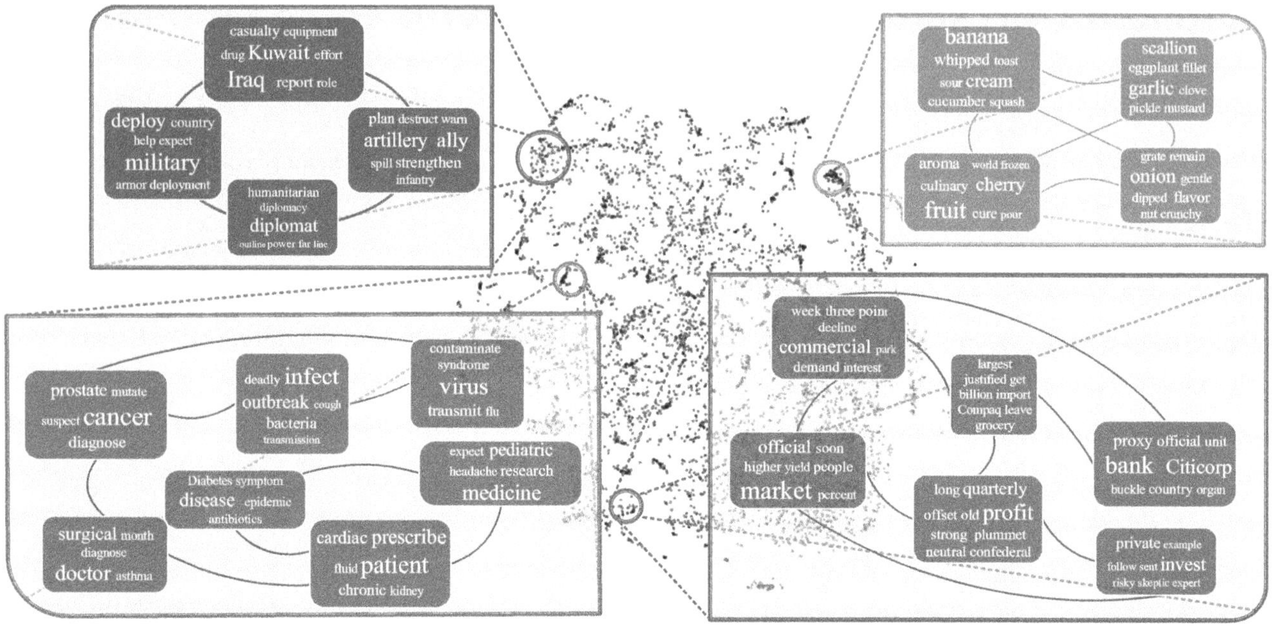

Figure 1: Visualization of 10K correlated topics on the NYTimes news corpus.Th e point cloud shows the 10K topic embeddings where each point represents a latent topic. Smaller distance indicates stronger correlation. We show four sets of topics which are nearby each other in the embedding space, respectively. Each topic is characterized by the top words according to the word distribution. Edge indicates correlation between topics with strength above some threshold.

or better performance than CTM in document classification and retrieval tasks.

The rest of the paper is organized as follows: section 2 briefly reviews related work; section 3 presents the proposed topic embedding model; section 4 shows extensive experimental ; and section 5 concludes the paper.

2 RELATED WORK

2.1 Correlated Topic Modeling

Topic models represent a document as a mixture of latent topics. Among the most popular topic models is the LDA model [6] which assumes conjugate Dirichlet prior over topic mixing proportions for easier inference. Due to its simplicity and scalability, LDA has extracted broad interest for industrial applications [40, 42].The Dirichlet prior is however incapable of capturing dependencies between topics.Th e classic CTM model provides an elegant extension of LDA by replacing the Dirichlet prior with a logistic-normal prior which models pairwise topic correlations with the Gaussian covariance matrix. However, the enriched extraction comes with computational cost.Th e number of parameters in the covariance matrix grows as square of the number of topics, and parameter estimation for the full-rank matrix can be inaccurate in high-dimensional space. More importantly, frequent matrix inversion operations during inference lead to $O(K^3)$ time complexity, which has significantly restricted the model and data scales. To address this, Chen et al. [9] derives a scalable Gibbs sampling algorithm based on data augmentation.Th ough bringing down the inference cost to $O(K^2)$ per document, the computation is still too expensive to be practical in real-world massive tasks. Putthividhya et al. [36] reformulates the correlation prior with independent factor models for faster inference. However, similar to many other approaches, the problem scale has still limited to thousands of documents and hundreds of topics. In contrast, we aim to scale correlated topic modeling to industrial level deployment by reducing the complexity to the LDA level which is linear to the topic size, while providing as rich extraction as the costly CTM model. We note that recent scalable extensions of LDA such as alias methods [28, 42] are orthogonal to our approach and can be applied in our inference for further speedup. We consider this as our future work.

Another line of topic models organizes latent topics in a hierarchy which also captures topic dependencies. However, the hierarchy structure is either pre-defined [7, 19, 30] or inferred from data using Bayesian nonparametric methods [4, 11] which are known to be computationally demanding [12, 17]. Our proposed model is flexible without sacrificing scalability.

2.2 Distributed Representation Learning

There has been a growing interest in distributed representation that learns compact vectors (a.k.a embeddings) for words [27, 33], entities [18, 31] , network nodes [14, 38], and others.Th e induced vectors are expected to capture semantic relatedness of the target items, and are successfully used in various applications. Compared to most work that induces embeddings for observed units, we learn distributed representations of latent topics which poses unique challenge for inference. Some previous work [25, 26] also induces compact topic manifold for visualizing large document collections. Our work is distinct in that we leverage the learned topic vectors

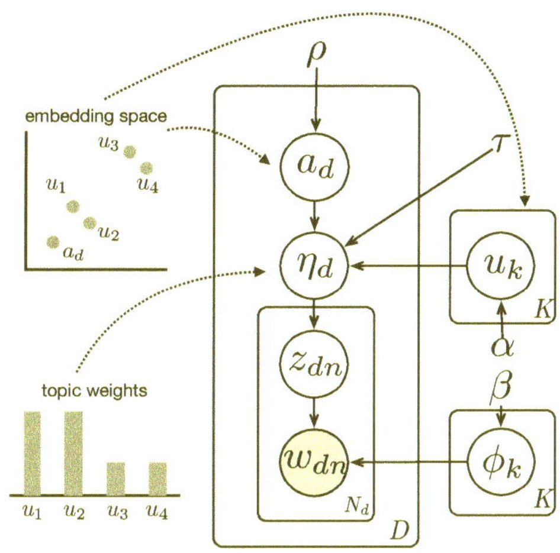

Figure 2: Graphical model representation.Th e leftpart schematically shows our correlation modeling mechanism, where nearby topics tend to have similar (either large or small) weights in a document.

for efficient correlation modeling and account for the uncertainty of correlations.

An emerging line of approaches [3, 10, 22, 29] incorporates word embeddings (either pre-trained or jointly inferred) with conventional topic models for capturing word dependencies and improving topic coherence. Our work differs since we are interested in the topic level, aiming at capturing topic dependencies with learned topic embeddings.

3 TOPIC EMBEDDING MODEL

This section proposes our topic embedding model for correlated topic modeling. Wefi rst give an overview of our approach, and present the model structure in detail. We then derive an efficient variational algorithm for inference.

3.1 Overview

We aim to develop an expressive topic model that discovers latent topics and underlying correlation structures. Despite this added representational power, we want to keep the model parsimonious and efficient in order to scale to large text data. As discussed above (section 2), CTM captures correlations between topic pairs with a Gaussian covariance matrix, imposing $O(K^2)$ parameter size and $O(K^3)$ inference cost. In contrast, we adopt a new modeling scheme drawing inspiration from recent work on distributed representations, such as word embeddings [33] which learn low-dimensional word vectors and have shown to be effective in encoding word semantic relatedness.

We induce continuous distributed representations for latent topics, and, as in word embeddings, expect topics with relevant semantics to be close to each other in the embedding space.Th e contiguity of the embedding space enables us to capture topical co-occurrence patterns conveniently—we further embed documents into the same vector space, and characterize document's topic proportions with its distances to the topics. Smaller distance indicates larger topic weight. By the triangle inequality of distance metric, intuitively, a document vector will have similar (either large or small) distances to the vectors of two semantically correlated topics which are themselves nearby each other in the space, and thus tend to assign similar probability mass to the two topics. Figure 2, left part, schematically illustrates the embedding based correlation modeling.

Symbol	Description
D, K, V	number of documents, latent topics, and vocabulary words
N_d	number of words in document d
M	embedding dimension of topic and document
$\boldsymbol{u}_k$	embedding vector of topic k
$\boldsymbol{a}_d$	embedding vector of document d
$\boldsymbol{\eta}_d$	(unnormalized) topic weight vector of document d
w_{dn}	the nth word in document d
z_{dn}	the topic assignment of word w_{dn}
$\boldsymbol{\phi}_k$	word distribution of topic k
K_s	number of non-zero entries of document's topic proportion
V_s	number of non-zero entries of topic word distribution

Table 1: Notations used in this paper.

We thus avoid expensive modeling of pairwise topic correlation matrix, and are enabled to perform inference in the low-dimensional embedding space, leading to significant reduction in model and inference complexity. We further exploit the intrinsic sparsity of topic occurrence, and develop stochastic variational inference with fast sparsity-aware sampling to enable high scalability. We derive the inference algorithm in section 3.3.

In contrast to word representation learning where word tokens are observed and embeddings can be induced directly from word collocation patterns, topics are hidden from the text, posing additional inferential challenge. We resort to generative framework as in conventional topic models by associating a word distribution with each topic. We also take into account uncertainty of topic correlations forfl exibility.Th us, in addition to the intuitive geometric interpretation of our embedding based correlation scheme, the full Bayesian treatment also endows connection to the classic CTM model, offering theoretical insights into our approach. We present the model structure in the next section. (Table 1 lists key notations; Figure 2 shows the graphical model representation of our model.)

3.2 Model Structure

Wefi rst establish the notations. Let $\boldsymbol{W} = \{\boldsymbol{w}_d\}_{d=1}^{D}$ be a collection of documents. Each document d contains N_d words $\boldsymbol{w}_d = \{w_{dn}\}_{n=1}^{N_d}$ from a vocabulary of size V.

We assume K topics underlying the corpus. As discussed above, for each topic k, we want to learn a compact distributed representation $\boldsymbol{u}_k \in \mathbb{R}^M$ with low dimensionality ($M \ll K$). Let $\boldsymbol{U} \in \mathbb{R}^{K\times M}$ denote the topic vector collection with the kth row $\boldsymbol{U}_{k\cdot} = \boldsymbol{u}_k^T$. As a common choice in word embedding methods, we use the vector inner product for measuring the closeness between embedding vectors. In addition to topic embeddings, we also induce document vectors in the same vector space. Let $\boldsymbol{a}_d \in \mathbb{R}^M$ denote the embedding of document d. We now can conveniently compute the affinity of a document d to a topic k through $\boldsymbol{u}_k^T\boldsymbol{a}_d$. A topic k' nearby, and thus semantically correlated to topic k, will naturally have similar distance to the document, as $|\boldsymbol{u}_k^T\boldsymbol{a}_d - \boldsymbol{u}_{k'}^T\boldsymbol{a}_d| \le \|\boldsymbol{u}_k - \boldsymbol{u}_{k'}\|\|\boldsymbol{a}_d\|$ and $\|\boldsymbol{u}_k - \boldsymbol{u}_{k'}\|$ is small.

We express uncertainty of the affinity by modeling the actual topic weights $\eta_d \in \mathcal{R}^K$ as a Gaussian variable centered at the affinity vector, following $\eta_d \sim \mathcal{N}(Ua_d, \tau^{-1}I)$. Here τ characterizes the uncertainty degree and is pre-specified for simplicity. As in logistic-normal models, we project the topic weights into the probability simplex to obtain topic distribution $\theta_d = \text{softmax}(\eta_d)$, from which we sample a topic $z_{dn} \in \{1, \ldots, K\}$ for each word w_{dn} in the document. As in conventional topic models, each topic k is associated with a multinomial distribution ϕ_k over the word vocabulary, and each observed word is drawn from respective word distribution indicated by its topic assignment.

Putting everything together, the generative process of the proposed model is summarized in Algorithm 1. A theoretically appealing property of our method is its intrinsic connection to conventional logistic-normal models such as the CTM model. If we marginalize out the document embedding variable a_d, we obtain $\eta_d \sim \mathcal{N}(0, UU^T + \tau^{-1}I)$, recovering the pairwise topic correlation matrix with low rank constraint, where each element is just the closeness of respective topic embeddings, coherent to the above geometric intuitions. Such covariance decomposition has been used in other context, such as sparse Gaussian processes [39] for efficient approximation and Gaussian reparameterization [23, 41] for differentiation and reduced variance. Here we relate low-dimensional embedding learning with low-rank covariance decomposition and estimation.

The low-dimensional representations of latent topics enable parsimonious correlation modeling with parameter complexity of $O(MK)$ (i.e., topic embedding parameters), which is efficient in terms of topic number K. Moreover, we are allowed to perform efficient inference in the embedding space, with inference cost *linear* in K, a huge advance compared to previous cubic complexity of vanilla CTM [5] and quadratic of recent improved version [9]. We derive our inference algorithm in the next section.

3.3 Inference

Posterior inference and parameter estimation is not analytically tractable due to the coupling between latent variables and the non-conjugate logistic-normal prior.Th is makes the learning difficult especially in our context of scaling to unprecedentedly large data and model sizes. We develop a stochastic variational method that (1) involves only compact topic vectors which are cheap to infer, and (2) includes a fast sampling strategy which tackles non-conjugacy and exploits intrinsic sparsity of both the document topic occurrence and the topical words.

Wefi rst assume a mean-field family of variational distributions:

$$q(u, \phi, a, \eta, z) = \prod_k q(u_k)q(\phi_k) \prod_d q(a_d)q(\eta_d) \prod_n q(z_{dn}). \quad (1)$$

where the factors have the parametric forms:

$$q(u_k) = \mathcal{N}(u_k|\mu_k, \Sigma_k^{(u)}), \quad q(a_d) = \mathcal{N}(a_d|\gamma_d, \Sigma_d^{(a)}),$$
$$q(\phi_k) = \text{Dir}(\phi_k|\lambda_k), \quad q(\eta_d) = \mathcal{N}(\eta_d|\xi_d, \Sigma_d^{(\eta)}), \quad (2)$$
$$q(z_{dn}) = \text{Multi}(z_{dn}|\kappa_{dn})$$

Variational algorithms aim to minimize KL divergence from q to the true posterior, which is equivalent to tightening the evidence lower bound (ELBO):

$$\mathcal{L}(q) = \sum_k \mathbb{E}_q\left[\log \frac{p(u_k)p(\phi_k)}{q(u_k)q(\phi_k)}\right] + \sum_{d,n} \mathbb{E}_q\left[\log \frac{p(a_d)p(\eta_d|a_d, U)p(z_{dn}|\eta_d)p(w_{dn}|z_{dn}, \phi)}{q(a_d)q(\eta_d)q(z_{dn})}\right] \quad (3)$$

Algorithm 1 Generative Process

1. For each topic $k = 1, 2, \cdots, K$,
   - Draw the topic word distribution $\phi_k \sim \text{Dir}(\beta)$
   - Draw the topic embedding $u_k \sim \mathcal{N}(0, \alpha^{-1}I)$
2. For each document $d = 1, 2, \cdots, D$,
   - Draw the document embedding $a_d \sim \mathcal{N}(0, \rho^{-1}I)$
   - Draw the document topic weight $\eta_d \sim \mathcal{N}(Ua_d, \tau^{-1}I)$
   - Derive the distribution over topics $\theta_d = \text{softmax}(\eta_d)$
   - For each word $n = 1, 2, \cdots, N_d$,
     (a) Draw the topic assignment $z_{dn} \sim \text{Multi}(\theta_d)$
     (b) Draw the word $w_{dn} \sim \text{Multi}(\phi_{z_{dn}})$

We optimize $\mathcal{L}(q)$ via coordinate ascent, interleaving the update of the variational parameters at each iteration. We employ stochastic variational inference which optimizes the parameters with stochastic gradients estimated on data minibatchs. Due to the space limitations, here we only describe key computation rules of the gradients (or closed-form solutions).Th ese stochastically estimated quantities are then used to update the variational parameters after scaled by a learning rate. Please refer to the supplementary material [1] for detailed derivations.

Updating topic and document embeddings. For each topic k, we isolate only the terms that contain $q(u_k|\mu_k, \Sigma_k^{(u)})$,

$$\mathcal{L}(q(u_k)) = \mathbb{E}_q[\log p(u_k)] + \sum_d \mathbb{E}_q[\log p(\eta_d|a_d, U)] - \mathbb{E}_q[\log q(u_k)]. \quad (4)$$

The optimal solution for $q(u_k)$ is then obtained by setting the gradient to zero, with the variational parameters computed as:

$$\mu_k = \tau\Sigma^{(u)} \cdot \left(\sum_d \xi_{dk}\gamma_d\right), \quad \Sigma^{(u)} = \left[\alpha I + \tau \sum_d \left(\Sigma_d^{(a)} + \gamma_d\gamma_d^T\right)\right]^{-1}, \quad (5)$$

where we have omitted the subscript k of the variational covariance matrix $\Sigma^{(u)}$ as it is independent with k. Intuitively, the optimal variational topic embeddings are the centers of variational document embeddings scaled by respective document topic weights and transformed by the variational covariance matrix.

By symmetry, the variational parameters of document embedding a_d is similarly updated as:

$$\gamma_d = \tau\Sigma^{(a)} \cdot \left(\sum_k \xi_{dk}\mu_k\right), \quad \Sigma^{(a)} = \left[\gamma I + \tau \sum_k \left(\Sigma^{(u)} + \mu_k\mu_k^T\right)\right]^{-1}, \quad (6)$$

where, again, $\Sigma^{(a)}$ is independent with d and thus the subscript d is omitted.

Learning low-dimensional topic and document embeddings is computationally cheap. Specifically, by Eq.(5), updating the set of variational topic vector means $\{\mu_k\}_{k=1}^K$ imposes complexity $O(KM^2)$, and updating the covariance $\Sigma^{(u)}$ requires only $O(M^3)$. Similarly, by Eq.(6), the cost of optimizing γ_d and $\Sigma^{(a)}$ is $O(KM)$ and $O(KM^2)$, respectively. Note that $\Sigma^{(a)}$ is shared across all documents and does not need updates per document. We see that all the updates cost only linearly w.r.t to the topic size K which is critical to scale to large-scale practical applications.

Sparsity-aware topic sampling. We next consider the optimization of the variational topic assignment $q(z_{dn})$ for each word w_{dn}. Letting $w_{dn} = v$, the optimal solution is:

$$q(z_{dn} = k) \propto \exp\{\xi_{dk}\} \exp\left\{\Psi(\lambda_{kv}) - \Psi\left(\sum_{v'} \lambda_{kv'}\right)\right\}, \quad (7)$$

where $\Psi(\cdot)$ is the digamma function; and ξ_d and λ_k are the variational means of the document's topic weights and the variational word weights (Eq.(2)), respectively. Direct computation of $q(z_{dn})$ with Eq.(7) has complexity of $O(K)$, which becomes prohibitive in the presence of many latent topics. To address this, we exploit two aspects of intrinsic sparsity in the modeling: (1)Th ough a whole corpus can cover a large diverse set of topics, a single document in the corpus is usually about only a small number of them. We thus only maintain the top K_s entries in each ξ_d, where $K_s \ll K$, making the complexity due to thefi rst term in the right-hand side of Eq.(7) only $O(K_s)$ for all K topics in total; (2) A topic is typically characterized by only a few words in the large vocabulary, we thus cut off the variational word weight vector λ_k for each k by maintaining only its top V_s entries ($V_s \ll V$). Such sparse treatment helps enhance the interpretability of learned topics, and allows cheap computation with on average $O(KV_s/V)$ cost for the second term[1]. With the above sparsity-aware updates, the resulting complexity for Eq.(7) with K topics is brought down to $O(K_s + KV_s/V)$, a great speedup over the original $O(K)$ cost.Th e top K_s entries of ξ_d are selected using a Min-heap data structure, whose computational cost is amortized across all words in the document, imposing $O(K/N_d \log K_s)$ computation per word.Th e cost forfi nding the top V_s entries of λ_k is similarly amortized across documents and words, and becomes insignificant.

Updating the remaining variational parameters will frequently involve computation of variational expectations under $q(z_{dn})$. It is thus crucial to speedup this operation. To this end, we employ sparse approximation by sampling from $q(z_{dn})$ a single indicator $\tilde{z}_{dn}$, and use the "hard" sparse distribution $\tilde{q}(z_{dn} = k) := \mathbf{1}(\tilde{z}_{dn} = k)$ to estimate the expectations. Note that the sampling operation is cheap, having the same complexity with computing $q(z_{dn})$ as above. As shown shortly, such sparse computation will significantly reduce our running cost.Th ough stochastic expectation approximation is commonly used for tackling intractability [24, 34], here we instead apply the technique for fast estimation of tractable expectations.

We next optimize the variational topic weights $q(\eta_d|\xi_d, \Sigma_d^{(\eta)})$. Extracting only the terms in $\mathcal{L}(q)$ involving $q(\eta_d)$, we get:

$$\begin{aligned}\mathcal{L}(q(\eta_d)) = \mathbb{E}_q\left[\log p(\eta_d|a_d, U)\right] + \mathbb{E}_q\left[\log p(z_d|\eta_d)\right] \\ - \mathbb{E}_q\left[\log q(\eta_d)\right],\end{aligned} \quad (8)$$

[1] In practice we also set a threshold s such that each word v needs to have at least s non-zero entries in $\{\lambda_k\}_{k=1}^K$.Th us the exact complexity of the second term is $O(\max\{KV_s/V, s\})$.

where the second term

$$\mathbb{E}_q\left[\log p(z_d|\eta_d)\right] = \sum_{k,n} q(z_{dn} = k)\mathbb{E}_q\left[\log(\text{softmax}_k(\eta_d))\right]$$

involves variational expectations of the logistic transformation which does not have an analytic form. We construct a fast Monto Carlo estimator for approximation. Particularly, we employ reparameterization trick byfi rst assuming a diagonal covariance matrix $\Sigma_d^{(\eta)} = \text{diag}(\sigma_d^2)$ as is commonly used in previous work [5, 23], where σ_d denotes the vector of standard deviations, resulting in the following sampling procedure:

$$\eta_d^{(t)} = \xi_d + \sigma_d \odot \epsilon^{(t)}; \quad \epsilon^{(t)} \sim \mathcal{N}(0, I), \quad (9)$$

where $\odot$ is the element-wise multiplication. With T samples of η_d, we can estimate the variational lower bound and the derivatives $\nabla\mathcal{L}$ w.r.t the variational parameters $\{\xi_d, \sigma_d\}$. For instance,

$$\begin{aligned}&\nabla_{\xi_d}\mathbb{E}_q\left[\log p(z_d|\eta_d)\right] \\ &\approx \sum_{k,n} q(z_{dn} = k)e_k - (N_d/T)\sum_{t=1}^T \mathbf{softmax}\left(\eta_d^{(t)}\right) \quad (10)\\ &\approx \sum_{k,n} \mathbf{1}(\tilde{z}_{dn} = k)e_k - (N_d/T)\sum_{t=1}^T \mathbf{softmax}\left(\eta_d^{(t)}\right)\end{aligned}$$

where e_k is an indicator vector with the kth element being 1 and the rest 0. In practice $T = 1$ is usually sufficient for effective inference. The second equation applies the hard topic sample mentioned above, which reduces the time complexity $O(KN_d)$ of the original standard computation (thefi rst equation) to $O(N_d + K)$ (i.e., $O(N_d)$ for the first term and $O(K)$ for the second).

Thefi rst term in Eq.(8) depends on the topic and document embeddings to encode topic correlations in document's topic weights. The derivative w.r.t to the variational parameter ξ_d is computed as:

$$\nabla_{\xi_d}\mathbb{E}_q\left[\log p(\eta_d|U, a_d)\right] = \tau(\tilde{U}\gamma_d - \xi_d). \quad (11)$$

Here $\tilde{U}$ is the collection of variational means of topic embeddings where the kth row $\tilde{U}_{k\cdot} = \mu_k^T$. We see that, with low-dimensional topic and document vector representations, inferring topic correlations is of low cost $O(KM)$ which grows only linearly w.r.t to the topic size.Th e complexity of the remaining terms in Eq.(8), as well as respective derivatives w.r.t the variational parameters, has complexity of $O(KM)$ (Please see the supplements [1] for more details). In summary, the cost of updating $q(\eta_d)$ for each document d is $O(KM + K + N_d)$.

Finally, the optimal solution of the variational topic word distribution $q(\phi_k|\lambda_k)$ is given by:

$$\lambda_{kv} = \beta + \sum_{d,n} \mathbf{1}(w_{dn} = v)\mathbf{1}(\tilde{z}_{dn} = k). \quad (12)$$

Algorithm summarization. We summarize our variational inference in Algorithm 2. As analyzed above, the time complexity of our variational method is $O(KM^2 + M^3)$ for inferring topic embeddings $q(u_d)$.Th e cost per document is $O(KM)$ for computing $q(a_d)$, $O(KM)$ for updating $q(\eta_d)$, and $O((K_s + KV_s/V)N_d)$ for maintaining $q(z_d)$.Th e overall complexity for each document is thus $O(KM + (K_s + KV_s/V)N_d)$, which is linear to model size (K), comparable to the LDA model while greatly improving over previous correlation methods with cubic or quadratic complexity.

The variational inference algorithm endows rich independence structures between the variational parameters, allowing straightforward parallel computing. In our implementation, updates of

Algorithm 2 Stochastic variational inference

Initialize variational parameters randomly
repeat
  Compute learning rate $\iota_{iter} = 1/(1 + iter)^{0.9}$
  Sample a minibatch of documents $\mathcal{B}$
  for all $d \in \mathcal{B}$ **do**
    repeat
      Update $q(z_d)$ with Eq.(7) and sample $\tilde{z}_d$
      Update $\boldsymbol{\gamma}_d$ with Eq.(6)
      Update $q(\boldsymbol{\eta}_d)$ using respective gradients computed with Eqs.(10),(11),and more in the supplements [1].
    until convergence
    Compute stochastic optimal values $\boldsymbol{\mu}^*, \Sigma^{(u)*}$ with Eq.(5)
    Compute stochastic optimal values $\boldsymbol{\lambda}^*$ with Eq.(12)
    Update $\boldsymbol{x} = (1 - \iota_{iter})\boldsymbol{x} + \iota_{iter}\boldsymbol{x}^*$ with $\boldsymbol{x} \in \{\boldsymbol{\mu}, \Sigma^{(u)}, \boldsymbol{\lambda}\}$
    Update $\Sigma^{(a)}$ with Eq.(6)
  end for
until convergence

variational topic embeddings $\{\boldsymbol{\mu}_k\}$ (Eq.(5)), topic word distributions $\{\boldsymbol{\lambda}_k\}$ (Eq.(12)), and document embeddings $\{\boldsymbol{\gamma}_d\}$ (Eq.(6)) for a data minibatch, are all computed in parallel across multiple CPU cores.

4 EXPERIMENTS

We demonstrate the efficacy of our approach with extensive experiments. (1) We evaluate the extraction quality in the tasks of document classification and retrieval, in which our model achieves similar or better performance than existing correlated topic models, significantly improving over simple LDA. (2) For scalability, our approach scales comparably with LDA, and handles massive problem sizes orders-of-magnitude larger than previously reported correlation results. (3)Qu alitatively, our model reveals very meaningful topic correlation structures.

4.1 Setup

Datasets. We use three public corpora provided in the UCI repository[2] for the evaluation: **20Newsgroups** is a collection of news documents partitioned (nearly) evenly across 20 different newsgroups. Each article is associated with a category label, serving as ground truth in the tasks of document classification and retrieval; **NYTimes** is a widely-used large corpus of New York Times news articles; and **PubMed** is a large set of PubMed abstracts.Th e detailed statistics of the datasets are listed in Table 2. We removed a standard list of 174 stop words and performed stemming. For NYTimes and Pubmed, we kept the top 10K frequent words in vocabulary, and selected 10% documents uniformly at random as test sets, respectively. For 20Newsgroups, we followed the standard training/test splitting, and performed the widely-used pre-processing[3] by removing indicative meta text such as headers and footers so that document classification is forced to be based on the semantics of plain text.

[2]http://archive.ics.uci.edu/ml
[3]http://scikit-learn.org/stable/datasets/twenty_newsgroups.html

Dataset	#doc (D)	vocab size (V)	doc length
20Newsgroups	18K	30K	130
NYTimes	1.8M	10K	284
PubMed	8.2M	10K	77

Table 2: Statistics of the three datasets, including the number of documents (D), vocabulary size (V), and average number of words in each document.

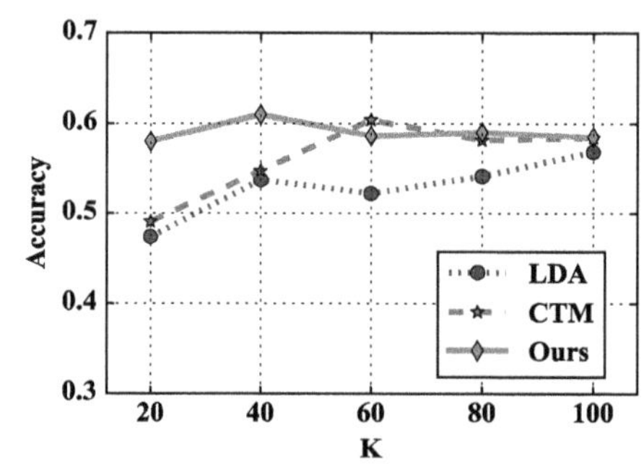

Figure 3: Classification accuracy on 20newsgroup.

Baselines. We compare the proposed model with a set of carefully selected competitors:

- **Latent Dirichlet Allocation (LDA)** [6] uses conjugate Dirichlet priors and thus scales linearly w.r.t the topic size but fails to capture topic correlations. Inference is based on the stochastic variational algorithm [16]. When evaluating scalability, we leverage the same sparsity assumptions as in our model for speeding up.
- **Correlated Topic Model (CTM)** [5] employs standard logistic-normal prior which captures pairwise topic correlations.Th e model uses stochastic variational inference with $O(K^3)$ time complexity.
- **Scalable CTM (S-CTM)** [9] developed a scalable sparse Gibbs sampler for CTM inference with time complexity of $O(K^2)$. Using distributed inference on 40 machines, the method discovers 1K topics from millions of documents, which to our knowledge is the largest automatically learned topic correlation structures so far.

Parameter Setting. Throughout the experiments, we set the embedding dimension to $M = 50$, and sparseness parameters to $K_s = 50$ and $V_s = 100$. We found our modeling quality is robust to these parameters. Following common practice, the hyperparameters arefi xed to $\beta = 1/K, \alpha = 0.1, \rho = 0.1$, and $\tau = 1$.The baselines are using similar hyper-parameter settings.

All experiments were performed on Linux with 24 4.0GHz CPU cores and 128GB RAM. All models are implemented using C/C++, and parallelized whenever possible using the OpenMP library.

4.2 Document Classification

Wefi rst evaluate the performance of document classification based on the learned document representations. We evaluate on the 20Newsgroups dataset where ground truth class labels are available. We compare our proposed model with LDA and CTM. For LDA

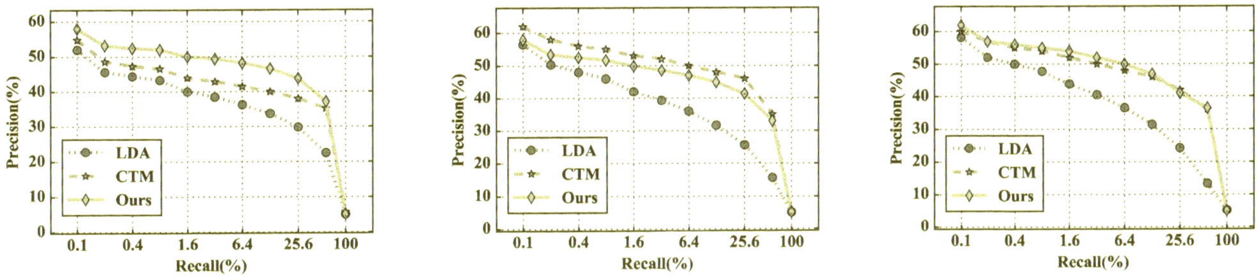

Figure 4: Precision-Recall curves on 20Newsgroups. Left: #topic $K = 20$. Middle: $K = 60$. Right: $K = 100$.

and CTM, a multi-class SVM classifier is trained for each of them based on the topic distributions of the training documents, while for the proposed model, the SVM classifier takes the document embedding vectors as input. Generally, more accurate modeling of topic correlations enables better document modeling and representations, resulting in improved document classification accuracy.

Figure 3 shows the classification accuracy as the number of topics varies. We see that the proposed model performs best in most of the cases, indicating that our method can discover high-quality latent topics and correlations. Both CTM and our model significantly outperforms LDA which treats latent topics independently, validating the importance of topic correlation for accurate text semantic modeling. Compared to CTM, our method achieves better or competitive accuracy as K varies, which indicates that our model, though orders-of-magnitude faster (as shown in the next), does not sacrifice modeling power compared to the complicated and computationally demanding CTM model.

4.3 Document Retrieval

We further evaluate the topic modeling quality by measuring the performance of document retrieval [15]. We use the 20Newsgroups dataset. A retrieved document is relevant to the query document when they have the same class label. For LDA and CTM, document similarity is measured as the inner product of topic distributions, and for our model we use the inner product of document embedding vectors.

Figure 4 shows the retrieval results with varying number of topics, where we use the test set as query documents to retrieve similar documents from the training set, and the results are averaged over all possible queries. We observe similar patterns as in the document classification task. Our model obtains competitive performance with CTM, both of which capture topic correlations and greatly improve over LDA.Th is again validates our goal that the proposed method has lower modeling complexity while at the same time is as accurate and powerful as previous complicated correlation models. In addition to efficient model inference and learning, our approach based on compact document embedding vectors also enables faster document retrieval compared to conventional topic models which are based on topic distribution vectors (i.e., $M \ll K$).

4.4 Scalability

We now investigate the efficiency and scalability of the proposed model. Compared to topic extraction quality in which our model achieves similar or better level of performance as the conventional complicated correlated topic model, here we want our approach to tackle large problem sizes which are impossible for existing correlation methods, and to scale as efficiently as the lightweight LDA, for practical deployment.

Dataset	K	Running Time			
		LDA	CTM	S-CTM	Ours
20Newsgroups	100	11 min	60 min	22 min	20 min
NYTimes	100	2.5 hr	–	6.4 hr	3.5 hr
	1K	5.6 hr	–	–	5.7 hr
	10K	8.4 hr	–	–	9.2 hr
PubMed	100K	16.7 hr	–	–	19.9 hr

Table 3: Total training time on various datasets with different number of topics K. Entries marked with "–" indicates model training is too slow to befi nished in 2 days.

Table 3 compares the total running time of model training with different sized datasets and models. As a common practice [16], we determine convergence of training when the difference between the test set per-word log-likelihoods of two consecutive iterations is smaller than some threshold. On small dataset like 20Newsgroups (thousands of documents) and small model (hundreds of topics), all approachesfi nish training in a reasonable time. However, with increasing number of documents and latent topics, we see that the vanilla CTM model (with $O(K^3)$ inference complexity) and its scalable version S-CTM (with $O(K^2)$ inference complexity) quickly becomes impractical, limiting their deployment in real-world scale tasks. Our proposed topic embedding method, by contrast, scales linearly with the topic size, and is capable of handling 100K topics on over 8M documents (PubMed)—a problem size several orders of magnitude larger than previously reported largest results [9] (1K topics on millions of documents). Notably, even with added model power and increased extraction performance compared to LDA (as has been shown in sections 4.2-4.3), our model only imposes negligible additional training time, showing strong potential of our method for practical deployment of real-world large-scale applications as LDA does.

Figure 5, left panel, shows the convergence curves on NYTimes as training goes. Using similar time, our model converges to a better point (higher test likelihood) than LDA does, while S-CTM is much slower, failing to arrive convergence within the time frame.

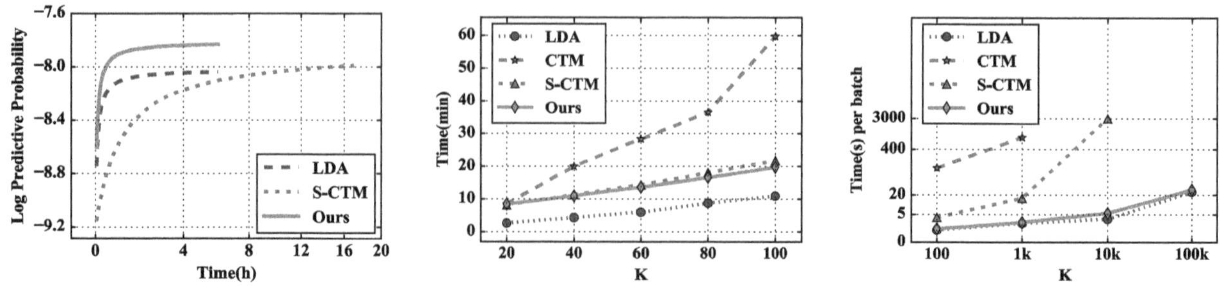

Figure 5: Left: Convergence on NYTimes with 1K topics. Middle: Total training time on 20Newsgroups. Right: Runtime of one inference iteration on a minibatch of 500 NYTimes articles, where the result points of CTM and S-CTM on large K are omitted as they fail to finish one iteration within 2 hours.

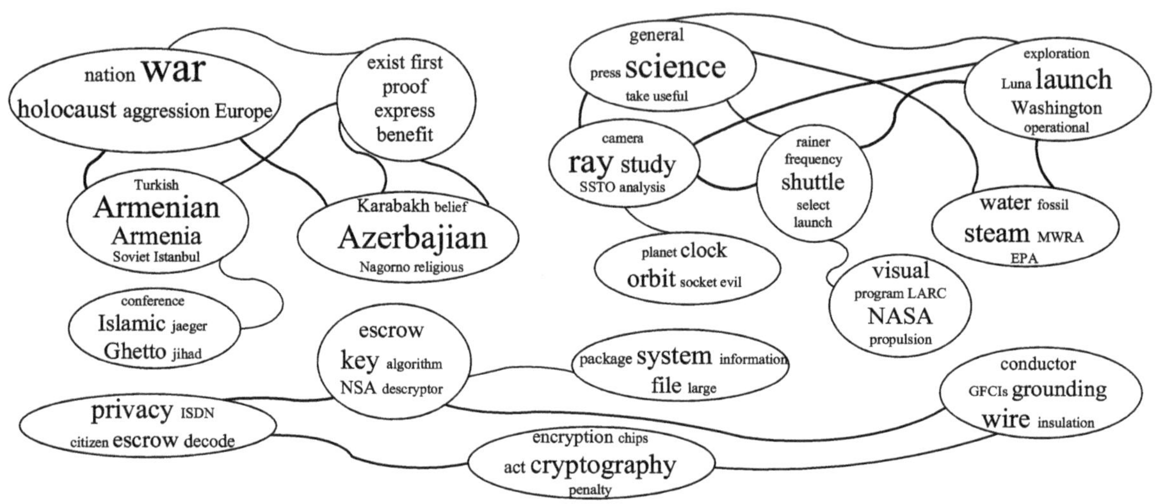

Figure 6: A portion of topic correlation graph learned from 20Newsgroups. Each node denotes a latent topic whose semantic meaning is characterized by the top words according to the topic's word distribution. The font size of each word is proportional to the word weight. Topics with correlation strength over some threshold are connected with edges. The thickness of the edges is proportional to the correlation strengths.

Figure 5, middle panel, measures the total training time with varying number of topics. We use the small 20Newsgroups dataset since on larger data (e.g., NYTimes and PubMed) the CTM and S-CTM models are usually too slow to converge in a reasonable time. We see that the training time of CTM increases quickly as more topics are used. S-CTM works well in this small data and model scale, but, as have been shown above, it is incapable of tackling larger problems. In contrast, our approach scales as efficiently as the simpler LDA model. Figure 5, right panel, evaluates the runtime of one inference iteration on a minibatch of 500 documents. when the topic size grows to a large number, CTM and S-CTM fail to finish one iteration in 2 hours. Our model, by contrast, keeps as scalable as LDA and considerably speeds up over CTM and S-CTM.

4.5 Visualization and Analysis

We qualitatively evaluate our approach by visualizing and exploring the extracted latent topics and correlation patterns.

Figure 6 visualizes the topic correlation graph inferred from the 20Newsgroups dataset. We can see many topics are strongly correlated to each other and exhibit clear correlation structure. For instance, the set of topics in the right upper region are mainly about astronomy and are interrelated closely, while their connections to information security topics shown in the lower part are weak. Figure 7 shows 100K topic embeddings and their correlations on the PubMed dataset. Related topics are close to each other in the embedding space, revealing diverse substructures of themes in the collection. Our model discovers very meaningful structures, providing insights into the semantics underlying the large text corpora and facilitating understanding of the large collection of topics.

5 CONCLUSIONS

We have developed a new correlated topic model which induces distributed vector representations of latent topics, and characterizes correlations with the closeness of topic vectors in the embedding

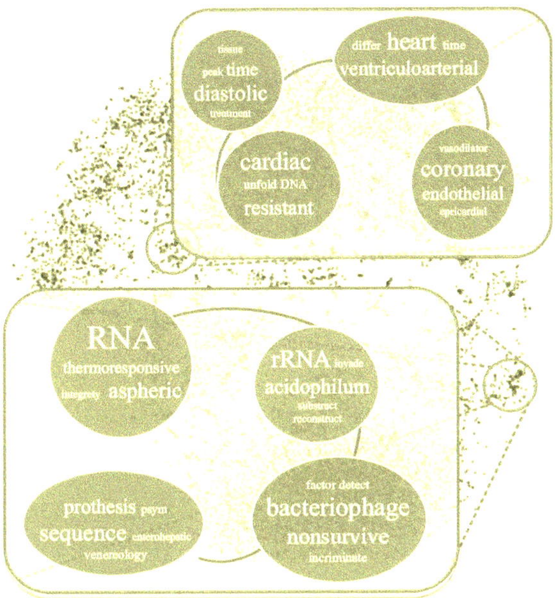

Figure 7: Visualization of 100K correlated topics on PubMed. See the captions of Figure 1 for more depictions.

space. Such modeling scheme, along with the sparsity-aware sampling in inference, enables highly efficient model training with linear time complexity in terms of the model size. Our approach scales to unprecedentedly large data and models, while achieving strong performance in document classification and retrieval.The proposed correlation method is generally applicable to other context, such as modeling word dependencies for improved topical coherence. It is interesting to further speedup of the model inference through variational neural Bayes techniques [13, 23] for amortized variational updates across data examples. Note that our model is particularly suitable to incorporate neural inference networks that, replacing the per-document variational embedding distributions, map documents into compact document embeddings directly. We are also interested in combining generative topic models with advanced deep text generative approaches [20, 21, 32] for improved text modeling.

ACKNOWLEDGMENTS

This research is supported by NSF IIS1447676, ONR N000141410684, and ONR N000141712463.

REFERENCES

[1] 2017. Supplementary material. (2017). www.cs.cmu.edu/~zhitingh/kddsupp

[2] Amr Ahmed and Eric Xing. 2007. On tight approximate inference of the logistic-normal topic admixture model. In *AISTATS*.

[3] Kayhan Batmanghelich, Ardavan Saeedi, Karthik Narasimhan, and Sam Gershman. 2016. Nonparametric Spherical Topic Modeling with Word Embeddings. In *ACL*.

[4] David M Blei,Th omas L Griffiths, and Michael I Jordan. 2010.Th e nested Chinese restaurant process and Bayesian nonparametric inference of topic hierarchies. *J. ACM* 57, 2 (2010), 7.

[5] David M Blei and John D Lafferty. 2007. A correlated topic model of science. *The Annals of Applied Statistics* (2007), 17–35.

[6] David M Blei, Andrew Y Ng, and Michael I Jordan. 2003. Latent Dirichlet allocation. *JMLR* 3, Jan (2003), 993–1022.

[7] Jordan L Boyd-Graber, David M Blei, and Xiaojin Zhu. 2007. A Topic Model for Word Sense Disambiguation.. In *EMNLP-CoNLL*. 1024–1033.

[8] Jianfei Chen, Kaiwei Li, Jun Zhu, and Wenguang Chen. 2016. WarpLDA: a Simple and Efficient O(1) Algorithm for Latent Dirichlet Allocation. In *VLDB*.

[9] Jianfei Chen, Jun Zhu, Zi Wang, Xun Zheng, and Bo Zhang. 2013. Scalable inference for logistic-normal topic models. In *NIPS*. 2445–2453.

[10] Rajarshi Das, Manzil Zaheer, and Chris Dyer. 2015. Gaussian LDA for topic models with word embeddings. In *ACL*.

[11] Kumar Dubey, Qirong Ho, Sinead A Williamson, and Eric P Xing. 2014. Dependent nonparametric trees for dynamic hierarchical clustering. In *NIPS*. 1152–1160.

[12] Yarin Gal and Zoubin Ghahramani. 2014. Pitfalls in the use of Parallel Inference for the Dirichlet Process.. In *ICML*. 208–216.

[13] Prasoon Goyal, Zhiting Hu, Xiaodan Liang, Chenyu Wang, and Eric Xing. 2017. Nonparametric Variational Auto-encoders for Hierarchical Representation Learning. *arXiv preprint arXiv:1703.07027* (2017).

[14] Aditya Grover and Jure Leskovec. 2016. node2vec: Scalable feature learning for networks. In *KDD*. ACM, 855–864.

[15] Geoffrey E Hinton and Ruslan R Salakhutdinov. 2009. Replicated softmax: an undirected topic model. In *NIPS*. 1607–1614.

[16] Matthew D Hoffman, David M Blei, Chong Wang, and John William Paisley. 2013. Stochastic variational inference. *JMLR* 14, 1 (2013), 1303–1347.

[17] Zhiting Hu, Qirong Ho, Avinava Dubey, and Eric P Xing. 2015. Large-scale Distributed Dependent Nonparametric Trees.. In *ICML*. 1651–1659.

[18] Zhiting Hu, Poyao Huang, Yuntian Deng, Yingkai Gao, and Eric P Xing. 2015. Entity Hierarchy Embedding.. In *ACL*. 1292–1300.

[19] Zhiting Hu, Gang Luo, Mrinmaya Sachan, Eric Xing, and Zaiqing Nie. 2016. Grounding topic models with knowledge bases. In *IJCAI*.

[20] Zhiting Hu, Zichao Yang, Xiaodan Liang, Ruslan Salakhutdinov, and Eric P Xing. 2017. Controllable Text Generation. *ICML* (2017).

[21] Zhiting Hu, Zichao Yang, Ruslan Salakhutdinov, and Eric P Xing. 2017. On Unifying Deep Generative Models. *arXiv preprint arXiv:1706.00550* (2017).

[22] Di Jiang, Rongzhong Lian, Lei Shi, and Hua Wu. 2016. Latent Topic Embedding. In *COLING*.

[23] Diederik P Kingma and Max Welling. 2013. Auto-encoding variational Bayes. *arXiv preprint arXiv:1312.6114* (2013).

[24] Miguel Lázaro-Gredilla. 2014. Doubly stochastic variational Bayes for non-conjugate inference. ICML.

[25] Tuan Le and Hady W Lauw. 2014. Semantic visualization for spherical representation. In *KDD*. ACM, 1007–1016.

[26] Tuan Minh Van LE and Hady W Lauw. 2014. Manifold learning for jointly modeling topic and visualization. (2014).

[27] Tao Lei, Yuan Zhang, Regina Barzilay, and Tommi Jaakkola. 2014. Low-rank tensors for scoring dependency structures. ACL.

[28] Aaron Q Li, Amr Ahmed, Sujith Ravi, and Alexander J Smola. 2014. Reducing the sampling complexity of topic models. In *KDD*. ACM, 891–900.

[29] Shaohua Li, Tat-Seng Chua, Jun Zhu, and Chunyan Miao. 2016. Generative topic embedding: a continuous representation of documents. In *ACL*.

[30] Wei Li and Andrew McCallum. 2006. Pachinko allocation: DAG-structured mixture models of topic correlations. In *ICML*. ACM, 577–584.

[31] Yuezhang Li, Ronghuo Zheng, Tian Tian, Zhiting Hu, Rahul Iyer, and Katia Sycara. 2016. Joint Embedding of Hierarchical Categories and Entities for Concept Categorization and Dataless Classification. In *COLING*.

[32] Xiaodan Liang, Zhiting Hu, Hao Zhang, Chuang Gan, and Eric P Xing. 2017. Recurrent Topic-Transition GAN for Visual Paragraph Generation. *arXiv preprint arXiv:1703.07022* (2017).

[33] Tomas Mikolov, Ilya Sutskever, Kai Chen, Greg Corrado, and Jeffrey Dean. 2013. Distributed Representations of Words and Phrases andTh eir Compositionality. In *NIPS*.

[34] David Mimno, MattHoff man, and David Blei. 2012. Sparse stochastic inference for latent Dirichlet allocation. *arXiv preprint arXiv:1206.6425* (2012).

[35] John Paisley, Chong Wang, David M Blei, et al. 2012.Th e discrete infinite logistic normal distribution. *Bayesian Analysis* 7, 4 (2012), 997–1034.

[36] Duangmanee Pew Putthividhya, Hagai T Attias, and Srikantan Nagarajan. 2009. Independent factor topic models. In *ICML*. ACM, 833–840.

[37] Rajesh Ranganath and David M Blei. 2016. Correlated random measures. *JASA* (2016).

[38] Jian Tang, MengQu , and Qiaozhu Mei. 2015. PTE: Predictive text embedding through large-scale heterogeneous text networks. In *KDD*. ACM, 1165–1174.

[39] Michalis K Titsias. 2009. Variational Learning of Inducing Variables in Sparse Gaussian Processes. In *AISTATS*, Vol. 5. 567–574.

[40] Yi Wang, Xuemin Zhao, Zhenlong Sun, Hao Yan, Lifeng Wang, Zhihui Jin, Liubin Wang, Yang Gao, Ching Law, and Jia Zeng. 2015. Peacock: Learning long-tail topic features for industrial applications. *TIST* 6, 4 (2015), 47.

[41] Andrew G Wilson, Zhiting Hu, Ruslan R Salakhutdinov, and Eric P Xing. 2016. Stochastic Variational Deep Kernel Learning. In *NIPS*. 2586–2594.

[42] Jinhui Yuan, Fei Gao, Qirong Ho, Wei Dai, Jinliang Wei, Xun Zheng, Eric Po Xing, Tie-Yan Liu, and Wei-Ying Ma. 2015. LightLDA: Big topic models on modest computer clusters. In *WWW*. ACM, 1351–1361.

Accelerating Innovation Through Analogy Mining

Tom Hope
The Hebrew University of Jerusalem
tom.hope@mail.huji.ac.il

Joel Chan
Carnegie Mellon University
joelchuc@cs.cmu.edu

Aniket Kittur
Carnegie Mellon University
nkittur@cs.cmu.edu

Dafna Shahaf
The Hebrew University of Jerusalem
dshahaf@cs.huji.ac.il

ABSTRACT

The availability of large idea repositories (e.g., the U.S. patent database) could significantly accelerate innovation and discovery by providing people with inspiration from solutions to analogous problems. However, finding useful analogies in these large, messy, real-world repositories remains a persistent challenge for either human or automated methods. Previous approaches include costly hand-created databases that have high relational structure (e.g., predicate calculus representations) but are very sparse. Simpler machine-learning/information-retrieval similarity metrics can scale to large, natural-language datasets, but struggle to account for structural similarity, which is central to analogy. In this paper we explore the viability and value of learning simpler structural representations, specifically, "problem schemas", which specify the purpose of a product and the mechanisms by which it achieves that purpose. Our approach combines crowdsourcing and recurrent neural networks to extract purpose and mechanism vector representations from product descriptions. We demonstrate that these learned vectors allow us to find analogies with higher precision and recall than traditional information-retrieval methods. In an ideation experiment, analogies retrieved by our models significantly increased people's likelihood of generating creative ideas compared to analogies retrieved by traditional methods. Our results suggest a promising approach to enabling computational analogy at scale is to learn and leverage weaker structural representations.

KEYWORDS

Computational analogy; innovation; creativity; product dimensions; text mining; text embedding

1 INTRODUCTION

The ability to find useful analogies is critical to driving innovation in a variety of domains. Many important discoveries in science were driven by analogies: for example, an analogy between bacteria and slot machines helped Salvador Luria advance the theory of bacterial mutation. Analogical reasoning forms the foundation of law, with the effectiveness of an argument often dependent on its legal precedents [32]. Innovation is often spurred by analogy as well: an analogy to a bicycle allowed the Wright brothers to design a steerable aircraft. Whether architecture, design, technology, art, or mathematics, the ability to find and apply patterns from other domains is fundamental to human achievement [9, 17, 22, 26].

The explosion of available online data represents an unprecedented opportunity to find new analogies and accelerate human progress across domains. For example, the US Patent database has full text for more than 9 million patents issued from 1976 to the present. InnoCentive[1] contains more than 40,000 business, social, policy, scientific, and technical problems and solutions. Quirky[2], a company that assists inventors in the development process, has had over 2 million product idea submissions. OpenIDEO[3] receives hundreds of solutions for a variety of social problems. Millions of scientific papers and legal cases are searchable on Google Scholar.

We believe these data form a treasure trove of analogies that can accelerate problem solving, innovation and discovery. In a striking recent example, a car mechanic invented a simple device to ease difficult childbirths by drawing an analogy to extracting a cork from a wine bottle, which he discovered in a YouTube video. This award-winning device could save millions of lives, particularly in developing countries. We imagine a future in which people could search through data based on deep analogical similarity rather than simple keywords; lawyers or legal scholars could find legal precedents sharing similar systems of relations to a contemporary case; and product or service designers could mine myriad potential solutions to their problem.

However, sifting through these massive data sources to find relevant and useful analogies poses a serious challenge for both humans and machines. In humans, memory retrieval is highly sensitive to surface similarity, favoring near, within-domain analogs that share object attributes over far, structurally similar analogs that share object relations [13–15, 20]. Analogical processing also incurs a heavy cognitive load, taxing working memory when even a few relations are required to be processed at once [16]. Thus searching through datasets with thousands or millions of items for structurally similar ones may be a daunting prospect.

Finding analogies is challenging for machines as well, as it is based on having an understanding of the deep relational similarity between two entities that may be very different in terms of surface attributes [12]. For example, Chrysippus' analogy between sound waves and water waves required ignoring many different surface features between the two [20]. Recent advances in data

KDD '17, August 13-17, 2017, Halifax, NS, Canada
 978-1-4503-4887-4/17/08...$15.00
DOI: 10.1145/3097983.3098038

[1] innocentive.com
[2] quirky.com
[3] OpenIDEO.com

mining and information retrieval include a variety of natural language techniques that use words, parts of speech or other language feature-based vector representations in order to calculate similarity measures (see [31]). Examples include word embedding models like Word2Vec [24], vector-space models like Latent Semantic Indexing [10], and probabilistic topic modeling approaches like Latent Dirichlet Allocation [4]. These approaches excel at detecting *surface similarity*, but are often unable to detect similarity between documents whose word distributions are disparate. The problem is especially acute when the source and target domains are different (for example, bacterial mutation and slot machines).

Another approach to finding analogies has been to use the structural similarity of sentences or texts, such as using coupled clustering for detecting structural correspondence of text [5, 35]. However, these approaches typically require rich data sets with clear substructures, whereas most descriptions of problems or ideas in existing online databases are short, sparse, or lack consistent structure. Other current methods focus on very narrow analogy tasks, such as four-term analogy problems (teacher:student = doctor:?), in particular with short strings (ABC:ABD = KJI:?) [19]. In contrast, we wish to find analogies in real world data, which involve complex representations and a diverse set of analogical relations.

In this paper, we are interested in **automatically discovering analogies in large, unstructured data sets**. In particular, we focus on a corpus of **product innovations**. There are two insights behind our approach that we believe may make this problem tractable despite its longstanding status as a "holy grail" in both cognitive science and AI. First, rather than trying to solve the problem of fully structured analogical reasoning, we instead explore the idea that for retrieving practically useful analogies, we can use weaker structural representations that can be learned and reasoned with at scale (in other words, there is a tradeoff between the ease of extraction of a structure and its expressivity). Specifically, we investigate the weaker structural representation of an idea's *purpose* and *mechanism* as a way to find useful analogies. The second insight is that advances in crowdsourcing have made it possible to harvest rich signals of analogical structure that can help machine learning models learn in ways that would not be possible with existing datasets alone.

This paper combines these two ideas to contribute a technique for computationally finding analogies from unstructured text datasets that go beyond surface features. At a high level, our approach uses the behavioral traces of crowd workers searching for analogies and identifying the purpose and mechanisms of ideas, then developing machine learning models that develop similarity metrics suited for analogy mining. We demonstrate that learning purpose and mechanism representations allows us to find analogies with higher precision and recall than traditional information-retrieval methods based on TF-IDF, LSA, LDA and GloVe, in challenging noisy settings. Furthermore, we use our similarity metrics to automatically find *far* analogies – products with high purpose similarity, and low mechanism similarity. In a user study, we show that we are able to "inspire" participants to generate more innovative ideas than alternative baselines, increasing the relative proportion of positively-rated ideas by at least 25%.

2 LEARNING A REPRESENTATION FOR ANALOGIES

2.1 Motivation

Much work in computation analogy has focused on fully structured data, often with logic-based representations. For example [11],

```
CAUSE(GREATER-THAN[TEMPERATURE(coffee),
      TEMPERATURE (ice-cube)],
      FLOW(coffee, ice-cube, heat, bar))
```

These representations, while very expressive, are notoriously difficult to obtain. In this section, we investigate a weaker structural representation. Our goal is to come up with a representation that can be *learned*, while still being expressive enough to allow analogical mining.

Analogies between product ideas are intricately related to their *purpose* and *mechanism*. Informally, we think of a product's purpose as "what it does, what it is used for", and a product's mechanism is "how it does it, how it works". The importance of a product's purpose and mechanism as core components of analogy are theoretically rooted in early cognitive psychology work on schema induction which define the core components of a schema as a goal and proposed solution to it (e.g., [15]). More recently, the practical value of defining a problem schema as a purpose and mechanism has been demonstrated to have empirical benefits in finding and using analogies to augment idea generation (e.g., [38–41]).

Separating an idea into purpose and mechanisms enables core analogical innovation processes such as re-purposing: For a given product (such as a kitchen-sink cleaner) and its purpose, finding another way to put it to use (cleaning windows). To that end, assume (for the moment) that we have for each product i two vectors, $\mathbf{p}_i$ and $\mathbf{m}_i$, representing the product's purpose and mechanism, respectively. Using this representation, we are able to apply rich queries to our corpus of products, such as:

- *Same purpose, different mechanism.* Given the corpus of all products $\mathcal{P}$, a product i with (normalized) purpose and mechanism vectors $\mathbf{p}_i, \mathbf{m}_i$, and distance metrics $d_p(\cdot,\cdot), d_m(\cdot,\cdot)$ between purpose and mechanism vectors (respectively), solve:

$$\begin{aligned} &\underset{\tilde{i}\in\mathcal{P}}{\operatorname{argmin}}\; d_p(\mathbf{p}_i, \mathbf{p}_{\tilde{i}}) \\ &\quad s.t. d_m(\mathbf{m}_i, \mathbf{m}_{\tilde{i}}) \geq \text{threshold}, \end{aligned} \tag{1}$$

- *Same Mechanism, different purpose.* Solve:

$$\begin{aligned} &\underset{\tilde{i}\in\mathcal{P}}{\operatorname{argmin}}\; d_m(\mathbf{m}_i, \mathbf{m}_{\tilde{i}}) \\ &\quad s.t. d_p(\mathbf{p}_i, \mathbf{p}_{\tilde{i}}) \geq \text{threshold}, \end{aligned} \tag{2}$$

The decomposition of products into purpose and mechanism also draws inspiration from engineering *functional models* and ontologies for describing products [18]. Although there is no set common definition of functions [25], much research on functionality has been conducted in areas such as functional representation, engineering design and value engineering. The scope of these ontologies, however, is highly "mechanistic" or engineering-oriented, while in many cases we observe in product data the purpose of a product is more naturally understood in others term – such as whether it is for entertainment, leisure, or more serious purposes, who is the target user (adults, children), and so forth.

Importantly, our dataset of product descriptions contains noisy texts, often written informally by non-professional people. In these texts product descriptions are often lacking detail or are ill-defined. To automatically describe a product in terms of a formal functional model would require an inordinate amount of meticulous data annotation and collection by professional engineers over a large number of product descriptions. We thus resort to a softer approach, hoping that a compromise on the level of detail will enable data-driven methods to automatically extract useful representations of product purpose and mechanism.

Finally, we also make note of the potentially wider applicability of automatically extracting these representations from real-word product descriptions. Identifying the key components and functions of products could conceivably improve (or augment) search capabilities in internal or external product databases, and perhaps enhance recommender systems by better understanding what a user is looking for in a product and what a product offers. This last idea is connected to a line of work on "product dimensions" [23], in which it is shown that *implicitly* identifying the properties of products (such as that Harry Potter is a book about wizards), helps in improving recommendations. The authors propose a method that combines ratings data with textual product reviews, hoping to implicitly recover topics in the text that inform recommendations. We too look at product dimensions, but target only two that are more abstract and broad, and directly learn them in a supervised fashion from annotated data.

2.2 Data

Innovation Corpus. We test our approach with a corpus of product descriptions from Quirky.com, an online crowdsourced product innovation website. Quirky is representative of the kinds of datasets we are interested in, because it is large (at the time of writing, it hosts upwards of 10,000 product ideas, of which our corpus included 8500), unstructured (ideas are described in natural language), and covers a variety of domains (invention categories) which makes cross-domain analogies possible. The following example illustrates the typical length and "messiness" of product ideas in this dataset:

```
Thirsty too
  Pet water bowl/dispenser for your vehicle cup holder.
  Over spill lip to catch water
  Has optional sleeve for larger cup holders
  Optional floor base
  One way valve so water cant over flow from bottle
  Small reservoir
  Reservoir acts as backsplash
  Water bottle attachment
  Holds water in your vehicle cupholder for pet
  Foldable handle to get unit out of holder
  Dishwasher safe
  Optional sleeve for larger cup holders
```

Collecting Purpose and Mechanism Data. In addition to the Quirky innovation corpus, we needed to collect analogy-specific data to train our model. Previous approaches to creating structured representations of items for analogical computation, for example predicate logic, are extremely heavyweight and can take tens of person-hours for complex items [37]. Instead, we aim to develop a lightweight task that avoids complex structure but instead relies on the cognitive expertise and intuitions of people to be able to separate the purpose of a product from its mechanism. By doing so we can

Figure 1: Collecting purpose and mechanism annotations from the crowd.

scale up the collection of purpose and mechanism labels through the use of microtasks and crowdsourcing markets [21]. Specifically, we show Amazon Mechanical Turk (AMT) crowd workers a product description, asking them to annotate the parts of the text they consider to be about the purposes of the product, and the parts related to mechanisms. We frame the problem in simple terms, guiding workers to look for words/phrases/chunks of text talking about "what the product does, what it is good for" (purposes), and "how it works, what are its components" (mechanisms). As seen in Figure 1, we juxtapose two copies of the product text side-by-side, to ease cognitive load and encourage workers not to give purpose and mechanism tags that are too similar or overlapping, thus capturing a potentially richer and more distinct signal. Our corpus consisted of 8500 products. Each product was annotated by four workers.

Collecting Analogies. In previous, preliminary work [7], we explored the use of crowdsourcing to label analogies, collecting labeled examples of analogies (product pairs) that were fed into a metric-learning deep learning model. While showing promising results, the process of collecting labeled analogies proved expensive, requiring considerable cognitive effort from workers and thus more time, limiting the number of labels that can realistically be collected. In addition, in that work, the deep learning model was blind to the rich structures of purpose and mechanism, and had no hope of recovering them automatically due to relative data scarcity. In this paper we take a different approach, focusing our resources on collecting purpose and mechanism annotations from the crowd, while collecting only a small number of curated labeled analogies strictly for the purpose of evaluation (see Section 3.1 for details).

2.3 Method

2.3.1 Extracting Purpose and Mechanism vectors. In this section, we describe our approach to learning to extract purpose and mechanism product representations. We begin with a set of N training product texts $\mathcal{X}_N = \{\mathbf{x}_1, \mathbf{x}_2, \ldots, \mathbf{x}_N\}$, where each $\mathbf{x}_i$ is a variable-length sequence of tokens $(x_i^1, x_i^2, \ldots, x_i^T)$. For each document $\mathbf{x}_i$, we collect a set of K purpose annotations and K mechanism annotations, where K is the number of workers who annotate each document. We define the *purpose annotation* to be a binary vector

$$\tilde{\mathbf{p}}_{i_k} = (\tilde{p}_{i_k}^1, \tilde{p}_{i_k}^2, \ldots, \tilde{p}_{i_k}^T)$$

of the same length as $\mathbf{x}_i$, with $\tilde{p}_{i_k}^j = 1$ if token x_i^j is annotated as purpose by annotator k, $\tilde{p}_{i_k}^j = 0$ if not. In the same way, we denote the *mechanism annotation* with

$$\tilde{\mathbf{m}}_{i_k} = (\tilde{m}^1_{i_k}, \tilde{m}^2_{i_k}, \ldots, \tilde{m}^T_{i_k})$$

While on the surface this setting appears to lend itself naturally to sequence-to-sequence learning [33], there are a few important differences. A key difference is that in our setting the problem of interest is not to learn to recover the latent $\tilde{\mathbf{p}}$ ($\tilde{\mathbf{m}}$) exactly for unseen products, but rather to extract some form of representation that captures the *overall* purpose and mechanism. That is, what we do care about is the semantic meaning or context our representation captures with respect to product purposes or mechanisms, rather than predicting any individual words. Additionally, sequence-to-sequence models typically involve heavier machinery and work well on large data sets, not suitable for our scenario were we have at most a few thousands of tagged examples.

On a more technical note, instead of one sequence in the output, we now have K. A simple solution is to aggregate the annotations, for example by taking the union or intersection of annotations, or considering a token x^j_i to be positively annotated if it has at least $\frac{K}{2}$ positive labels. Richer aggregations may also be used.

Considering that our focus here is to capture an overall representation (not predict a precise sequence), however, we resort to a simple and soft aggregation of the K annotations. In simple terms, we look at all words that were annotated, and take a TF-IDF-weighted average of their word vectors.

In more formal terms, let $\mathbf{w}_i = (w^1_i, w^2_i, \ldots, w^T_i)$ be the sequence of GloVe [27] word vectors (pre-trained on Common Crawl web data), representing $(x^1_i, x^2_i, \ldots, x^T_i)$. We select all x_i word vectors for which $\tilde{p}^j_{i_k} = 1$ ($\tilde{m}^j_{i_k} = 1$) for some k, and concatenate them into one sequence. We then compute the TF-IDF scores for tokens in this sequence, find the D tokens with top TF-IDF scores ($D = 5$ in our experiments), and take the TF-IDF-weighted average of their corresponding D GloVe vectors. We denote the resulting weighted-average vectors as $\mathbf{p}_i \in \mathbb{R}^{300}$ and $\mathbf{m}_i \in \mathbb{R}^{300}$ for purpose and mechanism annotations, respectively. We consider $\mathbf{p}_i, \mathbf{m}_i$ to be *target* vectors we aim to predict for unseen texts.

Embedding (short) texts with a weighted-average of word vectors (such as with TF-IDF) can lead to surprisingly good results across many tasks [2]. Furthermore, in our case this simple weighted-average has several advantages. As we will next see, it lends itself to a straightforward machine learning setting, suitable for our modestly-sized data set, and for the objective of finding an overall vector representation that can be used in multiple ways, chiefly the computation of **purpose-wise and mechanism-wise distances** between products. Additionally, by concatenating all annotations and weighting by TF-IDF, we naturally give more weight in the average vector to words that are more frequently annotated – thus giving higher impact to words considered important by all annotators with respect to purpose/mechanism.

2.3.2 Learning purpose and mechanism. We now have N training product texts $\mathcal{X}_N = \{\mathbf{x}_1, \mathbf{x}_2, \ldots, \mathbf{x}_N\}$, and N corresponding target tuples $\mathcal{Y}_N = \{(\mathbf{p}_1, \mathbf{m}_1), (\mathbf{p}_2, \mathbf{m}_2), \ldots, (\mathbf{p}_N, \mathbf{m}_N)\}$. We represent each $\mathbf{x}_i$ with its pre-trained GloVe vectors, $\mathbf{w}_i$. Our goal is to learn a function $f(\mathbf{w}_i)$ that predicts $(\mathbf{p}_i, \mathbf{m}_i)$. To this end, we model $f(\cdot)$ with a Recurrent Neural Network as follows. The network takes as input the variable-length sequence $\mathbf{w}_i$. This sequence is processed with a bidirectional RNN (BiRNN) [3] with one GRU layer. The BiRNN consists of the forward GRU $\overrightarrow{GRU}$ which reads the sequence $\mathbf{w}_i$ from w^1_i to w^T_i, and a backward GRU $\overleftarrow{GRU}$ which reads from w^T_i to w^1_i, thus in practice capturing the neighborhood of w^j_i from "both directions":

$$\overrightarrow{h^j_i} = \overrightarrow{GRU}(w^j_i),\ \overleftarrow{h^j_i} = \overleftarrow{GRU}(w^j_i),\ h^j_i = [\overrightarrow{h^j_i}, \overleftarrow{h^j_i}],$$

where we concatenate forward and backward GRU hidden states to obtain h^j_i, our representation for word j in product i. In our case, we are interested in h^T_i which captures the entire product text.

Next, let $\mathbf{W}_p$ and $\mathbf{W}_m$ be **purpose and mechanism weight matrices**, respectively. h^T_i is a *shared* representation of the document, which we now transform into two new vectors, $\hat{\mathbf{p}}_i, \hat{\mathbf{m}}_i$, forming our purpose and mechanism predictions for product i:

$$\hat{\mathbf{p}}_i = \mathbf{W}_p h^T_i,\ \hat{\mathbf{m}}_i = \mathbf{W}_m h^T_i. \tag{3}$$

Parameters in this network are then tuned to minimize the *MSE* loss averaged over $(\mathbf{p}_i, \mathbf{m}_i)$. In some scenarios, we may care more about predicting either purpose or mechanism, and in that case could incorporate a weight term in the loss function, giving more weight to either $\mathbf{p}_i$ or $\mathbf{m}_i$.

2.3.3 Purpose and Mechanism vector interpretations. Here, we give intuition about the kinds of representations extracted and the ability to interpret them with very simple tools. We first compute $\hat{\mathbf{p}}, \hat{\mathbf{m}}$ for held-out product texts. Then, in the first approach to interpreting purpose and mechanism predictions, we find the top 10 GloVe word vectors w most similar to each of $\hat{\mathbf{p}}, \hat{\mathbf{m}}$, among all vectors that appear in our vocabulary.

In the second approach, we aim to recover a set of 10 word vectors such that their sparse linear combination approximately gives $\hat{\mathbf{p}}$ or $\hat{\mathbf{m}}$. More formally, in the spirit of the sparse coding approach in [1], consider the collection of all word vectors in our vocabulary V, $w_1, w_2, \ldots, w_{|V|}$. We stack them into a matrix $\mathbf{W}$. We aim to solve the following optimization problem:

$$\underset{\mathbf{a}}{\operatorname{argmin}} ||\hat{\mathbf{p}}_i - \mathbf{W}\mathbf{a}||^2_2 \quad s.t. \quad ||\mathbf{a}||_0 \le 10, \tag{4}$$

where $\mathbf{a}$ is a weight vector. Optimization can be done with the Orthogonal Matching Pursuit (OMP) [6] greedy algorithm.

In Table 1, we display some examples of applying these two simple methods, to product texts in test data (not seen during training). The first product is a yogurt maker machine, *used for* concentrating yogurt under heat, and to *reduce* time and energy. We observe that words selected as most related to our purpose vector representation include *food, produce, concentrate, making, energy, reduce* and also words that are typical in the language used in describing advantages of products in our data, such as *especially, whole, enough, much.* Mechanism words, are indeed overall of a much more "mechanical" nature, including *liquid, heat, cooling, pump, steel, machine.* In the other examples too, we observe the same pattern: Words selected as most closely-related to purpose or mechanism representations, using simple techniques, empirically appear to reflect corresponding properties in the product text, both in language and in deeper meaning.

Table 1: Purpose and Mechanism vector interpretation examples. Descriptions shortened. Sparse coding shows only words with $|\alpha| \geq 0.1$

Product	Purpose words	Mechanism words
A small yogurt maker machine for concentrating yogurt under heat and vacuum. Has a round base in drum with customized scooper, washable stainless steel drum parts. Reduce time and energy used.	**Top similar:** concentrate, enough, food, even, much, especially, reduce, produce, whole **Sparse coding:** making, energy, yogurt, drum, concentrate, vacuum, heavy, foods, aches, service	**Top similar:** liquid, heat, cooling, pump, steel, machine, water, heating, electric **Sparse coding:** vacuum, cooled, drum, heavy, ingredients, design, renewable, stainless, vending
A cover placed on a car truck to protect from hail. Elastic perimeter to prevent wind from blowing under cover. Snap or velcro slits to open door without removing cover. Strong attachment so it wonfit blow away. Inflatable baffles that cover the top, front windshield, side.	**Top similar:** storm, hail, rain, roofs, doors, wind, front, winds, walls **Sparse coding:** roof, hail, padded, obstructing, defenses, diesel, windshield, wets	**Top similar:** roof, cover, lining, zipper, bottom, hood, plastic, flap, rubber **Sparse coding:** front, cover, insulation, hail, buckle, sling, watertight, cutter, blowing
A leash accessory with removable compartments for phone, cards cash, keys, poop bags, treats, bowl. Walk your dog and carry your essentials without pockets or a purse bag.	**Top similar:** bags, purse, wallet, carry, leash, backpack, pocket, dog, luggage **Sparse coding:** bag, leash, compartments, pets, phone, eats, practical, handing, pull	**Top similar:** leash, pouch, purse, pocket, bags, pockets, strap, compartment, backpack **Sparse coding:** leash, bag, compartments, hand, holders

3 EVALUATION: ANALOGIES

As typically done in the context of learning document representations, the key approach to quantitative evaluation is a down-stream task such as document classification. We now evaluate the predicted $\hat{\mathbf{p}}_i, \hat{\mathbf{m}}_i$ in the context of their ability to capture distances that reflect analogies, which is the primary focus of this paper. To do so, we first create a dataset of analogies and non-analogies.

3.1 Collecting analogies via crowdsourcing

We crowdsourced analogy finding within a set of about 8000 Quirky products. AMT crowd workers used our search interface to collect analogies – pairs of products – for about 200 seed documents. The search task is powered by a simple word-matching approach. To deal with word variants, we added lemmas for each word to the bag-of-words associated with each product. Each search query was also expanded with lemmas associated with each query term. Search results were ranked in descending order of number of matching terms. Median completion time for each seed was 7 minutes (workers could complete as many seeds as they wanted). Further, to deal with potential data quality issues, we recruited 3 workers for each seed (to allow for majority-vote aggregation).

Pairs that were tagged as **matches** became positive examples in our analogy dataset. However, coming up with negative examples was more difficult. Borrowing from information retrieval, we assume that people read the search results sequentially, and treat the **implicitly rejected** documents (i.e., documents that were not matches, despite appearing before matches) as negatives. It is important to remember that these documents are not necessarily real negatives. To further increase the chance that the document has actually been read, we restrict ourselves to the top-5 results.

Challenges. Getting workers to understand the concept of analogies and avoiding tagging products that are superficially similar (e.g., "both smartphone-based") as analogies proved a challenge. To address this, we scaffolded the search task by first requiring workers to generate a schema (or "pattern") to describe the core purpose and mechanism of the product, first in concrete terms, and then in more abstract terms (see an example pattern Figure 2). Workers were then instructed to find other products that matched the abstract schema they created. We found that this scaffolded workflow reduced the number of superficial matches; yet, a non-negligible portion of the pairs labeled as positive were either superficial matches or near analogies (i.e., analogies with many shared surface features), likely due to the strong tendency towards surface features in analogical retrieval [14]. Further, because products were multifaceted, search results may have been implicitly rejected even if they were analogous to the seed if the matching schema was different from the one initially identified by the worker.

3.2 Quantitative results

In Table 2, we present precision and recall @ K results. We rank all pairs in the test data ($N = 2500$, with training done on about 5500 products) based on their distances, according to various metrics, including our own. In summary, across all levels our approach outperformed the baselines, despite a challenging noisy setting. A considerable portion of test product pairs were tagged by workers as analogies despite having only surface similarity, creating mislabeled positive examples that favor the surface-based baselines. In addition to ranking by purpose-only and mechanism-only, we also concatenate both representations in a vector $[\mathbf{p}_i, \mathbf{m}_i]$ for product i, and observe an overall improvement in results, although the "one-dimensional" use of either purpose or mechanism alone still beats the baselines. Using $\mathbf{m}_i$ only led to considerably better results when looking at precision @ top 1%, perhaps indicating a tendency by workers to find more mechanism-based analogies.

4 EVALUATION: IDEATION BY ANALOGY

Since a major application of the enhanced search and retrieval capabilities of analogy is enhanced creativity, we now evaluate the **usefulness** of our algorithms. We examine the degree to which our model's retrieved output improves people's ability to generate

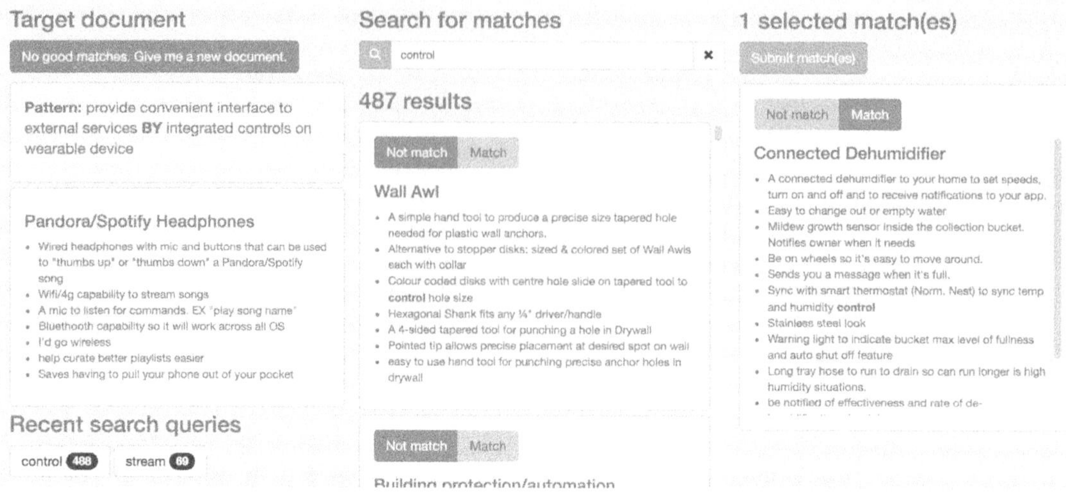

Figure 2: Screenshot of analogy search interface

Table 2: Model results. Precision, recall of positive labels @ top-scoring pairs (ranked by similarity).

Method	Top 1%	Top 5%	Top 10%	Top 15%	Top 20%	Top 25%
Glove + TF-IDF (top 5 words)	0.565, 0.018	0.515, 0.081	0.489, 0.153	0.468, 0.22	0.443, 0.277	0.434, 0.339
Glove + TF-IDF	0.609, 0.019	0.559, 0.087	0.487, 0.152	0.47, 0.22	0.449, 0.281	0.426 ,0.332
TF-IDF	0.63,0.02	0.537, 0.084	0.5 0.156	0.468, 0.22	0.464, 0.29	0.441, 0.344
LSA	0.413, 0.013	0.463, 0.072	0.446, 0.14	0.435, 0.204	0.413, 0.258	0.399, 0.312
LDA	0.435, 0.014	0.432, 0.067	0.414, 0.129	0.398, 0.187	0.384, 0.24	0.381, 0.298
Purpose only	0.674, 0.021	0.586, 0.092	0.535, 0.167	0.505, 0.237	0.496, 0.31	0.465, 0.363
Mechanism only	**0.739**, 0.023	0.586, 0.092	0.551, 0.172	**0.507**, 0.237	0.482, 0.301	0.47, 0.368
concat(Purpose, Mechanism)	0.696, 0.022	**0.612**, 0.096	**0.555**, 0.173	**0.507**, 0.237	**0.504**, 0.315	**0.478**, 0.373

creative ideas, compared to other methods. To do so we use a standard ideation task in which participants redesign an existing product [36], and are given inspirations to help them – either from our approach, a TF-IDF baseline, or a random baseline.

See Figure 3 for an example task given to crowdworkers. Here, the task was to redesign a cell phone case that can charge the phone. The middle part shows the top 3 inspirations per condition.

Our assumption is that our approach will provide participants with useful examples that are similar in purpose but provide diverse mechanisms that will help them explore more diverse parts of the design space in generating their ideas. We hypothesize that this approach will lead to better results than the TF-IDF baseline (highly relevant but non-diverse inspirations, focusing on surface features) and the random baseline (highly diverse but low relevance).

4.1 Generating near-purpose far-mechanism analogies

To generate inspirations for the redesign task, we start by using the learned purpose and mechanism representations $\mathbf{p}_i, \mathbf{m}_i$ for each document i (in the test set) to apply rich queries to our corpus of products. In particular, assuming all vectors are normalized to unit euclidean norm, we can find pairs of products i_1, i_2 such that $d_p(\mathbf{p}_{i_1}, \mathbf{p}_{i_2}) = \mathbf{p}_{i_1} \cdot \mathbf{p}_{i_2}$ is high (near purpose), while $d_m(\mathbf{m}_{i_1}, \mathbf{m}_{i_2}) = \mathbf{m}_{i_1} \cdot \mathbf{m}_{i_2}$ is low (far mechanism). This type of reasoning, as discussed above, is a core element of analogical reasoning.

We take this idea one step forward by *clustering* by purpose and *diversifying* by mechanism. In more detail, we take a set of 2500 products not seen during training, and follow a simple and intuitive procedure as follows. Let $\mathcal{P}_T$ denote our corpus of test-set products. Let S denote the number of seed products we wish to use in our experiment. Let M denote the number of inspirations we wish to produce for each seed $\{1, \ldots, P\}$.

Clustering by purpose. First, we find groups of products with similar purpose by clustering by our purpose representation.

- Run K-means ($K = 50$), based on vectors $\mathbf{p}_i, \forall i \in \mathcal{P}_T$. (Note that when all vectors are normalized, the euclidean norm on which K-means is based is equivalent to the cosine distance).
- For each cluster $k \in \{1, \ldots, K\}$, compute an intra-distance measure (purpose homogeneity) d_k. We use the *MSE*. Prune clusters with less than M instances. Rank clusters by d_k in descending order, pick top P. Call this set of clusters $\mathcal{K}_{\text{top-purpose}}$, with corresponding cluster centers $\bar{\mathbf{p}}_1, \ldots, \bar{\mathbf{p}}_S$.
- For each cluster k in $\mathcal{K}_{\text{top-purpose}}$, select the product i whose vector $\mathbf{p}_i$ is nearest to the cluster center $\bar{\mathbf{p}}_k$. This is our k^{th} **seed product**, denoted by s_k.

Result diversification by mechanism. We now have a set of seed products, each with a corresponding cluster of products with similar purposes. Next, we need to pick M inspirations per seed.

For each seed s_k, we have a set of *candidate matches* $\mathcal{U}_{s_k}$, all from the same purpose cluster. We empirically observe that in the purpose-clusters $\mathcal{K}_{\text{top-purpose}}$ we generate, some vectors are highly similar to the seed with respect to mechanism, and some less so. In order to generate far-mechanism results for each seed from candidate set $\mathcal{U}_{s_k}$, we now turn to diversification of results.

The problem of extracting a well-diversified subset of results from a larger set of candidates has seen a lot of work, prominently in the context of information retrieval (which is closely related to our setting). In our case, we assume to have found a set of relevant results $\mathcal{U}_{s_k}$ according to purpose metric $d_p(\cdot, \cdot)$, and diversify by mechanism metric $d_m(\cdot, \cdot)$.

There are many ways to diversify results, mainly differing by objective function and constraints. Two canonical measures are the MAX-MIN and MAX-AVG dispersion problems [28]. In the former, we aim to find a subset $\mathcal{M} \subseteq \mathcal{U}_{s_k}$ such that $|\mathcal{M}| = M$, and

$$\min_{\mathbf{m}_{i_1}, \mathbf{m}_{i_2} \in \mathcal{M}} d_m(\mathbf{m}_{i_1}, \mathbf{m}_{i_2})$$

is maximized. In the latter, we aim to find a subset $\mathcal{M} \subseteq \mathcal{U}_{s_k}$ such that $|\mathcal{M}| = M$, and

$$\frac{2}{M(M-1)} \sum_{\mathbf{m}_{i_1}, \mathbf{m}_{i_2} \in \mathcal{M}} d_m(\mathbf{m}_{i_1}, \mathbf{m}_{i_2})$$

is maximized. In other words, in the MAX-MIN problem we find a subset of products $\mathcal{M}$ such that the distance between the two nearest products is maximized. In the MAX-AVG problem, we find a subset such the average distance between pairs is maximized. Both problems admit simple greedy algorithms with constant-factor approximations [28]. We choose the MAX-MIN problem, since we want to avoid displaying too-similar results even once to a user (who may become frustrated and not proceed to read more inspirations).

We solve the problem using the GMM algorithm mentioned in [28]. Each iteration of GMM selects a candidate $m \in \mathcal{U}_{s_k} - \mathcal{M}$ such that the minimum distance from m to an already-selected product in $\mathcal{M}$ is the largest among remaining candidates in $\mathcal{U}_{s_k} - \mathcal{M}$, where we measure distance according to our mechanism metric $d_m(\cdot, \cdot)$.

In our experiments, we set $P = 12, M = 12$, for 12 seeds and 12 matches each, respectively.

4.2 Experiment design

We recruited 38 AMT workers to redesign an existing product, a common creative task in design firms [36]. To ensure robustness of effects, the experiment included 12 different "seed" products. Participants were paid $1.5 for their participation.

To maximize statistical power, we utilized a within-subjects design with a single manipulated factor, *inspiration_type*:

- ANALOGY: participants receive 12 product inspirations retrieved by our method detailed above, using near-purpose far-mechanism clustering and diversification.
- BASELINE: SURFACE: participants receive product inspirations retrieved using TF-IDF, by finding the top 12 products similar to the seed. This baseline is meant to simulate current search engines.
- BASELINE: RANDOM: participants receive 12 product inspirations sampled at random from our product corpus.

Since we used a within-subjects design, participants completed the redesign task under each of the 3 inspiration_type conditions.

Figure 3: Overview and excerpts of the ideation experiment. Top: Seed product. Workers were asked to solve the same problem in a different way. Middle: Top 3 inspirations for each of the conditions. Note that the TF-IDF baseline returns results from the same domain, while our method returns a broader range of products. Bottom: Ideas generated by users exposed to the different conditions.

The order of conditions was counterbalanced to prevent order effects. To ensure unbiased permutations, we used the Fisher-Yates shuffle to assign seeds to conditions, so that every seed would be seen in all conditions (by different users).

Since prior work has shown that people benefit more from analogies if they receive them after ideation has begun [34], the ideation task proceeded in two phases: 1) generating ideas unassisted for one minute, then 2) receiving 12 inspirations and generating more ideas for 6 minutes. The inspirations were laid out in four pages, 3 inspirations per page, and the users could freely browse them.

Figure 3 provides an overview of the experiment and an excerpt from the data. The original task was to redesign an existing product, in this case a cell phone charger case. The SURFACE baseline retrieves products that are very phone-related (or case related). In contrast, our algorithm retrieves diverse results such as a human pulley-powered electricity generator suit. The bottom of the figure shows ideas generated by users in each condition. Interestingly, the user exposed to our approach suggested a case that generates power using movement, potentially inspired by the suit.

4.3 Results

Measures. We are interested in the ability of our approach to enhance people's ability to generate creative ideas. Following [29], we measured creative output as the rate at which a participant generates good ideas. We recruited five graduate students to judge each idea generated by our participants as good or not. Our definition of "good" follows the standard definition of creativity in the literature as a combination of novelty, quality, and feasibility [30]. Each judge was instructed to judge an idea as good if it satisfied all of the following criteria: 1) it uses a different mechanism/technology than the original product (novelty), 2) it proposes a mechanism/technology that would achieve the same purpose as the original product (quality), and 3) could be implemented using existing technology and does not defy physics (feasibility).

Agreement between the judges was substantial, with a Fleiss kappa of 0.51, lending our measure of creativity acceptable inter-rater reliability. The final measure of whether an idea was good or not was computed by thresholding the number of votes, so that good = 1 if at least k judges rated it as good. We report results for both liberal and strict settings $k = 2, 3$.

Evaluation. For $k = 2$, out of 749 total ideas collected, 249 ideas were judged as good by this measure. As mentioned above, we use the Fisher-Yates shuffle to assign seeds to conditions. To take a conservative approach, as a first step we look only at seeds that appeared across all three conditions (9 such seeds), to put the conditions on par with one another. By this slicing of the data, there were 208 good ideas. The proportion of good ideas in our condition was 46% ($N = 105$). Next was the random baseline with 37% (49), and finally the TF-IDF baseline achieved 30% (N=54). These results are significant by a χ^2 proportion test ($p \leq .01$). We thus observe that both in terms of the absolute number of positively-rated ideas and in terms of proportions, our approach was able to generate a considerably large relative positive effect, leading to better ideas.

For $k = 3$ (the majority vote), out of 749 total ideas collected, 184 ideas were judged as good. Again, we start by looking only at seeds that appeared across all three conditions (9 such seeds). This leaves 154 good ideas. The proportion of good ideas in our condition was 38% ($N = 118$). Next-up was the random baseline with 22% (68), and finally the TF-IDF baseline achieved 21% (N=63), with $p < .01$. By looking at the more conservative majority-vote threshold, the observed effect of our method only increases.

Looking only at seeds that appeared across all conditions was a basic way to make sure we cancel out possible confounding factors. A more refined way is attempting to model these effects and condition on them, as follows.

We are interested in the likelihood that a given idea is good, or pr(good), as a function of inspiration condition. However, ideas are not independent: each participant generated multiple ideas, and ideas were proposed for different seeds. Failing to account for these dependencies would lead to inaccurate estimates of the effects of the inspirations: some participants may be better at generating ideas than others, while some seeds might be more easy/difficult than others. Therefore, we used a generalized linear mixed model,

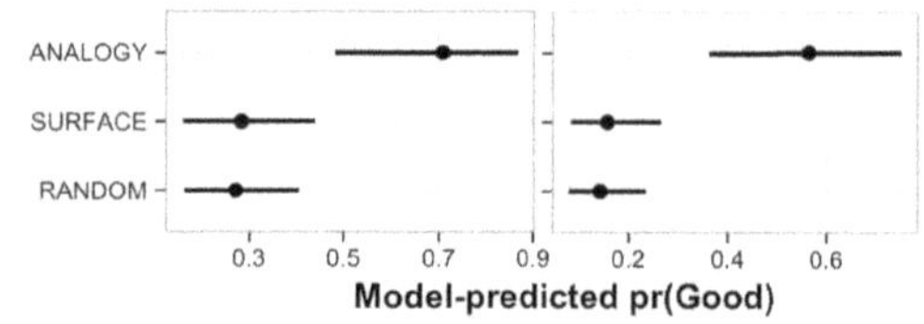

Figure 4: Showing proportion estimates by our random-effect logistic regression, for $k = 2$ (left) and $k = 3$ (right). Participants are significantly more likely to generate good ideas for the redesign ideation task when given inspirations from our analogy approach compared to baseline-surface and baseline-random approaches

with a fixed effect of inspiration condition, and random effects of participant and seed (to model within-participant and within-seed dependencies between ideas).

For $k = 2$, our resulting model (with fixed effect of inspiration condition) yields a significant reduction in variance compared to a null model with no fixed effects, Likelihood ratio $\chi^2(3) = 67.96$, $p < .01$. The model also yields a reduction in Akaike Information Criterion (AIC), from 682.28 in the null model to 620.32, indicating that the improved fit to the data is not due to overfitting.

For $k = 3$, the model also yields a significant drop in variance compared to a null model, Likelihood ratio $\chi^2(3) = 92.38$, $p < .01$, with AIC dropping from 682.28 in the null model to 595.90.

As Figure 4 shows, our method led to a significantly higher probability for good ideas. For $k = 2$, pr(Good) = 0.71, 95% confidence interval = [0.48, 0.87] in our condition. TF-IDF had pr(Good) = 0.28 [0.16, 0.44], and random had pr(Good) = 0.27 [0.16, 0.41]. The advantages of the analogy condition over each baseline are both substantial and statistically significant, B = −1.81, $p < .01$ vs. TF-IDF, and B = −1.88, $p < .01$ vs. random. For $k = 3$, we had pr(Good) = 0.56, [0.36, 0.75]. TF-IDF had pr(Good) = 0.16 [0.08, 0.27], and random had pr(Good) = 0.14 [0.08, 0.24], B = −1.94, $p < .01$ vs. TF-IDF, and B = −2.05, $p < .01$ vs. random.

Note that confidence intervals for the probability estimates are relatively wide (more so, unsurprisingly, for $k = 2$). Replications of this experiment, possibly with more data, could yield results somewhere in between, with more precise estimates on the true size of the effect. The main take-away of this study is that our approach yields a reliable increase in participants' creative ability.

5 DISCUSSION AND CONCLUSION

In this paper, we sought to develop a scalable approach to finding analogies in large, messy, real-world datasets. We explored the potential of learning and leveraging a weak structural representation (i.e., purpose and mechanism vectors) for product descriptions. We leverage crowdsourcing techniques to construct a training dataset with purpose/mechanism annotations, and use an RNN to learn purpose and mechanism vectors for each product. We demonstrate that these learned vectors allow us to find analogies with higher precision than traditional information-retrieval similarity metrics like TF-IDF, LSA, GloVe and LDA.

Our ideation evaluation experiment further illustrates the effectiveness of our approach: participants had a higher likelihood of generating good ideas for the redesign ideation task when they received inspirations sampled by our analogy approach (tuned to be similar in purpose, but different in mechanism), compared to a traditional (TF-IDF) baseline or random sampling approach. From a psychological perspective, the benefits of our inspirations are likely due to our approach's superior ability to sample diverse yet still structurally similar inspirations, since diversity of examples is a known robust booster for creative ability [8]. The TF-IDF approach yielded inspirations likely to be relevant, but also likely to be redundant and homogeneous, while the random sampling approach yields diversity but not relevance.

While moving to a "weak" structural representation based on purpose and mechanism significantly increased the feasibility of analogy-finding, extensions may be necessary to generalize to other domains besides product descriptions. For example, our purpose and mechanism vectors did not distinguish between higher and lower level purposes/mechanisms, or core/peripheral purposes/ mechanisms, and also did not encode dependencies between particular purposes/mechanisms. These are potentially fruitful areas for future work and may be especially important when moving from relatively simple product descriptions to more complex data such as scientific papers, in which purposes and mechanisms can exist at multiple hierarchical levels (e.g., "accelerate innovation" vs. "learn a vector representation of the purpose of an item"). More generally, we believe exploring the tradeoffs between degree of structure, learnability (including costs of generating training data, accuracy, and generalizability) and utility for augmenting innovation could lead to interesting points in the design space that could have both theoretical and practical value.

Acknowledgments. The authors thank the anonymous reviewers for their helpful comments. This work was supported by NSF grants CHS-1526665, IIS-1149797, IIS-1217559, Carnegie Mellon's Web2020 initiative, Bosch, Google, ISF grant 1764/15 and Alon grant. Dafna Shahaf is a Harry&Abe Sherman assistant professor.

REFERENCES

[1] Sanjeev Arora, Yuanzhi Li, Yingyu Liang, Tengyu Ma, and Andrej Risteski. 2016. Linear algebraic structure of word senses, with applications to polysemy. *arXiv preprint arXiv:1601.03764* (2016).

[2] Sanjeev Arora, Yingyu Liang, and Tengyu Ma. 2016. A simple but tough-to-beat baseline for sentence embeddings. (2016).

[3] Dzmitry Bahdanau, Kyunghyun Cho, and Yoshua Bengio. 2014. Neural machine translation by jointly learning to align and translate. *arXiv preprint arXiv:1409.0473* (2014).

[4] David M. Blei, Andrew Y. Ng, Michael I. Jordan, and John Lafferty. 2003. Latent Dirichlet Allocation. *Journal of Machine Learning Research* (2003), 993–1022.

[5] Danushka T Bollegala, Yutaka Matsuo, and Mitsuru Ishizuka. 2009. Measuring the similarity between implicit semantic relations from the web. In *Proceedings of the 18th international conference on World wide web.* ACM, 651–660.

[6] T Tony Cai and Lie Wang. 2011. Orthogonal matching pursuit for sparse signal recovery with noise. *IEEE Transactions on Information Theory* 57, 7 (2011).

[7] Joel Chan, Tom Hope, Dafna Shahaf, and Aniket Kittur. 2016. Scaling up Analogy with Crowdsourcing and Machine Learning. In *Workshop on Computational Analogy at ICCBR.*

[8] Joel Chan and Christian D. Schunn. 2015. The importance of iteration in creative conceptual combination. *Cognition* 145 (Dec. 2015), 104–115.

[9] Darren W Dahl and Page Moreau. 2002. The influence and value of analogical thinking during new product ideation. *Journal of Marketing Research* 39, 1 (2002).

[10] Scott Deerwester, Susan T. Dumais, Geroge W. Furnas, and Thomas K. Landauer. 1990. Indexing by Latent Semantic Analysis. *JASIST* 41, 6 (1990), 1990.

[11] Brian Falkenhainer, Kenneth D. Forbus, and Dedre Gentner. 1989. The structure-mapping engine: Algorithm and examples. *Artificial Intelligence* 41, 1 (1989).

[12] Dedre Gentner. 1983. Structure-Mapping: A Theoretical Framework for Analogy*. *Cognitive science* 7, 2 (1983), 155–170.

[13] Dedre Gentner, Russell Landers, and others. 1985. Analogical reminding: A good match is hard to find. In *Proceedings of the international conference on systems, man and cybernetics.* 607–613.

[14] Dedre Gentner, Mary Jo Rattermann, and Kenneth D Forbus. 1993. The roles of similarity in transfer: Separating retrievability from inferential soundness. *Cognitive psychology* 25, 4 (1993), 524–575.

[15] M. L. Gick and K. J. Holyoak. 1983. Schema induction and analogical transfer. *Cognitive Psychology* 15, 1 (1983), 1–38.

[16] Graeme S Halford, Rosemary Baker, Julie E McCredden, and John D Bain. 2005. How many variables can humans process? *Psychological science* 16, 1 (2005).

[17] Mary B Hesse. 1966. Models and analogies in science. (1966).

[18] Julie Hirtz, Robert B Stone, Daniel A McAdams, Simon Szykman, and Kristin L Wood. 2002. A functional basis for engineering design: reconciling and evolving previous efforts. *Research in engineering Design* 13, 2 (2002), 65–82.

[19] Douglas R Hofstadter, Melanie Mitchell, and others. 1994. The copycat project: A model of mental fluidity and analogy-making. *Advances in connectionist and neural computation theory* 2, 31-112 (1994), 29–30.

[20] Keith James Holyoak and Paul Thagard. 1996. *Mental leaps: Analogy in creative thought.* MIT press.

[21] Aniket Kittur, Ed H. Chi, and Bongwon Suh. 2008. Crowdsourcing User Studies with Mechanical Turk. In *Proceedings of the SIGCHI Conference on Human Factors in Computing Systems (CHI '08).* ACM, New York, NY, USA, 453–456.

[22] Arthur B Markman and Jeffrey Loewenstein. 2010. Structural comparison and consumer choice. *Journal of Consumer Psychology* 20, 2 (2010), 126–137.

[23] Julian McAuley and Jure Leskovec. 2013. Hidden factors and hidden topics: understanding rating dimensions with review text. In *Proceedings of the 7th ACM conference on Recommender systems.* ACM, 165–172.

[24] Tomas Mikolov, Kai Chen, Greg Corrado, and Jeffrey Dean. 2013. Efficient Estimation of Word Representations in Vector Space. *arXiv:1301.3781 [cs]* (Jan. 2013). http://arxiv.org/abs/1301.3781 arXiv: 1301.3781.

[25] Masanori Ookubo, Yusuke Koji, Munehiko Sasajima, Yoshinobu Kitamura, and Riichiro Mizoguchi. 2007. Towards Interoperability between Functional Taxonomies using an Ontology-based Mapping. In *Proc. of ICED 2007.*

[26] Colin Pask. 2003. Mathematics and the science of analogies. *American Journal of Physics* 71, 6 (2003), 526–534.

[27] Jeffrey Pennington, Richard Socher, and Christopher D Manning. 2014. Glove: Global Vectors for Word Representation. In *EMNLP*, Vol. 14. 1532–43.

[28] Sekharipuram S Ravi, Daniel J Rosenkrantz, and Giri Kumar Tayi. 1994. Heuristic and special case algorithms for dispersion problems. *Operations Research* 42, 2 (1994), 299–310.

[29] Bruce A. Reinig, Robert O. Briggs, and Jay F. Nunamaker. 2007. On the Measurement of Ideation Quality. *Journal of Management Information Systems* 23, 4 (May 2007), 143–161.

[30] Mark A. Runco and Garrett J. Jaeger. 2012. The Standard Definition of Creativity. *Creativity Research Journal* 24, 1 (Jan. 2012), 92–96.

[31] Ekaterina Shutova. 2010. Models of metaphor in NLP. In *Proceedings of the 48th annual meeting of the association for computational linguistics.* Association for Computational Linguistics, 688–697.

[32] Barbara A Spellman and Frederick Schauer. 2012. Legal reasoning. *Virginia Public Law and Legal Theory Research Paper* 2012-09 (2012).

[33] Ilya Sutskever, Oriol Vinyals, and Quoc V Le. 2014. Sequence to sequence learning with neural networks. In *Advances in neural information processing systems.* 3104–3112.

[34] Ian Tseng, Jarrod Moss, Jonathan Cagan, and Kenneth Kotovsky. 2008. The role of timing and analogical similarity in the stimulation of idea generation in design. *Design Studies* 29, 3 (2008), 203–221.

[35] Peter D Turney. 2006. Similarity of semantic relations. *Computational Linguistics* 32, 3 (2006), 379–416.

[36] D. Ullman. 2002. *The Mechanical Design Process* (3 ed.). New York, NY.

[37] Swaroop Vattam, Bryan Wiltgen, Michael Helms, Ashok K. Goel, and Jeannette Yen. 2011. DANE: Fostering Creativity in and through Biologically Inspired Design. In *Design Creativity 2010.*

[38] Lixiu Yu, Aniket Kittur, and Robert E Kraut. 2014. Searching for analogical ideas with crowds. In *Proceedings of the 32nd annual ACM conference on Human factors in computing systems.* ACM, 1225–1234.

[39] Lixiu Yu, Aniket Kittur, and Robert E Kraut. 2016. Encouraging fiOutside-the-boxfi Thinking in Crowd Innovation Through Identifying Domains of Expertise. In *Proceedings of the 19th ACM Conference on Computer-Supported Cooperative Work & Social Computing.* ACM, 1214–1222.

[40] L Yu, B Kraut, and A Kittur. 2014. Distributed analogical idea generation: innovating with crowds. In *CHI'14.*

[41] Lixiu Yu, Robert E Kraut, and Aniket Kittur. 2016. Distributed Analogical Idea Generation with Multiple Constraints. In *Proceedings of the 19th ACM Conference on Computer-Supported Cooperative Work & Social Computing.* ACM, 1236–1245.

Communication-Efficient Distributed Block Minimization for Nonlinear Kernel Machines*

Cho-Jui Hsieh
University of California, Davis
Davis, CA 95616
chohsieh@ucdavis.edu

Si Si†
Google Research
Mountain View, CA 94043
sisidaisy@google.com

Inderjit S. Dhillon
University of Texas at Austin
Austin, TX 78712
inderjit@cs.utexas.edu

ABSTRACT

Nonlinear kernel machines often yield superior predictive performance on various tasks; however, they suffer from severe computational challenges. In this paper, we show how to overcome the important challenge of speeding up kernel machines using multiple computers. In particular, we develop a parallel block minimization framework, and demonstrate its good scalability in solving nonlinear kernel SVM and logistic regression. Our framework proceeds by dividing the problem into smaller subproblems by forming a block-diagonal approximation of the Hessian matrix. The subproblems are then solved approximately in parallel. After that, a communication efficient line search procedure is developed to ensure sufficient reduction of the objective function value by exploiting the problem structure of kernel machines. We prove global linear convergence rate of the proposed method with a wide class of subproblem solvers, and our analysis covers strongly convex and some non-strongly convex functions. We apply our algorithm to solve large-scale kernel SVM problems on distributed systems, and show a significant improvement over existing parallel solvers. As an example, on the covtype dataset with half-a-million samples, our algorithm can obtain an approximate solution with 96% accuracy in 20 seconds using 32 machines, while all the other parallel kernel SVM solvers require more than 2000 seconds to achieve a solution with 95% accuracy. Moreover, our algorithm is the first distributed kernel SVM solver that can scale to massive data sets. On the kddb dataset (20 million samples and 30 million features), our parallel solver can compute the kernel SVM solution within half an hour using 32 machines with 640 cores in total, while existing solvers can not scale to this dataset.

KEYWORDS

Distributed Algorithm, Kernel Methods, Classification.

*The code is available in https://github.com/cjhsieh/Distributed-KSVM.
†Si Si is now working at Google Research; this work was done before she joined Google.

KDD '17, August 13-17, 2017, Halifax, NS, Canada

ACM ISBN 978-1-4503-4887-4/17/08...$15.00
https://doi.org/10.1145/3097983.3098080

1 INTRODUCTION

Kernel methods are a class of algorithms that map samples from input space to a high-dimensional feature space. The representative kernel machines include kernel SVM, kernel logistic regression and support vector regression. When a nonlinear kernel is used, all the above algorithms are hard to scale to large-scale problems due to the high computation cost and memory requirement of computing and storing the kernel matrix. Efficient sequential algorithms have been proposed for kernel machines, where the most widely-used one is the SMO algorithm [10, 18] implemented in LIBSVM and SVMLight. However, single-machine kernel SVM algorithms still cannot scale to larger datasets (e.g. LIBSVM takes 3 days on the MNIST dataset with 8 million samples), so there is a tremendous need for developing distributed algorithms for kernel machines.

Although many distributed algorithms have been proposed for solving linear SVM/logistic regression [9, 14, 34], they cannot be applied to nonlinear kernel machines since they synchronize information using primal variables. To the best of our knowledge, there are very few existing algorithms for distributed nonlinear kernel SVM training because of two challenges: How to deal with the huge kernel matrix and how to solve the large quadratic optimization problem in a distributed and communication-efficient manner. Most existing algorithms try to approximate kernel matrix in parallel to reduce the problem to a linear machine [3, 19], and then solve the resulting problem by a distributed optimization solver. However, due to the kernel approximation step, they cannot obtain the exact kernel SVM solution and this often leads to suboptimal prediction accuracy.

In this paper, we propose a distributed kernel SVM solver that is able to solve the quadratic optimization problem exactly by a Parallel Block Minimization (PBM) framework. At each iteration, PBM divides the whole problem into smaller subproblems by first forming a block-diagonal approximation of the kernel matrix. Each subproblem is much smaller than the original problem and they can be solved in parallel using existing serial solvers such as SMO (or greedy coordinate descent) [18] implemented in LIBSVM. After that, we develop a communication-efficient line search procedure to ensure a reduction of the objective function value.

Our contribution can be summarized below:

1. The paper is the first to apply the parallel block minimization (PBM) framework for training kernel machines, where each machine updates a block of dual variables. We develop an efficient line search procedure to synchronize the updates at the end of each iteration without any additional cost by exploiting the problem structure of kernel machines.

2. Our algorithm works for any partition of dual variables, and we show that the convergence speed can be significantly improved using a better partition (obtained by kmeans) .
3. We show that our proposed algorithm significantly outperforms existing kernel SVM and logistic regression solvers on a distributed system. In particular, our algorithm is the first distributed nonlinear SVM solver that scales to kddb dataset with 20 million samples and 30 million features. On this dataset, our parallel solver only takes half an hour to compute the kernel SVM solution with 32 machines containing 640 cores in total.
4. We prove a global linear convergence rate for PBM under mild conditions: we allow a wide range of inexact subproblem solvers, and our analysis covers many widely-used functions where some of them may not be strongly convex (e.g., SVM dual problem with a positive semi-definite kernel).

The rest of the paper is organized as follows. We discuss the related work in Section 2. In Section 3, we introduce the problem setting, and the proposed PBM framework is presented in Section 4. We prove a global linear convergence rate in Section 5. Experimental results are shown in Section 6, while Section 7 concludes the paper.

2 RELATED WORK

Algorithms for solving kernel machines. Several optimization algorithms have been proposed to solve kernel machines [10, 18]. Among them, decomposition methods [10, 11] have become widely-used in software packages such as LIBSVM [2] and SVMLight.

Parallelizing kernel SVM has also been studied in the literature. Recently an asynchronous greedy coordinate descent algorithm has been proposed for solving kernel SVM [30]. Although it achieves good performance on a multicore shared memory system, the algorithm cannot be used in distributed systems due to the need of asynchronous global parameter access. Several distributed SVM algorithms have been proposed: Cascade-SVM [4] proposed to randomly divide the problem into subproblems, but they still need to solve a global kernel SVM problem in the final stage; PSVM [3] uses an incomplete Cholesky factorization to approximate the original kernel SVM problem, and solves the resulting problem by an interior point method; P-pack SVM [35] applies a distributed SGD algorithm for training kernel SVM. Unfortunately, as shown in the experiments, none of the existing distributed kernel SVM algorithms can scale to extremely large datasets.

Two clustering based approaches for kernel SVM have been recently developed: Divide-and-conquer SVM (DC-SVM) [5] and Communication Avoiding SVM (CA-SVM) [29]. In DC-SVM, the global kernel SVM problem is hierarchically divided into smaller subproblems by kmeans or kernel kmeans, and the subproblems can be solved independently. The solutions from subproblems can be used directly for prediction (called DC-SVM early prediction) or can be used to initialize the global SVM solver. Although the subproblems can be solved in parallel, DC-SVM still needs a parallel solver for the global SVM problem in the final stage. Our idea of using clustering is similar to DC-SVM [5], but here we apply it to develop a distributed SVM solver, while DC-SVM is just a single-machine serial algorithm. The experimental comparisons between our proposed method and DC-SVM are shown in the experiments.

Kernel approximation approaches. Another line of approach for kernel machines aim to approximate the kernel matrix and then solve the reduced size problem. Nyström approximation [6, 22, 23, 27] and random Fourier features [19] can be used to form low-rank approximation of kernel matrices, and then the problem can be reduced to a linear SVM or logistic regression problem. To parallelize these algorithms, a distributed linear SVM or logistic regression solver is needed. The comparisons are in Figure 2. Using random Fourier features in kernel machine is also applied in [8] and [25]. Comparing with our proposed method, (1) they only consider solving linear systems, and it is nontrivial for them to solve kernel SVM and logistic regression problems; (2) they cannot obtain the exact solution of kernel machines, since they only use the approximate kernel.

Distributed linear SVM and logistic regression solvers. Several distributed algorithms have been proposed for solving the primal linear SVM problems [14, 15, 34], but they require synchronizing the primal variables at each iteration. Unfortunately, the primal variables cannot be explicitly formed in nonlinear kernel machines, so these methods cannot be directly applied to nonlinear kernel SVM or logistic regression. Distributed dual coordinate descent [9, 14, 28] and asynchronous dual coordinate descent [32] is also investigated for linear SVM.

Distributed Block Coordinate Descent. The main idea of our algorithm is similar to a class of Distributed Block Coordinate Descent (DBCD) parallel computing methods. As discussed recently in literature [17, 20, 21], different DBCD parallel algorithms have different ways to solve subproblems in each machine, and synchronize the results. However, no existing work has applied DBCD to kernel machines, partly due to the challenge of line search in distributed systems. Recent distributed dual coordinate descent linear SVM solvers [14, 34] also belongs to DBCD class.

Our Innovations. In contrast to the above algorithms, ours is the first one that adopts a block-partition based coordinate descent algorithm to kernel machines; previous work either focused on linear SVM [9, 14, 28] or primal ERM problems [17]. These approaches proposed to maintain and synchronize the vector $\boldsymbol{y} = X^T\boldsymbol{d}$ or $\boldsymbol{w} = X\boldsymbol{d}$, where $\boldsymbol{d}$ is the direction and X is the data matrix. Unfortunately, in kernel methods this strategy does not work since each sample may have infinite dimension after the nonlinear mapping. We overcome the challenges by synchronizing the $Q\boldsymbol{d}$ vector ($Q \in \mathbb{R}^{n\times n}$) and developing an efficient line search procedure. We further show that a better partition (obtained by kmeans) can speedup the convergence of the algorithm.

On the theoretical front: previous papers [9, 28] can only show linear convergence when the objective function is $f(x) = g(x) + h(x)$ and g is strongly convex. [14] considered some non-strongly convex functions, but they assume each subproblem is solved exactly. In this paper, we prove a global linear convergence even when g is not strongly convex and each subproblem is solved approximately. Our proof covers general DBCD algorithms for some non-strongly convex functions, for which previous analysis can only show sub-linear convergence.

3 PROBLEM SETUP

We focus on the following composite optimization problem:

$$\underset{\alpha \in \mathbb{R}^n}{\text{argmin}}\Big\{\alpha^T Q\alpha + \sum_i g_i(\alpha_i)\Big\} := f(\alpha) \text{ s.t. } a \le \alpha \le b, \quad (1)$$

where $Q \in \mathbb{R}^{n\times n}$ is positive semi-definite; each g_i is a univariate convex function; $a = [a_1, \cdots, a_n]$ and $b = [b_1, \cdots, b_n]$ are vectors. Note that we can easily handle the box constraint $a \le \alpha \le b$ by setting $g_i(\alpha_i) = \infty$ if $\alpha_i \notin [a_i, b_i]$, so we will omit the constraint in most parts of the paper.

An important application of (1) in machine learning is that it is the dual problem of ℓ_2-regularized empirical risk minimization. Given a set of instances $\{x_i, y_i\}_{i=1}^n$, we consider the following ℓ_2-regularized empirical risk minimization problem:

$$\arg\min_{w} \frac{1}{2} w^T w + C \sum_{i=1}^n \ell_i(w^T \Phi(x_i)), \quad (2)$$

where ℓ_i is the loss function depending on the label y_i, and $\Phi(\cdot)$ is the nonlinear feature mapping. For example, $\ell_i(u) = \max(0, 1-y_i u)$ for SVM with hinge loss. The dual problem of (2) can be written as

$$\arg\min_{\alpha} \frac{1}{2}\alpha^T Q\alpha + \sum_{i=1}^n \ell_i(-\alpha_i), \quad (3)$$

where $Q \in \mathbb{R}^{n\times n}$ in this case is the kernel matrix with $Q_{ij} = y_i y_j \Phi(x_i)^T \Phi(x_j)$. Our proposed approach works in the general setting, but we will discuss in more detail its applications to kernel SVM, where Q is the kernel matrix and α is the vector of dual variables. Note that, similar to [5], we ignore the bias term in (2). Indeed, in our experimental results we did not observe improvement in test accuracy by adding the bias term.

4 PROPOSED ALGORITHM

We describe our proposed framework PBM for solving (1) on a distributed system with k worker machines. We partition the variables α into k disjoint index sets $\{S_r\}_{r=1}^k$ such that

$$S_1 \cup S_2 \cup \cdots \cup S_k = \{1, \ldots, n\} \quad \text{and} \quad S_p \cap S_q = \phi \;\forall p \ne q,$$

and we use $\pi(i)$ to denote the cluster indicator that i belongs to. We associate each worker r with a subset of variables $\alpha_{S_r} := \{\alpha_i \mid i \in S_r\}$. Note that our framework allows any partition, and we will discuss how to obtain a better partition in Section 4.3.

At each iteration, we form the quadratic approximation of problem (1) around the current solution:

$$f(\alpha + \Delta\alpha) \approx \bar{f}_\alpha(\Delta\alpha) = \frac{1}{2}\alpha^T Q\alpha + \alpha^T Q\Delta\alpha + \frac{1}{2}\Delta\alpha^T \bar{Q}\Delta\alpha + \sum_i g_i(\alpha_i + \Delta\alpha_i), \quad (4)$$

where the second order term of the quadratic part ($\frac{1}{2}\Delta\alpha^T Q\Delta\alpha$) is replaced by $\frac{1}{2}\Delta\alpha^T \bar{Q}\Delta\alpha$, and $\bar{Q}$ is the block-diagonal approximation of Q such that

$$\bar{Q}_{ij} = \begin{cases} Q_{ij} & \text{if } \pi(i) = \pi(j) \\ 0 & \text{otherwise.} \end{cases} \quad (5)$$

By solving (4), we obtain the descent direction d:

$$d := \arg\min_{\Delta\alpha} \bar{f}_\alpha(\Delta\alpha). \quad (6)$$

Since $\bar{Q}$ is block-diagonal, problem (6) can be decomposed into k independent subproblems based on the partition $\{S_r\}_{r=1}^k$:

$$d_{S_r} = \underset{\Delta\alpha_{S_r}}{\text{argmin}}\Big\{\frac{1}{2}\Delta\alpha_{S_r}^T Q_{S_r,S_r}\Delta\alpha_{S_r} + \sum_{i\in S_r} \bar{g}_i(\Delta\alpha_i)\Big\} := f_\alpha^{(r)}(\Delta\alpha_{S_r}), \quad (7)$$

where $\bar{g}_i(\Delta\alpha_i) = g_i(\alpha_i + \Delta\alpha_i) + (Q\alpha)_i\Delta\alpha_i$. Subproblem (7) has the same form as the original problem (1), so can be solved by any existing kernel SVM/kernel regression solver on each machine. After solving the subproblems (7) independently for each r, the descent direction d is the concatenation of $d_{S_1}, \ldots d_{S_r}$. Since $f(\alpha + d)$ might even increase the objective function value $f(\alpha)$, we find the step size β to ensure the following sufficient decrease condition of the objective function value:

$$f(\alpha + \beta d) - f(\alpha) \le \beta\sigma\Delta, \quad (8)$$

where $\Delta = \nabla f(\alpha)^T d$, and $\sigma \in (0, 1)$ is a constant. We then update $\alpha \leftarrow \alpha + \beta d$. Now we discuss details of each step of our algorithm.

4.1 Solving the Subproblems

Note that subproblem (7) has the same form as the original problem (1), so we can apply any existing algorithm to solve it for each worker independently. In our implementation, we apply the following greedy coordinate descent method (a similar algorithm was used in LIBSVM). Assume the current subproblem solution is $\Delta\alpha_{S_r}$, we choose variable with the largest projected gradient:

$$i^* := \underset{i\in S_r}{\text{argmax}} \Big|\Pi\Big(\alpha_i + \Delta\alpha_i - (Q_{S_r,S_r}\Delta\alpha_{S_r})_i - \bar{g}_i'(\Delta\alpha_i)\Big) - \alpha_i - \Delta\alpha_i\Big| \quad (9)$$

where Π is the projection to the interval $[a_i, b_i]$. The selection only requires $O(|S_r|)$ time if $Q_{S_r,S_r}\Delta\alpha_{S_r}$ is maintained in local memory. Variable $\Delta\alpha_i$ is then updated by solving the following one-variable subproblem:

$$\delta^* = \underset{\delta}{\text{argmin}} \frac{1}{2}Q_{i^*,i^*}\delta^2 + (Q_{S_r,S_r}\Delta\alpha_{S_r})_{i^*}\delta + \bar{g}_{i^*}(\Delta\alpha_{i^*} + \delta) \quad (10)$$
$$\text{with } a_{i^*} \le \alpha_{i^*} + \Delta\alpha_{i^*} + \delta \le b_{i^*}.$$

For kernel SVM, the one-variable subproblem (10) has a closed form solution, while for logistic regression the subproblem can be solved by Newton's method (see [31] for the detailed discussions). The bottleneck of both (9) and (10) is to compute $Q_{S_r,S_r}\Delta\alpha_{S_r}$, which can be maintained after each update using $O(|S_r|)$ time.

Note that in our framework each subproblem does not need to be solved exactly. In Section 5 we will give theoretical analysis to the in-exact PBM method, and show that the linear convergence is guaranteed when each subproblem runs more than 1 coordinate update.

Communication Cost. There is no communication needed for solving the subproblems between workers; however, after solving the subproblems and obtaining the update direction d, each worker needs to obtain the updated $(Qd)_{S_r}$ vector for next iteration, where this term in (7) is the only "global information" needed for each machine. Since each worker only has the local update d_{S_r}, we compute $Q_{:,S_r}(d_{S_r})$ in each worker, and use a REDUCE_SCATTER collective communication to obtain updated $(Qd)_{S_r}$ for each worker. The communication cost for the collective REDUCE_SCATTER operation for an n-dimensional vector requires

$$\log(k)T_{\text{initial}} + nT_{\text{byte}} \tag{11}$$

communication time, where T_{initial} is the message startup time and T_{byte} is the transmission time per byte (see Section 6.3 of [1]). When n is large, the second term usually dominates, so we need $O(n)$ communication time and this *does not grow with the number of processors.*

4.2 Communication-efficient Line Search

After obtaining $(Q\boldsymbol{d})_{S_r}$ for each worker, we propose the following efficient line search approaches.

Armijo-rule based step size selection. For general $g_i(\cdot)$, a commonly used line search approach is to try step sizes $\beta \in \{1, \frac{1}{2}, \dots\}$ until β satisfies the sufficient decrease condition (8). The only cost is to evaluate the objective function value. For each choice of β, $f(\boldsymbol{\alpha} + \beta\boldsymbol{d})$ can be computed as

$$f(\boldsymbol{\alpha} + \beta\boldsymbol{d}) = f(\boldsymbol{\alpha}) + \sum_r \{\beta \boldsymbol{d}_{S_r}^T (Q\boldsymbol{\alpha})_{S_r} + \frac{1}{2}\beta^2 \boldsymbol{d}_{S_r}^T (Q\boldsymbol{d})_{S_r} + \sum_{i \in S_r} g_i(\alpha_i + \beta d_i) - g_i(\alpha_i)\},$$

so if each worker r has the vector $(Q\boldsymbol{d})_{S_r}$, we can compute $f(\boldsymbol{\alpha}+\beta\boldsymbol{d})$ using $O(n/k)$ time and $O(1)$ communication cost. In order to prove convergence, we add another condition that $f(\boldsymbol{\alpha} + \beta\boldsymbol{d}) \leq f(\boldsymbol{\alpha} + \boldsymbol{d}/k)$, although in practice we do not find any difference without adding this condition.

Optimal step size selection. If each g_i is a linear function with bounded constraint (such as for the kernel SVM case), the optimal step size can be computed without communication. The optimal step size is defined by

$$\beta^* := \arg\min_{\beta} f(\boldsymbol{\alpha} + \beta\boldsymbol{d}) \text{ s.t. } \boldsymbol{a} \leq \boldsymbol{\alpha} + \beta\boldsymbol{d} \leq \boldsymbol{b}. \tag{12}$$

If $\sum_i g_i(\alpha_i) = \boldsymbol{p\alpha}$, then $f(\boldsymbol{\alpha} + \beta\boldsymbol{d})$ with respect to β is a univariate quadratic function, and thus β_t^* can be obtained by the following closed form solution:

$$\beta = \min(\bar{\eta}, \max(\underline{\eta}, -(\boldsymbol{\alpha}^T Q\boldsymbol{d} + \boldsymbol{p}^T\boldsymbol{d})/(\boldsymbol{d}^T Q\boldsymbol{d}))), \tag{13}$$

where $\bar{\eta} := \min_{i=1}^n (b_i - \alpha_i)$ and $\underline{\eta} := \max_{i=1}^n (a_i - \alpha_i)$. This can also be computed in $O(n/k)$ time and $O(1)$ communication time. Our proposed algorithm is summarized in Algorithm 1.

4.3 Variable Partitioning

Our PBM algorithm converges for any choice of partition $\{S_r\}_{r=1}^k$. However, it is important to select a good partition in order to achieve faster convergence. Since our algorithm is solving an "approximate function" at each iteration, the difference between the approximate function $\bar{f}_{\boldsymbol{\alpha}}$ and the true function f controls the convergence rate of the algorithm. If $\bar{Q} = Q$ in subproblem (4) (no approximation error), then $\bar{f}_{\boldsymbol{\alpha}}(\Delta\boldsymbol{\alpha}) = f(\boldsymbol{\alpha} + \Delta\boldsymbol{\alpha})$ for any $\Delta\boldsymbol{\alpha}$, so our algorithm converges in one iteration. However, there is no parallelism in this case. On the other hand, if $\|Q - \bar{Q}\|$ is very large, the algorithm will converge slowly. Therefore, the convergence rate can be speed up

Algorithm 1: PBM: Parallel Block Minimization for solving (1)

Input : The objective function (1), initial $\boldsymbol{\alpha}_0$.
Output: The solution $\boldsymbol{\alpha}^*$.

```
Obtain a disjoint index partition {S_r}_{r=1}^k.
Compute Qα_0 in parallel (Qα_0 = 0 if α_0 = 0).
for t = 0, 1, ... (until convergence) do
    Obtain d_{S_r} by solving subproblems (7) in parallel.
    Compute Q_{:,S_r} d_{S_r} in parallel.
    Use REDUCE_SCATTER to obtain (Qd)_{S_r} in each worker.
    Obtain the step size β using line search (see Section 4.2 for details)
    α_{S_r} ← α_{S_r} + βd_{S_r} and (Qα)_{S_r} ← (Qα)_{S_r} + β(Qd)_{S_r} in parallel.
```

by finding a partition $\{S_r\}_{r=1}^k$ to minimize error

$$\|\bar{Q} - Q\|_F^2 = \sum_{i,j} Q_{ij}^2 - \sum_{r=1}^k \sum_{i,j \in S_r} Q_{ij}^2,$$

and the minimizer can be obtained by maximizing the second term. However, we also want to have a balanced partition in order to achieve better parallelization speedup.

The same problem has been encountered in [5, 24] for forming a good kernel approximation. They have shown that kernel kmeans can achieve a good partition for general kernel matrix, and if the kernels are shift-invariant (e.g., Gaussian, Laplacian, ...), we can use kmeans clustering on the data points to find a balanced partition with small kernel approximation error. Since we do not need the "optimal" partition, in practice we only run kmeans or kernel kmeans on a subset of 20000 training samples, so the overhead is very small compared with the whole training procedure.

We observe PBM with kmeans partition converges much faster compared to random partition. By random partition, we will assign each variable into a random partition. Due to randomness, each partition will roughly have the same number of variables. In Figure 1, we test the PBM algorithm on the kernel SVM problem with Gaussian kernel, and show that the convergence is much faster when the partition is obtained by kmeans clustering.

Local Prediction. We further propose a local prediction strategy for PBM when data is partitioned by kmeans clustering. Let $\boldsymbol{\alpha}_t$ be the solution before the t-th iteration of Algorithm 1, and $\boldsymbol{d}_t$ be the solution of the quadratic subproblem (4). The traditional way is to use $\boldsymbol{\alpha}_{t+1} = \boldsymbol{\alpha}_t + \beta_t \boldsymbol{d}_t$ for predicting new data.

However, we find the following procedure gives better prediction accuracy compared to using $\boldsymbol{\alpha}_{t+1}$: we first identify the cluster indicator of the test point $\boldsymbol{x}$ by choosing the nearest kmeans center. If $\boldsymbol{x}$ belongs to the r-th cluster, we then compute the prediction by the local model $\boldsymbol{\alpha}_t + (\boldsymbol{d}_t)_{<S_r>}$, where $(\boldsymbol{d}_t)_{<S_r>}$ is an n dimensional vector that sets all the elements outside S_r to be 0. Experimental results in Figure 1 show that this local prediction strategy is generally better than predicting by $\boldsymbol{\alpha}_{t+1}$. The main reason is that during the optimization procedure each local machine fits the local data by $\boldsymbol{\alpha}_t + (\boldsymbol{d}_t)_{<S_r>}$, so the prediction accuracy is better than the global model $(\boldsymbol{\alpha}_t + \boldsymbol{d}_t)$ which may not fit each local model that well.

Summary: Computational and Memory Cost: In Section 4.1, we showed that the greedy coordinate descent solver only requires

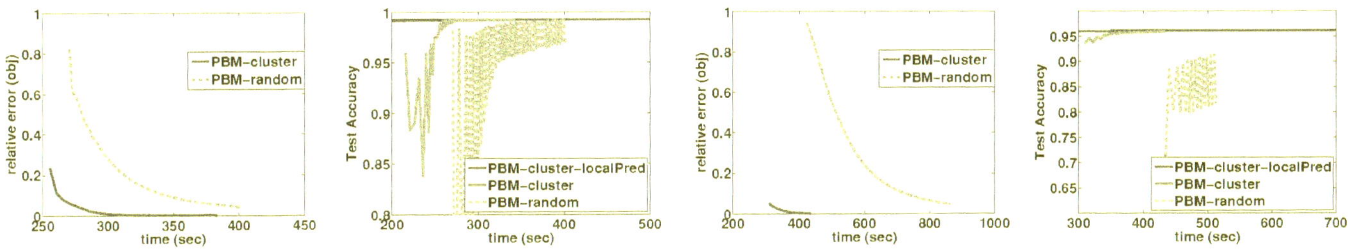

(a) webspam **obj** (b) webspam **accuracy** (c) covtype **obj** (d) covtype **accuracy**

Figure 1: Comparison of different variances of PBM. We observe PBM with kmeans partitioning converges faster than random partition, and the accuracy can further be improved by using our local prediction heuristic.

$O(|S_r|)$ time complexity per inner iteration. Before communication, we need to compute $Q_{:,S_r}\boldsymbol{d}_{S_r}$ in each machine, which requires $O(tn)$ time complexity, where t is number of inner iterations. The line search requires only $O(n/k)$ time. Therefore, the overall time complexity is $O(tn)$ for totally $O(tk)$ coordinate updates from all workers, so the average time per update is $O(n/k)$, which is k times faster than the original greedy coordinate descent (or SMO) algorithm for kernel SVM, where k is number of machines.

The time for running kmeans is $O(\bar{n}\bar{d})$ using k computers, where $\bar{n}$ is number subsamples (we set it to 20,000). This is a one time cost and is very small comparing to the cost of solving kernel machines. For example, on Covtype dataset the kmeans step only took 13 seconds, while the overall training time is 772 seconds. Note that **we include the clustering time in all the experimental results.**

Memory Cost: In kernel SVM, the main memory bottleneck is the memory needed for storing the kernel matrix. Without any trick (such as shrinking) to reduce the kernel storage, the space complexity is $O(n^2)$ for kernel SVM (otherwise we have to recompute kernel values when needed). Using our approach, (1) the subproblem solver only requires $O(n^2/k^2)$ space for the sub-matrix of kernel Q_{S_r,S_r} (2) Before synchronization, computing $Q_{:,S_r}\boldsymbol{d}_{S_r}$ requires $O(n^2/k)$ kernel entries. Therefore, the memory requirement will be reduced from n^2 to n^2/k using our algorithm. However, for large datasets the memory is still not enough. Therefore, similar to the LIBSVM software, we maintain a kernel cache to store columns of Q, and maintain the cache using the Least Recent Used (LRU) policy. In short, if memory is not enough, we use the kernel caching technique (implemented in LIBSVM) that computes the kernel values on-the-fly when it is not in the kernel cache and maintains recently used values in memory.

If each machine contains all the training samples, then $Q_{:,S_r}\boldsymbol{d}_{S_r}$ can be computed in parallel without any communication, and we only need one REDUCE_SCATTER mpi operation to gather the results. However, if each machine only contains a subset of samples, they have to broadcast $\{\boldsymbol{x}_i \mid i \in S_r, d_i \neq 0\}$ to other machines so that each machine q can compute $(Q\boldsymbol{d})_{S_q}$. In this case, we do not need to store the whole training data in each machine, and the communication time will be proportional to number of support vectors, which is usually much smaller than n.

5 CONVERGENCE ANALYSIS

In this section we show that PBM has a global linear convergence rate under certain mild conditions. Note that our result is stronger than some recent theoretical analysis of distributed coordinate descent. Compared to [9], we show linear convergence even when the objective function (1) is *not* strictly positive definite (e.g., for SVM with hinge loss), while [9] only has sub-linear convergence rate for those cases. In comparing to [14], they assume that the subproblems in each worker are solved exactly, while we allow an approximate subproblem solver (e.g., coordinate descent with ≥ 1 steps).

First we assume the objective function satisfies the following global error bound property. This is a weaker notion of strong convexity, in the sense that all the strongly convex functions satisfy this assumption (in those cases, κ is the condition number), but many other machine learning problems also satisfy this assumption even if they are not strongly convex [7, 26].

Definition 5.1 (Global error bound). Problem (1) admits a "global error bound" if there is a constant κ such that

$$\|\boldsymbol{\alpha} - P_S(\boldsymbol{\alpha})\| \leq \kappa \|T(\boldsymbol{\alpha}) - \boldsymbol{\alpha}\|, \quad (14)$$

where $P_S(\cdot)$ is the Euclidean projection to the set S of optimal solutions, and $T : \mathbb{R}^n \rightarrow \mathbb{R}^n$ is the operator defined by

$$T_i(\boldsymbol{\alpha}) = \arg\min_u f(\boldsymbol{\alpha} + (u - \alpha_i)\boldsymbol{e}_i), \ \forall i = 1, \ldots, n. \quad (15)$$

where $\boldsymbol{e}_i$ is the standard i-th unit vector and u is the variable to minimize. We say that the algorithm satisfies a global error bound from the beginning if (14) holds for the level set $\{\boldsymbol{\alpha} \mid f(\boldsymbol{\alpha}) \leq f(\mathbf{0})\}$.

Next, we discuss some problems that admit a global error bound:

Corollary 5.2. *Problem* (1) *satisfies a global error bound from the beginning if one of the following conditions is true.*

- *Q is positive definite (kernel is positive definite).*
- *For all $i = 1, \ldots, n$, $g_i(\cdot)$ is strongly convex for all the iterates (e.g., dual ℓ_2-regularized logistic regression with positive semi-definite kernel).*
- *Q is positive semi-definite and $g_i(\cdot)$ is linear for all i with a box constraint (e.g., dual hinge loss SVM with positive semi-definite kernel).*

Corollary 5.2 implies that many widely used machine learning problems, including dual formulation of SVM and ℓ_2-regularized logistic regression, admit a global error bound from the beginning even when the kernel has a zero eigenvalue. These have been proved in Theorem 1 of [7] and in [26].

We do not require the inner solver to obtain the exact solution of (7). Instead, we define the following condition for the inexact inner solver.

Definition 5.3. An inexact solver for solving the subproblem (7) achieves a "local linear improvement" if the inexact solution $\boldsymbol{d}_{S_r}$ satisfies

$$f_{\boldsymbol{\alpha}}^{(r)}(\boldsymbol{d}_{S_r}) - f_{\boldsymbol{\alpha}}^{(r)}(\hat{\boldsymbol{d}}_{S_r}) \leq \eta\big(f_{\boldsymbol{\alpha}}^{(r)}(0) - f_{\boldsymbol{\alpha}}^{(r)}(\hat{\boldsymbol{d}}_{S_r})\big), \tag{16}$$

for all iterates, where $f_{\boldsymbol{\alpha}}^{(r)}$ is the subproblem defined in (7), $\hat{\boldsymbol{d}}_{S_r} := \arg\min_\Delta f_{\boldsymbol{\alpha}}^{(r)}(\Delta)$ is the optimal solution of the subproblem, and $\eta \in (0,1)$ is a constant.

In the following we list some widely-used subproblem solvers that satisfy Definition 5.3.

Corollary 5.4. *The following subproblem solvers satisfy Definition 5.3 if the objective function admits a global error bound from the beginning: (1) Greedy Coordinate Descent with at least one step. (2) Cyclic coordinate descent with at least one epoch.*

The condition of (16) will be satisfied if an algorithm has a global linear convergence rate. The global linear convergence rate of cyclic coordinate descent has been proved in Section 3 of [26], and the linear convergence rate for greedy coordinate descent can be shown easily using the same analysis (see http://arxiv.org/abs/1608.02010).

We now show our proposed method PBM in Algorithm 1 has a global linear convergence rate in the following theorem.

Theorem 5.5. *Assume (1) the objective function admits a global error bound from the beginning (Definition 5.1), (2) the inner solver achieves a local linear improvement (Definition 5.3), (3)* $R_{min} = \min_i Q_{ii} \neq 0$, *and (4) the objective function is L-Lipschitz continuous for the level set. Then the following global linear convergence rate holds:*

$$f(\boldsymbol{\alpha}_{t+1}) - f(\boldsymbol{\alpha}^*) \leq \Big(1 - (1-\eta)\frac{R_{min}}{kBL\kappa^2}\Big)\big(f(\boldsymbol{\alpha}_t) - f(\boldsymbol{\alpha}^*)\big),$$

where $\boldsymbol{\alpha}^*$ *is an optimal solution, and* $B = \max_{r=1}^k |S_r|$ *is the maximum block size.*

Proof. We first define some notations that we will use in the proof. Let $\boldsymbol{\alpha}_t$ be the current solution of iteration t, $\boldsymbol{d}_t$ is the approximate solution of (7) satisfying Definition 5.3. For convenience we will omit the subscript t here (so $\boldsymbol{d} := \boldsymbol{d}_t$). We use $\boldsymbol{d}_{S_r}$ to denote the size $|S_r|$ subvector, and $\boldsymbol{d}_{<S_r>}$ to denote the n dimensional vector with

$$\boldsymbol{d}_{<S_r>} = \begin{cases} d_i & \text{if } i \in S_r \\ 0 & \text{otherwise} \end{cases}$$

By the definition of our line search procedure described in Section 4.2, we have

$$f(\boldsymbol{\alpha}_t + \beta \boldsymbol{d}) \leq f(\boldsymbol{\alpha}_t + \frac{1}{k}\sum_{r=1}^k \boldsymbol{d}_{<S_r>})$$

$$= f(\frac{1}{k}\sum_{r=1}^k(\boldsymbol{\alpha}_t + \boldsymbol{d}_{<S_r>})) \leq \frac{1}{k}\sum_{r=1}^k f(\boldsymbol{\alpha}_t + \boldsymbol{d}_{<S_r>}),$$

where the last inequality is from the convexity of $f(\cdot)$. We define $\hat{\boldsymbol{d}}$ to be the optimal solution of (4) (so each $\hat{\boldsymbol{d}}_{S_r}$ is the optimal solution of the r-th subproblem (7)). Then we have

$$f(\boldsymbol{\alpha}_t) - f(\boldsymbol{\alpha}_t + \boldsymbol{d}_t) \geq f(\boldsymbol{\alpha}_t) - \frac{1}{k}\sum_{r=1}^k f(\boldsymbol{\alpha}_t + \boldsymbol{d}_{<S_r>})$$

$$= \frac{1}{k}\sum_{r=1}^k \Big(f(\boldsymbol{\alpha}_t) - f(\boldsymbol{\alpha}_t + \hat{\boldsymbol{d}}_{<S_r>}) + f(\boldsymbol{\alpha}_t + \hat{\boldsymbol{d}}_{<S_r>}) - f(\boldsymbol{\alpha}_t + \boldsymbol{d}_{<S_r>})\Big)$$

$$\geq \frac{1}{k}\sum_{r=1}^k (1-\eta)\Big(f(\boldsymbol{\alpha}_t) - f(\boldsymbol{\alpha}_t + \hat{\boldsymbol{d}}_{<S_r>})\Big), \tag{17}$$

where the last inequality is from the local linear improvement of the in-exact subproblem solver (Definition 5.3). We then define a vector $\bar{\boldsymbol{d}}$ where each element is the optimal solution of the one variable subproblem:

$$\bar{d}_i = T_i(\boldsymbol{\alpha}_t) - (\boldsymbol{\alpha}_t)_i \ \ \forall i = 1, \ldots, n,$$

where $T_i(\boldsymbol{\alpha}_t)$ was defined in (15). First, by the definition of $\bar{Q}$ in (5), there is no approximation if the update vector is within one block, so we have $\bar{f}_{\boldsymbol{\alpha}}(\boldsymbol{d}_{<S_r>}) = f(\boldsymbol{\alpha} + \boldsymbol{d}_{<S_r>})$ for any block r. Since $\hat{\boldsymbol{d}}_{S_r}$ is the optimal solution of each subproblem, we have

$$f(\boldsymbol{\alpha}_t + \hat{\boldsymbol{d}}_{<S_r>}) \leq f(\boldsymbol{\alpha}_t + \bar{\boldsymbol{d}}_{<S_r>}/|S_r|), \ \forall r = 1, \ldots, k.$$

Combining with (17) we get

$$f(\boldsymbol{\alpha}_t) - f(\boldsymbol{\alpha}_t + \boldsymbol{d}_t) \geq \frac{1-\eta}{k}\sum_{r=1}^k \big(f(\boldsymbol{\alpha}_t) - f(\boldsymbol{\alpha}_t + \bar{\boldsymbol{d}}_{<S_r>}/|S_r|)\big)$$

$$\geq \frac{1-\eta}{k}\sum_{r=1}^k \Big(f(\boldsymbol{\alpha}_t) - \frac{1}{|S_r|}\sum_{i\in S_r} f(\boldsymbol{\alpha}_t + \bar{\boldsymbol{d}}_{<i>})\Big) \ \text{(by convexity)}$$

$$\geq \frac{1-\eta}{kB}\sum_{i=1}^n \big(f(\boldsymbol{\alpha}_t) - f(\boldsymbol{\alpha}_t + \bar{\boldsymbol{d}}_{<i>})\big),$$

where the last inequality is by the definition of B. Now consider the one variable problem $f(\boldsymbol{\alpha}_t + u\boldsymbol{e}_i)$. Since R_{min} is the lower bound of $f''(\boldsymbol{\alpha}_t + u\boldsymbol{e}_i)$ and $\bar{d}_i$ is the optimal for this single variate function, we have $f(\boldsymbol{\alpha}_t) \geq f(\boldsymbol{\alpha}_t + \bar{\boldsymbol{d}}_{<i>}) + \frac{1}{2}R_{min}\bar{d}_i^2$. As a result,

$$\sum_{i=1}^n \Big(f(\boldsymbol{\alpha}_t) - f(\boldsymbol{\alpha}_t + \bar{\boldsymbol{d}}_{<i>})\Big) \geq \sum_{i=1}^n R_{min}\bar{d}_i^2 = R_{min}\|\bar{\boldsymbol{d}}\|^2.$$

Therefore,

$$\begin{aligned} f(\boldsymbol{\alpha}_t) - f(\boldsymbol{\alpha}_t + \boldsymbol{d}_t) &\geq \frac{R_{min}(1-\eta)}{kB}\|T(\boldsymbol{\alpha}_t) - \boldsymbol{\alpha}_t\|^2 \\ &\geq \frac{R_{min}(1-\eta)}{kB\kappa^2}\|P_S(\boldsymbol{\alpha}_t) - \boldsymbol{\alpha}_t\|^2 \ \text{(by (14))} \\ &\geq \frac{LR_{min}(1-\eta)}{kB\kappa^2}\|f(\boldsymbol{\alpha}_t) - f(\boldsymbol{\alpha}^*)\|. \end{aligned}$$

Table 1: Dataset statistics

Dataset	# training samples	# testing samples	# features	C	γ
cifar	50,000	10,000	3072	2^3	2^{-22}
webspam	280,000	70,000	254	2^3	2^5
covtype	464,810	116,202	54	2^5	2^5
mnist8m	8,000,000	100,000	784	2^0	2^{-21}
kddb	19,264,097	748,401	29,890,095	2^1	2^{-1}

Therefore, we have

$$f(\boldsymbol{\alpha}_{t+1}) - f(\boldsymbol{\alpha}^*) = f(\boldsymbol{\alpha}_t) - \big(f(\boldsymbol{\alpha}_t) - f(\boldsymbol{\alpha}_{t+1})\big) - f(\boldsymbol{\alpha}^*)$$
$$\leq \left(1 - \frac{R_{min}(1-\eta)}{kBL\kappa^2}\right)\big(f(\boldsymbol{\alpha}_t) - f(\boldsymbol{\alpha}^*)\big).$$

□

Note that we do not make any assumption on the partition used in PBM, so our analysis works for a wide class of optimization solvers, including distributed linear SVM solver in [14] where they only consider that case when the subproblems are solved exactly.

To sum up, Theorem 5.5 shows that the proposed PBM framework converges linearly as long as the subproblem solver satisfies Definition 5.3, which means that the subproblem solver linearly reduces the approximate function $\bar{f}_{\boldsymbol{\alpha}}$. Since coordinate descent has linear convergence rate (Corollary 5.4), the PBM algorithm converges linearly if we run ≥ 1 greedy or random coordinate descent update in the inner iteration for solving the subproblem.

6 EXPERIMENTAL RESULTS

We conduct experiments on five public large-scale datasets listed in Table 1. We follow the procedure in [5, 33] to transform cifar and mnist8m into binary classification problems, and Gaussian kernel $K(\boldsymbol{x}_i, \boldsymbol{x}_j) = e^{-\gamma\|\boldsymbol{x}_i - \boldsymbol{x}_j\|^2}$ is used in all the comparisons. Our code can be downloaded from https://github.com/cjhsieh/Distributed-KSVM.

We follow the parameter settings in [5], where C and γ are selected by 5-fold cross validation on a grid of parameters. The experiments are conducted on Texas Advanced Computing Center Maverick cluster, where each machine has a 20-core CPU with 256GB memory. In this paper, we mainly focus on kernel SVM and kernel logistic regression.

We compare our PBM method with the following distributed kernel SVM solvers, where all of them are implemented in C++ and the inter-machine communication is using MPI:

1. P-pack SVM [35]: a parallel Stochastic Gradient Descent (SGD) algorithm for kernel SVM training. We set the pack size $r = 100$ according to the original paper.
2. Random Fourier features with distributed LIBLINEAR (RFF-LIBLINEAR): RFF-LIBLINEAR generates random Fourier features and solves the resulting problem by LIBLINEAR. In a distributed system, we can compute random features [19] for each sample in parallel (this is a one-time preprocessing step), and then solve the resulting linear SVM problem by distributed dual coordinate descent [14] implemented in MPI LIBLINEAR. Note that although Fastfood [13] can generate random features in a faster way, the bottleneck for RFF-LIBLINEAR is solving the resulting linear SVM problem after generating random features, so the performance is similar.
3. Nyström approximation with distributed LIBLINEAR (NYS-LIBLINEAR): We implemented the ensemble Nyström approximation [12] with kmeans sampling in a distributed system and solved the resulting linear SVM problem by MPI LIBLINEAR. The approach is similar to [16].
4. PSVM [3]: a parallel kernel SVM solver by in-complete Cholesky factorization and a parallel interior point method. We test the performance of PSVM with the rank suggested by the original paper ($n^{0.5}$ or $n^{0.6}$ where n is number of samples).

We also compare with the state-of-the-art single-thread nonlinear kernel SVM solver DC-SVM [5] and multi-core kernel SVM solver Asyn-GCD [30] in our experiments. Unfortunately, they cannot run on distributed systems (see our discussions in Section 2, so we just use them to serve as baselines for single-thread and single-machine multi-thread kernel SVM solvers respectively. For these two solvers we directly run the code released by the authors.

Comparison with other distributed kernel SVM solvers. We use 32 machines (each with 1 thread) and the best C, γ for all the solvers. Our parameter settings are exactly the same with [5] chosen by cross-validation in $[2^{-30}, 2^{10}]$. For cifar and mnist8m the samples are not normalized, so the averaged norm mean($\|\boldsymbol{x}_i\|$) is large (it is 876 on cifar). Since Gaussian kernel is $e^{-\gamma\|\boldsymbol{x}_i - \boldsymbol{x}_j\|^2}$, a good γ will be very small. We can normalize the data as well, and then a good γ will become larger. We mainly compare the *prediction accuracy* in the paper because most of the parallel kernel SVM solvers are "approximate solvers"—they solve an approximated problem, so it is not fair to evaluate them using the original objective function. In Figure 2 (a)-(d) we compare our proposed algorithm with other kernel SVM solvers. Note that in these figures, we vary the number random features for RFF-LIBLINEAR and the number of landmark points for NYS-LIBLINEAR. The results in Figure 2 (a)-(d) indicate that our proposed algorithm is much faster than other approaches. We further test the algorithms with varied number of workers and parameters in Table 2. Note that PSVM usually gets much lower test accuracy since it approximates the kernel matrix by incomplete Cholesky factorization, so we only show its results in Table 2.

MPI+OpenMP Hybrid Implementation. In the previous experiment, each machine only runs with one MPI worker. To exploit the power of each machine, we further implement an MPI+OpenMP hybrid version of our algorithm. In this setting, each machine can use multiple cores with OpenMP, and the between-machine communication is still done by MPI. Since cores in the same machine can access the shared memory space, the parallelism is often simpler because there is almost no communication cost.

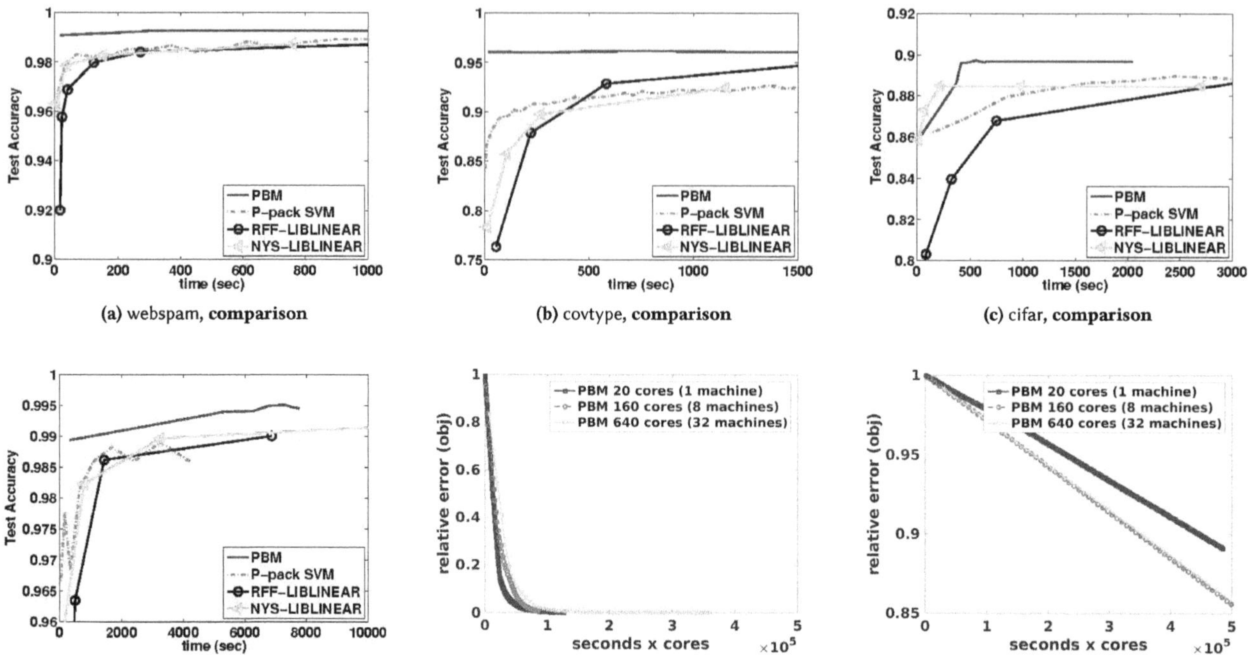

(a) webspam, **comparison** (b) covtype, **comparison** (c) cifar, **comparison**

(d) mnist8m, **comparison** (e) covtype, **scaling** (f) kddb, **scaling**

Figure 2: (a)-(d): Comparison with other distributed kernel SVM solvers using 32 workers. Markers for RFF-LIBLINEAR and NYS-LIBLINEAR are obtained by varying the number random features and landmark points respectively. (e)-(f): The objective function of PBM as a function of computation time (time in seconds × the number of workers), when the number of workers is varied. Results show that PBM has very good scalability on large datasets.

Table 2: Comparison on real datasets for kernel SVM. Here we use 32 machines (each machine with 1 thread) for all the distributed solvers (PBM, P-packSGD, PSVM), and 1 machine for the serial solver (DC-SVM). For kddb, we use 32 machines and 20 cores in each machine to test MPI+OpenMP Hybrid Implementation of PBM. The first column of PBM shows that PBM achieves good test accuracy after 1 iteration, and the second column of PBM shows PBM can achieve an accurate solution (with $\frac{f(\alpha)-f(\alpha^*)}{|f(\alpha^*)|} < 10^{-3}$) quickly and obtain even better accuracy. Note that "-" indicates the training time is more than 10 hours.

	PBM (first step)		PBM (10^{-3} error)		P-packSGD		PSVM $p = n^{0.5}$		PSVM $p = n^{0.6}$		DC-SVM (10^{-3} error)	
	time(s)	acc(%)	time(s)	acc(%)	time(s)	acc(%)	time(s)	acc(%)	time(s)	acc(%)	time(s)	acc(%)
webspam	**16**	99.07	360	**99.26**	1478	98.99	773	75.79	2304	88.68	8742	99.26
covtype	**14**	96.05	772	**96.13**	1349	92.67	286	76.00	7071	81.53	10457	96.13
cifar	**15**	85.91	540	**89.72**	1233	88.31	41	79.89	1474	69.73	13006	89.72
mnist8m	**321**	98.94	8112	**99.45**	2414	98.60	-	-	-	-	-	-
kddb	**1832**	88.59	32740	**88.76**	-	-	-	-	-	-	-	-

In our implementation, within each machine, we use OpenMP to compute the elements of kernel matrix in parallel. There are two places requiring kernel value computations: (1) When using the greedy coordinate descent algorithm to solve the subproblem (Step 4 in Algorithm 1), we need to access the i-th column of kernel matrix Q when updating the variable α_i, and (2) Step 5 in Algorithm 1 for computing $Q_{:,S_r} \boldsymbol{d}_{S_r}$. Note that we use the kernel cache strategy developed in LIBSVM for maintaining several columns of kernel matrix in memory, and remove the Least Recent Used (LRU) column when running out of memory space. Therefore, the OpenMP parallelism is used when the required kernel matrix column is not found in kernel cache (cache miss) and needed to be computed from scratch. Surprisingly, this simple hybrid implementation achieves superb speedup, especially in very large datasets when the memory can only cache a small portion of kernel matrix. For example, on covtype dataset, PBM with 32 machines and using 20 cores per machine is 8.9 times faster than its pure MPI implementation that only uses 1 core per machine; on kddb dataset, with the same setting, hybrid PBM is 15.2 times faster than its MPI version with 1 core per machine.

Scalability of PBM. For the second experiment we varied the number of machines from 1 to 32, and plot the scaling behavior of PBM. In Figure 2 (e)-(f), we set y-axis to be the relative error defined

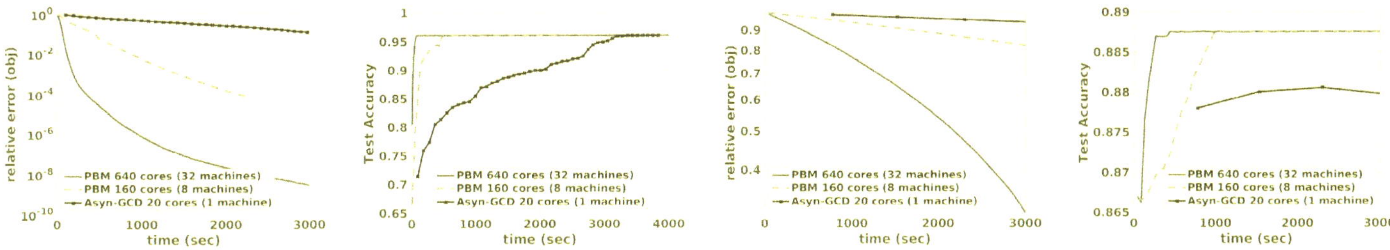

(a) covtype, obj (b) covtype, accuracy (c) kddb, obj (d) kddb, accuracy

Figure 3: Comparison with Asyn-GCD, the state-of-the-art multi-core single machine kernel SVM solver. Results show that our algortihm is uch faster than Asyn-GCD by using multiple computers.

by $(f(\alpha_t) - f(\alpha^*))/f(\alpha^*)$ where α^* is the optimal solution, and x-axis to be the total CPU time expended which is given by the number of seconds elapsed multiplied by the number of workers. We plot the convergence curves by changing number of machines (and using all the 20 cores in each machine). The perfect linear speedup is achieved if the curves overlap. This is indeed the case for both covtype and kddb.

Interestingly, in the kddb dataset, we observe a super-linear speedup when using 8 and 32 machines compared with the single-machine version. This is mainly due to the increasing amount of memory available for caching kernel values—for example, a single machine can only afford 100GB memory for storing the computed kernel values, while using 32 machines there will be a total amount of 3200GB memory for storing those values. Therefore, the "kernel cache miss rate" (portion of kernel values that needs to be recomputed) is much better as number of machine increases. As a result, the speedup of is almost linear and sometimes even super linear.

Comparison with single-machine solvers. We also compare PBM with state-of-the-art single machine solver for kernel SVM: Asyn-GCD [30] which uses multiple cores in a single machine, and DC-SVM [5] which can only run with a single thread. The results are in Table 2 and Figure 3. DC-SVM first computes the solutions in each partition, and then use the concatenation of local (dual) solutions to initialize a global kernel SVM solver (e.g., LIBSVM). However, the top level of DC-SVM is the bottleneck (taking 2/3 of the run time), so the speed is still slow in Table 2. Asyn-GCD is an asynchronous parallel coordinate descent algorithm for kernel SVM, and it performs much better than other single-machine SVM solvers including LIBSVM (see [30]). In Figure 3, we show that our distributed algorithm is much faster using multiple machines which might not be the case for some other distributed solvers. This confirms that our algorithm is much faster than the best single-machine kernel SVM solver.

Kernel logistic regression. We implement the PBM algorithm to solve the kernel logistic regression problem. Note that PSVM cannot be directly applied to kernel logistic regression. We use greedy coordinate descent proposed in [11] to solve each subproblem (7). The results are presented in Table 3, showing that our algorithm is faster than P-packSGD.

Table 3: Comparison on real datasets for kernel logistic regression. Here we use 32 machines (each machine with 1 thread).

	PBM (first step)		PBM (10^{-3} error)		P-packSGD	
	time(s)	acc(%)	time(s)	acc(%)	time(s)	acc(%)
webspam	**1679**	92.01	2131	**99.07**	4417	98.96
cifar	**471**	83.37	758	**88.14**	2115	87.07

7 CONCLUSION

We have proposed a parallel block minimization (PBM) framework for solving kernel machines on distributed systems. We show that PBM significantly outperforms other approaches on large-scale datasets, and prove a global linear convergence of PBM under mild conditions. By using 32 machines with totally 640 cores, our algorithm can solve the kddb dataset with 20 millions samples and 30 millions features in half hour.

Acknowledgments This research was supported by NSF grants CCF-1320746, IIS- 1546452 and CCF-1564000. Cho-Jui Hsieh also acknowledges support from XSEDE.

REFERENCES

[1] E. Chan, M. Heimlich, A. Purkayastha, and R. van de Geijn. 2007. Collective Communication: Theory, Practice, and Experience. *Concurrency and Computation: Practice and Experience* 19 (2007), 1749–1783.
[2] Chih-Chung Chang and Chih-Jen Lin. 2000. *LIBSVM: Introduction and Benchmarks.* Technical Report. Department of Computer Science and Information Engineering, National Taiwan University, Taipei, Taiwan.
[3] E. Chang, K. Zhu, H. Wang, H. Bai, J. Li, Z. Qiu, and H. Cui. 2008. Parallelizing Support Vector Machines on Distributed Computers. In *NIPS.*
[4] H. P. Graf, E. Cosatto, L. Bottou, I. Dundanovic, and V. Vapnik. 2005. Parallel Support Vector Machines: The Cascade SVM. In *NIPS.*
[5] C. J. Hsieh, S. Si, and I. S. Dhillon. 2014. A Divide-and-Conquer Solver for Kernel Support Vector Machines. In *ICML.*
[6] Cho-Jui Hsieh, Si Si, and Inderjit S Dhillon. 2014. Fast prediction for large-scale kernel machines. In *Advances in Neural Information Processing Systems.* 3689–3697.
[7] C.-J. Hsieh, H. F. Yu, and I. S. Dhillon. 2015. PASSCoDe: Parallel ASynchronous Stochastic dual Coordinate Descent. In *ICML.*
[8] P.-S. Huang, H. Avron, T. Sainath, V. Sindhwani, and B. Ramabhadran. 2014. Kernel Methods Match Deep Neural Networks on TIMIT. In *ICASSP.* 205–209.
[9] M. Jaggi, V. Smith, M. Takáč, J. Terhorst, T. Hofmann, and M. Jordan. 2014. Communication-efficient Distributed Dual Coordinate ascent. In *NIPS.*
[10] Thorsten Joachims. 1998. Making Large-scale SVM Learning Practical. In *Advances in Kernel Methods – Support Vector Learning.*
[11] S. Sathiya Keerthi, Kaibo Duan, Shirish Shevade, and Aun Neow Poo. 2005. A Fast Dual Algorithm for Kernel Logistic Regression. *Machine Learning* 61 (2005), 151–165.
[12] S. Kumar, M. Mohri, and A. Talwalkar. 2009. Ensemble Nyström Method. In *NIPS.*

[13] Q. Le, T. Sarlós, and A. Smola. 2013. Fastfood – Approximating Kernel Expansions in Loglinear Time. In *ICML*.

[14] C.-P. Lee and D. Roth. 2015. Distributed Box-Constrained Quadratic Optimization for Dual Linear SVM. In *ICML*.

[15] Chenxin Ma, Virginia Smith, Martin Jaggi, Michael I. Jordan, Peter Richtárik, and Martin Takáč. 2015. Adding vs. Averaging in Distributed Primal-Dual Optimization. In *ICML*.

[16] Dhruv Mahajan, S. Sathiya Keerthi, and Sundararajan Sellamanickam. 2014. A Distributed Algorithm for Training Nonlinear Kernel Machines. *arXiv:1405.4543* (2014).

[17] Dhruv Mahajan, S. Sathiya Keerthi, and Sundararajan Sellamanickam. 2014. A distributed block coordinate descent method for training L1 regularized linear classifiers. *arXiv:1405.4544* (2014).

[18] John C. Platt. 1998. Fast Training of Support Vector Machines using Sequential Minimal Optimization. In *Advances in Kernel Methods - Support Vector Learning*.

[19] Ali Rahimi and Benjamin Recht. 2008. Random Features for Large-scale Kernel Machines. In *NIPS*.

[20] P. Richtárik and M. Takáč. 2012. Parallel Coordinate Descent Methods for Big Data Optimization. *Mathematical Programming* (2012).

[21] C. Scherrer, A. Tewari, M. Halappanavar, and D. Haglin. 2012. Feature Clustering for Accelerating Parallel Coordinate Descent. In *NIPS*.

[22] Si Si, Kai-Yang Chiang, Cho-Jui Hsieh, Nikhil Rao, and Inderjit S. Dhillon. 2016. Goal-Directed Inductive Matrix Completion. In *KDD*. 1165–1174.

[23] Si Si, Cho-Jui Hsieh, and Inderjit S. Dhillon. 2016. Computationally Efficient Nyström Approximation using Fast Transforms. In *ICML*. 2655–2663.

[24] S. Si, C. J. Hsieh, and I. S. Dhillon. 2017. Memory Efficient Kernel Approximation. (2017).

[25] Stephen Tu, Rebecca Roelofs, Shivaram Venkataraman, and Benjamin Recht. 2016. Large Scale Kernel Learning using Block Coordinate Descent. *CoRR* abs/1602.05310 (2016).

[26] P.-W. Wang and C.-J. Lin. 2014. Iteration Complexity of Feasible Descent Methods for Convex Optimization. *Journal of Machine Learning Research* 15 (2014), 1523–1548.

[27] C. K. I. Williams and M. Seeger. 2001. Using the Nyström Method to Speed Up Kernel Machines. In *NIPS*.

[28] T. Yang. 2013. Trading Computation for Communication: Distributed Stochastic Dual Coordinate Ascent. In *NIPS*.

[29] Y. You, J. Demmel, K. Czechowski, L. Song, and R. Vuduc. 2015. CA-SVM: Communication-Avoiding Support Vector Machines on Clusters. In *IPDPS*.

[30] Yang You, Xiangru Lian, Ji Liu, Hsiang-Fu Yu, Inderjit Dhillon, James Demmel, and Cho-Jui Hsieh. 2016. Asynchronous Parallel Greedy Coordinate Descent. In *NIPS*.

[31] H.-F. Yu, F.-L. Huang, and C.-J. Lin. 2011. Dual Coordinate Descent Methods for Logistic Regression and Maximum Entropy Models. *Machine Learning* 85, 1-2 (2011), 41–75.

[32] Huan Zhang and Cho-Jui Hsieh. 2016. Fixing the convergence problems in parallel asynchronous dual coordinate descent. In *ICDM*.

[33] K. Zhang, L. Lan, Z. Wang, and F. Moerchen. 2012. Scaling up Kernel SVM on Limited Resources: A Low-rank Linearization Approach. In *AISTATS*.

[34] Y. Zhang and L. Xiao. 2015. DiSCO: Communication-Efficient Distributed Optimization of Self-Concordant Loss. In *ICML*.

[35] Zeyuan A. Zhu, Weizhu Chen, Gang Wang, Chenguang Zhu, and Zheng Chen. 2009. P-packSVM: Parallel Primal Gradient Descent Kernel SVM. In *ICDM*.

A Hierarchical Algorithm for Extreme Clustering

Ari Kobren*, Nicholas Monath*, Akshay Krishnamurthy, Andrew McCallum
akobren,nmonath,akshay,mccallum@cs.umass.edu
College of Information and Computer Sciences
University of Massachusetts Amherst

ABSTRACT

Many modern clustering methods scale well to a large number of data points, N, but not to a large number of clusters, K. This paper introduces Perch, a new non-greedy, incremental algorithm for hierarchical clustering that scales to both massive N and K—a problem setting we term *extreme clustering*. Our algorithm efficiently routes new data points to the leaves of an incrementally-built tree. Motivated by the desire for both accuracy and speed, our approach performs tree rotations for the sake of enhancing subtree purity and encouraging balancedness. We prove that, under a natural separability assumption, our non-greedy algorithm will produce trees with perfect dendrogram purity regardless of data arrival order. Our experiments demonstrate that Perch constructs more accurate trees than other tree-building clustering algorithms and scales well with both N and K, achieving a higher quality clustering than the strongest flat clustering competitor in nearly half the time.

CCS CONCEPTS

•Mathematics of computing → Cluster analysis; •Computing methodologies → Online learning settings;

KEYWORDS

Clustering; Large-scale learning

1 INTRODUCTION

Clustering algorithms are a crucial component of any data scientist's toolbox with applications ranging from identifying themes in large text corpora [12], to finding functionally similar genes [18], to visualization, pre-processing, and dimensionality reduction [22]. As such, a number of clustering algorithms have been developed and studied by the statistics, machine learning, and theoretical computer science communities. These algorithms and analyses target a variety of scenarios, including large-scale, online, or streaming settings [2, 41], clustering with distribution shift [3], and many more.

Modern clustering applications require algorithms that scale gracefully with dataset size and complexity. In clustering, dataset size is measured by the number of points N and their dimensionality d, while the number of clusters, K, serves as a measure of complexity. While several existing algorithms can cope with large datasets, very few adequately handle datasets with many clusters. We call problem instances with large N and large K *extreme clustering problems*–a phrase inspired by work in extreme classification [14].

Extreme clustering problems are increasingly prevalent. For example, in entity resolution, record linkage and deduplication, the number of clusters (i.e., entities) increases with dataset size [8] and can be in the millions. Similarly, the number of communities in typical real-world networks tends to follow a power-law distribution [15] that also increases with network size. Although used primarily in classification tasks, the ImageNet dataset also describes precisely this large N, large K regime ($N \approx 14M, K \approx 21K$) [17, 36].

This paper presents a new incremental clustering algorithm, called Perch, that scales mildly with both N and K and thus addresses the extreme clustering setting. Our algorithm constructs a tree structure over the data points in an incremental fashion by routing incoming points to the leaves, growing the tree, and maintaining its quality via simple *rotation* operations. The tree structure enables efficient (often logarithmic time) search that scales to large datasets, while simultaneously providing a rich data structure from which multiple clusterings at various resolutions can be extracted. The rotations provide an efficient mechanism for our algorithm to recover from mistakes that arise with greedy incremental clustering procedures.

Operating under a simple separability assumption about the data, we prove that our algorithm constructs a tree with perfect *dendrogram purity* regardless of the number of data points and without knowledge of the number of clusters. This analysis relies crucially on a recursive rotation procedure employed by our algorithm. For scalability, we introduce another flavor of rotations that encourage balancedness, and an approximation that enables faster point insertions. We also develop a leaf *collapsing* mode of our algorithm that can operate in memory-limited settings, when the dataset does not fit in main memory.

We empirically demonstrate that our algorithm is both accurate and efficient in clustering a variety of real-world datasets. In comparison to other tree-building algorithms (that are both incremental and multipass), Perch achieves the highest dendrogram purity in addition to being efficient. When compared to flat clustering algorithms where the number of clusters is given by an oracle, Perch with a pruning heuristic outperforms or is competitive with all other scalable algorithms. In both comparisons to flat and tree building algorithms, Perch scales best with the number of clusters.

*The first two authors contributed equally.

KDD '17, August 13-17, 2017, Halifax, NS, Canada

978-1-4503-4887-4/17/08...$15.00
DOI: 10.1145/3097983.3098079

2 THE CLUSTERING PROBLEM

In a *clustering problem* we are given a dataset $X = \{x_i\}_{i=1}^N$ of *points*. The goal is to partition the dataset into a set of disjoint subsets (i.e., clusters), C, such that the union of all subsets covers the dataset. Such a set of subsets is called a *clustering*. A high quality clustering is one in which the points in any particular subset are more similar to each other than the points in other subsets.

A clustering, C, can be represented as a map from points to clusters identities, $C : X \rightarrow \{1, \ldots, K\}$. However, structures that encode more fine-grained information also exist. For example, prior works construct a *cluster tree* over the dataset to compactly encode multiple alternative *tree-consistent partitions*, or clusterings [10, 25].

Definition 2.1 (Cluster tree [27]). A binary **cluster tree** $\mathcal{T}$ on a dataset $\{x_i\}_{i=1}^N$ is a collection of subsets such that $C_0 \triangleq \{x_i\}_{i=1}^N \in \mathcal{T}$ and for each $C_i, C_j \in \mathcal{T}$ either $C_i \subset C_j$, $C_j \subset C_i$ or $C_i \cap C_j = \emptyset$. For any $C \in \mathcal{T}$, if $\exists C' \in \mathcal{T}$ with $C' \subset C$, then there exists two $C_L, C_R \in \mathcal{T}$ that partition C.

As terminology, we often refer to the subsets of a cluster tree $\mathcal{T}$ as *nodes*, an internal node is one that is further refined in $\mathcal{T}$, and the leaves of a node are the data points in the corresponding subset. A tree-consistent partition is a subset of the nodes in the tree whose associated clusters partition the dataset, and hence is a valid clustering.

Cluster trees afford multiple advantages in addition to their representational power. For example, when building a cluster tree, it is typically unnecessary to specify the number of target clusters (which, in virtually all real-world problems, is unknown). Cluster trees also provide the opportunity for efficient cluster assignment and search, which is particularly important for large datasets with many clusters. In such problems, $O(K)$ search required by classical methods can be prohibitive, while a top down traversal of a cluster tree could offer $O(\log(K))$ search, which is exponentially faster.

Evaluating a cluster tree is more complex than evaluating a *flat clustering*. Assuming that there exists a ground truth clustering $C^\star = \{C_k^\star\}_{i=1}^K$ into K clusters, it is common to measure the quality of a cluster tree based on a single clustering extracted from the tree. We follow Heller et. al and adopt a more holistic measure of the tree quality, known as *dendrogram purity* [25]. Define

$$\mathcal{P}^\star = \{(x_i, x_j) \mid C^\star(x_i) = C^\star(x_j)\}$$

to be the pairs of points that are clustered together in the ground truth. Then, dendrogram purity is defined as follows.

Definition 2.2 (Dendrogram Purity). Given a cluster tree $\mathcal{T}$ over a dataset $X = \{x_i\}_{i=1}^N$, and a true clustering $C^\star$, the **dendrogram purity** of $\mathcal{T}$ is

$$\mathsf{DP}(\mathcal{T}) = \frac{1}{|\mathcal{P}^\star|} \sum_{k=1}^{K} \sum_{x_i, x_j \in C_k^\star} \mathsf{pur}(\mathsf{lvs}(\mathsf{LCA}(x_i, x_j)), C_k^\star)$$

where $\mathsf{LCA}(x_i, x_j)$ is the least common ancestor of x_i and x_j in $\mathcal{T}$, $\mathsf{lvs}(z) \subset X$ is the set of leaves for any internal node z in $\mathcal{T}$, and $\mathsf{pur}(S_1, S_2) = |S_1 \cap S_2| / |S_1|$.

In words, the dendrogram purity of a tree with respect to a ground truth clustering is the expectation of the following random process: (1) sample two points, x_i, x_j, uniformly at random from the pairs in the ground truth (and thus $C^\star(x_i) = C^\star(x_j)$), (2) compute their least common ancestor in $\mathcal{T}$ and the cluster (i.e. descendant leaves) of that internal node, (3) compute the fraction of points from this cluster that also belong to $C^\star(x_i)$. For large-scale problems, we use Monte Carlo approximations of dendrogram purity. More intuitively, dendrogram purity obviates the (often challenging) task of extracting the best tree-consistent partition, while still providing a meaningful measure of congruence with the ground truth flat clustering.

3 TREE CONSTRUCTION

Our work is focused on instances of the clustering problem in which the size of the dataset N *and* the number of clusters K are both very large. In light of the data structure's advantages with respect to efficiency and representation (Section 2), our method builds a cluster tree over data points. We are also interested in the *incremental* problem setting–in which data points arrive one at a time–because this resembles real-world scenarios in which new data is constantly being created. Well-known clustering methods based on cluster trees, like hierarchical agglomerative clustering, are often not incremental; there exist a few incremental cluster tree approaches, most notably BIRCH [41], but empirical results show that BIRCH typically constructs worse clusterings than most competitors [2, 31].

The following subsections describe and analyze several fundamental components of our algorithm, which constructs a cluster tree in an incremental fashion. The data points are assumed to reside in Euclidean space: $\{x_i\}_{i=1}^N \subset \mathbb{R}^d$. We make no assumptions on the order in which the points are processed.

3.1 Preliminaries

In the clustering literature, it is common to make various *separability assumptions* about the data being clustered. As one example, a set of points is ϵ-separated for K-means if the ratio of the clustering cost with K clusters to the cost with $K-1$ clusters is less than ϵ^2 [33]. While assumptions like these generally do not hold in practice, they motivate the derivation of several powerful and justifiable algorithms. To derive our algorithm, we make a strong separability assumption under $C^\star$.

Assumption 1 (Separability). *A dataset X is* ***separable*** *with respect to a clustering $C^\star$ if*

$$\max_{(x,y)\in\mathcal{P}^\star} \|x - y\| < \min_{(x',y')\notin\mathcal{P}^\star} \|x' - y'\|,$$

where $\|\cdot\|$ is the Euclidean norm. We assume that X is separable *with respect to $C^\star$.*

Thus under separability, the true clustering has all within-cluster distances smaller than any between-cluster distance. The assumption is quite strong, but it is not without precedent. In prior work, clusterings that obey this property are referred to as *nice clusterings* [1] or as *strictly separated* clusterings [7]. The NCBI uses a form of separability in their *clique*-based approach for protein clustering [35]. Separability also aligns well with existing clustering methods; for example under separability, agglomerative methods like complete, single, and average linkage are guaranteed to find $C^\star$, and $C^\star$ is guaranteed to contain the unique optimum of the

K-center cost function. Lastly, we use separability primarily for theoretically grounding the design of our algorithm, and we do not expect it to hold in practice. Our empirical analysis shows that our algorithm outperforms existing methods even when separability does not hold.

3.2 The Greedy Algorithm and Masking

The derivation of our algorithm begins from an attempt to remedy issues with greedy incremental tree construction. Consider the following greedy algorithm: when processing point x_i, a search is preformed to find its nearest neighbor in the current tree. The search returns a leaf node, ℓ, containing the nearest neighbor of x_i. A `Split` operation is performed on ℓ that: (1) disconnects ℓ from its parent, (2) creates a new leaf ℓ' that stores x_i, (3) creates a new internal node whose parent is ℓ's former parent and with children ℓ and ℓ'.

Fact 1. *There exists a separable clustering instance in 1-dimension with two balanced clusters where the greedy algorithm has dendrogram purity at most 7/8.*

Before turning to the proof, note that it is easy to generalize the construction to more clusters and higher dimension, although upper bounding the dendrogram purity may become challenging.

Proof. The construction has two clusters, one with half of its points near −1 and half of its points near +1, and another with all points around +4, so the instance is separable. If we show one point near −1, one point near +1, and then a point near +4, one child of the root contains the latter two points, so the true clustering is irrecoverable. To calculate the purity, notice that at least 1/2 of the pairs from cluster one have the root as the LCA, so their purity is 1/2 and the total dendrogram purity is at most 7/8. □

The impurity in this example is a result of the leaf at +1 becoming *masked* when +4 is inserted.

Definition 3.1 (Masking). A node v with sibling v' and aunt a in a tree $\mathcal{T}$ is **masked** if there exists a point $x \in \texttt{lvs}(v)$ such that

$$\max_{y \in \texttt{lvs}(v')} \|x - y\| > \min_{z \in \texttt{lvs}(a)} \|x - z\|. \quad (1)$$

Thus, v contains a point x that is closer to some point in the aunt a than some point in the sibling v'. Intuitively, masking happens when a point is misclustered. For example when a point belonging to the same cluster as v's leaves is sent to a, then v becomes masked. A direct child of the root cannot be masked since it has no aunt.

Under separability, masking is intimately related to dendrogram purity, as demonstrated in the following result.

Fact 2. *If X is separated w.r.t. $\mathcal{C}^\star$ and a cluster tree $\mathcal{T}$ contains no masked nodes, then it has dendrogram purity 1.*

Proof. Assume that $\mathcal{T}$ does not have dendrogram purity 1. Then there exists points x_i and x_j in $\texttt{lvs}(\mathcal{T})$ such that $C^\star(x_i) = C^\star(x_j)$ but $\texttt{lvs}(\texttt{LCA}(x_i, x_j))$ contains a point x_k in a different cluster. The least common ancestor has two children v_ℓ, v_r and x_i, x_j cannot be in the same child, so without loss of generality we have $x_i, x_k \in v_l$ and $x_j \in v_r$. Now consider $v = \texttt{LCA}(x_i, x_k)$ and v's sibling v'. If v' contains a point belonging to $C^\star(x_i)$, then the child of v that contains x_i is masked since x_i is closer to that point than it is to x_k. If the aunt of v contains a point belonging to $C^\star(x_i)$ then v is masked for the same reason. If the aunt contains only points that do not belong to $C^\star(x_i)$ then examine v's parent and proceed recursively. This process must terminate since we are below $\texttt{LCA}(x_i, x_j)$. Thus the leaf containing x_i or one of x_i's ancestors must be masked. □

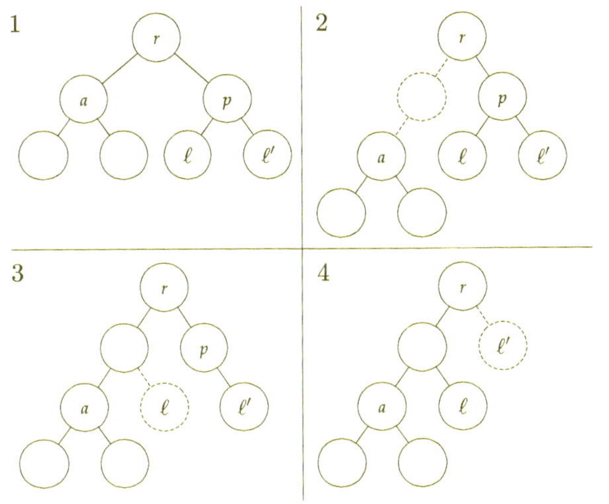

Figure 1: The `Rotate` procedure in four steps. In each step, the change to the tree is indicated by dotted lines.

3.3 Masking Based Rotations

Inspired by self-balancing binary search trees [38], we employ a novel *masking-based rotation* operation that alleviates purity errors caused by masking. In the greedy algorithm, after inserting a new point and creating the leaf ℓ' with sibling ℓ, the algorithm checks if ℓ is masked. If masking is detected, a `Rotate` operation is performed, which swaps the positions of ℓ' and its aunt in the tree (See Figure 1). After the rotation, the algorithm checks if ℓ's new sibling is masked and recursively applies rotations up the tree. If no masking is detected at any point in the process, the algorithm terminates (Algorithm 2).

At this point in the discussion, we check for masking exhaustively via Equation (1). In the next section we introduce approximations for scalability.

Theorem 3.2. *If X is separated w.r.t. $\mathcal{C}^\star$, the greedy algorithm with masking-based rotations constructs a cluster tree with dendrogram purity 1.0.*

Proof. Inductively, assume our current cluster tree $\mathcal{T}$ has dendrogram purity 1.0, and we process a new point x_i belonging to ground truth cluster $C^\star \in \mathcal{C}^\star$. In the first case, assume that $\mathcal{T}$ already contains some members of $C^\star$ that are located in a (pure) subtree, $\mathcal{T}[C^\star]$. Then, by separability x_i's nearest neighbor must be in $\mathcal{T}[C^\star]$ and if rotations ensue, no internal node $v \in \mathcal{T}[C^\star]$ can be rotated outside of $T[C^\star]$. To see why, observe that the children of $\mathcal{T}[C^\star]$'s root cannot be masked since this is a pure subtree and before insertion of v the full tree itself was pure (so no points from $C^\star$ can be outside of $\mathcal{T}[C^\star]$). In the second case, assume that T contains no points from cluster $C^\star$. Then, again by separability, recursive rotations must lift x_i out of the pure subtree that contains its nearest neighbor, which allows $\mathcal{T}$ to maintain perfect purity. □

4 SCALING

Two sub-procedures of the algorithm (described above) can render its naive implementation slow: finding nearest neighbors and checking whether a node is masked. Therefore, in this section we introduce several approximations that make our final algorithm, PERCH, scalable. First, we describe a *balance-based rotation* procedure that helps to balance the tree and makes insertion of new points much faster. Then we discuss a *collapsed mode* that allows our algorithm to scale to datasets that do not fit in memory. Finally, we introduce a bounding box approximation that makes both nearest neighbor and masking detection operations efficient.

4.1 Balance Rotations

While our rotation algorithm (Section 3.3) guarantees optimal dendrogram purity in the separable case, it does not make any guarantees on the depth of the tree, which influences the running time. Naturally, we would like to construct balanced binary trees, as these are conducive to logarithmic time search and insertion. We use the following notion of balance.

Definition 4.1 (Cluster Tree Balance). The balance of a cluster tree $\mathcal{T}$, denoted $\texttt{bal}(\mathcal{T})$, is the average *local balance* of all nodes in $\mathcal{T}$, where the local balance of a node v with children v_ℓ, v_r is $\texttt{bal}(v) = \frac{\min\{|\texttt{lvs}(v_\ell)|, |\texttt{lvs}(v_r)|\}}{\max\{|\texttt{lvs}(v_\ell)|, |\texttt{lvs}(v_r)|\}}$.

To encourage balanced trees, we use a balance-based rotation operation. A balance-rotation with respect to a node v with sibling v' and aunt a is identical to a masking-based rotation with respect to v, except that it is triggered when

1) the rotation would produce a tree $\mathcal{T}'$ with $\texttt{bal}(\mathcal{T}') > \texttt{bal}(\mathcal{T})$; and
2) there exists a point $x_i \in \texttt{lvs}(v)$ such that x_i is closer to a leaf of a than to some leaf of v' (i.e. Equation (1) holds).

Under separability, this latter check ensures that the balance-based rotation does not compromise dendrogram purity.

FACT 3. *Let X be a dataset that is separable w.r.t $C^\star$. If $\mathcal{T}$ is a cluster tree with dendrogram purity 1 and $\mathcal{T}'$ is the result of a balance-based rotation on some node in $\mathcal{T}$, then $\texttt{bal}(\mathcal{T}') > \texttt{bal}(\mathcal{T})$ and $\mathcal{T}'$ also has dendrogram purity 1.0.*

PROOF. The only situation in which a rotation could impact the dendrogram purity of a pure cluster tree $\mathcal{T}$ is when v and v' belong to the same cluster, but their aunt a belongs to a different cluster. In this case, separation ensures that

$$\max_{x \in \texttt{lvs}(v), y \in \texttt{lvs}(v')} \|x - y\| \leq \min_{x' \in \texttt{lvs}(v), z \in \texttt{lvs}(a)} \|x' - z\|,$$

so a rotation will not be triggered. Clearly, $\texttt{bal}(\mathcal{T}') > \texttt{bal}(\mathcal{T})$ since it is explicitly checked before performing a rotation. □

After inserting a new point and applying any masking-based rotations, we check for balance-based rotations at each node along the path from the newly created leaf to the root (Algorithm 2).

Algorithm 1 $\texttt{Insert}(x_i, \mathcal{T})$

```
t = NearestNeighbor(x_i)
l = Split(t)
for a in Ancestors(l) do
  a.AddPt(x_i)
end for
T = T.RotateRec(ℓ.Sibling(), CheckMasked)
T = T.RotateRec(ℓ.Sibling(), CheckBalanced)
if CollapseMode then
  T.TryCollapse().
end if
Output: T
```

4.2 Collapsed Mode

For extremely large datasets that do not fit in memory, we use a *collapsed mode* of PERCH. In this mode, the algorithm takes a parameter that is an upper bound on the number of leaves in the cluster tree, which we denote with L. After balance rotations, our algorithm invokes a `Collapse` procedure that merges leaves as necessary to meet the upper bound. This is similar to work in hierarchical extreme classification in which the depth of the model is a user-specified parameter [16].

The `Collapse` operation may only be invoked on an internal node v whose children are both leaves. The procedure makes v a *collapsed leaf* that stores the (ids, not the features, of the) points associated with its children along with sufficient statistics (Section 4.3), and then deletes both children. The points stored in a collapsed leaf are never split by any flavor of rotation. The `Collapse` operation may be invoked on internal nodes whose children are collapsed leaves.

When the cluster tree has $L + 1$ leaves, we collapse the node whose maximum distance between children is minimal among all collapsible nodes, and we use a priority queue to amortize the search for this node. Collapsing this node is guaranteed to preserve dendrogram purity in the separable case.

FACT 4. *Let X be a dataset separable w.r.t. $C^\star$ which has K clusters, if $L > K$, then collapse operations preserve perfect dendrogram purity.*

PROOF. Inductively, assume that the cluster tree has dendrogram purity 1.0 before we add a point that causes us to collapse a node. Since $L > K$ and all subtrees are pure, by the pigeonhole principle, there must be a pure subtree containing at least 2 points. By separability, all such pure 2-point subtrees will be at the front of the priority queue, before any impure ones, and hence the collapse will not compromise purity. □

4.3 Bounding Box Approximations

Many of the operations described thus far depend on nearest neighbor searches, which in general can be computationally intensive. We alleviate this complexity by approximating a set (or subtree) of points via a bounding box. Here each internal node maintains a bounding box that contains all of its leaves, like in R-Trees [24]. Bounding boxes are easy to maintain and update in $O(d)$ time.

Specifically, for any internal node v whose bounding interval in dimension j is $[v_-(j), v_+(j)]$, we approximate the squared minimum

Algorithm 2 RotateRec($v, \mathcal{T}$, func)

```
(ShouldRotate, ShouldStop) = func(v)
if ShouldRotate then
    T.Rotate(v)
end if
if ShouldStop then
    Output: T
else
    Output: T.RotateRec(v.Parent(), T, func)
end if
```

distance between a point x and $\texttt{lvs}(v)$ by

$$d_-(x,v)^2 = \sum_{j=1}^{d} \begin{cases} (x(j) - v_-(j))^2 & \text{if } x(j) \leq v_-(j) \\ (x(j) - v_+(j))^2 & \text{if } x(j) \geq v_+(j) \\ 0 & \text{otherwise} \end{cases} \tag{2}$$

We approximate the squared maximum distance by

$$d_+(x,v)^2 = \sum_{j=1}^{d} \max\left\{(x(j) - v_-(j))^2, (x(j) - v_+(j))^2\right\}. \tag{3}$$

It is easy to verify that these provide lower and upper bounds on the squared minimum and maximum distance between x and $\texttt{lvs}(v)$. Clearly when v consists of a single data point, the bounding box approximation is exact. See Figure 2 for a visual representation.

For the nearest neighbor search involved in inserting a point x into $\mathcal{T}$, we use the minimum distance approximation $d_-(x,v)$ as a heuristic in $A^\star$ search. Our implementation maintains a frontier of unexplored internal nodes of $\mathcal{T}$ and repeatedly expands the node v with minimal $d_-(x,v)$ by adding its children to the frontier. Since the approximation d_- is always a lower bound and it is exact for leaves, the heuristic is admissible, and thus the first leaf visited by the search is the nearest neighbor of x. This is similar to the nearest neighbor search in the Balltree data structure [32].

For masking rotations, we use a more stringent check based on Equation 1. Specifically, we perform a masking rotation on node v with sibling v' and aunt a if:

$$d_-(v,v') > d_+(v,a) \tag{4}$$

Note that $d_-(v,v')$ is a slight abuse of notation (and so is $d_+(v,a)$) because both v and v' are bounding boxes. To compute, $d_-(v,v')$, for each dimension in v's bounding box, use either the minimum or maximum along that dimension to minimize the sum of coordinate-wise distances (Equation 2). A similar procedure can be performed to compute $d_+(v,a)$ between two bounding boxes.

Note that if Equation 4 holds then v is masked and a rotation with respect to v will unmask v because, for all $x \in \texttt{lvs}(v)$:

$$\begin{aligned} \max_{y \in \texttt{lvs}(v')} ||x-y|| \geq \min_{y\in\texttt{lvs}(v')} ||x-y|| \\ \geq d_-(v,v') \geq d_+(v,a) &\geq \max_{z\in\texttt{lvs}(a)} ||x-z|| \\ &\geq \min_{z\in\texttt{lvs}(a)} ||x-z||. \end{aligned}$$

In words, we know that a rotation will unmask v because the upper bound on the distance from a point in v to a point in a is smaller than the lower bound on the distance from a point in v to a point in v'. However, the approximations lead to a conservative test that may not detect all instances of masking in the cluster tree.

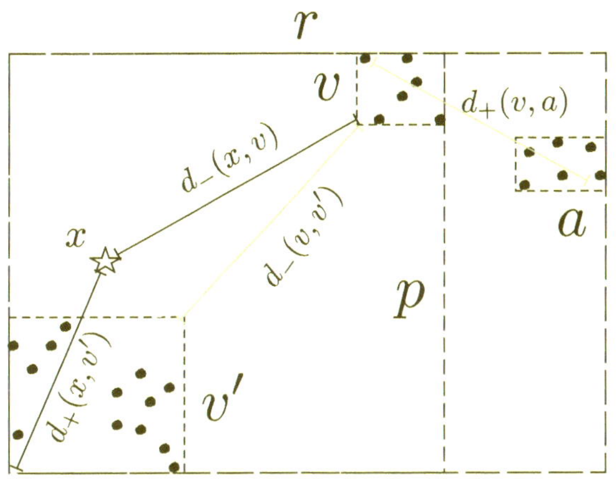

Figure 2: A subtree r with two children p and a; p is the parent of v and v' (all nodes indicated by boxes with dashed outlines). A point x is inserted and descends to v' because $d_+(x,v') < d_-(x,v)$ (black lines). The node v is masked because $d_+(v,a) < d_-(v,v')$ (gray lines).

5 PERCH

Our algorithm is called PERCH, for Purity Enhancing Rotations for Cluster Hierarchies.

PERCH can be run in several modes. All modes use bounding box approximations, masking-, and balance-based rotations. The standard implementation, simply denoted PERCH, only includes these features (See Algorithm 1). PERCH-C additionally runs in collapsed mode and requires the parameter L for the maximum number of leaves. PERCH-B replaces the $A^\star$ search with a breadth-first beam search to expedite the nearest neighbor lookup. This mode also takes the beam width as a parameter. Finally PERCH-BC uses the beam search and runs in collapsed mode.

We implement PERCH to mildly exploit parallelism. When finding nearest neighbors via beam or $A^\star$ search, we use multiple threads to expand the frontier in parallel.

6 EXPERIMENTS

We compare PERCH to several state-of-the-art clustering algorithms on large-scale real-world datasets. Since few benchmark clustering datasets exhibit a large number of clusters, we conduct experiments with large-scale classification datasets that naturally contain many classes and simply omit the class labels. Note that other work in large-scale clustering recognizes this deficiency of the standard clustering benchmarks [4, 8]. Although smaller datasets are not our primary focus, we also measure the performance of PERCH on standard clustering benchmarks.

6.1 Experimental Details

Algorithms. We compare the following 10 clustering algorithms:

- Perch - Our algorithm, we use various modes depending on the size of the problem. For beam search, we use a default width of 5 (per thread, 24 threads). We only run in collapsed mode for ILSVRC12 and ImageNet (100K) where $L = 50000$.
- BIRCH [41]- A top-down hierarchical clustering method where each internal node represents its leaves via mean and variance statistics. Points are inserted greedily using the node statistics; when the branching factor is exceeded, a powerful split operation is invoked. Importantly no rotations are performed.
- HAC - Hierarchical agglomerative clustering (various linkages). The algorithm repeatedly merges the two subtrees that are closest according to some measure, to form a larger subtree.
- Mini-batch HAC (MB-HAC) - HAC (various linkages) made to run online with mini-batching. The algorithm maintains a buffer of subtrees and must merge two subtrees in the buffer before observing the next point. We use buffers of size 2K and 5K and centroid (cent.) and complete (com.) linkages.
- K-means - LLoyd's algorithm, which alternates between assigning points to centers and recomputing centers based on the assignment. We use the K-means++ initialization [5].
- Stream K-means++ (SKM++) [2] - A streaming algorithm that computes a representative subsample of the points (a coreset) in one pass, runs K-means++ on the subsample, and in a second pass assigns points greedily to the nearest cluster center.
- Mini-batch K-means (MB-KM) [37] - An algorithm that optimizes the K-means objective function via mini-batch stochastic gradient descent. The implementation we use includes many heuristics, including several initial passes through the data to initialize centers via K-means++, random restarts to avoid local optima, and early stopping [34]. In robustness experiments, we also study a fully online version of this algorithm, with random initialization and without early stopping or reassignments.
- BICO [20] - An algorithm for optimizing the K-means objective that creates coresets via a streaming approach using a BIRCH-like data structure. K-means++ is run on the coresets and then points are assigned to the inferred centers.
- DBSCAN [19] - A density based method that computes nearest-neighbor balls around each point, merges overlapping balls, and builds a clustering from the resulting connected components.
- Hierarchical K-means (HKMeans) - top-down, divisive, hierarchical clustering. At each level of the hierarchy, the remaining points are split into two groups using K-means.

These algorithms represent hierarchical and flat clustering approaches from a variety of algorithmic families including coreset, stochastic gradient, tree-based, and density-based. Most of the algorithms operate incrementally and we find that most baselines exploit parallelism to various degrees, as we do with Perch. We also compare to the less scalable batch algorithms (HAC and K-means) when possible.

Datasets. We evaluate the algorithms on 9 datasets (See Table 1 for relevant statistics):

- ALOI - (Amsterdam Library of Object Images [21]) contains images and is used as an extreme classification benchmark [14].

	Name	Clusters	Points	Dim.
Large Data sets	ImageNet (100K)	17K	100K	2048
	Speaker	4958	36,572	6388
	ILSVRC12	1000	1.3M	2048
	ALOI	1000	108K	128
	ILSVRC12 (50K)	1000	50K	2048
	CoverType	7	581K	54
Small Benchmarks	Digits	10	200	64
	Glass	6	214	10
	Spambase	2	4601	57

Table 1: Dataset statistics.

- Speaker - The NIST I-Vector Machine Learning Challenge speaker detection dataset [23]. The goal is to cluster recordings from the same speaker together. We cluster the whitened development set (scripts provided by the challenge).
- ILSVRC12 - The ImageNet Large Scale Visual Recognition Challenge 2012 [36]. The class labels are used to produce a ground truth clustering. We generate representations of each image from the last layer of the Inception neural network [39].
- ILSVRC12 (50K) - a 50K subset of ILSVRC12.
- ImageNet (100K) - a 100K subset of the ImageNet database. Classes are sampled proportional to their frequency in the database.
- Covertype - forest cover types (benchmark).
- Glass - different types of glass (benchmark).
- Spambase - email data of spam and not-spam (benchmark).
- Digits - a subset of a handwritten digits dataset (benchmark).

The Covertype, Glass, Spambase and Digits datasets are provided by the UCI Machine Learning Repository [29].

Validation and Tuning. As the data arrival order impacts the incremental algorithms, we run each incremental algorithm on random permutations of each dataset. We tune hyperparameters for all methods and report the performance of the hyperparameter with best average performance over 5 repetitions for the larger datasets (ILSVRC12 and Imagenet (100K)) and 10 repetitions for the other datasets.

6.2 Hierarchical Clustering Evaluation

Perch and many of the other baselines build cluster trees, and, as such, they can be evaluated using dendrogram purity. In Table 2a, we report the dendrogram purity, averaged over random shufflings of each dataset, for the 6 large datasets, and for the hierarchical clustering algorithms (Perch, BIRCH, MB-HAC variants, HKMeans and HAC variants). Bold indicates the best performing scalable approach; italic indicates the best performing approach overall. The top 5 rows in the table correspond to incremental algorithms, while the bottom 4 are batch algorithms (with the two below the horizontal bar being unscalable to large N). The comparison demonstrates the quality of the incremental algorithms, as well as the degree of scalability of the batch methods. Unsurprisingly, we were not able to run some of the batch algorithms on the larger datasets.

Perch consistently produces trees with highest dendrogram purity amongst all incremental methods. Perch-B, which uses approximate nearest-neighbor search, is worse, but still consistently better than the baselines. For the datasets with 50K examples or

Method	CovType	ILSVRC12 (50k)	ALOI	ILSVRC 12	Speaker	ImageNet (100k)
Perch	***0.45 ± 0.004***	**0.53 ± 0.003**	***0.44 ± 0.004***	–	**0.37 ± 0.002**	***0.07 ± 0.00***
Perch-BC	***0.45 ± 0.004***	0.36 ± 0.005	0.37 ± 0.008	***0.21 ± 0.017***	0.09 ± 0.001	0.03 ± 0.00
BIRCH (incremental)	0.44 ± 0.002	0.09 ± 0.006	0.21 ± 0.004	0.11 ± 0.006	0.02 ± 0.002	0.02 ± 0.00
MB-HAC-Com.	–	0.43 ± 0.005	0.15 ± 0.003	–	0.01 ± 0.002	–
MB-HAC-Cent.	0.44 ± 0.005	0.02 ± 0.000	0.30 ± 0.002	–	–	–
HKMmeans	0.44 ± 0.001	0.12 ± 0.002	***0.44 ± 0.001***	0.11 ± 0.003	0.12 ± 0.002	0.02 ± 0.00
BIRCH (rebuild)	0.44 ± 0.002	0.26 ± 0.003	0.32 ± 0.002	–	0.22 ± 0.006	0.03 ± 0.00
HAC-Avg	–	*0.54*	–	–	*0.55*	–
HAC-Complete	–	0.40	–	–	0.40	–

(a) Dendrogram purity for hierarchical clustering.

Method	CoverType	ILSVRC 12 (50k)	ALOI	ILSVRC 12	Speaker	ImageNet (100K)
Perch	22.96 ± 0.7	**54.30 ± 0.3**	***44.21 ± 0.2***	–	**31.80 ± 0.1**	***6.178 ± 0.0***
Perch-BC	22.97 ± 0.8	37.98 ± 0.5	37.48 ± 0.7	25.75 ± 1.7	1.05 ± 0.1	4.144 ± 0.04
SKM++	23.80 ± 0.4	28.46 ± 2.2	37.53 ± 1.0	–	–	–
BICO	***24.53 ± 0.4***	45.18 ± 1.0	32.984 ± 3.4	–	–	–
MB-KM	24.27 ± 0.6	51.73 ± 1.8	40.84 ± 0.5	***56.17 ± 0.4***	1.73 ± 0.141	5.642 ± 0.00
DBSCAN	–	16.95	–	–	22.63	–
Kmeans	24.42 ± 0.00	*60.40 ± 0.5*	39.311 ± 0.3	–	32.185 ± 0.01	–
HAC-Avg	–	–	–	–	40.258	–
HAC-Complete	–	18.28	–	–	*44.297*	–

(b) Pairwise F1 for flat clustering.

Method	Round.	Sort.
Perch	0.446	0.351
MB-HAC (5K)	0.299	0.464
MB-HAC (2K)	0.171	0.451

(c) Dendrogram purity on adversarial input orders for ALOI.

Method	Round.	Sort.
Perch	44.77	35.28
o-MB-KM	41.09	19.40
SKM++	43.33	46.67

(d) Pairwise F1 on adversarial input orders for ALOI.

Table 2: Perch is the top performing algorithm in terms of dendrogram purity competitive in F1. Perch is nearly twice as fast as MB-KM on ImageNet (100K) (Section 6.4). Dashes represent algorithms that could not be run or produced low results.

fewer (ILSVRC12 50K and Speaker) we are able to run the less scalable algorithms. We find that HAC with average-linkage achieves a purity of 0.55 on the Speaker dataset and only outperforms Perch by 0.01 purity on ILSVRC12 (50K). HAC with complete-linkage only slightly outperforms Perch on Speaker with a purity of 0.40. This is somewhat unsurprising because HAC is allowed to examine the entire dataset in each iteration.

We hypothesize that the success of Perch in these experiments can largely be attributed to the rotation operations and the bounding box approximations. In particular, masking-based rotations help alleviate challenges with operating incrementally, by allowing the algorithm to make corrections caused by difficult arrival orders. Simultaneously, the bounding box approximation is a more effective search heuristic for nearest neighbors in comparison with using cluster means and variances as in BIRCH. We observe that MB-HAC with centroid-linkage performs poorly on some datasets, which is likely due to the fact that a cluster's mean can be an uninformative representation of its member points, especially in the incremental setting.

6.3 Flat Clustering Evaluation

We also compare Perch to the flat-clustering algorithms described above. Here we evaluate a K-way clustering via the Pairwise F1 score [30], which given ground truth clustering $C^\star$ and estimate $\widehat{C}$, is the harmonic mean of the precision and recall between $\mathcal{P}^\star$ and $\widehat{\mathcal{P}}$ (which are pairs of points that are clustered together in $C^\star, \widehat{C}$ respectively). In this section we compare Perch to MB-KM, SKM++, BICO, DBSCAN, K-means (with K-means++ initialization) and HAC where the tree construction terminates once K-subtrees remain. All algorithms, including Perch, use the true number of clusters as an input parameter (except DBSCAN, which does not take the number of clusters as input).

Since Perch produces a cluster tree, we extract a tree-consistent partition using the following greedy heuristic: while the tree $\mathcal{T}$ does not have K leaves, collapse the internal node with the smallest *cost*, where $\texttt{cost}(v)$ is the maximum length diagonal of v's bounding box multiplied by $|\texttt{lvs}(v)|$. $\texttt{cost}(v)$ can be thought of as an upper bound on the K-means cost of v. We also experimented with other heuristics, but found this one to be quite effective.

The results of the experiment are in Table 2b. Again, bold indicates the best performing scalable approach; italic indicates the best performing approach overall. As in the case of dendrogram purity, PERCH competes with or outperforms all the scalable algorithms (i.e., above the horizontal line) on all datasets, even though we use a naïve heuristic to identify the final flat clustering from the tree. K-means, which could not be run on the larger datasets, is able to achieve a clustering with 60.4 F1 on ILSVRC (50K) and 32.19 F1 on Speaker; HAC with average-linkage and HAC with complete-linkage achieve scores of 40.26 and 44.3 F1 respectively on Speaker. This is unsurprising because in each iteration of both K-means and HAC, the algorithm has access to the entire dataset. We were able to run K-means on the Covertype dataset and achieve a score of 24.42 F1. We observe that K-means is able to converge quickly, which is likely due to the K-means++ initialization and the small number of true clusters (7) in the dataset. Since PERCH performs well on each of the datasets in terms of dendrogram purity, it may be possible to extract better flat clusterings from the trees it builds with a different pruning heuristic.

We note that when the number of clusters is large, DBSCAN does not perform well, because it (and many other density based algorithms) assumes that some of the points are *noise* and keeps them isolated in the final clustering. This outlier detection step is particularly problematic when the number of clusters is large, because there are many small clusters that are confused for outliers.

6.4 Speed and Accuracy

We compare the best performing methods above in terms of running time and accuracy. We focus on PERCH-BC, BIRCH, and HKMeans. Each of these algorithms has various parameter settings that typically govern a trade-off between accuracy and running time, and in our experiment, we vary these parameters to better understand this trade-off. The specific parameters are:

- **PERCH-BC**: beam-width, collapse threshold,
- **BIRCH**: branching factor,
- **HKMeans**: number of iterations per level.

In Figure 3, we plot the dendrogram purity as a function of running time for the algorithms as we vary the relevant parameter. We use the ILSVRC12 (50K) dataset and run all algorithms on the same machine (28 cores with 2.40GHz processor).

The results show that PERCH-BC achieves a better trade-off between dendrogram purity and running time than the other methods. Except for in the uninteresting low purity regime, our algorithm achieves the best dendrogram purity for a given running time. HKMeans with few iterations can be faster, but it produces poor clusterings, and with more iterations the running time scales quite poorly. BIRCH with rebuilding performs well, but PERCH-BC performs better in less time.

Our experiments also reveal that MB-KM is quite effective, both in terms of accuracy and speed. When the number of clusters is fairly small, MB-KM achieves the best speed-accuracy trade-off. However, since the gradient computation in MB-KM are $O(K)$, the algorithm scales poorly when the number of clusters is large. In contrast, our algorithm, provided short trees are produced, has no dependence on K and is the fastest when the number of clusters is large. For example, for ImageNet (100K) (the dataset with the largest number of clusters), MB-KM runs in ~8007.93s (averaged over 5 runs) while PERCH runs nearly twice as fast in 4364.37s. Faster still (although slightly less accurate) is PERCH-BC which clusters the dataset in only 690.16s.

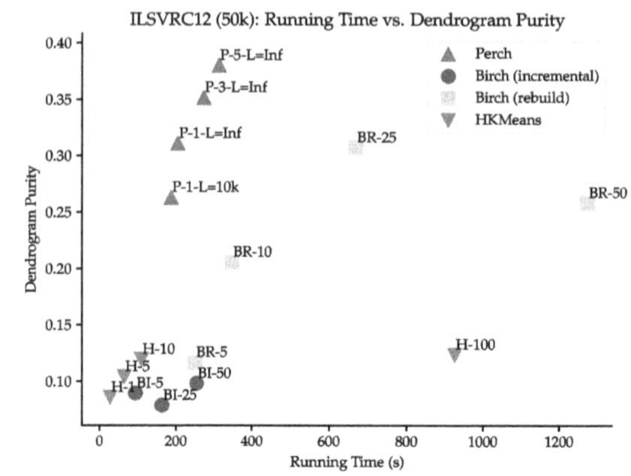

Figure 3: Speed vs. dendrogram purity on the ILSVRC12 50k dataset. PERCH (P) is always more accurate than BIRCH (B) even when tuned so the running times are comparable. HKmeans (H) is also depicted for comparison against a fast, batch, tree building algorithm.

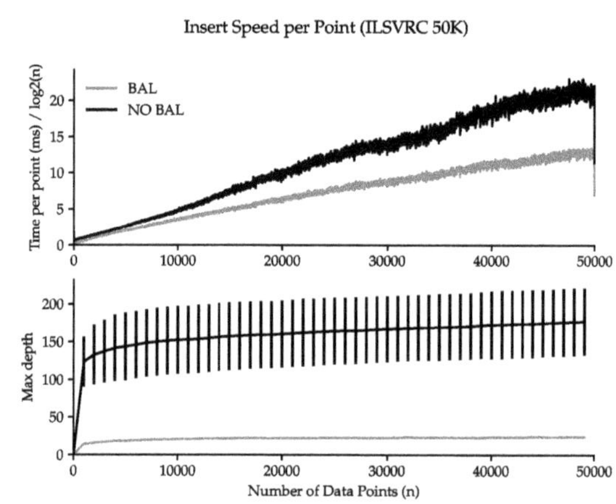

Figure 4: Insert speed divided by $\log_2(n)$ and max-depth as a function of the number of points inserted. PERCH is the red (bottom) line and PERCH without balance-rotations is black (top). Balancing helps to make insertion fast by keeping the tree short.

In Figure 4, we confirm empirically that insertion times scale with the size of the dataset. In the figure, we plot the insertion time and the maximum tree depth as a function of the number of data points on ILSVRC12 (50K). We also plot the same statistics for a variant of PERCH that does not invoke balance-rotations to understand how tree structure affects performance.

The top plot shows that PERCH's speed of insertion grows modestly with the number of points, even though the dimensionality of the data is high (which can make bounding box approximations worse). Both the top and bottom plots show that PERCH's balance rotations have a significant impact on its efficiency; in particular, the bottom plot suggests that the efficiency can be attributed to shallower trees. Recall that our analysis does not bound the depth of the tree or the running time of the nearest neighbor search. Thus in the worst case the algorithm may explore all leaves of the tree and have total running time scaling with $O(N^2d)$ where there are N data points. Empirically we observe that this is not the case.

6.5 Robustness

We are also interested in understanding the performance of PERCH and other incremental and online methods as a function of the arrival order. PERCH is designed to be robust to adversarial arrival orders (at least under separability assumptions), and this section empirically validates this property. On the other hand, many incremental and online implementations of batch clustering algorithms can make severe irrecoverable mistakes on adversarial data sequences. Our (non-greedy) masking-rotations explicitly and deliberately alleviate such behavior.

To evaluate robustness, we run the algorithms on two adversarial orderings of the ALOI dataset:

- **Sorted** - the points are ordered by class (i.e., all $x \in C_k^\star \subset C^\star$ are followed by all $x \in C_{i+1}^\star \subset C^\star$, etc.)
- **Round Robin** - the ith point to arrive is a member of $C_{i \bmod K}^\star$ where K is the true number of clusters.

The results in Tables 2a and 2b use a more benign random order.

Tables 2c and 2d contain the results of the robustness experiment. PERCH performs best on round-robin. While PERCH's dendrogram purity decreases on the sorted order, the degradation is much less than the other methods. Incremental versions of agglomerative methods perform quite poorly on round-robin but much better on sorted orders. This is somewhat surprising, since the methods use a buffer size that is substantially larger than the number of clusters, so in both orders there is always a good merge to perform. For flat clusterings, we compare PERCH with an online version of mini-batch K-means (o-MB-KM). This algorithm is restricted to pick clusters from the first mini-batch of points and not allowed to drop or restart centers. The o-MB-KM algorithm has significantly worse performance on the sorted order, since it cannot recover from separating multiple points from the same ground truth cluster. It is important to note the difference between this algorithm and the MB-KM algorithm used elsewhere in these experiments, which is robust to the input order. SKM++ improves since it uses a non-greedy method for the coreset construction. However, SKM++ is technically a streaming (not online) algorithm, since it makes two passes over the dataset.

6.6 Small-scale Benchmarks

Finally, we evaluate our algorithm on the standard (small-scale) clustering benchmarks. While PERCH is designed to be accurate and efficient for large datasets with many clusters, these results help us understand the price for scalability and provide a more exhaustive experimental evaluation. The results appear in Table 3 and show that PERCH is competitive with other batch and incremental algorithms (in terms of dendrogram purity), despite only examining each point once and being optimized for large-scale problems.

Method	Glass	Digits	Spambase
PERCH	0.474 ± 0.017	0.614 ± 0.033	0.611 ± 0.0131
BIRCH	0.429 ± 0.013	0.544 ± 0.054	0.595 ± 0.013
HKMeans	0.508 ± 0.008	0.586 ± 0.029	0.626 ± 0.000
HAC-C	0.47	0.594	0.628

Table 3: Dendrogram purity on small-scale benchmarks.

7 RELATED WORK

The literature on clustering is too vast for an in-depth treatment here, so we focus on the most related methods. These can be compartmentalized into hierarchical methods, incremental/online optimization of various clustering cost functions, and approaches based on coresets. We also briefly discuss related ideas in supervised learning and nearest neighbor search.

Standard hierarchical methods like single linkage are often the methods of choice for small datasets, but, with running times scaling quadratically with sample size, they do not scale to larger problems. As such, several incremental hierarchical clustering algorithms have been developed. A natural adaptation of these agglomerative methods is the mini-batch version that PERCH outperforms in our empirical evaluation. BIRCH [41] and its extensions [20] comprise state of the art online/incremental hierarchical methods that, like PERCH, insert points into a cluster tree data structure one at a time. However, unlike PERCH, these methods parameterize internal nodes with means and variances as opposed to bounding boxes, and they do not implement rotations, which our empirical and theoretical results justify. On the other hand, Widyantoro et al. [40] instead use a bottom-up approach.

A more thriving line of work focuses on incremental optimization of clustering cost functions. A natural approach is to use stochastic gradient methods to optimize the K-means cost [11, 37]. Liberty et al. [28] design an alternative online K-means algorithm that when processing a point, opts to start a new cluster if the point is far from the current centers. This idea draws inspiration from the algorithm of Charikar et al. [13] for the incremental k-center problem, which also adjusts the current centers when a new point is far away. Closely related to these approaches are several online methods for inference in a probabilistic model for clustering, such as stochastic variational methods for Gaussian Mixture Models [26]. As our experiments demonstrate, this family of algorithms is quite effective when the number of clusters is small, but for problems with many clusters, these methods typically do not scale.

Lastly, a number of clustering methods use coresets, which are small but representative data subsets, for scalability. For example, the StreamKM++ algorithm of Ackermann et al. [2] and the BICO algorithm of Fichtenberger et al. [20] run the K-means++ algorithm on a coreset extracted from a large data stream. Other methods with strong guarantees also exist [6], but typically coreset construction is expensive, and as above, these methods do not scale to the extreme clustering setting where K is large.

While not explicitly targeting the clustering task, tree-based methods for nearest neighbor search and extreme multiclass classification inspired the architecture of PERCH. In nearest neighbor search, the cover tree structure [9] represents points with a hierarchy while supporting online insertion and deletion, but it does not perform rotations or other adjustments that improve clustering performance. Tree-based methods for extreme classification can scale to a large number of classes, but a number of algorithmic improvements are possible with access to labeled data. For example, the recall tree [16] allows for a class to be associated with many leaves in the tree, which does not seem possible without supervision.

8 CONCLUSION

In this paper, we present a new algorithm, called PERCH, for large-scale clustering. The algorithm constructs a cluster tree in an incremental fashion and uses rotations to correct mistakes and encourage a shallow tree. We prove that under a separability assumption, the algorithm is guaranteed to recover a ground truth clustering and we conduct an exhaustive empirical evaluation. Our experimental results demonstrate that PERCH outperforms existing baselines, both in terms of clustering quality and speed. We believe these experiments convincingly demonstrate the utility of PERCH.

Our implementation of PERCH used in these experiments is available at: http://github.com/iesl/xcluster.

Acknowledgments

We thank Ackermann et. al [2] for providing us an implementation of StreamKM++ and BICO, and Luke Vilnis for many helpful discussions. We also thank the anonymous reviewers for their constructive feedback.

This work was supported in part by the Center for Intelligent Information Retrieval, in part by DARPA under agreement number FA8750-13-2-0020, in part by Amazon Alexa Science, in part by the National Science Foundation Graduate Research Fellowship under Grant No. NSF-1451512 and in part by the Amazon Web Services (AWS) Cloud Credits for Research program. The work reported here was performed in part using high performance computing equipment obtained under a grant from the Collaborative R&D Fund managed by the Massachusetts Technology Collaborative. Any opinions, findings and conclusions or recommendations expressed in this material are those of the authors and do not necessarily reflect those of the sponsor.

REFERENCES

[1] M. Ackerman and S. Dasgupta. 2014. Incremental clustering: The case for extra clusters. In *Advances in Neural Information Processing Systems.*
[2] M. R. Ackermann, M. Märtens, C. Raupach, K. Swierkot, C. Lammersen, and C. Sohler. 2012. StreamKM++: A clustering algorithm for data streams. In *Journal of Experimental Algorithmics.*
[3] C. C. Aggarwal, J. Han, J. Wang, and P. S. Yu. 2003. A framework for clustering evolving data streams. In *International Conference on Very Large Databases.*
[4] A. Ahmed, S. Ravi, A. J. Smola, and S. M. Narayanamurthy. 2012. Fastex: Hash clustering with exponential families. In *Advances in Neural Information Processing Systems.*
[5] D. Arthur and S. Vassilvitskii. 2007. k-means++: The advantages of careful seeding. In *Symposium on Discrete Algorithms.*
[6] M. Bădoiu, S. Har-Peled, and P. Indyk. 2002. Approximate clustering via core-sets. In *Symposium on Theory of Computing.*
[7] M. Balcan, A. Blum, and S. Vempala. 2008. A discriminative framework for clustering via similarity functions. In *ACM Symposium on Theory of Computing.*
[8] B. Betancourt, G. Zanella, J. W. Miller, H. Wallach, A. Zaidi, and R. C. Steorts. 2016. Flexible models for microclustering with application to entity resolution. In *Advances in Neural Information Processing Systems.*
[9] A. Beygelzimer, S. Kakade, and J. Langford. 2006. Cover trees for nearest neighbor. In *International Conference on Machine Learning.*
[10] C. Blundell, Y. W. Teh, and K. A. Heller. 2011. Discovering non-binary hierarchical structures with Bayesian rose trees. In *Mixture Estimation and Applications.*
[11] L. Bottou and Y. Bengio. 1995. Convergence properties of the k-means algorithms. In *Advances in Neural Information Processing Systems.*
[12] P. F. Brown, P. V. Desouza, R. L. Mercer, V. J. D. Pietra, and J. C. Lai. 1992. Class-based n-gram models of natural language. In *Computational Linguistics.*
[13] M. Charikar, C. Chekuri, T. Feder, and R. Motwani. 1997. Incremental clustering and dynamic information retrieval. In *Symposium on Theory of Computing.*
[14] A. E. Choromanska and J. Langford. 2015. Logarithmic time online multiclass prediction. In *Advances in Neural Information Processing Systems.*
[15] A. Clauset, M. E. Newman, and C. Moore. 2004. Finding community structure in very large networks. In *Physical Review E.*
[16] H. Daume III, N. Karampatziakis, J. Langford, and P. Mineiro. 2017. Logarithmic time one-against-some. In *International Conference on Machine Learning.*
[17] J. Deng, W. Dong, R. Socher, L. Li, K. Li, and L. Fei-Fei. 2009. Imagenet: A large-scale hierarchical image database. In *Computer Vision and Pattern Recognition.*
[18] M. B. Eisen, P. T. Spellman, P. O. Brown, and D. Botstein. 1998. Cluster analysis and display of genome-wide expression patterns. In *National Academy of Sciences.*
[19] M. Ester, H.-P. Kriegel, J. Sander, X. Xu, and others. 1996. A density-based algorithm for discovering clusters in large spatial databases with noise. In *International Conference on Knowledge Discovery and Data Mining.*
[20] H. Fichtenberger, M. Gillé, M. Schmidt, C. Schwiegelshohn, and C. Sohler. 2013. BICO: BIRCH meets coresets for k-means clustering. In *European Symposium on Algorithms.*
[21] J. Geusebroek, G. J. Burghouts, and A. W. Smeulders. 2005. The Amsterdam library of object images. In *International Journal of Computer Vision.*
[22] A. N. Gorban, B. Kégl, D. C. Wunsch, A. Y. Zinovyev, and others. 2008. *Principal Manifolds for Data Visualization and Dimension Reduction.* Springer.
[23] C. S. Greenberg, D. Bansé, G. R. Doddington, D. Garcia-Romero, J. J. Godfrey, T. Kinnunen, A. F. Martin, A. McCree, M. Przybocki, and D. A. Reynolds. 2014. The NIST 2014 speaker recognition i-vector machine learning challenge. In *Odyssey.*
[24] A. Guttman. 1984. R-trees: a dynamic index structure for spatial searching. In *International Conference on Management of Data.*
[25] K. A. Heller and Z. Ghahramani. 2005. Bayesian hierarchical clustering. In *International Conference on Machine Learning.*
[26] M. D. Hoffman, D. M. Blei, C. Wang, and J. W. Paisley. 2013. Stochastic variational inference. In *Journal of Machine Learning Research.*
[27] A. Krishnamurthy, S. Balakrishnan, M. Xu, and A. Singh. 2012. Efficient active algorithms for hierarchical clustering. In *International Conference on Machine Learning.*
[28] E. Liberty, R. Sriharsha, and M. Sviridenko. 2016. An algorithm for online k-means clustering. In *Workshop on Algorithm Engineering and Experiments.*
[29] M. Lichman. 2013. UCI Machine Learning Repository. http://archive.ics.uci.edu/ml
[30] C. D. Manning, P. Raghavan, H. Schütze, and others. 2008. *Introduction to Information Retrieval.* Cambridge University Press.
[31] L. O'callaghan, N. Mishra, A. Meyerson, S. Guha, and R. Motwani. 2002. Streaming-data algorithms for high-quality clustering. In *International Conference on Data Engineering.*
[32] S. M. Omohundro. 1989. *Five Balltree Construction Algorithms.* International Computer Science Institute Berkeley.
[33] R. Ostrovsky, Y. Rabani, L. J. Schulman, and C. Swamy. 2006. The effectiveness of Lloyd-type methods for the k-means problem. In *Foundations of Computer Science.*
[34] F. Pedregosa, G. Varoquaux, A. Gramfort, V. Michel, B. Thirion, O. Grisel, M. Blondel, P. Prettenhofer, R. Weiss, V. Dubourg, J. Vanderplas, A. Passos, D. Cournapeau, M. Brucher, M. Perrot, and E. Duchesnay. 2011. Scikit-learn: Machine learning in Python. In *Journal of Machine Learning Research.*
[35] K. D. Pruitt, T. Tatusova, G. R. Brown, and D. R. Maglott. 2012. NCBI reference sequences (RefSeq): Current status, new features and genome annotation policy. In *Nucleic Acids Research.*
[36] O. Russakovsky, J. Deng, H. Su, J. Krause, S. Satheesh, S. Ma, Z. Huang, A. Karpathy, A. Khosla, M. Bernstein, A. C. Berg, and L. Fei-Fei. 2015. ImageNet Large Scale Visual Recognition Challenge. In *International Journal of Computer Vision.*
[37] D. Sculley. 2010. Web-scale k-means clustering. In *International World Wide Web Conference.*
[38] R. Sedgewick. 1988. *Algorithms.* Pearson Education India.
[39] C. Szegedy, V. Vanhoucke, S. Ioffe, J. Shlens, and Z. Wojna. 2016. Rethinking the inception architecture for computer vision. In *Computer Vision and Pattern Recognition.*
[40] D. H. Widyantoro, T. R. Ioerger, and J. Yen. 2002. An incremental approach to building a cluster hierarchy. In *International Conference on Data Mining.*
[41] T. Zhang, R. Ramakrishnan, and M. Livny. 1996. BIRCH: An efficient data clustering method for very large databases. In *ACM Sigmod International Conference on Management of Data.*

Estimating Treatment Effect in the Wild via Differentiated Confounder Balancing

Kun Kuang*
Department of Computer Science
Tsinghua University
kk14@mails.tsinghua.edu.cn

Peng Cui
Department of Computer Science
Tsinghua University
cuip@tsinghua.edu.cn

Bo Li
School of Economics and Management
Tsinghua University
libo@sem.tsinghua.edu.cn

Meng Jiang
Department of Computer Science and Engineering, University of Notre Dame
mjiang2@nd.edu

Shiqiang Yang
Department of Computer Science
Tsinghua University
yangshq@tsinghua.edu.cn

ABSTRACT

The key challenge on estimating treatment effect in the wild observational studies is to handle confounding bias induced by imbalance of the confounder distributions between treated and control units. Traditional methods remove confounding bias by re-weighting units with supposedly accurate propensity score estimation under the unconfoundedness assumption. Controlling high-dimensional variables may make the unconfoundedness assumption more plausible, but poses new challenge on accurate propensity score estimation. One strand of recent literature seeks to directly optimize weights to balance confounder distributions, bypassing propensity score estimation. But existing balancing methods fail to do selection and differentiation among the pool of a large number of potential confounders, leading to possible underperformance in many high dimensional settings. In this paper, we propose a data-driven Differentiated Confounder Balancing (DCB) algorithm to jointly select confounders, differentiate weights of confounders and balance confounder distributions for treatment effect estimation in the wild high dimensional settings. The synergistic learning algorithm we proposed is more capable of reducing the confounding bias in many observational studies. To validate the effectiveness of our DCB algorithm, we conduct extensive experiments on both synthetic and real datasets. The experimental results clearly demonstrate that our DCB algorithm outperforms the state-of-the-art methods on treatment effect estimation.

KEYWORDS

Treatment Effect Estimation; Confounding Bias; Differentiated Confounder Balancing

*Tsinghua National Laboratory for Information Science and Technology (TNList).

KDD '17, August 13-17, 2017, Halifax, NS, Canada
© 2017 ACM. 978-1-4503-4887-4/17/08... $15.00
DOI: 10.1145/3097983.3098032

1 INTRODUCTION

Owing to the popularity of Big Data, abundant data are accumulated in various domains such as healthcare and advertising. At the same time, many machine learning and data mining methods are proposed to exploit these data for prediction, aiming to estimate the future outcome in the application of interest. These methods have been proved to be successful in prediction-oriented applications. However, the lack of interpretability of most predictive algorithms makes them less attractive in many settings, especially those requiring decision making. How to improve the explanability of learning algorithms is of paramount importance for both academic research and real applications.

Causal inference is a powerful statistical modeling tool for explanatory analysis. One fundamental problem in causal inference is treatment effect estimation, and its key challenge is to remove the confounding bias induced by the different confounder distributions between treated and control units. The gold standard approach for removing confounding bias is to conduct randomized experiments like A/B testing. But fully randomized experiments are usually expensive [14] and sometimes infeasible [5]. Therefore, many methods are proposed to estimate treatment effect directly from observational data under the unconfoundedness assumption [22]. Most of them adopt the propensity score to reweight units for removing confounding bias [3, 4, 6]. Although these methods are gaining ground in applied work, they require correct model specification on treatment assignment or accurate propensity score estimation. In big data scenarios, controlling high-dimensional variables may make the unconfoundedness assumption more plausible, but poses new challenge on accurate propensity score estimation. Recently, some researchers proposed to balance confounder distributions by directly optimizing the weights, without modeling or estimating the propensity scores [2, 7, 11, 26]. But they balance all observed variables equally without screening and differentiation of confounders, leading to poor performance in high-dimensional settings. Overall, the previous methods can work well in well-designed experimental settings or observational studies with grounded model assumptions and prior knowledge.

In the wild big data scenarios, however, there are almost always a large number of additional or mostly uncontrolled confounders and identified variables, and the correlations among them are complex and unknown in the real world [23]. Hence, we face the following challenges in estimating treatment effect in the wild observational studies: (1) **unknown model structure of the interactions among variables**: As stated in [23], pretty much everything in the real world interacts with everything else, to some degree, and their interactions are complicated due to the complex nature of the real world. We hardly know the real model structure among variables in the wild, so we cannot make any model specification a priori for removing confounding bias. (2) **high-dimensional and noisy variables**: In big data scenario, there are always a large number of observed variables, but not all these variables are confounders and different confounders contribute unequally to the confounding bias in data. Usually, we do not have sufficient prior knowledge to justify the inclusion of hundreds or even thousands of variables. How to differentiate the confounders and their confounding bias is quite difficult.

To address these challenges, we propose a data-driven method, named Differentiated Confounder Balancing (D-CB) algorithm. The method is based on the framework of confounder balancing, but in contrast with previous methods which balance all variables equally, we argue that some variables should not be regarded as confounders and we theoretically prove that the weights of confounders should be differentiated in confounder balancing. Motivated by this, we propose an integrated regularization algorithm to jointly select confounders, differentiate weights of confounders and balance confounder distributions for treatment effect estimation. During the treatment effect estimation, the selected confounders and their weights are used to adjust the weights of units, so that the confounder distributions, approximated by their moments, over all units can be balanced in treated and control groups. We validate our DCB algorithm with extensive experiments on both synthetic and real datasets. The results show that our algorithm outperforms the state-of-the-art methods on treatment effect estimation in observational studies.

The main contributions of this paper are:

- We address the new challenges of estimating treatment effect in big data scenarios with high-dimensional noisy variables and insufficient prior knowledge on variable interactions, which is beyond the capability of previous methods.
- We propose a novel DCB algorithm to jointly select confounders, optimize the confounder weights and sample weights for confounder balancing, and simultaneously estimate the treatment effect in the wild observational studies.
- The advantages of DCB algorithm are demonstrated in both synthetic and real datasets. We also show that our method can significantly help to improve the prediction performance with real online advertising dataset.

The rest of this paper is organized as follows. Section 2 reviews the related work. Section 3 introduces our differentiated confounder balancing estimator. Section 4 proposes the algorithm that accurately infers the treatment effect. Section 5 gives the experimental results. Finally, Section 6 concludes the paper.

2 RELATED WORK

Existing weighting based treatment effect estimation methods in observational studies either employ propensity score or optimize balance weights directly.

The propensity score was first proposed by Rosenbaum and Rubin [22], where it was estimated via a logistic regression. Then many other machine learning algorithms (e.g., lasso [8, 10], boosting regression [18], bagged CART and neural network [25]) are employed for propensity score estimation. Various estimators have been proposed based on propensity score, such as propensity score matching, inverse propensity weighting and double robust estimators [3, 4, 6, 16]. But these estimators require correct model specification on treatment assignment or precise estimation of the propensity score, which may not be the case in many applications [2].

Recently, researchers proposed new weighting based estimators by focusing on confounder balancing directly [2, 7, 11, 12, 26]. Hainmueller [11] introduced entropy balancing to directly adjust sample weights to the specified sample moments while moving the sample weights as little as possible. Athey et al. [2] proposed approximate residual balancing for sample weights learning via a lasso residual regression adjustment. Zubizarreta [26] learnt the stable balancing weights via minimizing its variance and adjusting for confounder balancing directly. Chan et al. [7] considered a wide class calibration weights constructed to attain confounder balancing directly. Imai et al. [12] introduced covariate balancing propensity score, which models treatment assignment while optimizing covariates balancing. Most of these methods are non-parametrical and require no propensity score estimation, but they do not differentiate the confounders by treating all observed variables as confounders and balanced all of them equally, leading to possible poor performance on treatment effect estimation in the setting of high dimensional variables.

Hence, it is very likely to improve the treatment effect estimation efficiency by fine-tuned selection and differentiated methods. To achieve the goal, we propose a differentiated confounder balancing algorithm to jointly optimize confounder weights and sample weights for precise treatment effect estimation.

3 PROBLEM AND OUR ESTIMATOR

In this section, we first give the notations and problem formulation, then revisit traditional confounder balancing estimators, and propose a novel estimator via differentiated confounder balancing.

3.1 Notations and Problem Formulation

Our goal is to estimate the treatment effect based on potential outcome framework [13, 22]. With the framework, we define a treatment as a random variable T and a potential outcome as $Y(t)$ which corresponds to a specific treatment $T = t$.

Table 1: Symbols and definitions.

Symbol	Definition
n_t (n_c)	Sample size for treated (control) group
n	Sample size ($n = n_t + n_c$)
p	Dimension of observed (augmented) variables
$T \in \mathbb{R}^{n\times 1}$	Treatment
$Y \in \mathbb{R}^{n\times 1}$	Outcome
$\mathbf{X} \in \mathbb{R}^{n\times p}$	Observed variables
$\mathbf{X_t} \in \mathbb{R}^{n_t\times p}$	Observed variables of treated units
$\mathbf{M_t} \in \mathbb{R}^{n_t\times p}$	Augmented variables of treated units
$\mathbf{M_c} \in \mathbb{R}^{n_c\times p}$	Augmented variables of control units
$W \in \mathbb{R}^{n_c\times 1}$	Sample weights on control units
$\beta \in \mathbb{R}^{p\times 1}$	Confounder weights

In this paper, we only focus on binary treatment, that is $t \in \{0, 1\}$. We define the units which received treatment ($T = 1$) as treated units and the other units with $T = 0$ as control units. Then, for each unit indexed by $i = 1, 2, \cdots, n$, we observe a treatment T_i, an outcome Y_i^{obs} and a vector of observed variables $X_i \in \mathbb{R}^{p\times 1}$, where the observed outcome Y_i^{obs} of unit i denotes by:

$$Y_i^{obs} = Y_i(T_i) = T_i \cdot Y_i(1) + (1 - T_i) \cdot Y_i(0). \quad (1)$$

The numbers of treated and control units are equal to n_t and n_c, and the dimension of all observed variables is p. In our paper, for any column vector $\mathbf{v} = (v_1, v_2, \cdots, v_m)^T$, let $\|\mathbf{v}\|_\infty = \max(|v_1|, \cdots, |v_m|)$, $\|\mathbf{v}\|_2^2 = \sum_{i=1}^m v_i^2$, and $\|\mathbf{v}\|_1 = \sum_{i=1}^m |v_i|$.

Throughout this paper, we assume the unconfoundedness [22] condition is satisfied.

Assumption 1: Unconfoundedness. The distribution of treatment is independent of potential outcome when given the observed variables. Formally, $T \perp (Y(0), Y(1)) | \mathbf{X}$.

In this paper, we focus on estimating the Average Treatment effect on the Treated (ATT), which represents the mean (average) difference between the potential outcomes under treated and control status among the treated subgroup. Formally, the ATT is defined as:

$$ATT = E[Y(1)|T = 1] - E[Y(0)|T = 1], \quad (2)$$

where $Y(1)$ and $Y(0)$ represent the potential outcome of units with treatment status as treated $T = 1$ and control $T = 0$, respectively. Our method proposed in this paper can be readily extended to estimate the Average Treatment effect on the Control (ATC) and hence the Average Treatment Effect (ATE) for the whole population.

In Eq. (2), $E[Y(1)|T = 1]$ can be straightforwardly estimated by the sample analog $\sum_{i:T_i=1} \frac{1}{n_t} \cdot Y_i^{obs}$. But it is cumbersome to estimate $E[Y(0)|T = 1]$, since we cannot observe the potential outcome $Y(0)$ for the treated units. Under Assumption 1, $E[Y(0)|T = 1]$ is usually estimated by re-weighting techniques for removing the confounding bias. The re-weighting methods form the surrogates of the unobserved potential outcome $(Y(0)|T = 1)$ by re-weighting the control units with sample weights W to make the confounder distributions on control units mimic the distributions on treated units. Then with the sample weights W on control units, we can estimate the ATT by:

$$\widehat{ATT} = \sum_{i:T_i=1} \frac{1}{n_t} \cdot Y_i^{obs} - \sum_{j:T_j=0} W_j \cdot Y_j^{obs}. \quad (3)$$

3.2 Revisiting on Confounder Balancing

It can been seen from Eq. (3) that the ATT estimation produces a sample weights learning problem. The classical approaches for sample weights learning are propensity score based methods [3, 4, 6]. The good performance of these methods hinges on the correct model specification for treatment assignment or accurate estimates of the propensity scores. Hence, the performance of these methods is often poor in the wild observational studies, where the model structure among variables is unknown.

To reduce the model dependency for applying on data in the wild, researchers proposed non-parametric methods to optimize the sample weights W by focusing on confounder balancing directly [2, 11]. The motivation behind these methods is that the confounders can be balanced by their moments, which uniquely determine their distributions. Therefore, they learn the sample weights W by:

$$W = \arg\min_W \|\overline{\mathbf{X}}_t - \textstyle\sum_{j:T_j=0} W_j \cdot X_j\|_2^2 \quad (4)$$

or

$$W = \arg\min_W \|\overline{\mathbf{X}}_t - \textstyle\sum_{j:T_j=0} W_j \cdot X_j\|_\infty^2, \quad (5)$$

where the $\overline{\mathbf{X}}_t$ represents the mean value of observed variables on treated units. The direct confounder balancing methods based on Eq. (4) or (5) can be applied on data in the wild. But they balance all observed variables equally without differentiating confounders, which results in poor performance in the setting of high dimensional variables.

3.3 Differentiated Confounder Balancing

To precisely estimate the treatment effect with high dimensional observational data in the wild, we propose to simultaneously learn confounder weights and sample weights. The confounder weights can determine which variable is included and its share of contribution on confounding bias, and the sample weights are designed for confounder balancing.

To be specific, we jointly optimize the confounder weights and sample weights by learning following optimization under some constraints to be clarified later.

$$W = \arg\min_W \left(\beta^T \cdot (\overline{\mathbf{X}}_t - \textstyle\sum_{j:T_j=0} W_j \cdot X_j)\right)^2, \quad (6)$$

where $W \in \mathbb{R}^{n_c\times 1}$ is sample weights and $\beta \in \mathbb{R}^{p\times 1}$ is the confounder weights. In Eq. (6), the confounder weights β differentiate the roles of each confounder in the balancing process, which helps for better removing the confounding bias in the wild observational studies.

Next, we give theoretical analysis on how to differentiate confounders weights with following proposition.

Proposition 3.1. *In observational studies, different confounders make unequal confounding bias on ATT with their own weights, and the weights can be learned via regressing potential outcome $Y(0)$ on observed variables $\mathbf{X}$.*

The general relationship among observed variables $\mathbf{X}$, treatment T and outcome Y can be represented as:

$$Y = f(\mathbf{X}) + T \cdot g(\mathbf{X}) + \epsilon, \quad (7)$$

where the *true* ATT is $E(g(\mathbf{X}_t))$, and the potential outcome $Y(0)$ can be represented by:

$$Y(0) = f(\mathbf{X}) + \epsilon. \tag{8}$$

We prove Proposition 3.1 with following assumption.

Assumption 2: Linearity. The regression of potential outcome $Y(0)$ on observed variables $\mathbf{X}$ is linear, that is $f(\mathbf{X}) = c + \alpha\mathbf{X}$.

Under assumption 2, we can rewrite estimator of $\widehat{ATT}$ as:

$$\begin{aligned}\widehat{ATT} &= \textstyle\sum_{i:T_i=1} \frac{1}{n_t} Y_i^{obs} - \sum_{j:T_j=0} W_j Y_j^{obs} \\ &= \textstyle\sum_{i:T_i=1} \frac{1}{n_t}(c + \alpha X_i + g(X_i) + \epsilon_i) - \sum_{j:T_j=0} W_j(c + \alpha X_j + \epsilon_j) \\ &= E(g(\mathbf{X}_t)) + (\textstyle\sum_{i:T_i=1} \frac{1}{n_t}\alpha X_i - \sum_{j:T_j=0} W_j \alpha X_j) + \phi(\epsilon) \\ &= ATT + \textstyle\sum_{k=1}^{p} \alpha_k (\sum_{i:T_i=1} \frac{1}{n_t} X_{i,k} - \sum_{j:T_j=0} W_j X_{j,k}) + \phi(\epsilon).\end{aligned}$$

where $\phi(\epsilon) = \sum_{i:T_i=1} \frac{1}{n_t}\epsilon_i - \sum_{j:T_j=0} W_j\epsilon_j$ refers to the difference of noises between treated and control units, and $\phi(\epsilon) \simeq 0$ with Gaussian noise. To reduce the bias of $\widehat{ATT}$, we need regulate the term $\sum_{k=1}^{p} \alpha_k \cdot (\sum_{i:T_i=1} \frac{1}{n_t} X_{i,k} - \sum_{j:T_j=0} W_j X_{j,k})$, where $(\sum_{i:T_i=1} \frac{1}{n_t} X_{i,k} - \sum_{j:T_j=0} W_j X_{j,k})$ means the difference of the kth confounder between treated and control units. The parameter α_k represents the confounding bias weight of the kth confounder, and it is the coefficient of X_k in the function $f(\mathbf{X})$. Hence, we can learn the confounder weights from the regression of potential outcome $Y(0)$ on observed variables $\mathbf{X}$ under *Linearity* assumption.

Actually, the regression of potential outcome $Y(0)$ against on observed variables $\mathbf{X}$ is infeasible, because of the counterfactual problem, that we cannot observe the potential outcome $Y(0)$ for treated units. Here we utilize the sample weights W again to facilitate the construction of surrogates for the potential outcomes $Y(0)$ of the treated units. We will elaborate on this later.

When the function $f(\mathbf{X})$ is nonlinear, that is $f(\mathbf{X})$ allows for powers and interactions among observed variables. It is conceptually easy to extend above results under *Linearity* assumption to bound the bias of ATT with Taylor expansion on $f(\mathbf{X})$ by balancing not only observed variables, but also their powers and interactions. Therefore, when $f(\mathbf{X})$ is nonlinear, we have to balance the augmented variables $\mathbf{M} = (\mathbf{X}, \mathbf{X}^2, X_iX_j, \mathbf{X}^3, X_iX_jX_k, \cdots)$, and learn the confounder weights by regressing the potential outcome $Y(0)$ on augmented variables $\mathbf{M}$.

The differentiated confounder balance strategy we propose focuses on mere bias control of the ATT estimator by mean modelling of the potential outcome. A possible refined strategy can be developed by incorporating variance modeling of the potential outcome, which allows one to control the variance and eventually the MSE of the resultant ATT estimator. We leave this extension to future work.

4 OPTIMIZATION

In this section, we give details of our DCB algorithm for treatment effect estimation, and introduce parameters tuning method for the "no ground truth" problem in observational causal inference.

4.1 Algorithm

With Proposition 3.1, we know the ATT estimator is affected by the unbalance of the observed variables, and their high order terms. That is the augmented variables $\mathbf{M}$:

$$\mathbf{M} = (\mathbf{X}, \mathbf{X}^2, X_iX_j, \mathbf{X}^3, X_iX_jX_k, \cdots). \tag{9}$$

Combining Eq. (6)&(9) and Proposition 3.1, we give our objective function to jointly optimize sample weights and confounder weights for ATT estimation in observational studies as:

$$\begin{aligned} \min \quad & (\beta^T \cdot (\overline{\mathbf{M}}_t - \mathbf{M}_c^T W))^2, \\ s.t. \quad & \textstyle\sum_{j:T_j=0}(1 + W_j) \cdot (Y_j - M_j \cdot \beta)^2 \le \lambda, \\ & \|W\|_2^2 \le \delta, \quad \|\beta\|_2^2 \le \mu, \quad \|\beta\|_1 \le \nu, \\ & \mathbf{1}^T W = 1 \quad and \quad W \succeq 0, \end{aligned} \tag{10}$$

where W is the sample weights and β is the confounder weights. $\overline{\mathbf{M}}_t$ represents the mean value of augmented variables on treated units. $\sum_{j:T_j=0}(1+W_j)\cdot(Y_j - M_j\cdot\beta)^2$ refers to the loss function of potential outcome $Y(0)$ when learning the confounder weights, including potential outcome loss on both control units $\sum_{j:T_j=0}(Y_j - M_j \cdot \beta)^2$ and treated units $\sum_{j:T_j=0} W_j \cdot (Y_j - M_j \cdot \beta)^2$, which is again a surrogate by weighting. With the constraints $\|\beta\|_2^2 \le \mu$ and $\|\beta\|_1 \le \nu$, we can remove the non-confounders and smooth the confounder weights. The formula $\mathbf{1}^T W = 1$ normalizes the sample weights on control units to add up to one, with the sample weights on treated units. The terms $W \succeq 0$ constraint each of sample weights is non-negative. With norm $\|W\|_2^2 \le \delta$, we can reduce the variance of the sample weights to achieve stability.

These lead to the following optimization problem, which is to minimize $\mathcal{J}(W, \beta)$ with constraints on parameters W.

$$\begin{aligned} \mathcal{J}(W,\beta) \quad = \quad & (\beta^T \cdot (\overline{\mathbf{M}}_t - \mathbf{M}_c^T W))^2 \\ & +\lambda \textstyle\sum_{j:T_j=0}(1 + W_j) \cdot (Y_j - M_j \cdot \beta)^2 \\ & +\delta\|W\|_2^2 + \mu\|\beta\|_2^2 + \nu\|\beta\|_1, \\ s.t. \quad & \mathbf{1}^T W = 1 \quad and \quad W \succeq 0. \end{aligned} \tag{11}$$

Here, we propose an iterative method to minimize the above objective function (11).

Firstly, we initialize sample weights $W = \{1/n_c, \cdots, 1/n_c\}^T$ and confounder weights $\beta = \{1/p, \cdots, 1/p\}^T$. Once the initial values are given, in each iteration, we first update β by fixing W, and then update W by fixing β. These steps are described below:

Update β: When fixing W, the problem (11) is equivalent to optimize following objective function:

$$\begin{aligned} \mathcal{J}(\beta) \quad = \quad & (\beta^T \cdot (\overline{\mathbf{M}}_t - \mathbf{M}_c^T W))^2 + \mu\|\beta\|_2^2 + \nu\|\beta\|_1 \\ & +\lambda \textstyle\sum_{j:T_j=0}(1 + W_j) \cdot (Y_j - M_j \cdot \beta)^2 \end{aligned} \tag{12}$$

which is a standard ℓ_1 norm regularized least squares problem and can be solved with any LASSO (or elastic net) solver. Here, we use the proximal gradient algorithm [19] with proximal operator to solve the objective function in (12).

Algorithm 1 Differentiated Confounder Balancing (DCB)

Input: Tradeoff parameters $\lambda > 0$, $\delta > 0$, $\mu > 0$, $\nu > 0$, Augmented Variables Matrix on treat units $\mathbf{M}_t$, Augmented Variables Matrix on control units $\mathbf{M}_c$ and Outcome Y.

Output: Confounder Weights β and Sample Weights W

Initialize Confounder Weights $\beta^{(0)}$ and Sample Weights $W^{(0)}$
Calculate the current value of $\mathcal{J}(W,\beta)^{(0)} = \mathcal{J}(W^{(0)},\beta^{(0)})$ with Equation (11)
Initialize the iteration variable $t \leftarrow 0$
repeat
  $t \leftarrow t+1$
  Update $\beta^{(t)}$ by solving $\mathcal{J}(\beta^{(t-1)})$ in Equation (12)
  Update $W^{(t)}$ by solving $\mathcal{J}(W^{(t-1)})$ in Equation (13)
  Calculate $\mathcal{J}(W,\beta)^{(t)} = \mathcal{J}(W^{(t)},\beta^{(t)})$
until $\mathcal{J}(W,\beta)^{(t)}$ converges or max iteration is reached
return β, W.

Update W: By fixing β, we can obtain W by optimizing (11). It is equivalent to optimize following objective function:

$$\begin{aligned} \mathcal{J}(W) &= (\beta^T\cdot(\overline{\mathbf{M}}_t - \mathbf{M}_c^T W))^2 + \delta\|W\|_2^2 \\ &\quad +\lambda\textstyle\sum_{j:T_j=0}(1+W_j)\cdot(Y_j - M_j\cdot\beta)^2, \\ s.t.&\quad \mathbf{1}^T W = 1 \quad and \quad W\succeq 0. \end{aligned} \tag{13}$$

For ensuring non-negative of W with constraint $W\succeq 0$, we let $W = \omega\odot\omega$, where $\omega\in\mathbb{R}^{n_c\times 1}$ and $\odot$ refers to the Hadamard product. Then the problem (13) can be reformulated as:

$$\begin{aligned} \mathcal{J}(\omega) &= (\beta^T\cdot(\overline{\mathbf{M}}_t - \mathbf{M}_c^T(\omega\odot\omega)))^2 + \delta\|\omega\odot\omega\|_2^2 \\ &\quad +\lambda\textstyle\sum_{j:T_j=0}(1+\omega_j\odot\omega_j)\cdot(Y_j - M_j\cdot\beta)^2, \\ s.t.&\quad \mathbf{1}^T(\omega\odot\omega) = 1. \end{aligned} \tag{14}$$

The partial gradient of term $\mathcal{J}(\omega)$ with respect to ω is:

$$\begin{aligned} \frac{\partial\mathcal{J}(\omega)}{\partial\omega} &= -4(\beta^T\cdot(\overline{\mathbf{M}}_t - \mathbf{M}_c^T(\omega\odot\omega)))\cdot\mathbf{M}_c\cdot\beta\odot\omega \\ &\quad +4\delta\omega\odot\omega\odot\omega + 2\lambda\omega\odot(Y_c - \mathbf{M}_c\cdot\beta)^2. \end{aligned}$$

Then we determine the step size a with line search, and update ω at t^{th} iteration as:

$$\omega^{(t)} = \omega^{(t-1)} - a\cdot\frac{\partial\mathcal{J}(\omega^{(t-1)})}{\partial\omega^{(t-1)}}.$$

With constraint $\mathbf{1}^T(\omega\odot\omega) = 1$, we normalize $\omega^{(t)}$ as:

$$\omega^{(t)} = \frac{\omega^{(t)}}{\sqrt{\mathbf{1}^T(\omega^{(t)}\odot\omega^{(t)})}}.$$

Then, we update $W^{(t)}$ at t^{th} iteration with:

$$W^{(t)} = \omega^{(t)}\odot\omega^{(t)}.$$

We update β and W iteratively until the objective function (11) converges. The whole algorithm is summarized in Algorithm 1.

Finally, with the optimized sample weights W by our DCB algorithm, we can estimate the ATT with Eq. (3).

REMARK 1. *The confounder weights β in our algorithm can be applied for outcome residual adjustment as [2] did. Then, with the optimized β and W in our algorithm, we can estimate the ATT by combining confounder balancing and residual adjustment as:*

$\widehat{ATT} = \sum_{i:T_i=1}\frac{1}{n_t}\cdot Y_i^{obs} - (\overline{\mathbf{M}}_t\cdot\beta + \sum_{j:T_j=0} W_j(Y_j^{obs} - M_i\cdot\beta))$.

4.2 Complexity Analysis

During the procedure of optimization, the main cost is to calculate the loss $\mathcal{J}(W,\beta)$, update confounder weights β and sample weights W. We analyze the time complexity of each of them respectively. For the calculation of the loss, its complexity is $O(np)$, where n is the sample size and p is the dimension of (augmented) variables. For updating β, this is standard LASSO problem and its complexity is $O(np)$. For updating W, the complexity is dominated by the step of calculating the partial gradients of function $\mathcal{J}(\omega)$ with respect to variable ω. The complexity of $\frac{\partial\mathcal{J}(\omega)}{\partial\omega}$ is $O(np)$.

In total, the complexity of each iteration in Algorithm 1 is $O(np)$.

4.3 Parameters Tuning

No ground truth for parameters tuning is the main challenge of causal inference in observational studies. To address this challenge, we apply matching method to estimate the ATT and set it as the "approximal ground truth" as [1, 15, 21] did. Specially, for each treated unit i, we find its closet match among control units as follow:

$$match(i) = \arg\min_{j:T_j=0}\|X_i - X_j\|_2^2. \tag{15}$$

To make the matching approximate to exactly matching, we drop unit i if $match(i) > \varepsilon$. Then, we can obtain the "approximal ground truth" by comparing the average outcome between the matched treated and control units.

With the "approximal ground truth", we can tune parameters for our algorithm and baselines with cross validation by grid searching.

5 EXPERIMENTS

In this section, we evaluate our algorithm on both synthetic and real world datasets, comparing with the state-of-the-art methods.

5.1 Baseline Estimators

We implement following baseline estimators to evaluate the ATT for comparison.

- *Directly Estimator* $\widehat{ATT}_{dir}$: It evaluates the ATT by directly comparing the average outcome between the treated and control units. It ignores the confounding bias in data.
- *IPW Estimator* $\widehat{ATT}_{IPW}$ [22]: It evaluates the ATT via reweighting units with inverse of propensity score. It relies on correct model specification on treatment assignment.
- *Doubly Robust Estimator* $\widehat{ATT}_{DR}$ [4]: It evaluates the ATT with combination of IPW and regression method. It relies on correct specification of propensity score or outcome regression models.

- *Entropy Balancing Estimator* $\widehat{ATT}_{ENT}$ [11]: It evaluates the ATT by directly balancing on confounders and entropy loss on sample weights. It ignores the confounder weights.
- *Approximate Residual Balancing Estimator* $\widehat{ATT}_{ARB}$ [2]: It evaluates the ATT by combining weighting adjustment via directly balancing on confounders and regression adjustment on outcome. It ignores the confounder weights.

In this paper, we implemented $\widehat{ATT}_{IPW}$ and $\widehat{ATT}_{DR}$ with **lasso regression** for variables selection.

5.2 Experiments on Synthetic Data

In this section, we introduce how to generate the synthetic datasets and demonstrate the effectiveness of our DCB algorithm with extensive experiments.

5.2.1 Dataset. To generate the synthetic datasets, we consider two sample sizes $n = \{2000, 5000\}$ and also vary the dimension of observed variables $p = \{50, 100\}$. We first generate the observed variables $\mathbf{X} = (\mathbf{x}_1, \mathbf{x}_2, \cdots, \mathbf{x}_p)$ with independent Gaussian distributions as:

$$\mathbf{x}_1, \mathbf{x}_2, \cdots, \mathbf{x}_p \overset{iid}{\sim} \mathcal{N}(0,1),$$

where $\mathbf{x}_i$ represents value of the ith variable in $\mathbf{X}$.

To test the robustness of all estimators, we generate the binary treatment variable T from a logistic function (T_{logit}) and a misspecified function (T_{missp}) as

$$T_{logit} \sim Bernoulli(1/(1+\exp(-\textstyle\sum_{i=1}^{p \cdot r_c} s_c \cdot x_i + \mathcal{N}(0,1)))), and$$
$$T_{missp} = 1 \; if \; \textstyle\sum_{i=1}^{p \cdot r_c} s_c \cdot x_i + \mathcal{N}(0,1) > 0, \; T_{missp} = 0 \; otherwise$$

where we vary both **confounding rate** r_c and **confounding strength** s_c from 0 to 1. The confounding rate represents the ration of confounders to all observed variables, and the confounding strength refers to the bias strength of confounders on treatment.

We generate the outcome Y from a linear function (Y_{linear}) and a nonlinear function (Y_{nonlin}) as:

$$Y_{linear} = T + \textstyle\sum_{j=1}^{p} \{I(mod(j,2) \equiv 0) \cdot (\frac{j}{2} + T) \cdot \mathbf{x}_j\} + \mathcal{N}(0,3),$$
$$Y_{nonlin} = T + \textstyle\sum_{j=1}^{p} \{I(mod(j,2) \equiv 0) \cdot (\frac{j}{2} + T) \cdot \mathbf{x}_j\} + \mathcal{N}(0,3)$$
$$+ \textstyle\sum_{j=1}^{p-1} \{I(mod(j,10) \equiv 1) \cdot \frac{p}{2} \cdot (x_j^2 + x_j \cdot x_{j+1})\},$$

where the $I(\cdot)$ is the indicator function and function $mod(x, y)$ returns the modulus after division of x by y.

Under different settings on treatment T and outcome Y, we know the *true ATT* in simulation. We evaluate the ATT with our algorithm, comparing with baselines.

5.2.2 Results. To evaluate the performance of our proposed method, we carry out the experiments for 100 times independently. Based on the estimated ATT ($\widehat{ATT}$), we calculate its $Bias$, standard deviations (SD), mean absolute errors (MAE) and root mean square errors ($RMSE$) with following definitions:

$$Bias = |\tfrac{1}{K}\textstyle\sum_{k=1}^{K} \widehat{ATT}_k - ATT|$$
$$SD = \sqrt{\tfrac{1}{K}\textstyle\sum_{k=1}^{K} (\widehat{ATT}_k - \tfrac{1}{K}\sum_{k=1}^{K} \widehat{ATT}_k)^2}$$
$$MAE = \tfrac{1}{K}\textstyle\sum_{k=1}^{K} |\widehat{ATT}_k - ATT|$$
$$RMSE = \sqrt{\tfrac{1}{K}\textstyle\sum_{k=1}^{K} (\widehat{ATT}_k - ATT)^2}$$

where K is the experimental times, $\widehat{ATT}_k$ is the estimated ATT in k^{th} experiment and ATT represents the *true treatment effect*.

We report the results in Table 2 for settings $T = T_{logit}, Y = Y_{linear}$ and $T = T_{missp}, Y = Y_{nonlin}$. The results under other settings are reported in the supplemental[1] to save space.

From Table 2, we have following observations and analyses:

- Directly estimator fails when confounders are associated with both treatment and outcome. From our results, we find Directly estimator makes huge error on ATT estimation, since it ignores the confounding bias in data.
- IPW and DR estimators have poor performance in the setting of high dimensional variables or when the model specifications are incorrect. IPW and DR estimators make huge error under setting 3 and setting 4, where $T = T_{missp}$ and $Y = Y_{nonlin}$.
- ENT estimator has good performance only when the parameters $s_c = 0.2$ under setting 2, where the confounding bias is small in data, but its performance deteriorates as the confounding bias increasing. Since it ignores the confounder weights, which makes it unable to effectively remove the confounding bias in data.
- ARB estimator achieves better performance than other baselines in most of time, since it is nonparametric method with regression adjustment. However, it is far inferior to our proposed estimator. The key reason is that it balances all observed variables equally.
- Our proposed DCB estimator, by jointly optimizing both sample weights and confounder weights, achieves significant improvements over the baselines in different settings, when varying sample size n, dimension of variables p, confounding rate r_c and confounding strength s_c.

We show the robustness of our estimator in Figure 1 by varying the sample size n, dimension of variables p, confounding rate r_c and confounding strength s_c. From Figure 1, we find that as we decrease n or increase p, r_c and s_c, the MAE of our estimator is consistent stable and small, while the MAE of baseline estimators increases continuously. This demonstrates that our proposed estimator is more precise and robust than the baselines.

5.2.3 Parameter Analysis. In our DCB algorithm, we have hype-parameters λ, δ, μ and ν. As mentioned before, we tuned these parameters in our experiments with cross validation by grid searching, and each parameter is uniformly varied from {0.001,0.01,0.1,1,10,100,1000}. We displayed the $Bias$ of treatment effect estimation with respect to λ, δ, μ and ν, respectively. As seen from Figure 2, the $Bias$ do not change too much and the performance are relatively stable when parameters $\lambda \geq 1$ and $\delta, \mu, \nu \leq 1$. From Figure 2a, we can see the $Bias$ is huge when parameter λ is too small. The main reason is that small value of λ would slack the

[1] https://www.dropbox.com/s/99s9rmkybo7jnbv/paper_supplemental.pdf

Table 2: Results on synthetic dataset in different settings. The *Bias* refers to the absolute error between the true and estimated ATT. The *SD*, *MAE* and *RMSE* represent the standard deviations, mean absolute errors and root mean square errors of estimated ATT ($\widehat{ATT}$) after 100 times independently experiments, respectively. The smaller *Bias*, *SD*, *MAE* and *RMSE*, the better.

Setting 1: $T = T_{logit}$, $Y = Y_{linear}$ **and** $s_c = 1$														
	n/p	$n = 2000, p = 50$			$n = 2000, p = 100$			$n = 5000, p = 50$			$n = 5000, p = 100$			
r_c	Estimator	*Bias* (SD)	MAE	RMSE	*Bias* (SD)	MAE	RMSE	*Bias* (SD)	MAE	RMSE	*Bias* (SD)	MAE	RMSE	
$r_c = 0.2$	$\widehat{ATT}_{dir}$	6.483 (3.460)	6.682	7.349	18.60 (8.859)	18.67	20.61	6.420 (2.050)	6.420	6.739	18.53 (5.148)	18.53	19.23	
	$\widehat{ATT}_{IPW}$	2.220 (6.224)	4.866	6.609	8.365 (15.40)	14.47	17.52	1.907 (4.092)	3.648	4.514	8.033 (9.852)	10.52	12.71	
	$\widehat{ATT}_{DR}$	0.118 (0.307)	0.253	0.329	1.591 (0.512)	1.591	1.672	0.059 (0.174)	0.145	0.183	1.446 (0.337)	1.446	1.485	
	$\widehat{ATT}_{ENT}$	0.371 (0.477)	0.453	0.605	4.924 (3.167)	5.052	5.855	0.046 (0.254)	0.210	0.258	2.425 (1.229)	2.429	2.719	
	$\widehat{ATT}_{ARB}$	0.074 (0.472)	0.376	0.477	0.868 (0.435)	0.881	0.971	0.027 (0.269)	0.217	0.270	0.365 (0.371)	0.447	0.520	
	$\widehat{ATT}_{DCB}$	**0.014** (0.121)	**0.099**	**0.122**	**0.006** (0.119)	**0.101**	**0.119**	**0.001** (0.073)	**0.053**	**0.073**	**0.001** (0.085)	**0.067**	**0.085**	
$r_c = 0.8$	$\widehat{ATT}_{dir}$	51.06 (3.725)	51.06	51.19	143.0 (9.389)	143.0	143.3	50.45 (1.900)	50.45	50.48	142.1 (5.647)	142.1	142.2	
	$\widehat{ATT}_{IPW}$	29.99 (4.048)	29.99	30.26	98.24 (8.462)	98.24	98.60	29.38 (2.216)	29.38	29.46	96.86 (5.899)	96.86	97.04	
	$\widehat{ATT}_{DR}$	0.345 (0.253)	0.367	0.428	4.492 (0.333)	4.492	4.504	0.338 (0.136)	0.338	0.365	4.306 (0.227)	4.306	4.312	
	$\widehat{ATT}_{ENT}$	15.06 (1.745)	15.06	15.16	63.02 (4.551)	63.02	63.19	10.09 (1.473)	10.09	10.19	51.99 (3.206)	51.99	52.09	
	$\widehat{ATT}_{ARB}$	0.231 (0.645)	0.553	0.685	2.909 (0.491)	2.909	2.951	0.189 (0.504)	0.428	0.538	2.259 (0.468)	2.259	2.307	
	$\widehat{ATT}_{DCB}$	**0.003** (0.127)	**0.102**	**0.127**	**0.020** (0.135)	**0.114**	**0.136**	**0.003** (0.088)	**0.072**	**0.088**	**0.012** (0.088)	**0.073**	**0.089**	
Setting 2: $T = T_{logit}$, $Y = Y_{linear}$ **and** $r_c = 0.5$														
	n/p	$n = 2000, p = 50$			$n = 2000, p = 100$			$n = 5000, p = 50$			$n = 5000, p = 100$			
s_c	Estimator	*Bias* (SD)	MAE	RMSE	*Bias* (SD)	MAE	RMSE	*Bias* (SD)	MAE	RMSE	*Bias* (SD)	MAE	RMSE	
$s_c = 0.2$	$\widehat{ATT}_{dir}$	11.80 (3.243)	11.80	12.24	43.38 (9.170)	43.38	44.34	11.53 (2.142)	11.53	11.73	42.64 (6.103)	42.64	43.07	
	$\widehat{ATT}_{IPW}$	3.897 (2.759)	4.144	4.775	18.37 (8.317)	18.38	20.17	3.873 (2.055)	3.875	4.384	17.13 (5.971)	17.13	18.14	
	$\widehat{ATT}_{DR}$	0.053 (0.150)	0.124	0.159	1.255 (0.265)	1.255	1.283	0.056 (0.104)	0.090	0.118	1.148 (0.180)	1.148	1.162	
	$\widehat{ATT}_{ENT}$	0.023 (0.168)	0.128	0.170	0.174 (0.193)	0.208	0.260	**0.001** (0.116)	0.090	0.116	0.089 (0.119)	0.120	0.149	
	$\widehat{ATT}_{ARB}$	**0.002** (0.170)	0.129	0.170	**0.011** (0.184)	0.151	0.185	0.004 (0.119)	0.094	0.120	0.006 (0.121)	0.093	0.122	
	$\widehat{ATT}_{DCB}$	0.011 (0.107)	**0.086**	**0.107**	0.013 (0.098)	**0.080**	**0.099**	0.003 (0.065)	**0.053**	**0.065**	**0.004** (0.073)	**0.060**	**0.073**	
$s_c = 0.8$	$\widehat{ATT}_{dir}$	22.81 (3.610)	22.81	23.09	69.28 (9.608)	69.28	69.94	21.91 (1.908)	21.91	21.99	68.72 (5.410)	68.72	68.93	
	$\widehat{ATT}_{IPW}$	9.984 (4.878)	10.15	11.11	40.64 (12.48)	40.64	42.51	9.263 (3.615)	9.263	9.943	40.31 (7.185)	40.31	40.94	
	$\widehat{ATT}_{DR}$	0.185 (0.256)	0.256	0.316	3.234 (0.449)	3.234	3.265	0.177 (0.166)	0.205	0.243	3.051 (0.245)	3.051	3.061	
	$\widehat{ATT}_{ENT}$	2.805 (1.153)	2.805	3.033	23.53 (4.432)	23.53	23.94	0.742 (0.447)	0.759	0.866	15.97 (2.519)	15.97	16.16	
	$\widehat{ATT}_{ARB}$	0.059 (0.564)	0.455	0.567	1.861 (0.491)	1.861	1.924	0.005 (0.408)	0.327	0.408	1.133 (0.451)	1.133	1.219	
	$\widehat{ATT}_{DCB}$	**0.007** (0.124)	**0.102**	**0.124**	**0.015** (0.123)	**0.102**	**0.124**	**0.001** (0.083)	**0.067**	**0.083**	**0.017** (0.076)	**0.063**	**0.078**	
Setting 3: $T = T_{missp}$, $Y = Y_{nonlin}$ **and** $s_c = 1$														
	n/p	$n = 2000, p = 50$			$n = 2000, p = 100$			$n = 5000, p = 50$			$n = 5000, p = 100$			
r_c	Estimator	*Bias* (SD)	MAE	RMSE	*Bias* (SD)	MAE	RMSE	*Bias* (SD)	MAE	RMSE	*Bias* (SD)	MAE	RMSE	
$r_c = 0.2$	$\widehat{ATT}_{dir}$	6.527 (5.367)	7.041	8.450	18.67 (14.04)	20.01	23.36	7.340 (3.425)	7.366	8.099	20.54 (9.992)	20.54	22.84	
	$\widehat{ATT}_{IPW}$	5.061 (8.998)	8.542	10.32	17.31 (19.22)	21.90	25.86	6.707 (6.494)	7.934	9.336	19.81 (15.04)	21.79	24.87	
	$\widehat{ATT}_{DR}$	6.334 (8.628)	8.562	10.70	23.65 (26.32)	29.16	35.38	6.493 (6.698)	7.637	9.329	23.44 (16.62)	24.77	28.74	
	$\widehat{ATT}_{ENT}$	3.770 (2.166)	3.842	4.348	13.46 (5.854)	13.58	14.68	3.096 (1.285)	3.102	3.352	12.16 (3.585)	12.16	12.68	
	$\widehat{ATT}_{ARB}$	0.643 (0.292)	0.647	0.706	3.757 (0.483)	3.757	3.788	0.512 (0.247)	0.517	0.569	3.288 (0.262)	3.288	3.299	
	$\widehat{ATT}_{DCB}$	**0.016** (0.316)	**0.263**	**0.317**	**0.021** (0.364)	**0.294**	**0.365**	**0.017** (0.169)	**0.139**	**0.169**	**0.082** (0.214)	**0.183**	**0.230**	
$r_c = 0.8$	$\widehat{ATT}_{dir}$	53.26 (5.308)	53.26	53.53	145.2 (13.47)	145.2	145.9	53.12 (3.673)	53.12	53.24	145.2 (9.247)	145.2	145.4	
	$\widehat{ATT}_{IPW}$	39.46 (6.404)	39.46	39.97	113.0 (16.91)	113.0	114.3	39.04 (4.424)	39.04	39.29	111.7 (10.19)	111.7	112.1	
	$\widehat{ATT}_{DR}$	15.12 (8.433)	15.40	17.31	34.07 (28.29)	37.09	44.28	14.26 (5.613)	14.28	15.33	30.92 (15.90)	31.70	34.77	
	$\widehat{ATT}_{ENT}$	29.83 (1.795)	29.83	29.89	97.32 (6.507)	97.32	97.54	25.73 (1.155)	25.73	25.76	85.63 (3.114)	85.63	85.68	
	$\widehat{ATT}_{ARB}$	1.342 (0.337)	1.342	1.384	7.440 (0.566)	7.440	7.462	1.102 (0.230)	1.102	1.126	6.526 (0.325)	6.526	6.535	
	$\widehat{ATT}_{DCB}$	**0.076** (0.321)	**0.255**	**0.330**	**0.024** (0.388)	**0.298**	**0.389**	**0.003** (0.207)	**0.171**	**0.207**	**0.021** (0.304)	**0.248**	**0.305**	
Setting 4: $T = T_{missp}$, $Y = Y_{nonlin}$ **and** $r_c = 0.5$														
	n/p	$n = 2000, p = 50$			$n = 2000, p = 100$			$n = 5000, p = 50$			$n = 5000, p = 100$			
s_c	Estimator	*Bias* (SD)	MAE	RMSE	*Bias* (SD)	MAE	RMSE	*Bias* (SD)	MAE	RMSE	*Bias* (SD)	MAE	RMSE	
$s_c = 0.2$	$\widehat{ATT}_{dir}$	18.01 (5.556)	18.01	18.84	59.49 (14.13)	59.49	61.15	18.01 (3.178)	18.01	18.29	60.34 (8.923)	60.34	60.99	
	$\widehat{ATT}_{IPW}$	7.288 (6.605)	8.429	9.836	32.24 (19.66)	33.23	37.76	7.372 (4.505)	7.516	8.639	33.39 (12.87)	33.39	35.78	
	$\widehat{ATT}_{DR}$	3.408 (5.953)	5.735	6.859	13.87 (21.90)	21.33	25.92	3.130 (4.146)	4.360	5.194	13.87 (12.53)	15.54	18.69	
	$\widehat{ATT}_{ENT}$	1.812 (0.818)	1.812	1.988	25.54 (6.241)	25.54	26.29	0.273 (0.160)	0.282	0.317	14.49 (2.800)	14.49	14.76	
	$\widehat{ATT}_{ARB}$	0.159 (0.254)	0.244	0.300	2.960 (0.385)	2.960	2.985	0.055 (0.150)	0.131	0.160	1.899 (0.241)	1.899	1.915	
	$\widehat{ATT}_{DCB}$	**0.005** (0.223)	**0.178**	**0.223**	**0.011** (0.288)	**0.228**	**0.288**	**0.012** (0.120)	**0.095**	**0.120**	**0.025** (0.158)	**0.125**	**0.160**	
$s_c = 0.8$	$\widehat{ATT}_{dir}$	24.58 (5.276)	24.58	25.14	72.30 (13.95)	72.30	73.63	24.10 (3.219)	24.10	24.31	71.20 (8.771)	71.20	71.74	
	$\widehat{ATT}_{IPW}$	18.34 (6.819)	18.34	19.56	57.07 (18.02)	57.07	59.85	17.65 (4.755)	17.65	18.28	54.95 (9.861)	54.95	55.83	
	$\widehat{ATT}_{DR}$	11.23 (8.757)	12.46	14.24	32.35 (26.22)	35.39	41.65	11.17 (5.492)	11.17	12.44	28.06 (14.24)	28.29	31.46	
	$\widehat{ATT}_{ENT}$	12.88 (1.956)	12.88	13.03	48.40 (5.818)	48.40	48.75	10.46 (1.315)	10.46	10.55	40.79 (2.773)	40.79	40.88	
	$\widehat{ATT}_{ARB}$	0.993 (0.343)	0.993	1.050	6.052 (0.525)	6.052	6.075	0.807 (0.255)	0.807	0.846	5.176 (0.279)	5.176	5.183	
	$\widehat{ATT}_{DCB}$	**0.042** (0.310)	**0.246**	**0.313**	**0.023** (0.364)	**0.306**	**0.365**	**0.006** (0.211)	**0.167**	**0.211**	**0.013** (0.237)	**0.194**	**0.238**	

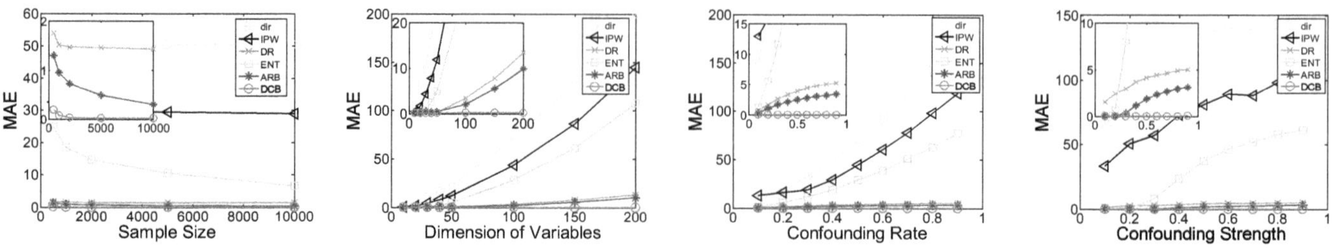

(a) sample size n (b) dimension of variables p (c) confounding rate r_c (d) confounding strength s_c

Figure 1: MAE on ATT estimation when varying different parameters, with setting $T = T_{logit}$, $Y = Y_{linear}$. The sub-figure on the top left corner of each main figure is plot by freezing MAE on Y-axis with a limit. The results show our proposed DCB estimator is more precise and robust than the baselines.

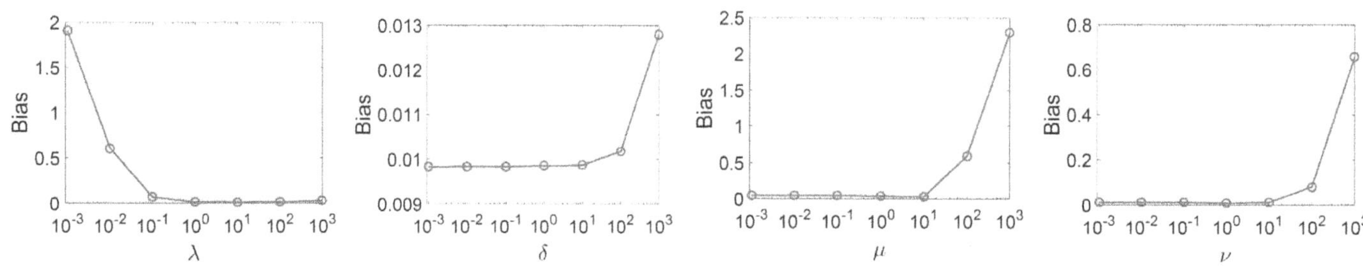

(a) (b) (c) (d)

Figure 2: The effect of hyper-parameters λ, δ, μ and ν.

constrain on confounder weights learning, resulting in imprecise confounder weights, even the trivial solution $\beta = 0$. From Figure 2c and 2d, we find that the *Bias* increased as the increasing of μ and ν. This is because that large value of μ and ν would enforce the confounder weights close to *zero*. The Figure 2b demonstrates that the performance is insensitive to the parameter δ. To sum up, we can easily obtain the best hype-parameters for our DCB algorithm.

5.3 Experiments on Real Data

In this section, we apply our DCB algorithm on two real datasets for ATT estimation and application, including the LaLonde dataset and an online advertising dataset.

5.3.1 LaLonde Dataset. First, we apply our DCB algorithm on the LaLonde [17] dataset[2], a canonical benchmark in the causal inference literature [9, 11]. The LaLonde dataset used in our paper consists of two parts. The first part comes from a randomized experiment on a large scale job training program, the National Support Work Demonstration (NSW)[3]. In the second part data, as [11] did, we replace the control group in randomized experiment with another control group drawn from the Current Population Survey-Social Security Administration file (CPS-1) where the measured covariates are the same with the experimental data. The treatment in this data is whether the participant attend the particular job training program or not, and the outcome is the earning in the year 1978. The data contains 10 raw observed variables, including earnings and employment status for year 1974 and 1975, education status (years of schooling and an indicator for completed high school degree), age, ethnicity (indicators for black and hispanic) and the married status.

Overall, there are *185* program participants (the treated units) and *260* nonparticipants (the control units) in the experimental data NSW. In the observational data CPS-1, we have *185* program participants and *15,992* nonparticipants. The randomized experimental data NSW provide the ground truth for estimating the ATT of the program. We estimate the ATT with the observational data CPS-1, comparing our proposed algorithm with the baselines.

Experimental Settings. In our experiments, we randomly split the observational data CPS-1 as 6 partitions, with the first 3 partitions, we train our model and baseline models for parameters tuning with cross validation by grid searching, and test model performance and robustness with the last 3 partitions. We conduct our DCB algorithm and baselines on two variables sets, V-RAW and V-INTERACTION. The V-RAW refers to the 10 raw observed variables, and the V-INTERACTION refers to the set of raw variables, their pairwise one-way interaction, and their squared terms.

Results. We report the results in Table 3, where the smaller *Bias* and *SD*, the better. From the results, we have following observations. (1) Directly estimator failed due to the existing of confounding bias in the LaLonde data. (2) IP-W generates a big error on ATT estimation in both V-RAW and V-INTERACTION settings. The main reason is that

[2]The dataset is available at http://users.nber.org/~rdehejia/data/nswdata2.html

[3]Notice that we focus on the Dehejia and Wahha sampled dataset of the LaLonde.

Table 3: ATT estimation results on LaLonde dataset, where the true ATT from randomized experiment is 1,794. The smaller *Bias* and SD, the better.

Variables Set	V-RAW		V-INTERACTION	
Estimator	$\widehat{ATT}$	*Bias* (SD)	$\widehat{ATT}$	*Bias* (SD)
$\widehat{ATT}_{dir}$	-8471	10265 (374)	-8471	10265 (374)
$\widehat{ATT}_{IPW}$	-4481	6275 (971)	-4365	6159 (1024)
$\widehat{ATT}_{DR}$	1154	639 (491)	1590	204 (812)
$\widehat{ATT}_{ENT}$	1535	259 (995)	1405	388 (787)
$\widehat{ATT}_{ARB}$	1537	257 (996)	1627	167 (957)
$\widehat{ATT}_{DCB}$	1958	**164** (728)	1836	**43** (716)

Table 4: Confounder weights learnt from our DCB algorithm with V-RAW variables set.

Rank	Confounder	Weight
1	Earnings 1975	0.335
2	Earnings 1974	0.241
3	Employed 1975	0.141
4	Education	0.138
5	Employed 1974	0.050
6	Married	0.039
7	High School Degree 1975	0.017
8	Age	-0.013
9	Black	-0.003
10	Hispanic	-0.001

the specification model of IPW is incorrect and the sample size between treated and control units is unbalanced. (3) Our proposed DCB estimator achieves the best performance compared with the baselines, since our estimator simultaneously optimizes sample weights and confounder weights, and requires no any model specification on treatment assignment. (4) Our estimator obtains a more accurate ATT estimation with V-INTERACTION variables set than V-RAW variables set. This demonstrates that our estimator can achieve a better confounder balancing with including the high order terms of observed variables in augmented variables.

In Table 4, we show the confounder weights optimized by our DCB algorithm with V-RAW variables set. From this table, we know that the confounders Earnings 1975 & 1974 and Education are very important for the outcome (Earning 1978), but the Black and Hispanic have few effects on the outcome. Thus the confounders of Earnings 1975 & 1974 and Education are more important, and should be balanced first.

5.3.2 Online Advertising Dataset. The real online advertising dataset we used is collected from Tencecnt WeChat App[4] during September 2015. In WeChat, each user can share (receive) posts to (from) his/her friends as like the Twitter and Facebook. Then the advertisers could push their advertisements to users, by merging them into the list of the user's wallposts. For each advertisement, there are two types of feedbacks: "Like" and "Dislike". When the user clicks the "Like" button, his/her friends will receive the advertisements with this action.

[4] http://www.wechat.com/en/

The online advertising campaign used in our paper is about LONGCHAMP handbags for young ladies[5]. This campaign contains 14,891 user feedbacks with Like and 93,108 Dislikes. For each user, we have 56 features including (1) demographic attributes, such as age, gender, (2) number of friends, (3) device (iOS or Android), and (4) the user settings on WeChat, for example, whether allowing strangers to see his/her album and whether installing the online payment service.

Experimental Settings. In our experiments, we set the feedback of users on the advertisement as outcome Y. Specifically, we set the outcome $Y_i = 1$ when user i likes the advertisement and $Y_i = 0$ when user i dislikes it. And we alternatively set one of the user features as the treatment T and others as the observed variables $\mathbf{X}$. Therefore, we can estimate the ATT for each user feature. We tuned the parameters in our algorithm and baseline methods with the "approximal ground truth" via cross validation by grid searching.

Evaluation and baselines. In this dataset, we have no ground truth about the treatment effect of each user feature, but we are interesting in whether the top k features ranked by our proposed DCB estimator is able to get good performance in predicting the Like and Dislike behaviors of users, comparing with all above ATT baseline estimators and two commonly used methods for correlation-based feature selection, including MRel (Maximum Relevance) [24] and mRMR (Maximum Relevance Minimum Redundancy) [20]. Our estimator and other ATT baseline estimator rank the user features by their absolute causal effect. We use MAE as the evaluation metric, which is defined as:

$$MAE = \frac{1}{m}\sum_{i=1}^{m}|\hat{Y}_i - Y_i|,$$

where m is the number of users in test data, $\hat{Y}_i$ and Y_i represent the predict and actual feedback of user i on the advertisement.

Results. We plot the results in Figure 3. From the results, we can find that our proposed DCB estimator achieves the best prediction accuracy with different number of features. Also, our method can get almost the optimal prediction performance with much less features than other baselines. The main reason is that with differentiating the confounders, our estimator can estimate the causal effect of each user feature more precise by better confounding bias removing. Another important observation is that the two commonly used correlation-based feature selection methods perform worse than our method and even the other causal estimators. This is because of the sample selection bias between the training and testing datasets, the correlation-based methods cannot handle this issue, while the causal estimators can solve the problem to a certain extent by balancing treated and control units and removing the confounding bias.

The results demonstrate that treatment effect estimation can significantly help to improve the prediction performance, as long as the confounding problems are appropriately addressed.

[5] http://en.longchamp.com/en/womens-bags

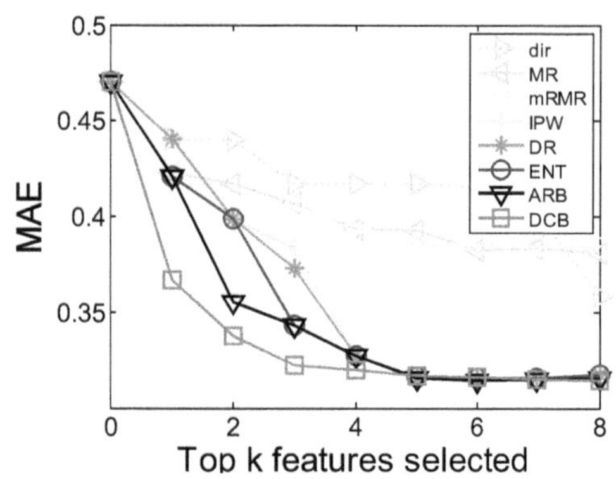

Figure 3: Our proposed DCB estimator outperforms the baselines when selecting the top k significant causal features to predict whether user will like or dislike an advertisement.

6 CONCLUSION

In this paper, we focus on how to estimate the treatment effect more precisely with high dimensional observational data in the wild. We argued that most previous weighting based estimators do not take confounder differentiation into account or require model specification, leading to poor performance in the setting of high dimensional variables or in the wild. Therefore, we proposed the concept of confounder weights for confounders differentiation with theoretical analysis. We proposed a differentiated confounder balancing algorithm to jointly optimize the confounder weights and sample weights for treatment effect estimation. Extensive experiments on both synthetic and real datasets demonstrated that our proposed algorithm can significantly and consistently outperforms the start-of-the-art methods. We also demonstrated that the top ranked features by our algorithm have the best prediction performance on an online advertising dataset.

Our future work will focus on causal inference with unobserved confounders in observational studies by data driven approach.

7 ACKNOWLEDGEMENT

This work was supported by National Program on Key Basic Research Project, No. 2015CB352300; National Natural Science Foundation of China, No. 61370022, No. 61521002, No. 61531006 and No. 61210008. Thanks for the research fund of Tsinghua-Tencent Joint Laboratory for Internet Innovation Technology. Bo Li's research was supported by the Tsinghua University Initiative Scientific Research Grant, No. 20165080091; National Natural Science Foundation of China, No. 71490723 and No. 71432004; Science Foundation of Ministry of Education of China, No. 16JJD630006.

REFERENCES

[1] S. Athey and G. W. Imbens. Machine learning methods for estimating heterogeneous causal effects. *stat*, 1050:5, 2015.
[2] S. Athey, G. W. Imbens, and S. Wager. Approximate residual balancing: De-biased inference of average treatment effects in high dimensions. *arXiv preprint arXiv:1604.07125*, 2016.
[3] P. C. Austin. An introduction to propensity score methods for reducing the effects of confounding in observational studies. *Multivariate behavioral research*, 46(3):399–424, 2011.
[4] H. Bang and J. M. Robins. Doubly robust estimation in missing data and causal inference models. *Biometrics*, 61(4), 2005.
[5] L. Bottou, J. Peters, J. Q. Candela, D. X. Charles, M. Chickering, E. Portugaly, D. Ray, P. Y. Simard, and E. Snelson. Counterfactual reasoning and learning systems: the example of computational advertising. *Journal of Machine Learning Research*, 14(1):3207–3260, 2013.
[6] D. Chan, R. Ge, O. Gershony, T. Hesterberg, and D. Lambert. Evaluating online ad campaigns in a pipeline: causal models at scale. In *Proceedings of the 16th ACM SIGKDD international conference on Knowledge discovery and data mining*, pages 7–16. ACM, 2010.
[7] K. C. G. Chan, S. C. P. Yam, and Z. Zhang. Globally efficient non-parametric inference of average treatment effects by empirical balancing calibration weighting. *Journal of the Royal Statistical Society: Series B (Statistical Methodology)*, 2015.
[8] V. Chernozhukov, D. Chetverikov, M. Demirer, E. Duflo, C. Hansen, et al. Double machine learning for treatment and causal parameters. *arXiv preprint arXiv:1608.00060*, 2016.
[9] A. Diamond and J. S. Sekhon. Genetic matching for estimating causal effects: A general multivariate matching method for achieving balance in observational studies. *Review of Economics and Statistics*, 95(3):932–945, 2013.
[10] M. H. Farrell. Robust inference on average treatment effects with possibly more covariates than observations. *Journal of Econometrics*, 189(1):1–23, 2015.
[11] J. Hainmueller. Entropy balancing for causal effects: A multivariate reweighting method to produce balanced samples in observational studies. *Political Analysis*, 20(1):25–46, 2012.
[12] K. Imai and M. Ratkovic. Covariate balancing propensity score. *Journal of the Royal Statistical Society: Series B (Statistical Methodology)*, 76(1):243–263, 2014.
[13] G. W. Imbens and D. B. Rubin. *Causal inference in statistics, social, and biomedical sciences.* Cambridge University Press, 2015.
[14] R. Kohavi and R. Longbotham. Unexpected results in online controlled experiments. *ACM SIGKDD Explorations Newsletter*, 12(2):31–35, 2011.
[15] K. Kuang, P. Cui, B. Li, M. Jiang, S. Yang, and F. Wang. Treatment effect estimation with data-driven variable decomposition. In *Proceedings of the 31st AAAI Conference on Artificial Intelligence.* AAAI, 2017.
[16] K. Kuang, M. Jiang, P. Cui, and S. Yang. Steering social media promotions with effective strategies. In *Data Mining (ICDM), 2016 IEEE 16th International Conference on.* IEEE, 2016.
[17] R. J. LaLonde. Evaluating the econometric evaluations of training programs with experimental data. *The American economic review*, pages 604–620, 1986.
[18] D. F. McCaffrey, G. Ridgeway, and A. R. Morral. Propensity score estimation with boosted regression for evaluating causal effects in observational studies. *Psychological methods*, 9(4):403, 2004.
[19] N. Parikh, S. P. Boyd, et al. Proximal algorithms. *Foundations and Trends in optimization*, 1(3):127–239, 2014.
[20] H. Peng, F. Long, and C. Ding. Feature selection based on mutual information criteria of max-dependency, max-relevance, and min-redundancy. *IEEE Transactions on pattern analysis and machine intelligence*, 27(8):1226–1238, 2005.
[21] C. A. Rolling and Y. Yang. Model selection for estimating treatment effects. *Journal of the Royal Statistical Society: Series B (Statistical Methodology)*, 76(4):749–769, 2014.
[22] P. R. Rosenbaum and D. B. Rubin. The central role of the propensity score in observational studies for causal effects. *Biometrika*, 70(1):41–55, 1983.
[23] R. M. Shiffrin. Drawing causal inference from big data, 2016.
[24] K. Torkkola. Feature extraction by non-parametric mutual information maximization. *Journal of machine learning research*, 3(Mar):1415–1438, 2003.
[25] D. Westreich, J. Lessler, and M. J. Funk. Propensity score estimation: neural networks, support vector machines, decision trees (cart), and meta-classifiers as alternatives to logistic regression. *Journal of clinical epidemiology*, 63(8):826–833, 2010.
[26] J. R. Zubizarreta. Stable weights that balance covariates for estimation with incomplete outcome data. *Journal of the American Statistical Association*, 110(511):910–922, 2015.

The Selective Labels Problem: Evaluating Algorithmic Predictions in the Presence of Unobservables

Himabindu Lakkaraju
Stanford University
himalv@cs.stanford.edu

Jon Kleinberg
Cornell University
kleinber@cs.cornell.edu

Jure Leskovec
Stanford University
jure@cs.stanford.edu

Jens Ludwig
University of Chicago
jludwig@uchicago.edu

Sendhil Mullainathan
Harvard University
mullain@fas.harvard.edu

ABSTRACT

Evaluating whether machines improve on human performance is one of the central questions of machine learning. However, there are many domains where the data is *selectively labeled* in the sense that the observed outcomes are themselves a consequence of the existing choices of the human decision-makers. For instance, in the context of judicial bail decisions, we observe the outcome of whether a defendant fails to return for their court appearance only if the human judge decides to release the defendant on bail. This selective labeling makes it harder to evaluate predictive models as the instances for which outcomes are observed do not represent a random sample of the population. Here we propose a novel framework for evaluating the performance of predictive models on selectively labeled data. We develop an approach called *contraction* which allows us to compare the performance of predictive models and human decision-makers without resorting to counterfactual inference. Our methodology harnesses the heterogeneity of human decision-makers and facilitates effective evaluation of predictive models even in the presence of unmeasured confounders (unobservables) which influence both human decisions and the resulting outcomes. Experimental results on real world datasets spanning diverse domains such as health care, insurance, and criminal justice demonstrate the utility of our evaluation metric in comparing human decisions and machine predictions.

1 INTRODUCTION

Machine learning models have been very effective at automating various perception and recognition tasks such as character recognition, sentiment detection, question answering, game playing, and image classification [13, 14, 27, 31]. In all these examples, when given the same set of input data and enough labeled training data, machines tend to outperform humans. There is a large set of domains, however, where evaluating whether machines improve on human performance has been much more challenging. Often, these are settings where humans have already performed the task, and where the the machine learning algorithm must be evaluated on data where the labels are themselves consequence of the existing choices of the human decision-makers.

We first dealt with issues of this form in an analysis of judicial bail decisions [17], an application which motivated the present paper. Since this is an important setting that illustrates the basic concerns, it is useful to briefly describe the underlying background of the application here. In a bail hearing, by law requires the judge to base their decision to release defendants on a prediction—if granted bail, will the defendant return for their court appearance without committing a crime in the intervening time. Given that millions of such prediction tasks are being performed each year, and the outcomes are highly consequential, it is natural to ask whether a machine learning algorithm could make these predictions better than the judge does.

In comparing the algorithm to the judge, one has to appreciate how different this type of task is from a more standard task such as image-based object recognition. First, judges' predictions rely on many informative features that are *unobservable* to the algorithm because they aren't recorded in available datasets; these may include information such as details of the defendant's behavior in the courtroom, and related behavioral inferences. Second, the *labels* we are trying to predict correspond to whether a defendant returned for their court appearance without committing a crime—the label is positive if they did, negative if they did not. But if a defendant is denied bail, then there is no opportunity for them to commit a crime or fail to show up for their court appearance, so we have no way to know what would have happened had they been released. So how do we evaluate an algorithm that proposes to release someone that the judge had jailed in the dataset? This results in a problem of *selective labels*: the process generates only a partial labeling of the instances, and the decision-maker's choices—the very decisions we wish to compare the algorithm to—determine which instances even have labels at all.

Judicial bail decisions represent just one of many fundamental examples of these types of questions, and the ubiquity of the phenomenon motivates our goal in the present work—to abstract the selective labels problem beyond any one application and study it as a general algorithmic question in itself, reaching across multiple domains. To begin with, here are some further basic examples of areas where the selective labels problem naturally arises. First, a common type of medical prediction question is whether a patient needs a costly treatment for a condition; not all patients need treatment, but the treatment is generally effective whenever it is prescribed.

KDD'17, August 13–17, 2017, Halifax, NS, Canada.
© 2017 ACM. 978-1-4503-4887-4/17/08...$15.00
http://dx.doi.org/10.1145/3097983.3098066

The problem is that if our training data comes from doctors who were prescribing treatment for the condition, then (i) we typically won't know all the features the doctor was able to observe when meeting a given patient in person, and (ii) there only exist labels for the people to whom treatment wasn't prescribed (since the people for whom treatment was prescribed had no subsequent symptoms, whether they needed the treatment or not). In a very different domain, suppose we wanted to predict which proposals for startup companies to fund, given data on early-stage investor decisions. Again, the challenge is that these investors generally obtain "soft information" from conversations with the founders that would be difficult to record as features, and we only learn the success or failure of the startup proposals that were in fact funded.

In this paper, we are interested in how to approach this class of prediction problems, which we characterize by the set of technical ingredients outlined in the examples above:

(1) The data comes from the judgments of decision-makers making a yes-no decision (e.g., granting bail, investing in a startup). In doing this, the decision-makers are basing their decisions on a set of features (X, Z) while the algorithm only observes features X; the Z are *unobservables*.
(2) The judgments of the decision-makers determines which instances have labels, leading to a *selective labels* problem.

There is a third aspect to these questions that is also relevant to how we think about them. A common strategy for addressing missing labels is to randomly acquire labels on hard-to-reach parts of the distribution, for example via experiments. (Consider for example the way in which one might acquire additional labels in a recommender system by showing suggestions that may not be ranked first by the underlying algorithm.) A key feature of our motivating applications, however, is that they arise in domains where such experimentation is simply infeasible. Exactly because these decisions—releasing a defendant or withholding treatments—is consequential, it is impractical and very often unethical to randomize decisions on a subset of instances simply to increase the variability in the evaluation data.[1]

Evaluating machine learning algorithms in these types of domains, without taking into account the issues above, can create misleading conclusions. For example, in the setting of bail, it could be that for young defendants, the presence of a defendant's family at the court hearing is highly predictive of a positive label (returning for their court appearance without committing a crime). If the judge accurately uses this feature, we obtain training data where young defendants have a much lower rate of negative labels. Now, suppose this feature isn't recorded in the administrative data available to an algorithm; then the algorithm trained on this data will falsely but confidently learn that young people commit no cime; if such an algorithm is then deployed, its error rate on young defendants will much higher than we expected. Similar issues can arise if a doctor is basing treatment decisions on symptoms that he or she observes in meeting a patient, but which aren't recorded and accessible to the algorithm.

While prior research has explored applications of machine learning to domains where human judgments are part of the data labeling process (crime [7, 21, 43], medical diagnosis [6, 22]), the selective labels problem is often overlooked, with evaluation of the models typically carried out by computing traditional metrics such as AUC or accuracy only on the data points for which ground truth labels are available [7]. This could potentially result in biased estimates of model's performance, because the labeled data is in fact a difficult-to-interpret non-random sample of the population. There has also been some work on inferring labels using counterfactual inference techniques [9, 12, 16, 36, 38] and leveraging these estimates when computing standard evaluation metrics. However, counterfactual inference techniques explicitly assume that there are no unmeasured confounders (that is, no unobservable variables Z) that could affect the outcome Y. This assumption does not typically hold in cases where human decisions are providing data labels [7, 21]. Thus, the combination of two ingredients—selective labels and non-trivial unobservables—poses problems for these existing techniques.

The present work. Here we propose a framework for developing and evaluating prediction algorithms in the presence of the selective labels problem. Our framework makes use of the fact that many domains involving selective labels have the following features:

(i) We have data on many decision-makers rather than just one;
(ii) These different decision-makers have a similar pool of cases, so that it is as if the instances had been randomly assigned across them; and
(iii) The decision-makers differ in the thresholds they use for their yes-no decisions.

If we think of a "yes" decision as producing a label for an instance (e.g. by granting bail), and a "no" instance as resulting in no label (e.g. by denying bail), then the decision-makers who have a lower threshold and say yes on more instances are labeling a larger fraction of their sample of population. The decision-maker is trying to avoid a particular bad outcome (e.g. a defendant not returning for their court appearance, or a company that receives an investment subsequently failing), and we note that the nature of task determines that only instances that receive a label can exhibit a bad outcome. Thus, for a particular decision-maker, we define their *acceptance rate* to be the fraction of instances on which their decision is yes, and their *failure rate* to be the fraction of instances on which the bad outcome occurs. This leads to a natural trade-off curve between acceptance rate and failure rate, and points (i), (ii), and (iii) mean that we can meaningfully construct such a curve over the population of decision-makers.[2]

To achieve this we make use of the heterogeneity among decision-makers via technique, which we call *contraction*. Starting with the decision-makers of high acceptance rates, we use algorithmic predictions to "contract" the set of instances they accept until it is scaled back to acceptance rates matching that of stricter decision-makers. In this way, we sweep out an algorithmic version of the curve that trades off between acceptance rate and failure rate, and

[1] If we truly tried using randomization to address these types of problems, we would be doing something very different from, say, a randomized drug trial. The ethics of drug trials rely crucially on the point that what's being tested is a treatment whose efficacy is uncertain. There is no corresponding basis for deliberately withholding treatments of known efficacy simply to create training data for prediction, which is essentially what we would need to address the problems here through randomization. One can offer similarly strong caveats about the other domains that we are considering.

[2] Note that the one-sidedness of the labeling implies that a decision-maker can always guarantee a failure rate of 0 by imposing an acceptance rate of 0; this is a concrete sense in which reducing the failure rate to 0 is not the overall goal of the process.

in the process evaluate the algorithm only on instances drawn from the population for which we have labels. Our contraction approach thus eliminates the need for imputation of labels for all those data points for which ground truth labels are not available. This makes our contraction technique ideal for judgment-based settings where unobservables may influence the outcomes.

To illustrate the intuition behind our contraction technique, let us consider the setting of judicial bail decisions. Let j be the judge with the highest acceptance rate, say 90%, and let $\mathcal{D}_j$ be the set of defendants who appear before j. Now, consider another judge k with a lower acceptance rate, say 80%, who sees a set of defendants $\mathcal{D}_k$. By point (ii), the sets $\mathcal{D}_j$ and $\mathcal{D}_k$ behave distributionally as if randomly assigned between j and k. Here is how we can evaluate a form of gain from algorithmic prediction relative to judge k. Suppose j and k each see 1000 defendants, and hence j grants bail to 900 while k grants bail to 800. We train a prediction algorithm on held-out labeled data, and then we apply it to 900 defendants in $\mathcal{D}_j$ who were granted bail. We use the algorithm to reverse the decision to grant bail on a subset of 100 of the defendants in $\mathcal{D}_j$ who had been granted bail by j. In this way, we now have a set of 800 defendants in $\mathcal{D}_j$ who have been granted bail by a hybrid human-algorithmic mechanism: judge j granted bail to 900 of the original 1000, and then the algorithm kept 800 of these for the final decision set. (This is the sense in which we "contract" judge j's set of 900 released defendants down to 800.) The point is that we can now compare the failure rate on this set of 800—the number of defendants who commit a crime or fail to return for their court appearance—to the failure rate on the set of 800 released by judge k. The extent to which the failure rate is lower for the hybrid human-algorithmic mechanism is a concrete type of performance guarantee provided by the contraction technique.

We demonstrate the utility of our contraction framework in comparing human judgments and model predictions across three diverse domains: criminal justice, health care, and insurance. We also show that our contraction technique accurately estimates the trade-off curve between acceptance rate and failure rate on synthetic datasets. Finally, we highlight the significance of the contraction technique by simulating the effects of unmeasured confounders (unobservables) and demonstrating how other counterfactual inference methods can result in overly optimistic—and hence inaccurate—estimates of a predictive model's performance.

2 RELATED WORK

Below we provide an overview of related research on selective labels and missing data. We further discuss how prior research handled these problems when evaluating predictive models. We then present a detailed overview of techniques proposed for counterfactual inference in causal inference literature.

Missing data problem. Recall that the selective labels problem is a form of missing data problem [1] which commonly arises in various settings where judgments of human decision-makers determine which instances have labels. A more commonly known variant of this problem is censoring in clinical trials where outcome labels of certain subjects are not recorded due to a variety of reasons including subjects dropping out from trials [25]. This problem has been studied extensively in the context of causal inference where the goal is to determine the effect of some treatment [2, 30, 32, 37, 38]. Since it is not always feasible to carry out randomized control trials to determine treatment effects, prior research has employed a variety of *imputation* techniques (discussed in detail below) to infer outcomes of counterfactual scenarios. For example, Freemantle et al. studied the effects of dosage of insulin on patients with type 2 diabetes using propensity score matching [11]. Similarly, McCormick et al. studied the effect of student-teacher relationships on academic performance using matching techniques [29]. The effectiveness of these techniques relies on the absence of unobservables, an assumption, which does not hold in our case.

Prior research also categorized missing data problems based on the reasons behind the missingness [26, 28]. A variable (label or a feature) value of some data point could be: (1) missing completely at random (MCAR) (2) missing at random (MAR), where the missingness can be accounted for by variables where there is complete information. For example, men are less likely to fill out depression surveys, but this is not dependent on their level of depression once we account for the fact that they are male [39]. (3) missing not at random (MNAR) [40], where the variable value that is missing is related to the reason why it's missing. For example, this would occur when people with high levels of depression failed to fill out the depression survey. Depending on the reason for missingness, various imputation techniques have been proposed to address the missing data problem. For instance, listwise deletion, where data points with missing values are removed from the dataset, was used when data was missing completely at random. and for regression modeling, nearest-neighbor matching, interpolation etc were adopted when the values are MAR (see Chapter 25 of [12], [18]). Note that there is a significant overlap between these methods and the techniques used for imputation in causal inference literature. These methods are not readily applicable to our setting as they assume that there are no unobservables influencing the occurrence of missing labels. MNAR problems are often addressed using approaches such as selection and pattern-mixture models [24] which require us to make assumptions about the underlying generative process of the data.

Evaluation in the presence of selective labels. There has been a lot of interest in developing accurate risk assessment models in health care [6], education [19], and criminal justice [7]. For example, Berk et al. [7] developed models to predict if a defendant is likely to commit a violent crime when released on parole. Selective labels problem arising in some of these settings makes it harder to train and evaluate predictive models. For instance, Berk et al. evaluated their model only on the set of defendants who have been granted parole. This evaluation could be potentially biased if the observed feature distribution or the conditional outcome distribution of the defendants who were released does not match that of defendants who were denied parole. This assumption is often violated in practice. There have been some attempts to work around this problem by using imputation to assign labels to those data points with missing labels [22, 43]. These imputed labels were then used in evaluating model performance. However, the imputation procedures adopted also make similar assumptions as above and are therefore not well suited to address the problem at hand ([43]). In earlier work [17] we explored techniques to overcome the presence of unobservables in one particular domain, judicial bail decisions. In contrast, here we study the issue of selective labels as a general problem in itself and explore in greater depth the performance of our proposed solution to address it across a broader set of domains.

Counterfactual inference. Counterfactual inference techniques have been used extensively to estimate treatment effects in observational studies. These techniques have found applications in a variety of fields such as machine learning, epidemiology, and sociology [3, 8–10, 30, 34]. Along the lines of Johansson et al. [16], counterfactual inference techniques can be broadly categorized as: (1) parametric methods which model the relationship between observed features, treatments, and outcomes. Examples include any type of regression model such as linear and logistic regression, random forests and regression trees [12, 33, 42]. (2) non-parametric methods such as propensity score matching, nearest-neighbor matching, which do not explicitly model the relationship between observed features, treatments, and outcomes [4, 15, 35, 36, 41]. (3) doubly robust methods which combine the two aforementioned classes of techniques typically via a propensity score weighted regression [5, 10]. The effectiveness of parametric and non-parametric methods depends on the postulated regression model and the postulated propensity score model respectively. If the postulated models are not identical to the true models, then these techniques result in biased estimates of outcomes. Doubly robust methods require only one of the postulated models to be identical to the true model in order to generate unbiased estimates. However, due to the presence of unobservables, we cannot guarantee that either of the postulated models will be identical to the true models.

3 PROBLEM FORMULATION

Here we formalize the notions of selective labels and unobservables, and formulate our problem statement.

Selective labels and unobservables. The goal of this work is to evaluate predictive models in a setting that is characterized by:

- *Selective labels:* The judgments of decision-makers determine which instances are labeled in the data(Figure 1).
- *Unobservables:* There exist unobservables (unmeasured confounders) which are available to the decision-makers when making judgments but are not recorded in the data and hence cannot be leveraged by the predictive models. Furthermore, these unobservables may influence the outcomes and are independent of the features recorded in the data.

Let $\boldsymbol{x}_i$ denote the feature values of subject i which are recorded in the data. Note that each observation i is also associated with unobservable features $\boldsymbol{z}_i$ that are not captured in the data. This means that the human decision-maker j_i who makes a *yes* ($t_i = 1$) or *no* decision ($t_i = 0$) on subject i has access to both $\boldsymbol{x}_i$ and $\boldsymbol{z}_i$. On the other hand, only $\boldsymbol{x}_i$ (but not $\boldsymbol{z}_i$) is available to predictive model. Let $y_i \in \{0, 1, NA\}$ denote the resulting outcome (that is, label). The selective labels problem(Figure 1) occurs because the observation of the outcome y_i is constrained based on the decision t_i made by the judge j_i:

$$y_i = \begin{cases} 0 \text{ or } 1, & \text{if } t_i = 1 \\ \textit{not observed } (NA), & \text{otherwise} \end{cases}$$

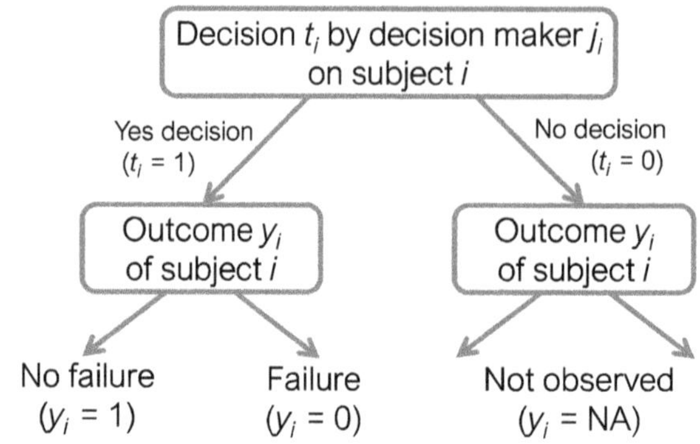

Figure 1: Selective labels problem.

Below, we discuss the characteristics of the observational data and the black box model which are inputs to our framework:

Input data. A dataset $\mathcal{D} = \{(\boldsymbol{x}_i, j_i, t_i, y_i)\}$ consisting of N observations, each of which corresponds to a subject (individual) from an observational study where $\boldsymbol{x}_i, j_i, t_i, y_i$ are as defined above.

Black box predictive model. Another input to our framework is a black box predictive model $\mathcal{B}$ which assigns risk scores to observations in $\mathcal{D}$. More specifically, $\mathcal{B}$ is a function which maps the characteristics (or feature values) $\boldsymbol{x}$ of an observation in $\mathcal{D}$ to a probability score $s \in [0, 1]$. This score indicates how confident the model is in assigning the observation to $t = 0$ (e.g., denying bail).

Problem statement. Given the observational data $\mathcal{D}$ and predictive model $\mathcal{B}$, our goal is to evaluate the performance of $\mathcal{B}$ and benchmark it against the performance of human decisions in $\mathcal{D}$, given the *selective labeling* of the data and the presence of *unobservables.*

4 OUR FRAMEWORK

In this section, we introduce *contraction,* a technique that allows us to address the selective labels problem in the presence of unobservables. We show how it can be used to compare the performance of a predictive model with a given human decision-maker. We then formally define the trade-off curve of *failure rate* versus *acceptance rate,* two quantities defined in the introduction: the acceptance rate is the fraction of individuals for whom the decision-maker makes a *yes* decision, thus providing them with a label and the *failure rate* is the fraction of bad outcomes in the full population of instances based on the decisions made.

Acceptance rate and failure rate. Decision making often involves optimizing for competing objectives. The goal is to not only minimize the chance of undesirable outcomes (e.g., crimes) but also to reduce the burden (physical, monetary, emotional) on the subjects and other resources (e.g., jail space). In order to quantify such competing objectives and assess the performance of a decision-maker (human or machine), we outline the following metrics:

(1) The *failure rate* of a decision-maker is defined as the ratio of the number of undesirable outcomes (e.g., crimes) occurring due to the decisions made to the total number of subjects judged by the decision-maker. For example, if a judge makes decisions concerning the bail petitions of 100

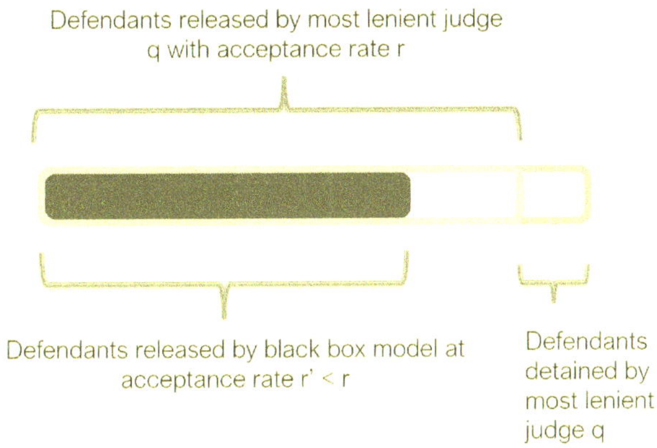

Figure 2: Pictorial representation of contraction technique.

defendants, releases 70 of them out of which 20 commit crimes, the failure rate of the judge is 0.2.

(2) The *acceptance rate* of a decision-maker is defined as the ratio of the number of subjects assigned to *yes* decision ($t = 1$) (e.g., release) by the decision-maker to the total number of subjects judged by the decision-maker. For instance, the acceptance rate of a judge who releases 70% of defendants who appear before him is 0.7.

The goal, given these definitions, is to achieve a high acceptance rate with a low failure rate.

Contraction technique. We can compare a black box predictive model to any given human decision-maker by forcing the acceptance rate of the model to be the same as that of the judge and measuring the corresponding failure rate. If the model exhibits a lower failure rate than the judge at the same acceptance rate, then we can claim that the model is better than that judge. There is, however, an important caveat to this. It is not straightforward to evaluate the failure rate of a model because the outcome labels of some of the observations might be missing due to the selective labels problem. As discussed earlier, imputation and other counterfactual inference techniques cannot be used due to the presence of the unobservables. Here, we discuss a new technique called *contraction* which allows us to compare the performance of a predictive model to any human judge even in the presence of the unobservables.

To illustrate the contraction technique(Figure 2), consider the bail setting where each judge decides on bail petitions of 100 defendants. Let us say our goal is to compare the performance of a black box model with that of some judge j' who releases 70% of the defendants who appear before him, i.e., judge j' releases 70 defendants and has a acceptance rate value of 0.7. In order to compare the model performance with j', we run the black box model on the set of defendants judged by the most lenient judge q who releases, say 90%, of the defendants. We achieve this by constraining the black box model to detain the same 10 defendants who were detained by q thus avoiding the missing labels. In addition to these 10 defendants, we allow the black box model to detain another 20 defendants deemed as highest risk by the model. We then compute the failure rate on the remaining 70 defendants who are considered as released by the model. Since the outcome labels (crime/no crime) of all

Algorithm 1 Contraction technique for estimating failure rate at acceptance rate r

Input: Observational data $\mathcal{D}$, Probability scores $\mathcal{S}$, Acceptance rate r
Procedure:
Let q be the decision-maker with highest acceptance rate in $\mathcal{D}$

$\mathcal{D}_q = \{(\boldsymbol{x}, j, t, y) \in \mathcal{D} | j = q\}$
▷ $\mathcal{D}_q$ is the set of all observations judged by q

$\mathcal{R}_q = \{(\boldsymbol{x}, j, t, y) \in \mathcal{D}_q | t = 1\}$
▷ $\mathcal{R}_q$ is the set of observations in $\mathcal{D}_q$ with observed outcome labels

Sort observations in $\mathcal{R}_q$ in descending order of confidence scores $\mathcal{S}$ and assign to $\mathcal{R}_q^{sort}$
▷ Observations deemed as high risk by $\mathcal{B}$ are at the top of this list

Remove the top $[(1.0 - r)|\mathcal{D}_q|] - [|\mathcal{D}_q| - |\mathcal{R}_q|]$ observations of $\mathcal{R}_q^{sort}$ and call this list $\mathcal{R}_\mathcal{B}$
▷ $\mathcal{R}_\mathcal{B}$ is the list of observations assigned to $t = 1$ by $\mathcal{B}$

Compute $u = \sum_{l=1}^{|\mathcal{R}_\mathcal{B}|} \frac{\mathbb{1}(y_l = 0)}{|\mathcal{D}_q|}$
Return u

of these defendants are observed, the failure rate can be easily computed from the data.

More generally, the idea behind the contraction technique is to simulate the black box model on the sample of observations judged by the decision-maker q with the highest acceptance rate by *contracting* the set of observations assigned to *yes* decision i.e., $t = 1$ by q while leveraging the risk scores (or probabilities) assigned to these observations by the model. The complete pseudo code formalizing the contraction technique discussed above is presented in Algorithm 1. The contraction technique exploits the following characteristics of the data and the problem setting:

(1) *Multiple decision-makers:* There are many different decision-makers, rather than just one.

(2) *Random assignment of subjects to decision-makers:* If the sample of observations on which we simulate the model is not identical to the sample seen by the judge with whom we are comparing the model, it is not possible to fairly compare the failure rate estimates of the two. We therefore require that observations/subjects are randomly assigned to decision-makers. We find that this requirement typically holds in practice in many decision making settings (more details provided in the experimental evaluation section).

(3) *Heterogeneity in acceptance rates:* The contraction technique relies on the fact that different decision-makers can vary significantly in the thresholds they use for their decisions, resulting in different acceptance rates.

It is important to note that the quality of the failure rate estimate obtained using contraction depends on the extent of agreement between the model and the most lenient judge q with respect to the instances that went unlabeled by q. In the above bail example, if the 10 defendants denied bail by judge q were also among the top 30 highest-risk defendants as ranked by the model, then the estimate of the failure rate would be equal to the true value. If, on the other hand, none of these 10 defendants were among the top 30 high risk defendants based on the model's confidence scores, then the estimated failure rate would not be the same as the true value.

We now describe how to provide a worst-case bound on the maximum difference between the estimate of failure rate obtained using contraction and its true value.

PROPOSITION 4.1. *Suppose the conditions (1)–(3) noted above for applying contraction are satisfied. The error in the estimate of failure rate u of* $\mathcal{B}$ *computed by the contraction algorithm (Algorithm 1) at any value of acceptance rate* $r \leq \psi$ *never exceeds* $\frac{(1.0-a)|\mathcal{D}_q - \mathcal{R}_q|}{|\mathcal{D}_q|}$. *The notation is defined in Algorithm 1. In addition, a is the fraction of observations in the set* $\mathcal{D}_q - \mathcal{R}_q$ *that both* $\mathcal{B}$ *and q agree on assigning to a no decision (t = 0), and* ψ *is the acceptance rate of q.*

We now briefly sketch the argument that justifies these bounds. The error in the estimate stems mainly from the disagreements between $\mathcal{B}$ and q about assigning defendants in the set $\mathcal{D}_q - \mathcal{R}_q$ to a *no* decision ($t = 0$). Given that $\mathcal{B}$ favors assigning $(1.0 - a)|\mathcal{D}_q - \mathcal{R}_q|$ subjects in that set to a *yes* decision i.e., $t = 1$ (e.g., release), in the worst case, all of these subjects might result in failures or undesirable outcomes. The upper bound on the failure rate is therefore $u + \frac{(1.0-a)|\mathcal{D}_q - \mathcal{R}_q|}{|\mathcal{D}_q|}$. Similarly in the best case, all the $(1.0 - a)|\mathcal{D}_q - \mathcal{R}_q|$ subjects that $\mathcal{B}$ chooses to assign to a *yes* decision ($t = 1$) result in no failures, and in addition, the same number of subjects that $\mathcal{B}$ chooses to assign to $t = 0$ (e.g., deny bail) turn out to be subjects with undesirable outcomes (failures). Therefore the lower bound on the failure rate is $u - \frac{(1.0-a)|\mathcal{D}_q - \mathcal{R}_q|}{|\mathcal{D}_q|}$. In either case, the difference between the failure rate estimated by the contraction algorithm and its true value does not exceed $\frac{(1.0-a)|\mathcal{D}_q - \mathcal{R}_q|}{|\mathcal{D}_q|}$.

Machine and human evaluation curves. We can use the contraction technique discussed above to compute the failure rate of the black box model $\mathcal{B}$ at various choices for the acceptance rate $r \in [0, \psi]$ where ψ is the acceptance rate of the decision-maker q with highest acceptance rate value. We can then plot the curve of failure rate vs. acceptance rate for $\mathcal{B}$ which we refer to as the *machine evaluation curve*.

Analogous to the machine evaluation curve, we can also plot the failure rate vs. acceptance rate curve for human decision-makers. This can be done by grouping decision-makers with similar values of acceptance rate into bins and treating each bin as a single hypothetical decision-maker. We can then compute the failure rate and acceptance rate values for each such bin and plot them as a curve. We refer to this curve as the *human evaluation curve*.

The machine and human evaluation curves together provide us with a useful way of benchmarking a given model's performance against human judgment. If the machine evaluation curve exhibits lower failure rates at all possible values of acceptance rate compared to the human evaluation curve, this suggests that the model may be able to make better decisions than expert human decision-makers.

5 EXPERIMENTAL EVALUATION

In this section, we discuss the detailed experimental evaluation of our framework. First, we analyze the accuracy of the estimates of model failure rates obtained using our contraction technique

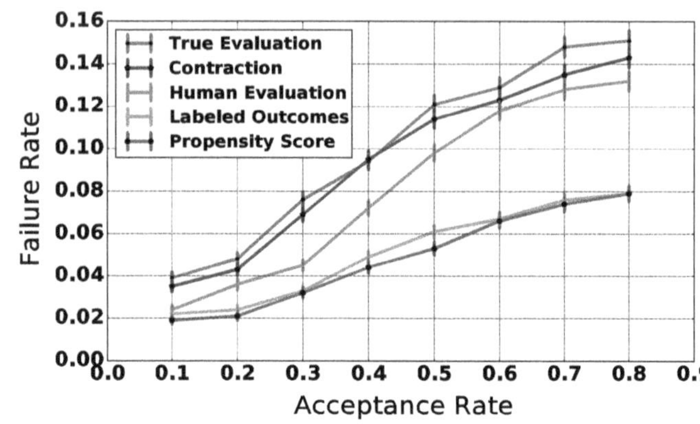

Figure 3: Effect of selective labels on estimation of predictive model failure rate (error bars denote standard errors): Green curve is the true failure rate of the predictive model and the machine evaluation using contraction (blue curve) follows it very closely. However, various imputation techniques heavily underestimate the failure rate. Based on the estimates of imputation, one would conclude that the predictive model outperforms human judges (red curve), while in fact its true performance is worse than that of the human judges.

by simulating the selective labels problem using synthetic data. We also compare the effectiveness of our contraction technique to various state-of-the-art baselines commonly used for counterfactual inference and imputation. Lastly, we analyze the utility of our framework in comparing human decisions and model predictions on real-world tasks which are all affected by the selective labels problem: judicial bail decisions, treatment recommendations in health care, and insurance application decisions.

5.1 Evaluation on Synthetic Data

Here we analyze how closely the estimates of failure rates obtained using contraction mimic the true values using synthetic data which captures the effect of selective labels.

Synthetic data. We generate a synthetic dataset with $M = 100$ human judges each judging 500 subjects (or observations) resulting in a total of $N = 50$k observations. We simulate three feature variables: X, Z, and W. X corresponds to observable information that is available to both predictive models and human decision-makers. Z represents an unobservable that is accessible only to the human decision-makers but not to the predictive models. In order to mimic real world settings, we include a variable W which represents information that is neither accessible to human decision-makers nor the predictive models but influences the outcome. We model these as independent Gaussian random variables with zero mean and unit variance.

We randomly assign subjects to decision-makers and assign an acceptance rate value r to each decision-maker by uniformly sampling from $[0.1, 0.9]$ and rounding to the nearest tenth decimal place. The outcome variable Y is simulated by modeling its conditional probability distribution as follows: $P(Y = 0|X, Z, W) = \frac{1}{1+\exp -(\beta_X X + \beta_Z Z + \beta_W W)}$ where the coefficients β_X, β_Z, and β_W

are set to 1.0, 1.0, and 0.2 respectively. The outcome value of an instance for which the variables X, Z, and W take the values x, z, and w respectively is set to 0 if $P(Y = 0|X = x, Z = z, W = w) \geq 0.5$, otherwise its outcome value is set to 1.

Analogously, we simulate the decision variable T by modeling its conditional probability distribution as: $P(T = 0|X, Z) = \frac{1}{1+\exp -(\beta_X X + \beta_Z Z)} + \epsilon$ where $\epsilon \sim N(0, 0.1)$ represents a small amount of noise. The decision variable corresponding to an instance for which $X = x, Z = z$ is set to 0 if the value of $P(T = 0|X = x, Z = z)$ lies within the top $(1 - r) * 100\%$ of instances assigned to the decision-maker j, otherwise it is set to 1.

Lastly, the selective labels problem is simulated by ensuring that the outcome labels of only those instances which are assigned to a *yes* decision ($t = 1$) are available in the data for the purposes of training the predictive models and computing our evaluation curves.

Model evaluation. We split the synthetic dataset randomly into two sets of 25k instances each and use one of these sets as a training set to train the predictive model and the other as an evaluation test set to which we apply our framework. We train logistic regression model on this training set. We also experimented with other predictive models and observed similar behavior. We use only the instances for which outcome labels are available (i.e., observations assigned to a *yes* decision) in the training set to train the predictive model. We then evaluate the predictive performance of the model using the following techniques:

- *True Evaluation* represents the true performance of the model. We evaluate the failure rate on the entire evaluation set using *all* outcome labels (both observed by the model as well as those hidden from the model) [3].
- *Contraction*: We apply contraction technique discussed in Section 4 to obtain this curve.
- *Labeled Outcomes Only*: To plot this curve, we first obtain all the subjects whose outcome labels are available in the evaluation set and rank them in ascending order based on the probability scores assigned by the predictive model. We then simulate the model at various values of acceptance rates r by assigning the observations corresponding to the top r fraction of the sorted list to *yes* decisions ($t = 1$). We then compute the failure rate on the observations assigned to *yes* decisions directly from their corresponding ground truth labels.
- *Imputation*: We use several commonly employed imputation techniques such as *gradient boosted trees, logistic regression, nearest neighbor matching* based on feature similarity, *propensity score matching*, and *doubly robust estimation* to impute all the missing outcomes in the evaluation set [26, 30]. We then use these imputed outcomes wherever true outcome labels are not available to compute the failure rates of the predictive model. All of the aforementioned approaches except for nearest neighbor matching require learning a regression/imputation model. We use the observations in the evaluation set for which outcome labels are available to learn these models.

[3]Note that selective labels problem does not allow us to compute true evaluation curves on real world datasets.

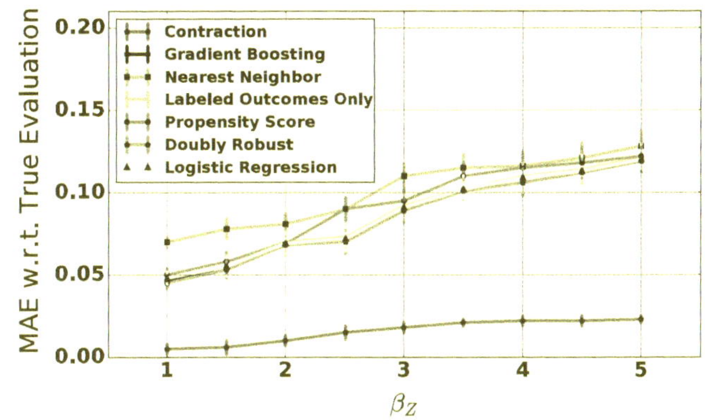

Figure 4: Effect of unobservables (error bars denote standard errors): As we increase the influence of unobservable Z on the outcome Y, imputation techniques result in erroneous estimates of model performance. Contraction, on the other hand, produces reliable estimates.

Results. Figure 3 shows evaluation curves for the predictive model as well as the human evaluation curve (Section 4). Note that the true evaluation curve (green curve) captures the true performance of the predictive model. It can be seen that the evaluation curve plotted using contraction (blue curve) closely follows the true evaluation curve demonstrating that contraction is very effective in estimating the true performance of the predictive model.

Figure 3 also shows the failure rates estimated by propensity score matching. It can be seen that this technique heavily underestimates the failure rate of the model. We also observed similar behavior in the case of other imputation techniques. This implies that the estimates of model performance obtained using imputation techniques in the presence of selective labels problem and unobservables are not reliable. Similar behavior is exhibited by the evaluation curve plotted using *labeled outcomes* only.

Lastly, Figure 3 also shows the failure rates of the human judges (red). Given that the judge has access both to variables X and Z we observe that the judge is making better predictions (lower failure rate) than the predictive model (which only has access to variable X). However, notice that imputation techniques so heavily overestimate the performance of the predictive model that it would lead us to wrongly conclude that the model is outperforming the human judges, while in fact its predictions are less accurate than those of the human judges.

To further demonstrate the effects of selective labels and unobservables on accurately estimating the failure rates of predictive models, we plot the discrepancy, i.e., mean absolute error computed across all possible acceptance rates between the true evaluation curve and the estimated performance of the model using various techniques including contraction(Figure 4). Here we vary the weight β_Z of the unobservable variable Z when generating the outcome labels in the synthetic dataset. As β_Z increases, the effect of unobservables becomes more pronounced. Notice, however, that contraction only slightly overestimates the performance of the model regardless of how strong the problem of selective labels and unobservables is. On the other hand, imputation techniques heavily overestimate the performance of the model and the degree of overestimation steadily increases with β_Z. The mean absolute error of contraction is 6.4 times smaller (at $\beta_Z = 1$) compared to the best performing imputation technique and this gap only increases with the increase in the value of β_Z.

Analyzing the error rate of contraction technique. Recall that the correctness of the failure rate estimates obtained using contraction technique depend on acceptance rate of the most lenient decision-maker, agreement rate of *no* decisions between the black box model $\mathcal{B}$ and the most lenient decision-maker, and the total number of subjects judged by the most lenient decision-maker. More specifically, higher values of each of these parameters result in tighter error bounds (Section 4) and consequently accurate estimates of failure rates. Next we empirically analyze the effect of each of the aforementioned aspects on the correctness of failure rate estimates obtained using contraction technique.

First, we analyze the effect of the acceptance rate of the most lenient decision-maker on the failure rate estimates obtained using contraction. We generate multiple synthetic datasets by varying the upper bound on the acceptance rate values which can be assumed by decision-makers and then plot the discrepancy (mean absolute error) between true evaluation curves and the estimates obtained using contraction(Figure 5(left)) across various possible acceptance rates of the most lenient decision-maker. It can be seen that the discrepancy increases as the acceptance rate of the most lenient decision-maker decreases. This is consistent with the error bound obtained in Section 4 and can be explained by the fact that the higher the acceptance rate of the most lenient decision-maker, the larger the number of outcome labels observed in the ground truth.

Next, we analyze the impact of the agreement rate of *no* decisions (e.g., who to jail) between the black box model and the most lenient decision-maker(s). In order to do so, we first generate a synthetic dataset and train a logistic regression model as described earlier. We then generate multiple instances of the logistic regression model by changing its predictions in such a way that we can obtain different values of agreement rates between this model and the most lenient decision-maker. Figure 5(center) shows the plot of the mean absolute error of the resulting estimates from contraction with respect to the true evaluation curve at various values of agreement rates. It can be seen that the mean absolute error is low when the agreement rate values are high and it increases with a decrease in the agreement rate. This is mainly because agreement rates are high when the black box model and the most lenient decision-makers make *no* decisions on the same set of subjects. In such a case, the failure rate estimates can be directly computed from the ground truth.

Lastly, we analyze the effect of the number of subjects judged by the most lenient decision-maker(s) on the correctness of the failure rate estimates obtained using contraction. We generate multiple synthetic datasets by varying the number of subjects judged by the most lenient decision-maker. This is achieved by generating the synthetic data using a similar process as discussed earlier but instead of setting $N = 50k$, we increase or decrease the value of N until the desired number of subjects are assigned to the most lenient decision-maker. Figure 5(right) shows the plot of mean absolute error of the contraction estimates with respect to the true evaluation curve at various values of the number of subjects judged by the most lenient decision-maker. It can be seen that the mean absolute error decreases steadily with an increase in the number of subjects assigned to the most lenient decision-maker.

5.2 Experiments on Real World Datasets

Next we apply our framework on real world datasets to compare the quality of human decisions and model predictions. We highlight the insights obtained using our evaluation metrics–human and machine evaluation curves on diverse domains such as criminal justice, health care, and insurance.

Dataset description. The bail dataset contains bail decisions of about 9k defendantscollected from an anonymous district court and comprises of decisions made by 18 judges. It captures information about various defendant characteristics such as demographic attributes, past criminal history for each of the 9k defendants. Further, the decisions made by judges in each of these cases (grant/deny bail) are also available. The outcome labels (if a defendant committed a crime when out on bail or not) of all the defendants who have been granted bail and released are also recorded. The selective labels problem in this case stems from the fact that the outcome labels of defendants who have been denied bail by judges cannot be observed.

The medical treatment dataset captures 60k patients suffering from coughing and/or wheezing collected by an online electronic health record company [20]. For each patient various attributes such as demographics, symptoms, past health history, test results have been recorded. Each patient in the dataset was prescribed either a milder treatment (quick relief drugs) or a stronger treatment (long term controller drugs). The outcome labels in this setting indicate if there was a relapse of patient symptoms within 15 days of treatment recommendation. If a patient experiences a relapse of symptoms within 15 days, we consider it a failure. Note that patients assigned to stronger treatment do not experience such a relapse, therefore the selective labels problem here is that we do not observe what would have happened to a patient who received the stronger treatment if he/she had been assigned to a milder treatment.

The insurance dataset comprises of decisions made by 74 managers of an insurance provider which insures large-scale corporations [21]. The dataset comprises of about 50k insurance requests filed by client companies. It captures information about various aspects of the client companies such as the domain they operate in (e.g., legal, chemical, tech etc.), losses and profits, assets owned, previous expertise etc. Each insurance request is either approved/denied by the manager in charge. The outcome labels (profit/loss to the insurance provider) of approved insurance requests are available in the data. The selective labels problem here stems from the fact that we do not observe profit/loss for insurance requests that were denied.

Experimental setup. We split each of the datasets into training and evaluation sets so that we can learn the predictive models on the training set and apply our framework to the evaluation set. In the bail decisions dataset, we use a subset of 4.8k defendants and 9 judges for evaluation. In case of asthma treatments, we use a subset of adult patients comprising of 28k instances and spanning 39 doctors as the evaluation set. Analogously, we use a set of 38k

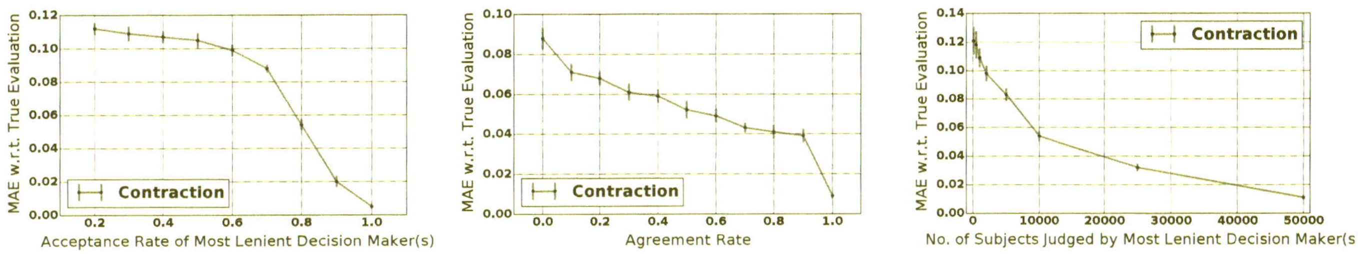

Figure 5: Analyzing the effect of acceptance rate of most lenient decision-makers(left), agreement rate between the black box model and the most lenient decision-makers(center), and number of subjects judged by the most lenient decision-makers(right) on the failure rate estimates obtained using contraction technique. Error bars denote standard errors.

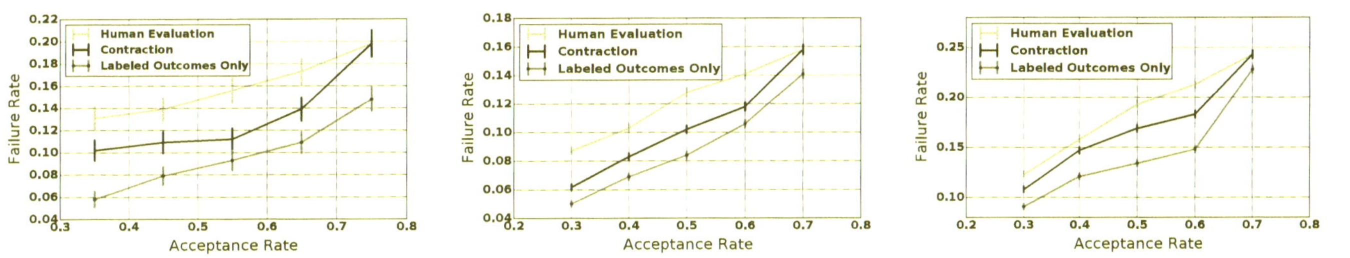

Figure 6: Comparing the performance of human decision-makers and predictive models on bail(left), medical treatment(center), and insurance(right) datasets(error bars denote standard errors). *Labeled outcomes only* curve results in over-optimistic estimates. *Contraction* produces more accurate estimates of model performance

subjects and 41 deciding managers associated with chemical domain as our evaluation set in the insurance requests data and leverage the rest to train the predictive models. We train the predictive models on those instances for which outcome labels are available in the training set. We experimented with various predictive models such as gradient boosted trees, random forests, decision trees, logistic regression, and SVMs. Due to space constraints, we only present results with gradient boosted trees (number of trees = 100) in this section.

Testing for random assignment:. Recall that the correctness of our contraction technique relies on the assumption that observations are randomly assigned to human decision-makers, i.e., there is no relationship between human decision-makers and characteristics of subjects. We utilized the following multiple hypothesis testing procedure [23] to validate this assumption:

(1) We fit a regression model (M1) which predicts the value of outcome variable y_i for each observation characterized by $\boldsymbol{x}_i$ in the evaluation set. We achieve this by training a regression model on the subjects in the evaluation set who were assigned to *yes* decisions ($t = 1$). Let $\hat{\boldsymbol{y}} = \{\hat{y}_1, \hat{y}_2 \cdots\}$ denote the estimates obtained for all the observations in the evaluation set using M1.
(2) We then fit another regression model (M2) to predict the estimate ($\hat{y}$) of M1 based only on the identifier information of human decision-makers.
(3) We then calculate the F-test statistic assuming that the null hypothesis that there is no relationship between the decision-makers and characteristics of subjects is true and call this statistic F_s.
(4) We determine the 95% confidence interval given the degrees of freedom of the regression model M2 and accept the null hypothesis if F_s falls within this interval. We reject the null hypothesis and assume that the random assignment assumption does not hold otherwise.

Based on the above test, we found that the null hypothesis holds on all our evaluation sets indicating that subjects are randomly assigned to decision-makers in our evaluation sets.

Evaluation and results. We plot human and machine evaluation curves for all the three real-world datasets(Figure 6). We plot all the machine and human evaluation curves as described in Section 5.1.

Figure 6 shows that both the machine evaluation curve plotted using contraction (black) as well as the one plotted only using only the labeled outcomes (blue) indicate that the predictive model is exhibiting lower failure rates than human decision-makers (red) at all possible values of acceptance rates on all the three datasets.

The estimates of model performance obtained using contraction are more reliable in practice because it turns out to be the case that the subjects assigned to *no* decisions ($t = 0$) by the decision-maker(s) with highest acceptance rate (let this decision-maker be denoted as j' with risk tolerance r') are often so risky that the model concurs with the decision-maker in assigning these subjects to *no* decision ($t = 0$). We found that the *agreement rate* (see Section 4) which is the ratio of the number of observations that both the predictive model at risk tolerance r' and j' agree on assigning to *no* decision

($t = 0$) to the total number of observations assigned to *no* decision by j' is 0.891, 0.932, and 0.718 on bail decisions, asthma treatments, and insurance requests datasets respectively. These high agreement rates ensure that the estimates of model performance obtained using contraction are close to the true values. It can be inferred from Figure 6 that the estimates of *labeled outcomes only* curve are overly optimistic about the model performance across all the datasets given that our contraction estimates accurately model the true values.

6 CONCLUSIONS AND FUTURE WORK

In this paper, we addressed the problem of evaluating predictive models in settings affected by the selective labels problem. More specifically, we developed an evaluation metric, *failure rate vs. acceptance rate*, which can be used to effectively compare human decisions and algorithmic predictions. Furthermore, we proposed a novel technique called *contraction* which can be used to estimate our evaluation metric without resorting to traditional imputation/counterfactual inference procedures which are not suitable for settings with unmeasured confounders (unobservables). This work marks an initial attempt at addressing the problem of selective labels in the presence of unmeasured confounders and paves way for several interesting future research directions. For instance, our framework can be readily applied to various domains where human decision making is involved ranging from public policy to health care and education. Furthermore, it would be interesting to explore how the contraction technique proposed in this work can be leveraged to improve the process of training machine learning models on selectively labeled data.

7 ACKNOWLEDGMENTS

This research has been supported in part by NSF IIS-1149837, SAP, Lightspeed, Stanford Data Science Initiative, and Chan Zuckerberg Biohub. Himabindu is supported by a Robert Bosch Stanford Graduate Fellowship, and a Google Anitaborg Scholarship. The authors would like to thank Stephen Bach, Cynthia Rudin, Rok Sosic, and the anonymous reviewers for insightful comments and feedback.

REFERENCES

[1] P. D. Allison. Missing data: Quantitative applications in the social sciences. *British Journal of Mathematical and Statistical Psychology*, 55(1):193–196, 2002.

[2] J. D. Angrist, G. W. Imbens, and D. B. Rubin. Identification of causal effects using instrumental variables. *JASA*, 91(434):444–455, 1996.

[3] J. D. Angrist and J.-S. Pischke. *Mostly harmless econometrics: An empiricist's companion.* Princeton university press, 2008.

[4] P. C. Austin. An introduction to propensity score methods for reducing the effects of confounding in observational studies. *Multivariate behavioral research*, 46(3):399–424, 2011.

[5] H. Bang and J. M. Robins. Doubly robust estimation in missing data and causal inference models. *Biometrics*, 61(4):962–973, 2005.

[6] M. Bayati, M. Braverman, M. Gillam, K. M. Mack, G. Ruiz, M. S. Smith, and E. Horvitz. Data-driven decisions for reducing readmissions for heart failure: General methodology and case study. *PloS one*, 9(10):e109264, 2014.

[7] R. Berk, L. Sherman, G. Barnes, E. Kurtz, and L. Ahlman. Forecasting murder within a population of probationers and parolees: a high stakes application of statistical learning. *JRSS*, 172(1):191–211, 2009.

[8] L. Bottou, J. Peters, D. X. Charles, M. Chickering, E. Portugaly, D. Ray, P. Y. Simard, and E. Snelson. Counterfactual reasoning and learning systems: the example of computational advertising. *JMLR*, 14(1):3207–3260, 2013.

[9] V. Chernozhukov, I. Fernández-Val, and B. Melly. Inference on counterfactual distributions. *Econometrica*, 81(6):2205–2268, 2013.

[10] M. Dudík, J. Langford, and L. Li. Doubly robust policy evaluation and learning. *arXiv preprint arXiv:1103.4601*, 2011.

[11] N. Freemantle, B. Balkau, and P. Home. A propensity score matched comparison of different insulin regimens 1 year after beginning insulin in people with type 2 diabetes. *Diabetes, Obesity and Metabolism*, 15(12):1120–1127, 2013.

[12] A. Gelman and J. Hill. *Data analysis using regression and multilevel/hierarchical models.* Cambridge university press, 2006.

[13] V. Govindan and A. Shivaprasad. Character recognitionfi!?a review. *Pattern recognition*, 23(7):671–683, 1990.

[14] P. Gupta and V. Gupta. A survey of text question answering techniques. *International Journal of Computer Applications*, 53(4), 2012.

[15] G. W. Imbens. Matching methods in practice: Three examples. *Journal of Human Resources*, 50(2):373–419, 2015.

[16] F. D. Johansson, U. Shalit, and D. Sontag. Learning representations for counterfactual inference. *arXiv preprint arXiv:1605.03661*, 2016.

[17] J. Kleinberg, H. Lakkaraju, J. Leskovec, J. Ludwig, and S. Mullainathan. Human decisions and machine predictions. *NBER working paper*, 2017.

[18] A. Kmetic, L. Joseph, C. Berger, and A. Tenenhouse. Multiple imputation to account for missing data in a survey: estimating the prevalence of osteoporosis. *Epidemiology*, 13(4):437–444, 2002.

[19] H. Lakkaraju, E. Aguiar, C. Shan, D. Miller, N. Bhanpuri, R. Ghani, and K. L. Addison. A machine learning framework to identify students at risk of adverse academic outcomes. In *KDD*, pages 1909–1918, 2015.

[20] H. Lakkaraju, S. H. Bach, and J. Leskovec. Interpretable decision sets: A joint framework for description and prediction. In *KDD*, pages 1675–1684, 2016.

[21] H. Lakkaraju and J. Leskovec. Confusions over time: An interpretable bayesian model to characterize trends in decision making. In *NIPS*, pages 3261–3269, 2016.

[22] H. Lakkaraju and C. Rudin. Learning cost-effective treatment regimes using markov decision processes. *CoRR*, abs/1610.06972, 2016.

[23] J. A. List, A. M. Shaikh, and Y. Xu. Multiple hypothesis testing in experimental economics. Technical report, NBER, 2016.

[24] R. J. Little. Selection and pattern-mixture models. *Longitudinal data analysis*, pages 409–431, 2008.

[25] R. J. Little, R. D'agostino, M. L. Cohen, K. Dickersin, S. S. Emerson, J. T. Farrar, C. Frangakis, J. W. Hogan, G. Molenberghs, S. A. Murphy, et al. The prevention and treatment of missing data in clinical trials. *New England Journal of Medicine*, 367(14):1355–1360, 2012.

[26] R. J. Little and D. B. Rubin. *Statistical analysis with missing data.* John Wiley & Sons, 2014.

[27] D. Lu and Q. Weng. A survey of image classification methods and techniques for improving classification performance. *International journal of Remote sensing*, 28(5):823–870, 2007.

[28] B. M. Marlin. *Missing data problems in machine learning.* PhD thesis, University of Toronto, 2008.

[29] M. P. McCormick, E. E. O'Connor, E. Cappella, and S. G. McClowry. Teacher–child relationships and academic achievement: A multilevel propensity score model approach. *Journal of School Psychology*, 51(5):611–624, 2013.

[30] S. L. Morgan and C. Winship. *Counterfactuals and causal inference.* Cambridge University Press, 2014.

[31] B. Pang, L. Lee, et al. Opinion mining and sentiment analysis. *Foundations and Trends® in Information Retrieval*, 2(1–2):1–135, 2008.

[32] J. Pearl. *Causality.* Cambridge university press, 2009.

[33] R. Prentice. Use of the logistic model in retrospective studies. *Biometrics*, pages 599–606, 1976.

[34] J. M. Robins, M. A. Hernan, and B. Brumback. Marginal structural models and causal inference in epidemiology, 2000.

[35] P. R. Rosenbaum. Observational studies. In *Observational Studies*, pages 1–17. Springer, 2002.

[36] P. R. Rosenbaum and D. B. Rubin. The central role of the propensity score in observational studies for causal effects. *Biometrika*, pages 41–55, 1983.

[37] D. B. Rubin. Estimating causal effects of treatments in randomized and nonrandomized studies. *Journal of educational Psychology*, 66(5):688, 1974.

[38] D. B. Rubin. Causal inference using potential outcomes: Design, modeling, decisions. *JASA*, 100(469):322–331, 2005.

[39] F. M. Shrive, H. Stuart, H. Quan, and W. A. Ghali. Dealing with missing data in a multi-question depression scale: a comparison of imputation methods. *BMC medical research methodology*, 6(1):57, 2006.

[40] H. Steck. Training and testing of recommender systems on data missing not at random. In *KDD*, pages 713–722, 2010.

[41] E. A. Stuart. Matching methods for causal inference: A review and a look forward. *Statistical science: a review journal of the Institute of Mathematical Statistics*, 25(1):1, 2010.

[42] S. Wager and S. Athey. Estimation and inference of heterogeneous treatment effects using random forests. *arXiv preprint arXiv:1510.04342*, 2015.

[43] J. Zeng, B. Ustun, and C. Rudin. Interpretable classification models for recidivism prediction. *JRSS*, 2016.

Constructivism Learning: A Learning Paradigm for Transparent Predictive Analytics

Xiaoli Li and Jun Huan
{xiaoli.li,jhuan}@ku.edu
Department of Electrical Engineering and Computer Science,
University of Kansas

ABSTRACT

Developing transparent predictive analytics has attracted significant research attention recently. There have been multiple theories on how to model learning transparency but none of them aims to understand the internal and often complicated modeling processes. In this paper we adopt a contemporary philosophical concept called "constructivism", which is a theory regarding how human learns. We hypothesize that a critical aspect of transparent machine learning is to "reveal" model construction with two key process: (1) the assimilation process where we enhance our existing learning models and (2) the accommodation process where we create new learning models. With this intuition we propose a new learning paradigm, constructivism learning, using a Bayesian nonparametric model to dynamically handle the creation of new learning tasks. Our empirical study on both synthetic and real data sets demonstrate that the new learning algorithm is capable of delivering higher quality models (as compared to base lines and state-of-the-art) and at the same time increasing the transparency of the learning process.

CCS CONCEPTS

•Mathematics of computing →Bayesian nonparametric models; •Computing methodologies →*Online learning settings;*

KEYWORDS

Constructivisim Learning; Transparent Machine Learning; Sequential Dirichlet Process; Dynamic Task Construction

ACM Reference format:

Xiaoli Li and Jun Huan. 2017. Constructivism Learning: A Learning Paradigm for Transparent Predictive Analytics. In *Proceedings of KDD'17, August 13–17, 2017, Halifax, NS, Canada.*, , 10 pages.
DOI: http://dx.doi.org/10.1145/3097983.3097994

1 INTRODUCTION

Developing transparent predictive analytics has attracted significant research attention recently [1, 5]. There are many applications where transparent models are critical for the successful deployment of such systems. For example in the medical domain, it is hard for a physician to use results from predictive modeling without knowing how the results are derived. To better train robots, Thomaz and Breazeal showed that if a learning algorithm can reveal its uncertainty of an action in reinforcement learning, that information provides great help for human to better train robots [27]. In addition in legal system for recidivism prediction, using black box predictive analytics may lead to unfair treatment of minority groups and thus commit illegal discrimination [31].

There is intensive discussion on how to define transparency and how to introduce transparency in a predictive analytics. A large body of literature focuses on explaining the results of the prediction [8, 13]. The premise is that if we are able to explain the model results, we improve the transparency of the model and in this sense interpretability and transparency are two closely interleaved concepts. Exemplar work in this category includes sparse linear models [28], prototype based methods such as Bayesian case models [12], and approximating opaque models using local and interpretable models with low complexity [20], among others. Additional theoretic model includes Situated Learning Theory [27], regarding human learning in the context of social interactions and "black box in a glass box" [6, 9] where different levels of modeling transparency are discussed.

The critical limitation of existing discussion is that all the aforementioned works focus on either making sense of the produced model to or delivering models that are easily understandable by end users (i.e. *model transparency*). They do not aim to understand the internal and often complicated modeling process (i.e. *modeling transparency*). We view machine learning decision process as a process of "trade-off" between model fitness (usually evaluated by a loss function) and modeler's experience (usually encoded as the prior distribution in Bayesian learning or the regularization in PAC learning). We argue that in order to achieve transparency we have to at least reveal the internal trade-off process that involves features, hyper-parameters, learning machines, and key results statistics, to the end user as advocated for example in [32].

Our work is motivated by a much broader philosophical discussion called "constructivism", which has profound impact of modern viewpoint about the nature of knowledge. In the constructivism theory, the learner constructs new knowledge through her interaction with the world with two key processes *assimilation* and *accommodation*. Through assimilation, a learner incorporates new experience into an existing knowledge framework without changing that framework. Through accommodation, a learner changes her internal representation of the external world according to the new experience.

With this intuition, we propose a new learning paradigm where when we have new interactions with the world (i.e. through a new

KDD'17, August 13–17, 2017, Halifax, NS, Canada.

DOI: http://dx.doi.org/10.1145/3097983.3097994

training sample), we evaluate whether existing knowledge can generalize well to this new interaction with minor modifications. If not we conclude that new knowledge should be constructed. Specifically in the context of data analytics, we assume samples arrive sequentially. For each newly introduced sample we evaluate our trained models and decide whether we should simply update the existing models (assimilation) or we should create a new learning model if we have sufficient evidence to believe that there is a new learning task in our data sets (accommodation). Here "we" is a machine learning algorithm. Modeling transparency in constructivism learning hence is specifically defined as the algorithm's ability to recognize assimilation and accommodation.

This new learning paradigm poses two challenges in designing an algorithm. First, the algorithm must have the capability to dynamically create models when needed (dynamic task construction). Secondly, the algorithm must have a way to determine which model a newly arrived sample should belong to (sample task assignment). We formalized a Bayesian nonparametric approach using sequential Dirichlet Process Mixture Models (DPMM) to support constructivism learning. The advantage of Bayesian nonparametric is that we do not need to specify the total number of classification models up front and we use data driven approaches to explore a set with potentially infinite number of models. Such Bayesian nonparametric models naturally support the dynamic construction of learning tasks. For sample task assignment we introduced a technique called the *selection principle* to improve the fitness principle, commonly used in traditional Dirichlet Process Mixture of models, which demonstrate significant empirical improvement.

In summary the major contributions that we made in this paper towards transparent predictive analytics are highlighted below.

- We introduced the theory of constructivism in order to offer transparency in the learning process using two concepts: assimilation and accommodation. Based on the theory, we designed a principled approach called *constructivism learning*.
- We performed a systematic investigation and formalized the related learning problem as a novel sequential Dirichlet Process Mixture of Classification Model problem (a.k.a. sDPMCM) where with new training samples we may either update existing learning models or identify a new learning task.
- We introduced a novel and efficient variational inference method for sDPMCM with a technique that we call selection principle.
- Our experimental study demonstrated the improved classification performance of the new learning paradigm. We showed that the new paradigm improved modeling transparency by revealing insights on two key components in a reasoning process: assimilation and accommodation.

2 RELATED WORK

We review related work in three highly relevant categories: transparent machine learning, constructivism (human) learning, and task construction in functional data analysis.

2.1 Transparent Machine Learning

We notice that there are a few recent efforts aiming to reveal the underlying reasoning mechanics of a machine learning algorithm. For example Krause et al. [14] employed a visual analytics to depict input-output relationship by treating the algorithm as a black-box. In this way the user gets a sense of internal learning process by observing how the output may change according to the change of input. Zhou et al. [32] developed a technique to improve transparency by revealing the internal status of a hierarchical beta process. In their study they visualize how output statistics (e.g. precision, recall) change according to different hyperparameter settings. However they lack principled and systematic approaches to address the problem. To initialize the discussion in this paper we adopted the theory of constructivism in human learning and designed an approach with comprehensive experimental study.

2.2 Constructivism Learning

We briefly review the constructivism theory in order to provide further background information and motivation of our work. The full treatment of the concept is clearly beyond this technical discussion and useful references can be found in [18]. Constructivism aims to better understand the nature of knowledge and thus it belongs to epistemology, a branch of philosophy dated back to Aristotle. In that constructivism is not merely a pedagogy though it has been widely used in designing education methods. Following constructivism in education, the focus is to change the role of an educator from a supervisor to a facilitator. Constructivism thus promotes active learning where instructor provide all the necessary information aiming to help students acquire new knowledge.

2.3 Learning with Task Construction

Dynamically identifying learning tasks using Bayesian nonparametric models have been discussed in different context, primarily in functional data clustering [11]. In functional data analysis, we have n sets of samples (labeled data or functional data) from different subjects, experiments, or object, functional clustering tries to construct and learn m regression functions (i.e. tasks) for those n sets of samples by clustering them so that the samples in the same cluster can be described using the same regression function.

Most of existing methods in learning with task construction were designed for batch data [4, 16, 17, 19, 21, 22, 25]. For the scenario of streaming data, the only existing work was proposed by Bastani et al. [3] in a recent paper for object trajectory clustering. In that work, a framework is presented for incremental clustering of object trajectories using DP mixtures of Gaussian processes. It is worth noting that the application of that method is specific to activity mining and analysis from surveillance video.

3 PRELIMINARY

Before presenting our method, we give a brief introduction to Dirichlet Process in order to be self-contained.

3.1 Notation

For clarity, we introduce the following notations. We use lowercase letters to represent scalar values, lowercase letters with bold font to represent vectors (e.g. $\boldsymbol{u}$), uppercase bold letters to represent

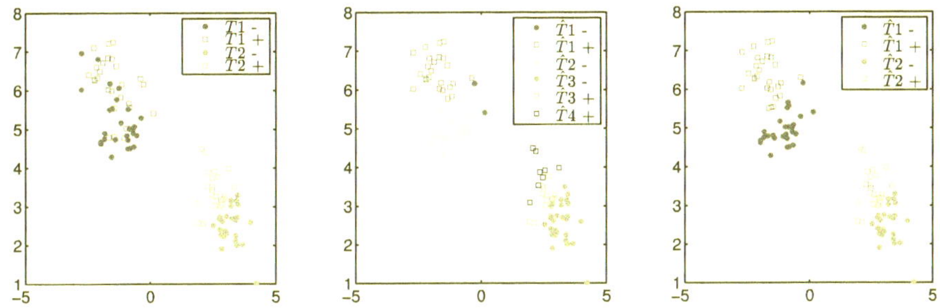

Figure 1: An Issue of the Fitness Principle: Left: Gound Truth; Middle: Tasks Constructed without Using the Selection Principle; Right: Tasks Constructed using the Selection Principle.

matrices (e.g. **A**), Greek letters $\{\alpha, \lambda, \gamma, \dots\}$ to represent parameters. Given a matrix $\mathbf{A} = (a_{i,j}) \in \mathbb{R}^{p \times k}$, $|\mathbf{A}|$ is the determinant of **A**. Unless stated otherwise, all vectors in this paper are column vectors. $\boldsymbol{u}^T$ is the transpose of the vector $\boldsymbol{u}$. We use $[1 : N]$ to denote the set $\{1, 2, \dots, N\}$.

3.2 Dirichlet Process Mixture Models (DPMM)

The Dirichlet process is a random probability measure defined using an concentration parameter α and a base distribution H over a set Θ, denoted as $\mathrm{DP}(\alpha, H)$. It is a distribution over distributions. Each draw G from a DP is a discrete distribution consists of weighted sum of point masses with locations drawn from H. It has the property that, for any finite set of measurable partitions $A_1, A_2, \cdots, A_k$ of Θ,

$$(G(A_1), G(A_2), \cdots, G(A_k)) \sim \mathrm{Dir}(\alpha H(A_1), \alpha H(A_2), \cdots, \alpha H(A_k))$$

Where *Dir* denotes a Dirichlet distribution.

Consider drawing i.i.d sequence $\theta_1, \theta_2, \cdots \theta_n \sim G$, the predictive distribution of θ_i conditioned on other $\theta_j, j < i$, written θ_{-i} is:

$$\theta_i | \theta_{-i} = \frac{1}{\alpha + n - 1} \sum_{j<i} \delta_{\theta_j} + \frac{\alpha}{\alpha + n - 1} H \tag{1}$$

Note that (1) implies clustering property of DP, i.e., θs in the same cluster have the same value, due to the positive probability that θ_i will take on the same value as other θ_{-i}.

Relying on this clustering property of DP, we formalize DP mixture of classification models (DPMCM) for data $(\boldsymbol{x}_i, y_i), i \in [1 : N]$, where $\boldsymbol{x}_i$ is a feature vector and y_i is a label, as follows:

$$\begin{aligned} y_i | \boldsymbol{x}_i, \boldsymbol{\beta}_i &\sim F_y(\cdot | \boldsymbol{x}_i, \boldsymbol{\beta}_i) \\ \boldsymbol{x}_i | \boldsymbol{\theta}_i &\sim F_x(\cdot | \boldsymbol{\theta}_i) \\ (\boldsymbol{\theta}_i, \boldsymbol{\beta}_i) | G &\sim G \\ G &\sim \mathrm{DP}(\alpha, H_\theta \times H_\beta) \end{aligned} \tag{2}$$

Here we model the joint distribution of $\boldsymbol{x}_i$ and y_i and assume that the base distribution $H_\theta \times H_\beta$ is independent between parameters $\boldsymbol{\theta}_i$ and $\boldsymbol{\beta}_i$. Through this formulation, data are grouped into different clusters with each cluster k represented by a generative model parameterized by $(\boldsymbol{\theta}_k^*, \boldsymbol{\beta}_k^*)$. We have $\boldsymbol{\theta}_i = \boldsymbol{\theta}_k^*$ and $\boldsymbol{\beta}_i = \boldsymbol{\beta}_k^*$ if $(\boldsymbol{x}_i, y_i)$ is generated using the model of cluster k. F_x and F_y are generative probabilistic models.

Note that (2) can be directly applied to constructivism learning since it allows dynamic task construction and sample task assignment. Specially, due to the infinite-dimensional space of Bayesian nonparametric models, the complexity of models adapts to data so that new tasks can be constructed as needed. In addition, the clustering property of DPMCM provides us a solution for determining which task a sample should be assigned to. However, the implementation of constructivism learning by directly using (2) may lead to some issues, for which a detailed discussion will be given in section 4.1.

4 ALGORITHM

In this section, we describe our proposed algorithm for constructivism learning (CL). We begin by formalizing the problem setting of CL. This is followed by the description of our sequential DP mixture of classification model(sDPMCM). Then we propose an improved version of sDPMCM , sequential DP mixture of classification model with selection (sDPMCM-s), which is enhanced using an approach we call the selection principle. In the last section, we present the sequential variational inference algorithm for sDPMCM-s adapted from [15].

4.1 Problem Setting and Challenges

We aim to design an algorithm with modeling transparency, i.e. the ability to recognize assimilation and accommodation, by building a set of models incrementally through dynamic task construction and sample task assignment. Specially, suppose that we have data that arrives sequentially, we try to determine whether newly arrived sample $(\boldsymbol{x}_i, y_i)$ can be well classified using existing tasks constructed from previous data $(\boldsymbol{x}_j, y_j), j = 1, 2, \dots, i-1$, or a new task needs to be constructed from scratch. Here $\boldsymbol{x}_i \in \mathbb{R}^d$ is a feature vector and $y_i \in \{0, 1\}$ its corresponding label. Giving a sequence of training samples $(\boldsymbol{x}_i, y_i)$, indexed by i, the outcome of our learning algorithm is a set of classification models. For clarity, we summarize the important notations in Table 1.

As we mentioned before, we can use DPMCM directly for CL. However, this may lead to two issues, short-sighted task assignment and high computational cost, which we discuss in the following.

First, In DPMCM, the decision of assigning a sample to a task is based on the *fitness principle*, i.e., evaluating the likelihood that the sample $(\boldsymbol{x}, y)$ is generated from the task k, which is calculated using:

$$w \int_\Theta F(\boldsymbol{x}, y | \Theta) V(d\Theta) \tag{3}$$

Table 1: Notations for CL

$\boldsymbol{x}_i, y_i$	The feature vector and label for the ith sample
μ_i^x, Σ_i^x	The Parameters for the distribution of $\boldsymbol{x}_i$
β_i^y	The parameter for the logistic function of the ith sample
α	The concentration parameter of DP
H	The base distribution of DP
ρ_i	Task assignment probability for the ith sample
$U(\beta^y; \boldsymbol{x}, y)$	Utility of the sample $(\boldsymbol{x}, y)$ for the task with the parameter β^y

where w is a weight determined by the parameter α and number of samples in the task k. F is the probability or density for $(\boldsymbol{x}, y)$ parameterized by Θ. V is a distribution for Θ. The drawback of this principle is that the contribution of a sample to a task is ignored. When DPMCM is applied to streaming data for classification models, this may lead to short-sighted task assignment and undesirable tasks since they are estimated in a single pass over the data.

We illustrate the problem of fitness principle using a synthetic data set as shown in Fig. 1. Here we have samples from two hidden tasks T_1 and T_2 (Left panel). We adopted a DPMCM, which outputted 4 tasks, rather than 2. In addition task $\hat{T}_4$ has only positive samples and $\hat{T}_2$ has only negative samples. Moreover the samples in $\hat{T}_1$ are highly unbalanced. We believe the reason why DPMCM produces large number of single-class tasks is that the samples in those tasks can be well classified and hence *well fitted*. However, those tasks constructed by DPMCM based only on fitness principle can hardly generalize well to unseen samples. Inspired by this observation, we develop a new DPMCM model enhanced with *selection principle* utilizing Kullback-Leibler divergence (KLD). It is a complement to the fitness principle. When making assignment decision, the contribution of a sample to a task is considered.

The second issue of employing DPMCM for CL is that we have to re-compute the inference for DPMCM when a new sample arrives, which is compute-intensive. To efficiently handle streaming data, we first adapt the sequential method proposed in [15] to DP mixture of classification models to achieve incrementally inference computation. Then we modify a variational approximation technique of logistic regression [10] for efficient task parameter updating.

4.2 Sequential DP Mixture of Classification Model

In this section, we first present a streaming inference method for Dirichlet process [15], which is the starting point of our formalization. Then we propose two new methods for CL, sequential DP mixture of classification models and its enhanced version by incorporating the selection principle.

4.2.1 Sequential DP Mixture Models (sDPMM). To handle streaming data for the following generic DP mixture model:

$$\boldsymbol{x}_i|\boldsymbol{\theta}_i \sim F(\cdot|\boldsymbol{\theta}_i)$$
$$\boldsymbol{\theta}_i|G \sim G$$
$$G \sim \mathrm{DP}(\alpha, H)$$

Lin proposed a sequential variational approximation method [15]. The advantage of Lin's method is that it is truncation free and a single pass over data can reliably estimate a DP mixture model. In this method suppose $\boldsymbol{\theta}$s are grouped into K clusters, and there is a cluster indicator c_i for each $\boldsymbol{\theta}_i, \forall i \in [1:N]$ such that $\boldsymbol{\theta}_i$ belongs to the kth cluster, i.e., $\boldsymbol{\theta}_i = \boldsymbol{\theta}_k^*$, if $c_i = k$. Lin proposed to approximate distribution:

$$p(G|\boldsymbol{x}_{1:N}) = \sum_{c_{1:N}} p(c_{1:N}|\boldsymbol{x}_{1:N})p(G|c_{1:N}, \boldsymbol{x}_{1:N})$$

using a tractable distribution with the following form:

$$q(G|\boldsymbol{x}_{1:N}) = \sum_{c_{1:N}} (\prod_{i=1}^{N} \rho(c_i)) q_v^{(c)}(G|c_{1:N}).$$

Here $\boldsymbol{\theta}_k^* \sim v_k$, which is an independent distribution. The task of inference is to optimize two sets of parameters $\rho \triangleq (\rho_1, \rho_2, \cdots, \rho_i)$ and $v_i \triangleq (v_1^i, v_2^i, \cdots, v_K^i)$ so that $q(G|\boldsymbol{x}_{1:N})$ best approximates the true posterior $p(G|\boldsymbol{x}_{1:N})$.

By using variational approximation technique to minimize the Kullback-Leibler divergence between the true posterior and the approximate posterior, we have sequential approximation for the optimal settings of ρ_{i+1} and v_k^{i+1} after processing i samples:

$$\rho_{i+1} \propto \begin{cases} w_k^i \int_{\boldsymbol{\theta}} F(\boldsymbol{x}_{i+1}|\boldsymbol{\theta}) v_k^i(d\boldsymbol{\theta}) & k \le K \\ \alpha \int_{\boldsymbol{\theta}} F(\boldsymbol{x}_{i+1}|\boldsymbol{\theta}) H(d\boldsymbol{\theta}) & k = K+1 \end{cases} \tag{4}$$

Where $w_k^i = \sum_{j=1}^{i} \rho_j(k)$.

$$v_k^{i+1}(d\boldsymbol{\theta}) \propto \begin{cases} H(d\boldsymbol{\theta}) \prod_{j=1}^{i+1} (F(\boldsymbol{x}_j|\boldsymbol{\theta}))^{\rho_j(k)} & k \le K \\ H(d\boldsymbol{\theta})(F(\boldsymbol{x}_{i+1}|\boldsymbol{\theta}))^{\rho_{i+1}(k)} & k = K+1 \end{cases} \tag{5}$$

$\rho_i(k), \forall k \in [1:K+1], i = 1, 2, \cdots$, are computed using:

$$\rho_i(k) = \frac{w_k^{i-1} \exp(h_i(k))}{\sum_{c=1}^{K+1} w_c^{i-1} \exp(h_i(c))} \tag{6}$$

Where $h_i(k)$ is marginal log-likelihood of $\boldsymbol{x}_i$ belonging to cluster k.

4.2.2 Sequential DP Mixture of Classification Models (sDPMCM). The DP Mixture of Classification Model (DPMCM) we use for CL is based on the general formulation (2). Here we model the joint distribution of $\boldsymbol{x}$ and y, $p(\boldsymbol{x}, y) = p(y|\boldsymbol{x})p(\boldsymbol{x})$, instead of only modeling the conditional distribution $p(y|\boldsymbol{x})$. This provide us the benefit of discovering hidden structure of data by clustering $\boldsymbol{x}$ [26]. Different from sDPMM model where only $\boldsymbol{x}$ is clustered, we cluster both $\boldsymbol{x}$ and y by modeling the joint distribution of $\boldsymbol{x}$ and y. Thus sDPMM cannot be directly applied to DP mixture of classification models. The main change required here is to modify the sequential approximation of ρ_{i+1} and v_k^{i+1} as follows :

$$\rho_{i+1} \propto \begin{cases} w_k^i \int_{\Theta} F(\boldsymbol{x}_{i+1}, y_{i+1}|\Theta) v_k^i(d\Theta) & k \le K \\ \alpha \int_{\Theta} F(\boldsymbol{x}_{i+1}, y_{i+1}|\Theta) H(d\Theta) & k = K+1 \end{cases} \tag{7}$$

$$v_k^{i+1}(d\boldsymbol{\Theta}) \propto \begin{cases} H(d\Theta) \prod_{j=1}^{i+1} (F(\boldsymbol{x}_j|\mu^x, \Sigma^x) F(y_j|\beta^y))^{\rho_j(k)} & k \le K \\ H(d\Theta)(F(\boldsymbol{x}_{i+1}|\mu^x, \Sigma^x) F(y_{i+1}|\beta^y))^{\rho_{i+1}(k)} & k = K+1 \end{cases} \tag{8}$$

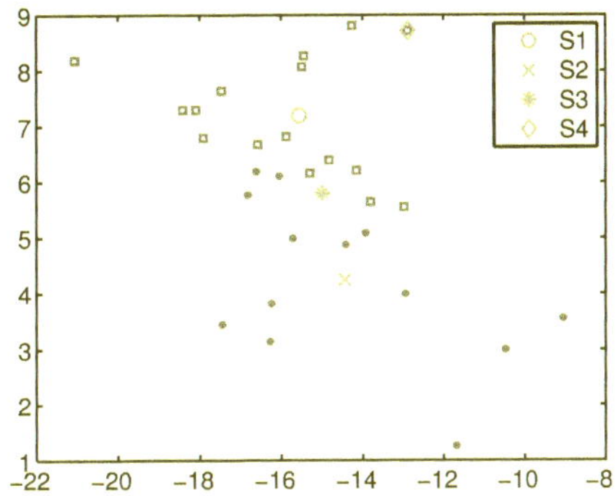

Figure 2: Function of Selection Principle: s_1: mean of positive samples; s_2: mean of negative samples; s_3: close to decision boundary; s_4: far away from decision boundary.

	s_1	s_2	s_3	s_4
KLD	4.485	4.486	4.547	4.491
Pr	0.972	0.967	0.729	0.953

Table 2: Comparison of KLD and Posterior Predictive Probability (Pr)

4.2.3 Sequential DP Mixture of Classification Model with Selection Principle (sDPMCM-s). In selection principle, we focus on evaluating the contribution of a sample to a task. Specially, we aim to measure the utility of an observation of a random variable, i.e. a sample, to other random variables, i.e., task parameters. To this end, we utilize Kullback-Leibler divergence (KLD). This technique has been used in Bayesian optimal experiment design (BOED) [24] to select the optimal design of experiment so that the expected utility of the experiment outcome can be maximized. Different from the general case in BOED, we focus on the utility of a given sample instead of the expected utility. Specifically, we assign a sample to a task so that KLD between the prior distribution of task parameters and the posterior given the sample is maximized. Suppose we have a sample $(\boldsymbol{x}, y)$ and task parameters $\boldsymbol{\beta}^y$, the utility is defined as:

$$U(\boldsymbol{\beta}^y; \boldsymbol{x}, y) = D_{KL}(p(\boldsymbol{\beta}^y | \boldsymbol{x}, y) \parallel p(\boldsymbol{\beta}^y))$$

The goal of selection principle is to assign a sample $(\boldsymbol{x}, y)$ to a task with parameter $\boldsymbol{\beta}^y$ such that $U(\boldsymbol{\beta}^y; \boldsymbol{x}, y)$ is maximized. To understand the function of selection principle, we illustrate it using Fig. 2 and Table 2. In this example we selected four representative samples in a task. s_1 and s_2 are mean of positive and negative samples separately. s_3 is close to decision boundary. s_4 is far away from decision boundary. We observe that although s_1, s_2, s_4 have higher posterior predictive probabilities, their utility to the task is lower than s_3. This example confirms our hypothesis that the selection principle can act as a regularization factor to regulate the range of a task to form more compact clusters.

To incorporate selection principle when making assignment decision, we modify the computation of task assignment probability ρ_{i+1} as follows:

$$\rho_{i+1} \propto \begin{cases} w_k^i s_k^{i+1} \int_\Theta F(\boldsymbol{x}_{i+1}, y_{i+1} | \Theta) \nu_k^i(d\Theta) & k \leq K \\ \alpha s_k^{i+1} \int_\Theta F(\boldsymbol{x}_{i+1}, y_{i+1} | \Theta) H(d\Theta) & k = K+1 \end{cases} \tag{9}$$

Where $s_k^{i+1} = \exp(\gamma U(\boldsymbol{\beta}^y; \boldsymbol{x}_{i+1}, y_{i+1}))$, where γ is a coefficient to regularize the effect of selection principle. Through s_k^{i+1}, the utility of $\boldsymbol{x}_{i+1}, y_{i+1}$ to the model parameter $\boldsymbol{\beta}^y$ is also considered when making task assignment decisions.

4.3 Inference

Several issues need to be addressed for the inference of the proposed sDPMCM-s for streaming data. First, posterior distribution for Θ and prediction distribution for $\boldsymbol{x}$ and y needs to be updated with relatively low complexity during streaming inference. Secondly, an efficient method is needed to compute $U(\boldsymbol{\beta}^y; (\boldsymbol{x}, y))$ when new samples arrive. Thirdly, the inference method, i.e. sDPMM, proposed by Lin was designed for DPMM instead of DPMCM. Thus some modification is needed to adapt it to DPMCM.

In the following, we first describe the details of classification models and variational approximation techniques used in sDPMCM-s for efficient model updating. Then we give the specific formula for utility computation. Lastly, we summarize the complete sequential inference for sDPMCM-s, and present the strategy we use for prediction.

4.3.1 Classification Model in sDPMCM. Within each task of the mixture, we assume that $\boldsymbol{x}$ follow a Multivariate Normal (MN) distribution with mean $\boldsymbol{m}^x$ and covariance matrix Σ^x. For simplicity of computation, we assume a conjugate prior, Normal-Inverse-Wishart(NIW), for $(\boldsymbol{m}^x, \Sigma^x)$. To model the relationship between $\boldsymbol{x}$ and y, we use logistic regression:

$$F_y(y | \boldsymbol{x}, \boldsymbol{\beta}) = \frac{\exp(y \boldsymbol{x}^T \boldsymbol{\beta})}{1 + \exp(\boldsymbol{x}^T \boldsymbol{\beta})} \tag{10}$$

Where $\boldsymbol{\beta} \in \mathbb{R}^d$. And we use a Multivariate Normal distribution for $\boldsymbol{\beta}^y$ with parameters $(\mu_0^\beta, \Psi_0^\beta)$. Note that we assume independence between $(\boldsymbol{m}^x, \Sigma^x)$ and $\boldsymbol{\beta}^y$, and the distribution of y does not depend on $(\boldsymbol{m}^x, \Sigma^x)$ given $\boldsymbol{x}$. This results in simplified computations.

The complete DPMCM for CL is summarized as follows:

$$G \sim \mathrm{DP}(\alpha, \mathrm{NIW}(\mu_0^x, \kappa_0^x, \Psi_0^x, \nu_0^x)\mathrm{MN}(\mu_0^\beta, \Psi_0^\beta)) \tag{11}$$

For $i = 1, 2, \ldots$, draw i.i.d using:

$$\begin{aligned} y_i | \boldsymbol{x}_i, \boldsymbol{\beta}_i^y &\sim F_y(\cdot | \boldsymbol{x}_i, \boldsymbol{\beta}_i^y) \\ \boldsymbol{x}_i | \boldsymbol{m}_i^x, \Sigma_i^x &\sim \mathrm{MN}(\cdot | \boldsymbol{m}_i^x, \Sigma_i^x) \\ (\boldsymbol{m}_i^x, \Sigma_i^x, \boldsymbol{\beta}_i^y) | G &\sim G \end{aligned} \tag{12}$$

Due to the clustering property of DP, $\Theta = (\boldsymbol{m}_i^x, \Sigma_i^x, \boldsymbol{\beta}_i^y)$ will be grouped into different clusters. Θs in the same cluster have an identical value.

4.3.2 Variational Approximation of Logistic Regression. Using logistic regression to model the relationship between $\boldsymbol{x}$ and y poses challenges for computing posterior distribution of model parameters and predictive distribution since they are computationally intractable. To tackle this, we adopt the variational approximation proposed in [10] to replace the logistic function with an adjustable lower bound that has a Gaussian form. This results in the Gaussian form of posterior due to the Gaussian prior of $\boldsymbol{\beta}^y$ and Gaussian variational form of $p(y|\boldsymbol{x}, \boldsymbol{\beta}^y, \xi)$. Here ξ is a variational parameter. To apply this variational approximation to DPMM in sequential setting, we need to modify the updating of parameters $\Psi^\beta, \mu^\beta, \xi$ in [10] so that the uncertainty of clustering brought by sequential inference can be incorporated. With straightforward calculation, we derive the following modification to the updating of parameters when $\rho_{i+1} > 0$:

$$\Psi^\beta_{i+1} = \left[(\Psi^\beta_i)^{-1} + 2\rho_{i+1} f(\xi)\boldsymbol{x}_{i+1}\boldsymbol{x}^T_{i+1}\right]^{-1}$$
$$\mu^\beta_{i+1} = \Psi^\beta_{i+1}\left[(\Psi^\beta_i)^{-1}\mu^\beta_i + (\rho_{i+1}y_{i+1} - \frac{1}{2})\boldsymbol{x}_{i+1}\right] \tag{13}$$
$$\xi^2 = \rho_{i+1}\left[\boldsymbol{x}^T_{i+1}\Psi^\beta_{i+1}\boldsymbol{x}_{i+1} + (\boldsymbol{x}^T_{i+1}\mu^\beta_{i+1})^2\right]$$

For the predictive lower bound for sample $\boldsymbol{x}_{i+1}, y_{i+1}$, it takes the form:

$$\begin{aligned}\ln q(y_{i+1}|\boldsymbol{x}_{i+1}, D) = &\ln g(\xi_{i+1}) - \frac{\xi_{i+1}}{2} + f(\xi_{i+1})\xi^2_{i+1}\\ &- \frac{1}{2}(\mu^\beta_i)^T(\Psi^\beta_i)^{-1}\mu^\beta_i\\ &+ \frac{1}{2}(\mu^\beta_{i+1})^T(\Psi^\beta_{i+1})^{-1}\mu^\beta_{i+1}\\ &+ \frac{1}{2}\ln\frac{|\Psi^\beta_{i+1}|}{|\Psi^\beta_i|}\end{aligned} \tag{14}$$

Where $D = (\boldsymbol{x}_1, y_1), (\boldsymbol{x}_2, y_2), \ldots, (\boldsymbol{x}_i, y_i)$.

4.3.3 Utility Computation. The computation of $U(\boldsymbol{\beta}^y; \boldsymbol{x}_{i+1}, y_{i+1})$ is straightforward after the variational approximation is used for logistic regression. Let denote the distribution as $p_i(\boldsymbol{\beta}^y \mid \mu^\beta_i, \Psi^\beta_i)$ before $(\boldsymbol{x}_{i+1}, y_{i+1})$ is assigned to a model and $p_{i+1}(\boldsymbol{\beta}^y \mid \mu^\beta_{i+1}, \Psi^\beta_{i+1})$ after assignment, we can calculate the KLD of two MN distributions p_i and p_{i+1}:

$$\begin{aligned}U(\boldsymbol{\beta}^y; \boldsymbol{x}_{i+1}, y_{i+1}) = &\frac{1}{2}\Bigg[\ln\frac{|\Psi^\beta_i|}{|\Psi^\beta_{i+1}|} - d + tr((\Psi^\beta_i)^{-1}\Psi^\beta_{i+1}) +\\ &(\mu^\beta_i - \mu^\beta_{i+1})^T(\Psi^\beta_i)^{-1}(\mu^\beta_i - \mu^\beta_{i+1})\Bigg]\end{aligned}$$

4.3.4 Sequential Inference for sDPMCM-s. To handle streaming data, we consider the method proposed in [15]. Specifically, when a new sample arrives, we first determine whether it will be assigned to an existing task or a new task. Then the model parameters of assigned task are updated. We describe these two steps separately in the following.

Task Assignment. To determine which task a newly arriving sample belongs to, we need to compute the assignment probability ρ_{i+1} based on (7) and (8). The probability of assigning newly arrived sample $(\boldsymbol{x}_{i+1}, y_{i+1})$ to task k, denoted as $\rho_{i+1}(k)$, is computed using:

$$\rho_{i+1}(k) = \frac{w^i_k s^{i+1}_k \exp(h_{i+1}(k))}{\sum^{K+1}_{c=1} w^i_c s^{i+1}_c \exp(h_{i+1}(c))} \tag{15}$$

Where $h_{i+1}(k)$ is the log posterior predictive of $(\boldsymbol{x}_{i+1}, y_{i+1})$ belonging to cluster k. It can be decomposed into two parts $h_{i+1}(k) = h^x_{i+1}(k) + h^y_{i+1}(k)$. Due to the conjugate property, the posterior predictive, i.e. $h^x_{i+1}(k)$, is a multivariate t distribution with density function:

$$\frac{\Gamma[(\delta_i + d)/2]}{\Gamma(\delta_i/2)\delta^{d/2}\pi^{d/2}|\Phi_i|^{1/2}}\left[1 + \frac{1}{\delta_i}(\boldsymbol{x} - \boldsymbol{v}_i)^T\Phi_i^{-1}(\boldsymbol{x} - \boldsymbol{v}_i)\right] \tag{16}$$

Where

$$\delta_i = v^x_i(k) - d + 1$$
$$\boldsymbol{v}_i = \mu^x_i(k)$$
$$\Phi_i = \frac{\kappa^x_i(k) + 1}{\kappa^x_i(k)(v^x_i(k) - d + 1)}\Psi^x_i(k)$$

$\mu^x_i(k), \Psi^x_i(k), \kappa^x_i(k), v^x_i(k)$ are posterior parameters of a NIW distribution for task k after receiving i samples. With (16), $h^x_{i+1}(k)$ can be computed directly.

For the computation of $h^y_{i+1}(k)$, we use the lower bound specified in (14) derived from a variational approximation of logistic regression.

Updating Model parameters. Relying on the conjugate property, posterior parameters of the NIW distribution of task k have a closed-form updating when receiving a new sample $\boldsymbol{x}_{i+1}$. For simplicity, we update natural parameters $\Lambda = (\eta^1_i(k), \eta^2_i(k), \eta^3_i(k), \eta^4_i(k))$ of NIW distribution for task k at each step. They can be derived from $\mu^x_i(k)$, $\Psi^x_i(k)$, $\kappa^x_i(k)$, $v^x_i(k)$ using:

$$\eta^1_i(k) = \kappa^x_i(k)\mu^x_i(k)$$
$$\eta^2_i(k) = \kappa^x_i(k)$$
$$\eta^3_i(k) = \Psi^x_i(k) + \kappa^x_i(k)\mu^x_i(k)(\mu^x_i(k))^T$$
$$\eta^4_i(k) = v^x_i(k) + d + 2$$

Modified from the sufficient statistics of the NIW distribution [7], the following form of updating for Λ with considering the uncertainty of task assignment are used:

$$\eta^1_{i+1}(k) = \eta^1_i(k) + \rho_{i+1}(k)\boldsymbol{x}_{i+1}$$
$$\eta^2_{i+1}(k) = \eta^2_i(k) + \rho_{i+1}(k)$$
$$\eta^3_{i+1}(k) = \eta^3_i(k) + \rho_{i+1}(k)\boldsymbol{x}_{i+1}(\boldsymbol{x}_{i+1})^T$$
$$\eta^4_{i+1}(k) = \eta^4_i(k) + \rho_{i+1}(k)$$

For the updating of parameters $\mu^\beta_i, \Psi^\beta_i$ for $\boldsymbol{\beta}^y_i$, we use the variational approximation in (13).

4.3.5 Prediction. For predicting the label of a test sample $\boldsymbol{x}$, we use the following strategy. First, we use all the K tasks learned from training data to predict the label of $\boldsymbol{x}$ to get K labels, $\hat{y}_1$, $\hat{y}_2, \ldots, \hat{y}_K$. Then we compare the posterior predictive of $P(\boldsymbol{x}, \hat{y}_k)$, $\forall k \in [1 : K]$ and set the label of $\boldsymbol{x}$ to $\hat{y}_{k^*}$ so that $P(\boldsymbol{x}, \hat{y}_{k^*}) = max(P(\boldsymbol{x}, \hat{y}_1), P(\boldsymbol{x}, \hat{y}_2), \ldots, P(\boldsymbol{x}, \hat{y}_K))$.

5 EXPERIMENTS

In this section, we first introduce the data sets and experimental protocol used in our experiments. Then we evaluate the performance of our proposed methods, sDPMCM and its variation sDPMCM-s, by comparing them with base-line methods SVM, Random Forest, and a state-of-the-art classification model based on enriched Dirichlet Process Mixture model (EDPMM) on 4 synthetic data sets and 3 real-world data sets. Lastly, we demonstrate how modeling transparency can be achieved by identifying assimilation and accommodation in a learning process.

5.1 Data Sets

For the experiments, we used both synthetic data sets and real-worlds data sets, as detailed below.

5.1.1 Synthetic Data Sets. we constructed 4 synthetic data sets with K hidden tasks each, where $K \in [2:5]$. For each task, we randomly draw its parameters from a NIW prior and a MN prior. For the NIW prior of $\boldsymbol{m}^x$ and Σ^x, we use zero mean and a diagonal scale matrix $\psi_0 I$, where $\psi_0 = 2$. We set $\kappa_0^x = 0.04$ and degree of freedom $\nu_0^x = d + 3$, where d is the dimension of $\boldsymbol{x}$. For the MN prior of $\boldsymbol{\beta}^y$, we use a MN distribution with zero mean and a unit diagonal covariance matrix. The data $\boldsymbol{x}, y$ are generated using the distribution described in (17). We summarize the statistics of 4 synthetic data sets in Table 3.

$$\begin{aligned} y_i|\boldsymbol{x}_i, \boldsymbol{\beta}_i^y &\sim F_y(\cdot|\boldsymbol{x}_i, \boldsymbol{\beta}_i^y) \\ \boldsymbol{x}_i|\boldsymbol{m}_i^x, \Sigma_i^x &\sim \text{MN}(\cdot|\boldsymbol{m}_i^x, \Sigma_i^x) \end{aligned} \tag{17}$$

Data Set	SDS1	SDS2	SDS3	SDS4
T	2	3	4	5
N	205	317	406	500

Table 3: Statistics of Synthetic Data Sets. T: Number of Hidden Tasks. N: Number of Samples.

5.1.2 Real-world Data Sets. We used 3 real-world data sets: WebKB, School Performance and Landmine.

WebKB. This data set contains a subset of the web pages collected from computer science departments of 4 universities in January 1997 by the World Wide Knowledge Base (WebKb) project of the CMU text learning group [1]. It is composed of 230 course pages and 821 non-course pages. For each web page, two types of representation are provided, text on the web page and anchor text of the hyperlinks to that page. We generate the features from text on the web pages using TF-IDF. Then we applied PCA to the features to keep the first 30 components. The classification goal here is to determine whether a web page is a course page or not.

School Performance. The school data set comes from the Inner London Education Authority (ILEA). It is composed of examination records from 140 secondary schools in years 1985,1986 and 1987. The original data includes the year of examination, 4 school-specific attributes and 3 student-specific attributes. In our experiments, we use the processed data set provided by [2], where categorical features are expressed as binary features. To use this data set for classification, we labeled those samples with examination scores larger than 30 as positive and others as negative. We use data from 123 schools by removing those schools with less than 5 positive or 5 negative samples.

LandMine. The land mine data set [23, 30] consists of 14,820 samples from 29 different geographical regions. The features are extracted from radar data, including four-moment based features, three correlation-based features, one energy-ratio feature, one spatial variance feature, and a bias term. The classification goal is to detect whether or not a land mine is present in an area. We used 20% of the data for our experiments.

For each data set, we randomly chose 50% of the data for training and the other 50% for testing. We applied bootstrap resampling to training data sets to create balanced data sets. The statistics about 3 data sets are summarized in Table 4.

Data Set	N	d
WebKB	1051	30
School	11966	17
LandMine	2972	9

Table 4: Statistics of Real Data Sets. N: number of samples d: number of features

5.2 Experiment Protocol

Baseline Methods. To the best of our knowledge, there is no previous work on learning with task construction for classification of streaming data. Thus we only compare our methods with two widely applied batch learning methods, SVM and Random Forest, and one state-of-the-art DP mixture of classification model, joint enriched Dirichlet process mixture model (EDPMM) proposed in [29]. For SVM, we used a SVM classifier with a RBF kernel provided in Matlab. For Random Forest, we used the algorithm implemented in scikit-learn python package. For EDPMM, we used the R code developed by the original authors. We implemented both sDPMCM and sDPMCM-s in Matlab.

Model Construction. We performed 10-fold cross validation to derive training and testing data.

Model Selection. We performed grid search to select optimal model parameters using 10-fold cross validation that was performed on the training data only.

Evaluation Metrics. We used AUC, the area under a ROC curve, calculated on testing data only, to compare the performance of different algorithms.

Significance Test. When we compared different methods, we made sure that these methods were trained using the same training data sets and were evaluated with the same testing data sets. We used paired student's t test to evaluate the statistical significance of the difference between different results.

5.3 Performance Evaluation Results

To evaluate the performance of our proposed methods, we compared them with 3 baseline methods on 4 synthetic data sets and 3 real-world data sets.

5.3.1 Comparison on Synthetic Data Sets. Table 5 presents the results of comparison on 4 synthetic data sets. Compared with SVM and RF, DP-based methods achieves competitive or better results on 4 data sets. As we expected, batch DP mixture model, EDPMM, outperforms sDPMCM and sDPMCM-s on the 3 synthetic data sets. However, the performance difference on SDS1 and SDS3 is not statistically significant according to the paired student's t test.

[1] http://www.cs.cmu.edu/afs/cs/project/theo-20/www/data/

Comparing sDPMCM and sDPMCM-s, we observe that sDPMCM-always outperforms sDPMCM. This demonstrates the effectiveness of selection principle on improving performance. It is worth noting that sDPMCM is comparable with EDPMM on SDS4 data set. And sDPMCM-s even performs significantly better than EDPMM on this data set. Our explanation is that the covariance structure may be more complicated with more hidden tasks. Compared with the Inverse-Gamma distribution adopted by EDPMM, the Inverse-Wishart distribution we used for sDPMCM and sDPMCM-s allows richer covariance structure.

DataSet	SVM	RF	EDPMM	sDPMCM	sDPMCM-s
SDS1	0.812	0.801	**0.860**	0.847	0.856
SDS2	0.787	0.748	**0.806***	0.788	0.798
SDS3	0.814	0.789	**0.823**	0.813	0.822
SDS4	0.823	0.814	0.839	0.838	**0.852***

Table 5: Comparison of Algorithms on Synthetic Data Sets. AUC is used for the performance metric.*: statistically significant with 5% significance level.

DataSet	SVM	RF	EDPMM	sDPMCM	sDPMCM-s
WebKB	0.873	0.896	0.894	0.897	**0.910***
School	**0.718**	**0.718**	0.676	0.715	0.717
LandMine	0.676	0.670	0.552	0.670	**0.687***

Table 6: Comparison of Algorithms on Real Data Sets. AUC is used for the performance metric.*: statistically significant with 5% significance level.

5.3.2 Comparison on Real Data Sets. We show the results of comparison of algorithms on real data sets in Table 6. Compared with base-line methods, EDPMM achieves similar performance on WebKB data set. However, its performance on LandMine data set is significantly worse than those of SVM and RF. There are two possible reasons. First, as we mentioned before, it is possible that the Inverse-Gamma prior adopted by EDPMM cannot explain the complicated covariance structure of data. Second, EDPMM used a nested structure to form hierarchical clusters, where X-clusters are nested into each y-cluster. This choice of ordering X and y may be inappropriate for this data set. Although it is possible to use a different ordering, this choice is problem specific and the work did not provide a way to guide this decision. For the school data set, EDPMM also has the worst performance among all algorithms. But note that we collect the result of EDPMM from one run of the experiment due to the high computation cost. For our proposed method, sDPMCM, it achieves comparable performance with random forest. Relying on selection principle, sDPMCM-s achieves statistically significant advantages over other algorithms on WebKB and Landmine data sets.

5.4 Transparency Evaluation

In this section, we conducted experiments to study whether our proposed methods sDPMCM and sDPMCM-s can achieve modeling transparency, i.e. the ability to recognize assimilation and accommodation in a learning process.

	SDS1		SDS5	
	Task 1	Task 2	Task 1	Task2
m	[-1.394;5.673]	[2.899;2.818]	[0.851;7.978]	[1.155;1.234]
Σ	[0.568,-0.345; -0.3454,0.8279]	[0.257,-0.178; -0.178,0.513]	[6.099,0.034; 0.034,5.932]	[5.116,0.023; 0.023;5.199]

Table 7: Statistics of SDS1 and SDS5

5.4.1 Evaluation Data Sets and Methods. We evaluate the modeling transparency of each algorithm using both synthetic data sets and real word data sets. For synthetic data sets, we first picked the data set SDS1, which consists of two well separated tasks. To further investigate the issue, we generated another synthetic data set, SDS5, containing two tasks with overlapping samples. We summarize the mean and variance of each task in each data set in Table 7. For real-world data sets, we conducted a case study using a subset of school data set, which consists of data from 5 schools.

For the evaluation on synthetic data sets, we adopt the following learning process. The number of samples is sequentially introduced in such way that the first n samples are all from one task, then we have samples from the second task. *Modeling transparency* in this context is the capacity that a learning algorithm recognizes the second learning task. Quantitatively, we define *constructivism modeling transparency, CMT*, as

$$CMT = 1/N_2, \tag{18}$$

where N_2 is the number of samples from the newly introduced task that the learning algorithm correctly recognizes the first time that there is a new task. Following this definition, we notice that MT must be a positive number between 0 and 1 (inclusively). CMT may take the value 1, if it only takes one sample from the newly introduced task in order for the learning algorithm to recognize that there is a new task. For those algorithms that can not recognize the existence of new tasks, the CMT value is zero (since "can not" is equivalent to that the algorithm needs infinite number of samples from the new task to recognize that there is a new task). CMT is undefined if the algorithm does not correctly recognize the newly arrived task. Apparently the higher the CMT value is, the more sensitive the learning task is for detecting a new task.

5.4.2 Results on Synthetic Data Sets. The two algorithms sDPMCM and sDPMCM-s are designed specifically to be able to recognize newly introduced tasks. For base line algorithms, we are not aware of any discussion on how to use those algorithms to answer the question regarding the number of learning tasks exists in the data set. To fill the gap, we collect the number of support vectors, denoted as S, for SVM and the number of tress, R, for Random Forest. It is our hope that we may see significant changes in S or R when accommodation happens.

The experiments results on SDS1 are shown in Fig. 3. For SVM and Random Forest, we observe that there is no correspondence between the change in modeling processes and the number of tasks. For SVM, the number of support vectors shows a steady increasing with increasing number of samples. For Random Forest, the number of trees tends to fluctuate with different number of samples. The arriving of samples from a new task did not trigger substantial changes in the modeling processes of both SVM and

	Task 1	Task 2
N	197	131
N1	63	102
N2	124	29
P	26%	45%

Table 8: N:Total number of students in the task; N1: number of students from schools funded by a grant from the central government; N2: number of students from church of England schools; P: average of percentage of students eligible for free school meals.

Random Forest. Following the discussion, we conclude that the constructivism modeling transparency, CMT, for SVM and Random Forest is zero. For sDPMCM and sDMCM-s, they can immediately identify that a new task was needed (accommodation) when the first sample (the 55th sample) of the second task arrived. In this case, CMT for both sDPMCM and sDPMCM-s are 1. However sDPMCM failed to identify the correct number of tasks. With selection principle, sDPMCM-s constructed exactly two tasks.

An additional experiment was performed on SDS5. SDS5 is more challenging since the samples from the two learning tasks overlap significantly. The result is displayed in Fig. 4. For this data set, SVM and Random Forest still could not identify the emergence of a new task. In this harder case, 10 samples were needed by sDPMCM-s to trigger an accommodation and hence its *CMT* is 1/10=0.1. We notice that sDPMCM-s can detect the change in the data set and constructed a new task to accommodate the change correctly. sDPMCM is more sensitive comparing to sDPMCM-s. It requires only 2 samples to recognize the existence of new task but sDPMCM does not do so correctly since it identifies many non-existing tasks as well. In this case its *CMT* is undefined.

5.4.3 Results on Real-World Data Sets. For real data sets, it is difficult, if impossible, to know precisely the number of learning tasks in the data set. Therefore we did a case study where we try to understand the tasks that constructed by the sDPMCM-s algorithm. Using 5 school data sets, sDPMCM-s constructed 2 tasks which we summarize in Table 8. From the results, we observe that about one-third of the students in task 1 are from schools funded by the central government while the ratio is more than two-thirds in task 2. In contrast, the number of students who are eligible for free school meals in task 2 is almost twice the number in task 1. The comparison reveals an obvious socioeconomic difference between the students from two tasks. Since socioeconomic status can have an non-negligible impact on student academic achievement, this difference between task 1 and task 2 may validate the accommodation identified by sDPMCM-s .

6 CONCLUSION

In this paper we proposed a new learning paradigm for transparent predictive analytics where we incorporate a contemporary philosophical concept of constructivism in machine learning. We developed a model formalization using Dirichlet Process Mixture Models for streaming data with efficient inference. Our experimental study demonstrated the utility of the proposed methods. Our future work is to extend the current algorithm to other learning scenarios such as semi-supervised learning.

REFERENCES

[1] Saleema Amershi, Maya Cakmak, William Bradley Knox, and Todd Kulesza. 2014. Power to the people: The role of humans in interactive machine learning. *AI Magazine* 35, 4 (2014), 105–120.

[2] Andreas Argyriou, Theodoros Evgeniou, and Massimiliano Pontil. 2008. Convex multi-task feature learning. *Machine Learning* 73, 3 (2008), 243–272.

[3] Vahid Bastani, Lucio Marcenaro, and Carlo S Regazzoni. 2016. Online Nonparametric Bayesian Activity Mining and Analysis From Surveillance Video. *IEEE Transactions on Image Processing* 25, 5 (2016), 2089–2102.

[4] J Bigelow and David B Dunson. 2005. Semiparametric classification in hierarchical functional data analysis. *Duke University ISDS Discussion paper* (2005), 05–18.

[5] Jenna Burrell. 2016. How the machine !!thinks??: Understanding opacity in machine learning algorithms. *Big Data & Society* 3, 1 (2016), 2053951715622512.

[6] Laura Chiticariu, Yunyao Li, and Fred Reiss. 2015. Transparent Machine Learning for Information Extraction. In *Proceedings of the 2015 Conference on Empirical Methods in Natural Language Processing*.

[7] Nicholas Foti, Jason Xu, Dillon Laird, and Emily Fox. 2014. Stochastic variational inference for hidden Markov models. In *Advances in Neural Information Processing Systems*. 3599–3607.

[8] Satoshi Hara and Kohei Hayashi. 2016. Making tree ensembles interpretable. In *ICML Workshop on Human Interpretability in Machine Learning (WHI 2016)*.

[9] Kristina Höök. 2000. Steps to take before intelligent user interfaces become real. *Interacting with computers* 12, 4 (2000), 409–426.

[10] Tommi S Jaakkola and Michael I Jordan. 2000. Bayesian parameter estimation via variational methods. *Statistics and Computing* 10, 1 (2000), 25–37.

[11] Julien Jacques and Cristian Preda. 2014. Functional data clustering: a survey. *Advances in Data Analysis and Classification* 8, 3 (2014), 231–255.

[12] Been Kim, Cynthia Rudin, and Julie A Shah. 2014. The Bayesian Case Model: A generative approach for case-based reasoning and prototype classification. In *Advances in Neural Information Processing Systems*. 1952–1960.

[13] Been Kim, Julie A Shah, and Finale Doshi-Velez. 2015. Mind the gap: A generative approach to interpretable feature selection and extraction. In *Advances in Neural Information Processing Systems*. 2260–2268.

[14] Josua Krause, Adam Perer, and Enrico Bertini. 2016. Using Visual Analytics to Interpret Predictive Machine Learning Models. In *ICML Workshop on Human Interpretability in Machine Learning (WHI 2016)*.

[15] Dahua Lin. 2013. Online learning of nonparametric mixture models via sequential variational approximation. In *Advances in Neural Information Processing Systems*. 395–403.

[16] Richard F MacLehose and David B Dunson. 2009. Nonparametric Bayes kernel-based priors for functional data analysis. *Statistica Sinica* (2009), 611–629.

[17] XuanLong Nguyen and Alan E Gelfand. 2011. The Dirichlet labeling process for clustering functional data. *Statistica Sinica* (2011), 1249–1289.

[18] Jean Piaget. 1985. *The equilibration of cognitive structures: The central problem of intellectual development.* University of Chicago Press.

[19] Shubhankar Ray and Bani Mallick. 2006. Functional clustering by Bayesian wavelet methods. *Journal of the Royal Statistical Society: Series B (Statistical Methodology)* 68, 2 (2006), 305–332.

[20] Marco Tulio Ribeiro, Sameer Singh, and Carlos Guestrin. 2016. Why Should I Trust You? Explaining the Predictions of Any Classifier. In *Proceedings of the 22nd ACM SIGKDD International Conference on Knowledge Discovery and Data Mining*. ACM, 1135–1144.

[21] Abel Rodriguez, David B Dunson, and Alan E Gelfand. 2008. The nested Dirichlet process. *J. Amer. Statist. Assoc.* 103, 483 (2008), 1131–1154.

[22] James C Ross and Jennifer G Dy. 2013. Nonparametric Mixture of Gaussian Processes with Constraints. In *Proceedings of the 30 th International Conference on Machine Learning*, Vol. 28. 1346–1354.

[23] Paul Ruvolo and Eric Eaton. 2013. ELLA: An Efficient Lifelong Learning Algorithm. *ICML (1)* 28 (2013), 507–515.

[24] Elizabeth G Ryan, Christopher C Drovandi, James M McGree, and Anthony N Pettitt. 2015. A review of modern computational algorithms for Bayesian optimal design. *International Statistical Review* (2015).

[25] Bruno Scarpa and David B Dunson. 2014. Enriched stick-breaking processes for functional data. *J. Amer. Statist. Assoc.* 109, 506 (2014), 647–660.

[26] Babak Shahbaba and Radford Neal. 2009. Nonlinear models using Dirichlet process mixtures. *Journal of Machine Learning Research* 10, Aug (2009), 1829–1850.

[27] Andrea L Thomaz and Cynthia Breazeal. 2006. Transparency and socially guided machine learning. In *Proceedings of 5th Intl. Conf. on Development and Learning (ICDL)*.

[28] Berk Ustun and Cynthia Rudin. 2016. Supersparse linear integer models for optimized medical scoring systems. *Machine Learning* 102, 3 (2016), 349–391.

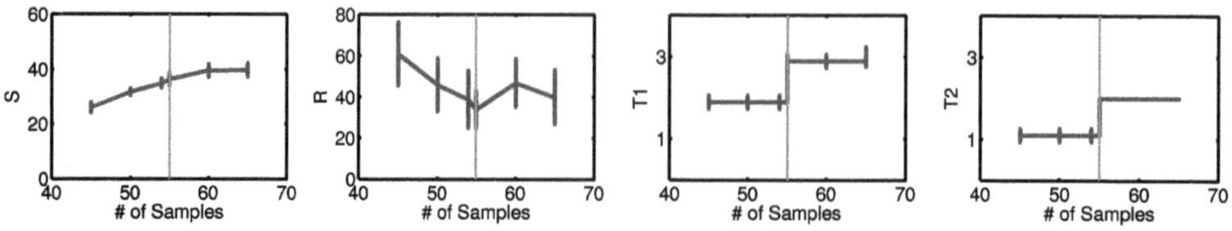

(a) Modeling Processes. S: number of support vectors; R: number of trees; T1,T2: number of tasks constructed by sDPMCM and sDPMCM-s. Red Line: the 1st sample from the 2nd task.

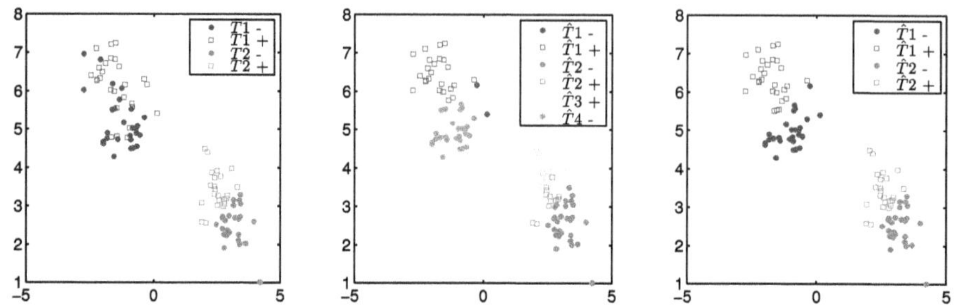

(b) Ground Truth

(c) Tasks constructed by sDPMCM

(d) Tasks constructed by sDPMCM-s

Figure 3: Transparency Evaluation with Non-overlapping Tasks

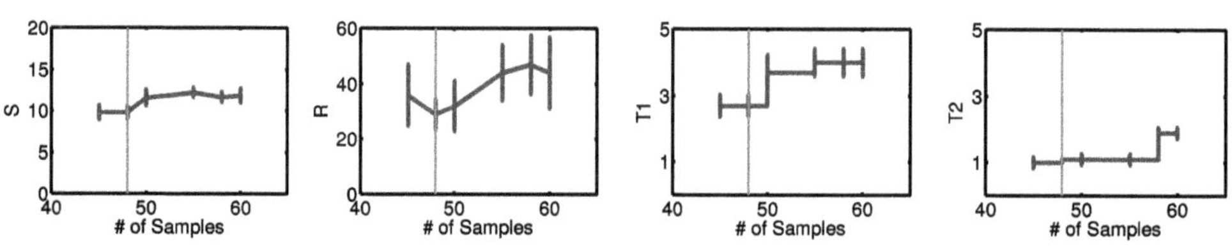

(a) Modeling Processes. S: number of support vectors; R: number of trees; T1,T2: number of tasks constructed by sDPMCM and sDPMCM-s. Red Line: the 1st sample from the 2nd task.

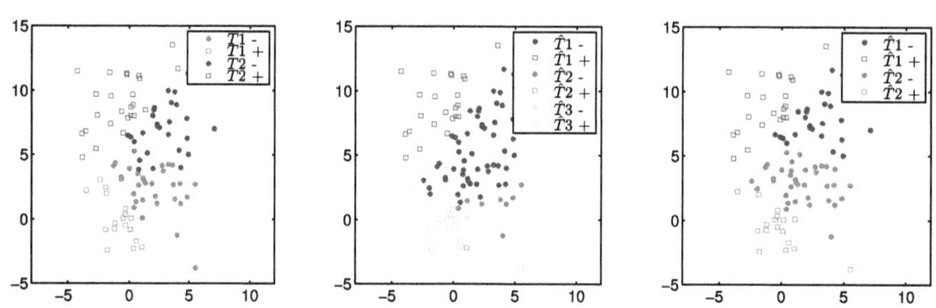

(b) Ground Truth

(c) Tasks constructed by sDPMCM

(d) Tasks constructed by sDPMCM-s

Figure 4: Transparency Evaluation with Overlapping Tasks

[29] Sara Wade, David B Dunson, Sonia Petrone, and Lorenzo Trippa. 2014. Improving prediction from dirichlet process mixtures via enrichment. *Journal of Machine Learning Research* 15, 1 (2014), 1041–1071.

[30] Ya Xue, Xuejun Liao, Lawrence Carin, and Balaji Krishnapuram. 2007. Multi-task learning for classification with dirichlet process priors. *Journal of Machine Learning Research* 8, Jan (2007), 35–63.

[31] Jiaming Zeng, Berk Ustun, and Cynthia Rudin. 2016. Interpretable classification models for recidivism prediction. *Journal of the Royal Statistical Society: Series A (Statistics in Society)* (2016).

[32] Jianlong Zhou, Zhidong Li, Yang Wang, and Fang Chen. 2013. Transparent Machine Learning–Revealing Internal States of Machine Learning. In *Proceedings of IUI2013 Workshop on Interactive Machine Learning*. 1–3.

Is the Whole Greater Than the Sum of Its Parts?

Liangyue Li
Arizona State University
liangyue@asu.edu

Hanghang Tong*
Arizona State University
hanghang.tong@asu.edu

Yong Wang
HKUST
ywangct@cse.ust.hk

Conglei Shi
IBM Research
shiconglei@gmail.com

Nan Cao
Tongji University
nan.cao@gmail.com

Norbou Buchler
US Army Research Laboratory
norbou.buchler.civ@mail.mil

ABSTRACT

The PART-WHOLE relationship routinely finds itself in many disciplines, ranging from collaborative teams, crowdsourcing, autonomous systems to networked systems. From the algorithmic perspective, the existing work has primarily focused on predicting the outcomes of the whole and parts, by either *separate* models or *linear joint* models, which assume the outcome of the parts has a linear and independent effect on the outcome of the whole. In this paper, we propose a joint predictive method named PAROLE to simultaneously and mutually predict the part and whole outcomes. The proposed method offers two distinct advantages over the existing work. First (*Model Generality*), we formulate joint PART-WHOLE outcome prediction as a generic optimization problem, which is able to encode a variety of complex relationships between the outcome of the whole and parts, beyond the linear independence assumption. Second (*Algorithm Efficacy*), we propose an effective and efficient block coordinate descent algorithm, which is able to find the coordinate-wise optimum with a linear complexity in both time and space. Extensive empirical evaluations on real-world datasets demonstrate that the proposed PAROLE (1) leads to consistent prediction performance improvement by modeling the non-linear part-whole relationship as well as part-part interdependency, and (2) scales linearly in terms of the size of the training dataset.

KEYWORDS

Joint predictive model; part-whole relationship

1 INTRODUCTION

The great Greek philosopher Aristotle articulated more than 2,000 years ago that "*the whole is greater than the sum of its parts*". This is probably most evident in *teams*, which, through appropriate synergy, promise a collective outcome (i.e., team performance) that is superior than the simple addition of what each individual team member could achieve (i.e., individual productivity). For example, in the scientific community, the new breakthrough is increasingly resulting from the teamwork, compared with individual researcher's sole endevour [20]; in professional sports (e.g., NBA), the peak performance of a grass-root team is often attributed to the harmonic teamwork between the team players rather than the individual player's capability. Beyond teams, the *part-whole* relationship also routinely finds itself in other disciplines, ranging from crowdsourcing (e.g., Community-based Question Answering (CQA) sites [23]), collective decision-making in autonomous system (e.g., a self-orchestrated swarm of drones[1]), to reliability assessment of a networked system of components [4, 24].

From the algorithmic perspective, an interesting problem is to predict the outcome of the whole and/or parts [7]. In organizational teams, it is critical to appraise the individual performance, its contribution to the team outcome as well as the team's overall performance [15]. In the emerging field of the "science of science", the dream of being able to predict breakthroughs, e.g. predicting the likelihood of a researcher making disruptive contributions and foreseeing the future impact of her research products (e.g., manuscripts, proposals, system prototypes) pervades almost all aspects of modern science [5]. In Community-based Question Answering (CQA) sites, predicting the long-term impact of a question (*whole*) and its associated answers (*parts*) enables users to spot valuable questions and answers at an early stage. Despite much progress has been

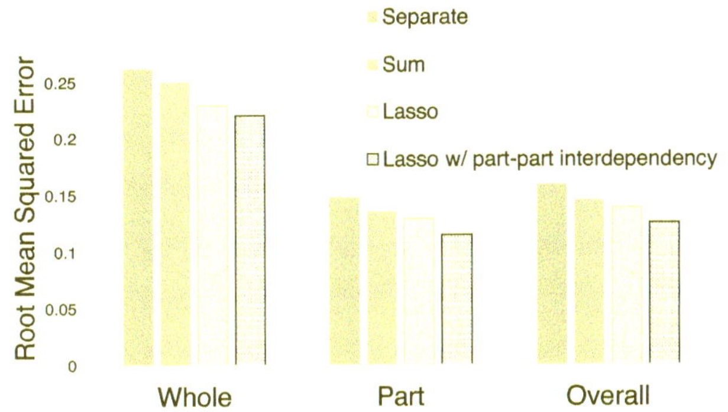

Figure 1: Prediction error comparison on *Movie* dataset. Lower is better. Best Viewed in Color. The right two bars are the proposed methods, which encode the non-linear part-whole relationship and the non-linearity with part-part interdependency respectively.

*To whom correspondence should be addressed.

[1] CBS 60 minutes report: http://www.cbsnews.com/news/60-minutes-autonomous-drones-set-to-revolutionize-military-technology/

KDD '17, August 13–17, 2017, Halifax, NS, Canada
© 2017 ACM. 978-1-4503-4887-4/17/08...$15.00
DOI: 10.1145/3097983.3098006

made, the existing work either develop separate models for predicting the outcome of whole and parts without explicitly utilizing the part-whole relationship [10, 14], or implicitly assume the outcome of the whole is a *linear* sum of the outcome of the parts [23], which might oversimplify the complicated part-whole relationships (e.g., non-linearity).

The key to address these limitations largely lies in the answers to the following questions, i.e., to what extent does the outcome of parts (e.g., individual productivity) and that of the whole (e.g., team performance) correlated, beyond the existing linear, independency assumption? How can we leverage such potentially non-linear and interdependent 'coupling' effect to mutually improve the prediction of the outcome of the whole and parts collectively? This is exactly the focus of this paper, which is highly challenging for the following reasons. First (*Modeling Challenge*), the relationship between the parts outcome and whole outcome might be complicated, beyond the simple addition or linear combination. For example, the authors in [22] empirically identified a non-linear correlation between the impacts of questions and the associated answers, that is, the impact of a question is much more strongly correlated with that of the *best* answer it receives, compared with the *average* impact of its associated answers. However, how to leverage such non-linear relationship between the parts and whole outcome has largely remained open. For teams, the team performance might be mainly dominated by a few top-performing team members, and/or be hindered by one or more struggling team members (i.e., the classic Wooden Bucket Theory, which says that "A bucket (whole) can only fill with the volume of water the shortest plank (parts) allows"). Moreover, the composing parts of the whole might not be independent with each other. In a networked system, the composing parts are connected with each other via an underlying network. Such part-part interdependency could have a profound impact on both the part outcome correlation as well as each part's contribution to the whole outcome. How can we mathematically encode the non-linear part-whole relationship as well as part-part interdependency? Second (*Algorithmic Challenge*), the complicated part-whole relationship (i.e., non-linearity and interdependency) also poses an algorithmic challenge, as it will inevitably increase the complexity of the corresponding optimization problem. How can we develop scalable algorithms whose theoretic properties are well-understood (e.g., the convergence, the optimality, and the complexity)?

To address these challenges, in this paper, we propose a joint predictive model named PAROLE to simultaneously and mutually predict the part and whole outcomes. First, *model generality*, the proposed model is flexible in admitting a variety of linear as well as non-linear relationships between the parts and whole outcomes, including *maximum aggregation, linear aggregation, sparse aggregation, ordered sparse aggregation* and *robust aggregation.* Moreover, it is able to characterize part-part interdependency via a graph-based regularization, which encourages the tightly connected parts to share similar outcomes as well as have similar effect on the whole outcome. Second, *algorithm efficacy*, we propose an effective and efficient block coordinate descent optimization algorithm, which converges to the coordinate-wise optimum with a linear complexity.

The main contributions of the paper can be summarized as follows:

Table 1: Table of symbols

Symbols	Definition
$\mathbf{F}^o, \mathbf{F}^p$	feature matrices for whole and part entities
$\mathbf{y}^o, \mathbf{y}^p$	impact vectors for whole and part entities
$\mathcal{O} = \{o_1, o_2, \ldots, o_{n_o}\}$	set of whole entities
$\mathcal{P} = \{p_1, p_2, \ldots, p_{n_p}\}$	set of part entities
$\phi(\cdot)$	whole to parts mapping function
G^p	the network connectivity among part entities
a_j^i	the contribution of part p_j to whole o_i
n_o/n_p	number of whole/part entities
$\text{Agg}(\cdot)$	the function that aggregates parts outcome
e_i	predicted whole outcome using whole feature vs. predicted whole outcome using aggregated parts outcome

- **Models.** We propose a joint predictive model (PAROLE) that is able to admit a variety of linear as well as non-linear part-whole relationships and encode the part-part interdependency.
- **Algorithms and Analysis.** We propose an effective and efficient block coordinate descent optimization algorithm that converges to the coordinate-wise optimum with a linear complexity in both time and space.
- **Empirical Evaluations.** We conduct extensive empirical studies on several real-world datasets and demonstrate that the proposed PAROLE achieves consistent prediction performance improvement and scales linearly. See Fig. 1 for some sampling results.

The rest of the paper is organized as follows. Section 2 formally defines the PART-WHOLE OUTCOME PREDICTION problem. Section 3 introduces the proposed PAROLE model and section 4 presents the optimization algorithm with analysis. The empirical evaluation results are given in Section 5. After reviewing related work in Section 6, we conclude the paper in Section 7.

2 PROBLEM DEFINITION

The main symbols are summarized in Table 1. We use bold capital letters (e.g., $\mathbf{A}$) for matrices and bold lowercase letters (e.g, $\mathbf{w}$) for vectors. We index the elements in a matrix using a convention similar to Matlab, e.g., $\mathbf{A}(:, j)$ is the jth column of $\mathbf{A}$, etc. The vector obtained by sorting the components in non-increasing order of $\mathbf{x}$ is denoted by $\mathbf{x}_{\downarrow}$. Such sorting operation can be defined by a permutation matrix $\mathbf{P_x}$, i.e., $\mathbf{P_x x} = \mathbf{x}_{\downarrow}$. We use $\mathcal{K}_{m+}$ to denote the *monotone non-negative cone*, i.e., $\mathcal{K}_{m+} = \{\mathbf{x} \in \mathbb{R}^n : x_1 \geq x_2 \geq \ldots x_n \geq 0\} \subset \mathbb{R}^n_+$. Similarly, we use $\mathcal{K}_m$ for the monotone cone.

We consider predicting the outcome for both the whole and their composing parts. Fig. 2 presents an illustrative example, which aims to predict the popularity (e.g., Facebook likes) of a particular movie (*whole*) and the popularities of the participating actors/actresses (*parts*). We denote the set of whole entities by $\mathcal{O} = \{o_1, o_2, \ldots, o_{n_o}\}$, and denote the set of part entities by $\mathcal{P} = \{p_1, p_2, \ldots, p_{n_p}\}$, where n_o and n_p are the number of the whole and parts, respectively. To specify the part-whole associations, we also define a mapping function ϕ that maps a whole entity to the set of its composing parts, e.g., $\phi(o_i) = \{p_{i_1}, p_{i_2}, \ldots, p_{i_{n_i}}\}$ (i.e., the edges between a movie and actors/actresses in Fig. 2). Note that the two sets $\phi(o_i)$ and $\phi(o_j)$ might have overlap. In the example of movies as whole entities, one actor could participate in multiple movies. Let $\mathbf{F}^o$ be the feature matrix for the whole entities, where the ith row $\mathbf{F}^o(i,:)$ is the feature vector for the ith whole entity. Similarly, let $\mathbf{F}^p$ be the feature matrix for the part entities, where the jth row $\mathbf{F}^p(j,:)$ is the feature vector for the jth part entity. The outcome vector of the whole entities is denoted as $\mathbf{y}^o$ and the outcome vector of the part entities is denoted as $\mathbf{y}^p$. In addition, we might also observe a network connectivity among the part entities, denoted as G^p. In the movie example, the network G^p could be the collaboration network among the actors/actresses (the connections among the actors/actresses in Fig. 2).

With the above notations, we formally define our Part-Whole Outcome Prediction problem as follows:

Problem 1. *Part-Whole Outcome Prediction*

Given: *the feature matrix for the whole/part entities* $\mathbf{F}^o/\mathbf{F}^p$*, the outcome vector for the whole/part entities* $\mathbf{y}^o/\mathbf{y}^p$*, the whole to part mapping function* ϕ*, and the parts' network* G^p *(optional);*

Predict: *the outcome of new whole and parts' entities.*

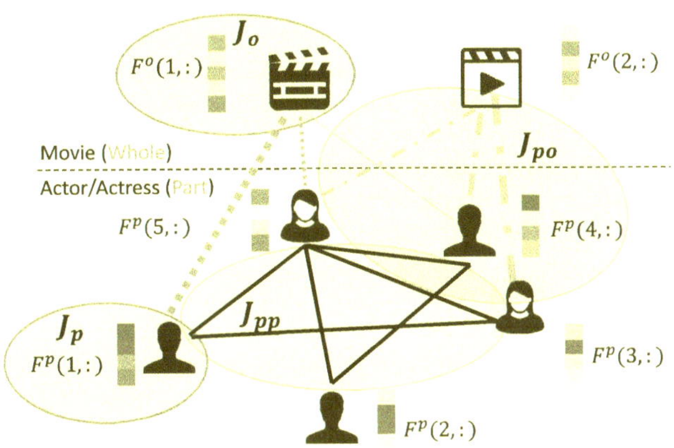

Figure 2: An illustrative example of part-whole outcome prediction where movies are the whole entities and the actors/actresses are the part entities. The four shadowed ellipses correspond to the key sub-objectives in our proposed PAROLE model (Eq. (1), Sec. 3.1.).

3 PROPOSED MODEL – PAROLE

In this section, we present our joint predictive model PAROLE to simultaneously and mutually predict the outcome of the whole and parts. We first formulate it as a generic optimization problem, and then present the details on how to instantiate the part-whole relationship and part-part interdependency, respectively.

3.1 A Generic Joint Prediction Framework

In order to fully embrace the complexity of the part-whole and part-part relationship, our joint predictive model should meet the following desiderata.

First (*part-whole relationship*), the outcome of the whole and that of the parts might be strongly correlated with each other. For example, the team outcome is usually a collective effort of the team members. Consequently, the team performance is likely to be correlated/coupled with each individual's productivity, which might be beyond a simple linear correlation. This is because a few top-performing team members might dominate the overall team performance, or reversely, a few struggling team members might drag down the performance of the entire team. Likewise, in scientific community, a scientist's reputation is generally built by one or a few of her highest-impact work. Our joint predictive model should have the capability to encode such non-linear part-whole relationships, so that the prediction of the parts outcome and that of the whole can mutually benefit from each other.

Second (*part-part interdependency*), the composing parts of a whole entity might be interdependent/interconnected via an underlying network, e.g., the collaboration network among the actors/actresses. The part-part interdependency could have a profound impact on the part-whole outcome prediction performance. That is, not only might the closely connected parts have similar effect on the whole outcome, but also these parts are very likely to share similar outcomes between themselves. Therefore, it is desirable to encode the part-part interdependency in the joint model to boost the prediction performance.

With these design objectives in mind, we propose a generic framework for the joint predictive model as follows:

$$\begin{aligned}
\min_{\mathbf{w}^o,\mathbf{w}^p} \mathcal{J} = & \underbrace{\frac{1}{n_o}\sum_{i=1}^{n_o}\mathcal{L}[f(\mathbf{F}^o(i,:),\mathbf{w}^o),\mathbf{y}^o(i))]}_{\mathcal{J}_o:\text{ predictive model for whole entities}} \\
& + \underbrace{\frac{1}{n_p}\sum_{i=1}^{n_p}\mathcal{L}[f(\mathbf{F}^p(i,:),\mathbf{w}^p),\mathbf{y}^p(i))]}_{\mathcal{J}_p:\text{ predictive model for part entities}} \\
& + \underbrace{\frac{\alpha}{n_o}\sum_{i=1}^{n_o}h(f(\mathbf{F}^o(i,:),\mathbf{w}^o),\mathrm{Agg}(\phi(o_i)))}_{\mathcal{J}_{po}:\text{ part-whole relationship}} \qquad (1) \\
& + \underbrace{\frac{\beta}{n_p}\sum_{i=1}^{n_p}\sum_{j=1}^{n_p}G^p_{ij}g(f(\mathbf{F}^p(i,:),\mathbf{w}^p),f(\mathbf{F}^p(j,:),\mathbf{w}^p))}_{\mathcal{J}_{pp}:\text{ part-part interdependency}} \\
& + \underbrace{\gamma(\Omega(\mathbf{w}^o)+\Omega(\mathbf{w}^p))}_{\mathcal{J}_r:\text{ parameter regularizer}}
\end{aligned}$$

where the objective function is a sum of five sub-objective functions. The first two sub-objectives $\mathcal{J}_o$ and $\mathcal{J}_p$ (the two blue shadowed ellipses in Fig. 2) minimize the training loss for whole and parts outcome predictions, where $f(\cdot,\cdot)$ is the prediction function parameterized by $\mathbf{w}^o$ and $\mathbf{w}^p$. The prediction function could be either linear or non-linear; and $\mathcal{L}(\cdot)$ is a loss function, e.g., squared loss for regression or logistic loss for classification. The core of the objective function is the third term $\mathcal{J}_{po}$ (the green shadowed ellipse in Fig. 2) and the fourth term $\mathcal{J}_{pp}$ (the pink shadowed ellipse in Fig. 2). $\mathcal{J}_{po}$ characterizes the part-whole relationship, where $\mathrm{Agg}(\cdot)$ is a function that aggregates the predicted outcomes of all the composing parts for the whole to a single outcome, e.g., maximum, summation/mean or more complicated aggregations; and $h(\cdot)$ function measures the correlation between the predicted whole outcome and the aggregated predicted parts outcome. In $\mathcal{J}_{pp}$, the function $g(\cdot)$ characterizes the relationship of the predicted outcomes of parts i and j based on their connectivity G^p_{ij}, such that tightly connected parts would share similar outcomes. Lastly, $\mathcal{J}_r$ regularizes $\mathbf{w}^o$ and $\mathbf{w}^p$ to prevent overfitting. The regularization parameters α, β and γ are used to balance the relative importance of each aspect.

Remarks: Depending on the specific choices of the aggregation function $\text{Agg}(\cdot)$ and the $h(\cdot)$ function, the proposed model in Eq. (1) is able to admit a variety of part-whole relationships, which we elaborate below.

3.2 Modeling Part-Whole Relationships

Overview. In this subsection, we give the instantiations for a variety of part-whole relationships. For each whole entity o_i, define e_i as follows:

$$e_i = \mathbf{F}^o(i,:)\mathbf{w}^o - \text{Agg}(o_i) \tag{2}$$

which measures the difference between the predicted whole outcome using whole features (i.e., $\mathbf{F}^o(i,:)\mathbf{w}^o$) and predicted whole outcome using aggregated parts outcome (i.e., $\text{Agg}(o_i)$). Our proposed model will be able to characterize a variety of part-whole relationship, by using (a) different aggregation functions $\text{Agg}(\cdot)$ with augmented regularizations; and (b) different loss functions on e_i (e.g., squared loss or robust estimator).

Maximum aggregation. Let us first consider using maximum as the aggregation function, which can model the correlation between the whole outcome and the maximum parts outcome. Given that the max function is not differentiable, we propose to approximate it with a differentiable function that will largely facilitate the optimization process. In details, we propose to use the smooth "soft" maximum function, which was first used in economic literature for consumer choice [17]: $\max(x_1, x_2, \ldots, x_n) \approx \ln(\exp(x_1)+\exp(x_2)+\ldots+\exp(x_n))$, where the maximum is approximated by summing up the exponential of each item followed by a logarithm. With this, we define the maximum aggregation function as follows:

$$\text{Agg}(o_i) = \ln\Big(\sum_{j\in\phi(o_i)} \exp(\mathbf{F}^p(j,:)\mathbf{w}^p)\Big) \tag{3}$$

which approximates the maximum predicted parts outcome. The part-whole relationship with maximum aggregation can be formulated as follows:

$$\mathcal{J}_{po} = \frac{\alpha}{2n_o}\sum_{i=1}^{n_o} e_i^2 \tag{4}$$

where we use the squared loss to measure the difference between the predicted whole outcome and the predicted approximated maximum parts outcome.

For the remaining part-whole relationships, we instantiate $\text{Agg}(o_i)$ using a linear function as follows:

$$\text{Agg}(o_i) = \sum_{j\in\phi(o_i)} a^i_j \mathbf{F}^p(j,:)\mathbf{w}^p \tag{5}$$

where each a^i_j is the weight of a particular part j's contribution to the whole o_i's outcome. Defining $\mathbf{a}_i$ as the vector whose components are a^i_j, $j \in \phi(o_i)$ and by imposing (i) different loss functions on e_i, and/or (ii) different norms on $\mathbf{a}_i$, we can model either linear or nonlinear part-whole relationships.

Linear aggregation. In this scenario, the whole outcome is a weighted linear combination of the parts outcome, where the weights determine each individual part's contribution to the whole outcome. The intuition of linear aggregation is that , in contributing to the final whole outcome, some parts play more important roles than the others. This part-whole relationship can be formulated as follows:

$$\mathcal{J}_{po} = \frac{\alpha}{2n_o}\sum_{i=1}^{n_o} e_i^2 \tag{6}$$

where we use the squared loss to measure the difference between the whole outcome and the aggregated parts outcome.

Remark: this formulation generalizes several special part-whole relationships. The expression that "*the whole is the sum of its parts*" is a special case of Eq. (6) where various a^i_j is 1, which we refer to as *Sum* in the empirical study. The average coupling formulated in [23] is also its special case with $a^i_j = \frac{1}{|o_i|}$. Instead of fixing the weights, Eq. (6) allows the model to learn to what extent each part contributes to the prediction of the whole outcome. Nonetheless, in all these variants, we have assumed that the part outcomes always have a *linear* effect on the whole outcome.

Sparse aggregation. The above linear aggregation assumes that each part would contribute to the whole outcome, which might not be the case as some parts have little or no effect on the whole outcome. This scenario can be seen in large teams, where the team performance could be primarily determined by a few members, who could either make or break the team performance. To encourage such a sparse selection among the composing parts of a whole entity, a natural choice is to introduce the l_1 norm on the vector $\mathbf{a}_i$ [18]:

$$\mathcal{J}_{po} = \frac{\alpha}{n_o}\sum_{i=1}^{n_o}\Big(\frac{1}{2}e_i^2 + \lambda|\mathbf{a}_i|_1\Big) \tag{7}$$

where the l_1 norm can shrink some part contributions to exactly zero and the parameter λ controls the degree of sparsity.

Ordered sparse aggregation. In some cases, the team performance (i.e., the whole outcome) is determined by not only a few key members, but also the structural hierarchy between such key members within the organization. To model such parts performance ranking in addition to the sparse selection, we adopt the ordered weighted l_1 norm (OWL) [25] that is able to give more weights to those parts with bigger effect on the whole outcome. Such part-whole relationship can be formulated as follows:

$$\mathcal{J}_{po} = \frac{\alpha}{n_o}\sum_{i=1}^{n_o}\Big(\frac{1}{2}e_i^2 + \lambda\Omega_{\mathbf{w}}(\mathbf{a}_i)\Big) \tag{8}$$

where $\Omega_{\mathbf{w}}(\mathbf{x}) = \sum_{i=1}^{n} |x|_{[i]} w_i = \mathbf{w}^T|\mathbf{x}|_\downarrow$ is the ordered weighted l_1 norm, where $|x|_{[i]}$ is the i-th largest component of the vector $|\mathbf{x}|$ and $\mathbf{w} \in \mathcal{K}_{m+}$ is a vector of non-increasing non-negative weights.

Robust aggregation. In all the above formulations, we model the difference between the whole outcome and the aggregated parts outcome using squared loss, which is prone to outlying parts/wholes.

To address this issue, we employ robust regression models [9] to reduce the effect of outliers as follows:

$$\mathcal{J}_{po} = \frac{\alpha}{n_o}\sum_{i=1}^{n_o}\rho(e_i) \tag{9}$$

where $\rho(\cdot)$ is a nonnegative and symmetric function that gives the contribution of each residual e_i to the objective function. In this paper, we consider two robust estimators, namely Huber and Bisquare estimators as follows:

Method \ Case	$\lvert e\rvert \le t$	$\lvert e\rvert > t$
Huber $\rho_H(e)$	$\frac{1}{2}e^2$	$t\lvert e\rvert - \frac{1}{2}t^2$
Bisquare $\rho_B(e)$	$\frac{t^2}{6}\{1-[1-(\frac{e}{t})^2]^3\}$	$\frac{t^2}{6}$

where the value t is a tuning constant. Smaller t values have more resistance to outliers.

3.3 Modeling Part-Part Interdependency

As mentioned in Sec. 3.1, the part-part interdependency, if exists, can play two roles in the part-whole outcome predictions, i.e., closely connected parts would (A) have similar effect on the whole outcome and (B) share similar part outcomes between themselves.

A - The effect on the whole outcome: the closely connected parts might have similar impact on the whole outcome. It turns out we can use the same method to model such a part-part effect for various aggregation methods in Sec. 3.2. Let us take *sparse aggregation* as an example and instantiate the term $\mathcal{J}_{po}$ in Eq. (1) as follows:

$$\mathcal{J}_{po} = \frac{\alpha}{n_o}\sum_{i=1}^{n_o}\left[\frac{1}{2}e_i^2 + \lambda\lvert \mathbf{a}_i\rvert_1 + \frac{1}{2}\sum_{k,l\in\phi(o_i)} G^p_{kl}(a^i_k - a^i_l)^2\right] \tag{10}$$

where if the two parts k and l of o_i are tightly connected, i.e., $G^p_{k,l}$ is large, then the difference between their impacts on the whole outcome, a^i_k and a^i_l, is small.

B - The effect on the parts' outcomes: the tightly connected parts might share similar outcomes themselves. Such parts outcome similarity can be instantiated by a graph regularization as follows:

$$\mathcal{J}_{pp} = \frac{\beta}{2n_p}\sum_{i=1}^{n_p}\sum_{j=1}^{n_p} G^p_{ij}(\mathbf{F}^p(i,:)\mathbf{w}^p - \mathbf{F}^p(j,:)\mathbf{w}^p)^2 \tag{11}$$

where tightly connected two parts i and j with large $G^p_{k,l}$ is encouraged to be closer to each other in the output space, i.e., with similar predicted outcomes.

4 OPTIMIZATION ALGORITHM

In this section, we propose an effective and efficient block coordinate descent optimization algorithm to solve the joint prediction framework in Eq. (1), followed by the convergence and complexity analysis.

4.1 Block Coordinate Descent Algorithm

The proposed Eq. (1) is general, being able to admit a variety of different separate models ($\mathcal{J}_o$ and $\mathcal{J}_p$) as well as part-whole relationship ($\mathcal{J}_{po}$). Let us first present our algorithm to solve a specific instance of Eq. (1) by instantiating it using linear predictive functions, squared loss and sparse aggregation as follows:

$$\begin{aligned}\min_{\mathbf{w}^o,\mathbf{w}^p} & \frac{1}{2n_o}\sum_{i=1}^{n_o}(\mathbf{F}^o(i,:)\mathbf{w}^o - \mathbf{y}^o(i))^2 + \frac{1}{2n_p}\sum_{i=1}^{n_p}((\mathbf{F}^p(i,:)\mathbf{w}^p - \mathbf{y}^p(i))^2 \\ & + \frac{\beta}{2n_p}\sum_{i=1}^{n_p}\sum_{j=1}^{n_p} G^p_{ij}(\mathbf{F}^p(i,:)\mathbf{w}^p - \mathbf{F}^p(j,:)\mathbf{w}^p)^2 + \frac{\gamma}{2}(\lVert\mathbf{w}^o\rVert_2^2 + \lVert\mathbf{w}^p\rVert_2^2) \\ & + \frac{\alpha}{n_o}\sum_{i=1}^{n_o}\left[\frac{1}{2}e_i^2 + \lambda\lvert\mathbf{a}_i\rvert_1 + \frac{1}{2}\sum_{k,l\in\phi(o_i)} G^p_{kl}(a^i_k - a^i_l)^2\right]\end{aligned} \tag{12}$$

In the formulation, we identify three coordinate blocks, namely $\mathbf{w}^o$, $\mathbf{w}^p$ and various a^i_j. We propose a block coordinate descent (BCD) algorithm to optimize Eq. (12) by updating one coordinate block while fixing the other two.

1. Updating $\mathbf{w}^o$ while fixing others: Observing that only $\mathcal{J}_o$, $\mathcal{J}_{po}$ and $\mathcal{J}_r$ are functions of $\mathbf{w}^o$, we have

$$\begin{aligned}\frac{\partial\mathcal{J}}{\partial\mathbf{w}^o} &= \frac{\partial\mathcal{J}_o}{\partial\mathbf{w}^o} + \frac{\partial\mathcal{J}_{po}}{\partial\mathbf{w}^o} + \frac{\partial\mathcal{J}_r}{\partial\mathbf{w}^o} \\ &= \frac{1}{n_o}(\mathbf{F}^o)'(\mathbf{F}^o\mathbf{w}^o - \mathbf{y}^o) + \gamma\mathbf{w}^o + \frac{\alpha}{n_o}(\mathbf{F}^o)'(\mathbf{F}^o\mathbf{w}^o - \mathbf{M}\mathbf{F}^p\mathbf{w}^p)\end{aligned} \tag{13}$$

where $\mathbf{M}$ is a n_o by n_p sparse matrix with $\mathbf{M}(i,j) = a^i_j$, for $j \in \phi(o_i)$. We then update $\mathbf{w}^o$ as $\mathbf{w}^o \leftarrow \mathbf{w}^o - \tau\frac{\partial\mathcal{J}}{\partial\mathbf{w}^o}$, where τ is the step size.

2. Updating $\mathbf{w}^p$ while fixing others: The sub-objective functions that are related to $\mathbf{w}^p$ are $\mathcal{J}_p$, $\mathcal{J}_{pp}$, $\mathcal{J}_{po}$ and $\mathcal{J}_r$. Therefore,

$$\begin{aligned}\frac{\partial\mathcal{J}}{\partial\mathbf{w}^p} &= \frac{\partial\mathcal{J}_p}{\partial\mathbf{w}^p} + \frac{\partial\mathcal{J}_{pp}}{\partial\mathbf{w}^p} + \frac{\partial\mathcal{J}_{po}}{\partial\mathbf{w}^p} + \frac{\partial\mathcal{J}_r}{\partial\mathbf{w}^p} \\ &= \frac{1}{n_p}(\mathbf{F}^p)'(\mathbf{F}^p\mathbf{w}^p - \mathbf{y}^p) + \frac{\beta}{n_p}(\mathbf{F}^p)'\mathcal{L}^p\mathbf{F}^p\mathbf{w}^p + \gamma\mathbf{w}^p \\ &\quad - \frac{\alpha}{n_o}(\mathbf{F}^p)'\mathbf{M}'(\mathbf{F}^o\mathbf{w}^o - \mathbf{M}\mathbf{F}^p\mathbf{w}^p)\end{aligned} \tag{14}$$

where $\mathcal{L}^p$ is the Laplacian of the graph G^p [1]. Similarly, $\mathbf{w}^p$ can be updated by $\mathbf{w}^p \leftarrow \mathbf{w}^p - \tau\frac{\partial\mathcal{J}}{\partial\mathbf{w}^p}$.

3. Updating a^i_j while fixing others: Let us fix a whole o_i and the sub-problem with respect to $\mathbf{a}_i$ becomes:

$$\min_{\mathbf{a}_i}\frac{1}{2}e_i^2 + \lambda\lvert\mathbf{a}_i\rvert_1 + \frac{1}{2}\sum_{k,l\in\phi(o_i)} G^p_{kl}(a^i_k - a^i_l)^2 \tag{15}$$

Observing that the sub-problem is a composite of a non-smooth convex function ($\lambda\lvert\mathbf{a}_i\rvert_1$) and a differentiable convex function (the remaining terms), we update $\mathbf{a}_i$ using the proximal gradient descent method [2]. We first take a gradient step by moving $\mathbf{a}_i$ along the negative direction of the derivative of the smooth part w.r.t. $\mathbf{a}_i$, as follows:

$$\mathbf{z} = \mathbf{a}_i - \tau[e_i(-\mathbf{F}^p(\phi(o_i),:)\mathbf{w}^p) + \mathcal{L}^p_i\mathbf{a}_i] \tag{16}$$

where $\mathcal{L}^p_i$ is a shorthand notation for the Laplacian of the subgraph $G^p(\phi(o_i),\phi(o_i))$. Next, we compute the proximal-gradient update for the l_1 norm using soft-thresholding as $\mathbf{a}_i \leftarrow \mathcal{S}_{\tau\lambda}(\mathbf{z})$, where the soft-thresholding operator is defined as follows:

$$[\mathcal{S}_t(\mathbf{z})]_j = \text{sign}(\mathbf{z}_j)(\lvert\mathbf{z}_j\rvert - t)_+, \tag{17}$$

where we use $(x)_+$ as a shorthand for $\max\{x, 0\}$.

We will cycle through the above three steps to update the three coordinate blocks until convergence. The algorithm is summarized in Algorithm 1.

Algorithm 1 PAROLE - Part-Whole Outcome Predictions

Input: (1) the feature matrix for whole/part entities $\mathbf{F}^o/\mathbf{F}^p$,
(2) outcome vector for the whole/part entities $\mathbf{y}^o/\mathbf{y}^p$,
(3) the whole to parts mapping function ϕ,
(4) the part-part network G^p (optional),
(5) parameters $\alpha, \beta, \gamma, \lambda, \tau$.
Output: Model parameters $\mathbf{w}^o$ and $\mathbf{w}^p$.
Initialize $\mathbf{w}^o$ and $\mathbf{w}^p$ and $a_j, j \in \phi(o_i), i = 1, \dots, n_o$
while Not converged **do**
  Update $\mathbf{w}^o \leftarrow \mathbf{w}^o - \tau \frac{\partial \mathcal{J}}{\partial \mathbf{w}^o}$
  Update $\mathbf{w}^p \leftarrow \mathbf{w}^p - \tau \frac{\partial \mathcal{J}}{\partial \mathbf{w}^p}$
  Update $\mathbf{a}_i$ via proximal gradient descent for $i = 1, \dots, n_o$

Remarks: we want to emphasize that Algorithm 1 provides a general optimization framework that not only works for the formulation with *sparse aggregation* in Eq. (12), but is also applicable to the other part-whole relationships introduced in Sec. 3.2. The only difference is that, since $\mathcal{J}_{po}$ varies for each part-whole relationship, its derivatives w.r.t. the coordinate blocks would also change. Next, for each of the other part-whole relationships, we give their derivative or proximal gradient w.r.t. the three coordinate blocks.

1. Maximum aggregation: the derivatives of $\mathcal{J}_{po}$ w.r.t. $\mathbf{w}^o$ and $\mathbf{w}^p$ are as follows:

$$\frac{\partial \mathcal{J}_{po}}{\partial \mathbf{w}^o} = \frac{\alpha}{n_o} \sum_{i=1}^{n_o} e_i (\mathbf{F}^o(i,:))'$$

$$\frac{\partial \mathcal{J}_{po}}{\partial \mathbf{w}^p} = \frac{\alpha}{n_o} \sum_{i=1}^{n_o} e_i \cdot \frac{\sum_{j \in \phi(o_i)} (\mathbf{F}^p(j,:))' \tilde{\mathbf{y}}_i^p}{\sum_{j \in \phi(o_i)} \tilde{\mathbf{y}}_i^p}$$

where we denote $\tilde{\mathbf{y}}_i^p = \exp(\mathbf{F}^p(j,:)\mathbf{w}^p)$.

2. Linear aggregation: the derivatives of $\mathcal{J}_{po}$ w.r.t. $\mathbf{w}^o$ and $\mathbf{w}^p$ are the same as in the *sparse aggregation* case. Its derivative w.r.t. $\mathbf{a}_i$ is same as in Eq. (16) without the following proximal-gradient update.

3. Ordered sparse aggregation: the only difference from the *sparse aggregation* lies in the proximal-gradient update for the OWL norm, which can be computed as follows [25]:

$$\text{prox}_{\Omega_\mathbf{w}}(\mathbf{v}) = \text{sign}(\mathbf{v}) \odot \left(\mathbf{P}_{|\mathbf{v}|}^T \text{proj}_{\mathbb{R}_+^n}(\text{proj}_{\mathcal{K}_m}(|\mathbf{v}|_\downarrow - \mathbf{w}))\right) \quad (18)$$

In the above equation, to compute $\text{prox}_{\Omega_\mathbf{w}}(\mathbf{v})$, we first compute the Euclidean project of $(|\mathbf{v}|_\downarrow - \mathbf{w})$ onto $\mathcal{K}_m$ using the linear time *pool adjacent violators* (PAV) algorithm [16]. This is followed by a projection onto the first orthant by a clipping operation. The resulting vector is sorted back according to the permutation matrix $\mathbf{P}_{|\mathbf{v}|}$ and then element-wisely multiplied by the signs of $\mathbf{v}$.

4. Robust aggregation: we compute the gradient of $\mathcal{J}_{po}$ using chain rule as follows:

$$\frac{\partial \mathcal{J}_{po}}{\partial \mathbf{w}^o} = \frac{\alpha}{n_o} \sum_{i=1}^{n_o} \frac{\partial \rho(e_i)}{\partial e_i} \frac{\partial e_i}{\partial \mathbf{w}^o}, \quad \frac{\partial \mathcal{J}_{po}}{\partial \mathbf{w}^p} = \frac{\alpha}{n_o} \sum_{i=1}^{n_o} \frac{\partial \rho(e_i)}{\partial e_i} \frac{\partial e_i}{\partial \mathbf{w}^p}$$

$$\frac{\partial \mathcal{J}_{po}}{\partial \mathbf{a}_i} = \frac{\alpha}{n_o} [\frac{\partial \rho(e_i)}{\partial e_i} \frac{\partial e_i}{\partial \mathbf{a}_i} + \mathcal{L}_i^p \mathbf{a}_i]$$

where $\frac{\partial e_i}{\partial \mathbf{w}^o} = \mathbf{F}^o(i,:)'$, $\frac{\partial e_i}{\partial \mathbf{w}^p} = -\sum_{j \in \phi(o_i)} a_j \mathbf{F}^p(j,:)'$, and $\frac{\partial e_i}{\partial \mathbf{a}_i} = -\mathbf{F}^p(\phi(o_i),:)\mathbf{w}^p$; and the gradient of the Huber and Bisquare estimator can be computed as follows:

Method \ Case	$\lvert e \rvert \le t$	$\lvert e \rvert > t$
Huber $\frac{\partial \rho_H(e)}{\partial e}$	e	$t \cdot \text{sign}(e)$
Bisquare $\frac{\partial \rho_B(e)}{\partial e}$	$e[1-(e/t)^2]^2$	0

4.2 Proofs and Analysis

In this subsection, we analyze the proposed PAROLE algorithm in terms of its convergence, optimality and complexity.

First, building upon the proposition from [19], we have the following theorem regarding the proposed Algorithm 1, which says that under a mild assumption, it converges to a local optimum (i.e., coordinate-wise minimum) of Eq. (12).

THEOREM 4.1. *(Convergence and Optimality of PAROLE). As long as $-\gamma$ is not an eigenvalue of $\frac{\alpha+1}{n_o}\mathbf{F}^{o'}\mathbf{F}^o$ or $\frac{1}{n_p}\mathbf{F}^{p'}\mathbf{F}^p + \beta\mathbf{F}^{p'}\mathcal{L}^p\mathbf{F}^p + \frac{\alpha}{n_o}\mathbf{F}^p\mathbf{M}'\mathbf{M}\mathbf{F}^p$, Algorithm 1 converges to a coordinate-wise minimum point.*

PROOF. Omitted for brevity. □

Next, we analyze the complexity of Algorithm 1, which is summarized in Lemma 4.2.

LEMMA 4.2. *(Complexity of PAROLE). Algorithm 1 takes $O(T(n_o d_o + n_p d_p + m_{po} + m_{pp}))$ time for linear aggregation, maximum aggregation, sparse aggregation, and robust aggregation, and it takes $O(T(n_o d_o + n_p d_p + C n_p d_p + m_{pp}))$ for ordered sparse aggregation, where d_o and d_p are the dimensionality of the whole and part feature vectors, $m_{po} = \sum_i |\phi(o_i)|$ is the number of associations between the whole and parts and m_{pp} is the number of edges in the part-part network, T is the number of iterations, $C = \max_i \log(|\phi(o_i)|)$ is a constant. The space complexity for Algorithm 1 is $O(n_o d_o + n_p d_p + m_{po} + m_{pp})$ for all the part-whole relationships.*

PROOF. Omitted for brevity. □

Remarks: suppose we have a conceptual part-whole graph $G = \{\mathcal{O}, \mathcal{P}\}$, which has n_o nodes for the whole entities and n_p nodes for the part entities, m_{po} links from whole nodes to their composing parts nodes and m_{pp} links in the part-part networks. The Lemma 4.2 says that PAROLE scales linearly w.r.t. the size of this part-whole graph in both time and space.

Table 2: Summary of Datasets.

Data	Whole	Part	# of whole	# of part
Math	Question	Answer	16,638	32,876
SO	Question	Answer	1,966,272	4,282,570
DBLP	Author	Paper	234,681	129,756
Movie	Movie	Actors/Actresses	5,043	37,365

5 EXPERIMENTS

In this section, we present the empirical evaluation results. The experiments are designed to evaluate the following aspects:

- *Effectiveness:* how accurate is the proposed PAROLE algorithm for predicting the outcomes of parts and whole?
- *Efficiency:* how fast and scalable is the proposed PAROLE algorithm?

5.1 Datasets

The real-world datasets used for evaluations are as follows:

CQA. We use Mathematics Stack Exchange (*Math*) and Stack Overflow (*SO*) data from [23]. The questions are whole and answers are parts both with voting scores as outcome. For each question, we treat all the answers it receives as its composing parts. The extracted features are described in [23].

DBLP. DBLP dataset provides the bibliographic information of computer science research papers. We treat authors as whole with h-index as outcome and papers as parts with citation counts as outcome. For each author, his/her composing parts are the papers s/he has co-authored. Paper features include temporal attributes and author features include productivity and social attributes.

Movie. We crawl the metadata of 5,043 movies with budget information[2] from IMDb website. The meta information includes movie title, genres, cast, budget, etc. We treat movies as whole and the actors/actresses as parts both with the number of Facebook likes as the outcome. For each movie, we treat its cast as the composing parts. Movie features include contextual attributes and actors/actresses features include productivity and social attributes.

The statistics of these datasets are summarized in Table 2. For each dataset, we first sort the whole in chronological order, gather the first x percent of whole and their corresponding parts as training examples and always test on the last 10% percent of whole and their corresponding parts. The percentage of training x could vary. The root mean squared error (RMSE) between the actual outcomes and the predicted ones is adopted for effectiveness evaluation. The parameters are set for each method on each dataset via a grid search.

Repeatability of experimental results: all the datasets are publicly available. We will release the datasets and code of the proposed algorithms through authors' website after the paper is published. The experiments are performed on a Windows machine with four 3.5GHz Intel Cores and 256GB RAM.

5.2 Effectiveness Results

We compare the effectiveness of the following methods:

(1) *Separate:* train a linear regression model for parts and whole separately.
(2) *Sum:* a joint model with Sum part-whole relationship.
(3) *Linear:* our PAROLE with linear aggregation.
(4) *Max:* our PAROLE with maximum aggregation.
(5) *Huber:* our PAROLE with robust Huber estimator.
(6) *Bisquare:* our PAROLE with robust Bisquare estimator.
(7) *Lasso:* our PAROLE with sparse aggregation.
(8) *OWL:* our PAROLE with ordered sparse aggregation.

A - Outcome prediction performance: the RMSE results of all the comparison methods for predicting the outcomes of parts and whole on all the datasets are shown from Fig. 3 to Fig. 6. We draw several interesting observations from these results. First, all the joint prediction models outperform the separate model in most cases, which suggests that the part outcome indeed has a profound impact on the whole outcome, and vice versa. Second, among the joint prediction models, in general, the linear methods (*Sum* and *Linear*) are not as good as the non-linear counterparts (*Max, Huber, Bisqaure, Lasso* and *OWL*), and in some cases (Fig. 3b, Fig. 5b), the linear joint models are even worse than the separate method, which indicates that the part-whole relationship is indeed more complicated than the linear aggregation. Third, among the non-linear methods, a consistent observation across all the datasets is that *Lasso* and *OWL* are the best two methods in almost all the cases. This suggests that the whole outcome is mostly dominated by a few, often high-performing, parts.

B - The effect of part-part interdependency: in the proposed joint prediction model, we have hypothesized that the part-part interdependency might help boost the predictions in two ways, i.e., regularizing the parts' contribution to the whole outcome as well as part outcome correlation. Here, we verify and validate to what extent these two aspects contribute to the performance gain, when such part-part interdependency information is available. Fig. 7 shows the results of *Lasso* on the *Movie* dataset with 50% training data. The network among the parts, i.e., actors/actresses, is their collaboration network. The "PAROLE-Basic" does not use the network information. The "PAROLE-GraphForWhole" applies the graph regularization on the parts' contribution to the whole, which brings a 8% overall prediction error reduction. On top of that, "PAROLE-GraphForWhole&Parts" uses the graph regularization on the parts' outcome, which brings a 14.5% decrease in the overall prediction error.

C - Convergence analysis: Fig. 8 shows the objective function value vs. the number of iterations on the *SO* dataset using *OWL* with 5% training data. As we can see, the proposed PAROLE algorithm coverges very fast, after 25-30 iterations.

D - Sensitivity analysis: to investigate the parameter sensitivity, we perform parametric studies with the two most important parameters in PAROLE, i.e., α that controls the importance of part-whole relationship and β that controls the importance of part-part interdependency on the parts outcome. The bowl shaped surface in Fig. 9 suggests that the proposed model can achieve good performance in a large volumn of the parameter space.

5.3 Efficiency Results

Fig. 10 shows the running time of all the proposed methods with varying size of training data ($n_o + n_p + m_{po}$). We can see that all the proposed methods scale linearly, which is consistent with Lemma 4.2. *OWL* takes the longest time due to the additional sorting operation in the proximal-gradient update for the OWL norm.

[2] http://www.the-numbers.com/movie/budgets/all

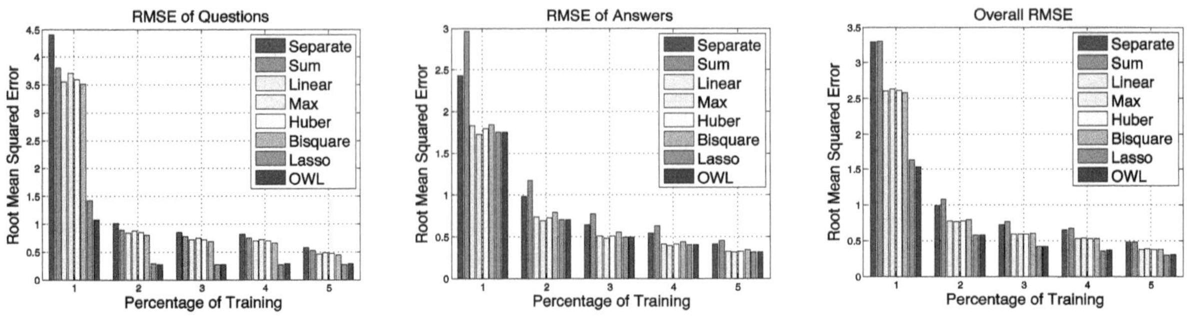

(a) RMSE of question outcome prediction. (b) RMSE of answer outcome prediction. (c) Overall RMSE.

Figure 3: RMSE comparisons on *Math*. Best viewed in color. From left to right: *Separate, Sum, Linear, Max, Huber, Bisquare, Lasso* and *OWL*.

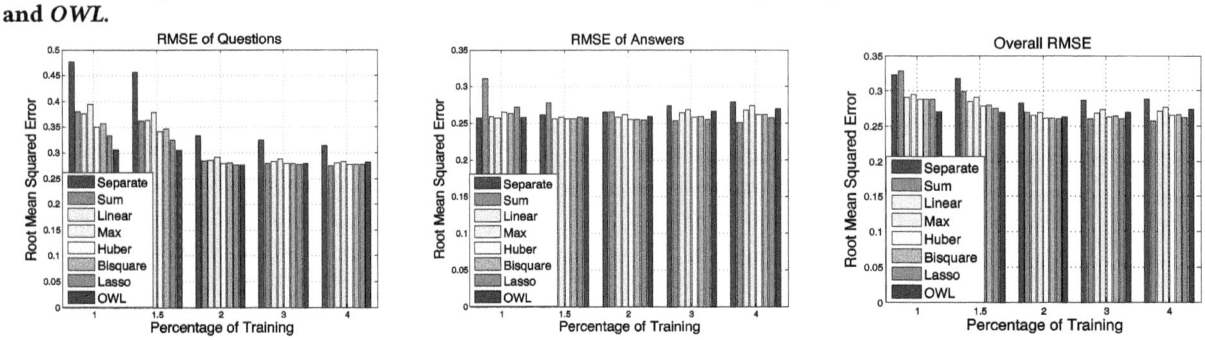

(a) RMSE of question outcome prediction. (b) RMSE of answer outcome prediction. (c) Overall RMSE.

Figure 4: RMSE comparisons on *SO*. Best viewed in color. From left to right: *Separate, Sum, Linear, Max, Huber, Bisquare, Lasso* and *OWL*.

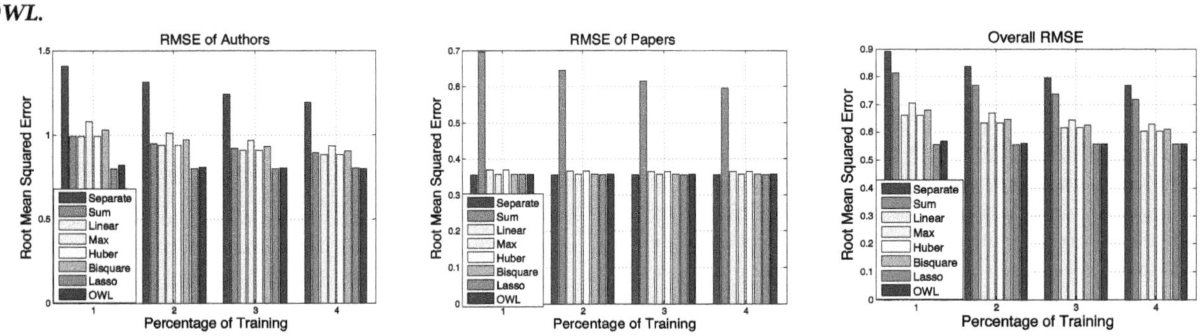

(a) RMSE of author outcome prediction. (b) RMSE of paper outcome prediction. (c) Overall RMSE.

Figure 5: RMSE comparisons on *DBLP*. Best viewed in color. From left to right: *Separate, Sum, Linear, Max, Huber, Bisquare, Lasso* and *OWL*.

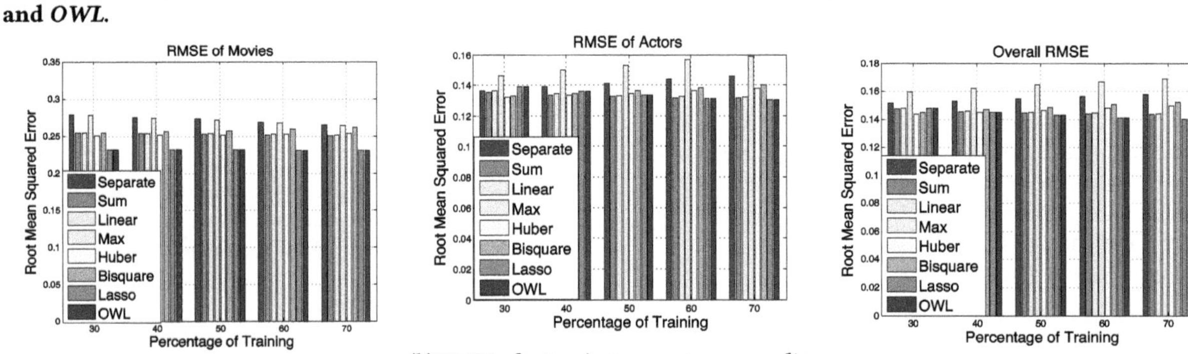

(a) RMSE of movie outcome prediction. (b) RMSE of actors/actress outcome prediction. (c) Overall RMSE.

Figure 6: RMSE comparisons on *Moive*. Best viewed in color. From left to right: *Separate, Sum, Linear, Max, Huber, Bisquare, Lasso* and *OWL*.

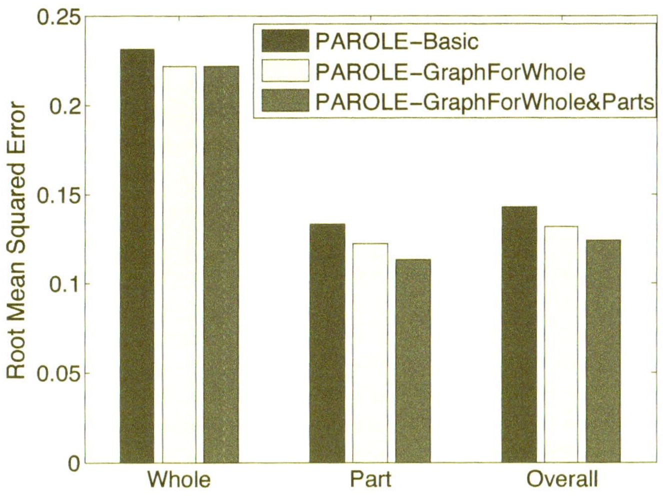

Figure 7: Performance gain analysis on *Movie.*

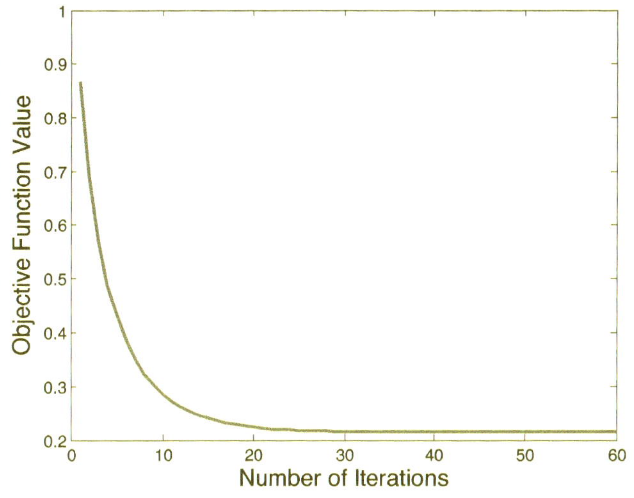

Figure 8: Convergence analysis on *SO.*

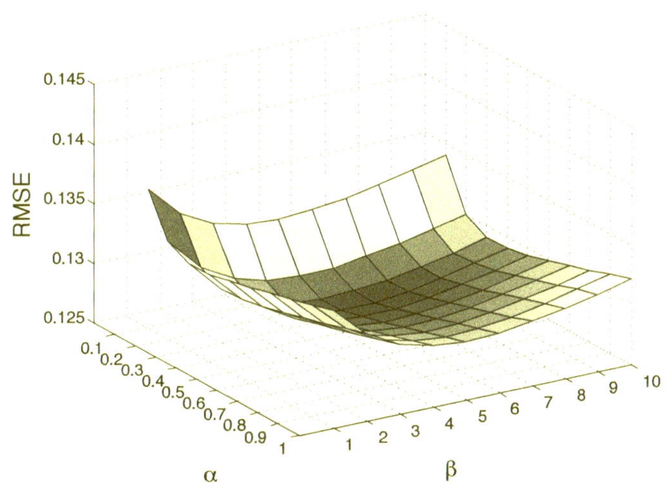

Figure 9: RMSE with varying α and β of *Lasso* on *Movie.*

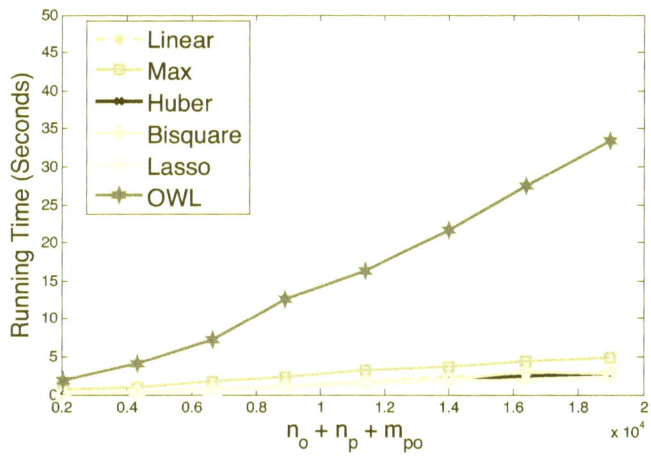

Figure 10: Scalability plot on *SO.*

6 RELATED WORK

Very few studies have quantitatively examined the part-whole relationships for the purpose of prediction. In CQA sites, empirical studies have shown a strong correlation between the question voting score and the average/maximum answer voting score [22]. Based on this observation, a joint predictive model that leverages question/answer coupling is proposed that is also able to capture the dynamics of the community posts [23]. Related to the part-whole relationship, there is a large body of literature on the collaborative teams. Along the line of team outcome prediction, the iBall [10] model focuses on the long-term impact forecasting of scholarly entities that exploits domain heterogeneity; going beyond the point prediction, the iPath [14] model aims to predict the pathway to impact. Though all the above predictive models can admit non-linear prediction functions for each separate model, they still assume a *linear* relationship between different models (e.g., part vs. whole).

On team formation and outcome optimization, the seminal work in [8] aims to form a team that can cover the required skill sets with strong team cohesion. Some recent work has been focusing on finding a good candidate to replace a team member [11] and enhance the team performance by allowing several enhancement operations, including refinement and expansion [13]. A visual interactive system is developed allowing users to explore and optimize teams [3, 12]. From the multi-task learning [6, 21] perspective, our method explicitly models two types of potentially non-linear task relatedness, i.e., part-whole relationship and part-part interdependency.

7 CONCLUSION

In this paper, we propose a joint predictive model PAROLE to simultaneously and mutually predict the parts and whole outcomes. First, *model generality*, the proposed model is able to (i) admit a variety of linear as well as non-linear relationship between the parts and whole outcome and (ii) characterize part-part interdependency. Second, *algorithm efficacy*, we propose an effective and efficient block coordinate descent optimization algorithm that converges to the coordinate-wise optimum with a linear complexity in both time and space. The empirical evaluations on real-world datasets demonstrate that (i) by modeling the non-linear part-whole relationship and part-part interdependency, the proposed method leads to consistent prediction performance improvement, and (ii) the proposed algorithm scales linearly w.r.t. the size of the training data. In the future, we would like to explore the dynamics of the proposed model as well as the hierarchy in the parts (i.e., the parts of the parts).

8 ACKNOWLEDGMENTS

This work is supported by National Science Foundation under Grant No. IIS-1651203, DTRA under the grant number HDTRA1-16-0017, Army Research Office under the contract number W911NF-16-1-0168, National Institutes of Health under the grant number R01LM011986, Region II University Transportation Center under the project number 49997-33 25, NSFC grant no. 61602306 and a Baidu gift.

REFERENCES

[1] Rie K Ando and Tong Zhang. 2006. Learning on Graph with Laplacian Regularization. In *NIPS*. 25–32.

[2] Amir Beck and Marc Teboulle. 2009. A fast iterative shrinkage-thresholding algorithm for linear inverse problems. *SIAM journal on imaging sciences* 2, 1 (2009), 183–202.

[3] Nan Cao, Yu-Ru Lin, Liangyue Li, and Hanghang Tong. 2015. g-Miner: Interactive Visual Group Mining on Multivariate Graphs. In *CHI*. 279–288.

[4] Chen Chen, Hanghang Tong, Lei Xie, Lei Ying, and Qing He. 2016. FASCINATE: Fast Cross-Layer Dependency Inference on Multi-layered Networks. In *KDD (KDD '16)*. 765–774.

[5] Aaron Clauset, Daniel B. Larremore, and Roberta Sinatra. 2017. Data-driven predictions in the science of science. *Science* 355, 6324 (2017), 477–480.

[6] Theodoros Evgeniou and Massimiliano Pontil. 2004. Regularized Multi-task Learning. In *KDD*. 109–117.

[7] Barbara R. Jasny and Richard Stone. 2017. Prediction and its limits. *Science* 355, 6324 (2017), 468–469. DOI: http://dx.doi.org/10.1126/science.355.6324.468

[8] Theodoros Lappas, Kun Liu, and Evimaria Terzi. 2009. Finding a team of experts in social networks. In *KDD*. ACM, 467–476.

[9] Kenneth D. Lawrence and Jeffrey L. Arthur. 1990. *Robust regression: analysis and applications*. Marcel Dekker Inc, New York.

[10] Liangyue Li and Hanghang Tong. 2015. The Child is Father of the Man: Foresee the Success at the Early Stage. In *KDD*. 655–664.

[11] Liangyue Li, Hanghang Tong, Nan Cao, Kate Ehrlich, Yu-Ru Lin, and Norbou Buchler. 2015. Replacing the Irreplaceable: Fast Algorithms for Team Member Recommendation. In *WWW*. 636–646.

[12] Liangyue Li, Hanghang Tong, Nan Cao, Kate Ehrlich, Yu-Ru Lin, and Norbou Buchler. 2016. TEAMOPT: Interactive Team Optimization in Big Networks. In *CIKM*. 2485–2487.

[13] Liangyue Li, Hanghang Tong, Nan Cao, Kate Ehrlich, Yu-Ru Lin, and Norbou Buchler. 2016. Enhancing Team Composition in Professional Networks: Problem Definitions and Fast Solutions. *TKDE* (2016).

[14] Liangyue Li, Hanghang Tong, Jie Tang, and Wei Fan. 2016. *iPath*: Forecasting the Pathway to Impact. In *SDM*. 468–476.

[15] Liwei Liu and Erdong Zhao. 2011. Team Performance and Individual Performance: Example from Engineering Consultancy Company in China. In *2011 International Conference on Management and Service Science*. 1–4.

[16] Patrick Mair, Kurt Hornik, and Jan de Leeuw. 2009. Isotone optimization in R: pool-adjacent-violators algorithm (PAVA) and active set methods. *Journal of statistical software* 32, 5 (2009), 1–24.

[17] David Schmeidler. 1989. Subjective probability and expected utility without additivity. *Econometrica: Journal of the Econometric Society* (1989), 571–587.

[18] Robert Tibshirani. 1996. Regression shrinkage and selection via the lasso. *Journal of the Royal Statistical Society. Series B (Methodological)* (1996), 267–288.

[19] Paul Tseng. 2001. Convergence of a block coordinate descent method for nondifferentiable minimization. *Journal of optimization theory and applications* 109, 3 (2001), 475–494.

[20] Stefan Wuchty, Benjamin F Jones, and Brian Uzzi. 2007. The increasing dominance of teams in production of knowledge. *Science* 316, 5827 (2007), 1036–1039.

[21] Jianpeng Xu, Pang-Ning Tan, Jiayu Zhou, and Lifeng Luo. 2017. Online Multi-task Learning Framework for Ensemble Forecasting. *TKDE* (2017).

[22] Yuan Yao, Hanghang Tong, Tao Xie, Leman Akoglu, Feng Xu, and Jian Lu. 2014. Joint voting prediction for questions and answers in CQA. In *ASONAM*. IEEE, 340–343.

[23] Yuan Yao, Hanghang Tong, Feng Xu, and Jian Lu. 2014. Predicting long-term impact of CQA posts: a comprehensive viewpoint. In *KDD*. ACM, 1496–1505.

[24] Petek Yontay and Rong Pan. 2016. A computational Bayesian approach to dependency assessment in system reliability. *Reliability Engineering & System Safety* 152 (2016), 104–114.

[25] Xiangrong Zeng and Mário A. T. Figueiredo. 2014. The Ordered Weighted l_1 Norm: Atomic Formulation, Dual Norm, and Projections. *CoRR* abs/1409.4271 (2014). http://arxiv.org/abs/1409.4271

Collaborative Variational Autoencoder for Recommender Systems

Xiaopeng Li
HKUST-NIE Social Media Lab
The Hong Kong University of Science and Technology
xlibo@connect.ust.hk

James She
HKUST-NIE Social Media Lab
The Hong Kong University of Science and Technology
eejames@ust.hk

ABSTRACT

Modern recommender systems usually employ collaborative filtering with rating information to recommend items to users due to its successful performance. However, because of the drawbacks of collaborative-based methods such as sparsity, cold start, etc., more attention has been drawn to hybrid methods that consider both the rating and content information. Most of the previous works in this area cannot learn a good representation from content for recommendation task or consider only text modality of the content, thus their methods are very limited in current multimedia scenario. This paper proposes a Bayesian generative model called collaborative variational autoencoder (CVAE) that considers both rating and content for recommendation in multimedia scenario. The model learns deep latent representations from content data in an unsupervised manner and also learns implicit relationships between items and users from both content and rating. Unlike previous works with denoising criteria, the proposed CVAE learns a latent distribution for content in latent space instead of observation space through an inference network and can be easily extended to other multimedia modalities other than text. Experiments show that CVAE is able to significantly outperform the state-of-the-art recommendation methods with more robust performance.

CCS CONCEPTS

•Human-centered computing →Collaborative filtering; Social recommendation; •Theory of computation →*Bayesian analysis; Social networks;*

KEYWORDS

Recommender systems; deep learning; generative models; Bayesian; variational inference; autoencoder

1 INTRODUCTION

With the rapid growth and high prevalence of Internet services and applications, people have access to large amounts of online multimedia content, such as movies, music, news and articles. While this growth has allowed users to be able to consume a huge number of resources with only one click, it has also made it more difficult for users to find information relevant to their interests. For example, users might be not aware of the existance of interesting movies they would like and researchers might find it difficult to search for important scientific articles related to their area of research. Therefore, recommender systems are becoming increasingly important to attract users, and make effective use of the information available. An application example of recommender systems is shown in Fig. 1. Generally, in recommendation applications, there are two types of information available: the rating and the item content, e.g., the posters of the movies or the plot descriptions. Existing methods for recommender systems can be roughly categorized into three classes [1]: content-based methods, collaborative-based methods, and hybrid methods. Content-based methods [12, 15, 17] make use of user profiles or item descriptions and the user will be recommended items similar to those the user has liked in the past. Collaborative-based methods [3, 21, 22] make use of usage or history data, such as user ratings on items, without using item content information, and the user will be recommended items that people with similar tastes and preferences have liked in the past. Collaborative-based methods generally achieve a better recommendation performance than content-based methods. Nevertheless, collaborative-based methods do have their limitations. The recommendation performance often drops significantly when the ratings are very sparse; moreover, they cannot be used for recommending new items that have not received any ratings from users, which is so-called cold-start problem. Consequently, hybrid methods [2, 14, 27] that use both content and collaborative information seek to get the best of both worlds.

Based on how tightly the rating information and auxilliary information are integrated, the hybrid methods may be further divided into two sub-categories: loosely coupled and tightly coupled methods [29]. Loosely coupled methods include the heuristic methods that implement separate collaborative and content-based systems and then combine the outputs obtained from individual recommender systems into final recommendations using a linear combination [6] or a voting scheme [18]. Yet, over the past years, researchers have been seeking to develop a unified model to incorporate both collaborative and content information in a tightly coupled way. Latent factor models have been proposed as such tightly coupled methods like [2, 14, 24], where auxilliary information is processed and regarded as a feature for the collaborative methods. However, all these methods assume that the features are good representations of the content considered, which is usually not the case. Even if the features are good representations of the content in general, they are not necessarily good representations for the recommendation tasks. Thus, the improvement often has to rely on a manual and tedious feature engineering process. Especially if the content of the items is multimedia content, e.g. texts

KDD '17, August 13-17, 2017, Halifax, NS, Canada

DOI: 10.1145/3097983.3098077

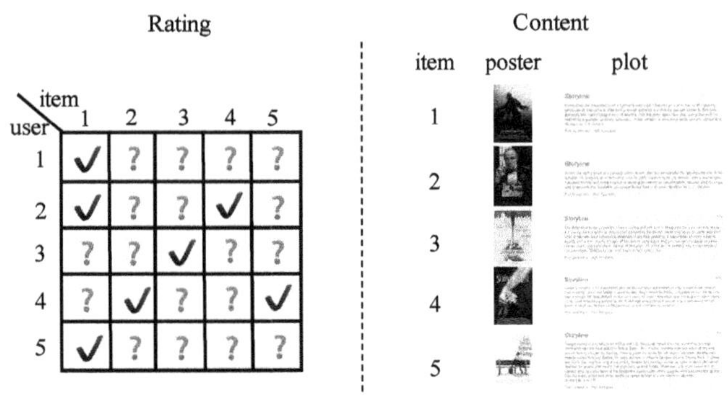

Figure 1: An example of recommendation application. Two types of information could exist: the rating and the item content, e.g., posters of movies or plot descriptions.

and images, a good representation for the recommendation tasks is hard to engineer but very crucial. Collaborative topic regression (CTR) [27] is a recently proposed method that explicitly links the learning of content to the recommendation task. It is a probabilistic graphical model that seamlessly integrates latent Dirichlet allocation (LDA) [4] and probabilistic matrix factorization (PMF) [22], and it produces promising and interpretable results. However, the representation capability of the model is limited to the topic model and the latent representation learned is often not effective enough especially when the auxiliary information is very sparse.

On the other hand, deep learning models have recently shown great potential for learning effective representations and achieved state-of-the-art performance in computer vision [13], natural language processing applications, etc. Though representation learning is appealing, few attempts have been made to develop deep learning models for recommendation. This is due partially to the fact that deep learning models, like many machine learning models, assume i.i.d. inputs. Thus it is difficult to develop deep learning models to capture and learn the implicit relationship between items (and users), which is, on the contrary, the strengh of probabilistic graphical models [10, 16]. This calls for the integration of Bayesian graphical models and deep learning models to benefit from the best of both worlds. [7, 23] use restricted Boltzmann machines instead of the conventional matrix factorization to perform collaborative filtering (CF). Although these models involve both deep learning models and CF, they actually belong to collaborative-based methods. There have also been some models that use a convolutional neural network (CNN) or deep belief network (DBN) for content-based recommendation [25, 31]. However, they use the latent factors learned through matrix factorization (MF) as the ground truth, instead of jointly learning representations and latent factors. Thus, it suffers greatly when the ratings are sparse and MF fails. Very recently, collaborative deep learning (CDL) [29] and collaborative recurrent autoencoder [30] have been proposed for joint learning a stacked denoising autoencoder (SDAE) [26] (or denoising recurrent autoencoder) and collaborative filtering, and they shows promising performance. Conceptually, both of the models try to learn a representation from content through some denoising criteria, either feedforwardly or recurrently. They first corrupt the input by masking out some parts or replacing them with wildcards, and then use neural networks to reconstruct the original input. The responses of the bottleneck layer are thus regarded as features to feed in the CTR model, and the neural network is optimized with additional finetuning. However, denoising autoencoders (DAEs) have in fact no Bayesian nature and the denoising scheme of the DAEs is in fact not from a probabilistic perspective but rather frequentist perspective. Thus, these models are difficult for Bayesian inference or require high computational cost. Furthermore, corrupting the input in observation space requires data specific corruption schemes, for example a corruption scheme with text content might not be a good corruption scheme for image content. The fixed noise level also degrades the robustness of representation learning.

To address above challenges, we propose a Bayesian deep generative model called collaborative variational autoencoder (CVAE) to jointly model the generation of content and the rating information in a collaborative filtering setting. The model learns deep latent representations from content data in an unsupervised manner and also learns implicit relationships between items and users from both content and rating. Unlike CTR, with the representation power of deep neural network, the CVAE model learns more effective representations for content than topic models. Unlike denoising autoencoders [26, 29], the CVAE model does not corrupt the input, but rather seeks for a probabilistic latent variable model for the content. It infers the stochastic distribution of the latent variable through an inference network, instead of point estimates, and it leads to more robust performance. Furthermore, because of the stochasticity in latent space instead of observation space, the CVAE model is not limited to the content data type. Different multimedia modalities, e.g. images and texts, are unified in the framework due to no data-specific corruption schemes in observation space. Note that although CVAE is presented with feedforward neural networks as the inference and generation networks, CVAE is also suitable for other deep learning models such as convolutional neural networks [11] and recurrent neural networks [8], depending on the data type of the content. The main contribution of this paper is summarized as follows:

- By formulating the recommendation problem in a probabilistic generative model with neural networks, the proposed CVAE model can simultaneously learn an effective latent representation for content and implicit relationships between items and users for recommendation tasks.
- By stochastically inferring the latent variable distribution in latent space instead of observation space, to the best of our knowledge, the proposed CVAE model is the first Bayesian generative model that provides a unified framework for recommendation with multimedia content.
- Unlike previous deep learning models, the proposed CVAE model is inherently a Bayesian probabilistic model. Besides maximum a posteriori (MAP) estimates, effecient variational inference is derived with Stochastic Gradient Variational Bayes, leading to efficient Bayesian learning with back-propagation.
- Experiments with two real-world datasets show that the proposed CVAE model significantly outperforms the state-of-the-art methods for recommendation with content.

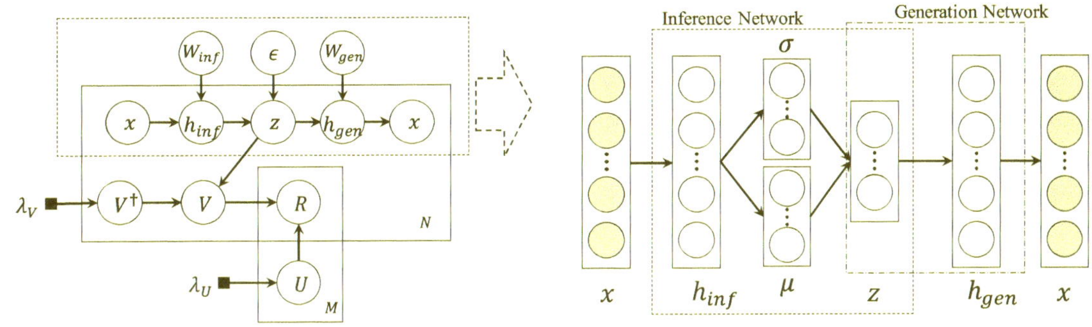

Figure 2: On the left is the proposed Collaborative Variational Autoencoder (CVAE); on the right is the zoom-in of the inference network and generation network in CVAE.

2 THE PROPOSED COLLABORATIVE VARIATIONAL AUTOENCODER

In this section, we describe the proposed collaborative variational autoencoder model (CVAE) for recommendation with content. CVAE, as shown in Fig. 2, is inherently a generative latent variable model, where the contents of the items are generated by their latent content variables and the ratings of the items by the users are generated through latent item variables. Latent item variables embed both content information through latent content variables and collaborative information through latent collaborative variables, bridging hybrid information together with deep architecture.

2.1 Collaborative Variational Autoencoder

In this paper, we represent users and items in a shared latent low-dimensional space of dimension K, where user i is represented by a latent variable $u_i \in \mathbb{R}^K$ and item j is represented by a latent variable $v_j \in \mathbb{R}^K$. Like probabilistic matrix factorization (PMF), we put Normal distribution as the prior. The latent variable for each user i is drawn from

$$u_i \sim \mathcal{N}(0, \lambda_u^{-1} I_K).$$

As with PMF, the collaborative information is important for predicting the ratings. For each item j, the collaborative information is embeded in the collaborative latent variable and is drawn from Normal distribution,

$$v_j^\dagger \sim \mathcal{N}(0, \lambda_v^{-1} I_K).$$

Traditional PMF only considers collaborative information for predicting rating and does not use the content of the items. The proposed CVAE model constructs a generative latent variable model for the content and assigns a latent content variable z_j to each item j. The content of the item x_j is generated from its latent variable z_j through generation neural network parameterized by θ:

$$x_j \sim p_\theta(x_j|z_j).$$

The generation network is illustrated in Fig. 2, where, given the latent variable z, x is generated through a multi-layer perception network (MLP). For example, if x is binary data, it can be generated from a multivariate Bernoulli distribution parameterized by the output of the generation network:

$$p_\theta(x|z) = \text{Ber}(f_\theta(z)).$$

Or if x is real-value data, it can be generated from Normal distribution $\mathcal{N}(f_\theta(z), \lambda^{-1} I)$. The generation process of the content through the generation network is defined as follows:

(1) For each layer l of the generation network
 (a) For each column n of the weight matrix W_l, draw

$$W_{l,*n} \sim \mathcal{N}(0, \lambda_w^{-1} I_{K_l}).$$

 (b) Draw the bias vector $b_l \sim \mathcal{N}(0, \lambda_w^{-1} I_{K_l})$.
 (c) For each row j of h_l, draw

$$h_{l,j*} \sim \mathcal{N}(\sigma(h_{l-1,j*} W_l + b_l), \lambda_s^{-1} I_K).$$

(2) For binary data, draw

$$x_j \sim \text{Ber}(\sigma(h_L W_{L+1} + b_{L+1}));$$

for real-value data, draw

$$x_j \sim \mathcal{N}(h_L W_{L+1} + b_{L+1}, \lambda_x^{-1} I).$$

Above, λ_w, λ_s and λ_x are hyperparameters. And generally, λ_s is taken to infinity so that normal neural network can be employed for computational efficiency. Beyond MLP, a deconvolutional network [19, 20] can be applied to model the generation of images, etc.

The prior distribution of the content variable is chosen to be a unit Normal distribution:

$$z_j \sim \mathcal{N}(0, I_K).$$

The item latent variables thus are composed with both the collaborative latent variable and the latent content variable:

$$v_j = v_j^\dagger + z_j.$$

The rating is thus drawn from the Normal distribution centered at the inner product between their latent representations,

$$R_{ij} \sim \mathcal{N}(u_i^T v_j, C_{ij}^{-1}),$$

where C_{ij} is the precision parameter. The precision parameter C_{ij} serves as confidence for R_{ij} similar to that in CTR [27] ($C_{ij} = a$ if $R_{ij} = 1$ and $C_{ij} = b$ otherwise) due to the fact that $R_{ij} = 0$ means the user i is either not interested in item j or not aware of it.

With the generative model constructed, the joint probability of both observations and latent variables is given by

$$p(R, X, U, V, Z) = \prod_{i,j} p(R_{ij}|u_i, v_j) p(u_i) p(v_j|z_j) p(x_j|z_j) p(z_j)$$

The inference of the model is not only apparently intractable but also difficult to perform normal variational inference, especially since $p(x_j|z_j)$ is determined by the generation network with non-linear units. To see that, we can use variational inference to approximate the posterior distribution with mean-field approximation:

$$q(U, V, Z) = \prod_{i=1}^{M} q(u_i|\theta_{u_i}) \prod_{j=1}^{N} q(v_j|\theta_{v_j}) q(z_j|\theta_{z_j})$$

However, the common mean-field approach requires an analytical solution of expectations with respect to the approximate posterior, which is not the case for the generation network since no conjugate probability distribution can be found. Instead, we can use the Stochastic Gradient Variational Bayes (SGVB) estimator for efficient approximate posterior inference of the latent content variable z by introducing an inference network parameterized by ϕ. The inference network is also an MLP corresponding to the MLP in the generation network, or convolutional network corresponding to the deconvolutional network. The variational distribution is thus chosen to be conjugate to the prior Normal distribution of z_j and is parameterized by ϕ and x_j, in replacement of θ_{z_j}, leading to per datapoint variational distributions with shared network parameters:

$$q(z_j|\theta_{z_j}) = q_\phi(z_j|x_j) = \mathcal{N}(\mu_\phi(x_j), \mathrm{diag}(\sigma^2_\phi(x_j))).$$

With the reparameterization trick similar to [9], it is straightforward to get a differentiable unbiased estimator of the lower bound and optimize it using standard stochastic gradient ascent techniques. The inference process of the latent content variable z through the inference network is defined as follows:

(1) For each layer l of the inference network
   (a) For each column n of the weight matrix W_l, draw

$$W_{l,*n} \sim \mathcal{N}(0, \lambda_w^{-1} I_{K_l}).$$

   (b) Draw the bias vector $b_l \sim \mathcal{N}(0, \lambda_w^{-1} I_{K_l})$.
   (c) For each row j of h_l, draw

$$h_{l,j*} \sim \mathcal{N}(\sigma(h_{l-1,j*} W_l + b_l), \lambda_s^{-1} I_{K_l}).$$

(2) For each item j
   (a) Draw latent mean and covariance vector

$$\mu_j \sim \mathcal{N}(h_L W_\mu + b_\mu, \lambda_s^{-1} I_K)$$
$$\log \sigma_j^2 \sim \mathcal{N}(h_L W_\sigma + b_\sigma, \lambda_s^{-1} I_K).$$

   (b) Draw latent content vector

$$z_j \sim \mathcal{N}(\mu_j, \mathrm{diag}(\sigma_j)).$$

The evidence lower bound (ELBO) can be obtained by

$$\begin{aligned}\mathcal{L}(q) =& \mathbb{E}_q[\log p(R, X, U, V, Z) - \log q(U, V, Z)] \\ =& \mathbb{E}_q[\log p(R|U, V) + \log p(U) + \log p(V|Z) + \log p(X|Z)] \\ &- \mathbb{KL}(q_\phi(Z|X)\|p(Z))\end{aligned}$$

In terms of $q_\phi(z|x)$, isolating the terms related to z, we have

$$\begin{aligned}\mathcal{L}(\theta, \phi; x_j) =& \mathbb{E}_{q_\phi(z_j|x_j)}[\log p_\theta(x_j|z_j)] + \mathbb{E}_{q_\phi(z_j|x_j)}[\log p(v_j|z_j)] \\ &- \mathbb{KL}(q_\phi(z_j|x_j)\|p(z_j)) + \text{const}.\end{aligned}$$

It is problematic to compute the two expectations above analytically, as well as the gradient of $\mathcal{L}$ with respect to ϕ. Instead, we can form Monte Carlo estimates of the two expectations by drawing samples from the variational distribution: $z_j \sim q_\phi(z_j|x_j)$. With the reparameterization trick[9], we can instead draw samples from $\epsilon \sim \mathcal{N}(0, I)$ and form the samples of z_j by $z_j = \mu_j + \sigma_j \odot \epsilon$. Thus, the above objective can be estimated using the SGVB estimator:

$$\begin{aligned}\mathcal{L}(\theta, \phi; x_j) \simeq& -\mathbb{KL}(q_\phi(z_j|x_j)\|p(z_j)) + \frac{1}{L}\sum_{l=1}^{L} \log p_\theta(x_j|z_j^{(l)}) \\ &+ \log p(v_j|z_j^{(l)}) + \text{const}.\end{aligned}$$

where $z_j^{(l)} = \mu_j + \sigma_j \odot \epsilon^{(l)}$ and $\epsilon \sim \mathcal{N}(0, I)$.

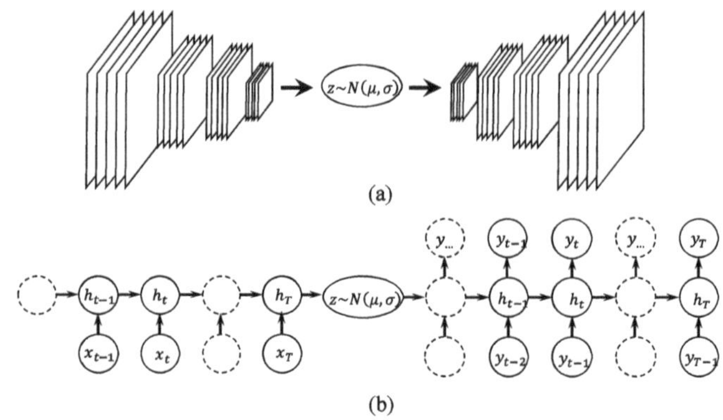

Figure 3: Extensions of inference networks and generation networks under the framework of CVAE for (a) image data and (b) sequential data for recommender systems.

Another interpretation of the proposed CVAE model is from the point of view of denoising. The inference network produces the posterior variational distribution for the latent content variable z. This can also be viewed as as corrupting the latent content vector with Gaussian noise. Unlike the stacked denoising autoencoder (SDAE) as proposed in [26, 29], where the input observations are first corrupted with various noise (masking noise, Gaussian noise, salt-and-peper noise, etc), the corruption of data in latent space avoids the diverse interpretation and corruption scheme of the observation space and provides a unified way of corruption. Also, the noise level is automatically learned through the inference network, instead of manually tuned like in SDAE. This leads to more robust and systematic learning of representation regardless of the data type it is trying to model.

For completeness, Fig. 3 shows the extensions of inference networks and generation networks under the framework of CVAE for other types of content data associated with items. For image data, a convolutional network and deconvolutional network pair can be used for inference network and generation network [19, 20]. For sequential data, such as text data in sequential form instead of bag-of-words representation, a recurrent neural network pair can be used [5]. Due to the stochasticity in latent space instead of the observation space, content data with different modalities are unified in the framework of CVAE for recommender systems.

2.2 Maximum A Posteriori Estimates

The MAP estimation can be performed by only considerring the variational distribution of $q_\phi(Z|X)$ and maximizing the objective with respect to $\{u_i\}$ and $\{v_j\}$ using block coordinate ascent. The objective thus becomes

$$\begin{aligned}\mathcal{L}^{\text{MAP}}(U,V,\theta,\phi) = &-\sum_{i,j}\frac{C_{ij}}{2}(R_{ij}-u_i^Tv_j)^2-\frac{\lambda_u}{2}\sum_i\|u_i\|_2^2\\&-\frac{\lambda_v}{2}\sum_j\mathbb{E}_{q_\phi(Z|X)}\|v_j-z_j\|_2^2\\&+\mathbb{E}_{q_\phi(Z|X)}\log p(X|Z)-\mathbb{KL}(q_\phi(Z|X)\|p(Z))\\&-\frac{\lambda_w}{2}\sum_l(\|W_l\|_F^2+\|b_l\|_2^2)\end{aligned} \tag{1}$$

The block coordinate ascent for $\{u_i\}$ and $\{v_j\}$ thus becomes

$$\begin{aligned}u_i &\leftarrow (VC_iV^T+\lambda_UI_K)^{-1}VC_iR_i\\v_j &\leftarrow (UC_jU^T+\lambda_VI_K)^{-1}(UC_iR_i+\lambda_v\mathbb{E}_{q_{\phi_Z}}[z_j])\end{aligned}$$

where it should be noted that $\mathbb{E}_{q_{\phi_Z}}[z_j]$ equals to μ_j produced by the inference network. And given U and V, the gradient with respect to μ and σ of z is

$$\begin{aligned}\nabla_{\mu_j}\mathcal{L}^{\text{MAP}}(\theta,\phi;x_j) \simeq &-\mu_j+\frac{1}{L}\sum_{l=1}^{L}\lambda_v(v_j-z_j^{(l)})\\&+\nabla_{z_j^{(l)}}\log p_\theta(x_j|z_j^{(l)})\\\nabla_{\sigma_j}\mathcal{L}^{\text{MAP}}(\theta,\phi;x_j) \simeq &\frac{1}{\sigma_j}-\sigma_j+\frac{1}{L}\sum_{l=1}^{L}[\lambda_v(v_j-z_j^{(l)})\\&+\nabla_{z_j^{(l)}}\log p_\theta(x_j|z_j^{(l)})]\odot\epsilon^{(l)}\end{aligned}$$

The last term $\log p_\theta(x_j|z_j^{(l)})$ depends on what the data type of x_j is. For binary data, $p_\theta(x|z)$ is a Bernoulli distribution. For categorical data, $p_\theta(x|z)$ could be a Categorical distribution. And for real-value data $p_\theta(x|z)$ could be a Normal distribution. Thus, the gradient of the generation network can be evaluated through backpropagation and so too the gradient of weights of the inference network. Furthermore, the number of samples L per datapoint can be set to 1 as long as the minibatch size M is large enough, e.g. $M = 128$. The weights of the inference network and generation network thus can be performed through backpropagation in a conventional manner.

2.3 Bayesian Inference

Previous works [23, 25, 29, 30] that also employ deep networks are difficult to conduct Bayesian inference, or they have to resort to computationally intensive Markov Chain Monte Carlo (MCMC). However, with the Bayesian nature of the proposed model, it is straightforward to perform efficient variational inference. The complete conditional of u_i is given by

$$p(u_i|R,V,X,Z)=\mathcal{N}(\mu_{u_in},\lambda_{u_in}^{-1}I_K)$$

where

$$\begin{aligned}\Lambda_{u_in} &= \sum_{j=1}^{N}C_{ij}v_jv_j^T+\lambda_uI_K\\\mu_{u_in} &= \Lambda_{u_in}^{-1}(\sum_{j=1}^{N}C_{ij}R_{ij}v_j)\end{aligned}$$

The complete conditional of v_j is given by

$$p(v_j|R,U,X,Z)=\mathcal{N}(\mu_{v_jn},\lambda_{v_jn}^{-1}I_K)$$

where

$$\begin{aligned}\Lambda_{v_jn} &= \sum_{i=1}^{M}C_{ij}u_iu_i^T+\lambda_vI_K\\\mu_{v_jn} &= \Lambda_{v_jn}^{-1}(\sum_{i=1}^{M}C_{ij}R_{ij}u_i+\lambda_vz_j)\end{aligned}$$

Taking the derivative of $\mathcal{L}$ with respect to θ_{u_i} and setting the gradient to zero, we have

$$\begin{aligned}\mu_{u_i} &\leftarrow (\mathbb{E}_{q_{\theta_V}}[VC_iV^T]+\lambda_UI_K)^{-1}(\mathbb{E}_{q_{\theta_V}}[V]C_iR_i)\\\Lambda_{u_i} &\leftarrow (\mathbb{E}_{q_{\theta_V}}[VC_iV^T]+\lambda_UI_K)\end{aligned}$$

where $\mathbb{E}_{q_{\theta_V}}[VC_iV^T]=\mathbb{E}_{q_{\theta_V}}[V]C_i\mathbb{E}_{q_{\theta_V}}[V]^T+\sum_jC_{ij}\Lambda_{v_j}^{-1}$. Likewise, for θ_{v_j}, we have

$$\begin{aligned}\mu_{v_j} &\leftarrow (\mathbb{E}_{q_{\theta_U}}[UC_jU^T]+\lambda_VI_K)^{-1}(\mathbb{E}_{q_{\theta_U}}[U]C_iR_i+\lambda_v\mathbb{E}_{q_{\phi_Z}}[z_j])\\\Lambda_{v_j} &\leftarrow (\mathbb{E}_{q_{\theta_U}}[UC_iU^T]+\lambda_VI_K)\end{aligned}$$

where $\mathbb{E}_{q_{\theta_U}}[UC_jU^T]=\mathbb{E}_{q_{\theta_U}}[U]C_i\mathbb{E}_{q_{\theta_U}}[U]^T+\sum_iC_{ij}\Lambda_{u_j}^{-1}$. Compared with the MAP estimates, it can be seen that the precision matrix further gauges our belief of the updates by introducing an additional term. The gradient of $\mathcal{L}$ with respect to μ and σ thus can be obtained:

$$\begin{aligned}\nabla_{\mu_j}\mathcal{L}(\theta,\phi;x_j) \simeq &-\mu_j+\frac{1}{L}\sum_{l=1}^{L}\Lambda_{v_j}(\mathbb{E}_{q_{\theta_V}}[v_j]-z_j^{(l)})\\&+\nabla_{z_j^{(l)}}\log p_\theta(x_j|z_j^{(l)})\\\nabla_{\sigma_j}\mathcal{L}(\theta,\phi;x_j) \simeq &\frac{1}{\sigma_j}-\sigma_j+\frac{1}{L}\sum_{l=1}^{L}[\Lambda_{v_j}(\mathbb{E}_{q_{\theta_V}}[v_j]-z_j^{(l)})\\&+\nabla_{z_j^{(l)}}\log p_\theta(x_j|z_j^{(l)})]\odot\epsilon^{(l)}.\end{aligned}$$

2.4 Prediction

Let D be the observed data. After all the parameters U, V (or μ, Λ), and the weights of the inference network and generation network are learned, the predictions can be made by

$$\mathbb{E}[R_{ij}|D]=\mathbb{E}[u_i|D]^T(\mathbb{E}[v_j^\dagger|D]+\mathbb{E}[z_j|D]).$$

For point estimation, the prediction can simplified as

$$R_{ij}^*=u_i^T(v_j^\dagger+\mathbb{E}[z_j])$$

where $\mathbb{E}[z_j]=\mu_j$, the mean vector obtained through the inference network for each item j. The items that have never been seen before will have no $v_j^\dagger$ term, but the $\mathbb{E}[z_j]$ can be inferred through the content. In this way, both the sparsity problem and cold start problem are alleviated, leading to robust recommendation performance.

3 EXPERIMENTS

In this section, we present both quantitative and qualitative experiment results on two real-word datasets to demonstrate the effectiveness of the proposed CVAE model for recommender systems[1].

3.1 Datasets

The two datasets are users and their libraries of articles with different scales and degrees of sparsity obtained from CiteULike[2], where users can create their own collections of articles. The first dataset, *citeulike-a*, is collected by [27], and there are 5,551 users and 16,980 articles with 204,986 observed user-item pairs. Users with fewer than 10 articles are not included in the dataset. The sparsity of the rating matrix is 99.78% (only 0.22% of the rating matrix have one entries). The second dataset, *citeulike-t*, is independently collected by [28] and is even larger and sparser. They manually selected 273 seed tags and collected all articles with at least one of the tags. There are 7,947 users and 25,975 articles with 134,860 observed user-item pairs. The sparsity of the rating matrix is 99.93% (only 0.07% of the rating matrix have one entries). Users with fewer than 3 artiles are not included in the dataset. Each article in the two datasets has a title and abstract. The content information of the articles is the concatenation of the titles and abstracts. We follow the same procedure as that in [27] to preprocess the text content information. After removing stop words, the vocabulary for each dataset is selected according to the tf-idf value of each word. The *citeulike-a* has a vocabulary size of 8,000 and the *citeulike-t* has a vocabulary size of 20,000. Each article is represented with a bag-of-words histogram vector and all the content vectors are then normalized over the maximum occurrences of each word in all articles.

3.2 Evaluation Scheme

For the recommendation task, we randomly select P items in the user's collection for each user to form the training set and use the rest of the items as the testing set. For the training, we consider both sparse setting ($P = 1$) and dense setting ($P = 10$) for each dataset. For the testing, each user is presented with M articles sorted by their predicted rating and evaluated based on which of these articles are actually in each users' collection. For each value of P, the evaluation is conducted five times with different random splits and the average performance is reported.

As in [27, 29], we use the recall as the evaluation metric since the zero ratings are in the form of implicit feedback. They may indicate that a user does not like an article or the user simply is not aware of it. This makes it difficult to accurately compute precision. However, since ratings of one explicitly mean true positive, we focus on recall. For each user, the definition of *recall@M* is

$$\text{recall@}M = \frac{\text{number of items that the user likes among the top } M}{\text{total number of items the user likes}}.$$

[1]Code is available at http://eelxpeng.github.io/research/

[2]http://www.citeulike.org

The recall for the entire system can be summarized using the average recall over all users.

3.3 Baselines and Experimental Settings

As already demonstrated in previous works [27, 29], hybrid recommendation with content performs significantly better than collaborative based methods, only hybrid models are used for comparison. The models included in our comparison are listed as follows:

- **CTR:** Collaborative Topic Regression [27] is a model performing latent dirichlet allocation (LDA) on the content and collaborative filtering on the rating with tighly coupled modeling.
- **DeepMusic:** DeepMusic [25] is a feedforward neural network model for music recommendation, where the objective is a linear regression and the latent factor vectors obtained by applying weighted matrix factorization (WMF) to the training rating data are used as groundtruth. We use the loosely coupled variant as our baseline.
- **CDL:** Collaborative Deep Learning [29] is a probabilistic feedforward model for joint learning of stacked denoising autoencoder (SDAE) and collaborative filtering. CDL is a very strong baseline and achieves the best performance among our baseline methods.
- **CVAE:** Collaborative Variational Autoencoder is our proposed model. The MAP estimates are conducted for fair comparison. It is a generative latent variable model that jointly models the generation of content and rating and uses variational Bayes with inference network for variational inference.

In the experiments, we first use a validation set to find the optimal hyperparameters for CTR, DeepMusic and CDL. For CTR, we find that it can achieve good performance when $a = 1$, $b = 0.01$, $\lambda_u = 0.1$, $\lambda_v = 1$, and $K = 50$, where a and b are the confidence value for C_{ij} under different ratings. The model is first pretrained with LDA to get the initial topic proportions and CTR is performed to jointly learn U, V and topic proportions iteratively. For DeepMusic, a two convolutional layers architecture is used. We tried our best to tune other hyperparameters. For CDL, we also set $a = 1$, $b = 0.01$, $K = 50$ and find that the best performance is achieved with $\lambda_u = 1$, $\lambda_v = 10$, $\lambda_n = 1000$ and $\lambda_w = 0.0001$. A two-layer SDAE network architecture is adopted to be the same as [29]. The weights of the network are first pretrained in a plain SDAE manner with the content of items and then fed into CDL for finetuning for another 200 epochs. The noise is set to be masking noise with a noise level of 0.3. For CVAE, the model with MAP estimation is used for fairness. The parameters of $a = 1$, $b = 0.01$, $K = 50$ are the same. The other hyperparameters are found through cross-validation on the validation set. The model is also pretrained in plain VAE manner to first learn initial starting points for the network weights. In terms of network architecture, it is found that the best performance is achieved by tying the weights of the inference network and the generation network (the weights of the inference network are set to be the transpose of the generation network). It is probably because by tying their weights together, it avoids many bad local minima, leading to more robust representation learning in the generation of the content part. This can also be verified through the result that

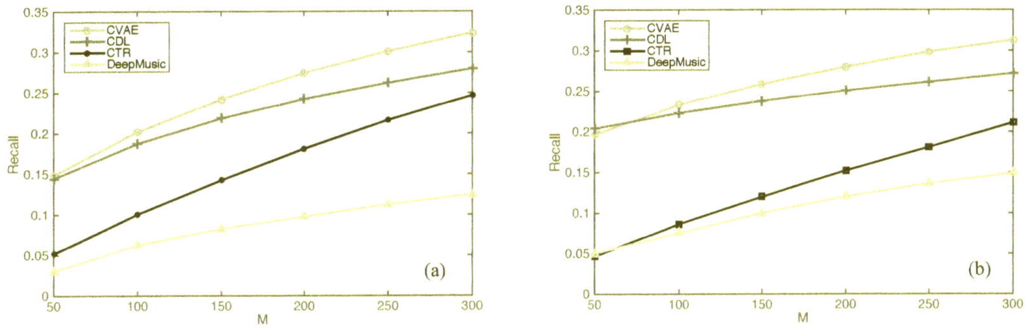

Figure 4: Performance comparison of CVAE, CDL, CTR and DeepMusic based on recall in the sparse setting for dataset (a) *citeulike-a* and (b) *citeulike-t*.

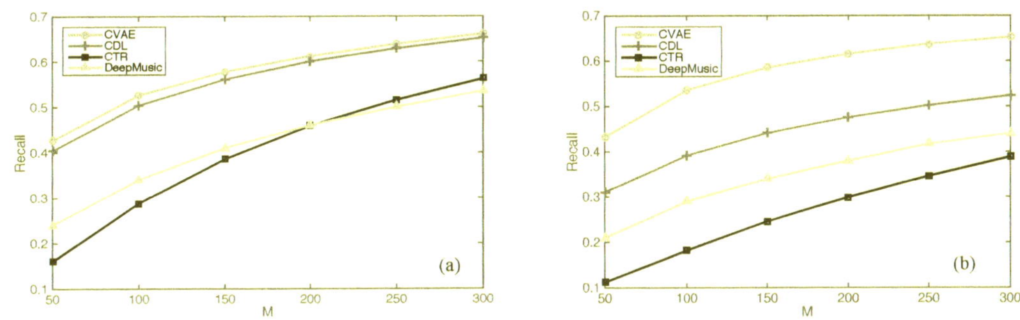

Figure 5: Performance comparison of CVAE, CDL, CTR and DeepMusic based on recall in the dense setting for dataset (a) *citeulike-a* and (b) *citeulike-t*.

tying weights together leads to lower reconstructure error. Both the inference network and the generation network are chosen to be a two-layer network architecture ('200-100' for inference network and '100-200' for generation network) with sigmoid activation function.

3.4 Performance Comparison

Fig. 4 and 5 show the results that compare CTR, DeepMusic, CDL and CVAE using the two datasets under both the sparse ($P = 1$) and dense ($P = 10$) settings. As it can be seen, CDL is a very strong baseline and outperforms the other baselines by a large margin. Compared with CTR, it can be seen that the deep learning structure of CDL learns better representations than topic modeling, leading to better performance. Although DeepMusic is also a deep learning model, it suffers badly from overfitting when the rating matrix is extremely sparse ($P = 1$) and achieves a comparable performance to CTR when the rating matrix is dense ($P = 10$). This is because DeepMusic uses the latent vector generated by WMF as the regression groundtruth, thus its performance highly relies on the WMF which fails when the rating matrix is sparse. By modeling the generation of content and rating simutaneously in a probabilistic generative latent variable model, CVAE is able to outperform all the baselines by a margin of 4.4%~20% (a relative boost of 15.7%~160%) in the sparse setting and 0.9%~10.8% (a relative boost of 1.4%~37.4%) in the dense setting for *citeulike-a*. For *citeulike-t*, since the dataset is even sparser, the improvement is more significant, 4.1%~16.39% (a relative boost of 15.1%~110%) in the sparse setting and 12.9%~26.4% (a relative boost of 24.7%~68.0%) in the dense setting. To focus more specifically on the comparison of CDL and CVAE, we can see that although both CDL and CVAE use deep learning models, the proposed CVAE achieves better and more robust recommendation, especially for larger M. This is because CVAE is inherent a Bayesian generative model and the distribution of latent content variable z is estimated, instead of point estimation. Thus it will lead to more robust performance. On the other hand, CDL is using some denoising criteria in observation space with a fixed noise level to learn a point estimate of latent representation, thus it is still easy to overfit the data.

To investigate the difference between focusing more on content and focusing more on ratings, we can add an factor of λ_r to the third line of Eq. 1 to adjust the penalty of reconstruction error with respect to rating-related terms. Fig. 6 shows the results of CVAE for different values of λ_r in *citeulike-a* under the sparse and dense setting while fixing $\lambda_u = 0.1$ and $\lambda_v = 10$. When λ_r is very small, e.g., 0.01, the penalty of reconstruction of the content is greatly reduced. It leads to degraded performance of representation learning of the content, thus the performance of the recommendation. While when λ_r is large, e.g., 100, the CVAE model would tend to degenerate into two independent models, one

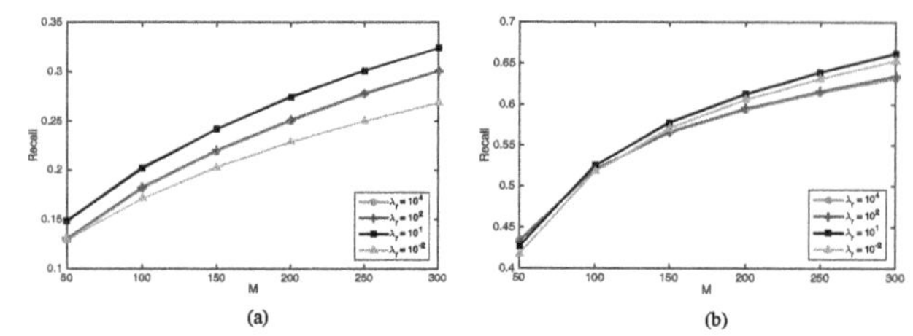

Figure 6: Performance comparison of CVAE for different values of λ_r based on recall for dataset *citeulike-a* in the sparse setting (a) and dense setting (b).

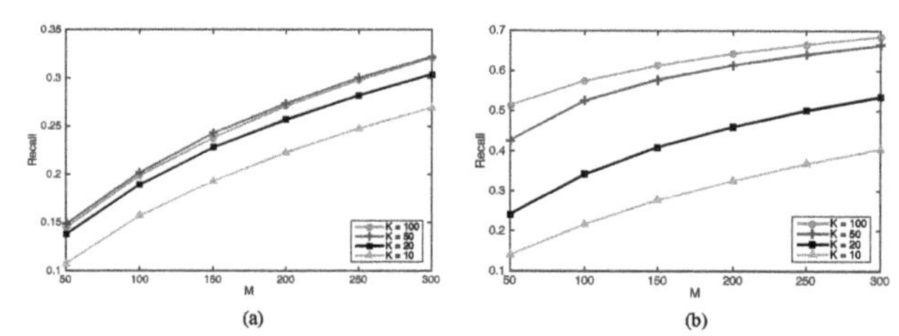

Figure 7: Performance comparison of CVAE for different values of K based on recall for dataset *citeulike-a* in the sparse setting (a) and dense setting (b).

for representation learning of the content, the other for probablistic matrix factorization. Yet, it can be seen that, $\lambda_r = 100$ and $\lambda_r = 10000$ have similar performance, showing that CVAE model is rather robust for preventing separate learning. It is because the CVAE is a generative model that learns the latent distribution, instead of point estimate. The Bayesian nature of the CVAE model makes it able to model the data better, leading to more robust performance. By comparing the influence of λ_r in the sparse setting and dense setting, it can be seen that joint learning content and rating is more important when dealing with very sparse data, and crucial for solving the cold-start problem.

Fig. 7 shows the results of CVAE for different values of the number of latent factors K. The influce of K depends on two parts, the latent variable for the representation of content and the latent variable for the matrix factorization model. It can be seen that when K is very small, e.g., 10, the CVAE is unable to learn a good representation from the content, thus it leads to degraded performance. On the other hand, when K is large enough, the influence of K is trivial since the representation capability is enough for the content it is trying to model. By comparing the influence of K in the sparse setting and dense setting, we can also see that the larger K has more influence in the dense setting. This is mainly because denser ratings offer more guidence for inference network to make variational inference, thus they need a larger representation capability to learn.

3.5 Qualitative Results

In order to gain better insight into CVAE, we train CVAE and CDL in the sparse setting ($P = 1$) with the dataset *citeulike-a* and use them to recommend articles for two example users. The corresponding rated articles for the target users and the top 10 recommended articles are shown in Table 1. As we can see, CVAE successfully identified user I as a researcher working on information retrieval with an interest in using language model. Consequently, CVAE achieves a high precision of 90% by focusing its recommendations on articles about language model based information retrieval, etc. On the other hand, the topics of articles recommended by CDL covers some purely natural language processing (Article 2, 5), and pure information retrieval (Article 6, 7, 8), instead of the interaction of both. For example, Article 6 recommended by CDL is content based 'image retrieval', which apparently has nothing to do with language models for information retrieval. A similar situation happens for user II. From the rated article, CVAE identifies the user as someone who is doing an overview of the area and is more interested in general methods and evaluation metrics for recommendation. Thus, the articles recommended by CVAE focus on some simpler methods and evaluation articles. Whereas, CDL recommends many articles focusing on some in-depth models for recommender systems, such as content-based or hybrid models (Article 1-4), which contradicts the intention of the user.

From these two users, we can see that the generative nature of the proposed CVAE model can capture the key points of articles and user preferences more accurately, due to its modeling of latent random variable distribution. From the other point of view, unlike CDL, which corrupts the input with fixed noise level at observation space, CVAE is more robust since it adaptively learns the stochastic noise to corrupt the data in latent space. Thus, generally CVAE achieves better recommendation performance.

4 CONCLUSIONS

This paper proposes the collaborative variational autoencoder that can jointly model the generation of item content while extracting the implicit relationships between items and users collaboratively. It is a Bayesian probabilistic generative model that unifies the collaborative and content information through stochastic deep learning models and graphical models, leading to robust recommendation performance. By its Bayesian nature, efficient variational inference is derived with stochastic gradient variational Bayes. To the best of our knowledge, CVAE is the first model that unifies the different modalities of multimedia for recommendation due to its inference of stochastic distribution in latent space instead of observation space. Experiments have shown that the proposed CVAE can significantly outperform the state-of-the-art methods for recommendation with content with more robust performance.

ACKNOWLEDGMENTS

This work is supported by the HKUST-NIE Social Media Lab., HKUST.

REFERENCES

[1] Gediminas Adomavicius and Alexander Tuzhilin. 2005. Toward the next generation of recommender systems: A survey of the state-of-the-art and possible extensions. *IEEE Transactions on Knowledge and Data Engineering* 17, 6 (2005), 734–749.

[2] Deepak Agarwal and Bee-Chung Chen. 2009. Regression-based latent factor models. In *Proceedings of the 15th ACM SIGKDD International Conference on Knowledge Discovery and Data Mining*. ACM, 19–28.

Table 1: Qualitative comparison between CVAE and CDL.

the rated article	Information retrieval as statistical translation	
	user I (CVAE)	in user's lib?
top 10 articles	**1. Linear discriminant model for information retrieval**	**yes**
	2. Probabilistic latent semantic indexing	**yes**
	3. Latent dirichlet allocation	**yes**
	4. Latent concept expansion using markov random fields	**yes**
	5. Document language models, query models, and risk minimization for information retrieval	**yes**
	6. Two-stage language models for information retrieval	**yes**
	7. Latent semantic indexing: a probabilistic analysis	no
	8. Relevance feedback for best match term weighting algorithms in information retrieval	**yes**
	9. Dependence language model for information retrieval	**yes**
	10. Probabilistic relevance models based on document and query generation	**yes**
	user I (CDL)	in user's lib?
top 10 articles	**1. Bayesian extension to the language model for ad hoc information retrieval**	**yes**
	2. PubMed related articles: a probabilistic topic-based model for content similarity	no
	3. Document language models, query models, and risk minimization for information retrieval	**yes**
	4. A probability ranking principle for interactive information retrieval	no
	5. Discriminative reranking for natural language parsing	no
	6. Relevance feedback: a power tool for interactive content-based image retrieval	no
	7. Some simple effective approximations to the 2-Poisson model for probabilistic weighted retrieval	no
	8. Combining approaches to information retrieval	no
	9. Language models for relevance feedback	**yes**
	10. Using language models for information retrieval	**yes**
the rated article	Methods and metrics for cold-start recommendations	
	user II (CVAE)	in user's lib?
top 10 articles	**1. Amazon.com recommendations: item-to-item collaborative filtering**	**yes**
	2. Evaluating collaborative filtering recommender systems	**yes**
	3. Empirical analysis of predictive algorithms for collaborative filtering	**yes**
	4. Item-based collaborative filtering recommendation algorithms	**yes**
	5. Trust in recommender systems	no
	6. The wisdom of the few: a collaborative filtering approach based on expert opinions from the web	**yes**
	7. Collaborative filtering with temporal dynamics	**yes**
	8. Taxonomy-driven computation of product recommendations	no
	9. Solving the apparent diversity-accuracy dilemma of recommender systems	no
	10. Modeling relationships at multiple scales to improve accuracy of large recommender systems	**yes**
	user II (CDL)	in user's lib?
top 10 articles	1. Content-based book recommending using learning for text categorization	no
	2. Unifying collaborative and content-based filtering	no
	3. Content-boosted collaborative filtering	no
	4. TrustWalker: a random walk model for combining trust-based and item-based recommendation	no
	5. A comprehensive evaluation of multicategory classification methods for microarray gene expression cancer diagnosis.	no
	6. Evaluating collaborative filtering recommender systems	**yes**
	7. AdaRank: a boosting algorithm for information retrieval	no
	8. Learning distance functions for image retrieval	no
	9. Opinion observer: analyzing and comparing opinions on the Web	yes
	10. Probabilistic models for unified collaborative and content-based recommendation in sparse-data environments	**yes**

[3] Daniel Billsus and Michael J Pazzani. 1998. Learning collaborative information filters.. In *Proceedings of the 15th International Conference on Machine Learning*, Vol. 98. 46–54.

[4] David M Blei, Andrew Y Ng, and Michael I Jordan. 2003. Latent dirichlet allocation. *Journal of Machine Learning Research* 3, Jan (2003), 993–1022.

[5] Samuel R Bowman, Luke Vilnis, Oriol Vinyals, Andrew M Dai, Rafal Jozefowicz, and Samy Bengio. 2016. Generating sentences from a continuous space. In *CONLL*. 10–21.

[6] Mark Claypool, Anuja Gokhale, Tim Miranda, Pavel Murnikov, Dmitry Netes, and Matthew Sartin. 1999. Combining content-based and collaborative filters in an online newspaper. In *Proceedings of ACM SIGIR workshop on recommender systems*, Vol. 60. Citeseer.

[7] Kostadin Georgiev and Preslav Nakov. 2013. A non-IID framework for collaborative filtering with restricted Boltzmann machines.. In *Proceedings of the 30th International Conference on Machine Learning*. 1148–1156.

[8] Alex Graves, Santiago Fernández, Faustino Gomez, and Jürgen Schmidhuber. 2006. Connectionist temporal classification: labelling unsegmented sequence data with recurrent neural networks. In *Proceedings of the 23rd International Conference on Machine Learning*. ACM, 369–376.

[9] Diederik P Kingma and Max Welling. 2013. Auto-encoding variational bayes. In *Proceedings of the 2nd International Conference on Learning Representations*.

[10] Daphne Koller and Nir Friedman. 2009. *Probabilistic graphical models: principles and techniques*. MIT press.

[11] Alex Krizhevsky, Ilya Sutskever, and Geoffrey E Hinton. 2012. Imagenet classification with deep convolutional neural networks. In *Advances in Neural Information Processing Systems*. 1097–1105.

[12] Ken Lang. 1995. Newsweeder: Learning to filter netnews. In *Proceedings of the 12th International Conference on Machine Learning*. 331–339.

[13] Yann LeCun, Yoshua Bengio, and Geoffrey Hinton. 2015. Deep learning. *Nature* 521, 7553 (2015), 436–444.

[14] Wu-Jun Li, Dit-Yan Yeung, and Zhihua Zhang. 2011. Generalized latent factor models for social network analysis. In *Proceedings of the 22nd International Joint Conference on Artificial Intelligence, Barcelona, Spain*. 1705.

[15] Xiaopeng Li, Ming Cheung, and James She. 2016. Connection Discovery using Shared Images by Gaussian Relational Topic Model. In *International Conference on Big Data*. IEEE, 931–936.

[16] Kevin P Murphy. 2012. *Machine learning: a probabilistic perspective*. MIT press.

[17] Michael Pazzani and Daniel Billsus. 1997. Learning and revising user profiles: The identification of interesting web sites. *Machine Learning* 27, 3 (1997), 313–331.

[18] Michael J Pazzani. 1999. A framework for collaborative, content-based and demographic filtering. *Artificial Intelligence Review* 13, 5-6 (1999), 393–408.

[19] Yunchen Pu, Zhe Gan, Ricardo Henao, Xin Yuan, Chunyuan Li, Andrew Stevens, and Lawrence Carin. 2016. Variational autoencoder for deep learning of images, labels and captions. In *Advances in Neural Information Processing Systems*. 2352–2360.

[20] Yunchen Pu, Xin Yuan, Andrew Stevens, Chunyuan Li, and Lawrence Carin. 2016. A deep generative deconvolutional image model. In *Proceedings of the 19th International Conference on Artificial Intelligence and Statistics*. 741–750.

[21] Steffen Rendle, Christoph Freudenthaler, Zeno Gantner, and Lars Schmidt-Thieme. 2009. BPR: Bayesian personalized ranking from implicit feedback. In *Proceedings of the 25th Conference on Uncertainty in Artificial Intelligence*. AUAI Press, 452–461.

[22] Ruslan Salakhutdinov and Andriy Mnih. 2007. Probabilistic matrix factorization.. In *Advances in Neural Information Processing Systems*, Vol. 1. 2–1.

[23] Ruslan Salakhutdinov, Andriy Mnih, and Geoffrey Hinton. 2007. Restricted Boltzmann machines for collaborative filtering. In *Proceedings of the 24th International Conference on Machine Learning*. ACM, 791–798.

[24] Ajit P Singh and Geoffrey J Gordon. 2008. Relational learning via collective matrix factorization. In *Proceedings of the 14th ACM SIGKDD International Conference on Knowledge Discovery and Data Mining*. ACM, 650–658.

[25] Aaron Van den Oord, Sander Dieleman, and Benjamin Schrauwen. 2013. Deep content-based music recommendation. In *Advances in Neural Information Processing Systems*. 2643–2651.

[26] Pascal Vincent, Hugo Larochelle, Isabelle Lajoie, Yoshua Bengio, and Pierre-Antoine Manzagol. 2010. Stacked denoising autoencoders: Learning useful representations in a deep network with a local denoising criterion. *Journal of Machine Learning Research* 11, Dec (2010), 3371–3408.

[27] Chong Wang and David M Blei. 2011. Collaborative topic modeling for recommending scientific articles. In *Proceedings of the 17th ACM SIGKDD International Conference on Knowledge Discovery and Data Mining*. ACM, 448–456.

[28] Hao Wang, Binyi Chen, and Wu-Jun Li. 2013. Collaborative topic regression with social regularization for tag recommendation.. In *International Joint Conference on Artificial Intelligence*.

[29] Hao Wang, Naiyan Wang, and Dit-Yan Yeung. 2015. Collaborative deep learning for recommender systems. In *Proceedings of the 21th ACM SIGKDD International Conference on Knowledge Discovery and Data Mining*. ACM, 1235–1244.

[30] Hao Wang, SHI Xingjian, and Dit-Yan Yeung. 2016. Collaborative recurrent autoencoder: Recommend while learning to fill in the blanks. In *Advances in Neural Information Processing Systems*. 415–423.

[31] Xinxi Wang and Ye Wang. 2014. Improving content-based and hybrid music recommendation using deep learning. In *Proceedings of the 22nd ACM International Conference on Multimedia*. ACM, 627–636.

Linearized GMM Kernels and Normalized Random Fourier Features

Ping Li
Department of Statistics and Biostatistics
Department of Computer Science
Rutgers University
Piscataway, NJ 08854, USA
pingli@stat.rutgers.edu

ABSTRACT

The method of "random Fourier features (RFF)" has become a popular tool for approximating the "radial basis function (RBF)" kernel. The variance of RFF is actually large. Interestingly, the variance can be substantially reduced by a simple normalization step as we theoretically demonstrate. We name the improved scheme as the "normalized RFF (NRFF)", and we provide a technical proof of the asymptotic variance of NRFF, as validated by simulations.

We also propose the "generalized min-max (GMM)" kernel as a measure of data similarity, where data vectors can have both positive and negative entries. GMM is positive definite as there is an associate hashing method named "generalized consistent weighted sampling (GCWS)" which linearizes this (nonlinear) kernel. We provide an extensive empirical evaluation of the RBF and GMM kernels on more than 50 datasets. For a majority of the datasets, the (tuning-free) GMM kernel outperforms the best-tuned RBF kernel.

We then conduct extensive classification experiments for comparing the linearized RBF kernel using NRFF with the linearized GMM kernel using GCWS. We observe that, in order to reach a similar accuracy, GCWS typically requires substantially fewer samples than NRFF, even on datasets where the original RBF kernel outperforms the original GMM kernel. As the training, storage, and processing costs are directly proportional to the sample size, our experiments can help demonstrate that GCWS would be a more practical scheme for large-scale machine learning applications.

The empirical success of GCWS (compared to NRFF) can also be explained theoretically, from at least two aspects. Firstly, the relative variance (normalized by the squared expectation) of GCWS is substantially smaller than that of NRFF, except for the very high similarity region (where the variances of both methods approach zero). Secondly, if we are allowed to make a general model assumption on the data, then we can show analytically that GCWS exhibits much smaller variance than NRFF for estimating the same object (e.g., the RBF kernel), except for the very high similarity region.

KDD '17, August 13-17, 2017, Halifax, NS, Canada

DOI: 10.1145/3097983.3098081

1 INTRODUCTION

It is popular in machine learning practice to use linear algorithms such as logistic regression or linear SVM. It is known that one can often improve the performance of linear methods by using nonlinear algorithms such as kernel SVMs, if the computational/storage burden can be resolved. In this paper, we introduce an effective measure of data similarity termed "generalized min-max (GMM)" kernel and the associated hashing method named "generalized consistent weighted sampling (GCWS)", which efficiently converts this nonlinear kernel into linear kernel. Moreover, we will also introduce what we call "normalized random Fourier features (NRFF)".

We start the introduction with the basic linear kernel. Consider two data vectors $u, v \in \mathbb{R}^D$. It is common to use the normalized linear kernel (i.e., the "cosine"):

$$\rho = \rho(u,v) = \frac{\sum_{i=1}^D u_i v_i}{\sqrt{\sum_{i=1}^D u_i^2}\sqrt{\sum_{i=1}^D v_i^2}} \tag{1}$$

This normalization step is in general a recommended practice. For example, when using LIBLINEAR or LIBSVM packages [8], it is suggested to first normalize the input data vectors to unit l_2 norm.

The popularity of the cosine can be explained by the fact that, if (u_i, v_i), $i = 1$ to D, are iid samples from a bivariate zero-mean normal distribution with a true (population) correlation parameter $\bar{\rho}$, then as $D \to \infty$, ρ converges to $\bar{\rho}$. However, when data are not exactly normal, as shown in [18], this convergence may not even hold. See Section 3 for more explanation on this important matter.

The proposed GMM kernel is defined on general data types which can have both negative and positive entries. The basic idea is to first transform the original data into nonnegative data and then compute the min-max kernel [11, 14, 19] on the transformed data.

1.1 Generalized Min-Max (GMM) Kernel

Consider the data vector u_i, $i = 1$ to D. We define the following transformation, depending on whether an entry u_i is positive or negative:

$$\begin{cases} \tilde{u}_{2i-1} = u_i, \quad \tilde{u}_{2i} = 0 & \text{if } u_i > 0 \\ \tilde{u}_{2i-1} = 0, \quad \tilde{u}_{2i} = -u_i & \text{if } u_i \leq 0 \end{cases} \tag{2}$$

For example, when $D = 2$ and $u = [-5 \;\; 3]$, the transformed data vector becomes $\tilde{u} = [0 \;\; 5 \;\; 3 \;\; 0]$. After this step of data transformation, the generalized min-max (GMM) similarity is defined as

$$GMM(u,v) = \frac{\sum_{i=1}^{2D} \min(\tilde{u}_i, \tilde{v}_i)}{\sum_{i=1}^{2D} \max(\tilde{u}_i, \tilde{v}_i)} \tag{3}$$

When the data are binary (0/1), GMM becomes the well-known "resemblance" similarity [4, 5, 16]. We will show in Section 4 that GMM is indeed an effective measure of data similarity through an extensive experimental study on kernel SVM classification. It is generally nontrivial to scale nonlinear kernels for large data [3]. In a sense, it is not practically meaningful to discuss nonlinear kernels without knowing how to compute them efficiently. This paper will focus on the "generalized consistent weighted sampling" (GCWS).

1.2 Generalized Consistent Weighted Sampling

Algorithm 1 summarizes the generalized consistent weighted sampling (GCWS). Given data vectors u and v, we transform them into nonnegative vectors $\tilde{u}$ and $\tilde{v}$ as in Eq. (2), then apply the original consistent weighted sampling (CWS) [11, 19] to generate tuples:

$$\left(i^*_{\tilde{u},j}, t^*_{\tilde{u},j}\right) \text{ and } \left(i^*_{\tilde{v},j}, t^*_{\tilde{v},j}\right), \quad j = 1, 2, ..., k \tag{4}$$

where $i^* \in [1,\ 2D]$ and t^* is unbounded. Following [11, 19], we have the basic probability result in Theorem 1.1.

THEOREM 1.1.

$$\mathbf{Pr}\left\{\left(i^*_{\tilde{u},j}, t^*_{\tilde{u},j}\right) = \left(i^*_{\tilde{v},j}, t^*_{\tilde{v},j}\right)\right\} = GMM(u, v) \tag{5}$$

Algorithm 1 Generalized Consistent Weighted Sampling (GCWS).

Input: Data vector $u = (i = 1 \text{ to } D)$
Transform: Generate vector $\tilde{u}$ in $2D$-dim by (2)
Output: Consistent uniform sample (i^*, t^*)

For i from 1 to $2D$
$r_i \sim Gamma(2,1)$, $c_i \sim Gamma(2,1)$, $\beta_i \sim Uniform(0,1)$
$t_i \leftarrow \lfloor \frac{\log \tilde{u}_i}{r_i} + \beta_i \rfloor$, $a_i \leftarrow \log(c_i) - r_i(t_i + 1 - \beta_i)$
End For
$i^* \leftarrow arg\min_i\ a_i$, $\quad t^* \leftarrow t_{i^*}$

Note that for sparse data, one will only need to deal with nonzero entries. The same random variables $\{r_i, c_i, \beta_i\}$ will be used for all data vectors (not just u). Algorithm 1 describes the procedure for generating one sample (i^*, t^*). With k independent samples, one can simply use the averaged indicator to estimate $GMM(u, v)$. The expectation (E) and variance (Var) of the indicator are

$$E\left[1\{i^*_{\tilde{u},j} = i^*_{\tilde{v},j} \text{ and } t^*_{\tilde{u},j} = t^*_{\tilde{v},j}\}\right] = GMM(u, v), \tag{6}$$

$$Var\left[1\{i^*_{\tilde{u},j} = i^*_{\tilde{v},j} \text{ and } t^*_{\tilde{u},j} = t^*_{\tilde{v},j}\}\right] = (1 - GMM(u, v))GMM(u, v) \tag{7}$$

The estimation variance, given k samples, will be $\frac{1}{k}(1-GMM)GMM$.

Practical Implementation: Based on intensive empirical observations [14], one can safely ignore t^* (which is unbounded) and simply use $\mathbf{Pr}\left\{i^*_{\tilde{u},j} = i^*_{\tilde{v},j}\right\} \approx GMM(u, v)$. Specifically, for each data vector u, we obtain k random samples $i^*_{\tilde{u},j}$, $j = 1$ to k. Then we store only the lowest b bits of i^*, based on the idea of [17]. We need to view those k integers as locations (of the nonzeros) instead of numerical values. For example, when $b = 2$, we should view i^* as a vector of length $2^b = 4$. If $i^* = 3$, then we code it as [1 0 0 0]; if $i^* = 0$, we code it as [0 0 0 1]. We then concatenate all k such vectors into a binary vector of length $2^b \times k$, with exactly k 1's.

For linear methods, the computational cost is largely determined by the number of nonzeros in each data vector, i.e., the k in our case. For the other parameter b, we recommend to use $b \geq 4$. When using batch algorithms (such as LIBLINEAR), a larger b will in general increase the training time but typically not much. Note that, with online learning [2], it would be obvious that the training time is determined by the number of nonzeros (and number of epoches).

The natural competitor of the GMM kernel is the RBF (radial basis function) kernel, and one competitor of the GCWS hashing method could be the RFF (random Fourier feature) algorithm.

2 RBF KERNEL AND NORMALIZED RANDOM FOURIER FEATURES (NRFF)

The radial basis function (RBF) kernel is widely used in machine learning and many fields. In this study, for convenience (e.g., parameter tuning), we recommend the following version:

$$RBF(u, v; \gamma) = e^{-\gamma(1-\rho)} \tag{8}$$

where $\rho = \rho(u, v)$ is the cosine defined in Eq. (1) and $\gamma > 0$ is a tuning parameter. Based on Bochner's Theorem [23], it is known [21] that, if we sample $w \sim uniform(0, 2\pi)$, $r_i \sim N(0, 1)$ i.i.d., and let $x = \sum_{i=1}^D u_i r_{ij}$, $y = \sum_{i=1}^D v_i r_{ij}$, where $\|u\|_2 = \|v\|_2 = 1$, we have

$$E\left(\sqrt{2}\cos(\sqrt{\gamma}x + w)\sqrt{2}\cos(\sqrt{\gamma}y + w)\right) = e^{-\gamma(1-\rho)} \tag{9}$$

This provides an elegant mechanism for linearizing the RBF kernel and the RFF method has become very popular in machine learning, computer vision, and beyond, e.g., [1, 6, 7, 9, 10, 20, 22, 24, 27, 28].

The result in Theorem 2.1 on the variance of RFF was known, for example, see [25]. In this paper, we provide a proof with general intermediate results which are needed for the proof of Theorem 2.2.

THEOREM 2.1. *Given $x \sim N(0, 1)$, $y \sim N(0, 1)$, $E(xy) = \rho$, and $w \sim uniform(0, 2\pi)$, we have*

$$E\left[\sqrt{2}\cos(\sqrt{\gamma}x + w)\sqrt{2}\cos(\sqrt{\gamma}y + w)\right] = e^{-\gamma(1-\rho)} \tag{10}$$

$$Var\left[\sqrt{2}\cos(\sqrt{\gamma}x + w)\sqrt{2}\cos(\sqrt{\gamma}y + w)\right] = \frac{1}{2} + \frac{1}{2}\left(1 - e^{-2\gamma(1-\rho)}\right)^2 \tag{11}$$

From Theorem 2.1, one can see that the variance of RFF might be large. Interestingly, the variance can be substantially reduced if we normalize the generated data, a procedure which we call "normalized RFF (NRFF)", as shown in Theorem 2.2.

THEOREM 2.2. *Consider k iid samples (x_j, y_j, w_j) where $x_j \sim N(0, 1)$, $y_j \sim N(0, 1)$, $E(x_j y_j) = \rho$, $w_j \sim uniform(0, 2\pi)$, $j = 1, 2, ..., k$. Let $X_j = \sqrt{2}\cos\left(\sqrt{\gamma}x_j + w_j\right)$ and $Y_j = \sqrt{2}\cos\left(\sqrt{\gamma}y_j + w_j\right)$. As $k \to \infty$, the following asymptotic normality holds:*

$$\sqrt{k}\left(\frac{\sum_{j=1}^k X_j Y_j}{\sqrt{\sum_{j=1}^k X_j^2}\sqrt{\sum_{j=1}^k Y_j^2}} - e^{-\gamma(1-\rho)}\right) \overset{D}{\Longrightarrow} N\left(0, V_{n,\rho,\gamma}\right) \tag{12}$$

where

$$V_{n,\rho,\gamma} = V_{\rho,\gamma} - \frac{1}{4}e^{-2\gamma(1-\rho)}\left[3 - e^{-4\gamma(1-\rho)}\right] \tag{13}$$

$$V_{\rho,\gamma} = \frac{1}{2} + \frac{1}{2}\left(1 - e^{-2\gamma(1-\rho)}\right)^2 \tag{14}$$

Obviously, $V_{n,\rho,\gamma} < V_{\rho,\gamma}$ (in particular, $V_{n,\rho,\gamma} = 0$ at $\rho = 1$), i.e., the variance of the normalized RFF is smaller than that of the original RFF. Figure 1 plots $\frac{V_{n,\rho,\gamma}}{V_{\rho,\gamma}}$ to visualize the improvement.

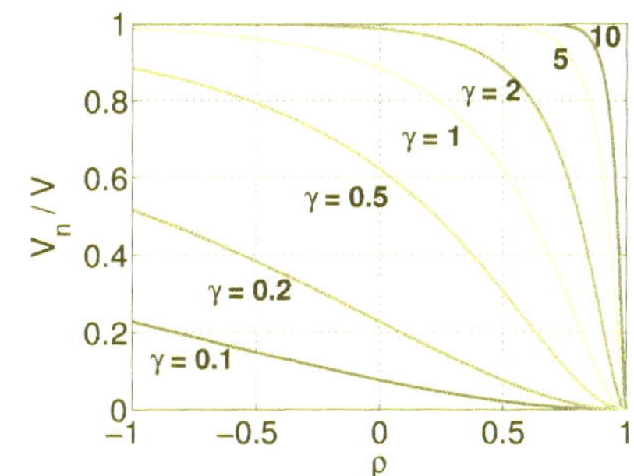

Figure 1: The ratio $\frac{V_{n,\rho,\gamma}}{V_{\rho,\gamma}}$ from Theorem 2.2 for visualizing the improvement due to the normalization step.

Note that the theoretical results in Theorem 2.2 are asymptotic (i.e., for larger k). With k samples, the variance of the original RFF is exactly $\frac{V_{\rho,\gamma}}{k}$, however the variance of the normalized RFF (NRFF) is written as $\frac{V_{n,\rho,\gamma}}{k} + O\left(\frac{1}{k^2}\right)$. It is thus important to understand the behavior when k is not large. For this purpose, Figure 2 presents the simulated mean square error (MSE) results for estimating the RBF kernel $e^{-\gamma(1-\rho)}$, confirming that a): the improvement due to normalization can be substantial, and b): the asymptotic variance formula (13) becomes accurate for merely $k > 10$.

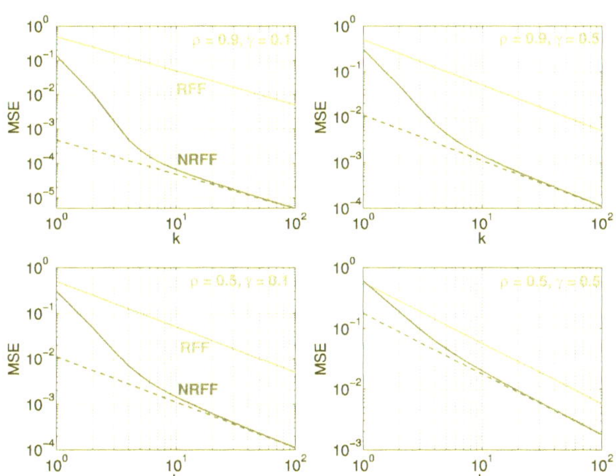

Figure 2: A simulation study to verify the asymptotic theoretical results in Theorem 2.2. With k samples, we estimate the RBF kernel $e^{-\gamma(1-\rho)}$, using both the original RFF and the normalized RFF (NRFF). With 10^5 repetitions at each k, we can compute the empirical mean square error: MSE = Bias^2+Var. Each panel presents the MSEs (solid curves) for a particular choice of (ρ, γ), along with the theoretical variances: $\frac{V_{\rho,\gamma}}{k}$ and $\frac{V_{n,\rho,\gamma}}{k}$ (dashed curves). The variance of the original RFF (curves above, or red if color is available) can be substantially larger than the MSE of the normalized RFF (curves below, or blue). When $k > 10$, the normalized RFF provides an unbiased estimate of the RBF kernel and its empirical MSE matches the theoretical asymptotic variance.

Next, we attempt to compare RFF (and NRFF) with GCWS. While ultimately we can rely on specific machine learning accuracy (e.g., classification, regression, or clustering) as a metric of performance, here we compare their variances (Var) relative to their expectations (E) in terms of Var/E^2, as shown in Figure 3. For example, for GCWS, we know $Var/E^2 = E(1-E)/E^2 = (1-E)/E$.

Figure 3 shows that the relative variance of GCWS is substantially smaller than that of the original RFF and NRFF, especially when E is not large. For the very high similarity region (i.e., $E \longrightarrow 1$), both NRFF and GCWS exhibit substantially smaller relative variances than the original RFF. Note that in the very high similarity region, the variances of both NRFF and GCWS approach zero.

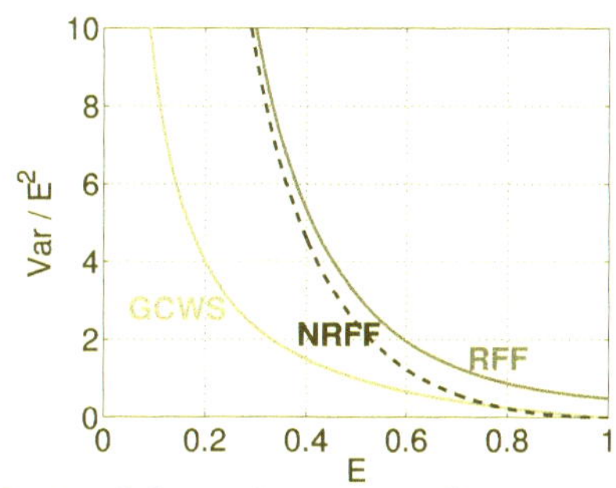

Figure 3: Ratio of the variance over the squared expectation, denoted as Var/E^2, for the convenience of comparing RFF & NRFF with GCWS. Also, see Section 3 and Figure 4.

The results from Figure 3 provide one plausible explanation why later we will observe that, in the classification experiments, GCWS typically needs substantially fewer samples than the normalized RFF, in order to achieve similar classification accuracies. Note that for practical data, the similarities among most data points are usually small (i.e., small E) and hence it is not surprising that GCWS may perform substantially better, according to Figure 3.

While Var/E^2 (known as the squared coefficient of variation) is a standard term in probability and statistics, there might be a concern that we are comparing two different methods which estimate different similarities. Interestingly, it is possible to connect the GMM kernel with cosine (and hence the RBF kernel) if we are allowed to make a gentle model assumption on the data. See Section 3 and Figure 4, which deliver a similar conclusion as Figure 3.

In a sense, this drawback of RFF is expected, due to nature of random projections. For example, as shown in [15], the linear estimator of ρ using random projections has variance $\frac{1+\rho^2}{k}$, where k is the number of projections. Understandably, in order to make the variance small, one will have to use a large number of projections.

Sketch Proof of Theorem 2.1: Firstly, we make use of a known integral: $\int_{-\infty}^{\infty} \cos(cx) e^{-x^2/2} dx = \sqrt{2\pi} e^{-c^2/2}$ to derive two basic integrals:

$$\int_{-\infty}^{\infty} \cos(c_1 x)\cos(c_2 x) e^{-x^2/2} dx = \frac{\sqrt{2\pi}}{2}\left[e^{-(c_1+c_2)^2/2} + e^{-(c_1-c_2)^2/2}\right]$$

$$\int_{-\infty}^{\infty} \sin(c_1 x)\sin(c_2 x) e^{-x^2/2} dx = \frac{\sqrt{2\pi}}{2}\left[e^{-(c_1-c_2)^2/2} - e^{-(c_1+c_2)^2/2}\right]$$

Next, we consider integers $b_1, b_2 = 1, 2, 3, ...,$ and, after some tedious algebra, we derive

$$
\begin{aligned}
&E\left(\cos(c_1x + b_1w)\cos(c_2y + b_2w)\right)\\
=&\frac{1}{2\pi}\int_0^{2\pi} E(\cos(c_1x + b_1t)\cos(c_2y + b_2t))dt\\
=&\frac{1}{2\pi}\frac{1}{\sqrt{2\pi}}e^{-\frac{c_2^2(1-\rho^2)}{2}}\int_0^{2\pi}\int_{-\infty}^{\infty} e^{-\frac{x^2}{2}}\cos(c_1x + b_1t)\cos(c_2\rho x + b_2t)dxdt\\
=&\frac{1}{2\pi}\frac{1}{\sqrt{2\pi}}e^{-\frac{c_2^2(1-\rho^2)}{2}}\int_{-\infty}^{\infty} e^{-\frac{x^2}{2}}\pi\cos((c_1 - c_2\rho)x)dx, \quad \text{when } b_1 = b_2\\
=&\frac{1}{2\pi}\frac{1}{\sqrt{2\pi}}e^{-\frac{c_2^2(1-\rho^2)}{2}}\pi\sqrt{2\pi}e^{-(c_1-c_2\rho)^2/2}\\
=&\frac{1}{2}e^{-\frac{c_1^2+c_2^2-2c_1c_2\rho}{2}} = \frac{1}{2}e^{-c^2(1-\rho)}, \quad \text{when } c_1 = c_2 = c
\end{aligned}
$$

The above integral is otherwise 0 if $b_1 \neq b_2$. This completes the proof of the first moment. Now, using the following fact

$$
\begin{aligned}
E\cos(2cx + 2w) =&\frac{1}{2\pi}\int_0^{2\pi}\frac{1}{\sqrt{2\pi}}\int_{-\infty}^{\infty}\cos(2cx + 2t)e^{-x^2/2}dxdt\\
=&\frac{1}{2\pi}\int_0^{2\pi}\frac{1}{\sqrt{2\pi}}\frac{1}{2}\sin 2t\int_{-\infty}^{\infty}\cos(2cx)e^{-x^2/2}dxdt\\
=&\frac{1}{4\pi}e^{-2c^2}\int_0^{2\pi}\sin 2tdt = 0
\end{aligned}
$$

we are ready to compute the second moment

$$
\begin{aligned}
&E\left[\cos(cx + w)\cos(cy + w)\right]^2\\
=&\frac{1}{4}E\left[\cos(2cx + 2w)\cos(2cy + 2w) + \cos(2cx + 2w) + \cos(2cy + 2w)\right] + \frac{1}{4}\\
=&\frac{1}{4}E\left[\cos(2cx + 2w)\cos(2cy + 2w)\right] + \frac{1}{4}\\
=&\frac{1}{8}e^{-4c^2(1-\rho)} + \frac{1}{4}
\end{aligned}
$$

and the variance

$$
Var\left[\cos(cx + w)\cos(cy + w)\right] = \frac{1}{8}e^{-4c^2(1-\rho)} + \frac{1}{4} - \frac{1}{4}e^{-2c^2(1-\rho)}
$$

This completes the proof of Theorem 2.1. □

Sketch Proof of Theorem 2.2: Define

$$
X_j = \sqrt{2}\cos(\sqrt{\gamma}x_j + w_j), \qquad Y_j = \sqrt{2}\cos(\sqrt{\gamma}y_j + w_j),
$$

$$
Z_k = \frac{\sum_{j=1}^k X_jY_j}{\sqrt{\sum_{j=1}^k X_j^2}\sqrt{\sum_{j=1}^k Y_j^2}}
$$

From Theorem 2.1, it is easy to see that, as $k \to \infty$, we have

$$
\frac{1}{k}\sum_{j=1}^k X_j^2 \to E\left(X_j^2\right) = e^{-\gamma(1-1)} = 1, \ a.s. \qquad \frac{1}{k}\sum_{j=1}^k Y_j^2 \to 1, \ a.s.
$$

$$
Z_k = \frac{\frac{1}{k}\sum_{j=1}^k X_jY_j}{\sqrt{\frac{1}{k}\sum_{j=1}^k X_j^2}\sqrt{\frac{1}{k}\sum_{j=1}^k Y_j^2}} \to e^{-\gamma(1-\rho)} = Z_\infty, \ a.s.
$$

We express the deviation $Z_k - Z_\infty$ as

$$
\begin{aligned}
Z_k - Z_\infty =& \frac{\frac{1}{k}\sum_{j=1}^k X_jY_j - Z_\infty + Z_\infty}{\sqrt{\frac{1}{k}\sum_{j=1}^k X_j^2}\sqrt{\frac{1}{k}\sum_{j=1}^k Y_j^2}} - Z_\infty\\
=&\frac{\frac{1}{k}\sum_{j=1}^k X_jY_j - Z_\infty}{\sqrt{\frac{1}{k}\sum_{j=1}^k X_j^2}\sqrt{\frac{1}{k}\sum_{j=1}^k Y_j^2}} + Z_\infty\frac{1 - \sqrt{\frac{1}{k}\sum_{j=1}^k X_j^2}\sqrt{\frac{1}{k}\sum_{j=1}^k Y_j^2}}{\sqrt{\frac{1}{k}\sum_{j=1}^k X_j^2}\sqrt{\frac{1}{k}\sum_{j=1}^k Y_j^2}}\\
=&\frac{1}{k}\sum_{j=1}^k X_jY_j - Z_\infty + Z_\infty\frac{1 - \frac{1}{k}\sum_{j=1}^k X_j^2\frac{1}{k}\sum_{j=1}^k Y_j^2}{2} + O_P(1/k)\\
=&\frac{1}{k}\sum_{j=1}^k X_jY_j - Z_\infty + Z_\infty\frac{1 - \frac{1}{k}\sum_{j=1}^k X_j^2}{2} + Z_\infty\frac{1 - \frac{1}{k}\sum_{j=1}^k Y_j^2}{2} + O_P(1/k)
\end{aligned}
$$

Thus, to analyze the asymptotic variance, it suffices to study:

$$
\begin{aligned}
&E\left(XY - Z_\infty + Z_\infty\frac{1 - X^2}{2} + Z_\infty\frac{1 - Y^2}{2}\right)^2\\
=&E\left(XY - Z_\infty(X^2 + Y^2)/2\right)^2\\
=&E(X^2Y^2) + Z_\infty^2E(X^4 + Y^4 + 2X^2Y^2)/4 - Z_\infty E(X^3Y) - Z_\infty E(XY^3)
\end{aligned}
$$

which can be obtained from the intermediate results in the proof of Theorem 2.1. In particular, if $b_1 = b_2$, then

$$
E\left(\cos(c_1x + b_1w)\cos(c_2y + b_2w)\right) = \frac{1}{2}e^{-\frac{c_1^2+c_2^2-2c_1c_2\rho}{2}}
$$

which is otherwise 0 if $b_1 \neq b_2$. We can now compute

$$
\begin{aligned}
E\left[\cos(cx + w)^3\cos(cy + w)\right] =& \frac{3}{8}e^{-c^2(1-\rho)}\\
E\left[\cos(cx + w)\cos(cy + w)\right]^2 =& \frac{1}{8}e^{-4c^2(1-\rho)} + \frac{1}{4}\\
E\left[\cos(cx + w)\right]^4 =& \frac{1}{8} + \frac{1}{4} = \frac{3}{8}
\end{aligned}
$$

$$
\begin{aligned}
V_{n,\rho,\gamma} =& E\left(XY - Z_\infty + Z_\infty\frac{1 - X^2}{2} + Z_\infty\frac{1 - Y^2}{2}\right)^2\\
=&E(X^2Y^2) + Z_\infty^2E(X^4 + Y^4 + 2X^2Y^2)/4 - Z_\infty E(X^3Y) - Z_\infty E(XY^3)\\
=&\frac{1}{2}e^{-4c^2(1-\rho)} + 1 + e^{-2c^2(1-\rho)}\left(\frac{3}{8} + \frac{3}{8} + \frac{1}{4}e^{-4c^2(1-\rho)} + \frac{1}{2}\right)\\
&- e^{-c^2(1-\rho)}\left(\frac{3}{2}e^{-c^2(1-\rho)} + \frac{3}{2}e^{-c^2(1-\rho)}\right)\\
=&V_{\rho,\gamma} - \frac{1}{4}e^{-2c^2(1-\rho)}\left[3 - e^{-4c^2(1-\rho)}\right]
\end{aligned}
$$

where $V_{\rho,\gamma}$ is the corresponding variance factor without the normalization step: $V_{\rho,\gamma} = \frac{1}{2} + \frac{1}{2}\left(1 - e^{-2c^2(1-\rho)}\right)^2$. □

3 COMPARING NRFF WITH GCWS USING ASYMPTOTIC OF GMM

The comparison might be more convincing if we can use both NRFF and GCWS to estimate the same object. This task would not be possible unless we can connect GMM with cosine in Eq. (1):

$$
\rho = \rho(u, v) = \frac{\sum_{i=1}^D u_iv_i}{\sqrt{\sum_{i=1}^D u_i^2}\sqrt{\sum_{i=1}^D v_i^2}}
$$

It is well understood that if (u_i, v_i), $i = 1$ to D, are iid samples from a bivariate zero-mean normal distribution with a true correlation parameter $\bar{\rho}$, then as $D \to \infty$, ρ converges to $\bar{\rho}$. However, when data are not exactly normal, as shown in [18], this convergence may not even hold.

For example, when (u_i, v_i), $i = 1$ to D, are iid samples from a bivariate centered t-distribution with ν degrees of freedom and a covariance matrix $\begin{bmatrix} 1 & \bar{\rho} \\ \bar{\rho} & 1 \end{bmatrix}$, the convergence $\rho \to \bar{\rho}$ holds only if $\nu \geq 2$. [18] provided a much more general result by assuming the data follow an "elliptical distribution" (which includes the t distribution). Simply speaking, the use of cosine ρ makes sense only when data have bounded second moments and it becomes reliable when data have bounded fourth (or higher) moments.

Under the same t-distribution assumption, [18] proved an interesting convergence result for the GMM kernel:

$$GMM(u, v) \to \frac{1 - \sqrt{(1-\bar{\rho})/2}}{1 + \sqrt{(1-\bar{\rho})/2}} = g, \qquad \text{as } D \to \infty \tag{15}$$

The convergence holds as long as $\nu \geq 1$, which is a much weaker assumption than that required for the convergence of cosine. The result was also generalized to the elliptical distribution family.

These theoretical results provide a mechanism to compare GMM with cosine. For example, if one uses both GMM and cosine to estimate the true correlation $\bar{\rho}$, it is more preferable to use GMM when $\nu < 8$. In fact, even when the data are perfectly normal, using GMM will not lose much statistical efficiency compared to using cosine. Since real-world data are virtually always heavy-tailed, the results in [18] appear to suggest one should essentially always use GMM.

In this section, we utilize the results in [18] to compare NRFF with GCWS. To simplify the discussion, we assume that the data dimension D is large enough and the data satisfy the convergence conditions for both GMM and cosine. This way, it is reasonable to assume

$$\rho = \bar{\rho}, \qquad GMM = g = \frac{1 - \sqrt{(1-\bar{\rho})/2}}{1 + \sqrt{(1-\bar{\rho})/2}} \tag{16}$$

Using the expression of g we can re-write RBF as

$$\rho = 1 - 2\left(\frac{1-g}{1+g}\right)^2, \qquad e^{-\gamma(1-\rho)} = e^{-2\gamma\left(\frac{1-g}{1+g}\right)^2} \tag{17}$$

This result provides us another estimator of the RBF kernel from GCWS hashing, which generates iid samples from a binomial distribution: $binomial(k,g)$, where g is the probability parameter.

Theorem 3.1. *Assume* $g = \frac{1-\sqrt{(1-\rho)/2}}{1+\sqrt{(1-\rho)/2}}$ *and* $X \sim binomial(k,g)$. *Then, denoting* $\bar{X} = \frac{1}{k}\sum_{i=1}^k X_i$, *we have*

$$E\left(e^{-2\gamma\left(\frac{1-\bar{X}}{1+\bar{X}}\right)^2}\right) = e^{-\gamma(1-\rho)} + O\left(\frac{1}{k}\right) \tag{18}$$

$$Var\left(e^{-2\gamma\left(\frac{1-\bar{X}}{1+\bar{X}}\right)^2}\right) = \frac{V_{g,\gamma}}{k} + O\left(\frac{1}{k^2}\right) \tag{19}$$

$$V_{g,\gamma} = e^{-2\gamma(1-\rho)}\frac{g(1-g)^3}{(1+g)^6}64\gamma^2 \tag{20}$$

Proof sketch: For an asymptotic analysis with large k, it suffices to consider $Z = \frac{1-\hat{X}}{1+\hat{X}}$ as a normal random variable, whose mean and variance can be calculated to be $\mu = \frac{1-g}{1+g}$, $\sigma^2 = \frac{1}{k}\frac{4g(1-g)}{(1+g)^4}$. A direct calculation shows that $E\left(e^{Z^2 t}\right) = \frac{1}{\sqrt{1-2\sigma^2 t}}e^{\frac{\mu^2 t}{1-2\sigma^2 t}}$. Then, by letting $\sigma^2 = \frac{1}{k}\lambda^2$, we have

$$\begin{aligned}
Var\left(e^{X^2 t}\right) =& E\left(e^{X^2 2t}\right) - E^2\left(e^{X^2 t}\right)\\
=&\frac{1}{\sqrt{1-2\sigma^2 2t}}e^{\frac{\mu^2 2t}{1-2\sigma^2 2t}} - \frac{1}{1-2\sigma^2 t}e^{\frac{\mu^2 2t}{1-2\sigma^2 t}}\\
=&\left(1 + \frac{2\lambda^2 t}{k} + O\left(\frac{1}{k^2}\right)\right)e^{2\mu^2 t\left(1+\frac{4\lambda^2 t}{k}+O\left(\frac{1}{k^2}\right)\right)}\\
&-\left(1 + \frac{2\lambda^2 t}{k} + O\left(\frac{1}{k^2}\right)\right)e^{2\mu^2 t\left(1+\frac{2\lambda^2 t}{k}+O\left(\frac{1}{k^2}\right)\right)}\\
=&\frac{4\mu^2\lambda^2 t^2}{k}e^{2\mu^2 t} + O\left(\frac{1}{k^2}\right)
\end{aligned}$$

The result follows by letting $t = -2\gamma$, $\mu = \frac{1-g}{1+g}$, and $\lambda^2 = \frac{4g(1-g)}{(1+g)^4}$. □

Theorem 3.1 and Theorem 2.2 provide a more direct comparison of GCWS with NRFF by visualizing $\frac{V_{n,\rho,\gamma}}{V_{g,\gamma}}$. As shown in Figure 4, when estimating the RBF kernel, the variance of GCWS is substantially smaller than the variance of NRFF, except for the very high similarity region (depending on γ). At high similarity, the variances of both methods approach zero. This provides another explanation for the superb empirical performance of GCWS compared to NRFF, as will be reported in Section 5.

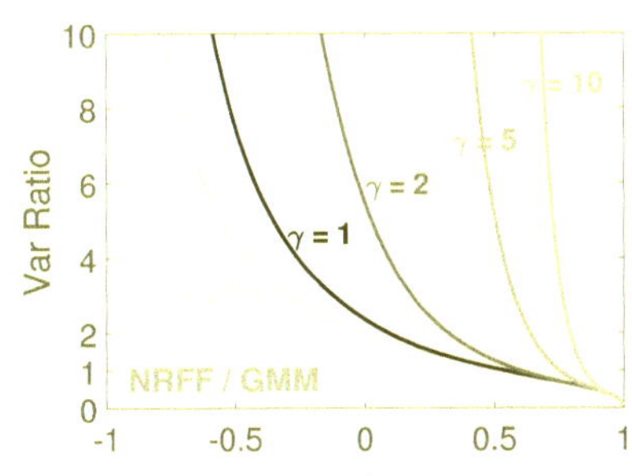

Figure 4: The variance ratio: $\frac{V_{n,\rho,\gamma}}{V_{g,\gamma}}$ provides another comparison of GCWS with NRFF. $V_{g,\gamma}$ is derived in Theorem 3.1 and $V_{n,\rho,\gamma}$ is derived in Theorem 2.2. The ratios are significantly larger than 1 except for the very high similarity region (where the variances of both methods are close to zero).

4 AN EXPERIMENTAL STUDY ON KERNELS

Table 1 lists datasets from the UCI repository. Table 2 presents datasets from the LIBSVM website as well as datasets which are fairly large. Table 3 contains datasets used in an empirical study on deep learning [12] and later for comparing deep nets with tree methods [13]. Except for the relatively large datasets in Table 2, we report the classification accuracies for using kernel SVM with RBF and kernel SVM with GMM, at their the best l_2-regularization

C values. More detailed results (for all regularization C values) are available in Figure 6. To ensure repeatability, we use the LIBSVM pre-computed kernel functionality. This also means we can not (easily) test nonlinear kernels on larger datasets (but then we can resort to hashing methods, e.g., GMM or NRFF).

Table 1: Public (UCI) classification datasets and l_2-regularized kernel SVM results. We report test classification accuracies for the linear kernel, the best-tuned RBF kernel (and the best γ), and the GMM kernel, at their individually- best SVM regularization C values.

Dataset	# train	# test	# dim	linear	RBF (γ)	GMM
Covertype25k	25000	25000	54	62.64	**82.66** (90)	82.65
CTG	1063	1063	35	60.59	**89.75** (0.1)	88.81
Car	864	864	6	71.53	94.91 (100)	**98.96**
DailySports	4560	4560	5625	77.70	97.61 (4)	**99.61**
Dexter	300	300	19999	92.67	93.00 (0.01)	**94.00**
Gesture	4937	4936	32	37.22	61.06 (9)	**65.50**
ImageSeg	210	2100	19	83.81	91.38 (0.4)	**95.05**
Isolet2k	2000	5797	617	93.95	**95.55** (3)	95.53
MSD20k	20000	20000	90	66.72	68.07 (0.1)	**71.05**
MHealth20k	20000	20000	23	72.62	82.65 (0.1)	**85.28**
Magic	9150	9150	10	78.04	84.43 (0.8)	**87.02**
Musk	3299	3299	166	95.09	**99.33** (1.2)	99.24
PageBlocks	2737	2726	10	95.87	**97.08** (1.2)	96.56
Parkinson	520	520	26	61.15	66.73(1.9)	**69.81**
PAMAP101	20000	20000	51	76.86	96.68 (15)	**98.91**
PAMAP102	20000	20000	51	81.22	95.67 (1.1)	**98.78**
PAMAP103	20000	20000	51	85.54	97.89 (19)	**99.69**
PAMAP104	20000	20000	51	84.03	97.32 (19)	**99.30**
PAMAP105	20000	20000	51	79.43	97.34 (18)	**99.22**
RobotNavi	2728	2728	24	69.83	90.69 (10)	**96.85**
Satimage	4435	2000	36	72.45	85.20 (200)	**90.40**
SEMG1	900	900	3000	26.00	**43.56** (4)	41.00
SEMG2	1800	1800	2500	19.28	29.00 (6)	**54.00**
Sensorless	29255	29254	48	61.53	93.01 (0.4)	**99.39**
Shuttle500	500	14500	9	91.81	99.52 (1.6)	**99.65**
SkinSeg10k	10000	10000	3	93.36	99.74 (120)	**99.81**
SpamBase	2301	2300	57	85.91	92.57 (0.2)	**94.17**
Splice	1000	2175	60	85.10	90.02 (15)	**95.22**
Thyroid2k	2000	5200	21	94.90	97.00 (2.5)	**98.40**
Urban	168	507	147	62.52	51.48 (0.01)	**66.08**
Vowel	264	264	10	39.39	94.70 (45)	**96.97**
YoutubeAudio10k	10000	11930	2000	41.35	48.63 (2)	**50.59**
YoutubeHOG10k	10000	11930	647	62.77	66.20 (0.5)	**68.63**
YoutubeMotion10k	10000	11930	64	26.24	28.81 (19)	**31.95**
YoutubeSaiBoxes10k	10000	11930	7168	46.97	49.31 (1.1)	**51.28**
YoutubeSpectrum10k	10000	11930	1024	26.81	33.54 (4)	**39.23**

Table 2: Datasets in groups 1 and 3 are from the LIBSVM website. Datasets in group 2 are from the UCI repository. Datasets in group 2 and 3 are fairly large and are used for testing hashing methods.

	Dataset	# train	# test	# dim	linear	RBF (γ)	GMM
	Letter	15000	5000	16	61.66	**97.44** (11)	97.26
1	Protein	17766	6621	357	69.14	70.32 (4)	**70.64**
	SensIT20k	20000	19705	100	80.42	83.15 (0.1)	**84.57**
	Webspam20k	20000	60000	254	93.00	**97.99** (35)	97.88
2	PAMAP101Large	186,581	186,580	51	79.19		
	PAMAP105Large	185,548	185,548	51	83.35		
	IJCNN	49990	91701	22	92.56		
3	RCV1	338,699	338,700	47,236	97.66		
	SensIT	78,823	19,705	100	80.55		
	Webspam	175,000	175,000	254	93.31		

When experimenting with the RBF kernel, we searched 58 different values of $\gamma \in \{0.001, 0.01, 0.1{:}0.1{:}2, 2.5, 3{:}1{:}20\ 25{:}5{:}50, 60{:}10{:}100, 120, 150, 200, 300, 500, 1000\}$, where for example 60:10:100 means the values are from 60 to 100 spaced at 10. Basically, Tables 1, 2, and 3 report the best RBF results among all γ and C values.

Table 3: Datasets from [12] for comparing deep learning methods with many learning algorithms such as kernel SVM. These datasets were later used by [13] to compare deep nets with tree methods.

Dataset	# train	# test	# dim	linear	RBF (γ)	GMM
M-Basic	12000	50000	784	89.98	**97.21** (5)	96.20
M-Image	12000	50000	784	70.71	77.84 (16)	**80.85**
M-Noise1	10000	4000	784	60.28	66.83 (10)	**71.38**
M-Noise2	10000	4000	784	62.05	69.15 (11)	**72.43**
M-Noise3	10000	4000	784	65.15	71.68 (11)	**73.55**
M-Noise4	10000	4000	784	68.38	75.33 (14)	**76.05**
M-Noise5	10000	4000	784	72.25	78.70 (12)	**79.03**
M-Noise6	10000	4000	784	78.73	**85.33** (15)	84.23
M-Rand	12000	50000	784	78.90	**85.39** (12)	84.22
M-Rotate	12000	50000	784	47.99	**89.68** (5)	84.76
M-RotImg	12000	50000	784	31.44	**45.84** (18)	40.98

The classification results indicate that, on these datasets, kernel (GMM and RBF) SVM classifiers often substantially improve over linear classifiers. Interestingly, For more than half of the datasets, the (tuning-free) GMM kernel outperforms the best-tuned RBF kernel. For a small number of datasets (e.g., "SEMG1" or "M-Rotate"), even though the RBF kernel performs better, we will show in Section 5 that GCWS can still be substantially better than NRFF.

For the datasets in Table 3, since [12] also conducted experiments on the RBF kernel, the polynomial kernel, and neural nets, we assembly the (error rate) results in Figure 5 and Table 4.

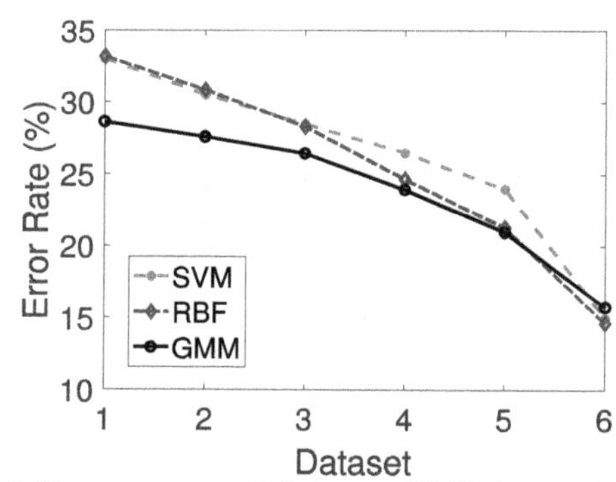

Figure 5: Error rates on 6 datasets: M-Noise1 to M-Noise6 as in Table 3. In this figure, the curve labeled as "SVM" represents the results on RBF kernel SVM conducted by [12], while the curve labeled as "RBF" presents our own experiments. The small discrepancies might be caused by the fact that we always use normalized data (i.e., ρ).

Table 4: Summary of test error rates of various algorithms on several datasets used in [12]. Results in group 1 are reported by [12] for using RBF kernel, polynomial kernel, and neural nets. Results in group 2 are from our own experiments.

Group	Method	M-Basic	M-Rotate	M-Image	M-Rand	M-RotImg
	SVM-RBF	3.05%	11.11%	22.61%	14.58%	55.18%
1	SVM-POLY	3.69%	15.42%	24.01%	16.62%	56.41%
	NNET	4.69%	18.11%	27.41%	20.04%	62.16%
	Linear	10.02%	52.01%	29.29%	21.10%	68.56%
2	RBF	**2.79%**	**10.30%**	22.16%	**14.61%**	**54.16%**
	GMM	3.80%	15.24%	**19.15%**	15.78%	59.02%

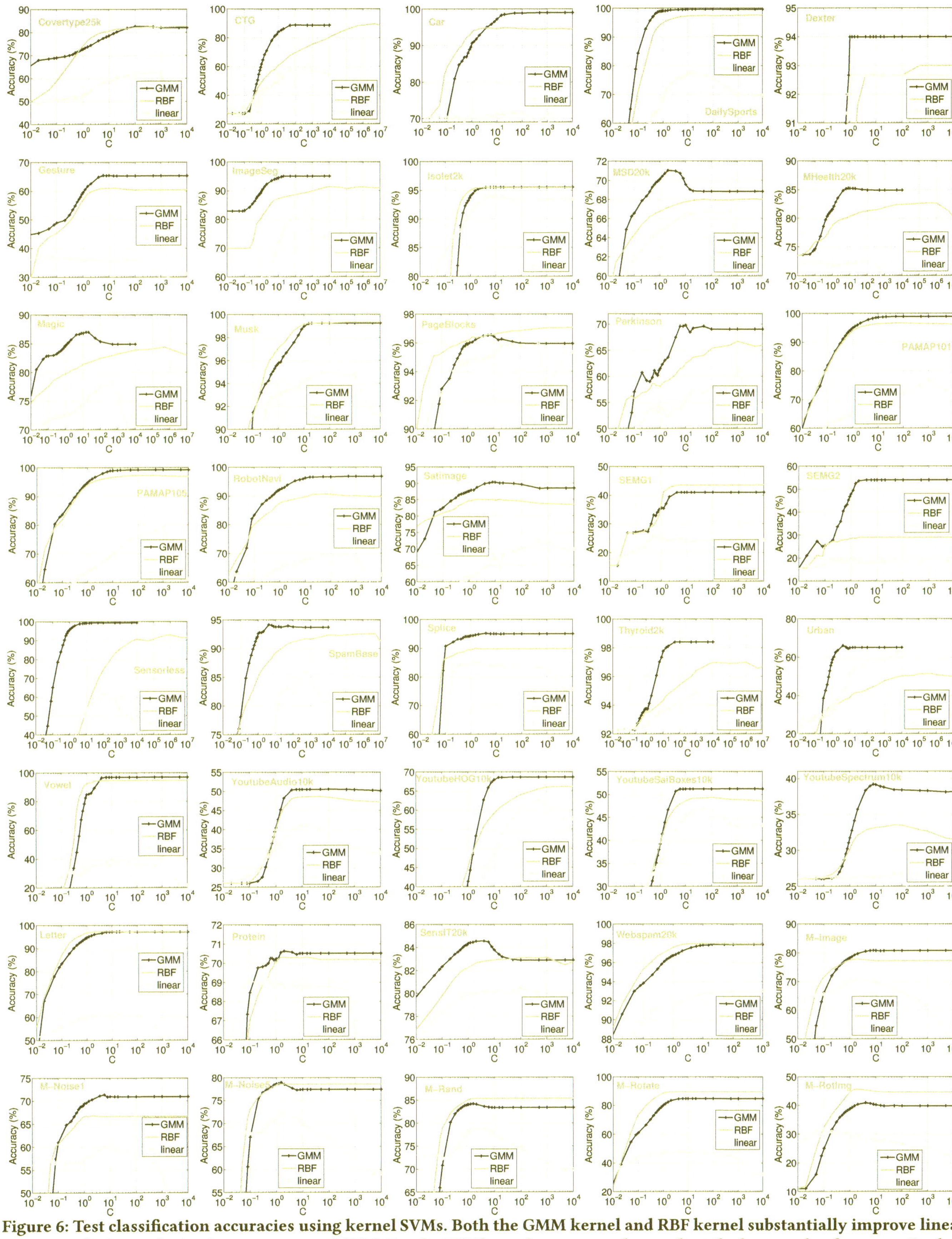

Figure 6: Test classification accuracies using kernel SVMs. Both the GMM kernel and RBF kernel substantially improve linear SVM. C is the l_2-regularization parameter of SVM. For the RBF kernel, we report the result at the best γ value for every C value.

5 HASHING FOR LINEARIZING KERNELS

It is known that a straightforward implementation of nonlinear kernels is difficult for large datasets [3]. For example, for a small dataset with merely 60,000 data points, the $60,000 \times 60,000$ kernel matrix has 3.6×10^9 entries. In practice, being able to linearize nonlinear kernels becomes highly beneficial, as that would allow us to easily apply efficient linear algorithms especially online learning [2]. Randomization (hashing) is a popular tool for linearization.

In the introduction, we have explained how to linearize both the RBF kernel and the GMM kernel. From practitioner's perspective, while the kernel classification results in Tables 1, 2, and 3 are informative, they are not sufficient for guiding the choice of kernels. For example, as we will show, for some datasets, even though the RBF kernel outperform the GMM kernel, the linearization algorithm (NRFF) requires substantially more samples (i.e., larger k).

We will report detailed experimental results on 4 datasets. As shown in Table 5, on the first two datasets, the RBF and GMM kernels perform similarly. In the second group, the RBF kernel noticeably outperforms the GMM kernel. We will show on all these 4 datasets, the GCWS hashing is substantially more accurate than NRFF at the same number of sample size (k). We will then present less detailed results on more datasets.

Table 5: 4 datasets for presenting detailed experimental results.

Group	Dataset	# train	# test	# dim	linear	RBF (γ)	GMM
1	Letter	15000	5000	16	61.66	**97.44** (11)	97.26
	Webspam20k	20000	60000	254	93.00	**97.99** (35)	97.88
2	SEMG1	900	900	3000	26.00	**43.56** (4)	41.00
	M-Rotate	12000	50000	784	47.99	**89.68** (5)	84.76

Figure 7 reports the test classification accuracies on the **Letter** dataset and **Webspam20k** dataset, for both linearized GMM kernel using GCWS and linearized RBF kernel (at the best γ) using NRFF, using the LIBLINEAR package. Obviously, the results obtained by GCWS hashing are noticeably better than the results of NRFF, especially when the number of samples (k) is not too large.

For the **Letter** dataset, the original dimension is merely 16. It is known that, for modern linear algorithms, the computational cost is largely determined by the number of nonzeros. Hence, the number of samples (i.e., k) is a crucial parameter which directly controls the training complexity. From Figure 7, we can see that with merely $k = 16$ samples, GCWS already produces better results than the original linear method. This phenomenon is exciting, because in industrial practice, the goal is often to produce better results than linear methods without consuming much more resources.

Figure 8 reports the test classification accuracies on the **SEMG1** dataset and **M-Rotate** dataset, respectively. For both datasets, the original RBF kernel considerably outperforms the original GMM kernel. Nevertheless, NRFF still needs substantially more samples than GCWS hashing on both datasets. Again, for GCWS, the results do not differ much once we use $b \geq 4$. Once again, these results confirm the advantage of GCWS hashing for large-scale learning.

Figure 9 reports test classification accuracies on more datasets, only for $b = 8$ and $k \geq 128$, which again confirm that linearization via GCWS works well for the GMM kernel. In contrast, the NRFF approach requires substantially more samples (i.e., larger k).

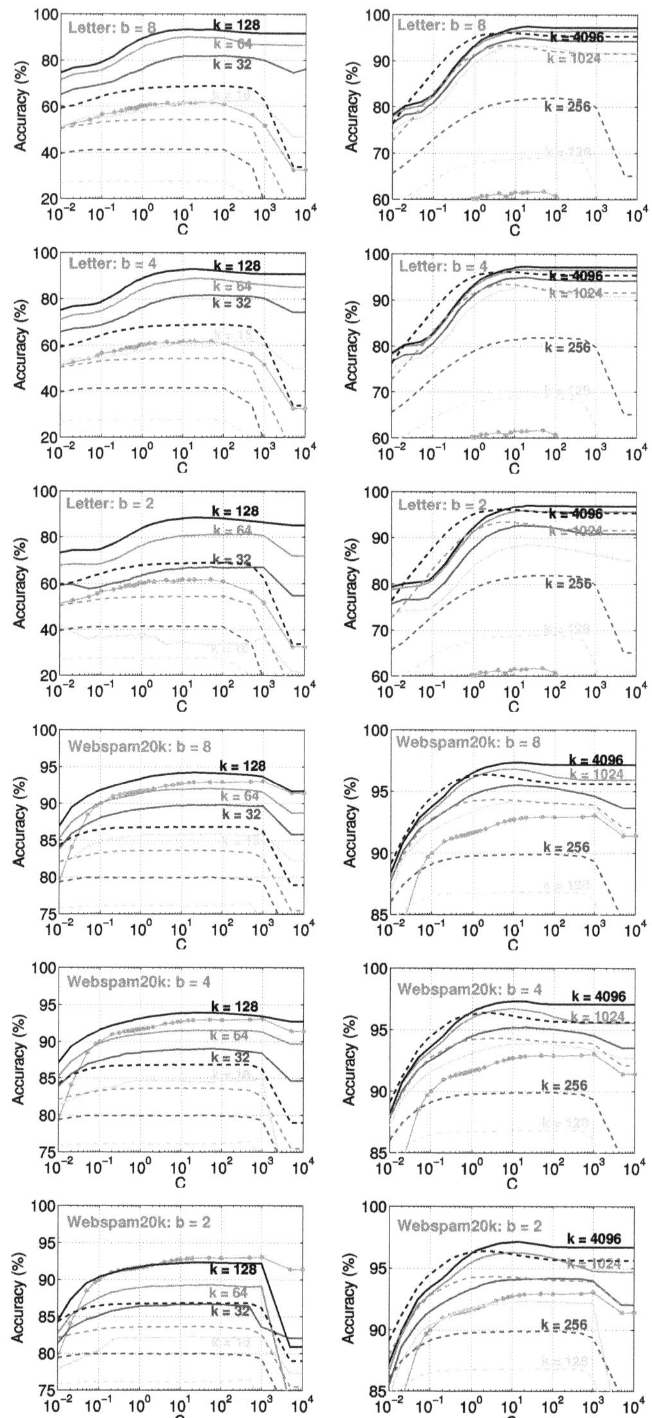

Figure 7: Letter and Webspam20k: Test classification accuracies of the linearized GMM kernel (solid, GCWS) and linearized RBF kernel (dashed, NRFF), using LIBLINEAR, averaged over 10 repetitions. In each panel, we report the results on 4 different k (sample size) values: 128, 256, 1024, 4096 (right panels), and 16, 32, 64, 128 (left panels). We can see that the linearized RBF (using NRFF) would require substantially more samples in order to reach the same accuracies as the linearized GMM kernel (using GCWS). In each panel, the solid curve marked by $*$ presents linear SVM results on the original data.

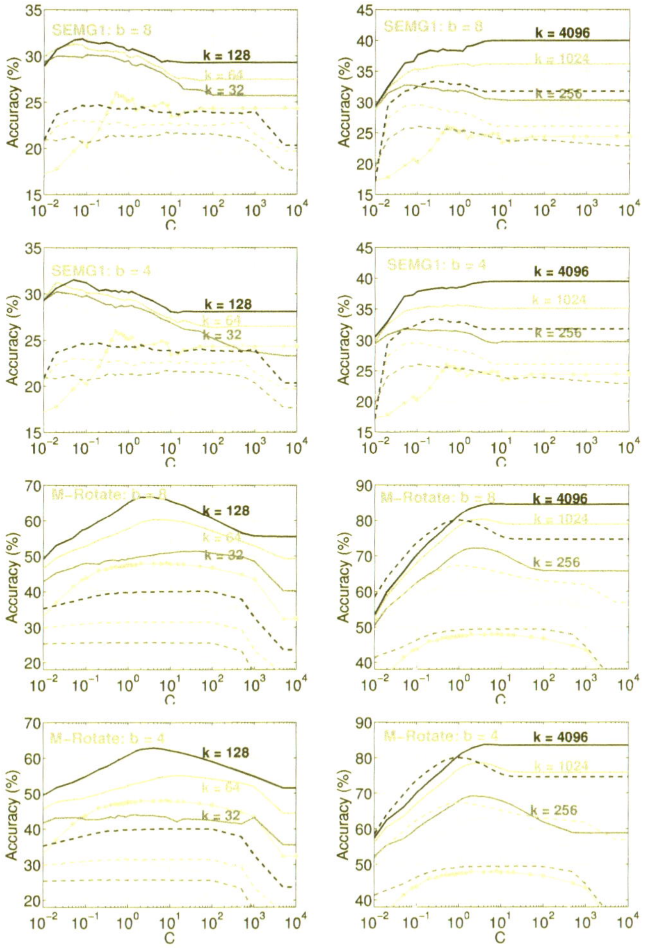

Figure 8: SEMG1 and M-Rotate: Test classification accuracies of the linearized GMM kernel (solid) and linearized RBF (dashed) kernel, using LIBLINEAR. Again, the linearized RBF would require substantially more samples in order to reach the same accuracies as the linearized GMM kernel. On these two datasets, the original RBF kernel outperforms the original GMM kernel as shown in Tables 1 and 3.

Figure 10 presents the hashing results on 6 larger datasets for which we cannot directly train kernel SVMs. We report only for $b = 8$ and k up to 1204. All these results confirm NRFF typically requires substantially more samples than GCWS. This phenomenon can be largely explained by the theoretical results in Theorem 2.2 and Theorem 3.1, which conclude that GCWS is considerably more accurate than NRFF, unless the similarity level is very high.

Training time: For linear algorithms, the training cost is largely determined by the number of nonzero entries per input data vector. In other words, at the same k, the training times of GCWS and NRFF will be roughly comparable. For GCWS and batch algorithms (e.g., LIBLINEAR), a larger b might increase the training time but often not much. See Figure 11 for an example, which in fact shows that NRFF consumed more time at high C (for achieving a good accuracy). Of course, with online learning, it would be more obvious that the training time is determined by the number of nonzeros and number of epoches (it is now common to use only one epoch).

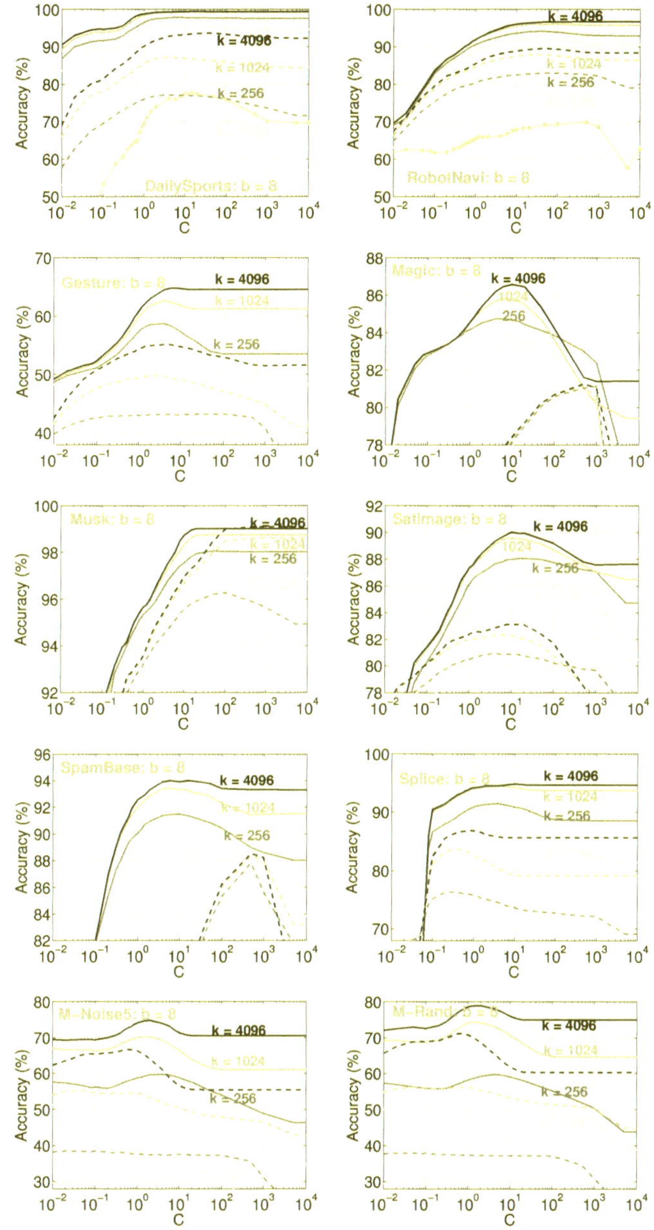

Figure 9: More Datasets: Test classification accuracies of the linearized GMM kernel (solid) and linearized RBF (dashed) kernel. Typically, the linearized RBF would require substantially more samples in order to reach the same accuracies as the linearized GMM kernel.

6 CONCLUSION

Large-scale machine learning has become increasingly important in practice. For many industrial applications, typically only linear methods are affordable, and it is practically beneficial to have methods which can provide substantially more accurate prediction results than linear methods, with no substantial increase of computational cost. The method of "random Fourier features" (RFF) has been a popular tool for linearizing the radial basis function (RBF) kernel, with numerous applications in machine learning, computer

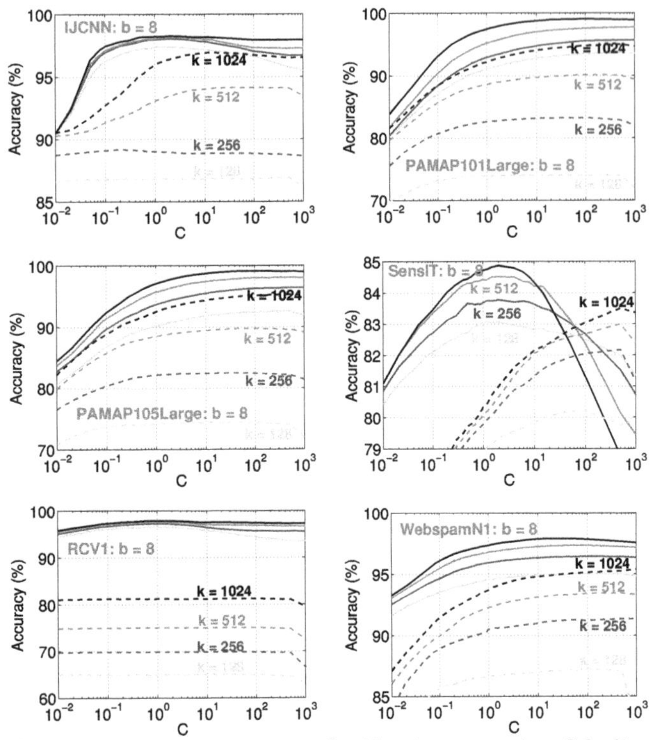

Figure 10: Larger Datasets: Test classification accuracies of the linearized GMM kernel (solid) and linearized RBF (dashed) kernel, on six larger datasets for which we cannot directly compute kernel SVM classifiers on the original data.

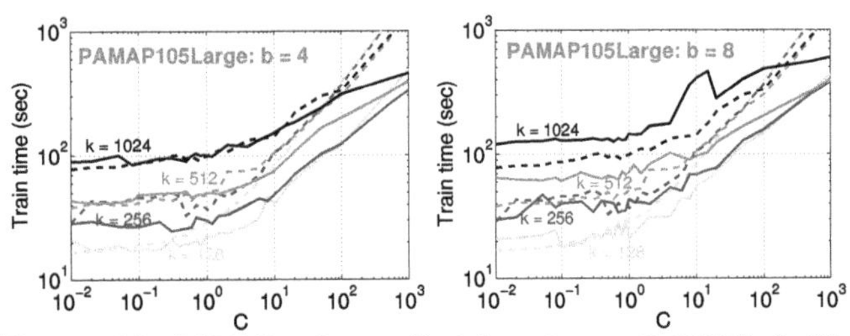

Figure 11: PAMAP105Large: Training times of GCWS (solid curves) and NRFF (dashed curves), for four sample sizes $k \in \{128, 256, 512, 1024\}$, and $b \in \{4, 8\}$.

vision, and beyond, e.g., [1, 6, 7, 9, 10, 20, 22, 24, 27, 28]. In this paper, we rigorously prove that a simple normalization step (i.e., NRFF) can substantially improve the original RFF procedure by considerably reducing the estimation variance.

This paper also proposes the "generalized min-max" (GMM) kernel as a measure of data similarity, to effectively capture data nonlinearity. The GMM kernel can be linearized via the "generalized consistent weighted sampling" (GCWS). Our experimental study demonstrates that usually GCWS does not need too many samples in order to achieve good accuracies. In particular, GCWS typically requires substantially fewer samples than NRFF, in order to reach a similar accuracy. This is practically important, because the training (and testing) cost is largely determined by the number of nonzeros (which is the same as the number of samples in NRFF or GCWS) per data vector of the dataset. The empirical success of GCWS can be explained by our theoretical analysis that the estimation variance of GCWS is usually much smaller than the variance of NRFF.

Given the popularity of the RBF kernel and RFF method, we expect that the GMM kernel and GCWS hashing will also be adopted in a broad range of applications, for example, computer vision [26].

Acknowledgement: NSF-Bigdata-1419210 and NSF-III-1360971.

REFERENCES

[1] Raja Hafiz Affandi, Emily Fox, and Ben Taskar. 2013. Approximate Inference in Continuous Determinantal Processes. In *NIPS*. Lake Tahoe, NV, 1430–1438.
[2] Leon Bottou. http://leon.bottou.org/projects/sgd.
[3] Léon Bottou, Olivier Chapelle, Dennis DeCoste, and Jason Weston (Eds.). 2007. *Large-Scale Kernel Machines*. The MIT Press, Cambridge, MA.
[4] Andrei Z. Broder, Moses Charikar, Alan M. Frieze, and Michael Mitzenmacher. 1998. Min-Wise Independent Permutations. In *STOC*. Dallas, TX, 327–336.
[5] Andrei Z. Broder, Steven C. Glassman, Mark S. Manasse, and Geoffrey Zweig. 1997. Syntactic clustering of the Web. In *WWW*. Santa Clara, CA, 1157 – 1166.
[6] Kacper P Chwialkowski, Aaditya Ramdas, Dino Sejdinovic, and Arthur Gretton. 2015. Fast Two-Sample Testing with Analytic Representations of Probability Measures. In *NIPS*. Montreal, Canada, 1981–1989.
[7] Bo Dai, Bo Xie, Niao He, Yingyu Liang, Anant Raj, Maria-Florina F Balcan, and Le Song. 2014. Scalable Kernel Methods via Doubly Stochastic Gradients. In *NIPS*. Montreal, Canada, 3041–3049.
[8] Rong-En Fan, Kai-Wei Chang, Cho-Jui Hsieh, Xiang-Rui Wang, and Chih-Jen Lin. 2008. LIBLINEAR: A Library for Large Linear Classification. *Journal of Machine Learning Research* 9 (2008), 1871–1874.
[9] José Miguel Hernández-Lobato, Matthew W Hoffman, and Zoubin Ghahramani. 2014. Predictive Entropy Search for Efficient Global Optimization of Black-box Functions. In *NIPS*. Montreal, Canada, 918–926.
[10] Cho-Jui Hsieh, Si Si, and Inderjit S Dhillon. 2014. Fast Prediction for Large-Scale Kernel Machines. In *NIPS*. Montreal, Canada, 3689–3697.
[11] Sergey Ioffe. 2010. Improved Consistent Sampling, Weighted Minhash and L1 Sketching. In *ICDM*. Sydney, AU, 246–255.
[12] Hugo Larochelle, Dumitru Erhan, Aaron C. Courville, James Bergstra, and Yoshua Bengio. 2007. An empirical evaluation of deep architectures on problems with many factors of variation. In *ICML*. Corvalis, Oregon, 473–480.
[13] Ping Li. 2010. Robust LogitBoost and Adaptive Base Class (ABC) LogitBoost. In *UAI*. Catalina Island, CA.
[14] Ping Li. 2015. 0-Bit Consistent Weighted Sampling. In *KDD*. Sydney, Australia, 665–674.
[15] Ping Li, Trevor J. Hastie, and Kenneth W. Church. 2006. Improving Random Projections Using Marginal Information. In *COLT*. Pittsburgh, PA, 635–649.
[16] Ping Li and Arnd Christian König. 2010. b-Bit Minwise Hashing. In *WWW*. Raleigh, NC, 671–680.
[17] Ping Li, Anshumali Shrivastava, Joshua Moore, and Arnd Christian König. 2011. Hashing Algorithms for Large-Scale Learning. In *NIPS*. Granada, Spain, 2672–2680.
[18] Ping Li and Cun-Hui Zhang. 2017. Theory of the GMM Kernel. In *WWW*. Perth, Australia, 1053–1062.
[19] Mark Manasse, Frank McSherry, and Kunal Talwar. 2010. *Consistent Weighted Sampling*. Technical Report MSR-TR-2010-73. Microsoft Research.
[20] Maxim Raginsky and Svetlana Lazebnik. 2009. Locality-sensitive binary codes from shift-invariant kernels. In *NIPS*. Vancouver, Canada, 1509–1517.
[21] A. Rahimi and B. Recht. 2007. Random features for large-scale kernel machines. In *NIPS*. Vancouver, Canada, 1177–1184.
[22] Emile Richard, Georges A Goetz, and E. J. Chichilnisky. 2015. Recognizing retinal ganglion cells in the dark. In *NIPS*. Montreal, Canada, 2476–2484.
[23] Walter Rudin. 1990. *Fourier Analysis on Groups*. John Wiley & Sons, New York, NY.
[24] Amar Shah and Zoubin Ghahramani. 2015. Parallel Predictive Entropy Search for Batch Global Optimization of Expensive Objective Functions. In *NIPS*. Montreal, Canada, 3330–3338.
[25] Dougal J. Sutherland and Jeff Schneider. 2015. On the Error of Random Fourier Features. In *UAI*. Amsterdam, The Netherlands.
[26] Jing Wang, Jie Shen, and Ping Li. 2017. Object proposal with kernelized partial ranking. *Pattern Recognition* 69 (2017), 299 – 309.
[27] Tianbao Yang, Yu-feng Li, Mehrdad Mahdavi, Rong Jin, and Zhi-Hua Zhou. 2012. Nyström Method vs Random Fourier Features: A Theoretical and Empirical Comparison. In *NIPS*. Lake Tahoe, NV, 476–484.
[28] Ian En-Hsu Yen, Ting-Wei Lin, Shou-De Lin, Pradeep K Ravikumar, and Inderjit S Dhillon. 2014. Sparse Random Feature Algorithm as Coordinate Descent in Hilbert Space. In *NIPS*. Montreal, Canada, 2456–2464.

Discrete Content-aware Matrix Factorization

Defu Lian
School of Computer Science and Engineering and Big Data Research Center, University of Electronic Science and Technology of China
dove.ustc@gmail.com

Rui Liu
Big Data Research Center, University of Electronic Science and Technology of China
ruiliu011@gmail.com

Yong Ge
Eller School of Management, University of Arizona
yongge@email.arizona.edu

Kai Zheng
University of Electronic Science and Technology of China
kevinzheng1983@gmail.com

Xing Xie
Microsoft Research
xingx@microsoft.com

Longbing Cao
University of Technology Sydney
longbing.cao@uts.edu.au

ABSTRACT

Precisely recommending relevant items from massive candidates to a large number of users is an indispensable yet computationally expensive task in many online platforms (e.g., Amazon.com and Netflix.com). A promising way is to project users and items into a Hamming space and then recommend items via Hamming distance. However, previous studies didn't address the cold-start challenges and couldn't make the best use of preference data like implicit feedback. To fill this gap, we propose a Discrete Content-aware Matrix Factorization (DCMF) model, 1) to derive compact yet informative binary codes at the presence of user/item content information; 2) to support the classification task based on a local upper bound of logit loss; 3) to introduce an interaction regularization for dealing with the sparsity issue. We further develop an efficient discrete optimization algorithm for parameter learning. Based on extensive experiments on three real-world datasets, we show that DCFM outperforms the state-of-the-arts on both regression and classification tasks.

CCS CONCEPTS

•**Information systems** →**Collaborative filtering;**

KEYWORDS

Recommendation, Discrete Hashing, Collaborative Filtering, Content-based Filtering

ACM Reference format:
Defu Lian, Rui Liu, Yong Ge, Kai Zheng, Xing Xie, and Longbing Cao. 2017. Discrete Content-aware Matrix Factorization. In *Proceedings of KDD'17, August 13–17, 2017, Halifax, NS, Canada.*, , 10 pages.
DOI: http://dx.doi.org/10.1145/3097983.3098008

DOI: http://dx.doi.org/10.1145/3097983.3098008

1 INTRODUCTION

Recommender systems aim to recommend relevant items (e.g., products and news) to users via mining and understanding their preferences for items. Thanks to the development of recommendation techniques over the past decades, they have been widely used in various web services such as Amazon.com and eBay.com for improving sale of products and increasing click-through rate of advertisements. However, within most of these web services, the number of customers and products is dramatically growing, making recommendation more challenging than ever before. For example, there are more than 300 million active Amazon customers and over 480 million products for sale till now. Consequently, it is challenging to generate immediate response to find out potentially-preferred products for customers via analyzing large-scale yet sparse browsing, purchasing and searching data.

In the past, a variety of recommendation approaches have been proposed, which include content-based methods, collaborative filtering algorithms, and the combination of both kinds [1]. Among these recommendation algorithms, dimension reduction techniques exemplified by matrix factorization demonstrate not only high effectiveness but also the best sole-model performance [1]. Matrix factorization algorithms factorize an $M \times N$ user-item rating matrix to map both users and items into a D-dimensional latent space, where one user's preference for an item is modeled by the inner product between their latent features. When content information of users and items is available, content-aware matrix factorization (CaMF) algorithms have been introduced [3, 16, 23], where extracted features from content information are also mapped into the same latent space. Such incorporation of content information usually leads to better recommendation performance [16]. In CaMF methods, users' preference for items could be still modeled as the inner product between the latent features of users and items [16]. The computational complexity for generating top-K preferred items for all users is $O(MND + MN \log K)$. Therefore, CaMF methods are often computationally expensive and lead to crucial low-efficiency issues when either M or N is large.

Upon the independence of generating top-K preferred items for different users, one way to solve the aforementioned challenge is to distribute the computation with parallel/distributed computing techniques [40]. Another promising solution for improving the efficiency is to encode real-valued latent factors with compact binary codes because the inner product between binary codes could be computed much more efficiently via bit operations. Furthermore, by indexing all items with special data structures, approximately querying top-K preferred items with user binary codes has logarithmic or even constant time complexity [21, 29]. The extensive efficiency study has been presented in [37]. However, learning compact binary codes is generally NP-hard [8] due to the discretization constraints. To tackle this problem, people resort to a two-stage procedure [19, 37, 39]. This procedure first solves a relaxed optimization algorithm via discarding the discrete constraints, and then performs direct binary quantization. However, according to [35], such a two-stage procedure results in a large quantization loss due to oversimplification. Consequently, a learning based framework was proposed for direct discrete optimization [35]. In spite of the advantages of such a framework, there are two important limitations. First, the content information of users and items is not taken into account, thus cold-start problems could not be well addressed. Second, they cannot make good use of preference data like binary feedback or implicit feedback (e.g., click data), which is often more prevalent in many recommendation scenarios.

To address these limitations, we propose Discrete Content-aware Matrix Factorization (DCMF) to learn hash codes for users and items at the presence of content information (such as user's age and gender, item's category and textual content). Without imposing discretization constraints on latent factors of content information, our framework requires the minimal number of discretization constraints. By additionally imposing balanced and de-correlated constraints, DCMF could derive compact yet informative binary codes for both users and items. Besides supporting the regression task, this framework can also handle the classification task based on a local variational bound of logistic regression when taking binary feedback or implicit feedback as input. In order to make better use of implicit feedback, an interaction regularizer is further introduced to address the sparsity challenge in implicit feedback. To solve the tractable discrete optimization of DCMF with all the challenging constraints, we develop an efficient alternating optimization method which essentially solves the mixed-integer programming subproblems iteratively. With extensive experiments on three real-world datasets, we show that DCMF outperforms the state-of-the-arts for both classification and regression tasks and verify the effectiveness of item content information, the logit loss for classification tasks, and the interaction regularization for sparse preference data.

To summarize, our contributions include:

- We study how to hash users and items at the presence of their respective content information for fast recommendation in both regression and classification tasks.
- We develop an efficient discrete optimization algorithm for tackling discretization, balanced and de-correlated constraints as well as interaction regularization.
- Through extensive experiments on three public datasets, we show the superiority of the proposed algorithm to the state-of-the-arts.

2 PRELIMINARIES

Matrix factorization operates on a user-item rating/preference matrix $\boldsymbol{R}$ of size $M \times N$, where M and N is the number of users and items, respectively. Each entry r_{ij} indicates rating/preference of a user i for an item j (using preference for subsequent presentation). All observed entries are denoted by $\Omega = \{(i,j)|r_{ij} \text{ is known}\}$. The set of items for which a user i have preference is $\mathbb{I}_i$ of size $N_i = |\mathbb{I}_i|$ and the set of users having preference for an item j is $\mathbb{U}_j$ of size $M_j = |\mathbb{U}_j|$. $\text{sgn}(\cdot) : \mathbb{R} \rightarrow \{\pm 1\}$ is a sign function. Below, upper case bold letters denote matrices, lower case bold letters denote column vectors, and non-bold letters represent scalars.

2.1 Content-aware Matrix Factorization

Matrix factorization maps both users and items onto a joint D-dimensional latent space ($D \ll \min(M, N)$), where each user is represented by $\tilde{\boldsymbol{p}}_i \in \mathbb{R}^D$ and each item is represented by $\tilde{\boldsymbol{q}}_j \in \mathbb{R}^D$. Thus, each user's predicted preference for each item is estimated by inner product. At the presence of their respective content information, encoded as $\boldsymbol{x}_i \in \mathbb{R}^{M\times F}$ and $\boldsymbol{y}_j \in \mathbb{R}^{N\times L}$ respectively, content-aware matrix factorization additionally maps their respective features into the same latent space via a matrix $\boldsymbol{U} \in \mathbb{R}^{F\times D}$ and a matrix $\boldsymbol{V} \in \mathbb{R}^{L\times D}$ respectively. Then each user (item) is represented by $\boldsymbol{p}_i = \tilde{\boldsymbol{p}}_i + \boldsymbol{U}'\boldsymbol{x}_i$ ($\boldsymbol{q}_j = \tilde{\boldsymbol{q}}_j + \boldsymbol{V}'\boldsymbol{y}_j$) according to [3, 4]. In this case, the predicted preference of user i for item j is $\hat{r}_{ij} = \boldsymbol{p}_i'\boldsymbol{q}_j = (\tilde{\boldsymbol{p}}_i + \boldsymbol{U}'\boldsymbol{x}_i)'(\tilde{\boldsymbol{q}}_j + \boldsymbol{V}'\boldsymbol{y}_j)$. Thus different from factorization machines [23], we don't take interaction between user (item) id and user (item) feature, and interaction between different user (item) features into account. However, such a prediction formula makes it possible to more easily leverage hash techniques for speeding up recommendation. To learn $\{\boldsymbol{p}_i\}, \{\boldsymbol{q}_j\}$, $\boldsymbol{U}$ and $\boldsymbol{V}$, we can minimize the following objective function [16]:

$$\sum_{(i,j)\in\Omega} \ell(r_{ij}, \boldsymbol{p}_i'\boldsymbol{q}_j) + \lambda_1 \sum_i \|\boldsymbol{p}_i - \boldsymbol{U}'\boldsymbol{x}_i\|^2 + \gamma_1\|\boldsymbol{U}\|_F^2 + \lambda_2 \sum_j \|\boldsymbol{q}_j - \boldsymbol{V}'\boldsymbol{y}_j\|^2 + \gamma_2\|\boldsymbol{V}\|_F^2 \quad (1)$$

where $\ell(r_{ij}, \boldsymbol{p}_i'\boldsymbol{q}_j)$ is a convex loss, like square loss $\ell(r_{ij}, \boldsymbol{p}_i'\boldsymbol{q}_j) = (r_{ij} - \boldsymbol{p}_i'\boldsymbol{q}_j)^2$ for rating prediction, logistic loss $\ell(r_{ij}, \boldsymbol{p}_i'\boldsymbol{q}_j) = \log(1 + e^{-r_{ij}\boldsymbol{p}_i'\boldsymbol{q}_j})$ for the classification task from binary feedback $r \in \{-1, 1\}$. When taking implicit feedback as input, an interaction regularization $\sum_{i,j}(\boldsymbol{p}_i'\boldsymbol{q}_j - 0)^2$, penalizing non-zero predicted preference, should be imposed for better recommendation performance. This is because the state-of-the-art objective function [10, 15, 17, 34] for implicit feedback could be decomposed into a Ω-dependent part and an interaction regularization. In particular, assuming $w_{ij} = \alpha + 1$ if $(i,j) \in \Omega$ and $w_{ij} = 1$ otherwise, then we have

$$\begin{aligned}
&\sum_{i,j} w_{ij}(r_{ij} - \boldsymbol{p}_i\boldsymbol{q}_j)^2 \\
=&(\alpha+1) \sum_{(i,j)\in\Omega} (r_{ij} - \boldsymbol{p}_i\boldsymbol{q}_j)^2 + \sum_{(i,j)\notin\Omega} (0 - \boldsymbol{p}_i'\boldsymbol{q}_j)^2 \\
=&\alpha \sum_{(i,j)\in\Omega} (\frac{\alpha+1}{\alpha} r_{ij} - \boldsymbol{p}_i'\boldsymbol{q}_j)^2 + \sum_{i,j}(0 - \boldsymbol{p}_i'\boldsymbol{q}_j)^2 - \frac{\alpha+1}{\alpha} r_{ij}^2 \\
\approx&\alpha \sum_{(i,j)\in\Omega} (r_{ij} - \boldsymbol{p}_i'\boldsymbol{q}_j)^2 + \sum_{i,j}(0 - \boldsymbol{p}_i'\boldsymbol{q}_j)^2 - r_{ij}^2
\end{aligned}$$

where the last approximation is derived since α is usually significantly larger than 1.

3 DISCRETE CONTENT-AWARE MATRIX FACTORIZATION

After obtaining latent representation for users and items, generating top-K preferred items for each user is considered as a similarity-based retrieval problem. In particular, treating a user's latent factor as a query, one can compute "similarity" score between user and item via inner product, and then extract the top-K preferred items through the max-heap data structure. However, such a similarity-based retrieval scheme, costing $O(ND + N\log K)$, leads to crucial low-efficiency issues for real practice when N is large.

If representing them by binary codes, this similarity-based search could be accelerated by more efficiently computing the inner product via the Hamming distance. Denoting $\Phi = [\phi_1, \cdots, \phi_M]' \in \{-1,1\}^{M\times D}$ and $\Psi = [\psi_1, \cdots, \psi_N]' \in \{-1,1\}^{N\times D}$ as user and item binary code, respectively, the inner product is represented as $\phi_i'\psi_j = 2\mathrm{H}(\phi_i, \psi_j) - D$, where $\mathrm{H}(\phi, \psi)$ denotes the Hamming distance between binary codes. Based on fast bit operations, Hamming distance computation is extremely efficient. If only conducting approximated similarity-based search, it has logarithmic or even constant time complexity based on advanced indexing techniques [21, 29]. For extensive efficiency study of hashing-based recommendation could be referred in [37]. Below, we investigate how to directly learn binary codes for users and items.

3.1 Loss Function

To derive the loss function, the first action is to convert continuous latent factors into binary ones. In order to assure that each bit carries as much information as possible, balanced constraints should be imposed on binary codes of users and items [39]. To make binary codes compact so that each bit should be as independent as possible, de-correlated constraints are also imposed on them. And they may lead to using shorter code for encoding more information [33]. Therefore, learning binary codes for users and items is to minimize the following objective function.

$$\begin{aligned}&\sum_{(i,j)\in\Omega} \ell(r_{ij}, \phi_i'\psi_j) + \lambda_1\|\Phi - XU\|_F^2 + \gamma_1\|U\|_F^2\\ &+\lambda_2\|\Psi - YV\|_F^2 + \gamma_2\|V\|_F^2 + \beta\sum_{ij}(\phi_i'\psi_j)^2\\ &\text{s.t. } \Phi \in \{-1,1\}^{M\times D}, \Psi \in \{-1,1\}^{N\times D},\\ &\underbrace{\mathbf{1}_M'\Phi = 0, \mathbf{1}_N'\Psi = 0}_{\text{balance}}, \underbrace{\Phi'\Phi = MI_D, \Psi'\Psi = NI_D}_{\text{de-correlation}}\end{aligned} \tag{2}$$

However, optimizing this objective function is a challenging task and it is generally NP-hard due to involving combinatorial optimization over space of size $(M+N)D$. Accordingly, we introduce an optimization framework that can minimize this objective function in a computationally tractable way by softening the balanced and de-correlated constraints. In particular, we can introduce a delegate continuous variable $P \in \mathcal{P}$ for Φ and a delegate continuous variable $Q \in \mathcal{Q}$ for Ψ, where $\mathcal{P} = \{P \in \mathbb{R}^{M\times D} | \mathbf{1}_M'P = 0, P'P = MI_D\}$ and $\mathcal{Q} = \{Q \in \mathbb{R}^{N\times D} | \mathbf{1}_N'Q = 0, Q'Q = NI_D\}$. Then the balanced and de-correlated constraints on users and items could be softened by $\min_{P\in\mathcal{P}} \|\Phi - P\|_F$ and $\min_{Q\in\mathcal{Q}} \|\Psi - Q\|_F$, respectively. It becomes a three-objective minimization problem. Applying scalarization techniques of multi-objective optimization problems, we formulate the tractable objective function of DCMF as follows:

$$\begin{aligned}&\sum_{(i,j)\in\Omega} \ell(r_{ij}, \phi_i'\psi_j) + \alpha_1\|\Phi - P\|_F^2 + \lambda_1\|\Phi - XU\|_F^2 + \gamma_1\|U\|_F^2\\ &+\alpha_2\|\Psi - Q\|_F^2 + \lambda_2\|\Psi - YV\|_F^2 + \gamma_2\|V\|_F^2 + \beta\sum_{ij}(\phi_i'\psi_j)^2\\ &\text{s.t. } \mathbf{1}_M'P = 0, P'P = MI_D, \mathbf{1}_N'Q = 0, Q'Q = NI_D\\ &\Phi \in \{-1,1\}^{M\times D}, \Psi \in \{-1,1\}^{N\times D}\end{aligned} \tag{3}$$

where α_1 and α_2 are tuning parameters. If there are feasible solutions in Eq (2), using very large values of α_1 and α_2 will enforce $\Phi = P$ and $\Psi = Q$, turning Eq (3) to Eq (2). The comparative small values of α_1 and α_2 allow a certain discrepancy between Φ and P, between Ψ and Q, making Eq (3) more flexible. Through jointly optimizing binary codes and delegate real variables, we can get nearly balanced and de-correlated hash codes for users and items.

Making use of $\mathrm{tr}(\Phi'\Phi) = \mathrm{tr}(P'P) = MD$ and $\mathrm{tr}(\Psi'\Psi) = \mathrm{tr}(Q'Q) = ND$, Eq (3) is equivalent to

$$\begin{aligned}&\sum_{(i,j)\in\Omega} \ell(r_{ij}, \phi_i'\psi_j) + \beta\sum_{ij}(\phi_i'\psi_j)^2 - 2\mathrm{tr}\big(\Phi'(\alpha_1 P + \lambda_1 XU)\big)\\ &+\lambda_1\mathrm{tr}\big(U'(X'X + \frac{\gamma_1}{\lambda_1}I_F)U\big) - 2\mathrm{tr}\big(\Psi'(\alpha_2 Q + \lambda_2 YV)\big)\\ &+\lambda_2\mathrm{tr}\big(V'(Y'Y + \frac{\gamma_2}{\lambda_2}I_L)V\big)\\ &\text{s.t. } \mathbf{1}_M'P = 0, P'P = MI_D, \mathbf{1}_N'Q = 0, Q'Q = NI_D\\ &\Phi \in \{-1,1\}^{M\times D}, \Psi \in \{-1,1\}^{N\times D}\end{aligned} \tag{4}$$

Note that we do not discard the discretization constraints but instead directly optimize discrete Φ and Ψ. It is worth mentioning that the norm of binary codes of both users and items are constant and don't take any effect of regularization, but the interaction regularization of binary codes between each user and each item is meaningful. Next, we develop an efficient learning solution for such a mixed-integer optimization problem.

3.2 Optimization

Generally speaking, alternating optimization is used, taking turns in updating each of Φ, Ψ, P, Q, U and V, given others fixed. Although the objective function in Eq (4) depends on the choice of loss function, it only affects the updating rules of Φ and Ψ since their update seeks binary latent representation to preserve the user-item intrinsic preference.

3.2.1 *Learning Φ and Ψ.*

We consider both regression and classification tasks for learning hash codes and thus elaborate the derivation for their updating rules, respectively.

- **Regression**: Ignoring the term irrelevant to Φ and Ψ, the loss function is

$$\begin{aligned}&\sum_{(i,j)\in\Omega} (r_{ij} - \phi_i'\psi_j)^2 - 2\mathrm{tr}\big(\Phi'(\alpha_1 P + \lambda_1 XU)\big)\\ &- 2\mathrm{tr}\big(\Psi'(\alpha_2 Q + \lambda_2 YV)\big) + \beta\sum_{i,j}\phi_i'\psi_j\psi_j'\phi_j,\end{aligned} \tag{5}$$

where summation is conducted over users independently, so we can update hash code for each user in parallel. In particular, learning hash code for a user i is to solve the following optimization problem:

$$\min_{\phi_i \in \{\pm 1\}^D} \phi_i'(\sum_{j \in \mathbb{I}_i} \psi_j \psi_j' + \beta \Psi' \Psi) \phi_i - 2\phi_i'(\sum_{j \in \mathbb{I}_i} r_{ij} \psi_j + \alpha_1 p_i + \lambda_1 U' x_i) \quad (6)$$

Due to the discrete constraints, such an optimization problem is generally NP-hard, we develop a coordinate-descent algorithm to take turns to update each bit of the hash code ϕ_i when other bits fixed. In particular, assuming the dth bit is represented by ϕ_{id} and the remaining codes by $\phi_{i\bar{d}}$, the coordinate-descent algorithm solves the following objective function:

$$\min_{\phi_{id} \in \{\pm 1\}} \phi_{id}(\phi_{i\bar{d}}' \sum_{j \in \mathbb{I}_i} \psi_{jd} \psi_{j\bar{d}} + \beta \phi_{i\bar{d}}' \Psi_{\bar{d}}' \psi_d - \sum_{j \in \mathbb{I}_i} r_{ij} \psi_{jd} - \alpha_1 p_{id} - \lambda_1 u_d' x_i),$$

where $\psi_{j\bar{d}}$ is the remaining set of item codes excluding ψ_{jd}, ψ_d is the dth column of the matrix Ψ while $\Psi_{\bar{d}}$ excludes the dth column from Ψ, u_d is the dth column of the matrix U. Thus we update ϕ_{id} based on the following rule:

$$\phi_{id}^* = \operatorname{sgn}(K(\hat{\phi}_{id}, \phi_{id})), \quad (7)$$

where $\hat{\phi}_{id} = \sum_{j \in \mathbb{I}_i} (r_{ij} - \hat{r}_{ij} + \phi_{id}\psi_{jd})\psi_{jd} + \alpha_1 p_{id} + \lambda_1 u_d' x_i - \beta \phi_i' \Psi' \psi_d + \beta N \phi_{id}$ while $\hat{r}_{ij} = \phi_i' \psi_j$ is prediction of preference, and $K(x, y)$ equals to x if x≠0 and y otherwise, meaning that we don't make an update if $\hat{\phi}_{id} = 0$. The update rule is applied among bits iteratively until convergence. Denoting the number of the bit-wise iteration as $\#iter$. Note that when the preference prediction of observed entries is cached, $\hat{r}_{ij}$ could be dynamically updated, i.e., $\hat{r}_{ij}^* = \hat{r}_{ij} + (\phi_{id}^* - \phi_{id})\psi_{jd}$. The third term except ϕ_i for all bits could be pre-computed before the user-level iteration, costing $O(ND^2)$. Therefore, excluding overhead of pre-computation, the complexity of updating the hash code for the user i is $O(\#iter(D^2 + N_i D))$, indicating that making update for all users in sequence costs $O(\#iter(MD^2 + |\Omega|D) + ND^2)$. If not considering interaction regularization, the complexity could be reduced to $O(\#iter|\Omega|D)$. When leveraging parallel computation, its complexity could decrease by a factor of the number of threads and (or) processes.

Similarly, we can learn hash code for an item j by solving

$$\min_{\psi_j \in \{\pm 1\}^D} \psi_j'(\sum_{i \in \mathbb{U}_j} \phi_i \phi_i' + \beta \Phi' \Phi) \psi_j - 2\psi_j'(\sum_{i \in \mathbb{U}_j} r_{ij} \phi_i + \alpha_2 q_j + \lambda_2 V' y_j)$$

Based on the coordinate-descent algorithm, we update ψ_j according to:

$$\psi_{jd}^* = \operatorname{sgn}(K(\hat{\psi}_{jd}, \psi_{jd})), \quad (8)$$

where $\hat{\psi}_{jd} = \sum_{i \in \mathbb{U}_j} (r_{ij} - \hat{r}_{ij} + \phi_{id}\psi_{jd})\phi_{id} + \alpha_2 q_{jd} + \lambda_2 v_d' y_j - \beta \psi_j' \Phi' \phi_d + \beta M \psi_{jd}$. Following the same analysis, the complexity is $O(\#iter(MD^2 + |\Omega|D) + ND^2)$ when updating all items in sequence.

- **Classification** We only consider the logistic loss $\ell(r_{ij}, \phi_i'\psi_j) = \log(1 + e^{-r_{ij}\phi_i'\psi_j})$ due to its wide use in practice [3, 13]. However, due to the non-linearity of this loss function, it is impossible to directly obtain the close form of updating rule for hash codes of users and items even based on the coordinate descent algorithm. Therefore, we seek its upper variational yet quadratic bound [11] and optimize the variational variable. In particular,

$$\begin{aligned} &\log(1 + e^{-r_{ij}\phi_i'\psi_j}) \\ &= \log(1 + e^{\phi_i'\psi_j}) - \frac{1 + r_{ij}}{2} \phi_i'\psi_j \\ &\le \lambda(\hat{r}_{ij})((\phi_i'\psi_j)^2 - \hat{r}_{ij}^2) - \frac{1}{2}(r_{ij}\phi_i'\psi_j + \hat{r}_{ij}) + \log(1 + e^{\hat{r}_{ij}}) \end{aligned} \quad (9)$$

where $\lambda(x) = \frac{1}{4x}\tanh(x/2) = \frac{1}{2x}(\sigma(x) - \frac{1}{2})$ and the equality holds only if $\hat{r}_{ij} = \phi_i'\psi_j$. Using this upper bound, learning hash code for user i is to solve

$$\min_{\phi_i \in \{\pm 1\}^D} \phi_i'(\sum_{j \in \mathbb{I}_i} \lambda(\hat{r}_{ij}) \psi_j \psi_j' + \beta \Psi' \Psi) \phi_i - \frac{1}{2} \phi_i' \sum_{j \in \mathbb{I}_i} r_{ij} \psi_j - 2\phi_i'(\alpha_1 p_i + \lambda_1 U' x_i), \quad (10)$$

where $\hat{r}_{ij}$ is the preference prediction based on the current value of ϕ_i and ψ_j. Through deviation, we can still apply Eq (7) for updating the dth bit ϕ_{id} but the first term of $\hat{\phi}_{id}$ should be $\sum_{j \in \mathbb{I}_i} (\frac{1}{4} r_{ij} - \lambda(\hat{r}_{ij})\hat{r}_{ij} + \lambda(\hat{r}_{ij})\phi_{id}\psi_{jd})\psi_{jd}$. Similarly, we can update hash codes for items according to Eq (8) after adjusting the first term of $\hat{\psi}_{id}$. The complexity of the updating rule remains the same as before.

3.2.2 *Learning* P *and* Q.

When fixing Φ, learning P could be solved via optimizing the following objective function:

$$\max_P \operatorname{tr}(P'\Phi), \text{ s.t. } \mathbf{1}_M' P = 0 \text{ and } P'P = MI_D. \quad (11)$$

An analytical solution can be obtained with the aid of a centering matrix $J_n = I_n - \frac{1}{n}\mathbf{1}_n\mathbf{1}_n'$. In particular, assume $J_M\Phi = S_P \Sigma_P T_P'$ as its Singular Value Decomposition, where each column of $S_P \in \mathbb{R}^{M \times \tilde{D}}$ and $T_P \in \mathbb{R}^{D \times \tilde{D}}$ contains the left- and right-singular vectors respectively, corresponding to $\tilde{D}$ non-zero singular values in the diagonal matrix Σ_P. Here, for generic purpose, the Φ is not assumed full column rank, i.e., $\tilde{D} \le D$. Note that $\mathbf{1}_M' J_M = 0$, so $\mathbf{1}_M' J_M \Phi = 0$, implying $\mathbf{1}_M' S_P = 0$. Then we construct matrices $\hat{S}_P$ of size $M \times (D - \tilde{D})$ and $\hat{T}_P$ of size $D \times (D - \tilde{D})$ by using a Gram-Schmidt orthogonalization process such that $\hat{S}_P'[S_P, \hat{S}_P, \mathbf{1}_M] = 0$ and $\hat{T}_P'[T_P, \hat{T}_P] = 0$. Then the analytical solution for updating P is determined as follows according to [18].

$$P = \sqrt{M}[S_P, \hat{S}_P][T_P, \hat{T}_P]'. \quad (12)$$

In practice, to compute such an analytical solution, we could first conduct eigendecomposition on the matrix $\Phi' J_M \Phi$ of size $D \times D$ to obtain T_P and $\hat{T}_P$, where each column of $\hat{T}_P$ corresponds to eigenvectors of zero eigenvalues. This only costs $O(D^3)$. Then, we can obtain $S_P = J_M \Phi T_P \Sigma_P^{-1}$ based on matrix multiplication of $O(MD\tilde{D})$ complexity. And $\hat{S}_P$ could be initialized to a random matrix followed by the aforementioned Gram-Schmidt orthogonalization process, costing $O(M(D^2 - \tilde{D}^2))$. Therefore, the overall complexity of updating P is $O(MD^2)$.

When fixing Ψ, learning Q could be solved in a similar way:

$$\max_{Q} \text{tr}(Q'\Psi), \text{ s.t. } \mathbf{1}'_N Q = 0 \text{ and } Q'Q = NI_D \tag{13}$$

Its analytical solution is

$$Q = \sqrt{N}[S_Q, \hat{S}_Q][T_Q, \hat{T}_Q]', \tag{14}$$

where each column of S_Q and T_Q contains the left- and right-singular vectors of $J_N\Psi$ respectively. And the construction of $\hat{S}_Q$ and $\hat{T}_Q$ is the same as that of $\hat{S}_P$ and $\hat{T}_P$ via the Gram-Schmidt process. Its overall complexity is $O(ND^2)$.

3.2.3 Learning U and V. When fixing P and Q, taking all terms related to U and V, the optimization problem with respect to U and V is then respectively formulated as:

$$\begin{aligned} &\min_{U} \text{tr}\big(U'(X'X + \frac{\gamma_1}{\lambda_1} I_F)U\big) - 2\text{tr}(\Phi' X U) \\ &\min_{V} \text{tr}\big(V'(Y'Y + \frac{\gamma_2}{\lambda_2} I_L)U\big) - 2\text{tr}(\Psi' Y V), \end{aligned} \tag{15}$$

The optimal solution for them is derived as:

$$\begin{aligned} U &= (X'X + \frac{\gamma_1}{\lambda_1} I_F)^{-1} X'\Phi \\ V &= (Y'Y + \frac{\gamma_2}{\lambda_2} I_L)^{-1} Y'\Psi. \end{aligned} \tag{16}$$

When the number of features is large, conjugate gradient descent could be applied. The time complexity only depends on the multiplication between matrices, costing $O((\|X\|_0 + \|Y\|_0)D\#iter)$, where $\|\cdot\|_0$ is the ℓ_0 norm of matrices, equaling to the number of non-zeros entries in the matrices, and #iter is the number of iterations of conjugate gradient descent to reach a given threshold of approximation error.

3.3 Learning Hashing Codes in Cold-Start Case

When items have no rating history in the training set but are associated with content information, it remains unknown to derive their hash codes. Accordingly, denoting feature representation, hash codes and delegate continuous variables of these N_1 items as X_1, Ψ_1 and Q_1, we can derive Ψ_1 by solving:

$$\begin{aligned} &\min_{\Psi_1, Q_1} -\text{tr}\big(\Psi_1'(\lambda_2 X_1 U + \alpha_2 Q_1)\big) \\ &\text{s.t. } Q_1'Q_1 = N_1 I_D \text{ and } \mathbf{1}'_{N_1} Q = 0. \end{aligned} \tag{17}$$

Resorting to the similar optimization techniques, we can easily obtain the hash codes of the cold-start items. The hash codes of cold-start users can be derived similarly.

3.4 Initialization

Note that the optimization problem involves a mixed-integer non-convex optimization, a better initialization strategy could be important for faster convergence and finding better local optimum. The solutions of two-stage learning schemes are promising. In particular, we first solve a relaxed optimization problem in Eq (3) by discarding the discretization constraints and apply binary quantization for obtaining hash codes for users and items. Note that such an objective function has imposed balanced and de-correlated constraints on latent factors of users and items, leading to a small quantization error according to [35].

To solve the relaxed optimization problem, we can also leverage alternating optimization for parameter learning. The update rules for all parameters are the same except Φ and Ψ because of discarding the discretization constraints. In particular, learning latent factors for a user i in case of the regression task is achieved by solving

$$\begin{aligned} \min_{\phi_i \in \mathbb{R}^D} \ &\phi_i'\big(\sum_{j\in\mathbb{I}_i} \psi_j\psi_j' + \beta\Psi'\Psi + \alpha_1 I_D\big)\phi_i \\ &- 2\phi_i'\big(\sum_{j\in\mathbb{I}_i} r_{ij}\psi_j + \alpha_1 p_i + \lambda_1 U'x_i\big) \end{aligned}$$

Thanks to its quadratics with respect to ϕ_i, there is a closed form of the updating rule. However, such a closed form costs $O(|\Omega|D^2 + MD^3)$ for updating latent factors of all users in sequence due to its existence of interaction regularization. Therefore, coordinate descent algorithm could be more appealing. In this case, the closed form for updating ϕ_{id} is

$$\begin{aligned} \phi_{id}^* = &\frac{\sum_{j\in\mathbb{I}_i}(r_{ij} - \hat{r}_{ij} + \phi_{id}\psi_{jd})\psi_{jd} - \beta\phi_i'\Psi'\psi_d}{\sum_{j\in\mathbb{I}_i}\psi_{jd}^2 + \beta\psi_d'\psi_d + \alpha_1} \\ &+ \frac{\beta\phi_{id}\psi_d'\psi_d + \alpha_1 p_{id} + \lambda_1 u_d' x_i}{\sum_{j\in\mathbb{I}_i}\psi_{jd}^2 + \beta\psi_d'\psi_d + \alpha_1} \end{aligned} \tag{18}$$

where $\hat{r}_{ij}$ is an aforementioned preference prediction and will be cached and updated dynamically. In the case of classification, resorting to the variational upper bound of logistic loss, the closed form of updating ϕ_{id} is very similar to Eq (18), except that the first term of numerator in the first part is replaced by $\sum_{j\in\mathbb{I}_i}\big(\frac{1}{4}r_{ij} - \lambda(\hat{r}_{ij})(\hat{r}_{ij} - \phi_{id}\psi_{jd})\big)\psi_{jd}$ and the first part of denominator is replaced by $\sum_{j\in\mathbb{I}_i}\lambda(\hat{r}_{ij})\psi_{jd}^2$.

In both cases, the updating rule for ψ_{jd} could be derived similarly. Following the same analysis as before, its complexity of each iteration could be reduced by a factor of D compared to a method which directly performs optimization with respect to ϕ_i. But the former one may require a larger number of iterations until convergence. After convergence, assuming the solution of the relaxed objective function is $(\Phi^*, \Psi^*, P^*, Q^*, U^*, V^*)$, the parameters (Φ, Ψ, P, Q, U, V) in Eq (3) could be initialized as a feasible solution $(\text{sgn}(\Phi^*), \text{sgn}(\Psi^*), P^*, Q^*, U^*, V^*)$. The effectiveness of the proposed initialization algorithm is illustrated in Fig 1.

4 EXPERIMENTS

4.1 Datasets

We evaluate the proposed algorithm on three public datasets of explicit feedback from different real-world online websites. In these three datasets, each user is assumed to have only one rating for an item, otherwise, the average value of multiple rating scores is assigned to this item.

The first dataset, denoted as **Yelp**, is the latest Yelp Challenge dataset, which originally includes 2,685,066 ratings from 409,117 users and 85,539 items (points of interest, such as restaurants, hotels and shopping malls). The rating scores are integers from 1 to 5. Most items are usually associated to a set of textual reviews. For

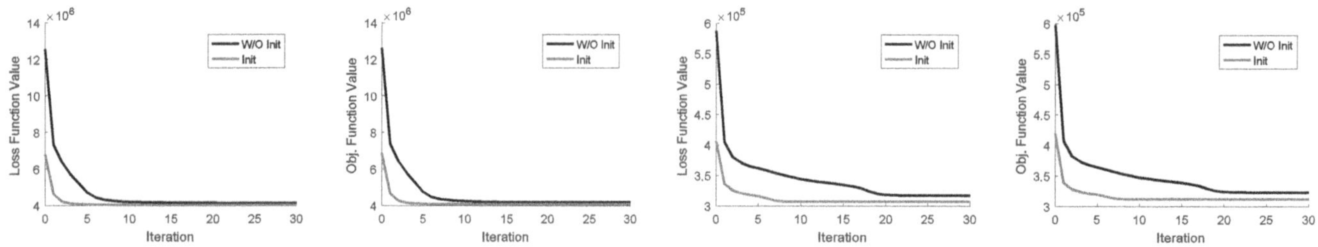

(a) Regression-Loss Function Value (b) Regression-Objective Function Value (c) Classification-Loss Function Value (d) Classification-Objective Function Value

Figure 1: Convergence curve of the overall objective function and loss (square loss and logit loss) function with/without initialization on the Yelp dataset. We see that it indeed helps to achieve faster convergence and lower objective/loss values.

each item, we aggregate all of its textual reviews and represent them by bag of words, after filtering stopping words and using tf-idf to choose the top 8,000 distinct words as the vocabulary according to [28].

The second dataset, denoted as **Amazon**, is a subset of 8,898,041 user ratings for Amazon books [20], where all users and all items originally have at least 5 ratings. All its rating scores are integers from 1 to 5. Similarly, most books are provided a set of textual reviews. A similar preprocessing procedure is applied for each book's reviews to obtain the content representation of each book.

The third one, denoted as **MovieLens**, is from the classic MovieLens 10M dataset, originally including 10,000,054 rating from 71,567 users for 10,681 items (movies). The rating scores are from 0.5 to 5 with 0.5 granularity. Most movies in this dataset are associated with 3-5 labels from a dictionary of 18 genre labels.

Due to the extreme sparsity of the Yelp and Amazon original datasets, we remove users who have less than 20 ratings and remove items which are rated by less than 20 users. Such a filtering strategy is also applied for the MovieLens dataset. Table 1 summaries the filtered datasets for evaluation.

Table 1: Data statistics of three datasets

Datasets	#users	#items	#ratings	Density
MovieLens	69,838	8,940	9,983,758	1.60%
Yelp	13,679	12,922	640,143	0.36%
Amazon	35,151	33,195	1,732,060	0.15%

4.2 Evaluation Framework

We will investigate the capability of the proposed algorithm for incorporating content information, the effectiveness of both logit loss and interaction regularization for the classification task. According to [28], there are two types of recommendation in practice: in-matrix recommendation and out-of-matrix recommendation, where the former task could be addressed by collaborative filtering and the latter task corresponds to the well-known cold-start problem in recommendation and cannot resort to collaborative filtering. Thus, it is sufficient that we evaluate the proposed algorithm from the following three perspectives for our investigation. Note that efficiency study of the hashing-based recommendation is not presented any more, since it has been extensively evaluated in previous work [37].

In-matrix regression. In this evaluation, we first randomly sample 50% ratings for each user as training and the rest 50% as testing. However, this task considers the case where each user has a set of items that she has not rated before, but that at least one other user has rated. Therefore, we carefully check this condition and always move items in the test set, which are not rated by any user in the training set, to the training set. We fit a model to the training set and evaluate it on the test set. We repeat five random splits and report the averaged results.

Out-matrix regression. This evaluation, corresponding to the cold-start problems, considers the case where a new collection of items appear but no one has rated them. In this case, we randomly sample 50% items and put all ratings for them into the training set, and then put the ratings for the rest items into the test set. This corresponds to randomly shuffling item column in the user-item matrix and then cutting matrix into two parts vertically. Hence this guarantees that none of these items in the test set are rated by any user in the training set.

In-matrix classification. This evaluation is similar to in-matrix regression, but converts the aforementioned training sets of ratings into binary like/dislike datasets. We follow the method proposed in [13, 26] for constructing the binary datasets from the rating datasets as follows. First, we treat only ratings of 4 stars or higher as "like" preference. And then for each user we add the same number of pseudo negative ("dislike") items to "like" ones by sampling in proportion to their popularity [6, 9, 25]. The popularity-based sampling is chosen to discourage trivial solutions. For each test set, only users' "like" preferences for items are kept.

4.3 Evaluation Measures

We use two measures for these evaluation tasks, respectively suitable for the regression and classification tasks.

For the regression task, error-based metrics such as root mean square error (RMSE) and mean absolute error (MAE) are diverged from the ultimate goal of practical recommender systems.

Thus we measure the recommendation performance with a widely-used NDCG (normalized Discounted Cumulative Gain) for evaluating recommendation algorithms (including most of hashing-based collaborative filtering algorithms) and information retrieval algorithms [32]. This metric has taken into account both ranking precision and the position of ratings. The average NDCG at cut off from 1 to 10 over all users is the final metric of the regression-based recommendation accuracy. The larger value of NDCG indicates higher accuracy of recommendation performance.

For the classification task, according to [13], MPR (mean percentile rank) is utilized for measuring the performance, since it is commonly used in the recommendations based on implicit feedback datasets [10, 27]. For a user i in the test set, we first rank all items not rated in the training set, and then compute the percentile rank PR_{ij} of each "like" item j in the test set with regard to this ranking:

$$PR_{ij} \triangleq \frac{1}{N - |\mathbb{I}_i(train)|} \sum_{j' \notin \mathbb{I}_i(train)} \mathbf{1}[p_{ij} < p_{ij'}],$$

where $\mathbf{1}[x] = 1$ if x is true and $\mathbf{1}[x] = 0$ otherwise, $\mathbb{I}_i(train)$ is a set of the rated items of the user i in the training set, and p_{ij} is the probability that the user i likes the item j. After that, we compute the average percentile rank over all "like" items of the user i in the test set and denoted it as PR_i. The final metric for the classification-based recommendation accuracy is computed by averaging PR_i over all users. Accordingly, the smaller MPR value indicates better rankings.

4.4 Baselines of Comparison

For hashing-based collaborative filtering, we only compare DCMF with the state-of-the-art method: **DCF** [35], which outperforms almost all two-stage binary code learning methods for collaborative filtering, include BCCF [39], PPH [37], CH [19]. Note that DCF also directly tackles a discrete optimization problem, subject to the de-correlated and balanced constraints, for seeking informative and compact binary codes for users and items. But it has not been designed for classification-based collaborative filtering, and for incorporating content information.

For feature-based recommendation system, we compare a very popular method: **libFM** [23], which has achieved the best sole-model for the track I challenge–link prediction–of KDDCup 2012 [24]. It supports both classification and regression tasks of recommendation, and provides several algorithms, including SGD, ALS and MCMC, for optimization. With the advantage of learning hyperparameters in MCMC, we choose MCMC for optimization.

4.5 Results

In three tasks, the algorithm is sensitive to the tuning parameters α_1 and α_2, so that they should not be set to large values. And we tune them on a validation set, which are randomly selected from the training data, by grid search over {1e-4, 1e-3, 1e-2, 1e-1, 1} and set both of them to 0.01. Our previous empirical studies showed that recommendation performance is insensitive to γ_1 and γ_2 [16], so we simply set $\frac{\gamma_1}{\lambda_1} = 1$ and $\frac{\gamma_2}{\lambda_2} = 1$. The most important parameter among three tasks is λ_2 since only item contents are considered. This parameter of the initialization algorithm, denoted as DCMFi, is different from DCMF. In the DCMFi, we tune it on the validation set by grid search over {100,1000,10000,100000,1000000} and respectively set them as 1000, 100000 and 1000000 on the Yelp, Amazon, and MovieLens dataset. In DCMF, it is simply set to 1. The interaction regularization, designed for implicit feedback datasets, is only put into use in the classification task. Its coefficient β is set to 0.01, 0.01 and 1e-6 on the Yelp, Amazon and MovieLens dataset after tuning on the validation set by grid search over {1e-6,1e-4,1e-2,1e-1}. β is much smaller on the MovieLens dataset since this dataset is denser than others.

4.5.1 Regression. In this task, in addition to comparing DCMF with DCF and libFM, we add DCMFi, representing the initialization algorithm with sign function applied, into the baselines. The comparison results with varying length of hash codes are shown in Fig 2, where DCF fails in the task of the out-matrix regression. From this figure, we observe that DCF works well for in-matrix regression, but adding item content through DCMF could improve the performance. Discrete constraints indeed lead to quantization loss by comparing DCMF with libFM, but their gap may also result from the adaptive learning of hyper-parameters using the MCMC inference. However, it is worth mentioning that in the task of the out-matrix regression, DCMF could outperform libFM, particularly on the MovieLens dataset. The reason still lies in the higher density of the dataset, so that libFM may overfit on the training set and put more emphasis on ratings than item content information. This could be further verified that with the increasing dimension of latent factor (or hash codes), the performance of DCMF could approach and even surpass that of libFM on three datasets. Finally, the superiority of DCMF to DCMFi demonstrates the effectiveness of the developed discrete optimization algorithm.

4.5.2 Classification. In this task, in addition to libFM and DCF, we also compare DCMF with several variants of the initialization algorithm – DCMFi, and show the results in Fig 4. We can observe that for ranking all candidate items, DCMFi(c), the initialization of DCMF with continuous latent factor, is better than DCMFi(c)/F, which removes item content, and DCMFi(c)/IF, which removes both interaction regularization and item content. Combining it with the superiority of DCMFi(c)/F to DCMFi(c)/IF, we can demonstrate the effectiveness of interaction regularization and item content for improving recommendation performance. The comparison of DCMFi(c)/IF with DCFi(c), the initialization of DCF with continuous latent factors, could reveal the benefit of using logit loss for modeling the classification task. The overall benefit of incorporating these three factors into the classification task could be further observed by the superiority of DCMF to DCF. The better performance of DCMF than DCMFi(d) shows the validity of the proposed discrete optimization algorithm. Finally, an interesting observation arises from the comparison of libFM with DCMF and DCMFi(c). On both Amazon and Yelp datasets, both DCMF and DCMFi(c) outperform libFM. This mainly depends on the consideration of interaction regularization. Due to the extremely small value of β, interaction regularization almost couldn't take effect on the MovieLens dataset. In other words, the high density of the MovieLens data is an important factor that leads libFM to demonstrating surprising recommendation performance.

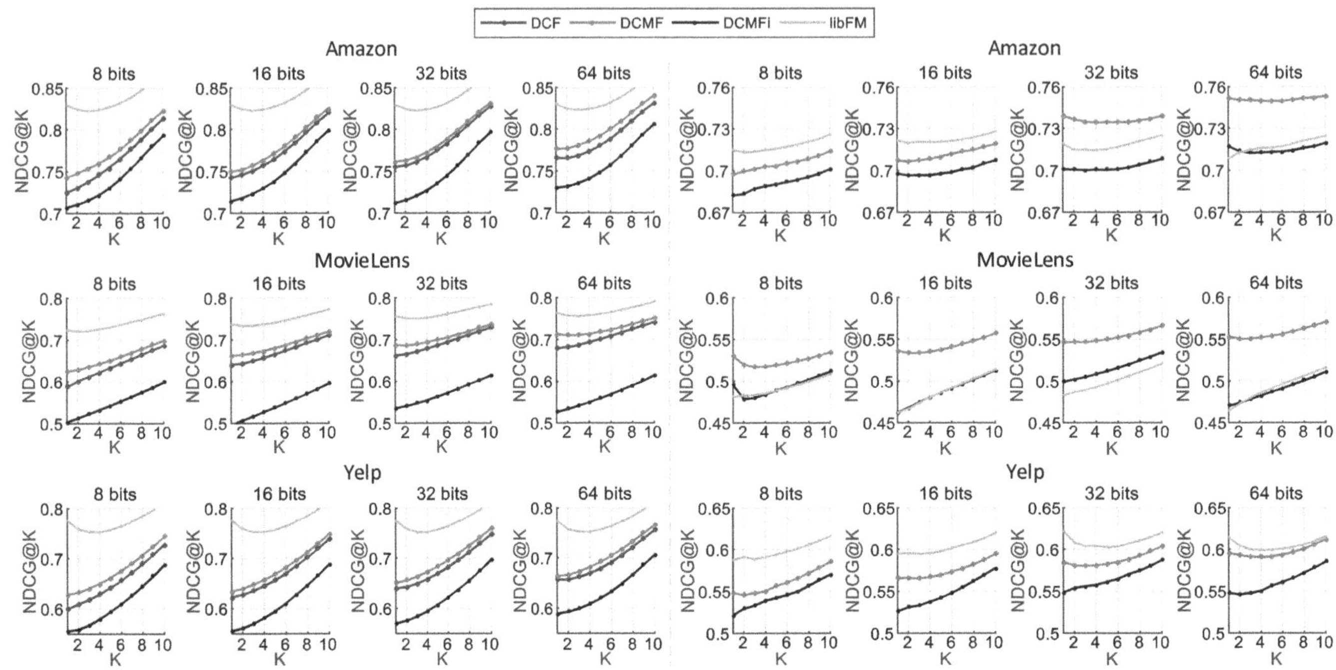

(a) In-matrix regression (b) Out-matrix regression

Figure 2: Item recommendation performance of hashing-based CF methods in the regression task given different code lengths

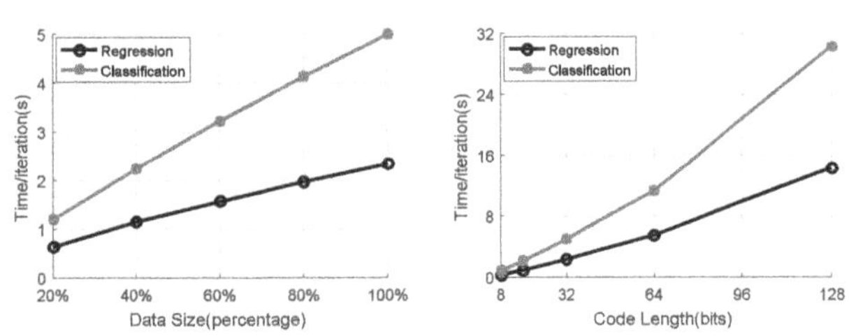

Figure 3: Efficiency v.s. data size and code length

4.6 Efficiency Study

After demonstrating the superior recommendation performance of DCMF, we further study its efficiency with the increase of data size and code length on the largest MovieLens dataset, and show them in Fig 3. When fitting DCMF of 32-D, each round of iteration costs several seconds and scales linearly with the increase of data size. When fitting DCMF on 100% training data, each round of iteration in case of classification scales quadratically with the increase of code length due to interaction regularization while the regression case is more efficient and scales linearly with code length.

5 RELATED WORK

This paper investigates hashing-based collaborative filtering at the presence of content information for regression and classification, so we mainly review recent advance of hashing-based recommendation algorithms. For comprehensive reviews of hashing techniques, please refer to [30, 31]. We also review some distributed/parallel recommender systems, since they share a similar spirit of improving recommendation efficiency.

5.1 Hashing-based Recommendation

As a pioneer work, Locality-Sensitive Hashing has been utilized for generating hash codes for Google News readers based on their click history [5]. Following this work, random projection is applied for mapping user/item learned latent representations from regularized matrix factorization into the Hamming space to obtain hash codes for users and items [12]. Similar to the idea of projection, Zhou et al. applied Iterative Quantization for generating binary code from rotated continuous user/item latent representation [39]. For the sake of deriving more compact binary codes from user/item continuous latent factors, the de-correlated constraint of different binary codes was imposed on user/item continuous latent factors [19]. However, since user/item's latent factors' magnitudes are lost due to binary discretization, hashing only preserves similarity between user and item rather than inner product based preference [37]. Thus they imposed a Constant Feature Norm (CFN) constraint on user/item continuous latent factors, and then separately quantized magnitudes and similarity. The relevant work could be summarized as two independent stages: relaxed learning of user/item latent factors with some specific constraints and subsequent binary discretization. However, such two-stage methods suffer from a large quantization loss according to [35], so direct optimization of matrix factorization with discrete constraints was proposed. To derive compact hash codes, the balanced and de-correlated constraints were further

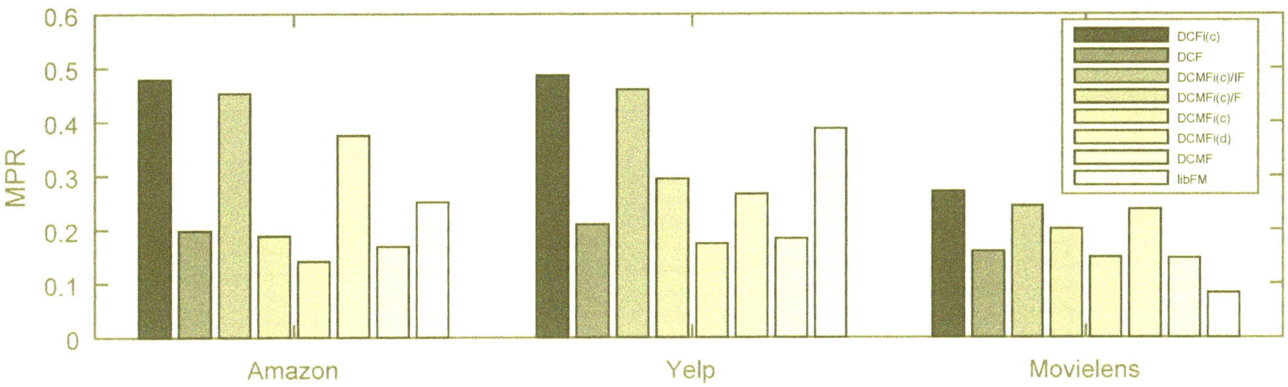

Figure 4: Item recommendation performance of hashing-based CF methods in the classification task, setting the length of hashing code to 32. DCMFi(c) and DCMFi(d) represent the initialization algorithm of DCMF using continuous latent factors and hash codes, DCFi(c) is the initialization algorithm of DCF using continuous latent factors. DCMFi(c)/F does not take content information into account. DCMFi(c)/IF does not take content information and interaction regularization into account.

imposed. For the sake of dealing with implicit feedback datasets, ranking-based loss function with binary constraints was proposed in [36].

5.2 Distributed/Parallel Recommender System

Due to superiority of matrix factorization algorithms for recommendation, their scalability has been extensively investigated recently. Based on the usage of optimization algorithms, there are mainly two lines of research. The first line is based on (block) coordinate descent. For example, user-wise (item-wise) block coordinate descent could be separated into many independent subproblems due to the independence of updating rules for different users (items) [40]. However, it is hard to be scaled up to very large-scale recommender systems since its parallelization in a distributed system requires a lot of communication cost. Instead, coordinate descent based parallel/distributed algorithm was proposed for updating rank-one factors one by one. By storing a part of residual $(r_{ij} - \phi_i'\psi_j)$ related to users and items in each machine, no communication of residual is required. The other line is based on stochastic gradient descent. For example, "delayed update" strategies were proposed in [2] and a lock-free approach called HogWild was investigated in [22]. In addition to proposing approximated but parallelized updating rules, exact distributed/parallel update among independent matrix blocks was proposed in [7]. When features of users and (or) items are available, feature-based matrix factorization such as Factorization Machine should be put into use. Its distributed optimization was also studied in [14, 38] based on parameter servers. However, the relevant work use continuous latent factors rather than hash codes. As an alternative way for improving the recommendation efficiency, the efficiency of hashing-based collaborative filtering in learning binary codes and online recommendation could be significantly improved with parallel/distributed techniques.

6 CONCLUSIONS

In this paper, we propose Discrete Content-aware Matrix Factorization for investigating how to learn informative and compact hash codes for users and items at the presence of content information, and extend the recommendation task from regression to classification. Simultaneously, we suggest an interaction regularization, which penalizes non-zero predicted preference, for dealing with the sparsity challenge. We then develop an efficient discrete optimization algorithm for learning hash codes for users and items. The evaluation results of the proposed algorithm on three public datasets not only demonstrates the capability of the proposed algorithm for incorporating content information, but also outperforms the state-of-the-art hashing-based collaborative filtering algorithms on both regression and classification tasks. And it is interestingly observed that the interaction regularization could greatly improve the recommendation performance when the user-item matrix is sparse, verifying the effect of the interaction regularization at addressing the sparsity issue.

ACKNOWLEDGMENTS

The work is supported by the National Natural Science Foundation of China (61502077,61631005,61602234,61572032,61502324,61532018) and the Fundamental Research Funds for the Central Universities (ZYGX2014Z012, ZYGX2016J087).

REFERENCES

[1] Gediminas Adomavicius and Alexander Tuzhilin. 2005. Toward the next generation of recommender systems: A survey of the state-of-the-art and possible extensions. *IEEE Trans. Know. Data. Eng.* 17, 6 (2005), 734–749.
[2] Alekh Agarwal and John C Duchi. 2011. Distributed delayed stochastic optimization. In *Proceedings of NIPS'11*. 873–881.
[3] Deepak Agarwal and Bee-Chung Chen. 2009. Regression-based latent factor models. In *Proceedings of KDD'09*. ACM, 19–28.
[4] Tianqi Chen, Weinan Zhang, Qiuxia Lu, Kailong Chen, Zhao Zheng, and Yong Yu. 2012. SVDFeature: a toolkit for feature-based collaborative filtering. *Journal of Machine Learning Research* 13, 1 (2012), 3619–3622.
[5] Abhinandan S Das, Mayur Datar, Ashutosh Garg, and Shyam Rajaram. 2007. Google news personalization: scalable online collaborative filtering. In *Proceedings of WWW'07*. ACM, 271–280.
[6] Gideon Dror, Noam Koenigstein, Yehuda Koren, and Markus Weimer. 2012. The Yahoo! Music Dataset and KDD-Cup'11.. In *KDD Cup*. 8–18.
[7] Rainer Gemulla, Erik Nijkamp, Peter J Haas, and Yannis Sismanis. 2011. Large-scale matrix factorization with distributed stochastic gradient descent. In *Proceedings of KDD'11*. ACM, 69–77.

[8] Johan Håstad. 2001. Some optimal inapproximability results. *Journal of the ACM (JACM)* 48, 4 (2001), 798–859.

[9] Xiangnan He, Hanwang Zhang, Min-Yen Kan, and Tat-Seng Chua. 2016. Fast matrix factorization for online recommendation with implicit feedback. In *Proceedings of SIGIR'16*, Vol. 16.

[10] Y. Hu, Y. Koren, and C. Volinsky. 2008. Collaborative filtering for implicit feedback datasets. In *Proceedings of ICDM'08*. IEEE, 263–272.

[11] T Jaakkola and M Jordan. 1997. A variational approach to Bayesian logistic regression models and their extensions. In *Sixth International Workshop on Artificial Intelligence and Statistics*, Vol. 82.

[12] Alexandros Karatzoglou, Alexander J Smola, and Markus Weimer. 2010. Collaborative Filtering on a Budget.. In *AISTATS*. 389–396.

[13] Noam Koenigstein and Ulrich Paquet. 2013. Xbox movies recommendations: Variational Bayes matrix factorization with embedded feature selection. In *Proceedings of RecSys'13*. ACM, 129–136.

[14] Mu Li, Ziqi Liu, Alexander J Smola, and Yu-Xiang Wang. 2016. DiFacto: Distributed factorization machines. In *Proceedings of WSDM'16*. ACM, 377–386.

[15] Defu Lian, Yong Ge, Nicholas Jing Yuan, Xing Xie, and Hui Xiong. 2016. Sparse Bayesian Content-Aware Collaborative Filtering for Implicit Feedback. In *Proceedings of IJCAI'16*. AAAI.

[16] Defu Lian, Yong Ge, Fuzheng Zhang, Nicholas Jing Yuan, Xing Xie, Tao Zhou, and Yong Rui. 2015. Content-Aware Collaborative Filtering for Location Recommendation based on Human Mobility Data. In *Proceedings of ICDM'15*. IEEE, 261–270.

[17] Defu Lian, Cong Zhao, Xing Xie, Guangzhong Sun, Enhong Chen, and Yong Rui. 2014. GeoMF: joint geographical modeling and matrix factorization for point-of-interest recommendation. In *Proceedings of KDD'14*. ACM, 831–840.

[18] Wei Liu, Cun Mu, Sanjiv Kumar, and Shih-Fu Chang. 2014. Discrete graph hashing. In *Proceedings of NIPS'14*. 3419–3427.

[19] Xianglong Liu, Junfeng He, Cheng Deng, and Bo Lang. 2014. Collaborative hashing. In *Proceedings of CVPR'14*. 2139–2146.

[20] Julian McAuley, Rahul Pandey, and Jure Leskovec. 2015. Inferring networks of substitutable and complementary products. In *Proceedings of KDD'15*. ACM, 785–794.

[21] Marius Muja and David G Lowe. 2009. Fast approximate nearest neighbors with automatic algorithm configuration. In *Proceedings of VISAPP'09*. 331–340.

[22] Benjamin Recht, Christopher Re, Stephen Wright, and Feng Niu. 2011. Hogwild: A lock-free approach to parallelizing stochastic gradient descent. In *Proceedings of NIPS'11*. 693–701.

[23] Steffen Rendle. 2012. Factorization machines with libFM. *ACM Trans. Intell. Syst. Tech.* 3, 3 (2012), 57.

[24] Steffen Rendle. 2012. Social network and click-through prediction with factorization machines. In *KDD-Cup Workshop*.

[25] Steffen Rendle and Christoph Freudenthaler. 2014. Improving pairwise learning for item recommendation from implicit feedback. In *Proceedings of WSDM'14*. ACM, 273–282.

[26] S. Rendle, C. Freudenthaler, Z. Gantner, and L. Schmidt-Thieme. 2009. BPR: Bayesian personalized ranking from implicit feedback. In *Proceedings of UAI'09*. AUAI Press, 452–461.

[27] Harald Steck. 2010. Training and testing of recommender systems on data missing not at random. In *Proceedings of KDD'10*. ACM, 713–722.

[28] Chong Wang and David M Blei. 2011. Collaborative topic modeling for recommending scientific articles. In *Proceedings of KDD'11*. ACM, 448–456.

[29] Jun Wang, Sanjiv Kumar, and Shih-Fu Chang. 2012. Semi-supervised hashing for large-scale search. *IEEE Trans. Pattern Anal. Mach. Intell.* 34, 12 (2012), 2393–2406.

[30] Jun Wang, Wei Liu, Sanjiv Kumar, and Shih-Fu Chang. 2016. Learning to hash for indexing big data – A survey. *Proc. IEEE* 104, 1 (2016), 34–57.

[31] Jingdong Wang, Ting Zhang, Jingkuan Song, Nicu Sebe, and Heng Tao Shen. 2016. A survey on learning to hash. *arXiv preprint arXiv:1606.00185* (2016).

[32] Markus Weimer, Alexandros Karatzoglou, Quoc Viet Le, and Alex Smola. 2007. Maximum margin matrix factorization for collaborative ranking. *Proceedings of NIPS'07* (2007), 1–8.

[33] Yair Weiss, Antonio Torralba, and Rob Fergus. 2009. Spectral hashing. In *Proceedings of NIPS'09*. 1753–1760.

[34] Fuzheng Zhang, Nicholas Jing Yuan, Defu Lian, Xing Xie, and Wei-Ying Ma. 2016. Collaborative knowledge base embedding for recommender systems. In *Proceedings of KDD'16*. ACM, 353–362.

[35] Hanwang Zhang, Fumin Shen, Wei Liu, Xiangnan He, Huanbo Luan, and Tat-Seng Chua. 2016. Discrete collaborative filtering. In *Proceedings of SIGIR'16*, Vol. 16.

[36] Yan Zhang, Defu Lian, and Guowu Yang. 2017. Discrete Personalized Ranking for Fast Collaborative Filtering from Implicit Feedback. In *Proceedings of AAAI'17*. 1669–1675.

[37] Zhiwei Zhang, Qifan Wang, Lingyun Ruan, and Luo Si. 2014. Preference preserving hashing for efficient recommendation. In *Proceedings of SIGIR'14*. ACM, 183–192.

[38] Erheng Zhong, Yue Shi, Nathan Liu, and Suju Rajan. 2016. Scaling Factorization Machines with Parameter Server. In *Proceedings of CIKM'16*. ACM, 1583–1592.

[39] Ke Zhou and Hongyuan Zha. 2012. Learning binary codes for collaborative filtering. In *Proceedings of KDD'12*. ACM, 498–506.

[40] Yunhong Zhou, Dennis Wilkinson, Robert Schreiber, and Rong Pan. 2008. Large-scale parallel collaborative filtering for the netflix prize. In *International Conference on Algorithmic Applications in Management*. Springer, 337–348.

Effective and Real-time In-App Activity Analysis in Encrypted Internet Traffic Streams

Junming Liu
Rutgers University, USA
jl1433@rutgers.edu

Yanjie Fu
Missouri U. of Science and Technology, USA
fuyan@mst.edu

Jingci Ming
Rutgers University, USA
jingci.ming@rutgers.edu

Yong Ren
Futurewei Tech. Inc, USA
Yong.Ren1@huawei.com

Leilei Sun
Tsinghua University, China
Dalian University of Technology
leisun@mail.dlut.edu.cn

Hui Xiong*
Rutgers University, USA
hxiong@rutgers.edu

ABSTRACT

The mobile in-App service analysis, aiming at classifying mobile internet traffic into different types of service usages, has become a challenging and emergent task for mobile service providers due to the increasing adoption of secure protocols for in-App services. While some efforts have been made for the classification of mobile internet traffic, existing methods rely on complex feature construction and large storage cache, which lead to low processing speed, and thus not practical for online real-time scenarios. To this end, we develop an iterative analyzer for classifying encrypted mobile traffic in a real-time way. Specifically, we first select an optimal set of most discriminative features from raw features extracted from traffic packet sequences by a novel *M*aximizing *I*nner activity similarity and *M*inimizing *D*ifferent activity similarity (MIMD) measurement. To develop the online analyzer, we first represent a traffic flow with a series of time windows, which are described by the optimal feature vector and are updated iteratively at the packet level. Instead of extracting feature elements from a series of raw traffic packets, our feature elements are updated when a new traffic packet is observed and the storage of raw traffic packets is not required. The time windows generated from the same service usage activity are grouped by our proposed method, namely, recursive time continuity constrained KMeans clustering (rCKC). The feature vectors of cluster centers are then fed into a random forest classifier to identify corresponding service usages. Finally, we provide extensive experiments on real-world traffic data from Wechat, Whatsapp, and Facebook to demonstrate the effectiveness and efficiency of our approach. The results show that the proposed analyzer provides high accuracy in real-world scenarios, and has low storage cache requirement as well as fast processing speed.

*Corresponding Author

KDD '17, August 13-17, 2017, Halifax, NS, Canada

ACM ISBN 978-1-4503-4887-4/17/08...$15.00
https://doi.org/10.1145/3097983.3098049

CCS CONCEPTS

• **Information systems → Mobile information processing systems**; **Data stream mining**; **Clustering and classification**;

KEYWORDS

Time Series Segmentation; Internet Traffic Analysis; In-APP Analytics; Service Usage Classification

1 INTRODUCTION

With the wide spread use of mobile devices, the messaging apps have been providing new ways of communication, such as text messaging, muti-media messaging, broadcast messaging, real-time chat, location sharing and moment post. This, in turn, motivates the emergence of in-App service usage analytics, which aims for understanding in-App user behaviors. Indeed, in-App service usage analytics has recently become critical for mobile companies to enhance user experiences and for Internet providers to provide intelligent network resource distributions [7]. A key task of In-App service usage analytics is to effectively classify mobile Internet traffic into different usage categories in a real-time manner. However, this is a challenging task due to the increasing adoption of secure protocols for in-App services. Moreover, as an online traffic analyzer, it should be able to handle millions of traffic flows from many users simultaneously. This requires fast processing speed and low storage cache requirement.

There are traditional packet inspection methods for the Internet traffic classification. These methods analyze the protocol types, port numbers or protocol signatures with the limited use of cache memory [9, 22, 29]. However, due to the limited available information and the complexity of packet encryption methods, the packet inspection method is not applicable for mobile messaging Apps with secure communication protocols. Recently, some researchers have tried to tackle these issues with data mining solutions [2, 6, 7], which first segment an Internet traffic flow into single-usage subsequences and then discover distinctive traffic patterns for single-usage classification. While the patterns discovered can help improve the classification accuracy, the feature extraction process is very slow and both of the segmentation algorithm and classifiers require the storage of a large set of raw traffic packet data. Moreover, the segmentation algorithm at the packet level is not accurate, and thus the segmented subsequence is not single usage due to the packet length variance. As a result, the features extracted from the inaccurately segmented subsequence are from mixed service usages that deteriorate classification performance.

To address these challenges, in this paper, we develop an online iterative mobile app traffic analyzer that comprises of a recursive time continuity constrained KMeans clustering (rCKC) algorithm for traffic flow segmentation and a Random Forest classifier for segmented traffic classification based on time window representation with adaptable features. Specifically, we first discretize the incoming traffic flows with a series of time windows, each of which is represented by the iterateable feature vector selected by our MIMD feature selection. The iterateable feature vector has the property that each feature element can be updated and the packet is released once a new traffic packet is received. The time window series are then grouped together by the rCKC segmentation algorithm that the time windows within one cluster represent the traffic flows generated from the same service usage. Finally, the cluster center feature vector is fed into a Random Forest classifier for service usage activity classification. As a result, the requirement for cache memory is reduced by more than 1000 times and the processing speed is increased by more than 10 times compared with existing studies. Moreover, we also demonstrate the applications of our method on two types of mobile Apps: Social Media Apps such as Facebook[1] and messaging Apps such as Wechat[2] and Whatsapp[3]. As shown in the results, the proposed analyzer provides high classification accuracy in real-world online scenarios, and has low cache requirement as well as fast processing speed.

2 PROBLEM FORMULATION

In this section, we first define some preliminaries. Then, we introduce the problem of Mobile App Traffic segmentation and classification.

2.1 Preliminaries

Here, we first introduce some preliminaries, which will be used throughout this paper.

Definition 1: *Internet traffic flow.* An internet traffic flow TF consists of a sequence of encrypted internet packets denoted by $TF = (\{t_i, P_i\})_{i=1}^{I}$ where I is the total number of packets and P_i represents the i-th packet received at time t_i. Each packet contains limited information including the packet length $P_i.l$, sender IP address $P_i.SIP$, receiver IP address $P_i.RIP$ and protocol type $P_i.Pr$. An internet traffic flow may contain one or more mobile user's usage activities.

[1]https://www.facebook.com/mobile/
[2]http://www.wechat.com/en/
[3]https://www.whatsapp.com/

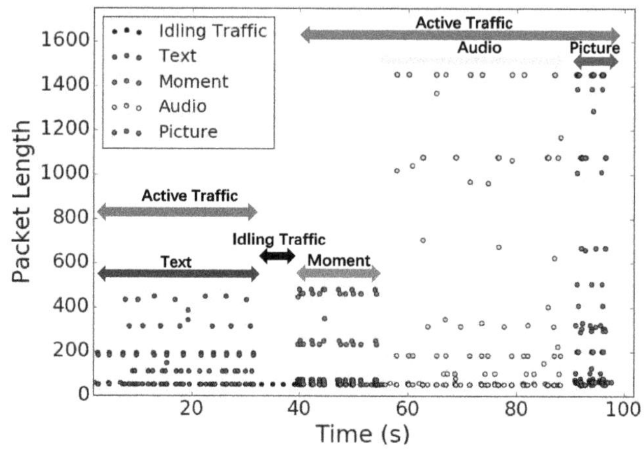

Figure 1: Examples of Wechat traffic flow

Definition 2: *Traffic Segment.* A traffic segment $S = < s_0, s_t >$ is a subsequence of an internet traffic flow from time s_0 to s_t. Segment operation $T(S)$ extracts the segment time duration $T(S) = s_t - s_0$. Operation $V(S)$ extracts the packet volume $V(S) = \sum_{P_i \in S} P_i.l$.

Figure 1 shows an example of traffic flow consisting of two activate traffic flows separated by a segment of idling traffic. The idling traffic represents the traffic flows of background packets when no service usage is activated. The second activate traffic flow includes three segments of traffic: browsing moment, sending audio note, and sending picture.

Definition 3: *Time Window Representation.* Instead of segmenting an internet traffic flow by comparing adjacent packets which is time-consuming and also introduces large variance, we divide a traffic flow into a set of continuous time windows. A time window W_n records a portion of traffic sequence starting from t_0^n to $t_{w_n}^n$. The size of a time window τ is fixed, s.t. $t_{w_n}^n - t_0^n \leq \tau$. There is a time gap Δ, s.t. $0 \leq t_0^{n+1} - t_{w_n}^n \leq \Delta$, between two adjacent time windows to ensure the smoothness of time window feature vector F_n.

2.2 Problem Definition

Given an incoming traffic flow $TF = (\{t_i, \bar{P}_i\})_{i=1}^{I}$, the mobile traffic analyzer is built to segment and classify a sequence of in-App usage activities denoted by $(\{b_n, e_n, \boldsymbol{u}_n\})_{n=1}^{N}$, where b_n, e_n, and $\boldsymbol{u}_n$ respectively represent the begin time, the end time, and the activity class. Essentially, there are two major tasks: traffic flow segmentation and traffic segment classification:

(1) *traffic flow segmentation*: the objective of our first task is to segment the origin traffic flow into multiple traffic segments $TF = \{S_1, S_2, ...S_n\}$, such that the traffic packets within each segment S are generated from the same single-usage activity.

(2) *traffic classification*: the second task is to classify the major usage activity given a segmented traffic.

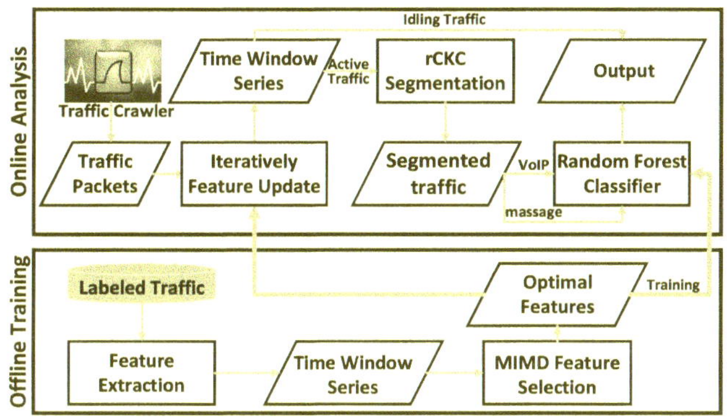

Figure 2: The Framework Overview.

2.3 Framework Overview

Figure 2 shows the framework of our proposed method which consists of two processes: offline training and online analysis. **Offline Training**. The offline process is conducted to learn the traffic patterns, test segmentation algorithm and train classifiers with labeled traffic flows. As shown in Figure 2, the offline process consists of four parts:
1) *Labeled traffic collection.* We collect the traffic flows of different mobile apps from a group of volunteers and employees of leading ICP provider company. Each traffic flow contains a sequence of packets with the corresponding packet receiving time, packet length, and packet protocol type. The service usage types, their start time and end time are reported by the data collectors.
2) *Traffic patterns extraction.* Mobile traffic patterns are extracted from a multi-view perspective: packet length related features and packet time delay related features. Totally 30 features are extracted as a full feature set in this part.
3) *MIMD feature selection.* To reduce the workload of feature extraction and save cache space for feature vectors, 6 most discriminative traffic patterns are selected as the optimal feature set using the MIMD feature selection criteria.
4) *Classifier Training.* The selected feature vectors and their labeled service activities are used for the Random Forest Classifier training. In this classifier, the major protocol types (TCP or UDP) are first used to filter the traffic into two major categories: VoIP (video call and voice call), and other usages (other usage activities including text, picture, audio, moment, etc). The usage services of each major category are then classified respectively.
Online Analysis. The online process is designed to analyze incoming streaming traffic flows. Different from the Offline process, the online process constructs the time windows and their feature vectors in an iterative way at traffic packet level. For each received traffic packets, its information (time stamp, packet length and protocol type) is collected to update the feature vector of the current time window. And the packet is released without the requirement of cache storage. Then the rCKC segmentation separates time windows into different groups and labels the time boundaries of single usage activity traffic segment. The segmented traffic can be easily inferred by incorporating the Random Forest Classifier learned in the offline process.

3 DATA COLLECTION

Table 1: Usage Activities of Different Mobile Apps

U#	Wechat	Whatsapp	Facebook
0	Audio	Audio	Moment
1	Location	Picture	Video upload
2	Picture	Voice Call	Video watch
3	Short Video	Text	Picture
4	Video Call	Short Video	New Video Upload
5	Moment	Location	
6	Text		
7	Voice Call		

To guarantee the data quality and facilitate our experiments, we design and deploy the data collection platform for off-line model training. With the cooperation of leading ICP provider company, we recruit volunteers and employees who are equipped with our specially configured smartphones with brand new Android or IOS. The traffic flows are captured by WireShark[4], a well-known traffic packet sniffing and analyzer tool, and we utilize it to crawl the packet information (packet time stamp, packet size, and protocol type) of traffic flows transmitted through our specific Internet access point. Meanwhile, data collectors report their corresponding usage types and activate time range as ground-truth. Finally, both the internet traffic and the reported usages are organized, archived and stored in our data repository.

4 METHODOLOGY

In this section, we first present our MIMD feature selection framework to select the most discriminative features. Then we provide the technical details of our rCKC algorithm for mobile APP traffic flow segmentation and Random Forest Classifier for segmented traffic classification.

4.1 MIMD Feature Selection

A set of 28 feature elements has been analyzed in our previous work [7] which provides the best usage activity classification accuracy. Here we list the 28 feature elements (more details of the feature element definitions can be found in [7]): **Packet length related features:** packet length maximal, minimal, mean, variance, kurtosis, skewness, hopping count, length of longest monotone (including increasing and decreasing) subsequences, size percentiles (4 subranges), 3 set of forward variances, 3 sets of backward variance, 3 most frequent subsequences; **Packet time delay related features:** time delay maximal, minimal, mean, variance, kurtosis, skewness. In addition, we add two more features: the traffic packet density (number of packet per second) and traffic speed (average

[4]www.wireshark.org

packet size per second) as our full feature set. However, although these feature elements can help achieve a high traffic flow classification accuracy, some of them are redundant and most of them are not iterateable. In other words, in order to extract the full set of features, the traffic analyzer needs to store all the raw traffic data, which makes the analyzer inapplicable as an online streaming traffic tool. In the following, we denote the feature set of 30 features as "full feature set" and conduct a feature selection algorithm to select the most representative feature set as our "optimal feature set". Besides that, the percentage of packets using TCP or UDP protocol is calculated for VoIP traffic filtering in order to reduce the problem complexity of the multi-class classification.

Motivated by the internal clustering validation measures [18, 25, 30], the optimal feature set for segmentation is selected to better group the packets that are generated from the same activity (Compactness) and to separate the packets from different activities (Separation) with the lowest time consumption. In this the following, we describe the two criteria of our recursive MIMD feature selection for the clustering based traffic flow segmentation.

Feature Similarity Function. After Z-score feature standardization, each feature element is rescaled to form a standard normal distribution. The similarity distance between any two feature vectors F, F' of dimension N are defined as:

$$SD(\mathbf{F}, \mathbf{F'}) = \frac{1}{N}\sum_{n=1}^{N} e^{-(F_n - F'_n)^2} \quad (1)$$

Maximal Inner Activity Similarity (IAS). For the packets generated from the same activity, their lengths and time intervals will vary. The features should not be sensitive to the inner cluster packet variance. In other words, for the time windows representing the continued activity, they should have high similarities in feature domain such that the segmentation algorithm will not mistakenly separate them as time windows from different activities. Mathematically, given a traffic flow from a single usage activity a_i represented by n_i^a time windows, the Maximal Inner Activity Similarity requires the maximal feature distance between the time windows $\mathbf{F}_{i,k}$, $k = 1, 2, ..., n_i^a$ and their segment center $\bar{\mathbf{F}}_i^a = \frac{1}{n_i^a}\sum_{k=1}^{n_i^a} \mathbf{F}_{i,k}$:

$$\max IAS(A; \mathbf{F}), \quad IAS(a_i; \mathbf{F}) = \frac{1}{n_i^a}\sum_{k=1}^{n_i^a} SD(\mathbf{F}_{i,k}^a, \bar{\mathbf{F}}_i^a) \quad (2)$$

Minimal Different Activity Similarity (DAS). The DAS measures how distinct that the feature vector representing one usage activity is from that representing another. For the packets generated from different activities, the selected features should be able to discriminate them by a large distance in the feature domain.

$$\min DAS(A \neq A'; \mathbf{F}), \quad DAS(a_i, a_j'; \mathbf{F}) = SD(\bar{\mathbf{F}}_i^a, \bar{\mathbf{F}}_j^{a'}) \quad (3)$$

Objective Function. We define the objective function Φ to combine the average IAS and DAS calculated from our off-line single activity traffic flows and optimize IAS and DAS simultaneously.

$$\max \Phi(IAS, DAS)), \quad \Phi(IAS, DAS) = IAS - DAS \quad (4)$$

Recursive Addition MIMD feature selection. When the full feature set is large, considering all feature subset is time costly. Therefore, we propose a recursive addition MIMD feature selection to select the optimal feature set. Specifically, we start with one feature that can maximize $\Phi(IAS, DAS)$ and recursively add one additional feature that can maximize the objective function. The addition step is repeated until the full set is reached. At last, we select the optimal feature set that has the maximal objective compared to all feature sets of different dimensions.

4.2 Traffic Flow Segmentation

Time series segmentation has been investigated to reduce the complexity of time series analysis. However, traditional time series segmentation algorithms such as Fourier Transforms, Wavelets, Symbolic Mappings and Piecewise Linear Representation are not applicable for mobile APP traffic time series due to the high density of Internet traffic flows and big variance of packet lengths. Motivated by the problem of image segmentation that the segmented pixel region must be spatial connected, in this paper, we propose a recursive Constrained KMeans Clustering (**rCKC**) algorithm with time continuity constraints for mobile App Internet traffic segmentation. To the best of our knowledge, such kind of constrained clustering algorithm has not been studied ever before in this problem.

After the time window representation, the problem of the traffic flow segmentation is to group a sequence of time windows $\{w_i(\mathbf{F}; t_i), i = 1, 2, ..., N\}$ into multiple clusters within which the time windows are the observation of traffic flows generated from the same usage service. In addition to the general clustering objective that within each cluster the distances between each time window are small and the distance between cluster centers are large, we add the time continuity constraints that the time windows within a cluster are timely connected as a link (w_i, w_{i+1}). Algorithm 1 presents the proposed CKC algorithm that recursively segments the origin traffic flows: Step 1 checks if the IAS of segment S is below the single activity IAS threshold δ. If the segment is identified as a single activity segment, no segment split is required and the feature vector of this segment center is output for classification. A segment with small IAS indicates a high probability that this segment contains more than one activity and should be split into sub-segment. The threshold δ is chosen as the lower bond of IAS that is calculated by the feature selection off-line. The segment split starts in step 4 with initiating K sub-segment centers by maximizing the distance between adjacent segment centers $D(c_j, c_{j+1})$. Step 7 assigns the time windows to each segment centers such that the average distance from the time windows to its segment center is minimized. Step 8 recalculates the segment center. Step 7 and 8 are repeated until the segment centers do not change and the segment is separated into K sub-segments $\{S_j, j = 1, 2, ..., K\}$. The algorithm acts on each sub-segment to check if further segment split is necessary in step 9 and 10. In our experiments, we set $K = 2$.

Algorithm 1 $rCKC(S = \{w_i, i = 1, 2, ..., N\}, K)$

Require: Input: $\{w_i(F_i; t_i), i = 1, 2, ..., N\}$
if $IAS(S) > \delta$ **then**
  output $S = \{w_i, i = 1, 2, ..., N; F(S)\}$
else
  Initial: $C^0 = \arg\max_{c_j \in \mathbf{W}} \sum_{j=1}^{K} DAS(c_j, c_{j+1})$
  while $C^p \neq C^{p+1}$ **do**
    $p \to p + 1$ %next iteration
    $b^p = \arg\max_{b^p} IAS(S(w_{b^p} : w_N))$;
    $C_1^p = \frac{1}{b^p} \sum_{i=1}^{b^p} (w_i)$
  end while
  for $j = 1 : K$ **do**
    rCKC(S_j, K)
  end for
end if

4.3 Segmented Traffic Classification

By feature extraction, we can output a set of vectorized traffic segments $S = (\boldsymbol{s}_j)_{j=1}^{J}$ where each is represented by a feature vector. To predict C types of service usages, we exploit the ensemble power of Random Forest with filtering (denoted as FRF). Specifically, by observing the traffic patterns, the traffic density and traffic speed can directly discriminative the VoIP activity (video call and voice call) from the rest. We first apply the filtering technology that separates the VoIP activity directly and the classification for the rest is conducted using the general technique of bagging of tree learners. By doing this, the C class classification task is simplified as a $C' < C$ class classification problem. Let B denote the number of trees, given a set of labeled traffic segments $S = (\boldsymbol{s}_j)_{j=1}^{J}$ with usage types $U = (u_j)_{j=1}^{J}$ where $u_j \in 1, 2, .., C'$, we repeatedly select a random sample with replacement of the labeled traffic segments, and respectively fit B decision trees to the B samples. After training, predictions for unknown traffic segment d' can be made by averaging the predictions from all the individual decision trees on the traffic segment d'. In particular, the random forest gives the probability estimation for each class c as follows:

$$P(c|s') = \frac{1}{B} \sum_{b=1}^{B} P_b(c|s') \tag{5}$$

where $P_b(c|s')$ is the probability estimation of usage type c given by the b-th tree. It is estimated by computing the ratio that usage type c gets votes from the leaves of the b-th tree. The overall decision function of random forest is defined as:

$$u' = argmax_c P(c|s') \tag{6}$$

5 EXPERIMENTAL RESULTS

To validate the efficiency and effectiveness of our proposed method, extensive experiments are performed on real-world traffic data from three mobile applications: Wechat, Whatsapp, and Facebook. For each application, we first collect a set of single activity traffic for feature selection and classifier training, and another set of traffic flows containing two activities (including one type activity with idling traffic) for traffic flow segmentation & classification testing. After the off-line model training and testing, an online performance test is conducted. All experiments are conducted on a PC with an Intel(R) Core i7-4790 CPU, 3.6 GHz, and 16 GB RAM running 64-bit Windows 10 system.

Table 2: Statistics of the WeChat Training data.

#	Usage Type	Records	Packets	Traffic	Tra/min
1	audio	136	44K	23.53M	208K
2	location	112	119K	31.79M	348K
3	picture	100	132K	103.2M	986K
4	sight	63	163K	141.11M	1.33M
5	video call	100	1,170K	239.76M	2.17M
6	moment	67	7K	1.18M	50K
7	text	229	30K	4.5M	32K
8	voice call	105	265K	32.54	758K

Table 3: Statistics of the Whatsapp Training data.

#	Usage Type	Records	Packets	Traffic	Tra/min
1	audio	176	72K	26.62M	436K
2	picture	197	178K	141.5M	2.26M
3	call	194	143K	21.64M	287K
4	text	202	34K	3.22M	42K
5	video	173	483K	472M	11.06M
6	location	80	11.52K	8.03M	47.77K

Table 4: Statistics of the Facebook Training data.

#	Usage Type	Records	Packets	Traffic	Tra/min
1	moment	101	40K	21.65M	607K
2	videoup	75	21K	6.56M	238K
3	video watch	108	1,216K	1,326M	42M
4	picture	97	57K	51M	2.26M
5	new video	77	844K	825M	10M

5.1 Experimental Data

Table 2, 3 and 4 show the basic statistics of our collected single activity traffic data of different types of service usages with respect to WeChat, WhatsApp and Facebook. In addition to this single activity traffic data, we collect two-activity traffic data that contains a segment of one activity traffic flow followed by another segment of traffic generated from a different service usage. Each activity-activity pair has 30 records and the time duration for each segment ranges from 5 seconds to 120 seconds.

5.2 Feature Engineering

Feature selection. The recursive addition MIMD feature selection progress is presented in Figure 3. As the dimension of the optimal feature set increases from 1 to 30 (full set), both of the IAS (red circle dot line) and the DAS (blue circle dot line) firstly increase and then decrease. The IAS reaches its maximum at the feature set of dimension 7 when the inner cluster time windows have the least variations. However, the DAS increases significantly which makes different segments less discriminative. By combining these two criterions, we find the objective (black circle dot line) Φ reaches its maximum at the feature set of dimension 6. Moreover, the cross-validation score (green square dot line) at dimension 6 is slightly lower (0.55%) than its highest value at dimension 25. Considering a higher dimension of features requires more memory and time consumption in feature extraction. Here in our following experiments, we use the feature set of dimension 6 as our optimal feature set. From a time window observation of N packets $\{(t_1, P_1), (t_2, P_2), ..., (t_N, P_N)\}$, the feature elements are defined and calculated as follows:

1 Percentile 25% P_{25}: percentage of packets with packet length smaller than 25% maximum packet length L_{max}. Mathematically, $P_{25} = \frac{1}{N}\sum_{i=1}^{N}\delta(P_i.l < 25\%L_{max})$. Where $\delta(.)$ is the delta function that equals to 1 if the condition is true.
2 Percentile 75% N_{75}: percentage of packets with packet length larger than 75% maximum packet length. Mathematically, $P_{75} = \frac{1}{N}\sum_{i=1}^{N}\delta(P_i.l > 75\%L_{max})$.
3 Top frequent continuous subsequence TCS: the highest repeating frequency of packet subsequence of length 3 (see detailed calculation in [7]).
4 Packet length variance var: the variance of packet length: $var = \frac{1}{N}(\sum_{i=1} NP_i.l^2) - (\frac{1}{N}\sum_{i=1}^{N} P_i)^2$
5 Traffic density TD: the average number of packets per unit time (second): $TD = \frac{N}{t_N - t_1}$.
6 Traffic speed TS: the average packet lengthes per unit time (second): $TS = \frac{\sum_{i=1}^{N} P_i.l}{t_N - t_1}$.

The ratio R_{pr} of packets number using UDP N_T and TCP N_U is collected for VoIP traffic filtering. After we determine the optimal feature set, the rCKC stopping threshold $\delta = 0.813$ is chosen to be the lower bond of IAS at dimension 6.

Iterative feature update. The iteratively time window feature update is illustrated in Algorithm 2. To achieve the feature iteration, two sets of small temporal vectors tem, tem' are iteratively updated. Once the analyzer receives a packet P, step 2 determines if a time window of packets (τ seconds of traffic flow) are observed. step 3 updates the tem vector to fill more packet information if the time window is not full. Step 5 updates the bottom half time window information for next time window updates. Once the time window is filled up, the feature vector is calculated and stored in Step 7~9. The bottom half time window information is used as the top half of the next new time window. After these updates, the packet P is released. As a result, the raw packets are not stored in the cache which significantly reduces the storage requirement. Once the memory stores a number of time window features, these time windows are used for traffic analysis (segmentation and classification) and the memory is released for new incoming time windows.

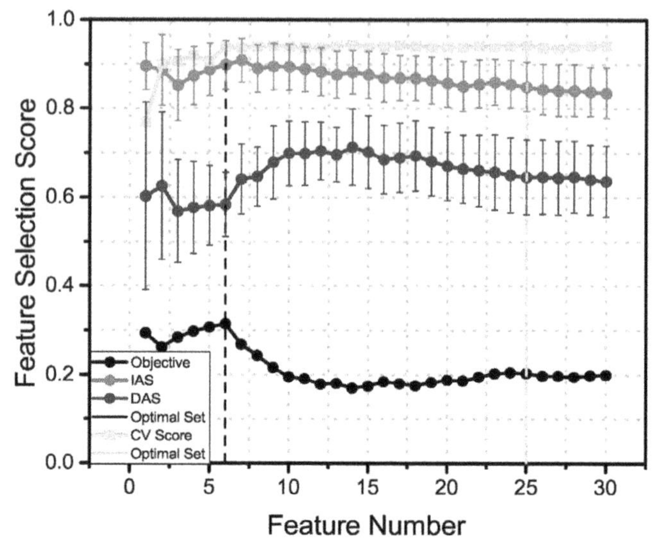

Figure 3: Feature Selection Progress.

The tem vector update function $Update(tem, P)$ works as follows: when a packet P of length $P.l$ arrives, variable N records the number of packets in current window and updates as $N+ = 1$; variable $N_{25}(N_{75})$ records the number of packets within $< 25\%$ ($> 75\%$) maximum packet length and updates as $N_{25}+ = \delta(P_i.l < 380)$, $N_{75}+ = \delta(P_i.l > 1135)$; variable FCS is a dictionary records the accumulate frequency of sequence $(P_{-2}.l, P_{-1}.l, P.l)$; variable N_T, N_U records the number of packet using $TCP(UDP)$ protocol and updates as $N_T+ = \delta(P.pr =' TCP')$, $N_U+ = \delta(P.pr =' UDP')$, where $\delta(.)$ is the delta function which equals to 1 if the condition is TRUE otherwise 0; L, L^2 records the summation of packet length and the square of packet length and updates as $L+ = P.l$, $L^2+ = P.l^2$. The packet is used for updating the tem vector only. Once the packet information is extracted, it is released without storage which significantly reduces the cache storage requirement for online traffic analyzer.

5.3 Baselines & Metric

5.3.1 Study of Single Activity Classifier. The single traffic flow activity classifier proposed in our work is denoted as the hierarchical random forest classifier (**HRF**). To confirm the effectiveness, we use the following four baseline algorithms for performance comparison: 1. Random Forest (**RF**); 2. Support Vector Classifier (**SVC**): The multi-class SVC builds a set of one-to-one classifiers and choose the class that is selected by the most classifiers [8]; 3. K-Nearest Neighbors classifier (**KNN**); and 4. Gaussian Naive Bayesian (**GNB**). The baselines are We measure the classification performance of different classifiers using the evaluation metrics of overall accuracy for all classes, and the Precision, Recall, F-Measure for each individual service usage category.

Algorithm 2 Iteratively update feature and time window

Require: Temple variable (initial 0):
tem=$(N, N_{25}, N_T, N_U, L, L^2, TCS)$
tem'=$(N', N'_{25}, N'_T, N'_U, L', L^2, TCS')$
while Receive packet P **do**
  if $P.t - T_0 \leq \tau$ **then**
    $Update(tem, P)$, $T_t = P.t$
    if $P.t - T_0 \geq \Delta$ **then**
      $Update(tem', P)$
    end if
  else
    $N_{25} = \frac{N_{25}}{N}$, $N_{75} = \frac{N_{75}}{N}$, $var = \frac{L^2}{N} - \mu^2$
    $TCS = \max_{L \in FCS} FCS(L)$
    $TS = \frac{L}{T.t - T_0}$, $TD = \frac{N}{T.t - T_0}$, $R_{pr} = \frac{N_U}{N_T}$
    Store feature: $N_{25}, N_{75}, var, TS, TD, R_{pr}$
    $tem = tem'$, $tem' = \mathbf{0}$, $Update(tem, P)$, T_0=$P.t$
  end if
end while

5.3.2 Study of traffic flow analyzer. The mobile traffic flow analyzer proposed in our work compromises of rCKC segmentation and Random Forest Classifier with filtering and is denoted as (**rCKC+FRF**). In order to confirm the effectiveness of our models, we conduct experiments to compare our methods with the following baselines:

- *AC+RF* [6]. This analyzer consists of an Agglomerative Connectivity Constrained Clustering (AC) and a Random Forest Classifier. The segmentation groups the timely adjacent time windows from bottom to up until a specific number of clusters is achieved.
- *CUMMA* [7]. The CUMMA traffic analyzer consists of adjacent packet merging strategy at packet level for traffic segmentation and a Random Forest Classifier for segmented traffic classification.
- *SW+RF* [11]. The sliding window (SW) based segmentation compares similarities between adjacent time windows in feature domain and combine the windows with a local search strategy. The average feature vector of adjacent time windows with high similarities are fed into the Random Forest Classifier.

The metrics we adopt to measure the performance are traffic duration accuracy (**TDA**) and traffic volume accuracy (**TVA**). The traffic duration accuracy evaluates the total correct service usage activity time durations and the traffic volume accuracy evaluates the total packet lengths that are correctly labeled. Given a traffic flow TF containing $\{\hat{S}\}$ traffic segments, their ground truth activities $\{\hat{a}_s\}$, our segmented traffic $\{S\}$ and predicted activities $\{a_s\}$, the two evaluation metrics **TDA** and **TVA** are formally formulated as follows:

$$TDA = \frac{1}{T(TF)} \sum_{S} \sum_{\hat{S}} \delta(a_s - \hat{a}_s) T(S \cap \hat{S}) \quad (7)$$

$$TVA = \frac{1}{V(TF)} \sum_{S} \sum_{\hat{S}} \delta(a_s - \hat{a}_s) V(S \cap \hat{S}) \quad (8)$$

Where $\delta(a_s - \hat{a}_s)$ is the delta function that equals to 1 if a_s equals $\hat{a}_s$ otherwise equals to 0. The intersection operation $S_1 \cap S_2$ captures the traffic segment shared by both segment S_1 and segment S_2.

5.4 Off-line Performance Test

Results on Wechat. The overall accuracy of different classifiers for Wechat single activity classification based on full feature set and optimal feature set is presented in Figure 4(a). As can be seen, our method outperforms the baselines with significant improvement using both feature sets. Moreover, by choosing the optimal feature set, our proposed method achieves an overall accuracy of 94.01%, slightly lower (-0.3%) than the overall accuracy using full feature set. Our *HRF* achieves a better accuracy than the *RF* algorithm indicates the VoIP-noVoIP separation can help boost the classifier performance by reducing the classes size. Figure 4(b) $\sim$ 4(d) shows the results of each approach in terms of precision, recall, and f-measure respectively using the optimal feature set. Comparing to the baseline algorithms, our method achieves the highest precision, recall and f-measure, indicating a balanced accuracy for each specific usage service. Among the eight usage activities, all classifiers have the worst performance on U5 (moment). The moment usage activity of Wechat APP is similar to that of browsers, and is the most challenging class for single activity prediction since it contains mixed traffics ranging from browsing (or posting) pictures to text only moment. Our method still achieves a f-measure of 0.7843 for this specific challenging task. Figure 4(e) presents the overall TDA and TVA of different traffic analyzer tests on the 2-activity pair traffic flows and our proposed analyzer significantly outperforms the state-of-the-art baselines with an overall TDA of 0.8366 and an overall TVA of 0.8935.

A more detailed TDA and TVA of 2-activity traffic flows are presented in Figure 5 that contains 8*8 sub-figures labeled by two usage activities. For example, the sub-figure "audio-picture" shows the performance test on two-activity traffic flow including a segment of audio traffic followed by a segment of picture traffic. The diagonal sub-figures shows the performance of our analyzer on short single activity traffic flows. As can be seen, our proposed traffic analyzer outperforms other baselines in all usage service environments.

Results on Whatsapp. The Whatsapp traffic flow has very similar traffic patterns compared to Wechat. The performance tests on Whatsapp is presented in Figure 6. The overall accuracy of our proposed classifier achieves an overall accuracy of 90.47% based on the optimal feature set and 93.56% based on the full feature set. Figure 6(b) $\sim$ 6(d) shows the significance of our classifier in terms of precision, recall and f-measure respectively using optimal feature set. Only 6 usage activities are tested for Whatsapp APP and our proposed classifier achieves the best performance on each single specific usage activity. Among all the 6 service usage classes, the test on Voice Call (U2) has the best performance since it is the only VoIP usage activity in our testing class.

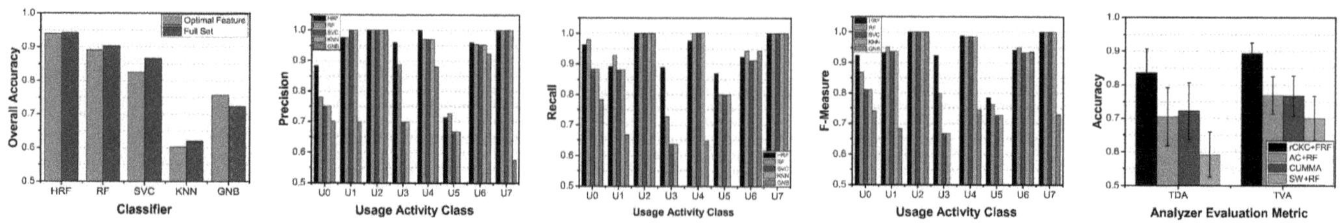

(a) Accuracy (b) Precision (c) Recall (d) F-Measure (e) TDA-TVA

Figure 4: Performance Comparison of Wechat

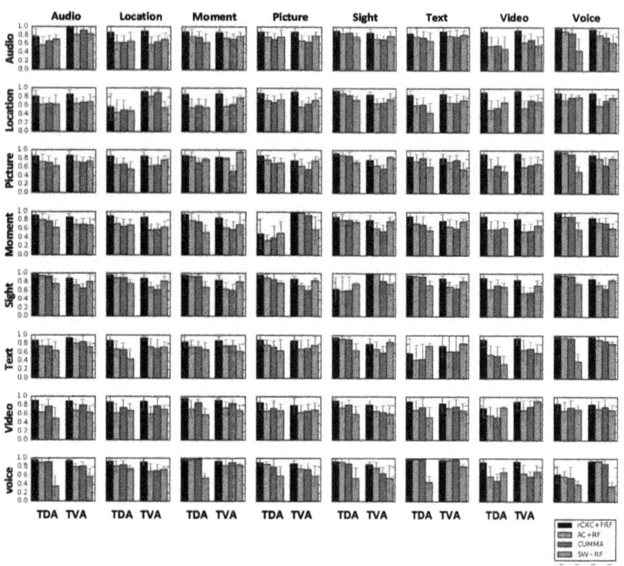

Figure 5: Performance Test on 2-activity traffic flows.

Similar to the Wechat performance test, we test our proposed analyzer on the 2-activity Whatsapp traffic flows. The analyzer performance comparison in Figure 6(e) illustrates that our analyzer improves the accuracy with an overall TDA of 0.9076 and an overall TVA of 0.966.

Results on Facebook. Figure 7 presents the offline test of our proposed classifier on Facebook Internet traffic flows. Different from the messaging APPs, there is no VoIP traffic flow tested on the Facebook APP and our HRF classifier is reduced to the traditional RF classifier. The overall accuracy of the RF classifier achieves the best overall accuracy of 92.48% among all other baselines based the optimal feature set and 95.87% based on the full feature set. The analyzer also works better on Facebook traffic flows with a high TDA(0.9147) and TVA(0.9654) present in Figure 7(e).

5.5 Online Performance Test

After we train and test our mobile traffic analyzer off-line with simple cases, we implement it online and test a continuous traffic flow of 2126 seconds during which the mobile user keeps switching service usage activities. The incoming traffic with labeled segment is shown in Figure 8(a). The average processing speed (number of packets processed per second) of different traffic analyzers is present in Figure 8(b). As can be seen, our designed analyzer is achieves an average processing speed of 8840 packets per second which is 14.3 times faster than the most competitive baseline, 7.14 times faster than CUMMA. Moreover, by choosing the optimal feature set, the processing speed increase almost 4 times for all analyzers. Figure 8(c) compares the TDA and TVA of different analyzers using the optimal feature set. Our proposed analyzer achieves a TDA of 86.82% and a TVA of 91.21%, which outperforms other baselines with significant margin. Due to the simplicity and local search strategy of SW+RF Internet traffic analyzer, it achieves a faster processing speed (1.94 times faster than our proposed method) but the overall TDA and TVA are only 35.42% and 53.96%.

6 RELATED WORK

Below we describe some related studies that have been accomplished on Internet traffic flow analysis.

Internet Traffic Segmentation. The mobile Internet traffic flow segmentation is basically a time series segmentation. In the past, several high level time series segmentation algorithms have been proposed, including Fourier Transformations [10], Wavelets [3], Symbolic Mappings [20], hierarchical bottom to up [13], top-down approach [15] and the most frequently used Piecewise Linear Representation (PLR) [14, 19]. These algorithms, based on time series element similarities, are supposed to support fast and dynamic implementation [12]. However, for the problem of Internet Streaming traffic flow segmentation, these algorithms are not applicable due to the large variance of the adjacent packet length and high traffic densities. To reduce the effect of packet level variance, a number of data mining techniques are proposed to extract time series patterns from a subset of traffic flows (time window representation) and calculate the traffic similarities based on the subflows. The most efficient one is the sliding window algorithm [4] that attempts to approximate the incoming subflows with similar traffic patterns. This algorithm works fast and can reduce the effect of packet length variances, however, as a local similarity search based algorithm, it suffers from the stability of Internet traffic flows. Most recently, a group of data mining researchers [1, 6, 16, 17, 23, 24] segment time series with clustering based algorithms in different time

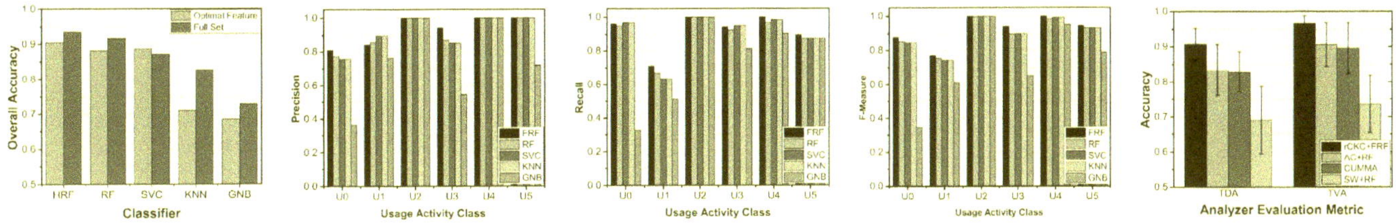

(a) Overall (b) Precision (c) Recall (d) F-Measure (e) TDA-TVA

Figure 6: Performance Comparison of Whatsapp

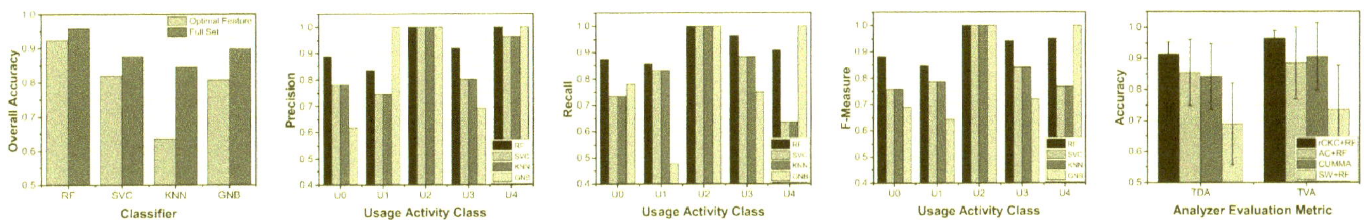

(a) Overall (b) Precision (c) Recall (d) F-Measure (e) TDA-TVA

Figure 7: Performance Comparison of Facebook

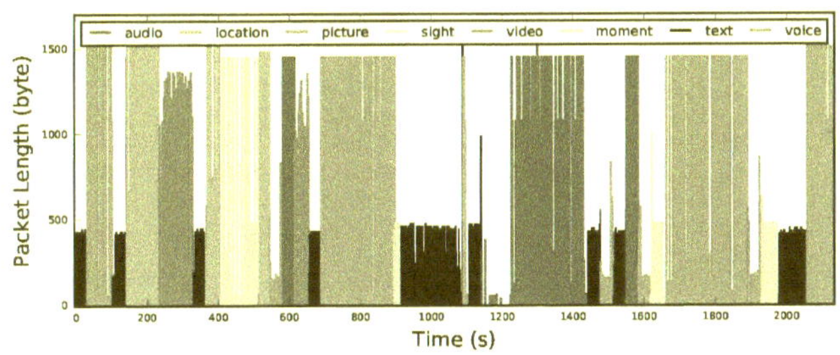

(a) Ground Truth Traffic Flow

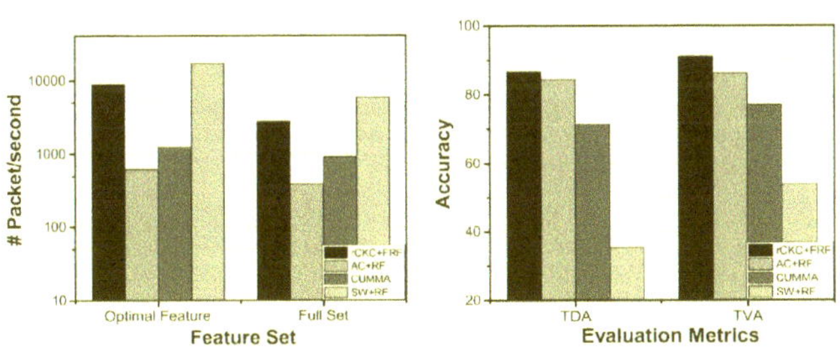

(b) Efficiency (c) Accuracy

Figure 8: Online Efficiency and Effectiveness Test

series analysis problems, however, most of these clustering based segmentation algorithms require a pre-specified number of segments and a set of complex high dimension feature vectors that can hardly be calculated iteratively as online time series segmentation algorithm. We further improve the time series segmentation algorithm with our rCKC algorithm that constructs time windows iteratively and finds the optimal number of segment recursively.

Mobile Service Activity Classification. Our work has a close connection with mobile service classification [27]. Falaki, etc. in [5] proposed a custom logging tool so as to enhance the classification of mobile App service usages. The authors also observed that the behaviors of people using mobile Apps are substantially diverse. Xu, etc. [28] collected the networking traces at anonymized IP-level from a large tier-1 cellular network and classified the traffic from different Apps by exploring signatures from HTTP headers. A novel approach that exploits the cross-layer interaction among various network layers for classifying usage of mobile Apps was developed by Qian, etc [21]. The work in [26] used the advertising traffic originating from the Apps as usage patterns for the classification of mobile service activities. The performances of these classifiers are limited due to the big variance of the traffic patterns extracted at packet level. Finally, our previous work in [7] proposed a step-by-step analytic method including traffic clustering, traffic classification using existing classifiers which provide a promising mobile service usage classification accuracy. However, since this classifier relies on a complex set of traffic patterns, the processing speed of this classifier is too low to meet the online efficiency requirement.

7 CONCLUSION

In this paper, we developed an online mobile app traffic analyzer for classifying mobile app traffic into different types of service usages. Specifically, we first proposed an optimal set of packet-level iterable features to reduce the cache memory requirement and to improve the processing speed. The received traffic packets from incoming traffic flows are then transferred into a series of time windows represented by the feature vectors, which is selected according to our MIMD criteria. Then, with the consideration of time continuity constraints, the time windows are clustered together with our rCKC clustering algorithm, by which the time windows generated from the same service activity traffic flow are grouped together. In this way, the service usage activities are identified for each segmented traffic flow. Finally, we provided the extensive experiments on real-world traffic flow data from Wechat, Whatsapp, and Facebook. The results show that the proposed method has the advantages of low storage cache requirement and fast processing speed. Also, our method can classify mobile app traffic with high accuracy in a real-time manner.

8 ACKNOWLEDGMENTS

This research was supported in part by the Natural Science Foundation of China (71329201) and Futurewei Technologies, Inc.

REFERENCES

[1] Saeed Aghabozorgi, Ali Seyed Shirkhorshidi, and Teh Ying Wah. 2015. Time-series clustering–A decade review. *Information Systems* 53 (2015), 16–38.
[2] Tengfei Bao, Huanhuan Cao, Enhong Chen, Jilei Tian, and Hui Xiong. 2012. An unsupervised approach to modeling personalized contexts of mobile users. *Knowledge and Information Systems* 31, 2 (2012), 345–370. https://doi.org/10.1007/s10115-011-0417-1
[3] Kin-Pong Chan and Ada Wai-Chee Fu. 1999. Efficient time series matching by wavelets. In *Data Engineering, 1999. Proceedings., 15th International Conference on.* IEEE, 126–133.
[4] Tak chung Fu. 2011. A review on time series data mining. *Engineering Applications of Artificial Intelligence* 24, 1 (2011), 164 – 181. https://doi.org/10.1016/j.engappai.2010.09.007
[5] Hossein Falaki, Ratul Mahajan, Srikanth Kandula, Dimitrios Lymberopoulos, Ramesh Govindan, and Deborah Estrin. 2010. Diversity in smartphone usage. In *Proceedings of the 8th international conference on Mobile systems, applications, and services.* ACM, 179–194.
[6] Y. Fu, J. Liu, X. Li, X. Lu, J. Ming, C. Guan, and H. Xiong. 2016. Service Usage Analysis in Mobile Messaging Apps: A Multi-label Multi-view Perspective. In *2016 IEEE 16th International Conference on Data Mining (ICDM).* 877–882. https://doi.org/10.1109/ICDM.2016.0106
[7] Y. Fu, H. Xiong, X. Lu, J. Yang, and C. Chen. 2016. Service Usage Classification with Encrypted Internet Traffic in Mobile Messaging Apps. *IEEE Transactions on Mobile Computing* 15, 11 (Nov 2016), 2851–2864. https://doi.org/10.1109/TMC.2016.2516020
[8] Mikel Galar, Alberto Fernández, Edurne Barrenechea, Humberto Bustince, and Francisco Herrera. 2011. An overview of ensemble methods for binary classifiers in multi-class problems: Experimental study on one-vs-one and one-vs-all schemes. *Pattern Recognition* 44, 8 (2011), 1761 – 1776. https://doi.org/10.1016/j.patcog.2011.01.017
[9] Patrick Haffner, Subhabrata Sen, Oliver Spatscheck, and Dongmei Wang. 2005. ACAS: Automated Construction of Application Signatures. In *Proceedings of the 2005 ACM SIGCOMM Workshop on Mining Network Data (MineNet '05).* ACM, New York, NY, USA, 197–202. https://doi.org/10.1145/1080173.1080183
[10] Eamonn Keogh, Kaushik Chakrabarti, Michael Pazzani, and Sharad Mehrotra. 2001. Dimensionality reduction for fast similarity search in large time series databases. *Knowledge and information Systems* 3, 3 (2001), 263–286.
[11] E. Keogh, S. Chu, D. Hart, and M. Pazzani. 2001. An online algorithm for segmenting time series. In *Proceedings 2001 IEEE International Conference on Data Mining.* 289–296. https://doi.org/10.1109/ICDM.2001.989531
[12] Eamonn Keogh, Selina Chu, David Hart, and Michael Pazzani. 2001. An online algorithm for segmenting time series. In *Data Mining, 2001. ICDM 2001, Proceedings IEEE International Conference on.* IEEE, 289–296.
[13] Eamonn J Keogh and Michael J Pazzani. 1998. An Enhanced Representation of Time Series Which Allows Fast and Accurate Classification, Clustering and Relevance Feedback.. In *KDD*, Vol. 98. 239–243.
[14] Victor Lavrenko, Matt Schmill, Dawn Lawrie, Paul Ogilvie, David Jensen, and James Allan. 2000. Mining of concurrent text and time series. In *KDD-2000 Workshop.* 37–44.
[15] Chung-Sheng Li, Philip S Yu, and Vittorio Castelli. 1998. MALM: a framework for mining sequence database at multiple abstraction levels. In *Proceedings of the 7th CIKM.*
[16] T Warren Liao. 2005. Clustering of time series data?a survey. *Pattern recognition* 38, 11 (2005), 1857–1874.
[17] T. Warren Liao. 2005. Clustering of time series dataąła survey. *Pattern Recognition* 38, 11 (2005), 1857 – 1874. https://doi.org/10.1016/j.patcog.2005.01.025
[18] Y. Liu, Z. Li, H. Xiong, X. Gao, and J. Wu. 2010. Understanding of Internal Clustering Validation Measures. In *2010 IEEE International Conference on Data Mining.* 911–916. https://doi.org/10.1109/ICDM.2010.35
[19] Sanghyun Park, Sang-Wook Kim, and Wesley W Chu. 2001. Segment-based approach for subsequence searches in sequence databases. In *Proceedings of the 2001 ACM symposium on Applied computing.* ACM, 248–252.
[20] C-S Perng, Haixun Wang, Sylvia R Zhang, and D Stott Parker. 2000. Landmarks: a new model for similarity-based pattern querying in time series databases. In *Data Engineering, 2000. Proceedings. 16th International Conference on.* IEEE, 33–42.
[21] Feng Qian, Zhaoguang Wang, Alexandre Gerber, Zhuoqing Mao, Subhabrata Sen, and Oliver Spatscheck. 2011. Profiling resource usage for mobile applications: a cross-layer approach. In *Proceedings of the 9th international conference on Mobile systems, applications, and services.* ACM, 321–334.
[22] B. Raahemi, W. Zhong, and J. Liu. 2008. Peer-to-Peer Traffic Identification by Mining IP Layer Data Streams Using Concept-Adapting Very Fast Decision Tree. In *2008 20th IEEE International Conference on Tools with Artificial Intelligence*, Vol. 1. 525–532. https://doi.org/10.1109/ICTAI.2008.12
[23] Stan Salvador and Philip Chan. 2004. Determining the number of clusters/segments in hierarchical clustering/segmentation algorithms. In *Tools with Artificial Intelligence, 2004. ICTAI 2004. 16th IEEE International Conference on.* IEEE, 576–584.
[24] Allou Samé, Faicel Chamroukhi, Gérard Govaert, and Patrice Aknin. 2011. Model-based clustering and segmentation of time series with changes in regime. *Advances in Data Analysis and Classification* 5, 4 (2011), 301–321.
[25] Pang-Ning Tan et al. 2006. *Introduction to data mining.* Pearson Education India.
[26] Alok Tongaonkar, Shuaifu Dai, Antonio Nucci, and Dawn Song. 2013. Understanding mobile app usage patterns using in-app advertisements. In *Passive and Active Measurement.* 63–72.
[27] Hannu Verkasalo. 2009. Contextual patterns in mobile service usage. *Personal and Ubiquitous Computing* 13, 5 (2009), 331–342.
[28] Qiang Xu, Jeffrey Erman, Alexandre Gerber, Zhuoqing Mao, Jeffrey Pang, and Shobha Venkataraman. 2011. Identifying diverse usage behaviors of smartphone apps. In *Proceedings of the 2011 ACM SIGCOMM conference on Internet measurement conference.* ACM, 329–344.
[29] S. Zander, T. Nguyen, and G. Armitage. 2005. Automated traffic classification and application identification using machine learning. In *The IEEE Conference on Local Computer Networks 30th Anniversary (LCN'05)l.* 250–257. https://doi.org/10.1109/LCN.2005.35
[30] Ying Zhao and George Karypis. 2002. Evaluation of Hierarchical Clustering Algorithms for Document Datasets. In *Proceedings of the Eleventh International Conference on Information and Knowledge Management (CIKM '02).* ACM, New York, NY, USA, 515–524. https://doi.org/10.1145/584792.584877

Functional Annotation of Human Protein Coding Isoforms via Non-convex Multi-Instance Learning

Tingjin Luo
tingjinluo@gmail.com
College of Science& Department of Computational Medicine and Bioinformatics, National University of Defense Technology
Changsha, Hunan 410073, China

Weizhong Zhang
zhangweizhongzju@gmail.com
College of Computer Science & Department of Computational Medicine and Bioinformatics & Tencent AI Lab
Zhejiang University
Hangzhou, Zhejiang 310058, China

Shang Qiu
qiush@umich.edu
Department of Electrical Engineering and Computer Science
University of Michigan
Ann Arbor, MI 48109, USA

Yang Yang
yangyangfuture@gmail.com
State Key Lab of Software Development Environment, School of Computer Science and Engineering
Beihang University
Beijing 100191, China

Dongyun Yi
dongyun.yi@gmail.com
College of Science & State Key Laboratory of High Performance Computing, National University of Defense Technology
Changsha, Hunan 410073, China

Guangtao Wang
gtwang@umich.edu
Department of Computational Medicine and Bioinformatics
University of Michigan
Ann Arbor, MI 48109, USA

Jieping Ye
jpye@umich.edu
Department of Electrical Engineering and Computer Science & Department of Computational Medicine and Bioinformatics
University of Michigan
Ann Arbor, MI 48109, USA

Jie Wang
jwangumi@umich.edu
Department of Computational Medicine and Bioinformatics
University of Michigan
Ann Arbor, MI 48109, USA

ABSTRACT

Functional annotation of human genes is fundamentally important for understanding the molecular basis of various genetic diseases. A major challenge in determining the functions of human genes lies in the functional diversity of proteins, that is, a gene can perform different functions as it may consist of multiple protein coding isoforms (PCIs). Therefore, differentiating functions of PCIs can significantly deepen our understanding of the functions of genes. However, due to the lack of isoform-level gold-standards (ground-truth annotation), many existing functional annotation approaches are developed at gene-level. In this paper, we propose a novel approach to differentiate the functions of PCIs by integrating sparse simplex projection—that is, a nonconvex sparsity-inducing regularizer—with the framework of multi-instance learning (MIL). Specifically, we label the genes that are annotated to the function under consideration as *positive bags* and the genes without the function as *negative bags*. Then, by sparse projections onto simplex, we learn a mapping that embeds the original bag space to a discriminative feature space. Our framework is flexible to incorporate various smooth and non-smooth loss functions such as logistic loss and hinge loss. To solve the resulting highly nontrivial non-convex and non-smooth optimization problem, we further develop an efficient block coordinate descent algorithm. Extensive experiments on human genome data demonstrate that the proposed approaches significantly outperform the state-of-the-art methods in terms of functional annotation accuracy of human PCIs and efficiency.

This work is partly supported by research grants from NSF China (No. 61473302, 61503396), NIH (R01 LM010730, U54 EB020403) and NSF (IIS- 0953662, III-1539991, III-1539722). Jieping Ye and Jie Wang are both corresponding authors.

KDD '17, August 13–17, 2017, Halifax, NS, Canada

978-1-4503-4887-4/17/08...$15.00
DOI: 10.1145/3097983.3097984

CCS CONCEPTS

•**Information systems** →**Data mining;** •**Computing methodologies** →**Optimization algorithms; Instance-based learning;** *Information extraction; Semi-supervised learning settings; Bagging;* •**Applied computing** →**Computational genomics; Bioinformatics;**

KEYWORDS

Non-Convex Problem; Key Instance Detection; Human PCIs; Multiple Instance Learning; Alternative Splicing

1 INTRODUCTION

Functional annotation of human protein coding isoforms (PCIs) is a central task in bioinformatics and plays a critical role in understanding the biological significance and underlying mechanisms of genes. Recent studies [6, 25] have shown that a gene can perform various functions as it may consist of multiple PCIs. According to the most recent GENCODE human annotation (version 19) [9, 11, 12, 19], a total of 57,820 genes consist of 196,520 PCIs. Moreover, PCIs can not only increase the protein functional diversity of mammalian genomes, but also is closely related to various human inherited diseases [9, 34, 40], such as colorectal cancer and spinal muscular atrophy. Therefore, differentiating the functions of PCIs [6, 15, 37] will accelerate our understanding of protein and gene functions.

However, due to the lack of isoform-level gold-standards (ground-truth), many existing functional annotation methods are developed at gene-level based on typical supervised learning algorithms, such as support vector machine (SVM) [20], logistic regression [21], Bayesian network [17] and Adaboost [32]. A major challenge in determining the functions of genes is the functional diversity of proteins, that is, a gene can perform different functions as it may consist of multiple PCIs. Without the ground-truth of isoforms, it is very difficult to build a suitable classification model and annotate the functions of PCIs by these supervised methods directly. Nevertheless, with development of recent bio-technologies, a large amount of gene expression data is obtained by deep sequencing of RNA and provides informative source for identifying the functions of PCIs. Thus the wide availability of RNA-seq data greatly increases our ability to differentiate the functions of isoforms. Furthermore, a suitable machine learning model can greatly improve the functional prediction performance of PCIs.

The main challenge for functional annotation task is how to use gene-level label information and a large number of gene expression features to predict isoform-level patterns. Lack of isoform-level gold standards prevents the functional annotation at isoform-level. Recently, the multiple instance learning (MIL) [15, 26, 31, 33] approaches have been adopted to tackle this kind of problem. R. Eksi et al. [15] developed a method named multiple instance support vector machine (miSVM) to differentiate functions of alternatively spliced isoforms on the mouse RNA-seq data. Recently, Panwar et al. [31] adopted miSVM to annotate the funtions of human isoforms. However, the optimal solution of miSVM was sensitive to the initial labels of isoforms inherited from positive genes and a threshold that represents a degree of strictness for assigning labels.

Recent studies [2, 7, 15] indicate that functional annotation of PCIs can be viewed as a new scenario of MIL. Although the rapid growth of RNA-seq data opens the door for functional annotation of human PCIs, the major challenges for differentiating functions of human PCIs still remain:

- Capturing the differential functions of human PCIs directly by existing experimental approaches is difficult.
- The annotated isoforms are unavailable. Annotations of different functions are commonly performed at the gene level in widely used databases such as Gene Ontology [4, 9] and KEGG [6, 22, 23] instead of isoform level. In addition, as each gene may contain more than one isoform, traditional supervised learning algorithms are inadequate to determine if a isoform is related to a specific function assigned at the gene level.
- The functional annotation task of human PCIs is unconventional. In fact, this task consists of two types of predictions. When given a positive gene with a function, the first task aims to determine which of its isoforms inherit this function. Another prediction task is to assign the functions of isoforms even for genes which are unknown to these functions and simultaneously predict the functions of genes. Nevertheless, few of MIL methods are suitable for these two predictions simultaneously.

To address these challenges, we propose a novel approach to differentiate PCIs' functions by integrating sparse simplex projection—that is, a nonconvex sparsity-inducing regularizer—with the framework of MIL. Specifically, a gene carries out a specific function by its key isoforms. To obtain a more discriminative feature representation of positive genes, we detect the key isoforms from them and introduce an isoform weight vector for each positive gene to measure the contribution of its isoforms. Based on the assumption that each positive gene consists of at least one of positive isoforms to carry out the function, we impose a nonconvex sparsity-inducing regularizer, which incorporates l_0-norm, l_1-norm and non-negative constraints on each isoform weight vector into our MIL framework. It enables our model better approximate the problem of key isoform detection. Finally, we learn these isoform weight vectors by sparse projections onto simplex and obtain the new feature representations of the positive genes. Our unified framework is flexible to incorporate various smooth and non-smooth loss functions such as logistic loss and hinge loss. Furthermore, under our framework, we propose a novel method named weighted logistic regression-based MIL method (WLRM). With the increase of gene expression features' dimensionality, elastic net regularization is employed in our methods to alleviate the over-fitting problem. To solve our formulated non-convex and non-smooth optimization problem, we further develop an efficient accelerated block coordinate decent (BCD) algorithm. Extensive experiments on human genome data show that our methods significantly outperform the state-of-the-art methods in terms of functional annotation accuracy of human PCIs and efficiency.

The rest of this paper is organized as follows. Section 2 reviews the background of MIL, and Section 3 presents our proposed MIL framework and efficient block coordinate descent algorithm with backtracking line search. Experiments on real human genome data are presented in Section 4, and the paper concludes with a summary in Section 5.

Notations: Matrices and vectors are written as boldface uppercase letters and italic boldface lowercase letters, respectively. For a matrix $\mathbf{M} = [m_{ij}]$, its ith row and jth column are denoted by $\boldsymbol{m}^i$ and $\boldsymbol{m}_j$, respectively. The l_p-norm of a vector $\boldsymbol{v} \in \mathbb{R}^n$ is defined as $\|\boldsymbol{v}\|_p = \left(\sum_i |v_i|^p\right)^{1/p}, p > 0$ and l_0-norm is the cardinality of nonzero elements in $\boldsymbol{v}$. The notations used in this paper are summarized in Table 1.

Table 1: Notations.

Notations	Description
d	Dimensionality of the original data
N	Number of genes
N_1	Number of positive genes
B_N	Index set of all negative bags or genes
B_P	Index set of all positive bags or genes
n_i	Number of instances in ith bag or gene
$\mathbf{1}(\cdot)$	Indicator function onto set C
$\mathbf{X}_i \in \mathbb{R}^{n_i \times d}$	Feature matrix of ith gene
$\boldsymbol{x}_j^i \in \mathbb{R}^d$	The jth feature vector of ith gene
$\boldsymbol{u}_i \in \mathbb{R}^{n_i}$	Isoform weight vector of ith gene
$\boldsymbol{w} \in \mathbb{R}^{d+1}$	Coefficients of the model

2 RELATED WORK

MIL was first introduced in [13] for drug activity prediction. Since then, many MIL methods have been proposed in the literature. Maron et.al. [29] proposed the diverse density (DD) method based on the elliptic target concept in feature space closely related to the peak density of positive instances. Zhang et al. [1] proposed a refinement of DD, named expectation maximization diverse density (EMDD) to learn the witness instances and perform multiple instance regression simultaneously by the EM method. Under the standard MI assumption, MIL could be viewed as a semi-supervised learning problem with the additional constraint that positive bags must contain at least one positive instance. In order to deal with large scale MIL problems, Wei et al. [38, 39] proposed MIL based on the Fisher Vector representation (miFV) and MIL based on the vector of locally aggregated descriptors representation (miVLAD) to convert the bag representation of an object to a simpler one, i.e., a vector representation. Thus, miFV and miVLAD only concern the classification of bags and cannot differentiate the function of instance. Besides, Andrews et al. [3] proposed multiple instance support vector machines (miSVM and MISVM) by encoding the positive constraints in the objective function of SVM. The aim of miSVM is to maximize the pattern margin of instances, while MISVM aims to maximize the margins at bag-level. It is possible for miSVM to predict the functions of isoforms based on the idea of selecting the witness instances. Recently, R. Eski et al. [15] applied miSVM and MISVM to annotate functions of mouse isoforms. Their experiments showed that miSVM performs better than MISVM. However, miSVM is sensitive to the initial labels of these isoforms extracted from positive genes.

The objective of these MIL methods is to predict the labels of bags, but not for instances. For a specific function, we have a set of positive genes annotated based on Gene Ontology (GO) and another set of negative genes that are unrelated to this function. Each gene consists of multiple isoforms. Differentiating functions of the genes can be tackled by traditional MIL methods. Nevertheless, the target of functional annotation of human PCIs consists of three tasks: key isoform detection, functional prediction of genes and PCIs. Due to the lack of the ground-truth of isoforms, it is very difficult to determine the functions of isoforms at given a multiple instance setting. In other words, functional annotation of human PCIs is very different from traditional MIL problems [33] and can be viewed as a new type of MIL. Therefore, it is necessary to develop a novel approach that can select key isoforms and differentiate the functions of PCIs simultaneously.

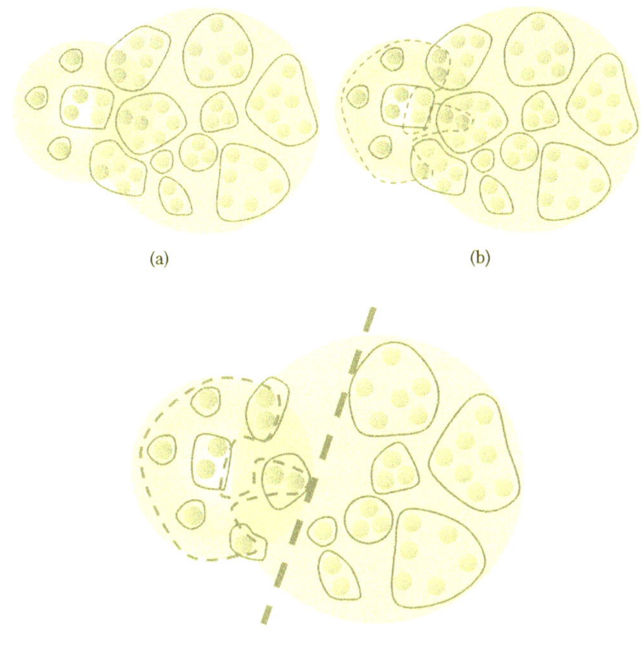

(a) (b) (c)

Figure 1: Illustration of key isoforms of positive genes for a certain function. (a) The green circles are the true positive isoforms and the remaining blue circles are negative isoforms. Each blue ring including at least one green circle represents the positive gene and others are negative genes. (b) The target of key isoform detection is to find all of the green circles in positive genes. (c) The classification hyperplane is learned by selected key isoforms.

3 A NOVEL MIL FRAMEWORK VIA NON-CONVEX PROGRAMING

We are given a set of genes $\mathbf{X} = \{\mathbf{X}_1, \mathbf{X}_2, ..., \mathbf{X}_n\}$, and their corresponding labels $\boldsymbol{y} = \{y_1, y_2, ..., y_n\} \in \{-1, +1\}^n$ for a specific biological process. The ith gene includes n_i isoforms whose feature vectors are $\mathbf{X}_i = [\boldsymbol{x}_1, ..., \boldsymbol{x}_{n_i}] \in \mathbb{R}^{d \times n_i}$. In our paper, a bag refers to a gene, which contains multiple PCIs. An instance refers to an individual isoform and a positive bag refers to a positive gene related to the specific function. We aim to detect key isoforms from positive genes and predict the functions of isoforms jointly by using the available gene label information.

3.1 Motivation and Formulation

Most existing MIL methods [8, 15, 26, 27, 29] assume that each instance in a bag plays an equal role when considering the similarity between two bags. However, for a specific biological process, only a few of positive genes carry out this function. For each positive gene, only its key isoforms are closely related to this function. In other words, the importance of isoforms for genes is not equal, especially for positive genes. As shown in Fig.1, only a few of key isoforms carry out this function and they are critical to functional annotation of genes. Meanwhile, as demonstrated in [3] and [28], key isoform detection is able to discriminate the functions of isoforms and thus help to improve the performance in real applications. This motivates us to develop a novel approach that is able to differentiate the functions of PCIs by integrating a nonconvex sparsity-inducing regularizer within the framework of MIL.

Without loss of generality, denote y and $\hat{y}$ as the true label and the predicted label for data point $\boldsymbol{x}$. Then the loss function is defined as $l(y, \hat{y})$. Similar to the typical supervised learning methods, we adopt the linear model to predict the functions of isoforms, that is, $\hat{y} = \boldsymbol{w}^T \boldsymbol{x} + b$. However, although the labels of all genes are known, the ground-truth of each isoform in positive genes remains unavailable, which renders the loss $l(y, \hat{y})$ difficult to compute. For the i-th positive gene, a positive gene carries out a specific function by its key isoforms. Thus we introduce an isoform weight vector $\boldsymbol{u}_i \in \mathbb{R}^{n_i}$ to measure the contribution of n_i isoforms to the function of this gene. If an isoform is negative, its weight will be zero. Note that the isoform weight vector does not only detect the key isoforms, but also eliminate the effect of negative isoforms in positive genes. Thus the isoform weight vector can enhance the discriminative power of our model. With the estimated isoform weight vector, we represent the positive gene by its selected key isoforms, that is, the new feature representation of the i-th positive gene is $\mathbf{X}_i \boldsymbol{u}_i$. The loss of the i-th positive gene is $l(y_i, \boldsymbol{w}^T \mathbf{X}_i \boldsymbol{u}_i + b)$. For isoforms of negative genes, their labels can inherit from the genes directly, and the loss of i-th negative gene is $\sum_{j=1}^{n_i} l(y_i, \boldsymbol{w}^T \boldsymbol{x}_j^i + b)$. Finally, the loss of our model is formulated as

$$\sum_{i \in B_P} l(y_i, \boldsymbol{w}^T \mathbf{X}_i \boldsymbol{u}_i + b) + \sum_{i \in B_N} \sum_{j=1}^{n_i} l(y_i, \boldsymbol{w}^T \boldsymbol{x}_j^i + b), \tag{1}$$

where $\boldsymbol{w}$ is the coefficients of the model, and B_P and B_N are the index vectors of positive genes and negative genes, respectively. For simplicity, the bias b can be absorbed into $\boldsymbol{w}$ when the constant value 1 is added as an additional dimension for each isoform $\boldsymbol{x}_i$. Thus the problem in Eq. (1) is rewritten as

$$\min_{\boldsymbol{w}, \boldsymbol{u}_i} \sum_{i \in B_P} l(y_i, \boldsymbol{w}^T \mathbf{X}_i \boldsymbol{u}_i) + \sum_{i \in B_N} \sum_{j=1}^{n_i} l(y_i, \boldsymbol{w}^T \boldsymbol{x}_j^i). \tag{2}$$

In practice, the RNA-seq data set is typically imbalanced, since the number of negative genes is much more than the number of positive genes. Similar to [20], we employ a weight parameter ρ/n_i for each negative gene to alleviate the imbalanced problem. The problem (2) is reformulated as

$$\min_{\boldsymbol{w}, \boldsymbol{u}_i} \sum_{i \in B_P} l(y_i, \boldsymbol{w}^T \mathbf{X}_i \boldsymbol{u}_i) + \sum_{i \in B_N} \frac{\rho}{n_i} \sum_{j=1}^{n_i} l(y_i, \boldsymbol{w}^T \boldsymbol{x}_j^i), \tag{3}$$

Based on the assumption [15] that each positive gene contains at least one key isoform to carry out the function and the remaining ones are negative isoforms, the cardinality (l_0-norm) constraint is a natural way to constrain the number of selected key isoforms. By definition, each element of the isoform weight vector represents the relationship between isoform and the function. It requires all elements of isoform weight vector to be non-negative. To some extent, the isoform weight vector can be viewed as a mapping which embeds the original bag space to a discriminative feature space. The new feature representation of a positive gene is the convex combination of all selected key isoforms. It is natural to constrain the summation of all elements to be equal to 1, that is, l_1-norm constraint. Therefore, the nonconvex sparsity-inducing regularizer, which incorporates l_0-norm, l_1-norm and non-negative constraints into the isoform weight vector, is employed in our formulation to better approximate the problem of key isoform detection. The formulation in Eq. (3) becomes

$$\begin{aligned} &\min_{\boldsymbol{w}, \boldsymbol{u}_i} \sum_{i \in B_P} l(y_i, \boldsymbol{w}^T \mathbf{X}_i \boldsymbol{u}_i) + \sum_{i \in B_N} \frac{\rho}{n_i} \sum_{j=1}^{n_i} l(y_i, \boldsymbol{w}^T \boldsymbol{x}_j^i) \\ &s.t. \ \forall i \in \{1, ..., N_1\}, \|\boldsymbol{u}_i\|_0 \le r, \|\boldsymbol{u}_i\|_1 = 1, \boldsymbol{u}_i \ge 0. \end{aligned} \tag{4}$$

Similar to SVM, when the dimensionality of expression features is large than the number of isoforms, Eq. (4) is also prone to over-fitting. A standard technique to alleviate over-fitting is regularization. Zou et al. [42] proposed the elastic net penalty which is a flexible regularization by mixing l_1-norm and l_2-norm regularization. Prior works have shown that the model with the elastic net penalty often outperforms the model with l_1-norm or l_2-norm regularization only. Thus our unified model incorporates the elastic net regularization to sparsify the coefficients $\boldsymbol{w}$. Finally, our unified framework can be formulated as

$$\begin{aligned} &\min_{\boldsymbol{w}, \boldsymbol{u}_i} \sum_{i \in B_P} l(y_i, \boldsymbol{w}^T \mathbf{X}_i \boldsymbol{u}_i) + \sum_{i \in B_N} \frac{\rho}{n_i} \sum_{j=1}^{n_i} l(y_i, \boldsymbol{w}^T \boldsymbol{x}_j^i) \\ &\quad + \lambda_1 \|\boldsymbol{w}\|^2 + \lambda_2 \|\boldsymbol{w}\|_1 \\ &s.t. \ \forall i \in \{1, ..., N_1\}, \|\boldsymbol{u}_i\|_0 \le r, \|\boldsymbol{u}_i\|_1 = 1, \boldsymbol{u}_i \ge 0. \end{aligned} \tag{5}$$

Note that our unified framework is flexible to incorporate various smooth and non-smooth loss functions. In this paper, we propose the weighted logistic regression-based MIL method (WLRM) by using logistic loss under this framework. Thus the basic loss function of WLRM can be formulated as

$$\begin{aligned} &\min_{\boldsymbol{w}, \boldsymbol{u}_i} \sum_{i \in B_P} \log\left(1 + \exp(-y_i \langle \boldsymbol{w}, \mathbf{X}_i \boldsymbol{u}_i \rangle)\right) + \\ &\sum_{i \in B_N} \frac{\rho}{n_i} \sum_{j=1}^{n_i} \log\left[1 + \exp(-y_i \langle \boldsymbol{w}, \boldsymbol{x}_j^i \rangle)\right]. \end{aligned} \tag{6}$$

in which by integrating the noncovex sparsity-inducing regularizers, we can finally obtain our WLRM model as follows

$$\begin{aligned} &\min_{\boldsymbol{w}, \boldsymbol{u}_i} \sum_{i \in B_P} \log\left(1 + \exp(-y_i \langle \boldsymbol{w}, \mathbf{X}_i \boldsymbol{u}_i \rangle)\right) + \lambda_1 \|\boldsymbol{w}\|^2 + \\ &\sum_{i \in B_N} \frac{\rho}{n_i} \sum_{j=1}^{n_i} \log\left[1 + \exp(-y_i \langle \boldsymbol{w}, \boldsymbol{x}_j^i \rangle)\right] + \lambda_2 \|\boldsymbol{w}\|_1 \\ &s.t. \ \forall i \in \{1, ..., N_1\}, \|\boldsymbol{u}_i\|_0 \le r, \|\boldsymbol{u}_i\|_1 = 1, \boldsymbol{u}_i \ge 0. \end{aligned} \tag{7}$$

It is worth noting that, although traditional logistic regression (LR) has been applied in many real applications, LR is not effective for functional annotation of PCIs, because there are no sufficient label information of isoforms, especially labels of true positive isoforms. Meanwhile, to solve our non-convex and non-smooth formulation, we further develop an efficient accelerated block coordinate decent (BCD) algorithm.

3.2 Optimization Methods

In this section, we develop an efficient algorithm based on the block coordinate descent (BCD) to solve this unified framework. Denote $\boldsymbol{x} = (\boldsymbol{w}, \boldsymbol{u}_1, ..., \boldsymbol{u}_{n_1})$ and $C_i = \{\boldsymbol{u}_i | \boldsymbol{u}_i \in \mathbb{R}^{n_i}, \|\boldsymbol{u}_i\|_1 = 1, \|\boldsymbol{u}_i\|_0 \leq r, \boldsymbol{u}_i \geq 0\}$, and the loss function is defined as

$$f(\boldsymbol{x}) = \sum_{i \in B_P} l(y_i, \boldsymbol{w}^T \mathbf{X}_i \boldsymbol{u}_i) + \sum_{i \in B_N} \frac{\rho}{n_i} \sum_{j=1}^{n_i} l(y_i, \boldsymbol{w}^T \boldsymbol{x}_j^i).$$

The problem (5) can be summarized as the following framework

$$\min_{\boldsymbol{x}} F(\boldsymbol{x}) = f(\boldsymbol{x}) + \sum_{i=1}^{n_s} r_i(\boldsymbol{x}_i), \tag{8}$$

where $n_s = N_1 + 1$ and the function $r_1(\boldsymbol{x}_1) = \lambda_1 \|\boldsymbol{w}\|^2 + \lambda_2 \|\boldsymbol{w}\|_1$ and $r_i(\boldsymbol{x}_i) = \mathbf{1}_{C_i}(\boldsymbol{u}_i)$ for $i = 2, ..., n_s$ is an indicator function of C_i. By allowing $\mathbf{1}_{C_i}$ to take the ∞-value, $\mathbf{1}_{C_i}$ can incorporate the constraints $\boldsymbol{u}_i \in C_i$ since enforcing the constraints is equivalent to minimize the indicator function of C_i. According to its definition, $\mathbf{1}_{C_i}$ is proper and closed.

We can observe that (1) our unified framework may include the smooth and non-smooth loss function; (2) $\boldsymbol{w}$ and $\boldsymbol{u}_i$ for $i = 1, 2, ..., N_1$ are coupled in the loss function and (3) the nonconvex sparsity-inducing regularizer is imposed to constrain each $\boldsymbol{u}_i$. Thus, each block of $\boldsymbol{x}$ may be non-convex and non-smooth and the problem (8) is a highly nontrivial nonconvex and non-smooth optimization problem. It is very difficult to solve the problem directly by the general gradient descent methods. Motivated by the idea [41], we develop an efficient block coordinate descent (BCD) algorithm to solve the problem (5). Specifically, we minimize F cyclically over each block of variables $\boldsymbol{x}_i$ by BCD method of Gauss-Seidel type, while fixing the remaining blocks at their last updated values. Let $\boldsymbol{x}_i^{k+1}$ denote the value of $\boldsymbol{x}_i$ after its k-th update and let $f_i^k(\boldsymbol{x}_i) \triangleq f(\boldsymbol{x}_1^k, ..., \boldsymbol{x}_{i-1}^k, \boldsymbol{x}_i, \boldsymbol{x}_{i+1}^k, ..., \boldsymbol{x}_{n_s}^k)$ for all i and k. At each iteration, we adopt a prox-linear surrogate function to approximate the upper bound of $F(\boldsymbol{x}^{k+1})$, and then each block of variables $\boldsymbol{x}_i$ can be updated as follows:

$$\begin{aligned}\boldsymbol{x}_i^{k+1} \in \arg\min_{\boldsymbol{x}_i} & f_i^k(\hat{\boldsymbol{x}}_i^{k+1}) + \langle \hat{g}_i^k, \boldsymbol{x}_i - \hat{\boldsymbol{x}}_i^{k+1} \rangle \\ & + \frac{1}{2\alpha_k} \|\boldsymbol{x}_i - \hat{\boldsymbol{x}}_i^{k+1}\|^2 + r_i(\boldsymbol{x}_i),\end{aligned} \tag{9}$$

Since $f_i^k(\hat{\boldsymbol{x}}_i^{k+1})$ is constant with respect to $\boldsymbol{x}_i$, the problem (9) is equivalent to the following problem

$$\boldsymbol{x}_i^{k+1} \in \arg\min_{\boldsymbol{x}_i} \langle \hat{g}_i^k, \boldsymbol{x}_i - \hat{\boldsymbol{x}}_i^{k+1} \rangle + \frac{1}{2\alpha_k} \|\boldsymbol{x}_i - \hat{\boldsymbol{x}}_i^{k+1}\|^2 + r_i(\boldsymbol{x}_i), \tag{10}$$

where $\alpha_k > 0$ is a step-size, $\hat{g}_i^k = \nabla f_i^k(\hat{\boldsymbol{x}}_i^k)$ and $\hat{\boldsymbol{x}}_i^{k+1}$ is the extrapolation

$$\hat{\boldsymbol{x}}_i^{k+1} = \boldsymbol{x}_i^k + \gamma_k(\boldsymbol{x}_i^k - \boldsymbol{x}_i^{k-1}),$$

where $\gamma_k \geq 0$ is an extrapolation weight. While we can simply set $\gamma_k = 0$, an appropriate $\gamma_k > 0$ can speed up the convergence of algorithm. Similar to the Nesterov's accelerated gradient descent [30], the extrapolation weight is given by $\gamma_k = \frac{t_k - 1}{t_{k+1}}$ with

$$t_0 = 0, t_k = \left(\sqrt{4t_{k-1}^2 + 1} + 1\right)/2.$$

Algorithm 1 Accelerated Block Coordinate Descent for Problem(5)

Initialize $\boldsymbol{w}^1 = \boldsymbol{w}^0$, $\boldsymbol{u}_i^1 = \boldsymbol{u}_i^0$, $\beta = 0.85$, $t_0 = 0$ and $k = 1$.
repeat
  1. Compute $t_k = \left(1 + \sqrt{4t_{k-1}^2 + 1}\right)/2$ and $\gamma_k = \frac{t_k - 1}{t_{k+1}}$;
  2. Find the smallest non-negative integer i_k by backtracking line search with $\bar{\alpha}_k(\boldsymbol{w}) = \beta^{i_k} \alpha_k(\boldsymbol{w})$;
  3. Update $\boldsymbol{w}^{k+1}$ by $\boldsymbol{w}^{k+1} = \hat{\boldsymbol{w}}^{k+1} - \alpha_k \nabla q(\hat{\boldsymbol{w}}^{k+1})$.
  for $i = 1, 2, ..., N_1$ **do**
    4. Find the smallest non-negative integer i_k by backtracking line search with $\bar{\alpha}_k(\boldsymbol{u}_i) = \beta^{i_k} \alpha_k(\boldsymbol{u}_i)$;
    5. Update each $\boldsymbol{u}_i^{k+1}$ by $\boldsymbol{u}_i^{k+1}(\mathcal{S}^*) = P_{C_i}(\tilde{\boldsymbol{u}}_i^{k+1}(\mathcal{S}^*))$.
  end for
  6. $k = k + 1$.
until Stopping criterion is satisfied.

When the Lipschitz constant L_k of $\hat{g}_i^k$ about $\boldsymbol{x}_i$ is known, we can set the step-size $\alpha_k = \frac{\beta}{L_k}$ with any $0 < \beta \leq 1$. However, L_k is often unknown or difficult to bound in practice, we will choose a proper step size α_k by backtracking line search method under the criterion:

$$f(\boldsymbol{x}^k) \leq f(\hat{\boldsymbol{x}}^{k-1}) + \langle \nabla f_i^k(\hat{\boldsymbol{x}}^{k-1}), \boldsymbol{x}_i^k - \hat{\boldsymbol{x}}_i^{k-1} \rangle + \frac{\beta}{2\alpha_k} \|\boldsymbol{x}_i^k - \hat{\boldsymbol{x}}_i^{k-1}\|^2.$$

Finally, the optimization details of solving the problem (5) by accelerated block coordinate descent under backtracking line search are listed in Algorithm 1.

3.3 Optimize model coefficients $\boldsymbol{w}$

When $\boldsymbol{u}_i$ is fixed, the problem (8) can be reformulated as:

$$q(\boldsymbol{w}) = f(\boldsymbol{w}) + \lambda_1 \|\boldsymbol{w}\|^2 + \lambda_2 \|\boldsymbol{w}\|_1. \tag{11}$$

Motivated by [5, 42], when fixed all of positive isoform weight vectors $[\boldsymbol{u}_1, ..., \boldsymbol{u}_{n_1}]$, the problem in (11) is a convex minimization problem with elastic net penalty. Therefore, we can obtain the optimal solution of the problem (11) by gradient-based methods. Denote $s(t) = \frac{1}{2}(1 + sign(1 - t))$ and let

$$\begin{aligned}\nabla q_{lr}(\boldsymbol{w}) = & \sum_{i \in B_N} \frac{\rho}{n_i} \sum_{j=1}^{n_i} \frac{-y_i \boldsymbol{x}_j^i}{1 + \exp(y_i \langle \boldsymbol{w}, \boldsymbol{x}_j^i \rangle)} + 2\lambda_1 \boldsymbol{w} \\ & + \sum_{i \in B_P} \frac{-y_i \mathbf{X}_i \boldsymbol{u}_i}{1 + \exp(y_i \langle \boldsymbol{w}, \mathbf{X}_i \boldsymbol{u}_i \rangle)} + \lambda_2 sign(\boldsymbol{w}),\end{aligned} \tag{12}$$

be the gradient of WLRM w.r.t. $\boldsymbol{w}$. According to Eq. (9), we derive a quadratic model to update $\boldsymbol{w}$ at each iteration:

$$\boldsymbol{w}^{k+1} \in \arg\min_{\boldsymbol{w}} \left\langle \nabla q_{lr}(\hat{\boldsymbol{w}}^{k+1}), \boldsymbol{w} - \hat{\boldsymbol{w}}^{k+1} \right\rangle + \frac{\|\boldsymbol{w} - \hat{\boldsymbol{w}}^{k+1}\|^2}{2\alpha_k}, \tag{13}$$

where $\hat{\boldsymbol{w}}^{k+1}$ is

$$\hat{\boldsymbol{w}}^{k+1} = \boldsymbol{w}^k + \gamma_k(\boldsymbol{w}^k - \boldsymbol{w}^{k-1}).$$

Moreover, the problem (13) has the closed form solution:

$$\boldsymbol{w}^{k+1} = \hat{\boldsymbol{w}}^{k+1} - \alpha_k \nabla q(\hat{\boldsymbol{w}}^{k+1}). \tag{14}$$

3.4 Optimize isoform weight vector u

When w is fixed, the problem (8) becomes

$$\min_{u_1,\ldots,u_{N_1}} \sum_{i=1}^{N_1} g_i(u_i) + 1_{C_i}(u_i), \tag{15}$$

where $g_i(u_i) = \log(1 + \exp(y_i \langle w, X_i u_i \rangle))$ for WLRM. The problem (15) is decoupled between different i, so we can solve the following problem for each i individually:

$$\min_{u_i} g_i(u_i) + 1_{C_i}(u_i).$$

Denote

$$\nabla g_i^{lr}(u_i) = \frac{\rho}{n_i} \frac{-y_i X_i^T w}{1 + \exp(y_i \langle w, X_i u_i \rangle)}, \tag{16}$$

as the partial derivatives of $g_i(u_i)$ of WLRM with respect to u_i. According to Eq. (9), we derive the following approximation model to update u_i at each iteration.

$$\begin{aligned} u_i^{k+1} \in \arg\min_{u_i} \frac{1}{2\alpha_k} \| u_i - \hat{u}_i^{k+1} \|^2 + 1_{C_i}(u_i) \\ + \langle \nabla g_i^{lr}(\hat{u}_i^{k+1}), u_i - \hat{u}_i^{k+1} \rangle, \end{aligned} \tag{17}$$

where $\hat{u}_i^{k+1} = u_i^k + \gamma_k (u_i^k - u_i^{k-1})$.

The formulation in (17) is a convex optimization problem with a nonconvex sparsity-inducing regularizer. Motivated by the idea in [14, 24], the problem (17) can be solved by the projected gradient descent algorithm. Finally, according to the greedy selector and simplex projector (GSSP) algorithm, the optimal solution of the problem (17) is the sparse Euclidean projections of $\hat{u}_i^{k+1}$ onto the positive simplex C_i, that is,

$$u_i^{k+1}(\mathcal{S}^*) = P_{C_i}(\tilde{u}_i^{k+1}(\mathcal{S}^*)), u_i^{k+1}(\overline{\mathcal{S}^*}) = 0, \tag{18}$$

where $P_{C_i}(\cdot)$ is a projection operator with respect to a collection of simpler sets C_i, $\tilde{u}_i^{k+1} = \hat{u}_i^{k+1} - \alpha_k \nabla g_i(\hat{u}_i^{k+1})$, $\mathcal{S}^*$ is the index set which keeps the r-largest positive entries of $\tilde{u}_i^{k+1}$ and $\overline{\mathcal{S}^*}$ is the complement of the set $\mathcal{S}^*$.

3.5 Key Instance Detection on Synthetic Data

We provide a toy example to illustrate the effectiveness of detecting key instances from positive bags in this section. The toy data set consists of two classes of instances, which are generated from two different Gaussian distributions (as shown in Fig. 2(a)). We randomly generate five positive bags and ten negative bags from two Gaussians. Fig. (2) (b) shows that, for each positive bag, we randomly sample a positive instance (the red point) from original positive class and certain negative instances from negtive class. Then we apply WLRM to detect the positive instances and learn the optimal classification model. In this experiment, we set $r = 1$. The results are displayed in Fig. (2)(c). The results verify that our WLRM is effective to detect the positive instances from bags and able to learn the optimal classification model by selected instances.

4 EXPERIMENTS

In this section, compared with the state-of-the-art methods miSVM, miFV and miVLAD, we present the experimental results on human RNA-seq data to demonstrate the effectiveness of our proposed WLRM. Meanwhile, we analyze the performance of WLRM in aspects of the parameter determination, convergence behavior and time complexity.

4.1 Experiment Settings

The dataset we used in our experiments is generated from a total of 573 human RNA-seq runs of ENCODE project [9]. We perform quality control on the original data.

(1) We used the human genome (build GRCh37.75) from Ensembl to align the short-reads of each RNA-seq dataset by TopHat (v.2.0.11) [35]. We removed the samples with less than 50% mapping reads coverage and 248 runs (of total 127 samples) remains. We then averaged expression values for each sample separately.

(2) We calculated the relative abundance of the transcript as Fragment Per Kilobase of exon per Million fragments (FPKM) by Cufflinks [36]. Then, we computed average expression values of of a total of 63,783 genes with 214,292 isoforms for each sample separately.

(3) As the extracted FPKM values for short transcripts (eg. tRNAs) were very high, we removed genes in which the average length of isoforms was less than 100 nucleotides. To ensure sufficient non-zero values for the subsequent machine learning step, we used only genes where more than half samples have larger than 1 FPKM values. Then, we used only genes marked as protein_coding (known, novel and putative) biotype in the Ensembl.

After these data preprocessing steps, we obtain a data set consisting of 11,946 genes with 59297 isoforms. We perform a $\log_2$-transformation of the FPKM values.

GO term based functional annotation [6, 9, 10, 36] has been well-studied in the past few years. Briefly speaking, a GO term (data-version:releases/2014-05-27) corresponds to a certain biological process and a set of "responsible" genes. Thus, for a given GO term, we label the genes that are annotated to this GO term as positive and the remaining genes as negative. The number of positive genes for these GO terms can be different, ranging from 20 to 300. In this paper, we focus on a list of 94 benchmark GO terms [1]. We follow the settings in [15] to divided all GO terms into five different groups according to the number of associated genes: (A) 20-27, (B) 28-40, (C) 41-64, (D) 65-114 and (E) 115-300.

For each GO term, we employ five fold cross validation [18] to estimate the model parameters and evaluate the performance of the proposed WLRM against miSVM[3, 31], miFV[38] and miVLAD[39] in terms of commonly used measures: classification accuracy (ACC), area under the ROC curve (AUC) [16], sensitivity, and specificity.

4.2 Functional Annotation of Human PCIs

In this experiment, we apply WLRM into human RNA-seq dataset to annotate the functions of PCIs. We compare our proposed WLRM with the state-of-art algorithm miSVM, miFV and miVLAD in this experiment. Due to the lack of ground-truth of annotated isoforms, we can only evaluate the performance of all compared methods at gene level by cross validation. Thus we calculate the prediction results by the label information of genes from Gene Ontology. Recall that, we employ 5-fold cross validation to estimate the optimal parameter values for all compared methods. We choose $r = 2$

[1] http://geneontology.org/page/go-slim-and-subset-guide

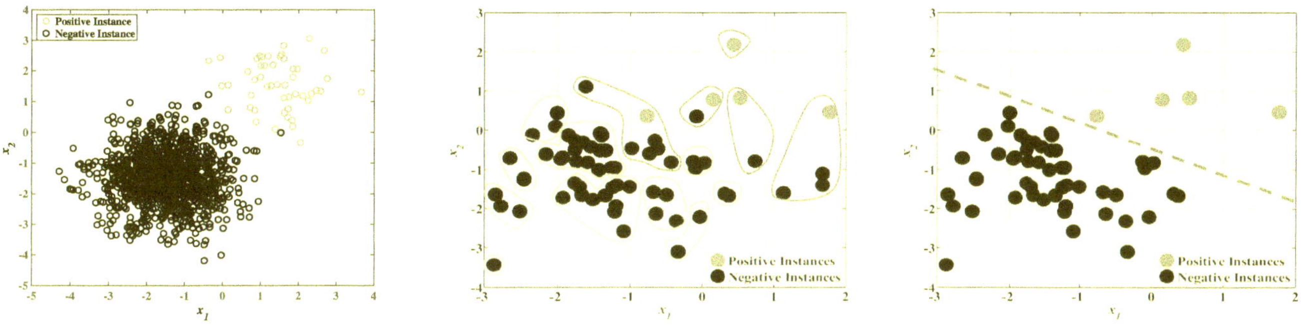

(a) (b) (c)

Figure 2: Example results of the proposed method on a two dimensional synthetic data. (a) The original distribution of the synthetic positive and negative instances. (b) Training Bags with true instance-level labels sampled from original distributed data. (c) The learned classification model and the selected instances by our method.

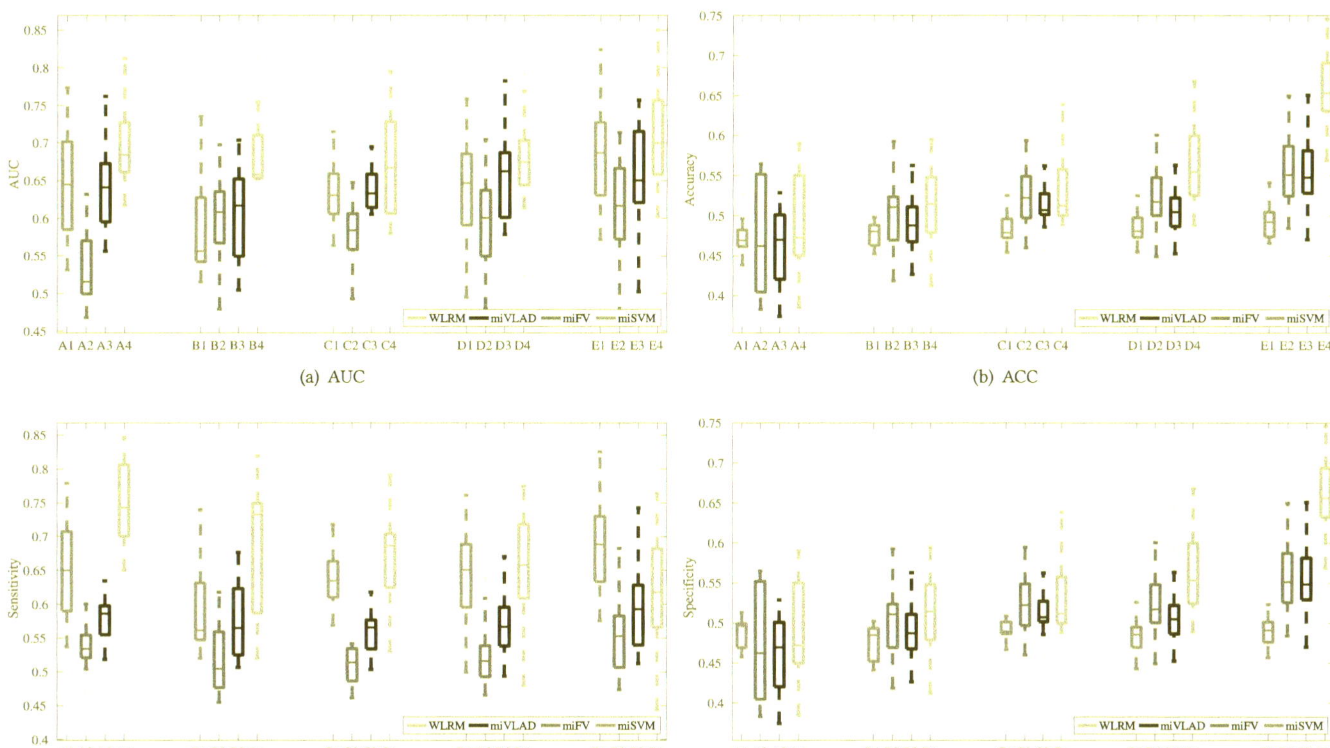

(a) AUC (b) ACC

(c) Sensitivity (d) Specificity

Figure 3: Performance of WLRM, miVLAD, miFV and miSVM for functional annotation of human PCIs. From (a) to (d) present the results of AUC, ACC, Sensitivity and Specificity, respectively.

for WLRM. The prediction performance is calculated for all of 94 GO terms. The experimental results of AUC, ACC, sensitivity and specificity are shown in Fig. 3.

The results in Fig. 3 show that the AUC, ACC, sensitivity and specificity results of WLRM are better than those of miSVM, miFV and miVLAD. Specifically, Fig. 3 (a) and (c) indicate that when the number of GO terms is very small, the performance of our methods is much better than the results of other methods, as shown in groups A and B. In group A, the median AUC values of WLRM is 0.691, which are better than 0.645 of miSVM, 0.518 of miFV and 0.635 of miVLAD. The median sensitivity values of WLRM is 0.745, which are much higher than 0.65 of miSVM, 0.533 of miFV and 0.589 of miVLAD. The main reason is that we use the weight $\frac{\rho}{n_i}$ to solve the unbalanced problem and enhance the performance of WLERM. On the other hand, as shown in Fig. 3 (b) and (d), the performance of ACC and specificity is slightly better with an increasing GO

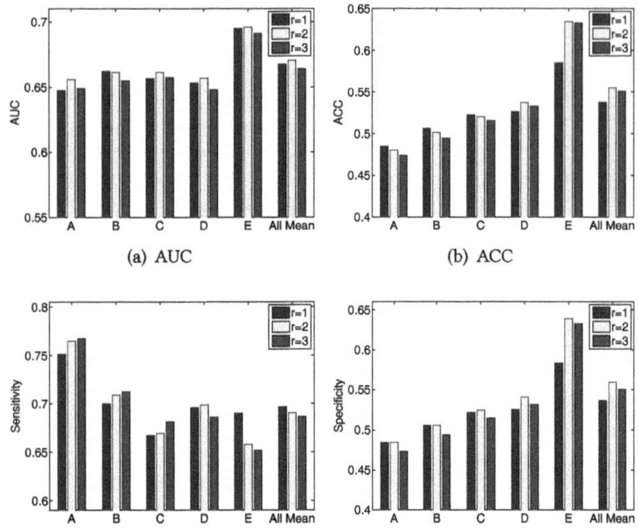

(a) AUC (b) ACC

(c) Sensitivity (d) Specificity

Figure 4: Performance variation of WLRM with respect to different values of the parameter r.

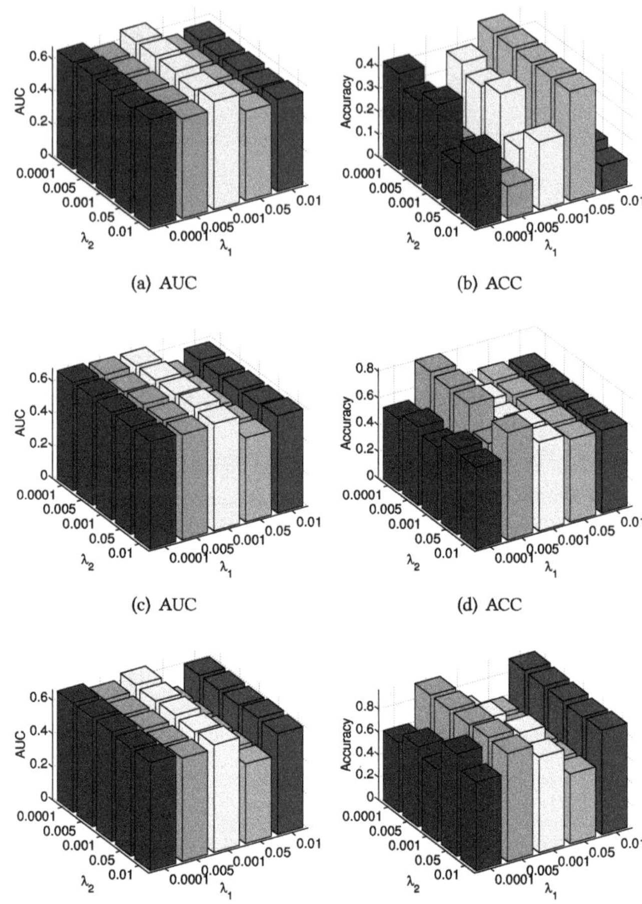

(a) AUC (b) ACC

(c) AUC (d) ACC

(e) AUC (f) ACC

Figure 5: Performance variation of WLRM with different values of ρ, λ_1 and λ_2. The top line is the mean AUC and ACC values of WLRM with $\rho = 1$. The middle line is the mean AUC and ACC values of WLRM with $\rho = 2$. The bottom line is the results of WLRM with $\rho = 3$.

term size. Because we obtain more information about positive genes with an increasing GO term size. Because WLRM is able to eliminate the effect of negative instances in positive bags by jointly selecting the positive instances and learning classification hyperplane. Overall, the performance of our proposed WLRM outperform other compared methods in most cases.

4.3 Effects of Parameters

In this experiment, we study the effects of different parameter values in terms of the classification performance. Recall that, our models have four parameters, i.e., r, ρ, λ_1 and λ_2. They can be separated two groups: first group is the parameter r, which control the number of selected positive instances; another group is parameters ρ, λ_1 and λ_2, which control the complexity of our WLRM.

We first study the effect of different values of r. The parameters r controls the cardinality of nonzero elements in each $\boldsymbol{u}_i$. The values of r is chosen from $\{1, 2, 3\}$. For other parameters, we adopt cross validation method to choose optimal values. The results of average AUC, ACC, sensitivity and specificity are shown in Fig. 4. We can observe that WLRM performs the best with $r = 2$. When $r = 3$, the performance of WLRM decreases. With the increse of r, the possibility of negative instance in positive bags is much more easily selected as positive instance.

We next show the effects of ρ, λ_1, and λ_2 for fixed $r = 2$. Fig. 5 shows the mean AUC and ACC results of WLRM with different values of ρ, λ_1 and λ_2. We can see from Fig. 5 that, parameter determination takes influence on the performance of WLRM. Different combinations of parameters may result in different classification models. Then, the AUC and ACC results change.

4.4 Convergence and Time Complexity

In this subsection, we take two groups of experiments. One group is convergence analysis experiments. We present the convergence characteristics of our WLRM on four different GO terms in Fig. 6. The objective function values are nonincreasing during the iterations. Our proposed method converges within 100 iterations.

Another group is the computational time of WLRM, miSVM, miFV and miVLAD on human genome dataset. All the algorithms are tested on a laptop with 4 processors (2.27 GHz for each) and 8 GB available RAM memory by Matlab implementations. The results are shown in Table 2. The results in Table 2 indicate that the running time of miSVM, miFV, miVLAD and WLRM increases linearly with the increase of the number of positive genes. Moreover, the running time of other MIL methods are at least 4.30 times of the running time of WLRM. When the number of positive genes is very small, i.e., the number in group A is from 20 to 27, the running time of other compared methods are at least 10.68 times of WLRM, especially the running time of miSVM is 31.39 times of WLRM. Overall, WLRM is much more efficient than others.

Table 2: Average running time ± the standard derivation (in seconds) of miSVM, miFV, miVLAD and WLRM for training the model on five groups of GO terms. The last row is the speedup of WLRM with respect to the runtime of the fastest one among other three methods.

Methods	Group A	Group B	Group C	Group D	Group E
miSVM	6340.0 ± 161.68	6385.5±243.14	6418.2±109.46	6455.2±215.87	6529.5±236.74
miFV	2872.0 ± 179.32	3169.7±198.71	4312.2±112.50	5693.5±197.89	8315.1±213.63
miVLAD	2157.6 ± 89.70	2661.5±135.43	3579.9±96.67	4939.3±110.87	6410.5±135.78
WLRM	**201.9±55.91**	**304.6±81.67**	**490.3±89.67**	**833.2±135.47**	**1489.7±283.67**
Speedup	**10.68**	**8.74**	**7.30**	**5.93**	**4.30**

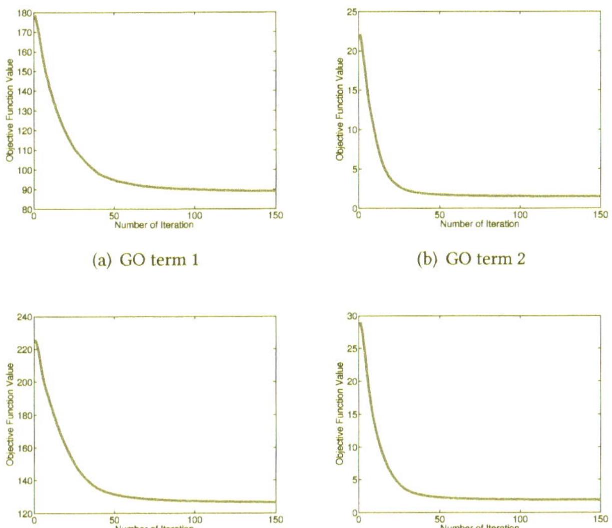

(a) GO term 1 (b) GO term 2

(c) GO term 3 (d) GO term 4

Figure 6: Number of iterations vs. the objective value of WLRM on two different GO terms.

5 CONCLUSIONS AND FUTURE WORK

In this paper, we develop a novel unified MIL framework to annotate functions of human PCIs. Based on this framework, we proposed a new method called WLRM based on the logistic loss. Specifically, we introduce an isoform weight vector for each positive gene and derive a nonconvex sparsity-inducing regularizes, which includes non-negative, l_0-norm and l_1-norm constraints on each isoform weights vector. The proposed method detects the key isoforms and embeds the original gene space into a discriminative feature space simultaneously. The isoform weight vectors can be obtained by sparse projections onto a simplex. Meanwhile, we develop an efficient block coordinate descent approach to solve our non-convex optimization problem. Finally, our WLRM is applied to predict the functions of human PCIs. There are several interesting directions to investigate in the future. First, we would like to find a more efficient and effective way of dealing with our non-convex optimization problem. Second, we would like to extend our model to the nonlinear case using kernel trick.

REFERENCES

[1] Robert A Amar, Daniel R Dooly, Sally A Goldman, and Qi Zhang. 2001. Multiple-instance learning of real-valued data. In *International Conference on Machine learning*. 3–10.
[2] Jaume Amores. 2013. Multiple instance classification: Review, taxonomy and comparative study. *Artificial Intelligence* 201 (2013), 81–105.
[3] Stuart Andrews, Ioannis Tsochantaridis, and Thomas Hofmann. 2002. Support vector machines for multiple-instance learning. In *Advances in Neural Information Processing Systems*. 561–568.
[4] Michael Ashburner, Catherine A Ball, Judith A Blake, David Botstein, Heather Butler, J Michael Cherry, Allan P Davis, Kara Dolinski, Selina S Dwight, Janan T Eppig, and others. 2000. Gene Ontology: tool for the unification of biology. *Nature Genetics* 25, 1 (2000), 25–29.
[5] Amir Beck and Marc Teboulle. 2009. A fast iterative shrinkage-thresholding algorithm for linear inverse problems. *SIAM Journal on Imaging Sciences* 2, 1 (2009), 183–202.
[6] Ko-Fan Chen and Damian C Crowther. 2012. Functional genomics in Drosophila models of human disease. *Briefings in Functional Genomics* 11, 5 (2012), 405–415.
[7] Yixin Chen, Jinbo Bi, and James Z Wang. 2006. MILES: Multiple-instance learning via embedded instance selection. *Pattern Analysis and Machine Intelligence, IEEE Transactions on* 28, 12 (2006), 1931–1947.
[8] Veronika Cheplygina, David MJ Tax, and Marco Loog. 2015. Multiple instance learning with bag dissimilarities. *Pattern Recognition* 48, 1 (2015), 264–275.
[9] ENCODE Project Consortium and others. 2012. An integrated encyclopedia of DNA elements in the human genome. *Nature* 489, 7414 (2012), 57–74.
[10] Melissa J Davis, Muhammad SB Sehgal, and Mark A Ragan. 2010. Automatic, context-specific generation of Gene Ontology slims. *BMC Bioinformatics* 11, 1 (2010), 498.
[11] Eleonora de Klerk and Peter A.C. 't Hoen. 2015. Alternative mRNA transcription, processing, and translation: insights from RNA sequencing. *Trends in Genetics* 31, 3 (2015), 128–139.
[12] Thomas Derrien, Rory Johnson, Giovanni Bussotti, Andrea Tanzer, Sarah Djebali, Hagen Tilgner, Gregory Guernec, David Martin, Angelika Merkel, David G Knowles, and others. 2012. The GENCODE v7 catalog of human long noncoding RNAs: analysis of their gene structure, evolution, and expression. *Genome Research* 22, 9 (2012), 1775–1789.
[13] Thomas G Dietterich, Richard H Lathrop, and Tomás Lozano-Pérez. 1997. Solving the multiple instance problem with axis-parallel rectangles. *Artificial Intelligence* 89, 1 (1997), 31–71.
[14] John Duchi, Shai Shalev-Shwartz, Yoram Singer, and Tushar Chandra. 2008. Efficient projections onto the l 1-ball for learning in high dimensions. In *Proceedings of the 25th International Conference on Machine learning*. ACM, 272–279.
[15] Ridvan Eksi, Hong-Dong Li, Rajasree Menon, Yuchen Wen, Gilbert S. Omenn, Matthias Kretzler, and Yuanfang Guan. 2013. Systematically Differentiating Functions for Alternatively Spliced Isoforms through Integrating RNA-seq Data. *PLoS Comput Biol* 9, 11 (11 2013), e1003314.
[16] Tom Fawcett. 2006. An introduction to ROC analysis. *Pattern Recognition Letters* 27, 8 (2006), 861–874.
[17] Robert Fung and Kuo-Chu Chang. 2013. Weighing and integrating evidence for stochastic simulation in Bayesian networks. *arXiv preprint arXiv:1304.1504* (2013).
[18] Gene H Golub, Michael Heath, and Grace Wahba. 1979. Generalized cross-validation as a method for choosing a good ridge parameter. *Technometrics* 21, 2 (1979), 215–223.
[19] Jennifer Harrow, Adam Frankish, Jose M Gonzalez, Electra Tapanari, Mark Diekhans, Felix Kokocinski, Bronwen L Aken, Daniel Barrell, Amonida Zadissa, Stephen Searle, and others. 2012. GENCODE: the reference human genome annotation for The ENCODE Project. *Genome Research* 22, 9 (2012), 1760–1774.
[20] Marti A. Hearst, Susan T Dumais, Edgar Osman, John Platt, and Bernhard Scholkopf. 1998. Support vector machines. *IEEE Intelligent Systems and their Applications* 13, 4 (1998), 18–28.
[21] David W Hosmer Jr and Stanley Lemeshow. 2004. *Applied logistic regression*. John Wiley & Sons.
[22] Minoru Kanehisa, Michihiro Araki, Susumu Goto, Masahiro Hattori, Mika Hirakawa, Masumi Itoh, Toshiaki Katayama, Shuichi Kawashima, Shujiro Okuda, Toshiaki Tokimatsu, and others. 2008. KEGG for linking genomes to life and the

environment. *Nucleic Acids Research* 36, suppl 1 (2008), D480–D484.
[23] Minoru Kanehisa, Susumu Goto, Yoko Sato, Miho Furumichi, and Mao Tanabe. 2011. KEGG for integration and interpretation of large-scale molecular data sets. *Nucleic Acids Research* (2011), gkr988.
[24] Anastasios T Kyrillidis, Stephen Becker, Volkan Cevher, and Christoph Koch. 2013. Sparse projections onto the simplex.. In *Proceedings of The 30th International Conference on Machine Learning*, Vol. 28. JMLR, 235–243.
[25] Hong-Dong Li, Rajasree Menon, Gilbert S Omenn, and Yuanfang Guan. 2014. The emerging era of genomic data integration for analyzing splice isoform function. *Trends in Genetics* 30, 8 (2014), 340–347.
[26] Wenyuan Li, Shuli Kang, Chun-Chi Liu, Xianghong Jasmine Zhou, and others. 2014. High-resolution functional annotation of human transcriptome: predicting isoform functions by a novel multiple instance-based label propagation method. *Nucleic Acids Research* 42, 6 (2014), e39.
[27] Yan Li, David MJ Tax, Robert PW Duin, and Marco Loog. 2013. Multiple-instance learning as a classifier combining problem. *Pattern Recognition* 46, 3 (2013), 865–874.
[28] Guoqing Liu, Jianxin Wu, and Zhi-Hua Zhou. 2012. Key instance detection in multi-instance learning. In *ACML*, Vol. 25. 253–268.
[29] Oded Maron and Tomás Lozano-Pérez. 1998. A framework for multiple-instance learning. *Advances in Neural Information Processing Systems* (1998), 570–576.
[30] Yurii Nesterov. 1983. A method of solving a convex programming problem with convergence rate $O(1/k^2)$. *Soviet Mathematics Doklady* 27 (1983). Issue 2.
[31] Bharat Panwar, Rajasree Menon, Ridvan Eksi, Hong-Dong Li, Gilbert S Omenn, and Yuanfang Guan. 2016. Genome-wide functional annotation of human protein-coding splice variants using multiple instance learning. *Journal of Proteome Research* 15, 6 (2016), 1747–1753.
[32] Gunnar Rätsch, Takashi Onoda, and K-R Müller. 2001. Soft margins for AdaBoost. *Machine Learning* 42, 3 (2001), 287–320.
[33] Burr Settles, Mark Craven, and Soumya Ray. 2008. Multiple-instance active learning. In *Advances in Neural Information Processing Systems*. 1289–1296.
[34] Timothy Sterne-Weiler and Jeremy R Sanford. 2014. Exon identity crisis: disease-causing mutations that disrupt the splicing code. *Genome Biology* 15, 1 (2014), 201.
[35] Cole Trapnell, Lior Pachter, and Steven L Salzberg. 2009. TopHat: discovering splice junctions with RNA-Seq. *Bioinformatics* 25, 9 (2009), 1105–1111.
[36] Cole Trapnell, Adam Roberts, Loyal Goff, Geo Pertea, Daehwan Kim, David R Kelley, Harold Pimentel, Steven L Salzberg, John L Rinn, and Lior Pachter. 2012. Differential gene and transcript expression analysis of RNA-seq experiments with TopHat and Cufflinks. *Nature Protocols* 7, 3 (2012), 562–578.
[37] Kai Wang, Mingyao Li, and Hakon Hakonarson. 2010. ANNOVAR: functional annotation of genetic variants from high-throughput sequencing data. *Nucleic Acids Research* 38, 16 (2010), e164–e164.
[38] Xiushen Wei, Jianxin Wu, and Zhihua Zhou. 2014. Scalable multi-instance learning. In *2014 IEEE International Conference on Data Mining (ICDM)*. IEEE, 1037–1042.
[39] Xiushen Wei, Jianxin Wu, and Zhihua Zhou. 2017. Scalable algorithms for multi-instance learning. *IEEE Transactions on Neural Networks and Learning Systems* 28, 4 (2017), 975–987.
[40] Hui Y Xiong, Babak Alipanahi, Leo J Lee, Hannes Bretschneider, Daniele Merico, Ryan KC Yuen, Yimin Hua, Serge Gueroussov, Hamed S Najafabadi, Timothy R Hughes, and others. 2015. The human splicing code reveals new insights into the genetic determinants of disease. *Science* 347, 6218 (2015).
[41] Yin Wotao Xu, Yangyang. 2017. A Globally Convergent Algorithm for Nonconvex Optimization Based on Block Coordinate Update. *Journal of Scientific Computing* (2017), 1–35.
[42] Hui Zou and Trevor Hastie. 2005. Regularization and variable selection via the elastic net. *Journal of the Royal Statistical Society: Series B (Statistical Methodology)* 67, 2 (2005), 301–320.

Discovering Reliable Approximate Functional Dependencies

Panagiotis Mandros
Max Planck Institute for Informatics and Saarland University, Germany
pmandros@mpi-inf.mpg.de

Mario Boley
Max Planck Institute for Informatics and Saarland University, Germany
mboley@mpi-inf.mpg.de

Jilles Vreeken
Max Planck Institute for Informatics and Saarland University, Germany
jilles@mpi-inf.mpg.de

ABSTRACT

Given a database and a target attribute of interest, how can we tell whether there exists a functional, or approximately functional dependence of the target on any set of other attributes in the data? How can we reliably, without bias to sample size or dimensionality, measure the strength of such a dependence? And, how can we efficiently discover the optimal or α-approximate top-k dependencies? These are exactly the questions we answer in this paper.

As we want to be agnostic on the form of the dependence, we adopt an information-theoretic approach, and construct a reliable, bias correcting score that can be efficiently computed. Moreover, we give an effective optimistic estimator of this score, by which for the first time we can mine the approximate functional dependencies from data with guarantees of optimality. Empirical evaluation shows that the derived score achieves a good bias for variance trade-off, can be used within an efficient discovery algorithm, and indeed discovers meaningful dependencies. Most important, it remains reliable in the face of data sparsity.

CCS CONCEPTS

•Information systems →Data mining; •Mathematics of computing →*Probability and statistics;*

KEYWORDS

Pattern discovery, Information theory

ACM Reference format:

Panagiotis Mandros, Mario Boley, and Jilles Vreeken. 2017. Discovering Reliable Approximate Functional Dependencies. In *Proceedings of KDD '17, August 13-17, 2017, Halifax, NS, Canada*, , 9 pages.
DOI: 10.1145/3097983.3098062

1 INTRODUCTION

Discovering dependencies is an important and well-studied topic in data mining. Most proposals, however, focus specifically on *symmetric* dependencies. That is, they aim to find variable sets that strongly correlate or associate with a target variable. In many applications, however, *asymmetric*, or targeted dependencies are of particular interest. When anonymizing a dataset, for example, we need to be certain a private attribute cannot be reconstructed given the public attribute, while we do not care for the opposite direction. Similarly, in scientific applications we want to hypothesize whether a certain target variable, say an effect, can be explained by the observed variables, the potential causes, and not the other way around. Generally, an effective procedure to detect functional dependencies from data allows us to rule out alternate theories about our domain and to determine whether finding concrete models, e.g., by statistical learning, is worthwhile, or if we rather should acquire more data or enrich our feature space first [6].

More formally, given a target variable Y and a set of attributes $\mathcal{X}$, we want to *measure* the degree at which Y has a functional, or an *approximate* functional dependence on $\mathcal{X}$, i.e., if $Y \approx f(\mathcal{X})$. Additionally, we want to efficiently discover whether any such $\mathcal{X}$ exists in our data. The database community studied how to infer *exact* functional dependencies, as these allow for normalization, i.e., reducing redundancy. These methods are not suited to our end, however, as they do not measure the approximation in terms of an intuitive score, and in addition, make implicit closed-world assumptions based on the schema of the data [7, 10, 14].

On the contrary, information theory provides an intuitive and interpretable measure to address these issues. The fraction of information quantifies functional dependence in terms of proportional reduction of uncertainty about Y when observing $\mathcal{X}$ [1, 3, 19]. Information-theoretic measures, however, are sensitive to data sparsity and as a result, the fraction of information overestimates the amount of dependence [21]. For large dimensionalities of $\mathcal{X}$, it is even possible that a functional dependence is indicated when $\mathcal{X}$ and Y are actually independent. This makes it a non-*reliable* score. In addition, maximizing it is **NP**-hard [12].

In this paper we propose a *reliable* measure for approximate functional dependencies based on the fraction of information. Even in extreme cases of data sparsity, it does not show dependence. In addition, we derive an effective optimistic estimator for this score, that allows for an admissible branch-and-bound algorithm to discover the top-k optimal, or α-approximate optimal strongest dependencies. Empirical evaluation shows that the derived score achieves a good bias for variance trade-off, and in addition, it does not favor spurious dependencies. The corresponding optimistic estimator is a data-dependent quantity, and by exploiting the structure of the data, leads to an effective search algorithm. Lastly, concrete findings in two exemplary application domains, AI and Materials Science, reproduce sensible domain information.

The main contributions of this paper are the following. We

(i) propose a consistent estimator for the fraction for information score that is not prone to spurious dependencies,
(ii) provide an efficient branch-and-bound algorithm for the discovery of optimal, and α-approximate optimal top-k dependencies, and

KDD '17, August 13-17, 2017, Halifax, NS, Canada

978-1-4503-4887-4/17/08...$15.00
DOI: 10.1145/3097983.3098062

(iii) provide empirical evaluation on a wide range of real and synthetic datasets.

The paper is structured as follows. We formally introduce the two problems we consider in Section 2. Next, in Section 3 we propose our fraction of information score, and in Section 4 we detail how to optimize it by deriving a bounding function for a branch-and-bound search scheme. Following, in Section 5 we evaluate the performance on a variety of tasks. Finally, we round up with conclusions in Section 6.

2 PROBLEM DEFINITION

We consider a discrete sample space governed by some probability mass function p for which we have defined $d+1$ discrete random variables $\mathcal{R} = \{X_1, \ldots, X_d, Y\}$ with domains $V(X_1), \ldots, V(X_d)$, and $V(Y)$, respectively. Subsets $\mathcal{S} \subseteq \mathcal{R}$ are identified with vector-valued random variables in the usual way with domain $\mathbf{V}(\mathcal{S}) = \times_{R \in \mathcal{S}} V(R)$. We consider the variable Y as the **output variable** and the remaining variables $\mathcal{I} = \{X_1, \ldots, X_d\}$ as the **input variables**, and our goal is to discover subsets of the input variables $\mathcal{X} \subseteq \mathcal{I}$ that approximately *determine* Y. In particular, we are interested in approximations to the concept of **functional dependencies**, i.e., the case when there is a function $f \colon \mathbf{V}(\mathcal{X}) \to V(Y)$ such that for all $\mathbf{x} \in \mathbf{V}(\mathcal{X})$ it holds that

$$p(Y = y \mid \mathcal{X} = \mathbf{x}) = \begin{cases} 1 & , \text{ if } y = f(\mathbf{x}) \\ 0 & , \text{ otherwise} \end{cases} . \quad (1)$$

Relaxing this rather strict concept is necessary because it is rare that such a completely deterministic relationship exists—if the random variables correspond to measurements of real-world quantities there are usually unobserved subtle effects or noise that cause Eq. (1) to not hold exactly.

One traditional approach to relax Eq. (1) is to use instead the condition $p(Y = y \mid \mathcal{X} = \mathbf{x}) \geq 1-\epsilon$ if $y = f(\mathbf{x})$, for some fixed value $\epsilon \in (0, 1]$, i.e., to allow a certain fraction of events to not obey the functional relation. However, as with any parameterization based on a hard threshold, this parameter is difficult to set in practice and additionally only provides a qualitative and not a quantitative relaxation [7]. That is, it does not allow us to express "how far" is Y from being determined by $\mathcal{X}$. In order to address these issues one can quantify the degree of functional dependence through information theoretic measures. A particularly useful way of doing this is to use the concept of **fraction of information** (F) [1, 3, 19], which is defined as

$$F(\mathcal{X}; Y) = \frac{H(Y) - H(Y \mid \mathcal{X})}{H(Y)}$$

where $H(Y) = -\sum_{y \in V(Y)} p(y) \log(p(y))$ denotes the **Shannon entropy** and $H(Y \mid \mathcal{X}) = \sum_{\mathbf{x} \in \mathbf{V}(\mathcal{X})} p(\mathbf{x}) H(Y \mid \mathcal{X} = \mathbf{x})$ the conditional Shannon entropy [23]. The numerator is referred to as **mutual information** $I(\mathcal{X}; Y) = H(Y) - H(Y \mid \mathcal{X})$. The entropy measures the uncertainty about Y, while the conditional entropy measures the uncertainty about Y after observing $\mathcal{X}$. The fraction of information then represents the proportional reduction of uncertainty about Y by knowing $\mathcal{X}$. Moreover, the extreme values, $F(\mathcal{X}; Y) = 1$ and $F(\mathcal{X}; Y) = 0$, correspond to a functional dependence and statistical independence, respectively. With this notion, we can go about discovering approximate functional dependencies from data.

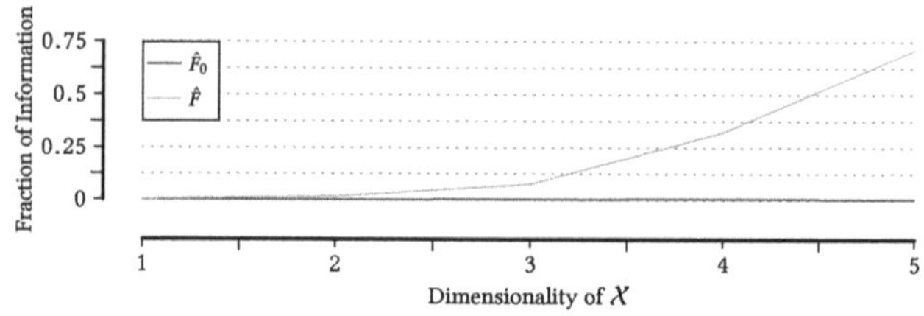

Figure 1: The fraction of information score against increasing dimensionality for $\mathcal{X}$; using $n = 1000$ samples from $\mathcal{R} = \{X_1, \ldots, X_5, Y\}$ where all variables are mutually independent and $|V(A)| = 4$ for all $A \in \mathcal{R}$. Since $\mathcal{X}$ and Y are independent, the reliable fraction of information should be constantly 0. However, the baseline estimator $\hat{F}$ shows increasing functional dependence. On the contrary, our proposed corrected score, $\hat{F}_0$, is always 0.

For that we assume that a dataset $\mathbf{D}_n \in \mathbf{V}(\mathcal{R})^n$ is given consisting of n i.i.d. samples $\mathbf{d}_1, \ldots, \mathbf{d}_n$ generated according to the joint distribution p. Such a dataset induces empirical probability estimates for all our random variables $\mathcal{S} \subseteq \mathcal{R}$ given by $\hat{p}(\mathcal{S} = \mathbf{v}) = c(\mathcal{S} = \mathbf{v})/n$ with the **empirical counts**

$$c(\mathcal{S} = \mathbf{v}) = |\{\mathbf{d} \in \mathbf{D}_n \colon \mathbf{d}(S) = \mathbf{v}(S) \text{ for all } S \in \mathcal{S}\}|$$

(where $\mathbf{d}(S)$ is the entry in $\mathbf{d}$ corresponding to variable S). In turn, these empirical probabilities give rise to empirical estimators $\hat{H}, \hat{I}, \hat{F}$ for our quantities of interest, H, I, and F. However, trying to directly discover approximate functional dependence using the empirical fraction of information $\hat{F}$ is bound to fail, because this estimator is not unbiased, i.e., we have $\mathbb{E}[\hat{F}(\mathcal{X}; Y)] \neq F(\mathcal{X}; Y)$ for finite n, as it is the case with many dependence measures [4, 9, 11, 17, 20, 26–28]. This holds in particular also for the case when $F(\mathcal{X}; Y) = 0$, i.e., when $\mathcal{X}$ contains no information about Y. This situation, which is referred to as the (lack of) zero-baseline property [21], can be misleading in practice. Even worse, independent of the true value $F(\mathcal{X}; Y)$, the bias depends on the number of attainable distinct values for $\mathcal{X}$, and favors larger attribute sets over smaller ones (which follows from the bias of the empirical mutual information, see, e.g., [22]). See Fig. 1 for a quantitative demonstration of both of these facts.

Even if a more suitable estimator was available, the challenge of which variable sets $\mathcal{X} \subseteq \mathcal{I}$ to test for high functional dependence scores remains—naively considering all 2^d options is practically infeasible. Thus, to derive a useful method for the reliable discovery of functional dependencies from data, we have to solve the following two problems:

(i) Find a more reliable empirical estimator $\hat{F}'$ for F; in particular one that satisfies the zero-baseline property and obtains better dimensionality bias.
(ii) Identify structural properties of $\hat{F}'$ that allow to derive an effective search algorithm for discovering the variable sets with the highest functional dependence scores.

We will present solutions to each of these problems in turn, in Sections 3 and 4, respectively.

3 RELIABLE FRACTION OF INFORMATION

Intuitively, the reason why $\hat{F}$ is unreliable as an estimator for F is that it does not take into account the confidence in the empirical estimates $\hat{H}(Y|\mathcal{X} = \mathbf{x})$. This is especially obvious in the extreme case when the empirical count $c(\mathcal{X} = \mathbf{x})$ is equal to 1. In this situation $c(Y = y, \mathcal{X} = x) = 1$ exactly for one value of $y \in V(Y)$ and, hence, $\hat{H}(Y|\mathcal{X} = \mathbf{x})$ is trivially equal to 0 independent of the true distribution p. Moreover, if the data size n is small compared to the observed domain of $\mathcal{X}$, this case is likely to occur for many of the sampled values for $\mathcal{X}$—even when $F(\mathcal{X}; Y) = 0$, which coincides with the highest error, because then $H(Y|\mathcal{X} = \mathbf{x}) = H(Y)$.

This last observation suggests a path to a more reasonable estimator: while it is hard to determine the bias in the general case, it is likely much easier under the assumption of independence $F(X; Y) = 0$, which, as pointed out above, corresponds exactly to the case of highest estimation error when the empirical observations are sparse. More concretely, let us denote by $b_0(\mathcal{X}, Y, n)$ the **bias under independence** defined as

$$b_0(\mathcal{X}, Y, n) = \mathbb{E}[\hat{F}(\mathcal{X}; Y) \mid F(\mathcal{X}; Y) = 0]$$

where the expectation is taken w.r.t. the random dataset $\mathbf{D}_n \sim p$ of size n. Let us assume that we have a good estimator $\hat{b}_0$ for this quantity. With this we can define a corrected estimator, let us refer to it as **reliable fraction of information** $\hat{F}_0$, as follows:

$$\hat{F}_0(\mathcal{X}; Y) = \hat{F}(\mathcal{X}; Y) - \hat{b}_0(\mathcal{X}, Y, n) \ .$$

This approach essentially trades the bias of $\hat{F}$ with that of $\hat{b}_0$ when $F(X; Y) = 0$. We have:

$$\begin{aligned}&\mathbb{E}[\hat{F}_0(\mathcal{X}; Y) - F(\mathcal{X}; Y) \mid F(\mathcal{X}; Y) = 0]\\ =&\mathbb{E}[\hat{F}(\mathcal{X}; Y) - \hat{b}_0(\mathcal{X}, Y, n) - 0 \mid F(\mathcal{X}; Y) = 0]\\ =&b_0(\mathcal{X}, Y, n) - \mathbb{E}[\hat{b}_0(\mathcal{X}, Y, n) \mid F(\mathcal{X}; Y) = 0] \ .\end{aligned}$$

A non-parametric choice for $\hat{b}_0$, which we use in this paper, corresponds to the *permutation model* (Lancaster [13, Chap. 11.2]), i.e., considering all possible datasets $\mathbf{D}'_n$ resulting from independently permuting the Y-values associated to the $\mathcal{X}$-values in the given empirical data $\mathbf{D}_n$. Formally, let S_n denote the symmetric group of degree n, i.e., S_n consists of all $n!$ bijections $\sigma \colon \{1, \dots, n\} \to \{1, \dots, n\}$. For a bijection $\sigma \in S_n$, let Y_σ denote the permuted version of Y, i.e., the variable with data entries $\mathbf{d}_i(Y_\sigma) = \mathbf{d}_{\sigma(i)}(Y)$. With this we can define the **permutation model** as the probabilities $\hat{\mathbb{P}}_0$ (and corresponding expectations $\hat{\mathbb{E}}_0$) resulting from permuting the empirical data of Y by a uniform random permutation from S_n. Using this model, the expectation of the empirical mutual information under independence, $\hat{m}_o$, is estimated as

$$\hat{m}_o(\mathcal{X}, Y, n) = \hat{\mathbb{E}}_0[\hat{I}(\mathcal{X}, Y_\sigma)] = \frac{1}{n!} \sum_{\sigma \in S_n} \hat{I}(\mathcal{X}, Y_\sigma) \ .$$

Clearly, a naive evaluation of this expression is computationally infeasible (order of $n!$). However, one can dramatically reduce the complexity by reformulating the above expression as a function of contingency table cell values and exploiting its symmetries [25]. More precisely, let the observed domains of $\mathcal{X}$ and Y be $\hat{\mathbf{V}}(\mathcal{X}) = \{\mathbf{x}_1, \dots, \mathbf{x}_R\}$ and $\hat{V}(Y) = \{y_1, \dots, y_C\}$, respectively. Moreover, we define shortcuts for the observed marginal counts $a_i = c(\mathcal{X} = \mathbf{x}_i)$ and $b_j = c(Y = y_j)$ as well as for the joint counts $c_{i,j} = c(\mathcal{X} = \mathbf{x}_i, Y = y_j)$. The complete joint count configuration $c = (c_{i,j} \colon 1 \leq i \leq C, 1 \leq j \leq R)$ we refer to as **contingency table**. Noting that $\hat{I}(\mathcal{X}, Y_\sigma)$ is a function of the contingency table c resulting from the random permutation, the estimator $\hat{m}_0$ can be rewritten as

$$\hat{m}_0(\mathcal{X}, Y, n) = \sum_{c \in \mathcal{T}} \hat{\mathbb{P}}_0[c]\hat{I}(c) = \sum_{c \in \mathcal{T}} \hat{\mathbb{P}}_0[c] \sum_{i=1}^{R} \sum_{j=1}^{C} \frac{c_{ij}}{n} \log \frac{c_{ij}n}{a_i b_j} \quad (2)$$

where $\mathcal{T} = \mathcal{T}(\mathcal{X}, Y)$ is the set of all possible contingency tables indexed by the values $\hat{\mathbf{V}}(\mathcal{X})$ and $\hat{V}(Y)$ (note that $\hat{\mathbb{P}}_0[c] > 0$ only for c resulting in the observed marginal counts a, b).

As this expression is still infeasible, Vinh et al. [25] propose to re-order the terms of the sum according to the possible count values that can be found in individual table cells. The permutation model implies that the empirical counts c_{ij} for the joint events $\mathcal{X} = \mathbf{x}_i, Y = y_j$ are generated according to the probabilities

$$\hat{\mathbb{P}}_0[c_{ij} = k] = h(k; a_i, b_j, n)$$

where h is the probability mass function of the hypergeometric distribution with c_{ij} the number of successes, a_i the number of draws, b_j the number of total successes, and n the population size. This allows us to group terms according to their count values for a specific table cell, which can be systematically enumerated from the support of the hypergeometric distribution, i.e., $k \in [\max(0, a_i + b_j - n), \min(a_i, b_j)]$. We can then compute $\hat{m}_0$ as

$$\hat{m}_0(\mathcal{X}, Y, n) = \sum_{i=1}^{R} \sum_{j=1}^{C} \sum_{k=\max(0, a_i+b_j-n)}^{\min(a_i, b_j)} h(k; a_i, b_j, n) \frac{k}{n} \log \frac{kn}{a_i b_j} \ .$$

Using the recurrence relation of the hypergeometric distribution, the computational complexity can be further reduced to the order of $\max(nR, nC)$ [20]. Moreover, it is easily parallelizable. Hence, we end up with an efficiently computable estimator for the bias under independence $\hat{b}_0(\mathcal{X}, Y, n) = \hat{m}_0(\mathcal{X}, Y, n)/\hat{H}(Y)$.

In addition to being computationally efficient, the resulting reliable functional dependence score $\hat{F}_0(\mathcal{X}; Y) = \hat{F}(\mathcal{X}; Y) - \hat{b}_0(\mathcal{X}, Y, n)$ satisfies several other properties. First of all, it is indeed a consistent estimator of F. One can show [26] that $\lim_{n \to \infty} \hat{m}_0(\mathcal{X}, Y, n) = 0$, which implies together with the consistency of $\hat{F}$ that

$$\lim_{n \to \infty} \hat{F}_0(\mathcal{X}; Y) = F(\mathcal{X}; Y) \ .$$

Moreover, $\hat{F}_0$ remains upper-bounded by 1, although this value is only attainable in the limit case $n \to \infty$ (for true functional dependencies). Most importantly, in contrast to the naive estimator, $\hat{F}_0$ approaches zero[1] as the data size relative to the empirical domain $\hat{\mathbf{V}}(\mathcal{X})$ approaches one. In other words, $\hat{b}_0(\mathcal{X}, Y, n)$ penalizes spurious dependencies that can easily appear for high dimensional $\mathcal{X}$—justifying the name *reliable* fraction of information.

4 SEARCH SCHEME

After deriving a suitably corrected empirical estimator for the fraction of information, we can now turn to the problem of using it for the discovery of approximate functional dependencies from a given dataset. Essentially, this is a combinatorial optimization problem

[1] It fact, it is principally not lower bounded by 0 since the empirical fraction of information can be less than the correction term. However, these are rare cases, which strongly indicate independence.

Algorithm 1: Best-first branch-and-bound; Given input and output variables $\mathcal{I}$ and Y, finds α-approximation to top-k result set $\mathcal{F}_k \subseteq \mathcal{P}(\mathcal{I})$ w.r.t. $f(\mathcal{X}) = \hat{F}_0(\mathcal{X}; Y)$ using optimistic estimator $\overline{f}(\mathcal{X}) = 1 - \hat{b}_0(\mathcal{X}; Y, n)$.

Bst-BB(Q,$\mathcal{F}_k$,k): **begin**
  if $Q = \emptyset$ **or** $\overline{f}(\text{top}(Q))/f(\mathcal{F}_k[k]) \leq \alpha$ **then**
    return $\mathcal{F}_k$
  else
    $R = \mathbf{r}(\text{top}(Q))$
    $\mathcal{F}_k' = \text{top-k}(\mathcal{F}_k \cup R)$
    $Q' = (Q \setminus \{\text{top}(Q)\}) \cup \{\mathcal{X} \in R\colon \overline{f}(\mathcal{X})/f(\mathcal{F}_k'[k]) \geq \alpha\}$
    return Bst-BB(Q',$\mathcal{F}_k$,k)

$\mathcal{F}_k$ = Bst-BB($\{\bot\}, \bot, k$)

where, given a dataset $\mathbf{D}_n$, the problem is to find a subset $\mathcal{X} \subseteq \mathcal{I}$ with maximal value of $\hat{F}_0$. However, as usual in pattern discovery, we are not just interested in one but several score maximizers—to produce more diverse insights into the data domain and to provide alternatives in subsequent applications. Hence, we end up with a top-k pattern search formulation:

Given *a dataset* $\mathbf{D}_n$ *consisting of n i.i.d. samples of random variables* $\mathcal{I}$ *and* Y *and a number k,* **find** *a family* $\mathcal{F}_k$ *of variable sets* $\mathcal{X}_1, \ldots, \mathcal{X}_k \subseteq \mathcal{I}$ *such that no variable set outside* $\mathcal{F}_k$ *has a higher* $\hat{F}_0$*-score than any of the sets in* $\mathcal{F}_k$*, i.e., for all* $\mathcal{X} \in \mathcal{F}_k$ *and* $\mathcal{Z} \in \mathcal{P}(\mathcal{I}) \setminus \mathcal{F}_k$ *it holds that* $\hat{F}_0(\mathcal{Z}; Y) \leq \hat{F}_0(\mathcal{X}; Y)$.

In the search for an algorithm solving the above problem, it is first important to note that maximizing mutual information is **NP**-hard [12]—even approximately and even in the restricted case when all $\mathcal{X}, \mathcal{Z} \subseteq \mathcal{I}$ are conditionally independent given Y. While it is an open question whether this result implies hardness of $\hat{F}_0$-maximization (the correction term changes maximization order), this is a substantial indication that no polynomial time algorithm for our problem exists (even with constant k). On the other hand, the branch-and-bound framework (see, e.g., Mehlhorn and Sanders [16, Chap. 12.4]), while not efficient in terms of the worst-case complexity, can often yield algorithms for hard optimization problems that are very effective in practice—particularly in the best-first search variant.

In a nutshell, best-first branch-and-bound maximizes an objective function $f : \Omega \to \mathbb{R}$ defined on some abstract search space Ω with the help of a **branch operator** $\mathbf{r} : \mathcal{P}(\Omega) \to \mathcal{P}(\Omega)$ and a matching auxiliary selection and **bounding function** $\overline{f} : \Omega \to \mathbb{R}$. The role of the branch operator is to non-redundantly generate the search space from some designated root element $\bot \in \Omega$, i.e., for all $\omega \in \Omega$ there must be a unique sequence $\bot = \omega_1, \ldots, \omega_l = \omega$ such that $\omega_{i+1} \in \mathbf{r}(\omega_i)$ for $i = 1, \ldots, l-1$. The bounding function must guarantee the property

$$\overline{f}(\omega) \geq \max\{f(\omega')\colon \omega' \in \mathbf{r}^*(\omega)\}$$

where $\mathbf{r}^*(\omega)$ denotes the set of all $\omega' \in \Omega$ that can be generated from ω by multiple applications of $\mathbf{r}$. Based on these ingredients, a branch-and-bound algorithm simply enumerates Ω starting from $\bot$, but uses $\overline{f}$ to avoid expanding elements that cannot yield an improvement over the best solution found so far.

For our problem the search space is $\mathcal{P}(\mathcal{I})$, for which a suitable branch operator is simply given by

$$\mathbf{r}(\mathcal{X}) = \{\mathcal{X} \cup \{X_i\}\colon i > \max\{j\colon X_j \in \mathcal{X}\}\}$$

i.e., we ensure non-redundant generation by creating a lexicographical order on the power set of the input variables and only enumerate lexicographically larger elements from a given set $\mathcal{X}$. In order to derive a bounding function $\overline{f}$ for our objective function $f(\mathcal{X}) = \hat{F}_0(\mathcal{X}; Y)$, we first need to establish another central property of the correction term $\hat{b}_0(\mathcal{X}, Y, n)$.

Theorem 4.1. *Given two sets of variables* $\mathcal{X} \subset \mathcal{X}' \subseteq \mathcal{I}$ *then* $\hat{b}_0(\mathcal{X}, Y, n) \leq \hat{b}_0(\mathcal{X}', Y, n)$*, i.e., the correction term is monotonically increasing with respect to the subset relation.*

Proof. It is sufficient to consider the case $\mathcal{X}' = \mathcal{X} \cup \{X\}$ for some $X \notin \mathcal{X}$, i.e. the cardinality differs by one variable. The general case follows inductively. Following the notation of Eq. (2), let the marginals of $Y, \mathcal{X}$, and $\mathcal{X}'$ be a_i for $i = 1, \ldots, R$, b_j for $j = 1, \ldots, C$, and b_j' for $j = 1, \ldots, C'$, respectively. Note that $C' \geq C$. We need to show that $\hat{m}_0(\mathcal{X}, Y, n) \leq \hat{m}_0(\mathcal{X}', Y, n)$, i.e., per definition $\sum_{c \in \mathcal{T}} \hat{\mathbb{P}}_0[c]\hat{I}(c) \leq \sum_{c' \in \mathcal{T}'} \hat{\mathbb{P}}_0[c']\hat{I}(c')$.

In order to do this, we first define a relation between the contingency tables of $\mathcal{T} = \mathcal{T}(\mathcal{X}, Y)$ and $\mathcal{T}' = \mathcal{T}(\mathcal{X}', Y)$. Let $\pi\colon \hat{\mathbf{V}}(\mathcal{X}') \to \hat{\mathbf{V}}(\mathcal{X})$ be the projection of values from $\mathcal{X}'$ to values of $\mathcal{X}$ defined by $\pi(\mathbf{x}') = \mathbf{x}$. We can extend this projection to the sets of contingency tables $\pi\colon \mathcal{T}' \to \mathcal{T}$ by finding the counts in the column corresponding to $\mathbf{x} \in \mathbf{V}(X)$ of $\pi(c')$ as the sum of the columns in c' corresponding to $\pi^{-1}(\mathbf{x})$. We will prove the claim by showing that for all $c \in \mathcal{T}$ we have $\hat{\mathbb{P}}_0[c]\hat{I}(c) \leq \sum_{c' \in \pi^{-1}(c)} \hat{\mathbb{P}}_0[c']\hat{I}(c')$.

First, it follows from the chain rule of information and from mutual information being non-negative [2] that $\hat{I}(c) \leq \hat{I}(c')$ for $c = \pi(c')$. Next we show that $\hat{\mathbb{P}}_0[c] = \sum_{c' \in \pi^{-1}(c)} \hat{\mathbb{P}}_0[c']$, which concludes the proof. For any contingency table $z \in \mathcal{T}(\mathcal{Z}, Y)$ let $S_n[z] = \{\sigma \in S_n : c(\mathcal{Z}, Y_\sigma) = c\}$ denote the set of permutations that result in z. Let $\sigma \in S_n \setminus S_n[c]$. This means that $c_{i,j}(\mathcal{X}, Y) \neq c_{i,j}(\mathcal{X}, Y_\sigma)$ for at least one cell i, j. Denoting by

$$\pi^{-1}(j) = \{j'\colon 1 \leq j' \leq C', \pi(\mathbf{x}_{j'}') = \mathbf{x}_j\}$$

the set of all indices of values of $\mathcal{X}'$ that are projected down to $\mathbf{x}$, it follows by the definition of π that

$$\sum_{j' \in \pi^{-1}(j)} c_{i,j'}'(\mathcal{X}', Y) \neq \sum_{j' \in \pi^{-1}(j)} c_{i,j'}'(\mathcal{X}', Y_\sigma) \ .$$

So for at least one $j' \in \pi^{-1}(j)$ it is $c_{i,j'}'(\mathcal{X}', Y) \neq c_{i,j'}'(\mathcal{X}', Y_\sigma)$, and, thus we also have that $\sigma \notin S_n[c']$ and can conclude

$$S_n[c] \supseteq \bigcup_{c' \in \pi^{-1}(c)} S_n[c'] \ . \qquad (3)$$

Now let $z' \in \mathcal{T}(\mathcal{X}', Y)$ with $\pi(z') \neq c$ and assume for a contradiction that $S_n[c] \supset S_n[c']$, i.e., there is an $\sigma \in S_n[c] \cap S_n[z']$. Let us denote $z = \pi(z')$. Since $S_n[c] \cap S_n[z] = \emptyset$, we know that $\sigma \notin S_n[z]$. However, it follows from Eq. (3) that $\sigma \notin S_n[z']$—a contradiction, and, hence $S_n[c] = \bigcup_{c' \in \pi^{-1}(c)} S_n[c']$. Thus, as desired

$$\hat{\mathbb{P}}_0[c] = \frac{|S_n(c)|}{|S_n|} = \sum_{c' \in \pi^{-1}(c)} \frac{|S_n(c')|}{|S_n|} = \sum_{c' \in \pi^{-1}(c)} \hat{\mathbb{P}}_0[c'] \ .$$

□

With this theorem (and the fact that the conditional entropy is bounded from below by 0), it follows for all $\mathcal{X} \subseteq \mathcal{X}' \subseteq \mathcal{I}$ that

$$\begin{aligned}\hat{F}_0(\mathcal{X}'; Y) =& \frac{\hat{H}(Y) - \hat{H}(Y \mid \mathcal{X}')}{\hat{H}(Y)} - \hat{b}_0(\mathcal{X}', Y, n) \\ \leq& 1 - \hat{b}_0(\mathcal{X}, Y, n) = \hat{F}'_0(\mathcal{X}; Y)\end{aligned}$$

Hence, since $\mathcal{X} \subseteq \mathcal{X}'$ for $\mathcal{X}' \in \mathbf{r}(\mathcal{X})$, we can use $\overline{f}(\mathcal{X}) = 1 - \hat{b}_0(\mathcal{X}, Y, n)$ as valid bounding function for the branch-and-bound search. Besides the features mentioned above, the search scheme also provides the option of relaxing the required result guarantee to that of an α-approximation for accuracy parameter $\alpha \in (0, 1]$. This means that the resulting family of variable sets $\mathcal{F}_k$ will satisfy the relaxed condition that for all $\mathcal{X} \in \mathcal{F}_k$ and $\mathcal{Z} \in \mathcal{P}(\mathcal{I}) \setminus \mathcal{F}_k$ it holds that $\alpha \hat{F}_0(\mathcal{Z}; Y) \leq \hat{F}_0(\mathcal{X}; Y)$. Hence, using α-values of less than 1 allows to trade accuracy for computation time.

The pseudocode in Algorithm 1 summarizes the resulting method for the discovery of approximate functional dependencies. The algorithm maintains a priority queue Q that holds the search frontier and a current result set $\mathcal{F}_k$ throughout the search. In the beginning of each iteration, it checks whether the search has terminated, which is the case either when the frontier is empty or the potential of top-potential element from the frontier (w.r.t. the bounding function) is less than the k-th best $\hat{F}_0$-value of the current result. As long as this condition is not satisfied, the search continuous by expanding the top-potential variable set (line 5), and using its successors to update the current result set (line 6), as well as the priority queue (line 7).

5 EMPIRICAL EVALUATION

In this section, we study the empirical performance of discovering approximate functional dependencies based on $\hat{F}_0$. This includes, the bias of $\hat{F}_0$ as an estimator of the true F functional, the performance of the bounding function $\overline{f}$ in branch-and-bound search, and two concrete examples of functional dependencies in real datasets.

5.1 Estimation Bias

In this section we evaluate the bias and variance of our corrected estimator $\hat{F}_0$. It is instructive to see the behavior of the bias for various amounts of dependence, and not in the particular case of independence, i.e., $F = 0$, where $\hat{F}_0$ aims to be unbiased (see Fig. 1 for an empirical confirmation of this fact). For that let us denote by P the set of all joint probability mass functions over two random variables X and Y with $|V(X)| = |V(Y)| = 3$, and by $P[a, b]$ all such probability mass functions for which we have a functional dependence score of $F_p(X; Y) \in (a, b]$. We are interested in the behavior of the estimation bias over P under a distribution that puts equal weight on the four different regimes "weak" ($P[0, 0.25]$), "low" ($P[0.25, 0.5]$), "high" ($P[0.5, 0.75]$), and "strong" ($P[0.75, 1]$).

More specifically, let $\tau(\mathbf{D}_n)$ be the result of the F-estimator τ computed on data $\mathbf{D}_n$ and $b(n)(p, \tau)$ the bias of τ when fixing the underlying pmf to p, i.e.,

$$b(n)(p, \tau) = \mathbb{E}_{\mathbf{D}_n \sim p}[\tau(\mathbf{D}_n)] - F_p(\mathcal{X}; Y) \ . \tag{4}$$

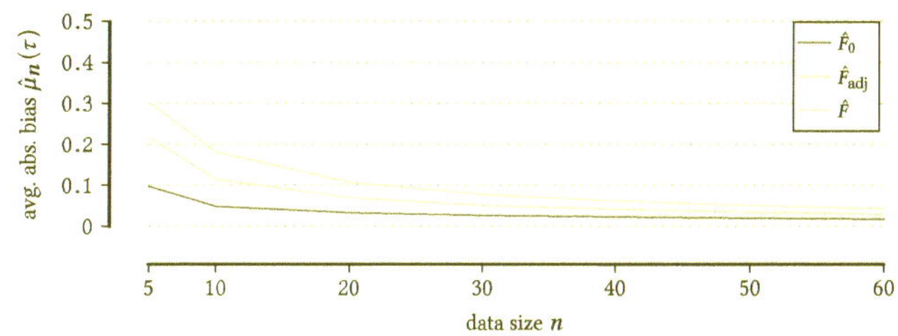

Figure 2: Estimated absolute bias $\hat{\mu}_n(\tau)$ of estimators $\tau = \hat{F}$, $\hat{F}_{\text{adj}}$, and the reliable fraction of information $\hat{F}_0$, averaged over all 100 pmfs $p \in P$ across different data sizes n.

To estimate the expected value $\mu_n(\tau)$ and standard variation $\sigma_n(\tau)$ of the absolute bias $|b(n)(p, \tau)|$ for the pmfs from P, we uniformly sample 100 pmfs $p^{(1)}, \ldots, p^{(100)}$ in equal proportions from the four different regimes, i.e., 25 each from $P[0, 0.25]$, $P[0.25, 0.5]$, $P[0.5, 0.75]$, and $P[0.75, 1]$. For each pmf $p^{(i)}$ we can calculate the true F value directly from its definition. To compute $b(n)(p^{(i)}, \tau)$ it then only remains to empirically estimate the expectation term in Eq. (4), for which we sample per pmf $p^{(i)}$ a total of 1000 datasets $D_n \sim p^{(i)}$ of size n. By averaging over all $p^{(i)}$, we end up with the desired estimates $\hat{\mu}_n(\tau)$ and $\hat{\sigma}_n(\tau)$ for the absolute bias of estimator τ with sample size n.

Equipped with this procedure we can go ahead and compare the performance of $\hat{F}_0$ to other estimators. In addition to the naive uncorrected estimator $\hat{F}$ we also introduce an alternative correction resulting from the application of the quantification adjustment framework proposed by Romano et al. [21]. This correction, which we denote by $\hat{F}_{\text{adj}}$, is defined as

$$\hat{F}_{\text{adj}}(\mathcal{X}; Y) = \frac{\hat{I}(\mathcal{X}, Y) - \hat{\mathbb{E}}_0[\hat{I}(\mathcal{X}, Y)]}{\hat{H}(Y) - \hat{\mathbb{E}}_0[\hat{I}(\mathcal{X}, Y)]} \ .$$

Thus, we consider $\tau \in \{\hat{F}, \hat{F}_{\text{adj}}, \hat{F}_0\}$. For each estimator, we compute $\hat{\mu}_n(\tau)$ and $\hat{\sigma}_n(\tau)$ for data sizes $n \in \{5, 10, 20, 30, 40, 50, 60\}$. We focus on small data sizes, because any consistent estimator converges to F for $n \to \infty$. Furthermore, we can expect the small data sizes for the small domain size $|V(\mathcal{X})| = 3$ of this experiment to behave similar to larger data sizes combined with the potentially huge domains occurring during the algorithmic search (resulting from the complex random variables $\mathcal{X}$).

In Figure 2 we present the results for the estimated absolute bias $\hat{\mu}_n(\tau)$ of estimators $\tau = \hat{F}$, $\hat{F}_{\text{adj}}$, and the reliable fraction of information $\hat{F}_0$, averaged over all 100 pmfs $p \in P$ across different data sizes n. We observe that our estimator $\hat{F}_0$ achieves a lower bias for all n compared to $\hat{F}$ and $\hat{F}_{\text{adj}}$, and converges fast to a bias close to zero after 10 samples. The differences in bias are apparent in the cases of $n = 5$ and $n = 10$ samples. These are cases where the insufficient data samples cause $\hat{H}(Y \mid \mathcal{X} = \mathbf{x})$ to approach 0, independent of the true distribution $\hat{p}$. In such scenarios, the estimators $\hat{F}$ and $\hat{F}_{\text{adj}}$ start to show functional dependence, while

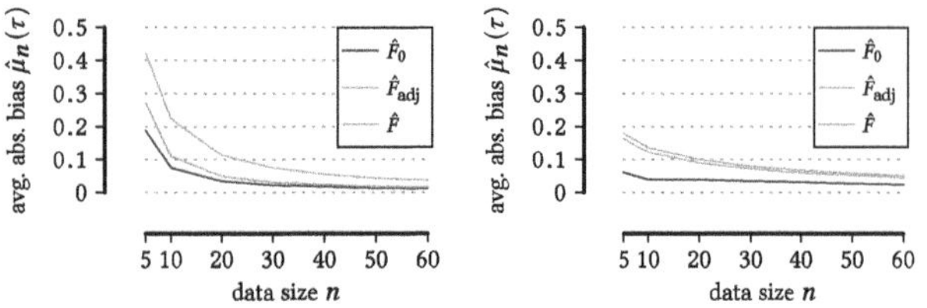

(a) Weak dependence (b) Strong dependence

Figure 3: Estimated absolute bias $\hat{\mu}_n(\tau)$ of estimators $\tau = \hat{F}$, $\hat{F}_{\text{adj}}$, and the reliable fraction of information $\hat{F}_0$, averaged over $p \in P[0, 0.25]$ (left) and over $p \in P[0.75, 1]$ (right), across different data sizes n.

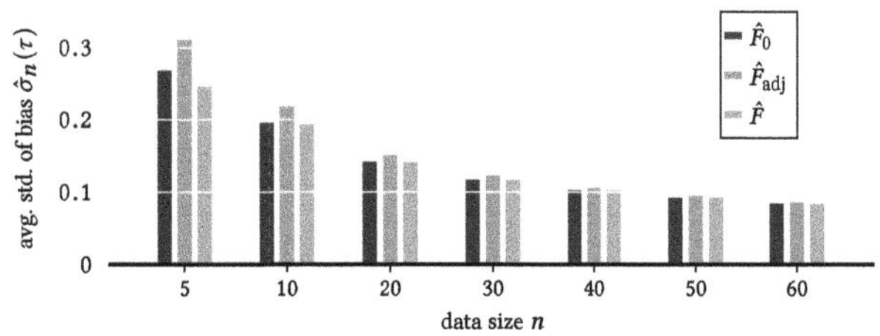

Figure 4: Estimated standard deviation $\hat{\sigma}_n(\tau)$ of estimators $\tau = \hat{F}$, $\hat{F}_{\text{adj}}$, and the reliable fraction of information $\hat{F}_0$, averaged over all 100 pmfs $p \in P$ across different data sizes n.

$\hat{F}_0$ is designed to show independence for reliability reasons. So it is useful to see that this design, also offers a better bias.

We can further draw conclusions about the behavior of $\hat{F}_0$ by considering only the "weak" and "strong" dependencies, i.e., where F is closer to independence and functional dependence respectively. As such, we present in Figure 3 the estimated absolute bias $\hat{\mu}_n(\tau)$, averaged over $p \in P[0, 0.25]$ (left), and $p \in P[0.75, 1]$ (right). We see that in both cases, i.e., when there is low and high functional dependence, $\hat{F}_0$ achieves a lower bias, as it was the case with $p \in P[0, 1]$. Since our score aims to be unbiased under the null hypothesis, we observe a high correction over the $\hat{F}$ for weak dependencies. Even for high dependencies, where one could expect to have less correction, we see that $\hat{F}_0$ is practically unbiased across all n.

For the standard deviation $\hat{\mu}_n(\tau)$, we present in Figure 4 the results after averaging over all 100 pmfs $p \in P$ across different data sizes n. We observe that $\hat{F}_0$ has an almost equal $\hat{\mu}_n$ for all n in comparison with $\hat{F}$, and a lower one with $\hat{F}_{\text{adj}}$. Estimators achieve better bias by trading variance, and from Figures 2, 3, and 4, we see that in comparison with $\hat{F}$ and $\hat{F}_{\text{adj}}$, we trade very little variance for a large bias correction. With the previous observations, we can conclude that $\hat{F}_0$ is a suitable estimator for the fraction of information F, as desired.

5.2 Optimization performance

In this section, we investigate the performance of the branch-and-bound algorithm combined with our optimistic estimator $\overline{f}(\mathcal{X}) = 1 - \hat{b}_0(\mathcal{X}, Y, n)$. Specifically, we are interested in the effects of having

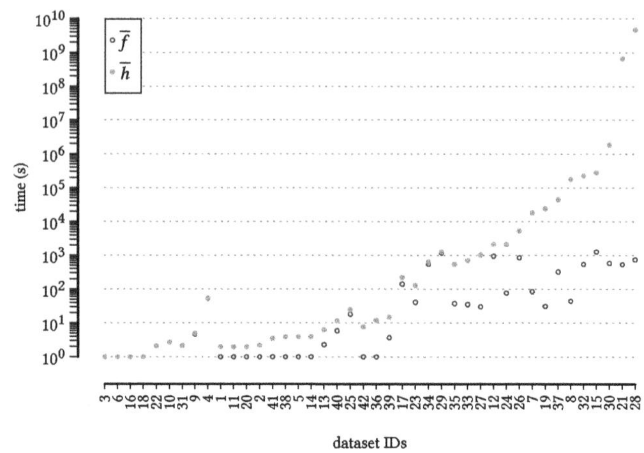

Figure 5: Computation time of branch-and-bound with $\overline{f}$ and $\overline{h}$ as bounding function respectively, across all datasets sorted according to speed-up.

a data dependent quantity in our bounding function, i.e., $\hat{b}_0(\mathcal{X}, Y, n)$, which in addition, acts as a penalty for non-reliable dependencies.

For this experiment we utilize the KEEL data repository.[2] We use all classification datasets with $n \in [100, 13000]$, $d \in [6, 90]$, without missing values, resulting in 42 datasets with an average number of 2800 data samples and 24 attributes.[3] All metric attributes are discretized using the method of Fayyad and Irani [5]. The datasets are summarized in Table 1. All experiments were executed on a dedicated Intel Xeon E5-2643 v3 machine with 256 GB memory. We make our code available online for research purposes.[4]

We employ the algorithm to retrieve the top dependence, and individually set the α for each dataset, such that the algorithm terminates in less than 30 minutes. We report time, α used, pruning percentage of the search space, depth of the solution, and the maximum depth the algorithm had to explore in Table 1.

The percentage of the datasets where $\alpha = 1$, i.e., 30 out of 42, show that an optimal solution can be discovered in under 30 minutes for the majority of the cases considered. In 28 datasets it takes a maximum of 6 minutes. For the rest, reasonable approximations to the optimal solution can be achieved, e.g., $\alpha = 0.9, 0.8$.

We observe that our bounding function $\overline{f}$, is effective in pruning a considerable amount of the search space, i.e., 67.9% on average. In addition, an average of 7.5 maximum depth combined with an average solution depth of 4.0, show that $\overline{f}$ is not simply pruning on set cardinality, but it is a data dependent quantity that selectively explores the search space based on the structure of the data. That is, it can potentially go to higher levels for promising candidates.

To further corroborate on the previous observation, we consider a hypothetical optimistic estimator $\overline{h}$ that prunes based solely on the cardinality of $\mathcal{X}$. For a meaningful comparison, we provide an oracle to this method and restrict the search space to the maximum depth that $\overline{f}$ had to explore, and not the complete space of size 2^d

[2] http://www.keel.es/

[3] Some attributes with obviously wrong type declarations were corrected, e.g., 'sex' was often corrected to be categoric and not metric.

[4] http://eda.mmci.uni-saarland.de/dora/

X_1	X_2	X_3
X_4	X_5	X_6
X_7	X_8	X_9

3	1	3
1	4	1
3	1	3

Figure 6: Tic-tac-toe board with input variables in corresponding board positions and variables contained in top approximate functional dependency marked in red (left); and number of winning combinations each position is involved in (right).

nodes. For example, if the maximum depth is l, then the branch-and-bound with $\bar{h}$ as bounding function will visit $q = \sum_{i=1}^{l} \binom{d}{i}$ nodes. The estimated time for every dataset is then $q \times t$, where t is a node processing time estimated by dividing the completion time of branch-and-bound with $\overline{f}$, with the number of nodes visited. We plot the computation time for both estimators in Figure 5. The datasets are sorted in ascending order of speed-up.

We see that in the majority of the datasets, taking into account the structure of the data is of crucial importance. This is most evident in the last two datasets, where it would take 20 and 146 years respectively to find the solution based on cardinality alone. This plot shows the potential of a data dependent optimistic estimator, as opposed to a simple function evaluating statistics as cardinality, in a potentially hard optimization problem.

Regarding reliability, useful conclusions can be drawn from the average solution dimensionality of 4.0, which is a reasonable number for the size of the data considered. Trying to maximize other estimators for example, such as $\hat{F}_{\text{adj}}$ or $\hat{F}$, would result in very large dimensionalities.

5.3 Exemplary discoveries

After investigating the statistical properties of $\hat{F}_0$ and its algorithmic performance, we close this section with examples of concrete approximate functional dependencies discovered in two different applications: determining the winner of a tic-tac-toe configuration and predicting the preferred crystal structure of octet binary semi-conductors. Both settings are examples of problems where elementary input features are available, but to correctly represent the input/output relation either non-linear models have to be used or—if interpretable models are sought—complex auxiliary feature have to be constructed from the given elementary features.

The tic-tac-toe application [15] is one of the earliest examples of this complex feature construction problem. Tic-tac-toe is a game of two players where each player picks a symbol from $\{x, o\}$ and, taking turns, marks his symbol in an unoccupied cell of a 3×3 game board. A player wins the game if he marks 3 consecutive cells in a row, column, or diagonal. A game can end in draw, if the board configuration does not allow for any winning move. The dataset consists of 958 end game, winning configurations (i.e., there are no draws). The 9 input variables $\mathcal{I} = \{X_1, \ldots, X_9\}$ represent the cells of the board, and can have 3 values $\{x, o, b\}$, where b denotes an empty

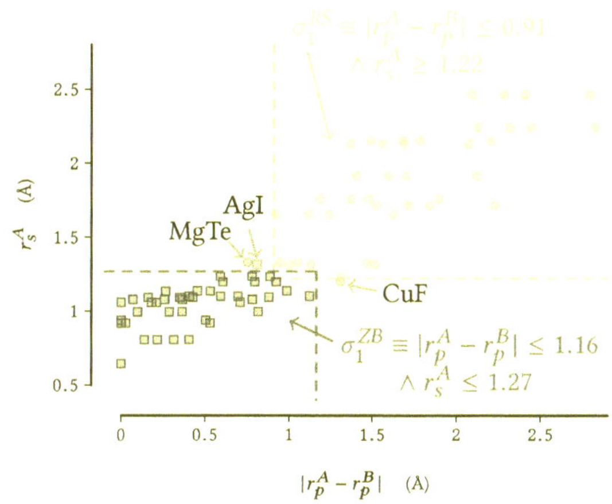

Figure 7: Binary semiconductors that crystalize as zinkblende (boxes) and rocksalt (circles); blue and green materials are correctly classified by subgroup-based prediction model—the involved rules (annotated) use elements of top functional dependency as two out of three variables. (source: Goldsmith et al. [8]).

cell (see Fig. 6). The output variable Y with $V(Y) = \{\text{win}, \text{loss}\}$ is the outcome of the game for player x.

Searching for approximate functional dependencies reveals as top pattern with empirical fraction of information $\hat{F} = 0.61$ and corrected score $\hat{F}_0 = 0.45$ the variable set

$$\mathcal{X} = \{X_1, X_3, X_5, X_7, X_9\}$$

i.e., the four corner cells and the middle one. This is a sensible discovery as these cells correspond exactly to those involved in the highest number of winning combinations (see Fig. 6). Knowing the state of these cell provides, therefore, a high amount of information about the outcome of the game. Moreover, removing a variable results in a loss of a considerable amount of information, while adding a variable would provide more information, but also redundancy. That is, the increase of fraction of information would not be higher than the increase of $\hat{b}_0$.

Our second example is a classical problem from Materials Science [24], which has meanwhile become a canonical example for the challenge of the automatic discovery of interpretable and "physically meaningful" prediction models of material properties [6, 8]. The task is to predict the symmetry or crystal structure, in which a given binary compound semi-conductor material will crystalize. That is, each of the 82 material involved consist of two atom types (A and B) and the output variable $Y = \{\text{rocksalt}, \text{zincblende}\}$ describes the crystal structure it prefers energetically. The input variables are 14 electro-chemical features of the two atom types considered in isolation: the radii of the three different electron orbitals shapes s, p, and d of atom type A denoted as $r_s(A), r_p(A), r_d(A)$ as well as four important energy quantities that determine its chemical properties (electron affinity, ionization potential, HOMO and LUMO energy levels); the same variables are defined for component B.

For this dataset the top approximate functional dependency with $\hat{F}_0 = 0.707$ and uncorrected empirical fraction of information $\hat{F} =$

0.735 is

$$\mathcal{X} = \{r_s(A), r_p(A)\}$$

i.e., the atomical s and p radii of component A. Again, this is a sensible finding, since these two variables constitute two out of three variables contained in the best structure prediction model that can be identified using the non-linear subgroup discovery approach [8]. Also both features are involved in the best linear LASSO model based on systematically constructed non-linear combinations of the elementary input variables [6]. The fact that not all variables of those models are identified by the functional dependency discovery algorithm can likely be explained by the facts that (a) the continuous input variables had to be discretized and (b) the dataset is extremely small with only 82 entries, which renders the discovery of reliable patterns with more than two variables very challenging.

6 CONCLUSION

We considered the dual problem of measuring and efficiently discovering approximate functional dependencies from data. We adopted an information theoretic approach, and proposed a fraction of information score that is reliable and achieves a good bias. In addition, we proposed an efficient optimistic estimator that allows for the effective discovery of the optimal, or α-approximate top-k dependencies of the target variable.

Although we carefully constructed the proposed correction term $\hat{b}_0$ such that bias under those regimes that are most problematic for searching for high-dimensional functional dependencies is removed, other scores could potentially be found that estimate the fraction of information with even less bias.

Other correction terms could also lead to other algorithms. The computational complexity for finding reliable functional dependencies is still open. Hence, polynomial time algorithm for this or adapted problem variants are a possibility. Similarly so, efficient tight(er) optimistic estimators would improve the runtime of branch-and-bound, as fewer nodes would have to be expanded to discover the optimal solution.

Both our score and optimistic estimator are specifically defined for discrete data. While in this paper we only considered univariate discrete targets, our scores can be trivially extended to multivariate discrete variables. Clearly, it is also of interest to discover approximate functional dependencies from continuous real-valued data. As entropy has been defined for such data, e.g. differential entropy [23] and cumulative entropy [18], it is possible to instantiate fraction of information scores. It will be interesting to see whether we can also efficiently correct these scores for chance, and whether optimistic estimators exist that allow for effective search.

ACKNOWLEDGMENTS

The authors wish to thank Luca Ghiringhelli and Brian Goldsmith for insightful discussions. Panagiotis Mandros is supported by the International Max Planck Research School for Computer Science (IMPRS-CS). The authors are supported by the Cluster of Excellence "Multimodal Computing and Interaction" within the Excellence Initiative of the German Federal Government.

REFERENCES

[1] Roger Cavallo and Michael Pittarelli. 1987. The Theory of Probabilistic Databases. In *Proceedings of the 13th International Conference on Very Large Data Bases (VLDB), Brighton, UK.* 71–81.
[2] Thomas M. Cover and Joy A. Thomas. 1991. *Elements of Information Theory.* Wiley-Interscience, New York, NY, USA.
[3] Mehmet M. Dalkilic and Edward L. Roberston. 2000. Information Dependencies. In *Proceedings of the 19th ACM SIGACT-SIGMOD-SIGART Symposium on Principles of Database Systems.* ACM, 245–253.
[4] Alin Dobra and Johannes Gehrke. 2001. Bias Correction in Classification Tree Construction. In *Proceedings of the 18th International Conference on Machine Learning (ICML), Williams College, MA.* Morgan Kaufmann, 90–97.
[5] Usama M. Fayyad and Keki B. Irani. 1993. Multi-Interval Discretization of Continuous-Valued Attributes for Classification Learning. In *Proceedings of the 13th International Joint Conference on Artificial Intelligence (IJCAI), Chambéry, France.* 1022–1029.
[6] Luca M Ghiringhelli, Jan Vybiral, Sergey V Levchenko, Claudia Draxl, and Matthias Scheffler. 2015. Big data of materials science: Critical role of the descriptor. *Physical review letters* 114, 10 (2015), 105503.
[7] Chris Giannella and Edward L. Robertson. 2004. On approximation measures for functional dependencies. *Information Systems* 29, 6 (2004), 483–507.
[8] Bryan R Goldsmith, Mario Boley, Jilles Vreeken, Matthias Scheffler, and Luca M Ghiringhelli. 2017. Uncovering structure-property relationships of materials by subgroup discovery. *New Journal of Physics* 19, Article 013031 (2017), 14 pages.
[9] Lawrence Hubert and Phipps Arabie. 1985. Comparing partitions. *Journal of Classification* 2, 1 (1985), 193–218.
[10] Ykä Huhtala, Juha Kärkkäinen, Pasi Porkka, and Hannu Toivonen. 1999. TANE: An efficient algorithm for discovering functional and approximate dependencies. *Comput. J.* 42, 2 (1999), 100–111.
[11] Igor Kononenko. 1995. On Biases in Estimating Multi-valued Attributes. In *Proceedings of the 14th International Joint Conference on Artificial Intelligence (IJCAI), San Francisco,CA,USA.* 1034–1040.
[12] Andreas Krause and Carlos E Guestrin. 2012. *Near-optimal nonmyopic value of information in graphical models.* Technical Report 1207.1394. arXiv.
[13] H.O. Lancaster. 1969. *The chi-squared distribution.* Wiley.
[14] Jixue Liu, Jiuyong Li, Chengfei Liu, and Yongfeng Chen. 2012. Discover dependencies from data–a review. *IEEE Transactions on Knowledge and Data Engineering* 24, 2 (2012), 251–264.
[15] Christopher J Matheus and Larry A Rendell. 1989. Constructive Induction On Decision Trees. In *Proceedings of the 11th International Joint Conference on Artificial Intelligence (IJCAI), Detroit, MI.* 645.
[16] Kurt Mehlhorn and Peter Sanders. 2008. *Algorithms and data structures: The basic toolbox.* Springer Science & Business Media.
[17] Hoang Vu Nguyen, Panagiotis Mandros, and Jilles Vreeken. 2016. Universal Dependency Analysis. In *Proceedings of the SIAM International Conference on Data Mining (SDM), Miami, FL.* SIAM, 792–800.
[18] Murali Rao, Yunmei Chen, Baba C. Vemuri, and Fei Wang. 2004. Cumulative Residual Entropy: A New Measure of Information. *IEEE Transactions on Information Technology* 50, 6 (2004), 1220–1228.
[19] Matthew Reimherr and Dan L Nicolae. 2013. On quantifying dependence: A framework for developing interpretable measures. *Statist. Sci.* 28, 1 (2013), 116–130.
[20] Simone Romano, James Bailey, Xuan Vinh Nguyen, and Karin Verspoor. 2014. Standardized Mutual Information for Clustering Comparisons: One Step Further in Adjustment for Chance.. In *Proceedings of the 31st International Conference on Machine Learning (ICML), Beijing, China.* 1143–1151.
[21] Simone Romano, Nguyen Xuan Vinh, James Bailey, and Karin Verspoor. 2016. A Framework to Adjust Dependency Measure Estimates for Chance. In *Proceedings of the SIAM International Conference on Data Mining (SDM), Miami, FL.* SIAM.
[22] Mark S Roulston. 1999. Estimating the errors on measured entropy and mutual information. *Physica D: Nonlinear Phenomena* 125, 3 (1999), 285–294.
[23] Claude E. Shannon. 1948. A Mathematical Theory of Communication. *The Bell System Technical Journal* 27, 3 (1948), 379–423.
[24] James A Van Vechten. 1969. Quantum dielectric theory of electronegativity in covalent systems. I. Electronic dielectric constant. *Physical Review* 182, 3 (1969), 891.
[25] Nguyen Xuan Vinh, Julien Epps, and James Bailey. 2009. Information theoretic measures for clusterings comparison: is a correction for chance necessary?. In *Proceedings of the 26th International Conference on Machine Learning (ICML), Montreal, Canada.* ACM, 1073–1080.
[26] Nguyen Xuan Vinh, Julien Epps, and James Bailey. 2010. Information theoretic measures for clusterings comparison: Variants, properties, normalization and correction for chance. *Journal of Machine Learning Research* 11, Oct (2010), 2837–2854.
[27] Yisen Wang, Simone Romano, Vinh Nguyen, James Bailey, Xingjun Ma, and Shu-Tao Xia. 2017. Unbiased Multivariate Correlation Analysis. In *Proceedings of the 31st AAAI Conference on Artificial Intelligence (AAAI).* AAAI.
[28] Allan P. White and Wei Zhong Liu. 1994. Technical Note: Bias in Information-Based Measures in Decision Tree Induction. *Machine Learning* 15, 3 (1994), 321–329.

ID	Name	#rows	#attrs.	#clases	α	time(s)	max dep.	sol. dep.	prune %
1	abalone	4174	8	28	1	2.1	8	3	0.00
2	appendicitis	106	7	2	1	1.0	6	3	50.00
3	tic	958	9	2	1	1.0	7	5	1.95
4	australian	690	14	2	1	3.7	11	5	75.01
5	bupa	345	6	2	1	1.0	1	1	96.88
6	car	1728	6	4	1	1.0	5	4	1.56
7	chess	3196	36	2	0.7	84.8	7	4	99.99
8	coil2000	9822	85	2	0.1	44.5	5	4	99.99
9	contraceptive	1473	9	3	1	1.0	7	4	75.00
10	ecoli	336	7	8	1	1.0	6	4	50.00
11	flare	1066	11	6	1	2.7	11	3	0.00
12	german	1000	20	2	1	76.9	11	7	97.29
13	glass	214	9	7	1	1.0	7	4	75.00
14	heart	270	13	2	1	1.0	9	5	75.34
15	ionosphere	351	33	2	1	1272.7	11	4	99.98
16	led7digit	500	7	10	1	1.0	7	5	0.00
17	lymphography	148	18	4	1	41.2	11	5	71.79
18	monk	432	6	2	1	1.0	4	3	10.94
19	movement-libras	360	90	15	0.4	31.2	5	3	99.99
20	nursery	12690	8	5	1	2.2	7	5	0.78
21	optdigits	5620	64	10	0.5	538.1	10	3	99.99
22	page	5472	10	5	1	4.7	8	4	7.23
23	penbased	10992	16	10	1	141.2	5	3	93.33
24	ring	7400	20	2	0.6	944.4	7	3	94.24
25	saheart	462	9	2	1	1.0	5	4	93.75
26	satimage	6435	36	7	0.9	850.9	5	3	99.99
27	segment	2310	19	7	1	35.3	8	2	98.37
28	sonar	208	60	2	1	744.7	13	6	99.99
29	spambase	4597	57	2	0.5	30.4	4	3	99.99
30	spectfheart	267	44	2	0.5	583.1	10	5	99.99
31	splice	3190	60	3	0.6	52.5	3	3	99.99
32	texture	5500	40	11	0.8	546.4	7	3	99.99
33	thyroid	7200	21	3	0.9	37.5	7	3	99.35
34	twonorm	7400	20	2	0.9	1160.2	6	4	94.74
35	vehicle	846	18	4	1	547.2	13	4	15.44
36	vowel	990	13	11	1	18.1	10	3	27.69
37	wdbc	569	30	2	1	326.1	10	4	99.96
38	wine	178	13	3	1	1.0	6	3	77.37
39	winequality red	1599	11	11	1	1.0	8	6	87.50
40	winequality white	4898	11	11	1	5.9	10	9	50.00
41	yeast	1484	8	10	1	1.0	7	7	50.00
42	zoo	101	15	7	1	2.3	9	5	84.41
Average		2800.0	24.0	5.6	0.89	194.0	7.5	4.0	67.9

Table 1: Datasets used in Section 5.2. The table contains information about the name and ID of the datasets used, number of rows, input variables, and classes, the α used for completion in less than 30 minutes, the time in seconds, the maximum depth of the algorithm, the depth of the best solution, and the percentage of the pruned search space.

Towards an Optimal Subspace for K-Means

Dominik Mautz[†], Wei Ye[†], Claudia Plant[§], Christian Böhm[†]
[†]Ludwig-Maximilians-Universität München, Munich, Germany
{mautz,ye,boehm}@dbs.ifi.lmu.de
[§]University of Vienna, Vienna, Austria
claudia.plant@univie.ac.at

ABSTRACT

Is there an optimal dimensionality reduction for k-means, revealing the prominent cluster structure hidden in the data? We propose SubKmeans, which extends the classic k-means algorithm. The goal of this algorithm is twofold: find a sufficient k-means-style clustering partition and transform the clusters onto a common subspace, which is optimal for the cluster structure. Our solution is able to pursue these two goals simultaneously. The dimensionality of this subspace is found automatically and therefore the algorithm comes without the burden of additional parameters. At the same time this subspace helps to mitigate the *curse of dimensionality*. The SubKmeans optimization algorithm is intriguingly simple and efficient. It is easy to implement and can readily be adopted to the current situation. Furthermore, it is compatible to many existing extensions and improvements of k-means.

KEYWORDS

clustering; k-means; subspace; dimensionality reduction

1 INTRODUCTION

The k-means clustering algorithm is one of, if not the, most often used partition based clustering algorithm. Our own community voted it second of the top 10 data mining algorithms [31]. Its popularity is largely a result of several intriguing properties: it is simple, it can readily be adopted to different situations, it is fast and can scale to very large datasets. Last but not least, its results are mostly sufficient for a first analysis.

However, the interpretation of what the algorithm finds becomes increasingly difficult with growing number of dimensions. Even in lower dimensional spaces it is sometimes hard to tell what structure the algorithm has found. In the following we propose SubKmeans, a technique, which extends k-means. It finds a clustering partition and simultaneously a transformation which highlights the structure found in the dataset.

Let us consider a small, five-dimensional synthetic dataset containing three clusters, as shown in Figure 1 (a). Let us assume for

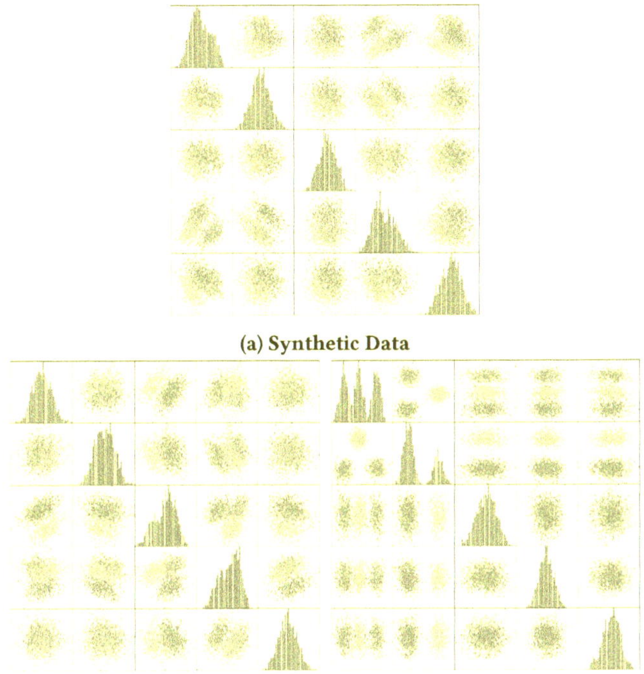

(a) Synthetic Data

(b) PCA (c) SubKmeans

Figure 1: Diagram (a) shows the scatter plots of artificial data set with color-coded ground truth. Diagram (b) shows the PCA transformation with ground truth. Diagram (c) shows the data transformed by SubKmeans. This method finds the correct cluster partition and automatically identifies the first two features in the transformed space—highlighted in yellow—as important for the cluster structure.

a moment that the ground truth would be unknown and the scatter plot monochrome. A data scientist inspecting these plots may assume that the data contains some structure as it shines through in some scatter plots. Yet, a clear structure does not present itself. Driven by this idea the data scientist now may try out a Principal Component Analysis (PCA) transformation, which reveals the directions of most variance within this dataset. Figure 1 (b) shows the result of this action. However, the result is somewhat disappointing. The new perspective onto the data does not reveal a clear structure. The next step may be to apply a simple clustering algorithm like k-means, to shed some light into the data. Let us further assume that this algorithm also finds the color-coded ground truth—which k-means indeed does for this simple dataset.

KDD '17, August 13-17, 2017, Halifax, NS, Canada

ACM ISBN 978-1-4503-4887-4/17/08...$15.00
https://doi.org/10.1145/3097983.3097989

At this point, our scientist may have a second look on both diagrams. But still, clear cluster boundaries are hardly visible and a clear cluster structure does not present itself. It is hard to tell what k-means actually found and if it is meaningful.

As a consequence, our researcher might turn to other, more sophisticated methods like Independent Component Analysis (ICA) or variants of non-linear manifold learning. These other techniques may even be able to find transformations in such a dataset, revealing more of the hidden structures. But, to the best of our knowledge, none of these techniques tries to find an optimal dimensionality reduction for k-means clustering. Therefore, in general, our data scientist will have a hard time identifying the feature combinations, which are most relevant for the overall found cluster structure.

The situation is completely different for the scatter plots shown in Figure 1 (c). The data shown in the figure was partitioned and transformed by our proposed algorithm SubKmeans. We can readily identify three clusters supported by the first two features. Further, we can see that only those two features provide relevant information for the overall cluster structure. The other three features only present unimodal structures and do not provide any crucial information. This algorithm takes—in contrast to a combination of PCA and k-means—the local structure into account and is not only able to partition the data, but also to simultaneously transform it such that its inner structure is revealed to the data scientist. Further, it identifies which of these newly revealed features are important to the clustering by splitting the transformed data into two subspaces. A *clustered* space, which contains all useful structure, and a *noise* space, which contains the irrelevant (unimodal) structures. Performing the partitioning in the *clustered* space has the additional advantage that it mitigates the problem of the meaningfulness of proximity in high-dimensional spaces.

Our **main contributions** are as follows:

(1) We extend k-means such that it incorporates a simultaneous dimensionality reduction step.
(2) The dimensionality of the *clustered* space is determined automatically.
(3) We do not introduce an additional parameter. The only parameter needed is the number of clusters k.
(4) We propose an optimization algorithm, SubKmeans, which is very easy to implement and can readily be adopted to different situations. It is fast, even without sophisticated performance optimizations.
(5) SubKmeans is compatible to many proposed extensions of k-means.

2 SUBSPACE K-MEANS

In the following we describe our proposed method SubKmeans.[1] We describe our algorithm, for the sake of brevity, as a simple extension of the well-known Lloyd's algorithm [21] with its EM-style alternating assignment and update steps. Though, it is possible to incorporate many other k-means extensions and modifications for performance optimization. A non-exhaustive list of these can be found in Section 4. Table 1 shows the used symbols and definitions.

[1]Implementation and supplementary available under: http://dmm.dbs.ifi.lmu.de/downloads/

Table 1: Symbols and Definitions

Symbol	Interpretation
$d \in \mathbb{N}$	Dimensionality of original space
$m \in \mathbb{N}$	Dimensionality of the *clustered* space
$k \in \mathbb{N}$	Number of Clusters
$\mathcal{D}$	Set of all objects
C_i	Set of objects assigned to cluster i
$\mathbf{x} \in \mathbb{R}^d$	A data point or object
$\mu_{\mathcal{D}} \in \mathbb{R}^d$	Dataset mean in the original space
$\mu_i \in \mathbb{R}^m$	Mean of cluster i in the original space
$S_{\mathcal{D}} \in \mathbb{R}^{d\times d}$	Scatter matrix of the dataset in the original space
$S_i \in \mathbb{R}^{d\times d}$	Scatter matrix of cluster i in the original space
$\Sigma \in \mathbb{R}^{d\times d}$	See definition in Formula 3
$P_C \in \mathbb{R}^{m\times d}$	Projection onto the first m attributes
$P_N \in \mathbb{R}^{d-m\times d}$	Projection onto the last $d - m$ attributes
$V \in \mathbb{R}^{d\times d}$	(orthonormal) matrix of a rigid transformation
$\mathbf{I}_l$	$l \times l$ identity matrix
$\mathbf{0}_{l,r}$	$l \times r$ zero matrix

2.1 Cost Function

In the classic version of the k-means algorithm, we want to find a set of k clusters C_i, which partitions the data such that the sum of squared errors is minimized,

$$\sum_{i=1}^{k} \sum_{\mathbf{x}\in C_i} \|\mathbf{x} - \mu_i\|^2,$$

where $\|\cdot\|$ represents the Euclidean norm.

We extend this basic idea in SubKmeans by the assumption that the cluster structure is contained in a lower dimensional subspace. That is, we assume that the data space can be split into two arbitrarily oriented subspaces. The first m-dimensional, subspace contains all structural information of the k clusters. We call this subspace the *clustered* space.

The orthogonal complement of this subspace builds a second, $(d - m)$-dimensional, subspace. It does not contain any structural information important for the clustering. The expectation within this subspace is that the data point values for each feature are drawn from the same unimodal symmetric distribution (See also Section 2.5). We call this the *noise* space, since its feature values do not help to distinguish between the different clusters in the *clustered* space. As we are not interested in the actual distribution of the *noise*, we assume that this space can be described by a single cluster.

Further, we assume that we can find an orthonormal (rigid) transformation matrix V, which rotates (and reflects) the original space in such a way that the first m features in the transformed space correspond to the *clustered* space and the last $(d-m)$ features correspond to the *noise* space. We can use two simple projections to split these features into their respective subspaces:

$$P_C = \begin{bmatrix} \mathbf{I}_m \\ \mathbf{0}_{d-m,m} \end{bmatrix}, \quad P_N = \begin{bmatrix} \mathbf{0}_{m,d-m} \\ \mathbf{I}_{d-m} \end{bmatrix}.$$

A data point $\mathbf{x}$ can then be projected onto the *clustered* space by $P_C^\top V^\top \mathbf{x}$. The projection onto the *noise* space is performed similarly using P_N.

Algorithm 1: SubKmeans

Input: dataset $\mathcal{D}$; number of clusters k
Output: clusters $\{C_1, \ldots, C_k\}$;
  rotation matrix V;
  dimensionality of *clustered* space m
`// Initialization:`
  $V \leftarrow$ random orthonormal matrix
  $m \leftarrow$ some initial value, e.g. $\frac{d}{2}$ or $\sqrt{d}$
  $\mu_{\mathcal{D}} \leftarrow \frac{1}{|\mathcal{D}|} \sum_{\mathbf{x} \in \mathcal{D}} \mathbf{x}$
  $S_{\mathcal{D}} \leftarrow \sum_{\mathbf{x} \in \mathcal{D}} (\mathbf{x} - \mu_{\mathcal{D}})(\mathbf{x} - \mu_{\mathcal{D}})^{\mathsf{T}}$
  $\forall i \in [1, k] : \mu_i \leftarrow$ random data point of $\mathcal{D}$
repeat
  `// Assignment step`
  $C_j \leftarrow \emptyset$
  $\forall \mathbf{x} \in \mathcal{D}$:
    $j \leftarrow \arg\min_{i \in [1,k]} \left\| P_C^{\mathsf{T}} V^{\mathsf{T}} \mathbf{x} - P_C^{\mathsf{T}} V^{\mathsf{T}} \mu_i \right\|^2$
    $C_j \leftarrow C_j \cup \{\mathbf{x}\}$
  `// Update step`
  $\forall i \in [1, k]$:
    $\mu_i \leftarrow \frac{1}{|C_i|} \sum_{\mathbf{x} \in C_i} \mathbf{x}$
    $S_i \leftarrow \sum_{\mathbf{x} \in C_i} (\mathbf{x} - \mu_i)(\mathbf{x} - \mu_i)^{\mathsf{T}}$
  `// Eigendecomposition:`
  `//` $\mathcal{E}$`: list of eigenvalues in ascending order`
  `//` V`: corresponding eigenvectors`
  $V, \mathcal{E} \leftarrow \mathrm{eig}\left(\left(\sum_{i=1}^{k} S_i\right) - S_{\mathcal{D}}\right)$
  $m \leftarrow |\{e | e \in \mathcal{E} \wedge e < 0\}|$
until *convergence*;

Combining these assumption we get the following cost function, which we want to minimize:

$$\mathcal{J} = \left[\sum_{i=1}^{k} \sum_{\mathbf{x} \in C_i} \left\| P_C^{\mathsf{T}} V^{\mathsf{T}} \mathbf{x} - P_C^{\mathsf{T}} V^{\mathsf{T}} \mu_i \right\|^2 \right] + \sum_{\mathbf{x} \in \mathcal{D}} \left\| P_N^{\mathsf{T}} V^{\mathsf{T}} \mathbf{x} - P_N^{\mathsf{T}} V^{\mathsf{T}} \mu_{\mathcal{D}} \right\|^2 . \tag{1}$$

This cost function builds a trade-off between the two subspaces. Our expectation is that this trade-off 'squeezes' all structural information out of the *noise* space into the *clustered* space. Combinations of features of the original space, which contain information regarding the clusters, are better represented by the first term. Yet, combinations of features that do not contain the structural information are better represented by the second term. Thus by optimizing this objective function, we can find the optimal subspace for k-means.

2.2 Optimization Algorithm

We can optimize this objective function with a modified version of Lloyd algorithm. The full algorithm is shown in Algorithm 1. Like the classic version, it is only able to find local minima and therefore has to be run multiple times—with different initializations—for a sufficient clustering solution.

As a first step we have to initialize V with an random orthonormal matrix. For instance, we could perform a QR decomposition of a random matrix and use the resulting orthonormal matrix Q as the initial value. Further, we need the initial dimensionality of the *clustered* space m. It should be noted that this value may not be chosen too big or too small, as it balances the probability that the initial *clustered* space contains parts of the cluster structure we want to find and the expressiveness of the similarity measure. For simplicity, we use in our implementation $d/2$ as it depends on d. Yet, it is also possible to let the user choose an initial value. The optimal value for m is subsequently found during the optimization. Last but not least, the initial cluster centers could for example be picked randomly from the dataset or set by k-means++.

The **assignment step** is nearly equivalent to the classic version. We keep the parameters of V, m, and μ_i fixed and assign each data point to the cluster for which the squared distance to the mean in the *clustered* space is minimized,

$$\arg\min_i \left\| P_C^{\mathsf{T}} V^{\mathsf{T}} \mathbf{x} - P_C^{\mathsf{T}} V^{\mathsf{T}} \mu_i \right\|^2 .$$

This minimizes the cost function with respect to the fixed parameters.

In the **update step** we keep the data point assignment fixed and determine the parameter values, for which the cost function is minimized. The following sections discuss in detail the steps taken and the correctness of each step.

2.2.1 Estimation of the cluster centers μ_i. We can determine the estimator for the cluster centers by setting the partial derivative with respect to μ_i equal to zero:

$$\frac{\partial}{\partial \mu_i} \mathcal{J} = \frac{\partial}{\partial \mu_i} \sum_{\mathbf{x} \in C_i} \left\| P_C^{\mathsf{T}} V^{\mathsf{T}} \mathbf{x} - P_C^{\mathsf{T}} V^{\mathsf{T}} \mu_i \right\|^2 \stackrel{!}{=} 0$$

We shorten this simple prove at this point for brevity. The result of this calculation shows what one would intuitively expect: the cluster mean $P_C^{\mathsf{T}} V^{\mathsf{T}} \mu_i$ in the *clustered* space is simply the mean value of all data points assigned to this cluster (in the original space) and can be calculated with the well-known formula:

$$\mu_i = \frac{1}{|C_i|} \sum_{\mathbf{x} \in C_i} \mathbf{x}.$$

We would like to emphasize that this formula is independent of V and m.

2.2.2 Estimation of the transformation matrix V. Next we need to estimate the value of V. For now, we assume that m is a fixed but arbitrary integer value in the range $[0 : d]$. Instead of taking the endeavor using a partial derivative, we prove that with some tricks we can rewrite the cost function such that it yields an eigen decomposition problem. Solving this eigenvalue problem also minimizes the objective function:

$$\begin{aligned}
\mathcal{J} &= \left[\sum_{i=1}^{k}\sum_{\mathbf{x}\in C_i}\left\|P_C^{\mathsf{T}}V^{\mathsf{T}}\mathbf{x} - P_C^{\mathsf{T}}V^{\mathsf{T}}\boldsymbol{\mu}_i\right\|^2\right] \\
&\quad + \sum_{\mathbf{x}\in\mathcal{D}}\left\|P_N^{\mathsf{T}}V^{\mathsf{T}}\mathbf{x} - P_N^{\mathsf{T}}V^{\mathsf{T}}\boldsymbol{\mu}_{\mathcal{D}}\right\|^2 \\
&= \left[\sum_{i=1}^{k}\sum_{\mathbf{x}\in C_i}\left(P_C^{\mathsf{T}}V^{\mathsf{T}}\mathbf{x} - P_C^{\mathsf{T}}V^{\mathsf{T}}\boldsymbol{\mu}_i\right)^{\mathsf{T}}\left(P_C^{\mathsf{T}}V^{\mathsf{T}}\mathbf{x} - P_C^{\mathsf{T}}V^{\mathsf{T}}\boldsymbol{\mu}_i\right)\right] \\
&\quad + \sum_{\mathbf{x}\in\mathcal{D}}\left(P_N^{\mathsf{T}}V^{\mathsf{T}}\mathbf{x} - P_N^{\mathsf{T}}V^{\mathsf{T}}\boldsymbol{\mu}_{\mathcal{D}}\right)^{\mathsf{T}}\left(P_N^{\mathsf{T}}V^{\mathsf{T}}\mathbf{x} - P_N^{\mathsf{T}}V^{\mathsf{T}}\boldsymbol{\mu}_{\mathcal{D}}\right) \\
&= \left[\sum_{i=1}^{k}\sum_{\mathbf{x}\in C_i}(\mathbf{x}-\boldsymbol{\mu}_i)^{\mathsf{T}}VP_CP_C^{\mathsf{T}}V^{\mathsf{T}}(\mathbf{x}-\boldsymbol{\mu}_i)\right] \\
&\quad + \sum_{\mathbf{x}\in\mathcal{D}}(\mathbf{x}-\boldsymbol{\mu}_{\mathcal{D}})^{\mathsf{T}}VP_NP_N^{\mathsf{T}}V^{\mathsf{T}}(\mathbf{x}-\boldsymbol{\mu}_{\mathcal{D}}) \\
&= \sum_{i=1}^{k}\sum_{\mathbf{x}\in C_i}\operatorname{Tr}\left((\mathbf{x}-\boldsymbol{\mu}_i)^{\mathsf{T}}VP_CP_C^{\mathsf{T}}V^{\mathsf{T}}(\mathbf{x}-\boldsymbol{\mu}_i)\right) \\
&\quad + \sum_{\mathbf{x}\in\mathcal{D}}\operatorname{Tr}\left((\mathbf{x}-\boldsymbol{\mu}_{\mathcal{D}})^{\mathsf{T}}VP_NP_N^{\mathsf{T}}V^{\mathsf{T}}(\mathbf{x}-\boldsymbol{\mu}_{\mathcal{D}})\right), \qquad (2)
\end{aligned}$$

where we apply in the last part of the equation the trace-trick. It exploits the fact that a scalar is also a 1×1 matrix. We can utilize the addition and cyclic permutation properties of trace to further rewrite the function:

$$\begin{aligned}
&= \operatorname{Tr}\left(P_CP_C^{\mathsf{T}}V^{\mathsf{T}}\underbrace{\left[\sum_{i=1}^{k}\sum_{\mathbf{x}\in C_i}(\mathbf{x}-\boldsymbol{\mu}_i)(\mathbf{x}-\boldsymbol{\mu}_i)^{\mathsf{T}}\right]}_{=:S_i}V\right) \\
&\quad + \operatorname{Tr}\left(P_NP_N^{\mathsf{T}}V^{\mathsf{T}}\underbrace{\left[\sum_{\mathbf{x}\in\mathcal{D}}(\mathbf{x}-\boldsymbol{\mu}_{\mathcal{D}})(\mathbf{x}-\boldsymbol{\mu}_{\mathcal{D}})^{\mathsf{T}}\right]}_{=:S_{\mathcal{D}}}V\right) \\
&= \operatorname{Tr}\left(P_CP_C^{\mathsf{T}}V^{\mathsf{T}}\left[\sum_{i=1}^{k}S_i\right]V\right) + \operatorname{Tr}\left(P_NP_N^{\mathsf{T}}V^{\mathsf{T}}S_{\mathcal{D}}V\right)
\end{aligned}$$

Next we have to apply a second trick. First we should note that $P_CP_C^{\mathsf{T}}$ is a diagonal matrix where the first m entries are ones and the rest are zeros:

$$P_CP_C^{\mathsf{T}} = \operatorname{diag}(\underbrace{1,\cdots 1}_{m-\text{times}},\ \underbrace{0,\cdots 0}_{(d-m)-\text{times}})$$

and equivalently for the noise projection:

$$P_NP_N^{\mathsf{T}} = \operatorname{diag}(\underbrace{0,\cdots 0}_{m-\text{times}},\ \underbrace{1,\cdots 1}_{(d-m)-\text{times}})$$

Since the trace of a matrix is the sum of its diagonal elements, we can use it to bring the two diagonal matrices $P_CP_C^{\mathsf{T}}$ and $P_NP_N^{\mathsf{T}}$ into a relationship:

$$\operatorname{Tr}(P_NP_N^{\mathsf{T}}A) = \operatorname{Tr}(A) - \operatorname{Tr}(P_CP_C^{\mathsf{T}}A),$$

where A is an arbitrary $d \times d$ matrix.

Further, we note that the trace of a matrix is also the sum of its eigenvalues and V is defined as an orthonormal matrix. Therefore, the transformation of the scatter matrix, $V^{\mathsf{T}}S_{\mathcal{D}}V$, only changes the direction of the eigenvectors, but does not change the eigenvalues itself. This means, that the trace of such a transformation, $\operatorname{Tr}(V^{\mathsf{T}}S_{\mathcal{D}}V)$, has to be constant for all possible values of the orthonormal matrix V, and we can ignore this term for the estimation of V. We can use these properties to further rewrite the cost function:

$$\begin{aligned}
&\operatorname{Tr}\left(P_CP_C^{\mathsf{T}}V^{\mathsf{T}}\left[\sum_{i=1}^{k}S_i\right]V\right) + \operatorname{Tr}\left(P_NP_N^{\mathsf{T}}V^{\mathsf{T}}S_{\mathcal{D}}V\right) \\
&= \operatorname{Tr}\left(P_CP_C^{\mathsf{T}}V^{\mathsf{T}}\left[\sum_{i=1}^{k}S_i\right]V\right) - \operatorname{Tr}\left(P_CP_C^{\mathsf{T}}V^{\mathsf{T}}S_{\mathcal{D}}V\right) + \operatorname{Tr}\left(V^{\mathsf{T}}S_{\mathcal{D}}V\right) \\
&= \underbrace{\operatorname{Tr}\left(P_CP_C^{\mathsf{T}}V^{\mathsf{T}}\left(\left[\sum_{i=1}^{k}S_i\right] - S_{\mathcal{D}}\right)V\right)}_{=:\Sigma} + \underbrace{\operatorname{Tr}\left(V^{\mathsf{T}}S_{\mathcal{D}}V\right)}_{\text{const. w.r.t. } V}. \qquad (3)
\end{aligned}$$

Since $P_CP_C^{\mathsf{T}}$ leaves the upper left $m \times m$ matrix untouched and sets all other values to zero, it is possible to minimize the function (1), for a fixed partition, fixed $\boldsymbol{\mu}_i$ and arbitrary but fixed m, by putting the eigenvectors of Σ into V's columns such that the m-eigenvectors corresponding to the m-smallest eigenvalues project the data into the *clustered* space and the other $(d-m)$ eigenvectors project the data onto the *noise* space. We therefore perform an eigenvalue decomposition of Σ and use the eigenvectors—sorted ascending to their corresponding eigenvalue—as columns in V. We should note that Σ is symmetric and therefore it is orthogonal diagonalizable and all its eigenvalues are real. Of course this only holds under the assumption that Σ has full rank, much like we assume for a Gaussian mixture model that its covariance matrices have full rank.

2.2.3 Estimation of the dimensionality m of the clustered *space.* Since we sort the eigenvalues in V in ascending order and the constant term in Formula 3 does not depend on m, the estimation of V is independent of the actual m (As long as we sort V ascending to the corresponding eigenvalues). This gives us the ability to also optimize m within each update step.

We can use the rewritten cost function in Formula 3 also to minimize the costs with respect to m. We note that the equation depends on m only through P_C. Since the trace is the sum of all eigenvalues and we want to minimize this sum, we can only minimize it, if we sum up all negative eigenvalues (which Σ may has because in general it is indefinite). This means, we let all eigenvectors corresponding to a negative eigenvalue project onto the *clustered* space. If the eigenvalues are all positive, we can minimize the trace only by setting m equal to zero. That is we do not have a *clustered* space because we cannot find any structure in the data following the current partition and the dataset is better explained by a single cluster. Eigenvectors with corresponding eigenvalues greater than zero have to project onto the *noise* space. If the eigenvalue is zero we are indifferent with respect to the cost function. Yet, from a clustering perspective we prefer to have a smaller *clustered* space and therefore it makes sense to let those eigenvectors also project onto the *noise* space. Consequently, we can optimize the cost function for a given V by setting m to the number of negative eigenvalues of Σ. Though, in practice, we might also want to assign eigenvectors with a negative eigenvalue close to zero (e.g. $\geq -1^{-10}$) to the *noise* space for the same reasons as components with an eigenvalue equal to zero.

We would like to note that the eigenvalues of Σ also give rise to a notion of how important the corresponding eigenvector is for the clustering structure: the smaller it is, the better the cluster structure is represented by it. Sorting the eigenvectors in V ascending by their eigenvalue therefore means that we also sort them by importance with respect to the cluster structure.

2.3 Convergence

The convergence of our modified algorithm is quite simple to see. The cost function is decreasing in each update and assignment step and it is bounded from below. Thus, the algorithm has to converge towards a (local) minimum.

2.4 Complexity

The complexity of our algorithm depends on the complexity of the classic Lloyd algorithm $O(Idk|\mathcal{D}|)$, where I is the number of iterations. Additionally, it depends on the complexity of eigenvalue decomposition $O(d^3)$ and the calculation of the scatter matrices $O(d^2|\mathcal{D}|)$ for each iteration of the loop. Combining these yields a total complexity of $O(I(mk|\mathcal{D}| + d^2|\mathcal{D}| + d^3))$ and is therefore comparable to most classical subspace clustering algorithms with respect to the cubic runtime in the dimensionality.

Yet, the cubic runtime of the eigen decomposition is nearly a non-issue with modern technology. Currrent GPUs provide high-level APIs for such tasks and distributed computing frameworks allow the decomposition of matrices with millions of entries in mere seconds.[2]

2.5 Relationship to Mixture Models

A further justification for our cost function can be found by exploring the relationships to Gaussian mixture models. It is quite easy to show that the standard k-means cost function is a limit to a Gaussian mixture model with the probability distribution

$$p(\mathbf{x}) = \Pi_i^k \pi_i \mathcal{N}(\mathbf{x}|\mu_i, \sigma\mathbf{I}),$$

where one lets the overall variance σ go to zero [20].

Following this approach, it can be shown that SubKmeans is also a limit to the mixture model with probability distribution:

$$p(\mathbf{x}) = \left[\sum_i^k \pi_i \mathcal{N}(P_C^\mathsf{T} V^\mathsf{T}\mathbf{x}|P_C^\mathsf{T} V^\mathsf{T}\boldsymbol{\mu}_i, \sigma\mathbf{I})\right] \mathcal{N}(P_N^\mathsf{T} V^\mathsf{T}\mathbf{x}|P_N^\mathsf{T} V^\mathsf{T}\boldsymbol{\mu}_{\mathcal{D}}, \sigma\mathbf{I})$$

This can easily be seen by taking the limit of the log-likelihood function with respect to $\sigma \leftarrow 0$, which yields the cost function shown in Eq. 1 (with additional constant terms). We would like to point out that the *clustered* and *noise* space in this mixture model are statistically independent.

3 EXPERIMENTS

We evaluated our method both with respect to its clustering results, as well as its dimensionality reduction properties based on eight real-world datasets of varying size and dimensionality. We got those datasets from the UCI[3] and UCR[4] repositories.

We compare SubKmeans to k-means in combination with two widely used preprocessing methods, which achieve a lower dimensional representation of the data, namely Principal Component Analysis (PCA)[19] and Independent Component Analysis (ICA) [17]. For PCA we used the widely used rule of thumb and kept components such that 90% of the total variance was retained. For ICA we used the method FastICA (with log cosh). As a sensible choice for the number of components in ICA we used k, since one might expect for each cluster that it should at least differ from the other clusters in one independent component. After this preprocessing we applied the classic k-means.

Further, we compare our method to four other proposed algorithms that perform some kind of dimensionality reduction during clustering, namely LDA-k-means, FOSSCLU, ORCLUS and 4C.

For ORCLUS and 4C we used the implementations of the ELKI[5] framework, for FOSSCLU we used the provided Java implementation. The LDA-k-means algorithm is a faithful translation of the repective Matlab version. The k-means and SubKmeans were implemented by the authors in Scala and Breeze. Thereby, we used simple implementations without any sophisticated performance optimization. All experiments were carried out on a computer with an Intel Core i7 3.40GHz, 32GB RAM, running Linux.

We applied standardization (zero mean and unit variance for all features) to all datasets as the sole common preprocessing step. For all algorithms (except for 4C), we set the number of clusters to the number of class labels of the respective dataset. We ran FOSSCLU, LDA-k-means, ICA-k-means, PCA-k-means and SubKmeans each in total 40 times. All of these algorithms are based on a cost function and may run into local minima. In order to account for those insufficient outcomes, we sorted the results by their costs of the respective cost function and removed the half with higher costs. Then we determined the average NMI-score for each algorithm.

ORCLUS has, besides k, the two additional parameters ϵ and a seeding parameter. For ϵ we ran a grid search over $[2; \min(20, d)]$ and tried this parameter 20 times with different seed values and selected the result that achieved the highest average NMI. 4C requires the user to set three parameters. We ran the algorithm for $\epsilon \in [2; 2 \times d]$, *minPts* $\in [1; 15]$ and $\lambda \in [2; \min(20, d)]$ and selected the overall best NMI.

Our *quantitative* results are presented in Table 2. We can see that SubKmeans is a promising clustering algorithm. It achieves with two exceptions the strongest NMI score. In the remaining lower-dimensional datasets, the advantages of the *clustered* space are not as visible as for the higher-dimensional datasets and SubKmeans is only ranked second.

Yet, even for lower dimensional datasets it may be of an advantage to use SubKmeans in terms of visualization. Figure 3 shows

[2] Compare http://docs.nvidia.com/cuda/ and https://databricks.com/blog/2014/07/21/distributing-the-singular-value-decomposition-with-spark.html
[3] https://archive.ics.uci.edu/ml/datasets.html
[4] http://www.timeseriesclassification.com/dataset.php
[5] https://elki-project.github.io/

Table 2: Real-world results (NMI-value). Results marked with † were either aborted after searching for 24 hours (per dataset) or failed due to memory constraints. In either case we show the best results we were able to achieve up to this point. The found dimensionality *m* of the *clustered* space for SubKmeans is shown in brackets.

	Wine ($\|\mathcal{D}\|$=178,k=3,d=9)	Pendigits ($\|\mathcal{D}\|$=7494,k=10,d=16)	Ecoli ($\|\mathcal{D}\|$=327,k=5,d=7)	Seeds ($\|\mathcal{D}\|$=210,k=3,d=7)	Soybean ($\|\mathcal{D}\|$=47,k=4,d=35)	Symbol ($\|\mathcal{D}\|$=995,k=6,d=398)	OliveOil ($\|\mathcal{D}\|$=60,k=4,d=570)	Plane ($\|\mathcal{D}\|$=210,k=7,d=144)
SubKmeans (m)	0.88 (2)	0.70 (9)	**0.68** (4)	**0.74** (2)	**1.00** (3)	**0.79** (5)	**0.75** (3)	**0.89** (6)
PCA-*k*-means	0.71	0.61	0.46	0.73	0.57	0.78	0.61	0.83
ICA-*k*-means	0.42	0.68	0.61	0.73	0.61	**0.79**	0.53	0.83
LDA-*k*-means	**0.93**	0.69	0.62	0.64	0.93	0.56	0.71	0.16
FOSSCLU	0.87	**0.77**	0.62	0.62	**1.00**	0.00†	0.00†	0.00†
ORCLUS	0.30	0.60	**0.68**	0.09	0.65	0.00†	0.40†	0.66
4C	0.52	0.55	0.09	0.53	0.64	0.21†	0.58†	0.78

a comparison between the transformation found by SubKmeans compared to PCA. We can see that the two most important features in the *clustered* space looks quite promising revealing relevant structures not only for synthetic datasets (like in Figure 1), but also for real-world applications. In contrast, the first two features of the *noise* space, do not reveal any major cluster structure to the naked eye and we come to the conclusion that the transformation is indeed able to separate important from unimportant features. If we compare these findings to the first two features of the PCA transformed data, we can see that this transformation reveals clear structures only in few cases (e.g. Wine and Symbol). Even for those datasets, the structural information revealed by SubKmeans often seems superior (e.g. Wine).

We performed additional experiments to reveal the effects of heavily overestimating the number of 'real' clusters in a dataset on the transformation matrix. The results show that the shape of the *clustered* space does not change greatly. Figure 4 shows two examples for Pendigits and Symbols, where *k* was set to twice the number of class labels. The first two dimensions of the clustered space look quite similar to the one shown in Figure 3—even with twice the number of clusters. This shows that SubKmeans indeed finds subspaces, in which the structural information of the clustering is most prominent and that our method also handles situation gracefully, in which the number of clusters is heavily overestimated.

This property may help identify the right number of clusters by visual inspection, even if the number of clusters for the first attempts were initially overestimated. Moreover, sometimes data scientists set a high value for *k* and process the found partition further to create non-spherical clusterings, for instance, by using the found partitions in combination with single-linkage agglomerative clustering [31]. Even in those situations the found transformation is very useful to verify these clusters visually.

Though, we do not want to conceal that the overestimation of *k* also has side effects on *m*. If we significantly overestimate the number of clusters, the algorithm will find more spurious structures within the noise space, with the consequence that *m* increases. Yet, since *V* is sorted by 'importance' this only has a rather small effect on the most significant components of *V* and by adjusting *k* accordingly or by inspecting the corresponding eigenvalues and choosing a threshold-value manually, this effect can be mitigated.

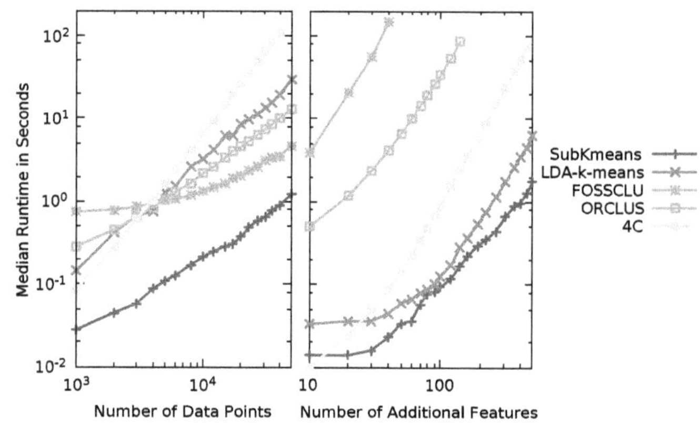

Figure 2: Runtime for varying *d* and $|\mathcal{D}|$

3.1 Runtime Experiments

We want to support our claim that, compared to other algorithms, incorporating some kind of dimensionality reduction, SubKmeans is indeed a fast algorithm. We compare it to FOSSCLU, LDA-*k*-means, ORCLUS and 4C. As basis we used a synthetic dataset containing data points, equally distributed over three well-separated Gaussian clusters. For all algorithms, we initially determined the parameter values yielding the best NMI score and kept them fixed.

We performed two experiments. In the first experiment, we wanted to evaluate the runtime behavior by sampling an increasing number of additional data points. In the second experiment, we wanted to evaluate how SubKmeans behaves for an increasing dimensionality. For this experiment we added additional *noise*-features drawn from a single Gaussian.

Figure 2 shows the results of both experiments. For each dataset and dimensionality configuration, we ran each algorithm ten times and present the median result. We can see that SubKmeans is indeed—among the tested—the fastest algorithm.

The closest competitor to SubKmeans for high-dimensional datasets is LDA-*k*-means. This can be expected, since this algorithm uses almost the same operations—assignment and update steps of *k*-means and the eigen-decomposition of scatter matrices—with an additional matrix inversion.

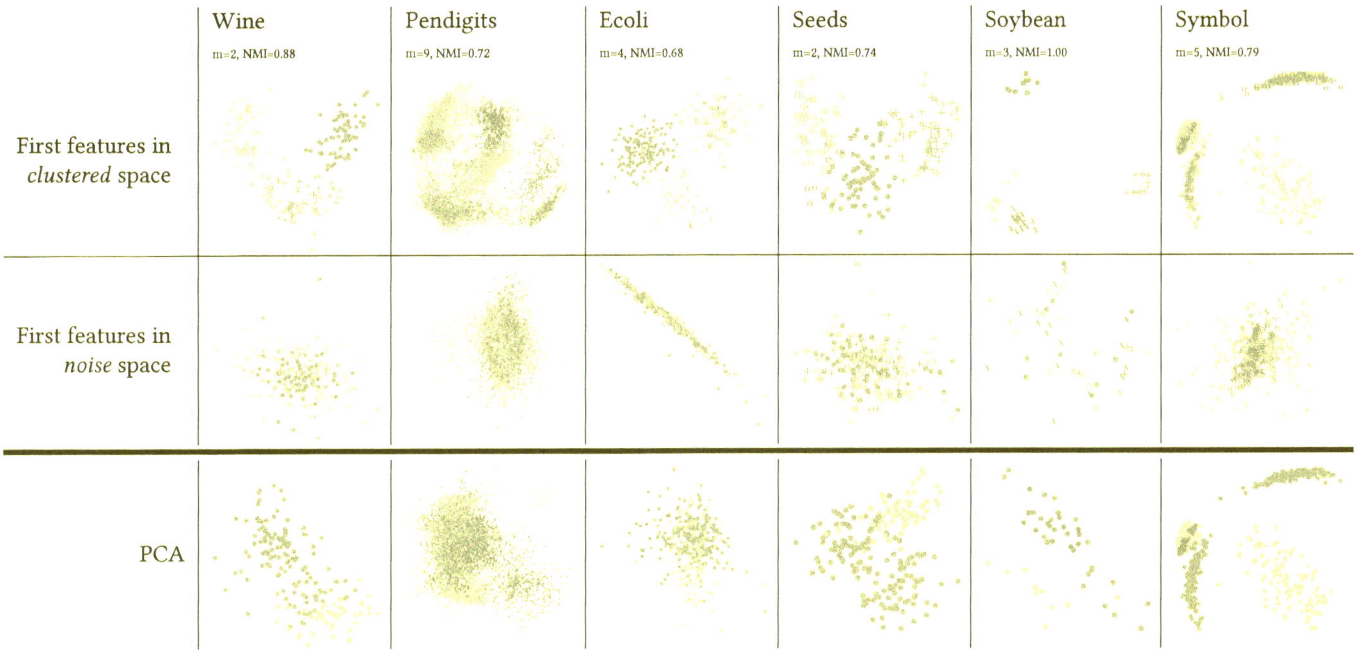

Figure 3: The diagrams show a comparison of PCA vs. the transformation by SubKmeans for the found solution with minimal costs for each dataset. The *clustered* space dimensionality m and the NMI of the model are given below the dataset name. Colors represent the class labels and symbol represent the predicted cluster labels. The first row shows the scatter plot of the first two dimensions of the *clustered* space. The second row shows the scatter plot of the first two dimensions of the *noise* space. The last row shows the first to two features found by PCA.

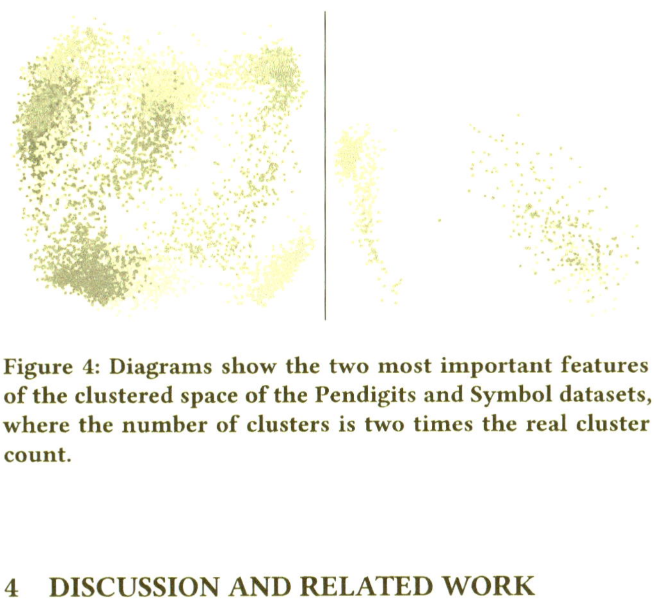

Figure 4: Diagrams show the two most important features of the clustered space of the Pendigits and Symbol datasets, where the number of clusters is two times the real cluster count.

4 DISCUSSION AND RELATED WORK

k-means gets its unbroken popularity from its simplicity, adaptability and execute speed. It has inspired numerous extensions and adaptations, many of which can also be combined in SubKmeans. We present some of these extensions in the following.

Further, we discuss SubKmeans in the context of other methods and algorithms, which either are or incorporate some kind of dimensional reduction or feature selection steps.

k-means Extensions

The simplicity and effectiveness of the k-means algorithm has inspired many adaptations and extensions of the basic idea. In the following we provide only a small, non-exhaustive overview.

The basic idea has been adopted to use the median instead of the mean [18]. The hard cluster assignment is weakened in Fuzzy-c-means [11], in which—much like in mixture models—each data point is proportionally assigned to multiple clusters.

There have been proposed different ways to initialize the cluster centers. The widely used k-means++ algorithm [4] contains an seeding technique, which selects data points as initial centers based on their proportional distance to the previous selected centers. This method has been shown to reduce the number of iterations and achieves, on average, better local minima compared to a random initialization. However, it also has been criticized for its inherent sequential nature. A more recent proposal is k-means|| [5]. In this proposal the initialization of the cluster centers is parallelized, which better fits the growing size of current datasets.

The automated estimation of the number of clusters k has been tackled by different researchers. Either by extending the cost function by a complexity term, like in X-means[25], or by using statistical tests, like in Q-means [16], as a cluster-split criteria. The Linde-Buzo-Gray algorithm [14] doubles the number of clusters for each iteration, but, towards a different end: finding a sufficient codebook for vector quantization. Bisecting k-means [28] follows a hierarchical top-down approach and in each step splits the clusters according to the 2-means.

Some proposals for accelerating the update step are based on kd-trees [23, 24]. Other researchers propose to exploit the triangle inequality [12, 15, 26] to minimize the number of clusters each data point has to be compared to. Further proposals, like [7], suggest exploiting the instruction sets of modern CPUs to parallelize the computation within each core.

A Bayesian treatment of k-means caRn for instance be found in [30], which reverses the roles of expectation and maximization in the classical EM algorithm. In [20] a nonparametric method is presented, which adapts the Dirichlet process together with a modified version of the Gibbs sampling method.

k-means can be extended to non-linearly separable input data via the kernel-trick. This idea was unified with spectral clustering into a common framework [9] and there seems to be a connection to SubKmeans as well, which we are planning to explore more in the future.

Some researchers [8, 10, 32] propose to combine k-means with Linear Discriminant Analysis (LDA), in order to perform a simultaneous dimensional reduction. We discuss the LDA-k-means algorithm ?? in more detail below.

Dimensionality Reduction Techniques

The goal of dimensionality reduction is to find a lower dimensional representation of a high-dimensional dataset. The proposed methods, thereby, make quite different assumptions and introduce a range of different optimization goals.

Probably the single most famous method falling into this category is PCA, which minimizes the reconstruction error. An alternative formulation searches for the directions with the highest variance. Kernel PCA [27] combines this idea with the kernel-trick.

Independent Component Analysis (ICA) [17] is not directly a dimensionality reduction mechanism, but aims at identifying statistically independent sources within the data.

Isomap [29] is a method, which finds a nonlinear lower dimensional representation based on the estimated geometric properties of the data's manifold.

Subspace and Projected Clustering

Many different proposals for clustering in high-dimensional datasets can be grouped under the banner of subspace and projected clustering algorithms. Algorithms in this family assign each cluster its own subspace, in which some cluster-criteria is fulfilled. This distinguishes them from the approach taken in SubKmeans, which identifies one common subspace. Algorithms like CLIQUE [3] or PROCLUS [1] identify only axis-parallel subspaces. This approach has the benefit that clusters are easily explainable by its subspace-features. Algorithms that try to find clusters in arbitrarily oriented subspaces encompass for instance ORCLUS [2] or 4C [6].

Common Subspace Clustering

Besides our own proposal SubKmeans, we identified two other algorithms following the same theme of identifying a single, common subspace for all clusters. The advantage of this approach is that it allows a researcher to interpret the relationship between data points within a cluster, as well as the relationship between clusters within the common subspace.

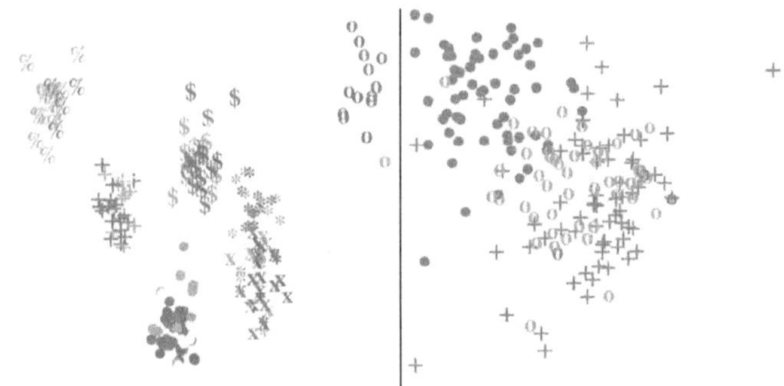

(a) LDA-k-means (b) FOSSCLU

Figure 5: The left scatter plot shows an example of the overfitting behavior of LDA-k-means for the Plane dataset. The right plot shows an example of FOSSCLU for the Wine dataset. It shows the first two features of the *clustered* space. We can see that the cluster structures are occluded, because the features are not sorted by 'importance'. Colors represent class labels. Clusters are symbol-coded.

LDA-k-means [10] combines the supervised Linear Discriminant Analysis (LDA) with k-means. Thereby, it iterates between partitioning the data using k-means and transforming the data into a subspace via LDA, in which the within cluster variance is minimized and the between cluster variance is maximized. However, we identified several drawbacks of this approach compared to SubKmeans. First the subspace is fixed to $(k-1)$-dimensions. Secondly, LDA is known to overfit with growing number of dimensions [22]. We also experienced this behavior in our experiments. Especially for the high-dimensional data sets, the found partition in the transformed space look very confident. The clusters in the respective subspaces are well separated yielding summed squared distances near zero. Yet, at the same time these results yield very bad NMI scores. Figure 5 (a) shows this behavior for the Plane dataset, where we show the scatter plot of the first two components. In that sense, LDA-k-means ignores structures disagreeing with the current partitioning assumption. SubKmeans chooses a different path: the ignored structure must be better explainable by the single noise cluster or otherwise has to be overcome by the clusters in the *clustered* space. Moreover, we see the maximization of the inter-cluster variance can be problematic in a situation, where the number of clusters is overestimated. In such a scenario the LDA tries to push sub-clusters apart that are actually part of a proper bigger cluster. In combination with the overfitting issue, this may not be recognized in high-dimensional datasets. It is possible to use a regularized version of LDA [32], however, this introduces a further parameter, which the user has to specify. At the same time such a regularization parameter would also be possible for SubKmeans—a further research area we are planning to explore.

FOSSCLU [13] is the second algorithm and shares many similarities with SubKmeans. It also searches for an orthonormal transformation, which projects the data onto a subspace. Simultaneously, it uses the EM-algorithm to optimize a crisp GMM. It uses the Minimum Description Length principle to automatically determines the values of k and m. Theoretically, compared to SubKmeans, it should better adapt to the data, much in the same way a classic GMM does compared to k-means. Yet, we determined several speed-related aspects, which speak for the use of SubKmeans over FOSSCLU. First, the transformation matrix is quite difficult to optimize and the proposed algorithm—based on the Jacobi transformation—is very time-consuming, providing only very few opportunities for further optimizations. This is why the proposed algorithm only optimizes the transformation between the two subspaces for a fixed m, but not within them. This means that the transformation matrix in FOSSCLU projects the for the GMM essential structure onto the subspace, but in an arbitrary orientation. The features are therefore not sorted by importance and essential structures within the *clustered* space might still be occluded from the viewer. Figure 5 (b) shows this behavior for the Wine dataset. Here the found solution yields an NMI score of 0.92 and $m = 7$. However, when the user fixes $m = 2$, the transformation yields a *clustered* space similar to that of SubKmeans in Figure 3. In SubKmeans on the other hand, the components of V are sorted corresponding to the feature importance, highlighting the most prominent structures by the first components. Additionally, SubKmeans brings the inherent property to optimize m within each iteration, whereas FOSSCLU has to start a whole EM-optimization for each possible value of m. In summary, FOSSCLU has a major speed disadvantage for datasets with more than twenty dimensions and our experiments confirm that SubKmeans is several orders of magnitude faster than FOSSCLU.

However, we should point out that—as there is no free lunch—SubKmeans has, like all clustering algorithms, its *limitations*. Specifically, it fails at the same well known examples as the classic k-means version.

5 CONCLUSION

In this paper, we propose SubKmeans, an extension of the k-means algorithm, which performs clustering and dimensionality reduction simultaneously without the need for additional parameters (except for k). Thereby, it finds a k-partition together with a—for this clustering—optimal subspace. It has many desirable properties. The most basic, non-optimized version is easy to implement and only uses standard features provided by all data computing frameworks. Even in this basic implementation, it is fast, though this could most likely further increased, for instance by a more sophisticated way of calculating the scatter matrices. Also, one could easily incorporate many other extensions proposed for k-means, e.g. for further speed-ups or estimation of k.

Future efforts may be directed towards the approximation of the transformation matrix V. We are very confident that this can be achieved quite easily by using a randomized singular value decomposition, resulting in further performance improvements for very high-dimensional datasets.

REFERENCES

[1] Charu C Aggarwal, Joel L Wolf, Philip S Yu, Cecilia Procopiuc, and Jong Soo Park. 1999. Fast algorithms for projected clustering. In *ACM SIGMoD Record*, Vol. 28. ACM, 61–72.

[2] Charu C. Aggarwal and Philip S. Yu. 2000. Finding Generalized Projected Clusters in High Dimensional Spaces. In *Proceedings of the 2000 ACM SIGMOD International Conference on Management of Data (SIGMOD '00)*. ACM, New York, NY, USA, 70–81. https://doi.org/10.1145/342009.335383

[3] Rakesh Agrawal, Johannes Gehrke, Dimitrios Gunopulos, and Prabhakar Raghavan. 1998. *Automatic subspace clustering of high dimensional data for data mining applications*. Vol. 27. ACM.

[4] David Arthur and Sergei Vassilvitskii. 2007. k-means++: The advantages of careful seeding. In *Proceedings of the eighteenth annual ACM-SIAM symposium on Discrete algorithms*. Society for Industrial and Applied Mathematics, 1027–1035.

[5] Bahman Bahmani, Benjamin Moseley, Andrea Vattani, Ravi Kumar, and Sergei Vassilvitskii. 2012. Scalable k-means++. *Proceedings of the VLDB Endowment* 5, 7 (2012), 622–633.

[6] Christian Böhm, Karin Kailing, Peer Kröger, and Arthur Zimek. 2004. Computing clusters of correlation connected objects. In *Proceedings of the 2004 ACM SIGMOD international conference on Management of data*. ACM, 455–466.

[7] Christian Böhm and Claudia Plant. 2015. Mining Massive Vector Data on Single Instruction Multiple Data Microarchitectures. In *Data Mining Workshop (ICDMW), 2015 IEEE International Conference on*. IEEE, 597–606.

[8] Fernando De la Torre and Takeo Kanade. 2006. Discriminative cluster analysis. In *Proceedings of the 23rd international conference on Machine learning*. ACM, 241–248.

[9] Inderjit S. Dhillon, Yuqiang Guan, and Brian Kulis. 2004. Kernel k-means: spectral clustering and normalized cuts. In *Proceedings of the Tenth ACM SIGKDD International Conference on Knowledge Discovery and Data Mining, Seattle, Washington, USA, August 22-25, 2004*. 551–556. https://doi.org/10.1145/1014052.1014118

[10] Chris Ding and Tao Li. 2007. Adaptive dimension reduction using discriminant analysis and k-means clustering. In *Proceedings of the 24th international conference on Machine learning*. ACM, 521–528.

[11] Joseph C Dunn. 1973. A fuzzy relative of the ISODATA process and its use in detecting compact well-separated clusters. (1973).

[12] Charles Elkan. 2003. Using the triangle inequality to accelerate k-means. In *ICML*, Vol. 3. 147–153.

[13] Sebastian Goebl, Xiao He, Claudia Plant, and Christian Böhm. 2014. Finding the optimal subspace for clustering. In *Data Mining (ICDM), 2014 IEEE International Conference on*. IEEE, 130–139.

[14] Robert M. Gray and David L. Neuhoff. 1998. Quantization. *IEEE transactions on information theory* 44, 6 (1998), 2325–2383.

[15] Greg Hamerly. 2010. Making k-means even faster. In *Proceedings of the 2010 SIAM international conference on data mining*. SIAM, 130–140.

[16] Greg Hamerly and Charles Elkan. 2004. Learning the k in k-means. (2004).

[17] Aapo Hyvärinen and Erkki Oja. 2000. Independent component analysis: algorithms and applications. *Neural networks* 13, 4 (2000), 411–430.

[18] Anil K Jain and Richard C Dubes. 1988. *Algorithms for clustering data*. Prentice-Hall, Inc.

[19] Ian Jolliffe. 2002. *Principal component analysis*. Wiley Online Library.

[20] Brian Kulis and Michael I Jordan. 2012. Revisiting k-means: New algorithms via Bayesian nonparametrics. *In Proceedings of the 23rd International Conference on Ma- chine Learning* (2012).

[21] Stuart Lloyd. 1982. Least squares quantization in PCM. *IEEE transactions on information theory* 28, 2 (1982), 129–137.

[22] Dijun Luo, Chris HQ Ding, and Heng Huang. 2011. Linear Discriminant Analysis: New Formulations and Overfit Analysis.. In *AAAI*.

[23] Andrew W Moore. 1999. Very fast EM-based mixture model clustering using multiresolution kd-trees. *Advances in Neural information processing systems* (1999), 543–549.

[24] Dan Pelleg and Andrew Moore. 1999. Accelerating exact k-means algorithms with geometric reasoning. In *Proceedings of the fifth ACM SIGKDD international conference on Knowledge discovery and data mining*. ACM, 277–281.

[25] Dan Pelleg, Andrew W Moore, and others. 2000. X-means: Extending K-means with Efficient Estimation of the Number of Clusters.. In *ICML*, Vol. 1.

[26] Steven J Phillips. 2002. Acceleration of k-means and related clustering algorithms. In *Workshop on Algorithm Engineering and Experimentation*. Springer, 166–177.

[27] Bernhard Schölkopf, Alexander Smola, and Klaus-Robert Müller. 1997. Kernel principal component analysis. In *International Conference on Artificial Neural Networks*. Springer, 583–588.

[28] Michael Steinbach, George Karypis, Vipin Kumar, and others. 2000. A comparison of document clustering techniques. In *KDD workshop on text mining*, Vol. 400. Boston, 525–526.

[29] Joshua B Tenenbaum, Vin De Silva, and John C Langford. 2000. A global geometric framework for nonlinear dimensionality reduction. *science* 290, 5500 (2000), 2319–2323.

[30] Max Welling and Kenichi Kurihara. 2006. Bayesian K-Means as a" Maximization-Expectation" Algorithm.. In *SDM*. SIAM, 474–478.

[31] Xindong Wu, Vipin Kumar, J Ross Quinlan, Joydeep Ghosh, Qiang Yang, Hiroshi Motoda, Geoffrey J McLachlan, Angus Ng, Bing Liu, S Yu Philip, and others. 2008. Top 10 algorithms in data mining. *Knowledge and information systems* 14, 1 (2008), 1–37.

[32] Jieping Ye, Zheng Zhao, and Mingrui Wu. 2007. Discriminative K-means for Clustering. In *Advances in Neural Information Processing Systems 20, Proceedings of the Twenty-First Annual Conference on Neural Information Processing Systems, Vancouver, British Columbia, Canada, December 3-6, 2007*. 1649–1656. http://papers.nips.cc/paper/3176-discriminative-k-means-for-clustering

SPARTan: Scalable PARAFAC2 for Large & Sparse Data

Ioakeim Perros
Georgia Institute of Technology
perros@gatech.edu

Evangelos E. Papalexakis
University of California, Riverside
epapalex@cs.ucr.edu

Fei Wang
Weill Cornell Medicine
feiwang03@gmail.com

Richard Vuduc
Georgia Institute of Technology
richie@cc.gatech.edu

Elizabeth Searles
Children's Healthcare Of Atlanta
elizabeth.searles@choa.org

Michael Thompson
Children's Healthcare Of Atlanta
michael.thompson@choa.org

Jimeng Sun
Georgia Institute of Technology
jsun@cc.gatech.edu

ABSTRACT

In exploratory tensor mining, a common problem is how to analyze a set of variables across a set of subjects whose observations do not align naturally. For example, when modeling medical features across a set of patients, the number and duration of treatments may vary widely in time, meaning there is no meaningful way to align their clinical records across time points for analysis purposes. To handle such data, the state-of-the-art tensor model is the so-called PARAFAC2, which yields interpretable and robust output and can naturally handle sparse data. However, its main limitation up to now has been the lack of efficient algorithms that can handle large-scale datasets.

In this work, we fill this gap by developing a scalable method to compute the PARAFAC2 decomposition of large and sparse datasets, called SPARTan. Our method exploits special structure within PARAFAC2, leading to a novel algorithmic reformulation that is both faster (in absolute time) and more memory-efficient than prior work. We evaluate SPARTan on both synthetic and real datasets, showing 22× performance gains over the best previous implementation and also handling larger problem instances for which the baseline fails. Furthermore, we are able to apply SPARTan to the mining of temporally-evolving phenotypes on data taken from real and medically complex pediatric patients. The clinical meaningfulness of the phenotypes identified in this process, as well as their temporal evolution over time for several patients, have been endorsed by clinical experts.

KEYWORDS

Sparse Tensor Factorization; PARAFAC2; Phenotyping; Unsupervised learning

ACM ISBN 978-1-4503-4887-4/17/08...$15.00
https://doi.org/10.1145/3097983.3098014

ACM Reference format:
Ioakeim Perros, Evangelos E. Papalexakis, Fei Wang, Richard Vuduc, Elizabeth Searles, Michael Thompson, and Jimeng Sun. 2017. SPARTan: Scalable PARAFAC2 for Large & Sparse Data. In *Proceedings of KDD '17, Halifax, NS, Canada, August 13-17, 2017,* 10 pages.
https://doi.org/10.1145/3097983.3098014

1 INTRODUCTION

This paper concerns tensor-based analysis and mining of multi-modal data where observations are difficult or impossible to align naturally along one of its modes. A concrete example of such data is electronic health records (EHR), our primary motivating application. An EHR dataset contains longitudinal patient information, represented as an event sequence of multiple modalities such as diagnoses, medications, procedures, and lab results. An important characteristic of such event sequences is that there is no simple way to align observations in time across patients. For instance, different patients may have varying length records between the first admission and the most recent hospital discharge; or, two patients whose records' have the same length may still not have a sensible chronological alignment as disease stages and patient progress vary.

For tensor methods, such data poses a significant challenge. Consider the most popular tensor analysis method in data mining, the canonical polyadic (CP) decomposition (also known as PARAFAC or CANDECOMP) [, ,]. A dataset with three modes might be stored as an $I \times J \times K$ tensor $\mathcal{X}$, which CP then decomposes into a sum of multi-way outer (rank-one) products, $\mathcal{X} \approx \sum_{r=1}^{R} \mathbf{u}_r \circ \mathbf{v}_r \circ \mathbf{w}_r$, where $\mathbf{u}_r, \mathbf{v}_r, \mathbf{w}_r$ are column vectors of size I, J, K, respectively, that effectively represents latent data concepts. Its popularity owes to its *intuitive output structure* and *uniqueness* property that makes the model reliable to interpret [, , , ,], as well as the existence of scalable algorithms and software [, ,]. However, to make, say, the irregular time points in EHR one of the input tensor modes would require finding some way to align time. This fact is an inherent limitation of applying the CP model: any preprocessing to aggregate across time may lose temporal patterns [, ,], while more sophisticated temporal feature extraction methods typically need continuous and sufficiently long temporal measures to work [ ]. Other proposed methods specific to healthcare applications may give some good results [, ,] but lack the *uniqueness*

Target Rank	10				40			
#nnz(Millions)	63	125	250	500	63	125	250	500
SPARTan	7.4	8.9	11.5	15.4	14	18.4	61	114
Sparse PARAFAC2	24.4	60.1	72.3	194.5	275.2	408.1	OoM	OoM

Table 1: Running time comparison: Time in minutes of one iteration for increasingly larger datasets (63m to 500m) and fixed target rank (two cases considered: $R = \{10, 40\}$). The mode sizes for the datasets constructed are: 1Mil. subjects, 5K variables and a maximum of 100 observations per subject. OoM (Out of Memory) denotes that the execution failed due to the excessive amount of memory requested. Experiments are conducted on a server with 1TB of RAM.

guarantee; thus, it becomes harder to reliably extract the actual latent concepts as an equivalent arbitrary rotation of them will provide the same fit. All of these weaknesses apply in the EHR scenario outlined above.

In fact, the type of data in the motivating example are quite general: consider that we have K subjects, for which we record J variables and we permit each k-th subject to have I_k observations, which are not necessarily comparable among the different subjects. For this type of data, Harshman proposed the *PARAFAC2 model* [17]. It is a more flexible version of CP: while CP applies the same factors across a collection of matrices, PARAFAC2 instead applies the same factor along one mode and allows the other factor matrix to vary [25]. At the same time, it preserves the desirable properties of CP, such as uniqueness [18, 24, 35, 37]. As shown in Figure 1, PARAFAC2 approximates each one of the input matrices as: $\mathbf{X}_k \approx \mathbf{U}_k \, \mathbf{S}_k \, \mathbf{V}^T$, where $\mathbf{U}_k$ is of size $I_k \times R$, $\mathbf{S}_k$ is a diagonal R-by-R, $\mathbf{V}$ is of size $J \times R$ and R is the target rank of the decomposition.

Despite its applicability, the lack of efficient PARAFAC2 decomposition algorithms has been cited as a reason for its limited popularity [6, 12]. Overall, PARAFAC2 has been mostly used for dense data (e.g., [24]) or sparse data with a small number of subjects [12]. To our knowledge, no work has assessed PARAFAC2 for large-scale sparse data, as well as the challenges arising by doing so.

In this paper, we propose SPARTan (abbreviated from Scalable PARafac Two) to fill this gap, with a focus on achieving scalability on large and sparse datasets. Our methodological advance is a new algorithm for scaling up the core computational kernel arising in the PARAFAC2 fitting algorithm. SPARTan achieves the best of both worlds in terms of speed and memory efficiency: *a)* it is *faster* than a highly-optimized baseline in all cases considered for both real (Figures 5, 6, 7) and synthetic (Table 1) datasets, achieving up to 22× performance gain; *b)* at the same time, SPARTan is *more scalable*, in that it can execute in reasonable time for large problem instances when the baseline fails due to excessive memory consumption (Table 1). We summarize our contributions as:

- **Scalable PARAFAC2 method:** We propose SPARTan, a scalable algorithm fitting the PARAFAC2 model on large and sparse data.
- **Evaluation on various datasets:** We evaluate the scalability of our approach using datasets originating from two different application domains, namely a longitudinal EHR and a time-evolving movie ratings' dataset, which is also publicly available. Additionally, we perform synthetic data experiments.
- **Real-world case study**: We performed a case study of applying SPARTan on temporal phenotyping over medically complex pediatric patients in collaboration with Children's Healthcare of Atlanta (CHOA). The phenotypes and temporal trends discovered were endorsed by a clinical expert from CHOA.

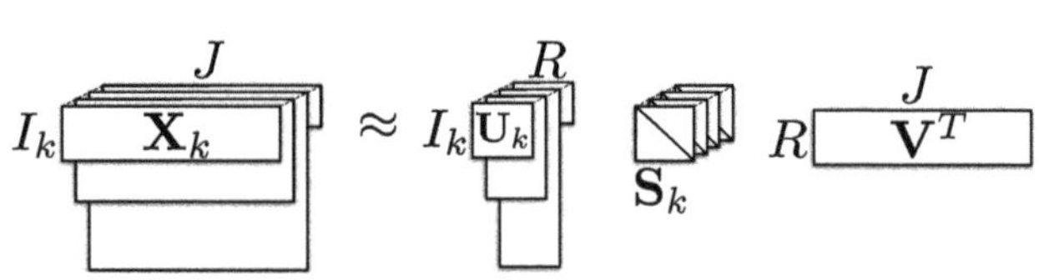

Figure 1: Illustration of the PARAFAC2 model.

To promote reproducibility, our code is open-sourced and publicly available at: https://github.com/kperros/SPARTan.

2 BACKGROUND

Next we describe the necessary terminology and operations regarding tensors. Then, we provide an overview of the CP model and relevant fitting algorithm. In Table 2, we summarize the notations used throughout the paper.

2.1 Tensors and Tensor Operations

The *order* of a tensor denotes the number of its dimensions, also known as ways or modes (e.g., matrices are 2-order tensors). A *fiber* is a vector extracted from a tensor by fixing all modes but one. For example, a matrix column is a mode-1 fiber. A *slice* is a matrix extracted from a tensor by fixing all modes but two. In particular, the $\mathbf{X}(:,:,k)$ slices of a third-order tensor $\mathcal{X}$ are called the frontal ones and we succinctly denote them as $\mathbf{X}_k$ [25]. *Matricization*, also called *reshaping* or *unfolding*, logically reorganizes tensors into other forms without changing the values themselves. The mode-n matricization of a N-order tensor $\mathcal{X} \in \mathbb{R}^{I_1 \times I_2 \times \cdots \times I_N}$ is denoted by

Symbol	Definition
$\mathcal{X}$, $\mathbf{X}$, $\mathbf{x}$, x	Tensor, matrix, vector, scalar
$\mathbf{X}^{\dagger}$	Moore-Penrose pseudoinverse
$\mathbf{X}(:, i)$	Spans the entire i-th column of $\mathbf{X}$ (same for tensors)
$\mathbf{X}(i, :)$	Spans the entire i-th row of $\mathbf{X}$ (same for tensors)
$diag(\mathbf{x})$	Diagonal matrix with vector $\mathbf{x}$ on the diagonal
$diag(\mathbf{X})$	Extract diagonal of matrix $\mathbf{X}$
$\mathbf{X}_k$	shorthand for $\mathbf{X}(:, :, k)$ (k-th frontal slice of tensor $\mathcal{X}$)
$\{\mathbf{X}_k\}$	the collection of $\mathbf{X}_k$ matrices, for all valid k
$\mathbf{X}_{(n)}$	mode-n matricization of tensor $\mathcal{X}$
$\circ$	Outer product
$\otimes$	Kronecker product
$\odot$	Khatri-Rao product
$*$	Hadamard (element-wise) product

Table 2: Notations used throughout the paper.

$\mathbf{X}_{(n)} \in \mathbb{R}^{I_n \times I_1 I_2 \ldots I_{n-1} I_{n+1} \ldots I_N}$ and arranges the mode-n fibers of the tensor as columns of the resulting matrix.

2.2 CP Decomposition

The CP decomposition [, ,] of a third-order tensor $\mathcal{X} \in \mathbb{R}^{I \times J \times K}$ is its approximation by a sum of three-way outer products:

$$\mathcal{X} \approx \sum_{r=1}^{R} \mathbf{u}_r \circ \mathbf{v}_r \circ \mathbf{w}_r \tag{1}$$

where $\mathbf{u}_r \in \mathbb{R}^I, \mathbf{v}_r \in \mathbb{R}^J$ and $\mathbf{w}_r \in \mathbb{R}^K$ are column vectors. If we assemble the column vectors $\mathbf{u}_r, \mathbf{v}_r, \mathbf{w}_r$ as: $\mathbf{U} = [\mathbf{u}_1\ \mathbf{u}_2\ \ldots\ \mathbf{u}_R] \in \mathbb{R}^{I \times R}, \mathbf{V} = [\mathbf{v}_1\ \mathbf{v}_2\ \ldots\ \mathbf{v}_R] \in \mathbb{R}^{J \times R}, \mathbf{W} = [\mathbf{w}_1\ \mathbf{w}_2\ \ldots\ \mathbf{w}_R] \in \mathbb{R}^{K \times R}$, then $\mathbf{U}, \mathbf{V}, \mathbf{W}$ are called the *factor matrices*. Interpretation of CP is very intuitive: we consider that the input tensor can be summarized as R latent concepts. Then, for each r-th concept, the vectors $(\mathbf{u}_r, \mathbf{v}_r, \mathbf{w}_r)$ are considered as soft-clustering membership indicators, for the corresponding I, J and K elements of each mode. An equivalent formulation of Relation ( ) w.r.t. the frontal slices $\mathbf{X}_k$ of the input tensor $\mathcal{X}$ is [ ]:

$$\mathbf{X}_k \approx \mathbf{U}\, \mathbf{S}_k\, \mathbf{V}^T \tag{2}$$

where $k = 1, 2, \ldots, K$ and $\mathcal{S} \in \mathbb{R}^{R \times R \times K}$ is an auxiliary tensor. Each frontal slice $\mathbf{S}_k$ of $\mathcal{S}$ contains the row vector $\mathbf{W}(k,:)$ along its diagonal: $\mathbf{S}_k = diag(\mathbf{W}(k,:))$. Relation ( ) provides another viewpoint of interpreting the CP model, through its correspondence to the Singular Value Decomposition (SVD): each slice $\mathbf{X}_k$ is decomposed to a set of factor matrices $\mathbf{U}, \mathbf{V}$ (similar to the singular vectors) which are common for all the slices, and a diagonal middle matrix (similar to the singular values) which varies for each k-th slice. Note, however, that no orthogonality constraints are imposed on $\mathbf{U}, \mathbf{V}$ of the CP model, as in the SVD [ ].

Uniqueness. A fundamental property of CP is uniqueness [,]. The issue with non-uniqueness can be exemplified via matrix factorization as follows [,]: If a matrix $\mathbf{X}$ is approximated by the product of $\mathbf{A}\mathbf{B}^T$, then it can also be approximated with the same error by $\mathbf{A}\mathbf{Q}\mathbf{Q}^{-1}\mathbf{B}^T = \tilde{\mathbf{A}}\tilde{\mathbf{B}}^T$, for any invertible $\mathbf{Q}$. Thus, we can easily construct two completely different sets of rank-one factors that sum to the original matrix. Inevitably, this hurts interpretability, since we cannot know whether our solution is an arbitrarily rotated version of the actual latent factors. In contrast to matrix factorization or Tucker decomposition [ ], Kruskal [ ] proved that CP is unique, under the condition: $k_{\mathbf{U}} + k_{\mathbf{V}} + k_{\mathbf{W}} \geq 2R + 2$, where $k_{\mathbf{U}}$ is the k-rank of $\mathbf{U}$, defined as the maximum value k such that any k columns are linearly independent. The only exception is related to elementary indeterminacies of scaling and permutation of the component vectors [,]. In sum, the CP decomposition is pursuing the true underlying latent information of the input tensor and provides reliable interpretation for unsupervised approaches.

Fitting the CP model. Perhaps the most popular algorithm for fitting the CP model is the CP-Alternating Least Squares (CP-ALS) [,], listed in Algorithm . The main idea is to solve for one factor matrix at a time, by fixing the others. In that way, each subproblem is reduced to a linear least-squares problem. In case the input tensor contains non-negative values, a non-negative least-squares solver (e.g., [ ]) can be used instead of an unconstrained one, to further improve the factors' interpretability [ ].

Due to the ever increasing need for CP decompositions in data mining, the parallel CP-ALS for sparse tensors has been extensively studied in the recent literature for both single-node and distributed settings (e.g., [, , , ,]). A pioneering work in addressing scalability issues for sparse tensors was provided by Bader and Kolda [ ] [1]. The authors identified and scaled up the algorithm's bottleneck, which is the materialization of the Matricized-Tensor-Times-Khatri-Rao-Product (MTTKRP). For example, in Algorithm , the MTTKRP corresponds to the computation of $\mathbf{X}_{(1)}(\mathbf{W} \odot \mathbf{V})$ when solving for $\mathbf{U}$. For large and sparse tensors, a naive construction of the MTTKRP requires huge storage and computational cost and has to be avoided.

Algorithm 1 CP-ALS

Require: $\mathcal{X} \in \mathbb{R}^{I \times J \times K}$ and target rank R
Ensure: $\lambda \in \mathbb{R}^R$, $\mathbf{U} \in \mathbb{R}^{I \times R}$, $\mathbf{V} \in \mathbb{R}^{J \times R}$, $\mathbf{W} \in \mathbb{R}^{K \times R}$
1: Initialize $\mathbf{V}, \mathbf{W}$
2: **while** convergence criterion is not met **do**
3: $\quad \mathbf{U} \leftarrow \mathbf{X}_{(1)}(\mathbf{W} \odot \mathbf{V})(\mathbf{W}^T\mathbf{W} * \mathbf{V}^T\mathbf{V})^{\dagger}$
4: $\quad$ Normalize columns of $\mathbf{U}$
5: $\quad \mathbf{V} \leftarrow \mathbf{X}_{(2)}(\mathbf{W} \odot \mathbf{U})(\mathbf{W}^T\mathbf{W} * \mathbf{U}^T\mathbf{U})^{\dagger}$
6: $\quad$ Normalize columns of $\mathbf{V}$
7: $\quad \mathbf{W} \leftarrow \mathbf{X}_{(3)}(\mathbf{V} \odot \mathbf{U})(\mathbf{V}^T\mathbf{V} * \mathbf{U}^T\mathbf{U})^{\dagger}$
8: $\quad$ Normalize columns of $\mathbf{W}$ and store norm in λ
9: **end while**

3 PARAFAC2 OVERVIEW & CHALLENGES

3.1 Model

As we introduced in Section , the PARAFAC2 model [ ] can successfully deal with an incomparable mode of each slice $\mathbf{X}_k$ [ ]. It does so, by introducing a set of $\mathbf{U}_k$ matrices replacing the $\mathbf{U}$ matrix of the CP model in Relation ( ). Thus, each slice $\mathbf{X}_k$ is decomposed as shown in Figure :

$$\mathbf{X}_k \approx \mathbf{U}_k\, \mathbf{S}_k\, \mathbf{V}^T \tag{3}$$

where $k = 1, \ldots, K, \mathbf{U}_k \in \mathbb{R}^{I_k \times R}, \mathbf{S}_k \in \mathbb{R}^{R \times R}$ is diagonal and $\mathbf{V} \in \mathbb{R}^{J \times R}$. To preserve uniqueness, Harshman [ ] imposed the constraint that the cross product $\mathbf{U}_k^T\mathbf{U}_k$ is invariant regardless which subject k is involved [,]. In that way, the CP model's invariance of the factor $\mathbf{U}_k$ itself (or $\mathbf{U}$ given its invariance to k), is relaxed [ ]. For the above constraint to hold, each $\mathbf{U}_k$ factor is decomposed as:

$$\mathbf{U}_k = \mathbf{Q}_k H \tag{4}$$

where $\mathbf{Q}_k$ is of size $I_k \times R$ and has orthonormal columns, and $\mathbf{H}$ is an $R \times R$ matrix, which does not vary by k [ ]. Then, the constraint that $\mathbf{U}_k^T\mathbf{U}_k$ is constant over k is implicitly enforced, as follows: $\mathbf{U}_k^T\mathbf{U}_k = \mathbf{H}^T\mathbf{Q}_k^T\mathbf{Q}_k\mathbf{H} = \mathbf{H}^T\mathbf{H} = \mathbf{\Phi}$.

There have been several results regarding the uniqueness property of PARAFAC2 [, ,]. The most relevant [ ] towards our large-scale data scenario (i.e., the number of K subjects can easily reach the order of hundreds of thousands) is that a rank-R PARAFAC2 model is unique if $\mathbf{\Phi}$ and $\mathbf{V}$ have rank R, $\mathbf{\Phi}$ has no zero entries and the number of K subjects is at least: $R\,(R+1)\,(R+2)\,(R+3)\,/\,24$ [ ]. Note that this bound on the number of K subjects is

[1] The contributions of [ ], among others, are summarized as the Tensor Toolbox [ ], which is widely acclaimed as the state-of-the-art package for single-node sparse tensor operations and algorithms.

sufficient but not necessary to achieve uniqueness; it is conjectured (as evaluated through simulation studies) that PARAFAC2 provides unique solutions as long as $K \geq 4$ [19, 24, 35].

3.2 Classical Algorithm for PARAFAC2

Below, we overview the classical algorithm for fitting PARAFAC2, proposed by Kiers et al. [24]. Their original algorithm expects dense data as input. Its objective function is as follows:

$$\min_{\{\mathbf{U}_k\},\{\mathbf{S}_k\},\mathbf{V}} \sum_{k=1}^{K} ||\mathbf{X}_k - \mathbf{U}_k\mathbf{S}_k\mathbf{V}^T||_F^2$$

subject to: $\mathbf{U}_k = \mathbf{Q}_k\mathbf{H}$, $\mathbf{Q}_k^T\mathbf{Q}_k = \mathbf{I}$ and $\mathbf{S}_k$ to be diagonal. Algorithm 2 follows an Alternating Least Squares (ALS) approach, divided in two distinct steps: first (lines 3-6), the set of column-orthonormal matrices $\{\mathbf{Q}_k\}$ is computed by fixing $\mathbf{H}, \mathbf{V}, \{\mathbf{S}_k\}$. This step can be derived by examining the pursuit of each $\mathbf{Q}_k$ as an individual Orthogonal Procrustes Problem [15] of the form:

$$\min_{\mathbf{Q}_k} ||\mathbf{X}_k - \mathbf{Q}_k\mathbf{H}\mathbf{S}_k\mathbf{V}^T||_F^2 \tag{5}$$

subject to $\mathbf{Q}_k^T\mathbf{Q}_k = \mathbf{I}$. Given the SVD of $\mathbf{H}\mathbf{S}_k\mathbf{V}^T\mathbf{X}_k^T$ as $\mathbf{P}_k\Sigma_k\mathbf{Z}_k$, the minimum of objective (5) over column-orthonormal $\mathbf{Q}_k$ is given by $\mathbf{Q}_k = \mathbf{Z}_k\mathbf{P}_k^T$ [15, 24].

Second, after solving for and fixing $\{\mathbf{Q}_k\}$, we find a solution for the rest of the factors as:

$$\min_{\mathbf{H},\{\mathbf{S}_k\},\mathbf{V}} \sum_{k=1}^{K} ||\mathbf{Q}_k^T\mathbf{X}_k - \mathbf{H}\mathbf{S}_k\mathbf{V}^T||_F^2 \tag{6}$$

where $\mathbf{S}_k$ is diagonal. Note the equivalence of the above objective with the CP "slice-wise" formulation of Relation (2). This equivalence implies that minimizing the objective (6) is achieved by executing the CP decomposition on a tensor $\mathcal{Y} \in \mathbb{R}^{R\times J\times K}$ with frontal slices $\mathbf{Y}_k = \mathbf{Q}_k^T\mathbf{X}_k$ (lines 7-10). In order to avoid executing all the costly CP iterations, Kiers et al. [24] propose to run a single CP-ALS iteration, since this suffices to decrease the objective.

The PARAFAC2 model can be extended so that non-negative constraints are imposed on $\{\mathbf{S}_k\}, \mathbf{V}$ factors [7]. This is a property inherited by the CP-ALS iteration, where we can constrain the factors $\mathbf{V}$ and $\mathbf{W}$ to be non-negative, as discussed in Section 2.2. Note that constraining the $\{\mathbf{U}_k\}$ factors to be non-negative as well is not as simple, and a naive approach would violate the model properties [8].

3.3 Challenges of PARAFAC2 on sparse data

Next, we summarize a set of crucial observations regarding the computational challenges, when executing Algorithm 2 on large, sparse data:

Bottleneck of Algorithm 2. Regarding the 1st step (lines 3-6), in practice for sparse $\mathbf{X}_k$, each one of the K sub-problems scales as $O(min(RI^2, R^2I))$, due to the SVD involved [38], where I is an upper bound for I_k. Note that this computation can be trivially parallelized for all K subjects. On the other hand, the 2nd step (lines 7-10) is dominated by the MTTKRP computation (which as we discussed in Section 2 is the bottleneck of sparse CP-ALS). Thus, it scales as $3R\ nnz(\mathcal{Y})$ [34], using state-of-the-art sparse tensor libraries for single-node [4]. Given that none of the input matrices $\mathbf{X}_k$ is

---

Algorithm 2 PARAFAC2-ALS [24]

Require: $\{\mathbf{X}_k \in \mathbb{R}^{I_k\times J}\}$ for $k = 1, \ldots, K$ and target rank R
Ensure: $\{\mathbf{U}_k \in \mathbb{R}^{I_k\times R}\}$, $\{\mathbf{S}_k \in \mathbb{R}^{R\times R}\}$ for $k = 1, \ldots, K$, $\mathbf{V} \in \mathbb{R}^{J\times R}$

1: Initialize $\mathbf{H} \in \mathbb{R}^{R\times R}$, $\mathbf{V}$, $\{\mathbf{S}_k\}$ for $k = 1, \ldots, K$
2: **while** convergence criterion is not met **do**
3:   **for** $k = 1, \ldots, K$ **do**
4:     $[\mathbf{P}_k, \Sigma_k, \mathbf{Z}_k] \leftarrow$ truncated SVD of $\mathbf{H}\mathbf{S}_k\mathbf{V}^T\mathbf{X}_k^T$ at rank R
5:     $\mathbf{Q}_k \leftarrow \mathbf{Z}_k\mathbf{P}_k^T$
6:   **end for**
7:   **for** k=1,…,K **do**
8:     $\mathbf{Y}_k \leftarrow \mathbf{Q}_k^T\mathbf{X}_k$ *// construct slice* $\mathbf{Y}_k$ *of tensor* $\mathcal{Y}$
9:   **end for**
10:   Run a single iteration of CP-ALS on $\mathcal{Y}$ to compute $\mathbf{H}$, $\mathbf{V}$, $\mathbf{W}$
11:   **for** $k = 1, \ldots, K$ **do**
12:     $\mathbf{S}_k \leftarrow diag(\mathbf{W}(k, :))$
13:   **end for**
14: **end while**
15: **for** $k = 1, \ldots, K$ **do**
16:   $\mathbf{U}_k \leftarrow \mathbf{Q}_k\mathbf{H}$ *// Assemble* $\mathbf{U}_k$
17: **end for**

---

completely zero, then: $3R\ nnz(\mathcal{Y}) \geq 3KR^2$. As a result, this step becomes the bottleneck of Algorithm 2 for large and sparse "irregular" tensors, since it cannot be parallelized w.r.t. the K subjects, as trivially happens with the 1st one.

Imbalance of mode sizes of $\mathcal{Y}$. The size of the intermediate tensor $\mathcal{Y}$ formed is $R \times J \times K$. For large-scale data, we expect that $R << K, J$ since R corresponds to the target rank of the overall PARAFAC2 decomposition. Note that this property of "size imbalance" may not hold for a general large tensor, thus generic CP-ALS solvers (e.g., [4]) cannot exploit it.

Structured sparsity of $\{\mathbf{X}_k\}$. First, we observe that even if the input slices $\{\mathbf{X}_k \in \mathbb{R}^{I_k\times J}\}$ are very sparse, all their I_k rows will contain at least one non-zero element. If this is not the case, we can simply filter the zero ones, without affecting the result. However, this does not hold for the J columns of each $\mathbf{X}_k$, which have to be aligned across all K subjects. A direct consequence of that in real datasets is that very few variables (relative to their total number) are typically recorded for each subject. For example, in the EHR data use case introduced in Section 1, very few medical features are recorded for each patient.

Driven by this observation, we are motivated to computationally exploit any column sparsity (i.e., cases where many columns will be completely zero) of each one of the input matrices $\mathbf{X}_k$.

4 THE SPARTAN APPROACH

4.1 Overview

Motivated by the challenges presented in Section 3, we propose a specialized version of the Matricized-Tensor-Times-Khatri-Rao-Product (MTTKRP) kernel, specifically targeting the intermediate tensor $\mathcal{Y} \in \mathbb{R}^{R\times J\times K}$ formed within the PARAFAC2-ALS algorithm. We first provide an overview of the properties that our approach exhibits:

- It is *fully parallelizable w.r.t. the K subjects.* This property is crucial towards scaling up for large-scale "irregular" tensors.
- It *exploits the structured sparsity* of the input frontal slices $\{\mathbf{X}_k\}$. This is possible due to the observation that the k-th frontal slice $\mathbf{Y}_k = \mathbf{Q}_k^T\mathbf{X}_k$ of $\mathcal{Y}$ follows precisely the column sparsity pattern of $\mathbf{X}_k$. In particular, if c_k is the number of columns of $\mathbf{X}_k$ containing

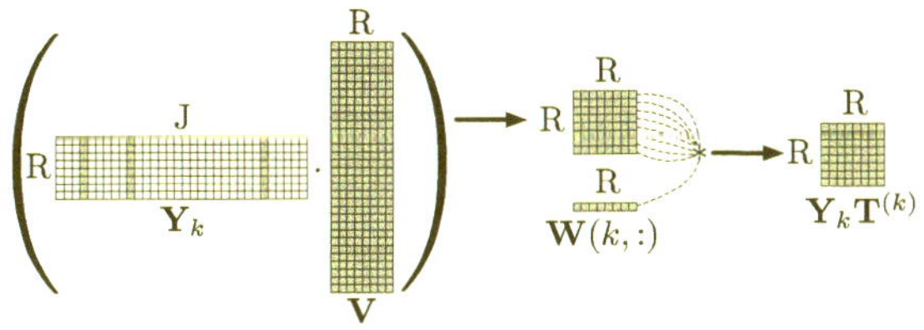

Figure 2: SPARTan computations for the MTTKRP w.r.t. the 1st mode. For each k-th partial result of Equation (8), we only use the rows of V factor matrix corresponding to the non-zero columns of Y_k. For each of the R rows of the resulting matrix, we compute the Hadamard product with $W(k, :)$, which is the k-th row of the factor matrix W. The described computations fulfill all of the desirable properties presented in Section 4.1.

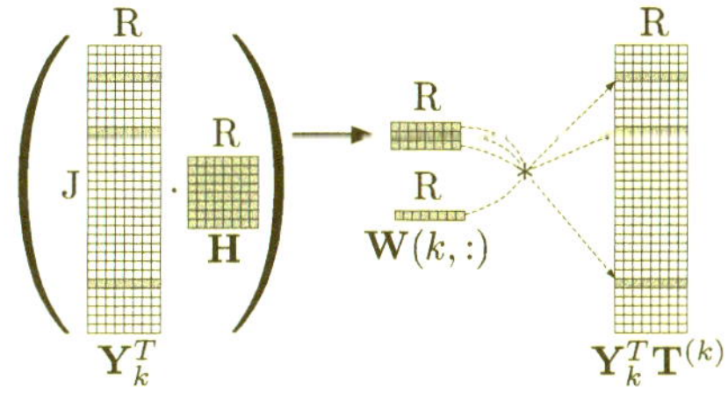

Figure 3: SPARTan computations for the MTTKRP w.r.t. the 2nd mode. For each k-th partial result of Equation (12), we perform the vector-matrix multiplications for each non-zero row of Y_k^T. Then, for each intermediate vector, the Hadamard product with $W(k, :)$ is computed. Finally, we distribute the vectors to their corresponding positions in $Y_k^T T^{(k)}$. As in the case w.r.t. the 1st mode, we limit computations to the necessary ones corresponding to the non-zero columns of Y_k and all the properties presented in Section 4.1 are preserved.

at least one non-zero element, then $\mathbf{Y}_k$ will contain $R\, c_k$ non-zero elements located in the positions of the non-zero columns of X_k. Exploiting structured sparsity is indispensable towards minimizing intermediate data and computations to the absolutely necessary ones.

- As a by-product of the above, SPARTan *avoids unnecessary data re-organization* (tensor reshaping/permutations), since all operations are formulated w.r.t. the frontal slices $\mathbf{Y}_k$ of tensor $\mathcal{Y}$. In fact, our approach never forms the tensor $\mathcal{Y}$ explicitly and directly utilizes the available collection of matrices $\{\mathbf{Y}_k\}$ instead.

4.2 Methodology

In the following, we describe the design of our MTTKRP kernel for each one of the tensor modes. We use the notation $\mathbf{M}^{(i)}$ to denote the MTTKRP corresponding to the i-th tensor mode. Note that our factor matrices are: $\mathbf{H} \in \mathbb{R}^{R \times R}, \mathbf{V} \in \mathbb{R}^{J \times R}$ and $\mathbf{W} \in \mathbb{R}^{K \times R}$ as in Line 10 of Algorithm 2.

Mode-1 MTTKRP. First, we re-visit the MTTKRP equation:

$$\mathbf{M}^{(1)} = \mathbf{Y}_{(1)} \left(\mathbf{W} \odot \mathbf{V}\right), \tag{7}$$

where $\mathbf{M}^{(1)} \in \mathbb{R}^{R \times R}, \mathbf{Y}_{(1)} \in \mathbb{R}^{R \times KJ}$. In order to attempt to parallelize the above computation w.r.t. the K subjects, we define the matrix $\mathbf{T}^{(k)} \in \mathbb{R}^{J \times R}$ to denote the k-th vertical block of the Khatri-Rao Product $\mathbf{W} \odot \mathbf{V} \in \mathbb{R}^{KJ \times R}$:

$$\mathbf{W} \odot \mathbf{V} = \begin{bmatrix} \mathbf{T}^{(1)} \\ \mathbf{T}^{(2)} \\ \vdots \\ \mathbf{T}^{(K)} \end{bmatrix}$$

We then remark that $\mathbf{Y}_{(1)}$ (i.e., mode-1 matricization of $\mathcal{Y}$) consists of an horizontal concatenation of the tensor's frontal slices $\mathbf{Y}_k$. Thus, we exploit the fact that the matrix multiplication in Equation (7) can be expressed as the sum of outer products or more generally, as a sum of block-by-block matrix multiplications:

$$\mathbf{M}^{(1)} = \sum_{k=1}^{K} \mathbf{Y}_k\, \mathbf{T}^{(k)} \tag{8}$$

Through Equation (8), the computation can be easily parallelized over K independent sub-problems and then sum the partial results. This directly utilizes the frontal slices $\mathbf{Y}_k$ without further tensor organization. However, it constructs the whole Khatri-Rao Product (in the form of blocks $\mathbf{T}^{(k)}$). In order to avoid that, we first state an expression for each i-th row of $\mathbf{T}^{(k)}$, which is a direct consequence of the Khatri-Rao Product definition:

$$\mathbf{T}^{(k)}(i, :) = \mathbf{V}(i, :) * \mathbf{W}(k, :), \tag{9}$$

where $*$ stands for the Hadamard (element-wise) product. Then, we express the j-th row of each partial result of Equation (8) as follows:

$$\begin{aligned} [\mathbf{Y}_k\, \mathbf{T}^{(k)}]_{j,:} &= \mathbf{Y}_k(j, :)\, \mathbf{T}^{(k)} \\ &\overset{Eq.(9)}{=} \sum_i \mathbf{Y}_k(j, i) * (\mathbf{V}(i, :) * \mathbf{W}(k, :)) \\ &\overset{(a)}{=} \left(\sum_i \mathbf{Y}_k(j, i) * \mathbf{V}(i, :)\right) * \mathbf{W}(k, :) \\ &\overset{(b)}{=} (\mathbf{Y}_k(j, :)\, \mathbf{V}) * \mathbf{W}(k, :), \end{aligned} \tag{10}$$

where (a) stems from the associative property of the Hadamard product and the fact that $\mathbf{W}(k, :)$ is independent of the summation and (b) from the calculation of matrix multiplication as a sum of outer-products (in particular, we encounter the sub-case of vector-matrix product).

Equation (10) suggests an efficient way to compute the partial results of Equation (8), which we illustrate in Figure 2. First, we compute the matrix product $\mathbf{Y}_k \mathbf{V}$ and for each row of the intermediate result of size $R \times R$, we compute the Hadamard product with $\mathbf{W}(k, :)$. Note that, as we discussed in Section 3, $\mathbf{Y}_k$ is expected to be column-sparse in practice, thus multiplying by $\mathbf{V}$ uses only those rows of $\mathbf{V}$ corresponding to the non-zero columns of $\mathbf{Y}_k$. Thus, we avoid the redundant and expensive computation of the full Khatri-Rao Product. Overall, the methodology described above enjoys all of the properties described in Section 4.1.

Mode-2 MTTKRP. The methodology followed for the Mode-2 case is similar to the one described for the 1st case. We state the corresponding MTTKRP equation:

$$\mathbf{M}^{(2)} = \mathbf{Y}_{(2)} \left(\mathbf{W} \odot \mathbf{H}\right) \tag{11}$$

where $\mathbf{M}^{(2)} \in \mathbb{R}^{J \times R}, \mathbf{Y}_{(2)} \in \mathbb{R}^{J \times RK}$. The main remark is that $\mathbf{Y}_{(2)}$ consists of an horizontal concatenation of the *transposed* frontal slices $\{\mathbf{Y}_k\}$ of the intermediate tensor $\mathcal{Y}$. Thus, if we denote as $\mathbf{T}^{(k)}$ the k-th vertical block of the Khatri-Rao Product $\mathbf{W} \odot \mathbf{H}$, we can

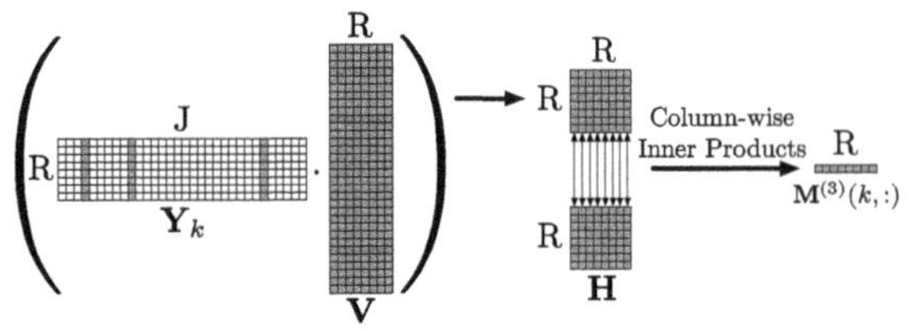

Figure 4: SPARTan computations for the MTTKRP w.r.t. the 3rd mode. We compute each row of the result $M^{(3)}(k,:)$ independently of others, enabling parallelization w.r.t. the K subjects. As in mode-1, mode-2 cases, we exploit the column sparsity of Y_k. In this case, we also leverage that H is a small R-by-R matrix in practice (due to the "size imbalance" of the intermediate tensor $\mathcal{Y}$). Thus, it is efficient to delay any computations on H until the R-by-R product of $Y_k V$ is formed, and then take column-wise inner products between those two matrices. The described operations fulfill all the properties outlined in Section 4.1.

formulate the problem as:

$$\mathbf{M}^{(2)} = \sum_{k=1}^{K} \mathbf{Y}_k^T \, \mathbf{T}^{(k)} \tag{12}$$

Given the above, it is easy to extend Equation (10) for this case, so as to compute a single row of each partial result of Equation (12):

$$[\mathbf{Y}_k^T \, \mathbf{T}^{(k)}]_{j,:} = \left(\mathbf{Y}_k(:,j)^T \, \mathbf{H}\right) * \mathbf{W}(k,:) \tag{13}$$

The corresponding operations are illustrated in Figure 3. A crucial remark is that we can focus on computing the relevant intermediate results only for the non-zero rows of $\mathbf{Y_k}^T$, since the rest of the rows of the result $\mathbf{Y_k}^T\mathbf{T}^{(k)}$ will be zero. In sum, we again avoid redundant computations of the full Khatri-Rao Product and preserve all of the properties described in Section 4.1.

Mode-3 MTTKRP. First, we state the equation regarding the Mode-3 case:

$$\mathbf{M}^{(3)} = \mathbf{Y}_{(3)} \, (\mathbf{V} \odot \mathbf{H}) \tag{14}$$

where $\mathbf{M}^{(3)} \in \mathbb{R}^{K \times R}$ and $\mathbf{Y}_{(3)} \in \mathbb{R}^{K \times JR}$. Note that in this case, we are pursuing the MTTKRP of the mode corresponding to the K subjects. Thus, an entirely different approach than the Mode-1, Mode-2 cases is needed so that we construct efficient independent sub-problems for each one of them. In particular, we need to design each k-th subproblem so that it computes the k-th row of $\mathbf{M}^{(3)}$. In addition, we want to operate only on $\{\mathbf{Y}_k\}$ without forming and reshaping the tensor $\mathcal{Y}$, as well as to exploit the frontal slices' sparsity. To tackle the challenges above, we leverage the fact that [14]:

$$\mathbf{M}^{(3)}(:,r) = \begin{bmatrix} \mathbf{H}(:,r)^T \, \mathbf{Y}_1 \, \mathbf{V}(:,r) \\ \vdots \\ \mathbf{H}(:,r)^T \, \mathbf{Y}_K \, \mathbf{V}(:,r) \end{bmatrix} \tag{15}$$

Then, we remark that in order to retrieve a certain element of the matrix $\mathbf{M}^{(3)}$, we have:

$$\begin{aligned} \mathbf{M}^{(3)}(k,r) &= \mathbf{H}(:,r)^T \, \mathbf{Y}_k \, \mathbf{V}(:,r) \\ &= \mathbf{H}(:,r)^T \, [\mathbf{Y}_k \mathbf{V}](:,r) \end{aligned}$$

The last line above reflects the inner product between the corresponding r-th columns of $\mathbf{H}$ and $[\mathbf{Y}_k \, \mathbf{V}]$, respectively. Thus, in order to retrieve a row $\mathbf{M}(k,:)$, we can simply operate as:

$$\mathbf{M}^{(3)}(k,:) = dot\,(\mathbf{H}, \mathbf{Y}_k\mathbf{V}) \tag{16}$$

Dataset	K	J	$max(I_k)$	#nnz
CHOA	464,900	1,328	166	12.3 Mil.
MovieLens	25,249	26,096	19	8.9 Mil.

Table 3: Summary statistics for the real datasets of our experiments. K is the number of subjects, J is the number of variables, I_k is the number of observations for the k-th subject and #nnz corresponds to the total number of non-zeros.

where the $dot()$ function extracts the inner product of the corresponding columns of its two matrix arguments. We illustrate this operation in Figure 4. Since $\mathbf{H}$ is a small R-by-R matrix (due to the tensor's "size imbalance"), it is very efficient to delay any computations on $\mathbf{H}$ until the R-by-R intermediate matrix is formed as a product of $\mathbf{Y}_k$ $\mathbf{V}$. Then, we simply take the column-wise inner products between those two R-by-R matrices. In that way, all the desirable properties we mentioned in Section 4.1 are also fulfilled.

In Algorithm 3, we list the pseudocode corresponding to the methodology proposed. Note that in lines 8,16, we can accumulate over the partial results in parallel, since the summation is independent of the iteration order.

Algorithm 3 MTTKRP for SPARTan

Require: $\{\mathbf{Y}_k \in \mathbb{R}^{R \times J}\}$ for $k = 1, \dots, K$, $\mathbf{H} \in \mathbb{R}^{R \times R}$, $\mathbf{V} \in \mathbb{R}^{J \times R}$, $\mathbf{W} \in \mathbb{R}^{K \times R}$, the target rank R and the mode n for which we are computing the MTTKRP

Ensure: $\mathbf{M}^{(n)}$

1: Initialize $\mathbf{M}^{(n)}$ with zeros
2: **if** $n == 1$ **then**
3:   **for** $k = 1, \dots, K$ **do**
4:     $temp \leftarrow \mathbf{Y}_k V$
5:     **for** $r = 1, \dots, R$ **do**
6:       $temp(r,:) \leftarrow temp(r,:) * \mathbf{W}(k,:)$
7:     **end for**
8:     $\mathbf{M}^{(1)} \leftarrow \mathbf{M}^{(1)} + temp$ *// sum in parallel* $\forall k = 1, \dots, K$
9:   **end for**
10: **else if** $n == 2$ **then**
11:   **for** $k = 1, \dots, K$ **do**
12:     Initialize $temp \in \mathbb{R}^{J \times R}$ with zeros
13:     **for** each j-th non-zero column of $\mathbf{Y}_k$ **do**
14:       $temp(j,:) \leftarrow (\mathbf{Y}_k(:,j)^T\mathbf{H}) * \mathbf{W}(k,:)$
15:     **end for**
16:     $\mathbf{M}^{(2)} \leftarrow \mathbf{M}^{(2)} + temp$ *// sum in parallel* $\forall k = 1, \dots, K$
17:   **end for**
18: **else if** $n == 3$ **then**
19:   **for** $k = 1, \dots, K$ **do**
20:     $\mathbf{M}^{(3)}(k,:) \leftarrow dot\,(\mathbf{H}, \mathbf{Y}_k\mathbf{V})$ *// in parallel* $\forall k = 1, \dots, K$
21:   **end for**
22: **end if**

5 EXPERIMENTS

5.1 Setup

Real Data Description. Table 3 provides summary statistics regarding the real datasets used.

The **CHOA** (Children Healthcare of Atlanta) dataset corresponds to EHRs of pediatric patients with at least 2 hospital visits. For each patient, we utilize the diagnostic codes and medication categories from their records, as well as the provided age of the patient (in days) at the visit time. The available International Classification of Diseases (ICD9) [ ] codes are summarized to Clinical Classification Software (CCS) [ ] categories, which is a standard step in healthcare analysis improving interpretability and clinical meaningfulness. We aggregate the time mode by week and all the medical events over each week are considered as a single observation. The resulting data are of 464,900 subjects by 1,328 features by maximum 166 observations with 12.3m non-zeros.

MovieLens 20M is another real dataset we used, which is *publicly available* [2]. We are motivated to use this dataset, because of the importance of the evolution of user preferences over time, as highlighted in recent literature [ ]. For this dataset, we consider that each year of ratings corresponds to a certain observation; thus, for each user, we have a year-by-movie matrix to describe her rating activity. We consider only the users having at least 2 years of ratings.

Implementation details. We used MatlabR2015b for our implementations, along with functionalities for sparse tensors from the Tensor Toolbox [ ] and the Non-Negative Least Squares (NNLS) approach [ ] from the N-way Toolbox [ ] [3]. In both the SPARTan and the baseline implementations, we adjust the CP-ALS iteration arising in the PARAFAC2-ALS, so that non-negative constraints are imposed on the $\{S_k\}$, V factors, as discussed in Section 3.2.

The baseline method corresponds to the standard fitting algorithm for the PARAFAC2 model [ ] adjusted for sparse tensors as in [ ]. We utilized the implementation from the most recent version of the Tensor Toolbox [ ] regarding both the manipulation of sparse tensors, as well as the CP-ALS iteration arising in the PARAFAC2-ALS.

Parallelism. We exploit the capabilities of the Parallel Computing Toolbox of Matlab, by utilizing its parallel pool in both SPARTan and the baseline approach, whenever this is appropriate. Regarding the size of the parallel pool, the number of workers of all the experiments regarding a certain dataset is fixed. For the movie-rating dataset we used the default of 12 workers. For the synthetic and the CHOA datasets, we increased the number of workers to 20 because of the data size increase.

Hardware. We conducted our experiments on a server running Ubuntu 14.04 with 1TB of RAM and four Intel E5-4620 v4 CPU's with a maximum clock frequency of 2.10GHz. Each one of the processors contains 10 cores, and each one of the cores can exploit 2 threads with hyper-threading enabled.

5.2 SPARTan is fast and memory-efficient

Synthetic Data. We assess the scalability of the approaches under comparison for sparse synthetic data. We considered a setup with 1,000,000 subjects, 5,000 variables and a maximum of 100 observations for each subject. The number of observations I_k for each subject is dependent on the number of rows of X_k containing non-zero elements; thus, I_k increases with the dataset density. Indicatively, the mean number of observations I_k for the sparsest dataset created ($\approx$ 63 mil.) is 46.9 and for the densest ($\approx$ 500 mil.) dataset, the mean I_k is 99.3. We randomly construct the factors of

[2] https://grouplens.org/datasets/movielens

[3] We also accredit the dense PARAFAC2 implementation by Rasmus Bro, from where we have adapted many functionalities.

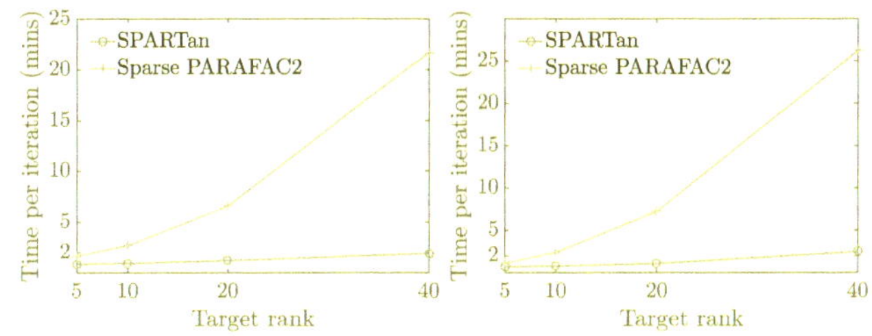

(a) CHOA dataset (b) MovieLens dataset

Figure 5: Time in minutes for one iteration (as an average over 10) for varying target rank for both the real datasets used. SPARTan achieves up to 12× and 11× speedup over the baseline approach for the CHOA and the MovieLens datasets respectively.

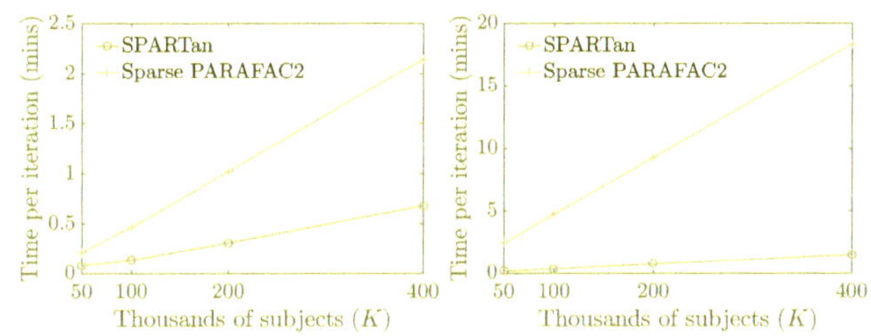

(a) Target Rank $R = 10$ (b) Target Rank $R = 40$

Figure 6: CHOA dataset: Time in minutes for one iteration (as an average over 10) for varying number of subjects (K) included and fixed target rank (two cases considered: $R = \{10, 40\}$).

a rank-40 (which is the maximum target rank used in our experiments) PARAFAC2 model. Based on this model, we construct the input slices $\{X_k\}$, which we then sparsify uniformly at random, for each sparsity level. The density of the sparsification governs the number of non-zeros of the collection of input matrices.

We provide the results in Table 1. First, we remark that SPARTan is *both more scalable* and *faster* than the baseline. In particular, the baseline approach fails to execute in the two largest problem instances for target rank $R = 40$, due to out of memory problems, during the creation of the intermediate sparse tensor $\mathcal{Y}$. Note that as we discussed in Section 4, SPARTan avoids the additional overhead of explicitly constructing a sparse tensor structure, since it only operates directly on the tensor's frontal slices $\{Y_k\}$. Regarding the baseline's memory issue, since the density of $\mathcal{Y}$ may grow (e.g., $\approx$ 10% in the densest case), we also attempted to store the intermediate tensor $\mathcal{Y}$ as a dense one. However, this also failed, since the memory requested for a dense tensor of size 40-by-5K-by-1Mil. exceeded the available RAM of our system (1TB). Overall, it is clear that the baseline approach cannot fully exploit the input sparsity. On the contrary, SPARTan properly executes for all the problem instances considered in a reasonable amount of time. In particular, for $R = 40$, SPARTan is up to 22× faster than the baseline. Even for a lower target rank of $R = 10$, SPARTan achieves up to 13× faster computation.

Real Data. We evaluate the scalability of the proposed SPARTan approach against the baseline method for the real datasets as well.

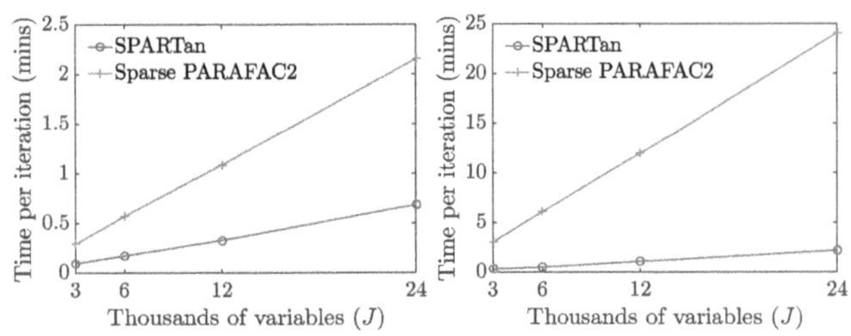

(a) Target Rank $R = 10$ (b) Target Rank $R = 40$

Figure 7: MovieLens dataset: Time in minutes for one iteration (as an average over 10) for varying number of variables (J) included and fixed target rank (two cases considered: $R = \{10, 40\}$).

In Figures 5, 6, 7, we present the results of the corresponding experiments. First, we target the full datasets and vary the pursued target rank (Figure 5). Note that for both datasets considered, the time per iteration of the baseline approach increases dramatically as we increase the target rank. On the contrary, the time required by SPARTan increases only slightly. Overall, our approach achieves up to over an order of magnitude gain regarding the time required per epoch for both datasets.

We also evaluate the scalability of the methods under comparison as we vary the subjects and the variables considered. Since the CHOA dataset (Figure 6) contains more subjects than variables, we vary the number of subjects for this dataset for two fixed target ranks (10, 40). In both cases, SPARTan scales better than the baseline. As concerns the MovieLens dataset (Figure 7), since it contains more variables than subjects, we examine the scalability w.r.t. increasing subsets of variables considered. In this case as well, we remark the favorable scalability properties of SPARTan, rendering it practical to use for large and sparse "irregular" tensors.

5.3 Phenotype discovery on CHOA EHR Data

Motivation. Next we demonstrate the usefulness of PARAFAC2 towards temporal phenotyping of EHRs. Phenotyping refers to the process of extracting meaningful patient clusters (i.e., phenotypes) out of raw, noisy Electronic Health Records [30]. An open challenge in phenotyping is to capture temporal trends or patterns regarding the evolution of those phenotypes for each patient over time. Below, we illustrate how SPARTan can be used to successfully tackle this challenge.

Model Interpretation: We propose the following model interpretation towards the target challenge:

- The common factor matrix $\mathbf{V}$ reflects the *phenotypes' definition* and the non-zero values of each r-th column indicate the membership of the corresponding medical feature to the r-th phenotype.
- The diagonal $\mathbf{S}_k$ provides the *importance membership indicators* of the k-th subject to each one of the R phenotypes/clusters. Thus, we can sort the R phenotypes based on the values of vector $diag(\mathbf{S}_k)$ and identify the most relevant phenotypes for the k-th subject.
- Each $\mathbf{U}_k$ factor matrix provides the *temporal signature* of each patient: each r-th column of $\mathbf{U}_k$ reflects the evolution of the expression of the r-th phenotype for all the I_k weeks of her medical history. Note that since all $\mathbf{X}_k, \mathbf{S}_k, \mathbf{V}$ matrices are non-negative, we only consider the non-negative elements of the temporal signatures in our interpretation.

Table 4: Phenotypes discovered by PARAFAC2. The title annotation for each phenotype is provided by the medical expert. The red color corresponds to diagnoses and the blue color corresponds to medications.

Cancer	**Weight**
Chemotherapy	0.35
Leukemias [39.]	0.27
Immunity disorders [57.]	0.23
HEPARIN AND RELATED PREPARATIONS	0.6
ANTIEMETIC/ANTIVERTIGO AGENTS	0.34
SODIUM/SALINE PREPARATIONS	0.32
TOPICAL LOCAL ANESTHETICS	0.19
ANTIHISTAMINES - 1ST GENERATION	0.16
Sickle Cell Anemia (SCA)	**Weight**
Sickle cell anemia [61.]	0.73
NSAIDS, CYCLOOXYGENASE INHIBITOR - TYPE	0.31
ANALGESICS NARCOTICS	0.26
FOLIC ACID PREPARATIONS	0.2
BETA-ADRENERGIC AGENTS	0.18
SODIUM/SALINE PREPARATIONS	0.16
Neurological System Disorders	**Weight**
Other nervous system symptoms and disorders	0.56
Rehabilitation care; fitting of prostheses; and adjustment of devices [254.]	0.5
Residual codes; unclassified; all E codes [259. and 260.]	0.46
Other connective tissue disease [211.]	0.33
Other and unspecified metabolic; nutritional; and endocrine disorders	0.18
Gastrointestinal Disorders	**Weight**
Residual codes; unclassified; all E codes [259. and 260.]	0.2
Other and unspecified metabolic; nutritional; and endocrine disorders	0.15
Other and unspecified gastrointestinal disorders	0.15
ANALGESIC/ANTIPYRETICS NON-SALICYLATE	0.32
POTASSIUM REPLACEMENT	0.26
BETA-ADRENERGIC AGENTS	0.23
ANALGESICS NARCOTICS	0.23
SODIUM/SALINE PREPARATIONS	0.22
SEDATIVE-HYPNOTICS NON-BARBITURATE	0.21
ANTIEMETIC/ANTIVERTIGO AGENTS	0.19
ANALGESICS NARCOTIC ANESTHETIC ADJUNCT AGENTS	0.18
NSAIDS, CYCLOOXYGENASE INHIBITOR - TYPE	0.16
IRRIGANTS	0.16
LAXATIVES AND CATHARTICS	0.15
GENERAL INHALATION AGENTS	0.15
Liver/Kidney System Disorders	**Weight**
Other aftercare [257.]	0.8
hronic kidney disease [158.]	0.39
Other and unspecified liver disorders	0.3
Immunity disorders [57.]	0.16

Temporal Phenotyping of Medically Complex Patients (MCPs) In order to illustrate the use of PARAFAC2 towards temporal phenotyping, we focus our analysis on a subset of pediatric patients from CHOA, which are classified by them as Medically Complex. These are the patients with high utilization, multiple specialty visits and high severity. Conceptually, those patients suffer from chronic and/or very severe conditions that are hard to treat. As a result, it becomes a very important challenge to accurately phenotype those patients, as well as provide a *temporal signature* for each one of them, which summarizes their phenotypes' evolution.

The number of MCPs in the CHOA cohort is 8,044, their diagnoses and medications sum up to 1,126, and the mean number of weekly observations for those patients is 28. We ran SPARTan for target rank $R = 5$ and the phenotypes discovered are provided in

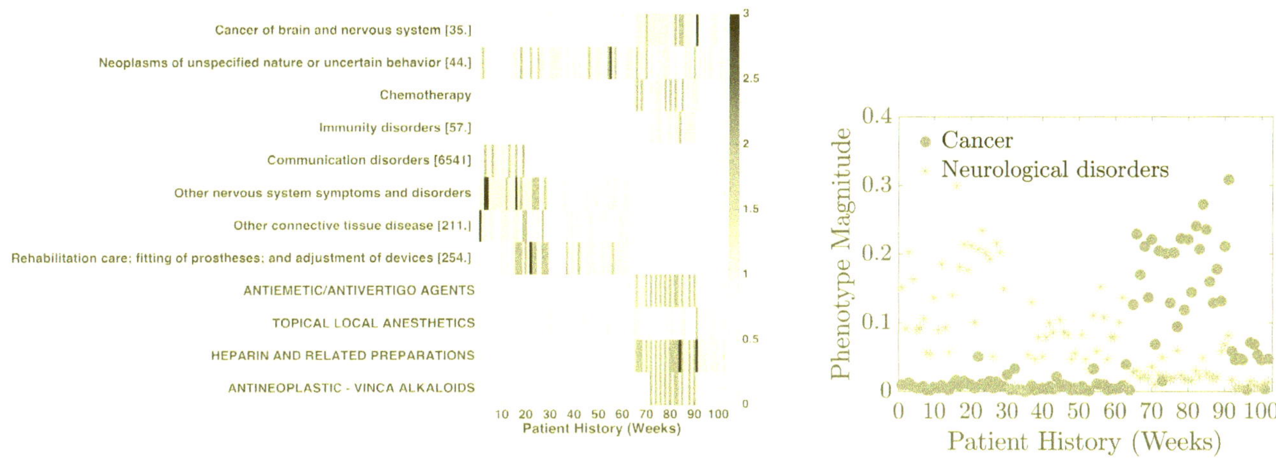

Figure 8: ***Left part:*** **Part of real EHR data of a Medically Complex Patient (MCP). For each week, it contains the occurrences of a diagnosis/medication in the patient's records.** ***Right part:*** **Temporal signature of the patient created by SPARTan. PARAFAC2 captures the stage where cancer treatment is initiated (week 65). At that point, indications of cancer treatment and diagnosis, such as cancer of brain, chemotherapy, heparin and antineoplastic drugs start to get recorded in the patient history. PARAFAC2 also captures the presence of neurological disorders during the first weeks of the patient history. The definition for each phenotype as produced by PARAFAC2 can be found in Table 4.**

Table 4 (*phenotypes' definition* matrix). The labels for each group are the definitions of the phenotypes provided by the medical expert, who endorsed their clinical meaningfulness.

In Figure 8, we provide part of the real EHR, as well as the temporal signature produced by SPARTan, for a certain medically complex patient. Regarding the EHR, we visualize the subset of diagnoses and medications for which the sum of occurrences for the whole patient history is above a certain threshold (e.g., 5 occurrences). This step ensures that the visualized EHR will only contain the conditions exhibiting some form of temporal evolution. For the patient example considered, we identify the top-2 relevant phenotypes through the importance membership indicator matrix S_k as discussed above. For those top-2 phenotypes, we present the resulting *temporal signature*, from which we easily detect intricate temporal trends of the phenotypes involved. Those trends were confirmed by the clinical expert as valuable towards fully understanding the phenotypic behavior of the MCPs.

6 DISCUSSION & CONCLUSIONS

PARAFAC2 has been the state-of-the-art model for mining "irregular" tensors, where the observations along one of its modes do not align naturally. However, it has been highly disregarded by practitioners, as compared to other tensor approaches. Bro [ ] has summarized the reason for that as:

> *The PARAFAC2 model has not yet been used very extensively maybe because the implementations so far have been complicated and slow.*

The methodology proposed in this paper renders this statement no longer true for large and sparse data. In particular, as tested over real and synthetic datasets, SPARTan is both fast and memory-efficient, achieving up to 22× performance gains over the best previous implementation and also handling larger problem instances for which the baseline fails due to insufficient memory.

The key insight driving SPARTan's scalability is the pursuit and exploitation of special structure in the data involved in intermediate computations; prior art did not do so, instead treating those computations as a black-box.

The capability to run PARAFAC2 at larger scales is, in our view, an important enabling technology. As shown in our evaluations on EHR data, the clinically meaningful phenotypes and temporal trends identified by PARAFAC2 reflect the ease of the model's interpretation and its potential utility in other application domains.

Future directions include, but are not limited to: *a)* development of PARAFAC2 algorithms for alternative models of computation, such as distributed clusters [ ], or supercomputing environments; *b)* extension of the methodology proposed for higher-order "irregular" tensors with more than one mismatched mode.

Finally, to enable reproducibility and promote further popularization of the PARAFAC2 modeling within the area of data mining, we open-source our implementations and make them *publicly available.*

ACKNOWLEDGMENTS

This work was supported by the National Science Foundation, award IIS-#1418511 and CCF-#1533768, Children's Healthcare of Atlanta, Google Faculty Award and UCB. E. Papalexakis was supported by the Bourns College of Engineering at UC Riverside. The work of Fei Wang is partially supported by NSF IIS-#1650723. This work has been funded in part by the Laboratory-Directed Research & Development (LDRD) program at Sandia National Laboratories. Sandia National Laboratories is a multimission laboratory managed and operated by National Technology and Engineering Solutions of Sandia, LLC. , a wholly owned subsidiary of Honeywell International, Inc. , for the U.S. Department of Energy's National Nuclear Security Administration under contract DE-NA-0003525.

The authors would like to thank Professor Rasmus Bro and Dr. Tamara Kolda for valuable conversations.

REFERENCES

- [1] 2017. Clinical Classifications Software (CCS) for ICD-9-CM. https://www.hcup-us.ahrq.gov/toolssoftware/ccs/ccs.jsp. (2017). Accessed: 2017-02-11.
- [2] Evrim Acar and Bülent Yener. 2009. Unsupervised multiway data analysis: A literature survey. *IEEE transactions on knowledge and data engineering* 21, 1 (2009), 6–20.
- [3] Claus Andersson and Rasmus Bro. 2000. The N-way toolbox for MATLAB. Available online. (January 2000). http://www.models.life.ku.dk/source/nwaytoolbox/
- [4] Brett W Bader and Tamara G Kolda. 2007. Efficient MATLAB computations with sparse and factored tensors. *SIAM Journal on Scientific Computing* 30, 1 (2007), 205–231.
- [5] Brett W. Bader, Tamara G. Kolda, and others. 2015. MATLAB Tensor Toolbox Version 2.6. Available online. (February 2015). http://www.sandia.gov/~tgkolda/TensorToolbox/
- [6] Rasmus Bro. 1997. PARAFAC. Tutorial and applications. *Chemometrics and intelligent laboratory systems* 38, 2 (1997), 149–171.
- [7] R Bro. 1998. Multi-way analysis in the food industry. (1998).
- [8] Rasmus Bro, Claus A Andersson, and Henk AL Kiers. 1999. PARAFAC2-Part II. Modeling chromatographic data with retention time shifts. *Journal of Chemometrics* 13, 3-4 (1999), 295–309.
- [9] Rasmus Bro and Sijmen De Jong. 1997. A fast non-negativity-constrained least squares algorithm. *Journal of chemometrics* 11, 5 (1997), 393–401.
- [10] J Douglas Carroll and Jih-Jie Chang. 1970. Analysis of individual differences in multidimensional scaling via an N-way generalization of "Eckart-Young" decomposition. *Psychometrika* 35, 3 (1970), 283–319.
- [11] Dehua Cheng, Richard Peng, Ioakeim Perros, and Yan Liu. 2016. SPALS: Fast Alternating Least Squares via Implicit Leverage Scores Sampling. In *Advances In Neural Information Processing Systems*. 721–729.
- [12] Peter A Chew, Brett W Bader, Tamara G Kolda, and Ahmed Abdelali. 2007. Cross-language information retrieval using PARAFAC2. In *Proceedings of the 13th ACM SIGKDD international conference on Knowledge discovery and data mining*. ACM, 143–152.
- [13] Eric C Chi and Tamara G Kolda. 2012. On tensors, sparsity, and nonnegative factorizations. *SIAM J. Matrix Anal. Appl.* 33, 4 (2012), 1272–1299.
- [14] Joon Hee Choi and S Vishwanathan. 2014. DFacTo: Distributed factorization of tensors. In *Advances in Neural Information Processing Systems*. 1296–1304.
- [15] Gene H Golub and Charles F Van Loan. 2013. *Matrix Computations*. Vol. 3. JHU Press.
- [16] Richard A Harshman. 1970. Foundations of the PARAFAC procedure: Models and conditions for an "explanatory" multi-modal factor analysis. (1970).
- [17] R. A. Harshman. 1972b. PARAFAC2: Mathematical and technical notes. *UCLA Working Papers in Phonetics* 22 (1972b), 30–44.
- [18] Richard A Harshman and Margaret E Lundy. 1996. Uniqueness proof for a family of models sharing features of Tucker's three-mode factor analysis and PARAFAC/CANDECOMP. *Psychometrika* 61, 1 (1996), 133–154.
- [19] Nathaniel E Helwig. 2013. The special sign indeterminacy of the direct-fitting Parafac2 model: Some implications, cautions, and recommendations for Simultaneous Component Analysis. *Psychometrika* 78, 4 (2013), 725–739.
- [20] Frank L Hitchcock. 1927. The expression of a tensor or a polyadic as a sum of products. *Studies in Applied Mathematics* 6, 1-4 (1927), 164–189.
- [21] Joyce C Ho, Joydeep Ghosh, Steve R Steinhubl, Walter F Stewart, Joshua C Denny, Bradley A Malin, and Jimeng Sun. 2014. Limestone: High-throughput candidate phenotype generation via tensor factorization. *Journal of biomedical informatics* 52 (2014), 199–211.
- [22] Joyce C Ho, Joydeep Ghosh, and Jimeng Sun. 2014. Marble: high-throughput phenotyping from electronic health records via sparse nonnegative tensor factorization. In *Proceedings of the 20th ACM SIGKDD international conference on Knowledge discovery and data mining*. ACM, 115–124.
- [23] U Kang, Evangelos Papalexakis, Abhay Harpale, and Christos Faloutsos. 2012. Gigatensor: scaling tensor analysis up by 100 times-algorithms and discoveries. In *Proceedings of the 18th ACM SIGKDD international conference on Knowledge discovery and data mining*. ACM, 316–324.
- [24] Henk AL Kiers, Jos MF Ten Berge, and Rasmus Bro. 1999. PARAFAC2-Part I. A direct fitting algorithm for the PARAFAC2 model. *Journal of Chemometrics* 13, 3-4 (1999), 275–294.
- [25] Tamara G Kolda and Brett W Bader. 2009. Tensor decompositions and applications. *SIAM review* 51, 3 (2009), 455–500.
- [26] Joseph B Kruskal. 1977. Three-way arrays: rank and uniqueness of trilinear decompositions, with application to arithmetic complexity and statistics. *Linear algebra and its applications* 18, 2 (1977), 95–138.
- [27] Neal Lathia, Stephen Hailes, Licia Capra, and Xavier Amatriain. 2010. Temporal diversity in recommender systems. In *Proceedings of the 33rd international ACM SIGIR conference on Research and development in information retrieval*. ACM, 210–217.
- [28] Evangelos E Papalexakis, Christos Faloutsos, and Nicholas D Sidiropoulos. 2015. ParCube: Sparse Parallelizable CANDECOMP-PARAFAC Tensor Decomposition. *ACM Transactions on Knowledge Discovery from Data (TKDD)* 10, 1 (2015), 3.
- [29] Evangelos E Papalexakis, Christos Faloutsos, and Nicholas D Sidiropoulos. 2016. Tensors for data mining and data fusion: Models, applications, and scalable algorithms. *ACM Transactions on Intelligent Systems and Technology (TIST)* 8, 2 (2016), 16.
- [30] Rachel L Richesson, Jimeng Sun, Jyotishman Pathak, Abel N Kho, and Joshua C Denny. 2016. Clinical phenotyping in selected national networks: demonstrating the need for high-throughput, portable, and computational methods. *Artificial Intelligence in Medicine* 71 (2016), 57–61.
- [31] Nicholas D Sidiropoulos and Rasmus Bro. 2000. On the uniqueness of multilinear decomposition of N-way arrays. *Journal of chemometrics* 14, 3 (2000), 229–239.
- [32] Nicholas D Sidiropoulos, Lieven De Lathauwer, Xiao Fu, Kejun Huang, Evangelos E Papalexakis, and Christos Faloutsos. 2016. Tensor decomposition for signal processing and machine learning. *arXiv preprint arXiv:1607.01668* (2016).
- [33] Vergil N Slee. 1978. The International classification of diseases: ninth revision (ICD-9). *Annals of internal medicine* 88, 3 (1978), 424–426.
- [34] Shaden Smith, Niranjay Ravindran, Nicholas D Sidiropoulos, and George Karypis. 2015. SPLATT: Efficient and parallel sparse tensor-matrix multiplication. In *Parallel and Distributed Processing Symposium (IPDPS), 2015 IEEE International*. IEEE, 61–70.
- [35] Alwin Stegeman and Tam TT Lam. 2015. Multi-set factor analysis by means of Parafac2. *Brit. J. Math. Statist. Psych.* (2015).
- [36] Jimeng Sun, Charalampos E Tsourakakis, Evan Hoke, Christos Faloutsos, and Tina Eliassi-Rad. 2008. Two heads better than one: pattern discovery in time-evolving multi-aspect data. *Data Mining and Knowledge Discovery* 17, 1 (2008), 111–128.
- [37] Jos MF ten Berge and Henk AL Kiers. 1996. Some uniqueness results for PARAFAC2. *Psychometrika* 61, 1 (1996), 123–132.
- [38] Lloyd N Trefethen and David Bau III. 1997. Numerical linear algebra. (1997).
- [39] Fei Wang, Noah Lee, Jianying Hu, Jimeng Sun, Shahram Ebadollahi, and Andrew F Laine. 2013. A framework for mining signatures from event sequences and its applications in healthcare data. *IEEE transactions on pattern analysis and machine intelligence* 35, 2 (2013), 272–285.
- [40] Fei Wang, Jiayu Zhou, and Jianying Hu. 2014. DensityTransfer: A Data Driven Approach for Imputing Electronic Health Records. In *Pattern Recognition (ICPR), 2014 22nd International Conference on*. IEEE, 2763–2768.
- [41] Yichen Wang, Robert Chen, Joydeep Ghosh, Joshua C Denny, Abel Kho, You Chen, Bradley A Malin, and Jimeng Sun. 2015. Rubik: Knowledge guided tensor factorization and completion for health data analytics. In *Proceedings of the 21th ACM SIGKDD International Conference on Knowledge Discovery and Data Mining*. ACM, 1265–1274.
- [42] Jiayu Zhou, Fei Wang, Jianying Hu, and Jieping Ye. 2014. From micro to macro: data driven phenotyping by densification of longitudinal electronic medical records. In *Proceedings of the 20th ACM SIGKDD international conference on Knowledge discovery and data mining*. ACM, 135–144.

struc2vec: Learning Node Representations from Structural Identity

Leonardo F. R. Ribeiro
Federal University of Rio de Janeiro
Systems Eng. and Comp. Science Dep.
leo@land.ufrj.br

Pedro H. P. Saverese
Federal University of Rio de Janeiro
Systems Eng. and Comp. Science Dep.
savarese@land.ufrj.br

Daniel R. Figueiredo
Federal University of Rio de Janeiro
Systems Eng. and Comp. Science Dep.
daniel@land.ufrj.br

ABSTRACT

Structural identity is a concept of symmetry in which network nodes are identified according to the network structure and their relationship to other nodes. Structural identity has been studied in theory and practice over the past decades, but only recently has it been addressed with representational learning techniques. This work presents *struc2vec*, a novel and flexible framework for learning latent representations for the structural identity of nodes. *struc2vec* uses a hierarchy to measure node similarity at different scales, and constructs a multilayer graph to encode structural similarities and generate structural context for nodes. Numerical experiments indicate that state-of-the-art techniques for learning node representations fail in capturing stronger notions of structural identity, while *struc2vec* exhibits much superior performance in this task, as it overcomes limitations of prior approaches. As a consequence, numerical experiments indicate that *struc2vec* improves performance on classification tasks that depend more on structural identity.

CCS CONCEPTS

•**Computing methodologies** → **Unsupervised learning;** *Learning latent representations;* •**Artificial Intelligence** → Learning;

KEYWORDS

feature learning; node embeddings; structural identity

1 INTRODUCTION

In almost all networks, nodes tend to have one or more functions that greatly determine their role in the system. For example, individuals in a social network have a social role or social position [11, 19], while proteins in a protein-protein interaction (PPI) network exert specific functions [1, 22]. Intuitively, different nodes in such networks may perform similar functions, such as interns in the social network of a corporation or catalysts in the PPI network of a cell. Thus, nodes can often be partitioned into equivalent classes with respect to their function in the network.

Although identification of such functions often leverage node and edge attributes, a more challenging and interesting scenario emerges when node function is defined solely by the network structure. In this context, not even the labels of the nodes matter but just their relationship to other nodes (edges). Indeed, mathematical sociologists have worked on this problem since the 1970s, defining and computing *structural identity* of individuals in social networks [11, 17, 19]. Beyond sociology, the role of webpages in the webgraph is another example of identity (in this case, hubs and authorities) emerging from the network structure, as defined by the celebrated work of Kleinberg [8].

The most common practical approaches to determine the structural identity of nodes are based on distances or recursions. In the former, a distance function that leverages the neighborhood of the nodes is used to measure the distance between all node pairs, with clustering or matching then performed to place nodes into equivalent classes [5, 9]. In the later, a recursion with respect to neighboring nodes is constructed and then iteratively unfolded until convergence, with final values used to determine the equivalent classes [3, 8, 26]. While such approaches have advantages and disadvantages, we provide an alternative methodology, one based on unsupervised learning of representations for the structural identity of nodes (to be presented). Recent efforts in learning latent representations for nodes in networks have been quite successful in performing classification and prediction tasks [6, 14, 16, 23]. In particular, these efforts encode nodes using as context a generalized notion of their neighborhood (e.g., w steps of a random walk, or nodes with neighbors in common). In a nutshell, nodes that have neighborhoods with similar sets of nodes should have similar latent representations. But neighborhood is a local concept defined by some notion of proximity in the network. Thus, two nodes with neighborhoods that are structurally similar but that are far apart will not have similar latent representations. Figure 1 illustrates the problem, where nodes u and v play similar roles (i.e., have similar local structures) but are very far apart in the network. Since their neighborhoods have no common nodes, recent approaches cannot capture their structural similarity (as we soon show).

Figure 1: An example of two nodes (u and v) that are structurally similar (degrees 5 and 4, connected to 3 and 2 triangles, connected to the rest of the network by two nodes), but very far apart in the network.

KDD '17, August 13-17, 2017, Halifax, NS, Canada
© 2017 ACM. 978-1-4503-4887-4/17/08...$15.00
DOI: 10.1145/3097983.3098061

It is worth noting why recent approaches for learning node representations such as *DeepWalk* [16] and *node2vec* [6] succeed in classification tasks but tend to fail in structural equivalence tasks. The key point is that many node features in most real networks exhibit a strong homophily (e.g., two blogs with the same political inclination are much more likely to be connected than at random). Neighbors of nodes with a given feature are more likely to have the same feature. Thus, nodes that are "close" in the network and in the latent representation will tend to share features. Likewise, two nodes that are "far" in the network will tend to be separated in the latent representation, independent of their local structure. Thus, structural equivalence will not properly be captured in the latent representation. However, if classification is performed on features that depend more on structural identity and less on homophily, then such recent approaches are likely to be outperformed by latent representations that better capture structural equivalence (as we soon show).

Our main contribution is a flexible framework for learning latent representations for the structural identity of nodes, called *struc2vec*. It is an alternative and powerful tool to the study of structural identity through latent representations. The key ideas of *struc2vec* are:

- Assess structural similarity between nodes independently of node and edge attributes as well as their position in the network. Thus, two nodes that have a similar local structure will be considered so, independent of network position and node labels in their neighborhoods. Our approach also does not require the network to be connected, and identifies structurally similar nodes in different connected components.
- Establish a hierarchy to measure structural similarity, allowing progressively more stringent notions of what it means to be structurally similar. In particular, at the bottom of the hierarchy, structural similarity between nodes depend only on their degrees, while at the top of the hierarchy similarity depends on the entire network (from the viewpoint of the node).
- Generates random *contexts* for nodes, which are sequences of structurally similar nodes as observed by a weighted random walk traversing a multilayer graph (and *not* the original network). Thus, two nodes that frequently appear with similar contexts will likely have similar structure. Such context can be leveraged by language models to learn latent representation for the nodes.

We implement an instance of *struc2vec* and show its potential through numerical experiments on toy examples and real networks, comparing its performance with *DeepWalk* [16] and *node2vec* [6] – two state-of-the-art techniques for learning latent representations for nodes, and with *RolX* [7] – a recent approach to identify roles of nodes. Our results indicate that while *DeepWalk* and *node2vec* fail to capture the notion of structural identity, *struc2vec* excels on this task – even when the original network is subject to strong random noise (random edge removal). We also show that *struc2vec* is superior in a classification task where node labels depends more on structural identity (i.e., air-traffic networks with labels representing airport activity).

The remainder of this paper is organized as follows. Section 2 briefly overviews the recent related work on learning latent representations of nodes in networks. Section 3 presents the *struc2vec* framework in detail. Experimental evaluation and comparison to other methods are shown in Section 4. Finally, Section 5 concludes the paper with a brief discussion.

2 RELATED WORK

Embedding network nodes in (Euclidean) space has received much attention over the past decades from different communities. The technique is instrumental for Machine Learning applications that leverage network data, as node embeddings can be directly used in tasks such as classification and clustering.

In Natural Language Processing [2], generating dense embeddings for sparse data has a long history. Recently, Skip-Gram [12, 13] was proposed as an efficient technique to learn embeddings for text data (e.g., sentences). Among other properties, the learned language model places semantically similar words near each other in space.

Learning a language model from a network was first proposed by *DeepWalk* [16]. It uses random walks to generate sequences of nodes from the network, which are then treated as sentences by Skip-Gram. Intuitively, nodes close in the network will tend to have similar contexts (sequences) and thus have embeddings that are near one another. This idea was later extended by *node2vec* [6]. By proposing a biased second order random walk model, *node2vec* provides more flexibility when generating the context of a vertex. In particular, the edge weights driving the biased random walks can be designed in an attempt to capture both vertex homophily and structural equivalence. However, a fundamental limitation is that structurally similar nodes will never share the same context if their distance (hop count) is larger than the Skip-Gram window.

subgraph2vec [14] is another recent approach for learning embeddings for rooted subgraphs, and unlike the previous techniques it does not use random walks to generate context. Alternatively, the context of a node is simply defined by its neighbors. Additionally, *subgraph2vec* captures structural equivalence by embedding nodes with the same local structure to the same point in space. Nonetheless, the notion of structural equivalence is very rigid since it is defined as a binary property dictated by the Weisfeiler-Lehman isomorphism test [21]. Thus, two nodes that are structurally very similar (but fail the test) and have non-overlapping neighbors may not be close in space.

Similarly to *subgraph2vec*, considerable effort has recently been made on learning richer representations for network nodes [4, 24]. However, building representations that explicitly capture structural identity is a relative orthogonal problem that has not received much attention. This is the focus of *struc2vec*.

A recent approach to explicitly identify the role of nodes using just the network structure is *RolX* [7]. This unsupervised approach is based on enumerating various structural features for nodes, finding the more suited basis vector for this joint feature space, and then assigning for every node a distribution over the identified roles (basis), allowing for mixed membership across the roles. Without explicitly considering node similarity or node context (in terms of structure), *RolX* is likely to miss node pairs that are structurally equivalent (to be shown).

3 *STRUC2VEC*

Consider the problem of learning representations that capture the structural identity of nodes in the network. A successful approach should exhibit two desired properties:

- The distance between the latent representation of nodes should be strongly correlated to their structural similarity. Thus, two nodes that have identical local network structures should have the same latent representation, while nodes with different structural identities should be far apart.
- The latent representation should not depend on any node or edge attribute, including the node labels. Thus, structurally similar nodes should have close latent representation, independent of node and edge attributes in their neighborhood. The structural identity of nodes must be independent of its "position" in the network.

Given these two properties, we propose *struct2vec*, a general framework for learning latent representations for nodes composed of four main steps, as follows:

(1) Determine the structural similarity between each vertex pair in the graph for different neighborhood sizes. This induces a hierarchy in the measure for structural similarity between nodes, providing more information to assess structural similarity at each level of the hierarchy.
(2) Construct a weighted multilayer graph where all nodes in the network are present in every layer, and each layer corresponds to a level of the hierarchy in measuring structural similarity. Moreover, edge weights among every node pair within each layer are inversely proportional to their structural similarity.
(3) Use the multilayer graph to generate context for each node. In particular, a biased random walk on the multilayer graph is used to generate node sequences. These sequences are likely to include nodes that are more structurally similar.
(4) Apply a technique to learn latent representation from a context given by the sequence of nodes, for example, Skip-Gram.

Note that *struct2vec* is quite flexible as it does not mandates any particular structural similarity measure or representational learning framework. In what follows, we explain in detail each step of *struct2vec* and provide a rigorous approach to a hierarchical measure of structural similarity.

3.1 Measuring structural similarity

The first step of *struct2vec* is to determine a structural similarity between two nodes without using any node or edge attributes. Moreover, this similarity metric should be hierarchical and cope with increasing neighborhood sizes, capturing more refined notions of structural similarity. Intuitively, two nodes that have the same degree are structurally similar, but if their neighbors also have the same degree, then they are even more structurally similar.

Let $G = (V, E)$ denote the undirected, unweighted network under consideration with vertex set V and edge set E, where $n = |V|$ denotes the number of nodes in the network and k^* its diameter. Let $R_k(u)$ denote the set of nodes at distance (hop count) exactly $k \geq 0$ from u in G. Note that $R_1(u)$ denotes the set of neighbors of u and in general, $R_k(u)$ denotes the ring of nodes at distance k. Let $s(S)$ denote the ordered degree sequence of a set $S \subset V$ of nodes.

By comparing the ordered degree sequences of the rings at distance k from both u and v we can impose a hierarchy to measure structural similarity. In particular, let $f_k(u, v)$ denote the *structural distance* between u and v when considering their k-hop neighborhoods (all nodes at distance less than or equal to k and all edges among them). In particular, we define:

$$f_k(u, v) = f_{k-1}(u, v) + g(s(R_k(u)), s(R_k(v))), \quad k \geq 0 \text{ and } |R_k(u)|, |R_k(v)| > 0 \tag{1}$$

where $g(D_1, D_2) \geq 0$ measures the distance between the ordered degree sequences D_1 and D_2 and $f_{-1} = 0$. Note that by definition $f_k(u, v)$ is non-decreasing in k and is defined only when both u or v have nodes at distance k. Moreover, using the ring at distance k in the definition of $f_k(u, v)$ forces the comparison between the degree sequences of nodes that are at the same distance from u and v. Finally, note that if the k-hop neighborhoods of u and v are isomorphic, and maps u onto v, then $f_{k-1}(u, v) = 0$.

A final step is determining the function that compares two degree sequences. Note that $s(R_k(u))$ and $s(R_k(v))$ can be of different sizes and its elements are arbitrary integers in the range $[0, n-1]$ with possible repetitions. We adopt Dynamic Time Warping (DTW) to measure the distance between two ordered degree sequences, a technique that can cope better with sequences of different sizes and loosely compares sequence patterns [18, 20].

Informally, DTW finds the optimal alignment between two sequences A and B. Given a distance function $d(a, b)$ for the elements of the sequence, DTW matches each element $a \in A$ to $b \in B$, such that the sum of the distances between matched elements is minimized. Since elements of sequence A and B are degrees of nodes, we adopt the following distance function:

$$d(a, b) = \frac{\max(a, b)}{\min(a, b)} - 1 \tag{2}$$

Note that when $a = b$ then $d(a, b) = 0$. Thus, two identical ordered degree sequences will have zero distance. Also note that by taking the ratio between the maximum and the minimum, the degrees 1 and 2 are much more different than degrees 101 and 102, a desired property when measuring the distance between node degrees. Finally, while we use DTW to assess the similarity between two ordered degree sequences, any other cost function could be adopted by our framework.

3.2 Constructing the context graph

We construct a multilayer weighted graph that encodes the structural similarity between nodes. Recall that $G = (V, E)$ denotes the original network (possibly not connected) and k^* its diameter. Let M denote the multilayer graph where layer k is defined using the k-hop neighborhoods of the nodes.

Each layer $k = 0, \ldots, k^*$ is formed by a weighted undirected complete graph with node set V, and thus, $\binom{n}{2}$ edges. The edge weight between two nodes in a layer is given by:

$$w_k(u, v) = e^{-f_k(u, v)}, \quad k = 0, \ldots, k^* \tag{3}$$

Note that edges are defined only if $f_k(u, v)$ is defined and that weights are inversely proportional to structural distance, and assume values smaller than or equal to 1, being equal to 1 only if $f_k(u, v) = 0$. Note that nodes that are structurally similar to u will have larger weights across various layers of M.

We connect the layers using directed edges as follows. Each vertex is connected to its corresponding vertex in the layer above and below (layer permitting). Thus, every vertex $u \in V$ in layer k is connected to the corresponding vertex u in layer $k+1$ and $k-1$. The edge weight between layers are as follows:

$$\begin{aligned} w(u_k, u_{k+1}) &= \log(\Gamma_k(u) + e), \quad k = 0, \ldots, k^* - 1 \\ w(u_k, u_{k-1}) &= 1, \quad k = 1, \ldots, k^* \end{aligned} \tag{4}$$

where $\Gamma_k(u)$ is number of edges incident to u that have weight larger than the average edge weight of the complete graph in layer k. In particular:

$$\Gamma_k(u) = \sum_{v \in V} \mathbb{1}(w_k(u, v) > \overline{w_k}) \tag{5}$$

where $\overline{w_k} = \sum_{(u,v) \in \binom{V}{2}} w_k(u, v) / \binom{n}{2}$. Thus, $\Gamma_k(u)$ measures the similarity of node u to other nodes in layer k. Note that if u has many similar nodes in the current layer, then it should change layers to obtain a more refined context. Note that by moving up one layer the number of similar nodes can only decrease. Last, the log function simply reduces the magnitude of the potentially large number of nodes that are similar to u in a given layer.

Finally, note that M has nk^* vertices and at most $k^* \binom{n}{2} + 2n(k^* - 1)$ weighted edges. In Section 3.5 we discuss how to reduce the complexity of generating and storing M.

3.3 Generating context for nodes

The multilayer graph M is used to generate structural context for each node $u \in V$. Note that M captures the structure of structural similarities between nodes in G using absolutely no label information. As in previous works, *struct2vec* uses random walks to generate sequence of nodes to determine the context of a given node. In particular, we consider a biased random walk that moves around M making random choices according to the weights of M. Before each step, the random walk first decides if it will change layers or walk on the current layer (with probability $q > 0$ the random walk stays in the current layer).

Given that it will stay in the current layer, the probability of stepping from node u to node v in layer k is given by:

$$p_k(u, v) = \frac{e^{-f_k(u,v)}}{Z_k(u)} \tag{6}$$

where $Z_k(u)$ is the normalization factor for vertex u in layer k, simply given by:

$$Z_k(u) = \sum_{\substack{v \in V \\ v \neq u}} e^{-f_k(u,v)} \tag{7}$$

Note that the random walk will prefer to step onto nodes that are structurally more similar to the current vertex, avoiding nodes that have very little structural similarity with it. Thus, the context of a node $u \in V$ is likely to have structurally similar nodes, independent of their labels and position in the original network G.

With probability $1-q$, the random walk decides to change layers, and moves to the corresponding node either in layer $k+1$ or layer $k-1$ (layer permitting) with probability proportional to the edge weights. In particular:

$$\begin{aligned} p_k(u_k, u_{k+1}) &= \frac{w(u_k, u_{k+1})}{w(u_k, u_{k+1}) + w(u_k, u_{k-1})} \\ p_k(u_k, u_{k-1}) &= 1 - p_k(u_k, u_{k+1}) \end{aligned} \tag{8}$$

Note that every time the walker steps within a layer it includes the current vertex as part of its context, independent of the layer. Thus, a vertex u may have a given context in layer k (determined by the structural similarity of this layer), but have a subset of this context at layer $k+1$, as the structural similarity cannot increase as we move to higher layers. This notion of a hierarchical context across the layers is a fundamental aspect of the proposed methodology.

Finally, for each node $u \in V$, we start a random walk in its corresponding vertex in layer 0. Random walks have a fixed and relatively short length (number of steps), and the process is repeated a certain number of times, giving rise to multiple independent walks (i.e., the multiple contexts of node u).

3.4 Learning a language model

Recent language modeling techniques have been extensively used to learn word embeddings, and only require sets of sentences in order to generate meaningful representations. Informally, the task can be defined as learning word probabilities given a context. In particular, Skip-Gram [12] has proven to be effective at learning meaningful representations for a variety of data. In order to apply it to networks, it suffices to use artificially generated node sequences instead of word sentences. In our framework, these sequences are generated by biased random walks on the multilayer graph M. Given a node, Skip-Gram aims to maximize the likelihood of its context in a sequence, where a node's context is given by a window of size w centered on it.

For this work we use Hierarchical Softmax, where conditional symbol probabilities are calculated using a tree of binary classifiers. For each node $v_j \in V$, Hierarchical Softmax assigns a specific path in the classification tree, defined by a set of tree nodes $n(v_j, 1), n(v_j, 2), \ldots, n(v_j, h)$, where $n(v_j, h) = v_j$. In this setting, we have:

$$P(v_j | v_i) = \prod_{k=1}^{h} C(n(v_j, k), v_i) \tag{9}$$

where C is a binary classifier present in every node in the tree. Note that since Hierarchical Softmax operates on a binary tree, we have that $h = O(\log |V|)$.

We train Skip-Gram according to its optimization problem given by equation (9). Note that while we use Skip-Gram to learn node embeddings, any other technique to learn latent representations for text data could be used in our framework.

3.5 Complexity and optimizations

In order to construct M, the structural distance between every node pair for every layer must be computed, namely, $f_k(u, v)$ for $u, v \in V$, and $0 \le k \le k^*$. However, $f_k(u, v)$ uses the result of a DTW calculation between two degree sequences. While classic implementation of DTW has complexity $O(\ell^2)$, fast techniques have complexity $O(\ell)$, where ℓ is the size of the largest sequence [20]. Let $d_{\max}$ denote the largest degree in the network. Then, the size of the degree sequence $|s(R_k(u))| \leq \min(d^k_{\max}, n)$, for any node u and layer k. Since in each layer there are $\binom{n}{2}$ pairs, the complexity of computing all distances for layer k is $O(n^2 \min(d^k_{\max}, n))$. The final complexity is then $O(k^* n^3)$. In what follows we describe a series of optimizations that will significantly reduce the computation and memory requirements of the framework.

Reducing the length of degree sequences (OPT1). Although degree sequences at layer k have lengths bounded by $\min(d^k_{\max}, n)$, for some networks this can be quite large even for small k (e.g., for $k = 3$ the sequences are already $O(n)$). To reduce the cost of comparing large sequences, we propose compressing the ordered degree sequence as follows. For each degree in the sequence, we count the number of occurrences of that degree. The compressed ordered degree sequence is a tuple with the degree and the number of occurrences. Since many nodes in a network tend to have the same degree, in practice the compressed ordered degree sequence can be an order of magnitude smaller than the original.

Let A' and B' denote the compressed degree sequences of A and B, respectively. Since the elements of A' and B' are tuples, we adapt the DTW pairwise distance function as follows:

$$\mathrm{dist}(\boldsymbol{a}, \boldsymbol{b}) = \left(\frac{\max(a_0, b_0)}{\min(a_0, b_0)} - 1\right) \max(a_1, b_1) \tag{10}$$

where $\boldsymbol{a} = (a_0, a_1)$ and $\boldsymbol{b} = (b_0, b_1)$ are tuples in A' and B', respectively; a_0 and b_0 are the degrees; a_1 and b_1 are the number of occurrences. Note that using the compressed degree sequence leads to comparisons between pieces of the original sequences that have the same degree (as opposed to comparing every degree). Thus, equation (10) leads to an approximation of the DTW on the original degree sequences, as given by equation (2). However, DTW now operates on A' and B', which are much shorter than A and B, respectively.

Reducing the number of pairwise similarity calculations (OPT2). While the original framework assesses the similarity between every node pair at every layer k, clearly this seems unnecessary. Consider two nodes with very different degrees (eg., 2 and 20). Their structural distance even for $k = 0$ will be large, and consequently the edge between them in M will have a very small weight. Thus, when generating context for these nodes, the random walk is unlikely to traverse this edge. Consequently, not having this edge in M will not significantly change the model.

We limit the number of pairwise similarity calculations to $\Theta(\log n)$ per node, for every level k. Let J_u denote the set of nodes that will be neighbors of u in M, which will be the same for every level. J_u should have the nodes most structurally similar to u. In order to determine J_u, we take the nodes that have degrees most similar to u. This can be computed efficiently by performing a binary search on the ordered degree sequence of all nodes in the network (for the degree of node u), and taking $\log n$ consecutive nodes on each direction after the search completes. Thus, computing J_u has complexity $\Theta(\log n)$. Computing J_u for all nodes has complexity $\Theta(n \log n)$ which is also needed for sorting the degrees of the network. As for memory requirements, each layer of M will now have $\Theta(n \log n)$ edges as opposed to $\Theta(n^2)$.

Reducing the number of layers (OPT3). The number of layers in M is given by the diameter of the network, k^*. However, for many networks the diameter can be much larger than the average distance. Moreover, the importance of assessing the structural similarity between two nodes diminishes with arbitrarily large values for k. In particular, when k is near k^* the length of the degree sequences of the rings become relatively short, and thus $f_k(u, v)$ is not much different from $f_{k-1}(u, v)$. Therefore, we cap the number the layers in M to a fixed constant $k' < k^*$, capturing the most important layers for assessing structural similarity. This significantly reduces the computational and memory requirements for constructing M.

Although the combination of the above optimizations affects the capacity of the framework in generating good representations for nodes that are structurally similar, we will show that their impact is marginal and sometimes even beneficial. Thus, the benefits in reducing computational and memory requirements of the framework greatly outweighs its drawbacks. Last, we make *struc2vec* available at: https://github.com/leoribeiro/struc2vec

4 EXPERIMENTAL EVALUATION

In what follows we evaluate *struct2vec* in different scenarios in order to illustrate its potential in capturing the structural identity of nodes, also in light of state-of-the-art techniques for learning node representations.

4.1 Barbell graph

We denote $B(h, k)$ as the (h, k)-barbell graph which consists of two complete graphs K_1 and K_2 (each having h nodes) connected by a path graph P of length k. Two nodes $b_1 \in V(K_1)$ and $b_2 \in V(K_2)$ act as the bridges. Using $\{p_1, \ldots, p_k\}$ to denote $V(P)$, we connect b_1 to p_1 and b_2 to p_k, thus connecting the three graphs.

The barbell graph has a significant number of nodes with the same structural identity. Let $C_1 = V(K_1) \setminus \{b_1\}$ and $C_2 = V(K_2) \setminus \{b_2\}$. Note that all nodes $v \in \{C_1 \cup C_2\}$ are structurally equivalent, in the strong sense that there exists an automorphism between any pair of such nodes. Additionally, we also have that all node pairs $\{p_i, p_{k-i}\}$, for $1 \leq i \leq k-1$, along with the pair $\{b_1, b_2\}$, are structurally equivalent in the same strong sense. Figure 2a illustrates a $B(10, 10)$ graph, where structurally equivalent nodes have the same color.

Thus, we expect *struct2vec* to learn vertex representations that capture the structural equivalence mentioned above. Every node pair that is structurally equivalent should have similar latent representation. Moreover, the learned representations should also capture structural hierarchies: while the node p_1 is not equivalent to neither nodes p_2 or b_1, we can clearly see that from a structural point of view it is more similar to p_2 (it suffices to compare their degrees).

Figure 2 shows the latent representations learned by *DeepWalk*, *node2vec* and *struct2vec* for $B(10, 10)$. *DeepWalk* fails to capture structural equivalences, which is expected since it was not designed to consider structural identities. As illustrated, *node2vec* does not capture structural identities even with different variations of its parameters p and q. In fact, it learns mostly graph distances, placing closer in the latent space nodes that are closer (in hops) in the graph. Another limitation of *node2vec* is that Skip-Gram's window size

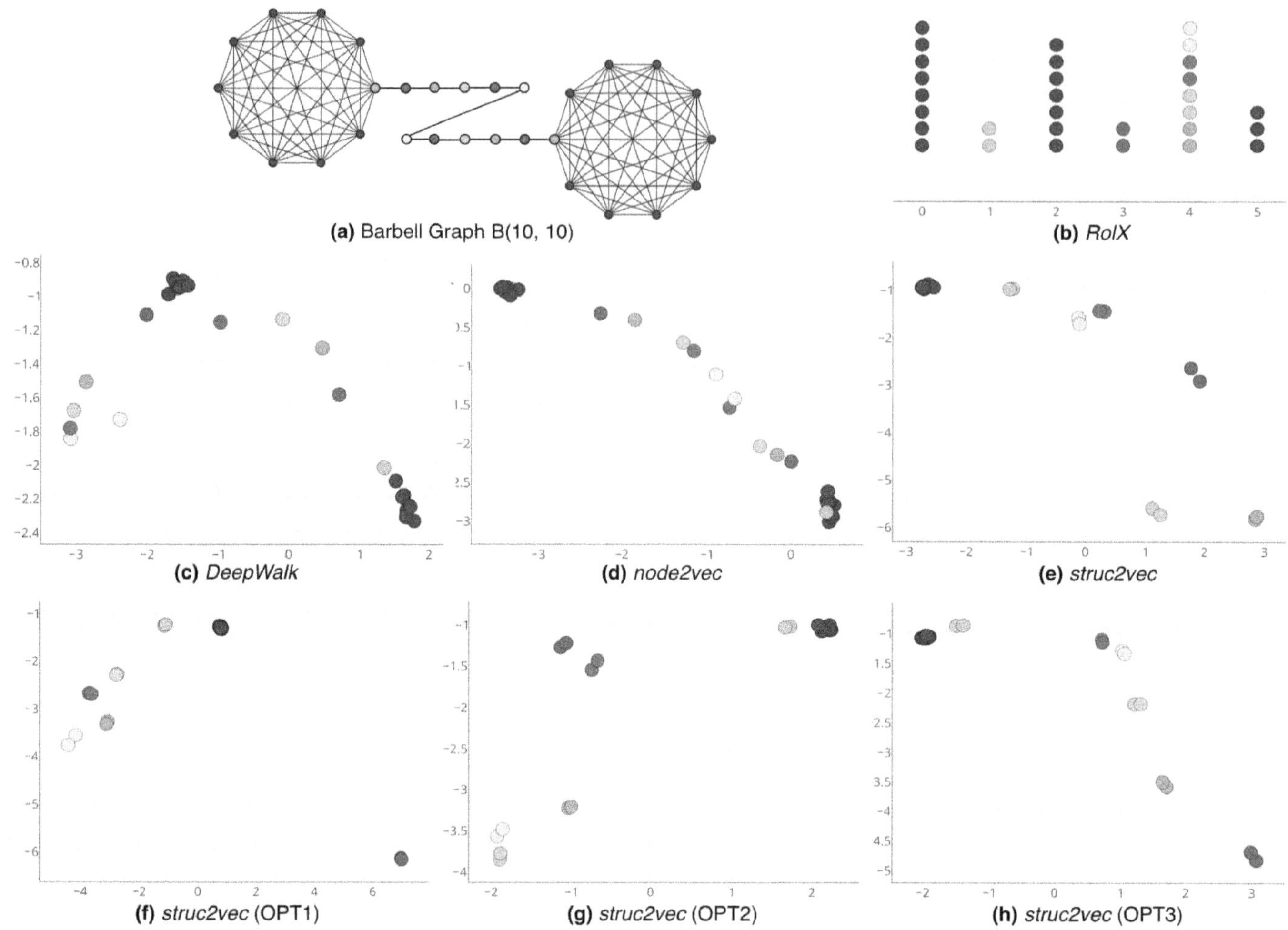

Figure 2: (a) Barbell graph $B(10, 10)$. (b) Roles identified by *RolX*. Latent representations in $\mathbb{R}^2$ learned by (c) DeepWalk, (d) *node2vec* and (e,f,g,h) *struc2vec*. Parameters used for all methods: number of walks per node: 20, walk length: 80, skip-gram window size: 5. For *node2vec*: $p = 1$ and $q = 2$.

makes it impossible for nodes in K_1 and K_2 to appear in the same context.

struct2vec, on the other hand, learns representations that properly separate the equivalent classes, placing structurally equivalent nodes near one another in the latent space. Note that nodes of the same color are tightly grouped together. Moreover, p_1 and p_{10} are placed close to representations for nodes in K_1 and K_2, as they are the bridges. Finally, note that none of the three optimizations have any significant effect on the quality of the representations. In fact, structurally equivalent nodes are even closer to one another in the latent representations under OPT1.

Last, we apply *RolX* to the barbell graph (results in Figure 2(b)). A total of six roles were identified and some roles indeed precisely captured structural equivalence (roles 1 and 3). However, structurally equivalent nodes (in K_1 and K_2) were placed in three different roles (role 0, 2, and 5) while role 4 contains all remaining nodes in the path. Thus, although *RolX* does capture some notion of structural equivalence when assigning roles to nodes, *struct2vec* better identifies and separates structural equivalence.

4.2 Karate network

The Zachary's Karate Club [25] is a network composed of 34 nodes and 78 edges, where each node represents a club member and edges denote if two members have interacted outside the club. In this network, edges are commonly interpreted as indications of friendship between members.

We construct a network composed of two copies G_1 and G_2 of the Karate Club network, where each node $v \in V(G_1)$ has a mirror node $u \in V(G_2)$. We also connect the two networks by adding an edge between mirrored node pairs 1 and 37. Although this is not necessary for our framework, *DeepWalk* and *node2vec* cannot place in the same context nodes in different connected components of the graph. Thus, we add the edge for a more fair comparison

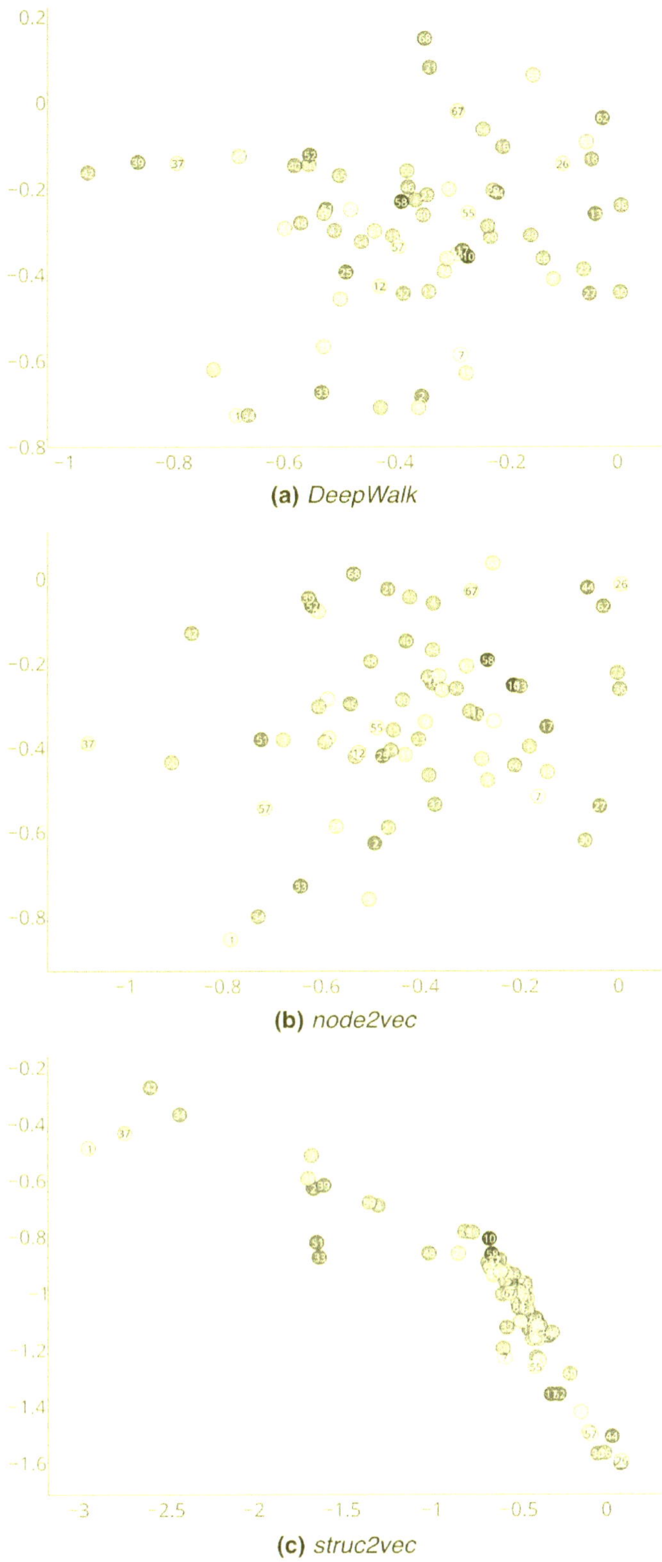

Figure 3: Node representations for the mirrored Karate network created by (a) *DeepWalk*, (b) *node2vec* and (c) *struc2vec*. Parameters used for all methods: number of walks per node: 5, walk length: 15, Skip-Gram window size: 3. For *node2vec*: $p = 1$ and $q = 2$.

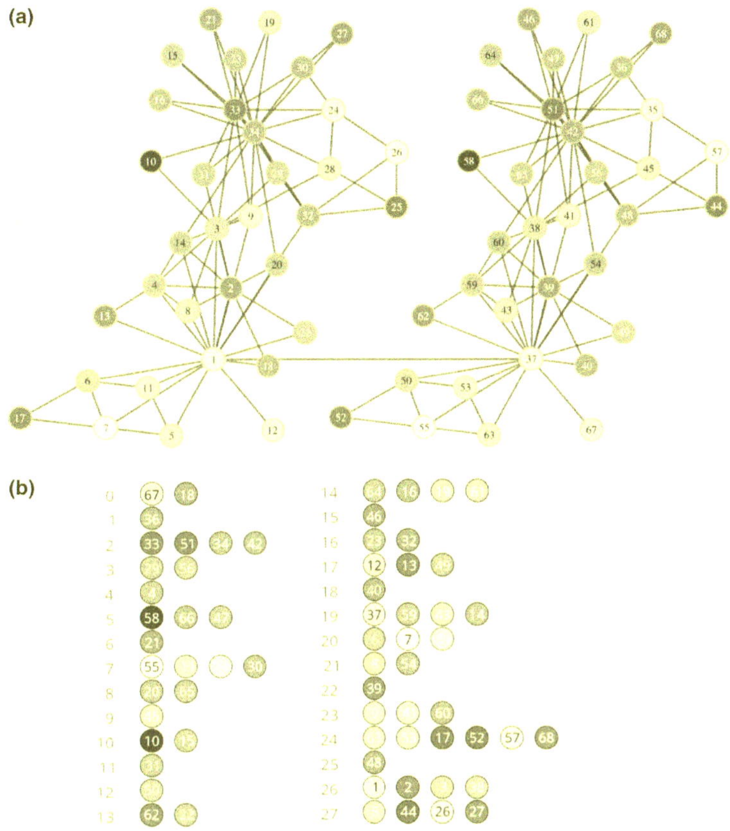

Figure 4: (a) Mirrored Karate network. Identical colors correspond to mirrored nodes. (b) Roles identified by *RolX*

with the two baselines. Figure 4a shows mirrored network with corresponding pairs having the same color.

Figure 3 shows the representations learned by *DeepWalk*, *node2vec* and *struct2vec*. Clearly, *Deepwalk* and *node2vec* fail to group in the latent space structurally equivalent nodes, including mirrored nodes.

Once again, *struct2vec* manages to learn features that properly capture the structural identity of nodes. Mirrored pairs – that is, nodes with the same color – stay close together in the latent space, and there is a complex structural hierarchy in the way the representations are grouped together.

As an example, note that nodes 1, 34 and their correspondent mirrors (37 and 42) are in a separate cluster in the latent space. Interestingly, these are exactly the nodes that represent the club instructor Mr. Hi and his administrator John A. The network was gathered after a conflict between the two split the members of the club into two groups – centered on either Mr. Hi or John A. Therefore, nodes 1 and 34 have the specific and similar role of leaders in the network. Note that *struct2vec* captures their function even though there is no edge between them.

Another visible cluster in the latent space is composed of nodes 2, 3, 4 and 33, also along with their mirrors. These nodes also have a specific structural identity in the network: all of them have high degrees and are also connected to at least one of the leaders. Lastly, nodes 26 and 25 (far right in the latent space) have extremely close representations, which agrees with their structural role: both have low degree and are 2 hops away from leader 34.

struct2vec also captures non-trivial structural equivalences. Note that nodes 7 and 50 (pink and yellow) are mapped to close points in the latent space. Surprisingly, these two nodes are structurally equivalent – there exists an automorphism in the graph that maps one into the other. This can be more easily seen once we note that nodes 6 and 7 are also structurally equivalent, and 50 is the mirrored version of node 6 (therefore also structurally equivalent).

Last, Figure 4b shows the roles identified by *RolX* in the mirrored Karate network (28 roles were identified). Note that leaders 1 and 34 were placed in different roles. The mirror for 1 (node 37) was also placed in a different role, while the mirror for 34 (node 42) was placed in the same role as 34. A total of 7 corresponding pairs (out of 34) were placed in the same role. However, some other structural similarities were also identified – e.g., nodes 6 and 7 are structurally equivalent and were assigned the same role. Again, *RolX* seems to capture some notion of structural similarities among network nodes but *struct2vec* can better identify and separate structural equivalences using latent representations.

Consider the distance between the latent representation for nodes. We measure the distance distribution between pairs corresponding to mirrored nodes and among all node pairs (using the representation shown in Figure 3). Figure 5 shows the two distance distributions for the representations learned by *node2vec* and *struc2vec*. For *node2vec* the two distributions are practically identical, indicating that distances between mirrored pairs blend well with all pairs. In contrast, *struc2vec* exhibits two very different distributions: 94% of mirrored node pairs have distance smaller than 0.25 while 68% of all node pairs have distance larger than 0.25. Moreover, the average distance between all node pairs is 5.6 times larger than that of mirrored pairs, while this ratio is about slightly *smaller* than 1 for *node2vec*.

To better characterize the relationship between structural distance and distances in the latent representation learned by *struc2vec*, we compute the correlation between the two distances for all node pairs. In particular, for each layer k we compute the Spearman and Pearson correlation coefficients between $f_k(u, v)$, as given by equation (1), and the euclidean distance between u and v in the learned representation. Results shown in Table 1 for the mirrored Karate network indeed corroborate that there is a very strong correlation between the two distances, for every layer, captured by both coefficients. This suggests that *struc2vec* indeed captures in the latent space the measure for structural similarity adopted by the methodology.

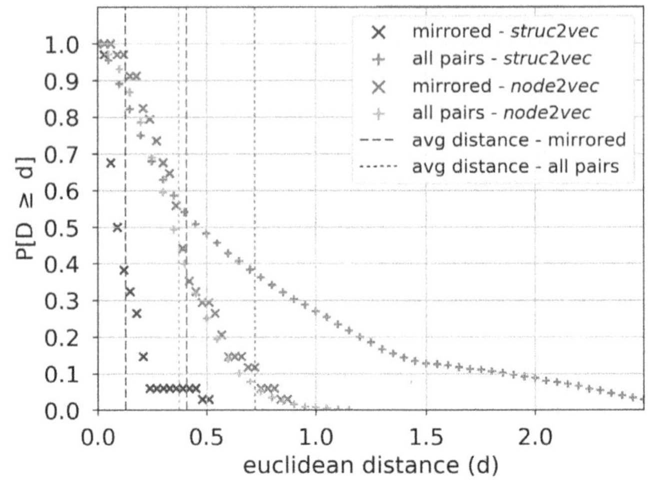

Figure 5: Distance distributions between node pairs (mirrored pairs and all pairs) in the latent space, for the mirrored Karate network learned by *node2vec* and *struc2vec* (as shown in Figure 3). Curves marked with × correspond to distances between mirrored pairs while + corresponds to all pairs; corresponding averages indicated by vertical lines.

Table 1: Pearson and Spearman correlation coefficients between structural distance and euclidean distance in latent space for all node pairs in the mirrored Karate network.

Layer	Pearson (p-value)	Spearman (p-value)
0	0.83 (0.0)	0.74 (0.0)
2	0.71 (0.0)	0.65 (0.0)
4	0.70 (0.0)	0.57 (0.0)
6	0.74 (0.0)	0.57 (2.37)

4.3 Robustness to edge removal

We illustrate the potential of the framework in effectively representing structural identity in the presence of noise. In particular, we randomly remove edges from the network, directly changing its structure. We adopt the parsimonious *edge sampling model* to instantiate two structurally correlated networks [15].

The model works by taking a fixed graph $G = (V, E)$ and generating a graph G_1 by sampling each edge $e \in E$ with probability s, independently. Thus, each edge of G is present in G_1 with probability s. Repeat the process again using G to generate another graph G_2. Thus, G_1 and G_2 are structurally correlated through G, and s controls the amount of structural correlation. Note that when $s = 1$, G_1 and G_2 are isomorphic, while when $s = 0$ all structural identity is lost.

We apply the edge sampling model to an *egonet* extracted from Facebook (224 nodes, 3192 edges, max degree 99, min degree 1) [10] to generate G_1 and G_2 with different values for s. We relabel the nodes in G_2 (to avoid identical labels) and consider the union of the two graphs as the input network to our framework. Note that this graph has at least two connected components (corresponding to G_1 and G_2) and every node (in G_1) has a corresponding pair (in G_2).

Figure 6 shows the distance (latent space with 2 dimensions) distribution between corresponding node pairs and all node pairs for various values for s (corresponding averages are shown in Table 2). For $s = 1$, the two distance distributions are strikingly different, with the average distance for all pairs being 21 times larger than that for corresponding pairs. More interestingly, when $s = 0.9$ the two distributions are still very different. Note that while further

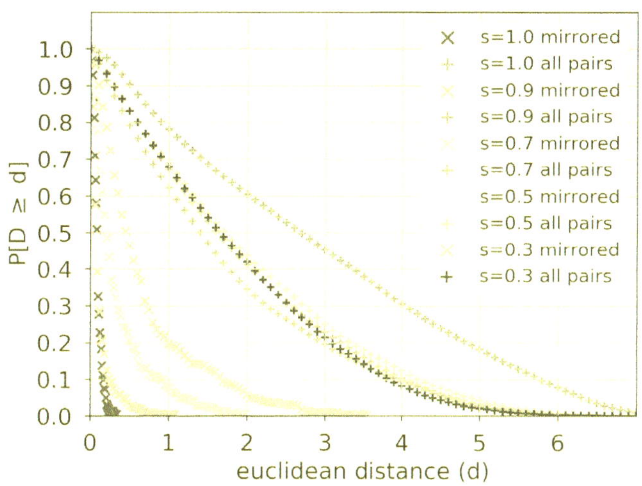

Figure 6: Distance distribution between node pairs in latent space representation (2 dimensions) under the edge sampling model (different values for s). Bottom curves (marked with $\times$) are for corresponding node pairs; top curves (marked with +) are for all node pairs.

decreasing s does not significantly affect the distance distribution of all pairs, it slowly increases the distribution of corresponding pairs. However, even when $s = 0.3$ (which means that the probability that an original edge appears both in G_1 and G_2 is 0.09, s^2), the framework still places corresponding nodes closer in the latent space.

This experiment indicates the robustness of the framework in uncovering the structural identity of nodes even in the presence of structural noise, modeled here through edge removals.

Table 2: Average and standard deviation for distances between node pairs in the latent space representation (see corresponding distributions in Figure 6).

s	Corresponding - avg (std)	All nodes - avg (std)
1.0	0.083 (0.05)	1.780 (1.354)
0.9	0.117 (0.142)	1.769 (1.395)
0.3	0.674 (0.662)	1.962 (1.445)

4.4 Classification

A common application of latent representations for network nodes is classification. *struc2vec* can be leveraged for this task when labels for nodes are more related to their structural identity than to the labels of their neighbors. To illustrate this potential, we consider air-traffic networks: unweighted, undirected networks where nodes correspond to airports and edges indicate the existence of commercial flights. Airports will be assigned a label corresponding to their level of activity, measured in flights or people (discussed below). We consider the following datasets (collected for this study):

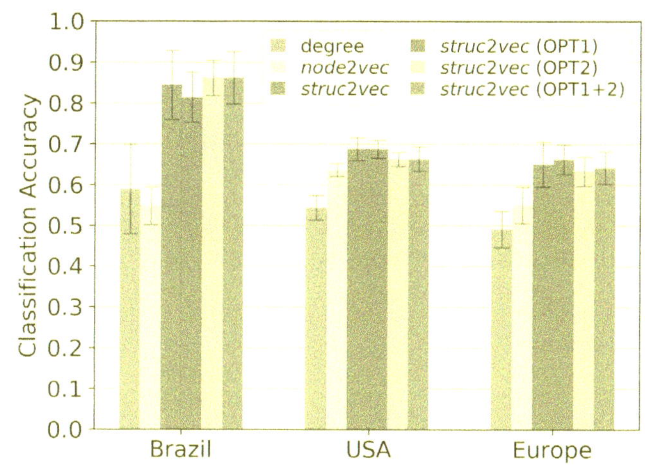

Figure 7: Average accuracy for multi-class node classification in air-traffic networks of Brazil, USA and Europe for different node features used in supervised learning.

- *Brazilian air-traffic network:* Data collected from the National Civil Aviation Agency (ANAC)[1] from January to December 2016. The network has 131 nodes, 1,038 edges (diameter is 5). Airport activity is measured by the total number of landings plus takeoffs in the corresponding year.
- *American air-traffic network:* Data collected from the Bureau of Transportation Statistics[2] from January to October, 2016. The network has 1,190 nodes, 13,599 edges (diameter is 8). Airport activity is measured by the total number of people that passed (arrived plus departed) the airport in the corresponding period.
- *European air-traffic network:* Data collected from the Statistical Office of the European Union (Eurostat)[3] from January to November 2016. The network has 399 nodes, 5,995 edges (diameter is 5). Airport activity is measured by the total number of landings plus takeoffs in the corresponding period.

For each airport, we assign one of four possible labels corresponding to their activity. In particular, for each dataset, we use the quartiles obtained from the empirical activity distribution to split the dataset in four groups, assigning a different label for each group. Thus, label 1 is given to the 25% less active airports, and so on. Note that all classes (labels) have the same size (number of airports). Moreover, classes are related more to the role played by the airport.

We learn latent representations for nodes of each air-traffic network using *struc2vec* and *node2vec* using a grid search to select the best hyperparameters for each case. Note that this step does not use any node label information. The latent representation for each node becomes the feature that is then used to train a supervised classifier (one-vs-rest logistic regression with L2 regularization). We also consider just the node degree as a feature since it captures a very basic notion of structural identity. Last, since classes have identical

[1] http://www.anac.gov.br/
[2] https://transtats.bts.gov/
[3] http://ec.europa.eu/

sizes, we use just the accuracy to assess performance. Experiments are repeated 10 times using random samples to train the classifier (80% of the nodes used for training) and we report on the average performance.

Figure 7 shows the classification performance of the different features for all air-traffic networks. Clearly, *struc2vec* outperforms the other approaches, and its optimizations have little influence. For the Brazilian network, *struc2vec* improves classification accuracy by 50% in comparison to *node2vec*. Interestingly, for this network *node2vec* has average performance (slightly) inferior to node degree, indicating the importance played by the structural identity of the nodes in classification.

4.5 Scalability

In order to illustrate its scalability, we apply *struc2vec* with the first two optimizations to instances of the Erdös-Rényi random graph model (using 128 dimensions, 10 walks per node, walk length 80, Skip-Gram window 10). We compute the average execution time for 10 independent runs on graphs with sizes from 100 to 1,000,000 nodes and average degree of 10. In order to speed up training the language model, we use Skip-Gram with Negative Sampling [13]. Figure 8 shows the execution time (in log-log scale) indicating that *struc2vec* scales super-linearly but closer to linear than to $n^{1.5}$ (dashed lines). Thus, despite its unfavorable worst case time and space complexity, in practice *struc2vec* can be applied to very large networks.

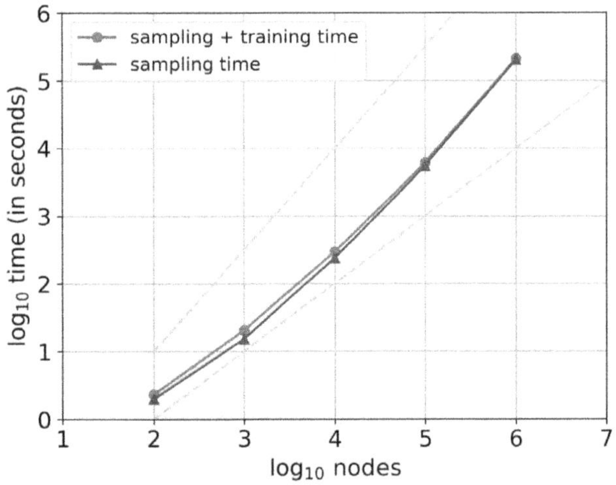

Figure 8: Average execution time of *struc2vec* on Erdös-Rényi graphs with average degree of 10. Training time refers to the additional time required by Skip-Gram.

5 CONCLUSION

Structural identity is a concept of symmetry in networks in which nodes are identified based on the network structure. The concept is strongly related to functions or roles played by nodes in the network, an important problem in social and hard sciences.

We propose *struc2vec*, a novel and flexible framework to learn representations that capture the structural identity of nodes in a network. *struc2vec* assesses the structural similarity of node pairs by considering a hierarchical metric defined by the ordered degree sequence of nodes and uses a weighted multilayer graph to generate context.

We have shown that *struc2vec* excels in capturing the structural identity of nodes, in comparison to state-of-the-art techniques such as *DeepWalk*, *node2vec* and *RolX*. It overcomes their limitation by focusing explicitly on structural identity. Not surprising, we also show that *struc2vec* is superior in classification tasks where node labels are more dependent on their role or structural identity. Last, different models to generate representations tend to capture different properties, and we argue that structural identity is clearly important when considering possible node representations.

REFERENCES

[1] Nir Atias and Roded Sharan. 2012. Comparative analysis of protein networks: hard problems, practical solutions. *Commun. ACM* 55 (2012).
[2] Yoshua Bengio, Réjean Ducharme, Pascal Vincent, and Christian Jauvin. 2003. A Neural Probabilistic Language Model. *JMLR* (2003).
[3] V Blondel, A Gajardo, M Heymans, P Senellart, and P Van Dooren. 2004. A measure of similarity between graph vertices: Applications to synonym extraction and web searching. *SIAM review* (2004).
[4] Shaosheng Cao, Wei Lu, and Qiongkai Xu. 2016. Deep Neural Networks for Learning Graph Representations. In *AAAI*.
[5] F Fouss, A Pirotte, J Renders, and M Saerens. 2007. Random-Walk Computation of Similarities Between Nodes of a Graph with Application to Collaborative Recommendation. *IEEE Trans. on Knowl. and Data Eng.* (2007).
[6] Aditya Grover and Jure Leskovec. 2016. node2vec: Scalable Feature Learning for Networks. In *ACM SIGKDD*.
[7] K Henderson, B Gallagher, T Eliassi-Rad, H Tong, S Basu, L Akoglu, D Koutra, C Faloutsos, and L Li. 2012. Rolx: structural role extraction & mining in large graphs. In *ACM SIGKDD*.
[8] Jon M Kleinberg. 1999. Authoritative sources in a hyperlinked environment. *Journal of the ACM (JACM)* (1999).
[9] Elizabeth A Leicht, Petter Holme, and Mark EJ Newman. 2006. Vertex similarity in networks. *Physical Review E* 73 (2006).
[10] Jure Leskovec and Julian J Mcauley. 2012. Learning to discover social circles in ego networks. In *NIPS*.
[11] Francois Lorrain and Harrison C White. 1971. Structural equivalence of individuals in social networks. *The Journal of mathematical sociology* 1 (1971).
[12] Tomas Mikolov, Kai Chen, Greg Corrado, and Jeffrey Dean. 2013. Efficient Estimation of Word Representations in Vector Space. In *ICLR Workshop*.
[13] T Mikolov, I Sutskever, K Chen, G Corrado, and J Dean. 2013. Distributed Representations of Words and Phrases and their Compositionality. In *NIPS*.
[14] A Narayanan, M Chandramohan, L Chen, Y Liu, and S Saminathan. 2016. subgraph2vec: Learning Distributed Representations of Rooted Sub-graphs from Large Graphs. In *Workshop on Mining and Learning with Graphs*.
[15] Pedram Pedarsani and Matthias Grossglauser. 2011. On the privacy of anonymized networks. In *ACM SIGKDD*.
[16] Bryan Perozzi, Rami Al-Rfou, and Steven Skiena. 2014. DeepWalk: Online Learning of Social Representations. In *ACM SIGKDD*.
[17] Narciso Pizarro. 2007. Structural Identity and Equivalence of Individuals in Social Networks Beyond Duality. *International Sociology* 22 (2007).
[18] T Rakthanmanon, B Campana, A Mueen, G Batista, B Westover, Q Zhu, J Zakaria, and E Keogh. 2013. Addressing big data time series: Mining trillions of time series subsequences under dynamic time warping. *ACM TKDD* (2013).
[19] Lee Douglas Sailer. 1978. Structural equivalence: Meaning and definition, computation and application. *Social Networks* (1978).
[20] S Salvador and P Chan. 2004. FastDTW: Toward accurate dynamic time warping in linear time and space. In *Workshop on Min. Temp. and Seq. Data, ACM SIGKDD*.
[21] N Shervashidze, P Schweitzer, E van Leeuwen, K Mehlhorn, and K Borgwardt. 2011. Weisfeiler-Lehman Graph Kernels. *JMLR* (2011).
[22] R Singh, J Xu, and B Berger. 2008. Global alignment of multiple protein interaction networks with application to functional orthology detection. *PNAS* (2008).
[23] Jian Tang, Meng Qu, Mingzhe Wang, Ming Zhang, Jun Yan, and Qiaozhu Mei. 2015. LINE: Large-scale Information Network Embedding. In *WWW*.
[24] Daixin Wang, Peng Cui, and Wenwu Zhu. 2016. Structural Deep Network Embedding. In *ACM SIGKDD*.
[25] Wayne W Zachary. 1977. An information flow model for conflict and fission in small groups. *Journal of anthropological research* (1977).
[26] Laura A Zager and George C Verghese. 2008. Graph similarity scoring and matching. *Applied mathematics letters* (2008).

Similarity Forests

Saket Sathe
IBM T. J. Watson Research Center
Yorktown Heights, NY 10598
ssathe@us.ibm.com

Charu C. Aggarwal
IBM T. J. Watson Research Center
Yorktown Heights, NY 10598
charu@us.ibm.com

ABSTRACT

Random forests are among the most successful methods used in data mining because of their extraordinary accuracy and effectiveness. However, their use is primarily limited to multidimensional data because they sample features from the original data set. In this paper, we propose a method for extending random forests to work with any arbitrary set of data objects, as long as similarities can be computed among the data objects. Furthermore, since it is understood that similarity computation between all $O(n^2)$ pairs of n objects might be expensive, our method computes only a very small fraction of the $O(n^2)$ pairwise similarities between objects to construct the forests. Our results show that the proposed similarity forest approach is very efficient and accurate on a wide variety of data sets. Therefore, this paper significantly extends the applicability of random forest methods to arbitrary data domains. Furthermore, the approach even outperforms traditional random forests on multidimensional data. We show that similarity forests are robust to the noisy similarity values that are ubiquitous in real-world applications. In many practical settings, the similarity values between objects are incompletely specified because of the difficulty in collecting such values. Similarity forests can be used in such cases with straightforward modifications.

CCS CONCEPTS

•Computing methodologies →Classification and regression trees; *Supervised learning by classification;* **•Information systems** →*Data mining;*

KEYWORDS

data mining; classification; random forests

1 INTRODUCTION

Random forests are among the most successful classifiers because of their tremendous accuracy and robustness in various domains. A recent study [8] evaluated 179 classifiers from 17 families on the *entire UCI collection of data sets,* and concluded that random forests were the best performing classifier among these families, and in most cases, their performance was better than other classifiers in a statistically significant way. In fact, multiple third-party implementations of random forests were tested by this study and virtually all implementations provided better performance than multiple implementations of other classifiers. The only other classifier that sometimes outperformed the random forest on a modest number of data sets was the support-vector machine; however, even in this case, the performance of random forests was superior in the aggregate. These results suggest that the random forest classifier is generally quite robust across a wide variety of settings, and is a good choice to use as a default classifier in the absence of domain-specific information.

Random forests are naturally designed to work with multidimensional data because they sample features from the original space in order to create the decision trees that form the ensemble components of the forest. In many applications, such as time-series data, discrete sequences, or graphs, a multidimensional representation might not exist. However, in such domains, the problem of similarity function computation is well studied, and it may be possible to compute similarities between objects. A further complication is that similarities are often incompletely specified when given by domain experts. In all these cases, one cannot use traditional random forests, which are inherently designed to work with multidimensional data sets.

A key problem is that similarity computations are often quite expensive in many domains [15], and it may not be feasible to compute all pairwise similarities from a computational point of view. Therefore, it is important to be able to construct the random forests efficiently while computing an extremely small subset of the pairwise similarities. After all, the number of pairwise similarities scales up quadratically with the number of points. Therefore, any method that requires the entire similarity matrix between pairs of objects to be specified up front is bound to face computational and storage challenges. Furthermore, in cases where all pairwise similarities are not specified (or even computable), this type of approach can still be used, albeit in a limited way.

One possible solution to this problem is to extract a multidimensional embedding from the similarity matrix. As we will discuss later, this approach is not only outrageously expensive (because the extraction of the embedding might require $O(n^3)$ time), but it also requires $O(n^2)$ space to materialize the similarity matrix. Just to provide an idea of the space required, a data set containing a million points would require space of the order of 10^{12}, which is already in the tera-byte order. On the other hand, the approach discussed in this paper requires no more than $O(n \cdot \log(n))$ time and $O(n)$ space for each component of the ensemble. It is also difficult to use traditional classification methods (like SVMs) when the similarities between pairs of data objects are incompletely specified. We show how our approach can be extended to such difficult cases.

KDD '17, August 13-17, 2017, Halifax, NS, Canada

DOI: 10.1145/3097983.3098046

In this paper, we propose the construction of random forests directly with similarity matrices *without assuming access to an explicit multidimensional representation of the data.* We refer to this approach as *SimForest,* which corresponds the fact that it is a *similarity forest.* The basic idea behind this approach is to assume that the data is embedded in some theoretical multidimensional space, and then use the similarities for computing the coordinates of data points along 1-dimensional projections. These 1-dimensional projections are created by sampling pairs of points belonging to different classes, and then for each pair projecting the remaining points along the theoretical multidimensional direction representing the line joining the pair. As we will show, this projection can be performed by using only the pairwise similarities. An important advantage of this approach is that by sampling pairs of points belonging to different classes, one often ends up selecting discriminating directions at least in a randomized sense. In other words, the bias characteristics of the individual components of the similarity forest are often very promising. In combination with the inherent robustness of an ensemble-centric approach, high-quality results are obtained. Therefore, much like the support vector machine, which uses pairwise similarities in order to perform the prediction (without explicitly materializing an embedding), we are able to use similarities in order to construct a random forest without materializing an embedding. However, as discussed in [8], random forests often have an advantage over the SVM in many data domains. The similarity forest approach extends these advantages to cases where traditional random forests cannot be used.

An additional advantage of the *SimForest* approach is that it can be naturally extended to settings where all pairs of similarity values are not available. This can happen in many cases where the number of data points is large, and the entire $O(n^2)$ matrix of similarity values cannot be reasonably materialized. Furthermore, the approach can be used even in domains (e.g., text) where the multidimensional representation is available, but traditional decision trees do not always enable good splits because of feature sparsity; in such cases, similarities can provide better splits.

This paper is organized as follows. The remainder of this section discusses the related work. In the next section, we will introduce the basic notations and definitions. We will also discuss the motivation and the basic idea underlying our approach. The *SimForest* algorithm is presented in section 3. The different variations and extensions of the *SimForest* approach are also discussed in this section. The experimental results are discussed in section 4. The conclusions are presented in section 5.

1.1 Related Work

A detailed survey of various data classification and ensemble algorithms is provided in [1]. A popular ensemble method is that of random forests. Random forests require the availability of a multidimensional representation up front in order to perform the classification. The support vector machine is one of the few classifiers that can work with similarity values in order to provide a classification with the use of the kernel trick [6, 7]. The kernel trick is equivalent to the use of a linear SVM on the transformed data, in a form that is computationally feasible [9, 19]. In general, it is impossible to fully materialize pairwise similarity matrices to perform transformations especially if the data size is large. This is the reason that the kernel trick is preferred over explicit transformation.

A feature bagging variant of the decision tree was first proposed in [11], and subsequently generalized to the present form of the random forest by Breiman [4, 5]. Interestingly, the work in [5, 17] shows that one can extract pairwise similarities from a random forest by counting the frequency with which two instances end up in the same leaf node. In this paper, we achieve the reverse, where we use the pairwise similarities for constructing the random forest. The work in [13, 18] constructs a rotation forest, in which a rotated axis system is constructed up front; the rotation directions are constructed using a combination of attribute partitioning and PCA. Several methods have been proposed for constructing oblique decision trees with [10] or without [12] the use of pairwise directions. However, these methods still need the original multidimensional feature space. The close relationship between random forests and kernel methods is provided in [16]. An extensive study showing the robustness of random forests is available in [8]. In this paper, we propose the use of a similarity-based approach for the direct construction of random forests, while materializing only a very small fraction of the pairwise similarities between objects.

2 DEFINITIONS AND MOTIVATION

We assume that we have a set of n objects denoted by $O_1 \dots O_n$. These n objects can be of any data type, and in most cases, we do not even need to know the specific object type, as long as it is possible to compute a similarity value between them. The similarity between the objects O_i and O_j is denoted by S_{ij}, and it may not necessarily be available up front to the algorithm. For example, in the time-series domain, a domain-specific similarity function may be used. In such cases, the similarity between objects are computed on the fly as needed by the algorithm; the algorithm design needs to minimize such computation. It is assumed that the labels are drawn from a set of c different possibilities denoted by $L = \{1 \dots c\}$. It is assumed that the ith object O_i in the training data is labeled as $l_i \in L$. We state the problem as follows:

PROBLEM 1 (SIMILARITY FOREST). *Given a set of n objects $O_1 \dots O_n$, which are labeled $l_1 \dots l_n$, construct a random forest with the use of only computed pairwise similarities between these objects and no access to the multidimensional representations (if any) of these objects.*

The resulting model is used for classification of objects with unknown labels. For a given test object O with computable similarities with other training objects, a principled method must be proposed in order to perform the classification. As we will show later in this paper, the testing process uses similar principles as the training phase.

For now, we assume that the similarity between any pair of objects can be computed, although we will discuss later how cases of incompletely available similarities can be effectively addressed. Furthermore, in some cases, one might be able to compute distances rather than similarities. For example, one might use distance functions such as the dynamic time-warping distance or edit distance in some domains. In such cases, the similarities can be computed from distances using the cosine law or (as an approximation) the distances can be used in lieu of the similarities with few implementation changes. These variations will also be discussed.

2.1 SimForest: The Motivation

Even though a multidimensional representation is not provided for the data objects, the basic idea is to assume that a multidimensional space exists in which the objects can be embedded. It is noteworthy that one can use kernel methods to extract a multidimensional representation of the objects, if all $O(n^2)$ pairs of similarities between the objects are provided. Such an approach can potentially use $O(n^2)$ space and $O(n^3)$ time, which is not practical for most real-world settings. Aside from this fact, all $O(n^2)$ pairs of similarities are not required to construct a similarity forest. This is because a similarity forest gains large accuracy advantages from the diversity of its individual components. Each ensemble component can often be constructed using a small number of pairwise similarities that are selected in randomized fashion. This is an important advantage of the approach when the similarity computations between pairs of objects are expensive and need to be performed on the fly.

Another point to keep in mind is that explicit embedding extractions do not always work well when the underlying space is very high-dimensional, and when individual dimensions capture little information. One advantage of directly constructing the random forest with similarities is that one can choose to select randomized splits that are biased towards more discriminative directions. Such an approach is able to retain excellent bias characteristics of the individual ensemble components without compromising too much on accuracy.

Let us assume that the objects $O_1 \dots O_n$ can be theoretically embedded in some multidimensional space as the points $\overline{X_1} \dots \overline{X_n}$. However, we do not assume that we explicitly know the representation of $\overline{X_1} \dots \overline{X_n}$; instead, we will work only with similarities between pairs of objects. In fact, we do not even assume that we know the dimensionality of the embedded data points $\overline{X_1} \dots \overline{X_n}$, because they are not required for constructing the similarity forest. Just as a random forest samples features from a multidimensional data set, the similarity-based approach samples pairs of objects in order to define directions in the multidimensional space. For example, sampling the object O_i and O_j results in the vector direction from $\overline{X_i}$ to $\overline{X_j}$. The data objects are then split into two groups using a hyperplane perpendicular to this direction. As we will show later, we do not need to explicitly project the data points along this direction, but the split can be fully executed only using pairwise similarities. This approach is applied recursively to construct each ensemble component of the similarity forest. During the testing phase, the traversal of the tree also requires such similarity computations. It is noteworthy that if the pairs of sampled objects $\overline{X_i}$ and $\overline{X_j}$ are chosen to belong to different classes, the randomized split directions will naturally tend to be more discriminating. The number of pairs of data objects that are required to be sampled at each node is analogous to the number of features that are sampled by the traditional random forest algorithm. Our experimental results show that a small number of pairs such as 2 or 3 can achieve a high level of accuracy.

3 THE SIMFOREST ALGORITHM

In order to describe the *SimForest* algorithm, we will denote the theoretical embeddings by $\overline{X_1} \dots \overline{X_n}$, although none of the algorithmic steps require the knowledge of these embeddings. Therefore, whenever we talk about "directions" in the data space, we are effectively talking about the theoretical embedding $\overline{X_1} \dots \overline{X_n}$. The approach constructs each decision tree in the similarity forest in top-down fashion by using recursive splits. This is similar to the traditional random forests approach. Like traditional random forests, which sample features for splitting, the *SimForest* algorithm samples directions from the original space. The notion of using multivariate directions in the data space for splitting is also used in traditional random forests [18]. However, in order to create a similarity-based approach, the *SimForest* method uses a completely different solution by defining the random directions in terms of *pairs of objects* to enable similarity-based splitting.

These pairs of objects are sampled from among the objects present at the node, which is to be split. One of our interesting and surprising discoveries was that a proper sampling of pairs of objects even improves the performance of *multidimensional* random forests. In other words, even if actual multidimensional representations of data points were given, it is still more accurate to use this approach over traditional random forests. Specifically, at each node, r pairs of objects are sampled in order to define r different random directions. The pairs of objects can be sampled in one of two ways:

(1) The pairs are selected randomly without paying any special attention to the class label.
(2) The pairs are always selected randomly to belong to different classes. In other words, the first object in the pair is selected randomly, whereas the second is selected from the objects belonging to a different class.

The second approach tends to lead to more discriminative splits and therefore reduces the height of the tree that is constructed. In our experiments, we always chose this option because it provided better results. In order to retain diversity, the value of r to be used should be small. Furthermore, using small values of r is beneficial for the efficiency of the method, and one can easily ensure accuracy by increasing the number of trees in the forest. In our experiments, we found that it was best to set the value of r to 1.

Next, we describe the process of evaluating the quality of a split used by the *SimForest* algorithm. Consider a pair of objects O_i and O_j that define the direction of the split. We would like to project each data point along the direction *from* O_i to O_j. Therefore, an object that is identical to O_i would obtain a coordinate of 0, and O_j should obtain a positive coordinate. Consider an object O_k that needs to be projected along this direction. As discussed earlier, the theoretical multidimensional embeddings of O_i, O_j, and O_k are, respectively, $\overline{X_i}$, $\overline{X_j}$ and $\overline{X_k}$. Then, the unit direction of the embedding is given by $\frac{\overline{X_j}-\overline{X_i}}{||\overline{X_j}-\overline{X_i}||}$. The projection $P(\overline{X_k})$ of $\overline{X_k}$ on this direction is therefore given by the dot product of $\overline{X_k} - \overline{X_i}$ on this unit direction. In other words, we have the following:

$$P(\overline{X_k}) = (\overline{X_k} - \overline{X_i}) \cdot \frac{\overline{X_j} - \overline{X_i}}{||\overline{X_j} - \overline{X_i}||} \quad (1)$$

We will show that this entire projection along the 1-dimensional line from $\overline{X_i}$ to $\overline{X_j}$ can be computed only in terms of similarities between pairs of objects. By expanding the product in the numerator of the aforementioned expression, we obtain the following:

$$P(\overline{X_k}) = \frac{\overline{X_k} \cdot \overline{X_j} - \overline{X_k} \cdot \overline{X_i} - \overline{X_i} \cdot \overline{X_j} + \overline{X_i} \cdot \overline{X_i}}{||\overline{X_j} - \overline{X_i}||}$$

$$= \frac{S_{kj} - S_{ki} - S_{ij} + S_{ii}}{||\overline{X_j} - \overline{X_i}||}$$

Here, S_{ij} represents the similarity between objects O_i and O_j. The main problem at this point is the denominator, which is not expressed as similarities. It is possible to also express the denominator in terms of similarities by using the following:

$$||\overline{X_j} - \overline{X_i}|| = \sqrt{||\overline{X_j}||^2 + ||\overline{X_i}||^2 - 2\overline{X_i} \cdot \overline{X_j}}$$

$$= \sqrt{S_{ii} + S_{jj} - 2S_{ij}}$$

However, in practice, it is not necessary to explicitly compute the denominator because (for a given pair) the denominator is independent of the specific data point O_k being projected. In other words, the denominator changes the embedded representation of each data point by only a constant factor, and the *ordering* of the projected points along the 1-dimensional line is not affected, whether or not one includes the denominator in the computation. In a decision tree, a split is computed by examining all $(n-1)$ possible partitions induced by this ordering. The $(n-1)$ potential split points are midway between the $(n-1)$ pairs of adjacent points in this aforementioned ordering. Therefore, we can compute the projection to within a constant of proportionality to achieve the same result. The corresponding projection $P(\overline{X_k})$ may be expressed as follows:

$$P(\overline{X_k}) \propto S_{kj} - S_{ki} - S_{ij} + S_{ii} \tag{2}$$

Furthermore, since the ith and jth objects are already fixed over all projections computed at the splitting node, the last two terms are constant for all data points within the node. In other words, we can write the following:

$$P(\overline{X_k}) \propto S_{kj} - S_{ki} + C \tag{3}$$

Here, C is a constant that does not affect the relative ordering of the points in the projection along the line from $\overline{X_i}$ to $\overline{X_j}$. One can view $S_{kj} - S_{ki}$ as a *scaled and translated proxy* for the projection of O_k on the line joining O_i to O_j. This proxy is used in lieu of the actual projection both in the training and in the testing phase. *Therefore, in order to compute a split for the direction defined by the pair (O_i, O_j), we need to sort the data objects $\{O_k\}_{k=1}^n$ in order of $(S_{kj} - S_{ki})$ and use it to evaluate various splitting points.*

Subsequently, the splitting point is chosen such that it minimizes the weighted Gini index of the children nodes. Specifically, if $p_1 \ldots p_c$ are the fractions of data points belonging to the c different classes in node N, then the Gini index of that node is given by the following:

$$G(N) = 1 - \sum_{i=1}^{c} p_i^2 \tag{4}$$

Then, if the node is split into two children N_1 and N_2, with n_1 and n_2 points, respectively, the weighted Gini quality $GQ(N_1, N_2)$ of the children nodes is given by the following:

$$GQ(N_1, N_2) = \frac{n_1 G(N_1) + n_2 G(N_2)}{n_1 + n_2} \tag{5}$$

When r different pairs of points are used at a node to define possible split directions, all $(n-1)$ possible splits along these r different directions are tested, and the best split is retained. In similarity forests, small values of r are typically used in order to ensure diversity. This is particularly important in cases where the pairs are chosen from different classes.

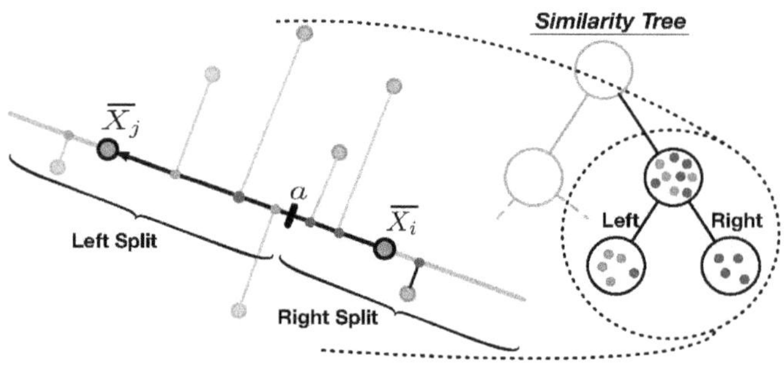

Figure 1: Conceptual illustration of splitting for similarity tree construction.

A conceptual illustration of the splitting process is shown in Figure 1. Each decision tree in the similarity forest is constructed recursively until the leaf nodes purely belong to a specific class. Although the construction of a decision tree often has a pruning phase in which the lower nodes of the tree are removed (to reduce overfitting), this is not done in all types of random forests, including the similarity forest. We construct the tree to full height without pruning, until each node only contains instances belonging to a particular class.

After the decision tree has been constructed, the relevant pairs of objects and the split points are stored at each node. These are required for the testing phase. It is important to note that the pair of objects (O_i, O_j) is *ordered* (for consistency with the testing phase) because the projection $S_{ij} - S_{ii}$ of object O_i is always negative, and the projection $S_{jj} - S_{ji}$ of object O_j is always positive. This holds true for most reasonable similarity functions in which the absolute magnitude of self-similarity S_{ii} is greater than the absolute magnitude of any cross-object similarity S_{ij}. This sign convention is caused by the fact that the direction of the projection vector is from O_i to O_j.

The testing phase uses an identical approach to project the test points on the line defined by the pairs of training points at each node. If (O_i, O_j) is the defining pair of objects for a given node, then the value of $S_{kj} - S_{ki}$ is computed for the test object O_k. The stored split point (say a) is used to determine which path in the decision tree to follow depending on whether or not $S_{kj} - S_{ki} \leq a$. This step is performed for each node on the path of the tree, until the object O_k is assigned to a leaf node. The label of the leaf node is reported as the prediction.

3.1 Implicit Assumptions

One of the implicit assumptions behind this approach is that the data points can be embedded in a multidimensional space. In order for this fact to be true, the $n \times n$ similarity matrix can be expressed as DD^T, where each row of D contains one of the embedded points $\overline{X_i}$. Any matrix that can be expressed as DD^T needs to be positive-semidefinite [2]. Many natural similarity functions satisfy this condition. However, *in practice*, one can still use this approach in a heuristic manner even if the underlying similarity matrix is not positive semi-definite. In particular, the use of the difference in similarities of pairs of objects (belonging to different classes) has a very natural and intuitive tendency to partition them into different classes. Therefore, even though the approach was *derived* assuming the existence of a multidimensional embedding, it can be used in virtually any setting.

3.2 Computational Complexity

One of the attractive features of this approach is its excellent computational complexity. Explicitly extracting a multidimensional embedding from the data might require $O(n^2)$ space and $O(n^3)$ time. Furthermore, at least $O(n^2)$ similarity computations will be required if the embedding is explicitly extracted. This can be prohibitive even when only a few thousand points are present in the data. A single split of *SimForest* requires time that is linear in the number of points *at the splitting node* in the tree. Since a decision tree strictly partitions the data points, the time required to construct *an entire level* of the decision tree is linear in the number of points. Assuming that the height of the tree is $O(\log(n))$, the time required to construct the entire decision tree is $O(n \cdot \log(n))$. Since a random forest typically contains a constant number of decision trees, the overall running time is still $O(n \cdot \log(n))$. The testing procedure requires $O(\log(n))$ time. This efficiency makes the approach an effective alternative to other competing methods.

3.3 Distances Instead of Similarities

In some settings, it is easier to compute distances rather than similarities. For example, in the sequence domain, one might naturally use the edit distance or the dynamic time-warping distance. In such cases, there are two ways in which one can convert distances to similarities:

(1) **Exact approach (computationally intensive):** One can use the *cosine law* to convert distances to similarities. Let U be an $n \times n$ matrix of 1s, and I be an $n \times n$ identity matrix. Let Δ be the $n \times n$ matrix of squared distances. According to the cosine law, a mean-centered similarity matrix S is constructed from the distance matrix Δ using the following rule [2]:

$$S = -\frac{1}{2}(I - U/n)\Delta(I - U/n) \tag{6}$$

The main disadvantage of this approach is that it requires the $O(n^2)$ distance matrix up front, which causes challenges from the point of view of computational and space efficiency.

(2) **Approximate approach (computationally efficient):** This approach uses the squared distances between points in lieu of the similarities. As we will show, this is equivalent to using the differences in similarities, if we make the *normalization* assumption that all points have the same squared norm. This is equivalent to saying that the self-similarity $\overline{X_i} \cdot \overline{X_i}$ of each object O_i is the same. In many domains, this is a reasonable assumption to make. For example, in the text domain, the cosine similarity between pairs of documents always lies in $(0, 1)$ and the self-similarity of a document to itself is always 1. This is because the cosine is a *normalized* similarity function. Similar normalizations are reasonable to assume in many data domains. Such an assumption provides an efficient heuristic approach to perform the splitting in cases where the affinities between objects are expressed in terms of distances rather than similarities.

Consider a setting in which the data points O_i and O_j are the pair of objects defining the direction along which all points are embedded. Let $D(O_i, O_j)$ be the distance between data points O_i and O_j. Then, the difference in squared distances of point O_k with respect to O_i and O_j is defined as follows:

$$\begin{aligned} D(O_k, O_i)^2 - D(O_k, O_j)^2 &= \\ &= ||\overline{X_k} - \overline{X_i}||^2 - ||\overline{X_k} - \overline{X_j}||^2 \\ &= 2\overline{X_k} \cdot \overline{X_j} - 2\overline{X_k} \cdot \overline{X_j} + \underbrace{(||\overline{X_i}||^2 - ||\overline{X_j}||^2)}_{\text{Zero (Because of Normalization)}} \\ &\propto S_{kj} - S_{ki} \end{aligned}$$

This is the same expression that we used for the case of similarities. Note that the expression $(||\overline{X_i}||^2 - ||\overline{X_j}||^2)$ is zero because it is assumed that all embedded points have the same self-similarity. Therefore, with this assumption *there is no difference* between using the squared distances or the similarities for splitting. This makes the approach quite general in many settings, because one can use either distances or similarities between objects, depending on what is available in the specific domain at hand.

3.4 Incompletely Specified Similarities

SimForest can also be used in cases where only a subset of pairwise similarities is observed. This is a particularly common problem in settings where similarity estimation is expensive. For example, if similarities between pairs of objects (such as images) are obtained using crowd-sourcing, a cost may be incurred for each pairwise similarity. Obviously, all pairwise similarities will be impossible to collect in a large data set.

This situation creates a problem from an algorithmic perspective. The problem is that not all objects can be partitioned between a pair of nodes at each split point because the projection of data points along arbitrary directions may require unobserved similarities to be available. The first algorithmic modification to address this issue is that the selected pairs of objects (O_i, O_j) for splitting should always be such that similarity between them is observed. However, this still does not solve the problem that the similarity of an arbitrary point O_k in that node may have unobserved similarities with either O_i or O_j. In such cases, since O_k cannot be assigned to one of the child nodes, we allow it to stay at the current node as its final destination. The class label of an internal node is defined by its majority class. Therefore, unlike the case of fully observed similarities, internal nodes also have a label.

When test instances are classified, the same procedure is applied in computing $S_{kj} - S_{ki}$ (when similarity is available) and assigning the point O_k to a child node, depending on the relationship of $S_{kj} - S_{ki}$ to the split point. Otherwise, if these similarities are not available, the point O_k is assigned to an internal node. The label of the corresponding node is reported as the prediction.

4 EXPERIMENTAL RESULTS

In this section we present extensive experimental results comparing *SimForest* with other competitive techniques. We start by describing the data sets in Section 4.1, followed by a description of the evaluation methodology in Section 4.2. Next, we extensively test *SimForest*'s resistance to noisy similarities in Section 4.3. In Section 4.4 we evaluate how missing similarity values effect the accuracy of *SimForest*. Lastly, in Section 4.5, we show results on multidimensional data.

4.1 Data Sets

We used several classification data sets for our experiments. The important characteristics of these data sets are given in Table 1. The data sets are of various sizes and have varying numbers of features. All of the data sets are obtained from the LibSVM Website repository of classification data sets[1]. All data sets were normalized to zero mean and unit variance.

Table 1: Summary of the Data Sets.

Data set	Points	Features	Classes
HEART	226	13	2
IONOSPHERE	295	34	2
BREAST-CANCER	573	10	2
AUSTRALIAN	579	14	2
DIABETES	645	8	2
GERMAN-NUMER	840	24	2
SVMGUIDE3	1035	22	2
A1A	32,240	123	2
MADELON	2200	500	2
SPLICE	2975	500	2
MUSHROOMS	6824	112	2

4.2 Evaluation Strategy

For every experiment we perform a 80-20 split of the data. 80% data is used for training the classifiers, while 20% data is used for testing its performance. In many experiments the training data is further divided into portions for model building and parameter tuning, in which 10% is used for tuning. Model performance is measured using *accuracy*. Accuracy is measured as the percentage of correctly classified test data points.

[1] https://www.csie.ntu.edu.tw/~cjlin/libsvmtools/datasets/

4.3 Performance with Noisy Similarity Matrices

The primary use case of *SimForest* is one in which only the similarities between objects are available, and the objects might not be multidimensional. In such cases, a traditional random forest cannot even be used, and the natural competitor to our approach is a kernel support vector machine. Therefore, this section will show results with respect to this natural competitor.

In many real settings, similarity matrices are noisy. For example, consider the use of crowdsourcing to measure image similarity, where a human crowdsourcer is tasked with assigning similarity to a pair of images. In such cases, it is natural for errors to occur in the similarity, which are partly due to error in judgment or even due to the inherent bias of different workers. In this section, we will show that *SimForest* is highly resistant to such noisy similarities, as compared to well-known classifiers, such as SVMs.

A key point here is in the availability of noisy similarity matrices, and that of testing the effect of a specific level of noise. Therefore, our approach was to use multidimensional data to construct the similarity matrices (with added noise), but not to assume access to the multidimensional features for building the classification model (either *SimForest* or baselines). This was achieved by constructing two types of similarity matrices, corresponding to the cosine similarity and the Gaussian RBF similarity. Note that both these similarity matrices are naturally used as kernels in support vector machines, and therefore the SVM approach[2] is well suited to these types of input similarity matrices. Noise was added[3] to the similarity matrices with the use of a *noise coefficient* α. For each similarity value, a noise value that was uniformly distributed between $[0, \alpha]$ was added. To mitigate the effect of random variations, ten different instantiations of the noise were generated, and the averaged results were reported. The bandwidth of the RBF kernel for computing the similarity matrix was selected by picking a point of optimum performance for the SVM (without added noise), but it was fed into both classifiers. This actually puts *SimForest* at a disadvantage because the similarity matrix that is given as part of the input data is biased towards working well with the (baseline) SVM. Note that the assumption here is that the similarity matrix is a part of the input data, and the analyst has no say in how it is chosen, computed, or obtained.

The similarity matrices were generated for six data sets, which were IONOSPHERE, HEART, GERMAN-NUMER, DIABETES, AUSTRALIAN, and A1A. A *SimForest* with 100 similarity trees is used for this experiment. In Table 2, we illustrate the accuracy obtained over various data sets with both types of similarity matrices at $\alpha = 2.5$. In all the data sets, *SimForest* has superior performance as compared to SVM. The best performance improvement of 14.7% and 12.6% is observed in the GERMAN-NUMER data set for RBF kernel and the IONOSPHERE data set for the cosine similarity, respectively. Overall, these experiments demonstrate that *SimForest* is highly noise resistant and can consistently produce superior results over

[2] In fact, *scikit-learn* has an option to input the similarity matrix rather than the multidimensional features in its SVM implementation. The details are available at http://scikit-learn.org/stable/modules/generated/sklearn.svm.SVC.html. We use this off-the-shelf implementation.

[3] It is assumed that the same noise is added to the (i, j)th and (j, i)th entries because the similarity matrix is symmetric.

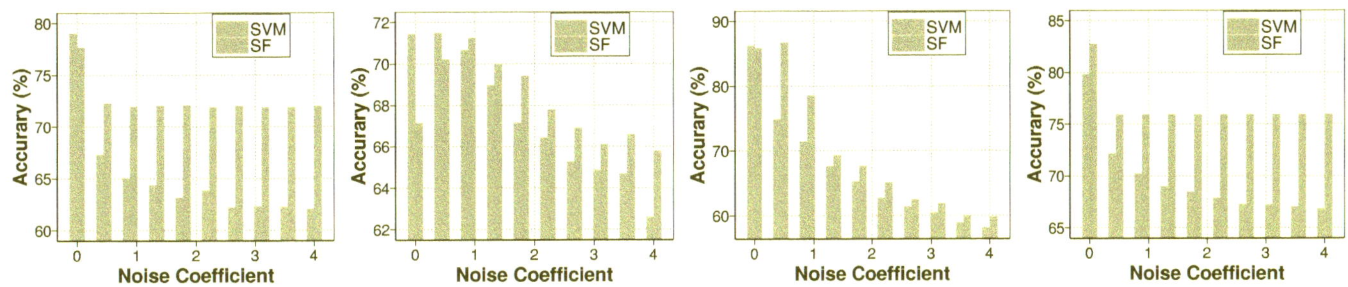

(a) GERMAN-NUMER (b) DIABETES (c) AUSTRALIAN (d) A1A

Figure 2: RBF Kernel: Comparing noise sensitivity of *SimForest* (SF) and SVM (best viewed in color).

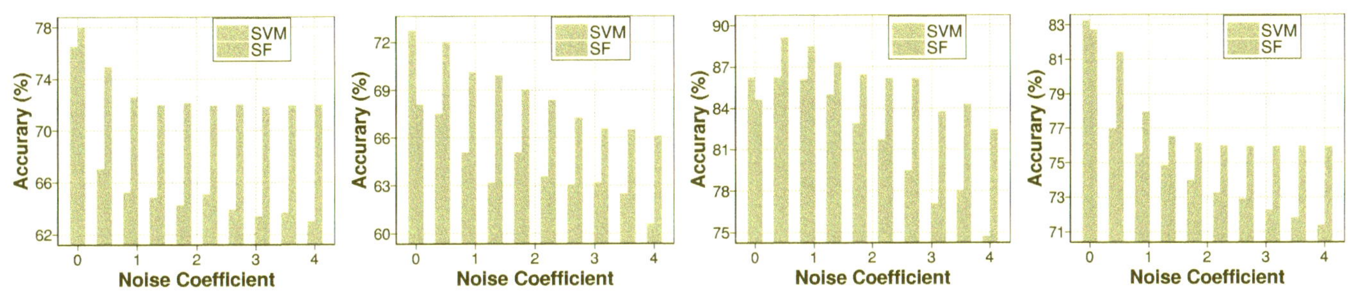

(a) GERMAN-NUMER (b) DIABETES (c) AUSTRALIAN (d) A1A

Figure 3: Cosine Similarity: Comparing noise sensitivity of *SimForest* (SF) and SVM (best viewed in color).

state-of-the-art methods like support vector machines. Most importantly, *SimForest* represents a natural generalization of the idea of random forests to the setting where only similarity matrices are available.

Table 2: Accuracy observed at a fixed value of the noise coefficient (α = 2.5).

Data set	RBF Kernel		Cosine Similarity	
	SimForest	SVM	*SimForest*	SVM
HEART	**68.14**	67.22	**72.96**	68.70
IONOSPHERE	**71.69**	68.59	**74.22**	65.91
AUSTRALIAN	**61.88**	61.23	**85.79**	79.49
DIABETES	**68.44**	64.87	**67.33**	62.85
GERMAN-NUMER	**72.00**	62.80	**71.85**	65.40
A1A	**75.94**	67.81	**75.97**	72.88

Further experiments were performed to compare the noise resistance of the proposed *SimForest* approach to SVMs, both of which can exclusively operate only on similarity matrices. The idea is to increase the noise coefficient α to examine the impact on the accuracy. Figures 2 and 3 show the comparison between *SimForest* and SVM for the RBF kernel and cosine similarity, respectively. For both types of similarity measures, *SimForest* exhibits extraordinary ruggedness to noise. One reason for this ruggedness is that SVMs attempt to maximize the inter-class margin by using a few select points known as *support vectors*. In other words, SVMs ignore points other than support vectors for prediction. It is particularly noteworthy that misclassified points and noise are usually support vectors that occur on the wrong side of the decision boundary. Therefore, addition of noise adversely affects the capability of the SVM to choose reliable support vectors, which results in a poor decision boundary. On the other hand, *SimForest* is inherently noise tolerant because of its robust approach in averaging out the noise. This results in higher overall accuracy of the *SimForest*.

The choice of the similarity matrix (cosine or RBF) does have some effect on the relative performance of the two methods, although the effect for high amounts of noise is similar. In all the plots shown in Figures 2 and 3, the *SimForest* classifier does much better than SVM when the value of α was set to large values. It is noteworthy that the similarity matrices in real applications are often highly noisy, which could be an artifact of the subjective way in which these matrices are extracted.

4.4 Handling Missing Similarities

Aside from the noise, an additional problem occurs when many entries of the similarity matrix are missing. The presence of missing entries is very natural when such matrices are derived from user feedback. Manual feedback is tedious and crowd-sourced feedback (e.g., *Amazon Mechanical Turk*) is expensive. Therefore, it is impractical to assume that all pairwise similarities will be available. Furthermore, even if the pairwise similarities can be computed, they are computationally expensive to evaluate. This approach is not feasible when the number of points is very large. For example, if a

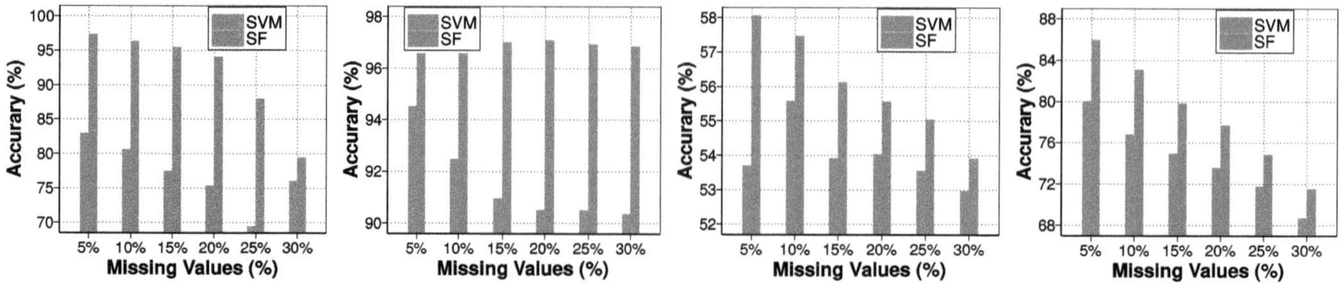

(a) Ionosphere (b) Breast-Cancer (c) Madelon (d) Splice

Figure 4: RBF Kernel: Impact of missing similarity values on *SimForest* (SF) and SVM (best viewed in color).

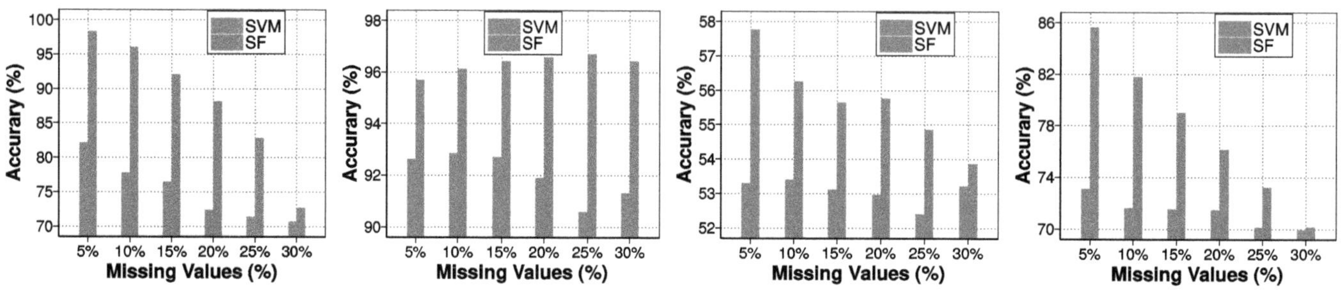

(a) Ionosphere (b) Breast-Cancer (c) Madelon (d) Splice

Figure 5: Cosine Similarity: Impact of missing similarity values on *SimForest* (SF) and SVM (best viewed in color).

matrix has 10^6 training points, one can hardly be expected to compute all 10^{12} similarity values between training pairs. At the end, one is often left to using simple extrapolation rules, such as the column-wise mean for imputation, when using a similarity-based classifier like an SVM. Very few classifiers have the ability to learn from incomplete data, particularly when the data is not specified in multidimensional form, but in the form of highly incomplete similarity matrices. A fundamental advantage of *SimForest* is that it can be built on similarity matrices with missing values (as discussed in section 3.4), without having to explicitly impute these values.

Table 3: Accuracy observed when 15% of similarity values are missing.

Data set	RBF Kernel		Cosine Similarity	
	SimForest	SVM	*SimForest*	SVM
German-Numer	**72.25**	67.60	**72.05**	64.25
Australian	**90.14**	83.47	**89.63**	86.23
Ionosphere	**95.49**	77.46	**92.11**	76.47
Breast-Cancer	**97.00**	90.94	**96.42**	92.07
Madelon	**56.11**	53.91	**55.65**	53.11
Splice	**79.81**	74.94	**79.02**	71.53

As in the previous section, we construct two different types of similarity matrices with the cosine and RBF similarity functions, and assume that only the similarity matrices are available without access to the multidimensional attributes. However, in this case, we drop a certain fraction of the similarity values, and allow access to only the retained values. The SVM model cannot work directly with missing values in the similarity matrix. Therefore, when such values were required by the SVM, the column-wise mean of the similarity matrix is used instead. In the case of the *SimForest*, the missing-value approach in Section 3.4 was used. The experiments were repeated for 10 different random samples of the missing entries for all methods and data sets, and the performance values were averaged to give stable results. Table 3 shows the results for the case when 15% of the entries are missing. The experiments are performed on the German-Numer, Australian, Ionosphere, Breast-Cancer, Madelon, and Splice data sets. The average improvement of *SimForest* across all data sets was 9.23% for the RBF kernel, while it was 9.42% for the cosine similarity. Thus, *SimForest* not only works in the presence of missing values without the need for imputation, but is also remarkably accurate when similarities are incompletely specified.

How do the fraction of the missing values affect the results? We show the sensitivity of *SimForest* to an increasing percentage of missing values. The sensitivity results are shown on four data sets, which are Ionosphere, Breast-Cancer, Madelon, and Splice. These results are shown in Figures 4 and 5 for the RBF kernel and cosine similarity, respectively. In both cases, it is evident that the *SimForest* approach is far more tolerant to missing values than SVMs. As the fraction of missing values increases, the *SimForest* approach performs much better than SVMs.

Table 4: Accuracy on multi-dimensional data sets.

Data set	HEART	IONOSPHERE	BREAST-CANCER	GERMAN-NUMER	SVMGUIDE3	A1A	MUSHROOMS
SimForest	**83.33**	**100.00**	**96.35**	**78.50**	**90.24**	82.81	**100.00**
Random Forest	79.62	94.36	**96.35**	77.00	87.80	82.63	**100.00**
SVM	81.48	87.32	**96.35**	76.00	58.53	**83.42**	**100.00**

4.5 Multidimensional Data

Next, we illustrate the performance of *SimForest* on multidimensional data, and we assume that access to the multidimensional attributes is available. Although the *SimForest* approach is designed for settings in which only similarities are available, it is easy to use it in cases where multidimensional features are available. There are no required changes to the implementation to adapt it to the multidimensional case, other than the fact that we explicitly compute the similarities (as needed) using the features. An additional advantage is that we can draw from a greater choice of similarity functions. We used the dot products between multidimensional features as the similarity values in the *SimForest*. Note that one can use other types of similarity values as well, although we used the simplest option in this case. To ensure comparability, we also used the dot product as the similarity for the SVM. A key difference in the comparison here is that we can now also include a traditional random forest because the underlying multidimensional feature representation is available. In this experiment, we include the traditional random forest with splits on individual attributes. The number of features sampled at each node for the traditional random forest is chosen as the square root of the data dimensionality, and 100 trees are grown for both random forest and *SimForest*. For the SVM, the value of the slack penalty was tuned using cross-validation. The results are shown in Table 4. Observe that *SimForest* is highly competitive to Random Forest and SVMs, even though *SimForest* was not originally designed for a multidimensional setting. The random forest, however, comes very close to matching the accuracy of *SimForest*. This is hardly surprising because the random forest is conceptually related to the *SimForest*, and is one of the best available classifiers. The key takeaway from the results on multidimensional data is not necessarily to advocate the use of *SimForest* in the multidimensional setting, but to emphasize the fact that it squeezes the most that is possible from a particular similarity matrix. This is evidenced by the fact that even direct access to the actual features does not help a traditional random forest win over *SimForest*. This indirectly suggests that the performance of *SimForest* is formidably strong for the case where one does not have access to the multidimensional features, and only the similarity matrices are available.

5 CONCLUSIONS AND SUMMARY

In this paper, we presented a method for constructing random forests from arbitrary object data types by using a similarity-centric approach to decision-tree construction. Our approach provides the ability to incorporate domain-specific similarity functions within the mining process. Only a small fraction of the pairwise similarities are computed, and therefore all pairwise similarities do not need to be materialized. Even where many of the pairwise similarities are missing, one can use such an approach for prediction. Although the approach is naturally designed for the case where the input is specified in the form of similarity matrices, it can be used for multidimensional data by using the derived similarity matrices of these objects. In these settings, the technique is competitive with off-the-shelf methods, which shows that *SimForest* gets the most out of any particular similarity function for the purposes of classification. The experimental results show that our approach has significant advantages over the baseline techniques of support vector machines and random forests, which are state-of-the-art methods for classification.

REFERENCES

[1] C. Aggarwal. Data Classification: Algorithms and Applications, *CRC Press*, 2014.
[2] C. Aggarwal. Data Mining: The Textbook, *Springer*, 2016.
[3] C. Aggarwal and S. Sathe. Outlier Ensembles: An Introduction, *Springer*, 2017.
[4] L. Brieman. Random Forests. *Journal Machine Learning archive*, 45(1), pp. 5–32, 2001.
[5] L. Brieman and A. Cutler. Random Forests Manual v4.0, *Technical Report, UC Berkeley*, 2003.
[6] C. Burges. A tutorial on support vector machines for pattern recognition. *Data mining and knowledge discovery*, 2(2), pp. 121–167, 1998.
[7] C. Cortes and V. Vapnik. Support-vector networks. *Machine Learning*, 20(3), pp. 273–297, 1995.
[8] M. Fernandez-Delgado, E. Cernadas, S. Barro, and D. Amorim. Do we Need Hundreds of Classifiers to Solve Real World Classification Problems?. *The Journal of Machine Learning Research*, 15(1), pp. 3133–3181, 2014.
[9] A. Graf, A. Smola, and S. Borer. Classification in a normalized feature space using support vector machines. *IEEE Transactions on Neural Networks*, 14(3), 2003.
[10] G. E. Hinton and M. Revow. Using pairs of data points to define splits for decision trees. In *NIPS* pp. 507-513, 1996.
[11] T. K. Ho. Random decision forests. *Third International Conference on Document Analysis and Recognition*, 1995. Extended version appears in *IEEE Transactions on Pattern Analysis and Machine Intelligence*, 20(8), pp. 832–844, 1998.
[12] M. Kretowski. An evolutionary algorithm for oblique decision tree induction. In *International Conference on Artificial Intelligence and Soft Computing*, pp. 432-437, 2004.
[13] L. Kuncheva and J. Rodrguez. An experimental study on rotation forest ensembles. In *Multiple Classifier Systems*, pp. 459–468, 2007.
[14] F. T. Liu, K. M. Ting, and Z.-H. Zhou. Isolation Forest. *ICDM Conference*, 2008. Extended version appears as "Isolation-based Anomaly Detection," *ACM Transactions on Knowledge Discovery from Data (TKDD)*, 6(1), 3, 2012.
[15] H. Lodhi, C. Saunders, J. Shawe-Taylor, N. Cristianini, and C. Watkins. Text classification using string kernels. *Journal of Machine Learning Research*, 2(Feb), pp. 419–444, 2002.
[16] E. Scornet. Random forests and kernel methods. *IEEE Transactions on Information Theory*, 62(3), pp. 1485-1500, 2016.
[17] Y. Qi, J. Klein-Seetharaman, and Z. Bar-Joseph. Random forest similarity for protein-protein interaction prediction from multiple sources. *Pacific Symposium on Biocomputing. Pacific Symposium on Biocomputing*, 2004.
[18] J. Rodriguez, L. Kuncheva, and C. Alonso. Rotation forest: A new classifier ensemble method. *IEEE Transactions on Pattern Analysis and Machine Intelligence*, 28(10), pp. 1619–1630, 2006.
[19] B. Schölkopf, A. Smola, K. Muller. Kernel principal component analysis. *International Conference on Artificial Neural Networks*, pp. 583–588, 1997.

Online Ranking with Constraints: A Primal-Dual Algorithm and Applications to Web Traffic-Shaping

Parikshit Shah Akshay Soni Troy Chevalier
{parikshit,akshaysoni,troyc}@yahoo-inc.com
Yahoo Research

ABSTRACT

We study the online constrained ranking problem motivated by an application to web-traffic shaping: an online stream of sessions arrive in which, within each session, we are asked to rank items. The challenge involves optimizing the ranking in each session so that local vs. global objectives are controlled: within each session one wishes to maximize a reward (local) while satisfying certain constraints over the entire set of sessions (global). A typical application of this setup is that of page optimization in a web portal. We wish to rank items so that not only is user engagement maximized in each session, but also other business constraints (such as the number of views/clicks delivered to various publishing partners) are satisfied.

We describe an online algorithm for performing this optimization. A novel element of our approach is the use of linear programming duality and connections to the celebrated Hungarian algorithm. This framework enables us to determine a set of *shadow prices* for each traffic-shaping constraint that can then be used directly in the final ranking function to assign near-optimal rankings. The (dual) linear program can be solved off-line periodically to determine the prices. At serving time these prices are used as weights to compute weighted rank-scores for the items, and the simplicity of the approach facilitates scalability to web applications. We provide rigorous theoretical guarantees for the performance of our online algorithm and validate our approach using numerical experiments on real web-traffic data from a prominent internet portal.

1 INTRODUCTION

This paper investigates the online constrained ranking problem — a collection of sessions arrive in an online manner. In each session we wish to make optimal decisions that balance local versus global trade-offs: locally we wish to maximize the engagement of that session, while globally we wish to satisfy certain constraints over the entire set of sessions. Each session involves a user interacting with a collection of items, and the decision-making task at hand is that of selecting a ranking of these items. The rankings chosen across all sessions influence the rewards collected in the sessions as well as whether or not the overall constraints are satisfied.

KDD'17, August 13–17, 2017, Halifax, NS, Canada.

978-1-4503-4887-4/17/08...$15.00
DOI: http://dx.doi.org/10.1145/3097983.3098025

While our main focus in this paper is to develop algorithms for the general online constrained ranking problem, the key motivating application involves webpage layout optimization and traffic-shaping. In this context, each session corresponds to a user interacting with a webpage (for example a web portal), and the decision-maker wishes to optimize the placement of content from an assortment of content (e.g. news articles, sports articles, ads, blogs, financial news, etc.).

The webpage is assumed to be divided into slots, and the problem of assigning content to slots may be viewed as an assignment or ranking problem. The natural locally optimal approach to optimizing a webpage involves computing an engagement score (e.g., a click probability or a predicted dwell-time) for each content, and displaying the content within slots on the page in descending order of the scores so that the highest (predicted) engaging content is in the most highly clicked slot, and so on.

However, in practice there are often other business constraints in place. For example we may wish to deliver a certain guaranteed number of clicks to different segments of the traffic. Business considerations may dictate that a certain number of clicks be delivered to a premium advertiser, or that a certain number of top-ranked page-views be delivered to certain premium news-agency partners over the entire collection of sessions in the traffic. These additional side constraints introduce trade-offs; performing a simple "locally optimal" ranking may violate these constraints. The challenge thus is to pick assignments in each session, online, in a way that satisfy the traffic-wide business constraints while maximizing user engagement. Since the traffic distribution is quite well-known in advance (and data is available for the same), the natural question to ask is whether we can optimize the pages in each session to maximize user engagement while satisfying the other traffic constraints. Our paper deals with developing a principled approach to deal with this traffic-shaping problem.

Note that our paper does not seek to address the learning-to-rank problem [8, 10], i.e. the problem of learning how to predict user engagement from data. Indeed, in many practical systems, a natural separation of concerns is assumed between learning-to-rank (or machine learning for predicting other user-engagement signals such as click-through rate, dwell-time etc.) and the traffic-shaping problem. The machine learned models are used as input signals to a *federation* layer that performs traffic-shaping, i.e. ingesting the signals and optimizing the ranking to maximize engagement and satisfying the constraints. However, the algorithm for traffic-shaping itself is completely agnostic to the details of how these signals are learned.

Comparison to related work: The traffic-shaping and click-shaping problems were studied by Agarwal et al. [1–3] using an optimization based framework that involved probabilistic sampling.

Several important features distinguish our work. The aforementioned work deals only with the single slot case (i.e. each session involves choosing a single item from a collection and picking the best one that satisfies a constraint), and they defer the multi-slot problem as an open problem. While they also adopt a linear programming approach, their model is substantially different; their optimization variables are probabilities of sampling items that maximize reward and satisfy traffic constraints. Moreover, they do not present theoretical guarantees on the solution quality. In contrast, our approach directly addresses the multi-slot situation (i.e. ranking items), our optimization involves optimizing over the set of permutations (i.e. assignments), and we tackle the online aspect of the problem by incorporating a learning phase followed by an online decision-making phase. We evaluate our method empirically and provide rigorous theoretical guarantees.

Our work draws on ideas and tools from the online optimization literature, specifically the primal-dual method for online linear programming [4] and its applications to online combinatorial optimization problems [7] such as the ad-words problem [12, 14], whole-page optimization problem for ads [13], combinatorial auctions [5], and extensions to the nonlinear case [11]. The aforementioned ideas have been used in online matching of ads to bidders under budget constraints – whereas our approach substantially uses ideas and tools from this literature, a key distinction is the nature of the decision-making problem. Each online session in the aforementioned lines of work involves a binary decision-making problem, i.e. whether or not to assign a unit of an item in the session. In contrast, in our problem, each session involves choosing a permutation (more specifically a perfect matching between the items and the slots).

Moreover, unlike [4] where the decision-maker must satisfy budget (upper bound) constraints, in our paper we have allocation (lower bound) constraints wherein a certain number of units (for e.g. clicks) must be delivered. Finally, we mention that within the literature, different lines of work arise from different distributional assumptions made on the sessions; e.g. [14] analyze the problem in the setting where the ordering of sessions may be adversarial with respect to the online decision maker. Another line of work [4, 12] assumes the *random permutation model*, wherein the distribution order of sessions may be assumed to exchangeable. Different theoretical guarantees are possible under different scenarios, and our work employs the random permutation model also. Our main contributions in this paper are the following:

- **Solution Form:** We present a new algorithm for the online constrained ranking problem. In the initial learning phase, dual prices λ_t corresponding to each traffic constraint t are learned. In the subsequent online phase, in each session, one is provided matrices C and A_t (see Sec. 2 for details) that capture the predictions for engagement and traffic-shaping units contributed for different possible rankings. The online ranking algorithm assumes the simple form:

$$\sigma = \texttt{MaxWeightMatching}\left(C + \sum_{t=1}^{T} \lambda_t A_t\right). \tag{1}$$

When $\lambda_t = 0$, one recovers the "greedy" solution, i.e. that of optimizing each session individually and disregarding the constraints. In order to satisfy the constraints, the session rankings must be re-optimized (over the space of permutations) as per (1). As a consequence of the connection to maximum-weight matching, we intimately use the Hungarian algorithm [16] and its analysis.
- **Scalability:** In the learning phase, data is collected and a single linear program needs to be solved offline to obtain the prices. Thereafter, the online aspect is extremely scalable as it involves computing a matching using the prices.
- **Evaluation and Guarantees:** We present detailed empirical validation of our algorithm on real data. We also theoretically analyze our algorithm using the primal-dual method. Specifically we show that our algorithm achieves a competitive ratio of $1 - O(\epsilon)$, where ϵ is the fraction of samples that are used in the learning phase.
- **Flexibility:** Another desirable feature of our algorithm is that it is flexible; indeed constraints can change, performance of the machine learned input signals can vary, and we would like a solution that is robust. Robustness is achieved by simply repeating the learning phase (with the new constraints in place, for instance), and obtaining the new prices. Thereafter, the implementation of the online algorithm remains the same, only the new prices need be propagated.

Notation: Throughout the paper, we will use the notation $[m] := \{1, \ldots, m\}$; this quantity will refer to the size of the list (of documents) to be ranked in each session. A permutation (or ranking), denoted by σ refers to a bijection between sets $\sigma : [m] \to [m]$. Usually the sets of interest are the set of documents (in a fixed session), and the different slots, and a permutation σ specifies the assignment of documents to slots. We will use the terms permutation, assignment, and ranking interchangeably throughout the paper. It will often be convenient to represent the ranking σ by a permutation matrix $P \in \mathbb{R}^{m \times m}$ where $(P)_{ij} = 1$ if $\sigma(i) = j$ and 0 otherwise. Such a matrix has a single entry equal to one in each row and column, with the remaining entries equal to zero. We will refer to the set of $m!$ permutation matrices as $\mathcal{P}$. The convex hull of $\mathcal{P}$, denoted by $co(\mathcal{P})$ is the Birkhoff polytope [16], which will play an important role.

Throughout the paper, the index k is reserved for sessions, i.e. $k \in [n]$, the index t is reserved for the T different traffic-shaping constraints, i.e. $t \in [T]$. In a session k, if document d is shown in position p, a user engagement of $(C_k)_{d,p}$ is assumed to be accrued. Given a permutation σ, the overall engagement reward is assumed to be additive, i.e. given by $\sum_{i=1}^{m} (C_k)_{i,\sigma(i)}$. The matrix C_k is conveniently represented by a bipartite graph with m nodes on the left and right and the edges having weights $(C_k)_{d,p}$. A matching σ achieves a weight of $\sum_{i=1}^{m} (C_k)_{i,\sigma(i)}$. A maximum-weight perfect matching is a permutation $\sigma \in \mathcal{P}$ with maximum possible weight. We remind the reader that a maximum-weight perfect matching in a bipartite graph is obtained via the Hungarian algorithm [16]. We will use the notation $P \geq 0$ to specify that the matrix P is entry-wise non-negative, and P' denotes the matrix transpose. We will use $\langle P, Q \rangle := \sum_{i=1}^{m} \sum_{j=1}^{m} P_{ij} Q_{ij}$ to denote the inner-product between the matrices $P, Q \in \mathbb{R}^{m \times m}$. When a ranking P is chosen, the engagement corresponding to that ranking is given by $\langle C_k, P\rangle$ due to the additive nature of the reward.

2 FORMULATION

Let $k \in [n]$ index a collection of sessions where different users interact with the content-delivery system of interest. In each session, a collection of m documents are made available. The task of the ranking system is, in each session k, to rank the documents, i.e. produce a permutation $\sigma_k : [m] \to [m]$.

For each session, we assume access to predictions of how each document would perform with respect to user engagement (e.g. clicks or dwell time) if document d was shown in the pth position. Let $C \in \mathbb{R}^{m\times m}$ be the matrix such that $C_{d,p}$ models the engagement when document d is shown in the pth position. (Typically, this type of information is available from the output of a machine-learned model that predicts the engagement for each document, personalized for each user corresponding to the session in question). For each session, the engagement is given by $\sum_{p=1}^{m} C_{p,\sigma(p)} = \langle C, P\rangle$, where P is the permutation matrix corresponding to σ. The total engagement across all sessions is therefore $\sum_{k=1}^{n}\langle C_k, P_k\rangle$, where k is the user engagement for the kth session and P_k is the corresponding permutation chosen.

Simultaneously, we assume that a number of traffic-shaping constraints are present. As an example, we may have constraints on the number of clicks that must be delivered to various publishing partners (in a fixed number of sessions). These can be captured as:

$$\sum_{k=1}^{n}\langle A_{kt}, P_k\rangle \geq b_t,$$

where the index k refers to the session, and t refers to t^{th} traffic-shaping constraint. The matrix $A_{kt} \in \mathbb{R}^{m\times m}$ is the matrix whose (d,p) entry captures the number of engagement units (e.g. clicks) delivered for the tth constraint in the kth session when document d is shown in position p (such estimates are also typically obtained as the output of a machine-learned click model)[1]. The constant b_t is the number of clicks that are committed to the publishing partner in n sessions contractually. The objective of the ranking system is to maximize the overall user-engagement while satisfying certain constraints.

The above description suggests a natural optimization formulation:

$$\begin{aligned} \underset{P_1,\dots,P_n}{\text{maximize}} \quad & \sum_{k=1}^{n}\langle C_k, P_k\rangle \\ \text{subject to} \quad & \sum_{k=1}^{n}\langle A_{kt}, P_k\rangle \geq b_t \quad t = 1,\dots,T \\ & P_k \in \mathcal{P} \quad k = 1,\dots,n. \end{aligned} \tag{2}$$

[1] As an aside, we note that in practice, C_k and A_{kt} are predictions obtained from a machine learned model, and the engagement (i.e., dwell-time and clicks) realized will likely be different from the predictions. We ignore this distinction in this paper, and make the simplifying assumption that the predictions are "perfect". When the models are consistent and a sufficiently large number of sessions are involved, the expected performance (being optimized here) will be close to that of the realized one.

While conceptually clean, working directly with this formulation has several disadvantages:

- Solving this formulation requires knowledge of the C_k, A_{kt} beforehand, whereas the problem is online in nature (i.e. the sessions arrive in an online manner).
- The above optimization formulation is combinatorial and therefore intractable, i.e. it involves optimizing over the set of permutations.

To address the last point, we perform a *convex relaxation* [6, Chapter 6] of the problem, i.e. relax the optimization constraints $P_k \in \mathcal{P}$ to $P_k \in co(\mathcal{P})$, where the $co(\mathcal{P})$ represents the convex hull of $\mathcal{P}$ [16, Chapter 18]. The resulting relaxation converts the optimization formulation (2) into a convex optimization problem (indeed, it is a linear programming problem), which can therefore be solved (in principle) in polynomial time. There are a number of difficulties pertaining to the relaxation:

- Linear programming is computationally intensive and solving one at serving-time is often infeasible due to the strict latency requirements. Hence we desire to avoid solving them at run-time (although solving offline on a periodic basis is acceptable).
- A problem associated with convex relaxations of combinatorial problems is that the resulting solution may be fractional (i.e. the solutions P_k may not be permutation matrices). We then have to devise a scheme to convert the optimal solution to a permutation matrix via a rounding scheme. As we will show in our subsequent analysis, we will not need to round solutions. The special structure of our problem and well-known results from graph matching and the analysis of the Hungarian algorithm [16, Chapter 17] actually guarantee that we can always produce a valid extremal solution, rather than a fractional one.
- In order to solve the convex relaxation, one needs a tractable representation of the set $co(\mathcal{P})$ in terms of a small number of equations and inequalities. It turns out that the convex hull of the set of permutation matrices has a compact description via the Birkhoff-von Neumann Theorem [16, Chapter 18], it is simply the set of so-called doubly stochastic matrices (sometimes also called the Birkhoff polytope) given by:

$$\mathcal{B} := co(\mathcal{P}) = \left\{P \in \mathbb{R}^{m\times m} \mid P\mathbf{1} = \mathbf{1}\ P'\mathbf{1} = \mathbf{1}\ P \geq 0\right\}. \tag{3}$$

We will be able to resolve the above difficulties by computing and analyzing the dual; indeed the analysis will reveal a natural and simple online algorithm which we will describe below.

We first explicitly state the primal and dual linear programs that result from the convex relaxation of (2).

$$\begin{aligned} \underset{P_1,\dots,P_n}{\text{maximize}} \quad & \sum_{k=1}^{n}\langle C_k, P_k\rangle \\ \text{subject to} \quad & \sum_{k=1}^{n}\langle A_{kt}, P_k\rangle \geq b_t \quad \forall\, t = 1,\dots,T \\ & P_k \in \mathcal{B} \quad k = 1,\dots,n \end{aligned} \tag{4}$$

$$\begin{aligned}
\underset{\lambda,\alpha_k,\beta_k}{\text{maximize}} \quad & \sum_{t=1}^{T} \lambda_t b_t + \sum_{k=1}^{n} \alpha_k' \mathbf{1} + \sum_{k=1}^{n} \beta_k' \mathbf{1} \\
\text{subject to} \quad & C_k + \sum_{t=1}^{T} \lambda_t A_{kt} + \mathbf{1}\alpha_k' + \beta_k \mathbf{1}' \leq 0 \;\; \forall k = 1,\ldots,n \\
& \lambda \geq 0
\end{aligned} \tag{5}$$

The dual linear program is of key interest in the paper — our algorithm will consist of solving (5) on historical data, and computing the optimal dual variables λ which have a natural price interpretation. We describe this in the next section.

3 THE ALGORITHM

Recall that in our setup, the n sessions arrive in a sequential manner online, and for each session k we have access to the matrices C_k (the engagement), and A_{tk} (corresponding to the traffic-shaping constraint). We denote the full set of sessions by N. Our approach involves using a subset of the sessions, S, initially to learn the dual prices. The corresponding primal/dual linear programs are called the *sample linear programs*. In these learning-phase sessions, we make arbitrary decisions — concretely we let $P_k = I$, the identity permutation. Let $\hat{n} := |S|$ be chosen and denote $\epsilon = \frac{\hat{n}}{n}$. Since the constraints require that a budget of b_t clicks are to be delivered over n sessions, it follows that when ϵn sessions are present, the corresponding commitment is only ϵb_t clicks for each traffic-constraint b_t. In this way, the b_t is rescaled. In order to be conservative, we instead require that for each constraint: $\sum_{k=1}^{\hat{n}} \langle A_{kt}, P_k \rangle \geq \nu \epsilon b_t$. The additional ν multiplicative factor ensures that the solution obtained is robust to random variations (we will discuss this in Section 5), and also to counter the conservative estimate that since the first ϵ fraction of sessions are used for learning, zero (or negligible) contributions to the constraints are made from it. Accordingly, the primal/dual sample linear programs are:

$$\begin{aligned}
\underset{P_1,\ldots,P_{\hat{n}}}{\text{maximize}} \quad & \sum_{k=1}^{\hat{n}} \langle C_k, P_k \rangle \\
\text{subject to} \quad & \sum_{k=1}^{\hat{n}} \langle A_{kt}, P_k \rangle \geq \nu \epsilon b_t \;\; \forall\, t = 1,\ldots,T \\
& P_k \in \mathcal{B} \;\; k = 1,\ldots,\hat{n}
\end{aligned} \tag{6}$$

$$\begin{aligned}
\underset{\lambda,\alpha_k,\beta_k}{\text{maximize}} \quad & \sum_{t=1}^{T} \nu\epsilon\lambda_t b_t + \sum_{k=1}^{\hat{n}} \alpha_k' \mathbf{1} + \sum_{k=1}^{\hat{n}} \beta_k' \mathbf{1} \\
\text{subject to} \quad & C_k + \sum_{t=1}^{T} \lambda_t A_{kt} + \mathbf{1}\alpha_k' + \beta_k \mathbf{1}' \leq 0 \;\; \forall k = 1,\ldots,\hat{n} \\
& \lambda \geq 0
\end{aligned} \tag{7}$$

In the theoretical anaylsis section we prove that when $\nu = 1 + 4\epsilon$, with high probability a feasible solution is returned. We also prove that when $\nu = 1 - \epsilon$, an almost feasible solution is returned, and that the objective is almost as large as the hindsight optimal feasible solution.

Algorithm 1 Algorithm for optimal traffic-shaping

1: **Input:** Data $\{(C_k, A_{k1}, \ldots, A_{kT})\}$ for sessions $k = 1, \ldots, n$ presented online for ranking, sample linear program parameters ν, ϵ.
2: For the first $\hat{n}$ sessions, let $P_k = I$ (arbitrary decisions) and log the session data $\{(C_k, A_{k1}, \ldots, A_{kT})\}$ corresponding to this sample set $k \in S$.
3: Solve the sample linear program (7) on S to obtain the dual prices $\hat{\lambda}_1, \ldots, \hat{\lambda}_m$.
4: **while** $\hat{n} < k \leq n$ **do**
5: Compute document score matrix $S_k = C_k + \sum_{t=1}^{T} \hat{\lambda}_t A_{kt}$ where $S_{d,p}$ represents the score when document d is shown in position p.
6: Set $\sigma_k :=$ `MaxWeightMatching`(S_k).
7: **Output:** Ranking σ_k for session k.
8: Increment session counter $k := k + 1$
9: **end while**

In words, the algorithm works as follows. First, using historical data, we offline solve the linear program (7) to obtain the optimal dual prices $\hat{\lambda}_t$ for each traffic shaping constraint. These prices are then made available to the online serving system for ranking. Once the learning phase is over, upon the arrival of new sessions, the matrices C_k, A_{kt} are computed, and the score matrix S_k is computed as per step 5. As mentioned before, the (d,p) entry of the matrix S_k represents the score when document d is shown in position p.

Once the score matrix is computed, we call a subroutine to compute the maximum-weight bipartite perfect matching with respect the weight matrix S_k, this perfect matching assigns documents to positions, and thereby yields the desired ranking σ_k for that session.

The run-time complexity is essentially the complexity of computing a perfect matching, for which a number of options are available. In order to compute a max-weight perfect matching exactly, one may use the celebrated Hungarian algorithm. The computational complexity of implementing the same is $O(m^3 \log m)$ [16]. In scenarios of interest to us, we are typically only interested in ranking of the order of 20 – 200 webpages in each session, and hence the algorithm is feasible to implement at run-time. When the scale is larger and the Hungarian algorithm is not a viable option, one can instead implement the naive greedy algorithm[2] as an alternative. The naive greedy algorithm is known to be a $\frac{1}{2}$-optimal algorithm for maximum matching, with a worst-case running time of $O(m^2)$. In our experiments, we use a position effects model called the "reference CTR" model, in which the greedy algorithm is actually optimal. The offline computational complexity is polynomial in the size of the problem — it involves the solution of the linear program (7), which scales with the sample size of the sampled linear program and is hence high. However, since offline computation is not a bottleneck, our approach is scalable to web applications.

While Algorithm 1 advocates choosing the first ϵ fraction of the traffic for solving the sampled linear program once (in advance)

[2] The greedy algorithm is simply the following: sort the edges of the bipartite graph in decreasing order. We maintain a set of edges M (initialized to be empty), and loop over the sorted edges. In each step, add the corresponding edge to M if it is possible to do so while maintaining the requirement that M is a (possibly partial) matching.

on historical data, this is mostly to simplify the analysis of the algorithm (in our experiments in the next section where data for 10^6 sessions were collected, we found $\epsilon = 0.001$ to work quite well for learning the correct prices). In practice, we recommend solving the dual linear program periodically (e.g. once daily) on all the historical data collected in that time period to refresh the prices to capture the random as well as seasonal variations in traffic. The analysis of periodically recomputing the solution is also possible (in the spirit of [4]), but the analysis is more complicated with only marginally better bounds — we leave this for future work.

4 NUMERICAL EXPERIMENTS

4.1 Experimental Setup

In this section we validate our algorithm via numerical experiments. Our numerical experiments are conducted on real data collected from session history on a major web-portal. We describe the setup for our experiment below.

Our data consists of 2000 sessions of web-traffic data. In each session, we are presented with 20 documents to rank on the web-page. Each document has associated with it the following attributes:

(1) The predicted dwell-time: This is a score generated by a machine-learned model on a large corpus of data that incorporates document features, user features, and document popularity signals. The predicted score is to be interpreted as a surrogate for the expected dwell-time when the user is shown that document.
(2) The click-through rate: This is again generated via a machine learned model, and is an estimate for the click-probability for a particular user to click on the document in question when that document is shown in the first position.
(3) Newsiness score: This is a normalized score that captures how newsy a particular document is. It is also obtained as the output of a machine-learned model. When a newsy article is shown in a highly clickable slot on the page, the overall page is deemed more newsy.
(4) Publisher A: This is a binary $\{0, 1\}$ score that captures whether a document is curated by Publisher A or not. Showing a Publisher A-curated document in a more clickable slot delivers more clicks to that publisher, and is hence more desirable to it.
(5) Publisher B: This is also a binary score (as above) corresponding to whether document is curated by Publisher B.

In our experiments, we implement Algorithm 1, i.e. use a subset of the data for learning the dual prices (making arbitrary decisions in the process), and in the remaining sessions making the optimal decisions with respect to the learned dual prices. In our experiments, the online optimization problem involves: (a) maximizing the dwell-time in each session, (b) delivering a fixed number of clicks to Publishers A and B, (c) achieving at least a certain average newsiness score over the entire set of sessions.

One of the key requirements of our framework is that we need the dwell-time, click probability, and newsiness score for each document when it is shown in any one of the 20 slots. The machine learned models generate these scores with respect to the first slot only. In order to address this, we utilize the (somewhat standard) Reference CTR model, which is explained below.

4.2 The Reference CTR

When users are presented with a list of content on a web-page, it is well-known [9] that there is a strong *position effect* for clicks, dwell-time, and other engagement metrics (such as the newsiness score of interest to us in this paper). It is commonly assumed [9], that a document d, when shown in slot p, has a CTR that depends on its CTR in position 1 (denoted by $c_1(d)$) and a factor that depends only on the position (denoted by ref_p). It is normalized so that $\text{ref}_1 = 1$. Hence the predicted CTR of document d in position p is given by:

$$c_p(d) = c_1(d) \times \text{ref}_p.$$

The quantity ref_p is computed by computing the aggregate CTR for each position, and normalizing by the aggregate CTR for position 1 [9]. We will also assume (for this experiment) that the dwell-time and newsiness have a similar position effect as above.

For a list of items presented to a user according to a permutation σ, the total number of (predicted) clicks generated by the session, and the clicks generated for publisher t (where $t \in \{A, B\}$) are respectively given by:

$$C(\sigma) = \sum_{p=1}^{m} c_p(\sigma(p)) \times \text{ref}_p$$

$$C_t(\sigma) = \sum_{p=1}^{m} c_p(\sigma(p)) \times \text{ref}_p \times \mathbf{1}\left(\sigma(p) \text{ of traffic type } t\right).$$

Similarly, we assume that the total dwell-time and newsiness respectively are:

$$D(\sigma) = \sum_{p=1}^{m} \texttt{dwell}(\sigma(p)) \times \text{ref}_p, \qquad N(\sigma) = \sum_{p=1}^{m} \texttt{news}(\sigma(p)) \times \text{ref}_p.$$

Figure 1 shows the reference CTR distribution.

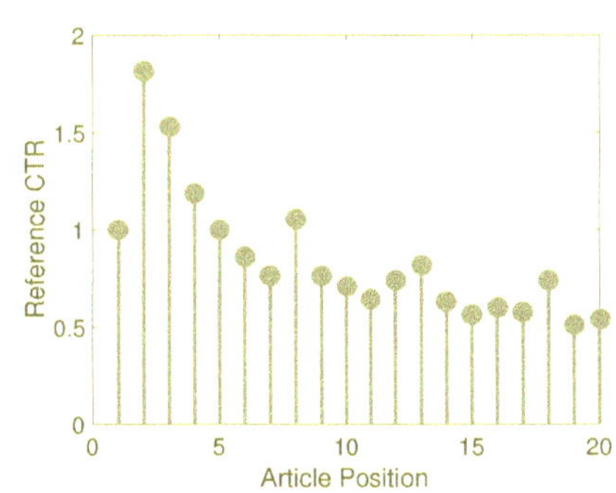

Figure 1: The reference CTR distribution for the slots on the page. Interestingly, the reference CTR distribution is not monotonically decreasing with the slot position due to various page presentation effects.

4.3 Observations

We first investigate the performance of sampled linear program when the size of the sample set increases to 2000 sessions (entire dataset). Figure 2a shows how the average (normalized) dwell-time per session varies as we increase the size of the sampled linear program. Note that when all 2000 sessions are used, we essentially obtain the hindsight-optimal solution. As Fig. 2a shows, this level of performance is approximately achieved by the sampled linear program within just 800 sessions, justifying our intuition that this quantity is distributionally stable with respect to the traffic.

Figure 2b shows how the dual prices change as a function of the number of sessions over which the sampled linear program is solved. Again, we see that the prices stabilize at approximately 800 sessions.

In Fig. 2c we investigate the trade-offs that are inevitable as a consequence of traffic-shaping. We fix the number of sessions to be 2000 and solve the corresponding linear program (i.e. the hindsight optimal solution). We fix the values of the constraints for clicks delivered to publisher B and the newsiness constraint. We vary the number of clicks deliverable to publisher A by changing a parameter θ (as θ increases, the corresponding click constraint commitment b_t increases multiplicatively). We study how the dwell-time per session changes as θ increases — the corresponding trade-off curve is shown in Fig. 2c.

In Fig. 2d we study the performance of the online algorithm. On the x-axis is the fraction of the 2000 sessions which were used for the sampled linear program. On the y-axis is the performance ratio for different metrics. A value of $\nu = 1.05$ (as required in (7)) was chosen for this experiment. The solid-blue curve is the competitive ratio (i.e. the ratio of the performance by the online algorithm to that of the hindsight optimal solution, see Sec. 5). Note that in the first ϵ fraction of the sessions (the price-learning phase), arbitrary suboptimal decisions are made, and hence the competitive ratio decreases as a function of ϵ (see Theorem 5.1). The yellow, purple, and green plots are the ratio of the clicks/newsiness delivered versus the value committed by the constraints (i.e. the b_t), and values under one indicate constraint violation. Note that for small values of ϵ, some of the constraints are actually violated – hence while the competitive ratio is high, training on that small subset of sessions yields infeasible solutions. The red dotted line indicates the online performance ratio as a function of ϵ. The online performance ratio is the ratio of the reward of the online algorithm to that of the hindsight optimal sessions, *restricted to the segment of the sessions where online decisions are made.* While the online performance ratio is close to 1 throughout, it attains this ratio by violating constraints at small values of ϵ.

Another interesting feature that we found was that, under the RefCTR model, the greedy algorithm (i.e. sorting documents by the price-weighted scores, and then matching them to positions in sorted order of their RefCTR value) achieve the *same ranking* compared to the Hungarian algorithm. This is simply a structural consequence of the RefCTR model (we omit the proof here), however the scalability implications are substantial; instead of implementing the Hungarian algorithm, the serving implementation only needs a sorting procedure.

We finally make a comment concerning comparing our approach to baseline approaches. To the best of our knowledge, there is no other work addressing the multi-slot traffic-shaping problem in the literature that would form a natural baseline to compare our approach with. Certain naive baselines that can be considered are:

- No traffic-shaping: we can simply apply the greedy approach and sort the sessions based on engagement scores only. Of course this is naive, and will likely violate the shaping constraints.
- A natural other baseline is to sort based on a weighted sum of the engagement scores and the constraint quantities. In the most general setting, this will be suboptimal compared to our approach (this approach is tantamount to the "greedy" approach for weighted matching, whereas the Hungarian algorithm yields the optimal solution). In the case of the RefCTR model considered in this section, the greedy approach actually yields optimal solutions when the weights are chosen judiciously. A typical heuristic to choose the weights is to perform a grid search over the weights (in which case the optimal weights will be learned), the main disadvantage being that this approach is not scalable when there are many competing constraints. Indeed, one interpretation of our work is that it provides a theoretical foundation and efficient approach for applying this popularly used weight-based heuristic.

5 THEORETICAL GUARANTEES

In order to describe the performance guarantees, we need to define a critical (and well-known) solution concept related to online algorithms, namely the notion of the competitive ratio of the algorithm.

Given online events $\{(C_k, A_{k1}, \ldots, A_{km})\}$ for sessions $k \in [n]$, let OPT denote the solution obtained by solving the linear program (4) on this data — we call the solution thus obtained the *optimal hindsight solution.* A hypothetical decision-maker with advance knowledge of the "future" sessions would make these optimal decisions, and this is the best performance achievable by any algorithm. Suppose Algorithm 1 (which is online) achieves a performance of $\widehat{\text{OPT}}$. We define the *competitive ratio* of the algorithm to be $\frac{\widehat{\text{OPT}}}{\text{OPT}}$. The competitive ratio measures how the performance of the online algorithm compares to the optimal hindsight solution. Our main result shows that, under certain assumptions, our algorithm achieves an $1 - O(\epsilon)$ competitive ratio. We state our assumptions next:

(1) **Assumption 1:** The sessions $\{(C_k, A_{k1}, \ldots, A_{kT})\}$ arrive in a random order, i.e. the matrices $\{(C_k, A_{k1}, \ldots, A_{kT})\}$ can be arbitrary, but every permutation of the indices k have an equal probability.
(2) **Assumption 2:** The optimization problems (4) and (6) are both strictly feasible.
(3) **Assumption 3:** The total number of sessions n is known a priori.
(4) **Assumption 4:** For every permutation P we have $\langle C_k, P\rangle \in [0,1]$ and $\langle A_{kt}, P\rangle \in [0,1]$ for all $k = 1, \ldots, n$ and $t = 1, \ldots, T$.

Theorem 5.1. *Consider the online traffic-shaping problem when the above assumptions hold true, and let $\epsilon \in (0, \frac{1}{3})$ be fixed. Define $B := \min_{t=1,\ldots,T} b_t$. Suppose the constraints satisfy the requirement that*

$$\epsilon \geq \left(\frac{\log\left(\frac{2C_0 T}{\epsilon}\right) + (T+1)\log\left(m^2 n\right)}{B} \right)^{\frac{1}{3}}. \tag{8}$$

Let the dual prices computed by the sampled linear program be denoted by $\hat{\lambda}$. Then the solution constructed by Algorithm 1, denoted by $P_k(\hat{\lambda})$, has the following properties:

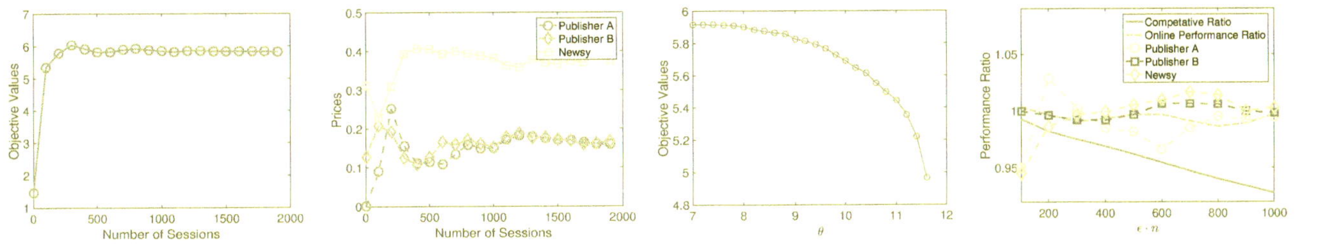

(a) (b) (c) (d)

Figure 2: (a) Average Dwell-time per session as a function of the sample size for the sampled linear program. The dwell-time per session stabilizes at approximately 800 sessions and is constant thereafter. (b) Dual prices for each of the constraints, as a function of the sample size for the sampled linear program. The dual prices also stabilize at approximately 800 sessions and are constant thereafter. (c) Trade-off between dwell-time per session and clicks delivered to Publisher A. (d) Different performance ratios as a function of ϵ.

(1) *In each session the optimal hindsight solution and the online approach via Algorithm 1 produce valid assignments P_k^* and $P_k^{online}(\hat{\lambda})$. Moreover, if the optimal hindsight prices, denoted λ^*, are given 1, then $P_k^* = P_k^{online}(\lambda^*)$.*

(2) *When $v = 1 + 4\epsilon$, With probability exceeding $1 - \epsilon$, the assignments satisfy the traffic-shaping constraints, i.e.*

$$\sum_{k=1}^{n} \langle A_{kt}, P_k(\hat{\lambda}) \rangle \geq b_t \quad \forall t = 1, \ldots, T$$

(3) *When $v = 1 - \epsilon$, with probability exceeding $1 - \epsilon$ the online solution satisfies*

$$\sum_{k=1}^{n} \langle A_{kt}, P_k(\hat{\lambda}) \rangle \geq (1 - 2\epsilon) b_t \quad \forall t = 1, \ldots, T$$

and objective attained by the online assignments $P_k(\hat{\lambda})$ satisfies:

$$\sum_{k=1}^{n} \langle C_k, P_k(\hat{\lambda}) \rangle \geq (1 - \epsilon) OPT,$$

(i.e. the competitive ratio is $1 - O(\epsilon)$ with high probability).

We give a detailed proof in Sec 7. We make the following remarks about the main result:

Remarks

(1) Note that the first part states that if the optimal prices are available to the online algorithm, then optimal decisions will be made in each session. Hence the prices λ^* are sufficient to make good decisions online. The second and third parts of the theorem quantify the intuition that if we use a small set of samples initially to learn the prices using the sampled linear program, the online algorithm will then perform almost optimally.

(2) Note that Algorithm 1 advocates using the Hungarian algorithm to compute the best matching in each session. Depending on the number of items to be ranked, this may or may not be feasible at run time – in the latter case a greedy algorithm may be used. The greedy algorithm, being a $\frac{1}{2}$-approximation in the worst case, can also be analyzed and bounds on the competitive ratio may be derived. In our experiments, we find that using the greedy algorithm does not lead to any loss of performance as a consequence of the RefCTR assumption (see Sec. 4).

(3) Assumption 4 requires that the for each permutation, the rewards and the influence to each traffic shaping is non-negative and bounded by 1. The non-negativity assumption is natural in our setting (since we are interested in quantities such as views and clicks). The upper bound of 1 is somewhat arbitrary, we merely need the rewards and influences to be bounded by some uniform quantity (say U). Our results would be more or less unaffected (modulo certain logarithmic factors in the statement of Theorem 5.1) if $U > 1$).

(4) We now comment on the qualitative relationship between ϵ, B and the competitive ratio. In order to make sense of the statement, let us study the setting when B increases linearly with the number of sessions n (note that this is the setting of most interest in practical applications; when traffic-size doubles, we hope to be able to commit twice as many clicks to a publishing partner). In this regime, $B = \rho n$ and as n increases, the right hand side of (8) decreases to zero and we may make ϵ arbitrarily small, thus yielding (a) a small fraction of the samples used for learning the prices (b) a better competitive ratio, and (c) a high probability of success simultaneously. Indeed (8) may be viewed as a "sample-complexity" type result.

Note that B growing super-linearly with respect to the number of sessions n would be problematic from a feasibility point of view – if we over-commit to a traffic-shaping constraint the optimization problem becomes infeasible violating Assumption 2).

The situation when B is small (e.g. $o(n)$) is a little more subtle. In this situation, the optimization problem itself is "easier" in the sense of finding a feasible solution. However, to get *multiplicative* bounds on the competitive ratio our proof techniques do need B to be large enough so that (8) is satisfied. The fact that we ask for multiplicative bounds (as opposed to additive ones) together with the fact that we make no distributional assumptions on the traffic beyond random arrival requires us to use a particular concentration inequality in the proof which in turn requires B to satisfy this condition. It is an interesting open problem to see whether this condition can be weakened.

(5) The competitive ratio decreases as the fraction of sessions ϵ used for learning increases. While on the one hand the prices are

learned more accurately as ϵ increases, on the other hand suboptimal decisions are made by the online algorithm in the learning phase. Indeed, we assume (somewhat pessimistically) that arbitrary decision are made in the learning phase with zero reward accrued, thus an ϵ-fraction of the possible reward is lost in this phase.
(6) While our formulation (4) only considers lower bound (satisfaction) constraints, our approach is amenable to upper bound (budget) constraints as well. As an example, if we wanted to optimize page-placement jointly for content and ads, with ads having budget constraints, we would encounter formulations with both upper and lower bound constraints. The corresponding linear inequalities can be incorporated into the optimization formulation of the sampled linear program, and the dual prices can be used as weights in weighted bipartite matching problem in the same manner. While we don't analyze this situation in this paper, we anticipate that an analogous analysis can be carried out.

6 CONCLUSION

In this paper we investigated the problem of online constrained ranking and its application to the web traffic-shaping problem. We developed a linear-programming based primal-dual algorithm for online ranking and demonstrated it's efficacy on real data. We also proved rigorous guarantees about the algorithm in terms of the achieved competitive ratio.

While the paper focuses on traffic-shaping as the motivating application, we believe this algorithm to have broad applicability to whole-page optimization and beyond. For instance, when optimizing the simultaneous placement of ads and organic content, additional constraints (or modifications to the objective) can be made to factor in the revenue considerations traffic-wide. More generally, this approach can be used for solving a variety of constrained online assignment problems such as matching customers to servers (e.g. matching drivers to passengers) subject to overall service-level constraints. We believe this approach will scale well to a variety of such application domains.

A number of further avenues for future work are worth mentioning:

- Our model involves optimizing (in the objective) subject to constraints the predicted dwell-time and the predicted clicks over a period of sessions. These predictions are obtained as the output of a machine-learned model. The number of actual clicks obtained, and the actual dwell-time realized will of course be different. As a practical strategy, we advocate re-solving the linear program periodically (and suitably altering the constraints) to capture these variations. However, there is an unavoidable feedback loop between the rankings and the machine learned models — the decisions made in the ranking phase affect the learning of these online models. Consequently, there is a natural exploration-exploitation trade-off that is unavoidable in this setup. Ranking unknown items in a highly clickable slot will lead to more exploration, whereas ranking more certain items will lead to exploitation. How one navigates this will likely be of key practical importance.
- Our approach assumes that the objective and the constraints can be expressed as linear functions of the ranking; the expected number of clicks and expected dwell time are assumed to be a weighted sum of the components derived from each slot. Other types of constraints may not be linearly expressible (e.g. suppose one wishes to enforce a certain notion of diversity in each ranking and enforce a certain minimum amount of average diversity across sessions). Working with non-linear constraints will likely enable us to enrich the quality of ranking in our traffic.
- Our approach makes weak assumptions about the traffic in order to achieve competitive ratio bounds, i.e. that the events arrive in a random order. If stronger independence assumptions are made, it is possible that stronger results might hold – for example it may be possible to prove that the optimal prices are learned and a sample complexity for the same might be characterizable.

7 PROOFS

We begin by stating two lemmas (their proofs are omitted due to space constraints) which follow as a standard consequence of the analysis of the Hungarian algorithm (we refer the reader to [16] for details).

LEMMA 7.1. *Let $C \in \mathbb{R}^{m\times m}$ be an entry-wise non-negative matrix. Consider the following optimization problems:*

$$\begin{aligned} \underset{P}{\text{maximize}} \quad & \langle C, P\rangle \\ \text{subject to} \quad & P \in \mathcal{B} \end{aligned} \tag{9}$$

$$\begin{aligned} \underset{\alpha,\beta}{\text{maximize}} \quad & \alpha'\mathbf{1} + \beta'\mathbf{1} \\ \text{subject to} \quad & C + \mathbf{1}\alpha' + \beta\mathbf{1}' \le 0 \end{aligned} \tag{10}$$

Then the following hold:

1. *The pair (9), (10) is a primal-dual pair, and strong duality holds.*
2. *An optimal solution P^* to (9) is attained at a permutation matrix, and this solution can be found using the Hungarian algorithm.*

LEMMA 7.2. *Let $\lambda = \bar{\lambda} \in \mathbb{R}^T$ be fixed such that $\bar{\lambda} \ge 0$. Consider the solution to the optimization problem*

$$\begin{aligned} \underset{\alpha_k,\beta_k}{\text{maximize}} \quad & \sum_{t=1}^{T} \bar{\lambda}_t b_t + \sum_{k=1}^{n} \alpha_k'\mathbf{1} + \sum_{k=1}^{n} \beta_k'\mathbf{1} \\ \text{subject to} \quad & C_k + \sum_{t=1}^{T} \lambda_t A_{kt} + \mathbf{1}\alpha_k' + \beta_k\mathbf{1}' \le 0 \;\; \forall k = 1,\dots,n \end{aligned} \tag{11}$$

A set of optimal dual solutions (w.r.t. the constraints of (11)) $P_k(\bar{\lambda})$ for $k = 1,\dots,n$ corresponding to (4) are achieved at extreme points of the Birkhoff polytope, (i.e. permutation matrices). Moreover each of the $P_k(\bar{\lambda})$ may be computed by computing a maximum-weight perfect matching with respect to the bipartite graph with weights $C_k + \sum_{t=1}^{T} \bar{\lambda}_t A_{kt}$ (using the Hungarian algorithm).

We will also need the following lemma concerning concentration of random variables. For a proof we refer the reader to [4, Lemma A.1], [12, Lemma 3] and the references therein.

Lemma 7.3. *Let $u_1, \ldots, u_r$ be a uniformly random sample without replacement from real numbers*

$$\left\{ |\sum_{i=1}^{r} u_i - r\bar{c}| \geq t \right\} \leq \exp\left(-\frac{t^2}{2r\sigma_R^2 + t\Delta_R} \right),$$

where $\Delta_R = \max_i c_i - \min_i c_i$, $\bar{c} = \frac{1}{R}\sum_{i=1}^{R} c_i$, *and* $\sigma_R^2 = \frac{1}{R}\sum_{i=1}^{R}(c_i - \bar{c})^2$.

We now provide a detailed proof of Theorem 1. Note that both our main result for online ranking, and our assumptions are of a similar flavor as existing literature in online algorithms [4, 12]. Indeed, it is known [4, 12], that in these related results, these assumptions are also tight, i.e. it is not possible to get $1 - O(\epsilon)$ competitive ratio if a single one of these assumptions is removed. While we do not show the tightness of the assumptions, we believe it likely that they are needed to achieve the stated competitive ratio.

Proof of Theorem 5.1. The main idea behind the proof, which mimics [4] with suitable adaptations, will be to use the complementary slackness conditions for linear programming. Let $\hat{\lambda}$ be a dual price vector obtained as the solution of the sampled linear program. We denote by $P_k(\hat{\lambda})$ the permutation that is chosen as per steps 5, 6 of the algorithm.

Part 1. The online assignments $P_k^{\text{online}}(\hat{\lambda})$ (and similarly $P_k^{\text{online}}(\lambda^*)$) are valid assignments since they are constructed via the Hungarian algorithm. Note that they are both trivially primal-feasible (since assignments are extreme points of the Birkhoff polytope).

Let λ^* be an optimal dual solution of (5). Note that when $\bar{\lambda} = \lambda^*$, the corresponding optimal solutions of (11) coincide with those of (5). By strong duality, a set of corresponding primal solutions also coincide. By Lemma 7.2, a dual variable corresponding to the constraints of (11) achieves optimality at permutation matrices $P_k(\lambda^*)$. Hence, $P_k(\lambda^*) = P_k^*$.

Part 2. Our proof strategy will be as follows. We will take a hypothetical optimal solution $\hat{\lambda}$ to the sampled linear program. It will be assumed to satisfy that the complementary slackness conditions of the primal dual pair (9),(10) - but otherwise arbitrary. We will show that as a consequence of complementary slackness and the assumptions, with high probability the solution yielded by $P_k(\hat{\lambda})$ are feasible for this hypothetical $\hat{\lambda}$. We will then take a union bound over all possible $\hat{\lambda}$ to obtain that the solution is feasible unconditionally.

Let us fix a constraint t and note that for the first ϵn sessions, arbitrary decisions are made and we thus assume that no contributions to the constraints are made from these. As a result we required that the sampled linear program satisfy:

$$\sum_{k \in S} \langle A_{kt}, P_k \rangle \geq (1 + 4\epsilon)\epsilon b_t,$$

where the additional $(1+4\epsilon)$ factor ensures that the solution robustly satisfies the constraints.

The bad event of interest to us is the event that a constraint is violated. We will call the set S bad when the solution λ leads us to a situation of such a constraint violation. Concretely, we consider the following set relations corresponding to a set S being bad:

$$\left\{ \sum_{k \in N \setminus S} \langle A_{kt}, P_k(\lambda) \rangle < b_t, \sum_{k \in S} \langle A_{kt}, P_k(\lambda) \rangle \geq (1 + 4\epsilon)\epsilon b_t \right\} \subseteq A_1 \cup A_2,$$

$$A_1 = \left\{ \sum_{k \in N \setminus S} \langle A_{kt}, P_k(\lambda) \rangle < b_t, \sum_{t \in S} \langle A_{kt}, P_k(\lambda) \rangle \geq (1 + 4\epsilon)\epsilon b_t, \sum_{k \in N} \langle A_{kt}, P_k(\lambda) \rangle \geq (1 + 3\epsilon) b_t \right\}$$

$$A_2 = \left\{ \sum_{k \in S} \langle A_{kt}, P_k(\lambda) \rangle \geq (1 + 4\epsilon)\epsilon b_t, \sum_{k \in N} \langle A_{kt}, P_k(\lambda) \rangle < (1 + 3\epsilon) b_t \right\}$$

Next we note that:

$$\begin{aligned}
\mathbb{P}(A_1) &\leq \mathbb{P}\left(\sum_{k \in N \setminus S} \langle A_{kt}, P_k(\lambda) \rangle < b_t, \sum_{k \in N} \langle A_{kt}, P_k(\lambda) \rangle \geq (1 + 3\epsilon) b_t \right) \\
&\leq \mathbb{P}\left(\sum_{k \in N \setminus S} \langle A_{kt}, P_k(\lambda) \rangle < b_t, \sum_{k \in N} \langle A_{kt}, P_k(\lambda) \rangle \geq \frac{1+\epsilon}{1-\epsilon} b_t \right) \\
&= \mathbb{P}\left(\sum_{k \in N \setminus S} \langle A_{kt}, P_k(\lambda) \rangle < b_t, (1-\epsilon) \sum_{k \in N} \langle A_{kt}, P_k(\lambda) \rangle \geq (1 + \epsilon) b_t \right) \\
&\leq 2\exp\left(-\frac{\epsilon^2 b_t}{2 - \epsilon} \right)
\end{aligned}$$

where the second inequality follows since $\frac{1+\epsilon}{1-\epsilon} < 1 + 3\epsilon$ for all $\epsilon \in (0, \frac{1}{3})$, and the last inequality follows from Lemma 7.3.

Defining $Y_k := \langle A_{kt}, P_k(\lambda) \rangle$, we also note that

$$\begin{aligned}
\mathbb{P}(A_2) &\leq \mathbb{P}\left(\sum_{t \in S} \langle A_{kt}, P_k(\lambda) \rangle \geq (1 + 4\epsilon)\epsilon b_t, \sum_{t \in N} \langle A_{kt}, P_k(\lambda) \rangle < (1 + 3\epsilon) b_t \right) \\
&\leq \mathbb{P}\left(|\sum_{t \in S} Y_t - \epsilon \sum_{t \in N} Y_t| \geq \epsilon^2 b_t \right) \\
&\leq 2\exp\left(-\frac{\epsilon^3 b_t}{2 + \epsilon} \right)
\end{aligned}$$

where the last inequality again follows from an application of Lemma 7.3.

Hence, the probability of a bad sample is bounded above by $4\exp\left(-\frac{\epsilon^3 b_t}{2+\epsilon}\right) \leq \delta$, where $\delta := \frac{\epsilon}{C_0 (m^2 n)^{T+1}}$

Since the solution λ obtained from the sampled linear program can be arbitrary, we take a union bound over all the possible "distinct" λ. We call two solutions λ_1 and λ_2 as distinct if $P_k(\lambda_1) \neq P_k(\lambda_2)$ for some session $k \in N$. Consider a dual constraint with complementary slackness:

$$\left(C_k + \sum_{t=1}^{T} \lambda_t A_{kt} + 1\alpha_k' + \beta_k 1' \right)_{ij} (P_k)_{ij} = 0.$$

and note that $(P_k)_{ij} > 0$ is only possible when

$$\left(C_k + \sum_{t=1}^{T} \lambda_t A_{kt} + 1\alpha_k' + \beta_k 1' \right)_{ij} \geq 0.$$

(Indeed, the set of possible solutions yielded by the Hungarian algorithm will be a subset of such possible P_k - by design the

Hungarian algorithm maintains the dual inequality as an invariant [16]). The set of possible P_k is thus bounded above by the number of unique separations of the points

$$\left\{\left((C_k)_{ij}, (A_{k1},)_{ij}, \ldots, (A_{kT},)_{ij}, 1\right)\right\}_{i,j,k\in[m]\times[m]\times[n]}$$

in $(T+1)$-dimensional space. By results from computational geometry [15], the number of such distinct hyperplanes, is bounded above by $C_0(m^2n)^{T+1}$ for some constant C_0. Applying a union bound over the possible different prices, and $t = 1, \ldots, T$ we obtain the required result.

Part 3. Given $\nu = 1 - \epsilon$, one can prove approximate feasibility in a similar manner as above by observing that

$$\mathbb{P}\left(\sum_{k\in N\setminus S} \langle A_{kt}, P_k(\lambda)\rangle < (1-2\epsilon)b_t, \sum_{k\in N} \langle A_{kt}, P_k(\lambda)\rangle \geq (1-\epsilon)b_t\right) \leq \delta,$$

where δ is the quantity used in the preceding part.

To bound the competitive ratio, our proof strategy will be to construct an auxiliary linear program for which the online solutions are optimal. We will show that a point P_k^* (the solution to (4)) is feasible with respect to this auxiliary linear program, and hence the objective function values between the online solution and that achieved by P_k^* cannot be too different.

Let $\hat{\lambda}$ be the solution of the sampled linear program (7) and $P_k(\hat{\lambda})$ the corresponding assignment. Consider the linear program:

$$\begin{aligned} \underset{P_1,\ldots,P_n}{\text{maximize}} \quad & \sum_{k=1}^{n} \langle C_k, P_k\rangle \\ \text{subject to} \quad & \sum_{k=1}^{n} \langle A_{kt}, P_k\rangle \geq \hat{b}_t \ \ \forall\, t = 1, \ldots, T \\ & P_k \in \mathcal{B} \ \ k = 1, \ldots, n \end{aligned} \tag{12}$$

where the quantity $\hat{b}_t$ is defined as $\hat{b}_t = \sum_{t\in N}\langle A_{kt}, P_k(\hat{\lambda})\rangle$ if $\hat{\lambda}_t > 0$ and $b_t = \min\left\{\sum_{t\in N}\langle A_{kt}, P_k(\hat{\lambda})\rangle, b_t\right\}$ if $\lambda_t = 0$. Since $\hat{\lambda}, P_k(\hat{\lambda})$ satisfy the complementary slackness conditions for (12) by construction, they are optimal solutions to it. Note that in general the solution of the sampled linear program could be fractional (i.e. $\hat{P}_k$ for some members of the Birkhoff polytope). However, as a consequence of Lemma 7.2, it is in fact the case that $\hat{P}_k = P_k(\hat{\lambda})$ are optimal.

Suppose $\hat{\lambda}_t > 0$, then the tth primal constraint is tight in the sampled linear program, i.e. $\sum_{k\in S}\langle A_{kt}, P_k(\hat{\lambda})\rangle = (1-\epsilon)\epsilon b_t$. By applying an argument along similar lines to part 2 above and applying concentration, it follows that with probability at least $1-\epsilon$,

$$\hat{b}_t = \sum_{t\in N}\langle A_{kt}, P_k(\hat{\lambda})\rangle \leq b_t.$$

Let P_k^* be the optimal solution to (6). It follows that P_k^* are also feasible solutions to (12). As a consequence, $\sum_{k\in N}\langle C_k, P_k(\hat{\lambda})\rangle \geq$ OPT, where OPT refers to the objective function value of the optimal solution to (6).

By again applying a concentration argument as above, we can argue that with probability exceeding $1-\epsilon$,

$$\sum_{k\in N\setminus S} \langle C_k, P_k(\hat{\lambda})\rangle \geq (1-\epsilon) \sum_{k\in N} \langle C_k, P_k(\hat{\lambda}) \geq (1-\epsilon)\text{OPT}.$$

Since the returns from the first $\hat{n}$ sessions are non-negative (under an arbitrary assignment), the online algorithm returns a reward of at least $(1-\epsilon)$OPT. □

REFERENCES

[1] Deepak Agarwal, Shaunak Chatterjee, Yang Yang, and Liang Zhang. 2015. Constrained Optimization for Homepage Relevance. In *Proceedings of the 24th International Conference on World Wide Web (WWW '15 Companion)*. ACM, New York, NY, USA, 375–384. DOI: http://dx.doi.org/10.1145/2740908.2745398

[2] Deepak Agarwal, Bee-Chung Chen, Pradheep Elango, and Xuanhui Wang. 2011. Click Shaping to Optimize Multiple Objectives. In *Proceedings of the 17th ACM SIGKDD International Conference on Knowledge Discovery and Data Mining (KDD '11)*. ACM, New York, NY, USA, 132–140. DOI: http://dx.doi.org/10.1145/2020408.2020435

[3] Deepak Agarwal, Bee-Chung Chen, Pradheep Elango, and Xuanhui Wang. 2012. Personalized Click Shaping Through Lagrangian Duality for Online Recommendation. In *Proceedings of the 35th International ACM SIGIR Conference on Research and Development in Information Retrieval (SIGIR '12)*. ACM, New York, NY, USA, 485–494. DOI: http://dx.doi.org/10.1145/2348283.2348350

[4] Shipra Agrawal, Zizhuo Wang, and Yinyu Ye. 2014. A Dynamic Near-Optimal Algorithm for Online Linear Programming. *Operations Research* 62, 4 (2014), 876–890. DOI: http://dx.doi.org/10.1287/opre.2014.1289

[5] M. F. Balcan, A. Blum, J. D. Hartline, and Y. Mansour. 2005. Mechanism design via machine learning. In *46th Annual IEEE Symposium on Foundations of Computer Science (FOCS'05)*. 605–614. DOI: http://dx.doi.org/10.1109/SFCS.2005.50

[6] Sébastien Bubeck. 2015. Convex Optimization: Algorithms and Complexity. *Foundations and Trends in Machine Learning* 8, 3-4 (2015), 231–357. DOI: http://dx.doi.org/10.1561/2200000050

[7] Niv Buchbinder and Joseph (Seffi) Naor. 2009. The Design of Competitive Online Algorithms via a Primal: Dual Approach. *Found. Trends Theor. Comput. Sci.* 3, 2–3 (Feb. 2009), 93–263. DOI: http://dx.doi.org/10.1561/0400000024

[8] Zhe Cao, Tao Qin, Tie yan Liu, and Hang Li. 2007. Learning to rank: from pairwise approach to listwise approach. In *In Proc. ICMLfi07*. 129–136.

[9] Olivier Chapelle and Ya Zhang. 2009. A Dynamic Bayesian Network Click Model for Web Search Ranking. In *Proceedings of the 18th International Conference on World Wide Web (WWW '09)*. ACM, New York, NY, USA, 1–10. DOI: http://dx.doi.org/10.1145/1526709.1526711

[10] Sougata Chaudhuri and Ambuj Tewari. 2016. Online Learning to Rank with Top-k Feedback. *CoRR* abs/1608.06408 (2016).

[11] Xiao Alison Chen and Zizhuo Wang. 2015. A dynamic learning algorithm for online matching problems with concave returns. *European Journal of Operational Research* 247, 2 (2015), 379 – 388. DOI: http://dx.doi.org/10.1016/j.ejor.2015.06.029

[12] Nikhil R. Devanur and Thomas P. Hayes. 2009. The adwords problem: Online keyword matching with budgeted bidders under random permutations. In *In Proc. 10th Annual ACM Conference on Electronic Commerge (EC.*

[13] Nikhil R. Devanur, Zhiyi Huang, Nitish Korula, Vahab S. Mirrokni, and Qiqi Yan. 2013. Whole-page Optimization and Submodular Welfare Maximization with Online Bidders. In *Proceedings of the Fourteenth ACM Conference on Electronic Commerce (EC '13)*. ACM, New York, NY, USA, 305–322. DOI: http://dx.doi.org/10.1145/2482540.2482603

[14] Aranyak Mehta, Amin Saberi, Umesh Vazirani, and Vijay Vazirani. 2005. Adwords and generalized on-line matching. In *In FOCS fi05: Proceedings of the 46th Annual IEEE Symposium on Foundations of Computer Science*. IEEE Computer Society, 264–273.

[15] Peter Orlik and Hiroaki Terao. 1992. *Arrangements of Hyperplanes*. Springer-Verlag.

[16] A. Schrijver. 2003. *Combinatorial Optimization - Polyhedra and Efficiency*.

On Finding Socially Tenuous Groups for Online Social Networks

Chih-Ya Shen
Department of Computer Science
National Tsing Hua Univ., Taiwan
chihya@cs.nthu.edu.tw

Liang-Hao Huang
Institute of Information Science
Academia Sinica, Taiwan
r90221003@gmail.com

De-Nian Yang
Institute of Information Science
Academia Sinica, Taiwan
dnyang@iis.sinica.edu.tw

Hong-Han Shuai
Department of Electrical and Computer Engineering
National Chiao Tung Univ., Taiwan
hhshuai@nctu.edu.tw

Wang-Chien Lee
Department of Computer Science and Engineering
The Pennsylvania State Univ., USA
wlee@cse.psu.edu

Ming-Syan Chen
Department of Electrical Engineering
National Taiwan Univ., Taiwan
mschen@ntu.edu.tw

ABSTRACT

Existing research on finding social groups mostly focuses on *dense* subgraphs in social networks. However, finding *socially tenuous groups* also has many important applications. In this paper, we introduce the notion of *k-triangles* to measure the tenuity of a group. We then formulate a new research problem, *Minimum k-Triangle Disconnected Group (MkTG)*, to find a socially tenuous group from online social networks. We prove that MkTG is NP-Hard and inapproximable within any ratio in arbitrary graphs but polynomial-time tractable in *threshold graphs*. Two algorithms, namely *TERA* and *TERA-ADV*, are designed to exploit graph-theoretical approaches for solving MkTG on general graphs effectively and efficiently. Experimental results on seven real datasets manifest that the proposed algorithms outperform existing approaches in both efficiency and solution quality.

1 INTRODUCTION

With the popularity and wide accessibility of online social networks (OSNs), e.g., Facebook, LiveJournal, LinkedIn, research on finding various *social groups* for community detection [14] and activity coordination [15, 17] has drawn increasing attention. Existing research works mostly focus on extracting *dense* groups of socially connected individuals from online social networks. However, *socially tenuous groups* (STGs), i.e., subgraphs with few social interactions and weak relationships among members, have not received much research attention[1]. We argue that STGs have many real needs, e.g., psychoeducational group formation and reviewer selection, and thus deserve more research effort.

[1]Reducing only the number of edges in the group is not sufficient for real applications (explained later).

KDD'17, August 13–17, 2017, Halifax, NS, Canada.
© 2017 ACM. 978-1-4503-4887-4/17/08...$15.00
DOI: http://dx.doi.org/10.1145/3097983.3097995

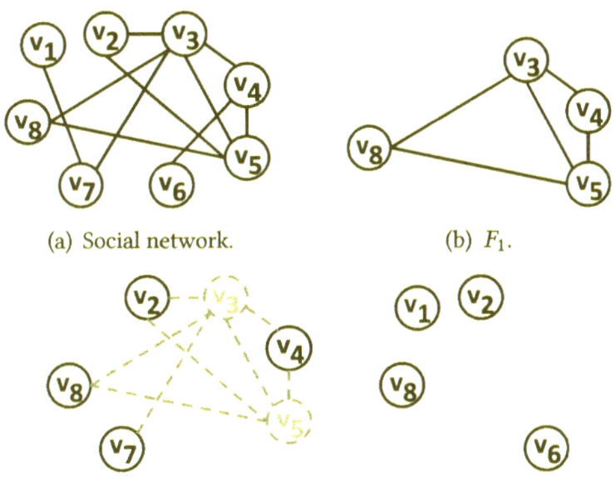

(a) Social network. (b) F_1. (c) F_2. (d) F_3.

Figure 1: Motivating example.

Psychoeducational group formation. For group therapy for substance abuse treatment, an important task is to form psychoeducational or cognitive-behavioral groups [9]. In addition to selecting individuals with similar disorder symptoms and behaviors, one essential criterion for group formation is to assign patients who do not know each other (and sometimes not even multi-hop friends) to form an STG [9]. Forming such an STG is critical for engaging the group members to share their feeling without hesitation. Moreover, it's less likely for members of such an STG to form *subgroups* which may act against other members during therapy sessions.

Consider a scenario where a clinical psychologist would like to select four patients from candidates in Figure 1(a) (their social relationships are illustrated) to form a psychoeducational therapy group. Note that $F_1 = \{v_3, v_4, v_5, v_8\}$ (see Figure 1(b)) may not be a good choice because there are many edges (social relationships) among them. While $F_2 = \{v_2, v_4, v_7, v_8\}$ (see Figure 1(c)) does not have direct social relationships, each pair of them forms a friend-of-friend relationship (through v_3 or v_5), which may lead to subgroups (due to common friends) or make them hesitate to share their private experiences (which may be leaked to common friends). As shown, $F_3 = \{v_1, v_2, v_6, v_8\}$ (see Figure 1(d)) is the best choice because the patients induce no direct or friend-of-friend relationships, minimizing the chance for private information shared in the therapy group to spread out.

Reviewer selection. STG also finds its applications in paper reviews. Conference program chairs need to assign experts to review papers. Besides matching the expertise of reviewers with the topics of submissions, it is crucial to avoid assigning reviewers socially close to each other and the authors of a paper in order to ensure unbiased assessments. While most review systems have utilized co-authorship, affiliations, and countries to avoid conflict of interests, current systems do not carefully consider social tenuity among the authors and reviewers[2]. STG can help!

To find socially tenuous subgraphs (STGs)[3], the tenuity of an STG needs to be properly modelled. Thus, we introduce the notion of *k-triangles* as the basis for measuring tenuity of STGs. A k-triangle in a social network exists when three individuals are located within k hops from each other. In the following, we first formally define the k-triangle and then discuss its properties and advantages.

Definition 1.1. A k-triangle is a triplet of vertices $\{u, v, w\}$, such that $d_G(u, v) \leq k$, $d_G(u, w) \leq k$, and $d_G(v, w) \leq k$, where $d_G(x, y)$ is the shortest path distance (in hops) between two vertices x, y on G.

It is worth clarifying that, for a k-triangle $\{u, v, w\}$ in a subgraph F, the shortest path distance between each pair of vertices is computed on the overall graph G instead of F, because the social relationships of the selected members go beyond F. For example, consider $F = \{v_1, v_3, v_6\}$ in Figure 1(a). The shortest path distance on F from v_1 to v_3 is infinite, but it's 2 on G.

Triangles serve well as a basic unit to measure various density relationships among the neighborhoods of vertices in a network, e.g., clustering coefficient, transitivity ratio, and k-trusses [8]. Countering the idea, the fewer k-triangles in a group, the more tenuous is the group. In fact, a $(k-1)$-triangle is a k-triangle. If a group has no k-triangle, it does not have any $(k-1)$-triangle, $(k-2)$-triangle,..., and 1-triangle. In fact, if a group does not have any k-triangle, it *does not* include any subgraph H with $|H| \geq 3$ in which $d_G(u, v) \leq k$ for $u, v \in H$[4]. Thus, the count of k-triangles serves very well for measuring the *group tenuity*.

Note that k-triangles have great advantages in measuring the group tenuity. First, k-triangles capture social relationships up to k hops. Two individuals with more common friends within k hops have more k-triangles. Consider Figure 1(c) as an example. $F_2 = \{v_2, v_4, v_7, v_8\}$ has no triangles (no 1-triangles) among them, but there exist four 2-triangles, i.e., each pair of vertices has a common friend. In contrast, in Figure 1(d), $F_3 = \{v_1, v_2, v_6, v_8\}$, which has no 2-triangle, is a better tenuous group than F_2. Second, k-triangles serve well as a basic block for many other graph structures, such as paths, trees, stars, or even cliques. Consider the example in Figure 1. Path $\{v_1, v_7, v_3\}$ is a 2-triangle, while $\{v_3, v_4, v_7, v_8\}$ (a tree rooted at v_4 as well as a star centered at v_3) contains four 2-triangles. Moreover, each clique of size p contains exactly C_3^p triangles. If the number of k-triangles is minimized in a subgraph, the aforementioned graph structures (which imply a certain degree of denseness) are also effectively minimized.

In this paper, we formulate a new research problem, namely *Minimum k-Triangle Disconnected Group (MkTG)*, which finds an STG by optimizing the group tenuity – *minimizing the number of k-Triangles normalized by the group size.* Given a social network $G = (V, E)$, MkTG finds a group F from G with the minimum number of k-triangles for each vertex subject to the following constraints. 1) F contains no fewer than n individuals (size constraint). 2) There is no edge in F (no-pair constraint). The size constraint can be specified based on practical need, e.g., finding at least three reviewers for paper review. The no-pair constraint guarantees that F does not contain any ego friends (directly connected friends), which is also important for forming psychoeducational groups and finding paper reviewers. Please note that F may still contain a lot of k-triangles ($k \geq 2$) even when F contains no directly connected friends. For example, in Figure 1(c), $F_2 = \{v_2, v_4, v_7, v_8\}$ contains no edge. However, there are four 2-triangles in F_2.

The MkTG problem is nontrivial due to the entangled group size constraint, no-pair constraint and social tenuity objective function. We prove that the MkTG problem is NP-Hard and inapproximable within any ratio. After the hardness analysis, we take steps to solve the MkTG problem systematically. We propose an efficient and effective algorithm, namely *Triangle and Edge Reduction Algorithm (TERA)*, for solving the MkTG problem on general graphs. Moreover, we devise advanced processing strategies for TERA, namely *TERA with Advanced Processing Strategies (TERA-ADV)*, which incorporate graph-theoretical strategies, i.e., *Simplicial Pruning* and *Vicinal Partition and Elimination*, to significantly avoid examining redundant vertices in the graph. Then, we consider the MkTG problem in *threshold graphs* [31]. We pay special attention on threshold graphs because the structural properties (e.g., degree distribution, largest component size, edge density, and local clustering coefficient) of many popular online social networks are similar to those of threshold graphs [32]. We propose a polynomial-time algorithm to find the optimal solution based on the notion of *vicinal pre-order*.

The contributions are summarized as follows.

- We identify a new problem of finding tenuous groups in online social networks and introduce a novel notion of k-triangle for measuring the tenuity of groups. Accordingly, we formulate the Minimum k-Triangle Disconnected Group (MkTG) problem, and prove it NP-Hard and inapproximable within any ratio.
- For MkTG in general graphs, we devise two algorithms, namely *Triangle and Edge Reduction Algorithm (TERA)* and *TERA with Advanced Processing Strategies (TERA-ADV)*. The latter employs *Simplicial Pruning* and *Vicinal Partition and Elimination* based on graph theory to find solutions efficiently and effectively.
- We study the MkTG problem in a special class of graphs, i.e., *threshold graphs*, which have graph properties very similar to many well-known online social networks. We show that our proposed algorithms can obtain the optimal solution in polynomial time according to the notion of vicinal pre-order.

[2] In fact, some people argue that double-blind review may not really be blind because the research community is small. Sometimes it is not difficult to guess the author identities during the paper bidding phase.
[3] In this paper, STG refers to both *socially tenuous group* and socially tenuous subgraph, which are used interchangeably under the context of this paper.
[4] For the case of $|H| = 2$, we can add a virtual vertex q linking through artificial paths to every vertex in the group. By controlling the hop number of the artificial paths, eliminating k-triangles in the original group can be transformed to eliminating the subgraphs H with $|H| = 2$.

- We perform extensive experiments on real datasets to evaluate the proposed algorithms and different baselines. Experimental results show that our algorithms outperform the baselines in both solution quality and efficiency.

The paper is organized as follows. Section 2 formulates the MkTG problem. Section 3 introduces the works relevant to this paper. Sections 4 and 5 present the algorithms for MkTG on general graphs and threshold graphs, respectively. Section 6 presents the experimental results, and Section 7 concludes this paper.

2 PROBLEM FORMULATION AND HARDNESS

Given a social network $G = (V, E)$, let $|F|$ denote the number of vertices in F, and $\Delta_k(F)$ denote the number of k-triangles in F. The MkTG problem is formulated as follows.

Problem: Minimum k-Triangle Disconnected Group (MkTG).
Given: A social network $G = (V, E)$, size constraint n, and tenuity parameter k.
Find: A subgraph $F \subseteq G$ where $|F| \geq n$ (size constraint) and $\nexists u, v \in F$ with edge $(u, v) \in E$ (no-pair constraint), such that $\frac{\Delta_k(F)}{|F|}$ is minimized.

When the group size $|F|$ (or the size constraint n) increases, it becomes harder to minimize the number of k-triangles, and it is more inclined for F to violate the no-pair constraint. Therefore, the objective function of the group includes a normalization term[5] to encourage exploring groups with different sizes, instead of always trying the smallest group (i.e., $|F| = n$). Intuitively, the tenuity objective above aims to *minimize the average number of k-triangles for each member in the group*. Therefore, one of the challenges for MkTG lies in achieving a good balance between the group size $|F|$ (or the size constraint n) and the number of k-triangles in F. On the other hand, the tenuity parameter k also has crucial impact on the number of k-triangles in F. As k increases, it becomes more challenging to find a subgraph with a small number of k-triangles because the number of k-hop friends increases for each vertex.

One approach for MkTG is to first construct the k-hop graph (detailed later), G_k of G, then construct the complement graph $\widehat{G}_k$ of G_k, and employ existing algorithms to extract dense subgraphs from $\widehat{G}_k$. Specifically, given input graph $G = (V, E)$ and parameter k, the k-hop graph $G_k = (V, E_k)$ retains the vertex set V and augments the edge set E into E_k. An edge $(u, v) \in E_k$ exists if and only if u and v are within k hops on G, i.e., $d_G(u, v) \leq k$. By transforming G into G_k, we ensure that a k-triangle $\{u, v, w\}$ exists in G if and only if $\{u, v, w\}$ is a 1-triangle in G_k. However, finding dense subgraphs on $\widehat{G}_k$ cannot obtain the good solutions for MkTG due to the interplay of k-triangles and the no-pair constraint.

A counterexample of the above approach is shown in Figure 2. Given G in Figure 2(a) and an MkTG with $k = 2$, $n = 3$, Figure 2(b) is the 2-hop graph, i.e., G_2, and Figure 2(c) is the complement graph of G_2, i.e., $\widehat{G}_2$. One optimal solution of this MkTG instance on G is $\{v_1, v_2, v_5\}$ with no 2-triangles which satisfies the no-pair constraint. In contrast, if we employ the algorithm to find the subgraph F_d with maximum density (i.e., to maximize $\frac{|E(F_d)|}{|V(F_d)|}$) on $\widehat{G}_2$ in Figure 2(c), we have $F_d = \{v_1, v_2, v_3, v_4, v_6\}$ with $\frac{|E(F_d)|}{|V(F_d)|} = 1$. However, there exists a 2-triangle ($\{v_2, v_3, v_6\}$) in F_d on the original graph G, and F_d does not satisfy the no-pair constraint. This example manifests that MkTG is very challenging and straightforward approaches cannot solve it properly.

[5]The normalization term could be $(|F|)^t$ with $t \geq 1$. Without loss of generality, we consider the case where = 1.

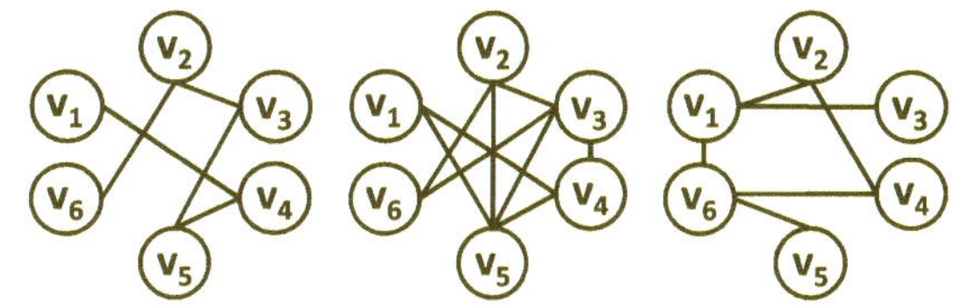

Figure 2: Counterexample to complementary graph approaches.

The proposed MkTG problem is *NP-Hard* and *inapproximable within any ratio*, which can be proved with a gap-introducing reduction from the Maximum Independent Set (MIS) problem (we present the hardness analysis in [10]). Therefore, it is impossible to design an approximation algorithm with any finite ratio for MkTG in an arbitrary graph. However, after carefully analyzing the problem, we observe that it is still possible to obtain the optimal solution to the MkTG problem in polynomial time for an important graph class, i.e., *threshold graphs* [31]. We are particularly interested in MkTG on threshold graphs due to their correspondence to many real-life social networks. For example, as reported in a recent study [32], the structural properties of the intergroup networks on online social networks (e.g., LiveJournal, Flickr, Youtube), including degree distribution, largest component size, edge density, and local clustering coefficient, match well with the structure of threshold graphs. Therefore, we also analyze the MkTG problem on threshold graphs.

3 RELATED WORKS

Extracting dense subgraphs or communities is an important research topic with many social applications. Various social cohesive measures have been proposed to find dense subgraphs, e.g., diameter [8], density [11], clique and its variations [12]. Moreover, community detection methods have been actively studied to extract densely connected subgraphs from social networks [13, 14], while research on organizing social groups based on tightness among existing friends and other crucial factors [15–17] has also been studied. GSGQ [15] and MRGQ [16] extract socially dense groups with spatial constraints, while user preference is also examined [17]. Although the above research covers various applications, they focus on extracting *dense* subgraphs from online social networks. In contrast, this paper explores a new problem of finding subgraphs with the minimum number of k-triangles. Therefore, the algorithms in prior works cannot be applied to the MkTG problem.

A recent line of research focuses on graph sparsification, simplification, sparse spanners, and sampling for massive networks [18–22]. These algorithms aim to find concise and representative subgraphs with the essential graph properties preserved so that the results are still informative for network analysis. For example, DEDS [18] processes the original graph into multiple smaller networks to improve the efficiency of link prediction, whereas the structure of a network is simplified for clustering [19]. In contrast, MkTG does not extract a subgraph with the graph properties preserved. It aims to find a subset of mutually remote vertices with the minimum number of k-triangles.

Some theoretical works analyze triangle-free graphs [23–26]. The number of independent sets in triangle-free graphs is studied in [23], while the number of pentagons in triangle-free graphs is derived in [24, 25]. Nevertheless, it is worth noting that, triangle-free graphs cannot ensure mutual tenuity. Even if a subgraph F contains no triangles, members of F may still be socially close to each other, e.g., friends-of-friends. Most importantly, the above works focus on analyzing the properties of triangle-free graphs, but apparently online social networks are not triangle-free. Some theoretical works [27–29] also analyze the properties of other sparse graphs, e.g., chordal graphs, interval graphs, and perfect graphs [27, 29]. Nevertheless, the above research does not aim to extract a subgraph from a social network.

4 MkTG ON GENERAL GRAPHS

In this section, we propose two new algorithms, namely *Triangle and Edge Reduction Algorithm (TERA)* and *TERA with Advanced Processing Strategies (TERA-ADV)*, for finding good solutions to the MkTG problem on general graphs efficiently. While it is inapproximable within any ratio as shown in Section 2, we prove later in Section 5 that the proposed TERA can find the optimal solution for MkTG on threshold graphs, which have similar properties with many online social networks, in polynomial time.

To solve MkTG, several crucial factors need to be carefully examined. The first factor is the tenuity objective and its interplay with the no-pair constraint, i.e., there must exist no edge in F. To minimize the number of k-triangles, one greedy approach is to iteratively select the vertices involved in few triangles. Nevertheless, these vertices may share common incident edges and thus are not able to ensure the no-pair constraint. The second factor is the trade-off between the minimum group size n and the number of k-triangles. The objective function aims to minimize the *average* number of k-triangles in F, i.e., to minimize $\frac{\Delta_k(F)}{|F|}$. As k and n increase, it is more likely to have k-triangles in F. Therefore, how to strike a balance between the group size and the number of k-triangles is crucial to minimizing the objective value.

To address the above factors, three ideas are considered in our algorithm design: 1) To include *isolated* vertices because isolated vertices ensure both the no-pair constraint and the minimization of the number of k-triangles. However, relying solely on the isolated vertices is not practical because the number of isolated vertices is usually small, especially in online social networks. 2) To identify the vertices appearing in many k-triangles. If these vertices are identified and removed from the resulting group F, the number of k-triangles can be significantly reduced. Note that a vertex with a great degree is not necessarily involved in many k-triangles in F since not all its neighboring vertices are always selected in F. 3) To generate multiple candidate groups of different sizes in order to extract the one with the best balance between the group size and the number of k-triangles.

In the following, we first present the basic TERA in Section 4.1 and then enhance it with advanced pre-processing and pruning techniques in Section 4.2. The proposed advanced techniques can pre-process the social networks offline to support arbitrary parameters k and n in MkTG issued by a user online.

4.1 Triangle and Edge Reduction Algorithm

In TERA, we first assign each vertex v with a weight $w(v)$, where $w(v)$ is the number of k-triangles v is involved in. Note that this step can be done efficiently offline by transforming G into the k-hop graph G_k (as mentioned in Section 2)[6] and then assigning the number of triangles each vertex v is involved in G_k as $w(v)$. Then, given the runtime parameters k and n, TERA iteratively removes a vertex v_i (and its incident edges) with the largest vertex weight from G. More specifically, let H_{i+1} denote the graph after removing vertex v_i from H_i in iteration i. Initially, H_1 is set as G. At each iteration afterwards, H_{i+1} represents the graph $H_i - \{v_i\}$.

Algorithm 1 Triangle and Edge Reduction (TERA)

Input: $G = (V, E)$, n, k
$H_1 \leftarrow G$, $i \leftarrow 1$, $\mathbb{U} \leftarrow \varnothing$
while $|H_i| > n$ **do**
  identify $v_i \in H_i$ as the vertex with the maximum $w(v_i)$ (break ties by selecting the vertex with larger degree in H_i)
  $H_{i+1} \leftarrow H_i - \{v_i\}$
  if H_{i+1} satisfies no-pair constraint **then**
    $\mathbb{U} \leftarrow \mathbb{U} \cup \{H_{i+1}\}$
  end if
  $i \leftarrow i + 1$
end while
$H^* \leftarrow \arg\min_{H_j \in \mathbb{U}} \frac{\Delta_k(H_j)}{|H_j|}$
if $H^* = \emptyset$ **then**
  $H^* \leftarrow \arg\min_{\forall j} \frac{\Delta_k(H_j)}{|H_j|}$
end if
output H^*

The intuition is that removing the vertices that are involved in a large number of k-triangles may likely reduce the number of k-triangles and keep isolated vertices in the remaining graph. Thus, v_i selected in the i-th iteration is the vertex which has the largest $w(v)$ in H_i, i.e., the remaining vertex that incurs the maximum number of k-triangles. Note that the vertex with a larger degree is more likely to violate the no-pair constraint. Thus, we prioritize the selection of the vertex with a larger degree on the induced subgraph of H_i on G if there are multiple vertices involved in the same number of k-triangles.

Accordingly, H_{i+1} is generated by removing v_i and its corresponding edges from H_i. Afterwards, H_{i+1} is processed in the next iteration $i+1$. The above procedure ends when $|H_i| \leq n$. Finally, we extract the graph $H^* \in \{H_1, H_2, \ldots\}$ with the minimum objective value that satisfies the no-pair constraint as the output solution. It

[6]For most networks, their k-hop graphs become complete graphs for $k \geq 6$. Therefore, we only need to consider the k-hop graphs for $2 \leq k \leq 5$. To reduce space consumption, we store only one copy of vertex set in the k-hop graph. Each edge e in the k-hop graph is marked with an integer k_e indicating e appears when $k \geq k_e$.

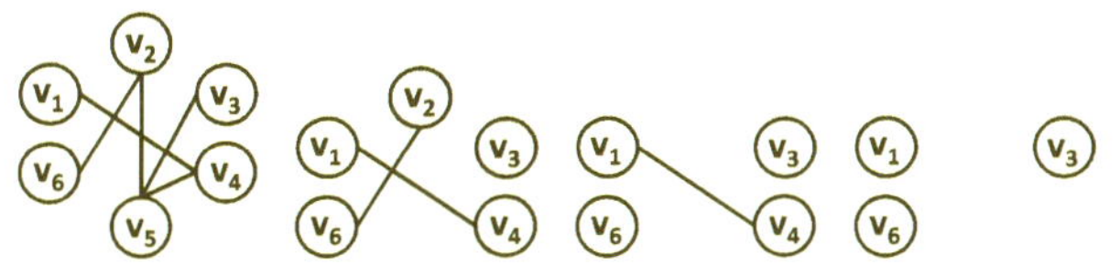

(a) $G = H_1$. (b) H_2. (c) H_3. (d) H_4.

Figure 3: Running example of TERA with $k = 2$ and $n = 3$.

is worth noting that as proved in the hardness analysis, deciding if MkTG has any feasible solution following the no-pair constraint is NP-Complete. Therefore, TERA and any other algorithm may not be able to find a feasible solution when an MkTG instance does not contain any feasible solution (otherwise, $P = NP$ holds)[7].

Example 4.1. Figure 3 is an example of TERA with $k = 2$ and $n = 3$. TERA starts with $H_1 = G$ (Figure 3(a)). Since v_5 is involved in the maximum number of 2-triangles, v_5 is removed from H_1 and produces H_2 (Figure 3(b)). Then, v_2 is removed from H_2 to create H_3 (Figure 3(c)). Finally, we remove v_4 and $H_4 = \{v_1, v_3, v_6\}$. The objective value of H_4 is minimum among all H_i, i.e., 0, and H_4 satisfies the no-pair constraint. Therefore, H_4 is returned by TERA.

Time Complexity Analysis of TERA. Given the input parameters k and n, TERA removes v_i and its incident edges in each iteration i, which requires $O(\delta_G)$ time, where δ_G is the maximum degree in G. Computing the number of k-triangles reduced by removing v_i takes $O(\delta_G^2)$ time. Since there are at most $O(|V|)$ iterations, the overall time complexity is $O(\delta_G^2|V|)$.

4.2 TERA with Advanced Strategies

Through the analysis and evaluation of TERA, we observe that it is not necessary to examine the whole vertex set in G, because many vertices will never satisfy the no-pair constraint. Moreover, many vertices are redundant and can be removed from G because these vertices can always be replaced to reduce the objective value. Therefore, we propose an advanced version of TERA, namely *TERA-ADV*, by exploring the above observations. TERA-ADV includes two main ideas: 1) we propose a pre-processing strategy, namely *Simplicial Pruning (SP)*, that significantly reduces the size of vertex set before TERA starts. 2) We partition the vertex set into several components based on graph theory and devise a strategy, namely *Vicinal Partition and Elimination (VPE)*, to eliminate redundant examinations in TERA. Conventional pruning strategies are usually performed at runtime. In contrast, Simplicial Pruning and Vicinal Partition and Elimination can be performed offline for arbitrary k and n in any problem instance before any query arrives. By removing a significant number of redundant vertices, these strategies reduce on-line computation cost and storage cost of the graph significantly. Let G_{SP} and G_V be the graphs after SP and VPE, respectively.

Simplicial Pruning (SP). Given a graph $G = (V, E)$ and a vertex $x \in V$, let $N(x)$ denote the 1-hop neighbors of x, and let $N[x]$ denote the *closed neighbors* of x, i.e., $N[x] = N(x) \cup \{x\}$. For example, $N[v_1] = \{v_1, v_3, v_9\}$ in Figure 4(a). A *simplicial vertex* $s \in V$ is a vertex where $N(s)$ forms a clique. For example, v_1, v_2, v_{10} are simplicial vertices. Simplicial vertices have nice properties and thus play important roles in the proposed Simplicial Pruning.

For the first nice property of simplicial vertices, given a feasible solution H (i.e., satisfying the no-pair constraint) of the MkTG problem and a simplicial vertex s, at most one vertex is overlapped by H and $N[s]$.

Lemma 4.2. *Given a feasible solution H and a simplicial vertex s, $|H \cap N[s]| \leq 1$ holds.*

Proof. Since s is a simplicial vertex and $N(s)$ forms a clique, $(x, y) \in E$ for any $x, y \in N[s]$. If more than one vertices in $N[s]$ are included in H, H must have at least one edge, and H will not be a feasible solution. □

Therefore, for a simplicial vertex s, we can select a vertex in $N[s]$ and trim others because at most one vertex in $N[s]$ would appear in any feasible solution to ensure the no-pair constraint. However, the identity of the chosen vertex is still not clear. Therefore, the second nice property of simplicial vertices states that, we can always choose the simplicial vertex s itself (and trim all other vertices in $N[s]$), which must satisfy the no-pair constraint and generates the minimal objective value.

Lemma 4.3. *Given a feasible solution H and a simplicial vertex s, if $y = H \cap N[s]$ and $H' = H - \{y\} \cup \{s\}$, then H' is no worse than H.*

Proof. Let $E(s)$ denote the set of incident edges of s. For a simplicial vertex s and $\forall u \in N[s]$, $|E(s)| = \min_{u \in N[s]} |E(u)|$ and $N[s] \subseteq N[u]$ must hold because each vertex $u \in N[s]$ also connects to every other vertex in $N[s]$, and u may have edges linking to other vertices outside $N[s]$. Since the number of edges incident on s is minimum among $N[s]$, and $N[s] \subseteq N[u], \forall u \in N[s]$, creating $H' = H - \{y\} \cup s$ by substituting y with s still allows H' to satisfy the no-pair constraint, if H already follows the no-pair constraint. Moreover, inequality $\frac{\Delta_k(H')}{|H'|} \leq \frac{\Delta_k(H)}{|H|}$ holds because 1) $|H'| = |H|$, and 2) every k-triangle connecting to s can be adjusted to connect to u (since $N(s) \subseteq N(u)$). □

Based on the above two properties, Simplicial Pruning proceeds as follows. Given the input graph $G = (V, E)$, we first extract the set of all simplicial vertices $\widehat{S} = \{s_1, s_2, ...\}$ according to [31]. Then, Simplicial Pruning removes $\bigcup_{s_i \in \widehat{S}} N(s_i)$ and their incident edges from G to produce G_{SP}. Therefore, for any feasible solution H obtained from G, we can always find a solution H' in G_{SP} no worse than H. That is, the vertices removed from G are indeed redundant and able to be safely removed. Moreover, if $|G_{SP}| < n$ in any instance of MkTG, we guarantee that the instance has no feasible solution.

Example 4.4. Consider the example in Figure 4(a) with $k = 2$ and $n = 4$ again. SP first identifies the set of simplicial vertices, i.e.,

[7] An alternative approach is to add the number of edges in a solution to the objective function, by replacing the tenuity objective of F with $\frac{\Delta_k(F)+E(F)}{|F|}$, where $E(F)$ is the number of edges in F. TERA can solve the above problem by including a set of *virtual nodes* R that links to every vertex in the k-hop graph G_k during the preprocessing step. In this case, if any two vertices $u, v \in F$ share an edge, the edge will be included in $|R|$ k-triangles, and the number of k-triangles thereby increases. Thus minimizing this new objective function would deter F from including edges.

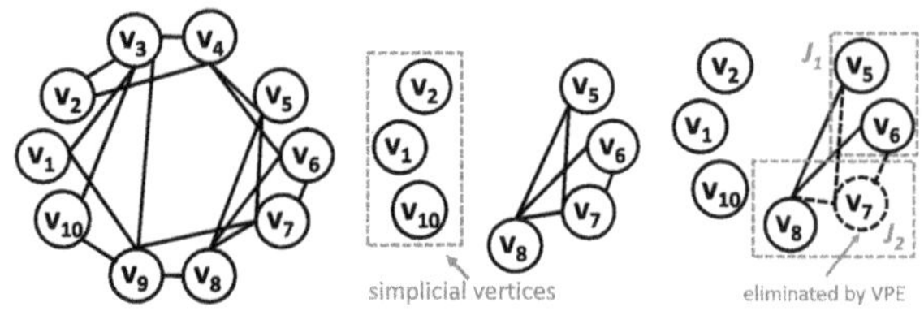

(a) Graph G. (b) After SP. (c) After VPE.

Figure 4: Running example of TERA-ADV.

$\widehat{S} = \{v_1, v_2, v_{10}\}$, and removes $N(v_1)$, $N(v_2)$, and $N(v_{10})$ from G to produce G_{SP}, where G_{SP} is shown in Figure 4(b).

Theorem 4.5. *For any feasible solution H obtained from G, there exists a solution H' in G_{SP} no worse than H. Moreover, if $|G_{SP}| < n$, there is no feasible solution to the MkTG problem.*

Proof. Let H be a feasible solution obtained from G, and assume $y \in N(s_i)$ and $y \in H$, where s_i is y's corresponding simplicial vertex. Based on Lemma 4.3, $H - \{y\} \cup \{s_i\}$ is a better solution than H. Therefore, there is always a solution H' in G_{SP} no worse than H.

On the other hand, if $|G_{SP}| < n$, suppose that the set of simplicial vertices in G_{SP} is $\bar{S} = \{\bar{s}_1, \bar{s}_2, ...\}$. That is, $G_{SP} = \bar{S} \cup W$, where W is the set of vertices that are neither simplicial vertices nor connected to any simplicial vertices (i.e., those not pruned from G). Then, $\bigcup_{\forall \bar{s}_i \in \bar{S}} N[\bar{s}_i] = G - W$ holds. For any feasible solution H, $H \cap N[\bar{s}_i]$ contains at most one vertex. Therefore, $H \cap (\bigcup_{\forall \bar{s}_i \in \bar{S}} N[\bar{s}_i])$ contains at most $|\bar{S}|$ vertices (otherwise, H violates the no-pair constraint). In other words, if $|G_{SP}| = |W \cup (\bigcup_{\forall \bar{s}_i \in \bar{S}} N[\bar{s}_i])| < n$, there is no solution for the instance of the MkTG. The theorem follows. □

Vicinal Partition and Elimination (VPE). We first use *vicinal pre-order* [31] to describe the relation of the common neighbors among two neighbor vertices x and y in any graph. The vicinal pre-order $x \lesssim y$ states that all vertices (except y) adjacent to x are also adjacent to y. In other words, $x \lesssim y$ holds if and only if $N(x) \subseteq N[y]$ holds, i.e., x's 1-hop neighbors are all included in y's closed neighbors. For example, $v_1 \lesssim v_{10}$ in Figure 4(a).

Based on vicinal pre-order, we partition the graph G_{SP} into a set of non-overlapping subgraphs $\{J_1, J_2, ...\}$, where $x \lesssim y$ and $y \lesssim x$ hold for any $x, y \in J_i$, i.e., x and y share the same neighbors. For example, $J_1 = \{v_5, v_6\}$ and $J_2 = \{v_7, v_8\}$ as shown in Figure 4(c). This enables TERA to further eliminate redundant vertices in G_{SP} (detailed later). Please note that an induced subgraph J_i either has no edges or forms a complete graph, where $w(x)$ is the number of k-triangles in which vertex x is involved for G_{SP}.

Based on the above observation, for each J_i that induces a complete graph, we can remove all the vertices in J_i except one vertex. The reason is that if a subgraph $\widehat{H}$ contains two vertices $x, y \in J_i$, $\widehat{H}$ is not a feasible solution because it violates the no-pair constraint. Therefore, since the incident edge sets of any vertices $x, y \in J_i$ are identical, we can remove any $|J_i| - 1$ vertices from J_i.

Vicinal Partition and Elimination (VPE) prunes the input graph and constructs G_V with the following two steps. In Step 1, the *Partition* step, VPE partitions the graph G_{SP} into $\{J_1, J_2, ...\}$ based on vicinal pre-order, i.e., each J_i contains vertices x, y if $x \lesssim y$ and $y \lesssim x$. Given G_{SP} produced by the SP strategy as shown in Figure 4(b), the vertices are partitioned into J_1 and J_2 by VPE, as shown in Figure 4(c). Then, in Step 2, the *Elimination* step, VPE identifies the set of subgraphs $\mathcal{J}_c = \{J_i : (x, y) \in E, \forall x, y \in J_i\}$ whose induced subgraphs are complete graphs. Then for those subgraphs in $\mathcal{J}_c$, VPE removes all the vertices (except one vertex) in each $J_i \in \mathcal{J}_c$ to form G_V. Please note that, VPE is performed offline, removing redundant vertices before the query comes. Moreover, if $|G_V| < n$, no feasible solution exists for the MkTG instance. This condition enables VPE to effectively prune redundant vertices.

Example 4.6. In Figure 4(c), vertex v_7 in J_2 is removed because J_2 induces a complete graph. After VPE, TERA starts on G_V, which contains vertices $\{v_1, v_2, v_5, v_6, v_8, v_{10}\}$, as shown in Figure 4(c). TERA then obtains the solution $\{v_1, v_2, v_8, v_{10}\}$ with objective value 0 following the no-pair constraint, which is an optimal solution.

Theorem 4.7. *If $|G_V| < n$, no feasible solution exists for the MkTG instance, where G_V is the output graph of VPE.*

Proof. Assume $\mathcal{J}_c = \{J_{c,1}, J_{c,2}, ..., J_{c,q}\}$ where each $J_{c,q}$ has its induced subgraph as a complete graph. After removing redundant vertices, let v_i denote a remaining vertex in $J_{c,i}$. Then, G_V can be represented as $G_V = W \cup \bigcup_{\forall i} v_i$, where $W = G_{SP} - J_c$, i.e., W is union of J_i with its induced subgraph having no edges. Since at most one vertex in each $J_{c,i}$ can be included in a feasible solution, if $|G_V| < n$, no solution exists for the MkTG instance. The theorem follows. □

Time Complexity Analysis of TERA-ADV (Offline Processing). Let δ_G denote the maximal degree of a vertex in G. Checking if a vertex v is a simplicial vertex requires $O(\delta_G^2)$ time. SP takes $O(\delta_G^2|V|)$ time, and VPE requires $O(|V|^2)$ time. The overall time complexity of performing SP and VPE is $O(\delta_G^2|V| + |V|^2)$.

5 SOLUTION OPTIMALITY OF MkTG ON THRESHOLD GRAPHS

In the following, we prove that TERA and TERA-ADV can find the optimal solutions of MkTG on *threshold graphs* [31], which are very similar to many well-known online social networks (e.g., LiveJournal, Flickr, Youtube) [32] in terms of important graph properties, such as the degree distribution, largest component size, edge density, and local clustering coefficient. Analyzing the tractability of MkTG on threshold graphs helps us understand the performance of the proposed algorithms on popular online social networks. We first define the threshold graph as follows.

Definition 5.1. A graph G is a threshold graph if there exists a weight $\widehat{w}_v$ for every vertex v in the graph and a real value τ (called the threshold value) such that for every edge (u, v), $\widehat{w}_v + \widehat{w}_u \geq \tau$ always holds.

Specifically, a threshold graph $G_C = (V_C, E_C)$ similar to online social networks can be constructed as follows [32]. For every vertex pair u, v, a larger weight is assigned to the vertex pair if u and v have more common or similar attributes (e.g., the number

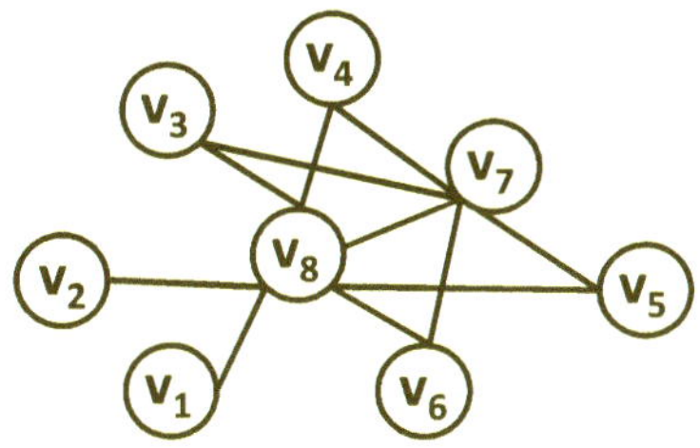

Figure 5: Running example of threshold graph.

of common neighbors). Then, given a threshold τ (not exceeding 10 in [32]), an edge (u, v) is constructed in E_C if the sum of vertex weights associated with u and v is at least τ. Therefore, it is not surprising that the threshold graph is similar to popular social networks because similar and close vertex pairs are inclined to be connected (the intuition is widely exploited in many link prediction algorithms, such as [36, 37]).

Example 5.2. Figure 5 presents an example of a threshold graph with $\tau = 6$, and vertex weights of $\{\widehat{w}_{v_1}, \ldots, \widehat{w}_{v_8}\}$ are $\{2, 2, 3, 3, 3, 3, 7, 7\}$, respectively. The parameters of MkTG are $k = 2$ and $n = 4$. After SP and VPE strategies, we have $G_V = \{v_1, v_2, v_3, v_4, v_5, v_6\}$ and the vertices are all simplicial vertices. Please note that G_V satisfies the no-pair constraint, indicating that the solutions generated by TERA-ADV (or TERA) afterwards all satisfy the no-pair constraint. TERA-ADV then sets $H_1 = G_V$. H_1 is a feasible solution with objective value $\frac{\Delta_2(H_1)}{6} = 3.3$. Then, v_6 is removed from H_1 to construct H_2, a feasible solution with $\frac{\Delta_2(H_2)}{5} = 2$. Finally, v_5 is removed from H_2 to create H_3, which is a feasible solution with $\frac{\Delta_2(H_3)}{4} = 1$. H_3 is returned by TERA-ADV as the solution (which is the optimal solution).

In the following, the vicinal pre-order of a graph is *linear* if for any two vertices x, y in the graph, $x \lesssim y$, or $y \lesssim x$, or both. The following lemma in the literature first presents the one-to-one correspondence between the vicinal pre-order and a threshold graph.

LEMMA 5.3. *[31] A graph G is a threshold graph if and only if the vicinal pre-order of G is linear.*

Lemma 5.3 indicates that the vertices in G to $\{v_1, \ldots v_{|G|}\}$ can be relabelled such that $v_1 \lesssim v_2 \lesssim \cdots \lesssim v_{|G|}$. To show the solution optimality of TERA, we first explore the relation of vicinal pre-order and the shortest path distances in a threshold graph.

LEMMA 5.4. *Given a threshold graph $G = (V, E)$, for any three vertices $x, y, z \in V$, if $x \lesssim y$, then $d_G(y, z) \leq d_G(x, z)$ holds.*

PROOF. We prove this lemma by the following two cases. Case i): if y is on the shortest path from x to z, denoted as $P_G(x, z)$, then $d_G(y, z) < d_G(x, z)$ holds. Case ii): if y is not on $P_G(x, z)$, then there exists a vertex $v \in N(x)$ and $v \in P_G(x, z)$. Since $v \in N(x)$ implies $v \in N(y)$ (because $x \lesssim y$), $d_G(y, z) \leq d_G(x, z)$ holds because the path $P_G(y, z) = \{y\} \cup \{v\} \cup d_G(v, z)$ must have length no larger than that of $P_G(x, z) = \{x\} \cup \{v\} \cup d_G(v, z)$. The lemma follows. □

Given a threshold graph $G = (V, E)$ and three arbitrary subgraphs of G, denoted as $S = (V_S, E_S)$, $B = (V_B, E_B)$, and $C = (V_C, E_C)$, where $V_B = \{b_1, .., b_r\}$, $V_C = \{c_1, .., c_r\}$. Also, $V_B \cap V_C = \varnothing$. Let $\Delta_k(S)$ denote the number of k-triangles in S. Based on the above lemmas, the following lemma connects vicinal pre-order to the number of k-triangles in a threshold graph.

LEMMA 5.5. *If $b_i, c_i \notin S$ and $c_i \lesssim b_i$ hold for every i in a threshold graph G, then $\Delta_k(S \cup C) \leq \Delta_k(S \cup B)$ for any k in MkTG.*

PROOF. Given a k-triangle $\{x, y, z\}$ in $S \cup C$, let $\lambda = |\{x, y, z\} \cap S|$. We prove the lemma by considering all possible cases of λ as follows.

Case 1: $\lambda = 0$. Let $\{x, y, z\} = \{c_h, c_i, c_j\}$. since $c_h \lesssim b_h$, $c_i \lesssim b_i$, and $c_j \lesssim b_j$, based on Lemma 5.4, we have $d_G(b_h, b_i) \leq d_G(b_h, c_i)$ (because $c_i \lesssim b_i$) and $d_G(b_h, c_i) \leq d_G(c_h, c_i)$ (because $c_h \lesssim b_h$). Therefore, $d_G(b_h, b_i) \leq d_G(c_h, c_i)$ holds. Similarly, after we substitute b_i with b_j and c_i with c_j, $d_G(b_h, b_j) \leq d_G(c_h, c_j)$. Again, if we substitute b_h with b_j and c_h with c_j, we have $d_G(b_i, b_j) \leq d_G(c_i, c_j)$.

Because $\{c_h, c_i, c_j\}$ is a k-triangle, the above inequality implies that each pair of vertices $s, t \in \{c_h, c_i, c_j\}$ must have their distance $d_G(s, t) \leq k$. According to the inequalities obtained above, we can conclude that for any pair of vertices $s', t' \in \{b_h, b_i, b_j\}$, $d_G(s', t') \leq k$ must also hold. For example, since $d_G(c_h, c_i) \leq k$ and $d_G(b_h, b_i) \leq d_G(c_h, c_i)$ (as proved above) hold, $d_G(b_h, b_i) \leq k$ holds. Therefore, $\{b_h, b_i, b_j\}$ is also a k-triangle in $S \cup B$.

Case 2: $\lambda = 1$. Let $\{x, y, z\} = \{s, c_i, c_j\}$ where, without loss of generality, we assume $\{s\} = \{s, c_i, c_j\} \cap S$. Based on Lemma 5.4, we have i) $d_G(b_i, s) \leq d_G(c_i, s) \leq k$ (because $c_i \lesssim b_i$), ii) $d_G(b_j, s) \leq d_G(c_j, s) \leq k$, and iii) $d_G(b_i, b_j) \leq d_G(c_i, b_j) \leq d_G(c_i, c_j) \leq k$. Therefore $\{s, b_i, b_j\}$ is a k-triangle in $S \cup B$.

Case 3: $\lambda = 2$. Let $\{x, y, z\} = \{s_1, s_2, c_i\}$ and $\{s_1, s_2\} = \{x, y, z\} \cap S$. Based on Lemma 5.4, we have i) $d_G(s_1, s_2) \leq k$, ii) $d_G(b_i, s_1) \leq d_G(c_i, s_1) \leq k$, and iii) $d_G(b_i, s_2) \leq d_G(c_j, s_2) \leq k$. Therefore $\{s_1, s_2, b_i\}$ is a k-triangle in $S \cup B$.

Case 4: $\lambda = 3$. let $\{x, y, z\} = \{s_1, s_2, s_3\}$ and $\{s_1, s_2, s_3\} = \{x, y, z\} \cap S$, $\{s_1, s_2, s_3\}$ is a k-triangle in $S \cup B$.

In summary, there is a one-to-one mapping of k-triangles from $S \cup C$ to $S \cup B$. Therefore, $\Delta_k(S \cup C) \leq \Delta_k(S \cup B)$. The lemma follows. □

Equipped with the above lemmas, we now prove that TERA acquires the optimal solution of the MkTG in a threshold graph G.

THEOREM 5.6. *Given a threshold graph $G = (V, E)$, TERA and TERA-ADV return the optimal solution of the MkTG problem on G.*

PROOF. We first analyze TERA as follows. Given $G = (V, E)$, the size constraint n, and the tenuity parameter k of the MkTG problem, we denote H^* as the subgraph generated by TERA. Let H^{OPT} be an optimal solution and $|H^{OPT}| = m \geq n$. We relabel the vertices in G to $\{v_1, \ldots v_{|G|}\}$ such that $v_1 \lesssim v_2 \lesssim \cdots \lesssim v_{|G|}$ according to Lemma 5.3, i.e., a vicinal pre-order is derived.

Suppose $v_i \lesssim v_j$. Given a k-triangle $\{v_i, a, b\}$, there are two cases. i) v_j is also a vertex of this k-triangle. ii) v_j is not a vertex of the k-triangle. In this case, since $d_G(a, b) \leq k$, $d_G(v_i, a) \leq k$, $d_G(v_i, b) \leq k$ (because $\{v_i, a, b\}$ is a k-triangle), while $d_G(v_j, a) \leq d_G(v_i, a)$ and $d_G(v_j, b) \leq d_G(v_i, b)$ hold (by Lemma 5.4), $\{v_j, a, b\}$ is a k-triangle. In summary, if $v_i \lesssim v_j$ holds, v_j must be involved in more k-triangles than v_i.

Note that TERA starts from G and then sequentially removes $v_{|G|}, v_{|G|-1}, ...,$ from G (TERA records the resulting subgraph once a vertex is removed) until there are n vertices left. The reason is that $v_{|G|} \gtrsim v_{|G|-1}$ and so on, indicating that $v_{|G|}$ is involved in more k-triangles than $v_{|G|-1}$ due to Lemma 5.5. Therefore, TERA will generate a subgraph $H^* = \{v_1, v_2, .., v_m\}$ in some iteration after removing $|V| - m$ vertices, and $|H^*| = |H^{OPT}| = m$.

In the following, we prove by contradiction that H^* is an optimal solution to MkTG according to Lemma 5.5. Suppose $|H^*| \neq |H^{OPT}|$ and let $H^{O\cap *} = H^{OPT} \cap H^*$, $H^{O-*} = H^{OPT} - H^*$, and $H^{*-O} = H^* - H^{OPT}$. Then $|H^{O-*}| = |H^{*-O}|$ holds since $|H^{OPT}| = |H^*|$. Moreover, for every $b \in H^{O-*}, c \in H^{*-O}$, we have $c \lesssim b$ because $\{v_1, v_2, .., v_m\}$ of H^* is the first m vertices in $v_1 \lesssim v_2 \lesssim .. \lesssim v_{|G|}$, and c is in H^*.

We first prove by contradiction that H^* follows the no-pair constraint. Suppose H^* does not follow the no-pair constraint. Then there exist $x, y \in H^*$ and $(x, y) \in E(G)$. Without loss of generality, we assume that $x \lesssim y$. We then consider every possible case of vertex x as follows.

Case 1: $x \in H^{*-O}$. We select two vertices $w, z \in H^{O-*}$ with $x \lesssim w$ and $y \lesssim z$. Since $(x, y) \in E(G)$ and $x \lesssim w$, $(w, y) \in E(G)$ holds by Lemma 5.4 because $d_G(w, y) \leq d_G(x, y)$. Since $(w, y) \in E(G)$ and $y \lesssim z$, $(w, z) \in E(G)$ holds because $d_G(w, z) \leq d_G(w, y)$, implying that the optimal solution H^{OPT} contains an edge and leads to a contradiction.

Case 2: $x \in H^{O\cap *}$ **or** $y \in H^{O\cap *}$. We select a vertex $z \in H^{O-*}$. Since $x \lesssim z$ and $y \lesssim z$. Similar to Case 1, we have $(x, z) \in E(G)$ and $(y, z) \in E(G)$. Therefore, for $x \in H^{O\cap *}$ or $y \in H^{O\cap *}$, the optimal solution H^{OPT} contains an edge and leads to a contradiction.

Based on the above two cases, H^* must satisfy the no-pair constraint. Also, since $|H^*| = |H^{OPT}| \geq n$ (i.e., the group size), H^* is a feasible solution.

Then, we prove that the number of k-triangles in H^* does not exceed the number of k-triangles in H^{OPT}. Our algorithm produces $H^* = \{v_1, v_2, ..., v_m\}$ with $v_1 \lesssim v_2 \lesssim ... \lesssim v_m$. Let $S = H^{OPT} \cap H^*$, $B = H^{OPT} - S$, $C = H^* - S$. Therefore, $H^{OPT} = S \cup B$, $H^* = S \cup C$, and $B \cap C = \emptyset$. Let $B = \{b_1, ..., b_{m-|S|}\}$ and $C = \{c_1, ..., c_{m-|S|}\}$. Since for each $b \in B$, the vertex ID of $b > m$, and for each $c \in C$, the vertex ID of $c \leq m$, $c_i \lesssim b_i$ for $i \in [1, m - |S|]$ holds. According to Lemma 5.5, we have $\Delta_k(H^*) \leq \Delta_k(H^{OPT})$. Since $|H^*| = |H^{OPT}|$ and H^{OPT} is an optimal solution, $\Delta_k(H^*)/|H^*| = \Delta_k(H^{OPT})/H^{OPT}$ holds, implying that H^* is also optimal.

The above analysis shows that if a feasible solution exists and thereby the optimal solution H^{OPT} also exists, our algorithm is able to obtain a feasible solution with the objective value identical to the one in H^{OPT}. Therefore, if TERA cannot find a subgraph which satisfies the no-pair constraint, it implies that the instance of MkTG problem on the threshold graph G has no feasible solution. For TERA-ADV, since SP and VPE strategies remove from G only the redundant vertices, TERA-ADV also finds the optimal solution for MkTG in threshold graphs. □

6 EXPERIMENTAL RESULTS

To evaluate the proposed algorithms, we conduct experiments on 5 real datasets. The first two datasets, *IG* and *FB*, are two social network datasets from Instagram and Facebook, respectively. FB contains 63K vertices and 817K edges [33], and IG includes 45K vertices and 678K edges [34]. The third dataset, DBLP, is a co-author network with 317K vertices and 1M edges[8]. The fourth dataset is the Pokec social network with 1.6M vertices and 30M edges[9]. Finally, Youtube video sharing dataset has 1.1M vertices and 3M edges, which is also employed to construct four threshold graphs with different thresholds $\tau = \{2, 4, 6, 8\}$ based on [32].

Table 1: Summary of datasets

Dataset	$\|V\|$	$\|E\|$	Avg. Deg.	$\frac{\Delta_1(G)}{\|V\|}$	CC	Diam
IG	45K	678K	15.1	132.6	0.24	7
FB	63K	817K	13	55.6	0.14	15
DBLP	317K	1M	3.2	7	0.63	21
Pokec	1.6M	30M	18.8	20	0.11	11
Youtube	1.1M	3M	2.6	2.7	0.08	24

Since no algorithm has been proposed for MkTG, we compare Triangle and Edge Reduction Algorithm (TERA) and TERA with Advanced Processing Strategies (TERA-ADV) with four baseline algorithms: Brute-Force (BF), Random (RND), BigClam [13] on the complement graph (BC), and Parallel Maximum Clique [38, 39] on the complement graph (PMC). BF finds the optimal solution of MkTG by enumerating all the subgraphs satisfying the no-pair constraint. RND selects random vertices from G to iteratively expand the subgraphs. It derives the tenuity objective value when a new vertex is added, and the best group following the no-pair constraint is returned.

BC is a community detection algorithm which detects overlapping communities by estimating non-negative latent factors. BC and PMC first construct the k-hop graph G_k of the original social network G and then transforms G_k into its complement graph $\widehat{G}_k$. We then employ BC to find the densest community in the complement graph, while PMC employs efficient heuristic approaches to find a clique of size n in the complement graph. The idea is to extract dense subgraphs (i.e., clique, community) in the complement graph and then return the corresponding tenuous subgraphs in the original social network[10].

In our experiments, the default parameters are $k = 2$ and $n = 20$. The algorithms are implemented on an HP DL580 server with Quadcore Intel X5450 3.0 GHz CPUs and 1TB RAM. Each result is averaged over 50 samples. The k-hop graphs for $2 \leq k \leq 5$ are constructed offline. Moreover, in TERA-ADV, the input graphs are filtered by Simplicial Pruning (SP) and Vicinal Partition and Elimination (VPE) offline as well.

6.1 Sensitivity Tests on Large Graphs

Figure 6 reports the results of TERA-ADV on FB, IG, DBLP, Pokec, and Youtube to help understand the behavior in different datasets. Figure 6(a) compares the objective values in different datasets. No k-triangle is created when $k = 1$. As k increases, the objective values increase because more vertices in F are within k hops on

[8] http://snap.stanford.edu/data/com-DBLP.html.
[9] http://snap.stanford.edu/data/soc-pokec.html.
[10] If no clique of size n can be found, PMC extracts the maximum clique C and randomly chooses other vertices from G to argument C until $|C| = n$.

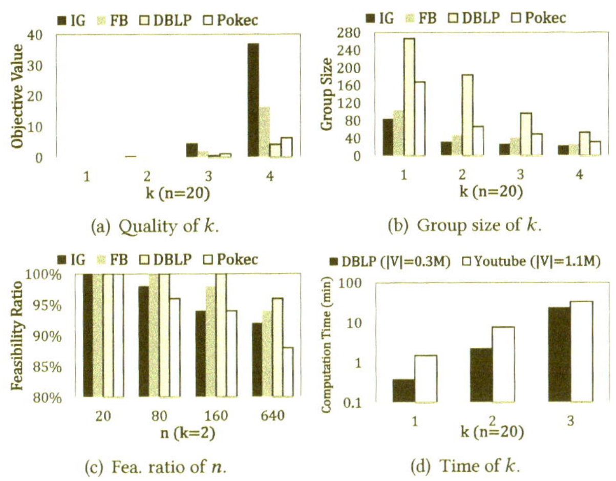

Figure 6: Comparisons on large datasets.

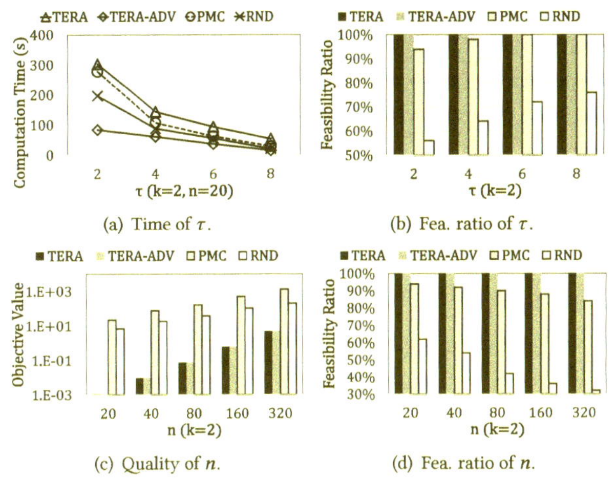

Figure 7: Comparisons on large threshold graphs (1.1M).

G. IG incurs the largest objective values because it is denser than others, i.e., the average number of 1-triangles is 132.6, and the average degree is 15. Figure 6(b) compares the group sizes obtained by TERA-ADV in different datasets. When k becomes large, small groups are preferred because larger groups in dense graphs tend to incur much more k-triangles. Moreover, TERA-ADV can find a larger group in DBLP without generating any k-triangle because the diameter is large, but the average degree is small in DBLP.

Figure 6(c) compares the feasibility ratios with different n (size constraint) in various datasets. Here, feasibility ratio is the ratio of the number of returned feasible solutions to the number of tested MkTG instances. For a small n, e.g., $n \leq 80$, the feasibility in each dataset is higher than 90%. TERA-ADV achieves the highest feasibility ratio in DBLP because DBLP has the smallest average degree, and TERA-ADV in this case tends to find large feasible groups easily. To understand the impact on computation time of different datasets, we compare the computation time of TERA-ADV in Figure 6(d) on DBLP (0.3M vertices) and Youtube (1.1M vertices). TERA-ADV is more efficient in DBLP because the number of vertices is only 1/3 that of Youtube. However, the computation time in the two datasets becomes closer when k increases. This is because the average degree and the clustering coefficient of Youtube is smaller than those of DBLP. In this case, SP and VPE can prune more redundant vertices in Youtube.

6.2 Comparisons on Large Threshold Graphs

Figure 7 compares the performance of different approaches in threshold graphs (with threshold $\tau = \{2, 4, 6, 8\}$) constructed from Youtube (1.1M vertices). As shown in Figure 7(a), the computation time drops when τ increases because the graph contains fewer edges in this case. The improvement of TERA-ADV over TERA becomes more significant for a smaller τ, because the SP and VPE strategies trim off more vertices from the original graph. Figure 7(b) compares the feasibility ratios of different τ. When τ decreases, the feasibility ratios of PMC and RND drop due to the larger number of edges. Please note that PMC does not achieve 100% feasibility ratio because sometimes it cannot find a clique of size n in the complement graph. However, the feasibility ratios of the proposed algorithms are both 100% because as shown in Section 5, TERA and TERA-ADV can obtain the optimal solution of MkTG on threshold graphs.

Figures 7(c) and 7(d) examine the objective values and the feasibility ratios of different approaches. The objective values of the optimal solutions obtained by TERA and TERA-ADV grow when n increases because more vertices lead to a greater number of k-triangles. In contrast, both PMC and RND incur much larger objective values, and RND has poor feasibility ratios. This is because PMC and RND do not well utilize the information brought by the vicinal pre-order in threshold graphs.

6.3 Different Approaches on Small Graphs

We compare the proposed TERA and TERA-ADV with other baseline approaches. Note that BF does not scale up to large social networks because it examines all possible combinations. Therefore, we randomly sample the IG dataset to generate small networks with different sizes. Figures 8(a) and 8(b) compare the execution time and the solution quality for all algorithms in IG. Figure 8(a) manifests that, even for tiny networks, BF still incurs unacceptable computation time to find the optimal solution, whereas TERA is very efficient. Moreover, TERA-ADV, equipped with Simplicial Pruning (SP) and Vicinal Partition and Elimination (VPE) to remove redundant vertices, requires small running time that is comparable to RND.

Figure 8(b) presents the pruning power of the SP and VPE strategies in TERA-ADV, where TERA-ADV can obtain high-quality solutions very close to the optimal solutions. In contrast, PMC and BC perform poorly because they cannot effectively minimize k-triangles. Therefore, the results confirm that finding dense subgraphs on complement graphs does not work for the MkTG problem. TERA-ADV obtains solutions with better quality than TERA because the SP and VPE strategies effectively remove the redundant vertices, which sometimes are considered by TERA and thus deteriorate the solution quality of TERA.

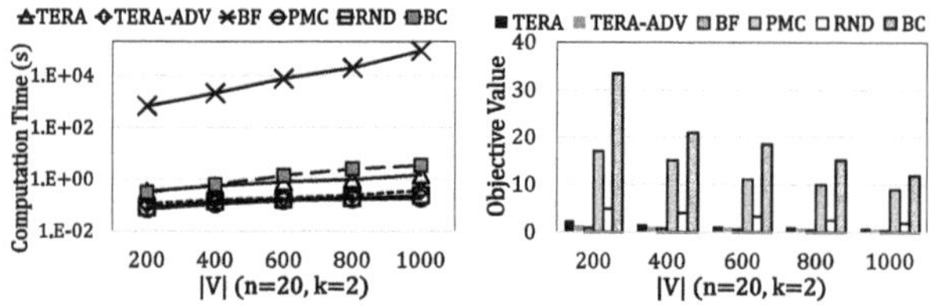

(a) Time of $|V|$ (IG). (b) Quality of $|V|$ (IG).

Figure 8: Comparisons of different approaches.

7 CONCLUSION

In contrast to previous works on identifying socially dense groups, research on finding socially tenuous groups has not received much attention in the research communities. This paper makes the first attempt to extract socially tenuous subgraphs from social networks. We introduce the notion of k-triangles for measuring group tenuity and formulate a new research problem, namely *Minimum k-Triangle Disconnected Group (MkTG)* that finds socially tenuous groups. We propose polynomial-time algorithms to obtain the optimal solutions for MkTG on threshold graphs, which are similar to many representative online social networks. We design two efficient and effective algorithms to solve MkTG on general graphs. Experimental results manifest that the proposed algorithms outperform baselines significantly in terms of computation time and solution quality. In the future work, we will incorporate other important dimensions, such as personal attributes, to ensure that the selected group members share similar or different attribute values to collaborate on the required tasks in various applications.

8 ACKNOWLEDGEMENTS

This work was supported in part by Ministry of Science and Technology (MOST), Taiwan, under MOST 105-2218-E-007 -032 -MY2, and MOST 105-2218-E-002 -035 -.

REFERENCES

[1] S. Seidman. Network structure and minimum degree. *Social Networks*, 1983.
[2] J. Cohen. Trusses: cohesive subgraphs for social network analysis, 2008.
[3] V. Batagelj and M. Zaversnik. Generalized cores. *arXiv:cs/0202039*, 2002.
[4] A. Goldberg. Finding a maximum density subgraph. *Technical Report*, 1984.
[5] D. Berlowitz, S. Cohen, B. Kimelfeld. Efficient enumeration of maximal k-plexes. *SIGMOD*, 2015.
[6] K. Reid. *Social work with groups*, 1997.
[7] J. Qiu, Z. Lin, C. Tang, and S. Qiao. Discovering organizational structure in dynamic social network. *ICDM*, 2009.
[8] S. Wasserman and K. Faust. Social network analysis: methods and applications. *Cambridge University Press*, 1994.
[9] Center for substance abuse treatment. Substance abuse treatment: group therapy. *Treatment improvement protocol (TIP) series 41*, 2005.
[10] On finding socially tenuous groups for online social networks (online full version). http://www.cs.nthu.edu.tw/~chihya/KDD2017/paper.pdf.
[11] U. Feige, G. Kortsarz, and D. Peleg. The dense k-subgraph problem. *Algorithmica*, 2001.
[12] R. Mokken. Cliques, clubs and clans. *Quality and Quantity: International Journal of Methodology*, 1979.
[13] J. Yang and J. Leskovec. Overlapping community detection at scale: a nonnegative matrix factorization approach. *WSDM*, 2013.
[14] J. Xie, S. Kelley, and B. Szymanski. Overlapping community detection in networks: The state-of-the-art and comparative study. *ACM Computing Survey*, 2013.
[15] Q. Zhu, H. Hu, J. Xu, and W.-C. Lee. Geo-social group queries with minimum acquaintance constraint. *arXiv:1406.7367v1*, 2014.
[16] C.-Y. Shen, D.-N. Yang, L.-H. Huang, W.-C. Lee, and M.-S. Chen. Socio-spatial group queries for impromptu activity planning. *TKDE*, 2016.
[17] H.-H. Shuai, D.-N. Yang, P. S. Yu, and M.-S. Chen. Willingness optimization for social group activity. *VLDB*, 2014.
[18] Y.-L. Chen, M.-S. Chen, and P. Yu. Ensemble of diverse sparsifications for link prediction in large-scale networks, *ICDM*, 2015.
[19] V. Satuluri, S. Parthasarathy, and Y. Ruan. Local graph sparsification for scalable clustering. *SIGMOD*, 2011.
[20] M. Mathioudakis, F. Bonchi, C. Castillo, A. Gionis, and A. Ukkonen. Sparsification of influence networks. *KDD*, 2011.
[21] N. Ruan, R. Jin, and Y. Huang. Distance preserving graph simplification. *ICDM*, 2011.
[22] P. Berman, S. Raskhodnikova, and G. Ruan. Finding sparser directed spanners. *FSTTCS*, 2010.
[23] M. Hujter and Z. Tuza. The number of maximal independent sets in triangle-free graphs. *SIAM Journal on Discrete Mathematics*, 1993.
[24] H. Hatami, J. Hladky, D. Kral, S. Norine, and A. Razborov. On the number of pentagons in triangle-free graphs. *Journal of Combinatorial Theory*, 2013.
[25] A. Grzesik. On the maximum number of five-cycles in a triangle-free graph. *Journal of Combinatorial Theory*, 2012.
[26] D. Brugmann, C. Komusiewicz, and H. Moser. On generating triangle-free graphs. *Electronic Notes in Discrete Mathematics*, 2009.
[27] M. Bougeret, N. Bousquet, R. Giroudeau, R. Watrigant. Parameterized complexity of the sparsest k-subgraph problem in chordal graphs. *SOFSEM*, 2014.
[28] A. Lee and I. Streinu. Pebble game algorithms and (k, l)-sparse graphs. *DMTCS*, 2005.
[29] R. Watrigant, M. Bougeret, and R. Giroudeau. The k-sparsest subgraph problem. *Tech. Rep.*, 2012.
[30] J. Cheng, Z. Shang, H. Cheng, H. Wang, and J. Yu. K-reach: who is in your small world. *VLDB*, 2012.
[31] N. Mahadev and U. Peled. Threshold graphs and related topics, New York, NY, USA: Elsevier, 1995.
[32] S. Saha, N. Ganguly, and A. Mukherjee. Intergroup networks as random threshold graphs. *Physical Review E*, 2014.
[33] B. Viswanath, A. Mislove, M. Cha, and K. Gummadi. On the evolution of user interaction in Facebook. *WOSN*, 2009.
[34] E. Ferrara, R. Interdonato, and A. Tagarelli. Online popularity and topical interests through the lens of Instagram. *HT*, 2014.
[35] U. Feige. Approximating maximum clique by removing subgraphs. *SIAM J. Discrete Math*, 2004.
[36] D. Liben-Nowell and J. Kleinberg. The link prediction problem for social networks. *Journal of the American Soceity for Information Science and Technology*, 2007.
[37] A. Clause, C. Moore, and M. Newman. Hierarchical structure and the prediction of missing links in network. *Nature*, 2008.
[38] R. A. Rossi, D. F. Gleich, A. H. Gebremedhin, and Md. M. A. Patwary. Fast maximum clique algorithms for large graphs. *WWW*, 2014.
[39] J. Xiang, C. Guo, and A. Aboulnaga. Scalable maximum clique computation using mapreduce. *ICDE*, 2013.

PReP: Path-Based Relevance from a Probabilistic Perspective in Heterogeneous Information Networks

Yu Shi
University of Illinois at Urbana-Champaign
yushi2@illinois.edu

Po-Wei Chan
University of Illinois at Urbana-Champaign
pchan12@illinois.edu

Honglei Zhuang
University of Illinois at Urbana-Champaign
hzhuang3@illinois.edu

Huan Gui
University of Illinois at Urbana-Champaign
huangui2@illinois.edu

Jiawei Han
University of Illinois at Urbana-Champaign
hanj@illinois.edu

ABSTRACT

As a powerful representation paradigm for networked and multi-typed data, the heterogeneous information network (HIN) is ubiquitous. Meanwhile, defining proper relevance measures has always been a fundamental problem and of great pragmatic importance for network mining tasks. Inspired by our probabilistic interpretation of existing path-based relevance measures, we propose to study HIN relevance from a probabilistic perspective. We also identify, from real-world data, and propose to model *cross-meta-path synergy*, which is a characteristic important for defining path-based HIN relevance and has not been modeled by existing methods. A generative model is established to derive a novel path-based relevance measure, which is data-driven and tailored for each HIN. We develop an inference algorithm to find the maximum a posteriori (MAP) estimate of the model parameters, which entails non-trivial tricks. Experiments on two real-world datasets demonstrate the effectiveness of the proposed model and relevance measure.

CCS CONCEPTS

•**Information systems** → **Data mining; Similarity measures;** •**Computing methodologies** → *Maximum a posteriori modeling;*

KEYWORDS

Heterogeneous information networks, graph mining, meta-paths, relevance measures.

1 INTRODUCTION

In real-world applications, objects of various types are often interconnected with each other. These objects, together with their relationship, form numerous heterogeneous information networks (HINs) [14, 16]. Bibliographical information network is a typical example, where researchers, papers, organizations, and publication venues are interrelated. A fundamental problem in HIN analysis is to define proper measures to characterize the relevance between node pairs in the network, which also benefits various downstream applications, such as similarity search, recommendation, and community detection [14, 16].

Most existing studies derive their HIN relevance measures on the basis of *meta-path* [14, 16, 17], which is defined as a concatenation of multiple node types linked by corresponding edge types. Based on the concept of *meta-path*, researchers have proposed PathCount, PathSim [17], and path constrained random walk [10] to measure relevance between node pairs. On top of these studies, people have explored the ideas of incorporating richer information [6, 21] and more complex typed structures [4, 7, 13] to define more effective relevance scoring functions, or adding supervision to derive task-specific relevance measures [2, 19, 23].

The probabilistic perspective. While building upon this powerful *meta-path* paradigm, we aim to additionally understand and model relevance from the probabilistic point of view. In this regard, we establish a probabilistic interpretation of existing HIN relevance measures, which is achieved by modeling the generating process of all path instances in an HIN and deriving the relevance of a node pair from the likelihood of observing the path instances connecting them. Relevance and likelihood can be connected by this approach because only a small portion of node pairs in an HIN are actually relevant; and a proper generating process has low likelihood to generate the path instances between each of these relevant node pairs. We will detailedly discuss this probabilistic interpretation in Sec. 3. Moreover, as a starting point for studying HIN relevance from the probabilistic perspective, we focus the scope of this paper on the basic *unsupervised* scenario. Meanwhile, we assume that the meta-paths of interest are already given. That is, we defer the study on the cases with label information and meta-path selection to future work.

In order to determine relevance between any pair of nodes, we have the key insight that a path-based HIN relevance should contain three characteristics – *node visibility*, *path selectivity*, and *cross-meta-path synergy* – which we describe in the following paragraphs.

Node visibility. One straightforward way to derive relevance in an HIN is PathCount [17]. For a meta-path $t \in \{1, \ldots, T\}$, PathCount is defined as the number of paths, P_{st} or equivalently $P_{\langle uv \rangle t}$, under this meta-path between a node pair $s = (u, v) \in \mathcal{V} \times \mathcal{V}$, *i.e.*,

KDD '17, August 13–17, 2017, Halifax, NS, Canada

978-1-4503-4887-4/17/08...$15.00
DOI: http://dx.doi.org/10.1145/3097983.3097990

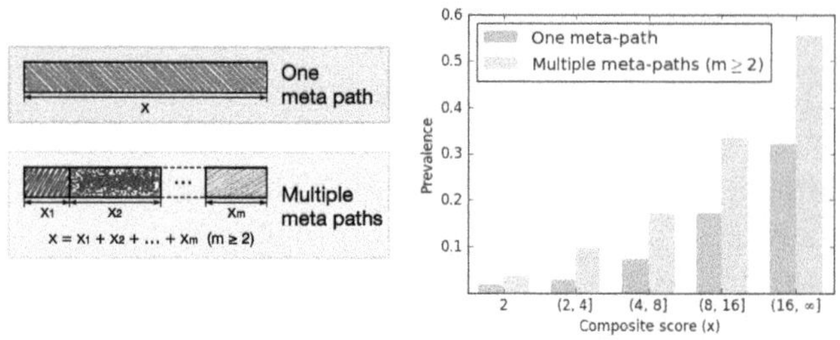

(a) (b)

Figure 1: (a) The same composite score (x) may be aggregated from different number of meta-paths, where score is represented by the length of the rectangles and each fill pattern represents a meta-path. (b) An observation made from an entity resolution task on the DBLP dataset that if linear combination is used to compute the composite score, node pairs with paths under multiple meta-paths are more likely to be relevant than those under only one meta-path. Prevalence is defined as the number of relevant node pairs divided by the total number of node pairs.

$PathCount^{(t)}(u,v) := P_{\langle uv \rangle t}$. One obvious drawback of this measure is that it favors nodes with high *node visibility*, *i.e.*, nodes with a large number of paths. To resolve this problem, [17] proposed to penalize PathCount by the arithmetic mean of the numbers of cycles attached to the two involved nodes, *i.e.*, $PathSim^{(t)}(u,v) := \frac{2 \cdot P_{\langle uv \rangle t}}{P_{\langle uu \rangle t} + P_{\langle vv \rangle t}}$. A similar design to model *node visibility* can be found in JoinSim [20], which is defined as PathCount penalized by geometric mean of the cycle numbers.

Path selectivity. Given any method defining relevance score under one meta-path, a natural question is how to combine multiple meta-paths to derive a unified relevance score – henceforth referred to as the *composite score.* To achieve this goal, Sun et al. [17] proposed to assign different weights to different meta-paths, and compute the composite score via linear combination. Let $\mathbf{w} = \{w_1, \ldots, w_T\}$ with w_t being the weight for meta-path t, the composite score of PathCount is given by $PathCount_{\mathbf{w}}(u,v) := \sum_{t=1}^{T} w_t \cdot PathCount^{(t)}(u,v)$. Similarly, one can define $PathSim_{\mathbf{w}}(u,v)$. This linear combination approach is adopted by follow-up works with multiple applications [14, 16], including personalized entity recommendation problem [22], outlier detection [9, 24], *etc.* The weights assigned or inferred in these cases specify how selective each meta-path is. The larger the *path selectivity*, the more significant this meta-path is in contributing to the composite score.

Cross-meta-path synergy. Suppose linear combination is used to find the composite score as in the previous paragraph, the two scenarios shown in Fig. 1a would receive the same composite score (x), where x_i equals to the score from the i-th meta-path multiplied by the corresponding weight. However, we have the observation that, when meta-paths do not clearly correlate, the latter scenario tends to imply a higher relevance. We take an entity resolution task on the DBLP dataset as example, which aims to merge author mentions that refer to the same entity. In this task, each node stands for an author mention, and each meta-path represents that two author mentions have both published papers in one particular research area. We label two author mentions as relevant if and only if they refer to the same entity, and we use PathCount with uniform weights as an example to compute the composite score. Results presented in Fig. 1 shows that with the same composite score, node pairs associated by paths under multiple meta-paths are more likely to be relevant than those under only one meta-path. We refer to this phenomenon as *cross-meta-path synergy.* We interpret this phenomenon as given the occurrence of one path, the happenstance of another path under the same meta-path may not be surprising, while the co-occurrence of two paths under two uncorrelated meta-paths may be a strong signal of relevance. Moreover, we should also realize that not necessarily all meta-path pairs are uncorrelated, which has been observed in a special type of HIN [15]. This implies *cross-meta-path synergy* does not necessarily exist between all pairs of meta-paths, and we deem a good relevance measure should reflect this difference.

Challenges and contributions. Regarding the three pivotal characteristics for path-based HIN relevance discussed above, the major challenge lies in how to integrate all these characteristics in a unified framework. We tackle this challenge by studying path-based relevance from a probabilistic perspective, and deriving relevance measure from a generative model. Since the model parameters are trained to fit each HIN, the derived relevance measure enjoys the property of being data-driven. That is, the derived relevance measure is tailored for each HIN. Lastly, we summarize our contributions as follows:

(1) We establish the probabilistic interpretation of existing path-based HIN relevance measures.
(2) We identify and propose to model *cross-meta-path synergy*, an important characteristic in path-based HIN relevance.
(3) We propose a novel relevance measure based on a generative model, which is data-driven and tailored for each HIN, and develop an inference algorithm with non-trivial tricks.
(4) Experiments on two real-world HINs corroborate the effectiveness of our proposed model and relevance measure.

2 PRELIMINERIES

In this section, we introduce the concepts and notations used in this paper.

Definition 2.1 (Heterogeneous Information Network). An **information network** is a directed graph $G = (\mathcal{V}, \mathcal{E})$ with a node type mapping $f : \mathcal{V} \rightarrow \mathcal{A}$ and an edge type mapping $g : \mathcal{E} \rightarrow \mathcal{R}$. Particularly, when the number of node types $|\mathcal{A}| > 1$ or the number of edge types $|\mathcal{R}| > 1$, the network is called a **heterogeneous information network** (HIN).

Due to the typed essence of HINs, paths that associate node pairs can be grouped under different meta-paths. We formally define meta-paths as follows.

Definition 2.2 (Meta-Path). A **meta-path** is a concatenation of multiple nodes or node types linked by edge types.

An example of a meta-path is [author] $\xrightarrow{\text{writes}}$ [paper] $\xrightarrow{\text{writes}^{-1}}$ [author], where a phrase in the brackets represents a node type and a phrase above the arrow refers to an edge type. When context is clear, we simply write [author]–[paper]–[author]. In this paper, we study the relevance problem when a set of meta-paths of interest is predefined by users.

To ease presentation, we focus on unweighted HINs, and model path count defined as follows. Note that the path-based model to be proposed in this paper can be extended to the weighted case.

Definition 2.3 (Path Count). The **path count** of a meta-path $t \in \{1, \ldots, T\}$ between a node pair $s = (u, v) \in \mathcal{V} \times \mathcal{V}$ is the number of concrete path instances under this meta-path that start from node u to node v, which is denoted by P_{st} or $P_{\langle uv \rangle t}$.

Note that the relevance score given by the PathCount measure [17] is exactly the path count of a meta-path between a node pair. Lastly, we introduce the probability distributions to be used.

Definition 2.4. The probability density functions of three probability distributions used in this paper are given as follows.

(1) Exponential distribution $\text{Exp}(\tilde{\lambda})$ with rate parameter $\tilde{\lambda} > 0$:

$$p(x) = \tilde{\lambda}\, e^{\tilde{\lambda} x} \quad (x > 0).$$

(2) Gamma distribution $\Gamma(\tilde{\alpha}, \tilde{\beta})$ with shape parameter $\tilde{\alpha} > 0$ and rate parameter $\tilde{\beta} > 0$:

$$p(x) = \frac{\tilde{\beta}^{\tilde{\alpha}}}{\Gamma(\tilde{\alpha})} x^{\tilde{\alpha}-1} e^{-\tilde{\beta} x} \quad (x > 0),$$

where $\Gamma(\tilde{\alpha}) = \int_0^\infty t^{\tilde{\alpha}-1} e^{-t}\, dt$ is the gamma function.

(3) Symmetric Dirichlet distribution $\text{Dir}_L(\tilde{\alpha})$ of order L and concentration parameter $\tilde{\alpha}$:

$$p(x_1, \ldots, x_L) = \frac{\Gamma(\tilde{\alpha} L)}{\Gamma(\tilde{\alpha})^L} \prod_{i=1}^{L} x_i^{\tilde{\alpha}-1} \quad (x_i > 0 \text{ and } \sum_{i=1}^{L} x_i = 1),$$

where $\Gamma(\cdot)$ is the gamma function.

We denote $\text{Exp}(x\,;\,\tilde{\lambda}) := p(x)$ the probability density function of $\text{Exp}(\tilde{\lambda})$, and denote $x \sim \text{Exp}(\tilde{\lambda})$ if x is generated from $\text{Exp}(\tilde{\lambda})$. Similar notations are also used for $\Gamma(\tilde{\alpha}, \tilde{\beta})$ and $\text{Dir}_L(\tilde{\alpha})$.

3 PROBABILISTIC INTERPRETATION OF EXISTING RELEVANCE MEASURES

In this section, we illustrate the probabilistic interpretation of existing path-based HIN relevance measures. We achieve this by studying the generating process of path counts between node pairs in an HIN, which contains a connection between relevance and the negative log likelihood. Suppose the path count under meta-path t between node pair s is generated from an exponential distribution

$$P_{st} \sim \text{Exp}(\lambda),$$

with fixed rate λ, then in terms of the rank it yields, the negative log likelihood of all observed paths under meta-path t between node pair s will be equivalent to the PathCount under meta-path t

$$-LL^{(t)}(s) = -\log(\lambda\, e^{-\lambda P_{st}}) = \lambda P_{st} - \log \lambda$$
$$\propto P_{st} + const = PathCount^{(t)}(s) + const.$$

Further, if we assume path instances under different meta-paths are generated from exponential distribution with meta-path-specific rates $\mathbf{w} = (w_1, w_2, \ldots, w_T)$, *i.e.*, $P_{st} \sim \text{Exp}(w_t)$, then the negative log likelihood of all observed path counts will be equivalent to PathCount with weights $\mathbf{w}$ for linear combination

$$-LL(s) = -\log(\prod_t w_t\, e^{-w_t P_{st}}) = \sum_t w_t P_{st} - \sum_t \log w_t$$
$$= \sum_t w_t P_{st} + const = PathCount_{\mathbf{w}}(s) + const.$$

Moreover, if we assume each node pair s has pair-specific generating rate proportional to a parameter κ_s, *i.e.*, $P_{st} \sim \text{Exp}(w_t/\kappa_s)$, then the negative log likelihood of observed path counts will be $-LL(s) = \sum_t w_t \cdot \frac{P_{st}}{\kappa_s} + T \log \kappa_s + const$. For node pair $s = (u, v)$, if we drop the logarithm term and set κ_s to be the arithmetic mean of the cycle count of the involved nodes u and v, the formula becomes

$$\sum_t w_t \cdot \frac{2 \cdot P_{\langle uv \rangle t}}{P_{\langle uu \rangle t} + P_{\langle vv \rangle t}} = PathSim_{\mathbf{w}}(s)$$

which is identical to PathSim with weights $\mathbf{w}$ for linear combination. In lieu of arithmetic mean, if we set κ_s to be the geometric mean of the same quantities, we get $\sum_t w_t \cdot \frac{P_{\langle uv \rangle t}}{\sqrt{P_{\langle uu \rangle t} \cdot P_{\langle vv \rangle t}}}$, which is identical to JoinSim with weights $\mathbf{w}$ for linear combination. Note that all the relevance measures discussed in this section are special cases of our relevance measure to be proposed in the next section.

Symbol	Definition
$\mathcal{V}$	The set of all nodes
$\mathcal{S}$	The set of all nontrivial node pairs
$T \in \mathbb{N}$	The number of meta-paths
$K \in \mathbb{N}$	The number of generating patterns
$P \in \mathbb{R}^{\lvert\mathcal{S}\rvert \times T}$	The observed path counts between node pairs over each meta-path
$\eta \in \mathbb{R}^T$	The *path selectivity*
$\tau \in \mathbb{R}^{\lvert\mathcal{S}\rvert}$	The *node pair visibility*
$\rho \in \mathbb{R}^{\lvert\mathcal{V}\rvert}$	The *node visibility*
$\Theta \in \mathbb{R}^{\lvert\mathcal{S}\rvert \times K}$	The generating patterns over meta-paths
$\Phi \in \mathbb{R}^{K \times T}$	The choices of generating patterns between node pairs
$\alpha \in \mathbb{R}_+$	The shape parameter of the gamma prior
$\beta \in (0, 1)$	The concentration parameter of the Dirichlet prior

Table 1: Summary of symbols

4 PROPOSED MODEL AND RELEVANCE

With the relevance–likelihood connection established in Sec. 3, we propose our **P**ath-based **Re**levance from **P**robabilistic perspective (PReP) likewise by modeling the generating process of path counts between node pairs, and further aim to model the three important characteristics. In a nutshell, the proposed generative-model-based relevance measure consists of two major parts: (i) inferring model parameters by finding the maximum a posteriori (MAP) estimate to fit the input HIN, and (ii) deriving relevance score between any node pair based on the learned model.

4.1 The PReP Model

Following the existing HIN relevance measures discussed in Sec. 3, we assume the path count, P_{st} or $P_{\langle uv \rangle t}$, between node pair $s =$

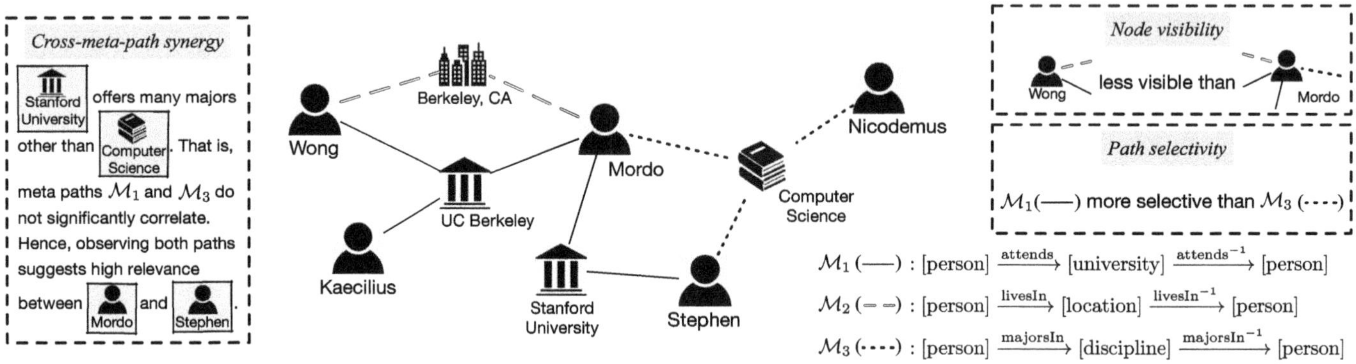

Figure 2: Toy example for one part of an HIN, consisting of four node types: person, university, location, and discipline.

(u, v) under meta-path t is generated from an exponential distribution with rate λ_{st}, *i.e.*, $P_{st} \sim \text{Exp}(\lambda_{st})$. To capture *node visibility*, *path selectivity*, and *cross-meta-path synergy*, we must design λ_{st} in a way that can model these three characteristics.

According to the property of exponential distribution, if a random variable X is generated from $\text{Exp}\left(\tilde{\lambda}\right)$, then the expectation of X will be $1/\tilde{\lambda}$. Bearing this in mind, we introduce three components to model the three characteristics as follows.

- Both the *node visibility* of u and that of v affect the generation of path instances. We consider the visibility of this pair of node as *node pair visibility*, τ_s, which is positively correlated with the expectation of P_{st}.
- We let path instances under the same meta-path share the same *path selectivity*. Denote η_t the *path selectivity* for meta-path t. η_t is negatively correlated with the expectation of P_{st}.
- Each node pair with paths in between can be linked by path instances under a different set of meta-paths. We assume an underlying *meta-path distribution* $\boldsymbol{\psi}_s = [\psi_{s1}, \ldots, \psi_{sT}]$ for node pair s, where $\sum_{t=1}^{T} \psi_{st} = 1$ and $\psi_{st} \geq 0$. As a distribution over meta-paths, $\boldsymbol{\psi}_s$ models the semantics of the relevance between this node pair, because each meta-path carries its own semantic meaning. With further design to be introduced, $\boldsymbol{\psi}_s$ also serves as the basis to capture *cross-meta-path synergy*. ψ_{st} is positively correlated with the expectation of P_{st}.

Putting the above three components together considering their correlation with the expectation of P_{st}, we find path count generating process as

$$P_{st} \sim \text{Exp}\left(\frac{\eta_t}{\tau_s \psi_{st}}\right), \tag{1}$$

where the detailed illustration and design of the three components are to be further discussed in this section. Note that while we only discuss unweighted HINs in this paper, the use of exponential distribution in Eq. (1) enables the model to handle weighted HINs, where paths are associated with real-valued path strengths, and P_{st} may not be integers to reflect the path strengths.

Since node pairs with no paths under any predefined meta-path should trivially receive the lowest possible relevance score, we only model the generation of path counts between node pairs with paths in between – henceforth referred to as nontrivial node pairs – and we denote $\mathcal{S}$ the set of all nontrivial node pairs.

Illustrative example. To better illustrate how each component design affects the path generation process, we present a toy example in Fig. 2, which shows a part of an HIN with four node types: person, university, location, and discipline. We concern three meta-paths in this network: $\mathcal{M}_1$: [person] $\xrightarrow{\text{attends}}$ [university] $\xrightarrow{\text{attends}^{-1}}$ [person], $\mathcal{M}_2$: [person] $\xrightarrow{\text{livesIn}}$ [location] $\xrightarrow{\text{livesIn}^{-1}}$ [person], $\mathcal{M}_3$: [person] $\xrightarrow{\text{majorsIn}}$ [discipline] $\xrightarrow{\text{majorsIn}^{-1}}$ [person].

Decoupling node pair visibility. To model *node visibility*, we decouple node pair visibility τ_s in Eq. (1) into two parts as in PathSim and JoinSim discussed in Sec. 3. The two parts correspond to the *node visibility* ρ_u and ρ_v, respectively, where $s = (u, v)$, and $\rho_z > 0$ for all $z \in \mathcal{V}$. In our design, we let

$$\tau_{(u,v)} = \rho_u \rho_v \tag{2}$$

as in JoinSim because decoupling by multiplication eases model inference, which will be made clear in the next paragraph.

Since a trivial rescaling – multiplying all ρ_z by a constant and multiplying all η_t by the square of the same constant – leads to exactly the same model (Eq. (1)), we further regularize ρ_z by a gamma prior with a constant rate parameter

$$\rho_z \sim \Gamma(\alpha, 1). \tag{3}$$

Note that we arbitrarily set the rate parameter to be 1 since the shape of the distribution is solely determined by the shape parameter α. We choose gamma distribution as the prior for ρ_z because it is the conjugate prior for the exponential distribution, and this fact will largely facilitate the inference algorithm as we will show in Sec. 5.2. To determine the shape parameter α, we fit the gamma distribution to the total path count each node has, $\{\sum_{t=1}^{T} \sum_{\tilde{z} \in \mathcal{V}} P_{\langle z\tilde{z} \rangle t}\}_{z \in \mathcal{V}}$, in the HIN as a rough prior information.

Path selectivity at meta-path level. We assume path instances under meta-path t share the same *path selectivity* η_t. In the scope of this paper, where supervision is not available, we assume uninformative prior on η_t. In future work where supervision is provided, we can further learn η_t by minimizing the difference between supervision and model output to derive a task-specific relevance measure.

Cross-meta-path synergy and generating patterns. As discussed in Sec. 1, we have observed the existence of *cross-meta-path*

Measure	Node Pair	$\mathcal{M}_1$	$\mathcal{M}_2$	$\mathcal{M}_3$	Composite	Truth
PathCount	*Mordo & Wong*	1	1	0	$w_1 + w_2$	−
	Mordo & Stephen	1	0	1	$w_1 + w_3$	+
PathSim	*Mordo & Wong*	0.67	1	0	$0.67w_1 + w_2$	−
	Mordo & Stephen	0.67	0	1	$0.67w_1 + w_3$	+
RWR ($C = 0.9$)	*Mordo & Wong*	0.29	0.47	0	$0.29w_1 + 0.47w_2$	−
	Mordo & Stephen	0.25	0	0.31	$0.25w_1 + 0.31w_3$	+
PReP	*Mordo & Wong*	1 generating pattern				−
	Mordo & Stephen	2 generating patterns				+

Table 2: Existing measures cannot yield desired relevance, unless we assert $\mathcal{M}_3$ (discipline) is always more selective than $\mathcal{M}_2$ (location), while PReP can achieve this by recognizing the co-occurrence of multiple generating patterns.

synergy in real-world HIN, and this characteristic has not been modeled by existing HIN relevance measures. In case meta-paths do not correlate, we may simply add a Dirichlet prior, with concentration parameter smaller than 1, over meta-path distribution $\boldsymbol{\psi}_s$ for all node pair s. This use of Dirichlet prior resembles latent Dirichlet allocation (LDA) [1], where the Dirichlet prior prefers sparse distributions, *i.e.*, most entries of $\boldsymbol{\psi}_s$ tend to be 0. Therefore, the co-occurrence of paths under different meta-paths gets a lower likelihood from this prior, and attains a higher relevance score under our relevance–likelihood connection.

However, in reality, it would not be surprising to see two people attending UC Berkeley also both live in the City of Berkeley. This implies *cross-meta-path synergy* does not necessarily exist between all pairs of meta-paths, *e.g.*, it may not exist between meta-path $\mathcal{M}_1$ and meta-path $\mathcal{M}_2$ in the toy example of Fig. 2. To address this situation, we introduce a new component – *generating patterns*. Each of a total of K generating patterns is a distribution over the T meta-paths, where meta-paths that often co-occur between node pairs will also be included in a common generating pattern, and when a node pair s generates a path instance in between, it would first choose generating pattern k with probability ϕ_{sk}, and then choose meta-path t from this generating pattern with probability θ_{kt}. Formally, we describe this process as

$$\psi_{st} = \sum_{k=1}^{K} \phi_{sk}\theta_{kt}, \tag{4}$$

where $\boldsymbol{\phi}_s = [\phi_{s1}, \ldots, \phi_{sK}]$ is node pair s's choices of generating patterns, such that $\sum_{k=1}^{K} \phi_{sk} = 1, \phi_{sk} \geq 0$; and $\boldsymbol{\theta}_k = [\theta_{k1}, \ldots, \theta_{kT}]$ is generating pattern k's distribution over meta-paths, such that $\sum_{t=1}^{T} \theta_{kt} = 1, \theta_{kt} \geq 0$.

A symmetric Dirichlet prior is then enforced on $\boldsymbol{\phi}_s$, so that synergy will be recognized between and only between meta-paths from different generating patterns

$$\boldsymbol{\phi}_s \sim \mathrm{Dir}_K(\beta), \tag{5}$$

where $\beta \in (0, 1)$ is the concentration hyperparameter.

With this design, our model gives a lower likelihood and higher relevance score to *Mordo* and *Stephen* (same university, same major) than *Mordo* and *Wong* (attending UC Berkeley and living in the City of Berkeley) in the toy example of Fig. 2 by learning a generating pattern that includes both $\mathcal{M}_1$ and $\mathcal{M}_2$. Whereas, other relevance measures cannot achieve this desired relationship as presented in Tab. 2, unless we set the weights $w_2 > w_3$, or equivalently assert $\mathcal{M}_2$ (location) is always less selective than $\mathcal{M}_3$ (discipline).

The unified model. For notation convenience, we use the bold italic form to represent the corresponding matrix or vector of each symbol with subscripts. For instance, the (s, t) element of $\boldsymbol{P}$ is P_{st} and the t-th element of $\boldsymbol{\eta}$ is η_t. Under this notation, combining Eq. (1), (3), and (5), with Eq. (2) and (4) substituted into Eq. (1), yields the total likelihood of the full PReP model

$$\begin{aligned}\mathcal{L} &= p(\boldsymbol{P}, \boldsymbol{\eta}, \boldsymbol{\rho}, \boldsymbol{\Phi}, \boldsymbol{\Theta} \mid \alpha, \beta) \\ &= \left\{\prod_{u \in \mathcal{V}} \Gamma\left(\rho_u \; ; \; (\alpha, 1)\right)\right\} \cdot \left\{\prod_{s \in \mathcal{S}} \mathrm{Dir}_K\left(\boldsymbol{\phi}_s \; ; \; \beta\right)\right\} \\ &\quad \cdot \left\{\prod_{\substack{s \in \mathcal{S} \\ (u,v)=s}} \prod_{t=1}^{T} \mathrm{Exp}\left(P_{st} \; ; \; \frac{\eta_t}{\rho_u \rho_v \sum_{k=1}^{K} \phi_{sk}\theta_{kt}}\right)\right\}\end{aligned} \tag{6}$$

4.2 The PReP Relevance Measure

Given the unified model (Eq. (6)), we have two options to derive relevance measure using likelihood: (i) find the maximum a posteriori estimate for all parameters and compute the total likelihood of the observed data, and (ii) consider all model parameters as hidden variables and define the relevance as the marginal likelihood of the observed data. However, the marginal likelihood does not have a closed-form representation in our case, nor can we approximate it with regular Markov chain Monte Carlo algorithms due to the large number of hidden variables. Therefore, we adopt the first option and defer the other to future work.

Once the model parameters $\{\boldsymbol{\eta}, \boldsymbol{\rho}, \boldsymbol{\Phi}, \boldsymbol{\Theta}\}$ are estimated, we define the PReP relevance for a node pair $s = (u, v)$ as the negative log-likelihood involving this node pair, $-\log p(\boldsymbol{P}_{s,:}, \boldsymbol{\phi}_s \mid \boldsymbol{\Theta}, \boldsymbol{\rho}, \boldsymbol{\eta}, \alpha, \beta)$, without the log term as in the derivation of PathSim in Sec. 3

$$r(s) = \sum_{t=1}^{T} \frac{P_{st}}{\rho_u \rho_v \eta_t \sum_{k=1}^{K} \phi_{sk}\theta_{kt}} + (1 - \beta) \sum_{k=1}^{K} \log \phi_{sk}. \tag{7}$$

Note that PathCount, PathSim, and JoinSim discussed in Sec. 3 are special cases of this PReP relevance measure, when $\{\boldsymbol{\eta}, \boldsymbol{\rho}, \boldsymbol{\Phi}, \boldsymbol{\Theta}\}$ are heuristically specified accordingly.

5 MODEL INFERENCE

In this section, we introduce the inference algorithm for the PReP model (Eq. (6)) proposed in Sec. 4.

5.1 The Optimization Problem

We find the maximum a posteriori (MAP) estimate for model parameters by minimizing the negative log-likelihood of the proposed model (Eq. 6), which, with an offset of a constant, is given by

Algorithm 1: Inference algorithm for the PReP model

Input : the observed path counts $\boldsymbol{P}$ and the hyperparameters
Output: the model parameters $\boldsymbol{\eta}$, $\boldsymbol{\rho}$, $\boldsymbol{\Phi}$, and $\boldsymbol{\Theta}$
begin
  Initialize $\boldsymbol{\rho}$, $\boldsymbol{\Phi}$, and $\boldsymbol{\Theta}$
  while *not converged* **do**
    Update $\boldsymbol{\eta}$ by the closed-form Eq. (10)
    while *not converged* **do**
      for $u \in \mathcal{V}$ **do**
        Update ρ_u by the closed-form solution to Eq. (11)
    Update $\boldsymbol{\Phi}$ via parallelized PGD with gradient in Eq. (13)
    Update $\boldsymbol{\Theta}$ via PGD with gradient in Eq. (12)

$$O = \sum_{u\in\mathcal{V}} (\rho_u - (\alpha-1)\log\rho_u) - (\beta-1)\sum_{s\in\mathcal{S}}\sum_{k=1}^{K}\log\phi_{sk}$$
$$+ T\sum_{(u,v)\in\mathcal{S}}(\log\rho_u + \log\rho_v) - |\mathcal{S}|\sum_{t=1}^{T}\log\eta_t$$
$$+ \sum_{\substack{s\in\mathcal{S}\\(u,v)=s}}\sum_{t=1}^{T}\left[\log\sum_{k=1}^{K}\phi_{sk}\theta_{kt} + \frac{\eta_t P_{st}}{\rho_u\rho_v\sum_{k=1}^{K}\phi_{sk}\theta_{kt}}\right], \quad (8)$$

and the optimization problem is therefore

$$\min_{\boldsymbol{\eta},\boldsymbol{\rho},\boldsymbol{\Phi},\boldsymbol{\Theta}} O(\boldsymbol{\eta},\boldsymbol{\rho},\boldsymbol{\Phi},\boldsymbol{\Theta}). \quad (9)$$

We solve the above minimization problem with an iterative algorithm to be detailed in the following Sec. 5.2.

5.2 The Inference Algorithm

We iteratively update one of $\boldsymbol{\eta}$, $\boldsymbol{\rho}$, $\boldsymbol{\Phi}$, and $\boldsymbol{\Theta}$ when the others are fixed. The inference algorithm is summarized in Algorithm 1.

Update $\boldsymbol{\eta}$ given $\{\boldsymbol{\rho},\boldsymbol{\Phi},\boldsymbol{\Theta}\}$. Once given $\boldsymbol{\rho}$, $\boldsymbol{\Phi}$, and $\boldsymbol{\Theta}$, the optimal $\boldsymbol{\eta}$ that minimizes O in Eq. (8) has a closed-form solution. One can derive this closed-form update formula by looking back to the total likelihood Eq. (6), since

$$\mathcal{L} \propto \prod_{s\in\mathcal{S}}\prod_{t=1}^{T}\mathrm{Exp}\left(P_{st}\,;\,\frac{\eta_t}{\tau_s\sum_{k=1}^{K}\phi_{sk}\theta_{kt}}\right)$$
$$= \prod_{t=1}^{T}\left[\mathrm{Exp}\left(\frac{1}{|\mathcal{S}|}\sum_{s\in\mathcal{S}}\frac{P_{st}}{\tau_s\sum_{k=1}^{K}\phi_{sk}\theta_{kt}}\,;\,\eta_t\right)\right]^{|\mathcal{S}|},$$

where $\tau_s = \rho_u\rho_v$ for node pair $s=(u,v)$. Using the property of exponential distributions, we find the $\boldsymbol{\eta}$ that maximizes $\mathcal{L}$, and hence minimizes O, can be computed by

$$\eta_t = \left(\frac{1}{|\mathcal{S}|}\sum_{s\in\mathcal{S}}\frac{P_{st}}{\tau_s\sum_{k=1}^{K}\phi_{sk}\theta_{kt}}\right)^{-1}. \quad (10)$$

Update $\boldsymbol{\rho}$ given $\{\boldsymbol{\eta},\boldsymbol{\Phi},\boldsymbol{\Theta}\}$. Unlike $\boldsymbol{\eta}$, closed-form formula for updating $\boldsymbol{\rho}$ does not exist because (i) $\boldsymbol{\rho}$ has an informative prior, and (ii) the generating process for paths between node pair (u,v) involves the coupling of ρ_u and ρ_v. Fortunately, the gamma distribution is the conjugate prior to the exponential distribution. Therefore, for each u, when the rest $\{\rho_v\}_{v\neq u}$ are fixed, the closed-form update formula for ρ_u can be derived as follows. Denote $\{\xi_s\}_{s\in\mathcal{S}}$ the following quantities that are fixed during the $\boldsymbol{\rho}$ update phase

$$\xi_s := \sum_{t=1}^{T}\frac{\eta_t P_{st}}{\sum_{k=1}^{K}\phi_{sk}\theta_{kt}},$$

and we have $\frac{\partial O}{\partial\rho_u} = \sum_{\substack{v\in\mathcal{V}\setminus\{u\}\\ s=(u,v)}}\left[\sum_{t=1}^{T}\frac{1}{\rho_u} - \frac{\xi_s}{\rho_u^2\rho_v}\right] - \frac{\alpha-1}{\rho_u} + 1$. Setting this partial derivative to 0 leads to

$$\rho_u^2 + [(|\mathcal{V}|-1)\cdot T - (\alpha-1)]\,\rho_u - \sum_{\substack{v\in\mathcal{V}\setminus\{u\}\\ s=(u,v)}}\frac{\xi_s}{\rho_v} = 0. \quad (11)$$

Note that Eq. (11) is a single-variable quadratic equation with one positive and one negative roots. Furthermore, O is convex *w.r.t.* ρ_u on the positive half-axis, and the positive root is a minimum of O. Therefore, the optimal ρ_u that minimizes O is given by the positive root of the quadratic equation (Eq. (11)), which has closed-form solution. Holistically, we update $\boldsymbol{\rho}$ by iterating through $u\in\mathcal{V}$ to update ρ_u with the aforementioned closed-form solution to Eq. (11).

Update $\boldsymbol{\Theta}$ given $\{\boldsymbol{\eta},\boldsymbol{\rho},\boldsymbol{\Phi}\}$. To update $\boldsymbol{\Theta}$, we use the projected gradient descent (PGD) algorithm [12]. The gradient is given by

$$\frac{\partial O}{\partial\boldsymbol{\Theta}} = \boldsymbol{\Phi}^\top\left[\frac{1}{\boldsymbol{\Phi}\boldsymbol{\Theta}} - \frac{\boldsymbol{P}}{(\boldsymbol{\tau}(\boldsymbol{\eta}^{\circ-1})^\top)\circ(\boldsymbol{\Phi}\boldsymbol{\Theta})^{\circ 2}}\right], \quad (12)$$

where $[\cdot]\circ[\cdot]$, $\frac{[\cdot]}{[\cdot]}$, and $[\cdot]^{\circ[\cdot]}$ are element-wise multiplication, division, and power. Additional constraint fed into PGD is that each row of $\boldsymbol{\Theta}$ lies in the standard $(T-1)$-simplex, *i.e.*, $\sum_{t=1}^{T}\theta_{kt}=1$ for all $k\in\{1,\ldots,K\}$ and $\theta_{kt}\geq 0$ for all $(k,t)\in\{1,\ldots,K\}\times\{1,\ldots,T\}$. Projection onto the standard simplex or the direct product of multiple standard simplices can be achieved efficiently using the method introduced in [3].

Update $\boldsymbol{\Phi}$ given $\{\boldsymbol{\eta},\boldsymbol{\rho},\boldsymbol{\Theta}\}$. Similarly, we use PGD to update $\boldsymbol{\Phi}$, where the gradient is given by

$$\frac{\partial O}{\partial\boldsymbol{\Phi}} = \left[\frac{1}{\boldsymbol{\Phi}\boldsymbol{\Theta}} - \frac{\boldsymbol{P}}{(\boldsymbol{\tau}(\boldsymbol{\eta}^{\circ-1})^\top)\circ(\boldsymbol{\Phi}\boldsymbol{\Theta})^{\circ 2}}\right]\boldsymbol{\Theta}^\top - \frac{\beta-1}{\boldsymbol{\Phi}}. \quad (13)$$

However, directly updating the entire $\boldsymbol{\Phi}$ using PGD can be problematic, because the row number of $\boldsymbol{\Phi}$ is the same as the number of nontrivial node pairs, $|\mathcal{S}|$, which can be significantly larger than that of $\boldsymbol{\Theta}$.

Fortunately, we can decompose the update scheme for $\boldsymbol{\Phi}$ by rows, because each row is independent from the others. Specifically, we update each row s using PGD in parallel, with gradient $\frac{\partial O}{\partial\boldsymbol{\Phi}_{s,:}} = \left[\frac{1}{\boldsymbol{\Phi}_{s,:}\boldsymbol{\Theta}} - \frac{\boldsymbol{P}_{s,:}}{(\tau_s(\boldsymbol{\eta}^{\circ-1})^\top)\circ(\boldsymbol{\Phi}_{s,:}\boldsymbol{\Theta})^{\circ 2}}\right]\boldsymbol{\Theta}^\top - \frac{\beta-1}{\boldsymbol{\Phi}_{s,:}}$, and constraints $\sum_{k=1}^{K}\phi_{sk}=1$ for all $s\in\mathcal{S}$ and $\phi_{st}\geq 0$ for all $(s,k)\in\mathcal{S}\times\{1,\ldots,K\}$.

5.3 Implementation Details

For program reproducibility, we provide details in parameter initialization and computational singularity handling.

Since the inference algorithm starts with updating η, no initialization for η is needed. ρ is initialized by drawing random samples from its prior distribution, $\Gamma(\alpha, 1)$, where α is estimated from data as discussed in Sec. 4. Φ is initialized uniformly at random within the row-wise simplex constraint. For Θ, the first T rows of this $K \times T$ matrix are initialized to be an identity matrix, because many node pairs with paths in between involve only one meta-path, and we initialize the rest $K - T$ rows uniformly at random within the row-wise simplex constraint. This choice is out of the consideration that the PReP model is not convex over all parameters.

Dirichlet distribution is defined over open sets with unbounded probability density function. As a result, when using MAP, certain components of Φ can be inferred to approach the singularities along the boundary. Therefore, in practice, we let Φ to be bounded away from the boundary with an infinitesimal quantity δ, *i.e.*, each of its entries must not only be positive, but also be greater or equal to δ. In this way, we keep the capability of Dirichlet distribution in modeling *cross-meta-path synergy*, while ensuring the model is computationally meaningful. In our experiment, we set $\delta = 10^{-50}$. With this constraint, the domain of definition for Φ is no longer a standard simplex as discussed in [3]. For this reason, we provide the algorithm for efficient projection onto this shrunken simplex, $\{\mathbf{x} \in \mathbb{R}^K | x_i \geq \delta, \sum_{i=1}^{K} x_i = 1\}$ in the Appendix, which is required by the inference algorithm. Note that if one wishes to evade the point estimation of parameters in the PReP model, Eq. (6), and thereby avoid computational singularity, they can treat all model parameters as hidden variables and derive relevance from the marginal likelihood of the observed data as discussed in Sec. 4.2. The exploration of this direction requires novel method, such as a sampling algorithm design for our model, to efficiently calculate marginal likelihood, and we defer this to future work.

6 EXPERIMENTS

In this section, we quantitatively evaluate the proposed model on two publicly available real-world HINs: Facebook and DBLP. We first describe the datasets and the unsupervised tasks used for evaluation. Baselines and model variations for comparison are then introduced. Afterward, we present experiment results together with discussions, which demonstrate the advantage of using probability as the backbone of relevance.

6.1 Data Description and Evaluation Tasks

In this section, we introduce the two publicly available real-world datasets and the evaluation tasks.

The Facebook dataset. This dataset [11] contains nodes of 11 types, including user, major, degree, school, hometown, surname, location, employer, work-location, work-project, and other. It consists of 5,621 nodes and 98,023 edges, among which 4,167 nodes are of the user type. We aim to determine the relevance between users, using 10 meta-paths, each of the form [user]–[X]–[user], where X is any of the above 11 node types except for other.

To derive ground truth label between user pairs for evaluation, we use being friends on Facebook as a proxy for being relevant. This dataset is collected by recruiting participants to label their own Facebook friends It consists of 10 distinct ego networks, where an ego network consists of one ego user and all her friends together with edges attached to these users. We hence perform one sub-task for each ego network, where the compared measures are used to calculate the relevance between all pairs of non-ego users in this ego network.

We use two evaluation metrics widely adopted for tasks with multiple relevant instances: the area under the receiver operating characteristic curve (ROC-AUC) and the area under precision-recall curve (AUPRC). The receiver operating characteristic curve (ROC) is created by plotting true positive rate against false positive rate as the threshold varies, while the precision-recall curve (PRC) is drawn by plotting precision against recall as the threshold varies. Higher values are more preferred for both ROC-AUC and AUPRC. We further average each of the above metrics across ego networks with the following methods – uni.: averaging over all ego networks uniformly; rel.: weighting by the number of relevant pairs in each ego network; tot.: weighting by the total number of pairs in each ego network.

The DBLP dataset. This dataset is derived from the DBLP dataset processed by Tang et al. [18] containing computer science research papers together with author names and publication venue associated to each paper. It consists of 13,697 nodes and 19,665 edges, among which 1,546 nodes are of the author type. Notably, in this dataset, the same author name associated with two papers may not necessarily be the same person. Based on this fact, we design an entity resolution task as follows. First, we use the labels made available by Tang et al. [18] to group all author name mentions corresponding to one person to define an author node. In this way, an author node is linked to multiple papers written by her. Then, for each author name, we split the author node with the most author name mentions into two nodes, and we define two nodes to be relevant if and only if they actually refer to the same person. Finally, we perform one sub-task for each author name, where the compared measures are used to calculate the relevance between all pairs of nodes with the same author name.

We use 14 meta-paths in this task, each of the form [author]–[paper]–[venue domain]–[paper]–[author], where a node of the venue domain type corresponds to one of the 14 computer science research areas. The definition of the 14 areas is derived from the Wikipedia page: List of computer science conferences[1]. Since only one relevant pair exists in each sub-task, the mean reciprocal rank (MRR) is used as the evaluation metric, where, for each sub-task, the reciprocal rank is the reciprocal of the rank of the relevant pair. Higher values indicate better results for MRR. We also average the above metrics across different sub-tasks using three methods: uni., rel., and tot. Note that uni. and rel. are equivalent in this entity resolution task because each sub-task has exactly one relevant pair.

6.2 Baselines and Variations

In this section, we describe the meta-path-based baseline methods and variations of the PReP model, which are used to compare with our proposed full PReP model. Existing meta-path-based unsupervised HIN measures define relevance computation method on each meta-path and then use linear combination to find the composite score. Therefore, each baseline consists of two parts: (i) the base

[1] https://en.wikipedia.org/wiki/List_of_computer_science_conferences

Dataset	Metric		PathCount		PathSim		JoinSim		SimRank		PReP			
			Mean	SD	Mean	SD	Mean	SD	Mean	SD	No-NV	No-PS	No-CS	(full)
Facebook	ROC-AUC	uni.	0.8056	0.8598	0.8367	0.8586	0.8326	0.8547	0.7977	0.8303	0.8310	0.6702	0.8689	**0.8850**
		rel.	0.8612	0.8879	0.8578	0.8888	0.8556	0.8872	0.8076	0.8596	0.8556	0.6713	0.8880	**0.9133**
		tot.	0.8558	0.8849	0.8577	0.8866	0.8557	0.8851	0.8096	0.8594	0.8547	0.6773	0.8893	**0.9139**
	AUPRC	uni.	0.2456	0.2832	0.2370	0.2845	0.2340	0.2803	0.2055	0.2435	0.2183	0.1650	**0.3273**	**0.3269**
		rel.	0.2496	0.3048	0.2142	0.2873	0.2117	0.2837	0.1764	0.2408	0.2067	0.1283	0.3354	**0.3486**
		tot.	0.2107	0.2542	0.1841	0.2460	0.1821	0.2432	0.1523	0.2071	0.1760	0.1089	0.3010	**0.3080**
DBLP	MRR	uni./rel.	0.8091	0.8130	0.6922	0.7003	0.7454	0.7538	0.6636	0.6738	0.8223	0.8494	0.8365	**0.8517**
		tot.	0.7839	0.7871	0.6612	0.6731	0.7128	0.7244	0.6302	0.6357	0.8234	**0.8407**	0.8264	0.8391

Table 3: Quantitative evaluation results on two real-world datasets using the proposed measure, PReP, and other measures.

measure that calculates the relevance score on one meta-path, and (ii) the weights assigned to different meta-paths used in the linear combination. The 4 base measures we used are:

- **PathCount** [17]. $PathCount_{\mathbf{w}}(s) := \sum_t w_t P_{st}$.
- **PathSim** [17]. $PathSim_{\mathbf{w}}(s) := \sum_t w_t \cdot \frac{2 \cdot P_{\langle uv \rangle t}}{P_{\langle uu \rangle t} + P_{\langle vv \rangle t}}$.
- **JoinSim** [20]. $JoinSim_{\mathbf{w}}(s) := \sum_t w_t \cdot \frac{P_{\langle uv \rangle t}}{\sqrt{P_{\langle uu \rangle t} \cdot P_{\langle vv \rangle t}}}$.
- **SimRank**. We adopt SimRank [8] with meta-path constraints. Let $\boldsymbol{A}$ be a matrix, where A_{uv} is the number of paths under this meta-path between node pair (u, v) after column normalization. The SimRank score is then given by S_{uv}, where S is the solution to $S = \max\{C \cdot (\boldsymbol{A}^\top S \boldsymbol{A}), \boldsymbol{I}\}$, and C is the decay factor to be specified. Note that we use SimRank instead of random walk with restart because SimRank is a symmetric relevance measure.

Without any supervision available, we use 2 heuristics to determine the weights $\mathbf{w}$ for linear combination.

- **Mean**. Let w_t be the reciprocal of the mean of all scores computed using the corresponding base measure on meta-path t.
- **SD**. Let w_t be the reciprocal of the standard deviation of all scores computed using the corresponding base measure on meta-path t. Note that this heuristic normalized the original score in the way similar to z-score.

Combining the aforementioned 4 base measures and 2 heuristic for setting weights, we have 8 baselines in total.

Additionally, we also experiment with three variations of PReP, which are partial models with one of the three components knocked out from the full PReP model.

- No *node visibility* (No-NV): Set $\boldsymbol{\rho} = \mathbf{1}_{|\mathcal{V}|}$, and do not update $\boldsymbol{\rho}$ during model inference.
- No *path selectivity* (No-PS): Set $\boldsymbol{\eta} = \mathbf{1}_T$, and do not update $\boldsymbol{\eta}$ during model inference.
- No *cross-meta-path synergy* (No-CS): Set $\boldsymbol{\Phi} = \mathbf{1}_{|\mathcal{V}| \times K}/K$, $\boldsymbol{\Theta} = \mathbf{1}_{|\mathcal{V}| \times T}/T$, and do not update $\boldsymbol{\Phi}$ and $\boldsymbol{\Theta}$ during model inference.

Note that $\mathbf{1}_M$ stands for all one column vector of size M and $\mathbf{1}_{M \times N}$ denotes all one matrix of size $M \times N$.

6.3 Effectiveness and Discussion

In this section, we present the quantitative evaluation results on both the Facebook and the DBLP datasets. We tune the decay factor C in the baseline measure, SimRank, to have the best performance with $C = 0.5$ for both SimRank-Mean and SimRank-SD on Facebook, and $C = 0.8$ for SimRank-Mean, $C = 0.7$ for SimRank-SD on DBLP. We set hyperparameters of PReP as $K = 15$ and $\beta = 10^{-4}$ for Facebook and $K = 14$ and $\beta = 10^{-2}$ for DBLP. The choice of hyperparameters will be further discussed in this section.

As presented in Tab. 3, PReP outperformed all 8 baselines under various metrics. Moreover, PReP outperformed its 3 variations under most metrics, suggesting each component of the model generally has a positive effect on the performance of the full PReP model. Note that under MRR (tot.), PReP performed slightly worse than PReP-No-PS, the partial model without η_t for *path selectivity*. This happened because, as discussed in Sec. 4, we cannot enforce task-specific design on *path selectivity* η_t due to the lack of supervision, and we expect *path selectivity* η_t to play a more important role in future work where relevance labels are provided as supervision.

Additionally, we have made the following observations.

Heuristic methods cannot yield robust relevance measures. Compared with PathCount, both PathSim and JoinSim further model *node visibility*, which penalizes the relevance with nodes that are highly visible. However, as Tab. 3 presents, PathSim and JoinSim cannot always outperform PathCount. Moreover, JoinSim performs better than PathSim on DBLP, while PathSim is slightly better than JoinSim on Facebook. We interpret these results as, PathSim and JoinSim model *node visibility* in a deterministic heuristic way. Unlike our generative-model-based measure that derives relevance measure based on parameters inferred from each HIN, the heuristic approaches adopted by PathSim and JoinSim have varying performance on different HINs. This suggests being data-driven is a favorable property of PReP.

Non-one-hot generating patterns help only when meta-paths correlate. In our experiment, we set $K = 14 = T$ for DBLP. Recall that we initialized the first T rows of $\boldsymbol{\Theta}$, the matrix representing the K generating patterns, to be T one-hot vectors corresponding to T meta-paths. We observed in the DBLP experiment that after model fitting, $\boldsymbol{\Theta}$ was still the same as its initialization, meaning each inferred generating pattern only generated path instances under exactly one meta-path. Moreover, by increasing the value of K, we did not see improvement in performance. This observation is inline with the situation that it is not frequently seen that two authors both publish papers in two distinct research areas, where the 14 areas on the Wikipedia page have been defined to be distinct areas including theory, software, parallel computing, *etc.* In this case, it is preferred to model synergy across every pair of meta-paths, and not to employ any non-one-hot generating patterns.

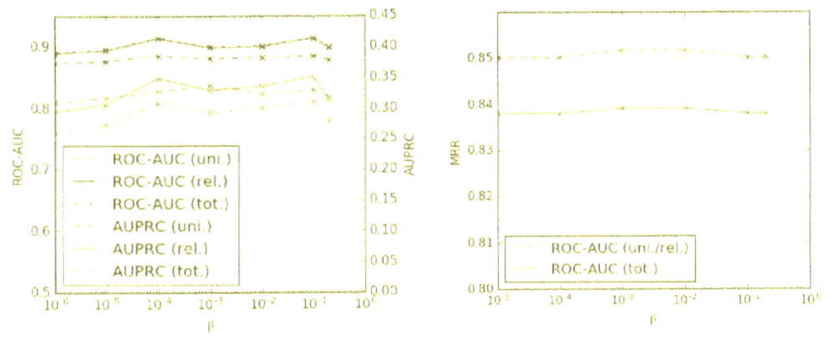

(a) Facebook (b) DBLP

Figure 3: Performance with varying β.

On the other hand, we used $K = 15 > T$ for Facebook, and we did observe non-one-hot generating patterns after model fitting. The most popular non-one-hot generating pattern consisted of three meta-paths: [user]–[hometown]–[user], [user]–[school]–[user], and [user]–[user]–[user], where we define popularity of a generating pattern as the fraction of node pairs adopting this pattern, *i.e.*, $pop(k) = \sum_{s \in S} \phi_{sk}$. This generating pattern corresponds to two users sharing the same hometown, the same school, and having common friends. This scenario is common for two people sharing similar friend group back in the hometown school.

Sensitivity of β in modeling *cross-meta-path synergy*. In the PReP model (Eq. (6)) and relevance measure (Eq. (7)), the concentration parameter β of the Dirichlet prior controls the extent to which we boost *cross-meta-path synergy*. Experiment results in Fig 3 shows performance of PReP do not significantly change around the values we have set for β, *i.e.*, 10^{-4} for Facebook and 10^{-2} for DBLP.

7 RELATED WORK

In this section, we review the study on HIN relevance. The problem of deriving relevance between node pairs has been extensively studied for homogeneous information networks. Relevance measures of this type include the random walk based *Personalized PageRank* and *SimRank* [8], the neighbor-based *common neighbors* and *Jaccard's coefficient*, the path-based *Katz* [5], *etc.* To generalize relevance from the homogeneous networks to the typed heterogeneous case, researchers have been exploring from multiple perspectives. One perspective, as in *PathCount* and *PathSim* from [17] and *Path-Constrained Random Walk* from [10], is to first compute relevance score along each meta-path, and then glue scores from all types together via linear combination to establish the composite measure. A great many applications [9, 14, 16, 22, 24] based on this meta-path paradigm with linear combination have been proposed. Our proposed method follows this meta-path paradigm, but goes beyond linear combination to model *cross-meta-path synergy* that we have observed from real-world HINs. Another perspective is to go beyond meta-path and derive relevance based on the more complex graph structures [4, 7]. While these approaches can yield good performance, they differ from our proposed methods for further entailing label information or expertise in designing graph structure. Also, they do not carry probabilistic interpretations. Besides, people have explored the idea of incorporating richer information [6, 21] to define more effective relevance scoring functions, or adding supervision to derive task-specific relevance measures [2, 19, 23]. While being valuable, these works are out of the scope of the problem we study in this paper, where we address the basic, unsupervised case with no additional information as our starting point of studying HIN relevance from the probabilistic perspective.

8 CONCLUSION AND FUTURE WORK

Inspired by the probabilistic interpretation of existing path-based relevance measures, we studied HIN relevance from a probabilistic perspective. We identified *cross-meta-path synergy* as one of the three characteristics that we deem important for HIN relevance. A generative model was proposed to derive a novel path-based relevance measure, PReP, which could capture the three important characteristics. An inference algorithm was also developed to find the maximum a posteriori (MAP) estimate of the model parameters, which entailed non-trivial tricks. Experiments on real-world HINs demonstrated the effectiveness of our relevance measure, which is data-driven and tailored for each HIN.

Future work includes the exploration of defining relevance from the proposed PReP model with marginal likelihood as discussed in Sec. 4.2. Further add-on designs to adapt the proposed model to a supervised setting are also worth exploring to unleash the potential of our model.

Acknowledgments. We thank our colleagues and friends for the enlightening discussions: Jason Jian Ge, Jiasen Yang, Carl Ji Yang, and many members of the Data Mining Group at UIUC. We also thank the anonymous reviewers for their insightful comments. This work was sponsored in part by the U.S. Army Research Lab. under Cooperative Agreement No. W911NF-09-2-0053 (NSCTA), National Science Foundation IIS-1320617 and IIS 16-18481, and grant 1U54GM114838 awarded by NIGMS through funds provided by the trans-NIH Big Data to Knowledge (BD2K) initiative (www.bd2k.nih.gov). The views and conclusions contained in this document are those of the author(s) and should not be interpreted as representing the official policies of the U.S. Army Research Laboratory or the U.S. Government. The U.S. Government is authorized to reproduce and distribute reprints for Government purposes notwithstanding any copyright notation hereon.

APPENDIX

We provide the algorithm for efficient projection onto the standard simplex shrunk by δ, $\{\mathbf{x} \in \mathbb{R}^K | x_i \geq \delta, \sum_{i=1}^K x_i = 1\}$, in Algorithm 2.

Algorithm 2: Efficient projection onto shrunk simplex

Input : the original vector $\mathbf{z} \in \mathbb{R}^K$ and the shrinking factor δ
Output: the projection $\mathbf{x} \in \mathbb{R}^K$
begin
  Sort $\mathbf{z}$ into $\mathbf{u}$: $u_1 \geq u_2 \geq \ldots \geq u_K$
  $\rho \leftarrow \max\{1 \leq j \leq K | u_j + \frac{1}{j}(1 - \delta K - \sum_{i=1}^j u_i) > 0\}$
  $\lambda \leftarrow \frac{1}{\rho}(1 - \delta K - \sum_{i=1}^\rho u_i)$
  $x_i \leftarrow \max\{z_i + \lambda, 0\} + \delta$

The validity of this algorithm can be established in a way similar to the proof of the algorithm for standard simplex [3].

REFERENCES

[1] David M Blei, Andrew Y Ng, and Michael I Jordan. 2003. Latent dirichlet allocation. *Journal of machine Learning research* 3, Jan (2003), 993–1022.

[2] Ting Chen and Yizhou Sun. 2017. Task-Guided and Path-Augmented Heterogeneous Network Embedding for Author Identification. In *WSDM*. ACM.

[3] John Duchi, Shai Shalev-Shwartz, Yoram Singer, and Tushar Chandra. 2008. Efficient projections onto the l 1-ball for learning in high dimensions. In *ICML*. ACM.

[4] Yuan Fang, Wenqing Lin, Vincent W Zheng, Min Wu, Kevin Chen-Chuan Chang, and Xiao-Li Li. 2016. Semantic Proximity Search on Graphs with Metagraph-based Learning. In *ICDE*. IEEE.

[5] Jiawei Han, Jian Pei, and Micheline Kamber. 2011. *Data mining: concepts and techniques*. Elsevier.

[6] Jiazhen He, James Bailey, and Rui Zhang. 2014. Exploiting transitive similarity and temporal dynamics for similarity search in heterogeneous information networks. In *DASFAA*. Springer.

[7] Zhipeng Huang, Yudian Zheng, Reynold Cheng, Yizhou Sun, Nikos Mamoulis, and Xiang Li. 2016. Meta Structure: Computing Relevance in Large Heterogeneous Information Networks. In *KDD*. ACM.

[8] Glen Jeh and Jennifer Widom. 2002. SimRank: a measure of structural-context similarity. In *KDD*. ACM.

[9] Jonathan Kuck, Honglei Zhuang, Xifeng Yan, Hasan Cam, and Jiawei Han. 2015. Query-based outlier detection in heterogeneous information networks. In *ICDE*. IEEE.

[10] Ni Lao and William W Cohen. 2010. Relational retrieval using a combination of path-constrained random walks. *Machine learning* 81, 1 (2010), 53–67.

[11] Julian J McAuley and Jure Leskovec. 2012. Learning to Discover Social Circles in Ego Networks. In *NIPS*. NIPS Foundation.

[12] Yurii Nesterov. 2013. *Introductory lectures on convex optimization: A basic course*. Vol. 87. Springer Science & Business Media.

[13] Chuan Shi, Xiangnan Kong, Yue Huang, S Yu Philip, and Bin Wu. 2014. Hetesim: A general framework for relevance measure in heterogeneous networks. *TKDE* 26, 10 (2014), 2479–2492.

[14] Chuan Shi, Yitong Li, Jiawei Zhang, Yizhou Sun, and S Yu Philip. 2017. A survey of heterogeneous information network analysis. *TKDE* 29, 1 (2017), 17–37.

[15] Yu Shi, Myunghwan Kim, Shaunak Chatterjee, Mitul Tiwari, Souvik Ghosh, and Rómer Rosales. 2016. Dynamics of Large Multi-View Social Networks: Synergy, Cannibalization and Cross-View Interplay. In *KDD*. ACM.

[16] Yizhou Sun and Jiawei Han. 2013. Mining heterogeneous information networks: a structural analysis approach. *SIGKDD Explorations* 14, 2 (2013), 20–28.

[17] Yizhou Sun, Jiawei Han, Xifeng Yan, Philip S Yu, and Tianyi Wu. 2011. Pathsim: Meta path-based top-k similarity search in heterogeneous information networks. In *Proceedings of VLDB*. VLDB Endowment.

[18] Jie Tang, Alvis CM Fong, Bo Wang, and Jing Zhang. 2012. A unified probabilistic framework for name disambiguation in digital library. *TKDE* 24, 6 (2012), 975–987.

[19] Chi Wang, Rajat Raina, David Fong, Ding Zhou, Jiawei Han, and Greg Badros. 2011. Learning relevance from heterogeneous social network and its application in online targeting. In *SIGIR*. ACM.

[20] Yun Xiong, Yangyong Zhu, and S Yu Philip. 2015. Top-k similarity join in heterogeneous information networks. *TKDE* 27, 6 (2015), 1710–1723.

[21] Kun Yao, Hoi Fong Mak, and others. 2014. PathSimExt: Revisiting pathsim in heterogeneous information networks. In *WAIM*. Springer.

[22] Xiao Yu, Xiang Ren, Yizhou Sun, Quanquan Gu, Bradley Sturt, Urvashi Khandelwal, Brandon Norick, and Jiawei Han. 2014. Personalized entity recommendation: A heterogeneous information network approach. In *Proceedings of WSDM*. ACM.

[23] Xiao Yu, Yizhou Sun, Brandon Norick, Tiancheng Mao, and Jiawei Han. 2012. User guided entity similarity search using meta-path selection in heterogeneous information networks. In *CIKM*. ACM.

[24] Honglei Zhuang, Jing Zhang, George Brova, Jie Tang, Hasan Cam, Xifeng Yan, and Jiawei Han. 2014. Mining query-based subnetwork outliers in heterogeneous information networks. In *ICDM*. IEEE.

Multi-Aspect Streaming Tensor Completion

Qingquan Song,[†] Xiao Huang,[†] Hancheng Ge,[†] James Caverlee,[†] Xia Hu[†,‡]
[†]Department of Computer Science and Engineering, Texas A&M University
[‡]Center for Remote Health Technologies and Systems, Texas A&M Engineering Experiment Station
{song_3134,xhuang,hge,caverlee,xiahu}@tamu.edu

ABSTRACT

Tensor completion has become an effective computational tool in many real-world data-driven applications. Beyond traditional static setting, with the increasing popularity of high velocity streaming data, it requires efficient online processing without reconstructing the whole model from scratch. Existing work on streaming tensor completion is usually built upon the assumption that tensors only grow in one mode. Unfortunately, the assumption does not hold in many real-world situations in which tensors may grow in multiple modes, i.e., multi-aspect streaming tensors. Efficiently modeling and completing these incremental tensors without sacrificing its effectiveness remains a challenging task due to the uncertainty of tensor mode changes and complex data structure of multi-aspect streaming tensors. To bridge this gap, we propose a Multi-Aspect Streaming Tensor completion framework (MAST) based on CANDECOMP/PARAFAC (CP) decomposition to track the subspace of general incremental tensors for completion. In addition, we investigate a special situation where time is one mode of the tensors, and leverage its extra structure information to improve the general framework towards higher effectiveness. Experimental results on four datasets collected from various real-world applications demonstrate the effectiveness and efficiency of the proposed framework.

1 INTRODUCTION

Tensors are multidimensional or N-way extensions of matrices. Given the increasing popularity of multi-modal information, data instances are often indexed with multiple variables and naturally derive high-order tensor objects [20]. Tensor completion, which aims at filling the missing entries of partially observed tensors, has become an effective computational tool in many real-world data mining applications such as social network analysis [7, 11], recommender systems [25, 26], image recovery [17], and clinical data analysis [9, 36].

Beyond traditional static setting, real-world applications are often imbued with high velocity streaming data. For example, due to the popularity of online information systems, large amounts of new data are produced rapidly. Facebook users update 684,478 messages and Twitter users post over 100,000 tweets every single minute.[1] With the large number of newly created data instances and features,

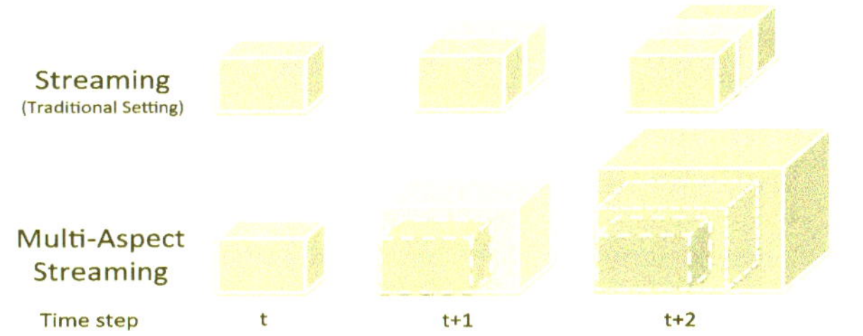

Figure 1: An illustration of traditional streaming tensors and multi-aspect streaming tensors.

model reconstruction from scratch is computationally expensive due to high time and space complexity [8]. The fast-evolving data motivates us to investigate dynamic tensor completion methods to timely model and incorporate newly emerging patterns.

Existing work has been conducted on developing dynamic tensor completion methods based on a widely used assumption that tensors will be developed in one mode (or dimension). Following this assumption, online completion methods have been proposed based on CP decomposition [15, 20]. The key idea is that, by iteratively updating the decompositions of static modes with partial decomposition of the incremental mode, the developed methods could efficiently track the low-rank subspace over time, and achieve comparable performance with batch learning methods for data imputation. The developed methods have shown effectiveness in dynamic data analysis applications such as video streams [15].

Unfortunately, in many real-world applications, a tensor may develop in multiple dimensions and traditional assumption does not hold. For example, given a dynamic tensor in recommender systems structured as $user \times movie \times actor$, the number of registered users, movies, and actors may all increase as time goes. This incremental property gives rise to a new streaming pattern, which we call multi-aspect streaming. Figure 1 depicts traditional streaming tensors and its generalized multi-aspect streaming tensors counterpart. As we can observe from the figure, from time t to $t + 2$, each mode of the multi-aspect streaming tensor increases while only one mode of the streaming tensor grows. To deal with the tensors with distinct data characteristics, in this paper, we propose to study the novel problem of effective multi-aspect streaming tensor completion.

Multi-aspect streaming tensor completion is a challenging task due to the following reasons. First, coordinating multidimensional dynamics is difficult given the uncertainty of tensor mode changes. It is too arbitrary to fix partial structure of a certain mode without accessing the data for an update. Second, the incremental part of multi-aspect streaming data may not be a complete tensor. This is different from streaming tensors in which the incremental part is well structured and can be directly decomposed. Third, the multi-aspect streaming pattern leads to much higher time and space complexity. Although some distributed and parallel algorithms could partially address the scalability issue [4, 24, 28], the problem

[1]http://mashable.com/2012/06/22/data-created-every-minute/

KDD'17, August 13–17, 2017, Halifax, NS, Canada.

DOI: http://dx.doi.org/10.1145/3097983.3098007

of non-adaptability still exists, meaning that the completion process of new data cannot directly benefit from the existing model without complete model reconstruction.

To tackle the aforementioned challenges, in this paper, we propose to investigate how to complete multi-aspect streaming tensors based on CP decomposition. Specifically, we mainly study: (1) How to build up an updatable framework based on CP decomposition for efficiently modeling multi-aspect streaming tensors? (2) How to effectively capture the low-rank subspace for completion purpose? Through answering the two questions, we propose a general Multi-Aspect Streaming Tensor completion algorithm (MAST). The main contributions are summarized as follows:

- Formally define the problem of multi-aspect streaming tensor completion;
- Propose a CP-based general algorithm MAST for multi-aspect streaming tensor completion;
- Propose a modified model T-MAST based on MAST for temporal multi-aspect streaming tensor completion, which is a special case of the general problem; and
- Empirically validate the effectiveness and efficiency of the proposed models on four real-world datasets with different real-world applications.

2 PRELIMINARIES

Notations and definitions in this paper are presented as follows. **Notations**: An Nth-order tensor is an N-way array, also known as N-dimensional or N-mode tensor. In this paper, tensors, matrices, vectors are denoted by Euler script letters (e.g., $\mathcal{X}$), boldface uppercase letters (e.g., $\mathbf{A}$), and boldface lowercase letters (e.g., $\mathbf{a}$), respectively. An entry of tensor $\mathcal{X}$ indexed by $[i_1^t, \ldots, i_N^t]$ is denoted as $\mathcal{X}[i_1^t, \ldots, i_N^t]$. We use $\mathbf{A}^{-1}$, $\mathbf{A}^\top$, and $\|\mathbf{A}\|_F$ to denote the transpose, inverse, and Frobenius norm of matrix $\mathbf{A}$, respectively. Let $[\![\cdot]\!]$ denote the Kruskal operator. Notations $\odot$ and $\circledast$ are used to represent the Khatri-Rao product and Hadamard product, respectively. The main symbols and operations are listed in Table 1.

Definition 1 (CP Decomposition). Given an Nth-order tensor $\mathcal{X}$, its CP decomposition is an approximation of N loading matrices $\mathbf{A}_n \in \mathbb{R}^{I_n \times R}, n = 1, \ldots, N$, such that,

$$\mathcal{X} \approx [\![\mathbf{A}_1, \ldots, \mathbf{A}_N]\!], \tag{1}$$

where R is a positive integer denoting an upper bound of the rank of $\mathcal{X}$. We can further unfold $\mathcal{X}$ along its nth mode as follows,

$$\begin{aligned} \mathcal{X} \overset{\text{unfold}}{\Longrightarrow} \quad \mathbf{X}_{(n)} &\approx \mathbf{A}_n(\mathbf{A}_N \odot \ldots \mathbf{A}_{n+1} \odot \mathbf{A}_{n-1} \ldots \odot \mathbf{A}_1)^\top \\ &= \mathbf{A}_n[(\mathbf{A}_k)^{\odot k \neq n}]^\top. \end{aligned} \tag{2}$$

Definition 2 (Coupled Tensor). If two tensors share one or more modes, then they are coupled with each other and called coupled tensors. For example, in recommender systems, two tensors structured as *user×movie×time* and *movie×actor×director* are coupled on the *movie* mode.

Definition 3 (Tensor Sequence). A sequence of Nth-order tensors $\mathcal{X}^{(1)}, \ldots, \mathcal{X}^{(T)}, \ldots$ is called a tensor sequence denoted as $\{\mathcal{X}^{(T)}\}$, where each $\mathcal{X}^{(T)} \in \mathbb{R}^{I_1^T \times I_2^T \times \ldots \times I_N^T}, T \in \mathbb{Z}^+$.

Definition 4 (Multi-aspect streaming Tensor Sequence). A sequence of Nth-order tensors $\{\mathcal{X}^{(T)}\}$ is called multi-aspect streaming tensor sequence if for any $T \in \mathbb{Z}^+$, $\mathcal{X}^{(T-1)}$ is the sub-tensor of $\mathcal{X}^{(T)}$, denoted as $\mathcal{X}^{(T-1)} \subseteq \mathcal{X}^{(T)}$. T increases with time, and $\mathcal{X}^{(T)}$ is the snapshot tensor of this sequence taken at time T.

Notations	Definitions
$\mathcal{X} \in \mathbb{R}^{I_1 \times I_2 \times \ldots \times I_N}$	N^{th}-order tensor
$\mathbf{X}_{(n)} \in \mathbb{R}^{I_n \times (\Pi_{i \neq n}^N I_i)}$	Mode-n unfolding matrix of tensor $\mathcal{X}$
$[\![\cdot]\!]$	Kruskal operator, e.g., $\mathcal{X} \approx [\![\mathbf{A}_1, \ldots, \mathbf{A}_N]\!]$
$\odot$	Khatri-Rao product
$\circledast$	Hadamard product
$(\mathbf{A}_k)^{\odot k \neq n}$	$\mathbf{A}_N \odot \ldots \odot \mathbf{A}_{n+1} \odot \mathbf{A}_{n-1} \odot \ldots \odot \mathbf{A}_1$
$(\mathbf{A}_k)^{\circledast k \neq n}$	$\mathbf{A}_N \circledast \ldots \circledast \mathbf{A}_{n+1} \circledast \mathbf{A}_{n-1} \circledast \ldots \circledast \mathbf{A}_1$

Table 1: Main symbols and operations.

In fact, any tensor sequence $\{\mathcal{X}^{(T)}\}$ can be modeled as a multi-aspect streaming one by adding an additional mode, i.e., defining an $(N+1)^{\text{th}}$-order new tensor sequence $\{\mathcal{Y}^{(T)}\}$, where $\mathcal{Y}^{(T)} \in \mathbb{R}^{J_1^T \times J_2^T \times \ldots \times J_N^T \times T}$, $J_n = \max_t\{I_n^t\}$. Entries of $\mathcal{Y}^{(T)}$ are defined as:

$$\mathcal{Y}^{(T)}[i_1^t, \ldots, i_N^t, t] = \begin{cases} \mathcal{X}^{(t)}[i_1^t, \ldots, i_N^t], & \text{if } 1 \leq i_n^t \leq I_N^t, \\ 0, & \text{otherwise}, \end{cases} \tag{3}$$

where $1 \leq t \leq T$, and then $\mathcal{Y}^{(T-1)} \subseteq \mathcal{Y}^{(T)}$ is satisfied.

Based on the terminologies, the multi-aspect streaming tensor completion problem can be formally defined as follows.

Given a multi-aspect streaming tensor sequence $\{\mathcal{X}^{(T)}\}$ with missing entries, we aim at recovering the missing data in current snapshot $\mathcal{X}^{(T)}$. Since $\mathcal{X}^{(T-1)} \subseteq \mathcal{X}^{(T)}$, and we have recovered $\mathcal{X}^{(T-1)}$ in previous time step, the problem is equivalent to completing the relative complement of $\mathcal{X}^{(T-1)}$ in $\mathcal{X}^{(T)}$ which is denoted as $\mathcal{X}^{(T)} \backslash \mathcal{X}^{(T-1)}$.

3 MULTI-ASPECT STREAMING TENSOR COMPLETION

In this section, we introduce the proposed framework MAST to solve the general multi-aspect streaming completion problem. By taking advantage of the learned model in previous time step, MAST can accelerate the completion process while preserving comparable completion accuracy to traditional batch learning methods. To achieve this, we begin with designing a dynamic tensor decomposition (DTD) algorithm to model the incremental pattern of multi-aspect streaming tensor sequence and track its low-rank subspace. Then, based on the DTD algorithm, we conduct the completion task via the nuclear norm constraint. At the end, we discuss a special case in which "time" is one mode of the tensors and further improve our framework for a better completion effectiveness.

3.1 Dynamic Tensor Decomposition

CP decomposition is a widely used tool for tensor completion [11, 17, 18]. By decomposing a tensor into multiple low-rank matrices using its observed entries, the underlying low-rank subspace structure can be tracked for filling the missing entries. There are two intuitive solutions for our main problem. At each time step, we can either reconstruct the batch CP model for the entire snapshot, or decompose $\mathcal{X}^{(T)} \backslash \mathcal{X}^{(T-1)}$ only. The former solution is both time and space consuming since the snapshots are increasing dramatically. In contrast, the latter fails to exploit the information in $\mathcal{X}^{(T-1)}$ to help achieve desirable imputation.

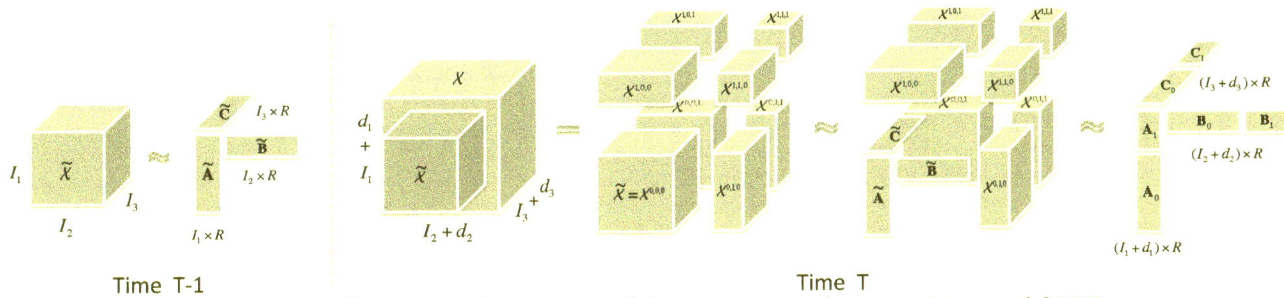

Figure 2: An illustration of the proposed dynamic tensor decomposition model DTD.

To accelerate completion process while preserving effectiveness, a dynamic CP decomposition method DTD is proposed. It is based on two ideas. First, CP decomposition enjoys the good partitioning property which means if $\mathcal{X}^{(T)}$ is approximated by $[\![\mathbf{A}_1,\ldots,\mathbf{A}_N]\!]$, then its sub-tensor $\mathcal{X}^{(T-1)}$ could be approximated by $[\![\widetilde{\mathbf{A}}_1,\ldots,\widetilde{\mathbf{A}}_N]\!]$ where $\widetilde{\mathbf{A}}_n$ is a sub-matrix of $\mathbf{A}_n$, for $n=1,\ldots,N$. This enables us to partition the current snapshot $\mathcal{X}^{(T)}$ to take advantage of the foregone acquired decomposition of its sub-tensor $\mathcal{X}^{(T-1)}$. Second, partial calculation complexity of decomposing $\mathcal{X}^{(T)}$ can be reduced one order lower by substituting acquired decompositions for $\mathcal{X}^{(T-1)}$. These two ideas are separately used in following two steps of our proposed method for information preservation and optimization acceleration, respectively.

3.1.1 Tensor partition and substitution. For the ease of presentation, we use a third-order tensor with steady growth on all three modes as an example. It is straightforward to extend to general N^{th}-order tensors. We use $\widetilde{\mathcal{X}} \in \mathbb{R}^{I_1\times I_2\times I_3}$ and $\mathcal{X} \in \mathbb{R}^{(I_1+d_1)\times(I_2+d_2)\times(I_3+d_3)}$ to represent two consecutive snapshots $\mathcal{X}^{(T-1)}$ and $\mathcal{X}^{(T)}$, $(T\in\mathbb{Z}^+)$, respectively. $\widetilde{\mathcal{X}}=0$ if $T=0$. We now introduce the details.

Let $\mathbf{A}\in\mathbb{R}^{(I_1+d_1)\times R}, \mathbf{B}\in\mathbb{R}^{(I_2+d_2)\times R}, \mathbf{C}\in\mathbb{R}^{(I_3+d_3)\times R}$ be the CP factor matrices of $\mathcal{X}$, the CP loss function under gaussian noise is:

$$\mathcal{L}(\mathbf{A},\mathbf{B},\mathbf{C}) = \|\mathcal{X}-[\![\mathbf{A},\mathbf{B},\mathbf{C}]\!]\|_F^2. \tag{4}$$

After partitioning $\mathcal{X}$ into eight sub-tensors according to $\widetilde{\mathcal{X}}$, we use a binary tuple $(i,j,k)\in\{0,1\}^3 \triangleq \Theta$ to denote these eight sub-tensors as shown in Figure 2, with $\widetilde{\mathcal{X}}=\mathcal{X}^{0,0,0}$. Each pair of adjacent sub-tensors are coupled with each other. Based on the partitioning property of CP decomposition, each sub-tensor of $\mathcal{X}$ could also be approximated via the sub-matrices of A, B and C, i.e., $\mathcal{X}^{i,j,k}\approx[\![\mathbf{A}_i,\mathbf{B}_j,\mathbf{C}_k]\!]$. $\mathbf{A}_0\in\mathbb{R}^{I_1\times R}$ and $\mathbf{A}_1\in\mathbb{R}^{d_1\times R}$ are the partitioned sub-matrices of A, i.e., $\mathbf{A}^\top=[\mathbf{A}_0^\top,\mathbf{A}_1^\top]$. Similarly to $\mathbf{B}_j$ and $\mathbf{C}_k$. Then Equation (4) could be rewritten as follows.

$$\begin{aligned}\mathcal{L}(\mathbf{A},\mathbf{B},\mathbf{C}) &= \sum_{(i,j,k)\in\Theta}\|\mathcal{X}^{i,j,k}-[\![\mathbf{A}_i,\mathbf{B}_j,\mathbf{C}_k]\!]\|_F^2\\ &= \|\mathcal{X}^{0,0,0}-[\![\mathbf{A}_0,\mathbf{B}_0,\mathbf{C}_0]\!]\|_F^2 + \mathcal{L}_0,\end{aligned} \tag{5}$$

where $\mathcal{L}_0 \triangleq \sum_{(i,j,k)\in\Theta\setminus(0,0,0)}\|\mathcal{X}^{i,j,k}-[\![\mathbf{A}_i,\mathbf{B}_j,\mathbf{C}_k]\!]\|_F^2$.

Let $[\![\widetilde{\mathbf{A}},\widetilde{\mathbf{B}},\widetilde{\mathbf{C}}]\!]$ denote the CP decomposition of $\widetilde{\mathcal{X}}$ obtained at time $T-1$. It represents the low-rank subspace which preserves the information of former snapshot. Based on this, we can approximately replace $\mathcal{X}^{0,0,0}$ by $[\![\widetilde{\mathbf{A}},\widetilde{\mathbf{B}},\widetilde{\mathbf{C}}]\!]$ and get the loss function as follows:

$$\mathcal{L}(\mathbf{A},\mathbf{B},\mathbf{C}) \approx \mu\|[\![\widetilde{\mathbf{A}},\widetilde{\mathbf{B}},\widetilde{\mathbf{C}}]\!]-[\![\mathbf{A}_0,\mathbf{B}_0,\mathbf{C}_0]\!]\|_F^2 + \mathcal{L}_0, \tag{6}$$

where weight $\mu\in[0,1]$ is the forgetting factor [20] used to alleviate the influence of the previous decomposition error. If $\mu=1$, then $[\![\widetilde{\mathbf{A}},\widetilde{\mathbf{B}},\widetilde{\mathbf{C}}]\!]$ is considered as a perfect decomposition of $\widetilde{\mathcal{X}}$. If $\mu=0$, then the former-step information is considered as independent to current decomposition. As our final goal is to complete this tensor sequence, this inequality $(0<\mu<1)$ is quite effective to alleviate the substitution errors especially when the percentage of missing data is high. In other words, this forgetting factor degrades the status of old data and upgrades the power of newly arrived data, so that we can more effectively incorporate newly emerged information to update the foregone decomposition and ensure the substitution error not continuously accumulated.

3.1.2 Alternating least square updating. The optimization is based on alternating least squares (ALS), for its fast and easy implementation with high accuracy [16, 38]. The update rule for $\mathbf{A}_0$ is:

$$\begin{aligned}\frac{\partial\mathcal{L}}{\partial\mathbf{A}_0} =& -2\mu(\widetilde{\mathbf{A}}(\widetilde{\mathbf{C}}\odot\widetilde{\mathbf{B}})^\top(\mathbf{C}_0\odot\mathbf{B}_0)-\mathbf{A}_0(\mathbf{C}_0\odot\mathbf{B}_0)^\top(\mathbf{C}_0\odot\mathbf{B}_0))\\ &-2\sum_{j,k}(\mathbf{X}_{(1)}^{0,j,k}(\mathbf{C}_k\odot\mathbf{B}_j)-\mathbf{A}_0(\mathbf{C}_0\odot\mathbf{B}_0)^\top(\mathbf{C}_0\odot\mathbf{B}_0)),\\ \mathbf{A}_0 \leftarrow& \frac{\mu\widetilde{\mathbf{A}}\left[(\widetilde{\mathbf{C}}^\top\mathbf{C}_0)\circledast(\widetilde{\mathbf{B}}^\top\mathbf{B}_0)\right]+\sum_{(j,k)\neq(0,0)}\mathbf{X}_{(1)}^{0,j,k}(\mathbf{C}_k\odot\mathbf{B}_j)}{(\sum_{k=0}^1\mathbf{C}_k^\top\mathbf{C}_k)\circledast(\sum_{j=0}^1\mathbf{B}_j^\top\mathbf{B}_j)}.\end{aligned} \tag{7}$$

The main difference between the above update rule and static CP-ALS method is the first term of the numerator. Following the property of Khatri-Rao product, the space and time complexity of calculating the Khatri-Rao products $\odot$ in equation $(\widetilde{\mathbf{C}}\odot\widetilde{\mathbf{B}})^\top(\mathbf{C}_0\odot\mathbf{B}_0)$ can be reduced using the element-wise Hadamard product, i.e., $\widetilde{\mathbf{C}}^\top\mathbf{C}_0\circledast\widetilde{\mathbf{B}}^\top\mathbf{B}_0$. Hence, by substituting $\mathcal{X}^{0,0,0}$ with $[\![\widetilde{\mathbf{A}},\widetilde{\mathbf{B}},\widetilde{\mathbf{C}}]\!]$, this term is changed from $\mathbf{X}_{(1)}^{0,0,0}(\mathbf{C}_0\odot\mathbf{B}_0)$ to $\mu\widetilde{\mathbf{A}}\left[(\widetilde{\mathbf{C}}^\top\mathbf{C}_0)\circledast(\widetilde{\mathbf{B}}^\top\mathbf{B}_0)\right]$ leading to a reduction of time complexity from $O(RI_1I_2I_3)$ to $O(R^2(I_1+I_2+I_3))$.

The update rules of the incremental matrix $\mathbf{A}_1$ can be derived as:

$$\mathbf{A}_1 \leftarrow \frac{\sum_{j,k}\mathbf{X}_{(1)}^{1,j,k}(\mathbf{C}_k\odot\mathbf{B}_j)}{(\sum_{k=0}^1\mathbf{C}_k^\top\mathbf{C}_k)\circledast(\sum_{j=0}^1\mathbf{B}_j^\top\mathbf{B}_j)}. \tag{8}$$

Similar update rules for matrices $\mathbf{B}_0$, $\mathbf{C}_0$, $\mathbf{B}_1$, and $\mathbf{C}_1$ can be easily derived. The proposed DTD model enjoys several nice properties. First, it is capable of handling any-mode-change dynamic pattern. Second, it has a fast updating process for the purpose of scalability. Third, it well preserves the information acquired from old data as well as captures the new data characteristics through the updated process. Besides, the idea of partitioning also benefits methods in solving large-scale tensor decomposition problems [4, 24, 28].

3.2 Proposed Completion Framework - MAST

The proposed DTD method balances the trade-off between efficiency and effectiveness in modeling the multi-aspect streaming pattern. As CP decomposition is an effective way in addressing static tensor completion problem, the DTD model also paves the way of solving the multi-aspect streaming tensor completion problem. In this section, we show how MAST is applied to this problem. We start with introducing the nuclear norm based method on low-rank tensor completion problem in batch setting and then combine it with the DTD model for completing multi-aspect streaming tensor sequences.

3.2.1 Low-rank tensor completion (LRTC). Generalized from matrix completion problem, the LRTC problem can be formulated as an equivalent rank-minimization problem as follows [9]:

$$\underset{\mathcal{X}}{\text{minimize}}\ rank(\mathcal{X}) \quad \text{subject to } \mathbf{\Omega} \circledast \mathcal{X} = \mathcal{T}, \tag{9}$$

where $\mathcal{X}$ denotes the complete tensor, $\mathcal{T}$ denotes the practical observations of $\mathcal{X}$. $\mathbf{\Omega}$ is a binary tensor with the same size as $\mathcal{X}$ indicating whether each corresponding entry in $\mathcal{X}$ is observed or not.

As calculating the tensor rank is an NP-hard problem [12], one way is to relax the tensor rank by replacing it with the summation of the nuclear norm of its factorized matrices [17, 18]. The modified relaxation objective function is described as follows:

$$\begin{aligned} \underset{\mathcal{X},\mathbf{A}_1,\mathbf{A}_2,\ldots,\mathbf{A}_N}{\text{minimize}} \quad & \sum_{n=1}^{N} \alpha_n \|\mathbf{A}_n\|_* + \|\mathcal{X} - [\![\mathbf{A}_1, \mathbf{A}_2, \ldots, \mathbf{A}_N]\!]\| \\ \text{subject to} \quad & \mathbf{\Omega} \circledast \mathcal{X} = \mathcal{T}, \end{aligned} \tag{10}$$

where $\{\alpha_n\}$ are trade-offs to balance the significance of each mode.

3.2.2 Combine LRTC with DTD. Since multi-aspect streaming tensor completion problem can be treated as a dynamic LRTC problem, a natural solution is to combine DTD with LRTC approach. By extending Equation (6) to N^{th}-order tensor and combining it with Equation (10), the proposed loss function for N^{th}-order multi-aspect streaming tensor completion problem is formulated as:

$$\begin{aligned} \mathcal{L} = & \sum_{(i_1,\ldots,i_N)\in\Theta_N\setminus\{0\}^N} \|\mathcal{X}^{(i_1,\ldots,i_N)} - [\![\mathbf{A}_1^{(i_1)}, \ldots, \mathbf{A}_N^{(i_N)}]\!]\|_F^2 \\ & + \sum_{n=1}^{N} \alpha_n \|\mathbf{A}_n\|_* + \mu \|[\![\widetilde{\mathbf{A}}_1, \ldots, \widetilde{\mathbf{A}}_N]\!] - [\![\mathbf{A}_1^{(0)}, \ldots, \mathbf{A}_N^{(0)}]\!]\|_F^2 \\ \triangleq & \ \mathcal{L}_1 + \sum_{n=1}^{N} \alpha_n \|\mathbf{A}_n\|_*, \end{aligned} \tag{11}$$

where $\mathbf{A}_n = \begin{bmatrix} \mathbf{A}_n^{(0)} \\ \mathbf{A}_n^{(1)} \end{bmatrix} \begin{matrix} \in \mathbb{R}^{I_n \times R} \\ \in \mathbb{R}^{d_n \times R} \end{matrix}$. $[\![\widetilde{\mathbf{A}}_1, \ldots, \widetilde{\mathbf{A}}_N]\!]$ is the decomposition of recovered tensor $\widetilde{\mathcal{X}}$ in the previous step, and $\Theta_N = \{0, 1\}^N$.

A tensor-based Alternating Direction Method of Multipliers (ADMM) algorithm is employed to solve this optimization problem. ADMM is an efficient optimization scheme for accommodating various constraints [14, 23]. Following the similar optimization scheme described in [11, 18], we induce auxiliary variables $\mathbf{Z}_n = \begin{bmatrix} \mathbf{Z}_n^{(0)} \\ \mathbf{Z}_n^{(1)} \end{bmatrix} \begin{matrix} \in \mathbb{R}^{I_n \times R} \\ \in \mathbb{R}^{d_n \times R} \end{matrix}$, $n = 1, \ldots, N$ into Equation (11), then the corresponding partial augmented Lagrangian function is:

Algorithm 1: The proposed framework MAST

Input: $\mathcal{T}, \Omega, \{\widetilde{\mathbf{A}}_n\}_{n=1}^N, R, \{\alpha_n\}_{n=1}^N, \mu, \eta, \eta_{\max}, \rho, tol$;
Output: $\mathcal{X}, \{\mathbf{A}_n\}_{n=1}^N$

Initialize $\mathbf{A}_n^{(0)} = \widetilde{\mathbf{A}}_n, \mathbf{A}_n^{(1)} = rand(\mathbf{d_n}, R), \mathbf{Z}_n = \mathbf{Y}_n = \mathbf{0}$;
repeat
  $\eta = \min\{\eta * \rho, \eta_{\max}\}$ (accelerate optimization process);
  for $n = 1 : N$ **do**
    Update $\mathbf{A}_n^{(0)}$ and $\mathbf{A}_n^{(1)}$ using Equation (13);
  Update $\mathcal{X}$ using Equation (15);
  for $n = 1 : N$ **do**
    Update $\mathbf{Z}_n$ using Equation (14);
    Update $\mathbf{Y}_n$ using Equation (16);
until $\|\mathcal{X}_{pre} - \mathcal{X}\|_F / \|\mathcal{X}_{pre}\|_F < tol$;

$$\begin{aligned} \underset{\mathcal{X},\{\mathbf{A}_n\},\{\mathbf{Z}_n\},\{\mathbf{Y}_n\}}{\text{minimize}} \quad & \mathcal{L}_1 + \sum_{n=1}^{N} \left(\alpha_n \|\mathbf{Z}_n\|_* + < \mathbf{Y}_n, \mathbf{Z}_n - \mathbf{A}_n > + \frac{\eta}{2} \|\mathbf{Z}_n - \mathbf{A}_n\|_F^2 \right) \\ \text{subject to} \quad & \mathbf{\Omega} \circledast \mathcal{X} = \mathcal{T}, \ \ \mathbf{Z}_n = \mathbf{A}_n, \ \ n = 1, 2, \ldots, N, \end{aligned} \tag{12}$$

where $\mathbf{Y}_n = \begin{bmatrix} \mathbf{Y}_n^{(0)} \\ \mathbf{Y}_n^{(1)} \end{bmatrix} \begin{matrix} \in \mathbb{R}^{I_n \times R} \\ \in \mathbb{R}^{d_n \times R} \end{matrix}$ is the Lagrange multiplier matrix, $\eta > 0$ is a penalty parameter. Based on Equations (7) and (8), by calculating the derivatives of matrices $\{\mathbf{A}_n^{(0)}\}$ and $\{\mathbf{A}_n^{(1)}\}(n = 1, 2, \ldots, N)$, we can get their update rules as follows:

$$\begin{aligned} \mathbf{A}_n^{(0)} & \leftarrow \frac{\mu \widetilde{\mathbf{A}}_n \left[(\widetilde{\mathbf{A}}_k^\top \mathbf{A}_k^{(0)})^{\circledast k \neq n} \right] + \sum_{i \in S_n^0} \mathbf{X}_{(n)}^i (\mathbf{A}_k^{(i_k)})^{\odot k \neq n} + \eta \mathbf{Z}_n^{(0)} + \mathbf{Y}_n^{(0)}}{(\mathbf{A}_k^{(0)\top} \mathbf{A}_k^{(0)} + \mathbf{A}_k^{(1)\top} \mathbf{A}_k^{(1)})^{\circledast k \neq n} + \eta \mathbf{I}_R}, \\ \mathbf{A}_n^{(1)} & \leftarrow \frac{\sum_{i \in S_n^1} \mathbf{X}_{(n)}^i (\mathbf{A}_k^{(i_k)})^{\odot k \neq n} + \eta \mathbf{Z}_n^{(1)} + \mathbf{Y}_n^{(1)}}{(\mathbf{A}_k^{(0)\top} \mathbf{A}_k^{(0)} + \mathbf{A}_k^{(1)\top} \mathbf{A}_k^{(1)})^{\circledast k \neq n} + \eta \mathbf{I}_R}, \end{aligned} \tag{13}$$

where $S_n^0 = \{(s_1, \ldots, s_N) | \sum_{k=1}^N s_k \neq 0, s_k \in \{0, 1\}, s_n = 0\}$ and $S_n^1 = \{(s_1, \ldots, s_N) | \forall\, k \in \{1, \ldots, N\}\ s_k \in \{0, 1\}, s_n = 1\}$.

In each iteration, the auxiliary matrices $\{\mathbf{Z}_n\}$ has a closed-form solution as follows[6]:

$$\mathbf{Z}_n = SVT_{\frac{\alpha_n}{\eta}}(\mathbf{A}_n - \frac{\mathbf{Y}_n}{\eta}), \ n = 1, 2, \ldots, N. \tag{14}$$

where $SVT_{\frac{\alpha_n}{\eta}}$ is the singular value thresholding operator [6] defined as $SVT_\delta(\mathbf{A}) = \mathbf{U}(diag\{\sigma_i - \delta\})_+ \mathbf{V}^\top$, where $\mathbf{U}(diag\{\sigma_i\}_{1 \le i \le r})\mathbf{V}^\top$ is the singular value decomposition of matrix $\mathbf{A}$. For any matrix $\mathbf{X}$, $\mathbf{X}_+ = \max\{\mathbf{X}, 0\}$, where $\max\{\cdot, \cdot\}$ is an element-wise operator.

To mask the missing values and iteratively completing tensor $\mathcal{X}$, $\mathcal{X}$ is updated as follows:

$$\mathcal{X} \leftarrow \mathcal{T} + \mathbf{\Omega}^c \circledast [\![\mathbf{A}_1, \mathbf{A}_2, \ldots, \mathbf{A}_N]\!]. \tag{15}$$

Finally, $\mathbf{Y}_n$ is updated as follows:

$$\mathbf{Y}_n \leftarrow \mathbf{Y}_n + \eta(\mathbf{Z}_n - \mathbf{A}_n), \ n = 1, 2, \ldots, N. \tag{16}$$

By using this optimization scheme, we can get the decomposition matrices and completed tensor $\mathcal{X}$ simultaneous. The entire optimization process of MAST is summarized in Algorithm 1. The termination criterion is that the relative changing of tensor $\mathcal{X}$ in two contiguous iterations is smaller than the tolerance.

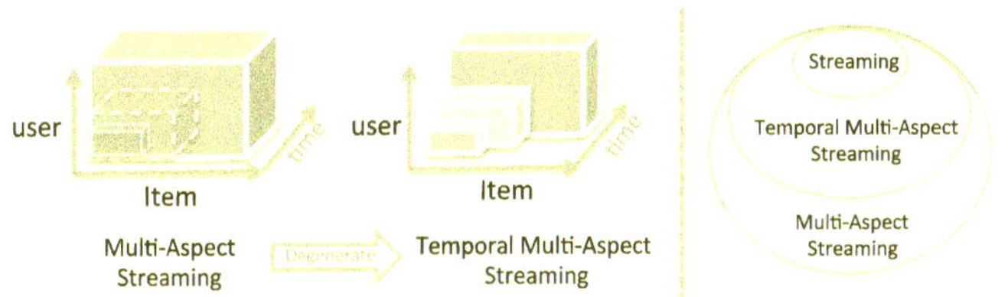

Figure 3: Degeneration of multi-aspect streaming tensor.

3.3 Temporal Multi-Aspect Streaming Tensor Completion

In some real-world applications, time is one mode of each tensor in a multi-aspect streaming tensor sequence. Take a recommender system structured as a *user* × *movie* × *time* tensor as an example. If a new user or a new item joins the system at time T, their past-time information would not exist during $t \in (0, T)$. This information shortage renders the snapshot tensor degenerated to a ladder-type structure shown in Figure 3. If we treat this structure as a combination of slices $\{\mathcal{X}^{(T)}\}$, then the original multi-aspect streaming tensor sequence can be reconstructed using the incremental tensor slices with zero-paddings. We call these slices $\{\mathcal{X}^{(T)}\}$ temporal multi-aspect streaming tensor sequence. This special structure provides us a way to improve MAST model for a better effectiveness by alleviating the quantity of substitution on missing entries.

3.3.1 Connection of Different Dynamic Patterns. Figure 3 depicts the relationships between different dynamic patterns. The temporal multi-aspect steaming is a special scenario. If the sizes of the tensor slices are the same at each time step, it will further degenerate into the traditional streaming tensor situation. Although the general framework MAST can be directly applied to the temporal case, the ladder-type structure provides extra information that could help.

We propose to reduce the quantity of substitution on missing entries to improve one of the key manipulations of MAST, i.e., tensor substitution. Different from DTD, because of data missing, the substitution of $\mathcal{X}^{(T-1)}$ at time T is composed of two parts: (1) using former-step predicted values to impute the missing entries; (2) using fitting values to substitute the existed entries. The substitution of existed part often has much smaller error and usually provides more convincing information than the prediction of missing part. As the degeneration process naturally centralizes the existed data in the ladder-type object, all of the extra parts can be treat as missing data and their substitution errors are easy to reduce. Thus, besides forgetting factor μ, this special structure paves another way to reduce the accumulated error in MAST framework towards effectively capturing fast and dramatically changed subspaces.

3.3.2 Temporal Multi-Aspect Streaming CP Completion Algorithm. Inspired by the coupled tensor factorization [2], we tailor the general MAST framework and use Figure 4 to illustrate the main idea of the variation model T-MAST. Let $\mathcal{X}^{(T)}$ denote the new tensor slice arrives at time T. $\mathcal{T}^{(T)}$ represents its observed entries. $\{[\![\widetilde{\mathbf{A}}_1^{(t)}, \begin{bmatrix}\widetilde{\mathbf{A}}_2^{(1)}\\ \vdots \\ \widetilde{\mathbf{A}}_2^{(t)}\end{bmatrix}, \ldots, \begin{bmatrix}\widetilde{\mathbf{A}}_N^{(1)}\\ \vdots \\ \widetilde{\mathbf{A}}_N^{(t)}\end{bmatrix}]\!]\}_{(1\le t\le T-1)}$ is the set of CP decompositions of the recovered tensor slices $\{\mathcal{X}^{(t)}\}_{(1\le t\le T-1)}$ at time $T-1$. We use $\mathbf{A}_n^{(T)}, n = 1, \ldots, N$ to represent the incremental part of the decomposition matrix on mode-n at time T and use $\mathbf{A}_n^{(t)}$ $(1 \le t \le T-1)$ to represent the updated result of $\widetilde{\mathbf{A}}_n^{(t)}$ at current timestamp T. At each time step T, the problem is converted to how to recover $\mathcal{X}^{(T)}$ based on the decompositions of former recovered slices $\{\mathcal{X}^{(t)}\}_{(1\le t\le T-1)}$ and get the updated CP decomposition set $\{[\![\mathbf{A}_1^{(t)}, \begin{bmatrix}\mathbf{A}_2^{(1)}\\ \vdots \\ \mathbf{A}_2^{(t)}\end{bmatrix}, \ldots, \begin{bmatrix}\mathbf{A}_N^{(1)}\\ \vdots \\ \mathbf{A}_N^{(t)}\end{bmatrix}]\!]\}_{(1\le t\le T)}$.

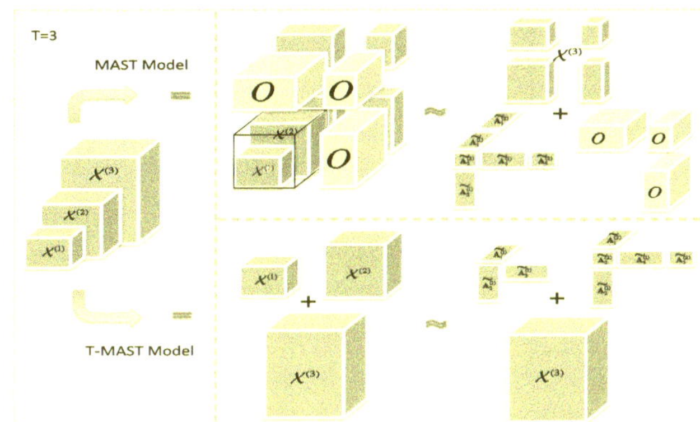

Figure 4: An illustration of T-MAST comparing with MAST.

Comparing to MAST, which requires zero-paddings to redefine a multi-aspect sequence shown in Figure 4, for T-MAST, rather than reconstructing it as a whole tensor, we directly treat this ladder type object as coupled tensor slices and use the decomposition of each slice to substitute it. Since newly added zero-padding tensors and the block operation of $\mathcal{X}^{(T)}$ has no influence on the current update, the difference between MAST and T-MAST models is how we substitute the former existed slices. Owing to the slice-based substitution in T-MAST model, the substitution of the former zero-padding parts can be omitted compared with the tensor-based substitution used in MAST model. Thus, it successfully reduces the proportion of missing data substitution as described before. The modified loss function is defined as follows:

$$\mathcal{L} = \left\|\mathcal{X}^{(T)} - [\![\mathbf{A}_1^{(T)}, \mathbf{A}_2, \mathbf{A}_3, \ldots, \mathbf{A}_N]\!]\right\|_F^2 + \sum_{n=1}^{N} \alpha_n \left\|\mathbf{A}_n\right\|_* + \sum_{t=1}^{T-1} \mu_t \left\| [\![\widetilde{\mathbf{A}}_1^{(t)}, \begin{bmatrix}\widetilde{\mathbf{A}}_2^{(1)}\\ \vdots \\ \widetilde{\mathbf{A}}_2^{(t)}\end{bmatrix}, \ldots, \begin{bmatrix}\widetilde{\mathbf{A}}_N^{(1)}\\ \vdots \\ \widetilde{\mathbf{A}}_N^{(t)}\end{bmatrix}]\!] - [\![\mathbf{A}_1^{(t)}, \begin{bmatrix}\mathbf{A}_2^{(1)}\\ \vdots \\ \mathbf{A}_2^{(t)}\end{bmatrix}, \ldots, \begin{bmatrix}\mathbf{A}_N^{(1)}\\ \vdots \\ \mathbf{A}_N^{(t)}\end{bmatrix}]\!] \right\|_F^2, \quad (17)$$

where $\mathbf{A}_n = \begin{bmatrix}\mathbf{A}_n^{(1)}\\ \vdots \\ \mathbf{A}_n^{(T)}\end{bmatrix}, n = 1, \ldots, N.$

3.3.3 Optimization Scheme. By comparing Equation (17) with Equation (11), we can easily find that their first and second terms are correspondingly equivalent when dealing with the temporal-mode-involved scenario. The different is the last term. Hence, we can still use ADMM algorithm to solve the above optimization problem and the only difference lies in the optimization of $\{\mathbf{A}_n\}_n$. For the sake of brevity, we omit other repetitive derivation and only focus on the update of matrices $\{\mathbf{A}_n^{(t)}\}_{t,n}$. For each non-temporal mode $n =$

$2, \ldots, N$, we calculate the partial derivatives of matrices $\{\mathbf{A}_n^{(t)}\}, t = 1, \ldots, T$, and define intermediate recursive matrix sequences $\{\mathbf{B}_n^{(t)}\}$, $\{\mathbf{D}_n^{(t)}\}$, $\{\mathbf{P}_n^{(t)}\}$, and $\{\mathbf{Q}_n^{(t)}\}$ to update them in each iteration. Assume $\widetilde{\mathbf{A}_k^{(T)}} = 0$, $\mathbf{P}_k^{(T)} = \sum_{j=1}^{T} \widetilde{\mathbf{A}_k^{(j)}}^\top \mathbf{A}_k^{(j)}$, and $\mathbf{Q}_k^{(T)} = \sum_{j=1}^{T} \mathbf{A}_k^{(j)\top} \mathbf{A}_k^{(j)}$, $k = 2, \ldots, N$. For any $k = 2 \ldots, N$, we have:

$$\mathbf{P}_k^{(t)} = \mathbf{P}_k^{(t+1)} - \widetilde{\mathbf{A}_k^{(t)}}^\top \mathbf{A}_k^{(t)}; \quad \mathbf{Q}_k^{(t)} = \mathbf{Q}_k^{(t+1)} - \mathbf{A}_k^{(t)\top} \mathbf{A}_k^{(t)}, \ t = T-1, \ldots, 1.$$

Based on $\{\mathbf{P}_n^{(t)}\}$ and $\{\mathbf{Q}_n^{(t)}\}$, if we define $\mathbf{D}_n^{(T+1)} = 0$, $\mu_T = 1$, and $\mathbf{B}_n^{(T+1)} = 0$, we have:

$$\begin{cases} \mathbf{D}_n^{(t)} = \mathbf{D}_n^{(t+1)} + \mu_t (\widetilde{\mathbf{A}_1^{(t)}}^\top \mathbf{A}_1^{(t)}) \circledast (\mathbf{P}_k^{(t)})^{\circledast k \neq 1, n}, \\ \mathbf{B}_n^{(t)} = \mathbf{B}_n^{(t+1)} + \mu_t (\mathbf{A}_1^{(t)\top} \mathbf{A}_1^{(t)}) \circledast (\mathbf{Q}_k^{(t)})^{\circledast k \neq 1, n}, \ t = T, \ldots, 1. \end{cases}$$

Then we can get the update rules for $\{\mathbf{A}_n^{(t)}\}$ as follows:

$$\mathbf{A}_n^{(t)} \leftarrow \frac{\mathbf{C}_n^{(t)} + \widetilde{\mathbf{A}_n^{(t)}} \mathbf{D}_n^{(t)} + \eta \mathbf{Z}_n^{(t)} + \mathbf{Y}_n^{(t)}}{\mathbf{B}_n^{(t)} + \eta \mathbf{I}_R}, \ t = T, \ldots, 1, \ n = 2, \ldots, N, \tag{18}$$

where $\{\mathbf{Y}_n^{(t)}\}_{t,n}$ are the Lagrange matrix multipliers. $\{\mathbf{C}_n^{(t)}\}_t$ are the block sub-matrices of $\mathbf{C}_n \triangleq \mathbf{X}_{(n)}^{(T)} \left[\mathbf{A}_1^{(T)} \odot \left(\mathbf{A}_k \right)^{\odot k \neq 1, n} \right]$ based on the size of $\{\mathbf{A}_n^{(t)}\}_t$.

For each mode n, only $2(N-1)R^2$ extra space is needed comparing to the MAST model if we follow the updating order below:

$$\begin{aligned} \mathbf{C}_n \rightarrow \ & \{\mathbf{P}_k^{(T)}\}_{k \in [2,N]} \rightarrow \{\mathbf{Q}_k^{(T)}\}_{k \in [2,N]} \rightarrow \mathbf{D}_n^{(T)} \rightarrow \mathbf{B}_n^{(T)} \rightarrow \mathbf{A}_n^{(T)} \\ \rightarrow \ & \{\mathbf{P}_k^{(T-1)}\}_{k \in [2,N]} \rightarrow \{\mathbf{Q}_k^{(T-1)}\}_{k \in [2,N]} \rightarrow \mathbf{D}_n^{(T-1)} \rightarrow \mathbf{B}_n^{(T-1)} \rightarrow \mathbf{A}_n^{(T-1)} \\ \rightarrow \ldots \rightarrow \ & \{\mathbf{P}_k^{(1)}\}_{k \in [2,N]} \rightarrow \{\mathbf{Q}_k^{(1)}\}_{k \in [2,N]} \rightarrow \mathbf{D}_n^{(1)} \rightarrow \mathbf{B}_n^{(1)} \rightarrow \mathbf{A}_n^{(1)}. \end{aligned}$$

The temporal mode ($n = 1$) could be updated by:

$$\mathbf{A}_1^{(t)} \leftarrow \frac{\mu_t \mathbf{C}_n^{(t)} + \eta \mathbf{Z}_1^{(t)} + \mathbf{Y}_1^{(t)}}{\mu_t (\mathbf{Q}_k^{(t)})^{\circledast k \neq 1} + \eta \mathbf{I}_R}, \ t = T, \ldots, 1, \ \mu_T = 1, \tag{19}$$

where $\mathbf{C}_n^{(T)} = \mathbf{X}_{(1)}^{(T)} \left(\mathbf{A}_k \right)^{\odot k \neq 1}$, $\mathbf{C}_n^{(t)} = (\mathbf{P}_k^{(t)})^{\circledast k \neq 1}$. The rest matrices $\{\mathbf{Y}_n^{(t)}\}$, $\{\mathbf{Z}_n^{(t)}\}$ and tensor $\mathcal{X}^{(T)}$ are updated similarly as MAST.

From model perspective, although T-MAST can not handle the general multi-aspect streaming situation as MAST, both of them can be applied to the traditional streaming case. Not surprisingly, comparing Equations (11) and (17), using the traditional streaming setting, these two models are equivalent to each other.

4 EXPERIMENTS

In this section, we empirically evaluate the performance of the proposed framework MAST. Three major aspects are analyzed.

Q1: How effective is MAST compared with static and dynamic CP completion methods on different real-world datasets with different dynamic variation patterns?

Q2: How efficient is MAST compared with the state-of-the-art methods on datasets with different length of time segments?

Q3: What is the influence of the forgetting factor μ on the general model MAST?

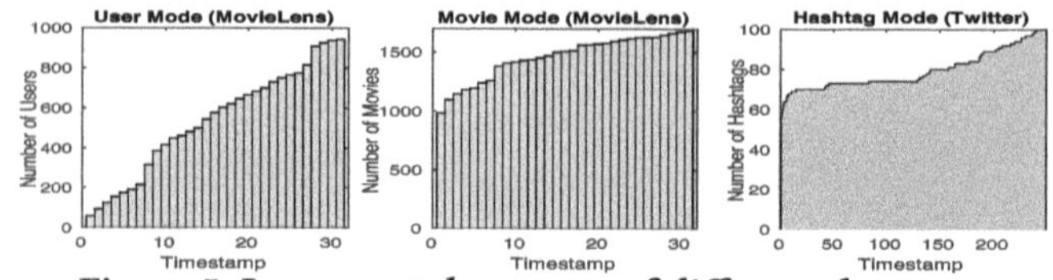

Figure 5: Incremental patterns of different datasets.

	Total Size	Initial Size	Increased Modes
Twitter Topic	$500 \times 500 \times 20$	$50 \times 50 \times 20$	1,2
Youtube	$1066 \times 1066 \times 5$	$100 \times 100 \times 5$	1,2
MovieLens	$943 \times 1682 \times 31$	$57 \times 983 \times 1$	1,2,3
Twitter Hashtag	$100 \times 1000 \times 249$	$57 \times 1000 \times 1$	1,3

Table 2: Characteristics of the four datasets.

4.1 Datasets and Tasks

To evaluate the validity of MAST, we apply it to four datasets with different applications. Their basic information is shown in Table 2.

Twitter Topic [10] (Recommendation): It is a third-order tensor with binary entries of size $500(user) \times 500(expert) \times 20(topic)$. Experts represent the high-quality content producers of 20 topics. It starts from $50 \times 50 \times 20$ and increases 2% of total users and experts at each time step. The task is to recommend the personalized expert of each topic to each user.

Youtube[2] [33] (Link Prediction): It includes 1,066 users which have the most interactions among original 15,088 users sharing five interactions, including contact, co-contact, co-subscription, co-subscribed, and favorite networks. It starts from $100(user) \times 100(user) \times 5(interaction)$ and increases 2% of total users in each timestamp. The task is to predict missing links at each time step.

MovieLens[3] (Recommendation): It is a benchmark dataset for movie recommendation structured as a temporal multi-aspect streaming tensor sequence of size $943(user) \times 1{,}682(item) \times 31(week)$. Instead of predicting concrete movie rates, the task is to predict what movies a user may rate.

Twitter Hashtag [11] (Information Diffusion): This is a spatial-temporal dataset structured as a temporal multi-aspect streaming tensor sequence of size $100(hashtag) \times 1000(city) \times 249(day)$. Each binary entry indicates whether the corresponding hashtag emerges at the corresponding city on a specific day or not. Hashtag mode is increased as time goes. The task is to predict the emergence of previously appeared hashtags in each city at each time step.

The MovieLens and Twitter Hashtag follow the natural evolvement of a ladder-type increment. To give a better understanding of the incremental process, we depict the sectional views of the user and item modes of MovieLens, as well as the hashtag mode of Twitter Hashtag in Figure 5. The incremental pattern of Twitter Hashtag dataset is relatively gentle comparing with MovieLens.

4.2 Baseline Methods

Three state-of-the-art CP completion methods are employed including two categories, i.e., static and dynamic algorithms.

- Static CP-ALS [5]: It is a traditional CP-based method also called EM-ALS [1]. To enhance the learning process, the former-step decomposition is utilized as the initialization for the current step. We implement it with the help of [3].

[2] http://socialcomputing.asu.edu/datasets/YouTube
[3] http://movielens.umn.edu

Tensor Type		General Multi-Aspect Streaming Tensor						Temporal Multi-Aspect Streaming Tensor					
Dataset		Twitter Topic			Youtube			MovieLens			Twitter Hashtag		
Missing Percentage		20%	50%	80%	20%	50%	80%	20%	50%	80%	20%	50%	80%
Static	CP-ALS	0.8394	0.7810	0.6238	**0.9390**	**0.9209**	0.8609	0.9304	0.9057	0.8605	0.9257	0.9236	0.9133
	TNCP	**0.8443**	**0.7936**	**0.6661**	0.9384	0.9199	**0.8659**	**0.9344**	**0.9139**	**0.8790**	**0.9258**	**0.9238**	**0.9137**
Dynamic	OLSTEC	0.6670	0.5035	0.5028	0.8601	0.7315	0.7225	0.7048	0.6550	0.6227	0.7449	0.6716	0.6314
	MAST	**0.8392**	**0.7714**	**0.6493**	**0.9326**	**0.9141**	**0.8618**	0.8393	0.8354	0.8099	0.9160	0.9019	0.8641
	T-MAST	$N.A.$	$N.A.$	$N.A.$	$N.A.$	$N.A.$	$N.A.$	**0.9294**	**0.9023**	**0.8586**	**0.9233**	**0.9153**	**0.8881**

Table 3: Performance in terms of RA-AUC metric. (Results of the best dynamic and static methods are highlighted.)

- Static TNCP [18]: It is one of the state-of-the-art static completion methods. It employs trace norm constraints optimized by ADMM algorithm. Similar initialization approach is employed to accelerate the convergence.
- OLSTEC [15]: It is a state-of-the-art streaming tensor completion method. We extend it for multi-aspect streaming tensor completion by splitting the multi-aspect incremental process into several streaming ones and update them in random order in each iteration until it converges.
- T-MAST: This is a variation of MAST tailored towards temporal multi-aspect streaming tensor sequence. It cannot be applied to the Twitter Topic and Youtube.

4.3 Experimental Setup

Following widely used settings [15, 20], for all datasets, we randomly cover a fixed percentage of data and consider the remaining entries as observed information. The hidden data is used as ground truth. To further study the impact of the missing ratio, we vary it as {20%,50%,80%}. To evaluate the performance, a widely used metric is employed for all tasks, i.e., running-average Area Under Curve (RA-AUC). For the first two datasets, we focus on the incremental part $\mathcal{X}^{(t)}\backslash\mathcal{X}^{(t-1)}$ at time step t to avoid double counting and calculate the Area Under Curve (AUC) score of each topic slice or interaction slice based on the prediction. The average AUC at time t among topics or interaction slices is denoted as AUC_t. For the last two datasets which are two multi-aspect streaming tensor sequences, AUC_t is calculated using the prediction of missing data in slice $\mathcal{X}^{(t)}$. The running-average AUC score is defined as: $\text{RA-AUC} = \frac{1}{T}\sum_{t=1}^{T}\text{AUC}_t$, where T is the total number of time steps. The efficiency is measured by average running time defined as $\frac{1}{T}\sum_{t=1}^{T}\text{RT}_t$, where RT_t is the running time at time step t.

Parameter Setting: We set the tolerance rate to 10^{-5}, the maximum number of iteration to 500 for all the algorithms. By testing the performance of static methods on whole four datasets using 10 different ranks varying from 5 to 50, we set $R = 10$ in all the experiment considering of both accuracy and speed for fair comparison. In the implementation of our proposed method, default parameters are set as $\alpha_n = \frac{1}{10N}$ $n = 1,\ldots,N$, $\eta = 10^{-4}$, $\rho = 1.05$ and $\eta_{\max} = 10^6$. The forgetting factors are fine-tuned according to the missing ratio f (usually $\mu = \mu_t = 1-f$ $(\forall\, t > 0)$). For baselines, we follow the suggestions of original papers to set parameters. The initial completion and warm start matrices are calculated using TNCP method for two reasons: (1) MAST framework degenerates to static TNCP when $T = 1$. (2) For fair comparison, we use the same best warm start at initial time for all methods. All experimental results are the arithmetic average of five runs and are ran on a Dell OptiPlex 9030 i7-16GB desktop with MATLAB R2016b.

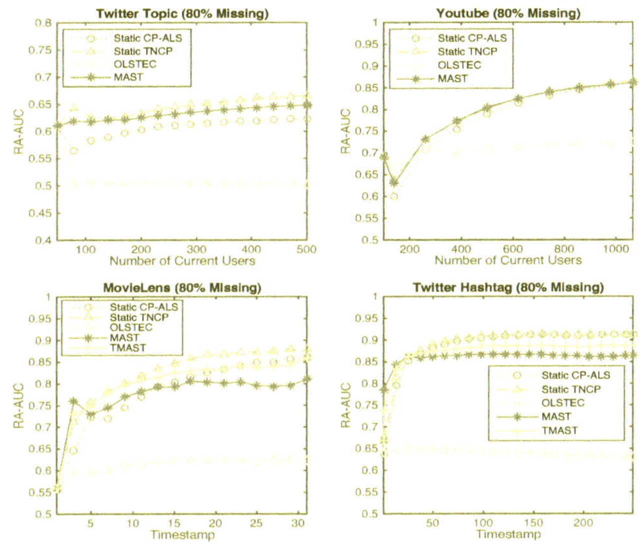

Figure 6: Performance of different methods on the four datasets with different timestamps.

4.4 Evaluation of Effectiveness

Table 3 shows the performance of MAST and baselines on different datasets in terms of RA-AUC. Three main conclusions are observed.

First, MAST has commensurate performance comparing with the two static models and higher performance than dynamic baseline method OLSTEC with different percentages of random missing entries on the first two datasets. To illustrate the performance of different models over time, we display the RA-AUC variation curve of MAST compared with baselines on four datasets with 80% missing entries in Figure 6. The results show that, with time goes, the increase of users leads to a fluctuant increasing RU-AUC for all the methods except OLSTEC. MAST has comparable performance to the static baselines and has higher accuracy than OLSTEC.

Second, on both MovieLens and Twitter Hashtag, which have different dynamic patterns shown in Figure 5, the variation model T-MAST outperforms MAST. This result empirically validates our analysis in Section 3.3 that the ladder-type structure of temporal multi-aspect streaming pattern could help to reduce the quantity of substitution on missing entries thereby improving general MAST framework. Besides, as can be seen from the results, the difference between T-MAST and MAST on MovieLens is larger than the one on Twitter Hashtag. This is because MovieLens dataset has fewer snapshots and sharper changes on the size of tensor slices than Twitter Hashtag as shown in Figure 5. The dramatically increased ladder-type structure leads to a larger ratio of missing data substitution at each time step. This further results in a hysteresis effect for capturing characteristics of the new data during the update.

Dataset		Twitter Topic			Youtube			MovieLens			Twitter Hashtag		
Missing Percentage		20%	50%	80%	20%	50%	80%	20%	50%	80%	20%	50%	80%
Static	CP-ALS	305.20	307.42	302.85	504.77	502.73	500.72	1189.9	1223.3	1170.2	257.16	468.13	582.38
	TNCP	110.73	118.69	117.92	371.33	368.56	365.67	509.87	511.34	456.59	172.01	194.78	193.59
Dynamic	OLSTEC	14.042	14.150	13.903	29.592	27.272	27.216	144.18	143.59	140.81	9.2601	9.6796	9.3625
	MAST	**8.7937**	**8.3523**	**7.6398**	**28.270**	**26.443**	**25.626**	118.13	113.74	110.72	**8.9186**	**8.5487**	**7.0420**
	T-MAST	$N.A.$	$N.A.$	$N.A.$	$N.A.$	$N.A.$	$N.A.$	**113.65**	**105.29**	**103.56**	19.1785	18.6397	16.3826

Table 4: Average running time of different methods on the four datasets.

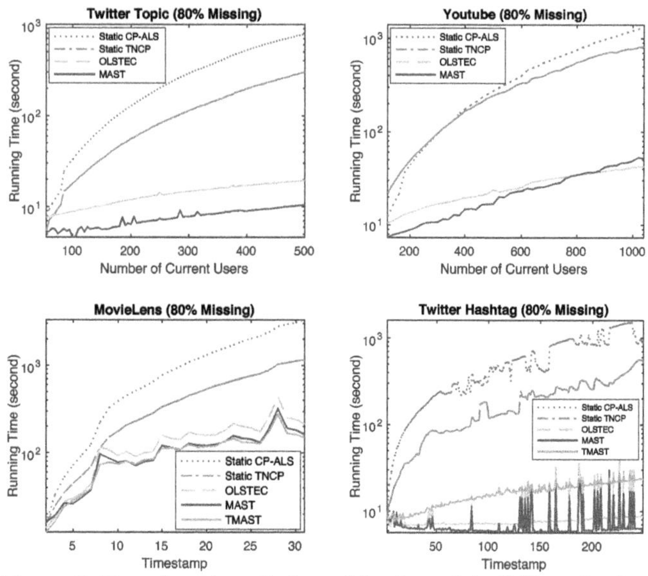

Figure 7: Running time (in logarithmic scale) of all methods.

Third, MAST shows strong stability on different datasets of different dynamic patterns. Furthermore, for different ratios of missing data and different length of time steps, our proposed framework retains comparable performance with static models. Theses results demonstrate the capability of our model in capturing low-rank subspace of dynamically changed tensor objects.

4.5 Evaluation of Efficiency

To study the efficiency of the proposed framework, we compare the average running time of all five models shown in Table 4. For better visualization, Figure 7 displays the computation time (RT_t) in logarithmic scale as a function of timestamps or user numbers on four datasets with 80% missing. From these results, we can come to the conclusion that (1) For general multi-aspect streaming tensor, MAST model takes much less running time than static models and outperforms OLSTEC. (2) T-MAST model shows comparable efficiency with MAST on short-term datasets. Although it sacrifices the time complexity to some degree on long-term datasets for the sake of higher effectiveness, it is still significantly faster than static models. If we assume $R \ll I_n$, $n = 1, \ldots, N$, and define $S^t = \prod_{n=1}^{N} I_n^t$, where I_n^t is size of the Nth mode of slice $\mathcal{X}^{(t)}$ in a temporal multi-aspect streaming tensor sequence, the complexities per iteration of all three dynamic models at time t would be $O((N+1)R(S^t - S^{(t-1)}))$ comparing to $O((N+1)RS^t)$ of two static models. Moreover, a dramatic change in the size of the tensor will cause a violent fluctuation on the completion time. For instance, the structures of Youtube and Twitter Topic datasets changed more steadily than MovieLens and Twitter Hashtag datasets resulting in less violent fluctuations on the running-time curves. If we focus on one dataset such as Twitter Hashtag, the time curve fluctuates more acutely when the size of the newly slice increases sharply.

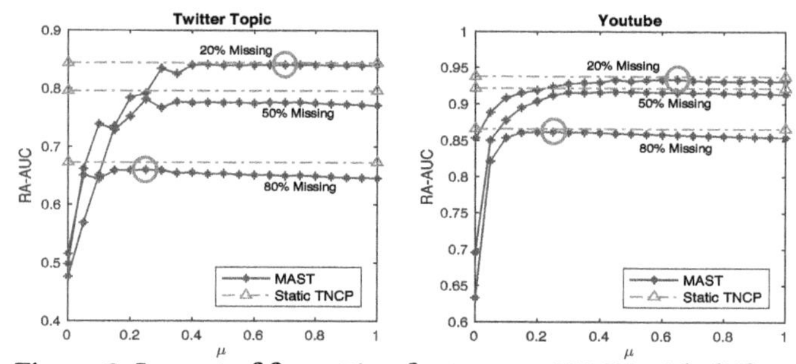

Figure 8: Impact of forgetting factor μ on MAST with different missing percentages.

4.6 Influence of Forgetting Factor μ

To investigate the effect of forgetting factor μ on our proposed framework, we vary it from 0 to 1 with a step size 0.05 and compare the performance of MAST model on Twitter Topic and Youtube datasets. Results shown in Figure 8 demonstrate that with the decreasing of forgetting factor, the performance of MAST increases at first and then decreases. With the increase of the missing ratio, the turning point becomes closer to 0, which inspires us to choose a smaller μ to alleviate the substitution error. In sum, these observations illustrate that: (1) A suitable shrinkage on the approximately substituted tensor could alleviate the previous fitting error and result in better completion effectiveness. (2) The higher the missing ratio is, the smaller the forgetting factor we should choose to alleviate the hysteresis effect of our framework in capturing the low-rank subspace for multi-aspect streaming tensor completion.

5 RELATED WORK

The related work can be categorized into two main topics as follows: **Dynamic Tensor Factorization.** Tensor factorization methods have received widespread concerns and achievements under static setting [16, 23]. Increasingly massive amount of real-world dynamic data nowadays requires an extensive concern on the problem of dynamic tensor factorization [15]. Nion and Sidiropoulos [22] proposed two adaptive PARAFAC algorithms adopting the recursive least square and simultaneous diagonalization tracking methods to solve the online third-order tensor factorization. Phan et al. [24] partitioned a large-scale tensor into small grids and proposed a grid-based scalable tensor factorization method which could also be used in dynamic tensor factorization. Zhou et al. [38] proposed an accelerated online algorithm that can track the CP decompositions of incremental N^{th}-order tensors. However, all of them are not directly applicable to multi-aspect streaming situations and the completion task. Kasai [15] substituted the stochastic gradient descent method with recursive least square method and improved the algorithm proposed by Mardani et al. [20] focusing on the problem of subspace learning and imputation for streaming tensors. Besides CP decomposition, dynamic tucker decomposition methods were also proposed [31, 32, 37]. Some of them were not only focusing on one-mode increasing condition [13, 30], but also giving possible solutions for all-mode incremental update using matrix-based online methods such as incremental SVD [19] without considering about missing entries. Finally, it is worth to mention that though not a factorization method, the histogram-based approach [8] conducted on multi-aspect streaming tensor analysis can be treated as one of the pioneer researches on the multi-aspect streaming pattern.

Low-Rank Tensor Completion. Since the real-world multidimensional datasets are oftentimes raw and incomplete because of missing at random and limited permissions [11, 18], low-rank tensor completion problem has been attractive to researchers and practitioners in data mining, online learning, computer vision, signal processing, etc. Generalized from matrix cases, a wide range of approaches have been proposed such as trace-norm based methods [9, 17, 29, 35], factorization-based approaches [1, 5, 34], tensor completion with auxiliary information [2, 11, 21], and online tensor imputation [15, 20]. Although both theoretical analysis and various practical applications have been considered, to our best knowledge, no existing work has been conducted on the low-rank tensor completion with general multi-aspect streaming patterns.

6 CONCLUSION AND FUTURE WORK

In this paper, we focus on the multi-aspect streaming tensor completion problem and propose an updatable CP completion framework MAST. The proposed framework can effectively capture the low-rank subspace of multi-aspect streaming tensor sequences so as to achieve the completion purpose. To further enhance the effectiveness, we also tailor the general framework toward a special case where time is one mode of the multi-aspect streaming tensors. By conducting experiments on various real-world applications, we empirically validate the effectiveness and efficiency of our proposed framework. Future work will center on investigating dynamic Tucker-based tensor completion methods and incorporating scalable tensor mining techniques [27, 28] into our framework.

ACKNOWLEDGMENTS

This work is, in part, supported by DARPA (#W911NF-16-1-0565) and NSF (#IIS-1657196). The views, opinions, and/or findings expressed are those of the author(s) and should not be interpreted as representing the official views or policies of the Department of Defense or the U.S. Government.

REFERENCES

[1] Evrim Acar, Daniel M Dunlavy, Tamara G Kolda, and Morten Mørup. 2011. Scalable tensor factorizations for incomplete data. *Chemometrics and Intelligent Laboratory Systems* (2011).

[2] Evrim Acar, Tamara G Kolda, and Daniel M Dunlavy. 2011. All-at-once optimization for coupled matrix and tensor factorizations. *arXiv* (2011).

[3] Brett W Bader, Tamara G Kolda, and others. 2015. MATLAB Tensor Toolbox Version 2.6, Available online,. (2015).

[4] Alex Beutel, Partha P Talukdar, Abhimanu Kumar, Christos Faloutsos, Evangelos E Papalexakis, and Eric P Xing. 2014. Flexifact: scalable flexible factorization of coupled tensors on hadoop. *ICDM* (2014).

[5] Rasmus Bro. 1998. Multi-way analysis in the food industry: models, algorithms, and applications. *MRI, EPG and EMA," Proc ICSLP* (1998).

[6] Jian-Feng Cai, Emmanuel J Candès, and Zuowei Shen. 2010. A singular value thresholding algorithm for matrix completion. *SIOPT* (2010).

[7] Daniel M Dunlavy, Tamara G Kolda, and Evrim Acar. 2011. Temporal link prediction using matrix and tensor factorizations. *TKDD* (2011).

[8] Hadi Fanaee-T and João Gama. 2015. Multi-aspect-streaming tensor analysis. *Knowledge-Based Systems* (2015).

[9] Silvia Gandy, Benjamin Recht, and Isao Yamada. 2011. Tensor completion and low-n-rank tensor recovery via convex optimization. *Inverse Problems* (2011).

[10] Hancheng Ge, James Caverlee, and Haokai Lu. 2016. Taper: a contextual tensor-based approach for personalized expert recommendation. *Proc. of RecSys* (2016).

[11] Hancheng Ge, James Caverlee, Nan Zhang, and Anna Squicciarini. 2016. Uncovering the spatio-temporal dynamics of memes in the presence of incomplete information. *CIKM* (2016).

[12] Johan Håstad. 1990. Tensor rank is NP-complete. *Journal of Algorithms* (1990).

[13] Weiming Hu, Xi Li, Xiaoqin Zhang, Xinchu Shi, Stephen Maybank, and Zhongfei Zhang. 2011. Incremental tensor subspace learning and its applications to foreground segmentation and tracking. *IJCV* (2011).

[14] Xiao Huang, Jundong Li, and Xia Hu. 2017. Accelerated attributed network embedding. *SDM* (2017).

[15] Hiroyuki Kasai. 2016. Online low-rank tensor subspace tracking from incomplete data by CP decomposition using recursive least squares. *ICASSP* (2016).

[16] Tamara G Kolda and Brett W Bader. 2009. Tensor decompositions and applications. *SIAM review* (2009).

[17] Ji Liu, Przemyslaw Musialski, Peter Wonka, and Jieping Ye. 2013. Tensor completion for estimating missing values in visual data. *TPAMI* (2013).

[18] Yuanyuan Liu, Fanhua Shang, Licheng Jiao, James Cheng, and Hong Cheng. 2015. Trace norm regularized CANDECOMP/PARAFAC decomposition with missing data. *IEEE Transactions on Cybernetics* (2015).

[19] Xiang Ma, Dan Schonfeld, and Ashfaq Khokhar. 2009. Dynamic updating and downdating matrix SVD and tensor HOSVD for adaptive indexing and retrieval of motion trajectories. *ICASSP* (2009).

[20] Morteza Mardani, Gonzalo Mateos, and Georgios B Giannakis. 2015. Subspace learning and imputation for streaming big data matrices and tensors. *IEEE TSP* (2015).

[21] Atsuhiro Narita, Kohei Hayashi, Ryota Tomioka, and Hisashi Kashima. 2011. Tensor factorization using auxiliary information. *ECML PKDD* (2011).

[22] Dimitri Nion and Nicholas D Sidiropoulos. 2009. Adaptive algorithms to track the PARAFAC decomposition of a third-order tensor. *IEEE TSP* (2009).

[23] Evangelos E. Papalexakis, Christos Faloutsos, and Nicholas D. Sidiropoulos. 2016. Tensors for data mining and data fusion: models, applications, and scalable Algorithms. *TIST* (2016).

[24] Anh Huy Phan and Andrzej Cichocki. 2011. PARAFAC algorithms for large-scale problems. *Neurocomputing* (2011).

[25] Steffen Rendle, Leandro Balby Marinho, Alexandros Nanopoulos, and Lars Schmidt-Thieme. 2009. Learning optimal ranking with tensor factorization for tag recommendation. *KDD* (2009).

[26] Steffen Rendle and Lars Schmidt-Thieme. 2010. Pairwise interaction tensor factorization for personalized tag recommendation. *WSDM* (2010).

[27] Lee Sael, Inah Jeon, and U Kang. 2015. Scalable tensor mining. *Big Data Research* (2015).

[28] Kijung Shin and U Kang. 2014. Distributed methods for high-dimensional and large-scale tensor factorization. *ICDM* (2014).

[29] Marco Signoretto, Lieven De Lathauwer, and Johan AK Suykens. 2010. Nuclear norms for tensors and their use for convex multilinear estimation. *Linear Algebra and Its Applications* (2010).

[30] Andrews Sobral, Christopher G Baker, Thierry Bouwmans, and El-hadi Zahzah. 2014. Incremental and multi-feature tensor subspace learning applied for background modeling and subtraction. *ICIAR* (2014).

[31] Jimeng Sun, Dacheng Tao, and Christos Faloutsos. 2006. Beyond streams and graphs: dynamic tensor analysis. *KDD* (2006).

[32] Jimeng Sun, Dacheng Tao, Spiros Papadimitriou, Philip S Yu, and Christos Faloutsos. 2008. Incremental tensor analysis: theory and applications. *TKDD* (2008).

[33] Lei Tang, Xufei Wang, and Huan Liu. 2009. Uncoverning groups via heterogeneous interaction analysis. *ICDM* (2009).

[34] Giorgio Tomasi and Rasmus Bro. 2005. PARAFAC and missing values. *Chemometrics and Intelligent Laboratory Systems* (2005).

[35] Ryota Tomioka, Kohei Hayashi, and Hisashi Kashima. 2010. Estimation of low-rank tensors via convex optimization. *arXiv* (2010).

[36] Yichen Wang, Robert Chen, Joydeep Ghosh, Joshua C Denny, Abel Kho, You Chen, Bradley A Malin, and Jimeng Sun. 2015. Rubik: Knowledge guided tensor factorization and completion for health data analytics. *KDD* (2015).

[37] Rose Yu, Dehua Cheng, and Yan Liu. 2015. Accelerated online low-rank tensor learning for multivariate spatio-temporal streams. *ICML* (2015).

[38] Shuo Zhou, Nguyen X Vinh, James Bailey, Yunzhe Jia, and Ian Davidson. 2016. Accelerating online CP decompositions for higher order tensors. *KDD* (2016).

Scalable and Sustainable Deep Learning via Randomized Hashing

Ryan Spring
Rice University
Department of Computer Science
Houston, Texas, USA 43017-6221
rdspring1@rice.edu

Anshumali Shrivastava
Rice University
Department of Computer Science
Houston, Texas, USA 43017-6221
anshumali@rice.edu

ABSTRACT

Current deep learning architectures are growing larger in order to learn from complex datasets. These architectures require giant matrix multiplication operations to train millions of parameters. Conversely, there is another growing trend to bring deep learning to low-power, embedded devices. The matrix operations, associated with the training and testing of deep networks, are very expensive from a computational and energy standpoint. We present a novel hashing-based technique to drastically reduce the amount of computation needed to train and test neural networks. Our approach combines two recent ideas, Adaptive Dropout and Randomized Hashing for Maximum Inner Product Search (MIPS), to select the nodes with the highest activations efficiently. Our new algorithm for deep learning reduces the overall computational cost of the forward and backward propagation steps by operating on significantly fewer nodes. As a consequence, our algorithm uses only 5% of the total multiplications, while keeping within 1% of the accuracy of the original model on average. A unique property of the proposed hashing-based back-propagation is that the updates are always sparse. Due to the sparse gradient updates, our algorithm is ideally suited for asynchronous, parallel training, leading to near-linear speedup, as the number of cores increases. We demonstrate the scalability and sustainability (energy efficiency) of our proposed algorithm via rigorous experimental evaluations on several datasets.

CCS CONCEPTS

• **Computing methodologies → Neural networks**; • **Theory of computation → Streaming, sublinear and near linear time algorithms**; **Parallel algorithms**;

KEYWORDS

Neural Networks; Deep Learning; Locality-Sensitive Hashing; Randomized Algorithms; Parallel Computing

KDD'17, August 13–17, 2017, Halifax, NS, Canada.

ACM ISBN 978-1-4503-4887-4/17/08...$15.00
https://doi.org/10.1145/3097983.3098035

1 INTRODUCTION

Deep learning is revolutionizing big-data applications, after being responsible for groundbreaking improvements in image classification [12] and speech recognition [9]. With the recent upsurge in data, at a much faster rate than our computing capabilities, neural networks are growing larger to process information more effectively. In 2012, state-of-the-art convolutional neural networks contained at most 10 layers. Afterward, each successive year has brought deeper architectures with greater accuracy. Microsoft's deep residual network [8], which won the ILSVRC 2015 competition with a 3.57% error rate, had 152 layers and 11.3 billion FLOPs. To handle such large neural networks, researchers usually train them on large computer clusters with high-performance graphics cards.

Due to the growing size and complexity of networks, efficient algorithms for training massive deep networks in a distributed, parallel environment is currently the most sought-after problem in both academia and the commercial industry. For example, Google [5] used a 1-billion parameter neural network, which took three days to train on a 1000-node cluster, totaling over 16,000 CPU cores. Each instantiation of the network spanned 170 servers. In distributed computing environments, the parameters of giant deep networks are required to be split across multiple nodes. However, this setup requires costly communication and synchronization between the parameter server and processing nodes in order to transfer the gradient and parameter updates. The sequential and dense nature of gradient updates prohibits any efficient splitting (sharding) of the neural network parameters across computer nodes. There is no clear way to avoid the costly synchronization without resorting to some ad-hoc breaking of the network. This ad-hoc breaking of deep networks is not well-understood and is likely to hurt performance. Synchronization is one of the major hurdles in scalability. Asynchronous training is the ideal solution, but it is sensitive to conflicting, overlapping parameter updates, which leads to poor convergence.

While deep networks are growing larger and more complex, there is also push for greater energy efficiency to satisfy the growing popularity of machine learning applications on mobile phones and low-power devices. For example, there is recent work by McMahan et al. [22] aimed at leveraging the vast data of mobile devices. This work has the users train neural networks on their local data, and then periodically transmit their models to a central server. This approach preserves the privacy of the user's personal data, but still allows the central server's model to learn effectively. Their work is dependent on training neural networks locally. Back-propagation is the most popular algorithm for training deep networks. Each iteration of the back-propagation algorithm is composed of giant matrix multiplications. These matrices are very large, especially for massive networks with millions of nodes in the hidden layer, which are common in industrial practice. Large matrix multiplications are parallelizable on GPUs, but not energy-efficient. Users require their phones and tablets to have long battery life. Reducing the computational costs of neural networks, which directly translates into longer battery life, is a critical issue for the mobile industry.

The current challenges for deep learning illustrate a great demand for algorithms that reduce the amount of computation and energy usage. To reduce the bottleneck matrix multiplications, there has been a flurry of works around reducing the amount of computations associated with them. Most of them revolve around exploiting low-rank matrices or low precision updates (See Section 6.2 for details). However, updates with these techniques are hard to parallelize making them unsuitable for distributed and large scale applications. On the contrary, our proposal capitalizes on the sparsity of the activations to reduce the computation complexity. To the best of our knowledge, this is the first proposal that exploits sparsity to reduce the amount of computation associated with deep networks. We further show that our approach admits asynchronous parallel updates leading to perfect scaling with increasing parallelism.

Recent machine learning research has focused on techniques for dealing with the famous problem of over-fitting with deep networks. A notable line of work [2, 20, 21] improved the accuracy of neural networks by only updating the neurons with the highest activations. Adaptive dropout [2] sampled neurons in proportion to an affine transformation of the neuron's activation. The Winner-Take-All (WTA) approach [20, 21] kept only the top-k% neurons by using a hard threshold. It was found that such a selective choice of nodes and sparse updates provide a natural regularization [30]. However, these approaches rely on inefficient, brute-force techniques to find the best neurons. Thus, these techniques are equally as expensive as the standard back-propagation method leading to no computational savings.

Our idea is to index the neurons (the weights of each neuron as a vector) in a hash table using locality sensitive hashing. These hash tables allow us to select (or sample) the neurons with the highest activations in sub-linear time. Moreover, since our approach results in a sparse active set of neurons randomly, the gradient updates are unlikely to overwrite each other because of their sparsity. Sparse updates are ideal for asynchronous and parallel gradient updates. It is known that asynchronous stochastic gradient descent (ASGD) [23] will converge if the number of simultaneous parameter updates is small. We heavily leverage this sparsity which unique to our proposal. On several deep learning benchmarks, we show that our approach outperforms standard algorithms including vanilla dropout [30] at high sparsity levels and matches the performance of adaptive dropout [2] and winner-take-all [20, 21] while needing less computation (only 5%).

1.1 Our Contributions:

(1) We present a scalable and sustainable algorithm for training and testing fully-connected neural networks. Our idea capitalizes on the recent, successful technique of adaptive dropouts and locality sensitive hashing (LSH) for maximum inner product search (MIPS) [25]. We show significant reductions in the computational requirement for training deep networks without any significant loss in accuracy (within 1% of the accuracy of the original model on average). In particular, our method achieves the performance of other state-of-the-art regularization methods such as Dropout, Adaptive Dropout, and Winner-Take-All when using only 5% of the neurons in a standard neural network.
(2) Our proposal reduces computations associated with both the training and testing (inference) of deep networks by reducing the multiplications needed for the feed-forward and back-propagation operations.
(3) The key idea in our algorithm is to associate LSH hash tables [7, 11] with every layer. These hash tables support constant-time $O(1)$ insertion and deletion operations.
(4) Our scheme naturally leads to sparse gradient updates. Sparse updates are ideally suited for massively parallelizable asynchronous training [23]. We demonstrate that this sparsity opens room for truly asynchronous training without any compromise with accuracy. As a result, we obtain near-linear speedup when increasing number of cores.
(5) The code for training and running our randomized-hashing approach is available online [1]

2 RELATED WORK

There have been several recent advances aimed at improving the performance of neural networks. Courbariaux et al. [4], Lin et al. [17] reduced the number of floating point multiplications by mapping the network's weights stochastically to {-1, 0, 1} during forward propagation. Reducing the precision of the weights and activations is an orthogonal approach. In addition, binary quantization only gives a constant factor of improvement, while our approach is sub-linear in the size of the network. Therefore, the improvements will be significantly more for larger networks.

Sindhwani et al. [28] uses structured matrix transformations with low-rank matrices to reduce the number of parameters for the fully-connected layers of a neural network. This low-rank constraint leads to a smaller memory footprint. However, such an approximation is not well suited for asynchronous, parallel training, limiting its scalability. We instead use random but sparse activations that are easily parallelized by leveraging advances in approximate query processing. (See Section 6.2 for details)

We briefly review Dropout and its variants, which are popular sparsity promoting techniques for neural networks. Although such randomized, sparse activations improve the generalization of neural networks, to the best of our knowledge, this sparsity has not been adequately exploited to make deep networks computationally cheap and parallelizable. We provide first such evidence.

Dropout [30] is primarily a regularization technique that addresses the issue of over-fitting by randomly dropping half of the nodes in a hidden layer while training the network. The nodes are independently sampled for every mini-batch of training data [30]. We reinterpret Dropout as a technique for reducing the number of multiplications during forward and back-propagation phases, by ignoring nodes randomly in the network. It is known that the

[1] https://github.com/rdspring1/LSH_DeepLearning

network's performance becomes worse when too many nodes are dropped from the network. Usually, only 50% of the nodes in the network are dropped when training the network. At test time, the network takes the average of the thinned networks to form a prediction from the input data, which involves computing the activations for all of the nodes in the network.

Adaptive dropout [2] is an enhancement to the dropout technique that adaptively chooses the nodes based on their activations. The methodology samples a small subset of nodes from the network, where the sampling is in proportion to the node activations. Adaptive dropouts demonstrate better performance than vanilla dropout [30]. A notable feature of Adaptive Dropout is that you can drop significantly more nodes than the standard Dropout technique while still retaining superior performance.

Winner-Take-All [20, 21] is an extreme form of Adaptive Dropouts that uses mini-batch statistics to enforce a sparsity constraint. With this technique, only the k% largest, non-zero activations are used during the forward and back-propagation phases of training. This approach requires computing the forward propagation step before selecting the k% nodes with a hard threshold. Unfortunately, all of these techniques require full computation of the activations to sample nodes selectively. Therefore, they are only intended for better generalization and not for reducing computational cost. Our approach uses the insight that selecting a very sparse set of hidden nodes with the highest activations can be reformulated as dynamic approximate query processing problem, which can solve efficiently using locality sensitive hashing. The differentiating factor between our approach and the two other algorithms, Adaptive Dropout and Winner-Take-All (WTA), is that we use sub-linear time, randomized hashing to determine the active set of nodes instead computing the activation for each node individually.

There is also another orthogonal line of work which uses universal hashing to reduce the network's memory footprint [3]. Unlike our objective, theirs was to reduce the number of parameters in a neural network by using a hash function to tie virtual weights together to the same real weight. The HashedNet architecture is more computational expensive than the standard neural network because it incurs an additional overhead when either rebuilding the weight matrix or looking up the value of corresponding weight. Hashed nets are complementary to our approach because we focus on reducing the computational cost of neural networks rather than its memory size.

3 BACKGROUND

3.1 Locality-Sensitive Hashing (LSH)

Locality-Sensitive Hashing (LSH) [6, 7, 10] is a popular, sub-linear time algorithm for approximate nearest-neighbor search. The main idea is to place similar items into the same bucket of a hash table with high probability. An LSH hash function maps an input data vector to an integer key - $h(x) : \mathbb{R}^D \mapsto [0, 1, 2, \ldots, N]$. A collision occurs when the hash values for two elements are equal - $h(x) = h(y)$. The collision probability for an LSH hash function is proportional to the similarity metric between the two elements - $Pr[h(x) = h(y)] \propto sim(x, y)$. Essentially, similar items are more likely to collide with each other under the same hash function.

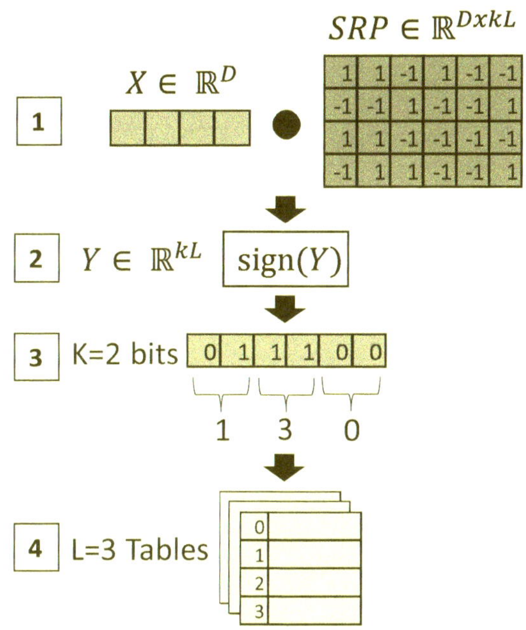

Figure 1: Locality Sensitive Hashing: (1) Compute the projection using a signed, random matrix $\mathcal{R}^{D \times kL}$ and the item $x \in \mathcal{R}^D$. (2) Generate a bit from the sign of each entry in the projection $\mathcal{R}^{kL}$ (3) From the kL bits, we create L integer fingerprints with k bits per fingerprint. (4) Add the item x into each hash table using the corresponding integer key

Sub-linear Time Search using (K, L) LSH Algorithm. To be able to answer approximate nearest-neighbor queries in sub-linear time, the idea is to create hash tables that have constant-time insert and search operations (See Figure 1). Given the collection C, which we are interested in querying for the set of nearest-neighbors, the hash tables are generated using some locality sensitive hash (LSH) family. We assume that we have access to the appropriate locality sensitive hash (LSH) family $\mathcal{F}$ for the given similarity metric.

The classic LSH algorithm uses two parameters - (K, L) to improve the precision and recall of nearest-neighbors for a collection C. Each hash table has a meta-hash function H that is formed by concatenating K random hash functions from $\mathcal{F}$. Now, under the meta-hash function H, all of the K independent hash function values must match in order for two items to have the same fingerprint. $[H(x) = H(y)] \iff [h_i(x) = h_i(y)]$ for all $[i = 0, 1, 2, \ldots, K]$. L hash tables are constructed from the collection C. Given a query, we collect one buckets from each hash table and return the union of L buckets. Intuitively, the meta-hash function reduces the amount of false positives because valid nearest-neighbor items are more likely to match all K hash values for a given query. The union of the L buckets decreases the number of false negatives by increasing the number of potential buckets that could hold valid nearest-neighbor items. The probability that at least one of the L meta-hash fingerprints match and the two items form a candidate pair [15] is

$$Pr[H(x) = H(y)] = 1 - (1 - p^k)^L$$

The overall algorithm works in two phases:

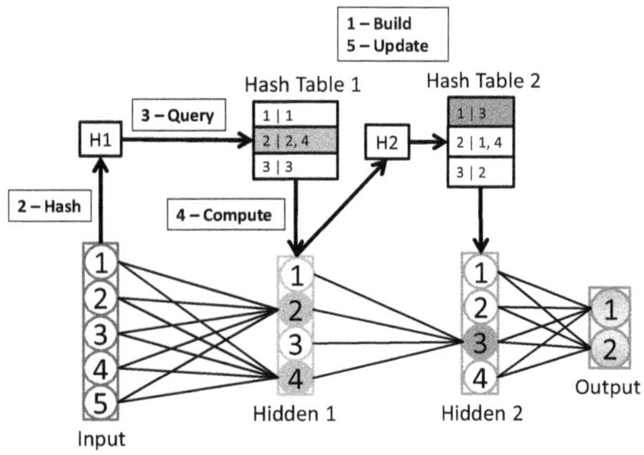

Figure 2: A visual representation of a neural network using randomized hashing: (1) Build the hash tables by hashing the weights of each hidden layer (Pre-processing operation) (2) Hash the layer's input (3) Query the layer's hash table(s) for the active set *AS* (4) Only perform forward and back-propagation on the neurons in the active set. The solid-colored neurons in the hidden layer are the active neurons. (5) Update the *AS* weights via gradient descent and the hash tables by rehashing the updated *AS* weights.

(1) **Pre-processing Phase:** We construct L hash tables from the data by storing all elements $x \in C$. (See Figure 2 for an illustration) We only store pointers to the vector in the hash tables because storing whole data vectors is very memory inefficient.
(2) **Query Phase:** Given a query q, we will search for its nearest-neighbors. We report the union from all of the buckets collected from the L hash tables. Note, we do not scan all of the elements in C, we only probe L different buckets, one bucket per hash table. **Note:** For nearest-neighbor search, we need to filter these candidates further. However, our algorithm does not require such filtering, because we want to perform adaptive sampling and not exact nearest-neighbor search. (explained in section 6.1)

Multi-Probe LSH. One common complaint with the classical LSH algorithm is that it requires a significant number of hash tables. Large L increases the processing time and memory cost. A simple solution is to probe multiple "close-by" buckets in each hash table rather than probing only one bucket [19]. Thus, for a given query q, in addition to probing bucket $H_j(q)$ in hash table $j \in L$, we also generate several new addresses to probe by slightly perturbing values of $H_j(q)$. This simple idea significantly reduces the number of tables needed with LSH, allowing us to work with only a few hash tables. (See Lv et al. [19] for more details)

4 PROPOSED METHODOLOGY

4.1 Intuition

The Winner-Take-All [20, 21] technique shows that we should only consider a few nodes with large activations (top k%) and to ignore the rest while computing the feed-forward pass. Furthermore, the back-propagation updates should only be performed on those top k% nodes. Let n denote the total number of nodes in the neural network. Let *AS* (Active Set) define the subset of top k% nodes with significant activations where $|AS| \ll n$. For each gradient update, Winner-Take-All needs to first perform $O(n \log n)$ work to sort the activations to find the *AS*, and then to update the $O(AS)$ weights. $O(n \log n)$ seems quite wasteful. In particular, finding the active set *AS* is a search problem that can be solved well using smart data structures. Furthermore, if the data structure is dynamic and efficient, then the gradient updates will also be efficient.

For a node i with weight w_i and input x, its activation is a monotonic function of the inner product $w_i^T \cdot x$. Thus, selecting the active set *AS* is equivalent to searching through a collection of weight vectors for the ones that have large inner products with the input x. Equivalently, from a query processing perspective, if we treat the input x as a query, then the search problem of selecting top k% nodes can be solved in sub-linear time using the recent advances in maximum inner product search (MIPS) [25]. Our proposal is to create hash tables with indexes generated by asymmetric locality sensitive hash functions tailored for inner products. With such hash tables, we can very efficiently approximate the active set *AS* for a given query input x.

One last implementation challenge is how to update the nodes (weights associated with them) in the *AS*, during the gradient update. If we can perform these updates in $O(AS)$ instead of $O(n)$, then we save a significant amount of computation. Therefore, we need a data structure where updates are also efficient. We describe our the details of our system in Section 4.2.

4.2 Hashing-Based Back-Propagation

We use randomized hash functions to build hash tables from the nodes in each hidden layer. We sample nodes from the hash table with probability proportional to the node's activation in sub-linear time. We then perform forward and back propagation only on the active nodes retrieved from the hash tables. We later update the hash tables to reorganize only the modified weights.

Figure 2 illustrates an example neural network with two hidden layers, five input nodes, and two output nodes. Hash tables are built for each hidden layer, where the weighted connections for each node are hashed to place the node in its corresponding bucket. Creating hash tables to store all the initial parameters is a one-time operation which requires cost linear in the number of parameters.

During a forward propagation pass, the input to the hidden layer is hashed with the same hash function used to build the hidden layer's hash table. The input's fingerprint is used to collect the active set *AS* nodes from the hash table. The hash table only contains pointers to the nodes in the hidden layer. Then, forward propagation is performed only on the nodes in the active set *AS*.

Note: As argued, unlike exact nearest-neighbor search, we report everything retrieved from buckets as the active set *AS*, without any filtration of the candidates. Our randomized hashing approach

Algorithm 1 Deep Learning with Randomized Hashing

```
// HF_l - Layer l Hash Function
// HT_l - Layer l Hash Tables
// AS_l - Layer l Active Set
// θ^l_AS ∈ W^l_AS, b^l_AS - Layer l Active Set parameters
Randomly initialize parameters W^l, b^l for each layer l
HF_l = constructHashFunction(k, L)
HT_l = constructHashTable(W^l, HF_l)
while not stopping criteria do
  for each training epoch do
    // Forward Propagation
    for layer l = 1 ... N do
      fingerprint_l = HF_l(a_l)
      AS_l = collectActiveSet(HT_l, fingerprint_l)
      for each node i in AS_l do
        a_i^{l+1} = f(W_i^l a_i^l + b_i^l)
      end for
    end for
    // Backpropagation
    for layer l = 1 ... N do
      ΔJ(θ^l_AS) = computeGradient(θ^l_AS, AS_l)
      θ^l_AS = updateParameters(θ^l_AS, ΔJ(θ_AS))
    end for
    for each Layer l -> updateHashTables(HF_l, HT_l, θ^l)
  end for
end while
```

adaptively samples [29] from all of the candidates. (See Section 6.1 for the sampling view of our algorithms)

The rest of the hidden layer's nodes, which are not part of the active set, are ignored and automatically switched off. On the back-propagation pass, the active set is reused to determine the gradient and to update the parameters. We rehash the nodes in each hidden layer to account for the changes in the network during training.

In detail, the hash function for each hidden layer is composed of K randomized hash functions. We use the sign of an asymmetrically transformed random projection to generate the K bits for each data vector. (See Shrivastava and Li [27] for details) The K bits are stored together efficiently as an integer, forming a fingerprint for the data vector. We create a hash table of 2^K buckets, but we only keep the nonempty buckets to minimize the memory footprint (analogous to hash-maps in Java). Each bucket stores pointers to the nodes whose fingerprints match the bucket's id instead of the node itself. In figure 2, we showed only one hash table, which is likely to miss valuable nodes in practice. In our implementation, we generate L hash tables for each hidden layer, and each hash table has an independent set of K random projections. Our final active set from these L hash tables is the union of the buckets selected from each hash table. For each layer, we have L hash tables. Effectively, we have two tunable parameters, K bits and L tables to control the size and the quality of the active sets. The K bits increase the precision of the fingerprint, meaning the nodes in a bucket are more likely to generate higher activation values for a given input. The L tables increase the probability of finding useful nodes that are missed because of the randomness in the hash functions.

Efficient Query and Updates: Our algorithm critically depends on the efficiency of the query and update procedure. The hash table is one of the most efficient data structures, so this is not a difficult challenge. We only store references to the weight vectors, which makes the hash table a very light entity. Furthermore, we reduce the number of hash tables L by using Multi-Probe LSH [19]. A large number of tables L increases the hashing time and memory cost. A simple solution is to probe multiple "nearby" buckets in every hash table rather than probing only a single bucket. Multi-Probe LSH for a binary hash function is quite straightforward. We just have to randomly flip a few bits of the meta-hash fingerprint to generate more addresses.

The gradient update to a weight vector associated with a node may change its location in the hash table. Updating the node's location only requires one insertion and one deletion in the respective buckets. There are plenty of data structures available for representing the buckets that have efficient insert and delete operations. In theory, we can use a red-black-tree to ensure both insertion and deletion cost is logarithmic in the size of the bucket. However, in our implementation, the buckets are represented by simple arrays because they are easy to parallelize, and the buckets are relatively sparse. Arrays have constant-time $O(1)$ insertion and linear-time $O(b)$ deletion, where b is the size of buckets.

Overall Cost: For each layer, during every Stochastic Gradient Descent (SGD) update, we compute $K \times L$ hashes of the input data, probe several buckets per hash table, and then take their union. In our experiments, we use $K = 6$ and $L = 5$ – only 30 hash computations per data point. There are many other techniques to further reduce this hashing cost [1, 16, 24, 26]. The process gives us the active set AS of nodes, which is significantly smaller than the total number of nodes n. During SGD, we update all of the nodes in the AS and then rebuild the hash tables. Overall, the cost is on the order of the number of nodes in the active set AS. For 1000 nodes per layer and an AS containing only 5% of the layer's nodes, we only have to update around 50 nodes. The primary bottleneck is calculating the activation for each node in the AS. The performance benefits will be even more significant for larger neural networks.

Bonus: Sparse Updates can be Parallelized: As mentioned, we only need to update the set of weights associated with nodes in the active set AS. If each AS is very sparse, then it is unlikely that a group of active sets will significantly overlap. Small overlaps imply fewer conflicts while updating the parameters. Fewer conflicts while updating is an ideal ground where SGD updates can be parallelized without any overhead. In fact, it was shown both theoretically and experimentally that random, sparse SGD updates can be parallelized without compromising with the convergence [23]. Vanilla SGD is a sequential operation, and parallel updates lead to poor convergence, due to significant overwrites among the gradient updates. Our experimental results, in Section 5.3, support this known phenomenon. Exploiting this unique property, we show near-linear scaling without hurting convergence using our algorithm, while increasing the number of concurrently running models.

5 EVALUATIONS

We design experiments to answer the following six important questions:

(1) How much can we reduce computation without affecting the neural network's accuracy?
(2) How effective is adaptive sampling compared to a random sampling of nodes?
(3) How does the accuracy of our approximate hashing-based approach compare with the expensive, exact approaches of adaptive dropouts [2] and Winner-Takes-all [20, 21]?
(4) How is the network's convergence effected by increasing number of cores when using asynchronous SGD?
(5) Is the sparse gradient update necessary? Is there any deterioration in performance, if we perform standard, dense updates in parallel?
(6) How much does the walk-clock time decrease, as a function of increasing number of cores?

For evaluation, we implemented the following five approaches to compare and contrast against our approach.

- Standard (NN) : A full-connected neural network
- Dropout (VD) [30]: A neural network that disables the nodes of a hidden layer using a fixed probability threshold
- Adaptive Dropout (AD) [2]: A neural network that disables the nodes of a hidden layer using a probability threshold based on the inner product of the node's weights and the input.
- Winner Take All (WTA) [20, 21]: A neural network that sorts the activations of a hidden layer and selects the k% largest activations
- Randomized Hashing (LSH): A neural network that selects nodes using randomized hashing. A hard threshold limits the active node set to k% sparsity

Dataset	Train Size	Test Size
MNIST8M	8,100,000	10,000
NORB	24,300	24,300
Convex	8,000	50,000
Rectangles	12,000	50,000

Figure 3: Dataset - Training + Test Size

5.1 Datasets

To test our neural network implementation, we used four publicly available datasets - MNIST8M [18], NORB [14], CONVEX, and RECTANGLES [13]. The statistics of these datasets are summarized in Table 3. The MNIST8M, CONVEX, and RECTANGLES datasets contain 28×28 images, forming 784-dimensional feature vectors. The MNIST8M task is to classify each handwritten digit in the image correctly. It is derived by applying random deformations and translations to the MNIST dataset. The CONVEX dataset objective is to identify if a single convex region exists in the image. The goal for the RECTANGLES dataset is to discriminate between tall and wide rectangles overlaid on a black and white background image. The NORB dataset [14] contains images of 50 toys, belonging to 5 categories under various lighting conditions and camera angles.

5.2 Sustainability

5.2.1 Experimental Setting. All of the experiments for our approach and the other techniques were run on a 6-core Intel i7-3930K machine with 16 GB of memory. Our approach uses stochastic gradient descent with Momentum and Adagrad [5]. Since our approach uniquely selects an active set of nodes for each hidden layer, we focused on a CPU-based approach to simplify combining randomized hashing with neural networks. The ReLU activation function was used for all methods. The learning rate for each approach ranged between 10^{-2} and 10^{-4}. The parameters for the randomized hash tables were K = 6 bits and L = 5 tables with multi-probe LSH [19]. For the experiments, we use a fixed threshold to cap the number of active nodes selected from the hash tables to guarantee the amount of computation is within a certain level.

5.2.2 Effect of computation levels. Figures 4, 5 show the accuracy of each method on neural networks with 2 and 3 hidden layers with the percentage of active nodes ranging from [0.05, 0.10, 0.25, 0.5, 0.75, 0.9]. The standard neural network is our baseline in these experiments and is marked with a dashed black line. Each hidden layer contains 1000 nodes. The x-axis represents the average percentage of active nodes per epoch selected by each technique. Our approach only performs the forward and back propagation steps on the nodes selected in each hidden layer. The other baseline techniques except for Dropout (VD) perform the forward propagation step for all of the nodes first, before setting node activations to zero based on the corresponding algorithm. Therefore, Dropout (VD) and our proposal (LSH) require fewer multiplications than the standard neural network training procedure.

Figures 4 and 5 summarizes the accuracy of different approaches at various computations levels.

- Our method (LSH) gives the best overall accuracy with the fewest number of active nodes. The fact that our approximate method is even slightly better than WTA and adaptive dropouts is not surprising, as it is long known that a small amount of random noise leads to better generalization. (See Srivastava et al. [30] for examples)
- As the number of active nodes decreases from 90% to 5%, LSH experiences the smallest drop in performance and less performance volatility.
- VD experiences the greatest drop in performance when reducing the number of active nodes from 50% to 5%.
- WTA performed better than VD when the percentage of active nodes is less than 50%
- As the number of active nodes approaches 100%, the performance stabilizes for each method.

Lowering the computational cost of running neural networks and running fewer operations reduces the energy consumption and heat produced by the processor. However, large neural networks provide better accuracy and arbitrarily reducing the number of active nodes hurts performance. Our experiments show that our method (LSH) provides the best of both worlds - high performance and low processor computation. This approach is ideal for mobile phones because reducing the processor's load directly translates into longer battery life.

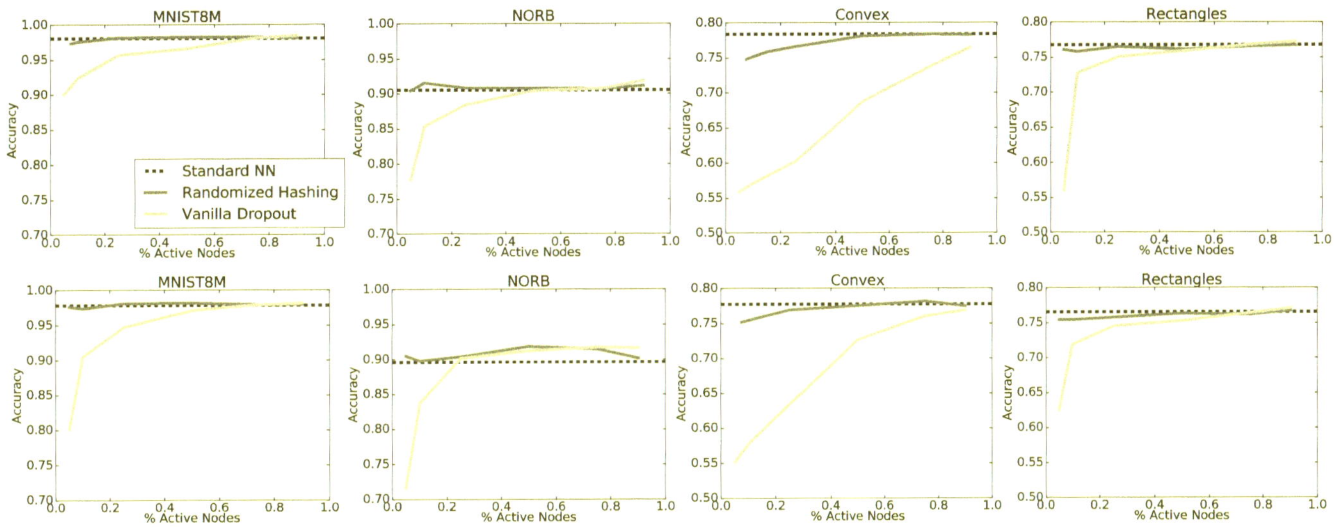

Figure 4: Classification accuracy under different levels of active nodes with networks on the MNIST (1st), NORB (2nd), Convex (3rd) and Rectangles (4th) datasets. The standard neural network (dashed black line) is our baseline accuracy. We can clearly see that adaptive sampling with hashing (LSH) is significantly more effective than random sampling (VD). Top Panels: 2 hidden Layers. Bottom Panels: 3 hidden Layers

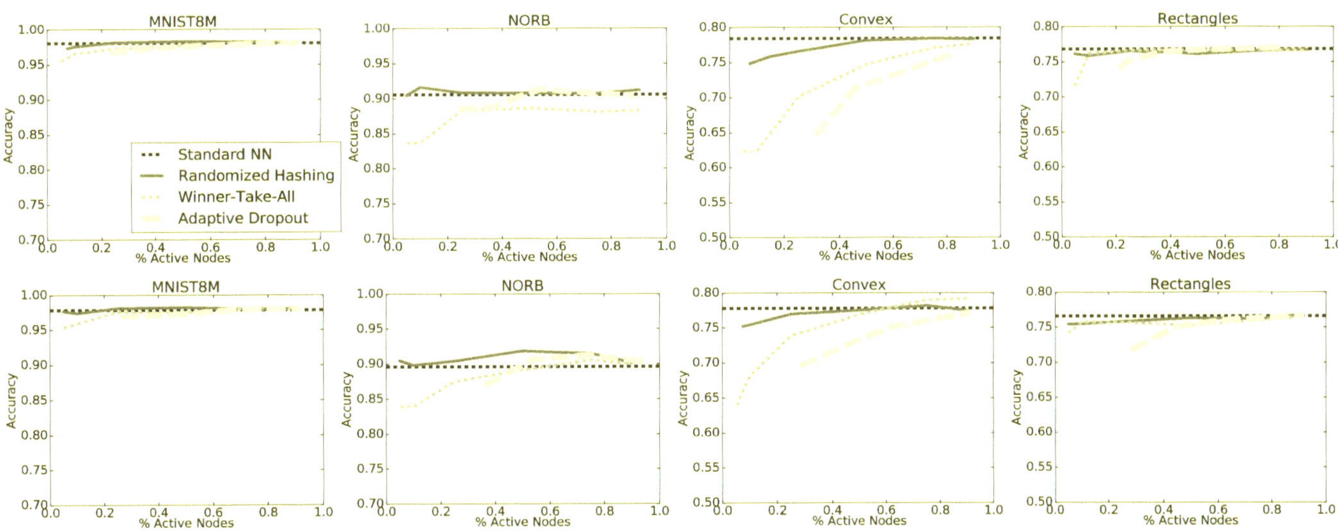

Figure 5: Classification accuracy under different levels of active nodes with networks on the MNIST (1st), NORB (2nd), Convex (3rd) and Rectangles (4th) datasets. The standard neural network (dashed black line) is our baseline accuracy. WTA and AD (dashed red and yellow lines) perform the same amount of computation as the standard neural network. Those two techniques select nodes with high activation values to achieve better accuracy, but they require computing the activation for every node in the hidden layer. We compare our LSH approach to determine whether our randomized algorithm achieves comparable performance, while reducing the total amount of computation. We do not have data for adaptive dropout at the 5% and 10% computation levels because those models diverged when the number of active nodes dropped below 25%. Top Panels: 2 hidden Layers. Bottom Panels: 3 hidden Layers

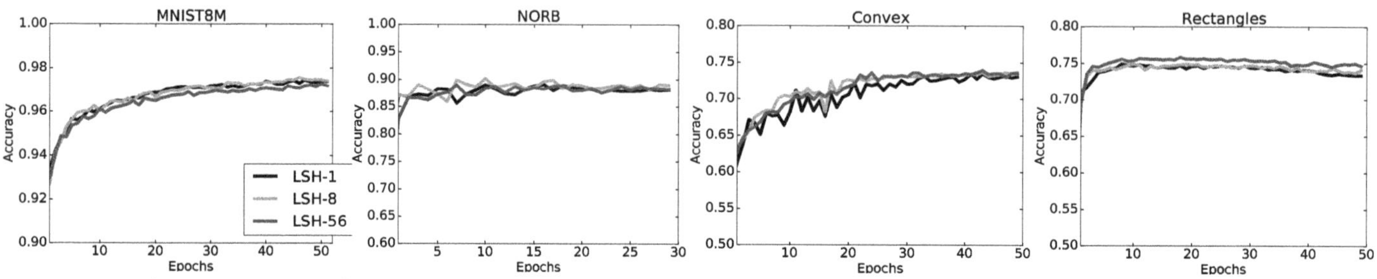

Figure 6: The convergence of our randomized hashing approach (LSH-5%) over several training epochs using asynchronous stochastic gradient (ASGD) with 1, 8, 56 cores. We used a (3 hidden layer) network on the MNIST (1st), NORB (2nd), Convex (3rd) and Rectangles (4th) datasets. Only 5% of the standard network's computation was performed in this experiment. ASGD has no effect on convergence with the sparse, random gradient updates.

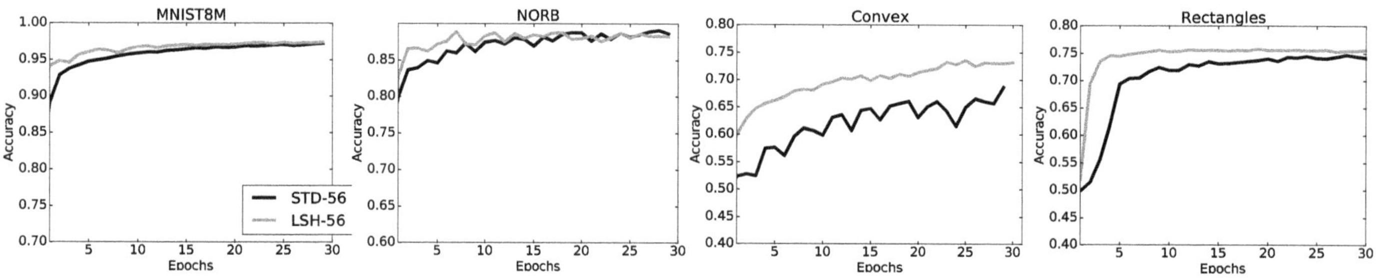

Figure 7: Performance comparison between our randomized hashing approach and a standard network using asynchronous stochastic gradient descent (ASGD) on an Intel Xeon ES-2697 machine with 56-cores. We used (3 hidden layer) networks on MNIST (1st), NORB (2nd), Convex (3rd) and Rectangles (4th). All networks were initialized with the same settings for this experiment. We see that parallelizing the non-sparse gradient updates leads to poor convergence.

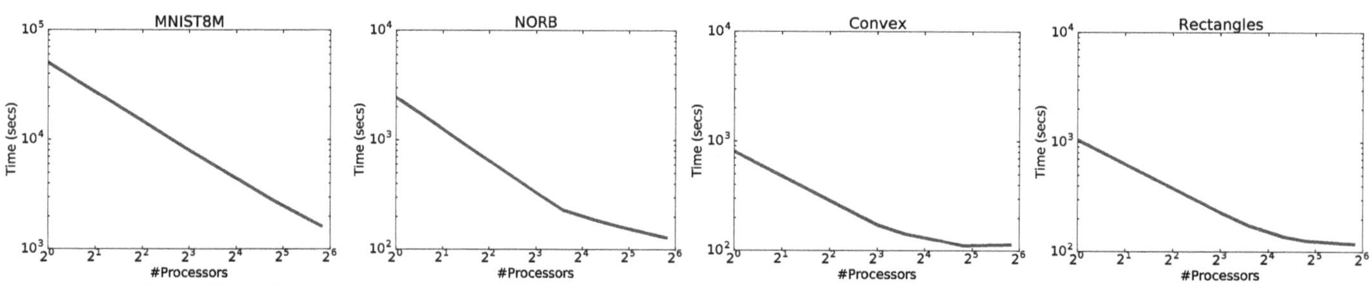

Figure 8: The wall-clock per epoch for our approach (LSH-5%) gained by using asynchronous stochastic gradient descent. We used a (3 hidden layer) network on the MNIST (1st), NORB (2nd), Convex (3rd) and Rectangles (4th). We see smaller performance gains with the Convex and Rectangles datasets because there are not enough training examples to use of all of the cores effectively. Only 5% of the standard network's computation was performed in this experiment.

5.3 Scalability

5.3.1 Experimental Setting. We now show experiments to demonstrate the scalability of our approach to large-scale, distributed computing environments. Specifically, we are testing if our approach maintains accuracy and improves training time, as we increase the number of cores. We use asynchronous stochastic gradient descent with momentum and adagrad [5, 23]. Our implementation utilizes data parallelism by running the same model on multiple training examples concurrently. The gradient is applied without synchronization to maximize performance. We run all of the experiments on an Intel Xeon ES-2697 machine with 56 cores and 256 GB of memory. The ReLU activation was used for all models, and the learning rate ranged between 10^{-2} and 10^{-3}.

5.3.2 Results with different number of cores. Figure 6 shows how our method performs with asynchronous stochastic gradient descent (ASGD) using only 5% of the neurons of a full-sized neural network. The neural network has three hidden layers, and each hidden layer contains 1000 neurons. The x-axis represents the number of epochs completed, and the y-axis shows the test accuracy for the given epoch. We compare how our model converges with multiple cores working concurrently. Since our ASGD implementation does not use locks, it depends on the sparsity of the gradient to ensure the model converges and performs well [23]. From our experiments, we see that our method converges at a similar rate and obtains the same accuracy regardless of the number of cores running ASGD.

Figure 8 illustrates how our method scales with multiple cores. The inherent sparsity of our randomized hashing approach reduces the number of simultaneous updates and allows for more asynchronous models without any performance penalty. We show the corresponding drop in wall-clock computation time per epoch while adding more cores. We achieve roughly a 31x speed up while running ASGD with 56 cores.

5.3.3 ASGD Performance Comparison with Standard Neural Network. Figure 7 compares the performance of our LSH approach against a standard neural network (STD) when running ASGD with 56-cores. We clearly out-perform the standard network for all of our experimental datasets. However, since there is a large number of models running concurrently, their gradients are constantly being overridden, preventing ASGD from converging to an optimal local minimum. Our approach produces a spare gradient that reduces the number of conflicts between the different models, while keeping enough valuable gradients for ASGD to progress towards the local minimum efficiently.

From Figures 6, 7 and 8, we conclude the following:

(1) The gradient updates are quite sparse with 5% LSH and running them in parallel does not affect the convergence rate of our hashing-based approach. Even when running 56 cores in parallel, the convergence is indistinguishable from the sequential update (1 core) on all the four datasets.
(2) If we instead run vanilla SGD in parallel, then the convergence is affected. The convergence is in general slower compared the sparse 5% LSH. This slow convergence is due to dense updates which leads to overwrites. Parallelizing dense updates affects the four datasets differently. For convex dataset, the convergence is very poor.
(3) As expected, we obtain near-perfect decrease in the wall clock times with increasing the number of cores with LSH-5%. Note, if there are too many overwrites, then atomic overwrites are necessary, which will create additional overhead and hurt the parallelism. Thus, the near-perfect scalability also indicates fewer gradient overwrites.
(4) On the largest dataset - MNIST8M, the running time per epoch for the 1-core implementation is 50,254 seconds. The 56-core implementation runs in 1,637 seconds. Since the convergence is not affected, there is a 31x speedup in the training process while using 56 cores.
(5) We see that the performance gains from data parallelism become flat with the Convex and Rectangle datasets, especially while using a large number of cores. This poor scaling occurs because the two datasets have fewer training examples than MNIST8M or NORB, so there is less parallel work for a large number of cores. We do not see such behaviors with MNIST8M which has around 8 million training examples.

6 DISCUSSIONS

Machine learning with a huge parameter space is becoming a common phenomenon. Stochastic Gradient Descent (SGD) remains the most popular optimization algorithm due to its effectiveness and simplicity. Each SGD update is expected to alter only a small subset of the parameters significantly. Identifying that subset of parameters is a search problem. We can exploit the rich literature in approximate query processing to find this active set of parameters efficiently. Of course, the approximate active set contains a small amount of random noise, which is often good for generalization. Sparsity and randomness enhance data parallelism because the gradient updates are unlikely to overwrite each other. In conclusion, we are reformulating the machine learning problem into an approximate query processing problem, and then leveraging the decades of research from the systems and database communities. We have demonstrated one concrete example, by showing how neural networks can be scaled-up using randomized hashing. We believe that the combination of sparsity with approximate query processing is the future of large-scale machine learning.

6.1 Equivalence with Adaptive Dropouts

From a statistical perspective, Asymmetric Locality-Sensitive Hashing (ALSH) [25] for finding nodes with large inner products is equivalent to Adaptive Dropout [2] with a non-trivial sampling distribution.

The Adaptive Dropout technique uses the Bernoulli distribution to sample nodes with large activation. In theory, any distribution assigning probabilities in proportion to the node's activation is sufficient. We argue that the Bernoulli distribution is sub-optimal. There is another non-intuitive, but a very efficient distribution. This distribution comes from the theory of Locality-Sensitive Hashing (LSH) [11], which is primarily considered a black-box technique for fast sub-linear search. Our core idea comes from the observation that, for a given search query q, the LSH algorithm inherently samples, in sub-linear time, points from a distribution with probability proportional to $1 - (1 - p^K)^L$ [29]. Here, the collision probability p is a monotonic function of the similarity between the query and the retrieved point.

Theorem 6.1. **Hashing-Based Efficient Sampling** - *For a given input x to any layer of the neural network, any (K, L) parameterized LSH algorithm selects a node i, associated with weight vector w_i, with probability proportional to $1 - (1 - p^K)^L$. Here, the collision probability of the associated locality-sensitive hash function is $p = Pr[h(x) = h(w_i)]$. Thus, the sampling probability $1 - (1 - p^K)^L$ is monotonic with respect to p.*

6.2 Low-Rank vs Sparsity

The low-rank (or structured) assumption is very convenient for reducing the complexity of general matrix operations. However, low-rank, dense updates do not promote sparsity and are not friendly for distributed computing. The same principle holds with deep networks. We illustrate it with a simple example.

Consider a layer of the first network (left) shown in Figure 9. The insight is that if the weight matrix $W \in \mathbb{R}^{mxn}$ for a hidden layer has low-rank structure where rank $r \ll min(m, n)$, then it has a representation $W = UV$ where $U \in \mathbb{R}^{mxr}$ and $V \in \mathbb{R}^{rxn}$. This low-rank structure improves the storage requirements and matrix-multiplication time from $O(mn)$ to $O(mr + rn)$. As shown in Figure 9, there is an equivalent representation of the same network using an intermediate hidden layer that contains r nodes and uses the identity activation function. The weight matrices for the hidden layers in the second network (right) map to the matrix decomposition, U and V.

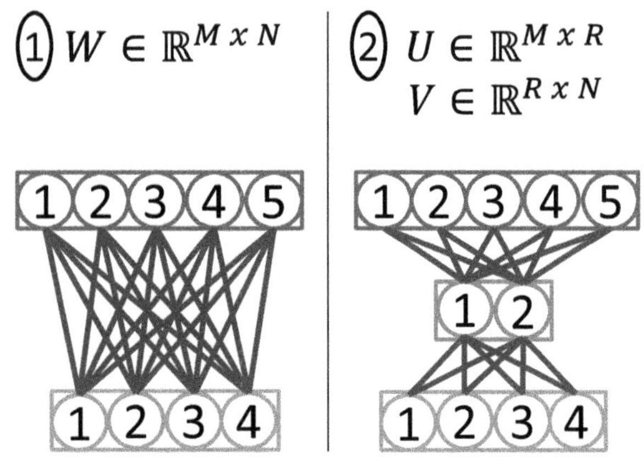

Figure 9: (1) The single-layer network is characterized by the weight matrix $W \in R^{M \times N}$ of constrained rank R such that $W = UV$ with $U \in \mathbb{R}^{M \times R}$ and $V \in \mathbb{R}^{R \times N}$. (2) An equivalent network contains two layers, represented by the matrices, U and V. The first layer uses the identity activation function I. (3) Both networks produce the same output. $a = f(W^T x) = f((UV)^T x) = f((V^T U^T)x) = f(V^T I(U^T x))$

Sindhwani et al. [28] uses structured matrix transformations with low-rank matrices to reduce the number of parameters for the fully-connected layers of a neural network. The low-rank, structured matrices require dense gradient updates, which is not ideally suited for data parallelism [23]. In this work, we move away from the low-rank assumption. Instead, we make use of sparsity to reduce the amount of computation. We showed that due to random sparsity, our approach is well-suited for Asynchronous Stochastic Gradient Descent (ASGD), leading to near-linear scaling.

7 FUTURE WORK

One future direction is to optimize our approach for low-power, mobile processors. There are many platforms including the Nvidia Tegra, Qualcomm Snapdragon, and Movidius Myriad. The other direction is to leverage the power of GPUs and distributed computing. GPUs are commonly used to train deep networks because of their high performance. The next logical step is to harness the computational savings via randomized hashing on GPUs.

8 ACKNOWLEDGMENTS

The work was supported by NSF Awards IIS-1652131 and DMS-1547433. We would like to thank reviewers of ICML 2016, NIPS 2016 and KDD 2017 for their encouraging remarks and suggestions.

REFERENCES

[1] Dimitris Achlioptas. 2003. Database-friendly Random Projections: Johnson-Lindenstrauss with Binary Coins. *J. Comput. Syst. Sci.* 66, 4 (June 2003), 671–687. https://doi.org/10.1016/S0022-0000(03)00025-4

[2] Jimmy Ba and Brendan Frey. 2013. Adaptive dropout for training deep neural networks. In *Advances in Neural Information Processing Systems 26.* 3084–3092.

[3] Wenlin Chen, James Wilson, Stephen Tyree, Kilian Weinberger, and Yixin Chen. 2015. Compressing Neural Networks with the Hashing Trick. In *Proceedings of the 32nd International Conference on Machine Learning.* 2285–2294.

[4] Matthieu Courbariaux, Itay Hubara, Daniel Soudry, Ran El-Yaniv, and Yoshua Bengio. 2016. Binarized neural networks: Training deep neural networks with weights and activations constrained to +1 or-1. *arXiv preprint arXiv:1602.02830* (2016).

[5] Jeffrey Dean, Greg Corrado, Rajat Monga, Kai Chen, Matthieu Devin, Mark Mao, Andrew Senior, Paul Tucker, Ke Yang, Quoc V Le, et al. 2012. Large scale distributed deep networks. In *Advances in Neural Information Processing Systems.* 1223–1231.

[6] Jinyang Gao, Hosagrahar Visvesvaraya Jagadish, Wei Lu, and Beng Chin Ooi. 2014. DSH: data sensitive hashing for high-dimensional KNN search. In *Proceedings of the 2014 ACM SIGMOD.* ACM, 1127–1138.

[7] Aristides Gionis, Piotr Indyk, Rajeev Motwani, et al. 1999. Similarity search in high dimensions via hashing. *VLDB* 99, 6 (1999), 518–529.

[8] Kaiming He, Xiangyu Zhang, Shaoqing Ren, and Jian Sun. 2016. Deep Residual Learning for Image Recognition. In *The IEEE Conference on Computer Vision and Pattern Recognition (CVPR).*

[9] Geoffrey Hinton, Li Deng, Dong Yu, George E Dahl, Abdel-rahman Mohamed, Navdeep Jaitly, Andrew Senior, Vincent Vanhoucke, Patrick Nguyen, Tara N Sainath, et al. 2012. Deep neural networks for acoustic modeling in speech recognition: The shared views of four research groups. *Signal Processing Magazine, IEEE* 29, 6 (2012), 82–97.

[10] Qiang Huang, Jianlin Feng, Yikai Zhang, Qiong Fang, and Wilfred Ng. 2015. Query-aware locality-sensitive hashing for approximate nearest neighbor search. *Proceedings of the VLDB Endowment* 9, 1 (2015), 1–12.

[11] Piotr Indyk and Rajeev Motwani. 1998. Approximate Nearest Neighbors: Towards Removing the Curse of Dimensionality. In *STOC.* Dallas, TX, 604–613.

[12] Alex Krizhevsky, Ilya Sutskever, and Geoffrey E Hinton. 2012. Imagenet classification with deep convolutional neural networks. In *Advances in neural information processing systems.* 1097–1105.

[13] Hugo Larochelle, Dumitru Erhan, Aaron Courville, James Bergstra, and Yoshua Bengio. 2007. An empirical evaluation of deep architectures on problems with many factors of variation. In *Proceedings of the 24th international conference on Machine learning.* ACM, 473–480.

[14] Yann LeCun, Fu Jie Huang, and Leon Bottou. 2004. Learning methods for generic object recognition with invariance to pose and lighting. In *Computer Vision and Pattern Recognition, 2004. CVPR 2004. Proceedings of the 2004 IEEE Computer Society Conference on,* Vol. 2. IEEE, II–97.

[15] Jure Leskovec, Anand Rajaraman, and Jeffrey David Ullman. 2014. *Mining of massive datasets.* Cambridge University Press.

[16] Ping Li, Trevor J Hastie, and Kenneth W Church. 2006. Very sparse random projections. In *Proceedings of the 12th ACM SIGKDD international conference on Knowledge discovery and data mining.* ACM, 287–296.

[17] Zhouhan Lin, Matthieu Courbariaux, Roland Memisevic, and Yoshua Bengio. 2015. Neural Networks with Few Multiplications. *arXiv preprint arXiv:1510.03009* (2015).

[18] Gaëlle Loosli, Stéphane Canu, and Léon Bottou. 2007. Training Invariant Support Vector Machines using Selective Sampling. In *Large Scale Kernel Machines,* Léon Bottou, Olivier Chapelle, Dennis DeCoste, and Jason Weston (Eds.). MIT Press, Cambridge, MA., 301–320. http://leon.bottou.org/papers/loosli-canu-bottou-2006

[19] Qin Lv, William Josephson, Zhe Wang, Moses Charikar, and Kai Li. 2007. Multi-probe LSH: efficient indexing for high-dimensional similarity search. In *Proceedings of the 33rd international conference on Very large data bases.* VLDB Endowment, 950–961.

[20] Alireza Makhzani and Brendan Frey. 2013. k-Sparse Autoencoders. *arXiv preprint arXiv:1312.5663* (2013).

[21] Alireza Makhzani and Brendan J Frey. 2015. Winner-Take-All Autoencoders. In *Advances in Neural Information Processing Systems 28.* 2791–2799.

[22] H. Brendan McMahan, Eider Moore, Daniel Ramage, Seth Hampson, and Blaise Aguera y Arcas. 2016. Communication-Efficient Learning of Deep Networks from Decentralized Data. In *Proceedings of the 20th International Conference on Artificial Intelligence and Statistics (AISTATS).* http://arxiv.org/abs/1602.05629

[23] Benjamin Recht, Christopher Re, Stephen Wright, and Feng Niu. 2011. Hogwild: A lock-free approach to parallelizing stochastic gradient descent. In *Advances in Neural Information Processing Systems.* 693–701.

[24] Anshumali Shrivastava. 2016. Simple and Efficient Weighted Minwise Hashing. In *Advances in Neural Information Processing Systems 29.* 1498–1506.

[25] Anshumali Shrivastava and Ping Li. 2014. Asymmetric LSH (ALSH) for sublinear time maximum inner product search (MIPS). In *Advances in Neural Information Processing Systems.* 2321–2329.

[26] Anshumali Shrivastava and Ping Li. 2014. Improved Densification of One Permutation Hashing. In *UAI.* Quebec, CA.

[27] Anshumali Shrivastava and Ping Li. 2015. Improved Asymmetric Locality Sensitive Hashing (ALSH) for Maximum Inner Product Search (MIPS). In *Conference on Uncertainty in Artificial Intelligence (UAI).*

[28] Vikas Sindhwani, Tara Sainath, and Sanjiv Kumar. 2015. Structured transforms for small-footprint deep learning. In *Advances in Neural Information Processing Systems.* 3070–3078.

[29] Ryan Spring and Anshumali Shrivastava. 2017. A New Unbiased and Efficient Class of LSH-Based Samplers and Estimators for Partition Function Computation in Log-Linear Models. *arXiv preprint arXiv:1703.05160* (2017).

[30] Nitish Srivastava, Geoffrey Hinton, Alex Krizhevsky, Ilya Sutskever, and Ruslan Salakhutdinov. 2014. Dropout: A simple way to prevent neural networks from overfitting. *The Journal of Machine Learning Research* 15, 1 (2014), 1929–1958.

AnnexML: Approximate Nearest Neighbor Search for Extreme Multi-label Classification

Yukihiro Tagami
Yahoo Japan Corporation
Department of Intelligence Science and Technology, Kyoto University
yutagami@yahoo-corp.jp

ABSTRACT

Extreme multi-label classification methods have been widely used in Web-scale classification tasks such as Web page tagging and product recommendation. In this paper, we present a novel graph embedding method called "AnnexML". At the training step, AnnexML constructs a k-nearest neighbor graph of label vectors and attempts to reproduce the graph structure in the embedding space. The prediction is efficiently performed by using an approximate nearest neighbor search method that efficiently explores the learned k-nearest neighbor graph in the embedding space. We conducted evaluations on several large-scale real-world data sets and compared our method with recent state-of-the-art methods. Experimental results show that our AnnexML can significantly improve prediction accuracy, especially on data sets that have larger a label space. In addition, AnnexML improves the trade-off between prediction time and accuracy. At the same level of accuracy, the prediction time of AnnexML was up to 58 times faster than that of SLEEC, which is a state-of-the-art embedding-based method.

CCS CONCEPTS

•**Computing methodologies** →**Supervised learning by classification;**

KEYWORDS

Extreme multi-label classification, k-nearest neighbor graph, approximate nearest neighbor search, learning-to-rank.

1 INTRODUCTION

Extreme multi-label classification has recently been receiving much attention. Its objective is to learn a classifier that can automatically annotate a data point with the most relevant subset from an extremely large label set (10^4 to 10^6) [4, 18]. In one example, an extreme multi-label classifier is learned to tag a new Wikipedia article by using a subset of the most relevant Wikipedia categories [17]. In another example, a classifier is built to display a subset of online advertisements to Web users, given the users' Web browsing histories and search keywords.

When a label space is extremely large, a traditional baseline approach that builds a one-versus-rest classifier for each label is computationally expensive [2, 27]. More specifically, this naive approach needs to train an extremely large number of binary classifiers. Thus, some methods of dealing with this problem attempt to reduce the effective number of labels. Some "embedding-based" approaches rely on the low-rank label matrix assumption [15, 26, 30]. This assumption means that there are correlations between labels, so these approaches learn a small number of "latent" factors of labels. Regressors are learned to perform prediction on these "latent" factors of labels with features and project them back onto the original high-dimensional label space. However, this assumption is violated in many real-world data sets because of the number of "tail" labels that only a few data points have [4, 26].

To address this problem, Sparse Local Embeddings for Extreme Classification (SLEEC) [4] was developed. SLEEC is also an embedding-based method, but is free of any low-rank label matrix assumptions. This method first partitions data points by using k-means clustering and then learns a projection matrix (or regressor) for each partition by preserving distances from a relatively small number of nearest neighbors in the label space. In other words, SLEEC reduces the effective number of labels by converting a multi-label classification problem into a set of regression problems by using nearest neighbors in the label space. The number of these regression problems is independent from the number of labels, whereas the above naive one-versus-rest approach needs to train the same number of classifiers as labels. Prediction is performed by using the labels of training points close to the test point in the embedding space. In other words, SLEEC uses a k-nearest neighbor classifier in the embedding space.

However, SLEEC also has three problems. The first problem is learning to partition data. SLEEC partitions training points with k-means clustering before learning embeddings. This means SLEEC only uses feature vectors and does not access label information in this procedure. Therefore, data points that have similar label vectors are not guaranteed to be assigned to the same partition. This partitioning could affect the quality of embeddings learned in subsequent steps. The second is learning embeddings. In the prediction step, SLEEC predicts labels of the test point by using the nearest training points in the embedding space, as described above. Hence, the order of distance plays a crucial role, whereas the values themselves are not very important. Thus, the objective function of SLEEC is somewhat indirect for this purpose. In addition, SLEEC's optimization process for learning regressors is slightly complicated because of sparsity-induced and rank-constraint regularization terms. The third problem is prediction speed. The authors [4] reported that SLEEC made predictions in 8 milliseconds

KDD'17, August 13–17, 2017, Halifax, NS, Canada.

978-1-4503-4887-4/17/08...$15.00
DOI: 10.1145/3097983.3097987

per test point compared with 0.5 milliseconds for the tree-based FastXML [18] on a WikiLSHTC-325K data set, but SLEEC made predictions much more accurately than FastXML. Although this prediction time would be acceptable for most real-world applications, much faster prediction is preferable for scaling up to solve Web-scale classification problems.

In this paper, we present a novel graph embedding method named "AnnexML[1]," which copes with the all three problems in a comprehensive and more direct way based on the k-nearest neighbor graph (KNNG). The key idea of AnnexML is reproducing the KNNG of label vectors in the embedding space to improve both the prediction accuracy and speed of the k-nearest neighbor classifier. The KNNG consists of training points as vertices. A directed edge connects from the i-th vertex to the j-th one if the j-th point is included in the set of the nearest neighbors of the i-th point in a certain metric space.

More specifically, AnnexML tackles the above three problems as follows. For the first problem, AnnexML learns a multiclass classifier, which partitions the approximate KNNG of the label vectors in order to preserve the graph structure as much as possible. Then, for the second problem, AnnexML projects the each divided subgraph into an individual embedding space by formulating this problem as a ranking problem instead of regression one. This objective function is easily optimized with simple stochastic gradient descent. For the third problem, AnnexML efficiently retrieves approximate nearest neighbors of a test point by exploring the learned KNNG in the embedding space. This technique improves the trade-off between prediction time and accuracy.

To summarize, our main contributions are as follows.

- We present a novel method of learning to partition data points by using an approximate KNNG as weak supervision, instead of unsupervised k-means clustering (Section 3.1)
- For learning embeddings, we formulate this problem as a ranking one and optimize the objective function by using simple stochastic gradient descent (Section 3.2)
- For faster prediction, we use an approximate k-nearest neighbor search technique by efficiently traversing the learned KNNG in the embedding space (Section 3.3)
- We conducted experiments on several large-scale real-world data sets and compared our method with recent state-of-the-art methods in terms of prediction accuracy and time (Section 4)

2 PROBLEM FORMULATION

In this paper, we consider a data set $\mathcal{D} = \{(\boldsymbol{x}_i, \boldsymbol{y}_i)\}_{i=1}^N$, which consists of N training points, where $\boldsymbol{x}_i \in \mathcal{X} \subseteq \mathbb{R}^M$ is an M-dimensional feature vector and $\boldsymbol{y}_i \in \mathcal{Y} \subseteq \{0,1\}^L$ is the corresponding L-dimensional label vector. $y_{ij} = 1$ if the i-th sample has the j-th label, and $y_{ij} = 0$ otherwise. Multi-label learning aims to build a classifier, $f : \mathbb{R}^M \to \{0,1\}^L$, that accurately predicts the label vector for a given sample.

In the context of extreme multi-label learning, the number of labels L is large and in the same order as the numbers of training points N and features M (see Table 2 for the statistics of the data sets used in the experiments). For example, a naive approach, which uses the one-versus-rest technique where an independent classifier is learned for each label, needs to train a massive number of binary classifiers. In addition, at the prediction time of this approach, all binary classifiers are applied to each test point. Thus, this naive approach might be computationally expensive in terms of both training and prediction time.

To overcome the above problem, some methods developed for extreme multi-label classification attempt to reduce the effective number of labels. We briefly describe these methods in Section 5.

[1] Approximate Nearest Neighbor Search for EXtreme Multi-Label Classification

Algorithm 1 Overview of training single learner

Require: Training data: $\mathcal{D} = \{(\boldsymbol{x}_i, \boldsymbol{y}_i)\}_{i=1}^N$
Partition $\mathcal{D}$ into K subsets $\mathcal{D}_1, \ldots, \mathcal{D}_K$ ▷ Section 3.1
for each parition c **do**
  Learn projection matrix $\boldsymbol{V}_c$ using $\mathcal{D}_c$ ▷ Section 3.2
  $\boldsymbol{Z}_c \leftarrow \boldsymbol{V}_c \boldsymbol{X}_c$
end for
return $\{(\mathcal{D}_1, \boldsymbol{V}_1, \boldsymbol{Z}_1), \ldots, (\mathcal{D}_K, \boldsymbol{V}_K, \boldsymbol{Z}_K)\}$

Algorithm 2 Overview of prediction with single learner

Require: Test point: $\boldsymbol{x}_t$, number of nearest neighbors: n
$c_t \leftarrow$ partition closest to $\boldsymbol{x}_t$
$\boldsymbol{z}_t \leftarrow \boldsymbol{V}_{c_t} \boldsymbol{x}_t$
$\tilde{\mathcal{N}}_{Z_{c_t}}^{(t)} \leftarrow$ approximate n-nearest neighbors of $\boldsymbol{z}_t$ in $\boldsymbol{Z}_{c_t}$ ▷ Section 3.3
$\hat{\boldsymbol{y}}_t \leftarrow$ empirical label distribution for points in $\tilde{\mathcal{N}}_{Z_{c_t}}^{(t)}$
return $\hat{\boldsymbol{y}}_t$

3 PROPOSED METHOD

In this section, we introduce our proposed method, AnnexML.

Hereafter, we represent an index set of entire training points as $\mathcal{I} = \{1, 2, \ldots, N\}$. Let $\boldsymbol{X} = [\boldsymbol{x}_1; \ldots; \boldsymbol{x}_N] \in \mathbb{R}^{M \times N}$ be the data matrix and $Y = [\boldsymbol{y}_1; \ldots; \boldsymbol{y}_N] \in \mathbb{R}^{L \times N}$ be the label matrix.

First, we describe training and prediction overviews. These high-level overviews are similar to those of SLEEC [4]. However, we stress that AnnexML is a graph embedding method that copes with the three problems of SLEEC in a comprehensive and straightforward way based on KNNG, which consists of training points as vertices.

Algorithm 1 shows an overview of the training procedure. First, AnnexML splits the data points into K partitions and then learns a linear map $\boldsymbol{V}_c \in \mathbb{R}^{d \times M}$ that projects the data points to a low-dimensional subspace for each partition $c \in \{1, \ldots K\}$, instead of a global projection map. The embedding vector $\boldsymbol{z}_i \in \mathbb{R}^d$ is mapped from the feature vector $\boldsymbol{x}_i$ by using $\boldsymbol{V}_c$ for each $i \in \mathcal{I}_c$. Here, $\mathcal{I}_c$ is the index set of data points in the partition c. The data matrix of partition c is denoted as $\boldsymbol{X}_c$. In a similar way, $\boldsymbol{Y}_c$ and $\boldsymbol{Z}_c$ represent the label and embedding matrix, respectively. AnnexML is able to improve its prediction accuracy by learning an ensemble of multiple learners with different random initializations, as described later (Section 3.1).

Algorithm 2 shows an overview of the prediction procedure. AnnexML first determines the partition to which a test point $\boldsymbol{x}_t$

Table 1: Label frequency of training data used in experiments. For example, more than 174,000 labels occur in at most five training points in WikiLSHTC-325K data set.

Frequency	WikiLSHTC-325K		Amazon-670K	
1	79,732	(24.82%)	71,817	(10.76%)
≤ 2	112,788	(35.11%)	309,976	(46.45%)
≤ 3	137,596	(42.84%)	435,442	(65.25%)
≤ 4	157,541	(49.04%)	509,203	(76.31%)
≤ 5	174,341	(54.27%)	555,905	(83.30%)
≤ 10	226,956	(70.65%)	637,379	(95.51%)
All	321,222	(100.00%)	667,317	(100.00%)

belongs, finds approximate k-nearest neighbors (training points) in the low-dimensional subspace corresponding to the partition c_t, and finally predicts labels on the basis of the labels of neighbors. To make predictions with an ensemble of multiple learners, first, all sets of nearest neighbors obtained by learners are aggregated; then, AnnexML outputs an empirical label distribution of points in the aggregated nearest neighbors.

In the following subsections, we give details on the training and prediction procedures. The key point of AnnexML is reproducing the structure of the KNNG of the label vectors as much as possible in the embedding space. In Section 3.1, we represent a novel method of learning to partition data. AnnexML learns a multi-class classifier to divide the KNNG of the label vectors into subgraphs. Then, in Section 3.2, we learn a projection matrix in order to preserve the edge connections of each subgraph in an individual embedding space. Regarding this problem as ranking one, we apply a learning-to-rank technique that uses cosine similarity. Finally, in Section 3.3, we present an approximate nearest neighbor search method that efficiently explores the learned KNNG in the embedding space. Replacing the naive brute-force calculation with this method, AnnexML successfully speeds up the prediction time without a noticeable drop in accuracy.

3.1 Learning to Partition Data Points

AnnexML partitions data points before learning embeddings for efficient training and prediction, like SLEEC does. While SLEEC simply uses k-means clustering for this purpose, AnnexML aims to allocate the data points that have similar label vectors to the same partition. This means that AnnexML utilizes label information $\boldsymbol{y}$ but SLEEC only accesses feature vectors $\boldsymbol{x}$. The label frequency of an extreme multi-label classification data set follows a "heavy tailed" distribution [4, 26]. Table 1 shows the label frequency in the training data of WikiLSHTC-325K and Amazon-670K data sets. About 54% and 83% of the labels occur in at most five training points on each data set. Without label information, the data points that have the same tail label might be allocated to different partitions as the number of partitions increases. Thus, this difference between AnnexML and SLEEC could affect the quality of the embeddings learned in the subsequent steps and the final prediction results.

From the perspective of reproducing the KNNG of the label vectors, AnnexML divides the graph into K subgraphs while keeping the structure as much as possible. Hence, this problem can be regarded as finding the minimum K-way graph cut [1]. However, in contrast with the common minimum K-cut problem, we need to learn a multi-class classifier to predict the partition of an unknown test point. Thus, we use a novel sequential maximization procedure for learning the classifier.

To construct the KNNG of the label vectors, we find the nearest neighbors $\mathcal{N}_Y^{(i)}$ for each i-th data point from the indices of all training points $\mathcal{I}$. The set of nearest neighbors $\mathcal{N}_Y^{(i)}$ is defined by using the inner product between normalized label vectors $\boldsymbol{y}/|\boldsymbol{y}|$ as:

$$\mathcal{N}_Y^{(i)} := \underset{S:S\subseteq\mathcal{I},\,|S|=n,\,i\notin S}{\arg\max} \sum_{j\in S} \frac{\boldsymbol{y}_i^{\mathrm{T}}\boldsymbol{y}_j}{|\boldsymbol{y}_i||\boldsymbol{y}_j|}, \tag{1}$$

where S is the index set in which the number of elements equals n and $|\boldsymbol{y}_i| = \sum_j y_{ij}$ is the number of labels that a data point has.

The computational cost of naively finding $\mathcal{N}_Y^{(i)}$ for all data points is $O(N^2)$. Thus, this naive approach is infeasible for a large $N \sim 10^6$. If the label vectors $\boldsymbol{y}$ are sufficiently sparse, we can efficiently find the nearest neighbors $\mathcal{N}_Y^{(i)}$ by using an inverted index. The estimated computational cost is $\sum_{j=1}^{L} n_j(n_j-1)/2$, where n_j is the number of data points that have the j-th label. However, if a few n_j corresponding to "head" labels are near N, which means almost all data points have the same label, the above cost reaches $O(N^2)$. Efficient algorithms for top-k retrieval on an inverted index [9] or finding approximate k-nearest neighbors [7] can be applied to this situation. However, we focus on tail labels and ignore head labels in some cases. In other words, we expect that the number of data points corresponding to head labels in each partition is enough not to affect the subsequent step, even if head labels are ignored in this step. Thus, we only consider the l tail labels under the conditions $\sum_{j=1}^{l} n_j(n_j-1)/2 \le \alpha N,\ n_1 \le n_2 \le \ldots \le n_L$ to find approximate nearest neighbors $\tilde{\mathcal{N}}_Y^{(i)}$ in order to keep the computational cost within $O(N)$ by using the adjusting parameter $\alpha \ll N$.

After approximate nearest neighbors $\tilde{\mathcal{N}}_Y^{(i)}$ are obtained for all data points, we learn the weight vector $\boldsymbol{w}_c$ for each partition c in order that the data points having the same tail labels are allocated in the same partition while the data points are divided almost equally among partitions. Using a sequential maximization procedure like stochastic k-means clustering [6], we sequentially maximize the following objective function for each i-th sample.

$$\max_{\boldsymbol{w}_{c_i}} \sum_{j\in\tilde{\mathcal{N}}_Y^{(i)}} \log\sigma(\boldsymbol{w}_{c_i}^{\mathrm{T}}\boldsymbol{x}_j) + \sum_{k\in S^-} \log\sigma(-\boldsymbol{w}_{c_i}^{\mathrm{T}}\boldsymbol{x}_k) - \lambda|\boldsymbol{w}_c|_1, \tag{2}$$

where $c_i = \arg\max_c \boldsymbol{w}_c^{\mathrm{T}}\boldsymbol{x}_i$ is the partition to which the i-th point belongs at this time step, S^- is the set of indices randomly selected from $\mathcal{I}$, $\sigma(z) = 1/(1+\exp(-z))$ is a sigmoid function, and λ is a regularization parameter. We learn the linear classifier $\boldsymbol{w}_c$'s by using the FTRL-Proximal algorithm [14] with AdaGrad [8] learning rate adjustment.

The first term of the above objective function is intended to assign the approximate nearest neighbors $\tilde{\mathcal{N}}_Y^{(i)}$ to the same partition c_i to which the i-th point belongs. The second term aims for the randomly selected points S^- to not be included in the partition c_i.

Since some partitions that have a lot of data points cause the training and prediction time to become long, this term prevents a lot of data points from being allocated in a single partition. The last term is the L_1-regularization term to make $\boldsymbol{w}_c$'s sparse. Sparse $\boldsymbol{w}_c$'s are also preferable for faster prediction.

The above L_1-regularization term reduces the final model size as well as the prediction time. At training time, $\boldsymbol{w}_c$'s are favored to to be stored in dense vectors for faster training. These vectors use $O(KM)$ space. Note that the number of partitions K depends on the number of entire training points N (see Section 4). Thus, this space complexity is infeasible for large N and M. To remedy this problem, we use a hashing trick [25] for storing $\boldsymbol{w}_c$'s in 24-bit space (approximately 16.7 millions of bins) instead of $O(KM)$ space. In practice, we did not notice a drop in accuracy when using this technique.

Since the above objective function is non-convex (when c_i is not fixed), AnnexML is also able to improve its prediction accuracy by learning an ensemble of multiple learners with different random initializations of $\boldsymbol{w}_c$, like the k-means clustering of SLEEC.

At the prediction step (line 1 in Algorithm 2), the partition c_t to which a test point $\boldsymbol{x}_t$ belongs is determined by using the learned $\boldsymbol{w}_c$'s as:

$$c_t = \arg\max_c \boldsymbol{w}_c^{\mathrm{T}} \boldsymbol{x}_t.$$

3.2 Learning Embeddings

For learning embedding vector $\boldsymbol{z}_i$ and projection matrix $\boldsymbol{V}_c$, AnnexML employs a pairwise learning-to-rank approach. This is because the learning objective of AnnexML is to reconstruct the KNNG of label vectors in the embedding space. In other words, arranging the k-nearest neighbors of the i-th sample is regarded as a ranking problem if we consider an i-th point and other points as a query and items, respectively. Thus, we use the pairwise learning-to-rank approach similar to S2Net [29] and DSSM [10] in order to optimize k-nearest neighbors in the embedding space more directly.

To represent the objective function of AnnexML, we first define the relevance score between $\boldsymbol{x}_i$ and $\boldsymbol{x}_j$ as cosine similarity between embedding vectors $\boldsymbol{z}_i = \boldsymbol{V}_c\boldsymbol{x}_i$ and $\boldsymbol{z}_j = \boldsymbol{V}_c\boldsymbol{x}_j$:

$$R(\boldsymbol{x}_i, \boldsymbol{x}_j) := \cos(\boldsymbol{z}_i, \boldsymbol{z}_j) = \frac{\boldsymbol{z}_i^{\mathrm{T}}\boldsymbol{z}_j}{\|\boldsymbol{z}_i\|\|\boldsymbol{z}_j\|} = \frac{\boldsymbol{x}_i^{\mathrm{T}}\boldsymbol{V}_c^{\mathrm{T}}\boldsymbol{V}_c\boldsymbol{x}_j}{\|\boldsymbol{V}_c\boldsymbol{x}_i\|\|\boldsymbol{V}_c\boldsymbol{x}_j\|}.$$

We also represent the conditional probability by using the above relevance score and softmax function as follows:

$$\begin{aligned} P(\boldsymbol{x}_j \mid \boldsymbol{x}_i) &:= \frac{\exp(\gamma R(\boldsymbol{x}_i, \boldsymbol{x}_j))}{\exp(\gamma R(\boldsymbol{x}_i, \boldsymbol{x}_j)) + \sum_{k\in S_c^-} \exp(\gamma R(\boldsymbol{x}_i, \boldsymbol{x}_k))} \\ &= \frac{\exp(\gamma \cos(\boldsymbol{z}_i, \boldsymbol{z}_j))}{\exp(\gamma \cos(\boldsymbol{z}_i, \boldsymbol{z}_j)) + \sum_{k\in S_c^-} \exp(\gamma \cos(\boldsymbol{z}_i, \boldsymbol{z}_k))}, \end{aligned}$$

where γ is a scaling parameter that magnifies $\cos(\boldsymbol{z}_i, \boldsymbol{z}_j)$ from $[-1, +1]$ to the range of larger values and $S_c^- \subseteq \mathcal{I}_c$ is the set of indices randomly selected from data points in the corresponding partition c. Then, we minimize the negative log likelihood:

$$\min_{\boldsymbol{V}_c} \sum_{i\in\mathcal{I}_c} \sum_{j\in\mathcal{N}_{Y_c}^{(i)}} -\log P(\boldsymbol{x}_j \mid \boldsymbol{x}_i).$$

Here, the set of nearest neighbors $\mathcal{N}_{Y_c}^{(i)}$ is almost the same as $\mathcal{N}_Y^{(i)}$ (see Equation 1) but is selected from $\mathcal{I}_c$ rather than $\mathcal{I}$. Note that the computational cost of finding exact $\mathcal{N}_{Y_c}^{(i)}$ for all i is not very large since the number of data points in a cluster $|\mathcal{I}_c|$ is much smaller than that of all training points $N = |\mathcal{I}|$ (the number of clusters to which K should be set to fulfill this condition). Thus, we can use the exact $\mathcal{N}_{Y_c}^{(i)}$ for learning embeddings. The above negative log likelihood is transformed as:

$$\begin{aligned} &-\log P(\boldsymbol{x}_j \mid \boldsymbol{x}_i) \\ &= -\log\left(\frac{\exp(\gamma\cos(\boldsymbol{z}_i, \boldsymbol{z}_j))}{\exp(\gamma \cos(\boldsymbol{z}_i, \boldsymbol{z}_j)) + \sum_{k\in S_c^-} \exp(\gamma\cos(\boldsymbol{z}_i, \boldsymbol{z}_k))}\right) \\ &= -\log\left(\frac{1}{1 + \sum_{k\in S^-} \exp(\gamma(\cos(\boldsymbol{z}_i, \boldsymbol{z}_k) - \cos(\boldsymbol{z}_i, \boldsymbol{z}_j)))}\right) \\ &= \log\left(1 + \sum_{k\in S_c^-} \exp(-\gamma\Delta_{ijk})\right), \end{aligned}$$

where $\Delta_{ijk} = \cos(\boldsymbol{z}_i, \boldsymbol{z}_j) - \cos(\boldsymbol{z}_i, \boldsymbol{z}_k)$ is the difference between two cosine values. Hence, this objective function aims to increase the difference between these cosine values.

We learn the projection matrix $\boldsymbol{V}_c$ by using stochastic gradient descent with AdaGrad [8]. Let a, b, and c be $\boldsymbol{z}_i^{\mathrm{T}}\boldsymbol{z}_j$, $1/\|\boldsymbol{z}_i\|$, and $1/\|\boldsymbol{z}_j\|$, respectively. The gradient of the $\cos(\boldsymbol{z}_i, \boldsymbol{z}_j)$ is derived as:

$$\begin{aligned} \frac{\partial \cos(\boldsymbol{z}_i, \boldsymbol{z}_j)}{\partial \boldsymbol{V}_c} &= \frac{\partial}{\partial \boldsymbol{V}_c}\left(\frac{\boldsymbol{z}_i^{\mathrm{T}}\boldsymbol{z}_j}{\|\boldsymbol{z}_i\|\|\boldsymbol{z}_j\|}\right) \\ &= -abc^3\boldsymbol{z}_i\boldsymbol{x}_i^{\mathrm{T}} - acb^3\boldsymbol{z}_j\boldsymbol{x}_j^{\mathrm{T}} + bc(\boldsymbol{z}_i\boldsymbol{x}_j^{\mathrm{T}} + \boldsymbol{z}_j\boldsymbol{x}_i^{\mathrm{T}}). \end{aligned}$$

Using cosine similarity instead of the inner product has some advantages. First, the objective function is regularized by the normalizing factor of a cosine. Hence, the explicit regularization term of $\boldsymbol{V}_c$ is not needed, so this learning procedure is simple. Second, we can easily apply an approximate nearest neighbor search technique that uses the learned KNNG for speeding up the prediction. We give the details of this technique in Section 3.3.

In the rest of this subsection, we clarify the difference between AnnexML and SLEEC. First, we briefly describe the learning procedure of SLEEC. The objective function of SLEEC is defined as:

$$\min_{\boldsymbol{V}_c} \sum_{i\in\mathcal{I}_c} \sum_{j\in\mathcal{N}_{Y_c}^{(i)}} \left\|\boldsymbol{y}_i^{\mathrm{T}}\boldsymbol{y}_j - \boldsymbol{x}_i^{\mathrm{T}}\boldsymbol{V}_c^{\mathrm{T}}\boldsymbol{V}_c\boldsymbol{x}_j\right\|^2 + \lambda \sum_{i\in\mathcal{I}_c} |\boldsymbol{V}_c\boldsymbol{x}_i|_1 + \mu\|\boldsymbol{V}_c\|_F^2.$$

The first term indicates the sum of squared errors between the inner product of label vectors and that of embedding vectors. The second term is an L_1-regularization term for embedding vectors $\boldsymbol{z}_i = \boldsymbol{V}_c\boldsymbol{x}_i$, which leads to sparse embeddings for reducing the size of models and the prediction time as well as avoiding overfitting. The last is the L_2-regularization term of $\boldsymbol{V}_c$. λ and μ are regularization parameters corresponding to the second and last terms, respectively. This objective function is non-convex and non-differentiable. Thus, the optimization process is divided into two phases and done using singular value projection and ADMM.

Obviously, the above objective function of SLEEC is a regression problem of minimizing the sum of squared errors. This means SLEEC learns the projection matrix $\boldsymbol{V}_c$ to reproduce the inner product values of label vectors by using embedding vectors. However,

Algorithm 3 ANNSearch(Query $\boldsymbol{q}$, Ball tree T, KNNG G)

```
H ← empty heap
TreeSearch(q, T.root, H)
GraphSearch(q, G, H)
return H
```

at the prediction step, these learned values are used only for retrieving k-nearest neighbors. In comparison, the objective function of AnnexML focuses on whether a data point is included in the set of k-nearest neighbors or not. Thus, the learning procedure of AnnexML is more intuitive and consistent with the prediction procedure.

3.3 Faster Prediction using Approximate Nearest Neighbor Search on KNNG

The prediction of AnnexML mostly relies on the k-nearest neighbor search in the embedding space (see Algorithm 2). Thus, for faster prediction, we need to speed up this nearest neighbor search task. Instead of SLEEC's naive brute-force search, we apply an approximate k-nearest neighbor search method to this task. This method efficiently explores the learned KNNG in the embedding space by using an additional tree structure and a pruning technique via the triangle inequality.

Representing the nearest neighbor search task more concretely, we find the following index set $\mathcal{N}^{(t)}_{Z_c}$ from training points $\mathcal{I}_c$ in a certain partition c with cosine similarity:

$$\mathcal{N}^{(t)}_{Z_c} = \mathop{\arg\max}_{S:S\subseteq\mathcal{I}_c,\,|S|=n} \sum_{j\in S} \cos(\boldsymbol{z}_t, \boldsymbol{z}_j) = \mathop{\arg\max}_{S:S\subseteq\mathcal{I}_c,\,|S|=n} \sum_{j\in S} \frac{\boldsymbol{z}_t^{\mathrm{T}}\boldsymbol{z}_j}{\|\boldsymbol{z}_j\|},$$

where $\boldsymbol{z}_t = \boldsymbol{V}_c\boldsymbol{x}_t$ is the embedding vector that corresponds to a test point $\boldsymbol{x}_t$.

For efficient indexing in a metric space, the triangle inequality is a key element, as suggested by Sugawara et al. [22]. We also want to utilize the triangle inequality for efficient retrieval, but the cosine distance $1 - \cos(\boldsymbol{z}_t, \boldsymbol{z}_j)$ cannot satisfy this inequality. Fortunately, if the indexed vectors $\boldsymbol{z}_j$ are normalized in advance, that is, $\|\boldsymbol{z}_j\| = 1$ for all j, the above $\mathcal{N}^{(t)}_{Z_c}$ becomes the same as the following index set of nearest neighbors by using Euclidean distance:

$$\mathop{\arg\min}_{S:S\subseteq\mathcal{I}_c,\,|S|=n} \sum_{j\in S} \|\boldsymbol{z}_t - \boldsymbol{z}_j\|^2 = \mathop{\arg\min}_{S:S\subseteq\mathcal{I}_c,\,|S|=n} \sum_{j\in S} \left(\|\boldsymbol{z}_j\|^2 - 2\boldsymbol{z}_t^{\mathrm{T}}\boldsymbol{z}_j\right).$$

Thus, we use Euclidean distance between normalized vectors as metrics for searching. Note that this transformation does not change the structure (or edge connections) of the learned KNNG.

Algorithms 3, 4, 5, and 6 are the pseudo codes that represent the approximate k-nearest neighbor search procedure using the KNNG. In these pseudo codes, the embedding of a test point $\boldsymbol{z}_t$ is represented as query vector $\boldsymbol{q}$. To efficiently find reasonable starting points from the graph, our method combines the KNNG with a ball tree. Please refer to the papers [16, 19] for the indexing method of the ball tree.

A query $\boldsymbol{q}$ first traverses from the root to the leaf nodes of the ball tree (Algorithm 4). At each internal node, the test point determines which child node (left or right) is to be followed by using the distances from the centers of the balls. After the test point reaches a leaf node, the distance from each indexed point corresponding to the node is calculated and pushed into the heap (Algorithm 5). Using these data points as seeds, the KNNG is explored (Algorithm 6). In the exploration step, if a data point is satisfied with the condition and pushed into the heap, the nearest neighbors are also pushed into the queue of candidates for the subsequent evaluation.

To summarize, we first obtain a reasonable set of approximate nearest neighbors by using a ball tree and then improve the approximation quality by exploring the KNNG on the basis of local search. Since we only need to calculate the distances to a small number of balls' centers and subset of training points, we can speed up this search task.

Note that the brute-force calculation of SLEEC cannot be directly replaced with the above search procedure because it does

Algorithm 4 TreeSearch(Query $\boldsymbol{q}$, Tree node N, Heap H)

```
if N is a leaf node then
    LineSearch(q, N.S, H)
else
    ldist ← d(q, N.left.center)
    rdist ← d(q, N.right.center)
    if ldist < rdist then
        TreeSeach(q, N.left, H)     ▹ follow the left child node
    else
        TreeSeach(q, N.right, H)    ▹ follow the right child node
    end if
end if
```

Algorithm 5 LineSearch(Query $\boldsymbol{q}$, Index set S, Heap H)

```
for i ∈ S do
    dist ← d(q, z_i)
    if dist < LargestDistance(H) then
        PopAndPushHeap(H, i, dist)
    end if
end for
```

Algorithm 6 GraphSearch(Query $\boldsymbol{q}$, KNNG G, Heap H)

```
C ← index of H                  ▹ a queue of candidates
D ← empty set                   ▹ a set of already evaluated
while C is not empty do
    i ← pop from C
    if i in D then
        continue
    end if
    D ← D ∪ {i}
    dist ← d(q, z_i)
    if dist < LargestDistance(H) then
        PopAndPushHeap(H, i, dist)
        for j in N^(i)_{Z_c} do     ▹ nearest neighbors in G
            push j to C
        end for
    end if
end while
```

not use cosine similarity (or Euclidean distance) but rather the inner product as the metric in the embedding space. Some Maximum Inner-Product Search (MIPS) methods [3, 19, 20] might be applicable to SLEEC for faster prediction. However, such a study is beyond the scope of this paper. We leave this direction as future work.

4 EXPERIMENTS

In this section, we evaluated our method on six large scale multi-label data sets. These data sets were provided by the Extreme Classification Repository [5] and had already been pre-processed and separated into training and test sets. We did not use any additional meta data. The statistics for the data sets are summarized in Table 2.

We compared AnnexML with several state-of-the-art methods: SLEEC [4], FastXML [18], PfastreXML [12], PLT [13], and PD-Sparse [27]. To represent the prediction difficulty of each data set, we also show the performance of a naive baseline that makes predictions by using the k-most common labels in the training data.

We evaluated the performance of the methods with precision at k ($k \in \{1, 3, 5\}$), which is a widely used metric for extreme multi-label classification and ranking tasks:

$$\mathrm{P@}k := \frac{1}{kN_{test}} \sum_{i=1}^{N_{test}} \sum_{l=1}^{k} y_{i\pi(l)}.$$

Here, $\pi(k) = j$ means that the j-th label is ranked in the k-th position by the predicted score. We also evaluated the performances with normalized Discounted Cumulative Gain (nDCG) at k. However, since the results showed the same tendency, we only report those with P@k. At least, by definition, the value of nDCG@1 is the same as that of P@1.

We implemented AnnexML in C++. In all experiments, we used ten default hyper-parameters for training AnnexML: the number of partitions in a learner: $K = \lfloor N/6000 \rfloor$, the embedding dimension: $d = 50$, the number of learners: 15, the number of (approximate) nearest neighbors and randomly sampled points used in learning both partitionings and embeddings: $n = 10$, the number of epochs for learning both partitionings and embeddings: 10, the initial learning rate of AdaGrad: $\eta_0 = 0.1$, the L_1-regularization parameter in Equation 2: $\lambda = 4$, the scaling parameter for cosine: $\gamma = 10$, the adjustment parameter for finding approximate nearest neighbors: $\alpha = 5000$, and the number of edges in the KNNG for prediction: 50. These default values of hyper-parameters were determined in preliminary experiments with small-scale data sets. Thus, we avoided hyper-parameter tuning for the large-scale data sets and significantly reduced the total training time.

For the other baseline methods, if P@k on each data set is reported in the original papers, we used those values for fair comparison. Otherwise, we used the C++ and MATLAB implementations for SLEEC, FastXML, PfastreXML and PD-Sparse, provided by the authors [5]. In this case, the suggested hyper-parameters were used. Since we use ordinary (not propensity scored) precision at k as the evaluation metrics, the propensity scores of PfastreXML were set to the same value for all labels. For PLT, we referred only to the values reported in the original paper because hyper-parameters were tuned by an off-the-shelf optimizer in the experiments.

4.1 Results

The experimental results are summarized in Table 3. The **bold** elements indicate the best performance of the methods. For PLT, since we referred only to the values reported in the original paper [13], as mentioned above, the scores on Wikipedia-500K data set are not available. The scores of PD-Sparse on three data sets are also unavailable because of excessive memory usage and training time in our experimental setting. Thus, we referred to the scores on Delicious-200K and WikiLSTHC-325K data sets reported in the Extreme Classification Repository [5].

AnnexML performed the best in almost all cases. There were especially large improvements for data sets that have larger label spaces. For example, AnnexML improved over SLEEC by about 8% and 6% in absolute terms of P@1 and P@5 on WikiLSHTC-325K data set. On Amazon-670K data set, AnnexML was also superior to SLEEC by approximately 7% and 4% in absolute terms of P@1 and P@5. These substantial improvements indicate AnnexML is not just a minor updated version of SLEEC. There is still much room to improve the prediction accuracy of AnnexML by tuning the hyper-parameters for each data set, like SLEEC does. However, we leave this as future work.

Table 4 compares the results of the three improvements proposed in Section 3. Method E+P+A equals AnnexML in Table 3. If we did not use the proposed partitioning or approximate nearest neighbor search, we used k-means clustering and a brute-force cosine calculation, like SLEEC does. Method E outperformed SLEEC on almost all data sets. Thus, our learning procedure that uses the learning-to-rank approach successfully improved the embedding quality. In comparison with E and E+P, the proposed partitioning method significantly improved P@k on the data sets that have a larger label space. In comparison with E and E+A, the approximate nearest neighbor search technique for faster prediction had slightly poorer accuracy on all data sets except Delicious-200K. One possible explanation for the unexpected improvement on Delicious-200K was that the number of nearest neighbors retrieved for prediction was small (set to be 10 for all data sets). The number suggested by SLEEC's authors is 70 for this data set. Hence, the approximate nearest neighbor search retrieved more diverse samples, and these samples could fortunately stabilize the prediction result. Next, we present the speed-up effect of the approximate nearest neighbor search.

Figure 1 plots the prediction time and performances of AnnexML, AnnexML-BF, SLEEC, FastXML, and PfastreXML when the number of learners changes. A higher precision at the same prediction time (upper left line) indicates better results. This experiment was conducted by using a single CPU thread on a machine with two Xeon E5-2680v3 processors and 128 GB of RAM that ran the Linux operating system. AnnexML-BF is the same method as E+P in Table 4, which uses a brute-force cosine calculation for prediction. We chose SLEEC, FastXML and PfastreXML for comparison since these methods are also ensemble methods, and we can easily control the trade-off between prediction time and accuracy by just changing the number of learners. To conduct a fair comparison, we used our own C++ implementation for SLEEC's prediction, instead of the provided MATLAB codes. This is almost the same as the implementation of AnnexML-BF. For FastXML and PfastreXML, we

Table 2: Statistics of datasets used in experiments

Dataset	#Train N	#Test N_{test}	#Features M	#Labels L	Avg. points per label	Avg. labels per point
AmazonCat-13K	1,186,239	306,782	203,882	13,330	448.57	448.57
Wiki10-31K	14,146	6,616	101,938	30,938	8.52	18.64
Delicious-200K	196,606	100,095	782,585	205,443	72.29	75.54
WikiLSHTC-325K	1,778,351	587,084	1,617,899	325,056	17.46	3.19
Wikipedia-500K	1,813,391	783,743	2,381,304	501,070	24.75	4.77
Amazon-670K	490,449	153,025	135,909	670,091	3.99	5.45

Table 3: Experimental results. Unavailable values are denoted as "–" (see text for details).

Dataset		AnnexML	SLEEC	FastXML	PfastreXML	PLT	PD-Sparse	Most common
AmazonCat-13K	P@1	**0.9355**	0.8919	0.9310	0.8994	0.9147	0.8931	0.2988
	P@3	**0.7838**	0.7517	0.7818	0.7724	0.7584	0.7403	0.1878
	P@5	0.6332	0.6109	0.6338	**0.6353**	0.6102	0.6011	0.1486
Wiki10-31K	P@1	**0.8650**	0.8554	0.8295	0.8263	0.8434	0.7771	0.8079
	P@3	**0.7428**	0.7359	0.6756	0.6874	0.7234	0.6573	0.5050
	P@5	**0.6419**	0.6310	0.5770	0.6006	0.6272	0.5539	0.3675
Delicious-200K	P@1	0.4666	**0.4703**	0.4320	0.3762	0.4537	0.3437	0.3873
	P@3	0.4079	**0.4167**	0.3868	0.3562	0.3894	0.2948	0.3675
	P@5	0.3764	**0.3888**	0.3621	0.3403	0.3588	0.2704	0.3552
WikiLSHTC-325K	P@1	**0.6336**	0.5557	0.4975	0.5810	0.4567	0.6126	0.1588
	P@3	**0.4066**	0.3306	0.3310	0.3761	0.2913	0.3948	0.0603
	P@5	**0.2979**	0.2407	0.2445	0.2769	0.2195	0.2879	0.0380
Wikipedia-500K	P@1	**0.6386**	0.5839	0.4934	0.5891	–	–	0.1529
	P@3	**0.4269**	0.3788	0.3351	0.3937	–	–	0.0583
	P@5	**0.3237**	0.2821	0.2586	0.3005	–	–	0.0368
Amazon-670K	P@1	**0.4208**	0.3505	0.3697	0.3919	0.3665	0.3370	0.0028
	P@3	**0.3665**	0.3125	0.3332	0.3584	0.3212	0.2962	0.0027
	P@5	0.3276	0.2856	0.3053	**0.3321**	0.2885	0.2684	0.0023

used the provided C++ implementations with careful coding optimizations for improving efficiency.

Comparing AnnexML and AnnexML-BF, we see that the approximate nearest neighbor search technique successfully sped up prediction time with a slight drop in accuracy. On WikiLSHTC-325K data set, AnnexML made predictions more than four times faster than AnnexML-BF when using the same number of learners. In other words, the prediction time with an ensemble of four AnnexML learners was almost the same as that of a single AnnexML-BF model. In this case, AnnexML made predictions in approximately 0.34 milliseconds per test point and achieved an about 5% higher P@1 than that of AnnexML-BF in absolute terms (0.6121 vs. 0.5657). Compared with FastXML and PfastreXML, AnnexML also achieved a higher P@k at a 1 millisecond budget per test point in almost all cases. AnnexML achieved the same prediction accuracy as SLEEC with an ensemble of at most four learners, which also made predictions within 1 millisecond per test point. In particular, on WikiLSHTC-325K data set, a single model of AnnexML achieved almost the same P@1 as an ensemble of 15 SLEEC learners. This AnnexML's prediction time was about 58 times faster than that of SLEEC (0.08 milliseconds vs. 4.66 milliseconds).

5 RELATED WORK

Extreme multi-label learning typically follows two major types of approaches: tree based [12, 13, 18] and embedding based [4, 15, 26, 30].

Tree-based methods are common in extreme multi-label classification because of their fast prediction. FastXML [18] is a state-of-the-art tree-based classifier. At the training phase, FastXML recursively partitions the feature space corresponding to the internal node by using a linear classifier optimized for nDCG-based ranking loss. A test point traverses the tree from the root node to a leaf node, and FastXML then makes predictions by using the labels of training points that correspond to the leaf node. PfastreXML [12] is an improved version of FastXML, made by replacing the nDCG loss with its propensity scored variant and using additional classifiers designed for tail labels. Jasinska et al. [13] developed PLT, which is a tree-based classifier that maximizes the F-measure. More recently, we gave a brief overview of a simple tree-based approach in a work-in-progress paper [23].

Most embedding-based approaches reduce the effective number of labels on the basis of the low-rank label matrix assumption. LEML [30] learns a low-rank projection matrix, which maps features to labels, by using a generic empirical risk minimization

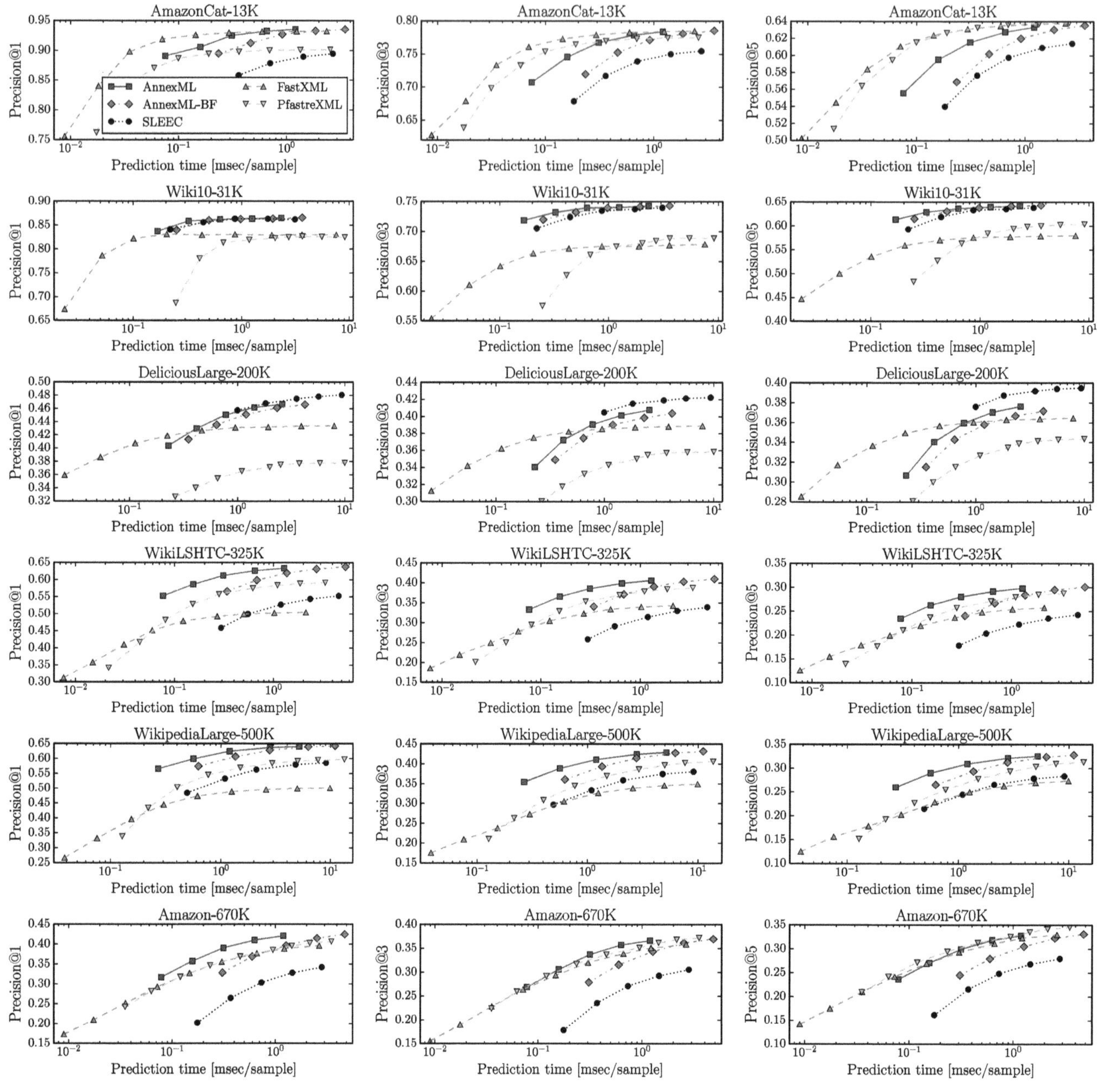

Figure 1: Precision versus prediction time when the number of learners changes. Number of learners was {1, 2, 4, 8, 15} for AnnexML, AnnexML-BF, and SLEEC, and {1, 2, 4, ..., 128, 256} for FastXML and PfastreXML. This experiment was conducted with C++ implementations on single CPU thread of the same machine for fair comparison.

framework. Mineiro and Karampatziakis developed another embedding-based method, named "Rembrandt" [15], by using techniques of randomized linear algebra. REML [26] decomposes the label matrix into a low-rank structure and sparse component, which represents label correlations and outliers, respectively. Si et al. proposed Goal-directed Inductive Matrix Completion (GIMC) [21] and also applied this method to multi-label classification. In this paper, since SLEEC was reported to achieve better or comparable performance to the above embedding-based methods on larger data sets [4, 15, 21, 26], we only compared our method with SLEEC.

PD-Sparse [27] uses primal and dual-sparse formulation, which consists of the dual-sparse loss and the primal-sparse regularizer. Using these two types of sparsity and hashing techniques, PD-Sparse can be efficiently learned and achieves fast prediction.

Table 4: Comparing results of our three improvements proposed in Section 3.

		E	E+P	E+A	E+P+A
Learning Embeddings		✓	✓	✓	✓
Learning to Partition data		✗	✓	✗	✓
ANN search for prediction		✗	✗	✓	✓
AmazonCat-13K	P@1	**0.9381**	0.9353	0.9374	0.9355
	P@3	0.7835	**0.7853**	0.7809	0.7838
	P@5	0.6320	**0.6353**	0.6289	0.6332
Wiki10-31K	P@1	**0.8703**	0.8655	0.8690	0.8650
	P@3	**0.7448**	0.7431	0.7446	0.7428
	P@5	**0.6454**	0.6435	0.6447	0.6419
Delicious-200K	P@1	**0.4670**	0.4660	0.4669	0.4666
	P@3	0.4018	0.4038	0.4077	**0.4079**
	P@5	0.3705	0.3717	**0.3770**	0.3764
WikiLSHTC-325K	P@1	0.6108	**0.6378**	0.6024	0.6336
	P@3	0.3907	**0.4102**	0.3836	0.4066
	P@5	0.2875	**0.3008**	0.2819	0.2979
Wikipedia-500K	P@1	0.6323	**0.6410**	0.6215	0.6386
	P@3	0.4156	**0.4299**	0.4048	0.4269
	P@5	0.3144	**0.3261**	0.3056	0.3237
Amazon-670K	P@1	0.3670	**0.4248**	0.3631	0.4208
	P@3	0.3190	**0.3698**	0.3161	0.3665
	P@5	0.2862	**0.3309**	0.2834	0.3276

Distributed learning is another approach to extreme multi-label classification. Babbar and Schölkopf proposed DiSMEC [2], which is a large-scale distributed framework for learning one-versus-rest linear classifiers. Using a distributed framework, DiSMEC learns a L_2-regularized L_2-loss SVM for each label in parallel. To reduce the model size and make prediction faster, they pruned *ambiguous* weights in the region near zero after training. They reported that the model for an entire WikiLSHTC-325K data set can be trained in approximately 6 hours on 400 cores and 3 hours on 1,000 cores. In this paper, we did not compare our method with DiSMEC because we focus on non-distributed approaches. Note that the ensemble of 15 AnnexML models on the aforementioned data set were trained within 4 hours by using 24 cores on the single machine described in Section 4.1.

In an approximate similarity search task for neural word embeddings, Sugawara et al. [22] compared hash-based, tree-based, and graph-based algorithms. They reported that a graph-based indexing method (NGT [11]) outperformed other methods. NGT is an indexing method that combines a variant of a vantage point tree [28] with an approximate KNNG. In our experiments, the KNNG combined with the ball tree also successfully accelerated the prediction speed without a noticeable drop in accuracy.

Tang et al. developed LargeVis [24] for visualizing large-scale and high-dimensional data (100 to 784 dimensions in their experiments) in 2 or 3 dimensional space. First, LargeVis constructs an approximate KNNG. Then, the model allocates the data points in low-dimensional space by preserving the structures of the graph. Thus, LargeVis is somewhat similar to AnnexML. However, AnnexML tries to find approximate k-nearest neighbors in the label space $\mathcal{Y}$ for classification, whereas LargeVis attempts to find them on feature space $\mathcal{X}$ for (unsupervised) visualization. Furthermore, AnnexML learns the projection matrix $\boldsymbol{V}_c$ that maps feature vectors $\boldsymbol{x}$ to embeddings $\boldsymbol{z}$ to predict unseen test points, although LargeVis directly learns the $\boldsymbol{z}$ of data points.

6 CONCLUSION

In this paper, we presented AnnexML by dealing with three problems affecting SLEEC. The key idea of AnnexML is reproducing the KNNG of label vectors in the embedding space to improve both the prediction accuracy and time of the k-nearest neighbor classifier. Experimental results on several large-scale data sets showed that AnnexML can significantly improve prediction accuracy, especially on larger data sets. In addition, the prediction time of AnnexML was up to 58 times faster than that of SLEEC at the same level of accuracy.

As future work, we plan to incorporate some of the ideas of approximate nearest neighbor search methods into an extreme multi-label classifier based on more complex nonlinear models, such as kernel machines and deep neural networks.

We released our implementation of AnnexML on the Yahoo! Japan Research page[2]. Our code would be useful for both researchers who compare their results with ours and practitioners who try to solve real-world Web-scale classification problems.

ACKNOWLEDGMENTS

We would like to thank Professor Hisashi Kashima, members of his laboratory at Kyoto University, and our colleagues at the Yahoo Japan Corporation for the many insightful discussions and helpful comments.

REFERENCES

[1] Kevin Aydin, MohammadHossein Bateni, and Vahab Mirrokni. 2016. Distributed Balanced Partitioning via Linear Embedding. In *Proceedings of the Ninth ACM International Conference on Web Search and Data Mining*.

[2] Rohit Babbar and Bernhard Schölkopf. 2017. DiSMEC: Distributed Sparse Machines for Extreme Multi-label Classification. In *Proceedings of the Tenth ACM International Conference on Web Search and Data Mining*.

[3] Yoram Bachrach, Yehuda Finkelstein, Ran Gilad-Bachrach, Liran Katzir, Noam Koenigstein, Nir Nice, and Ulrich Paquet. 2014. Speeding Up the Xbox Recommender System Using a Euclidean Transformation for Inner-product Spaces. In *Proceedings of the 8th ACM Conference on Recommender Systems*.

[4] Kush Bhatia, Himanshu Jain, Purushottam Kar, Manik Varma, and Prateek Jain. 2015. Sparse Local Embeddings for Extreme Multi-label Classification. In *Proceedings of the 28th International Conference on Neural Information Processing Systems*.

[5] Kush Bhatia, Himanshu Jain, Yashoteja Prabhu, and Manik Varma. 2016. The Extreme Classification Repository. (2016). Retrieved January 15, 2017 from https://manikvarma.github.io/downloads/XC/XMLRepository.html

[6] Leon Bottou, Yoshua Bengio, and others. 1995. Convergence properties of the k-means algorithms. In *Advances in neural information processing systems*.

[7] Wei Dong, Charikar Moses, and Kai Li. 2011. Efficient K-nearest Neighbor Graph Construction for Generic Similarity Measures. In *Proceedings of the 20th International Conference on World Wide Web*.

[8] John Duchi, Elad Hazan, and Yoram Singer. 2011. Adaptive Subgradient Methods for Online Learning and Stochastic Optimization. *J. Mach. Learn. Res.* (2011).

[9] Marcus Fontoura, Vanja Josifovski, Jinhui Liu, Srihari Venkatesan, Xiangfei Zhu, and Jason Zien. 2011. Evaluation Strategies for Top-k Queries over Memory-Resident Inverted Indexes. In *The 37th International Conference on Very Large Databases*.

[10] Po-Sen Huang, Xiaodong He, Jianfeng Gao, Li Deng, Alex Acero, and Larry Heck. 2013. Learning Deep Structured Semantic Models for Web Search using Clickthrough Data. In *Proceedings of the 22nd ACM international conference on Conference on information & knowledge management*.

[2] https://research-lab.yahoo.co.jp/en/software/

[11] Masajiro Iwasaki. 2016. Pruned Bi-directed K-nearest Neighbor Graph for Proximity Search. In *International Conference on Similarity Search and Applications.*
[12] Himanshu Jain, Yashoteja Prabhu, and Manik Varma. 2016. Extreme Multi-label Loss Functions for Recommendation, Tagging, Ranking & Other Missing Label Applications. In *Proceedings of the 22Nd ACM SIGKDD International Conference on Knowledge Discovery and Data Mining.*
[13] Kalina Jasinska, Krzysztof Dembczyński, Róbert Busa-Fekete, Karlson Pfannschmidt, Timo Klerx, and Eyke Hüllermeier. 2016. Extreme F-Measure Maximization using Sparse Probability Estimates. In *Proceedings of The 33rd International Conference on Machine Learning.*
[14] H Brendan McMahan. 2011. Follow-the-Regularized-Leader and Mirror Descent: Equivalence Theorems and L1 Regularization. In *Proceedings of the Fourteenth International Conference on Artificial Intelligence and Statistics.*
[15] Paul Mineiro and Nikos Karampatziakis. 2015. Fast Label Embeddings via Randomized Linear Algebra. In *Joint European Conference on Machine Learning and Knowledge Discovery in Databases.*
[16] Stephen M. Omohundro. 1989. *Five Balltree Construction Algorithms.* Technical Report. International Computer Science Institute.
[17] Ioannis Partalas, Aris Kosmopoulos, Nicolas Baskiotis, Thierry Artieres, George Paliouras, Eric Gaussier, Ion Androutsopoulos, Massih-Reza Amini, and Patrick Galinari. 2015. LSHTC: A benchmark for large-scale text classification. *arXiv preprint arXiv:1503.08581* (2015).
[18] Yashoteja Prabhu and Manik Varma. 2014. FastXML: A Fast, Accurate and Stable Tree-classifier for Extreme Multi-label Learning. In *Proceedings of the 20th ACM SIGKDD International Conference on Knowledge Discovery and Data Mining.*
[19] Parikshit Ram and Alexander G. Gray. 2012. Maximum Inner-product Search Using Cone Trees. In *Proceedings of the 18th ACM SIGKDD International Conference on Knowledge Discovery and Data Mining.*
[20] Anshumali Shrivastava and Ping Li. 2014. Asymmetric LSH (ALSH) for Sublinear Time Maximum Inner Product Search (MIPS). In *Advances in Neural Information Processing Systems.*
[21] Si Si, Kai-Yang Chiang, Cho-Jui Hsieh, Nikhil Rao, and Inderjit S. Dhillon. 2016. Goal-Directed Inductive Matrix Completion. In *Proceedings of the 22Nd ACM SIGKDD International Conference on Knowledge Discovery and Data Mining.*
[22] Kohei Sugawara, Hayato Kobayashi, and Masajiro Iwasaki. 2016. On Approximately Searching for Similar Word Embeddings. In *Proceedings of the 54th Annual Meeting of the Association for Computational Linguistics (Volume 1: Long Papers).*
[23] Yukihiro Tagami. 2017. Learning Extreme Multi-label Tree-classifier via Nearest Neighbor Graph Partitioning. In *Proceedings of the 26th International Conference on World Wide Web Companion.*
[24] Jian Tang, Jingzhou Liu, Ming Zhang, and Qiaozhu Mei. 2016. Visualizing Large-scale and High-dimensional Data. In *Proceedings of the 25th International Conference on World Wide Web.*
[25] Kilian Weinberger, Anirban Dasgupta, John Langford, Alex Smola, and Josh Attenberg. 2009. Feature Hashing for Large Scale Multitask Learning. In *ICML.*
[26] Chang Xu, Dacheng Tao, and Chao Xu. 2016. Robust Extreme Multi-label Learning. In *Proceedings of the 22Nd ACM SIGKDD International Conference on Knowledge Discovery and Data Mining.*
[27] Ian EH Yen, Xiangru Huang, Kai Zhong, Pradeep Ravikumar, and Inderjit S Dhillon. 2016. PD-Sparse: A Primal and Dual Sparse Approach to Extreme Multiclass and Multilabel Classification. In *Proceedings of The 33rd International Conference on Machine Learning.*
[28] Peter N. Yianilos. 1993. Data Structures and Algorithms for Nearest Neighbor Search in General Metric Spaces. In *Proceedings of the Fourth Annual ACM-SIAM Symposium on Discrete Algorithms.*
[29] Wen-tau Yih, Kristina Toutanova, John C Platt, and Christopher Meek. 2011. Learning Discriminative Projections for Text Similarity Measures. In *Proceedings of the Fifteenth Conference on Computational Natural Language Learning.*
[30] Hsiang-Fu Yu, Prateek Jain, Purushottam Kar, and Inderjit S Dhillon. 2014. Large-scale Multi-label Learning with Missing Labels. In *Proceedings of The 31st International Conference on Machine Learning.*

Interpretable Predictions of Tree-based Ensembles via Actionable Feature Tweaking

Gabriele Tolomei
Yahoo Research
London, UK
gtolomei@yahoo-inc.com

Fabrizio Silvestri*
Facebook
London, UK
fsilvestr@fb.com

Andrew Haines
Yahoo Research
London, UK
haines@yahoo-inc.com

Mounia Lalmas
Yahoo Research
London, UK
mounia@acm.org

ABSTRACT

Machine-learned models are often described as "black boxes". In many real-world applications however, models may have to sacrifice predictive power in favour of human-interpretability. When this is the case, feature engineering becomes a crucial task, which requires significant and time-consuming human effort. Whilst some features are inherently static, representing properties that cannot be influenced (*e.g.*, the age of an individual), others capture characteristics that could be *adjusted* (*e.g.*, the daily amount of carbohydrates taken). Nonetheless, once a model is learned from the data, each prediction it makes on new instances is irreversible - assuming every instance to be a static point located in the chosen feature space. There are many circumstances however where it is important to understand *(i)* why a model outputs a certain prediction on a given instance, *(ii)* which adjustable features of that instance should be modified, and finally *(iii)* how to alter such a prediction when the mutated instance is input back to the model.

In this paper, we present a technique that exploits the internals of a tree-based ensemble classifier to offer *recommendations* for transforming true negative instances into positively predicted ones. We demonstrate the validity of our approach using an online advertising application. First, we design a Random Forest classifier that effectively separates between two types of ads: *low* (negative) and *high* (positive) quality ads (instances). Then, we introduce an algorithm that provides recommendations that aim to transform a low quality ad (negative instance) into a high quality one (positive instance). Finally, we evaluate our approach on a subset of the active inventory of a large ad network, *Yahoo Gemini*.

*The author has contributed to this work while he was employed at Yahoo Research.

KDD '17, August 13-17, 2017, Halifax, NS, Canada

ACM ISBN 978-1-4503-4887-4/17/08...$15.00
https://doi.org/10.1145/3097983.3098039

CCS CONCEPTS

• Theory of computation → Machine learning theory; • Computing methodologies → Ensemble methods; • Information systems → Online advertising;

KEYWORDS

Model interpretability; Actionable feature tweaking; Recommending feature changes; Altering model predictions; Random forest

ACM Reference format:
Gabriele Tolomei, Fabrizio Silvestri, Andrew Haines, and Mounia Lalmas. 2017. Interpretable Predictions of Tree-based Ensembles via Actionable Feature Tweaking. In *Proceedings of KDD '17, Halifax, NS, Canada, August 13-17, 2017,* 10 pages.
https://doi.org/10.1145/3097983.3098039

1 INTRODUCTION

An increasing number of organisations and governments rely on *Machine Learning* (ML) techniques to extract knowledge from the large volumes of data they collect every day to optimise their operational effectiveness.

ML solutions are usually considered as "black boxes"; they take some inputs and produce desired outputs, especially when their ultimate goal is *prediction* rather than *inference.* As long as ML models work properly, "everybody" is happy and little attention is devoted to understand why such surprisingly good results are obtained. Still, it is beneficial to have available techniques supporting humans in interpreting and "debugging" these models, particularly when they fail [23] or lead to some oddities.[1]

Excluding recent trends in ML such as Deep Learning [13], typically the initial effort when designing an ML solution consists in modelling the objects of a given domain of interest, *i.e., feature engineering.* This step aims to describe each object in the domain using an appropriate set of properties (*features*), which define a so-called *feature space.* For a given dataset, each object can be considered as a static point located in the feature space since each feature value is deemed to be fixed; once a model is learned from the data, each prediction it makes on new objects is irreversible.

Let us assume that we disagree with a prediction that the model returns for a given object or that we would like to enforce switching

[1] http://www.telegraph.co.uk/technology/2016/03/24/microsofts-teen-girl-ai-turns-into-a-hitler-loving-sex-robot-wit/

such a prediction. The research question we ask in this work is *how can we understand what can be changed in the feature vector in order to modify the prediction accordingly?*

To better understand this challenge with an example, consider an ML application in the healthcare domain, where patients (objects) are mapped to a vector of clinical indicators (features), such as age, blood pressure, daily carbohydrates taken, *etc.* Assume next that an ML model has been designed to accurately predict from these features whether a patient is at risk of a heart attack or not. If for a given patient our model predicts that there is a high risk of a heart attack it would be of great advantage for medical physicians to also have a tool that suggests the most appropriate clinical treatment by offering targeted adjustments to specific indicators (*e.g.*, reducing the daily amount of carbohydrates). In other words, to recommend the clinical treatment to switch a patient from being of high risk (negative instance) to low risk (positive instance).

In this work, we propose an algorithm for *tweaking* input features so as to change the output predicted by an existing machine-learned model. Our method is designed to operate on top of any tree-based ensemble binary classifier, although it can be extended to multi-class classification. Our proposed algorithm exploits the internals of the model to generate recommendations for transforming true negative instances into positively predicted ones (or vice versa).

We describe the theoretical framework along with experiments designed to validate the proposed algorithm. Our approach is then evaluated in the commercial and more implementable setting of online advertisement recommendations to illustrate the generic nature of our framework and the many and varied domains it can be applied to.

After presenting an effective Random Forest classifier that is able to separate between *low* and *high* quality advertisements [12], we show how our algorithm can be used to automatically generate "interpretable" and "actionable" suggestions on how to convert a low quality ad (negative instance) into a high quality one (positive instance). Such insights can be provided to advertisers who may turn them into actual changes to their ad campaigns with the aim of improving their return on investment. Finally, we assess the quality of recommendations that our algorithm generates out of a dataset of advertisements served by the *Yahoo Gemini* ad network.

2 PROBLEM STATEMENT

We start by considering the typical binary classification problem and focus on an ensemble of tree-based classifiers as an effective solution to the above problem. Additionally, we define how the internals of an existing ensemble of trees can be used to derive a feedback loop for recommending how true negative instances can be turned into positively predicted ones (or vice versa).

The approach we propose can be easily extended to the more general multi-class classification problem. We plan to present this result in future extended work.

2.1 Notation

Let $\mathcal{X} \subseteq \mathbb{R}^n$ be an n-dimensional vector space of real-valued features. Any $\mathbf{x} \in \mathcal{X}$ is an n-dimensional feature vector, *i.e.*, $\mathbf{x} = (x_1, x_2, \ldots, x_n)^T$, representing an object in the vector space $\mathcal{X}$. Suppose that each $\mathbf{x}$ is associated with a binary *class label* – either neg (*negative*) or pos (*positive*) – and let $\mathcal{Y} = \{-1, +1\}$ be the set encoding all such possible class labels.

We assume there exists an *unknown target* function $f : \mathcal{X} \longmapsto \mathcal{Y}$ that maps any feature vector to its corresponding class label. In addition, we let $\hat{f} \approx f$ which is learned from a labelled dataset of m instances $\mathcal{D} = \{(\mathbf{x_1}, y_1), (\mathbf{x_2}, y_2), \ldots, (\mathbf{x_m}, y_m)\}$. More specifically, $\hat{f}$ is the estimate that best approximates f on $\mathcal{D}$, according to a specific *loss function* ℓ. Such a function measures the "cost" of prediction errors we would make if we replaced the true target f with the estimate $\hat{f}$.

The flexibility *vs.* interpretability of $\hat{f}$ depends on the *hypothesis space* which $\hat{f}$ has been picked from by the learning algorithm. In this work, we focus on $\hat{f}$ represented as an *ensemble* of K tree-based classifiers, $\hat{f} = \phi(\hat{h}_1, \ldots, \hat{h}_K)$. Each $\hat{h}_k : \mathcal{X} \longmapsto \mathcal{Y}$ is a base estimate, and ϕ is the function responsible for combining the output of all the individual base classifiers into a single prediction.

A possible implementation of ϕ could use a *majority voting* strategy. In this setting, a given instance $\mathbf{x}$ would obtain a predicted class label $\hat{f}(\mathbf{x})$ based on the result of the majority of the base classifiers; this is the *mode* of the base predictions. Although other strategies may be used, this does not impact our proposed approach.

2.2 Enforcing Positive Prediction

In any ensemble of tree-based classifiers, each base estimate $\hat{h}_k$ is encoded by a decision tree T_k, and the ensemble is represented as a forest $\mathcal{T} = \{T_1, \ldots, T_K\}$.

Our aim is to identify how to transform a true negative instance into a positively predicted one. Let $\mathbf{x} \in \mathcal{X}$ be a true negative instance such that $f(\mathbf{x}) = \hat{f}(\mathbf{x}) = -1$. The task can now be defined as transforming the original input feature vector $\mathbf{x}$ into a new feature vector $\mathbf{x}'$ ($\mathbf{x} \rightsquigarrow \mathbf{x}'$) such that $\hat{f}(\mathbf{x}') = +1$. Moreover, we accomplish an optimised form of the problem by choosing $\mathbf{x}'$ as the best transformation among all the possible transformations $\mathbf{x}^*$, according to a *cost function* $\delta : \mathcal{X} \times \mathcal{X} \longmapsto \mathbb{R}$. This is defined as follows:

$$\mathbf{x}' = \arg\min_{\mathbf{x}^*} \left\{ \delta(\mathbf{x}, \mathbf{x}^*) \mid \hat{f}(\mathbf{x}) = -1 \wedge \hat{f}(\mathbf{x}^*) = +1 \right\}$$

The cost function measures the "effort" of transforming $\mathbf{x}$ into $\mathbf{x}'$. A possible choice of such a function is the number of features affected by the transformation or the Euclidean distance between the original and the transformed vector.

2.3 Positive and Negative Paths

Any root-to-leaf path of a single decision tree can be interpreted as a cascade of *if-then-else* statements, where every internal (non-leaf) node is a boolean test on a specific feature value against a threshold. We restrict the tree decisions to be binary representations as any multiway decision can be represented in a binary form and there is little performance benefit in n-ary splits. An instance's feature value is then evaluated at each node to determine which branch to traverse. This is repeated until the leaves are reached whereby the pos/neg classification labels are defined and assigned.

Given a forest of K decision trees $\mathcal{T} = \{T_1, \ldots, T_K\}$, we denote by $p_{k,j}$ the j-th path of the k-th tree T_k. We refer to $p^+_{k,j}$ (or $p^-_{k,j}$) as the j-th path of T_k that leads to a leaf node labelled as pos (or neg) – a *positive* (or *negative*) path. For simplicity, we assume that each path of a decision tree contains at most n non-leaf nodes, which correspond to n boolean conditions, one for each distinct feature.[2] We thus represent a root-to-leaf path as follows:

$$p_{k,j} = \{(x_1 \lesseqgtr \theta_1), (x_2 \lesseqgtr \theta_2), \ldots, (x_n \lesseqgtr \theta_n)\} \quad (1)$$

Let $P_k^+ = \bigcup_{j \in T_k} p_{k,j}^+$ describe the set of all positive paths, and $P_k^- = \bigcup_{j \in T_k} p_{k,j}^-$ the set of all the negative paths in T_k. Also, let $P_k = P_k^+ \cup P_k^-$ be the set of *all* the paths in T_k.

We thus enumerate the possible paths in a single decision tree. Even under the assumption that each $p_{k,j} \in P_k$ is at most a length-n path then T_k is a depth-n binary tree, whose number of leaves is therefore bounded to 2^n. As the total number of leaves coincides with the total number of possible paths, we obtain $|P_k| \leq 2^n$.

In general, we cannot ensure a bound on each $|P_k|$, as there might exist some paths $p_{k,j} \in P_k$ whose length is greater than n. In practice though, we can specify the maximum number of paths at training time by bounding the depth of the generated trees to the number n of features. Even with such a relaxed condition, the total number of possible paths encoded by the forest $\mathcal{T}$ is equal to $\sum_{k=1}^{K} |P_k| \leq K2^n$, therefore still exponential in n. We see later how this does not disrupt computational efficacy in practice, as our algorithm operates on a subset of those paths.

2.4 Tweaking Input Features

Given our input feature vector $\mathbf{x}$, we know from our hypothesis that $f(\mathbf{x}) = \hat{f}(\mathbf{x}) = -1$. If the overall prediction is obtained using a majority voting strategy, it follows:

$$\hat{f}(\mathbf{x}) = -1 \iff \left(\sum_{k=1}^{K} \hat{h}_k(\mathbf{x})\right) \leq 0$$

Furthermore, there must be at least $\lceil \frac{K}{2} \rceil$ decision trees (base classifiers) of the forest $\mathcal{T}$ whose output is -1. That is, there exists $K^- \subseteq \{1, \ldots, K\}$ with $|K^-| \geq \lceil \frac{K}{2} \rceil$, such that:

$$\hat{h}_{k^-}(\mathbf{x}) = -1, \ \forall k^- \in K^-$$

As we are operating in a binary classification setting, there must also exist $K^+ = \{1, \ldots, K\} \setminus K^-$, which denote the set of classifier indices that output a positive label when input with $\mathbf{x}$, *i.e.*, $\hat{h}_{k^+}(\mathbf{x}) = +1, \ \forall k^+ \in K^+$.

Our goal is to tweak the original input feature vector $\mathbf{x}$ so as to adjust the prediction made by the ensemble from negative (-1) to positive $(+1)$. We can skip all the trees indexed by K^+, as these are already encoding the (positive) prediction we ultimately want. We therefore focus on each tree T_k where $k \in K^-$, and consider the set P_k^+ of all its positive paths. With each $p_{k,j}^+ \in P_k^+$ we associate an instance $\mathbf{x}_j^+ \in \mathcal{X}$ that *satisfies* that path – *i.e.*, an instance whose adjusted feature values meet the boolean conditions encoded in $p_{k,j}^+$ to finish on a pos-labelled leaf, and therefore $\hat{h}_k(\mathbf{x}_j^+) = +1$.

Among all the possibly infinite instances satisfying $p_{k,j}^+$, we restrict to $\mathbf{x}_{j(\epsilon)}^+$ to be feature value changes with a "tolerance" of at most ϵ. We call it the ϵ-satisfactory instance of $p_{k,j}^+$. We consider $p_{k,j}^+$ containing at most n boolean conditions, as specified by Equation 1. Therefore, for any (small) fixed $\epsilon > 0$, we build a feature vector $\mathbf{x}_{j(\epsilon)}^+$ as follows:

$$\mathbf{x}_{j(\epsilon)}^+[i] = \begin{cases} \theta_i - \epsilon & \text{if the } i\text{-th condition is } (x_i \leq \theta_i) \\ \theta_i + \epsilon & \text{if the } i\text{-th condition is } (x_i > \theta_i) \end{cases} \quad (2)$$

Having a single *global* tolerance ϵ for all the features works as long as we standardise every feature (*e.g.*, using z-score or min-max). If we use standard z-score for each feature, the actual magnitude of the change cannot just depend on ϵ but instead needs to be considered a multiple of a unit of standard deviation from the feature mean. Let $\theta_i = \frac{t_i - \mu_i}{\sigma_i}$ be the z-score of the threshold on the i-th feature value, where t_i is the non-standardised value, μ_i and σ_i are the mean and standard deviation of the i-th feature respectively.[3] Now, suppose that $x_i = \theta_i \pm \epsilon$ is the tweaked value of the i-th feature according to the ongoing transformation of the input vector $\mathbf{x}$. Therefore, $x_i = \frac{t_i - \mu_i}{\sigma_i} \pm \epsilon$. Returning to the original (*i.e.*, non-standardised) feature scale, we obtain $x_i = t_i - \mu_i \pm \epsilon\sigma_i$. Depending on the sign, the tweaked feature is either moving closer to or farther away from the original feature mean μ_i, pivoting around t_i.

For each $p_{k,j}^+ \in P_k^+$ we transform our input feature vector $\mathbf{x}$ into the ϵ-satisfactory instance $\mathbf{x}_{j(\epsilon)}^+$ that validates $p_{k,j}^+$. This leads us to a set of transformations $\Gamma_k = \bigcup_{j \in P_k^+} \mathbf{x}_{j(\epsilon)}^+$, associated with the k-th tree T_k.

Each resulting transformation in Γ_k may have an impact on other trees of the forest. There might exist $l \in K^+$ whose corresponding tree already provides the correct prediction when this is input with $\mathbf{x}$, $\hat{h}_l(\mathbf{x}) = +1$. It may also happen that by changing $\mathbf{x}$ into $\mathbf{x}'$ the prediction of the l-th tree is incorrect and now $\hat{h}_l(\mathbf{x}') = -1$. In other words, by changing $\mathbf{x}$ into another instance $\mathbf{x}' \in \Gamma_k$ we are only guaranteed that the prediction of the k-th base classifier is correctly fixed, *i.e.*, from $\hat{h}_k(\mathbf{x}) = -1$ to $\hat{h}_k(\mathbf{x}') = +1$. The overall prediction for $\mathbf{x}'$ may or may not be fixed, where $\hat{f}(\mathbf{x}')$ may still output -1, exactly as $\hat{f}(\mathbf{x})$ did.

If the change from $\mathbf{x}$ to $\mathbf{x}'$ also leads to $\hat{f}(\mathbf{x}') = +1$, then $\mathbf{x}'$ will be a *candidate* transformation for $\mathbf{x}$. More formally, let $\Gamma = \bigcup_{k=1}^{K} \Gamma_k$ be the set of *all* the ϵ-satisfactory transformations of the original $\mathbf{x}$ from the positive paths of all the trees in the forest. Our feature tweaking problem can then be generally defined as follows:

$$\mathbf{x}' = \operatorname*{arg\,min}_{\mathbf{x}_{j(\epsilon)}^+ \in \Gamma \ | \ \hat{f}(\mathbf{x}_{j(\epsilon)}^+) = +1} \left\{\delta(\mathbf{x}, \mathbf{x}_{j(\epsilon)}^+)\right\}$$

In [6], it has already been proven that a problem similar to the one we define above is NP-hard as it reduces to DNF-MAXSAT. Our version, in fact, introduces an additional constraint (ϵ) on the possible way features can be tweaked and thus it is itself NP-hard. This problem definition is still valid for the base case when $K = 1$. There, the additional condition requiring $\hat{f}(\mathbf{x}_{j(\epsilon)}^+) = +1$ is not necessary because it is implicitly true by definition. In that scenario, the ensemble is composed of a single base classifier – *i.e.*, the forest contains a single decision tree and tweaking its prediction also results in changing the overall prediction. Note that when there is only one decision tree, our problem can be solved *optimally*:

[2] In general, there can be multiple boolean conditions associated with a single feature.

[3] In practice, μ_i and σ_i are often unknown, so the sample mean and the sample standard deviation are used instead.

```
Input :
  ▷ An estimate function f̂ resulting from an ensemble of decision trees
  𝒯 = {T_1, ..., T_K}, each one associated with a base estimate
  ĥ_k, k = 1, ..., K
  ▷ A feature vector x representing a true negative instance, such that
  f(x) = f̂(x) = −1
  ▷ A cost function δ
  ▷ A (small) threshold ε > 0
Output:
  ▷ The optimal transformation x' with respect to δ, such that
  f̂(x') = +1
begin
    x' ⟵ x;
    δ_min ⟵ +∞;
    for k = 1, ..., K do
        if f̂(x) == ĥ_k(x) and ĥ_k(x) == −1 then
            /* retrieve the set of positive paths of the k-th decision tree
               */
            P_k^+ ⟵ getPositivePaths(T_k);
            foreach p_{k,j}^+ ∈ P_k^+ do
                /* generate the ε-satisfactory instance associated with
                   the j-th positive path of the k-th decision tree   */
                x_{j(ε)}^+ ⟵ buildPositiveInst(x, p_{k,j}^+, ε);
                if f̂(x_{j(ε)}^+) == +1 then
                    if δ(x, x_{j(ε)}^+) < δ_min then
                        x' ⟵ x_{j(ε)}^+;
                        δ_min ⟵ δ(x, x_{j(ε)}^+);
                    end
                end
            end
        end
    end
    return x';
end
```

Algorithm 1: The Feature Tweaking Algorithm

We can enumerate all the positive paths, choose the one with the minimum cost, and check if the threshold of tolerance ϵ is satisfied on each feature. Because base trees are interconnected through the features they share, simply enumerating positive paths does not work for an ensemble of trees since the output of a base tree may affect outputs of its sibling trees. The presence of the condition $\hat{f}(\mathbf{x}^+_{j(\epsilon)}) = +1$ circumvents this issue by querying the model itself on the correctness of the ϵ-transformation of an instance.

2.5 The Feature Tweaking Algorithm

Our approach takes as input 4 key components: *(i)* The trained ensemble model $\hat{f}$; *(ii)* A feature vector $\mathbf{x}$ that represents a true negative instance; *(iii)* A cost function δ measuring the "effort" required to transform the true negative instance into a positive one; and *(iv)* A positive threshold ϵ that bounds the tweaking of each single feature to pass every boolean test on a positive path of each tree. The result being the transformation $\mathbf{x}'$ of the original $\mathbf{x}$ that exhibits the minimum cost according to δ. The detailed description is presented in Algorithm 1.

In the worst case, our algorithm examines all K trees of the forest, although it investigates only those trees whose base predictions are negatives (neg-labelled). Then, all the positive paths of each tree are considered, and for each of those a potential candidate ϵ-transformation is built according to the scheme proposed in Equation 2. As such, the number of steps depends on the number of positive paths on each tree, which in turn is related to the number of leaves.

We stated in Section 2.3 that we cannot provide *apriori* any limit to the depth of a decision tree, and therefore to its number of leaves. However, in practice these can be bounded whilst training the model. We therefore set the maximum length of each root-to-leaf path, *i.e.*, the depth of each tree, to be at most equal to the number of input features n. Considering our goal, this is not a limitation as each transformation should at most affect each feature exactly once. The total number of positive paths to be examined will then be limited by $K2^n$, and so the worst case complexity is $O(2^n)$. It follows that our method might be unsuitable for dealing with high-dimensional datasets, such as text, images, or videos. In reality such a setting would not really make sense when transforming input instances in the original feature space (*e.g.*, change a few words on a document or a few pixels of an image).

Although the search space can be exponential in the number of features, in practice the number of positive paths of each tree is significantly smaller. This makes our method feasible on average input sizes (*i.e.*, below 100 features). For example, in our experiments we found that the maximum depth of each tree leading to the best classification results is significantly smaller than the total number $n = 45$ of features (see Table 2). In addition, many positive paths may share several boolean conditions, especially when extracted from the same decision tree. This allows us to avoid tweaking the same input feature multiple times according to the same condition by using some caching mechanism.

Finally, our algorithm can be easily parallelised since each tree can be explored independently from the others for any given instance – *i.e.*, we can adjust the k-th tree while keeping the remaining $K \setminus k$ trees simultaneously fixed for all $k \in \{1, \ldots, K\}$.

3 USE CASE: IMPROVING AD QUALITY

We demonstrate the utility of our method when applied to a real-world use case in online advertising. We investigate how our algorithm can be used to improve the *quality* of advertisements served by the *Yahoo Gemini* ad network.

3.1 Why Ad Quality?

A main source of monetisation for online web services comes in the form of advertisements (*ads* for short) impressed in dedicated real estate units of rendered web pages. Online publishers operating these web services typically reserve predefined slots within their streams, utilising a third party ad network to deliver ad inventory to impress within them. Ad networks free publishers from running their own ad servers as they decide for them which ads should be placed at which slots, when and to whom. Advertisers rely on ad networks to optimise their *return on investment* – for example through targeting the right audience according to the advertiser budget and marketing strategy.

A trustworthy relationship between advertisers, publishers and ad networks is instrumental to the success of online advertising. On the advertiser side, ad networks provide advertisers with tools for monitoring key performance indicators (*e.g.*, number of ad *impressions*, *click-through rate* or CTR, *bounce rate*) as well as effective mechanisms to overcome fraudulent activities such as *click spam* [7, 22]. On the publisher side, ad networks provide mechanisms that allow users to hide ads they dislike and indicate the reasons for doing so. This information can be used by ad networks to ensure that the ads they serve do not negatively affect user engagement on a publisher website, as well as reporting to advertisers on the *quality* of their ads.

As with any self served content delivery platform, an ad network has a varying distribution of quality with many ads being of low quality. Not serving them may not be an option when supply is exhausted. Therefore, another approach to positively shift the inventory quality distribution is to leverage the interpretability of the internal machinery of existing ad quality prediction models – *i.e.*, binary classifiers – so as to offer actionable *recommendations*. The intention of these programmatically-computed recommendations is to provide advertisers with guidance on how they can improve their ad quality at scale. Such a system yields value for all beneficiaries in this advertising ecosystem ultimately culminating with a better user experience.

Returning to our work, by applying our feature tweaking algorithm introduced in Section 2.5, we show in the rest of this paper how we can transform a low quality ad into a set of new "proposed" high quality ads by shifting their position in an ad quality feature space. The algorithm employs the internals of a learned binary classifier to *tweak* the feature-based representation of a low quality ad so that the new "proposed" ads are promoted to high quality ones when re-input to the classifier. Each transformation is associated with a *cost*, allowing us to generate actionable suggestions from the "proposed" instances with the least cost, so as to improve low quality ads. We validate our approach on a dataset of mobile native ads served by the *Yahoo Gemini*[4] ad network.

3.2 A Definition of Ad Quality

Many factors can affect the quality of an ad: its *relevance*, *i.e.*, whether the ad matches the user interest [19]; the *pre-click* experience, *i.e.*, whether the ad annoys a user [27]; and finally the *post-click* experience, *i.e.*, whether the *ad landing page*[5] meets the user click intent that brought them to the landing page [12]. We focus on the latter, the post-click experience, following from [1, 12].

Inspired by these studies, we define and measure the quality of ads using the time spent on their landing pages as a proxy, referred to as *dwell time*. We know from [12] that ad landing pages exhibiting long dwell times promote a positive long-term post-click experience. Based on this definition of ad quality, we design a binary classifier that effectively separates between *low* and *high* quality ads, *i.e.*, ad landing pages whose dwell time is below or above a threshold τ, respectively. We compute τ as the median of all the sample means of dwell times observed for a large set of ad landing pages. Intuitively, an ad landing page is of high quality if its average dwell time is greater than τ – *i.e.*, if the average time users spent on the page is greater than the average time users spent on at least 50% of any other ad landing page. Although more sophisticated approaches can be designed [1], this is not the main goal of this research, and we leave it for future work.

[4] https://gemini.yahoo.com

[5] We refer to *ad landing page* as the web page of the advertiser that a user is redirected to after clicking on an *ad*.

3.3 Predicting Ad Quality

To apply our algorithm to our use case, we first need to learn a binary classifier that predicts whether an ad is of high quality or not, given a feature-based representation of the ad creative and the landing page.

3.3.1 Ad Feature Engineering. A sample of the set of features used in this work is listed in Table 1. This is based on the same set used in [1], with the additional "Language" category (marked with "†" in the Table). Due to space constraints we do not show all the features, and invite the reader to refer to [1] for a complete description of them.

Each feature in the table is associated with a *category* and a *source*. The former indicates the type of features whilst the latter specifies whether the feature is computed from the ad *landing page* (LP), the ad *creative* (CR), or a combination of the two (CR-LP). Although our focus is on the post-click experience (*i.e.*, ad landing page), we aim to obtain the best performing model for predicting the quality of the ads, and hence include both pre-click (*i.e.*, ad creative) and historical features; the latter not participating in the tweaking process as – by definition – they cannot be altered.

3.3.2 Learning Binary Classifiers. As our feature tweaking algorithm is designed to work on tree-based ensemble classifiers, we train the following learning models to find our best estimate $\hat{f}$: Decision Trees (DT) [18], which can be thought of as a special case of an ensemble with a single tree; Gradient Boosted Decision Trees (GBDT) [9], and Random Forests (RF) [2].

The original dataset $\mathcal{D} = \{(\mathbf{x_1}, y_1), (\mathbf{x_2}, y_2), \dots, (\mathbf{x_m}, y_m)\}$ is split into two datasets $\mathcal{D}_{\text{train}}$ and $\mathcal{D}_{\text{test}}$ using stratified random sampling. $\mathcal{D}_{\text{train}}$ is used for training the models and accounts for 80% of the total number of instances in $\mathcal{D}$, whilst $\mathcal{D}_{\text{test}}$ contains the remaining held-out portion used for evaluating the models. $\mathcal{D}_{\text{train}}$ is also used to perform model selection, which is achieved by tuning the hyperparameters specific for each.

With every combination of model and corresponding hyperparameters, we run a 10-fold cross validation to find the best settings for each model – *i.e.*, the one with the best cross validation performance. We measure this performance using the *Area Under the Curve of the Receiver Operating Characteristic* (ROC AUC). Each model is in turn re-trained on the whole $\mathcal{D}_{\text{train}}$ using the best hyperparameter setting. Finally, the overall best model is deemed to be the one that best performs on the test set $\mathcal{D}_{\text{test}}$.

3.3.3 Labelled Dataset of Ads. We collect a random sample of 1,500 ads served by the *Yahoo Gemini* ad network on a mobile app during one month. To ensure reliable estimates of dwell time, we only consider ads clicked at least 500 times. We saw that the distribution was skewed with around 80% of the instances having an average dwell time within approximately 100 seconds, whereas the remaining 20% sat in the long tail of very long dwell times. The

Table 1: Set of features used to characterise ad *creative* (CR), ad *landing page* (LP), or both (CR-LP).

Category	Source	Description
Language[†]	CR	This set of features capture the extent to which the text of the ad creative may include adult, violent, or spam content (*e.g.*, ADULT_SCORE, HATE_SCORE, and SPAM_SCORE)
DOM	LP	This set of features are derived from the elements extracted from the HTML DOM of the ad landing page, such as the main textual content (LANDING_MAIN_TEXT_LENGTH), the total number of internal and external hyperlinks (LINKS_TOTAL_COUNT), the ratio of main text length to the total number of hyperlinks on the page (LINKS_MAIN_LENGTH_TOTAL_RATIO), *etc.*
Readability	CR-LP	These features range from a simple count of tokens (words) in the text of the ad creative and landing page to well-known scores for measuring the summarisability/readability of a text (*e.g.*, READABILITY_SUMMARY_SCORE), *etc.*
Mobile Optimising	LP	This set of features describe the degree of mobile optimisation of the ad landing page by measuring the ability of it to be tuned to different screen sizes (VIEW_PORT), testing for the presence of a click-to-call button (CLICK_TO_CALL), *etc.*
Media	LP	These features refer to any media content displayed within the ad landing page, such as the number of images (NUM_IMAGES), *etc.*
Input	LP	This set of features represent all the possible input types available on the ad landing page, such as the number of checkboxes, drop-down menus, and radio buttons (NUM_INPUT_CHECKBOX, NUM_INPUT_DROPDOWN, NUM_INPUT_RADIO), *etc.*
Content & Similarity	CR-LP	These features extract the set of Wikipedia *entities* from the ad creative and landing page (NUM_CONCEPT_ANNOTATION), and measure the *Jaccard* similarity between those two sets (SIMILARITY_WIKI_IDS), *etc.*
History	LP	These features measure historical indicators, such as the median *dwell time* as computed from the last 28 days of observed ad clicks (HISTORICAL_DWELLTIME), and the *bounce rate* – *i.e.*, the proportion of ad clicks whose dwell time is below 5 seconds (HISTORICAL_BOUNCE_RATE), *etc.*

median τ of those averages, calculated as described in Section 3.2, is equal to $\approx$ 62.5 seconds. We therefore reach an evenly balanced ground truth, where 50% of the instances have an average dwell time at most equal to τ and the remaining 50% above τ.

To build our labelled dataset $\mathcal{D}$, for each ad we extract the features listed in Section 3.3.1. As these are a mix of categorical (*i.e.*, discrete) and continuous features, we apply *one-hot encoding* to transform each k-valued categorical feature into a k-dimensional binary vector. The i-th component of such a vector evaluates to 1 if and only if the value of the original feature is i, and 0 otherwise. We also standardise continuous features by transforming their original values into their corresponding *z-scores* [11]. Finally, we obtain a set of 45 features.

3.3.4 Offline Evaluation. From the balanced labelled dataset above we derive two random partitions $\mathcal{D}_{\text{train}}$ and $\mathcal{D}_{\text{test}}$, which contain 80% and 20% of the total samples respectively. We again validate our performance by running a 10-fold cross validation on $\mathcal{D}_{\text{train}}$ selecting between different models and their varying hyperparameter settings.

For DT, we test two different node-splitting criteria s: *Gini index* and *entropy*. We also set the maximum depth of the tree d to the total number of features. For GBDT, we use four values of the number K of base trees in the ensemble, with $K = \{10, 100, 500, 1{,}000\}$ in combination with the learning rates α, 0.001, 0.01, 0.05, 0.1, 1. Finally, for RF we test the same number of base trees as for GBDT whilst again bounding the maximum depth of each base tree to the total number of features. For each learning model we report

Model	s	α	d	K	ROC AUC
RF	–	–	16	1,000	**0.93**
GBDT	–	0.1	–	100	0.92
DT	*entropy*	–	3	–	0.84

Table 2: Best cross validation hyperparameter settings for each learning model ("–" if the hyperparameter is not considered).

	RF	GBDT	DT
F_1	**0.84**	0.81	0.75
MCC	**0.66**	0.63	0.49

Table 3: Evaluation of best performing models on the test set $\mathcal{D}_{\text{test}}$.

in Table 2 the hyperparameter settings leading to the best cross validation ROC AUC. The overall best performing model is RF with an ensemble of 1,000 base trees and maximum depth 16.

To avoid mixing model selection with model evaluation, we re-train each model on $\mathcal{D}_{\text{train}}$ using its best hyperparameter setting, and assess its validity on the held-out and unseen test set $\mathcal{D}_{\text{test}}$. We measure two standard quality metrics, F_1 and Matthews Correlation Coefficient (MCC) [17]. Table 3 shows the results. RF is the best performing model also with respect to the ability of generalising its predictive power to previously unseen examples.

Compared with the results reported in [12], we notice a remarkable increase of ROC AUC (+10.7%) and a small improvement of F_1 (+1.2%). In their work, Logistic Regression (LogReg) [26] was the

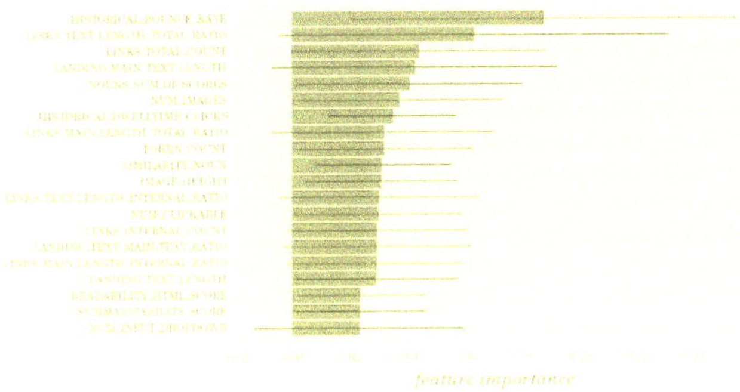

Figure 1: Top-20 most important features of our RF model.

best model (ROC AUC = 0.84 and F_1 = 0.83). Our increased performance comes from a combination of a more rigorous procedure for determining the threshold τ.[6] a more effective learning model, RF, and a larger set of features.

We also calculate the "importance" of each feature from the learned RF model. Figure 1 lists the top-20 most important ones. As in [1, 12], historical features have significant predictive power. We keep historical features because we want the learned model for which we run our feature tweaking algorithm to be the most effective possible. However, our feature tweaking algorithm will ignore historical features when generating recommendations, as it only considers *adjustable* ad features, *i.e.*, features that advertisers can actively alter to improve the quality of their ads.

From now on, we use RF as our learned model to generate actionable suggestions on which features to tweak to turn a low quality ad into a high quality one.

4 EXPERIMENTS: AD FEATURE RECOMMENDATIONS

We validate the recommendations generated with our approach, by applying our feature tweaking algorithm to our learned RF model. Any $\mathbf{x}'$ that results from a valid (*i.e.*, positive) ϵ-transformation of the original negative instance $\mathbf{x}$ encapsulates a set of directives on how to positively change the ad features. We compute the vector $\mathbf{r}$ resulting from the component-wise difference between $\mathbf{x}'$ and $\mathbf{x}$, which is $\mathbf{r}[i] = \mathbf{x}'[i] - \mathbf{x}[i]$. Then for each feature i, such that $\mathbf{r}[i] \neq 0$ (*i.e.*, $\mathbf{x}'[i] \neq \mathbf{x}[i]$), this vector provides the *magnitude* and the *direction* of the changes that should be made on feature i. The magnitude denotes the absolute value of the change (*i.e.*, $|\mathbf{x}'[i] - \mathbf{x}[i]|$), whilst the direction indicates whether this is an *increase* or a *decrease* of the original value of feature i (*i.e.*, $\text{sgn}(\mathbf{x}'[i] - \mathbf{x}[i])$). Finally, to derive the final list of recommendations, we sort $\mathbf{r}$ according to the feature ranking, as shown in Figure 1.

4.1 The impact of hyperparameters δ and ϵ

Our approach depends on a *tweaking cost* (δ) associated with transforming a negative instance (low quality ad) into a positive instance (high quality ad), and a *tweaking tolerance* (ϵ) used to change each individual ad feature. We first explore how ϵ impacts on the ad

[6] In their work, the threshold was set as the *flat* median of the observed dwell times of all ads.

ϵ	0.01	0.05	0.10	0.50	1.00
ad coverage (%)	58.5	64.2	72.3	**77.4**	63.2

Table 4: The impact of tolerance threshold ϵ on ad coverage.

coverage, which is the percentage of ads for which our approach is able to provide recommendations. We experiment with five values of ϵ: 0.01, 0.05, 0.1, 0.5, and 1. These values can be thought of as multiples of a unit of standard deviation from each individual feature mean, as discussed in Section 2.4. Table 4 shows the highest coverage is when $\epsilon = 0.5$.

Although some low quality ads cannot be transformed, those that can are often associated with multiple transformations. Figure 2 shows the distribution of ϵ-transformations across the set of ads, generated using different values of ϵ (except $\epsilon = 1$ which is similar to $\epsilon = 0.05$). All the distributions are skewed offering a high number of transformations proposed for few ads. Interestingly, the number of transformations is more evenly distributed across the ads when ϵ increases. This is in agreement with the finding above, where larger values of ϵ result in a higher coverage before decreasing again between $\epsilon = 0.5$ and 1.

To choose the most appropriate transformation for an ad, we experiment with several tweaking cost functions δ, each taking as input the original ($\mathbf{x}$) and the transformed ($\mathbf{x}'$) feature vectors:

- tweaked_feature_rate: proportion of features affected by the transformation of $\mathbf{x}$ into $\mathbf{x}'$ (range = $[0, 1]$);
- euclidean_distance: Euclidean distance between $\mathbf{x}$ and $\mathbf{x}'$ (range = $\mathbb{R}$);
- cosine_distance: 1 minus the cosine of the angle between $\mathbf{x}$ and $\mathbf{x}'$ (range = $[0, 2]$);
- jaccard_distance: one's complement of the Jaccard similarity between $\mathbf{x}$ and $\mathbf{x}'$ (range = $[0, 1]$);
- pearson_correlation_distance: 1 minus the Pearson's correlation coefficient between $\mathbf{x}$ and $\mathbf{x}'$ (range = $[0, 2]$).

Up to a certain value, the tolerance ϵ is positively correlated with the ad coverage. We explore how it impacts the five tweaking cost functions. Figure 3(a) plots the micro-average costs and Figure 3(b) shows the median of all the individual per-ad average costs. In general, the greater the tolerance the higher the cost (except for tweaked_feature_rate and jaccard_distance when $\epsilon = 1$); thus a trade-off between ϵ (*i.e.*, ad coverage) and the cost of ad transformations δ is desirable.

4.2 Evaluating Recommendations

We first present descriptive statistics on the recommendations obtained with our approach on a set of 100 low quality ad landing pages, the true negative instances in $\mathcal{D}_{test}$. Each recommendation either suggests to *increase* or *decrease* the value of a given feature. Overall, the recommendations are almost evenly distributed over the two cases above.

In Figure 4, we list the top-5 most frequent features recommended to be tweaked according to the top-1, top-2 and top-3 proposed ϵ-transformations by measuring the relative frequency of each feature appearing among each of the ϵ-transformations. The most frequent feature is LINKS_TEXT_LENGTH_TOTAL_RATIO in all settings, which measures the ratio of text length to the total number of hyperlinks

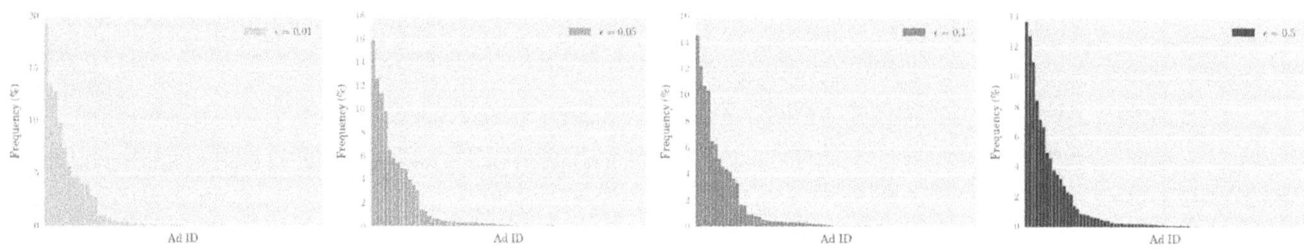

(a) (b) (c) (d)

Figure 2: Distribution of per-ad ϵ-transformations.

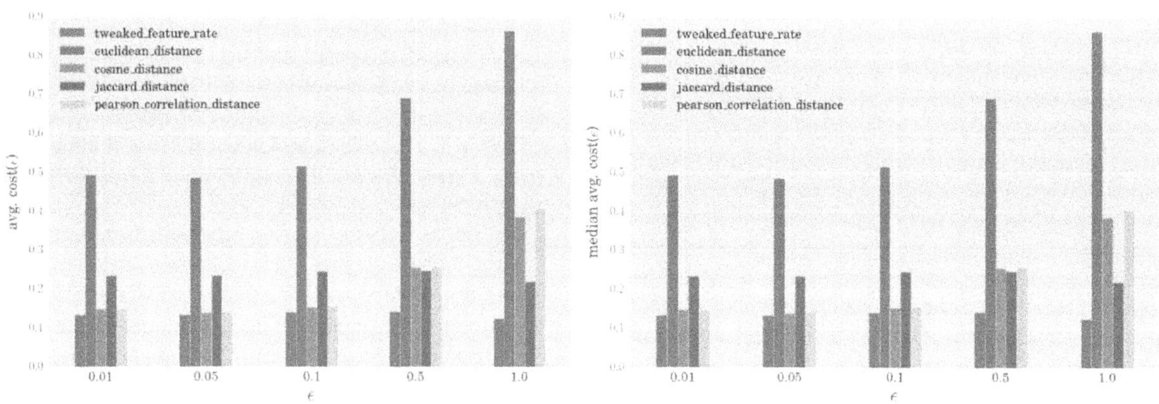

(a) (b)

Figure 3: The impact of tolerance threshold ϵ on costs δ.

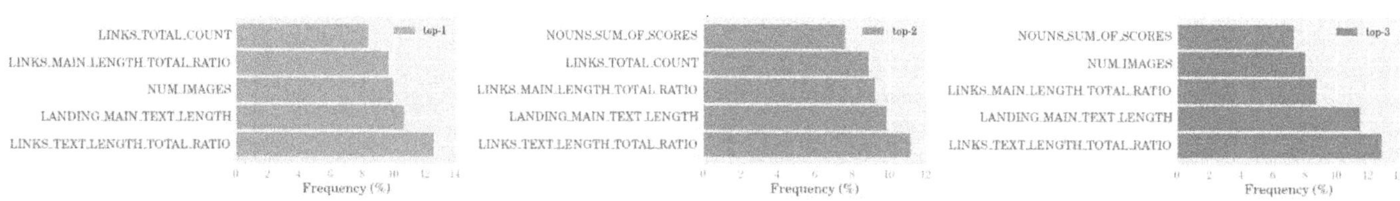

(a) (b) (c)

Figure 4: Top-5 most frequent features appearing in the top-1, top-2 and top-3 ϵ-transformations (ϵ = 0.05).

in the ad landing page. Interestingly, *all* the recommendations concerning this feature suggest to *decrease* its value. This indicates that low quality ad landing pages generally exhibit an unbalanced ratio of text to hyperlinks suggesting that saturating a page in links rather than content has negative effects on dwell time.

We measure the Pearson's correlation coefficient (ρ) between feature rankings appearing in the top-1, top-2 and top-3 ϵ-transformations. All three rankings are strongly related with each other, with top-1 reaching $\rho = 0.93$ and 0.81 when compared to top-2 and top-3, respectively. Similarly, top-2 is highly correlated to top-3 ($\rho = 0.79$).[7] We also compute the correlation coefficient between top-1 ϵ-transformations for all values of ϵ, and δ = cosine_distance. The top-1 rankings derived from $\epsilon = 0.05$ and 0.1 are the highest correlated ($\rho = 0.92$). However, there is no statistical significant correlation between top-1 rankings when $\epsilon = 0.1$ and 0.5, indicating that higher values of tolerance may impact more on the features requiring change.

We now perform a *qualitative* and *quantitative* assessment of such recommendations. For each low quality landing page, we focus on its top-k ϵ-transformations, *i.e.*, the k less costly transformations according to the cost function δ. In turn, each transformation contains a list of recommendations, sorted by the feature rank they refer to. We set the hyperparameters to $\epsilon = 0.05$ and δ = cosine_distance,

[7]All values are statistically significant at $\alpha = 0.01$.

as this combination provides the best trade-off between ad coverage and average cost. We consider the top-3 ϵ-transformations suggested for each ad landing page. Around 91.0% of landing pages can be associated with all three ϵ-transformations, whereas our algorithm provides the remaining 7.5% and 1.5% with two and one ϵ-transformation, respectively.

We also asked an internal team of creative strategists (CS)[8] to validate the recommendations generated by our approach. Each CS was assigned a set of ad landing pages with the corresponding ϵ-transformations, and additional metadata useful for assessing the recommendations within each transformation. The same set of ad landing pages – and therefore the same list of recommendations – was assessed by two CSs, who were asked to rate each recommendation as *helpful*, *non-helpful*, or *non-actionable*. A recommendation is deemed *helpful* when it is likely to help the advertiser to improve the user experience of the ad, and *non-helpful* otherwise. A *non-actionable* recommendation is one that cannot be practically implemented. Whenever a disagreement occurred, a third CS was called to resolve the conflict.

Overall, 57.3% of all the generated recommendations are rated helpful with an inter-agreement rate of 60.4% and only 0.4% result in a non-actionable suggestion. We also look at the 42.3% non-helpful recommendations, and saw that about 25% can be considered "neutral"; that is, they would not hurt the user experience if discarded as well as not adding any positive value if implemented.

Non-helpful tweaks might occur due to two reasons. First, the learned model we leverage for generating feature recommendations – no matter how accurate it is – is not perfect; therefore, a true negative instance that is transformed into a positive prediction does not necessarily mean it is *actually* positive. Second, tuning the hyperparameters (δ and ϵ) of our algorithm affects the set of candidate transformations. As such, limiting non-helpful tweaks can be achieved by improving the accuracy of the learned model and choosing values of the hyperparameters to minimize errors.

Furthermore, when we further look into the non-actionable recommendations we see that these are related to the features ADULT_SCORE and NUM_INPUT_DROPDOWN. Our algorithm suggests to decrease the value of those features; however, the ad landing pages do not contain adult words nor drop-downs. Most likely, the ad copies and landing pages used to generate recommendations have changed before the CSs performed their assessment.

Finally, we measure the "helpfulness" of each feature recommendation as follows:

$$\text{helpfulness}(i) = \frac{|\text{helpful}(i)|}{|\text{helpful}(i)| + |\neg\text{helpful}(i)|}$$

This computes the relative frequency of recommendations for feature i as being described as helpful by the CS team. In Figure 5, we report the ranked list of features involved in the top-10 most helpfulness recommendations. A similar ranking is obtained if we weight the helpfulness score on the basis of the *overall* relative recommendation frequency. The majority of the most helpful recommendations were features extracted from the DOM structure and content of the ad landing page, indicating that high quality landing pages should exhibit a good balance between textual content and hyperlinks. Those features were the most predictive in our RF ad quality model (Figure 1).

[8]Creative strategists work with advertisers' web masters on strategic choices to help them developing effective advertising messages.

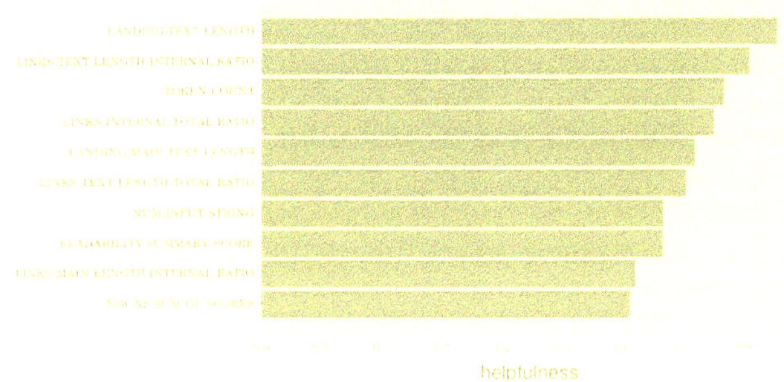

Figure 5: Top-10 most helpful feature recommendations according to the helpfulness score.

5 RELATED WORK

The research challenge addressed in this work is largely unexplored. Although machine learning has received a lot of attention in recent years, the focus has been mainly on the accuracy, efficiency, scalability, and robustness of the proposed various techniques. Works on extracting actionable knowledge from machine-learned models have been mostly conducted within the business and marketing domains. Early works have focused on the development of interestingness metrics as proxy measures of knowledge actionability [3, 10].

Another line of research on actionable knowledge discovery concerns post-processing techniques. Liu *et al.* propose methods for pruning and summarizing learned rules, as well as matching rules by similarity [14, 15]. Cao *et al.* present domain-driven data mining; a paradigm shift from a research-centered discipline to a practical tool for actionable knowledge [4, 5]. The authors discuss several frameworks for handling different problems and applications.

Many works discuss post-processing techniques specifically tailored to decision trees [8, 16, 24, 25]. Yang *et al.* study the problem of proposing actions to maximise the expected profit for a group of input instances based on a single decision tree, and introduce a greedy algorithm to approximately solve such a problem [25]. This is significantly different from our work; in fact, our work is more related to the one presented by Cui *et al.* [6]. Here, the authors propose a method to support actionability for additive tree models (ATMs), which is to find the set of actions that can change the prediction of an input instance to a desired status with the minimum cost. The authors formulate the problem as an instance of integer linear programming (ILP) and solve it using existing techniques.

Similarly to Cui *et al.*, we also consider transforming the prediction for a given instance output by an ensemble of trees, and we introduce an algorithm that finds the *exact* solution to the problem. Our work differs from theirs in several aspects: *(i)* We tackle the theoretical intractability (NP-hardness) of the problem by designing an algorithm that creates a feedback loop with the original model to build a set of candidate transformations without the need, in practice, to explore the entire exponential search space; *(ii)* We introduce another hyperparameter (ϵ) to govern the amount of change that each feature can sustain; *(iii)* We experiment with five concrete functions describing the cost of each transformation (δ); *(iv)* We leverage on the importance of each feature derived from the model to rank the final list of recommendations; *(v)* We focus on the actual recommendations generated, and how they impact in practice on a real use case, if properly implemented.

More recent work on related topics are those of Ribeiro *et al.* [20, 21]. In particular, [21] presents LIME, a method that aims to explain the predictions of any classifier by learning an interpretable model that is specifically built around the predictions of interest. They frame this task as a submodular optimization problem, which the authors solved using a well-known greedy algorithm achieving performance guarantees. They test their algorithm on different models for text (*e.g.*, random forests) and image classification (*e.g.*, neural networks), and validate the utility of generated explanations both via simulated and human-assessed experiments.

6 CONCLUSIONS

Machine-learned models are often designed to favour accuracy of prediction at the expense of human-interpretability. However, in some circumstances it becomes important to understand why the model returns a certain prediction on a given instance and how such an instance could be transformed in such a way that the model changes its original prediction. We investigate this problem within the context of general ensembles of tree-based classifiers, which has been proven to be NP-hard. We then introduce an algorithm that is able to transform a true negative instance into a set of new "proposed" positive instances by shifting their position in the feature space. The algorithm leverages the internals of the learned ensemble to *tweak* the feature-based representation of a true negative instance so that the new "proposed" ones are promoted to a positive classification when re-input to the classifier.

Despite computationally intractable in the worst case, we demonstrate the applicability of our approach on a real-world use case in online advertising. The feasibility of our approach has been achieved by *(i)* setting an upper bound to the maximum number of changes affecting each instance (*i.e.*, at most equivalent to the number of features), which can be controlled at training time, and by *(ii)* creating a feedback loop with the original model to build a set of candidate transformations without the need, in practice, to explore the entire exponential search space.

After designing an effective Random Forest classifier able to separate between *low* and *high* quality ads – our application scenario – we automatically provide "actionable" suggestions on how to optimally convert a low quality ad (negative instance) into a high quality one (positive instance) using our approach. To illustrate the outcomes of our algorithm, we assess the quality of the recommendations that our method generates from a dataset of ads served by a large ad network, *Yahoo Gemini*. An evaluation conducted by an internal team of creative strategists shows that 57.3% of the provided recommendations are indeed helpful, and likely to improve the ad quality, if implemented.

In future work, we plan to extend the approach presented in this work to multi-class setting as well as to other learning models, and to encapsulate it into a reinforcement learning framework.

ACKNOWLEDGMENTS

The authors would like to thank Huw Evans, Mahlon Chute, and all the Yahoo's internal team of creative strategists for their invaluable contributions in evaluating the quality of the method presented in this work.

REFERENCES

[1] Nicola Barbieri, Fabrizio Silvestri, and Mounia Lalmas. 2016. Improving Post-Click User Engagement on Native Ads via Survival Analysis. In *WWW '16*. International World Wide Web Conferences Steering Committee, 761–770.

[2] Leo Breiman. 2001. Random Forests. *Machine Learning* 45, 1 (Oct. 2001), 5–32.

[3] Longbing Cao, Dan Luo, and Chengqi Zhang. 2007. Knowledge Actionability: Satisfying Technical and Business Interestingness. *International Journal of Business Intelligence and Data Mining* 2, 4 (Dec. 2007), 496–514.

[4] Longbing Cao and Chengqi Zhang. 2006. Domain-Driven Actionable Knowledge Discovery in the Real World. In *PAKDD '06*. Springer-Verlag, 821–830.

[5] Longbing Cao, Huaifeng Zhang, E.K. Park, Dan Luo, Yanchang Zhao, and Chengqi Zhang. 2013. Flexible Frameworks for Actionable Knowledge Discovery. *IEEE TKDE* 22, 9 (Sep. 2013), 1299–1312.

[6] Zhicheng Cui, Wenlin Chen, Yujie He, and Yixin Chen. 2015. Optimal Action Extraction for Random Forests and Boosted Trees. In *KDD '15*. ACM, 179–188.

[7] Neil Daswani and Michael Stoppelman. 2007. The Anatomy of Clickbot.A. In *HotBots '07*. USENIX Association, 11–11.

[8] Jianfeng Du, Yong Hu, Charles X. Ling, Ming Fan, and Mei Liu. 2011. Efficient Action Extraction with Many-to-Many Relationship between Actions and Features. In *LORI '11*. Springer Berlin Heidelberg, 384–385.

[9] Jerome H. Friedman. 2002. Stochastic Gradient Boosting. *Computational Statistics and Data Analysis* (2002).

[10] Robert J. Hilderman and Howard J. Hamilton. 2000. Applying Objective Interestingness Measures in Data Mining Systems. In *PKDD '00*. Springer Berlin Heidelberg, 432–439.

[11] E. Kreyszig. 1979. *Introductory Mathematical Statistics: Principles and Methods*. Wiley.

[12] Mounia Lalmas, Janette Lehmann, Guy Shaked, Fabrizio Silvestri, and Gabriele Tolomei. 2015. Promoting Positive Post-Click Experience for In-Stream Yahoo Gemini Users. In *KDD '15*. ACM, 1929–1938.

[13] Yann LeCun, Yoshua Bengio, and Geoffrey Hinton. 2015. Deep Learning. *Nature* 521 (May 2015), 436–444. Issue 7553.

[14] Bing Liu and Wynne Hsu. 1996. Post-analysis of Learned Rules. In *AAAI '96*. AAAI Press, 828–834.

[15] Bing Liu, Wynne Hsu, and Yiming Ma. 1999. Pruning and Summarizing the Discovered Associations. In *KDD '99*. ACM, 125–134.

[16] Karim Masud and M. Rahman Rashedur. 2013. Decision Tree and Naïve Bayes Algorithm for Classification and Generation of Actionable Knowledge for Direct Marketing. *Journal of Software Engineering and Applications* 6, 4 (2013), 196–206.

[17] B. W. Matthews. 1975. Comparison of the predicted and observed secondary structure of T4 phage lysozyme. *Biochimica et Biophysical Acta* 405 (Oct. 1975), 442–451.

[18] J. R. Quinlan. 1986. Induction of Decision Trees. *Machine Learning* 1, 1 (March 1986), 81–106.

[19] Hema Raghavan and Dustin Hillard. 2009. A Relevance Model Based Filter for Improving Ad Quality. In *SIGIR '09*. ACM, 762–763.

[20] Marco Tulio Ribeiro, Sameer Singh, and Carlos Guestrin. 2016. Model-agnostic interpretability of machine learning. In *2016 ICML Workshop on Human Interpretability in Machine Learning (WHI 2016)*. 91–95.

[21] Marco Tulio Ribeiro, Sameer Singh, and Carlos Guestrin. 2016. "Why Should I Trust You?": Explaining the Predictions of Any Classifier. In *KDD '16*. ACM, 1135–1144.

[22] Brett Stone-Gross, Ryan Stevens, Apostolis Zarras, Richard Kemmerer, Chris Kruegel, and Giovanni Vigna. 2011. Understanding Fraudulent Activities in Online Ad Exchanges. In *IMC '11*. ACM, 279–294.

[23] Christian Szegedy, Wojciech Zaremba, Ilya Sutskever, Joan Bruna, Dumitru Erhan, Ian Goodfellow, and Rob Fergus. 2013. Intriguing properties of neural networks. *CoRR* (2013).

[24] Qiang Yang, Jie Yin, Charles Ling, and Rong Pan. 2007. Extracting Actionable Knowledge from Decision Trees. *IEEE TKDE* 19, 1 (Jan. 2007), 43–56.

[25] Qiang Yang, Jie Yin, Charles X. Ling, and Tielin Chen. 2003. Postprocessing Decision Trees to Extract Actionable Knowledge. In *ICDM '03*. IEEE Computer Society, 685–688.

[26] Hsiang-Fu Yu, Fang-Lan Huang, and Chih-Jen Lin. 2011. Dual Coordinate Descent Methods for Logistic Regression and Maximum Entropy Models. *Machine Learning* 85, 1-2 (Oct. 2011), 41–75.

[27] Ke Zhou, Miriam Redi, Andrew Haines, and Mounia Lalmas. 2016. Predicting Pre-click Quality for Native Advertisements. In *WWW '16*. International World Wide Web Conferences Steering Committee, 299–310.

Structural Deep Brain Network Mining

Shen Wang
University of Illinois at Chicago
Chicago, USA
swang224@uic.edu

Lifang He*
Shenzhen University
Shenzhen, China
lifanghescut@gmail.com

Bokai Cao
University of Illinois at Chicago
Chicago, USA
caobokai@uic.edu

Chun-Ta Lu
University of Illinois at Chicago
Chicago, USA
clu29@uic.edu

Philip S. Yu
University of Illinois at Chicago
Chicago, USA
Tsinghua University
Beijing, China
psyu@cs.uic.edu

Ann B. Ragin
Northwestern University
Chicago, USA
ann-ragin@northwestern.edu

ABSTRACT

Mining from neuroimaging data is becoming increasingly popular in the field of healthcare and bioinformatics, due to its potential to discover clinically meaningful structure patterns that could facilitate the understanding and diagnosis of neurological and neuropsychiatric disorders. Most recent research concentrates on applying subgraph mining techniques to discover connected subgraph patterns in the brain network. However, the underlying brain network structure is complicated. As a shallow linear model, subgraph mining cannot capture the highly non-linear structures, resulting in sub-optimal patterns. Therefore, how to learn representations that can capture the highly non-linearity of brain networks and preserve the underlying structures is a critical problem.

In this paper, we propose a Structural Deep Brain Network mining method, namely SDBN, to learn highly non-linear and structure-preserving representations of brain networks. Specifically, we first introduce a novel graph reordering approach based on module identification, which rearranges the order of the nodes to preserve the modular structure of the graph. Next, we perform structural augmentation to further enhance the spatial information of the reordered graph. Then we propose a deep feature learning framework for combining supervised learning and unsupervised learning in a small-scale setting, by augmenting Convolutional Neural Network (CNN) with decoding pathways for reconstruction. With the help of the multiple layers of non-linear mapping, the proposed SDBN approach can capture the highly non-linear structure of brain networks. Further, it has better generalization capability for high-dimensional brain networks and works well even for small sample learning. Benefit from CNN's task-oriented learning style, the learned hierarchical representation is meaningful for the clinical task. To evaluate the proposed SDBN method, we conduct extensive experiments on four real brain network datasets for disease diagnoses. The experiment results show that SDBN can capture discriminative and meaningful structural graph representations for brain disorder diagnosis.

*Corresponding author. This work was done while the author was at the University of Illinois at Chicago.

KDD'17, August 13–17, 2017, Halifax, NS, Canada.
© 2017 ACM. ISBN 978-1-4503-4887-4/17/08...$15.00
DOI: http://dx.doi.org/10.1145/3097983.3097988

CCS CONCEPTS

•Information systems →Data mining; •Computing methodologies →Machine learning;

KEYWORDS

brain network, deep learning, graph reordering

1 INTRODUCTION

In many neurological and neuropsychiatric disorders, brain involvement, including irreversible loss of brain tissue and deterioration in cognitive function [19], has deleterious consequences for judgment and function. Early detection in subclinical periods is critical for aiding clinical diagnosis, clarifying underlying mechanisms and informing neuroprotective interventions to slow or reverse neural injury for a broad spectrum of brain disorders, e.g., HIV infection, attention-deficit/hyperactivity disorder (ADHD), and bipolar disorder (BP). The last several decades have witnessed rapid progress in noninvasive neuroimaging techniques, e.g., functional resting-state magnetic resonance imaging (fMRI) and structural diffusion tensor imaging (DTI), from which an underlying brain connectivity network (a.k.a, connectome [42]) can be interrogated. New capacilities for investigating the vast patterns of connectivity involving billions of neurons, promise to yield new insights concerning the normal brain and many disorders. Brain connectomes are often represented as graphs, where nodes represent brain regions and edges represent connections between pairs of regions.

Learning discriminative and clinically meaningful representations from brain networks has the following challenges:

- **High non-linearity**: [30] found that the underlying structure of graph data is often non-linear. Brain network, as a typical example of graph data, has highly non-linear interactions between cortical regions [36]. How to build the model to capture these highly non-linear structure is challenging.

- **Structure preserving**: The structure of brain network plays a key role in brain network analysis. However underlying structure of brain network is highly complicated [37]. Therefore, preserving the structure is difficult during the brain network mining.
- **Noise**: The analysis of real brain networks usually suffers from noise. For example, some brain connections may be wrongly placed during fMRI analysis. This kind of noise may introduce errors into diagnosis of the brain disorders.
- **Limited quantity and high dimensionality**: imaging studies of neurological disorders often involve a limited number of samples due to the limited number of available patients of interest and the high costs of acquiring the data, which significantly limits the graph mining method that can be used.

In the literature, many brain network mining methods have been proposed. Most of them concentrate on selecting frequent substructures, such as connected subgraph patterns[6, 9, 22, 26]. However, since connections between brain regions are characterized by massive complexity, it is difficult for traditional subgraph mining models to accurately capture or approximate the complicated highly non-linear structure of brain networks. Moreover, these methods only search for most frequent simple patterns, and do not consider any underlying structural information of brain networks. Additionally, as the number of subgraph patterns is exponential to the size of graphs, the subgraph mining process is both time consuming and memory intensive. Recently, some researchers leverage kernel techniques as a way to perform brain network learning [23, 46], where graph kernel is used to integrate local connectivity and global topological properties of brain networks. From the perspective of model architecture depth, all the above methods are shallow models. As stated in [47] and [50], shallow models are recognized as encountering the curse of dimensionality, and having limited capability in learning the feature representation in complex situations.

To address the above challenges, we propose a Structural Deep Brain Network Mining method, namely SDBN, to learn highly non-linear and structure-preserving representations of brain networks. Specifically, we consider to extract the locally connected ROIs as the receptive fields in the brain network and construct a multilayer convolutional neural network (CNN) architecture, which consists of multiple non-linear gating functions, for learning the graph representation in the highly non-linear latent space. To solve the issues of structural preserving and graph noise, we exploit the underlying graph structure in threefold. First, we propose a novel graph reordering approach based on spectral clustering to rearrange the order of the nodes, which can preserve the modular structure of the graph. Second, we perform structural augmentation to further enhance the spatial information of the reordered graph for structure-preserving and noise-robust feature learning. Third, we propose a deep feature learning framework for joint supervised and unsupervised learning in a small-scale setting by augmenting multilayer CNN with decoding pathways for reconstruction. Benefiting from the multiple layers of non-linear mapping, the proposed SDBN method can capture the highly non-linear structure of brain networks. With the help of the regularization power of unsupervised learning augmentation, the proposed deep model is robust to small datasets. Moreover, CNN learns features in a task-oriented style and can capture the meaningful feature for clinical tasks.

In summary, this paper makes the following contributions:

- We propose a Structural Deep Brain Network mining method, namely SDBN, to learn discriminative and meaningful graph representation from brain networks. The learned graph representation residing in the highly non-linear latent space can preserve the graph structure and be robust to the noise.
- A graph reordering technique for brain networks is proposed with the help of spectral clustering. This technique corresponds brain networks from different subjects and makes them comparable. The CNN-based deep feature learning method becomes more reliable and the underlying graph structure can be exposed.
- A structural augmentation is introduced to enhance the structure information by adding the spatial information and to alleviate the effect of the noise.
- A deep feature learning framework for joint supervised and unsupervised learning is proposed in a small-scale setting by augmenting existing neural networks with decoding pathways for reconstruction. The unsupervised learning augmentation has a regularization effect to make the learned features have better generalization from the high dimensional data.
- The proposed method is extensively evaluated on brain disorder detection with four real brain network datasets. The experiments show that SDBN can capture discriminative and meaningful structural graph representations for brain disorder diagnosis.

2 PRELIMINARY AND PROBLEM FORMULATION

In this section, we first establish the key notational conventions that we will use in the sequel. We then define the problem we are concerned with brain network mining.

Notations. Throughout this paper, vectors are denoted by boldface lowercase letters (*e.g.*, $\mathbf{a}$), matrices are denoted by boldface capital letters (*e.g.*, $\mathbf{A}$), and cubes are denoted by calligraphic letters (*e.g.*, $\mathcal{A}$). For a matrix $\mathbf{A} \in \mathbb{R}^{I \times J}$, its elements are denoted by a_{ij}, and its i-th row and j-th column are denoted by $\mathbf{a}_i$ and $\mathbf{a}^j$, respectively. We denote a weighted graph by a triple $G = (V, E, \mathbf{W})$, where $V = \{v_1, v_2, \cdots, v_N\}$ is the set of nodes, $E \subseteq V \times V$ is the set of edges connecting nodes, and $\mathbf{W}$ is the connectivity weight matrix encoding connectivity strengths of the edges. In particular, $N = |V|$ denotes the number of nodes and $M = |E|$ denotes the number of edges of the graph. We will often use calligraphic letters $(\mathcal{G}, \mathcal{H}, \cdots)$ to denote general sets or spaces, regardless of their specific nature.

Before proceeding to define our problem, we first introduce some related concepts of brain network. Hereafter we use "brain network" and "graph" interchangeably whenever there is no ambiguity.

Definition 2.1. **(Brain Network)** A brain network (or connectome), is a weighted graph $G = (V, E, \mathbf{W})$ with $|V|$ nodes and $|E|$ edges reflecting brain regions of interest (ROIs) and connectivities between ROIs, respectively. The weights or adjacency matrix in $\mathbf{W}$ represent the connectivity degree, where a larger weight corresponds to a higher connectivity degree, reflecting stronger functional correlations in fMRI and tighter fiber connections in DTI.

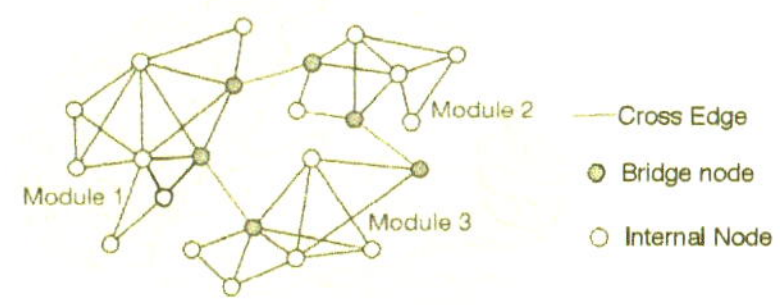

Figure 1: A brain network example, associated with modules, cross edges, internal and bridge nodes

The module structure of brain network is critical in the study of brain. To facilitate brain analysis, brain network mining is required to preserve the module structure. It can be characterized by locality and similarity. The locality describes that nodes in the same module are connected tightly while the similarity describes that nodes in the same module often have similar neighborhood structure. The definition of "module" is given as follows.

Definition 2.2. **(Module)** A module (also called community or group) in a graph is a subset of nodes which are densely connected to each other, but sparsely connected to the nodes in other modules. The node with all its neighboring nodes in the same module is internal node. The node with neighboring nodes belong to the different modules is bridge node.

To better understand and illustrate the module structure, an example of brain network is shown in Figure 1, in which lobe Frontal, lobe Parietal, lobe Temporal are represented by the modules in blue, yellow and green respectively. There are a number of nodes representing brain regions and a number of edges representing connections between pairs of regions. Among these nodes, white nodes indicate the internal nodes and red nodes indicate the bridge nodes. Between different modules, bridge nodes are connected by cross edge marked in blue. One can notice that within each module, the nodes are connected tightly to each other than the nodes in other regions, which performs strong locality and similarity.

Now we formally define the problem studied in this paper. Given N brain networks $\mathcal{G} = \{G_1, G_2, \cdots, G_N\}$, we denote their corresponding connectivity matrices $\mathcal{W} = \{\mathbf{W}_1, \mathbf{W}_2, \cdots, \mathbf{W}_N\}$, where $\mathbf{W}_i \in \mathbb{R}^{N \times N}$. Let $\mathcal{H} = \{\mathbf{h}_1, ..., \mathbf{h}_N\}$. We are concerned with discovering a good vector representation $\mathbf{h}_i$ for each brain network G_i. Specifically, we are interested in learning a representation function $f : \mathcal{G} \to \mathcal{H}$, which maps each brain network $G_i \in \mathcal{G}$ into a discriminative, highly-nonlinear, structure-preserving, and clinically meaningful representation $\mathbf{h}_i \in \mathcal{H}$. The representation function is estimated on a collection of brain networks and their connectivity matrices.

Deep learning methods have powerful representation learning capability, especially in capturing the highly-nonlinear representation. Among them Convolutional Neural Network (CNN) provides an efficient framework to discover the highly-nonlinear, discriminative and task-focus representation. It can capture the local stationary structures hierarchically, which has achieved successes in many fields, such as computer vision, signal processing and nature language processing. However, applying CNN straightforwardly to brain network is not reliable. The connection between different brain regions lies on an irregular or non-Euclidean domain. This kind of edge is a universal representation of heterogeneous pairwise relation. In terms of the connectivity matrices, the receptive field of CNN can not encode the module structure well. Therefore it is usually difficult to identify common patterns and different patterns among different subjects. Here we formulate a graph reordering technique to generalize CNN to learn a structure-preserving representation $\mathcal{H}$. Its definition is as follows.

Definition 2.3. **(Graph Reordering)** Given a collection of unlabeled graphs $\mathcal{G} = \{G_1, G_2, \cdots, G_N\}$, the goal of graph reordering is to find a labeling ℓ such that for any two graphs $G_i, G_j \in \mathcal{G}$ drawn uniformly at random from $\mathcal{G}$, the expected difference between the distance of the graph connectivity matrices based on ℓ and the distance of the graphs in graph space is minimized. Let $\mathbf{d}_{\mathrm{G}}$ be a distance measure on graphs $\mathcal{G}$, and $\mathbf{d}_{\mathrm{W}}$ be a distance measure on connectivity matrices $\mathcal{W}$. It can be formulated as the following optimization problem:

$$\arg\min_{\ell} \mathbb{E}_{\mathrm{G}}[||\mathbf{d}_{\mathrm{W}}(\mathbf{W}_i^{\ell}, \mathbf{W}_j^{\ell}) - \mathbf{d}_{\mathrm{G}}(G_i, G_j)||] \quad (1)$$

Graph reordering is essentially a graph labeling procedure, which assigns labels to the nodes or edges, or both. In general, Eq. (1) is a difficult combinatorial problem. Solving this problem would require $n!$ trials in the worst case. Therefore optimal graph reordering is NP-hard and computationally infeasible. Alternatively, we borrow the idea of graph compression [8], handling this problem by performing module identification in brain.

In the following, we will elaborate our approach towards above concepts.

3 PROPOSED METHOD

As discussed in the introduction, learning good feature representations from brain networks is challenging due to its complex and non-linear structure. To overcome these challenges, we propose a structural deep brain network mining (SDBN) method. An overview of SDBN is shown in Figure 2, which consists of three main steps: (1) Graph Reordering; (2) Structural Augmentation; and (3) Convolutional Deep Feature Learning. These steps collectively address the challenges of brain network representation learning.

3.1 Graph Reordering

The objective of graph reordering is to leverage graph labeling procedure to reorder the nodes in the connectivity matrix, where the difference of distances from the connectivity matrices of graphs is minimized, in the sense that nodes close to each other are more likely to have strong connections. In this way, a permutation of the nodes across different brain networks is established. By graph reordering, nodes belonging to the same module will be located close to each other [13] and the structural topology within the graphs is very similar [33]. This would make CNN more able to bring out the latent network structures shared by the different networks. However, as the optimal graph reordering is NP-hard, it is infeasible to solve Eq. (1) directly. Alternatively, we borrow the idea from graph compression [2] to address this problem. The intuitive idea of graph compression is to produce a compressed graph of a given weighted graph by finding an ordering of nodes, such that the connectivity matrix is close to block-diagonal. Specifically, it was noted that finding modules is a useful conceptual tool for analyzing

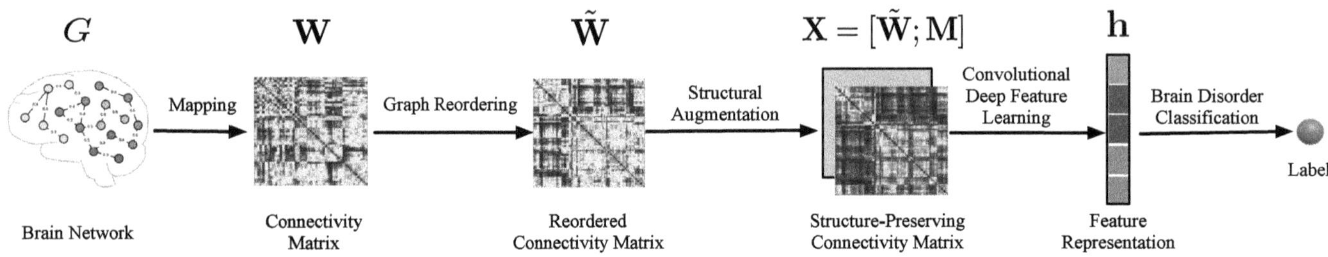

Figure 2: An overview of the proposed SDBN method. Connectivity matrix, reordered connectivity matrix and structure-preserving connectivity matrix are represented in heat map, where high heat color indicates strong connection. The structure-preserving connectivity matrix consists of two channels: the first channel is the reordered connectivity matrix with the weights of the off-block diagonal regions being lowered. The second channel is the module identification matrix M

relations between the original and compressed graphs. Based on this insight, we identify the modules among brain networks to approximate the optimal graph reordering.

Currently various methods have been used for module identification. Among the existing methods, spectral clustering often yields more superior performance compared to other methods. Spectral methods have also been successfully applied to graph reordering problems [24]. Therefore, we employ the spectral clustering to perform module identification. The key idea of spectral clustering is to convert a clustering problem into a graph partitioning problem and then solve this problem by means of matrix theory. Let K be the number of modules to be identified, and $\hat{\mathbf{W}} \in \mathbb{R}^{N\times N}$ be the average connectivity matrix across all graphs. Then, spectral clustering can be formulated as follows:

$$\min_{\mathbf{F}} \sum_{i,j=1}^{N} \hat{w}_{ij} \left\|\mathbf{f}_i - \mathbf{f}_j\right\|_2^2 = \mathrm{tr}\left(\mathbf{F}^{\mathrm{T}}\mathbf{L}\mathbf{F}\right)$$
$$\text{s.t. } \mathbf{F}^{\mathrm{T}}\mathbf{F} = \mathbf{I}_K \quad (2)$$

where $tr(\cdot)$ denotes the trace function, a superscript T denotes transposition, $\mathbf{I}_K$ denotes the identity matrix with size K, and $\mathbf{L}$ is the Laplacian matrix [45] obtained from $\hat{\mathbf{W}}$.

By applying K-means to the eigenvectors of the Laplacian matrix $\mathbf{L}$, we can obtain K modules $\mathcal{M} = \{M_1, M_2, \cdots, M_K\}$, with $V = M_1 \cup M_2 \cup \cdots \cup M_K$ and $M_i \cap M_j = \varnothing$ for every pair i, j with $i \neq j$. We treat the module sequence $1, 2, \cdots, K$ as a permutation of nodes. Based on this, the reordered connectivity matrix $\tilde{\mathbf{W}}$ for each brain network can be established. Since all reordered connectivity matrices are obtained according to the global module structure, different subjects are more comparable. An example of the reordered connectivity matrices for abnormal and normal subjects is shown in the second column (b) and (e) of Figure 3.

3.2 Structural Augmentation

According to the graph reordering procedure above, we obtain the reordered connectivity matrix for each brain network. This representation is more meaningful and beneficial to CNN architecture. However, there are still two problems affecting the use of CNN. The first one is the spatial information loss caused by CNN itself. The second one is the noise in brain network. To address these problems, we propose a structural augmentation approach to further enhance the spatial information of the reordered graph for structure-preserving and noise-robust feature learning.

CNN adopts max pooling to perform invariant properties to translation, rotation and shifting, which results in the spatial information loss. However, the spatial relation of each receptive field is also important structure information for brain network mining. Given the top layer of the network, the original spatial information is lost. Naturally, the clinical structure patterns only occur in specific brain regions and those occurring in the other brain regions are usually invalid.

To tackle this problem, we augment the reordered connectivity matrix with an additional channel. Specifically, we define a module identification matrix $\mathbf{M}$ to further encode the module structure information, whose element is:

$$m_{ij} = \begin{cases} k & \text{for} \quad v_i, v_j \in M_k, i, j = 1, ..., N \\ 0 & \text{for} \quad otherwise \end{cases} \quad (3)$$

The constructed $\mathbf{M}$ is a block-diagonal matrix. It is concatenated with the reordered connectivity matrix as an additional channel as shown in Figure 2. With such an information augmentation, we could preserve the spatial information during the feature learning procedure.

On the other hand, brain networks usually suffer from noise, which is introduced by the error in the acquisition and in the image analysis. For the reordered connectivity matrix obtained from graph reordering, the intra-module neighbor edges reside in the block-diagonal region and the cross edges lie in the off-diagonal region. The intra-module neighbor edges preserve the structure within each module, which are more reliable to learn structure-preserving graph representation, while the cross edges are more complicated which may have negative effects to study the modular structure and some of them may be invalid connections [18]. To alleviate the effects of cross edges, we further augment the reordered connectivity matrix $\tilde{\mathbf{W}}$ by lowering the weights of the off-block diagonal regions such that

$$\tilde{w}_{ij} = \begin{cases} 1 & \text{for} \quad i, j \in M_k, k = 1, ..., K \\ \epsilon & \text{for} \quad i, j \notin M_k, k = 1, ..., K \end{cases} \quad (4)$$

An example of the resulted new reordered connectivity matrices for abnormal and normal subjects is shown in the third column (c) and

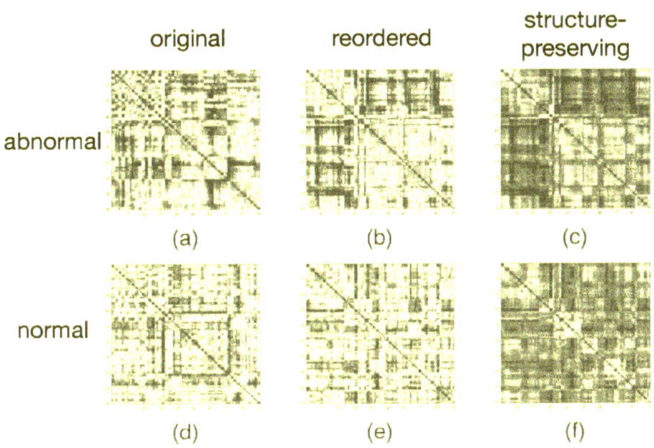

Figure 3: The first row and second row show the connectivity matrices of the abnormal subjects and that of the normal subjects, respectively. From left to right, the first column Figures (a) and (d) present the original connectivity matrices mapped from the brain network, the second column Figures (b) and (e) indicate the reordered connectivity matrices after the graph reordering and the third column Figures (c) and (f) show the first channel of structure preserving connectivity matrices.

(f) of Figure 3. Together with module information augmentation, we obtain the structure-preserving connectivity matrix $\mathbf{X} = [\tilde{\mathbf{W}}; \mathbf{M}]$ as shown in Figure 2, which encodes more structural information and is beneficial for CNN.

3.3 Unsupervised Learning Augmented CNN

In this section, the resulting connectivity matrices are fed into the CNN architecture for feature learning. Specifically, we introduce a novel CNN architecture to learn highly non-linear feature representations from the brain network data while dealing with the problem of small sample size and high dimensionality.

CNN is a supervised feature learning technique, which has demonstrated state-of-the-art performance for image analysis [27]. Recent works [14] [39] [43] commonly nest a group of convolutional layers and a pooling layer to construct the basic feature extractor in different scales. The extracted internal representation preserves highly-nonlinear properties. Consider the feature extractors in different scales as cells, the input data goes over a number of convolution-pooling cells and fully connected layer. Finally, they are fed to the top-layer classifier. The CNN with L cells can be defined as follows

$$\mathbf{X}^l = f_l(\mathbf{X}^{l-1}; \Theta_l) \quad \text{for} \quad l = 1, 2, ..., L+1 \tag{5}$$

where $\mathbf{X}^0 = \mathbf{X}$ is the input,which is the resulted structure-preserving connectivity matrix. $f_l(\cdot)$ for $l = 1, 2, ..., L$ are the feature mapping functions of the $l-th$ cell with the parameter Θ_l. The final classification loss can be represented as follows

$$C(\mathbf{X}^0, y) = \ell(\mathbf{X}^{L+1}, y) \tag{6}$$

where y corresponds to the ground truth label, which indicates the patients' disease diagnose result, and ℓ indicates the classification loss function.

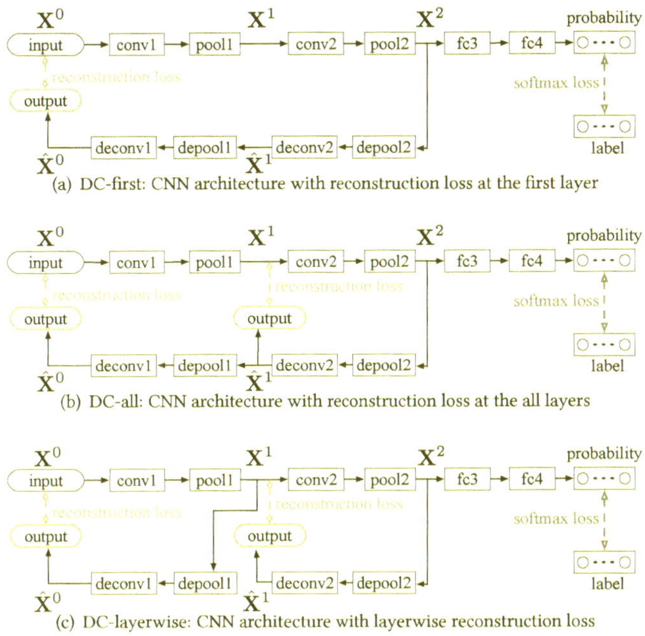

Figure 4: CNN architecture with three types of unsupervised learning augmentation

Given a set of subject data $\mathbf{X}_1, \mathbf{X}_2, ..., \mathbf{X}_N$ with corresponding labels $y_1, y_2, ..., y_N$, the CNN is trained by minimizing the objective function as follows

$$\frac{1}{N}\sum_{i=1}^{N} C(\mathbf{X}_i, y_i) \tag{7}$$

However, CNN usually requires a large amount of labeled data for training, which is infeasible for current brain health research, due to the limited number of available patients of interest and the high costs of acquiring the data. It could potentially limit the performance of CNN.

Motivated by the recent attempts [28, 35, 41, 49] to couple the unsupervised and supervised learning in the same phase, making the unsupervised objective being able to impact the network training after supervised learning took place, we augment the auxiliary unsupervised learning objective function to the supervised learning objective function to address the above problem. The joint objective function is as follows

$$\frac{1}{N}\sum_{i=1}^{N}(C(\mathbf{X}_i, y_i) + \lambda U(\mathbf{X}_i)) \tag{8}$$

where $U(\cdot)$ indicates the unsupervised objective function, which can be one or more auxiliary pathways that are attached to the convolution-pooling cells in the original CNN.

Specifically, given the CNN architecture for classification, we take the sub-network consists of all the convolution-pooling cells as the encoding pathway, and build a mirrored decoder network as an auxiliary pathway of the original network. The fully connected layers are not used for reconstruction, since they are more related to supervised learning objective. For a CNN with 2 convolution-pooling cells, we consider three types of unsupervised learning augmentation via decoding: DC-first, DC-all and DC-layerwise. Their frameworks are shown in Figure 4. The decoding pathway is defined as follows

$$\hat{X}^L = X^L, \quad \hat{X}^{l-1} = f_l^{dec}(\hat{X}^l; \Theta_l'), \quad \hat{X} = \hat{X}^0 \tag{9}$$

where Θ_l' are decoder parameters.

Figure 4(a) shows the framework of DC-first. In DC-first, the CNN is just augmented with a stacked autoencoder. The decoding starts from the pooled feature generated by the second pooling layer and goes to reconstruct the original input. Reconstruction errors are measured between the final reconstruction input and the CNN input. The auxiliary training signals of DC-first come from the bottom of the decoding pathway and are incorporated with the top-down signals from the supervised learning into the encoder pathway. The corresponding unsupervised loss is as follows:

$$U_{DC-first}(X) = ||\hat{X} - X||_2^2 \tag{10}$$

Figure 4(b) shows the framework of DC-all. Different from DC-first, it allows more gradients to flow directly to the previous cells. This model makes the autoencoder perform better mirrored architecture by matching activations for all the cells. Its unsupervised learning loss is as follows:

$$U_{DC-all}(X) = \sum_{l=1}^{L-1} ||\hat{X}^l - X^l||_2^2 \tag{11}$$

Figure 4(c) shows the framework of DC-layerwise, which is another autoencoder variant with layerwise decoding architecture. It reconstructs the output activations of every cell to its input. Its unsupervised learning loss is the same as DC-all. Different from DC-all, its decoding pathway is defined as follows:

$$\hat{X}^{l-1} = f_l^{dec}(X^l; \Theta_l') \tag{12}$$

The first two methods encourage top-level convolution features to preserve as much information as possible. In contrast, the decoding pathways in DC-layerwise concentrates on inverting the clean intermediate activations to the input of the associated cell-layer, performing parallel layerwise training.

The training procedure of our proposed method is as follows: (1) Train the CNN with labels; (2) Train "layerwise" decoding pathways; (3) Train the top-down decoding pathways; and (4) Fine-tune the entire augmented network. With the help of the proposed deep convolutional feature learning framework, we can address the three problems above and learn discriminative graph feature representations.

4 EXPERIMENTS AND RESULTS

In this section, we evaluate the proposed methods on four real-world datasets. We first introduce the datasets used in the experiments, the compared methods and the experimental setting. Next, we show the performance of compared methods on four brain network datasets described below. We further conduct several case studies, including the effectiveness of graph reordering using different spectral clustering configurations (corresponding to different Laplacian matrices) and the effectiveness of unsupervised learning augmentation.

Table 1: The statistics for each dataset

Name	HIV-fMRI	HIV-DTI	BP-fMRI	ADHD-fMRI
Category	fMRI	DTI	fMRI	fMRI
Quantity	77	77	97	776
Size	90 x 90	90 x 90	82 x 82	90 x 90

4.1 Data Collection

In the experiments, we evaluate the proposed methods on four brain network datasets from three different neurological disorders.

- **HIV-fMRI-77 & HIV-DTI-77**: Chicago Early HIV Infection Study at Northwestern University [34] collected both fMRI and DTI data for 56 HIV (positive) and 21 seronegative controls (negative). By propagating the Automated Anatomical Labeling (AAL) to each image [44], each brain is represented as a graph with 90 nodes corresponding to cerebral regions (45 for each hemisphere). A detailed description about data acquisition and preprocessing is available in [5].
- **BP-fMRI-97**: This dataset consists of 52 bipolar I subjects who are currently in euthymia and 45 age and gender matched healthy controls. Using the Freesurfer-generated cortical/subcortical gray matter regions, functional brain networks were derived using pairwise BOLD signal correlations of 82 brain regions. A detailed description about data acquisition and preprocessing is available in [6].
- **ADHD-fMRI-776**: This dataset is collected from ADHD-200 global competition dataset[1]. The dataset contains records of resting-state fMRI images for 776 subjects, which are labeled as real patients (positive) and normal controls (negative). Similarly, each brain is parcellated into 90 brain regions.

The statistics for each dataset is summarized in Table 1. The HIV-fMRI, HIV-DTI, BP-fMRI are relatively small datasets, while the ADHD-fMRI is a relatively big dataset.

4.2 Compared Methods

To evaluate the performance of the proposed method, we compare it with other state-of-the-art methods. All the compared methods are summarized as follows:

- **gSSC**: It is a semi-supervised subgraph feature selection method [25] based upon both labeled and unlabeled graphs.
- **Freq**: This method is an unsupervised subgraph feature selection method based upon frequency. The top-*n* frequent subgraph features are selected.
- **Conf, Ratio, Gtest, HSIC**: These methods are supervised subgraph selection [26] based upon confidence, frequency ratio, G-test score and HSIC, respectively. The top-*n* discriminative subgraph features are selected in terms of different discrimination criteria.
- **AE**: It is an unsupervised feature learning method based on autoencoder [48] which learns the latent representation of all the connectivity data without considering any structural information.

[1] http://neurobureau.projects.nitrc.org/ADHD200

- **CNN**: It is a plain vanilla convolutional architecture stacking the convolution layer, pooling layer, non-linear gating layer and fully connected layer. The graph reordering and structural augmentation is not applied.

Since the proposed SDBN consists of several components, we consider several variations of SDBN as follows:

- **CNN-GN**: It is a convolutional architecture with graph reordering of nodes. It has three versions: **SP**, **NJW** and **SM** [45], each of which uses a different spectral clustering method. SP indicates the graph reordering using the unnormalized spectral clustering, which aims to minimize ratio cut. NJW indicates the graph reordering with the normalized spectral clustering by Ng-Jordan-Weiss Algorithm [32]. SM indicates the graph reordering with normalized spectral clustering by Shi and Malik [38], which aims to minimize normalized cut.
- **CNN-GN-A**: It is a convolutional architecture with graph reordering and structural augmentation.
- **CNN-GN-A-DC**: It is a convolutional architecture with graph reordering, structural augmentation and unsupervised learning augmentation. It has three variations: **DC-first**, **DC-all**, **DC-layerwise**. DC-first uses the augmentation with reconstruction loss at the first layer. DC-all uses the augmentation with reconstruction loss at all layers. DC-layerwise uses the augmentation with a layerwise architecture.
- **SDBN**: It is the method proposed in this work which can learn structural-preserving graph feature representation that lies in a highly non-linear latent space. There are two versions of SDBN: one with a shallow architecture (**SDBN-S**) and one with a deep architecture (**SDBN-D**). We select the best parameter configuration for them.

4.3 Experimental Setting

To evaluate the quality of the learned brain network representation, we feed the learned feature representation to a softmax classifier for each compared method. For the subgraph mining methods, the threshold for four dataset is 0.9, 0.3, 0.5, 0.5, respectively. We select top-100 features for classification as in [48].

For SDBN, we first select the configuration of the graph reordering. By empirical study, we choose the SM spectral clustering method and set the cluster size $K = 9$. Then we choose the configurations to build CNN. We build a convolutional architecture with different layers as shown in Table 2. It stacks the convolution layer, pooling layer, non-linear gating layer and fully connected layer. For a fair comparison, we set the number of the neurons in the fully connected layer to 100. SDBN-S has the following setup: LayerC-LayerP-LayerN-LayerF-Layer-N, while SDBN-D has the following setup: LayerC-LayerP-LayerN-LayerC-LayerP-LayerN-LayerF-LayerN. To prevent the overfiting problem, the dropout is added after the fully connected layer with dropout rate being 0.5. In the experiment, we apply AdaGrad [11], an adaptive gradient-based optimization approach that automatically determines a per-parameter learning rate, for parameter learning. Since there are limited number of subjects in the datasets, we perform a 3-fold cross validation as in [3] on balanced datasets and report the average results.

Table 2: The configuration of different cell-layers in the convolution architecture. LayerC, LayerP, LayerN and LayerF indicate the convolution layer, the pooling layer, the non-linear gating function and the fully connected layer, respectively.

Name	LayerC	LayerP	LayerN	LayerF
Type	conv	max-pool	gating	fc
Parameter	$5 \times 5 \times 50$	2×2	relu	100

4.4 Performance on Brain Disorder Detection

In this section, we investigate the effectiveness of the learned structure-preserving graph feature representations for brain disease detection. The average classification performance are shown in Table 3. Two evaluation metrics are used, including accuracy and F1 score. It is easy to see that SDBN outperforms all the other baseline methods on all four datasets. Compared with subgraph mining methods that search in a potentially exponential space, the proposed methods achieve better performance and consume around 83% less memory and computation resources. In additional we can see that AE has a little better performance than the subgraph mining methods in most of cases. This is probably because, the connectivity patterns learned from AE can capture the non-linear complex structure in brain network. CNN is nearly the worst one among all the models, since applying CNN directly to brain network is not reliable. Compared with the shallow feature learning methods, our shallow model SDBN-S outperforms AE. This is due to the fact that SDBN can identify more complex graph representations, while AE can only identify simple representations. It supports our premise that more discriminative graph feature representation can be identified by SDBN. Considering the deepness, our deep architecture SDBN-D achieves a better result than the shallow architecture SDBN-S, since the features learned from the deep architecture can capture hierarchical and highly non-linear structure patterns. It is also worth noticing that deep model has limited improvement compared with shallow model on small data set such as HIV-fMRI, HIV-DIT, BP-fMRI, while shows significant improvement in the a relative big dataset such as ADHD-fMRI. When the size of dataset is big, the deep learning methods show their superiority.

4.5 Case Study of Graph Reordering

In this part, we study the importance of graph reordering in the proposed method. We compare the performance of CNN with and without graph reordering. In addition, we study how the graph reordering using different spectral clustering methods and cluster sizes affects the quality of learned feature representation.

We conduct experiments for brain disorder detection with three different spectral clustering methods and two cluster numbers on all four datasets. The clustering methods used in the experiments include SP, NJW, and SM [45] as mentioned above. Two cluster sizes 6 and 9 are considered. The average accuracies are reported in Figure 5. Compared the CNN without graph reordering, CNNs with graph reordering have a significant gain except for the ones using SP. It indicates the importance of graph reordering. As an unnormalized spectral clustering method, SP has a limited clustering ability, especially for brain networks. It has limited improvement

Table 3: Performances of the compared methods. The results are reported as "average performance + (rank)".

Dataset	Measure	Method									
		gSSC	Freq	Conf	Ratio	Gtest	HSIC	AE	CNN	SDBN-S	SDBN-D
HIV-fMRI-77	ACC	60.0 (4)	54.3 (8)	58.6 (6)	54.3 (8)	50 (9)	58.7 (5)	62.9 (3)	55.2 (9)	65.3 (2)	**66.5 (1)**
	F1	62.5 (4)	58.2 (8)	64.2 (3)	62.0 (5)	52.5 (10)	59.5 (7)	60.4 (6)	56.7 (9)	65.4 (2)	**66.7 (1)**
HIV-DIT-77	ACC	59.5 (4)	64.6 (3)	52.4 (9)	59.3 (5)	59.3 (5)	57.9 (6)	57.8 (7)	54.3 (8)	64.7 (2)	**65.9 (1)**
	F1	59.6 (4)	63.9 (3)	46.1 (10)	57.9 (7)	58.5 (5)	58.3 (6)	56.8 (8)	53.5 (9)	64.5 (2)	**65.6 (1)**
BP-fMRI-97	ACC	56.7 (5)	56.8 (4)	50.8 (10)	54.2 (8)	55.2 (6)	54.9 (7)	60.4 (3)	53.8 (9)	63.0 (2)	**64.8 (1)**
	F1	57.8 (4)	57.6 (5)	49.1 (10)	53.7 (8)	53.9 (7)	55.8 (6)	59.8 (3)	52.1 (9)	62.5 (2)	**63.7 (1)**
ADHD-fMRI-776	ACC	55.7 (4)	48.5 (7)	54.5 (6)	48.5 (7)	54.5 (6)	46.1 (8)	61.3 (3)	55.3 (5)	68.9 (2)	**71.2 (1)**
	F1	55.9 (4)	55.0 (5)	51.4 (7)	55.0 (5)	51.4 (7)	50.5 (8)	60.1 (3)	54.2 (6)	67.6 (2)	**69.9 (1)**

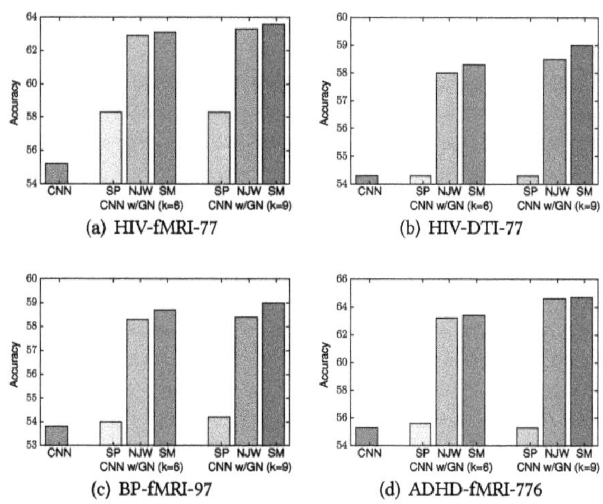

Figure 5: Case study of graph reordering. In each bar chart, the CNN methods with and without graph reordering (GR) are compared. For CNN w/GN, different cluster numbers m are tested.

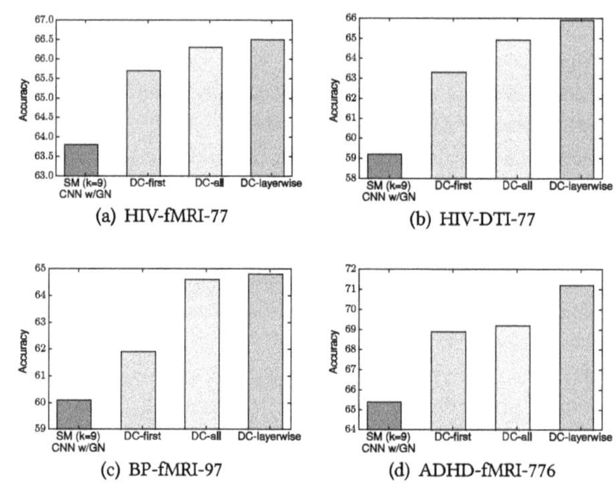

Figure 6: Case study of unsupervised learning augmentation. In each bar chart, the method with good graph reordering (SM, k=9), and the methods with additional unsupervised learning augmentation are compared.

on HIV-DTI, BP-fMRI and ADHD-fMRI compared with CNN without graph reordering. The clusters it produces cannot preserve the underlying structure well and are not helpful for CNN feature learning. For the rest of two clustering methods, SM is slightly better than NJW, due to its better clustering ability. Hence, the spectral clustering method is the key to graph reordering. Compared with graph reordering using different cluster sizes, the ones with 9 clusters are slightly better than the ones with 6 clusters, which confirms the same observation in [31]. It indicates that the cluster size is also an important factor for graph reordering. Overall, the quality of spectral clustering is important to graph reordering and good spectral clustering will produce a graph reordering close to the optimal graph reordering.

Spectral clustering not only supports graph reordering but also exposes the rich graph structure of brain networks. The generated clustering information can be reused for structural augmentation. In order to test its effectiveness, we add the modular structure matrix during the feature learning process. It is found that with structural augmentation, we usually have about 1% improvement based on CNN with good graph reordering.

In conclusion, graph reordering is critical to learn graph representation directly from the brain network data using CNN architecture. After graph reordering, the structure-preserving locally connectivity regions can be extracted and serve as the receptive fields of CNN, allowing the CNN framework to learn effective graph representations.

4.6 Case Study of Unsupervised Learning Augmentation

In this part, we investigate the effectiveness of unsupervised learning augmentation in the proposed method. With the best reordering configuration from previous section, we compare CNN with and without unsupervised learning augmentation. We conduct experiments for brain disease detection with three different unsupervised learning augmentations on all four datasets. We take the sub-network of CNN composed of all the convolution-pooling layers as the encoder and generate a fully mirrored decoder network as an auxiliary pathway of the original network. We measure the reconstruction loss in three ways: DC-first, DC-all, DC-layerwise as described above and augment the supervised loss with these reconstruction loss. The average accuracies are shown as in Figure 6. We can see that on four datasets, CNNs with unsupervised learning augmentation outperform the ones without augmentation. It demonstrates the effectiveness of unsupervised learning augmentation, and the performance of different augmentation methods are comparable. Among them, the DC-layerwise is slightly better than the other two methods, the DC-all is slightly better than DC-first.

Overall, unsupervised learning augmentation is helpful for learning graph representation. This can be explained in two folds. First, the spatial information is critical for brain network analysis. The clinical disrupted conductivities is module inspired and usually happens among certain ROIs. The traditional CNN's max pooling operation preserves the spatial invariance properties but removes the spatial information. Reconstruction objective is spatial corresponded, which can help to keep the spatial information. Second, the decoding pathways help the supervised objective reach a better optimum and regularize the final objective solution. Third, the layer-wise reconstruction loss is an effective way to regularize the network training.

5 RELATED WORK

Our work is related to deep learning, graph reordering and brain data mining. We briefly discuss them in the followings.

5.1 Deep Learning

Representation learning has long been an important problem of machine learning and many works aim at learning representations for samples [1]. Recent years, deep learning is becoming more and more popular, due to its powerful ability of learning feature with different kinds properties and can be applied for different kind of data. It made success in different fields, such as computation vision [14, 27, 39, 43], nature language processing [40] and speech recognition [21]. Several recent works have been proposed which show neural architectures for graph input data [12, 20, 29], these methods are trying to apply the convolutional neural network on the simple graph structure data. However, to the best of our knowledge, there have been few deep learning works on brain network [48], especially learning brain network representations.

5.2 Graph Reordering

Graph Reordering is very active in the field of data base and data mining. It is widely used for the graph compression task. which focus on finding homogeneous regions in the graph so that nodes inside a region are tightly connected to each other than to nodes in other regions. In terms of the adjacency matrix, the target was to find an ordering of nodes so that the adjacency matrix is close to block-diagonal, containing more "square" blocks. Spectral clustering [32, 38], co-clustering [10], cross-associations [7], and shingle-ordering [8] are typical examples for such approaches. Graph reordering also has some other applications. Recently, [33] proposed a reordering method for the nodes of the neighborhood graph so as to map from the unordered graph space to a vector space with a linear order and try to learn from graph with the help of CNN with considering the node attribute.

5.3 Brain Data Mining

Applications of data mining techniques to brain network data analysis are related to our work as well. Wee et al. used clustering coefficients of each brain region and a multi-kernel SVM for early detection of brain abnormalities in Alzheimer's disease [46]. Jie et al. used a graph kernel and integrate local connectivity and global topological properties of fMRI brain networks [23]. Kong et al. proposed a discriminative subgraph selection approach for uncertain fMRI networks [6, 26]. Cao et al. proposed a supervised tensor factorization technique to analyze EEG brain networks [4]. Ma et al. investigate the interior-node topology of brain networks [31]. Zhang et al. presented an autoencoder architecture with the guidance of side information for brain network analysis [48]. He et al. proposed several tensor based methods to analyze brain data [15–17]. In contrast to the existing works, this work presents a novel approach to discover highly non-linear patterns from brain network data based on a deep convolutional architecture.

6 CONCLUSION AND OUTLOOK

In this paper, a structural deep brain network mining method, namely SDBN, is proposed to learn structural preserving and clinically meaningful representation from brain network. SDBN consists of several components: (1) Graph Reordering (2) Structural Augmentation, and (3) Convolutional Deep Feature Learning. Based on spectral clustering, graph reordering is proposed to impose an order on the nodes of the neighborhood graph so as to preserve the global and local structure of the brain network. Next, we perform structural augmentation to further enhance the spatial information of the reordered graph. Then a deep feature learning framework is introduced, which joint supervised and unsupervised learning in a small-scale setting by augmenting existing supervised CNN with decoding pathways for unsupervised reconstruction. With the help of the multiple layers of non-linear mapping, it can capture the highly non-linear network structure of the brain network. To evaluate our methods, we conduct the experiment on four real brain network datasets for disease diagnoses. The experiments show that SDBN can discover discriminative and meaningful structural graph representation for brain disorder diagnosis. Since the proposed deep feature learning framework is end-to-end and task-oriented, its application is not limited to binary disease classification. It can be easily extended to the other clinical task with objectives such as multi-class classification, clustering, regression and ranking. We plan to apply our framework for the other medical task.

7 ACKNOWLEDGEMENTS

This work is supported in part by NSF through grants IIS-1526499 and CNS-1626432, and NSFC through grants 61503253 and 61672313, and NIH through grant R01-MH080636. We gratefully acknowledge the support of NVIDIA Corporation with the donation of the Titan X GPU used for this research.

REFERENCES

[1] Yoshua Bengio, Aaron Courville, and Pascal Vincent. Representation learning: A review and new perspectives. *IEEE Transactions on Pattern Analysis and Machine Intelligence*, 35(8):1798–1828, 2013.
[2] Paolo Boldi and Sebastiano Vigna. The webgraph framework i: compression techniques. In *Proceedings of the 13th International Conference on World Wide*

Web, pages 595–602, 2004.
[3] Bokai Cao, Lifang He, Xiangnan Kong, Philip S. Yu, Zhifeng Hao, and Ann B. Ragin. Tensor-based multi-view feature selection with applications to brain diseases. In *IEEE International Conference on Data Mining*, pages 40–49, 2014.
[4] Bokai Cao, Lifang He, Xiaokai Wei, Mengqi Xing, Philip S. Yu, Heide Klumpp, and Alex D Leow. t-bne: Tensor-based brain network embedding. In *Proceedings of the SIAM International Conference on Data Mining*, 2017.
[5] Bokai Cao, Xiangnan Kong, Jingyuan Zhang, Philip S. Yu, and Ann B. Ragin. Identifying HIV-induced subgraph patterns in brain networks with side information. *Brain Informatics*, 2015.
[6] Bokai Cao, Liang Zhan, Xiangnan Kong, Philip S. Yu, Nathalie Vizueta, Lori L Altshuler, and Alex D Leow. Identification of discriminative subgraph patterns in fmri brain networks in bipolar affective disorder. In *International Conference on Brain Informatics and Health*, pages 105–114, 2015.
[7] Deepayan Chakrabarti, Spiros Papadimitriou, Dharmendra S Modha, and Christos Faloutsos. Fully automatic cross-associations. In *Proceedings of the 10th ACM SIGKDD International Conference on Knowledge Discovery and Data Mining*, pages 79–88, 2004.
[8] Flavio Chierichetti, Ravi Kumar, Silvio Lattanzi, Michael Mitzenmacher, Alessandro Panconesi, and Prabhakar Raghavan. On compressing social networks. In *Proceedings of the 15th ACM SIGKDD International Conference on Knowledge Discovery and Data Mining*, pages 219–228, 2009.
[9] Ian Davidson, Sean Gilpin, Owen Carmichael, and Peter Walker. Network discovery via constrained tensor analysis of fmri data. In *Proceedings of the 19th ACM SIGKDD International Conference on Knowledge Discovery and Data Mining*, pages 194–202, 2013.
[10] Inderjit S Dhillon, Subramanyam Mallela, and Dharmendra S Modha. Information-theoretic co-clustering. In *Proceedings of the 9th ACM SIGKDD International Conference on Knowledge Discovery and Data Mining*, pages 89–98, 2003.
[11] John Duchi, Elad Hazan, and Yoram Singer. Adaptive subgradient methods for online learning and stochastic optimization. *Journal of Machine Learning Research*, 12:2121–2159, 2011.
[12] David K Duvenaud, Dougal Maclaurin, Jorge Iparraguirre, Rafael Bombarell, Timothy Hirzel, Alán Aspuru-Guzik, and Ryan P Adams. Convolutional networks on graphs for learning molecular fingerprints. In *Advances in Neural Information Processing Systems*, pages 2224–2232, 2015.
[13] Daniel Gamermann, Arnau Montagud, RA Infante, Julian Triana, PF de Córdoba, and JF Urchueguía. Pynetmet: Python tools for efficient work with networks and metabolic models. *arXiv preprint arXiv:1211.7196*, 2012.
[14] Kaiming He, Xiangyu Zhang, Shaoqing Ren, and Jian Sun. Deep residual learning for image recognition. *arXiv preprint arXiv:1512.03385*, 2015.
[15] Lifang He, Xiangnan Kong, Philip S. Yu, Xiaowei Yang, Ann B. Ragin, and Zhifeng Hao. Dusk: A dual structure-preserving kernel for supervised tensor learning with applications to neuroimages. In *Proceedings of the SIAM International Conference on Data Mining*, pages 127–135, 2014.
[16] Lifang He, Chun-Ta Lu, Hao Ding, Shen Wang, Linlin Shen, Philip S. Yu, and Ann B. Ragin. Multi-way multi-level kernel modeling for neuroimaging classification. In *Proceedings of the IEEE Conference on Computer Vision and Pattern Recognition*, 2017.
[17] Lifang He, Chun-Ta Lu, Guixiang Ma, Shen Wang, Linlin Shen, Philip S. Yu, and Ann B. Ragin. Kernelized support tensor machines. In *Proceedings of the 34th International Conference on Machine Learning*, 2017.
[18] Lifang He, Chun-Ta Lu, Jiaqi Ma, Jianping Cao, Linlin Shen, and Philip S. Yu. Joint community and structural hole spanner detection via harmonic modularity. In *Proceedings of the 22nd ACM SIGKDD International Conference on Knowledge Discovery and Data Mining*, pages 875–884, 2016.
[19] RK Heaton, DB Clifford, DR Franklin, SP Woods, C Ake, F Vaida, RJ Ellis, SL Letendre, TD Marcotte, JH Atkinson, et al. Hiv-associated neurocognitive disorders persist in the era of potent antiretroviral therapy charter study. *Neurology*, 75(23):2087–2096, 2010.
[20] Mikael Henaff, Joan Bruna, and Yann LeCun. Deep convolutional networks on graph-structured data. *arXiv preprint arXiv:1506.05163*, 2015.
[21] Geoffrey Hinton, Li Deng, Dong Yu, George E Dahl, Abdel-rahman Mohamed, Navdeep Jaitly, Andrew Senior, Vincent Vanhoucke, Patrick Nguyen, Tara N Sainath, et al. Deep neural networks for acoustic modeling in speech recognition: The shared views of four research groups. *IEEE Signal Processing Magazine*, 2012.
[22] Shuai Huang, Jing Li, Jieping Ye, Adam Fleisher, Kewei Chen, Teresa Wu, and Eric Reiman. Brain effective connectivity modeling for alzheimer's disease by sparse gaussian bayesian network. In *Proceedings of the 17th ACM SIGKDD International Conference on Knowledge Discovery and Data Mining*, pages 931–939, 2011.
[23] Biao Jie, Daoqiang Zhang, Wei Gao, Qian Wang, Chong-Yaw Wee, and Dinggang Shen. Integration of network topological and connectivity properties for neuroimaging classification. *IEEE Transactions on Biomedical Engineering*, 2014.
[24] Martin Juvan and Bojan Mohar. Optimal linear labelings and eigenvalues of graphs. *Discrete Applied Mathematics*, 36(2):153–168, 1992.
[25] Xiangnan Kong and Philip S. Yu. Semi-supervised feature selection for graph classification. In *Proceedings of the 16th ACM SIGKDD International Conference on Knowledge Discovery and Data Mining*, pages 793–802, 2010.
[26] Xiangnan Kong, Philip S. Yu, Xue Wang, and Ann B. Ragin. Discriminative feature selection for uncertain graph classification. In *Proceedings of the SIAM International Conference on Data Mining*, pages 82–93, 2013.
[27] Alex Krizhevsky, Ilya Sutskever, and Geoffrey E Hinton. Imagenet classification with deep convolutional neural networks. In *Advances in Neural Information Processing Systems*, pages 1097–1105, 2012.
[28] Hugo Larochelle and Yoshua Bengio. Classification using discriminative restricted boltzmann machines. In *Proceedings of the 25th International Conference on Machine Learning*, pages 536–543, 2008.
[29] Yujia Li, Daniel Tarlow, Marc Brockschmidt, and Richard Zemel. Gated graph sequence neural networks. *arXiv preprint arXiv:1511.05493*, 2015.
[30] Dijun Luo, Feiping Nie, Heng Huang, and Chris H Ding. Cauchy graph embedding. In *Proceedings of the 28th International Conference on Machine Learning*, pages 553–560, 2011.
[31] Guixiang Ma, Lifang He, Bokai Cao, Jiawei Zhang, Philip S. Yu, and Ann B. Ragin. Multi-graph clustering based on interior-node topology with applications to brain networks. In *Joint European Conference on Machine Learning and Knowledge Discovery in Databases*, pages 476–492, 2016.
[32] Andrew Y Ng, Michael I Jordan, and Yair Weiss. On spectral clustering: Analysis and an algorithm. In *Advances in Neural Information Processing Systems*, pages 849–856, 2002.
[33] Mathias Niepert, Mohamed Ahmed, and Konstantin Kutzkov. Learning convolutional neural networks for graphs. In *Proceedings of the 33rd International Conference on Machine Learning*, 2016.
[34] Ann B. Ragin, Hongyan Du, Renee Ochs, Ying Wu, Christina L Sammet, Alfred Shoukry, and Leon G Epstein. Structural brain alterations can be detected early in hiv infection. *Neurology*, 2012.
[35] Marc'Aurelio Ranzato and Martin Szummer. Semi-supervised learning of compact document representations with deep networks. In *Proceedings of the 25th International Conference on Machine Learning*, pages 792–799, 2008.
[36] Mikail Rubinov, Stuart A Knock, Cornelis J Stam, Sifis Micheloyannis, Anthony WF Harris, Leanne M Williams, and Michael Breakspear. Small-world properties of nonlinear brain activity in schizophrenia. *Human Brain Mapping*, 30(2):403–416, 2009.
[37] Blake Shaw and Tony Jebara. Structure preserving embedding. In *Proceedings of the 26th International Conference on Machine Learning*, pages 937–944, 2009.
[38] Jianbo Shi and Jitendra Malik. Normalized cuts and image segmentation. *IEEE Transactions on Pattern Analysis and Machine Intelligence*, 22(8):888–905, 2000.
[39] Karen Simonyan and Andrew Zisserman. Very deep convolutional networks for large-scale image recognition. *arXiv preprint arXiv:1409.1556*, 2014.
[40] Richard Socher, Alex Perelygin, Jean Y Wu, Jason Chuang, Christopher D Manning, Andrew Y Ng, Christopher Potts, et al. Recursive deep models for semantic compositionality over a sentiment treebank. In *Proceedings of the Conference on Empirical Methods in Natural Language Processing*, volume 1631, page 1642, 2013.
[41] Kihyuk Sohn, Guanyu Zhou, Chansoo Lee, and Honglak Lee. Learning and selecting features jointly with point-wise gated boltzmann machines. In *Proceedings of the 30th International Conference on Machine Learning*, pages 217–225, 2013.
[42] Olaf Sporns, Giulio Tononi, and Rolf Kötter. The human connectome: a structural description of the human brain. *PLoS Comput Biol*, 2005.
[43] Christian Szegedy, Wei Liu, Yangqing Jia, Pierre Sermanet, Scott Reed, Dragomir Anguelov, Dumitru Erhan, Vincent Vanhoucke, and Andrew Rabinovich. Going deeper with convolutions. In *Proceedings of the IEEE Conference on Computer Vision and Pattern Recognition*, pages 1–9, 2015.
[44] Nathalie Tzourio-Mazoyer, Brigitte Landeau, Dimitri Papathanassiou, Fabrice Crivello, Olivier Etard, Nicolas Delcroix, Bernard Mazoyer, and Marc Joliot. Automated anatomical labeling of activations in spm using a macroscopic anatomical parcellation of the mni mri single-subject brain. *Neuroimage*, 2002.
[45] Ulrike Von Luxburg. A tutorial on spectral clustering. *Statistics and computing*, 2007.
[46] Chong-Yaw Wee, Pew-Thian Yap, Daoqiang Zhang, Kevin Denny, Jeffrey N Browndyke, Guy G Potter, Kathleen A Welsh-Bohmer, Lihong Wang, and Dinggang Shen. Identification of mci individuals using structural and functional connectivity networks. *Neuroimage*, 2012.
[47] Zhaoquan Yuan, Jitao Sang, Changsheng Xu, and Yan Liu. A unified framework of latent feature learning in social media. *IEEE Transactions on Multimedia*, 16(6):1624–1635, 2014.
[48] Jingyuan Zhang, Bokai Cao, Sihong Xie, Chun-Ta Lu, Philip S. Yu, and Ann B. Ragin. Identifying connectivity patterns for brain diseases via multi-side-view guided deep architectures. In *Proceedings of the SIAM International Conference on Data Mining*, pages 36–44, 2016.
[49] Yuting Zhang, Kibok Lee, Honglak Lee, and UMICH EDU. Augmenting supervised neural networks with unsupervised objectives for large-scale image classification. In *Proceedings of the 33rd International Conference on Machine Learning*, 2016.
[50] Jinfeng Zhuang, Ivor W Tsang, and Steven CH Hoi. Two-layer multiple kernel learning. In *AISTATS*, pages 909–917, 2011.

Randomized Feature Engineering as a Fast and Accurate Alternative to Kernel Methods

Suhang Wang
Arizona State University
Tempe, AZ 85281
suhang.wang@asu.edu

Charu Aggarwal
IBM T.J. Watson Research Center
Yorktown Heights, NY 10598
charu@us.ibm.com

Huan Liu
Arizona State University
Tempe, AZ 85281
huan.liu@asu.edu

ABSTRACT

Feature engineering has found increasing interest in recent years because of its ability to improve the effectiveness of various machine learning models. Although tailored feature engineering methods have been designed for various domains, there are few that simulate the consistent effectiveness of kernel methods. At the core, the success of kernel methods is achieved by using similarity functions that emphasize local variations in similarity. Unfortunately, this ability comes at the price of the high level of computational resources required and the inflexibility of the representation as it only provides the similarity of two data points instead of vector representations of each data point; while the vector representations can be readily used as input to facilitate various models for different tasks. Furthermore, kernel methods are also highly susceptible to overfitting and noise and it cannot capture the variety of data locality. In this paper, we first analyze the inner working and weaknesses of kernel method, which serves as guidance for designing feature engineering. With the guidance, we explore the use of randomized methods for feature engineering by capturing multi-granular locality of data. This approach has the merit of being time and space efficient for feature construction. Furthermore, the approach is resistant to overfitting and noise because the randomized approach naturally enables fast and robust ensemble methods. Extensive experiments on a number of real world datasets are conducted to show the effectiveness of the approach for various tasks such as clustering, classification and outlier detection.

CCS CONCEPTS

•Information systems →Data mining;

KEYWORDS

Randomized Feature Engineering; Unsupervised Feature Learning

ACM Reference format:
Suhang Wang, Charu Aggarwal, and Huan Liu. 2017. Randomized Feature Engineering as a Fast and Accurate Alternative to Kernel Methods. In *Proceedings of KDD'17, August 13–17, 2017, Halifax, NS, Canada.*, , 10 pages.
DOI: http://dx.doi.org/10.1145/3097983.3098001

KDD'17, August 13–17, 2017, Halifax, NS, Canada.

ISBN 978-1-4503-4887-4/17/08...$15.00
DOI: http://dx.doi.org/10.1145/3097983.3098001

1 INTRODUCTION

Machine learning algorithms are highly sensitive to the specific feature representation of the data used [3]. Selecting the proper feature representation is important because a good set of features enables the use of fast and simple models, whereas overly compact representations often necessitate the use of complex models that are slow to train and semantically opaque. For example, a well-chosen set of features can often be used in conjunction with a linear support vector machine, which can be trained in time that is linear in the size of the input [14]. The importance of the specific representations has been pointed out quite forcefully [9]: "At the end of the day, some machine learning projects succeed and some fail. What makes the difference? Easily the most important factor is the features used." *Therefore, our first goal of feature engineering is to design discriminative engineered features which can enable the use of fast and simple models.*

Kernel methods [1, 2, 11, 22, 30, 32] are among the most popularly used feature transformation methods, which have been successfully incorporated in different algorithms for better performance such as kernel SVMs for classification [20], kernel PCA for dimensionality reduction [17] and kernel K-means for clustering [7]. The essential idea of kernel methods is to transform a non-linearly separable data to a discriminative and linearly separable feature space, in which the discriminative nature of the feature space is primarily ensured by tuning the parameters of the kernel.

Kernel methods use an implicit transformation by working with the similarity of the data points in the input space, but not the explicit representation in the transformed feature space. Explicit features can be readily used as input for off-the-shelf methods, such as linear SVMs for classification and k-means for clustering. On the other hand, customized kernel algorithms need to be developed for different tasks, such as kernel SVMs for classification and kernel K-means for clustering. *Thus, the second goal of feature engineering is to construct/learn explicit features* to enable wider applicability across many problems.

Kernel algorithms could also be interpreted as a two-step approach of first learning explicit features and then applying simple models on the features. However, such an explicit approach is not practical. Consider a data set $\mathbf{X} \in \mathbb{R}^{n \times d}$ containing n data points and d dimensions. Let $\mathbf{S} \in \mathbb{R}^{n \times n}$ be the kernel similarity matrix with the (i, j)-th entry equal to the kernel similarity between the ith and jth data points, i.e., $\mathbf{S}_{ij} = k(\mathbf{x}_i, \mathbf{x}_j)$, where $k(\cdot, \cdot)$ is the kernel function such as RBF. Then, any kernel SVM can be implemented using the following two-step process:

- Diagonalizing the positive semi-definite similarity matrix $\mathbf{S}$ as $\mathbf{S} = \mathbf{Q}\Sigma^2\mathbf{Q}^T$, where $\mathbf{Q}$ is an $n \times n$ matrix with orthonormal columns and Σ^2 contains the non-negative eigenvalues.

Then, an n-dimensional embedding of the data is given by $Q\Sigma$; and
- Applying a linear SVM on training data with features as $Q\Sigma$, and class labels in the n-dimensional vector $\mathbf{y}$.

The dual problem of linear SVMs is to maximize $\sum_{i=1}^{n} a_i - \frac{1}{2}\sum_{i=1}^{n}\sum_{j=1}^{n} a_i a_j y_i y_j \mathbf{q}_i \Sigma(\mathbf{q}_j \Sigma)^T$, where a_i are the Lagrange multipliers and $\mathbf{q}_i$ is the i-th row of Q. It is evident that $\mathbf{q}_i\Sigma(\mathbf{q}_j\Sigma)^T = \mathbf{q}_i\Sigma^2\mathbf{q}_j^T = k(\mathbf{x}_i, \mathbf{x}_j)$, and thus the above two-step process is equivalent to kernel SVMs. Furthermore, one can also make a similar argument about the kernel k-means algorithm [7, 8].

The transformed features $Q\Sigma$ in the two-step approach are explicit features, which is also referred to as the *data-specific Mercer kernel map*. The explicit features $Q\Sigma$ provide several advantages, such as the ability to manipulate explicit features, drop irrelevant features from $Q\Sigma$, provide better interpretability, or be used as input to different models for different tasks. These flexibilities are not available when using the kernel trick. However, calculating $Q\Sigma$ is rarely used in kernel SVMs or kernel PCAs because of (i) the large dimensionality of the matrix $Q\Sigma$, which is potentially as large as the number of training points n; and (2) the large computational cost, which is of $O(n^3 + n^2 d)$. The fact that the n-dimensional transformation is so cumbersome and space-inefficient limits its practical usage. Furthermore, kernel transformations have several weaknesses from a *modeling* point of view, such as its sensitivity to the multi-locality of the data and noise [23], which will be discussed in detail in Section 2. *Thus, our third goal is to design a feature engineering method that is space and time efficient, and robust to noise.*

Therefore, in this paper, we investigate the problem of designing explicit robust engineered features with lower space and time requirements, which can capture multi-granular locality of the data and thus facilitate classification and clustering with simple models such as linear SVM and K-means. The main contributions of the paper are as follows:

- We investigate the inner working and weaknesses of kernel methods, which inspires a principled way to design engineered features;
- We propose a novel feature engineering method with low space and time requirement called RandLocal, which learns robust features that capture multi-granular locality and is efficient for various tasks with simple models; and
- We conduct extensive experiments to demonstrate the effectiveness of the proposed framework for tasks such as clustering, classification and outlier detection.

The rest of the paper are organized as follows. In Section 2, we investigate inner working and weaknesses of kernel methods. In Section 3, we introduce the proposed framework RandLocal with time/space complexity and connection to nearest neighbor based methods. In Section 5, we conduct experiments to show effectiveness of RandLocal. In Section 6, we conclude with future work.

2 THE INNER WORKING OF A KERNEL TRANSFORMATION AND ITS WEAKNESSES

In this section, we introduce the working and weaknesses of a kernel transformation, which serves as a guidance for designing RandLocal.

2.1 Inner Working of Kernel Transformations

At its core, a kernel method uses a similarity function between two points that is more sensitive to data locality than the dot product. For example, when one uses a Gaussian kernel with small bandwidth h (relative to average inter-point distance), i.e., $k(\mathbf{x}_i, \mathbf{x}_j = \exp^{-\|\mathbf{x}_i - \mathbf{x}_j\|_2^2/h}$, the similarities between many pairs of points are nearly 0 because of the exponential drop-off in similarity with inter-point distance. However, this decay is relatively slow for distances that are much smaller than the bandwidth. It is not the case with the dot-product, which is linearly related to the squared distance between points. Therefore, in high-dimensional embeddings, *pairwise kernel similarity is often extremely sensitive within small data localities of the original representation (depending on the parameters of the kernel such as bandwidth), whereas it is extremely insensitive outside that small locality.*

For example, consider the 9 clusters which belongs two classes illustrated in Figure 1(a). In this case, it is evident that the two classes are perfectly separable using a nonlinear boundary, but they cannot be separated with a linear boundary. This is because the class distributions are localized into small clusters that cannot be linearly separated from one another. However, if we used a Gaussian kernel with bandwidth of about half the radius of each cluster, the resulting embedding, i.e., $Q\Sigma$, would be such that the dot products across clusters would be nearly zero, except at the boundary regions. This can be approximately achieved in a non-negative embedding in which the top-9 components of this representation will be dominated by points from the nine different clusters. In other words, points from each cluster will have a significantly positive component only along one of these nine features and will have zero values across the other eight features. However, to achieve this goal, one has to increase the dimensionality of the original data from two features to nine features in sparse format. This observation is important and therefore we emphasize it below:

> *Increasing the similarity sensitivity to data locality in a kernel function often creates new features that describe the behavior of small data localities. One can simulate this type of pairwise similarity with feature engineering by defining features specific to small data localities. The feature values are set to 0 (or roughly constant values) if the data point lies outside that locality.*

Parameters such as the kernel bandwidth implicitly control the size of this locality in kernel transformations. The aforementioned feature engineering creates a sparse data representation that is sensitive to data locality. Co-incidentally, this type of *sparse* transformation also makes the data linearly separable by a support-vector machine because the linear SVM is now able to put together the small local pieces represented by each feature on the appropriate side of the linear separator (irrespective of the shape of the original

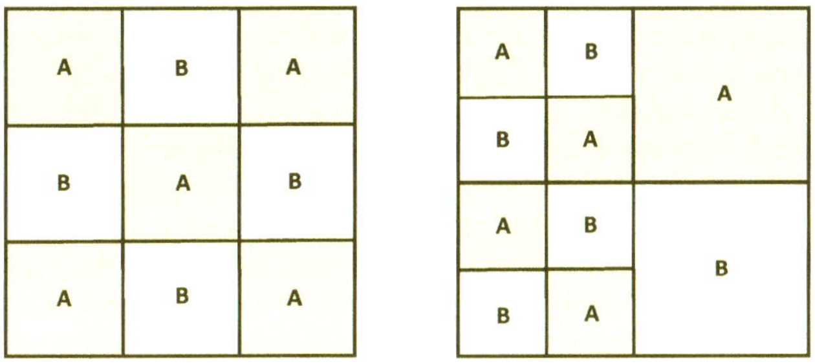

(a) Classes A and B are not linearly separable

(b) Different localities of data are prone to overfitting/underfitting

Figure 1: Examples of different localities of data points

decision boundary). For example, if we create a 3×3 grid of regions in Figure 1(a), such that each region of the grid contains one of the clusters, then we can create nine binary features depending on the presence or absence of a point in each cluster. It can be easily shown that this binary representation is linearly separable. Although this particular example is a little too clean as compared to real settings, it nevertheless sets up the intuition we need for the feature engineering step.

2.2 Weaknesses of Kernel Transformations

With knowing the working of kernel transformations, we will now discuss what they lack. Some key weaknesses are *in addition to* the space- and time-inefficiency of kernel methods.

2.2.1 Inflexibility in Locality of Representation. The most important problem with kernel representations is that one cannot control the granularity of the resulting data locality because it is "baked into the cake" once the parameters of the kernel (e.g., Gaussian bandwidth) have been chosen. In many cases, different bandwidths are more appropriate for different data localities, and kernel functions cannot fully express these factors. An example is illustrated in Figure 1(b), in which a smaller kernel bandwidth is appropriate for the data points on the left, and a larger kernel bandwidth is appropriate for data points towards the right. Choosing a small kernel bandwidth will cause overfitting in some parts of the data, whereas choosing a large kernel bandwidth will cause underfitting in other parts of the data. Therefore, one of our goals will be to design a sparse representation of the data with randomized feature engineering, which is sensitive to data-locality in a multi-granular way. As we will see later, this type of flexibility is one of the major advantages that explicit feature engineering methods have over kernel transformations, because the learning algorithm can now pick and choose the *relevant* granularity of feature representation in each data locality, rather than an opaque use of all transformed features with the kernel method. Although some recent methods partially address this problem [5], they are highly prone to overfitting, which is common with kernel methods.

2.2.2 Irrelevant Input Features and the Curse of Dimensionality. Kernel methods are not immune to the curse of dimensionality. Even though the margin-based approach of an SVM can reduce the impact of irrelevant features in the *transformed space*, the transformation itself includes the impact of irrelevant features in the *input space*. Often small subsets of (input) features may be relevant for various data localities in which the remaining features may not add much information. In fact, it has been shown [4] that the Gaussian kernel, which uses the squared distance in its exponent, is susceptible to poor results with an increasing number of irrelevant (input) features. This is because the Gaussian kernel can be expanded into interactions of various orders between input features. It has been shown that in many data sets, only the lower-order interactions between features are relevant [10], and the use of all features adds noise. For example, in Figure 1(a), if 10 noisy features are added to the data set, a Gaussian kernel would work very poorly because of the impact of noisy features.

2.2.3 Locally Relevant Features. This problem of irrelevant input features is particularly significant when the relevant features vary with data locality. Even though many input features may be relevant on a global basis, only small subsets of input features are often relevant when examining various data localities. For example, rule-based classifiers are often able to provide high-quality classification, even when the antecedents are allowed to contain a maximum of two or three features. This is primarily because rule-based classifiers typically model small localities of the data in their antecedents, in which small subsets of dimensions are effective. A kernel methods such as kernel SVM usually uses all the dimensions and their higher-order interactions while computing similarities and thus cannot capture the multi-level data locality. For sparse representations, even the modeling of second-order interactions is sufficient, as is evident from the recent success of second-order factorization machines [19]. Correspondingly, we will construct a feature representation that is able to model such lower-order interactions among input features, *in addition to* the global patterns.

2.2.4 Opaque Trade-Off between Overfitting and Underfitting. The lack of interpretability of the kernel features makes the trade-off between overfitting and underfitting (with the use of parameters such as the kernel bandwidth). As mentioned earlier, such representations are often inappropriately global in using a single parameter to control the sensitivity of data locality to parameters such as the bandwidth. On the other hand, we will show that randomized feature engineering is able to extract a large number of features of multiple levels of granularity. Because of the multi-granular representation, under-fitting is always avoided in each data locality. Furthermore, it naturally enables ensemble-centric approach to learning, which also avoids overfitting.

2.2.5 Efficiency Issues. Kernel methods are extremely slow because they work with an $n \times n$ matrix of similarities between pairs of points. Therefore, the complexity of a kernel method is somewhere between $O(n^2 d)$ and $O(n^3)$. Therefore, it is useful to examine randomized feature engineering methods that can be extremely efficient in comparison. In fact, we will propose a method whose complexity is linear in to number of data points.

2.2.6 Interpretability. The features produced by a kernel method are often not very interpretable. This precludes their use to make diagnostic inferences about specific predictions.

Given the inner working and weaknesses of kernel transformation, in next section, we will propose RandLocal, a more flexible approach of feature engineering which incorporate these characteristics.

3 RANDOMIZED FEATURE ENGINEERING TO CREATE LOCAL FEATURES

As discussed in section 2, feature engineering methods can simulate greater sensitivity in pairwise similarity in small localities by creating features that correspond to local regions defined by *anchor points* sampled from the data set. The basic idea is to create a nonnegative representation of the data, in which each features are associated with anchor points. A data point takes on a strictly positive value for a particular feature only if it is a nearest neighbor for that particular anchor point. Otherwise it takes on a value of 0 for that feature. Therefore, only one feature is activated by a given data point for a particular group of anchors. Each set of anchor points induces a Voronoi partition of the data space, and the granularity of this Voronoi partition depends on the number of anchor points. When a linear classifier is applied to this representation, it implicitly uses the class distribution of each of the local regions to define the relevance of that (engineered) feature to the corresponding class. A larger number of anchor points helps in defining more detailed decision boundaries but runs a risk of greater overfitting.

Multiple features are made to take on non-zero values by repeatedly sampling different groups of anchor points. The resulting representation is sparse and nonnegative with a high degree of local information captured by the features. The degree of locality (i.e., granularity) is captured by the number of anchor points. Since, the appropriate granularity cannot be known in advance (and may, in fact, vary with data locality), we propose to vary the number of anchor points in the range [32, 1024] using a geometric distribution. The overall process of creating each set of features (from a particular anchor group) is summarized in Algorithm 1.

Algorithm 1 RandFea

Input: Dataset: $\mathbf{X} \in \mathbb{R}^{N \times d}$, ϵ
Output: Engineered features **F**

- Sample the real number p uniformly at random between $\log_2(32) = 5$, and $\log_2(1024) = 10$.
- Set the number of anchors r to $\lfloor 2^p \rfloor$, and sample r anchors
- Calculate the distance of N points to r anchors
- Let the average of the $r \times N$ anchor-point distances be D_{avg}.
- Initialize a sparse all zero matrix $\mathbf{F} \in \mathbb{R}^{N \times r}$.
- **for** each data point $\mathbf{x}_i$ **do**
  - Let the minimum distance of $\mathbf{x}_i$ to the r anchors be $D_{min}(\mathbf{x}_i)$, and the nearest anchor be k. If the nearest anchor is $\mathbf{x}_i$ itself, use second nearest anchor.
  - Set $\mathbf{F}_{ik} = \max\{D_{avg} - D_{min}(\mathbf{x}_i), \epsilon \cdot D_{avg}\}$
- **end for**
- return the engineered feature **F**

In Algorithm 1, ϵ is a small number such as 0.0001, and is meant to add regularization and smoothing to the process against the presence of outliers. Euclidean distance is used to calculate the anchor-point distance while other distance metrics can also be adopted. Any data point $\mathbf{x}_i$ that is also an anchor is always assigned to its nearest other anchor (in order to avoid overfitting) and therefore the value of $D_{min}(\mathbf{x}_i)$ is not necessarily 0. Note that this description implicitly assumes that the data set contains significantly more than 1024 points because the number of anchors needs to be smaller than the number of points by a factor of at least 2 or 3. To ensure that the number of anchors is significantly less than the number of points, we can set the upper limit of sampling the real number p to $\min\{\log_2(N/2), \log_2(1024)\}$. The value $\mathbf{F}_{ik} = \max\{D_{avg} - D_{min}(\mathbf{x}_i), \epsilon \cdot D_{avg}\}$ captures the locality information, i.e., its nearest neighbor is k-th anchor and the distance to it is $D_{avg} - D_{min}(\mathbf{x}_i)$. Thus, the resulting feature **F** is informative. The reason we use only the nearest anchor is: (i) to make **F** sparse which can reduce space requirement and advance classification or clustering models such as SVM and K-means; and (2) the nearest anchor is more informative.

The anchors essentially divide the data space into a set of *Voronoi regions*, which also correspond to the features. Data points lying within these Voronoi regions activate these features. When a linear SVM is applied to this feature representation, it "pieces together" these Voronoi regions in order to create a decision boundary. The Voronoi regions with the use of 50, 200, and 1000 anchor points are illustrated in Figures 2(a), (b), and (c), respectively. In the figure, each dot represents an anchor point. The line surrounding an anchor point forms a Voronoi region for the anchor point. Any data point within the Voronoi region of an anchor point will be closer to it than other anchor points. For example, if we superimposed these Voronoi regions, with the class distributions shown in Figures 1(a) or 1(b), the only errors would be caused by edge effects of the irregular Voronoi boundaries. As a result, the decision boundary would be somewhat jagged, but would still approximate the true decision boundary well. Clearly, a larger number of anchors provides decision boundaries that conform more closely with the training data, but the trade-off is that it could overfit to the specific vagaries of a particular training data set. This is the reason that we vary the number of anchors in order to provide multigranular analysis. Note that using multiple sets of anchors will always result in a smoother decision boundary because of its implicit ensemble-centric approach in hiding the complexity within the feature representation, but using a low-variance linear model at the very end. This type of feature representation can use the features with the appropriate relevance and granularity from each data locality. For example, if a particular combination of low-dimensional features is relevant in a particular data locality, the local features in the anchor points using the closest possible combination of features will be automatically identified by a supervised learning algorithm. Of course, since sampling is used, the precise combination of features may not be available; however, in many cases, a close enough combination of locally engineered features may be available for learning.

The approach can also address the problem in a kernel SVM that it uses a global bandwidth (and corresponding granularity of analysis) in cases different bandwidths are suitable to different data localities. For example, in the case of Figure 1(b), a linear SVM should use coarse features to classify data points in the right-hand side of Figure 1(b), whereas it should use fine-grained features to classify data points on the left-hand side. This is possible in the case of our

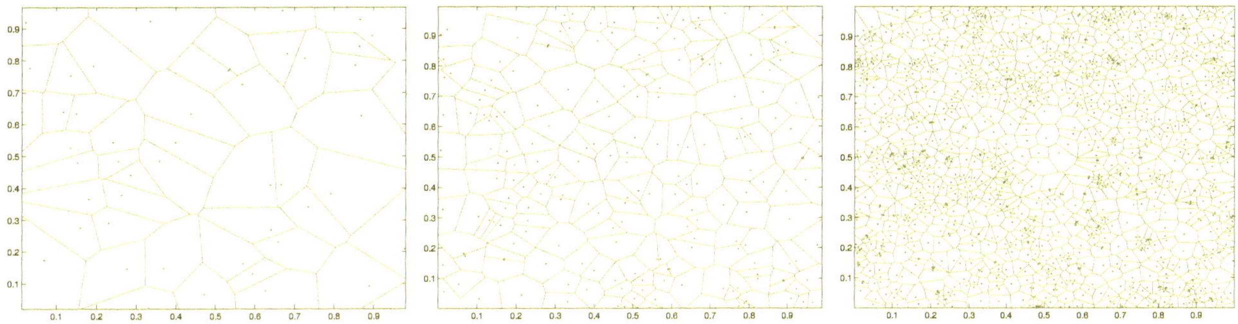

(a) 50 anchors (b) 200 anchors (c) 1000 anchors

Figure 2: The anchors define the level of granularity covered by the new feature set. The number of anchors defines the trade-off between bias and variance of a learning method. A smaller number of anchors corresponds to larger bandwidths of the Gaussian kernel, whereas a larger number of anchors corresponds to smaller bandwidths of the Gaussian kernel.

approach because the features are associated with anchors with varying levels of granularity. In fact, an L_1-regularization can even be used to select the appropriate features for each data locality, since the coefficients of irrelevant features (in the transformed space) would be set to 0. Note that this type of locally adaptive learning is not possible for a kernel learning method that typically uses a single value of the bandwidth to learn the features.

It is also noteworthy that the local regions created by the features are highly interpretable. For example, if a particular feature has a weight of a particular sign in the coefficient vector of a linear SVM (with labels +1 and −1), the sign of the coefficient defines the class affinity of the data locality of that specific anchor. Similarly, if a k-means algorithm is applied to the engineered feature representation for clustering, it will piece together the dense regions of arbitrary shape in the input space by using the local regions defined by the various features. The dominant features in the centroid of a cluster define the regions relevant to that cluster as well.

3.1 Addressing Locally Irrelevant Features in the Input Space

Most kernel methods perform poorly when many features in the *input space* are globally or locally irrelevant. This is because the kernel method uses all (input) features within the kernel similarity function irrespective to their relevance [4, 10]. The explicit methodology of feature engineering provides a natural way to sample the input space for features, while constructing the overall feature representation by repeated anchor sampling. While sampling each set of anchor points, an additional step is added up front to sample subsets of features. Then, the overall process of feature engineering (which we refer to as *RandLocal*) are summarized in Algorithm 2.

In Algorithm 2, the number of sets of anchors T is an input parameter to the algorithm. **parfor** means *parallel for loop*. The approach starts with a null set of features and progressively samples anchors to add sets of sparse features for T iterations. The value of T defines the dimensionality of the feature representation. Although the precise dimensionality depends on the vagaries of the sampling process, exactly T features will always be non-zero in each data point. Therefore, the representation is very sparse. The value of T is

Algorithm 2 RandLocal

Input: Dataset: $\mathbf{X} \in \mathbb{R}^{n \times d}$, Iterations: T
Output: engineered feature **F**

Initialize $\mathbf{F} = \emptyset$
parfor t=1 to T **do**
  Sample a number m_t between 1 and d
  Create $\mathbf{X}_t \in \mathbb{R}^{n \times m_t}$ by sampling m_t features from **X**
  Create engineered features as $\mathbf{F}_t$ = RandFea($\mathbf{X}_t$)
  Concatenate $\mathbf{F}_t$ to **F**
end parfor
return engineered feature **F**

selected to be somewhere between 100 and 500. It is noteworthy that sparse representations like text are also almost always separable with linear SVMs and other low-variance models [14]. Although the subspace sampling process of *RandLocal* is quite safe in the supervised setting (because of the ability to detect the relevance of engineered features a posteriori), one needs to be careful of subspace sampling in the unsupervised setting. We discuss this issue below.

3.1.1 Difference between Supervised and Unsupervised Settings. The aforementioned description of *RandLocal* is appropriate for the supervised setting. In supervised settings, low-dimensional combinations of features in the input space often have a high level of predictive power because of the ability to learn them from the *labeled* training data. However, in unsupervised problems, it is difficult to learn the relevance of engineered features, and randomly sampling subspaces often leads to dropping relevant (input) features that cannot be detected a posteriori. Therefore, in order to avoid this problem, one minor change is made to the algorithm *RandLocal* above to make it more appropriate for unsupervised problems. In particular, instead of sampling between 1 and d dimensions in the first step of *RandLocal*, we only sample between $\lceil d/2 \rceil$ and d dimensions. This reduces the likelihood of losing a very large proportion of the relevant input features. This type of subspace sampling is similar to the feature bagging approach [15] that is commonly used in unsupervised outlier detection (albeit in a different context). In the following, it is assumed that supervised applications of *RandLocal* always sample between 1 and d dimensions, whereas unsupervised applications of *RandLocal* sample between $\lceil d/2 \rceil$ and d dimensions.

3.2 Time and Space Complexity

Now we'll demonstrate that RandLocal is time and space efficient.
Time Complexity Let's consider the t-th time we call RandLocal with $\mathbf{X}_t \in \mathbb{R}^{n \times m_t}$ as input. Assume that the number of anchors we sampled is r_t. Then The complexity of calculating the distance of the n data point to r_t anchor points is $O(nm_t r_t)$. For each data point $\mathbf{x}_i$, getting $D_{min}(\mathbf{x}_i)$ and setting the feature of $\mathbf{x}_i$ cost $O(nr_t)$. Thus, the total time complexity is $O(\sum_{t=1}^{T} nm_t r_t)$ where T is the number of times we perform RandFea. Note that r_t is a small number within 32 and 1024 and performing RandFea T times is embarrassingly parallel. Therefore, RandLocal is efficient for distributed or multi-thread computation.
Space Complexity Similarly, for each call of RandFea with $\mathbf{X}_t \in \mathbb{R}^{n \times m_t}$ as input, the $r_t \times n$ distance matrix takes $O(nr_t)$ space. Since $\mathbf{F}_t \in \mathbb{R}^{n \times r_t}$ is very sparse, i.e., only n nonzero entries, the space complexity of $\mathbf{F}_t$ is $O(n)$. Therefore, the total space complexity of RandLocal in Algorithm 2 is $O(\sum_{t=1}^{T} nr_t)$. The space complexity of the returned high-dimensional sparse engineered feature $\mathbf{F}$ is $O(nT)$. Therefore, RandLocal is also space efficient.

3.3 Connections with Weighted Nearest Neighbor Methods

In addition to the aforementioned discussion, it is possible to show another interesting connection between the feature engineering method discussed earlier and kernel methods. Since the engineered representation uses nearest neighbors in conjunction with anchor points, dot products between pairs of engineered representation can be shown to be heavily localized similarities. It is also well known that kernel SVMs are weighted nearest neighbor classifiers [31]. In other words, one can show that both kernel SVMs and linear SVMs on the engineered representation approximately behave like weighted nearest neighbor classifiers in the original input space. The only difference is that the engineered method has better diversity because of its ability to select different numbers of anchors in various subspaces of the input space, and it can also drop the irrelevant (engineered and input) features in various phases of the learning process. As a result the engineered method is more adaptive and less prone to overfitting.

4 EXPERIMENTS

In this section, we conduct experiments to show the effectiveness of the engineered features by RandLocal for different tasks. Specifically, we aim to answer the following three questions:

- With the sparse representation that captures multi-locality, can RandLocal improve classification performance with linear SVMs and clustering performance with K-means?
- How robust is RandLocal in constructing features from noisy datasets?
- Can RandLocal construct effective features for detecting outliers?

We begin by introducing the datasets and representative state-of-the-art feature engineering methods; we then compare RandLocal with these feature engineering methods on classification and clustering to answer the first question and we investigate the ability of RandLocal in handling noisy datasets to answer the second question. We also study the RandLocal for outlier detection to answer the third question. Finally, further experiments are conducted to investigate the sensitivity of RandLocal to the parameters.

Table 1: Statistics of Datasets for Classification & Clustering

Dataset	IJCNN	COVTYPE	MNIST	GISETTE
# instances	141,691	581,012	70,000	7,000
# features	22	54	780	5,000
# classes	2	7	10	2

Table 2: Statistics of Datasets for Outlier Detection

Dataset	ALOI	KDDCup99	SPAMBASE	PB
# instances	50,000	100,655	4,601	5,473
# features	64	98	57	10
# outliers	1,508	3,377	1,813	560

4.1 Datasets

The classification and clustering experiments are conducted on 4 publicly available benchmark datasets, which includes IJCNN, COVTYPE, MNIST and GISETTE [1]. The statistics of the datasets are summarized in Table 1. From the table we can see that the number of data points varies from 7,000 to 581,012 and the features vary from 22 to 5,000. It also includes binary class and multi-class datasets. In this way, we aim to give a comprehensive understanding of how RandLocal performs with datasets of various conditions.

The outlier detection experiments are conducted on 4 widely used outlier detection benchmark datasets [6], which includes ALOI [2], KDDCup99 [3], SPAMBASE and PageBlock (PB) [4]. The statistics of the datasets are summarized in Table 2. From the table we note that the datasets are extremely imbalanced, and thus can check the ability of RandLocal in dealing with extremely imbalanced datasets.

4.2 Compared Feature Engineering Methods

The representative state-of-the-art feature engineering algorithms RandLocal compare to are listed as follows:

- RAW: Raw features. It is a baseline to understand the performance without feature engineering.
- RBF Kernel: We use RBF kernel transformation to learn feature map $\mathbf{Q}\Sigma$ from the RBF similarity matrix S. This is used as representative kernel transformation method.
- DAE: Denoising autoencoder [24] is a variant of autoencoder which is to learn a feature representation that is able to reconstruct the input data. Specifically, DAE is trained to reconstruct a clean "repaired" input from a corrupted version, which makes it able to extract more robust features. The encoded feature is used as feature representation.
- SDAE: Stacked denoising autoencoder [25] is a deep network based on stacking layers of DAE. Compared with the

[1] The 4 datasets are available from https://www.csie.ntu.edu.tw/ cjlin/libsvmtools/datasets/
[2] https://elki-project.github.io/datasets/multi_view
[3] http://scikit-learn.org/stable/modules/generated/sklearn.datasets.fetch_kddcup99.html
[4] SPAMBASE and PB are avaliable from https://archive.ics.uci.edu/ml/datasets/

Table 3: Classification performance comparison on four datasets in terms of Micro-F1 and Macro-F1.

Dataset	IJCNN		COVTYPE		MNIST		GISETTE	
Name	Micro-F1	Macro-F1	Micro-F1	Macro-F1	Micro-F1	Macro-F1	Micro-F1	Macro-F1
RAW	92.08±0.25	69.20±0.25	63.28±0.08	28.98±0.09	91.61±0.11	91.19±0.11	92.91±0.77	92.91±0.77
RBF Kernel	97.06±0.37	90.71±0.39	75.04±0.10	51.50±0.11	97.08±0.14	97.06±0.13	97.13±0.81	97.19±0.79
DAE	93.19±0.31	71.51±0.38	67.97±0.07	36.81±0.20	97.53±0.07	97.47±0.07	92.99±1.09	92.99±1.09
SDAE	93.88±0.34	72.47±0.40	66.13±0.07	41.02±0.19	97.75±0.09	97.68±0.09	94.24±1.13	94.26±1.13
RandLocal	**98.84**±0.27	**93.80**±0.35	**89.52**±0.06	**84.78**±0.20	**98.02**±0.05	**97.98**±0.05	**97.60**±0.96	**97.60**±0.97

DAE, features learned in a purely unsupervised fashion by SDAE are higher-level and could boost the performance of classification/clustering. We used a three-layer stacked DAE and the third layer feature representation is used for experiments. SDAE is used as a representative deep learning algorithm for unsupervised representation learning.

4.3 Classification Performance

To answer the first question, we first compare RandLocal with representative feature engineering algorithms introduced in Section 4.2 in terms of classification.

Two widely used classification evaluation metrics, i.e., Micro-F1 and Macro-F1, are adopted to evaluate the classification ability of the proposed framework RandLocal. The larger the Micro-F1 and Macro-F1 scores are, the better the classification results is, which indicates the dicriminativeness of the features.

For each feature learning algorithm, we first learn the representation from **X**. We then use linear SVM to perform classification with the learned representation. We fix the classifier to be linear SVM as our goal is to test the dicriminativeness of the features learned by each method, not the effectiveness of the classifier. It is noteworthy that learning RBF kernel feature $\mathbf{Q}\Sigma$ (see section 1) is intractable for large datasets due to the huge space and time requirement of creating the RBF kernel similarity matrix and performing eigen decomposition. Thus, instead of explicitly learning $\mathbf{Q}\Sigma$ and applying a linear SVM, we used kernel SVMs to simulate this two step-approach. The equivalence of these two procedures is well known (see section 1).

There are some parameters to be set for the feature engineering methods and linear/kernel SVMs. In the experiment, we use 10-fold cross validation on the training data to set the parameters. Note that no test data are involved in the parameter tuning. Specifically, for RBF kernel, we do a grid search of the bandwidth from $[1e-5, 1e-4, \ldots, 10]$. For DAE and SDAE, we search the dimension of latent features from $[\lceil 0.1d \rceil, \lceil 0.2d \rceil, \ldots, \lceil 0.6d \rceil]$, where d is number of features. For RandLocal, we empirically set ϵ to be 0.0001 and T to be 400. The sensitivity of parameters ϵ and T on the classification performance of RandLocal will be analyzed in Section 4.7. The experiments are conducted using 5-fold cross validation and the average performance with standard deviation in terms of Macro-F1 and Micro-F1 are reported in Table 3. From the table, we make the following observations

- The transformed features outperforms RAW feature, which implies the importance of feature engineering; and
- Generally, RBF kernel outperforms or has close performance with DAE and SDAE, while RandLocal outperforms RBF kernel and the other compared method.

We also conducted the t-test on all performance comparisons and it is evident from t-test that all improvements are significant, which indicates the effectiveness of RandLocal.

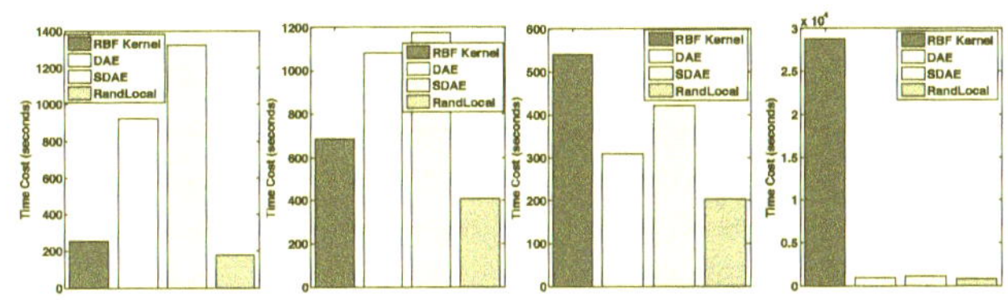

(a) GISETTE (b) MNIST (c) IJCNN (d) COVTYPE

Figure 3: Time cost of feature learning

Table 4: Time cost (Seconds) of training using linear SVM

Dataset	GISETTE	IJCNN	MNIST	COVTYPE
RAW	2.12	2.29	8.55	39.86
RandLocal	1.89	2.49	12.06	98.48

Running Time Comparison: As stated previously, RandLocal is time efficient for both feature construction and model learning.

To show the time efficiency of RandLocal in feature construction, we plot the time cost of learning features for RBF Kernel, DAE, SDAE and RandLocal in Figure 3. From the figure, we can see that: (i) Generally, as the dataset becomes large, the time cost of RBF kernel increases dramatically. For example, on COVTYPE, which has around 580,000 samples, the time cost of RBF is of order 10^4 seconds, which is very time consuming; and (ii) Among the compared methods, RandLocal is time efficient as it's time complexity is linear to number of samples n and feature size d.

To show the efficiency of running linear SVM with the sparse engineered features from RandLocal, we compare the time of training and testing linear SVM with RandLocal features and that of RAW features in Table 4. From the table, we can see that the time cost of training SVM for RandLocal features is similar to that of RAW. Both of them are fast.

4.4 Clustering Performance

To further check the effectiveness of RandLocal, we use datasets in Table 1 for clustering. We first learn features and then perform clustering with K-means on learned features. Following the previous

Table 5: Clustering performance comparison (ACC±std). N/A means the result is not available due to large memory requirement to run RBF Kernel

Dataset	COVTYPE	MNIST	GISETTE
RAW	0.4092±0.0239	0.4642±0.0016	0.6842±0.0014
RBF Kernel	N/A	0.5329±0.0082	0.7059±0.0013
DAE	0.4214±0.0256	0.4843±0.0077	0.7027±0.0047
SDAE	0.4312±0.0267	0.5244±0.0035	0.7157±0.0036
RandLocal	**0.4574**±0.0198	**0.6872**±0.0054	**0.8322**±0.0163

Table 6: Clustering performance comparison (NMI±std)

Dataset	COVTYPE	MNIST	GISETTE
RAW	0.1612±0.0136	0.4016±0.0013	0.1219±0.0010
RBF Kernel	N/A	0.5017±0.0046	0.1351±0.0011
DAE	0.1746±0.0149	0.4320±0.0055	0.1311±0.0056
SDAE	0.1788±0.0157	0.4853±0.0024	0.1257±0.0045
RandLocal	0.2011±0.0129	0.6685±0.0042	0.3652±0.0409

work [27], two widely used evaluation metrics, accuracy (ACC) and normalized mutual information (NMI), are employed to evaluate the quality of clusters. Note that labels are only used to evaluate the clustering results and are not used for feature construction or parameter tuning. The larger ACC and NMI are, the better the performance is. We use grid search to select parameters for each method and report the best results. For RandLocal, we empirically set $\epsilon = 0.0001$ and $T = 400$. Since K-means depends on initialization, we repeat the experiments 20 times and the average results are reported in Table 5 and 6. Note that due to the large memory requirement, we cannot learn RBF kernel features for COVTYPE and IJCNN, which we denote as N/A. We only report the results of COVTYPE, MNIST and GISETTE as we have similar observations for IJCNN. From the two tables, we find that RandLocal significantly outperforms RBF Kernel, DAE and SDAE, which indicates the effectiveness of the features constructed by RandLocal.

The experiments on classification and clustering answers our first question, i.e., by creating a sparse representation that captures multi-level granularity , RandLocal can significantly improves classification/clustering performance using a simple model.

4.5 Robustness to Noise

To answer the second question, i.e., the robustness of RandLocal to noise, we create two sets of synthetic datasets by adding and appending noise, respectively, to IJCNN, COVTYPE, MNIST and GISETTE. Specifically, for each dataset, $\mathbf{X} \in \mathbb{R}^{n \times d}$, in Table 1, we first create a noise matrix $\mathbf{G} \in \mathbb{R}^{n \times \tilde{d}}$ by randomly sampling from the uniform distribution $[f_{min}, f_{max}]$, where $\tilde{d} = \lceil 0.1d \rceil$, f_{min} is the minimal value in $\mathbf{X}$ and f_{max} is the maximal value. To add noise to $\mathbf{X}$, we randomly select $\tilde{d}$ features, which we denote as $\mathcal{I}$. Then the synthetic data is created by adding $\mathbf{G}$ to the selected $\tilde{d}$ features, i.e., $\tilde{\mathbf{X}} = \mathbf{X}, \tilde{\mathbf{X}}(:, \mathcal{I}) = \tilde{\mathbf{X}}(:, \mathcal{I}) + \mathbf{G}$. We do this for each dataset in Table 1, which generates four synthetic datasets. To append noise to $\mathbf{X}$, we directly concatenate $\mathbf{G}$ at the end of $\mathbf{X}$, i.e., $\hat{\mathbf{X}} = [\mathbf{X}, \mathbf{G}]$, which gives us another four datasets. With the noisy datasets, we then learn features and use linear SVM to perform classification.

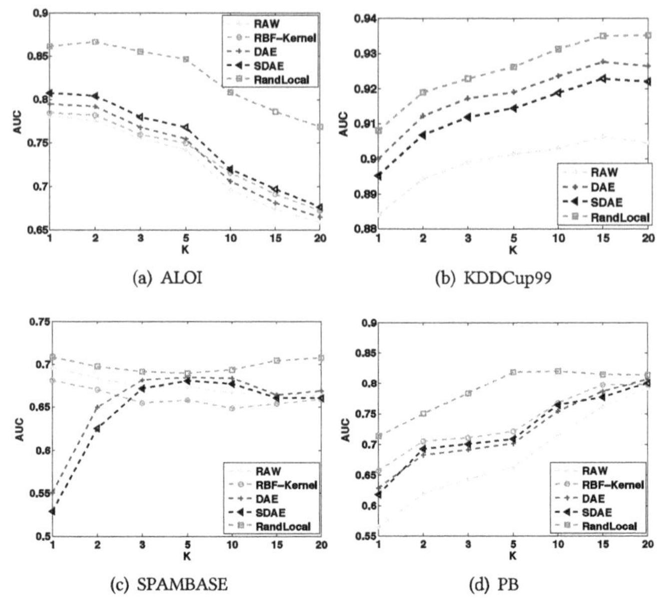

Figure 4: Outlier detection performance in terms of AUC

All the experimental settings and compared algorithms are the same as Section 4.3, i.e., we use 10 fold cross validation to tune parameters and perform 5 fold cross validation for classification. For RandLocal, we set $\epsilon = 0.0001$ and $T = 400$. To avoid the randomness of the results, the operations of adding and appending noise are carried out 5 times for each dataset and we report the average results. We only report the classification performance in terms of Micro-F1 as we have similar observations for Macro-F1. The average Micro-F1 with standard deviation on the two sets of synthetic datasets are shown in Table 7. From the table, we make the following observations: (i) In presence of noise, the performance of all the feature learning methods decreases, which satisfies our expectation that noisy features will degrade the classification performance; and (ii) RandLocal outperforms the compared feature engineering methods. In addition, generally, the performance decrease of RandLocal is smaller than that of RBF Kernle, DAE and SDAE, which shows the effectiveness of RandLocal in handling noisy features. This is because RandLocal randomly sample a subset of features to calculate the distance to anchors, which reduces the probability of including lots of noisy features; while the kernel methods uses all the noisy features to calculate the distance and DAE, SDAE tries to learn latent features that are good at reconstructing noise features, which amplifies the affects of noise. Furthermore, RandLocal repeats the feature construction T times, which can be seen as ensembling many feature sets and thus alleviate the problem caused by noise.

4.6 Outlier Detection

To answer the third question, we perform outlier detection using the datasets listed in Table 2. From Table 2 we can see that the datasets are extremely imbalanced, thus, it will be difficult to learn features for classes with few points. Therefore, by performing outlier detection, we aim to see the ability of RandLocal in learning

Table 7: Classification performance in presence of noise. Note that numbers inside parentheses in the table denote the performance reductions compared to the performance without noise in Table 3

Dataset	Add 10% Noise				Append 10% Noise			
Name	IJCNN	COVTYPE	MNIST	GISETTE	IJCNN	COVTYPE	MNIST	GISETTE
SVM-linear	91.39(0.75%)	61.31(3.12%)	89.90(0.49%)	91.89(1.10%)	91.84(0.26%)	61.32(3.10%)	90.35(1.38%)	91.91(1.07%)
SVM-rbf	93.36(3.81%)	49.12(34.54%)	92.15(5.08%)	95.29(1.90%)	93.62(3.54%)	49.12(34.54%)	92.65(4.56%)	95.20(1.99%)
DAE	90.26(3.15%)	63.11(7.15%)	91.64(6.04%)	75.36(18.96%)	90.14(3.27%)	63.54(6.52%)	91.13(6.56%)	67.74(27.15%)
SDAE	90.59(3.50%)	63.08(4.62%)	85.54(12.49%)	77.30(17.98%)	90.27(3.85%)	63.04(4.67%)	83.61(14.47%)	70.31(25.39%)
RandLocal	**96.00**(2.88%)	**80.62**(9.94%)	**93.63**(4.47%)	**96.86**(0.76%)	**95.62**(3.26%)	**78.80**(11.98%)	**93.80**(4.30%)	**96.24**(1.39%)

features from imbalanced datasets. Next, we introduce experimental settings and performances with comparison to other feature learning methods.

For outlier detection, we use the popular evaluation metric, areas under curve (AUC), which is a standard way to measure the effectiveness of outlier detection [18].

Note that our focus is to measure the effectiveness of the features for outlier detection, not the quality of outlier detection algorithms. Thus, for fair comparison, we first learn features using feature learning algorithms and then apply the same outlier detection algorithm on the learned features. In the experiments, we use the popular k-nearest neighbor distance based outlier detection [12], which uses the distance to the k-nearest neighbor as the outlier score. With the outlier score, we calculate AUC using the ground truth. Due to large memory requirement in calculating RBF kernel transformation on KDDCup99, we don't compare RandLocal with it on KDDCup99. We use grid search to tune the parameters for each feature learning algorithm. Each experiment is conducted 10 times and the average performance in terms of AUC is shown in Figure 4. From the figure, we make the following observations: (i) Generally, SDAE and DAE outperforms RAW, which implies that SDAE and DAE can learn useful features for outlier detection. SDAE is slightly better than DAE as SDAE can learn higher level features; and (ii) RandLocal outperforms the compared methods on the four outlier detection datasets. Especially on ALOI, compared to SDAE, the performance increases by more than 7.5%, which shows the strong ability of RandLocal in handling outliers. In addition, we can see that when K increases, the performance increase/decrease pattern of RandLocal is very similar to K while DAE and SDAE has different pattern to DAE on spambase. That's because RandLocal directly captures the multi-granularity of datasets while DAE and SDAE transforms the raw feature to latent space.

The result shows the strong ability of RandLocal in handling outliers. This is because outliers will typically be far away from their nearest anchors, and the feature values are chosen to be $\max\{D_{avg} - D_{min}(\mathbf{x}_i), \epsilon D_{avg}\}$, Therefore, all feature values are nonnegative, but the feature values of outliers are unusually small.

4.7 Parameter Analysis

The proposed framework has two important parameters, ϵ and T, where ϵ is a small number meant to add regularization and smoothing to the process against the presence of outliers and T is an inter specifies the number of random feature sets we want to get, which controls the level of granularity. In this section, we investigate the impact of the parameters ϵ and T on the performance

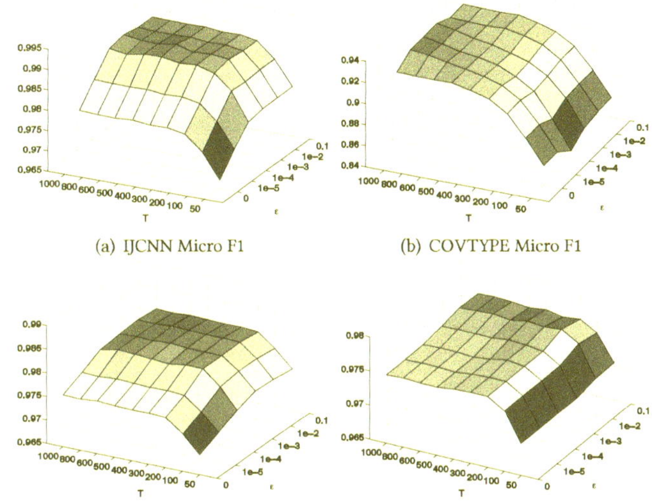

(a) IJCNN Micro F1 (b) COVTYPE Micro F1

(c) MNIST Micro F1 (d) GISETTE Micro F1

Figure 5: Parameter Analysis

of RandLocal. We only show the classification results since we have similar observations with clustering and outlier detection. We vary the values of ϵ as $\{0, 1e-5, 1e-4, 1e-3, 1e-2, 0.1\}$ and the values of T as $\{50, 100, 200, 300, 400, 500, 600, 800, 1000\}$. For each datasets, we first learn the features with RandLocal then perform 5-fold cross validation using linear SVM on the features. The average results are shown in Figure 5. It can be observed from the figure that: (i) Generally, with the increment of α, the performance tends to first increase then become stable. When we increase T from 50, each new feature sets are likely to introduce new granularity as there are few feature sets, which provides richer locality information that can improve performance a lot. When T is large enough, increasing T doesn't help as it is more likely to provide redundant features to the rich features we already have with large T. A value of T around 200 to 400 can give relatively good performance and save computational cost; and (ii) When we set $\epsilon = 0$, $\max\{D_{avg} - D_{min}(\mathbf{x}_i), \epsilon \cdot D_{avg}\}$ reduces to $D_{avg} - D_{min}(\mathbf{x}_i)$ and the performance is not as good as the performance when ϵ is not $1e-5$, which shows that adding ϵ can add regularization and smoothing to the process against the presence of outliers. When we increase ϵ from $1e-5$ to 0.1, there are slightly performance increment. In other words, RandLocal is relatively more stable to ϵ, which eases the parameter selection.

5 CONCLUSION

The performance of machine learning algorithms i highly sensitive to the specific feature representation of the data used [3]. Good feature representations can significantly improve the machine learning and data mining performance such as classification [21] and recommender systems [13, 16, 29]. In this paper, we propose a novel unsupervised feature engineering method, RandLocal, as an accurate and efficient alternative to kernel methods. RandLocal is space and time efficient and learns features that capture multi-granular locality. Extensive experiments on real-world datasets demonstrate the effectiveness of RandLocal for various applications such as classification and clustering. The analysis of RandLocal on noisy datasets and outlier detection shows the robustness of RandLocal in dealing imbalanced datasets and noisy features. Further experiments are conducted to analyze the sensitivity of the hyper-parameters.

There are several interesting directions need further investigation. First, in this paper, we employ Euclidean distance to calculate the distance between data points and anchor points. One direction is to study if other distance metrics can improve the performance of RandLocal. Second, in this paper, we randomly select subset of features to calculate the distance between anchor points. In practice, features may have correlations [28]. For example, for image datasets, nearby pixels are more likely to have similar values. Thus, another direction is to investigate the structures/correlations of features to improve RandLocal performance. Finally, linked data such as linked documents [26] are very pervasive. We also would like to extend RandLocal to include link information.

6 ACKNOWLEDGEMENTS

This material is based upon work supported by, or in part by, the National Science Foundation (NSF) under the grant #1614576.

REFERENCES

[1] Charu C Aggarwal. 2015. *Data mining: the textbook.* Springer.
[2] Francis R Bach, Gert RG Lanckriet, and Michael I Jordan. 2004. Multiple kernel learning, conic duality, and the SMO algorithm. In *Proceedings of the twenty-first international conference on Machine learning.* ACM, 6.
[3] Yoshua Bengio, Aaron Courville, and Pascal Vincent. 2013. Representation learning: A review and new perspectives. *IEEE transactions on pattern analysis and machine intelligence* 35, 8 (2013), 1798–1828.
[4] Yoshua Bengio, Olivier Delalleau, and Nicolas Le Roux. 2006. The curse of highly variable functions for local kernel machines. *Advances in neural information processing systems* 18 (2006), 107.
[5] Michael Brockmann, Theo Gasser, and Eva Herrmann. 1993. Locally adaptive bandwidth choice for kernel regression estimators. *J. Amer. Statist. Assoc.* 88, 424 (1993), 1302–1309.
[6] Guilherme O Campos, Arthur Zimek, Jörg Sander, Ricardo JGB Campello, Barbora Micenková, Erich Schubert, Ira Assent, and Michael E Houle. 2016. On the evaluation of unsupervised outlier detection: measures, datasets, and an empirical study. *Data Mining and Knowledge Discovery* 30, 4 (2016), 891–927.
[7] Inderjit S Dhillon, Yuqiang Guan, and Brian Kulis. 2004. Kernel k-means: spectral clustering and normalized cuts. In *Proceedings of the tenth ACM SIGKDD international conference on Knowledge discovery and data mining.* ACM, 551–556.
[8] Chris Ding and Xiaofeng He. 2004. K-means clustering via principal component analysis. In *Proceedings of the twenty-first international conference on Machine learning.* ACM, 29.
[9] Pedro Domingos. 2012. A few useful things to know about machine learning. *Commun. ACM* 55, 10 (2012), 78–87.
[10] David K Duvenaud, Hannes Nickisch, and Carl E Rasmussen. 2011. Additive gaussian processes. In *Advances in neural information processing systems.* 226–234.
[11] Jerome Friedman, Trevor Hastie, and Robert Tibshirani. 2001. *The elements of statistical learning.* Vol. 1. Springer series in statistics Springer, Berlin.
[12] Ville Hautamaki, Ismo Karkkainen, and Pasi Franti. 2004. Outlier detection using k-nearest neighbour graph. In *Pattern Recognition, 2004. ICPR 2004. Proceedings of the 17th International Conference on*, Vol. 3. IEEE, 430–433.
[13] Xiangnan He, Lizi Liao, Hanwang Zhang, Liqiang Nie, Xia Hu, and Tat-Seng Chua. 2017. Neural collaborative filtering. In *Proceedings of the 26th International Conference on World Wide Web.* International World Wide Web Conferences Steering Committee, 173–182.
[14] Thorsten Joachims. 2006. Training linear SVMs in linear time. In *Proceedings of the 12th ACM SIGKDD international conference on Knowledge discovery and data mining.* ACM, 217–226.
[15] Aleksandar Lazarevic and Vipin Kumar. 2005. Feature bagging for outlier detection. In *Proceedings of the eleventh ACM SIGKDD international conference on Knowledge discovery in data mining.* ACM, 157–166.
[16] Xinyue Liu, Chara Aggarwal, Yu-Feng Li, Xiaugnan Kong, Xinyuan Sun, and Saket Sathe. 2016. Kernelized matrix factorization for collaborative filtering. In *Proceedings of the 2016 SIAM International Conference on Data Mining.* SIAM, 378–386.
[17] Sebastian Mika, Bernhard Schölkopf, Alexander J. Smola, Klaus-Robert Müller, Matthias Scholz, and Gunnar Rätsch. 1998. Kernel PCA and De-Noising in Feature Spaces. In *Advances in Neural Information Processing Systems 11, [NIPS Conference, Denver, Colorado, USA, November 30 - December 5, 1998].* 536–542.
[18] Miloš Radovanović, Alexandros Nanopoulos, and Mirjana Ivanović. 2015. Reverse nearest neighbors in unsupervised distance-based outlier detection. *IEEE transactions on knowledge and data engineering* 27, 5 (2015), 1369–1382.
[19] Steffen Rendle. 2012. Factorization machines with libfm. *ACM Transactions on Intelligent Systems and Technology (TIST)* 3, 3 (2012), 57.
[20] Bernhard Schölkopf and Alexander J Smola. 2002. *Learning with kernels: support vector machines, regularization, optimization, and beyond.* MIT press.
[21] Ali Sharif Razavian, Hossein Azizpour, Josephine Sullivan, and Stefan Carlsson. 2014. CNN features off-the-shelf: an astounding baseline for recognition. In *Proceedings of the IEEE Conference on Computer Vision and Pattern Recognition Workshops.* 806–813.
[22] John Shawe-Taylor and Nello Cristianini. 2004. *Kernel methods for pattern analysis.* Cambridge university press.
[23] Sören Sonnenburg, Gunnar Rätsch, Christin Schäfer, and Bernhard Schölkopf. 2006. Large scale multiple kernel learning. *Journal of Machine Learning Research* 7, Jul (2006), 1531–1565.
[24] Pascal Vincent, Hugo Larochelle, Yoshua Bengio, and Pierre-Antoine Manzagol. 2008. Extracting and composing robust features with denoising autoencoders. In *Proceedings of the 25th international conference on Machine learning.* ACM, 1096–1103.
[25] Pascal Vincent, Hugo Larochelle, Isabelle Lajoie, Yoshua Bengio, and Pierre-Antoine Manzagol. 2010. Stacked denoising autoencoders: Learning useful representations in a deep network with a local denoising criterion. *Journal of Machine Learning Research* 11, Dec (2010), 3371–3408.
[26] Suhang Wang, Jiliang Tang, Charu Aggarwal, and Huan Liu. 2016. Linked Document Embedding for Classification. In *Proceedings of the 25th ACM International on Conference on Information and Knowledge Management.* ACM, 115–124.
[27] Suhang Wang, Jiliang Tang, and Huan Liu. 2015. Embedded Unsupervised Feature Selection. In *Proceedings of the Twenty-Ninth AAAI Conference on Artificial Intelligence, January 25-30, 2015, Austin, Texas, USA.* 470–476.
[28] Suhang Wang, Yilin Wang, Jiliang Tang, Charu Aggarwal, Suhas Ranganath, and Huan Liu. 2017. Exploiting hierarchical structures for unsupervised feature selection. In *Proceedings of the 2017 SIAM International Conference on Data Mining.*
[29] Suhang Wang, Yilin Wang, Jiliang Tang, Kai Shu, Suhas Ranganath, and Huan Liu. 2017. What Your Images Reveal: Exploiting Visual Contents for Point-of-Interest Recommendation. In *Proceedings of the 26th International Conference on World Wide Web, WWW 2017, Perth, Australia, April 3-7, 2017.* 391–400.
[30] Brian J Worton. 1989. Kernel methods for estimating the utilization distribution in home-range studies. *Ecology* 70, 1 (1989), 164–168.
[31] Hao Zhang, Alexander C Berg, Michael Maire, and Jitendra Malik. 2006. SVM-KNN: Discriminative nearest neighbor classification for visual category recognition. In *Computer Vision and Pattern Recognition, 2006 IEEE Computer Society Conference on*, Vol. 2. IEEE, 2126–2136.
[32] Ding-Xuan Zhou. 2003. Capacity of reproducing kernel spaces in learning theory. *IEEE Transactions on Information Theory* 49, 7 (2003), 1743–1752.

Human Mobility Synchronization and Trip Purpose Detection with Mixture of Hawkes Processes

Pengfei Wang*
CNIC, Chinese Academy of Sciences
Beijing, China
wpf@cnic.cn

Yanjie Fu*†
Missouri U. of Sci. and Tech.
MO, USA
fuyan@mst.edu

Guannan Liu
Beihang University
Beijing, China
liugn@buaa.edu.cn

Wenqing Hu
Missouri U. of Sci. and Tech.
MO, USA
huwenqing.pku@gmail.com

Charu Aggarwal
IBM T. J. Watson Research Center
NY, USA
charu@us.ibm.com

ABSTRACT

While exploring human mobility can benefit many applications such as smart transportation, city planning, and urban economics, there are two key questions that need to be answered: (i) What is the nature of the spatial diffusion of human mobility across regions with different urban functions? (ii) How to spot and trace the trip purposes of human mobility trajectories? To answer these questions, we study large-scale and city-wide taxi trajectories; and furtherly organize them as arrival sequences according to the chronological arrival time. We figure out an important property across different regions from the arrival sequences, namely *human mobility synchronization effect*, which can be exploited to explain the phenomenon that two regions have similar arrival patterns in particular time periods if they share similar urban functions. In addition, the arrival sequences are mixed by arrival events with distinct trip purposes, which can be revealed by the regional environment of both the origins and destinations. To that end, in this paper, we develop a joint model that integrates Mixture of Hawkes Process (MHP) with a hierarchical topic model to capture the arrival sequences with mixed trip purposes. Essentially, the human mobility synchronization effect is encoded as a synchronization rate in the MHP; while the regional environment is modeled by introducing latent *Trip Purpose* and *POI Topic* to generate the Point of Interests (POIs) in the regions. Moreover, we provide an effective inference algorithm for parameter learning. Finally, we conduct intensive experiments on synthetic data and real-world data, and the experimental results have demonstrated the effectiveness of the proposed model.

KEYWORDS

Human mobility, synchronization, trip purpose, Hawkes process, variational inference

*These two authors contributed equally to this work.
†Corresponding author.

KDD'17, August 13–17, 2017, Halifax, NS, Canada.
© 2017 ACM. ISBN 978-1-4503-4887-4/17/08...$15.00
DOI: http://dx.doi.org/10.1145/3097983.3098067

1 INTRODUCTION

The pervasiveness of GPS-equipped devices have accumulated large-scale human mobility data, such as taxicab GPS trajectories, cell-phone traces, geo-tagged posts and photos. Such fine-grained trajectory data, including where and when people leave, where and when they arrive, represent an invaluable source of information for understanding the nature of and exploring the semantics of human mobility, which can be benefit many applications such as smart transportation, city planning and governance, and urban economics [7, 21, 26, 27].

In most cases, people's mobility behaviors after they leave the taxi remains un-tracked, and we have no clues about their specific destinations and afterward activities. Therefore, in order to extend the analysis of human mobility, the focus of this paper is to develop a general probabilistic model to describe the arrival events at a region and spot trip purposes simultaneously. Then, the following two key questions need to be answered: (i) What is the spatial diffusion of human mobility across functional regions? (ii) How to spot and trace the latent trip purposes of taxi trajectories?

To answer these questions, we study the large-scale and city-wide taxi trajectories. We observe and identify a very important property of human mobility, which is, *human mobility synchronization*. In other words, if two regions share similar spatial configurations and urban functions in a particular time period, the two regions are likely to have similar patterns of arrival events. For instance, in the Greater New York area, there are two famous international airports (Newark and JFK) providing domestic and international flight services. It is likely that trips to the two places usually share similar purposes: to fly out or to pick up others; as Figure 1 shows, the distributions of arrival events around the two places in a common workday shares similar temporal patterns, with peaks in the early morning and afternoon.

In particular, a trajectory can be regarded as a mobility arrival event consisting of three elements: the destination region, the origin region, and the time period and each arrival event is associated with a trip purpose. However, it is difficult to identify the trip purpose of a single arrival event with high confidence, if each trip is analyzed individually and independently. Alternatively, we organize arrival events as a sequence in terms of chronological arrival times, so as to obtain higher confidence for identifying trip purposes at an aggregate level. For instance, if we observe

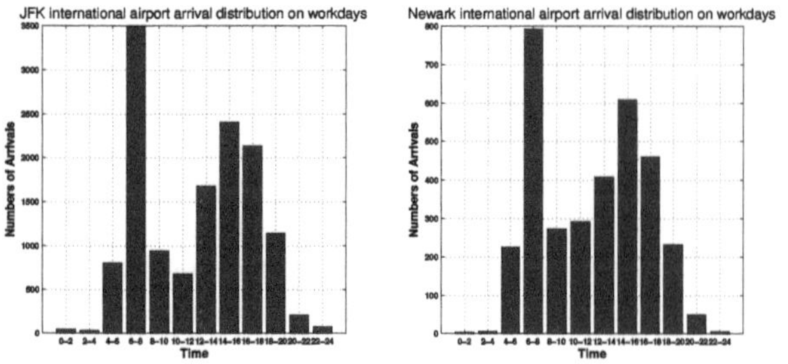

Figure 1: Taxi arrival distribution of JFK Airport and Newark Airport

massive arrival events from 7AM to 9AM in a specific region, it is *likely* that the trip purposes are to work. Moreover, suppose this region has many companies, banks, office buildings, then the function of the region is likely to be office function, and we have *higher confidence* to identify the trip purposes of arrival events as to work. Furthermore, assuming there are two regions of office function, we observe massive arrival events in both regions from 7AM to 9AM. Based on the synchronization property, we have *much higher confidence* to identify the trip purposes of the arrival events in both regions are to work. While the above intuition demonstrates the correlations among mobility arrivals, functional regions, and trip purposes, how to jointly model the correlations for describing mobility arrivals and tracing trip purposes is still a technical question.

In addition, trip purposes are not only relevant to the urban function of the destinations but also related to the origins. For example, a trajectory from a residential region to an office region is likely to be associated with a working purpose. However, a region in urban areas contains different types of POIs and thus is usually mixed with multiple functionalities [33], making it difficult to exploit functional regions for spotting trip purposes. For example, the Times Square is one famous scenic spot mixed with numerous office buildings. The arrival events in Times Square then can be attributed to various purposes. To overcome the challenge, we exploit a topic modeling method, where origin and destination regions are regarded as documents and POIs are regarded as words, for profiling the portfolios of POI topics in each region.

Along this line, we provide a unique perspective of modeling human mobility data as a stochastic process for simultaneously capturing mobility arrival events and trip purposes. Specifically, we develop a unified probabilistic model by combining a multivariate Hawkes mixture model with a hierarchical POI topic model. First, the Hawkes mixture model exploits the synchronization property to describe mobility arrivals and trace trip purposes. In particular, we first organize trajectories as a sequence of chronological arrival events, with each having a specific trip purpose. We then introduce a mixture of Hawkes processes to track the arrival sequences with distinct trip purposes, by assuming each Hawkes process corresponds to a kind of trip purposes. Essentially, in modeling the arrival sequences, the emergence of arrival events with a specific purpose at a region can possibly synchronize to other similar regions, such effect is modeled with a synchronization rate. Second, the trip purpose of an arrival can be inferred by its POI topics of origin and the POI topics of destination. Then, we introduce a latent variable *POI Topic* to model the mixture of regional functionalities with regards to POI distributions. Therefore, a hierarchical topic model can be extended by establishing connections between POI Topic and the latent trip purpose. Also, we provide an effective learning algorithm for estimating the parameters. Finally, we conduct intensive experiments on both synthetic data and real-world data, and the experimental results have demonstrated the effectiveness of our proposed model.

2 PRELIMINARY

2.1 Arrival Sequences

In order to distinguish the traffic flow into different purposes and identify the corresponding arrival patterns in aggregate, we firstly transform the independent arrival events into arrival sequences. To be more specific, we firstly divide the map according to the latitude and longitude, resulting in multiple divided small regions in the city. Then, each taxi trajectory from one region to another can be regarded as an event, with each consisting of the origin and destination, as well as the time. Considering the arrival time chronologically, we can organize the events as an arrival sequence.

Usually the events in time sequences are homogeneous and only the underlying temporal patterns can be extracted from the sequences. Nevertheless, the arrival events are assumed to have distinct types or goals, and in order to reveal the hidden purposes of the taxi trips, we resort to the regional environment, which can be further depicted by the POIs located in the regions, since the POIs in a region can be viewed as a set of independent functionalities, and together reflecting the functional mixtures of the regions. Therefore, the arrival events are heterogeneous with the information about the POIs around the origins and destinations, as well as the arrival time, which can be defined as a three-element tuple: $(POI^{origin}, POI^{destination}$, arrival time).

Furthermore, the events are assumed to be inter-correlated with each other because different regions with similar functionality may synchronize with each other on the arrival events. For example, in holiday seasons, when we see people flock in one particular business area of a city, the other region with shopping malls assembled has higher probability to have a great number of arrival events at the same time. In this paper, we define such effect across different regions as *human mobility synchronization effect.*

Definition 1. ***(Human mobility synchronization)*** *Human mobility synchronization refers to the phenomenon that the arrival events with a particular trip purpose at two or more regions has similar arrival rate at the same time.*

By discovering the synchronization effect across different regions, the arrival patterns with a specific trip purpose can be mutually learned from the synchronized regions, and to better reveal the distribution of urban functions in the city. Therefore, the arrival sequence with several different trip purposes contains heterogeneous events which are also self-correlated.

2.2 Problem Definition

Given a city map and taxi trajectories, along with the accurate positions of POIs on the map, we can organize the taxi trajectories as arrival sequences accordingly. The arrival sequence consists of a set of arrival events $E = \{E_1, E_2, \cdots, E_N\}$, in which each event corresponds to a three-element tuple (W_n^o, W_n^d, t_n), representing the POIs around the origin and the destination, and the arrival time respectively. Here $W_n^o = \{w_{n1}^o, w_{n2}^o, \cdots, w_{ni}^o, \cdots\}$ indicates the set of POIs in the regions of the origin point O_n, with each element in the set w_{ni}^o representing one particular POI in the region. Assume that there are M trip purposes underlying all the taxi trajectories, and then the problem can then be defined as follows, i) modeling the heterogeneous and self-correlated arrival sequences; ii) identifying the M types of trip purposes from the arrival sequences; iii) revealing the traffic flow with different trip purposes at different time periods for each region.

3 MODEL

3.1 Hawkes Process

Before we introduce the model for the arrival sequences, we briefly introduce the Hawkes Process [12]. Point process models the events in a time sequence with N events $\{E_1, \cdots, E_N\}$. It generally assumes that historical events before time t, which is $\mathcal{H}(t)$, can influence the future events with a conditional intensity function as follows,

$$\lambda(t|\mathcal{H}(t)) = \lim_{\Delta t \to 0} \frac{\mathbb{E}[N(t + \Delta t)|\mathcal{H}_t]}{\Delta t}. \tag{1}$$

The above intensity function simply depicts the expected rates conditioned on the past events. Obviously, Hawkes Process does not follow Markovian property since the events at t are not only influenced by the events at time $t - 1$. More formally, the univariate Hawkes Process $N(t)$ is defined by,

$$\lambda(t) = \mu(t) + \int_{-\infty}^{t} g(t - s)\mathrm{d}N(s), \tag{2}$$

where μ is the base intensity, $g(\cdot)$ is a kernal function describing the time decay effect of past events on current events. With the Hawkes Process, the *self-exciting* property can be captured, and such property is indeed a common phenomenon in different types of sequences. In our previously defined arrival sequences, such property may not hold if the events are treated as a univariate Hawkes Process with same intensity function, because the influence across different regions cannot be encoded through the *self-exciting* process.

Obviously, the univariate Hawkes Process can be extended to handle multi-dimensional random processes, which is know for multivariate Hawkes Process (MHP). In the multivariate case, different dimensions are correlated with each other, and a kernal function $g_{d'd}$ is introduced to model the triggering effect between a pair of dimensions. To be more specific, suppose the sequence can be described by a D-dimensional variable, then for each dimension d, the intensity function can be defined separately as follows,

$$\lambda_d(t) = \mu_d(t) + \sum_{d'=1}^{D} \int_{\infty}^{t} g_{d'd}(t - s)\mathrm{d}N_{d'}(s). \tag{3}$$

Considering the arrival sequences, each region i can be treated as a separate dimension; however, the arrival events at the same region may show distinct arrival patterns if trip purposes are considered separately, thus we have to exploit mixture of Hawkes Process (MHP) to incorporate the latent trip purposes in modeling the heterogeneous arrival sequences.

3.2 Mixture of Hawkes Processes in Modeling Arrival Sequences

In this paper, we aim to model the previously defined arrival sequences in terms of the arrival time at different regions of the city, and meanwhile with distinct trip purposes. Moreover, the inter-correlations between the events, or the *synchronization effect* across different regions are considered to uncover the arrival patterns of the trip. Since we assume that there are M types of trip purposes underlying all the arrival sequence, we then exploit MHP to model the heterogeneous arrival sequences.

We partition the city map into different regions, and let the "regions" be labeled as $i = 1, 2, ..., I$. Then, the arrival sequence can be regarded as a series of events at these I regions. We assume that there are M trip purposes underlying the taxi trajectories, then for each region i, the arrival events with purpose m can be modeled as one particular Hawkes Process. Therefore, we introduce a set of latent variables $\{G_n\}$ to represent the purpose of each event E_n respectively. Specifically, $G_n = \{G_{n1}, ..., G_{nM}\}$ is a binary vector with $G_{nm} = 1$ if and only if the arrival event E_n belongs to purpose m.

Meanwhile, according to the definition of *human mobility synchronization*, the arrival patterns of trips with similar purposes can synchronize across different regions. Therefore, suppose there is a *synchronization structure* for trip purpose m between the regions, which can be represented as a set of non-negative weights $\{\alpha_{ij}^m\}$, $i, j = 1, 2, ..., I$, $m = 1, 2, ..., M$ over all the regions distributed in the map.

Therefore, we model the arrival sequence with *synchronization structure* in the framework of mixture of Hawkes Process [32]. Specifically, we have a multivariate Hawkes Process $\{N_{m,i}(t)\}$, representing the number of arrival events at region i, with trip purpose m at time t, and the intensity can be defined as,

$$\lambda_{i,m}(t) = \mu_{i,m} + \sum_{j=1}^{I} \alpha_{ji}^m \int_{-\infty}^{t} g(t - s)dN_{m,j}(s) . \tag{4}$$

Here $\mu_{i,m}$ specifies the rate that region i got visited spontaneously with trip purpose m. The base rate of visiting with purpose m is given by γ_m, and the specific rate related to the region with node i is μ_i, thus $\mu_{i,m} = \mu_i \gamma_m$. The function $g(t) : \mathbb{R}_+ \to \mathbb{R}_+$ is a kernel function expressing the time-decay effect. We can pick $g(t)$ to be a function that is equal to zero when $t \geq 2$ (hours), such that we capture the temporal regularity of human mobility.

We can further extend Eq. (4) in a more practical form as follows,

$$\lambda_{i,m}(t) = \mu_i \gamma_m + \sum_{t_l \leq t} G_{lm} \alpha_{i_l i}^m g(t - t_l) . \tag{5}$$

3.3 Hierarchical Topic Modeling for Trip Purposes

As discussed previously, the trip purpose can be reflected by the neighborhood environment of both the origin place and the destination place, because the POIs in the neighborhood corresponds to travelers' afterward activities when they leave the taxi in an aggregate level. However, the regional environment is usually mixed with multiple categories of POIs, in order to better uncover the urban functionality of a region, we introduce a latent variable *POI*

Topic$\in \{1, \cdots, r, \cdots, R\}$ to represent the mixture of POIs, which is indeed in spirit of traditional topic model such as LDA [1]. Then, the POIs W^o located in the origin neighborhood and the POIs W^d in the destination neighborhood can be regarded as words in documents, which can be generated from *POI Topic* specific probability distribution.

Then, the purpose of a trip G_n can be recovered from the POI Topics of both ends of the trajectories. For example, if the origin place is identified to be a residential area with houses, gardens, and supermarkets, while the destination region consists of many office buildings, the trip purpose can be inferred as pairwise POI Topics ("*residential*"→ "*office*"), which can be semantically explained as a working purpose trip. Since the trip purpose is a latent variable itself, the POI Topics of both ends are generated from a purpose-specific probability distribution respectively. Furthermore, we assume that each G_n is sampled i.i.d from a multinomial distribution parameterized by a multinomial distribution $\pi = [\pi_1, ..., \pi_M]$.

In a nutshell, we can construct a hierarchical topic model with the two latent variables, *i.e.*, trip purpose and POI Topic. Then, for each trip from origin point o to destination point d, the POIs locate in the origin and destination regions are generated as follows,

- Generate a purpose $m \sim \texttt{Multi}(\pi)$
- Generate the POI Topic for the origin $z_o \sim Multi(\Phi_{mz})$
  - For each POI w^o in the origin neighborhood
  - Generate the POI $w^o \sim Multi(\beta_{zw})$
- Generate the POI Topic for the destination $z_d \sim Multi(\Phi_{mz})$
  - For each POI w^d in the origin neighborhood
  - Generate the POI $w^d \sim Multi(\beta_{zw})$

Therefore, the POIs around the origin point o and destination point d generated by the trip purpose G can be written as,

$$p(\mathbf{W}^o, \mathbf{W}^d|G) = \sum_{z^o}\sum_{z^d} p(\mathbf{W}^o|z^o)p(\mathbf{W}^d|z^d)p(z^o, z^d|G). \quad (6)$$

3.4 Joint MHP for Arrival Sequences

Considering both the mixture of Hawkes Processes and the hierarchical topic modeling for trip purposes, we can jointly model the arrival sequences by incorporating the temporal arrival events and the regional environment. Here, we provide a toy example to show how the arrival sequences with multiple trip purposes are modeled. As shown in Figure 2, in modeling the arrival sequences at *Time Square* and *Wall Street*, both the regional environment of the origins and destinations are taken into account, which are generated from the latent trip purposes. Because both *Time Square* and *Wall Street* are mixed with scenic spots and office buildings, the arrival sequences show different patterns with regards to specific latent trip purposes. For example, in the early morning, the arrival events are mostly for working purpose coming from residential areas such as *Newport*, *Brooklyn*, etc. While in later time of the day, travelers may also arrive at the spots for sightseeing purpose, and their origin places are usually mixed with hotel, and other scenic spots. Furthermore, since the arrival events are similar at the two places, a *synchronization effect* between the two areas will collaboratively influence the arrival events of each other.

Specifically, given the sequence E, each event n is represented by $\{t_n, i_n, <\mathbf{W}^o_n, \mathbf{W}^d_n>\}$, and suppose the latent trip purpose G_n is given, then the likelihood of the arrival sequences can be written

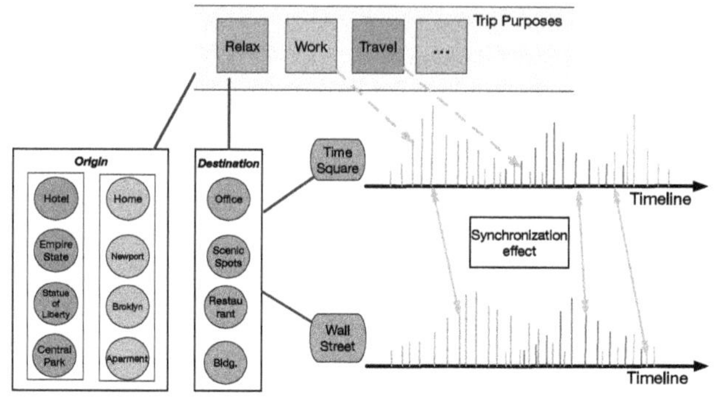

Figure 2: Toy example of Joint MHP for modeling arrival sequences

as,

$$L(G, t, \mathbf{W}) = \prod_{n=1}^{N} p(G_n)p(\mathbf{W}^o_n, \mathbf{W}^d_n|G_n)p(t_n|G_n). \quad (7)$$

3.5 Model Inference

Assuming that the latent variable G and then z are observed, then the likelihood function for the complete data $(G, z, t, W) = \{(G_n, z_n, t_n, W$ with $t_0 = 0$ and $t_N = T$, is given by

$$\begin{aligned} L(G, z, t, W) = &\prod_{n=1}^{N}\prod_{m=1}^{M} p(\mathbf{W}^o_n, \mathbf{W}^d_n, z_o, z_d|G_{nm}) \\ &\times[\pi_m \lambda_{i_n, m}(t_n)]^{G_{nm}} \times \exp\left(-\sum_{i=1}^{I}\sum_{m=1}^{M}\int_0^T \lambda_{i,m}(s)ds\right). \end{aligned} \quad (8)$$

We introduce a mean-field fully factorized variational distribution parametrized by multinomial distribution ϕ's and ζ's as follows:

$$q(G_{1:N}, Z|\phi, \zeta) = \prod_{n=1}^{N} q(G_n|\phi_n) \times \prod_{m=1}^{M} q(z^o_n|\zeta^o_m) \times q(z^d_n|\zeta^d_m). \quad (9)$$

Thus, by using the concavity of log-function, a tight lower bound of the log likelihood can be introduced

$$\begin{aligned} \mathcal{L}(t, W) &\equiv \log\left(\int_{\{(G,z)\}} L(G, z, t, W)d\{(G, z)\}\right) \\ &\geq \int_{\{(G,z)\}} \log\left(L(G, z, t, W)\frac{d\{(G, z)\}}{dq(\{(G, z)\})}\right) dq(\{(G, z)\}) \\ &= \mathbf{E}_q[\mathcal{L}(G, z, t, W)] + \mathcal{E}[q] \equiv \mathfrak{L}, \end{aligned} \quad (10)$$

where $\mathcal{L}(G, z, t, W) = \log L(G, z, t, W)$ is the log-likelihood and

$$\begin{aligned} \mathcal{E}[q] &= -\mathbf{E}[\log q(\phi)] - \mathbf{E}[\log q(\zeta^o)] - \mathbf{E}[\log q(\zeta^d)] \\ &= -\sum_{n=1}^{N}\sum_{m=1}^{M} \phi_{nm}\log\phi_{nm} \\ &\quad -\sum_{m=1}^{M}\sum_{r^o=1}^{R} \zeta^o_{mr^o}\log\zeta^o_{mr^o} - \sum_{m=1}^{M}\sum_{r^d=1}^{R} \zeta^d_{mr^d}\log\zeta^d_{mr^d} \end{aligned} \quad (11)$$

The right-hand side $\mathfrak{L}$ in (10) is the so-called evidence lower bound (ELBO), which will be used as the surrogate to the true log-likelihood in inference and in learning. We then have,

$$
\begin{aligned}
\mathfrak{L} &= \sum_{n=1}^{N}\sum_{m=1}^{M}\phi_{nm}(\log\pi_m + \mathbf{E}_q[\log\lambda_{i_n,m}(t_n)] + \mathbf{E}_q\log p_m(W_n)) \\
&- \sum_{i=1}^{I}\sum_{m=1}^{M}\int_0^T \mathbf{E}_q[\lambda_{i,m}(s)]ds + \mathcal{E}[q] \,.
\end{aligned} \tag{12}
$$

To calculate (12) more explicitly, we make use of the formula (5) and we further have

$$
\begin{aligned}
&\sum_{i=1}^{I}\sum_{m=1}^{M}\int_0^T \mathbf{E}_q[\lambda_{i,m}(s)]ds \\
=& \sum_{i=1}^{I}\sum_{m=1}^{M}\left[\gamma_m\mu_i T + \int_0^T \sum_{t_l\le s}\phi_{lm}\alpha^m_{i_l i}g(s-t_l)ds\right] \\
=& \; T\sum_{i=1}^{I}\sum_{m=1}^{M}\gamma_m\mu_i + \sum_{n=1}^{N}\mathcal{G}(T-t_n)\sum_{m=1}^{M}\phi_{nm}\sum_{i=1}^{I}\alpha^m_{i_n i} \,.
\end{aligned} \tag{13}
$$

To deal with the sum involving $\mathbf{E}_q[\log\lambda_{i_n,m}(t_n)]$, we make use of the formula (5) and we write $\mathbf{E}_q[\log\lambda_{i_n,m}(t_n)] = \mathbf{E}_q[\log(\gamma_m\mu_i + \sum_{t_l<t_n} G_{lm}\alpha^m_{i_l i_n}g(t_n-t_l))]$, after that we apply Jensen's inequality:

$$
\begin{aligned}
&\mathbf{E}_q[\log\lambda_{i_n,m}(t_n)] \\
=& \; \mathbf{E}_q[\log(\gamma_m\mu_i + \sum_{t_l<t_n} G_{lm}\alpha^m_{i_l i_n}g(t_n-t_l))] \\
\ge& \; \eta^m_{nn}\log\left(\frac{\gamma_m\mu_i}{\eta^m_{nn}}\right) + \sum_{l=1}^{n-1}\phi_{lm}\eta^m_{ln}\log\left(\frac{\alpha^m_{i_l i_n}g(t_n-t_l)}{\eta^m_{ln}}\right) \\
=& \; \eta^m_{nn}\log(\gamma_m\mu_{i_n}) + \sum_{l=1}^{n-1}\phi_{lm}\eta^m_{ln}\log(\alpha^m_{i_l i_n}g(t_n-t_l)) \\
&-\eta^m_{nn}\log(\eta^m_{nn}) - \sum_{l=1}^{n-1}\phi_{lm}\eta^m_{ln}\log(\eta^m_{ln}) \,.
\end{aligned} \tag{14}
$$

Here the set of branching variables $\{\eta^m, m = 1,2,\ldots.,M\}$ are chosen such that each η^m is a $N\times N$ lower-triangular matrix with n-th row $\eta^m_n = [\eta^m_{1n},\ldots,\eta^m_{nn}]^T$. The branchings η also satisfies the following conditions

$$
\eta^m_{ln} \ge 0 \,,\; l = 1,2,\ldots,n \,, \tag{15}
$$

$$
\eta^m_{nn} + \sum_{l=1}^{n-1}\phi_{lm}\eta^m_{ln} = 1 \,. \tag{16}
$$

While for $\mathbf{E}_q[\log p(\mathbf{W}^o_n, \mathbf{W}^d_n|G_n)]$, since we introduce the fully factorized variational distribution (9), we now have

$$
\begin{aligned}
&\mathbf{E}_q[\log p(\mathbf{W}^o_n, \mathbf{W}^d_n, z_o, z_d|G_n)] \\
=& \; \mathbf{E}_q[\log p(z_o|G_n)] + \mathbf{E}_q[\log p(\mathbf{W}^o_n|z_o)] \\
+& \; \mathbf{E}_q[\log p(\mathbf{z}_d|G_n)] + \mathbf{E}_q\log p(\mathbf{W}^d_n|z_d) \\
=& \sum_{z_o=1}^{R}\zeta^o_{mz_o}\log\zeta^o_{mz_o} + \sum_{z_o=1}^{R}\sum_{w=1}^{C}\zeta^o_{m,z^o}\log\beta_{z^o,c^o_w} \\
+& \sum_{z_d=1}^{R}\zeta^d_{mz^d}\log\zeta^d_{mz^d} + \sum_{z_d=1}^{R}\sum_{w=1}^{C}\zeta^d_{m,z^d}\log\beta_{z^d,w} \,.
\end{aligned} \tag{17}
$$

Summarizing (12), (13), (14), and (17), we can maximize the ELBO by introducing the constraints $\sum_{m=1}^{M}\phi_{nm} = 1$ as Lagranging multiplier. Then, the variational distribution ϕ can be inferred as follows,

$$
\begin{aligned}
&\phi_{nm} \propto \pi_m : \text{prior} \\
&\times \prod_{r_o=1}^{R}(\zeta^o_{mr^o})^{\zeta^o_{mr^o}} \prod_{r^d=1}^{R}(\zeta^d_{mr^d})^{\zeta^d_{mr^d}} : \text{POI topics} \\
&\times \prod_{r^o=1}^{R}\prod_{c^o=1}^{C}(\beta^o_{r^o c^o})^{\zeta^o_{mr^o}W^o_{nc^o}} \prod_{r^d=1}^{R}\prod_{c^d=1}^{C}(\beta^d_{r^d c^d})^{\zeta^d_{mr^d}W^d_{nc^d}} : \text{POIs} \\
&\times(\gamma_m\mu_{i_n})^{\eta^m_{nn}} : \text{ self triggering} \\
&\times\prod_{l=1}^{n-1}(\alpha^m_{i_l i_n}g(t_n-t_l))^{\phi_{lm}\eta^m_{ln}} : \text{ influences from the past} \\
&\times\prod_{l=n+1}^{N}(\alpha^m_{i_n i_l}g(t_l-t_n))^{\phi_{lm}\eta^m_{nl}} : \text{ influences to the future} \\
&\times\exp\left(-\mathcal{G}(T-t_n,t_n)\sum_{i=1}^{I}\alpha^m_{i_n i}\right) : \text{ influences by trip purpose.}
\end{aligned} \tag{18}
$$

We can see from (18) that the inference for ϕ can be decomposed to different building blocks of the joint model including the influence in MHP and the purposes inferred from the regional environment.

Furthermore, we can infer the variational multinomial ζ^o and ζ^d by taking the derivative with respect to ELBO with the normalization condition as Lagrangian, and let $\epsilon = \frac{\sum_{n=1}^{N}\phi_{nm}}{1-\sum_{n=1}^{N}\phi_{nm}}$, we can get

$$
\zeta^o_{m,r} \propto \prod_{c=1}^{C}(\beta_{rc})^{\epsilon W^o_{nc}} \,, \tag{19}
$$

$$
\zeta^o_{m,r} \propto \prod_{c=1}^{C}(\beta_{rc})^{\epsilon W^d_{nc}} \,. \tag{20}
$$

After updating the variational parameters ϕ and ζ, we can proceed to estimate and update the parameters involved in the joint model including the self-instantaneous visit rates μ_i, the per-region visit rates γ_i, the synchronization rates $\alpha^m_{ij} \in \mathbb{R}^{12}_+$, the regularization prior for sampling the purposes π_m, and the multinomial distribution of POIs over topics β_{rc},

$$
\pi_m \propto \sum_{n=1}^{N}\phi_{nm} \,, \tag{21}
$$

$$
\mu_i \propto \frac{\sum_{m=1}^{M}\phi_{nm}\sum_{n=1}^{N}\delta_{i_n,i}\eta^m_{nn}}{\sum_{m=1}^{M}\gamma_m T} \,, \tag{22}
$$

$$
\gamma_m \propto \frac{\sum_{n=1}^{N}\phi_{nm}\eta^m_{nn}}{\sum_{i=1}^{I}\mu_i T} \,, \tag{23}
$$

$$
\alpha^m_{ij} = \frac{\sum_{n=1}^{N}\sum_{l=1}^{n-1}\phi_{nm}\phi_{lm}\eta^m_{ln}\delta_{i_l i}\delta_{i_n j}}{\sum_{n=1}^{N}\mathcal{G}(T-t_n)\phi_{nm}\delta_{i_n i}} \,, \tag{24}
$$

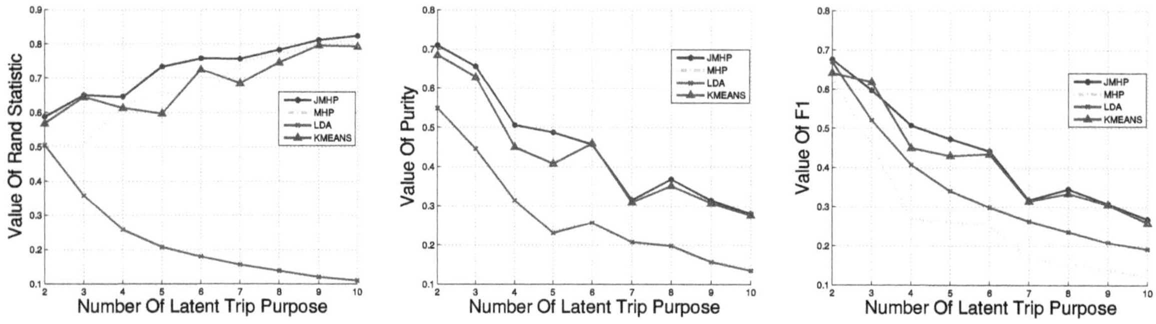

(a) (b) (c)

Figure 3: Experiments on synthetic data. (a): Comparison of Rand Statistic. (b): Comparison of purity. (c): Comparison of F1-Value

$$\beta_{rc} \propto \sum_n \sum_m \phi_{nm}(\zeta^o_{m,c} W^o_{m,c} + \zeta^d_{m,c} W^d_{m,c}). \quad (25)$$

4 EXPERIMENT

4.1 Synthetic Data

We simulate data with pre-defined M trip purposes by running Ogata's modified thinning algorithm [23]. Specifically, given model dimensions (M, I, T), the parameters $(\mu, \gamma, \alpha, \beta)$ can be drawn. Then, we can randomly generate the distribution of the arrival events, including the arrival time, and the corresponding POI distribution of the origin and destination points. We mix the trips with different purposes into one arrival sequence by ordering the events chronologically. The POIs located in the regions were sampled from the hierarchical topic models. In this experiment, 2,000-50,000 events involving $M = 10$ purposes, $Z = 10$ latent topics, $C = 50$ words and $I = 50$ nodes are generated.

Since the simulated data has the "label" of trip purposes, we can then testify whether our model can accurately distinguish traffic flow with particular purposes from all the trajectories. More specifically, the parameter ϕ inferred from the joint model reveal the trip purpose distribution of each arrival event, and we can label an event by the purpose with the largest value of ϕ, *i.e.*, $m^*_n = \text{argmax}_m \phi_{n,m}$. Thus, the task can be regarded as clustering the trajectories into different types.

Baseline Methods. We compare our proposed approach with the following baseline methods:

- MHP: In MHP, we only model the time sequence without considering the particular POIs of the regions. Similar to the joint MHP model, we can also estimate the parameters concerning the purpose distribution of each trip.
- LDA: Given the POIs in the origin and destination region, we can regard each trip as a document with each POI as a word. Then, we can use topic model LDA to learn the topic distribution of each trip and categorize the trip into one particular cluster.
- K-means: K-means is exploited to cluster the related POI vectors of each trip.

Evaluation metrics. Since the task of identifying trip purposes can be regarded as clustering, and we also simulate the labels, we can use several external measures to evaluate the performance.

Purity. Purity represents the extent to which a cluster can represent a particular labeled class, which can be computed by

$$\text{purity} = \sum_j^K \frac{N_j}{N} max(\frac{N_{ij}}{N_j}), \quad (26)$$

where $N_{ij} = |P_i \bigcap C_j|$ and $N_j = |C_j|$, P_i is a set of data which are labeled with class i, and C_j is the jth cluster in the clustering results.

F1-Measure. We firstly calculate the precision and recall with respect to the clustering results, and

$$F_1 = 2 * precision * recall/(precision + recall) \quad (27)$$

Rand Statistics. Rand statistics can be computed by

$$\text{RS} = \frac{2 * (N_{11} + N_{00})}{N(N-1)}, \quad (28)$$

where N_{11} is the number of data pairs that are in the same class both in the origin data set and the clustering outcome, N_{00} is the number that events pair are in the different clusters both in the origin data set and the clustering results, and N is the number of data points.

In Figure 3, we show the performances of different methods in identifying distinct trip purposes with regards to the above evaluation metrics. It is shown that the joint MHP model achieves the best performance among all the methods. Meanwhile, we also vary the number of latent trip purposes to show the performance. Obviously, the performance of the proposed model still performs best.

4.2 NYC Data

We also apply the model to a real world dataset, which consists of taxi trajectories and the POI information collected from 01/2015 to 06/2015 in New York City. In the raw data set, there are more than 70,000,000 trajectories from about 700,000 pickup points to more than 1,000,000 dropoff points. First, we divide the NYC map into regions which consists of a square with 0.008 longitude as width and 0.008 latitude as height, and we also filter out the obviously incorrect trajectories and points. Then, we retain the regions which

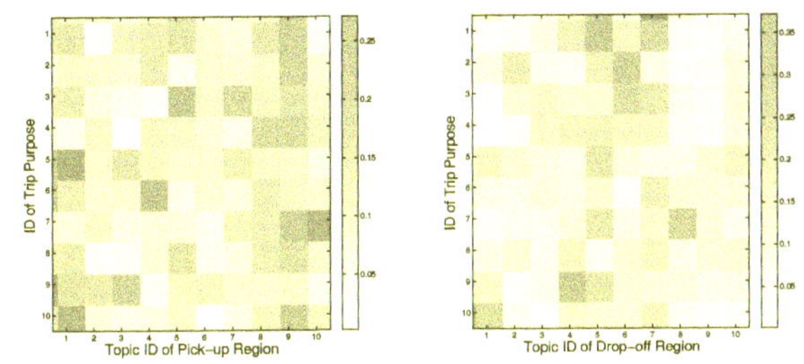

Figure 4: POI Topic distribution over latent trip purposes for origin and destination

Figure 5: The locations of regions A, B, and C on the city map of NYC.

have at least 10 POIs and 36000 arrival events during the time period. Thus, we obtain about 55,000,000 taxi trajectories and 152 regions. In addition, the arrival events are sampled from the original dataset randomly, resulting in 31630 arrival events between the 152 regions in total.

Identifying POI Topics. In order to discover the underlying semantic meanings of POI Topics, we analyze the parameters β_r^c, and list the most representative POIs for each POI topic, which are shown in Table 1. We can see from Table 1 that each POI Topic is mixed with several related POIs but show particular urban functionality in overall. Specifically, we see representative POIs such as bar, nightclub and restaurant in Topic 1, which refers to a nightlife related POI Topic. Both Topic 2 and Topic 3 can be inferred as dining related topics, but there still exist some differences regarding the types of restaurants. Topic 4 is mixed with office, hotel and entertainment places, which corresponds to the fact that some regions in the city play the role of both working areas and scenic spots, *e.g.*, Time Square. Topic 5 indicates shopping related urban functions and Topic 6 is regarded as school oriented because it mostly consists of POIs concerning schools. Obviously, Topic 7 should be identified as a mixture of travelers' visited places including scenic spots, traffic centers, etc. Topic 8 can be viewed as a general entertainment function while Topic 9 consists of fast food related POIs, as well as offices; since a working place is usually blended with many fast food restaurants. Topic 10 refers to the residential areas with apartment buildings and dining restaurants.

Spotting Trip Purposes. As discussed previously, the trip purpose can be detected by integrating the regional environment of both the origins and destinations, which can be estimated from the POI Topic distribution over trip purposes. As shown in Figure 4, we can see that each trip purpose focuses on particular POI topics, and the purpose can be inferred in combination of the topics at both ends of the trips. Then, several interesting trip purposes are identified as follows:

Shopping purpose. In purpose 1, we see topics of the origins concentrate on Topic 1 and 9, while the destinations are mainly composed of Topic 5 and 7. Considering the urban functionality of both ends, such trips can be inferred as shopping and outdoors activities.

Dining purpose. Purpose 2 consists of office related topics (Topic 4 and 9) as the origins and the restaurant related topics (Topic 6) as destinations, thus such trips can be inferred as for dining purpose.

Homing purpose. In purpose 5, the topics of the destinations are composed of topic 10, which corresponds to residential areas, while the topics of the origins are much more diverse. Then, the trips annotated with purpose 5 can be regarded as homing from various regions in the city.

Synchronization Effect. We further use a case to illustrate the *synchronization effect* discovered from the model. In the joint MHP model, we introduce a synchronization effect to when the correlation index is bigger, the relationship between the pair of regions is bigger. We choose three regions A, B, and C and plot them on the map 5. Region A and B are located at the two sides of the Central Park, while region C locates in Brooklyn. By estimating the synchronization rate between these regions, we can obtain $\alpha_{AB} = 8.27066832, \alpha_{AC} = 0.00711464$, indicating that region A and B has a strong synchronization effect while A and C has weak connections in terms of arrival events. Then, we further analyze the POI distribution and the arrival sequences at these regions. As shown in Figure 6, the POI distribution of region A and B are very similar, which are mainly mixed with educational buildings, residential apartments, restaurants, and shops. However, the POIs in region C show different distribution with few shopping related POIs. In view of the arrival sequences, region A and B show extremely similar patterns, while region C has a different arrival patterns. This case illustrates that the synchronization effect is strong among the regions with similar urban functions.

5 RELATED WORK

This paper is related to the following categories of prior work including discovering the urban functionality and trip purposes from human mobility data, traffic flow prediction, as well as the application of Hawkes Process in various fields.

Urban functionality and trip purpose discovery. With the rapid development of mobile and GPS technologies, large-scale footstep data has been accumulated and attracted lots of studies in discovering functional blocks and trip purposes [36]. The work in [30] proposed a semantic model, along with a computation and annotation platform for developing a semantic approach to understand the trip purpose better. Rinku *et al.* [3] proposed a method to determine the destinations of trips using only speed and time data from real world driving trips without accessing GPS traces. The work in [8] proposed a method to automatically annotate raw trajectories with the activities of users during their movement when tracked by a GPS device. The work in [37] proposed an approach

Table 1: Representative POIs for POI Topics

TOPIC 1	prob.	TOPIC 2	prob.	TOPIC 3	prob.	TOPIC 4	prob.	TOPIC 5	prob.
Bar	0.1884	Chinese Rest.	0.1286	Bar	0.0933	Office	0.3331	Clothing Store	0.0995
Home	0.0953	Italian Rest.	0.0913	Italian Rest.	0.0565	General Entertain	0.1035	Cafe	0.0693
Nightclub	0.0571	Asian Rest.	0.0541	American Rest.	0.0442	Hotel	0.1023	Office	0.0574
Event Space	0.0495	Tea Room	0.0481	Wine Bar	0.0373	Building	0.0869	Coffee Shop	0.0535
Cocktail Bar	0.0495	Bar	0.0472	Sushi Rest.	0.0319	Event Space	0.0593	Cosmetics Shop	0.0419
Lounge	0.0495	Spa or Massage Parlor	0.0416	Mexican Rest.	0.0306	Sandwich Place	0.0376	General Entertain	0.0408
Speakeasy	0.0471	Salon or Barbershop	0.0403	Lounge	0.0297	Hotel Bar	0.0342	French Rest.	0.0406
Breakfast Spot	0.0382	Vietnamese Rest.	0.039	Pizza Place	0.0278	Lounge	0.0342	High Tech Outlet	0.0388
French Rest.	0.0334	Art Gallery	0.0342	Coffee Shop	0.0256	Other Outdoors	0.0298	Salon or Barbershop	0.0368
Boat or Ferry	0.0316	Cocktail Bar	0.0316	Salon or Barbershop	0.0256	Performing Arts Venue	0.0289	Miscellaneous Shop	0.0331
TOPIC 6	**prob.**	**TOPIC 7**	**prob.**	**TOPIC 8**	**prob.**	**TOPIC 9**	**prob.**	**TOPIC 10**	**prob.**
College Acad.	0.0808	Park	0.1343	Art Gallery	0.2773	American Rest.	0.1023	Home	0.2005
Food Truck	0.0756	Other Outdoors	0.1	Park	0.1021	Deli or Bodega	0.0619	Building	0.0591
University	0.0653	Scenic Lookout	0.0767	Other Outdoors	0.0892	Office	0.0569	Deli or Bodega	0.0471
College Library	0.0639	General Travel	0.0753	Cafe	0.0555	Pizza Place	0.0464	Pizza Place	0.0442
General College/University	0.0573	Building	0.074	Playground	0.049	Bar	0.0448	Laundromat or Dry Cleaner	0.0342
College Dorm	0.0565	Airport	0.074	Automotive Shop	0.0386	Food Truck	0.0434	Coffee Shop	0.0317
Cafe	0.0499	Harbor or Marina	0.0616	Event Space	0.033	Sandwich Place	0.0392	Drugstore or Pharmacy	0.0291
Plaza	0.0485	Taxi	0.0534	Strip Club	0.0265	Coffee Shop	0.0346	Chinese Rest.	0.0256
Park	0.0382	Government Building	0.048	Sculpture Garden	0.0241	Burger Joint	0.0326	Mexican Rest.	0.0236
College Classroom	0.0374	Seafood Rest.	0.0343	Plaza	0.0233	Cafe	0.0307	Apartment Building	0.0206

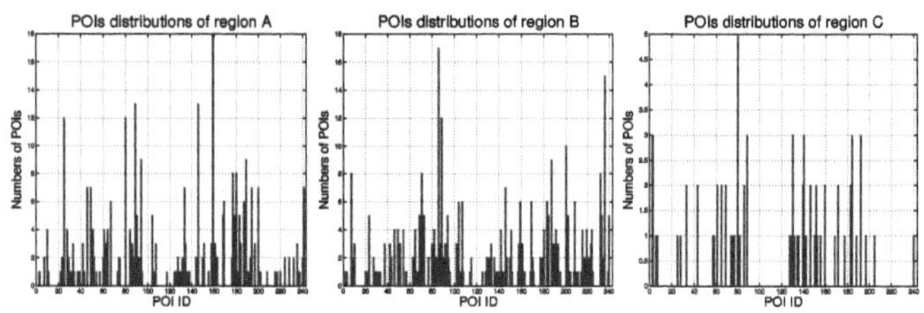

(a) POIs distribution in region A, B and C

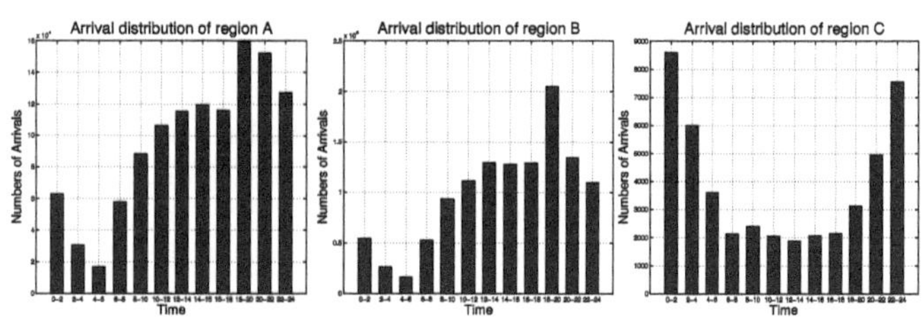

(b) Arrival sequences in region A, B and C

Figure 6: Synchronization effect with different synchronization rates (α_{AB} = 8.27066832, α_{AC} = 0.00711464).

which focused on model and infer the purpose of travel, or the activity at the destination of a trip during daily life scenarios. The work in [18] constructed a effective recommendation system by the analysis of the historical check-in data. Specifically, they studied the exploration prediction problem and converted it into a classification problem and proposed a novel future location prediction model called CEPR to make a location prediction more efficiently. The work in [19] proposed a collective iterative classification algorithm to classify the purpose of passengers. The general idea of this work is to first form groups based on the extracted mobility features and collectively classify the purposes of group passengers sharing same destination and same purposes. The work in [28] used the historical mobility data records to spot user preferences to annotate venue to mobility records of mobile users.

Traffic flow prediction. Traffic flow prediction has been one of major challenges for developing intelligent transportation system [35]. [15] uses regime-switching space-time models and selection operator (LASSO) to predict the real-time road traffic and verifies the method on a real data set. [20] compares a few typical methods on forecasting traffic flow and then proposes a seasonal support vector machine function to improve the accuracy and computing efficiency. [11] uses a method, adaptive Kalman filter, to improve the performance of short term traffic flow forecasting. [13] constructs framework with a deep belief network at the bottom to achieve the effective features and a multi-task regression layer at the top. The work in [25] proposed four methods by using Kalman filtering theory to solve the multi-step ahead predicting of short-term traffic flow and evaluated the approaches with other prediction methods.

Applications of Hawkes Processes. Recently Hawkes process [12] has been widely used in many fields, including earthquake [22, 24], finance [5], crime [2], streaming texts [4, 31, 32, 34], social network [6, 9, 10, 14, 17], and marketing [29], etc. For example, [22] describes a generalized model which focuses on space-time clustering for historical earthquakes by Hawkes process. Also, [24] applies the Hawkes process for earthquake occurrences with clustering and interpretation. Yang et al [32] propose a generalized model to track the meme and the corresponding diffusion network by combining mixture of Hawkes processes and a language model. Li et al. [16] combine topic model with Hawkes process to simultaneously identify and label the searching tasks. [34] constructs a self-exciting point process model with the re-sharing information in the social network to predict the popularity of Tweets.

6 CONCLUSIONS

Summary. Modeling mobility arrivals and spotting trip purposes have been two key challenges in the semantic exploration of human mobility data. By studying large-scale human mobility data, we observe and identify the synchronization property of human mobility. Human mobility synchronization indeed jointly captures the correlations among functional regions, mobility arrivals, and trip purposes; that is, if two regions share similar spatial configurations and urban functions, given a particular time period, the two regions show arrival events with similar arrival rates with respect to specific trip purposes. In addition, we construct the latent factor POI topics of both the origin and destination to reflect the latent trip purpose. Along this line, we develop a probabilistic method via modeling human mobility data as stochastic point processes, by exploiting both human mobility synchronization and POI topics of origin and destination regions. This probabilistic model combines both a mixture of Hawkes point processes and a topic modeling where POIs are regarded as words and regions are regarded as documents. The model can effectively model mobility arrivals, spot trip purposes, and learn the spatiotemporal synchronization rates among region pairs through the variational inference. Finally, we present extensive experiments on synthetic data and real world human mobility data of NYC to demonstrate the effectiveness of the proposed model.

Acknowledgment. This research was partially supported by University of Missouri Research Board (proposal number: 4991). This work was also partially supported by the National Key Research Program of China under Grant No. 2016YFB1000600, No. 2016YFB0501900 and Natural Science Foundation of China under Grant No. 61402435.

REFERENCES

[1] David M Blei, Andrew Y Ng, and Michael I Jordan. 2003. Latent dirichlet allocation. *Journal of machine Learning research* 3, Jan (2003), 993–1022.

[2] Aaron Clauset, Ryan Woodard, and others. 2013. Estimating the historical and future probabilities of large terrorist events. *The Annals of Applied Statistics* 7, 4 (2013), 1838–1865.

[3] Rinku Dewri, Prasad Annadata, Wisam Eltarjaman, and Ramakrishna Thurimella. 2013. Inferring trip destinations from driving habits data. In *Proceedings of the 12th ACM workshop on Workshop on privacy in the electronic society*. ACM, 267–272.

[4] Nan Du, Mehrdad Farajtabar, Amr Ahmed, Alexander J Smola, and Le Song. 2015. Dirichlet-hawkes processes with applications to clustering continuous-time document streams. In *Proceedings of the 21th ACM SIGKDD International Conference on Knowledge Discovery and Data Mining*. ACM, 219–228.

[5] Paul Embrechts, Thomas Liniger, Lu Lin, and others. 2011. Multivariate Hawkes processes: an application to financial data. *Journal of Applied Probability* 48 (2011), 367–378.

[6] Eric W Fox, Martin B Short, Frederic P Schoenberg, Kathryn D Coronges, and Andrea L Bertozzi. 2016. Modeling e-mail networks and inferring leadership using self-exciting point processes. *J. Amer. Statist. Assoc.* just-accepted (2016).

[7] Yanjie Fu, Guannan Liu, Spiros Papadimitriou, Hui Xiong, Yong Ge, Hengshu Zhu, and Chen Zhu. 2015. Real estate ranking via mixed land-use latent models. In *Proceedings of the 21th ACM SIGKDD International Conference on Knowledge Discovery and Data Mining*. ACM, 299–308.

[8] Barbara Furletti, Paolo Cintia, Chiara Renso, and Laura Spinsanti. 2013. Inferring human activities from GPS tracks. (2013).

[9] Manuel Gomez-Rodriguez, Jure Leskovec, and Bernhard Schölkopf. 2013. Modeling Information Propagation with Survival Theory.. In *ICML (3)*. 666–674.

[10] Manuel Gomez Rodriguez, Jure Leskovec, and Bernhard Schölkopf. 2013. Structure and dynamics of information pathways in online media. In *Proceedings of the sixth ACM international conference on Web search and data mining*. ACM, 23–32.

[11] Jianhua Guo, Wei Huang, and Billy M. Williams. 2014. Adaptive Kalman filter approach for stochastic short-term traffic flow rate prediction and uncertainty quantification. *Transportation Research Part C Emerging Technologies* 43 (2014), 50–64.

[12] Alan G Hawkes. 1971. Spectra of some self-exciting and mutually exciting point processes. *Biometrika* 58, 1 (1971), 83–90.

[13] W. Huang, G. Song, H. Hong, and K. Xie. 2014. Deep Architecture for Traffic Flow Prediction: Deep Belief Networks With Multitask Learning. *IEEE Transactions on Intelligent Transportation Systems* 15, 5 (2014), 2191–2201.

[14] David Hunter, Padhraic Smyth, Duy Q Vu, and Arthur U Asuncion. 2011. Dynamic egocentric models for citation networks. In *Proceedings of the 28th International Conference on Machine Learning (ICML-11)*. 857–864.

[15] Yiannis Kamarianakis, Wei Shen, and Laura Wynter. 2012. Real-time road traffic forecasting using regime-switching space-time models and adaptive LASSO. *Applied Stochastic Models in Business and Industry* 28, 4 (2012), 297–315.

[16] Liangda Li, Hongbo Deng, Anlei Dong, Yi Chang, and Hongyuan Zha. 2014. Identifying and labeling search tasks via query-based hawkes processes. In *Proceedings of the 20th ACM SIGKDD international conference on Knowledge discovery and data mining*. ACM, 731–740.

[17] Liangda Li and Hongyuan Zha. 2013. Dyadic event attribution in social networks with mixtures of hawkes processes. In *Proceedings of the 22nd ACM international conference on Conference on information & knowledge management*. ACM, 1667–1672.

[18] Defu Lian, Xing Xie, Vincent W Zheng, Nicholas Jing Yuan, Fuzheng Zhang, and Enhong Chen. 2015. CEPR: A collaborative exploration and periodically returning model for location prediction. *ACM Transactions on Intelligent Systems and Technology (TIST)* 6, 1 (2015), 8.

[19] Youfang Lin, Huaiyu Wan, Rui Jiang, Zhihao Wu, and Xuguang Jia. 2015. Inferring the travel purposes of passenger groups for better understanding of passengers. *Intelligent Transportation Systems, IEEE Transactions on* 16, 1 (2015), 235–243.

[20] Marco Lippi, Matteo Bertini, and Paolo Frasconi. 2013. Short-Term Traffic Flow Forecasting: An Experimental Comparison of Time-Series Analysis and Supervised Learning. *IEEE Transactions on Intelligent Transportation Systems* 14, 2 (2013), 871–882.

[21] Yu Liu, Zhengwei Sui, Chaogui Kang, and Yong Gao. 2014. Uncovering patterns of inter-urban trip and spatial interaction from social media check-in data. *PloS one* 9, 1 (2014), e86026.

[22] Fabio Musmeci and David Vere-Jones. 1992. A space-time clustering model for historical earthquakes. *Annals of the Institute of Statistical Mathematics* 44, 1 (1992), 1–11.

[23] Yosihiko Ogata. 1981. On Lewis' simulation method for point processes. *IEEE Transactions on Information Theory* 27, 1 (1981), 23–31.

[24] Yosihiko Ogata. 1998. Space-time point-process models for earthquake occurrences. *Annals of the Institute of Statistical Mathematics* 50, 2 (1998), 379–402.

[25] Luis Leon Ojeda, Alain Y Kibangou, and Carlos Canudas De Wit. 2013. Adaptive Kalman filtering for multi-step ahead traffic flow prediction. In *American Control Conference (ACC), 2013*. IEEE, 4724–4729.

[26] Meng Qu, Hengshu Zhu, Junming Liu, Guannan Liu, and Hui Xiong. 2014. A cost-effective recommender system for taxi drivers. In *Proceedings of the 20th ACM SIGKDD international conference on Knowledge discovery and data mining*. ACM, 45–54.

[27] Zuchao Wang, Min Lu, Xiaoru Yuan, Junping Zhang, and Huub Van De Wetering. 2013. Visual traffic jam analysis based on trajectory data. *IEEE Transactions on Visualization and Computer Graphics* 19, 12 (2013), 2159–2168.

[28] Fei Wu and Zhenhui Li. 2016. Where did you go: Personalized annotation of mobility records. In *Proceedings of the 25th ACM International on Conference on Information and Knowledge Management*. ACM, 589–598.

[29] Lizhen Xu, Jason A Duan, and Andrew Whinston. 2014. Path to purchase: A mutually exciting point process model for online advertising and conversion. *Management Science* 60, 6 (2014), 1392–1412.

[30] Zhixian Yan, Dipanjan Chakraborty, Christine Parent, Stefano Spaccapietra, and Karl Aberer. 2013. Semantic trajectories: Mobility data computation and annotation. *ACM Transactions on Intelligent Systems and Technology (TIST)* 4, 3 (2013), 49.

[31] Jaewon Yang and Jure Leskovec. 2011. Patterns of temporal variation in online media. In *Proceedings of the fourth ACM international conference on Web search and data mining*. ACM, 177–186.

[32] Shuang-Hong Yang and Hongyuan Zha. 2013. Mixture of Mutually Exciting Processes for Viral Diffusion. *ICML (2)* 28 (2013), 1–9.

[33] Jing Yuan, Yu Zheng, and Xing Xie. 2012. Discovering regions of different functions in a city using human mobility and POIs. In *ACM SIGKDD International Conference on Knowledge Discovery and Data Mining*. 186–194.

[34] Qingyuan Zhao, Murat A Erdogdu, Hera Y He, Anand Rajaraman, and Jure Leskovec. 2015. Seismic: A self-exciting point process model for predicting tweet popularity. In *Proceedings of the 21th ACM SIGKDD International Conference on Knowledge Discovery and Data Mining*. ACM, 1513–1522.

[35] Yu Zheng. 2015. Trajectory data mining: an overview. *ACM Transactions on Intelligent Systems and Technology (TIST)* 6, 3 (2015), 29.

[36] Yu Zheng, Licia Capra, Ouri Wolfson, and Hai Yang. 2014. Urban computing: concepts, methodologies, and applications. *ACM Transactions on Intelligent Systems and Technology (TIST)* 5, 3 (2014), 38.

[37] Zack Zhu, Ulf Blanke, and Gerhard Tröster. 2014. Inferring travel purpose from crowd-augmented human mobility data. In *Proceedings of the First International Conference on IoT in Urban Space*. ICST (Institute for Computer Sciences, Social-Informatics and Telecommunications Engineering), 44–49.

FORA: Simple and Effective Approximate Single-Source Personalized PageRank

Sibo Wang*
University of Queensland
sibo.wang@uq.edu.au

Renchi Yang
Nanyang Technological University
rcyang@ntu.edu.sg

Xiaokui Xiao
Nanyang Technological University
xkxiao@ntu.edu.sg

Zhewei Wei†
Renmin University of China
zhewei@ruc.edu.cn

Yin Yang
Hamad Bin Khalifa University
yyang@hbku.edu.qa

ABSTRACT

Given a graph G, a source node s and a target node t, the *personalized PageRank* (*PPR*) of t with respect to s is the probability that a random walk starting from s terminates at t. A *single-source PPR* (*SSPPR*) query enumerates all nodes in G, and returns the top-k nodes with the highest PPR values with respect to a given source node s. SSPPR has important applications in web search and social networks, e.g., in Twitter's Who-To-Follow recommendation service. However, SSPPR computation is immensely expensive, and at the same time resistant to indexing and materialization. So far, existing solutions either use heuristics, which do not guarantee result quality, or rely on the strong computing power of modern data centers, which is costly.

Motivated by this, we propose FORA, a simple and effective index-based solution for approximate SSPPR processing, with rigorous guarantees on result quality. The basic idea of FORA is to combine two existing methods Forward Push (which is fast but does not guarantee quality) and Monte Carlo Random Walk (accurate but slow) in a simple and yet non-trivial way, leading to an algorithm that is both fast and accurate. Further, FORA includes a simple and effective indexing scheme, as well as a module for top-k selection with high pruning power. Extensive experiments demonstrate that FORA is orders of magnitude more efficient than its main competitors. Notably, on a billion-edge Twitter dataset, FORA answers a top-500 approximate SSPPR query within 5 seconds, using a single commodity server.

KEYWORDS

Personalized PageRank, Forward Push, Random Walk

*Work done while at NTU.
†Corresponding author.

KDD'17, August 13-17, 2017, Halifax, NS, Canada

ACM ISBN 978-1-4503-4887-4/17/08...$15.00
https://doi.org/10.1145/3097983.3098072

1 INTRODUCTION

Personalized PageRank (*PPR*) is a fundamental operation first proposed by Google [19], a major search engine. Specifically, given a graph G and a pair of nodes s, t in G, the PPR value $\pi(s, t)$ is defined as the probability that a random walk starting from s (called the *source node*) terminates at t (the *target node*), which reflects the importance of t with respect to s. One particularly useful variant of PPR is the *single-source PPR* (*SSPPR*), which takes as input a source node s and a parameter k, and returns the top-k nodes in G with the highest PPR values with respect to s. According to a recent paper [12], Twitter, a leading microblogging service, applies SSPPR in their Who-To-Follow application, which recommends to a user s (who is a node in the social graph) a number of other users (with high PPR values with respect to s) that user s might want to follow. Clearly, such an application computes SSPPR for every user in the social graph on a regular basis. Hence, accelerating PPR computation may lead to improved user experience (e.g., faster response time), as well as reduced operating costs (e.g., lower power consumption in the data center).

Similar to PageRank [19], PPR computation on a web-scale graph is immensely expensive, which involves extracting eigenvalues of a $n \times n$ matrix, where n is the number of nodes that can reach millions or even billions in a social graph. Meanwhile, unlike PageRank, PPR values cannot be easily materialized: since each pair of source/target nodes lead to a different PPR value, storing all possible PPR values requires $O(n^2)$ space, which is infeasible for large graphs. For these reasons, much previous work focuses on *approximate PPR* computation (defined in Section 2.1), which provides a controllable tradeoff between the execution time and result accuracy. Meanwhile, compared to heuristic solutions, approximate PPR provides rigorous guarantees on result quality.

However, even under the approximate PPR definition, SSPPR computation remains a challenging problem, since it requires sifting through all nodes in the graph. To our knowledge, the majority of existing methods (e.g., [15, 16, 22]) focus on approximate pair-wise (i.e., with given source and target nodes) PPR computations. A naive solution is to compute pair-wise PPR $\pi(s, v)$ for each possible target node v, and subsequently applies top-k selection. Clearly, the running time of this approach grows linearly to the number of nodes in the graph, which is costly for large graphs.

Motivated by this, we propose *FORA* (short for **FO**ward Push and **RA**ndom Walks), an efficient algorithm for approximate SSPPR computation. The basic idea of FORA is to combine two existing solutions in a simple and yet non-trivial way, which are (i) Forward Push [1], which can either computes the exact SSPPR results at a high cost, or terminate early but with no guarantee at all on the result quality, and (ii) Monte Carlo [8], which samples and executes random walks and provides rigorous guarantees on the accuracy of SSPPR results, but is rather inefficient. In fact, this idea is so effective that even without any indexing, basic FORA already outperforms its main competitors BiPPR [15] and HubPPR [22]. Then, we describe a simple and effective indexing scheme for FORA, as well as a novel algorithm for top-k selection. Extensive experiments using several real graphs demonstrate that FORA is more than two orders of magnitude faster than BiPPR, and more than an order of magnitude faster than HubPPR. In particular, on a billion-edge Twitter graph, FORA answers top-500 SSPPR query within 5 seconds, using a single commodity server.

2 BACKGROUND

2.1 Problem Definition

Let $G = (V, E)$ be a directed graph. In case the input graph is undirected, we simply convert it to a directed one by treating each edge as two directed edges of opposing directions. Given a source node $s \in V$ and a decay factor α, a random walk (or more precisely, random walk with restart [10]) from s is a traversal of G that starts from s and, at each step, either (i) terminates at the current node with α probability, or (ii) proceeds to a randomly selected out-neighbor of the current node. For any node $v \in V$, the personalized PageRank (PPR) $\pi(s, v)$ of v with respect to s is then the probability that a random walk from s terminates at v [19].

A *single-source PPR (SSPPR)* query takes as input a graph G, a source node s, and a parameter k, and returns the top-k nodes with the highest PPR values with respect to s, together with their respective PPR values. This paper focuses on approximate SSPPR processing, and we first define a simpler version of the approximate SSPPR without top-k selection (called approximate whole-graph SSPPR), as follows.

Definition 2.1 (Approximate Whole-Graph SSPPR). Given a source node s, a threshold δ, an error bound ϵ, and a failure probability p_f, an approximate whole-graph SSPPR query returns an estimated PPR $\hat{\pi}(s, v)$ for each node $v \in V$, such that for any $\pi(s, v) > \delta$,

$$|\pi(s,v) - \hat{\pi}(s,v)| \le \epsilon \cdot \pi(s,v) \tag{1}$$

holds with at least $1 - p_f$ probability. □

The above definition is consistent with existing work, e.g., [15, 16, 22]. Next we define the approximate top-k SSPPR, as follows.

Definition 2.2 (Approximate Top-k SSPPR). Given a source node s, a threshold δ, an error bound ϵ, a failure probability p_f, and a positive integer k, an approximate top-k SSPPR query returns a sequences of k nodes, $v_1, v_2, \cdots, v_k$, such that with probability $1 - p_f$, for any $i \in [1, k]$ with $\pi(s, v_i^*) > \delta$,

$$|\hat{\pi}(s,v_i) - \pi(s,v_i)| \le \epsilon \cdot \pi(s,v_i) \tag{2}$$

$$\pi(s,v_i) \ge (1-\epsilon) \cdot \pi(s,v_i^*) \tag{3}$$

hold with at least $1 - p_f$ probability, where v_i^* is the node whose actual PPR with respect to s is the i-th largest. □

Notation	Description
G=(V, E)	The input graph G with node set V and edge set E
n, m	The number of nodes and edges in G, respectively
$N^{out}(v)$	The set of out-neighbors of node v
$N^{in}(v)$	The set of in-neighbors of node v
$\pi(s, t)$	The exact PPR value of t with respect to s
α	The probability that a random walk terminates at a step
δ, ϵ, p_f	Parameters of an approximate PPR query, as in Definitions 2.1 and 2.2
r_{max}	The residue threshold for local update
$r(s, v)$	The residue of v during a local update process from s
$\pi^\circ(s, v)$	The reserve of v during a local update process from s
r_{sum}	The sum of all nodes' residues during a local update process from s

Table 1: Frequently used notations.

Note that Equation 2 ensures the accuracy of the estimated PPR values, while Equation 3 guarantees that the i-th result returned has a PPR value close to the i-th largest PPR score. This definition is consistent with previous work [22]. Following previous work [15, 16, 22], we assume that $\delta = O(1/n)$, where n is the number of nodes in G. The intuition is that, we provide approximation guarantees for nodes with above-average PPR values.

In addition, most applications of personalized PageRank concern web graphs and social networks, in which case the underlying input graphs are generally *scale-free*. That is, for any $k \ge 1$, the fraction $f(k)$ of nodes in G that have k edges satisfies

$$f(k) = c \cdot k^{-\gamma}, \tag{4}$$

where γ is a parameter with $2 \le \gamma \le 3$, and c is a constant smaller than 1. It can be verified that, in a scale-free graph with $2 \le \gamma \le 3$, the average node degree $m/n = O(\log n)$. We will analyze the asymptotic performance of our algorithm on both general graphs and scale-free graphs. Table 1 lists the frequently-used notations throughout the paper.

Remark. Our algorithms can also handle SSPPR queries where the source s is not fixed but sampled from a node distribution. Interested readers are referred to Appendix B.2 for details.

2.2 Main Competitors

Monte-Carlo. A classic solution for approximate PPR processing is the *Monte-Carlo (MC)* approach [8]. Given a source node s, MC generates ω random walks from s, and it records, for each node v, the fraction of random walks $f(v)$ that terminate at v. It then uses $f(v)$ as an estimation of the PPR $\hat{\pi}(s, v)$ of v with respect to s. According to [8], MC satisfies Definition 2.1 with a sufficiently large number of random walks: $\omega = \Omega\left(\frac{\log(1/p_f)}{\epsilon^2\delta}\right)$. According to Refs. [15, 16, 22] as well as our experiments in Section 5, MC is rather inefficient. Specifically, the time complexity of MC is $O\left(\frac{\log(1/p_f)}{\epsilon^2\delta}\right)$. As will be explained later in Section 3.2, when $\delta = O(1/n)$ and the

Algorithm 1: Forward Push

Input: Graph G, source node s, probability α, residue threshold r_{max}
Output: $\pi^{\circ}(s, v)$, $r(s, v)$ for all $v \in V$
1 $r(s, s) \leftarrow 1$; $r(s, v) \leftarrow 0$ for all $v \neq s$;
2 $\pi^{\circ}(s, v) \leftarrow 0$ for all v;
3 **while** $\exists v \in V$ *such that* $r(s, v)/|N^{out}(v)| > r_{max}$ **do**
4   **for** *each* $u \in N^{out}(v)$ **do**
5     $r(s, u) \leftarrow r(s, u) + (1 - \alpha) \cdot \frac{r(s,v)}{|N^{out}(v)|}$
6   $\pi^{\circ}(s, v) \leftarrow \pi^{\circ}(s, v) + \alpha \cdot r(s, v)$;
7   $r(s, v) \leftarrow 0$;

graph is scale-free, in which case $m/n = O(\log n)$, this time complexity is a factor of $1/\epsilon$ larger than that of *FORA* even without indexing or top-k pruning.

BiPPR and HubPPR. *BiPPR* [15] and its successor *HubPPR* [22] are currently the states of the art for answering *pairwise* PPR queries, in which both the source node s and the target node t are given, and the goal is to approximate the PPR value $\pi(s, t)$ of t with respect to s. The main idea of BiPPR is a bi-direction search on the input graph G. The forward direction simply samples and executes random walks, akin to MC described above. Unlike MC, however, BiPPR requires a much smaller number of random walks, thanks to additional information provided by the backward search.

The backward search in BiPPR (dubbed as *reverse push*) is originally proposed in [1], and is rather complicated. In a nutshell, the reverse push starts from the target node t, and recursively propagate *residue* and *reserve* values along the reverse directions of edges in G. Initially, the residue is 1 for node t, and 0 for all other nodes. The original reverse push [1] requires complete propagation until the residues of all nodes become very small, which is rather inefficient as pointed out in [15]. BiPPR performs the same backward propagations, but terminates early when the residues of all nodes are below a pre-defined threshold. Then, the method performs forward search, i.e., random walks, utilizing the residue and reserve information computed during backward search. The main tricky part in BiPPR is how to set this residue threshold to minimize computation costs, while satisfying Inequality 1. Intuitively, if the residue threshold is set too high, then the forward search requires numerous random walks to reach the approximation guarantee; conversely, if the residue threshold is too low, then the cost of backward search dominates. Ref. [15] provides a careful analysis, and reports that a residue threshold of $O\left(\epsilon \cdot \sqrt{\frac{m \cdot \delta}{n \cdot \log(1/p_f)}}\right)$ strikes a good balance between forward and backward searches, and achieves a low overall cost for pair-wise PPR computation.

To extend BiPPR to SSPPR, one simple method is to enumerate all nodes in G, and compute the PPR value for each of them with respect to the source node s. The problem, however, is that the residue threshold designed in [15] is not optimized for SSPPR, leading to poor performance. To explain, observe that applying BiPPR for SSPPR involves one backward search at each node in G, but only one single forward search from s. Therefore, we improve the performance of BiPPR by tuning down overhead of each backward search at the cost of a less efficient forward search. This optimization turns out to be non-trivial, and we present it in Appendix B.1. Nevertheless, the properly optimized version of BiPPR still involves high costs since it either *(i)* degrades to the Monte-Carlo approach if the residue threshold is large or *(ii)* incurs a large number of backward searches if the residue threshold is small.

HubPPR [22] is an index structure based on BiPPR that features an improved algorithm for top-k queries. Since HubPPR inherits the deficiencies of the BiPPR, it is not suitable for SSPPR, either. We will demonstrate this in our experiments in Section 5.

Forward Push. *Forward Push* [2] is an earlier solution that is not as efficient as BiPPR and HubPPR. We describe it in detail here since the proposed solution FORA uses its components. Specifically, Forward Push can compute the *exact* PPR values at a high cost. It can also be configured to terminate early, but without any guarantee on result quality. Algorithm 1 shows the pseudo-code of Forward Push for whole-graph SSPPR processing. It takes as input G, a source node s, a probability value α, and a threshold r_{max}; its output consists of two values for each node v in G: a *reserve* $\pi^{\circ}(s,v)$ and a *residue* $r(s,v)$. The reserve $\pi^{\circ}(s,v)$ is an approximation of $\pi(s,v)$, while the residue $r(s,v)$ is a by-product of the algorithm. In the beginning of the algorithm, it sets $r(s,s) = 1$ and $\pi^{\circ}(s,s) = 0$, and sets $r(s,v) = \pi^{\circ}(s,v) = 0$ for any $v \neq s$ (Lines 1-2 in Algorithm 1). Subsequently, the residue of s is converted into other nodes' reserves and residues in an iterative process (Lines 3-7).

Specifically, in each iteration, the algorithm first identifies every node v with $\frac{r(s,v)}{|N^{out}(v)|} > r_{max}$, where N^{out} denotes the set of out-neighbors of v (Line 3). After that, it *propagates* part of v's residue to each u of v's out-neighbors, increasing u's residue by $(1-\alpha) \cdot \frac{r(s,v)}{|N^{out}(v)|}$. Then, it increases v's reserve by $\alpha \cdot r(s,v)$, and resets v's residue to $r(s,v) = 0$. This iterative process terminates when every node v has $\frac{r(s,v)}{|N^{out}(v)|} \leq r_{max}$ (Line 3).

Andersen et al. [2] show that Algorithm 1 runs in $O(1/r_{max})$ time, and that the reserve $\pi^{\circ}(s,v)$ can be regarded as an estimation of $\pi(s,v)$. This estimation, however, does not offer any worst-case assurance in terms of absolute or relative error. As a consequence, Algorithm 1 itself is insufficient for addressing the problem formulated in Definitions 2.1 and 2.2.

3 FORA

This section presents the proposed FORA algorithm. We first describe a simpler version of FORA for whole-graph SSPPR (Definition 2.1) without indexing in Sections 3.1 and Sections 3.2. Then, we present the indexing scheme of FORA in Section 3.3, and top-k selection in Section 3.4.

3.1 Main Idea

As reviewed in Section 2.2, (i) MC is inefficient due to a large number of random walks required to satisfy the approximation guarantee, (ii) BiPPR and HubPPR either degrade to MC, or require fewer forward random walks but still incur high cost due to numerous backward search operations, and (iii) Forward Push with early termination provides no formal guarantee on result quality. The proposed solution FORA can be understood as a combination of these methods. In particular, FORA first performs Forward Push with

Algorithm 2: *FORA* for Whole-Graph SSPPR

Input: Graph G, source node s, probability α, threshold r_{max}
Output: Estimated PPR $\hat{\pi}(s, v)$for all $v \in V$

1 Invoke Algorithm 1 with input parameters G, s, α, and r_{max}; let $r(s, v_i)$, $\pi^{\circ}(s, v_i)$ be the returned residue and reserve of node v_i;
2 Let $r_{sum} = \sum_{v_i \in V} r(s, v_i)$ and $\omega = r_{sum} \cdot \frac{(2\epsilon/3+2)\cdot\log(2/p_f)}{\epsilon^2 \cdot \delta}$;
3 Let $\hat{\pi}(s, v_i) = \pi^{\circ}(s, v_i)$ for all $v_i \in V$;
4 **for** $v_i \in V$ *with* $r(s, v_i) > 0$ **do**
5   Let $\omega_i = \lceil r(s, v_i) \cdot \omega / r_{sum} \rceil$;
6   Let $a_i = \frac{r(s,v_i)}{r_{sum}} \cdot \frac{\omega}{\omega_i}$;
7   **for** $i = 1$ *to* ω_i **do**
8   Generate a random walk W from v_i;
9   Let t be the end point of W;
10         $\hat{\pi}(s, t) += \frac{a_i \cdot r_{sum}}{\omega}$;
11 return $\hat{\pi}(s, v_1), \cdots, \hat{\pi}(s, v_n)$;

early termination, and subsequently runs random walks. Similar to BiPPR and HubPPR, FORA utilizes information obtained through Forward Push to significantly cut down the number of required random walks while satisfying the same result quality guarantees. But unlike BiPPR and HubPPR, in FORA there is a single invocation of Forward Push starting from the source node s, while BiPPR and HubPPR invokes numerous backward search operations. The tricky part in FORA is how to combine Forward Push with MC, explained below.

Specifically, the reason that Forward Push with early termination fails to obtain any result quality guarantee is that it uses $\pi^{\circ}(s, v)$ to approximate $\pi(s, v)$, and yet, the two values are not guaranteed to be close. To mitigate this deficiency, we aim to utilize the residue $r(s, v)$ to improve the accuracy of $\pi^{\circ}(s, v)$. Towards this end, we utilize the following result from [2]:

$$\pi(s, t) = \pi^{\circ}(s, t) + \sum_{v \in V} r(s, v) \cdot \pi(v, t), \tag{5}$$

for any s, t, v in G. Our idea is to derive a rough approximation of $\pi(v, t)$ for each node v (denoted as $\pi'(v, t)$), and then combine it with the reserve of each node to compute an estimation of $\pi(s, t)$:

$$\pi(s, t) = \pi^{\circ}(s, t) + \sum_{v \in V} r(s, v) \cdot \pi'(v, t).$$

In particular, we derive $\pi'(v, t)$ by performing a number of random walks from v, and set $\pi'(v, t)$ to the fraction of walks that ends at t.

It remains to answer two key questions in FORA: (i) how many random walks do we need for each node v? and (ii) how should we set the residue threshold r_{max} in Forward Push? It turns out that although the FORA algorithm itself is simple, deriving the proper values for its parameters is rather challenging, since they must optimize efficiency while satisfying the result quality guarantee. In the following, we first present the complete FORA and answer question (i); then we answer question (ii) in Section 3.2.

Algorithm 2 illustrates the pseudo-code of FORA. Given G, a source node s, a probability value α, and a residue threshold r_{max}, FORA first invokes Algorithm 2 on G to obtain a reserve $\pi^{\circ}(s, v_i)$ and a residue $r(s, v_i)$ for each node v_i (Line 1 in Algorithm 2). After that, it computes the total residue of all nodes r_{sum}, based on which it derives a value ω that will be used to decide the number of random walks required from each node v_i (Line 2). Then, it initializes the PPR estimation of each v_i to be $\hat{\pi}(s, v_i) = \pi^{\circ}(s, v_i)$, and it proceeds to inspect the nodes whose residues are larger than zero (Line 3-4).

For each v_i of those nodes, it performs ω_i random walks from v_i, where

$$\omega_i = \left\lceil \frac{r(s, v_i)}{r_{sum}} \cdot \omega \right\rceil.$$

If a random walk ends at a node t, then FORA increases $\hat{\pi}(s, v_i)$ by $\frac{a_i \cdot r_{sum}}{\omega}$, where

$$a_i = \frac{r(s, v_i)}{r_{sum}} \cdot \frac{\omega}{\omega_i}.$$

After all v_i are processed, the algorithm returns $\hat{\pi}(s, v_i)$ as the approximated PPR value for v_i (Line 11).

To explain why FORA can provide accurate results, let us consider the ω_i random walks that it generates from a node v_i. Let $X_j(t)$ be a Bernoulli variable that takes value 1 if the j-th random walk terminates at t, and value 0 otherwise. By definition,

$$\mathbb{E}[X_j] = \pi(v_i, t).$$

Then, based on the definition of ω, ω_i, and a_i, we have

$$\mathbb{E}\left[\frac{r_{sum}}{\omega} \cdot \sum_{j=1}^{\omega_i} (a_i \cdot X_j)\right] = r(s, v_i) \cdot \pi(v_i, t). \tag{6}$$

Observe that $\frac{r_{sum}}{\omega} \cdot \sum_{j=1}^{\omega_i} (a_i \cdot X_j)$ is exactly the amount of increment that $\hat{\pi}(s, t)$ receives when FORA processes v_i (see Lines 7-10 in Algorithm 2). We denote this increment as ψ_i. It follows that

$$\mathbb{E}\left[\sum_{i=1}^{n} \psi_i\right] = \sum_{i=1}^{n} r(s, v_i) \cdot \pi(v_i, t). \tag{7}$$

Combining Equations 5 and 7, we can see that FORA returns, for each node v, an estimated PPR $\hat{\pi}(s, v)$ whose expectation equals $\pi(s, v)$. Next, we will show that $\hat{\pi}(s, v)$ is very close to $\pi(s, v)$ with a high probability. For this purpose, we utilize the following concentration bound:

Theorem 3.1 ([7]). *Let $X_1, \cdots, X_\omega$ be independent random variables with*

$$\Pr[X_i = 1] = p_i \;\; and \;\; \Pr[X_i = 0] = 1 - p_i.$$

Let $X = \frac{1}{\omega} \cdot \sum_{i=1}^{\omega} a_i X_i$ with $a_i > 0$, and $\nu = \frac{1}{\omega} \sum_{i=1}^{\omega} a_i^2 \cdot p_i$. Then,

$$\Pr[|X - \mathbb{E}[X]| \geq \lambda] \leq 2 \cdot \exp\left(-\frac{\lambda^2 \cdot \omega}{2\nu + 2a\lambda/3}\right),$$

where $a = \max\{a_1, \cdots, a_\omega\}$. □

To apply Theorem 3.1, let us consider the $\omega' = \sum_{i=1}^{n} \omega_i$ random walks generated by FORA. Let $b_j = a_i$ if the j-th random walk starts from v_i. Then, we have $\max_j b_j = 1$, and $b_j^2 \leq b_j$ for any j. In addition, let $Y_j(t)$ be the a random variable that equals 1 if the j-th walk terminates at t, and 0 otherwise. Then, by Theorem 3.1 and Equations 5 and 7, we have the following result.

Lemma 3.2. *For any node v with $\pi(s,v) > \delta$, Algorithm 2 returns an approximated PPR $\hat{\pi}(s,v)$ that satisfies Equation 1 with at least $1-p_f$ probability.* □

3.2 Choosing r_{max}

Recall from Sections 2.2 and 3.1 that parameter r_{max} determines how quickly we can terminate Forward Push. A high value for r_{max} leads to low cost for Forward Push (since it can terminate early), but high cost for random walks (since a large number of them are required), and vice versa. Thus, finding the appropriate value of r_{max} requires modelling the overall running time of *FORA*. Recall that, the Forward Push runs in $O\left(\frac{1}{r_{max}}\right)$ time. In addition, the expected time complexity of the random walk phase is $O\left(r_{sum}\cdot\frac{(2\epsilon/3+2)\cdot\log(2/p_f)}{\epsilon^2}\right)$, since each random walk takes $O(1)$ expected time to generate. Observe that

$$r_{sum} = \sum_{v_i\in V} r(s,v_i) \le \sum_{v_i\in V} r_{max}\cdot|N^{out}(v_i)| = m\cdot r_{max}.$$

Therefore, the expected running time of Algorithm 2 is

$$O\left(\frac{1}{r_{max}} + m\cdot r_{max}\cdot\frac{(2\epsilon/3+2)\cdot\log(2/p_f)}{\epsilon^2\cdot\delta}\right).$$

Using the method of Lagrange multipliers, we can see that the above time complexity is minimized when

$$r_{max} = \frac{\epsilon}{\sqrt{m}}\cdot\sqrt{\frac{\delta}{(2\epsilon/3+2)\cdot\log(2/p_f)}}. \quad (8)$$

Accordingly, the expected time complexity of Algorithm 2 becomes

$$O\left(\frac{1}{\epsilon\cdot\sqrt{\delta}}\sqrt{m\cdot(2\epsilon/3+2)\cdot\log(2/p_f)}\right).$$

When $\delta = O(1/n)$, $p_f = O(1/n)$, the above time complexity becomes $O\left(\frac{1}{\epsilon}\sqrt{m\cdot n\cdot\log n}\right)$ for general graphs. When the graph is scale-free, in which case $m/n = O(\log n)$, the time complexity becomes $O\left(\frac{1}{\epsilon}n\cdot\log n\right)$, improving over the MC approach by $1/\epsilon$.

3.3 Indexing Scheme

Based on FORA, we propose a simple and effective index structure to further improve the efficiency of whole-graph SSPPR queries. The basic idea is to pre-compute a number of random walks from each node v, and then store the destination of each walk. During query processing, if FORA requires x performing random walks from v, we would inspect the set S of random walk destinations pre-computed for v, and then retrieve the first x nodes in S. As such, we avoid generating any random walks on-the-fly, which considerably reduces query overheads.

A natural question to ask is: how many random walks should we pre-compute for each node v? To answer this question, we first recall that, when the local update phase of FORA terminates, the residue of each node v is at most $|N^{out}(v)|\cdot r_{max}$. Combining this with Lemma 3.2, we can see that the number of random walks from v required by FORA is

$$\left\lceil |N^{out}(v)|\cdot r_{max}\cdot\frac{(2\epsilon/3+2)\cdot\log(2/p_f)}{\epsilon^2\cdot\delta}\right\rceil. \quad (9)$$

Since we set r_{max} according to Equation 8, we have

$$\text{Eqn. } 9 = \left\lceil |N^{out}(v)|\cdot\frac{1}{\epsilon\cdot\sqrt{m\cdot\delta}}\cdot\sqrt{(2\epsilon/3+2)\cdot\log(2/p_f)}\right\rceil$$

We use $\omega_{max}(v)$ to denote the r.h.s. of the above equation.

In summary, we pre-compute $\omega_{max}(v)$ random walks from each node v, and record the last nodes of those walks in our index structure. The total space overhead incurred is

$$\sum_v \omega_{max}(v) = \sum_v \left\lceil |N^{out}(v)|\cdot\frac{\sqrt{(2\epsilon/3+2)\cdot\log(2/p_f)}}{\epsilon\cdot\sqrt{m\cdot\delta}}\right\rceil$$
$$\le n + \frac{\sqrt{m}}{\epsilon\cdot\sqrt{\delta}}\cdot\sqrt{(2\epsilon/3+2)\cdot\log(2/p_f)}.$$

Therefore, we have the following lemma.

Lemma 3.3. *The space consumption of our index structure is*

$$O\left(n + \frac{1}{\epsilon}\sqrt{\frac{m\log(1/p_f)}{\delta}}\right). \quad (10)$$

When $\delta = O(1/n)$, $p_f = O(1/n)$, and $m/n = O(\log n)$, the above space complexity becomes $O\left(\frac{1}{\epsilon}n\cdot\log n\right)$. □

Remark. One may wonder whether we can also pre-compute the Forward Push result for each node, so that we can answer each query by a simple combination of pre-processed Forward Push and random walks, which could lead to higher query efficiency. However, we note that storing the Forward Push results for all nodes incurs significant space overheads. In particular, it requires $O(\min\{n, 1/r_{max}\})$ space for each node, where r_{max} is set according to Equation 8. As such, the total space consumption for preprocessing Forward Push results is

$$O\left(\min\left\{n^2, \frac{n}{\epsilon}\cdot\sqrt{\frac{m\cdot\log(1/p_f)}{\delta}}\right\}\right),$$

which is prohibitive for large graphs. Therefore, we do not store Forward Push results in our index structure.

3.4 Top-k SSPPR

In this section, we discuss how FORA handles approximate top-k SSPPR queries.

Rationale. A straightforward approach to answer a top-k SSPPR query with FORA is to first apply it to perform a whole-graph SSPPR query, and then returns the k nodes with the largest approximate PPR values. However, if we are to satisfy the accuracy requirement described in Definition 2.2, we would need to set the parameters of FORA according to the exact k-th largest PPR value $\pi(s,v_k^*)$, which is unknown in advance. To address this, a naive solution is to conservatively set $\pi(s,v_k^*) = 1/n$, which, however, would lead to unnecessary overheads.

To avoid the aforementioned overheads, we propose a trial-and-error approach as follows. We first assume that $\pi(s,v_k^*)$ is a large value (e.g., 1/2), and we set the parameters of FORA accordingly to perform a whole-graph SSPPR query. After that, we inspect the results obtained to check whether the estimated PPR values are indeed large. If they are not as large as we have assumed, then we re-run FORA with more conservative parameters, and check the new results returned. This process is conducted iteratively, until

Algorithm 3: Top-k FORA

Input: Graph G, source node s, probability α
Output: k nodes with the highest approximate PPR scores

1 **for** $\delta = \frac{1}{2}, \cdots, \frac{1}{n}$ **do**
2 Invoke Algorithm 2 with G, s, α, and r_{max} set by Equation 8 and fail probability $p'_f = \frac{p_f}{n \cdot \log n}$;
3 Let $C = \{v'_1, \cdots, v'_k\}$ be the set that contains the k nodes with the top-k largest lower bounds (from Theorem 3.1);
4 Let $LB(u)$ and $UB(u)$ be the lower and upper bounds of $\pi(s, u)$ (from Theorem 3.1);
5 **if** $UB(v'_i) < (1+\epsilon) \cdot LB(v'_i)$ *for* $i \in [1, k]$ ***and*** $LB(v'_k) \geq \delta$ **then**
6 Let U be the set of nodes $u \in V \setminus C$ such that $UB(u) > (1+\epsilon) \cdot LB(v'_k)$;
7 **if** $\nexists u \in U$ ***such that*** $UB(u) < (1+\epsilon) \cdot LB(u)/(1-\epsilon)$ **then**
8 return $v'_1, v'_2, \cdots, v'_k$ and their estimated PPR;

we are confident that the results from FORA conform to the requirements in Definition 2.2.

Algorithm. Algorithm 3 shows the pseudo-code of the top-k extension of FORA. The algorithm consists of at most $\log n$ iterations. In the i-th iteration, we invoke Algorithm 2 with δ set to $1/2^i$, and the failure probability set to $p'_f = \frac{p_f}{n \log n}$ (Lines 1-2 in Algorithm 3. (The reason for this setting will be explained shortly). After we obtain the results from *FORA*, we compute an upper bound and a lower bound of each node's PPR value, and use them to decide whether the current top-k results are sufficiently accurate (Lines 3-8). If the top-k results are accurate, then we return them as the top-k answers (Line 8); otherwise, we proceed to the next iteration. In the following, we elaborate how the upper and lower bounds of each node's PPR value is derived.

Define $LB_0(v) = 0$ and $UB_0(v) = 1$ for any $v \in V$. We have the following theorem that establishes the lower bound $LB_j(v)$ and upper bound $UB_j(v)$ of $\pi(s, v)$ in the j-th iteration of Algorithm 3:

Theorem 3.4. *In the j-th iteration of Algorithm 3, let ω_j be the ω calculated by FORA (Algorithm 2 Line 2) in this iteration, and $\pi^\circ_j(s, v)$ and $\hat{\pi}_j(s, v)$ be the reserve and estimated PPR of v. Define*

$$\epsilon_j = \sqrt{\frac{3r_{sum} \cdot \log(2/p'_f)}{\omega_j \cdot \max\{\pi^\circ_j(s, v), LB_{j-1}(s, v)\}}}, \text{ and } \lambda_j = \frac{2/3 \log(2/pf')}{2\omega_j}$$

$$+ \frac{\sqrt{\frac{4}{9} r^2_{sum} \cdot \log^2(2/p'_f) + 8r_{sum} \cdot \omega_j \cdot \log(2/p'_f) \cdot UB_{j-1}(v)}}{2\omega_j}$$

Then, with at least $1 - p'_f$ probability, the following two inequalities hold simultaneously:

$$\hat{\pi}_j(s, v)/(1+\epsilon_j) \leq \pi(s, v) \leq \hat{\pi}_j(s, v)/(1-\epsilon_j)$$

$$\hat{\pi}_j(s, v) - \lambda_i \leq \pi(s, v) \leq \hat{\pi}_j(s, v) + \lambda_i.$$

Theorem 3.4 enables us to derive tight lower and upper bounds of each node's PPR value in each iteration. In particular, we set

$$UB_j(v) = min\{1, \hat{\pi}_j(s, v)/(1-\epsilon), \hat{\pi}_j(s, v) + \lambda_i\},$$

$$LB_j(v) = \max\{\hat{\pi}_j(s, v)/(1+\epsilon), \hat{\pi}_j(s, v) - \lambda_i, 0\}.$$

With these upper and lower bounds, the following theorem shows that if Lines 5 and 7 in Algorithm 3 holds, then Algorithm 3 returns the answer for the approximate top-k SSPPR query.

Theorem 3.5 (Approximate Top-k). *Let $v'_1, \cdots, v'_k$ be the k nodes with the largest lower bounds in the j-th iteration of Algorithm 3. Let U be the set of nodes $u \in V \setminus C$ such that $UB_j(u) > (1+\epsilon) \cdot LB_j(v'_k)$, If $UB(v'_i) < (1+\epsilon) \cdot LB(v'_i)$ for $i \in [1, k]$, $LB_j(v'_k) \geq \delta$, and there exists no $u \in U$ such that $UB_j(u) < (1+\epsilon) \cdot LB_j(u)/(1-\epsilon)$, then returning $v'_1, \cdots, v'_k$ and their estimated PPR values would satisfy the requirements in Definition 2.2 with at least $1 - j \cdot n \cdot p'_f$ probability.*

Now recall that the number of iterations in Algorithm 3 is $\log n$, and in each iteration, we assume that the upper and lower bounds are correct. Hence, by applying union bound, the failure probability will be at most $n \log n \cdot p'_f$. Note that $p'_f = \frac{p_f}{n \log n}$. The failure probability is hence no more than p_f, and we guarantee that the returned answer has approximation with at least $1 - p_f$ probability.

4 OTHER RELATED WORK

Apart from the methods discussed in Section 2.2 , there exists a plethora of techniques for whole-graph and top-k SSPPR queries. Those techniques, however, are either subsumed by *BiPPR* and *HubPPR* or unable to provide worst-case accuracy guarantees. In particular, a large number of techniques adopt the *matrix-based* approach, which formulates PPR values with the following equation:

$$\boldsymbol{\pi_s} = \alpha \cdot \boldsymbol{e_s} + (1-\alpha) \cdot \boldsymbol{\pi_s} \cdot D^{-1} A, \tag{11}$$

where $\boldsymbol{\pi_s}$ is a vector whose i-th element equals $\pi(s, v_i)$, $A \in \{0, 1\}^{n \times n}$ is the adjacency matrix of G, and $D \in R^{n \times n}$ is a diagonal matrix in which each i-th element on its main diagonal equals the out-degree of v_i. Matrix-based methods typically start from an initial guess of $\boldsymbol{\pi_s}$, and then iteratively apply Equation 11 to refine the initial guess, until converge is achieved. Recent work that adopts this approach [10, 17, 21, 24] propose to decompose the input graph into tree structures or sub-matrices, and utilize the decomposition to speed up the PPR queries. The state-of-the-art approach for the single-source and top-k PPR queries in this line of research work is *BEAR* proposed by Shin et al. [21]. However, as shown in [22], the best of these methods is still inferior to *HubPPR* [22] in terms of query efficiency and accuracy.

There also exist methods that follow similar approaches to the forward search method [2] described in Section 2.2. Berkin et al. [6] propose to pre-compute the Forward Push results from several important nodes, and then use these results to speed up the query performance. Ohsaka et al. [18] and Zhang et al. [23] further design algorithms to update the stored Forward Push results on dynamic graphs. Jeh et al. [13] propose the backward search algorithm, which (i) is the reverse variant of the Forward Push method, and (ii) can calculates the estimated PPRs from all nodes to a target node t. Zhang et al. [23] also design the algorithms to update the stored backward push results on dynamic graphs. Nonetheless, none of these solutions in this category provide approximation guarantees for single-source or top-k PPR queries on directed graphs.

Name	n	m	Type	Linking Site
DBLP	613.6K	2.0M	undirected	www.dblp.com
Web-St	281.9K	2.3M	directed	www.stanford.edu
Pokec	1.6M	30.6M	directed	pokec.azet.sk
LJ	4.8M	69.0M	directed	www.livejournal.com
Orkut	3.1M	117.2M	undirected	www.orkut.com
Twitter	41.7M	1.5B	directed	twitter.com

Table 2: Datasets. ($K = 10^3, M = 10^6, B = 10^9$)

	MC	*BiPPR*	*HubPPR*	*FORA*	*FORA+*
DBLP	12.9	3.5	2.4	0.7	0.07
Web-St	5.0	3.5	1.5	0.03	0.01
Pokec	66.4	23.7	19.2	12.1	0.8
LJ	144.7	57.8	48.3	21.0	1.8
Orkut	241.4	168.7	133.2	46.4	4.9
Twitter	4.6K	3.3K	2.8K	891.5	103.1

Table 3: Whole-graph SSPPR performance (s). ($K = 10^3$)

In addition, there are techniques based on the Monte-Carlo framework. Fogaras et al. [8] propose techniques to pre-store the random walk results, and use them to speed up the query processing. Nonetheless, the large space consumption of the technique renders it applicable only on small graphs. Bahmani et al. [4] and Sarma et al. [20] investigate the acceleration of the Monte-Carlo approach in distributed environments. Lofgren et al. propose *FastPPR* [16], which significantly outperforms the Monte-Carlo method in terms of query time. However, *FastPPR* in turn is subsumed by *BiPPR* [15] in terms of query efficiency. In [14], Lofgren further proposes to combine a modified version of Forward Push, random walks, and the back search algorithm to reduce the processing time of pairwise PPR queries. Nevertheless, the time complexity of the method remains unclear, since [14] does not provide any theoretical analysis on the asymptotic performance of the method.

Finally, Ref. [3, 5, 9–11, 15] present studies on the top-k PPR queries. Gupta et al. [11] propose to use Forward Push to return the top-k answers. However, their solutions do not provide any approximation guarantee. Avrachenkov et al. [3] study how to use Monte-Carlo approach to find the top-k nodes. Nevertheless, the solution does not return estimated PPR values and does not provide any worst-case assurance. Fujiwara et al. [9, 10] and Shin et al.[21] investigate how to speed up the top-k PPR queries with the matrix decomposition approach. These approaches either cannot scale to large graphs or do not provide approximation guarantees.

5 EXPERIMENTS

In this section, we experimentally evaluate *FORA* and its index-based variant, referred to as *FORA+*, against the states of the art. All experiments are conducted on a Linux machine with an Intel 2.6GHz CPU and 64GB memory.

5.1 Experimental Settings

Datasets and query sets. We use 6 real graphs: *DBLP*, *Web-St*, *Pokec*, *LJ*, *Orkut*, and *Twitter*, which are benchmark datasets used in recent work [15, 22]. Table 2 summarizes the statistics of the data. For each dataset, we choose 50 source nodes uniformly at random, and we generate an SSPPR query from each chosen node. In addition, we also generate 5 top-k queries from each source node, with k varying in $\{100, 200, 300, 400, 500\}$. Note that the maximum k is set to 500 in accordance to Twitter's Who-To-Follow service [12], whose first step requires deriving top-500 PPR results.

Methods. For whole-graph SSPPR queries, we compare our proposed *FORA* and *FORA+* against three methods: (i) the *Monte-Carlo* approach, dubbed as *MC*; (ii) the optimized *BiPPR* for SSPPR queries described in Appendix B.1; (iii) *HubPPR*, which is the indexed version of *BiPPR*. For fair comparison, the index size of *HubPPR* is set to be the same as that of *FORA+*. For top-k SSPPR queries, we compare our algorithm with the existing approximate solutions: the single-source MC, the single-source *BiPPR*, as well as the top-k algorithm for *HubPPR* in [22]. We also include the *Forward Push* as a baseline for top-k SSPPR queries, and we tune its parameter r_{max} on each dataset separately, so that its precision for top-k PPR queries is the same as *FORA* on each dataset. Following previous work[15, 16, 22], we set $\delta = 1/n, p_f = 1/n$, and $\epsilon = 0.5$.

5.2 Whole-Graph SSPPR Queries

In our first set of experiments, we evaluate the efficiency of each method for whole-graph SSPPR queries. Table 3 reports the average query time of each method. Observe that both *FORA* and *BiPPR* achieve better query performance than *MC*, which is consistent with our analysis that the time complexity of *FORA* and *BiPPR* is better than that of *MC*. Moreover, *FORA* is at least 3 times faster than *BiPPR* on most of the datasets.

The reason, as we explain in Section 3.2, is that *BiPPR* either degrades to the *MC* approach when the backward threshold is large, or requires conducting a backward search from each node v in G, even if $\pi(s, v)$ is extremely small. In contrast, *FORA* avoids degrading to *MC* and tends to omit nodes with small PPR values, which helps improve efficiency.

In addition, *FORA+* achieves significant speedup over *FORA*, and is around 10 times faster than the latter on most of the datasets. The *HubPPR* also improves over *BiPPR*, but the improvement is far less than what *FORA+* achieves over *FORA*. Moreover, even without any index, *FORA* is still more efficient than *HubPPR*.

5.3 Top-k SSPPR Queries

In our second set of experiments, we evaluate the efficiency and accuracy of each method for top-k SSPPR queries. Figures 1 reports the average query time of each method on four representative datasets: *DBLP*, *Pokec*, *Orkut*, and *Twitter*. (The results on the other two datasets are qualitatively similar, and are omitted due to the space constraint.) Note that the y-axis is in log-scale. The main observation is that *FORA* and *FORA+* both considerably outperform competitors. In particular, *FORA* is up to two orders of magnitude faster than *MC* and *BiPPR*. This is expected since our top-k algorithm applies an iterative approach to refine the top-k answers and terminates immediately whenever the answer could provide the desired approximation guarantee. *HubPPR*'s top-k algorithm has a similar early-termination mechanism, but it is still outperformed by our *FORA* by more than an order of magnitude, since

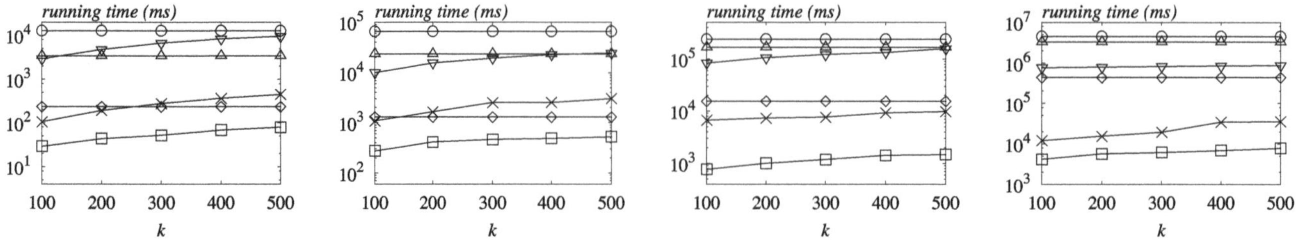

(a) DBLP (b) Pokec (c) Orkut (d) Twitter

Figure 1: Top-k SSPPR query efficiency: varying k.

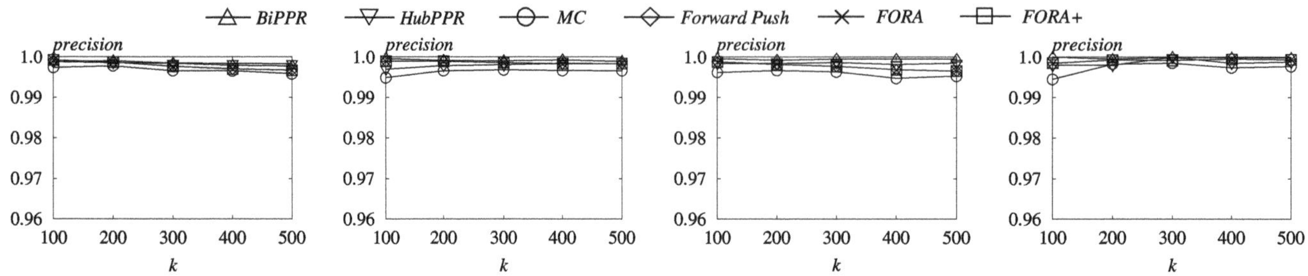

(a) DBLP (b) Pokec (c) Orkut (d) Twitter

Figure 2: Top-k SSPPR query accuracy: varying k.

Datasets	Preprocessing time (sec)		Space overhead of *HubPPR* & *FORA+*	
	HubPPR	*FORA+*	Index size	Graph size
DBLP	28.7	4.9	90.8MB	18.4MB
Web-St	11.8	2.0	45.5MB	10.4MB
Pokec	112.3	38.6	411.9MB	130.8MB
LJ	307.9	97.1	1.1GB	295.2MB
Orkut	582.2	204.9	1.6GB	950.1MB
Twitter	5849.0	3335.1	12.6GB	6.2GB

Table 4: Preprocessing costs.

HubPPR inherits the deficiences of *BiPPR* on SSPPR queries. Recall that *Forward Push* provides no approximation guarantee, and we tune the r_{max} on each dataset separately, so that it provides the same precison for top-500 SSPPR queries as our *FORA* algorithm does. Observe that, when both algorithms provide the identical precision, the performance of the proposed *FORA* and *Forward Push* is roughly comparable on small and medium size graphs, e.g., on *DBLP*, *Pokec*, and *Orkut*. When the graph size increases, however, *FORA* dominates the *Forward Push* in terms of the query efficiency. In particular, on *Twitter*, *FORA* is faster than *Forward Push* by an order of magnitude.

To compare the accuracy of the top-k results returned by each method, we first calculate the ground-truth answer of the top-k queries using the *Power Iteration* [19] method with 100 iterations. Afterwards, we evaluate the top-k results of each algorithm by their precision with respect to the ground truth. Note that the precision and recall are the same for the top-k SSPPR queries. Figure 2 shows the accuracy of the top-k query algorithms on four datasets: *DBLP*, *Pokec*, *Orkut*, and *Twitter*. Observe that all methods provide high precisions, and *FORA*, *FORA+*, *BiPPR*, and *HubPPR* are all slightly more accurate than *MC*.

5.4 Preprocessing Costs

Finally, we inspect the preprocessing costs of the two index-based methods, *FORA+* and *HubPPR*. Recall that we set the index size of *HubPPR* the same as the proposed *FORA+*. As shown in Table 4, the preprocessing time of *FORA* and *HubPPR* are both moderate, and the cost of *FORA* is much smaller than that of *HubPPR*. In addition, even on the largest dataset Twitter, *FORA+* can finish the index construction in less than an hour. Table 4 also reports the index size of *FORA+* and *HubPPR*. We also add the space consumption of the input graph as the reference values. As we can observe, the index size of *FORA+* is no more than 4 times the original graph in general. In particular, on *Orkut*, the index size of *FORA+* is only 1.7 times the input graph, and yet, as we show in Sections 5.2 and 5.3, it can speed up the query efficiency of whole-graph and top-k SSPPR queries by around 10 times. This demonstrates the effectiveness and efficiency of our indexing scheme.

6 CONCLUSION

We present FORA, a novel algorithm for approximate single-source personalized PageRank computation. The main ideas include (i) combining Monte-Carlo random walks with Forward Push in a non-trivial and optimized way (ii) pre-computing and indexing random walk results and (iii) additional pruning based on top-k selection. Compared to existing solutions, FORA involves a reduced number of random walks, avoids expensive backward searches, and provides rigorous guarantees on result quality. Extensive experiments demonstrate that FORA outperforms existing solutions by a large margin, and enables fast responses for top-k SSPPR searches on very large graphs with little computational resource.

7 ACKNOWLEDGMENTS

This research is supported by the DSAIR center at NTU, Singapore, as well as grants MOE2015-T2-2-069 from MOE, Singapore,

NSFC.61502503 from NSCF, China, and NPRP9-466-1-103 from QNRF, Qatar.

REFERENCES

[1] Reid Andersen, Christian Borgs, Jennifer T. Chayes, John E. Hopcroft, Vahab S. Mirrokni, and Shang-Hua Teng. 2007. Local Computation of PageRank Contributions. In *WAW*. 150–165.

[2] Reid Andersen, Fan R. K. Chung, and Kevin J. Lang. 2006. Local Graph Partitioning using PageRank Vectors. In *FOCS*. 475–486.

[3] Konstantin Avrachenkov, Nelly Litvak, Danil Nemirovsky, Elena Smirnova, and Marina Sokol. 2011. Quick Detection of Top-k Personalized PageRank Lists. In *WAW*. 50–61.

[4] Lars Backstrom and Jure Leskovec. 2011. Supervised random walks: predicting and recommending links in social networks. In *WSDM*. 635–644.

[5] Bahman Bahmani, Kaushik Chakrabarti, and Dong Xin. 2011. Fast personalized PageRank on MapReduce. In *SIGMOD*. 973–984.

[6] Pavel Berkhin. 2005. Survey: A Survey on PageRank Computing. *Internet Mathematics* 2, 1 (2005), 73–120.

[7] Fan R. K. Chung and Lincoln Lu. 2006. Survey: Concentration Inequalities and Martingale Inequalities: A Survey. *Internet Mathematics* 3, 1 (2006), 79–127.

[8] Dániel Fogaras, Balázs Rácz, Károly Csalogány, and Tamás Sarlós. 2005. Towards scaling fully personalized pagerank: Algorithms, lower bounds, and experiments. *Internet Mathematics* 2, 3 (2005), 333–358.

[9] Yasuhiro Fujiwara, Makoto Nakatsuji, Hiroaki Shiokawa, Takeshi Mishima, and Makoto Onizuka. 2013. Efficient ad-hoc search for personalized PageRank. In *SIGMOD*. 445–456.

[10] Yasuhiro Fujiwara, Makoto Nakatsuji, Takeshi Yamamuro, Hiroaki Shiokawa, and Makoto Onizuka. 2012. Efficient personalized pagerank with accuracy assurance. In *KDD*. 15–23.

[11] Manish S. Gupta, Amit Pathak, and Soumen Chakrabarti. 2008. Fast algorithms for topk personalized pagerank queries. In *WWW*. 1225–1226.

[12] Pankaj Gupta, Ashish Goel, Jimmy Lin, Aneesh Sharma, Dong Wang, and Reza Zadeh. 2013. Wtf: The who to follow service at twitter. In *WWW*. 505–514.

[13] Glen Jeh and Jennifer Widom. 2003. Scaling personalized web search. In *WWW*. 271–279.

[14] Peter Lofgren. 2015. Efficient Algorithms for Personalized PageRank. *CoRR* abs/1512.04633 (2015).

[15] Peter Lofgren, Siddhartha Banerjee, and Ashish Goel. 2016. Personalized pagerank estimation and search: A bidirectional approach. In *WSDM*. 163–172.

[16] Peter A Lofgren, Siddhartha Banerjee, Ashish Goel, and C Seshadhri. 2014. Fast-ppr: Scaling personalized pagerank estimation for large graphs. In *KDD*. 1436–1445.

[17] Takanori Maehara, Takuya Akiba, Yoichi Iwata, and Ken-ichi Kawarabayashi. 2014. Computing personalized PageRank quickly by exploiting graph structures. *PVLDB* 7, 12 (2014), 1023–1034.

[18] Naoto Ohsaka, Takanori Maehara, and Ken-ichi Kawarabayashi. 2015. Efficient PageRank Tracking in Evolving Networks. In *SIGKDD 2015*. 875–884.

[19] Lawrence Page, Sergey Brin, Rajeev Motwani, and Terry Winograd. 1999. The PageRank citation ranking: bringing order to the web. (1999).

[20] Atish Das Sarma, Anisur Rahaman Molla, Gopal Pandurangan, and Eli Upfal. 2013. Fast Distributed PageRank Computation. In *ICDCN*. 11–26.

[21] Kijung Shin, Jinhong Jung, Lee Sael, and U. Kang. 2015. BEAR: Block Elimination Approach for Random Walk with Restart on Large Graphs. In *SIGMOD*. 1571–1585.

[22] Sibo Wang, Youze Tang, Xiaokui Xiao, Yin Yang, and Zengxiang Li. 2016. HubPPR: Effective Indexing for Approximate Personalized PageRank. *PVLDB* 10, 3 (2016), 205–216. http://www.vldb.org/pvldb/vol10/p205-wang.pdf

[23] Hongyang Zhang, Peter Lofgren, and Ashish Goel. 2016. Approximate Personalized PageRank on Dynamic Graphs. In *KDD*. 1315–1324.

[24] Fanwei Zhu, Yuan Fang, Kevin Chen-Chuan Chang, and Jing Ying. 2013. Incremental and Accuracy-Aware Personalized PageRank through Scheduled Approximation. *PVLDB* 6, 6 (2013), 481–492.

APPENDIX

A PROOF OF THEOREM

Proof of Lemma 3.2. Firstly, let X_j be the j-th random walk. Define $Y' = \frac{1}{\omega'}\sum_{j=1}^{\omega'} b_j X_j$, and $\nu = \frac{1}{\omega'}\sum_{j=1}^{\omega'} b_j^2 \mathbb{E}[X_j]$. Let $a = \max\{b_1, \cdots, b_{\omega'}\}$. By definition, $b_j^2 \le 1$, and hence, $\nu \le \mathbb{E}[Y']$ and $a \le 1$. By Theorem 3.1, $\Pr[|Y' - \mathbb{E}[Y']| \ge \lambda] \le 2 \cdot \exp\left(-\frac{\lambda^2 \cdot \omega'}{2\nu + 2a\lambda/3}\right)$.

Apply $\nu \le \mathbb{E}[Y']$, we have

$$\Pr[|Y' - \mathbb{E}[Y']| \ge \lambda] \le 2 \cdot \exp\left(-\frac{\lambda^2 \cdot \omega'}{2\mathbb{E}[Y'] + 2a\lambda/3}\right).$$

By Equation 6 and $\mathbb{E}[Y'] \le \frac{\omega}{\omega' \cdot r_{sum}} \cdot \pi(s,t)$,

$$\Pr[|\pi(s,t) - \hat{\pi}(s,t)| \ge \frac{\omega' \cdot r_{sum}}{\omega}\lambda] \le 2 \cdot \exp\left(-\frac{\lambda^2 \cdot \omega'}{2\frac{\omega \cdot \pi(s,t)}{\omega' \cdot r_{sum}} + 2a\lambda/3}\right).$$

Let $\lambda = \frac{\omega \cdot \epsilon \cdot \pi(s,t)}{\omega' \cdot r_{sum}}$, we have

$$\Pr[|\pi(s,t) - \hat{\pi}(s,t)| \ge \epsilon \cdot \pi(s,t)] \le 2 \cdot \exp\left(-\frac{\epsilon^2 \cdot \omega \cdot \pi(s,t)}{r_{sum} \cdot (2 + 2a \cdot \epsilon/3)}\right).$$

As we only consider approximation for $\pi(s,t) > \delta$ and $a \le 1$,

$$\Pr[|\pi(s,t) - \hat{\pi}(s,t)| \ge \epsilon \cdot \pi(s,t)] \le 2 \cdot \exp\left(-\frac{\epsilon^2 \cdot \omega \cdot \delta}{r_{sum} \cdot (2 + 2\epsilon/3)}\right).$$

Since $\omega = r_{sum} \cdot \frac{(2\epsilon/3+2) \cdot \log(2/p_f)}{\epsilon^2 \cdot \delta}$, we can conclude that

$$\Pr[|\pi(s,t) - \hat{\pi}(s,t)| \ge \epsilon \cdot \pi(s,t)] \le p_f$$

holds for $\pi(s,t) > \delta$. Also notice that the target t is arbitrarily chosen, and we can derive this bound for all nodes $v \in V$. Hence, the returned answer for the single-source PPR query satisfies Definition 2.1, which finishes the proof. □

Proof of Theorem 3.4. Given ω_j, we can derive that:

$$\Pr[|\pi(s,t) - \hat{\pi}(s,t)| \ge \epsilon \cdot \pi(s,t)] \le 2 \cdot \exp\left(-\frac{\epsilon^2 \cdot \omega_j \cdot \pi(s,t)}{2 + 2a \cdot \epsilon/3}\right).$$

Since $a \le 1$ and $\pi(s,t) \ge \pi^{\circ}(s,t)$, and $\pi(s,t) \ge LB_{j-1}(t)$, we can derive that:

$$\Pr[|\pi(s,t) - \hat{\pi}(s,t)| \ge \epsilon \cdot \pi(s,t)] \le$$
$$2\exp\left(-\frac{\epsilon^2 \cdot \omega_j \cdot \max\{\pi_j^{\circ}(s,v), LB_{j-1}(s,v)\}}{2 + 2\epsilon/3}\right).$$

Let p_f' equal the RHS of the above inequality. We have $\epsilon \ge \sqrt{\frac{3\log(2/p_f')}{\omega_j \cdot \max\{\pi_j^{\circ}(s,v), LB_{j-1}(s,v)\}}}$.

By setting $\epsilon_j = \sqrt{\frac{3\log(2/p_f')}{\omega_j \cdot \max\{\pi_j^{\circ}(s,v), LB_{j-1}(s,v)\}}}$, we can derive that $\hat{\pi}_j(s,v)/(1+\epsilon_j) \le \pi(s,v) \le \hat{\pi}_j(s,v)/(1-\epsilon_j)$ holds with $1 - p_f'$ probability. Similarly, we have

$$\Pr[|\pi(s,t) - \hat{\pi}(s,t)| \ge \epsilon \cdot \pi(s,t)] \le 2\exp\left(-\frac{\lambda^2 \cdot \omega}{r_{sum} \cdot (2\pi(s,t) + 2\lambda/3)}\right)$$

Let p_f' equal the RHS of the above inequality, and note that $\pi(s,t) \le UB_{j-1}(t)$. This helps us derive the designed bound for λ_j. □

Proof of Theorem 3.5. We apply a similar technique in [22]. If $LB_j(v_i') \cdot (1+\epsilon) > UB_j(v_i')$. Then, it can be derived that

$$\hat{\pi}(v_i') \le UB_j(v_i') \le LB_j(v_i') \cdot (1+\epsilon) \le (1+\epsilon) \cdot \pi(s, v_i').$$
$$\hat{\pi}(v_i') \ge LB_j(v_i') \ge UB_j(v_i')/(1+\epsilon) \ge (1-\epsilon) \cdot \pi(s, v_i').$$

Hence, $v_1', \cdots, v_k'$ satisfy Equation 2. Let $v_1, \cdots, v_k$ be the k nodes that have the top-k exact PPR values. Assume that all bounds are correct, then as $LB(v_l') \ge \delta$, it indicates that the top-k PPR values are no smaller than δ. In this case, all the top-k nodes should satisfy ϵ-approximation guarantee, i.e., they satisfy that $UB(v_i) < (1+\epsilon)\cdot LB(v_i)/(1-\epsilon)$.

Let $UB'_j(1), UB'_j(2), \cdots UB'_j(k)$ be the top-k largest PPR upper bounds in the j-th iteration. Note that, the i-th largest PPR satisfy that $UB'_j(i) \geq \pi(s, v_i) \geq LB_j(s, v'_i)$.

Now assume that one of the upper bounds say $UB'_j(i)$ is not from $UB(v_1), \cdots, UB(v_k)$. If it satisfies that $LB_j(v'_k)\cdot(1+\epsilon) \geq UB'_j(i)$, it indicates that $LB_j(v'_i)\cdot(1+\epsilon) \geq UB'_j(i)$ for all nodes. Hence, we update the node whose upper bound is minimum among $UB_j(v'_1), \cdots, UB_j(v'_1)$, we can still guarantee that $LB_j(v'_i)\cdot(1+\epsilon) > UB_j(v'_i)$. We repeat this process until $UB_j(v'_1), \cdots, UB_j(v'_k)$ are the top-k upper bounds. On the other hand, let U be the set of nodes such that, the node $u \in U$ satisfies that $UB_j(u) < LB_j(v'_k)$. Then it is still possible that these nodes are from the exact top−k answers. However, recall that if a node $u \in U$ is from the top-k, it should satisfy that $UB(u) < (1+\epsilon)\cdot LB(u)/(1-\epsilon)$. As a result, if there exists no node $u \in U$ such that $UB(u) < (1+\epsilon)\cdot LB(u)/(1-\epsilon)$, then no node $u \in U$ is from the top-k answers, in which case it will not affect the approximation guarantee.

Afterwards, we proceed a bubble sort on the top-k upper bounds in decreasing order. If we replace two upper bounds $UB_j(v'_x)$ and $UB_j(v'_y)$ with $x < y$, then $UB_j(v'_x) < UB_j(v'_y)$. Also $LB_j(v'_x) > LB_j(v'_y)$ from the definition. As

$$UB_j(v'_x)/LB_j(v'_y) < UB_j(v'_y)/LB_j(v'_y) \leq (1+\epsilon)$$
$$UB_j(v'_y)/LB_j(v'_x) < UB_j(v'_y)/LB_j(v'_y) \leq (1+\epsilon)$$

When the sort finishes, the inequations still hold. We then have

$$UB'_j(1) \leq (1+\epsilon)\cdot LB_j(v'_i)\cdots, UB'_j(k) \leq (1+\epsilon)\cdot LB_j(v'_k).$$

Also note that

$$\hat{\pi}(v'_i) \geq LB_j(v'_i) \geq \frac{1}{1+\epsilon} UB'_j(i) \geq (1-\epsilon)\cdot \pi(s, v_i),$$

for all $i \in [1, k]$. So, the answer provides approximation guarantee if the bounds from the first to the j-th iteration are all correct. By applying the union bound, we can obtain that the approximation is guaranteed with probability at least $1 - n\cdot j\cdot p'_f$.

B EXTENSIONS

B.1 Extending *BiPPR* to Whole-Graph SSPPR

Recall from Section 2.2 that in BiPPR, it includes both a forward phase and a backward phase. It is proved in [1] that the amortized time complexity for the backward phase is $O\left(\frac{m}{n\cdot r_{max}}\right)$, and in [15], it shows that the forward phase requires $O\left(\frac{r_{max}\cdot\log(1/p_f)}{\epsilon^2\cdot\delta}\right)$ time, given the backward phase threshold r_{max}. Afterwards, they choose $r_{max} = O\left(\epsilon\cdot\sqrt{\frac{m\cdot\delta}{n\cdot\log(1/p_f)}}\right)$ to minimize the time complexity for the pairwise PPR query, which is $O\left(\frac{1}{\epsilon}\sqrt{\frac{m\cdot\log(1/p_f)}{n\cdot\delta}}\right)$. To apply BiPPR for whole-graph SSPPR queries, a straightforward approach is to use it to answer n point-to-point PPR queries (i.e., from s to every other node). This, however, leads to a total time complexity of $O\left(\frac{1}{\epsilon}\sqrt{\frac{mn\cdot\log(1/p_f)}{\delta}}\right)$, which is a factor of $\sqrt{n}$ larger than that of the whole-graph SSPPR FORA.

To improve this, we observe that the n point-to-point PPR queries share the same forward phase, and hence, we can conduct the forward phase once and then re-use its results for all n backward phase. In addition, to reduce the total cost of n backward phases, we can set r_{max} to a larger value; although it would require more random walks to be generated in the forward phase, the tradeoff is still favorable as the overhead of the forward phase has been significantly reduced by the re-usage of results. Since the backward phase (for all target nodes) has a cost of $O\left(\frac{m}{r_{max}}\right)$, it can be verified that, by setting $r_{max} = O\left(\epsilon\cdot\sqrt{\frac{m\cdot\delta}{\log(1/p_f)}}\right)$, the expected time complexity of this optimized version of BiPPR (for SSPPR queries) is

$$O\left(\frac{1}{\epsilon\cdot\sqrt{\delta}}\sqrt{m\cdot\log(1/p_f)}\right),$$

which is identical to that of single-source FORA.

However, as we show in Section 5, the optimized *BiPPR* is significantly outperformed by Whole-Graph SSPPR FORA. The reason is that, even after the aforementioned optimization, BiPPR either degrades to MC when r_{max} is large, or still requires performing a backward phase from each node v in G, even if $\pi(s, v)$ is extremely small and can be omitted. In contrast, single-source FORA does not suffer from these deficiencies, and avoid examining nodes with very small PPR values. Instead, it performs a forward search phase, followed by a number of random walks from the nodes visited in the search; this process tends to avoid examining nodes with very small PPR values, since those nodes are unlikely to be visited by the forward push or the random walks.

B.2 Extending FORA to Source Distributions

In many real applications of the personalized PageRank, the source s can be a distribution (e.g., on a set of bookmark pages) instead of a single node. We show that our algorithms for single-source-node *FORA* can be extended to the case of arbitrary source distributions.

Let σ be the node distribution that the source node s is sampled from. For any target node t, its personalized PageRank with respect to σ is defined as [15]:

$$\pi(\sigma, t) = \sum_{v\in V} \sigma(v)\cdot\pi(v, t),$$

where $\sigma(v)$ is the probability that a sample from σ equals v. To apply our algorithms, we modify Line 1 of Algorithm 1 to set the initial residue of each node v as $\sigma(v)$. Let $\pi^\circ(\sigma, v)$ (resp. $r(\sigma, v)$) denote the reserve (resp. residue) of node v in the modified version of Forward Push. Then, it is easy to prove that the following invariant holds for the modified version of Forward Push:

$$\pi(\sigma, t) = \pi^\circ(\sigma, t) + \sum_{v\in V} r(\sigma, v)\cdot\pi(v, t).$$

In particular, the initial states satisfy the above invariant, and by induction, it can be proved that the invariant still holds after every push operation. Given the above invariant, our algorithms can be applied to compute $\pi(\sigma, t)$ without compromising their asymptotic guarantees. Besides, the indexing scheme presented in Section 3.3 is still applicable, since the maximum number of random walks required for each node is identical to that in the single-source-node algorithms.

Large-scale Collaborative Ranking in Near-Linear Time

Liwei Wu
Depts. of Statistics and Computer Science
University of California, Davis
liwu@ucdavis.edu

Cho-Jui Hsieh
Depts. of Statistics and Computer Science
University of California, Davis
chohsieh@ucdavis.edu

James Sharpnack
Dept. of Statistics
University of California, Davis
jsharpna@ucdavis.edu

ABSTRACT

In this paper, we consider the Collaborative Ranking (CR) problem for recommendation systems. Given a set of pairwise preferences between items for each user, collaborative ranking can be used to rank un-rated items for each user, and this ranking can be naturally used for recommendation. It is observed that collaborative ranking algorithms usually achieve better performance since they directly minimize the ranking loss; however, they are rarely used in practice due to the poor scalability. All the existing CR algorithms have time complexity at least $O(|\Omega|r)$ per iteration, where r is the target rank and $|\Omega|$ is number of pairs which grows quadratically with number of ratings per user. For example, the Netflix data contains totally 20 billion rating pairs, and at this scale all the current algorithms have to work with significant subsampling, resulting in poor prediction on testing data.

In this paper, we propose a new collaborative ranking algorithm called Primal-CR that reduces the time complexity to $O(|\Omega|+d_1\bar{d}_2r)$, where d_1 is number of users and $\bar{d}_2$ is the averaged number of items rated by a user. Note that $d_1\bar{d}_2$ is strictly smaller and often much smaller than $|\Omega|$.

Furthermore, by exploiting the fact that most data is in the form of numerical ratings instead of pairwise comparisons, we propose Primal-CR++ with $O(d_1\bar{d}_2(r + \log \bar{d}_2))$ time complexity. Both algorithms have better theoretical time complexity than existing approaches and also outperform existing approaches in terms of NDCG and pairwise error on real data sets. To the best of our knowledge, this is the first collaborative ranking algorithm capable of working on the full Netflix dataset using all the 20 billion rating pairs, and this leads to a model with much better recommendation compared with previous models trained on subsamples. Finally, compared with classical matrix factorization algorithm which also requires $O(d_1\bar{d}_2r)$ time, our algorithm has almost the same efficiency while making much better recommendations since we consider the ranking loss.

KEYWORDS

Collaborative Ranking, Recommendation Systems, Large-Scale.

KDD'17, August 13–17, 2017, Halifax, NS, Canada.

DOI: http://dx.doi.org/10.1145/3097983.3098071

1 INTRODUCTION

In online retail and online content delivery applications, it is commonplace to have embedded recommendation systems– algorithms that recommend items to users based on previous user behaviors and ratings. Online retail companies develop sophisticated recommendation systems based on purchase behavior, item context, and shifting trends. The Netflix prize [2], in which competitors utilize user ratings to recommend movies, accelerated research in recommendation systems. While the winning submissions agglomerated several existing methods, one essential methodology, latent factor models, emerged as a critical component. The latent factor model means that the approximated rating for user i and item j is given by $u_i^\top v_j$ where u_i, v_j are k-dimensional vectors. One interpretation is that there are k latent topics and the approximated rating can be reconstructed as a combination of factor weights. By minimizing the square error loss of this reconstruction we arrive at the incomplete SVD,

$$\min_{U,V} \sum_{i,j\in\Omega} (R_{i,j} - u_i^\top v_j)^2 + \frac{\lambda}{2}(\|U\|_F^2 + \|V\|_F^2), \tag{1}$$

where Ω contains sampled indices of the rating matrix, R.

Often the performance of recommendation systems is not measured by the quality of rating prediction, but rather the ranking of the items that the system returns for a given user. The task of finding a ranking based on ratings or relative rankings is called Collaborative Ranking. Recommendation systems can be trained with ratings, that may be passively or actively collected, or by relative rankings, in which a user is asked to rank a number of items. A simple way to unify the framework is to convert the ratings into rankings by making pairwise comparisons of ratings. Specifically, the algorithm takes as input the pairwise comparisons, $Y_{i,j,k}$ for each user i and item pairs j, k. This approach confers several advantages. Users may have different standards for their ratings, some users are more generous with their ratings than others. This is known as the calibration drawback, and to deal with this we must make a departure from standard matrix factorization methods. Because we focus on ranking and not predicting ratings, we can expect improved performance when recommending the top items. Our goal in this paper is to provide a collaborative ranking algorithm that can scale to the size of the full Netflix dataset, a heretofore open problem.

The existing collaborative ranking algorithms, (for a summary see section 2), are limited by the number of observed ratings per user in the training data and cannot scale to massive datasets, therefore, making the recommendation results less accurate and less useful in practice. This motivates our algorithm, which can make use of the entire Netflix dataset without sub-sampling. Our contribution can be summarized below:

- For input data in the form of pairwise preference comparisons, we propose a new algorithm Primal-CR that alternatively minimizes latent factors using Newton's method in the primal space. By carefully designing the computation of gradient and Hessian vector product, our algorithm reduces the sample complexity per iteration to $O(|\Omega|+d_1\bar{d}_2 r)$, while the state-of-the-art approach [17] have $O(|\Omega|r)$ complexity. Here $|\Omega|$ (total number of pairs), is much larger than $d_1\bar{d}_2$ (d_1 is number of users and $\bar{d}_2$ is averaged number of items rated by a user). For the Netflix problem, $|\Omega| = 2 \times 10^{10}$ while $d_1\bar{d}_2 = 10^8$.
- For input data in the form of ratings, we can further exploit the structure to speedup the gradient and Hessian computation. The resulting algorithm, Primal-CR++, can further reduce the time complexity to $O(d_1\bar{d}_2(r + \log \bar{d}_2))$ per iteration. In this setting, our algorithm has time complexity near-linear to the input size, and have comparable speed with classical matrix factorization model that takes $O(d_1\bar{d}_2 r)$ time, while we can achieve much better recommendation by minimizing the ranking loss.

We show that our algorithms outperform existing algorithms on real world datasets and can be easily parallelized.

2 RELATED WORK

Collaborative filtering methodologies are summarized in [20] (see [6] for an early work). Among them, matrix factorization [13] has been widely used due to the success in the Netflix Prize. Many algorithms have been developed based on matrix factorization [5, 11, 18, 19, 22], and many scalable algorithms have been developed [8, 13]. However, they are not suitable for ranking top items for a user due to the fact that their goal is to minimize the mean-square error (MSE) instead of ranking loss. In fact, MSE is not a good metric for recommendation when we want to recommend the top K items to a user. This has been pointed out in several papers [1] which argue normalized discounted cumulative gain (NDCG) should be used instead of MSE, and our experimental results also confirm this finding by showing that minimizing the ranking loss results in better precision and NDCG compared with the traditional matrix factorization approach that is targeting squared error.

Ranking is a well studied problem, and there has been a long line of research focuses on learning one ranking function, which is called Learning to Rank. For example, RankSVM [12] is a well-known pair-wise model, and an efficient solver has been proposed in [4] for solving rankSVM. [3] is a list-wise model implemented using neural networks. Another class of point-wise models fit the ratings explicitly but has the issue of calibration drawback (see [10]).

The collaborative ranking (CR) problem is essentially trying to learn multiple rankings together, and several models and algorithms have been proposed in literature. The Cofirank algorithm [25], which tailors maximum margin matrix factorization [23] for collaborative ranking, is a point-wise model for CR, and is regarded as the performance benchmark for this task. If the ratings are 1-bit, a weighting scheme is proposed to improve the usual point-wise Matrix Factorization approach [15]. List-wise models for Learning to Rank can also be extended to many rankings setting, [21]. However it is still quite similar to a point-wise approach since they only consider the top-1 probabilities.

For pairwise models in collaborative ranking, it is well known that they do not encounter the calibration drawback as do point-wise models, but they are computationally intensive and cannot scale well to large data sets [21]. The scalability problem for pairwise models is mainly due to the fact that their time complexity is at least proportional to $|\Omega|$, the number of pairwise preference comparisons, which grows quadratically with number of rated items for each user. Recently, [17] proposed a new Collrank algorithm, and they showed that Collrank has better precision and NDCG as well as being much faster compared with other CR methods on real world datasets, including Bayesian Personalized Ranking (BPR) [19]. Unfortunately their scalability is still constrained by number of pairs, so they can only run on subsamples for large datasets, such as Netflix. In this paper, our algorithm Primal-CR and Primal-CR++ also belong to the family of pairwise models, but due to cleverly re-arranging the computation, we are able to have much better time complexity than existing ones, and as a result our algorithm can scale to very large datasets.

There are many other algorithms proposed for many rankings setting but none of these mentioned below can scale up to the extent of using all the ratings in the full Netflix data. There are a few using Bayesian frameworks to model the problem [19], [16], [24], the last of which requires many specified parameters. Another one proposed retargeted matrix factorization to get ranking by monotonically transforming the ratings [14]. [9] proposes a similar model without making generative assumptions on ratings besides assuming low-rank and correctness of the ranking order.

3 PROBLEM FORMULATION

We first formally define the collaborative ranking problem using the example of item recommender system. Assume we have d_1 users and d_2 items, the input data is given in the form of "for user i, item j is preferred over item k" and thus can be represented by a set of tuples (i, j, k). We use Ω to denote the set of observed tuples, and the observed pairwise preferences are denoted as $\{Y_{ijk} \mid (i, j, k) \in \Omega\}$, where $Y_{ijk} = 1$ denotes that item j is preferred over item k for a particular user i and $Y_{ijk} = -1$ to denote that item k is preferred over item j for user i.

The goal of collaborative ranking is to rank all the unseen items for each user i based on these partial observations, which can be done by fitting a scoring matrix $X \in \mathbb{R}^{d_1 \times d_2}$. If the scoring matrix has $X_{ij} > X_{ik}$, it implies that item j is preferred over item k by the particular user i and therefore we should give higher rank for item j than item k. After we estimate the scoring matrix X by solving the optimization problem described below, we can then recommend top k items for any particular user.

The Collaborative Ranking Model referred to in this paper is the one proposed recently in [17]. It belongs to the family of pairwise models for collaborative ranking because it uses pairwise training losses [1]. The model is given as

$$\min_X \sum_{(i,j,k)\in\Omega} \mathcal{L}(Y_{ijk}(X_{ij} - X_{ik})) + \lambda \|X\|_*, \tag{2}$$

where $\mathcal{L}(.)$ is the loss function, $\|X\|_*$ is the nuclear norm regularization defined by the sum of all the singular value of the matrix X, and λ is a regularization parameter. The ranking loss defined in the first term of (2) penalizes the pairs when $Y_{ijk} = 1$ but $X_{ij} - X_{ik}$ is positive but small, and penalizes even more when the difference is negative. The second term in the loss function is based on the assumption that there are only a small number of latent factors contributing to the users' preferences which is analogous to the idea behind incomplete SVD for matrix factorization mentioned in the introduction. In general we can use any loss function, but since $\mathcal{L}_2$-hinge loss defined as

$$\mathcal{L}(a) = \max(0, 1 - a)^2 \tag{3}$$

gives the best performance in practice [17] and enjoys many nice properties, such as smoothness and differentiable, we will focus on L_2-hinge loss in this paper. In fact, our first algorithm Primal-CR can be applied to any loss function, while Primal-CR++ can only be applied to L_2-hinge loss.

Despite the advantage of the objective function in equation (2) being convex, it is still not feasible for large-scale problems since d_1 and d_2 can be very large so that the scoring matrix X cannot be stored in memory, not to mention how to solve it. Therefore, in practice people usually transform (2) to a non-convex form by replacing $X = UV^T$, and in that case since $\|X\|_* = min_{X=U^TV} \frac{1}{2}(\|U\|_F^2 + \|V\|_F^2)$ [23], problem (2) can be reformulated as

$$\min_{U,V} \sum_{(i,j,k)\in\Omega} \mathcal{L}(Y_{ijk} \cdot u_i^T(v_j - v_k)) + \frac{\lambda}{2}(\|U\|_F^2 + \|V\|_F^2), \tag{4}$$

We use u_i and v_j denote columns of U and V respectively. Note that [17] also solves the non-convex form (4) in their experiments, and in the rest of the paper we will propose a faster algorithm for solving (4).

4 PROPOSED ALGORITHMS

4.1 Motivation and Overview

Although collaborative ranking assumes that input data is given in the form of pairwise comparisons, in reality almost all the datasets (Netflix, Yahoo-Music, MovieLens, etc) contain user ratings to items in the form of $\{R_{ij} \mid (i,j) \in \bar{\Omega}\}$, where $\bar{\Omega}$ is the subset of observed user-item pairs. Therefore, in practice we have to transform the rating-based data into pair-wise comparisons by generating all the item pairs rated by the same user:

$$\Omega = \{(i,j,k) \mid j,k \in \bar{\Omega}_i\}, \tag{5}$$

where $\bar{\Omega}_i := \{j \mid (i,j) \in \bar{\Omega}\}$ is the set of items rated by user i. Assume there are averagely $\bar{d}_2$ items rated by a user (i.e., $\bar{d}_2 =$ mean$(|\bar{\Omega}_i|)$), then the collaborative ranking problem will have $O(d_1\bar{d}_2{}^2)$ pairs and thus the size of Ω grows quadratically.

Unfortunately, all the existing algorithms have $O(|\Omega|r)$ complexity, so they cannot scale to large number of items. For example, the AltSVM (or referred to asCollrank) Algorithm in [17] will run out of memory when we subsample 500 rated items per user on Netflix dataset since its implementation[1] stores all the pairs in memory and therefore requires $O(|\Omega|)$ memory. So it cannot be used for the full Netflix dataset which has more than *20 billion pairs* and requires 300GB memory space. To the best of our knowledge, no collaborative ranking algorithms have been applied to the full Netflix data set. But in real life, we hope to make use of as much information as possible to make better recommendation. As shown in our experiments later, using full training data instead of sub-sampling (such as selecting a fixed number of rated items per user) achieves higher prediction and recommendation accuracy for the same test data.

To overcome this scalability issue, we propose two novel algorithms for solving problem (4), and both of them significantly reduce the time complexity over existing methods. If the input file is in the form of $|\Omega|$ pairwise comparisons, our proposed algorithm, Primal-CR, can reduce the time and space complexity from $O(|\Omega|r)$ to $O(|\Omega| + d_1\bar{d}_2r)$, where $\bar{d}_2$ is the average number of items compared by one user. If the input data is given as user-item ratings (e.g., Netflix, Yahoo-Music), the complexity is reduced from $O(d_1\bar{d}_2{}^2r)$ to $O(d_1\bar{d}_2r + d_1\bar{d}_2{}^2)$.

If the input file is given in ratings, we can further reduce the time complexity to $O(d_1\bar{d}_2r + d_1\bar{d}_2\log\bar{d}_2)$ using exactly the same optimization algorithm but smarter ways to compute gradient and Hessian vector product. This time complexity is much smaller than the number of comparisons $|\Omega| = O(d_1\bar{d}_2^2)$, and we call this algorithm Primal-CR++.

We will first introduce Primal-CR in Section 4.2, and then present Primal-CR++ in Section 4.3.

4.2 Primal-CR: the proposed algorithm for pairwise input data

Algorithm 1 Primal-CR/ Primal-CR++: General Framework

```
Input: Ω, {Y_ijk : (i,j,k) ∈ Ω}, λ ∈ R+                ▷ for Primal-CR
Input: M ∈ R^{d1×d2}, λ ∈ R+                             ▷ for Primal-CR++
Output: U ∈ R^{r×d1} and V ∈ R^{r×d2}
 1: Randomly initialize U, V from Gaussian Distribution
 2: while not converged do
 3:     procedure Fix U and update V
 4:         while not converged do
 5:             Apply truncated Newton update (Algorithm 2)
 6:         end while
 7:     end procedure
 8:     procedure Fix V and update U
 9:         while not converged do
10:             Apply truncated Newton update (Algorithm 2)
11:         end while
12:     end procedure
13: end while
14: return U, V                                          ▷ recover score matrix X
```

In the first setting, we consider the case where the pairwise comparisons $\{Y_{ijk} \mid (i,j,k) \in \Omega\}$ are given as input. To solve problem (4), we alternatively minimize U and V in the primal space (see Algorithm 1). First, we fix U and update V, and the subproblem

[1] Collrank code is available on https://github.com/dhpark22/collranking.

Algorithm 2 Truncated Newton Update for V (same procedure can be used for updating U)

Input: Current solution U, V
Output: V

Compute $g = \text{vec}(\nabla f(V))$
Let $H = \nabla^2 f(V)$ (do not explicitly compute H)
procedure LINEAR CONJUGATE GRADIENT(g, F)
  Initialize $\delta_0 = 0$
  $r_0 = H\delta_0 - g, p_0 = -r_0$
  for $k = 0, 1, ..., maxiter$ **do**
    Compute the Hessian-vector product $q = Hp_k$
    $\alpha_k = -r_k^T p_k / p_k^T q$
    $\delta_{k+1} = \delta_k + \alpha_k p_k$
    $r_{k+1} = r_k + \alpha_k q$
    if $||r_{k+1}||_2 < ||r_0||_2 \cdot 10^{-2}$ **then**
      break
    end if
    $\beta_{k+1} = (r_{k+1} q)/p_k^T q$
    $p_{k+1} = -r_{k+1} + \beta_{k+1} p_k$
  end for
  return δ
end procedure
$V = V - s\delta$ (stepsize s found by line search)
return U or V

for V while U is fixed can be written as follows:

$$V = \underset{V \in \mathbb{R}^{r \times d_2}}{\text{argmin}} \left\{ \frac{\lambda}{2} ||V||_F^2 + \sum_{(i,j,k) \in \Omega} \mathcal{L}(Y_{ijk} \cdot u_i^T (v_j - v_k)) \right\} := f(V) \tag{6}$$

In [17], this subproblem is solved by stochastic dual coordinate descent, which requires $O(|\Omega|r)$ time and $O(|\Omega|)$ space complexity. Furthermore, the objective function decreases for the dual problem sometimes does not imply the decrease of primal objective function value, which often results in slow convergence. We therefore propose to solve this subproblem for V using the primal truncated Newton method (Algorithm 2).

Newton method is a classical second-order optimization algorithm. For minimizing a vector-valued function $f(x)$, Newton method iteratively updates the solution by $x \leftarrow x - (\nabla^2 f(x))^{-1} \nabla f(x)$. However, the matrix inversion is usually hard to compute, so a truncated Newton method computes the update direction by solving the linear system $\nabla^2 f(x) a = \nabla f(x)$ up to a certain accuracy, usually using a linear conjugate gradient method. If we vectorized the problem for updating V in eq (6), the gradient is a (rd_2)-sized vector and the Hessian is an (rd_2)-by-(rd_2) matrix, so explicitly forming the Hessian is impossible. Below we discuss how to apply the truncated Newton method to solve our problem, and discuss efficient computations for each part.

Derivation of Gradient. When applying the truncated Newton method, the gradient $\nabla f(V)$ is a $\mathbb{R}^{r \times d_2}$ matrix and can be computed explicitly:

$$\nabla f(V) = \sum_{i=1}^{d_1} \sum_{(j,k) \in \Omega_i} \mathcal{L}'(Y_{ijk} \cdot u_i^T (v_j - v_k))(u_i e_j^T - u_i e_k^T) Y_{ijk} + \lambda V, \tag{7}$$

where $\nabla f(V) \in \mathbb{R}^{r \times d_2}$, $\Omega_i := \{(j,k) \mid (i,j,k) \in \Omega\}$ is the subset of pairs that associates with user i, and e_j is the indicator vector used to add the u_i vector to the j-th column of the output matrix. The first derivative for L_2-hinge loss function (3) is

$$\mathcal{L}'(a) = 2\min(a - 1, 0) \tag{8}$$

For convenience, we define $g := \text{vec}(\nabla f(V))$ to be the vectorized form of gradient. One can easily see that computing g naively by going through all the pairwise comparisons (j, k) and adding up arrays is time-consuming and has $O(|\Omega|r)$ time complexity, which is the same with Collrank [17].

Fast computation for gradient. Fortunately, we can reduce the time complexity to $O(|\Omega| + d_1 \bar{d}_2 r)$ by smartly rearranging the computations, so that the time is only linear to $|\Omega|$ and r, but not to $|\Omega|r$. The method is described below.

First, for each i, the first term of (7) can be represented by

$$\sum_{(j,k) \in \Omega_i} \mathcal{L}'(Y_{ijk} \cdot u_i^T (v_j - v_k))(u_i e_j^T - u_i e_k^T) Y_{ijk} = \sum_{j \in \bar{d}_2(i)} t_j u_i e_j^T, \tag{9}$$

where $\bar{d}_2(i) := \{j \mid \exists k \text{ s.t. } (i,j,k) \in \Omega\}$ and t_j is some coefficient computed by summing over all the pairs in Ω_i. If we have t_j, the overall gradient can be computed by $O(\bar{d}_2(i)r)$ time for each i. To compute t_j, we first compute $u_i^T v_j$ for all $j \in \bar{d}_2(i)$ in $O(\bar{d}_2(i)r)$ time, and then go through all the (j, k) pairs while keep adding the coefficient related to this pair to t_j and t_k. Since there is no vector operations when we go through all pairs, this step only takes $O(\Omega_i)$ time. After getting all t_j, we can then conduct $\sum_{j \in \bar{d}_2(i)} t_j u_i e_j^T$ in $O(\bar{d}_2(i)r)$ time. Therefore, the overall complexity can be reduced to $O(|\Omega| + d_1 \bar{d}_2 r)$. The pseudo code is presented in Algorithm 3.

Algorithm 3 Primal-CR: efficient way to compute $\nabla f(V)$

Input: Ω, $\{Y_{ijk} : (i,j,k) \in \Omega\}$, $\lambda \in \mathbb{R}^+$, current variables U, V
Output: g, m ▷ $g \in \mathbb{R}^{d_2 r}$ is the gradient for $f(V)$

Initialize $g = 0$ ▷ $g \in \mathbb{R}^{r \times d_2}$
for $i = 1, 2, \ldots, d_1$ **do**
  for all $j \in \bar{d}_2(i)$ **do**
    precompute $u_i^T v_j$ and store in a vector m_i
  end for
  Initialize a zero array t of size d_2
  for all $(j, k) \in \bar{d}_2(i)$ **do**
    if $Y_{ijk}(m_i[j] - m_i[k]) < 1$ **then**
      $s = 2(Y_{ijk}(m_i[j] - m_i[k]) - 1)$
      $t[j] \mathrel{+}= Y_{ijk} s$
      $t[k] \mathrel{-}= Y_{ijk} s$ ▷ O(1) time per for loop iteration
    end if
  end for
  for all $j \in \bar{d}_2(i)$ **do**
    $g[:, j] \mathrel{+}= t[j] \cdot u_i$
  end for
end for
$g = vec(g + \lambda V)$ ▷ vectorize matrix $g \in \mathbb{R}^{r \times d_2}$
Form a sparse matrix $m = [m_1 \ldots m_{d_1}]$ ▷ m can be reused later
return g, m

Derivation of Hessian-vector product. Now we derive the Hessian $\nabla^2 f(V)$ for $f(V)$. We define $\nabla_j f(V) := \frac{\partial}{\partial v_j} f(V) \in \mathbb{R}^r$ and $\nabla^2_{j,k} f(V) := \frac{\partial^2}{\partial v_j \partial v_k} f(V) \in \mathbb{R}^{r\times r}$ in the following derivations. From the gradient derivation, we have

$$\nabla_j f(V) = \sum_{i:j\in\bar{d}_2(i)} \sum_{\substack{k\in\bar{d}_2(i)\\ k\neq j}} \mathcal{L}'(Y_{ijk} \cdot u_i^T(v_j - v_k)) u_i Y_{ijk} + \lambda v_j.$$

Taking derivative again we can obtain

$$\nabla^2_{j,k} f(V) =$$

$$\begin{cases} \sum_{i:(j,k)\in\bar{d}_2(i)} \mathcal{L}''(Y_{ijk} \cdot u_i^T(v_j - v_k))(-u_i u_i^T) & \text{if } j \neq k \\ \sum_{i:j\in\bar{d}_2(i)} \sum_{k\in\bar{d}_2(i), k\neq j} \mathcal{L}''(Y_{ijk} \cdot u_i^T(v_j - v_k)) u_i u_i^T + \lambda I_{r\times r} & \text{if } j = k \end{cases}$$

and the second derivative for $\mathcal{L}_2$ hinge loss function is given by:

$$\mathcal{L}''(a) = \begin{cases} 2 & \text{if } a \leq 1 \\ 0 & \text{if } a > 1. \end{cases} \quad (10)$$

Note that if we write the full Hessian H as a $(d_2 r)$ by $(d_2 r)$ matrix, then $\nabla^2_{j,k} f(V)$ is an $r \times r$ block in H, where there are totally d_2^2 of these blocks. In the CG update for solving $H^{-1}g$, we only need to compute $H \cdot a$ for some $a \in \mathbb{R}^{d_2 r}$. For convenience, we also partition this a into d_2 blocks, each subvector a_j has size r, so $a = [a_1; \cdots; a_j]$. Similarly we can use subscript to denote the subarray $(H \cdot a)_j$ of the array $H \cdot a$, which becomes

$$(H \cdot a)_j = \sum_{k\neq j} \nabla^2_{j,k} f(V) \cdot a_k + \nabla^2_{j,j} f(V) \cdot a_j$$

$$= \lambda a_j + \sum_{i:j\in\bar{d}_2(i)} u_i \sum_{\substack{k\in\bar{d}_2(i)\\ k\neq j}} \mathcal{L}''(Y_{ijk} \cdot u_i^T(v_j - v_k))(u_i^T a_j - u_i^T a_k).$$

Therefore, we have

$$H \cdot a = \sum_j E_j (H \cdot a)_j$$

$$= \lambda a + \sum_i \sum_{j\in\bar{d}_2(i)} E_j u_i \sum_{\substack{k\in\bar{d}_2(i)\\ k\neq j}} \mathcal{L}''(Y_{ijk} \cdot u_i^T(v_j - v_k))(u_i^T a_j - u_i^T a_k) \quad (11)$$

where E_j is the projection matrix to the j-th block, indicating that we are only adding $(H \cdot a)_j$ to the j-th block of matrix, and setting 0 elsewhere.

Fast computation for Hessian-vector product . Similar to the case of gradient computation, using a naive way to compute $H \cdot a$ requires $O(|\Omega| r)$ time since we need to go through all the (i, j, k) tuples, and each of them requires $O(r)$ time. However, we can apply the similar trick in gradient computation to reduce the time complexity to $O(|\Omega| + d_1 \bar{d}_2 r)$ by pre-computing $u_i^T a_j$ and caching the coefficient using the array t. The detailed algorithm is given in Algorithm 4.

Note that in Algorithm 4, we can reuse the m (sparse array storing the current prediction) which has been pre-computed in the gradient computation (Algorithm 3), and that will cost only $O(d_1 \bar{d}_2)$ memory. Even without storing the m matrix, we can compute m in the loop of line 4 in Algorithm 4, which will not increase the overall computational complexity.

Algorithm 4 Primal-CR: efficient way to compute Hessian vector product

Input: Ω, $\{Y_{ijk} : (i, j, k) \in \Omega\}$, $\lambda \in \mathbb{R}^+$, $a \in \mathbb{R}^{d_2 r}$, m, U, V
Output: Ha ▷ $Ha \in \mathbb{R}^{d_2 r}$ is needed in Linear CG

```
1:  Ha = 0                                              ▷ Ha ∈ R^{d2 r}
2:  for i = 1, 2, ..., d1 do
3:      for all j ∈ d̄2(i) do
4:          precompute u_i^T a_j and store it in array b
5:      end for
6:      Initialize a zero array t of size d2
7:      for all (j, k) ∈ d̄2(i) do
8:          if Y_ijk(m_i[j] − m_i[k]) < 1.0 then
9:              s_jk = 2.0 · (b[j] − b[k])
10:             t[j] += s_jk
11:             t[k] −= s_jk          ▷ O(1) time per for loop iteration
12:         end if
13:     end for
14:     for all j ∈ d̄2(i) do
15:         (Ha)[(p − 1) · r + 1 : p · r] += t[j] · u_i
16:     end for
17: end for
18: return Ha
```

Fix V and Update U. After updating V by truncated Newton, we need to fix V and update U. The subproblem for U can be written as:

$$U = \underset{U\in\mathbb{R}^{r\times d_2}}{\operatorname{argmin}} \{\frac{\lambda}{2}\|U\|_F^2 + \sum_{i=1}^{d_1} \sum_{(j,k)\in\bar{d}_2(i)} \mathcal{L}(Y_{ijk} \cdot u_i^T(v_j - v_k))\} \quad (12)$$

Since u_i, the i-th column of U, is independent from the rest of columns, equation 12 can be decomposed into d_1 independent problems for u_i:

$$u_i = \underset{u\in\mathbb{R}^r}{\operatorname{argmin}} \frac{\lambda}{2}\|u\|_2^2 + \sum_{(j,k)\in\bar{d}_2(i)} \mathcal{L}(Y_{ijk} \cdot u^T(v_j - v_k)) := h(u) \quad (13)$$

Eq (13) is equivalent to an r-dimensional rankSVM problem. Since r is usually small, the problems are easy to solve. In fact, we can directly apply an efficient rankSVM algorithm proposed in [4] to solve each r-dimensional rankSVM problem. This algorithm requires $O(|\Omega_i| + r|\bar{d}_2(i)|)$ time for solving each subproblem with respect to u_i, so the overall complexity is $O(|\Omega| + r d_1 \bar{d}_2)$ time per iteration.

Summary of time and space complexity. When updating V, we first compute gradient by Algorithm 3, which takes $O(|\Omega| + d_1 \bar{d}_2 r)$ time, and each Hessian-vector product in 4 also takes the same time. The updates for U takes the same time complexity with updating V, so the overall time complexity is $O(|\Omega| + d_1 \bar{d}_2 r)$ per iteration. The whole algorithm only needs to store size $d_1 \times r$ and $d_2 \times r$ matrices for gradient and conjugate gradient method. The m matrix in Algorithm 3 is not needed, but in practice we find it can speedup the code by around 25%, and it only takes $d_1 \bar{d}_2 \leq |\Omega|$ memory space (less than the input size). Therefore, our algorithm is very memory-efficient.

Before going to Primal-CR++, we discuss the time complexity of Primal-CR when the input data is the user-item rating matrix. Assume $\bar{d}_2$ is the averaged number of rated items per user, then there will be $|\Omega| = O(d_1\bar{d}_2^2)$ pairs, leading to $O(d_1\bar{d}_2^2 + d_1\bar{d}_2 r)$ time complexity for Primal-CR. This is much better than the $O(d_1 d_2^2 r)$ complexity for all the existing algorithms.

Algorithm 5 Primal-CR++: compute gradient part for $f(V)$

Input: $M \in \mathbb{R}^{d_1 \times d_2}$, $\lambda \in \mathbb{R}^+$, current U, V
Output: g ▷ $g \in \mathbb{R}^{d_2 r}$ is the gradient for $f(V)$
Initialize $g = 0$ ▷ $g \in \mathbb{R}^{r \times d_2}$
for $i = 1, 2, ..., d_1$ **do**
  Let $\bar{d}_2 = |\bar{d}_2(i)|$ and $r_j = R_{i,j}$ for all j.
  Compute $m[j] = u_i^T v_j$ for all $j \in \bar{d}_2(i)$
  Sort $\bar{d}_2(i)$ according to the ascending order of m_i, so $m[\pi(1)] \leq \cdots \leq m[\pi(\bar{d}_2)]$
  Initialize $s[1], \ldots, s[L]$ and $c[1], \ldots, c[L]$ with 0
  (Store in segment tree or Fenwick tree.)
  $p \leftarrow 1$
  for all $j = 1, \ldots, \bar{d}_2$ **do**
    while $m[\pi(p)] \leq m_j + 1$ **do**
      $s[r_{\pi(p)}] += m[\pi(p)]$, $c[r_{\pi(p)}] += 1$
      $p += 1$
    end while
    $S = \sum_{\ell \geq r_{\pi(p)}} s[\ell]$, $C = \sum_{\ell \geq r_{\pi(p)}} c[\ell]$
    $t^+[\pi(j)] = 2(C \cdot (m[\pi(j)] + 1) - S)$
  end for
  Do another scan j from $\bar{d}_2$ to 1 to compute $t^-[\pi(j)]$ for all j
  $g[:, j] += (t^+[j] + t^-[j]) \cdot u_i$ for all j
end for
$g = vec(g + \lambda V)$ ▷ vectorize matrix $g \in \mathbb{R}^{r \times d_2}$
return g

4.3 Primal-CR++: the proposed algorithm for rating data

Now we discuss a more realistic scenario, where the input data is a rating matrix $\{R_{ij} \mid (i,j) \in \bar{\Omega}\}$ and $\bar{\Omega}$ is the observed set of user-item ratings. We assume there are only L levels of ratings, so $R_{ij} \in \{1, 2, \ldots, L\}$. Also, we use $\bar{d}_2(i) := \{j \mid (i,j) \in \bar{\Omega}\}$ to denote the rated items for user i.

Given this data, the goal is to solve the collaborative ranking problem (4) with all the pairwise comparisons in the rating dataset as defined in (5). There are totally $O(d_1\bar{d}_2^2)$ pairs, and the question is: Can we have an algorithm with near-linear time with respect to number of observed ratings $|\bar{\Omega}| = d_1\bar{d}_2$? We answer this question in the affirmative by proposing Primal-CR++, a near-linear time algorithm for solving problem (4) with L2-hinge loss.

The algorithm of Primal-CR++ is exactly the same with Primal-CR, but we use a smarter algorithm to compute gradient and Hessian vector product in near-linear time, by exploiting the structure of the input data.

We first discuss how to speed up the gradient computation of (7), where the main computation is to compute (9) for each i. When the loss function is L2-hinge loss, we can explicitly write down the coefficients t_j in (9) by

$$t_j = \sum_{k \in \bar{d}_2(i)} 2(m_j - m_k - Y_{ijk}) I[Y_{ijk}(m_j - m_k) \leq 1], \tag{14}$$

where $m_j := u_i^T v_j$ and $I[\cdot]$ is an indicator function such that $I[a \leq b] = 1$ if $a \leq b$, and $I[a \leq b] = 0$ otherwise. By splitting the cases of $Y_{ijk} = 1$ and $Y_{ijk} = -1$, we get

$$\begin{aligned} t_j &= t_j^+ + t_j^- \\ &= \sum_{\substack{k \in \bar{d}_2(i) \\ m_k \leq m_j + 1,\ Y_{ijk} = -1}} 2(m_j - m_k + 1) + \sum_{\substack{k \in \bar{d}_2(i) \\ m_k \geq m_j - 1,\ Y_{ijk} = 1}} 2(m_j - m_k - 1). \end{aligned} \tag{15}$$

Assume the indexes in $\bar{d}_2(i)$ are sorted by the the ascending order of m_j. Then we can scan from left to right, and maintain the current accumulated sum $s_1, ..., s_L$ and the current index counts $c_1, ..., c_L$ for each rating level. If the current pointer is p, then

$$s_\ell[p] = \sum_{j : m_j \leq p, R_{ij} = \ell} m_j \text{ and } c_\ell[p] = |\{j : m_j \leq p, R_{ij} = \ell\}|.$$

Since we scan from left to right, these numbers can be maintained in constant time at each step. Now assume we scan over the numbers $m_1 + 1, m_2 + 1, \ldots$, then at each point we can compute

$$t_j^+ = \sum_{\ell = R_{i,j}+1}^{L} 2\{(m_j + 1)c_\ell[m_j + 1] - s_\ell[m_j + 1]\},$$

which can be computed in $O(L)$ time.

Although we observe that $O(L)$ time is already small in practice (since L usually smaller than 10), in the following we show there is a way to remove the dependency on L by using a simple Fenwick tree [7], F+tree [26] or segment tree. If we store the set $\{s_1, \ldots, s_L\}$ in Fenwick tree, then each query of $\sum_{\ell \geq r} s_i$ can be done in in $O(\log L)$ time, and since each step we only need to change one element into the set, the updating time is also $O(\log L)$. Note that t_j^- can be computed in the same way by scanning from largest m_j to the smallest one.

To sum up, the algorithm first computes all m_j in $O(\bar{d}_2 r)$ time, then sort these numbers using $O(\bar{d}_2 \log \bar{d}_2)$ time, and then compute t_j for all j using two linear scans in $O(\bar{d}_2 \log L)$ time. Here $\log L$ is dominated by $\log \bar{d}_2$ since L can be the number of unique rating levels in the current set $\bar{d}_2(i)$. Therefore, after computing this for all users $i = 1, \ldots, d_1$, the time complexity for computing gradient is

$$O(d_1\bar{d}_2 \log \bar{d}_2 + d_1\bar{d}_2 r) = O(|\bar{\Omega}|(\log \bar{d}_2 + r)).$$

A similar procedure can also be used for computing the Hessian-vector product, and the computation of updating U with fixed V is simplier since the problem becomes decomposable to d_1 independent problems, see eq (13). Due to the page limit we omit the details here; interesting readers can check our code on github.

Compared with the classical matrix factorization, where both ALS and SGD requires $O(|\bar{\Omega}|r)$ time per iteration [13], our algorithm has almost the same complexity, since $\log \bar{d}_2$ is usually smaller than r (typically $r = 100$). Also, since all the temporary memory when computing user i can be released immediately, the

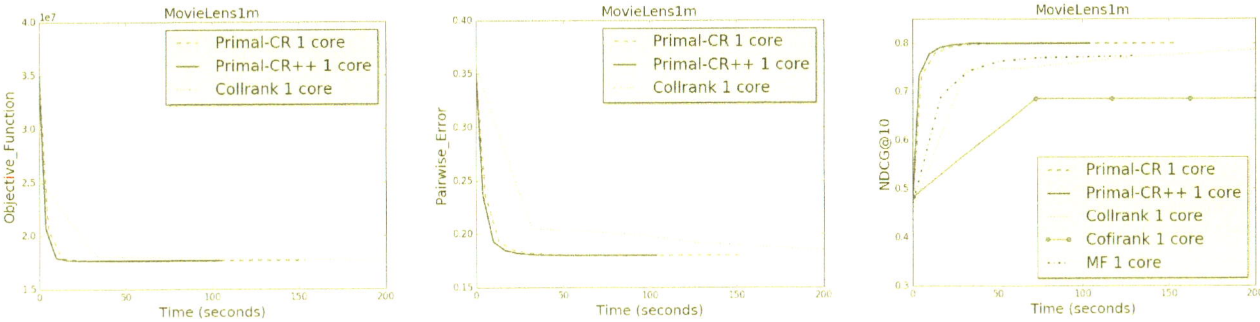

Figure 1: Comparing Primal-CR, Primal-CR++ and Collrank, MovieLens1m data, 200 ratings/user, rank 100, lambda = 5000

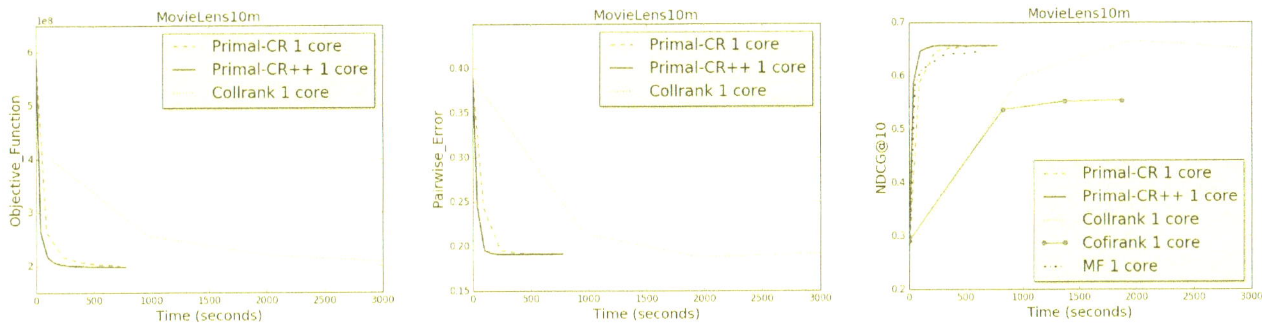

Figure 2: Comparing Primal-CR, Primal-CR++ and Collrank, MovieLens10m data, 500 ratings/user, rank 100, lambda = 7000

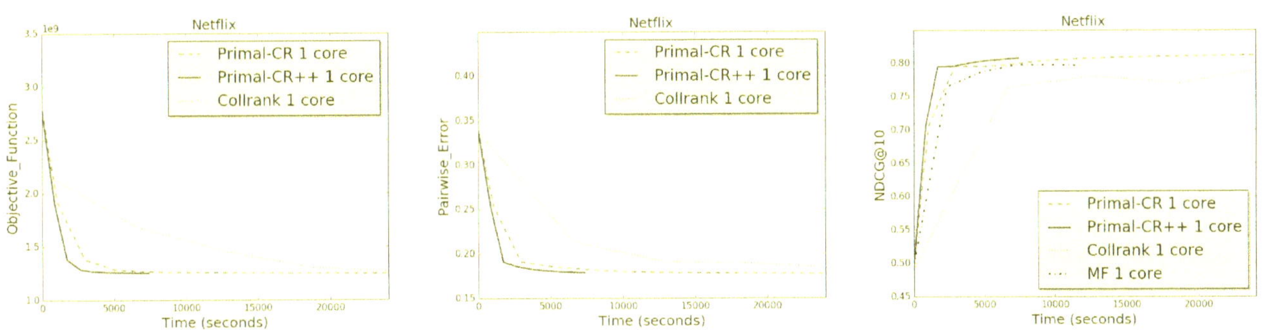

Figure 3: Comparing Primal-CR, Primal-CR++ and Collrank, Netflix data, 200 ratings/user, rank 100, lambda = 10000

only memory cost is still the same with Primal-CR++, which is $O(d_1 r + d_2 r)$.

4.4 Parallelization

Updating U while fixing V can be parallelized easily because each column of U is independent and we can actually solve d_1 independent subproblems at the same time. For the other side, updating V while fixing U can also be parallelized by parallelizing "computing g" part and "computing Ha" part respectively. We implemented the algorithm using parallel computing techniques in Julia by computing g and Ha distributedly and summing them up in the end. We show in section 5.2 that our parallel version of the proposed new algorithm works better than the paralleled version of Collrank algorithm [17].

5 EXPERIMENTS

In this section, we test the performance of our proposed algorithms Primal-CR and Primal-CR++ on real world datasets, and compare with existing methods. All experiments are conducted on the UC Davis Illidan server with an Intel Xeon E5-2640 2.40GHz CPU and 64G RAM. We compare the following methods:

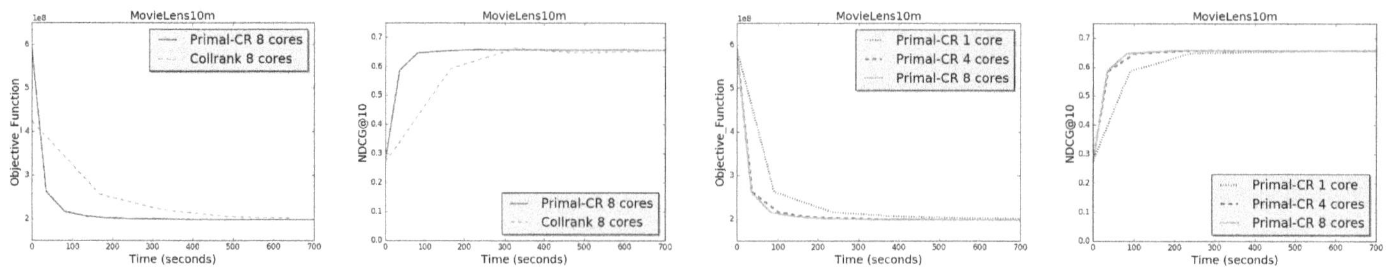

Figure 4: Comparing parallel version of Primal-CR and Collrank and Speedup of Primal-CR, MovieLens10m data, 500 ratings/user, rank 100, lambda = 7000

- Primal-CR and Primal-CR++: our proposed methods implemented in Julia. [2]
- Collrank: the collaborative ranking algorithm proposed in [17]. We use the C++ code released by the authors, and they parallelized their algorithm using OpenMP.
- Cofirank: the classical collaborative ranking algorithm proposed in [25]. We use the C++ code released by the authors.
- MF: the classical matrix factorization model in (1) solved by SGD [13].

We used three data sets (MovieLens1m, Movielens10m, Netflix data) to compare these algorithms. The dataset statistics are summarized in Table 1. The regularization parameter λ used for each datasets are chosen by a random sampled validation set. For the pair-wise based algorithms, we covert the ratings into pair-wise comparisons, by saying that item j is preferred over item k by user i if user i gives a higher rating to item j over item k, and there will be no pair between two items if they have the same rating.

We compare the algorithms in the following three different ways:

- Objective function: since Collrank, Primal-CR, Primal-CR++ have the same objective function, we can compare the convergence speed in terms of the objective function (4) with squared hinge loss.
- Predicted pairwise error: the proportion of pairwise preference comparisons that we predicted correctly out of all the pairwise comparisons in the testing data:

$$\text{pairwise error} = \frac{1}{|\mathcal{T}|} \sum_{\substack{(i,j,k)\in\mathcal{T}\\ Y_{ijk}=1}} 1(X_{ij} > X_{ik}), \tag{16}$$

  where $\mathcal{T}$ represents the test data set and $|\mathcal{T}|$ denotes the size of test data set.
- NDCG@k: a standard performance measure of ranking, defined as:

$$\text{NDCG@}k = \frac{1}{d_1} \sum_{i=1}^{d_1} \frac{\text{DCG@}k(i,\pi_i)}{\text{DCG@}k(i,\pi_i^*)}, \tag{17}$$

  where i represents i-th user and

$$\text{DCG@}k(i,\pi_i) = \sum_{l=1}^{k} \frac{2^{M_{i\pi_i(l)}} - 1}{log_2(l+1)}. \tag{18}$$

  In the DCG definition, $\pi_i(l)$ represents the index of the l-th ranked item for user i in test data based on the score matrix $X = U^T V$ generated, M is the rating matrix and M_{ij} is the rating given to item j by user i. π_i^* is the ordering provided by the underlying ground truth of the rating.

5.1 Compare single thread versions using the same subsamples

Since Collrank cannot scale to the full dataset of Movielens10m and Netflix, we sub-sample data using the same approach in their paper [17] and compare all the methods using the smaller training sets. More specifically, for each data set, we subsampled N ratings for training data and used the rest of ratings as test data. For this subsampled data, we discard users with less than $N + 10$ ratings, since we need at least 10 ratings for test data to compute the NDCG@10.

As shown in Figure 1, 2, 3, both Primal-CR and Primal-CR++ perform considerably better than the existing Collrank algorithm. As data size increases, the performance gap becomes larger. As one can see, for Netflix data where $N = 200$, the speedup is more than 10 times compared to Collrank.

For Cofirank, we observe that it is even slower than Collrank, which confirms the experiments conducted in [17]. Furthermore, Cofirank cannot scale to larger datasets, so we omit the results in Figure 2 and 3.

We also include the classical matrix factorization algorithm in the NDCG comparisons. As shown in our complexity analysis, our proposed algorithms are competitive with MF in terms of speed, and MF is much faster than other collaborative ranking algorithms. Also, we observe that MF converges to a slightly worse solution in MovieLens10m and Netflix datasets, and converges to a much worse solution in MovieLens1m. The reason is that MF minimizes a simple mean square error, while our algorithms are minimizing ranking loss. Based on the experimental results, our algorithm Primal-CR++ should be able to replace MF in many real world recommender systems.

5.2 Compare parallel versions

Since Collrank can be implemented in a parallel fashion, we also implemented the parallel version of our algorithm in Julia. We want to show our algorithm scales up well and is still much faster than Collrank in the multi-core shared memory setting. As shown

[2] Our code is available on https://github.com/wuliwei9278/ml-1m.

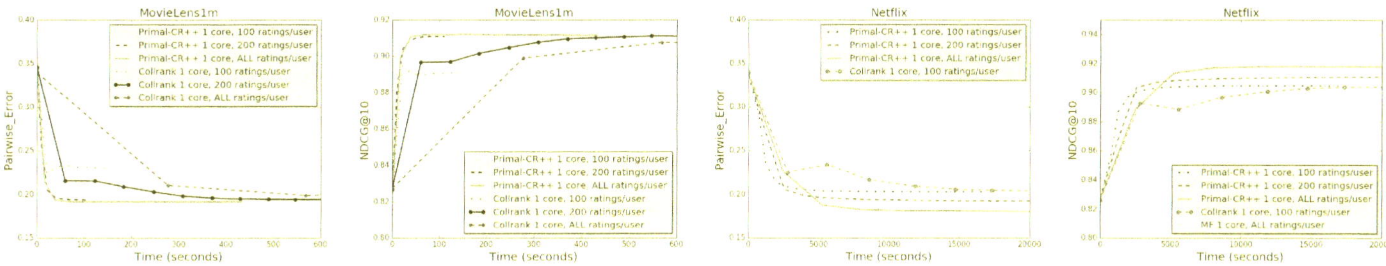

Figure 5: Varies number of ratings per user in training data, MovieLens1m and Netflix data, rank 100

	MovieLens1m	Movielens10m	Netflix
Users	6,040	71,567	2,649,430
Items	3,952	65,134	17,771
Ratings	1,000,209	10,000,054	99,072,112
λ	5,000	7,000	10,000

Table 1: Datasets used for experiments

# cores	1	4	8
Speedup for Primal-CR	1x	2.46x	3.12x
Speedup for Collrank	1x	2.95x	3.47x

Table 2: Scability of Primal-CR and Collrank on Movielens10m

in Figure 4, Primal-CR is still much faster than Collrank when 8 cores are used. Comparing our Primal-CR algorithm in 1 core, 4 cores and 8 cores on the same machine in Figure 4, the speedup is desirable. The speedup of Primal-CR and Collrank is summarized in the Table 2. One can see from the table that the speedup of our Primal-CR algorithm is comparable to Collrank.

5.3 Performance using Full Training Data

Due to the $O(|\Omega|k)$ complexity, existing algorithms cannot deal with large number of pairs, so they always sub-sample a limited number of pairs per user when solving MovieLens10m or Netflix data. For example, for Collrank, the authors fixed number of ratings per user in training as N and only reported N up to 100 for Netflix data. When we tried to apply their code for $N = 200$, the algorithm gets very slow and reports memory error for $N = 500$.

Using our algorithm, we have the ability to solve the full Netflix problem, so a natural question to ask is: Does using more training data help us predict and recommend better? The answer is yes! We conduct the following experiments to verify this: For all the users with more than 20 ratings, we randomly choose 10 ratings as test data and out of the rest ratings we randomly choose up to C ratings per user as training data. One can see in Figure 5, for the same test data, more training data leads to better prediction performance in terms of pairwise error and NDCG. Using all available ratings ($C = d_2$) gives lowest pairwise error and highest NDCG@10, using up to 200 ratings per user ($C = 200$) gives second lowest pairwise error and second highest NDCG@10, and using up to 100 ratings per user ($C = 100$) has the highest pairwise error and lowest NDCG@10. Similar phenomenon is observed for Netflix data in Figure 5. Collrank code does not work for $C = 200$ and $C = d_2$ and even for $C = 100$, it takes more than 20,000 secs to converge while our Primal-CR++ takes less than 5,000 secs for the full Netflix data. The speedup of our algorithm will be even more for a larger C or larger data size d_1 and d_2. We tried to create input file without subsampling for Collrank, we created 344GB input data file and Collrank reported memory error message "Segmentation Fault". We also tried $C = 200$, still got the same error message. It is possible to implement Collrank algorithm by directly working on the rating data, but the time complexity remains the same, so it is clear that our proposed Primal-CR and Primal-CR++ algorithms are much faster.

To the best of our knowledge, our algorithm is the first ranking-based algorithm that can scale to full Netflix data set using a single core, and without sub-sampling. Our proposed algorithm makes the Collaborative Ranking Model in (4) a clear better choice for large-scale recommendation system over standard Matrix Factorization techniques, since we have the same scalability but achieve much better accuracy. Also, our experiments suggest that in practice, when we are given a set of training data, we should try to use all the training data instead of doing sub-sampling as existing algorithms do, and only Primal-CR and Primal-CR++ can scale up to all the ratings.

6 CONCLUSIONS

We considered the collaborative ranking problem setting in which a low-rank matrix is fitted to the data in the form of pairwise comparisons or numerical ratings. We proposed our new optimization algorithms Primal-CR and Primal-CR++ where the time complexity is much better than all the existing approaches. We showed that our algorithms are much faster than state-of-the-art collaborative ranking algorithms on real data sets (MovieLens1m, Movielens10m and Netflix) using same subsampling scheme, and moreover our algorithm is the only one that can scale to the full Movielens10m and Netflix data. We observed that our algorithm has the same efficiency with matrix factorization, while achieving better NDCG since we minimize ranking loss. As a result, we expect our algorithm to be able to replace matrix factorization in many real applications.

REFERENCES

[1] Suhrid Balakrishnan and Sumit Chopra. 2012. Collaborative ranking. In *Proceedings of the fifth ACM international conference on Web search and data mining*. ACM, 143–152.

[2] James Bennett, Stan Lanning, and Netflix Netflix. 2007. The Netflix Prize. In *In KDD Cup and Workshop in conjunction with KDD.*

[3] Zhe Cao, Tao Qin, Tie-Yan Liu, Ming-Feng Tsai, and Hang Li. 2007. Learning to rank: from pairwise approach to listwise approach. In *Proceedings of the 24th international conference on Machine learning.* ACM, 129–136.

[4] Olivier Chapelle and S Sathiya Keerthi. 2010. Efficient algorithms for ranking with SVMs. *Information Retrieval* 13, 3 (2010), 201–215.

[5] Kai-Yang Chiang, Cho-Jui Hsieh, and Inderjit S Dhillon. 2015. Matrix completion with noisy side information. In *Advances in Neural Information Processing Systems.* 3447–3455.

[6] Mukund Deshpande and George Karypis. 2004. Item-based top-n recommendation algorithms. *ACM Transactions on Information Systems (TOIS)* 22, 1 (2004), 143–177.

[7] P. M. Fenwick. 1994. A new data structure for cumulative frequency tables. *Software: Practice and Experience* (1994).

[8] Rainer Gemulla, Erik Nijkamp, Peter J Haas, and Yannis Sismanis. 2011. Large-scale matrix factorization with distributed stochastic gradient descent. In *Proceedings of the 17th ACM SIGKDD international conference on Knowledge discovery and data mining.* ACM, 69–77.

[9] Suriya Gunasekar, Oluwasanmi O Koyejo, and Joydeep Ghosh. 2016. Preference Completion from Partial Rankings. In *Advances in Neural Information Processing Systems.* 1370–1378.

[10] Severin Hacker and Luis Von Ahn. 2009. Matchin: eliciting user preferences with an online game. In *Proceedings of the SIGCHI Conference on Human Factors in Computing Systems.* ACM, 1207–1216.

[11] Cho-Jui Hsieh, Nagarajan Natarajan, and Inderjit S Dhillon. 2015. PU Learning for Matrix Completion. In *ICML.*

[12] T. Joachims. 2002. Optimizing search engines using clickthrough data. In *ACM SIGKDD.*

[13] Yehuda Koren, Robert Bell, and Chris Volinsky. 2009. Matrix factorization techniques for recommender systems. *Computer* 42, 8 (2009).

[14] Oluwasanmi Koyejo, Sreangsu Acharyya, and Joydeep Ghosh. 2013. Retargeted matrix factorization for collaborative filtering. In *Proceedings of the 7th ACM conference on Recommender systems.* ACM, 49–56.

[15] Rong Pan, Yunhong Zhou, Bin Cao, Nathan N Liu, Rajan Lukose, Martin Scholz, and Qiang Yang. 2008. One-class collaborative filtering. In *Data Mining, 2008. ICDM'08. Eighth IEEE International Conference on.* IEEE, 502–511.

[16] Weike Pan and Li Chen. 2013. GBPR: Group Preference Based Bayesian Personalized Ranking for One-Class Collaborative Filtering.. In *IJCAI*, Vol. 13. 2691–2697.

[17] Dohyung Park, Joe Neeman, Jin Zhang, Sujay Sanghavi, and Inderjit S Dhillon. 2015. Preference Completion: Large-scale Collaborative Ranking from Pairwise Comparisons. *stat* 1050 (2015), 16.

[18] Steffen Rendle. 2010. Factorization machines. In *Data Mining (ICDM), 2010 IEEE 10th International Conference on.* IEEE, 995–1000.

[19] Steffen Rendle, Christoph Freudenthaler, Zeno Gantner, and Lars Schmidt-Thieme. 2009. BPR: Bayesian personalized ranking from implicit feedback. In *Proceedings of the twenty-fifth conference on uncertainty in artificial intelligence.* AUAI Press, 452–461.

[20] J Ben Schafer, Dan Frankowski, Jon Herlocker, and Shilad Sen. 2007. Collaborative filtering recommender systems. In *The adaptive web.* Springer, 291–324.

[21] Yue Shi, Martha Larson, and Alan Hanjalic. 2010. List-wise learning to rank with matrix factorization for collaborative filtering. In *Proceedings of the fourth ACM conference on Recommender systems.* ACM, 269–272.

[22] Si Si, Kai-Yang Chiang, Cho-Jui Hsieh, Nikhil Rao, and Inderjit S Dhillon. 2016. Goal-directed inductive matrix completion. In *KDD.*

[23] Nathan Srebro, Jason DM Rennie, and Tommi S Jaakkola. 2004. Maximum-Margin Matrix Factorization.. In *NIPS*, Vol. 17. 1329–1336.

[24] Maksims Volkovs and Richard S Zemel. 2012. Collaborative ranking with 17 parameters. In *Advances in Neural Information Processing Systems.* 2294–2302.

[25] Markus Weimer, Alexandros Karatzoglou, Quoc Viet Le, and Alex Smola. 2007. Maximum margin matrix factorization for collaborative ranking. *Advances in neural information processing systems* (2007), 1–8.

[26] Hsiang-Fu Yu, Cho-Jui Hsieh, Hyokun Yun, SVN Vishwanathan, and Inderjit S Dhillon. 2015. A scalable asynchronous distributed algorithm for topic modeling. In *Proceedings of the 24th International Conference on World Wide Web.* ACM, 1340–1350.

HoORaYs: High-order Optimization of Rating Distance for Recommender Systems

Jingwei Xu
State Key Laboratory for Novel Software Technology
China 210023
jingwei.xu@smail.nju.edu.cn

Yuan Yao*
State Key Laboratory for Novel Software Technology
China 210023
y.yao@nju.edu.cn

Hanghang Tong
Arizona State University
Phoenix, Arizona
hanghang.tong@asu.edu

Xianping Tao
State Key Laboratory for Novel Software Technology
China 210023
txp@nju.edu.cn

Jian Lu
State Key Laboratory for Novel Software Technology
China 210023
lj@nju.edu.cn

ABSTRACT

Latent factor models have become a prevalent method in recommender systems, to predict users' preference on items based on the historical user feedback. Most of the existing methods, explicitly or implicitly, are built upon the *first-order rating distance* principle, which aims to minimize the difference between the estimated and real ratings. In this paper, we generalize such first-order rating distance principle and propose a new latent factor model (HoORaYs) for recommender systems. The core idea of the proposed method is to explore *high-order rating distance*, which aims to minimize not only (i) the difference between the estimated and real ratings of the same (user, item) pair (i.e., the first-order rating distance), but also (ii) the difference between the estimated and real rating difference of the same user across different items (i.e., the second-order rating distance). We formulate it as a regularized optimization problem, and propose an effective and scalable algorithm to solve it. Our analysis from the geometry and Bayesian perspectives indicate that by exploring the high-order rating distance, it helps to reduce the *variance* of the estimator, which in turns leads to better generalization performance (e.g., smaller prediction error). We evaluate the proposed method on four real-world data sets, two with explicit user feedback and the other two with implicit user feedback. Experimental results show that the proposed method consistently outperforms the state-of-the-art methods in terms of the prediction accuracy.

CCS CONCEPTS

•**Information systems** →**Information systems applications; Collaborative filtering;** *Data mining;*

KDD '17, August 13-17, 2017, Halifax, NS, Canada

DOI: 10.1145/3097983.3098019

KEYWORDS

High-order distance, recommender systems, latent factor model, collaborative filtering

1 INTRODUCTION

In recent years, researchers have devoted great efforts to the development of recommender systems in many real-world applications [4, 6, 11]. The key task of recommender systems is to predict the users' preference on items. Collaborative filtering (CF) methods and content-based methods have been widely used to achieve this task. For example, matrix factorization [11] takes ratings as input and outputs the latent vectors for users and items; it becomes a popular base for recommender systems, largely due to its great success at the Netflix Prize. To further improve the recommendation accuracy, Wang et al. [20] propose the collaborative topic regression (CTR) rating model to incorporate item content; Ma et al. [12] model social trust (Sorec) by incorporating social relationships and ratings. The combination of CTR and Sorec is also explored [2, 17].

A line of existing work has focused on employing different types of data (e.g., ratings, item content, social relationships, etc.) so as to make more informed and accurate recommendations. In this work, we focus on an orthogonal line work, i.e., the optimization formulation aspect.

From the optimization viewpoint, most of the existing methods, explicitly or implicitly, are built upon the *first-order rating distance* principle. That is, these methods seek for an 'optimal' latent representations for users and items, which minimize the differences between the estimated and real ratings of the *same* (user, item) pair. Conceptually, minimizing the first-order distance (between the real rating to estimated rating) can be viewed as a self-calibration process. However, the solution space of the optimization problem could be large, especially when the available user feedback information is sparse, which might result in a *biased* estimator for the latent vectors of users and items.

In this paper, we generalize the first-order distance principle and propose to leverage the high-order distance to improve the recommendation performance. The core idea of the proposed method is to explore *high-order rating distance*, which aims to minimize not only (i) the difference between the estimated and real ratings of the same (user, item) pair (i.e., the first-order rating distance), but also (ii) the difference between the estimated and real rating difference of the same user across different items (i.e., the second-order rating distance). We hypothesize that by exploring high-order distance, it will help shrink the solution space of the corresponding optimization problem. By doing so, the *variance* of the estimator (i.e., the latent representations of users and items) could be mitigated, which will in turn lead to better generalization performance (e.g., a smaller prediction error).

The main contributions of this paper include:

- **New Model and Algorithm** that embrace the high-order rating distance in the latent factor methods for recommender systems. The proposed model HoORaYs can handle both explicit and implicit user feedback, as well as the case when content information is available. The proposed algorithm is able to find local optima with a linear time complexity.
- **Analysis** from both the geometric perspective and the Bayesian perspective for the proposed model, which provides key insight on how the high-order distance reduces the variance, and how to generalize the high-order distance based optimization to other recommendation models.
- **Experimental evaluations** on four real-world data sets showing the effectiveness of the proposed method. For example, the proposed method outperforms the best competitors by up to 24.3% improvement in terms of the prediction accuracy.

The rest of the paper is organized as follows. In Section 2, we present the problem statement. In Section 3, we describe the proposed model with the geometric interpretation, Bayesian interpretation, and algorithm analysis. In Section 4, we present the experimental results. In Section 5, we review the related work. Finally, we conclude the paper in Section 6.

2 PROBLEM STATEMENT

In this section, we provide the problem statement and some background knowledge of our proposed model.

2.1 The Recommendation Problem

In recommender systems, the two kinds of fundamental elements are users and items. We assume there are M users and N items in the recommender system. We denote the latent vectors for users as $U = \{u_i\}_{i=1}^{m}$, and the latent vectors for items as $V = \{v_j\}_{j=1}^{n}$. The length of these latent vectors is K. The observed ratings are usually denoted as $R = \{r_{ij} | r_{ij} \in [1, r_{max}]\}$, where r_{ij} represents the rating that user i gives to item j, and the value r_{max} is the scale of rating in the target recommender system (e.g., 5 stars on *MovieLens*).

Based on the above notations, we define the target problem as follows

Problem 1. *The Recommendation Problem*

Given: *(1) the set of existing ratings R from users to items, (2) a user i, and (3) an item j;*

Find: *the estimated rating $\hat{r}_{ij}$ from user i to item j.*

As we can see from the definition, the input of our problem includes the existing ratings. Our focus is on the optimization aspect instead of employing more types of data, although the proposed method can be similarly applied when more types data are available. The goal is to predict the unobserved ratings from users to items, and we can directly obtain the ratings as long as we have learned the latent vectors U and V.

2.2 Latent Factor Models: Matrix Factorization

In recent years, matrix factorization based collaborative filtering [11] becomes one of the most popular methods to solve the recommendation problem. In the view of matrix factorization, the users and items could be represented by factors in the same latent factor space. For example, user i is represented by a latent factor vector u_i, and item j is represented by a latent factor vector v_j. So we predict the rating that user i gives to item j with the inner product of the two corresponding latent factor vectors

$$\hat{r}_{ij} = u_i^T v_j \quad (1)$$

We use the observed ratings to learn the latent factor vectors. Commonly, we minimize the following optimization function

$$\min_{U^*, V^*} \sum_{r_{ij} \in R} (r_{ij} - u_i^T v_j)^2 \quad (2)$$

where square loss is used as the loss function, and R is the set of the observed ratings.

2.3 Model Variance Reduction

From statistical learning perspective, a good estimator (e.g., latent vectors in our recommendation problem) should have small prediction errors (*PE*) on both training and the new data. With the bias-variance decomposition [5], the expected prediction error is the sum of three terms: the *irreducible errors*, *Bias*, and *Variance*

$$PE = \sigma^2 + Bias^2 + Variance \quad (3)$$

It is well known that the local curvature can be picked up to fit the training data when the model becomes more complex. However, such a complex model suffers from the high *variance*, and hence to a high *PE* when estimating on the new data (overfitting). To deal with the overfitting in Eq. (1), researchers added ridge constraints (i.e., L2-regularization) on the parameters u_i and v_j by controlling their sum of squares, so that the original unconstrained optimization problem becomes

$$minimize \sum_{r_{ij} \in R} (r_{ij} - u_i^T v_j)^2 \ \ s.t. \sum_{i=1}^{m} (u_i)^2 \le t_u, \sum_{j=1}^{n} (v_j)^2 \le t_v \quad (4)$$

where $t_u > 0$ and $t_v > 0$. The above optimization problem can be re-written as

$$\mathcal{L} = \sum_{r_{ij} \in R} (r_{ij} - u_i^T v_j)^2 + \lambda_u \sum_{i=1}^{m} ||u_i||^2 + \lambda_v \sum_{j=1}^{n} ||v_j||^2 \quad (5)$$

where λ_u and λ_v are the parameters to control the L2 regularization terms. With the proper λ_u and λ_v, Eq. (5) balances *bias* and *variance* to reach the lower *PE*.

3 HIGH-ORDER OPTIMIZATION OF RATING DISTANCE

In this section, we describe the proposed HoORaYs model (Subsection 3.1). Then, we analyze why the proposed model can reduce the *variance* of the estimator from two different perspectives, including geometric interpretation (Subsection 3.2) and Bayesian interpretation (Subsection 3.3). Finally, we present a brief algorithm analysis in terms of its optimality and complexity (Subsection 3.4).

3.1 The HoORaYs Model

The core idea of HoORaYs is to use high-order rating distance to reduce the *variance* of the estimator (i.e., the latent factors for users and items) by shrinking the solution space of the optimization problem in Eq. (4). The intuition is as follows. By optimizing the first-order distance, we basically want to find a good estimator which matches a user's *preference* on each of the observed *items*. By introducing the additional high-order distance, we require the learnt latent factors to *also* capture the subtle *preference difference* of a user across different *item pairs*.

In particular, the error between the real rating r_{ij} and the estimated rating $\hat{r}_{ij}$ in Eq. (4) can be treated as the distance between two ratings. In addition the rating distance of $< r_{ij}, \hat{r}_{ij} >$ pair, other rating errors from different kinds of pairs (e.g., $< r_{ij'}, \hat{r}_{ij} >$, $< r_{ij'}, r_{ij} >$, and so on) can also be measured as rating distances. These rating distances have their own meaning in the context of recommender systems. For example, the distance between $r_{ij'}$ and r_{ij} (denoted by D) means the real difference between item j and item j' under user i; the distance between $r_{ij'}$ and $\hat{r}_{ij}$ (denoted by $\hat{D}$) means the estimated difference between item j and item j' under user i after estimating $\hat{r}_{ij}$. Furthermore, when $r_{ij'}$ is fixed for both D and $\hat{D}$, we can measure the distance between D and $\hat{D}$. The error between D and $\hat{D}$ reflects the accuracy of learned latent vectors of user i and item j. This error is the distance between two rating distances, and we call this distance of distance as second-order rating distance.

As we can see, both first-order and second-order distances reflect the learned latent vectors of user/items. If we add second-order rating distance to the optimization problem in Eq. (4) as an additional constraint, we could further reduce the *variance* of the latent vectors of users/items in recommender systems. The optimization problem of our proposed HoORaYs is written as below

$$\begin{aligned} minimize & \sum_{r_{ij}\in R} (r_{ij} - u_i^T v_j)^2 \\ s.t. & \sum_{i=1}^{m} (u_i)^2 \leq t_u, \sum_{j=1}^{n} (v_j)^2 \leq t_v \\ & \sum_{r_{ij}} \sum_{r_{i'j'}} I_{iji'j'} (\sigma(u_i^T v_j, r_{i'j'}) - \sigma(r_{ij}, r_{i'j'}))^2 = 0 \end{aligned} \tag{6}$$

where $\sigma(x, y) = 1/(1 + e^{-(x-y)})$, and $I_{iji'j'} = 1$ if ratings r_{ij} and $r_{i'j'}$ exist with $i' = i \bigwedge j' \neq j \bigvee i' \neq i \bigwedge j' = j$. The optimization problem with second-order rating distance constraint can be re-written as follow

$$\begin{aligned} \underset{U^*, V^*}{\text{argmin}} & \sum_{r_{ij}} (r_{ij} - u_i^T v_j)^2 + \lambda_u \sum_{i=1}^{m} ||u_i||^2 + \lambda_v \sum_{j=1}^{n} ||v_j||^2 \\ & + \lambda_d \sum_{r_{ij}} \sum_{r_{i'j'}} I_{iji'j'} (\sigma(u_i^T v_j, r_{i'j'}) - \sigma(r_{ij}, r_{i'j'}))^2 \end{aligned} \tag{7}$$

where λ_d is the parameter to control the effect of second-order rating distance.

Speed Gear. Since the complexity of second-order distance in Eq. (7) is roughly $O(|R|(|\overline{R_u}| + |\overline{R_v}|))$, we propose to speedup the model learning process based on two key observations: (i) the rating scale is usually small for recommender systems (e.g., 1-5 stars), and (ii) the contributions of different ratings from other users/items are equal to each other if they share the same rating value. Hence, the loss function in Eq. (7) could be re-written as

$$\begin{aligned} \underset{U^*, V^*}{\text{argmin}} & \sum_{r_{ij}} (r_{ij} - u_i^T v_j)^2 + \lambda_u \sum_{i=1}^{m} ||u_i||^2 + \lambda_v \sum_{j=1}^{n} ||v_j||^2 \\ & + \lambda_d \sum_{r_{ij}} \sum_{r=1}^{r_{max}} |\Omega_{r_{ij},r}| (\sigma(u_i^T v_j, r) - \sigma(r_{ij}, r))^2 \end{aligned} \tag{8}$$

where r_{max} is the maximal rating value (e.g., $r_{max} = 5$ in *MovieLens*), and $|\Omega_{r_{ij},r}|$ is the total number of ratings that the user i rated to other items with value r or the item j received from other users with value r.

Update Rules. We use stochastic gradient descent to optimize Eq. (8). In detail, we alternatively optimize U, V in each iteration. In each iteration, we take the partial derivatives of Eq. (8) with respect to u_i and v_j, which lead to the following update rules

$$\begin{aligned} u_i \leftarrow & - \lambda_u u_i + (r_{ij} - u_i^T v_j) v_j \\ & + \lambda_d \sum_{r=1}^{r_{max}} |\Omega_{r_{ij},r}| (\sigma(r_{ij}, r) \sigma(u_i^T v_j, r)(1 - \sigma(u_i^T v_j, r)) v_j \\ & - \sigma(u_i^T v_j, r)^2 (1 - \sigma(u_i^T v_j, r)) v_j) \end{aligned} \tag{9}$$

$$\begin{aligned} v_j \leftarrow & - \lambda_v v_j + (r_{ij} - u_i^T v_j) u_i \\ & + \lambda_d \sum_{r=1}^{r_{max}} |\Omega_{r_{ij},r}| (\sigma(r_{ij}, r) \sigma(u_i^T v_j, r)(1 - \sigma(u_i^T v_j, r)) u_i \\ & - \sigma(u_i^T v_j, r)^2 (1 - \sigma(u_i^T v_j, r)) u_i) \end{aligned} \tag{10}$$

We summarize our fast learning algorithm in Alg. 1, where α is the learning rate, ∇ is the partial derivative operator, and we use stochastic gradient descent method to learn the parameters.

3.2 Geometric Interpretation of HoORaYs

Here we present the geometric interpretation of the proposed HoORaYs. By adding the constraint of second-order rating distance to the optimization problem in Eq. (4), the solution space to U and V can be further shrunk, which leads to the decrease on *variance*.

The illustrative example in Fig. 1 shows how the constraint of second-order rating distance could shrink the original solution space. Suppose that the latent factor space is 2-dimensional, and each user/item has its place, which is presented as the latent vector in the space. In Fig. 1(a), taking user i and item j for example

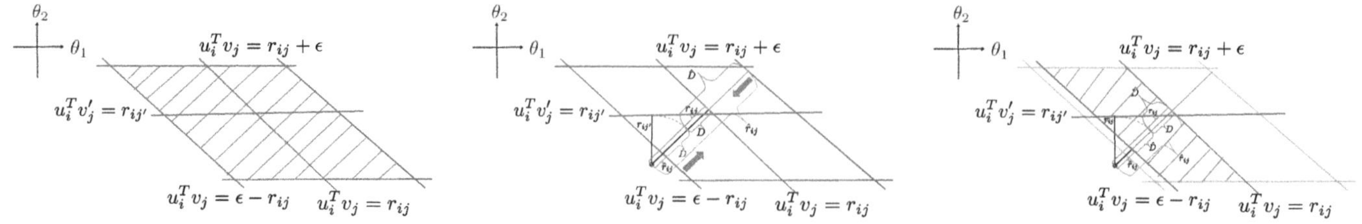

(a) The solution space of matrix factorization

(b) The solution space with the constraint of second-order rating distance (before optimization)

(c) The solution space with the constraint of second-order rating distance (after optimization)

Figure 1: The illustrative example of applying the constraint of second-order rating distance to matrix factorization. We can see that second-order distance further shrinks the solution space, which means to reduce *variance* of prediction error for the optimization problem. Notice that, the second-order distance will also shrink the solution space on the other side, for clarify, we do not indicate that in the figure.

Algorithm 1: Learning HoORaYs

Input: the set of observed ratings R, and the maximal rating scale r_{max}
Output: latent vectors of users U, latent vectors of items V

initialize U, V
repeat
  for $r_{ij} \in R$ **do**
    for $r \leftarrow 1, ..., r_{max}$ **do**
      for $f \leftarrow 1, ..., k$ **do**
        update $u_{i,f} \leftarrow u_{i,f} - \alpha \nabla_{u_{i,f}}$ as defined in Eq. (9)
        update $v_{j,f} \leftarrow v_{j,f} - \alpha \nabla_{v_{j,f}}$ as defined in Eq. (10)
until *convergence*;
return U^*, V^*

and by assuming that v_j and r_{ij} are given, we want to find u_i by first-order rating distance (e.g., matrix factorization). Ideally, $u_i^T v_j = r_{ij}$ exists for the perfect u_i, and this line could be plotted in the space. As shown in Fig. 1(a), any point in this line is a solution to u_i, and all points satisfy the best condition to r_{ij}. Then, we allow the error to u_i, e.g., $|u_i^T v_j - r_{ij}| < \epsilon$. With the two paralleled lines $u_i^T v_j = r_{ij} + \epsilon$ and $u_i^T v_j = r_{ij} - \epsilon$ (two red lines in Fig. 1(a)), any point inside the two bounded lines is a solution that satisfies to the error ϵ. Now, we consider another item j' with the given $v_{j'}$ into the space, and the solution space of u_i is then bounded by the four red lines in the Fig. 1(a). In Fig. 1(b), the black point is the origin of the latent factor space, and the length of perpendicular distance from origin to line $u_i^T v_j = r_{ij}$ is r_{ij} when u_i is normalized. $r_{ij'}$, denoted as a black line segment, can also measured in the space. After coinciding line segment $r_{ij'}$ to line segment r_{ij}, several second-order distances appear. In Fig. 1(b), the second-order distance between r_{ij} and $r_{ij'}$ is denoted as D. Based on the two worst estimated $\hat{r}_{ij}$ bounded by ϵ, we could point out two second-order distances between $\hat{r}_{ij}$ and $r_{ij'}$ as $\hat{D}$ in Fig. 1(b). By the constraint of $|\hat{D} - D|^2 = 0$, the error bounds would shrink from both sides. Ideally, as the optimization problem in Eq. (6) reaches the optima, the shaded area will be compressed by the constraint of second-order rating distance. Shrinking the solution space reduces the *variance* (e.g., almost half of original solution space is shrunk in Fig. 1(c)), and might reduce the prediction error (*PE*) of the rating model in Eq. (1).

3.3 Bayesian Interpretation of HoORaYs

In addition to the geometric interpretation, we present our proposed HoORaYs from Bayesian perspective. Minh et al. [14] presented a probabilisitic model for matrix factorization. In probabilistic matrix factorization, they assumed that ratings are generated by a specific generative process. In order to leverage information from content (e.g., reviews, tags), researchers used topic modeling approaches to extract latent topics from items. Collaborative topic regression (CTR) model was proposed by Wang et al. [20] to deal with recommendation problem by considering the merit of both probabilistic topic modeling and collaborative filtering.

The proposed HoORaYs can apply to both MF and CTR. Take CTR model as the rating model, The graphical model of HoORaYs is shown in Fig. 2. We treat the constraint of second-order distance as an observed random variable after observing the rating. Next, instead of simply using the distance between the real r_{ij} and estimated $\hat{r}_{ij}$ as the optimization target in CTR, we optimize over the second-order distance $d_{iji'j'}$ which is the distance between the real rating distance (between r_{ij} and $r_{i'j'}$) and the estimated rating distance (between $\hat{r}_{ij}$ and $r_{i'j'}$). The generative process of HoORaYs is as follows

- For each user i, draw the latent vector $u_i \sim \mathcal{N}(0, \lambda_u^{-1} \mathbf{I}_K)$
- For each item j
  - Draw topic proportions $\theta_j \sim Dirichlet(\alpha)$
  - Draw the latent offset $\epsilon_j \sim \mathcal{N}(0, \lambda_v^{-1} \mathbf{I}_K)$ and set the item latent vector as $v_j = \epsilon_j + \theta_j$
  - For each word w_{jn_w},

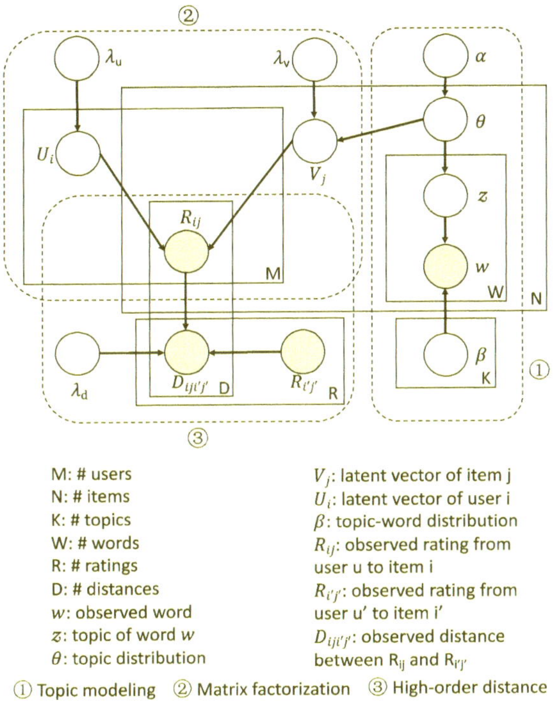

Figure 2: The probabilistic graphical model of HoORaYs.

  - ∗ Draw topic assignment $z_{jn_w} \sim \text{Mult}(\theta_j)$
  - ∗ Draw word $w_{jn_w} \sim \text{Mult}(\beta_{z_{jn_w}})$
- For each pair of user and item, draw the rating

$$r_{ij} \sim \mathcal{N}(u_i^T v_j, c_{ij}^{-1})$$

- For each second-order rating distance of r_{ij} vs. $r_{i'j'}$ ($i' = i \wedge j' \neq j \vee i' \neq i \wedge j' = j$), draw the distance

$$d_{iji'j'} \sim \mathcal{N}(\sigma(u_i^T v_j, r_{i'j'}), \lambda_d^{-1})$$

where $\mathcal{N}(x|\mu, \sigma^2)$ is the Gaussian distribution with mean μ and variance σ^2, $\mathbf{I_K}$ is the $K * K$ identity matrix, the function g is the sigmoid function where $\sigma(x, y) = 1/(1 + e^{-(x-y)})$, and c_{ij} is the confidence parameter for the rating r_{ij}, which is introduced by Wang et al. [20] to solve the *one-class* collaborative filtering problem with implicit feedback. Specifically, we set c_{ij} a higher value if $r_{ij} = 1$, and we give c_{ij} a lower value if $r_{ij} = 0$.

The conditional distribution over the observed high-order distance is

$$P(D|R, U, V, \lambda_d^{-1}) = \prod_i^m \prod_j^n \prod_{i'}^m \prod_{j'}^n \mathcal{N}(\sigma(u_i^T v_j, r_{i'j'}), \lambda_d^{-1})^{I_{iji'j'}} \quad (11)$$

where $I_{iji'j'} = 1$ if ratings r_{ij} and $r_{i'j'}$ exist with $i' = i \wedge j' \neq j \vee i' \neq i \wedge j' = j$. Then, we have the following equation for the posterior probability of the latent vectors of HoORaYs by the Bayesian inference

$$p(U, V|D, R, C, \lambda_d, \lambda_u, \lambda_v) \propto p(D|R, \lambda_d) p(R|U, V, C) p(U|\lambda_u) p(v|\lambda_v) \quad (12)$$

Given the topic parameter β, computing the full posterior of u_i, v_j, and θ_j directly is intractable. Here, we develop an EM-style algorithm to learn the maximum a posteriori estimates. Notice that, maximizing the posterior in Eq. (12) is equivalent to maximizing the complete log likelihood of θ, U, V, R and D, given λ_u, λ_v, λ_d, C, and β.

$$\begin{aligned} \mathcal{L}^* = &- \frac{\lambda_u}{2} \sum_{i=1}^m u_i^T u_i - \frac{\lambda_v}{2} \sum_{j=1}^n (v_j - \theta_j)^T (v_j - \theta_j) \\ &+ \sum_{j=1}^n \sum_{n_w=1}^W \log(\sum_k \theta_{jk} \beta_{k, w_{jn_w}}) \\ &- \frac{\lambda_d}{2} \sum_{r_{ij}} \sum_{r=1}^{r_{max}} |\Omega_{r_{ij}, r}| (\sigma(r_{ij}, r) - \sigma(u_i^T v_j, r))^2 \\ &- \sum_{r_{ij}} \frac{c_{ij}}{2} (r_{ij} - u_i^T v_j)^2 \end{aligned} \quad (13)$$

where r_{max} is the maximal rating value (e.g., $r_{max} = 5$ in *MovieLens*), and $|\Omega_{r_{ij}, r}|$ is the total number of ratings that the user i rated to other items with value r or the item j received from other users with value r.

We use stochastic gradient ascent to optimize Eq. (13). In detail, we iteratively optimize U, V, and the topic proportions θ. Given the current estimate of θ_j, we could find optima of U and V via similar equations to Eq. (9) and Eq. (10). Given the current U and V, we update the topic proportions θ as follows. We first define $q(z_{jn_w} = k) = \phi_{jn_w k}$, and then separate the items that contain θ_j and apply Jensen's inequality as follows

$$\begin{aligned} \mathcal{L}(\theta_j) \geq &- \frac{\lambda_v}{2} (v_j - \theta_j)^T (v_j - \theta_j) \\ &+ \sum_{n_w=1} \sum_k \phi_{jn_w k} (\log \theta_{jk} \beta_{k, w_{jn_w}} - \log \phi_{jn_w k}) \\ &= \mathcal{L}(\theta_j, \Phi_j) \end{aligned} \quad (14)$$

Let $\Phi_j = (\phi_{jn_w k})_{n_w=1, k=1}^{W \times K}$. $\mathcal{L}(\theta_j)$ has a tight lower bound $\mathcal{L}(\theta_j, \Phi_j)$. Analytically, we cannot optimize θ_j. Hence, we use projection gradient approach to optimize the other parameters U, V, $\theta_{1:N}$, and $\phi_{1:N}$. After estimating U, V, and ϕ, we could optimize β as follows

$$\beta_{kw} \propto \sum_j \sum_{n_w} \phi_{jn_w k} [w_{jn_w} = w] \quad (15)$$

After the optimal parameters U^*, V^*, $\theta_{1:N}^*$, and β^* are learned, each rating r_{ij} can be estimated as

$$r_{ij} \approx (u_i^*)^T v_j^* \quad (16)$$

3.4 Algorithm Analysis

In this part, we analyze the effectiveness and efficiency of our algorithms.

The effectiveness of the proposed HoORaYs is summarized in Lemma 3.1. Overall, it finds local optima in the solution space of the latent vectors from users and items. The proposed optimization problem (Eq. (8)) is not convex wrt the coefficients (u_i, v_j), and such a local minimum is acceptable in practice.

Lemma 3.1 (**Effectiveness of HoORaYs**). *Fixing the ratings in R, HoORaYs finds the local minimum for the optimization problem in Eq. (8).*

Table 1: The statistics of the four data sets.

Data	*Lastfm*	*Delicious*	*MovieLens*	*Google Play*
#users	1,892	1,867	2,113	170,781
#items	17,632	69,226	10,197	104,061
#tags	11,946	53,388	13,222	N/A
#taggings	186,479	437,593	47,957	N/A
#words	N/A	N/A	N/A	10,569
#reviews	N/A	N/A	N/A	3,367,435
#ratings/hits	92,834	104,799	855,598	3,367,435
rating Scale	[1]	[1]	[0.5-5]	[1-5]

PROOF SKETCH. If we fix either the U matrix or the V matrix, the optimization problem becomes convex and the corresponding step in Alg. 1 can find the global optima. Next, based on the alternating procedure of learning parameters U and V in Alg. 1, we have that Alg. 1 finds a local minimum for the optimization problem in Eq. (8).

The time complexity of the proposed HoORaYs is summarized in Lemma 3.2. This Lemma shows that HoORaYs requires *linear time* for learning latent vectors of users and items (e.g., step 3-7 in Alg. 1); and it scales linearly wrt the number of observed ratings in the training phase (e.g., step 2-7 in Alg. 1).

LEMMA 3.2 (**Time Complexity of HoORaYs**). *Fixing the set of ratings R, and r_{max}, HoORaYs requires $O(|R|)$ time for each iteration in Alg. 1*

PROOF. For each iteration in Alg. 1, we need $O(|R|)$ time for the loop that starts from step 3. The time cost for the loop that starts from step 4 is r_{max}, and step 5-7 costs $O(k)$ time for updating parameters. Therefore, the total time cost of the iteration of step 2-7 is $O(|R| \cdot r_{max} \cdot k \cdot m)$, where m is the maximum iteration number for Alg. 1. Notice that, r_{max}, k and m are small constants, so the total time cost of Alg. 1 can be written as $O(|R|)$. □

4 EXPERIMENTS

In this section, we present the experimental evaluations. All the experiments help us to answer the following questions:

- How accurate is the proposed method compared to the state-of-the-art methods?
- How efficient is the proposed method compared to the state-of-the-art methods? How scalable is the proposed method?
- How do the parameters affect the performance of our model?

4.1 Experimental Setup

4.1.1 Data Sets. In this paper, we use four real-world data sets, i.e., *Google Play*, *MovieLens*, *Lastfm*, and *Delicious*. The first data set was collected by Chen et al. [3], and the other three data sets were provided by Cantador et al. [1]. Table 1 shows the statistics of the four data sets. For the *Lastfm* and *Delicious* data, the user feedback is implicitly given by listening to a song (on *Lastfm*) and bookmarking an item (on *Delicious*), respectively. Following typical implicit feedback setting, we set the user rating as '1' if the implicit feedback is observed, and '0' otherwise. For the *MovieLens* and *Google Play* data, there are explicit ratings from users to items. The rating scale is $[0.5 \sim 5]$ with step 0.5 for *MovieLens* data, and $[1 \sim 5]$ with step 1 for *Google Play* data. As for the content information, we use the aggregated review content in the first data set. We follow standard processing steps including stop-words removal, short-words removal, low-frequency words removal, high-frequency words removal, and stemming. For the other three data sets, we directly use the tag information on items as content input.

4.1.2 Evaluation Metrics. In this paper, we use the following four evaluation metrics. Specially, we use Root Mean Square Error (*RMSE*) and Mean Absolute Error (*MAE*) for the case of explicit feedback, and use *Recall@N* and Area Under the Curve (*AUC*) for the case of implicit feedback. In other words, *RMSE* and *MAE* are used for the *Google Play* and *MovieLens* data, and they are defined as

$$RMSE = \sqrt{\frac{\sum_{r_{ij} \in T} (\hat{r}_{ij} - r_{ij})^2}{|T|}}$$

$$MAE = \frac{\sum_{r_{ij} \in T} |\hat{r}_{ij} - r_{ij}|}{|T|}$$

where T is the set of ratings to be evaluated as the test set.

Recall@N and *AUC* are used for *Lastfm* and *Delicious*. For a given user, *Recall@N* is defined as the ratio between the number of items that the user likes in Top N ranking list, and the total number of items that the user likes; *AUC* indicates the probability that a randomly chosen observed example is ranked higher than a randomly chosen unobserved example. For these two metrics, we average them over all the users as the final result.

4.1.3 Compared methods. In the experiment section, we use HoORaYs to denote the proposed model that considers content information, and use HoORaYs$_0$ to denote the proposed model without content information. We compare our methods (HoORaYs$_0$ and HoORaYs) with some state-of-the-art recommendation algorithms including probabilistic matrix factorization (PMF) [14], collaborative topic regression (CTR) [20], and Bayesian personalized ranking (BPR) [18]. Note that BPR is specially designed for the implicit feedback, and we only compare with BPR in the implicit feedback case. As for parameters, the dimension of the latent vectors is set to 200 for the proposed methods and all the competitors. The reported results come from the best parameters tuned for each model. For HoORaYs$_0$ and HoORaYs, we set $\alpha = 0.01$, $\lambda_u = 0.1$, and $\lambda_v = 0.1$ ($\lambda_v = 0.5$ for *Google Play*), where α is the learning rate. Since λ_d is more sensitive to data, we set $\lambda_d = 0.01$ on *Google Play* and *MovieLens* data sets, $\lambda_d = 0.1$ on *Lastfm* data, and $\lambda_d = 5$ on *Delicious* data.

For all the four data sets, we randomly select 75% of the user feedback as training data, the use the remaining data as test set.

4.1.4 Reproducibility of experiments. All the datasets are publicly available. All the parameter settings are stated in the previous subsection. We will release the code of the proposed algorithm through the first author's website* upon the publication of the paper.

4.2 Evaluation Results

Here, we present the experimental results.

*http://moon.nju.edu.cn/people/jingweixu/

Table 2: The comparisons of *RMSE* results on *Google Play* and *MovieLens* data. The proposed methods (HoORaYs$_0$ and HoORaYs) outperform the compared methods.

Data set	PMF	CTR	HoORaYs$_0$	HoORaYs
Google Play	1.2958	1.2842	1.2747	**1.2733**
MovieLens	0.7764	0.7724	0.7645	**0.7620**

Table 3: The comparisons of *MAE* results on for *Google Play* and *MovieLens* data. The proposed methods (HoORaYs$_0$ and HoORaYs) outperform the compared methods.

Data set	PMF	CTR	HoORaYs$_0$	HoORaYs
Google Play	1.0132	0.9997	0.9855	**0.9827**
MovieLens	0.5977	0.5952	0.5814	**0.5808**

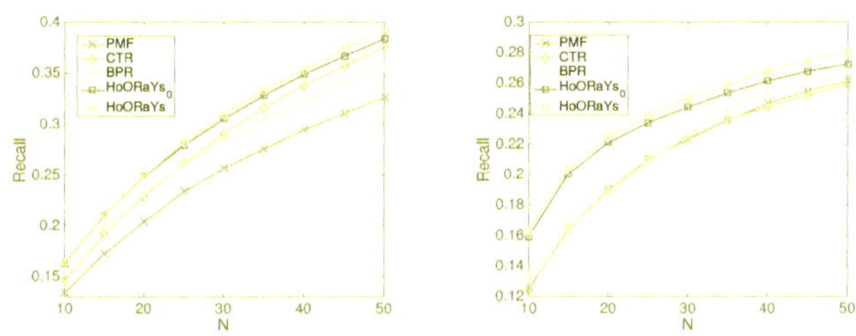

(a) *Lastfm* data (b) *Delicious* data

Figure 3: The comparisons of *Recall@N* results on *lastfm* and *Delicious* data.The proposed methods outperform the compared methods on both data sets.

Explicit user feedback. We first show the performance of the proposed methods for explicit feedback. Table 2 and Table 3 show the results on *Google Play* and *MovieLens* with *RMSE* and *MAE*, respectively.

We can first observe from the tables that, the proposed HoORaYs$_0$ and HoORaYs significantly outperform PMF and CTR in terms of both *RMSE* and *MAE*. For example, in Table 2, HoORaYs achieves 0.85% and 1.35% improvement over the best competitor (CTR) wrt *RMSE* on *Google Play* and *MovieLens*, respectively. As for the *MAE* metric in Table. 3, HoORaYs outperforms the best competitor (CTR) by 1.70% v.s. 2.42% on *Google Play* and *MovieLens*, respectively.

Second, we can see that HoORaYs$_0$ also outperforms CTR on both data sets, although CTR considers content information while HoORaYs$_0$ does not. This indicates the importance of using high-order distance during the optimization process.

Third, the performance on the *MovieLens* data is better than that on the *Google Play* data. This is due to the fact that the *Google Play* data is much sparser than the *MovieLens* data (0.02% sparsity on *Google Play* and 3.97% sparsity on *MovieLens*).

Overall, the above results indicate that the proposed methods are more accurate than the compared methods for the case of explicit feedback, and that the high-order rating distance plays an important role for improving the prediction accuracy of recommendation.

Table 4: The comparisons of *AUC* results on *Lastfm* and *Delicious* data. The proposed methods (HoORaYs$_0$ and HoORaYs) outperform the compared methods on both data sets.

Data set	PMF	CTR	BPR	HoORaYs$_0$	HoORaYs
Lastfm	0.880	0.897	0.896	0.905	**0.905**
Delicious	0.644	0.657	0.655	0.663	**0.667**

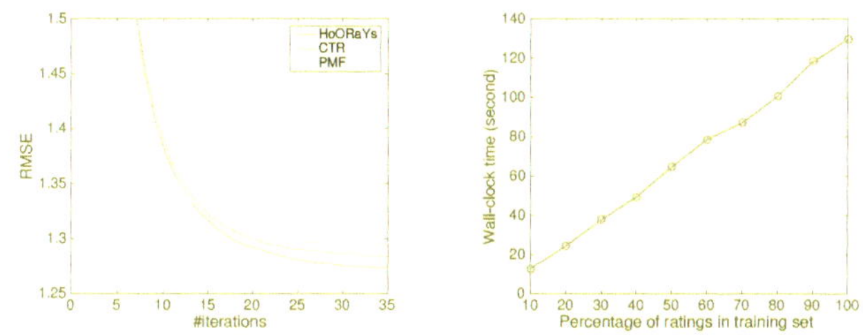

(a) Efficiency evaluation on *Google Play* data, x-axis is #iterations and y-axis is RMSE. (b) Scalability evaluation on *Google Play* data, x-axis is time cost and y-axis is ratings used for training.

Figure 4: Efficiency and scalability evaluation on *Google Play* data.

Implicit user feedback. Next, we present the results of the proposed methods for the implicit feedback case. We compare the proposed methods with PMF, CTR, and BPR, and show the results in Fig. 3 and Table 4.

In Fig. 3, we show the *Recall* results with top N from 10 to 50 with fixed step 5. As we can see, the two proposed methods HoORaYs$_0$ and HoORaYs significantly outperform the compared methods in all cases on both *Lastfm* and *Delicious* data. In Fig. 3(a), both HoORaYs$_0$ and HoORaYs are consistently better than the best competitors on *Lastfm* with 7% improvement on average. In Fig. 3(b), the proposed methods outperform the compared methods especially when number of N is small. For example, when N is 15, HoORaYs$_0$ and HoORaYs achieve 21.7% and 24.3% improvement over the best competitor. Overall, the proposed methods outperform the best competitors with averagely 12.6% improvement in this series of evaluation.

Similar results are observed in Table 4 which shows the *AUC* scores. Specially, we can observe that HoORaYs$_0$ outperforms the BPR method. This again indicates the usefulness of the proposed high-order distance minimization as BPR uses an *AUC*-like optimization target. We also notice that the results on *Lastfm* is better than that on *Delicious*. Again, this is due to the data sparsity (0.08% sparsity on *Delicious* v.s. 0.28% sparsity on *Lastfm*).

Together with the results in Table 2, Table 3, Table 4, and Fig. 3, we can conclude that the proposed methods outperform the compared methods in both explicit feedback case and implicit feedback case. Moreover, the proposed methods can outperform the compared methods even when the content information is unavailable.

Efficiency and Scalability. Next, we present the results of the proposed methods in terms of efficiency and scalability. All the

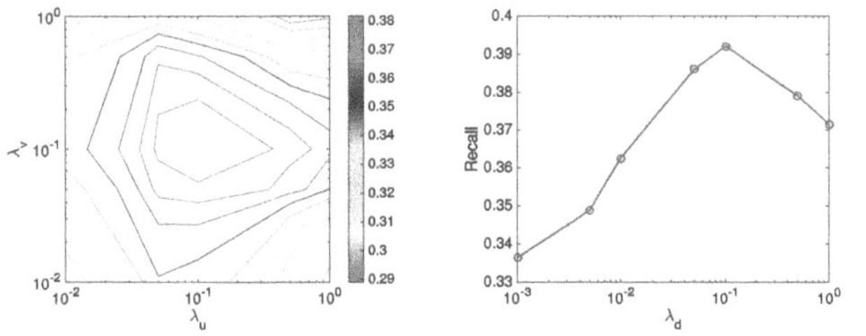

(a) The effects of λ_u and λ_v

(b) The effects of λ_d

Figure 5: The effects of λ_u, λ_v, and λ_d of the proposed HoORaYs with *Recall@50* on *Lastfm* data.

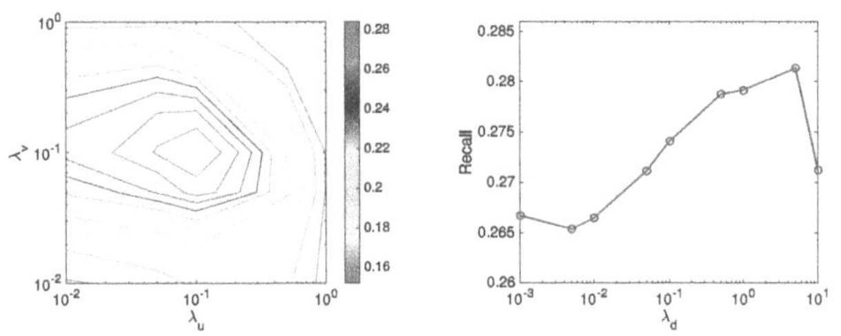

(a) The effects of λ_u and λ_v

(b) The effects of λ_d

Figure 6: The effects of λ_u, λ_v, and λ_d of the proposed HoORaYs with *Recall@50* on *Delicious* data.

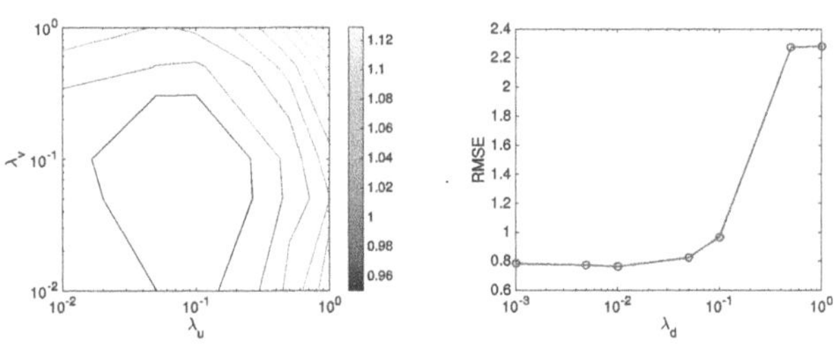

(a) The effects of λ_u and λ_v

(b) The effects of λ_d

Figure 7: The effects of λ_u, λ_v, and λ_d of the proposed HoORaYs on *MovieLens* data.

experiments are run on a Macbook Pro. The machine has four 2.5GHz Intel i7 Cores and 16 GB memory.

In Fig 4(a), we show the efficiency of HoORaYs on *Google Play* data. Compared to MF and CTR, the RMSE of the proposed HoORaYs decreases faster than that of the other two methods. Especially after 13th iteration, HoORaYs still keeps high gradient descent ratio, and the RMSE value reaches the bottom as fast as MF and CTR do. Compared to MF and CTR, the proposed model reveals the equivalent ability in terms of efficiency in practice. Fig 4(b) presents the scalability evaluation for HoORaYs on *Google Play* data. We plot the wall-clock time of each iteration with different number of ratings in training set. As we can see from the figures,

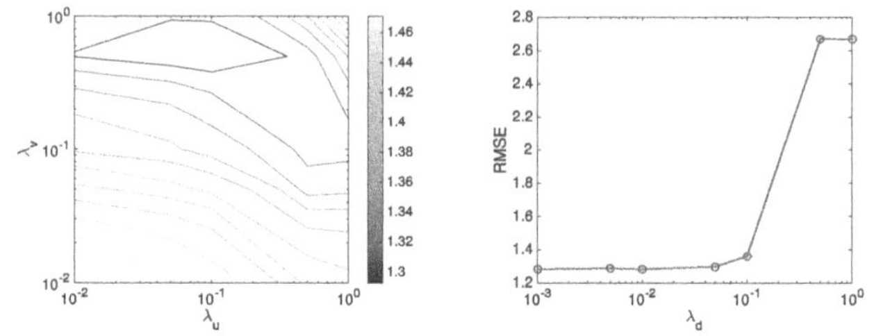

(a) The effects of λ_u and λ_v

(b) The effects of λ_d

Figure 8: The effects of λ_u, λ_v, and λ_d of the proposed HoORaYs on *Google Play* data.

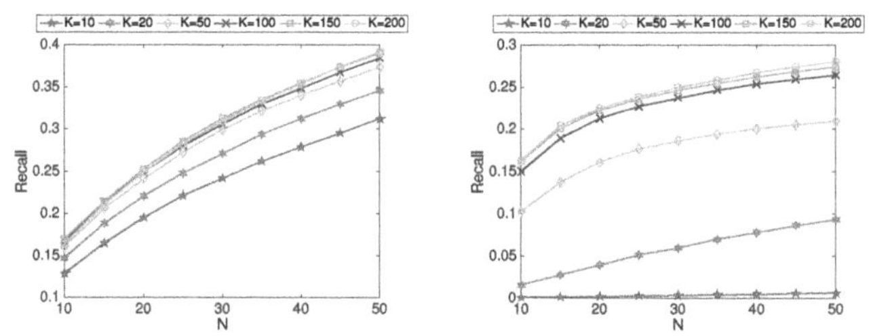

(a) *Lastfm* data

(b) *Delicious* data

Figure 9: The effects of the latent vector dimension K of the proposed HoORaYs with *Recall* on *Lastfm* and *Delicious* data sets.

our proposed HoORaYs scales linearly when number of ratings increases.

Study of Parameters. Finally, we conduct a parameter study of the proposed methods. We first study the parameters of λ_u, λ_v, and λ_d. We use *Recall@50* as an example, and plot the results on *Lastfm* and *Delicious* data in Fig. 5 and Fig. 6, respectively. As we can see from the figures, HoORaYs can achieve best performance when $\lambda_u = \lambda_v = 0.1$ for both data sets. As for λ_d, HoORaYs is sensitive to this parameter, and it achieves the best performance with different λ_d for different data sets. In practice, we suggest to set $\lambda_u = \lambda_v = 0.1$ by default, and tune the λ_d parameter when using the proposed models. For the effects of parameters on data set with explicit feedback, we study the parameters of λ_u, λ_v, and λ_d on *MovieLens* and *Google Play* data, and the results are plotted In Fig. 7 and Fig. 8. For *MovieLens* data, HoORaYs have the best performance when $\lambda_u = \lambda_v = 0.1$ in Fig 7(a). As for λ_d in Fig 7(b), HoORaYs can achieve good performance when $\lambda_d < 0.05$. As a result, we select $\lambda_d = 0.01$ in our evaluation. As we can see from Fig. 8(a), HoORaYs can achieve best performance when $\lambda_u = 0.1$ and $\lambda_v = 0.5$. For λ_d, we can find the similar results in Fig. 8(b) to the results on *MovieLens* data. In practice, we select $\lambda_d = 0.01$ for the evaluation.

Another parameter of the proposed method is the latent vector's dimension K. Fig. 9 presents the effects of K with *Recall@N* on *Lastfm* and *Delicious* data. We vary the size of K with $K = 10, 20, 50, 100, 150, 200$. In general, as shown in Fig. 9(a) and Fig. 9(b), a larger K usually brings better performance before it overfits the data set. Fig. 9(a) shows the performance with different K selection on *Lastfm* data. We can also observe from the figures that, the *Recall* performance improves significantly when we increase K from 10 to 100, and the improvement becomes minor when K is larger than 100. In practice, we suggest to set K between 100 and 200 for the proposed HoORaYs.

5 RELATED WORK

In this section, we briefly review some related work.

Collaborative filtering approaches with user feedback as input have been widely used in recommender systems [7, 10, 11, 14]. For example, matrix factorization methods [11, 14] take ratings as input, and learn the latent vectors of users and items for recommendation. To improve recommendation accuracy, side information is also widely explored. For example, Wang et al. [20] and McAuley and Leskovec [13] incorporate content information; Ma et al. [12] and Tang et al. [19] incorporate social relationships; Chen et al. [2] and Purushotham et al. [17] consider both content and social information.

While many recommendation algorithms are designed for explicit user feedback, several researchers put their focus on case of implicit user feedback. For example, Rendle et al. [18] propose Bayesian personalized ranking to optimize the rankings instead of ratings. Formulating the problem as one-class collaborative filtering, traditional approaches are also adapted for implicit feedback [8, 15, 16], and side information is also considered in this one-class setting [23, 24].

Different from and orthogonal to most of the existing recommendation methods, we propose a new regularized optimization problem by involving high-order rating distance as the constraint for shrinking the solution space. By reducing the *variance*, the better recommendation accuracy could be reached. Similar strategies are also explored in some related problems. For example, Rendle et al. [18] and Kabbur et al. [9] propose an *AUC*-like optimization function. Our high-order optimization problem is different from the *AUC*-like optimization as we use the other existing ratings to shrink the solution space while *AUC* focuses on the order of observed-unobserved examples; additionally, we have experimentally shown that the proposed method outperforms BPR with same input. This work generalizes the rating comparison strategy [21, 22], which can be viewed as a second-order rating distance, primarily designed for the cold-start case. Moreover, it also justifies the rationality behind the higher-order rating distance from two complementary perspectives (the geometric vs. Bayesian interpretations).

6 CONCLUSION

In this paper, we have proposed a high-order optimization of rating distance for recommender systems HoORaYs to further reduce the solution space of latent vectors for users and items. The proposed HoORaYs model used second-order rating distance as the constraint to the optimization problem. HoORaYs can be applied for both explicit and implicit user feedback. We presented a geometric interpretation to show how HoORaYs helps reduce the *variance* of the estimated latent factors. Based on the Bayesian interpretation, we further explained the HoORaYs from the generative model perspective. By connecting to CTR rating model, our HoORaYs can naturally handle the case when content information is available. The experimental evaluations on four real-world data sets show that the proposed method consistently outperforms the state-of-the-art methods in terms of prediction accuracy.

ACKNOWLEDGMENTS

This work is supported by the National 863 Program of China (No. 2015AA01A203), National Key Research and Development Program of China (No. 2016YFB1000802), National Natural Science Foundation of China (No. 61373011, 61690204), the Collaborative Innovation Center of Novel Software Technology and Industrialization. This work is supported by NSF (IIS-1651203), DTRA (HDTRA1-16-0017), ARO (W911NF-16-1-0168), NIH (R01LM011986), and a Baidu gift.

REFERENCES

[1] Iván Cantador, Peter Brusilovsky, and Tsvi Kuflik. 2011. 2nd Workshop on Information Heterogeneity and Fusion in Recommender Systems (HetRec 2011). In *Proceedings of the 5th ACM conference on Recommender systems (RecSys 2011)*. ACM, New York, NY, USA.

[2] Chaochao Chen, Xiaolin Zheng, Yan Wang, Fuxing Hong, Zhen Lin, and others. 2014. Context-Aware Collaborative Topic Regression with Social Matrix Factorization for Recommender Systems.. In *AAAI*, Vol. 14. 9–15.

[3] Ning Chen, Steven CH Hoi, Shaohua Li, and Xiaokui Xiao. 2015. SimApp: A framework for detecting similar mobile applications by online kernel learning. In *Proceedings of the Eighth ACM International Conference on Web Search and Data Mining*. ACM, 305–314.

[4] Abhinandan S Das, Mayur Datar, Ashutosh Garg, and Shyam Rajaram. 2007. Google news personalization: scalable online collaborative filtering. In *Proceedings of the 16th international conference on World Wide Web*. ACM, 271–280.

[5] Stuart Geman, Elie Bienenstock, and René Doursat. 1992. Neural networks and the bias/variance dilemma. *Neural computation* 4, 1 (1992), 1–58.

[6] Pankaj Gupta, Ashish Goel, Jimmy Lin, Aneesh Sharma, Dong Wang, and Reza Zadeh. 2013. Wtf: The who to follow service at twitter. In *Proceedings of the 22nd international conference on World Wide Web*. ACM, 505–514.

[7] Jonathan L Herlocker, Joseph A Konstan, Al Borchers, and John Riedl. 1999. An algorithmic framework for performing collaborative filtering. In *Proceedings of the 22nd annual international ACM SIGIR conference on Research and development in information retrieval*. ACM, 230–237.

[8] Yifan Hu, Yehuda Koren, and Chris Volinsky. 2008. Collaborative filtering for implicit feedback datasets. In *Data Mining, 2008. ICDM'08. Eighth IEEE International Conference on*. IEEE, 263–272.

[9] Santosh Kabbur, Xia Ning, and George Karypis. 2013. FISM: factored item similarity models for top-N recommender systems. In *ACM SIGKDD International Conference on Knowledge Discovery and Data Mining*. ACM, 659–667.

[10] George Karypis. 2001. Evaluation of item-based top-n recommendation algorithms. In *Proceedings of the tenth international conference on Information and knowledge management*. ACM, 247–254.

[11] Yehuda Koren, Robert Bell, and Chris Volinsky. 2009. Matrix factorization techniques for recommender systems. *Computer* 42, 8 (2009), 30–37.

[12] Hao Ma, Tom Chao Zhou, Michael R Lyu, and Irwin King. 2011. Improving recommender systems by incorporating social contextual information. *ACM Transactions on Information Systems (TOIS)* 29, 2 (2011), 9.

[13] Julian McAuley and Jure Leskovec. 2013. Hidden factors and hidden topics: understanding rating dimensions with review text. In *Proceedings of the 7th ACM conference on Recommender systems*. ACM, 165–172.

[14] Andriy Mnih and Ruslan Salakhutdinov. 2007. Probabilistic matrix factorization. In *NIPS*. 1257–1264.

[15] Rong Pan, Yunhong Zhou, Bin Cao, Nathan Nan Liu, Rajan Lukose, Martin Scholz, and Qiang Yang. 2008. One-class collaborative filtering. In *Data Mining, 2008. ICDM'08. Eighth IEEE International Conference on*. IEEE, 502–511.

[16] Ulrich Paquet and Noam Koenigstein. 2013. One-class collaborative filtering with random graphs. In *Proceedings of the 22nd international conference on World Wide Web*. ACM, 999–1008.

[17] Sanjay Purushotham, Yan Liu, and C-C Jay Kuo. 2012. Collaborative topic regression with social matrix factorization for recommendation systems. *arXiv preprint arXiv:1206.4684* (2012).

[18] Steffen Rendle, Christoph Freudenthaler, Zeno Gantner, and Lars Schmidt-Thieme. 2009. BPR: Bayesian personalized ranking from implicit feedback. In

Proceedings of the twenty-fifth conference on uncertainty in artificial intelligence. AUAI Press, 452–461.
[19] Jiliang Tang, Xia Hu, Huiji Gao, and Huan Liu. 2013. Exploiting Local and Global Social Context for Recommendation.. In *IJCAI.* 264–269.
[20] Chong Wang and David M Blei. 2011. Collaborative topic modeling for recommending scientific articles. In *Proceedings of the 17th ACM SIGKDD international conference on Knowledge discovery and data mining.* ACM, 448–456.
[21] Jingwei Xu, Yuan Yao, Hanghang Tong, Xianping Tao, and Jian Lu. 2015. Icebreaking: mitigating cold-start recommendation problem by rating comparison. In *Proceedings of the 24th International Conference on Artificial Intelligence.* AAAI Press, 3981–3987.
[22] Jingwei Xu, Yuan Yao, Hanghang Tong, Xianping Tao, and Jian Lu. 2016. RaPare: A Generic Strategy for Cold-Start Rating Prediction Problem. *IEEE Transactions on Knowledge and Data Engineering* (2016).
[23] Yuan Yao, Hanghang Tong, Guo Yan, Feng Xu, Xiang Zhang, Boleslaw K Szymanski, and Jian Lu. 2014. Dual-regularized one-class collaborative filtering. In *Proceedings of the 23rd ACM International Conference on Conference on Information and Knowledge Management.* ACM, 759–768.
[24] Xiaodong Zheng, Hao Ding, Hiroshi Mamitsuka, and Shanfeng Zhu. 2013. Collaborative matrix factorization with multiple similarities for predicting drug-target interactions. In *Proceedings of the 19th ACM SIGKDD international conference on Knowledge discovery and data mining.* ACM, 1025–1033.

Collaboratively Improving Topic Discovery and Word Embeddings by Coordinating Global and Local Contexts

Guangxu Xun[1], Yaliang Li[1,2], Jing Gao[1], Aidong Zhang[1]
[1]Department of Computer Science and Engineering, SUNY at Buffalo, New York, USA
[2]Baidu Research Big Data Lab, Sunnyvale, CA USA
[1]{guangxux, yaliangl, jing, azhang}@buffalo.edu, [2]yaliangli@baidu.com

ABSTRACT

A text corpus typically contains two types of context information – global context and local context. Global context carries topical information which can be utilized by topic models to discover topic structures from the text corpus, while local context can train word embeddings to capture semantic regularities reflected in the text corpus. This encourages us to exploit the useful information in both the global and the local context information. In this paper, we propose a unified language model based on matrix factorization techniques which 1) takes the complementary global and local context information into consideration simultaneously, and 2) models topics and learns word embeddings collaboratively. We empirically show that by incorporating both global and local context, this collaborative model can not only significantly improve the performance of topic discovery over the baseline topic models, but also learn better word embeddings than the baseline word embedding models. We also provide qualitative analysis that explains how the cooperation of global and local context information can result in better topic structures and word embeddings.

CCS CONCEPTS

• **Information systems → Data mining**; • **Computing methodologies → Topic modeling**; *Natural language processing*;

KEYWORDS

Topic modeling, word embeddings, global context, local context, unified language model

ACM Reference format:
Guangxu Xun, Yaliang Li, Jing Gao, and Aidong Zhang. 2017. Collaboratively Improving Topic Discovery and Word Embeddings by Coordinating Global and Local Contexts. In *Proceedings of KDD '17, August 13-17, 2017, Halifax, NS, Canada*, 9 pages.
DOI: 10.1145/3097983.3098009

1 INTRODUCTION

Topic models [2, 6, 11, 29] and word embedding models [1, 4, 20] are two of the most successful and prevalent language models nowadays. They model languages from two different but complementary points of view — the global viewpoint and the local viewpoint. Topic models, such as Probabilistic Latent Semantic Analysis (PLSA) [11] and Latent Dirichlet Allocation (LDA) [2], are usually built upon the document-level global context information in a text corpus. Topic models follow the bag-of-word assumption that a document is represented as a bag of its words (disregarding grammar and even word order, but keeping multiplicity). Documents are modeled as mixtures of latent topics, where latent topics are formulated as multinomial distributions over words. Bayesian methods are then employed to infer the topic structures based on the global document-word frequency matrix of the corpus. In contrast to topic models utilizing the document-level global context information, most of the word embedding models, such as Neural Probabilistic Language Model (NPLM) [1] and Skip-Gram [20], are based on the local context information. Word embedding models follow the distributional hypothesis [9] that words occurring in similar local contexts tend to have similar syntactic and semantic properties. Semantically related words ought to be projected close to each other in the word embedding space. Word embeddings can then be constructed using internal representations from neural network architectures of local word sequences.

While local context can help disambiguate word meanings, global context can also provide useful topical information. Therefore, it is natural to expect more sufficient input information and better performance if a language model is able to utilize these two complementary context information collaboratively. In addition, both topic structures and word embeddings can be discovered from the corpus. However, it is difficult to develop a unified language model in depth which can absorb both the idea of globality from topic models and the idea of locality from word embedding models, because topic models are usually statistical generative models while word embedding models are mostly based on artificial neural networks.

Instead of developing a unified language model, researchers tend to combine global and local context by using the pre-trained result based on one type of context information to assist in modeling language on the other type of context information [5, 18, 27, 28]. For example, Gaussian-LDA [5] uses pre-trained word embeddings learned from large external corpora such as Wikipedia and then models topics with Gaussian distributions in the word embedding space; in contrast, Topical Word Embedding (TWE) [18] uses pre-trained topic structures to learn topic embeddings and improve word embeddings.

However, there are several limitations in combining topic models and word embedding models in this separate and heuristic manner. The first limitation stems from the difference of semantics in different datasets. One popular way to model topics upon word embeddings is to replace discrete word types in the target dataset (e.g. ESPN sports news) with continuous word embeddings learned from

978-1-4503-4887-4/17/08...$15.00
DOI: 10.1145/3097983.3098009

an external corpus (e.g. Wikipedia). But the difference of semantics in ESPN sports news and Wikipedia would probably result in poor performance. The second limitation is that external corpus is not always available. In some research domains such as biomedicine, there are no such knowledge bases as comprehensive as Wikipedia. However, if we want to directly train word embeddings on the target dataset and the target dataset is relatively small, we have to face the third limitation, i.e., the lack of local context information, as training word embeddings typically requires a large amount of local contexts.

The aforementioned limitations inspire us to develop a unified language model which is able to make use of both the global and the local context information collaboratively. We propose to unify the process of modeling topics and learning word embeddings via matrix factorization, and take advantage of both the idea of globality from topic models and the idea of locality from word embedding models. The new model is named Collaborative Language Model (CLM). In CLM, the global context information is encoded in the document-word matrix and the local context information is encoded in the word co-occurrence matrix. In addition to topic structures and word embeddings, we also introduce topic embeddings for topics and assume that the importance of a word in a topic is proportional to the inner product value of the corresponding word embedding and topic embedding. By fully exploiting the context information in a text corpus, CLM has the following advantages:

- CLM is able to discover topic structures and learn word embeddings collaboratively.
- CLM does not rely on pre-trained topic structures or pre-trained word embeddings learned from external corpora.
- When the text corpus is not large enough, with the help of global context information, CLM can overcome the lack of local context information and learn good word embeddings.
- With the help of local context information, CLM can discover more coherent latent topics.

To evaluate how well CLM discovers topics and learns word embeddings, we perform four quantitative evaluation tasks including two topic structure evaluation tasks and two word embedding evaluation tasks. We show that by taking both global and local context information into consideration, CLM outperforms the baselines on both the topic structure evaluation tasks and the word embedding evaluation tasks. We also provide qualitative assessment and case studies to explain how topic structures and word embeddings can collaboratively enhance the quality of each other.

2 RELATED WORK

Topic models are a powerful unsupervised tool to reveal the latent semantic structure from a text corpus based on its global document-word context information. Latent Semantic Analysis (LSA) [6] is proposed as a dimensionality reduction technique by projecting the document-word matrix to a linear subspace with Singular Value Decomposition (SVD). PLSA [11] introduces latent variables which can be viewed as 'topics' between documents and words, where each document is a multinomial distribution over topics and each topic is also a multinomial distribution over words. LDA [2] further extends PLSA to a complete probabilistic model by adding Dirichlet priors at the document level. Non-negative Matrix Factorization (NMF) [14] is a useful matrix decomposition technique for multivariate data and its non-negativity makes the resulting matrices easy to explain in many application domains. Ding et al. [7] have proven the equivalence between PLSA and NMF as they optimize the same objective function of the global document-word matrix.

Word embeddings, also known as word vectors and distributed representations of words, have proven to be able to capture semantic regularities in language by learning the local word co-occurrence context information. Specifically, NPLM [1] first introduces word embeddings into natural language processing. Many variants have been proposed since then to improve the efficiency of NPLM [4, 20]. In particular, the popular Continuous Bag Of Words (CBOW) and Skip-Gram models proposed by Mikolov et al. [20] are efficient to train and obtain state-of-the-art results on various linguistic tasks. The training methods of CBOW and Skip-Gram are highly popular, but not well understood until Levy et al. [15] proved that Skip-Gram with negative sampling training method is implicitly factorizing the pointwise mutual information (PMI) matrix of the local word co-occurrence patterns.

In order to make use of both the global context and the local context information, many composite models have been proposed to combine topic models and word embedding models. One common way is to use pre-trained word embeddings and replace the multinomial distribution over words with a probability function defined in the word embedding space to generate a focus word given its topic and neighboring words. Among them, Latent Feature Topic Modeling (LFTM) [23] defines the probability function as a mixture of the conventional multinomial distribution and a link function between the embeddings of the focus word and topics. TopicVec [17] adds context word embeddings to the link function in addition to the focus word embeddings and topic embeddings. Gaussian-LDA [5] models topics as Gaussian distributions over the continuous word embeddings. The other common way to combine topic models and word embedding models is to use pre-trained LDA topic structures to learn topic embeddings and assist in training word embeddings. For example, Topic2Vec [24] treats the pre-trained topic labels as special words and learns embeddings for topics by including the topic labels in the neural network architecture. Topical Word Embedding (TWE) [18] further concatenates the topic embedding with the word embedding to form the topical word embedding for each word.

However, all of these composite models combine topic models and word embedding models in a separate and heuristic manner – they either utilize pre-trained word embeddings or pre-trained topic structures. In contrast, our CLM model proposes to make the topic model and the word embedding model work collaboratively, and fully exploit the complementary global and local context information in a text corpus. Huang et al. [12] and Le et al. [13] propose to incorporate global information to help the learning of word embeddings by assigning an embedding to each document. Their ideas can be viewed as special cases of our model, with the number of topics set to the number of documents.

3 NOTATIONS AND DEFINITIONS

Table 1 shows the notations used in this paper. We use bold uppercase letters such as $\boldsymbol{D}$ to represent matrices, bold lowercase

Table 1: Table of Notations

Notation	Meaning
V	Vocabulary size
N	Number of documents
K	Number of topics
M	Dimensionality of the embedding space
$\boldsymbol{D} \in \mathbb{R}^{V\times N}$	Document-word matrix $[\boldsymbol{d}_1, ..., \boldsymbol{d}_N]$
$\boldsymbol{W} \in \mathbb{R}^{V\times V}$	Word co-occurrence matrix
$\boldsymbol{T} \in \mathbb{R}^{K\times V}$	Topic-word matrix $[\boldsymbol{t}_1, ..., \boldsymbol{t}_V]$
$\boldsymbol{\Theta} \in \mathbb{R}^{K\times N}$	Document-topic matrix $[\boldsymbol{\theta}_1, ..., \boldsymbol{\theta}_N]$
$\boldsymbol{A} \in \mathbb{R}^{M\times K}$	Topic embedding matrix $[\boldsymbol{\alpha}_1, ..., \boldsymbol{\alpha}_K]$
$\boldsymbol{B} \in \mathbb{R}^{M\times V}$	Word embedding matrix $[\boldsymbol{\beta}_1, ..., \boldsymbol{\beta}_V]$
$\boldsymbol{C} \in \mathbb{R}^{M\times V}$	Context word embedding matrix $[\boldsymbol{c}_1, ..., \boldsymbol{c}_V]$
$\boldsymbol{d}_n$	The nth document
$\boldsymbol{\theta}_n$	Topic representation for the nth document
$\boldsymbol{t}_v$	Topic distribution for the vth word
$\boldsymbol{\alpha}_k$	Topic embedding for the kth topic
$\boldsymbol{\beta}_v$	Word embedding for the vth word
$\boldsymbol{c}_v$	Context embedding for the vth word
d_{ij}, w_{ij}, t_{ij}	The ij^{th} entry in matrix $\boldsymbol{D}, \boldsymbol{W}, \boldsymbol{T}$ respectively

letters such as $\boldsymbol{d}_n$ to represent vectors or embeddings, regular uppercase letters such as V to represent scalar constants, and regular lowercase letters such as d_{ij} to represent scalar variables.

Given a text corpus, its document-level global context information is encoded in the document-word matrix $\boldsymbol{D}$ and its local context information is encoded in the word co-occurrence matrix $\boldsymbol{W}$. The word co-occurrence matrix $\boldsymbol{W}$ is constructed from small fixed-sized text intervals in the documents. Each text interval is composed of a focus word and its neighboring context words falling in a fix-sized window centered at the focus word. The value of entry w_{ij} is the number of times that a context word w_j appears in word w_i's contexts.

Given the global context matrix $\boldsymbol{D}$ and the local context matrix $\boldsymbol{W}$, our goal is to discover topic structures and learn word embeddings collaboratively based on both context information.

4 METHODOLOGY

Our CLM model follows three basic assumptions: (1) each document focuses on only a small amount of topics and each topic assigns high probability to only a small number of words; (2) words appearing in similar local context tend to have similar syntactic and semantic properties and should be mapped to nearby areas in the embedding space; and (3) words close to each other in the embedding space tend to have similar topic distributions and vice versa.

We will introduce our CLM model according to how CLM is formulated based on these assumptions as well as how CLM utilizes the global and the local context information.

4.1 Our Proposed Model

The three aforementioned assumptions correspond to three building blocks of CLM. We first introduce the three building blocks. Then we describe our proposed model CLM and its relationship with other existing composite models.

4.1.1 Exploiting global context information. Given the global document-word matrix $\boldsymbol{D}$, NMF decomposes it into the product of document-topic matrix $\boldsymbol{\Theta}$ and topic-word matrix $\boldsymbol{T}$. The non-negativity of NMF ensures the explainability of document-topic distribution and topic-word distribution. The objective function to factorize $\boldsymbol{D}$ with regularization is:

$$\begin{aligned} L_{glo} &= ||\boldsymbol{D} - \boldsymbol{T}^T\boldsymbol{\Theta}||_2^2 + \lambda_s||\boldsymbol{\Theta}||_2^2 + \lambda_s||\boldsymbol{T}||_2^2, \\ &subject\ to: \\ &\boldsymbol{\Theta} \geq 0\ and\ \boldsymbol{T} \geq 0, \end{aligned} \quad (1)$$

where $||\boldsymbol{\Theta}||_2^2$ denotes the l_2 norm regularization we use on document-topic matrix $\boldsymbol{\Theta}$, $||\boldsymbol{T}||_2^2$ denotes the l_2 norm regularization we use on topic-word matrix $\boldsymbol{T}$, and λ_s is the parameter to prevent overfitting: the larger value of λ_s, the larger amount of shrinkage on $\boldsymbol{\Theta}$ and $\boldsymbol{T}$. In our model, instead of the raw frequency matrix, we use the document-word matrix with TF-IDF weights as $\boldsymbol{D}$.

4.1.2 Exploiting local context information. Based on the local context information, word embedding models can learn a low-dimensional representation for each word. In the Skip-Gram model [20], the objective of each training step is to predict neighboring words within a fixed window given a focus word. Stochastic gradient descent with negative sampling is a regular way to train Skip-Gram. Levy et al. [15] have proven an equivalence between Skip-Gram trained with negative sampling value of k and the factorization of the positive PMI word co-occurrence matrix shifted by $\log k$, i.e., the shifted positive pointwise mutual information matrix (SPPMI). Therefore, in our model, instead of the raw frequency matrix, we use the SPPMI word co-occurrence matrix as $\boldsymbol{W}$.

The PMI value between a pair of discrete outcomes x and y is defined as:

$$PMI(x, y) = \log \frac{P(x, y)}{P(x)P(y)}.$$

Empirically, the PMI value between a word w and its context word c can be estimated by considering the actual number of their co-occurrence times in the corpus:

$$PMI(w, c) = \log \frac{\#(w, c) \cdot E}{\#(w) \cdot \#(c)},$$

where $\#(w, c)$ is the number of times words w and c co-occur, $\#(w) = \sum_c \#(w, c)$, $\#(c) = \sum_w \#(w, c)$, and E is the total number of word-context pairs. The SPPMI matrix is then constructed as:

$$SPPMI_k(w, c) = \max(PMI(w, c) - \log k, 0).$$

Following the similar idea, CLM exploits local context information and learns word embeddings by factorizing matrix $\boldsymbol{W}$:

$$L_{loc} = ||\boldsymbol{W} - \boldsymbol{B}^T\boldsymbol{C}||_2^2 + \lambda_s||\boldsymbol{B}||_2^2 + \lambda_s||\boldsymbol{C}||_2^2. \quad (2)$$

4.1.3 Collaboration. By exploiting the global context information of a text corpus, we can discover the topic structures; and by exploiting the local context information, we can learn the word embeddings. However, these two parts should not be isolated from each other: semantically related words usually belong to similar topics and they are also close to each other in the embedding space. Hence we assume that the distances between word embeddings correlate with their topical similarities. As with exploiting the local context information, we realize this assumption by factorizing topic-word matrix T into the product of topic embedding matrix A and context word embedding matrix C:

$$L_{com} = ||T - A^T C||_2^2 + \lambda_s||A||_2^2 + \lambda_s||C||_2^2. \tag{3}$$

Hence the probability of word w being grouped into topic z can be measured by the inner product of the corresponding topic embedding and word embedding: $p(z|w) \propto t_{zw} = \alpha_z^T c_w$. Therefore, besides achieving the topic embeddings, Eq. 3 also regulates words with similar topic distributions to be close in the embedding space and nearby words to have similar topic distributions.

4.1.4 Unifying the three assumptions. Both the global context information and the local context information contain useful patterns in a text corpus. We propose to utilize both types of context information jointly, and to discover topic structures and learn word embeddings collaboratively:

$$\begin{aligned} L = &\underbrace{\lambda_d||D - T^T\Theta||_2^2}_{global} + \underbrace{\lambda_w||W - B^T C||_2^2}_{local} + \underbrace{||T - A^T C||_2^2}_{joint} \\ &+ \underbrace{\lambda_s||\Theta||_2^2 + \lambda_s||T||_2^2 + \lambda_s||A||_2^2 + \lambda_s||B||_2^2 + \lambda_s||C||_2^2}_{regularization}, \\ &subject\ to: \\ &\Theta \geq 0\ and\ T \geq 0, \end{aligned} \tag{4}$$

where λ_d and λ_w are the parameters controlling the weights of the global and local modeling parts. Eq. 4 is the objective function of our model. Topic-word distribution matrix T is shared by both the global modeling and the joint modeling parts of the objective function. Context word embedding matrix C is shared by both the local modeling and the joint modeling parts of the objective function. Therefore, the topic structures and word embeddings we obtained must account for both the global and the local context information of a text corpus.

4.1.5 Relationship with other composite models. As we discussed in Section 2, two popular ways to combine topic models and word embedding models are 1) modeling topics based on pre-trained word embeddings and 2) learning word embeddings based on pre-trained topic structures. These models can be viewed as special cases of CLM that keep either topic structures or word embeddings fixed. More specifically, if we use pre-trained word embeddings and keep them fixed, then CLM considers only the combination of Eq. 1 and Eq. 3. This results in CLM becoming functionally equivalent to the composite models that discover topic structures with the help of pre-trained word embeddings, such as Gaussian-LDA [5] and TopicVec [17]. In contrast, if we use pre-trained topic structures and keep them fixed, then CLM considers only the combination of Eq. 2 and Eq. 3. Again CLM becomes functionally equivalent to the composite models that learn word embeddings and topic embeddings with the help of pre-trained topic structures, such as TWE [18] and Topic2Vec [24].

4.2 Parameter Inference

In this subsection, we will introduce how to do parameter estimation and inference for our proposed CLM model via collective matrix factorization. First the objective function of CLM in Eq. 4 is expanded as:

$$\begin{aligned} L = &\lambda_d \sum_{v=1,n=1}^{V,N} (d_{vn} - t_v^T\theta_n)^2 + \lambda_w \sum_{v=1,v'=1}^{V,V} (w_{vv'} - \beta_v^T c_{v'})^2 \\ &+ \sum_{k=1,v=1}^{K,V} (t_{kv} - \alpha_k^T c_v)^2 + \lambda_s \sum_{n=1}^{N}(\theta_n^T\theta_n) + \lambda_s \sum_{v=1}^{V}(t_v^T t_v) \\ &+ \lambda_s \sum_{k=1}^{K}(\alpha_k^T\alpha_k) + \lambda_s \sum_{v=1}^{V}(\beta_v^T\beta_v) + \lambda_s \sum_{v=1}^{V}(c_v^T c_v), \\ &subject\ to: \\ &\Theta \geq 0\ and\ T \geq 0. \end{aligned} \tag{5}$$

Then we compute the gradient of our objective function Eq. 5 with respect to each vector $\{\theta_{1:N}, t_{1:V}, \alpha_{1:K}, \beta_{1:V}, c_{1:V}\}$:

$$\begin{aligned} \frac{\partial L}{\partial \theta_n} &= 2\lambda_d \sum_{v=1}^{V}(d_{vn} - t_v^T\theta_n)(-t_v) + 2\lambda_s\theta_n \\ \frac{\partial L}{\partial t_v} &= 2\lambda_d \sum_{n=1}^{N}(d_{vn} - t_v^T\theta_n)(-\theta_n) + 2(t_v - A^T c_v) + 2\lambda_s t_v \\ \frac{\partial L}{\partial \alpha_k} &= 2\sum_{v=1}^{V}(t_{kv} - \alpha_k^T c_v)(-c_v) + 2\lambda_s\alpha_k \\ \frac{\partial L}{\partial \beta_v} &= 2\lambda_w \sum_{v'=1}^{V}(w_{vv'} - \beta_v^T c_{v'})(-c_{v'}) + 2\lambda_s\beta_v \\ \frac{\partial L}{\partial c_{v'}} &= 2\lambda_w \sum_{v=1}^{V}(w_{vv'} - \beta_v^T c_{v'})(-\beta_v) + 2\lambda_s c_{v'} \\ &+ 2\sum_{k=1}^{K}(t_{kv'} - \alpha_k^T c_{v'})(-\alpha_k) \end{aligned}$$

Similar to the Alternating Least Squares (ALS) matrix factorization method, we obtain the following closed-form updates by iteratively setting the gradient to zero:

$$\begin{aligned} \theta_n &= (\lambda_d \sum_{v=1}^{V} t_v t_v^T + \lambda_s I)^{-1}(\lambda_d \sum_{v=1}^{V} d_{vn} t_v) \\ t_v &= (\lambda_d \sum_{n=1}^{N} \theta_n\theta_n^T + (1+\lambda_s)I)^{-1}(\lambda_d \sum_{n=1}^{N} d_{vn}\theta_n + A^T c_v) \\ \alpha_k &= (\sum_{v=1}^{V} c_v c_v^T + \lambda_s I)^{-1}(\sum_{v=1}^{V} t_{kv} c_v) \\ \beta_v &= (\sum_{v'=1}^{V} c_{v'} c_{v'}^T + \lambda_s I)^{-1}(\sum_{v'=1}^{V} w_{vv'} c_{v'}) \\ c_{v'} &= (\lambda_w \sum_{v=1}^{V} \beta_v\beta_v^T + \sum_{k=1}^{K} \alpha_k\alpha_k^T + \lambda_s I)^{-1} \\ &* (\lambda_w \sum_{v=1}^{V} w_{vv'}\beta_v + \sum_{k=1}^{K} t_{kv'}\alpha_k) \end{aligned} \tag{6}$$

Note that this update does not guarantee the non-negativity of θ_n and t_v. Since our objective function is continuous, the minimum should be either at the points where the gradient is zero or on the boundary. Hence, if Eq. 6 assigns $\boldsymbol{\theta}_n$ and $\boldsymbol{t}_v$ negative entries, we can just set the negative entries to zeros. The main difference between our updates and ALS is that many variables are associated with more than one matrix factorization term. For example, context word embeddings $\boldsymbol{c}_v$ is associated with both local context matrix $\boldsymbol{W}$ and topic-word matrix $\boldsymbol{T}$. Iteratively performing these updates achieves a stationary point of our model's objective function L.

5 EXPERIMENTS

We carry out experiments on two real-world text corpora to demonstrate the efficacy of our CLM model in two aspects: modeling topics and learning word embeddings. To investigate the quality of the topic structures discovered by CLM, we compare its performance with existing topic modeling methods on two topic evaluation tasks, the topic coherence evaluation task and the document classification task. To investigate the quality of the word embeddings learned by CLM, we compare its performance with existing word embedding models on two word embedding evaluation tasks, the word similarity task and the word analogy task. Moreover, we provide case studies to show the advantages of exploiting both types of context information.

The 20 Newsgroups dataset[1] and the Reuters-21578 dataset[2] are used in our experiments. 20News contains approximately 20,000 newsgroup documents evenly partitioned into 20 different categories. Reuters contains about 10,000 documents, but the numbers of documents in each category are highly imbalanced. We select only the largest 8 categories in Reuters, leaving us with 7,674 documents in total. In the preprocessing step, stop words and words with total frequency lower than 10 get removed, and all words are converted to lowercase. When constructing the local context matrix $\boldsymbol{W}$, we set the context window size to 10, i.e., 5 preceding words and 5 following words are considered as local context words for a focus word. For the parameters controlling the weights and regularization, we set $\lambda_d = 1e-2$, $\lambda_w = 2e-2$, and $\lambda_s = 1e-7$.

The source code of our implementation is available at https://github.com/XunGuangxu/2in1.

5.1 Evaluation on Topic Coherence

5.1.1 Baselines and experimental settings. The topic modeling methods we use as our baselines are the vanilla LDA [2], NMF [14], PLSI [11], Gaussian-LDA [5] and LFTM [23], among which Gaussian-LDA and LFTM are composite topic models that are built upon pre-trained word embeddings. For 20News and Reuters, we set the number of topics K to 20 and 8, respectively, as there are 20 newsgroups and 8 categories. We set the number of iterations to 100 for all the methods. For LDA, we set the hyperparameters alpha to $50/K$ and beta to 0.01. For the sake of fairness, the word embeddings used in Gaussian-LDA and LFTM are trained on the same dataset using word2vec toolkit [20]. And we set the dimensionality of word embeddings to 50 for Gaussian-LDA, LFTM and CLM.

5.1.2 Evaluation metrics. In order to quantitatively assess the topic coherence, we adopt an automated metric, called coherence score of topics proposed by [22], which is able to automatically evaluate the coherence of each topic. Given a topic z and its top U words $V^z = \{v_1^z, v_2^z, ..., v_U^z\}$, the coherence score of this topic with respect to its top U words is defined as:

$$C(z; V^z) = \sum_{u=2}^{U} \sum_{l=1}^{u} \log \frac{D(v_u^z, v_l^z) + 1}{D(v_l^z)},$$

where $D(v_l^z)$ is the document frequency of word v_l^z and $D(v_u^z, v_l^z)$ is the number of documents in which words v_u^z and v_l^z co-occurred. The coherence score follows the intuition that top words in the same topic tend to frequently co-occur in documents. A topic coherence score closer to zero means a higher co-occurrence rate of the topic words, indicating a more coherent topic. This topic coherence score shows high consistency with human judgements on topic qualities [22]. In order to investigate the overall quality of the discovered topic set, we use the average topic coherence score: $\bar{C} = \frac{1}{K} \sum_z C(z; V^z)$.

Table 2: Topic Coherence Scores on 20News

Top U words	5	10	20	50
NMF	-18.051	-85.538	-417.199	-2796.776
PLSI	-15.151	-78.597	-365.693	-2684.952
LDA	-15.308	-80.482	-368.820	-2694.437
Gaussian-LDA	-19.450	-94.523	-435.903	-3407.968
LFTM	-16.589	-78.541	-385.734	-2807.011
CLM	**-11.624**	**-60.303**	**-282.799**	**-2275.523**

Table 3: Topic Coherence Scores on Reuters

Top U words	5	10	20	50
NMF	**-11.281**	-66.412	-335.619	-2705.525
PLSI	-13.226	-70.078	-333.570	-2767.808
LDA	-12.093	-69.806	-352.296	-2840.746
Gaussian-LDA	-24.223	-108.453	-478.433	-3688.172
LFTM	-13.268	-71.352	-369.009	-2982.395
CLM	-11.483	**-63.083**	**-313.459**	**-2683.163**

5.1.3 Experimental results. The topic coherence results of each method on 20News and Reuters are reported in Table 2 and Table 3, respectively. To make this evaluation more comprehensive, we vary the number of topic words $U = \{5, 10, 20, 50\}$. The best scores are highlighted in boldface. As generative models, PLSI and LDA achieve similar topic coherence scores. Gaussian-LDA does not perform well and this is probably because this topic coherence metric is more appropriate for measuring frequent words in a topic while Gaussian-LDA ranks words according to their Gaussian probabilities in each topic. LFTM outperforms Gaussian-LDA because LFTM takes advantage of both the conventional Dirichlet multinomial and the link function in the embedding space. As with CLM, NMF also factorizes the document-word matrix to learn topic structures, but our CLM model is able to utilize the additional semantic information in word embeddings learned from local context and this semantic information helps CLM discover more coherent topics. CLM ranks words in each topic according to their values in the topic-word matrix $\boldsymbol{T}$. We can see that CLM achieves significantly higher coherence scores than the baselines.

[1] http://qwone.com/ jason/20Newsgroups/
[2] http://www.daviddlewis.com/resources/testcollections/reuters21578/

Table 4: Document Classification on 20News

	Precision	Recall	F1
NMF	0.704	0.701	0.697
PLSI	0.722	0.712	0.709
LDA	0.727	0.722	0.719
Gaussian-LDA	0.309	0.265	0.227
LFTM	0.716	0.714	0.709
TWE	0.525	0.466	0.437
PV-DBOW	0.510	0.491	0.459
PV-DM	0.428	0.386	0.361
CLM	**0.825**	**0.818**	**0.816**

Table 5: Document Classification on Reuters

	Precision	Recall	F1
NMF	0.911	0.877	0.891
PLSI	0.919	0.896	0.906
LDA	0.888	0.870	0.879
Gaussian-LDA	0.462	0.315	0.353
LFTM	0.893	0.591	0.661
TWE	0.794	0.512	0.626
PV-DBOW	0.755	0.505	0.549
PV-DM	0.681	0.434	0.507
CLM	**0.944**	**0.916**	**0.929**

5.2 Evaluation on Document Classification

5.2.1 Baselines and experimental settings. In addition to the baselines used in Subsection 5.1, we also include TWE [18] and two Doc2Vec models [13]: PV-DBOW and PV-DM, as they can provide document-level representations for this document classification task. TWE is a composite model built upon pre-trained topic structures, so we feed the output of the vanilla LDA to TWE as the pre-trained topic structures. We keep the same experimental settings as in Subsection 5.1, except that, for 20News we set the number of topics to 280 for the topic models and the dimensionality of document embeddings to 280 for TWE, PV-DBOW and PV-DM, and for Reuters we set them to 110.

5.2.2 Evaluation metrics. In the document classification task on 20News, each newsgroup document is represented as a 280 dimensional vector. Hence, 20,000 newsgroup documents are classified into 20 classes according to their document-topic distributions or document embeddings. The reason why we change the number of topics from 20 to 280 is that the number of classes is already 20 and the number of features (topics) should be larger than that. Similarly, we set the number of features (topics) to 110 for Reuters. In order to evaluate the overall performance across all the document classes, we adopt the macro-averaged precision, recall and F1 measures as the evaluation metrics, as macro-averaging gives equal weight to each class.

5.2.3 Experimental results. Table 4 and Table 5 present the classification performance of the different methods on 20News and Reuters, respectively. The highest scores are highlighted in boldface. The document-topic representation used here corresponds to the document-topic matrix $\boldsymbol{\Theta}$ in our model. We can see that CLM outperforms the baselines significantly. On this task, PLSI, LDA and LFTM still obtain similar and better scores than the other baselines. As with CLM, NMF is also based on matrix factorization techniques, but NMF does not achieve as good performance as CLM due to its inability to utilize both context information. Gaussian-LDA performs considerably inferior to all other methods. By checking its output variables manually, we find that the Gaussian distributions for different topics are highly similar and hence its document-topic representations are not discriminative enough. TWE, PV-DBOW and PV-DM assign a low-dimensional embedding to each document based on the word embeddings in it, but the classification results on these document embeddings are inferior to the results on document topic proportions.

5.3 Evaluation on Word Similarity

Having shown the superiority of CLM in topic discovery, we now evaluate the quality of word embeddings learned from the 20 Newsgroups dataset by CLM in the following two tasks. As we know, training word embeddings requires a large amount of local context information to capture language regularities. Hence, Wikipedia, the largest online encyclopedia, is the most frequently used training dataset for word embeddings due to its sheer range of topics and ample local context information. However, for experiment domains involving smaller corpus size such as the 20 Newsgroups dataset, gathering the local context information is quite a challenge. We will show that our CLM model is able to overcome the challenge of lacking local context information by taking the complementary global context information into consideration.

5.3.1 Baselines and experimental settings. The word embedding methods we include as our baselines are the SPPMI matrix without dimensionality reduction [15], SVD of the SPPMI matrix [15], GloVe [25], CBOW [20], Skip-Gram [20], PV-DBOW [13], PV-DM [13] and TWE [18], among which TWE is a composite model that is built upon pre-trained LDA topic structures, and PV-DBOW and PV-DM take the influence of documents on word embeddings into consideration. Different from the others, GloVe constructs word co-occurrence matrix and learns word embeddings purely based on document-level global context information. For uniformity, we set the number of context window size to 10, the number of negative samples to 5, and the dimensionality of the embedding space to 50 for all the methods. And we set the number of topics to 20 for TWE and CLM. We then perform 100 iterations of training for all the methods.

5.3.2 Evaluation metrics. We use several test datasets to evaluate the word pair similarities calculated by word embeddings: WordSim353 (WS353) [8] (including WordSim Relatedness (WS Sim) and WordSim Similarity (WS Rel)), MEN [3], Turk [26], SimLex-999 [10], and Rare [19]. These datasets contain word pairs associated with human-assigned similarity scores. After ranking the word pairs according to their cosine similarities in the embedding space and human-assigned similarity scores respectively, the word embeddings are evaluated by measuring the Spearman's rank correlation with the human ratings. We exclude word pairs that contain out-of-vocabulary words from the test datasets. A higher correlation value indicates it is more consistent with human judgements on word similarities.

Table 6: Comparison of Word Similarity Results

	WS353	WS Rel	WS Sim	Men	Turk	SimLex-999	Rare
SPPMI	0.461	0.444	0.465	0.444	**0.551**	0.131	0.245
SPPMI + SVD	0.451	0.435	0.449	0.426	0.489	0.166	0.349
GloVe	0.300	0.279	0.320	0.192	0.268	0.049	0.230
Skip-Gram	0.492	0.479	0.473	0.456	0.512	0.155	0.407
CBOW	0.488	0.451	0.494	0.432	0.529	0.151	0.407
PV-DBOW	0.477	0.442	0.486	0.449	0.488	0.139	0.285
PV-DM	0.297	0.304	0.310	0.236	0.339	0.013	0.157
TWE	0.317	0.231	0.407	0.190	0.260	0.084	0.184
CLM	**0.526**	**0.486**	**0.550**	**0.477**	0.525	**0.189**	**0.411**

5.3.3 Experimental results. The results are summarized in Table 6. The highest correlation scores are highlighted in boldface. Similar performances are achieved by the SPPMI matrix and SVD of SPPMI; however, the dimensionality of SPPMI word representations is the vocabulary size – 20,678 – much higher than 50 dimensions for the other methods. As with CLM, SVD also learns word embeddings by factorizing the local SPPMI matrix, but its inability to utilize the additional global topical information results in inferior performance to ours. Skip-Gram and CBOW yield better results than SPPMI and SVD of SPPMI. PV-DBOW performs on a par with Word2Vec models. GloVe performs inferior to the other methods. This may be due to the fact that GloVe utilizes only global context information but there is inadequate global context information to train word embeddings in the 20 Newsgroups dataset. As one can see, the SPPMI matrix obtains the best correlation score on the Turk test dataset, and CLM outperforms the baselines on all the other test datasets.

5.4 Evaluation on Word Analogy

5.4.1 Baselines and experimental settings. For the second evaluation task on the quality of word embeddings, we use the same baselines and keep the same experimental settings as in the previous word similarity task in Subsection 5.3.

5.4.2 Evaluation metrics. The word analogy task refers to questions of the form "a is to a* as b is to b*", where b* is hidden and needs to be inferred from the vocabulary. We use two test datasets for the word analogy task: MSR [21], which contains 8000 morphosyntactic analogy questions, such as "good is to better as rich is to richer", and Google [20], which contains 19544 questions, about half of the same syntactic type as in MSR, and the other half of a semantic nature, such as "king is to queen as man is to woman". We filter out questions involving out-of-vocabulary words. The hidden words b* can be inferred by optimizing 3CosAdd [16]:

$$\arg\max_{b*\in V}(cos(b*, b - a + a*)).$$

The evaluation metric for the word analogy task is the percentage of questions for which the 3CosAdd result is the correct answer b*.

5.4.3 Experimental results. Table 7 shows the results on the word analogy task. As can be seen, the lack of local context information in the 20 Newsgroups dataset heavily limits the performance of the different methods on such a difficult task as word analogies. Linguistically speaking, the word analogy task relies more on contextual information from common words and auxiliary verbs to correctly infer b*. Word embeddings learned from larger dataset which provides sufficient local context such as Wikipedia can achieve better performance on this task. For word embeddings learned from the 20 Newsgroups dataset, SVD of the SPPMI matrix performs on a par with the raw SPPMI matrix. CBOW, Skip-Gram and PV-DBOW yield better results than SPPMI and SVD of SPPMI because their training procedures give more influence to frequent pairs. GloVe does not perform well since it only explores global context information. TWE does not achieve good results because it is heavily limited by the sparsity issue and influenced by the pre-trained topic structures. We can still see that, by exploiting both the global and the local context information, CLM overcomes the lack of local context information and outperforms the baselines significantly.

Table 7: Comparison of Word Analogy Results

	Google	MSR
SPPMI	6.60%	5.40%
SPPMI + SVD	4.93%	7.32%
GloVe	2.67%	3.51%
Skip-Gram	6.62%	10.70%
CBOW	5.61%	12.00%
PV-DBOW	7.12%	11.77%
PV-DM	2.84%	7.55%
TWE	3.76%	5.38%
CLM	**8.28%**	**14.20%**

5.5 Qualitative Assessment of Topic Embeddings

Besides topic structures and word embeddings, CLM can also learn topic embeddings for each topic, i.e., the topic embedding matrix $\boldsymbol{A}$. Those topic embeddings are of the same dimensionality as word embeddings. The relationships between topic embeddings and word embeddings are modeled in Eq. 3: the larger inner product value a word embedding and a topic embedding get, the more important that word is in the topic. After convergence, the similarities and correlations among topics are also captured in the embedding space. Figure 2 shows the two-dimensional PCA projection of the topic embeddings related to religions and Mideast. Each topic embedding is annotated with its topic name and top 5 words. We can observe that the semantic similarities between topics correlate with the

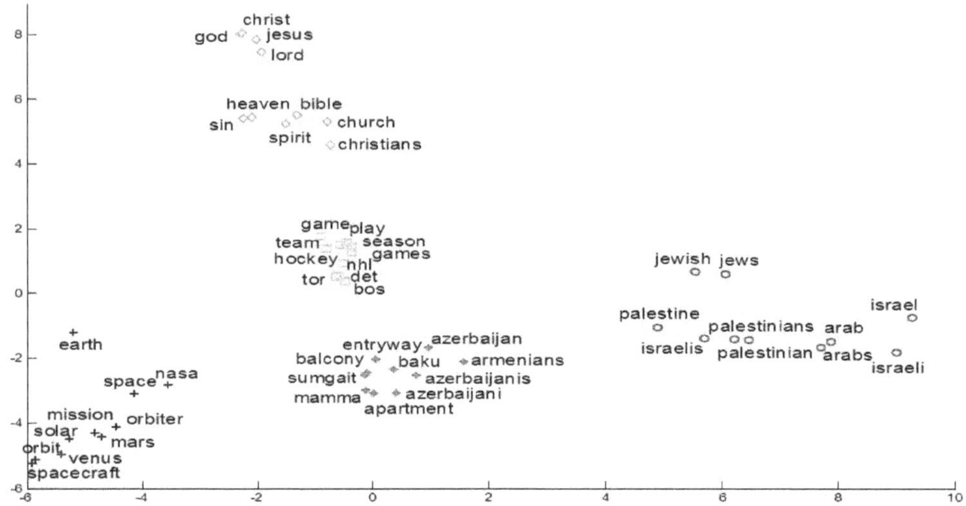

Figure 1: Two-dimensional PCA projection of word embedding clusters.

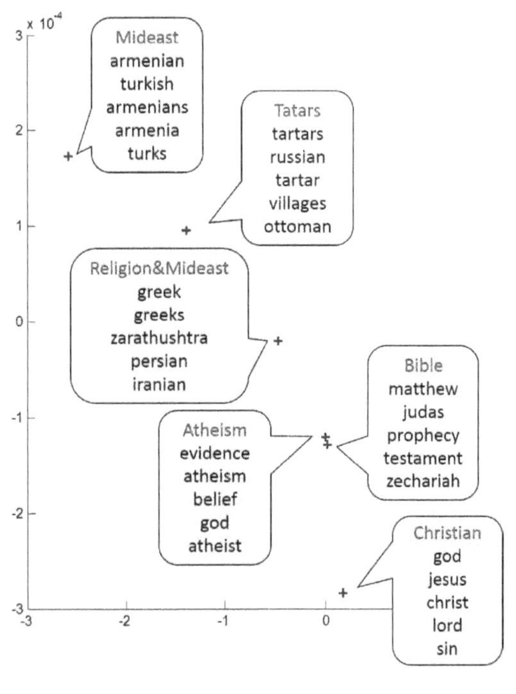

Figure 2: Two-dimensional PCA projection of the topic embeddings related to religions and mideast.

Euclidean distances between the corresponding topic embeddings. The correlations among topics can also be captured in this embedding space. For example, Figure 2 illustrates how the topic of Christian transitions to the topic of Mideast through the topics of Bible and religions.

5.6 Case Studies

5.6.1 How local context information assists global context information in discovering topic structures. Having shown the superiority of CLM in discovering topic structures in Subsections 5.1 and 5.2, we now take the topic of astronomy as an example to illustrate how word embeddings can help discover more coherent topics. Word embeddings learned from local context information are able to capture semantic regularities in language: words with similar semantic properties are found to be close to each other in the embedding space. And we are encouraged to group semantically related words (words that are geographically close in the embedding space) into same topics. This intuition is illustrated in Figure 1: words belonging to same topics tend to locate in nearby areas.

Table 8: Case Study 1

	Coherence score	Avg cosine distance
10 random words	-171.641	0.026
NMF	-102.422	0.570
CLM	**-89.731**	**0.728**

To verify our assumption, we quantitatively show that the average cosine distance of words in a topic is consistent with the topic coherence score. As our closest competitor in topic discovery, NMF is equivalent to our CLM model without considering word embeddings. The top 10 words in the topic of astronomy discovered by CLM are *{'space', 'orbit', 'solar', 'spacecraft', 'mission', 'mars', 'earth', 'venus', 'nasa', 'orbiter'}* as shown on the bottom left corner in Figure 1. The top 10 words in the topic of astronomy discovered by NMF are *{'space', 'earth', 'planet', 'system', 'spacecraft', 'solar', 'venus', 'surface', 'moon', 'kilometers'}*. We then calculate the average cosine distance of words and the topic coherence score for CLM and NMF respectively. Table 8 justifies the consistency between the topic coherence score and the average cosine distance. Therefore, by considering the spatial information of word embeddings, more coherent topics can be discovered by CLM.

5.6.2 How global context information assists local context information in learning word embeddings. In Subsections 5.3 and 5.4, we have shown that the word embeddings learned by CLM are closer to human judgements in terms of word similarities. We now take

Table 9: Case Study 2

Word pairs	Ground truth ranking	SPPMI +SVD ranking	CLM ranking	Cosine similarity of $p(z\|w)$
king – queen	13	135	118	0.733
money – currency	7	79	41	0.851
planet – space	42.5	201	143	0.918
mile – kilometer	12	94	62	0.879
man – woman	24	70	44	0.731

several word pairs in the WS353 test dataset to illustrate how global topical information can help us learn better word embeddings. We compare our rankings for these example words with the rankings of our closest competitor SPPMI+SVD which is equivalent to our CLM model without considering global topical information. As we can see in Table 9, due to the lack of sufficient local context information, these word pairs are not ranked properly by SPPMI+SVD. With the help of global topical information, CLM can improve the similarity ranking as words' topic distribution regulates. If two words have similar topic distributions (measured by the cosine similarity between their $p(z|w)$), such as planet and space, CLM would adjust the two corresponding word embeddings closer to each other accordingly and assign them a higher position in the similarity ranking.

6 CONCLUSION

We present a unified language model CLM based on matrix factorization techniques which is able to collaboratively discover topic structures and learn word embeddings. Moreover, building our model on both the global and the local context enables it to make use of more sufficient information. The proposed CLM model formulates documents as admixtures of topics, where each topic is a multinomial distribution over words and is influenced by word embeddings in the way that words close to each other in the embedding space should be grouped into same topics. At the same time, CLM also assumes that words appearing in similar local contexts and having similar topic distributions tend to get mapped to nearby areas in the embedding space. Topics and words are jointly trained and embedded in the vector space that preserves semantic regularities, while sparse and interpretable document-topic distributions are achieved simultaneously. The experiments on the real-world datasets validate the effectiveness of CLM.

ACKNOWLEDGMENTS

We thank Wayne Xin Zhao and Sheng Li for their help and useful discussions. This work was supported in part by the US National Science Foundation under grants NSF IIS-1218393, IIS-1514204 and IIS 1319973. Any opinions, findings, and conclusions or recommendations expressed in this material are those of the author(s) and do not necessarily reflect the views of the National Science Foundation.

REFERENCES

[1] Yoshua Bengio, Holger Schwenk, Jean-Sébastien Senécal, Fréderic Morin, and Jean-Luc Gauvain. 2006. Neural probabilistic language models. In *Innovations in Machine Learning*. Springer, 137–186.

[2] David M Blei, Andrew Y Ng, and Michael I Jordan. 2003. Latent dirichlet allocation. *the Journal of machine Learning research* 3 (2003), 993–1022.

[3] Elia Bruni, Gemma Boleda, Marco Baroni, and Nam-Khanh Tran. 2012. Distributional semantics in technicolor. In *Proceedings of the 50th Annual Meeting of the Association for Computational Linguistics: Long Papers-Volume 1*. Association for Computational Linguistics, 136–145.

[4] Ronan Collobert, Jason Weston, Léon Bottou, Michael Karlen, Koray Kavukcuoglu, and Pavel Kuksa. 2011. Natural language processing (almost) from scratch. *The Journal of Machine Learning Research* 12 (2011), 2493–2537.

[5] Rajarshi Das, Manzil Zaheer, and Chris Dyer. 2015. Gaussian LDA for Topic Models with Word Embeddings.. In *ACL (1)*. 795–804.

[6] Scott Deerwester, Susan T Dumais, George W Furnas, Thomas K Landauer, and Richard Harshman. 1990. Indexing by latent semantic analysis. *Journal of the American society for information science* 41, 6 (1990), 391.

[7] Chris Ding, Tao Li, and Wei Peng. 2006. Nonnegative matrix factorization and probabilistic latent semantic indexing: Equivalence chi-square statistic, and a hybrid method. In *AAAI*, Vol. 6. 137–143.

[8] Lev Finkelstein, Evgeniy Gabrilovich, Yossi Matias, Ehud Rivlin, Zach Solan, Gadi Wolfman, and Eytan Ruppin. 2001. Placing search in context: The concept revisited. In *Proceedings of the 10th international conference on World Wide Web*. ACM, 406–414.

[9] Zellig S Harris. 1954. Distributional structure. *Word* 10, 2-3 (1954), 146–162.

[10] Felix Hill, Roi Reichart, and Anna Korhonen. 2016. Simlex-999: Evaluating semantic models with (genuine) similarity estimation. *Computational Linguistics* (2016).

[11] Thomas Hofmann. 1999. Probabilistic latent semantic indexing. In *Proceedings of the 22nd annual international ACM SIGIR conference on Research and development in information retrieval*. ACM, 50–57.

[12] Eric H Huang, Richard Socher, Christopher D Manning, and Andrew Y Ng. 2012. Improving word representations via global context and multiple word prototypes. In *ACL (1)*. 873–882.

[13] Quoc V Le and Tomas Mikolov. 2014. Distributed Representations of Sentences and Documents.. In *ICML*, Vol. 14. 1188–1196.

[14] Daniel D Lee and H Sebastian Seung. 2001. Algorithms for non-negative matrix factorization. In *Advances in neural information processing systems*. 556–562.

[15] Omer Levy and Yoav Goldberg. 2014. Neural word embedding as implicit matrix factorization. In *Advances in neural information processing systems*. 2177–2185.

[16] Omer Levy, Yoav Goldberg, and Israel Ramat-Gan. 2014. Linguistic Regularities in Sparse and Explicit Word Representations.. In *CoNLL*. 171–180.

[17] Shaohua Li, Tat-Seng Chua, Jun Zhu, and Chunyan Miao. 2016. Generative topic embedding: a continuous representation of documents. In *Proceedings of The 54th Annual Meeting of the Association for Computational Linguistics (ACL)*.

[18] Yang Liu, Zhiyuan Liu, Tat-Seng Chua, and Maosong Sun. 2015. Topical Word Embeddings.. In *AAAI*. 2418–2424.

[19] Thang Luong, Richard Socher, and Christopher D Manning. 2013. Better word representations with recursive neural networks for morphology.. In *CoNLL*. 104–113.

[20] Tomas Mikolov, Ilya Sutskever, Kai Chen, Greg S Corrado, and Jeff Dean. 2013. Distributed representations of words and phrases and their compositionality. In *Advances in neural information processing systems*. 3111–3119.

[21] Tomas Mikolov, Wen-tau Yih, and Geoffrey Zweig. 2013. Linguistic Regularities in Continuous Space Word Representations.. In *Hlt-naacl*, Vol. 13. 746–751.

[22] David Mimno, Hanna M Wallach, Edmund Talley, Miriam Leenders, and Andrew McCallum. 2011. Optimizing semantic coherence in topic models. In *Proceedings of the Conference on Empirical Methods in Natural Language Processing*. Association for Computational Linguistics, 262–272.

[23] Dat Quoc Nguyen, Richard Billingsley, Lan Du, and Mark Johnson. 2015. Improving topic models with latent feature word representations. *Transactions of the Association for Computational Linguistics* 3 (2015), 299–313.

[24] Liqiang Niu, Xinyu Dai, Jianbing Zhang, and Jiajun Chen. 2015. Topic2Vec: learning distributed representations of topics. In *Asian Language Processing (IALP), 2015 International Conference on*. IEEE, 193–196.

[25] Jeffrey Pennington, Richard Socher, and Christopher D Manning. 2014. Glove: Global Vectors for Word Representation.. In *EMNLP*, Vol. 14. 1532–1543.

[26] Kira Radinsky, Eugene Agichtein, Evgeniy Gabrilovich, and Shaul Markovitch. 2011. A word at a time: computing word relatedness using temporal semantic analysis. In *Proceedings of the 20th international conference on World wide web*. ACM, 337–346.

[27] Guangxu Xun, Vishrawas Gopalakrishnan, Fenglong Ma, Yaliang Li, Jing Gao, and Aidong Zhang. 2016. Topic Discovery for Short Texts Using Word Embeddings. In *Data Mining (ICDM), 2016 IEEE 16th International Conference on*. IEEE, 1299–1304.

[28] Guangxu Xun, Yaliang Li, Wayne Xin Zhao, Jing Gao, and Aidong Zhang. 2017. A Correlated Topic Model Using Word Embeddings. In *Proceedings of the 26th International Joint Conference on Artificial Intelligence*.

[29] Wayne Xin Zhao, Jing Jiang, Jianshu Weng, Jing He, Ee-Peng Lim, Hongfei Yan, and Xiaoming Li. 2011. Comparing twitter and traditional media using topic models. In *Advances in Information Retrieval*. Springer, 338–349.

PPDSparse: A Parallel Primal-Dual Sparse Method for Extreme Classification

Ian E.H. Yen[†] Xiangru Huang[‡] Wei Dai[†,*] Pradeep Ravikumar[†] Inderjit Dhillon[‡] Eric Xing[†,*]

[†]Carnegie Mellon University [‡]University of Texas at Austin *Petuum Inc.

{eyan, pradeepr}@cs.cmu.edu, {xrhuang,inderjit}@cs.utexas.edu, {wei.dai, eric.xing}@petuum.com

ABSTRACT

Extreme Classification comprises multi-class or multi-label prediction where there is a large number of classes, and is increasingly relevant to many real-world applications such as text and image tagging. In this setting, standard classification methods, with complexity linear in the number of classes, become intractable, while enforcing structural constraints among classes (such as low-rank or tree-structure) to reduce complexity often sacrifices accuracy for efficiency. The recent *PD-Sparse* method addresses this via an algorithm that is sub-linear in the number of variables, by exploiting *primal-dual* sparsity inherent in a specific loss function, namely the max-margin loss. In this work, we extend PD-Sparse to be efficiently parallelized in large-scale distributed settings. By introducing separable loss functions, we can scale out the training, with network communication and space efficiency comparable to those in one-versus-all approaches while maintaining an overall complexity sub-linear in the number of classes. On several large-scale benchmarks our proposed method achieves accuracy competitive to the state-of-the-art while reducing the training time from days to tens of minutes compared with existing parallel or sparse methods on a cluster of 100 cores.

KEYWORDS

Extreme Classification, Primal Dual Method, Sparse Optimization.

1 INTRODUCTION

Extreme Classification comprises Multiclass and Multilabel prediction with a large number of classes, and has become increasingly prevalent in real-world applications such as text and image tagging, where the number of tags can easily go beyond tens or even hundreds of thousands.

In such a setting, standard approaches such as one-versus-all and one-versus-one become intractable due to their high training and prediction complexity (that is at least linear) w.r.t. the number of classes. On a benchmark data set with hundreds of thousand of classes, the training time of the one-versus-all approach could take a few months [11, 34], with a model taking hundreds of gigabytes to store.

Structural Constraints. Many approaches have since been proposed to address this space and computational complexity by imposing structural constraints among the sub-models for each class, such as embedding or hierarchy based, among others. One of the most commonly used structural constraint is based on *low-rank embedding* [5, 17, 36], which projects parameters of different classes to a low-dimensional subspace, and thus reduces the effective number of classes. However, such a low-rank assumption could often be violated in real-world data, for instance data with a power-law label distribution, and thus leads to lower accuracy [1, 34]. One remedy to this caveat is to find *local embeddings* instead of a *global embedding*, which entails a much weaker structural constraint, and leads to higher accuracy [2]. However, to find such local embeddings, one needs to find *nearest neighbors*, which either leads to a high complexity w.r.t. the number of samples, or introduces additional dependency on the quality of clustering, which could be unstable for high dimensional data. Thus despite its superior accuracy on some data sets, the local embedding algorithm [2] could be unstable, and moreover has many more tuning parameters than other methods.

Another commonly used structural constraint is based on a tree hierarchy [7, 14, 24], which finds a tree or a forest that filters a fraction of classes as candidates at each tree node visited. This leads to a *logarithmic* prediction time w.r.t. the number of classes. However, finding an optimal tree that maximizes performance measure is computationally hard; note that a greedy partitioning method could potentially have large cumulative error due to cascading effects. As a result, one often needs to train a large number of trees to get reasonable performance. Moreover, in practice, a good hierarchy might not exist in the first place, so that the tree-based approach often has to trade accuracy for efficiency.

Primal and Dual Sparsity. As [34] pointed out, when the number of classes become large, the collection of model parameters is under-determined, so that a simple structural constraint of sparsity might be practically useful. For the specific max-margin loss, [34] showed that there exists a naturally sparse solution to the Extreme Classification problem with sub-linear number of non-zeros in both primal and dual variables, which can be exploited to develop an estimation algorithm with sub-linear dependency on the number of classes. Since primal-dual sparsity is naturally satisfied in the Extreme Classification setting, the estimation algorithm often leads to higher accuracy on problems with larger number of classes. However, the max-margin loss employed in [34] has several disadvantages:

KDD '17, August 13-17, 2017, Halifax, NS, Canada

DOI: 10.1145/3097983.3098083

(i) it is not separable w.r.t. classes and thus requires optimizing parameters of all classes together, which can lead to a high memory consumption that prohibits its application to larger problems, (ii) the non-separability w.r.t. classes prevents a simple parallelization scheme that the one-versus-all methods enjoy, (iii) the max-margin loss focuses on the margin between the most confusing classes, which as a criterion is sensitive to *mis-labeling*, such as missing positive labels.

A recent work [1] shows that an one-versus-all based approach with weight truncation (for model compression) can reduce the training time substantially via parallelization, albeit the approach has no theoretical guarantee on the resulting model quality. This leads to the question: can we develop a method that enjoys both the *parallelizability, small memory footprint* of the one-versus-all technique and the sub-linear complexity of *primal-dual sparse* method?

In this work, we propose a *greedy algorithm* that enjoys both the low runtime complexity inherent in the primal-dual sparse approach *and* one-versus-all's simple parallelization training with small memory footprint. Our specific contributions are as follows:

- We show that the loss optimized by the common one-versus-all technique also enjoys a similar *primal-dual sparse* structure presented in [34] when a class-wise bias is added.
- We propose a *greedy active-set algorithm* that optimizes parameters of each class separately *without communication* and thus enjoys both parallelizability and primal-dual sparsity.
- We extend the analysis in [34] in two ways: (i) we bound the number of non-zero dual variables in terms of the *number of positive samples* instead of the *number of confusing samples* that could be growing linearly with the total number of samples for the separable loss considered; (ii) the bound holds not only for the optimal solution but also for any descent iterates during the optimization, which leads to a more realistic analysis for the sub-linear complexity of the algorithm.
- In our experiments on several benchmark data sets with hundreds of thousands of classes, our proposed method achieves accuracy competitive with state-of-the-art. On a cluster of 100 cores, our method is orders of magnitude faster than the existing parallel one-versus-all methods and the sequential PD-Sparse.

2 PROBLEM SETUP AND BACKGROUND

We consider the standard *Empirical Risk Minimization (ERM)* framework for Multilabel/Multiclass classification, where we are given a collection of training samples $\{(\boldsymbol{x}_i, \boldsymbol{y}_i)\}_{i=1}^N$ with $\boldsymbol{x}_i \in \mathbb{R}^D$ denoting D-dimensional feature vectors that encode relevant information about the instances, and $\boldsymbol{y}_i \in \{-1, 1\}^K$ denoting label vectors such that $y_{ik} = 1$ if k is a correct label for the i-th sample and $y_{ik} = -1$ otherwise. We denote $\mathcal{P}(\boldsymbol{y}) = \{k | y_k = 1\}$ as the set of positive labels and $\mathcal{N}(\boldsymbol{y}) = \{k | y_k = -1\}$ as the set of negative ones for each sample.

Extreme Classification refers to cases when K is extremely large, sometimes as large as N. On the other hand, the number of positive labels per sample $|\mathcal{P}(\boldsymbol{y}_i)|$ is usually pretty small. In Multiclass classification, we have $|\mathcal{P}(\boldsymbol{y}_i)| = 1$, and in most Mulitlabel prediction problems, $|\mathcal{P}(\boldsymbol{y}_i)|$ is typically in the order of tens or less than 10.

In this work we consider classifiers $h : \mathbb{R}^D \rightarrow \{-1, 1\}^K$ of the form

$$h_W(\boldsymbol{x}) = sign(W^T \boldsymbol{x} + \boldsymbol{b})$$

where W is a $D \times K$ matrix. Each column of W is denoted as $\boldsymbol{w}_k$, which corresponds to the model parameters of k-th class. For such linear classifiers, given a loss function $L : \mathbb{R}^K \times \{-1, 1\}^K$, we are interested in the ERM approach to classification that solves the following problem

$$W^* \in arg \min_{W \in \mathbb{R}^{D \times K}} \sum_{i=1}^{N} L(W^T \boldsymbol{x}_i, \boldsymbol{y}_i). \tag{1}$$

2.1 Primal & Dual Sparsity

The estimation problem (1) is said to have *primal sparsity* if the solution W^* has a small number of non-zeros $nnz(W^*)$. Interestingly, for specific loss functions, the optimization problem could also have *dual sparsity.*

[34] specifically considered the max-margin loss [8, 9]:

$$L(\boldsymbol{z}, \boldsymbol{y}) = \max_{k_n \in \mathcal{N}(\boldsymbol{y})} \max_{k_p \in \mathcal{P}(\boldsymbol{y})} (1 + z_{k_n} - z_{k_p})_+. \tag{2}$$

For a given $(\boldsymbol{z}, \boldsymbol{y})$, define the set of *active labels* as those labels k that attain the maximum of (2). In other words, a label is active if it is *most confusing*; note that a negative label is more confusing if it gets a higher score, while a positive label is more confusing if its score is lower. Letting k_a denote the average number of active labels ranging over the training dataset, the optimization problem in (1) with the max-margin loss (2) is said to be *dual sparse* if k_a is small relative to K, which entails that only few of the dual variables are non-zeros at a minimizer of the ERM problem. [34] showed that this is indeed typically the case in extreme classification settings, and proposed a method they called *PD-Sparse* that exploits this fact.

[34] further show that, under the loss (2), if one has k_a average number of active labels, there exists a minimizer of the ERM problem (1) with $nnz(W^*) \leq Nk_a$, which can moreover be the unique solution by augmenting the objective (1) with an arbitrarily small ℓ_1-penalty. In other words, the *dual sparsity* (small k_a) implies *primal sparsity* (small $nnz(W^*)$) if

$$k_w := \frac{nnz(W^*)}{D} \leq \frac{Nk_a}{D} \ll K,$$

This results in a model of both primal and dual sparse structure as long as $DK \gg Nk_a$. Note this result is significant since the sparse solution is *not enforced* but *identified.* In other words, it is not a trade-off between accuracy and sparsity. Instead, when $DK \gg Nk_a$, there are many more parameters than constraints in the problem (1), and there exits a very sparse solution among the many possible solutions.

3 FORMULATION: PRIMAL-DUAL SPARSITY WITH SEPARABILITY

A significant disadvantage of the loss (2) is that it is not separable w.r.t. the class parameters $\boldsymbol{w}_1, ..., \boldsymbol{w}_K$, and therefore it requires training all parameters W together. This incurs a much larger memory consumption than the *one-versus-all* approach even in the presence of sparsity. This prohibits *PD-Sparse* from using a simple parallelization scheme that assigns the training of different classes to different cores—a scheme that could enjoy nearly linear speedup to even a thousand of cores in [1].

To achieve parallelizability and space efficiency, we consider the following *class-separable hinge loss*

$$L(z, y) := \sum_{k=1}^{K} \ell(z_k, y_k) = \sum_{k=1}^{K} \max(1 - y_k z_k, 0) \tag{3}$$

One-versus-all method can be interpreted as minimizing (3) since

$$\min_{W \in \mathbb{R}^{D \times K}} \sum_{i=1}^{N} \sum_{k=1}^{K} \ell(w_k^T x_i, y_{ik}) = \sum_{k=1}^{K} \left(\sum_{i=1}^{N} \ell(w_k^T x_i, y_{ik}) \right) \tag{4}$$

The goal of this section is to show that (4) also permits a *primal-dual sparse* structure similar to [34] when a *bias* term is added to the parameters of each class. We first note that showing (3) has dual sparsity is more difficult, since unlike (2), it penalizes each class separately, so there could potentially be many more active labels for each sample as we discuss below. We thus take two different approaches to show the desired dual sparsity structure.

3.1 Dual Sparsity: Active Labels

We first employ an approach similar to [34], and try to establish dual sparsity in terms of the number of active labels of each sample i. In our case, the set of active labels are characterized as

$$C_i := \{k \mid y_{ik} \langle \mathbf{w}_k, \mathbf{x}_i \rangle \leq 1\},$$

that is, labels of either wrong predictions or confidence scores ≤ 1 for a particular sample i. This is related to the set of support vectors of each class $\mathcal{S}_k := \{i \mid y_{ik} \langle \mathbf{w}_k, \mathbf{x}_i \rangle \leq 1\}$. Denote $k_a := \frac{1}{N} \sum_{i=1}^{N} |C_i|$ and $n_a := \frac{1}{K} \sum_{k=1}^{K} |S_k|$ as the average number of active labels and support vectors. We have

$$N k_a = K n_a.$$

Note when the number of active labels k_a is constant, we have $n_a = N k_a / K$ decreases with K, which results in the *dual sparsity* when $K \gg k_a$.

The following theorem then shows that the dual sparsity also implies a primal-sparse solution when $n_a \ll D$.

Theorem 3.1. *Let $\lambda > 0$ be an arbitrarily small constant and*

$$\mathbf{w}^* \in \underset{\mathbf{w} \in \mathbb{R}^D}{argmin}\ \lambda \|\mathbf{w}\|_1 + \sum_{i=1}^{N} \ell(\mathbf{w}^T \mathbf{x}_i, y_i). \tag{5}$$

Then for $\{\mathbf{x}_i\}_{i=1}^N$ drawn from a continuous distribution *we have*

$$d_k := nnz(\mathbf{w}^*) \leq n_a. \tag{6}$$

where $n_a := \{i \mid y_i \langle \mathbf{w}^*, \mathbf{x}_i \rangle \leq 1\}$ is the number of support vectors.

Proof. Let X be an $N \times D$ feature matrix with rows $\{\mathbf{x}_i\}_{i=1}^N$. Any optimal solution of (5) satisfies

$$\lambda \boldsymbol{\rho}^* + \sum_{i=1}^{N} \alpha_i^* \mathbf{x}_i = \lambda \boldsymbol{\rho}^* + X^T \boldsymbol{\alpha}^* = 0 \tag{7}$$

for some $\boldsymbol{\rho}^* \in \partial(\|\mathbf{w}^*\|_1)$ and $\alpha_i^* \in \partial_{z_i} \ell(z_i, y_i)$ with $z_i := \langle \mathbf{w}^*, \mathbf{x}_i \rangle + b$. Then since hinge loss (and square hinge loss) has $\alpha_i^* \neq 0$ only when $y_i z_i^* \leq 1$, there are at most n_a non-zeros α_i^* in the linear system (7). On the other hand, the subgradient $\boldsymbol{\rho}^*$ of $\|\mathbf{w}^*\|_1$ satisfies

$$\boldsymbol{\rho}^* = \begin{cases} 1, & w_j^* > 0 \\ -1, & w_j^* < 0 \\ \nu, & \nu \in [-1, 1], w_j^* = 0. \end{cases}$$

Let $\mathcal{B} := \{j \mid w_j^* \neq 0\}$ be the indexes with non-zeros weights. Then consider equations given by the non-zeros α_is and $|\mathcal{B}|$ rows in (7)

$$-\lambda\ sign([\mathbf{w}^*]_{\mathcal{B}}) = X^T \boldsymbol{\alpha}^*.$$

It has $nnz(\mathbf{w}^*)$ equations and n_a variables, which, for a feature matrix at *general position*, can be satisfied only if

$$nnz(\mathbf{w}^*) = |\mathcal{B}| \leq n_a.$$

A feature matrix X is always at *general position* if its rows $\{\mathbf{x}\}_{i=1}^N$ are drawn from a continuous distribution [28]. □

Note the Theorem 3.1 implies that when the number of active labels k_a is constant, both the number of non-zeros in the primal variables d_k and dual variables n_a are proportional to $\frac{N k_a}{K}$. However, there are several drawbacks with Theorem 3.1. First, the loss (3) does not *force* k_a to be small as the max-margin loss (2) does, so in our case k_a could actually increase linearly with K. Second, Theorem 3.1 only analyzes the optimal solution $(\boldsymbol{\alpha}^*, \mathbf{w}^*)$, which cannot however guarantee the sparsity of $\mathbf{w}$ during the intermediate iterates of the training algorithm. Finally, the result (6) holds only for a purely ℓ_1-regularized objective, which is known to yield a non-smooth dual objective that can be hard to optimize in a coordinate-wise fashion. In next section, we thus employ a different approach to resolve these caveats.

3.2 Dual Sparsity: Positive Examples

In this section, we take a more realistic approach which bounds the ℓ_1-norm of primal and dual variables by the *number of positive examples* of each class, which decreases as a function of K even under the separable loss (3). Denote n_p as the average number of positive samples per class, and k_p as the average number of positive labels per sample. We have

$$n_p := \left(\frac{k_p}{K} \right) N \ll N. \tag{8}$$

when K is large. Note unlike the number of active labels k_a, the number of positive labels k_p is a constant that does not grow with K in most of Extreme Classification problems. Therefore, the number of positive samples per class n_p is decreasing with K since $n_p = N k_p / K$.

Now consider a model that incorporates the bias term, where we have an additional feature $x_{i,0} = 1$ for all samples, and an additional weight $w_{k,0}$ for all classes. For ease of optimization in the dual, we consider the following ℓ_1-ℓ_2 (Elastic-Net) regularized objective :

$$\min_{\mathbf{w}_k \in \mathbb{R}^D} F(\mathbf{w}_k) := \lambda \sum_{j=1}^{D} |w_{jk}| + \frac{1}{2} \|\mathbf{w}_k\|^2 + \sum_{i=1}^{N} \ell(\mathbf{w}_k^T \mathbf{x}_i, y_{ik}), \tag{9}$$

which has a dual objective of the form

$$\begin{aligned} \min_{\boldsymbol{\alpha}_k \in \mathbb{R}^N} \quad & G(\boldsymbol{\alpha}_k) := \frac{1}{2}\|\mathbf{w}(\boldsymbol{\alpha}_k)\|^2 - \sum_{i=1}^{N} \alpha_{ik} \\ s.t. \quad & \mathbf{w}(\boldsymbol{\alpha}_k) = \mathbf{prox}_\lambda(\hat{X}^T \boldsymbol{\alpha}_k), \\ & 0 \le \alpha_{ik} \le 1. \end{aligned} \tag{10}$$

where $\hat{X}$ is $N \times D$ matrix with rows $\{y_{ik}\boldsymbol{x}_i\}_{i=1}^N$, and $\mathbf{prox}_\lambda(.)$ is the proximal operator of the function $\lambda \sum_{j=1}^D |w_j|$. Note we do not penalize bias term in the ℓ_1 regularization, so $w_0 = [\hat{X}^T \boldsymbol{\alpha}_k]_0$. Then the following two theorems bound the ℓ_1-norm of primal and dual parameters respectively.

Theorem 3.2 (ℓ_1-norm of primal variables). *Let $\hat{\mathbf{w}} = (\hat{w}_0 = -1, \hat{\mathbf{w}}_{-0} = 0)$ be a trival solution. For any $\mathbf{w}_k$ with $F(\mathbf{w}_k) \le F(\hat{\mathbf{w}})$, we have*

$$\|\mathbf{w}_k\|_1 \le \frac{2n_p^k}{\lambda}. \tag{11}$$

where n_p^k is the number of positive samples of k-th class.

Proof. $\hat{\mathbf{w}}$ satisfies

$$F(\hat{\mathbf{w}}) = \frac{1}{2} + n_p^k \le 2n_p^k$$

since $\ell(-1, y_{ik}) = 0$ for $y_{ik} = -1$ and $\ell(0, y_{ik}) = 1$ for $y_{ik} = 1$. Then for any $\mathbf{w}_k$ of better objective than $\hat{\mathbf{w}}$,

$$\lambda\|\mathbf{w}_k\|_1 \le F(\mathbf{w}_k) \le F(\hat{\mathbf{w}}) \le 2n_p^k$$

which yields the result. □

Theorem 3.3 (ℓ_1-norm of dual variables). *Any optimal solution $\boldsymbol{\alpha}_k$ of (10) satisfies*

$$\|\boldsymbol{\alpha}_k^*\|_1 \le 4n_p^k.$$

Proof. Let $\mathbf{w}$, $\boldsymbol{\alpha}$ be the primal and dual variables for a particular class. By strong duality, the optimal dual objective (in its maximization form) equals to the optimal primal objective

$$\max_{\boldsymbol{\alpha}} -G(\boldsymbol{\alpha}) = \min_{\mathbf{w}} F(\mathbf{w})$$

and therefore, any optimal solution $(\mathbf{w}^*, \boldsymbol{\alpha}^*)$ satisfies

$$-\frac{1}{2}\|\mathbf{w}^*\|^2 + \sum_i \alpha_i^* = \frac{1}{2}\|\mathbf{w}^*\|^2 + \lambda\sum_{j=1}^{D}|w_j^*| + \sum_{i=1}^{N}\ell(\langle\mathbf{w}^*, \boldsymbol{x}_i\rangle, y_{ik}),$$

which yields the bound

$$\begin{aligned} \|\boldsymbol{\alpha}^*\|_1 &= \|\mathbf{w}^*\|^2 + \lambda\sum_{j=1}^{D}|w_j^*| + \sum_{i=1}^{N}\ell(\langle\mathbf{w}^*, \boldsymbol{x}_i\rangle, y_{ik}) \\ &\le 2\left(\frac{1}{2}\|\mathbf{w}^*\|^2 + \lambda\sum_{j=1}^{D}|w_j^*| + \sum_{i=1}^{N}\ell(\langle\mathbf{w}^*, \boldsymbol{x}_i\rangle, y_{ik})\right) \le 4n_p^k \end{aligned}$$

where the last inequality is due to the existence of $\hat{\mathbf{w}} = (\hat{w}_0 = -1, \hat{\mathbf{w}}_{-0} = 0)$ with primal objective $F(\hat{\mathbf{w}}) \le 2n_p^k$. □

Theorem 3.2 and 3.3 successfully bound the ℓ_1-norm of primal, dual variables by $n_p = O(N/K)$. Although a small ℓ_1-norm does not imply small number of non-zeros in general, we show in the next section that the *complexity* of our algorithm is determined by the ℓ_1 norm of primal and dual variables. In particular, in Section 4.2, we propose a random sparsification procedure that finds a sparse approximation to $\mathbf{w}_k$ in order to perform efficient greedy search of active coordinates. The procedure is guaranteed to find a sparse solution with number of non-zeros proportional to $\|\mathbf{w}_k\|_1^2$. Further, Section 4.3 gives an iteration complexity, and thus a bound on the active size, proportional to $\|\boldsymbol{\alpha}^*\|_1^2$, where $\boldsymbol{\alpha}^*$ is an optimal solution of (10).

4 ALGORITHM

In this section, we propose a greedy algorithm that alternates between the search of potential support vectors and the optimization over a small set of active samples. Note we have an objective (9) for each class k independent of other classes, so in the following we simply use $\boldsymbol{\alpha}$ to denote $\boldsymbol{\alpha}_k$ and $\mathbf{w}$ to denote $\mathbf{w}_k$ for a particular class k being solved. The algorithm will be performed for each class independently *without communication*, and thus it is inherently easy to parallelize.

4.1 A Greedy Active-Set Method

Instead of searching for the *confusing labels* of each sample as in [34], we propose a greedy algorithm that optimizes (10) by looking for *active samples* of each class. Note the domain of our objective (10) has box constraints $0 \le \alpha_i \le 1$ instead of simplex constraints as in [34], so a Frank-Wolfe-based algorithm used in [34] does not lead to sparse iterates. Here we propose a *greedy active-set coordinate descent* algorithm that alternates between the greedy search of novel active variables and the optimization over an active set.

The objective (10) has gradient of the form

$$\nabla G(\boldsymbol{\alpha}) = \hat{X}^T \mathbf{w}(\boldsymbol{\alpha}) - 1, \tag{12}$$

which can be evaluated in time $O(nnz(\mathbf{w})\bar{n})$ if the vector $\mathbf{w}(\boldsymbol{\alpha})$ is maintained whenever any dual coordinate α_i is changed, where $\bar{n}$ is an upper bound on the number of non-zero in each column of X. On the other hand, when $\boldsymbol{\alpha}$ is changed by $\Delta\boldsymbol{\alpha}$, the maintenance of

$$\mathbf{w}(\boldsymbol{\alpha} + \Delta\boldsymbol{\alpha}) = \mathbf{prox}_{\lambda\|.\|_1}(\hat{X}^T\boldsymbol{\alpha} + \hat{X}^T\Delta\boldsymbol{\alpha}) \tag{13}$$

requires a cost of $O(nnz(\Delta\boldsymbol{\alpha})\bar{d})$ where $\bar{d}$ is an upper bound on the number of non-zeros for each row of $\hat{X}$. Note one can exploit the sparsity of both $\hat{X}$ and $\mathbf{w}(\boldsymbol{\alpha})$ simultaneously when computing the gradients of all coordinates together as

$$\nabla G(\boldsymbol{\alpha}) = \sum_{j=0}^{D} w_j \hat{X}_{:,j}. \tag{14}$$

Therefore, an efficient algorithm exploits (14) to compute gradients of all coordinate simultaneously while updates only a small number of them to ensure a small $nnz(\Delta\alpha)$. This suggests a greedy strategy that optimizes only coordinates α_i leading to the most progress. The resulting algorithm is summarized in Algorithm 1, where we perform an inner minimization over active set via Randomized Dual Coordinate Descent (Algorithm 2) [13]. The cost of one epoch of Algorithm 2 over the active set is $O(|\mathcal{A}|\bar{d})$. Therefore, each iteration of Algorithm 1 has an overall cost of $O(nnz(\mathbf{w})\bar{n} + |\mathcal{A}|\bar{d})$. Note this is a cost sublinear to the size of data matrix $nnz(X)$ if $nnz(\mathbf{w}) \ll D$ and $nnz(\boldsymbol{\alpha}) \ll N$. In section 4.2 and 4.3, we give bounds on $nnz(\mathbf{w})$ and $|\mathcal{A}|$ that decreases with number of classes K.

Algorithm 1 Greedy Active-Set Algorithm

---

0. $\boldsymbol{\alpha} = 0, \boldsymbol{b} = \boldsymbol{1}, \mathcal{A} = \{i|y_{ik} = 1\}$ and $H_{ii} = \|\boldsymbol{x}_i\|^2, i \in [N]$.
for t=1.....T **do**
  1. Compute $\nabla G(\boldsymbol{\alpha})$ via random sparsification (Algorithm 3).
  2. $\mathcal{A} \leftarrow$ Pick κ variables $\notin \mathcal{A}$ of largest $-\nabla_{\alpha_i} G(\boldsymbol{\alpha})$.
  3. Minimize (10) w.r.t. coordinates in $\mathcal{A}$ via Algorithm 2.
  4. Eliminate $\{i \mid \alpha_i = 0 \;\&\; y_{ik} \neq 1\}$ from $\mathcal{A}$.
end for

Algorithm 2 Coordinate Descent for Acitve Subproblem

---

for s=1.....S **do**
  1. Draw $i \in \mathcal{A}$ uniformly at random.
  2. Compute $\nabla_i G(\boldsymbol{\alpha}) = y_i\langle \boldsymbol{w}, \boldsymbol{x}_i\rangle - 1$.
  3. $\Delta\alpha_i \leftarrow \min(\max(\alpha_i - \nabla_i G(\boldsymbol{\alpha})/H_{ii}, 0), U) - \alpha_i$
  4. Maintain (13) with update $\Delta\alpha_i$.
end for

4.2 Sublinear-Time Search via Random Sparsification

Given an ℓ_1 norm bounded by (11), we show that the maximum negative gradient found in Step 2 of Algorithm 1 can be approximated with δ precision when replacing $\boldsymbol{w}(\boldsymbol{\alpha})$ with its random sparsified version $\tilde{\boldsymbol{w}}$ obtained from Algorithm 3, where the number of non-zeros in $\tilde{\boldsymbol{w}}$ is bounded by the square of ℓ_1-norm as stated in the following theorem.

THEOREM 4.1. *Running the Random Sparsification procededure 3 for* $R = \lceil \frac{2\|\boldsymbol{w}\|_1^2}{\delta^2} \rceil$ *iterations gives a* $\tilde{\boldsymbol{w}}$ *satisfying*

$$nnz(\tilde{\boldsymbol{w}}) \leq \left(\frac{4n_p^2}{\lambda^2}\right)\frac{1}{\delta^2}, \tag{15}$$

with

$$\mathbb{E}[\min_i \; y_i\langle \tilde{\boldsymbol{w}}, \boldsymbol{x}_i\rangle] - \min_i \; y_i\langle \boldsymbol{w}, \boldsymbol{x}_i\rangle \leq \delta, \tag{16}$$

PROOF. Since the function $f(z) = \min_i \; z_i$ is 1-Lipschitz-continuous, we have

$$\min_i \; y_i\langle \tilde{\boldsymbol{w}}, \boldsymbol{x}_i\rangle - \min_i \; y_i\langle \boldsymbol{w}, \boldsymbol{x}_i\rangle \leq |\langle \tilde{\boldsymbol{w}}, \boldsymbol{x}_i\rangle - \langle \boldsymbol{w}, \boldsymbol{x}_i\rangle|.$$

Taking expectation over $\tilde{\boldsymbol{w}}$ on both sides, we have

$$\begin{aligned}\mathbb{E}[\min_i \; y_i\langle \tilde{\boldsymbol{w}}, \boldsymbol{x}_i\rangle] - \min_i \; y_i\langle \boldsymbol{w}, \boldsymbol{x}_i\rangle &\leq \mathbb{E}[|\langle \tilde{\boldsymbol{w}}, \boldsymbol{x}_i\rangle - \langle \boldsymbol{w}, \boldsymbol{x}_i\rangle|] \\ &\leq \sqrt{\mathbb{E}[|\langle \tilde{\boldsymbol{w}}, \boldsymbol{x}_i\rangle - \langle \boldsymbol{w}, \boldsymbol{x}_i\rangle|^2]}\end{aligned} \tag{17}$$

from Jensen's inequality. Since $\mathbb{E}[\langle \tilde{\boldsymbol{w}}, \boldsymbol{x}_i\rangle] = \langle \boldsymbol{w}, \boldsymbol{x}_i\rangle$ by the construction of $\tilde{\boldsymbol{w}}$ in Algorithm 3, the RHS of (17) corresponds to the square root of variance

$$\mathbb{E}[\min_i \; \langle \tilde{\boldsymbol{w}}, \boldsymbol{x}_i\rangle] \leq \sqrt{Var[\langle \tilde{\boldsymbol{w}}, \boldsymbol{x}_i\rangle]} = \frac{\|\boldsymbol{w}\|_1}{\sqrt{R}}.$$

The conclusion follows by noticing that $nnz(\tilde{\boldsymbol{w}}) \leq R$ and $\|\boldsymbol{w}\|_1$ satisfies (11). □

Note (16) implies that the greedy coordinate $\hat{i}$ found by approximate search and the coordinate found by exact search $i^* =$

Algorithm 3 Random Sparsification

INPUT: a vector $\boldsymbol{w} \in \mathbb{R}^D$.
0. $\tilde{\boldsymbol{w}}^0 = 0$.
for $r = 1...R$ **do**
  1. Draw $j \in [D]$ with probability $|w_j|/\|\boldsymbol{w}\|_1$.
  2. $\tilde{\boldsymbol{w}}^{(r)} \rightarrow \tilde{\boldsymbol{w}}^{(r-1)} + sign(w_j)\boldsymbol{e}_j$
end for
OUTPUT: $\tilde{\boldsymbol{w}} := \frac{\|\boldsymbol{w}\|_1}{R}\tilde{\boldsymbol{w}}^{(R)}$

$arg\min_i \; y_i\langle \boldsymbol{w}, \boldsymbol{x}_i\rangle - 1$ satisfy

$$\mathbb{E}[\nabla_{\hat{i}} G(\boldsymbol{\alpha})] \leq \nabla_{i^*} G(\boldsymbol{\alpha}) + 2\delta \tag{18}$$

Therefore, by replacing $\boldsymbol{w}$ with $\tilde{\boldsymbol{w}}$, we reduce the cost of gradient computation from the worst-case $O(nnz(\boldsymbol{w})\bar{n}) = O(D\bar{n})$ to $O(nnz(\tilde{\boldsymbol{w}})\bar{n})$ with a 2δ approximation error. In the next section, we will show that setting $\delta = O(N\hat{\epsilon})$ suffices for the global convergence of our Greedy Algorithm 1 to $\frac{1}{N}(G(\boldsymbol{\alpha}) - G^*) \leq \hat{\epsilon}$ for some $\hat{\epsilon} \in (0, 1)$. Therefore, we have

$$nnz(\tilde{\boldsymbol{w}}) = O(\frac{n_p^2}{\lambda^2 N^2 \hat{\epsilon}^2}) = O(\frac{k_p^2}{\lambda^2 K^2 \hat{\epsilon}^2}).$$

which could be much less than D in the Extreme Classification setting.

4.3 Convergence Analysis

In this section, we give an iteration complexity of Algorithm 1 that depends on the ℓ_1 norm of the optimal solution $\boldsymbol{\alpha}^*$. For simplicity of the analysis, we assume that a normalized feature matrix with $\|\boldsymbol{x}_i\| \leq 1$.

THEOREM 4.2. *Let* $\boldsymbol{\alpha}^*$ *be an optimal solution of* (10). *The iterates* $\{\boldsymbol{\alpha}^t\}_{t=1}^{\infty}$ *given by Algorithm 1 with Random Sparsification tolerance* $\delta \leq \frac{\epsilon}{4\|\boldsymbol{\alpha}^*\|_1}$ *has* $\mathbb{E}[G(\boldsymbol{\alpha}^t)] - G(\boldsymbol{\alpha}^*) \leq \epsilon$ *for any iterate*

$$t \geq \frac{4\|\boldsymbol{\alpha}^*\|_1^2}{\epsilon} + \frac{G(0) - G^*}{\|\boldsymbol{\alpha}^*\|_1^2}.$$

PROOF. Our dual objective (10) is of the form

$$g(\boldsymbol{\alpha}) + h(\boldsymbol{\alpha})$$

where $h(\boldsymbol{\alpha}) := \sum_{i=1}^N h_i(\alpha_i)$ and

$$h_i(\alpha) = \begin{cases} 0, & 0 \leq \alpha \leq 1 \\ \infty, & o.w. \end{cases}$$

and $g(\boldsymbol{\alpha}) = \frac{1}{2}\|\boldsymbol{w}(\boldsymbol{\alpha})\|^2 - \sum_{i=1}^N \alpha_i$ is smooth with Lipschitz-continuous gradient $\nabla g(\boldsymbol{\alpha})$. To see this, let $B_\alpha = \{j|w_j(\boldsymbol{\alpha}) \neq 0\}$. The generalized Hessian of $g(\boldsymbol{\alpha})$ is

$$\nabla^2 g(\boldsymbol{\alpha}) = X_{:,B_\alpha} X_{:,B_\alpha}^T$$

which has diagonal elements $\|\boldsymbol{x}_{i,B_\alpha}\|^2$ bounded by $\|\boldsymbol{x}_i\|^2 \leq 1$ and thus a spectral norm bounded by N. Then for any coordinate i, we have the following descent amount since the second derivative of the smooth part of objective is bounded by $\|\boldsymbol{x}_i\|^2 \leq 1$.

$$\min_\eta \; G(\boldsymbol{\alpha} + \eta\boldsymbol{e}_i) - G(\boldsymbol{\alpha}) \leq \min_\eta \; \nabla_i G * \eta + \frac{1}{2}\eta^2 + h_i(\alpha_i + \eta) \tag{19}$$

where $\boldsymbol{e}_i$ is an indicator vector. Note for $i \in \mathcal{A}$, the minimizer of RHS of (19) is 0 since the previous iteration already minimizes our objective w.r.t. the active set $\mathcal{A}$. And for $i \notin \mathcal{A}$, the minimizer of the RHS of (19) is $-[-\nabla_i G(\alpha)]_+^2/2$, which corresponds to the selection criteria at Step 2 of Algorithm 1. Therefore, at each iteration, the coordinate $\hat{i}$ and i^* found by the approximate and exact greedy search respectively satisfy

$$\begin{aligned}\mathbb{E}[G(\alpha+\Delta\alpha)]-G(\alpha) &\leq \mathbb{E}[\min_{\eta}\ G(\alpha+\eta e_{\hat{i}})]-G(\alpha)\\ &\leq \min_{\eta}\ \nabla_{i^*}G*\eta+\frac{1}{2}\eta^2+h_i(\alpha_i+\eta)+2\delta\eta\\ &\leq \min_{\eta}\ \langle\nabla G,\eta\rangle+\frac{1}{2}\|\eta\|_1^2+h(\alpha+\eta)+2\delta\sum_i\eta_i\end{aligned}$$

where the first inequality is because the update $\Delta\alpha$ is obtained by minimizing objective w.r.t. a working set $\mathcal{A}^{r+1}$ containing $\hat{i}$, and the second, third inequalities follow from (18) and the fact that a linear objective subject to ℓ_1 ball has minimizer at the corner respectively. Then we use convexity to obtain a global estimate of descent amount relative to the suboptimality $G(\alpha)-G(\alpha^*)$:

$$\mathbb{E}[G(\alpha+\Delta\alpha)]-G(\alpha) \tag{20}$$

$$\leq \min_{\eta}\ \langle\nabla G,\eta\rangle+\frac{1}{2}\|\eta\|_1^2+h(\alpha+\eta)+2\delta\sum_i\eta_i \tag{21}$$

$$\leq \min_{q\in[0,1]}\ q(\nabla G,\alpha^*-\alpha)+\frac{q^2}{2}\|\alpha^*\|_1^2+2q\delta\|\alpha^*\|_1 \tag{22}$$

$$\leq \min_{q\in[0,1]}\ -q(G(\alpha)-G(\alpha^*))+\frac{q^2}{2}\|\alpha^*\|_1^2+2q\delta\|\alpha^*\|_1 \tag{23}$$

where the last ineqaulity is from convexity, and the second inequality is from a restriction of optimization space to $\eta = q(\alpha^*-\alpha)$ and the fact that for $i\in\mathcal{A}$ the minimizer of (21) has $\eta_i=0$. Then choosing $\delta \leq \frac{G(\alpha)-G(\alpha^*)}{4\|\alpha^*\|_1}$ and minimizing the RHS w.r.t. q leads to

$$\mathbb{E}[G(\alpha+\Delta\alpha)]-G(\alpha) \leq -\frac{(G(\alpha)-G(\alpha^*))^2}{4\|\alpha^*\|_1^2} \tag{24}$$

for iterates with $G(\alpha)-G(\alpha^*)\leq 2\|\alpha^*\|_1^2$ and has

$$\mathbb{E}[G(\alpha+\Delta\alpha)]-G(\alpha)\leq -\|\alpha^*\|_1^2/2 \tag{25}$$

for iterates with $G(\alpha)-G(\alpha^*) > 2\|\alpha^*\|_1^2$. Note the constant descent amount (25) happens only in the beginning iterates when $G(\alpha)-G(\alpha^*)$ and can happen at most $2(G(0)-G(\alpha^*))/\|\alpha^*\|_1^2$ times. Considering those iterates of case (24), we have recursive relation $\Delta G^{t+1}-\Delta G^t \leq -\frac{(\Delta G^t)^2}{4\|\alpha^*\|_1^2}$ where $\Delta G^t := \mathbb{E}[G(\alpha^t)\mid\alpha^{t-1}]-G(\alpha^*)$. The recursion leads to the conclusion by, for example, Theorem 1 of [26]. □

Theorem 4.2 is significant when combined with Theorem 3.3, which gives us an iteration complexity of

$$t=\frac{4\|\alpha\|_1^2}{\epsilon}\leq\frac{64n_p^2}{\epsilon},$$

and also a bound on the active size $|\mathcal{A}|\leq\kappa t\leq\kappa\frac{64n_p^2}{\epsilon}$ that depends only on the number of positive examples. Considering the average case where $n_p = Nk_p/K$, for achieving $\frac{1}{N}(G(\alpha)-G^*)\leq\hat{\epsilon}\in(0,1)$, we have

$$|\mathcal{A}| = O(\frac{Nk_p^2}{K^2\hat{\epsilon}}).$$

Then the complexity for running Algorithm 1 on all classes is:

$$K*O(nnz(\tilde{w})\bar{n}+|\mathcal{A}|\bar{d}) = O\left(\frac{k_p^2\bar{n}}{K\lambda^2\hat{\epsilon}^2}+nnz(X)\frac{k_p^2}{K\hat{\epsilon}}\right),$$

times the number of iterations, which is a cost proportional to the factor k_p^2/K.

5 PRACTICAL ISSUES

5.1 Parallelization Architecture

The dual objective (10) comprises independent sub-objectives for different classes, and which moreover only differ by the set of labels $\{y_{ik}\}_{i=1}^N$. Under a shared-memory architecture each thread can share the same copy of data matrix X. In our implementation, we employ a two-layer parallelization with 10 computational nodes and 10 threads per node. Dynamic load balancing is performed by one of the thread which assigns new labels to a thread once it finishes its current job. Usually one can enjoy a nearly linear speedup as long as the number of parallel jobs is an order of magnitude less than K. More sophisticated communication and load balancing can also be achieved through distributed shared memory [10, 29] and scheduler [19].

5.2 Loss and Regularization Variants

In practice, we found replacing the hinge loss in (9) with a square hinge loss

$$\ell(z,y) := \frac{1}{2}\max(1-yz,0)^2$$

yields a better performance in our empirical evaluation. One can also introduce an additional tuning parameter τ for the ℓ_2 regularization in (9), although in our experiments we found $\tau = 1$ to be the optimal choice out of $\{0.1, 1, 10\}$ for most of the data sets.

5.3 Two-Level Sparsification

The sparsification of $\mathbf{w}$ described in section 4.2 reduces the cost of computing (14) from $O(nnz(X))$ to $O(nnz(\tilde{w})\bar{n})$. For some data sets, each column of X is dense ($\bar{n}\approx N$), but most of entries have small magnitude which contribute little to $\nabla G(\alpha)$. A trick to further speed up the greedy search is to consider only entries in X with magnitude larger than a threshold. Then by sorting each column of X in descending order of magnitude, one can stop traversing the sorted list once processed all entries of magnitude larger than the threshold. This trick improves the efficiency of the proposed method signficantly for a number of text data sets in our experiments.

6 EXPERIMENTS

In this section, we compare our proposed algorithm with state-of-the-art approaches on multiclass and multilabel problems chosen based on the experimental results shown in the Extreme Classification Repository [1] and [1, 34]. The compared methods are:

[1]https://manikvarma.github.io/downloads/XC/XMLRepository.html

Table 1: Results and statistics for large-scale Multilabel data sets, N_{train}= number of training samples, N_{test}= number of testing samples, T_{train} = training time, T_{test} = testing time, K = number of classes, D = number of features. P@k = top-k accuracy. DiSMEC and PPDSparse are parallelized with 100 cores. We highlight the best result for each metric, except that for T_{train} we highlight best results among single-core solvers (left four) and parallel solvers. For all experiments, we set a memory limit to be 100G. Experiments that exceeded limits are marked *Memory Limit Exceeded* (MLE).

Data	Metrics	FastXML	PfastreXML	SLEEC	PDSparse	DiSMEC	PPDSparse
Amazon-670K	T_{train}	**5624s**	6559s	20904s		174135s	**921.9s**
N_{train}=490449	P@1 (%)	33.12	32.87	35.62		43.00	**43.04**
N_{test}=153025	P@3 (%)	28.98	29.52	31.65	MLE	38.23	**38.24**
D=135909	P@5 (%)	26.11	26.82	28.85		34.93	**34.94**
K=670091	model size	**4.0G**	6.3G	6.6G		8.1G	5.3G
	T_{test}/N_{test}	**1.41ms**	1.98ms	6.94ms		148ms	20ms
WikiLSHTC-325K	T_{train}	**19160s**	20070s	39000s	94343s	271407s	**353s**
N_{train}=1778351	P@1 (%)	50.01	57.17	58.34	60.70	64.00	**64.13**
N_{test}=587084	P@3 (%)	32.83	37.03	36.7	39.62	**42.31**	42.10
D=1617899	P@5 (%)	24.13	27.19	26.45	29.20	**31.40**	31.14
K=325056	model size	14G	16G	650M	**547M**	8.1G	4.9G
	T_{test}/N_{test}	**1.02ms**	1.47ms	4.85ms	3.89ms	65ms	290ms
Delicious-200K	T_{train}	8832.46s	8807.51s	**4838.7s**	5137.4s	38814s	**2869s**
N_{train}=196606	P@1 (%)	**48.85**	26.66	47.78	37.69	44.71	45.05
N_{test}=100095	P@3 (%)	**42.84**	23.56	42.05	30.16	38.08	38.34
D=782585	P@5 (%)	**39.83**	23.21	39.29	27.01	34.7	34.90
K=205443	model size	1.3G	20G	2.1G	**3.8M**	18G	9.4G
	T_{test}/N_{test}	1.28ms	7.40ms	2.685ms	**0.432ms**	311.4ms	275ms
AmazonCat-13K	T_{train}	11535s	13985s	119840s	**2789s**	11828s	**122.8s**
N_{train}=1186239	P@1 (%)	**94.02**	86.06	90.56	87.43	92.72	92.72
N_{test}=306782	P@3 (%)	**79.93**	76.24	76.96	70.48	78.11	78.14
D=203882	P@5 (%)	**64.90**	63.65	62.63	56.70	63.40	63.41
K=13330	model size	9.7G	11G	12G	**15M**	2.1G	355M
	T_{test}/N_{test}	1.21ms	1.34ms	13.36ms	0.87ms	**0.20ms**	1.82ms

- **FastXML** [24]: An efficient and scalable tree-based algorithm. We adopted parameter setting suggested by the solver.
- **PfastreXML** [14]: An efficient and scalable tree ensemble based method improving upon FastXML by minimizing propensity-scored loss at each tree node, which leads to better performance on tail labels. Since all other methods are not adjusted based on the propensity, in our experiment we still measure performance via traditional top-k accuracy.
- **SLEEC** [2]: A non-linear solver that 1) partitions training sample into clusters and 2) compute local embeddings that preserves nearest neighbor structure within each cluster. Because of this composition of components, its performance highly relies on its parameter setting. We adopted settings suggested by the authors for each data set.
- **PDSparse** [34]: A Primal-Dual sparse method that minimizes a max-margin loss with ℓ_1-ℓ_2 regularization and enjoys sublinear complexity w.r.t. the number of classes.
- **DiSMEC** [1]: A distributed and parallelized method that learns one-versus-all classifiers with heuristic model compression (weight truncation). We run this method with 100 cores using the same parallelization framework to our solver.
- **PPDsparse**: The proposed method with 100 cores (10 machines with 10 cores on each machine).

All compared solvers are available from Extreme Classification Repository[1]. Other solvers not compared in this paper are i) *one-vs-all logistic regression, one-vs-all SVM, multiclass SVM, one-vs-all ℓ_1-regularized logistic regression*, implemented in *LibLinear* [12], ii) *Vowpal-Wabbit* [7], iii) *LEML* [36], iv) *RobustXML* [33], v) *PLT* [15], vi) *LPSR-NB* [30]. All of these have been shown less competitive in a number of previous papers [1, 34].

Experiments are conducted on four large-scale multilabel data sets, four medium-scale multilabel data sets and three large-scale multiclass data sets. We adopt data sets used by [1, 14, 24, 34] and also that from the Extreme Classification Repository [1]. Large-scale multilabel data sets are *WikiLSHTC-325K, Delicious-200K, Amazon-670K* and *AmazonCat-13K*. Medium-scale Multilabel data sets are *Mediamill, Bibtex, RCV1-2K* and *EURLex-4K*. They can be found at Extreme Classification Repository[1]. Multiclass data sets *LSHTC1, Dmoz* and *aloi.bin* are available [2] from authors of [34].

The data statistics and results are shown in Table 1, 2 and 3. For all experiments, we select our hyperparameter λ from $\{0.01, 0.1, 1\}$ and τ from $\{0.1, 1, 10\}$ to maximize the heldout performance. However, we observed that for most of data sets, $\tau = 1, \lambda = 0.01$ consistently gives the best performance. For large-scale multilabel datasets

[2] http://www.cs.utexas.edu/~xrhuang/PDSparse/

Table 2: Results and statistics for small Multilabel data sets, N_{train}= number of training samples, N_{test}= number of testing samples, T_{train} = training time, T_{test} = testing time, K = number of classes, D = number of features. P@k = top-k accuracy. DiSMEC and PPDSparse are parallelized with 100 cores. We highlight the best result for each metric, except that for T_{train} we highlight best results among single-core solvers (left four) and parallel solvers.

Data	Metrics	FastXML	PfastreXML	SLEEC	PDSparse	DiSMEC	PPDSparse
Mediamill	T_{train}	276.4s	293.2s	9504s	**23.8s**	**12.15s**	34.1s
N_{train}=30993	P@1 (%)	84.27	84.08	**87.37**	83.64	84.83	84.42
N_{test}=12914	P@3 (%)	67.34	67.45	**72.60**	66.13	67.17	67.26
D=120	P@5 (%)	53.06	53.23	**58.39**	50.90	52.80	52.78
K=101	model size	87M	88M	104M	**20K**	412K	412K
	T_{test}/N_{test}	0.27ms	0.37ms	4.95ms	**0.004ms**	0.142ms	0.078ms
Bibtex	T_{train}	21.68s	21.47s	296.86s	**7.71s**	**0.203s**	0.232s
N_{train}=4880	P@1 (%)	63.66	63.18	**64.77**	62.36	63.69	63.69
N_{test}=2515	P@3 (%)	39.42	**39.67**	38.97	36.50	38.80	39.43
D=1836	P@5 (%)	28.60	**29.47**	28.50	26.50	28.30	28.67
K=159	model size	34M	37M	5.2M	**20K**	2.1M	2.5M
	T_{test}/N_{test}	0.64ms	0.73ms	0.70ms	**0.007ms**	0.28ms	0.094ms
RCV1-2K	T_{train}	4874.4s	4947.2s	85212s	**709.5s**	641.1s	**35.0s**
N_{train}=623847	P@1 (%)	91.14	89.79	**91.36**	90.02	90.52	91.08
N_{test}=155962	P@3 (%)	73.35	72.65	**73.38**	71.92	72.31	72.93
D=47236	P@5 (%)	**52.69**	52.23	52.50	51.23	51.25	52.10
K=2456	model size	3.9G	4.1G	1.1G	**1.6M**	209M	23M
	T_{test}/N_{test}	0.87ms	1.08ms	53.95ms	**0.066ms**	1.72ms	0.338ms
EURLex-4K	T_{train}	**315.9s**	324.4s	4543.4s	773.2s	76.07s	**9.95s**
N_{train}=15539	P@1 (%)	70.86	70.33	**79.15**	75.90	70.61	74.61
N_{test}=3809	P@3 (%)	59.06	58.61	**64.09**	61.16	57.56	59.56
D=5000	P@5 (%)	49.58	49.69	**52.09**	50.83	47.33	48.43
K=3993	model size	384M	455M	121M	25M	15M	**9.5M**
	T_{test}/N_{test}	3.65ms	5.43ms	3.67ms	**0.73ms**	2.26ms	1.5ms

Table 3: Results and statistics for Multiclass data sets, N_{train}= number of training samples, N_{test}= number of testing samples, T_{train} = training time, T_{test} = testing time, K = number of classes, D = number of features. DiSMEC and PPDSparse are parallelized with 100 cores. We highlight the best result for each metric, except that for T_{train} we highlight best results among single-core solvers (left four) and parallel solvers.

Data	Metrics	FastXML	PfastreXML	SLEEC	PDSparse	DiSMEC	PPDSparse
aloi.bin	T_{train}	1900.9s	1901.6s	16193s	**139.8s**	92.0s	**7.05s**
N_{train}=100000	accuracy (%)	95.71	93.43	93.74	96.2	96.28	**96.38**
N_{test}=8000	model size	1.3G	1.3G	3.7G	19M	16M	**14M**
D=636911	T_{test}/N_{test}	5.05ms	5.10ms	28.00ms	0.064ms	0.02ms	**0.0178ms**
K=1000							
LSHTC1	T_{train}	1398.2s	1422.4s	5919.3s	**196.6s**	298.8s	**45.8s**
N_{train}=88806	accuracy (%)	22.04	**23.32**	12.2	22.46	22.74	22.70
N_{test}=5000	model size	937M	1.1G	631M	**88M**	142M	381M
D=347255	T_{test}/N_{test}	5.73ms	8.81ms	14.66ms	**0.40ms**	3.7ms	6.94ms
K=12294							
Dmoz	T_{train}	6475.1s	6619.7s	47490s	**2518.9s**	1972.0s	**170.60s**
N_{train}=345068	accuracy (%)	**40.76**	39.78	33.03	39.91	39.38	39.32
N_{test}=38340	model size	3.5G	3.8G	1.5G	**680M**	369M	790M
D=833484	T_{test}/N_{test}	3.29ms	3.20ms	40.43ms	**1.87ms**	4.58ms	6.58ms
K=11947							

(Table 1), we use tf-idf features with sample-wise normalization as suggested by the author of [1].

Our experimental results confirmed several comments from previous work [1, 34]: 1) Among single-core solvers (PDSparse, FastXML, PfastreXML, SLEEC), PDSparse can achieve orders of magnitude speed up in terms of training time without significantly downgrading performance compared to the direct one-vs-all approach (except on Delicious-200k, a data set of missing labels) . 2) Given enough computing resources, DiSMEC is able to achieve significantly higher accuracy than other approaches on some data sets. However, their training on the largest data sets typically take few days even with 100 cores.

From Table 1-3, we illustrate how our proposed PPDSparse method combines the strength from both PDSparse and DiSMEC. By adopting one-versus-all loss, PPDSparse can achieve accuracy as good as DiSMEC on most of data sets and resolve drawbacks of the max-margin loss used by PDSparse in three ways: (i) PPDSparse reduces the memory requirement of PDSparse by orders of magnitude due to the separation of training of each class, which clears the MLE issue of PDSparse on Amazon-670K, (ii) By embarassingly parallelized to 100 cores, PPDSparse is orders of magnitude faster than both PDSparse and parallel 1-vs-all (DiSMEC), (iii) the performance of PPDSparse is less sensitive to data set of mislabeling. On Delicious-200K, a data set of missing positive labels, PPDsparse improves accuracy of PDSparse significantly.

The training of PPDSparse is consistently faster than tree-based and local embedding methods by orders of magnitude while maintaining a competitive accuracy on most of data sets. On Amazon-670K and WikiLSHTC-325K, PPDSparse (and DisMEC) enjoy a significant increase in accuracy compared to tree-based approaches. On the other hand, the prediction speed of Primal Dual sparse approaches (PPDSparse, PDSparse) are slower than tree-based methods (FastXML, PfastreXML) on problems of more than 10^5 classes, while being comparable on medium-sized data sets of $10^3 - 10^4$ classes (Table 3), presumably because tree-based methods enjoy logarithmic-time prediction w.r.t. the number of classes.

7 ACKNOWLEDGEMENT

I.D. is supported by NSF via CCF-1320746, IIS-1546452, and CCF-1564000. W.D. is supported by ONR via N000141410684, and NSF via CCF-1629559. P.R. is supported by ARO via W911NF-12-1-0390 and NSF via IIS-1149803, IIS-1320894, IIS-1447574, and DMS-1264033, and NIH via R01 GM117594-01 as part of the Joint DMS/NIGMS Initiative to Support Research at the Interface of the Biological and Mathematical Sciences.

REFERENCES

[1] R. Babbar and B. Schölkopf. 2017. DiSMEC: Distributed Sparse Machines for Extreme Multi-label Classification. In *Proceedings of the Tenth ACM International Conference on Web Search and Data Mining (WSDM 2017)*.
[2] Kush Bhatia, Himanshu Jain, Purushottam Kar, Manik Varma, and Prateek Jain. 2015. Sparse local embeddings for extreme multi-label classification. In *Advances in Neural Information Processing Systems*. 730–738.
[3] Koby C. and Yoram S. 2002. On the algorithmic implementation of multiclass kernel-based vector machines. *The Journal of Machine Learning Research* (2002).
[4] Jie Chen and others. 2016. Efficient one-vs-one kernel ridge regression for speech recognition. In *Acoustics, Speech and Signal Processing (ICASSP), 2016 IEEE International Conference on*. IEEE, 2454–2458.
[5] Y.N. Chen and H.T. Lin. 2012. Feature-aware label space dimension reduction for multi-label classification. In *Advances in Neural Information Processing Systems*.
[6] Anna Choromanska, Alekh Agarwal, and John Langford. 2013. Extreme multi class classification. In *NIPS Workshop: eXtreme Classification, submitted*.
[7] Anna E Choromanska and John Langford. 2015. Logarithmic time online multiclass prediction. In *Advances in Neural Information Processing Systems*. 55–63.
[8] K. Crammer and Y. Singer. 2001. On the algorithmic implementation of multiclass kernel-based vector machines. *JMLR* (2001).
[9] Koby Crammer and Yoram Singer. 2003. A family of additive online algorithms for category ranking. *Journal of Machine Learning Research* 3, Feb (2003), 1025–1058.
[10] Wei Dai, Abhimanu Kumar, Jinliang Wei, Qirong Ho, Garth Gibson, and Eric P. Xing. 2015. Analysis of High-Performance Distributed ML at Scale through Parameter Server Consistency Models. In *Proceedings of the 29th AAAI Conference on Artificial Intelligence*.
[11] J. Deng, A.C. Berg, K. Li, and Li F-F. What does classifying more than 10,000 image categories tell us? In *ECCV 2010*.
[12] Rong-En Fan, Kai-Wei Chang, Cho-Jui Hsieh, Xiang-Rui Wang, and Chih-Jen Lin. 2008. LIBLINEAR: A library for large linear classification. *The Journal of Machine Learning Research* 9 (2008), 1871–1874.
[13] Cho-Jui Hsieh, Kai-Wei Chang, Chih-Jen Lin, S Sathiya Keerthi, and Sellamanickam Sundararajan. 2008. A dual coordinate descent method for large-scale linear SVM. In *Proceedings of 25th international conference on Machine learning*.
[14] Himanshu Jain, Yashoteja Prabhu, and Manik Varma. 2016. Extreme Multi-label Loss Functions for Recommendation, Tagging, Ranking & Other Missing Label Applications. In *Proceedings of the 22nd ACM SIGKDD International Conference on Knowledge Discovery and Data Mining*. ACM.
[15] Kalina Jasinska, Krzysztof Dembczynski, Róbert Busa-Fekete, Karlson Pfannschmidt, Timo Klerx, and E Hüllermeier. 2016. Extreme f-measure maximization using sparse probability estimates. In *Proceedings of the 33nd International Conference on Machine Learning*. 1435–1444.
[16] Sham Kakade, Shai Shalev-Shwartz, and Ambuj Tewari. 2009. On the duality of strong convexity and strong smoothness: Learning applications and matrix regularization. *Unpublished Manuscript, http://ttic. uchicago. edu/shai/papers/KakadeShalevTewari09. pdf* (2009).
[17] A. Kapoor, R. Viswanathan, and P. Jain. Multilabel classification using bayesian compressed sensing. In *NIPS 2012*.
[18] S Sathiya Keerthi and others. 2008. A sequential dual method for large scale multi-class linear SVMs. In *Proceedings of the 14th ACM SIGKDD international conference on Knowledge discovery and data mining*. ACM, 408–416.
[19] Jin Kyu Kim and others. 2016. STRADS: a distributed framework for scheduled model parallel machine learning. In *Proceedings of the Eleventh European Conference on Computer Systems*. ACM, 5.
[20] Simon Lacoste-Julien, Martin Jaggi, Mark Schmidt, and Patrick Pletscher. 2013. Block-Coordinate Frank-Wolfe Optimization for Structural SVMs. In *ICML 2013 International Conference on Machine Learning*. 53–61.
[21] P. Langley. 2000. Crafting Papers on Machine Learning. In *Proceedings of the 17th International Conference on Machine Learning (ICML 2000)*, Pat Langley (Ed.). Morgan Kaufmann, Stanford, CA, 1207–1216.
[22] O. Meshi, M. Mahdavi, and A. Schwing. Smooth and Strong: MAP Inference with Linear Convergence. In *NIPS 2015*.
[23] Ioannis Partalas and others. 2015. Lshtc: A benchmark for large-scale text classification. *arXiv preprint arXiv:1503.08581* (2015).
[24] Yashoteja Prabhu and Manik Varma. 2014. Fastxml: A fast, accurate and stable tree-classifier for extreme multi-label learning. In *Proceedings of the 20th ACM SIGKDD international conference on Knowledge discovery and data mining*.
[25] Ali Rahimi and Benjamin Recht. 2007. Random features for large-scale kernel machines. In *Advances in neural information processing systems*. 1177–1184.
[26] P. Richtárik and M. Takáč. 2014. Iteration complexity of randomized block-coordinate descent methods for minimizing a composite function. *Mathematical Programming* (2014).
[27] Shai Shalev-Shwartz and Tong Zhang. 2013. Stochastic dual coordinate ascent methods for regularized loss. *The Journal of Machine Learning Research* (2013).
[28] Ryan J Tibshirani and others. 2013. The lasso problem and uniqueness. *Electronic Journal of Statistics* 7 (2013), 1456–1490.
[29] Jinliang Wei, Wei Dai, Aurick Qiao, Qirong Ho, Henggang Cui, Gregory R Ganger, Phillip B Gibbons, Garth A Gibson, and Eric P Xing. 2015. Managed communication and consistency for fast data-parallel iterative analytics. In *Proceedings of the Sixth ACM Symposium on Cloud Computing*. ACM, 381–394.
[30] Jason Weston, Ameesh Makadia, and Hector Yee. 2013. Label Partitioning For Sublinear Ranking.. In *ICML (2)*. 181–189.
[31] Lingfei Wu and Andreas Stathopoulos. 2015. A preconditioned hybrid svd method for accurately computing singular triplets of large matrices. *SIAM Journal on Scientific Computing* 37, 5 (2015), S365–S388.
[32] Lingfei Wu, Ian EH Yen, Jie Chen, and Rui Yan. 2016. Revisiting random binning features: Fast convergence and strong parallelizability. In *Proceedings of the 22nd ACM SIGKDD International Conference on Knowledge Discovery and Data Mining*.
[33] Chang Xu, Dacheng Tao, and Chao Xu. 2016. Robust extreme multi-label learning. In *Proceedings of the 22nd ACM SIGKDD International Conference on Knowledge Discovery and Data Mining, San Francisco, CA, USA August*. 13–17.
[34] I.E.H. Yen, X. Huang, K. Zhong, P. Ravikumar, and I.S Dhillon. 2016. Pd-sparse: A primal and dual sparse approach to extreme multiclass and multilabel classification. In *Proceedings of the 33nd International Conference on Machine Learning*.
[35] I.E.H. Yen, T.W. Lin, S.D. Lin, P. Ravikumar, and I.S. Dhillon. Sparse random feature algorithm as coordinate descent in Hilbert space. In *NIPS 2014*.
[36] H.F. Yu, P. Jain, P. Kar, and I. S Dhillon. 2013. Large-scale multi-label learning with missing labels. *arXiv:1307.5101* (2013).
[37] Hui Zou and Trevor Hastie. 2005. Regularization and variable selection via the elastic net. *Journal of the Royal Statistical Society: Series B* (2005).

Local Higher-Order Graph Clustering

Hao Yin
Stanford University
yinh@stanford.edu

Austin R. Benson
Stanford University
arbenson@stanford.edu

Jure Leskovec
Stanford University
jure@cs.stanford.edu

David F. Gleich
Purdue University
dgleich@purdue.edu

ABSTRACT

Local graph clustering methods aim to find a cluster of nodes by exploring a small region of the graph. These methods are attractive because they enable targeted clustering around a given seed node and are faster than traditional global graph clustering methods because their runtime does not depend on the size of the input graph. However, current local graph partitioning methods are not designed to account for the higher-order structures crucial to the network, nor can they effectively handle directed networks. Here we introduce a new class of local graph clustering methods that address these issues by incorporating higher-order network information captured by small subgraphs, also called network motifs. We develop the Motif-based Approximate Personalized PageRank (MAPPR) algorithm that finds clusters containing a seed node with minimal *motif conductance*, a generalization of the conductance metric for network motifs. We generalize existing theory to prove the fast running time (independent of the size of the graph) and obtain theoretical guarantees on the cluster quality (in terms of motif conductance). We also develop a theory of node neighborhoods for finding sets that have small motif conductance, and apply these results to the case of finding good seed nodes to use as input to the MAPPR algorithm. Experimental validation on community detection tasks in both synthetic and real-world networks, shows that our new framework MAPPR outperforms the current edge-based personalized PageRank methodology.

1 INTRODUCTION

The goal of graph clustering—also called community detection or graph partitioning—is to identify clusters of densely linked nodes given only the graph itself [15]. The vast majority of algorithms optimize a function that captures the edge density of the cluster (a set of nodes), for instance, conductance or modularity. Most methods for clustering are *global* and seek to cluster all nodes of the network. *Local graph clustering*—also known as seeded or targeted graph clustering—is a specific case of this problem that takes an additional input in the form of a seed set of vertices. The idea is to identify a single cluster nearby the seed set without ever exploring the entire graph, which makes the local clustering methods much faster than their global counterparts. Because of its speed and scalability, this approach is frequently used in applications including ranking and community detection on the Web [13, 16], social networks [22], and bioinformatics [24]. Furthermore, the seed-based targeting is also critical to many applications. For example, in the analysis of protein-protein interaction networks, local clustering aids in determining additional members of a protein complex [45].

The theory and algorithms for local approaches are most well developed when using conductance as the cluster quality measure [2, 50]. Conductance, however, is only defined for simple undirected networks. Using principled local clustering methods for networks involving signed edges, multiple edge types, and directed interactions has remained an open challenge. Moreover, current cluster quality measures simply count individual edges and do not consider how these edges connect to form small network substructures, called network motifs. Such *higher-order connectivity structures* are crucial to the organization of complex networks [5, 35, 48], and it remains an open question how network motifs can be incorporated into local clustering frameworks. Designing new algorithms for *local higher-order graph clustering* that incorporate higher-order connectivity patterns has the potential to lead to improved clustering and knowledge discovery in networks.

There are two main advantages to local higher-order clustering. First, it provides new types of heretofore unexplored local information based on higher-order structures. Second, it provides new avenues for higher-order structures to guide seeded graph clustering. In our recent work, we established a framework that generalizes global conductance-based clustering algorithms to cluster networks based on higher-order structures [5]. However, there are multiple issues that arise when this framework is applied to local graph clustering methodologies that we address here.

Present work: Local higher-order clustering. In this paper we develop local algorithms for finding clusters of nodes based on higher-order network structures (also called *network motifs*, Figure 1). Our local methods search for a cluster (a set of nodes) S with minimal *motif conductance*, a cluster quality score designed to incorporate the higher-order structure and handle edge directions [5]. More precisely, given a graph G and a motif M, the algorithm aims to find a set of nodes S that has good motif conductance (for motif M) such that S contains a given set of seed nodes. Cluster S has good (low) motif conductance for some motif M if the nodes in S participate in many instances of M and there are few instances of M that cross the set boundary defined by S. Figure 2 illustrates the concept of motif conductance, where the idea is that we do not count the number of edges that are cut, but the number of times

KDD'17, August 13–17, 2017, Halifax, NS, Canada.

DOI: 10.1145/3097983.3098069

a given network motif M gets cut. This way edges that do not participate in a given motif (say, a triangle) do not contribute to the conductance. Motif conductance has the benefit that it allows us to focus the clustering on particular network substructures that are important for networks of a given domain. For example, triangles are important higher-order structures of social networks [19] and thus focusing the clustering on such substructures can lead to improved results.

Our main approach is to generalize Approximate Personalized PageRank (APPR) [2] to finding sets of provably small motif conductance (Theorem 4.3). The APPR method is a graph diffusion that "spreads" mass from a seed set to identify the cluster. It has an extremely fast running time, which is roughly proportional to the size of the output cluster. Our generalization, the motif-based APPR method, or MAPPR, uses a pre-processing step that transforms the original network into a weighted undirected graph where the weights depend on the motif of interest. This procedure finds all instances of the motif, but does not store the enumeration, which helps to scale to larger networks (for example, if the motif is a clique such as a triangle, no additional memory is needed by our method). We show that running APPR on this weighted network maintains the provably fast running time and has theoretical guarantees on cluster output quality in terms of motif conductance. An additional benefit of our MAPPR method is that it naturally handles directed graphs on which graph clustering has been a longstanding challenge. The original APPR method can only be used for undirected graphs, and existing local approaches for APPR on directed graphs are challenging to interpret [3].

We use MAPPR on a number of community detection tasks and show improvements over the corresponding edge-based methods. We show that using the triangle motif improves the detection of ground truth communities in synthetic networks. In addition, we identify important directed triangle motifs for recovering community structure in directed graphs.

We also show how to identify good seeds for finding local higher-order clusters when the motif is a clique. To do this, we develop a theory around the relationship between 1-hop neighborhoods, motif conductance, and a recently developed higher-order generalization of the network clustering coefficient. Essentially, we show that if the network has a large ℓth-order clustering coefficient C_ℓ, then there exists some node whose 1-hop neighborhood has small ℓ-clique conductance. We use a notion of local optimality in node neighborhood conductances to identify many good seed nodes for MAPPR and find that the resulting clusters capture global trends in the clustering structure of the graph.

In summary, our paper develops simple and flexible methods for local higher-order graph clustering with theoretical guarantees. By going beyond the old edge-based community detection objective functions, our work opens a new door to higher-order clustering and community detection problems that apply to a broad set of network clustering problems.

2 PRELIMINARIES

Before deriving our algorithms, we first go over the basic notation and cluster quality scores that we use throughout the paper. Our datasets will be simple, unweighted, possibly directed graphs $G = (V, E)$ with adjacency matrix A. We denote $n = |V|$ as the number of nodes and $m = |E|$ as the number of edges. Our algorithms will sometimes use a weighted graph $G_w = (V, E, W)$.

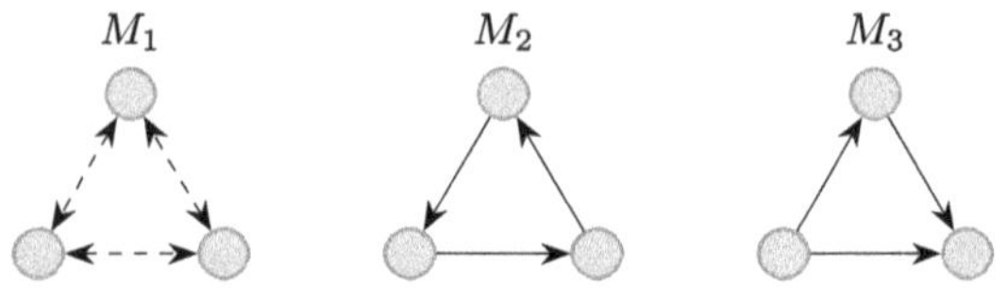

Figure 1: Examples of three directed motifs: a triangle in any direction (M_1), a cycle (M_2), and a feed-forward loop (M_3).

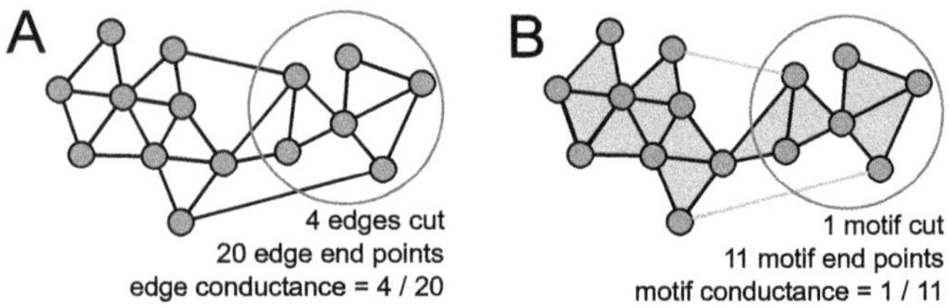

Figure 2: Illustration of (edge) conductance (A) and motif conductance (B) for the same set of nodes in the same graph, where the motif M is the triangle. Our methods finds clusters of nodes based on the motif conductance, where the user can decide which motif M to use for the clustering.

Cut, volume, and conductance. The *cut* of a set of nodes $S \subset V$, denoted by $\text{cut}(S)$, is the number of edges with one end point in S and the other end point in the complement set $\bar{S} = V \backslash S$. The *volume* of a set of nodes S, denoted by $\text{vol}(S)$, is the number of edge end points in S, i.e. $\text{vol}(S) = \sum_{u \in S} d_u$, where d_u is the degree of node u. The *conductance* of a set of nodes $S \subset V$ is

$$\phi(S) = \frac{\text{cut}(S)}{\min(\text{vol}(S), \text{vol}(\bar{S}))}.$$

Figure 2A illustrates the concept. When $\text{vol}(S) \leq \text{vol}(\bar{S})$, the conductance measures the ratio of the number of edges leaving S to the number of edges in S. Note that conductance is symmetric—$\phi(S) = \phi(\bar{S})$ since $\text{cut}(S) = \text{cut}(\bar{S})$. Conductance generalizes to weighted networks where $\text{cut}(S)$ is the sum of weights cut and $\text{vol}(S)$ is the sum of weighted degrees. Small conductance indicates a good cluster, and we will use this metric (and the motif conductance defined next) for evaluating cluster quality.

Conductance is recognized as one of the most important graph clustering criterions [39] and is empirically effective at capturing ground-truth communities compared to other popular measures used in community detection [47]. Although minimizing conductance is NP-hard [46], there are approximation algorithms with theoretical guarantees for finding clusters with small conductance [2, 9]. A known issue of using conductance as a global clustering criterion is cluster imbalance, i.e., the detected clusters tend to be of uneven sizes [29, 31]. In local clustering, we seek small clusters containing a seed node, so the imbalance works in our favor.

Motif cut, motif volume, and motif conductance. Benson et al. recently generalized the cut, volume, and conductance measures to account for network motifs [5]. For this paper, we define a network motif M to be any small connected graph (such as a triangle), and an *instance* of M in a graph G is some induced subgraph H of G

that is isomorphic to M. Given a motif M, the *motif cut* of a set of nodes S, denoted by $\text{cut}_M(S)$, is the number of instances of M that have at least one end point (i.e., node) in S and at least one end point in $\bar{S}$ (Figure 2B). The *motif volume* of a set of nodes S, denoted by $\text{vol}_M(S)$ is the number of motif instance end points in S, i.e., the number of times a node is in S, counted over each node in every instance of M. The *motif conductance* for a given motif M is then

$$\phi_M(S) = \frac{\text{cut}_M(S)}{\min(\text{vol}_M(S), \text{vol}_M(\bar{S}))}.$$

In the case that M is an edge, these definitions are simply the original cut, volume, and conductance measures described above. These definitions also accommodate mixtures of motifs (e.g., triangles *and* edges) by counting over the union of instances of each motif type.

Comparing edge and motif conductance. We often compare values of motif conductance to edge conductance (see Figure 2). Although these two objective functions measure different (but related) quantities, they both represent a probability. Edge conductance is equivalently the probability that traversing a random edge adjacent to a randomly selected node from the cluster leads outside the cluster (provided that the volume of the cluster is less than half of the total graph volume). Motif conductance is the probability that a traversing to a random end point of a randomly chosen motif adjacent to a randomly selected node from the cluster leaves the cluster (provided that the motif volume of the cluster is less than half of the total graph volume). Thus, a motif conductance much smaller than an edge conductance is evidence that the higher-order structured exposed by the motif characterizes the cluster structure more clearly.

3 RELATED WORK

We now summarize some additional related work. There are a few methods for global partitioning based on motifs [4, 5, 27, 38, 43]. This paper instead focuses on local clustering methods that examine local regions of the network. There are several methods for finding clusters containing a seed node beyond the personalized PageRank method considered here, including other graph diffusions [8, 26], local spectral methods [32, 33], local modularity maximization [10], flow-based algorithms [36], and minimum degree maximization [11, 40]. All of these local methods optimize edge-based criteria to find clusters, whereas we are focused on finding clusters based on motifs. We generalize the personalized PageRank method because of the algorithm's simplicity, scalability, and theoretical underpinnings. Most related to our approach are a couple of local clustering methods based on triangle frequencies through finding k-trusses containing a seed node [20] or by greedily growing a cluster from a seed node to avoid cutting triangles [38]. In the latter method, the notion of cutting a triangle is a special case of the motif cut discussed above.

Higher-order structures (under the names motifs, graphlets, or subgraphs) are crucial in many domains including neuroscience [41], biology [37], and social networks [44]. Many of our experiments use triangle motifs, which have long been studied for their frequency in social networks [19]. The algorithmic problem of counting or estimating the frequency of various higher-order patterns has also drawn a large amount of attention [1, 6, 12, 23].

4 MOTIF CONDUCTANCE MINIMIZATION

We now develop our local higher-order clustering methodology. We begin by generalizing the Approximate Personalized PageRank (APPR) algorithm of Andersen et al. [2] to quickly find a cluster containing a given seed node with minimal motif conductance. Our algorithm has theoretical guarantees on cluster quality and running time. We then show how the motif conductance of 1-hop neighborhoods in a network can be used to identify many good seed nodes.

4.1 Motif-based Approximate Personalized PageRank (MAPPR)

We now adapt the classical Approximate Personalized PageRank (APPR) method to account for motifs. The essential idea of our approach is to transform the input graph, which is unweighted and possibly directed, into a weighted undirected graph where the weights depend on the motif [5]. We then prove that the fast Approximate Personalized PageRank method on this weighted graph will efficiently find a set with small motif conductance that contains a given seed node. We also explain how previous theoretical results are applicable to this approach, which gives us formal guarantees on running time and cluster output quality in terms of motif conductance.

Background on APPR. The personalized PageRank (PPR) vector represents the stationary distribution of a particular random walk. At each step of the random walk, with a parameter $\alpha \in (0, 1)$, the random walker "teleports" back to a specified seed node u with probability $1 - \alpha$; and with probability α, the walker performs a random walk step. The key idea is that the stationary distribution of this process for a seed node u (the PPR vector p_u) will have large values for nodes "close" to u. We can write the stationary distribution as the solution to the following system of equations $(I - \alpha P)p_u = (1 - \alpha)e_u$, where I is the identity matrix, P is the column-stochastic transition matrix representing the random walk over the graph, and e_u is the indicator vector for node u. Formally, $P = AD^{-1}$, where A is the adjacency matrix, $D = \text{diag}(Ae)$ is the diagonal degree matrix, and e is the vector of all ones.

Andersen et al. developed a fast algorithm for approximating p_u by a vector $\tilde{p}_u$ where $0 \leq D^{-1}p_u - D^{-1}\tilde{p}_u \leq \varepsilon$ component-wise [2]. To obtain a cluster with small conductance from this approximation, a *sweep* procedure is used: (i) sort the nodes by descending value in the vector $D^{-1}\tilde{p}_u$, (ii) compute the conductance of each prefix in this sorted list, (iii) output the prefix set with smallest conductance. Overall, this algorithm is fast (it runs in time proportional to the size of the output cluster) and is guaranteed to have small conductance provided that node u is in a set with small conductance. We will be more specific with the guarantees in the following section, when we derive the analogous theory for the motif-based approach.

Adapting APPR for motifs. We now propose the motif-based APPR (MAPPR) algorithm that finds a cluster with small motif conductance by finding an approximate PPR vector on a weighted graph based on the motif. Given a motif M, MAPPR has three steps: (i) construct a weighted graph W, where W_{ij} is the number of instances of M containing nodes i and j, (ii) compute the approximate PPR vector for this weighted graph, (iii) use the sweep procedure to output the set with minimal conductance. Algorithm 1 formally

Algorithm 1: Motif-PageRank-Nibble method for finding localized clusters with small motif conductance.

Input: Unweighted graph $G = (V, E)$, motif M, seed node u, teleportation parameter α, tolerance ε
Output: Motif-based cluster (set $S \subset V$)
1 $W_{ij} \leftarrow$ #(instances of M containing nodes i and j)
2 $\tilde{p} \leftarrow$ Approximate-Weighted-PPR($W, u, \alpha, \varepsilon$) (Algorithm 2)
3 $D_W \leftarrow \text{diag}(We)$
4 $\sigma_i \leftarrow$ ith smallest entry of $D_W^{-1}\tilde{p}$
5 **return** $S \leftarrow \arg\min_\ell \phi_M(S_\ell)$, where $S_\ell = \{\sigma_1, \ldots, \sigma_\ell\}$

Algorithm 2: Approximate-Weighted-PPR

Input: Undirected edge-weighted graph $G_w = (V_w, E_w, W)$, seed node u, teleportation parameter α, tolerance ε
Output: an ε-approximate weighted PPR vector $\tilde{p}$
1 $\tilde{p}(v) \leftarrow 0$ for all vertices v
2 $r(u) \leftarrow 1$ and $r(v) \leftarrow 0$ for all vertices v except u
3 $d_w(v) \leftarrow \sum_{e \in E_w : v \in e} W(v)$
4 **while** $r(v)/d_w(v) \geq \varepsilon$ *for some node* $v \in V_w$ **do**
5 /* push operation */
6 $\rho \leftarrow r(v) - \frac{\varepsilon}{2} d_w(v)$; $\tilde{p}(v) \leftarrow \tilde{p}(v) + (1-\alpha)\rho$; $r(v) \leftarrow \frac{\varepsilon}{2} d_w(v)$
7 **for** *each* $x : (v, x) \in E_w$ **do** $r(x) \leftarrow r(x) + \frac{W(v,x)}{d_w(v)} \cdot \alpha\rho$
8 **return** $\tilde{p}$

describes this method. Note that step (i) needs to be done only once, whereas steps (ii) and (iii) would be repeated for multiple subsequent runs.

This method is motivated by the following result of Benson et al. [5], which says that for motifs on three nodes, standard conductance in the weighted graph is equal to motif conductance in the original graph.

Theorem 4.1 ([5], Theorem 5). *Denote the edge conductance in a graph H by $\phi^{(H)}(S)$. Let M be a motif on three nodes, and let G_W be the weighted graph where W_{ij} is the number of instances of M in graph G containing nodes i and j. Then $\phi_M^{(G)}(S) = \phi^{(G_W)}(S)$.*

(When the motif has more than 3 nodes, the weighted graph serves as a principled heuristic for motif conductance [5].) We interpret this result for our purposes: if we can find a set with low *edge* conductance in the weighted graph using APPR, then this set will have small *motif* conductance.

The APPR method is designed for *unweighted* graphs, whereas we want to use the method for weighted graphs. Mathematically, this corresponds to replacing the column stochastic matrix P in the linear system with the column stochastic matrix $P_W = WD_W^{-1}$, where $D_W = \text{diag}(We)$ is the diagonal weighted degree matrix. For the purposes of implementation, this modification is simple. We just need to change the algorithm's push method to push residual weights to neighbors proportional to edge weights (instead of evenly). We state the procedure in Algorithm 2.

For the purposes of theoretical analysis with motifs, it is important that our edge weights are integers so that we can interpret an edge with weight k as k parallel edges. Since all the analysis of APPR permits parallel edges in the graph, we can combine previous results for theoretical guarantees on Algorithm 1. The following result says that our algorithm runs in time proportional to the size of the output set.

Theorem 4.2. *Algorithm 1, after line 1, runs in $O(\frac{1}{\varepsilon(1-\alpha)})$ time, and the number of nodes with non-zero values in the output approximated PPR vector is at most $\frac{1}{\varepsilon(1-\alpha)}$.*

Proof. This follows from Andersen et al. [2, Lemma 2], where we translate G_w into a unweighted graph with parallel edges. □

Although APPR with weighted edges has used before [3, 17], there was never a runtime bound. This result is the first (albeit straightforward) theoretical bound on the runtime of APPR with weighted edges when they arise from integers.

Our next result is a theoretical guarantee on the quality of the output of Algorithm 1 in terms of motif conductance. The proof of the result follows from combining Theorem 4.1 and the analysis of Zhu et al. [50] (an improvement over the analysis of Andersen et al.). The result says that if there is some set T with small motif conductance, then there are several nodes in T for which Algorithm 1 outputs a set with small motif conductance. For notation, let η be the inverse mixing time of the random walk on the subgraph induced by T.

Theorem 4.3. *Let $T \subset V$ be some unknown targeted community we are trying to retrieve from an unweighted graph using motif M. Then there exists $T^g \subseteq T$ with $\text{vol}_M(T^g) \geq \text{vol}_M(T)/2$, such that for any seed $u \in T^g$, Algorithm 1 with $1 - \alpha = \Theta(\eta)$ and $\varepsilon \in [\frac{1}{10\text{vol}_M(T)}, \frac{1}{5\text{vol}_M(T)}]$ outputs a set S with*

$$\phi_M(S) \leq \tilde{O}\left(\min\left\{\sqrt{\phi_M(T)}, \phi_M(T)/\sqrt{\eta}\right\}\right).$$

The final piece we need to consider is the complexity of forming the weighted graph in line 1 of Algorithm 1. For ℓ-clique motifs, we use the method of Chiba and Nishizeki to compute the adjacency matrix W in $O(\ell a^{\ell-2} m)$ time, where a is the arboricity of the graph [7] and m is the number of edges in the graph. This is sufficient for the motifs considered in this paper, and there are also efficient algorithms for counting other types of motifs [34]. Note that this computation can be reused for many subsequent evaluations of the clustering algorithm for different seeds.

Towards purely local methods. Our method precomputes the number of motif instances containing each pair of nodes. Computing W is a (possibly large) upfront cost, but subsequently finding local clusters for any given seed node is fast. The graph weighting procedure could also be done locally by having the push procedure compute W_{vx} "on the fly" for all nodes x adjacent to node v. This suffices for Algorithm 2, but Algorithm 1 needs to know the total volume of the weighted graph to compute the motif conductance scores. To address this, one might use recent techniques for quickly estimating the total ℓ-clique volume on large graphs [21]. We leave the runtime analysis of this purely local method for future work.

Practical considerations. The formal theory underlying the methods (Theorem 4.3) requires multiple apriori unknowable parameters including the inverse mixing time η of the target community and the volume of the output. As practical guidance, we suggest using $\alpha = 0.98$, computing the PPR vector for $\varepsilon = 10^{-2}/\bar{d}_M$, $10^{-3}/\bar{d}_M$, $10^{-4}/\bar{d}_M$, where $\bar{d}_M = \frac{1}{n}\text{vol}_M(G)$ is the average motif-degree of all nodes, and outputting the set of best motif conductance. The reason for scaling by $\bar{d}_M$ is as follows. Theorem 4.2 bounds the running time by volume as if accessing an edge (i, j) with weight W_{ij} takes $\Theta(W_{ij})$ time (i.e., as if the edges are parallel). However, we merely need to access the value W_{ij}, which takes $O(1)$ time. Scaling ε by $\bar{d}_M$ accounts for the average effect of parallel edges present due to the weights of the motifs and permits the algorithm to do more computation with roughly the same running time guarantees.

Rather than using the global minimum in the sweep procedure in the last step of the Nibble method, we apply the common heuristic of finding the first local minimum [47]. The first local minimum is the smallest set where the PageRank vector suggests a border between the seed and the rest of the graph. It also better models the small size scale of most ground truth communities that we encounter in our experiments.

4.2 Finding many good seed nodes

So far we have proposed MAPPR to find a *single* cluster containing a *given* seed with minimal motif conductance. Now we consider the problem of how to quickly find *many* clusters with small motif conductance. Our approach will examine small network neighborhoods of nodes to identify good seeds for the targeted cluster expansion of MAPPR. We justify the use of these neighborhoods from a technical result that establishes a relationship between 1-hop neighborhoods and clusters of small motif conductance.

Informally, our key theorem is: Real world graphs with large clustering coefficients have a 1-hop neighborhood with small motif conductance for clique motifs. We can find this set since we can compute the motif conductance of all 1-hop neighborhoods efficiently. The result holds for undirected graphs only, so we will be concerned only with undirected graphs in this section. We establish our result in theory in this section and demonstrate the result in practice in Section 5.

The formal theory rests on the idea of higher-order clustering coefficients, which we developed in recent work [49] and briefly review below. As an extreme case of our theory, consider a graph with clustering coefficient 1. Then that graph will be a union of cliques, and any 1-hop neighborhood in that graph is a cluster with motif conductance of zero. The theory developed in this section relaxes this extreme setting and relates large clustering coefficients to finding node neighborhoods with small motif conductance. Our experiments in Section 5.3 show that these node neighborhoods are even better than our theory would predict.

Background on higher-order clustering coefficients. First, we introduce the definition of higher-order clustering coefficients proposed by Yin et. al [49]. The classical clustering coefficient is the fraction of wedges (length-2 paths) in the graph that are closed (i.e., induce a 3-clique, or a triangle). We can alternatively interpret each wedge as a (2-clique, adjacent edge) pair, where the "adjacent edge" shares a single node with the 2-clique (edge). The clustering coefficient is formally $C = 6|K_3|/|W|$, where K_3 is the set of 3-cliques, W is the set of (2-clique, adjacent edge) wedges, and the constant 6 comes from the fact that each 3-clique closes 6 wedges.

The generalization to higher-order clustering coefficients follows by simply looking at the fraction of (ℓ-clique, adjacent edge) pairs, or *ℓ-wedges*, that are "closed", i.e., induce an $(\ell+1)$-clique. Formally, the *ℓth-order clustering coefficient* is

$$C_\ell = (\ell^2 + \ell)|K_{\ell+1}|/|W_\ell|,$$

where $K_{\ell+1}$ is the set of $(\ell+1)$-cliques, W_ℓ is the set of ℓ-wedges, and the $(\ell^2 + \ell)$ comes from the fact that each $(\ell + 1)$-clique closes that many wedges. We can also measure local clustering with respect to a node u. Formally, the *local ℓth-order clustering coefficient* of node u is

$$C_\ell(u) = \ell|K_{\ell+1}(u)|/|W_\ell(u)|,$$

where $K_{\ell+1}(u)$ is the set of $(\ell + 1)$-cliques containing node u and $W_\ell(u)$ is the set of ℓ-wedges centered at u, i.e., the set of (ℓ-clique, adjacent edge) pairs whose intersection is node u.

Theory. Next, we state our main result of this section, which says that if the network exhibits higher-order clustering, i.e., C_ℓ is large, then there is a 1-hop neighborhood with small ℓ-clique conductance. For notation, let $N(u)$ denote the nodes in the 1-hop neighborhood of node u, i.e., $N(u) = \{v \in V \mid (u, v) \in E\} \cup \{u\}$.

THEOREM 4.4. *Let graph $G = (V, E)$ have ℓth-order clustering coefficient C_ℓ. Suppose that $\mathrm{vol}_{K_\ell}(N(u)) \leq \mathrm{vol}_{K_\ell}(V)/2$ for each node u. Then there exists a node $u \in V$ such that*

$$\phi_{K_\ell}(N(u)) \leq \frac{1 - C_\ell}{1 - C_\ell + [C_\ell/(1 + \sqrt{1 - C_\ell})]^2} \quad (1)$$

$$\leq \min\{2(1 - C_\ell), 1\}. \quad (2)$$

The bound in Theorem 4.4 is monotonically decreasing and approaches 0 as C_ℓ approaches 1. This result is a generalization of a similar statement for edge conductance [18], but prior results contain only the case of $\ell = 2$ and only use the weaker bound (2) of Theorem 4.4.

We now prove this result via several technical results relating higher-order clustering coefficients and motif conductance, where the motif is a clique. We note that many of the results are generalizations of previous theory developed by Gleich and Seshadhri [18].

The following lemma relates the higher-order clustering coefficient with neighborhood cuts, which we use to prove Theorem 4.4.

LEMMA 4.5. $\sum_{v \in V} \mathrm{cut}_{K_\ell}(N(v)) \leq (1 - C_\ell) \cdot |W_\ell|$.

PROOF. If an ℓ-clique $(u_1, \ldots u_\ell)$ gets cut from $N(v)$, then v must directly connect with one of $u_1, \ldots, u_\ell$, say u_1. Note that the clique $(u_1, \ldots u_\ell)$ and adjacent edge (u_1, v) form an open $(\ell + 1)$-wedge since v can not connect to all of $u_1, \ldots, u_\ell$. Therefore, we have an injective map from any cut clique on the left-hand side of the inequality to an open ℓ-wedge. □

Next, we define a probability distribution on the nodes, $p_\ell(u) = |W_\ell(u)|/|W_\ell|$, which connects the global and local ℓth-order clustering coefficient in the following lemma.

LEMMA 4.6. $\sum_{u \in V} p_\ell(u) C_\ell(u) = C_\ell$.

PROOF.

$$\sum_{u \in V} p_\ell(u) C_\ell(u) = \sum_{u \in V} \frac{|W_\ell(u)|}{|W_\ell|} \cdot \frac{\ell \cdot |K_{\ell+1}(u)|}{|W_\ell(u)|}$$

$$= \frac{\ell}{|W_\ell|} \cdot \sum_{u \in V} |K_{\ell+1}(u)| = \frac{\ell}{|W_\ell|} \cdot (\ell + 1)|K_{\ell+1}| = C_\ell. \quad \square$$

The following lemma creates a random variable whose expectation is bounded by $1 - C_\ell$, which we use in the proof of Theorem 4.4.

LEMMA 4.7. $\sum_{u \in V} p_\ell(u) \frac{\mathrm{cut}_{K_\ell}(N(u))}{|W_\ell(u)|} \leq 1 - C_\ell$.

Proof. Using Theorem 4.5, $\sum_{u \in V} p_\ell(u) \frac{\text{cut}_{K_\ell}(N(u))}{|W_\ell(u)|}$ $= \frac{1}{|W_\ell|} \sum_{u \in V} \text{cut}_{K_\ell}(N(u)) \le \frac{1}{|W_\ell|}(1 - C_\ell) \cdot |W_\ell| = 1 - C_\ell$. □

We are finally ready to prove our main result, and we will prove the existence using the probabilistic method. Suppose we choose a node u according to the probability distribution $p_\ell(u)$. Let $X = \text{cut}_{K_\ell}(N(u))/|W_l(u)|$ be a random variable. According to Lemma 4.7, $\mathbb{E}[X] \le 1 - C_\ell$. Then for any constant $a > 1$, by Markov's inequality, we have $\mathbb{P}[X > a(1-C_\ell)] \le 1/a$. Let $b = (aC_\ell - 1)/(a-1)$, and $p = \mathbb{P}[C_\ell(u) < b]$. Now according to Lemma 4.6, we have that

$$C_\ell = \sum_{C_\ell(u)<b} p_\ell(u)C_\ell(u) + \sum_{C_\ell(u)\ge b} p_\ell(u)C_\ell(u) < bp + (1-p).$$

Thus $p < (1 - C_\ell)/(1 - b) = 1 - 1/a$. By the union bound, the probability that $\text{cut}_{K_\ell}(N(u))/|W_\ell(u)| > a(1 - C_\ell)$ or $C_\ell(u) < b$ is less than 1. Therefore, there exists some node u such that $\text{cut}_{K_\ell}(N(u)) \le a(1 - C_\ell) \cdot |W_\ell(u)|$ and $C_\ell(u) \ge b$. Now we show that, for this u, we have

$$\phi_\ell(N(u)) \le [1 - C_\ell] \,/\, [1 - C_\ell + (aC_\ell - 1)/(a-1)]\,.$$

We first find a lower bound on $\text{vol}_{K_\ell}(N(u))$. First, each ℓ-clique cut would contribute at least one into $\text{vol}_{K_\ell}(N(u))$. Second, each $(\ell + 1)$-clique in $K_{\ell+1}(u)$ uniquely corresponds to an ℓ-clique in $N(u)$ which is induced by the ℓ nodes in the $(\ell + 1)$-clique other than u, thus will contribute ℓ into $\text{vol}_{K_\ell}(N(u))$. Note that each $(\ell + 1)$-clique in $K_{\ell+1}(u)$ closes ℓ different ℓ-wedges in $W_\ell(u)$, and there are $C_\ell(u)|W_\ell(u)|$ closed ℓ-wedges. Therefore, by combining all the observations here, we have

$$\begin{aligned}\text{vol}_{K_\ell}(N(u)) &\ge \text{cut}_{K_\ell}(N(u)) + \ell \cdot C_\ell(u)|W_\ell(u)|/\ell \\ &\ge \text{cut}_{K_\ell}(N(u)) + b|W_\ell(u)|.\end{aligned}$$

Now combining that $\text{cut}_{K_\ell}(N(u)) \le a(1 - C_\ell) \cdot |W_\ell(u)|$ and our assumption that $\text{vol}_{K_\ell}(N(u)) \le \text{vol}_{K_\ell}(\overline{N(u)})$,

$$\begin{aligned}\phi_{K_\ell}(N(u)) &= \frac{\text{cut}_{K_\ell}(N(u))}{\text{vol}_{K_\ell}(N(u))} \le \frac{\text{cut}_{K_\ell}(N(u))}{\text{cut}_{K_\ell}(N(u)) + b|W_\ell(u)|} \\ &\le \frac{a(1-C_\ell)\cdot|W_\ell(u)|}{a(1-C_\ell)|W_\ell(u)| + b|W_\ell(u)|} = \frac{1-C_\ell}{1 - C_\ell + \frac{aC_\ell - 1}{a(a-1)}}.\end{aligned}$$

Finally, (1) is obtained by setting $a = (1 + \sqrt{1 - C_\ell})/C_\ell$. □

Local minima as good seeds. Theorem 4.4 says that there must be at least one node whose 1-hop neighborhood has small motif conductance for clique motifs, provided there is higher-order clustering in the network. We use this as motivation to consider nodes whose 1-hop neighborhoods have small motif conductance as candidate seed nodes for MAPPR. Following the terminology of Gleich and Seshadhri [18], we say that a node u is a *locally minimal* if $\phi_M(N(u)) \le \phi_M(N(v))$ for all neighbors v of u. Between between 1% and 15% of nodes are local minima in the datasets we consider in Section 5.3. In that section, we verify that these local minima are in fact better seeds for MAPPR compared to random nodes, and we show that running MAPPR with all of these seeds is sufficient for reconstructing the global structure of the network.

5 EXPERIMENTS

In this section, we first evaluate the performance of our MAPPR algorithm on networks with ground truth communities or clusters, both on synthetic networks in Section 5.1 and on real-world networks in Section 5.2.[1] Our evaluation procedure of both the edge-based APPR and MAPPR is the following. For each ground truth community, we use every node as a seed to obtain a set and then pick the set with the highest F_1 score for recovering the ground truth. Next, we average of the F_1 scores over all detected communities for the detection accuracy of the method. This measurement captures how well the community can be recovered, and has previously been used to compare seeded clustering algorithms [26].

In Section 5.3, we empirically evaluate the theory of Section 4.2 for finding good seed nodes. We first show the existence of 1-hop neighborhood clusters of small motif conductances in real-world networks, and then use this idea to find seeds upon which running MAPPR will output many clusters with small motif conductance.

5.1 Recovering communities in synthetic networks with MAPPR

We first evaluate our MAPPR method for recovering ground truth in two common synthetic random graph models—the planted partition model and the LFR model. In both cases, we find that using triangle motifs increases the range of parameters in which we are able to recover the ground truth communities.

Planted partition model. The planted partition model generates an undirected unweighted graph with kn_1 nodes. Nodes are partitioned into k built-in communities, each of size n_1. Between any pair of nodes from the same community, an edge exists with probability p and between any pair of nodes from different communities, an edge exists with probability q. Each edge exists independently of all other edges.

In our experiment, we examine the behavior of MAPPR and the edge-based APPR methods by fixing parameters $n_1 = 50$, $k = 10$, $p = 0.5$, and takings different values of q such that the community mixing level $\mu = [(k - 1)q]/[p + (k - 1)q]$, which measures the fraction of neighbors of a node that cross cluster boundary, varies from 0.1 to 0.9. For each value of μ, we computed the average of the "mean best" F_1 score described above over 20 random instances of the graph. For MAPPR, we used the triangle motif. We are motivated in part by recent theoretical results of Tsourakakis et al. showing that with high probability, the triangle conductance of a cluster in the planted partition model is smaller than the edge conductance [43]. Here we take an empirical approach and study recovery instead of conductance.

Figure 3A illustrates the results. Using triangles with MAPPR significantly outperforms the edge-based APPR method when $\mu \in [0.4, 0.6]$. In this regime, for any given node, the expected number of intra-community edges and inter-community edges is roughly the same. Thus, the edge-based method degrades in performance. However, the number of intra-community triangles remains greater than the number of inter-community triangles, so the triangle-based method is able to recover the planted partition.

LFR model. The LFR model also generates random graphs with planted communities, but the model is designed to capture several properties of real-world networks with community structure such as skew in the degree and community size distributions and overlap in community membership for nodes [28]. For our purposes, the

[1] As part of this paper, real-world datasets and implementations of the MAPPR algorithms are available at http://snap.stanford.edu/mappr.

Table 1: Recovery of ground truth community structure in undirected graphs using edge-based and motif-based APPR (MAPPR), where the motif is the triangle. Bold numbers denote better recovery or smaller conductance with 5+% relative difference. F_1 score, precision, and recall are all averages over the 100 ground truth communities.

				F_1 score		Precision		Recall		Motif conductance	
Network	$\|V\|$	$\|E\|$	# comms. (sizes)	edge	triangle	edge	triangle	edge	triangle	edge	triangle
com-DBLP	317K	1.05M	100 (10–36)	0.264	0.269	0.342	**0.366**	0.310	**0.329**	0.393	0.384
com-Amazon	335K	926K	100 (10–178)	**0.620**	0.556	0.634	0.660	**0.704**	0.567	0.163	**0.065**
com-YouTube	1.13M	2.99M	100 (10–200)	0.140	**0.165**	0.233	**0.390**	0.147	**0.188**	**0.536**	0.739
com-LiveJournal	4.00M	34.7M	100 (10–10)	0.255	**0.274**	0.216	**0.280**	0.606	**0.672**	0.498	**0.409**
com-Orkut	3.07M	117M	100 (10–200)	0.063	**0.078**	0.072	**0.117**	**0.212**	0.166	0.702	**0.510**
com-Friendster	65.6M	1.81B	100 (10–191)	0.095	**0.114**	0.103	**0.158**	0.204	**0.234**	0.747	**0.622**

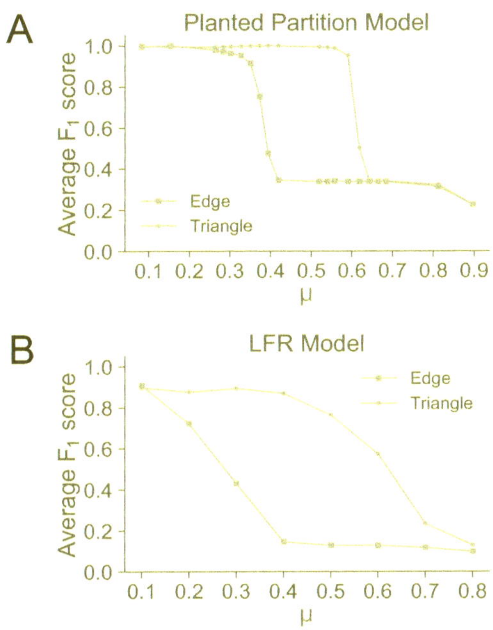

Figure 3: Average F_1 score on detected clusters in the planted partition model (A) and LFR model (B) as a function of the mixing parameter μ that specifies the fraction of neighbors of a node that cross cluster boundaries. We use the classical edge-based APPR and our triangle-based MAPPR to recover ground truth clusters. There is a large parameter regime where the triangle-based approach significantly outperforms the edge-based approach in both models.

most important model parameter is the mixing parameter μ, which is the fraction of a node's edges that connect to a node in another community. We fix the other parameters as follows: $n = 1000$ is the number of nodes, where 500 nodes belong to 1 community and 500 belong to 2; the number of communities is randomly chosen between 43 and 50; the average degree is 20; and the community sizes range from 20 to 50.

We again use the edge-based APPR method and MAPPR with the triangle motif. Figure 3B shows the results. The performance of the edge-based method decays as we increase the mixing parameter μ from 0.1 to 0.4, while the triangle-based method maintains an F_1 score of approximately 0.9 in this regime. For mixing parameters as large as 0.6, the F_1 score for MAPPR is still three times larger than that of the edge-based method, and throughout nearly the entire parameter space, using triangles improves performance.

To summarize, incorporating triangles into personalized PageRank dramatically improves the recovery of ground truth community structure in synthetic models. In the next section, we run experiments on both undirected and directed real-world networks.

5.2 Recovering communities in real-world networks with MAPPR

We now compare the edge- and motif-based APPR methods on real-world networks with ground truth communities. Although these graphs have as many as 1.8 billion edges, the APPR method takes at most a few seconds per seed once the graph is in memory.

Undirected graphs. We analyzed several well-known networks with ground truth community structure constructed from Web data: com-Amazon, com-DBLP, com-YouTube, com-LiveJournal, com-Orkut, and com-Friendster [47]. For each network, we examined 100 communities whose sizes ranged between 10 and 200 nodes. Summary statistics of the datasets and our experiment are in Table 1. In 5 out of 6 networks, MAPPR achieves a higher F_1 score than edge-based APPR. In 3 of the 5 networks, the F_1 score provides a relative improvement of over 5%. In all 6 networks, the average precision of the recovered clusters is larger, and in 4 of these networks, the change is greater than 5%. We suspect this arises from triangles encouraging more tight-knit clusters. For example, dangling nodes connected by one edge to a cluster are ignored by the triangle-based method, whereas such a node would increase the edge-based conductance of the set. In 4 of the 6 networks, recall in the triangle-based method provides relative improvements of at least 5%.

Directed graphs. A major advantage of MAPPR is that it easily handles directed graphs; we simply need to specify the directed motifs. Here, we use the three different directed triangle motifs in Figure 1 (M_1, the undirected triangle; M_2, the cycle; and M_3, the feed-forward loop). We form our motif weighted matrix W with respect to general subgraphs (i.e., *not* induced subgraphs). Thus, a triangle with all six directed edges contains 1 instance of motif M_1, 2 instances of motif M_2, and 2 instances of motif M_3.

We analyze two directed networks. The first is an e-mail network between members of a European research institution (email-Eu), where department membership of researchers are the ground truth

Table 2: Recovery of ground truth communities in directed graphs using edge-based and motif-based APPR for the three triangular motifs in Figure 1. Bold numbers denote (i) cases where a motif-based method's score is a 5+% relative improvement over the edge-based method and (ii) cases where the edge-based method out-performs all 3 motif-based methods by 5+%.

				F_1 score				Precision				Recall			
Network	$\|V\|$	$\|E\|$	# comms. (sizes)	edge	M_1	M_2	M_3	edge	M_1	M_2	M_3	edge	M_1	M_2	M_3
EMAIL-EU	1.00K	25.6K	28 (10–109)	0.398	**0.496**	**0.443**	**0.483**	0.502	**0.580**	**0.605**	**0.660**	**0.754**	0.685	0.577	0.594
WIKI-CATS	1.79M	28.5M	100 (21–192)	0.239	0.246	0.234	0.231	0.334	**0.368**	**0.391**	**0.360**	**0.377**	0.327	0.226	0.328

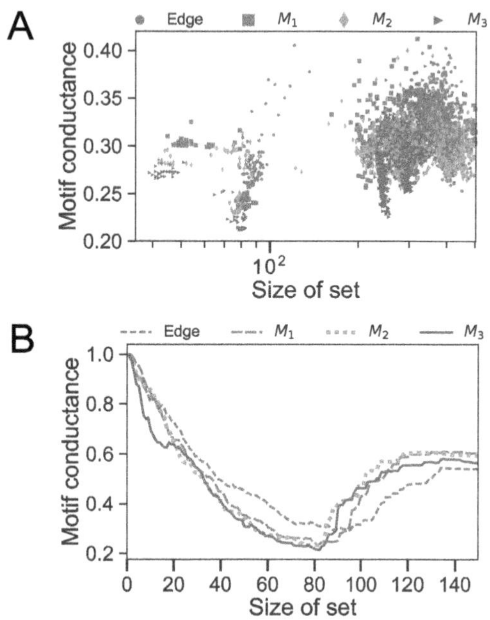

Figure 4: A: Distribution of set size and conductance from using each node in EMAIL-EU as a seed for edge-based APPR and motif-based APPR (MAPPR) with the three motifs in Figure 1. Smaller edge-based cluster concentrate in sizes of 70–100, a regime where also containing many motif-based clusters with smaller conductance. B: Sweep profile for a single seed in EMAIL-EU for edge and the same three motifs. The shape of the curves is similar, but the minima for the 3 motif-based curves occur for smaller set sizes and have smaller motif conductances compared to the curve for edges.

communities. The second network is the English Wikipedia hyperlink network (WIKI-CATS), where the article categories are the ground truth communities (we only consider 100 categories for our analysis). The datasets and recovery results are summarized in Table 2. For both networks, using motif M_1 provides an improvement in F_1 score over the edge-based method. The improvement is drastic in EMAIL-EU (25% relative improvement). In fact, all three motifs lead to substantial improvements in this network. We also see that in both networks, the motifs provide additional precision but sacrifice recall. These tighter clusters are expected for the same reasons as for the undirected networks.

We investigate the results for EMAIL-EU in more detail, as the use of motifs dramatically improves the recovery of ground truth clusters with respect to F_1 score. First, we used every node in the network as a seed for the APPR methods with edges and the three motifs (Figure 4A). The clusters bifurcate into small (< 100 nodes) and large (> 200 nodes) sizes. For the small clusters, the edge-based ones concentrate in sizes of 70–100. In this range, there are several clusters with much smaller motif-based conductance for all three motifs. This provides evidence that the 3 motifs are better models for the community structure in the network. We also see that of the large clusters, the edge-based ones tend to be the largest. Since these sets are larger than the sizes of the communities in the network, this observation provides evidence for why precision is better when using triangle motifs with MAPPR.

Next, we examined the sweep profile for a single seed node in the EMAIL-EU network (Figure 4B). The sweep profile highlights key differences between the output of the motif-based and edge-based algorithms. Although the general shape of the sweep profile is the same across the 3 motifs and edges, the minimum of the curves occurs for a smaller set and at a smaller conductance value for the motifs. A plausible explanation is that the edge-based and motif-based APPR methods are capturing roughly the same set, but the constraint of triangle participation excludes some nodes. The smaller motif conductance values indicate that these motifs are better models for the cluster structure in the network.

5.3 Finding many good seed nodes

We now empirically analyze the theory of Section 4.2. The goal of our experiments here is (i) to demonstrate that there are 1-hop neighborhood clusters of small motif conductance as a test of how well Theorem 4.4 holds in practice, and (ii) to use this idea to quickly find many clusters with minimal motif conductance by running targeted cluster expansion around a subset of the 1-hop neighborhood clusters. Regarding (i), we find that real-world networks exhibit much better results than predicted by the theory and the 1-hop neighborhood with minimal motif conductance is competitive with spectral graph theory approaches. Regarding (ii), we show that locally minimal nodes are better seeds than random nodes. We use this insight to find the global structure of clique conductance clusters more quickly than exhaustive enumeration.

We evaluate 1-hop neighborhood cluster quality in terms of motif conductance for 2-clique (edge), 3-clique (triangle), and 4-clique motifs using four undirected networks where we can exhaustively sample targeted clusters easily: CA-CONDMAT, a co-authorship network constructed from papers posted to the condensed matter category on arXiv [30]; FB-HARVARD1, a snapshot of the friendships network between Harvard students on Facebook in September 2005 [42]; EMAIL-ENRON, an e-mail communication network of the employees of Enron Corporation and their contacts [25]; and WEB-GOOGLE, a Web graph released by Google for a programming contest [31]. Summary statistics for the networks are in Table 4.

Table 3: Comparison of Fiedler clusters and the best 1-hop neighborhood clusters in terms of motif conductance. A star (⋆) denotes when 1-hop neighborhood clusters are the same across different clique sizes, a dagger (†) denotes when Fiedler clusters are the same, and a bullet (•) denotes when the neighborhood and Fiedler clusters are the same.

	M = 2-cliques (edges)				M = 3-cliques (triangles)				M = 4-cliques			
	Neighborhood		Fiedler		Neighborhood		Fiedler		Neighborhood		Fiedler	
	$\|S\|$	$\phi_M(S)$	$\|S\|$	$\phi_M(S)$	$\|S\|$	$\phi_M(S)$	$\|S\|$	$\phi_M(S)$	$\|S\|$	$\phi_M(S)$	$\|S\|$	$\phi_M(S)$
CA-CONDMAT	23•	$1.1\cdot10^{-2}$	23•	$1.1\cdot10^{-2}$	17⋆	$2.0\cdot10^{-3}$	18†	$1.5\cdot10^{-3}$	17⋆	$1.4\cdot10^{-4}$	18†	$1.1\cdot10^{-4}$
EMAIL-ENRON	21⋆	$2.4\cdot10^{-2}$	25†	$1.7\cdot10^{-2}$	21⋆	$1.3\cdot10^{-2}$	25†	$6.7\cdot10^{-3}$	8	$3.6\cdot10^{-3}$	25†	$1.6\cdot10^{-3}$
FB-HARVARD1	4	$2.0\cdot10^{-1}$	1,470	$1.1\cdot10^{-1}$	5⋆	$1.4\cdot10^{-1}$	1,429	$4.9\cdot10^{-2}$	5⋆	$7.7\cdot10^{-2}$	1,299	$2.2\cdot10^{-2}$
WEB-GOOGLE	203	$1.5\cdot10^{-3}$	5,335	$9.2\cdot10^{-5}$	62⋆	$1.8\cdot10^{-4}$	10,803	$5.9\cdot10^{-5}$	62⋆	$1.1\cdot10^{-5}$	8,001	$2.2\cdot10^{-6}$

Table 4: Summary statistics of datasets. The C_ℓ are the higher-order clustering coefficients [49].

Dataset	$\|V\|$	$\|E\|$	C_2	C_3	C_4
CA-CONDMAT	15,147	75,623	0.30	0.25	0.26
EMAIL-ENRON	18,561	156,139	0.11	0.06	0.05
FB-HARVARD1	13,319	793,410	0.14	0.07	0.07
WEB-GOOGLE	393,582	2,905,337	0.07	0.06	0.07

1-hop neighborhoods have small motif conductance. Plugging the higher-order clustering coefficients from Table 4 into the bound from Theorem 4.4 yields weak, albeit non-trivial bounds on the smallest neighborhood conductance (all bounds are ≥ 0.9 for the networks we consider). However, the spirit of the theorem rather than the bound itself motivates our experiments: with large higher-order clustering, there should be a neighborhood with small clique conductance. We indeed find this to be true in our results.

Table 3 compares the neighborhood with smallest motif conductance for the 2-clique, 3-clique, and 4-clique motifs with the Fiedler cluster obtained by a sweep procedure on the second eigenvector of the normalized Laplacian matrix [14]. Here, the Fiedler cluster represents a method that uses the global structure of the network to compare against the local neighborhood clusters. In all cases, the best neighborhood cluster has motif conductance far below the upper bound of Theorem 4.4. For all clique orders, the best neighborhood cluster always has conductance within a factor of 3.5 of the Fiedler cluster in CA-CONDMAT, EMAIL-ENRON, and FB-HARVARD1. With WEB-GOOGLE, the conductances are much smaller but the best neighborhood still has conductance within an order of magnitude of the Fiedler set. We conclude that the best neighborhood cluster in terms of conductance, which comes from purely local constructs, is competitive with the Fiedler vector that takes into account the global graph structure. This motivates our next set of experiments that uses nodes that induce small neighborhood conductance as seeds for the APPR method.

Local minima are good seeds. So far, we have used our theory to find a single node whose 1-hop neighborhood has small motif conductance for clique motifs. We examine this further by using nodes whose neighborhoods induce good clusters as seeds for MAPPR. Recall that we defined a node u to be locally minimal if $\phi_M(N(u)) \leq \phi_M(N(v))$ for all neighbors v of u. To test whether local minima are good seeds for APPR, we first exhaustively computed MAPPR clusters using every node in each of our networks as a seed. Next, we used a one-sided Mann Whitney U test to test the null hypothesis that the local minima yield APPR clusters with motif conductances that are *not less than* motif conductances from using non-local minima as seeds (Table 5). The p-values from these tests say that we can safely reject the null hypothesis at significance level < 0.003 for all cliques and networks considered except for 2-cliques in CA-CONDMAT. In other words, local minima are better seeds than non-local minima.

Table 5: The p-values from Mann-Whitney U tests of the null hypothesis that the motif conductances of sets from MAPPR seeded with local minima are *not less than* the motif conductances of sets from MAPPR seeded with non-local minima. In all but CA-CONDMAT with the standard edge motif, we reject the null at a significance level < 0.003.

motif	CA-CONDMAT	EMAIL-ENRON	FB-HARVARD1	WEB-GOOGLE
edge	0.87	$< 1\cdot10^{-16}$	$8.17\cdot10^{-05}$	$< 1\cdot10^{-16}$
triangle	$2.07\cdot10^{-03}$	$< 1\cdot10^{-16}$	$4.32\cdot10^{-04}$	$< 1\cdot10^{-16}$
4-clique	$7.20\cdot10^{-10}$	$< 1\cdot10^{-16}$	$1.55\cdot10^{-05}$	$< 1\cdot10^{-16}$

Finally, we use these local minimum seeds to construct network community profile (NCP) plots for different motifs. NCP plots are defined as the optimal conductance over all sets of a fixed size k as a function of k [31]. The shapes of the curves reveal the cluster structure of the networks. In practice, these plots are generated by exhaustively using every node in the network as a seed for the APPR method [31]. Here, we compare this approach to two simpler ones: (i) using the neighborhood sizes and conductances and (ii) using only local minima as seeds for APPR. In the latter case, between 1% and 15% of nodes are local minima, depending on the network, so this serves as an economical alternative to the typical exhaustive approach.

Figure 5 shows the NCP plots for CA-CONDMAT and FB-HARVARD1 with the triangle and 4-clique motifs. Seeding with local minima is sufficient for capturing the major trends of the NCP plot. In general, the curves constructed from neighborhood information capture the first downward spike in the plot, but do not capture larger sets with small conductance. Finally, the triangle and 4-clique NCP plots are quite similar for both networks. Thus, we suspect that local minima for lower-order cliques could also be used as good seeds when looking for sets based on higher-order cliques.

6 DISCUSSION

Our work enables fast local clustering of graphs in terms of rich, higher-order structures with theoretical guarantees on cluster quality. Our method is also an effective technique for finding clusters in directed graphs, a common data type with relatively few analytic

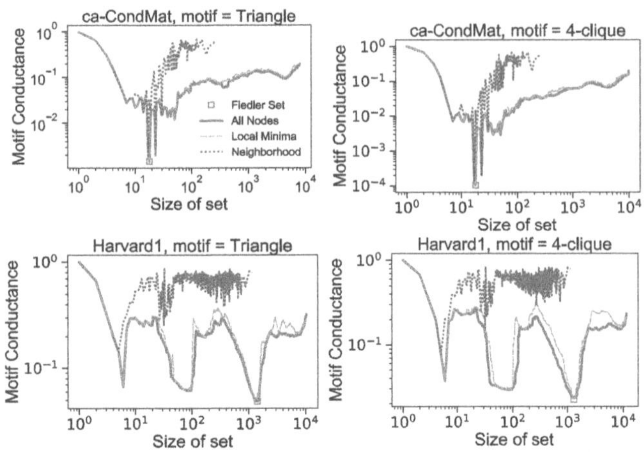

Figure 5: NCP plots for two networks with two different clique sizes. Curves are constructed from MAPPR with all nodes as seeds (blue), MAPPR with just local minima as seeds (green), and all 1-hop neighborhoods (purple). Using local minima as seeds captures the trends of exhaustive PPR using only a fraction of the seeds.

tools, and we found that using directed triangle motifs provided substantial improvements in recovery of communities in a directed e-mail network. We also found triangles critical for recovery in common synthetic models. Lastly, we computed local motif-based clusters for clique motifs through 1-hop neighborhoods and found the centers of 1-hop neighborhoods with small motif conductance to be good seeds. Neighborhoods also revealed correlations between cliques of different orders—in several cases, the same neighborhood has the smallest motif conductance for different clique motifs. Exploring this structure is an interesting avenue for future research.

ACKNOWLEDGMENTS

This research has been supported in part by NSF CCF-1149756, NSF IIS-1422918, NSF IIS-1546488, NSF Center for Science of Information STC CCF-093937, NSF IIS-1149837, Sloan Research Fellowship, DARPA SIMPLEX, Stanford Data Science Initiative, Chan Zuckerberg Biohub, Tencent, and Huawei.

REFERENCES

[1] N. K. Ahmed, J. Neville, R. A. Rossi, and N. Duffield. Efficient graphlet counting for large networks. In *ICDM*, 2015.
[2] R. Andersen, F. Chung, and K. Lang. Local graph partitioning using pagerank vectors. In *FOCS*, 2006.
[3] R. Andersen, F. Chung, and K. Lang. Local partitioning for directed graphs using PageRank. *Internet Mathematics*, 2008.
[4] A. R. Benson, D. F. Gleich, and J. Leskovec. Tensor spectral clustering for partitioning higher-order network structures. In *SDM*, 2015.
[5] A. R. Benson, D. F. Gleich, and J. Leskovec. Higher-order organization of complex networks. *Science*, 2016.
[6] M. Bressan, F. Chierichetti, R. Kumar, S. Leucci, and A. Panconesi. Counting graphlets: Space vs time. In *WSDM*, 2017.
[7] N. Chiba and T. Nishizeki. Arboricity and subgraph listing algorithms. *SIAM Journal on Computing*, 1985.
[8] F. Chung and O. Simpson. Solving linear systems with boundary conditions using heat kernel pagerank. In *WAW*, 2013.
[9] F. R. Chung. Four proofs for the cheeger inequality and graph partition algorithms. In *ICCM*, 2007.
[10] A. Clauset. Finding local community structure in networks. *Phys. Rev. E*, 72(2), 2005.
[11] W. Cui, Y. Xiao, H. Wang, and W. Wang. Local search of communities in large graphs. In *SIGMOD*, 2014.
[12] L. De Stefani, A. Epasto, M. Riondato, and E. Upfal. Trièst: Counting local and global triangles in fully-dynamic streams with fixed memory size. In *KDD*, 2016.
[13] A. Epasto, J. Feldman, S. Lattanzi, S. Leonardi, and V. Mirrokni. Reduce and aggregate: similarity ranking in multi-categorical bipartite graphs. In *WWW*, 2014.
[14] M. Fiedler. Algebraic connectivity of graphs. *Czechoslovak Mathematical J.*, 1973.
[15] S. Fortunato. Community detection in graphs. *Physics Reports*, 2010.
[16] U. Gargi, W. Lu, V. Mirrokni, and S. Yoon. Large-scale community detection on youtube for topic discovery and exploration. In *ICWSM*, 2011.
[17] D. F. Gleich and M. W. Mahoney. Using local spectral methods to robustify graph-based learning algorithms. In *KDD*, 2015.
[18] D. F. Gleich and C. Seshadhri. Vertex neighborhoods, low conductance cuts, and good seeds for local community methods. In *KDD*, 2012.
[19] M. S. Granovetter. The strength of weak ties. *American J. of Sociology*, 1973.
[20] X. Huang, H. Cheng, L. Qin, W. Tian, and J. X. Yu. Querying k-truss community in large and dynamic graphs. In *SIGMOD*, 2014.
[21] S. Jain and C. Seshadhri. A fast and provable method for estimating clique counts using turán's theorem. In *WWW*, 2017.
[22] L. G. S. Jeub, P. Balachandran, M. A. Porter, P. J. Mucha, and M. W. Mahoney. Think locally, act locally: Detection of small, medium-sized, and large communities in large networks. *Physics Review E*, 91, 2015.
[23] M. Jha, C. Seshadhri, and A. Pinar. Path sampling: A fast and provable method for estimating 4-vertex subgraph counts. In *WWW*, 2015.
[24] B.-B. Jiang, J.-G. Wang, Y. Wang, and J. Xiao. Gene prioritization for type 2 diabetes in tissue-specific protein interaction networks. *Systems Biology*, 2009.
[25] B. Klimt and Y. Yang. Introducing the Enron corpus. In *CEAS*, 2004.
[26] K. Kloster and D. F. Gleich. Heat kernel based community detection. In *KDD*, 2014.
[27] C. Klymko, D. F. Gleich, and T. G. Kolda. Using triangles to improve community detection in directed networks. In *ASE BigData Conference*, 2014.
[28] A. Lancichinetti and S. Fortunato. Benchmarks for testing community detection algorithms on directed and weighted graphs with overlapping communities. *Physical Review E*, 2009.
[29] K. J. Lang. Fixing two weaknesses of the spectral method. In *NIPS*, 2005.
[30] J. Leskovec, J. Kleinberg, and C. Faloutsos. Graph evolution: Densification and shrinking diameters. *TKDD*, 2007.
[31] J. Leskovec, K. J. Lang, A. Dasgupta, and M. W. Mahoney. Community structure in large networks: Natural cluster sizes and the absence of large well-defined clusters. *Internet Mathematics*, 2009.
[32] Y. Li, K. He, D. Bindel, and J. E. Hopcroft. Uncovering the small community structure in large networks: A local spectral approach. In *WWW*, 2015.
[33] M. W. Mahoney, L. Orecchia, and N. K. Vishnoi. A local spectral method for graphs: With applications to improving graph partitions and exploring data graphs locally. *JMLR*, 2012.
[34] D. Marcus and Y. Shavitt. Efficient counting of network motifs. In *ICDCSW*, 2010.
[35] R. Milo, S. Shen-Orr, S. Itzkovitz, N. Kashtan, D. Chklovskii, and U. Alon. Network motifs: simple building blocks of complex networks. *Science*, 2002.
[36] L. Orecchia and Z. A. Zhu. Flow-based algorithms for local graph clustering. In *SODA*, 2014.
[37] N. Pržulj. Biological network comparison using graphlet degree distribution. *Bioinformatics*, 2007.
[38] K. Rohe and T. Qin. The blessing of transitivity in sparse and stochastic networks. *arXiv:1307.2302*, 2013.
[39] S. E. Schaeffer. Graph clustering. *Computer Science Rev.*, 2007.
[40] M. Sozio and A. Gionis. The community-search problem and how to plan a successful cocktail party. In *KDD*, 2010.
[41] O. Sporns and R. Kötter. Motifs in brain networks. *PLOS Biology*, 2004.
[42] A. L. Traud, P. J. Mucha, and M. A. Porter. Social structure of facebook networks. *Physica A: Statistical Mechanics and its Applications*, 2012.
[43] C. Tsourakakis, J. Pachocki, and M. Mitzenmacher. Scalable motif-aware graph clustering. In *WWW*, 2017.
[44] J. Ugander, L. Backstrom, and J. Kleinberg. Subgraph frequencies: Mapping the empirical and extremal geography of large graph collections. In *WWW*, 2013.
[45] K. Voevodski, S.-H. Teng, and Y. Xia. Spectral affinity in protein networks. *BMC Systems Biology*, 2009.
[46] D. Wagner and F. Wagner. Between min cut and graph bisection. In *MFCS*, 1993.
[47] J. Yang and J. Leskovec. Defining and evaluating network communities based on ground-truth. *Knowledge and Information Systems*, 2015.
[48] Ö. N. Yaveroğlu, N. Malod-Dognin, D. Davis, Z. Levnajic, V. Janjic, R. Karapandza, A. Stojmirovic, and N. Pržulj. Revealing the hidden language of complex networks. *Scientific Reports*, 2014.
[49] H. Yin, A. R. Benson, and J. Leskovec. Higher-order clustering in networks. *arXiv:1704.03913*, 2017.
[50] Z. A. Zhu, S. Lattanzi, and V. S. Mirrokni. A local algorithm for finding well-connected clusters. In *ICML*, 2013.

Long Short Memory Process: Modeling Growth Dynamics of Microscopic Social Connectivity

Chengxi Zang*
Computer Science Department, Tsinghua University
zangcx13@mails.tsinghua.edu.cn

Peng Cui
Computer Science Department, Tsinghua University
cuip@tsinghua.edu.cn

Christos Faloutsos
Computer Science Department, Carnegie Mellon University
christos@cs.cmu.edu

Wenwu Zhu
Computer Science Department, Tsinghua University
wwzhu@tsinghua.edu.cn

ABSTRACT

How do people make friends dynamically in social networks? What are the temporal patterns for an individual increasing its social connectivity? What are the basic mechanisms governing the formation of these temporal patterns? No matter cyber or physical social systems, their structure and dynamics are mainly driven by the connectivity dynamics of each individual. However, due to the lack of empirical data, little is known about the empirical dynamic patterns of social connectivity at microscopic level, let alone the regularities or models governing these microscopic dynamics.

We examine the detailed growth process of "WeChat", the largest online social network in China, with 300 million users and 4.75 billion links spanning two years. We uncover a wide range of long-term power law growth and short-term bursty growth for the social connectivity of different users. We propose three key ingredients, namely average-effect, multiscale-effect and correlation-effect, which govern the observed growth patterns at microscopic level. As a result, we propose the long short memory process incorporating these ingredients, demonstrating that it successfully reproduces the complex growth patterns observed in the empirical data. By analyzing modeling parameters, we discover statistical regularities underlying the empirical growth dynamics. Our model and discoveries provide a foundation for the microscopic mechanisms of network growth dynamics, potentially leading to implications for prediction, clustering and outlier detection on human dynamics.

KEYWORDS

Human dynamics; Social dynamics; Social network; Power law growth; Burst;

*Tsinghua National Laboratory for Information Science and Technology (TNList)

KDD '17, August 13-17, 2017, Halifax, NS, Canada
© 2017 ACM. 978-1-4503-4887-4/17/08... $15.00
DOI: 10.1145/3097983.3098055

1 INTRODUCTION

In recent years, much effort has been made to model the growth of social networks, ranging from reproducing the statistical properties of structures [4], to modeling the growth dynamics of nodes and links [25], aiming to enhance our understanding on complex social systems. In microscopic view, the structures and dynamics of complex social systems are mainly driven by the growth dynamics of individual's social connectivity. However, little is known about this microscopic dynamics in reality, mainly due to the lack of large scale datasets recording the detailed social network evolution. Thus, fundamental questions as follows are largely unknown: What are the dynamic growth patterns of an individual's connectivity in social networks? What are the plausible regularities governing these microscopic growth dynamics? Can we unify the connectivity growth dynamics of largely heterogeneous individuals into a simple mathematic model? Answering to these questions not only advances our understanding on the evolution of complex social systems, but also delivers models to capture human dynamics at microscopic level, leading to applications for predicting future growth, clustering typical modes of human dynamics, and detecting outliers.

In literature, the studies on microscopic connectivity dynamics are mainly conducted theoretically. The Barabási-Albert model [4] which generates scale-free network, predicts the scaling relationship between the connectivity and the time with exponent 0.5. The fitness model [5] extends this exponent to a fitness function with range < 1. However, these theoretical hypotheses ignore the ubiquitous densification phenomenon [15], and the empirical growth dynamics may have exponent value ≥ 1. Recently, a paucity of empirical studies are conducted. Ref.[14] finds the rate of connectivity grows with current degree in a mean-field setting, indicating a superlinear growth in average, but they ignore the large heterogeneity among different users. Ref.[2] reports that the rate of connectivity is constant, indicating a linear growth in average, but the result is also from a mean-field setting and the connectivity timestamps are simulated from user behavior logs rather than explicitly recorded. Thus, the growth dynamics of social connectivity of each individual has not been empirically explored or theoretically studied.

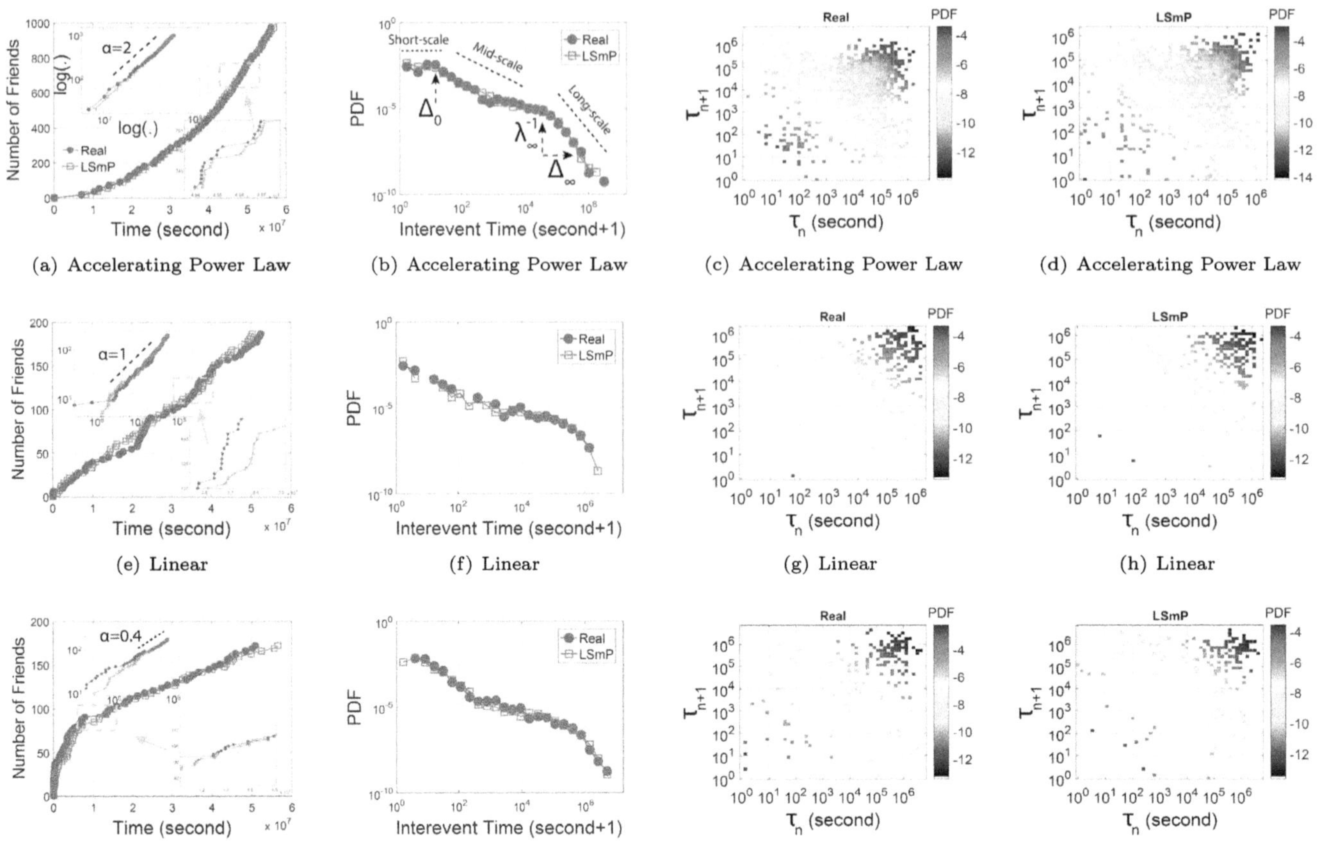

(a) Accelerating Power Law (b) Accelerating Power Law (c) Accelerating Power Law (d) Accelerating Power Law

(e) Linear (f) Linear (g) Linear (h) Linear

(i) Decelerating Power Law (j) Decelerating Power Law (k) Decelerating Power Law (l) Decelerating Power Law

Figure 1: *Microscopic social connectivity features various power law growth in the long term and bursts in the short term. LSmP fits reality well.* (a)(e)(i) plot three instances of different growth patterns: the accelerating power law growth, linear growth, and decelerating power law growth, respectively. The same plots on log-log scale are shown in the upper insets, while the lower insets illustrate short-term bursts. Each row describes different aspects of the same empirical dynamics. (b) (f) (j) plot inter-event time (IET) distributions. (c)(g)(k) plot the empirical joint distributions of consecutive IETs, while (d)(h)(l) are the counterparts generated by LSmP. Our model fits the reality well on all the aspects.

In this paper, we study the detailed evolution traces of WeChat from zero to 300 million users and 4.75 billion friendships spanning two years. The dataset explicitly records when and how a link is established between whom and whom, serving as one of the largest datasets which support this study. From this dataset, we find the growth dynamics of social connectivity exhibit rich complexities which are far beyond our current understanding. Figure 1 showcases the growth dynamics of three individuals over two years, we find: *i)* a wide range of power law growth in the long term, and *ii)* stochastic bursts in the short term. Based on these empirical observations, we propose three ingredients, i.e., average-effect, multiscale-effect, and correlation-effect, which govern the growth dynamics. We then propose a stochastic model, **Long-Short-memory Process (LSmP)**, incorporating these ingredients, to characterize the empirical dynamics. The effectiveness of LSmP is validated in multiple aspects. By analyzing the modeling parameters, we find statistical regularities underlying these growth dynamics. By clustering in the parameter space, we find three typical modes of social connectivity growth in the long term, and two typical modes in the short term. We also illustrate that outliers can be easily detected with clear explanation in the parameter space. In summary, the contributions of this work are as follows:

- **Findings:** The growth dynamics of social connectivity features long-term power law growth and short-term bursts. We find three ingredients, i.e., average-effect, multiscale-effect, and correlation-effect accounting for the power law and bursty growth dynamics.

- **LSmP model:** A stochastic model captures above findings. It is parsimonious, and the parameters have clear physical meanings.
- **Accuracy:** LSmP accurately fits the growth dynamics.
- **Usefulness:** LSmP provides insightful understandings on human dynamics, and implies applications in prediction, clustering, pattern discovery, and outlier detection, etc.

Reproducibility: Our code is open-sourced at github.com/calvin-zcx/LSMP

The outline of the paper is the typical one: survey, proposed method, experiments, and conclusions.

2 RELATED WORK

As the investigated problem is closely related to network evolution and human behavior dynamics, we mainly review the related works in these two fields.

Network evolution. The Barabási-Albert model (BA) [4] predicts the dynamics of individual's connectivity scales against time with exponent $\alpha = 0.5$ ($k(t) \sim t^{1/2}$). The fitness model [5] extends the BA model to heterogeneous connectivity dynamics, with scaling exponent $\alpha < 1$. However, we find empirical connectivity dynamics are more complex: the dynamics with scaling exponent $\alpha >= 1$ are prevalent. Recently, a paucity of empirical studies are conducted. [14] finds the rate of connectivity grows with current degree in a mean-field setting, and ignores the large heterogeneity among different users. [2] reports that the rate of connectivity is constant, but the result is also from a mean-field setting and the connectivity timestamps are simulated from user behavior logs rather than explicitly recorded. [25] examines several large social networks and finds the power law growth for both nodes and links over time, implying that the average connectivity scales with time. In all, how the connectivity dynamics grows at *an individual level* is largely unaddressed.

Human dynamics. Human dynamics often exhibit bursts and heavy-tailed inter-event time (IET) distribution [3]. Priority queue model [23] and modulated Poission model [16] may account for IET's fat-tail nature. Recently, evidences of multiscale nature of IET distribution [27] have been found, including bimodal distribution [24] at long-scale, and quick actions at short-scale [27]. However, they treat the IETs independent identically distributed, ignoring their correlations [12]. Two lines of works try to capture the bursts and correlations: the self-exciting process [7, 11, 20], and the self-feeding process [1, 10, 22]. However, none of them can generate both power law growth with arbitrary exponent and mutiscale IET distribution as we observed in the empirical dataset.

3 PROPOSED METHOD

In this section, we present the ingredients accounting for the long-term power law growth and short-term bursts, and then propose our stochastic model based on these ingredients.

Table 1: Symbols and Definitions

Symbols	Definitions
$n(t)$	Cumulative number of events by time t for a specific user
t_i	The time of event i
τ_i	The interevent time (IET) between event i and $i-1$
$\mathcal{H}_t$	The history of previous events by t, a list of event times
$\lambda(t\|\mathcal{H}_t)$	The hazard function of LSmP
$\Phi_\infty(t)$	The hazard function for long-term memory
λ_∞	The long-term event rate
α	The long-term growth exponent
Δ_∞	The long-term time scale
$\Phi_0(t)$	The hazard function for short-term memory
λ_0	The short-term event rate
θ	The short-term fizzling exponent
Δ_0	The short-term time scale
m	Memory length of short-term memory

3.1 Model Intuition

Here we introduce the intuition and backgrounds to motivate the model design.

Ingredients for power law growth. Zang et al. [25] proposed a dynamic model to capture the growth dynamics of the number of nodes $n(t)$ in social networks: $\frac{dn(t)}{dt} = \frac{\beta}{t^\theta} n(t)(N - n(t))$, where N is the ceiling size and β is the growth rate. It generates a variety of growth patterns, including power law growth as a special case when $\theta = 1$ and $n(t) \ll N$. By defining $\alpha = \beta N$, we get the equation which generates power law growth for $n(t)$:

$$\frac{dn(t)}{dt} = \frac{\alpha}{t} n(t). \quad (1)$$

Thus, when the fizzling exponent $\theta = 1$, this equation indicates the physical meaning at microscopic level: *the rate of making friends* $\frac{dn(t)}{dt}$ *at present is proportional to the long-term average rate* $\frac{n(t)}{t}$, and this long-term memory is kept by the behavior of making $n(t)$ friends so far. We name it **average-effect** which generates the power law growth.

Ingredients for bursts. Human behaviors often exhibit multiscale IET distribution [27] as shown in Fig.1b, taking on flat short-scale, fat-tailed middle-scale, and the exponential-like long-scale. When we i.i.d. sample IETs from a multiscale distribution, a sequence of small value IETs occur in short-scale, followed by large value IET in the middle-scale and long-scale, generating intense activities followed by long vacation, namely, bursts. Thus, the multiscale IET distribution, which captures the short-term memory since last event, generates bursts. We denotes this ingredient as **multiscale-effect**.

Given a Poisson process exhibiting non-bursty growth, if we rearrange the IET sequence as follows: make small value IET followed by smaller IET, and make large value IET followed by larger IET, and then we also get bursty behaviors. Thus, the correlations between IETs can also generate bursts. Figures 1cg&k plot the joint distribution of two consecutive IETs from real data. If the IETs are independent, the points on joint distribution should spread out, while in reality the dots are clustered, e.g., red dots, which support our conjecture of correlated IETs. Indeed, the corresponding growth dynamics in Figs. 1ae&i, along with the lower insets, exhibit bursts in the short-term. We name this ingredient as **correlation-effect**.

Model framework: temporal point process. The process that a user will add friends at a specific time epoch is a (stochastic) temporal point process. Mathematically, we want to know the time t of the next event, and let $f(t|\mathcal{H}_t)$ be the conditional probability density function of the time of the $(n+1)^{th}$ event conditioned on all the events in history $\mathcal{H}_t$, and its corresponding cumulative distribution function is $F(t|\mathcal{H}_t)$. This temporal point process is intuitively and uniquely specified by the hazard function $\lambda(t|\mathcal{H}_t)$ [8]. The hazard function $\lambda(t|\mathcal{H}_t) = \mathbb{E}[n(dt)|\mathcal{H}_t]/dt$ describes the rate of the occurrence of the event given the history $\mathcal{H}_t = (t_1, ..., t_{n-1}, t_n)$ of previous events, where $n(dt)$ denotes the number of events falling in $[t, t + dt)$ and $n(t)$ stands for the cumulative number of events falling in $(-\infty, t)$. The relationship between hazard function and the conditional probability density function is $\lambda(t|\mathcal{H}_t) = \frac{f(t|\mathcal{H}_t)}{1-F(t|\mathcal{H}_t)}$ and $f(t|\mathcal{H}_t) = \lambda(t|\mathcal{H}_t)e^{-\int_{t_n}^{t} \lambda(s|\mathcal{H})_t ds}$.

3.2 The LSmP model

Here we propose the **L**ong-**S**hort-**m**emory **P**rocess (LSmP), which is based fundamentally on the average-effect, multiscale-effect, and correlation-effect to capture the long-term power-law growth and short-term bursts of social connectivity. The hazard function specifying the LSmP is:

$$\lambda(t|\mathcal{H}_t) = \underbrace{\lambda_\infty \alpha(\frac{t}{\Delta_\infty} + 1)^{\alpha-1}}_{\text{Long-term memory } \Phi_\infty(t|\mathcal{H}_t)} + \underbrace{\sum_{i=n(t)-m+1}^{n(t)} \lambda_0(\frac{t-t_i}{\Delta_0} + 1)^{-\theta}}_{\text{Short-term memory } \Phi_0(t|\mathcal{H}_t)}$$
$$= \Phi_\infty(t|\mathcal{H}_t) + \Phi_0(t|\mathcal{H}_t) \quad (2)$$

3.2.1 Long-term memory.

We first show the average-effect generates power-law stochastic growth, taking on long-term memory.

LEMMA 3.1. *The average-effect, namely the present hazard rate $\Phi_\infty(t|\mathcal{H}_t)$ is the the mean value of its previous hazard rate from $-\Delta_\infty$, generates power law dynamics with arbitrary exponent α.*

PROOF. We formulate the average-effect as:

$$\Phi_\infty(t|\mathcal{H}_t) = \frac{\alpha}{t + \Delta_\infty} \int_{-\Delta_\infty}^{t} \Phi_\infty(s|\mathcal{H}_t)ds, \quad (3)$$

and replace the integral term by the equation $\int_{-\Delta_\infty}^{t} \Phi_\infty(s)ds = \lambda_\infty\Delta_\infty(\frac{t}{\Delta_\infty} + 1)^\alpha$, we get:

$$\Phi_\infty(t|\mathcal{H}_t) = \lambda_\infty\alpha(\frac{t}{\Delta_\infty} + 1)^{\alpha-1}. \quad (4)$$

□

The $\Phi_\infty(t|\mathcal{H}_t) = \lambda_\infty\alpha(\frac{t}{\Delta_\infty} + 1)^{\alpha-1}$ captures the long-term power law growth dynamics of adding friends in the temporal point process framework, serving as the stochastic counterpart of the dynamic differential equation 1 in Sec. 3.1.

Justification of the model:

Various power law growth. As shown in Sec. 3.1, the α is the average number of new friends introduced by one existing friend in $n(t)$ at time interval $(t, t+dt)$. When $\alpha > 1$, the accelerating power law growth appears, implying a rich-get-richer phenomenon: more friends you have, much more friends you will have in the future. When $\alpha = 1$, $\Phi_\infty(t|\mathcal{H})$ equals to λ_∞, indicating that $n(t)$ is supposed to have a constant growth rate without long-term memory. In contrast, when $\alpha < 1$, $n(t)$ exhibits decelerating power law growth. Three instances are shown in Figs. 1ae&i.

Long-scale of multiscale-effect. The range of long-scale is controlled by λ_∞ and α. When $\alpha = 1$, $\Phi_\infty(t|\mathcal{H}_t)$ degenerates to the Poisson process, which captures the routine activities of adding friends. Specifically, an event is expected to occur with an average inter-event time λ_∞^{-1} with deviation controlled by Δ_∞, as shown in Fig. 1b. When α increases, the exponential mode in the tail part moves towards left, implying a smaller τ and thus an accelerating $n(t)$. In contrast, when a decreases, the second mode of $f(\tau)$ moves to right, implying a larger τ and thus a decelerating $n(t)$.

Long-term correlation of IETs. When $\alpha \neq 1$, the long-term memory appears, taking on long-term IETs' correlations. Indeed, when $\alpha \geq 1$, IETs tend to become shorter and shorter, while when $\alpha \leq 1$, IETs become larger and larger, implying an increasing and a saturated circle of friends, respectively.

3.2.2 Short-term memory.

The short-term memory $\Phi_0(t|\mathcal{H}_t)$ captures the multiscale-effect and correlation-effect, which generate bursty dynamics.

LEMMA 3.2. *The $\lambda(t|\mathcal{H}_t)$ generates constant short-scale, power law middle-scale and exponential long-scale when $\alpha = m = \theta = 1$.*

PROOF. The conditional probability density function of the time of the next event, say $(n + 1)^{th}$ event, is (refer to Sec. 3.1):

$$f(t|\mathcal{H}_t) = \lambda(t|\mathcal{H}_t)e^{-\int_{t_n}^{t} \lambda(s|\mathcal{H}_t)ds}$$
$$= (\Phi_\infty(t|\mathcal{H}_t) + \Phi_0(t|\mathcal{H}_t))e^{-\int_{t_n}^{t} \Phi_\infty(s|\mathcal{H}_t)ds}e^{-\int_{t_n}^{t} \Phi_0(s|\mathcal{H}_t)ds}$$
$$= [\lambda_\infty\alpha(\frac{t}{\Delta_\infty} + 1)^{\alpha-1} + \sum_{i=n-m+1}^{n} \lambda_0(\frac{t-t_i}{\Delta_0} + 1)^{-\theta}]$$
$$\times e^{-\lambda_\infty\Delta_\infty[(\frac{t}{\Delta_\infty}+1)^\alpha - (\frac{t_n}{\Delta_\infty}+1)^\alpha]}$$
$$\times \prod_{i=n-m+1}^{n} e^{-\int_{t_n}^{t} \lambda_0(\frac{s-t_i}{\Delta_0}+1)^{-\theta}ds}$$

The condition $\alpha = 1$ excludes the effect of long-term memory. When $m = 1$, the short-term memory is solely determined by the fizzling effect, indicating the independency between any two consecutive events. Thus $\lambda(t|\mathcal{H}_t)$ describes a **renewal process** where $f(t|\mathcal{H}_t) = f(\tau_{n+1}) = f(\tau)$. When $\theta = 1$,

$$f(t|\mathcal{H}_t) = [\lambda_\infty + \lambda_0(\frac{t-t_n}{\Delta_0} + 1)^{-1}]e^{-\lambda_\infty(t-t_n)}(\frac{t-t_n}{\Delta_0} + 1)^{-\lambda_0\Delta_0}$$
$$\approx \lambda_0(\frac{t-t_n}{\Delta_0} + 1)^{-(1+\lambda_0\Delta_0)}e^{-\lambda_\infty(t-t_n)}, \quad \text{when } \lambda_\infty \ll \lambda_0$$

Thus, when $\alpha = m = \theta = 1$, the IET distribution is:

$$f(\tau) \approx \lambda_0(\frac{\tau}{\Delta_0} + 1)^{-(1+\lambda_0\Delta_0)}e^{-\lambda_\infty\tau}, \quad (5)$$

which exhibits constant rate λ_0 at short scale ($\tau < \Delta_0$), power law distribution with exponent $1+\lambda_0\Delta_0$ at middle scale, and the exponential mode at long scale (τ in the vicinity of λ_∞^{-1}) .

□

Justification of the model:

Multiscale IET distribution. The multiscale pattern of IET distribution also holds in other parameter settings:

i) The range of short scale is controlled by Δ_0, as shown in Fig. 1b. When Δ_0 increases, the range of short-scale expands to right, and vice verse. When $\Delta_0 \to 0$, the short-scale of IET distribution disappears.

ii) The slope of the middle range is primarily controlled by θ. When $\alpha = m = 1$, the the situation when $\theta = 1$ is shown in lemma 3.2; when $\theta \neq 1$, the $e^{-\int_{t_n}^{t} \lambda_0(\frac{s-t_n}{\Delta_0}+1)^{-\theta} ds}$ is a stretched exponential distribution which exhibits fat-tail IET distribution at middle scale. Thus, the larger θ is, the sharper slope is.

Short-term correlation of IETs. Both correlation-effect and multiscale-effect have impact on the short-term correlation of IETs:

i) When $\alpha = m = 1$, the LSmP denotes a renew process, indicating no correlation between IETs. When $m > 1$, the correlation appears. When $m = \infty$, $\Phi_0(t|\mathcal{H}_t)$ behaves like Hawkes process with power-law-like kernel, and the supercritical state ($\int \Phi_0(s|\mathcal{H}_t)ds > 1$) generates exponential growth, implying the strongest correlation.

ii) The larger value of θ, the quicker temporal fizzling of previous influence, and thus the weaker IETs' correlation.

Bursts. The bursts are governed by the multiscale effect and the correlation-effect:

i) As shown in Fig. 1b, Δ_0 is critical point between small IET (quick activities) in short-scale and fat-tailed IET in middle-scale. Thus, the larger Δ_0 is, the more bursty $n(t)$ is. The smaller θ, the more bursty of $n(t)$. Because the smaller θ, the fatter IET distributions at middle-scale, and thus more IETs with relatively small values appear.

ii) A longer memory length induces the stronger short-term IETs' correlation due to the superposition influence of previous events, leading to a sudden large rate/burst.

3.3 Parameter estimation

We learn the parameters of LSmP by maximizing log-likelihood function. The log-likelihood function of observing a point process $\{t_1, ..., t_{n-1}, t_n\}$ on time period $[0, T)$ is given by:

$$\begin{aligned}\log L(t_1, ..., t_n) &= -\int_0^T \lambda(t|\mathcal{H}_t)dt + \int_0^T \log \lambda(t|\mathcal{H}_t)dN(t) \\ &= -\lambda_\infty \Delta_\infty [(\frac{t_n}{\Delta_\infty} + 1)^\alpha - 1] \\ &- \sum_{i=1}^{n} \frac{\lambda_0 \Delta_0}{1-\theta} [(\frac{t_{i+m} - t_i}{\Delta_0} + 1)^{1-\theta} - 1] \\ &+ \sum_{i=1}^{n} \log[\lambda_\infty \alpha (\frac{t_i}{\Delta_\infty} + 1)^{\alpha-1} + \lambda_0 A(i)]\end{aligned} \tag{6}$$

where $A(i) = \sum_{t_{i-m} \leq tj < t_i} (\frac{t_i - t_j}{\Delta_0} + 1)^{-\theta}$ for $i \geq 2$, and t_i denotes the time of occurrence of the ith event, and $A(1) = 0$. For convenience, we assume $T = t_n$. Maximizing Eq. 6 regarding $\{\lambda_\infty, \alpha, \Delta_\infty, \lambda_0, \theta, \Delta_0, m\}$, subject to $\{\alpha, \Delta_\infty, \theta, \Delta_0, \lambda_\infty, \lambda_0 \geq 0; m \in \mathcal{N}\}$ leads to estimated modeling parameters.

A good advantage of LSmP is that all the parameters have closed-form gradients. The gradients for the long-memory part are:

$$\frac{\partial \log L}{\partial \lambda_\infty} = -\Delta_\infty [(\frac{t_n}{\Delta_\infty} + 1)^\alpha - 1] + \sum_{i=1}^{n} \frac{\alpha(\frac{t_i}{\Delta_\infty} + 1)^{\alpha-1}}{D(i)} \tag{7}$$

$$\begin{aligned}\frac{\partial \log L}{\partial \alpha} &= -\lambda_\infty \Delta_\infty (\frac{t_n}{\Delta_\infty} + 1)^\alpha \ln(\frac{t_n}{\Delta_\infty} + 1) \\ &+ \sum_{i=1}^{n} \frac{\lambda_\infty (\frac{t_i}{\Delta_\infty} + 1)^{\alpha-1} [\alpha \ln(\frac{t_i}{\Delta_\infty} + 1) + 1]}{D(i)}\end{aligned} \tag{8}$$

$$\begin{aligned}\frac{\partial \log L}{\partial \Delta_\infty} &= -\lambda_\infty [(\frac{t_i}{\Delta_\infty} + 1)^\alpha - 1] + \lambda_\infty \alpha \frac{t_n}{\Delta_\infty} (\frac{t_n}{\Delta_\infty} + 1)^{\alpha-1} \\ &- \sum_{i=1}^{n} \frac{\lambda_\infty \alpha (\alpha - 1) \frac{t_i}{\Delta_\infty^2} (\frac{t_i}{\Delta_\infty} + 1)^{\alpha-2}}{D(i)}\end{aligned} \tag{9}$$

where $D(i) = \lambda_\infty \alpha (\frac{t_i}{\Delta_\infty} + 1)^{\alpha-1} + \lambda_0 A(i)$. When $\theta \neq 1$, the gradients for the short-memory part are:

$$\frac{\partial \log L}{\partial \lambda_0} = -\frac{\Delta}{1-\theta} \sum_{i=1}^{n} [(\frac{t_{i+m} - t_i}{\Delta} + 1)^{1-\theta} - 1] + \sum_{i=1}^{n} \frac{A(i)}{D(i)} \tag{10}$$

$$\begin{aligned}\frac{\partial \log L}{\partial \Delta_0} &= -\frac{\lambda_0}{1-\theta} \sum_{i=1}^{n} [(\frac{t_{i+m} - t_i}{\Delta_0} + 1)^{-\theta} (\theta \frac{t_{t+m} - t_i}{\Delta_0} + 1) - 1] \\ &+ \sum_{i=1}^{n} \frac{\lambda_0 B(i)}{D(i)}\end{aligned} \tag{11}$$

$$\begin{aligned}\frac{\partial \log L}{\partial \theta} &= -\frac{\lambda_0 \Delta_0}{(1-\theta)^2} \sum_{i=1}^{n} [(\frac{t_{i+m} - t_i}{\Delta_0} + 1)^{1-\theta} - 1 \\ &- (1-\theta)(\frac{t_{i+m} - t_i}{\Delta_0} + 1)^{1-\theta} \ln(\frac{t_{i+m} - t_i}{\Delta_0} + 1)] \\ &- \sum_{i=1}^{n} \frac{\lambda_0 C(i)}{D(i)}\end{aligned} \tag{12}$$

where $B(i) = \sum_{t_{i-m} \leq tj < t_i} \frac{\theta(t_i - t_j)}{\Delta_0^2} (\frac{t_i - t_j}{\Delta_0} + 1)^{-\theta-1}$ for $i \geq 2$ and $B(1) = 0$, and $C(i) = \sum_{t_{i-m} \leq tj < t_i} (\frac{t_i - t_j}{\Delta_0} + 1)^{-\theta} \ln(\frac{t_i - t_j}{\Delta_0} + 1)$ for $i \geq 2$ and $C(1) = 0$. The counterparts when $\theta = 1$ can easily get, and we leave it for brevity. In numerical calculation when $\theta = 1$, we could add a very small error, say 10^{-8}, to θ to reuse above formulas.

For a specific m, we solve the constrained optimization problem by the trust-region-reflective algorithm [6], and then choose the best results by enumerating m according to the maximum likelihood principle [14]. For reproducibility, we open our code, see Section 5.

3.4 Simulation of LSmP dynamics

We design the simulation method of LSmP by the inverse method [8] (P260, Algorithm 7.4.III.) due to unbounded nature of $\lambda(t|\mathcal{H}_t)$ when $\alpha > 1$. The basic operation of the inverse method is solving the equation $\log u + \int_{t_n}^{t} \lambda(s|\mathcal{H}_t)ds = 0$ for t where u is generated from uniform distribution $U(0, 1)$. When $\alpha \leq 1$, the adapting Ogata's thining algorithm [19] can be applied for speeding up. For brevity, we only present the inverse method here. We open our simulation code, see Section 5.

4 EXPERIMENTS

In this section, we evaluate the effectiveness of LSmP on the real data at large scale. We introduce the dataset in Sec.4.1. In Sec.4.2, we validate the accuracy of matching real data in three aspects. What's more, our LSmP can be applied in

Algorithm 1: Simulation algorithm for the Long-Short-Memory Process (LSmP)

Input : Hazard function of LSmP$\lambda(t|\mathcal{H}_t) = \Phi_\infty(t|\lambda_\infty, \Delta_\infty, \alpha) + \Phi_0(t|\lambda_0, \Delta_0, \theta)$, total event number N

Output : $\{t_1, ..., t_N\}$

Set current number of events $n = 1$, and current time $t = 0$;
while $n \leq N$ **do**
  Sample $u \sim Uniform([0, 1])$;
  Solve $\log u + \int_t^x \lambda(s|\mathcal{H}_t)ds = 0$ for x by Algorithm 2.;
  $t = t + x$;
  $t_n = t$;
  $n = n + 1$;
end

Algorithm 2: Newton's iterative method

Input : Equation $F(x) = \log u + \int_{tn}^x \lambda(s|\mathcal{H}_t)ds$.

Output : x

Set $\epsilon = 10^{-8}$, $x = t_n - t_{n-1}$;
while $|F(x)| \leq \epsilon$ **do**
  $x = x - \frac{F(x)}{F'(x)}$;
end

many data mining tasks. In Sec.4.2.3, by analyzing the modeling parameters, we find statistical regularities underlying the empirical growth dynamics. In Sec.4.4, we cluster typical growth patterns of human connectivity and detect outliers.

4.1 Datasets

Our experiments are conducted on WeChat, which is the largest online social network in China with more than 806 million monthly active users by June 30, 2016. We collected the history data of WeChat consisting of complete records of all the node and link growth from January 21, 2011 (the release day of WeChat), to January 16, 2013 when the registered users reached 300 million. In total, there are 300 million registered users and more than 4.75 billion friendships. The records are (u, t_u) and $(u, v, t_{u,v})$ where u and v represent the users' ID, and t_u, $t_{u,v}$ are the timestamps of the birth of node and link respectively. In order to get enough friendships to study connectivity dynamics for each individual, we select the first 1 million users sorted by degree (with degree ≥ 143) and random select 10% of this population for the following experiments. All the WeChat data that we could access were anonymized for strict privacy policy.

4.2 Accuracy

We validate the accuracy of our LSmP by answering if our model can capture the empirical growth dynamics for each individual. The experiments are conducted by validating the accuracy of following three aspects: *(i)* the growth shape, *(ii)* the multiscale IET distribution, and *(iii)* the IETs' correlation.

4.2.1 Baselines for human dynamics. We consider following four representative human dynamic models for comparison:

1) Poisson process (PP) has a constant hazard function $\lambda(t|\mathcal{H}_t) = \lambda$, which generates linear growth.

2) Hawkes process with exponential kernel (HWK-E) has hazard function $\lambda(t|\mathcal{H}_t) = \mu + \sum_{t_i<t} \alpha e^{-\beta(t-t_i)}$ [9].

3) Hawkes process with power law kernel (HWK-P) has a fat-tailed kernel is used in HWK-P. The hazard function of this model is $\lambda(t|\mathcal{H}_t) = \mu + \sum_{t_i<t} \alpha(t - t_i)^{-\beta}$ [13]. HWK-P owns critical phenomena [7].

4) Self-feeding process (SFP) [1, 22] captures the Markovian dependency of IETs. The hazard function of this model is $\lambda(t|\mathcal{H}_t) = \frac{1}{\mu/e+\tau_i}$.

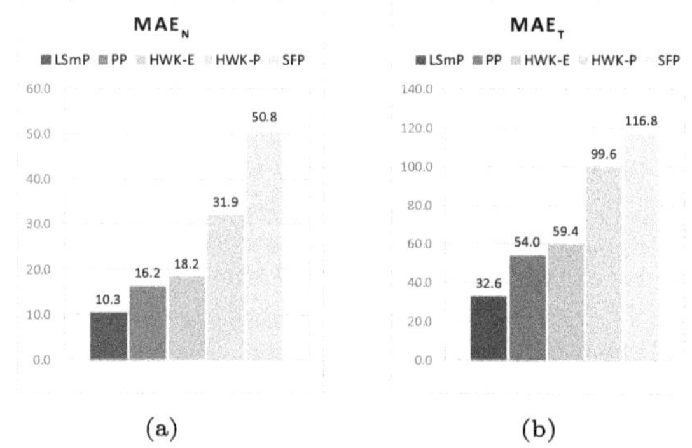

Figure 2: *LSmP fits reality much better than competitors in both settings.* Median value of the Mean Average Error (MAE) for cumulative number of events over time $n_i(t)$, i.e., $MAE_N(i)$, and the event time epochs t, i.e., $MAE_T(i)$ are shown in (a) and (b), respectively.

4.2.2 Accuracy of growth curve shape. We evaluate the shape accuracy between the empirical dynamics $n_i(t) = |\{t_j < t|t_j \in \mathcal{H}_t = (t_1, ..., t_{n_i})\}|$ and the estimated dynamics $\hat{n_i(t)} = |\{\hat{t_j} < \hat{t}|\hat{t_j} \in \hat{\mathcal{H}_t} = (\hat{t_1}, ..., \hat{t_{n_i}})\}|$ of each individual i by considering the average mean error of the cumulative count: $MAE_N(i) = \frac{\sum_{j=1}^{n_i} |n(t_j) - n(\hat{t_j})|}{n_i}$, and the average mean error of the event time epochs: $MAE_T(i) = \frac{\sum_{j=1}^{n_i} |t_j - \hat{t_j}|}{n_i}$. For each individual, we compute $MAE_N(i)$ and $MAE_T(i)$, and Figure 2 plots the median of MAEs for the $n_i(t)$.

The proposed LSmP model fits the reality much better than the baselines for both the metrics. In average, LSmP captures the number of event $n(t)$ at each event time epoch t_i with error 10.3. In contrast, the MAE_N given by the PP, HWK-E, HWK-P, SFP are 1.6, 1.8, 3.1, 4.9 times of the LSmP's, respectively. Similar results go with the error of the event time t_i: the MAE_T given by the PP, HWK-E, HWK-P, SFP are 1.7, 1.8, 3.1, 18.7 times of the LSmP's, respectively. The worst results are given by the SFP due to the fact that it may generate extremely overestimated IET. The HWK-P gives the second largest error due to the fact that the Hawkes process with power law kernel is easily in the supercritical regime, which generates exponential growth. The PP and the HWK-E give similar results because they generate linear growth.

Table 2: KS-Test of models. Our LSmP model captures the multiscale IET distribution. Winner in bold.

	KS-Test (Sig. $\alpha = 5\%$)				
τ	LSmP	PP	HWK-E	HWK-P	SFP
Pass Rate	**87.1%**	7.8%	62.9%	37.0%	2.4%
Error Statistic	**0.098**	0.256	0.134	0.162	0.291
$\log(\tau)$	LSmP	PP	HWK-E	HWK-P	SFP
Pass Rate	**87.1%**	7.8%	62.9%	37.0%	2.4%
Error Statistic	**0.098**	0.256	0.134	0.162	0.291

4.2.3 Accuracy of multiscale IET distribution. We then demonstrate that the LSmP accurately captures the multiscale IET distribution of the growth dynamics. We compare the IETs of each individual's connectivity dynamics $\tau_i = \{\tau_1, ..., \tau_{n_i}\}$ and the generated counterpart $\hat{\tau}_i = \{\hat{\tau}_1, ..., \hat{\tau}_{n_i}\}$ by testing whether τ_i and $\hat{\tau}_i$ are from the same continuous distribution. The two-sample Kolmogorov-Smirnov test (KS -Test) is applied for this standard statistical test mission. The fitting results of the model are shown by the indicator of passing the test, and a statistic representing the extent of difference between empirical data and the fitting results.

Table 2 presents the average pass rate and the error statistic for LSmP and the baselines with the significance level $\alpha = 5\%$. Our LSmP model outperforms all the baselines significantly in both the metrics: 87.1% of the generated dynamics by LSmP passes the KS-Test with average error 0.098. The pass rate of LSmP increases to 94.1% if we loose the significance level to 1%. We also conduct the hypothesis test on the logarithmically transformed IET $\log(\tau)$. We get same results for the $\log(\tau)$ as the τ. All the baselines fail to capture the multiscale IET distribution: *i)* the PP, which only generates exponential distribution in the long-scale, fails the short-scale and middle-scale; *ii)* the HWK-E exhibits a mixture of two exponential distributions at short-scale and long-scale, neglecting the fat-tail in middle-scale; *iii)* the HWK-H misses the flat short-scale; *iv)* the SFP cannot generate flat short-scale and exhibits large bias in the middle scale.

4.2.4 Accuracy of IETs' correlation. We further show that our LSmP captures the correlation between the IETs by comparing the joint distribution of consecutive IETs $p(\tau_{i,j}, \tau_{i,j+1})$ from empirical data, and the generated results $p(\hat{\tau}_{i,j}, \hat{\tau}_{i,j+1})$. We apply the two-dimensional version of the Kolmogorov-Smirnov test (2D-KS-Test) [21] to test whether $p(\tau_{i,j}, \tau_{i,j+1})$ and $p(\hat{\tau}_{i,j}, \hat{\tau}_{i,j+1})$ are same. We set the significance level to 5%. Table 3 presents the average pass rate and the error statistic for LSmP and other baselines. Again, LSmP beats all the baselines significantly in both metrics. We further examine to what extent the goodness-of-fit by the 2D-KS-Test are dominated by the marginal distributions. By shuffling the IET of the generated growth dynamics, we test the shuffled $p_s(\hat{\tau}_{i,j'}, \hat{\tau}_{i,j'+1})$ against the empirical $p(\hat{\tau}_{i,j}, \hat{\tau}_{i,j+1})$. We find LSmP gets the largest pass rate 77.5% (as shown in the second panel of Table 3) due to the nice characterization of the marginal distribution. What's more, LSmP also has the maximum additional increase 8% (=85.5% − 77.5%) due to the characterization of the correlation between IETs. Same conclusions can be drawn from the logarithmically transformed IET $\log(\tau)$.

Table 3: 2D-KS-Test of models. Our LSmP model captures the IETs' correlation. Winner in bold.

	2D-KS-Test (Sig. $\alpha = 5\%$)				
τ	LSmP	PP	HWK-E	HWK-P	SFP
Pass Rate	**85.5%**	7.9%	61.1%	34.1%	2.0%
Error Statistic	**0.145**	0.329	0.189	0.220	0.371
Shuffled τ	LSmP	PP	HWK-E	HWK-P	SFP
Pass Rate	**77.5%**	7.9%	57.2%	27.3%	1.9%
Error Statistic	**0.159**	0.329	0.194	0.231	0.384
$\log(\tau)$	LSmP	PP	HWK-E	HWK-P	SFP
Pass Rate	**85.4%**	6.7%	62.0%	34.0%	2.6%
Error Statistic	**0.145**	0.329	0.189	0.220	0.371

In all, only our LSmP correctly approximates the empirical growth dynamics of individuals' connectivity with respect to the shape of curves, the multiscale IET distribution and the IETs' correlation.

4.3 Discovering statistical regularity by parameter analysis

One good advantage of LSmP is that all the modeling parameters have clear physical meanings. In this section, we find statistical regularities underlying the empirical growth patterns through parameter analysis. To our best knowledge, this is the first empirical study of the profound exponents, α and θ, which govern human dynamics.

Figure 3 plots the distributions of the six parameters of LSmP. We fit the distributions of each parameter by Levenberg-Marquardt algorithm [17] and report their coefficients' values with confidence bounds 95%. We get following findings for the human dynamics of adding friends in the long-term:

Rich complexities and heterogeneities in power law growth. Figure 3a plots the distribution of the exponent α of power law growth, we find that it's a mixture of three distributions as follows, taking on complexity:

i) A skewed normal distribution ($\mu = 0.70$, $\sigma = 0.57$, $s = 2.6$) near 1 where μ is the mean location, the σ is the standard deviation and s is the skewness. The location value indicates in average users show decelerating power law growth with exponent $\alpha \sim t^{0.7}$. The positive skewness value shows that there exist a large number of linear growth($\alpha = 1$) and accelerating power law growth ($\alpha > 1$). A relatively large variance implies the heterogeneity of human growth patterns in the long-term. Besides, these findings at microscopic level are consistent with our previous finding [25] that at macroscopic level nodes grow over time $n(t) \sim t^{2.15}$, links grow over time $e(t) \sim t^3$ and thus average connectivity grows $\frac{e(t)}{n(t)} \sim t^{0.85}$.

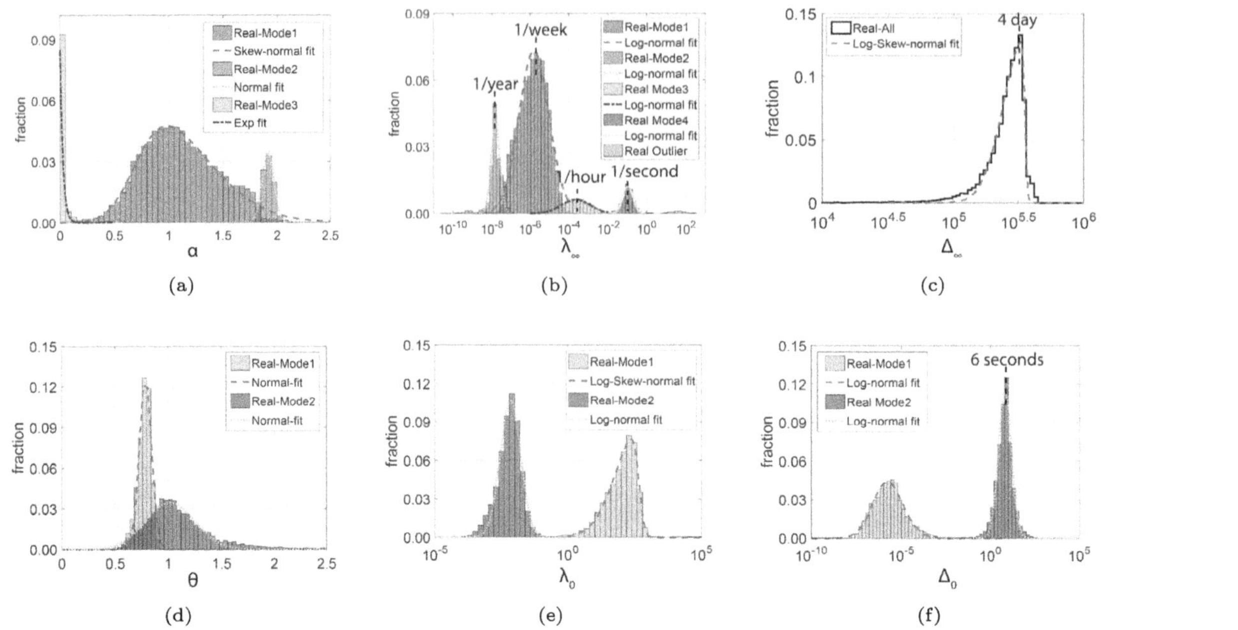

Figure 3: *Parameter distributions.* Short-term parameters: (a) α, (b) λ_∞, (c) Δ_∞, and long-term parameters: (d) θ, (e) λ_0, (f) Δ_0. The colored bars represent the sub-clusters, and the same colors denotes same population. The overall distribution is marked by black stairs. The fitting curves for each cluster are denoted by colored lines.

ii) A normal distribution ($\mu = 1.9$, $\sigma = 0.077$) near 2 implies that there exist some users with large power law exponents with upper-bound near ≈ 2. The reason of this bound might origin from the fact that the maximum number of links to be linked in a social network is proportional to the square of the number of nodes so far.

iii) An exponential distribution ($\alpha \propto e^{-39.4x}$) near 0, indicates that the growth dynamics in this regime decelerate significantly in the long-term. The finite size effect of friendships, possibly derived from the limited human cognition may account for this deceleration.

Log-normal distribution governing the multiscale long-term rate and human adds a friend per week. Figure 3b plots the distribution of growth rate λ_∞, and we find a mixture of four log-norm distributions spanning more than 8 order of magnitude, ranging from 1/second, 1/hour, 1/week to 1/year. The majority of human growth lie in the mode 1, with best log-norm fitting (for $\log(\lambda_\infty)$, $\mu = -5.80$, $\sigma = 1.11$), indicating that humans add friends in a cycle of 7.3 days in average. The small λ_∞ in mode 2 ($\mu = -3.65$, $\sigma = 1.04$) implies a long period of time without events at initial lifetime, while large λ_∞ in mode 3 ($\mu = -0.97$, $\sigma = 0.37$) and mode 4 ($\mu = -0.97$, $\sigma = 0.37$) imply a burst of events at the initial lifetime. We discuss the correlation between λ_∞ and α and their implications in the next subsection.

Typical time scale in the long-term is 4 days. Figure 3c plots the distribution of Δ_∞, best fitted by a skewed log-norm distribution ($\mu = 5.55$, $\sigma = 0.17$, $s = -12.00$), implying that the typical time scale of human dynamics of adding friends is near 4 days ($= 10^\mu$ s). For example, when you start a new job on Monday and establish a set of connections to your workmates until Friday (four days later!).

The findings for the human dynamics in the short-term are as follows:

Gaussian mixture of fizzling exponent. Figure 3d plots the the fizzling exponent θ, which follows a Gaussian mixture distribution with two modes: mode 1 ($\mu = 0.79$, $\sigma = 0.080$) and mode 2 ($\mu = 1.02$, $\sigma = 0.32$). The case when $\theta = 1$ in mode 2 is in line with the prediction of the priority queue model [23], indicating a power law decay (See Lemma 3.2). But we find rather than the power law decay in the critical state when $\theta = 1$, $\theta \neq 1$ is more general, indicating a stretched exponential decay. Especially we find the mode 1 with mean value 0.79, indicating a fatter tail of the IET distribution.

Bimodal short-term rate. Figure 3e plots the distribution of the short-term growth rate λ_0, which follows a bimodal distribution, where the skewed log-normal distribution ($\mu = 2.68$, $\sigma = 0.88$, $s = -5.63$) best fits the mode 1, and the log-normal distribution ($\mu = -2.16$, $\sigma = 0.56$) best explains the mode 2. The separated two modes show clear two clusters for human dynamics in the short IET scale. We discuss it in next section.

Bimodal critical time in the short-term, and adding friends as soon as 6 seconds. Figure 3f plots the distribution of short-term scale Δ_0, which also follows a bimodal distribution. The mode 2 is best fitted by log-normal distribution ($\mu = 0.81$,$\sigma = 0.51$), with mean value 6 seconds, indicating the critical time between the quick actions and the fat-tailed patterns of the IET distribution. Indeed, the WeChat offers multiple methods for adding friends as soon as possible, e.g.,"shake it". By shaking the mobile phone, user can add strangers who is shaking at the same, and thus a random link is built. The mode 1 follows log-normal distribution ($\mu = -6.03$,$\sigma = 1.3$) with mean value $10^{-5.77}$ (~ 0) seconds, indicating that the IET distribution of this users consisting of only middle-scale and long-scale (Fig. 1d). In addition, we find strong correlations between these three short-term parameters: the population in Δ_0-model correspond to the large λ_0 value in λ_0-model1 and the 0.79 fizzling exponent in θ-model.

4.4 Clustering growth dynamics and detecting outliers

The LSmP's ability of pattern finding is further examined in the joint distribution of modeling parameters.

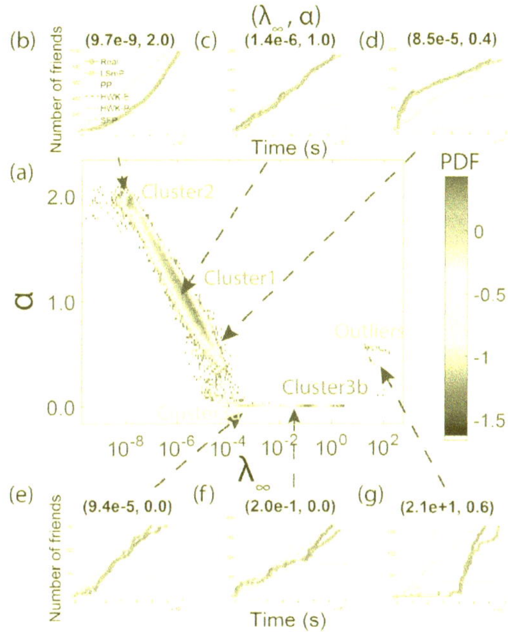

Figure 4: *Growth modes in the long-term.* (a) The joint distribution of the long-term rate λ_∞ and the power law growth exponent α, on a log-linear scale. The corresponding marginal distributions are shown in Figs. 3. Instances of growth are shown in (b-g).

Due to the prevailing of the (skewed/log) normal distribution in our data, we apply the Gaussian mixture model to the long-term parameter space $(\alpha, \lambda_\infty, \Delta_\infty)$ and short-term parameter space $(\theta, \lambda_0, \Delta_0)$ respectively, and find clusters, as shown in Fig. 3. Bars with different color represent different clusters, while the same color in different marginal distributions represent same cluster. We further examine the cluster patterns in the high-order parameter space [26], as shown in the joint distributions in Fig. 4 and Fig. 5. Different modes in the long-term and short-term are found by these joint distributions.

Long-term growth modes. Figure 4 plots the growth dynamics projected into the long-term (λ_∞, α)-space, we find

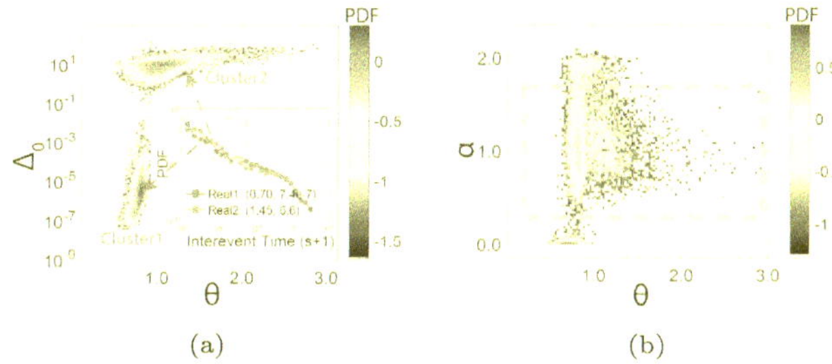

Figure 5: *Growth modes in the short-term.* (a) The joint distribution of the short-term fizzling the exponent θ and the short-term time scale δ_0, on a linear-log scale. The inset plots two representative IET distribuions in cluster 1 and cluster 2, respectively. (b) The joint distribution of θ and α on a linear-linear plot.

three major growth modes of human connectivity dynamics as our LSmP predicts:

Linear growth is in the vicinity of the $\alpha = 1$ region, consisting of the population near the mode of Cluster1. The $\alpha = 1$ features linear growth as shown in Fig. 4c.

Accelerating power law growth is in the $\alpha > 1$ regime, containing the top half part of the Cluster1, and the quadratic growth dynamics in Cluster2. The quadratic growth ($\alpha = 2$) is a special case of accelerating power law growth, as shown in Fig. 4b.

Decelerating power law growth is in the regime with $\alpha < 1$, consisting of the bottom half of the Cluster1 (one instance in Fig. 4d) and Cluster3a and 3b. Figures 4e&f plot two instances in Cluster3a and Cluster3b respectively. Along the λ_∞ axis, the Cluster3a exhibits a large delay at initial time and then decelerating power law growth followed at the small λ_∞ value region, while the Cluster3b shows initial burst then followed by decelerating power law growth growth at the large λ_∞ value region.

Short-term growth modes. Figure 5a plots the joint distribution of the short-term (θ, Δ_0)-space. We find the two modes of the short-term dynamics are separated by whether they show short-scale in IET distributions, as shown in the inset of fig. 5a.

Correlation between long-term and short-term. We further examine the correlation between the long-term parameters and the short-term parameters. The Figure 5b plots the joint distribution of the short-term fizzling exponent θ and long-term power law growth exponent α. We find the majority of dynamics (in Cluster1) show large variance with respect to θ, implying the relatively small correlations between the long-term memory and short-term memory.

Outlier detection. In addition, we showcase the outlier detection in the parameter space. By examining the joint profile for the λ_∞ and α, we also find outliers. Figure 4g plots one growth instance in the outlier point cloud, featuring long time vacation and large burst. A couple of actions for this user within first 1.3 year, he/she then added 50 friends in few minutes. We find the baselines can not capture these phenomena at all, but our LSmP even captures this outlier to some extent. Furthermore, the parsimonious feature dimension and the clear physical meanings facilitate the design of more elaborated outlier detection method for future work.

5 CONCLUSIONS

In this paper, we studied the growth dynamics of individual's social connectivity in WeChat. We find various power law growth in the long-term and bursts in the short-term. We find the average-effect to account for power law growth and multiscale-effect and correlation-effect to account for bursts. Based fundamentally on these ingredients, we propose LSmP to capture the individual's social connectivity dynamics. Our LSmP gives a unified but parsimonious model which can accurately match and comprehensively explain growth dynamics of microscopic social connectivity. The main contributions are:

- **Novel findings**: We analyze the social connectivity dynamics in real social network at microscopic level and discover power law growth in the long-term and bursts in the short-term. We find three ingredients, i.e., average-effect, multiscale-effect and correlation-effect accounting for the power law and bursty growth.
- **Novel LSmP model**: We propose a stochastic model to capture above findings. LSmP is parsimonious and all the parameters have clear physical meanings.
- **Accuracy**: We present experiments on real social networks. Our LSmP model matches the real growth patterns accurately.
- **Usefulness**: Our LSmP provides insightful understandings on human dynamics, and implies applications in prediction, clustering, pattern discovery, and outlier detection, etc.

Limitation and future work. The sociological theories underlying the observed behaviors need further examination. Due to the ubiquity of growth phenomena, it's also interesting to see if our model can be applied to the growth dynamics of other systems, ranging from the connectome of C.elegans [18] to the growth of a company.

Reproducibility. We open-source our code of the LSmP at https://github.com/calvin-zcx/LSMP.

Acknowledgement

The authors thank anonymous reviewers for many useful discussions and insightful suggestions. This work was supported by National Program on Key Basic Research Project, No. 2015CB352300; National Natural Science Foundation of China, No. 61370022, No. 61521002, No. 61531006 and No. 61210008. Thanks for the research fund of Tsinghua-Tencent Joint Laboratory for Internet Innovation Technology.

REFERENCES

[1] Rodrigo Augusto da Silva Alves, Renato Martins Assuncao, and Pedro Olmo Stancioli Vaz de Melo. 2016. Burstiness Scale: A Parsimonious Model for Characterizing Random Series of Events. In *Proceedings of the 22nd ACM SIGKDD*. ACM, 1405–1414.

[2] Valerio Arnaboldi, Marco Conti, Andrea Passarella, and Robin Dunbar. 2013. Dynamics of personal social relationships in online social networks: a study on twitter. In *Proceedings of the first ACM conference on Online social networks*. ACM, 15–26.

[3] Albert-Laszlo Barabasi. 2005. The origin of bursts and heavy tails in human dynamics. *Nature* 435, 7039 (2005), 207–211.

[4] Albert-László Barabási and Réka Albert. 1999. Emergence of scaling in random networks. *science* 286, 5439 (1999), 509–512.

[5] Ginestra Bianconi and A-L Barabási. 2001. Competition and multiscaling in evolving networks. *EPL (Europhysics Letters)* 54, 4 (2001), 436.

[6] Thomas F Coleman and Yuying Li. 1996. An interior trust region approach for nonlinear minimization subject to bounds. *SIAM Journal on optimization* (1996).

[7] Riley Crane and Didier Sornette. 2008. Robust dynamic classes revealed by measuring the response function of a social system. *PNAS* 105, 41 (2008), 15649–15653.

[8] Daryl J Daley and David Vere-Jones. 2003. *An introduction to the theory of point processes: volume I: Elementary Theory and Methods*. Springer Science & Business Media.

[9] Angelos Dassios, Hongbiao Zhao, and others. 2013. Exact simulation of Hawkes process with exponentially decaying intensity. *Electronic Communications in Probability* 18, 62 (2013), 1–13.

[10] Alceu Ferraz Costa, Yuto Yamaguchi, Agma Juci Machado Traina, Caetano Traina Jr, and Christos Faloutsos. 2015. Rsc: Mining and modeling temporal activity in social media. In *SIGKDD'15*. ACM.

[11] Alan G Hawkes. 1971. Spectra of some self-exciting and mutually exciting point processes. *Biometrika* 58, 1 (1971), 83–90.

[12] Hang-Hyun Jo, Juan I Perotti, Kimmo Kaski, and János Kertész. 2015. Correlated bursts and the role of memory range. *Physical Review E* (2015).

[13] Patrick J Laub, Thomas Taimre, and Philip K Pollett. 2015. Hawkes processes. *arXiv preprint arXiv:1507.02822* (2015).

[14] Jure Leskovec, Lars Backstrom, Ravi Kumar, and Andrew Tomkins. 2008. Microscopic evolution of social networks *(KDD '08)*. ACM, 462–470.

[15] Jure Leskovec, Jon Kleinberg, and Christos Faloutsos. 2007. Graph evolution: Densification and shrinking diameters. *TKDD* (2007).

[16] R Dean Malmgren, Daniel B Stouffer, Adilson E Motter, and Luís AN Amaral. 2008. A Poissonian explanation for heavy tails in e-mail communication. *PNAS* 105, 47 (2008), 18153–18158.

[17] Jorge J Moré. 1978. The Levenberg-Marquardt algorithm: implementation and theory. In *Numerical analysis*. Springer, 105–116.

[18] Vincenzo Nicosia, Petra E Vértes, William R Schafer, Vito Latora, and Edward T Bullmore. 2013. Phase transition in the economically modeled growth of a cellular nervous system. *PNAS* 110, 19 (2013), 7880–7885.

[19] Yosihiko Ogata. 1981. On Lewis' simulation method for point processes. *IEEE Transactions on Information Theory* 27, 1 (1981), 23–31.

[20] Tohru Ozaki. 1979. Maximum likelihood estimation of Hawkes' self-exciting point processes. *Annals of the Institute of Statistical Mathematics* 31, 1 (1979), 145–155.

[21] JA Peacock. 1983. Two-dimensional goodness-of-fit testing in astronomy. *Monthly Notices of the Royal Astronomical Society* 202, 3 (1983), 615–627.

[22] Pedro Olmo S Vaz de Melo, Christos Faloutsos, Renato Assunção, and Antonio Loureiro. 2013. The self-feeding process: a unifying model for communication dynamics in the web. In *Proceedings of the 22nd international conference on World Wide Web*. ACM, 1319–1330.

[23] Alexei Vázquez, Joao Gama Oliveira, Zoltán Dezsö, Kwang-Il Goh, Imre Kondor, and Albert-László Barabási. 2006. Modeling bursts and heavy tails in human dynamics. *Physical Review E* 73, 3 (2006), 036127.

[24] Ye Wu, Changsong Zhou, Jinghua Xiao, Jürgen Kurths, and Hans Joachim Schellnhuber. 2010. Evidence for a bimodal distribution in human communication. *PNAS* 107, 44 (2010), 18803–18808.

[25] Chengxi Zang, Peng Cui, and Christos Faloutsos. 2016. Beyond Sigmoids: The NetTide Model for Social Network Growth, and Its Applications. In *Proceedings of the 22Nd ACM SIGKDD (KDD '16)*. ACM, 2015–2024.

[26] Chengxi Zang, Peng Cui, Chaoming Song, Christos Faloutsos, and Wenwu Zhu. 2017. Quantifying Structural Patterns of Information Cascades. In *Proceedings of the 26th International Conference on WWW Companion*. 867–868.

[27] Tianyang Zhang, Peng Cui, Chaoming Song, Wenwu Zhu, and Shiqiang Yang. 2016. A multiscale survival process for modeling human activity patterns. *PloS one* 11, 3 (2016), e0151473.

Weisfeiler-Lehman Neural Machine for Link Prediction

Muhan Zhang
Department of Computer Science and Engineering
Washington University in St. Louis
muhan@wustl.edu

Yixin Chen
Department of Computer Science and Engineering
Washington University in St. Louis
chen@cse.wustl.edu

ABSTRACT

In this paper, we propose a next-generation link prediction method, Weisfeiler-Lehman Neural Machine (WLNM), which learns topological features in the form of graph patterns that promote the formation of links. WLNM has unmatched advantages including higher performance than state-of-the-art methods and universal applicability over various kinds of networks. WLNM extracts an enclosing subgraph of each target link and encodes the subgraph as an adjacency matrix. The key novelty of the encoding comes from a fast hashing-based Weisfeiler-Lehman (WL) algorithm that labels the vertices according to their structural roles in the subgraph while preserving the subgraph's intrinsic directionality. After that, a neural network is trained on these adjacency matrices to learn a predictive model. Compared with traditional link prediction methods, WLNM does not assume a particular link formation mechanism (such as common neighbors), but learns this mechanism from the graph itself. We conduct comprehensive experiments to show that WLNM not only outperforms a great number of state-of-the-art link prediction methods, but also consistently performs well across networks with different characteristics.

CCS CONCEPTS

• Information systems → Data mining; • Computing methodologies → Supervised learning;

KEYWORDS

link prediction; graph labeling; color refinement; neural network

ACM Reference format:

Muhan Zhang and Yixin Chen. 2017. Weisfeiler-Lehman Neural Machine for Link Prediction. In *Proceedings of KDD '17, Halifax, NS, Canada, August 13-17, 2017,* 9 pages.
https://doi.org/10.1145/3097983.3097996

1 INTRODUCTION

Link prediction [1] is attracting increasing interests among data mining and machine learning communities. It has many applications, such as friend recommendation in social networks [2], product recommendation in e-commerce [3], knowledge graph completion [4], finding interactions between proteins [5], and recovering missing reactions in metabolic networks [6]. While many sophisticated models such as stochastic block models [5] and probabilistic matrix factorization [7] have been developed, some simple heuristics such as common neighbors and Katz index work surprisingly well in practice and are often more interpretable and scalable. For instance, the common neighbor heuristic assumes that two nodes are more likely to have a link if they have more common neighbors. Although simple, this heuristic has been shown to perform very well on social networks [1]. Other successful heuristics include AA [2], RA [8], Katz [9] as well as many carefully calculated node proximity scores based on network topology or random walks.

However, a significant limitation of these heuristics is that they lack universal applicability to different kinds of networks. For example, common neighbors may work well when predicting friendships in social networks or predicting coauthorships in collaboration networks, but has been shown to have poor performance on electrical grids and biological networks [10]. On the other hand, Average Commute Time, a.k.a. resistance distance [11], has exceptional performance on predicting power grids and router-level Internets, but has poor results on social networks. A survey paper compared over 20 different heuristics and found that none of them performs consistently well across all networks [10]. This implies the need to manually choose different heuristics for different networks based on prior beliefs or expensive trial and error.

Can we automatically learn suitable heuristics from a network itself? The answer is yes, since these heuristics are after all extracted from the network topology. By extracting local patterns for each link, we should be able to learn which patterns foster the formation of a link. This way, various heuristics embedded in the local patterns can be learned automatically, avoiding the need to manually select heuristics. Moreover, for those networks on which no existing heuristic works well, we can learn new heuristics that suit them. Our goal in this paper is to design such a universal model.

We propose a new link prediction method called Weisfeiler-Lehman Neural Machine (WLNM). For each target link, WLNM first extracts a subgraph in its neighborhood, which we call the *enclosing subgraph* of a link. WLNM then represents the enclosing subgraph as an adjacency matrix. After that, a neural network is trained on these adjacency matrices to learn a link prediction model. Figure 1 illustrates the proposed framework.

To encode each enclosing subgraph, the key issue is to decide the ordering of graph vertices. The goal of *graph labeling* is to assign nodes of two different enclosing subgraphs to similar indices in respective adjacency matrices if and only if their structural roles within the graphs are similar. Since machine learning models read data sequentially, a stable ordering based on structural roles of vertices is crucial for learning meaningful models.

The Weisfeiler-Lehman (**WL**) algorithm [12] is a graph labeling method which determines vertex ordering based on graph topology. The classical WL algorithm works as follows. Initially, all vertices get the same label. Then, vertices iteratively concatenate their own

ACM ISBN 978-1-4503-4887-4/17/08...$15.00
https://doi.org/10.1145/3097983.3097996

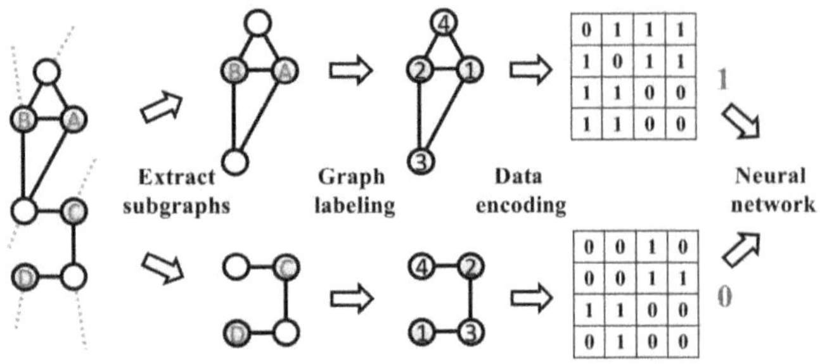

Figure 1: An illustration of WLNM. Given a network, WLNM first samples a set of positive links (illustrated as link (A, B)) and negative links (illustrated as link (C, D)) as training links, and extracts an enclosing subgraph for each link. Graph labeling is used to decide the vertex ordering and adjacency matrix. The resulting (matrix, label) pairs are fed into a neural network for link prediction.

labels and their direct neighbors' labels as their signature strings and compress these signature strings into new, short labels until convergence. In the end, vertices with identical structural roles will get the same labels.

A limitation of the classical WL algorithm is that it requires the storing and sorting of possibly long signature strings in each iteration, which is time consuming. On the other hand, a hashing-based WL [13] is much faster, but is no longer stable: the vertex ordering is not preserved between iterations. To address the above challenge, we propose a novel PALETTE-WL graph labeling algorithm, which combines the efficiency of the hashing-based WL and the order-preserving property of the classical WL. PALETTE-WL first colors subgraph vertices according to their distance to the target link, and then iteratively refines the initial colors so that the relative color ordering is preserved. Our results prove that the PALETTE-WL algorithm leads to very good enclosing subgraph representations and is computationally efficient.

To learn nonlinear topological features from the enclosing subgraphs, neural network is used for its exceptional expressing power. Our experiments show that neural networks achieve superior link prediction performance than heuristic methods, especially on some datasets where all existing methods perform poorly.

WLNM has a few distinctive advantages. 1) **Higher performance**—WLNM uses neural networks to learn sophisticated topological features which simple heuristics cannot express. It outperforms all baseline methods in almost all datasets we have tested; 2) **Universality**—WLNM automatically learns topological features, avoiding the need to choose heuristics or do feature selection/engineering for different networks. Empirical results confirm that WLNM consistently performs well across various networks, while most other methods perform well only on a few networks and poorly on others.

We summarize our contributions as follows. 1) We propose Weisfeiler-Lehman Neural Machine (WLNM), a novel link prediction framework to automatically learn topological features from networks. 2) We propose a novel graph labeling method, PALETTE-WL, to efficiently encode enclosing subgraphs into adjacency matrices so that neural networks can learn meaningful patterns. 3) We conduct extensive experiments on various kinds of real-world networks and compare WLNM to 12 heuristic and latent feature methods. WLNM outperforms state-of-the-art link prediction methods and offers great universality across various networks.

Table 1: Popular Heuristics for Link Prediction

Name	Formula	Order
common neighbors	$\|\Gamma(x) \cap \Gamma(y)\|$	first
Jaccard	$\frac{\|\Gamma(x)\cap\Gamma(y)\|}{\|\Gamma(x)\cup\Gamma(y)\|}$	first
preferential attachment	$\|\Gamma(x)\| \cdot \|\Gamma(y)\|$	first
Adamic-Adar	$\sum_{z\in\Gamma(x)\cap\Gamma(y)} \frac{1}{\log\|\Gamma(z)\|}$	second
resource allocation	$\sum_{z\in\Gamma(x)\cap\Gamma(y)} \frac{1}{\|\Gamma(z)\|}$	second
Katz	$\sum_{l=1}^{\infty} \beta^l \|\text{path}(x, y) = l\|$	high
PageRank	$q_{xy} + q_{yx}$	high
SimRank	$\gamma \frac{\sum_{a\in\Gamma(x)}\sum_{b\in\Gamma(y)}\text{score}(a,b)}{\|\Gamma(x)\|\cdot\|\Gamma(y)\|}$	high
resistance distance	$\frac{1}{l^+_{xx}+l^+_{yy}-2l^+_{xy}}$	high

Notes: $\Gamma(x)$ denotes the neighbor set of vertex x. $\beta < 1$ is a damping factor. $|\text{path}(x, y) = l|$ counts the number of length-l paths between x and y. q_{xy} is the stationary distribution probability of y under the random walk from x with restart, see [14]. SimRank score is a recursive definition. l^+_{xy} is the (x, y) entry of the pseudoinverse of the graph's Laplacian matrix.

2 PRELIMINARIES

In this section, we introduce some background knowledge in link prediction and graph theory, which are important for understanding the proposed WLNM method.

2.1 Heuristic methods for link prediction

A large category of link prediction methods are based on some heuristics that measure the proximity between nodes to predict whether they are likely to have a link. Popular heuristics include: common neighbors (CN), Adamic-Adar (AA) [2], preferential attachment (PA) [15], resource allocation (RA) [8], Katz [9], PageRank [14], SimRank [16], resistance distance [11], and their numerous variants. Liben-Nowell and Kleinberg [1] first studied their link prediction performance on social networks. Empirical comparisons of these heuristics on different networks can be found in [10, 17]. We group link prediction heuristics into three classes: first-order, second-order and high-order methods, based on the most distant node necessary for computing the heuristic. For example, common neighbor is a first-order heuristic, since it only involves the direct neighbors of the two nodes. Katz index is a high-order heuristic, because one needs to search the entire graph for all possible paths between two vertices. Table 1 summarizes nine popular heuristics, which will be used as baselines in our experiments.

2.2 Graphs

A network can be represented as a graph $G = (V, E)$, where $V = \{v_1, ..., v_n\}$ is the set of vertices and $E \subseteq V \times V$ is the set of links. A graph can be represented by an adjacency matrix A, where $A_{i,j} = 1$ if there is a link from i to j and $A_{i,j} = 0$ otherwise. We say i and j are adjacent if $A_{i,j} = 1$. If the links are undirected, A will be symmetric. In this paper, we consider undirected networks, although our model can be easily generalized to directed networks. We use $\Gamma(x)$ or $\Gamma^1(x)$ to denote the set of 1-hop neighbors of a vertex $x \in V$. We use

Algorithm 1 Weisfeiler-Lehman Graph Labeling

```
input: graph G = (V, E), initial colors c^0(v) = 1 for all v ∈ V
output: final colors c(v) for all v ∈ V
let c(v) = c^0(v) for all v ∈ V
while c(v) has not converged do
    for each v ∈ V do
        collect a multiset {c(v')|v' ∈ Γ(v)} containing its neighbors' colors
        sort the multiset in ascending order
        concatenate the sorted multiset to c(v) to generate a signature string s(v) = ⟨c(v), {c(v')|v' ∈ Γ(v)}_sort⟩
    end for
    sort all s(v) in lexicographical ascending order
    map all s(v) to new colors 1,2,3,... sequentially; same strings get the same color
end while
```

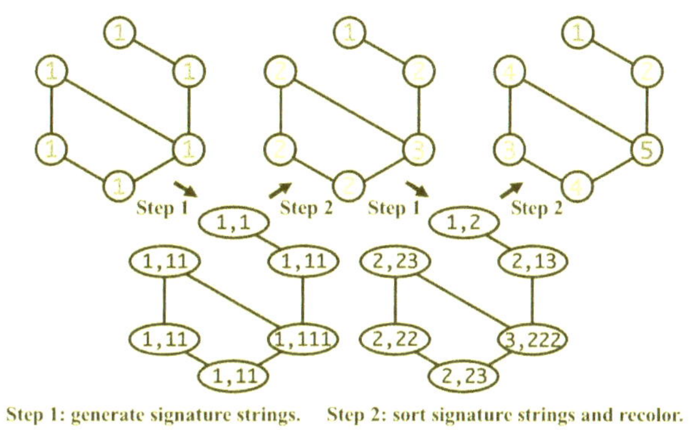

Figure 2: Illustration of two iterations of the WL algorithm for a graph. The vertices in the upper left graph are initially all colored 1. In each iteration, step 1 calculates the WL signature string for each vertex by concatenating the color of the vertex and the (sorted) colors of the vertex's neighbors. Step 2 recolors the graph according to these WL signatures.

$\Gamma^d(x)$ to denote the set of vertices whose distance to x is less than or equal to d, $d = 1, 2, 3, \cdots$.

2.3 The Weisfeiler-Lehman algorithm

A **graph labeling** function is a map $l : V \rightarrow C$ from vertices V to an ordered set C, conventionally called **colors** in literature. In this paper, we adopt the set of integer colors starting from 1. If l is injective, then C can be used to uniquely determine the vertex order in an adjacency matrix.

Our proposed Palette-WL graph labeling method is based on the 1-dimensional Weisfeiler-Lehman (WL) algorithm [12], shown in Algorithm 1. Widely used in graph isomorphism checking, WL belongs to a class of **color refinement** algorithms that iteratively update vertex colors until a fixed point is reached.

The main idea of WL is to iteratively augment vertex labels using their neighbors' labels and compress the augmented labels into new labels until convergence. At first, all vertices are set to the same color 1. For each vertex, it gets a *signature string* by concatenating its own color and the sorted colors of its immediate neighbors. Vertices are then sorted by the ascending order of their signature strings and assigned new colors $1, 2, 3, \cdots$. Vertices with the same signature strings get the same color.

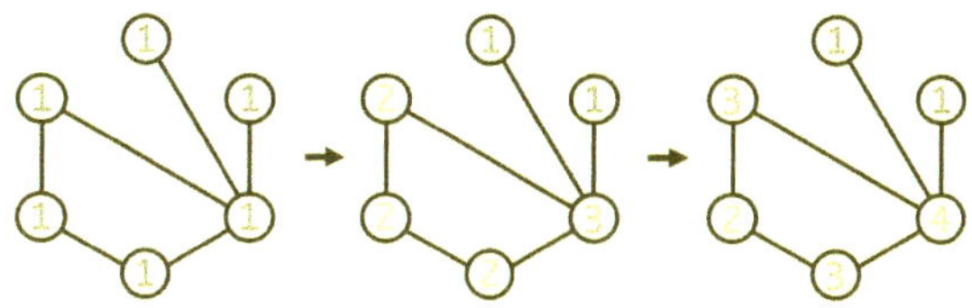

Figure 3: Illustration of the WL coloring for another graph. Comparing the vertex orderings in Figure 2 and Figure 3, we see that vertices with similar structural roles have similar relative rankings.

For example, assume vertex x has color 2 and its neighbors have colors $\{3, 1, 2\}$ respectively, and vertex y has color 2 and its neighboring colors are $\{2, 1, 2\}$. The signature strings for x and y are $\langle 2, 123 \rangle$ and $\langle 2, 122 \rangle$, respectively. Since $\langle 2, 122 \rangle$ is smaller than $\langle 2, 123 \rangle$ lexicographically, y will be assigned a smaller color than x in the next iteration. Such process is iterated until vertex colors stop changing. Figure 2 shows an example. All vertices are initially colored 1 and finally colored by a richer set $\{1, \cdots, 5\}$.

One key benefit of the WL algorithm is that the final colors encode the structural roles of vertices inside a graph and define a relative ordering for vertices (with ties)—vertices with the same final color share the same structural role within a graph. Moreover, this relative ordering for vertices is consistent across different graphs—e.g., if vertex v in G and vertex v' in G' share similar structural roles in their corresponding graphs, they will have similar relative positions in their respective orderings, which is shown in Figure 3. The structure-encoding property of WL is essential for its success in graph kernel design [18], which measures graph similarity by counting vertices' matching WL colors. Recently, WL is also used in graph CNNs to define a global ordering for sequentially moving convolutional filters along vertices and a local ordering for reading each receptive field [19].

3 WEISFEILER-LEHMAN NEURAL MACHINE (WLNM)

In this section, we propose our Wlnm model. Wlnm is a neural network model combined with encoded subgraph patterns. It automatically learns topological features that promote the formation of links from each link's local subgraph pattern.

To encode the subgraph patterns, we propose Palette-WL, a variant of WL that is fast and order-preserving. Palette-WL leverages the ability of the classical WL to label vertices according to their structural roles, but also preserves vertices' initial relative ordering defined by their distance to the target link, a property that is crucial for link prediction. Wlnm further leverages the superior expressive power of neural networks to learn possibly complicated link formation mechanisms which are difficult to model by heuristic scores. As a result, Wlnm has remarkable prediction performance and universality.

Wlnm includes the following three main steps:

(1) Enclosing subgraph extraction, which generates K-vertex neighboring subgraphs of links.

Algorithm 2 ENCLOSING SUBGRAPH EXTRACTION

```
input: target link (x, y), network G, integer K
output: enclosing subgraph G(V_K) for (x, y)
V_K = {x, y}
fringe = {x, y}
while |V_K| < K and |fringe| > 0 do
    fringe = (∪_{v∈fringe} Γ(v)) \ V_K
    V_K = V_K ∪ fringe
end while
return enclosing subgraph G(V_K)
```

(2) Subgraph pattern encoding, which represents each subgraph as an adjacency matrix whose vertex ordering is given by our PALETTE-WL graph labeling algorithm.
(3) Neural network training, which learns nonlinear graph topological features for link prediction.

3.1 Enclosing subgraph extraction

To learn topological features from a network, WLNM extracts an enclosing subgraph for each link, and use these ⟨subgraph, link⟩ pairs as training data. The enclosing subgraph of each link describes the "surrounding environment" of that link, which we assume contains topological information deciding whether a link is likely to exist.

For a given link, its **enclosing subgraph** is a subgraph within the neighborhood of that link. The size of the neighborhood is described by the number of vertices in the subgraph, which is denoted by a user-defined integer K. We describe the procedure for extracting the enclosing subgraph in the following.

For a given link between x and y, we first add their 1-hop neighbor vertices $\Gamma(x)$ and $\Gamma(y)$ to an ordered node list V_K. Then, vertices in $\Gamma^2(x), \Gamma^2(y), \Gamma^3(x), \Gamma^3(y), \cdots$, are iteratively added to V_K until $|V_K| \geq K$ or there are no more neighbors to add. Algorithm 2 shows the enclosing subgraph extraction process.

After running the extraction algorithm, the number of vertices in V_K may not be exactly K. One way to unify the size is to discard the last added $|V_K| - K$ vertices if $|V_K| > K$. In this paper, we adopt a different strategy. Inspired by [19], we first use graph labeling to impose an ordering for V_K, and then reorder V_K using this order. After that, if $|V_K| > K$, the bottom $|V_K| - K$ vertices are discarded. If $|V_K| < K$, we add $K - |V_K|$ dummy nodes to V_K. This way, the sizes of different enclosing subgraphs are unified to K.

When $K \geq |\Gamma(x) \cup \Gamma(y) \cup x \cup y|$, the enclosing subgraph contains all the information needed for calculating first-order heuristics in Table 1. When $K \geq |\Gamma^2(x) \cup \Gamma^2(y) \cup x \cup y|$, it contains the information needed for second-order heuristics. When K equals $|V|$, the extracted subgraph encompasses all first-order, second-order and high-order heuristics. This gives an intuitive explanation why WLNM outperforms heuristic methods.

3.2 Subgraph pattern encoding

Subgraph pattern encoding is to represent each enclosing subgraph as an adjacency matrix with a particular vertex ordering, so that the neural network in WLNM can read the data in sequence. We illustrate the process of subgraph pattern encoding in Figure 4, and explain the details below.

3.2.1 PALETTE-WL for vertex ordering. We use graph labeling to determine the vertex ordering for each enclosing subgraph. To facilitate the training of neural networks, the vertex orderings generated by the graph labeling algorithm should be consistent across different subgraphs, e.g., vertices receive similar rankings if their relative positions and structural roles within their respective subgraphs are also similar. We will describe our proposed PALETTE-WL algorithm and explain why we adopt it in the following.

We first formally state our two intuitive requirements for the graph labeling algorithm used here as follows.

(1) It should impose vertex orderings such that two nodes with similar structural roles in their respective enclosing subgraphs have similar rankings.
(2) It should distinguish the "target link" in each enclosing subgraph and preserve the topological directionality within the enclosing subgraph.

The first requirement is important, since it allows machine learning models to sequentially read vertices of enclosing subgraphs in a stable order. It can be satisfied by the classical WL algorithm, since WL ranks vertices according to their structural roles (as exemplified by Figure 2 and 3). However, the classical WL does not meet the second requirement. Namely, it cannot **distinguish the target link** from other parts of the enclosing subgraph. This is because WL treats all vertices equally in the beginning. From the final WL colors, we cannot tell which colors encode the two nodes of the target link. Such a limitation will make the training meaningless.

We further explain the importance of the second requirement as follows. Unlike ordinary graphs, enclosing subgraphs have intrinsic directionality: at the center is the target link, other vertices and edges are iteratively added outwards based on their distance to the central link. A good graph labeling algorithm should be able to reflect this directionality, e.g., 1) the two central vertices always have the smallest colors; 2) vertices closer to the center link have smaller colors than farther ones. Such directionality is crucial for defining meaningful vertex orderings. If a graph labeling method does not keep this directionality, the generated vertex representation may be very poor for link prediction.

We will propose a PALETTE-WL algorithm that meets both requirements above. To formalize our analysis, we first give the definition of *color-order preservingness.*

Definition 3.1. An iterative graph labeling algorithm is color-order preserving if: given any two vertices v_a and v_b, if v_a has a smaller color than v_b at an iteration, then v_a gets a smaller color than v_b in the next iteration.

A color-order preserving algorithm has the following benefit when used as a graph labeling method:

COROLLARY 3.2. *If a graph labeling algorithm is color-order preserving, then the vertices' final color ordering still observes their initial color ordering. In other words, if vertex v_a's initial color is smaller than v_b's, v_a's final color is still smaller than v_b's final color.*

Remember that we need the final vertex ordering of an enclosing subgraph to reflect the vertices' distance to the target link. This can be achieved if we initially label vertices based on the ascending order of their distance to the target link, and then run a color-order preserving algorithm to refine their labels.

For instance, we can initially assign color 1 to the two vertices of the target link, color 2 to the link's 1-hop neighbors, color 3 to

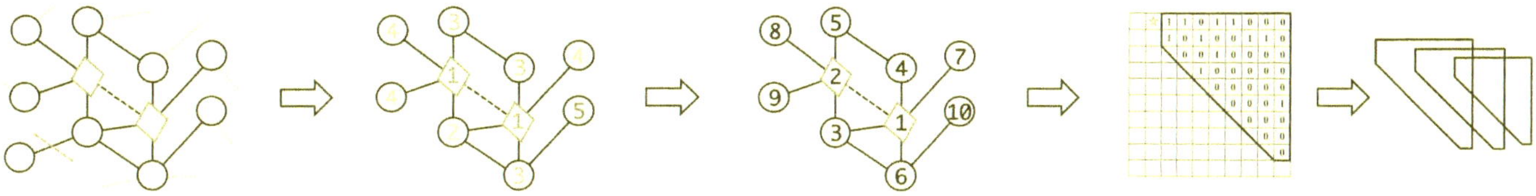

Figure 4: Illustration of the WLNM procedure: enclosing subgraph extraction (the leftmost figure), subgraph pattern encoding (the middle three figures), and neural network training (the rightmost figure).

the link's 2-hop neighbors, etc., and then run color refinement on these initial colors. The color-order preserving property ensures that the final labels still observe the distance ordering. Moreover, since the two vertices from the target link have the smallest initial color, they are guaranteed to have smaller final colors than all other vertices. This means that a target link is always encoded as $A_{1,2}$ in its enclosing subgraph.

Color-order preservingness is a much desired property for the graph labeling algorithm in WLNM to have. Fortunately, we have the following theorem.

THEOREM 3.3. *The classical 1-dimensional WL algorithm is color-order preserving.*

PROOF. At the ith iteration of the WL algorithm (given in Algorithm 1), consider any pair of vertices v_a and v_b, and assume their current colors are $c^i(v_a)$ and $c^i(v_b)$, respectively. Their signature strings $s^i(v_a)$ and $s^i(v_b)$ are $\langle c^i(v_a), \{c^i(x)|x \in \Gamma(v_a)\}_{\text{sort}}\rangle$ and $\langle c^i(v_b), \{c^i(x)|x \in \Gamma(v_b)\}_{\text{sort}}\rangle$, respectively. If $c^i(v_a) < c^i(v_b)$, then $s^i(v_a)$ is lexicographically smaller than $s^i(v_b)$ regardless of their latter letters. Therefore, we have $c^{i+1}(v_a) < c^{i+1}(v_b)$. □

Thus, the classical WL algorithm is an eligible graph labeling algorithm for WLNM. However, it requires storing, reading, and sorting of the vertices' signature strings, which is often prohibitively expensive since the signature strings can be very long for nodes with high degree.

Recently, a fast hashing-based WL algorithm was proposed [13]. It uses a perfect hash function $h(x)$ to map unique signatures to unique real values. As a result, vertices can be iteratively partitioned using their hash values instead of the signature strings, which is shown to be much faster than the classical WL algorithm [13].

The hash function for vertex x is as follows:

$$h(x) = c(x) + \sum_{z \in \Gamma(x)} \log(\mathcal{P}(c(z))), \tag{1}$$

where $c(x)$ and $c(z)$ are integer colors, $\mathcal{P}$ is the list of all primes, where $\mathcal{P}(n)$ is the nth prime number. It can be shown that, given two vertices x and y, $h(x) = h(y)$ if and only if: 1) $c(x) = c(y)$; and 2) $\Gamma(x)$ and $\Gamma(y)$ contain the same colors with the same cardinality (same WL signature ⇔ same new color).

Albeit much faster than the classical WL, the above hashing-based WL is not color-order preserving. In other words, although vertices can be partitioned according to structural roles, their final colors do not define a meaningful ordering. Besides, the colors generated by the above WL sometimes do not converge in our experiments. That is, two vertices may start to exchange their colors from some iteration on and never stop. To address the above issues as well as preserving the efficiency of the hashing-based WL, we propose the PALETTE-WL algorithm. It is a color refinement method equipped with a modified hash function:

$$h(x) = c(x) + \frac{1}{\left\lceil \sum_{z' \in V_K} \log(\mathcal{P}(c(z'))) \right\rceil} \cdot \sum_{z \in \Gamma(x)} \log(\mathcal{P}(c(z))), \tag{2}$$

where $\lceil \cdot \rceil$ is the ceiling operation that gives the smallest integer greater than the input, V_K is the vertex set of the enclosing subgraph to be labeled.

Now we prove that PALETTE-WL is color-order preserving.

THEOREM 3.4. *The WL algorithm with the hash function in (2) (PALETTE-WL)*

(1) *has perfect hashing, i.e., $h(x) = h(y)$ if and only if: 1) $c(x) = c(y)$; and 2) $\Gamma(x)$ and $\Gamma(y)$ contain the same colors with the same cardinality; and*
(2) *is color-order preserving.*

PROOF. We first prove the perfect hashing property, following a similar argument as in [13]. To prove the first direction ($h(x) = h(y) \Rightarrow$ two conditions), we see that $h(x) = h(y)$ means:

$$c(x) - c(y) = \frac{\sum_{z \in \Gamma(y)} \log(\mathcal{P}(c(z))) - \sum_{z \in \Gamma(x)} \log(\mathcal{P}(c(z)))}{\left\lceil \sum_{z' \in V_K} \log(\mathcal{P}(c(z'))) \right\rceil}. \tag{3}$$

We exponentiate both sides and write $N_x := \Pi_{z \in \Gamma(x)} \mathcal{P}(c(z))$, $N_y := \Pi_{z \in \Gamma(y)} \mathcal{P}(c(z))$, $Z := \left\lceil \sum_{z' \in V_K} \log(\mathcal{P}(c(z'))) \right\rceil$ (note that they are all integers). Then we have

$$e^{Z(c(x)-c(y))} = N_y / N_x. \tag{4}$$

On the left-hand side of the above equation, $Z(c(x) - c(y))$ is an integer. We know that all integral powers of e are irrational except for e^0. On the right-hand side, N_y/N_x is rational, which means that we must have $c(x) = c(y)$ (the first condition) and $e^{Z(c(x)-c(y))} = 1$. Thus we have $N_x = N_y$. Since N_x and N_y are integers, their prime factorizations must be the same. This implies that the two multisets $\{c(z)|z \in \Gamma(x)\}$ and $\{c(z)|z \in \Gamma(y)\}$ coincide (the second condition). This proves the first direction. The opposite direction can be easily proved using the definition of $h(x)$.

To prove that it is color-order preserving, we consider any pair of vertices x and y. Assume their colors at the ith iteration have $c^i(x) < c^i(y)$. Note that $c^i(x)$ and $c^i(y)$ are integers, which implies that $c^i(x) + 1 \le c^i(y)$.

Algorithm 3 THE PALETTE-WL ALGORITHM

input: enclosing subgraph $G(V_K)$ centered at target link (x, y), which is extracted by Algorithm 2
output: final colors $c(v)$ for all $v \in V_K$
calculate $d(v) := \sqrt{d(v, x) \cdot d(v, y)}$ for all $v \in V_K$
get initial colors $c(\mathbf{v}) = f(d(\mathbf{v}))$
while $c(\mathbf{v})$ has not converged **do**
  calculate hashing values $h(v)$ for all $v \in V_K$ by (2)
  get updated colors $c(\mathbf{v}) = f(h(\mathbf{v}))$
end while[1]
return $c(\mathbf{v})$

We have:

$$h^i(x) = c^i(x) + \frac{1}{\left\lceil \sum_{z' \in V_K} \log(\mathcal{P}(c^i(z'))) \right\rceil} \cdot \sum_{z \in \Gamma(x)} \log(\mathcal{P}(c^i(z))) < c^i(x) + 1 \le c^i(y) \le h^i(y), \tag{5}$$

which means $h^i(x) < h^i(y)$. Therefore, in the next iteration we are guaranteed to have $c^{i+1}(x) < c^{i+1}(y)$. □

We call it PALETTE-WL because the labeling process is like to draw initial colors from a palette to vertices, and then iteratively refine them by mixing their original colors and nearby colors in such a way that the colors' relative ordering is preserved. We show the complete steps of PALETTE-WL in Algorithm 3. Vertices are first assigned initial colors according to their geometric mean distance to the vertices x and y of the target link. Then the initial colors are iteratively refined using the hash function in (2). To facilitate expression, we define $f : \mathbb{R}^K \to C^K$, which maps K real numbers to K colors. f first maps the smallest real number to color 1, and then maps the second smallest real number to color 2, and so on. If two or more real numbers are equal to each other, they are mapped to the same color. Such process is repeated until every real number is mapped to a color. We use $d(v_a, v_b)$ to denote the length of the shortest path between v_a and v_b.

Finally, we sort the vertices in V_K using their PALETTE-WL colors in ascending order. If there are vertices with the same color, we use NAUTY, a graph canonization tool, to break the ties [20].

3.2.2 Represent enclosing subgraphs as adjacency matrices. Given an enclosing subgraph $G(V_K)$, WLNM represents it as an upper triangular adjacency matrix whose vertex ordering is decided by V_K's PALETTE-WL colors. After that, the adjacency matrix is vertically read and input to a fully-connected neural network.

To further increase the flexibility of WLNM, we can relax the 1/0 entries of adjacency matrix by letting them encode other information. In our experiments, we set $A_{i,j} = 1/d((i, j), (x, y))$ where $d((i, j), (x, y))$ is the length of the shortest path to reach link (i, j) from link (x, y).

3.3 Neural network learning

Training. After we encode the enclosing subgraphs, the next step in WLNM is to train a classifier. To learn sophisticated nonlinear patterns, we resort to neural networks due to their unprecedented representation capability. For a given network $G = (V, E)$, we first construct the positive samples by selecting all edges $(x, y) \in E$. Then, we construct negative samples by randomly selecting $\alpha|E|$ pairs of $x, y \in V$ such that $(x, y) \notin E$. For a given training link (x, y) (positive or negative), WLNM first extracts its enclosing subgraph and then encodes the enclosing subgraph into an adjacency matrix using the proposed PALETTE-WL algorithm. The adjacency matrices are vertically fed into a feedforward neural network together with their labels (1: $(x, y) \in E$, 0: $(x, y) \notin E$).

Note that the entry $A_{1,2}$ (shown as a star in Figure 4) should not be fed into the neural network, because it records the existence of the link (x, y). Although $A_{1,2}$ can be either 1 or 0 during training, $A_{1,2}$ is always 0 when we are predicting an unknown link. Adding this "class label" in our inputs will make the prediction on all testing links biased towards 0 (nonexistence).

Testing (link prediction). After training the neural network, we can predict the existence of a testing link by extracting its enclosing subgraph, encoding it using PALETTE-WL, and feeding the resulting adjacency matrix to the neural network. Finally, a prediction score between 0 and 1 is output for each testing link, which represents the estimated probability of the testing link being positive.

3.4 Discussions

The following analysis shows that 1) the colors generated by PALETTE-WL are guaranteed to converge; and 2) the adjacency matrices can be constructed efficiently.

THEOREM 3.5. *If a color refinement algorithm is color-order preserving, then given any vertex v, its color is non-decreasing over iterations.*

PROOF. Consider any vertex v whose color $c(v) = k$. We can prove the result by induction on k. When $k = 1$, v already has the smallest color, so its color is non-decreasing in the next iteration. Now consider the case when $c(v) = k + 1$ and, in the next iteration, its color is reduced to a color $l < k + 1$. Since every color in $\{1, 2, ..., k + 1\}$ has been assigned to at least one vertex, let v' be one such vertex whose color is l. By the induction hypothesis, v' will get a color larger than or equal to l, which contradicts the color-order preserving requirement. □

LEMMA 3.6. *For a graph with K vertices, the PALETTE-WL algorithm takes at most K iterations to converge.*

PROOF. Theorem 3.5 implies that the total number of colors does not decrease. Assume the algorithm has not converged at an iteration, there must be a vertex that has its current color c changed. By Theorem 3.5, it must increase its color. If c is already the largest color, increasing it will increase the color number. Otherwise, the vertex must increase c to some existing color c'. Due to the color-order preserving property, vertices that originally have color c' must increase their colors, too. Repeating this argument we see that finally the total number of colors must be increased. In either case, the color number increases at least by 1 in each iteration. Since there are at most K different colors in the end, the iteration number is bounded by K. □

In each iteration, we need to compute the hash function for each vertex by (2), which takes at most $O(K)$ time. Evaluating K hash functions needs $O(K^2)$ time (or $O(|E|)$ time if using sparse matrix-matrix multiplications, where E is the edge set of this graph). And the sorting needs $O(K \log K)$ time. Thus, the time complexity of each iteration is $O(K^2)$. Given Lemma 3.6, we have the following.

[1] There will be at most K iterations; see Lemma 3.6

Figure 5: Visualization experiments for a 3-regular graph (left), a preferential attachment graph (middle), and a USAir network (right). In each block, the top left figure depicts the network, the bottom left visualizes the weight matrix trained on the network's enclosing subgraphs. Four example enclosing subgraphs are displayed beside them, including two most frequent positive enclosing subgraphs (the first row) and two randomly generated negative enclosing subgraphs (the second row). In each enclosing subgraph, two red diamonds correspond to the target link. The enclosing subgraph size K is set to 6, 9, 6 for the three networks, respectively.

THEOREM 3.7. *For a graph with K vertices, the PALETTE-WL algorithm has $O(K^3)$ time complexity.*

The above results show that we can encode the enclosing subgraphs efficiently. We have three additional notes. First, after running PALETTE-WL, ties can be broken by running NAUTY, which has an average time complexity of $O(K)$ [21]. Second, there exists $O((|E| + |V|) \log |V|)$ time implementation of WL using some special data structure [22]. However, the resulting WL is not color-order preserving. Third, subgraph pattern encoding is naturally parallelizable, which can further promote the scalability of WLNM.

4 RELATED WORK

Link prediction [1] has been a hot topic for the past decade in data mining. Existing link prediction methods can be mainly categorized into two types: topological feature-based and latent feature-based. Topological feature-based methods predict links based on some local or global node similarity heuristics. Popular measures include common neighbors [1], Katz index [9], Adamic-Adar index [2], and PageRank [1]. We have surveyed them in Table 1. These heuristics do not perform well when the similarity scores do not capture the network's latent formation mechanisms. Latent feature-based methods predict links based on their latent features or latent groups, which can be extracted through low-rank decomposition of network's adjacency matrix [3], or trained by fitting some probabilistic models [5]. Popular latent feature-based methods include: matrix factorization [23]; ranking methods [24] which treat link prediction as a learning to rank problem; and stochastic block models [5, 25], which assume that nodes have latent groups and links are determined by the group memberships of nodes. Latent feature-based methods focus more on individual nodes than network topologies, thus cannot explain how networks are formed.

There has been research studying extracting local patterns from graphs to build graph kernels [26]. However, to the best of our knowledge, no existing research extracts subgraphs for link prediction. The use of graph labeling methods to impose a vertex ordering is introduced in [19]. In that paper, local subgraphs are extracted for nodes to define receptive fields around node pixels in order to learn a convolutional neural network for graph classification. Our paper extracts local subgraphs around links instead of node pixels, and our task is to predict the existence of links instead of classifying graphs. Moreover, we analyzed in-depth a particular graph labeling method, the Weisfeiler-Lehman algorithm, and proposed a new efficient and color-order preserving variant, PALETTE-WL, to meet the special requirements for link prediction learning. Graph labeling, especially WL, has also been used to design efficient graph kernels [18].

5 EXPERIMENTAL RESULTS

In this section, we conduct two types of experiments: a visualization on small datasets, and a performance comparison on real-world networks. All codes and datasets are publicly available at https://github.com/muhanzhang/LinkPrediction.

5.1 Visualization

We use two small artificial datasets and a real-world air line network [27] to visualize the learning ability of WLNM. Here, for visualization purpose, we only train a logistic regression model on the enclosing subgraphs. Figure 5 depicts the networks, some extracted enclosing subgraphs, and the learned weights.

As we can see, WLNM successfully extracts the building blocks for each network, and the weight patterns indicate how links in different networks are likely to form. For example, we observe that the most frequent positive enclosing subgraph of the USAir network is a clique. This makes sense since big cities tend to establish dense airline connections with other big cities too. The second most frequent one is also illustrative, as it depicts the pattern of four small cities connecting to two big cities.

We also display the PALETTE-WL labels for vertices of the enclosing subgraphs. As we can see, vertices 1 and 2 always correspond to the target link. Other vertices' labels characterize their structural roles within the subgraph and also preserve the enclosing subgraph's directionality.

Note that the visualized weights for the toy datasets are merely learned from a linear classifier. When the link formation mechanisms are complex, the need to learn sophisticated nonlinear features urges us to use neural networks in real-world experiments.

5.2 Experiments on real-world networks

To evaluate the performance of WLNM, we compare it with 12 baselines on eight real-world networks.

Table 2: AUC results of 12 baseline methods, WLLR, and WLNM

Data	CN	Jac.	AA	RA	PA	Katz	RD	PR	SR	SBM	MF-c	MF-r	WLLR^{10}	WLNM^{10}	WLNM^{20}
USAir	0.940	0.903	0.950	0.956	0.894	0.931	0.898	0.944	0.782	0.944	0.918	0.849	0.896	**0.958**	**0.961**
NS	0.938	0.938	0.938	0.938	0.682	0.940	0.582	0.940	0.940	0.920	0.636	0.720	0.862	**0.984**	**0.981**
PB	0.919	0.873	0.922	0.923	0.901	0.928	0.883	0.935	0.773	0.938	0.930	**0.943**	0.827	0.933	0.939
Yeast	0.891	0.890	0.891	0.892	0.824	0.921	0.880	0.927	0.914	0.914	0.831	0.881	0.854	**0.956**	**0.951**
C.ele	0.848	0.792	0.864	0.868	0.755	0.864	0.740	**0.901**	0.760	0.867	0.832	0.844	0.803	0.859	0.854
Power	0.590	0.590	0.590	0.590	0.441	0.657	0.845	0.664	0.763	0.665	0.524	0.517	0.778	**0.848**	**0.874**
Router	0.561	0.561	0.561	0.561	0.471	0.378	0.926	0.380	0.367	0.857	0.779	0.783	0.897	**0.944**	0.915
E.coli	0.932	0.806	0.952	0.958	0.912	0.929	0.889	0.954	0.637	0.939	0.909	0.916	0.894	**0.971**	**0.976**
Ranking	7.875	10.625	7.500	6.875	12.875	7.125	10.375	5.125	11.000	5.625	10.500	9.500	10.125	2.500	2.375

Datasets. We use eight datasets: USAir, NS, PB, Yeast, C.ele, Power, Router, and E.coli. USAir is a network of US Air lines [27]. NS is a collaboration network of researchers who publish papers on network science [28]. PB is a network of US political blogs [29]. Yeast is a protein-protein interaction network in yeast [30]. C.ele is a neural network of C. elegans [31]. Power is an electrical grid of western US [31]. Router is a router-level Internet [32]. E.coli is a pairwise reaction network of metabolites in E. coli [33]. We include the dataset statistics in Table 3. In each dataset, all existing links are randomly split into a training set (90%) and a testing set (10%). Other potential edges are treated as unknown links. Area under the ROC curve (AUC) is adopted to measure the link prediction performance, which can be understood as the probability that a random positive link from the testing set has a higher score than a random unknown link.

Baselines and experimental setting. We compared WLNM with nine heuristic methods in Table 1. They are: common neighbors (CN), Jaccard (Jac.), Adamic-Adar (AA), resource allocation (RA), preferential attachment (PA), Katz, resistance distance (RD), PageRank (PR), and SimRank (SR). In addition, we also compared WLNM with three latent feature models: stochastic block model (SBM) [5], matrix factorization using a classification loss function (MF-c), and matrix factorization using a regression loss function (MF-r). For Katz, we set the damping factor β to 0.001. For PageRank, we set the damping factor d to 0.85 as suggested by [14]. For Katz and PageRank, we also tested $\beta = 0.01$ and $d = 0.7$. The results are very similar and thus not reported. For SBM, we use the implementation of [25]. For MF, we use the libFM [34] software. The number of latent groups of SBM is searched in $\{4, 6, 8, 10, 12\}$. The number of latent factors of MF is searched in $\{5, 10, 15, 20, 50\}$. The best result is reported for each dataset.

For the proposed WLNM, we report subgraph sizes $K = 10$ (WLNM^{10}) and $K = 20$ (WLNM^{20}). We randomly sample from the unknown links to construct negative examples. We set the number of sampled negative links to be twice of the given positive training links. The link prediction performance is evaluated on the testing set as well as a sampled set of unknown links which is also twice as large. The sampling is performed so that the training and testing links do not overlap. For the neural network structure, we use three fully-connected hidden layers with 32, 32, 16 hidden neurons respectively and a softmax layer as the output layer. Rectified linear unit (ReLU) is adopted as the activation function for all hidden layers. We adopt the Adam update rule [35] for optimization with a learning rate of 0.001 and a mini-batch size of 128. We set the number of training epochs to be 100. The model parameters with the best results on 10% validation splits of the training set are used to predict the testing links. The neural network is implemented using Torch [36]. To demonstrate the strength of neural networks, we also train a logistic regression model on the same enclosing subgraphs (under $K = 10$, we call this model WLLR^{10}).

Table 3: Comparison of different graph labeling methods (K=10). Palette-WL (PWL^c) performs the best on all datasets.

Data	$\lvert V \rvert$	$\lvert E \rvert$	PWL^c	PWL^1	HWL^c	Nauty	Rand
USAir	332	2126	**0.958**	0.777	0.758	0.767	0.607
NS	1589	2742	**0.984**	0.896	0.881	0.896	0.738
PB	1222	16714	**0.933**	0.730	0.726	0.725	0.609
Yeast	2375	11693	**0.956**	0.774	0.743	0.764	0.654
C.ele	297	2148	**0.859**	0.609	0.634	0.631	0.555
Power	4941	6594	**0.848**	0.647	0.665	0.641	0.550
Router	5022	6258	**0.944**	0.557	0.622	0.555	0.640
E.coli	1805	14660	**0.971**	0.863	0.857	0.838	0.773

All experiments are ran 10 times on a 12-core Linux server which has two NVIDIA TITAN GPUs with 6GB memory each. Under this configuration, 10 runs of WLNM on all datasets finish in 2.5 hours. The average AUC results are reported in Table 2.

Results. From Table 2, we can observe the following. WLNM generally performs much better than other baselines in terms of AUC. It outperforms all 12 baselines on USAir, NS, Yeast, Power, Router, and E.coli by a large margin. **Most remarkably**, WLNM performs very well on the two difficult datasets: Power and Router, on which most other methods can only perform slightly better than random guessing. This suggests that WLNM is able to learn "novel" topological features which current heuristics cannot express. Another interesting finding is that, for all the 12 baseline methods, none of them can perform well on all datasets. In comparison, WLNM performs consistently well—it has an AUC greater than 0.85 across all datasets, and often, the result is over 0.95. We also find that WLNM is robust under the variation of K. Its performance is similarly good for K=10, 20, 30, and 40 (not all reported).

To demonstrate the universality of WLNM, we calculate the rankings of all the methods based on AUC for each dataset, and append the average ranking of each method (over all datasets) to Table 2. Compared to other methods, WLNM shows substantial overall advantages, having the best average ranking of less than 2.5.

To further show the importance of PALETTE-WL in subgraph pattern encoding, we compare it to other four graph labeling methods under $K = 10$ in Table 3. Here, PWL^c denotes our PALETTE-WL method with initial distance-based colors. To show the usefulness of distance-based initial coloring, we compare PALETTE-WL with all vertices colored 1 initially PWL^1. To show the consequence of a WL that is not color-order preserving, we report the performance of HWL^c, which uses the hashing function in (1). As we can see, its performance is much worse than PWL^c, since it cannot preserve the relative ordering of vertices and thus resulting in chaotic final labelings. Finally, we also report the results by directly applying NAUTY to get a canonical labeling for each subgraph (Nauty), and randomly ordering the vertices (Rand). We also did experiments using the classical WL algorithm and saw very similar results to PWL^c. However, on datasets PB and E.coli, WL cannot finish in 2 hours whereas PALETTE-WL finishes in minutes. Thus we do not list the results here. From Table 3, we can see that PWL^c outperforms all other variants by a large margin.

6 CONCLUSIONS

In this paper, we have proposed a next-generation link prediction method, Weisfeiler-Lehman Neural Machine (WLNM), which learns topological features from networks by extracting links' local enclosing subgraphs. To properly encode a link's enclosing subgraph, we have proposed an efficient graph labeling algorithm called PALETTE-WL to impose an order on subgraph vertices based on their structural roles and the subgraph's intrinsic directionality. After that, a neural network is trained on the adjacency matrices to learn nonlinear topological features for link prediction. Experimental results have shown that WLNM gives unprecedentedly strong performance compared to 12 state-of-the-art methods. Moreover, WLNM exhibits great generality, i.e. the ability to automatically learn complex network topological features, as it performs consistently well across different networks.

ACKNOWLEDGMENTS

The authors would like to thank Roman Garnett, Sanmay Das, and Zhicheng Cui for the helpful discussions. The authors would also like to thank the anonymous reviewers for their valuable comments. The work is supported in part by the DBI-1356669, SCH-1343896, III-1526012, and SCH-1622678 grants from the National Science Foundation of the United States.

REFERENCES

[1] David Liben-Nowell and Jon Kleinberg. The link-prediction problem for social networks. *Journal of the American society for information science and technology*, 58(7):1019–1031, 2007.

[2] Lada A Adamic and Eytan Adar. Friends and neighbors on the web. *Social networks*, 25(3):211–230, 2003.

[3] Yehuda Koren, Robert Bell, and Chris Volinsky. Matrix factorization techniques for recommender systems. *Computer*, (8):30–37, 2009.

[4] Maximilian Nickel, Kevin Murphy, Volker Tresp, and Evgeniy Gabrilovich. A review of relational machine learning for knowledge graphs. *arXiv preprint arXiv:1503.00759*, 2015.

[5] Edoardo M Airoldi, David M Blei, Stephen E Fienberg, and Eric P Xing. Mixed membership stochastic blockmodels. *Journal of Machine Learning Research*, 9 (Sep):1981–2014, 2008.

[6] Tolutola Oyetunde, Muhan Zhang, Yixin Chen, Yinjie Tang, and Cynthia Lo. Boostgapfill: Improving the fidelity of metabolic network reconstructions through integrated constraint and pattern-based methods. *Bioinformatics*, 2016.

[7] Ruslan Salakhutdinov and Andriy Mnih. Bayesian probabilistic matrix factorization using markov chain monte carlo. In *Proceedings of the 25th international conference on Machine learning (ICML)*, pages 880–887. ACM, 2008.

[8] Tao Zhou, Linyuan Lü, and Yi-Cheng Zhang. Predicting missing links via local information. *The European Physical Journal B*, 71(4):623–630, 2009.

[9] Leo Katz. A new status index derived from sociometric analysis. *Psychometrika*, 18(1):39–43, 1953.

[10] Linyuan Lü and Tao Zhou. Link prediction in complex networks: A survey. *Physica A: Statistical Mechanics and its Applications*, 390(6):1150–1170, 2011.

[11] Douglas J Klein and Milan Randić. Resistance distance. *Journal of Mathematical Chemistry*, 12(1):81–95, 1993.

[12] Boris Weisfeiler and AA Lehman. A reduction of a graph to a canonical form and an algebra arising during this reduction. *Nauchno-Technicheskaya Informatsia*, 2 (9):12–16, 1968.

[13] Kristian Kersting, Martin Mladenov, Roman Garnett, and Martin Grohe. Power iterated color refinement. In *AAAI*, pages 1904–1910, 2014.

[14] Sergey Brin and Lawrence Page. Reprint of: The anatomy of a large-scale hypertextual web search engine. *Computer networks*, 56(18):3825–3833, 2012.

[15] Albert-László Barabási and Réka Albert. Emergence of scaling in random networks. *Science*, 286(5439):509–512, 1999.

[16] Glen Jeh and Jennifer Widom. Simrank: a measure of structural-context similarity. In *Proceedings of the eighth ACM SIGKDD international conference on Knowledge discovery and data mining*, pages 538–543. ACM, 2002.

[17] William Cukierski, Benjamin Hamner, and Bo Yang. Graph-based features for supervised link prediction. In *The 2011 International Joint Conference on Neural Networks (IJCNN)*, pages 1237–1244. IEEE, 2011.

[18] Nino Shervashidze, Pascal Schweitzer, Erik Jan van Leeuwen, Kurt Mehlhorn, and Karsten M Borgwardt. Weisfeiler-lehman graph kernels. *Journal of Machine Learning Research*, 12(Sep):2539–2561, 2011.

[19] Mathias Niepert, Mohamed Ahmed, and Konstantin Kutzkov. Learning convolutional neural networks for graphs. In *Proceedings of the 33rd annual international conference on machine learning. ACM*, 2016.

[20] Practical graph isomorphism, {II}. *Journal of Symbolic Computation*, 60(0):94 – 112, 2014. ISSN 0747-7171.

[21] László Babai, Paul ErdoËİ s, and Stanley M Selkow. Random graph isomorphism. *SIAM Journal on Computing*, 9(3):628–635, 1980.

[22] Christoph Berkholz, Paul Bonsma, and Martin Grohe. Tight lower and upper bounds for the complexity of canonical colour refinement. In *European Symposium on Algorithms*, pages 145–156. Springer, 2013.

[23] Kurt Miller, Michael I Jordan, and Thomas L Griffiths. Nonparametric latent feature models for link prediction. In *Advances in neural information processing systems*, pages 1276–1284, 2009.

[24] Steffen Rendle, Christoph Freudenthaler, Zeno Gantner, and Lars Schmidt-Thieme. Bpr: Bayesian personalized ranking from implicit feedback. In *Proceedings of the twenty-fifth conference on uncertainty in artificial intelligence*, pages 452–461. AUAI Press, 2009.

[25] Christopher Aicher, Abigail Z Jacobs, and Aaron Clauset. Learning latent block structure in weighted networks. *Journal of Complex Networks*, 3(2):221–248, 2015.

[26] S Vichy N Vishwanathan, Nicol N Schraudolph, Risi Kondor, and Karsten M Borgwardt. Graph kernels. *Journal of Machine Learning Research*, 11(Apr):1201–1242, 2010.

[27] Vladimir Batagelj and Andrej Mrvar. http://vlado.fmf.uni-lj.si/pub/networks/data/, 2006.

[28] Mark EJ Newman. Finding community structure in networks using the eigenvectors of matrices. *Physical review E*, 74(3):036104, 2006.

[29] Robert Ackland et al. Mapping the us political blogosphere: Are conservative bloggers more prominent? In *BlogTalk Downunder 2005 Conference, Sydney*. BlogTalk Downunder 2005 Conference, Sydney, 2005.

[30] Christian Von Mering, Roland Krause, Berend Snel, Michael Cornell, Stephen G Oliver, Stanley Fields, and Peer Bork. Comparative assessment of large-scale data sets of protein–protein interactions. *Nature*, 417(6887):399–403, 2002.

[31] Duncan J Watts and Steven H Strogatz. Collective dynamics of âĂŸsmall-worldâĂŹnetworks. *Nature*, 393(6684):440–442, 1998.

[32] Neil Spring, Ratul Mahajan, David Wetherall, and Thomas Anderson. Measuring isp topologies with rocketfuel. *IEEE/ACM Transactions on networking*, 12(1):2–16, 2004.

[33] Muhan Zhang, Zhicheng Cui, Tolutola Oyetunde, Yinjie Tang, and Yixin Chen. Recovering metabolic networks using a novel hyperlink prediction method. *arXiv preprint arXiv:1610.06941*, 2016.

[34] Steffen Rendle. Factorization machines with libfm. *ACM Transactions on Intelligent Systems and Technology (TIST)*, 3(3):57, 2012.

[35] Yoshua Bengio, Jérôme Louradour, Ronan Collobert, and Jason Weston. Curriculum learning. In *Proceedings of the 26th International Conference on Machine Learning (ICML)*, pages 41–48. ACM, 2009.

[36] R. Collobert, K. Kavukcuoglu, and C. Farabet. Torch7: A matlab-like environment for machine learning. In *BigLearn, NIPS Workshop*, 2011.

EmbedJoin: Efficient Edit Similarity Joins via Embeddings*

Haoyu Zhang
Indiana University Bloomington
Bloomington, IN 47408, USA
hz30@umail.iu.edu

Qin Zhang
Indiana University Bloomington
Bloomington, IN 47408, USA
qzhangcs@indiana.edu

ABSTRACT

We study the problem of edit similarity joins, where given a set of strings and a threshold value K, we want to output all pairs of strings whose edit distances are at most K. Edit similarity join is a fundamental problem in data cleaning/integration, bioinformatics, collaborative filtering and natural language processing, and has been identified as a primitive operator for database systems. This problem has been studied extensively in the literature. However, we have observed that all the existing algorithms fall short on long strings and large distance thresholds.

In this paper we propose an algorithm named `EmbedJoin` which scales very well with string length and distance threshold. Our algorithm is built on the recent advance of metric embeddings for edit distance, and is very different from all of the previous approaches. We demonstrate via an extensive set of experiments that `EmbedJoin` significantly outperforms the previous best algorithms on long strings and large distance thresholds.

1 INTRODUCTION

Given a collection of strings, the task of similarity join is to find all pairs of strings whose similarities are above a predetermined threshold, where the similarity of two strings is measured by a specific distance function. Similarity join is a fundamental problem in data cleaning and integration (e.g., data deduplication), bioinformatics (e.g., find similar protein/DNA sequences), collaborative filtering (e.g., find user pairs of similar interests), natural language processing (e.g., automatic spelling corrections), etc. It has been studied extensively in the literature (see [12] for a survey), and has been identified as one of the primitive operators for database systems [7].

In this paper we study similarity join under edit distance. The edit distance between two strings x and y, denoted by $\mathrm{ED}(x, y)$, is defined to be the minimum number of edit operations (insertion, deletion and substitution) to transfer x to y. Formally, given a collection of strings $\mathcal{S} = \{s_1, s_2, \ldots, s_n\}$ over alphabet Σ, a similarity threshold K, edit similarity (self)join outputs

$$\{(s_i, s_j) \mid s_i, s_j \in \mathcal{S}; i \neq j; \mathrm{ED}(s_i, s_j) \leq K\}.$$

*Both authors are supported in part by NSF CCF-1525024 and IIS-1633215.

KDD'17, August 13–17, 2017, Halifax, NS, Canada.

ISBN 978-1-4503-4887-4/17/08...$15.00
DOI: http://dx.doi.org/10.1145/3097983.3098003

For example, given strings `ACCAT`, `CCAAT`, `GCCCT`, `CACGA`, `AACGG` and $K = 2$, the output pairs will be (`ACCAT, CCAAT`), (`ACCAT, GCCCT`), (`CACGA, AACGG`).

Compared with the Hamming distance and token-based distances such as Cosine, Jaccard, Overlap and Dice, edit distance retains the information of the orderings of characters, and captures the best alignment of the two strings, which is critical to applications in bioinformatics, natural language processing and information retrieval. On the other hand, edit distance is computationally more expensive than Hamming and token-based distances: computing edit distance takes at least quadratic time under the SETH conjecture [2], while Hamming, Cosine, Jaccard, Overlap and Dice can be computed in linear time.

Due to its difficulty and usefulness, a large portion of the similarity join literature has been devoted to edit distance [1, 3, 5, 10, 15, 16, 18, 22–25]. However, we have observed that all the existing approaches fall short on long strings and relatively large thresholds. In the recent string similarity search/join competition, it was reported that "an error rate of 20% ~ 25% pushes today's techniques to the limit" [21]. By 20% errors we mean that the distance threshold is set to be 20% of the string length. In fact the limit is reached much earlier on strings that are longer than those tested in the competition.

However, long strings and large thresholds are critical to many applications. For example, documents can contain hundreds of thousands of characters; the lengths of DNA sequences range from thousands to billions of bases. If we set a threshold that is too small, then we may end up getting zero output pair which is certainly not interesting.

Our Contribution. The main contribution of this paper is a novel approach of computing edit similarity joins that scales very well with the string length and the distance threshold. Different from all previous approaches which directly perform computations on the edit distance, we first embed the input strings from the edit space to the Hamming space, and then perform a filtering in the Hamming space using locality sensitive hashing.

Our algorithm, named `EmbedJoin`, is randomized and may introduce a small number of errors (95% - 99% recall, 100% precision in all of our experiments), but it significantly outperforms all the previous algorithms in both running time and memory usage on long strings and large thresholds. In particular, `EmbedJoin` scales very well up to error rate 20% on large datasets which is beyond the reach of existing algorithms.

Overview of Our Approach. Given two strings $x, y \in \Sigma^N$, the Hamming distance between x and y is defined to be $\mathrm{Ham}(x, y) = \sum_{i=1}^{N} \mathbf{1}(x_i \neq y_i)$. Our approach is built on the recent advance of metric embeddings for edit distance, and is very different from all of the previous approaches. In [6], it has been shown that there exists an embedding function $f : \Sigma^N \to \Sigma^{3N}$ such that given $x, y \in \Sigma^N$, we have with probability $1 - o(1)$ that [1]

$$\mathrm{ED}(x,y) \quad \leq \quad \mathrm{Ham}(f(x), f(y)),$$

and with probability at least 0.999 that

$$\mathrm{Ham}(f(x), f(y)) \quad \leq \quad O\left((\mathrm{ED}(x,y))^2\right).$$

We call this scheme the *CGK-embedding*, named after the initials of the authors in [6]. The details of the embedding algorithm will be illustrated in Section 3.1. We call

$$D(x,y) = \mathrm{Ham}(f(x), f(y))/\mathrm{ED}(x,y)$$

the *distortion* of the CGK-embedding on input (x, y). Note that if $\mathrm{ED}(x,y) \leq K$, then $1 \leq D(x,y) \leq O(K)$ with probability at least 0.99.

The high level idea of our approach is fairly simple: we first embed using CGK all the strings from the edit space to the Hamming space, and then perform a filtering step on the resulting vectors in the Hamming space using locality sensitive hashing (LSH) [9, 11]. LSH has the property that it will map a pair of items of small Hamming distance to the same bucket in the hash table with good probability, and map a pair of items of large Hamming distance to different buckets with good probability. The final step is to verify for each hash bucket B, and for all the strings hashed into B, whether their pairwise edit distances are at most K or not, by an exact dynamic programming based edit distance computation.

One may observe that the worst-case distortion of the CGK-embedding can be fairly large if the threshold K is large. However, we have observed that the practical performance of CGK-embedding is much better. We will give more discussions on this phenomenon in Section 3.1. To further reduce the distortion, we choose to run the embedding multiple times, and then for each pair of strings we choose the run with the minimum Hamming distance for the filtering. This minimization step does not have to be performed explicitly since we do not have to compute $\mathrm{Ham}(f(x), f(y))$ for all pairs of strings which is time consuming. We instead integrate this step with LSH for a fast filtering.

Finally, we note that since LSH is a dimension reduction step, LSH-based filtering naturally fits long strings (e.g., DNA sequences) which are our main interest. For short strings LSH-based filtering may not be the most effective approach and one may want to use different filtering methods. We also note Satuluri et al. [19] used LSH-based filtering for computing similarity joins under the Jaccard distance and the Cosine distance. Unfortunately there is no efficient LSH for edit distance, which is the motivation for us to first embed the strings to vectors in the Hamming space and then perform LSH.

2 RELATED WORK

Similarity Joins for Edit Distance. The edit similarity join problem has been studied extensively in the literature. We refer the readers to [12] for a comprehensive survey. A widely adopted approach to this problem is to first generate for each string a set of signatures/substrings. For example, in the q-gram signature, we generate all substrings of length q (e.g., when $q = 2$, the 2-grams of `ACCAT` is {`AC, CC, CA, AT`}). We then perform a filtering step based on the frequencies, positions and/or the contents of these substrings. The filtering step will give a set of candidate (similar) pairs, for each of which we use a dynamic programming algorithm for edit distance to verify its *exact* similarity. Concrete algorithms of signature-based approach include `GramCount` [10], `AllPair` [3], `FastSS` [5], `ListMerger` [15], `EDJoin` [25], `QChunk` [18], `VChunk` [24], `PassJoin` [16], and `AdaptJoin` [23]. We will briefly describe in Section 4.1 the best ones among these algorithms which we use as competitors to `EmbedJoin` in the experiments.

While different signature-based algorithms use different filtering methods, their common feature is to first compute some upper or lower bounds, and then prune those pairs (x, y) for which $g(sig(x), sig(y))$ is above or below the predetermined upper/lower bounds, where g is a predefined function, and $sig(x), sig(y)$ are signatures of x and y respectively. The main drawback of signature-based approach is that the information about the sequence ordering is somewhat lost when converting strings to a set of substrings. Another issue is that the precomputed upper/lower bounds may be too loose for effective pruning.

There are a few other approaches for computing edit similarity joins, such as trie-based algorithm `TrieJoin` [22], tree-based algorithm `M-Tree` [8], enumeration-based algorithm `PartEnum` [1]. However, as reported in [12], these algorithms are not very effective on datasets of long strings.

Similarity Joins for Other Metrics. Similarity joins have been studied for a number of other metrics [1, 3, 10, 15, 16, 23, 26, 27], including Cosine, Jaccard, Overlap and Dice. A survey of these works is beyond the scope of this paper, and we again refer reader to [12] for an overview.

Other Related Work on Edit Distance. Edit distance is also a notoriously difficult metric for sketching and embeddings, and very little is known in these frontiers. As mentioned, embedding enables us to study the similarity join problem in an easier metric space. On the other hand, if we can efficiently obtain small sketches of the input strings, then we can solve the similarity join problem on smaller inputs. Ostrovsky and Rabani proposed an embedding from the edit metric to the ℓ_1 metric with an $\exp(O(\sqrt{\log N \log\log N}))$ distortion [17] where N is the length of the string. A corresponding distortion lower bound of $\Omega(\log N)$ has been obtained by Kraughgamer and Rabani [13]. Recently Chakraborty et al. gives a weak embedding to the Hamming space [6] with an $O(K)$ distortion,[2] which serves as the main tool in our algorithm. For sketching, very recently Belazzougui and Zhang [4] proposed the first almost linear time sketching algorithm that gives a sketch of sublinear size (more precisely, $O(K^8 \log^5 N)$), which, unfortunately, is still too large to be useful in practice in its current form.

Computing edit distance in the RAM model has been studied for decades. It is well-known that the edit distance verification problem under distance threshold K can be solved in time $O(NK)$ by dynamic programming [20]. It has been further improved to

[1] The analysis in [6] in fact only gives $\mathrm{ED}(x, y)/2 \leq \mathrm{Ham}(f(x), f(y))$. However, as we shall describe in Algorithm 1, if we pad the embedded strings using a character that is not in the dictionary, then it is easy to show that $\mathrm{ED}(x, y) \leq \mathrm{Ham}(f(x), f(y))$ with probability $1 - o(1)$.

[2] In a "weak" embedding, the distortion holds for *each* pair of strings with constant probability, say, 0.99. In contrast, in a "strong" embedding, with probability 0.99 the distortion holds for *all* pairs of strings simultaneously.

Notation	Definition
$[n]$	$[n] = \{1, 2, \ldots, n\}$
K	Edit distance threshold
$\mathcal{S}$	The set of input strings
s_i	The i-th string in $\mathcal{S}$
$\lvert x\rvert$	Length of string x
n	Number of input strings, i.e., $n = \lvert\mathcal{S}\rvert$
N	Maximum length of strings in $\mathcal{S}$
Σ	Alphabet of strings in $\mathcal{S}$
r	Number of CGK-embeddings for each input string
t_i^ℓ	The output string generated by the ℓ-th CGK-embedding of s_i
z	Number of hash functions used in LSH for each string generated by CGK-embedding
m	Length of the LSH signature
f_j^ℓ	$f_j^\ell : \Sigma^N \to \Sigma^m$, the j-th ($j \in [z]$) LSH function for each string generated by the ℓ-th CGK-embedding
$\mathcal{D}_j^\ell$	The hash table corresponding to the LSH function f_j^ℓ

Table 1: Summary of Notations

Algorithm 1 CGK-Embedding(s, R) [6]

Input: A string $x \in \Sigma^\eta$ for some $\eta \leq N$, and a random string $R \in \{0,1\}^{3N|\Sigma|}$

Output: A string $x' \in \Sigma^{3N}$

```
Interpret R as a set of functions
        π_1, ..., π_3N : Σ → {0,1}; for the k-th char σ_k in Σ,
        π_j(σ_k) = R[(j − 1) · |Σ| + k]
i ← 1
x' ← ∅
for j ∈ [3N] do
    if i ≤ |x| then
        x' ← x' ⊙ x[i]            ▹ the "⊙" denotes concatenation
        i ← i + π_j(x[i])
    else
        x' ← x' ⊙ ⊥               ▹ "⊥" can be an arbitrary character outside Σ
    end if
end for
```

$O(N + K^2)$ [14], but the algorithm in [14] employs suffix trees and thus may not have advantage in practice.

3 THE ALGORITHM

In this section we present our algorithm EmbedJoin. We will first illustrate the CGK-embedding and the LSH for the Hamming distance; these are the main tools that we shall use in EmbedJoin. We list in Table 1 a set of notations that will be used in the presentation.

3.1 The CGK-Embedding

We describe the CGK-embedding in Algorithm 1. Below we illustrate the main idea behind the CGK-embedding, which we believe is useful and important to understand the intuition of EmbedJoin. We note that the original algorithm in [6] was only described for binary strings, and it was mentioned that we can encode an alphabet Σ into binary codes using $\log|\Sigma|$ bits for each character. In our rewrite (Algorithm 1) we choose to use the alphabet Σ directly without the encoding. This may give some performance gain when the size of the alphabet is small.

Let N be the maximum length of all input strings in $\mathcal{S}$. The CGK-embedding maps a string $x \in \mathcal{S}$ to an output string $x' \in \Sigma^{3N}$ using a random bit string $R \in \{0,1\}^{3N|\Sigma|}$. We maintain a counter $i \in [1..|x|]$ pointing to the input string x, initialized to be 1. The embedding proceeds by steps $j = 1, \ldots, 3N$. At the j-th step, we first copy $x[i]$ to $x'[j]$. Next, with probability $1/2$, we increase i by 1, and with the rest of the probability we keep i to be the same. At the point when $i > |x|$, if j is still no more than $3N$, we simply pad an arbitrary character outside the dictionary Σ (denoted by "$\perp$" in Algorithm 1) to make the length of x' to be $3N$. In practice this may introduce quite some overhead for short strings in the case that the string lengths vary significantly. We will discuss in Section 3.4 how to efficiently deal with input strings of very different lengths.

Now consider two input stings x and y. We use i_0 and i_1 as two counters pointing to x and y respectively. At the j-th step, we first copy $x[i_0]$ to $x'[j]$, and $y[i_1]$ to $y'[j]$, and then decide whether to increment i_0 and i_1 using the random bit string R. There are four possibilities: (1) only i_0 increments; (2) only i_1 increments; (3) both i_0 and i_1 increment; and (4) neither i_0 nor i_1 increments. Let $d = i_0 - i_1$ be the position *shift* of the two counters/pointers on the two strings. Note that if $x[i_0] = y[i_1]$, then only the cases (3) and (4) can happen, so that d will remain the same. Otherwise if $x[i_0] \neq y[i_1]$, then each case can happen with probability $1/4$ – whether i_0 or i_1 will increment depends on the two random hash values $\pi_j(x[i_0])$ and $\pi_j(y[i_1])$. Thus with probability $1/4$, $1/2$ and $1/4$, the value d will increment, remain the same, or decrement, respectively. Ignoring the case when the value d remains the same, we can view d as a (different) *simple random walk* on the integer line with 0 as the origin.

We now try to illustrate the high level idea of why CGK-embedding gives an $O(K)$ distortion. Let $u = |x|$ and $v = |y|$. Suppose that at some step j, letting $p = i_0(j)$ (the value of i_0 at step j) and $q = i_1(j)$, we have two tails $x[p..u] = \alpha \circ \tau$ and $y = y[q..v] = \tau$ where α, τ are two substrings and $|\alpha| = k \leq K$. That is, we have k consecutive deletions in the optimal alignment of the two tails. Now if after a few random walk steps, at step $j' > j$, we have $p' = i_0(j') \geq p + k$, $q' = i_1(j') \geq q$ and $p' - q' = (p - q) + k$, then the two tails $x[p'..u]$ and $y[q'..v]$ can be perfectly aligned, and consequently the pairs of characters in the output strings x', y' will always be the same; in other words, they will *not* contribute to the Hamming distance from step j'.

Now observe that since the value of d changes according to a simple random walk, by the theory of random walk, with probability 0.999 it takes at most $O(k^2)$ steps for d to go from $(p - q)$ to $(p' - q')$ where $|(p - q) - (p' - q')| = k$. Therefore the number of steps j where $x'[j] \neq y'[j]$ is bounded by $O(k^2)$. This is roughly why $\mathrm{Ham}(x', y')$ can be bounded by $O(K^2)$ if $\mathrm{ED}(x, y) \leq K$, and consequently the distortion can be bounded by $O(K)$.

Small Distortion is Good for Edit Similarity Join. We now explain why the distortion of the embedding matters. If we have an embedding f such that for any pair of input strings (x, y), the distortion of the embedding is upper bounded by D, then the set $\{(x, y) \mid \text{Ham}(f(x), f(y)) \leq D \cdot K\}$ will include all pairs (x, y) such that $\text{ED}(x, y) \leq K$. Therefore a small D can help to reduce the number of false positives, and consequently reduce the verification time which typically dominates the total running time.

Why CGK-embedding Does Better in Practice? Although the worst-case distortion of CGK-embedding can be large when $\text{ED}(x, y)$ is large, we have observed that its practical performance on the datasets that we have tested is much better. While it is difficult to fully understand this phenomenon without a thorough investigation of the actual properties of the datasets, we can think of the following reasons.

First, if a set of z edits fall into an interval of length $O(z)$, *and* the difference between the numbers of insertions and deletions among the z edits is at most $O(\sqrt{z})$ (substitutions do not matter), then with probability 0.999 after $O(z)$ walk steps the random walk will re-synchronize. In other words, the distortion of the embedding is $O(1)$ with probability 0.999 on this cluster of edits. We have observed that in our protein/genome datasets (Section 4.1) the edits are often clustered into small intervals; in each cluster most edits are substitutions, and consequently the difference between the numbers of insertions and deletions is small.

Second, in the task of differentiating similar pairs of strings and dissimilar pairs of strings, as long as the distance gap between strings is preserved after the embedding, the distortion of CGK-embedding will not affect the performance by much. In particular, when the distortion of CGK-embedding is $\Theta(k)$ (which is very likely when edits are well separated), the embedding actually *amplifies* the distance gap between similar and dissimilar pairs, which makes the next LSH step easier.

To further improve the effectiveness of the CGK-embedding, we run the embedding multiple times and then take the one with the minimum Hamming distance. That is, we choose the run with the best distortion. This is just a heuristic, and cannot improve the distortion by much in theory, but we have observed that for the real-world datasets that we have tested, repeating and then taking the minimum does help to reduce the distortion. In Figure 1 we depicted the best distortions under different numbers of runs of the CGK-embedding on a real-world genome dataset.

3.2 LSH for the Hamming Distance

Our second tool is the LSH for the Hamming distance, introduced in [9, 11] for solving nearest neighbor problems. We first give the definition of LSH. By $h \in_r \mathcal{H}$ we mean sampling a hash function h randomly from a hash family $\mathcal{H}$.

Definition 3.1. (Locality Sensitive Hashing [9]) Let U be the item universe, and $d(\cdot, \cdot)$ be a distance function. We say a hash family $\mathcal{H}$ is (l, u, p_1, p_2)-sensitive if for any $x, y \in U$

- if $d(x, y) \leq l$, then $\mathbf{Pr}_{h \in_r \mathcal{H}}[h(x) = h(y)] \geq p_1$,
- if $d(x, y) \geq u$, then $\mathbf{Pr}_{h \in_r \mathcal{H}}[h(x) = h(y)] \leq p_2$.

We have the following LSH for the Hamming distance.

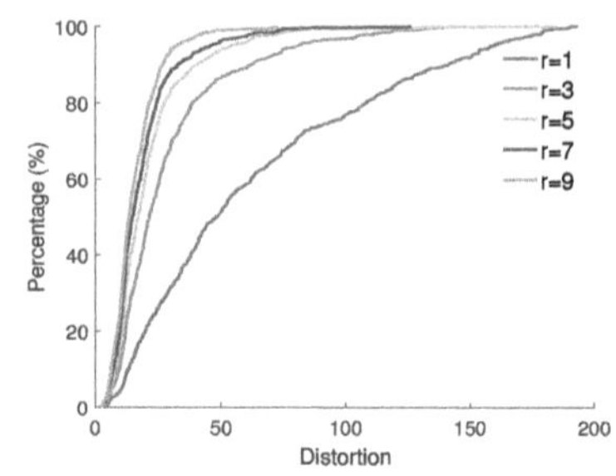

Figure 1: The CDF of the best distortions of 1000 random pairs strings from the GEN50kS dataset, under different numbers of CGK-embeddings (value r)

THEOREM 3.2. *(Bit-sampling LSH for Hamming [9]) For the Hamming distance over vectors in Σ^N, for any $d > 0, c > 1$, the family*

$$\mathcal{H}_N = \{v_i : v_i(b_1, \ldots, b_N) = b_i \mid i \in [N]\}$$

is $(d, cd, 1 - d/N, 1 - cd/N)$-sensitive.

We can use the standard AND-OR amplification method[3] to amplify the gap between p_1 and p_2. We first concatenate m (m is a parameter) hash functions, and define

$$f = h_1 \circ h_2 \circ \ldots \circ h_m \text{ where } \forall i \in [m], h_i \in_r \mathcal{H},$$

such that for $x \in U$, $f(x) = (h_1(x), h_2(x), \ldots, h_m(x))$ is a vector of m bits. Let $\mathcal{F}(m)$ be the set of all such hash functions f. We then define (for a parameter z)

$$g = f_1 \vee f_2 \vee \ldots \vee f_z, \text{ where } \forall j \in [z], f_j \in_r \mathcal{F}(m),$$

such that for $x, y \in U$ $g(x) = g(y)$ if and only if there is at least one $j \in [z]$ for which $f_j(x) = f_j(y)$. Easy calculation shows that g is

$$\left(d, cd, 1 - \left(1 - (d/N)^m\right)^z, 1 - \left(1 - (cd/N)^m\right)^z\right)$$

sensitive. By appropriately choosing the parameters m, z we can amplify the gap between p_1 and p_2.

We comment that this vanilla version of LSH is enough for our applications, and its fast time performance fits our needs well.

3.3 Our EmbedJoin Algorithm

Now we are ready to describe EmbedJoin, which is presented in Algorithm 3 using Algorithm 2 as a subroutine. We explain them in words below; a running example for EmbedJoin can be found in the Appendix of the full version [28].

In the preprocessing we generate $r \times z$ hash tables $\mathcal{D}_j^\ell$ ($\ell \in [r], j \in [z]$) implicitly by sampling $r \times z$ random hash functions f_j^ℓ ($\ell \in [r], j \in [z]$) from $\mathcal{F}(m)$ (defined in Section 3.2). We then CGK-embed each string $s_i \in \mathcal{S}$ for r times, getting t_i^ℓ ($\ell \in [r]$).

We now describe our main algorithm. As previous algorithms, EmbedJoin has two stages: it first finds a small set of candidate pairs, and then verifies each of them using exact edit-distance computation via dynamic programming. We use the algorithm for computing edit distance in [16] for the second step. In the rest of this section we explain the first filtering step.

[3] See, for example, https://en.wikipedia.org/wiki/Locality-sensitive_hashing.

Algorithm 2 Preprocessing $(\mathcal{S}, r, z, m)$

Input: Set of input strings $\mathcal{S} = \{s_1, \ldots, s_n\}$, and parameters r, z and m described in Table 1
Output: Strings in $\mathcal{S}$ in the sorted order, strings after CGK-embedding $\{t_i^\ell \mid \ell \in [r], i \in [n]\}$, and hash tables $\{\mathcal{D}_j^\ell \mid \ell \in [r], j \in [z]\}$.
Sort $\mathcal{S}$ first by string length increasingly, and second by the alphabetical order.
for each $\ell \in [r]$ **do**
  for each $j \in [z]$ **do**
    Initialize hash table $\mathcal{D}_j^\ell$ by generating a random hash function $f_j^\ell \in \mathcal{F}(m)$
  end for
end for
for each $\ell \in [r]$ **do**
  Generate a random string $R^\ell \in \{0, 1\}^{3N|\Sigma|}$
  for each $s_i \in \mathcal{S}$ **do**
    $t_i^\ell \leftarrow$ CGK-Embedding(s_i, R^ℓ)
  end for
end for

Algorithm 3 EmbedJoin $(\mathcal{S}, K, r, z, m)$

Input: Set of input strings $\mathcal{S} = \{s_1, \ldots, s_n\}$, distance threshold K, and parameters r, z and m described in Table 1
Output: $O \leftarrow \{(s_i, s_j) \mid s_i, s_j \in \mathcal{S}; i \neq j; \mathrm{ED}(s_i, s_j) \leq K\}$
1: Preprocessing$(\mathcal{S}, r, z, m)$ ▷ Using Algorithm 2
2: $C \leftarrow \emptyset$ ▷ Collection of candidate pairs
3: **for each** $s_i \in \mathcal{S}$ (in the sorted order) **do**
4:   **for each** $\ell \in [r]$ **do**
5:     **for each** $j \in [z]$ **do**
6:       **for each** string s stored in the $f_j^\ell(t_i^\ell)$-th bucket of table $\mathcal{D}_j^\ell$ **do**
7:         **if** $|s_i| - |s| \leq K$ **then**
8:           $C \leftarrow C \cup (s, s_i)$
9:         **else**
10:           Remove s from $\mathcal{D}_j^\ell$
11:         **end if**
12:       **end for**
13:       Store s_i in the $f_j^\ell(t_i^\ell)$-th bucket of $\mathcal{D}_j^\ell$
14:     **end for**
15:   **end for**
16:   Remove duplicate pairs in C
17: **end for**
18: **for each** $(x, y) \in C$ **do**
19:   **if** $\mathrm{ED}(x, y) \leq K$ **then** ▷ Using the algorithm in [16]
20:     $O \leftarrow O \cup (x, y)$
21:   **end if**
22: **end for**

The main idea of the filtering step is fairly straightforward. We use LSH to find all pairs (s_i, s_j) for which there exists an $\ell \in [r]$ such that t_i^ℓ and t_j^ℓ are hashed into the same bucket by at least one of the hash functions $f_j^\ell \in \mathcal{F}(m)$ $(j \in [z])$. In other words, for at least one of the r CGK-embeddings, the output pairs corresponding to s_i and s_j are identified to be similar by at least one of the z LSH functions. Recall that we do r repetitions of CGK-embedding to achieve a good distortion ratio (see the discussion in Section 3.1), and we use z LSH functions from $\mathcal{F}(m)$ to amplify the gap between p_1 and p_2 in the definition of LSH to reduce false positives/negatives (see the discussion in Section 3.2).

In the actual implementation, we use a sliding window to speed-up the filtering: We first sort the input strings in $\mathcal{S}$ according to their lengths increasingly (breaking ties by the alphabetical orders of the strings). We then process them one by one. If $s_i \in S$ is hashed into some bucket B in the hash table, when fetching each string s in B we first test whether $|s_i| - |s| \leq K$ (Line 7). If not, we can immediately conclude $\mathrm{ED}(s, s_i) > K$, and consequently $\mathrm{ED}(s, s_{i'}) > K$ $(i' > i)$ for all the future strings $s_{i'} \in \mathcal{S}$, since we know for sure that $|s_{i'}| - |s| > K$ due to the sorted order. We thus can safely delete s from bucket B (Line 10). Otherwise we add (s, s_i) to our candidate set C. After these we store s_i in bucket B for future comparisons. Note that each pair (s_i, s_j) can potentially be added into C multiple times by different LSH collisions, we thus do a deduplication at Line 16.

There are two implementation details that we shall mention. First, in the preprocessing we do not need to generate the whole t_i^ℓ, but just those m bits that will be used by each of the z LSH functions. This reduces the space usage from $3N \cdot r \cdot n$ to $z \cdot m \cdot r \cdot n$. Second, It is time/space prohibited to generate the hash table $\mathcal{D}_j^\ell$ whose size is $|\Sigma|^m$. We adopt the standard two-level hashing implementation of LSH: For a signature in Σ^m, we first convert it into a vector $u \in \{1, \ldots, |\Sigma|\}^m$ in the natural way. We then generate a random vector $v \in \{0, \ldots, P-1\}^m$ where $P > 1,000,000$ is a prime we choose that fits our datasets in experiments. Finally, the second level hash function returns $\langle u, v \rangle \bmod P$, where $\langle \cdot, \cdot \rangle$ denotes the inner product.

Choices of parameters. There are three parameters m, z, r in `EmbedJoin` that we need to specify. Recall that m is the length of the LSH signature, or, the number of primitive hash functions $h \in \mathcal{H}$ we use in each $f \in \mathcal{F}(m)$; and z is the number of LSHs we use for each string generated by CGK-embedding. The larger z and m are, the better LSH performs in terms of accuracy and filtering effectiveness. The product $m \cdot z$ will contribute to the total running time of the algorithm. On the other hand, r is number of CGK-embeddings we perform for each input string. The larger r we use, the smaller distortion we will get (see Figure 1).

The concrete choices of m, z and r depend on the data size, distance thresholds, computation time/space budget and accuracy requirements. For our datasets we have tested a number of parameter combinations. We refer readers to Section 4.2 for some statistics. We have observed that $r = z = 7$, and $m = 15 - \lfloor \log_2 \frac{100K}{N} \rfloor$ are good choices to balance the resource usage and the accuracy.

Running time. The preprocessing step takes time $O(r \cdot z \cdot P + r \cdot n \cdot 3N|\Sigma|)$. The time cost of LSH-based filtering depends on the usefulness of the sliding window pruning; in the worst case it is $O(nrzm)$ where m counts the cost of evaluating a hash function $f \in \mathcal{F}(m)$. Finally, the verification step costs $O(NK \cdot Z)$ where Z is the number of candidate pairs after LSH-based filtering.

3.4 Further Speed-up

Note that in the CGK-Embedding (Algorithm 1), we always pad the output strings x' up to length $3N$, where $N = \max_{i\in[n]}\{|s_i|\}$. This approach is not very efficient for datasets containing strings with very different lengths (for example, our datasets UNIREF and TREC; see Section 4.1), since we need to pad a large number of "$\perp$" to the output strings which can be a waste of time. For example, for two strings s_1 and s_2 where $|s_1|, |s_2| \ll N$, if we map them to bit vectors s_1' and s_2' of size $3N$, then most of the aligned pairs in s_1' and s_2' are $(\perp, \perp)$s which carry almost no information. Then if we use bit-sampling LSH for the Hamming distance we need a lot of samples in order to hit the interesting region, that is, the coordinates of strings in s_1' and s_2' where at least one of the two characters is *not* "$\perp$". This is time and space expensive. We propose two ways to handle this issue.

Grouping. We first partition the set of strings of $\mathcal{S}$ to $(N'/K - 1)$ groups where $N' = \lceil N/K \rceil \cdot K$. The i-th group contains all the strings of lengths $((i-1)K, (i+1)K]$. Note that each string will be included in two groups (the redundancy), and every pair of strings with distance at most k will both be included in at least one of the groups. We then apply EmbedJoin on each group, and union the outputs at the end. Due to the redundancy this approach may end up evaluating at most twice of the total number of candidates.

Truncation. The second method is to use truncation, that is, we truncate each embedded string of size $3N$ to $3 \cdot avg(\mathcal{S})$, where $avg(\mathcal{S})$ is the average length of the strings in $\mathcal{S}$. We then apply EmbedJoin on all the truncated strings. Note that after truncation we essentially assume that all the bits after the $(3avg(\mathcal{S}))$-th position in the embedded strings are the same, and thus truncation will *not* increase the Hamming distance of any pair of strings, and consequently will not introduce any false negative. It can introduce some false positives but this is not a problem since we have a verification step at the end to remove all the false positives.

Our experimental results (see the full version [28]) show that truncation always has the better performance than grouping on our tested datasets. Therefore in the rest of the paper we always use truncation.

4 EXPERIMENTS

In this section we present our experimental studies. After listing the datasets and tested algorithms, we first give an overview of the performance of EmbedJoin. We then compare it with the existing best algorithms. Finally, we show the scalability of EmbedJoin in the ranges that the existing best algorithms cannot reach.

4.1 The Setup

Datasets. We tested the algorithms in three publicly available real world datasets.

UNIREF: a dataset of UniRef90 protein sequence data from UniProt project.[4] Each sequence is an array of amino acids coded in uppercase letters. We first remove sequences whose lengths are smaller than 200, and then extract the first 400,000 protein sequences.

[4] Available in http://www.uniprot.org/

Datasets	n	Avg Len	Min Len	Max Len	$\|\Sigma\|$
UNIREF	400000	445	200	35213	25
TREC	233435	1217	80	3947	37
GEN50kS	50000	5000	4844	5109	4
GEN20kS	20000	5000	4847	5109	4
GEN20kM	20000	10000	9849	10090	4
GEN20kL	20000	20000	19838	20098	4
GEN80kS	80000	5000	4844	5109	4
GEN320kS	320000	5000	4841	5152	4

Table 2: Statistics of tested datasets

TREC: a dataset of references from Medline (an online medical information database) consisting of titles and abstracts from 270 medical journals.[5] We first extract and concatenate title, author, and abstract fields, and then convert punctuations into white spaces and letters into their upper cases.

GEN50kS GEN20kS GEN20kM GEN20kL GEN80kS GEN320kS: datasets of human genome sequences of 50 individuals obtained from the *personal genomes project*,[6] and the reference sequence is obtained from GRCh37 assembly. We choose to use Chromosome 20. We partition the long DNA sequences into shorter substrings according to the indices of the reference sequence to construct the datasets listed above. The names of datasets can be read as 'GEN $\circ$ number of strings ($20k$ to $320k$) $\circ$ string length (S $\approx$ 5k, M $\approx$ 10k, L $\approx$ 20k)'.

We summarize the statistics of our datasets in Table 2.

Tested Algorithms. We implemented our algorithm EmbedJoin in C++, and complied using GCC 5.4.0 with O3 flag. We compared our algorithms with PassJoin[16], EDJoin[25], AdaptJoin[23], and QChunk[18], whose binary codes were downloaded from the authors' project websites. We choose these competing algorithms based on the recommendations of the experimental study [12] and the similarity search/join competition [21]. We believe that these are the best existing algorithms for edit similarity joins.

Measurements. We report three types of measurements in our experiments: *accuracy*, *memory usage* and *running time*. Recall that EmbedJoin only have false negatives; the *accuracy* we report is number of output pairs returned by EmbedJoin divided by the ground truth returned by other exact competing algorithms. The memory usage we report is the maximum memory usage of a program during its execution. As mentioned, the competing algorithms may use different filtering methods or different parameters. We always choose the *best* combinations for comparisons. To make the comparison fair we have counted the time used for all the preprocessing steps.

Computing Environment. All experiments were conducted on a Dell PowerEdge T630 server with 2 Intel Xeon E5-2667 v4 3.2GHz CPU with 8 cores each, and 256GB memory.

4.2 Performance Overview of EmbedJoin

In this section we present an overview of the performance of EmbedJoin. All the results are the average of five independent runs.

[5] Available in http://trec.nist.gov/data/t9_filtering.html
[6] Available in http://personalgenomes.org/

	$r=5$			$r=7$			$r=9$		
Accuracy	$z=3$	$z=5$	$z=7$	$z=3$	$z=5$	$z=7$	$z=3$	$z=5$	$z=7$
$m=5$	94.5%	97.4%	98.6%	96.9%	99.0%	99.5%	98.5%	99.4%	99.7%
$m=7$	91.6%	94.0%	95.6%	95.2%	97.2%	98.4%	96.4%	98.4%	99.1%
$m=9$	90.1%	90.9%	92.9%	90.7%	94.7%	96.1%	92.9%	96.2%	97.6%

Table 3: Accuracy of EmbedJoin, UNIREF **dataset,** $K = 20$

	$r=5$			$r=7$			$r=9$		
Accuracy	$z=3$	$z=5$	$z=7$	$z=3$	$z=5$	$z=7$	$z=3$	$z=5$	$z=7$
$m=8$	91.3%	94.2%	95.6%	91.3%	94.2%	95.6%	95.6%	95.6%	98.6%
$m=10$	90.0%	92.8%	92.8%	91.3%	94.2%	94.2%	92.8%	94.2%	95.6%
$m=12$	90.0%	90.0%	91.3%	90.0%	90.0%	91.3%	91.3%	92.8%	94.2%

Table 4: Accuracy of EmbedJoin, TREC **dataset,** $K = 40$

	$r=5$			$r=7$			$r=9$		
Accuracy	$z=3$	$z=5$	$z=7$	$z=3$	$z=5$	$z=7$	$z=3$	$z=5$	$z=7$
$m=11$	99.1%	99.5%	99.6%	99.5%	99.6%	99.8%	99.6%	99.8%	99.8%
$m=13$	99.0%	99.3%	99.4%	99.3%	99.5%	99.6%	99.5%	99.7%	99.8%
$m=15$	98.8%	99.1%	99.3%	99.1%	99.4%	99.5%	99.4%	99.6%	99.7%

Table 5: Accuracy of EmbedJoin, GEN50kS **dataset,** $K = 100$

Due to the space constraints we delay some of the experimental results (e.g., Figures and Tables) of this section to the full version [28], and only summarize the performance of our algorithms.

Accuracy. In Table 3, 4 and 5 we study how different parameters (r, z, m) influence the accuracy of EmbedJoin. We vary r in $\{5, 7, 9\}$, z in $\{3, 5, 7\}$, and choose slightly different values for m on different datasets (the choices of m largely depend on the string length and the distance threshold K). We observe that the accuracy of EmbedJoin is 90.1 ~ 99.7% on UNIREF, 90.0 ~ 98.6% on TREC, and 98.8 ~ 99.8% in GEN50kS.

We note that the accuracy of EmbedJoin increases with r and z, and decreases with m. This is consistent with the theory. When r and z increase, we use more hash functions (recall that the total number of hash functions used is $r \cdot z$), and thus each pair of strings have more chance to be hashed into the same bucket in at least one of the hash tables. Similarly, when m decreases, each LSH function has larger collision probability. Of course, the increase of the collision probability will always introduce more false positives, and consequently increase the verification time. Using more hash functions/tables will also increase the space usage.

Time and Space. In Table 6 we study how different parameters (r, z, m) influence the running time of EmbedJoin in the GEN50kS dataset. We note that the running time increases when r and z increase, decreases when m increases. This is just the opposite to what we have observed for accuracy, and is consistent to the theory that increasing the collision probability will introduce more false positives/candidates and thus increase the verification time.

Due to the space constraints we refer readers to the full version for the statistics of memory usage of EmbedJoin under different parameters (r, z, m). We observe that the memory usage increases when r and z increases. This is because when r and z increase we need to store more hash tables *and* we will have more candidate pairs to verify. When m increases, the memory usage stays the same or slightly increases. There are two kinds of mutually exclusive forces that affect this. On the one hand, when m increases the size of each hash signature increases. On the other hand, when m increases the number of candidate pairs decreases. From what we have observed, the first force generally dominates the second.

More Studies. We also did the followings. (1) Recorded the change of accuracy of EmbedJoin under different thresholds K and parameters (r, z, m). (2) Recorded and compared the running time of EmbedJoin on different modules of the algorithms: reading the input and CGK-embedding, performing LSH, and verification. (3) Studied how different parameters (r, z, m) influence the number of candidates generated by EmbedJoin. Due to the space constraints we refer readers to the full version [28] for details.

4.3 A Comparison with Existing Algorithms

In this section we compare EmbedJoin with the existing best algorithms introduced in Section 4.1. We note that in some figures some data points for competing algorithms are missing, which is either because these algorithms have implementation limitations (returned wrong answers or triggered memory overflow) or they cannot finish in 24 hours.

Scalability on the Threshold Distance. Figure 2 shows the running time of different algorithms when varying the distance threshold K on UNIREF, TREC and GEN50kS. In all experiments we always guarantee the accuracy of EmbedJoin is above 95% on UNIREF and TREC, and is above 99% on GEN50kS.

Time(s)	$r = 5$			$r = 7$			$r = 9$		
	$z = 3$	$z = 5$	$z = 7$	$z = 3$	$z = 5$	$z = 7$	$z = 3$	$z = 5$	$z = 7$
$m = 11$	143.9	149.1	159.2	152.4	159.8	172.3	158.8	174.4	191.4
$m = 13$	132.6	134.1	137.3	138.4	140.9	145.5	143.4	147.0	154.0
$m = 15$	131.6	133.5	134.0	134.2	138.3	139.0	137.6	142.6	147.6

Table 6: Running time of EmbedJoin, GEN50kS dataset, K = 100

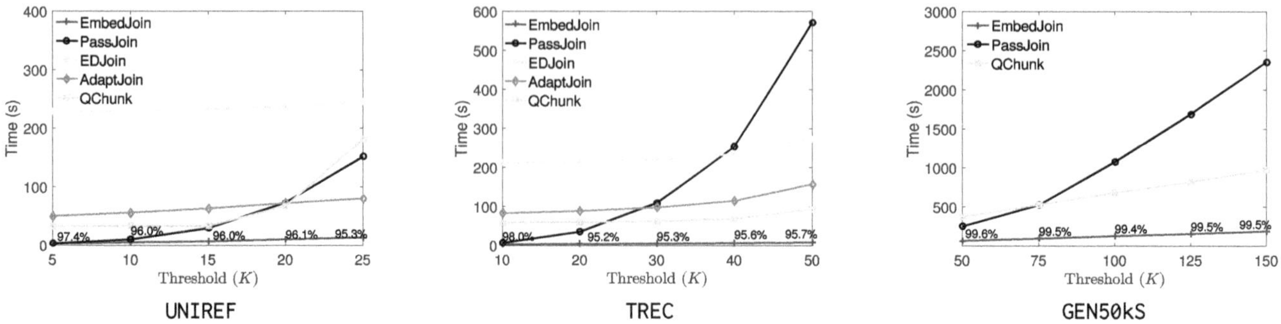

Figure 2: Running time, varying K. Percentages on the curves for EmbedJoin are its accuracy

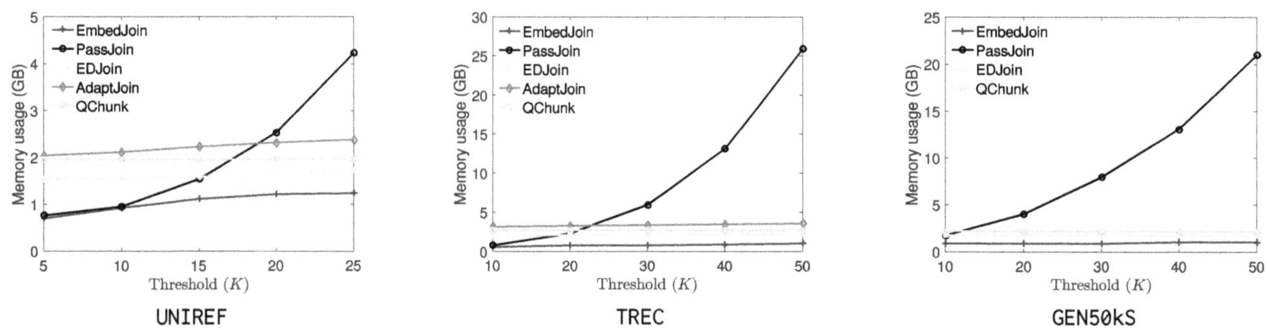

Figure 3: Memory usage, varying K

We observe that EmbedJoin always has the best performance: the running time of EmbedJoin is better than the best existing algorithm by a factor of 6.2 on UNIREF ($K = 25$), 12.1 in TREC ($K = 50$), and 5.2 on GEN50kS ($K = 150$). The PassJoin algorithm does not scale well on K: when K increases, the running time jumps sharply. This may due to the fact that the time complexity in the filtering step of PassJoin is $O(nK^3)$ – a cubic dependence on K. The other three algorithms, EDJoin, AdaptJoin and QChunk, are all based on q-gram or its variants; they generally have similar running time curves, which rise much slower compared with PassJoin when K increases. One exception is that on the UNIREF dataset the running time of QChunk increases sharply when K passes 20, which may due to the sudden increase of the number of candidate pairs that QChunk produces. On GEN50kS, the running time of EDJoin is too large (> 10000s when $K = 50$) and thus does not fit the figure, and AdaptJoin reports erroneous results.

We would like to comment that the *output size* has little to do with the running time of the algorithms. For example, for the five distance thresholds on the UNIREF dataset in Figure 2, the corresponding output sizes are 707, 1377, 2154, 3184, 5864; the numbers increase quickly. On the other hand, for the five distance thresholds on the TREC dataset the corresponding output sizes are 52, 63, 64, 69, 70; the numbers increase slowly. But the running time curves of the test algorithms on the two datasets generally follow the similar trends. The major components that affect the running time are the time spent on the filtering and the number of *candidate pairs* after the filtering step for verification. We refer readers to the full version of this paper for statistics on the running time of EmbedJoin on different modules.

Figure 3 shows the memory usages of different algorithms in the same settings as Figure 2. We note that the memory used by EmbedJoin is always the smallest among all. This is largely because the hash tables used by EmbedJoin take less space than the signatures and indexes built by other algorithms. The memory usage of PassJoin is also small at the beginning, but deteriorates fast when K increases. The three q-gram based algorithms have similar trends in memory usage.

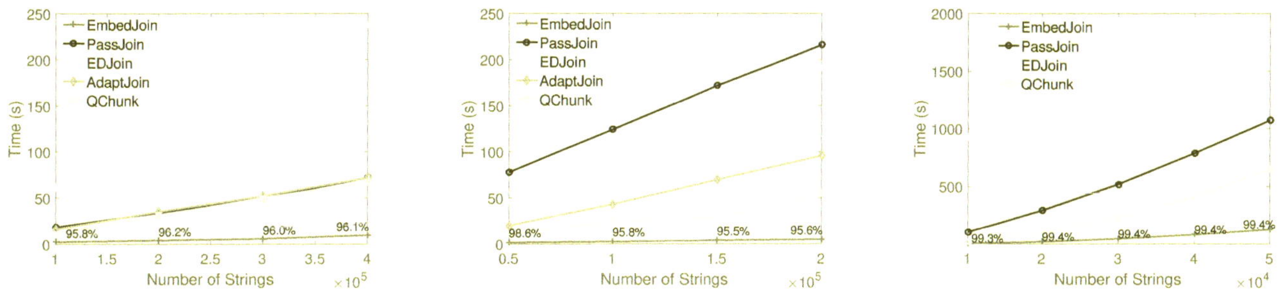

UNIREF ($K = 20$) TREC ($K = 40$) GEN50kS ($K = 100$)

Figure 4: Running time, varying n. Percentages on the curves for EmbedJoin are its accuracy

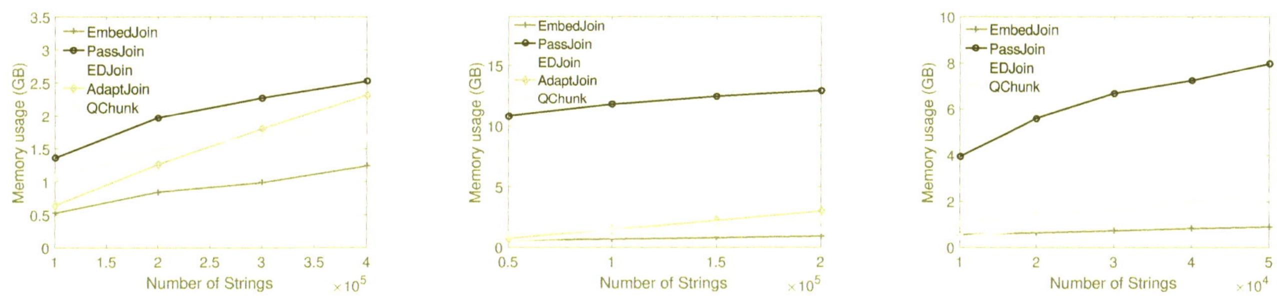

UNIREF ($K = 20$) TREC ($K = 40$) GEN50kS ($K = 100$)

Figure 5: Memory usage, varying the input size n

Scalability on the Input Size. Figure 4 shows the running time of different algorithms on the UNIREF, TREC and GEN50kS datasets when varying input size n. The trends of the running time of all algorithms are similar; they increase almost linearly with respect to n. It is clear that EmbedJoin performs much better than all the other algorithms: EmbedJoin performs better than the best existing algorithm by a factor of 6.8 on UNIREF ($N = 4 \times 10^5$), 11.5 on TREC ($N = 2 \times 10^5$), and 5.1 on GEN50kS ($N = 5 \times 10^4$).

Figure 5 shows the memory usages of different algorithms in the same settings as Figure 4. The trends of the memory usages of all algorithms are similar; they increase almost linearly with respect to n. It is clear that EmbedJoin always performs the best.

The Ultimate Scalability of EmbedJoin. Finally, we present a set of experiments that distinguish EmbedJoin from all the competing algorithms. We test all the algorithms on longer strings (length ranges from 5,000 to 20,000) with larger distance thresholds (1% ~ 20% of the corresponding string length). The numbers of strings in the datasets range from 20,000 to 320,000. For EmbedJoin we fix $r = z = 7$, and set $m = 15 - \lfloor \log_2 x \rfloor$ where $x\%$ is the threshold. Result points are only depicted for those that can finish in 24 hours, *and* return correct answers.

When varying the string length N (see Figure 6), there are three algorithms that can produce data points in the GEN20kS dataset: EDJoin can report answer up to the 2% distance threshold, and PassJoin and QChunk can go up to 8%. We observe a sharp time jump of QChunk from 4% to 8% – at the 8% distance threshold QChunk barely finished within 24 hours. On GEN20kL, unfortunately, the program for QChunk that we have used cannot produce any data point due to memory overflow. PassJoin only succeeds at the 1% distance threshold.

When varying the number of input strings n (see Figure 7; the first subfigure of Figure 7 is simply a repeat of the first subfigure of Figure 6), all the other computing algorithms cannot produce anything on GEN320kS. PassJoin manages to produce results on GEN80kS up to 4% distance threshold. On the other hand, EmbedJoin scales smoothly on all the datasets.

To summarize, it is clear that on large datasets with long string, EmbedJoin performs much better than all the competing algorithms, and scales well up to distance threshold 20%. Unfortunately, we do not know the exact accuracy of EmbedJoin in many points since other exact computation algorithms cannot finish, but from what we have observed on shorter strings and smaller distance thresholds, we would expect that its accuracy will be consistently high.

5 CONCLUSION

We propose an algorithm named EmbedJoin for computing edit similarity join, one of the most important operations in database systems. Different from all previous approaches, we first embed the input strings from the edit space to the Hamming space, and then try to perform a filtering (for reducing candidate pairs) in the Hamming space where efficient tools like locality sensitive hashing are available. Our experiments have shown that EmbedJoin significantly outperforms, at a very small cost of accuracy, all previous best algorithms on long strings and large thresholds.

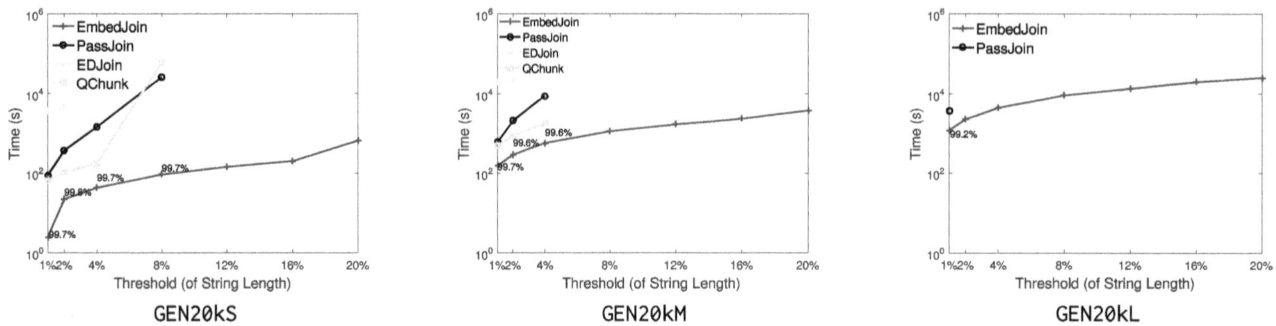

Figure 6: Scalability on string length. Percentages on the curves for `EmbedJoin` **are its accuracy**

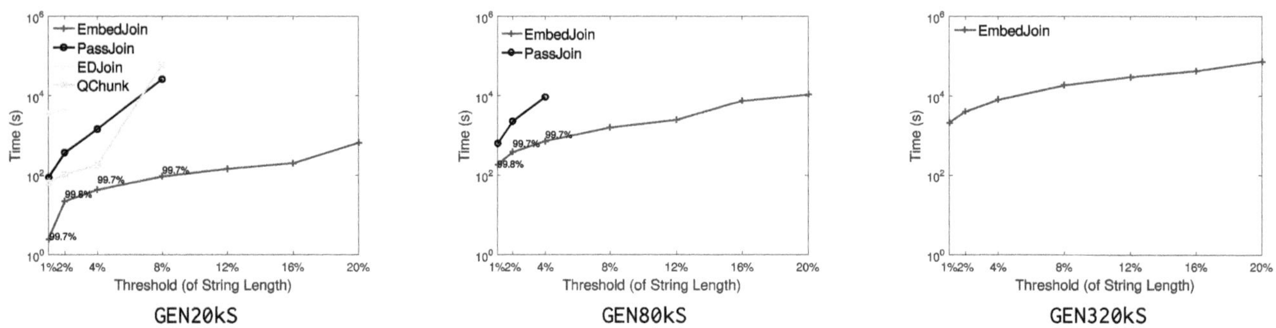

Figure 7: Scalability on number of strings. Percentages on the curves for `EmbedJoin` **are its accuracy**

6 ACKNOWLEDGMENT

The authors would like to thank Djamal Belazzougui for many helpful discussions, and Haixu Tang and Diyue Bu for their help on preparing the human genome datasets.

REFERENCES

[1] Arvind Arasu, Venkatesh Ganti, and Raghav Kaushik. 2006. Efficient Exact Set-Similarity Joins. In *VLDB*. 918–929.

[2] Arturs Backurs and Piotr Indyk. 2015. Edit Distance Cannot Be Computed in Strongly Subquadratic Time (unless SETH is false). In *STOC*. 51–58.

[3] Roberto J. Bayardo, Yiming Ma, and Ramakrishnan Srikant. 2007. Scaling up all pairs similarity search. In *WWW*. 131–140.

[4] Djamal Belazzougui and Qin Zhang. 2016. Edit Distance: Sketching, Streaming and Document Exchange. In *FOCS*. to appear.

[5] Thomas Bocek, Ela Hunt, Burkhard Stiller, and Fabio Hecht. 2007. *Fast similarity search in large dictionaries.* University.

[6] Diptarka Chakraborty, Elazar Goldenberg, and Michal Koucký. 2016. Streaming algorithms for embedding and computing edit distance in the low distance regime. In *STOC*. 712–725.

[7] Surajit Chaudhuri, Venkatesh Ganti, and Raghav Kaushik. 2006. A Primitive Operator for Similarity Joins in Data Cleaning. In *ICDE*. 5.

[8] Paolo Ciaccia, Marco Patella, and Pavel Zezula. 1997. M-tree: An Efficient Access Method for Similarity Search in Metric Spaces. In *VLDB*. 426–435.

[9] Aristides Gionis, Piotr Indyk, and Rajeev Motwani. 1999. Similarity Search in High Dimensions via Hashing. In *VLDB*. 518–529.

[10] Luis Gravano, Panagiotis G. Ipeirotis, H. V. Jagadish, Nick Koudas, S. Muthukrishnan, and Divesh Srivastava. 2001. Approximate String Joins in a Database (Almost) for Free. In *VLDB*. 491–500.

[11] Piotr Indyk and Rajeev Motwani. 1998. Approximate Nearest Neighbors: Towards Removing the Curse of Dimensionality. In *STOC*. 604–613.

[12] Yu Jiang, Guoliang Li, Jianhua Feng, and Wen-Syan Li. 2014. String Similarity Joins: An Experimental Evaluation. *PVLDB* 7, 8 (2014), 625–636.

[13] Robert Krauthgamer and Yuval Rabani. 2009. Improved Lower Bounds for Embeddings into L_1. *SIAM J. Comput.* 38, 6 (2009), 2487–2498.

[14] Gad M. Landau, Eugene W. Myers, and Jeanette P. Schmidt. 1998. Incremental String Comparison. *SIAM J. Comput.* 27, 2 (1998), 557–582.

[15] Chen Li, Jiaheng Lu, and Yiming Lu. 2008. Efficient Merging and Filtering Algorithms for Approximate String Searches. In *ICDE*. 257–266.

[16] Guoliang Li, Dong Deng, Jiannan Wang, and Jianhua Feng. 2011. PASS-JOIN: A Partition-based Method for Similarity Joins. *PVLDB* 5, 3 (2011), 253–264.

[17] Rafail Ostrovsky and Yuval Rabani. 2007. Low distortion embeddings for edit distance. *J. ACM* 54, 5 (2007).

[18] Jianbin Qin, Wei Wang, Yifei Lu, Chuan Xiao, and Xuemin Lin. 2011. Efficient exact edit similarity query processing with the asymmetric signature scheme. In *SIGMOD*. 1033–1044.

[19] Venu Satuluri and Srinivasan Parthasarathy. 2012. Bayesian Locality Sensitive Hashing for Fast Similarity Search. *PVLDB* 5, 5 (2012), 430–441.

[20] Esko Ukkonen. 1985. Algorithms for Approximate String Matching. *Information and Control* 64, 1-3 (1985), 100–118.

[21] Sebastian Wandelt, Dong Deng, Stefan Gerdjikov, Shashwat Mishra, Petar Mitankin, Manish Patil, Enrico Siragusa, Alexander Tiskin, Wei Wang, Jiaying Wang, and Ulf Leser. 2014. State-of-the-art in string similarity search and join. *SIGMOD Record* 43, 1 (2014), 64–76.

[22] Jiannan Wang, Guoliang Li, and Jianhua Feng. 2010. Trie-Join: Efficient Trie-based String Similarity Joins with Edit-Distance Constraints. *PVLDB* 3, 1 (2010), 1219–1230.

[23] Jiannan Wang, Guoliang Li, and Jianhua Feng. 2012. Can we beat the prefix filtering?: an adaptive framework for similarity join and search. In *SIGMOD*. 85–96.

[24] Wei Wang, Jianbin Qin, Chuan Xiao, Xuemin Lin, and Heng Tao Shen. 2013. VChunkJoin: An Efficient Algorithm for Edit Similarity Joins. *IEEE Trans. Knowl. Data Eng.* 25, 8 (2013), 1916–1929.

[25] Chuan Xiao, Wei Wang, and Xuemin Lin. 2008. Ed-Join: an efficient algorithm for similarity joins with edit distance constraints. *PVLDB* 1, 1 (2008), 933–944.

[26] Chuan Xiao, Wei Wang, Xuemin Lin, and Jeffrey Xu Yu. 2008. Efficient similarity joins for near duplicate detection. In *WWW*. 131–140.

[27] Jiaqi Zhai, Yin Lou, and Johannes Gehrke. 2011. ATLAS: a probabilistic algorithm for high dimensional similarity search. In *SIGMOD*. 997–1008.

[28] Haoyu Zhang and Qin Zhang. 2017. EmbedJoin: Efficient Edit Similarity Joins via Embeddings. *CoRR* abs/1702.00093 (2017).

TrioVecEvent: Embedding-Based Online Local Event Detection in Geo-Tagged Tweet Streams

Chao Zhang[1], Liyuan Liu[1], Dongming Lei[1], Quan Yuan[1], Honglei Zhuang[1], Tim Hanratty[2], and Jiawei Han[1]
[1]Dept. of Computer Science, University of Illinois at Urbana-Champaign, Urbana, IL, USA
[2]U.S. Army Research Laboratory, Adelphi, MD, USA
[1]{czhang82, ll2, dlei5, qyuan, hzhuang3, hanj}@illinois.edu
[2]timothy.p.hanratty@mail.mil

ABSTRACT

Detecting local events (*e.g.*, protest, disaster) at their onsets is an important task for a wide spectrum of applications, ranging from disaster control to crime monitoring and place recommendation. Recent years have witnessed growing interest in leveraging geo-tagged tweet streams for online local event detection. Nevertheless, the accuracies of existing methods still remain unsatisfactory for building reliable local event detection systems. We propose TrioVecEvent, a method that leverages multimodal embeddings to achieve *accurate* online local event detection. The effectiveness of TrioVecEvent is underpinned by its two-step detection scheme. First, it ensures a high coverage of the underlying local events by dividing the tweets in the query window into coherent geo-topic clusters. To generate quality geo-topic clusters, we capture short-text semantics by learning multimodal embeddings of the location, time, and text, and then perform online clustering with a novel Bayesian mixture model. Second, TrioVecEvent considers the geo-topic clusters as candidate events and extracts a set of features for classifying the candidates. Leveraging the multimodal embeddings as background knowledge, we introduce discriminative features that can well characterize local events, which enable pinpointing true local events from the candidate pool with a small amount of training data. We have used crowdsourcing to evaluate TrioVecEvent, and found that it improves the performance of the state-of-the-art method by a large margin.

1 INTRODUCTION

Detecting local events (*e.g.*, disaster, protest, sport game) at their onsets is in pressing need for many applications. For example, in disaster control, it is highly important to build a real-time disaster detector that constantly monitors a geographical region. By sending out timely alarms when emergent disasters outbreak, the detector can help people take timely actions to alleviate huge life and economic losses. Another example is public order maintaining. For local governments, it is desirable to monitor people's activities in the city and know about social unrests (*e.g.*, protest, crime) as soon as possible. With a detector that discovers social unrests upon their onsets, the government can respond timely to prevent severe social riots.

While the task of online local event detection is extremely challenging years ago due to the lack of data sources, it has been recently made possible by the proliferation of geo-tagged social media. As a local event outbreaks, a considerable number of geo-tagged records (*e.g.*, tweets, Instagram posts) often emerge instantly [1, 10, 22, 24, 32, 44], created by the participants and/or witnesses who broadcast it right on the spot. Such records, as a result of human sensing, not only provide a comprehensive view of the event with multi-dimensional information (location, time, and text), but also serve as first-hand reports because of their real-time nature.

A handful of studies [1, 44] have investigated leveraging geo-tagged tweet streams for online local event detection. Typically, they cluster the keywords/tweets in the query window into candidate events, and then rank the candidates to select the top-K locally bursty ones. Despite the compelling results achieved by these studies, their detection accuracies remain unsatisfactory. For example, the state-of-the-art method [44] achieves only ~30% precision, which is inadequate for building reliable local event detection systems in practice.

Indeed, online local event detection from continuous geo-tagged tweet streams is by no means a trivial task. It has several unique challenges that largely limit the performance of existing methods: 1) *Capturing short-text semantics.* To effectively extract local events, it is key to carefully capture the text semantics, such that the tweets discussing about the same event can be grouped. Existing methods, however, fall short in capturing short-text semantics. They either consider each keyword as an independent item [1], or rely on measures (*e.g.*, random walk [44]) that could suffer severely from text sparsity; 2) *Filtering uninteresting activities.* Many geo-tagged tweets just reflect routine activities (*e.g.*, dining, shopping) instead of any interesting events. To identify true local events, existing methods rely on heuristic ranking functions to select the top-K bursty candidates. However, it is hard — if not impossible — to manually design a gold-standard ranking function for accurate candidate filtering. Worse still, some query windows contain more than K events, while some (*e.g.*, the early morning) contain no events at all. The rigid top-K selection can incur severe detection accuracy loss due to its inflexibility; and 3) *Fast online detection.* When a local event outbreaks, our goal is to report the event instantly to allow for timely actions. Hence, it is desirable to continuously monitor the massive geo-tagged tweet stream and report local events on

KDD '17, August 13-17, 2017, Halifax, NS, Canada

978-1-4503-4887-4/17/08...$15.00
DOI: http://dx.doi.org/10.1145/3097983.3098027

the fly. Such a requirement renders existing batch-wise detection methods [8, 22, 36] inapplicable.

We propose TrioVecEvent, an embedding-based detector that enables *accurate* online local event detection from continuous geo-tagged tweet streams. The foundation of TrioVecEvent is a multimodal embedding learner that maps all the regions, hours, and keywords into the same space with their correlations preserved. If two units are highly correlated (*e.g.*, 'Pats' and 'Patriots', or the 5th Ave region and the keyword 'shopping'), their representations in the latent space tend be close. Such multimodal embeddings not only allow us to capture the subtle semantic similarities between tweets, but also serve as background knowledge by revealing the typical keywords in different regions and hours.

Built upon the multimodal embeddings, TrioVecEvent employs a two-step scheme to achieve high detection accuracy. First, *it performs online clustering to divide the tweets in the query window into coherent geo-topic clusters.* We develop a novel Bayesian mixture model that jointly models the tweet locations in the Euclidean space and the semantic embeddings in the spherical space. The model can generate quality candidates to ensure a high coverage of the underlying events. Second, *it extracts a set of discriminative features for accurate candidate classification.* Based on the multimodal embeddings, we design features that can well characterize local events, which enable pinpointing true positives from the candidate pool with a small amount of training data. Compared with existing top-K candidate selection schemes, the classification-based candidate filtering not only frees us from designing heuristic ranking functions, but also eliminates the inflexibility of rigid top-K selection. Furthermore, as the query window shifts continuously, TrioVecEvent does not need to detect the local events in the new window from scratch, but just needs to update the previous results with little cost to enable fast online detection.

Our main contributions are summarized as follows:

(1) We develop a multimodal embedding learner that jointly maps the location, time, and text into the same latent space with their correlations preserved. The multimodal embeddings not only capture the subtle semantics of tweet messages, but also serve as background knowledge to extract discriminative features for candidate filtering.
(2) We propose a novel Bayesian mixture clustering model that finds geo-topic clusters as candidate events. It generates quality geo-topic clusters without specifying the number of clusters a priori, and continuously updates the clustering results as the query window shifts.
(3) We design an effective candidate classifier that judges whether each candidate is indeed a local event. Relying on the multimodal embeddings, we extract a set of discriminative features for the candidates, which enable training a reliable classifier with a small amount of training data.

We have performed extensive experiments on two large-scale geo-tagged tweet data sets. Our effectiveness studies based on crowdsourcing show that TrioVecEvent improves the detection precision of the state-of-the-art method [44] by a large margin. Meanwhile, TrioVecEvent demonstrates excellent efficiency, making it suitable to be deployed for monitoring large geo-tagged tweet streams in practice.

2 RELATED WORK

In this section, we review existing work related to our problem, including: (1) event detection and forecasting; and (2) geo-tagged social media mining.

2.1 Event Detection and Forecasting

2.1.1 Global Event Detection. A larger number of methods have been proposed for extracting global events that are bursty in the entire data stream. Generally, existing global event detection approaches can be classified into two categories: *document-based* and *feature-based.* Document-based approaches [3, 4, 33] consider each document as a basic unit. They group similar documents into clusters and then find the bursty ones as events. For instance, Allan *et al.* [4] perform online clustering and use a similarity threshold to determine whether a new document should form a new topic or be merged into an existing one; Aggarwal *et al.* [3] also detect events via online clustering, but with a similarity measure that considers both tweet content relevance and user proximity; Sankaranarayanan *et al.* [33] train a Naïve Bayes filter to obtain news-related tweets and cluster them based on TF-IDF similarity. Feature-based approaches [17, 20, 23, 26, 37] identify a set of bursty features (*e.g.*, keywords) and cluster them to form events. Various techniques for extracting bursty features have been proposed, such as Fourier transform [17], Wavelet transform [37], and phrase-based burst detection [14, 23]. For example, Fung *et al.* [13] model feature occurrences with binomial distribution to extract bursty features; He *et al.* [17] construct the time series for each feature and perform Fourier Transform to identify bursts; Weng *et al.* [37] use wavelet transform and auto-correlation to measure word energy and extract high-energy words; Li *et al.* [23] segment each tweet into meaningful phrases and extract bursty phrases based on frequency; Giridhar *et al.* [14] extract an event as a group of tweets that contain at least one pair of bursty keywords.

The above methods are all designed for detecting globally bursty events. A local event, however, is usually bursty in a local region instead of the entire stream. Hence, directly applying these methods to our problem can miss many local events.

2.1.2 Local Event Detection. Local event detection has been receiving increasing research interest in the past few years [1, 8, 11, 12, 22, 30, 32, 44]. Watanabe *et al.* [36] and Quezada *et al.* [30] extract location-aware events in the social media, but their focus is on geo-locating the tweets/events. Sakaki *et al.* [32] achieve real-time earthquake detection, by training a classifier to judge whether an incoming tweet is earthquake-related. Li *et al.* [24] detect crime and disaster events (CDE) with a self-adaptive crawler for CDE-related tweets. Our work differs from these studies in that we aim to detect all kinds of local events, whereas they focus on specific event types. Quite a few generic local event detection methods have been proposed [1, 8, 22, 44]. Chen *et al.* [8] use Wavelet transform to extract spatiotemporally bursty Flickr tags, and then cluster them based on their co-occurrences and spatiotemporal distributions. Krumm *et al.* [22] discretize the time into equal-size bins and compare the number of tweets in the same bin across different days to extract local events.

Nevertheless, the above methods can only handle static data and detect local events in batch. While online methods have been gaining increasing attention in the data mining community [7, 18, 25, 39], few methods exist for supporting online local event detection. To the best of our knowledge, there are only two studies that have investigated the online local event detection problem [1, 44]. Abdelhaq *et al.* [1] first extract bursty and localized keywords in the query window, then cluster such keywords based on their spatial distributions, and finally select the top-K locally bursty clusters. Zhang *et al.* [44] detect geo-topic clusters based on random walk, and later rank these clusters to select spatiotemporally bursty ones. While these two methods support online local event detection, their accuracies are limited because of two reasons: 1) the clustering step does not capture short-text semantics well; and 2) the candidate filtering effectiveness is limited by heuristic ranking functions and the inflexibility of top-K selection.

2.1.3 Local Event Forecasting. Local event forecasting is another line of research that is related to our problem. Foley *et al.* [12] use distant supervision to extract future local events from Web pages, but the proposed method can only extract local events that are well advertised in advance on the Web. Zhao *et al.* [45–47] formulate local event forecasting as a binary prediction problem, *i.e.*, predicting whether a specific type of event (*e.g.*, civil unrest) will occur on a given day. Their methods combine social media with other data sources (*e.g.*, gold standard report, news articles) to train reliable predictors. Our problem is orthogonal to their studies in that, instead of performing binary prediction for a specific event type, we attempt to extract all types of local events at their onsets.

2.2 Geo-Tagged Social Media Mining

The emergence of geo-tagged social media has enabled progresses in various location-based mining tasks besides local event detection, including location recommendation [35], link prediction [9], mobility modeling [43], and spatiotemporal activity modeling [42]. Among such tasks, spatiotemporal activity modeling is mostly related to the local event detection problem, thus we detail existing approaches to it in the following.

Spatiotemporal activity modeling aims at detecting the typical activities in different geographical regions [6, 16, 21, 34]. Early approaches incorporate spatiotemporal information into classic topic models for this problem. In particular, Sizov *et al.* [34] extend LDA [6] by assuming each latent topic has a multinomial distribution over text and two Gaussians over latitudes and longitudes; Yin *et al.* [40] extend PLSA by assuming each region has a Gaussian distribution that generates locations, as well as a multinomial distribution over the latent topics that generate text; Guo *et al.* [16] use Dirichlet Process to extract activities that freely span several regions and peak multiple time periods; Hong *et al.* [19] and Yuan *et al.* [41] introduce the user factor in the modeling process to capture user preferences. Recently, representation learning has attracted much attention for mobile data mining tasks [38, 42, 48]. Among them, Zhang *et al.* [42] propose a multimodal representation learning method for the spatiotemporal activity modeling problem. By embedding geographical regions, time periods, and keywords into the same latent space, the proposed approach is capable of capturing their cross-modal correlations and outperforming previous geographical topic models. Although spatiotemporal activity modeling and local event detection are two closely related tasks, there is a clear difference between them. The former attempts to summarize the typical activities in different regions, whereas the latter aims at detecting unusual activities bursted in local areas.

3 PRELIMINARIES

3.1 Problem Description

Let $\mathcal{D} = (d_1, d_2, \ldots, d_n, \ldots)$ be a continuous stream of geo-tagged tweets that arrive in chronological order. Each tweet d is a tuple $\langle t_d, l_d, x_d \rangle$, where t_d is its post time, l_d is its geo-location, and x_d is a bag of keywords that denote the tweet message. Consider a query time window $Q = [t_s, t_e]$ where t_s and t_e are the start and end timestamps satisfying $t_{d_1} \le t_s < t_e \le t_{d_n}$. The online local event detection problem aims at extracting all the local events that occur during Q and updating the event list online as Q shifts continuously.

3.2 The Framework of TrioVecEvent

A local event often results in relevant tweets around its occurring location. For example, suppose a protest occurs at the JFK Airport in New York City, many participants post tweets on the spot to express their attitude, with keywords like 'protest' and 'rights'. Such tweets form a geo-topic cluster as they are geographically close and semantically relevant. However, not necessarily does every geo-topic cluster correspond to a local event. It is because a geo-topic cluster may correspond to just routine activities in the region, *e.g.*, taking flights at JFK, shopping at the 5th Ave, *etc.*. We claim that a local event often leads to a *bursty and unusual geo-topic cluster*. The cluster is bursty in that it consists of a considerable number of tweets, and unusual in that its semantics deviates from routine activities significantly.

Motivated by the above, we design an embedding-based detection method TrioVecEvent. At the foundation of TrioVecEvent is a multimodal embedding learner [42] that maps all the regions, hours, and keywords into a latent space. If two units are highly correlated (*e.g.*, 'flight' and 'airport', or the JFK Airport region and the keyword 'flight'), their embeddings in the latent space tend be close. Figure 1 shows two real examples in Los Angeles and New York City, where we learn multimodal embeddings using millions of geo-tagged tweets in these cities and perform similarity searches. One can see that given the example queries, the multimodal embeddings well capture the correlations between different units. The usage of such embeddings is two-fold: 1) they allow us to capture the semantic similarities between tweets and further group the tweets into coherent geo-topic clusters; and 2) they reveal the typical keywords appearing in different regions and hours, which serve as background knowledge to help identify unusual and bursty geo-topic clusters.

Figure 2 shows the framework of TrioVecEvent. As shown, *the embedding learner* embeds the location, time, and text using massive data from the geo-tagged tweet stream. It maintains a cache for keeping newly arrived tweets and updating the embeddings periodically. Based on the multimodal embeddings, TrioVecEvent employs a two-step detection scheme: 1) in *the online clustering step*, we develop a Bayesian mixture model that jointly models geographical locations and semantic embeddings to extract coherent geo-topic clusters in the query window; 2) in *the candidate classification* step, we extract a set of discriminative features for the

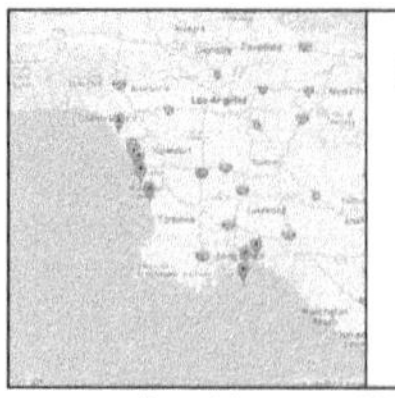

"33.942, -118.409"	"nba"	"baseball"	"beach"
lax	lakers	dodgers	beachlife
international	kobe	ladders	sand
losangeles	bryant	dogerstadium	boardwalk
united	bulls	itfdb	ocean
people	cavs	letsgododgers	wave
tsa	kevin	game	beachday
sfo	knicks	dodgergame	pacificocean
food	clipper	play	santamonica
flight	lebron	losdoyers	pier
travel	cp3	win	wave

"beach"

(a) Examples on LA (the second query is the location of the LAX Airport).

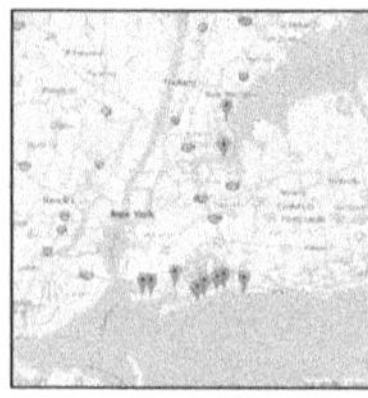

"40.641, -73.778"	"nba"	"baseball"	"beach"
jfk	knicks	mlb	rockaway
airport	melo	yankees	beachday
international	lebron	mets	howard_beach
johnfkennedy	durant	yanks	brighton
burger	basketball	inning	longbeach
terminal	kobe	yankee	coney
john	cavs	ballpark	atlantic
kennedy	theknicks	pitch	island
sfo	game	jeter	boardwalk
flight	lakers	game	long

"beach"

(b) Examples on NY (the second query is the location of the JFK Airport).

Figure 1: Example similarity queries based on the multimodal embeddings learned from the geo-tagged tweets in Los Angeles and New York City. In each city, the first query retrieves regions relevant to the keyword 'beach'; the second retrieves keywords relevant to the airport location; and the last three retrieve relevant keywords for the given query keywords. For each query, we use the learned embeddings to compute the cosine similarities between different units, and retrieve the top ten most similar units without including the query itself.

candidates and determine whether each candidate is a true local event.

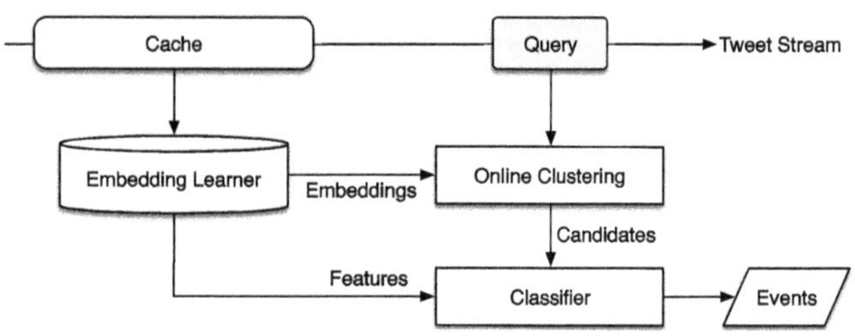

Figure 2: The framework of TrioVecEvent.

Now the key questions about TrioVecEvent are: 1) how to generate embeddings that can well capture the correlations between different units? 2) how do we perform online clustering to obtain quality geo-topic clusters in Q? and 3) what are the features that can discriminate true local events from non-events? In what follows, we introduce the multimodal embedding learner in Section 4, and then describe the two-step detection process of TrioVecEvent in Section 5.

4 MULTIMODAL EMBEDDING

The multimodal embedding module jointly maps all the spatial, temporal, and textual units into the same low-dimensional space with their correlations preserved. While the keywords are natural textual units for embedding, the space and time are are continuous and there are no natural embedding units. To address this issue, we break the geographical space into equal-size regions (300m*300m) and consider each region as a spatial unit. Similarly, we break one day into 24 hours and consider every hour as a basic temporal unit.

The multimodal embedding learner consumes the continuous tweet stream and learns D-dimensional representations for all the regions, hours, and keywords. As aforementioned, we maintain a cache C for keeping newly arrived tweets, and use it to periodically update the embeddings. To effectively incorporate the information in C without overfitting, we take the embeddings learned before the arrival of C as initialization, and optimize the embeddings over C for one full epoch. Such a simple strategy efficiently incorporates the tweets in the cache C, while largely preserving the information in the historical stream.

Our embedding procedure is inspired by the CBOW model [27] that predicts one unit given its context. Specifically, given a tweet d, for any unit $i \in d$ with type X (region, hour, or keyword), let $\mathbf{v}_i$ be the embedding of unit i, then we model the likelihood of observing i as

$$p(i|d_{-i}) = \exp(s(i, d_{-i})) / \sum_{j \in X} \exp(s(j, d_{-i})),$$

where d_{-i} is the set of all the units in d except i; and $s(i, d_{-i})$ is the similarity score between i and d_{-i}, defined as

$$s(i, d_{-i}) = \mathbf{v}_i^T \sum_{j \in d_{-i}} \mathbf{v}_j / |d_{-i}|.$$

For a cache C of geo-tagged tweets, the objective is to predict all the units of the tweets in C:

$$J_C = -\sum_{d \in C} \sum_{i \in d} \log p(i|d_{-i}).$$

To efficiently optimize the above objective function, we follow the idea of negative sampling [27] and use stochastic gradient descent (SGD) for updating. At each time, we randomly sample a tweet d from C and a unit $i \in d$. With negative sampling, we randomly select K negative units that have the same type with i but do not appear in d. Then we minimize the following function for the selected samples:

$$J_d = -\log \sigma(s(i, d_{-i})) - \sum_{k=1}^{K} \log \sigma(-s(k, d_{-i})),$$

where $\sigma(\cdot)$ is the sigmoid function. The updating rules for different variables can be easily derived by taking the derivatives of the above objective and then applying SGD, we omit the details here due to the space limit.

5 TWO-STEP LOCAL EVENT DETECTION

In this section, we describe the two-step detection process of TrioVecEvent. We first develop a Bayesian mixture clustering model in Section 5.1, and then design a candidate classifier in Section 5.2. For clarity, Table 1 summarizes the notations used in this section.

Table 1: The notations used in Section 5.

$\mathcal{X}$	the set of semantic embeddings for the tweets in Q
$\mathcal{Z}$	the set of cluster memberships for the tweets in Q
$\mathcal{L}$	the set of geo-location vectors for the tweets in Q
$\boldsymbol{\kappa}$	the set of κ for all the clusters
$\boldsymbol{\kappa}^{\neg k}$	the subset of $\boldsymbol{\kappa}$ excluding the one for cluster k
$\mathbf{A}^{\neg d}$	the subset of any set $\mathbf{A}$ excluding element d
$\mathbf{A}^{k}$	the subset of elements that are assigned to cluster k in set $\mathbf{A}$
$\mathbf{x}^{k}$	the sum of the semantic embeddings in cluster k
$\mathbf{x}^{k,\neg d}$	the sum of the semantic embeddings in cluster k excluding d
n^{k}	the number of tweets in cluster k
$n^{k,\neg d}$	the number of tweets in cluster k excluding d

5.1 Candidate Generation

5.1.1 A Bayesian Mixture Clustering Model. We develop a Bayesian mixture clustering model to divide the tweets in the query window Q into a number of geo-topic clusters, such that the tweets in the same cluster are geographically close and semantically relevant. We consider each tweet d as a tuple $(\mathbf{l}_d, \mathbf{x}_d)$. Here, $\mathbf{l}_d$ is a 2-dimensional vector denoting d's geo-location; and $\mathbf{x}_d$ is the D-dimensional semantic embedding of d, derived by averaging the embeddings of the keywords in d's message.

The key idea behind our model is that every geo-topic cluster implies a coherent activity (*e.g.*, protest) around a certain geo-location (*e.g.*, the JFK Airport). The location acts as a *geographical center* that triggers geo-location observations around it in the Euclidean space; while the activity serves as a *semantic focus* that triggers semantic embedding observations around it in the spherical space. We assume there are at most K geo-topic clusters in the query window Q. Note that assuming the maximum number of clusters is a weak assumption that can be readily met in practice. At the end of the clustering process, some of these K cluster may become empty. As such, the appropriate number of clusters in any ad-hoc query window can be automatically discovered.

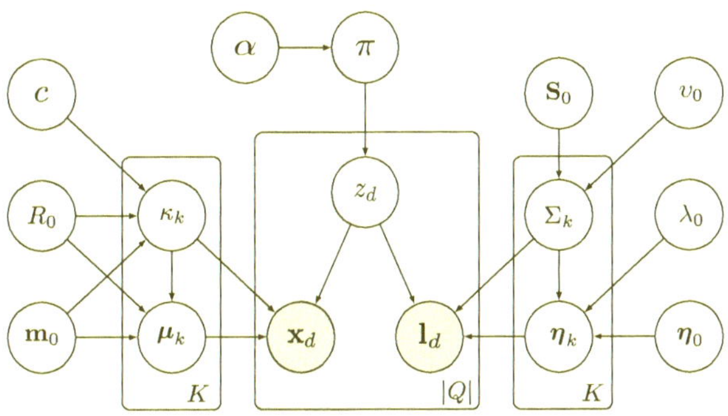

Figure 3: The graphical model of geo-topic clustering.

Figure 3 shows the generative process for all the tweets in the query window Q. As shown, we first draw a multinomial distribution π from a Dirichlet prior $\mathbf{Dirichlet}(.|\alpha)$ [28]. Meanwhile, for modeling the geo-locations, we draw K normal distributions from a Normal-Inverse-Wishart (NIW) prior $\mathbf{NIW}(.|\boldsymbol{\eta}_0, \lambda_0, \mathbf{S}_0, \upsilon_0)$ [28], which is a conjugate prior of the normal distribution; and for modeling the semantic embeddings, we draw K von Mises-Fisher (vMF) distributions from its conjugate prior $\Phi(\boldsymbol{\mu}, \kappa|\mathbf{m}_0, R_0, c)$ [29]. For each tweet $d \in Q$, we first draw its cluster membership z_d from π. Once the cluster membership is determined, we draw its geo-location $\mathbf{l}_d$ from the respective normal distribution, and its semantic embedding $\mathbf{x}_d$ from the respective vMF distribution.

While using normal distributions for modeling the geo-location $\mathbf{l}_d$ is intuitive, we justify the choice of the vMF distribution for modeling the semantic embedding $\mathbf{x}_d$ as follows. For a D-dimensional unit vector $\mathbf{x}$ that follows vMF distribution, its probability density function is given by

$$p(\mathbf{x}|\boldsymbol{\mu}, \kappa) = C_D(\kappa) \exp(\kappa \boldsymbol{\mu}^T \mathbf{x}),$$

where $C_D(\kappa) = \frac{\kappa^{D/2-1}}{I_{D/2-1}(\kappa)}$ and $I_{D/2-1}(\kappa)$ is the modified Bessel function. The vMF distribution has two parameters: the mean direction $\boldsymbol{\mu}$ ($\boldsymbol{\mu} = 1$) and the concentration parameter κ ($\kappa > 0$). The distribution of $\mathbf{x}$ on the unit sphere concentrates around the mean direction $\boldsymbol{\mu}$, and is more concentrated if κ is large. Our choice of the vMF distribution is motivated by the effectiveness of the cosine similarity [27, 42] in quantifying the similarities between multimodal embeddings. The mean direction $\boldsymbol{\mu}$ acts as a semantic focus on the unit sphere, and produces relevant semantic embeddings around it, where concentration degree is controlled by the parameter κ. The superiority of the vMF distribution over other alternatives (*e.g.*, Gaussian) for modeling textual embeddings has also been demonstrated in recent studies on clustering [15] and topic modeling [5].

To summarize the above generative process, we have:

$$\begin{aligned}
&\pi \sim \mathbf{Dirichlet}(.|\alpha)\\
&\{\boldsymbol{\eta}_k, \Sigma_k\} \sim \mathbf{NIW}(.|\boldsymbol{\eta}_0, \lambda_0, \mathbf{S}_0, \upsilon_0) \quad k = 1, 2, \ldots, K\\
&\{\boldsymbol{\mu}_k, \kappa_k\} \sim \Phi(.|\mathbf{m}_0, R_0, c) \quad k = 1, 2, \ldots, K\\
&z_d \sim \mathbf{Categorical}(.|\pi) \quad d \in Q\\
&\mathbf{l}_d \sim \mathcal{N}(.|\boldsymbol{\eta}_{z_d}, \Sigma_{z_d}) \quad d \in Q\\
&\mathbf{x}_d \sim \mathbf{vMF}(.|\boldsymbol{\mu}_{z_d}, \kappa_{z_d}) \quad d \in Q
\end{aligned}$$

where $\Lambda = \{\alpha, \mathbf{m}_0, R_0, c, \boldsymbol{\eta}_0, \lambda_0, \mathbf{S}_0, \upsilon_0\}$ are the hyper-parameters for the prior distributions.

5.1.2 Parameter Estimation. The key to obtain the geo-topic clusters is to estimate the posterior distributions for $\{z_d\}_{d \in Q}$. We use Gibbs sampling for this purpose. Since we have chosen conjugate priors for π and $\{\boldsymbol{\mu}_k, \boldsymbol{\eta}_k, \Sigma_k\}_{k=1}^{K}$, these parameters can be integrated out during the Gibbs sampling process, resulting in a collapsed Gibbs sampling procedure. Due to the space limit, we directly give the conditional probabilities for $\{\kappa_k\}_{k=1}^{K}$ and $\{z_d\}_{d \in Q}$:

$$p(\kappa_k|\boldsymbol{\kappa}^{\neg k}, \mathcal{X}, \mathcal{Z}, \alpha, \mathbf{m}_0, \mathcal{R}_0, c) \propto \frac{(C_D(\kappa_k))^{c+n^k}}{C_D(\kappa_k \| R_0 \mathbf{m}_0 + \mathbf{x}^k \|)}, \tag{1}$$

$$\begin{aligned}
p(z_d = k|\mathcal{X}, \mathcal{L}, \mathcal{Z}^{\neg d}, \boldsymbol{\kappa}, \Lambda) &\propto p(z_d = k|\mathcal{Z}^{\neg d}, \alpha)\cdot\\
&p(\mathbf{x}_d|\mathcal{X}^{\neg d}, \mathcal{Z}^{\neg d}, z_d = k, \Lambda) \cdot p(\mathbf{l}_d|\mathcal{L}^{\neg d}, \mathcal{Z}^{\neg d}, z_d = k, \Lambda). \quad (2)
\end{aligned}$$

The three quantities in Equation 2 are given by:

$$p(z_d = k|\cdot) \propto (n^{k,\neg d} + \alpha), \quad (3)$$

$$p(\mathbf{x}_d|\cdot) \propto \frac{C_D(\kappa_k) C_D(\|\kappa_k(R_0 \mathbf{m}_0 + \mathbf{x}^{k,\neg d})\|_2)}{C_D(\|\kappa_k(R_0 \mathbf{m}_0 + \mathbf{x}^{k,\neg d} + \mathbf{x}_d)\|_2)}, \quad (4)$$

$$p(\mathbf{l}_d|\cdot) \propto \frac{\lambda^{k,\neg d}(\upsilon^{k,\neg d} - 1)|\mathbf{S}^{\mathcal{L}^k \cap \mathcal{L}^{\neg d}}|^{\upsilon^{k,\neg d}/2}}{2(\lambda^{k,\neg d} + 1)|\mathbf{S}^{\mathcal{L}^k \cup \{\mathbf{l}_d\}}|^{(\upsilon^{k,\neg d}+1)/2}}, \quad (5)$$

where $\lambda^{\cdot}$, $\upsilon^{\cdot}$, and $\mathbf{S}^{\cdot}$ are the posterior estimations for the parameters of the NIW distribution [28].

From Equation 2, 3, 4, and 5, we observe that our Bayesian mixture model enjoys several nice properties when determining the cluster membership for a tweet d: 1) With Equation 3, d tends to join a cluster that has more members, resulting in a rich-get-richer effect; 2) With Equation 4, d tends to join a cluster that is more semantically similar to its textual embedding $\mathbf{x}_d$, leading to semantically coherent clusters; and 3) With Equation 5, d tends to join a cluster that is more geographically close to its geo-location $\mathbf{l}_d$, resulting in geographically compact clusters.

5.1.3 Incremental Updating. When the query window Q shifts, it is undesirable to re-compute the geo-topic clusters in the new query window from scratch for the purpose of fast online detection. We employ an incremental updating strategy that efficiently approximates the clustering results in the new window. As shown in Figure 4, assume the query window shifts from Q to Q', we denote by $D_- = \{d_1, \ldots, d_m\}$ the outdated tweets, and $D_+ = \{d_{n-k+1}, \ldots, d_n\}$ the new tweets. Instead of performing Gibbs sampling for all the tweets in Q', we simply drop D_- and sample the cluster memberships for the tweets in D_+. Such an incremental updating strategy achieves excellent efficiency and yields quality geo-topic clusters in practice as the memberships of the remaining tweets are mostly stable.

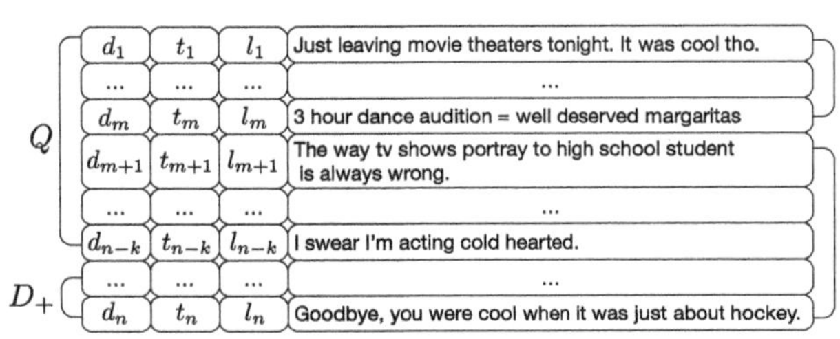

Figure 4: Incremental updating as the query window shifts.

5.2 Candidate Classification

We have so far obtained a set of coherent geo-topic clusters in the query window as candidates. Now we proceed to describe the candidate classifier for pinpointing the true local events. The key is to define a set of features that can well discriminate true local events from non-events. We introduce the following set of features for this purpose:

(1) **Spatial unusualness** quantifies how unusual a candidate is in its geographical region. As the multimodal embeddings can unveil the typical keywords in different regions, we use them as background knowledge to measure the spatial unusualness of a candidate C. Specifically, we compute the spatial unusualness as $f_{su}(C) = \sum_{d \in C} \cos(\mathbf{v}_{l_d}, \mathbf{x}_d)/|C|$, where $\mathbf{v}_{l_d}$ is the embedding of the region of tweet d, and $\mathbf{x}_d$ is the semantic embedding of tweet d.
(2) **Temporal unusualness** quantifies how temporally unusual a candidate is. We define the temporal unusualness of a candidate C as $f_{tu}(C) = \sum_{d \in C} \cos(\mathbf{v}_{t_d}, \mathbf{x}_d)/|C|$, where $\mathbf{v}_{t_d}$ is the embedding of the hour of tweet d.
(3) **Spatiotemporal unusualness** jointly considers the space and time to quantify how unusual a candidate C is: $f_{stu}(C) = \sum_{d \in C} \cos((\mathbf{v}_{l_d} + \mathbf{v}_{t_d})/2, \mathbf{x}_d)/|C|$.
(4) **Semantic concentration** computes how semantically coherent C is: $f_{su}(C) = \sum_{d \in C} \cos(\overline{\mathbf{x}}_d, \mathbf{x}_d)/|C|$, where $\overline{\mathbf{x}}_d$ is the average semantic embedding of the tweets in C.
(5) **Spatial and temporal concentrations** quantify how concentrated a candidate C is over the space and time. We compute three quantities for the tweets in C: 1) the standard deviation of the longitudes; 2) the standard deviation of the latitudes; and 3) the standard deviation of the creating timestamps.
(6) **Burstiness** quantifies how bursty a candidate C is. We define it as the number of tweets in C divided by the time span of C.

The Classification Procedure. To summarize, for each candidate C, we extract the following features: 1) the spatial unusualness; 2) the temporal unusualness; 3) the spatiotemporal unusualness; 4) the semantic concentration; 5) the longitude concentration; 6) the latitude concentration; 7) the temporal concentration; and 8) the burstiness. With the above features, we use logistic regression to train a binary classifier and judge whether each candidate is indeed a local event. We choose the logistic regression classifier because of its robustness when there is limited training data. We have also tried other classifiers like Random Forest, and find that the logistic regression classifier has slightly better performance in our experiments. The training instances are collected over 100 query windows in a crowdsourcing platform. We will shortly describe the labeling process in Section 6.

5.3 Complexity Analysis

We analyze the time complexities of the candidate generation step and the candidate classification step separately. For candidate generation, to extract geo-topic clusters in the new query window, the time complexity is $O(INKD)$, where I is the number of Gibbs sampling iterations, N is the number of new tweets, K is the maximum number of clusters; and D is the latent embedding dimension. Note that I, K and D are usually fixed to moderate values in practice, thus the candidate generation step scales roughly linearly with N and has good efficiency. For candidate classification, the major overhead lies in feature extraction. Let N_c be the maximum number of tweets in each candidate, then the time complexity of feature extraction is $O(KN_cD)$.

6 EXPERIMENTS

6.1 Experimental Settings

6.1.1 Baselines. We compare TrioVecEvent with all the existing online local event detection methods that we are aware of, described as follows:

- EVENTWEET [1] extracts bursty and localized keywords from the query window, then clusters these keywords based on spatial distributions, and finally selects top-K locally bursty clusters.
- GEOBURST [44] is the state-of-the-art method for online local event detection. It first uses random walk on a keyword co-occurrence graph to detect geo-topic clusters, and then ranks all the clusters by the weighted combination of spatial burstiness and temporal burstiness.
- GEOBURST+ is an upgraded version of GEOBURST by replacing the ranking module with a classifier. Instead of heuristically ranking the candidates, we train a classifier to determine whether each candidate is a local event. The used features include spatial burstiness, temporal burstiness [44], as well as spatial and temporal concentrations (Section 5.2).

6.1.2 Parameters. As EVENTWEET and GEOBURST both perform top-K selection to identify local events from the candidate pool, we set $K = 5$ for them to achieve a tradeoff between precision and recall. Meanwhile, EVENTWEET requires to partition the whole space into $M \times M$ small grids. After tuning, we set $M = 50$. In GEOBURST and GEOBURST+, there are three additional parameters: the kernel bandwidth h; (2) the restart probability α; and (3) the RWR similarity threshold δ. Following the original paper [44], we set them as $h = 0.01, \alpha = 0.2$, and $\delta = 0.02$. All the baseline methods require a reference window that precedes the query to quantify the burstiness of the candidates, we follow [44] and set the reference duration to one week.

TRIOVECEVENT involves the following major parameters: (1) the latent dimension D for embedding; and (2) the maximum number of clusters K; and (3) the number of Gibbs sampling iterations I. After tuning, we set $D = 100$, $K = 500$, and $I = 10$, as we find such a setting can produce geo-topic clusters that are fine-grained enough while achieving good efficiency. In addition, the Bayesian mixture model involves several hyper-parameters, as shown in Figure 3. In general, we observe that our model is not very sensitive to them. We set $\alpha = 1.0, c = 0.01, R_0 = 0.01, \mathbf{m}_0 = 0.1 \cdot \mathbf{1}, \lambda_0 = 1.0, \eta_0 = 0, \upsilon_0 = 2.0, \mathbf{S}_0 = 0.01 \cdot \mathbf{I}$, which are commonly adopted values for the prior distributions used in our model. We conduct the experiments on a computer with Intel Core i7 2.4GHz CPU and 8GB memory.

6.1.3 Data Sets and Groundtruth. Our experiments are based on the same data sets as in [44]. The first data set LA consists of the geo-tagged tweets in Los Angeles collected during 2014.08.01 – 2014.11.30; and the second data set NY consists of the geo-tagged tweets in New York City during the same period. For each data set, we use an off-the-shelf tool [31] to preprocess the text messages by preserving entities and nouns, and then remove the keywords that appear less than 100 times in the entire corpus.

To evaluate the methods and collect training data for GEOBURST+ and TRIOVECEVENT, we randomly generate 200 non-overlapping query windows with four different lengths: 3-hour, 4-hour, 5-hour, and 6-hour. After ranking these windows in chronological order, we run each the method online by shifting a fixed-length (3h, 4h, 5h, 6h) query window on a 5-minute basis, and save the results falling in each target query window. After collecting labeled data with crowdsourcing, we use the groundtruth in the first 100 windows for training the classifiers of GEOBURST+ and TRIOVECEVENT; and that in the rest 100 windows for comparing all the methods.

Now we describe the labeling process based on crowdsourcing. For all the methods, we upload their results to CrowdFlower[1] for human judging. Since EVENTWEET and GEOBURST are top-K methods with $K = 5$, we upload five results for each of them in each query window. GEOBURST+ and TRIOVECEVENT are classification-based methods, and the raw numbers of candidate events could be large. To limit the number of candidates while ensuring the coverages of the two methods, we employ a simple heuristic for eliminating negative candidates. It removes the candidates that have too few users (*i.e.*, the number of users is less than five) or too dispersed spatial distributions (*i.e.*, the longitude or latitude standard deviation is larger than 0.02). After filtering such trivial negatives, we upload the remaining candidates for evaluation.

On CrowdFlower, we represent each event with five tweets and ten keywords, and ask three CrowdFlower workers to judge whether the event is indeed a local event. To ensure the quality of the workers, we label 20 queries as groundtruth judgments on each data set, such that only the workers who can achieve no less than 80% accuracy on the groundtruth can submit their answers. Finally, we use majority voting to aggregate the workers' answers. The representative tweets and keywords are selected as follows: (1) For GEOBURST and GEOBURST+, we select five tweets having the largest authority scores, and ten keywords having the largest TF-IDF weights. (2) EVENTWEET represents each event as a group of keywords. We select ten keywords with the highest scores in each event. Then we regard the group of keywords as a query to retrieve the top five most similar tweets using the BM25 retrieval model. (3) TRIOVECEVENT represents a candidate as a group of tweets. We first compute the average semantic embedding, and then select the closest keywords and tweets using cosine similarity.

6.1.4 Metrics. As aforementioned, we use the groundtruth in the last 100 query windows to evaluate all the methods. To quantify the performance of all the methods, we report the following metrics: (1) *Precision.* The detection precision is $P = N_{\text{true}}/N_{\text{report}}$, where N_{true} is the number of true local events and N_{report} is the total number of reported events. (2) *Pseudo Recall.* The true recall is hard to measure due to the lack of the comprehensive set of events in the physical world. We thus measure the pseudo recall for each method. Specifically, for each query window, we aggregate the true positives of different methods. Let N_{total} be the total number of distinct local events detected by all the methods; we compute the pseudo recall of each method as $R = N_{\text{true}}/N_{\text{total}}$. (3) *Pseudo F1-Score.* Finally, we also report the pseudo F1 score of each method, which is computed as $F1 = 2 * P * R/(P + R)$.

6.2 Illustrative Cases

Before reporting the quantitative results, we first present several examples for TRIOVECEVENT. Figure 5 and 6 show several exemplifying geo-topic clusters detected by TRIOVECEVENT on LA and NY, respectively. For each cluster, we plot the locations of the member tweets and show the top five representative tweets. The clusters in Figure 5(a) and 5(b) correspond to two positive local events in LA: 1) a protesting rally held at the LAPD Headquarter for making voice for Mike Brown and Ezell Ford; and 2) Katy Perry's concert at the Staples Center. For each event, one can see the generated geo-topic

[1] http://www.crowdflower.com/

- Standing for **justice**! @ LAPD Headquarters http://t.co/YxNUAloQcE
- At the LAPD **protest** downtown **#EzellFord #MikeBrown** http://t.co/kWphv6dXOr
- Hands Up. Don't **Shoot**. @ Los Angeles City Hall
- Black, Brown, poor white, ALL **oppressed** people **unite**. #ftp #lapd **#ferguson** #lapd **#mikebrown #ezellford** http://t.co/szf3mJRJwV
- Finished **marching** now **gathered** back at LAPD police as organizers speak some truth **#EzellFord #MikeBrown #ferguson** http://t.co/M33n9lMOzC

(a) LA local event I: a protest rally at the LAPD Headquarter.

- Thanks for making my Teenage Dreams come true @arjanwrites!! AHHH **@KATYPERRY**!! (at **@STAPLESCenter** for **Katy Perry**) https://t.co/TVEaghr1Tt
- **Katy perry** with my favorite. http://t.co/FpfPYAQNBR
- @MahoganyLOX are you at the **Katy perry concert**?
- One of the beeeeest **concerts** in history!
- My two minutes of fame was me and my friends picture getting put on the TV screens at the **Katy Perry concert**.

(b) LA local event II: Katy Perry's concert at the Staples Center.

- #beachlife @ Long Beach Shoreline Marina
- Downtown LB at night #DTLB #LBC #Harbor @ The Reef Restaurant
- Jambalaya @ California Pizza Kitchen at Rainbow Harbor http://t.co/9XbDhQAVsN
- #coachtoldmeto @ Octopus Long Beach http://t.co/lYQc8u2m1F
- El Sauz tacos are the GOAT.

(c) LA non-event: enjoying beach life at the Long Beach.

Figure 5: Example geo-topic clusters on LA. The first two are classified as positive local events and the third as negative.

- **Hoboken Fall Arts & Music Festival** with bae @alli_holmes93 @ Washington St. Hoboken
- On Washington Street. (at **Hoboken Music And Arts Festival**) https://t.co/YbLSdZhLZV
- Sweeeeet. Bonavita **Guitars**, at the **Hoboken festival**. http://t.co/2Cw1Qz4UGo
- I'm at **Hoboken Music And Arts Festival** in Hoboken, NJ https://t.co/l4bSM3mrjb
- It's a **festy music** day.

(a) NY local event I: the Hoboken Music and Arts Festival in Hoboken, NJ.

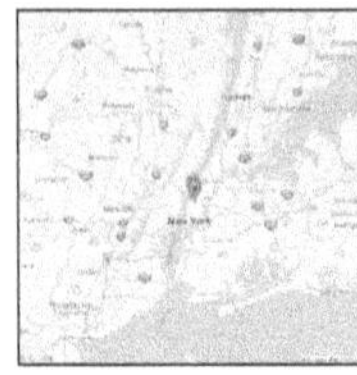

- **Knicks game** w literally a person. http://t.co/hxVYidpCzs
- **Knicks game** with my main man.
- It has been one of my dream to watch **NBA game**!! Let's go! http://t.co/GRJRvFw6vd
- Watching @nyknicks at @TheGarden for for the first time! Go **Knicks**! #nyk4troops
- I was outside of **msg** today pretending I liked the **Knicks**. It's that bad.

(b) NY local event II: The Knicks' basketball game at the Madison Square Garden.

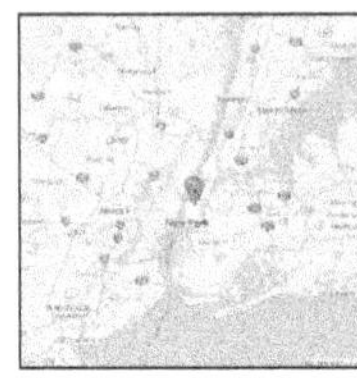

- Happiness is a shroom burger from Shake Shack. @ Shake Shack Times Square http://t.co/tvYqYbsKOo
- Just A Taco in the City ya Know #TimeSquare#DallasBBQ @ Dallas BBQ http://t.co/hyCNkpSrSd
- Craving a lobster roll, aka I must get to RI NOW.
- Rainbow Set Sushi dulu dan menikmati midtown manhattan sebelum kembali ke??? (at Wasabi Sushi & Bento) https://t.co/uC9rt8yCoC
- Pork carnitas tacos & blood orange margaritas w my favorite rican @ Lucys Cantina

(c) NY non-event: having food aroun the Time Square.

Figure 6: Example geo-topic clusters detected on NY. The first two are classified as positive local events; while the third as negative.

cluster is of high quality — the tweets in each cluster are highly geographically compact and semantically coherent. Even if there are tweets discussing about the event with different keywords (*e.g.*, 'shoot', 'justice', and 'protest'), TrioVecEvent can group them into the same cluster. This is because the multimodal embeddings can effectively capture the subtle semantic correlations between the keywords. While the first two clusters are classified as true local events by TrioVecEvent, the last one in Figure 5(c) is marked as negative. Although the last one is also a meaningful geo-topic cluster, it reflects routine activities around the long beach instead of any unusual events. TrioVecEvent is able to capture this fact and classify it into the negative class.

Figure 6(a) and 6(b) show two example local events detected by TrioVecEvent on NY. The first is the Hoboken Arts and Music Festival; and the second is the basketball game between the Knicks and the Hawks. Again, we can see the member tweets are highly relevant both geographically and semantically. As they represent interesting and unusual activities in their respective areas, TrioVecEvent successfully classifies them as true local events. In contrast, the third cluster just reflects the everyday activity of having food around the Time Square, and is returned as a non-event.

To further understand why TrioVecEvent is capable of generating high-quality geo-topic clusters and eliminating non-event candidates, we can re-examine the cases in Figure 1. As shown, the retrieved results based on the learned embeddings are highly meaningful. For instance, given the query 'beach', the top locations are all beach-life areas in LA and NYC; given the location of the airport, the top keywords reflect typical flight-related activities around the airport; and given different keywords as queries, the retrieved keywords are semantically relevant. Such results explain why TrioVecEvent is capable of grouping relevant tweets into the same geo-topic cluster and why the embeddings can serve as useful knowledge for extracting discriminative features (*e.g.*, spatial and temporal unusualness, semantic concentration).

6.3 Quantitative Results

6.3.1 Effectiveness Comparison. Table 2 reports the precision, pseudo recall, and pseudo F1 of all the methods on LA and NY. We find that TrioVecEvent significantly outperforms the baseline methods on both data sets. Compared with the strongest baseline GeoBurst+, TrioVecEvent yields around 118% improvement in precision, 26% improvement in pseudo recall, and 66% improvement in pseudo F1-score. The huge improvements are attributed to the two advantages of TrioVecEvent: (1) the embedding-based clustering model capture short-text semantics more effectively, and generate high-quality geo-topic clusters to achieve a good coverage of all the potential events; and (2) the multimodal embeddings enable the classifier to extract discriminative features for the candidates, and thus accurately pinpoint true local events.

Comparing GeoBurst and its upgraded version GeoBurst+, we find that GeoBurst+ outperforms GeoBurst by a considerable margin. Such a phenomenon further verifies that classification-based candidate filtering is superior to the ranking-based strategy, even with moderately-sized training data. EvenTweet performs much poorer than the other methods on our data. After investigating the results, we find that although EvenTweet can extract

Table 2: The performance of different methods. 'P' is precision, 'R' is pseudo recall; and 'F1' is pseudo F1 score.

Method	LA			NY		
	P	R	F1	P	R	F1
EVENTWEET	0.132	0.212	0.163	0.108	0.196	0.139
GEOBURST	0.282	0.451	0.347	0.212	0.384	0.273
GEOBURST+	0.368	0.483	0.418	0.351	0.465	0.401
TRIOVECEVENT	**0.804**	**0.612**	**0.695**	**0.765**	**0.602**	**0.674**

spatiotemporally bursty keywords in the query window, clustering these keywords merely based on the spatial distributions often leads to semantically irrelevant keywords in the same cluster, which yields suboptimal detection accuracies.

6.3.2 Efficiency Comparison. We proceed to report the efficiency of different methods. Since the time cost of GEOBURST+ is almost the same as GEOBURST, we only show the cost of GEOBURST for brevity. First, we study the convergence rate of the Gibbs sampler for the Bayesian mixture model. For this purpose, we randomly select a three-hour query window, and apply the Bayesian mixture model for extracting geo-topic clusters in the query window. Figure 7(a) shows the log-likelihood as the number of Gibbs sampling iterations increases. We observe that the log-likelihood quickly converges after a few iterations. Hence, it is usually sufficient to set the number of iterations to a relatively small value (*e.g.*, 10) in practice for better efficiency.

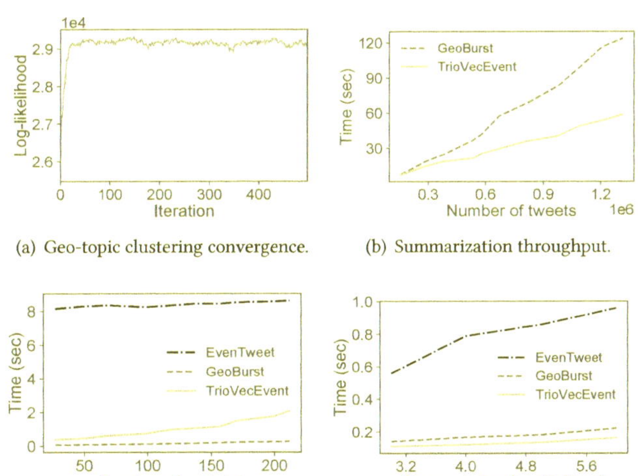

(a) Geo-topic clustering convergence. (b) Summarization throughput.

(c) Online clustering time. (d) Candidate filtering time.

Figure 7: Efficiency study on LA. Figure 7(a) shows the convergence rate of the Bayesian mixture model; Figure 7(b) shows the summarization throughputs for GEOBURST and TRIOVECEVENT; Figure 7(c) shows the cost of online clustering; and Figure 7(d) shows the cost of candidate filtering.

Both GEOBURST and TRIOVECEVENT require summarizing the continuous tweet stream for obtaining background knowledge: the summarization of GEOBURST is done by extending the Clustream algorithm [2]; while that of TRIOVECEVENT is achieved with multimodal embedding. In this set of experiments, we compare the throughputs of the summarization modules in these two methods. Specifically, we apply the two methods to process LA and record the accumulated CPU time for summarization in the process. As depicted in Figure 7(b), the summarization of both methods scales well with the number of tweets, and TRIOVECEVENT is about 50% faster than GEOBURST. Meanwhile, we observe that the embedding learner scales roughly linearly with the number of processed tweets, making it suitable for large-scale tweet streams.

Now we investigate the efficiency of online clustering and candidate filtering for different methods. To this end, we randomly generate 1000 3-hour query window, and continuously shift each query window on a basis of 1, 2, . . ., 10 minutes. In Figure 7(c), we report the averaged running time of different methods in terms of the number of new tweets. As shown, both GEOBURST and TRIOVECEVENT are much more efficient than EVENTWEET, while GEOBURST is the fastest. In terms of candidate filtering, Figure 7(d) reports the running time of the three methods as the query window length changes. Among the three methods, TRIOVECEVENT achieves the best efficiency for candidate filtering. This is because TRIOVECEVENT needs to extract only a small set of features for candidate classification. With the learned multimodal embeddings, all of the features are quite cheap to compute.

6.3.3 Feature Importance. Finally, we measure the importance of different features for candidate classification. Our measurement is based on the Random Forest Classifier, by computing how many times a feature is used for dividing the training samples in the learned tree ensemble. Figure 8 plots the normalized fractions of all the features, where larger values indicate higher importance. As shown, the spatial concentrations turn out to be the most important features on both data sets. This is expected, as a local event usually occurs at a specific point-of-interest, resulting in a geo-topic cluster that is spatially compact. The unusualness measures also serve as important indicators for the classifier, which clearly shows that the embeddings serve as useful knowledge for distinguishing unusual events from routine activities. The other four features (burstiness, semantic concentration, spatiotemporal unusualness, and temporal concentration) act as useful indicators as well, receiving considerable weights for candidate classification.

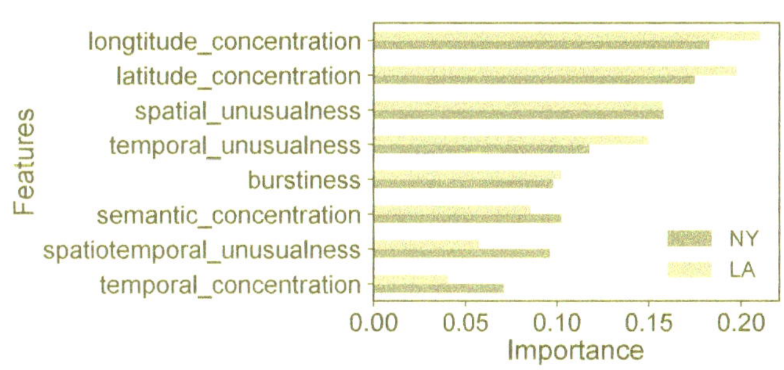

Figure 8: The importance of different features for candidate classification on LA and NY.

7 CONCLUSION

We have proposed the TrioVecEvent method to enable accurate online local event detection in continuous geo-tagged tweet streams. With the multimodal embeddings of the location, time, and text, TrioVecEvent first obtains quality geo-topic clusters in the query window to ensure a high coverage of the underlying events. It then extracts a set of features to characterize the candidates, such that the true local events can be accurately identified. Our extensive experiments have demonstrated that TrioVecEvent improves the accuracy of the state-of-the-art method significantly while achieving good efficiency. In the future, we are interested in extending the method for assigning true local events into fine-grained types, thus allowing the end users to take different actions for different event types.

8 ACKNOWLEDGEMENTS

We would like to thank the reviewers for their insightful comments. This work was sponsored in part by the U.S. Army Research Lab. under Cooperative Agreement No. W911NF-09-2-0053 (NSCTA), National Science Foundation IIS-1017362, IIS-1320617, and IIS-1354329, HDTRA1-10-1-0120, and Grant 1U54GM114838 awarded by NIGMS through funds provided by the trans-NIH Big Data to Knowledge (BD2K) initiative (www.bd2k.nih.gov), and MIAS, a DHS-IDS Center for Multimodal Information Access and Synthesis at UIUC. The views and conclusions contained in this document are those of the authors and should not be interpreted as representing any funding agencies.

REFERENCES

[1] H. Abdelhaq, C. Sengstock, and M. Gertz. Eventweet: Online localized event detection from twitter. *PVLDB*, 6(12):1326–1329, 2013.
[2] C. C. Aggarwal, J. Han, J. Wang, and P. S. Yu. A framework for clustering evolving data streams. In *VLDB*, pages 81–92, 2003.
[3] C. C. Aggarwal and K. Subbian. Event detection in social streams. In *SDM*, pages 624–635, 2012.
[4] J. Allan, R. Papka, and V. Lavrenko. On-line new event detection and tracking. In *SIGIR*, pages 37–45, 1998.
[5] K. Batmanghelich, A. Saeedi, K. Narasimhan, and S. Gershman. Nonparametric spherical topic modeling with word embeddings. In *ACL*, 2016.
[6] D. M. Blei, A. Y. Ng, and M. I. Jordan. Latent dirichlet allocation. *Journal of Machine Learning Research*, 3(1):993–1022, 2003.
[7] L. Cao, M. Wei, D. Yang, and E. A. Rundensteiner. Online outlier exploration over large datasets. In *KDD*, pages 89–98, 2015.
[8] L. Chen and A. Roy. Event detection from flickr data through wavelet-based spatial analysis. In *CIKM*, pages 523–532, 2009.
[9] J. Cranshaw, E. Toch, J. I. Hong, A. Kittur, and N. M. Sadeh. Bridging the gap between physical location and online social networks. In *UbiComp*, pages 119–128, 2010.
[10] S. Doan, B.-K. H. Vo, and N. Collier. An analysis of twitter messages in the 2011 tohoku earthquake. In *Electronic Healthcare*, pages 58–66. Springer, 2012.
[11] W. Feng, C. Zhang, W. Zhang, J. Han, J. Wang, C. Aggarwal, and J. Huang. Streamcube: Hierarchical spatio-temporal hashtag clustering for event exploration over the twitter stream. In *ICDE*, pages 1561–1572, 2015.
[12] J. Foley, M. Bendersky, and V. Josifovski. Learning to extract local events from the web. In *SIGIR*, pages 423–432, 2015.
[13] G. P. C. Fung, J. X. Yu, P. S. Yu, and H. Lu. Parameter free bursty events detection in text streams. In *VLDB*, pages 181–192, 2005.
[14] P. Giridhar, S. Wang, T. F. Abdelzaher, J. George, L. Kaplan, and R. Ganti. Joint localization of events and sources in social networks. In *DCOSS*, pages 179–188, 2015.
[15] S. Gopal and Y. Yang. Von mises-fisher clustering models. In *ICML*, pages 154–162, 2014.
[16] J. Guo and Z. Gong. A nonparametric model for event discovery in the geospatial-temporal space. In *CIKM*, pages 499–508, 2016.
[17] Q. He, K. Chang, and E.-P. Lim. Analyzing feature trajectories for event detection. In *SIGIR*, pages 207–214, 2007.
[18] X. He, H. Zhang, M. Kan, and T. Chua. Fast matrix factorization for online recommendation with implicit feedback. In *SIGIR*, pages 549–558, 2016.
[19] L. Hong, A. Ahmed, S. Gurumurthy, A. J. Smola, and K. Tsioutsiouliklis. Discovering geographical topics in the twitter stream. In *WWW*, pages 769–778, 2012.
[20] W. Kang, A. K. H. Tung, W. Chen, X. Li, Q. Song, C. Zhang, F. Zhao, and X. Zhou. Trendspedia: An internet observatory for analyzing and visualizing the evolving web. In *ICDE*, pages 1206–1209, 2014.
[21] C. C. Kling, J. Kunegis, S. Sizov, and S. Staab. Detecting non-gaussian geographical topics in tagged photo collections. In *WSDM*, pages 603–612, 2014.
[22] J. Krumm and E. Horvitz. Eyewitness: Identifying local events via space-time signals in twitter feeds. In *SIGSPATIAL*, 2015.
[23] C. Li, A. Sun, and A. Datta. Twevent: segment-based event detection from tweets. In *CIKM*, pages 155–164, 2012.
[24] R. Li, K. H. Lei, R. Khadiwala, and K.-C. Chang. Tedas: A twitter-based event detection and analysis system. In *ICDE*, pages 1273–1276, 2012.
[25] S. Liang, E. Yilmaz, and E. Kanoulas. Dynamic clustering of streaming short documents. In *KDD*, pages 995–1004, 2016.
[26] M. Mathioudakis and N. Koudas. Twittermonitor: trend detection over the twitter stream. In *SIGMOD*, pages 1155–1158, 2010.
[27] T. Mikolov, I. Sutskever, K. Chen, G. S. Corrado, and J. Dean. Distributed representations of words and phrases and their compositionality. In *NIPS*, pages 3111–3119, 2013.
[28] K. P. Murphy. *Machine learning: a probabilistic perspective*. MIT press, 2012.
[29] G. Nunez-Antonio and E. Gutiérrez-Pena. A bayesian analysis of directional data using the von mises–fisher distribution. *Communications in StatisticsfiSimulation and Computation®*, 34(4):989–999, 2005.
[30] M. Quezada, V. Peña-Araya, and B. Poblete. Location-aware model for news events in social media. In *SIGIR*, pages 935–938, 2015.
[31] A. Ritter, S. Clark, Mausam, and O. Etzioni. Named entity recognition in tweets: An experimental study. In *EMNLP*, pages 1524–1534, 2011.
[32] T. Sakaki, M. Okazaki, and Y. Matsuo. Earthquake shakes twitter users: real-time event detection by social sensors. In *WWW*, pages 851–860, 2010.
[33] J. Sankaranarayanan, H. Samet, B. E. Teitler, M. D. Lieberman, and J. Sperling. Twitterstand: news in tweets. In *GIS*, pages 42–51, 2009.
[34] S. Sizov. Geofolk: latent spatial semantics in web 2.0 social media. In *WSDM*, pages 281–290, 2010.
[35] W. Wang, H. Yin, L. Chen, Y. Sun, S. W. Sadiq, and X. Zhou. Geo-sage: A geographical sparse additive generative model for spatial item recommendation. In *KDD*, pages 1255–1264, 2015.
[36] K. Watanabe, M. Ochi, M. Okabe, and R. Onai. Jasmine: a real-time local-event detection system based on geolocation information propagated to microblogs. In *CIKM*, pages 2541–2544, 2011.
[37] J. Weng and B.-S. Lee. Event detection in twitter. In *ICWSM*, pages 401–408, 2011.
[38] S. Yao, S. Hu, Y. Zhao, A. Zhang, and T. F. Abdelzaher. Deepsense: A unified deep learning framework for time-series mobile sensing data processing. In *WWW*, pages 351–360, 2017.
[39] J. Yin and J. Wang. A text clustering algorithm using an online clustering scheme for initialization. In *KDD*, pages 1995–2004, 2016.
[40] Z. Yin, L. Cao, J. Han, C. Zhai, and T. S. Huang. Geographical topic discovery and comparison. In *WWW*, pages 247–256, 2011.
[41] Q. Yuan, G. Cong, Z. Ma, A. Sun, and N. M. Thalmann. Who, where, when and what: discover spatio-temporal topics for twitter users. In *KDD*, pages 605–613, 2013.
[42] C. Zhang, K. Zhang, Q. Yuan, H. Peng, Y. Zheng, T. Hanratty, S. Wang, and J. Han. Regions, periods, activities: Uncovering urban dynamics via cross-modal representation learning. In *WWW*, pages 361–370, 2017.
[43] C. Zhang, K. Zhang, Q. Yuan, L. Zhang, T. Hanratty, and J. Han. Gmove: Group-level mobility modeling using geo-tagged social media. In *KDD*, pages 1305–1314, 2016.
[44] C. Zhang, G. Zhou, Q. Yuan, H. Zhuang, Y. Zheng, L. Kaplan, S. Wang, and J. Han. Geoburst: Real-time local event detection in geo-tagged tweet streams. In *SIGIR*, pages 513–522, 2016.
[45] L. Zhao, F. Chen, C.-T. Lu, and N. Ramakrishnan. Multi-resolution spatial event forecasting in social media. In *KDD*, 2016.
[46] L. Zhao, Q. Sun, J. Ye, F. Chen, C. Lu, and N. Ramakrishnan. Multi-task learning for spatio-temporal event forecasting. In *KDD*, pages 1503–1512, 2015.
[47] L. Zhao, J. Ye, F. Chen, C. Lu, and N. Ramakrishnan. Hierarchical incomplete multi-source feature learning for spatiotemporal event forecasting. In *KDD*, pages 2085–2094, 2016.
[48] S. Zhao, T. Zhao, I. King, and M. R. Lyu. Geo-teaser: Geo-temporal sequential embedding rank for point-of-interest recommendation. In *WWW*, pages 153–162, 2017.

Graph Edge Partitioning via Neighborhood Heuristic

Chenzi Zhang*†
University of Hong Kong
czzhang@cs.hku.hk

Fan Wei†
Stanford University
fanwei@stanford.edu

Qin Liu‡
Huawei Noah's Ark Lab
karlqliu@gmail.com

Zhihao Gavin Tang
University of Hong Kong
zhtang@cs.hku.hk

Zhenguo Li§
Huawei Noah's Ark Lab
li.zhenguo@huawei.com

ABSTRACT

We consider the edge partitioning problem that partitions the edges of an input graph into multiple balanced components, while minimizing the total number of vertices replicated (one vertex might appear in more than one partition). This problem is critical in minimizing communication costs and running time for several large-scale distributed graph computation platforms (e.g., PowerGraph, Spark GraphX). We first prove that this problem is NP-hard, and then present a new partitioning heuristic with polynomial running time. We provide a worst-case upper bound of replication factor for our heuristic on general graphs. To our knowledge, we are the first to provide such bound for edge partitioning algorithms on general graphs. Applying this bound to random power-law graphs greatly improves the previous bounds of expected replication factor. Extensive experiments demonstrated that our partitioning algorithm consistently produces much smaller replication factors on various benchmark data sets than the state-of-the-art. When deployed in the production graph engine, PowerGraph, in average it reduces replication factor, communication, and running time by 54%, 66%, and 21%, respectively.

CCS CONCEPTS

• **Information systems → Computing platforms**; • **Mathematics of computing → Graph algorithms**;

KEYWORDS

Graph edge partitioning; distributed graph mining

*Work performed during the author's internship at Noah's Ark Lab, Huawei.
†Equal contribution.
‡Work performed during the author's graduate study at the Chinese University of Hong Kong.
§Corresponding author.

KDD'17, August 13-17, 2017, Halifax, NS, Canada

ACM ISBN 978-1-4503-4887-4/17/08...$15.00
https://doi.org/10.1145/3097983.3098033

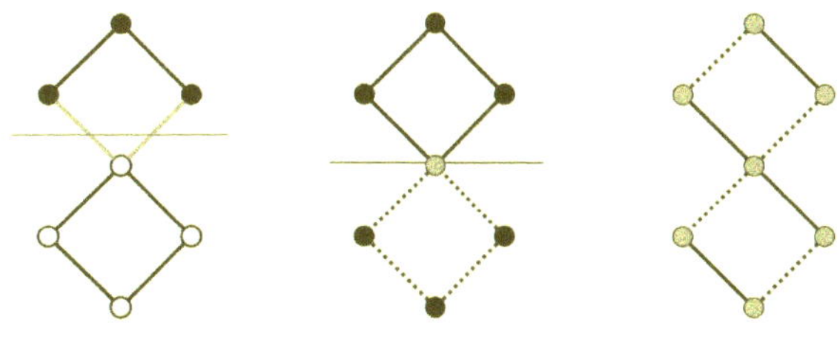

Figure 1: Vertex vs edge partitioning. (a) Ideal vertex partitioning cuts two edges; (b) Ideal edge partitioning cuts only one vertex, Replication Factor=1.14 (solid edges for one partition, dashed edges for the other); (c) Worst edge partitioning, Replication Factor=2.

1 INTRODUCTION

To handle large-scale graphs, distributed graph engines [11, 12, 16] partition the input graph and parallelize the computation on a cluster of machines. A traditional approach to graph partitioning is *vertex partitioning*: a distributed graph engine partitions the vertex set of a graph into balanced partitions such that the number of edges across different partitions is minimized. However, for most of the large real-world graphs, *edge partitioning* (Fig. 1) is found to be more effective in advanced distributed graph engines [6, 7, 16], which evenly assigns edges to machines in a way that minimizes the number of times each vertex is cut (i.e., replicated). Because most real-world graphs (e.g., social networks, web graphs) have *skewed power-law degree distribution*, which means that most vertices have relatively few neighbors while a few have many neighbors (e.g., celebrities on Facebook's social network). The power-law degree distribution can lead to substantial work imbalance in distributed graph systems that adopt vertex partitioning. Since the storage, communication, and computation complexity of a partition is linear in the number of edges in the partition, the running time of each vertex partition can vary widely. Not surprisingly, researchers demonstrated that edge partitioning performs better on many large real-world graphs [6, 7]. This important finding attracts great interests in edge partitioning recently [3, 6, 13, 15, 17].

Edge partitioning has been widely adopted in recent graph systems including PowerGraph [6], Spark GraphX [7], and Chaos [16], to divide the graph across machines. It turns out that the overall system performance depends greatly on the quality of graph partitioning. To understand what makes a good edge partitioning, two issues should be addressed. Firstly, the jobs should be distributed evenly across machines, in order to minimize delay caused by stragglers during each round or superstep of computations. More critically, the communication between machines should be minimized, which is often a bottleneck in graph computing due to the intrinsic dependency and expensive random access in the graph [6]. While it is relatively easy to solve the first issue by partitioning the edges evenly, the second issue can be highly challenging, which asks to minimize the so-called *vertex replication* (Section 2.2) that is caused when two adjacent edges (join at the same vertex) are allocated to different machines.

Quite a few methods have been proposed for edge partitioning. Chaos [16] distributes the edges randomly (RAND) under high network bandwidth. RAND ignores all graph structure and incurs high vertex replication (Section 5). The density-based hashing method (DBH) [17] first partitions the vertices randomly, and then assigns each edge (x, y) by following one of its end vertices (i.e., x and y) of smaller degree. DBH can exploit the skewed degree distribution of power-law graphs, but it leverages little graph structure, like RAND. Oblivious [6] is a streaming algorithm that considers the distribution of previously assigned edges when assigning an incoming edge – an edge is more likely to be assigned to the partition with more adjacent edges. HDRF [15] is another streaming algorithm that extends Oblivious by further exploiting the power-law degree distribution, like DBH. Both HDRF and Oblivious rely only on historical data, and thus use the graph structure only partially. Sheep [13] partitions the graph in a divide and conquer manner, which uses more graph structure than Oblivious and HDRF, but it works well only for tree-like graphs. Those methods mentioned above, due to their not attempting to exploit the graph structure, typically yield high replication factor. The notable multi-level vertex partitioning algorithm METIS [8] is extended for edge partitioning [3], which makes full access to the graph structure by partitioning the graph entirely in memory. This does lead to the state-of-the-art replication factors on a great number of graphs [13], but it is not applicable to large graphs.

In this paper, we present a heuristic called *NE (Neighbor Expansion)* that is developed based on a new, theoretically sound partitioning model that greedily maximizes edge locality. Our main contributions are summarized as follows:

- We establish theoretical understanding of the edge partitioning problem, including proving its NP-hardness and showing that every graph can be p-edge partitioned with replication factor $O(\sqrt{p})$.
- We propose a new edge partitioning heuristic called NE, and provide a worst-case upper bound of replication factor for our heuristic on general graphs. To the best of our knowledge, we are the first to provide such bound for edge partitioning algorithms on general graphs. We also show that it improves over existing bounds on random power-law graphs. We conduct extensive experiments which show that it significantly reduces the replication factor.
- We apply our partitioner to a distributed graph engine, PowerGraph. In average it reduces replication factor, communication, and running time by 54%, 66%, and 21%, respectively.

2 GRAPH EDGE PARTITIONING

In this section, we first formalize the graph edge partitioning problem. We then show it is NP-hard and prove a sharp bound of replication factors (Section 2.2) for general graphs.

2.1 Notation

Let $G = (V, E)$ be an undirected, unweighted graph with $n = |V|$ vertices and $m = |E|$ edges. An edge connecting vertices x and y is denoted as (x, y) or $e_{x,y}$. For a vertex x, denote by $N(x) = \{y | (x, y) \in E\}$ the set of vertices adjacent to x. For a vertex set S, denote by $N(S) = \cup_{x \in S} N(x)$ and $E_S = \{(x, y) \in E : x, y \in S\}$. For an integer $p \geq 2$, denote by $[p] = \{1, 2, \ldots, p\}$. For an edge set E_i, denote $V(E_i) = \{x | \{x, y\} \in E_i\}$ as the set of vertices covered by E_i.

2.2 Problem Statement

A p-edge partitioning of G refers to a disjoint partitioning of its edge set E into p subsets E_i, such that $E_i \subseteq E, \cup_{i \in [p]} E_i = E$, and $E_i \cap E_j = \emptyset$ for $i \neq j$. A p-edge partitioning is α-balanced if

$$\max_{i \in [p]} \{|E_i|\} \leq \lceil \alpha |E| / p \rceil. \quad (1)$$

The *replication factor* [3] of a partitioning is defined as

$$\mathrm{RF}(E_1, \ldots, E_p) := \frac{1}{|V|} \sum_{i \in [p]} |V(E_i)|. \quad (2)$$

Definition 1 (MIN-RF(p, α)). *The MIN-RF(p, α) problem is to find an α-balanced p-edge partitioning $\{E_i\}_{i \in [p]}$ to minimize the replication factor RF$(E_1, \ldots, E_p)$.*

2.3 NP-Hardness

The p-edge partitioning problem has been proved to be NP-hard in [3] when p grows with $n = |V|$. To our best knowledge, it has not been proved elsewhere that this problem is NP-hard when p is constant[1]. We fill this gap and give the following NP-hardness result (proof in Appendix A).

Theorem 2.1. *For any $\alpha \geq 1, p \geq 2$, the MIN-RF(p, α) problem is NP-hard with respect to the number of vertices. In particular, the MIN-RF$(2, \alpha)$ problem is NP-hard.*

2.4 Bound for General Graphs

In this section, we show that it is always possible to achieve $O(\sqrt{p})$ replication factor for any MIN-RF(p, α) problem (though it may take exponentially long time to find such a partitioning). We also show that this bound is tight up to constant factors. These results mean that $O(\sqrt{p})$ is the best replication factor we can hope for if we are dealing with general graphs. However, for certain graphs like power-law graphs, it is possible to obtain a tighter bound (Section 4.2).

[1] In [3], the NP-hardness is proved by a reduction from 3-partition problem. When p is constant, the 3-partition problem, hence the derived edge partitioning problem, is polynomial time solvable.

Lemma 2.2. *For any graph G and any positive integer p, there always exists a 1-balanced p-edge partitioning such that the replication factor is at most $2\sqrt{p} + \frac{p}{n}$, which is $2\sqrt{p} + o(1)$ if $p = o(n)$.*

Proof. We first prove the following claim.

Claim 1. *Given any graph H with t vertices and m edges, and let k be a positive integer, there must exist a subset of vertices U such that $|U| \leq \frac{t-1}{\sqrt{k}} + 1$, and the number of edges in the induced subgraph by U is at least m/k.*

Proof. We use an averaging argument. Consider all subsets of size $l = \frac{t-1}{\sqrt{k}} + 1$. If none of them is such that the induced graph on the vertex set has more than m/k edges, we would have $\sum_{U \subset V(H):|U|=l} |E(U)| \leq m/k \cdot \binom{t}{l}$. On the other hand, each edge in H is counted in $\binom{t-2}{l-2}$ vertex sets of cardinality l. Therefore we have $\sum_{U \subset V(H):|U|=l} |E(U)| = m \cdot \binom{t-2}{l-2}$. Combining the two formulas above, we have

$$m/k \cdot \binom{t}{l} \geq m \cdot \binom{t-2}{l-2},$$

which is equivalent to $t(t-1)/l(l-1) \geq k$. However, $l > t/\sqrt{k}$, which means

$$\frac{t(t-1)}{l(l-1)} < \left(\frac{t-1}{l-1}\right)^2 = k. \qquad \square$$

Given the claim, in $G_0 = G$, we can find a vertex set U_1 such that the number of edges induced by U_1, i.e., the number of edges in $G_0[U_1]$ is at least $|E(G_0)|/p$. By the claim, we know $|U_1| \leq \frac{n-1}{\sqrt{p}} + 1$. Then we remove $|E(G_0)|/p$ edges in $G_0[U_1]$ from G_0, obtaining G_1. By a similar argument, we can find a vertex set U_2 such that the number of edges induced by U_2, i.e., the number of edges in $G_1[U_2]$ is at least $|E(G_1)|/(p-1) = |E(G)|/p$. By the claim, we know $|U_2| \leq \frac{n-1}{\sqrt{p-1}} + 1$. Removing $|E(G_1)|/(p-1)$ edges in $G_1[U_2]$ from G_1, obtaining G_2. Repeating this process, eventually we have obtained $U_1, U_2, \ldots, U_p$ that exhaust all the edges in G, while

$$|U_i| \leq \frac{n-1}{\sqrt{p-(i-1)}} + 1.$$

Therefore the replication factor is

$$\sum_{1 \leq i \leq p} |U_i|/n \leq \frac{1}{n} \sum_{1 \leq i \leq p} \left(\frac{n-1}{\sqrt{p-(i-1)}} + 1 \right) \leq 2\sqrt{p} + \frac{p}{n}. \qquad \square$$

Remark 1. *For a graph, the lemma gives a 1-balanced p-partitioning, which is also a valid partitioning of MIN-RF(p,α) problem for $\alpha \geq 1$.*

Lemma 2.3. *There exists a graph such that the replication factor is at least $\sqrt{p/2}\sqrt{(n-1)/n} = \sqrt{p/2}(1 - o_n(1))$ for any 2-balanced partitioning.*

The proof also generalizes to α-partitioning for any $\alpha \geq 1$.

Proof. Consider a complete graph on n vertices. After partitioning into p parts, we have the vertex sets being $V_1, \ldots, V_p$. Suppose $|V_i| = n_i$ and the edges in the i-th machine is e_i. Therefore $\binom{n_i}{2} \geq e_i$, which means $n_i \geq \sqrt{2e_i}$. We know $\sum_{i=1}^{p} e_i = \binom{n}{2}$ and $e_i \leq 2\binom{n}{2}/p$ by the definition of 2-balancedness. Therefore

$$\sum_{i=1}^{p} n_i \geq \sum_{i=1}^{p} \sqrt{2e_i} \geq p/2 \cdot \sqrt{2 \cdot 2\binom{n}{2}/p} = \sqrt{p/2}\sqrt{n(n-1)},$$

where the last inequality is by Jensen inequality. Thus the replication factor is at least

$$\frac{1}{n}\sum_{i=1}^{p} n_i \geq \frac{1}{n}\sqrt{p/2}\sqrt{n(n-1)} = \sqrt{p/2}\sqrt{(n-1)/n}. \qquad \square$$

3 ALGORITHM

In this section, we propose a new edge partitioning algorithm, which partitions the graph iteratively in p rounds. In each round, one edge set is generated (for one machine). Specifically, in round i, edge set E_i is selected from the working graph G_i containing all un-assigned edges so far, i.e., $G_i = (V, E \setminus \cup_{j<i} E_j)$. Empty initially, E_i is expanded in steps until $|E_i| > \alpha m/p$. In each step, one vertex x is selected according to a neighbor expansion heuristic discussed below. Then, adjacent edges of x are added to E_i, and x is added to *core set* C. *Boundary set* $S = V(E_i)$ is the vertex set covered by E_i. Since edges covered by S are not necessarily in E_i, we also add those edges to E_i without increasing vertex replication. The above step is repeated until $|E_i| > \alpha m/p$. We now elaborate the heuristic to select the core vertex x.

Neighbor Expansion. By construction the core set C is always contained in the boundary set S. In case $S \setminus C = \emptyset$, x is picked randomly from $V \setminus C$. Otherwise, it is selected as follows,

$$x := \arg\min_{v \in S \setminus C} |N(v) \setminus S|.$$

The objective $|N(v) \setminus S|$ is the number of vertices that will be assigned to machine i, if v is selected as core vertex and its adjacent edges are added to E_i. Our heuristic is to select x to minimize the number of vertices to be added to the boundary set S, thereby to minimize the increment of replication factor due to adjacent edges of x.

Example. We illustrate one step of our algorithm in Fig. 2. The left and right figures stand for the graph before and after this step. Allocated edges are denoted in solid line and edges in dashed line have not been allocated yet. At the beginning, there are 2 vertices in the core set C, 4 vertices in the boundary set S, and there are 4 allocated edges. Now we need to choose the next core vertex to expand the core set C. Among the candidates $S \setminus C = \{x, z\}$, vertex x is selected because $|N(x) \setminus S| = 1 < |N(z) \setminus S| = 3$. Then, vertex x is added to C and S, and its neighbor y is added to S. Two edges $e_{x,y}$ and $e_{y,z}$ are allocated in this step.

We summarize our heuristic in Algorithm 1, where for ease of presentation the sub-routine of core set update and boundary set update is described in Algorithm 2.

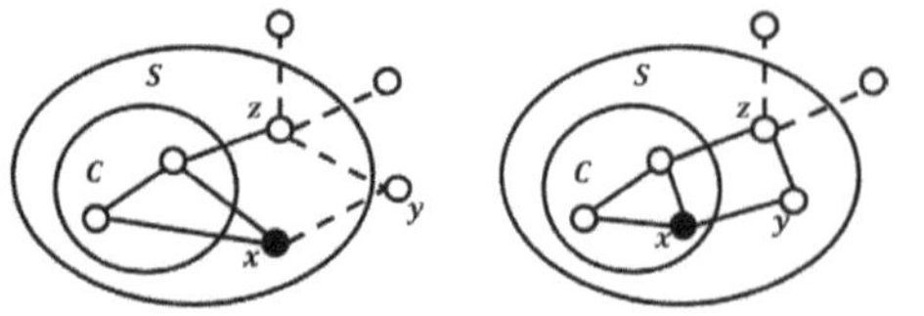

Figure 2: Illustrating a step in our algorithm. Left: a core vertex x is selected. Right: the core vertex set C, the boundary vertex set S, and the edge set E_i are updated.

Algorithm 1 Generate one edge partition E_k.

1: **procedure** EXPAND(E, δ) ▷ $\delta = \alpha m/p$
2: $C, S, E_k \leftarrow \emptyset$
3: **while** $|E_k| \le \delta$ **do**
4: **if** $S \setminus C = \emptyset$ **then**
5: x is selected randomly in $V \setminus C$
6: **else**
7: $x \leftarrow \arg\min_{v \in S \setminus C} |N(v) \setminus S|$
8: ALLOCEDGES(C, S, E_k, x)

Algorithm 2 Allocate edges for core vertex x.

1: **procedure** ALLOCEDGES(C, S, E_k, x)
2: $C \leftarrow C \cup \{x\}, S \leftarrow S \cup \{x\}$
3: **for** $y \in N(x) \setminus S$ **do**
4: $S \leftarrow S \cup \{y\}$
5: **for** $z \in N(y) \cap S$ **do**
6: $E_k \leftarrow E_k \cup \{e_{y,z}\}$
7: $E \leftarrow E \setminus \{e_{y,z}\}$
8: **if** $|E_k| > \delta$ **then return**

4 ANALYSIS

4.1 Upper bound of replication factor

We analyze the replication factor for Algorithm 1. Let $S_k = V(E_k)$ be the covered vertex set when the algorithm terminates for partition k. To the best of our knowledge, we are the first to provide a worst-case upper bound of replication factor on general graphs.

THEOREM 4.1. *Suppose G has no isolated vertex, and let E_i's be the edge sets produced by Algorithm 1 solving MIN-RF(p, α) and $S_i = V(E_i)$. Then, we have*

$$RF = \frac{1}{n} \sum_{i \in [p]} |S_i| \le \frac{1}{n} \left(\frac{3}{2}|E| + \frac{1}{2}\sigma + p - 1 \right), \tag{3}$$

where σ is the number of connected components in the original graph.

REMARK 2. *A trivial bound for the replication factor is $\frac{1}{n}\sum_{i \in [p]} |S_i| \le \frac{2|E|}{n}$ as each edge corresponds to 2 vertices. To our best knowledge, our bound is the first improvement for general graphs that brings down the constant from 2 to 3/2.*

PROOF. Observe that Alg. 1 contains p rounds of iterations. In the i-th iteration, a new vertex in $S_i \setminus C_i$ is added to the core C_i and some edges are added to E_i until $|E_i| > \frac{\alpha m}{k}$. Recall $S_i = V(E_i)$. We analyze how these variables change as the number of steps t increase. We rename the variables and sets above in terms of t for convenience. Let $s_0 = 0$. At each step $t \ge 1$, a new vertex is added to the core C_{s_t}. Thus $1 \le s_t \le p$. Let $C_{i,t}, S_{i,t}$, and $E_{i,t}$ be the sets C_i, S_i, E_i at the beginning of step t respectively. Let σ_t be the number of connected components of $G_t = G \setminus \bigcup_{j=1}^{p} E_{j,t}$ removing the isolated vertices. Let $|G_t|$ be the number of edges in G_t.

We define a potential function $\Phi_t = \frac{3}{2}|G_t| + \frac{1}{2}\sigma_t + p - s_t + \sum_{i \in [p]} |S_{i,t}|$. Initially, all $S_{i,0} = \emptyset$. We will show that when the algorithm terminates at $t = T$, $\Phi_T \le \Phi_0$. We show this by showing (1) $\Phi_1 \le \Phi_0$, and (2) $\Phi_t \le \Phi_{t-1}$ or $\Phi_t \le \Phi_{t-2}$. For simplicity, denote $s_t = i$. Define the difference operator Δ as $\Delta(\cdot) = (\cdot)_{t+1} - (\cdot)_t$. In step t, a vertex x is added to $C_{i,t}$; then one of the four following cases happens. Let k be the number of x's adjacent edges added to $E_{i,t}$, and let h be the number of non-adjacent edges of x added to $E_{i,t}$. We analyze Φ_t in each of the cases.

C1. *When $E_{i,t}$ is full (i.e., the i-th machine is full); x is the first vertex added to $S_{i+1,t+1}$:* Thus $s_{t+1} = s_t + 1$. Counting x and k of its adjacent neighbor vertices, we have $\Delta|S_{i+1}| = k + 1$. The total number of edges allocated is $\Delta|G| = -(k+h)$. However, $\Delta\sigma \le k + h$ as deleting each edge can increase the number of connected components by at most 1. Then we have $\Delta\Phi = \frac{3}{2}\Delta|G| + \frac{1}{2}\Delta\sigma - \Delta s + \Delta|S_{i+1}| \le -\frac{3(k+h)}{2} + \frac{k+h}{2} - 1 + (1+k) = -h \le 0$. (thus $\Phi_1 \le \Phi_0$).

C2. *When $E_{i,t}$ is not full; $x \in S_{i,t} \setminus C_{i,t}$. At the end of step $t+1$, there are still edges in the same connected component as x in G_t not assigned:* Similarly $\Delta|G| = -(k+h)$, $\Delta\sigma_t \le k + h$, and $\Delta|S_{i,t}| = k$. Hence, $\Delta\Phi = \frac{3}{2}\Delta|G| + \frac{1}{2}\Delta\sigma + \Delta|S_i| \le -\frac{3(k+h)}{2} + \frac{k+h}{2} + k = -h \le 0$.

C3. *When $E_{i,t}$ is not full; $x \in S_{i,t} \setminus C_{i,t}$. At the end of step $t+1$, all edges in the same connected component as x in G_t are assigned to $E_{i,t}$:* We have $\Delta|G| = -(h+k)$ and $\Delta|S_i| = k$. By assumption, this step removes fully in G_t the connected component containing x, meaning $\Delta\sigma = -1$. Therefore $\Delta\Phi = \frac{3}{2}\Delta|G| + \frac{1}{2}\Delta\sigma + \Delta|S_i| = -\frac{3(k+h)}{2} - \frac{1}{2} + k \le -\frac{k+1}{2} \le 0$.

C4. *When $E_{i,t}$ is not full but $S_{i,t} \setminus C_{i,t} = \emptyset$. Thus x is a random node chosen in Step 5:* Notice this case happens only when previous step is in Case 3. Similarly $\Delta|G| = -(k+h)$, $\Delta\sigma \le k + h$ and $\Delta|S_i| = k + 1$. Note that Φ will not decrease in this step. However, if take into consideration $\Phi_t - \Phi_{t-1} \le \frac{-(k'+1)}{2}$ for $k' \ge 1$, we have $\Phi_{t+1} - \Phi_{t-1} = (\Phi_{t+1} - \Phi_t) + (\Phi_t - \Phi_{t-1}) \le \left(\frac{-3(k+h)}{2} + \frac{k+h}{2} + 1 + k\right) + \left(\frac{-(k'+1)}{2}\right) \le 0$.

Moreover, right before Alg. 1 terminates, we are in Case 3. Therefore $\Phi_T - \Phi_{T-1} \le \frac{-(k+1)}{2} \le -1$. Furthermore, since $\Phi_{T-1} \le \Phi_0$, we have that $\Phi_T \le \Phi_0 - 1$. In other words $\Phi_0 = \frac{3}{2}|G_0| + \frac{1}{2}\sigma + p \ge \Phi_{\text{end}} + 1 = \sum_{i \in [p]} |S_i| + 1$, which finishes the proof. □

We construct the following example, showing that the analysis for Algorithm 1 (Theorem 4.1) is tight.

Example. In this example, our algorithm is required to partition the edges (in Fig. 3) into four parts. In the worst case, the edge set E_1 can be selected as the green edges, by first including the two green edges in the first line and then the middle edge in the second line. Similarly, E_2, E_3, E_4 may be partitioned as the blue, brown, and red edges respectively. In this case, $|E| = 12, \sigma = 6, p = 4$, while $|S_{\text{green}}| = |S_{\text{blue}}| = |S_{\text{red}}| = |S_{\text{brown}}| = 6$. Hence $\sum_i |S_i| = 24 = \frac{3}{2} \cdot 12 + \frac{1}{2} \cdot 6 + 4 - 1 = \frac{3}{2}|E| + \frac{1}{2}\sigma + p - 1$, which achieves equality in Theorem 4.1. This example can be easily extended to any p.

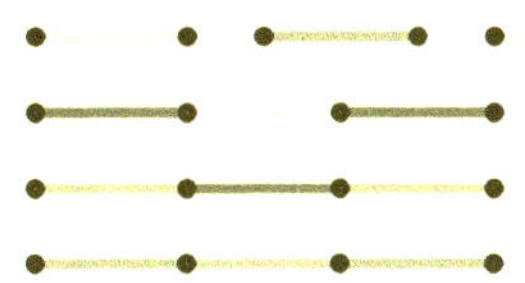

Figure 3: Bound in Theorem 4.1 is tight.

4.2 Upper bound for random power-law graphs

Prior to this work, DBH [17] and HDRF [15] give upper bounds of expected replication factor of their graph edge partitioners for random power-law graphs. In this section, we apply Theorem 4.1 to give an improved numerical upper bound of replication factor for a "typical" random power-law graph, and compare our upper bound with the existing ones in literature.

Power-law graphs specify the degree distribution in the way that the fraction of k-degree vertices p_k is proportional to $k^{-\tau}e^{-k/\kappa}$, where τ and κ are constants. $\tau > 2$ controls the skewness of the distribution, and κ gives a soft upper bound of the vertex degree, i.e., p_k decreases exponentially when $k \geq \kappa$.

To apply Theorem 4.1, we need to estimate the expectation of $|E|/n$ and σ/n. Here we apply the elegant treatment of random power-law graphs by Newman [14] using generating functions, and derive the expected number of connected components and the expected number of edges. Recall that a generating function carries a sequence of numbers as coefficients of a series expansion. The following is a generating function that carries the degree distribution,

$$G_0(x) = \sum_{k=1}^{\infty} p_k x^k,$$

where $p_k = Ck^{-\tau}e^{-k/\kappa}$, with C being a normalization constant so that $G_0(1) = 1$.

Computing $\mathbb{E}[|E|/n]$. We can calculate the expectation of $|E|/n$ as $\mathbb{E}\left[\frac{|E|}{n}\right] = 1/2 \sum_{k\geq 1} kp_k = 1/2 G_0'(1)$.

Computing $\mathbb{E}[\sigma/n]$. We now estimate the term $\mathbb{E}[\sigma/n]$. When $\tau > 2$, it is almost sure that the graph is not fully connected [14]; when $2 < \tau < 3.4785$ and $\kappa \to \infty$, besides small connected components the graph contains a giant component of constant fraction of vertices [1]. To give a quantitative argument, we define the following terms. If we pick an edge and go to one of its end vertices uniformly at random, then the probability $\hat{q}_k$ that the end vertex has degree k is proportional to kp_k. Let $q_k = \hat{q}_{k+1}$ be the probability that the end vertex has outgoing degree k, not counting the edge we come from. This sequence q_k is expressed in the following generating function

$$G_1(x) = \sum_{k=0}^{\infty} q_k x^k = \sum_{k=1}^{\infty} \hat{q}_k x^{k-1} = \frac{\sum_{k=1}^{\infty} kp_k x^{k-1}}{\sum_{k=1}^{\infty} kp_k} = \frac{G_0'(x)}{G_0'(1)},$$

where the last two steps normalize the sequence so that $G_1(1) = 1$. We study the size of a component reached by choosing a random

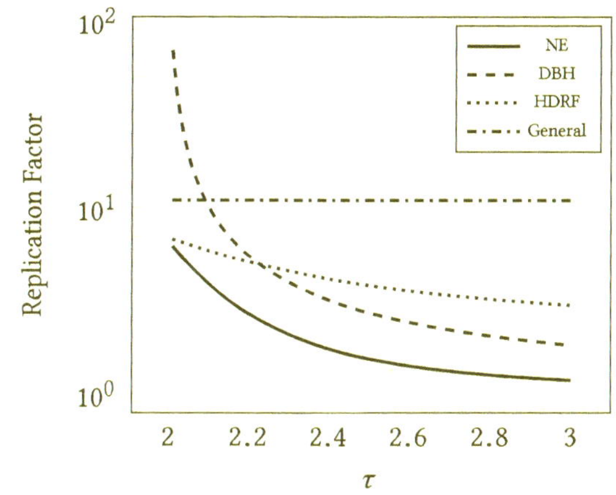

Figure 4: Theoretical bounds of NE, DBH, HDRF and the bound (Lemma 2.2) for general graphs ($p = 30$).

edge and following it to one of its ends. Let $H_1(x)$ be the generating function for the component size distribution, excluding the giant one, i.e., $H_1(x) = a \cdot 0 + \sum t_k x^k$, where a is the probability that this edge leads to the giant component, and t_k is the probability that this edge leads to a small component of size k. Here we follow Newman's assumption [14] that there is no loop in the small components. Hence we have

$$H_1(x) = a \cdot 0 + xq_0 + xq_1 H_1(x) + xq_2[H_1(x)]^2 + \ldots \quad ,$$

and thus

$$H_1(x) = xG_1(H_1(x)). \tag{4}$$

Combining $H_1(1) + a = 1$ and $H_1(1) = G_1(H_1(1))$ we can solve $G_1(1-a) = 1 - a$ for $a \in (0,1)$. Knowing a, we can approximate $H_1(x)$ by solving Equation 4 numerically for the first few hundred terms. Similarly, if we start with a randomly chosen vertex, the size of the small component reached by this vertex is encoded by the generating function

$$H_0(x) = xG_0(H_1(x)) = \sum_{k=2}^{\infty} h_k x^k.$$

The term $\mathbb{E}[\sigma/n]$ can be expressed as

$$\mathbb{E}\left[\frac{\sigma}{n}\right] = \frac{1}{n} + \sum_{k\geq 2} \frac{h_k}{k},$$

where the first term $1/n$ stands for the giant component. As we can numerically compute the first few hundred coefficients of $H_1(x)$, we can numerically compute the coefficients for $H_0(x)$, which are the h_k's.

Expected Upper Bound. Plugging $\mathbb{E}[\sigma/n]$ and $\mathbb{E}[|E|/n]$ into the bound in Theorem 4.1, we obtain an upper bound of expected replication factor for a random power-law graph.

Comparison with Existing Bounds. Let us compare our theoretical bounds with the ones in literature. Prior to ours, DBH [17] and HDRF [15] give upper bounds of expected replication factor for random power-law graphs. In HDRF [15], an average-case analysis

Table 1: Real-world graphs.

Graph	Alias	$\|V\|$	$\|E\|$
com-LiveJournal	LJ	3,997,962	34,681,189
com-Orkut	Orkut	3,072,441	117,185,083
Twitter [9]	TW	41,652,230	1,468,364,884
com-Friendster	FS	65,608,366	1,806,067,135
uk-union [2]	UK	133,633,040	5,507,679,822

is applied to their streaming method to give a bound for power-law graphs. In DBH [17], an upper bound on expected replication factor is derived for their randomized algorithm. However, they only study the case when $\kappa \to \infty$. To apply these bounds, we let $\kappa = \infty$, and consider the graph $n = 10^6$, i.e. set $p_k = 0$ for $k > 10^6$. The results in Fig. 4 indicate that our upper bound is consistently lower than theirs for $\tau \in (2,3)$ with a wide margin. We also plot the general bound derived in Lemma 2.2. As expected, it is worse than the bound we derived in this section that relies on special properties of random power-law graphs.

5 EXPERIMENTAL RESULTS

In this section, we evaluate our *neighbor expansion (NE)* algorithm and compare it against other state-of-the-art partitioners.

To evaluate a partitioner, we consider the following metrics: *workload balance, replication factor,* and *time consumption.* For workload balance, we ensure results of each partitioner are 1.1-balanced and do not report the detailed values. We compare the replication factor and running time in Section 5.1. Since one important application of edge-partitioning algorithms is to partition graphs for distributed graph processing systems, we also evaluate whether the given partitioner can reduce the communication cost and execution time on distributed graph processing systems like PowerGraph [6] and PowerLyra [4] in Section 5.2.

Testbed. We evaluate all partitioners and run graph analytic applications (Section 5.2) on a cluster of nine machines, each with 24 Intel E5-2620 2.40 GHz cores and 125 GB RAM connected via Gigabit Ethernet.

Datasets. Five real-world benchmark graphs of various scales are used for our evaluation. Most of the graphs can be found in SNAP [10]. The statistics of the graphs are listed in Table 1.

Competing partitioners. We compare our NE algorithm with six existing edge partitioners, including METIS [8], RAND [6], DBH [17], Oblivious [6], HDRF [15], and Sheep [13]. **METIS** is the state-of-the-art method for vertex partitioning which minimizes edge cut and balances user-defined vertex weight. One can turn a vertex-partitioner into an edge-partitioner while preserving its performance [3]. To transform METIS to an edge-partitioner, we first call METIS with the vertex weight equal to its degree. Then based on the vertex partitioning produced by METIS, each edge is randomly assigned to one of its adjacent vertices' partition. For **Oblivious** and **HDRF**, following [15], we feed the edges in a random order, to balance the resulting partitions.

Table 2: Replication factors for real-world graphs ($p = 30,\ \alpha = 1.1$).

	LJ	Orkut	TW	FS	UK
METIS	2.16	5.24	-	-	-
RAND	8.27	19.48	11.68	11.84	15.99
DBH	5.18	11.97	3.67	6.88	5.14
Oblivious	3.43	6.94	8.60	8.82	2.03
HDRF	3.33	7.27	7.90	8.87	1.62
Sheep	3.33	7.94	2.34	4.45	1.29
NE	**1.55**	**2.48**	**1.88**	**1.98**	**1.04**

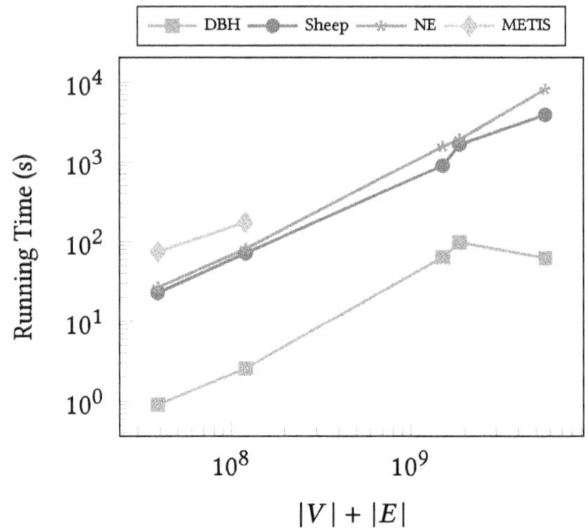

Figure 5: Running time of different partitioning methods.

5.1 Experiments on real-world graphs

In this section, we compare the performance of partitioners on real-world graphs.

Replication factor. As shown in Table 2, our NE algorithm[2] outperforms all existing methods with large margins. Among existing partitioners, METIS gives the lowest replication factor which is consistent with literature [3, 13]. However, METIS runs out of memory when partitioning the Twitter, Friendster and UK-union graphs on our 125 GB RAM machine. This result also echoes the fact reported by [13].

Running time. Fig. 5 plots the running time of all partitioners for a variety of input graphs. As expected, DBH is the fastest since they only scan the input graph once. We did not report the running time of RAND, Oblivious and HDRF since they are integrated in PowerGraph and we cannot get the standalone running time. But their performance should be similar to DBH since they all scan the input graph once sequentially [17]. Using only a single thread, NE and Sheep [13] have similar running time. But Sheep can be speeded up significantly by multi-threading, which is not directly applicable to NE due to the difference in memory access pattern.

[2]Since there is randomness in the NE algorithm, we report the average replication factor, with relative standard error less than 1%.

Table 3: Replication factor, network communication cost (GB), and running time (second) for distributed graph mining.

Task	Graph	PowerGraph + RAND			PowerGraph + Oblivious			PowerLyra + Hybrid_Ginger			PowerGraph + NE		
		RF	Comm.	Time	RF	Comm.	Time	RF	Comm.	Time	RF	Comm.	Time
PageRank	LJ	4.81	40.51	101.07	3.25	26.37	80.77	2.98	12.24	43.12	**1.35**	**3.65**	**39.23**
	Orkut	8.04	54.65	123.37	5.79	37.05	94.67	5.99	25.63	64.90	**1.75**	**6.66**	**44.93**
	TW	6.18	509.96	851.30	2.43	209.46	335.53	2.76	152.25	311.40	**1.38**	**51.45**	**297.97**
	FS	5.39	768.33	1183.90	3.40	411.82	670.10	3.60	294.54	589.24	**1.48**	**92.16**	**392.70**
	UK	6.89	1535.57	2582.93	1.86	540.48	764.10	2.12	386.41	759.26	**1.02**	**55.89**	**554.77**
Triangle Count	LJ	4.81	4.10	3.90	3.25	3.05	3.01	2.99	3.76	3.02	**1.35**	**0.88**	**1.39**
	Orkut	8.04	9.24	9.93	5.79	7.59	8.08	6.02	11.69	10.41	**1.75**	**2.53**	**4.36**
	TW	6.18	91.63	154.73	2.43	56.52	**119.97**	2.74	97.77	188.36	**1.38**	**30.45**	154.91
	FS	5.39	128.12	138.05	3.40	99.22	111.82	3.60	152.69	234.71	**1.48**	**41.29**	**84.18**
	UK	6.89	344.13	2166.17	1.86	157.32	185.54	2.13	299.49	1207.06	**1.02**	**72.34**	**166.07**

5.2 Experiments on graph analytics

Table 3 compares our NE algorithm against two partitioners, RAND and Oblivious, in PowerGraph and one partitioner, Hybrid_Ginger, in PowerLyra, in terms of replication factor, communication cost, and execution time for running the PageRank (100 iterations) and triangle counting applications on a cluster of nine machines. Each result reported in Table 3 is an average of three runs to ensure that their relative standard error is less than 5%. We observe that the communication cost is closely related to the replication factor, roughly as a linear function. This is not surprising because replication factor is designed to model the communication cost. Our NE algorithm optimizes the replication factor and successfully reduces the communication cost for all cases.

Running time depends on replication factor in a similar pattern. For most cases, a reduction of replication factor (hence the communication cost) means a reduction in running time. The only exception is the triangle counting application on Twitter graph. In this case, comparing the NE and the Oblivious methods, we find that a reduction of replication factor dose not reduce the running time. Based on our understanding of the PowerGraph system, this may be explained by several factors. One factor is that, in PowerGraph, the computation and network communication happen concurrently, so the reduction of the communication cost can only reduce the running time when the network communication is the bottleneck of the whole system. Another factor is the potential unbalanced computation workload on each machine. For each vertex with multiple replicas in PowerGraph, one replica is nominated as the master, while others are mirrors. The computation in PowerGraph is conducted on each edge and each master replica. Since our algorithm only guarantees the edge partitioning is balanced, the unbalanced allocation of master replicas may cause congestion on some machines.

In conclusion, compared with other existing methods, our partitioner NE successfully reduces the communication cost for all graphs and reduces the running time for most graphs. In average[3] NE reduces replication factor, communication, and running time by 54%, 66%, and 21%, respectively.

[3]We report the average decrease of ten cases (five from PageRank and five from triangle counting). Each decrease is calculated as $(y-x)/y$, where x is the value of NE and y is the lowest value of existing methods.

6 CONCLUSION AND FUTURE WORK

In this paper, we proposed a new graph edge partitioner Neighbor Expansion (NE) that outperforms other state-of-the-art ones including METIS [8] and Sheep [13] in terms of replication factors. Applying the NE algorithm to distributed graph mining effectively reduces communication cost and running time for applications such as PageRank and triangle counting.

Our algorithm can be further improved in several aspects. Firstly, it will be very interesting if any theoretical approximation results can be proved for the NE algorithm, to explain its good performance in the experiments. Secondly, we might need new data structures to support the NE heuristic in a distributed, multi-thread environment. Thirdly, the NE algorithm needs to load the whole graph edge set in main memory, while other methods like Sheep or DBH only store vertex set. For instance, our implementation of NE takes about 90 GB RAM to partition uk-union [2]. We have made some preliminary attempts to extend the NE algorithm to a streaming algorithm via sampling methods (Appendix B), which is able to partition the clueweb graph [2] ($|V|$ = 978M, $|E|$ = 42.5B) whose edge set exceeds the volume of main memory.

REFERENCES

[1] William Aiello, Fan Chung, and Linyuan Lu. A random graph model for massive graphs. In *STOC*, pages 171–180, 2000.
[2] Paolo Boldi, Massimo Santini, and Sebastiano Vigna. A large time-aware web graph. In *ACM SIGIR Forum*, volume 42, pages 33–38. ACM, 2008.
[3] Florian Bourse, Marc Lelarge, and Milan Vojnovic. Balanced graph edge partition. In *SIGKDD*, pages 1456–1465, 2014.
[4] Rong Chen, Jiaxin Shi, Yanzhe Chen, and Haibo Chen. Powerlyra: Differentiated graph computation and partitioning on skewed graphs. In *Proceedings of the Tenth European Conference on Computer Systems*, page 1. ACM, 2015.
[5] Uriel Feige and Mohammad Mahdian. Finding small balanced separators. In *STOC*, pages 375–384, 2006.
[6] Joseph E Gonzalez, Yucheng Low, Haijie Gu, Danny Bickson, and Carlos Guestrin. Powergraph: Distributed graph-parallel computation on natural graphs. In *OSDI*, pages 17–30, 2012.
[7] Joseph E Gonzalez, Reynold S Xin, Ankur Dave, Daniel Crankshaw, Michael J Franklin, and Ion Stoica. Graphx: Graph processing in a distributed dataflow framework. In *OSDI*, pages 599–613, 2014.
[8] George Karypis and Vipin Kumar. A fast and high quality multilevel scheme for partitioning irregular graphs. *SIAM Journal on scientific Computing*, 20(1):359–392, 1998.
[9] Haewoon Kwak, Changhyun Lee, Hosung Park, and Sue Moon. What is twitter, a social network or a news media? In *WWW*, pages 591–600, 2010.
[10] Jure Leskovec and Andrej Krevl. SNAP Datasets:Stanford large network dataset collection. 2014.

[11] Yucheng Low, Danny Bickson, Joseph Gonzalez, Carlos Guestrin, Aapo Kyrola, and Joseph M Hellerstein. Distributed graphlab: a framework for machine learning and data mining in the cloud. *VLDB*, 5(8):716–727, 2012.

[12] Grzegorz Malewicz, Matthew H Austern, Aart JC Bik, James C Dehnert, Ilan Horn, Naty Leiser, and Grzegorz Czajkowski. Pregel: a system for large-scale graph processing. In *SIGMOD*, pages 135–146, 2010.

[13] Daniel Margo and Margo Seltzer. A scalable distributed graph partitioner. *VLDB*, 8(12):1478–1489, 2015.

[14] Mark EJ Newman, Steven H Strogatz, and Duncan J Watts. Random graphs with arbitrary degree distributions and their applications. *Physical review E*, 64(2):026118, 2001.

[15] Fabio Petroni, Leonardo Querzoni, Khuzaima Daudjee, Shahin Kamali, and Giorgio Iacoboni. Hdrf: Stream-based partitioning for power-law graphs. In *CIKM*, pages 243–252, 2015.

[16] Amitabha Roy, Laurent Bindschaedler, Jasmina Malicevic, and Willy Zwaenepoel. Chaos: Scale-out graph processing from secondary storage. In *SOSP*, pages 410–424, 2015.

[17] Cong Xie, Ling Yan, Wu-Jun Li, and Zhihua Zhang. Distributed power-law graph computing: Theoretical and empirical analysis. In *NIPS*, pages 1673–1681, 2014.

A MIN-RF(p,α) PROBLEM IS NP-HARD

Notation. Given a graph $G = (V,E)$, two vertex sets A,B, let $E(A,B) = \{\{u,v\} : u \in A, v \in B\}$, let $e(A,B) = |E(A,B)|$. Furthermore, we define $E(S) = E(S,S)$ and $e(S) = e(S,S)$.

THEOREM A.1. *For any $\alpha \geq 1$, MIN-RF(p,α) problem is NP-hard with respect to n. In particular, we show that MIN-RF($2,\alpha$) problem is NP-hard.*

PROOF. We claim that MIN-RF($2,\alpha$) problem is equivalent to the following MIN-β-separator problem which we will prove to be NP-hard.

DEFINITION 2 (MIN-β-SEPARATOR PROBLEM). *Given a graph $G = (V,E)$, a β-separator is a vertex subset S such that $V(G) \setminus S$ can be partitioned into two vertex sets W_1, W_2 such that W_1, W_2 are disconnected from each other and $e(W_i) + e(W_i,S) \leq \lceil \beta e(G) \rceil$ for $i = 1,2$. The MIN-β-separator problem is to find the smallest β-separator S.*

LEMMA A.2. *MIN-RF($2,\alpha$) problem is equivalent to MIN-β-separator problem with $\beta = \alpha/2$.*

PROOF. Given a graph $G = (V,E)$, let $\{E_1^*, E_2^*\}$ be the optimal solution to the MIN-RF($2,\alpha$) problem. Let S^* be the optimal solution to the MIN-β-separator problem with $\beta = \alpha/2$. We show that $|V(E_1^*)| + |V(E_2^*)| = |V| + |S^*|$, and this will infer that two problems are equivalent.

Given E_1^*, E_2^*, let $S = V(E_1^*) \cap V(E_2^*)$. Let $W_i = V(E_i^*) \setminus S$ for $i = 1,2$. There is no edge between W_1 and W_2 because E_1^*, E_2^* is a edge partition. And $e(W_i) + e(W_i,S) \leq |E_i^*| \leq \lceil \alpha|E|/2 \rceil = \lceil \beta|E| \rceil$, hence S is a β-separator. Therefore, we get $|V(E_1^*)| + |V(E_2^*)| \geq |V| + |S^*|$.

Given S^* which separates $V(G) \setminus S^*$ into two vertex sets W_1^*, W_2^*, we obtain α-balanced 2-edge partition E_1, E_2 as follows. Let $e_i = e(W_i^*) + e(W_i^*, S)$. Then we know $e_i \leq \beta e(G)$. The β-separator gives a natural edge partition for our problem: the first machine contains the vertices $W_1^* \cup S^*$ and the second machine contains the vertices $W_2^* \cup S^*$. The edges in the first machine are $e(W_1^*) \cup e(W_1^*, S^*)$ and x number of edges in $E(S^*)$ with $0 \leq x \leq e(S^*) = e(G) - e_1 - e_2$. Thus there are $e_1 + x$ edges in the first machine. The edges in the second machine are $e(W_2^*) \cup e(W_2^*, S^*)$ and the rest of the edges in $e(S^*)$, thus the number of edges in the second machine is $e_2 + e(S^*) - x = e(G) - e_1 - x$. We show that we can find an x such that $|E_i| \leq \lceil \alpha|E|/2 \rceil$.

WOLG, we assume $e_1 \geq e_2$. We separate it into two cases:

(1) If $e_1 \geq e(G)/2$, we choose $x = 0$. Then the number of edges in the first machine is e_1 and the number of edges in the second machine is $e(G) - e_1 \leq e_1$. Because S^* is β-separator, we know $\max\{|E_1|, |E_2|\} \leq e_1 \leq \lceil \beta|E| \rceil = \lceil \alpha|E|/2 \rceil$.

(2) If $e_1 < e(G)/2$, we choose $x = \lfloor e(G)/2 \rfloor - e_1$. Thus the number of edges in the first machine is $\lfloor e(G)/2 \rfloor$, and the number of edges in the second machine is $\lceil e(G)/2 \rceil$. Clearly E_1, E_2 is α-balanced.

Therefore we have obtained an α-balanced 2-edge partition from S^*, which means $|V(E_1^*)| + |V(E_2^*)| \leq |V| + |S^*|$.

Thus we have shown that MIN-RF($2,\alpha$) problem is equivalent to MIN-β-separator problem. □

LEMMA A.3. *MIN-β-separator problem is NP-hard.*

PROOF. The proof is motivated by [5] which proves that a vertex constraint MIN-separator problem is NP-hard. To the best of our knowledge, our work here is the first focusing on the edge constraint of separator and showing that MIN-β-separator problem is NP-hard.

We reduce MAX-CLIQUE problem to MIN-β-separator problem. Given a graph G on n vertices $v_1, \ldots, v_n$, we show that checking whether there is a clique in G containing a fixed v_1 with size k can be reduced to our problem of checking whether there is a separator of size k that satisfies the edge β-separator constraint. (Notice that there are at most n choices of v_1 and at most n choices of k).

We create an auxiliary graph H from G. First create a vertex set W of order $|W| = \max\left(\frac{1-\beta}{\beta}\left(\binom{n}{2} + 2e(G)\right) - \frac{3}{\beta}\binom{k}{2}, 0\right)$. When $k \leq n-1$ as n is large enough, $|W| > 0$. Let the vertex set of H be $\{v_1, \ldots, v_n\} \cup \bigcup_{v_i \sim v_j} u_{ij} \cup W$, where u_{ij} are newly created vertices corresponding to each un-ordered pair i,j with v_i, v_j adjacent in G. Thus $|V(H)| = n + e(G) + |W|$. The edges in H are as follows. Within $\{v_1, \ldots, v_n\}$ all edges are connected (thus it is a clique on n vertices). Vertex u_{ij} is only connected to v_i, v_j. There is a complete bipartite graph between W and v_1 while within W it is an independent set. Thus the number of edges in H is $e(H) = |W| + \binom{n}{2} + 2e(G)$.

We show that finding the β-separator of size k containing v_1 in H is equivalent to finding a k-clique containing v_1 in G. Suppose $V(H) \setminus S$ can be partitioned into two connected components (each connected components might be disconnected) V_1, V_2. If $v_1 \notin S$, then WOLG assume $v_1 \in V_1$. Suppose the separator of size k consists of s vertices $U \subseteq \{v_2, \ldots, v_n\}$, x vertices X in W, and y vertices Y in $\{u_{ij}\}$. By the construction, we know that v_1 is connected to all the vertices in $\{v_2, \ldots, v_n\} \setminus U$, and it is connected to all the vertices in $\bigcup_{i,j \text{ not all in } U}\{u_{ij}\}$. Since V_1, V_2 are not connected to each other, all the neighbors of v_1 excluding S should be in V_1. Therefore the following edges are known to be in $E(V_1) \cup E(V_1, S)$: the $|W| - |X|$ edges from v_1 to $W \setminus Y$, the $\binom{n}{2} - \binom{s}{2}$ edges within $\{v_1, v_2, \ldots, v_n\}$ excluding the edges within U, and the edges coming out from u_{ij} with v_i, v_j not both in U and not including the edges coming from vertices in X. The latter case consists of $2(e(G) - e(U)) - 2y$ edges. Thus we have

$$|E(V_1) \cup E(V_1,S)| \geq |W| - x + \binom{n}{2} - \binom{s}{2} + 2(e(G) - e(U)) - 2y. \quad (5)$$

Since $x+y+s=k$ we know $x+2y \leq 2(k-s)$. Also $e(U) \leq \binom{|U|}{2} = \binom{s}{2}$. Therefore (5) satisfies

$$\begin{aligned}
&|E(V_1) \cup E(V_1, S)| \\
\geq &|W| + \binom{n}{2} - \binom{s}{2} + 2\left(e(G) - \binom{s}{2}\right) - 2(k-s) \\
\geq &|W| + \binom{n}{2} - \binom{k}{2} + 2\left(e(G) - \binom{k}{2}\right) \quad (6)\\
= &e(H) - 3\binom{k}{2}. \quad (7)
\end{aligned}$$

The second to last inequality holds because to minimize the expression over $0 \leq s \leq k$ we should choose $s = k$ for $k \geq 2$ by simple computation. The last equality holds because $e(H) = |W| + \binom{n}{2} + 2e(G)$.

However, by our choice of $|W|$, we have that $(1-\beta)e(H) = |W| + 3\binom{k}{2}$. Thus $e(H) - 3\binom{k}{2} > \beta e(H)$. However, if this is the case, then (7) tells us that $|E(V_1) \cup E(V_1, S)| > \beta e(H)$. This is a contradiction.

Therefore $v_1 \in S$. Suppose the separator of size k consists of s vertices $U \subseteq \{v_1, v_2, \ldots, v_n\}$ and $v_1 \in U$, x vertices X in W, and y vertices Y in $\{u_{ij}\}$. Suppose $v \in \{v_1, v_2, \ldots, v_n\} \setminus \{v_1\}$. Then similarly, by the construction, we know that v is connected to all the vertices in $\{v_1, v_2, \ldots, v_n\} \setminus U$, and it is connected to all the vertices in $\bigcup_{i,j \text{not all in } U} \{u_{ij}\}$. Since V_1, V_2 are not connected to each other, we know all the neighbors of v excluding S should be in V_1. Therefore the edges we are certain to be in $E(V_1) \cup E(V_1, S)$ include the $\binom{n}{2} - \binom{s}{2}$ edges within $\{v_1, v_2, \ldots, v_n\}$ excluding the edges within U, and the edges coming out from u_{ij} with v_i, v_j not both in U and not including the edges coming from vertices in X. The latter case consists of $2(e(G) - e(U)) - 2y$ edges. Thus we have

$$\begin{aligned}
&|E(V_1) \cup E(V_1, S)| \\
\geq &\binom{n}{2} - \binom{s}{2} + 2(e(G) - e(U)) - 2y \\
\geq &\binom{n}{2} - \binom{s}{2} + 2(e(G) - e(U)) - 2(k-s)
\end{aligned}$$

where the last inequality holds because $x+y+s=k$ and thus $-2y \geq -2(k-s)$. If $1 \leq s \leq k-1$, we know

$$\begin{aligned}
&|E(V_1) \cup E(V_1, S)| \\
\geq &\binom{n}{2} - \binom{s}{2} + 2(e(G) - e(U)) - 2(k-s) \\
\geq &\binom{n}{2} - \binom{s}{2} + 2\left(e(G) - \binom{s}{2}\right) - 2(k-s) \\
\geq &\binom{n}{2} - \binom{k-1}{2} + 2\left(e(G) - \binom{k-1}{2}\right) - 2,
\end{aligned}$$

where the last inequality is by optimizing the quadratic in s. However,

$$\begin{aligned}
&\binom{n}{2} - \binom{k-1}{2} + 2\left(e(G) - \binom{k-1}{2}\right) - 2 \\
> &\beta e(H) \\
= &\binom{n}{2} - \binom{k}{2} + 2\left(e(G) - \binom{k}{2}\right).
\end{aligned}$$

Thus we have that $s = k$. Thus we must have

$$\begin{aligned}
\beta e(H) = &\binom{n}{2} - \binom{k}{2} + 2\left(e(G) - \binom{k}{2}\right) \quad (8)\\
\geq &|E(V_1) \cup E(V_1, S)| \quad (9)\\
\geq &\binom{n}{2} - \binom{k}{2} + 2(e(G) - e(U)). \quad (10)
\end{aligned}$$

This means that U must be a clique of size k and it contains v_1. Therefore we reduce MAX-CLIQUE problem to MIN-β-separator problem. Since MAX-CLIQUE problem is NP-hard, we have that MIN-β-separator problem is NP-hard. □

The claim is a direct consequence of the two lemmas. □

B THE STREAMING ALGORITHM

Based on Alg. 1, we propose a streaming algorithm (Alg. 3) that considers the trade-off between the partitioning quality and memory consumption. This algorithm only requires $O(|V|)$ memory, hence can process graphs whose edge set exceeds main memory. Our technique is to sample edges uniformly from the original graph, and then run Alg. 1 on the sampled graph.

In total, we need to scan through the edge list[4] from the hard disk twice. In the first scan, we randomly shuffle the edge list, and record the number of vertices, the number of edges, and the degree of each vertex. In the second scan, we stream in the edges one by one from the shuffled edge list, and maintain *CacheSize* number of edges in memory. The value of CacheSize is determined mostly by the memory budget. In general the larger of CacheSize the better the partitioning quality. In practice, we find that CacheSize $= 2\times|V|$ produces balanced partitions of good replication factor.

Like Alg. 1, the streaming algorithm produces edge partition for each machine in turn. In round i, it constructs the working graph consisting of the sampled edges (denoted as $\hat{E}$), and then applies Alg. 1 to allocate a $|\hat{E}|/p-i+1$ fraction of edges for machine i. The allocated edges E_i are immediately stored to the hard disk, while the core set C_i and the boundary set S_i are stored in the main memory for partitioning the unallocated edges.

Prior to round i, the *CheckEdge* procedure (Alg. 4) is used to add extra unallocated edges to the edge set E_j for $|E_j| \leq \alpha m/p$ and $j < i$. The reason is that by the time E_j is established, the sampled edge set $\hat{E}$ does not contain the full information of the graph and E_j has fewer edges than expected. The edges allocated to E_j is based on its core set C_j and boundary set S_j. The CheckEdge procedure is applied to the current sampled edge set $\hat{E}$, and also the edges to be loaded into memory. An edge $e = \{x, y\}$ is allocated to E_j if one of the following two conditions is true.

(1) if e is covered by S_j, i.e., $e \subseteq S_j$, or
(2) if e is touched by C_j, i.e., $|e \cap C_j| = 1$, and the degree of each adjacent vertex is less than the average degree of the original graph, i.e., $\max\{d_x, d_y\} \leq 2m/n$. (In this case, when edge e is added to E_j the boundary set S_j is augmented as $S_j \leftarrow S_j \cup e$.)

[4]We assume the graph is stored in edge list format. Each line represents an edge as a pair of vertex IDs.

Algorithm 3 Partitioning via sampling.

Randomly shuffle edge list, record n, m, d
$\hat{E} \leftarrow \emptyset$, $E \leftarrow$ shuffled edge list
for $i \in [p]$ **do**
  $\tilde{E} \leftarrow \hat{E}$, $\hat{E} \leftarrow \emptyset$
  for $e \in \tilde{E}$ **do**
    $\hat{E} \leftarrow \hat{E} \cup$ CheckEdge(e, i)
  while $|\hat{E}| \leq$ CacheSize AND $E \neq \emptyset$ **do**
    pick next edge $e \in E$, $E \leftarrow E \setminus \{e\}$
    $\hat{E} \leftarrow \hat{E} \cup$ CheckEdge(e, i)
  $C_i, S_i, E_i \leftarrow$ Expand$(\hat{E}, |\hat{E}|/p-i+1)$
  $\hat{E} \leftarrow \hat{E} \setminus E_i$
  update d, remove degree due to E_i

Algorithm 4 Allocating edges for partitions.

procedure CheckEdge$(e = \{x, y\}, i)$
  for $j \in \{1 \leq t < i : |E_j| \leq \alpha m/p\}$ **do**
    if $e \cap C_j \neq \emptyset$ AND $\max\{d_x, d_y\} \leq 2m/n$ **then**
      $S_j \leftarrow S_j \cup e$
    if $e \subseteq S_j$ **then**
      $E_j \leftarrow E_j \cup \{e\}$
      $d_x \leftarrow d_x - 1$
      $d_y \leftarrow d_y - 1$
      return $\emptyset$
  return $\{e\}$

Memory Consumption. Note that Alg. 3 needs to maintain and work on an edge set of size $|\hat{E}|$ = CacheSize, while the NE algorithm works on the whole edge set of size $|E|$. Both algorithms need to store the core set C_i and boundary set S_i in memory for all the p machines. They also need to maintain the vertex degree d_x in memory. So the total memory consumptions of the NE algorithm and the streaming algorithm are $O(|E| + p|V|)$ and $O(\text{CacheSize} + p|V|)$, respectively. Given that CacheSize $= O(|V|)$ and $p = O(1)$, we show that, by running our NE algorithm on a sampled graph, we can reduce the memory consumption from $O(|E| + |V|)$ to $O(|V|)$. Next, we use the experiments to study the partitioning quality of our streaming algorithm.

Experiments. We compare the replication factor of NE and the streaming algorithm (Alg. 3) in Table 4. To evaluate the scalability of the streaming algorithm we add a new graph *clue-web* [2] of 978,408,098 vertices and 42,574,107,469 edges. Comparing with NE, the streaming algorithm enables us to process much larger graphs with some compromise on replication factor.

Table 4: Replication factors ($p = 30, \alpha = 1.1$).

	LJ	Orkut	TW	FS	UK	clue-web
NE	1.55	2.48	1.88	1.98	1.04	Out of memory
Alg. 3	1.88	4.49	2.83	3.00	1.65	1.94

Randomization or Condensation? Linear-Cost Matrix Sketching Via Cascaded Compression Sampling

Kai Zhang*
Department of Computer and Information Sciences
Temple University, Philadelphia PA
kzhang980@gmail.com

Chuanren Liu*
Decision Sciences and MIS
Drexel University
Philadelphia, PA
chuanren.liu@drexel.edu

Jie Zhang*
Institute of Science and Technology for Brain-Inspired Intellegence
Fudan University, Shanghai
jzhang080@gmail.com

Hui Xiong
Management Science and Information Systems Department, Rutgers
1 Washington Park, Newark NJ
hxiong@rutgers.edu

Eric Xing
Machine Learning Department
Carnegie Mellon University
5000 Forbes Ave, Pittsburgh, PA
epxing@cs.cmu.edu

Jieping Ye
Department of Computational Medicine and Bioinformatics
University of Michigan, Ann Arbor
jpye@umich.edu

ABSTRACT

Matrix sketching is aimed at finding compact representations of a matrix while simultaneously preserving most of its properties, which is a fundamental building block in modern scientific computing. Randomized algorithms represent state-of-the-art and have attracted huge interest from the fields of machine learning, data mining, and theoretic computer science. However, it still requires the use of the entire input matrix in producing desired factorizations, which can be a major computational and memory bottleneck in truly large problems. In this paper, we uncover an interesting theoretic connection between matrix low-rank decomposition and *lossy signal compression*, based on which a cascaded compression sampling framework is devised to approximate an $m \times n$ matrix in only $O(m + n)$ time and space. Indeed, the proposed method accesses only a small number of matrix rows and columns, which significantly improves the memory footprint. Meanwhile, by sequentially teaming two rounds of approximation procedures and upgrading the sampling strategy from a uniform probability to more sophisticated, encoding-orientated sampling, significant algorithmic boosting is achieved to uncover more granular structures in the data. Empirical results on a wide spectrum of real-world, large-scale matrices show that by taking only linear time and space, the accuracy of our method rivals those state-of-the-art randomized algorithms consuming a quadratic, $O(mn)$, amount of resources.

KEYWORDS

Randomized algorithms, Matrix sketching, Low-rank decomposition, Cascaded compression sampling

* Equal contribution.

KDD '17, August 13-17, 2017, Halifax, NS, Canada

978-1-4503-4887-4/17/08...$15.00
DOI: 10.1145/3097983.3098050

1 INTRODUCTION

Matrix arises in many modern disciplines as a popular tool for data representation and modelling. Identifying structures of the matrix allows researchers to uncover important patterns in the data, which in turn translates into actionable decisions or scientific discoveries. Matrix low rank decomposition [15] is one such structure-finding technique. It is aimed at approximating an input matrix $\mathbf{A} \in \mathbb{R}^{m \times n}$ by $\mathbf{A} \approx \mathbf{P}\mathbf{Q}^{\top}$, where $\mathbf{P}$ and $\mathbf{Q}$ have a low column rank $k \ll m, n$. Such reduced representation can provide a universal computational platform to solve problems in various scientific computing and data analysis applications, with important applications in optimization, machine learning, information retrieval, computer vision, and bioinformatics [1, 9, 12, 13, 17, 19, 20, 22, 24, 25, 33].

Recent advances in randomized algorithms have made it state-of-the-art in solving low-rank approximation problems. These algorithms fully exploit stochastic properties of random sampling and projection to extract key structures from the data. Abundant literature exists, with examples including monte-carlo sampling [10, 14], adaptive sampling [3], CUR matrix decomposition [5, 25], random projection method [7, 11, 17], sparse embedding and fast transforms [8, 27]. These algorithms are computationally more efficient than singular value decomposition, the latter taking $O(n^2m)$ time if $m \geq n$. In the meantime, important probabilistic error bounds are provided that fully characterize the behaviour of various sampling/randomization schemes. See reviews in [17, 24].

With unprecedented amount of electronic data acquired in modern scientific and engineering applications, however, existing randomized methods can still be computationally demanding on large data. In particular, these algorithms need to fully access and manipulate the entire input matrix, either in identifying an informative subspace for subsequent projection [17], or in computing high-quality sampling probabilities [10, 14, 25]. This necessitates $O(mn)$ time and space for an $m \times n$ dense matrix. Yet in case of exceptionally high dimensions, storing matrix alone already becomes onerous, not to mention complicated operations on top of it.

In this paper, we aim to combat the computational and memory bottlenecks of matrix low-rank decomposition on large data. Our main philosophy has a notable difference compared with existing randomized algorithms. In these algorithms, extensive theoretic studies have been performed on probabilistic error bounds that various randomization schemes can achieve when sampling a desired volume of data, often taking $O(mn)$ time and space. In comparison, we consider the scenario that available computing resource (time and memory) is only linear for an $m \times n$ input matrix, i.e., $O(m+n)$. Under such condition, our goal is to fully optimize the sampling scheme subject to available computing resources, so as to make the best of what is given and maximally reduce approximation error.

We initiate this new problem setting because in big data applications, achieving a desired sampling rate and manipulating the entire input matrix (as is often needed in existing randomized algorithms) can be intractable. A linear-cost constraint, on the other hand, is much easier to accomplish. Of course, such a constraint poses significant challenges, because it only allows accessing a small, constant number of rows/columns of the data; also, a linear amount of resources hardly affords any advanced sampling scheme other than uniform; finally, approximation of general rectangular matrices with linear cost is much harder than for positive semi-definite (PSD) matrices that lie on a Riemannian manifold [12, 13, 30].

To solve these problems, we propose a new computational framework called cascaded compression sampling. Our key innovation is an interesting, theoretic connection between the quality of low-rank approximation and the encoding powers of sampling. This allows us to study low-rank approximation from a novel, lossy data compression point of view, where the choice of good sampling schemes can thus benefit naturally from the design of the code-books. In particular, we show that sampled columns/rows should correspond to representative code-vectors in the low-rank embeddings of the matrix. Motivated by this, we employ cascaded sampling procedures that upgrade from simple, random sampling to more sophisticated, compression-based sampling, so as to progressively uncover granular structures in the data. Theoretically, the rise of approximation quality is proven to be lower-bounded by the improvement of encoding powers through the compression sampling, thus guaranteeing the algorithmic boosting property. Computationally, both rounds of operations take only linear time and space, thus more efficient on large data. The performance of our approach rivals the quality of state-of-the-art randomized algorithms while being one to two orders of magnitude faster with only a small fraction of their memory costs. The performance gains are more significant on large, sparse matrices.

The rest of the paper is organized as follows. Section 2 reviews existing work. Section 3 presents our key theorem linking matrix low-rank approximation and lossy singal compression. Section 4 introduces the cascaded compression sampling framework, and proves its algorithmic boosting property. Section 5 reports experimental results, and the last section concludes the paper.

2 RELATED WORK

2.1 Quadratic-Cost Algorithms

We first review state-of-the-art randomized algorithms that take a quadratic, $O(mn)$ amount of time and space for an $m \times n$ matrix.

Monte-Carlo sampling method [10, 14] approximates an input matrix $\mathbf{A}$ by selecting a subset of columns with data-dependent probabilities p_j's. The rank-k basis of selected columns (often rescaled by p_j's) $\mathbf{Q}_k$ is then used for final decomposition. If the probabilities satisfy $p_j \geq \beta \cdot \|\mathbf{A}_{[:,j]}\|^2 / (\sum_{i=1}^{n} \|\mathbf{A}_{[:,i]}\|^2)$, then with probability at least $1-\delta$, one has $\|\mathbf{A} - \mathbf{Q}_k\mathbf{Q}_k^\top \mathbf{A}\|_F^2 \leq \|\mathbf{A} - \mathbf{A}_k\|_F^2 + \epsilon\|\mathbf{A}\|_F^2$, where $\mathbf{A}_k$ is the best rank-k approximation, $\epsilon = 2\eta/\sqrt{k/\beta c}$, with $\beta \leq 1, \eta = 1 + \sqrt{(8/\beta)\log(1/\delta)}$.

Random projection methods [17] project $\mathbf{A}$ using $\mathbf{Q} \in \mathbf{R}^{m\times k}$ with orthonormal columns such that $\mathbf{A} \approx \mathbf{Q}\mathbf{Q}^\top \mathbf{A}$. Computing $\mathbf{Q}$ requires multiplying $\mathbf{A}$ with a Gaussian test matrix Ω with q steps of power iterations, $\mathbf{Y} = (\mathbf{A}\mathbf{A}^\top)^q \mathbf{A}\Omega$, and then a QR-decomposition $\mathbf{Y} = \mathbf{QR}$. Using a template $\Omega \in \mathbb{R}^{m\times(k+p)}$ with over-sampling parameter p, $\mathbb{E}\|\mathbf{A} - \mathbf{Q}\mathbf{Q}^\top\mathbf{A}\| = [1 + 4\sqrt{(k+p)}\cdot \min(m,n)/(p-1)]\Sigma_{k+1}$, where $\mathbb{E}$ is expectation with Ω, Σ_{k+1} is the $(k+1)$th singular value. New projection methods are explored in [7, 11].

Using structured templates (sub-sampled randomized Hard-amard transform (SRHT) [4] or random Fourier transform [17]), the complexity of random projection reduces from $O(mnk)$ $O(mn\log k)$. More recently, sparse embedding is introduced for low-rank decomposition in input sparsity time [8], which allows approximation $\|\mathbf{A} - \hat{\mathbf{A}}\|_F = (1 \pm \epsilon)\|\mathbf{A} - \mathbf{A}_k\|_F$ with high probability in $O(nnz(\mathbf{A})) + O(nk^2/\epsilon + k^3/\epsilon^5)$ time. Here $nnz(\mathbf{A})$ is the number of non-zeros. It can be more efficient for sparse input matrices.

CUR matrix decomposition was proposed in [25] to improve the interpretability of low-rank matrix decomposition. As shown in Figure 1(a), it samples a subset of columns and rows from $\mathbf{A}$, as $\mathbf{C} \in \mathbb{R}^{m\times k_c}$ and $\mathbf{R} \in \mathbb{R}^{k_r \times n}$, and then solve

$$\min_{\mathbf{U}} \|\mathbf{A} - \mathbf{CUR}\|_F^2 \rightarrow \mathbf{U}^* = \mathbf{C}^\dagger \mathbf{A} \mathbf{R}^\dagger, \tag{1}$$

where † is pseudo-inverse. If leverage scores are used for sampling, then with high probability, $\|\mathbf{A} - \mathbf{CUR}\|_F \leq (2+\epsilon)\|\mathbf{A} - \mathbf{A}_k\|_F$ [25]. The leverage scores are computed by top-r singular vectors, taking $O(mn)$ space and $O(mnr)$ time. Computing $\mathbf{U}$ in (1) involves multiplying $\mathbf{A}$ with $\mathbf{C}^\dagger$ and $\mathbf{R}^\dagger$.

2.2 Linear-Cost Algorithms

The randomized algorithms discussed in Section 2.1 take at least quadratic time and space. One way to reduce the cost is to restrict the calculations to only a small fraction of rows and columns. We use a general variant of CUR, called *Bilateral Re-sampled CUR* (BR-CUR), to initiate discussion.

Algorithm 1: Bilateral Resampled CUR (BR-CUR)

Input: $\mathbf{A}$, base sampling $\mathcal{I}_r^b, \mathcal{I}_c^b$, target sampling $\mathcal{I}_r^t, \mathcal{I}_c^t$;
Output: $\mathbf{C}, \mathbf{U}, \mathbf{R}$

1: Compute base rows and columns $\mathbf{C} = \mathbf{A}_{[:,\mathcal{I}_c^b]}$, $\mathbf{R} = \mathbf{A}_{[\mathcal{I}_r^b,:]}$.
2: Sample on base rows and columns $\bar{\mathbf{C}} = \mathbf{C}_{[\mathcal{I}_r^t,:]}$, $\bar{\mathbf{R}} = \mathbf{R}_{[:,\mathcal{I}_c^t]}$.
3: Compute target block matrix $\mathbf{M} = \mathbf{A}_{[\mathcal{I}_r^t,\mathcal{I}_c^t]}$.
4: Solve intersection matrix $\mathbf{U}^* = \arg\min_{\mathbf{U}} \|\mathbf{M} - \bar{\mathbf{C}}\mathbf{U}\bar{\mathbf{R}}\|_F^2$.
5: Reconstruct the input matrix by $\mathbf{A} \approx \mathbf{C}\mathbf{U}^*\mathbf{R}$.

As illustrated in Figure 1(b), BR-CUR has two rounds of samplings: blue "base"-sampling $\mathcal{I}_r^b$ (row) and $\mathcal{I}_c^b$ (column) to construct $\mathbf{C}$ and $\mathbf{R}$, and green "target"-sampling $\mathcal{I}_r^t$ (row) and $\mathcal{I}_c^t$ (column) to specify a sub-matrix from $\mathbf{A}$. In computing $\mathbf{U}$ (step 4), it only minimizes the error on the target sub-matrix, therefore computationally quite efficient. Let k_1 and k_2 be the number of samples

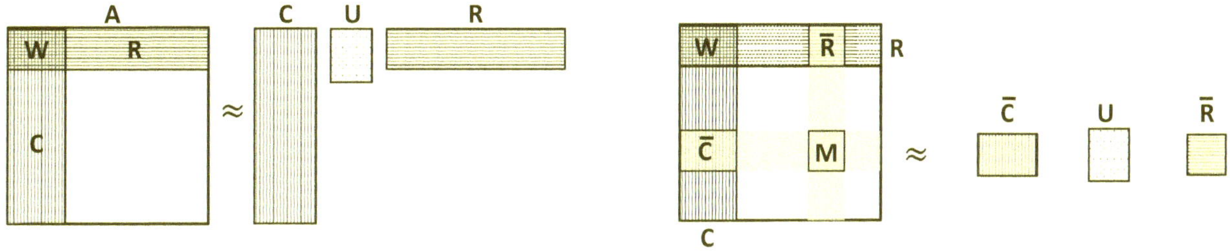

(a) Illustration of CUR method.

(b) Illustration of Re-sampled CUR.

Figure 1: Graphical illustration of the CUR matrix decomposition and the bilateral re-sampled CUR method.

selected in the base and target sampling. Then BR-CUR only takes $O((m+n)(k_1+k_2))$ space and $O\left((m+n)\max(k_1,k_2)^2\right)$ time.

The BR-CUR procedure subsumes most linear-cost algorithms for matrix low-rank decomposition in the literature.

1. Nyström method [12, 13, 30]: for PSD matrix $\mathbf{A}$, upon using the same base and target sampling, and the same row and column sampling, i.e., $\mathcal{I}_c^b = \mathcal{I}_r^b = \mathcal{I}_c^t = \mathcal{I}_c^t$.

2. Pseudo-skeleton [16] or bilateral projection [35]: for rectangular matrix $\mathbf{A}$, and using the same base and target sampling, i.e., $\mathcal{I}_r^b = \mathcal{I}_r^t$ and $\mathcal{I}_c^b = \mathcal{I}_c^t$. It generalizes Nyström method from symmetric to rectangular matrices. Let $\mathbf{W}$ be the intersection of $\mathbf{C}$ and $\mathbf{R}$, then it has compact form,

$$\mathbf{A} \approx \mathbf{C}\mathbf{W}^{\dagger}\mathbf{R}. \tag{2}$$

3. Sketch-CUR [29]: in case of rectangular $\mathbf{A}$ and independent base/target sampling (with different rates).

These algorithms only access a small fraction of rows and columns to reconstruct the input matrix. However, the performance can be inferior, in particularly on general, rectangular matrices (Section 4.2 for detail). More recently, online streaming algorithms began to draw increasing attention for matrix decomposition [21, 26, 31]. Their memory cost is much smaller, but the whole matrix still needs to be fully accessed and the time complexity is at least $O(m \cdot n)$.

3 THEORETIC ANALYSIS OF MATRIX BILATERAL DECOMPOSITION

In this section, we present a novel theoretic analysis on bilateral decomposition of general, rectangular matrices. It links the quality of matrix approximation with the encoding powers of bilateral sampling, and inspires a novel, encoding-orientated sampling scheme.

3.1 A New Error Bound

As discussed in Section 2.1, for most randomized algorithms in the literature, the randomization scheme is pre-determined and then probabilistic theoretical guarantees are derived, specifying how many samples should be selected to achieve a desired accuracy [3, 10, 14, 17, 25]. In this work, our goal is different: *we want to maximally reduce the approximation error given a fixed rate of sampling.* Therefore, our error bound is expressed in terms of the numerical properties of sampling, instead of a pre-selected sampling scheme. Our error bound will shed important light on the design of effective sampling schemes that fully exploits a limited computing resource, thus quite useful to practitioners.

Given an input matrix $\mathbf{A} \in \mathbb{R}^{m\times n}$, assume $\mathbf{A} = \mathbf{P}\mathbf{Q}^{\top}$, where $\mathbf{P} \in \mathbb{R}^{m\times r}$ and $\mathbf{Q} \in \mathbb{R}^{n\times r}$ are exact decomposition, say, from an SVD. Without loss of generality suppose we select k columns $\mathbf{C} = \mathbf{A}_{[:,\mathcal{Z}^c]}$ and k rows $\mathbf{R} = \mathbf{A}_{[\mathcal{Z}^r,:]}$, where $\mathcal{Z}^c$ and $\mathcal{Z}^r$ are sampling indices. These indices locate representative instances (rows) in $\mathbf{P}$ and $\mathbf{Q}$, denoted by $\mathbf{Z}^r = \mathbf{P}_{[\mathcal{Z}^r,:]}$ and $\mathbf{Z}^c = \mathbf{Q}_{[\mathcal{Z}^c,:]}$, respectively. In order to study how the bilateral sampling affects matrix approximation result, we adopt a data-encoding model. Let the m rows of $\mathbf{P}$ be segmented into k groups, where the group representatives are rows in $\mathbf{Z}^r$; similarly, let the n rows in $\mathbf{Q}$ fall into k groups, where the group representatives are rows in $\mathbf{Z}^c$. Let the $s^r(i)$ be the group assignment function that maps the i-th row in $\mathbf{P}$ to the $s^r(i)$-th row in $\mathbf{Z}^r$; similarly, $s^c(i)$ maps the i-th row in $\mathbf{Q}$ to the $s^c(i)$-th row in $\mathbf{Z}^c$. Then, the errors of reconstructing $\mathbf{P}$ and $\mathbf{Q}$ using representatives in $\mathcal{Z}^r$ and $\mathcal{Z}^c$ via respective mapping function $s^r(\cdot)$ and $s^c(\cdot)$ can be defined as

$$e^r = \sum_{l=1}^{m} \|\mathbf{P}_{[l,:]} - \mathbf{Z}^r_{[s^r(l),:]}\|^2, \quad e^c = \sum_{l=1}^{n} \|\mathbf{Q}_{[l,:]} - \mathbf{Z}^c_{[s^c(l),:]}\|^2. \tag{3}$$

We also define T^r and T^c as the maximum cluster sizes in $\mathbf{P}$ and $\mathbf{Q}$, respectively, as

$$T^r = \max_{1\le y\le k} |\{i : s^r(i) = y\}|, \; T^c = \max_{1\le y\le k} |\{i : s^c(i) = y\}|. \tag{4}$$

We can then analyze how matrix approximation error is associated with the encoding powers of bilateral sampling (in reconstructing the decompositions $\mathbf{P}$ and $\mathbf{Q}$) as follows.

Theorem 1. *Given an input matrix* $\mathbf{A}$*, and suppose one samples* k *columns* $\mathbf{C}$ *and* k *rows* $\mathbf{R}$*, with the intersection* $\mathbf{W}$*. Then we can bound the approximation error (2) as follows.*

$$\left\|\mathbf{A} - \mathbf{C}\mathbf{W}^{\dagger}\mathbf{R}\right\|_F \le \left(\sqrt{6k\theta T^{\frac{3}{2}}}\right)\cdot\sqrt{\mathrm{e^r + e^c}} + \left(k\theta T\|\mathbf{W}^{\dagger}\|_F\right)\cdot\sqrt{\mathrm{e^c e^r}}$$

Here $T = \max(T^r, T^c)$, T^r *and* T^c *are defined in (4),* e^r *and* e^c *are defined in (3);* θ *is a data dependent constant (see Appendix). Proof can be found in the Appendix.*

From Theorem 1, we can see that given a fixed sampling rate k the key quantities affecting the matrix approximation error are e^r and e^c (3), the encoding errors of reconstructing $\mathbf{P}$ and $\mathbf{Q}$ with their representative rows whose indices are specified in the bilateral sampling. In case both e^c and e^r approach zero, the approximation error will also approach zero. Namely, choosing a bilateral sampling that can reduce the encoding errors (3) is an effective way to

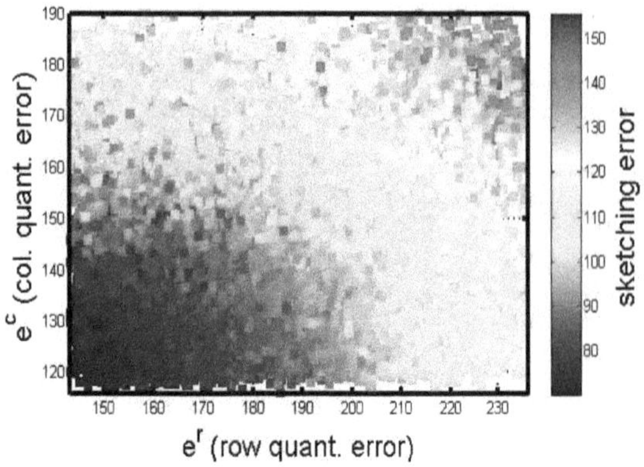

Figure 2: Matrix approximation error vs. row and column encoding errors.

bound matrix approximation error. We visualize their relations in Figure 2. Here, given A with exact decomposition $\mathbf{PQ}^\top$, we perform bilateral samplings many times on rows of P and Q, each time using different choices such as uniform sampling, vector quantization with different number of iterations, and so on, such that resultant encoding errors vary a lot. Then we plot the encoding errors (e^r, e^c) and color-code it with the corresponding matrix approximation error $\mathcal{E}$. As can be seen, $\mathcal{E}$ shows a clear correlation with e^c and e^r. Only when both e^c and e^r are small (blue), $\mathcal{E}$ will be small; if either e^c or e^r is large, $\mathcal{E}$ will be large too.

3.2 Low-rank Compression Sampling

Theorem 1 provides an important criterion for sampling: the selected rows and columns of A should be representative code-vectors in the low-rank embeddings P and Q, in order for the approximation error to be well bounded. To achieve this goal, we propose to use k-means to select representative rows in P and Q. The k-means algorithm, a.k.a. vector quantization [23], is a lossy data compression technique that has been widely used in signal processing. The algorithm can iteratively compute a set of representative code-vectors by finding a local optimal of the encoding error (or distortion) as defined in (3). Of course, exact decompositions P and Q are impractical and possibly high dimensional. Therefore, we resort to an alternative low-dimensional embedding $\mathbf{P} \in \mathbb{R}^{m \times k}, \mathbf{Q} \in \mathbb{R}^{n \times k}$ that will be discussed in more detail in the cascaded compression sampling framework in Section 4.

We shall first examine behaviour of the k-means sampling on the low-rank embeddings of the input matrix. For dense matrices, their energy spreads across all the rows and columns, so the embedding has a fairly uniform distribution (Figure 3(a)). For sparse matrices, energy distribution tends to concentrate around a small number of rows/columns; and hence the embedding collapses towards the origin (Figure 3(b). The k-means algorithm assigns more code-vectors in densely distributed regions. Therefore the code-vectors are uniform for dense matrices (Figure 3(a)), but will be attracted to the origin for sparse matrices (Figure 3(b)).

In order to prevent k-means sampling from picking too many points close to the origin (e.g. low-energy rows/columns whose entries are mostly zeros), we propose a general, importance weighted k-means sampling as follows

$$e^r = \sum_{l=1}^{m} \|\mathbf{P}_{[l,:]} - \mathbf{Z}^r_{[s^r(l),:]}\|^2 \cdot \Upsilon(\|\mathbf{P}_{[l,:]}\|_2) \quad (5)$$

$$e^c = \sum_{l=1}^{n} \|\mathbf{Q}_{[l,:]} - \mathbf{Z}^c_{[s^c(l),:]}\|^2 \cdot \Upsilon(\|\mathbf{Q}_{[l,:]}\|_2). \quad (6)$$

Here we use the norm of $\mathbf{P}_{[l,:]}$ (or $\mathbf{Q}_{[l,:]}$) to re-weight the objective of k-means in (3), because it is an upper-bound of the energy of the ith row in A (up to a constant scaling), as $\|\mathbf{A}_{[i,:]}\| = \|\mathbf{P}_{[i,:]} \cdot \mathbf{Q}\| \leq \|\mathbf{P}_{[i,:]}\| \cdot \|\mathbf{Q}\|$. The $\Upsilon(\cdot)$ is a monotonous function adjusting the weights (e.g. power or step function). By doing this, the k-means code-vectors will be pushed away from the origin (Figure 3(c)). For dense matrices, the weighting function can be simply chosen as constant. In practice, the k-means code-vector is replaced with its closest in-sample point. Finally, the weighing can be deemed a prior knowledge (preference) on approximating rows and columns of the input matrix, which can be incorporated trivially into Theorem 1.

4 CASCADED COMPRESSION SAMPLING

Theorem 1 suggests that one perform weighted k-means sampling (5) and (6) on the bilateral embeddings of the input matrix to effectively control the approximation error. Since computing an exact embedding is impractical, we will resort to approximate embeddings discussed in the following framework.

Algorithm 2: Cascaded Compression Sampling (CCS)

Input: A; **Output**: $\mathbf{A} \approx \bar{\mathbf{U}}\bar{\mathbf{S}}\bar{\mathbf{V}}^\top$

1: *Pilot Sampling*: randomly select k columns and k rows $\mathbf{C} = \mathbf{A}_{[:,\mathcal{I}^c]}, \mathbf{R} = \mathbf{A}_{[\mathcal{I}^r,:]}, \mathbf{W} = \mathbf{A}_{[\mathcal{I}^r,\mathcal{I}^c]}$.

2: *Pilot approximation*: run [U, S, V] = `sketching`(C, R, W), let $\mathbf{P} = \mathbf{US}^{\frac{1}{2}}$, and $\mathbf{Q} = \mathbf{VS}^{\frac{1}{2}}$.

3: *Follow-up sampling*: perform weighted k-means on P and Q, respectively, to obtain row index $\bar{\mathcal{I}}^r$ and column index $\bar{\mathcal{I}}^c$; let $\bar{\mathbf{C}} = \mathbf{A}_{[:,\bar{\mathcal{I}}^c]}, \bar{\mathbf{R}} = \mathbf{A}_{[\bar{\mathcal{I}}^r,:]}, \bar{\mathbf{W}} = \mathbf{A}_{[\bar{\mathcal{I}}^r,\bar{\mathcal{I}}^c]}$.

4: *Follow-up approximation*: $[\bar{\mathbf{U}}, \bar{\mathbf{S}}, \bar{\mathbf{V}}]$= `sketching`($\bar{\mathbf{C}}, \bar{\mathbf{R}}, \bar{\mathbf{W}}$).

The CCS framework has two rounds of computations. First, we perform simple random sampling (step 1) and compute a pilot approximation of the input matrix (step 2). Although it can be less accurate, it provides a compact embedding of the input matrix (P and Q). Then, as guided by Theorem 1, we apply weighted k-means on P and Q to identify representative samples (step 3); resultant sampling is used for final approximation (step 4). As will be shown both theoretically (Section 4.2) and empirically (Section 5), it is exactly the follow-up sampling that allows us to extract more informative samples to significantly improve approximation quality.

The CCS algorithm takes only $O((m+n)(k_1+k_2))$ space and $O((m+n)k_1k_2c)$ time, where k_1 and k_2 is the pilot and follow-up sampling rate, respectively, and c is the number of k-means iterations. In practice, $k_1 = k_2 \ll m, n$ and $c = 5$ in all our experiment, so the complexities are linear in $m+n$. In case of sparse input matrices, the complexity will be further reduced since only non-zero entries will be involved in the pilot sampling and approximation steps. As will be shown in Section 5, impressively, that our method is computationally more efficient than those algorithms taking only input-sparsity time [8, 27] on large sparse input matrices.

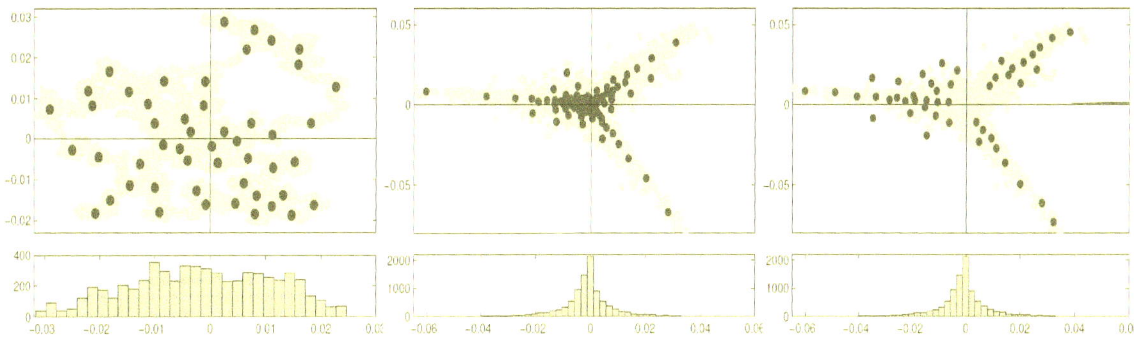

(a) dense matrix, k-means sampling (b) sparse matrix, k-means sampling (c) sparse matrix, weighted k-means

Figure 3: Top-2 dimensions of the low-rank embedding P, histogram on horizontal dimension, and (weighted) k-means sampling results.

4.1 The sketching Routine

This section discusses the `sketching` routine in Algorithm 2. Given a subset of rows **R**, columns **C**, and intersection **W** from **A**, it returns $\mathbf{A} \approx \mathbf{U}\mathbf{S}\mathbf{V}^\top$. Both Sketch-CUR and Pseudo-skeleton method are candidates. Empirically, their performance can be sensitive to the choice of the number of singular vectors used in computing the pseudo-inverse (1,2), as shown in Figure 4. In particular, the optimal rank can be quite small and varies from data to data.

In the following we propose a stabilized, parameter-free version of Pseudo-skeleton method (2). Assuming an SVD $\mathbf{W} = \mathbf{U}_w\Sigma_w\mathbf{V}_w^\top$, then $\mathbf{W}^\dagger = \mathbf{V}_w\Sigma_w^{-1}\Sigma_w\Sigma_w^{-1}\mathbf{U}_w^\top$. Plug this into $\mathbf{A} \approx \mathbf{C}\mathbf{W}^\dagger\mathbf{R}$, we have

$$\mathbf{A} \approx \left(\mathbf{C}\mathbf{V}_w\Sigma_w^{-1}\right)\Sigma_w\left(\Sigma_w^{-1}\mathbf{U}_w^\top\mathbf{R}\right).$$

Here, $\mathbf{U}_w$ and $\mathbf{V}_w$ are left and right singular vectors of **W**, extrapolated via $\mathbf{U}_w^\top\mathbf{R}$ and $\mathbf{C}\mathbf{V}_w$, respectively, and then normalized by the singular values Σ_w. In case $\Sigma_w(i,i)$ approaches zero, the normalization becomes numerically unstable. To avoid this ambiguity, we use the norms of the extrapolated singular-vectors for normalization,

$$\mathbf{A} \approx \left(\mathbf{C}\mathbf{V}_w\mathbf{N}_c^{-1}\right)\sqrt{\frac{mn}{k^2}}\Sigma_w\left(\mathbf{N}_r^{-1}\mathbf{U}_w^\top\mathbf{R}\right), \quad (7)$$

$$s.t.\ \ \mathbf{N}_c = \mathrm{diag}(\|\mathbf{C}\mathbf{V}_w\|_\otimes),\ \mathbf{N}_r = \mathrm{diag}(\|\mathbf{R}^\top\mathbf{U}_w\|_\otimes). \quad (8)$$

Here $diag(\cdot)$ fills a diagonal matrix with given vector, $\|\cdot\|_\otimes$ returns column-wise norms, namely $\mathbf{N}_r$ and $\mathbf{N}_c$ are norms of extrapolated singular vectors. The constant $\sqrt{mn}/k$ adjusts scale of solution, which can also be computed adaptively using a small validation set. We can then define the `sketching()` routine with $\mathbf{U} = \mathbf{C}\mathbf{V}_w\mathbf{N}_c^{-1}$, $\mathbf{V} = \mathbf{N}_r^{-1}\mathbf{U}_w^\top\mathbf{R}$, and $\Sigma = \Sigma_w\sqrt{mn}/k$, see Algorithm 3. As can be seen from Figure 4, it gives stable result though using all singular vectors. In practice, this can be more convenient than choosing the best rank (or threshold) through validation on a hold-out data set.

In positive semi-definite (PSD) matrices, intriguingly, numerical sensitivity diminishes by sampling the same subset of rows and columns, reducing to the Nyström method [12, 13, 30]. We speculate that PSD matrix resides in a Riemannian manifold [2], so symmetric sampling better captures its structure. However, rectangular matrix is not endowed with any structural constraint. This makes the approximation of rectangular matrices particularly challenging and abundant results of the Nyström method may not be borrowed here directly [12, 13, 18, 30, 34].

Algorithm 3: Stabilized sketching

Input: Sampled columns (**C**), rows (**R**), and intersection (**W**)
Output: Stable factorization

1: Compute singular value decomposition $\mathbf{W} = \mathbf{U}_w\Sigma_w\mathbf{V}_w^\top$.
2: Extrapolate left and right singular vectors as $\mathbf{C}\mathbf{V}_w$ and $\mathbf{U}_w^\top\mathbf{R}$.
3: Compute column norms of $\mathbf{C}\mathbf{V}_w$ and $\mathbf{R}^\top\mathbf{U}_w$, load them in diagonal matrices $\mathbf{N}_c$ and $\mathbf{N}_r$, respectively (8).
4: Normalize singular vectors as $\mathbf{C}\mathbf{V}_w\mathbf{N}_c^{-1}$ and $\mathbf{N}_r^{-1}\mathbf{U}_w^\top\mathbf{R}$.
5: Reconstruct by $(\mathbf{C}\mathbf{V}_w\mathbf{N}_c^{-1})\,\Sigma_w\,(\mathbf{N}_r^{-1}\mathbf{U}_w^\top\mathbf{R})$.
6: Re-scale by (7) or data-dependent factor through validation.

4.2 Algorithmic Boosting Property

In the literature, many two-step methods were designed for fast CUR decomposition. They start from an initial decomposition (fast JL-transform [11], random projection [3, 28, 29]), and then compute a sampling probability for subsequent CUR [3, 28]. Note that these two-step methods focus more on theoretic guarantees of the final approximation, but not the improvement of approximation quality between the two steps; in comparison, we target on algorithmically boosting the approximation accuracy from the first step to the second step, both of which are computationally quite cheap.

How to quantify the rise of approximation quality in a two-step method? How to choose the right pilot and follow-up sampling to save computations and maximize performance gains? By cascading random sampling with weighted k-means, we have derived a working example of "algorithmic boosting". Next, we show that, decrement of the error bound from the pilot to the follow-up approximation in CCS, is lower bounded by the drop of encoding errors achieved through the follow-up k-means sampling. Namely, the better the encoding based sampling, the larger the performance gain.

Theorem 2. *Let the error bound of the pilot and follow-up sketching in CABS be Ψ_p and Ψ_f, respectively. Then the error bound will drop by at least the following amount*

$$\Psi_p - \Psi_f \geq \sqrt{\frac{3k\theta T_p^c T_p^r (T_p^r + T_p^c)}{2(e_p^r + e_p^c)}}\left|\Delta_e^r + \Delta_e^c\right| + k\theta\left\|\mathbf{W}_p^\dagger\right\|_F\sqrt{\frac{T^c T^r}{e_p^r e_p^c}}\left|\Delta_e^r e_f^c + \Delta_e^c e_f^r + \Delta_e^r\Delta_e^c\right|.$$

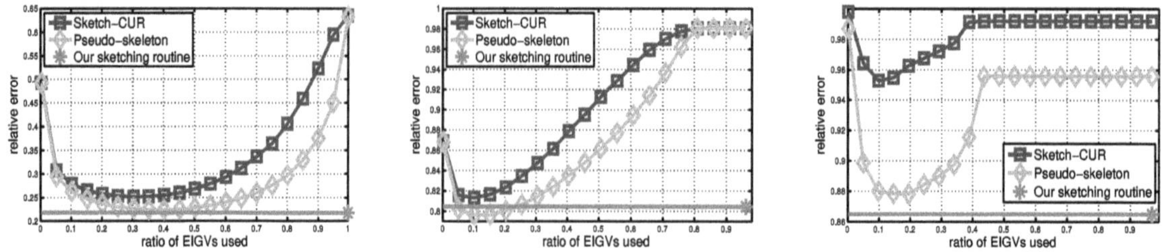

(a) galaxy image (b) movie-lens (c) 20newsgroup

Figure 4: Performance of sketch-CUR and pseudo-skeleton method can be rank sensitive.

Parameters are defined in the same way as in Theorem 1, and sub-index $\{p, f\}$ denotes pilot or follow-up; Δ_e^r (Δ_e^c) is the drop of row (column) encoding error in the follow-up k-means sampling. Proof of Theorem 2 can be found in the Appendix.

The boosting effect is not dependent on specific `sketching` routine. Empirically, using Pseudo-skeleton or Sketch-CUR can also achieve significant performance gains, showing the generality of our framework in achieving the goal of algorithmic boosting.

4.3 Relation with Matrix Coherence

Matrix coherence is a useful index to describe how easy it is to recover an input matrix through random sampling or matrix completion algorithms [6]. Let $\mathbf{U} \in \mathbb{R}^{m\times r}$ be the top r left singular vectors, then coherence can be defined as

$$\mu_0(\mathbf{U}) = \max_{ij} |\mathbf{U}_{ij}|, \quad or \quad \mu_1(\mathbf{U}) = \max_{i=1,2,\ldots,m} \|\mathbf{U}_{[i,:]}\|_2^2. \tag{9}$$

Our error bound is also related to matrix singular vectors: it depends on the quantization error induced in grouping/encoding the rows of the re-scaled singular vectors. According to [32], the quantization error can be written as

$$e = tr(\mathbf{U}\Delta\mathbf{U}^\top) - tr(\Pi\mathbf{U}\Delta\mathbf{U}^\top\Pi^\top) \tag{10}$$

where Δ is the singular value matrix, and $\Pi \in \mathbb{R}^{m\times k}$ is a partition matrix encoding the k-means sampling. For both the coherence (9) and quantization error (10), the lower value, the easier the approximation. An important difference is that the quantization error hinges on both the singular-vector structures and (unknown) sampling scheme, instead of a pre-defined, random sampling.

5 EXPERIMENTS

Our experiments run on a server with 2.6GHZ processor and 64G RAM. Benchmark data sets are described in Table 1. All codes are written in matlab and *fully optimized* by vectorized operations and matrix computations, to guarantee a fair comparison in case time consumption is considered.

First we compare the performance of linear-cost algorithms, including: (a) Sketch-CUR [29], where target sampling rate is three times as much as the base sampling rate; (b) Pseudo-skeleton [16], which is a generalized version of the Nyström method; (c) Ours (`pilot`), step 2 of Algorithm 2; (d) Ours (`follow-kmeans`,

Table 1: Summary of benchmark data sets.

data	#row	#column	sparsity	content
heic0707a	18000	18000	dense	image (galaxy)
heic1206a	29566	14321	dense	image (galaxy)
mnist	60000	60000	dense	RBF kernel
a8a	22696	22696	dense	RBF kernel
movielens	69878	10677	0.56%	movie rating
20news	18774	61188	0.22%	word document
reuters	8293	18933	0.25%	word document
TDT2	10212	36771	0.35%	word document

`wkmeans`, `hdthd`), step 4 of Algorithm 2, using constant weighting, power function weighting (power equals 5), and step function weighting, respectively[1]. In Figure 5, we gradually increase sampling rate from 1% to 15%, and report averaged error[2] $\|\mathbf{A} - \tilde{\mathbf{A}}\|_F / \|\mathbf{A}\|_F$ (for sparse matrices, only non-zero entries are considered) over 20 repeats. The number of selected rows and columns are both k for simplicity, with the sampling rate defined as $k/\sqrt{mn}$.

We can see that our pilot approximation result is already more accurate than Pseudo-skeleton and Sketch-CUR, demonstrating the stability of our sketching routine proposed in Section 4.1. Our follow-up sampling is consistently better than pilot sampling, which demonstrates the "algorithmic boosting" effect; in particular, the boosting effect is more significant on sparse matrices (larger improvement of accuracy between the pilot and follow-up approximations). We also observe that on sparse matrices, the step function (`follow-hdthd`) is slightly better than the power function (`follow-wkmeans`) when used as weighting in k-means sampling.

Then we compare our approach with state-of-the-art randomized algorithms (with quadratic costs), including (a) Adaptive-CUR [28], which uses error distribution of an initial approximation to guide subsequent sampling; (b) CUR Method, a two-step method using fast JL-transform to compute leverage scores and then perform CUR [11]; (c) Random projection [17], with $q = 1$ step of power iteration; (d) Input-sps-time: sparse embedding method by [8]; (e) Ours (`k-means`) for dense matrices with constant weighting function; and (f) Ours (`hd-thd`) for sparse matrices with step weighting function. Averaged performance over 20 repeats is shown in Fig 6. The

[1]For step function, $\Upsilon_i = 1$ if $\|P_{[i,:]}\|_2$ is among the top-k largest for $i = 1, 2, \ldots, m$, and $\Upsilon_i = 0$ otherwise; so we also call this "hard-threshold" (hdthd). In other words, only top-k points are sampled under such weighting scheme.

[2]For all methods under comparison, when computing the error, the approximation $\tilde{\mathbf{A}}$ is first fit to $\mathbf{A}$ by linear transform to remove global scaling and translation factors.

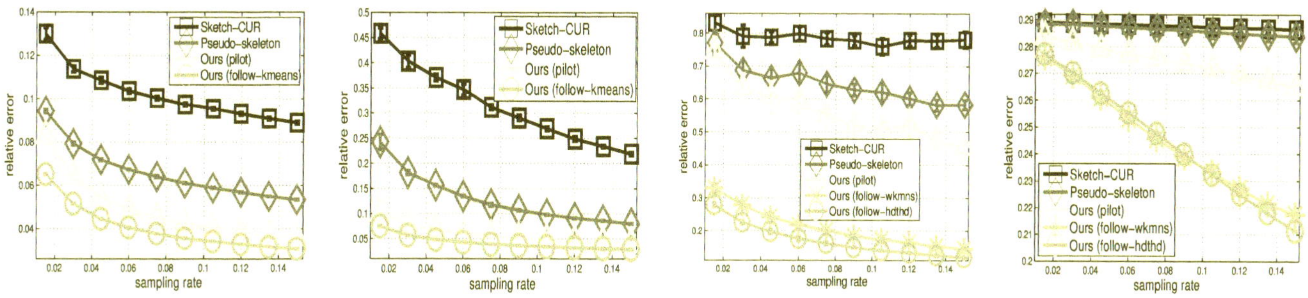

(a) image (b) image (c) 20newsgroup (d) movie-lens

Figure 5: Relative error of our method and other randomized algorithms (with linear costs).

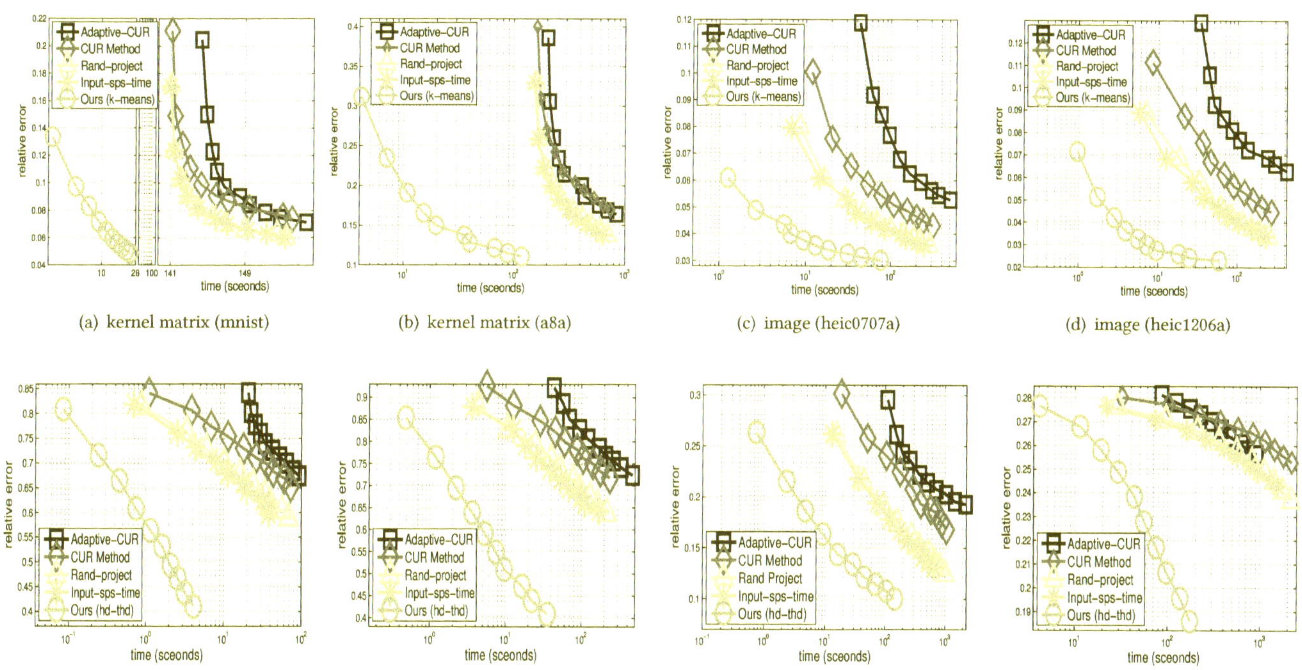

(a) kernel matrix (mnist) (b) kernel matrix (a8a) (c) image (heic0707a) (d) image (heic1206a)

(e) Reuters (f) TDT2 (g) 20Newsgroup (h) movie-lens

Figure 6: Relative approximation error of our method and randomized algorithms (with quadratic costs).

sampling rate for our method is chosen higher than quadratic-cost methods so that their time consumptions are more comparable.

We can see that the Adaptive-CUR can be slower, which we speculate is due to the computation of the residue of approximation on the whole input matrix. The sparse embedding method (input-sparsity-time) is faster and more accurate than the random projection with a (dense) Gaussian template matrix, but the difference can be insignificant on both dense and sparse matrices. The fast CUR method has a similar time cost compared with random projection, but is less accurate. Our approach has significant performance gains on both dense and sparse matrices; its advantage is most obvious on kernel matrices by only computing a small subset of its rows and columns; in comparison, all other methods need to compute the entire kernel matrix. Overall, our approach can be one to two orders of magnitude faster than existing algorithms in order to attain similar accuracies. In the meantime, our memory cost is only a small fraction of theirs. The larger the data, the higher the performance gains that can be expected.

6 CONCLUSIONS

In this work, by unravelling the interesting underlying connection between matrix decomposition and lossy data compression, we proposed cascaded compression sampling for linear-cost low-rank decomposition of large matrices. Our method outperfroms existing randomized algorithms using either dense or sparse projection schemes, demonstrating the power of data encoding in solving large-scale matrix sketching problems. We are currently investigating how to characterize the behaviour of compression-based sampling more precisely using sharp probabilistic error bounds.

APPENDIX

Proof of Theorem 1

We partition $\mathbf{A}$ into equal-sized blocks, by the clusters defined in Section 3.1. Remind that rows in $\mathbf{P}$ are grouped into k clusters with cluster size $T^r_{(i)}$. We add virtual instances to $\mathbf{P}$ such that all clusters have the same size, i.e., $T^r = \max T^r_{(i)}$. Virtual instances added to the qth cluster are chosen as the qth representative in $\mathbf{Z}^r$, so they induce no extra quantization errors. Then, we can re-partition $\mathbf{P}$ into T^r partitions each containing exactly k instances. We use $\mathcal{I}^r_i$ to denote the indexes of these partitions for $i = 1, 2, ..., T^r$; similarly rows in $\mathbf{Q}$ are completed by virtual rows, falling in partitions $\mathcal{I}^c_j$ for $j = 1, 2, ..., T^c$. Finally $\mathbf{A}$ is augmented to kT^r-by-kT^c matrix, forming a number of T^cT^r blocks each is of size k-by-k. The approximation error on each of these blocks is bounded as

$$\frac{1}{\sqrt{k\theta}}\left\|\mathbf{A}_{[\mathcal{I}^r_i,\mathcal{I}^c_j]} - \mathbf{C}_{[\mathcal{I}^r_i,:]}\mathbf{W}^{\dagger}\mathbf{R}^{\top}_{[\mathcal{I}^c_j,:]}\right\|_F \le \sqrt{e^r_j + e^c_j}$$
$$+\sqrt{e^r_i} + \sqrt{e^c_i} + \sqrt{k\theta e^r_i e^c_j}\left\|\mathbf{W}^{\dagger}\right\|_F. \tag{11}$$

Here $e^r_i = \sum_{l\in\mathcal{I}^r_i}\|\mathbf{P}_{[l,:]} - \mathbf{Z}^r_{[s(l),:]}\|^2$ is the error of encoding rows of $\mathbf{P}$ (via $\mathcal{I}^r_i$) with representative $\mathbf{Z}^r$ via the mapping s^r. Similarly, $e^c_i = \sum_{l\in\mathcal{I}^c_i}\|\mathbf{P}_{[l,:]} - \mathbf{Z}^c_{[s(l),:]}\|^2$ is the error of encoding rows in $\mathbf{Q}$ (specified by $\mathcal{I}^c_j$) with representative $\mathbf{Z}^c$.

To prove this inequality, define $\langle\mathbf{X},\mathbf{Y}\rangle = \mathbf{X}\mathbf{Y}^{\top}$ for matrices $\mathbf{X}, \mathbf{Y}$ with proper dimensions

$$\mathbf{C}_{[\mathcal{I}^r_i,:]} = \left\langle\mathbf{P}_{[\mathcal{I}^r_i,:]}, \mathbf{Q}_{[\mathcal{Z}^c,:]}\right\rangle, \mathbf{R}_{[\mathcal{I}^c_j,:]} = \left\langle\mathbf{P}_{[\mathcal{I}^c_j,:]}, \mathbf{Q}_{[\mathcal{Z}^r,:]}\right\rangle, \tag{12}$$
$$\mathbf{A}_{[\mathcal{I}^r_i,\mathcal{I}^r_j]} = \left\langle\mathbf{P}_{[\mathcal{I}^r_i,:]}, \mathbf{Q}_{[\mathcal{I}^c_j,:]}\right\rangle, \mathbf{W} = \left\langle\mathbf{P}_{[\mathcal{Z}^r,:]}, \mathbf{Q}_{[\mathcal{Z}^c,:]}\right\rangle. \tag{13}$$

Here we use transposed version of $\mathbf{R}$ for convenience of proof. The change of representation won't affect the correctness of our proofs. We also define the following difference matrices

$$\Delta_C = \mathbf{C}_{[\mathcal{I}^r_i,:]} - \mathbf{W}, \Delta_R = \mathbf{R}_{[\mathcal{I}^c_j,:]} - \mathbf{W}, \Delta_A = \mathbf{A}_{[\mathcal{I}^r_i,\mathcal{I}^c_j]} - \mathbf{W}, \tag{14}$$

We will also need the following inequality,

$$(\phi(\mathbf{x}_1,\mathbf{y}_1) - \phi(\mathbf{x}_2,\mathbf{y}_2))^2 \le \theta\cdot(\|\mathbf{x}_1 - \mathbf{x}_2\|^2 + \|\mathbf{y}_1 - \mathbf{y}_2\|^2), \tag{15}$$

where $\mathbf{x}_1, \mathbf{x}_2, \mathbf{y}_1, \mathbf{y}_2$ are $1\times d$ vectors, $\phi(\cdot,\cdot)$ be the inner product between two such vectors, $\theta = 2f'(\xi)^2$ (using Lagrangian mean-value theorem). Using Proposition 2, we can bound norms of the difference matrices

$$\|\Delta_A\|^2_F = \left\|\mathbf{A}_{[\mathcal{I}^r_i,\mathcal{I}^c_j]} - \mathbf{W}\right\|^2_F$$
$$= \left\|\left\langle\mathbf{P}_{[\mathcal{I}^r_i,:]}, \mathbf{Q}_{[\mathcal{I}^c_j,:]}\right\rangle - \left\langle\mathbf{P}_{[\mathcal{Z}^r,:]}, \mathbf{Q}_{[\mathcal{Z}^c,:]}\right\rangle\right\|^2_F$$
$$= \sum_{p,q=1}^{k}\left[\phi\left(\mathbf{P}_{[\mathcal{I}^r_i(p),:]}, \mathbf{Q}_{[\mathcal{I}^c_j(q),:]}\right) - \phi\left(\mathbf{P}_{[\mathcal{Z}^r(p),:]}, \mathbf{Q}_{[\mathcal{Z}^c(q),:]}\right)\right]^2$$
$$\le \theta\sum_{p,q=1}^{k}\left(\left\|\mathbf{P}_{[\mathcal{I}^r_i(p),:]} - \mathbf{P}_{[\mathcal{Z}^r(p),:]}\right\|^2 + \left\|\mathbf{Q}_{[\mathcal{I}^c_j(q),:]} - \mathbf{Q}_{[\mathcal{Z}^c(q),:]}\right\|^2\right)$$
$$= k\theta\left(e^r_i + e^c_j\right).$$

Here we have used the pre-defined relation $s^r(\mathcal{I}^r_i(p)) = p$, and $s^c(\mathcal{I}^c_j(q)) = q$, since the partition index $\mathcal{I}^c_i$ and $\mathcal{I}^c_j$ has the corresponding representative set $\mathcal{Z}$. Similarly,

$$\|\Delta_C\|^2_F = \left\|\mathbf{C}_{[\mathcal{I}^r_i,:]} - \mathbf{W}\right\|^2_F\left\|\left\langle\mathbf{P}_{[\mathcal{I}^r_i,:]}, \mathbf{Q}_{[\mathcal{Z}^c,:]}\right\rangle - \left\langle\mathbf{P}_{[\mathcal{Z}^r,:]}, \mathbf{Q}_{[\mathcal{Z}^c,:]}\right\rangle\right\|^2_F$$
$$\le \theta\sum_{p,q=1}^{k}\left\|\mathbf{P}_{[\mathcal{I}^r_i(p),:]} - \mathbf{P}_{[\mathcal{Z}^r(p),:]}\right\|^2 = \theta k e^r_i,$$

and $\|\Delta_R\|^2_F \le \theta k e^c_j$. By using above three inequalities, and combining them with (13), we can prove (11). With this proposition, and by using the inequality $\sum_i^n\sqrt{x_i} \le \sqrt{n\sum_i x_i}$, the overall approximation error can be bounded as follows

$$\frac{1}{\sqrt{k\theta}}\left\|\mathbf{A} - \mathbf{C}\mathbf{W}^{\dagger}\mathbf{R}^{\top}\right\|_F \le \frac{1}{\sqrt{k\theta}}\sum_{i=1}^{T^r}\sum_{j=1}^{T^c}\left\|\mathbf{A}_{[\mathcal{I}^r_i,\mathcal{I}^c_j]} - \mathbf{C}_{[\mathcal{I}^r_i,:]}\mathbf{W}^{\dagger}\mathbf{R}_p[\mathcal{I}^c_j,:]^{\top}\right.$$
$$\le \sqrt{T^c}\sum_i\sqrt{\sum_j(e^c_j + e^r_j)} + \sqrt{T^r}\sum_j\sqrt{\sum_i e^r_i} + \sqrt{T^c}\sum_i\sqrt{\sum_j e^c_j}$$
$$+\sqrt{k\theta}\left\|\mathbf{W}^{\dagger}\right\|_F\sqrt{T^c}\sum_i\sqrt{\sum_j e^r_i e^c_j}$$
$$\le \sqrt{T^cT^r(T^re^c + T^ce^r)} + T^c\sqrt{T^re^r} + T^r\sqrt{T^ce^c} + \sqrt{k\theta}\sqrt{T^cT^re^ce^r}\left\|\mathbf{W}^{\dagger}\right\|$$
$$\le \sqrt{3(T^c + T^r)(e^c + e^r)} + \sqrt{k\theta}\sqrt{T^cT^re^ce^r}\|\mathbf{W}^{\dagger}\|_F.$$

By using $T = \max(T^r, T^c)$, we can easily prove Theorem 1.

Proof of Theorem 2

The CCS algorithm uses only the k-dimensional embedding instead of the exact embedding as stated in Theorem 1. The consequence is that the resultant error bound will be loosened by the trailing singular values of the input matrix, as follows

$$\left\|\mathbf{A} - \mathbf{C}\mathbf{W}^{\dagger}\mathbf{R}^{\top}\right\|_F \le \left\|\mathbf{A}_k - \mathbf{C}\mathbf{W}^{\dagger}\mathbf{R}^{\top}\right\|_F + \left\|\mathbf{A}_{\bar{k}}\right\|_F$$
$$\le \sqrt{T^cT^r}\left(\sqrt{3k\theta(e^r + e^c)(T^r + T^c)} + k\theta\sqrt{e^ce^r}\left\|\mathbf{W}^{\dagger}\right\|_F\right) + \|\mathbf{A}_{\bar{k}}\|_F$$
$$= \mu\sqrt{e^r + e^c} + \nu\sqrt{e^r\cdot e^c} + \|\mathbf{A}_{\bar{k}}\|_F,$$

where we have $\mu = \sqrt{3k\theta T^cT^r(T^r + T^c)}$, $\nu = k\theta\sqrt{T^cT^r}\|\mathbf{W}^{\dagger}\|_F$, and $\|\mathbf{A}_{\bar{k}}\|_F = \sqrt{\sum_{i=k+1}^{\min(m,n)}\sigma_i^2}$ is a constant which is the l_2-norm of the $\min(m,n) - k$ singular values. In case singular-value spectrum decays rapidly, this constant can be quite small. In other words the error bound is only slightly loosened if rank-k embeddings are used for the follow-up sampling.

In the following we will use the updated error bound for the pilot and follow-up sketching, as

$$\Psi_p = \mu_p\sqrt{e^r_p + e^c_p} + \nu_p\sqrt{e^r_p\cdot e^c_p} + \|\mathbf{A}_{\bar{k}}\|$$
$$\Psi_f = \mu_p\sqrt{e^r_f + e^c_f} + \nu_f\sqrt{e^r_f\cdot e^c_f} + \|\mathbf{A}_{\bar{k}}\|,$$

where

$$\mu_p = \sqrt{3k\theta T^c_pT^r_p(T^r_p + T^c_p)}, \nu_p = k\theta\sqrt{T^c_pT^r_p}\left\|\mathbf{W}^{\dagger}_p\right\|_F$$
$$\mu_f = \sqrt{3k\theta T^c_fT^r_f(T^r_f + T^c_f)}, \nu_f = k\theta\sqrt{T^c_fT^r_f}\left\|\mathbf{W}^{\dagger}_f\right\|_F.$$

Here the sub-index $\{p, f\}$ denotes the pilot and the follow-up step, and all parameters are defined in the same way as in Theorem 1. For example, $T^c_{p,f}$ and $T^r_{p,f}$ are the maximum cluster sizes in the column and row embeddings; $e^c_{p,f}$ and $e^r_{p,f}$ are the encoding errors for the column and row embeddings. The above relation holds because the random sampling in the pilot step can be deemed as equivalently running on the the rank-k embeddings of the input matrix. This instantly gives the following guarantee

$$\Delta^r_e = e^r_p - e^r_f \geq 0, \Delta^c_e = e^c_p - e^c_f \geq 0.$$

Here Δ^r_e and Δ^c_e are exactly the drop of the encoding errors achieved by the k-means sampling algorithm in the follow-up sampling step. Next, we will show that, the drop of the error bounds from the pilot sketching step to the follow-up sketching step in CCS, can be exactly quantified by the drop of the encoding errors Δ^r_e and Δ^c_e.

We also use the inequality $g(x) - g(y) \geq (x - y) \cdot g'(x)$ for the function $g(x) = \sqrt{x}$ and any pair of numbers $x \geq y \geq 0$. Namely $\sqrt{x} - \sqrt{y} \geq (x - y)\frac{1}{2\sqrt{x}}$. We assume that $T^r_p = T^r_f = T^r$, and $T^c_p = T^c_f = T^c$. This is justified because the pilot random sampling and the follow-up k-means sampling can be deemed as running on the same, rank-k embedding of the input matrix. Namely the maximum cluster sizes in the two rounds of samplings are the same. So we can write $\mu_p = \mu_f = \mu$. On other hand, we assume that $\|\mathbf{W}^\dagger_f\|_F \leq \|\mathbf{W}^\dagger_p\|_F$. This is because the follow-up sampling selects highly non-redundant rows and columns as representatives, so the norm of $\|\mathbf{W}^\dagger\|_F$ typically drops. In other words,

$$\nu_p\sqrt{e^r_p e^c_p} - \nu_f\sqrt{e^r_f e^c_f} \geq k\theta\sqrt{e^r_p e^c_p}\sqrt{T^c T^r}\left\|\mathbf{W}^\dagger_p\right\|_F - k\theta\sqrt{e^r_f e^c_f}\sqrt{T^c T^r}\left\|\mathbf{W}^\dagger_p\right\|_F$$
$$= k\theta\sqrt{T^c T^r}\left\|\mathbf{W}^\dagger_p\right\|_F\left(\sqrt{e^r_p e^c_p} - \sqrt{e^r_f \cdot e^c_f}\right) \geq 0.$$

So we further bound the difference as follows

$$\Psi_p - \Psi_f = \left(\mu_p\sqrt{e^r_p + e^c_p} - \mu_p\sqrt{e^r_f + e^c_f}\right) + \left(\nu_p\sqrt{e^r_p \cdot e^c_p} - \nu_f\sqrt{e^r_f \cdot e^c_f}\right)$$
$$\geq \mu\left(\sqrt{e^r_p + e^c_p} - \sqrt{e^r_f + e^c_f}\right) + k\theta\sqrt{T^c T^r}\left\|\mathbf{W}^\dagger_p\right\|_F\left(\sqrt{e^r_p \cdot e^c_p} - \sqrt{e^r_f \cdot e^c_f}\right)$$
$$\geq \mu\frac{1}{2\sqrt{e^r_p + e^c_p}}\left(e^r_p - e^r_f + e^c_p - e^c_f\right) + \left\|\mathbf{W}^\dagger_p\right\|_F\frac{k\theta\sqrt{T^c T^r}}{\sqrt{e^r_p \cdot e^c_p}}\left(e^r_p e^c_p - e^r_f \cdot e^c_f\right)$$
$$= \frac{\sqrt{3k\theta T^c T^r(T^r + T^c)}}{2\sqrt{e^r_p + e^c_p}}(\Delta^r_e + \Delta^c_e) + \left\|\mathbf{W}^\dagger_p\right\|_F\frac{k\theta\sqrt{T^c T^r}}{\sqrt{e^r_p \cdot e^c_p}}\left(\Delta^r_e e^c_f + \Delta^c_e e^r_f + \Delta^r_e \Delta^c_e\right).$$

This completes the proof of Theorem 2.

REFERENCES

[1] O. Alter, P.O. Brown, and D. Botstein. 2000. Singular value decomposition for genome-wide expression data processing and modeling. *Proceedings of the National Academy of Sciences* 97, 18 (2000), 10101–10106.

[2] R. Bhatia. 2015. *Positive Definite Matrices.* Princeton University Press.

[3] C. Boutsidis, P. Drineas, and M. Magdon-Ismail. 2004. Near-Optimal Column-Based Matrix Reconstruction. *SIAM J. Comput.* 43, 2 (2004), 687–717.

[4] C. Boutsidis and A. Gittens. 2013. Improved matrix algorithms via the Subsampled Randomized Hadamard Transform. *SIAM Journal of MAtrix Analysis and Applications* 34, 3 (2013), 1301–1340.

[5] C. Boutsidis and D.P. Woodruff. 2014. Optimal CUR matrix decompositions. In *Proceedings of the forty-sixth annual ACM symposium on Theory of computing.* 353–362.

[6] E.J. Candes and B. Recht. 2009. Exact Matrix Completion via Matrix Completion. *Foundations of Computational Mathematics* 9 (2009), 717–772.

[7] K.L. Clarkson, P. Drineas, M. Magdon-Ismail, M.W. Mahoney, X. Meng, and D.P. Woodruff. 2013. The Fast Cauchy Transform and Faster Robust Linear Regression. In *Annual ACM-SIAM Symposium on Discrete Algorithms.* 466–477.

[8] K.L. Clarkson and D.P. Woodruff. 2013. Low rank approximation and regression in input sparsity time. In *Annual ACM Symposium on theory of computing.*

[9] S. Deerwester, S.T. Dumais, G.W. Furnas, T.K. Landauer, and R. Harshman. 1990. Indexing by latent semantic analysis. *Journal of the American Society for Information Science* 41, 6 (1990), 391–407.

[10] P. Drineas, R. Kannan, and M.W. Mahoney. 2006. Fast Monte Carlo algorithms for matrices II: computing a low-rank approximation to a matrix. *SIAM Journal of Computing* 36, 1 (2006), 158–183.

[11] P. Drineas, M. Magdon-Ismail, M.W. Mahoney, and D.P. Woodruff. 2012. Fast approximation of matrix coherence and statistical leverage. *Journal of Machine Learning Research* 13, 1 (2012), 3475–3506.

[12] P. Drineas and M.W. Mahoney. 2005. On the Nyström Method for Approximating a Gram Matrix for Improved Kernel-Based Learning. *Journal of Machine Learning Research* 6 (2005), 2153–2175.

[13] C. Fowlkes, S. Belongie, F. Chung, and J. Malik. 2004. Spectral grouping using the Nyström method. *IEEE Transactions on Pattern Analysis and Machine Intelligence* 26, 2 (2004), 214–225.

[14] A. Frieze, R. Kannan, and S. Vempala. 2004. Fast monte-carlo algorithms for finding low-rank approximations. *J. ACM* 51, 6 (2004), 1025–1041.

[15] G. H. Golub and C. F. Van Loan. 1996. *Matrix Computation.* Johns Hopkins University Press.

[16] S.A. Goreinov, E.E. Tyrtyshnikov, and N.L. Zamarashki. 1997. A theory of pseudoskeleton approximations. *Linear Algebra Appl.* 261, 1 (1997), 1–21.

[17] N. Halko, P.G. Martinsson, and J.A. Tropp. 2011. Finding Structure with Randomness: Probabilistic Algorithms for Constructing Approximate Matrix Decompositions. *SIAM Rev.* 53, 2 (2011), 217–288.

[18] S. Kumar, M. Mohri, and A. Talwalkar. 2012. Sampling methods for the Nyström method. *Journal of Machine Learning Research* 13, 1 (2012), 981–1006.

[19] L. Lan, K. Zhang, H. Ge, W. Cheng, J. Liu, A. Rauber, X. Li, J. Wang, and H. Zha. 2017. Low-rank Decomposition Meets Kernel Learning: A Generalized Nyström Method. *Artificial Intelligence* 250 (2017), 1–15.

[20] D.D. Lee and H.S. Seung. 1999. Learning the parts of objects by non-negative matrix factorization. *Nature* 401, 6755 (1999), 788 – 791.

[21] E. Liberty. 2013. Simple and deterministic matrix sketching. In *ACM SIGKDD international conference on Knowledge discovery and data mining.* 581–588.

[22] E. Liberty, F. Woolfe, P. Martinsson, V. Rokhlin, and M. Tygert. 2007. Randomized algorithms for the low-rank approximation of matrices. *Proceedings of National Academy of Sciences* 104, 51 (2007), 20167–20172.

[23] Y. Linde, A. Buzo, and R.M. Gray. 1980. An Algorithm for Vector Quantizer Design. *IEEE Transactions on Communications* 28, 1 (1980), 84–95.

[24] M.W. Mahoney. 2011. Randomized Algorithms for Matrices and Data. *Foundations and Trends in Machine Learning* 3, 2 (2011), 123 – 224.

[25] M.W. Mahoney and P. Drineas. 2009. CUR matrix decompositions for improved data analysis. *Proceedings of National Academy of Sciences* 106 (2009), 697–702.

[26] I. Mitliagkas, C. Caramanis, and P. Jain. 2013. Memory limited, streaming PCA. In *Advances in Neural Information Processing Systems.* 2886–2894.

[27] J. Nelson and H.L. Nguyên. 2015. OSNAP: Faster Numerical Linear Algebra Algorithms via Sparser Subspace Embeddings. In *IEEE Annual Symposium on Foundations of Computer Science (FOCS).* 135–143.

[28] S. Wang and Z. Zhang. 2012. A Scalable CUR Matrix Decomposition Algorithm: Lower Time Complexity and Tighter Bound. In *Advances in Neural Information Processing Systems 25.* 647–655.

[29] S. Wang, Z. Zhang, and T. Zhang. 2016. Towards More Efficient Nystrom Approximation and CUR Matrix Decomposition. *Journal of Machine Learning Research* 17 (2016), 1–49.

[30] C.K. I. Williams and M. Seeger. 2001. Using the Nystrom Method to Speed Up Kernel Machines. In *Advances in Neural Information Processing Systems 13.* 682–688.

[31] S. Yun, M. lelarge, and A. Proutiere. 2015. Fast and Memory Optimal Low-Rank Matrix Approximation. In *Advances in Neural Information Processing Systems 28.* 3177–3185.

[32] H. Zha, C. Ding, M. Gu, X. He, and H. Simon. 2002. Spectral relaxation for K-means clustering.. In *Neural Information Processing Systems 14.*

[33] K. Zhang, L. Lan, Z. Wang, and F. Moerchen. 2012. Scaling up Kernel SVM on Limited Resources: A Low-rank Linearization Approach. In *Proceedings of the Fifteenth International Conference on Artificial Intelligence and Statistics (Proceedings of Machine Learning Research),* Vol. 22. 1425–1434.

[34] K. Zhang, I. Tsang, and J. Kwok. 2008. Improved Nyström low-rank approximation and error analysis. In *International conference on Machine learning.* 1232–1239.

[35] T. Zhou and D. Tao. 2011. Godec: Randomized low-rank & sparse matrix decomposition in noisy case (2011). In *International Conference on Machine Learning.*

Tracking the Dynamics in Crowdfunding

Hongke Zhao, Hefu Zhang
Anhui Province Key Laboratory of Big Data Analysis and Application, University of Science and Technology of China
{zhhk,zhf2011}@mail.ustc.edu.cn

Yong Ge
Eller College of Management, University of Arizona
yongge@email.arizona.edu

Qi Liu, Enhong Chen*
Anhui Province Key Laboratory of Big Data Analysis and Application, University of Science and Technology of China
{qiliuql,cheneh}@ustc.edu.cn

Huayu Li
College of Computing and Informatics, UNC Charlotte
hli38@uncc.edu

Le Wu
School of Computer and Information, Hefei University of Technology
lewu@hfut.edu.cn

ABSTRACT

Crowdfunding is an emerging Internet fundraising mechanism by raising monetary contributions from the crowd for projects or ventures. In these platforms, the dynamics, i.e., daily funding amount on *campaigns* and *perks* (backing options with rewards), are the most concerned issue for creators, backers and platforms. However, tracking the dynamics in crowdfunding is very challenging and still under-explored. To that end, in this paper, we present a focused study on this important problem. A special goal is to forecast the funding amount for a given campaign and its perks in the future days. Specifically, we formalize the dynamics in crowdfunding as a hierarchical time series, i.e., *campaign level* and *perk level*. Specific to each level, we develop a special regression by modeling the decision making process of the crowd (visitors and backing probability) and exploring various factors that impact the decision; on this basis, an enhanced switching regression is proposed at each level to address the heterogeneity of funding sequences. Further, we employ a revision matrix to combine the two-level base forecasts for the final forecasting. We conduct extensive experiments on a real-world crowdfunding data collected from Indiegogo.com. The experimental results clearly demonstrate the effectiveness of our approaches on tracking the dynamics in crowdfunding.

KEYWORDS

Crowdfunding, Dynamics, Hierarchical time series

ACM Reference format:

Hongke Zhao, Hefu Zhang, Yong Ge, Qi Liu, Enhong Chen, Huayu Li, and Le Wu. 2017. Tracking the Dynamics in Crowdfunding. In *Proceedings of KDD'17, August 13-17, 2017, Halifax, NS, Canada.*, 10 pages.
DOI: http://dx.doi.org/10.1145/3097983.3098030

*The corresponding author.

KDD'17, August 13-17, 2017, Halifax, NS, Canada.

DOI: http://dx.doi.org/10.1145/3097983.3098030

Figure 1: An example of raising-money campaign.

1 INTRODUCTION

Crowdfunding, as a particular form of crowdsourcing, is the practice of funding a project or venture by raising monetary contributions from a large number of people. Recent years have witnessed the rapid development of crowdfunding platforms, such as Kickstarter.com[1], Indiegogo.com[2]. In 2015, it was estimated by *Forbes* that over US $34 billion were raised worldwide in this way, compared with that the venture capital industry invests $30 billion on average each year [3].

As the most popular type of crowdfunding, reward-based platforms (e.g., Indiegogo.com) enable people to create projects for raising money they need, in return for "rewards" (often vowing future products). When an individual (or a team) wants to raise money on these platforms, she will create a *campaign* for her project. Figure 1 shows the snapshot for one raising-money campaign on Indiegogo.com. From the campaign page, we can see some basic properties of this campaign, e.g., *creator, goal, story* and also the dynamic funding progress, e.g., *funded/remaining amount, remaining days*. A campaign often sets several (e.g., 10) types of "rewards" (i.e., perks) with different prices, thus backers could make different monetary contributions by selecting different perks. The funding sequence is shown in the green rectangle of Figure 1, which is indeed a two-level time series, i.e., the dynamic of funding amount on perks and dynamic of summarized-funding amount on this campaign.

In the literature, there are a number of studies on crowdfunding [4, 27, 29]. Most of these existing works focus on predicting the campaign success, i.e., reaching the fixed funding goals or

[1] https://www.kickstarter.com
[2] https://www.indiegogo.com

not [22, 27, 29], with small-scale datasets. However, many platforms, such as Indiegogo.com, encourage the "flexible goal" instead of the "fixed goal" [10], where the success of a campaign is no longer a big concern of creators. In fact, for creators, backers and platform operators, they all want to understand and forecast the dynamics of campaigns and perks every day, rather than just predict the final funding results. Specifically, successful forecasting of the dynamics could benefit all three parties: (1) creators can update their campaigns and adjust the perk settings in time based on the dynamics; (2) backers can make better decisions according to the current popularities and future dynamics; (3) platform operators can provide better services, such as management and recommendation of campaigns based on the dynamics. Unfortunately, less effort has been made towards this goal. To this end, in this paper, we propose a focused study on tracking and forecasting the dynamics in crowdfunding in a holistic view. To the best of our knowledge, this is the first attempt in this area.

However, it is a very challenging task. First, there are hierarchical dynamics in longitudinal crowdfunding data, i.e., multiple time series of funding amount for a given campaign and its multiple perks. How to model the hierarchical dynamics is a nontrivial problem. Second, funding dynamics are potentially affected by the visiting crowd's decision making and various factors, such as social features, prices, and time. To track and forecast the dynamics, how to model the effects of these factors in the decision making of crowd is very challenging. At last, the dynamics vary a lot among different campaigns, perks, and even different funding phases. Thus, how to address such heterogeneity is also difficult.

To conduct this study, we first collect massive real-world crowdfunding data with detailed daily transaction information from Indiegogo.com [3]. After carefully exploring the data, we identify important factors that affect the decision making of crowd and the dynamics of crowdfunding, and construct useful features at both campaign and perk levels. To address the hierarchy of crowdfunding dynamics, we propose a two-layer framework for modeling the dynamics at both campaign and perk levels. Specific to each level, we first develop a single regression model to capture the impacts of various factors (e.g., financial features, social features, time) on the decision making of the crowd (i.e., visitors and backing probability). Further, to address the aforementioned heterogeneity of funding sequences, we propose an enhanced switching regression at each level. Then we employ a revision matrix to combine the two-level base forecasts in order to achieve an optimal final forecasting. Finally, we evaluate our approaches by conducting extensive experiments with our collected data. The experimental results clearly demonstrate the effectiveness of our proposed approaches for tracking and forecasting the dynamics in crowdfunding. Specifically, the contributions of this paper can be summarized as follows:

- We propose a focused study on tracking and forecasting the dynamics of crowdfunding at both campaign and perk levels using a unique dataset collected from Indiegogo.com.
- We develop a special regression at each level for dynamics in crowdfunding by modeling the funding process. Further, we introduce an enhanced switching regression to better handle the heterogeneity of dynamics among different campaigns, perks and different funding phases.
- We develop a novel two-layer framework that could capture the intrinsic relationship between campaign-level dynamics and perk-level dynamics, and employ a revision matrix to combine the base forecasts at two levels for achieving better final forecasting of dynamics.
- We conduct extensive experiments to validate the effectiveness of our method by comparing with several state-of-the-art methods, and report some interesting findings.

[3]The data is publicly available in http://home.ustc.edu.cn/%7Ezhhk/DataSets.html

2 RELATED WORK

The related work can be grouped into two categories, i.e., the work on crowdfunding and the studies on time series forecasting.

2.1 Crowdfunding

Since crowdfunding is a recently emerging market, many problems are still under-explored in the literature. In the past, some prior studies focused on an important issue: predicting the funding results, i.e., success or failure of a campaign, and identifying the influence factors [14, 22, 27]. For example, to predict the success or failure of campaigns and also estimate the time of success, [22] formulated the campaign success prediction as a survival analysis problem and applied the censored regression approach where one could perform regression in the presence of partial information. Lu et al. [27] inferred the impacts of social media on crowdfunding and found the social features could help predict the success rate of project. Mitra and Gilbert [28] explored the factors which lead to successfully funding a crowdfunding project. They found the language used in the project has surprisingly predictive power accounting for 58.56% of the variance around successful funding. Besides the studies of predicting final funding results, some researchers studied the fundraising dynamics for campaigns in their complete funding durations [19]. However, these studies are mainly from the statistical and empirical perspectives to understand the backers' behaviors, and are still lack of deep and quantitative explorations. In fact, creators, backers and platform operators all want to track the dynamics of both campaigns and perks every day, rather than just to predict their final funding results. Unfortunately, less effort has been made towards this goal.

Besides the task of predicting success, a few studies have explored the other problems in crowdfunding or the similar service, e.g., P2P lending, from data mining perspectives, such as campaign recommendations [30], loan recommendations [36, 38], investor (backer) recommendations [2], market state modeling [37] and backing motivation classifications [26].

2.2 Time Series Forecasting

In the literature, time series forecasting has been widely studied [5, 6]. Models for time series forecasting have many forms and can describe different stochastic processes. For example, the autoregressive model [1, 8] and vector autoregression model [18] assume that the current value linearly depends on the previous values. However, conventional autoregressive models only include the response variables without exogenous variables. To address

Table 1: A Summary of data.

Entity	Amount
Campaign	14,143 (13,227 flexible, 916 fixed Campaigns)
Perk	83,450
Member	27,721 Creators (Belong to 14,137 Teams), 211,812 Backers
Contribution	1,862,097 Counts, $ 206,151,977 Amount
Comment	172,824 Comments, 68,189 Replies

the non-linear dependency of input variables and output variables, some other models were applied, such as support vector machine [7] and neural networks [33, 34]. In particular, with the development of deep learning in recent years, many studies found that the recurrent neural network (RNN) can provide satisfactory results for nonstationary time series forecasting [9, 13]. However, most of these methods work as a black box, and are lack of explanatory.

Indeed, developing a forecasting model could not only predict the funding amount but also interpret the decision making of the crowd and the factors impacting the decision, which is very needed for crowdfunding. Unfortunately, little effort has been made to track and forecast the dynamics of crowdfunding in this way.

3 PRELIMINARIES

In this section, we first introduce the working mechanism of Indiegogo.com, and also the collected dataset from this website. Then we introduce the constructed features from the data.

3.1 Indiegogo.com and Dataset

In crowdfunding services, there are generally three types of actors: the individual *creators* or teams who propose the *campaigns to* be funded for their ideas, the visiting individuals (i.e., potential *backers*) who look for campaigns to support, and a *platform* (e.g., Indiegogo.com) that brings these two parties together [12]. Based on the different types of rewards for backers, crowdfunding platforms can be mainly classified into four categories, i.e., *donation-based, reward-based, equity-based* and *lending-based* platforms [21]. As the most popular type, reward-based platforms follow a mode in which a backer's primary objective for funding is to gain a non-financial reward, i.e., *perk* in Indiegogo.com. Indiegogo.com also encourages the "flexible goal" instead of the "fixed goal" and "all-or-nothing" rule [10, 36, 37] for campaigns, which is very different from other common crowdfunding platforms, such as Kickstarter.com [2, 14, 22, 27, 30]. That is to say, for one flexible campaign, it is not necessary to raise a fixed amount of money in the declared durations in order to make this campaign effective. Even a less amount of fund (than the flexible goal) is collected eventually, the funding transaction of this campaign will still be effective. Also, one campaign can continue collecting fund after the flexible goal is reached or over time. In other words, for the flexible-goal campaigns in Indiegogo.com, the declared goals and durations are only for informational purposes.

Indiegogo data contains a variety of heterogeneous information about all entities as shown in Table 1. Entities of each type include various information in the form of unstructured data, such as image, video, and text, and structured data, such as geo-spatial, numerical, categorical, and ordinal data. From these entities, we can obtain the hierarchical dynamics (e.g., daily funding amount time series)

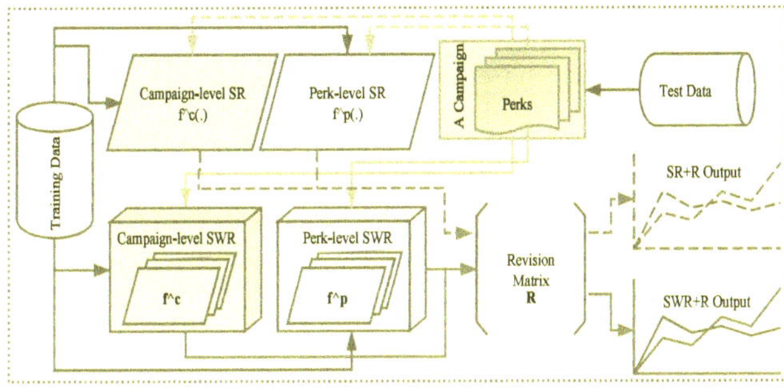

Figure 2: Overview of our solution.

for both campaigns and perks, and also construct various features including both static and time-varying ones.

3.2 Constructed Features

From this dataset, we construct 24 features for campaigns and 30 features for perks. A summary of them is shown in Table 2.

3.2.1 Campaign Features. The campaign features can be grouped into 4 categories, i.e., campaign profile, social media, perk summary and funding progress. The features of campaign profile and social media are extracted from campaign entities. The features of perk summary, i.e., *Perk Option, Claimed Num*, are extracted from the corresponding perk entities of a campaign. The features of funding progress and also *Available Num* are extracted from contribution entities, which are time-varying.

These features are very heterogeneous, including both numerical, categorical data and also text. For consistency, we represent all features as numerics or numerical vectors [25]. Specifically, for the categorical data with less than 10 dimensions, such as *Type, Owner Type, Currency,* and *Verification,* we adopt the **one-hot encoding** [36], i.e., converting a categorical variable with n categories into a n-dimensional binary vector, in which only the value in the corresponding category is set to one and the other values are set to zero. For the categorical data with more than 10 dimensions, such as *Category* and geo-spatial data, i.e., *Country, City,* we use the **count encoding**, i.e., replacing the variables by the respective count frequencies of the variables in the dataset. For text data, such as *Title, Story,* we adopt a **doc2vec** tool [20] to convert them into numerical vectors. Specifically, the numerical vector for *title* is 10-dimensional and the vector for *story* is 100-dimensional.

3.2.2 Perk Features. The perk features can be grouped into three categories, i.e., perk profile, funding progress and the features from its campaign. In particular, the funding dynamic of a perk is highly related to its campaign features. Thus, we also include the features of the corresponding campaign as a part of each perk's feature. We preprocess them in the same way as introduced for campaigns, except the perk description is represented by a 10-dimensional numerical vector.

4 PROBLEM AND METHOD OVERVIEW

In this section, we first introduce the problem of tracking the dynamics in crowdfunding, and then overview our proposed method. For better illustration, Table 3 lists the mathematical notations used in this paper.

Table 2: The description of features.

Feature level	Category	Feature Type	Feature	Description
Campaign Feature	Campaign Profile	Static	Title	Title of the campaign
			Story	Detailed description of the campaign in text
			Team Size	Number of members in the crowdfunding team
			Type	Flexible or fixed goal
			Duration	Declared funding duration of the campaign
			Goal	Amount the campaign wants to fund
			Country	Country of the creator
			City	City of the creator
			Category	Category of the campaign, such as Technology, Education
			Owner Type	Purpose of the campaign, such as business, individual, non-profit
			Currency	Currency for paying the perks, such USD
	Social or Media		Image Num	Number of images provided by the campaign
			Video Num	Number of videos provided by the campaign
			Social Exposure	Number of exposure places, e.g.,Facebook, Twitter, Youtube, website
			Friend Num	Number of friends of funding team in Facebook
			Verification	Whether the campaign was verified in Facebook
	Perk Summary		Perk Option	Number of perk options
			Claimed Num	Total claimed number of perks
		Time-varying	Available Num	Total available number of perks
	Funding Progress		Backer Num	Number of backers who has contributed to the campaign
			Funded Amount	Amount the campaign has collected
			Funded Percentage	Percentage the campaign has funded
			Comment Num	Number of comments the campaign received
			Reply Num	Number of replies the creator has made
Perk Feature	Perk Profile	Static	Description	Short description of the perk
			Featured	Whether this perk is recommended by the campaign
			Price	Unit price of the perk
			Claimed Num	Claimed number of the perk
	Funding progress	Time-varying	Sales Num	Number of perks have sold
			Available Num	Available number of the perk
	Campaign	-	Campaign Features	All the features of the campaign which this perk belongs to

Table 3: Mathematical notations.

Symbol	Size	Description
$Y^c(Y^p)$	$I(K) \times T$	Daily funding amount matrix for I campaigns (K perks), T funding days;
B	$I \times T$	Daily backer number matrix for I campaigns;
$\mathcal{X}^c(\mathcal{X}^p)$	$I(K) \times T \times M^c(M^p)$	Campaign (perk) covariant/feature tensor, $M^c(M^p)$ is the length of covariant/feature vector;
$\mathcal{Z}^p$	$K \times T \times J$	Unobservable cluster tensor for perks, J is the cluster number of perk sequences;
$f^p(.)(f^c(.))$	1	Base forecasts in SR for perks (campaigns);
$\boldsymbol{f}^p(\boldsymbol{f}^c)$	$J(J') \times 1$	Base forecasts in SWR for perks (campaigns), $\boldsymbol{f}^p = \{f_j^p(.)\vert j \in \{1,\dots,J\}\}, \boldsymbol{f}^c = \{f_{j'}^c(.)\vert j' \in \{1,\dots,J'\}\}$;
$\boldsymbol{R}_i$	$(K_i+1)^2$	Revision matrix for campaign i and its K_i perks.

4.1 Problem Statement

For I campaigns with T funding days[4], we have the daily funding amount time series $Y^c = (Y^c(i,t))_{I\times T}$, backer number time series $B = (B(i,t))_{I\times T}$, and the campaign features $\mathcal{X}^c = ((\mathcal{X}^c(i,t))_{I\times T}$. K_i represents the number of perks of i-th campaign, and $k_i \in \{1,\dots,K_i\}$ represents the k_i-th perk of this campaign. For all the K ($K = \sum_{i=1}^{I} K_i$) perks, we also have their daily funding amount time series $Y^p = (Y^p(k,t))_{K\times T}$, and perk features $\mathcal{X}^p = (\mathcal{X}^p(k,t))_{K\times T}$. Each $Y^c(i,t)$ or $Y^p(k,t)$ represents the funding amount of i-th campaign or k-th perk at its t-th funding day.

Our goal is to learn a model $\mathbb{F}(.)$ which can be used to forecast the daily funding amount, i.e., $Y^c(i,t+h), Y^p(k_i,t+h)$, for i-th campaign and its perks in next h days, when given their funding amount sequences, i.e., $Y^c(i,\tau), B(i,\tau)$ in previous τ days before t and their current features $\mathcal{X}^c(i,t)$ and $\mathcal{X}^p(k_i,t)$, where τ represents $(t-\tau : t)$. Please note that, we do not use the previous-days series of funding amount and backer number on perks, i.e., Y^p, B^p, as the input variables even though they are available in our data. The reason is that the time series of funding amount and backer number on perks are sparser compared with those on campaigns. More importantly, according to the crowdfunding mechanism, all the backers of perks come from their campaign visitors. The rationality will be demonstrated in the experiments. Formally, the task can be formulated as:

$$\begin{Bmatrix} \widehat{Y^c}(i,t+h) \\ \widehat{Y^p}(1,t+h) \\ \cdots \\ \widehat{Y^p}(K_i,t+h) \end{Bmatrix} = \mathbb{F}(Y^c(i,\tau), B(i,\tau), \mathcal{X}^c(i,t), \mathcal{X}^p(k_i,t)) + \epsilon,$$

[4]For better presentation in matrix, we use a notation T to represent the funding days for all campaigns though their durations may be different.

where $k_i \in \{1, ..., K_i\}$ and ϵ is the error vector. To forecast the time series in next h days, we first focus on predicting the values at current day t and the estimations in following days $t + h$ can also be derived by taking the current estimations as input variables.

4.2 Method Overview

Since the dynamics in crowdfunding are two-level time series, we propose a hierarchical model $\mathbb{F}(.)$ for fully considering the characteristics of hierarchy and making full use of the available information. Specifically, $\mathbb{F}(.)$ contains the campaign-level base forecasts (i.e., $f^c(.)$, $\boldsymbol{f^c}$), the perk-level base forecasts (i.e., $f^p(.)$ or $\boldsymbol{f^p}$), and a combination of them using a revision matrix $\boldsymbol{R}$. Figure 2 shows the overview of our method. Specifically, we first independently learn the base forecasts for campaigns (gray shapes) and perks (white shapes). At each level, we propose two kinds of structures for the base forecasts, i.e., **S**ingle **R**egression (denoted as SR, $f^c(.)$ and $f^p(.)$) and **SW**itching **R**egression (denoted as SWR, $\boldsymbol{f^c}$ and $\boldsymbol{f^p}$) based on the understanding of decision making of the crowd (visitors and backing probability) and assumptions on funding sequences. Then for a target campaign (purple) and its perks (blue), we use a revision matrix to get the final results by combining the estimations of these two-level forecasts.

5 STRUCTURES OF BASE FORECASTS

In this section, we define the structures of base forecasts: the single regression model, i.e., $f^c(.)$ and $f^p(.)$, and the switching regression model, i.e., $\boldsymbol{f^c}$ and $\boldsymbol{f^p}$. Specifically, we define the structures of base forecasts by exploring the mechanism of crowdfunding and modeling the decision making of "crowd". The two-level base forecasts have the similar forms. Thus, we detail the structures of perk-level base forecasts, and then directly give the structures of campaign-level base forecasts.

5.1 Single Regression Model, $f^p(.), f^c(.)$

In SR, we suppose the funding amount time series of campaigns or perks can be modeled by a single model. Specifically, at perk level, SR has the form of $f^p(.)$. In fact, SR can explore the previous-days funding dynamics and also capture the impacts of time-varying covariants (perk features) and time by an inbuilt parametric Hazard function [11, 23].

Different from other conventional time series problems, crowdfunding is a financial service in which a complete funding activity contains two processes, i.e., *user visiting* and *visitor backing*. That is, a campaign may obtain more contributions if it can attract frequent visits. Also, not all the visitors will contribute her visiting campaigns. A visitor of campaign i will contribute to this campaign only if her evaluation on this campaign is higher than a threshold. If so, this visitor will back this campaign by selecting a perk based on her evaluation and comparison of perks. Therefore, in $f^p(.)$, we try to model the funding process by two components, i.e., *current visitors*, and *backing probability of selecting a perk*.

5.1.1 Modeling Visitors. We assume the current visitors of a campaign come from two ways: *infected by previous backers*, and *the spontaneous visitors*. The visitors of a perk are essentially the current visitors on its campaign, because all users first access campaigns rather than perks.

Infected Visitors. The intrinsic objective of crowdfunding is to attract massive contributions from the "crowd", thus the propagation is crucial for a campaign. Crowdfunding mechanism encourages the backers to share their backed campaigns to their friends via virtual social relations, e.g., Facebook, Twitter, or real-life relations, and indeed, backers are also willing to do that. What's more, researchers have found that the prior fundings on a campaign have great effects on its dynamics in the following durations [32]. Thus, previous backers influence the current and following propagation of a specific campaign and also its current underlying visitors. Specifically, we model the infected visitors PU_t^i at current time t by the propagation of the backers in previous τ days on campaign i as:

$$PU_t^i = (\boldsymbol{\alpha^p})^T \cdot \boldsymbol{B}(i, \tau), \tag{1}$$

where $\boldsymbol{\alpha^p}$ is the coefficient vector to weight the propagation influences of backers in previous τ days.

Spontaneous Visitors. Besides the visitors infected by the propagation of previous-days backers, there are also some spontaneous visitors arriving at any funding days of a campaign. The spontaneously arriving visitors may be attracted by the properties of a campaign. Specifically, we suppose that the spontaneous visitors on campaign i at time t, SU_t^i, follow a *Poisson* distribution [23] as follows:

$$Pois(SU_t^i = m|\lambda_i) = \frac{\exp(-\lambda_i)\lambda_i}{m!}, \tag{2}$$

where λ_i is the parameter for mean visiting in a unit time. As described above, to capture the impacts of time-varying covariants of perks, we allow parameter λ_i to be a function of the time-varying campaign covariants $\boldsymbol{X}^c(i, t)$ [23]:

$$\lambda_i = (\boldsymbol{\xi^p})^T \cdot \boldsymbol{X}^c(i, t), \tag{3}$$

where $\boldsymbol{\xi^p}$ is the coefficient vector to weight the covariants. Thus, the spontaneous visitors of a campaign SU_t^i can be computed as:

$$\mathrm{E}(SU_t^i) = \int_0^\infty Pois(SU_t^i)\, d(SU_t^i) = \lambda_i. \tag{4}$$

In summary, we can infer the underlying visitors U_t^i of campaign i at time t by:

$$U_t^i = \mathrm{E}(PU_t^i + SU_t^i) = (\boldsymbol{\alpha^p})^T \cdot \boldsymbol{B}(i, \tau) + (\boldsymbol{\xi^p})^T \cdot \boldsymbol{X}^c(i, t). \tag{5}$$

After modeling the current visitors of one campaign, in the following, we will introduce the second factor which influences the funding dynamics, i.e., backing probability of selecting a perk.

5.1.2 Backing Probability of Selecting a Perk: $g(.)$. In this study, we explore the Hazard model [11, 23] to approximate the backing probability of crowd, i.e, $g(t, \boldsymbol{x})$, where $\boldsymbol{x}$ is the abbreviation of $\boldsymbol{X}^p(k_i, t)$. Hazard function is widely-used in COX of survival analysis, which is the instantaneous rate of occurrence of the event. Specifically, we explore the density function, i.e., $g(t, \boldsymbol{x})$, for the probability of event. In our study, the event refers to the backing behavior [23]. The reason for exploring proportional Hazard to approximate the backing probability is that Hazard can reflect the impacts of both time and features on event which are all important in the dynamics of crowdfunding. In survival analysis, the probability density function can be derived from the definition of Hazard model $h(t)$:

$$h(t) = \lim_{\Delta t \to 0} \frac{P(t \leq Tb \leq t + \Delta t | Tb \geq t)}{\Delta t} = \frac{g(t)}{1 - G(t)} = \frac{g(t)}{S(t)},$$

where Tb is the random variable which represents the time until the event occurs, i.e., backing the campaign by selecting a specific perk, and $g(t), G(t), S(t)$ are respectively the probability density function, cumulative distribution function and survivor function of Tb. Specific to perk k_i of campaign i at time t, Hazard function has the following form:

$$h(t|\boldsymbol{x}) = h_0(t) \exp((\boldsymbol{\beta^p})^T \cdot \boldsymbol{X^p}(k_i, t)), \tag{6}$$

where $h_0(t)$ is a baseline function, which is perk independent and a function of time. Hazard function can capture the impacts of both time and time-varying covariants by the baseline function and the risk proportion. A campaign and its perks share a same $h_0(t)$ function since they conform a same funding timeline. Term $\exp((\boldsymbol{\beta^p})^T \boldsymbol{X^p}(k_i, t))$ is the proportional risk associated with the covariates. The baseline function is arbitrary nonnegative perk-independent of time for parameter functions. In our study, we adopt a Gompertz distribution form [17, 31]:

$$h_0(t) = \exp(\gamma_0 + \gamma_1 t). \tag{7}$$

After defining the form of proportional Hazard model $h(t)$, the density function, i.e., $g(t, \boldsymbol{x})$, can be derived. The details of derivation are shown in Appendix A. In summary, we can get the form of the base forecast, i.e., $f^p(.)$, as follows.

$$\begin{aligned}\widehat{Y^p}(k_i, t) &= f^p(\boldsymbol{B}(i, \tau), \boldsymbol{X^c}(i, t), \boldsymbol{X^p}(k_i, t)|\boldsymbol{\Theta^p}) + \epsilon_t^p \\ &= p_{k_i}((\boldsymbol{\alpha^p})^T \boldsymbol{B}(i, \tau) + (\boldsymbol{\xi^p})^T \boldsymbol{X^c}(i, t)) g(t|\boldsymbol{X^p}(k_i, t)) + \epsilon_t^p,\end{aligned}$$

where p_{k_i} is the unit price of perk k_i, $\boldsymbol{\Theta^p} = (\boldsymbol{\alpha^p}, \boldsymbol{\xi^p}, \boldsymbol{\beta^p}, \boldsymbol{\gamma})$. Parameters $\boldsymbol{\Theta^p}$ can be learned by maximum likelihood estimation or equally least square when the error follows Gaussian distribution:

$$\begin{aligned}\mathcal{L}(\boldsymbol{\Theta^p}) = \arg\min_{\boldsymbol{\Theta^p}} \frac{1}{2} \sum_{i=1}^{I} \sum_{k_i=1}^{K_i} \sum_{t=\tau}^{T} (Y^p(k_i, t) - \widehat{Y^p}(k_i, t))^2 \\ + \lambda^p ||\boldsymbol{\Theta^p}||_2,\end{aligned} \tag{8}$$

where λ^p is a regularization parameter and $||.||_2$ denotes the $L2$ norm, which is used to avoid overfitting.

Now, we have given the specific structure of $f^p(.)$. Similarly, we define the structure of base forecast $f^c(.)$ for campaign level as:

$$\begin{aligned}\widehat{Y^c}(i, t) &= f^c(\boldsymbol{Y^c}(i, \tau), \boldsymbol{X^c}(i, t)|\boldsymbol{\Theta^c}) + \epsilon_t^c \\ &= ((\boldsymbol{\alpha^c})^T \boldsymbol{Y^c}(i, \tau) + (\boldsymbol{\xi^c})^T \boldsymbol{X^c}(i, t)) g(t|\boldsymbol{X^c}(i, t)) + \epsilon_t^c.\end{aligned}$$

Please note that, in the campaign-level modeling, there is not a declared price for each campaign. Thus, for consistency, we use the funding amount observation $\boldsymbol{Y^c}(i, \tau)$ rather than the backer number observation $\boldsymbol{B}(i, \tau)$ in $f^c(.)$.

5.2 Switching Regression Model

According to our observations, different campaigns and perks have great heterogeneities, and even for one campaign or perk, its funding dynamic at different funding phases may vary a lot. Thus, training a single model, i.e., $f^c(.)$ or $f^p(.)$ is inadequate. Also, some studies have found that the time series have the clustering characteristics, that is, the sequences in the same cluster have the similar growth pattern [24]. Thus, in this subsection, we introduce an enhanced switching regression model, i.e., SWR, based on a more reasonable assumption, i.e., funding amount sequences of campaigns and perks respectively form different clusters in which sequences have different dynamic patterns. We also take the perk-level base forecasts $\boldsymbol{f^p} = \{f_j^p(.)|j \in \{1, ..., J\}\}$ as examples to introduce SWR, where $f_j^p(.)$ is the base forecast for j-th perk sequence cluster and J is the number of clusters. $f_j^p(.)$ has the similar form with $f^p(.)$ in SR, but each $f_j^p(.)$ has its own parameters.

Besides the observable variables, i.e., $\boldsymbol{Y^c}, \boldsymbol{Y^p}, \boldsymbol{B}, \boldsymbol{X^c}, \boldsymbol{X^p}$, in $\boldsymbol{f^p}$, we also assume there are some unobservable cluster indicator variables, such that $\boldsymbol{\mathcal{Z}^p} = (\mathcal{Z}^p(k, t))_{K \times T}$, where $\mathcal{Z}^p(k_i, t))$ can be abbreviated as z and $z = (z_1, ..., z_J)$. Specifically, $z_j \in \{0, 1\}$ and $|z| = 1$, where $z_j = 1$ means the funding amount sequence $(\boldsymbol{Y^p}(k_i, \tau), Y^p(k_i, t))$ of k_i-th perk at time slice t belongs to the j-th sequence cluster of perks, and vice versa. That is to say, a funding sequence at a given specific time only belongs to one specific cluster. Please note that, the clustering object is sequence segments rather than complete funding sequences of perks so that a perk may belong to different clusters in different time slices. Thus, for perk k_i at time t, we have:

$$\widehat{Y^p}(k_i, t) = \prod_{j=1}^{J} f_j^p(\boldsymbol{B}(i, \tau), \boldsymbol{X^c}(i, t), \boldsymbol{X^p}(k_i, t)|\boldsymbol{\Theta_j^p})^{z_j} + \epsilon_t^p, \tag{9}$$

where $\boldsymbol{\Theta_j^p}$ are the parameters learned from the sequence segments in j-th cluster. Similarly, we can also get the campaign-level base forecasts $\boldsymbol{f^c}$.

6 MODEL LEARNING AND FORECAST

In this section, we first detail the learning process for $\boldsymbol{f^p}$, in the same way, $f^p(.), f^c(.), \boldsymbol{f^c}$ can also be learned. Then, for a given target campaign and its perks, we propose to revise the forecasts by an optimization combination of the two-level base forecasts for the final forecasting.

6.1 Learning Base Forecasts in SWR

Because $\boldsymbol{\mathcal{Z}^p}$ in $\boldsymbol{f^p}$ is unobservable, we can learn $\boldsymbol{\Theta_j^p}$ and cluster the sequence segments simultaneously by an EM-process. Since the clusters are hard restraint, we can achieve learning through two steps, i.e., estimating the cluster variables $\boldsymbol{\mathcal{Z}^p}$, optimizing the parameters $\boldsymbol{\Theta_j^p}$ with current $\boldsymbol{\mathcal{Z}^p}$.

Estimating $\boldsymbol{\mathcal{Z}^p}$. Donate $\boldsymbol{\Theta_j^p}(o)$ as the parameters in o-th iteration. In each iteration, we estimate $\boldsymbol{\mathcal{Z}^p}$, i.e., let each $z_j = 1$ iff:

$$j = \arg\min_{j'=1}^{J} |Y^p(k_i, t) - f_{j'}^p(.|\boldsymbol{\Theta_{j'}^p}(o))|. \tag{10}$$

Optimizing Θ_j^p. After estimating $\mathcal{Z}^p$, we optimize the current parameters $\Theta_j^p(o)$. In each iteration, the loss function $\mathcal{L}(\Theta_j^p(o))$ is defined as:

$$\mathcal{L}(\Theta_j^p(o)) = \arg\min_{\Theta_j^p(o)} \frac{1}{2}\sum_{i=1}^{I}\sum_{k_i=1}^{K_i}\sum_{t=\tau}^{T}\sum_{j=1}^{J} z_j(Y^p(k_i,t) - \widehat{Y^p}(k_i,t))^2 + \lambda_j^p||\Theta_j^p(o)||_2. \tag{11}$$

For optimizing the above function, we adopt the alternating least squares (ALS) [39]. ALS is a popular optimization method with accurate parameter estimation and fast convergence rate, which computes each parameter by fixing the other parameters when minimizing the object function. Specifically, the updating rules for some representative parameters in $\mathcal{L}(\Theta_j^p(o))$ are as follows:

$$\alpha_j^p(o) \leftarrow \alpha_j^p(o) - \eta_\alpha \frac{\partial\mathcal{L}}{\partial\alpha_j^p(o)}, \quad \xi_j^p(o) \leftarrow \xi_j^p(o) - \eta_\xi \frac{\partial\mathcal{L}}{\partial\xi_j^p(o)},$$
$$\gamma(o) \leftarrow \gamma(o) - \eta_\gamma \frac{\partial\mathcal{L}}{\partial\gamma(o)}, \quad \beta_j^p(o) \leftarrow \beta_j^p(o) - \eta_\beta \frac{\partial\mathcal{L}}{\partial\beta_j^p(o)},$$

where $\Theta_j^p(o) = (\alpha_j^p(o), \xi_j^p(o), \gamma(o), \beta_j^p(o))$ are the parameters in o-th iteration, and $\eta = (\eta_\alpha, \eta_\xi, \eta_\gamma, \eta_\beta)$ are the learning rates. The details of gradients are given in Appendix B. Repeat these two steps until convergence.

6.2 Revise Forecasts by Optimal Combination

We have learned the campaign-level and perk-level base forecasts, i.e., f^c and f^p, respectively. Next we introduce how to get the final forecasting for given target campaign i and its K_i perks by combining the independent estimations of the two-level base forecasts.

In the literature, researchers have proposed some combination strategies, such as "bottom-up" and "top-down" strategies for hierarchical time series data [15]. Specifically, bottom-up strategies attempt to produce forecasts at the lowest level and aggregate them to the upper levels of the hierarchy, while top-down methods produce forecast at the top level and then disaggregate to the lower levels using proportions. These two types of strategies are not suitable for the problem in crowdfunding, because processing base forecasts at lower (perk) level suffers the sparsity while processing base forecasts at campaign level will not consider the relations of perks in a same campaign. To this end, we propose to produce independent forecasts at both campaign and perk levels, and then use a revision matrix to get the final estimations. The proof of optimality of this combination strategy can be found in [15, 16].

Specifically, we denote $(\widehat{Y^c}(i,t), \widehat{Y^p}(1,t), ..., \widehat{Y^p}(K_i,t))^T$ as $\widehat{Y}(i,t)$ which represent the estimations for target campaign i and its perks at t by the base forecasts. $\widetilde{Y}(i,t)$ are the final estimations for them after the revision. That is,

$$\widetilde{Y}(i,t) = R_i\widehat{Y}(i,t), \tag{12}$$

where R_i is the revision matrix for campaign i and its perks which can provide an optimal combination of the independent estimations of base forecasts. Specifically, R_i has the following form:

$$R_i = \frac{1}{K_i+1}\begin{Bmatrix} K_i & 1 & 1 & \cdots & \cdots & 1 \\ 1 & K_i & \text{-1} & \text{-1} & \cdots & \text{-1} \\ 1 & \text{-1} & K_i & \text{-1} & \cdots & \text{-1} \\ \vdots & \vdots & \ddots & \ddots & \ddots & \vdots \\ 1 & \text{-1} & \cdots & \text{-1} & K_i & \text{-1} \\ 1 & \text{-1} & \cdots & \cdots & \text{-1} & K_i \end{Bmatrix}.$$

Thus, the final estimations for campaign i and perk k_i are:

$$\widetilde{Y^c}(i,t) = \frac{1}{K_i+1}(K_i\widehat{Y^c}(i,t) + \sum_{k_i=1}^{K_i}\widehat{Y^p}(k_i,t)),$$
$$\widetilde{Y^p}(k_i,t) = \frac{1}{K_i+1}(\widehat{Y^c}(i,t) - \sum_{k_i'}\widehat{Y^p}(k_i',t) + K_i\widehat{Y^p}(k_i,t)),$$

where $k_i' = \{1, ..., k_{i-1}, k_{i+1}, ..., K_i\}$ represent the other perks of the target campaign except current perk k_i. We can see that, the matrix revises the final estimations by considering both perk-perk and perks-campaign relations. The revision optimizes the final estimations especially when the individual base forecasting for target campaign or perk performs bad. We will empirically examine that in the experiments.

7 EXPERIMENT

In this section, we construct experiments with the collected dataset to evaluate the performances of our approaches.

7.1 Experimental Setup

We partition the dataset into subsets based on the declared funding durations of campaigns and construct experiments mainly on two subsets whose durations are 30 and 60 days. Specifically, for 30-days campaigns and perks, we construct observations and features in their duration (30 days) and the following 15 days after that. Similarly, for 60-days campaigns and perks, we construct observations and features in their durations (60 days) and the following 30 days. For each subset, we partition the data into a training set and a test set, i.e., we randomly select 20% elements from Y^c as the test set. Consequently, the other variables in the corresponding places, e.g., B, $\mathcal{X}^c$, $\mathcal{X}^p$, will also be selected. The remaining elements are used for training. We process each subset five times in this way. The reported results are averaged over five-round tests. Table 4 shows one-round data partitioning.

Table 4: Data partitioning.

Sub_sets	#Training Sequences		#Test Sequences	
	Campaign	Perk	Campaign	Perk
30_days	8,000	88,663	2,000	23,204
60_days	8,000	93,986	2,000	22,984

7.1.1 Comparison Methods. We compare the following methods on forecasting the dynamics, i.e., daily funding amount, for campaigns and perks.

- **Switching Regression with Revision (SWR+R)**: training switching regression models (i.e., f^c, f^p) for campaigns and perks independently and then using the revision matrix to combine them for the final results. Empirically, the cluster numbers for campaigns and perks are respectively set as 4 and 8.

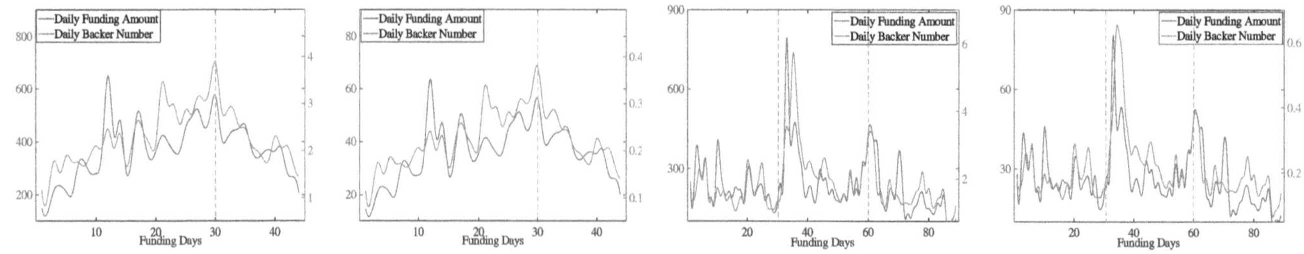

(a) Campaign_30days (b) Perk_30days (c) Campaign_60days (d) Perk_60days

Figure 3: Funding series display.

- **Switching Regression (SWR)**: training switching regression models (i.e., f^c, f^p) for campaigns and perks independently. The settings of SWR are the same as those in SWR+R.
- **Single Regression with Revision (SR+R)**: training single regression models (i.e., $f^c(.), f^p(.)$) for campaigns and perks independently and then using the revision matrix to combine them for the final results.
- **Single Regression (SR)**: training single regression models (i.e., $f^c(.), f^p(.)$) for campaigns and perks.
- **Random Forest (RF)**: training random forest regressions for campaigns and perks, in which the input variables are the same as those in SR and SWR.
- **Autoregressive Model (AR)**: training autoregressive models [1, 8] for campaigns and perks using the daily funding observations.
- **Average (AVE)**: using the averages of funding amount in previous τ days to predict the current funding. In these methods, the parameters τ are all set as 5.

7.1.2 Evaluation Metrics. To evaluate the forecasting performances, here we select two widely-used metrics, i.e., the *Root Mean Squared Error* (RMSE) [34] and *Mean Relative Squared Error* (MRSE) [8] for evaluation. Specifically, their definitions are:

$$RMSE = \sqrt{\frac{\sum_{i=1}^{N}(y_i - \hat{y_i})^2}{N}}, \quad MRSE = \frac{1}{N}\sum_{i=1}^{N}(\frac{\hat{y_i}}{y_i} - 1)^2,$$

where N is the number of predictions, y_i is the i-th real observation value and $\hat{y_i}$ is the corresponding estimated value.

7.2 Experimental Results

We first plot the funding time series and analyze the characteristics, and then report the forecasting results.

7.2.1 Funding Series Analysis. We mainly have two types of time series observations, *daily contributions* (backer numbers), and *daily funding amount* for both campaigns and perks. The funding time series of campaigns and perks are shown in Figure 3. From these figures, we can see that: 1) the adjacent daily funding amount is highly correlated, so that we exploit the variables in previous days (e.g., $\boldsymbol{Y^c}(i, \tau)$ and $\boldsymbol{B}(i, \tau)$) in our approaches; 2) the series of both campaigns and perks at different funding time have different dynamic patterns, e.g., 30-days campaigns and perks have observable peaks at the end of their declared durations, 60-days campaigns and perks have observable peaks at both the end and middle of their durations. Besides, in the start-up days, the funding amount is relatively small and grows slowly, while after the declared durations, the funding time series decays over time. These inspire us to explore the time effect (i.e., $h_0(t)$) and cluster the time series at the granularity of sequence segments rather than the complete series of campaigns and perks.

Table 5: The running time (seconds).

Methods	SWR+R	SWR	SR+R	SR	RF	AR	AVE
Training	1,860	1,860	254	254	1.52	9.69	-
Test	0.73	0.18	0.59	0.12	0.25	0.09	0.05

7.2.2 Efficiency Results. Table 5 records the running time (seconds) of different methods for training and test on all the constructed datasets. We can see that our models need more time than others for training. However, in tests, our two-level base forecasts, i.e., SWR and SR, run faster than RF.

7.2.3 Forecasting Performances. For better training and forecasting, we scaled the time series variables using ln(.) function, i.e., $Y^c(i, t) = \ln(Y^c(i, t) + 1)$. Figure 4 shows the forecasting performances with respect to the predicting days, i.e., h. Overall, our methods, i.e., SWR+R, SWR, SR+R, SR and the ensemble method, i.e., RF, perform significantly better than AR and AVE which lose the predicting abilities with the accumulation of errors over time. Second, in the campaign-level tests, SWR+R performs best; while in the perk-level tests, SWR performs best. The possible reason is that the base forecasts SWR (also SR) predict more accurately for perks, i.e., perk-level base forecasts work better than campaign-level ones (the perk instances for training are much more than campaigns'), so that, after revising, the performances on campaigns become better while performances on perks turn to a little worse. Even so, clearly, both SWR+R and SWR have the satisfactory performances compared with other methods, e.g., the values of RMSE or MRSE are reduced by more than 50% in most cases. Third, from the comparisons of SR and SWR, we can see the effectiveness of clustering for funding sequences. Finally, our methods perform much better for perks while AR and AVE have worse results for perks. That is because the time series of perks are much sparser and more unstable so that it is more difficult to predict for AR and AVE in which only the response variables are taken into consideration. Differently, our models explore the relations of perks and campaigns so that they work well for perks.

7.2.4 Parameter Effects. We also test the effects of the common parameter, i.e., τ, of the corresponding methods. We report the

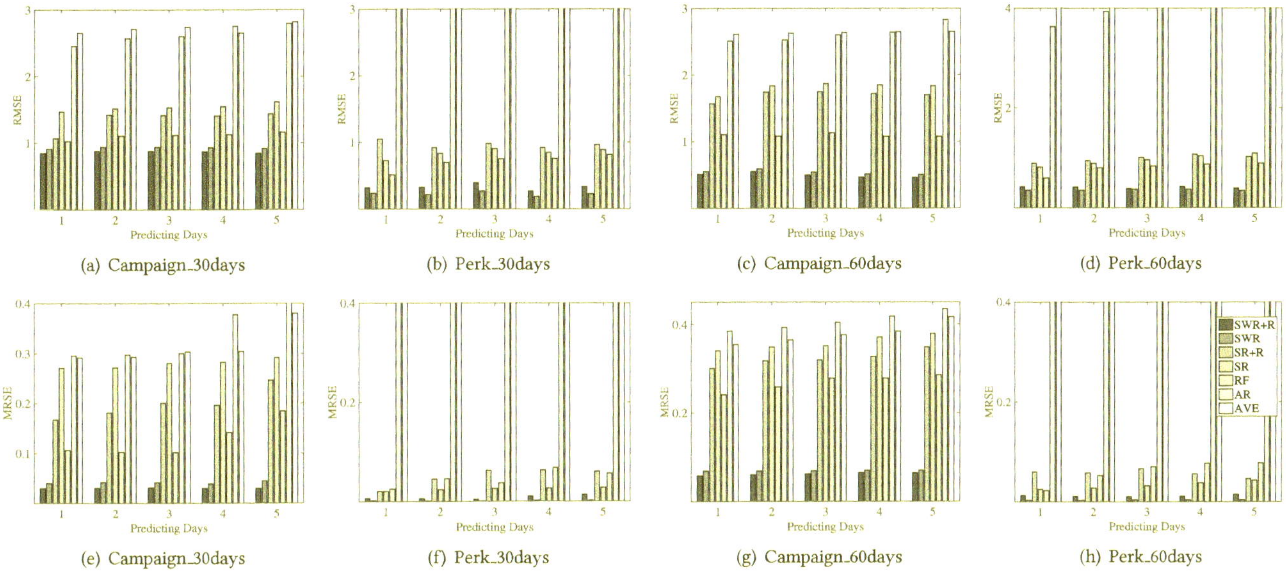

Figure 4: Forecasting performances.

results when forecasting the dynamics only in next one days in Figure 5. In most cases, all methods will achieve better results, i.e., smaller RMSE and MRSE, as τ becomes larger. Please note that, in all cases, our model, i.e., SWR, has the best performances. The comparison results between SR, SWR, RF, AR and AVE clearly demonstrate the robustness of SWR and also the importance of our constructed features on tracking and forecasting the dynamics of funding time series in crowdfunding.

8 CONCLUSION

In this paper, we presented a focused study on tracking and forecasting the dynamics in crowdfunding in a holistic view. For constructing this study, we first collected massive real-world crowdfunding data with detailed daily transaction information from Indiegogo.com and generated various features at both campaign and perk levels. We then formalized the problem as the prediction with hierarchical time series and proposed a two-layer solution framework. Specifically, for both campaign and perk levels, we developed two regression models, i.e., SR and SWR, by exploring the decision making of crowd and the clustering characteristic of funding sequences. For a given target campaign and perks, we employed a revision matrix to combine the independent estimations of two-level base forecasts. Finally the experimental results on our collected data clearly demonstrated the effectiveness of our solutions, especially SWR and the combination.

In the future, we will test other combination strategies for the two-level base forecasts, e.g., bottom-up strategies, which produces forecasts at the perk level and aggregates them to the campaigns.

ACKNOWLEDGMENTS

This research was partially supported by grants from the National Science Foundation for Distinguished Young Scholars of China (Grant No. 61325010), the National Natural Science Foundation of China (Grants No. 61672483, U1605251, 61602234, 61572032) and the Anhui Provincial Natural Science Foundation (No.1708085QF140). Qi Liu gratefully acknowledges the support of the Youth Innovation Promotion Association of CAS (No. 2014299).

REFERENCES

[1] Hirotugu Akaike. 1969. Fitting autoregressive models for prediction. *Annals of the institute of Statistical Mathematics* 21, 1 (1969), 243–247.

[2] Jisun An, Daniele Quercia, and Jon Crowcroft. 2014. Recommending investors for crowdfunding projects. In *23rd WWW*. ACM, 261–270.

[3] Chance Barnett. 2015. Trends show crowdfunding to surpass VC in 2016. *Forbes, June* 9 (2015).

[4] Paul Belleflamme, Thomas Lambert, and Armin Schwienbacher. 2014. Crowdfunding: Tapping the right crowd. *Journal of Business Venturing* 29, 5 (2014), 585–609.

[5] George EP Box, Gwilym M Jenkins, Gregory C Reinsel, and Greta M Ljung. 2015. *Time series analysis: forecasting and control*. John Wiley & Sons.

[6] Peter J Brockwell and Richard A Davis. 2006. *Introduction to time series and forecasting*. Springer Science & Business Media.

[7] Li-Juan Cao and Francis Eng Hock Tay. 2003. Support vector machine with adaptive parameters in financial time series forecasting. *IEEE Trans. on NN* 14, 6 (2003), 1506–1518.

[8] Biao Chang, Hengshu Zhu, Yong Ge, Enhong Chen, Hui Xiong, and Chang Tan. 2014. Predicting the popularity of online serials with autoregressive models. In *23rd CIKM*. ACM, 1339–1348.

[9] Jerome T Connor, R Douglas Martin, and Les E Atlas. 1994. Recurrent neural networks and robust time series prediction. *IEEE trans. on NN* 5, 2 (1994), 240–254.

[10] Douglas J Cumming, Gaël Leboeuf, and Armin Schwienbacher. Crowdfunding models: Keep-it-all vs. all-or-nothing. In *Paris December 2014 finance meeting*.

[11] Lloyd D Fisher and Danyu Y Lin. 1999. Time-dependent covariates in the Cox proportional-hazards regression model. *Annual review of public health* 20, 1 (1999), 145–157.

[12] Raymond P Fisk, Lia Patrício, Andrea Ordanini, Lucia Miceli, Marta Pizzetti, and A Parasuraman. 2011. Crowd-funding: transforming customers into investors through innovative service platforms. *Journal of service management* 22, 4 (2011), 443–470.

[13] C Lee Giles, Steve Lawrence, and Ah Chung Tsoi. 2001. Noisy time series prediction using recurrent neural networks and grammatical inference. *Machine learning* 44, 1-2 (2001), 161–183.

[14] Michael D Greenberg and Elizabeth M Gerber. 2014. Learning to fail: experiencing public failure online through crowdfunding. In *SIGCHI Conference on Human Factors in Computing Systems*. ACM, 581–590.

[15] Rob J Hyndman, Roman A Ahmed, George Athanasopoulos, and Han Lin Shang. 2011. Optimal combination forecasts for hierarchical time series. *Computational Statistics & Data Analysis* 55, 9 (2011), 2579–2589.

[16] Rob J Hyndman, Alan J Lee, and Earo Wang. 2016. Fast computation of reconciled forecasts for hierarchical and grouped time series. *Computational Statistics &*

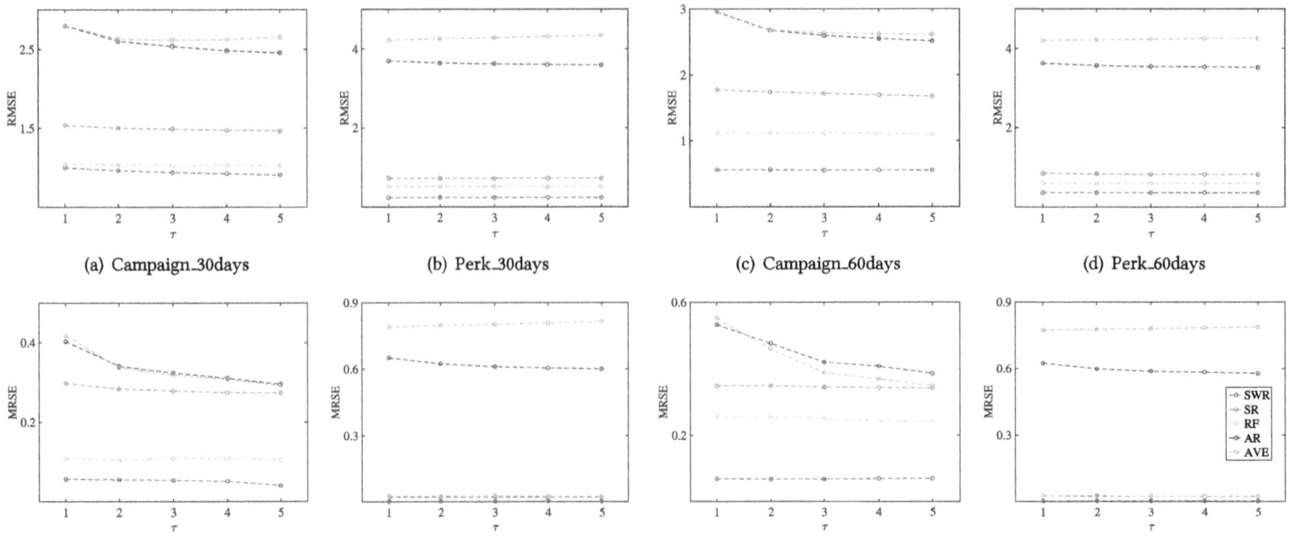

(a) Campaign_30days (b) Perk_30days (c) Campaign_60days (d) Perk_60days

(e) Campaign_30days (f) Perk_30days (g) Campaign_60days (h) Perk_60days

Figure 5: Effects of parameter τ.

Data Analysis 97 (2016), 16–32.

[17] Dipak C Jain and Naufel J Vilcassim. 1991. Investigating household purchase timing decisions: A conditional hazard function approach. *Marketing Science* 10, 1 (1991), 1–23.

[18] Søren Johansen. 1995. *Likelihood-based inference in cointegrated vector autoregressive models.* Oxford University Press on Demand.

[19] Venkat Kuppuswamy and Barry L Bayus. 2015. Crowdfunding creative ideas: The dynamics of project backers in Kickstarter. *UNC Kenan-Flagler Research Paper* 2013-15 (2015).

[20] Quoc Le and Tomas Mikolov. 2014. Distributed representations of sentences and documents. In *Proceedings of the 31st International Conference on Machine Learning (ICML-14).* 1188–1196.

[21] Othmar M Lehner. 2013. Crowdfunding social ventures: a model and research agenda. *Venture Capital* 15, 4 (2013), 289–311.

[22] Yan Li, Vineeth Rakesh, and Chandan K Reddy. 2016. Project success prediction in crowdfunding environments. In *9th WSDM.* ACM, 247–256.

[23] Zhuoxin Li and Jason A Duan. 2014. Dynamic strategies for successful online crowdfunding. *Available at SSRN 2506352* (2014).

[24] T Warren Liao. 2005. Clustering of time series data-a survey. *Pattern recognition* 38, 11 (2005), 1857–1874.

[25] Qi Liu, Guifeng Wang, Hongke Zhao, Chuanren Liu, Tong Xu, and Enhong Chen. 2017. Enhancing Campaign Design in Crowdfunding: A Product Supply Optimization Perspective. In *26th IJCAI.*

[26] Yang Liu, Roy Chen, Yan Chen, Qiaozhu Mei, and Suzy Salib. 2012. I loan because...: Understanding motivations for pro-social lending. In *5th WSDM.* ACM, 503–512.

[27] Chun-Ta Lu, Sihong Xie, Xiangnan Kong, and Philip S Yu. 2014. Inferring the impacts of social media on crowdfunding. In *7th WSDM.* ACM, 573–582.

[28] Tanushree Mitra and Eric Gilbert. 2014. The language that gets people to give: Phrases that predict success on kickstarter. In *17th CSCW.* ACM, 49–61.

[29] Ethan Mollick. 2014. The dynamics of crowdfunding: An exploratory study. *Journal of business venturing* 29, 1 (2014), 1–16.

[30] Vineeth Rakesh, Wang-Chien Lee, and Chandan K Reddy. 2016. Probabilistic Group Recommendation Model for Crowdfunding Domains. In *9th WSDM.* ACM, 257–266.

[31] Germán Rodrıguez. 2010. *Parametric Survival Models.* Technical Report. Technical report, Princeton, NJ: Princeton University.

[32] Jacob Solomon, Wenjuan Ma, and Rick Wash. 2015. Don't Wait!: How Timing Affects Coordination of Crowdfunding Donations. In *18th CSCW.* ACM, 547–556.

[33] Weizhong Yan. 2012. Toward automatic time-series forecasting using neural networks. *IEEE Trans. on NN and LS* 23, 7 (2012), 1028–1039.

[34] Guoqiang Zhang, B Eddy Patuwo, and Michael Y Hu. 1998. Forecasting with artificial neural networks:: The state of the art. *International journal of forecasting* 14, 1 (1998), 35–62.

[35] Jianfei Zhang, Lifei Chen, Alain Vanasse, Josiane Courteau, and Shengrui Wang. 2016. Survival Prediction by an Integrated Learning Criterion on Intermittently Varying Healthcare Data. In *30th AAAI.*

[36] Hongke Zhao, Qi Liu, Guifeng Wang, Yong Ge, and Enhong Chen. Portfolio Selections in P2P Lending: A Multi-Objective Perspective. In *22nd SIGKDD.* ACM, 2075–2084.

[37] Hongke Zhao, Qi Liu, Hengshu Zhu, Yong Ge, Enhong Chen, Yan Zhu, and Junping Du. 2017. A Sequential Approach to Market State Modeling and Analysis in Online P2P Lending. *IEEE Transactions on Systems, Man, and Cybernetics: Systems* (2017).

[38] Hongke Zhao, Le Wu, Qi Liu, Yong Ge, and Enhong Chen. 2014. Investment recommendation in p2p lending: A portfolio perspective with risk management. In *Data Mining (ICDM), 2014 IEEE International Conference on.* IEEE, 1109–1114.

[39] Xiaodong Zheng, Hao Ding, Hiroshi Mamitsuka, and Shanfeng Zhu. 2013. Collaborative matrix factorization with multiple similarities for predicting drug-target interactions. In *19th SIGKDD.* ACM, 1025–1033.

Appendix A. Derivation for $g(.)$ From the definition of proportional Hazard model, we have: $g(t|\boldsymbol{x}) = h(t|\boldsymbol{x})S(t|\boldsymbol{x})$; also, from [23, 35], we know: $S(t|\boldsymbol{x}) = \exp(-\int_0^t h(t_x|\boldsymbol{x})\, d(t_x))$; thus, $g(t|\boldsymbol{x}) = h_0(t)\exp((\boldsymbol{\beta^p})^T \boldsymbol{X^p}(k_i, t))\exp((-\int_0^t h(t_x|\boldsymbol{x})\, d(t_x))$.

Appendix B. Gradients for parameters in $f_j^p(.)$

$$\frac{\partial \mathcal{L}}{\partial \alpha_j^p(o)} = -\sum_{i=1}^{I}\sum_{k_i=1}^{K_i}\sum_{t=\tau}^{T}\sum_{j=1}^{J} AB(i,\tau)C + \frac{\lambda_j^p \alpha_j^p(o)}{||\Theta_j^p(o)||_2},$$

$$\frac{\partial \mathcal{L}}{\partial \xi_j^p(o)} = -\sum_{i=1}^{I}\sum_{k_i=1}^{K_i}\sum_{t=\tau}^{T}\sum_{j=1}^{J} A\boldsymbol{X^c}(i,t)C + \frac{\lambda_j^p \xi_j^p(o)}{||\Theta_j^p(o)||_2},$$

$$\frac{\partial \mathcal{L}}{\partial \gamma_0(o)} = -\sum_{i=1}^{I}\sum_{k_i=1}^{K_i}\sum_{t=\tau}^{T}\sum_{j=1}^{J} ACDE + \frac{\lambda_j^p \gamma_0(o)}{||\Theta_j^p(o)||_2},$$

$$\frac{\partial \mathcal{L}}{\partial \beta_j^p(o)} = -\sum_{i=1}^{I}\sum_{k_i=1}^{K_i}\sum_{t=\tau}^{T}\sum_{j=1}^{J} ACDE\boldsymbol{x} + \frac{\lambda_j^p \beta_j^p(o)}{||\Theta_j^p(o)||_2};$$

where

$$A = z_j(Y^{\boldsymbol{p}}(k_i,t) - \widehat{Y^{\boldsymbol{p}}}(k_i,t))p_{k_i},$$

$$C = \exp(\gamma_0 + \gamma_1 t + (\boldsymbol{\beta^p})^T\boldsymbol{x} - \frac{1}{\gamma_1}\exp(\gamma_0 + (\boldsymbol{\beta^p})^T\boldsymbol{x})(\exp(\gamma_1 t) - 1)),$$

$$E = 1 - \frac{1}{\gamma_1}\exp(\gamma_0 + (\boldsymbol{\beta^p})^T\boldsymbol{x})(\exp(\gamma_1 t) - 1),$$

$$D = (\boldsymbol{\alpha^p})^T B(i,\tau) + (\boldsymbol{\xi^p})^T \boldsymbol{X^c}(i,t).$$

Meta-Graph Based Recommendation Fusion over Heterogeneous Information Networks

Huan Zhao, Quanming Yao, Jianda Li, Yangqiu Song and Dik Lun Lee
{hzhaoaf,qyaoaa}@cse.ust.hk;jlicy@connect.ust.hk;{yqsong,dlee}@cse.ust.hk
Department of Computer Science and Engineering
Hong Kong University of Science and Technology
Clear Water Bay, Hong Kong

ABSTRACT

Heterogeneous Information Network (HIN) is a natural and general representation of data in modern large commercial recommender systems which involve heterogeneous types of data. HIN based recommenders face two problems: how to represent the high-level semantics of recommendations and how to fuse the heterogeneous information to make recommendations. In this paper, we solve the two problems by first introducing the concept of meta-graph to HIN-based recommendation, and then solving the information fusion problem with a "matrix factorization (MF) + factorization machine (FM)" approach. For the similarities generated by each meta-graph, we perform standard MF to generate latent features for both users and items. With different meta-graph based features, we propose to use FM with Group lasso (FMG) to automatically learn from the observed ratings to effectively select useful meta-graph based features. Experimental results on two real-world datasets, Amazon and Yelp, show the effectiveness of our approach compared to state-of-the-art FM and other HIN-based recommendation algorithms.

CCS CONCEPTS

•Information systems → Collaborative filtering; Recommender systems; •Computer systems organization → *Heterogeneous (hybrid) systems;*

KEYWORDS

Recommendation system; Collaborative filtering; Heterogeneous information networks; Factorization machine.

1 INTRODUCTION

Recommendation on the platforms like Amazon or Yelp refers to the problem of recommending items, such as products or businesses, to users so that the platforms can make more revenue when users consume more items. Essentially if we consider users and items as a bipartite graph, this is a link prediction problem on heterogeneous types of entities, i.e., *User* and *Item*. Nowadays large commercial recommender systems often incorporate richer heterogeneous information. For example, on Amazon, the products have categories, or they can belong to brands, and users can write reviews to products. On Yelp, users can follow other users to form a social network, the location based businesses have categories, and users can write reviews to businesses as well. Then, real-world recommender systems often need to consider richer semantics with different types of information that are enabled and collected by the platforms. This richer heterogeneity thus requires the development of a mathematical representation to formulate it and a tool to compute over it.

Heterogeneous information networks (HINs) [30] have been proposed as a general data representation for many different types of data, such as scholar network data [32], social network data [13], patient network data [3], or knowledge graph data [5]. At the beginning, HINs were used to handle entity search and similarity measure problems [32], where the query and result entities are assumed to be of the same type (e.g., using *Person* to search *Person*). Later, it was extended to handle heterogeneous entity recommendation problems (i.e., recommending *Items* to *Users*) [29, 39, 40]. To incorporate rich semantics, HINs first builds a network schema of the heterogeneous network. For example, for Yelp, a network schema is defined over the entity types *User, Review, Word, Business*, etc. Then, the semantic relatedness constrained by the entity types can be defined by the similarities between two entities along meta-paths [32]. For traditional collaborative filtering, if we want to recommend businesses to users, we can build a simple meta-path *Business→User* and learn from this meta-path to make generalizations. From HIN's schema, we can define more complicated meta-paths like *User → Review → Word → Review → Business*. This meta-path defines a similarity to measure whether a user tends to like a business if his/her reviews are similar to those written by other users for the same business.

When applying meta-path based similarities to recommender systems, there are two major challenges. First, meta-path may not be the best way to characterize the rich semantics. Figure 1 shows a concrete example, where a meta-path *User → Review → Word → Review → Business* is used to capture users' similarity since they both write reviews and mention the seafood it serves. However, if we want to capture the semantic that U_1 and U_2 rate the same type of business (such as *Restaurant*), and at the same time, they mention the same aspect (such as *seafood*), the meta-path fails. Thus, we need a better way to capture such complicated semantics. Recently, Fang et al. [6] and Huang et al. [10] have proposed to use meta-graph (or meta-structure) to compute similarity between homogeneous type of entities (e.g., using *Person* to search *Person*) over HINs, which can capture more complex semantics that meta-path cannot. However, they didn't explore entities of heterogeneous

KDD'17, August 13–17, 2017, Halifax, NS, Canada.

DOI: http://dx.doi.org/10.1145/3097983.3098063

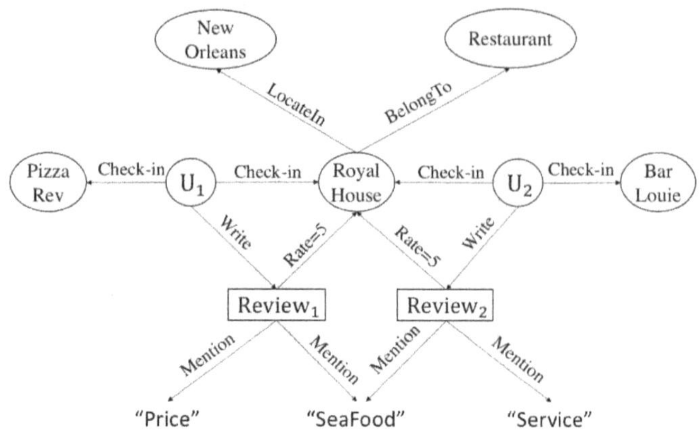

Figure 1: Example of HIN, which is built based on the web page for Royal House on Yelp.

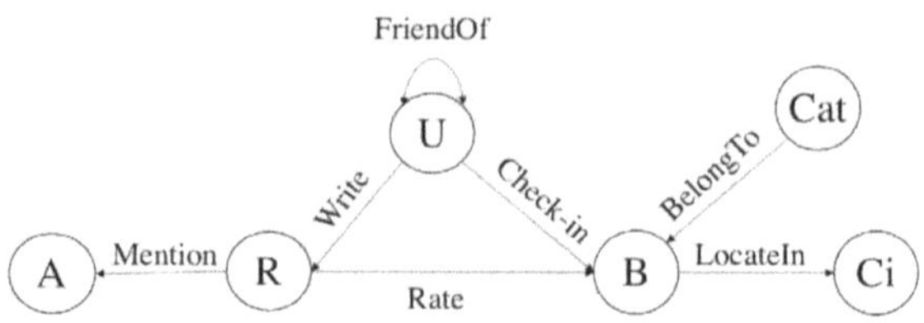

Figure 2: Example of HIN Schema. A: aspect extracted from reviews; R: reviews; U: users; B: business; Cat: category of item; Ci: city.

types with meta-graph. Thus in this paper, we extend this idea to heterogeneous recommendation problem. However, how to use the similarities between heterogeneous types of entities developed from HINs in recommendation is still unclear, which results in the second challenge.

Second, different meta-paths or meta-graphs result in different similarities. How to assemble them in an effective way is another challenge. Currently, there are two principled ways. Considering our goal is to achieve accurate prediction of *User* and *Item* ratings, which can be formulated as a matrix completion problem of the user-item rating matrix. One way to predict the missing ratings based on HIN is to use meta-paths to generate a lot of ad-hoc alternative similarities for user-item matrix, and then learn a weighting mechanism for different meta-paths to combine the similarities explicitly to approximate the user-item rating matrix [29]. This approach does not consider implicit factors of each meta-path, and each alternative similarity matrix could be very sparse to contribute to the final ensemble. The other way is to first factorize each user-item similarity matrix computed based on each meta-path, and then use the latent features to recover a new user-item matrix, which is used for ensemble [40]. This method resolves the sparsity problem of each similarity matrix. However, it does not fully make use of the latent features since when ensemble is performed, each meta-path cannot see others' variables but only the single value predicted by the others.

To address the above challenges, we propose a new principled way to fully combine different latent features. First, instead of using meta-paths for heterogeneous recommendation [29, 40], we introduce the concept of meta-graph to the recommendation problem, which allows us to incorporate more complex semantics into our prediction problem. Second, instead of computing the recovered matrices directly, we use all of the latent features of all meta-graphs. Inspired by the famous work PCA+LDA used for face recognition [2], which first uses PCA (principle component analysis) to perform unsupervised dimensionality reduction, and then applies LDA (linear discriminant analysis) to discover further reduced dimensions guided by supervision, we apply matrix factorization (MF) + factorization machine (FM) [25] to our recommendation problem. For each meta-graph, we first compute the user-item similarity matrix under the guidance of the meta-graph, and then use unsupervised (without seeing the ratings) MF to factorize it into a set of user and item latent vectors. Then, with many different sets of user and item vectors computed from different meta-graphs, we use FM to assemble them to learn from the rating matrix. To effectively select useful meta-graphs, we propose to use FM with Group lasso (FMG), i.e. the $\ell_{2,1}$-norm regularization, to learn the parameters. In this way, we can automatically determine for new incoming problems which meta-graph should be used, and for each meta-graph generated user and item vectors, how they should be weighted. Experimental results on two large real-world datasets, Amazon and Yelp, show that our approach can successfully outperform other MF-based, FM-based, and existing HIN-based state-of-the-arts for recommendation. Our code is available at https://github.com/HKUST-KnowComp/FMG.

2 FRAMEWORK

In this section, we introduce our framework to handle HIN-based recommendation.

2.1 Meta-graph based Similarity

The definitions of HIN and HIN Schema (a schema graph of entity types and their relations) have been introduced in [32]. Here we skip the formal definition and only illustrate the original HIN in Figure 1 and the corresponding schema in Figure 2. Here we focus on the concepts related to our paper. First, we formally define the meta-graph in HIN for recommendation.

Definition 2.1. **Meta-graph.** A meta-graph $\mathcal{M}$ is a directed acyclic graph (DAG) with a single source node n_s (i.e., with in-degree 0) and a single sink (target) node n_t (i.e., with out-degree 0), defined on an HIN $\mathcal{G} = (\mathcal{V}, \mathcal{E})$ with schema $\mathcal{T}_G = (\mathcal{A}, \mathcal{R})$, where $\mathcal{V}$ is the node set, $\mathcal{E}$ is the edge set, $\mathcal{A}$ is the node type set, and $\mathcal{R}$ is the edge type set. Then we define a meta-graph as $\mathcal{M} = (\mathcal{V}_M, \mathcal{E}_M, \mathcal{A}_M, \mathcal{R}_M, n_s, n_t)$, where $\mathcal{V}_M \subseteq \mathcal{V}$, $\mathcal{E}_M \subseteq \mathcal{E}$ constrained by $\mathcal{A}_M \subseteq \mathcal{A}$ and $\mathcal{R}_M \subseteq \mathcal{R}$, respectively.

We show all of the meta-graphs used in this paper for both Amazon and Yelp in Figure 3. We can see that they are DAGs with U (*User*) as the source node and B (*Business* for Yelp and *Product* for Amazon) as the target node. Here we use $\mathcal{M}_3$ and $\mathcal{M}_9$ used on Yelp data to illustrate the computation problem.

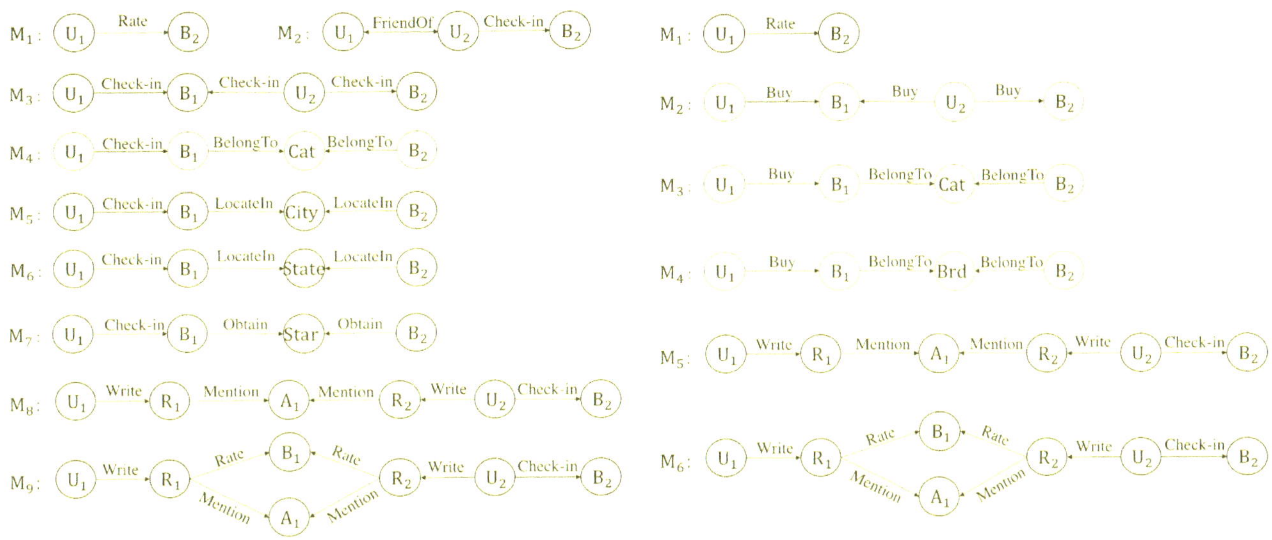

(a) Yelp-200K (Star: the average stars a business obtained).

(b) Amazon-200K (Brd: brand of the item).

Figure 3: Meta-graphs used for Amazon and Yelp datasets.

Given the above definition of meta-graph, we want to compute the similarities between the source and the target nodes. Originally, commuting matrices [32] have been used to compute the counting-based similarity matrix of a meta-path. Suppose we have a meta-path $\mathcal{P} = (A_1, A_2, \ldots, A_l)$, where A_i's are node types in $\mathcal{A}$. Then we can define a matrix $\mathbf{W}_{A_iA_j}$ as the adjacency matrix between type A_i and type A_j. Then, the commuting matrix for path $\mathcal{P}$ is $\mathbf{C}_P = \mathbf{W}_{A_1,A_2} \cdot \mathbf{W}_{A_2,A_3} \cdot \ldots \cdot \mathbf{W}_{A_{l-1},A_l}$. For example, for $\mathcal{M}_3$ in Figure 3(a), $\mathbf{C}_{\mathcal{M}_3} = \mathbf{W}_{UB} \cdot \mathbf{W}_{UB}^\top \cdot \mathbf{W}_{UB}$, where $\mathbf{W}_{UB}$ is the adjacency matrix between type U and type B. This shows that the counting-based similarities for a meta-path can be computed by the multiplication of a sequences of matrices like the above $\mathbf{W}_{UB}$. In practice, we can implement this in a very efficient way if the adjacency matrices $\mathbf{W}$'s are sparse.

For meta-graphs, the problem becomes more complicated. For example, for $\mathcal{M}_9$ in Figure 3(a), there are two ways to pass through the meta-graph, which are (U, R, A, R, U, B) and (U, R, B, R, U, B). Note that R represents the entity type *Review* in HIN. Here in the path (U, R, A, R, U, B), (R, A, R) means that if two reviews both mention the same A (*Aspect*), then they have some similarity. Similarly, in (U, R, B, R, U, B), R, B, R means that if two reviews both rate the same B (*Business*), then they have some similarity as well. We should define our logic of similarity when there are multiple ways for a flow passing through the meta-graph from source node to the target one. When there are two paths, we can allow a flow to pass through either path, or we constrain a flow to satisfy both of them. By analyzing the former strategy, we find that it is similar to simply split such meta-graph into multiple meta-paths and then adopt our later computation. Thus, we choose the latter, which requires one more matrix operation than simple multiplication, i.e., the Hadamard product, or element-wise product. Algorithm 1 depicts the algorithm for computing the counting-based similarity for $\mathcal{M}_9$ in Figure 3(a), where $\odot$ is the Hadamard product. After obtaining $\mathbf{C}_{S_r}$, it is easier to obtain the whole commuting matrix $\mathbf{C}_{\mathcal{M}_9}$ by the multiplication of a sequence of matrices. In practice, not limited to $\mathcal{M}_9$ in Figure 3(a), the meta-graph defined in this paper can be computed by two operations (Hadamard product and multiplication) on the corresponding matrices.

Algorithm 1 Computing commuting matrix for $\mathbf{C}_{\mathcal{M}_9}$.

Compute $\mathbf{C}_{P_1}$: $\mathbf{C}_{P_1} = \mathbf{W}_{RB} \cdot \mathbf{W}_{RB}^\top$;
Compute $\mathbf{C}_{P_2}$: $\mathbf{C}_{P_2} = \mathbf{W}_{RA} \cdot \mathbf{W}_{RA}^\top$;
Compute $\mathbf{C}_{S_r}$: $\mathbf{C}_{S_r} = \mathbf{C}_{P_1} \odot \mathbf{C}_{P_2}$;
Compute $\mathbf{C}_{\mathcal{M}_9}$: $\mathbf{C}_{\mathcal{M}_9} = \mathbf{W}_{UR} \cdot \mathbf{C}_{S_r} \cdot \mathbf{W}_{UR}^\top \cdot \mathbf{W}_{UB}$.

By computing the similarities between all users and items along the meta-graph $\mathcal{M}$, we can obtain a user-item similarity matrix $\hat{\mathbf{R}} \in \mathbb{R}^{m \times n}$, where $\hat{\mathbf{R}}_{ij}$ represents the similarity between user u_i and item b_j along the meta-graph $\mathcal{M}$, and m and n are the number of users and items, respectively. Then by designing L meta-graphs, we can get L different user-item similarity matrices, denoted by $\hat{\mathbf{R}}^1, \ldots, \hat{\mathbf{R}}^L$.

2.2 Meta-graph based Latent Features

After we obtain L different user-item similarity matrices, we use matrix factorization to obtain the latent features of users and items to reduce the noise and fix the sparsity problem of the original similarity matrices. State-of-the-art MF techniques can be used for the task [14, 22, 36]. Based on the assumption that the users' preferences are controlled by a small number of factors, the similarity matrix $\mathbf{R}$ can be factorized into two low-rank matrices, $\mathbf{U}$ and $\mathbf{B}$, which represent the latent features of users' preferences and items, respectively. By solving the optimizing problem in (1), the low dimensional representations of users and items can be obtained:

$$\min_{\mathbf{U},\mathbf{B}} \frac{1}{2}||P_\Omega(\mathbf{U}\mathbf{B}^\top - \mathbf{R})||_F^2 + \frac{\lambda_u}{2}||\mathbf{U}||_F^2 + \frac{\lambda_b}{2}||\mathbf{B}||_F^2, \quad (1)$$

where observed positions are indicated by 1's in $\Omega \in \{0,1\}^{u_m \times b_n}$, and $[P_\Omega(\mathbf{X})]_{ij} = \mathbf{X}_{ij}$ if $\Omega_{ij} = 1$, and 0 otherwise. λ_u and λ_b are the hyper-parameters that control the influence of Frobenius norm regularization to avoid overfitting. For L meta-graph based similarities between users and items, we can obtain L groups of latent features of users and items, denoted as $\mathbf{U}^{(1)}, \mathbf{B}^{(1)}, ..., \mathbf{U}^{(L)}, \mathbf{B}^{(L)}$.

2.3 Recommendation Model

After we obtain L groups of user and item latent features, for a sample $\mathbf{x}^n$ in the observed ratings, i.e., a pair of user and item, denoted by $\mathbf{u}_i$ and $\mathbf{b}_j$, we concatenate all of the corresponding user and item features from all of the L meta-graphs:

$$\mathbf{x}^n = \underbrace{\mathbf{u}_i^{(1)}, ..., \mathbf{u}_i^{(l)}, ..., \mathbf{u}_i^{(L)}}_{L \times F} \underbrace{\mathbf{b}_j^{(1)}, ..., \mathbf{b}_j^{(l)}, ..., \mathbf{b}_j^{(L)}}_{L \times F}, \quad (2)$$

where F is the rank used to factorize every similarity matrix by (1), and $\mathbf{u}_i^{(l)}$ and $\mathbf{b}_j^{(l)}$, respectively, represent user and item latent features generated from l-th meta-graph. Note that F can be different for different matrices, but we keep it constant for simplicity. $\mathbf{x}^n$ represents the feature vector of the n-th sample after concatenation. Then each user and item can be represented by the $L \times F$ latent features, respectively.

Given all of the features in (2), the rating for the sample $\mathbf{x}^n$ based on FM [25] is computed as follows:

$$\hat{y}^n(\mathbf{w}, \mathbf{V}) = w_0 + \sum_{i=1}^{d} w_i x_i^n + \sum_{i=1}^{d} \sum_{j=i+1}^{d} \langle \mathbf{v}_i, \mathbf{v}_j \rangle x_i^n x_j^n, \quad (3)$$

where w_0 is the global bias, $\mathbf{w} \in \mathbb{R}^d$, representing the first-order weights for the features, and $\mathbf{V} = [\mathbf{v}_i] \in \mathbb{R}^{d \times K}$ represents the second-order weights to model the interactions across different features. $\langle \cdot, \cdot \rangle$ is the dot product of two vectors of size K. $\mathbf{v}_i$ is the i-th row of the matrix $\mathbf{V}$, which describes the i-th variable with K factors. $d = 2LF$ represents the total number of features generated by the L meta-graph based similarity matrices. F is the rank used to factorize every similarity matrix. $\mathbf{x}_i^n$ is the i-th feature in $\mathbf{x}^n$. The parameters can be learned by minimizing the mean square loss:

$$\min_{\mathbf{w},\mathbf{V}} \sum_{n=1}^{N} (y^n - \hat{y}^n(\mathbf{w}, \mathbf{V}))^2, \quad (4)$$

where y^n is an observed rating for the n-th sample. N is the number of all the observed ratings.

There are two problems when applying the FM model to the meta-graph based latent features. The first problem is that it may bring noise when working with many meta-graphs thus impairing the predicting capability of the model. Moreover, in practice, some meta-graphs can be useless since information provided by some meta-paths can be covered by others. The second problem is the computational cost. All of the features are generated by standard matrix factorization, which means that the design matrix, i.e., features fed to FM, are dense. It increases the computational cost for learning the parameters of the model as well as that of online recommendation.

To alleviate the above two problems, we propose a novel regularization for FM, i.e., the group lasso regularization [42], which is a feature selection method on a group of variables. The group lasso regularization of parameters $\mathbf{p}$ is defined as follows:

$$\Phi(\mathbf{p}) = \sum_{g=1}^{G} ||\mathbf{p}_{\mathcal{I}_g}||_2, \quad (5)$$

where $\mathcal{I}_g$ is the index set belonging to the predefined g-th group of variables, $g = 1, 2, ..., G$, and $|| \cdot ||_2$ is the ℓ_2-norm. In our model, the groups correspond to the meta-graph based features. For example, $\mathbf{U}^{(l)}$ and $\mathbf{B}^{(l)}$ are the user and item latent features generated by the l-th meta-graph. For a pair of user i and item j, the latent features are $\mathbf{u}_i^{(l)}$ and $\mathbf{b}_j^{(l)}$. There are two corresponding groups of variables in $\mathbf{w}$ and $\mathbf{V}$ according to (3). With L meta-graphs, the features of users and items from every single meta-graph can be put in a group. We have in total $2L$ groups of variables in $\mathbf{w}$ and $\mathbf{V}$, respectively.

For the first-order parameters $\mathbf{w}$ in (3), which is a vector, the group lasso is applied to the subset of variables in $\mathbf{w}$. Then we have:

$$\Phi_{\mathbf{w}}(\mathbf{w}) = \sum_{l=1}^{2L} ||\mathbf{w}_l||_2, \quad (6)$$

where $\mathbf{w}_l \in \mathbb{R}^F$, which models the weights for a group of user or item features from one meta-graph. For the second-order parameters $\mathbf{V}$ in (3), we have the regularizer as:

$$\Phi_{\mathbf{V}}(\mathbf{V}) = \sum_{l=1}^{2L} ||\mathbf{V}_l||_F, \quad (7)$$

where $\mathbf{V}_l \in \mathbb{R}^{F \times K}$, the l-th block of $\mathbf{V}$ corresponding to the l-th meta-graph based features in a sample, and $|| \cdot ||_F$ is the Frobenius norm.

With group lasso regularizations, during the training process, our model can automatically select useful features and remove redundant ones in group, i.e. generated by different meta-graphs. In the selection process, unuseful features are removed in the unit of a group.

2.4 Comparison with Previous Latent Feature based Model

Previous approaches of recommendation based on HIN [40] also applied matrix factorization to generate latent features from different meta-paths and predict the rating by a weighted ensemble of dot product of user and item latent features from every single meta-path:

$$\hat{r}(\mathbf{u}_i, \mathbf{b}_j) = \sum_{l=1}^{L} \theta_l \cdot \hat{\mathbf{u}}_i^{(l)} \cdot \hat{\mathbf{b}}_j^{(l)T}, \quad (8)$$

where $\hat{r}(\mathbf{u}_i, \mathbf{b}_j)$ is the predicted rating for user $\mathbf{u}_i$ and $\mathbf{b}_j$, L is the number of meta-paths used, and θ_l is the weight for the l-th meta-path latent features. However, here the predicting method is not adequate, as it fails to capture the interactions between inter-meta-graph features, i.e. features across different meta-graphs, as well as the intra-meta-graph features, i.e. features inside a single meta-graph. It may decrease the prediction ability of all of the user and item features.

3 MODEL OPTIMIZATION

In this section, we introduce how to solve the optimization problem. We define our FM over meta-graph (FMG) model with the following objective function:

$$h(\mathbf{w},\mathbf{V}) = \sum_{n=1}^{N} (y^n - \hat{y}^n(\mathbf{w},\mathbf{V}))^2 + \lambda_w \Phi_{\mathbf{w}}(\mathbf{w}) + \lambda_v \Phi_{\mathbf{V}}(\mathbf{V}). \quad (9)$$

Note that in (3) we merge all of the superscripts (l)'s into subscript without introducing confusion of the original FM model. Here, we can see that h is non-smooth due to the use of $\Phi_{\mathbf{w}}$ and $\Phi_{\mathbf{V}}$. Besides, as (3) is not convex on $\mathbf{V}$, h is also not convex.

3.1 Optimization

To tackle the non-convex non-smooth objective function, we propose to use the proximal gradient algorithm [23], which is a powerful tool to handle non-convex problems, in the form of (9). Specifically, the state-of-the-art nonmonotonous accelerated proximal gradient (nmAPG) algorithm [17] is used. The motivation comes from two facts. First, nonsmoothness comes from the proposed regularizers, which can be efficiently handled since the corresponding proximal steps have cheap closed-form solution. Second, the acceleration technique is useful for significantly speeding up first order optimization algorithms [17, 37], and nmAPG is the only technique which can deal with general non-convex problems with sound convergence guarantee. The whole procedure is given in Algorithm 2.

Note that while both $\Phi_{\mathbf{w}}$ and $\Phi_{\mathbf{V}}$ are nonsmooth in (9), they are imposed on $\mathbf{w}$ and $\mathbf{V}$ separately. Thus, we can also perform proximal step independently for these two regularizers [23] as follows.

$$\mathbf{prox}_{\lambda_w \Phi_{\mathbf{w}} + \lambda_V \Phi_{\mathbf{V}}}(\mathbf{w},\mathbf{V}) = \left(\mathbf{prox}_{\lambda_w \Phi_{\mathbf{w}}}(\mathbf{w}), \mathbf{prox}_{\lambda_V \Phi_{\mathbf{V}}}(\mathbf{V})\right).$$

These are performed at lines 6-7 and 12-13. The closed-form solution of $\mathbf{prox}_{\alpha\Phi_{\mathbf{w}}}(\cdot)$ and $\mathbf{prox}_{\alpha\Phi_{\mathbf{V}}}(\cdot)$ can be obtained easily from Lemma 3.1 below. Thus, each proximal step can be solved in one pass of all groups.

LEMMA 3.1 ([41]). *The closed-form solution of* $\mathbf{p}^* = \mathbf{prox}_{\lambda\Phi}(z)$ *(Φ is defined in (5)) is given by*

$$\mathbf{p}^*_{\mathcal{I}_g} = \max\left(1 - \frac{\lambda}{\|\mathbf{z}_{\mathcal{I}_g}\|_2}, 0\right)\mathbf{z}_{\mathcal{I}_g},$$

for all $g = 1, \ldots, G$.

Finally, it is easy to verify that the assumptions on the convergence of nmAPG in [17] are satisfied. Thus, Algorithm 2 is guaranteed to produce a critical point of (9).

3.2 Complexity Analysis

The major computational cost in the training process is to update the gradients of all parameters including gradient calculation and evaluation of proximal operators. In [25], the author shows that for every single sample, computing each gradient is $O(1)$ time, which leads to $O(Kd)$ time in total for one sample, where K is the dimensions for factorizing the second order parameters, as shown in (3), and $d = 2LF$ is the number of features in every sample. For evaluating the proximal operator Φ, according to Lemma 3.1, for each sample, each gradient also costs $O(1)$, thus achieving $O(Kd)$ time by updating all gradients in one sample. Then, the total time in one iteration is $O(N(Kd + Kd)) = O(NKd)$, where N is the number of all observations. Assuming T iterations are used in total, the overall time of the learning process is $O(TNKd)$.

Algorithm 2 nmAPG [17] algorithm for (9).

1: Initiate $\mathbf{w}_0$, $\mathbf{V}_0$ as Gaussian random matrices;
2: $\bar{\mathbf{w}}_1 = \mathbf{w}_1 = \mathbf{w}_0$, $\bar{\mathbf{V}}_1 = \mathbf{V}_1 = \mathbf{V}_0$, $c_1 = h(\mathbf{w}_1, \mathbf{V}_1)$; $q_1 = 1$, $\delta = 10^{-3}$, $a_0 = 0$, $a_1 = 1$, $\alpha = 10^{-7}$;
3: **for** $t = 1, 2, 3, \ldots, T$ **do**
4: $\quad \mathbf{y}_t = \mathbf{w}_t + \frac{a_{t-1}}{a_t}(\bar{\mathbf{w}}_t - \mathbf{w}_t) + \frac{a_{t-1}-1}{a_t}(\mathbf{w}_t - \mathbf{w}_{t-1})$;
5: $\quad \mathrm{Y}_t = \mathbf{V}_t + \frac{a_{t-1}}{a_t}(\bar{\mathbf{V}}_t - \mathbf{V}_t) + \frac{a_{t-1}-1}{a_t}(\mathbf{V}_t - \mathbf{V}_{t-1})$;
6: $\quad \bar{\mathbf{w}}_{t+1} = \mathbf{prox}_{\alpha\lambda\Phi_{\mathbf{w}}}(\mathbf{w}_t - \alpha\nabla_{\mathbf{w}} h(\mathbf{w}_t, \mathbf{V}_t))$;
7: $\quad \bar{\mathbf{V}}_{t+1} = \mathbf{prox}_{\alpha\lambda\Phi_{\mathbf{V}}}(\mathbf{V}_t - \alpha\nabla_{\mathbf{V}} h(\mathbf{w}_t, \mathbf{V}_t))$;
8: $\quad \Delta_t = \|\bar{\mathbf{w}}_{t+1} - \mathbf{y}_t\|_2^2 + \|\bar{\mathbf{V}}_{t+1} - \mathrm{Y}_t\|_F^2$
9: $\quad$ **if** $h(\bar{\mathbf{w}}_{t+1}, \bar{\mathbf{V}}_{t+1}) \leq c_t - \delta\Delta_t$; **then**
10: $\quad\quad \mathbf{w}_{t+1} = \bar{\mathbf{w}}_{t+1}$, $\mathbf{V}_{t+1} = \bar{\mathbf{V}}_{t+1}$;
11: $\quad$ **else**
12: $\quad\quad \hat{\mathbf{w}}_{t+1} = \mathbf{prox}_{\alpha\lambda\Phi_{\mathbf{w}}}(\mathbf{w}_t - \alpha\nabla_{\mathbf{w}} h(\mathbf{w}_t, \mathbf{V}_t))$;
13: $\quad\quad \hat{\mathbf{V}}_{t+1} = \mathbf{prox}_{\alpha\lambda\Phi_{\mathbf{V}}}(\mathbf{V}_t - \alpha\nabla_{\mathbf{V}} h(\mathbf{w}_t, \mathbf{V}_t))$;
14: $\quad\quad$ **if** $h(\hat{\mathbf{w}}_{t+1}, \hat{\mathbf{V}}_{t+1}) < h(\bar{\mathbf{w}}_{t+1}, \bar{\mathbf{V}}_{t+1})$ **then**
15: $\quad\quad\quad \mathbf{w}_{t+1} = \hat{\mathbf{w}}_{t+1}$;
16: $\quad\quad\quad \mathbf{V}_{t+1} = \hat{\mathbf{V}}_{t+1}$;
17: $\quad\quad$ **else**
18: $\quad\quad\quad \mathbf{w}_{t+1} = \bar{\mathbf{w}}_{t+1}$;
19: $\quad\quad\quad \mathbf{V}_{t+1} = \bar{\mathbf{V}}_{t+1}$;
20: $\quad\quad$ **end if**
21: $\quad$ **end if**
22: $\quad a_{t+1} = \frac{1}{2}(\sqrt{4a_t^2 + 1} + 1)$
23: $\quad q_{t+1} = \eta q_t + 1$;
24: $\quad c_{t+1} = \frac{1}{q_{t+1}}(\eta q_t c_t + h(\mathbf{w}_{t+1}, \mathbf{V}_{t+1}))$;
25: **end for**
26: **return** $\mathbf{w}_{T+1}, \mathbf{V}_{T+1}$.

4 EXPERIMENTS

In this section, we first introduce the datasets, evaluation metric and experimental settings. And then show the experimental results.

4.1 Datasets

To demonstrate the effectiveness of HIN for recommendation, we conduct experiments on four datasets with rich heterogeneous information. The first dataset is Yelp, which is provided for the Yelp challenge.[1] Yelp is a website where a user can rate local businesses or post photos and reviews about them. The rates fall in the range of 1 to 5, where higher ratings mean users like the businesses while lower rates mean users' negative feedbacks to the businesses. Based on the information collected, the website can recommend businesses according to the users' preferences. Another dataset is Amazon Electronics,[2] which is provided in [8]. As we know, Amazon highly relies on recommendations to present interesting items to users who are surfing on the website. In [8] many domains

[1] https://www.yelp.com/dataset_challenge
[2] http://jmcauley.ucsd.edu/data/amazon/

Table 1: Statistics of Yelp and Amazon datasets.

Yelp-200K				
Relations(A-B)	Number of A	Number of B	Number of (A-B)	Avg Degrees of A/B
User-Business	36,105	22,496	191,506	5.3/8.5
User-Review	36,105	191,506	191,506	5.3/1
User-User	17,065	17,065	140,344	8.2/8.2
Business-Category	22,496	869	67,940	3/78.2
Business-Star	22,496	9	22,496	1/2,499.6
Business-State	22,496	18	22496	1/1,249.8
Business-City	22,496	215	22,496	1/104.6
Review-Business	191,506	22,496	191,506	1/8.5
Review-Aspect	191,506	10	955,041	5/95,504.1
Amazon-200K				
Relations(A-B)	Number of A	Number of B	Number of (A-B)	Avg Degrees of A/B
User-Business	59,297	20,216	183,807	3.1/9.1
User-Review	59,297	183,807	183,807	3.1/1
Business-Category	20,216	682	87,587	4.3/128.4
Business-Brand	95,33	2,015	9,533	1/4.7
Review-Business	183,807	20,216	183,807	1/9.1
Review-Aspect	183,807	10	796,392	4.3/79,639.2

Table 2: The density of rating matrices in the four datasets Density $= \frac{\#Ratings}{\#Users \times \#Items}$.

	Amazon-200K	Yelp-200K	CIKM-Yelp	CIKM-Douban
Density	0.015%	0.024%	0.086%	0.630%

of Amazon dataset are provided, and we choose the electronics domain for our experiments. We extract subsets of entities from Yelp and Amazon to build the HIN, which includes diverse types and relations. The subsets of the two datasets both include around 200,000 ratings in the user-item rating matrices. Thus, we identify them as Yelp-200K and Amazon-200K, respectively. Besides, we also use the datasets provided in the CIKM paper [29], which we call CIKM-Yelp and CIKM-Douban. The statistics of our datasets are shown in Table 1. For the detailed information of CIKM-Yelp and CIKM-Douban, we refer the user to [29]. Note that i) the number of types and relations in the first two datasets, i.e. Amazon-200K and Yelp-200K, we used in this paper are much more than those used in previous works [29, 39, 40]; ii) We give the sparsity of the four datasets in Table 2. The sparsity of the rating matrices is more severe than those used in [29, 39, 40].

4.2 Evaluation Metric

To evaluate the recommendation performance, we adopt the root-mean-square-error (RMSE) as our metric, which is the most popular one for rating prediction in the recommendation literature [14, 20, 22]. RMSE is defined as follows

$$\text{RMSE} = \sqrt{\frac{\sum_{(i,j)\in\mathcal{R}_{test}} (\mathbf{R}_{ij} - \hat{\mathbf{R}}_{ij})^2}{|\mathcal{R}_{test}|}}, \tag{10}$$

where $\mathcal{R}_{test}$ is the set of all user-item pairs (i, j) in the test set, $\hat{\mathbf{R}}_{ij}$ is the predicted rate of user u_i to item b_j, and $\mathbf{R}_{ij}$ is the observed rate of user u_i to item b_j in the test set. For RMSE, smaller value means better performance.

4.3 Baseline Models

We compare the following models to our approach.

- **RegSVD** [15]: RegSVD is the basic matrix factorization with L_2 regularization, which uses only the user-item rating matrix. We run the implementation in Librec [7].[3]
- **FMR** [25]: FMR is the factorization machine with only the user-item rating matrix. We adopt the method in Section 4.1.1 of [25] to model the rating prediction task. We use the code provided by the authors.[4]
- **HeteRec** [40]: HeteRec method is based on meta-path based similarity between users and items. A weighted ensemble model is learned from the latent features of users and items generated by applying matrix factorization to the similarity matrices of different meta-paths. We implemented it based on [40].
- **SemRec** [29]: SemRec is a meta-path based recommendation on weighted HIN, which is built by connecting users and items with the same ratings. Different models are learned from different meta-paths, and a weight ensemble method is used to predict the users' ratings. We use the code provided by the authors.[5]

Note that in [39], the meta-path based similarities are used as regularization terms in the matrix factorization framework. And in [29], the authors reported that SemRec outperforms this method. Thus, we do not report the experimental results of [39] here.

4.4 Experimental Settings

To demonstrate the capability of our model, we use the meta-graphs shown in Figure 3. The meanings of the nodes are given in the figures. To get the aspects from review texts, we use Gensim [24], a topic model software to extract topics. The number of topics is set to 10 empirically. We also try other numbers and they showed similar results. Thus, we fix the number of topics to 10 for all experiments to make fair comparisons.

In terms of designing the experiments, we randomly split the datasets into training and test ones by the ratio 8:2, i.e., 80% of the whole data are used for training and the remaining 20% are for testing. The process is repeated five times and the average RMSE of the five rounds are reported. Our framework is implemented with Python 2.7, and all experiments run in a Linux server with Intel i7 CPU and 32GB RAM.

4.5 Recommendation Effectiveness

We show our results in Table 3. As shown in Table 2, the sparsity of the rating matrices of our data is severe. This is important for the rating prediction task. By comparing RMSEs of Yelp-200K and CIKM-Yelp, we can see that the denser training data results in lower RMSE, i.e., better performance can be obtained. This is because with more observations in the training set, we can get more information about the whole matrix, leading to more accurate predicted ratings of the users to the items. Note that the reason why we did not report the result of SemRec on Amazon-200K is that the programs

[3] https://www.librec.net/
[4] http://www.libfm.org/
[5] https://github.com/zzqsmall/SemRec

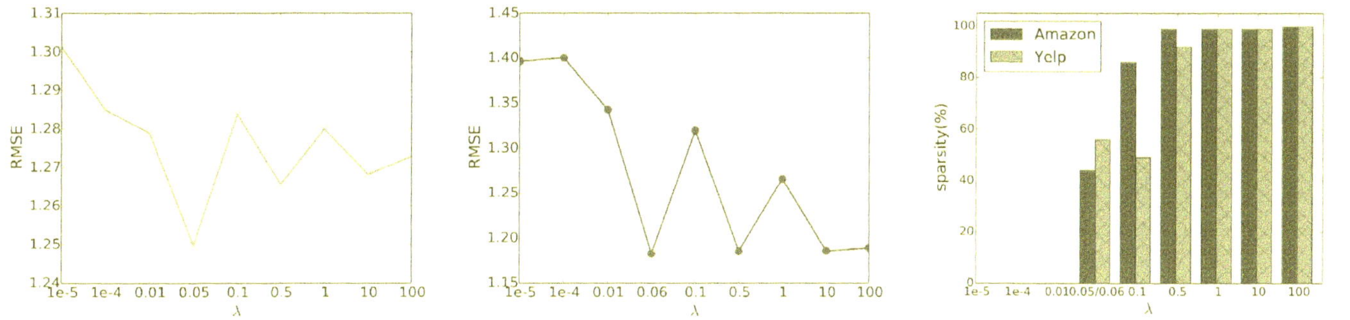

(a) Yelp. (b) Amazon. (c) Sparsity of w, V.

Figure 4: Effects of λ. (a) and (b) show RMSEs with different λ's. (c) shows the trend of sparsity. Note that at the fourth point of x-axis we have $\lambda = 0.05$ for Yelp and $\lambda = 0.06$ for Amazon, respectively.

Table 3: Recommending performance in terms of RMSE. Percentages in the brackets are the reduction of RMSE comparing our approach with the corresponding approaches in the table header.

	Amazon-200K	Yelp-200K	CIKM-Yelp	CIKM-Douban
RegSVD	2.9656 (+60.0%)	2.5141 (+50.5%)	1.5323 (+27.7%)	0.7673 (+9.0%)
FMR	1.3462 (+11.9%)	1.7637 (+29.4%)	1.4342 (+22.8%)	0.7524 (+7.2%)
HeteRec	2.5368 (+53.2%)	2.3475 (+47.0%)	1.4891 (+25.6%)	0.7671 (+9.0%)
SemRec	- -	1.4603 (+14.7%)	1.1559 (+4.2%)	0.7216 (+3.2%)
FMG	**1.1864**	**1.2456**	**1.1074**	**0.6985**

crashed on Amazon-200K in a server with 128G memory due to the large numbers of users and items as shown in Table 1.

From Table 3, we can see that comparing to RegSVD and FMR, which only use the rating matrix, SemRec and FMG, which use additional heterogeneous information by meta-graphs, are significantly better. Especially, the sparser the rating matrix, the more useful the additional information incorporated. For example, on Amazon-200K, FMG outperforms RegSVD by 60%, while for CIKM-Douban, the percentage of RMSE decreasing is 9%. Note that the performance of HeteRec is worse than FMR, despite the fact that we have tried our best to tune the models. The reason is that, as we show in Section 2.3, using a weighting ensemble of dot product of latent features may lose information among the meta-graphs and fail to avoid noise caused by too many meta-graphs.

When comparing the results of FMG and SemRec, we find that the performance gap between them are not that large, which means that SemRec is still a good method for rating prediction, especially when comparing SemRec to the other three baselines. The good performance of SemRec may be attributed to two reasons. First, incorporating rating values into HIN leads to a weighted HIN, which may better capture the meta-graph or meta-path based similarity. Currently, FMG ignores the rating values, so it remains unknown whether it can further decrease RMSE if we adopt a similar approach to incorporate rating values into HIN. We leave it as future work. Second, the meta-graphs SemRec exploits are all of the style like $U \rightarrow * \leftarrow U \rightarrow B$, which have a good capability of predication. In the Section 4.6, we will show that FMG can automatically select features constructed by meta-graphs like $U \rightarrow * \leftarrow U \rightarrow B$ while removing those by meta-graphs like ($U \rightarrow B \rightarrow * \leftarrow B$). In Section 4.7, we further study the prediction ability of each meta-graph, and also show that meta-graphs with style like $U \rightarrow * \leftarrow U \rightarrow B$ are better than those like $U \rightarrow B \rightarrow * \leftarrow B$.

4.6 The Parameter λ

In this part, we show the influence of parameter λ, with $\lambda = \lambda_w = \lambda_v$, which controls the effects of group lasso. The experiments were conducted on Yelp-50k and Amazon-50k, where only 50,000 ratings are sampled and thus is a smaller version of Yelp-200K and Amazon-200K for the sake of efficiency of parameter tuning. The RMSEs of Yelp-50k and Amazon-50K are shown in Figures 4(a) and (b), respectively. We can see that with λ increasing, RMSE decreases first and then increases, demonstrating that λ values that are too large or too small are not good for the performance of rating prediction. Specifically, on Yelp, the best is $\lambda = 0.05$, and on Amazon, the best is $\lambda = 0.06$. Next, we give further analysis of these two parameters in terms of sparsity and the selected meta-graphs by group lasso.

Sparsity of $\mathbf{w}, \mathbf{V}$. We now study the sparsity of the learned parameters, i.e., ratio of zeros in $\mathbf{w}, \mathbf{V}$ after learning. Sparsity is defined as sparsity $= \frac{z}{w_n + v_n}$, where z is the total number of zeros in $\mathbf{w}$ and $\mathbf{V}$, and w_n and v_n are the number of entries in $\mathbf{w}$ and $\mathbf{V}$, respectively. The larger sparsity is, the more zeros are in $\mathbf{w}$ and $\mathbf{V}$, which will reduce the time of online prediction. The trend of sparsity with different λ's is shown in Figure 4(c). We can see that with λ increasing, the sparsity becomes greater, which aligns with the effects of group lasso. Note that the trend is non-monotonous due to the non-convexity of the objective function w.r.t. $\mathbf{w}$ and $\mathbf{V}$ and the fact that we set $\lambda_w = \lambda_v$ for the convenience of parameter tuning.

The Selected Meta-graphs. In this part, we analyze the selected features by group lasso. From Figure 4, we can see that $\mathbf{w}$ and $\mathbf{V}$

Table 4: Selected Meta-graphs for Yelp and Amazon datasets.

		User-Part		Item-Part	
		W	V	W	V
Yelp	Important	$M_1 - M_4, M_6, M_8$	$M_1 - M_3, M_5, M_8$	$M_1 - M_5, M_8, M_9$	M_3, M_8
	Useless	M_5, M_7, M_9	M_4, M_6, M_7, M_9	M_6, M_7	$M_1, M_2, M_4 - M_7, M_9$
Amazon	Important	$M_1 - M_3, M_5$	$M_1 - M_6$	M_2, M_3, M_5, M_6	M_2, M_5, M_6
	Useless	M_4, M_6	-	M_1, M_4	M_1, M_3, M_4

are good in terms of RMSE and sparsity when $\lambda = 0.05$ on Yelp and $\lambda = 0.06$ on Amazon. Thus, we show the most important meta-graphs with this configuration for user and item latent features. The results of Amazon and Yelp are shown in Table 4.

From Table 4, we can observe that both the first-order and second-order interactions are important for overall performance, which demonstrates that the second-order interactions are necessary for better recommendation performance. As we mentioned in Section 1, previous works do not fully make use of the latent features, like the second-order interactions.

Another discovery is that the meta-graphs with style like $U \rightarrow * \leftarrow U \rightarrow B$ are better than those like $U \rightarrow B \rightarrow * \leftarrow B$. Here we use $U \rightarrow * \leftarrow U \rightarrow B$ to represent meta-graphs like M_2, M_3, M_8, M_9 in Figure 3(a) and M_2, M_5, M_6 in Figure 3(b), while use $U \rightarrow B \rightarrow * \leftarrow B$ to represent meta-graphs like M_4, M_5, M_6, M_7 in Figure 3(a) and M_3, M_4 in Figure 3(b). For Yelp, we can see that meta-graphs like M_2, M_3, M_8, M_9 tend to be selected while $M_4 - M_7$ are removed, which means that on Yelp, recommendations by friends or similar users are better than those by similar items. Similar cases exist on Amazon, i.e., M_3, M_4 tend to be removed.

Finally, on both datasets, complex structures like M_9 in Figure 3(a) and M_6 in Figure 3(b) are determined to be important for item latent features, which demonstrates the importance of capturing these kinds of relations, which are ignored by previous meta-path based recommendation methods [29, 39, 40].

4.7 Recommending Performance with Single Meta-Graph

In this part, we compare the performances of different meta-graphs separately. In the training process, we use only one meta-graph for user and item features and then predict and evalute the results obtained by the corresponding meta-graph. Specifically, we run experiments to compare RMSEs of all of the meta-graphs in Figure 3. The RMSE of each meta-graph is shown in Figure 5. Note that we show as comparison the RMSEs of all the meta-graphs used, denoted by M_{all}.

From Figure 5, we can see that on both Yelp and Amazon, the performances are the best when all meta-graph based user and item features are used, which demonstrates the usefulness of the semantics captured by the designed meta-graphs in Figure 3. Besides, we can see that on Yelp, the performances of $M_4 - M_7$ are the worst, and on Amazon, the performances of $M_3 - M_4$ are also among the worst three. Note that they are both meta-graphs with style like $U \rightarrow B \rightarrow * \leftarrow B$. Thus, it aligns with the observation in Section 4.6 that meta-graphs with style like $U \rightarrow * \leftarrow U \rightarrow B$ are better than those like $U \rightarrow B \rightarrow * \leftarrow B$.

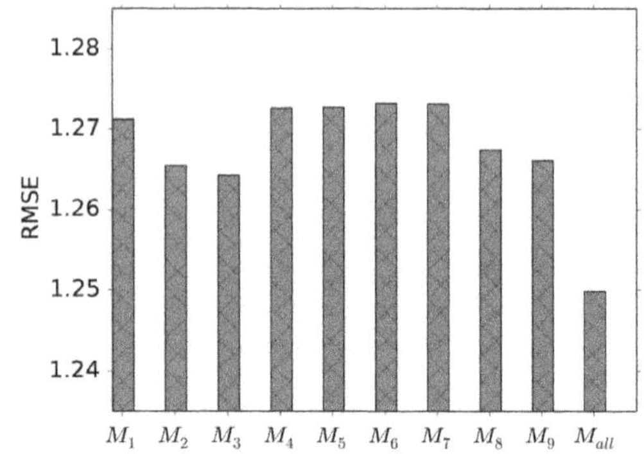

(a) Yelp.

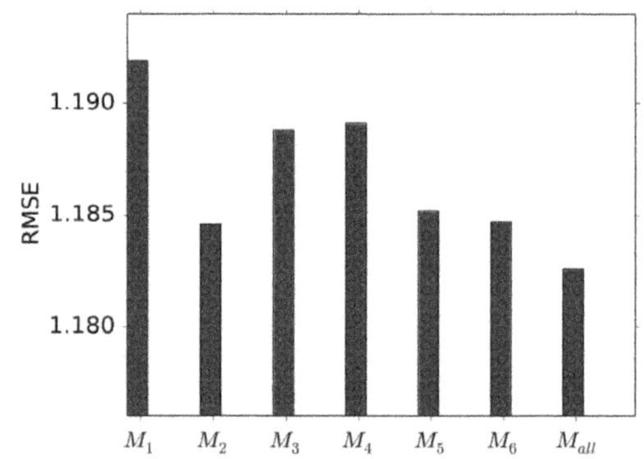

(b) Amazon.

Figure 5: RMSE of single meta-graph on Yelp and Amazon datasets. M_{all} is our model trained with all meta-graphs.

Finally, for M_9 on Yelp and M_6 on Amazon, we can see that the performances of these two meta-graphs are among the best three, which demonstrates the usefulness of the complex semantics captured in M_9 on Yelp and M_6 on Amazon. In future work, we will try to design more complex meta-graphs like these two, and study if they can further improve recommending performance.

4.8 The Parameters F and K

In this part, we study the influence of the two parameters: F and K. F is the rank used to factorize meta-graph based user-item similarity matrices to obtain user and item latent features (see

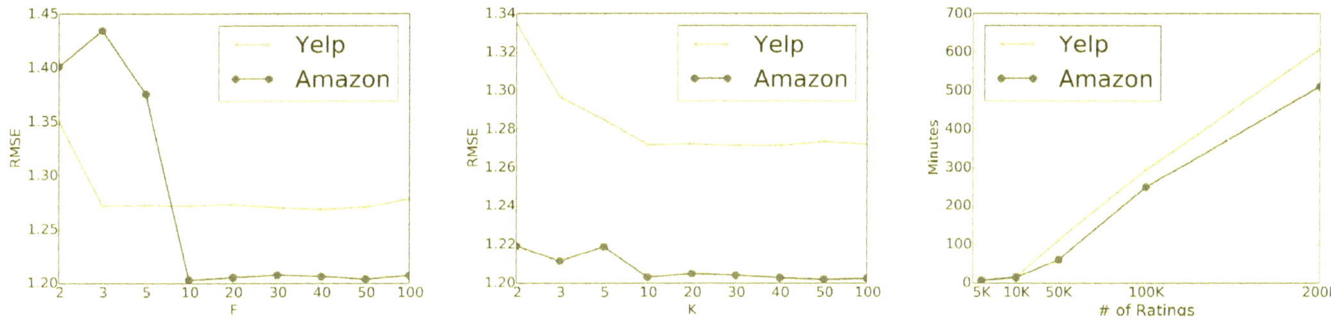

(a) Varying F with $K = 10$. (b) Varying K with $F = 10$. (c) Scalability.

Figure 6: (a) and (b) show RMSEs with different K's and F's, (c) shows the execution time with different sizes of datasets.

Section 2.2). K is the number of factors to factorize the second-order weights $\mathbf{V}$ in the FMG model (see Section 2.3). For the sake of efficiency, we conduct extensive experiments using the smaller datasets, Yelp-50K and Amazon-50K. We set F and K to values in the range of $[2, 3, 5, 10, 20, 30, 40, 50, 100]$. The results are shown in Figures 6(a) and (b). We can see that the performances get better with larger F or K in both datasets. After a threshold value, i.e., 10, the performance becomes stable. In practice, the performance gains are marginal when the two parameters are greater than 10, and larger values mean higher computational cost. Therefore, it is enough to obtain a good performance to set $F = 10$ and $K = 10$ for these two datasets, which are the adopted settings of these two parameters of the experimental results reported in Section 4.5.

4.9 Scalability

In this part, we study the scalability of our FMG model. We extract a series of datasets of different scales from Yelp-200K and Amazon-200K according to the number of observations in the user-item rating matrix. The specific values are $[5K, 10K, 50K, 100K, 200K]$. The time cost of Amazon and Yelp datasets are shown in Figure 6(c), for which we set $\lambda = 0.05$ for Yelp and $\lambda = 0.06$ for Amazon and number of iterations to 3,000. We can see from the figure that the training time is almost linear to the number observed ratings.

5 RELATED WORK

In this section, we briefly introduce the related work of HINs and recommendation.

5.1 Heterogeneous Information Networks

HINs have been proposed as a general representation for many real-world graphs or networks. Meta-path has been developed as a sequence of entity types defined by the HIN network schema. Based on a meta-path, several similarity measures, such as PathCount [32], PathSim [32], and Path Constrained Random Walk [16] have been proposed. These measures have been shown to be useful for entity search and similarity measure in many real networks. After the development of meta-path, many data mining tasks have been enabled or enhanced including recommendation [29, 39, 40], similarity search [27, 28, 32], clustering [33, 35], classification [1, 12, 18], and link prediction [31, 43]. Recently, meta-graph (or meta-structure) has been proposed to define more complicated semantics in HIN [6, 10]. They still applied meta-graph to entity similarity problem where entities are constrained to be of the same type. In this paper, we extend this idea to recommendation problem. The problem of recommendation requires us to approximate the large-scale user-item rating matrix. Thus, instead of computing each similarity efficiently online, we consider to compute the matrices offline, and design the best way to use the user-item matrices generated by different meta-graphs for the final prediction.

5.2 Recommendation in HIN

Modern e-commerce websites allow us to incorporate heterogeneous information in making recommendations. Traditional recommendation systems must be enhanced to make use of the rich semantics provided by the heterogeneous information. For example, Ma et al. [20] incorporated social relations as regularization sterm into the matrix factorization in recommendation systems. In [4, 34], items' meta-data are modeled to improve the recommendation task. In [19, 21], the review texts are analyzed together with the ratings in the rating prediction task. Ye et al. [38] proposed a probabilistic model to incorporate users' preferences, social network and geographical information to enhance the point-of-interests recommendation. These previous approaches have demonstrated the importance and effectiveness of heterogeneous information in improving recommendation accuracy. However, most of these approaches dealt with different heterogeneous information disparately, hence losing important information that exist across them.

HIN-based recommendation has been proposed to avoid the disparate treatment of different types of information. Based on meta-path, several approaches have attempted to tackle the recommendation task based on HIN. In [39], meta-path based similarities are used as regularization terms in the matrix factorization framework. In [40], multiple meta-paths are used to learn user and item latent features, which are then used to recover similarity matrices combined by a weighted mechanism. In [29], users' ratings to items are used to build a weighted HIN, based on which meta-path based methods are used to measure the similarities of users for recommendation. The combination of different meta-paths are explicit, using the similarities instead of latent features. As discussed in the introduction, all of the above approaches do not make full use of the meta-path based features, whereas our approach based on the factorization machine can do.

5.3 Factorization Machine

Factorization Machine [25] is a state-of-the-art recommendation framework, which can model the interactions among features, e.g., the rating information, categories of items, texts, time, etc. Therefore, it is a powerful framework to integrate content features for collaborative-filtering-based recommendation. Many approaches and systems have been developed based on FMs [9, 11, 26]. Different from previous approaches which only consider explicit features, we generate latent features by matrix factorization based on different meta-graphs. For FM using the original explicit features, MF can be regarded as a step similar to PCA to perform dimensionality reduction to reduce the noise of the original features.

6 CONCLUSION

In this paper, we present a heterogeneous information network (HIN) based recommendation method. We introduce a principled way of fusing heterogeneous information in the network. By using meta-graphs derived from the HIN schema, we can formulate complicated semantics between users and items. Then, we use matrix factorization to obtain latent features of user and item from each meta-path in an unsupervised way. After that, we use a group lasso regularized factorization machine to fuse different groups of semantic information extracted from different meta-graphs to predict the links. Experimental results demonstrate the effectiveness of our approach. In the future, we plan to explore richer information to enrich the features and semantics in the network, and use parallel computing and deep learning to further improve our system.

7 ACKNOWLEDGMENT

Research in this paper was partially supported by the Research Grants Council HKSAR GRF (No.615113 and No.614513), China 973 Fundamental R&D Program (No.2014CB340304) and Hong Kong ITF Grant (No. ITF/391/15FX). We also thank the anonymous reviewers for their valuable comments and suggestions that help improve the quality of this manuscript.

REFERENCES

[1] P. Bangcharoensap, T. Murata, H. Kobayashi, and N. Shimizu. Transductive classification on heterogeneous information networks with edge betweenness-based normalization. In *WSDM*, pages 437–446, 2016.
[2] P. Belhumeur, J. Hespanha, and D. Kriegman. Eigenfaces vs. Fisherfaces: Recognition using class specific linear projection. *IEEE Transactions on Pattern Analysis and Machine Intelligence*, 19(7):711–720, 1997.
[3] J. C. D. Chapter 13: Mining electronic health records in the genomics era. *PLoS Computational Biology*, 8(12), 2012.
[4] A. Deepak and B. Chen. fLDA: Matrix factorization through latent dirichlet allocation. In *WSDM*, pages 91–100, 2010.
[5] X. Dong, E. Gabrilovich, G. Heitz, W. Horn, N. Lao, K. Murphy, T. Strohmann, S. Sun, and W. Zhang. Knowledge vault: A web-scale approach to probabilistic knowledge fusion. In *KDD*, pages 601–610, 2014.
[6] Y. Fang, W. Lin, V. W. Zheng, M. Wu, K. C.-C. Chang, and X. Li. Semantic proximity search on graphs with meta graph-based learning. In *ICDE*, pages 277–288, 2016.
[7] G. Guo, J. Zhang, Z. Sun, and N. Yorke-Smith. Librec: A Java library for recommender systems., 2015.
[8] R. He and J. McAuley. Ups and downs: Modeling the visual evolution of fashion trends with one-class collaborative filtering. In *WWW*, pages 507–517, 2016.
[9] L. Hong, A. S. Doumith, and B. D. Davison. Co-factorization machines: Modeling user interests and predicting individual decisions in twitter. In *WSDM*, pages 557–566, 2013.
[10] Z. Huang, Y. Zheng, R. Cheng, Y. Sun, N. Mamoulis, and X. Li. Meta Structure: Computing relevance in large heterogeneous information networks. In *KDD*, pages 1595–1604, 2016.
[11] Y. Juan, Y. Zhuang, W. Chin, and C. J. Lin. Field-aware factorization machines for CTR prediction. In *RecSys*, pages 43–50, 2016.
[12] X. Kong, B. Cao, and P. S. Yu. Multi-label classification by mining label and instance correlations from heterogeneous information networks. In *KDD*, pages 614–622, 2013.
[13] X. Kong, J. Zhang, and P. S. Yu. Inferring anchor links across multiple heterogeneous social networks. In *CIKM*, pages 179–188, 2013.
[14] Y. Koren. Factorization meets the neighborhood: a multifaceted collaborative filtering model. In *KDD*, pages 426–434, 2008.
[15] Y. Koren, R. Bell, and C. Volinsky. Matrix factorization techniques for recommender systems, 2009.
[16] N. Lao and W. W. Cohen. Relational retrieval using a combination of path-constrained random walks. *Machine Learning*, 81(1):53–67, 2010.
[17] H. Li and Z. Lin. Accelerated proximal gradient methods for nonconvex programming. In *NIPS*, pages 379–387, 2015.
[18] X. Li, B. Kao, Y. Zheng, and Z. Huang. On transductive classification in heterogeneous information networks. In *CIKM*, pages 811–820, 2016.
[19] G. Ling, M. R. Lyu, and I. King. Ratings meet reviews, a combined approach to recommend. In *RecSys*, pages 105–112, 2014.
[20] H. Ma, D. Zhou, C. Liu, M. R. Lyu, and I. King. Recommender systems with social regularization. In *WSDM*, pages 287–296, 2011.
[21] J. McAuley and J. Leskovec. Hidden factors and hidden topics: understanding rating dimensions with review text. In *RecSys*, pages 165–172, 2013.
[22] A. Mnih and R. Salakhutdinov. Probabilistic matrix factorization. In *NIPS*, pages 1257–1264, 2007.
[23] N. Parikh and S. Boyd. Proximal algorithms. *Foundations and Trends in Optimization*, 1(3):127–239, 2014.
[24] R. Řehůřek and P. Sojka. Software Framework for Topic Modelling with Large Corpora, May 2010.
[25] S. Rendle. Factorization machines with libFM. *ACM Transactions on Intelligent Systems and Technology*, 3(3):57:1–57:22, 2012.
[26] S. Rendle and L. S. T. Pairwise interaction tensor factorization for personalized tag recommendation. In *WSDM*, pages 81–90, 2010.
[27] C. Shi, X. Kong, Y. Huang, Y. P. S., and B. Wu. HeteSim: A general framework for relevance measure in heterogeneous networks. *IEEE Transactions on Knowledge and Data Engineering*, 26(10):2479–2492, 2014.
[28] C. Shi, X. Kong, P. S. Yu, S. Xie, and B. Wu. Relevance search in heterogeneous networks. In *ICEDT*, pages 180–191, 2012.
[29] C. Shi, Z. Zhang, P. Luo, P. S. Yu, Y. Yue, and B. Wu. Semantic path based personalized recommendation on weighted heterogeneous information networks. In *CIKM*, pages 453–462, 2015.
[30] Y. Sun and J. Han. Mining heterogeneous information networks: a structural analysis approach. *ACM SIGKDD Explorations Newsletter*, 14(2):20–28, 2013.
[31] Y. Sun, J. Han, C. C. Aggarwal, and N. V. Chawla. When will it happen?: Relationship prediction in heterogeneous information networks. In *WSDM*, pages 663–672, 2012.
[32] Y. Sun, J. Han, X. Yan, P. S. Yu, and T. Wu. PathSim: Meta path-based top-k similarity search in heterogeneous information networks. *VLDB*, 4(11):992–1003, 2011.
[33] Y. Sun, B. Norick, J. Han, X. Yan, P. S. Yu, and X. Yu. PathSelClus: Integrating meta-path selection with user-guided object clustering in heterogeneous information networks. *ACM Transactions on Knowledge Discovery from Data*, 7(3):11, 2013.
[34] F. Vasile, E. Smirnova, and A. Conneau. Meta-Prod2Vec: Product embeddings using side-information for recommendation. In *RecSys*, pages 225–232, 2016.
[35] C. Wang, Y. Song, A. El-Kishky, D. Roth, M. Zhang, and J. Han. Incorporating world knowledge to document clustering via heterogeneous information networks. In *KDD*, pages 1215–1224, 2015.
[36] Q. Yao and J. Kwok. Accelerated inexact soft-impute for fast large-scale matrix completion. In *AAAI*, pages 4002–4008, 2015.
[37] Q. Yao and J. Kwok. Efficient learning with a family of nonconvex regularizers by redistributing nonconvexity. In *ICML*, pages 2645–2654, 2016.
[38] M. Ye, P. Yin, W. C. Lee, and D. L. Lee. Exploiting geographical influence for collaborative point-of-interest recommendation. In *SIGIR*, pages 325–334, 2011.
[39] X. Yu, X. Ren, Q. Gu, Y. Sun, and J. Han. Collaborative filtering with entity similarity regularization in heterogeneous information networks. *IJCAI HINA*, 27, 2013.
[40] X. Yu, X. Ren, Y. Sun, Q. Gu, B. Sturt, U. Khandelwal, B. Norick, and J. Han. Personalized entity recommendation: A heterogeneous information network approach. In *WSDM*, pages 283–292, 2014.
[41] L. Yuan, J. Liu, and J. Ye. Efficient methods for overlapping group lasso. In *NIPS*, pages 352–360, 2011.
[42] M. Yuan and Y. Lin. Model selection and estimation in regression with grouped variables. *Journal of the Royal Statistical Society: Series B*, 68(1):49–67, 2006.
[43] J. Zhang, P. S. Yu, and Z. Zhou. Meta-path based multi-network collective link prediction. In *KDD*, pages 1286–1295, 2014.

Coresets for Kernel Regression

Yan Zheng
University of Utah
Salt Lake City, UT 84108
yanzheng@cs.utah.edu

Jeff M. Phillips
University of Utah
Salt Lake City, UT 84108
jeffp@cs.utah.edu

ABSTRACT

Kernel regression is an essential and ubiquitous tool for non-parametric data analysis, particularly popular among time series and spatial data. However, the central operation which is performed many times, evaluating a kernel on the data set, takes linear time. This is impractical for modern large data sets.

In this paper we describe coresets for kernel regression: compressed data sets which can be used as proxy for the original data and have provably bounded worst case error. The size of the coresets are independent of the raw number of data points; rather they only depend on the error guarantee, and in some cases the size of domain and amount of smoothing. We evaluate our methods on very large time series and spatial data, and demonstrate that they incur negligible error, can be constructed extremely efficiently, and allow for great computational gains.

ACM Reference format:
Yan Zheng and Jeff M. Phillips. 2017. Coresets for Kernel Regression. In *Proceedings of KDD '17, Halifax, NS, Canada, August 13-17, 2017,* 10 pages.
https://doi.org/10.1145/3097983.3098000

1 INTRODUCTION

Kernel regression [14, 25] is a powerful non-parametric technique for understanding scalar-valued 1-dimensional (and higher dimensional) data sets. It has distinct advantages over linear or polynomial regression techniques in that it does not impose a possibly restrictive or over-fitting model on the data. Rather it uses a kernel similarity function to describe a smooth weighted average over the points. This allows the predicted function to locally adapt to the values of the data. These advantages have led to wide use of the kernel regression to predict, model, and visualize data from stocks [27] to weather monitoring [21] to quantified self [23].

However, as these data sets have grown to enormous scale, these kernel regression techniques have hit computational bottlenecks. Just to evaluate the model at a single query point takes $O(|P|)$ time. This runtime is completely infeasible in comparison to parametric models where it takes $O(1)$ time, especially in a common situation where many (perhaps $O(|P|)$ queries) are made. This paper explores near-linear and sub-linear techniques to compress data for kernel regression, to bring these powerful approaches to large data.

Thanks to NSF CCF-1350888, IIS-1251019, ACI-1443046, CNS-1514520, CNS-1564287.

KDD '17, August 13-17, 2017, Halifax, NS, Canada

ACM ISBN 978-1-4503-4887-4/17/08...$15.00
https://doi.org/10.1145/3097983.3098000

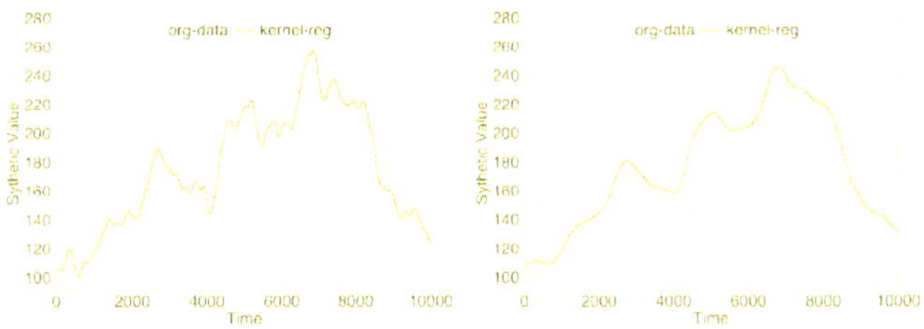

Figure 1: Kernel regression of synthetic data with bandwidth 50 (left) and 200 (right).

1.1 Basic Definitions

Kernel regression is based on a *kernel*, which is a bivariate function $K : \mathbb{R}^d \times \mathbb{R}^d \to [0, 1]$ which in this setting we can restrict to map to a range of $[0, 1]$ without loss of generality. As input points get closer, the kernel value should get larger. In this paper we will focus on Gaussian kernels so $K(p, q) = \exp(-\|p - q\|^2/\sigma^2)$ for a smoothing *bandwidth* parameter σ. These kernels have nice properties since they are smooth, but other kernels such as Laplace, Epanechnikov, or Triangle which have Lipschitz bounds should be perfectly suited for any of our results.

We consider an input data sets $P \subset \mathbb{R}^{d+1}$. We decompose this into the first d explanatory coordinates denoted $P_x \subset \mathbb{R}^d$ and the last dependent one $P_y \subset \mathbb{R}$. Most examples we discuss have $d = 1$ where it is common to think of these data items P_x as times, but many approaches generalize for larger values of d. Then each data item $p \in P$ is also associated with a scalar data value p_y (the set of these comprises P_y).

A *kernel density estimate* (KDE) is a smooth function defined by convolving the data set with the kernel, for a query point $q \in \mathbb{R}^d$ as

$$\textsc{kde}_P(q) = \frac{1}{|P|} \sum_{p \in P} K(p_x, q).$$

We say a *weighted kernel density estimate* (WKDE) replaces this with a weighted sum

$$\textsc{wkde}_P(q) = \frac{1}{|P|} \sum_{p \in P} K(p_x, q) p_y.$$

Finally, the (Nadaraya-Watson) *kernel regression* function is defined for a query point $q \in \mathbb{R}^d$ as

$$\textsc{kr}_P(q) = \frac{\sum_{p \in P} K(p_x, q) p_y}{\sum_{p \in P} K(p_x, q)} = \frac{\textsc{wkde}_P(q)}{\textsc{kde}_P(q)}.$$

This maps each domain point in $\mathbb{R}^d$ to an estimate in the space $\mathbb{R}$ of scalar values; it takes a weighted average (defined by kernel similarity) of the scalar values nearby. Figure 1 visualizes, for $d = 1$, the kernel regression and its original data of a synthetic time series dataset (see Section 4) with bandwidth 50 and 200. The query q can be any time point between 0 and 10,000.

There are various other forms of kernel regression [19]. But in this paper we focus on the Nadaraya-Watson variety [14, 25] as it has an important long history and has been widely used in areas such as image processing [22] and economics [3]. Moreover, since it does not try to pass through every data point, it is the most robust to outliers that are pervasive in large data, which often by necessity cannot be carefully filtered.

1.2 Coresets

The brute force solution of kernel regression is time consuming as each computation calculates KDE and WKDE, which takes $O(|P|)$ time. In this paper, we show how to scalably apply kernel regression to massive scalar-valued data sets. The main idea is to approximate P with a *coreset* S where S_x can for instance be a subset of P_x, but each $s \in S$ can potentially be given a scalar value s_y different from the associated original point. In particular, the coreset S should act as a proxy for P, so that for any q the value $\text{KR}_S(q)$ should approximate $\text{KR}_P(q)$.

The coreset S should be substantially smaller than P, while also preserving the strong approximation guarantees. Any query to KR_S takes time at most proportional to $|S|$ instead of $|P|$, so the size of S directly impacts the efficiency of interacting with KR_S. Moreover, if the construction of S is efficient (and ours is roughly as fast as reading the data, or sorting if needed), then the time to compute m values of the kernel regression (common for say visualization) is also reduced by $|P|/|S|$, after factoring the build time. Here are a list of scenarios where such coresets are essential.

- The data is too big to store. For example, Square Kilometer Array, the world's largest radio telescope, receives several terabytes of data per second. Most of the data is in scalar values, such as baseline-corrected power flux density, sensitivity, and receiver temperature, so kernel regression is a good way to track those scalar values over time. However storing all of this data is a challenging problem, let alone analyzing it. Instead of storing all of it, a coreset for kernel regression would keep relevant data that provably behaves like the original data, but needs much less space.
- The data is large and the older parts requires less accuracy. For instance in analyzing trends in system log data, we want more accurate recent data, but allow more imprecision in historical data. For example, in the CloudLab [20] central power database, power data serves as a way to monitor the cloud performance. It has scalar values and changes gradually overtime but may have noisy fluctuations. Kernel regression is a good way to track this, and older data can be kept with less precision.
- The data is for interactive analysis. To interact with very large data stored on disk one can first analyze a small coreset, and then refine to a larger coresets with more accuracy as more precision is needed; this is much more efficient than bringing all relevant data to disk for each query. Instead we can maintain several layers of different sized coresets. For instance, in spatial data systems, such as Mesowest [11], temperature is connected with each geo-coordinate, to show temperature across the United States, a coarse level coreset is sufficient. But to zoom the map to see the temperature at the state or city level, then a more detailed coreset is required.

1.3 Our Approach

To formalize the meaning of $\text{KR}_S(q)$ is "close" to $\text{KR}_P(q)$, we focus on worst-case error guarantees (L_∞ as opposed to L_2 or L_1 more common to KDEs); this ensures we do not have any spurious regression values. This is essential for data analysis, since we want to be able to find important trends and detect outlier points, and also not be fooled into thinking we observe a non-existent trend or a non-existent outlier.

Beyond that, the error function should not be affected by either a shift or a scaling of a scalar value, since this is equivalent to changing the units (e.g., Celsius to Fahrenheit). As such a natural bound will be absolute error difference with the bound depending on some quantity that depends on the scaling. We will use $M = \max_{p,p' \in P} |p_y - p'_y|$, the maximum difference between scalar values, so as the scale of the units on p_y changes, M does at the same rate. In particular, we are interested in a coreset S of a data set P such that for some domain $\mathcal{U} \subset \mathbb{R}^d$ that

$$\max_{q \in \mathcal{U}} |\text{KR}_P(q) - \text{KR}_S(q)| \leq \varepsilon M.$$

Our coresets S have size depending linearly on $1/\varepsilon$ and sometimes $\Delta = \max_{p,p' \in P} \|p_x - p'_x\|/\sigma$.

It is worth noting that in setting $\mathcal{U} = \mathbb{R}^d$, such a result may not be possible. The kernel regression definition $\text{KR}_P(q)$ has in its denominator $\text{KDE}_P(q)$, so when $\text{KDE}_P(q)$ is very close to 0, then $\text{KR}_P(q)$ is very unstable. So we consider a domain $\mathcal{U}$ which is defined by a mild condition on $\text{KDE}_P(q)$; in particular that $\text{KDE}_P(q)$ is above some very small value ρ.

To further put this error bound in perspective, consider instead the relative error $\max_{q \in \mathcal{U}} \frac{\text{KR}_S(q)}{\text{KR}_P(q)}$. This is unstable whenever $\text{KR}_P(q)$ is close to 0. And, furthermore, the q where $\text{KR}_P(q)$ is small, depends entirely on the units chosen for the p_y values. For instance, we could have $p_y = 32°$ Fahrenheit (not be close to 0) or $p_y = 0°$ Celsius which is exactly 0 and makes *any* relative error requirement imply no error at all. Since the change of units is meaningless, this error measure is not feasible.

1.4 Our Results

Our results focus mainly on $P_x \subset \mathbb{R}^1$ and $P_x \subset \mathbb{R}^2$ (so the x-coordinate(s) naturally represent time or spatial coordinates), although many aspects extend naturally to high dimensions.

We first bound the accuracy of a kernel regression coreset formed by random sampling; these are the first known bounds for the *sample complexity* of kernel regression. It is of particular interest since in many cases the data set provided on input is itself a random sample from some much larger data set or distribution we do not have access to (e.g., a 1% stream from Twitter). So if the input data is indeed sampled, our bounds measure the error present before any analysis is applied. However, random sampling performs poor compared to most other methods we consider, so it makes sense to further compress them.

We analyze (theoretically and empirically) several straight-forward aggregation techniques to construct coresets. These are of particular interest since they mimic common online aggregation techniques [5]. We also propose some modifications which demonstrate sizable empirically improvements. Interestingly, effective coresets for KDEs [29], do not perform the best for kernel regression.

Algorithm 1 Z-order (Z)

```
1: Sort data P_x in Z-order; set h = |P|/|S|
2: Choose a random number in r = [0, h − 1]
3: for i ← 1 to |S| do
4:     Put P_{r+h·(i−1)} into S
5: return S
```

Algorithm 2 Z-Aggregate (ZA)

```
1: Sort data P_x in Z-order; set h = |P|/|S|
2: for i ← 1 to |S| do
3:     P_i = [P_{h·(i−1)}, ···, P_{h·i}]
4:     Put average of all the points in P_i into S
5: return S
```

Algorithm 3 G-Aggregate (GA)

```
1: Map P_x into grid G_γ
2: for g ∈ G_γ(P) do
3:     Put average of all the points in P_g into S
4: return S
```

Algorithm 4 Aggregate-Neighbor (AN)

```
1: Map P_x into grid G_γ
2: for g ∈ G_γ(P) do
3:     Put average of all the points in P_g into S
4: for g ∈ G_γ(P̄) adjacent to G_γ(P) do
5:     For center c of g, put (c, KR_P(c)) in S
6: return S
```

In particular, our recommended method **G-Aggregate** for $P_x \subset \mathbb{R}^1$, carefully aggregates data over a fixed size non-empty grid cells; it takes $O(|P|)$ after sorting the data. For $P_x \subset \mathbb{R}^2$, we recommend **Aggregate-Neighbor**, which carefully adds a few points to the coreset from **G-Aggregate**. For a data sets $P_x \subset \mathbb{R}^d$, these both produce a coreset S of size $O(\Delta/\varepsilon\rho)^d$, where $\Delta = \max_{p,p' \in P} \|p_x - p'_x\|/\sigma$, and guarantees for any $q \in \mathbb{R}^d$ with $\text{KDE}_{P_x}(q) > \rho$ that $|\text{KR}_P(q) - \text{KR}_S(q)| \leq \varepsilon M$, where $M = \max_{p,p' \in P} |p_y - p'_y|$. Moreover, these methods are simple to implement and work extremely well on real and synthetic data sets.

1.5 Related Work

This is the first work to address sample complexity and coreset size for Nadaraya-Watson kernel regression. There is an enormous body of work on other types of coresets, see the recent survey on coresets [17], including many for parametric regression variants like least-square regression [4] and l_p regression [7].

The only non-parametric regression coreset we are aware of is a form of kernel regression [26] related to the smallest enclosing ball. It predicts the value at a point $q \in \mathbb{R}^d$ as $f(q) = \beta + \sum_{p \in P} \alpha_p K(p_x, q)$ with loss function $\sum_{p \in P} \max\{0, |f(p_x) - p_y| - \bar{\varepsilon}\}$, for a parameter $\bar{\varepsilon}$. Then it finds a set of $O(1/\varepsilon)$ non-zero α_p parameters (corresponding with points in the coreset) so many points satisfy $|f(p_x) - p_y| \leq \bar{\varepsilon}(1+\varepsilon)$. No implementations were attempted.

Rather, we believe the most related work involves coresets for kernel density estimates [2, 12, 16, 29] as mentioned above. We extend some of these results and show others do not work well when translated to the regression variant of this problem.

2 SUBSET SELECTION METHODS

We next describe several natural approaches to compress scalar-valued spatial data. Some of these are likely in use in existing data aggregation frameworks (e.g., RFF [5]), but as far as we know have not been analyzed in how they preserve kernel regression values.

Random sampling (RS): This method simply draws a uniform random sample S from the data set P. This is probably the most common data aggregation method anywhere. In other cases, it is often assumed that even before aggregating data, the data is only a random sample of some unseen larger "true" dataset. This is known to approximate kernel density estimates [2, 9, 12], and we will show extends to kernel regression.

k-Center (kCen): This method creates a k-center clustering of P_x using the greedy Gonzalez algorithms [8]; that finds a set of k center points which (with a factor 2) minimizes the distance to the furthest data point. This is inspired by both a recent way to approximate the kernel mean (equivalent to the KDE) [1] and also the initial step in (improved) fast Gauss transforms [28]. It takes $O(kn)$ time to find the center set, and then data points can be aggregated to the closest center in as much time.

Sorting-based approaches: For $P_x \subset \mathbb{R}^1$, these methods just sort the points, and choose S as evenly spaced points in the sorted order. Inspired by a coreset for KDEs, we can extend to higher dimensions using the Z-order space-filling curve to implicitly define a single ordering over the data points which attempts to preserve spatial locality. Hence we refer to it as **Z-order (Z)**. Also, inspired by this approach we take a random point from each block in the sorted order instead of the first or last of each block deterministically.

As an extension, we propose **Z-Aggregate (ZA)** which is more careful on how it represents each interval. It again sorts the x-coordinate(s) of P by Z-order, and then for a set of consecutive points P_i of size h, $[h(i-1), hi)$ for $i = 1, 2, \ldots, k$, choose $s_x = \frac{1}{|P_i|} \sum_{p \in P_i} p_x$ and $s_y = \frac{1}{|P_i|} \sum_{p \in P_i} p_y$ as the ith point in S.

Grid-based approaches: Define a grid G_γ into square grid cells (intervals for $P_x \subset \mathbb{R}$) of side length γ. It will be convenient to designate $G_\gamma(P)$ as the non-empty grid cells, and $G_\gamma(\bar{P})$ as the empty grid cells. For a grid g, define $P_g \subset P = \{p \in P \mid p_x \in g\}$, the points in g. In the basic method **Grid (G)**, for each $g \in G_\gamma(P)$, randomly place one point from P_g into S, and give it a weight $|P_g|$.

In an extension **G-Aggregate (GA)**, for each $g \in G_\gamma(P)$ we create a new point to place in S as (s_x, s_y) defined $s_x = \frac{1}{|P_g|} \sum_{p \in P_g} p_x$ and $s_y = \frac{1}{|P_g|} \sum_{p \in P_g} p_y$.

The above algorithms can be subtly further improved by adding extra points in the empty grids with non-empty grids as neighbors, we call this **Aggregate-Neighbor (AN)**. Specifically these empty, but adjacent cells generate a point at the cell center c with value equal to the kernel regression value $\text{KR}_P(c)$. This takes a bit longer than just performing an aggregate, but these empty, but adjacent cells are few so the time burden is negligible. This is inspired by the work [6] and the illustrative toy example in Figure 2. We will see the improvement is especially significant for $P_x \subset \mathbb{R}^2$.

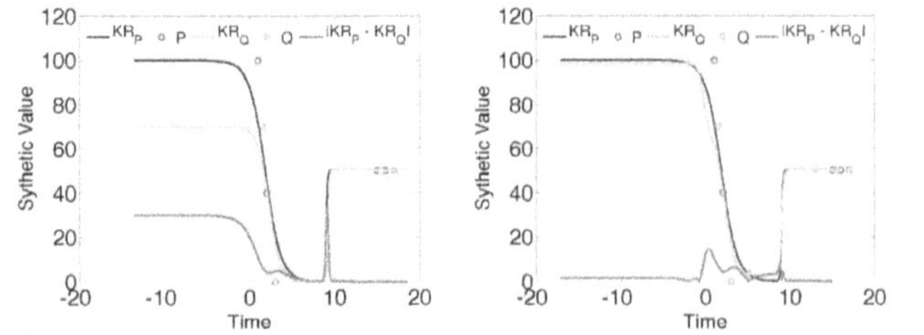

Figure 2: Example improvement of Aggregate-Neighbor (right) over G-Aggregate (left). Input $P = \{(1\ 100), (2\ 40), (3\ 0), (15\ 50), (16\ 50), (17\ 50)\}$. With G-Aggregate with $\gamma = 2$, the coreset $Q = \{(1.5\ 70), (3\ 0), (15.5\ 50), (17\ 50)\}$. The largest errors occur at $x < 0$ and around $x = 9$. If we add the extra points at the empty grid cells with non-empty neighbor grids, i.e., Aggregate-Neighbor, then L_∞ is significantly reduced. We add three points $(-2.06\ 98.3124)$, $(5\ 3.2559)$ and $(13\ 50)$.

2.1 Progressive Grid-based approaches

In many scenarios, $P_x \subset \mathbb{R}$ and this coordinate represents time. Let the current time $t_{\text{NOW}} : x = 0$, and so all other values are negative (say 5 hours ago is $x = -5$). In these settings, we might only examine windows of the data over $x \in [-T, 0]$, that is including now, and up to T time units into the past. Further we can assume over any view we would set the bandwidth σ so that $\Delta = \max_{p,p' \in P} \|p_x - p'_x\|/\sigma = T/\sigma$ is upper bounded; otherwise the smoothing is below the resolution of the what can fit in a view window (its too noisy).

For these scenarios, we design a progressive approach where we allow more errors for older data points. Extending the grid-based approaches, as data becomes older (new points arrive) we increase the grid resolution γ, and further compress the data. Specifically, we divide P into regions $R_1, \ldots, R_r$ so the resolution γ_i used in region R_i is $\gamma_i = a^{i-1}\gamma_1$, where a is a constant (we use $a = 1.5$ in our experiments). Setting the width of region $\text{width}(R_i) = a^{i-1}\text{width}(R_1)$ ensures that there are the same number of grid cells in each region. Then for a fixed resolution in the first region, the size of the coreset will grow only logarithmically with time.

3 ANALYSIS

We start by providing some structural lemmas that relate approximations of kernel density estimates and weighted kernel density estimates to kernel regression. Then we will use these results to bound the accuracy of specific techniques.

Our goal in each case is to show that the coreset S approximates the full data set P in the following sense for parameters $\rho, \varepsilon \in (0, 1)$. For any $q \in \mathbb{R}^d$ such that $\text{KDE}_P(q) > \rho$, then

$$|\text{KR}_P(q) - \text{KR}_S(q)| \le \varepsilon M,$$

where $M = \max_{p,p' \in P} |p_y - p'_y|$. Then call S an *(ρ, ε)-coreset* of P.

We believe such strong worst case bounds should be surprising. If we revisit Figure 2 we can observe that removing one point can cause error in $\text{KR}_P(q) - \text{KR}_S(q)$ on the order of M (in this case $M/4$).

Structural results: We need a few definitions and previous results before we can begin stating our new structural tools. A data set X and a family of subsets $\mathcal{R}$ define a *range space* $(X, \mathcal{R})$, and the range space's VC-dimension ν [24] (informally) describes the combinatorial complexity of the ranges; typically $\nu = \Theta(d)$. A kernel $K : \mathbb{R}^d \times \mathbb{R}^d \to \mathbb{R}^+$ is *linked* to a range space if for every threshold τ and subset $Y_x \subset X$ defined $Y_x = \{y \in X \mid K(x, y) \ge \tau,\ x \in \mathbb{R}^d\}$ there exists a range $R \in \mathcal{R}$ such that $R \cap X = Y_x$. Importantly, all centrally symmetric kernels (including Gaussians) are linked to a range space where $\mathcal{R} = \mathcal{B}$, meaning all subsets are defined by inclusion in balls.

A *relative (ρ, ε)-approximation* of $(X, \mathcal{R})$ is a set Y

$$\max_{R \in \mathcal{R}} \left| \frac{|R \cap X|}{|X|} - \frac{|R \cap Y|}{|Y|} \right| \le \varepsilon \max\left\{ \frac{|R \cap X|}{|X|}, \rho \right\}.$$

Similarly, define a *relative (ρ, ε)-approximation* of (P, K) for kernel K as a set S such that

$$\max_{x \in \mathbb{R}^d} |\text{KDE}_P(x) - \text{KDE}_S(x)| \le \varepsilon \max\{\text{KDE}_P(x), \rho\}.$$

Define a *(ρ, ε)-approximation for kernel regression of P* as a set S such that $\text{KDE}_P(q) \ge \rho$, then

$$|\text{KR}_S(q) - \text{KR}_P(q)| \le \varepsilon M,$$

where $M = \max_{p,p' \in P} |p_y - p'_y|$. Define a (non-relative) ε-approximation Y of a range space $(X, \mathcal{R})$, so

$$\max_{R \in \mathcal{R}} \left| \frac{|R \cap X|}{|X|} - \frac{|R \cap Y|}{|Y|} \right| \le \varepsilon.$$

It is know an ε-approximation can be constructed, with probability at least $1-\delta$ via a random sample S of size $O((1/\varepsilon^2)(\nu + \log 1/\delta))$, and a relative (ρ, ε)-approximation with size $O((1/\rho\varepsilon^2)(\nu \log(1/\rho) + \log(1/\delta)))$ [10, 13]. Given an ε-approximation S of a range space linked to K, then it is known [12] that it is also a (non-relative) ε-approximation of (P, K). In this paper (in the Appendix A) we generalize this linking result (roughly following the structure of the proof in [12]) to relative (ρ, ε)-approximations.

Theorem 3.1. *For any kernel $K : \mathbb{R}^d \times \mathbb{R}^d \to \mathbb{R}^+$ linked to a range space $(\mathbb{R}^d, \mathcal{A})$, a relative (ρ, ε)-approximation S of $(P, \mathcal{A})$ is a $(\rho K^+, 2\varepsilon)$-approximation of (P, K), where $K^+ = \max_{p,q \in P} K(p, q)$.*

Next we provide a sufficient condition for (ρ, ε)-approximation for kernel regression.

Lemma 3.2. *For error parameters $\alpha, \beta, \rho > 0$, with $\alpha \le 1/2$, consider a point set $P \subset \mathbb{R}^{d+1}$. Let S be a coreset of P so that for any query point $q \in \mathbb{R}^d$, both*

$$|\text{KDE}_P(q) - \text{KDE}_S(q)| < \alpha \max\{\text{KDE}_P(q), \rho\}$$
$$|\text{WKDE}_P(q) - \text{WKDE}_S(q)| < \beta M.$$

Then for any $q \in \mathbb{R}^d$ such that $\text{KDE}_P(q) \ge \rho$, then $|\text{KR}_S(q) - \text{KR}_P(q)| \le 4(\alpha + \beta/\rho)M$.

Proof. Change the units of p_y so all values lie between 1 and 2. The shifting of these values does not change the approximation factor βM, but the rescaling of the range changes the bound to $|\text{WKDE}_P(q) - \text{WKDE}_S(q)| \le \beta$, and also ensures $1 \le \text{KR}_P(q) \le 2$. And recall, p_y values have no bearing on $\text{KDE}_P(q)$.

By using the Gaussian kernel we have $\text{KDE}_S(q) > 0$ and also $0 \le \text{WKDE}_P(q) \le 2$. Thus we can consider relative error bounds, using $\text{KDE}_P(q) > \rho$, and hence also $\text{WKDE}_P(q) > \rho$.

$$\begin{aligned}\frac{\text{KR}_S(q)}{\text{KR}_P(q)} &= \frac{\text{WKDE}_S(q)}{\text{WKDE}_P(q)}\frac{\text{KDE}_P(q)}{\text{KDE}_S(q)}\\ &\geq \left(1-\frac{\beta}{\text{WKDE}_P(q)}\right)\left(1-\frac{\alpha}{1+\alpha}\right)\\ &= 1-\frac{\beta}{\text{WKDE}_P(q)}-\frac{\alpha}{1+\alpha}+\frac{\alpha\beta}{(1+\alpha)\text{WKDE}_P(q)}\\ &\geq 1-\frac{\beta}{\rho}-\alpha\end{aligned}$$

Next we see the relative error bound is slightly different in the other direction.

$$\begin{aligned}\frac{\text{KR}_S(q)}{\text{KR}_P(q)} &= \frac{\text{WKDE}_S(q)}{\text{WKDE}_P(q)}\frac{\text{KDE}_P(q)}{\text{KDE}_S(q)}\\ &\leq \left(1+\frac{\beta}{\text{WKDE}_P(q)}\right)\left(1+\frac{\alpha}{1-\alpha}\right)\\ &= 1+\frac{\beta}{\text{WKDE}_P(q)}+\frac{\alpha}{1-\alpha}+\frac{\alpha\beta}{(1-\alpha)\text{WKDE}_P(q)}\\ &\leq 1+\frac{\beta}{\rho}+\frac{\alpha}{1-\alpha}+\frac{\alpha\beta}{(1-\alpha)\rho}\\ &= 1+\frac{\beta}{(1-\alpha)\rho}+\frac{\alpha}{1-\alpha}\\ &\leq 1+\frac{2\beta}{\rho}+2\alpha\end{aligned}$$

Together these imply $\frac{\text{KR}_S(q)}{\text{KR}_P(q)} \in [1-\beta/\rho-\alpha, 1+2\beta/\rho+2\alpha]$. This translates to the following additive error

$$\begin{aligned}|\text{KR}_P(q)-\text{KR}_S(q)| &\leq 2(\beta/\rho+\alpha)\text{KR}_P(q)\\ &\leq 2(\beta/\rho+\alpha)2M = 4(\alpha+\beta/\rho)M. \qquad \square\end{aligned}$$

We also need another property about the slope of the Gaussian kernel. This is the only bound specific to the Gaussian kernel, so for any other kernels with a similar bound (e.g., Triangle, Epanechnikov) the remaining analysis and algorithms can apply.

Lemma 3.3. *A unit Gaussian kernel $K(x) = \exp(-x^2/2\sigma^2)$ is $1/\sigma$-Lipschitz.*

Proof. By taking the first derivative of K with respect to x, we have $\frac{dK(x)}{dx} = \exp(-\frac{x^2}{2\sigma^2})(-\frac{x}{\sigma^2})$. Take the second derivative $\frac{d^2K(x)}{dx^2} = \exp(-\frac{x^2}{2\sigma^2})(\frac{x^2}{\sigma^4}-\frac{1}{\sigma^2})$ and set $\frac{d^2K(x)}{dx^2} = 0$. We get $x = \pm\sigma$, and thus $|\frac{dK(x)}{dx}|$ has the maximum values on $x = \pm\sigma$, equals to $\exp(-\frac{1}{2})(\frac{1}{\sigma}) \leq 1/\sigma$. So a unit Gaussian kernel is $1/\sigma$-Lipschitz. $\square$

3.1 Accuracy of Random Sampling

We start by analyzing how kernel regression is preserved under random sampling. In many cases the "input" data to a problem should actually be modeled as a random sample of some much larger set, or it may be done as a first pass on data to reduce its complexity.

The key structural result will be on sampling weighted sets.

Lemma 3.4. *For a weighted point set (P, w) with $P \subset \mathbb{R}^d$ of size n, then a random sample of points $Q \subset P$ of size $s = O((1/\varepsilon^2)(d + \log(1/\delta)))$, with probability at least $1-\delta$, satisfies for any $B \in \mathcal{B}$*

$$\left|\frac{1}{n}\sum_{p\in P\cap B} w(p) - \frac{1}{s}\sum_{p\in Q\cap B} w(p)\right| \leq \varepsilon M,$$

where $M = \max_{p\in X} w(p) - \min_{p\in X} w(p)$.

Proof. First assume $\max_{p\in X} w(p) = 1$ and that $\min_{p\in X} w(p) = 0$; then $M = 1$. Otherwise, we can simply "change the units" by uniformly shifting and scaling all w values to reach this scenario.

We first consider (X, w) as a point set $P \subset \mathbb{R}^{d+1}$, where the y-coordinate is $w(p)$. Then we consider the range space $(P, \mathcal{R})$ where $\mathcal{R}$ defines the set of subsets induced by ranges which are balls in the first d coordinates, and an interval in the y-coordinate; we refer to them as hypercylinders. The range space has VC-dimension $O(d)$. For a given query $B \in \mathcal{B}$ on X (B is the ball in $\mathbb{R}^d$ on the x-coordinates), we are interested hypercylinders $R \in \mathcal{R}$ so that the x-coordinates are restricted to those in our query choice of B.

In fact, we can break the hypercylinder R, which implicitly has a y-interval of $[0, 1]$, up into $\eta = c/\varepsilon$ disjoint hypercylinders (design constant c so that c/ε is an integer), each with the same ball B in x-coordinates and a y width of ε/c. Let P_i be the set P restricted to ith such y interval. We can round all values within the interval to a value $v_i = i \cdot (c/\varepsilon)$, incurring at most ε/c error. Then if each ith piece's sample Q_i is off in count by α_i and $|\sum_i \alpha_i| \leq \varepsilon n/2$, then we can say the total error is at most $|P|\varepsilon/c + n\varepsilon/2$. Setting $c \geq 2$, ensures the total as is at most εn as desired.

However, *individually* bounding each α_i to be small is hard. If there are few points in one of the levels, then we get a poor estimate on the count in Q_i using standard techniques. Instead we can bound $\sum_i \alpha_i$ *in aggregate*. By the definition of ε-samples, if Q is an $\varepsilon/2$-sample of $(P, \mathcal{R})$, then $|\sum_{r=i}^{j} \alpha_i| \leq \varepsilon/2 \cdot n$ for all $i, j \in [1, \eta]$. And this holds by our random sample with probability at least $1-\delta$.

Now we can write the total error from (P, w) to (Q, w) in an ball $B \in \mathcal{B}$ as

$$\begin{aligned}\frac{1}{n}\sum_{p\in P\cap I} w(p) &= \frac{1}{n}\sum_{i=1}^{\eta}\sum_{p\in P_i\cap B} w(p)\\ &\leq \frac{1}{n}\sum_{i=1}^{\eta}\sum_{p\in P_i\cap B}(v_i+\varepsilon/c)\\ &= \frac{\varepsilon}{c}+\frac{1}{n}\sum_{i=1}^{\eta} v_i|P_i\cap B|\\ &\leq \frac{\varepsilon}{c}+\frac{1}{n}\sum_{i=1}^{\eta} v_i\left(\alpha_i+\frac{n}{s}|Q_i\cap B|\right)\\ &= \frac{\varepsilon}{c}+\frac{1}{n}\sum_{i=1}^{\eta} v_i\alpha_i+\frac{1}{s}\sum_{1=1}^{\eta}\sum_{p\in Q_i\cap B} v_i\\ &\leq \frac{\varepsilon}{c}+\frac{1}{n}\sum_{i=1}^{\eta}\alpha_i+\frac{1}{s}\sum_{i=1}^{\eta}\sum_{p\in Q_i\cap B}(w(p)+\varepsilon/c)\\ &\leq \frac{2\varepsilon}{c}+\frac{\varepsilon}{2}+\frac{1}{s}\sum_{p\in Q\cap B} w(p).\end{aligned}$$

Setting $c \geq 4$, and repeating the argument symmetrically to show the lower bound, we obtain that for any $B \in \mathcal{B}$

$$\left| \frac{1}{n} \sum_{p \in P \cap B} w(p) - \frac{1}{s} \sum_{p \in Q \cap B} w(p) \right| \leq \varepsilon. \qquad \square$$

This results generalizes to weighted kernel density estimates, for centrally-symmetric and non-increasing (as function of distance from center) kernels, following [12]. The only change is using the weighted bound in Lemma 3.4, in place of where Joshi *et.al.* used the unweighted bound in the definition of a ball-range space linked with the aforementioned kernels.

Theorem 3.5. *Consider any kernel* $K : \mathbb{R}^d \times \mathbb{R}^d \to \mathbb{R}^+$ *linked to* $(\mathbb{R}^d, \mathcal{B})$. *For a weighted point set* (X, w) *with* $X \subset \mathbb{R}^d$, *then a random sample* $Q \subset X$ *of size* $s = O((1/\varepsilon^2)(d + \log(1/\delta)))$, *with probability at least* $1 - \delta$, *for any* $x \in \mathbb{R}^d$ *satisfies*

$$\left| \text{WKDE}_{X,w}(x) - \text{WKDE}_{Q,w}(x) \right| \leq \varepsilon M,$$

where $M = \max_{p \in X} w(p) - \min_{p \in X} w(p)$.

Now we are ready to show the main result.

Theorem 3.6. *Consider a point set* $P \subset \mathbb{R}^{d+1}$ *of arbitrary size, and parameters* $\rho, \varepsilon \in (0, 1)$. *Let* S *be a uniform sample from* P *of size* $O(\frac{1}{\varepsilon^2 \rho^2}(d \log(1/\rho) + \log(2/\delta)))$, *with probability at least* $1 - \delta$, *the set* S *is a* (ρ, ε)*-approximation for kernel regression on* P.

Proof. For a binary range space (such as $(P, \mathcal{B})$) with constant VC-dimension [24] ν, a random sample S of size $k = O(\frac{1}{(\varepsilon')^2 \rho}(\nu \log(1/\rho) + \log(2/\delta)))$ provides an (ρ, ε')-sample with probability at least $1-\delta/2$ [10, 13]. Theorem 3.1 gives a linking result for kernel density estimate, implying that this is also a relative $(\rho, 2\varepsilon')$-coreset for a kernel where $K(x, x) = 1$. This satisfies the first condition of Lemma 3.2 with $\alpha = 2\varepsilon'$.

Second we invoke Theorem 3.5 so that we have with probability at least $1 - \delta/2$ that $|\text{WKDE}_P(q) - \text{WKDE}_S(q)| \leq (\varepsilon' \rho)M$, hence satisfying the second condition of Lemma 3.2 with $\beta = \varepsilon' \rho$.

Setting $\varepsilon' = \varepsilon/16$ invoking Lemma 3.2, then with probability at least $1-(\delta/2+\delta/2) = 1-\delta$, for any $q \in \mathbb{R}^d$ that $|\text{KR}_S(q) - \text{KR}_P(q)| \leq 4(\varepsilon/8 + (\varepsilon\rho/16)/\rho)M \leq \varepsilon M$. $\square$

3.2 Accuracy of Grid-Based Approaches

We first bound the error in **Grid**. This implies other related algorithms (**G-Aggregate**, **Aggregate-Neighbor**) will have have the same asymptotic error bounds for d constant.

Theorem 3.7. ***Grid*** *with* $\gamma = \frac{\varepsilon \sigma \rho}{8\sqrt{d}}$ *produces* S, *a* (ρ, ε)*-coreset for the kernel regression of* $P \subset \mathbb{R}^{d+1}$.

Proof. We will prove bounds on both error in KDE_P and WKDE_P separately, then combine them with Lemma 3.2. This algorithm maps all points P_g for a grid cell $g \in G_\gamma$ to a single point, and by reweighting, changes each points location by at most $\gamma\sqrt{d}$. Using that K is $(1/\sigma)$-Lipschitz, this changes KDE_P by at most $\gamma\sqrt{d}/\sigma$ in KDE_S. Only considering $\text{KDE}_P(q) \geq \rho$, then $|\text{KDE}_P(q) - \text{KDE}_S(q)| \leq \frac{\gamma\sqrt{d}}{\rho\sigma} \max\{\rho, \text{KDE}_P(q)\}$.

For WKDE_P the analysis is similar, but we may also replace p_y for a point $p \in P_g$ with a different s_y. We can bound $|p_y - s_y| \leq M = \max_{p,p' \in P} |p_y - p'_y|$. Hence for all $q \in \mathbb{R}^d$, then $|\text{WKDE}_P(q) - \text{WKDE}_S(q)| \leq \gamma\sqrt{d}M/\sigma$.

Combining these two bounds together with Lemma 3.2 we obtain (for q with $\text{KDE}_P(q) \geq \rho$) that $|\text{KR}_P(q) - \text{KR}_S(q)| \leq 4(\frac{\gamma\sqrt{d}}{\rho\sigma} + \frac{\gamma\sqrt{d}}{\sigma}/\rho)M = 4(\frac{\varepsilon}{8} + \frac{\varepsilon\rho}{8}/\rho)M = \varepsilon M$. $\square$

By aggregating on each relevant grid cell, we bound coreset size with $\Delta = \max_{p,p' \in P} \|p_x - p'_x\|/\sigma$.

Corollary 3.8. *For* $P \subset \mathbb{R}^{d+1}$ *for constant* d, *methods* ***Grid***, ***G-Aggregate***, *and* ***Aggregate-Neighbor***, *run in* $O(|P|)$ *time, and return* S *a* (ρ, ε)*-coreset for kernel regression of* P *of size at most* $O((\Delta/\varepsilon\rho)^d)$.

Accuracy of progressive grid-based methods: If the size width(R_1) of the first region in the progressive methods is a constant, there are at most $O(\log \Delta)$ regions. Set $\gamma = \varepsilon\sigma\rho/8 \cdot a^{i-1}$, so each region has a grid with $O(1/\varepsilon\rho)$ cells.

Corollary 3.9. *For* $P \subset \mathbb{R}^2$, *under any allowable view window of size* T *and scaling so* T/σ *is fixed, then the progressive Grid approach achieves an* (ρ, ε)*-coreset for kernel regression of* P *of size at most* $O((1/\varepsilon\rho) \log \Delta)$.

Accuracy bounds for other methods: Despite bounds for $|\text{KDE}_P(q) - \text{KDE}_S(q)|$ for other methods (e.g., **Z-order**) we are not able to show these for WKDE_P and hence KR_P. For example, there exists simple examples with wildly varying density where the Z-order techniques approximates the density well, but not the function values. Hence, we either cannot bound the accuracy or the size for this method.

4 EXPERIMENTS

Here we run an extensive set of experiments to validate our methods. We compare KR_P where $P_x \subset \mathbb{R}^1$, $P_x \subset \mathbb{R}^2$, and $P_x \subset \mathbb{R}^6$ with kernel regression under smaller coreset KR_S for both synthetic and real data. To show our methods work well in large data sets, we use large real data set (n = 2 million and 24 million) and synthetic data (n = 1 million) for $P_x \subset \mathbb{R}^1$, and real data set (n = 1 million) for $P_x \subset \mathbb{R}^2$. Our algorithms scale well beyond these sizes, but evaluating error was prohibitive.

4.1 Data Sets

For real data we consider "Individual Household Electric Power Consumption" data set on UCI Machine Learning Repository. The number of instances is 2,075,259, we use the first three attributes to do kernel regression. Date, time (together for x-value), and global active power (for y-value): household global minute-averaged active power (in kilowatt). This data set has gaps on the x-axis, and kernel regression does a nice job of interpolating those gaps.

To demonstrate the effectiveness of progressive grids, we use a "CloudLab" dataset. CloudLab [20] is cloud computing platform, and we have obtained a trace of power usage from the Utah site with 400 million values. We use the most recent 10-month window which has size 24,351,363.

The time series synthetic data $P_x \subset \mathbb{R}^1$ is generated using formula: $y_i = c + \phi y_{i-1} + N(0, \sigma)$, where the x-coordinates are $i = 0, 1, \cdots$ and y_i is the corresponding y coordinates. It mimics a stock price so the next data depends on the previous one plus some

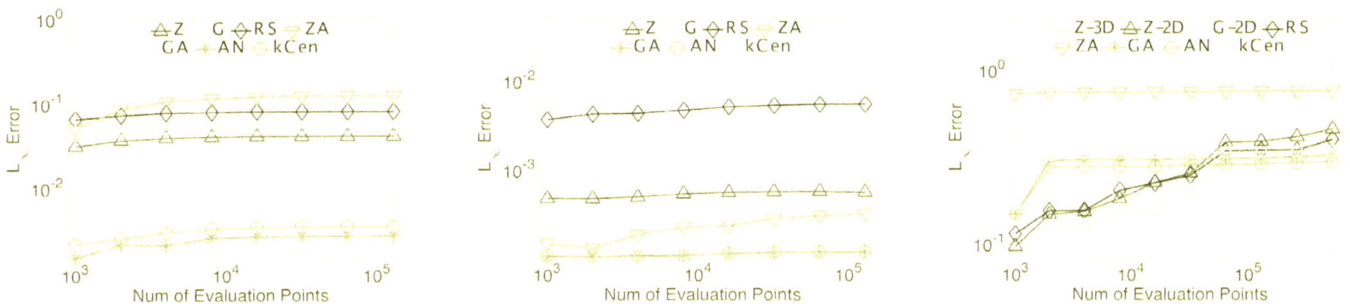

Figure 3: The maximum L_∞ error found based on the number of evaluation points on real (left) and synthetic data(middle) when $P_x \subset \mathbb{R}^1$, and real data(right) when $P_x \subset \mathbb{R}^2$.

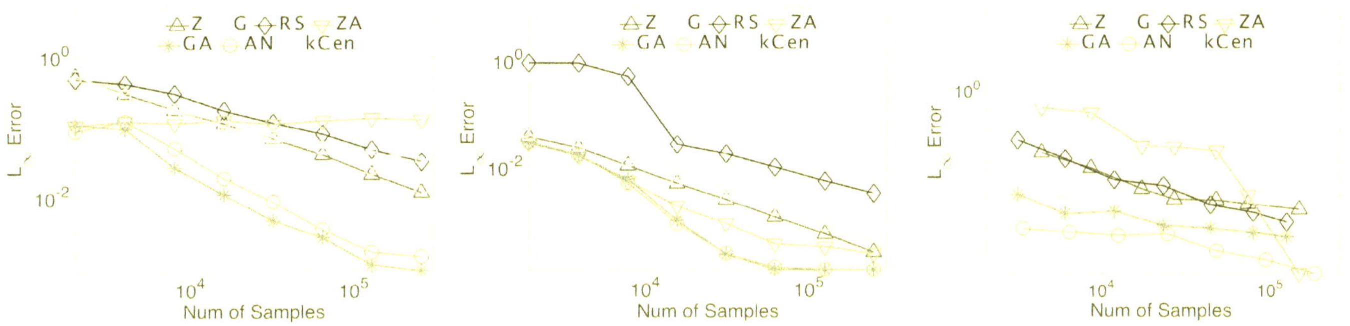

Figure 4: L_∞ error for coresets when also testing sparse regions on real data(left) and synthetic data(middle) when $P_x \subset \mathbb{R}$, and real data(right) when $P_x \subset \mathbb{R}^2$.

random noise. In the experiment, we set $c = 0, \phi = 1, y_0 = 10, \sigma = 1$ and generate 1 million points. The first 10,000 points and kernel regression with bandwidth 50 and 200 are shown in Figure 1.

For $P_x \subset \mathbb{R}^2$ real dataset, we consider OpenStreetMap data from the state of Iowa. Specifically, we use the longitude and latitude of all highway data points as P_x and time stamp as P_y. Kernel regression on this dataset can give a good approximation of when the highway data point is added.

For high dimension experiment, we consider two datasets. One is house price dataset (CAD) in StatLib [15] and the other is Physicochemical Properties of Protein Tertiary Structure Dataset (CASP) from UCI machine learning repository. CAD dataset contains 20,640 observations on housing prices with 9 economic covariates and CASP dataset has 45,730 data points for 10 random variables. For both datasets, we use first 6 features to do the kernel regression.

4.2 Effectiveness of Coresets

Coresets guarantee that kernel regression error is bounded for *all* values of $q \in \mathbb{R}$ (as long as the data is not too sparse). But evaluating at all of these points, is by definition, impossible. As a result, we evaluate over a very fine covering of evaluation points (in our case 128,000 for $P_x \subset \mathbb{R}^1$ and 512,000 for $P_x \subset \mathbb{R}^2$). We have plotted error as the number of evaluation points increase and observed that all methods clearly converge well before this many samples.

In more detail, we randomly generate a evaluation point q in the domain $\mathbb{R}$ for $P_x \subset \mathbb{R}$ and q in the domain $\mathbb{R}^2$ for $P_x \subset \mathbb{R}^2$, without the restriction $\text{KDE}_P(q) > \rho$. With fixed coreset size 64,000, we experiment on the number of evaluation points from 1,000 to 128,000 for $P_x \subset \mathbb{R}$ and 1,000 to 512,000 for $P_x \subset \mathbb{R}^2$ in Figure 3. As the number of evaluation points increases, the value of maximum error in the domain will consistently approach some error value and we can then have some confidence that we have the correct worst case error as this processes plateaus. Under all the subset selection methods (Figure 3), the errors are steady at size 128,000 for $P_x \subset \mathbb{R}$ and 512,000 for $P_x \subset \mathbb{R}^2$, so we use evaluation points of size 128,000 for $P_x \subset \mathbb{R}$ and 512,000 for $P_x \subset \mathbb{R}^2$ in the following experiments.

Since all the methods are randomized algorithms, we run all the subset selection methods ten times and use the average errors as the final results. The bandwidth is set to 400 for the real dataset in $\mathbb{R}^1$, 50 for the synthetic dataset in $\mathbb{R}^1$, and 50 for real data in $\mathbb{R}^2$; other bandwidths have similar performance.

Figure 4 shows all the methods converge as the size of the coreset increases. The exception is **Z-Aggregate** on real data in $\mathbb{R}$; on inspection, the problem occurs in sparse regions, similar to Figure 2. **G-Aggregate** and **Aggregate-Neighbor** (and sometimes **Z-Aggregate**) work significantly better compared to all the other methods in all datasets with $P_x \subset \mathbb{R}$. They consistently decrease, at certain sizes have one or two orders of magnitude less error, and obtain virtually no error at size about 50,000. Even when the size of the coreset is small, **G-Aggregate** and **Aggregate-Neighbor** have very small errors and converge very fast when the size increases. For $P_x \subset \mathbb{R}^2$, **Aggregate-Neighbor** achieve noticeably smaller error, but **G-Aggregate** (and **Grid**) perform well and are simpler.

In particular **G-Aggregate** and **Aggregate-Neighbor** stay *at least* one order of magnitude smaller in error than **Random Sampling**. This indicates it is much better to aggregate based on x-value than just randomly sample. It also justifies further thinning the

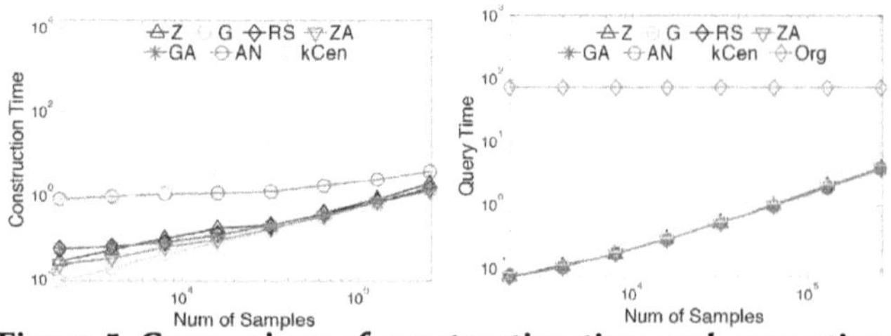

Figure 5: Comparison of construction time and query time for real dataset with $P_x \subset \mathbb{R}$.

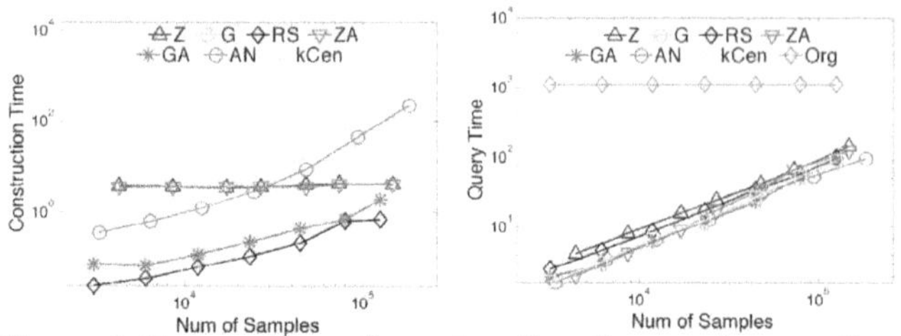

Figure 6: Comparison of construction time and query time for real dataset with $P_x \subset \mathbb{R}^2$.

data with these methods if the data should be modeled as a random sample since the additional error introduced would be negligible compared to what was already present due to the sampling.

The grid-based methods also consistently outperform the (z-order) sorting-based methods, so it is better to compress based on the x-coordinate change, rather than on the number of points.

Filling in a few neighbor values (the **-Neighbor** method) can also result in significant gains in accuracy for $P_x \subset \mathbb{R}^2$, but for $P_x \subset \mathbb{R}$ it does not show much improvement, and sometimes performs worse. The larger error per points (Figure 4, real data) is mainly due to the extra points added without much error reduction. It seems just aggregating does a good enough job for $P_x \subset \mathbb{R}$, but for $P_x \subset \mathbb{R}^2$ more complicated situations arise where this extra step is helpful.

4.3 Efficiency of Coresets

To show the efficiency of our methods, we compare the construction time and query time based on the coreset compared to the original dataset (denoted Org) for the dataset $P_x \subset \mathbb{R}$. For both comparisons, inspired by the Improved Fast Gauss Transform [28] and other fast kernel evaluation methods, for each query point, only the neighbor points within ten bandwidth are queried to calculate the kernel regression values. The construction time includes building the tree structure for the local data query, plus the time to generate the coreset. The query time are based on 128,000 evaluation points.

From Figure 5 for $P_x \subset \mathbb{R}$, **Grid**, **G-Aggregate**, **Random Sample**, **Z-order** and **Z-Aggregate** have the most efficient construction times, roughly as fast as just reading the data. Note that **k-Center** becomes quite slow for large coreset size. Similarly, **Grid**, **G-Aggregate**, and **Random Sample** are very efficient for $P_x \subset \mathbb{R}^2$ (Figure 6), but **Z-order** and **Z-Aggregate** have noticeable overhead compared to the grid-based methods (and have no accuracy or analysis advantage). In both settings, there is also considerable time overhead to running **Aggregate-Neighbor**, which has a slight accuracy advantage for $P_x \subset \mathbb{R}^2$ – this it is probably only worth it if pre-processing time on these scales are not of much importance but accuracy for $P_x \subset \mathbb{R}^2$ is.

For the query time, all the methods improve at least 2 orders of magnitude over using the original data. Their query times are all about the same; this is as expected since they all produce a coreset of the same size, which can be used as proxy for the full data set in precisely the same way.

Main take-away: In conclusion, **G-Aggregate** is the best algorithm in terms of effectiveness and efficiency for $P_x \subset \mathbb{R}$, with **Aggregate-Neighbor** has better accuracy in $P_x \subset \mathbb{R}^2$, but has some increased overhead in construction time. They are orders of magnitude faster than using the original data (and best among all proposed methods) and have extremely small error even for small coreset sizes (again the best among all proposed methods). For data sets of size 1 or 2 million, they achieves very small error using only 10,000 points and almost no error around 100,000 points. They (especially **G-Aggregate**) are very simple to implement, and about as fast to construct as reading the data. As seen in Section 3 we prove very strong error guarantees for these methods.

4.4 Consistency with Bandwidth

In Figure 7, we test the consistency of the algorithms by varying the bandwidth. We fix the number of evaluation point as 128,000 and the median coreset size as 62,500. By varying the bandwidth from 40 to 800 for real data (left) of $P_x \subset \mathbb{R}$, 10 to 160 for synthetic data (middle) for $P_x \subset \mathbb{R}$ and real data (right) for $P_x \subset \mathbb{R}^2$, the errors are decreasing for all the methods. This matches with our analysis in Section 3 and aligns with the notion that the more we smooth the data, the more stable it is, and the fewer data points we actually need. Again, **G-Aggregate** consistently performs the best or among the best of our methods. The exception is the real data in $\mathbb{R}^2$ (right), where for very large bandwidths, the simple methods **Z-order** and **Random Sample** dominate. In this setting, the data is so smoothed these methods, which in this setting exactly or roughly amount to a random sample, work better than trying to fit gridded data to circularly smoothed estimates. We do not attempt to automatically choose the bandwidth, as this should be a choice of the user to determine the scale they examine the data [18].

4.5 Progressive grid-based approaches

We evaluate the progressive grid-based approach on the CloudLab data. The total coreset size is 316,485, using **G-Aggregate** in each region. And we use 256,000 evaluation points. We evaluate the algorithm at four smoothing choices $\sigma = \{10, 15, 30, 45\}$. For each σ, we gradually increase the window size T, starting at 1 day (86,400), up to 10 months($2.5 \cdot 10^7$), as shown in Figure 8. We see that as a new region is reached, and the grid size enlarges, then so does the error. Also, as long as T/σ is bounded by $4 \cdot 10^4$, the error stays under 0.01.

4.6 High dimension

For simplicity, we only compare **G-Aggregate** and **Random Sampling**. When increasing the grid size, the number of empty grid increases as well, so we observe that, the size of coreset doesn't increase exponentially. By increasing the number of grids cells from 10 to 20, that is a factor 2 in each dimension, the average number of non-empty grids for CAD dataset are $\{902, 1367, 1863, 2538, 3150, 3791\}$ and for CASP dataset are $\{1034, 1554, 2122, 2742, 3543, 4342\}$. The relationship of L_∞ error and coreset size is shown in the left Figure 9, using bandwidths 3 and 3.8 respectively. The error decreases when

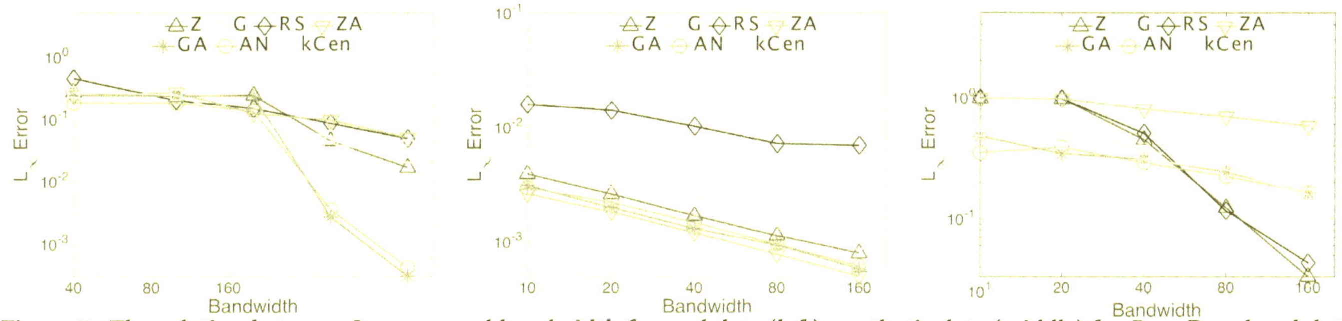

Figure 7: The relation between L_∞ error and bandwidth for real data (left), synthetic data (middle) for $P_x \subset \mathbb{R}$ and real data (right) for $P_x \subset \mathbb{R}^2$.

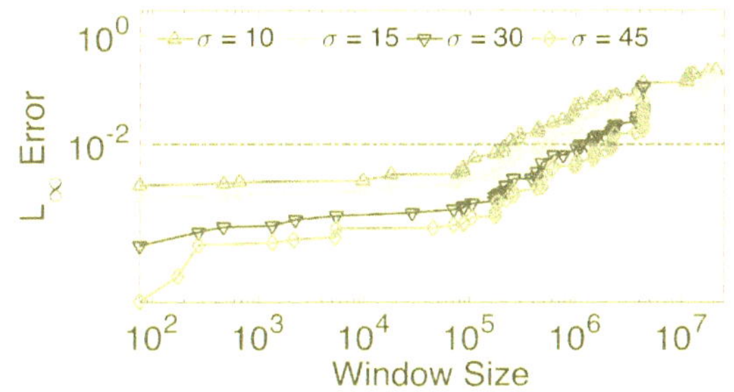

Figure 8: The relation between window size and L_∞ error for progressive G-Aggregate method.

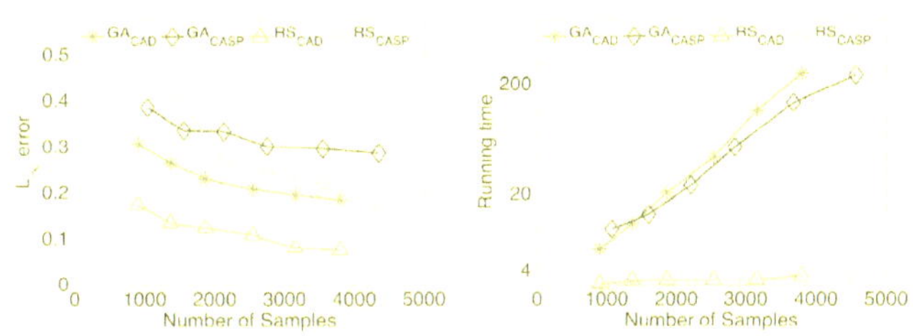

Figure 9: Left: L_∞ error for coresets of high dimensional datasets. Right: Running time to generate the coresets.

the size of coreset increases for both methods. For the same coreset size, **Random Sampling** perform better than **G-Aggregate**, and its running time (right figure in Figure 9) is much less. This aligns with our theoretical bounds. For example, for grid size 20^6, the **G-Aggregate** method takes about 250s, while the **Random Sampling** takes only around 3s. So we recommend the simple and fast method **Random Sampling** to generate coreset for kernel regression for high dimension datasets.

5 CONCLUSION

We describe several algorithms for coresets for kernel regression. Many (random sampling, order-based thinning, and grid-based thinning) are common heuristics. As we demonstrate on data sets with millions of points, those based on grids work much better, and that small modification of aggregating and sometimes filling in sparse-neighborhood boundaries can make large difference in error reduction. With our best methods, massive data sets can be drastically reduced in size and have negligible error. Find our code and data at: http://www.cs.utah.edu/~jeffp/students/kernel-reg/.

REFERENCES

[1] T. Arnold. Sparse density representations for simultaneous inference on large spatial datasets. *arXiv preprint arXiv:1510.00755*, 2015.

[2] S. Balakrishnan, B. T. Fasy, F. Lecci, A. Rinaldo, A. Singh, and L. Wasserman. Statistical inference for persistent homology. *Annals of Statistics*, 2014.

[3] R. Blundell and A. Duncan. Kernel regression in empirical microeconomics. *Journal of Human Resources*, pages 62–87, 1998.

[4] C. Boutsidis, P. Drineas, and M. Magdon-Ismail. Near-optimal coresets for least-squares regression. *IEEE Trans. Information Theory*, 59(10), 2013.

[5] J. D. Brutlag. Aberrant behavior detection in time series for network monitoring. In *System Administration Conference (LISA)*. USENIX, 2000.

[6] S. Chan, I. Diakonikolas, R. A. Servedio, and X. Sun. Efficient density estimation via piecewise polynomial approximation. In *STOC*, 2014.

[7] A. Dasgupta, P. Drineas, B. Harb, R. Kumar, and M. W. Mahoney. Sampling algorithms and coresets for ℓ_p regression. *SICOMP*, 38:2060–2078, 2009.

[8] T. F. Gonzalez. Clustering to minimize the maximum intercluster distance. *Theoretical Computer Science*, 38:293–306, 1985.

[9] A. Gretton, K. M. Borgwardt, M. J. Rasch, B. Schölkopf, and A. Smola. A kernel two-sample test. *JMLR*, 13:723–773, 2012.

[10] S. Har-Peled. *Geometric approximation algorithms*. AMS, 2011.

[11] J. Horel, M. Splitt, L. Dunn, J. Pechmann, B. White, C. Ciliberti, S. Lazarus, J. Slemmer, D. Zaff, and J. Burks. Mesowest: Cooperative mesonets in the western united states. *Bulletin of the American Meteorological Society*, 83(2):211–225, 2002.

[12] S. Joshi, R. V. Kommaraju, J. M. Phillips, and S. Venkatasubramanian. Comparing distributions and shapes using the kernel distance. *SoCG*, 2011.

[13] Y. Li, P. M. Long, and A. Srinivasan. Improved bounds on the samples complexity of learning. *J. Comp. and Sys. Sci.*, 62:516–527, 2001.

[14] E. A. Nadaraya. On estimating regression. *Theory of Probability and its Applications*, 9:141–142, 1964.

[15] R. K. Pace and R. Barry. Sparse spatial autoregressions. *Statistics & Probability Letters*, 33(3):291–297, 1997.

[16] J. M. Phillips. eps-samples for kernels. *SODA*, 2013.

[17] J. M. Phillips. Coresets and sketches. In *Handbook on Discrete and Computational Geometry*, chapter 47. CRC Press, 3rd edition, 2016.

[18] J. M. Phillips and Y. Zheng. L_infty error and bandwith selection for kernel density estimates of large data. In *KDD*, 2015.

[19] C. E. Rasmussen and C. K. I. Williams. *Gaussian Processes for Machine Learning*. MIT Press, 2006.

[20] R. Ricci, E. Eide, and The CloudLab Team. Introducing CloudLab: Scientific infrastructure for advancing cloud architectures and applications. *USENIX ;login:*, 39(6), Dec. 2014.

[21] N. Sharma, P. Sharma, D. Irwin, and P. Shenoy. Predicting solar generation from weather forecasts using machine learning. In *SmartGridComm*, 2011.

[22] H. Takeda, S. Farsiu, and P. Milanfar. Kernel regression for image processing and reconstruction. *IEEE Trans Image Processing*, 16:349–366, 2007.

[23] F. Tom. Mining the quantified self: Personal knowledge discovery as a challenge for data science. *Big Data*, 3:249–266, 2016.

[24] V. Vapnik and A. Chervonenkis. On the uniform convergence of relative frequencies of events to their probabilities. *Th. of Prob. Applic.*, 16:264–280, 1971.

[25] G. S. Watson. Smooth regression analysis. *Indian Journal of Statistics, Series A*, 26:359–372, 1964.

[26] X. Wei and Y. Li. Theoretical analysis of a rigid coreset minimum enclosing ball algorithm for kernel regression estimation. In *International Symposium on Neural Networks*, pages 741–752, 2008.

[27] J. R. Wolberg. *Expert Trading Systems: Modeling Financial Markets with Kernel Regression*. Wiley, 2000.

[28] C. Yang, R. Duraiswami, N. Gumerov, and L. Davis. Improved fast Gauss transform and efficient kernel density estimation. In *ICCV*, 2003.

[29] Y. Zheng, J. Jestes, J. M. Phillips, and F. Li. Quality and efficiency in kernel density estimates for large data. In *SIGMOD*, 2012.

A LINKING AND (ρ, ε)-APPROXIMATIONS FOR KERNEL REGRESSION

Theorem A.1. *For any kernel $K : \mathbb{R}^d \times \mathbb{R}^d \to \mathbb{R}^+$ linked to a range space $(\mathbb{R}^d, \mathcal{A})$, a (ρ, ε)-approximation S of $(P, \mathcal{A})$ for $S \subset \mathbb{R}^d$ is a $(\rho K^+, 2\varepsilon)$-approximation of (P, K), where $K^+ = \max_{p,q \in P} K(p, q)$.*

Proof. We first give the definition of κ. For two point sets P, S, define a *similarity* between the two point sets as

$$\kappa(P, S) = \frac{1}{|P|}\frac{1}{|S|}\sum_{p \in P}\sum_{s \in S} K(p, s),$$

and when the point set S only contains one single point s and a subset $P' \subset P$, we have $\kappa_P(P', s) = (1/|P|)\sum_{p \in P'} K(p, s)$.

Then we follow the same technique in proof of Theorem 5.1 in [12], suppose q is any query point, we can sort all $p_i \in P$ in similarity to q so that $p_i < p_j$ (and by notation $i < j$) if $K(p_i, q) > K(p_j, q)$. Thus any super-level set containing p_j also contains p_i for $i < j$. We can now consider the one-dimensional problem on this sorted order from q.

We now count the deviation $D(P, S, q) = \text{KDE}_P(q) - \text{KDE}_S(q)$ from p_1 to p_n using a charging scheme. That is each element $s_j \in S$ is charged to $g = |P|/|S|$ points in P. For simplicity we will assume that g is an integer, otherwise we can allow fractional charges. We now construct a partition of P slightly differently, for positive and negative $D(P, S, q)$ values, corresponding to undercounts and overcounts, respectively.

Undercount of $\text{KDE}_S(q)$: For undercounts, we partition P into $2|S|$ sets $\{P'_1, P_1, P'_2, P_2, \ldots, P'_{|S|}, P_{|S|}\}$ of consecutive points by the sorted order from q. Starting with p_1, we place points in set P'_j or P_j following their sorted order. Recursively on j and i, starting at $j = 1$ and $i = 1$, we place each p_i in P'_j as long as $K(p_i, q) > K(s_j, q)$ (this may be empty). Then we place the next g points p_i into P_j. After g points are placed in P_j, we begin with P'_{j+1}, until all of P has been placed in some set. Let $t \le |S|$ be the index of the last set P_j such that $|P_j| = g$. Note that for all $p_i \in P_j$ (for $j \le t$) we have $K(s_j, q) \ge K(p_i, q)$, thus $\kappa_S(\{s_j\}, q) \ge \kappa_P(P_j, q)$. We can now bound the undercount as

$$D(P, S, q) = \sum_{j=1}^{|S|}\left(\kappa_P(P_j, q)\right) - \kappa_S(\{s_j\}, q) + \sum_{j=1}^{|S|}\kappa_P(P'_j, q) \le \sum_{j=1}^{t+1}\kappa_P(P'_j, q)$$

since the first term is at most 0 and $|P'_j| = 0$ for $j > t + 1$. Now consider a super-level set $H \in \mathcal{A}$ containing all points before s_{t+1}; H is the smallest range that contains every non-empty P'_j. Because (for $j \le t$) each set P_j can be charged to s_j, then $\sum_{j=1}^{t} |P_j \cap H| = g|S \cap H|$. And because S is an (ρ, ε)-approximation of $(P, \mathcal{A})$, then

$$\frac{|P \cap H|}{|P|} - \frac{|S \cap H|}{|S|} \le \varepsilon \max\left\{\frac{|P \cap H|}{|P|}, \rho\right\}.$$

Hence

$$\begin{aligned}\frac{1}{|P|}\sum_{j=1}^{t+1}|P'_j| &= \frac{1}{|P|}\sum_{j=1}^{t+1}|P'_j \cap H| \\ &= \frac{1}{|P|}\Big(\sum_{j=1}^{t+1}|P'_j \cap H| + \sum_{j=1}^{t}|P_j \cap H| - g|S \cap H|\Big) \\ &= \frac{|P \cap H|}{|P|} - \frac{|S \cap H|}{|S|} \le \varepsilon \max\left\{\frac{|P \cap H|}{|P|}, \rho\right\}.\end{aligned}$$

We can now bound

$$D(P, S, q) \le \sum_{j=1}^{t+1}\kappa_P(P'_j, q) = \sum_{j=1}^{t+1}\sum_{p \in P'_j}\frac{K(p, q)}{|P|}.$$

When $\frac{|P \cap H|}{|P|} \ge \rho$, and $\rho \ge \sum_{p \in P'_1}\frac{K(p,q)}{|P|}\Big/\varepsilon$,

$$\begin{aligned}D(P, S, q) &\le \sum_{j=1}^{t+1}\sum_{p \in P'_j}\frac{K(p, q)}{|P|} \le \frac{\varepsilon}{|P|}\sum_{p \in P}K(p, q) + \sum_{p \in P'_1}\frac{K(p, q)}{|P|} \\ &\le \varepsilon \text{KDE}_P(q) + \varepsilon\rho \le 2\varepsilon \max\{\text{KDE}_P(q), \rho\}.\end{aligned}$$

The second inequality is because, all the points in P_j has larger $K(\cdot, q)$ values than the points in P'_{j+1} and $\frac{1}{|P|}\sum_{j=1}^{t+1}|P'_j| \le \varepsilon\frac{|P \cap H|}{|P|}$.

Finally, when $\frac{|P \cap H|}{|P|} \le \rho$,

$$D(P, S, q) \le \sum_{j=1}^{t+1}\sum_{p \in P'_j}\frac{K(p, q)}{|P|} \le \frac{1}{|P|}\sum_{j=1}^{t+1}|P'_j|K^+ \le \varepsilon\rho K^+.$$

Overcount of $\text{KDE}_S(q)$: The analysis for overcounts is similar to undercounts, but we partition the data in a reverse way: we partition P into $2|S|$ sets $\{P_1, P'_1, P_2, P'_2, \ldots, P_{|S|}, P'_{|S|}\}$ of consecutive points by the sorted order from q (some of the sets may be empty). Starting with p_n (the furthest point from q) we place points in sets P'_j or P_j following their reverse-sorted order. Recursively on j and i, starting at $j = |S|$ and $i = n$, we place each p_i in P'_j as long as $K(p_i, q) < K(s_j, q)$ (this may be empty). Then we place the next g points p_i into P_j. After g points are placed in P_j, we begin with P'_{j-1}, until all of P has been placed in some set. Let $t \le |S|$ be the index of the last set P_j such that $|P_j| = g$ (the smallest such j). Note that for all $p_i \in P_j$ (for $j \ge t$) we have $K(s_j, q) \le K(p_i, q)$, thus $\kappa_S(\{s_j\}, q) \le \kappa_P(P_j, q)$. We can now bound the (negative) overcount as

$$\begin{aligned}D(P, S, q) &= \sum_{j=|S|}^{t}\left(\kappa_P(P_j, q)\right) - \kappa_S(\{s_j\}, q) \\ &+ \sum_{j=t-1}^{1}\left(\kappa_P(P_j, q)\right) - \kappa_S(\{s_j\}, q) + \sum_{j=1}^{|S|}\kappa_P(P'_j, q) \\ &\ge \kappa_P(P_{t-1}, q) - \sum_{j=t-1}^{1}\kappa_S(\{s_j\}, q),\end{aligned}$$

and using a similar approach as with the undercount, we can show

$$D(P, S, q) \ge -\varepsilon\rho K^+.$$

So when $\frac{|P \cap H|}{|P|} \ge \rho$, S is an $(\rho, 2\varepsilon)$-approximation of $(P, \mathcal{K})$, and when $\frac{|P \cap H|}{|P|} \le \rho$, it is a $(\varepsilon\rho K^+)$-approximation of $(P, \mathcal{K})$. □

A Local Algorithm for Structure-Preserving Graph Cut

Dawei Zhou
Arizona State University
dzhou23@asu.edu

Si Zhang
Arizona State University
szhan172@asu.edu

Mehmet Yigit Yildirim
Arizona State University
yigityildirim@asu.edu

Scott Alcorn
Early Warnings LLC.
scott.alcorn@earlywarning.com

Hanghang Tong
Arizona State University
hanghang.tong@asu.edu

Hasan Davulcu
Arizona State University
HasanDavulcu@asu.edu

Jingrui He*
Arizona State University
jingrui.he@asu.edu

ABSTRACT

Nowadays, large-scale graph data is being generated in a variety of real-world applications, from social networks to co-authorship networks, from protein-protein interaction networks to road traffic networks. Many existing works on graph mining focus on the vertices and edges, with the first-order Markov chain as the underlying model. They fail to explore the high-order network structures, which are of key importance in many high impact domains. For example, in bank customer personally identifiable information (PII) networks, the star structures often correspond to a set of synthetic identities; in financial transaction networks, the loop structures may indicate the existence of money laundering. In this paper, we focus on mining *user-specified high-order* network structures and aim to find a *structure-rich* subgraph which does not break many such structures by separating the subgraph from the rest.

A key challenge associated with finding a *structure-rich* subgraph is the prohibitive computational cost. To address this problem, inspired by the family of local graph clustering algorithms for efficiently identifying a low-conductance cut without exploring the entire graph, we propose to generalize the key idea to model high-order network structures. In particular, we start with a generic definition of high-order conductance, and define the high-order diffusion core, which is based on a high-order random walk induced by *user-specified high-order* network structure. Then we propose a novel **H**igh-**O**rder **S**tructure-**P**reserving **LO**cal **C**ut (*HOSPLOC*) algorithm, which runs in polylogarithmic time with respect to the number of edges in the graph. It starts with a seed vertex and iteratively explores its neighborhood until a subgraph with a small high-order conductance is found. Furthermore, we analyze its performance in terms of both effectiveness and efficiency. The experimental results on both synthetic graphs and real graphs demonstrate the effectiveness and efficiency of our proposed *HOSPLOC* algorithm.

*To whom correspondence should be addressed

KDD '17, August 13-17, 2017, Halifax, NS, Canada

ACM ISBN 978-1-4503-4887-4/17/08...$15.00
https://doi.org/10.1145/3097983.3098015

KEYWORDS

Local Clustering Algorithm, High-Order Network Structure

1 INTRODUCTION

Given a massive graph and an initial vertex, to identify a good partition from the original graph - a subset of vertices with minimum conductance, is an *NP-complete problem* [19]. Graph-based local clustering algorithms [2, 3, 29] provide an important class of tools to efficiently discover a dense subgraph that contains or is close to a given vertex without exploring the whole graph. Despite the elegant theoretical analysis, most existing works are inherently limited to simple network structures, i.e., vertices and edges, with the first-order Markov chain as the underlying model.

However, in many real-world applications, high-order network structures, e.g., triangles, loops, and cliques, are essential for exploring useful patterns on networks. For example, the multi-hop loop structure may indicate the existence of money laundering in financial networks [11]; the star structure may correspond to a set of synthetic identities in PII networks of bank customers [18]. Therefore, an intriguing research question is whether graph-based local clustering algorithms can be generalized to model *user-specified* network structures in an efficient way. Specifically, the traditional graph-based local clustering algorithms aim to find a cut by exploring the first-order connectivity patterns on the level of vertices and edges, while we aim to find the best cut based on high-order connectivity patterns on the level of network motifs.

Despite its key importance, it remains a challenge to generalize graph-based local clustering algorithms to model high-order network structures. Specifically, we need to answer the following questions. First (***Q1. Model***), it is not clear that how to conduct the generalized random walk with respect to high-order network structures. Some existing works [5, 23, 32] have studied the second-order random walks based on the 3rd-order network structures. However, it is unknown how to construct high-order random walks on the basis of the *user-specified* network structures. Second (***Q2. Algorithm***), how can we design a high-order local clustering algorithm that produces a graph cut rich in the *user-specified* network structures in an efficient way? This question has been largely overlooked in the previous researches. Third (***Q3. Generalization***), how can we generalize our proposed algorithm to solve the real-world problems on various types of graphs, such as signed graphs, bipartite graphs and multipartite graphs?

To address these problems, in this paper, we propose a novel local algorithm for structure-preserving graph clustering named *HOSPLOC*. The core of *HOSPLOC* is to approximately compute the distribution of high-order random walk [23] that is directly based on *user-specified high-order* network structures, and then utilize the idea of vector-based graph partition methods [24, 25, 29] to find a cut with a small high-order conductance. Our algorithm operates on the tensor representation of graph data which allows the users to specify what kind of network structures should be preserved in the returned cluster. In addition, we provide analyses regarding the effectiveness and efficiency of the proposed algorithm. Furthermore, we present how *HOSPLOC* can be applied to the applications with various types of networks, e.g., signed networks, bipartite networks and multipartite networks. Finally, we evaluate the performance of *HOSPLOC* from multiple aspects using various real-world networks. Figure 1 compares the clusters returned by the proposed *HOSPLOC* algorithm and the Nibble algorithm [29], which shows that *HOSPLOC* is better at partitioning a subgraph with the rich *user-specified high-order* network structure.

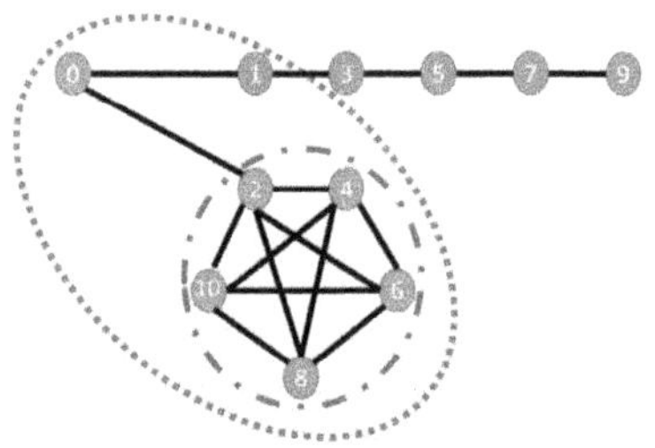

Figure 1: A synthetic network where vertex 0 is connected with two kinds of network structures: clique and line. The local clusters found by *HOSPLOC* (within the blue dash-dot line) and the Nibble algorithm [29] (within the red dotted line) with the same initial vertex, i.e., vertex 0, where *HOSPLOC* is conducted on the basis of 3-node line (illustrated in Table 1).

The main contributions of the paper are summarized below.

(1) Definitions of adjacency tensor and transition tensor for high-order random walk induced by high-order network structures.
(2) A local algorithm named *HOSPLOC* for structure-preserving graph cut with *polylogorithmic* time complexity regarding the number of edges.
(3) Theoretical analyses regarding the effectiveness and efficiency of *HOSPLOC*.
(4) Generalizations and applications of *HOSPLOC* on signed networks, bipartite networks and multipartite networks.
(5) Extensive experimental results on both synthetic and real networks demonstrating the performance of the proposed *HOSPLOC* algorithm.

The rest of our paper is organized as follows. Related works are reviewed in Section 2, followed by the introduction of notation and preliminaries in Section 3. In Section 4, we present our proposed *HOSPLOC* algorithm as well as the analyses regarding its effectiveness and efficiency. Then we introduce its generalizations and applications in Section 5. Experimental results are presented in Section 6 before we conclude the paper in Section 7.

2 RELATED WORK

2.1 Local Spectral Clustering on Graphs

Nowadays, large-scale networks data appear in a broad spectrum of disciplines, from social networks [21, 22] to collaborative networks[8, 9], from rare category detection [34–37] to crowdsourcing [38, 39]. Local spectral clustering techniques provide a simple, efficient time alternative to recursively identify a local sparse cut C with an upper-bounded conductance. In [29], the authors introduce an almost-linear Laplacian linear solver and a local clustering algorithm, i.e., Nibble, which conducts cuts that can be combined with balanced partitions. In [2, 3], the authors extend Nibble algorithm [29] by using personalized PageRank vector to produce cuts with less running time on undirected and directed graphs. More recently, [14] proposes a local graph clustering algorithm with the same guarantee as the Cheeger inequalities, of which time complexity is slightly super linear in the size of the partition. In [4], the authors introduce randomized local partitioning algorithms that find sparse cuts by simulating the volume-biased evolving set process. However, to my best of knowledge, this paper is the first local clustering framework that focuses on modeling high-order network structures and aims to find a *structure-rich* subgraph with a *polylogarithmic* time complexity in the number of edges.

2.2 High-order Markov Chain Models

There are many cases that one would like to model observed data as a high-order Markov chain in different real-world problems, such as airport travel flows [27], web browsing behavior [10] and wind turbine design [26]. To solve these problems, many previous works [1, 26, 30] approximate the limiting probability distribution of high-order Markov chain as a linear combination of transition probability matrix. More recently, in [23], the authors introduce a rank-1 approximation of high-order Markov chain limiting distribution and propose a recursive algorithm to compute it. Later on, [15] introduces a computationally tractable approximation of the high-order PageRank named multi-linear PageRank, where the underlying stochastic process is a vertex-reinforced random walk. In [6], the authors introduce a novel stochastic process, i.e., spacey random walk, whose stationary distribution is given by the tensor eigenvector, and show the convergence properties of these dynamics. In [5, 32], the authors propose the similar spectral clustering frameworks that allow for modeling third-order network structures and conduct partition while preserving such structures on the given graph. Followed by [5], [33] proposes a tensor spectral co-clustering method by modeling higher-order data with a novel variant of a higher-order Markov chain, i.e., the super-spacey random walk. Compared to the existing high-order Markov chain models, we propose a novel scalable local clustering algorithm that can identify clusters with a small conductance and also preserve the *user-specified high-order* network structures in a *polylogarithmic* time complexity. Besides, we also provide provable theoretical bounds on the effectiveness and efficiency of the proposed *HOSPLOC* algorithm.

3 NOTATIONS AND PRELIMINARIES

In this section, we review the basics of random walks with the Markov chain interpretation and the Nibble algorithm for local clustering on graphs [29], which pave the way for the proposed structure-preserving graph cut algorithm to be introduced in the next section.

3.1 Notations

Given an undirected graph $G = (V, E)$, where V consists of n vertices, and E consists of m edges, we let $A \in \mathbb{R}^{n \times n}$ denote the adjacency matrix of graph G, $D \in \mathbb{R}^{n \times n}$ denote the diagonal matrix of vertex degrees, and $d(v) = D(v, v)$ denote the degree of vertex $v \in V$. The transition matrix of a lazy random walk on graph G is $M = (A^T D^{-1} + I)/2$, where $I \in \mathbb{R}^{n \times n}$ is an identity matrix. For convenience, we define the indicator vector χ_C as follows.

$$\chi_C(v) = \begin{cases} 1 & v \in C \\ 0 & \text{Otherwise} \end{cases}.$$

In particular, the initial distribution of a random walk starting from vertex v could be denoted as χ_v.

The volume of a subset $C \subseteq V$ is defined as the summation of vertex degrees in C, i.e., $\mu(C) = \sum_{v \in C} d(v)$. We let $\bar{C}$ be the complementary set of C, i.e., $\bar{C} = \{v \in \bar{C} | v \in V, v \notin C\}$. The conductance of subset $C \subseteq V$ is therefore defined as $\Phi(C) = \frac{|E(C,\bar{C})|}{\min(\mu(C),\mu(\bar{C}))}$ [7], where $E(C, \bar{C}) = \{(u, v) | u \in C, v \in \bar{C}\}$, and $|E(C, \bar{C})|$ denotes the number of edges in $E(C, \bar{C})$. Besides, we represent the elements in a matrix or a tensor using the convention similar to Matlab, e.g., $M(i, j)$ is the element at the ith row and j^{th} column of the matrix M, and $M(i, :)$ is the ith row of M, etc.

3.2 Markov Chain Interpretation

The oth order Markov chain S describes a stochastic process that satisfies [15]

$$\begin{aligned} &Pr(S_{t+1} = i_1 | S_t = i_2, \ldots, S_{t-o+1} = i_{o+1}, \ldots, S_1 = i_{t+1}) \\ =&Pr(S_{t+1} = i_1 | S_t = i_2, \ldots, S_{t-o+1} = i_{o+1}) \end{aligned} \tag{1}$$

where $i_1, \ldots, i_{t+1}$ denote the set of states associated with different time stamps. Specifically, this means the future state only depends on the past o states. If each vertex in graph G corresponds to a distinct state, we can interpret the transition matrix M as the transition matrix of the 1st-order Markov chain. Specifically, the transition probability between vertex i and vertex j is given by $M(i, j) = Pr(S_{t+1} = i | S_t = j)$. In Section 4.1, we introduce the idea of adjacency tensor and transition tensor for modeling the high-order network structures, which will lead to the high-order Markov chains and high-order random walks.

3.3 Nibble Algorithm

Given an undirected graph G and a parameter $\phi > 0$, to find a cut C from G such that $\Phi(C) \leq \phi$ or to determine no such C exists is an NP-complete problem [28]. Nibble algorithm [29] is one of the earliest attempts to partition a graph with a bounded conductance in polylogarithmic time. Starting from a given vertex, Nibble provably finds a local cluster in time $(O(2^b log^6 m)/\phi^4))$, where b is a constant which controls the lower bound of the output volume. This is proportional to the size of the output cluster. The key idea behind Nibble is to conduct truncated random walks by using the following truncation operator

$$[q]_\epsilon(u) = \begin{cases} q(u) & \text{if } q(u) \geq d(u)\epsilon \\ 0 & \text{Otherwise} \end{cases} \tag{2}$$

where $q \in \mathbb{R}^n$ is the distribution vector over all the vertices in the graph, and ϵ is the truncation threshold that can be computed as follows [29]

$$\epsilon = \frac{1}{(1800 \cdot (l+2) t_{last} 2^b)} \tag{3}$$

where l can be computed as $l = \lceil log_2(\mu(V)/2) \rceil$, and t_{last} can be computed as $t_{last} = (l+1)\left\lceil \frac{2}{\phi^2} ln\left(c_1(l+2)\sqrt{\mu(V)/2}\right)\right\rceil$.

Then, Nibble applies the vector-based partition method [24, 25, 29] that sorts the probable nodes based on the ratio of function I_x to produce a low conductance cut. To introduce function I_x mathematically, we first define $S_j(q)$ to be the set of top j vertices u that maximizes $q(u)/d(u)$. That is $S_j(q) = \{\pi(1), \ldots, \pi(j)\}$, where π is the permutation that follows $\frac{q(\pi(i))}{d(\pi(i))} \geq \frac{q(\pi(i+1))}{d(\pi(i+1))}$. In addition, we let $\lambda_j(q) = \sum_{u \in S_j(q)} d(u)$ denote the volume of the set $S_j(q)$. Finally, the function I_x is defined as follows

$$I_x(q, \lambda_j(q)) = \frac{q(\pi(i))}{d(\pi(i))}. \tag{4}$$

In the next section, we will introduce the high-order structure preserving graph cut framework, i.e., *HOSPLOC*. Compared to Nibble, *HOSPLOC* can model the *user-specified* network structure and conduct a *structure-rich* cut with a small conductance. Moreover, similar to Nibble, *HOSPLOC* runs in polylogarithmic time with respect to the number of edges in the graph.

4 HIGH-ORDER NETWORK STRUCTURE AND THE HOSPLOC ALGORITHM

In the previous section, we introduced the notations and preliminaries. Now, we generalize the idea of truncated local clustering to produce clusters that preserve the *user-specified high-order* network structures. We start by introducing the adjacency tensor and the associated transition tensor based on the *user-specified high-order* network structures, followed by the discussion on the stationary distribution of high-order random walk. Then, we introduce the definitions of high-order conductance and high-order diffusion core. Finally, we present the proposed high-order local clustering algorithm *HOSPLOC* with theoretical analyses on the effectiveness and efficiency.

4.1 Adjacency Tensor and Transition Tensor

For an undirected graph G, the corresponding adjacency matrix A could be considered as a matrix representation of the existing edges on G. However, in many real applications, we may want to explore and capture more complex and high-order network structures. Table 1 summarizes the examples of network structures $\mathbb{N}$ of different orders and the corresponding Markov chain. Notice that the order

$\mathbb{N}$	Example	Illustration	Markov Chain
1st-order	Vertex		0th-order
2nd-order	Edge	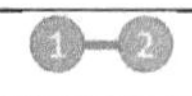	1st-order
3rd-order	3-node Line	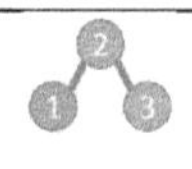	2nd-order
	Triangle	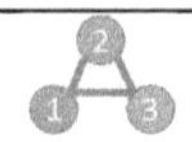	
k^{th}-order	k-node Star	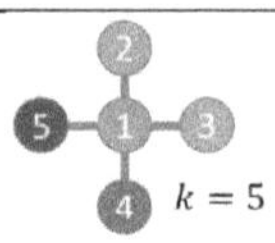	$(k-1)^{th}$-order

Table 1: Network Structures $\mathbb{N}$ and Markov Chains.

of the network structure is different from the order of the Markov chain (or random walk). For example, the edges in E are considered as the 2nd-order network structures, and they correspond to the 1st-order Markov Chain (random walk) due to the matrix representation of E. We use k to denote the order of the network structure $\mathbb{N}$. As what will be explained next, the kth-order network structures correspond to the $(k-1)^{th}$-order Markov chain (random walk).

To model the *user-specified* network structure $\mathbb{N}$, we introduce the definition of adjacency tensor $\mathbf{T}$ and the transition tensor $\mathbf{P}$ to represent the high-order random walk induced by the high-order network structures $\mathbb{N}$.

*Definition 4.1 (**Adjacency Tensor**).* Given a graph $G = (V, E)$, the kth-order network structure $\mathbb{N}$ on G could be represented in a k-dimensional adjacency tensor $\mathbf{T}$ as follows

$$T(i_1, i_2, \ldots, i_k) = \begin{cases} 1 & \{i_1, i_2, \ldots, i_k\} \subseteq V \text{ and form } \mathbb{N}. \\ 0 & \text{Otherwise.} \end{cases} \tag{5}$$

*Definition 4.2 (**Transition Tensor**).* Given a graph $G = (V, E)$ and the adjacency tensor $\mathbf{T}$ for the kth-order network structure $\mathbb{N}$, the corresponding transition tensor $\mathbf{P}$ could be computed as

$$P(i_1, i_2, \ldots, i_k) = \frac{T(i_1, i_2, \ldots, i_k)}{\sum_{i_1=1}^{n} T(i_1, i_2, \ldots, i_k)} \tag{6}$$

By the above definition, we have $\sum_{i_1} P(i_1, \ldots, i_k) = 1$. Therefore, if each vertex in G is a distinguishable state, we can interpret the kth-order transition tensor $\mathbf{P}$ as a $(k-1)^{th}$-order Markov chain (random walk), i.e., $Pr(S_{t+1} = i_1 | S_t = i_2, \ldots, S_{t-k+2} = i_k) = P(i_1, \ldots, i_k)$. Intuitively, if $i_1 \neq i_1'$, and they both form $\mathbb{N}$ together with $i_2, \ldots, i_k$, then the probabilities of the next state being i_1 and being i_1' are the same given $S_t = i_2, \ldots, S_{t-k+2} = i_k$. Notice that the transition matrix M of a lazy random walk defined in Subsection 3.1 can be considered as a special case of Definition 4.2 with the 2nd-order network structure $\mathbb{N}$, if we allow self-loops.

4.2 Stationary Distribution

For the kth-order network structure $\mathbb{N}$ and the corresponding $(k-1)^{th}$-order random walk with transition tensor $\mathbf{P}$, if the stationary distribution $\mathbf{X}$ exists, where $\mathbf{X}$ is a $(k-1)$-dimensional tensor, then it satisfies [15]

$$X(i_1, i_2, \ldots, i_{k-1}) = \sum_{i_k} P(i_1, i_2, \ldots, i_k) X(i_2, \ldots, i_k). \tag{7}$$

where $X(i_1, \ldots, i_{k-1})$ denotes the probability of being at states $i_1, \ldots, i_{k-1}$ in consecutive time steps upon convergence of the random walk, and $\sum_{i_1, \ldots, i_{k-1}} X(i_1, \ldots, i_{k-1}) = 1$.

However, for this system, storing the stationary distribution requires $O(n^{(k-1)})$ space complexity. For the sake of computational scalability, in high-order random walks, a commonly held assumption is 'rank-one approximation' [5, 23], i.e.,

$$X(i_2, \ldots, i_k) = q(i_2) \ldots q(i_k) \tag{8}$$

where $q \in \mathbb{R}_+^{n \times 1}$ with $\sum_i q(i) = 1$. Then, we have

$$\sum_{i_2, \ldots, i_k} P(i_1, \ldots, i_k) q(i_2) \ldots q(i_k) = q(i_1).$$

In this way, the space complexity of the stationary distribution of high-order random walk is reduced to $O(n)$. Although q is an approximation of the true stationary distribution of the high-order random walk, [23] theoretically demonstrates the convergence and effectiveness of the nonnegative vector q if $\mathbf{P}$ satisfies certain properties.

Following [5, 23], in this paper, we also adopt 'rank-one approximation' and assume the stationary distribution of the high-order random walk satisfies Eq. 8. To further simplify the notation, we let $\bar{P}$ denote the $(k-2)$-mode unfolding matrix of the k-dimensional transition tensor P. Thus, the $(k-1)^{th}$-order random walk satisfies:

$$q = \bar{P}(q \otimes \ldots \otimes q) \tag{9}$$

where $\otimes$ denotes the Kronecker product symbol. For example, for the third-order network structure $\mathbb{N}$ (e.g., triangle), the transition tensor $\mathbf{P} \in \mathbb{R}^{n \times n \times n}$ can be constructed based on Definition 4.2. Then, the 1-mode unfolding matrix $\bar{P}$ of $\mathbf{P}$ can be written as follows

$$\bar{P} = [P(:, :, 1), P(:, :, 2), \ldots, P(:, :, n)]$$

where $\bar{P} \in \mathbb{R}^{n \times n^2}$. In this way, the associated second-order random walk with respect to the triangle network structure satisfies

$$q = \bar{P}(q \otimes q).$$

4.3 High-Order Conductance

Given a high-order network structure $\mathbb{N}$, it is usually the case that the user would like to find a local cluster C on the graph G such that: (1) C contains a rich set of network structures $\mathbb{N}$; (2) by partitioning all the vertices into C and $\bar{C}$, we do not break many such network structures. For example, in financial fraud detection, directed loops may refer to money laundering activities. In this case, we want to ensure the partition preserves rich directed loops inside the cluster and breaks such structure as less as possible. It is easy to see that the traditional definition of the conductance $\Phi(C)$ introduced in Subsection 3.1 does not serve this purpose. Therefore, we introduce the following generalized definition of conductance to preserve user-defined high-order network structure $\mathbb{N}$.

Definition 4.3 (k^{th}-order Conductance). For any cluster C in graph G and the kth-order network structure $\mathbb{N}$, the kth-order conductance $\Phi(C, \mathbb{N})$ is defined as

$$\Phi(C,\mathbb{N}) = \frac{cut(C,\mathbb{N})}{min\{\mu(C,\mathbb{N}), \mu(\bar{C},\mathbb{N})\}} \tag{10}$$

where $cut(C, \mathbb{N})$ denotes the number of network structures broken due to the partition of G into C and $\bar{C}$, i.e.,

$$cut(C,\mathbb{N}) = \sum_{i_1,\ldots,i_k \in V} T(i_1,\ldots,i_k) - \sum_{i_1 i_2,\ldots,i_k \in C} T(i_1,\ldots,i_k) - \sum_{i_1,\ldots,i_k \in \bar{C}} T(i_1,\ldots,i_k) \tag{11}$$

and $\mu(C, \mathbb{N})$ ($\mu(\bar{C}, \mathbb{N})$) denotes the total number of network structures $\mathbb{N}$ incident to the vertices within C ($\bar{C}$), i.e.,

$$\mu(C,\mathbb{N}) = \sum_{i_1 \in C; i_2,\ldots,i_k \in V} T(i_1, i_2, \ldots, i_k)$$
$$\mu(\bar{C},\mathbb{N}) = \sum_{i_1 \in \bar{C}; i_2,\ldots,i_k \in V} T(i_1, i_2, \ldots, i_k). \tag{12}$$

Claim 1. *Definition 4.3 provides a generic definition of network conductance with respect to any network structure, and it subsumes existing measures of network conductance. In particular.*

- *When $\mathbb{N}$ represents edges, $\Phi(C, \mathbb{N})$ is twice the traditional conductance $\Phi(C)$ introduced in Subsection 3.1.*
- *When $\mathbb{N}$ represents triangles, $\Phi(C, \mathbb{N})$ is the same as the 'high-order conductance' ϕ_3 introduced in [5].*

4.4 High-Order Diffusion Core

Similar to the Nibble algorithm, we are given a seed vertex v, and our goal is to find a cluster C containing or near v without looking at the whole graph. The main advantage of our proposed work is that, given the *user-specified high-order* network structure $\mathbb{N}$, we are able to produce a local cluster that preserves such structure within the cluster C and does not break many such structures by partitioning the graph into C and $\bar{C}$.

To this end, we perform high-order random walk with transition tensor $\mathbf{P}$ defined in Definition 4.2, starting from the seed vertex v. Let $q^{(t)}$ denote the distribution vector over all the vertices after the tth iteration of the high-order random walk. Ideally, a seed vertex chosen within a cluster C with low conductance should lead to the discovery of this cluster. However, as pointed out in [29], for the 2nd-order network structure and the associated 1st-order random walk, if the vertices within the cluster are more strongly attached to vertices outside the cluster than inside it, they may not be good candidates for the seed, as the random walk will have a relatively high chance of escaping the cluster after a few iterations. Therefore, they propose the definition of the diffusion core to characterize the subset of vertices within the cluster, such that the random walks starting from such vertices stay inside the cluster for a long time. Here, we generalize the definition of a diffusion core to high-order network structures as follows.

Definition 4.4 (k^{th}-Order ξ-Diffusion Core). For any cluster C, we define $C^{k,\xi} \in C$ to be the kth-order ξ-diffusion core of C, such that

$$\chi^T_{\bar{C}^{k,\xi}} q^{(t)} \leq \xi \frac{cut(C,\mathbb{N})}{\mu(C,\mathbb{N})} \tag{13}$$

where $q^{(t)}$ denotes the diffusion distribution of t-step high-order random walks, and ξ is a positive constant that controls the compactness of the diffusion core.

Note that the left hand side of Eq. 13, $\chi^T_{\bar{C}^{k,\xi}} q^{(t)}$, represents the probability that a high-order random walk terminates outside the cluster C after t steps, which is also called the escaping probability of the cluster C. On the right hand side of Eq. 13, the numerator could be considered as the total number of the kth-order random walk paths to escape cluster C, while the denominator could be regarded as the total number of the kth-order random walk paths starting from C. It is easy to see that $\chi^T_{\bar{C}^{k,\xi}} q^{(t)}$ is positively correlated with $\frac{cut(C,\mathbb{N})}{\mu(C,\mathbb{N})}$. Since, for a given C, $\chi^T_{\bar{C}^{k,\xi}} q^{(t)}$ is a computable constant, we consider Eq. 13 as the compactness constraint for the kth-order ξ-diffusion core $C^{k,\xi} \in C$.

Proposition 4.5. *For any cluster C and the kth-Order ξ-diffusion core $C^{k,\xi} \in C$, we have*

$$\chi^T_{\bar{C}^{k,\xi}} q^{(t)} \leq \xi \Phi(C,\mathbb{N}). \tag{14}$$

Proof. Given a cluster $C \in V$ and a kth-order network structure $\mathbb{N}$, the corresponding k^{th}-order conductance can be computed as

$$\Phi(C,\mathbb{N}) = \frac{cut(C,\mathbb{N})}{min\{\mu(C,\mathbb{N}), \mu(\bar{C},\mathbb{N})\}}.$$

Obviously, we can divide the proof into the following two cases.
Case 1 : when $\mu(C,\mathbb{N}) \geq \mu(\bar{C},\mathbb{N})$, $\Phi(C,\mathbb{N}) = \frac{cut(C,\mathbb{N})}{\mu(\bar{C},\mathbb{N})} \geq \frac{cut(C,\mathbb{N})}{\mu(C,\mathbb{N})}$.
Case 2 : when $\mu(C,\mathbb{N}) < \mu(\bar{C},\mathbb{N})$, $\Phi(C,\mathbb{N}) = \frac{cut(C,\mathbb{N})}{\mu(C,\mathbb{N})}$.

Thus, we have $\Phi(C,\mathbb{N}) \geq \frac{cut(C,\mathbb{N})}{\mu(C,\mathbb{N})}$. Meanwhile, by Definition. 4.4, it turns out that

$$\chi^T_{\bar{C}^{k,\xi}} q^{(t)} \leq \xi \frac{cut(C,\mathbb{N})}{\mu(C,\mathbb{N})} \leq \xi \Phi(C,\mathbb{N}).$$

□

4.5 The Proposed *HOSPLOC* Algorithm

Basically, the proposed *HOSPLOC* could be decomposed into three main steps: (1) approximately compute the distribution of high-order random walk starting at any vertex from which the walk does not mix rapidly; (2) truncate all small entries in $q^{(t)}$ to 0, thus we can limit the computation to the neighborhood of the seed; (3) apply the vector-based graph partition method [24, 25, 29] to search for a *structure-rich* cut with a small conductance.

Now, we are ready to present our proposed *HOSPLOC* algorithm. The given input are the transition tensor $\mathbf{P}$, the transition matrix M, the seed vertex v, the conductance upper-bound ϕ, the maximum iteration number $t_{\max}$, and the constants b, c_1, ξ. Note that constant b controls the volume lower bound of the returned set C, i.e., $2^b \leq \mu(C)$, and c_1 is a constant which guarantees that the elements in C have a large probability of staying within C. Step 1 to Step 4 are the initialization process. Step 1 constructs unfolding matrix $\bar{P}$ of the transition tensor $\mathbf{P}$. Step 2 to Step 4 compute the truncation constant ϵ and the truncated initial distributions vectors $r^{(m)}$, $m = 1, \ldots, k-1$. The iterative process between Step 5 and Step 16 aims to identify the proper high-order local cluster C: Step 6 calculates the updated distribution over all the vertices in current iteration; Step 7 calculates the truncated local distribution $r^{(t)}$; the iterative process stops when it finds a proper cluster which satisfies the three constraints in Step 9 to Step 11, where condition (a) guarantees that the conductance of C is upper-bounded by ϕ, condition (b) ensures that the volume of C is lower-bounded by 2^b, and condition (c) enforces that elements in C have a large probability mass.

Algorithm 1 High-Order Structure-Preserved Local Cut (*HOSPLOC*)

Input:
(1) Transition tensor $\mathbf{P}$ and transition matrix M,
(2) Initial vertex v,
(3) Conductance upper bound ϕ,
(4) Maximum iteration number $t_{\max}$,
(5) Parameters b, c_1, ξ.
Output:
Local cluster C;
1: Construct the unfolding matrix $\bar{P}$ of the transition tensor $\mathbf{P}$.
2: Compute constant ϵ based on Eq. 3.
3: Set initial distribution vectors $q^{(t)} = M^{(t-1)}\chi_v$, where $t = 1, \ldots, k-1$.
4: Compute truncated initial local distribution vectors $r^{(t)} = [q^{(t)}]_\epsilon$, $t = 1, \ldots, k-1$.
5: **for** $t = k : t_{\max}$ **do**
6: Update distribution vector $q^{(t)} = \bar{P}(r^{(t-1)} \otimes \ldots \otimes r^{(t-k+1)})$.
7: Update truncated distribution vectors $r^{(t)} = [q^{(t)}]_\epsilon$.
8: **if** there exists a j such that:
9: (a)$\Phi(S_j(q^{(t)})) <= \phi$,
10: (b)$2^b <= \lambda_j(q^{(t)})$,
11: (c)$I_x(q^{(t)}, 2^b) >= \frac{\xi}{c_1(l+2)2^b}$. **then**
12: return $C = S_j(q^{(t)})$ and quit.
13: **else**
14: Return $C = \emptyset$.
15: **end if**
16: **end for**

Next, we analyze the proposed *HOSPLOC* algorithm in terms of effectiveness and efficiency. Regarding the effectiveness, we will show that for any cluster C, if the seed vertex comes from the kth-order ξ-diffusion core, i.e., $v \in C^{k,\xi}$, then the non-empty set C' returned by *HOSPLOC* has a large overlap with C. To be specific, we have the following theorem.

Theorem 4.6 (**Effectiveness of *HOSPLOC***). *Let C be a cluster on graph G such that $\Phi(C, \mathbb{N}) \leq \frac{1}{c_2(l+2)}$, where $2c_1 \leq c_2$. If* HOSPLOC *runs with starting vertex $v \in C^{k,\xi}$ and returns a non-empty set C', then we have $\mu(C' \cap C) \geq 2^{b-1}$.*

Proof. Let $q^{(t)}$, $t \leq t_{\max}$, be the distribution of $t-step$ high-order random walk when the set $C' = S_j(q^{(t)})$ is obtained. Then, based on Proposition 4.5, we have the following inequality

$$\chi_{\bar{C}}^T q^{(t)} \leq \chi_{\bar{C}^{k,\xi}}^T q^{(t)} \leq \xi\Phi(C, \mathbb{N}) \leq \frac{\xi}{c_2(l+2)}. \tag{15}$$

In Step 11 of Algorithm 1, condition (c) guarantees that

$$I_x(u) = \frac{q^{(t)}(u)}{d(u)} \geq \frac{\xi}{c_1(l+2)2^b} \tag{16}$$

where $u \in S_j(q^{(t)})$. Since $d(u) \geq 0$ and $c_1(l+2)2^b \geq 0$, we can infer the following inequality from Eq. 16

$$d(u) \leq \frac{1}{\xi} c_1(l+2)2^b q^{(t)}(u). \tag{17}$$

Let j' be the smallest integer such that $\lambda_{j'}(q^{(t)}) \geq 2^b$. In Step 10 of Algorithm 1, condition (b) guarantees that $j' \leq j$. By Eq. 15 and Eq. 17, we have

$$\begin{aligned} &\mu(S_{j'}(q^{(t)}) \cap \bar{C}) \\ &= \sum_{u \in S_{j'}(q^{(t)}) \cap \bar{C}} d(u) \\ &\leq \sum_{u \in S_{j'}(q^{(t)}) \cap \bar{C}} \frac{1}{\xi} c_1(l+2)2^b q^{(t)}(u) \\ &\leq \frac{1}{\xi} c_1(l+2)2^b (\chi_{\bar{C}}^T q^{(t)}) \\ &\leq \frac{\xi c_1(l+2)2^b}{\xi c_2(l+2)} \leq 2^{b-1}. \end{aligned} \tag{18}$$

Due to $2^b <= \lambda_j'(q^{(t)})$, it turns out that $\mu(S_{j'}(q^{(t)}) \cap C) \geq 2^{b-1}$. Since $j \geq j'$, we have the final conclusion

$$\mu(S_j(q^{(t)}) \cap C) \geq \mu(S_{j'}(q^{(t)}) \cap C) \geq 2^{b-1}. \tag{19}$$

□

Regarding the efficiency of *HOSPLOC*, we provide the following lemma to show the *polylogarithmic* time complexity of *HOSPLOC* with respect to the number of edges in the graph.

Lemma 4.7 (**Efficiency of *HOSPLOC***). *Given Graph G and the kth-order network structure $\mathbb{N}$, $k \geq 3$, the time complexity of* HOSPLOC *is bounded by $O\left(t_{max}\frac{2^{bk}}{\phi^{2k}}log^{3k}m\right)$.*

Proof. To bound the running time of *HOSPLOC*, we first show that each iteration in Algorithm 1 takes time $O(\frac{1}{\epsilon^k})$. Instead of conducting dense vector multiplication or Kronecker product, we track the nonzeros in both matrixes and vectors. Here, we let V^t denote the set of vertices such that $\{u \in V^{(t)} | r^{(t)}(u) > 0\}$, and $V^{(\hat{t})}$ be the set with the maximum number of nonzero elements in $\{V^{(t)} | 1 \leq t \leq t_{max}\}$. In Step 6, the Kronecker product chain $r^{(t-1)} \otimes \ldots \otimes r^{(t-k+1)}$ can be performed in time proportion to

$$|V^{(t-1)}| \ldots |V^{(t-k+1)}| \leq |V^{(\hat{t})}|^{(k-1)} \leq \mu(V^{(\hat{t})})^{(k-1)}.$$

Also, [29] shows that $\mu(V^{(t)}) \leq 1/\epsilon$ for all t. Therefore, to compute $r^{(t-1)} \otimes \ldots \otimes r^{(t-k+1)}$ takes $O(\mu(V^{(\hat{t})})^{(k-1)}) \leq O(1/\epsilon^{(k-1)})$ time. After that, the matrix vector product can be computed in

$$O(\mu(V^{(t)}, \mathbb{N})) \leq O(\mu(V^{(\hat{t})}, \mathbb{N})) \leq O(\mu(V^{(\hat{t})}))^k \leq O(\frac{1}{\epsilon^k}).$$

The truncation in Step 7 can be computed in time $O(|V^{(\hat{t})}|)$. Step 8 to Step 15 require sorting the vertices in $|V^t|$ according to $r^{(t)}$, which takes time $O(|V^{(\hat{t})}| \log |V^{(\hat{t})}|)$. In sum, the time complexity of each iteration in *HOSPLOC* is $O(\frac{1}{\epsilon^k})$.

Since the algorithm runs at most t_{max} iterations, the overall time complexity of *HOSPLOC* is $O(\frac{t_{max}}{\epsilon^k})$. By Eq. 3, we can expand $O(\frac{t_{\max}}{\epsilon^k})$ as follows

$$O\left(\frac{t_{\max}}{\epsilon^k}\right) = O\left(t_{max}\left(\frac{2^b log^3 \mu(V)}{\phi^2}\right)^k\right) = O\left(t_{max}\frac{2^{bk}}{\phi^{2k}} log^{3k} m\right).$$

□

Remark 1: The major computation overhead of Algorithm 1 comes from Step 6. Note that $O\left(t_{max}\frac{2^{bk}}{\phi^{2k}} log^{3k} m\right)$ is a strict upper-bound for considering extreme cases. While, due to the power law distribution in real networks, we may usually have $|V^{(t)}| \le \sqrt{\mu(V^{(t)})}$. Then, the time complexity of Algorithm 1 can be reduced to $O(t_{max}/\epsilon^{k/2}) = O(t_{max}(2^b/\phi^2)^{k/2} log^{3k/2} m)$.

Remark 2: Suppose the maximum iteration number of Nibble and *HOSPLOC* are both upper-bounded by t_{max}, then the time complexity of Nibble is $O\left(\frac{t_{max} 2^b log^4 m}{\phi^2}\right)$. Considering the $k = 3$ case, the time complexity of *HOSPLOC* is $O\left(t_{max}\frac{2^{3b}}{\phi^6} log^9 m\right)$. Without considering the impact from the other constants, we can see that similar to Nibble, *HOSPLOC* also runs in *polylogarithmic* time complexity with respect to the number of edges in the graph.

5 GENERALIZATIONS AND APPLICATIONS

In this section, we will to introduce several generalizations and applications of our proposed *HOSPLOC* algorithm on signed networks, bipartite networks and multipartite networks.

5.1 Community Detection on Signed Network

First, we extend our proposed framework, i.e., *HOSPLOC*, to solve problems on signed graphs. In many real applications, the high-order network structures of interest to us are presented with signed edges. For instance, Fig. 2 presents an unstable 3-node network structure and a stable 3-node network structure based on social status theorem [17]. In community detection [13], we may want to ensure (1) the stable configurations to be rich within communities and sparse in-between different communities; (2) the unstable configurations to be sparse within communities and rich in-between different communities. For this purpose, the adjacency tensor can be constructed as follows

$$T(i_1, i_2, \ldots, i_k) = \begin{cases} 1 & \{i_1, i_2, \ldots, i_k\} \text{ is stable structure} \\ 0 & \{i_1, i_2, \ldots, i_k\} \text{ is unstable structure} \\ \alpha & \text{Otherwise} \end{cases} \quad (20)$$

where $\{i_1, i_2, \ldots, i_k\} \in V$ and constant $0 < \alpha < 1$. By this way, we can ensure: (1) the returned cluster of *HOSPLOC* contains rich stable structures; (2) the partition would most likely break unstable structures.

5.2 Adversarial Learning on Bipartite Network

We now turn our attention to the problem of user behavior modeling on the adversarial networks. Given an adversarial network $B = (V_B, E_B)$, the bipartite graph B contains two types of nodes, i.e., user nodes V_U and advertiser campaign nodes V_A, i.e., $V_B = \{V_U, V_A\}$. The edges E_B only exist between user nodes V_U and advertiser campaign nodes V_A. Intuitively, the customers with similar activities on the adversarial network should be included in the same cluster. For this reason, we choose 4-node loop as the base network structure for *HOSPLOC* algorithm. Specifically, suppose both user nodes u_1, u_2 have user-campaign interactions with the advertiser campaign nodes a_1 and a_2, then we have a 4-node loop, i.e., $u_1 \longrightarrow a_1 \longrightarrow u_2 \longrightarrow a_2 \longrightarrow u_1$. In this problem, we consider the adversarial network as an undirected graph, and the adjacency tensor can be constructed as follows

$$T(i_1, i_2, i_3, i_4) = \begin{cases} 1 & \{i_1, i_2, i_3, i_4\} \text{ form a 4-nodes loop} \\ 0 & \text{Otherwise} \end{cases} \quad (21)$$

where $\{i_1, i_2, i_3, i_4\} \in V_B$. Starting from an initial vertex, the returned cluster C_B by *HOSPLOC* would represent a local user-campaign community, which consists of both similar users and the users' favorite advertiser campaigns.

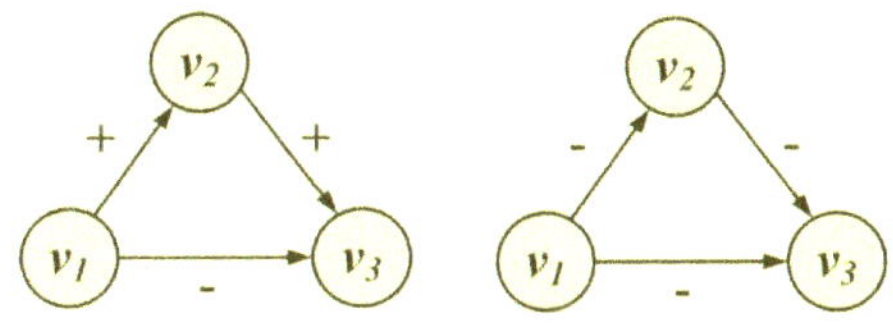

Figure 2: Social Status Theory Example: (Left) A directed "+" edge from node v_1 to node v_2 shows that v_2 has a higher status than v_1. (Right) A directed "-" edge from node v_1 to node v_2 shows vice versa.

5.3 Synthetic ID Detection on Multipartite Network

Now we will explain how to detect synthetic IDs on PII network by using our proposed *HOSPLOC* algorithm. PII network is a typical multipartite network, where each partite set of nodes represents a particular type of PII, such as users' names, users' accounts, and email addresses, and the edges only exist between different partite sets of nodes. In synthetic ID fraud [18], criminals often use modified identity attributes, such as phone number, home address and email address, to combine with real users' information and create synthetic IDs to do malicious activities. Hence, for the synthetic IDs, there is a high possibility that their PIIs would be shared by multiple identities, which may compose rich star-shaped structures. In this case, the adjacency tensor can be constructed as

$$T(i_1, i_2, \ldots, i_k) = \begin{cases} 1 & \{i_1, i_2, \ldots, i_k\} \text{ form a } k\text{-node star} \\ 0 & \text{Otherwise} \end{cases} \quad (22)$$

where $\{i_1, i_2, \ldots, i_k\} \in V_B$. Note that the returned partition may consist of various types of nodes. However, it is viable to trace back from the extracted PII nodes and discover the set of synthetic identities.

6 EXPERIMENTAL RESULTS

Now, we demonstrate the performance of our proposed *HOSPLOC* algorithm in the sense of effectiveness, efficiency, and parameter

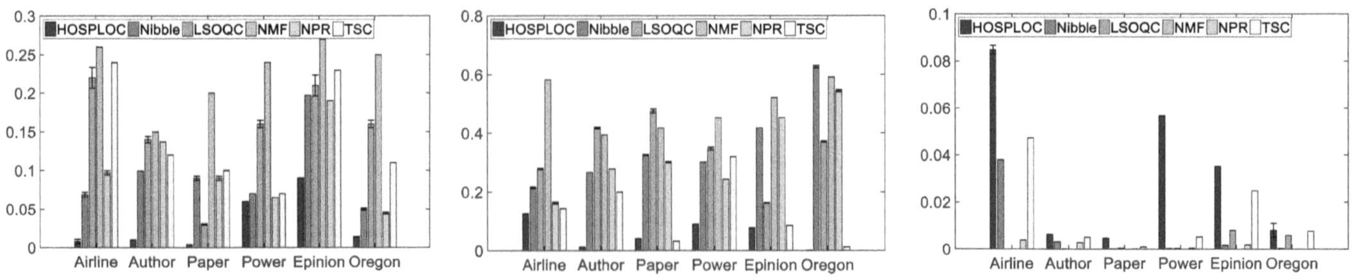

(a) Conductance (b) The 3rd-Order Conductance (c) Triangle Density

Figure 3: Effectiveness.

sensitivity. Moreover, we also present two interesting case studies on bipartite graph and multipartite graph.

6.1 Experiment Setup

Category	Network	Type	Nodes	Edges
Citation	Author	Undirected	61,843	402,074
	Paper	Undirected	62,602	10,904
Infrastructure	Airline	Undirected	2,833	15,204
	Oregon	Undirected	7,352	15,665
	Power	Undirected	4,941	13,188
Social	Epinion	Undirected	75,879	508,837
Review	Rating	Bipartite	8724	90962
Financial	PII	Multipartite	375	519

Table 2: Statistics of the Networks.

Data sets: We evaluate our proposed algorithm on both synthetic and real-world network graphs. The statistics of all real data sets are summarized in Table 2.

- *Collaboration Network:* We use two collaboration networks from*. In network (Author), the nodes are authors, and an edge only exists when two authors have a co-authored paper. In network (Paper), the nodes are distinct papers, and an edge only exists when one paper cites another paper.
- *Infrastructure Network:* In network (Airline)†, the nodes represent 2,833 airports, and the edges represent the U.S. flights in a one-month interval. Network (Oregon) [20] is a network of routers in Autonomous Systems inferred from Oregon route-views between March 31, 2001, and May 26, 2001. Network (Power) ‡ contains the information of the power grid of the western states of U.S. A node represents a generator, a transformator or a substation, and an edge represents a power supply line.
- *Social Network:* Network (Epinion) [20] is a who-trust-whom online social network. Each node represents a user, and one edge exits if and only if when one user trusts another user.
- *Review Network:* Network (Rating) [16] is a bipartite graph, where one side of nodes represent 643 users, and another side of nodes represent 7,483 movies. Edges refer to the positive ratings, i.e., rating score larger than 2.5, on MovieLens website. Note that this network is a subgraph from the original one, due to storing the 4th-order transition tensor of the original graph, i.e., 100s K vertices and millions edges, requires too much memory.
- *Financial Network:* Network (PII) is a multipartite graph, which consists of five types of vertices, i.e., 112 bank accounts, 71 names, 80 emails, 35 addresses, and 77 phone numbers. Edges only exist between account vertices and PII vertices.

Comparison Methods: In our experiments, we compare our methods with both local and global graph clustering methods. Specifically, the comparison algorithm includes three local algorithms, i.e., (1) Nibble [29]; (2) NPR [2]; (3) LS-OQC [31], and two global clustering algorithms, i.e., (1) NMF [12]; (2) TSC [5]. Among these five baseline algorithms, TSC algorithm is designed based on high-order Markov chain, which can model high-order network structures, i.e., triangle.

Repeatability: Most of the data sets are publicly available. The code of the proposed algorithms will be released on the authors' website. For all the results reported, we set $c_1 = 140$ and $\xi = 1$. The experiments are mainly performed on a Windows machine with four 3.5GHz Intel Cores and 256GB RAM.

6.2 Effectiveness Comparison

The effectiveness comparison results conducted on six real undirected graphs by the following three evaluation metrics are shown in Fig. 3. Among them, (1) **Conductance** [7] measures the general quality of a cut on graph, which quantitatively indicates the compactness of a cut; (2) **The 3rd-Order Conductance** could be computed based on Eq. 10 by treating triangle as the network structure $\mathbb{N}$, which estimates how well the network structure $\mathbb{N}$ is preserved in the returned cut from being broken by the partitions; (3) **Triangle Density** [7] computes the ratio of how rich the triangle is included in the returned cluster.

Moreover, to evaluate the convergence of local algorithms, we randomly select 30 vertices from one cluster on each testing graph and run all the local algorithms multiple times by treating each of these nodes as an initial vertex. In Fig. 3, the heights of bars indicate the average value of evaluation metrics, and the error bars (only for local algorithms) represent the standard deviation of evaluation metrics in multiple runs. We have the following observations: (1) In general, local algorithms perform better than the global algorithm, and our *HOSPLOC* algorithm consistently outperforms the others on all the evaluation metrics. For example, compared to the best competitor, i.e., TSC, on network (Airline), *HOSPLOC* algorithm is

*https://aminer.org/data
†http://www.levmuchnik.net/Content/Networks/ NetworkData.html
‡http://konect.uni-koblenz.de/networks/opsahl-powergrid

97% smaller on conductance, 12.2% smaller on the 3rd-order conductance, 80% larger on triangle density. (2) High-order Markov chain models, i.e., *HOSPLOC* and TSC, could better preserve triangles in the returned cluster. For example, on network (Epinion), both *HOSPLOC* and TSC return a cluster with much higher triangle density and much lower the 3rd-order conductance. (3) *HOSPLOC* algorithm shows a more robust convergence property than the other local clustering algorithm by comparing the size of error bars. For example, among the three local algorithms, only *HOSPLOC* algorithm returns the identical cluster on network (Paper) with different initial vertexes.

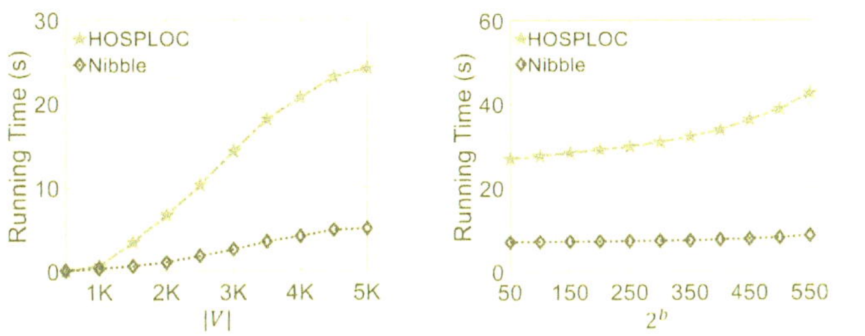

(a) The number of vertices (b) The lower bound of C's volume

Figure 4: Scalability Analysis.

6.3 Scalability Analysis

Here, we evaluate the efficiency of our proposed *HOSPLOC* algorithm with triangle as the specified network structure, by comparing with Nibble algorithm on synthetic graphs. Since our method is built on higher order of random walk than Nibble, we consider Nibble as the running time lower bound of *HOSPLOC* algorithm. Notice that all the results in Fig. 4 are the average values of multiple runs by using 30 different initial vertexes on the same graph. In Fig. 4 (a), we show the running time of *HOSPLOC* and Nibble on a series of synthetic graphs with increasing number of vertices but fixed edge density of 0.5%. We observe that although *HOSPLOC* requires more time than Nibble in each run, the running time of *HOSPLOC* increases *polylogarithmically* with the size of the graph $|V|$. In Fig. 4 (b), we show the running time of *HOSPLOC* and Nibble versus the lower bound of output volume on the synthetic graph with 5000 vertices and 0.5% edge density, by keeping the other parameters fixed. We can see that the running time of *HOSPLOC* is polynomial with respect to 2^b, which is consistent with our time complexity analysis.

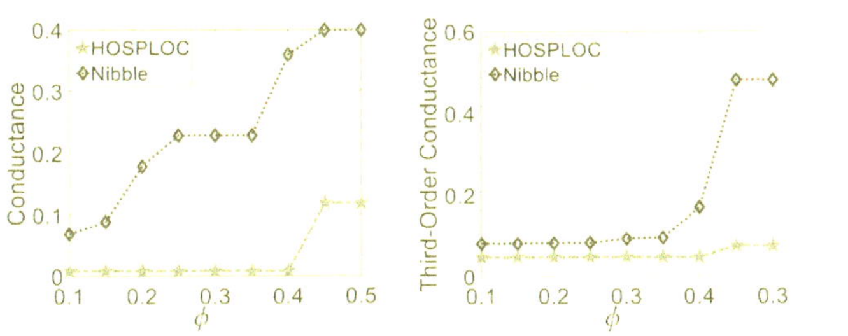

(a) Conductance (b) The 3rd-order conductance

Figure 5: Parameter Analysis w.r.t. Conductance Upper-bound ϕ.

6.4 Parameter Analysis

In this subsection, we analyze the parameter sensitivity of our proposed *HOSPLOC* algorithm with triangle as the specified network structure, by comparing with Nibble algorithm on the synthetic graph with 5000 vertices and 0.5% edge density. In the experiments, we evaluate the conductance and the 3rd-order conductance of the returned cut with different values of input parameter ϕ. In Fig. 5, we have the following observations: (1) *HOSPLOC* returns the optimal cut even with a very lose conductance upper bound ϕ. In Fig. 5 (a), we can see the output conductance of *HOSPLOC* converges to the minimum value when $\phi = 0.4$, while the output conductance of Nibble converges to its minimum value until $\phi = 0.1$. (2) Both the conductance and the 3rd-order conductance of *HOSPLOC*'s cut are always smaller than Nibble's cut with different ϕ.

6.5 Case Study

In this subsection, we will consider more complex network structures and perform our proposed *HOSPLOC* algorithm on bipartite and multipartite networks.

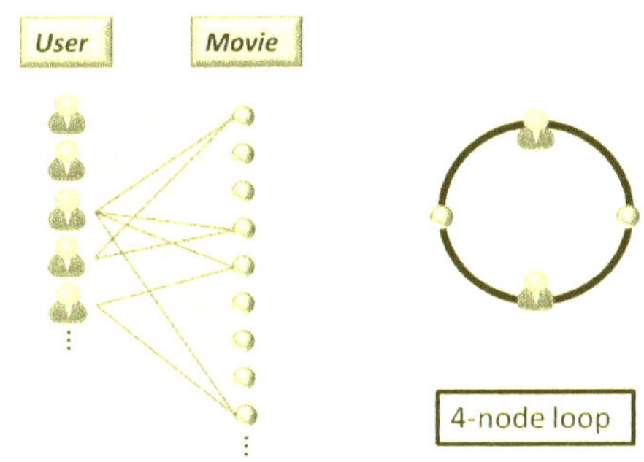

(a) (b)

Figure 6: Case study on bipartite network Rating. (a) An example of detected community by *HOSPLOC* on Rating. (b) An example of 4-node loop on Rating.

Case Study on Bipartite Graph. We conduct a case study on the network (Rating) to find a local community consisting of similar taste users and their favorite movies. In this case study, we construct the transition tensor on the basis of 4-node loop based on Eq. 21. Fig. 6 (a) presents a miniature of the cluster identified by our proposed *HOSPLOC* algorithm regarding 4-node loop that illustrated in Fig. 6 (b). For example, in Fig. 6, the highlighted red loop shows that both of the third and the fourth users like the first and the fourth movies, while the highlighted blue loop represents that both of the third and the fifth users like the fifth and the last movies. It seems the fifth user does not like the first movie due to no direct connection between them. While the interesting part is the first, the fifth and the last movies are from the same series, i.e., Karate Kid I, II, III. Moreover, the fourth movie, i.e., Back to School, and Karate Kid I, II, III, are all from the category of comedy. It turns out that our *HOSPLOC* algorithm returns a community of comedy movies and their fans.

Case Study on Multipartite Graph. Here, we conduct a case study on the network (PII) to identify suspicious systemic IDs. In this case, we treat 5-node star as the underlying network structure, and the corresponding transition tensor could be generated by Eq. 22. Fig. 7 (a) presents a subgraph of the returned cut by our proposed *HOSPLOC* algorithm regarding 5-node star that illustrated in Fig. 7 (b). We can see that many PIIs are highly shared by different accounts. For example, the account connected with blue lines shares the home address and email address with the account connected with purple lines, while the account connected with red lines shares the holder's name and phone number with the account connected with blue lines. Comparing with the regular dense subgraph detection methods, our method can better identify the IDs who share their PIIs with others, by exploring the nature structure of PII, i.e., 5-node star, on the given graph.

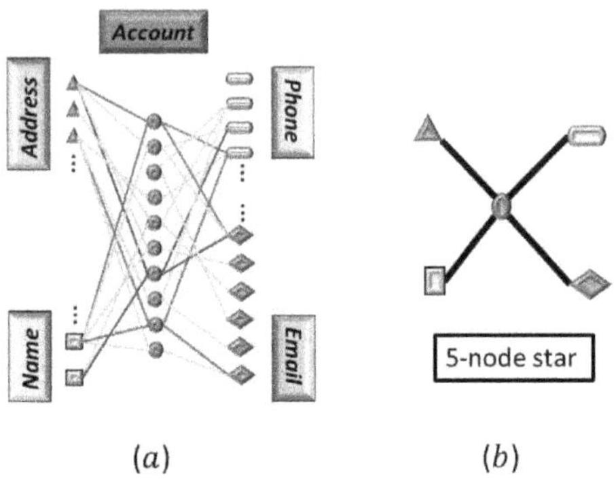

Figure 7: Case study on multipartite network PII. (a) An example of detected community by *HOSPLOC* on PII. (b) An example of 5-node star on PII.

7 CONCLUSION

In this paper, we propose a local clustering framework, i.e., *HOSPLOC*, that gives users the flexibility to model any high-order network structures and returns a small high-order conductance cluster which largely preserves the *user-specified* network structures. Besides, we analyze its performance in terms of the optimality of the obtained cluster and the *polylogarithmic* time complexity on massive graphs. Furthermore, we generalize the proposed *HOSPLOC* algorithm and try to solve multiple real problems on signed networks, bipartite networks and multipartite networks, by exploring the useful high-order network connectivity patterns, such as loops and stars. Finally, the extensive empirical evaluations on a diverse set of networks demonstrate the effectiveness and scalability of our proposed *HOSPLOC* algorithm.

ACKNOWLEDGMENT

This work is supported by National Science Foundation under Grant No. IIP-1430144, No. IIS-1552654 and No. IIS-1651203, ONR under Grant No. N00014-15-1-2821 and No. N00014-16-1-2015, DTRA under Grant No. HDTRA1-16-0017, Army Research Office under the contract number No. W911NF-16-1-0168, National Institutes of Health under the grant number No. R01LM011986, Region II University Transportation Center under the project number No. 49997-33 25, an IBM Faculty Award and a Baidu gift.

REFERENCES

[1] SR A and SR D. 1988. Limit distribution of a high order Markov chain. *J R Stat Soc* (1988).
[2] R. Andersen, F. Chung, and K. Lang. 2006. Local graph partitioning using pagerank vectors. In *IEEE FOCS (2006)*.
[3] R. Andersen, F. Chung, and K. Lang. 2007. Local partitioning for directed graphs using PageRank. In *International Workshop on Algorithms and Models for the Web-Graph*. Springer.
[4] R. Andersen, S. O. Gharan, Y. Peres, and L. Trevisan. 2016. Almost Optimal Local Graph Clustering Using Evolving Sets. *JACM* (2016).
[5] A. R Benson, D. F Gleich, and J. Leskovec. 2015. Tensor spectral clustering for partitioning higher-order network structures. In *SIAM SDM (2015)*.
[6] A. R Benson, D. F Gleich, and L.-H. Lim. 2016. The Spacey Random Walk: A stochastic Process for Higher-Order Data. *arXiv preprint arXiv:1602.02102* (2016).
[7] B Bollobás. 2013. *Modern graph theory*. Springer Science & Business Media (2013).
[8] C. Chen, J. He, N. Bliss, and H. Tong. 2015. On the connectivity of multi-layered networks: Models, measures and optimal control. In *IEEE ICDM (2015)*.
[9] C. Chen, H. Tong, L. Xie, L. Ying, and Q. He. 2016. FASCINATE: Fast Cross-Layer Dependency Inference on Multi-layered Networks. In *ACM SIGKDD (2016)*.
[10] F. Chierichetti, R. Kumar, P. Raghavan, and T. Sarlos. 2012. Are web users really markovian?. In *ACM WWW (2012)*.
[11] K.-K. R. Choo. 2008. *Money laundering risks of prepaid stored value cards*. Australian Institute of Criminology (2008).
[12] C. Ding, T. Li, and M. I Jordan. 2008. Nonnegative matrix factorization for combinatorial optimization: Spectral clustering, graph matching, and clique finding. In *IEEE ICDM (2008)*.
[13] S. Fortunato. 2010. Community detection in graphs. *Physics reports* (2010).
[14] S. O. Gharan and L. Trevisan. 2012. Approximating the expansion profile and almost optimal local graph clustering. In *IEEE FOCS (2012)*.
[15] D. F Gleich, L.-H. Lim, and Y. Yu. 2015. Multilinear PageRank. *SIMAX* (2015).
[16] F M. Harper and J. A Konstan. 2016. The movielens datasets: History and context. *TiiS* (2016).
[17] A. B Hollingshead et al. 1975. Four factor index of social status. (1975).
[18] C. J. Hoofnagle. 2007. Identity theft: Making the known unknowns known. *Harv. JL & Tech.* (2007).
[19] T. Leighton and S. Rao. 1999. Multicommodity max-flow min-cut theorems and their use in designing approximation algorithms. *JACM* (1999).
[20] J. Leskovec and A. Krevl. 2014. SNAP Datasets: Stanford Large Network Dataset Collection. http://snap.stanford.edu/data. (June 2014).
[21] J. Li, H. Dani, X. Hu, and H. Liu. 2017. Radar: Residual Analysis for Anomaly Detection in Attributed Networks. In *IJCAI (2017)*.
[22] J. Li, X. Hu, L. Jian, and H. Liu. 2016. Toward Time-Evolving Feature Selection on Dynamic Networks. In *IEEE ICDM (2016)*.
[23] W. Li and M. K Ng. 2014. On the limiting probability distribution of a transition probability tensor. *Linear and Multilinear Algebra* (2014).
[24] L. Lovász and M. Simonovits. 1990. The mixing rate of Markov chains, an isoperimetric inequality, and computing the volume. In *IEEE FOCS (1990)*.
[25] L. Lovász and M. Simonovits. 1993. Random walks in a convex body and an improved volume algorithm. *Random structures & algorithms* (1993).
[26] A. E Raftery. 1985. A model for high-order Markov chains. *J R Stat Soc Series B Stat Methodol* (1985).
[27] M. Rosvall, A. V Esquivel, A. Lancichinetti, J. D West, and R. Lambiotte. 2014. Memory in network flows and its effects on spreading dynamics and community detection. *Nature communications* (2014).
[28] J. Šíma and S. E. Schaeffer. 2006. On the NP-completeness of some graph cluster measures. In *Springer SOFSEM (2006)*.
[29] D. A Spielman and S.-H. Teng. 2013. A local clustering algorithm for massive graphs and its application to nearly linear time graph partitioning. *SICOMP* (2013).
[30] J. L Teugels. 2008. Markov Chains: Models, Algorithms and Applications. *JASA* (2008).
[31] C. Tsourakakis, F. Bonchi, A. Gionis, F. Gullo, and M. Tsiarli. 2013. Denser than the densest subgraph: extracting optimal quasi-cliques with quality guarantees. In *ACM SIGKDD (2013)*.
[32] C. E Tsourakakis, J. Pachocki, and M. Mitzenmacher. 2017. Scalable motif-aware graph clustering. In *WWW (2017)*.
[33] T. Wu, A. R Benson, and D. F Gleich. 2016. General tensor spectral co-clustering for higher-order data. In *NIPS (2016)*.
[34] D. Zhou, J. He, K.-S. Candan, and H. Davulcu. 2015. MUVIR: Multi-View Rare Category Detection.. In *IJCAI (2015)*.
[35] D. Zhou, J. He, Y. Cao, and J. Seo. 2016. Bi-level Rare Temporal Pattern Detection. In *IEEE ICDM (2016)*.
[36] D. Zhou, A. Karthikeyan, K. Wang, N. Cao, and J. He. 2016. Discovering rare categories from graph streams. *Springer DMKD* (2016).
[37] D. Zhou, K. Wang, N. Cao, and J. He. 2015. Rare category detection on time-evolving graphs. In *IEEE ICDM (2015)*.
[38] Y. Zhou and J. He. 2016. Crowdsourcing via tensor augmentation and completion. In *IJCAI (2016)*.
[39] Y. Zhou, L. Ying, and J. He. 2017. MultiC2: an Optimization Framework for Learning from Task and Worker Dual Heterogeneity. In *SIAM SDM (2017)*.

Anomaly Detection with Robust Deep Autoencoders

Chong Zhou
Worcester Polytechnic Institute
100 Institute Road
Worcester, MA 01609
czhou2@wpi.edu

Randy C. Paffenroth
Worcester Polytechnic Institute
100 Institute Road
Worcester, MA 01609
rcpaffenroth@wpi.edu

ABSTRACT

Deep autoencoders, and other deep neural networks, have demonstrated their effectiveness in discovering non-linear features across many problem domains. However, in many real-world problems, large outliers and pervasive noise are commonplace, and one *may not have access to clean training data* as required by standard deep denoising autoencoders. Herein, we demonstrate novel extensions to deep autoencoders which not only maintain a deep autoencoders' ability to discover high quality, non-linear features but can also eliminate outliers and noise *without access to any clean training data*. Our model is inspired by Robust Principal Component Analysis, and we split the input data X into two parts, $X = L_D + S$, where L_D can be effectively reconstructed by a deep autoencoder and S contains the outliers and noise in the original data X. Since such splitting increases the robustness of standard deep autoencoders, we name our model a "Robust Deep Autoencoder (RDA)". Further, we present generalizations of our results to grouped sparsity norms which allow one to distinguish random anomalies from other types of structured corruptions, such as a collection of features being corrupted across many instances or a collection of instances having more corruptions than their fellows. Such "Group Robust Deep Autoencoders (GRDA)" give rise to novel anomaly detection approaches whose superior performance we demonstrate on a selection of benchmark problems.

KEYWORDS

Autoencoders; Robust Deep Autoencoders; Group Robust Deep Autoencoder; Denoising; Anomaly Detection

1 INTRODUCTION

Deep learning is part of a broad family of methods for representation learning [11], and it has been quite successful in pushing forward the state-of-the-art in multiple areas [9–11, 29]. In particular, herein we focus on deep autoencoders which construct representations based on non-linear combinations of input features, and where the non-linearity is classically introduced by way of some non-linear activation function [11]. Unfortunately, outliers and noise may reduce the quality of representations discovered by deep autoencoders [15, 16]. There is a large extent literature which attempts to address this challenge and two approaches include *denoising autoencoders* and *maximum correntropy autoencoders*. Denoising autoencoders [9, 17, 23, 30, 31], require access to a source of clean, noise-free data for training, and such data is not always readily available in real-world problems [28]. On the other hand, maximum correntropy autoencoders replace the reconstruction cost with a noise-resistant criteria *correntropy* [22]. However, such a model still trains the hidden layer of the autoencoder on corrupted data, and the feature quality of the hidden layer may still be influenced by training data with a large fraction of corruptions.

As we will detail, our model isolates noise and outliers in the input, and the autoencoder is trained after this isolation. Thus, our method promises to provide a representation at the hidden layers which is more faithful to the true representation of the noise-free data.

1.1 Contribution

Herein we show how denoising autoencoders can be generalized to the case where no clean, noise-free data is available, and we demonstrate the superior performance of our proposed methods using standard benchmark problems such as the MNIST data set [12]. We call such algorithms *"Robust Deep Autoencoders (RDA)"*, and our proposed models improve upon normal deep autoencoders by introducing an anomaly regularizing penalty based upon either ℓ_1 or $\ell_{2,1}$ norms. Using such a regularizing penalty, we derive a training algorithm for the proposed model by combining ideas from proximal methods [4], backpropagation [24], and the Alternating Direction of Method of Multipliers (ADMM) [3]. As an interesting consequence of the development of such RDAs, we have also derived a novel family of unsupervised anomaly detection algorithms. We demonstrate the effectiveness of these anomaly detection algorithm, as compared to a baseline approach, on a number of challenging benchmark problems.

In particular, we emphasize that our proposed methods differ from standard techniques in two important ways.

- First, our methods *differ from standard denoising autoencoders* [28] in that they do not require any noise-free training data. Rather, our methods compute the entries on which the autoencoder loss function is enforced *on-the-fly* based upon the performance of the underlying autoencoder algorithm.
- Second, our methods *differ from standard sparse autoencoders* [13] in that we do not penalize the sparsity of the hidden layer. Rather, our methods allow for a sparse set

KDD '17, August 13-17, 2017, Halifax, NS, Canada

978-1-4503-4887-4/17/08...$15.00
DOI: 10.1145/3097983.3098052

of *exceptions* to the enforcement of the autoencoder loss function.

2 BACKGROUND

We begin the derivation of our methods by providing a brief introduction to non-linear feature representation by way of deep autoencoders. We also present a few foundational ideas from Robust Principal Component Analysis (RPCA) which are classically used to construct low-dimensional *linear* features by filtering out outlying measurements using a convex relaxation of the rank operator [6, 20].

2.1 Deep Autoencoders

A deep autoencoder is a feed-forward multi-layer neural network in which the desired output is the input itself. Upon first glance, this process may seem trivial since the identity mapping would have no reconstruction error. However, autoencoders become non-trivial when the identity map is disallowed either by way of some type of regularization or, more importantly for the current derivation, by having hidden layers which are a *low-dimensional*, non-linear representation of the input data.

In particular, autoencoders learn a map from the input to itself through a pair of encoding and decoding phases

$$\overline{X} = D(E(X)) \tag{1}$$

where X is the input data, E is an encoding map from the input data to the hidden layer, D is a decoding map from the hidden layer to the output layer, and $\overline{X}$ is the recovered version of the input data. The idea is to train E and D to minimize the difference between X and $\overline{X}$.

In particular, an autoencoder can be viewed as a solution to the following optimization problems:

$$\min_{D,E} ||X - D(E(X))|| \tag{2}$$

where $|| \cdot ||$ is commonly chosen to be the ℓ_2-norm.

Usually, an autoencoder with more than one hidden layers is called a deep autoencoder [11]and each additional hidden layer requires an additional pair of encoders $E(\cdot)$ and decoders $D(\cdot)$. By allowing many layers of encoders and decoders, a deep autoencoder can effectively represent complicated distributions over the input X. In the sequel, our focus will be on deep autoencoders with all autoencoders assumed to be deep.

2.2 Robust Principal Component Analysis

Robust Principal Component Analysis (RPCA) [6, 7, 20] is a generalization of Principal Component Analysis (PCA) [8] that attempts to reduce the sensitivity of PCA to outliers. In particular, RPCA allows for the careful teasing apart of sparse outliers so that the remaining low-dimensional approximation is faithful to the noise-free low-dimensional subspace describing the bulk of the raw data [6, 7, 20].

Specifically, RPCA splits a data matrix X into a low-rank matrix L and a sparse matrix S such that

$$X = L + S. \tag{3}$$

The matrix L contains a low-dimensional representation of X [6, 7, 20] and the matrix S consists of element-wise outliers, which can not be efficiently captured by the low-dimensional representation L.

Naively, this matrix decomposition can be computed by way of the following optimization problem [6, 7]

$$\begin{aligned} &\min_{L,S} \rho(L) + \lambda||S||_0 \\ &\text{s.t. } ||X - L - S||_F^2 = 0, \end{aligned} \tag{4}$$

where $\rho(L)$ is the rank of L, $||S||_0$ is the number of non-zero entries in S, and $|| \cdot ||_F$ is the Frobenius norm. However, the non-convex optimization (4) is NP-hard [6, 7] and only computationally tractable for small matrices X. However, there is a large literature [6, 7, 20] on convex relaxations of this class of problems, such as

$$\begin{aligned} &\min_{L,S} ||L||_* + \lambda||S||_1 \\ &\text{s.t. } ||X - L - S||_F^2 = 0, \end{aligned} \tag{5}$$

where the $|| \cdot ||_*$ is the nuclear norm (i.e., the sum of the singular values of the matrix) and $|| \cdot ||_1$ is the one norm (i.e., the sum of the absolute values of the entries).

While optimization (4) is NP-hard, optimization (5) is convex and can be solved for large data matrices X. With this idea, the key insight of our method can be succinctly described. It is well known [10] that, when one considers a Frobenius loss function and constrains the autoencoder D and E (2) to be linear maps, that PCA is an optimal autoencoder. *Accordingly, our method can be viewed as replacing the nuclear norm in (5), which results in a linear projection to a low-dimensional hidden layer, with a non-linear autoencoder, which results in a non-linear projection to a low-dimensional hidden layer.*

Of course, one must therefore solve (5) but with a more complicated objective function. However, using ideas such as the Alternating Direction Method of Multipliers [3], we demonstrate how one can address such problems by combining standard off-the-shelf solvers for optimizing a deep autoencoder with standard techniques for optimizing proximal problems involving the ℓ_1 or other similar penalties [4, 20].

3 METHODOLOGY

In this section we provide the derivation of our proposed methodologies for constructing *Robust Deep Autoencoders*, which we view as a combination of autoencoders and robust principal component analysis. The central idea is that a RDA inherits the non-linear representation capabilities of autoencoders combined with the anomaly detection capabilities of RPCA. The key insight is that noise and outliers[1] are essentially incompressible and therefore cannot effectively be projected to a low-dimensional hidden layer by an autoencoder. In particular, if exceptions could be allowed to the autoencoder loss function, then the low-dimensional hidden layer could provide accurate reconstruction, with a low-dimensional hidden layer, *except for those few exceptions.* Just as in RPCA, when the noise and outliers are isolated into S, the remaining data L_D

[1]In this paper, the term "noise" implies the element-wise noise, the "outlier" implies the row-wise outlying instance and the "anomalies" implies both.

can be accureately reconstructed by an autoencoder with such a low-dimensional hidden layer.

3.1 Robust Deep Autoencoders with ℓ_1 Regularization

Inspired by RPCA, we augment autoencoders with a filter layer. The filter layer culls out the anomalous parts of the data that are difficult to reconstruct, and the remaining portion of the data can be represented by the low-dimensional hidden layer with small reconstruction error.

Similar to RPCA, a Robust Deep Autoencoder also splits input data X into two parts $X = L_D + S$, where L_D represents the part of the input data that is well represented by the hidden layer of the autoencoder, and S contains noise and outliers which are difficult to reconstruct. By removing the noise and outliers from X, the autoencoder can more perfectly recover the remaining L_D. To achieve this property, our loss function for a given input X could be thought of as the ℓ_0 norm of S, which counts the number of non-zero entries in S, balanced against the reconstruction error of L_D, as in the optimization problem

$$\begin{aligned} \min_{\theta} \; & ||L_D - D_\theta(E_\theta(L_D))||_2 + \lambda||S||_0 \\ \text{s.t. } & X - L_D - S = 0, \end{aligned} \tag{6}$$

where $E_\theta(\cdot)$ denotes an encoder, $D_\theta(\cdot)$ denotes a decoder, and S captures the anomalous data, L_D is a low dimension manifold and λ is a parameter that tunes the level of sparsity in S. *λ plays an essential role in our analysis.* In particular, a small λ will encourage much of the data to be isolated into S as noise or outliers, and therefore minimize the reconstruction error for the autoencoder. Similarly, a large λ will discourage data from being isolated into S as noise or outliers, and therefore increase the reconstruction error for the autoencoder.

Foreshadowing our results in Section 5, we note that we make extensive use of the λ parameter in our numerical results. In particular, one can tune λ depending on the desired use of the robust autoencoder. For example, λ can be tuned to maximize the performance of the features provided by the hidden layer in some supervised learning problems or λ can be tuned to optimize false alarm rates in unsupervised anomaly detection problems.

Unfortunately, the optimization problem in (6) is not computationally tractable, just as is (4). However, following the RPCA literature [6, 7, 20], one can relax the combinatorial $||S||_0$ term of the optimization (6) by replacing it with a convex relaxation $||S||_1$, giving rise to the optimization

$$\begin{aligned} \min_{\theta} \; & ||L_D - D_\theta(E_\theta(L_D))||_2 + \lambda||S||_1 \\ \text{s.t. } & X - L_D - S = 0. \end{aligned} \tag{7}$$

Notice that in the constraint of (7) we split the input data X into two parts, L_D and S. L_D is the input to an autoencoder $D_\theta(E_\theta(L_D))$ and we train this autoencoder by minimizing the reconstruction error $||L_D - D_\theta(E_\theta(L_D))||_2$ through back-propagation. S, on the other hand, contains noise and outliers which are difficult to represent using the autoencoder $D_\theta(E_\theta(\cdot))$.

Note, while the objective $||L_D - D_\theta(E_\theta(L_D))||_2$ does not specify any particular form for the encoding and decoding pair E and D, herein we follow the standard practice of having

$$E_\theta(x) = E_{W,b}(x) = \text{logit}(Wx + b_E)$$

and

$$D_\theta(x) = D_{W,b}(x) = \text{logit}(W^T E_{W,b}(x) + b_D)$$

[11].

3.2 Robust Deep Autoencoders with $\ell_{2,1}$ Regularization

Our basic RDA in Section 3.1 assumes that the noise and outliers are unstructured, and thus we have used a generic ℓ_1 penalty on S to introduce element-wise sparsity. However, in many cases we may have anomalies that are structured.

In particular, we can view our training data as a matrix where each row is a data *instance*, such as a picture in an image processing application or a packet in a network analysis application, while each column is a *feature*, such as a pixel in an image or a particular byte in a packet. An example of such a data matrix is shown in Figure 1.

Accordingly, we treat two different types of *group anomalies*. First, we have the case where a particular feature is corrupted across many instances. For example, perhaps a digital camera has a bad pixel in its image plane. Second, we have the case where a particular instance is anomalous across many different features. For example, one may have a picture of a 7 mixed into a group of pictures all of which are otherwise pictures of 2s, as in Figure 1. As a consequence, we have developed additional techniques that group errors across elements in S to enhance anomaly detection. In particular, both cases can easily be treated by our methods by generalizing the ℓ_1 penalty to a grouped $\ell_{2,1}$ norm [2].

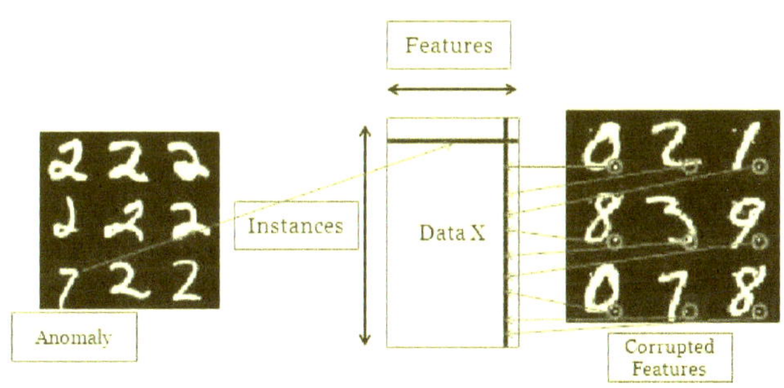

Figure 1: This figure shows two examples of group anomalies. For example, on the left, we see a collection of 2s corrupted by a single 7. This corresponds to a row of X being anomalous. Similarly, on the right, we see a collection of digits where a particular pixel is always on. This corresponds to a column of X being anomalous. Our structured $\ell_{2,1}$ penalty is intended to address both of these cases.

3.3 Anomalous Feature and Instance Detection

In particular, the $\ell_{2,1}$ norm can be defined as

$$||X||_{2,1} = \sum_{j=1}^{n} ||x_j||_2 = \sum_{j=1}^{n} (\sum_{i=1}^{m} |x_{ij}|^2)^{1/2} \tag{8}$$

and, it can be viewed as inducing a ℓ_2 norm regularizer over members of each group and then a ℓ_1 norm regularizer between groups [19]. Similarly, if we want to group the elements of a row and then look for sparse anomalies among the collection of rows, we merely need to look at the transpose of X and use $||X^T||_{2,1}$.

With definition (8) in mind, we can pose the following optimization problem

$$\begin{aligned} \min_{\theta,S} & \ ||L_D - D_\theta(E_\theta(L_D))||_2 + \lambda||S||_{2,1} \\ \text{s.t.} & \ X - L_D - S = 0, \end{aligned} \tag{9}$$

where the terms are defined as in (7) except the ℓ_1 norm has been replaced by the grouped norm $\ell_{2,1}$.

Similarly, if we are interested in analyzing data with anomalous data instances, then we merely need to consider the following optimization problem using the grouped penalty $\ell_{2,1}$ on S^T:

$$\begin{aligned} \min_{\theta,S} & \ ||L_D - D_\theta(E_\theta(L_D))||_2 + \lambda||S^T||_{2,1} \\ \text{s.t.} & \ X - L_D - S = 0. \end{aligned} \tag{10}$$

4 ALGORITHM TRAINING

In this section we provide the details of our methodology for solving problems such as (7), (9), and (10). In particular, we are inspired by ideas such as the Alternating Direction Method of Multipiers [4] and R. L. Dykstra's alternating projection method [5][2]. As we will detail, we iteratively optimize each of the terms in (7), (9), and (10) separately, interspersed with projections onto the constraint manifold. Note, since our full objective is not convex, the convergence of the method to a global minimum is non-trivial to guarantee. In particular, even the minimization of just the autoencoder $||L_D - D_\theta(E_\theta(L_D))||_2$ cannot, in full generality, be guaranteed to find a global minimizer [29]. However, as we will demonstrate in Section 5, we have substantial empirical evidence that the optimization algorithm we present below provides high-quality solutions.

4.1 Alternating Optimization for ℓ_1 and $\ell_{2,1}$ Robust Deep Autoencoder

The key insight of the Alternating Direction Method of Multipliers (ADMM) [4] is to divide the objective we wish to minimize into two (or more) pieces. One then optimizes with respect to one of the pieces while keeping the other pieces fixed. Accordingly, as inspired by the RPCA literature [6, 7, 20] we split the objective in (7), (9), and (10) into a first piece which depends on L_D and is independent of S, namely $||L_D - D_\theta(E_\theta(L_D))||_2$, and a second piece which depends on S and is independent of L_D.

Back-propagation [10] is a typical training algorithm for deep learning and it is precisely the method we use for optimizing the term $||L_D - D_\theta(E_\theta(L_D))||_2$ when S is held constant. However, the terms such as $||S||_1$, $||S||_{2,1}$, and $||S^T||_{2,1}$ are more delicate since they are not differentiable. However, such non-differentiable terms can be phrased as proximal gradient problems [4], whose solution we will detail in Sections 4.2 and 4.3. To combine these two parts, we follow the idea of an ADMM [3, 4] and Dykstra's alternating projection method [5]. In effect, we use a back-propagation method to train an autoencoder to minimize $||L_D - D(E(L_D))||_2$ with S fixed, a proximal gradient to minimize the penalty term $||S||_1$ or $||S||_{2,1}$ with L_D fixed, and after each minimization we use element-wise projections $S = X - L_D$ and $L_D = X - S$ to enforce the constraints.

[2] Not to be confused with E. W. Dijkstra's algorithm for shortest paths in graphs

The following is our proposed optimizing method:

Input: $X \in R^{N \times n}$
Initialize $L_D \in R^{N\times n}, S \in R^{N\times n}$ to be zero matrices, $LS = X$, and an autoencoder $D(E(\cdot))$ with randomly initialized parameters.

while(True):
1. Remove S from X, using the remainder to train the autoencoder. (In the first iteration, since S is the zero matrix, the autoencoder $D(E(\cdot))$ is given the input X):
$L_D = X - S$
2. Minimize the first term $||L_D - D(E(L_D))||_2$ using back-propagation.
3. Set L_D to be the reconstruction from the trained autoencoder:
$L_D = D(E(L_D))$
4. Set S to be the difference between X and L_D:
$S = X - L_D$
5. Optimize S using a proximal operator:
$S = prox_{\lambda, l_{2,1}}(S)$
or:
$S = prox_{\lambda, l_1}(S)$
6.1 Check the convergence condition that L_D and S are close to the input X thereby satisfying the constraint:
$c_1 = ||X - L_D - S||_2 \ / \ ||X||_2$
6.2 Check the convergence condition that L_D and S have converged to a fixed point:
$c_2 = ||LS - L_D - S||_2 \ / \ ||X||_2$
if $c_1 < \varepsilon$ or $c_2 < \varepsilon$:
break
7. Update LS for convergence checking in the next iteration:
$LS = L_D + S$
Return L_D and S

4.2 Proximal Method for ℓ_1 Norm

The ℓ_1 norm can be optimized efficiently through the use of a proximal method [3, 4] such as

$$prox_{\lambda, l_1}(x_i) = \begin{cases} x_i - \lambda, & x_i > \lambda \\ x_i + \lambda, & x_i < -\lambda \\ 0, & x_i \in [-\lambda, \lambda]. \end{cases} \tag{11}$$

Such a function is known as a *shrinkage* operator and is quite common in ℓ_1 optimization problems. For additional details see [4].

The following pseudo-code provides an implementation of proximal operator $prox_{\lambda, l_1}(S)$:

Input: $S \in R^{m\times n}, \lambda$

```
For i in 1 to m × n:
    if S[i] > λ :
        S[i] = S[i] − λ
        continue
    if S[i] < −λ :
        S[i] = S[i] + λ
        continue
    if −λ <= S[i] <= λ :
        S[i] = 0
        continue
Return S
```

4.3 Proximal Method for $\ell_{2,1}$ Norm

Similar to (11) the $\ell_{2,1}$ norm minimization problem can also be phrased as a proximal problem, but in a slightly more complicated form. In particular, the proximal operator for the $\ell_{2,1}$ norm is a block-wise soft-thresholding function [3, 18, 19]

$$(prox_{\lambda,l_{2,1}}(x))^j = \begin{cases} x_g^j - \lambda \frac{x_g^j}{||x_g||_2}, & ||x_g||_2 > \lambda \\ 0, & ||x_g||_2 <= \lambda, \end{cases} \quad (12)$$

where the g is a group index and j is a within-group index. This optimization combines elements x_j into blocks and thus the element-wise sparsity from (11) becomes block-wise sparsity. For additional details see [4].

The following pseudo-code provides an implementation of proximal operator $prox_{\lambda,l_{2,1}}(S)$:

```
Input: S ∈ R^{m×n}, λ
For j in 1 to n:
    e_j = ( Σ_{i=1}^{m} |S[i,j]|^2 )^{1/2}
    if e_j > λ :
        For i in 1 to m:
            S[i,j] = S[i,j] − λ S[i,j]/e_j
        continue
    if e_j <= λ :
        For i in 1 to m:
            S[i,j] = 0
        continue
Return S
```

5 NUMERICAL RESULTS

In this section we demonstrate the effectiveness of our propose robust autoencoders using the well-known image recognition MNIST data set [12]. The training set consists of 50,000 instances, and each instance is a 28×28 pixel image. Each image is labeled as a digit ranging from "0" to "9". However, as we will detail in the sequel, rather than merely considering the original MNIST data set, we corrupt the base images with noise and outliers to demonstrate and validate the various capabilities of our approaches.

5.1 Implementation Details

We build our implementation of a RDA using the Google machine learning library, Tensorflow, version 0.12.0rc0 [1] and Theano version 0.9 [26]. We ran our experiments on a virtual machine running an Ubuntu 14.04.3 image with 2 CPUs, and 4 GB memory. The image is run on hardware provided the NSF Jetstream Cloud [25, 27].

As is standard in the literature [11], we specify the encoder $E(\cdot)$ of each layer as $E(X) = g(X \cdot W + b_E)$, where X is our input data, g is an activation function, W is a projection from the input dimension to a lower dimensional hidden layer and b is a bias term. The decoder $D(\cdot)$ of each decoding layer is $\overline{X} = D(X) = g(E(X) \cdot W^T + b_D)$, where W^T projects a low-dimensional hidden layer back to the higher input dimension. We choose $g(\cdot)$ to be the sigmoid function $g(t) = \frac{1}{1+\exp^{-t}}$.

The TensorFlow based autoencoder is the building block of our implementation and makes use of the following pseudo-code interface:

```
Initialize an autoencoder with sizes of each layer
    .init(layer_sizes)
Training the autoencoder, given data X
    .fit(X, iter, batch_size)
After training, get the hidden layer value
    .transform(X)
```

Our code is available on Github at: https://github.com/zc8340311/RobustAutoencoder/tree/master/lib

5.2 ℓ_1 Robust Deep Autoencoder for Denoising

In Figure 2, we show the key results for our proposed ℓ_1 penalized Robust Deep Autoencoder as compared against a standard autoencoder. Our experiment consists of taking the digits from the MNIST data set and corrupting them with various levels of noise. In particular, we randomly pick a certain number of the pixels for each instance, and we set the pixel value to 0 if the original pixel value is larger than 0.5, and we set the pixel value to 1 otherwise.

Then, these corrupted images are used to train a normal autoencoder and a RDA each with exactly the same number and breadth of layers. In particular, we use two hidden layers which project the input data from 784 dimensions to 196 dimensions, and then project 196 dimensions to 49 dimensions.

Both models are only trained on corrupted images and neither of them has any extra information, e.g. the labels of the images or any clean images. After training, we extract the dimension reduced features from their hidden layers.

To judge the quality of the features produced by our hidden layers we use the following procedure. In particular, we use the values in the hidden layer as features for a supervised classifier. We split the data with 1/3 of the instances as a testing set and the remaining 2/3 as a training set. The quality of features produced by the various autoencoders are judged by the prediction accuracy of the classifier on the test set. For our supervised classifier, we choose a random forest as implemented in the scikit-learn package, version 0.18, [21]. We use 50 trees in the forest and leave the remaining parameters for the classifier at their default values (e.g., each tree has access to a number features equal to the square root of the total number of input features). Note, we do not choose a state-of-the-art supervised learning method for this problem since the supervised learning method is merely used to assess the performance of the features provided by the (robust) autoencoder's hidden layers. We leverage the random forest to offer a fair comparison environment, which is consistent through all experiments.

For a fixed supervised classifier, we presume that higher test error rates are indicative of lower feature quality. With the above details in mind, Figure 2 demonstrates how the features provided by an autoencoder's hidden layer are corrupted by the noise in the images, while the robust autoencoder's hidden layers are more faithful representations of the original noiseless images, even though the RDA was trained using *only corrupted imagery*.

In the Figure 2, from left to right, the input X has a larger and larger fraction of corrupted pixels. As specified by our noise model, the number of corrupted pixels ranges from 10 to 350 (out of 784) per image. From bottom to top, the λ value grows from 0.1 to 100. In particular, we can see the Robust Deep Autoencoders and normal autoencoders get similar test errors when there are few corruptions, e.g. 10 to 50 corrupted pixels for each image (as shown in Figure 2 by case ①). This fact should not be surprising, since for such images the ℓ_1 penalty does not play a pivotal role.

However, when the noise increases, for example in the cases of area ② in Figure 2, and one has from 80 to 300 corrupted pixels per image, and *the normal autoencoder has up to 30% higher error rates than the Robust Deep Autoencoders!* The red areas in Figure 2 indicate those experiments where noise has significantly reduced the feature quality provided by the autoencoder's hidden layer, while the Robust Deep Autoencoder's hidden layer is immune to the noise, due to S and the ℓ_1 penalty. Also, from a more qualitative point of view, one also finds that the reconstructed images from the Robust Deep Autoencoders are *cleaner* digits and might be more desirable for consumption by a human analyst. Finally, when the fraction of corrupted pixels continues to grow, say about above 300 corrupted pixels per image, in the cases of area ③ in Figure 2, neither model can produce high-quality features and the testing accuracy of both methods is again the same.

5.3 $\ell_{2,1}$ Robust Deep Autoencoder for Outlier Detection

Our anomaly detection experiments begin by gathering images of the digit "4" from the MNIST dataset, and these images will comprise our nominal data. This nominal data is then corrupted by mixing in images which are randomly sampled from other digit's images (e.g. "0", "7","9" etc.). The mixed data contains 4859 nominal instances and 265 anomalies. Accordingly, the ratio of anomalies to total number of instances in this set is about 5.2%. Our experimental setup is shown in Figure 3.

We train an $\ell_{2,1}$ RDA using the mixed data without providing any side information (such as which images are actually "4"). It is our goal that the $\ell_{2,1}$ RDA should automatically pick out the high reconstruction error anomalies and isolate these outliers into S. The performances of the $\ell_{2,1}$ RDA can then be assessed by comparing the predicted outlying instances in S and the true outliers whose label we know.

Figure 3: This figure shows the first 100 image instances for our outlier detection task. In this experiment, the "4" digits are nominal, and all other digits are considered as anomalies.

In this instance, the layer sizes of the RDA are 784, 400, and 200. [3] To get the optimal value of λ, we search a range from $1e-05$ to $1.5e-04$ with layer sizes fixed and only judge the λ value based on its F1-score for detecting outliers [8]. Figure 4 shows a set of examples that are intended to provide the reader within intuition as to how λ influences the predictions and sparsity of S when using the $\ell_{2,1}$ norm.

Figure 5 shows the results of our anomaly detection experiment. We wish to emphasize that the entire experiment is unsupervised, except for the training of *the single parameter λ*.

In particular, the training of the $\ell_{2,1}$ RDA is fully unsupervised, and the $\ell_{2,1}$ RDA is only trained with unlabeled images. Tuning the λ parameter makes the algorithm semi-supervised in that we use the F1-score to select the optimal λ value. The idea is that the optimal choice for λ does not revolve around the particular form of the anomalies. Rather, the choice of λ revolves around ensuring that all nominal instances are represented by L_D. In other words, λ is not chosen based on the anomalous instances, it is chosen based on the normal instances.

As shown in Figure 4 our experiment proceeds as follows. λ is used to control the sparsity of S. In particular, a small λ places a small penalty on S, and the RDA emphasizes minimizing the reconstruction error by marking many images as anomalous and giving rise to many false-positives. λ then can be increased to trade-off false-positives for false-negatives. Accordingly, the optimal λ should balance both false-positive and false-negative rates. Thus, we use the F1-score to select the optimal λ.

To validate the performance of our outlier and anomaly detection methods, we compare our model against a state-of-the-art outlier detection method, namely the Isolation Forest [14]. The key idea of Isolation forests is that anomalies are

[3]Note, for this experiment we do not use a normal autoencoder.

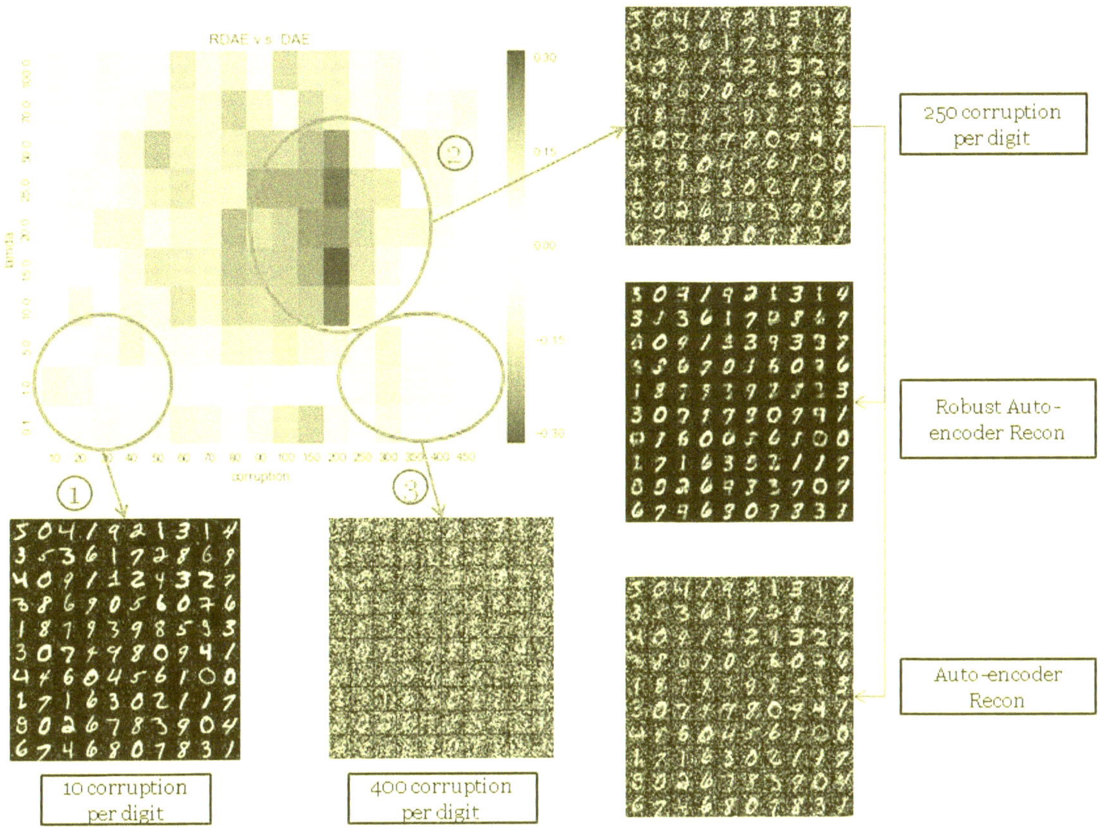

Figure 2: This figure shows the difference between error rates for the features constructed by a normal autoencoder and a RDA. Red indicates where the error rates of the RDA are superior to those of the normal autoencoder, and blue indicates where the converse is true. The errors rates are bases upon the prediction of image labels with respect to different degrees of corruption and different values of λ in the Robust Deep Autoencoders. The x-axis shows different corruption levels, and the y-axis shows different λ values. The two images on the bottom, indicated with ① and ③, show examples of images with the designated amount of corrupted pixels. As can be seen, the images range from very modest corruptions to those in which the original digits cannot be seen. Most importantly, the area marked by ② shows a large region, covering many different levels of corruption and values of λ, in which the RDA performs better than the standard autoencoder on the image classification task. In particular, for some levels of corruption, and values of λ, the robust auto-encode performs up to 30% better. On the right, we show several examples of images from the red area. As can be seen, the original images on top are quite corrupted, while the images in the middle, produced from the Robust Deep Autoencoder's output layer, are largely noise free. However, the standard autoencoder, as it only has noisy imagery on which to train, faithfully, but inappropriately, reproduces the noise.

'few and different', which make them more susceptible to isolation than normal points [14].

We use the Isolation Forests model as implemented by version 0.18.1 of the scikit-learn package [21]. The isolation forest model take two variables: the number of trees and the fraction of outliers. We fix the number of trees to 100 and optimize over the outlier fraction from 0.01 to 0.69 (similiar to the optimization of λ in the RDA). We pick the best fraction number based on the F1-score.

We compare the $\ell_{2,1}$ RDA and isolation forest on their best F1-score and on how they perform across a range of parameters. From Figures 5 and 6, we can see the RDA gets as F1 score of 0.64 with its optimal λ parameter, while the highest F1-score achieved by the Isolation Forest is 0.37, which is a 73.0% improvement.

5.4 Convergence of Training Method

As we mentioned in Section 4, since the objective function of both an ℓ_1 RDA and an $\ell_{2,1}$ RDA is not convex, the convergence of our model to a global minimum is non-trivial to guarantee. However, in our experiments, we have empirically observed the convergence rates of our algorithm, and in this section, we provide some of

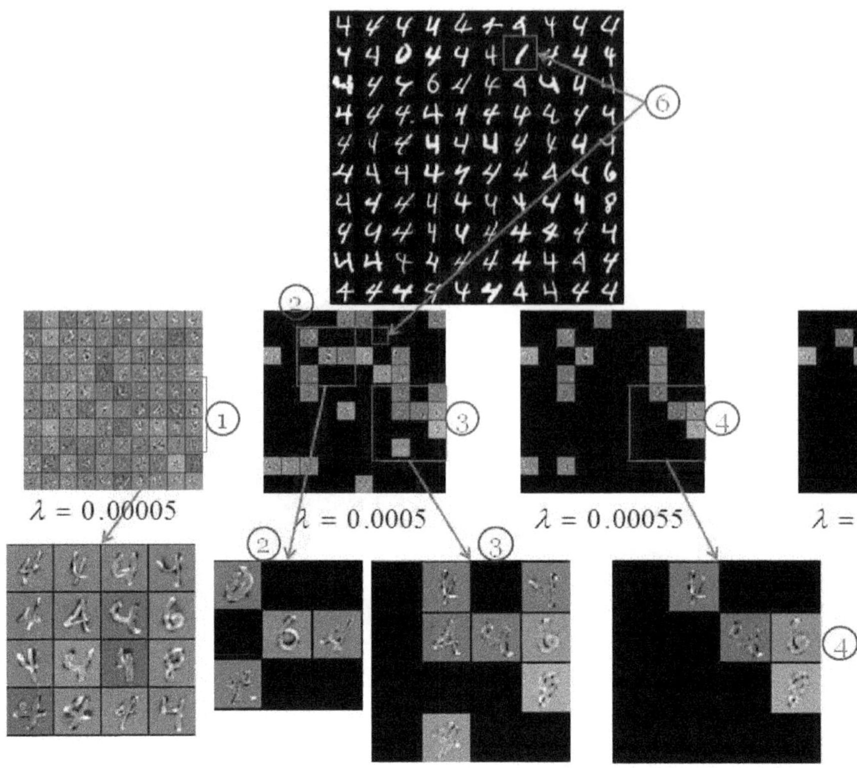

Figure 4: This figure shows how the sparsity of S changes with different λ values. ① shows a small λ, namely λ = 0.00005, which levies a small penalty on S, and the robust autoencoder emphasizes minimizing the reconstruction error by marking many images as anomalous. Accordingly, S is dense and every instance is non-zero. Since non-zero rows in S are marked as anomalies, the RDA has a high false-positive rate. In the case of ②, ③, and ④ the λ value is larger, placing a heavier penalty on S, and forcing S to be sparser. Many rows are shrunk to zero which reduces the false-positive rate, but also increases the false-negative rate. For example, ⑥ indicates an example of a false-negative; a "1" digit is supposed to be picked out as an outlier, but is marked as nominal. When the λ value gets even larger, as in ⑤, the large penalty on S causes every row of S to be shrunk to zero. In this cases, S is the zero matrix and thus no instance will be marked as anomalies. Accordingly, the optimal λ should balance both false-positive and false-negative rates. Thus, we use the F1-score to select the optimal λ.

our observations. Our proposed training algorithm, following the idea of an ADMM, minimizes one part of the objective with the other parts fixed. In particular, with S fixed, we use 30 instances as a training batch and 5 epochs to train the autoencoder part $|L_D - D_\theta(E_\theta(L_D))\|_2$. With L fixed, solving the proximal problem for S is deterministic and only takes one step. Accordingly, in Figure 7, one can see a "stair case" pattern where 5 epochs of minimization for the autoencoder is followed by a single solve of the proximal problem for S. As one can see, the largest decrease in objective function is achieved by each proximal solve.

As we discussed in Section 3, λ is also essential to the convergence of the problem. Accordingly, Figure 7 shows convergence histories for several values of λ. As one can see, our proposed ADMM algorithm converges quickly in many cases of interest. A theoretical justification of these convergence properties will be a subject of future work.

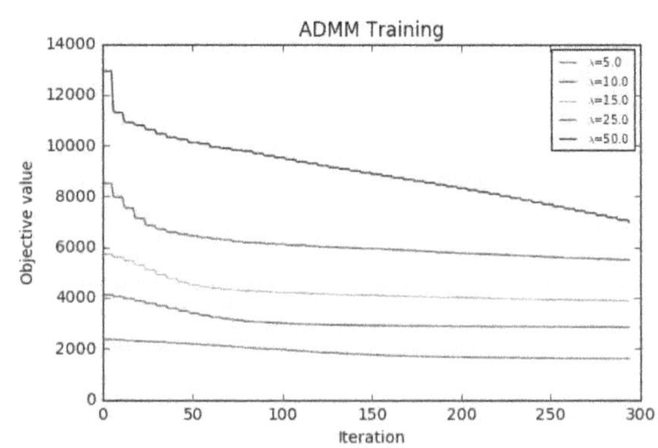

Figure 7: This figure shows the convergence of our optimization algorithm for (7). The objective descends quickly in the first 50 iterations and archives convergences after 200 iterations when λ is small. Convergence is slower for large λ values but still reasonable for our problems of interest.

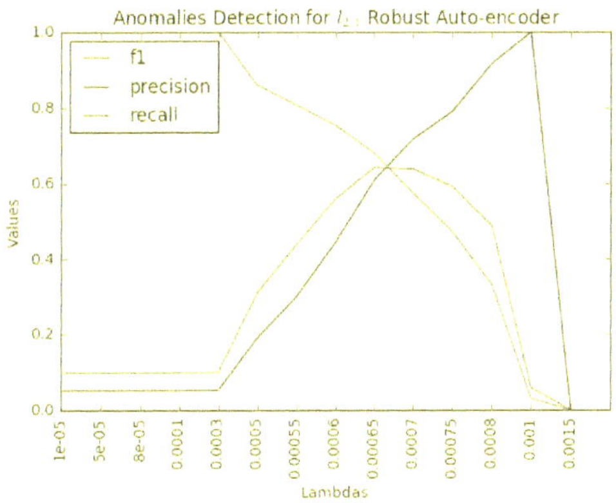

Figure 5: This figure shows the precision, recall and F1-scores with different λ values for the RDA. In the cases of a small λ, every row is non-zero and all the rows are marked as anomalies. We get high recall scores but very low precision and F1-scores. As the λ values increase, the F1-score and score increase reaching a maximum at $\lambda = 0.00065$ with an F1-score of 0.64.

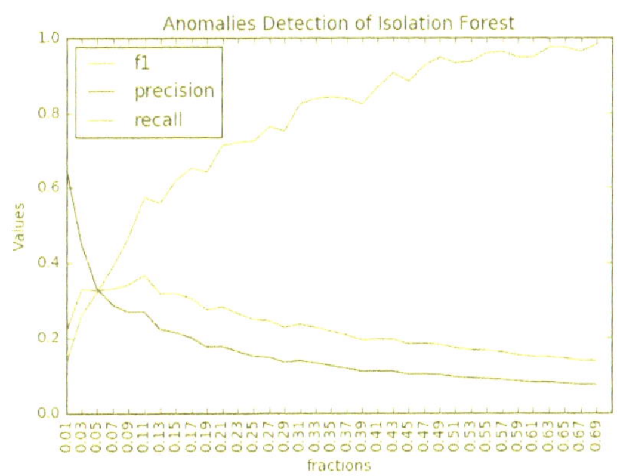

Figure 6: This figure shows the precision, recall and F1-score as we vary the fraction ratio for the Isolation Forest algorithm from 0.01 to 0.69. The optimal F1-score that the Isolation Forest achieves is about 0.37 when the fraction is equal to 0.11. This F1-score is approximately 73.0% worse than the score achieve by the RDA.

6 CONCLUSION

In this paper, we have shown how denoising autoencoders can be generalized to the case where no clean, noise-free data is available, creating a new family of methods that we call *"Robust Deep Autoencoders"*. These methods use an anomaly regularizing penalty based upon either ℓ_1 or $\ell_{2,1}$ norms. The resulting optimization problem was solved using ideas from proximal methods [4], backpropagation [24], and the Alternating Direction of Method of Multipliers (ADMM) [3]. We demonstrated the effectiveness of our approaches based upon noisy versions of the MNIST data set [12], where we achieved an approximately 30% improvement over standard autoencoders. As an interesting consequence of the development of such robust deep autoencoders, we also derived a novel family of unsupervised anomaly detection algorithms (parameterized by λ) and the effectiveness of these methods was demonstrated by comparing against Isolation Forests where we achieved a 73% improvement over that method. It is worth mentioning that in this paper we focus on improving autoencoders, however the $X = L_D + S$ framework, which is inspired by the RPCA, could be generalized where the autoencoder part is exchanged for other cost functions.

In the future, we would like to test our model on additional data sets from multiple areas, especially for the detection of cyber-attacks in network data. In addition, while we have substantial empirical evidence as to the convergence of our training algorithm for constructing high quality solutions, we would like to derive a theoretical basis for our training algorithm including convergence rates.

REFERENCES

[1] Martín Abadi, Ashish Agarwal, Paul Barham, Eugene Brevdo, Zhifeng Chen, Craig Citro, Greg S. Corrado, Andy Davis, Jeffrey Dean, Matthieu Devin, Sanjay Ghemawat, Ian Goodfellow, Andrew Harp, Geoffrey Irving, Michael Isard, Yangqing Jia, Rafal Jozefowicz, Lukasz Kaiser, Manjunath Kudlur, Josh Levenberg, Dan Mane, Rajat Monga, Sherry Moore, Derek Murray, Chris Olah, Mike Schuster, Jonathon Shlens, Benoit Steiner, Ilya Sutskever, Kunal Talwar, Paul Tucker, Vincent Vanhoucke, Vijay Vasudevan, Fernanda Viegas, Oriol Vinyals, Pete Warden, Martin Wattenberg, Martin Wicke, Yuan Yu, and Xiaoqiang Zheng. 2016. TensorFlow: Large-Scale Machine Learning on Heterogeneous Distributed Systems. (mar 2016). arXiv:1603.04467 http://arxiv.org/abs/1603.04467

[2] Christopher M Bishop. 2006. Pattern recognition. *Machine Learning* 128 (2006), 1–58.

[3] Stephen Boyd. 2010. Distributed Optimization and Statistical Learning via the Alternating Direction Method of Multipliers slide (Alternating Direction Method of Multipliers). (2010). http://dl.acm.org/citation.cfm?id=2185816

[4] S.P. Boyd and L. Vandenberghe. 2004. *Convex optimization*. Vol. 25. DOI: http://dx.doi.org/10.1080/10556781003625177

[5] James P Boyle and Richard L Dykstra. 1986. A method for finding projections onto the intersection of convex sets in Hilbert spaces. In *Advances in order restricted statistical inference*. Springer, 28–47.

[6] E J Candès, X Li, Y Ma, and J Wright. 2009. Robust Principal Component Analysis? *Preprint: arXiv:0912.3599* (2009).

[7] David L. Donoho. 2006. For most large underdetermined systems of linear equations the minimal ??? 1-norm solution is also the sparsest solution. *Communications on Pure and Applied Mathematics* 59, 6 (2006), 797–829. DOI: http://dx.doi.org/10.1002/cpa.20132 arXiv:0912.3599

[8] J. Friedman, T. Hastie, and R. Tibshirani. 2008. *The Elements of Statistical Learning*. Vol. 2. http://www-stat.stanford.edu/

[9] Jonas Gehring, Yajie Miao, Florian Metze, and Alex Waibel. 2013. Extracting deep bottleneck features using stacked auto-encoders. *ICASSP, IEEE International Conference on Acoustics, Speech and Signal Processing - Proceedings* (2013), 3377–3381. DOI: http://dx.doi.org/10.1109/ICASSP.2013.6638284

[10] Ian Goodfellow, Yoshua Bengio, and Aaron Courville. 2016. Deep Learning. (2016). DOI: http://dx.doi.org/10.1038/nmeth.3707 arXiv:arXiv:1312.6184v5

[11] Y LeCun, Y Bengio, and G Hinton. 2015. Deep learning. *Nature* (2015). http://www.nature.com/nature/journal/v521/n7553/abs/nature14539.html

[12] Y LeCun, L Bottou, and Y Bengio. 1998. Gradient-based learning applied to document recognition. *Proceedings of the* (1998). http://ieeexplore.ieee.org/abstract/document/726791/

[13] Honglak Lee, Alexis Battle, Rajat Raina, and Andrew Y Ng. 2007. Efficient sparse coding algorithms. *Advances in neural information processing systems* 19 (2007), 801.

[14] Fei Tony Liu and Kai Ming Ting. 2008. Isolation Forest. *2008 Eighth IEEE International* (2008). http://ieeexplore.ieee.org/xpls/abs

[15] O Lyudchik. 2016. Outlier detection using autoencoders. (2016). http://cds.cern.ch/record/2209085

[16] Yunlong Ma, Peng Zhang, Yanan Cao, and Li Guo. 2013. Parallel auto-encoder for efficient outlier detection. In *Proceedings - 2013 IEEE International Conference on Big Data, Big Data 2013*. 15–17. DOI: http://dx.doi.org/10.1109/BigData.2013.6691791

[17] Lingheng Meng, Shifei Ding, and Yu Xue. 2016. Research on denoising sparse autoencoder. *International Journal of Machine Learning and Cybernetics* (2016), 1–11. DOI: http://dx.doi.org/10.1007/s13042-016-0550-y

[18] Sofia Mosci, Lorenzo Rosasco, Matteo Santoro, Alessandro Verri, and Silvia Villa. 2010. Solving structured sparsity regularization with proximal methods. In *Joint European Conference on Machine Learning and Knowledge Discovery in Databases*. Springer, 418–433.

[19] Ulric Neisser. 2004. Pattern Recognition. *Cognitive psychology: Key readings.* (2004). DOI: http://dx.doi.org/10.1016/j.patcog.2011.03.019 arXiv:arXiv:1011.1669v3

[20] Randy C. Paffenroth, Philip C. Du Toit, Louis L Scharf, Anura P Jayasumana, Vidarshana Bandara, and Ryan Nong. 2012. Space-time signal processing for distributed pattern detection in sensor networks. *Proceedings of SPIE - The International Society for Optical Engineering* 8393 (2012), The Society of Photo-Optical Instrumentation Engin. DOI: http://dx.doi.org/10.1117/12.919711

[21] Fabian Pedregosa, Gaël Varoquaux, Alexandre Gramfort, Vincent Michel, Bertrand Thirion, Olivier Grisel, Mathieu Blondel, Peter Prettenhofer, Ron Weiss, Vincent Dubourg, and others. 2011. Scikit-learn: Machine learning in Python. *Journal of Machine Learning Research* 12, Oct (2011), 2825–2830.

[22] Yu Qi, Yueming Wang, Xiaoxiang Zheng, and Zhaohui Wu. 2014. Robust feature learning by stacked autoencoder with maximum correntropy criterion. In *ICASSP, IEEE International Conference on Acoustics, Speech and Signal Processing - Proceedings*. 6716–6720. DOI: http://dx.doi.org/10.1109/ICASSP.2014.6854900

[23] Salah Rifai, Pascal Vincent, Xavier Muller, Xavier Glorot, and Yoshua Bengio. 2011. Contractive auto-encoders: Explicit invariance during feature extraction. In *Proceedings of the 28th international conference on machine learning (ICML-11)*. 833–840.

[24] David E. Rumelhart, Geoffrey E. Hinton, and Ronald J. Williams. 1986. Learning representations by back-propagating errors. *Nature* 323, 6088 (oct 1986), 533–536. DOI: http://dx.doi.org/10.1038/323533a0 arXiv:arXiv:1011.1669v3

[25] Craig A. Stewart, George Turner, Matthew Vaughn, Niall I. Gaffney, Timothy M. Cockerill, Ian Foster, David Hancock, Nirav Merchant, Edwin Skidmore, Daniel Stanzione, James Taylor, and Steven Tuecke. 2015. Jetstream: A self-provisioned, scalable science and engineering cloud environment. *Proceedings of the 2015 XSEDE Conference on Scientific Advancements Enabled by Enhanced Cyberinfrastructure - XSEDE '15* (2015), 1–8. DOI: http://dx.doi.org/10.1145/2792745.2792774

[26] Theano Development Team. 2016. Theano: A Python framework for fast computation of mathematical expressions. *arXiv e-prints* abs/1605.02688 (May 2016). http://arxiv.org/abs/1605.02688

[27] John Towns, Timothy Cockerill, Maytal Dahan, Ian Foster, Kelly Gaither, Andrew Grimshaw, Victor Hazlewood, Scott Lathrop, Dave Lifka, Gregory D. Peterson, Ralph Roskies, J. Ray Scott, and Nancy Wilkens-Diehr. 2014. XSEDE: Accelerating scientific discovery. *Computing in Science and Engineering* 16, 5 (sep 2014), 62–74. DOI: http://dx.doi.org/10.1109/MCSE.2014.80 arXiv:http://dx.doi.org/10.1109/MCSE.2014.80

[28] Pascal Vincent, Hugo Larochelle, Yoshua Bengio, and Pierre-Antoine Manzagol. 2008. Extracting and composing robust features with denoising autoencoders. *Proceedings of the 25th international conference on Machine learning - ICML '08* (2008), 1096–1103. DOI: http://dx.doi.org/10.1145/1390156.1390294 arXiv:arXiv:1412.6550v4

[29] Pascal Vincent, Hugo Larochelle, Isabelle Lajoie, Yoshua Bengio, and Pierre-Antoine Manzagol. 2010. Stacked denoising autoencoders: Learning useful representations in a deep network with a local denoising criterion. *Journal of Machine Learning Research* 11, Dec (2010), 3371–3408.

[30] J Xie, L Xu, and E Chen. 2012. Image denoising and inpainting with deep neural networks. *Advances in Neural Information Processing* (2012), 1–9. http://papers.nips.cc/paper/4686-image-denoising-and-inpainting-with-deep-neural-networkshttp://papers.nips.cc/paper/4686-image-denoising

[31] Dan Zhao, Baolong Guo, Jinfu Wu, Weikang Ning, and Yunyi Yan. 2015. Robust feature learning by improved auto-encoder from non-Gaussian noised images. In *IST 2015 - 2015 IEEE International Conference on Imaging Systems and Techniques, Proceedings*. DOI: http://dx.doi.org/10.1109/IST.2015.7294537

Author Index

NOTES

NOTES

NOTES

NOTES

NOTES

NOTES

www.ingramcontent.com/pod-product-compliance
Ingram Content Group UK Ltd.
Pitfield, Milton Keynes, MK11 3LW, UK
UKHW051420290926
15471UKWH00009B/1693

9 781450 356695